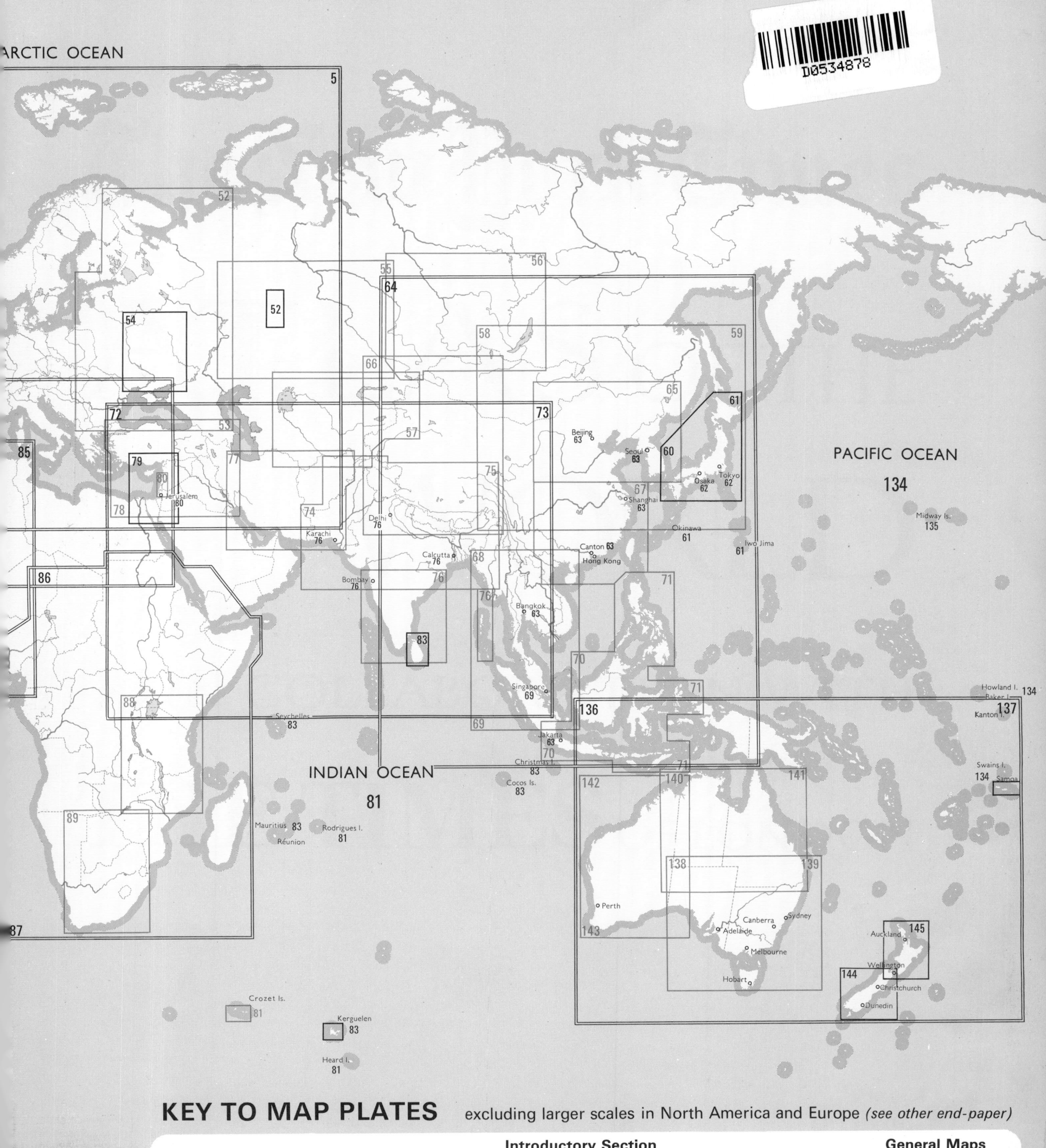

ARCTIC OCEAN

PACIFIC OCEAN
134

Midway Is.
135

Howland I. 134
Baker I.
Kanton I. 137

Swains I.
134 Samoa

INDIAN OCEAN
81

Beijing 63
Seoul 63
Osaka 62 Tokyo 62
Shanghai 63
Okinawa 61
Iwo Jima
Canton 63
Hong Kong 63

Delhi 76
Karachi 76
Calcutta 76
Bombay 76
Bangkok 63
Jerusalem 80

Singapore 69
Jakarta 63
Christmas I. 83
Cocos Is. 83

Seychelles 83

Mauritius 83
Rodrigues I. 81
Réunion

Perth
Canberra Sydney
Adelaide
Melbourne
Hobart

Auckland 145
Wellington
Christchurch
Dunedin

Crozet Is. 81

Kerguelen 83

Heard I. 81

KEY TO MAP PLATES excluding larger scales in North America and Europe *(see other end-paper)*

| 114 1:12 000 000 and smaller | 83 1:3 000 000 |
| 116 1:6 000 000 and smaller | 80 1:1 000 000 and larger |

Inset maps of islands, cities, etc. are named

Maps prepared in Great Britain
by Bartholomew,
a Division of HarperCollins*Publishers*,
Edinburgh, Scotland

Maps printed by Bartholomew,
HarperCollins*Manufacturing*,
Edinburgh, Scotland

Conurbation maps compiled and drawn by
Fairey Surveys Limited, Maidenhead;
A.W. Gatrell; and
Hunting Surveys Limited, Borehamwood

Preliminary section designed by
Ivan Dodd.
Cartography by
Thames Cartographic Services,
Maidenhead.
Typesetting by
Swanston Graphics Limited, Derby

Physical Earth maps and cover
illustrations by Duncan Mackay

States and Territories of the World
and Metropolitan Areas prepared by
Geographical Research Associates,
Maidenhead

Index processed and typeset by
Stibo Datagrafik, Århus, Denmark

Index printed by
Courier International Limited,
Tiptree, England

Books bound by
Sigloch, Künzelsau, Germany

Published in Great Britain by
Times Books,
an Imprint of HarperCollins*Publishers*,
77-85 Fulham Palace Road,
Hammersmith,
London W6 8JB
under the title
The Times Concise Atlas of the World.

Published in the United States of America
by TIMES BOOKS, a division of Random
House, Inc., New York, NY 10022

Copyright © 1991 by Times Books and
Bartholomew
Reprinted with revisions 1985
Second revised edition 1986
Reprinted 1988, 1989
Reprinted with revisions 1991

**Library of Congress Cataloging-in-
Publication Data**

The New York Times atlas of the world.

  Includes index.
  1. Atlases. I. John Bartholomew and
Son. II. New York times. III. Times
(London, England). IV. Title.
V. Atlas of the world. VI. Times atlas of
the world.
G1021. N57 1987 912   86-675048
ISBN 0-8129-1626-3

Manufactured in the
United Kingdom/Germany

9 8 7 6 5 4

FOREWORD

This new edition of *The New York Times Atlas of the World* will, it is hoped, find as much favour with those who acquire a copy for the first time as it has with those familiar with the earlier editions.

Every effort has been made to ensure that the maps are as up-to-date as possible. The index of names has, in consequence, been augmented. It now contains some 100,000 entries but it still does not contain all the names which appear on the maps. The reader may, however, rest assured that the names of all important inhabited places and physical features are included together with the page number, country name and grid reference.

Great attention has been paid to the spelling of geographical names, a matter of great complexity due to the multiplicity of the World's languages, the diverse forms of writing or the absence of any writing system whatsoever. For want of a standard way of spelling names a variety of spellings has been used over the centuries establishing in each of the major languages of the world its own conventional way of spelling which differs greatly from the name found locally. In this atlas the name taken is always the name used by the official administering body. Where necessary that name has been converted into the Roman alphabet by systems which follow English language usage. Those systems accord with the transcription and transliteration systems accepted for official use in the United States and the United Kingdom. For added reference the English language conventional names have been added parenthetically e.g. Roma (Rome), Moskva (Moscow).

Names like maps often invoke political protestations. The status of areas, the international boundaries and the names associated with them as shown in this edition are those which reflect the situation pertaining on the ground at the time of publication: where boundaries are the subject of international dispute this portrayal will not win the approval of the contending parties but, in the view of the publishers, the function of an atlas is to show facts and not to adjudicate between the rights and wrongs of political issues.

Preceding the index is a list of countries of the World. It shows a world re-cast in a mould unforeseen and unforeseeable at the end of the Second World War. Yet the changes in the political scene are small in comparison with the way science has altered the pattern of life. No century in the world's history has witnessed changes so fundamental and widespread. Of more significance than the magnitude of the change is its rate, now such that any reliable prediction of the future beyond a decade or two cannot be made.

The trend is vividly demonstrated in the diagram showing the demand for energy but it is no less apparent under other subject headings.

Unabated growth of that kind cannot continue indefinitely. The maps which make up the body of the atlas show the physical and political world of to-day. How the same maps will look in the future depends on the size of the world's population; the pattern of settlement; the spread of industry; the availability of food, minerals and sources of energy; the world's vegetation, atmosphere and climate all of which are in risk of catastrophic change.

To sustain ever increasing numbers of people requires constant stock-taking of natural resources. Remote-sensing, a product of the space age, is now beginning to reveal its eventual capacity for the kind of global monitoring required.

The space age has barely dawned yet it has already stretched the confines of our world to include the solar system and embrace more and more of the universe.

Our atlas, therefore, includes the Earth we live on, the solar system and the universe beyond. May it bring pleasure and interest to all who use it.

CONTRIBUTORS

John C. Bartholomew
Cartographic Consultant
Bartholomew, Edinburgh

Ronald Jones
Department of Geography
Queen Mary College, London

H.A.G. Lewis OBE
Geographical Consultant
to *The London Times*

Stephen Lippard
Department of Earth Sciences,
The Open University, Milton Keynes

David Rothery
Department of Earth Sciences,
The Open University, Milton Keynes

David Whitehouse
Space Scientist
Farnborough, Hants

Editorial direction by
Janet Christie
Alison M. Ewington
H.A.G. Lewis OBE
Paul Middleton
Barry Winkleman

CONTENTS

GEOGRAPHICAL COMPARISONS

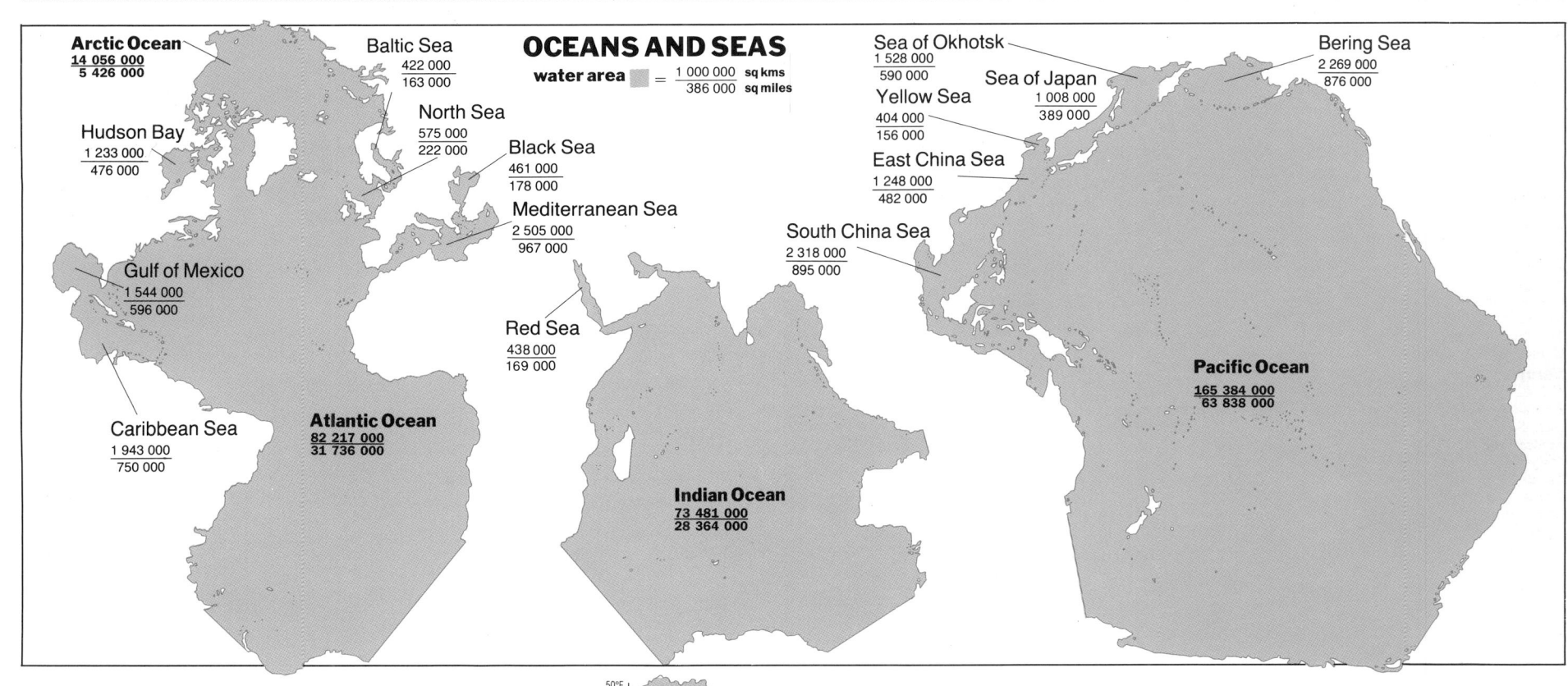

OCEANS AND SEAS

water area ▨ = 1 000 000 sq kms / 386 000 sq miles

Arctic Ocean 14 056 000 / 5 426 000

Baltic Sea 422 000 / 163 000

Hudson Bay 1 233 000 / 476 000

North Sea 575 000 / 222 000

Black Sea 461 000 / 178 000

Gulf of Mexico 1 544 000 / 596 000

Mediterranean Sea 2 505 000 / 967 000

Red Sea 438 000 / 169 000

Caribbean Sea 1 943 000 / 750 000

Atlantic Ocean 82 217 000 / 31 736 000

Indian Ocean 73 481 000 / 28 364 000

Sea of Okhotsk 1 528 000 / 590 000

Bering Sea 2 269 000 / 876 000

Sea of Japan 1 008 000 / 389 000

Yellow Sea 404 000 / 156 000

East China Sea 1 248 000 / 482 000

South China Sea 2 318 000 / 895 000

Pacific Ocean 165 384 000 / 63 838 000

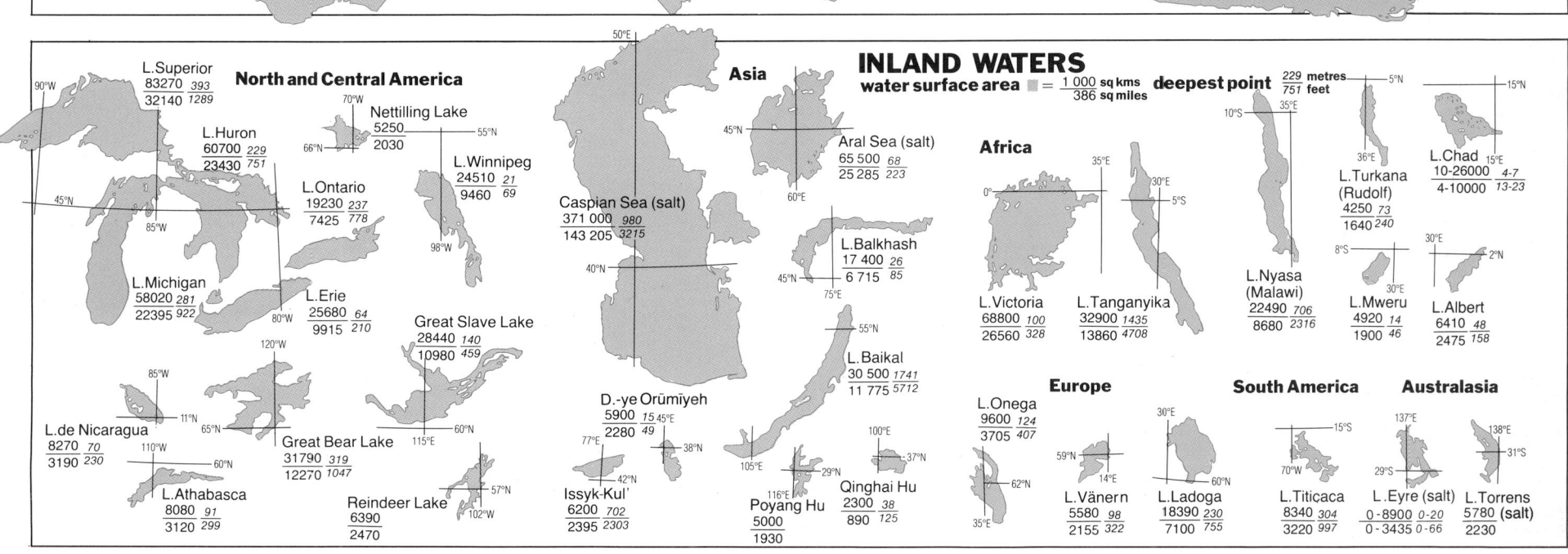

INLAND WATERS

water surface area ▨ = 1 000 sq kms / 386 sq miles   deepest point 229 metres / 751 feet

North and Central America

L.Superior 83270 / 32140 *393 / 1289*
L.Huron 60700 / 23430 *229 / 751*
Nettilling Lake 5250 / 2030
L.Winnipeg 24510 / 9460 *21 / 69*
L.Ontario 19230 / 7425 *237 / 778*
L.Michigan 58020 / 22395 *281 / 922*
L.Erie 25680 / 9915 *64 / 210*
Great Slave Lake 28440 / 10980 *140 / 459*
L.de Nicaragua 8270 / 3190 *70 / 230*
Great Bear Lake 31790 / 12270 *319 / 1047*
L.Athabasca 8080 / 3120 *91 / 299*
Reindeer Lake 6390 / 2470

Asia

Aral Sea (salt) 65 500 / 25 285 *68 / 223*
Caspian Sea (salt) 371 000 / 143 205 *980 / 3215*
L.Balkhash 17 400 / 6 715 *26 / 85*
L.Baikal 30 500 / 11 775 *1741 / 5712*
D.-ye Orūmīyeh 5900 / 2280 *15 / 49*
Issyk-Kul' 6200 / 2395 *702 / 2303*
Poyang Hu 5000 / 1930
Qinghai Hu 2300 / 890 *38 / 125*

Africa

L.Victoria 68800 / 26560 *100 / 328*
L.Tanganyika 32900 / 13860 *1435 / 4708*
L.Nyasa (Malawi) 22490 / 8680 *706 / 2316*
L.Turkana (Rudolf) 4250 / 1640 *73 / 240*
L.Chad 10-26000 / 4-10000 *4-7 / 13-23*
L.Mweru 4920 / 1900 *14 / 46*
L.Albert 6410 / 2475 *48 / 158*

Europe

L.Onega 9600 / 3705 *124 / 407*
L.Vänern 5580 / 2155 *98 / 322*
L.Ladoga 18390 / 7100 *230 / 755*

South America

L.Titicaca 8340 / 3220 *304 / 997*

Australasia

L.Eyre (salt) 0-8900 / 0-3435 *0-20 / 0-66*
L.Torrens 5780 (salt) / 2230

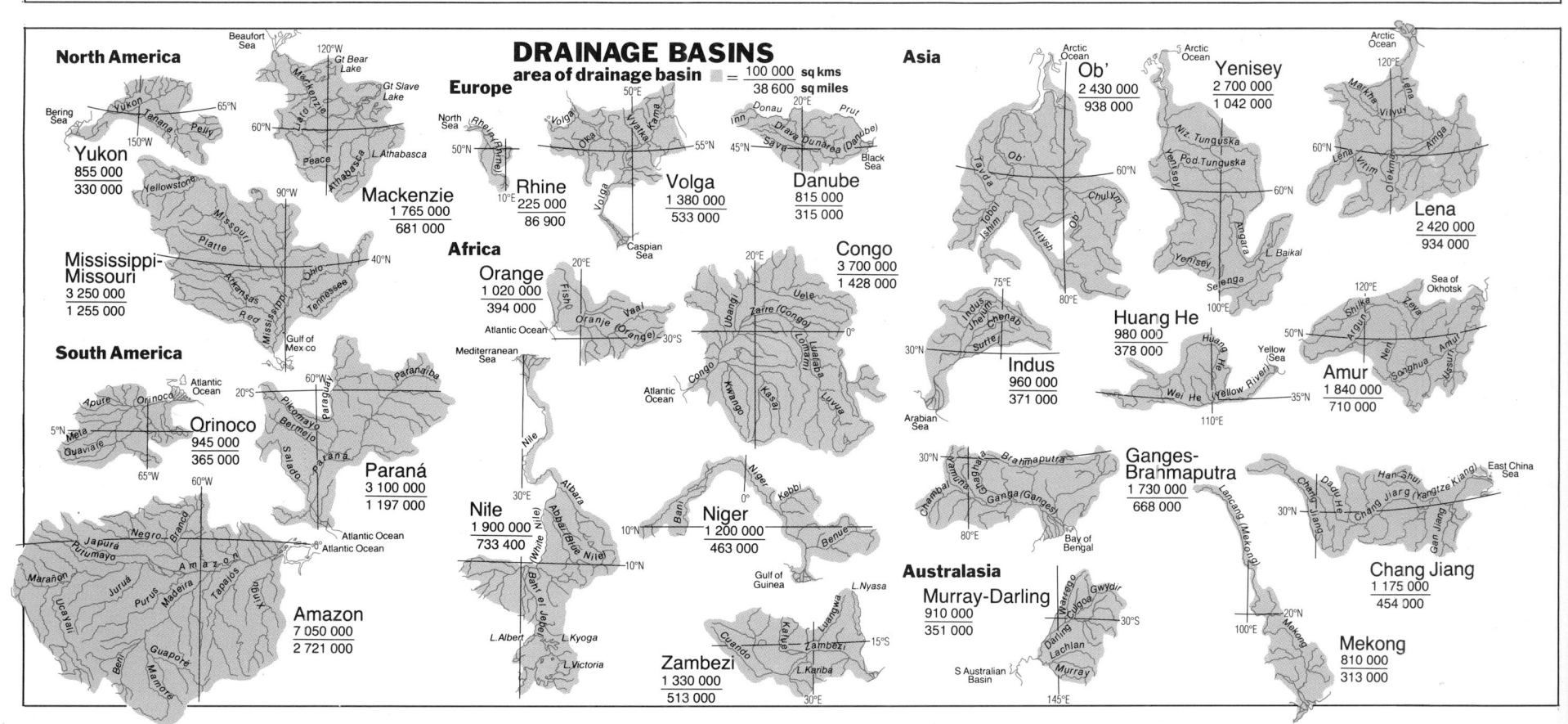

DRAINAGE BASINS

area of drainage basin ▨ = 100 000 sq kms / 38 600 sq miles

North America

Yukon 855 000 / 330 000
Mackenzie 1 765 000 / 681 000
Mississippi-Missouri 3 250 000 / 1 255 000

South America

Orinoco 945 000 / 365 000
Paraná 3 100 000 / 1 197 000
Amazon 7 050 000 / 2 721 000

Europe

Rhine 225 000 / 86 900
Volga 1 380 000 / 533 000
Danube 815 000 / 315 000

Africa

Orange 1 020 000 / 394 000
Nile 1 900 000 / 733 400
Niger 1 200 000 / 463 000
Congo 3 700 000 / 1 428 000
Zambezi 1 330 000 / 513 000

Asia

Ob' 2 430 000 / 938 000
Yenisey 2 700 000 / 1 042 000
Lena 2 420 000 / 934 000
Indus 960 000 / 371 000
Huang He 980 000 / 378 000
Amur 1 840 000 / 710 000
Ganges-Brahmaputra 1 730 000 / 668 000
Chang Jiang 1 175 000 / 454 000
Mekong 810 000 / 313 000

Australasia

Murray-Darling 910 000 / 351 000

MOUNTAIN HEIGHTS

	Metres	Feet	Mountain
North and Central America			
U.S.A.	6,194	20,320	McKinley
Canada	5,951	19,524	Logan
Mexico	5,699	18,697	Citlaltépetl (Orizaba)
U.S.A.	4,418	14,495	Whitney
U.S.A.	4,398	14,431	Elbert
U.S.A.	4,392	14,410	Rainier
Hawaii, U.S.A.	4,205	13,796	Mauna Kea
South America			
Argentina	6,960	22,834	Aconcagua
Argentina–Chile	6,880	22,572	Ojos del Salado
Argentina	6,872	22,546	Bonete
Peru	6,768	22,205	Huascarán
Bolivia	6,542	21,463	Sajama
Bolivia	6,485	21,276	Illampu
Ecuador	6,310	20,702	Chimborazo
Ecuador	5,896	19,344	Cotopaxi
Africa			
Tanzania	5,895	19,340	Kilimanjaro
Kenya	5,200	17,058	Kirinyaga (Kenya)
Uganda-Zaire	5,110	16,763	Stanley (Margherita)
Tanzania	4,565	14,979	Meru
Ethiopia	4,533	14,872	Ras Dashen
Rwanda-Zaire	4,507	14,786	Karisimbi
Kenya-Uganda	4,321	14,178	Elgon
Morocco	4,165	13,664	Toubkal
Cameroon	4,095	13,435	Caméroun
Europe			
U.S.S.R.	5,642	18,510	El'brus
France-Italy	4,807	15,770	Mont-Blanc
Italy-Switzerland	4,634	15,203	Monte Rosa (Dufour)
Switzerland	4,545	14,910	Dom (Mischabel)
Italy-Switzerland	4,478	14,690	Matterhorn
Canary Is	3,718	12,198	Teide
Spain	3,482	11,424	Mulhacén
Sicily, Italy	3,323	10,902	Etna
Asia			
China-Nepal	8,848	29,028	Everest (Qomolangma Feng)
India-China	8,611	28,250	K2 (Qogir Feng) (Godwin Austen)
India-Nepal	8,586	28,170	Kangchenjunga
China-Nepal	8,463	27,766	Makalu
China-Nepal	8,201	26,906	Cho Oyu
Nepal	8,167	26,795	Dhaulagiri
Nepal	8,163	26,781	Manaslu
India	8,125	26,657	Nanga Parbat
Nepal	8,091	26,545	Annapurna
Kashmir	8,068	26,470	Gasherbrum
China	8,012	26,286	Xixabangma Feng (Gosainthan)
Kashmir	7,885	25,869	Distaghil Sar
Kashmir	7,821	25,659	Masherbrum
Kashmir	7,816	25,643	Nanda Devi
China-India	7,756	25,446	Kamet
China	7,723	25,338	Muztag
Pakistan	7,690	25,230	Tirich Mir
U.S.S.R.	7,495	24,590	Pik Kommunizma
U.S.S.R.-China	7,439	24,406	Pik Pobedy (Tomur Feng)
Iran	5,671	18,605	Damävand
Turkey	5,123	16,808	Büyükağri (Ararat)
Indonesia	5,030	16,503	Jaya (Carstensz)
Malaysia	4,094	13,431	Kinabalu
Japan	3,776	12,388	Fuji
Australasia			
New Zealand	3,764	12,349	Cook
Australia	2,230	7,316	Kosciusko
Antarctica			
Antarctica	5,140	16,860	Vinson Massif
Antarctica	4,528	14,855	Kirkpatrick
Antarctica	3,794	12,447	Erebus

RIVER LENGTHS

	Kms	Miles	River
North and Central America	6,019	3,740	Mississippi-Missouri
	4,250	2,640	Mackenzie
	3,969	2,466	Missouri
	3,779	2,348	Mississippi
	3,185	1,980	Yukon
	3,058	1,900	St Lawrence
	2,870	1,785	Rio Grande
	2,570	1,600	Nelson-Saskatchewan
	2,348	1,459	Arkansas
	2,333	1,450	Colorado
South America	6,515	4,050	Amazon
	4,500	2,800	Paraná
	3,200	1,990	Madeira
	2,900	1,800	São Francisco
	2,750	1,710	Pará-Tocantins
	2,600	1,615	Paraguay
	2,500	1,555	Orinoco
Africa	6,695	4,160	Nile
	4,667	2,900	Zaire (Congo)
	4,030	2,505	Niger
	2,650	1,650	Zambezi
	2,490	1,550	Shabeelle
	1,860	1,155	Orange
Europe	3,688	2,290	Volga
	2,850	1,770	Danube
	2,285	1,420	Dnepr
	1,870	1,162	Don
	1,320	820	Rhine
	1,159	720	Elbe
	1,014	630	Wisła (Vistula)
	1,012	629	Loire
	1,006	625	Tejo (Tagus)
Asia	6,380	3,965	Chang Jiang (Yangtze)
	5,570	3,460	Ob'-Irtysh
	5,550	3,450	Yenisey-Angara
	5,464	3,395	Huang He (Yellow R.)
	4,425	2,750	Mekong
	4,416	2,744	Amur
	4,400	1,730	Lena
	3,180	1,975	Indus
	3,078	1,913	Syrdar'ya
	3,060	1,901	Salween
	2,840	1,765	Brahmaputra
	2,815	1,750	Euphrates
	2,620	1,630	Amudar'ya
	2,534	1,575	Ural
	2,510	1,560	Ganga (Ganges)
	2,150	1,335	Irrawaddy
Australasia	3,750	2,330	Murray-Darling

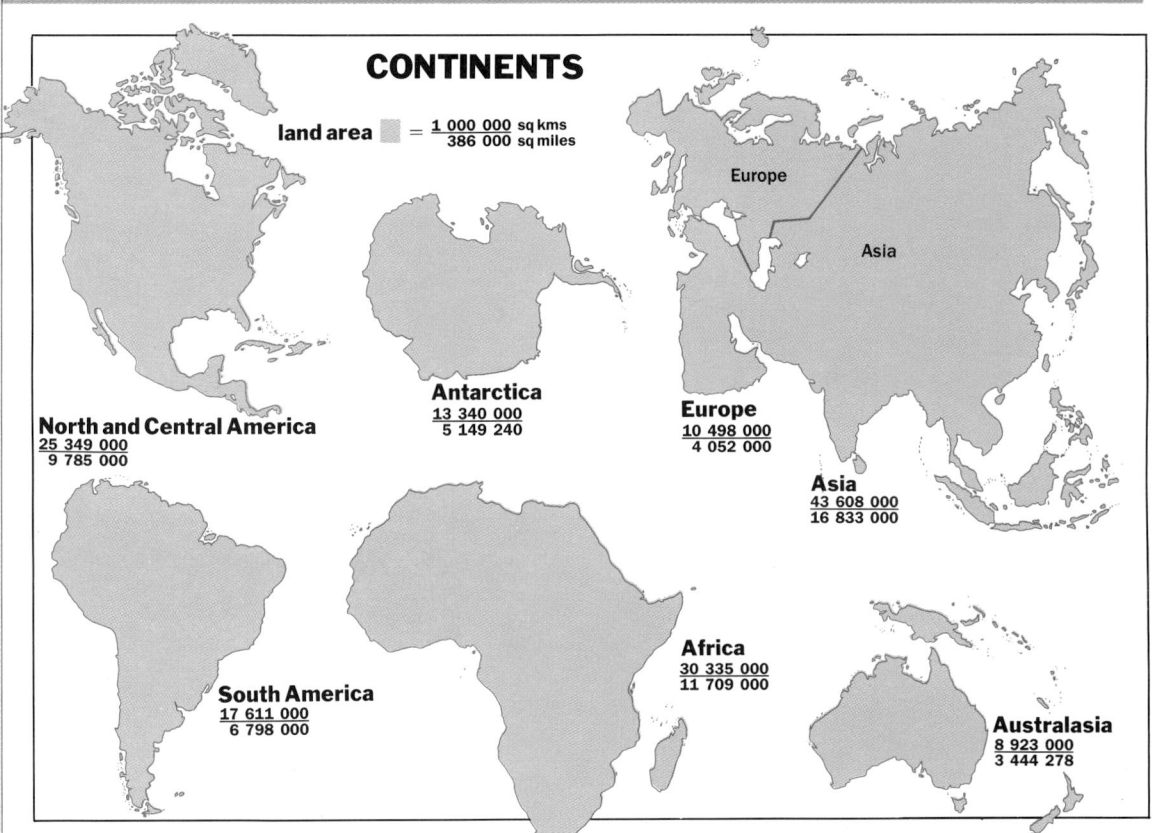

CONTINENTS

land area ■ = 1 000 000 sq kms / 386 000 sq miles

North and Central America
25 349 000
9 785 000

Antarctica
13 340 000
5 149 240

Europe
10 498 000
4 052 000

Asia
43 608 000
16 833 000

South America
17 611 000
6 798 000

Africa
30 335 000
11 709 000

Australasia
8 923 000
3 444 278

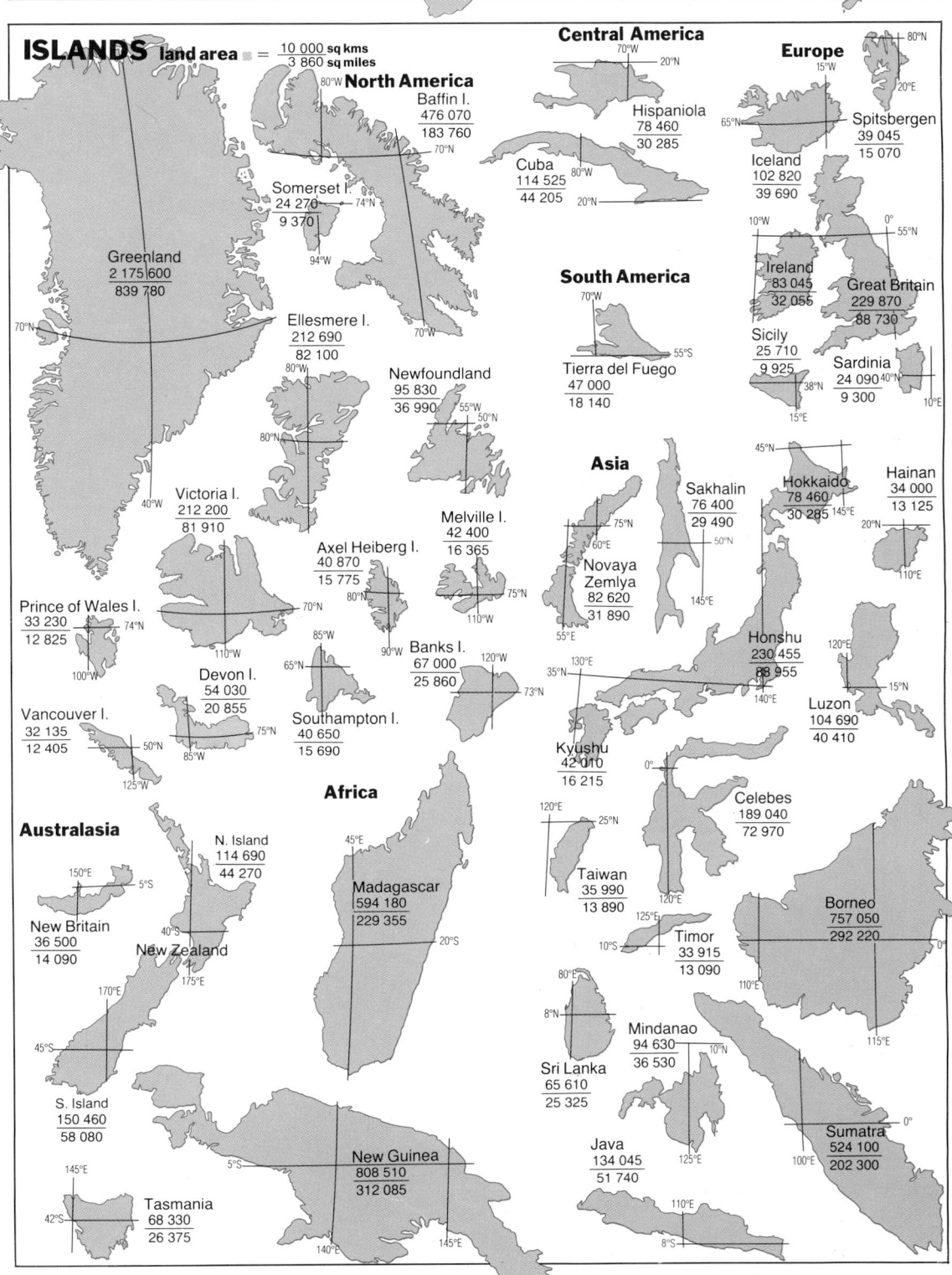

ISLANDS

land area ■ = 10 000 sq kms / 3 860 sq miles

North America

Greenland 2 175 600 / 839 780
Baffin I. 476 070 / 183 760
Somerset I. 24 270 / 9 370
Ellesmere I. 212 690 / 82 100
Newfoundland 95 830 / 36 990
Victoria I. 212 200 / 81 910
Melville I. 42 400 / 16 365
Axel Heiberg I. 40 870 / 15 775
Prince of Wales I. 33 230 / 12 825
Banks I. 67 000 / 25 860
Devon I. 54 030 / 20 855
Vancouver I. 32 135 / 12 405
Southampton I. 40 650 / 15 690

Central America

Cuba 114 525 / 44 205
Hispaniola 78 460 / 30 285

South America

Tierra del Fuego 47 000 / 18 140

Europe

Spitsbergen 39 045 / 15 070
Iceland 102 860 / 39 690
Ireland 83 045 / 32 055
Great Britain 229 870 / 88 730
Sicily 25 710 / 9 925
Sardinia 24 090 / 9 300

Asia

Sakhalin 76 400 / 29 490
Hokkaido 78 460 / 30 285
Hainan 34 000 / 13 125
Novaya Zemlya 82 620 / 31 890
Honshu 230 455 / 88 955
Luzon 104 690 / 40 410
Kyūshū 42 010 / 16 215
Celebes 189 040 / 72 970
Taiwan 35 990 / 13 890
Timor 33 915 / 13 090
Borneo 757 050 / 292 220
Mindanao 94 630 / 36 530
Sri Lanka 65 610 / 25 325
Java 134 045 / 51 740
Sumatra 524 100 / 202 300

Africa

Madagascar 594 180 / 229 355

Australasia

N. Island 114 690 / 44 270
New Zealand
New Britain 36 500 / 14 090
S. Island 150 460 / 58 080
Tasmania 68 330 / 26 375
New Guinea 808 510 / 312 085

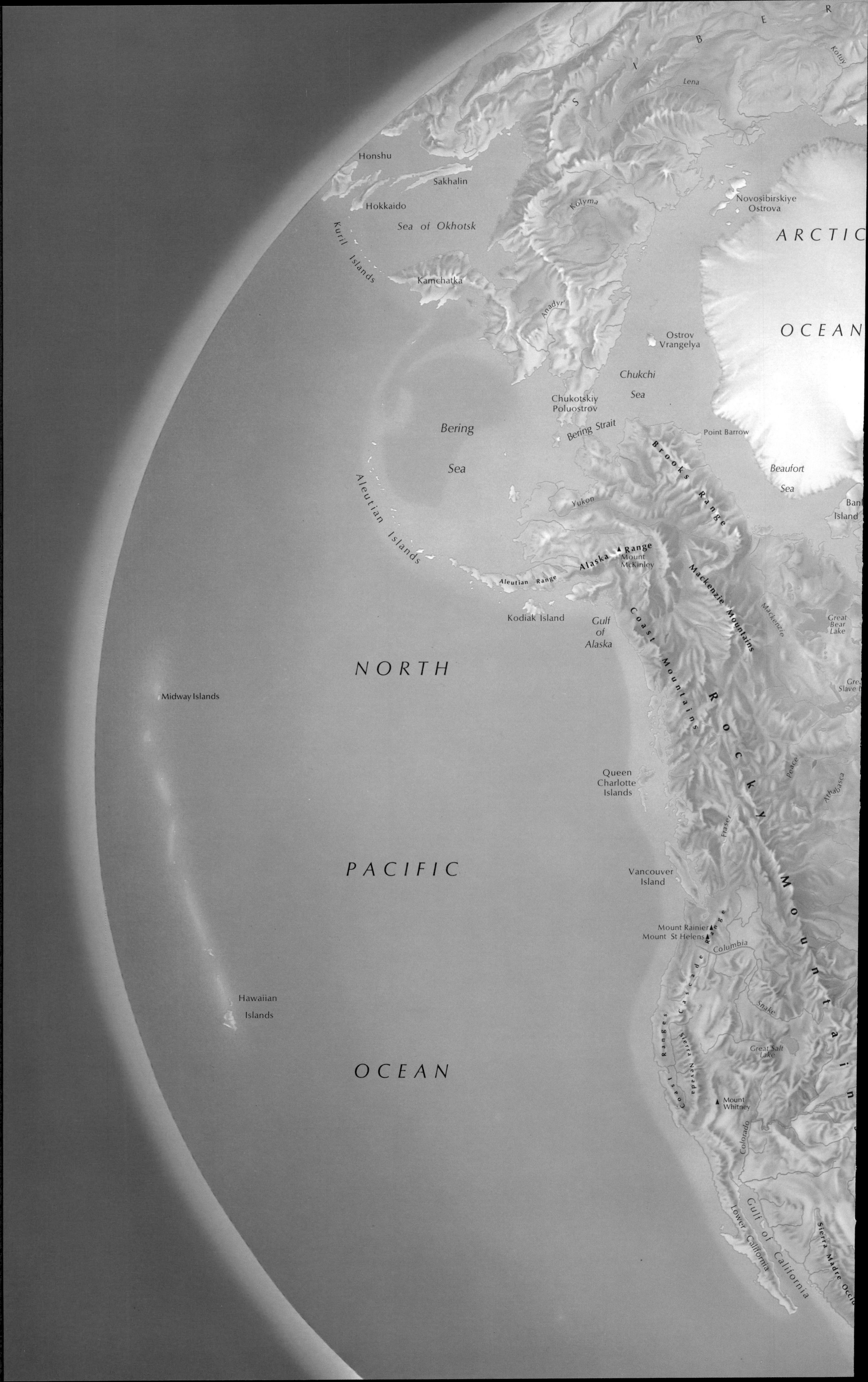

S I B E R I A

Kotuy

Lena

Honshu

Sakhalin

Kolyma

Novosibirskiye
Ostrova

Hokkaido

Sea of Okhotsk

Kuril Islands

Kamchatka

Anadyr'

Ostrov
Vrangelya

ARCTIC

OCEAN

Chukchi
Sea

Chukotskiy
Poluostrov

Bering

Sea

Bering Strait

Point Barrow

Brooks Range

Beaufort
Sea

Ban
Island

Aleutian Islands

Yukon

Mackenzie Mountains

Great
Bear
Lake

Alaska Range
Mount
McKinley

Aleutian Range

Mackenzie

Kodiak Island

Gulf
of
Alaska

Coast Mountains

R O C K Y

Gre
Slave

NORTH

Peace

Athabasca

Midway Islands

Queen
Charlotte
Islands

Fraser

M o u n t a i n s

PACIFIC

Vancouver
Island

Mount Rainier
Mount St Helens

Cascade Range

Columbia

Hawaiian
Islands

Snake

OCEAN

Coast Ranges

Sierra Nevada

Great Salt
Lake

Mount
Whitney

Colorado

Gulf of California

Lower California

Sierra Madre Occid

6

Yenisey
Ob'
Urals
Novaya Zemlya
Severnaya Zemlya
Black Sea
SCANDINAVIA
North Cape
Limit of permanent pack ice
Svalbard
Norwegian Sea
NORTH POLE
Jan Mayen
North Sea
Mediterranean Sea
BRITISH ISLES
Bay of Biscay
Greenland
Denmark Strait
Iceland
Ellesmere Island
Queen Elizabeth Islands
Parry Islands
Baffin Bay
NORTH AFRICA
Davis Strait
Cape Farewell
Madeira
Victoria Island
Baffin Island
NORTH
Canary Islands
Foxe Basin
Southampton Island
Hudson Strait
Cape Chidley
Labrador Sea
Azores
Hudson Bay
Labrador
Lake Athabasca
Churchill
Reindeer Lake
Southern Indian Lake
La Grande Rivière
Laurentian Highlands
Newfoundland
Cape Race
James Bay
Rupert
ATLANTIC
Saskatchewan
Lake Winnipeg
Nova Scotia
Lake Manitoba
Lake of the Woods
Lake Superior
St. Lawrence
Cape Cod
Lake Huron
Lake Ontario
Missouri
Mississippi
Lake Michigan
Lake Erie
Great Plains
Platte
Ohio
Appalachian Mountains
Bermuda
OCEAN
Cape Hatteras
Ozark Plateaus
Arkansas
Tennessee
Savannah
Red River
Florida
Bahamas
Rio Grande
West Indies
Gulf of Mexico
Sierra Madre Oriental
Caribbean Sea
Orinoco
Yucatan

Colo

Sierra Madre Occidental

Lower California

Gulf of California

Rio Grande

Sierra Madre Oriental

GULF

OF

MEXICO

Popocatépetl ▲

Gulf of Campeche

Yucatan

Florida

W

C

G R E

Islas Revillagigedo

Sierra Madre del Sur

*Gulf
of
Honduras*

*Lake
Nicaragua*

Clipperton
Island

Isthmus

P A C I F I C

Isla del Coco

Isla de Malpelo

Galapagos Islands

O C E A N

BAHAMAS

W E S T

Cuba

Jamaica

G R E A T E R   A N T I L L E S

Hispaniola

Puerto
Rico

I N D I E S

C A R I B B E A N

S E A

L E S S E R   A N T I L L E S

N O R T H

A T L A N T I C

O C E A N

Bermuda

Trinidad

Gulf
of
Darien

Gulf
of
Panama

Panama

Cordillera   Occidental

Cordillera   Oriental

Cauca

Magdalena

Lake
Maracaibo

L L A N O S

Orinoco

Guiana

Roraima ▲

Highlands

Branco

Mouths
of the
Amazon

▲ Cotopaxi

Chimborazo

Negro

Japurá

Putumayo

Amazon

Amazon

Marañón

A
N
D
E
S

Ucayali

Juruá

Purus

Madeira

▲ Huascarán

Tapajós

Xingu

Tocantins

Araguaia

Parnaíba

São Francisco

Madre de Dios

Lake
Titicaca

▲ Ancohuma

M A T O

G R O S S O

Lake
Poopó

Salar
de
Uyuni

Atacama Desert

G R A N   C H A C O

Paraguay

Pilcomayo

B r a z i l i a n   H i g h l a n d s

Paraná

Galapagos Islands

Lake
Titicaca
Salar de
Uyuni
Lake
Poopó

Gran Chaco
Pilcomayo
Paraguay
Bermejo
Salado
Paraná
Uruguay
Plate

Pampas

San Félix · San Ambrosio
Aconcagua

Juan Fernández

Colorado
Negro

S O U T H

Patagonia
Chubut
Chico
Deseado

Sala y Gomez

Falkland
Islands

Easter Island

Tierra del
Fuego

Cape Horn

Drake   Passage

Elephant Island

P A C I F I C

South
Shetland
Islands

Ducie Island

Graham Land

PENINSULA

Palmer Land

Henderson Island

Pitcairn Island

ANTARCTIC

O C E A N

Peter I Island

Bellingshausen
Sea

Ellsworth
Land

Rapa

A   N

Marie Byrd
Land

S O U T H E R N

Ross
Ice
Shelf

Ross

Sea

Mount Erebus

Scott Island

Chatham
Islands

Balleny Islands

Bounty
Islands   Antipodes

New Zealand

Campbell Island

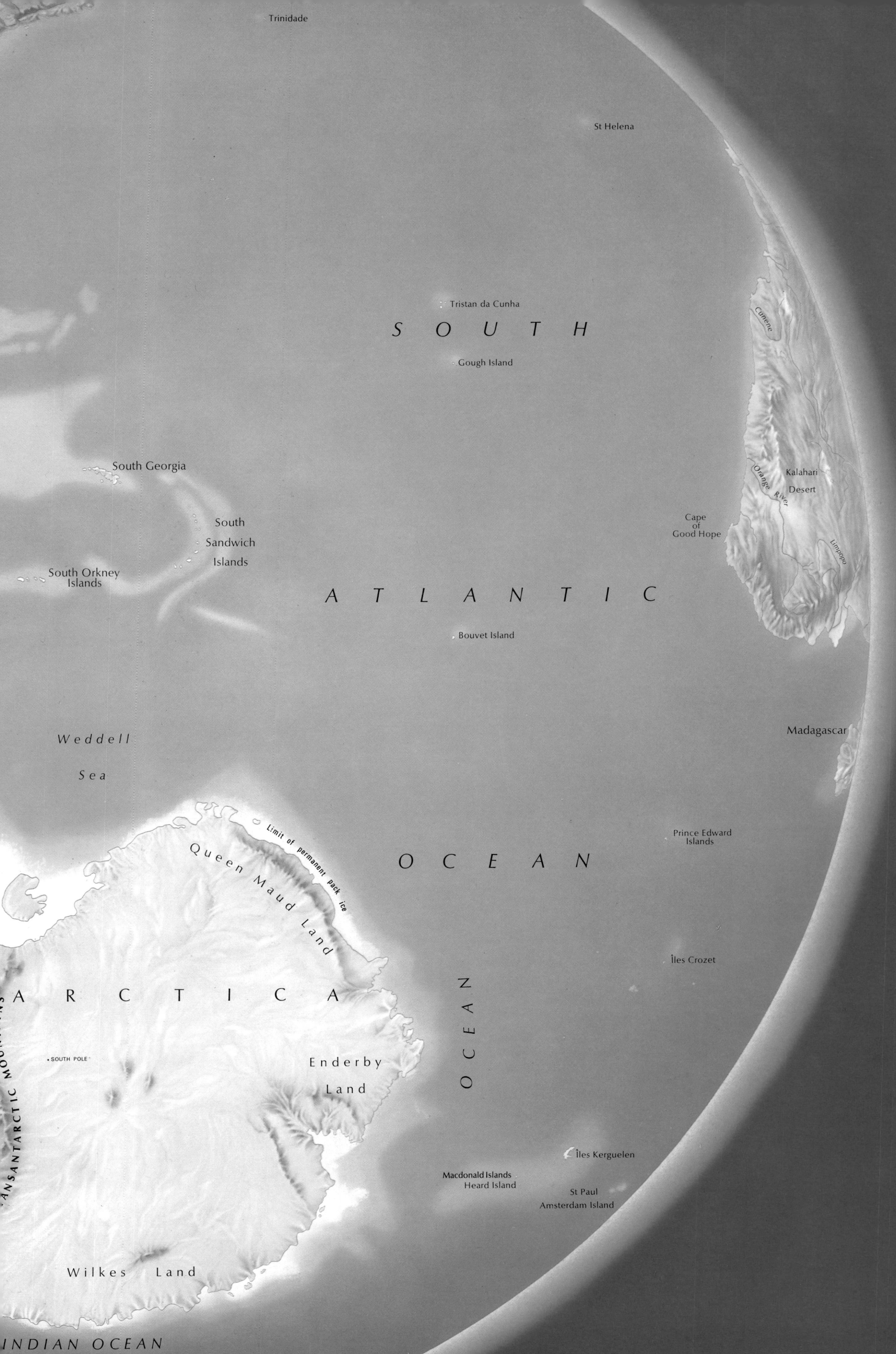

Trinidade

St Helena

Tristan da Cunha

S O U T H

Gough Island

Cunene

South Georgia

Kalahari
Desert

Orange River

South
Sandwich
Islands

A T L A N T I C

Cape
of
Good Hope

Limpopo

South Orkney
Islands

Bouvet Island

Madagascar

Weddell

Sea

O C E A N

Prince Edward
Islands

Limit of permanent pack ice

Queen Maud Land

A R C T I C A

O
C
E
A
N

Îles Crozet

•SOUTH POLE•

Enderby
Land

TRANSANTARCTIC MOUNTAINS

Îles Kerguelen

Macdonald Islands
Heard Island

St Paul
Amsterdam Island

Wilkes   Land

INDIAN OCEAN

Sicily

Malta

Iberian Peninsula

Medi

Azores

Strait of Gibraltar

Chott
Melrhir

El Jerid

Gulf of
Sirte

Madeira

ATLAS MOUNTAINS

L

Canary Islands

NORTH

ATLANTIC

OCEAN

Hoggar

Tibesti

S   A   H   A   R   A

Lac Faguibine

Senegal

Cape Verde
Islands

S   A   H   E   L

Niger

Lake
Chad

Cape
Verde

Gambia

Benue

Adamawa
Highlands

Lake
Volta

Ubangi

Grain Coast

Slave Coast
Bight of
Benin

Ivory Coast Gold Coast

Mouths
of the Niger

Sanaga

Bioko

Gulf of Guinea

Príncipe

St Paul Rocks

São Tomé

Lac
Mai-Ndombe

Pagalu

Congo

Kasai

SOUTH   AMERICA

Cuango

Ascension

S   O   U   T   H

Bié
Plateau

St Helena

Cunene

Okavango

A   T   L   A   N   T   I   C

Etosha Pan

Okava

Namib Desert

Lake
Ngami

K a l a h

D e s e

O   C   E   A   N

Orange River

Cape of Good Hope

Tristan da Cunha

Lake Urmia
Caspian Sea
Crete
Cyprus
rranean Sea
Euphrates
Tigris
Zagros Mountains
Amudar'ya
Pamirs
Tarim
Daryācheh-ye-Namak
Hindu Kush
Karakoram
Dead Sea
Plateau of Iran
Plateau of Tibet
Qattâra
Sinai
Gulf of Suez
Gulf of Aqaba
Helmand
HIMALAYAS
yan
Desert
Nile
RED SEA
Persian Gulf
ARABIAN
Brahmaputra
The Great Oasis
Lake Nasser
Indus
Thar Desert
PENINSULA
Al Liwā'
Gulf of Oman
Nubian Desert
Umm as Samim
Ganges (Ganga)
Maṣirah
RUB AL KHĀLĪ
ARABIAN SEA
Godavari
Deccan
Krishna
Jebel Marra
Blue Nile
White Nile
Bab el Mandeb
Lake Tana
Danakil Desert
Gulf of Aden
Socotra
Ethiopian Plateau
Laccadive Islands
Ogaden
Rift Valley
Shabeelle
Ceylon
Uele
Lake Turkana
Maldive Islands
Lake Kyoga
Lake Albert
Mt Stanley
Mount Kenya
Tana
Jubba
Lake Edward
Lake Victoria
INDIAN
Lake Kivu
Lake Natron
Kilimanjaro
Lake Eyasi
Lualaba
Seychelles
Pemba Island
Lake Tanganyika
Zanzibar
Amirante Islands
Chagos Archipelago
Coëtivy Island
Mafia Island
Lake Rukwa
Lake Upemba
Lake Mweru
Aldabra Islands
Providence Islands
Lake Bangweulu
Agalega Islands
Lake Nyasa
Comoro Islands
OCEAN
Mozambique Channel
Madagascar
Lake Chilwa
Zambezi
Tromelin
Lake Kariba
Makgadikgadi Pan
Rodrigues
Mauritius
Réunion
Limpopo
Vaal
Drakensberg

NORTH POL

ARCTIC

Ellesmere Island

Hudson Bay

Baffin Island

Davis Strait

Greenland

Greenland Sea

Jan Mayen

LABRADOR

Norwegian Sea

Cape Farewell

Denmark Strait

Iceland

Faeroe Islands

N O R T H

British Isles

Grampians

North Sea

S C A N D

Vänern

Vättern

Irish Sea

A T L A N T I C

Severn

Thames

English Channel

Rhine

Elbe

N O

Seine

Loire

Bay of Biscay

Massif Central

Mt. Blanc

A L P S

Po

O C E A N

Garonne

Rhône

Apennin

Adriat

Azores

Cantabrian Mts

Pyrenees

Corsica

Ebro

Tagus

Balearic Islands

Sardinia

Guadalquivir

M E D I T E R

Strait of Gibraltar

Sicily

Madeira

R

Malta

A T L A S   M O U N T A I N S

Chott Melrhir

El Jerid

Canary Islands

OCEAN

Novosibirskiye
Ostrova

Severnaya
Zemlya

Limit of permanent pack ice

Franz
Josef
Land

Svalbard

Barents
Sea

Kara
Sea

Novaya
Zemlya

North Cape

Lena

CENTRAL
SIBERIAN
PLATEAU

Nizhnyaya Tunguska

Lena

Yenisey

Angara

Lake
Baikal

WEST
SIBERIAN
PLAIN

SIBERIA

Pechora

URAL MOUNTAINS

White
Sea

Severnaya Dvina

Onega

Ladoga

Gulf of Bothnia

SCANDINAVIA

Gulf of Finland

THE EUROPEAN PLAIN

Baltic Sea

Dvina

Vistula

Neisse

Central
Russian
Uplands

Volga

Ob

Ob

Irtysh

KIRGHIZ STEPPE

Lake
Balkhash

CARPATHIANS

Hungarian Plain

Danube

Dinaric Alps

Tisza

Dniester

Dnieper

Danube

Balkan Mountains

Rhodope

Thrace

Pindus

Bosporus

Sea of Marmara

Dardanelles

Aegean
Sea

Sea of Azov

Don

Volga

Ural

Kura

KIZIL

Aral
Sea

Kyzylkum

Syrdar'ya

Amudar'ya

Karakumy

Caucasus

Araxes

Lake
Van

Lake
Urmia

Daryācheh-ye-Namak

Caspian Sea

Zagros Mountains

Plateau
of
Iran

Helmand

Black Sea

ASIA MINOR

Tuz
Gölü

Kizil Irmak

Taurus

Cyprus

Crete

MEDITERRANEAN SEA

Mesopotamia

Tigris

Euphrates

Syrian Desert

Jordan

Dead Sea

Gulf of
Sirte

Libyan Desert

Nile

Gulf
of
Suez

Gulf
of
Aqaba

ARABIAN
PENINSULA

Persian Gulf

Gulf
of
Oman

Barents Sea

Kheta

Scandinavia

Baltic Sea

White Sea

Pechora

CENTRAL

SIBERIAN

PLATEAU

Lake Ladoga

Lake Onega

NORTH EUROPEAN PLAIN

Ural Mountains

Ob

WEST

SIBERIAN

PLAIN

Nizhnyaya Tunguska

S I B

Dnieper

Volga

Tobol

Yenisey

Angara

Le

Don

Ural

Ishim

Ozero Tengiz

Ob

Black Sea

Caucusus

Volga

Caspian Sea

Kirghiz

Steppe

Irtysh

Lake Baikal

Hövsgöl Nuur

Selenga

Aral Sea

Syrdar'ya

Ozero Zaysan

ALTAI

MONGO

Kyzylkum

Amudar'ya

Lake Balkhash

Ozero Alakol'

Ebinur Hu

GOBI

Karakumy

Ili

Dzungaria

Issyk Kul

Tien Shan

Bosten Hu

Turfan Depression

Yellow River (Huang He)

Plateau of Iran

Pik Kommunizma

Pamirs

Tarim

Lop Nur

Hindu Kush

Karakoram

Takla Makan

Altun Shan

Qaidam Pendi

K2

Kunlun Shan

Qinghai Hu

Helmand

H I M A L A Y A

Plateau of Tibet

Yangtze Kiang (Chang Jiang)

Yellow River (Huang He)

Qin Ling

Chenab

Indus

Sutlej

Salween

Red Basin

Indo-Gangetic Plain

Brahmaputra

Yangtze Kiang (Chang Jiang)

Thar Desert

Ganges (Ganga)

Mekong

Narmada

Khasi Hills

Naga Hills

Nan Ling

Arabian Sea

Mahanadi

Mouths of the Ganges

Arakan

Irrawaddy

Red River (Song Hong)

Western Ghats

Deccan

Godavari

Gulf of Tongking

Krishna

Eastern Ghats

Bay of Bengal

Salween

Hainan

INDOCHINA

Laccadive Islands

Cauvery

Andaman Islands

Andaman Sea

Chao Phraya

Palk Strait

Maldive Islands

Ceylon

Nicobar Islands

Gulf of Thailand

Mekong

Kra Isthmus

Malay Peninsula

Strait of Malacca

INDIAN OCEAN

Sumatra

Laptev Sea
Novosibirskiye Ostrova
Bering Strait
Alaska
Anadyr
Nunivak Island
Yana
Kolyma
Indigirka
Verkhoyanskiy Khrebet
Lena
Bering Sea
Aleutian Islands
Vilyuy
Kamchatka
Komandorskiye Ostrova
Aldan
Khr. Dzhungdzhur
Sea of Okhotsk
Yablonovyy Khrebet
Shilka
Sakhalin
Tatarskiy Proliv
Kuril Islands
Greater Khingan Range
Amur
Sikhote Alin
Hulun Nur
Ussuri
Manchuria
Songhua
Oz Khanka
Hokkaido
NORTH
Midway Islands
Sea of Japan
Changbai Shan
Honshu
Bo Hai
Korea
Yellow River (Huang He)
PACIFIC
Yellow Sea
Great Plain of China
Korea Strait
Shikoku
Kyushu
Yangtze Kiang (Chang Jiang)
Bonin Islands
OCEAN
East China Sea
Dongting Hu
Poyang Hu
Ryukyu Islands
Volcano Islands
Taiwan Strait
Taiwan
Marianas
Marshall Islands
PHILIPPINES
South China Sea
Guam
Kiribati
Paracel Islands
Luzon
Caroline Islands
Mindoro
Samar
Panay
Palawan
Negros
Sulu Sea
Mindanao
Spratly Islands
Celebes Sea
Borneo
Admiralty Islands
New Ireland

South
China
Sea

N O R

Malay Peninsula

Strait of Malacca

S u m a t r a

B
o
r
n
e
o

C e l e b e s

Sea

C a

Makassar Strait

Celebes

M
o
l
u
c
c
a
s

B a n d a

Sea

J a v a

Sea

E
A
S
T

J a v a

Bali

Christmas Island

Cocos (Keeling) Islands

I
N
D
I
E
S

Timor

T i m o r

Sea

A r a f u r

Sea

Arnhem Land

Victoria

Bark

I N D I A N

Fitzroy

Kimberley
Plateau

Tanami
Desert

Great
Sandy
Desert

Ashburton

Macdonnell Ranges

Si
D

Gascoyne

Gibson
Desert

Lake
Amadeus

Fink

Great Victoria Desert

Lake
Moore

Lake
Barlee

Nullarbor Plain

Lake
Gardner

Great Australian Bight

O C E A N

St Paul

S O U T H E R N

Kerguelen

Heard Island
Macdonald Islands

A N T A R C T I C A

roline Islands Pohnpei MICRONESIA Marshall
Islands

TH PACIFIC OCEAN SOUTH

M E L Nauru POLY

E L Admiralty Islands Banaba

New Guinea New Ireland Kiribati

N Bismarck
Sea New Britain Bougainville Solomon Islands E

S I Tokelau
Islands

Torres Strait Great Barrier Santa
Cruz
Islands Tuvalu

Cape
York
Peninsula Coral PACIFIC A

Gulf of
arpentaria Reef Vanuatu Samoan
Islands

ableland Sea Fiji N
E
S
I

Flinders Tahiti

Georgina New
Caledonia Tonga Society
Islands

n
t Diamantina OCEAN

Cooper Creek Great Dividing Range

Lake
Eyre Barwon Norfolk Island

Lake
Torrens Darling Lord Howe Island Kermadec Islands

Murray Lachlan

Murrumbidgee

Murray

Mount Kosciusko Australian Alps Tasman

Bass Strait Sea New Zealand

Tasmania Cook
Strait

Chatham Islands

OCEAN Bounty Islands

Antipodes Islands

Aucklanc Islands

Campbell Island

Macquarie Island

STAR CHARTS

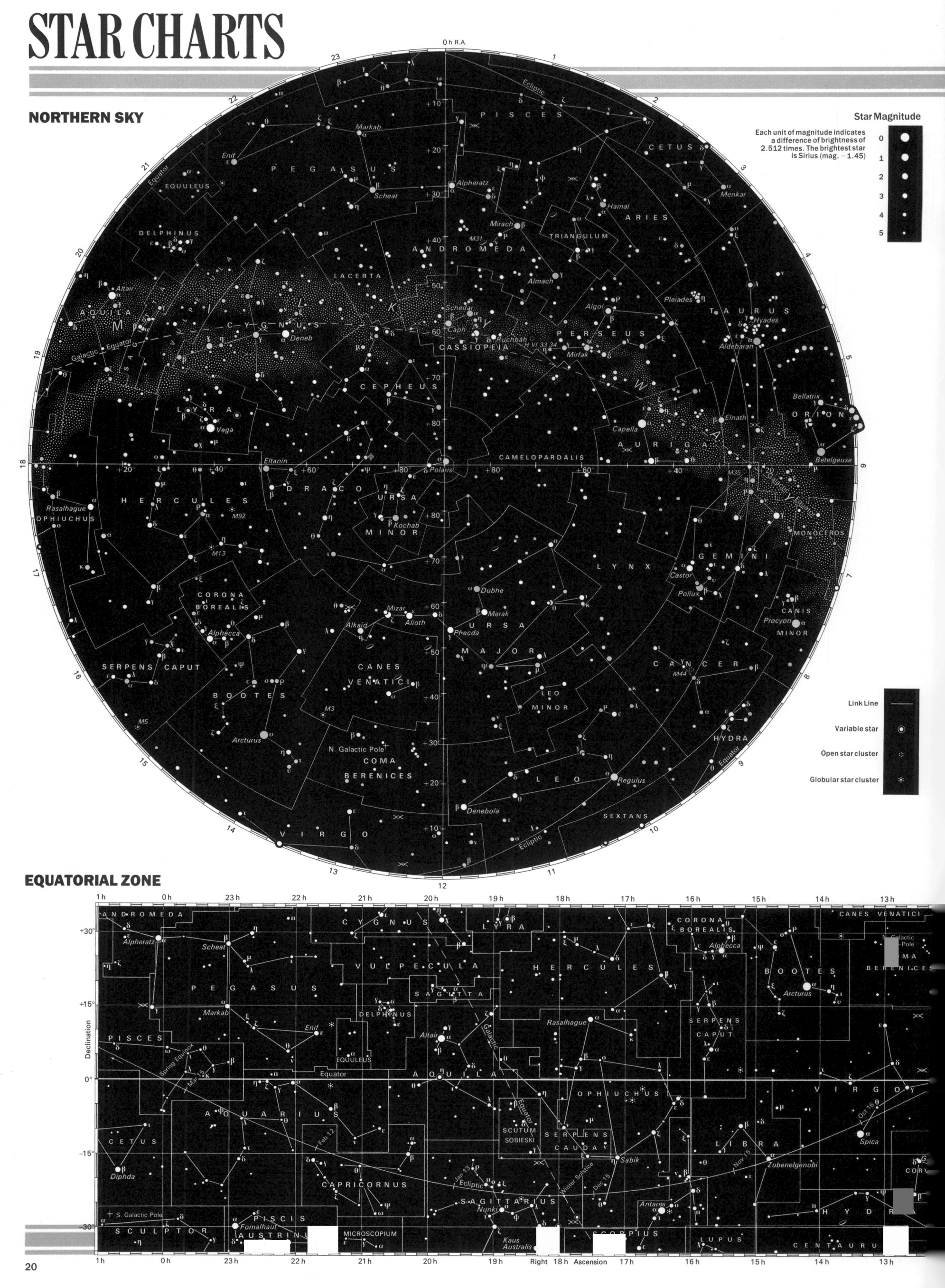

NORTHERN SKY

EQUATORIAL ZONE

Star Magnitude

Each unit of magnitude indicates a difference of brightness of 2.512 times. The brightest star is Sirius (mag. −1.45)

0 1 2 3 4 5

Link Line ———
Variable star ⊙
Open star cluster ✳
Globular star cluster ✳

Star Colours and Spectral Types

		*Temp in 000°C
O-B		50.0–25.0
A		11.0
F		7.5
G		6.0
K		5.0
M		3.5

The surface temperature of a star is indicated both by its colour and its spectrum

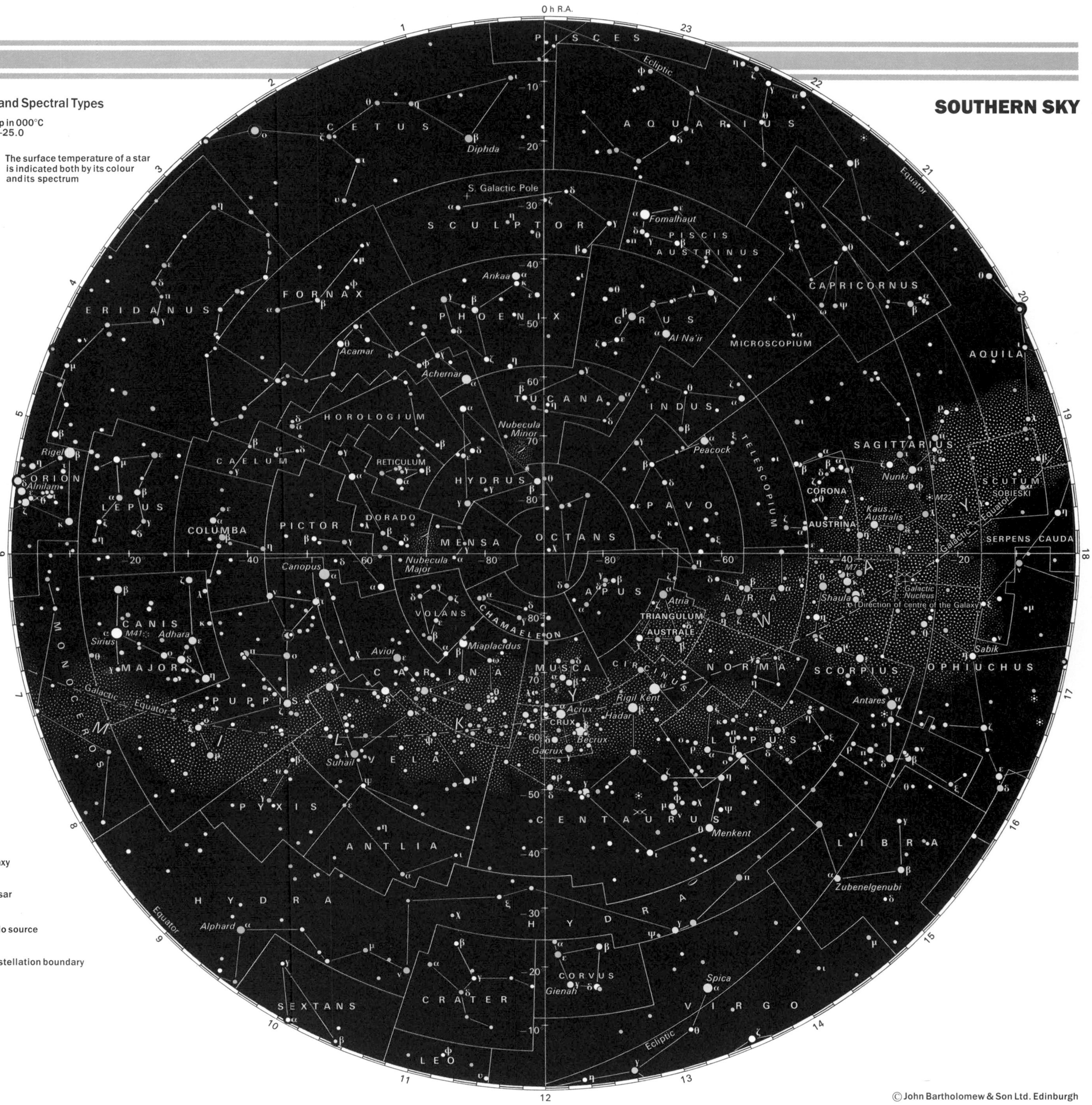

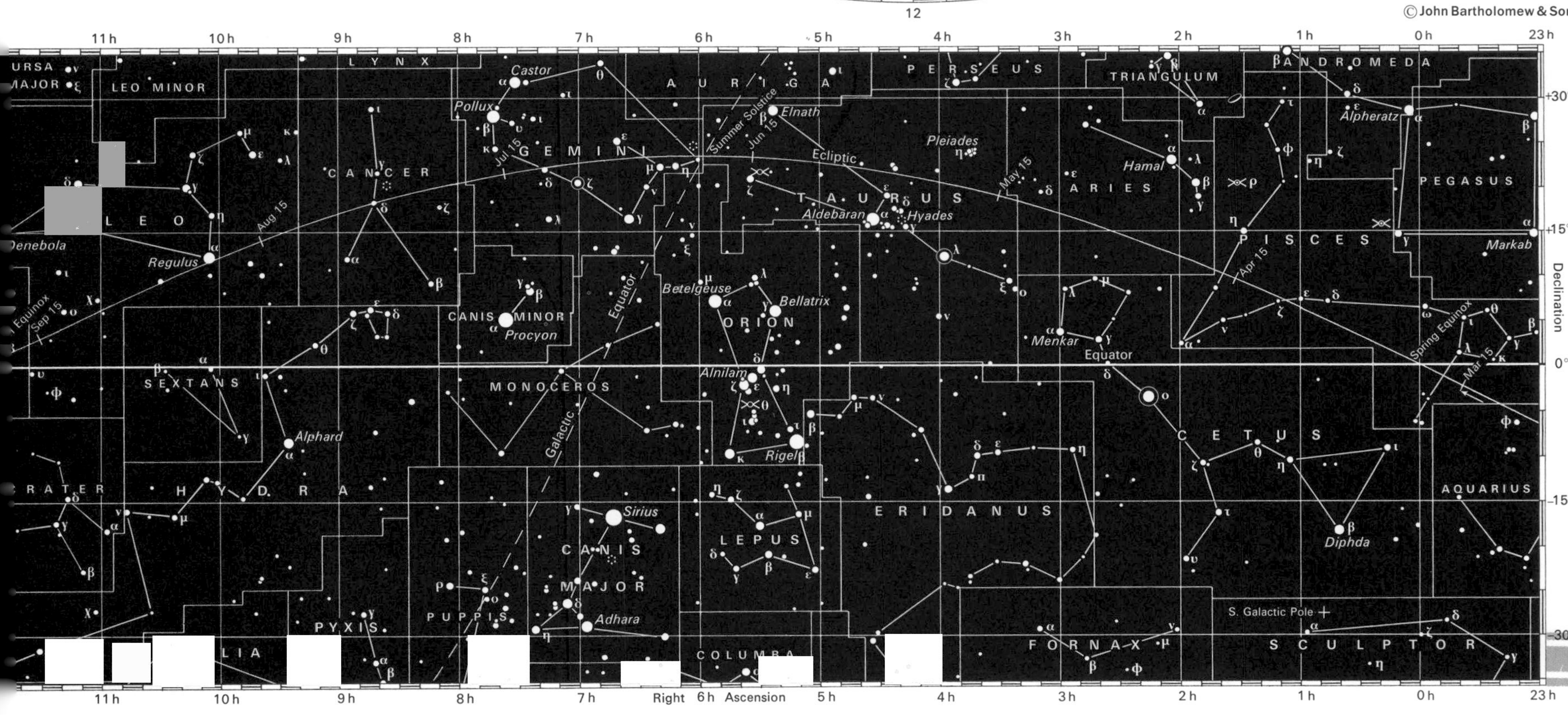

Galaxy
Quasar
Radio source
Constellation boundary

© John Bartholomew & Son Ltd. Edinburgh

Right Ascension

Declination

21

UNIVERSE

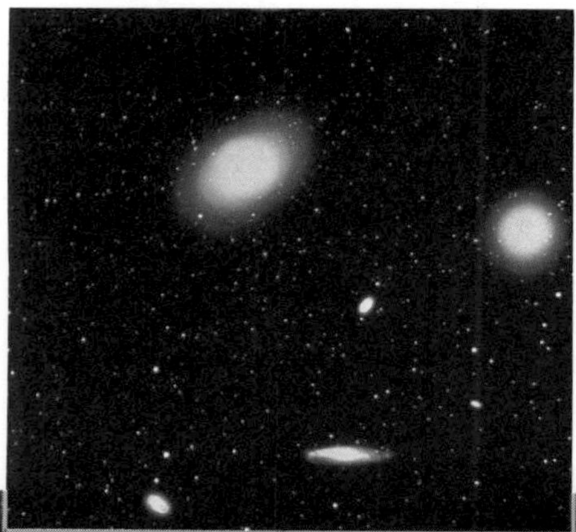

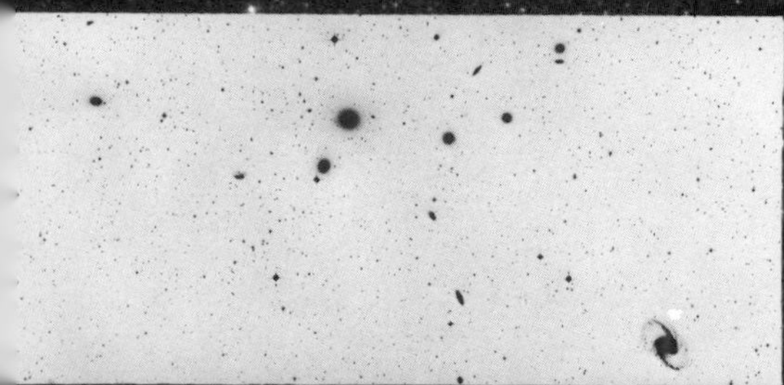

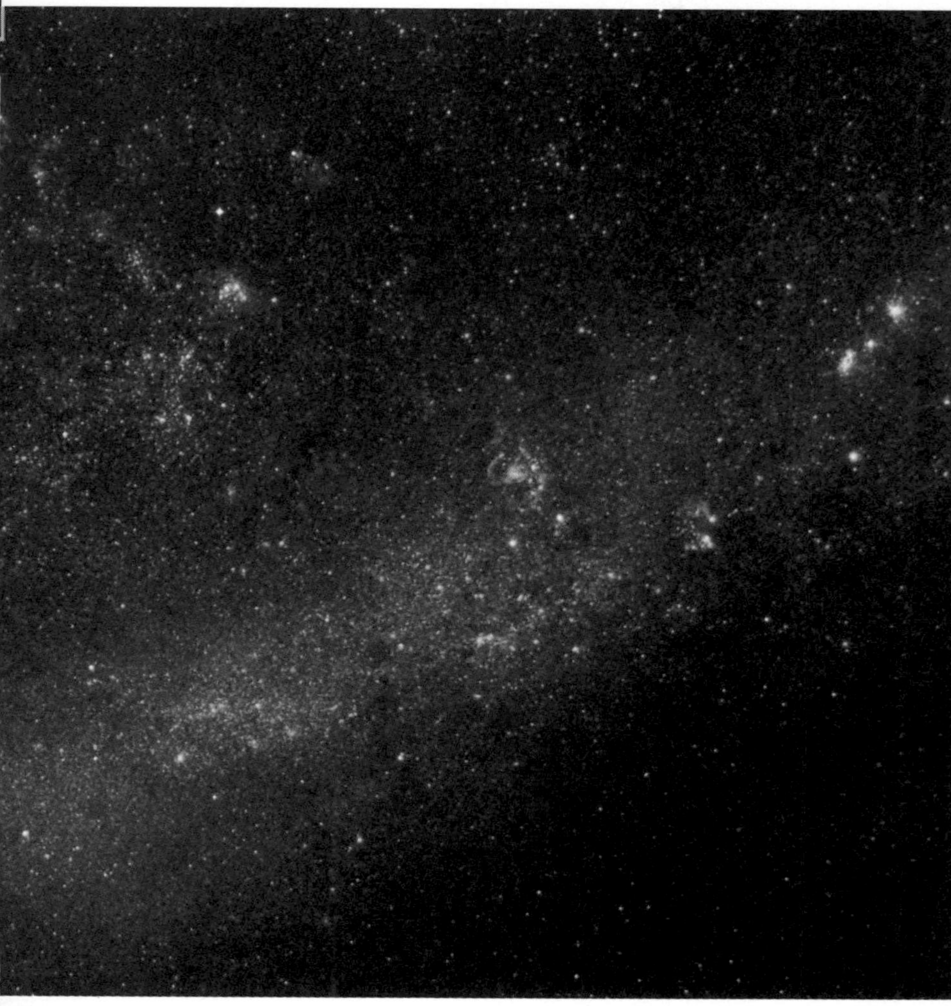

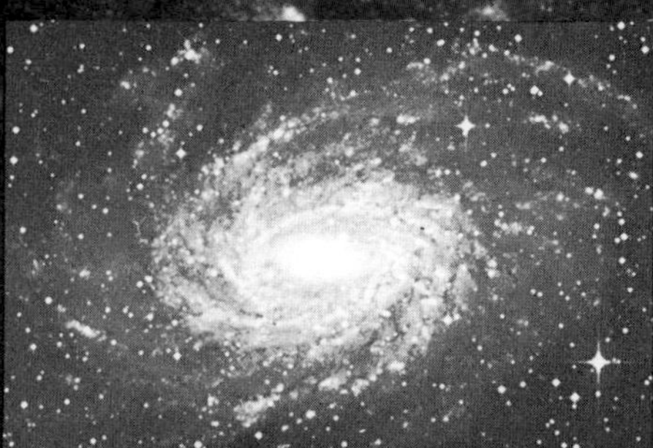

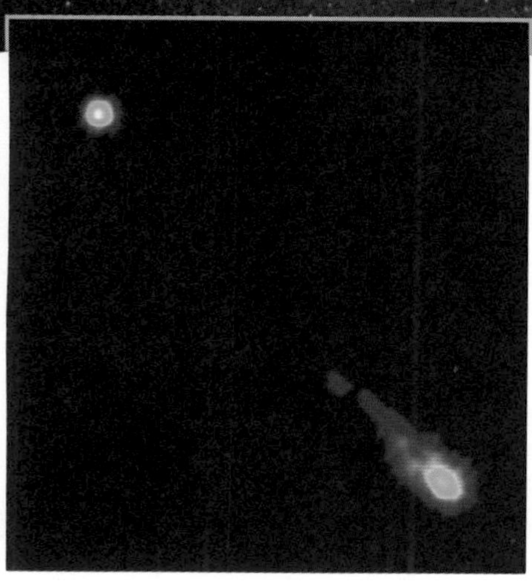

ORIGINS OF THE UNIVERSE

According to some astronomers our universe may have begun some ten or twenty thousand million years ago in an event astronomers have called the big bang. Not only might all the matter and energy we now see in the universe have been created then but also the fabric of space and time itself.

The conditions in the universe shortly after the big bang were far removed from those prevalent today. Temperatures were so high that all matter and energy were reduced to their constituent common particles. From the first instant, the universe began expanding with an expansion of space itself. This resulted in the universe becoming larger and cooler.

Recent progress in physics has advanced our understanding of this unique event. Every event must have a cause, but such concepts do not apply when one considers the particles that make up atoms. Scientists can now envisage a situation where matter is created out of nothing, with dimensions of space and time in which to exist. This is because events happening without a cause are acceptable to quantum physics.

As the universe expanded it cooled until matter and radiation could no longer interact so freely with each other. From that time, the recombination era, matter began to cool and form lumps that were the forerunners of primitive galaxies. Pulled in by their own force of gravity these lumps grew smaller and began to spin faster. In so doing they flattened out into the rough disc shapes that became giant rotating wheels of matter. Within these galaxies smaller clouds were also experiencing gravitational collapse, and these eventually formed clusters of hot young stars.

STRUCTURE OF THE UNIVERSE

When astronomers look at the universe they see a hierarchy of structures. On the largest scale are clusters of galaxies and perhaps clusters of clusters. Our own group of galaxies, the Local Group, is an insignificant collection of two large galaxies with a few minor ones. In turn our Local Group is part of the Virgo supercluster containing tens of thousands of galaxies.

We inhabit a universe of galaxies, numbering perhaps a hundred billion. We see normal spiral galaxies at all angles of inclination; barred spirals with gas, dust and stars connecting spiral arms at opposite ends of the galaxy; and elliptical galaxies with no obvious structure. Such galaxies may grow through mergers with other galaxies. All types of galaxies orbit each other and are sometimes distorted by the gravitational pull of their companion, producing streams of stars that sometimes bridge the space between galaxies.

Because the evolution of galaxies takes place over hundreds of millions of years we have to determine how they change by studying many galaxies each at a different stage of evolution. With the advance of large computers, galaxy evolution and even the development of clusters of galaxies can be simulated. These computers make possible the simulation of the collective motions of thousands of points, each representing a star under the gravitational influence of all the other points. It is possible to simulate the apparent collision of two galaxies. Since galaxies are mostly empty space, stars will seldom actually collide: in fact, the galaxies will tend to pass through one another without contact, but nevertheless the form of the galaxies can be altered. For instance, when a small galaxy runs into a large one face on, the result is a temporary ring galaxy, a rare and beautiful sight.

Each galaxy is composed of thousands of millions of stars most of which occur in multiple systems, particularly pairs. In the great dark between the stars there are vast clouds of gas and dust. Some of this makes new stars. In these clouds molecules of astonishing complexity have been found, some so complex as to be classified as organic, so the abundance of these molecules, suggests that the basis of life may be universal and not restricted to the Earth.

QUASARS

Until the 1950s astronomers had gleaned all they knew about the universe from studies with optical telescopes. Their achievements included the measurements of the distances of the stars, the nature of stars and their life cycles, the broad features of galaxies, and the observation that the universe was expanding. The large radio receiving dishes such as the one at Jodrell Bank were also built for this purpose. Their wide collecting areas were able to collect the weak radio signals from objects almost on the other side of the universe. It required several years to develop the precise methods needed to pinpoint these objects on the sky and look for their optical counterparts. These coun-

terparts were obviously at large distances yet they appeared small and starlike, and therefore were called quasi-stellar objects or quasars. In quasars the energy of thousands of normal galaxies is concentrated in a region of space not much larger than our own solar system. We see such objects not as they are now but as they were in the distant past. This is because of lookback time. As light travels at a finite speed it takes time to traverse the enormous distances of space. Hence the light we receive from a distant object set off on its journey some time in the past. The effect of lookback time is severe when we consider the distant quasars. We are seeing light that was sent off when the universe was only a tenth of its present age and size. By looking deeper and deeper into space astronomers can look further back in time and are consequently able to determine what the universe was like during the period of its youth and how it has since developed.

Quasars appear to be a phenomenon of the early universe. We believe they are points of violent activity occurring near supermassive black holes at the centres of galaxies. It may be that most, if not all, galaxies that are well behaved today have at their core a dormant black hole. This idea is confirmed when deep photograph images are taken of some quasars. Almost swamped by the brilliance of the central object is a faint fuzzy halo of ordinary stars.

Above Our nearest galaxy, the Large Magellanic Cloud, because of its proximity, is the most extended object visible in the sky apart from the Milky Way.

Top left Part of the Virgo cluster of galaxies which contains the Local Group in which our galaxy resides.

Upper left The Fornax 1 group of galaxies is thought to contain the barred spiral NGC 1365 lower right. Fornax 1 is centred upon the elliptical galaxy NGC 1399.

Lower left NGC 6744 in the constellation Pavo, is a particularly bright barred spiral galaxy similar to our own, containing about 200 million stars like the Sun.

Bottom left In 1963 observations from Cambridge, England of radio source 3C 273 led to the discovery of the first of the quasars.

BLACK HOLE

As galactic material is drawn from a companion star towards the black hole by gravity it becomes very hot and gives off vast amounts of radiation. Material circulates around the black hole like a whirlpool forming a disc of accretion. Once this material is drawn beyond the horizon it cannot escape.

Whether the black hole was there first and the galaxy of stars formed around it or whether the black hole is the result of stellar collisions at the galaxy's heart, we do not know. We suspect the matter that fuels the black hole will only be available during the galaxy's youth and eventually the supply will run out and the black hole will decline.

horizon

accretion disc

flow of material from star to Black Hole

companion star

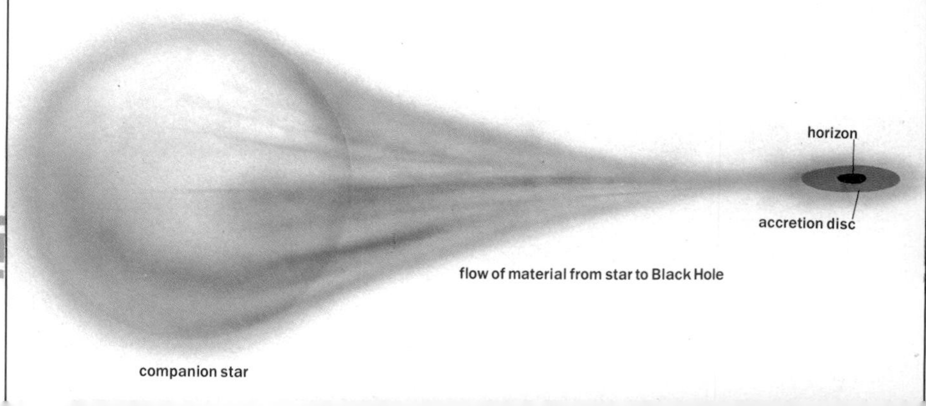

STARS

Stars are born out of vast clouds of gas and dust in space. This process is happening in numerous stellar nurseries throughout the galaxy. Fragments of the gas cloud break off and start to collapse under their own gravity. In becoming smaller the clouds grow hotter and become a protostar. Protostars shine because of energy liberated by the collapse. Eventually the temperature at the centre attains a critical level and nuclear reactions commence. The star is then born. In a million years the collapse is halted when the weight of the outer layer is supported by the high temperatures and pressure generated by nuclear reactions.

In the clouds of gas and dust stars are formed in large numbers. Such stellar birthsites appear dark when seen from the outside but from the inside they are brilliantly illuminated by newborn stars. When a large number have formed their combined effect is to disperse the remaining material in the gas cloud. The star cluster thus formed will spread out into space. Because of this, the relations of our Sun, formed from the same gas cloud, could well be on the other side of the galaxy.

Stars come in many different forms. The brightest stellar luminaries in our galaxy are some ten million times brighter than our Sun. These objects are rare; far more common are stars feebler than our Sun. It would take an entire galaxy of them to equal in brilliance the brightest stars. It is a difficult task to determine how faint are the faintest stars, but they probably only have one or two per cent of the mass of our Sun and radiate about a hundred thousandth of its luminosity.

A star's consumption of its nuclear fuel, and therefore its lifetime, depends upon its mass. The brightest stars use their fuel in about a million years. However, stars like our Sun make their supply last much longer, about ten thousand million years. Before our Sun runs out of nuclear fuel completely it will undergo dramatic changes. It will swell up and change from a yellow dwarf star into a red giant. As it swells it will increase in brightness. At this stage the nuclear reactions sustaining the Sun will be the conversion of helium into heavier elements. But there are only a limited number of nuclear reactions that can produce starlight and the Sun will run through a range of instabilities. It may blow off its atmosphere into space in one or more concentric rings of gas. Eventually, when exhausted of nuclear fuel, it will collapse to become a white dwarf, a cosmic cinder the size of the Earth and made of nuclear ash weighing a ton per teaspoonful. It will then cool and fade until our universe dies.

The more massive stars evolve faster and have a different fate in store. If they are more massive than about 1.4 solar masses they are not stable at the white dwarf stage and will collapse into a tighter configuration called a neutron star. With this star most of

the material is compressed into a few cubic kilometres. A neutron star cannot have a mass greater than about four times the mass of our Sun. This is because it cannot support itself against its own gravity and will collapse. There is not a state of matter able to resist this collapse and the star will become a black hole.

Some of the more massive stars end their lives more dramatically in a supernova explosion. During such an explosion one star can outshine a galaxy of its companions for many days. It is believed that the core of a giant star suddenly collapses to a neutron star, leaving the rest of the star to fall inwards to become explosively heated and ejected into space.

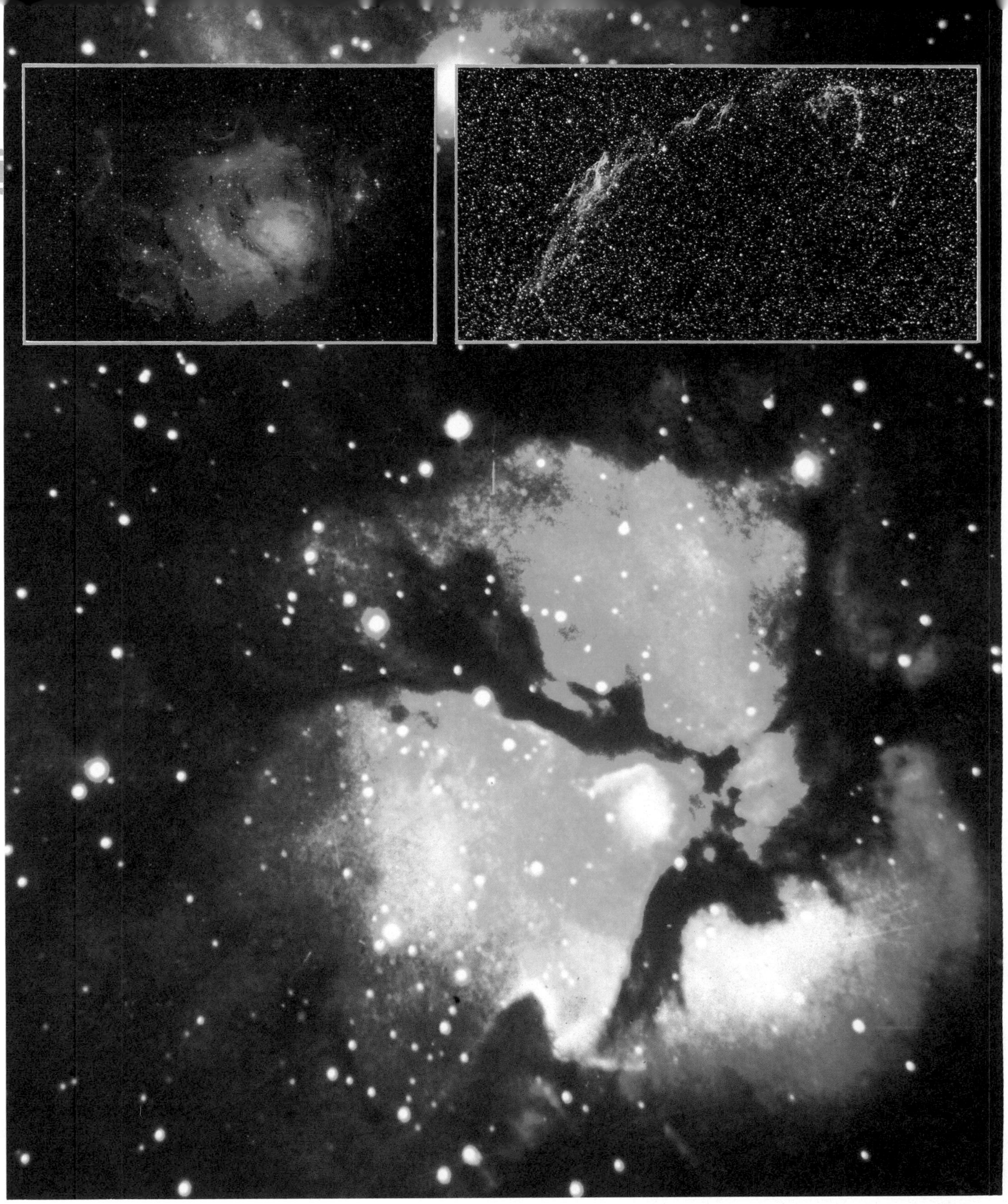

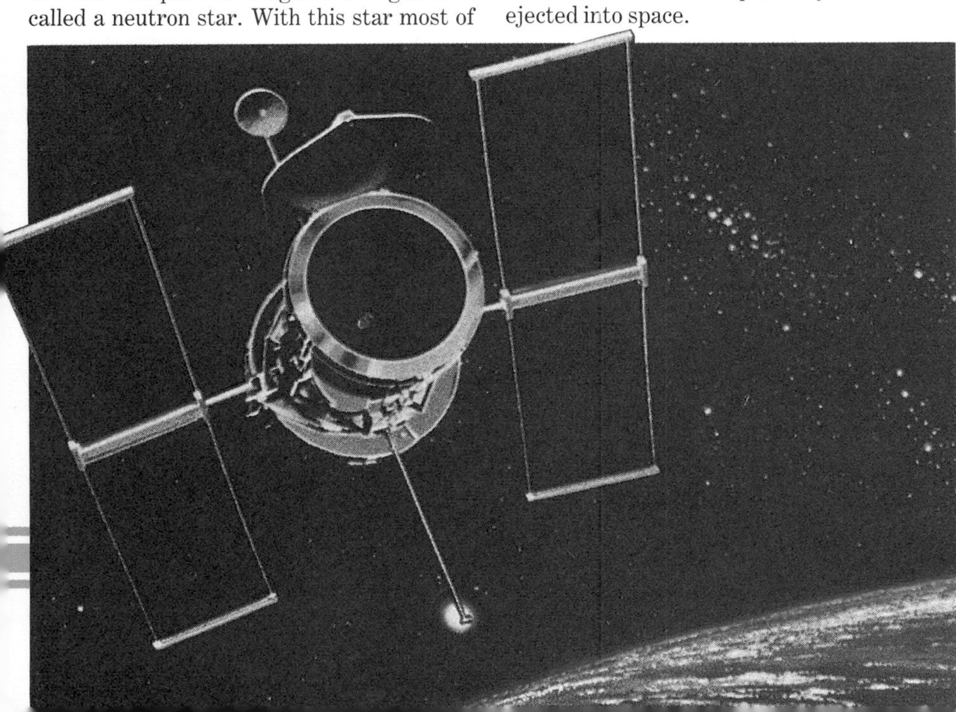

Above The Trifid Nebula is an example of a vast cloud of gas and dust. Globules of cold gas develop and condense and form new stars.
Below The Space Telescope, when launched, will help astronomers to study objects fifty times fainter and seven times further away than observed from Earth.

THE FUTURE OF THE UNIVERSE

Galaxies and clusters of galaxies recede from each other as they take part in the expansion of the universe after the big bang. Will this expansion continue forever, or could the universe slow down, the expansion halt and start collapsing, reinacting the events of the early universe in reverse? The universe will either expand or collapse, but if it does continue to expand, all its matter will end up spread thinly throughout space. All sources of energy will eventually be played out: the universe will become featureless and totally and completely inactive. This is the so called heat death.

For any form of life the alternative is just as depressing. The expansion of the universe may one day slow down and halt. Then instead of receding the galaxies will start to approach each other. When closely packed, galaxies will coalesce and stars collide. All matter will become gaseous and the temperature will be ever increasing as the space contracts. Becoming hotter and denser unimaginable temperatures may be attained. Eventually space, time and all of the matter in the universe will be compressed to a

Top left The Lagoon Nebula in the constellation of Sagittarius consists of a cloud of hydrogen and dust. The brightest region includes the new star Herschel 36, less than 10 000 years old.
Top right The Veil Nebula in Cygnus is the remnant of a supernova. The dust will eventually break up into small cold clouds.

single point. Events will have come full circle because it was from such a point that the big bang was thought to have originated in the first place.

Some scientists, looking for a certain symmetry, have postulated that out of this compression will emerge a new big bang and that the universe is cyclic with expansion and compression followed by expansion again. We may one day be able to know the fate of the universe, although we will never know if there are other cycles.

Such questions as the fate of the universe and the nature of the ninety per cent of the universe we cannot see could be answered by the space telescope. When this is placed in orbit by the American space shuttle it will remain operational until at least the end of the century. It will be a large telescope in orbit high above the Earth's turbulent and murky atmosphere and will obtain clearer and deeper pictures than ever before. It will be able to peer some seven times further into space than any instrument before it. Its prospects for finding the unexpected and solving some of the mysteries of the universe are immense.

SOLAR SYSTEM

Current theory suggests that the solar system condensed from a primitive solar nebula of gas and dust during an interval of a few tens of millions of years about 4600 million years ago. Gravity caused this nebula to contract, drawing most of its mass into the proto-sun at the centre. Turbulence gave the original cloud a tendency to rotate, and as it contracted conservation of angular momentum caused the proto-sun to spin faster and faster, forcing the remainder of the cloud into a disc shape.

The centre of the cloud heated up as it compressed, and so eventually became hot enough for the Sun to begin to shine, through nuclear energy released at its core. Meanwhile the surrounding disc cooled, allowing material to condense into solid form. Particles stuck together as they col-

lided and progressively larger bodies were built up. These swept up most of the debris to form the planets, which orbit the Sun close to the plane of the now vanished disc. The first materials to condense were the least volatile refractory compounds such as oxides of iron, nickel and aluminium. Decreasing temperature allowed rocky silicate material to appear followed by more volatile compounds such as water and methane. Thus composition of the planets progressed from less refractory cores to more volatile outer layers.

The planets nearest to the Sun are dense with metallic cores mantled by rocky silicate materials; planets further from the Sun accreted and retained large volumes of volatiles and are thus much more massive. They may have cores of rock and ice, surround-

ed by solid or liquid hydrogen enveloped in thick gassy atmospheres. These Gas Giants are accompanied by captured rocky and icy satellites which are mostly too small to have accreted and held atmospheres.

The subsequent evolution of the solar system was dominated by continuing chemical segregation within the planets and surface bombardment by waning numbers of smaller bodies. This bombardment was over by 3–4000 million years ago, although minor impacts still occur. Traces of these events remain on the surfaces of those bodies which have insufficient internal heat to drive any kind of resurfacing process.

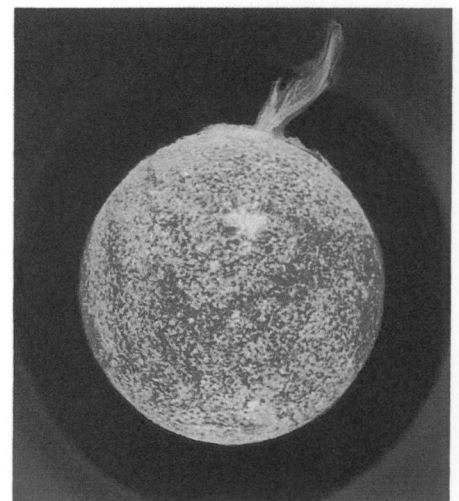

Right An ultra-violet image of the Sun from Skylab in 1973. A spectacular eruption of gas rises for half a million kilometres, channelled by the Sun's magnetic field.

	SUN	MERCURY	VENUS	EARTH	(MOON)	MARS	JUPITER	SATURN	URANUS	NEPTUNE	PLUTO
Mass (Earth=1)	333 400	0.055	0.815	1 (5.97 10²⁴kg)	0.012	0.107	317.8	95.2	14.5	17.2	0.003
Volume (Earth=1)	1 306 000	0.06	0.88	1	0.020	0.150	1 319	751	62	54	0.015?
Density (water=1)	1.41	5.43	5.24	5.52	3.34	3.94	1.33	0.70	1.30	1.76	1.1?
Equatorial diameter (km)	1 392 000	4878	12 104	12 756	3476	6 787	142 796	120 000	50 800	48 600	3 000?
Polar flattening	0	0	0	0.003	0	0.005	0.065	0.108	0.030	0.026	?
'Surface' gravity (Earth=1)	27.9	0.37	0.88	1	0.16	0.38	2.64	1.15	1.17	1.18	0.45?
Number of satellites greater than 100 km diameter	—	0	0	1	—	0	4	10	6	6	1
Total number of satellites	—	0	0	1	—	2	16	17	c.15	8	1
Period of rotation (in Earth days)	25.38	58.65	−243 (retrograde)	23hr 56m 4 secs	27.32	1.03	0.414	0.438	−0.72 (retrograde)	0.67	−6.39 (retrograde)
Length of year (in Earth days and years)	—	88 days	224.7 days	365.26 days	—	687 days	11.86 years	29.46 years	84.01 years	164.8 years	247.7 years
Distance from Sun (max) Mkm	—	69.7	109	152.1	—	249.1	815.7	1 507	3 004	4 537	7 375
Distance from Sun (min) Mkm	—	45.9	107.4	147.1	—	206.7	740.9	1 347	2 735	4 456	4 425
Distance from Sun (mean) Mkm	—	57.9	108.2	149.6	—	227.9	778.3	1 427	2 870	4 497	5 900
Mean orbital velocity km/sec	—	47.9	35.0	29.8	—	24.1	13.1	9.6	6.8	5.4	4.7
Inclination of axis	7.25°	0.0°	177.3°	23.45°	6.68°	25.19°	3.12°	26.73°	97.86°	29.56°	118°?
Inclination of orbit to ecliptic	—	7.01°	3.39°	0°	5.15°	1.85°	1.30°	2.48°	0.77°	1.77°	17.13°

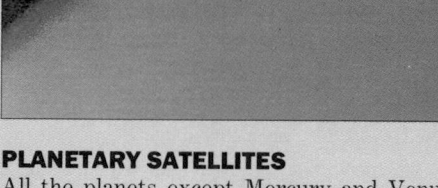

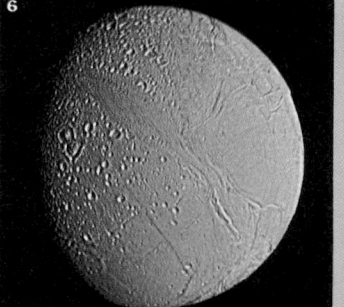

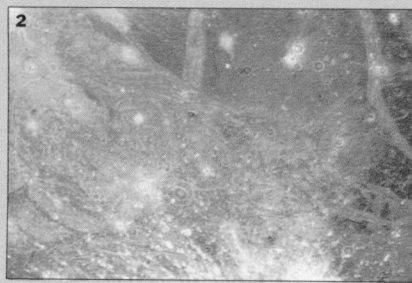

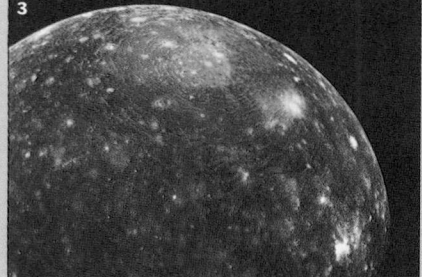

PLANETARY SATELLITES

All the planets except Mercury and Venus have other bodies in orbit around them. The Earth–Moon system can be described as a double planet, whereas Mars' two minute companions appear to be captured asteroids. The satellite systems of the Gas Giants present a quite different story: there are smaller moons (100km across or less) in the form of roughly spherical icy bodies, less regular rocky bodies (probably captured asteroids), and larger moons around 1000km in diameter which are layered bodies with rocky cores and usually icy crusts.

A few of the more interesting bodies are described here; the tables give the full list.

1 Deimos is the smaller, outer irregular shaped moon of Mars. The ancient surface is covered by about 10 metres of loose rock or regolith.
2 The dark background material of **Ganymede** shows a high density of impact craters, and is therefore very old. The lighter network of grooves may have been formed by movements of the ice crust.
3 Callisto is among the most cratered bodies in the Solar System with a surface at least 4 billion years old.
4 This Voyager 1 image of **Io** shows a plume of vaporized sulphur (upper left) rising for 300km above the first known active extraterrestrial volcano, Pele.
5 Titan is Saturn's largest moon and holds an extremely dense atmosphere of nitrogen and methane above a surface of rock and ice.

6 Enceladus has experienced recent geological activity which has modified the cratered landscape.
7 The surface of **Mimas** is heavily cratered and shows no sign of geological activity. This image shows craters as little as 2km across.
8 This Voyager 2 mosaic of **Miranda** shows varied geological areas from compressional ridges in curvilinear patterns to extensional (pulled apart) faults.
9 Much of **Ariel**'s surface is densely pitted with craters 5 to 10 kms across, and criss-crossed by valleys and fault scarps.
10 Titania displays many impact scars and also evidence of geological activity.
11 On **Oberon**'s icy surface several large impact craters are clearly visible surrounded by bright rays similar to those on Callisto.

Left Io and Europa are clearly visible as they transit the face of Jupiter. The Great Red Spot of Jupiter has been observed for 300 years but the white ovals nearby did not appear until the 1930s. They are all centres of high pressure in this turbulent atmosphere.

Lower left The rings of Saturn lie in the equatorial plane and consist of countless small ice-covered particles. Tethys and Dione orbit Saturn at less than 400000km.

Below These 2 photographs of Uranus (true colour left, false colour right), were taken from 9.1 million km by Voyager 2. The planet's atmosphere is deep, cold and remarkably clear, but the false colours enhance the polar region. Here, the suggestion is that a brownish haze of smog is concentrated over the pole.

GAS GIANTS

Jupiter has at least 16 satellites and a debris ring system about 50000km above the cloud tops. The outer atmosphere is all that can be directly observed of the planet itself. It is mostly hydrogen with lesser amounts of helium, ammonia, methane, water vapour and more exotic compounds. Jupiter's rapid rotation causes it to be flattened towards the poles. This rotation and heat flow convection from the interior cause complex weather patterns. Liquid droplets and solid particles of ammonia and other compounds, cause the clouds to be opaque. Where cloud systems interact vast storms can occur in the form of vortices. Some last only a few days, but the most persistent of these, the Great Red Spot, has been present since it was first detected in the 17th century.

The internal structure of Jupiter can be deduced. At about 1000km below the cloud tops hydrogen and helium may liquify to form a 10000km layer. Convection currents in this region generate the planet's intense magnetic field. The denser core, about 4% of the planet's mass, is mostly of rock and ice, with a little iron near the centre.

Saturn is the least dense of the planets. It has a stormy atmosphere situated above a 30000km layer of liquid molecular hydrogen and helium distorted by the planet's rotation. Below is a thin shell of liquid metallic hydrogen wrapped around a rock and ice core containing 25% of Saturn's mass.

The rings of Saturn are thought to be mostly made of icy debris, from 10m down to a few microns in size, derived from the break-up of a satellite. The rings are less than 1km thick but extend from above the cloud layer out to about 170000km from the centre. The rings are divided by gaps swept clear by complex gravitational interaction.

Uranus was little known until Voyager 2 flew by it in 1986. It has a cloud cover more featureless than either Jupiter or Saturn and

consists mostly of hydrogen. Unique among the planets, its axis is tilted almost into the plane of its orbit, with the north pole presently facing towards the Sun. Voyager 2 provided detailed images of the planet's eleven rings of icy debris.

Neptune provided a number of surprises when Voyager 2 flew by, on 24 August 1989, passing within 5,000km of the planet's north pole. The planet rotates in 16 hours 3 minutes, one hour faster than was believed to be the rate. Six new satellites were discovered, all mis-shapen and meteor-marked, little changed since soon after their

formation. Neptune has four rings varying from 17km to 2,500km thick. The magnetic axis is inclined 50° to the axis of rotation and displaced 10,000km from the centre.

Neptune's atmosphere, a mixture of hydrogen, helium and methane, exhibits great turbulence. There is a great dark spot at 22°S latitude and a smaller dark spot nearer the south pole. Triton was found to be smaller than previous estimates.

Pluto, usually the most distant planet, is temporarily within the orbit of Neptune. The atmosphere is thought to be composed mostly of methane.

EARTHLIKE PLANETS

Mercury is the nearest planet to the Sun, spinning three times for every two orbits around the Sun. It has an exceptionally large metallic core which may be responsible for Mercury's weak magnetic field. Mercury is an airless world subject to vast extremes of temperature, from –180°C at night to 430°C near the middle of its long day.

The Mariner 10 space probe during the mid-1970s, revealed the surface to be dominated by heavily cratered areas dating from the early meteorite bombardment of the inner solar system. As the bombardment was tailing off Mercury's radius contracted by 1–2km, forming compressional features (lobate scarps) which may have been caused by a change in the core from liquid to solid.

Venus has a dense atmosphere of 96% carbon dioxide mixed with nitrogen, oxygen, sulphur dioxide and water vapour which hides the surface under permanent cloud and maintains a mean surface temperature of about 480°C. The planet's slow rotation means that weather systems are driven mostly by solar heat, rather than by spin. As a result, beyond 10 kilometres above the surface, westerly winds of up to 100 m/sec cause a bulk rotation of the atmosphere in about four days.

Much of the globe has been mapped by radar altimetry revealing a range in height of 13.7km with no clear distinction between high (continents) and low areas (oceans). Some highs may be large, still active shield volcanoes.

The surface has been seen directly only by two Russian probes which landed. A Russian probe in orbit used an imaging radar which showed features interpreted as impact craters, fault systems and fold belts.

Mars has a thin atmosphere of about 95% carbon dioxide mixed with other minor constituents. The polar caps consist of semi-permanent water ice and ephemeral solid carbon dioxide. Day and night surface temperatures vary between about –120°C and –20°C. Mars has two small satellites, each less than about 25km across, probably captured asteroids.

A variety of landscapes has been identified, including ancient heavily cratered terrains and plains which may consist of lava flows. There are several large volcanoes; the best preserved of these, Olympus Mons, rises 23km above the surface and is 500km across at its base.

Mars shows evidence of erosional processes. The effect of winds is seen in the degraded form of the older craters and the deposition of sand dunes. Dust storms frequently obscure the surface. The large channels, such as the 5000km long Valles Marineris, may have been cut by flowing water. Water is abundant in the polar caps and may be widespread held in as permafrost below the surface.

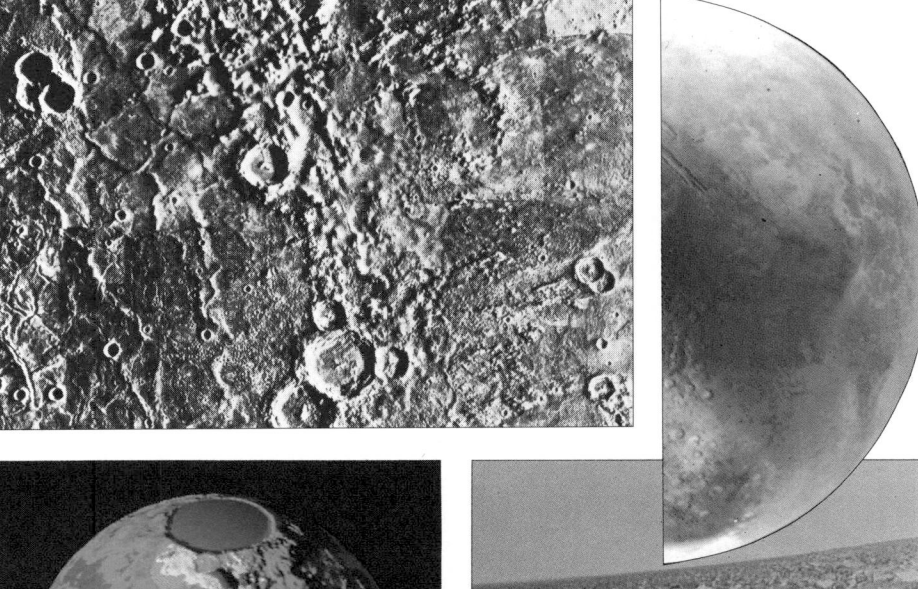

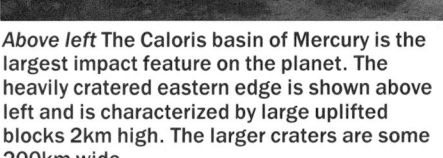

Above left The Caloris basin of Mercury is the largest impact feature on the planet. The heavily cratered eastern edge is shown above left and is characterized by large uplifted blocks 2km high. The larger craters are some 200km wide.

Left The two hemispheres of Venus constructed from radar altimetry data from Pioneer. High areas are yellow and green and low areas blue in these false colour images. There is no data for the polar regions.

Above right The relatively recent plains of Mars appear bright; the dark area is ancient cratered terrain. The long straight canyon Valles Marineris, 5000km long, is clearly visible.

Above This Viking Lander 2 photograph shows a thin coating of ice that has accumulated at the base of rocks on the Martian soil. The ice is probably less than a few microns in thickness and is suspected to be water ice.

	radius of orbit (1000km)	orbital period (days)	diameter (km)
EARTH			
Moon	384.40	27.322	3 476
MARS			
Phobos	9.38	0.319	(14x11x9)†
Deimos	23.46	1.262	(8x6x6)
JUPITER			
Metis	128.0	0.295	40
Adastrea	129.0	0.297	24
Amalthea	181.0	0.498	(135x83x75)
Thebe	221.0	0.675	80
Io	421.8	1.769	3 630
Europa	671.1	3.551	3 138
Ganymede	1 070.4	7.155	5 262
Callisto	1 882.6	16.689	4 800
Leda	11 094.0	239	16
Himalia	11 480.0	250.566	186
Lysithea	11 720.4	259.219	36
Elara	11 736.9	259.653	76
Ananke	21 200.0	631R	30
Carme	22 600.0	692R	40
Pasiphae	23 500.0	735R	50
Sinope	23 700.0	758R	36
SATURN			
Atlas	137.7	0.602	(20x10)
1980 S 27	139.4	0.613	(70x50x40)
1980 S 26	141.7	0.629	(55x45x35)
Epimetheus	151.4	0.694	(70x60x50)
Janus	151.5	0.695	(110x100x80)
Mimas	185.5	0.942	392
Enceladus	238.0	1.370	500
Tethys	294.7	1.888	1 060
Telesto	294.7	1.888	(17x14x13)
Calypso	294.7	1.888	(17x11x11)
1980 S 6	377.4	2.737	(18x16x15)
Dione	377.4	2.737	1 120
Rhea	527.0	4.518	1 530
Titan	1 221.8	15.945	5 150
Hyperion	1 481.1	21.277	(205x130x110)
Iapetus	3 561.3	79.330	1 460
Phoebe	12 592.0	550.480R	220
URANUS			
Miranda	129.9	1.414	484
Ariel	190.8	2.520	1160
Umbriel	265.8	4.144	1190
Titania	436.1	8.706	1610
Oberon	583.1	13.463	1550
10 further satellites discovered 1986			
NEPTUNE			
Triton	355.3	5.877R	3 800
Nereid	5 511.0	360.200	300
6 further satellites discovered 1989			
PLUTO			
Charon	19.7	6.387	1 000

† Many satellites are ellipsoidal in shape, in which case the 3 major axes are quoted. R = Retrograde

EARTH'S MOON

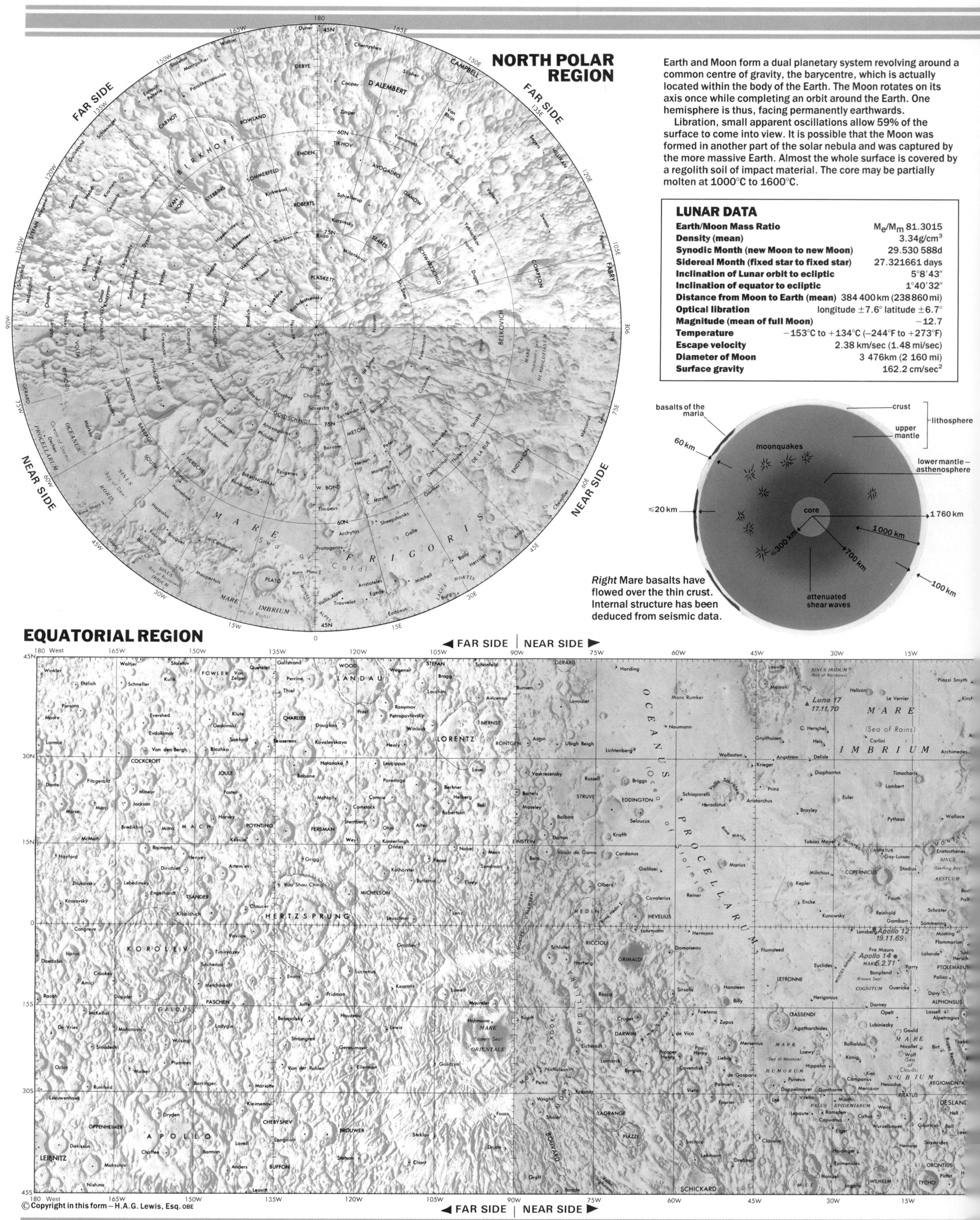

NORTH POLAR REGION

Earth and Moon form a dual planetary system revolving around a common centre of gravity, the barycentre, which is actually located within the body of the Earth. The Moon rotates on its axis once while completing an orbit around the Earth. One hemisphere is thus, facing permanently earthwards.

Libration, small apparent oscillations allow 59% of the surface to come into view. It is possible that the Moon was formed in another part of the solar nebula and was captured by the more massive Earth. Almost the whole surface is covered by a regolith soil of impact material. The core may be partially molten at 1000°C to 1600°C.

LUNAR DATA

Earth/Moon Mass Ratio	M_e/M_m 81.3015
Density (mean)	3.34g/cm³
Synodic Month (new Moon to new Moon)	29.530 588d
Sidereal Month (fixed star to fixed star)	27.321661 days
Inclination of Lunar orbit to ecliptic	5°8′43″
Inclination of equator to ecliptic	1°40′32″
Distance from Moon to Earth (mean)	384 400 km (238 860 mi)
Optical libration	longitude ±7.6° latitude ±6.7°
Magnitude (mean of full Moon)	−12.7
Temperature	−153°C to +134°C (−244°F to +273°F)
Escape velocity	2.38 km/sec (1.48 mi/sec)
Diameter of Moon	3 476km (2 160 mi)
Surface gravity	162.2 cm/sec²

Right Mare basalts have flowed over the thin crust. Internal structure has been deduced from seismic data.

EQUATORIAL REGION

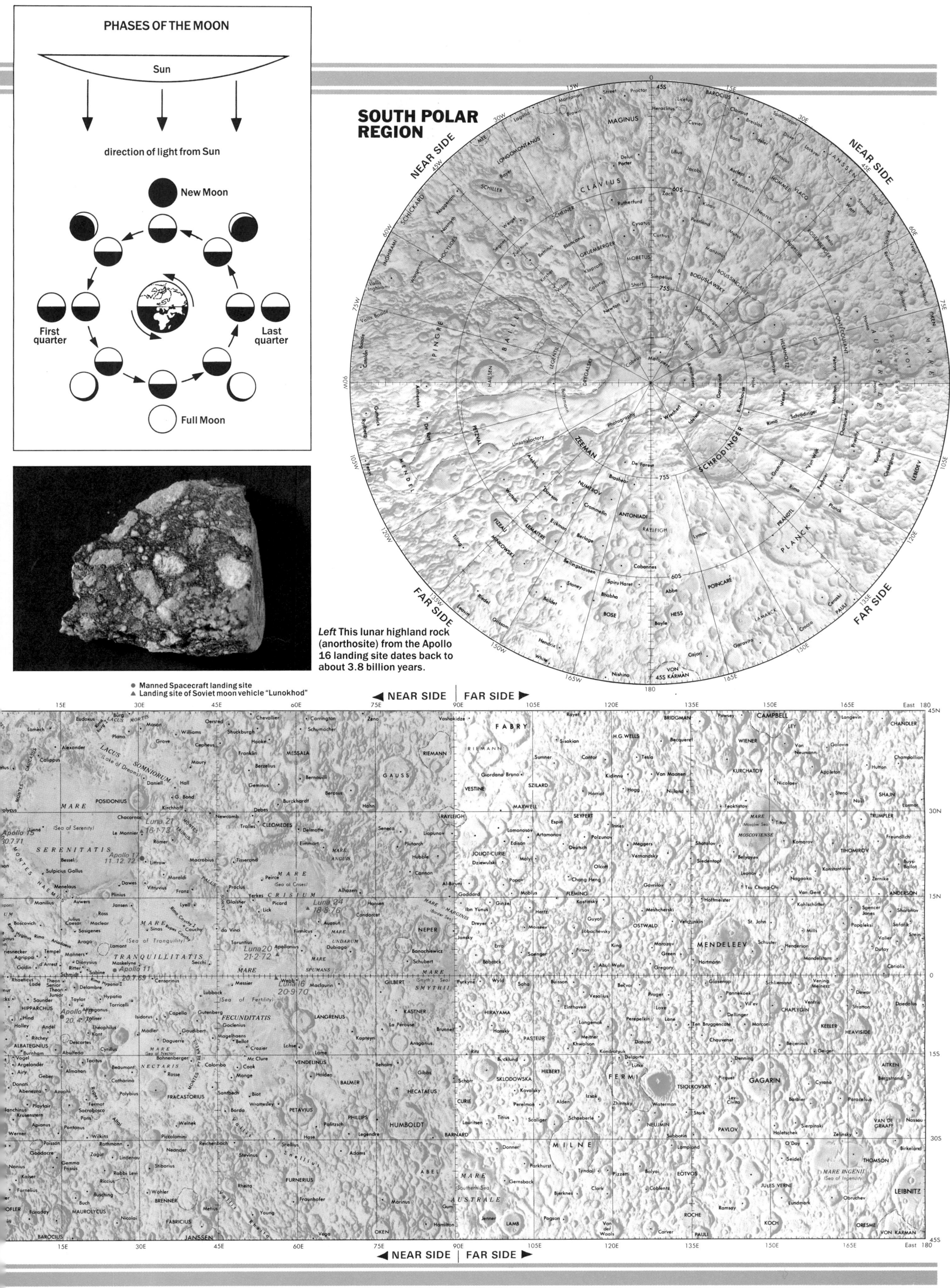

PHASES OF THE MOON

Sun

direction of light from Sun

New Moon

First quarter

Last quarter

Full Moon

SOUTH POLAR REGION

Left This lunar highland rock (anorthosite) from the Apollo 16 landing site dates back to about 3.8 billion years.

● Manned Spacecraft landing site
▲ Landing site of Soviet moon vehicle "Lunokhod"

◀ NEAR SIDE │ FAR SIDE ▶

◀ NEAR SIDE │ FAR SIDE ▶

SPACE FLIGHT

The space age began on 4 October 1957 when the U.S.S.R. launched the first artificial satellite, Sputnik 1. The first American satellite, Explorer 1, followed within four months and discovered the Van Allen radiation belts. Luna 3 (1959) acquired the first pictures of the far side of the moon. Yuri Gagarin became the first man in space (1961). At this time the U.S.A. was developing specialist satellites such as TIROS 1 (the first weather satellite), Transit 1B (the first navigation satellite), and Echo 1 (the first communications satellite), all launched in 1960. During the 1960s and 70s the nearby planets began to be investigated by flybys, orbiting probes and hard (crash) or soft landings, the U.S.S.R. on Venus; the U.S.A. on Mars. On 20 July 1969 the first manned landing on the Moon was achieved (U.S. astronauts Armstrong, Aldrin and Collins, Apollo XI) while the lunar studies by the U.S.S.R. were made by unmanned spacecraft which returned small samples.

The American probe Pioneer 10, launched in 1972, was the first vehicle to traverse the asteroid belt. It transmitted pictures as it flew by Jupiter and continued on its way at a speed sufficient to make it the first spaceship to leave the solar system (1983). In 1977 the automatic space probes Voyager 1 and 2 were launched to explore Jupiter, Saturn, Uranus and Neptune detecting planetary atmospheres, ring systems, volcanic activity and new satellites. Voyager 2 after having explored Neptune in 1989 is now heading out of the solar system.

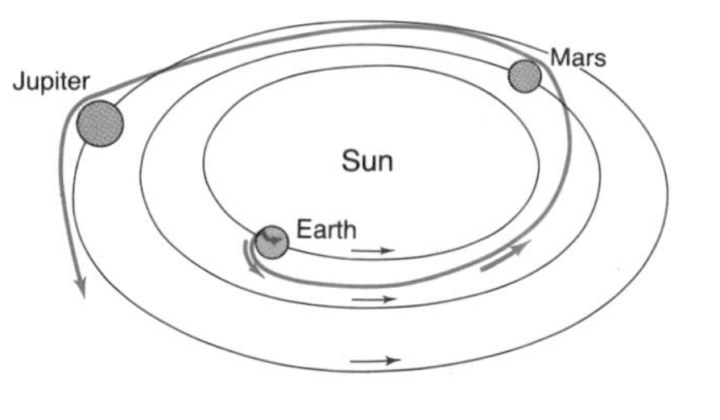

Above The gravitational slingshot effect may be used to swing a spacecraft past a major planet and speed it on its way to the next.

Right In April 1984 Space Shuttle Challenger successfully recaptured the Solar Maximum satellite for repair in the cargo bay, using the Remote Manipulation System Arm.

REMOTE SENSING

From orbit a camera or other imaging system is ideally placed to record and monitor large areas of the Earth on a regular basis. Photography is still useful in that it can provide a high resolution record, but it is restricted to visible and near infra-red wavelengths and requires return of the film to Earth. Images recorded in digital form are not restricted to the photographic region of the spectrum, can be transmitted to a ground receiving station while the satellite continues in orbit, and are in a form suitable for computerised image processing.

Digital images are recorded using electronic sensors. Usually the forward motion of the satellite is used to build up a picture line by line. Each line is recorded either by using a mirror vibrating at a right angle to the satellite's motion which reflects onto an individual sensor for each waveband, or by using large sensor arrays to record whole lines at a time (pushbroom systems). The data within each line is broken into a string of numbers, each representing the brightness of one spot (or pixel) on the ground. This digital data may be transmitted in real time or recorded on board to be transmitted later.

Right River and stream channels in Irian Jaya (Indonesia) revealed by a radar image taken from the Space Shuttle. This region of lowland forest and mangrove swamp is perennially cloud covered. The colours have been added artifically.

In order to cover most of the globe, remote sensing satellites are usually placed in polar orbits, highly inclined to the equator, passing over a wide latitude range. Most are put in Sun-synchronous orbit arranged so that the Earth rotates beneath them at a rate sufficient to keep the satellites overhead at approximately the same local time throughout their north–south passage. The orbit then takes them from south to north on the nightside of the Earth before beginning another north–south passage further west at the same local time.

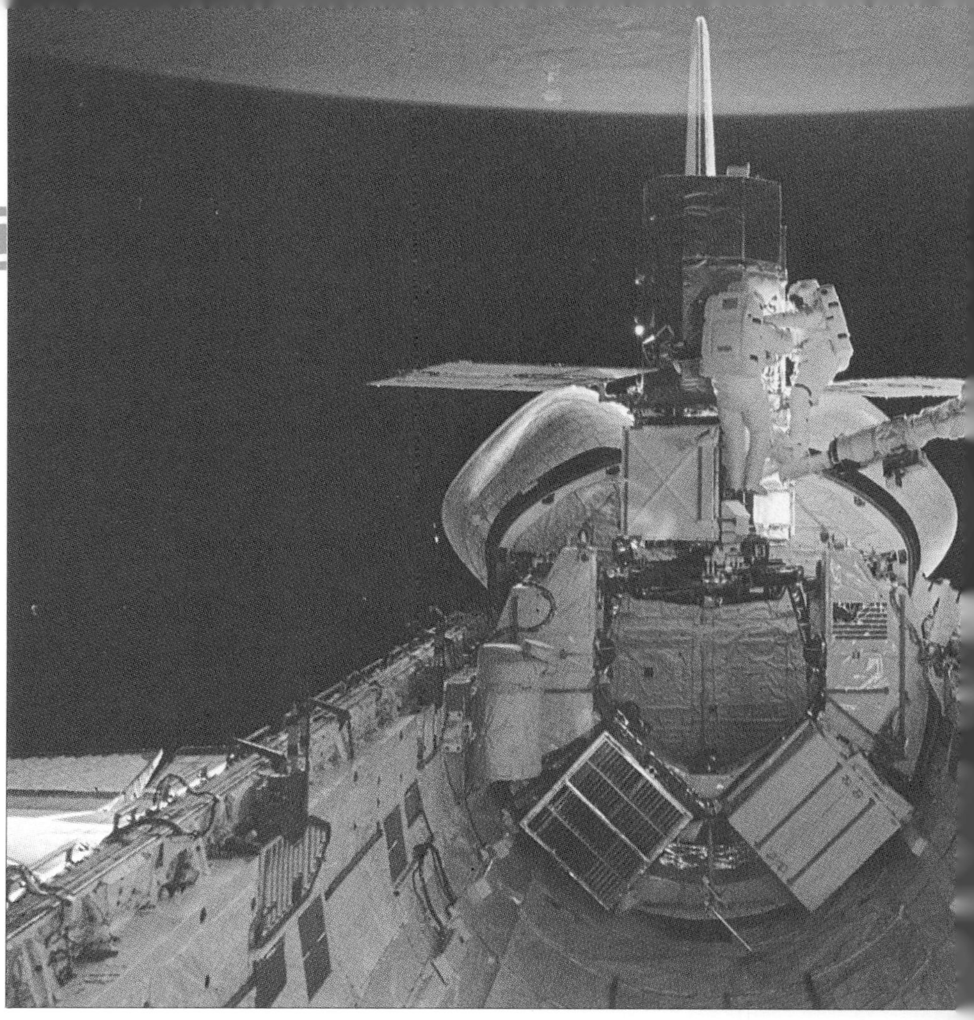

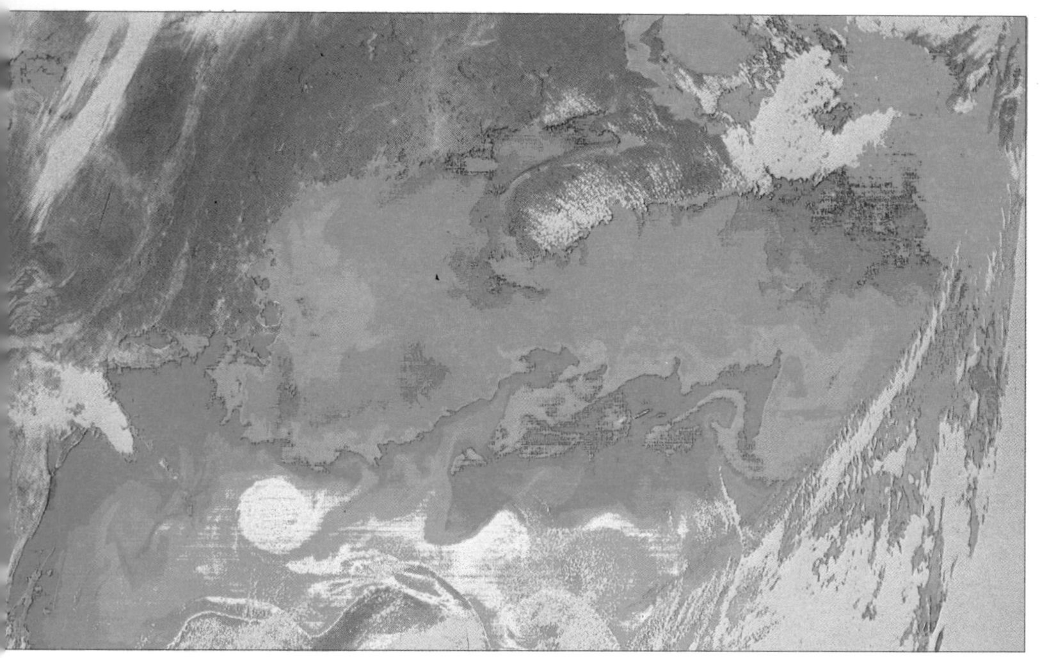

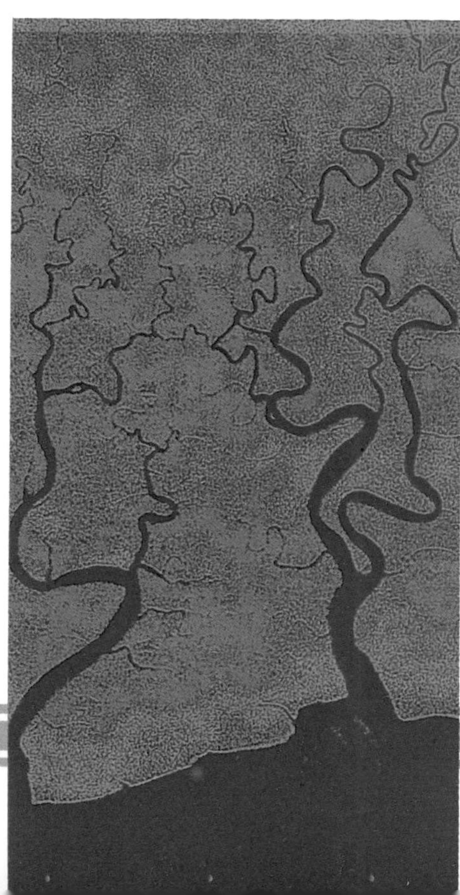

Landsat has provided by far the most widely used multi-spectral imagery. When first launched in 1972 Landsat was known as the Earth Resources Technology Satellite (ERTS). More will be said of Landsat later.

Seasat was the first oceanography satellite. Instrument failure ended its life after 100 days. It was a radar satellite equipped to measure wave height, wind-speed and surface roughness. Synthetic aperture radar provided high-quality images rather like a conventional photograph. Among other satellites dedicated to the oceans is the Nimbus-7 Coastal Zone Colour scanner.

Salyut 6 satellites of the U.S.S.R. operating from 1978 acquired photography from 1978 onwards in orbits at 260km and 340km. Film removal and replenishment was made by Soyuz and Progress spacecraft. A multi-spectral capability was included. Digital systems were introduced later.

The European Space Agency collaborated in Spacelab and a number of space applications but its main effort was devoted to the Ariane launcher and, for remote-sensing, SPOT (Système Probataire d'Observation de la Terre). The first SPOT imagery became available in March, 1986. SPOT has two identical imagers and either may be used to acquire multi-spectral data with 20m

WEATHER SATELLITES

In June 1979 the Nimbus-7 Coastal Zone Colour scanner produced this false-colour image (*left*) of ocean currents off the east coast of the United States. The scanner measures sea-surface temperatures using the infra-red channels. The warm Gulf Stream is orange, the warm circular eddy is shown in yellow, and the cold Labrador current east of Nova Scotia, is dark blue.

The TIROS (Television and Infra-red Observation Satellites) first launched in 1960 continue in highly advanced form today. They are placed in non-synchronous orbits to give repeat coverage of middle and lower latitudes, and their complex equipment measures sea-surface temperatures, identifies ice and snow, and acquires images in the visible parts of the spectrum by day and in the infra red after dark.

Other satellites, such as Meteosat, are in much higher geosynchronous orbits and provide effectively continuous coverage of almost complete hemispheres.

NAVIGATION SATELLITES

Navigation satellites came into being as a system used by Polaris submarines to ascertain their exact coordinates when at sea in any part of the world. By comparing the change in frequency of signals received from a satellite with the transmitted frequency the position of the submarine in relation to the satellite is obtained. The system was first applied in 1964 in the US Navy's Transit satellites which transmitted precise ephemeris data for military use and less accurate 'broadcast' data for general use.

There was an immediate non-military demand for such a means of ascertaining to a high order of accuracy the position of installations on land or oil rigs at sea. If a sufficient number of passes of a satellite can be observed a positional accuracy of 1m or so can be obtained. Navstar/Global Positioning System will be far more accurate when in operation in the 1990's. Navstar and GPS are synonymous. The titles distinguish the navigation uses from other general uses.

resolution or panchromatic with 10m resolution. Operating in an orbit of 832km each swath is 60km wide. Two adjacent swaths increase the swath width to 120km. Alternatively, one scanner may be swung up to 27° to either side. The advantage is two-fold. Repeat coverage may be obtained after 2 days instead of the 26 days for the satellite to return to the same pass. Viewing a scene from two angles gives stereoscopy and, therefore, allows contours to be plotted.

A further type of imaging is by radar, which can be processed to give a picture resembling a black and white photograph. This has been used over land to map tropical regions which are permanently cloud covered and to see through very dry sand deserts to the rocky structures beneath, and over the sea to determine roughness and wave patterns. In the early 1990s, Canada plans to launch such a satellite (Radarsat) to monitor sea-ice in Arctic waters.

There are too many applications of satellite technology by individual nations to be discussed here. Of relevance in the present context of Earth-resources satellite is India's Bhaskara spacecraft, launched by the U.S.S.R. in 1979. It operated two TV cameras with 1km resolution in two spectral bands and a radiometer for ocean study. Japan has a strong oceanography interest. Canada, with UK cooperation, will operate a radar satellite designed for arctic and sub-arctic areas and the study of ice.

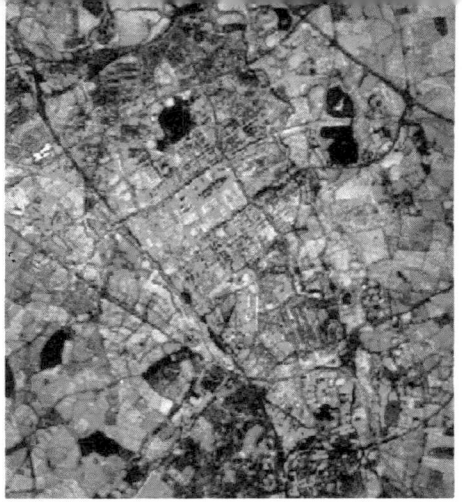

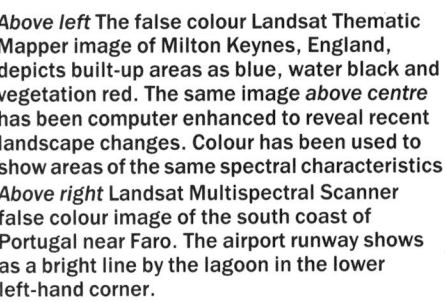
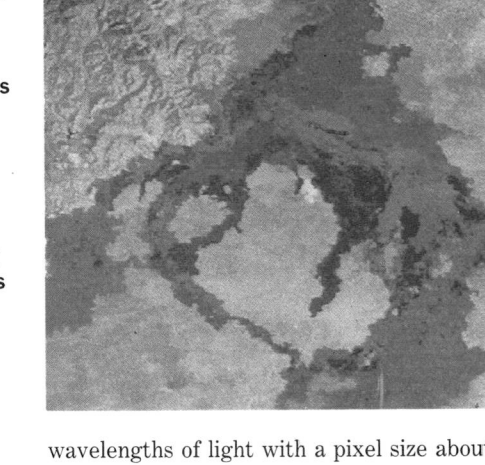

Above left The false colour Landsat Thematic Mapper image of Milton Keynes, England, depicts built-up areas as blue, water black and vegetation red. The same image *above centre* has been computer enhanced to reveal recent landscape changes. Colour has been used to show areas of the same spectral characteristics
Above right Landsat Multispectral Scanner false colour image of the south coast of Portugal near Faro. The airport runway shows as a bright line by the lagoon in the lower left-hand corner.
Left Another multi-spectral Landsat image showing Gunung Muryo (1602m) and Tanjung (Cape) Bugel on the island of Java. This area is shown on page 70—N9.
Right Landsat Multispectral Scanner false colour image of Craters of the Moon in Idaho, U.S.A. There is little vegetation except in and near the mountainous area in the north-west.

VOYAGER PROBE

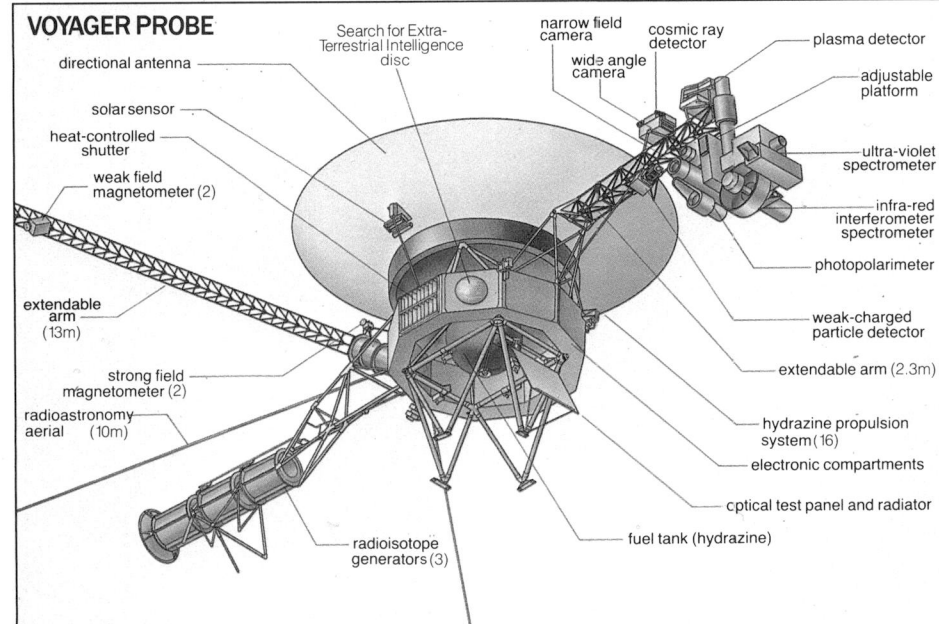

Labels: directional antenna; solar sensor; heat-controlled shutter; weak field magnetometer (2); extendable arm (13m); strong field magnetometer (2); radioastronomy aerial (10m); Search for Extra-Terrestrial Intelligence disc; narrow field camera; wide angle camera; cosmic ray detector; plasma detector; adjustable platform; ultra-violet spectrometer; infra-red interferometer spectrometer; photopolarimeter; weak-charged particle detector; extendable arm (2.3m); hydrazine propulsion system (16); electronic compartments; optical test panel and radiator; fuel tank (hydrazine); radioisotope generators (3)

THE FUTURE

Space technology is still in its infancy. In the next 30 years manned stations will be established on the Moon and Mars. No one can say what scientific and technological innovations will have been introduced between then and now. Nearer to the present there promises to be a wider application of photography from satellite than has been the case at present except in military circles from which the world at large is excluded.

Metric cameras have been operated by Russian spacecraft and the U.S. Space Shuttle. The Shuttle has also carried the Large Format Camera which has very high resolution. There is no possibility that photography of this type will replace airborne systems for the plotting of detailed relief. Its potential is in the ability to provide repetitive photographic cover. New films and processing systems will improve the resolution still more.

Whether or not precise ephemeris data is released the future of position-fixing by satellite is assured. An immediate benefit will be the continuous read-out of latitude, longitude and speed of ships at sea. Ship positions will be given with an accuracy of 5–10m and speed to 3–6cm/sec. Land vehicles can be navigated to even greater accuracy. On land also property and other surveys will use satellite positioning systems to give locations with an accuracy of a few centimetres.

Above The two Voyager space probes have recorded pictures of Jupiter, Saturn, Uranus and their satellites. Voyager 2 reached Neptune in 1989. Apart from the imaging experiments, the probes have detected magnetic fields, charged particles, planetary atmospheres, ring systems, volcanic activity and new satellites. After 1990 the probes will be beyond the orbit of Pluto heading out of the Solar System. The data sent back could never have been acquired from Earth.

LANDSAT

It soon became apparent in the 1960s that sensors in space could contribute an enormous volume of specialised data about the surface and sub-surface of the planet. A series of unmanned satellites proved that infra-red and radar photography could discriminate between diseased and healthy crops, direct shipping from ice-hazardous water, monitor oil pollution, plot geological fault lines and help discover new fossil fuel resources.

In 1972 Landsat–1 (initially known as ERTS or Earth Resources Technology Satellite) was launched carrying 218 kilos of sensory equipment, into a sun-synchronous orbit at a height of about 920km. The path partially overlapped with its neighbour on each successive day (14 orbits per day), and took 18 days before repeating its ground coverage. Landsat–2 (1975) and Landsat–3 (1978) continued the series. The main instrument on all these was the Multispectral Scanner (MSS) which was sensitive in four

Below SPOT's multi-spectral image with 20m resolution of the Djebel Amour-Oued Mzi area (west of Laghouat), Algeria, – page 85, E2. Bare ground appears blue, sparse vegetation, reddish; cultivation and palm groves, bright red.
Below right The panchromatic image has 10m resolution. It shows Savigliano (south of Turin), Italy, and the snow-covered Po valley. The communications network, isolated buildings and small agricultural plots are clearly visible. The area is shown on page 44, C2.

wavelengths of light with a pixel size about 80m across.

In 1982 Landsat–4 replaced Landsat–3. The satellite at 700km now contained a Thematic Mapper which could differentiate between seven wavelengths of light, with pixels only 30m across. This was specifically designed to analyse agricultural and vegetation characteristics and discriminate between rock types and formations for mineral exploration. The information received could now be transmitted direct to 15 major ground receiving stations by an improved communications programme, but the very complexity and volume of data was, in many ways, detrimental to its effective use. In 1984 Landsat–5 was launched to replace the faulty Landsat–4. Landsat operations have now been transferred to the private enterprise Eosat company.

Images from Landsat using various wavelengths can be used to map cultural features, to measure the depth of shallow water, to monitor the health and development of forestry and agricultural crops and as an aid in oil and mineral exploration. This series of satellites now provides earth scientists with a means of gathering data on a global scale. Interpretation methods have advanced rapidly. As well as private industry benefitting from this technology, many agencies of the United Nations use Landsat data in a wide variety of applications.

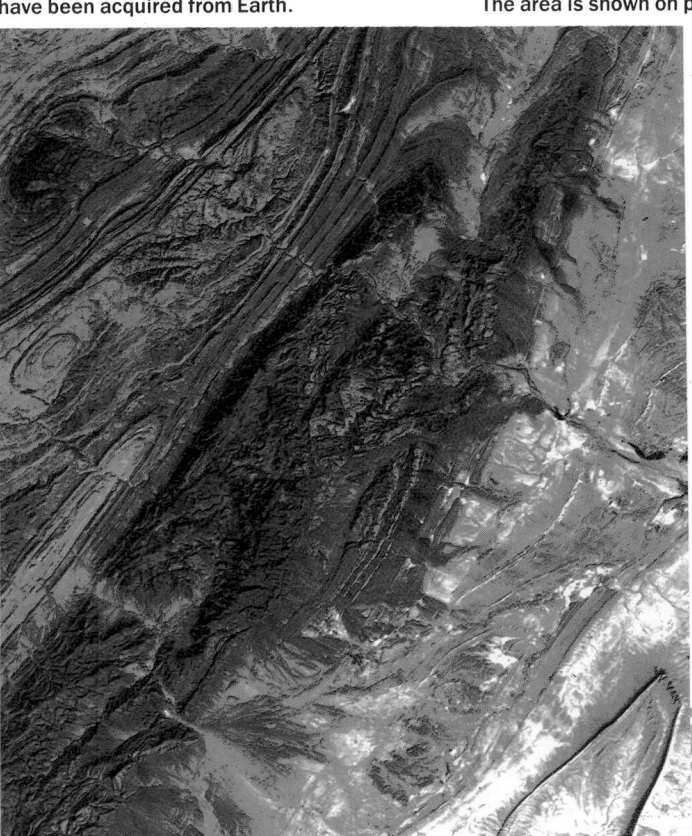
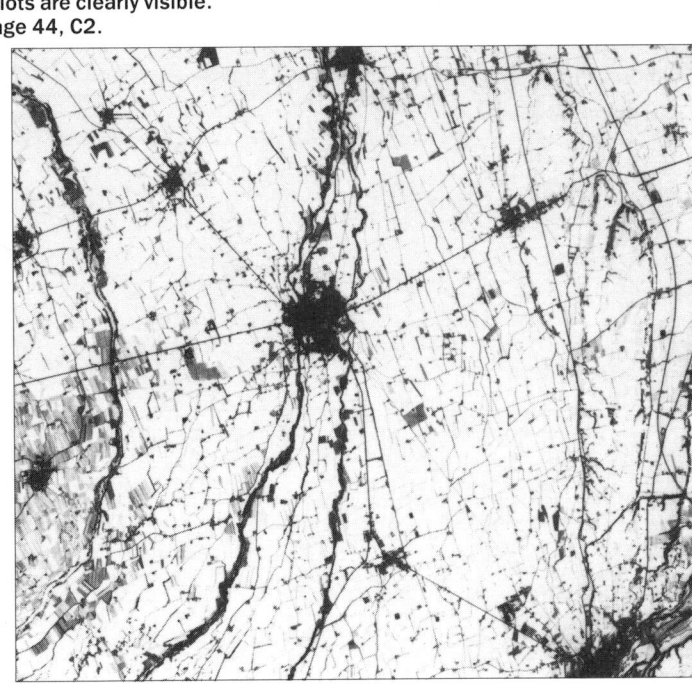

EARTH STRUCTURE

Internally the earth may be divided broadly into crust, mantle and core.

The crust is a thin shell constituting only 0.2% of the mass of the Earth. The continental crust varies in thickness from 20 to 90km and is less dense than ocean crust. Two-thirds of the continents are overlain by sedimentary rocks of average thickness less than 2km but attaining 20km. Ocean crust is on average 7km thick. It is composed of igneous rocks, basalts and gabbros.

Crust and mantle are separated by the Mohorovičić Discontinuity (Moho). The mantle differs from the crust. It is largely igneous. The upper mantle extends to 350km. There is a low velocity zone between 50km and 150km indicating a partial melting. The lower mantle has a more uniform composition. A sharp discontinuity defines the meeting of mantle and core. The inability of the outer core to transmit seismic waves suggests it is liquid. It is probably of metallic iron with other elements – sulphur, silicon, oxygen, potassium and hydrogen have all been suggested. The inner core is solid and probably of nickel-iron.

Temperature at the core-mantle boundary is about 3700°C and 4000°–4500°C in the inner core.

Evolution of the lithosphere, hydrosphere and atmosphere has been strongly influenced by the biosphere – the sphere of living things. The ancestral atmosphere lacked free oxygen. Plant life added oxygen to the atmosphere and transferred carbon dioxide to the crustal rocks and the hydrosphere. The composition of air at 79% nitrogen and 20% oxygen remains stable by the same mechanism.

Solar energy is distributed around the Earth by the atmosphere. Most of the weather and climate processes occur in the troposphere. The atmosphere also shields the Earth. Ozone which exists to the extent of 2 parts per million is at its maximum at 30km. It is the only gas which absorbs ultra-violet radiation. Water-vapour and CO_2 keep out infra-red radiation.

Above 80km nitrogen and oxygen cannot retain their molecular form. They tend to separate into atoms which become ionized (an ion is an atom lacking one or more of its electrons).

The ionosphere is a zone of ionized belts which reflect radio waves back to earth. These electrification belts change their position dependent on light and darkness and external factors.

Beyond the ionosphere, the magnetosphere extends to outer space. Ionized particles form a plasma (a fourth state of matter i.e. other than solid, liquid, gas) constrained by the Earth's magnetic field.

THE EARTH'S SHELLS

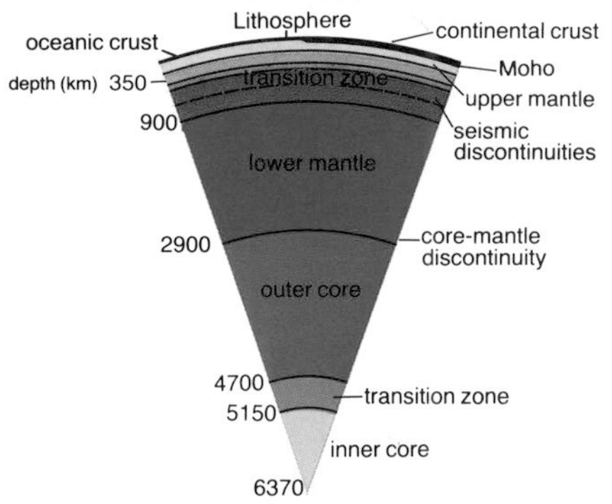

SEISMIC WAVES

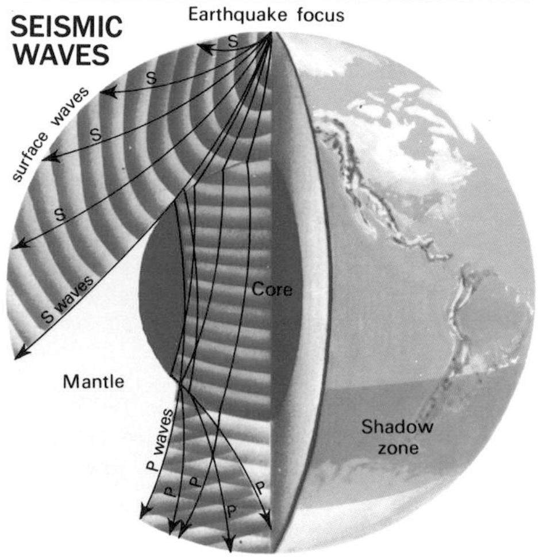

Above In an earthquake the shock generates vibrations, or seismic waves, which radiate in all directions from the focus. Surface waves travel close to the surface of the Earth. They cause most motion in the ground and, therefore, most damage to structures.

Other waves known as body waves pass through the body of the Earth. They are of two kinds. Primary (P) waves are compressional waves. They are able to travel through solids and fluids and cause the particles of the Earth to vibrate in the direction of travel of the wave. Secondary (S) waves are transverse, or shear, waves. They can only pass through solids. They travel at about half the velocity of 'P' waves and they vibrate at right angles to the path travelled by the wave.

Both types of wave obey normal rules of reflection and refraction. Their velocities depend on the nature of the medium through which they pass. Where the physical or chemical properties of the Earth change, the velocity and path of the waves are changed too. From the way the waves travel the nature of the internal layers of the Earth is revealed. By the same means the fluid nature of the outer core is confirmed. Because of the different paths followed by the two types of waves, there is a 'shadow zone' at 105° to 142° from the earthquake focus where waves of both kinds fail to reach the surface.

EARTH'S GRAVITY AND MAGNETIC FIELDS

The Earth is spheroidal in form because it is a rotating body. Were it not so it would take the form of a sphere. The shape is determined by the mass of the Earth and its rate of rotation. Centrifugal force acting outwards reduces the pull of gravity acting inwards so that gravity at the equator is less than at the poles. In theory gravity would be expected to vary progressively from the equator to the poles. In fact, it does not. Uneven distribution of matter within the Earth distorts the shape taken up by the mean sea-level surface (the geoid). In consequence a plumb-line or spirit-level may depart from the assumed vertical or horizontal. Moreover, the orbits of artificial satellites are perturbed by the irregularity of the Earth's gravity.

MAGNETISM

Like gravity, magnetism is strongest at the poles and weakest at the equator. The magnetic field of the Earth resembles that of a bar magnet displaced slightly from the geographical poles. It was long believed that the core being made of iron acted as a magnet but the temperatures prevailing there would destroy such magnetism. Today the belief is that electric currents generated in the semi-molten outer core are responsible for the magnetic field. The magnetic poles are not coincident with the geographical poles. Were a bar magnet substituted for the Earth's field it would not pass through the centre of the Earth but through a point in the plane of the equator about 1200km from the centre in the direction of Indonesia. The bar itself would be inclined at about 12° to the Earth's axis. The magnetic poles change their position from year to year so maps of magnetic declination used for navigation need to be updated annually.

Magnetism is expressed scientifically in three components, intensity, declination (departure from true north), and dip (the inclination in the vertical plane).

When molten rocks cool and solidify materials which are magnetic acquire the alignment of the Earth's local magnetic field at the time they solidified. The magnetism becomes frozen in the rocks. From this historic record the geographical position of the rocks at the time can be estimated from the magnetic alignments within the rocks. From such rock it was discovered that the Earth's magnetic poles had experienced a number of reversals the north pole becoming the south and vice-versa. A system of classification of the field allowed the ages of the various parts of the ocean floor to be deduced thus providing the evidence for sea-floor spreading and plate tectonics.

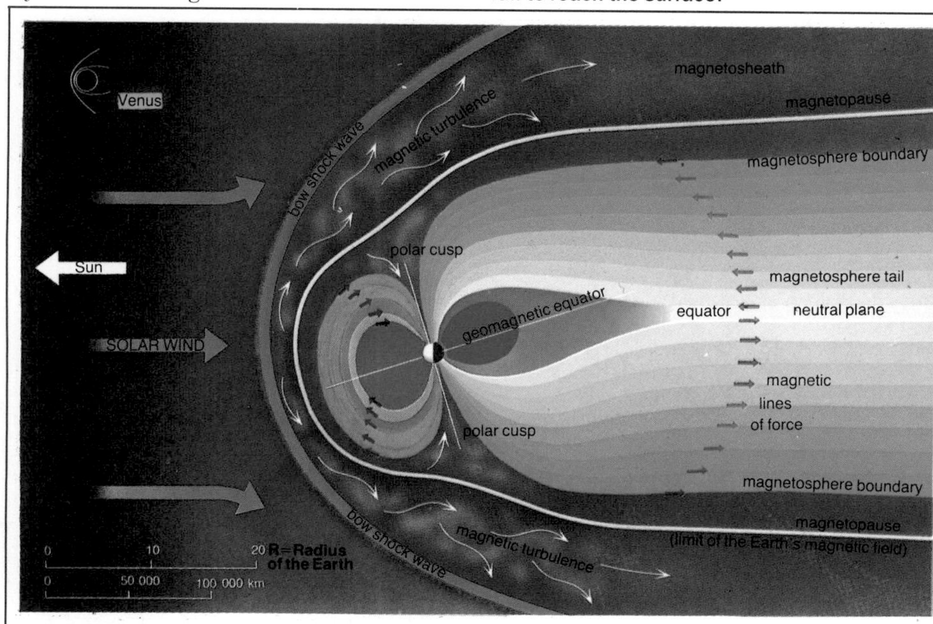

THE MAGNETOSPHERE

A stream of ionized gas, or plasma, the solar wind pours out from the Sun. Travelling at 1000km/sec its encounter with the Earth's magnetic field creates a bow shock wave. The magnetopause, the effective limit of the magnetic field, is pushed back to within 10 Earth radii measured in the direction of the Sun. It is stretched out in a long tail on the opposite side of the Earth. Between the bow-wave and magnetopause is the magnetosheath a region of charged particles producing fluctuations in the magnetic field. On the inner side of the magnetopause is a transition zone where charged particles react with the magnetic field and the magnetosheath. From this zone particles enter the internal magnetic field by the magnetic poles to produce aurorae. Particles trapped by the Earth's magnetism are deflected at the polar cusps and become trapped to form the Van Allen belts at about 5 Earth radii measured from the magnetic equator.

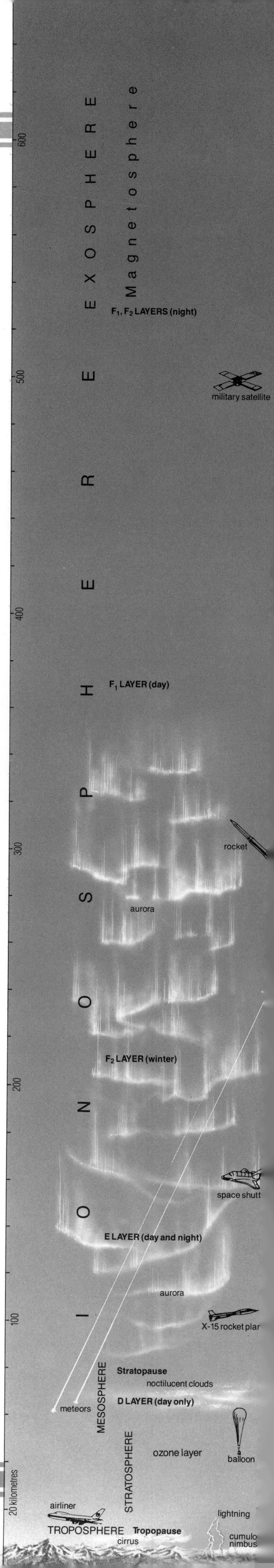

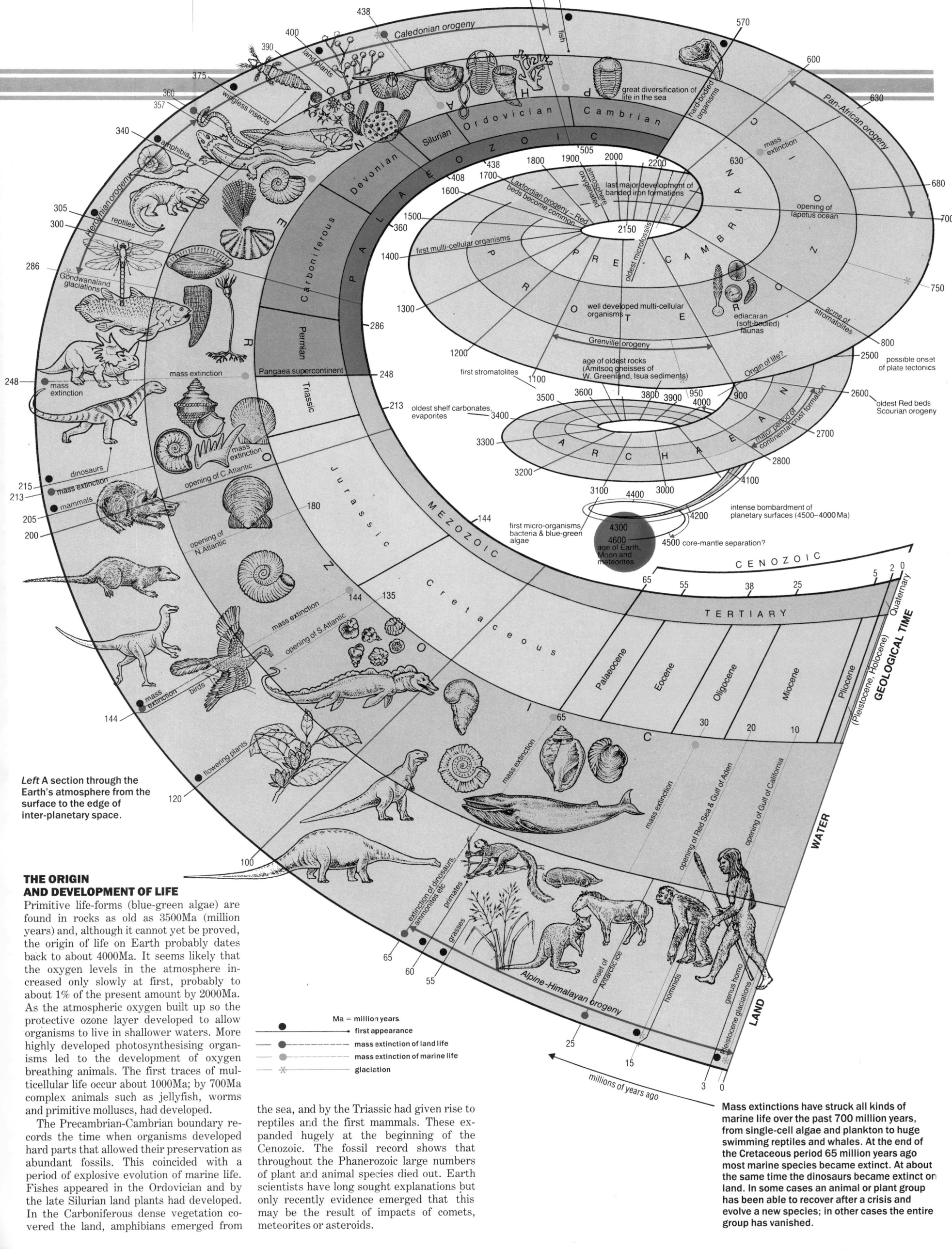

Left A section through the Earth's atmosphere from the surface to the edge of inter-planetary space.

THE ORIGIN AND DEVELOPMENT OF LIFE

Primitive life-forms (blue-green algae) are found in rocks as old as 3500Ma (million years) and, although it cannot yet be proved, the origin of life on Earth probably dates back to about 4000Ma. It seems likely that the oxygen levels in the atmosphere increased only slowly at first, probably to about 1% of the present amount by 2000Ma. As the atmospheric oxygen built up so the protective ozone layer developed to allow organisms to live in shallower waters. More highly developed photosynthesising organisms led to the development of oxygen breathing animals. The first traces of multicellular life occur about 1000Ma; by 700Ma complex animals such as jellyfish, worms and primitive molluscs, had developed.

The Precambrian-Cambrian boundary records the time when organisms developed hard parts that allowed their preservation as abundant fossils. This coincided with a period of explosive evolution of marine life. Fishes appeared in the Ordovician and by the late Silurian land plants had developed. In the Carboniferous dense vegetation covered the land, amphibians emerged from the sea, and by the Triassic had given rise to reptiles and the first mammals. These expanded hugely at the beginning of the Cenozoic. The fossil record shows that throughout the Phanerozoic large numbers of plant and animal species died out. Earth scientists have long sought explanations but only recently evidence emerged that this may be the result of impacts of comets, meteorites or asteroids.

Mass extinctions have struck all kinds of marine life over the past 700 million years, from single-cell algae and plankton to huge swimming reptiles and whales. At the end of the Cretaceous period 65 million years ago most marine species became extinct. At about the same time the dinosaurs became extinct on land. In some cases an animal or plant group has been able to recover after a crisis and evolve a new species; in other cases the entire group has vanished.

Ma = million years.
- first appearance
- mass extinction of land life
- mass extinction of marine life
- glaciation

DYNAMIC EARTH

Map 1
50 million years ago

Map 2
100 million years ago

Map 3
150 million years ago

Map 4
200 million years ago

PLATE TECTONICS

Tectonics means the act of building. As applied to geology, the word, which comes from Greek, refers to study of the processes which produce faults, joints, folds and cleavage or cause magma to rise to the surface as the Earth's crust reacts to forces from below. Plate tectonics attribute such tectonic effects to the movement of the parts of the lithosphere. The lithosphere is defined as the rigid outer layer of the Earth consisting of the crust and the part of the upper mantle immediately below. Together they form a rigid layer which is split into a number of plates all in motion, like rafts, carrying the continents and the oceans with them to drift apart, to collide, to unite or sub-divide in a process of destruction and renewal. There are six major plates and a number of minor ones diverging, converging or sliding past each other at varying rates.

The plates are able to move because the rigid lithosphere rests on a less rigid asthenosphere a zone where the mantle is hotter and less resistant. Temperature increases at the rate of 20°C to 40°C with each km of depth in the outer parts of the Earth.

At mid-ocean ridges, a continuous chain some 40000km in length running through all the oceans, new crust is created. Magma (hot molten rock) rises to flow out of the rift and solidify as pillow lavas or gabbros without reaching the crustal surface. The intrusion of new material forces the rift sides to move outwards and they are pushed further apart as still more magma injects itself into the rift. The rifts are regions of low seismic activity with a high heat flow.

Evidence of sea-floor spreading is provided by the magnetism locked into the rocks at the time they solidified. Evidence is also provided by the ocean sediments which become increasingly thicker outwards from the rift indicating a longer period of time for their deposition and consequently a greater age of the ocean floor on which they lie.

At mid-ocean ridges the plate margins are divergent (or extensional), new crust is formed and the boundary is said to be constructive. Where two plates meet the margins are convergent (or compressional) and are destructive. One plate slides under the other the plate margin descending at a steep angle, sometimes to a depth of 700km, into the asthenosphere, until melting occurs. Lighter material rises to attach itself to the underside of the continents. Continental plates containing much lighter material float over the ocean plates. Where the ocean plate is subducted, the subduction zone is marked by an ocean trench. Island areas are also formed in the oceans and young folded mountain ranges at the edge of a continent.

At some plate boundaries crust is neither created nor destroyed: the plates slide past each other at transform faults. The margins are translational and by type, conservative.

From study of all the oceans it can be said that the ocean floors are less than 200M years old. The Pacific plate contains only ocean crust. The other major plates consist of both continental and ocean crust. A fairly authoritative account can be given of the way the continents have drifted, divided and collided over the past 200M years. A very incomplete picture can be drawn of the course of events in the preceding 400M years and only a sketchy picture before that.

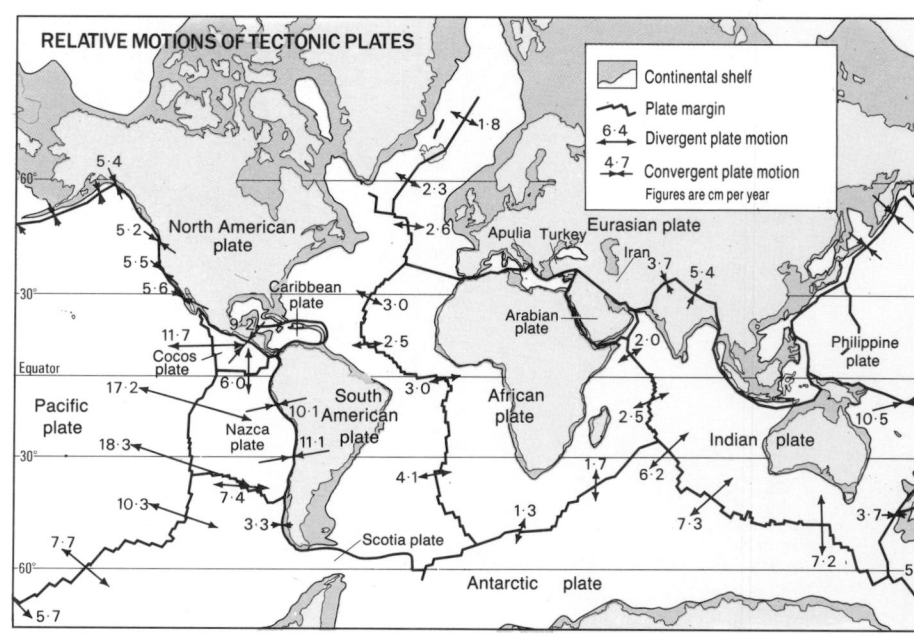

RELATIVE MOTIONS OF TECTONIC PLATES

Continental shelf
Plate margin
6·4 → Divergent plate motion
4·7 → Convergent plate motion
Figures are cm per year

PLATE TECTONIC CYCLE

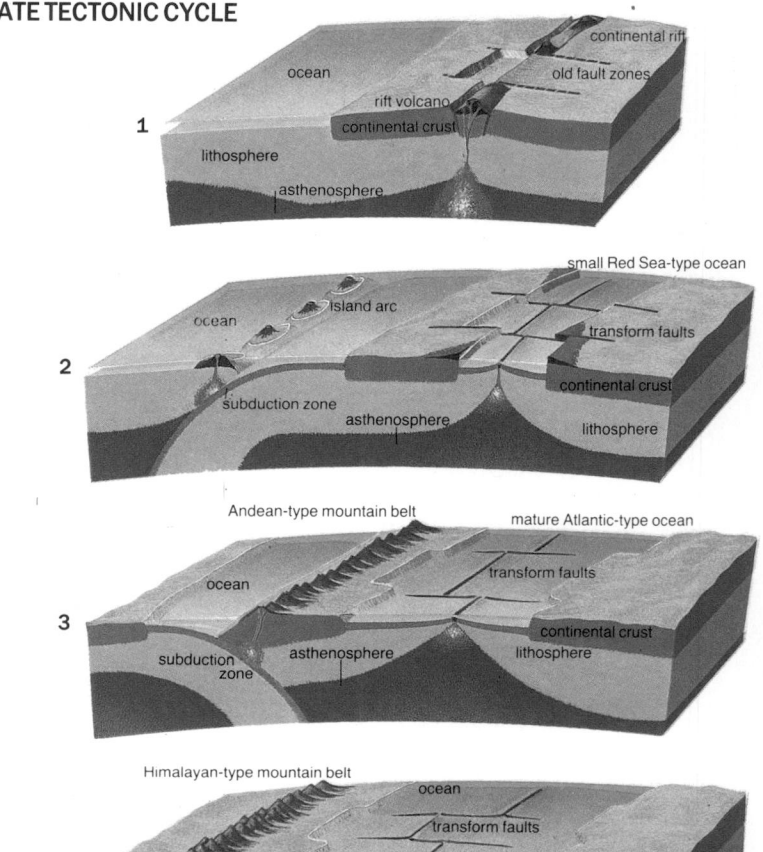

Above When continental lithosphere is subjected to tensional forces, it can become so attenuated that fault zones develop and crustal rocks subside. Hot magma rises from the asthenosphere to fill the space and that increases the heat flow through the lithosphere. Partial melting of mantle material ensues in the process of basaltic volcanism at a mid-ocean ridge. A rift develops in the continent and the two sides of the rift are forced further apart. Separation may be arrested after a while as in the case of the Rio Grande of south-west USA and the rift valley of East Africa. Should the process not be arrested, the rift will lengthen until the continent is split into two diverging plates.

1 Continental rifting in part following old faults in the continental basement.
2 Continental break-up with the formation of new oceanic crust in a small Red Sea-type ocean basin. Transform faults follow continental fractures.
3 A large mature Atlantic-type ocean basin has now formed on the site of the former continent. The subduction zone changes in direction (flips) to dip beneath the continent, forming a cordillera-type mountain belt.
4 Where continental collision occurs one continent partly underthrusts the other producing a Himalayan-type mountain belt underlain by thick continental crust (75-90km).

MAJOR TECTONIC FEATURES

Right Particular features are associated with different types of mineral deposits: continental rifts with tin and fluorine, mid-ocean ridges with marine metallic sulphides, island arcs and cordilleran-type mountains with a variety of metallic deposits.

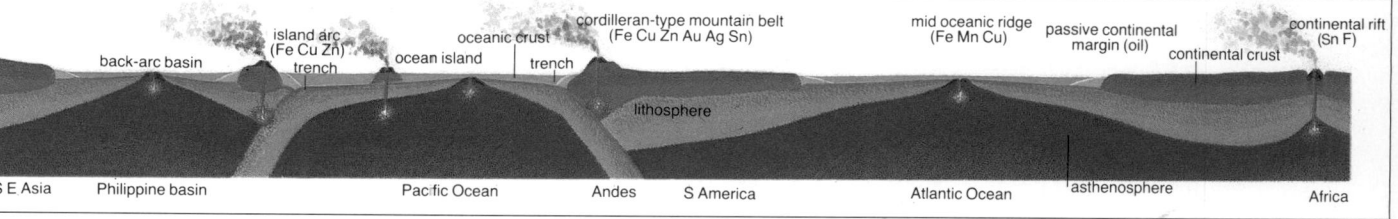

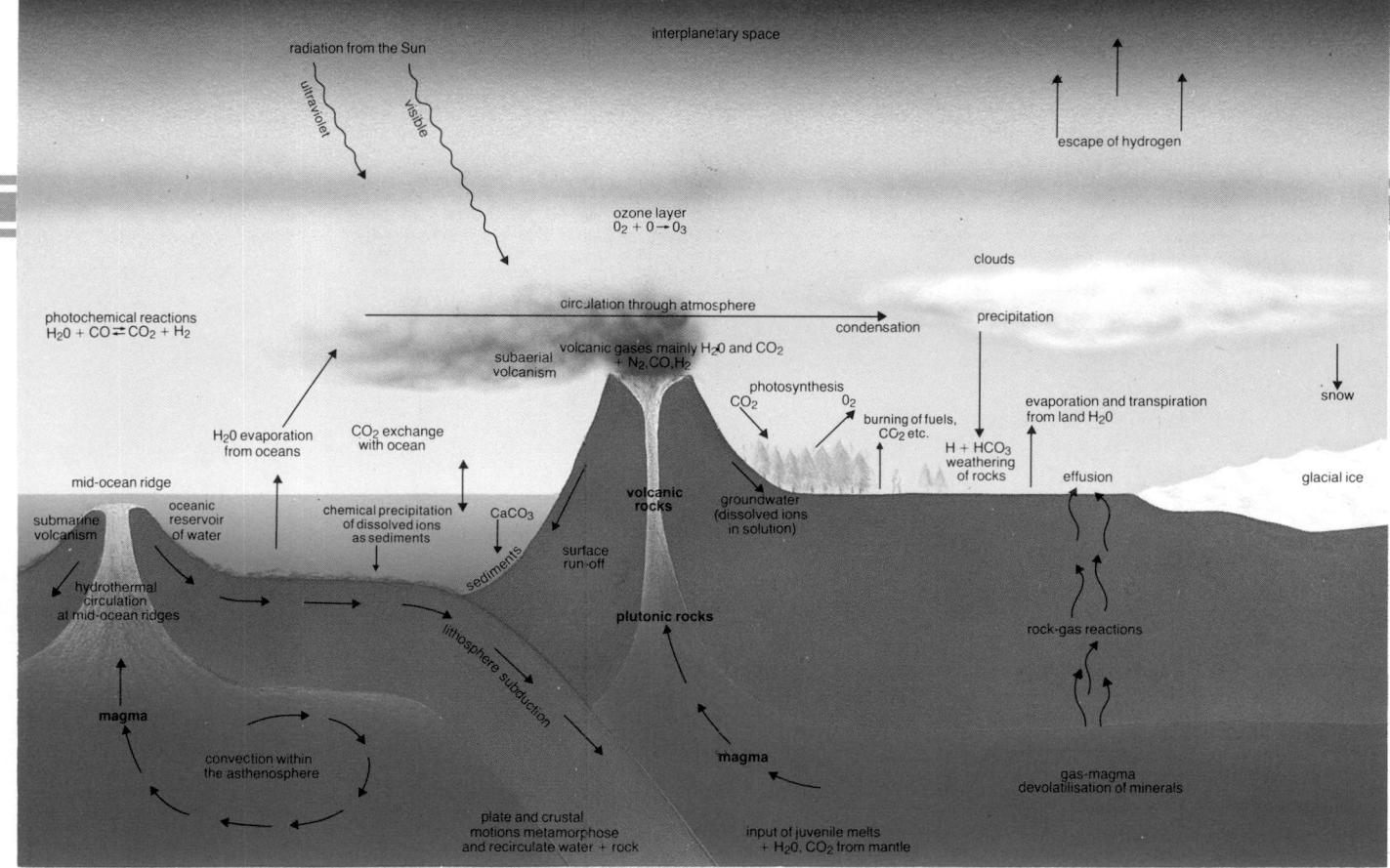

Labels in diagram: radiation from the Sun, ultraviolet, visible, interplanetary space, escape of hydrogen, ozone layer $O_2 + O \rightarrow O_3$, clouds, circulation through atmosphere, precipitation, condensation, snow, photochemical reactions $H_2O + CO \rightleftharpoons CO_2 + H_2$, subaerial volcanism, volcanic gases mainly H_2O and CO_2 + N_2, CO, H_2, photosynthesis CO_2 O_2, burning of fuels, CO_2 etc., evaporation and transpiration from land H_2O, H_2O evaporation from oceans, CO_2 exchange with ocean, $H + HCO_3$ weathering of rocks, effusion, glacial ice, mid-ocean ridge, submarine volcanism, oceanic reservoir of water, chemical precipitation of dissolved ions as sediments, $CaCO_3$, volcanic rocks, surface run-off, groundwater (dissolved ions in solution), hydrothermal circulation at mid-ocean ridges, sediments, plutonic rocks, rock-gas reactions, lithosphere subduction, magma, magma, convection within the asthenosphere, gas-magma devolatilisation of minerals, plate and crustal motions metamorphose and recirculate water + rock, input of juvenile melts + H_2O, CO_2 from mantle

ROCK AND HYDROLOGICAL CYCLES

Left In the most familiar cycle rain falls onto the land, drains to the sea, evaporates, condenses into cloud and is precipitated onto the land again. Water is also released and recirculated as a result of plate movements and volcanic activity. In the rock cycle rocks are weathered and eroded, forming sediments which are in turn compacted into rocks that are eventually exposed and then weathered again. Man's industrial activity has modified the atmosphere by increasing the amount of CO_2 and adding other gases that may affect the vital ozone layer that shields the Earth from the Sun's ultra-violet rays. In the oceans, CO_2 and calcium are converted into calcium carbonate which forms sedimentary rocks which are re-cycled by the action of plate tectonics. In the atmosphere, CO_2, dust and water-vapour absorb infra-red energy and re-radiate it both to space and the atmosphere. If the level of CO_2 is increased, less of the Earth's own heat escapes to space, more is returned to the atmosphere and the Earth becomes warmer.

SURFACE PROCESSES

The lithosphere, the outermost layer of the Earth; the hydrosphere of salt and fresh water and the atmosphere composed of gases are all closely connected. There is a constant transfer of material from one to the other. The air in the atmosphere does not remain motionless. Convection and other influences impart complex patterns of motion in which matter is conveyed from one area to another. Atmospheric water vapour deposited on the lithosphere as water containing dissolved gases, reacts physically and chemically with surface rocks.

Variation in temperature, particularly frost, precipitation and winds cause a gradual fragmentation of surface rocks and physical decay in the process called weathering. Vegetation also plays its part in the alteration of surface rocks, by adding organic matter to weathered rocks to create soils and by resisting erosion. Water, however, is the major factor since it also acts as a transport medium.

Rivers transport enormous quantities of material varying from large boulders to particles of sand or clay carried in suspension. Where rivers overflow their banks, sand, gravel and clays are deposited in the flood plains to produce fertile valleys. On reaching the ocean or a lake the carrying capacity of the current is dissipated and material carried in suspension is deposited to form a delta.

Slumping of ocean floor material or earthquakes can put large quantities of fine sediments into suspension as a turbid layer which erodes the continental slope, thereby gathering more material all of which is deposited on the continental rise or the floor of the abyssal plain as "turbidites".

VOLCANOES

Almost all the world's active volcanoes, numbering 500–600 are located at convergent plate boundaries. Those are the volcanoes which give spectacular demonstrations of volcanic activity. Yet far greater volcanic activity continues unnoticed and without cessation at mid-ocean ridges where magma from the upper mantle is quietly being extruded on to the ocean floor to create new crustal material. The basalts erupted there are derived more or less directly from material of the mantle. Similar lavas are seen in the Columbia plateau, U.S.A. and the Deccan, India.

Chemical composition of magmas and the amount of gas they contain are important factors in determining the nature of a volcanic eruption. Gas-charged basalts produce cinder cones. Mount Etna in Italy has numerous such cinder cones. Violent eruptions usually occur when large clouds of lava come into contact with water to produce fine-grained ash. The name Surtseyan is given to this type after the volcanic island which appeared off Iceland in 1963. Andesites are more viscous. When charged with gas they erupt with explosive violence. Volcanoes like Fujiyama, Vesuvius and most of the other renowned volcanoes with steep sides are of this type.

Nuées ardentes (burning clouds) are extremely destructive. They are produced by rhyolitic magmas which erupt explosively sending molten lava fragments and gas at great speed down the mountain sides.

In spite of the destructiveness of many volcanoes people still live in their vicinity because of the fertile volcanic soils. Geothermal energy in regions of volcanic activity is another source of attraction.

EARTHQUAKES

Earthquakes are the manifestation of a slippage at a geological fault. The majority occur at tectonic plate boundaries. The interior of a plate tends to be stable and less subject to earthquakes. When plates slide past each other strain energy is suddenly released. Even though the amount of movement is very small the energy released is colossal. It is transferred in shock waves.

Most earthquakes originate at not very great depths – 5km or so. At the San Andreas fault earthquakes originate at about 20km depth. Over 70% of all foci are at depths of less than 70km. Some, however, may be as deep as 700km. The precise cause of those very deep earthquakes is not known. The point from which the earthquake is generated is the focus and the point on the surface immediately above the focus is the epicentre. Plotting the foci of deep earthquakes at convergent plate boundaries allows the path of the subducted plate to be traced.

Two types of scale are used to define the magnitude of earthquakes. In the logarithmic Richter Scale each unit is ten times the intensity of the next lower on the scale. The intensity is recorded by seismographs. There is no upper limit but the greatest magnitude yet recorded is 8·9.

The Modified Mercalli Earthquake Intensity Scale is in common use. It is based on the observed effects of an earthquake. At the lowest end the numeral I means the shock is felt by only a few people under special circumstances. A shock felt generally, with minor breakages indoors is classed as V. General alarm is equivalent to VIII and 'Panic' with varying categories of total destruction are graded IX to XII.

EXTERNAL INFLUENCES

Every day over a million tons of extra-terrestrial material falls on the Earth. Most of this material is ultra-fine cosmic dust. Only a small proportion of the incoming material actually reaches the surface of the Earth. Most is burned up by friction with the atmosphere where it vaporises after being heated to incandescence when it may be seen as so-called shooting stars.

Meteors come both sporadically and in showers. They are part of the solar system and rotate round the Sun. When the Earth comes in contact with them a meteor display occurs.

Occasionally a larger body survives passage through the atmosphere and strikes the ground. One very large meteorite fell in Arizona about 25,000 years ago. Meteor Crater is the result. Another devastating impact occurred in 1908 when an object struck the Tunguska area of Siberia, devastating an area of several kilometres radius in which all the trees were felled.

Tektites are curious objects. They are small and glassy and are found lying on the surface in several places – Australia, South-East Asia, Ivory Coast and Czechoslovakia. Terrestrial and extra-terrestrial origins have been ascribed to them. They have the appearance of melted rocks formed as the result of meteorite impact but no local evidence of such impact has been detected at any of the sites.

It seems inevitable that a comet or an asteroid will, in the course of time, collide with the Earth. Both comets and asteroids pass within the Earth's orbit. A collision will occur if the Earth happens to be located in that part of its orbit when one or the other crosses it.

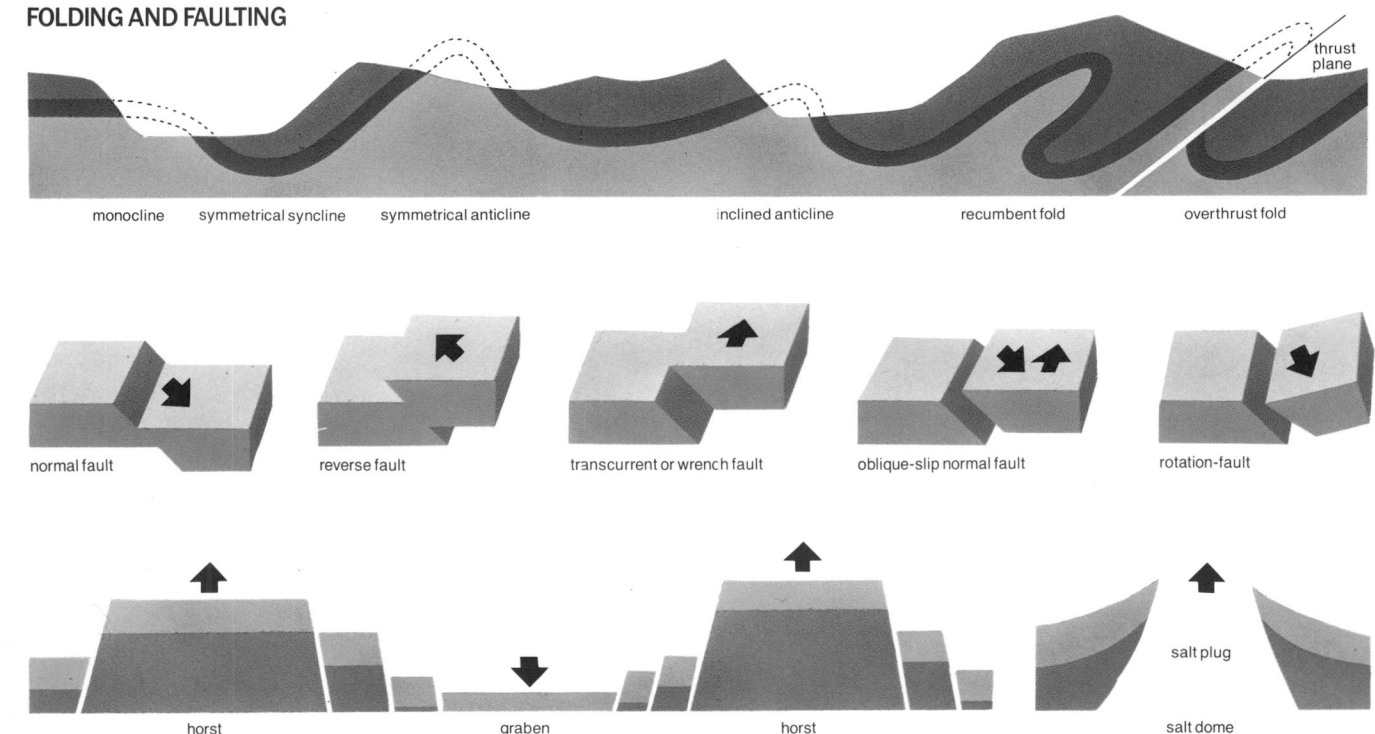

FOLDING AND FAULTING

Labels: thrust plane, monocline, symmetrical syncline, symmetrical anticline, inclined anticline, recumbent fold, overthrust fold, normal fault, reverse fault, transcurrent or wrench fault, oblique-slip normal fault, rotation-fault, horst, graben, horst, salt plug, salt dome

Left When the Earth's crust bends under compression, folds develop. The simplest of these is a monocline, a one-sided fold, although downfolds (synclines) and upfolds (anticlines) are more usual. Increasing pressure steepens the side facing the pressure until one side is pushed under the other, to form a recumbent fold. Finally it may break along its axis, one limb being thrust over the other. Mountain chains often demonstrate intense folding between converging plates.

Faults occur when the Earth's crust breaks, often causing earthquakes. When tension stretches the crust normal faulting occurs and the rocks on one side of the fault-plane override those on the other.

A horst is a block of the crust thrust up between faults; the reverse is a graben or rift valley. Repeated horst and graben forms give basin and range topography as in Nevada, USA.

The upward movement of a plug of salt, some thousands of feet in depth, may force up strata and the surface layers to form a salt dome, often associated with oil and gas.

CLIMATE

Climate is generally said to be the average weather conditions observed over a long period. The factors which determine climate are temperature and rainfall.

Although heated slightly by the passage of the Sun's rays the atmosphere is warmed by the re-radiation of solar heat energy stored in the oceans and continents. Air which contains as much water vapour as possible (i.e. the air is saturated) is said to have a relative humidity of 100 and half-saturated air, 50. Air at a temperature of 32°C (90°F) can hold more than nine times as much water vapour as air at 0°C (32°F). For this reason polar regions have low precipitation.

Near the equator where the north-east and south-east trade winds meet is a zone known as the Inter-tropical Convergence Zone. Here warm, water-laden air rises to some 12-15km in altitude, its high content of water-vapour visible as cumulonimbus clouds. On cooling with altitude rain falls. This low-pressure doldrum zone of light winds has daily afternoon rains.

The two tropics are zones of descending air and, therefore, high atmospheric pressure and low rainfall. On the other hand, the arctic and antarctic circles are low pressure zones and between them and the tropics the winds are 'anti-trade' i.e. blowing from the SW and NW respectively in the northern and southern hemispheres. This is the zone of the 'westerlies' in which weather is determined by depressions (low-pressure centres) and anti-cyclones (high pressure centres), the first rain-bearing, the second dry. In the polar regions the winds tend to be easterly. The poles themselves are high-pressure areas.

But for the rotation of the Earth, winds would blow south or north from high-pressure zones at the poles and tropics towards the polar circles and equator. Rotation and centrifugal force impart a west or east motion. The system of pressure belts moves from 6° to 10° north or south following the seasonal movements of the Sun.

Continents and oceans also influence the global pattern especially in the northern hemisphere where most land lies. The interiors of N. America and Eurasia become very hot in summer and very cold in winter causing air to flow respectively from and to the oceans. Monsoons are an expression of this seasonal reversal of direction.

Tropical cyclones (typhoons and hurricanes and many local names) are highly destructive systems. They occur in a belt between 5° and 30° latitude, the majority in the northern hemisphere. They can be 800km in diameter, rotating clockwise in the southern hemisphere and counter-clockwise in the northern. Wind speeds above Force

BEAUFORT SCALE OF WIND FORCE

†wind velocity	0	4	9	16	23	31	40	50	60	72
*maximum waveheight	0	0.1	0.2	0.3	1.0	1.0–1.7	2.5	3.5	6.0	10.0
Beaufort scale no.	**0**	**1**	**2**	**3**	**4**	**5**	**6**	**7**	**8**	**9**
	Smoke rises vertically. Leaves on trees still.	Smoke rises straight but not vertically. Leaves rustle.	Smoke blown out of vertical still more.	Flags flutter. Leaves and small twigs in motion. Ripple on ponds.	Small flags flying fully. Small branches in motion even when leafless. Paper and dust blown about.	Large flags stretched. Tops of large trees shake. Small waves on ponds. Wind whistles.	Large bare branches in motion. Wind whistles around buildings. Humming of telephone wires.	Trunks of small (leafless) trees in motion. White tops on waves in ponds.	Large trees in motion; twigs and branches break off. Wind impedes walking.	Large boughs break off. Light objects lifted o ground. Roof tiles blown off.

† km/hr
* trough to crest in metres

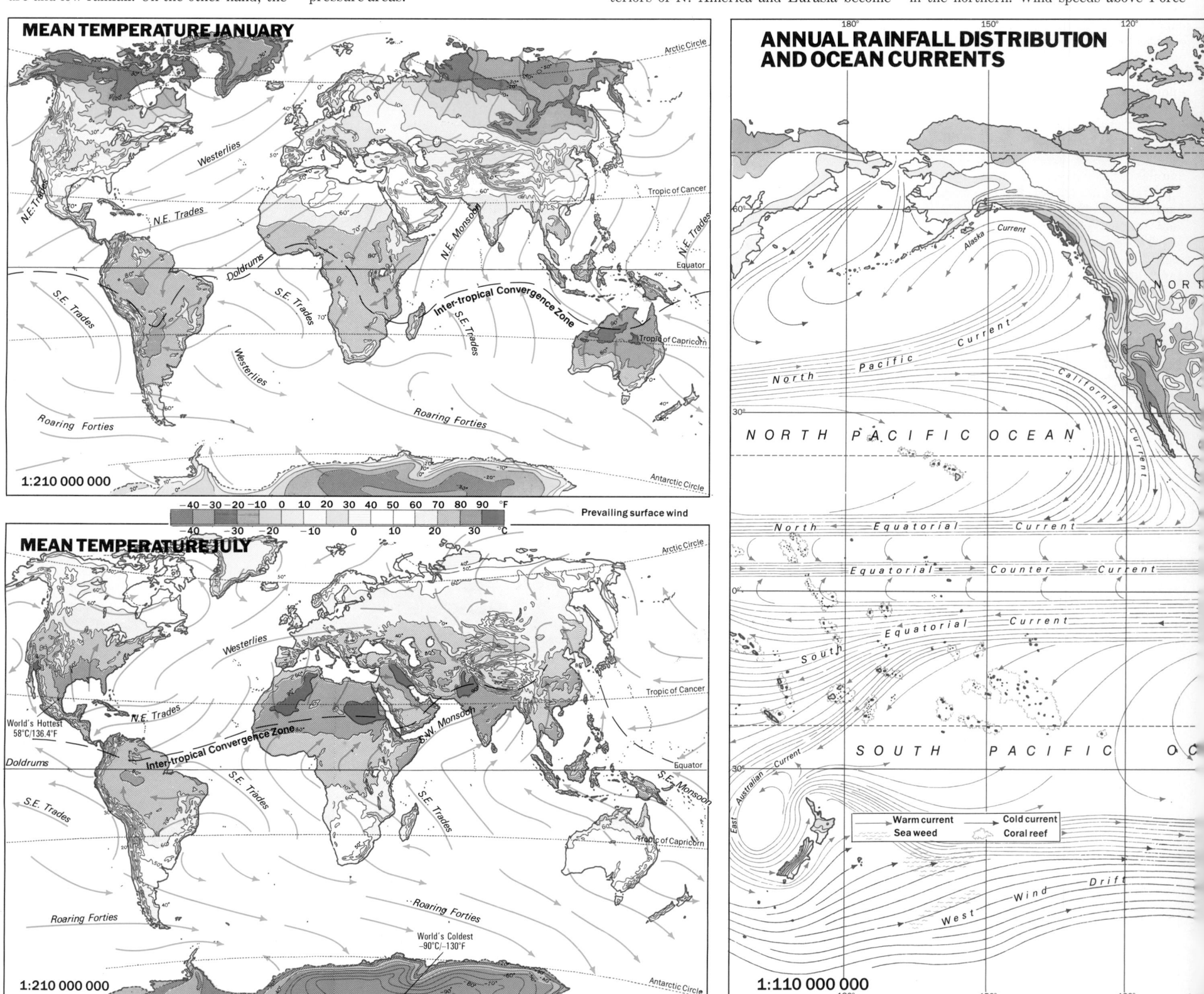

MEAN TEMPERATURE JANUARY

1:210 000 000

Westerlies
N.E. Trades
N.E. Trades
Doldrums
S.E. Trades
S.E. Trades
Westerlies
Roaring Forties
Roaring Forties
N.E. Monsoon
Inter-tropical Convergence Zone
Arctic Circle
Tropic of Cancer
Equator
Tropic of Capricorn
Antarctic Circle

-40 -30 -20 -10 0 10 20 30 40 50 60 70 80 90 °F
-40 -30 -20 -10 0 10 20 30 °C

Prevailing surface wind

MEAN TEMPERATURE JULY

1:210 000 000

Westerlies
World's Hottest 58°C/136.4°F
N.E. Trades
Doldrums
Inter-tropical Convergence Zone
S.E. Trades
S.E. Trades
S.E. Trades
S.W. Monsoon
S.E. Monsoon
Roaring Forties
World's Coldest -90°C/-130°F
Arctic Circle
Tropic of Cancer
Equator
Tropic of Capricorn
Antarctic Circle

ANNUAL RAINFALL DISTRIBUTION AND OCEAN CURRENTS

1:110 000 000

Alaska Current
North Pacific Current
California Current
NORTH PACIFIC OCEAN
North Equatorial Current
Equatorial Counter Current
Equatorial Current
South Equatorial Current
SOUTH PACIFIC OC
East Australian Current
West Wind Drift

Warm current → Cold current
Sea weed → Coral reef

84	97	104
12.0	over 16.0	over 16.0
10	**11**	**12**
Trees uprooted considerable damage.	Major destruction.	Disastrous destruction

Left In 1805, the British admiral, Francis Beaufort, devised a sequence of numbers to indicate the force of winds at sea. Associated effects at sea and on land were added later to show that 'white horses' occasional at Force 3 became widespread at Force 6, that waves became higher and longer, that spray and foam increased with turbulence until visibility was affected. Wind speeds were added later still. More scientific methods exist but the scale is easily assimilable and the Beaufort number with temperature; pressure; precipitation; visibility and outlook together provide a concise weather summary.

12, seas rising to 16–17m and torrential rain cause the destruction.

Far from destructive are the Chinook of N. America and the Föhn winds of the Alps. Air, depleted of moisture, is warmed in its descent of the rain-shadow side of high mountain ranges.

Tsunamis, destructive ocean waves, are not the result of weather but of submarine seismic activity. A wave of no more than 1m but travelling at 650km/hr can rise to 16m or more on impact with the shore.

Right Waterspouts are sea tornadoes, short-lived phenomena lasting from one minute to half-an-hour. A rapidly gyrating vortex descends from a cumulus or cumulonimbus cloud whipping the sea and sucking up a column of water from 1m to 300m diameter which travels with the cloud but with the base moving at a different speed. High velocity peripheral winds, the disturbed sea-surface and descent of water inflict the damage. It should be noted that the African tornado, also highly destructive, is actually a violent squall.

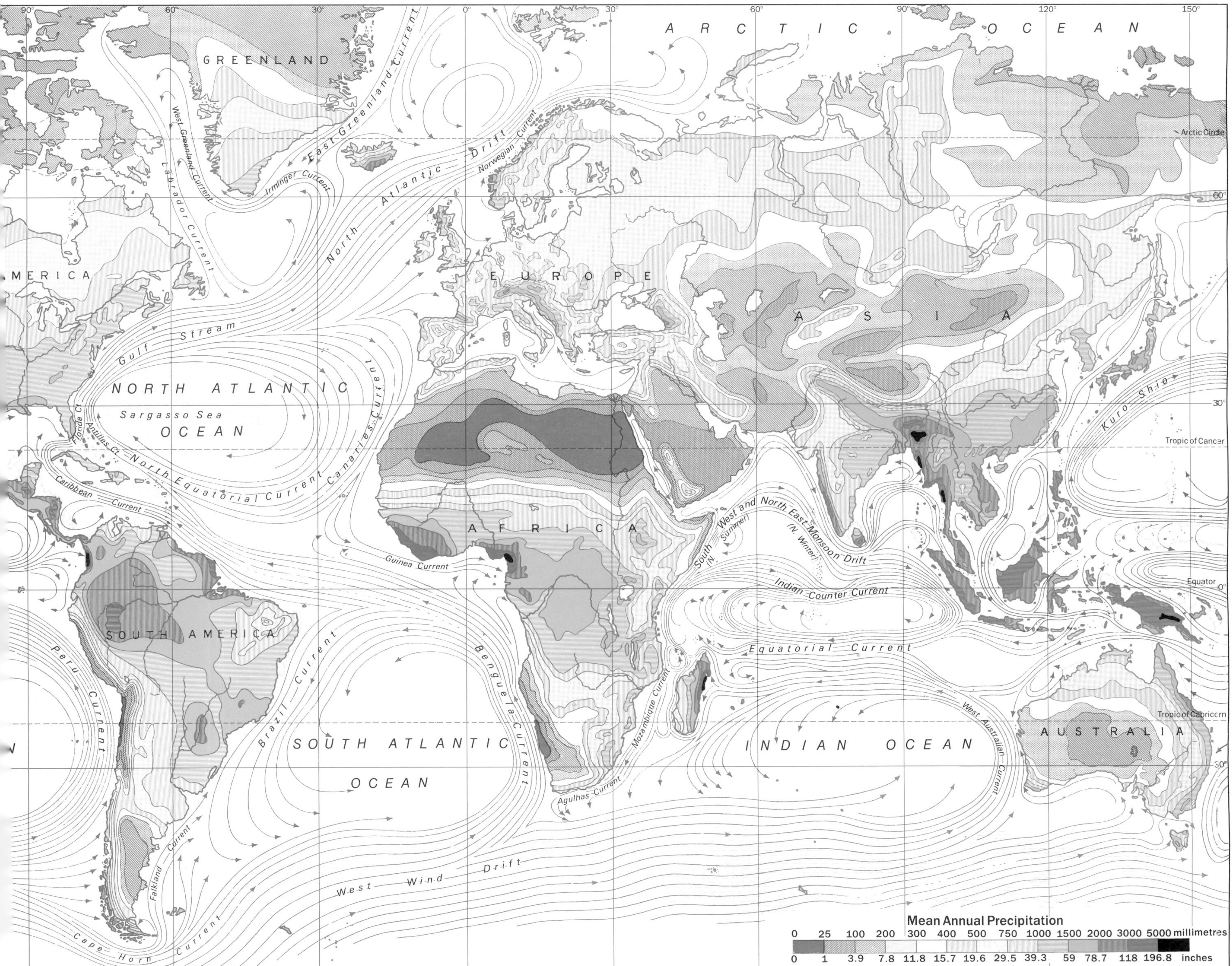

Mean Annual Precipitation

0	25	100	200	300	400	500	750	1000	2000	3000	5000 millimetres
0	1	3.9	7.8	11.8	15.7	19.6	29.5	39.3	59	78.7	118 196.8 inches

VEGETATION

In a world so subordinated to human beings, it is salutory to be reminded that the atmosphere itself and fertile soils which support agriculture are the creations of plant life. Yet there is far less general concern for the preservation of plants threatened with extinction than there is over endangered animal species.

Perhaps the most remarkable feature of plant life is its almost complete ubiquity. Unless inhibited by ice, plants establish themselves wherever conditions allow and once established encourage the formation or collection of soil and the means to generate their species. The type of plant is determined primarily by climate and soil. Soil is composed of solid, liquid and gas, the solid part being the primary parent rock with secondary rock material changed through moisture and chemical reaction. Humus, decayed vegetable matter, is both solid and liquid. The gas is air.

Russian research first linked soil type to climate, so Russian terms are used for soils. Vegetation zones broadly match soil classes. Thus in the tundra, low temperature and a permanently frozen sub-soil retard organic decay. Thaw in the peaty surface produces swamps. Trees and shrubs are sparse and stunted. South of the tundra is the boreal forest (taiga) of coniferous trees, largely evergreen with some deciduous trees. Their resinous leaves protect against extreme cold and limit transpiration. Soils are podzols, a name applied to whitish-grey sandy soils in which leaching has taken place, a process by which water percolates downwards carrying organic and other matter in solution. These soils are acid. The coniferous vegetation does not produce a rich humus when it decays. Because Siberian rivers flow north the lower reaches are still frozen when the upper reaches thaw. Floods then ensue.

SOIL GROUPS

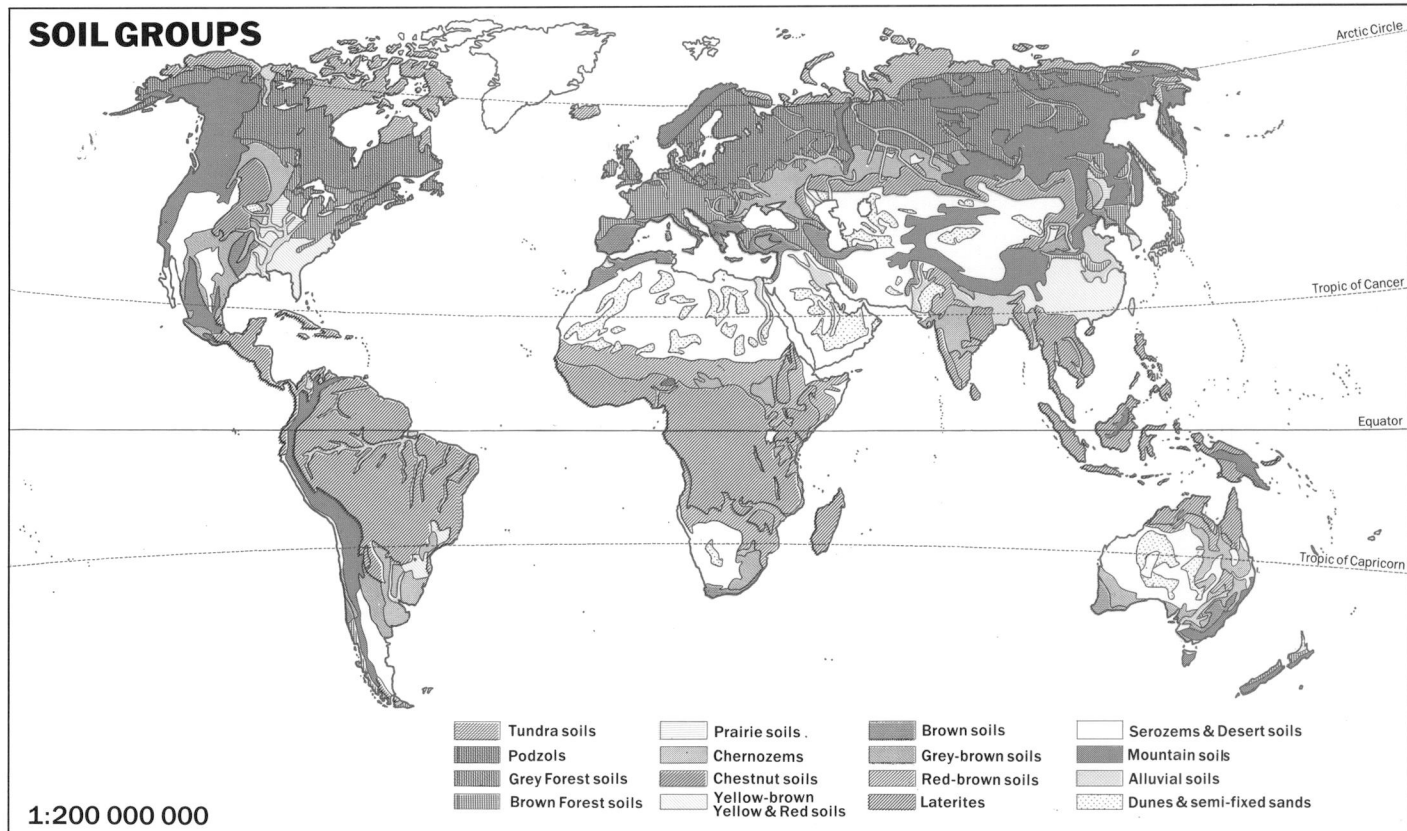

1:200 000 000

Tundra soils	Prairie soils
Podzols	Chernozems
Grey Forest soils	Chestnut soils
Brown Forest soils	Yellow-brown Yellow & Red soils

Brown soils	Serozems & Desert soils
Grey-brown soils	Mountain soils
Red-brown soils	Alluvial soils
Laterites	Dunes & semi-fixed sands

Trees of the taiga are, therefore, less healthy than those of N. America.

South of the taiga the mixed coniferous and deciduous temperate forests merge into a zone of deciduous forests where trees have a resting period in winter and summers are dry enough and warm enough to allow humus to form. Further south again are the chernozems, fine-grained loams rich in humus hence their name 'black-earth'. This is the zone of the naturally occurring wooded grassy steppes. The soils are of various kinds but they are very like the loess of northern China where the cohesive properties of the soil allow it to form vertical faces. These fertile soils which are found in Europe, Asia and N. & S. America have all been given over to agriculture.

South again are the rather less fertile chestnut soils of the true steppes. Next follow red and grey soils of the semi-desert and desert steppes.

Beyond the hot deserts are the tropical grasslands and finally at the equator the rain forests (selva) where very tall evergreen trees form a dense forest, denser in S. America than in Africa or Asia. The resting period in which the trees shed their leaves occurs at various times throughout the year.

More than two fifths of all living things on earth are found in the rain forests and there is a tremendous variety of trees and other forms of life in even a small area of forest.

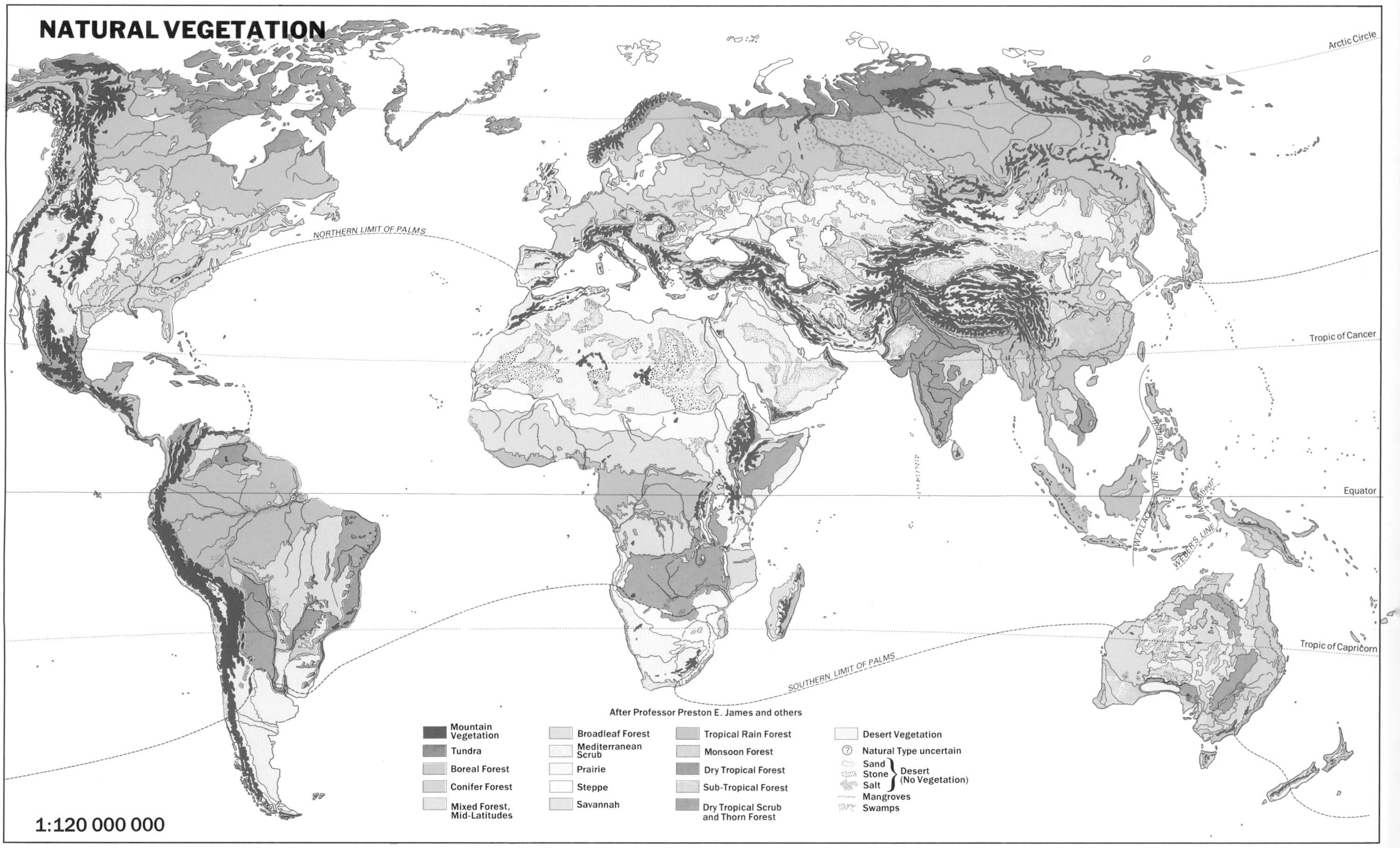

NATURAL VEGETATION

After Professor Preston E. James and others

Mountain Vegetation	Broadleaf Forest	Tropical Rain Forest	Desert Vegetation
Tundra	Mediterranean Scrub	Monsoon Forest	Natural Type uncertain
Boreal Forest	Prairie	Dry Tropical Forest	Sand / Stone / Salt — Desert (No Vegetation)
Conifer Forest	Steppe	Sub-Tropical Forest	Mangroves
Mixed Forest, Mid-Latitudes	Savannah	Dry Tropical Scrub and Thorn Forest	Swamps

1:120 000 000

important in the manufacture of fertilizers. Phosphate rock is exploited widely, though the main volume of production is from U.S.A., U.S.S.R. and Morocco. U.S.S.R., North America, Germany and France are the leading suppliers of potash. Sources of **borax, fluorite** and **sulphur** occur throughout N. America, Europe and western Asia, with U.S.A. a leading producer of all three.

Other Industrial minerals

Asbestos, well-known as a fibrous insulating material; it is produced in U.S.S.R., Canada, Southern Africa, China and Italy. **China clay**, a fine white clay used in the paper, ceramic and cosmetic industries is found in China, northern Europe and U.S.A.
Magnesite, a magnesium ore comes particularly from U.S.S.R., central Europe and China for use in the production of refractories and chemicals.
Mica, used as an electrical insulator, is principally produced in U.S.A. and in smaller quantities throughout Europe and Asia.
Talc, a soft greasy mineral is used as a lubricant and in paper manufacture, paint and cosmetics. Production is mainly from eastern U.S.A., U.S.S.R., France and Italy.

Light metals

Aluminium is extracted from bauxite, an ore occurring in feldspars and other silicates which readily breaks down in tropical conditions. It is therefore often found as a surface crust in tropical areas. Principal producers are Australia, Guinea and Jamaica with smaller but substantial amounts from S.E. Europe, U.S.S.R. and the northern regions of South America. **Titanium** is a heat resistant metal used in high grade steel alloys largely in the aircraft and aerospace industries. The two main ores, rutile and ilmenite, are widespread and plentiful; the main sources include Brazil, Canada and Norway.

Iron

Iron is the second most abundant metallic element in the Earth's crust after aluminium. Rarely found as a free metal it exists in ores of varying constitutions which are smelted to produce metallic iron. Further processing produces steel and combination with other metals makes special steels and alloys with specific properties. Iron ore is mined in many locations but the principal producing areas are U.S.S.R. (the world's leading producer) especially the Ukraine, Australia, Brazil and U.S.A. followed by Canada, China and India. Many other countries produce smaller but nonetheless substantial tonnages.

Ferro-alloy metals

These metals are variously mined in many locations throughout the world but, taken collectively, the most important producing areas are U.S.S.R., South Africa and Canada followed by U.S.A. and China. All of these metals offer specific qualities and properties for the manufacture of a variety of special steels and alloys. **Nickel** and **chromium**, for example, are necessary for the production of high quality stainless steel whilst **vanadium** and **tungsten** help produce very hard steels.

Base metals

Generally mined as ores and compounds the free metal is released after smelting. **Antimony, copper, tin** and **zinc** are important in the making of alloys but each has individual uses related to its specific properties. Copper, **lead, tin** and **zinc** for example, are corrosion resistant under certain conditions, and the liquidity of **mercury** has obvious uses. Often found together or in combination with other metals, they are distributed widely over the Earth's surface and there are many significant producing countries.

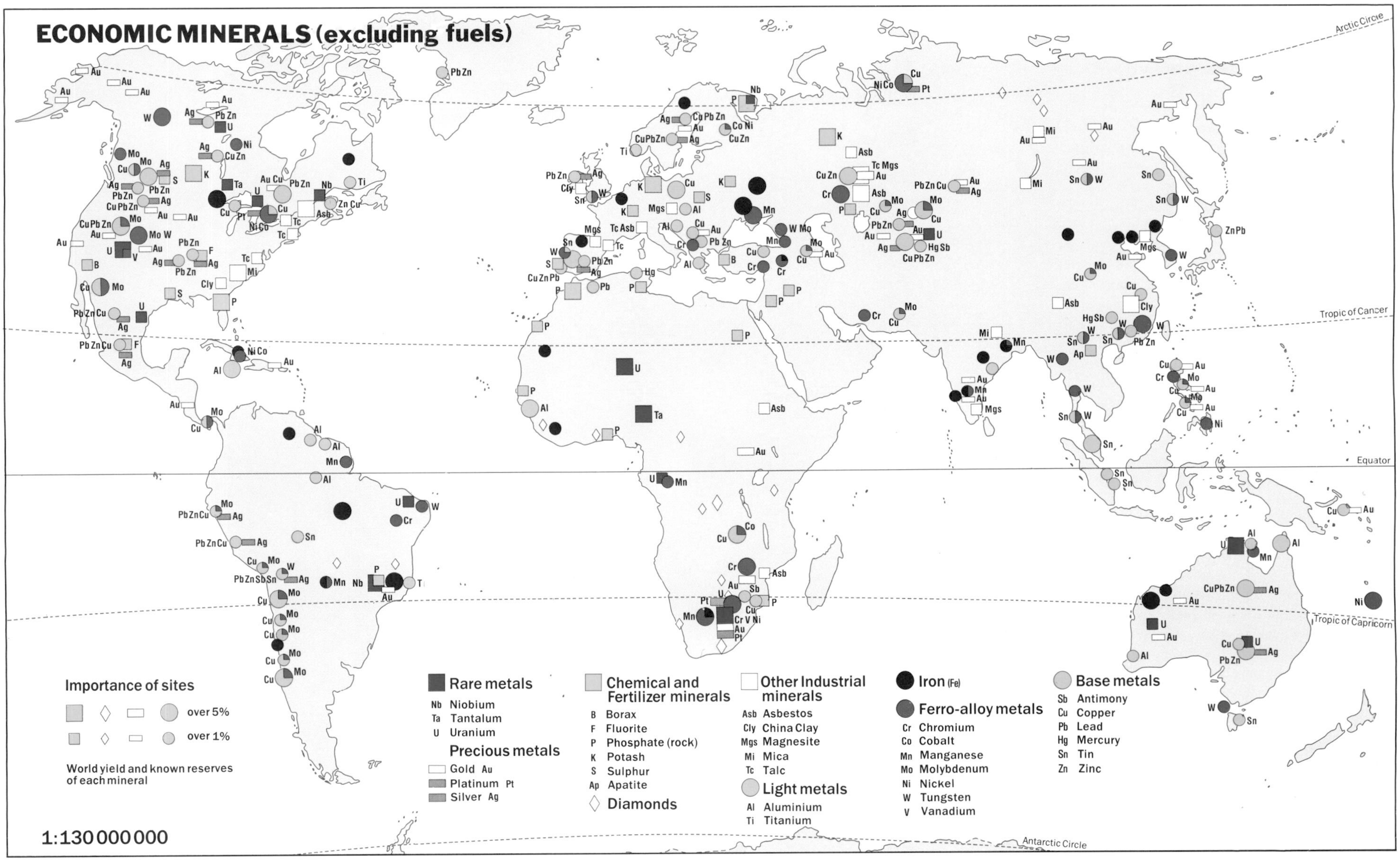

Rare metals

Uranium, the best known and most important of the rare metals owes the expansion of its production to the development of nuclear power and related industries. North America is the largest producer but there are significant deposits in Australia, South Africa, U.S.S.R., Niger, Zaire and Brazil. **Niobium**, a metal used in alloys and toolmaking is mined mainly in Brazil, Canada and U.S.S.R., while **Tantalum**, a corrosion resistant metal valuable to the electronic and chemical industries is found in N. America and Nigeria.

Precious metals

Over and above their more glamorous associations, gold, platinum and silver have a wide range of applications within industry including electronics, chemicals and photography. South Africa dominates the western world's production of **gold** and **platinum**,

Above Manganese nodules form gradually over millions of years around a foreign body. Although they occur over 20% of the ocean floor, only in limited areas are they of economic importance.

accounting for at least two thirds of total output (the major platinum mines are located in Bophuthatswana). U.S.S.R., also a substantial producer of platinum is the other major gold producing country while smaller amounts are found in North America and several other localities worldwide. **Silver** production is less dominated by any one country and is mined throughout the Americas, U.S.S.R. and Australia.

Chemical and Fertilizer minerals

This grouping embraces a variety of minerals occurring in a range of forms and requiring very different recovery techniques. Their usage is widespread in chemical processes throughout industry, **apatite, potash** and **phosphate rock** being especially

ECONOMIC MINERALS (excluding fuels)

Importance of sites

over 5%
over 1%

World yield and known reserves of each mineral

Rare metals
Nb Niobium
Ta Tantalum
U Uranium

Precious metals
Gold Au
Platinum Pt
Silver Ag

Diamonds

Chemical and Fertilizer minerals
B Borax
F Fluorite
P Phosphate (rock)
K Potash
S Sulphur
Ap Apatite

Other Industrial minerals
Asb Asbestos
Cly China Clay
Mgs Magnesite
Mi Mica
Tc Talc

Light metals
Al Aluminium
Ti Titanium

Iron (Fe)

Ferro-alloy metals
Cr Chromium
Co Cobalt
Mn Manganese
Mo Molybdenum
Ni Nickel
W Tungsten
V Vanadium

Base metals
Sb Antimony
Cu Copper
Pb Lead
Hg Mercury
Sn Tin
Zn Zinc

1:130 000 000

ENERGY

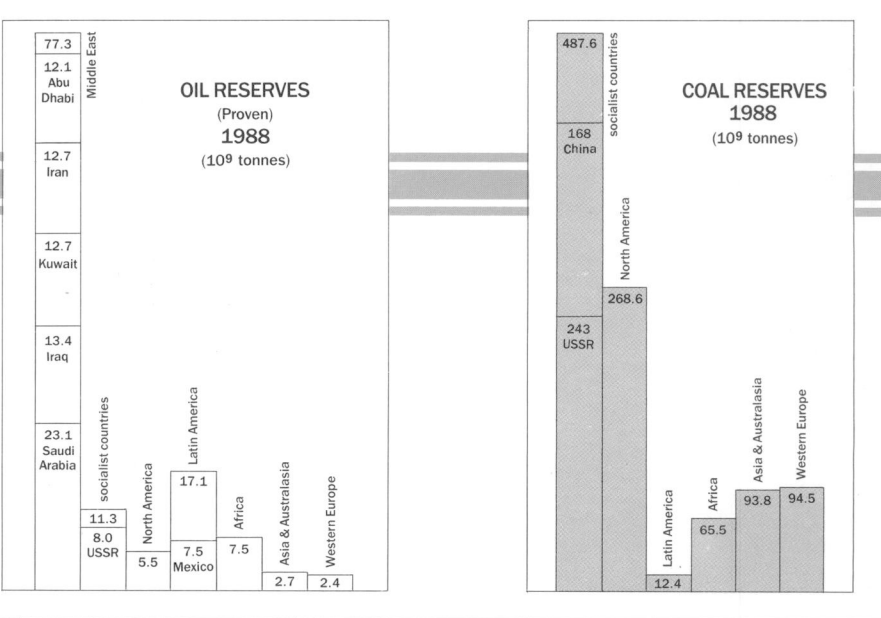

Taken together, the maps and diagrams though concerned with energy, give in graphic form, a summary of two centuries of economic growth.

Coal powered the industrial revolution and replaced wood as the primary source for industrial and domestic heat.

From the end of World War I another economic transformation began. Oil which had been used since remotest times to provide light and heat began to achieve major industrial importance. The last coal-fired ships vanished from the seas and with them the coal-bunkering stations disposed around the world. On land the internal-combustion engine replaced the horse; oil-fired electricity generation began to challenge coal-fired plants.

The end of World War II marked the start of unparalleled economic growth. Between 1950 and 1984 world energy demand increased four-fold, the steepest rise occurring between 1960 and 1970. In this period coal lost its pre-eminence as a source of energy. An oil industry developed to produce a variety of fuels and lubricants. It contained a large petro-chemical element.

Eighty per cent of this stupendous industrial expansion was based in North America (particularly the U.S.A.), W. Europe, the U.S.S.R. and Japan. Oil and gas were the sources of the additional energy required for the expansion and the Middle East was the source of half the oil consumed.

The oil producing and exporting nations (OPEC) decided to raise the price of oil in 1973 thus bringing to an end the era of low-price energy. Revolution in Iran and the outbreak of war between Iraq and Iran caused a further escalation in price in 1979. Oil was then 17 times dearer than in 1972. Demand fell. The continued search for alternative sources was intensified. Rate of production fell below rate of discovery once more. Middle East share of world oil production fell from 50% to 32% by 1984. However, the Middle East still possesses over 50% of proved reserves.

Off-shore technology in exploration and exploitation have created a new oil technology. Operations in Alaska and Siberia have taxed the ingenuity of the oil-industry in combating severe climatic conditions.

Oil and gas reserves are constantly reviewed as new discoveries are made but the life of both is relatively short. Coal reserves are probably adequate for the next 250 years. In the coming decades the use of oil will increasingly be restricted to areas like transport where no alternative exists. Coal will once more be in the ascendancy. Coal gas which has been virtually replaced by natural gas may once more be used. Extraction of oil from coal may also be practised. Other sources of oil and gas are bituminous shales and tar sands.

Among the possible alternative energy sources are those in which the energy expended is renewed. Wind-generation and tidal power are two such examples. Although they may well be economically operated the installation costs are prodigious.

Nuclear energy alone promises to be capable of meeting future demands. Early promises of this form of generation providing abundant and cheap energy were not fulfilled. Fears that the supply of uranium would run out have been dispelled by enrichment techniques which yield 50 to 60 times the output. Strong opposition from those concerned for the environment has been the principle reason why the nuclear industry has been retarded. The accident at Three-Mile Island in the United States in 1979 had a profound effect on public opinion which will be reinforced by that at Chernobyl' in the Ukraine in April 1986.

Still further options remain. All nuclear energy at the moment is based on nuclear fission. If nuclear fusion techniques were developed an unlimited supply of energy could be provided by the oceans. The process would be the same as that by which the Sun creates its energy. Geothermal power is practical and feasible. Another source is the transformation of the Sun's light into electricity by photovoltaique techniques. Alternatively, solar energy can be converted into micro-waves by satellite. Such methods are for the next century, not this.

SOURCES OF ENERGY

Oil

Gas

Coal

Lignite

Uranium

Hydro-Electric

Oil pipeline

Gas pipeline

COMPARATIVE DEVELOPMENT
as shown by Energy Consumption

Percentage of total world population

Energy consumption per head (metric tons coal equivalent)

High — 8.0
6.3%
21.3% — 2.0
64.3%
7.8% — 0.2
Low

1:59 000 000

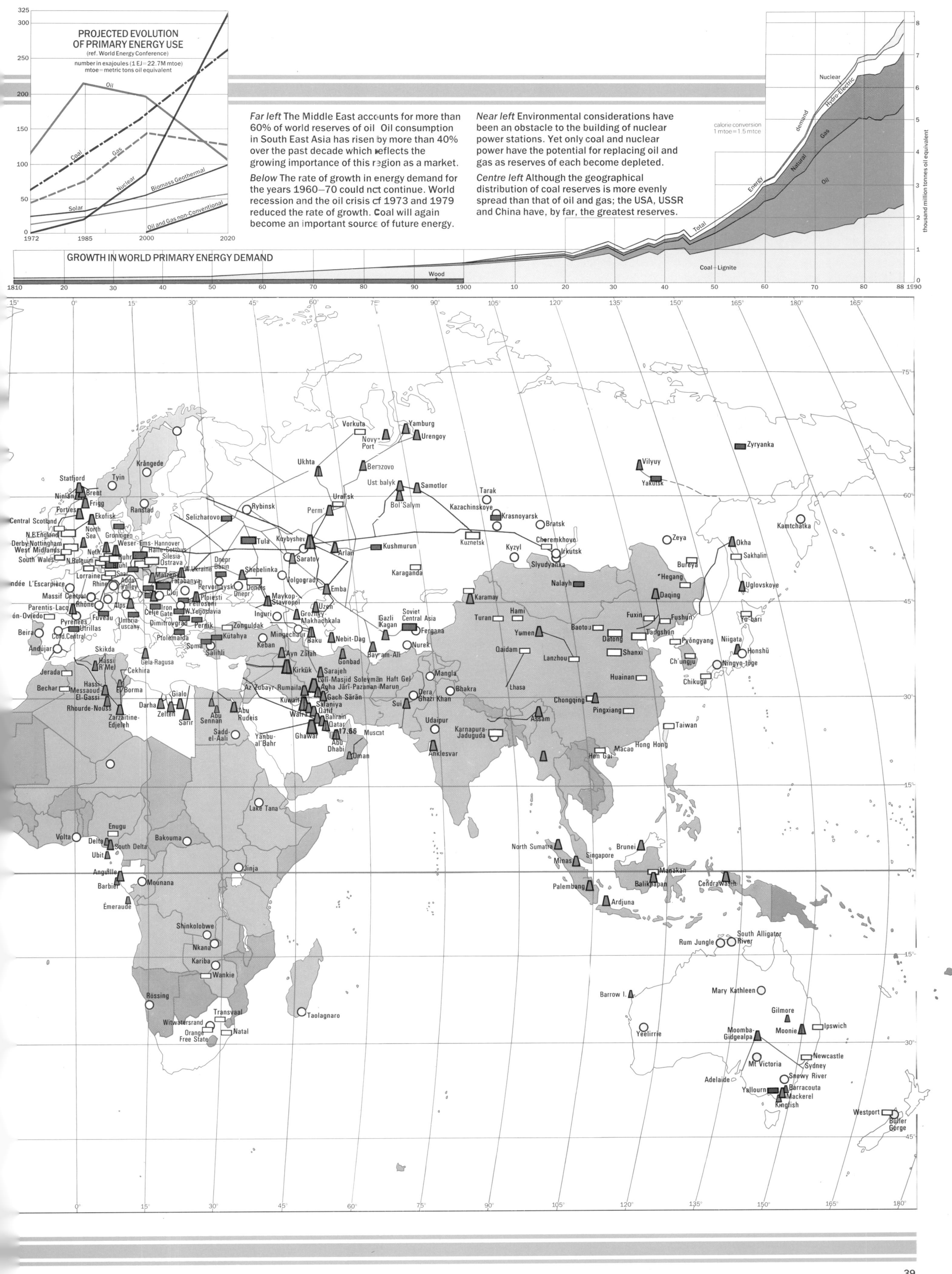

PROJECTED EVOLUTION OF PRIMARY ENERGY USE
(ref. World Energy Conference)
number in exajoules (1 EJ = 22.7M mtoe)
mtoe = metric tons oil equivalent

Oil
Coal
Gas
Nuclear
Solar
Biomass Geothermal
Oil and Gas non-Conventional

1972 1985 2000 2020

Far left The Middle East accounts for more than 60% of world reserves of oil. Oil consumption in South East Asia has risen by more than 40% over the past decade which reflects the growing importance of this region as a market.

Below The rate of growth in energy demand for the years 1960–70 could not continue. World recession and the oil crisis of 1973 and 1979 reduced the rate of growth. Coal will again become an important source of future energy.

Near left Environmental considerations have been an obstacle to the building of nuclear power stations. Yet only coal and nuclear power have the potential for replacing oil and gas as reserves of each become depleted.

Centre left Although the geographical distribution of coal reserves is more evenly spread than that of oil and gas; the USA, USSR and China have, by far, the greatest reserves.

GROWTH IN WORLD PRIMARY ENERGY DEMAND

Wood

1810 20 30 40 50 60 70 80 90 1900 10 20 30 40 50 60 70 80 88 1990

Nuclear
Hydro-Electric
Energy demand
Natural Gas
Oil
Total
Coal – Lignite

calorie conversion
1 mtoe = 1.5 mtce

thousand million tonnes oil equivalent

39

FOOD

With a world population which has doubled in the half-century between 1925 and 1975, it is a source of wonderment that more people are not starving. Especially since a further increase of 25% in the number of mouths to feed occurred in the decade up to 1985. It is still more remarkable when it is remembered that only about 11% of the Earth's land surface is under cultivation and that includes areas of non-food products like rubber. The credit for this achievement must be given to the development of artificial fertilizers; the conditioning of plants to alien climates; the development of high-yield seeds and new strains and generally improved agricultural technology. There is no great reserve of land ready to be brought into crop production. The outlook for the future is of a world in which the poorest areas have the highest population growth and the greatest difficulty in producing sufficient food. Matters of immediate concern are the current rate of soil erosion through the felling of trees, over-cropping, and the loss of fertility of world soils through unwise use of artificial fertilizers. Animal manure and vegetable waste are frequently used as fuel. Cash crops are planted where food · crops are needed. Even if organic matter were returned to the soil and all the land were devoted to food crops, the required yields would not necessarily be achieved. In many of the poorest areas improved seeds and fertilizers would still be required. Food provision is not therefore, simply a matter of agricultural technology and distribution. Political and social factors are also involved.

From the land now under cultivation 98% of all food is produced. The other 2% comes from the sea. Unless, through some miracle of laboratory science, protein can be artificially created in sufficient quantities, the sea is the only major source available in the immediate future for supplementing the food potential of the land. Fish-farming, practised in East Asia for four thousand years, has been taken up in several parts of the world but it has been restricted to certain types of fish and shell-fish. The land, however, remains the main source of food and future yields depend on soil conservation and recovery; the development of new strains; conservation of food plants now under threat of extinction; elimination of pests and diseases; improved animal husbandry; investigating new sources of vegetable protein and synthetic food production.

Nutritional standards vary from nation to nation as do diets. North America, Western Europe, Australia and New Zealand are the great meat-eaters; East Asia consumes more fish and less meat but much of the world is dependent on cereal crops, beans and pulses. In overall calorie terms the best-fed nations take in on average, daily, almost three times the average of the worst-fed. Comparing the daily calorie intake of average low-calorie groups of countries with Canada, the United States, Argentina, Western Europe, Australia, and New Zealand there is a gap of more than 1300 calories. Reducing this disparity must depend on improved local food production provided at the same time the present high rate of population growth can be abated.

Arctic Circle
Tropic of Cancer
Equator
Tropic of Capricorn
Calorie Sources
Wheat
Maize
Barley
Millet, Sorghum
Rice
Starchy Roots
Sugar
Potatoes
Protein Sources
3
2
1
Choice of Meats Beef, Pork, Mutton
Dairy Produce
Fish
3 or 4
1 or 2
Choice of Pulses Beans, Peas, etc.
Animal Fat
Limits of Hunger Belt (less than 2750 calories per day)

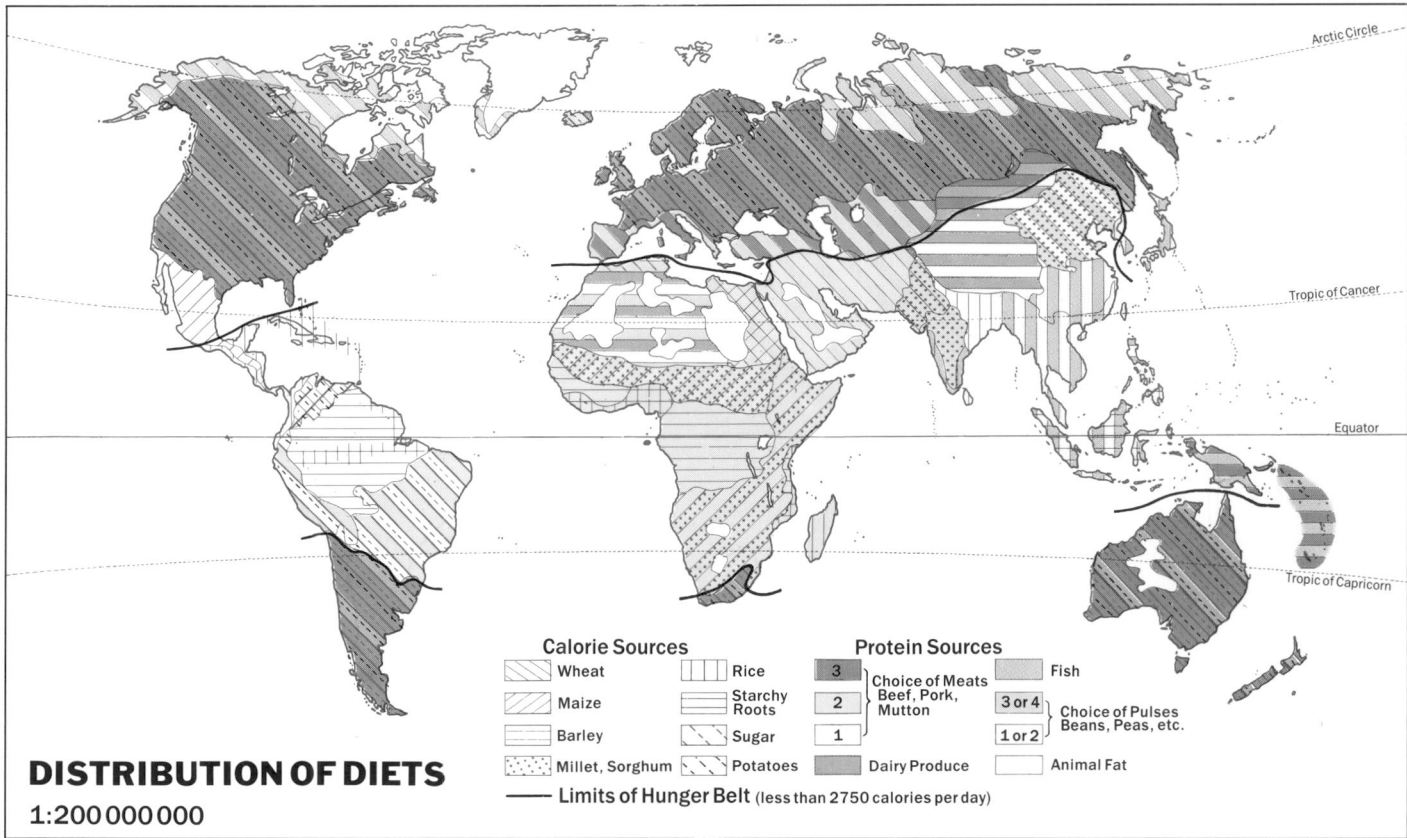

DISTRIBUTION OF DIETS
1:200 000 000

FOOD SOURCES

Arctic Circle
Tropic of Cancer
Equator
Tropic of Capricorn
High Yield Zones
Wheat
Maize
Barley, Oats, Rye
Rice
Millets
Sea fishing
Livestock
Dairy farming
Cattle
Sheep
Pigs
Major Specialised Crops
Sugar beet/cane
Apples
Bananas
Citrus fruit
Vine growing
Coffee
Cocoa
Tea
1 2 Soybeans/Groundnuts
3 4 Cottonseed/Sunflower
Low Yield Zones
Tundra, Ice-cap
Forest
Mountain
Extensive grassland
Desert, semi-desert

1:150 000 000

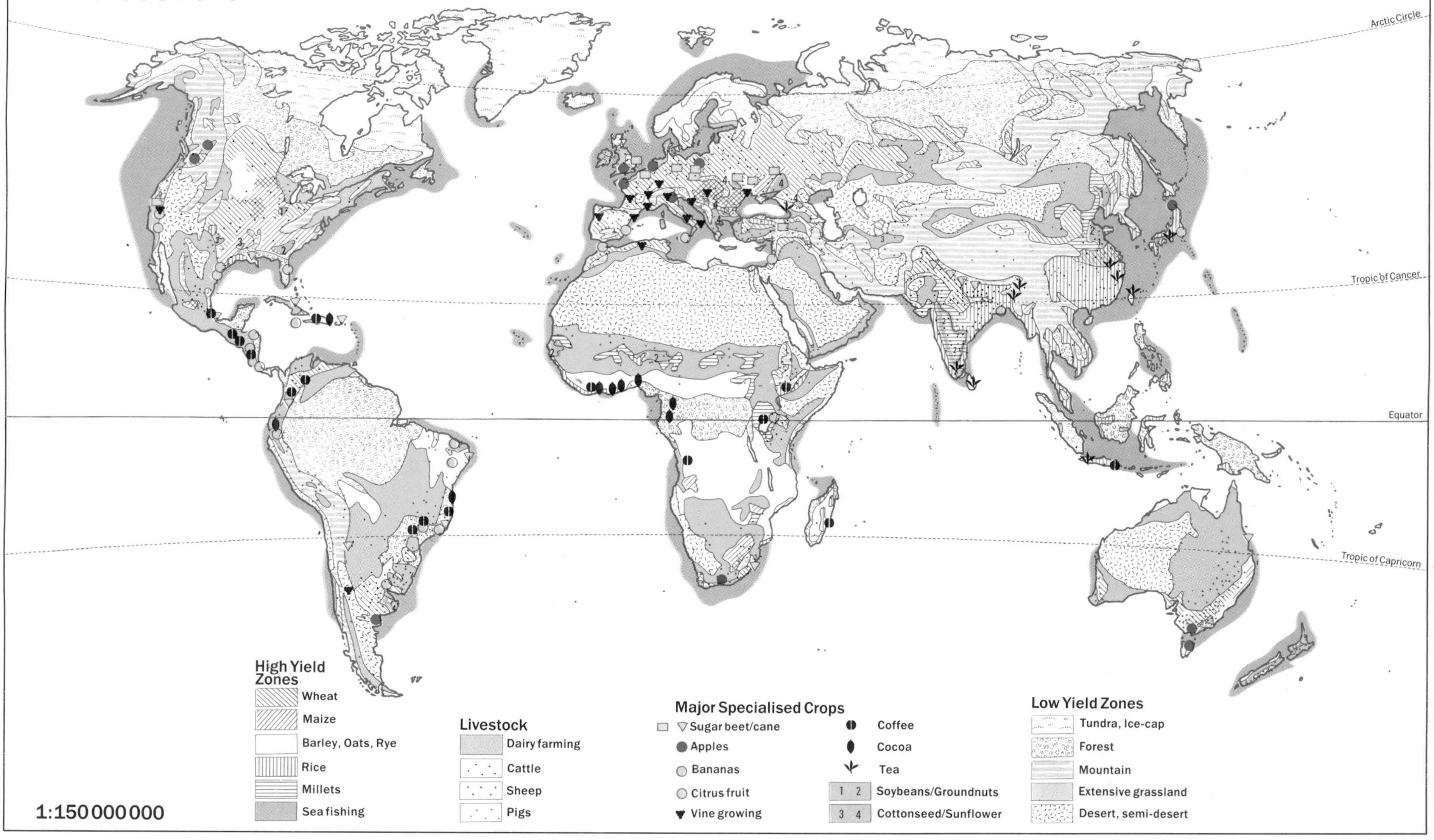

In the view of many people, proliferation of the human race is, in itself and its environmental consequences, a threat to the future of all life on this planet. The twentieth century promises to close with 3.6 times as many people as there were at the beginning. Fortunately, the high rate of annual increase (1.99%) of the period up to 1975 has been reduced, and consequently, there will be almost 1.5 billion fewer people at the end of the century than was at one time anticipated. Assuming that the present growth (1.67%) continues, there will be 6.1 billion people by AD2000.

For any country a growth rate in excess of 2% can spell disaster: 2% means a doubling of population in 35 years, 2.5% gives a doubling in 28 years and a growth of 3.5% doubles in only 20 years. Rate of growth is dependent on the number of live births, infant mortality and the death rate. The increase in numbers has been largely the result of reduction in infant mortality and the death rate in adults. People are living longer and a reduction in the number of live births may well be counter-balanced by prolonged life.

There is a kind of north-south divide, if one excludes Australia and New Zealand, with the technologically developed world approaching zero growth while the rest of the world continues to increase, in some areas at an alarming rate. Kenya's sustained annual growth rate of over 4% makes it the highest in Africa although most countries in this continent have a growth rate of more than 2%. This growth rate is high in spite of shorter life expectancy and high infant mortality (114 per 1000 compared with 16 for Europe and 12 for North America).

Today, Albania alone in Europe has a rate of growth in excess of 2%. The United Kingdom, Sweden, Denmark, Luxembourg,

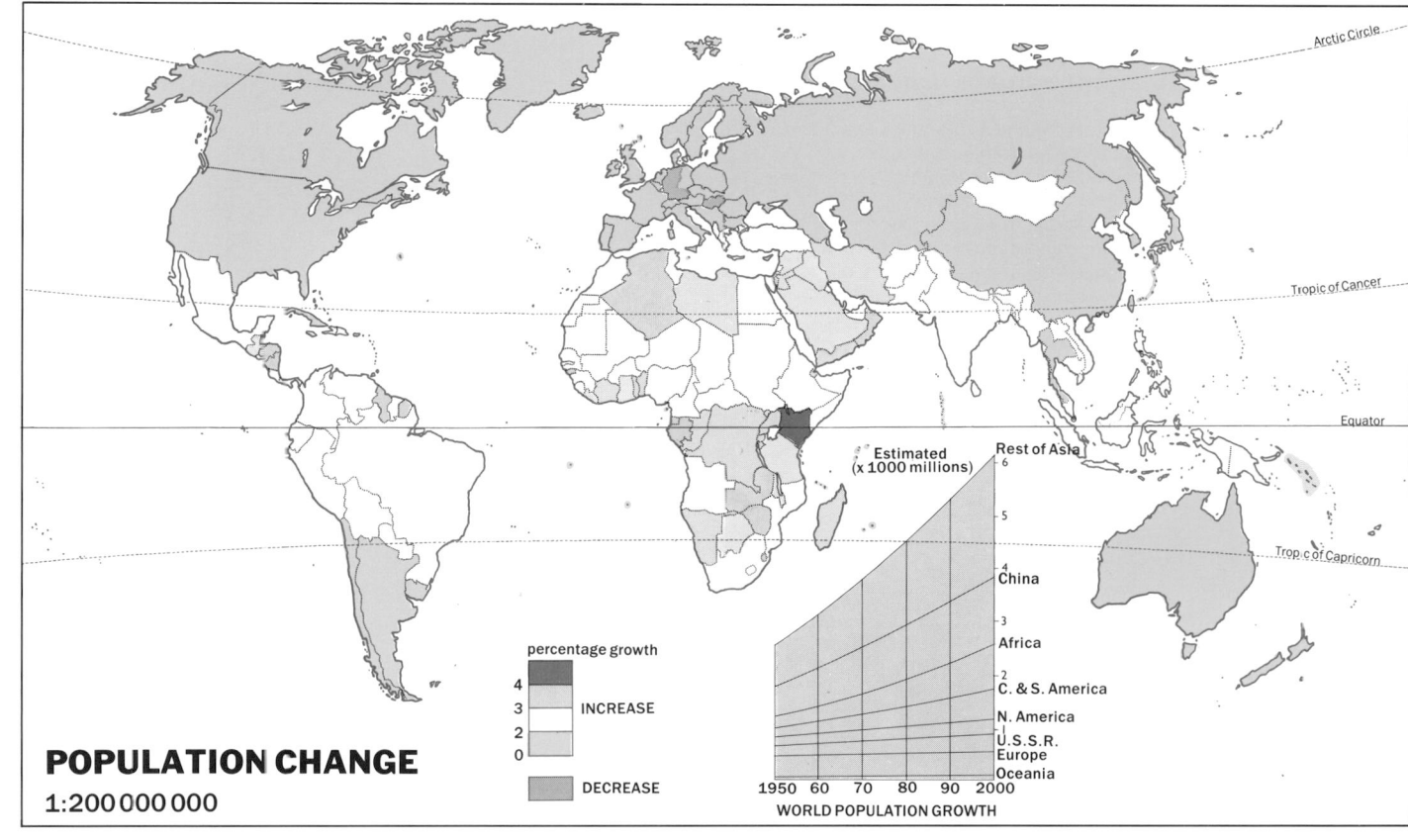

POPULATION CHANGE
1:200 000 000

percentage growth

4
3
2   INCREASE
0

DECREASE

Estimated (x 1000 millions)

Rest of Asia
China
Africa
C. & S. America
N. America
U.S.S.R.
Europe
Oceania

WORLD POPULATION GROWTH

1950 60 70 80 90 2000

Hungary, Switzerland, Austria, and East and West Germany have achieved zero or negative growth. Japan, U.S.A. and the U.S.S.R. have achieved a rate below 1%.

China's policy of population control has brought the growth rate down to 1.17% not far removed from Ireland (1.11%) and from Canada (1.2%) the highest of the northern nations. India, likewise has, by its birth control policy, slowed its rate of growth yet at present rates the combined populations of China and India will exceed 2½ billion by the end of the century at which time the population of Asia will have equalled or surpassed the total world population of 1975.

In Central and South America a high average birth-rate by country is accompanied by a general lowering of the death-rate which for most of the area is about the same as that of Canada and U.S.A., Europe, U.S.S.R., Japan, China, Australia and New Zealand all of which are either 10 or less per 1000 compared with 10 to 20 for Africa and Southern Asia (except Malaysia, Thailand and Philippines). Life expectancy is lowest in parts of Africa and Asia – below 40 years compared with over 70 for almost all the developed world.

Increased longevity, reduced infant mortality and a high birth rate will inevitably change the numbers of young and old who live as dependants. Providing for them is a great challenge for the next few generations.

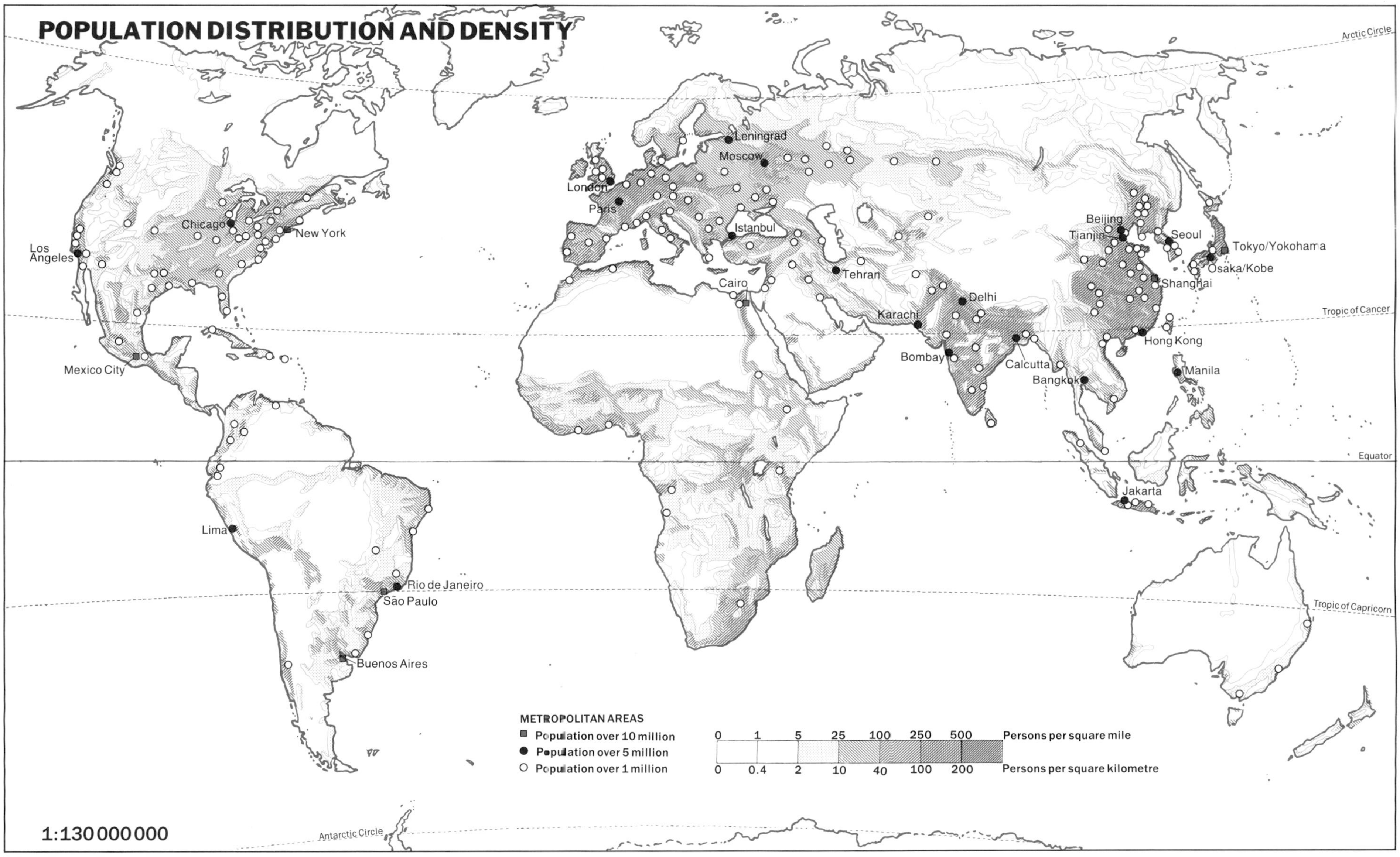

POPULATION DISTRIBUTION AND DENSITY

Leningrad
Moscow
London
Paris
Chicago
New York
Los Angeles
Istanbul
Tehran
Cairo
Beijing
Tianjin
Seoul
Tokyo/Yokohama
Osaka/Kobe
Shanghai
Delhi
Karachi
Bombay
Calcutta
Hong Kong
Bangkok
Manila
Mexico City
Lima
Rio de Janeiro
São Paulo
Buenos Aires
Jakarta

METROPOLITAN AREAS
■ Population over 10 million
● Population over 5 million
○ Population over 1 million

0 1 5 25 100 250 500   Persons per square mile

0 0.4 2 10 40 100 200   Persons per square kilometre

1:130 000 000

PATTERNS OF HUMAN SETTLEMENT

1 Carnoet, France Farmsteads widely dispersed on compact holdings, with scattered hamlets and small villages containing community facilities like churches, schools and shops. In western Europe such a pattern occurs especially in regions where Celtic traditions survive.

2 Ierstedt, Germany Highly nucleated rural settlement. Few farmsteads occur outside the large, rather formless villages, because traditionally farms are composed of separate scattered strips, although land consolidation is now widespread.

3 Middelburg, Holland Medieval towns in western Europe were small and compact by modern standards. Winding, narrow streets led to a central market square, around which were the town's chief public buildings (town hall, guildhall, the main church). Walls usually protected the town, but when later demolished, their line is often shown by roughly circular streets. Many present-day large cities have such medieval towns as a historic core, but Middelburg has not expanded greatly due to a restricted economic basis.

4 Heerhugowaard, Holland Strongly linear rural settlement of high density in a region of intensive farming. Land reclamation confines building to the elevated dikes that line major drainage canals. Villages are large, extending considerable distances along roadsides.

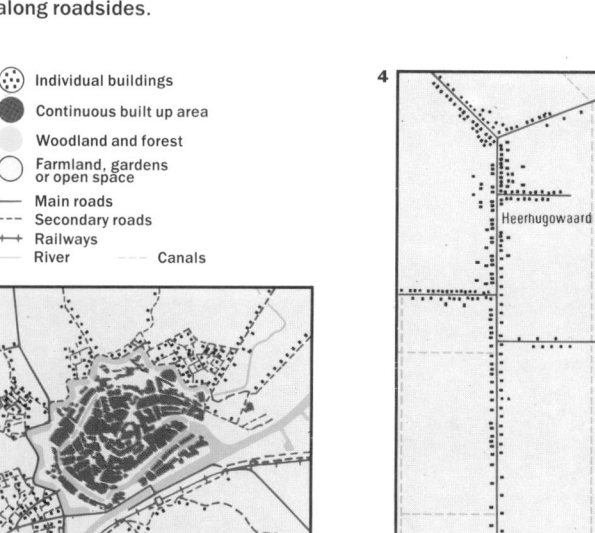

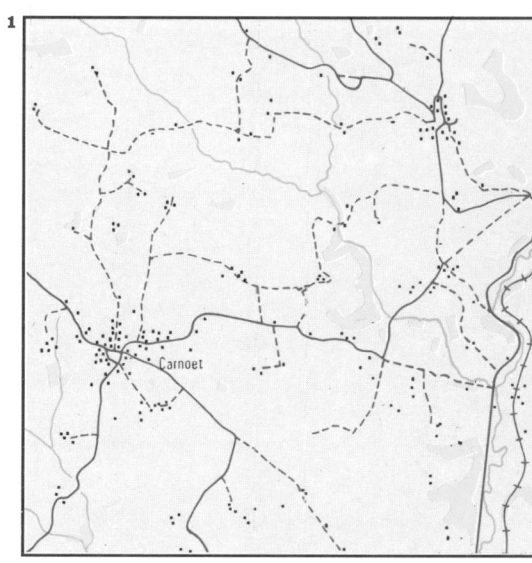

Individual buildings
Continuous built up area
Woodland and forest
Farmland, gardens or open space
— Main roads
--- Secondary roads
+++ Railways
— River   === Canals

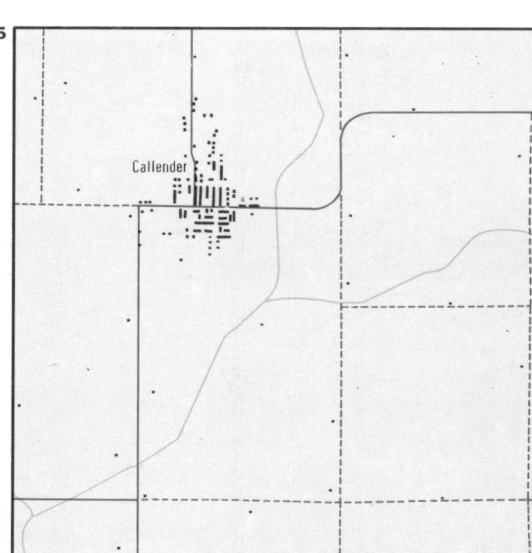

Scale of all maps: 1 inch to 1 mile

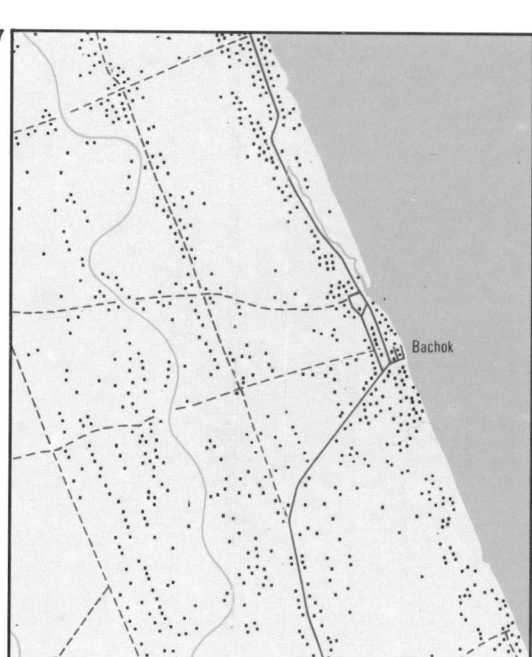

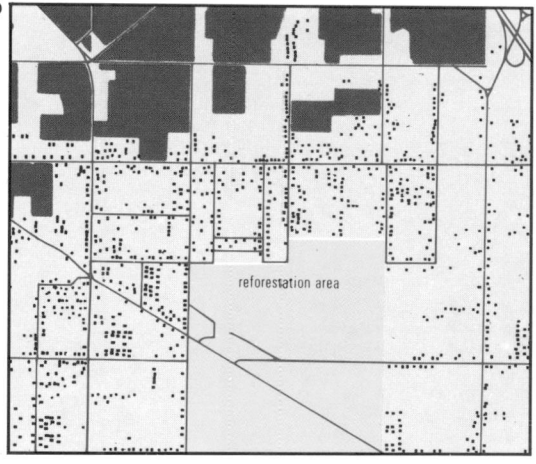

5 Callender, Iowa, USA To dispose of public land to settlers, US government surveys after 1785 created 1-mile square farm units ('sections'), though many have since been subdivided. Dispersed rural settlement thus appeared from the outset, with small nucleated villages at intervals throughout the area. Roads were built along most section boundaries, giving a characteristic checkerboard pattern.

6 Kangundo, Kenya Moderately dense pattern of dispersed settlement in a tribal farming economy. Community facilities like markets and schools stand on isolated sites, not having formed, here at least, nuclei around which villages have evolved.

7 Bachok, Malaysia This linear arrangement of houses and villages has been strongly influenced by the existence of parallel sandy beach ridges. These are elevated slightly above the flat intervening tracts that are seasonally flooded for paddy (rice) cultivation.

8 Gentilly, Quebec French colonists in North America divided land into narrow plots, initially running back from rivers, with farms close together for safety, and along the river banks for access to water transport. This 'long lot' system later developed to incorporate other rows of farms along roads, often parallel to the rivers. Villages grew up especially around churches.

9 Fort Mann, BC, Canada The characteristic sprawl of the North American 'rural-urban fringe'. Without tight control on development, and often with intense land speculation, sporadic growth of this kind occurs commonly around American cities. Housing appears in small clusters, or along roads, or on scattered individual lots. Non-residential uses develop, especially those needing ample space, e.g. shopping centres, factories, motels, drive-in cinemas or schools. Set among all these are recreational open spaces such as golf courses and country clubs. What is left of earlier farmsteads forms another component in this highly diversified area.

10 East Kilbride, Scotland The British New Towns, all established since 1946, are planned urban communities drawing population chiefly from conurbations (London and Clydeside especially), for which by intention they relieve housing pressures. Local employment is simultaneously created to make each New Town as independent as possible economically and socially. Earlier New Towns are composed of several neighbourhood units around the town centre, each neighbourhood containing a range of facilities for the everyday needs of its residents (primary schools, shops, churches, doctors, meeting halls, etc.). East Kilbride, Scotland (designated 1947) is an excellent example.

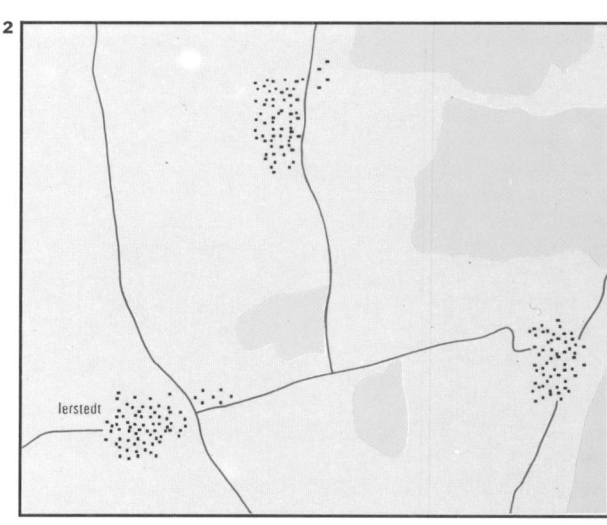

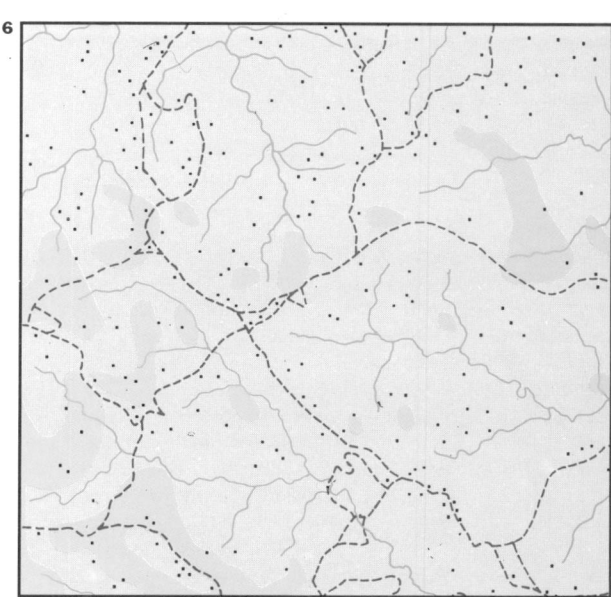

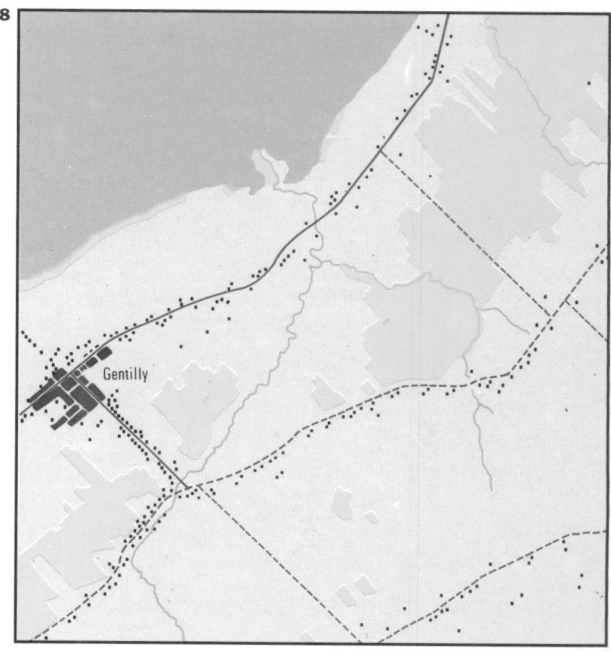

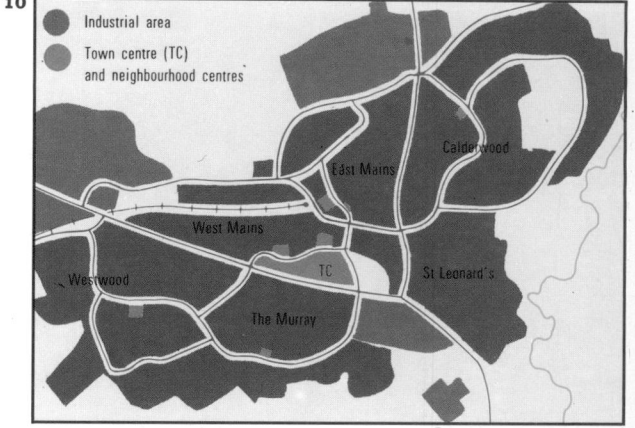

Industrial area
Town centre (TC) and neighbourhood centres

Taking the world as a whole 41% of people are said to be urban. In the technologically developed world the figure is 72% and for the less developed world 31%. Such figures give no idea of the concentrations of the population. In the developed world urban population tends to be distributed between many towns and cities. In the developing world there has been a trend over the past three or four decades for the population to migrate towards a single city, the capital, and the area immediately adjacent. The overall trend is migration from a rural to urban way of life, a movement which began when the first cities were founded. For most of history the transfer has been slow. However, today in much of the developing world it is proceeding at an extremely high rate.

Rural settlement has always depended for its character on a number of factors: climate; type of land-use; water supply; method of land allocation; transport and communications; history and tradition. Patterns vary from total dispersion to linear arrangements or clustering. Density of population depends on the type of land-use, being very sparse in cold temperate forest land to extremely dense settlements in the river valleys of southern and eastern Asia, the Nile Valley and delta and the large rivers of China, the criterion being how many people the type of land-use will support.

The cities of early history were founded on trade and commerce. They became centres of administration, wealth and power. Mining and the extractive industries in general, led to the foundation of other urban communities. In the industrial revolution the number and size of such communities increased rapidly and, linked by the supporting communications networks, developed into conurbations. The industrial areas of N. America, Britain, Germany and later Japan are examples. Interconnection of conurbations created the megalopolis of the eastern U.S.A.; Tokyo-Osaka; the Midlands and the South-East of England and the Ruhr in Germany. Above all, the industrial centres and their infra-structure grew at the pace required for the accommodation of an expanding work-force, the built-up areas of towns increasing at least as fast as the growth of population. New towns were built before the influx of population attracted by the newly developed industries. It was a period of high birth-rate and the subsequent fall in birth-rate reduced the pressure on housing. This process contrasts sharply with the developing world today. Great though the

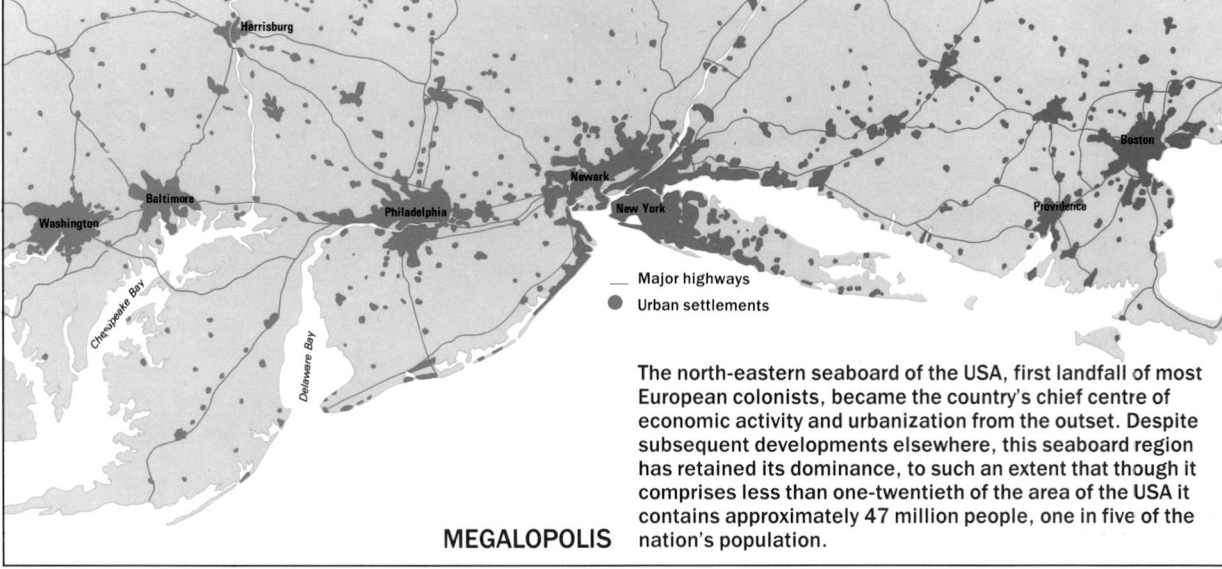

_ Major highways
● Urban settlements

MEGALOPOLIS

The north-eastern seaboard of the USA, first landfall of most European colonists, became the country's chief centre of economic activity and urbanization from the outset. Despite subsequent developments elsewhere, this seaboard region has retained its dominance, to such an extent that though it comprises less than one-twentieth of the area of the USA it contains approximately 47 million people, one in five of the nation's population.

overall changes were, they took place over a long period in comparison with the rate of growth of urban population which has been occurring in the developing world over the past forty years.

In the U.S.S.R. there are 22 cities with more than 1 million population where there were only 8 or so in 1964. Alma-Ata had 456,000 inhabitants in 1964. It had almost 1.1 million in 1985. In the 1930s there were few cities with more than 100,000 inhabitants; there are 276 today. In 1940, just under 33% of the total population was classified as urban. In 1985, the percentage was 68%. By way of comparison, the Federal Republic of Germany has 94% urban and Belgium 95% compared with 88% for the Netherlands, 76% for the United Kingdom; 74% for the U.S.A.

Although the growth of the urban population of the U.S.S.R. has been rapid, the extra number of people living in towns and cities since 1959 almost exactly equals the increase in total population of the U.S.S.R. in the same period. In other words the extra people added are urban. However, they are distributed among a great many urban communities.

Comparing the U.S.S.R. with Egypt, between 1932 and 1985 the population of Egypt increased from 14.2 million to 47 million, whereas Cairo, in the same period grew from 1,060,000 to 3.6 million by 1947 and 12 million by 1985, an overall rate of growth of more than three times the national rate. In spite of extreme congestion the city continues to grow in defiance of inducements to go to Asyût or Alexandria and other cities.

The lure of the capital city is widespread throughout the developing world. Seoul in South Korea increased its population from 3.6 million in 1955 to over 14 million in 1981 and today more than half S. Korea's population of 43 million lives in or around Seoul. Mexico City has continued to grow long after it was thought to have reached saturation point at 14 million. In 1985 there was an estimated 17.5 million in the city and its peripheral areas. This growth of Mexico City, too is despite government inducements to settle in other provincial capitals. The population of Tehran has grown to approximately 9 million in 1985. Its population in 1933 was only 350,000.

Jakarta and its metropolitan area doubled in population from 1961–1981. A programme of transmigration is operating to transfer people from overcrowded Java to Sumatra and others of the 13,500 islands which make up the Indonesian archipelago. No such large-scale plan exists in other developing countries in some of which more than half the population now lives around the periphery of the capital city. In the communist world of centrally planned economies the growth of the capital city is restricted. Pyongyang was re-built after the Korean War and the population remains approximately static at 1.8 million. Saigon (Ho Chi Minh City) in Vietnam has experienced a reduction in population of more than one-third to approximately 3 million. It is evident that migration to the capital city tends to occur unless there is government control on the movements of people. Growth of cities like Cairo in Egypt and the Quito-Guayaquil urban complex in Ecuador which has also exhibited a growth rate exceeding the natural population rate, continue as long as the opportunities for employment or greater wealth remain.

In the developed world the tendency for the past three decades has been a movement of de-centralization made possible by the creation of new industries in provincial regions and re-location of existing commerce and industry as part of central planning. Tokyo-Osaka and the metropolitan area of London are examples. The re-location of commerce and industry and the migration of the population from an urban environment to the surrounding rural areas are particularly marked in the United States.

In the case of the developing world increased services, housing, water supply, energy, communications and transport place a considerable burden on the economy.

As long as the population of the developing world continues to increase at its present high rate so long will urban population continue to grow. There is no possibility of agriculture or forestry assimilating large numbers of extra people. They will become urban dwellers adding to the populations of the largest of a small number of cities.

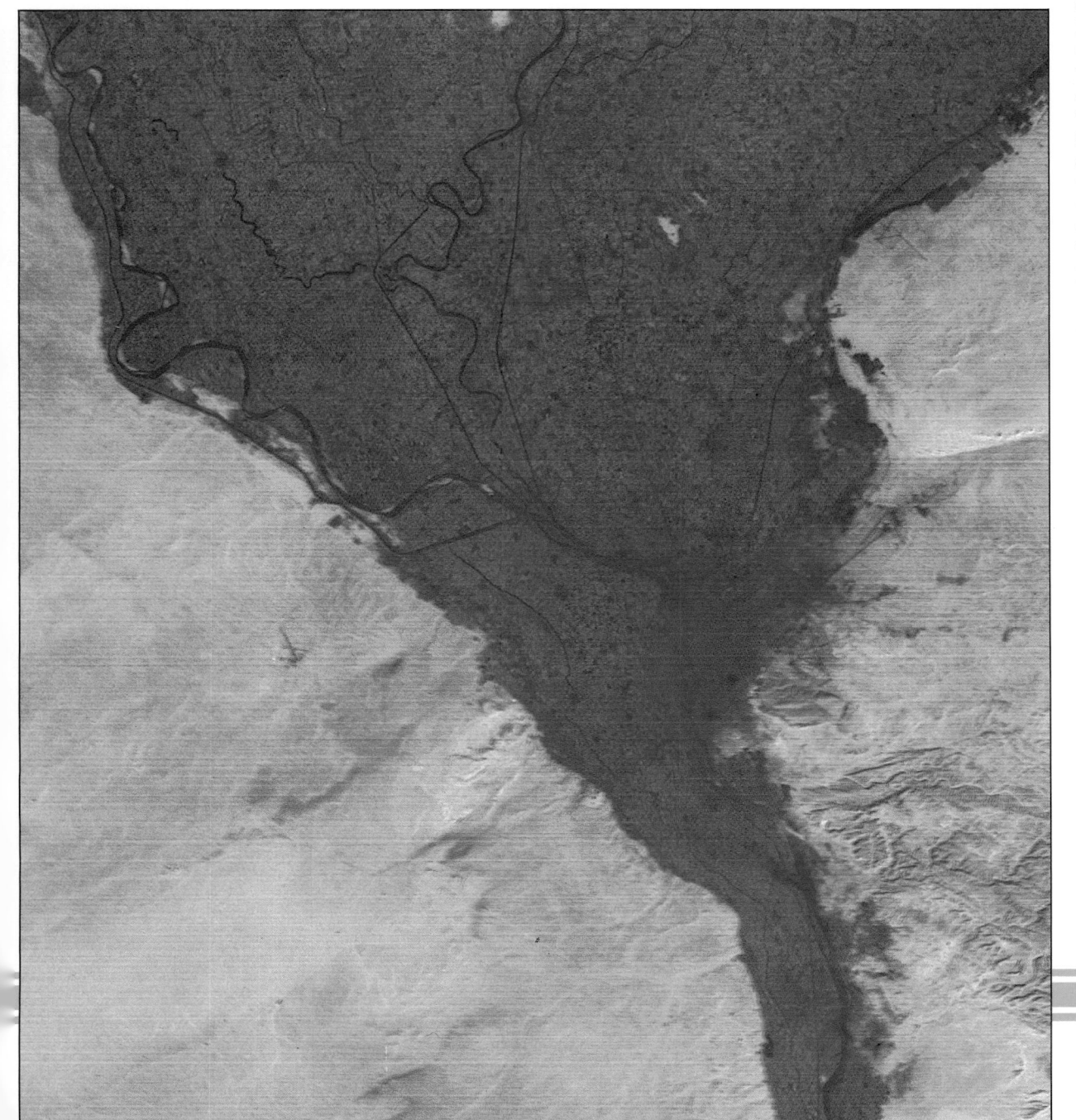

Left Landsat satellite imagery of the Nile delta shows clearly the abrupt boundary between cultivated land and barren desert. The Cairo conurbation has spread to fill all the available land between the river and the desert. This is visible because enhancement of the image using false colour has aided identification: vegetation is coloured red, water is black and built-up areas and roads are dark purple. The desert areas have retained their natural grey-brown colour.

MAP PROJECTIONS

Map projection is the means by which the imaginary lines of latitude and longitude (the graticule) on a three-dimensional globe are transferred to two-dimensional paper. This transfer cannot be made without error of some kind. Most map projections are no more than a mathematical arrangement of the lines of latitude and longitude to try to achieve a specified result but their underlying principles are firmly based on the concept of perspective projection from a view-point, or light-source onto a plane, a cone or a cylinder tangent to (touching) the globe or secant to (cutting) it.

tangent cylinder — tangent cone — tangent plane
secant cylinder — secant cone — secant plane
increasing distortion

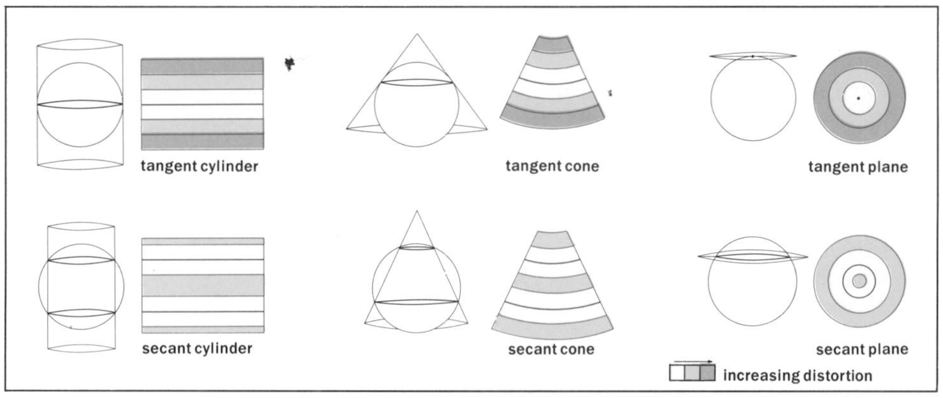

The cylinder and the cone can be opened to form a plane and, therefore, serve for projection of the graticule. Either may be tangent, with one standard parallel, or be secant, with two in order to reduce scale-errors overall. Projections may preserve shape (be *conformal*) or area (when they are called *equal-area*) or preserve distance from a central point (be *equidistant*). No two of those properties can exist in a single projection. A projection may dispense with all three in favour of another property e.g. minimum scale-error. It may just aim at good general shape for land, ocean or a region.

MAPS OF THE HEMISPHERE

Orthographic projection gives the view as seen from an infinite distance. It is most used for the visible face of the Moon. Other azimuthal projections are best explained by their polar case. In the *stereographic* the projection is from one pole on to a plane tangent at the other. Meridians and parallels plot as circles, arcs of circles or straight lines. In the *equidistant*, the straight, radiating meridians are true to scale. The parallels are equally-spaced concentric circles. Distances are correct along a meridian (but not in other directions). In *Lambert's Equal-Area*, the parallels are so spaced that the area enclosed by two meridians and any two parallels is in true proportion to the corresponding area on the globe.

Orthographic — Stereographic — Equidistant — Lambert azimuthal equal-area

REGIONAL MAPS

In the *conic with one standard parallel*, the parallel of tangency is made true to scale. Others are concentric circles drawn from the apex of the cone, usually at their correct spacing. Scale errors are reduced with *two standard parallels* of true length and spacing. Neither projection is conformal or equal-area but they can be made so. The conformal version of both has been widely used in topographic maps and aeronautical charts. *Bonne*, a modified conic with one standard parallel is equal-area. The central meridian and all parallels are correctly subdivided. The standard parallel is true to scale. Other parallels are arcs of circles concentric with it. Meridians are curved lines where they are straight in the other two.

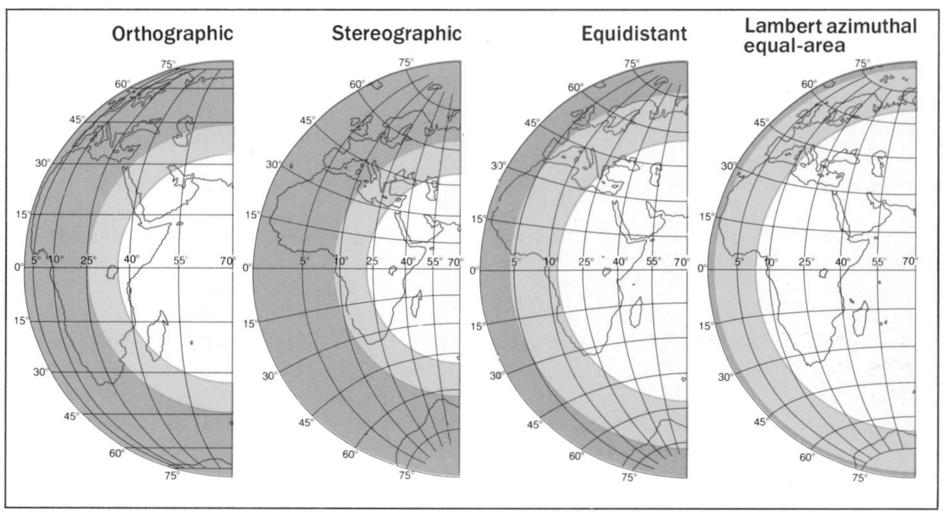

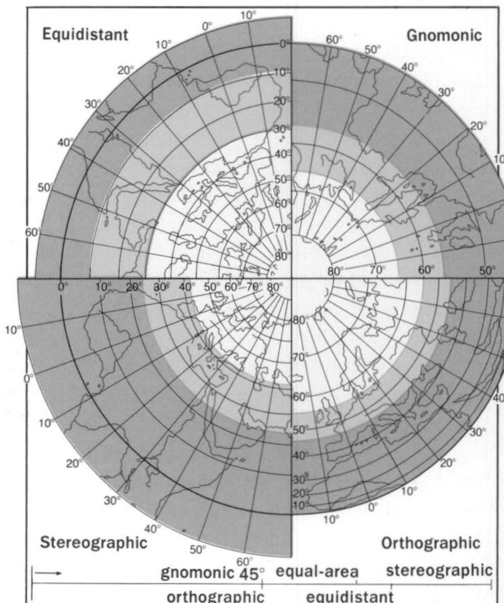

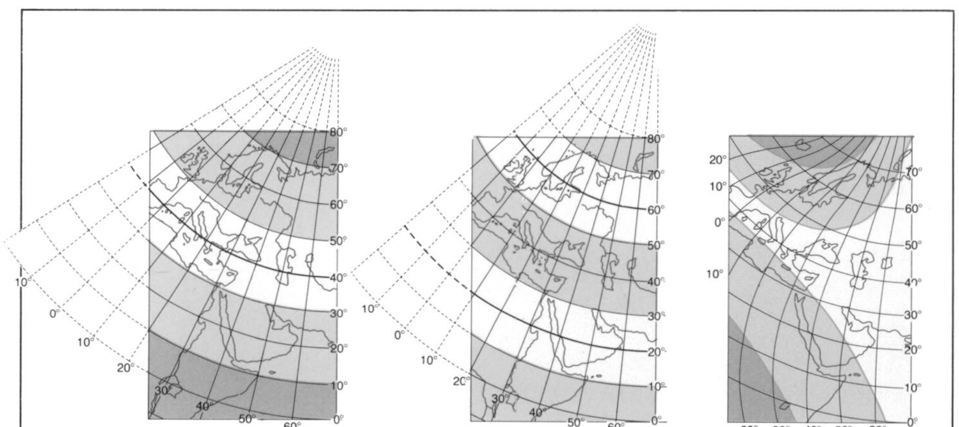

Conic projection with 1 standard parallel — Conic projection with 2 standard parallels — Bonne projection

Equidistant — Gnomonic
Stereographic — Orthographic
gnomonic 45° equal-area
orthographic — stereographic
orthographic — equidistant

The bar scale shows the comparative lengths of half-meridians (90°) in four projections. To these, Lambert's Equal-Area has been added.

POLAR PROJECTIONS

The *gnomonic* is the projection (view) from the centre of the Earth. The limit plotted here is 45° from the tangent point (the pole). This gives a circle equal in radius to 90° (the equator) on the *orthographic* projection. The other two projections are plotted on this same equator. They are, therefore, not to scale but they show the way the parallels are equally spaced in the *equidistant*; are increasingly spaced in the *stereographic* and become very crowded near the equator in the *orthographic* projection.

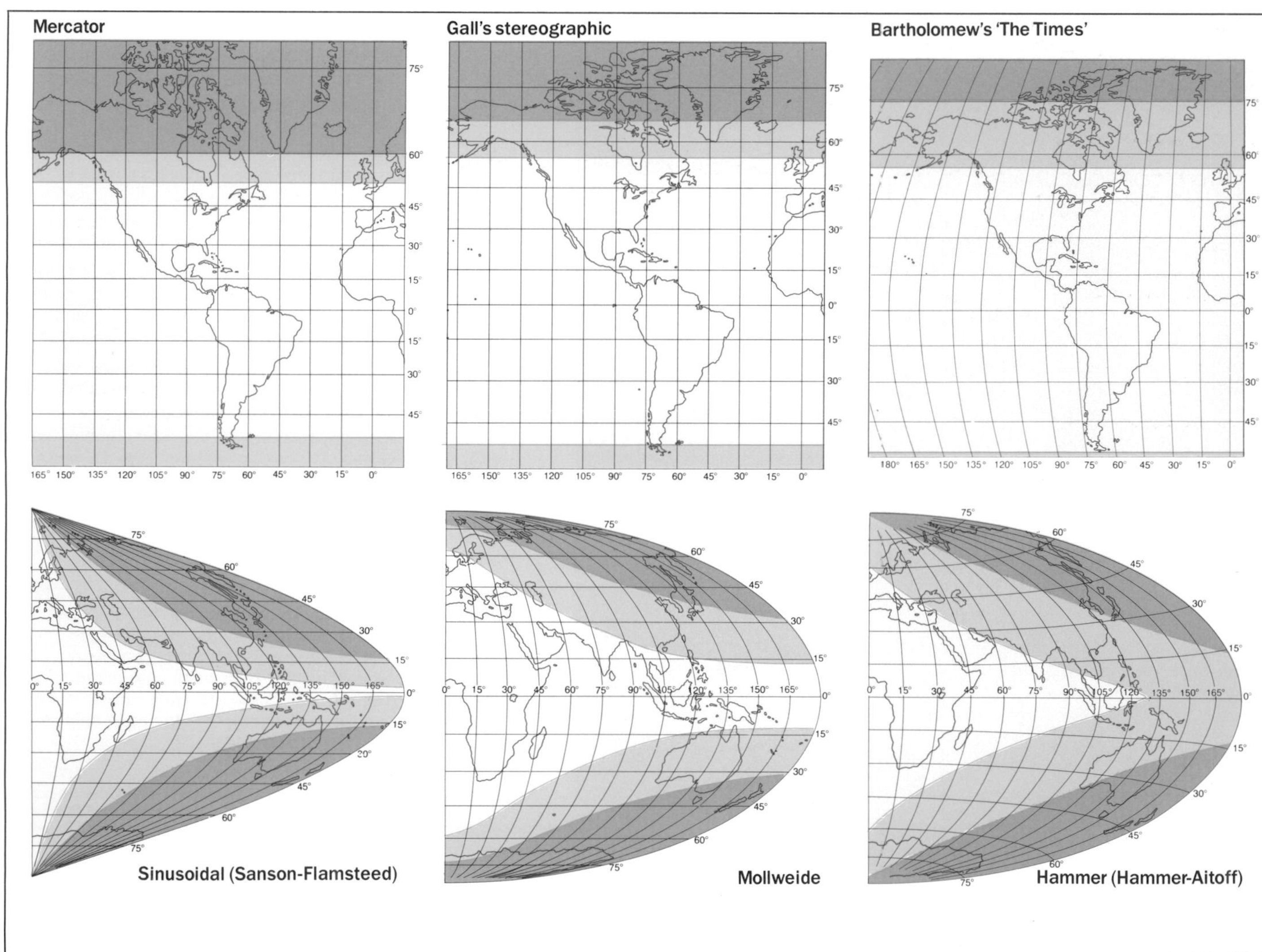

WORLD MAPS

Mercator is conformal (scale at any point is the same in all directions). Lines of constant bearing (loxodromes or rhumb lines) plot as straight lines, hence its importance to navigators. *Gall's* projection, a kind of stereographic is neither conformal nor equal-area. A cylinder is secant at 45°N and S. Projection is from a point on the equator diametrically opposite. *"The Times"* projection has Gall's parallels but the meridians are modified from the sinusoidal and considerably less curved. In the *sinusoidal* projection, the central meridian is perpendicular to the equator and half its length. Parallels are straight, equally spaced and equally subdivided. Meridians drawn through the subdivisions are sine curves. In *Mollweide*, the central meridian cuts the equator and all parallels at right angles. All are subdivided equally. Meridians 90° east and west of centre form a circle equal in area to a hemisphere. From that equation the spacing of the parallels can be calculated. *Hammer's* projection, derived from Lambert's equal-area, has the equator doubled in length. All three projections are equal-area. *Winkel Tripel* is the mean of Hammer and Plate Carrée. It is not equal-area. *Plate Carrée*, the simplest projection (not shown here) is a system of squares based on the equator.

Mercator — Gall's stereographic — Bartholomew's 'The Times'

Sinusoidal (Sanson-Flamsteed) — Mollweide — Hammer (Hammer-Aitoff)

SYMBOLS & ABBREVIATIONS 1

BOUNDARIES

- International
- International, Undefined or Alignment Uncertain
- Limits of Sovereignty across Water Areas
- Autonomous, Federal State
- Main Administrative
- Other Administrative
- Offshore Administrative
- Armistice, Cease-Fire Line
- Demilitarised Zone
- National Park
- Reserve, Reservation

COMMUNICATIONS

- Main Railways
- Other Railway
- Light Railway
- Projected Railways
- Railway Tunnels
- Road Tunnel
- Special Highway *Projected*
- Main Road *Projected*
- Other Road *Projected*
- Tracks
- Car Ferries
- Rail Ferries
- Navigable Canals *Locks*
- Projected or Disused Canal
- Drainage or Irrigation Canal
- Canal Tunnel
- Tunnel Aqueduct

LAKE TYPES

- Fresh-water
- Reservoir *Dam*
- Seasonal Fresh
- Seasonal Brackish
- Salt-lake, Lagoon
- Ferennial Salt-lake
- Seasonal Salt-lake
- Saline Mud-flat
- Salt-flat

LANDSCAPE FEATURES

- Ice-field and Glaciers
- Ice-cap, Ice-sheet
- Lava-fields
- Lava-fields
- Sand Desert, Dunes
- Saline Marsh, Salt Desert
- Marsh, Swamp
- Swamp, Flood-area
- Mangrove Swamp
- Tidal Area
- Atoll

OTHER FEATURES

- River, Stream
- Seasonal Watercourses
- Seasonal Flood-plain
- Undefined Course of River
- Pass; Gorges
- Waterfalls, Rapids
- Dam, Barrage
- Escarpments
- Flood Dyke
- Limits of Ice-shelf
- Reefs
- Rocks
- Spot Depth
- · 9650
- Lighthouse
- Lightship; Beacon
- Waterhole, Well
- Active Volcano
- Summit, Peak
- Oil Wells
- Oil or Natural Gas Pipeline
- Mine
- Site of Battle
- Historic Site
- Historic Ruin
- Ancient Walls
- Mosque, Sheikh's Tomb
- Cathedral, Monastery, Church
- International or Main Airport
- Airport, Airfield

CITY MAPS

- State Boundary
- County, Department Boundary
- City Limits
- Borough, District Boundary
- Main Railways *Station*
- Other Railways *Bridge*
- Projected Railways
- Underground Railway *Station*
- Special Highway *Projected*
- Main Road
- Secondary Road
- Other Road, Street
- Track
- Road Tunnel
- Bridge; Flyover
- Seaway *Locks*
- Canals
- Drainage Canal
- Waterfalls, Rapids
- Historic Walls
- Airports
- Racecourses
- Stadium
- Cemetery; Churches
- Woodland, Park
- Built-up Area

STYLES OF LETTERING

TOGO	Country Name
ALBERTA	-Major, Administrative Divisions
KENT CHER	-Other
PARIS Bern	National Capitals
Omsk	
Denver	Administrative Centres
Krakow	
GANDER Gatwick	Airports

M O A B	Historic Region
D E C C A N	
S I N A I	Physical Regions
Mato Grosso	
ATLAS Nile	
Mt Blanc Thames	Physical Features
BASIN Ridge	Ocean Bottom Features
M A S A I	Tribal Name

PRINCIPAL MAP ABBREVIATIONS

A.	1. Alp, Alpen, Alpi. 2. Alt	Ch^e	Chaine	H^n	Horn	Mkt.	Markt
Abb^e	Abbaye	Ch^le	Chapelle	Hosp.	1. Hospice, Hospiz. 2. Hospital	Mon.	Monasterio, Monastery
A.C.T.	Australian Capital Territory	C^ma	Cima	Ht.	Haut		3. Prince
Aig.	Aiguille	C^no	Corno	Hte.	Haute	Mont.	Monument
Akr.	Akra, Akrotirion	C^o	Cerro	H^er	Hinter	Mt.	Mont, Mount, Mountain
Anch.	Anchorage	Const^n	Construction	H^y	Highway	Mte.	Monte
A.O.	Avtonomnaya Oblast'	Cord.	Cordillera	I.	Ile, Ilha, Insel, Isla, Island, Isle, Isola, Isole	M^tes	Montes
App^no	Appennino	Cr.	Creek			Mti.	Monti, Munţi
Aqued.	Aqueduct	Cuch.	Cuchilla			Mts.	Monts, Mountains
Ar.	Arroyo	Cuc^lo	Cuccuru	IJ.	IJssel	N.	1. Nam. 2. Neu, Ny.
Arch.	Archipel, Archipelago, Archipiélago	Cy.	City	im.	imeni		2. Nevado, Nudo.
		Czo.	Cozzo	In.	1. Inder, Indre, Inre. 2. Inlet		3. Pont
Arr.	Arrecife	D.	1. Da, Dag, Dagh, Dağı, Dağları. 2. Danau. 3. Darreh. 4. Daryácheh	IND.	India		4. Noord, Nord, Nörre, Nerre, North. 5. Nos
A.S.S.R.	Avtonomnaya Sovetskaya Sotsialisticheskaya Respublika			Inf.	Inferior, -e, Inférieure	N^a	Nuestra
		-d.	-dake	Int.	International	Nat.	National
		D.C.	District of Columbia	I^s	Iles, Ilhas, Islands, Islas, Isles	N.D.	Notre Dame
Ay.	Ayia, Ayioi, Áyion, Áyios	Den.	Denmark	ISR.	Isrzel	N.E.	Neder, Nieder
		Dists.	Districts	Isth.	Isthmus	Neth.	North East
B.	1. Baai, Bahia, Baia, Baje, Baja, Bay, Bucht, Bukhta, Bukt. 2. Bad. 3. Ban. 4. Barazh, Barrage, Barragem. 5. Bayou. 6. Bir. 7. Bonto. 8. Bulu	Div.	Division	J.	1. Jabal, Jebel, Jibál. 2. Järvi, Ja₁re, Jazira, Jezero, Jezioro. 3. Jökull	Nizm.	Netherlands
		Dj.	Djebel				Nizhne, -neye, -niy, -nyaya
		Dns.	Downs			Nizm.	Nizmennost
		Dz.	Dzong			N.O.	Noord Oost, Nord Ost
		E.	East			Nor.	Norway, Norwegian
		Eil.	Eiland, Eilanden			N^os	Nudos
		Escarp.	Escarpment	Jap.	Japan, Japanese	Nov.	Novyy, -aya, -iye, -oye
		Est.	Estación	Jct.	Junction	N^r	Nether
B^c	Banc	E^ta	Etang	K.	1. Kaap, Kap, Kapp. 2. Kaikyō. 3. Kato. 4. Kerang, Kering. 5. Kiang. 6. Kirke. 7. Ko. 8. Koh, Küh, Kūhha. 9. Kólpos. 10. Kopf. 11. Kuala. 12. Kyst	N.W.	North West
B^ca	Boca	F.	Firth			N.W.	New West
Bel.	Belgium, Belgian	F.D.	Federal District			N.Z.	New Zealand
Bg.	Berg	Fj.	1. Fjell. 2. Fjord, Fjördur			O.	1. Old. 2. Oost, Ost.
Bge	Barrage						3. Ostrov
Bgt.	Bight, Bugt	F^k	Fork			Ö.	1. Östre. 2. Öy
B^i	Bani, Beni	Fl.	Fleuve			Ø.	1. Östre. 2. Öy
B^j	Burj	Fr.	France, French			Ob.	Ober
B^k	Bank	Ft.	Fort			O^d	Oude
Bk.	Bank	F^te	Fonte	Kan.	Kanal, Kanaal	O^et	Oguilet
B^n	Basin	Fy.	Ferry	Kap.	Kapelle	Ogl.	Oglat
B^o	Bol'shoy, -oye, -aya, -iye	-g	-gawa	Kep.	Kepulauan	O.L.V.	Onze Lieve Vrouw
		G.	1. Gebel. 2. Ghedir. 3. Göl, Gölü, Göl. 4. Golfe, Golfo, Gulf. 5. Gompa. 6. Gora, Gory. 7. Guba, 8. Gunung	Kg.	Kompong, Kompong,	Or.	Ori, Oros
Bos.	Bosanski			Kh.	1. Khawr.	Orm.	Ormos
Br.	1. Branch. 2. Bredning. 3. Bridge, Brücke. 4. Britain, British. 5. Burun				2. Khirbet, Khirbet, Khirbat, Khābān, -e. 3. Khowr	Os(t)	Ostrova
		G^a	Gara			Ot.	Olet
		G^d	Grand			O^v	Over, Övre
		G^de	Grande			O^va	Ostrov, -a
Bt.	Bukit	Geb.	Gebergte, Gebirge	Khr.	Khrebet	Oz.	Ozero
Bü.	Büyük	Geog^l	Geographical	Kl.	1. Kechil. 2. Klein, -e	P.	1. Pass. 2. Pic, Pico, Piz. 3. Pulau. 4. Pou
Bukh^r	Bukhta	Gez.	Gezira	Kör.	Köfez, -i		
C.	1. Cabo, Cap, Cape. 2. Ceská, -é, -y. 3. Col.	Ghub.	Ghubba	Kr.	Kangar	Pal.	Palace, Palacio, Palais
		Gl.	1. Gamle, Gammel. 2.Glacier	Kü.	Küçük	Pass.	Passage
Ç	Çay			L.	1. Lac, Lago, Lagôa, Lake, Liman, Limni, Liqen, Loch, Lough. 2. Lam	Peg.	Pegunungan
Cab^o	Cabeço	Gp.	Group			Pen.	Peninsula, Penisola
Cach.	Cachoeira, -o	Gr.	1. Graben. 2. Gross, -e, Grande			Per.	Pereval
Can.	1. Canal. 2. Canale. 3. Canavese. 4. Cañon, Canyon	G^i	Gasr			Ph.	Phum
		G^les	Grottes	Lag.	Lagoon, Laguna, -e	Ph^m	Phnom
Cas.	Castle	H.	1. Hawr. 2. Hill. 3. Hoch. 4. Hora, Hory	Land.	Land	P^gio	Poggio
Cat.	1. Cataract. 2. Catena			Ldg.	Landing	Plosk.	Ploskogor'ye
		Halv.	Halvey	Lit.	Little	Pk.	1. Peak, Pik
Cath.	Cathedral	Har.	Harbour	Ll.	Lille	Pkwy.	Parkway
C^d	Ciudad	H^d	Head	M.	1. Mae. 2. Meer. 3. Muang. 4. Muntil. 5. Muong. 6. Mys. 7. Monte	Pl.	1. Planina, Planinski. 2. Plei
Cerv.	Cervená, -é	H.E.P.	Hydro-Electric Power			P^la	Playa
Ch.	1. Chapel, Chapelle, Church. 2. Chaung. 3. Chott.	H^g	Hegység			P^ta	Puerta
		H^ts	Heights			P^te	Pointe
		H^y	Hasi, Hasy	m	metre's	Pol.	Poluostrov
Chan.	Channel	Hist.	Historic	Mal.	Melyy, -aya, -oye	P^ov	Poluostrov
Ch^au	Château			Mem.	Memorial		
				Mex.	Mexico, Mexican		
				M^gna	Mcntagna		
				M^t	Messif		
				M^gne	Mcntagne		

P.P.	Pulau-pulau	S.S.R.	Sovetskaya Sotsialisticheskaya Respublika
Pr.	1. Proliv. 2. Przyladek. 3. Prince		
Prom^y	Promontory	S^t	Saint, Sint, Staryy
Prop.	Proposed	S^e	1. State 2. Stor, Store. 3. Stung
PRÖT.	Protectorate	Sta	Santa
PROV.	Provincial	Sta.	Station
Psa	Presa	Stby.	Staby, Statsjonsby
P^so	Passo	S^e	Sainte
Pt.	1. Point. 2. Point	Ste.	Store
P^t	1. Petit. 2. Point. 3. Pont	Sten.	Stenón, Stenós
		S^to	Santo
P^ta	1. Ponta, Punta. 2. Puerta	Str.	Strait
P^te	1. Pointe. 2. Ponte, Puente	S^tu	Stuvina
		Sv.	Svaty, Sveti
P^to	1. Porto, Puerto. 2. Ponto, Punto	S.W.	South West
		T.	1. Tal. 2. Tal, Tall, Tell. 3. Tepe, Tepesi
Pizzo	Pizzo		
Q.	Qala, Qara, Qarn	Talsp.	Talsperre
R.	1. Reka, Rio, River, Rivière, Rud, Rzeka. 2. Ria	Tel.	Teluk
		Terr.	Terrace
Ra.	Range	Terr^y	Territory
Rap.	Rapids	Tg.	Tanjung
R^d	Road	Thwy.	Throughway, Thruway
REC.	Recreation	Tk.	Teluk
Res.	Reservoir	T^mt	Tablemount
R^f	Reef	T^o	Tando
R^ge	Ridge	Tpk.	Turnpike
Rib^a	Ribeira	Tr.	Trench, Trough
Rly.	Railway	Torre	Torre
R.S.F.S.R.	Rossiyskaya Sovetskaya Federativnaya Sotsialisticheskaya Respublika	Tun.	Tunnel
		U	Uad
		U.A.E.	United Arab Emirates
R^te	Route	Ug.	Udjung
Rom.	Romania, Romanian	U.K.	United Kingdom
		Unt.	Unter
		Up^r	Upper
R.S.R.		U.S.A.	United States of America
Sab.	Sabkhat	U.S.S.R.	Union of Soviet Socialist Republics
Sc.	Scoglio	V.	1. Val, Valle. 2. Väster, Vest, Vester. 3. Vatn. 4. Ville. 5. Vorder. 6. Volcán
S^e	Sound, Sund		
S.E.	South East		
Seb.	Sebjet, Sebkhat, Sebkra	Vila	Vila
Sev.	Sever, -naya, -nyy	Vdkhr.	Vodokhranilishche
		Vel.	Velikiy, -aya, -iye
S^no	Stagno	Ven.	Venezuela, Venezuelan
Sh.	1. Shan. 2. Sharif. 3. Shatt 4. Shima. 5. Shankou	Verkh.	Verkhniy, -neye, -ne, -nyaya
Si.	Sidi	Vn.	Volcán
S^noll	Seaknoll	Vol.	Volcán, Volcano, Vulkán
S^t	Sankt	Vost.	Vostochnyy
Sl.	Slieve	Vozv.	Vozvyshennost'
S^mt	Seamount	W.	1. Wad. 2. Wald. 3. Wan. 4. Water. 5. Well. 6. West
Snr^a	Senhora		
Snr^o	Senhoro		
Sp.	1. Spain, Spanish. 2. Spitze	W^r	Wester
S^pk	Seapeak	-y	-yama
Spr.	Spring	Y.	Ytre, Ytter, Ytri
S^r	Sönder, Sender	Z.	Zaliv
Sr.	Sredniy, -nyaya	Zal.	Zaliv
		Zap.	Zapadnyy, -aya, -o, -oye
		Zem.	Zemlya

Population Key

Capitals	Cities & Towns	
■	●	over 3 mill.
■	●	over 1 mill.
□	○	under 1 mill.

Communications
— Roads
— Railways
Main Shipping Routes
Other Shipping Routes

Limits of Pack-ice
Permanent Pack-ice
Average Winter Limit

West of 90° Greenwich

Independence gained since 1939
from former sovereign powers:

UK	France
Belgium	Italy
Denmark	Japan

Netherlands
Spain
USA

G910

Year of Independence
60 = 1960:

Territory ceded or annexed since 1939
Boundary adjustments
Transfers of territory
Independent before 1939
Dependent territory

CHANGES OF SOVEREIGNTY
since World War II
1:125 000 000

BARTHOLOMEWS "THE TIMES" PROJECTION

1:66 000 000
(45° N. & S.)

TIME ZONES
1:125 000 000

'Zone Times are the Standard Times
kept on land and sea compared with
12 hours (noon) Greenwich Mean Time.
Daylight Saving Time (normally one
hour in advance of local Standard
Time), which is observed by certain
countries for part of the year,
is not shown on the map.

John Bartholomew & Son Ltd. Edinburgh

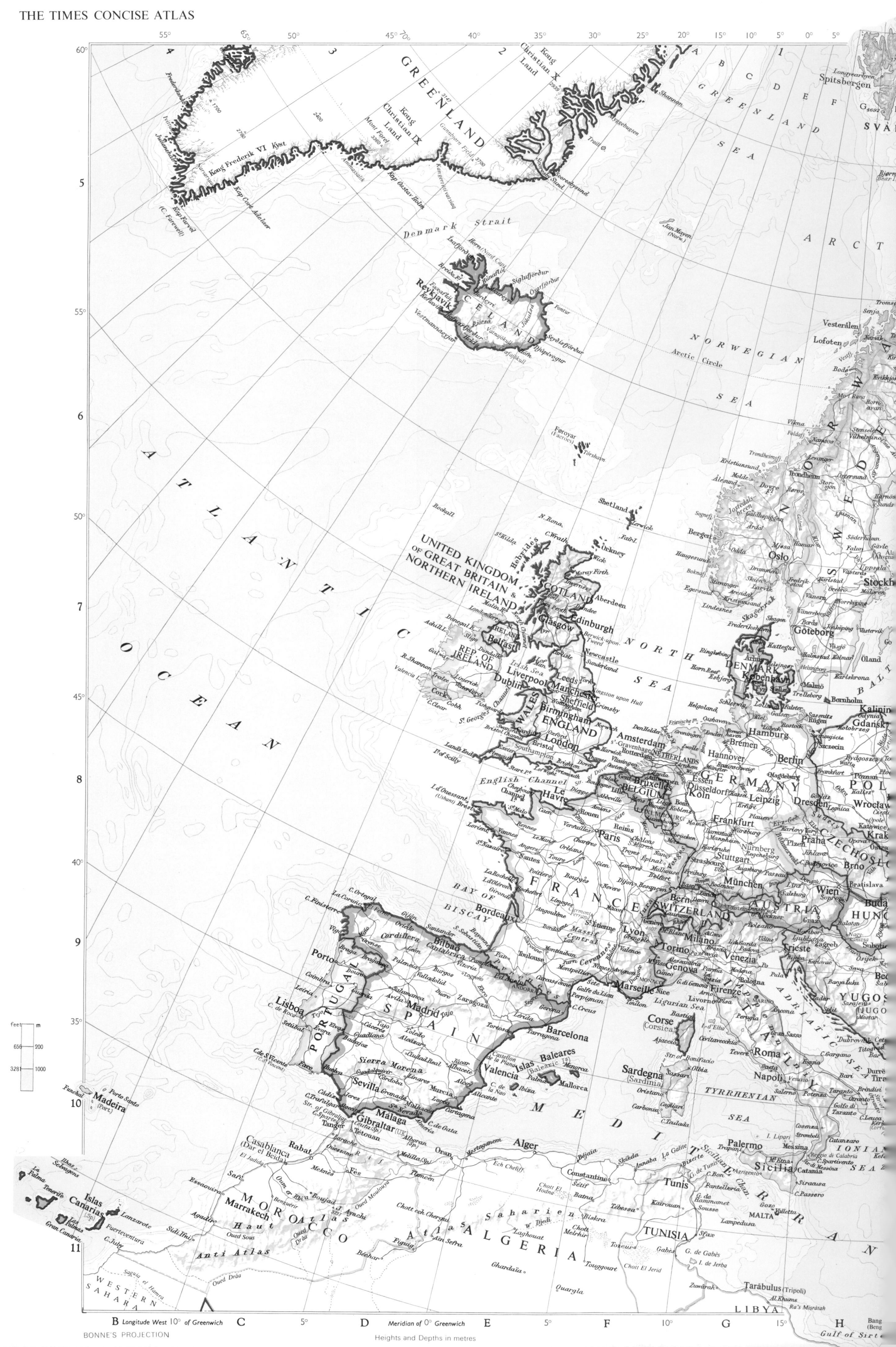

BONNE'S PROJECTION
Heights and Depths in metres

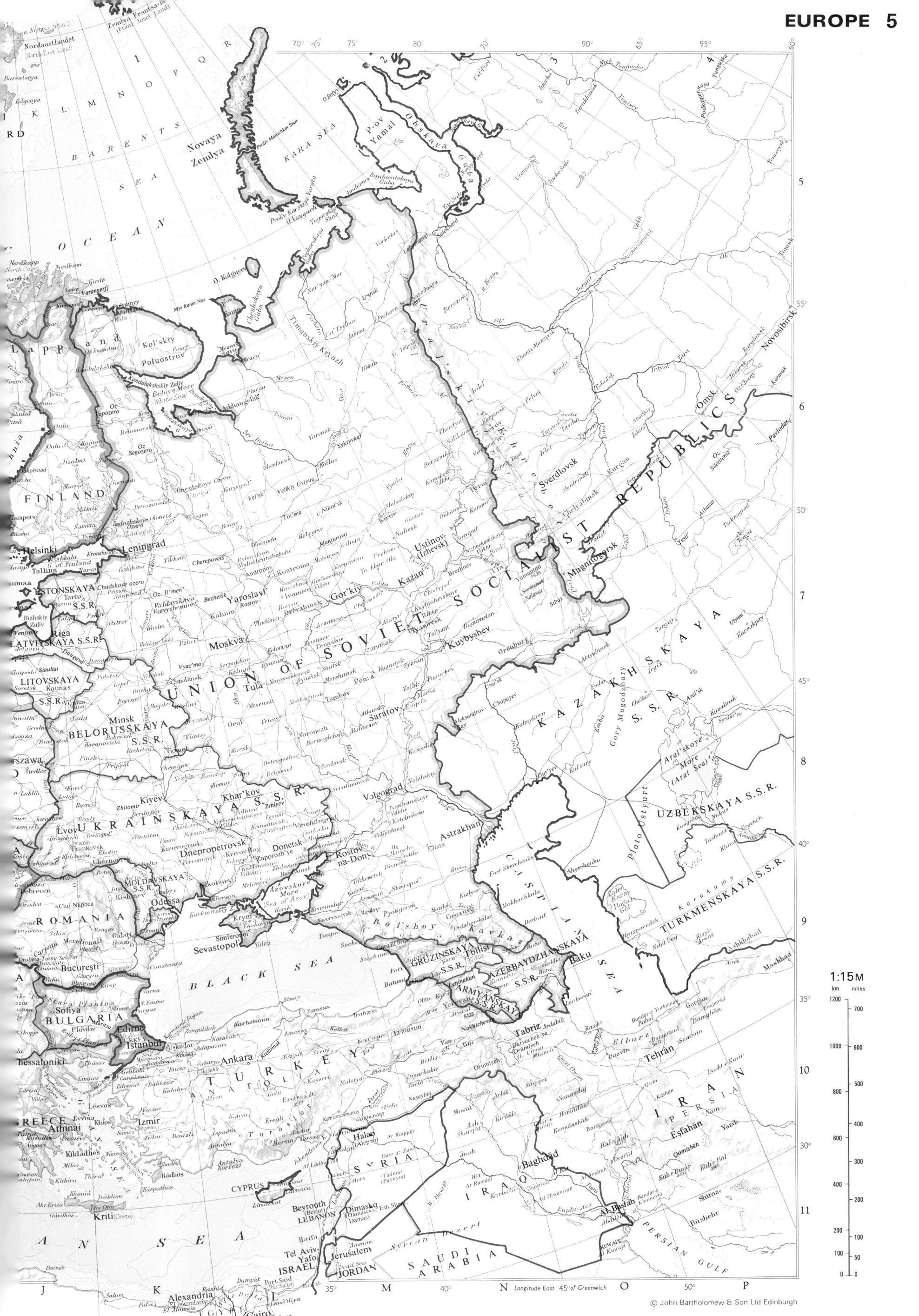

1:15M

© John Bartholomew & Son Ltd Edinburgh

UNION OF SOVIET SOCIALIST REPUBLICS
BARENTS SEA
OCEAN
KARA SEA
Novaya Zemlya
P-ov Yamal
Obskaya Guba
Kol'skiy Poluostrov
Beloye More (White Sea)
FINLAND
Helsinki
Leningrad
Tallinn
ESTONSKAYA S.S.R.
Riga
LATVIYSKAYA S.S.R.
LITOVSKAYA S.S.R.
Vilnius
Minsk
BELORUSSKAYA S.S.R.
Warszawa
Moskva
Yaroslavl'
Gor'kiy
Kazan'
Ustinov (Izhevsk)
Kuybyshev
Saratov
Volgograd
Astrakhan'
Sverdlovsk
Chelyabinsk
Magnitogorsk
Orenburg
Omsk
Novosibirsk
Pavlodar
Arkhangel'sk
Kiyev
Khar'kov
UKRAINSKAYA S.S.R.
Dnepropetrovsk
Donetsk
Rostov-na-Donu
L'vov
Odessa
MOLDAVSKAYA S.S.R.
Kishinev
Sevastopol'
Simferopol'
Yalta
Azovskoye More (Sea of Azov)
BLACK SEA
ROMANIA
Bucureşti
BULGARIA
Sofiya
Istanbul
Edirne
Ankara
TURKEY
Izmir
GREECE
Athinai
Kriti (Crete)
CYPRUS
Beyrouth (Beirut)
LEBANON
Dimashq (Damascus)
SYRIA
Halab (Aleppo)
ISRAEL
Tel Aviv-Yafo
Jerusalem
JORDAN
Alexandria
Cairo
EGYPT
SAUDI ARABIA
IRAQ
Baghdad
Al Basrah
KUWAIT
PERSIAN GULF
IRAN (PERSIA)
Tehran
Tabriz
Eşfahān
Mashhad
Ashkhabad
TURKMENSKAYA S.S.R.
UZBEKSKAYA S.S.R.
KAZAKHSKAYA S.S.R.
Aral'skoye More (Aral Sea)
CASPIAN SEA
Baku
AZERBAYDZHANSKAYA S.S.R.
GRUZINSKAYA S.S.R.
Tbilisi
ARMYANSKAYA S.S.R.
Yerevan
Bol'shoy Kavkaz
Gur'yev
Ural'sk
Longitude East 45° of Greenwich
km miles

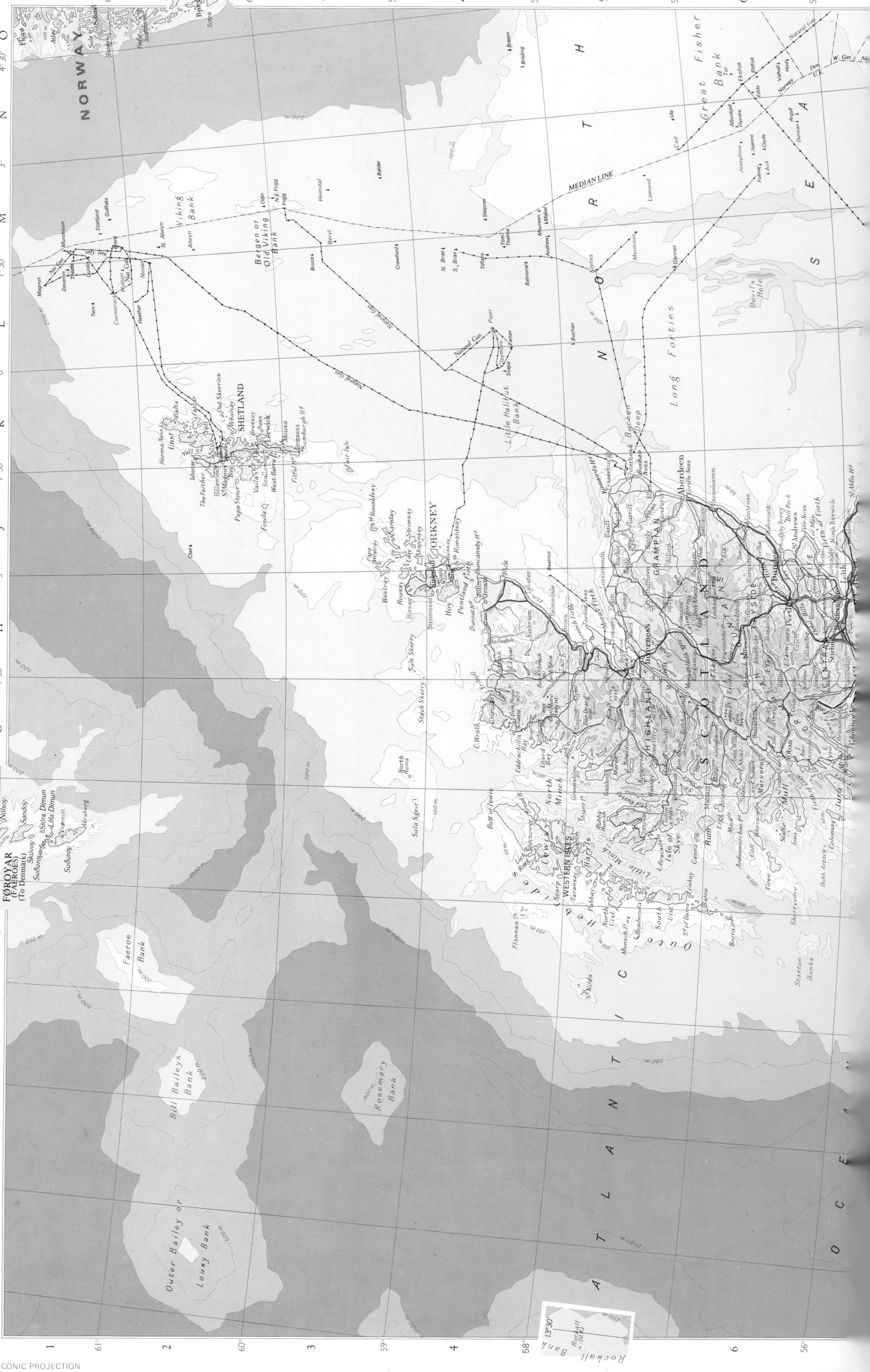
NORWAY
SHETLAND
ORKNEY
SCOTLAND
HIGHLAND
GRAMPIAN
TAYSIDE
WESTERN ISLES
FØROYAR (FAEROES) (To Denmark)
MEDIAN LINE
Natural Gas
Viking Bank
Bergen or Old Viking Bank
Little Halibut Bank
Buchan Deep
Long Forties
Great Fisher Bank
Devils Hole
Faeroe Bank
Bill Baileys Bank
Rosemary Bank
Outer Bailey or Lousy Bank
Stanton Banks
Rockall Bank
Aberdeen
Dundee
Inverness
Perth
Pentland Firth
North Minch
Little Minch
Outer Hebrides
Isle of Skye
Lewis
Harris
North Uist
South Uist
Mull
Jura
Fair Isle
Foula
Sula Sgeir
North Rona
Sule Skerry
Stack Skerry
Flannan Is.
St Kilda
Butt of Lewis
C. Wrath
Unst
Yell
Hoy
Westray
Sanday
Stronsay
Wick
Stornoway
ATLANTIC OCEAN
NORTH SEA
CONIC PROJECTION

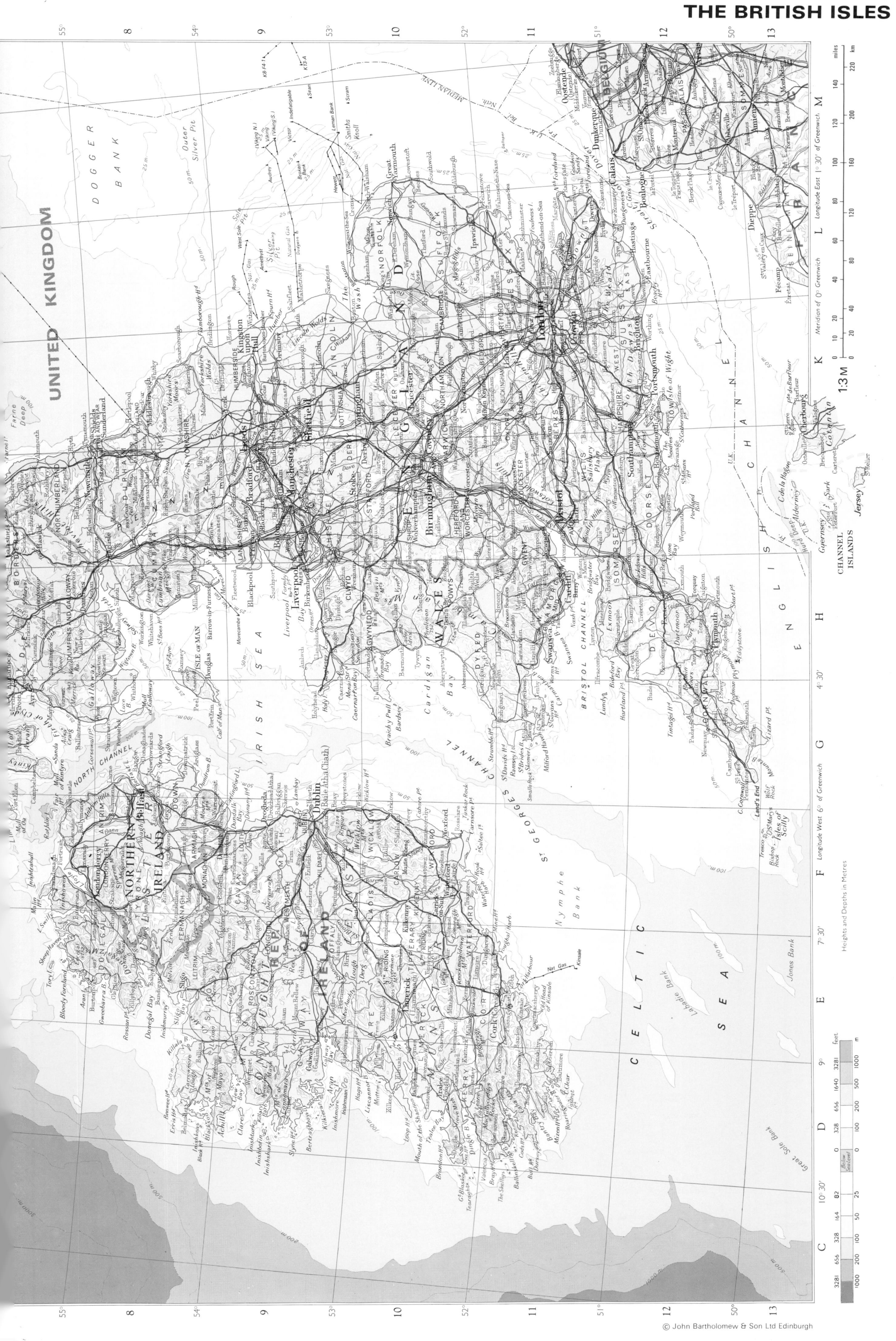
UNITED KINGDOM
IRELAND
NORTHERN IRELAND
ENGLAND
WALES
FRANCE
BELGIUM
DOGGER BANK
IRISH SEA
CELTIC SEA
ENGLISH CHANNEL
BRISTOL CHANNEL
ST GEORGES CHANNEL
NORTH CHANNEL
CHANNEL ISLANDS
Nymphe Bank
Jones Bank
Labadie Bank
Great Sole Bank
London
Dublin
Belfast
Manchester
Liverpool
Birmingham
Bristol
Cardiff
Plymouth
Southampton
Cork
Galway
Limerick
Meridian of 0° Greenwich
Longitude West 6° of Greenwich
Longitude East 1° 30' of Greenwich
Heights and Depths in Metres
1:3M
miles
km
feet
m

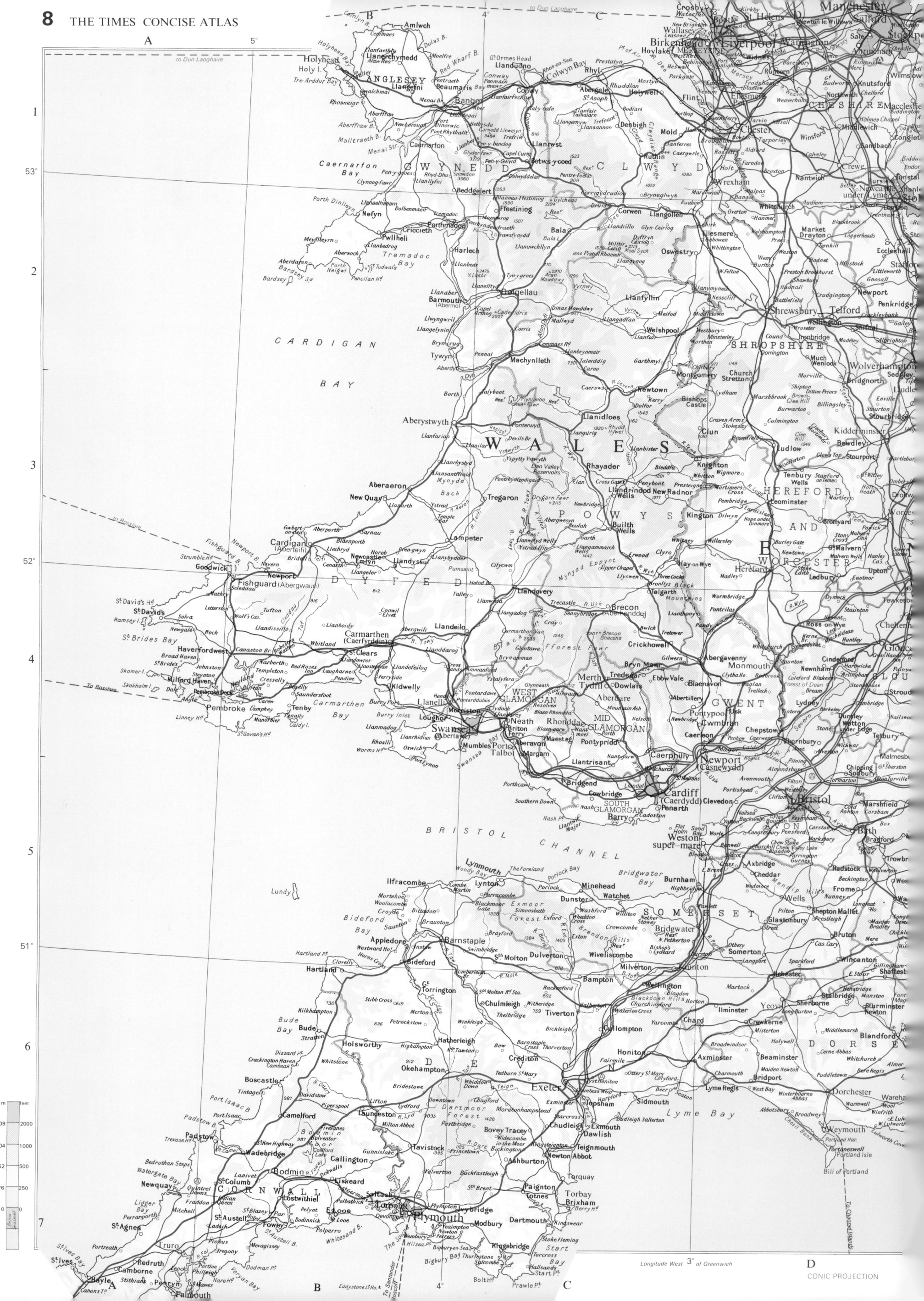

A
B
C
D
E
5°
4°
3°
53°
52°
51°
1
2
3
4
5
6
7
to Dun Laoghaire
to Rosslare
To Rosslare
To Santander Roscoff
To Channel Islands
ANGLESEY
GWYNEDD
CLWYD
WALES
POWYS
DYFED
WEST GLAMORGAN
MID GLAMORGAN
SOUTH GLAMORGAN
GWENT
SHROPSHIRE
HEREFORD AND WORCESTER
CHESHIRE
MERSEYSIDE
SOMERSET
DEVON
CORNWALL
DORSET
CARDIGAN BAY
BRISTOL CHANNEL
Caernarfon Bay
Tremadoc Bay
St Brides Bay
Carmarthen Bay
Swansea Bay
Bideford Bay
Bridgwater Bay
Porlock Bay
Lyme Bay
Start Bay
Lundy
Holyhead
Bangor
Caernarfon
Llandudno
Colwyn Bay
Rhyl
Chester
Wrexham
Liverpool
Birkenhead
Manchester
Dolgellau
Aberystwyth
Machynlleth
Newtown
Shrewsbury
Telford
Wolverhampton
Rhayader
Llandrindod Wells
Builth Wells
Hereford
Cardigan
Fishguard
St Davids
Haverfordwest
Milford Haven
Pembroke
Tenby
Carmarthen
Llanelli
Swansea
Neath
Port Talbot
Merthyr Tydfil
Brecon
Abergavenny
Monmouth
Newport
Cardiff
Bristol
Bath
Weston-super-mare
Minehead
Ilfracombe
Barnstaple
Bideford
Taunton
Bridgwater
Wells
Yeovil
Exeter
Torquay
Plymouth
Bodmin
Truro
Falmouth
Penzance
St Ives
Newquay
Dorchester
Weymouth
Bill of Portland
Longitude West 3° of Greenwich
CONIC PROJECTION
m
feet
609
2000
304
1000
152
500
76
250
0
0
Below Sea Level

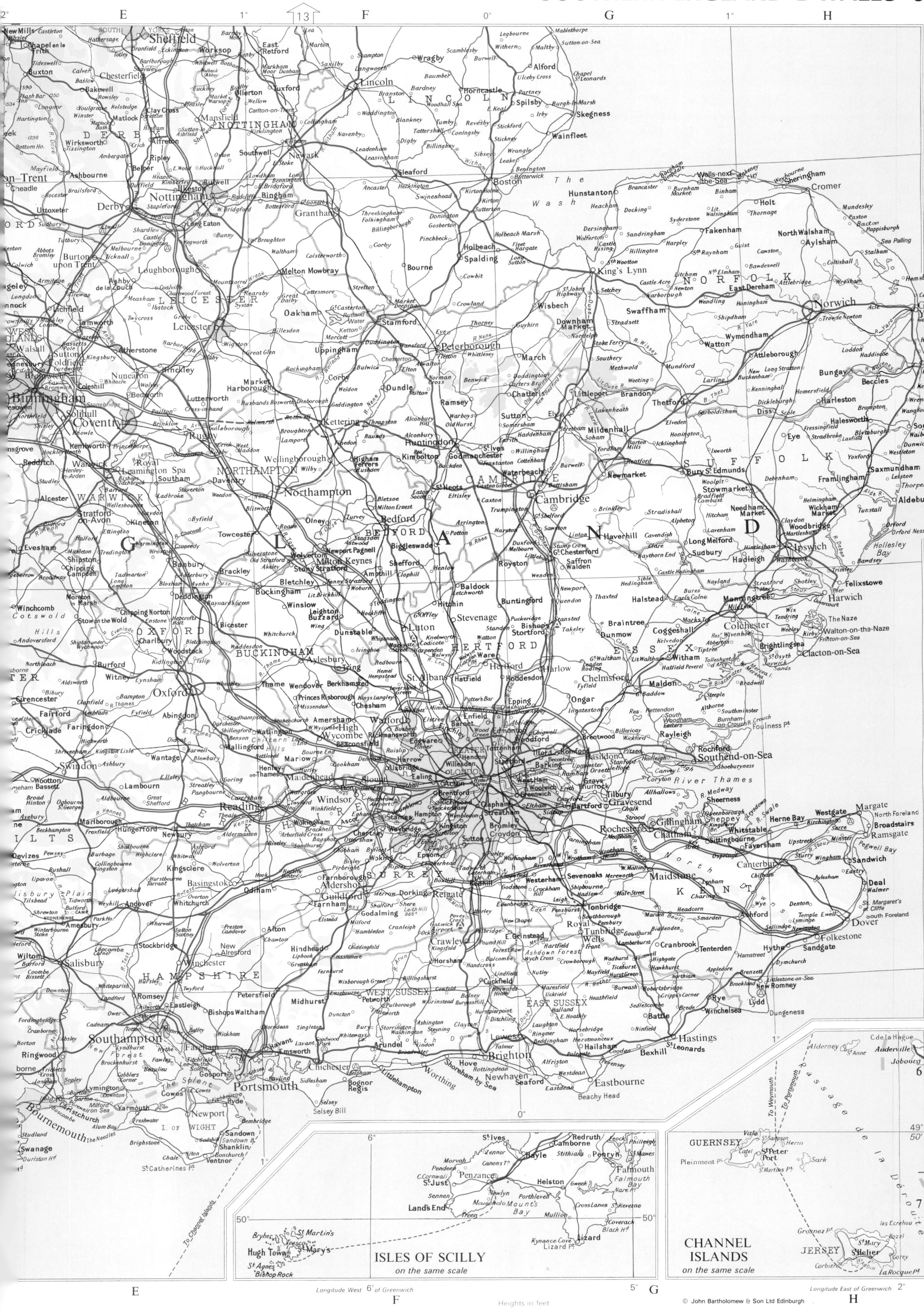

ISLES OF SCILLY
on the same scale

CHANNEL ISLANDS
on the same scale

GUERNSEY

JERSEY

1:1 M

Heights in feet

Longitude West of Greenwich

Longitude East of Greenwich

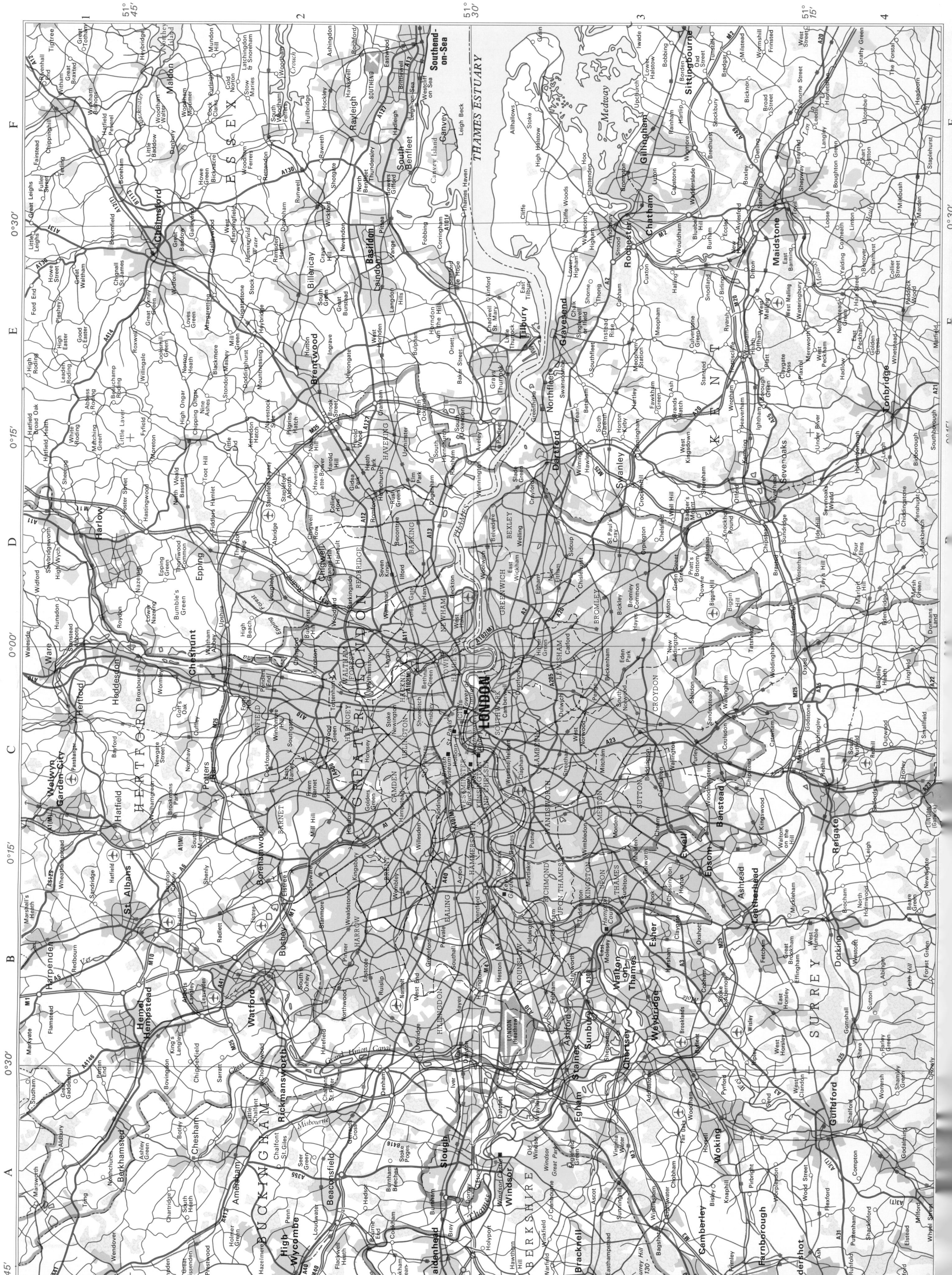

© Times Books Ltd

1:300 000

ESSEX · HERTFORD · BUCKINGHAM · BERKSHIRE · SURREY · KENT · GREATER LONDON

Southend-on-Sea · Chelmsford · Basildon · Brentwood · Tilbury · Gravesend · Rochester · Chatham · Gillingham · Sittingbourne · Maidstone · Tonbridge · Sevenoaks · Dartford · Swanley · Bromley · Croydon · Reigate · Dorking · Guildford · Woking · Aldershot · Farnborough · Camberley · Bracknell · Maidenhead · Windsor · Slough · High Wycombe · Beaconsfield · Amersham · Chesham · Berkhamsted · Hemel Hempstead · Harpenden · St Albans · Welwyn Garden City · Hatfield · Hertford · Hoddesdon · Ware · Cheshunt · Harlow · Epping · Potters Bar · Barnet · Borehamwood · Bushey · Watford · Rickmansworth · Harrow · Hillingdon · Staines · Sunbury · Walton on Thames · Weybridge · Chertsey · Esher · Leatherhead · Epsom · Banstead · Sutton · Merton · Kingston upon Thames · Richmond upon Thames · Hounslow · Ealing

LONDON

London Heathrow

THAMES ESTUARY

10 20 30 40 50 60 70 80 90 100

0   5   10   15 km
0   5   10 miles

SOUTH LANCASHIRE

A 3°00' B 2°45' C 2°30' D 2°15' E

IRISH SEA

Southport

LANCASHIRE

Chorley

Ormskirk

Wigan

Bolton

Bury

Rochdale

Oldham

GREATER MANCHESTER

MANCHESTER

Ashton-under-Lyne

Salford

Stretford

Sale

Stockport

Altrincham

Cheadle

St. Helens

MERSEYSIDE

Kirkby

Bootle

Wallasey

Birkenhead

LIVERPOOL

Huyton

Roby

Prescot

Newton-le-Willows

Warrington

Widnes

Runcorn

Ellesmere Port

LIVERPOOL BAY

MERSEY

CHESHIRE

Northwich

Macclesfield

Knutsford

Wilmslow

PEAK DISTRICT NATIONAL PARK

CLWYD

DEE

53° 30'

53° 15'

1

2

3

WEST MIDLANDS

A 2°15' B 2°00' C 1°45' D 1°30' E 1°15'

STAFFORD

Cannock

Lichfield

Brownhills

Walsall

Aldridge

Sutton Coldfield

Tamworth

Wolverhampton

Willenhall

Wednesfield

Wednesbury

Tipton

West Bromwich

Dudley

Oldbury

Smethwick

Rowley Regis

Halesowen

Stourbridge

SALOP

Kidderminster

WEST MIDLANDS

BIRMINGHAM

Edgbaston

Solihull

LEICESTER

Atherstone

Nuneaton

Hinckley

Bedworth

Coventry

WARWICK

Royal Leamington Spa

Kenilworth

Warwick

Rugby

WORCESTER AND HEREFORD

Bromsgrove

Redditch

52° 30'

52° 15'

4

5

1:300 000

5 10 15 km

5 10 miles

© Times Books Ltd

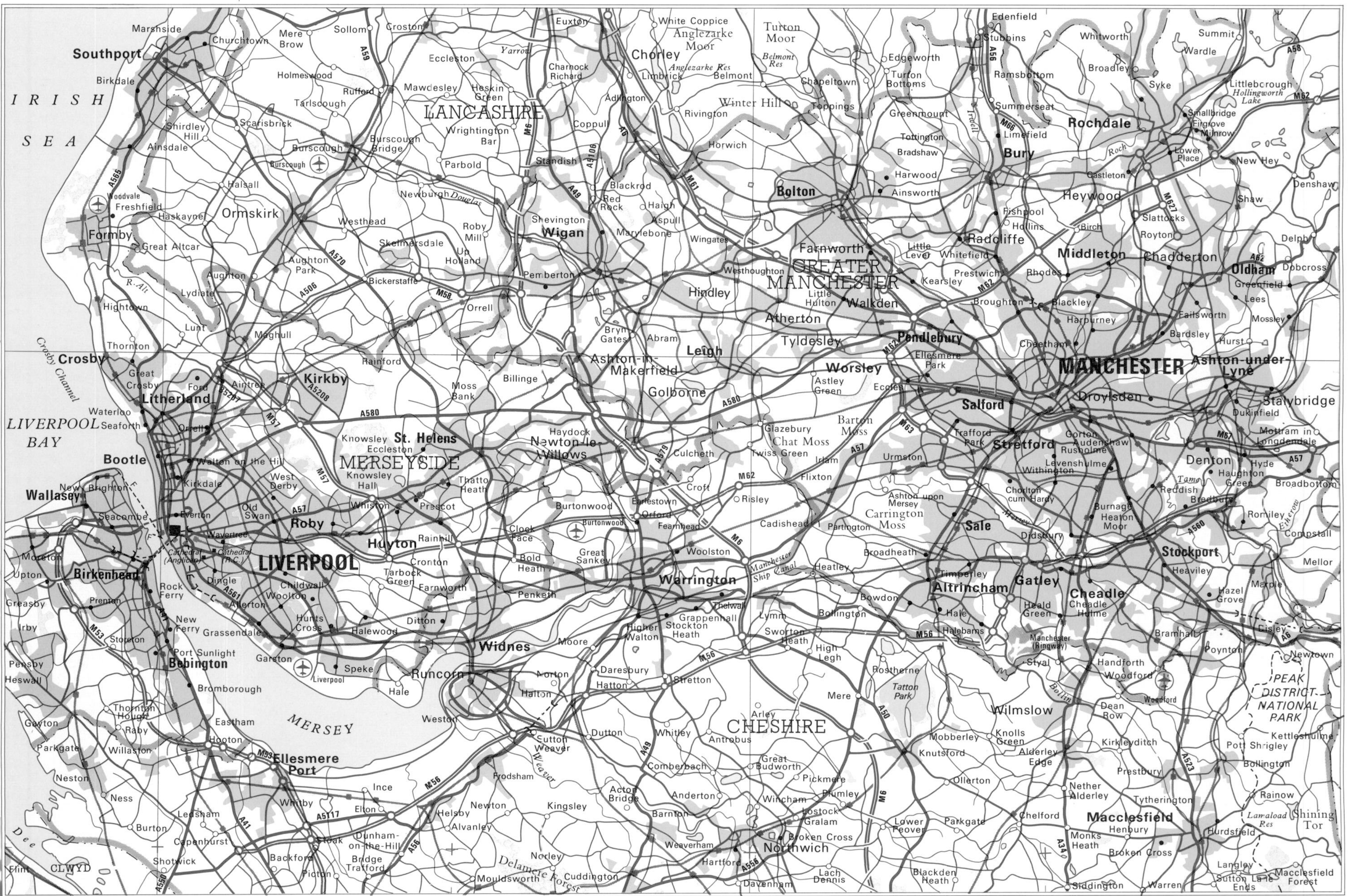

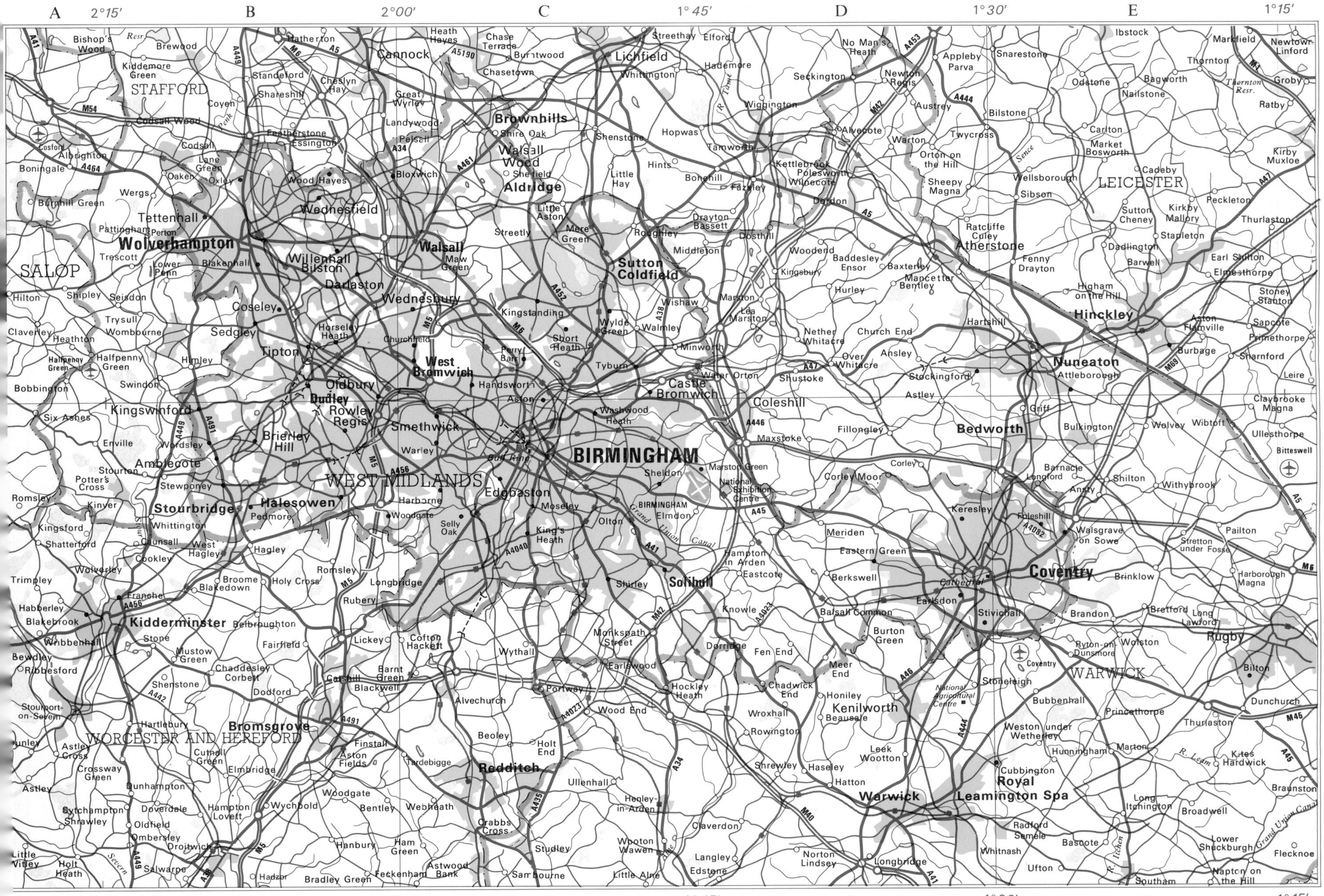

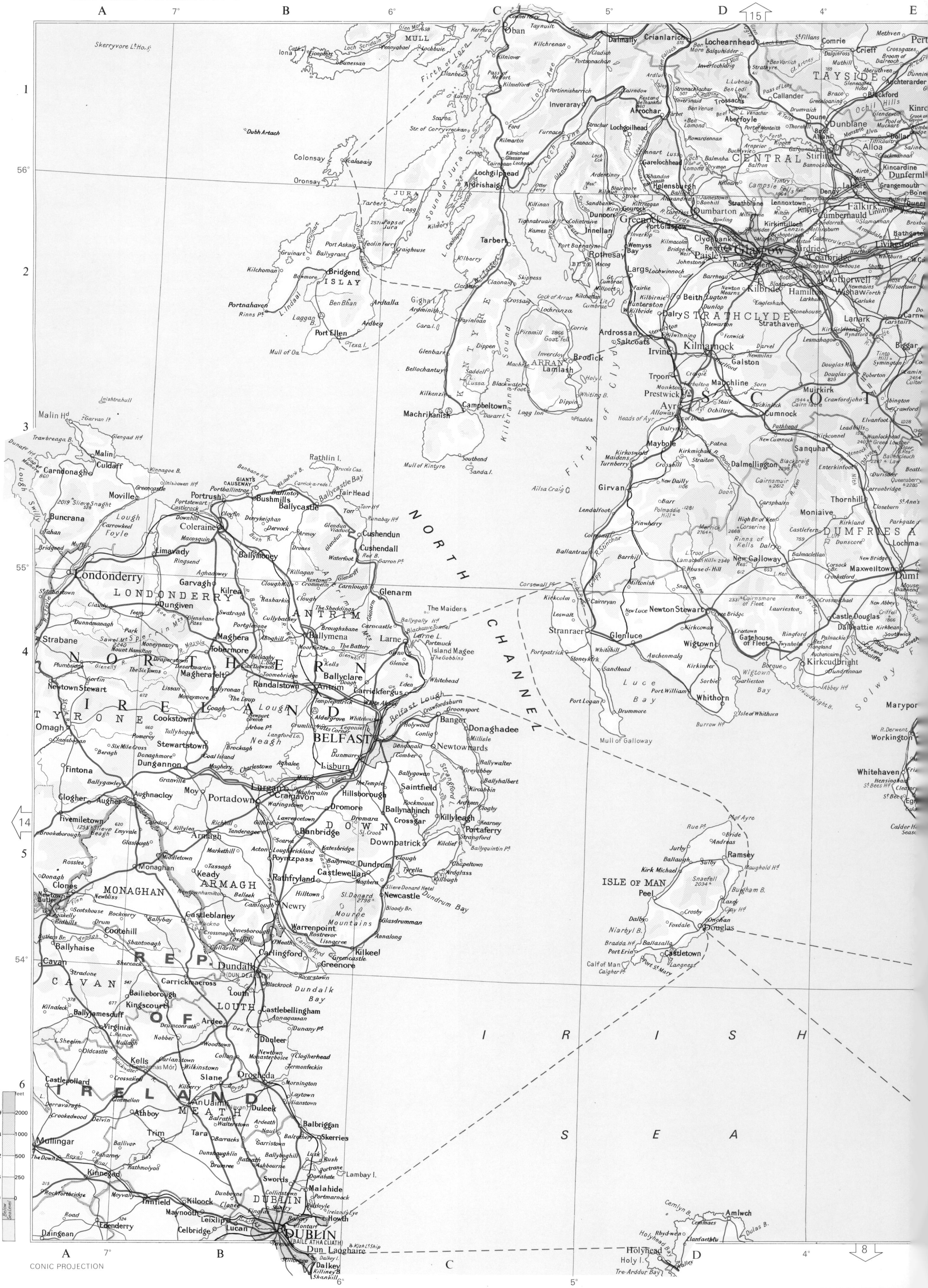

CONIC PROJECTION

NORTH CHANNEL
IRISH SEA
NORTHERN IRELAND
REP. OF IRELAND
SCOT
ISLE OF MAN
ISLAY
JURA
MULL
ARRAN
KINTYRE
ANTRIM
DOWN
ARMAGH
LONDONDERRY
TYRONE
MONAGHAN
CAVAN
LOUTH
MEATH
TAYSIDE
CENTRAL
STRATHCLYDE
DUMFRIES
BELFAST
DUBLIN
Londonderry
Glasgow
Oban
Campbeltown
Stranraer
Ayr
Kilmarnock
Douglas
Ramsey
Peel
Dundalk
Drogheda
Newry
Armagh
Portadown
Lisburn
Larne
Coleraine
Omagh
Strabane
Bangor
Downpatrick
Holyhead
Belfast Lough
Solway F
Firth of Clyde
Sound of Jura
Dundalk Bay
Dundrum Bay
Luce Bay
Mull of Kintyre
Mull of Galloway
Rathlin I.
Lough Neagh
Lough Foyle
Lambay I.
15
14
8
A
B
D
1
2
3
4
5
6
7°
6°
5°
4°
56°
55°
54°
m
feet
609
304
152
76
0
2000
1000
500
250
0

Heights in feet

Meridian of 0° Greenwich

© John Bartholomew & Son Ltd Edinburgh

A 10° B 9° C 8° D 7° E 6° F

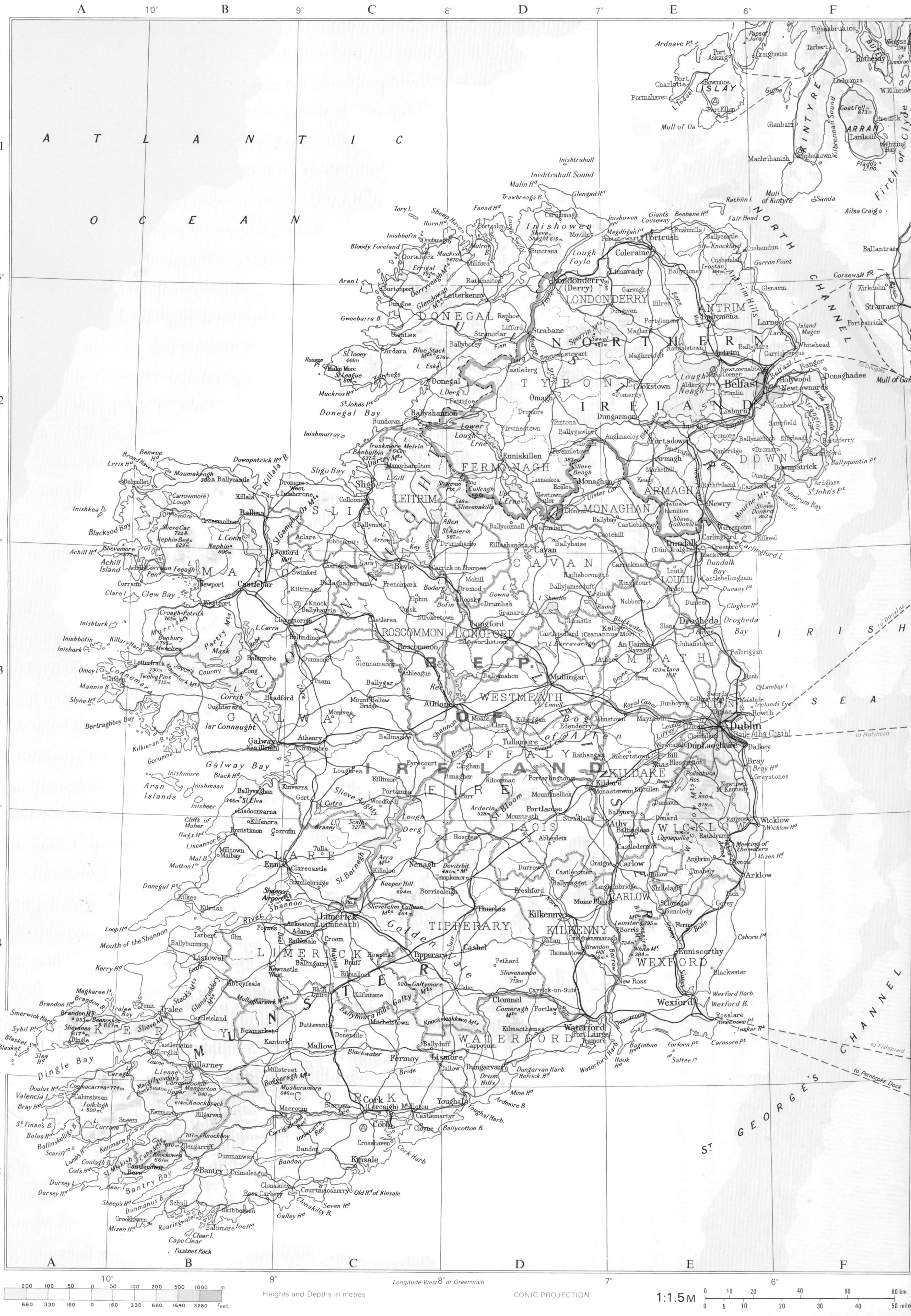

ATLANTIC OCEAN

NORTHERN IRELAND

REP. OF IRELAND — EIRE

DONEGAL · LONDONDERRY · ANTRIM · TYRONE · FERMANAGH · DOWN · ARMAGH · MONAGHAN · CAVAN · LEITRIM · SLIGO · MAYO · ROSCOMMON · LONGFORD · WESTMEATH · MEATH · LOUTH · GALWAY · OFFALY · KILDARE · DUBLIN · WICKLOW · CLARE · LAOIS · CARLOW · KILKENNY · TIPPERARY · LIMERICK · KERRY · CORK · WATERFORD · WEXFORD

Belfast · Londonderry (Derry) · Dublin · Baile Átha Cliath · Dun Laoghaire · Cork (Corcaigh) · Limerick (Luimneach) · Galway (Gaillimh) · Waterford (Port Lairge) · Wexford · Sligo · Dundalk (Dun Dealgan) · Drogheda

IRISH SEA

NORTH CHANNEL

ST. GEORGE'S CHANNEL

Firth of Clyde

ISLAY · ARRAN · KINTYRE

to Douglas · to Holyhead · to Fishguard · to Pembroke Dock

Heights and Depths in metres

CONIC PROJECTION

1 : 1.5 M

Longitude West 8° of Greenwich

| 200 | 100 | 50 | 0 | 50 | 100 | 200 | 500 | 1000 | m |
| 660 | 330 | 160 | 0 | 160 | 330 | 660 | 1640 | 3280 | feet |

| 0 | 10 | 20 | 40 | 60 | 80 km |
| 0 | 5 | 10 | 20 | 30 | 40 | 50 mile |

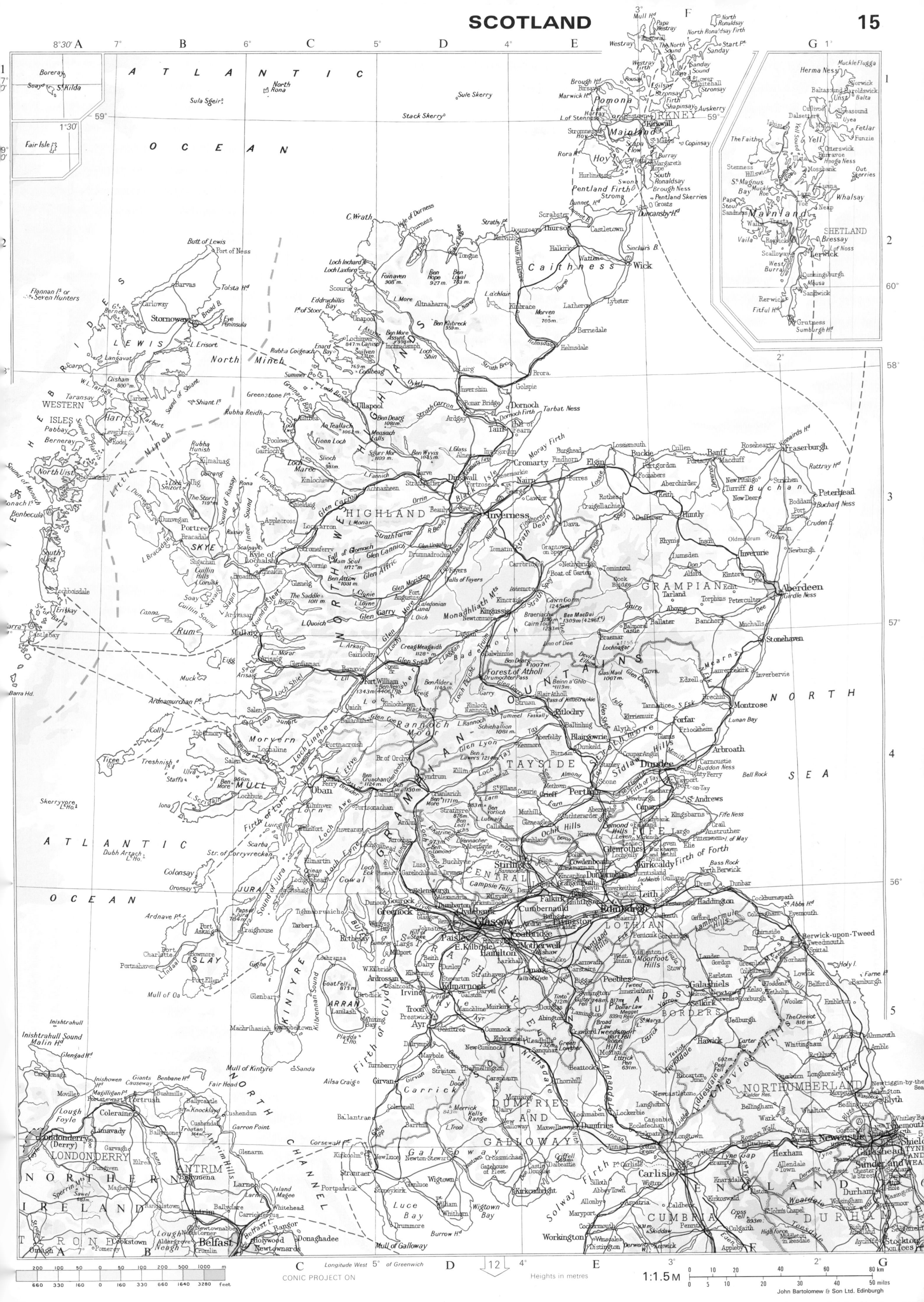

CONIC PROJECTION Longitude West 5° of Greenwich

Heights in metres 200 100 50 0 50 100 200 500 1000 m / 660 330 160 0 160 330 660 1640 3280 feet

1:1.5M 0 10 20 40 60 80 km / 0 5 10 20 30 40 50 miles

12

John Bartolomew & Son Ltd. Edinburgh

CONIC PROJECTION

F
G
H
J
K
L
1° 30′
0°
1° 30′
3°
4° 30′
GOLFE DE GASCOGNE
(GOLFO DE GASCUÑA)
F R A N C E
GOLFE DU LION
Toulouse
Montpellier
Nimes
Arles
Marseille
Narbonne
Perpignan
Carcassonne
Béziers
Bayonne
Biarritz
St. Jean de Luz
San Sebastián
Pamplona
Logroño
Zaragoza
Lérida
Barcelona
Tarragona
Gerona
Andorra
Tortosa
Castellón de la Plana
Sagunto
Valencia
Golfo de Valencia
Alicante
Murcia
Cartagena
Albacete
Almería
Teruel
MALLORCA
Palma
MENORCA
Mahón
Ciudadela
IBIZA
Formentera
ISLAS BALEARES
(BALEARIC ISLANDS)
(To Spain)
M E D I T E R R A N E A N   S E A
A L G E R I A
Oran
Mostaganem
Sidi Bel Abbès
Tlemcen
Mascara
Longitude East 3° of Greenwich
Meridian of 0° Greenwich
1
2
3
4
5
6
7
8
9
10
43°
42°
41°
40°
39°
38°
37°
36°
35°
MADRID
1:60 000
TETUAN
CHAMARTIN
CIUDAD UNIVERSITARIA
Parque del Oeste
CHAMBERI
SALAMANCA
MONCLOA
Casa de Campo
Palacio Real
Puerta del Sol
Plaza Mayor
Museo del Prado
Parque del Retiro
RETIRO
LATINA
ARGANZUELA
CARABANCHEL
VALLECAS
1:3 M
km miles
© John Bartholomew & Son Ltd Edinburgh

Conic Projection

Longitude West 1° 30' of Greenwich   Meridian of 0° Greenwich   1° 30'   Heights and Depths in metres

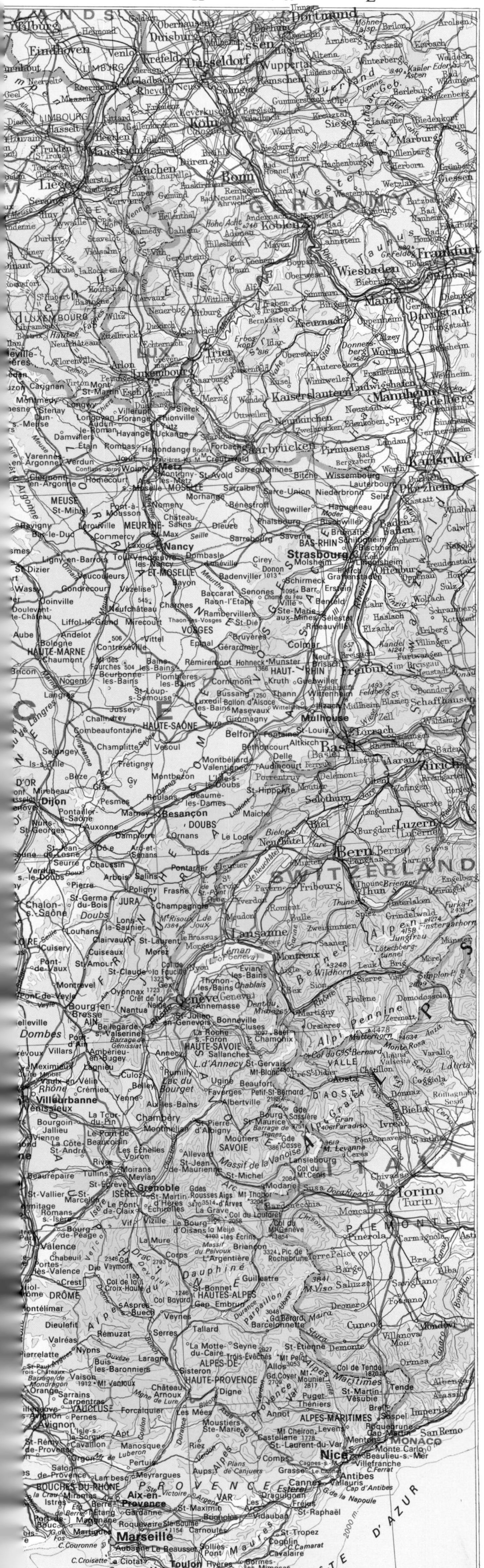

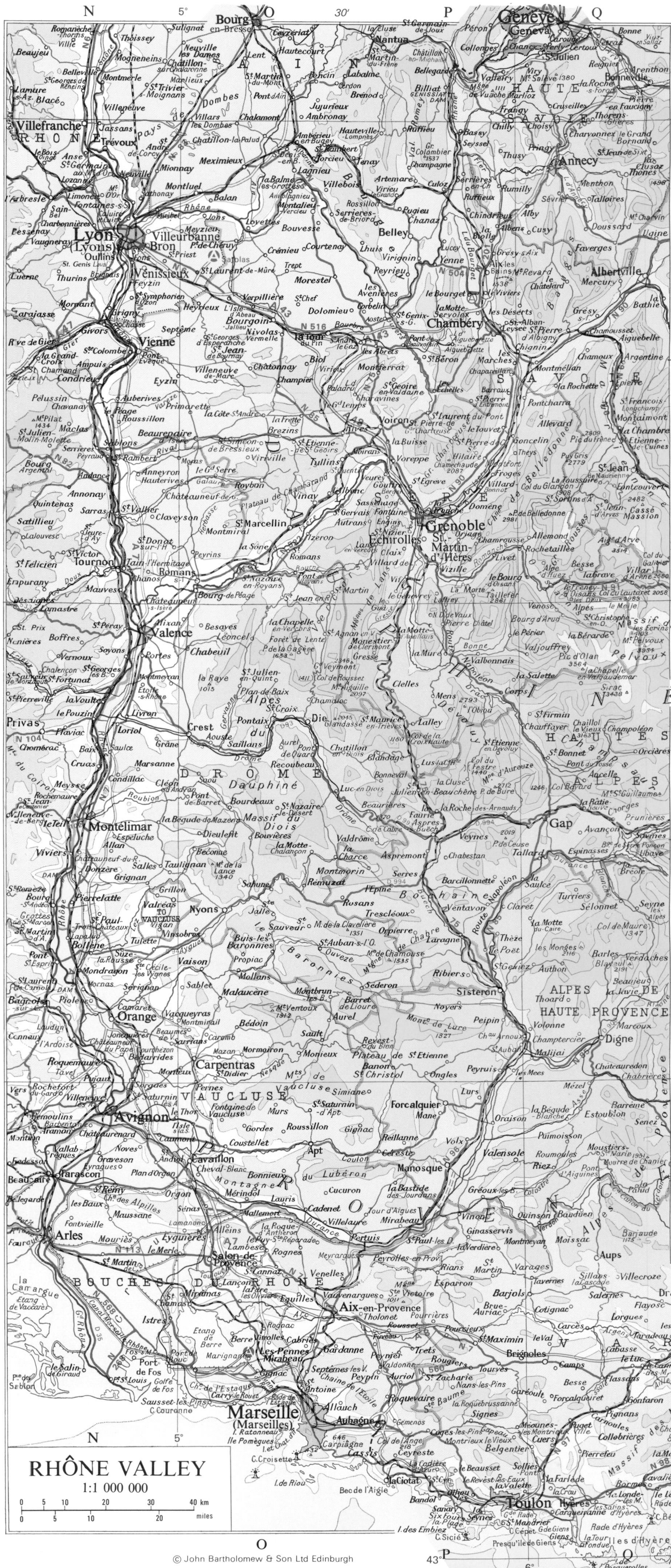

RHÔNE VALLEY

1:1 000 000

0 5 10   20   30   40 km

0 5 10   20   miles

Longitude East 6° of Greenwich

© John Bartholomew & Son Ltd Edinburgh

CONIC PROJECTION

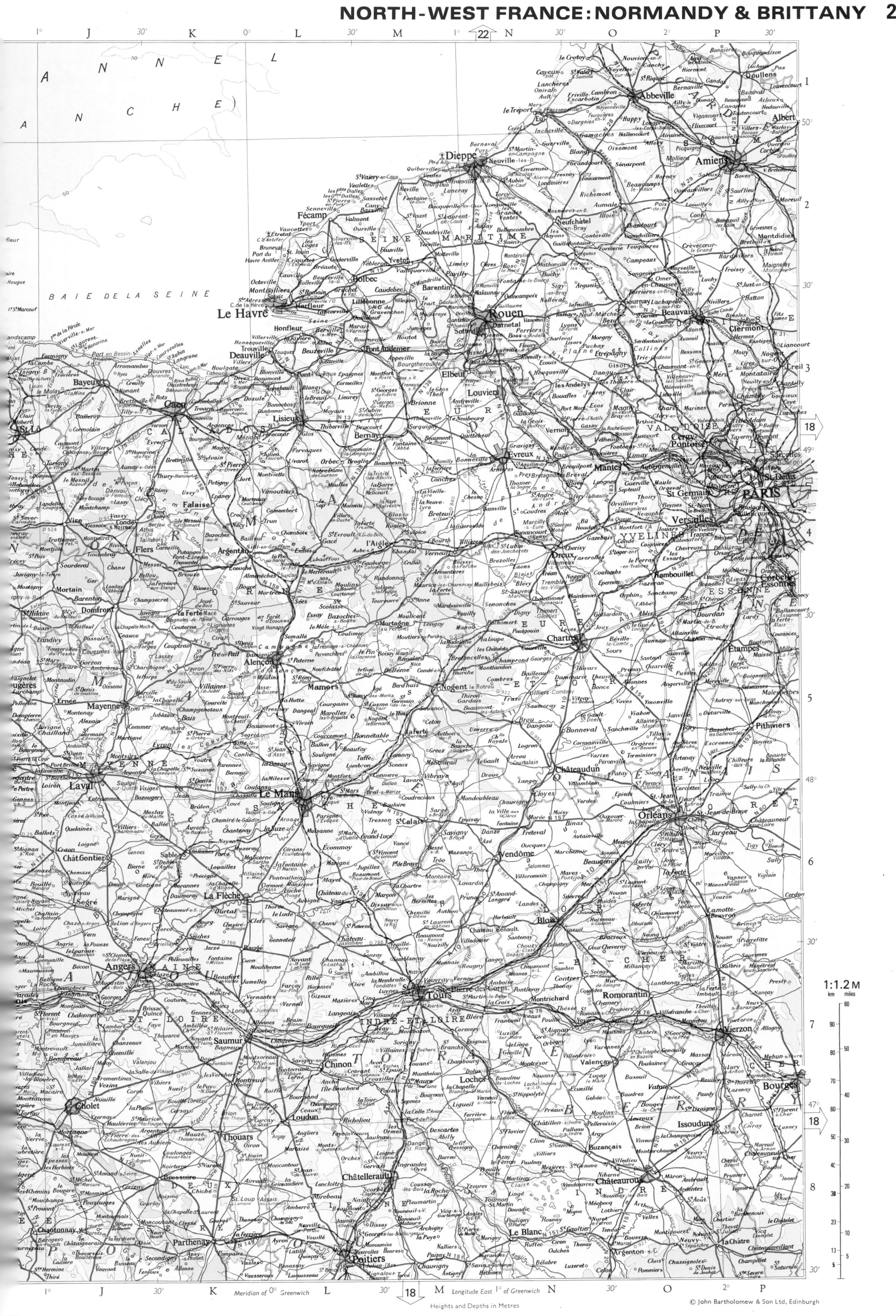
22
18
18
18
Meridian of Greenwich
Longitude East of Greenwich
Heights and Depths in Metres
1:1.2 M
km miles
LA MANCHE
BAIE DE LA SEINE
SEINE MARITIME
CALVADOS
EURE
ORNE
MAYENNE
SARTHE
EURE-ET-LOIR
VAL D'OISE
YVELINES
ESSONNE
LOIRET
LOIR-ET-CHER
INDRE-ET-LOIRE
MAINE-ET-LOIRE
CHER
INDRE
DEUX SÈVRES
SOMME
PARIS
Le Havre
Rouen
Dieppe
Abbeville
Amiens
Beauvais
Caen
Lisieux
Évreux
Chartres
Alençon
Le Mans
Laval
Angers
Tours
Orléans
Blois
Vendôme
Châteaudun
Saumur
Chinon
Cholet
Poitiers
Châtellerault
Châteauroux
Bourges
Vierzon
Issoudun
Romorantin
Versailles
Dreux
Rambouillet
Étampes
Pithiviers
Mayenne
Flers
Argentan
Falaise
Bayeux
St Lô
Deauville
Honfleur
Fécamp
Bolbec
Yvetot
Elbeuf
Louviers
Bernay
Mantes
Pontoise
Cergy
Nogent le Rotrou
La Flèche
Château Gontier
Parthenay
Thouars
Bressuire
Loudun
Loches
Le Blanc
La Châtre
Sablé
Segré
Domfront
Mortagne
L'Aigle

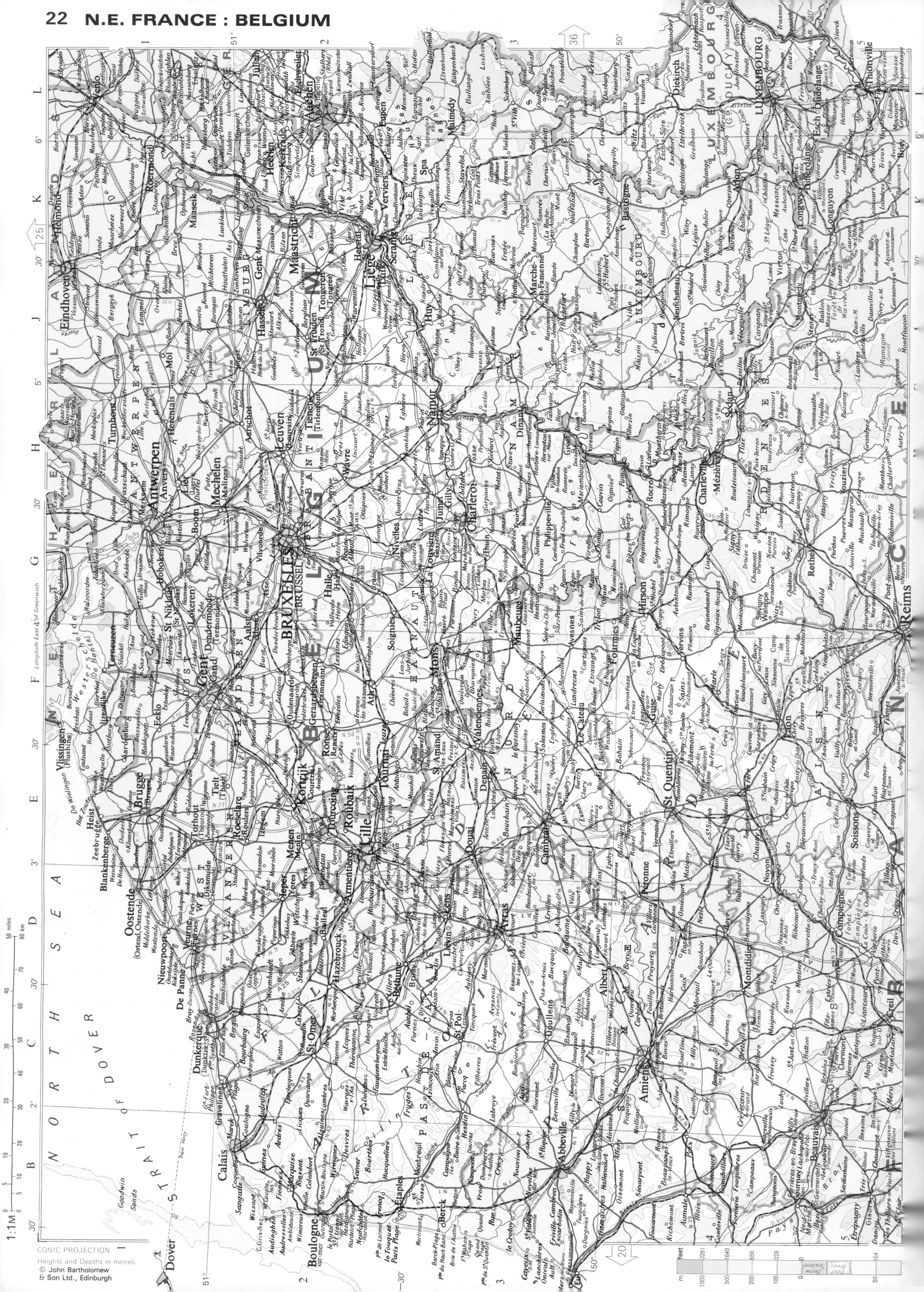
NORTH SEA
STRAIT OF DOVER
BELGIUM
FRANCE
LUXEMBOURG
BRUXELLES BRUSSEL
Antwerpen (Anvers)
Gent (Gand)
Brugge (Bruges)
Oostende (Ostend, Ostende)
Liège
Namur
Charleroi
Mons
Lille
Calais
Dunkerque
Boulogne sur-mer
Amiens
Arras
Reims
St Quentin
Abbeville
Dover
Longitude East 4° of Greenwich
1:1M
CONIC PROJECTION
Heights and Depths in metres
© John Bartholomew & Son Ltd., Edinburgh

PARIS

1:300 000

© Times Books Ltd

0 5 10 15 km
0 5 10 miles

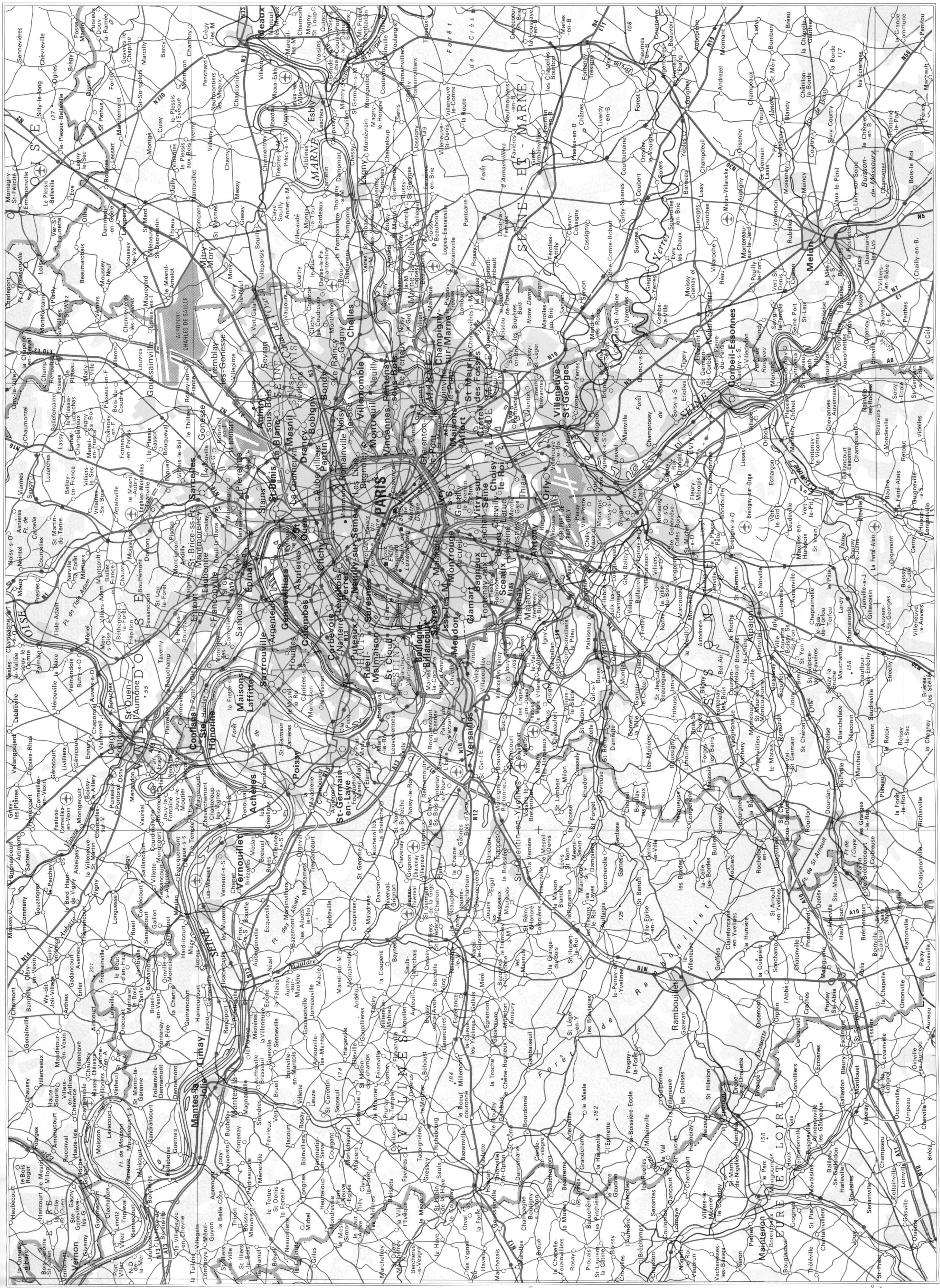

NORTH SEA

NOORDHOLLAND

AMSTERDAM

ZUID-HOLLAND

UTRECHT

ZUIDELIJK - FLEVOLAND

MARKERWAARD

IJMEER

GOOIMEER

IJmuiden
Zaandam
Haarlem
Heemstede
Zandvoort
Amstelveen
Weesp
Naarden
Huizen
Bussum
Hilversum
Hillegom
Lisse
Noordwijk aan Zee
Katwijk aan Zee
Oegstgeest
Valkenburg
Wassenaar
Voorschoten
Scheveningen

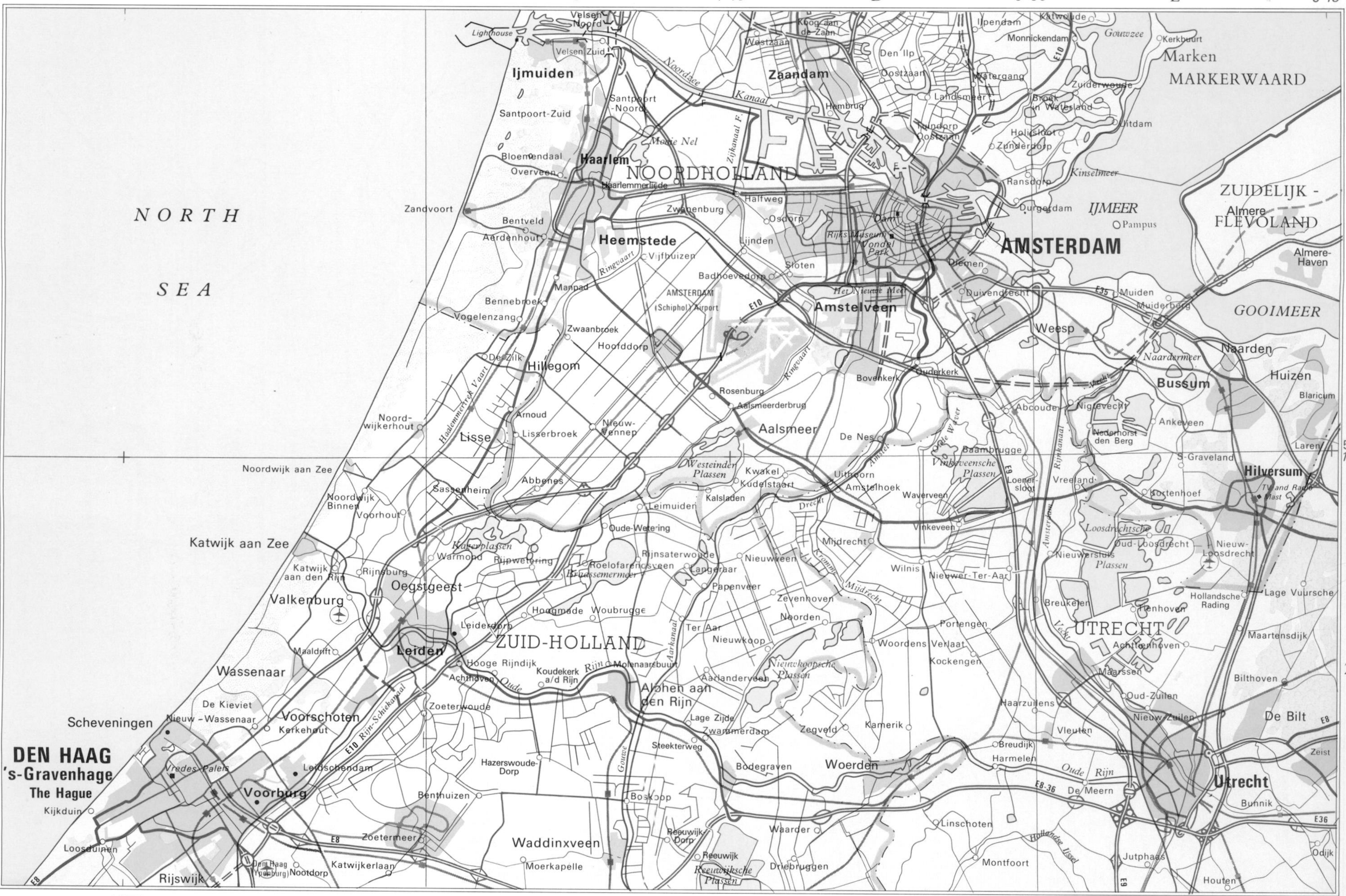

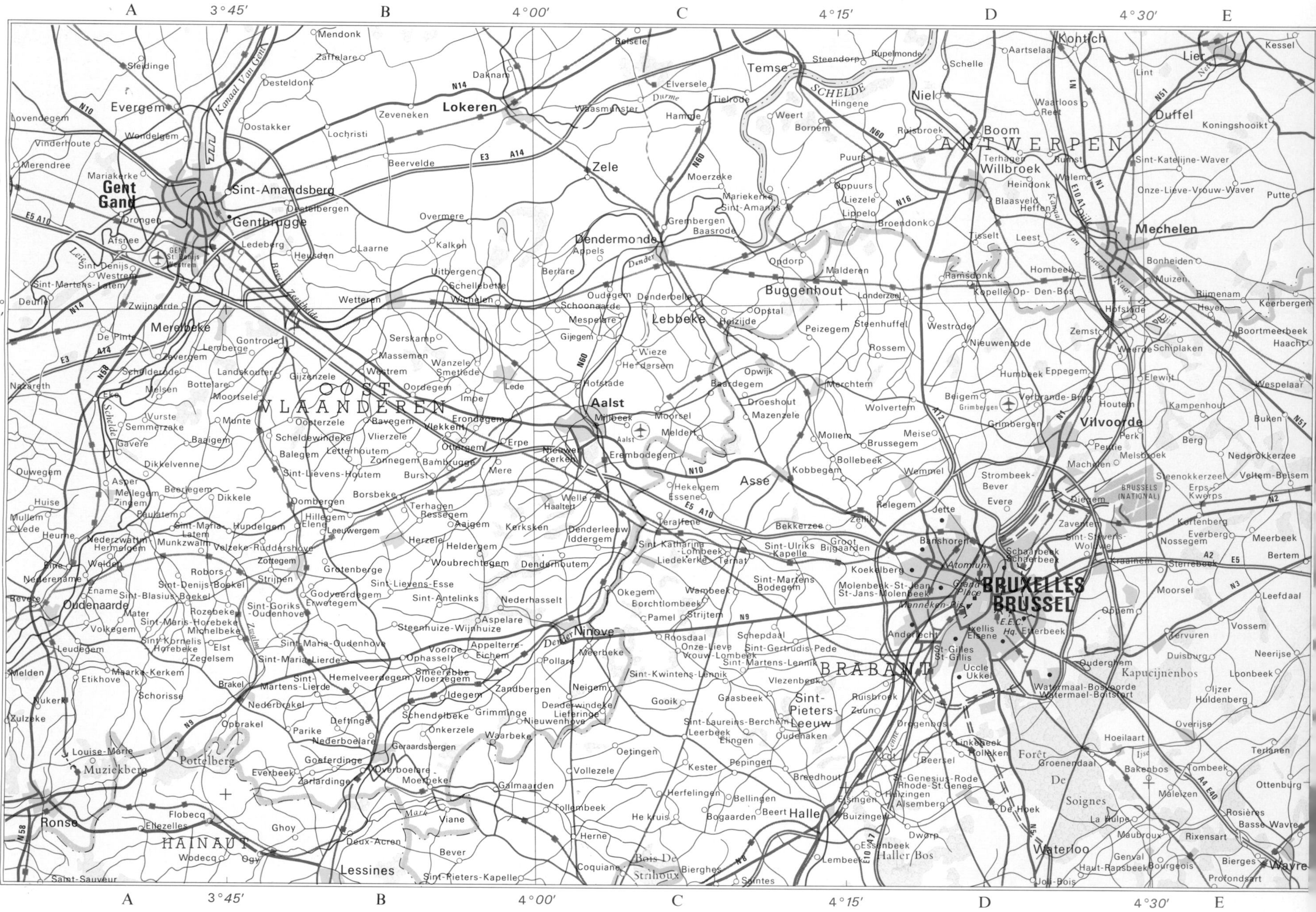

DEN HAAG
's-Gravenhage
The Hague
Voorburg
Rijswijk
Zoetermeer
Waddinxveen
Leiden
Alphen aan den Rijn
Woerden
Utrecht
De Bilt

BRUSSELS

OOST VLAANDEREN

ANTWERPEN

BRABANT

HAINAUT

SCHELDE

Gent / Gand
Genthrugge
Sint-Amandsberg
Merelbeke
Lokeren
Zele
Dendermonde
Aalst
Asse
Ninove
Mechelen
Willebroek
Boom
Vilvoorde

BRUXELLES BRUSSEL

Waterloo
Ronse
Oudenaarde

ONIC PROJECTION

164 | 0 | 328 | 656 | 1640 | 3281 feet
Tidal Areas | Below Sea Level
50 | 0 | 100 | 200 | 500 | 1000 m

1:1M
0 5 10 20 30 miles
0 5 10 20 30 40 50 60 km

NORWEGIAN
SEA
Arctic Circle
Vestfjorden
Lofoten
NORD-TRØNDELAG
SØR-TRØNDELAG
Trondheim
Kristiansund
Ålesund
Molde
Bodø
Narvik
Tromsø
Hammerfest
FINNMARKSVIDDA
U.S.S.R.

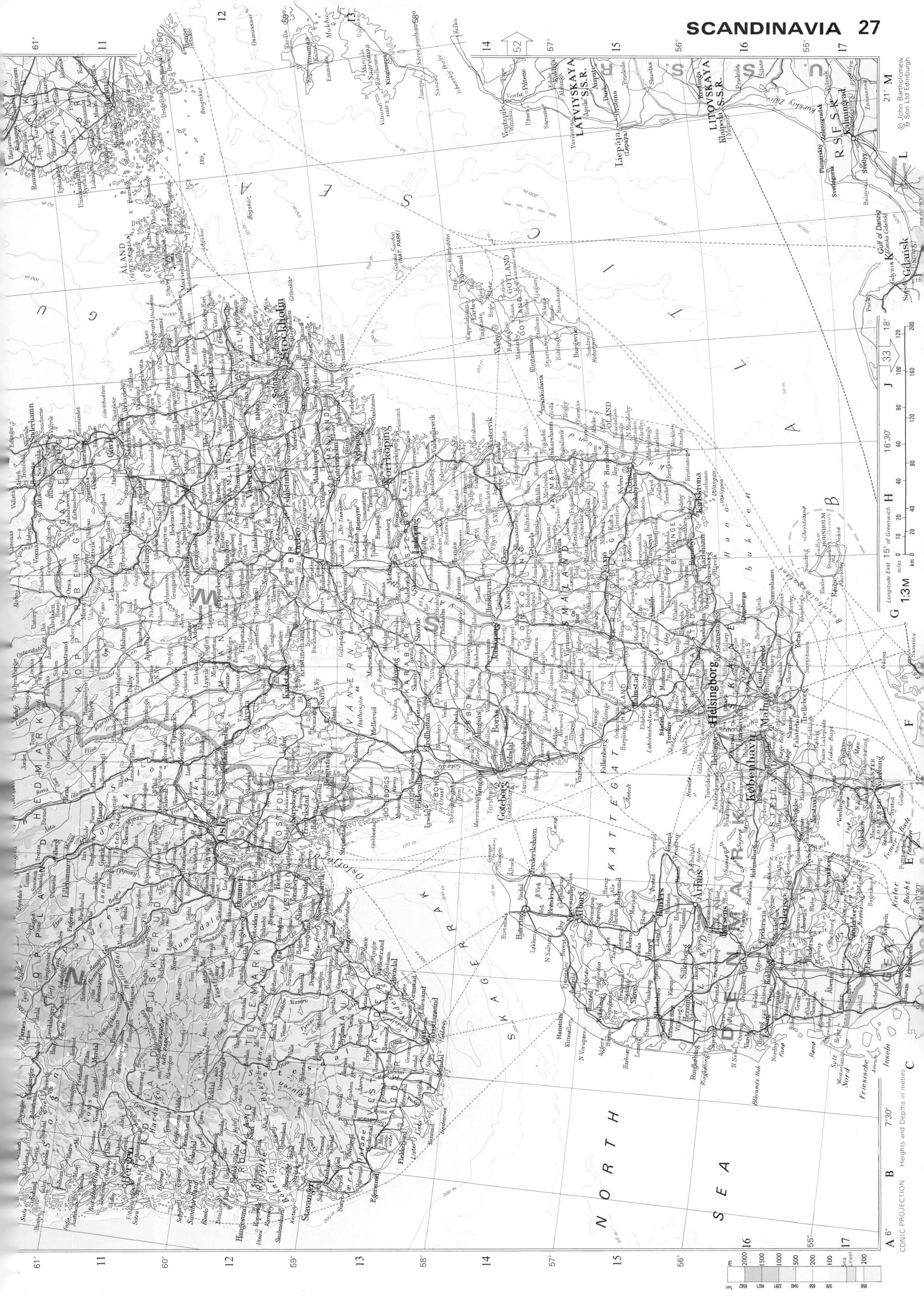
NORTH SEA
SKAGERRAK
KATTEGAT
BALTIC SEA
Oslo
Stockholm
Göteborg
København
Malmö
Helsingborg
Bergen
Stavanger
Kristiansand
Norrköping
Linköping
Örebro
Västerås
Uppsala
Karlstad
Jönköping
Gävle
Visby
GOTLAND
ÖLAND
BORNHOLM
ÅLAND
Gdańsk
Kaliningrad
Liepāja
LATVIYSKAYA S.S.R.
LITOVSKAYA S.S.R.
Gulf of Danzig
Longitude East 15° of Greenwich
1:3M
CONIC PROJECTION
Heights and Depths in metres
© John Bartholomew & Son Ltd Edinburgh

SKAGERRAK
KATTEGAT
DENMARK
JYLLAND
SJÆLLAND
(ZEALAND)
FYN
(FÜNEN)
LOLLAND
FALSTER
LANGELAND
ALS
MORS
NORDJYLLAND
VIBORG
ÅRHUS
RINGKØBING
VEJLE
RIBE
SØNDERJYLLAND
Vendsyssel
Himmerland
Djursland
Limfjorden
Jammerbugt
Tannis Bugt
Ålbæk Bugt
Ålborg Bugt
Læsø
Anholt
Samsø
Samsø Bælt
Store Bælt
Lille Bælt
Smålandsfarvandet
Femer Bælt
Skagen
Hirtshals
Hjørring
Frederikshavn
Sæby
Brønderslev
Ålborg
Nørresundby
Thisted
Skive
Viborg
Randers
Grenå
Hobro
Mariager
Holstebro
Struer
Ringkøbing
Herning
Silkeborg
Århus
Ebeltoft
Skanderborg
Horsens
Vejle
Fredericia
Kolding
Middelfart
Esbjerg
Varde
Ribe
Haderslev
Åbenrå
Sønderborg
Tønder
Odense
Nyborg
Svendborg
Fåborg
Assens
Kalundborg
Holbæk
Slagelse
Korsør
Næstved
Vordingborg
Ringsted
Sorø
Nakskov
Maribo
Nykøbing
Rudkøbing
Marstal
Ærø
Fanø
Rømø
Sylt
Westerland
Föhr
NORDFRIESISCHE INSELN
Flensburg
GERMANY
Fehmarn
To Göteborg
To Varberg
ICELAND
REYKJAVÍK
Akureyri
Húnaflói
Faxaflói
Breidha fjördhur
Ísafjördhur
Siglufjördhur
Hafnarfjördhur
Keflavík
Reykjanesta
Arctic Circle
Grimsey
Longitude East 10° of Greenwich
1:1M
feet 656 164 0 328 656 1640 3281 4921 6562
m 200 50 0 100 200 500 1000 1500 2000
km 0 5 10 20 30 40 50 60 70 80
miles 0 5 10 20 30 40 50

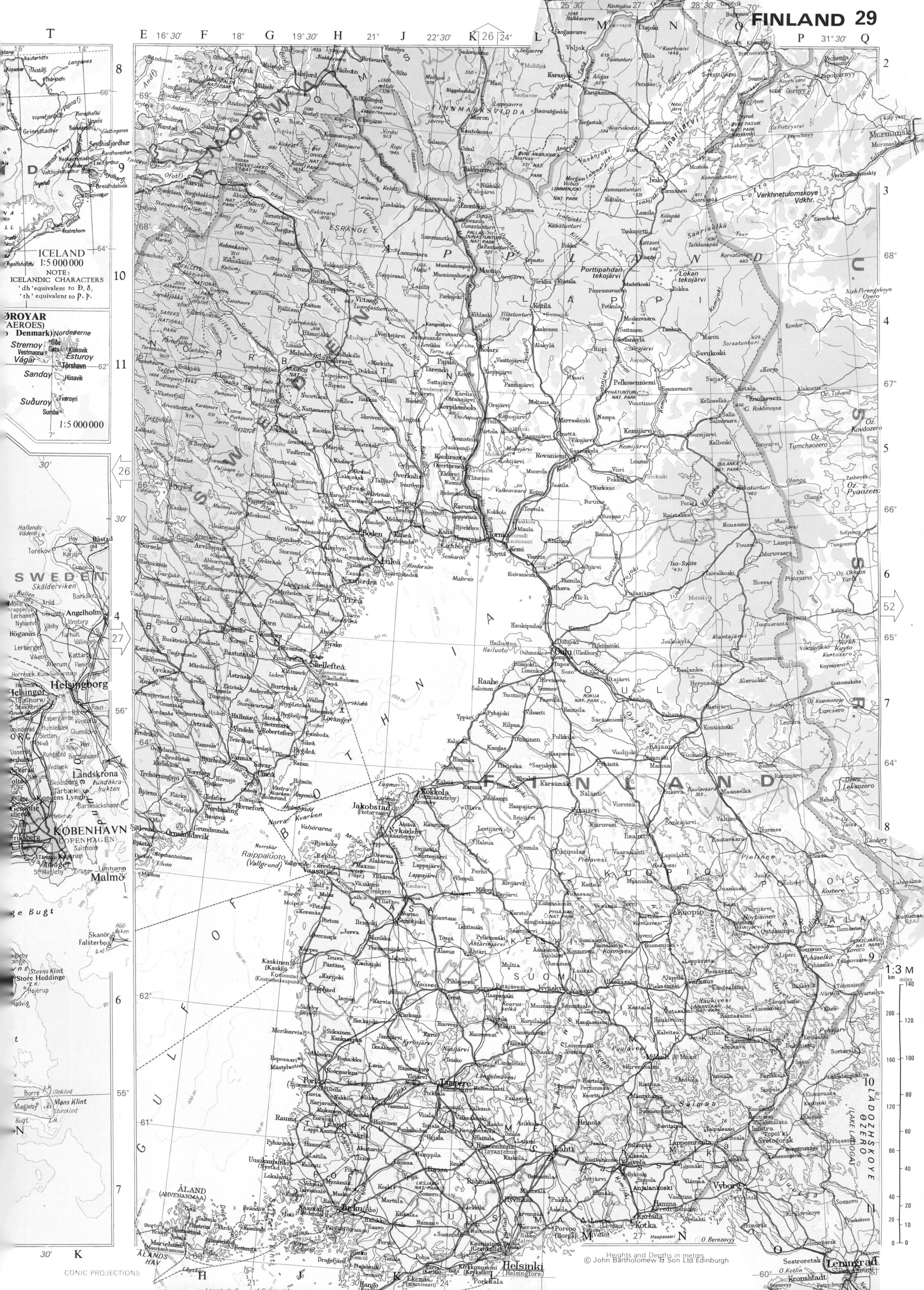
ICELAND
1:5 000 000
NOTE:
ICELANDIC CHARACTERS
'dh' equivalent to Đ, ð,
'th' equivalent to Þ, þ.
FØROYAR
(FAEROES)
(to Denmark)
1:5 000 000
SWEDEN
NORWAY
SWEDEN
FINLAND
LAPPI
OULU
KUOPIO
VAASA
KESKI SUOMI
TURKU-PORI
HÄME
MIKKELI
KYMI
UUSIMAA
POHJOIS KARJALA
ÅLAND (AHVENANMAA)
GULF OF BOTHNIA
GULF OF FINLAND
U.S.S.R.
LADOZHSKOYE OZERO (LAKE LADOGA)
Helsinki (Helsingfors)
Tampere
Turku (Åbo)
Oulu (Uleåborg)
Vaasa
Kuopio
Lahti
Jyväskylä
Pori (Björneborg)
Rovaniemi
Leningrad
Vyborg
Murmansk
København
Malmö
Helsingborg
Kiruna
Luleå
Umeå
Skellefteå
Narvik
1:3 M
Heights and Depths in metres
© John Bartholomew & Son Ltd Edinburgh
CONIC PROJECTIONS

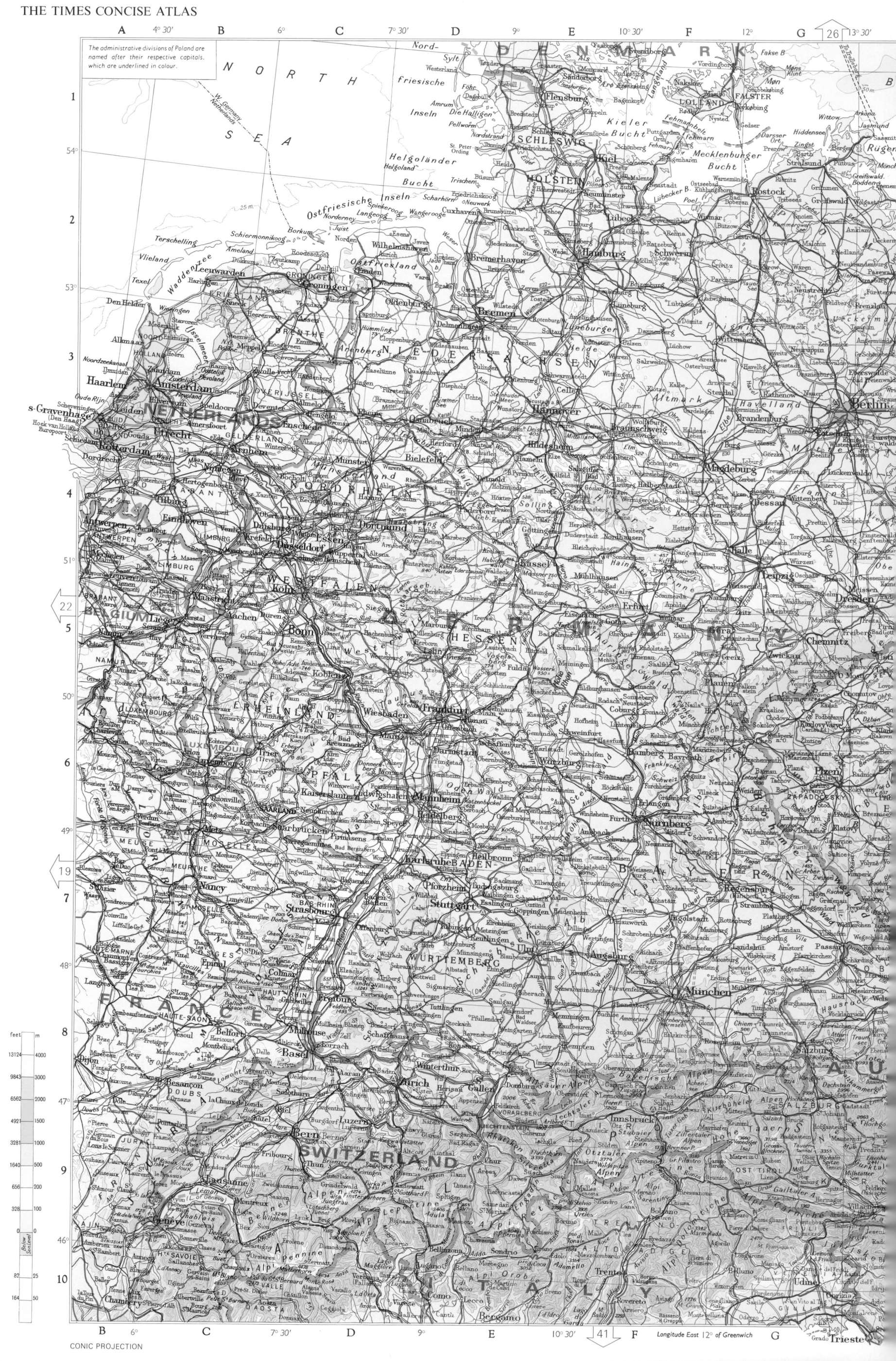

Longitude East 12° of Greenwich

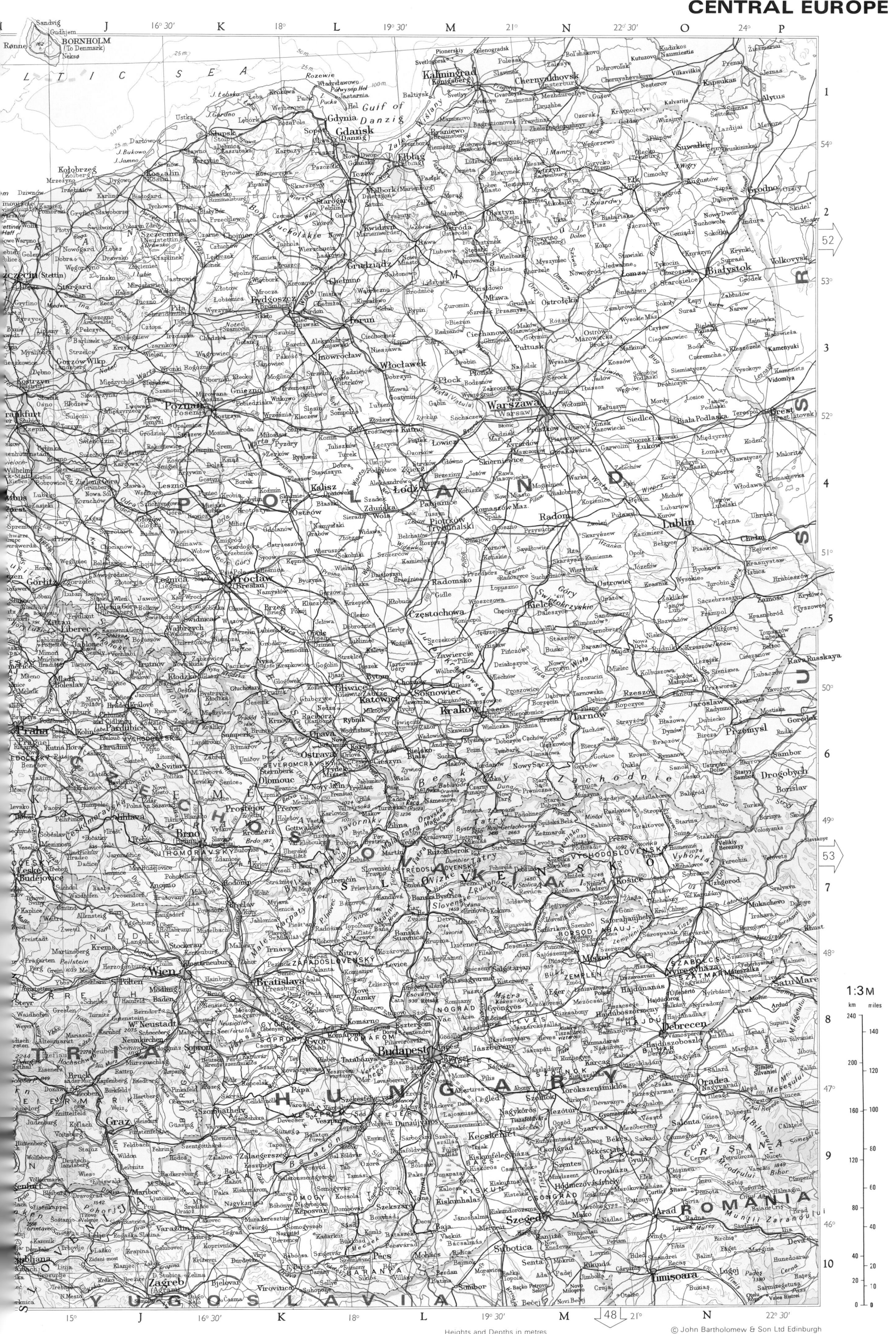

Heights and Depths in metres

© John Bartholomew & Son Ltd Edinburgh

1:3M

km miles

NORTH SEA

HELGOLÄNDER BUCHT

OSTFRIESISCHE INSELN

OSTFRIESLAND

NIEDERSACHSEN

SCHLESWIG-HOLSTEIN

NETHERLANDS

NORDRHEIN-WESTFALEN

HESSEN

Groningen · Hamburg · Bremen · Bremerhaven · Cuxhaven · Wilhelmshaven · Emden · Oldenburg · Delmenhorst · Hannover · Osnabrück · Münster · Bielefeld · Dortmund · Essen · Duisburg · Düsseldorf · Wuppertal · Hagen · Kassel · Göttingen · Hildesheim · Hameln · Paderborn · Detmold · Herford · Minden · Nienburg · Verden · Celle · Rendsburg · Heide · Neumünster · Pinneberg · Harburg · Stade · Buxtehude

NOTE: 'ß'-German equivalent to 'ss'

feet
3281
1640
656
328
0
32
65
m
1000
500
200
100
Below Sea Level · Areas
10
20

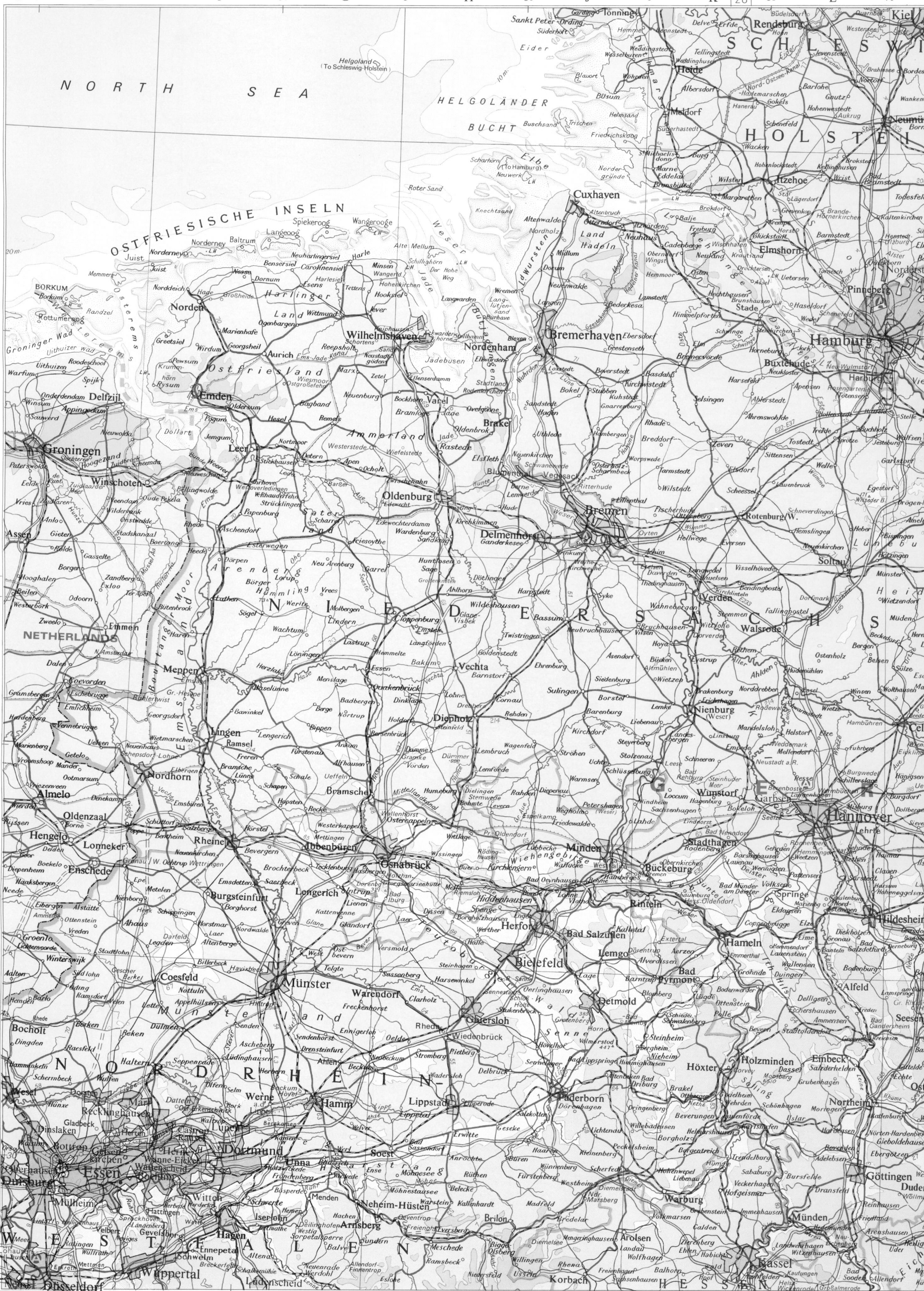

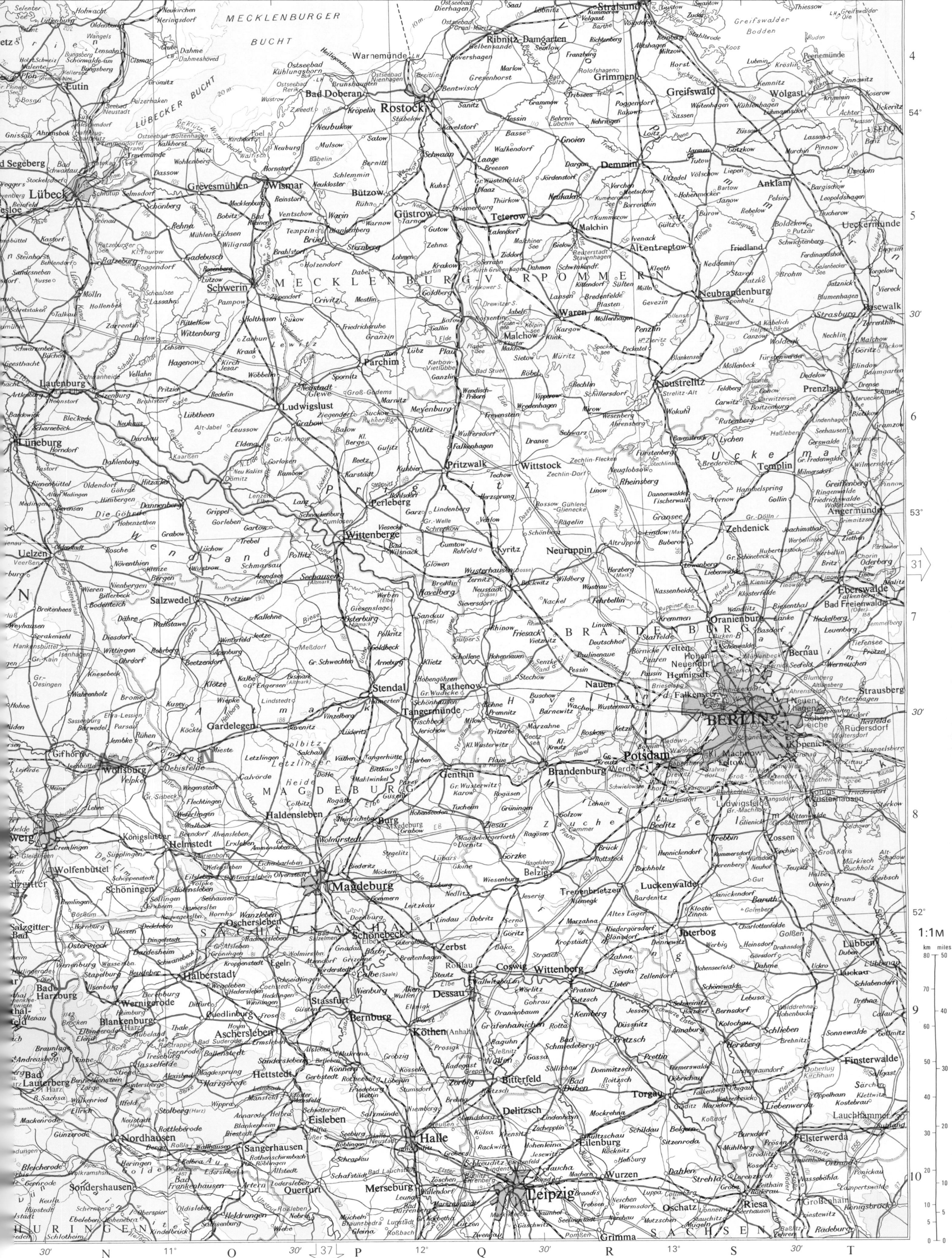

Heights and Depths in metres

SCHLESWIG-HOLSTEIN

HAMBURG

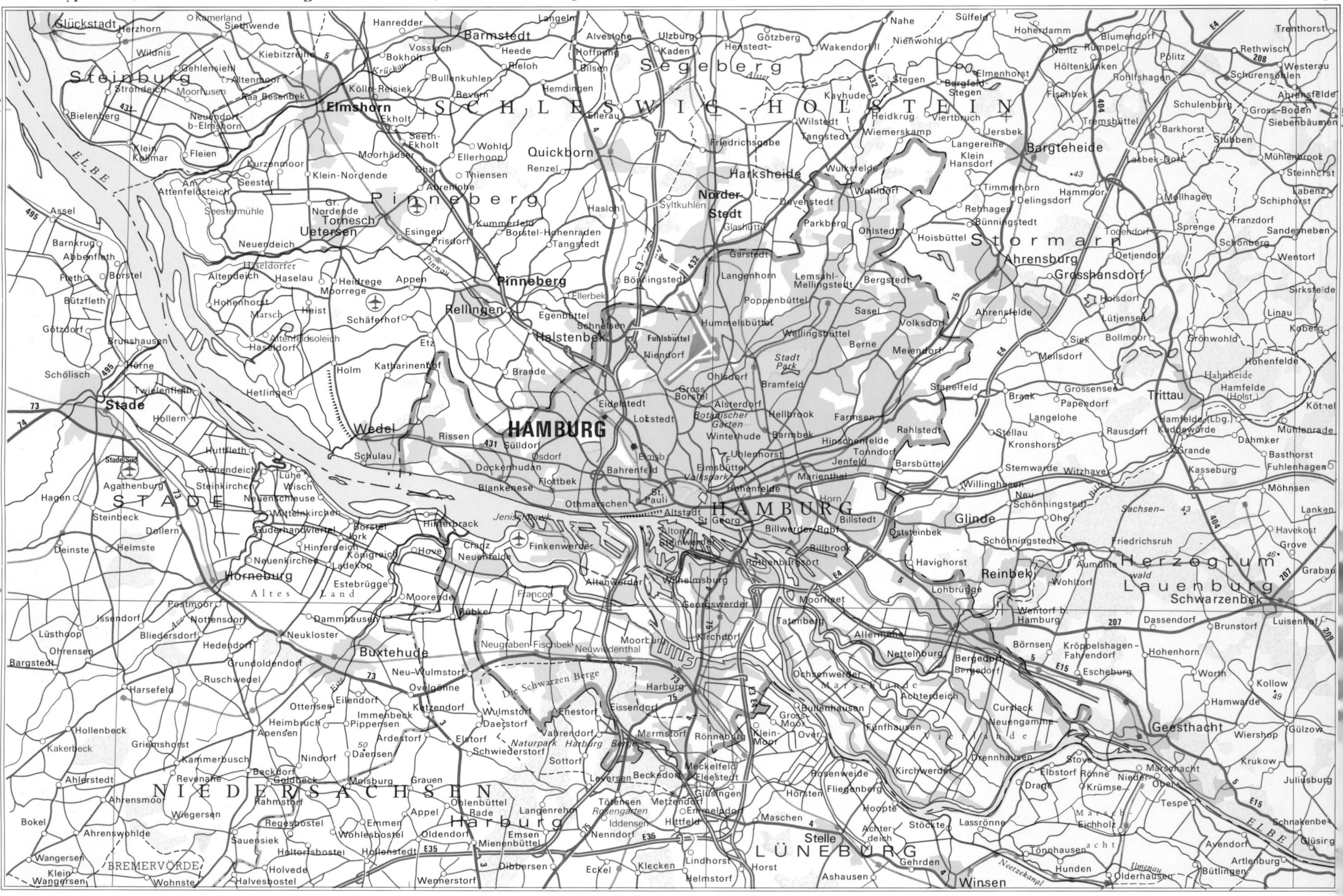

STADE

NIEDERSACHSEN

Harburg

LÜNEBURG

Stormarn

Segeberg

Pinneberg

Herzogtum Lauenburg

BREMERVÖRDE

BERLIN

BERLIN

Mitte

POTSDAM

Potsdam

FRANKFURT

Charlottenburg

Spandau

Köpenick

Wilmersdorf

Steglitz

Zehlendorf

Tempelhof

Neukölln

Königs Wusterhausen

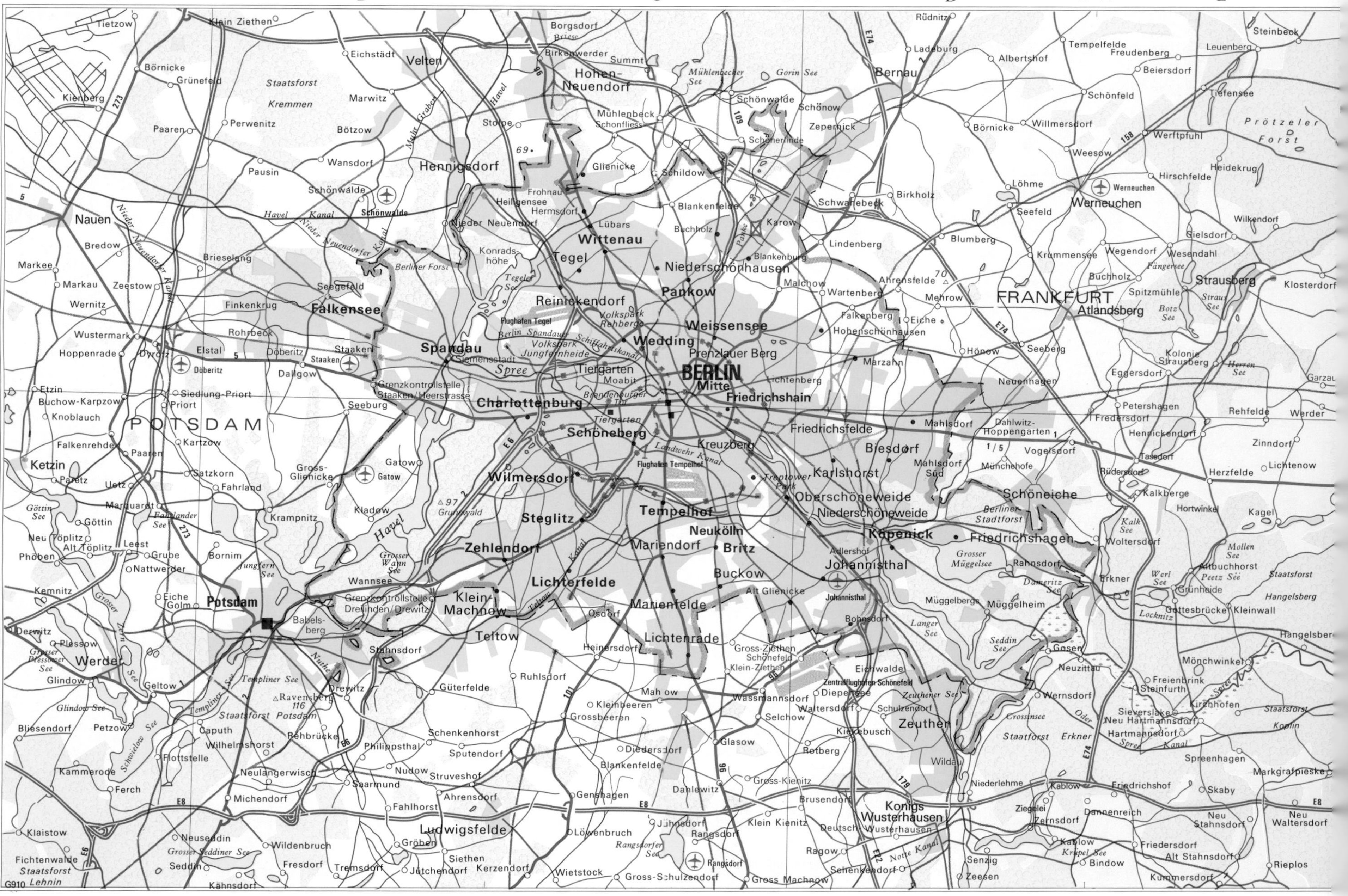

© Times Books Ltd

1:300 000

1:300 000

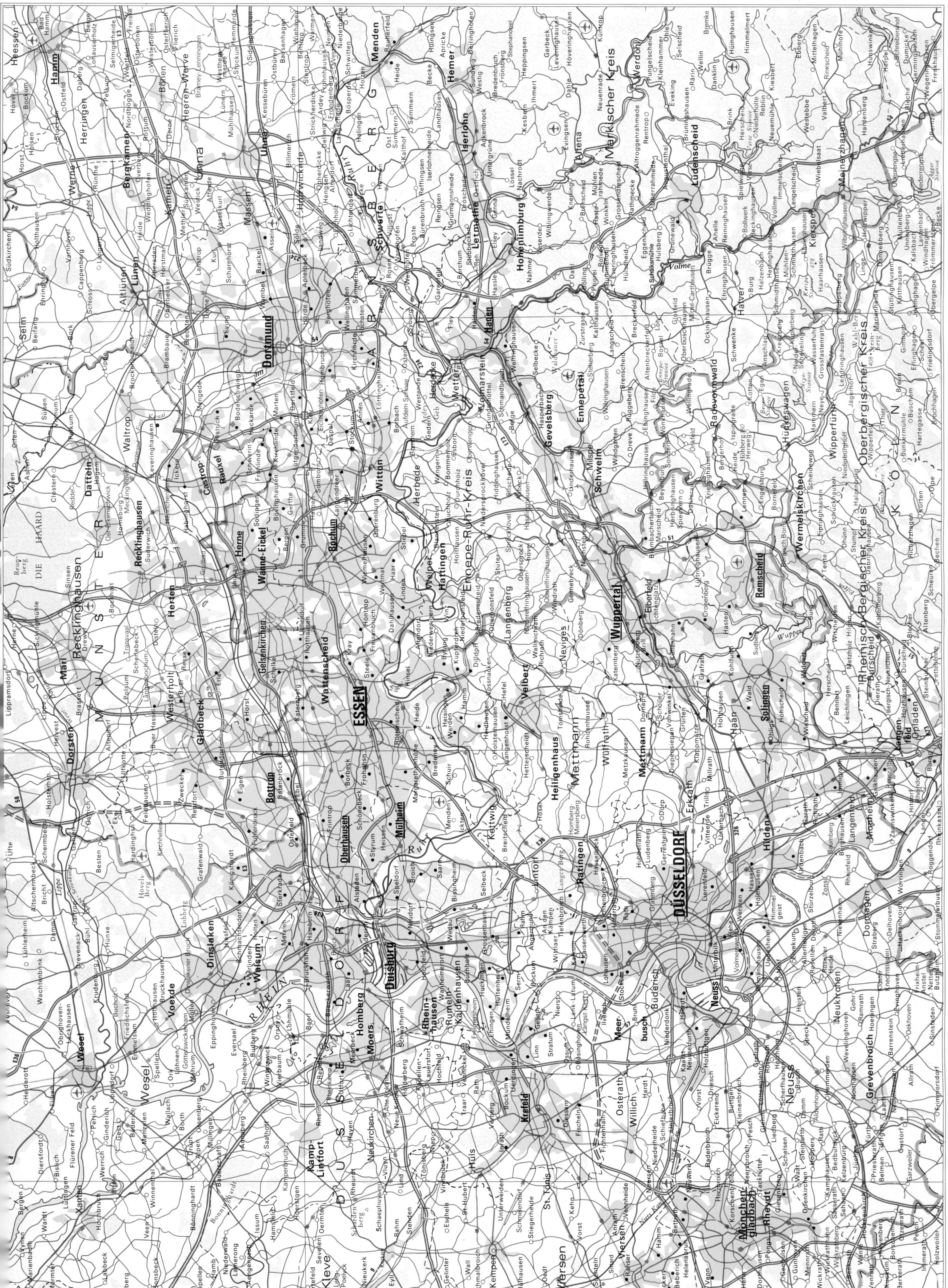

N O R D R H E I N

CONIC PROJECTION

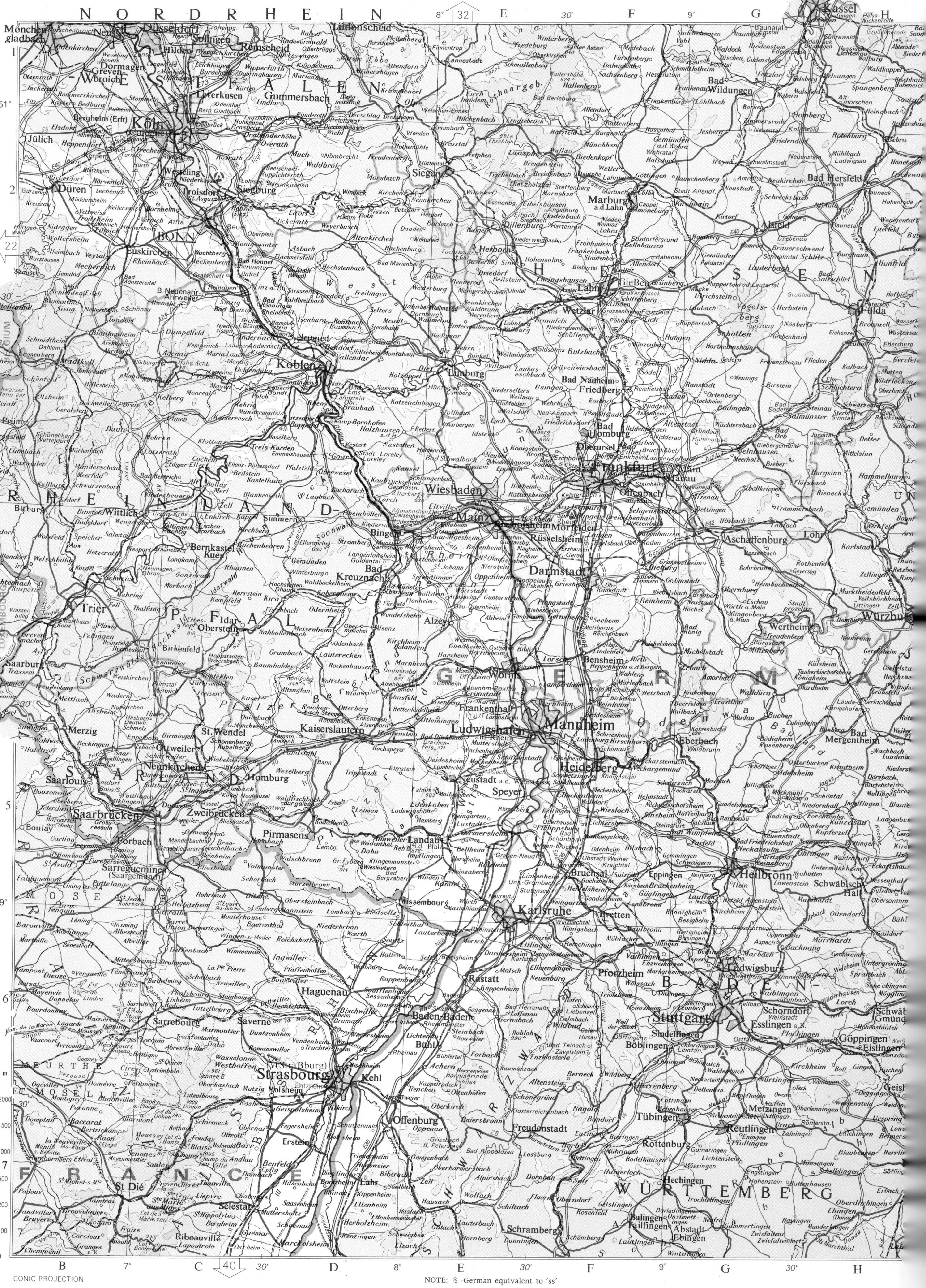

NOTE: ß -German equivalent to 'ss'

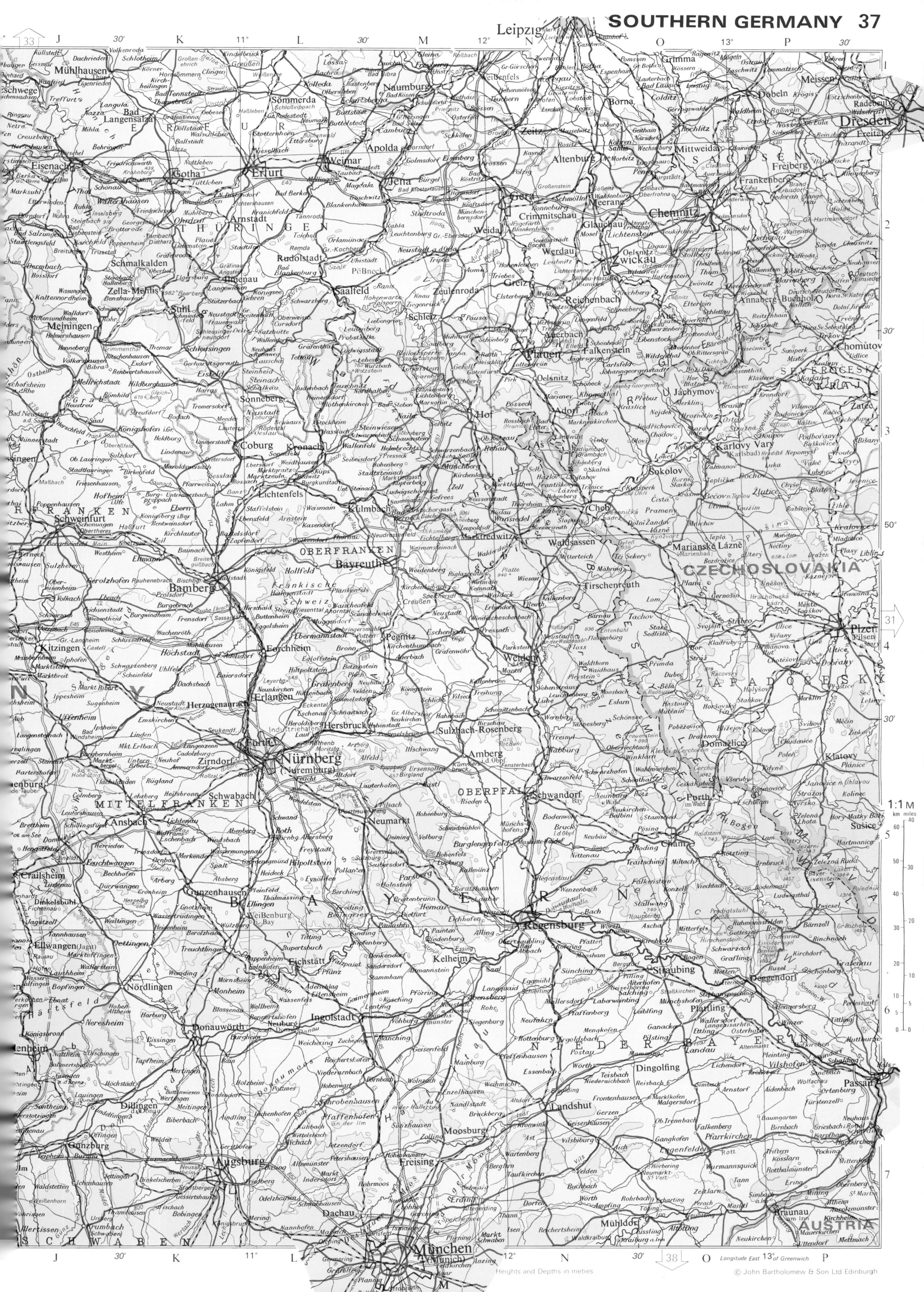

Heights and Depths in metres
Longitude East 13° of Greenwich

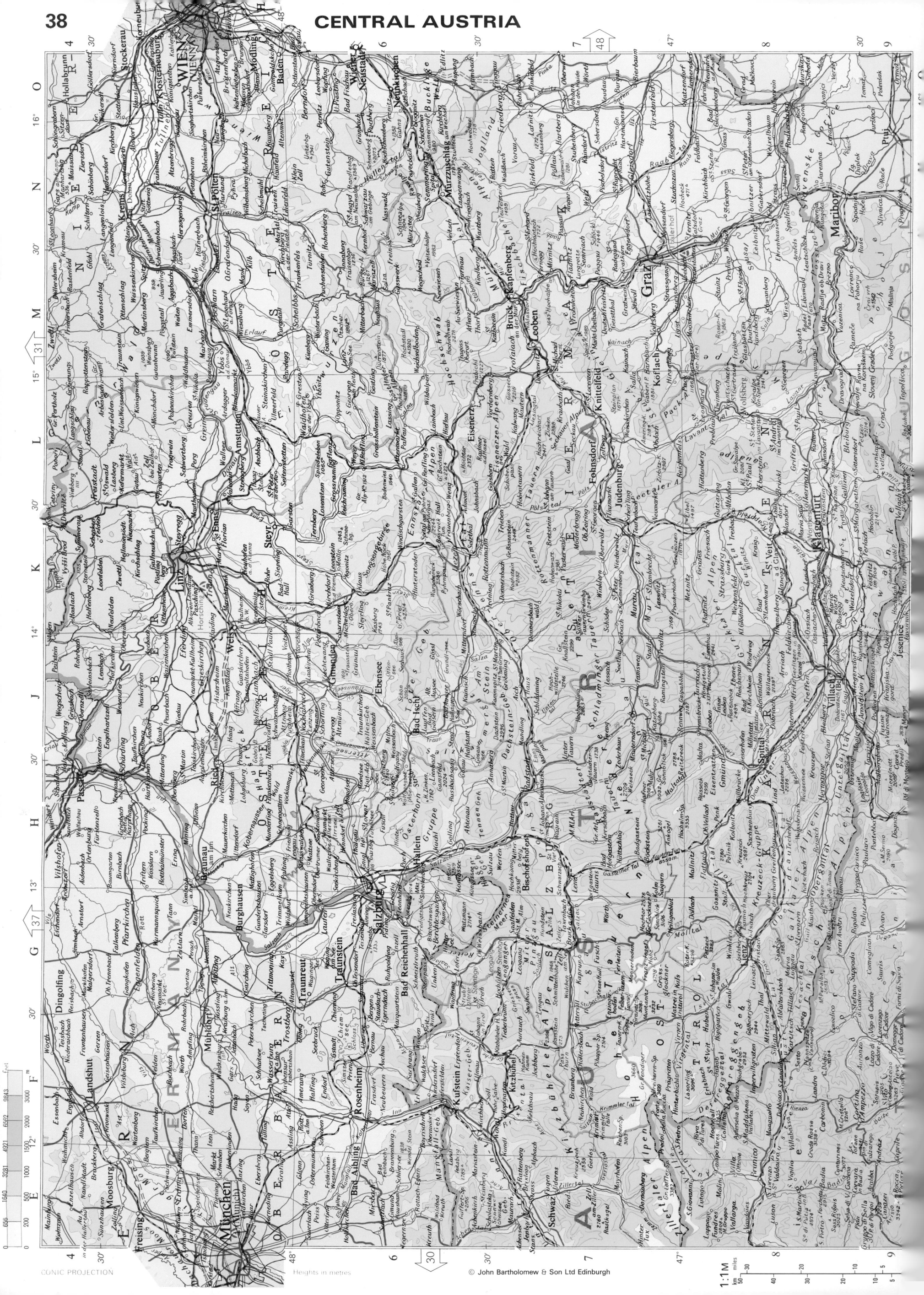

Heights in metres

© John Bartholomew & Son Ltd Edinburgh

1:1 M

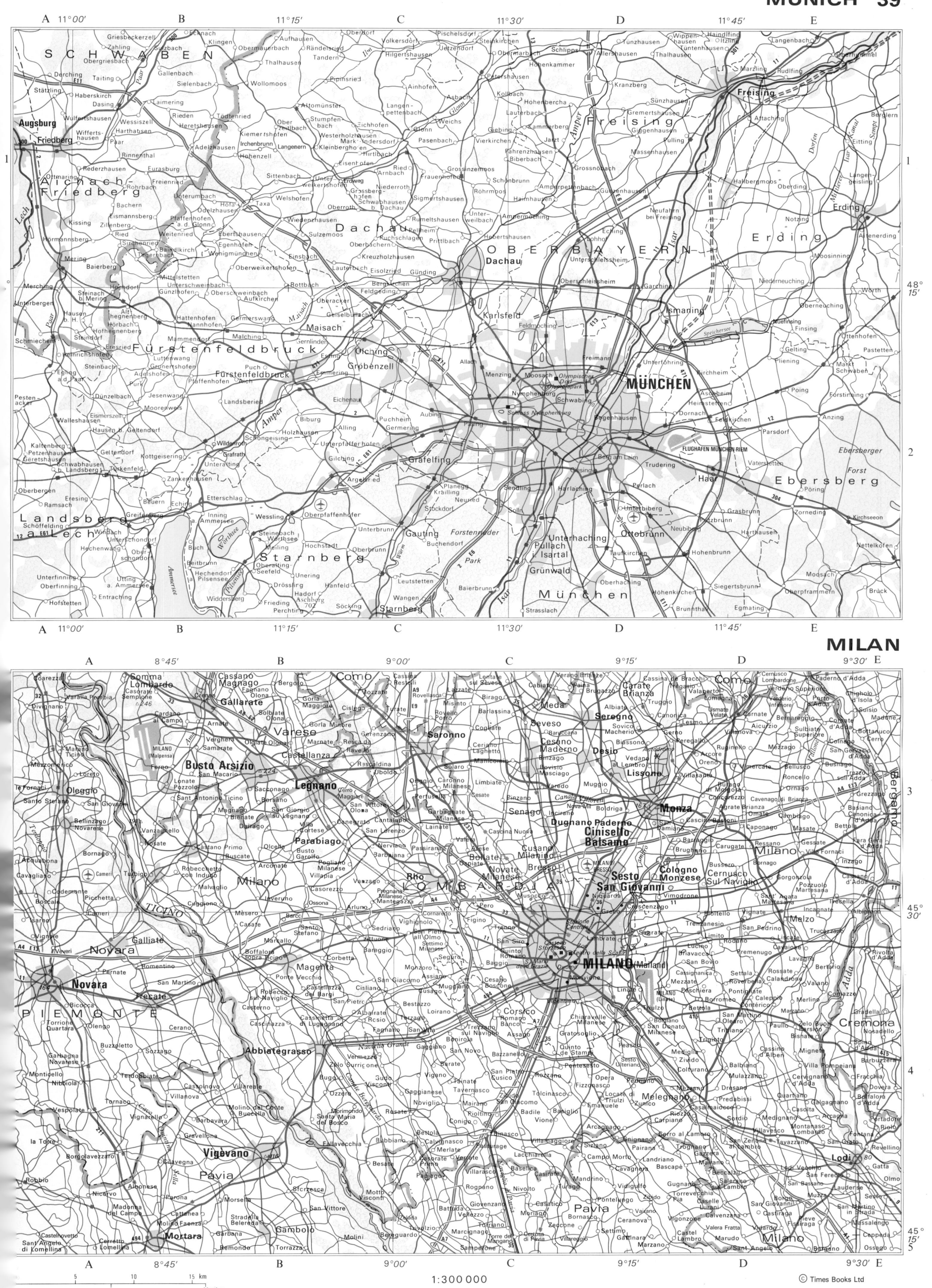

1:300 000

© Times Books Ltd

Heights and Depths in metres

| 0 | 328 | 656 | 1640 | 1381 | 4921 | 6562 | 9843 | 13124 | feet |
| 0 | 100 | 200 | 500 | 1000 | 1500 | 2000 | 3000 | 4000 | m |

München
Augsburg
Memmingen
Kempten
Kaufbeuren
Landsberg
Starnberg
Weilheim
Garmisch-Partenkirchen
Innsbruck
Bad Tölz
Konstanz
Friedrichshafen
Ravensburg
Bregenz
Dornbirn
Feldkirch
Bludenz
Landeck
St. Gallen
Winterthur
Zürich
Schaffhausen
Sigmaringen
Tuttlingen
Schwenningen
Rottweil
Ebingen
Überlingen
Singen
Glarus
Schwyz
Altdorf
Chur
Davos
St. Moritz
Bellinzona
Locarno
Lugano
Como
Lecco
Bergamo
Brescia
Milano
Novara
Varese
Monza
Sondrio
Tirano
Bormio
Merano
Bolzano
Trento
Rovereto
Riva
Verona
Mantova
Pavia
Lodi
Cremona
Vigevano
Vercelli
Bodensee (L. Constance)
Lago Maggiore
Lago di Como
Lago d'Iseo
Lago di Garda
AUSTRIA
TIROL
VORARLBERG
LIECHTENSTEIN
GRAUBÜNDEN
TICINO
LOMBARDIA
TRENTINO
ALTO ADIGE
SCHWABEN
ITALY
Longitude East 9° of Greenwich
1:1M
0 5 10 20 30 40 50 km
0 5 10 20 30
© John Bartholomew & Son Ltd Edinburgh

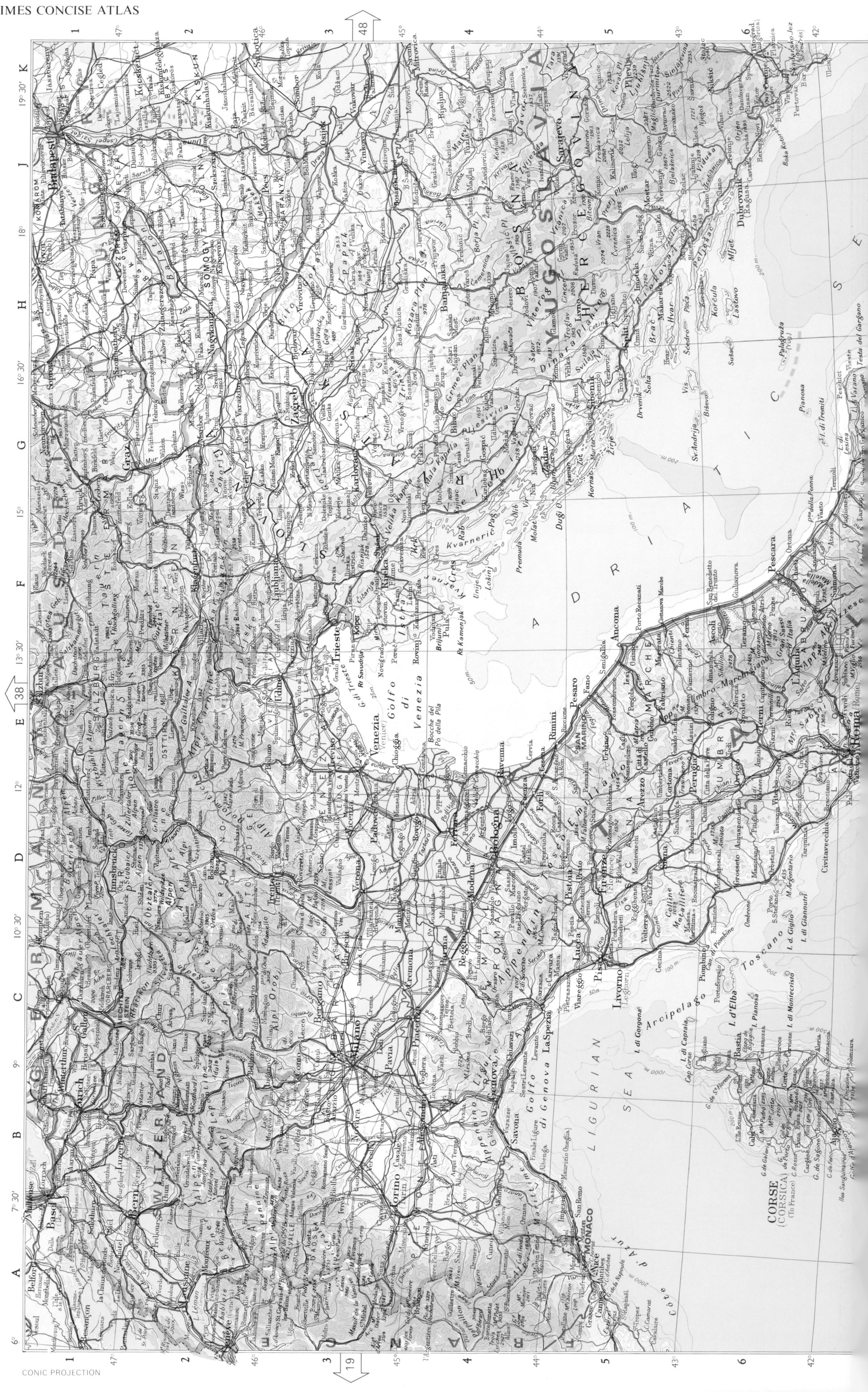
48
38
19
Budapest
Zagreb
Ljubljana
Trieste
Venezia
Milano
Torino
Genova
Bologna
Firenze
Roma
Sarajevo
Split
Dubrovnik
Ancona
Pescara
Bern
Zürich
Innsbruck
Graz
CORSE
(CORSICA)
MONACO

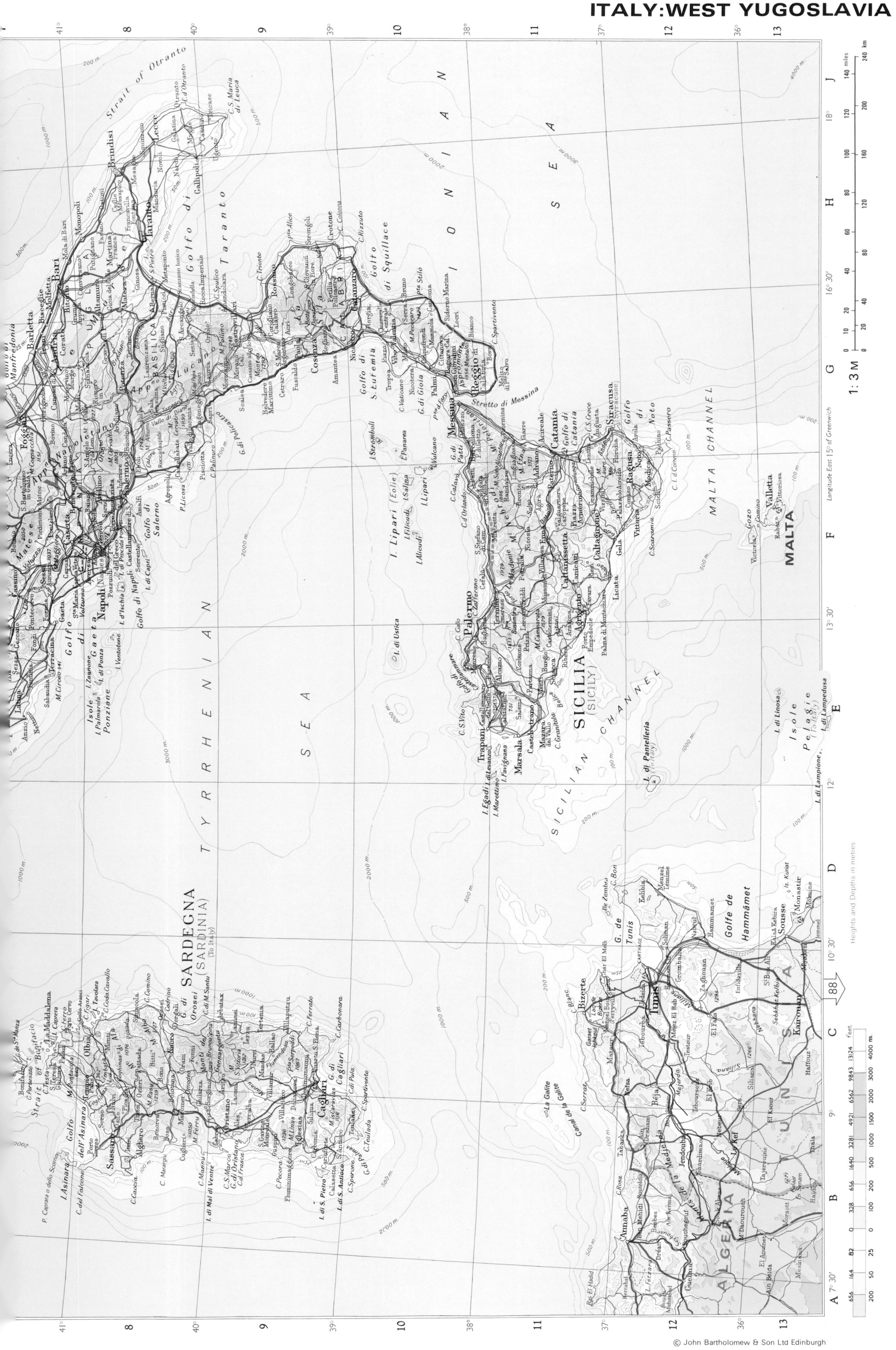
TYRRHENIAN SEA
IONIAN SEA
SARDEGNA (SARDINIA) (To Italy)
SICILIA (SICILY)
MALTA
TUNISIA
ALGERIA
SICILIAN CHANNEL
MALTA CHANNEL
Strait of Otranto
Strait of Bonifacio
Golfo di Taranto
Golfo di Squillace
Stretto di Messina
Golfe de Hammâmet
G. de Tunis
Isole Ponziane
I. Lipari (Eolie)
Isole Pelagie
I. di Pantelleria
I. di Lampedusa
I. di Linosa
I. di Ustica
Napoli
Bari
Brindisi
Lecce
Taranto
Foggia
Barletta
Potenza
Cosenza
Catanzaro
Reggio di Calabria
Messina
Palermo
Catania
Siracusa
Ragusa
Trapani
Marsala
Agrigento
Caltanissetta
Cagliari
Sassari
Olbia
Nuoro
Oristano
Tunis
Bizerte
Sousse
Kairouan
Annaba
Valletta
Gozo
1: 3 M
Longitude East 15° of Greenwich
Heights and Depths in metres

FRANCE

Torino, Turin
Milano, Milan
Novara
Vercelli
Asti
Alessandria
Pavia
Piacenza
Cremona
Lodi
Crema
Tortona
Voghera
Stradella
Cuneo
Pinerolo
Carmagnola
Bra
Alba
Acqui Terme
Ovada
Savona
Genova (Genoa)
Rapallo
Chiavari
Sestri Levante
La Spezia
Sarzana
Carrara
Marina di Carrara
Imperia
San Remo
Ventimiglia
Bordighera
Monte-Carlo
MONACO
Nice
Menton
Antibes
Cannes
Finale Lig.
Albenga
Alassio
Diano Marina
Oneglia
Porto Maurizio

GOLFO DI GENOVA

RIVIERA DI PONENTE

RIVIERA DI LEVANTE

LIGURIAN SEA

Viareggio

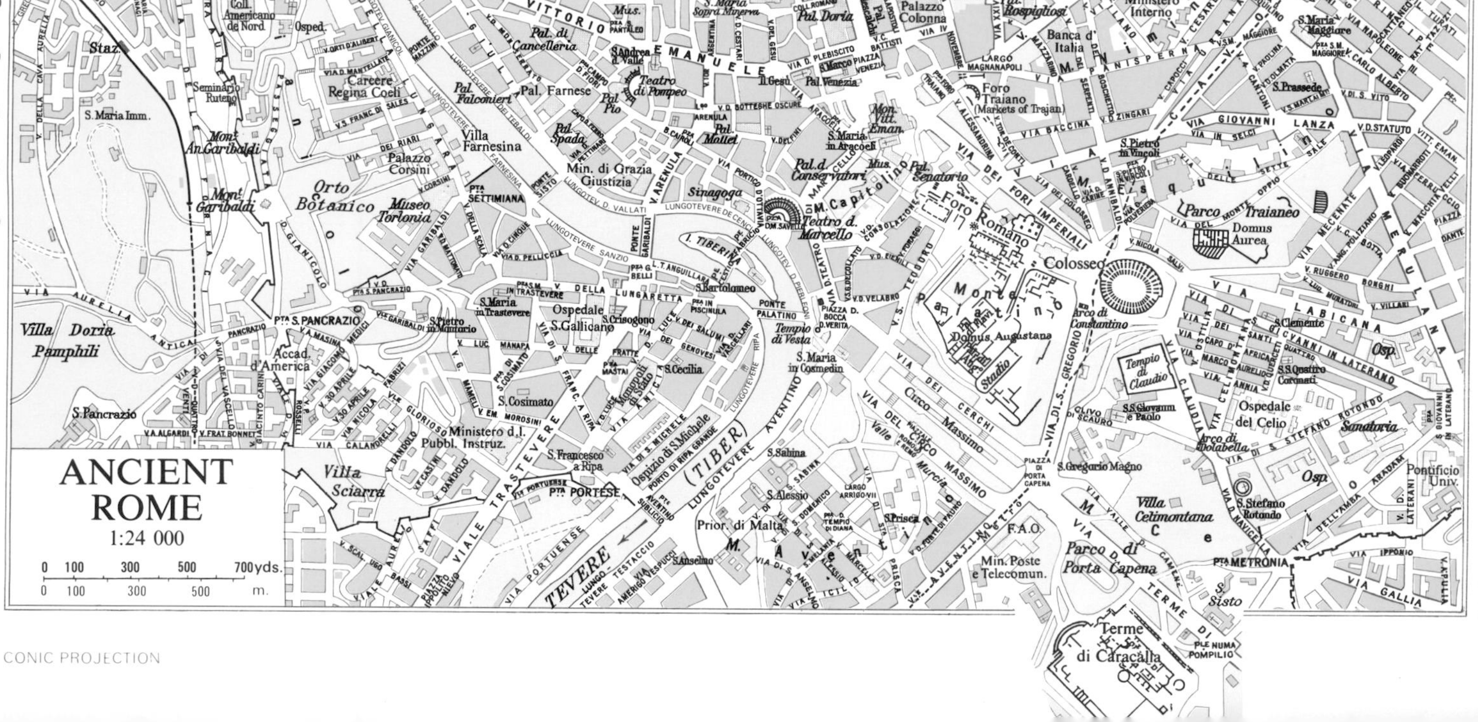

ANCIENT ROME
1:24 000

0   100   300   500   700 yds.
0   100   300   500   m.

feet
13124   4000
9843   3000
6562   2000
4921   1500
3281   1000
1640   500
656   200
328   100
164   50
0   0
656   200

CITTÀ DEL VATICANO
S. Pietro in Vaticano
Castel S. Angelo
TEVERE (TIBER)
Villa Doria Pamphili
Orto Botanico

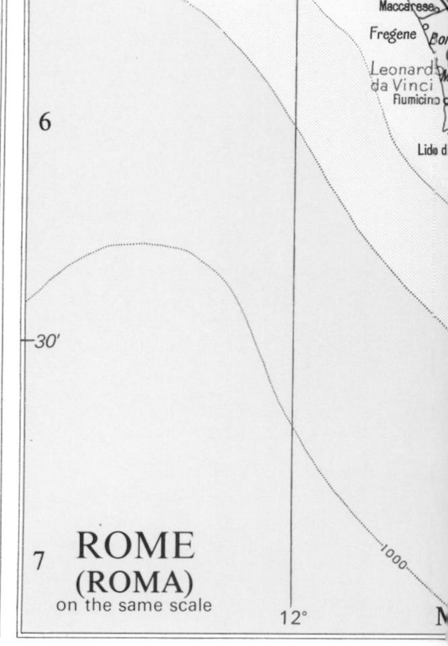

ROME (ROMA)
on the same scale

Civitavecchia
Tarquinia
Bracciano

Conic Projection

GOLFO DI VENEZIA
ADRIATIC SEA
Venezia (Venice)
Verona
Vicenza
Padova
Mantova
Ferrara
Bologna
Modena
Reggio nell'Emilia
Parma
Ravenna
Forlì
Rimini
SAN MARINO
Pesaro
Fano
Senigallia
Ancona
Firenze (Florence)
Pistoia
Prato
Lucca
Pisa
Livorno
Arezzo
ROMA
ROME
Frascati
Tivoli
Latina
Frosinone
Avezzano
Terracina
Gaeta
Formia
NAPLES (NAPOLI)
on the same scale
Napoli (Naples)
Caserta
Benevento
Avellino
Salerno
Golfo di Napoli
Golfo di Salerno
Golfo di Gaeta
Golfo di Terracina
Capri
I.d'Ischia
1:1M
km
miles

A 16° 30' B 18° C 19° 30' D 21° E 22° 30' 48 F 24° G 25° 30'

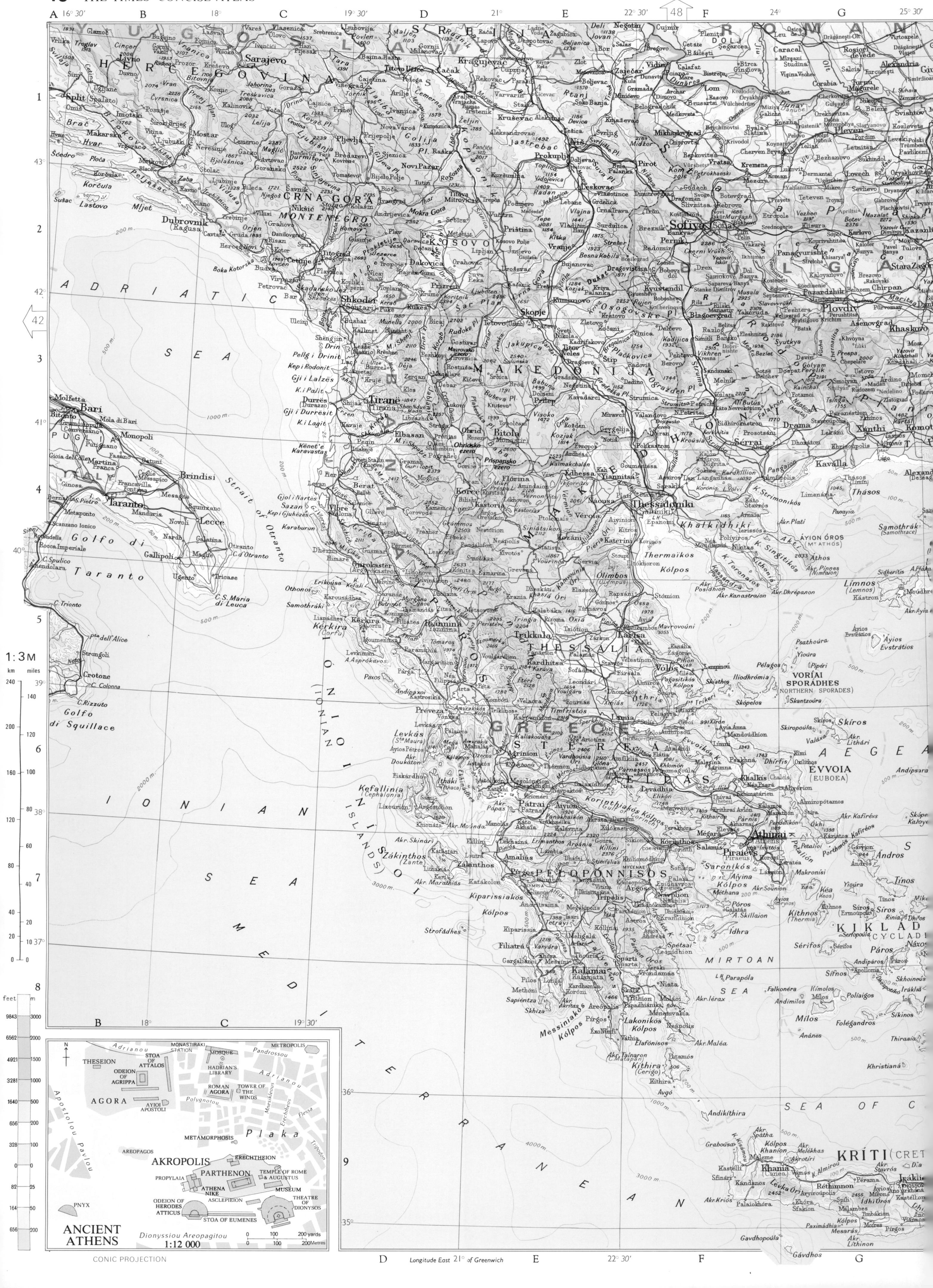

Y U G O S L A V I A

H E R C E G O V I N A

Sarajevo

C R N A   G O R A
M O N T E N E G R O

Niksić

Dubrovnik
(Ragusa)

A D R I A T I C   S E A

Shkodër
(Scutari)

Prishtina

K O S O V O

Skopje

M A K E D O N I J A

S O F I Y A
Sofia

B U L G A R I A

Plovdiv

Khaskovo

Tiranë
(Tirana)

Durrës
(Durazzo)

Elbasan

Bitola
(Monastir)

Ohridsko
ezero

Bari

Brindisi

Taranto

Lecce

Gallipoli

Golfo di Taranto

Strait of Otranto

P U G L I A

I T A L Y

A L B A N I A

Korçë

Kastoria

Ioánnina

Flórina

Édhessa

Yiannitsá

Naousa

Véroia

Thessaloníki

Sérrai

Kaválla

Dráma

Xánthi

Komotiní

Thásos

Khalkidhikí

ÁYION ÓROS
(Mt Áthos)

I O N I A N   S E A

Kérkira
(Corfu)

Igoumenítsa

Préveza

Árta

E P I R O S

T H E S S A L I A

Tríkkala

Lárisa

Kardhítsa

Vólos

Ólimbos
(Olympus)

Kateríni

Lárisa

Pagasitikós
Kólpos

VORÍAI
SPORÁDHES
(NORTHERN SPORADES)

Skíathos

Iliodhrómia

Skíros

Skópelos

A E G E A N

E V V O I A
(EUBOEA)

Khalkís
(Chalcis)

G R E E C E

S T E R E A   E L L A S

Agrínion

Mesolóngion

Pátrai
(Patras)

Levádhia

Thívai
(Thebes)

Athínai
Athens

Piraiévs
(Piraeus)

K E F A L L I N I A
(Cephalonia)

Zákinthos
(Zante)

Pírgos

P E L O P O N N I S O S

Trípolis

Kalámai
(Kalamata)

Spárti
(Sparta)

Náfplion

Árgos

Kórinthos
(Corinth)

Sími

K I K L A D H E S
(CYCLADES)

Ándros

Tínos

Síros

Páros

Náxos

Mílos

Sífnos

M I R T O A N   S E A

Kíthira
(Cerigo)

Andikíthira

K R Í T I   (CRETE)

Khaniá
(Canea)

Iráklion

SEA OF C...

M E D I T E R R A N E A N   S E A

1 : 3 M

km miles
240   140
200   120
160   100
120   80
 80   60
 40   40
        20
  0   0

1 : 3 M

feet   m
9843 3000
6562 2000
4921 1500
3281 1000
1640   500
 656   200
 328   100
  82   50
 164   — (sea level)
 656 —

ANCIENT ATHENS

THESEION

STOA OF ATTALOS

MONASTIRAKI
STATION

MOSQUE

METROPOLIS

ODEION OF
AGRIPPA

HADRIAN'S
LIBRARY

ROMAN
AGORA

TOWER OF
THE WINDS

A G O R A

AYIOI
APOSTOLI

METAMORPHOSIS

P l a k a

AREOPAGOS

AKROPOLIS

PARTHENON

ERECHTHEION

TEMPLE OF ROME
& AUGUSTUS

ATHENA
NIKE

PROPYLAIA

ASCLEPIEION

MUSEUM

PNYX

ODEION OF
HERODES
ATTICUS

STOA OF EUMENES

THEATRE
OF
DIONYSOS

Dionyssiou Areopagitou

1:12 000

0   100   200 yards
0   100   200 Metres

CONIC PROJECTION

Longitude East 21° of Greenwich

B 18° C 19° 30' D E 22° 30' F G

The names of provinces in Bulgaria are named after their respective capitals, which are underlined in colour.

İSTANBUL (CONSTANTINOPLE)
1 : 110 000

BOSPORUS
1:1 100 000

CORFU (KÉRKIRA)
(To Greece)
1:1 200 000

RHODES (RÓDHOS)
(To Greece)
1:1 200 000

ATHENS – PIRÆUS (ATHÍNAI – PIRAIÉVS)
1:150 000

© John Bartholomew & Son Ltd Edinburgh

Heights and Depths in metres

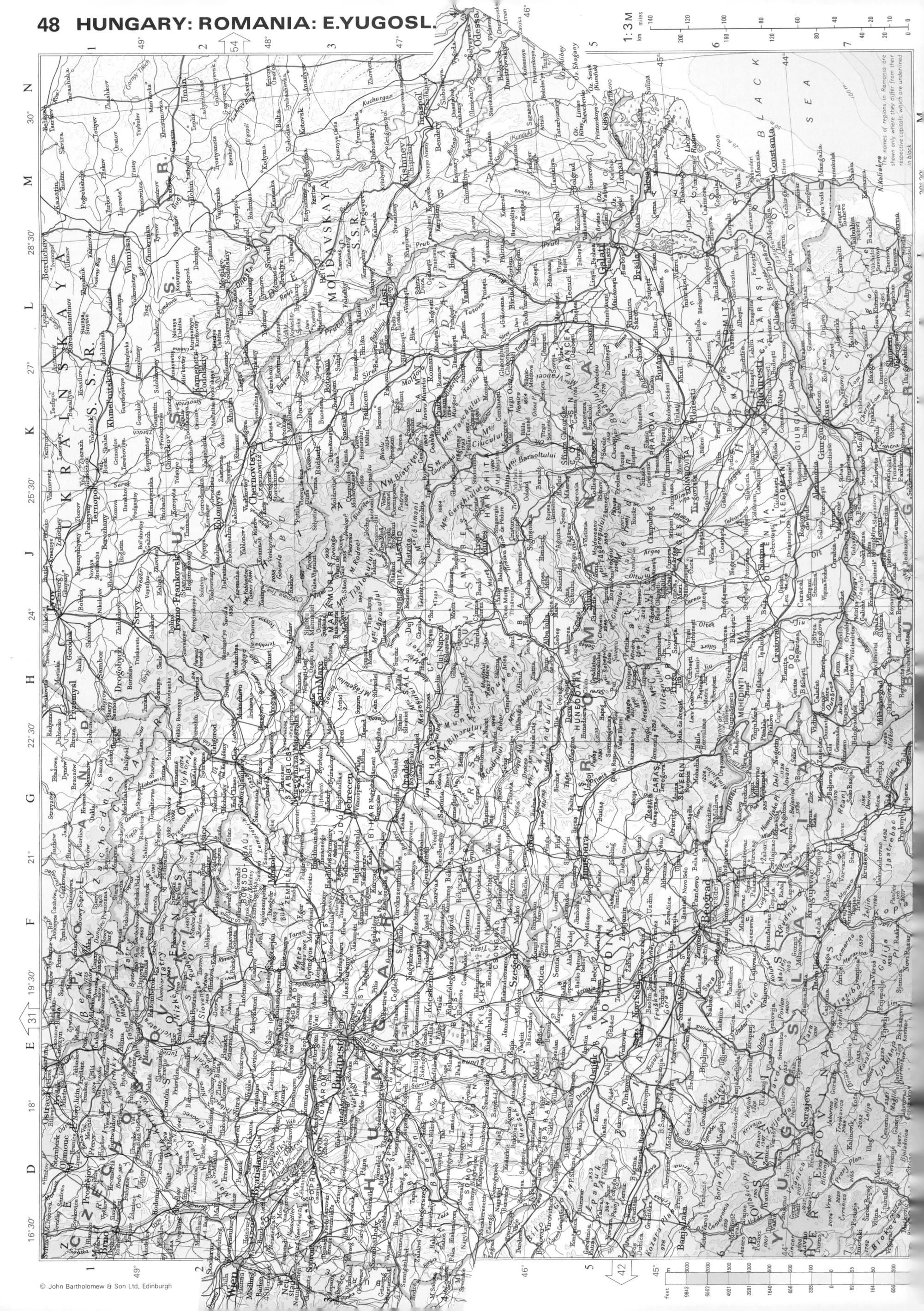

Leningrad map

LENINGRAD

GULF OF FINLAND

Kronshtadt

Ostrov Kotlin

Sestroretsk · Levashovo · Pargolovo · Vsevolozhsk

Lomonosov · Petrodvorets · Strel'na

Ostrov Krestovskiy · Ostrov Vasilyevskiy

GOROD · LENINGRAD

LENINGRAD AIRPORT

Krasnoye Selo · Shushary · Kolpino · Pontonnyy · Pavlovo · Otradnoye

Pushkin · Sofiya · Pavlovsk · Taytsy

NEVA

Top border: A 29°45′ B 30°00′ C 30°15′ D 30°30′ E 30°45′ F

Right border: 1 · 60°00′ · 2 · 59°45′ · 3

Moscow map

MOSKVA

GOROD MOSKVA

Bolshoi Theatre · Red Square · Kremlin

SHEREMET'YEVO AIRPORT · VNUKOVO AIRPORT

Kryukovo · Skhodnya · Khimki · Dolgoprudnyy · Mytishchi · Kaliningrad · Shchelkovo · Ivanteyevka · Fryazino

Dedovsk · Krasnogorsk · Tushino · Babushkin · Balashikha

Odintsovo · Kuntsevo · Reutov · Zheleznodorozhnyy · Lyubertsy · Elektrougli

Lenino · Biryulevo · Lyublino · Oktyabr'skiy · Lytkarino · Zhukovskiy

Aprelevka · Ramenskoye

M O S K V A

Top border: A 37°15′ B 37°30′ C 37°45′ D 38°00′ E 38°15′

Bottom border: A 37°15′ B 37°30′ C 37°45′ D 38°00′ E 38°15′

Right border: 4 · 55°45′ · 5

Scale: 1:300 000

0 5 10 15 km
0 5 10 miles

© Times Books Ltd

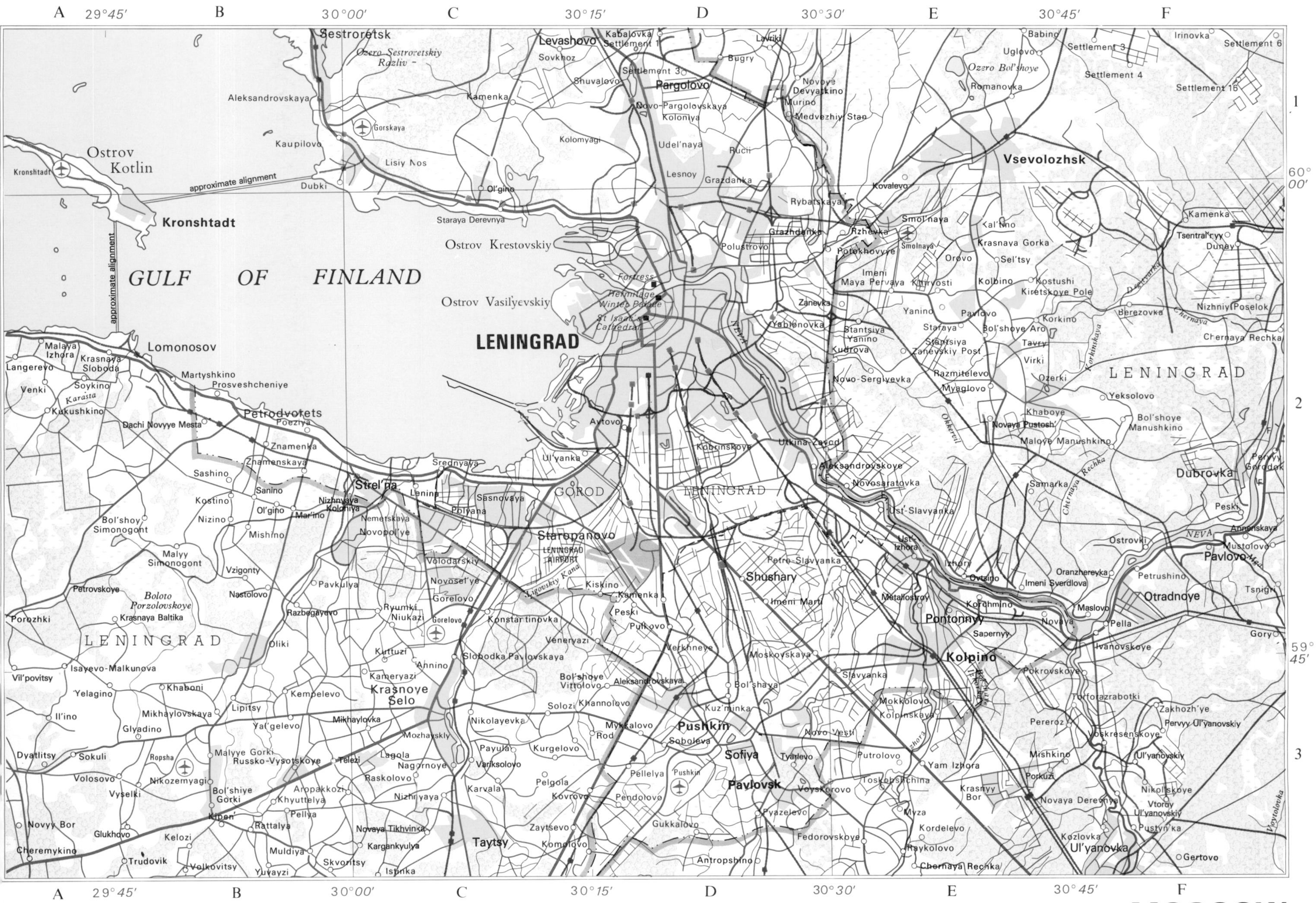

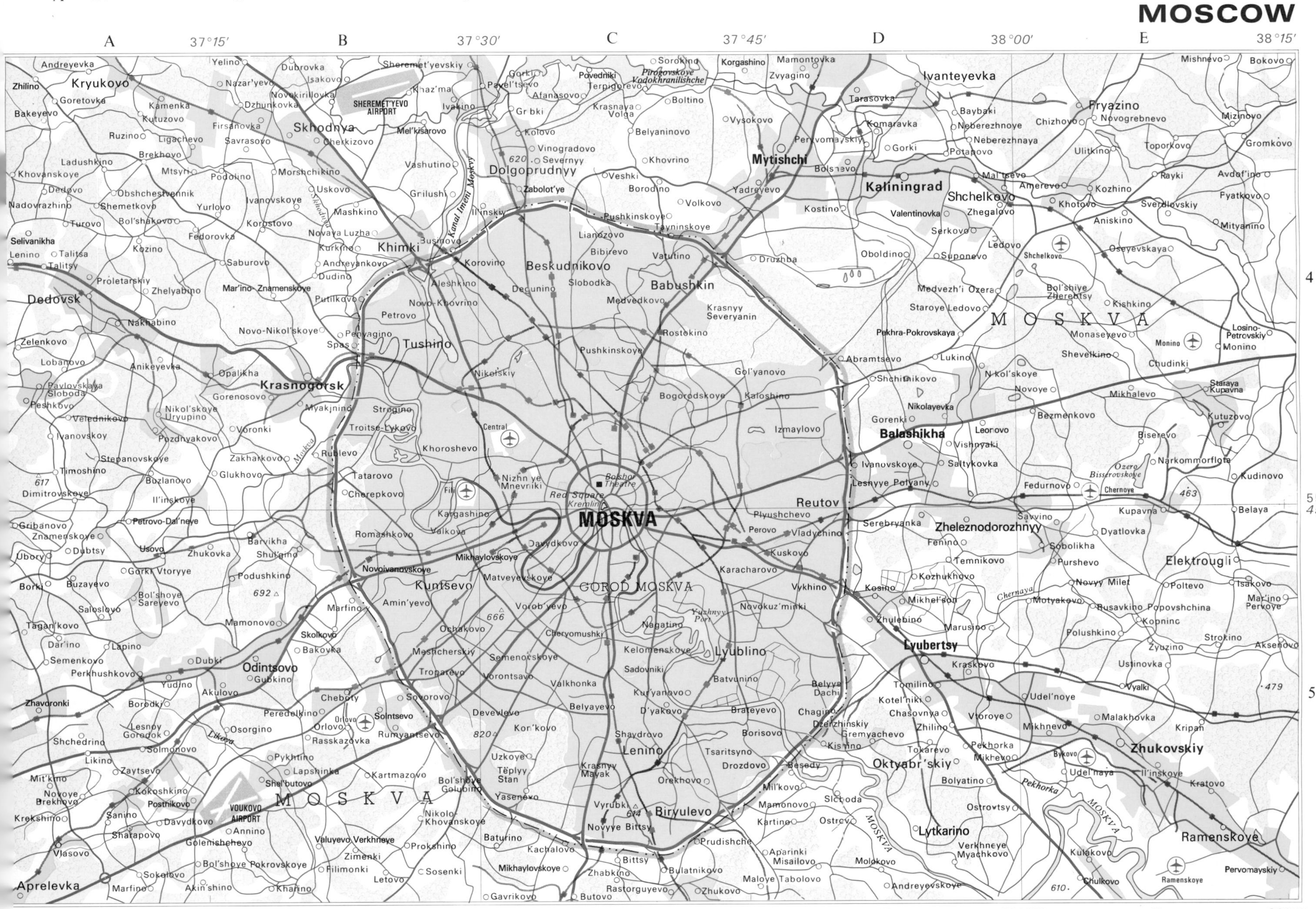

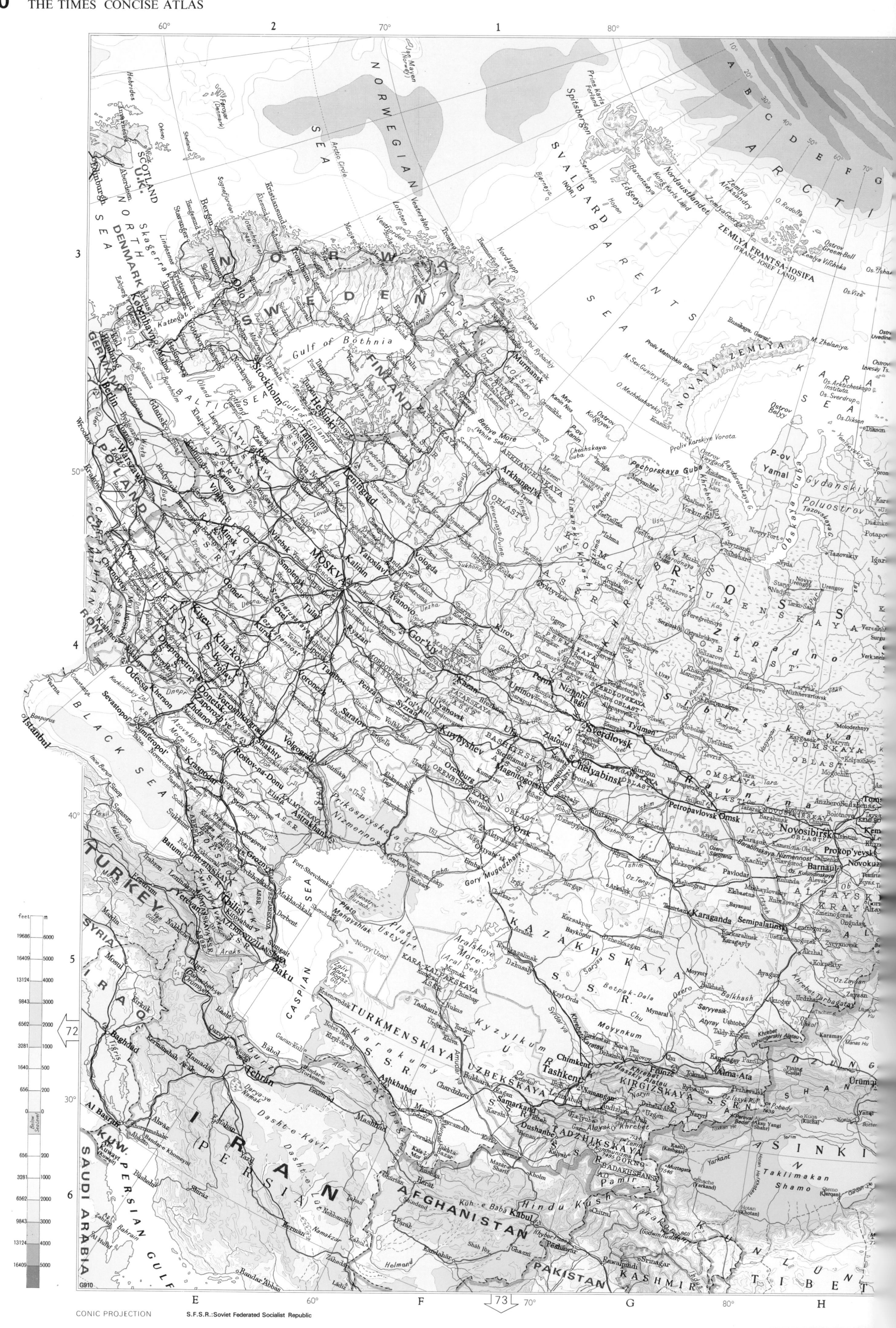

ALASKA (USA)

ARCTIC OCEAN

SEVERNAYA ZEMLYA
(NORTH LAND)

NOVOSIBIRSKIYE OSTROVA
(NEW SIBERIAN ISLANDS)

EAST SIBERIAN SEA

LAPTEV SEA

CHUKCHI SEA

BERING SEA

POLUOSTROV TAYMYR

Y A K U T S K A Y A A.S.S.R.

Yakutsk

Khrebet Cherskogo

Verkhoyanskiy Khrebet

Plato Putorana

KAMCHATSKAYA OBLAST'

Petropavlovsk-Kamchatskiy

SEA OF OKHOTSK

MAGADANSKAYA OBLAST'

Magadan

SAKHALIN

SAKHALINSKAYA OBLAST'

Kurilskiye Ostrova (Kuril Is.)

Krasnoyarsk

IRKUTSKAYA OBLAST'

Irkutsk

Ulan Ude

BURYATSKAYA A.S.S.R.

CHITINSKAYA OBLAST'

Chita

Stanovoy Khrebet

AMURSKAYA OBLAST'

KHABAROVSKIY KRAY

Khabarovsk

PRIMORSKIY KRAY

Vladivostok

HOKKAIDO

SEA OF JAPAN

TUVINSKAYA A.S.S.R.

Kyzyl

MONGOLIA

Ulaanbaatar (Ulan Bator)

GOBI

INNER MONGOLIA

MANCHURIA

Harbin

Qiqihar

Changchun

Shenyang (Mukden)

Fushun

Anshan

N. KOREA

S. KOREA

JAPAN

Tokyo

Yokohama

Nagoya

Kyoto

Osaka

HONSHU

SHIKOKU

KYUSHU

Nagasaki

Fukuoka

Hiroshima

Hami (Kumul)

C H I N A

Lanzhou

Xi'an

Beijing (Peking)

Tianjin (Tientsin)

Bo Hai

Qingdao

Jinan

Taiyuan

Shijiazhuang

Zhengzhou

Luoyang

Nanjing (Nanking)

Shanghai

Hangzhou

Ningbo

Wenzhou

Wuhan

Hefei

YELLOW SEA

EAST CHINA SEA

Qilian Shan

Nan Shan

Qaidam Pendi

Qinghai Hu

Min Shan

1:18M
km   miles

700
1000   600
      500
800   400
600   300
      200
400
      100
200   50
100

Longitude East 100° of Greenwich

Heights and Depths in metres

© John Bartholomew & Son Ltd Edinburgh

INDUSTRIAL URALS
Central Area
1:3 000 000
Statute Miles
Kilometres
MURMANSKAYA OBLAST'
FINLAND
ESTONSKAYA S.S.R.
LATVIYSKAYA S.S.R.
LITOVSKAYA S.S.R.
BELOYE MORE (WHITE SEA)
Leningrad
MOSKVA
Arkhangel'sk
Sverdlovsk
Chelyabinsk
Gor'kiy
Kazan'
Perm'
Riga
Helsinki (Helsingfors)

CASPIAN SEA

BLACK SEA (CHERNOYE MORE) (KARA DENIZ)

SEA OF AZOV (AZOVSKO MORE)

POLAND

BELORUSSKAYA S.S.R.

UKRAINSKAYA S.S.R.

R.S.F.S.R.

KAZAKHSKAYA S.S.R.

KALMYTSKAYA

ROSTOV

KRASNODAR

GRUZINSKAYA S.S.R.

AZERB.

DAGESTAN

ROMANIA

BULGARIA

TURKEY

CRIMEA (KRYM)

Moskva

WARSZAWA

Kuybyshev
Ulyanovsk
Saratov
Engels
Penza
Ryazan
Tula
Orel
Kursk
Voronezh
Lipetsk
Tambov
Michurinsk
Kharkov
Belgorod
Sumy
Poltava
Kiev (Kiyev)
Zhitomir
Vinnitsa
Chernovtsy
Kishinev
Odessa
Nikolayev
Kherson
Krivoy Rog
Dnepropetrovsk
Zaporozhye
Melitopol
Simferopol
Sevastopol
Yalta
Donetsk
Zhdanov
Kramatorsk
Konstantinovka
Lugansk
Shakhty
Novocherkassk
Rostov-na-Donu
Taganrog
Volgograd
Astrakhan
Stavropol
Armavir
Maykop
Sochi
Sukhumi
Batumi
Tbilisi
Makhachkala
Grozny
Ordzhonikidze
Derbent
Novorossiysk
Tuapse
Kerch
Smolensk
Mogilev
Bobruysk
Gomel
Bryansk
Chernigov
Vilnius
Minsk
Lublin
Istanbul (Constantinople)
Zonguldak
Sinop
Samsun
Trabzon
Constanța
București (Bucharest)
Varna
Sibiu
Brașov

1:6 M
CONIC PROJECTION

400 km
400 miles

feet 13124 9843 6562 3281 1640 656 0
m 4000 3000 2000 1500 1000 500 200 100 0

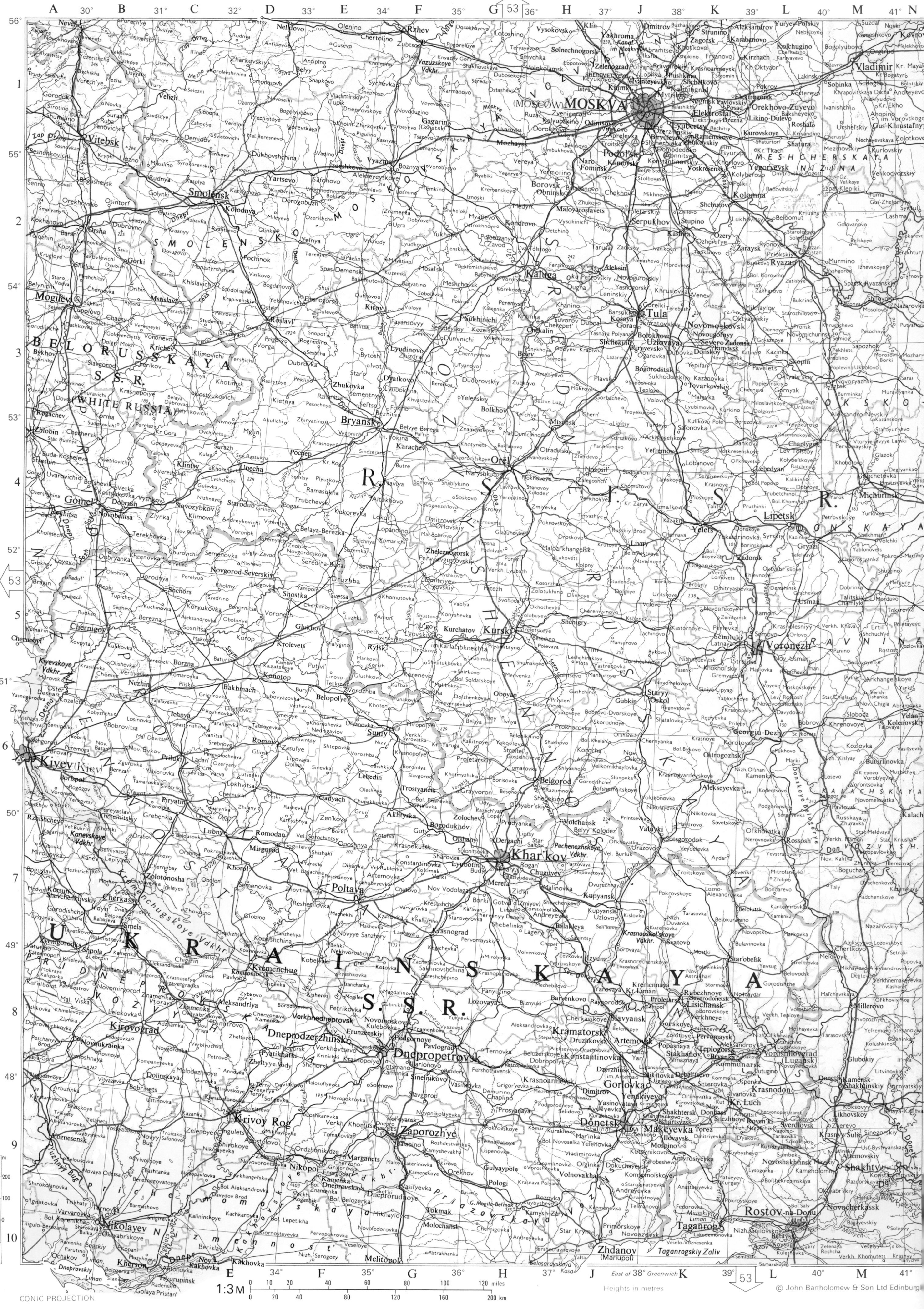

CONIC PROJECTION

1:3 M

East of 38° Greenwich

Heights in metres

© John Bartholomew & Son Ltd Edinburgh

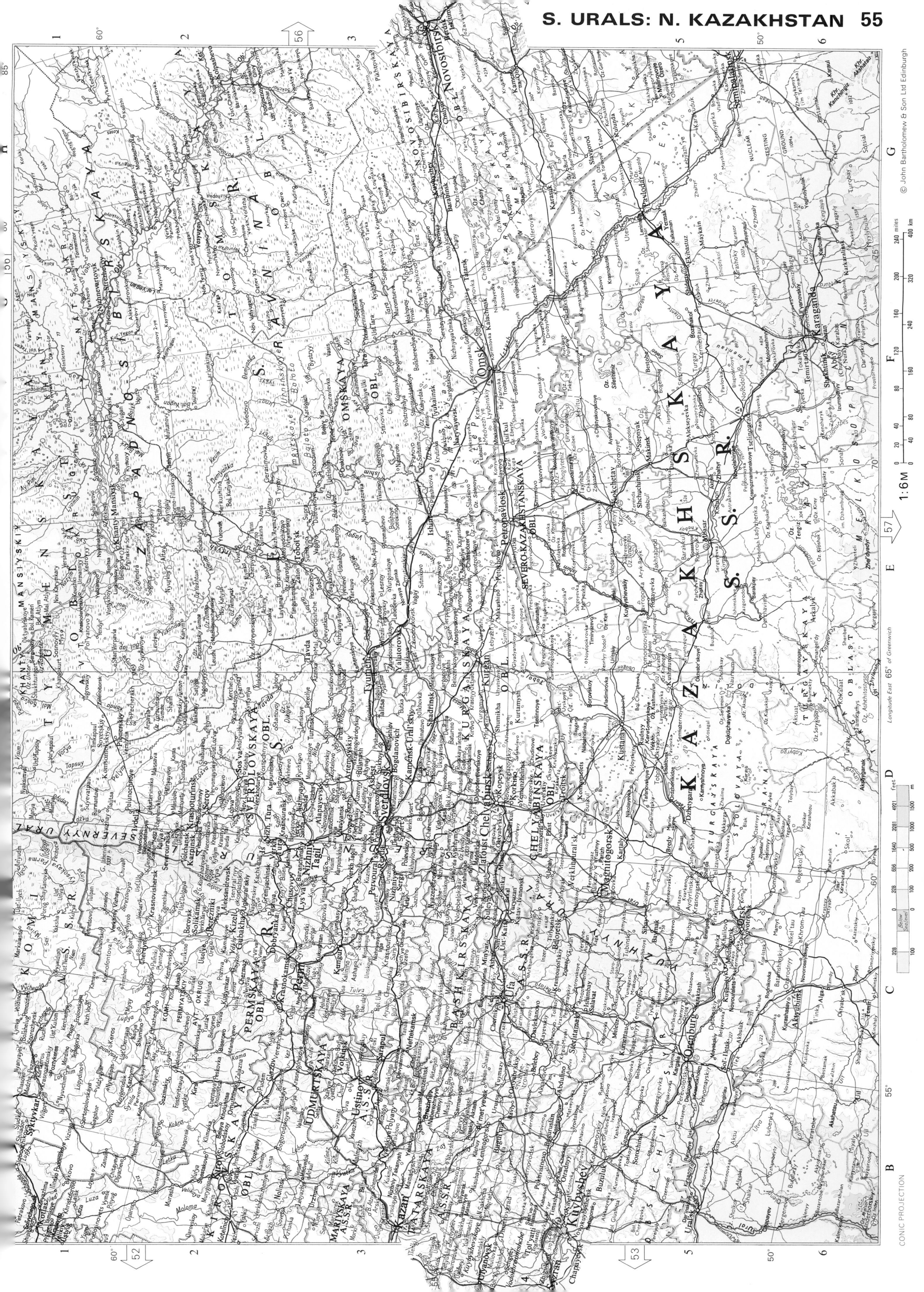
Sverdlovsk
Chelyabinsk
Perm'
Ufa
Kuybyshev
Orenburg
Omsk
Novosibirsk
Karaganda
Tselinograd
Semipalatinsk
Pavlodar
Kustanay
Petropavlovsk
Kurgan
Tyumen'
Tobol'sk
Magnitogorsk
Zlatoust
Nizhniy Tagil
Kazan'
Izhevsk
Syktyvkar
Aktyubinsk
Uralsk
Orsk
Kokchetav
SVERDLOVSKAYA OBL.
CHELYABINSKAYA OBL.
KURGANSKAYA OBL.
OMSKAYA OBL.
NOVOSIBIRSKAYA OBL.
PERMSKAYA OBL.
SEVERO-KAZAKHSTANSKAYA OBL.
UDMURTSKAYA A.S.S.R.
TATARSKAYA A.S.S.R.
BASHKIRSKAYA A.S.S.R.
KAZAKHSKAYA S.S.R.
ZAPADNO SIBIRSKAYA
NUCLEAR TESTING GROUND
TURGAYSKAYA STOLOVAYA STRANA
Longitude East 65° of Greenwich
CONIC PROJECTION
1:6M
52
53
56
57

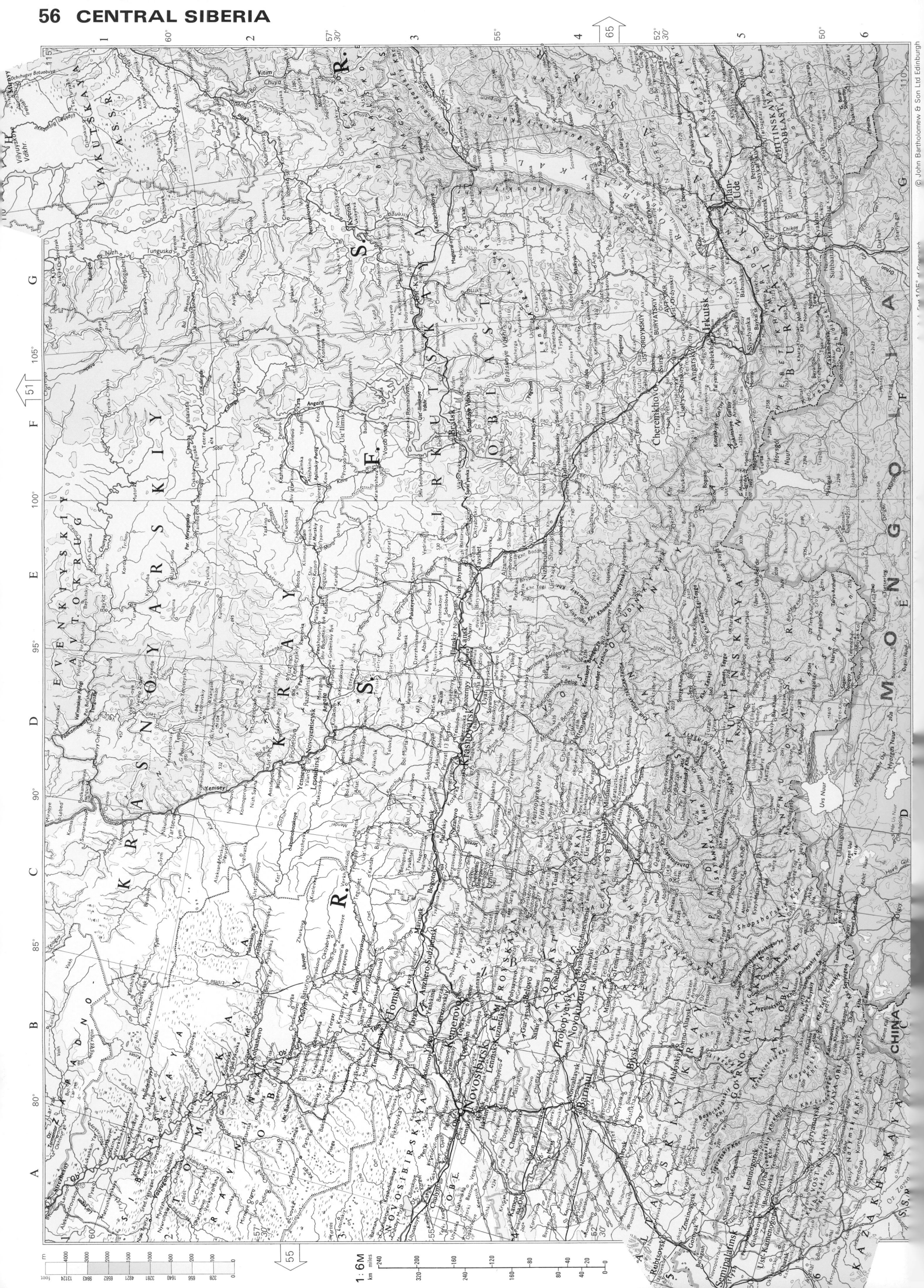

MONGOLIA
CHINA
Irkutsk
Krasnoyarsk
Novosibirsk
Tomsk
Kemerovo
Barnaul
Ulan-Ude
1:6M
© John Bartholomew & Son Ltd Edinburgh

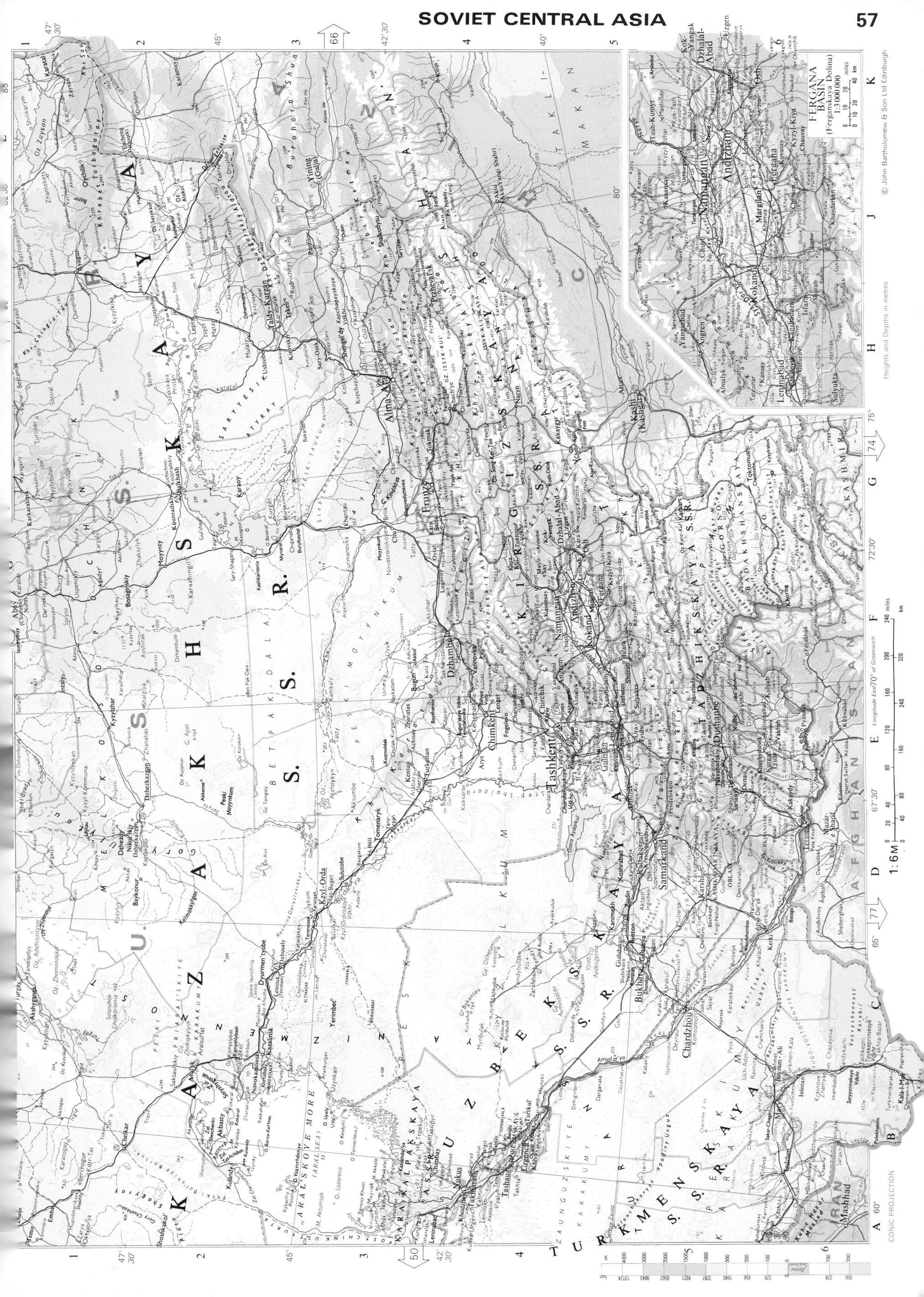

FERGANA
BASIN
(Ferganskaya Dolina)
1:3 000 000

Heights and Depths in metres

1:6M

1:6 000 000

Longitude East 70° of Greenwich

CONIC PROJECTION

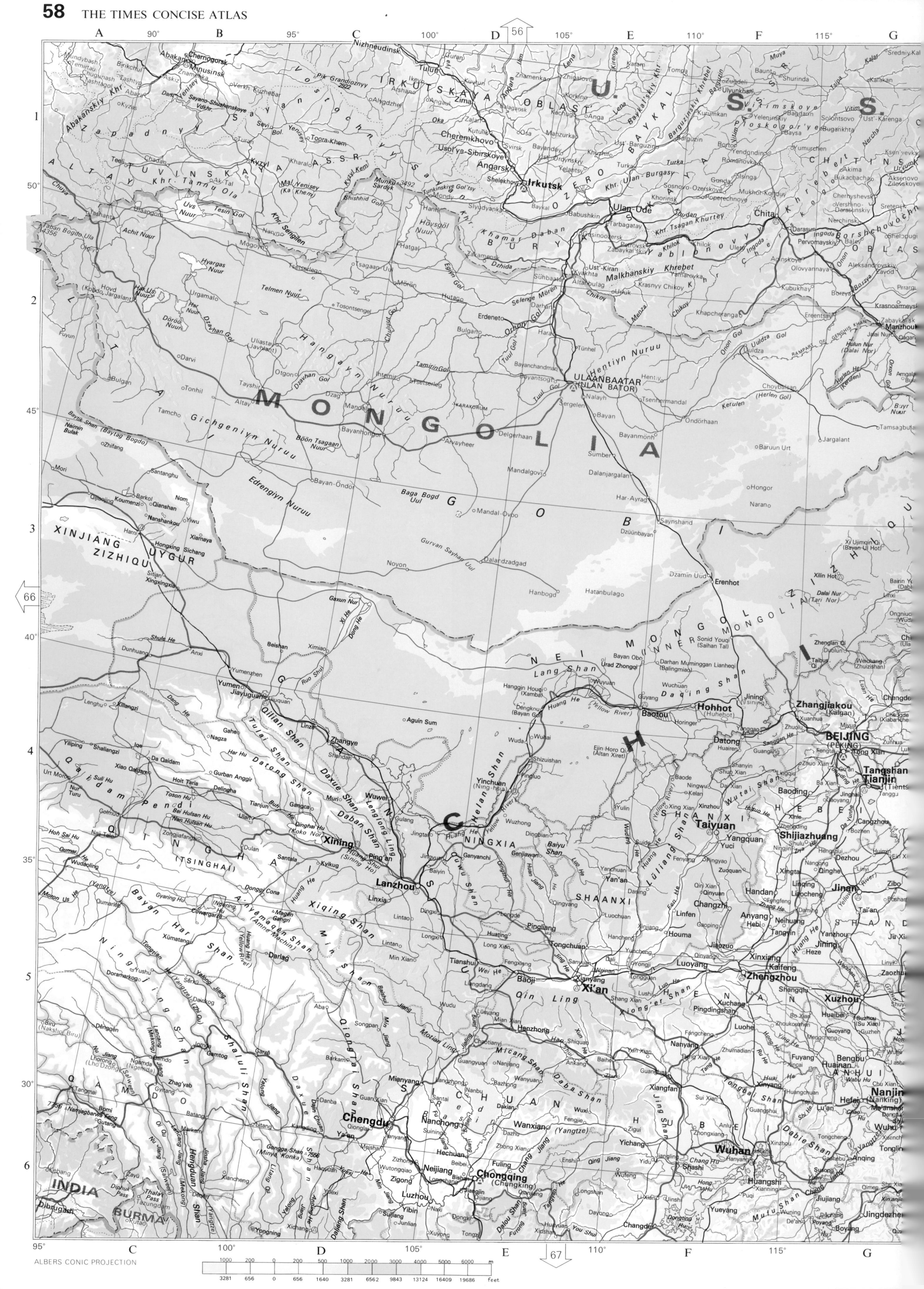

ALBERS CONIC PROJECTION

m	1000	200	0	200	500	1000	2000	3000	4000	5000	6000
feet	3281	656	0	656	1640	3281	6562	9843	13124	16409	19686

Heights and Depths in metres
1:9 M
0 50 100 200 300 miles
0 50 100 200 300 400 500 600 km

SEA OF JAPAN

SEA OF OKHOTSK

Continuation on the same scale

U.S.S.R.

HOKKAIDO

SORACHI

ISHIKARI

ABASHIRI

KUSHIRO

NEMURO

SHIRIBESHI

IBURI

HIDAKA

TOKACHI

Sapporo

Asahikawa

Otaru

Muroran

Hakodate

Aomori

Shiretoko misaki

Abashiri

Nemuro

Kushiro

Obihiro

Erimo-misaki

SOUTH KOREA

Pusan

Masan

Chinju

Tsushima

KOREA STRAIT (Tsushima-kaikyō)

Oki

Dōgo

Dōzen

Matsue

Tottori

SHIMANE

TOTTORI

OKAYAMA

HIROSHIMA

YAMAGUCHI

HYOGO

Himeji

Kōbe

Hiroshima

Okayama

Kurashiki

Fukuyama

Yamaguchi

Kita-Kyushu

Fukuoka

Ube

Shimonoseki

FUKUOKA

NAGASAKI

Sasebo

Nagasaki

Saga

Kurume

Omuta

Kumamoto

Beppu

Oita

Uwajima

Matsuyama

Kōchi

TOKUSHIMA

KAGAWA

EHIME

KŌCHI

SHIKOKU

KYŪSHŪ

Miyazaki

Nobeoka

Kagoshima

Kanoya

Sata-misaki

Muroto-zaki

Ashizuri-misaki

CONIC PROJECTION

feet	m
9843	3000
6562	2000
4921	1500
3281	1000
1640	500
656	200
328	100
0	0
656	200
6562	2000
13124	4000
26248	8000

1 : 3 M

OKINAWA
1:1 200 000

IWO JIMA
1:300 000

Heights and Depths in metres

OSAKA

Tokyo map:

139°30′ 139°45′ 140°00′

SAITAMA-KEN

Iruma · Shiki · Warabi · Hatogaya · Sōka · Misato · Izumi · Minowa

Tokorozawa · Niiza · Asaka · Kawaguchi · Yashio · CHIBA-KEN

Higashi-Murayama · Kiyose · Wako · Toda · Adachi · Matsudo · Kamagaya

Musashi-Murayama · Kodaira · Tanashi · Nerima · Toshima · Katsushika · Ichikawa

TŌKYŌ-TO · Nakano · Shinjuku · Bunkyō · Taitō · Sumida · Edogawa · Funabashi · Yachiyo

Fussa · Akishima · Tachikawa · Koganei · Musashino · Mitaka · Shibuya · **TOKYO** · Chūō · Kōtō · Urayasu · Narashino

Hachiōji · Kunitachi · Fuchū · Chōfu · Setagaya · Minato · Meguro

Hino · Tama · Inagi · Komae · Yōga · Shinagawa

Sagamihara · Machida · Midori · Ōta · Ōmori

KANAGAWA-KEN · Kamata · TŌKYŌ INTERNATIONAL AIRPORT HANEDA · **TŌKYŌ-WAN**

Zama · Yamato · Seya · Asahi · Kanagawa · **Kawasaki** · Tsurumi · Ichihara

Atsugi · Ebina · Hodogaya · Nishi · **YOKOHAMA** · Kisarazu

Chōgo · Totsuka · Naka · Minami Isogo · Sodegaura · Umatate

Osaka map:

135°15′ 135°30′ 135°45′

KYŌTO-FU · SHIGA-KEN · Biwa-ko · Fushimi

HYŌGO-KEN · Nagaoka · Uji

Inada · Sanda · Ōsaka-fu · Ōyamazaki · Kumiyama · Yawata · Jōyō

Kawanishi · Ikeda · Minoo · Senri · Ibaraki · Takatsuki · Hirakata · KYŌTO-FU

Takarazuka · Arima · Itami · Toyonaka · Yamada · Settsu · Kōri · Katano

Nishinomiya · Suita · Neyagawa · Shijōnawate

Ashiya · Amagasaki · Higashi-Yodogawa · Moriguchi · Kadoma · Daitō · Ikoma

KŌBE · Nada · **ŌSAKA** · Jōto · Higashinari · Higashi-Ōsaka · NARA-KEN

Hyōgo · Suma · Minato · Nishi · Ikuno · Tennōji · Abeno · Yao · Nara

ŌSAKA-WAN · Taishō · Higashi-Sumiyoshi · Yamato-Kōriyama · Kashiwara

Sakai · Matsubara · Fujidera · Habikino · Kokubu

Takaishi · Ōtori · Yamato-Takada

Inset: KYŌTO-FU · **KYŌTO** · Higashiyama · Minami · Mukō · Nagaoka

© Times Books Ltd.

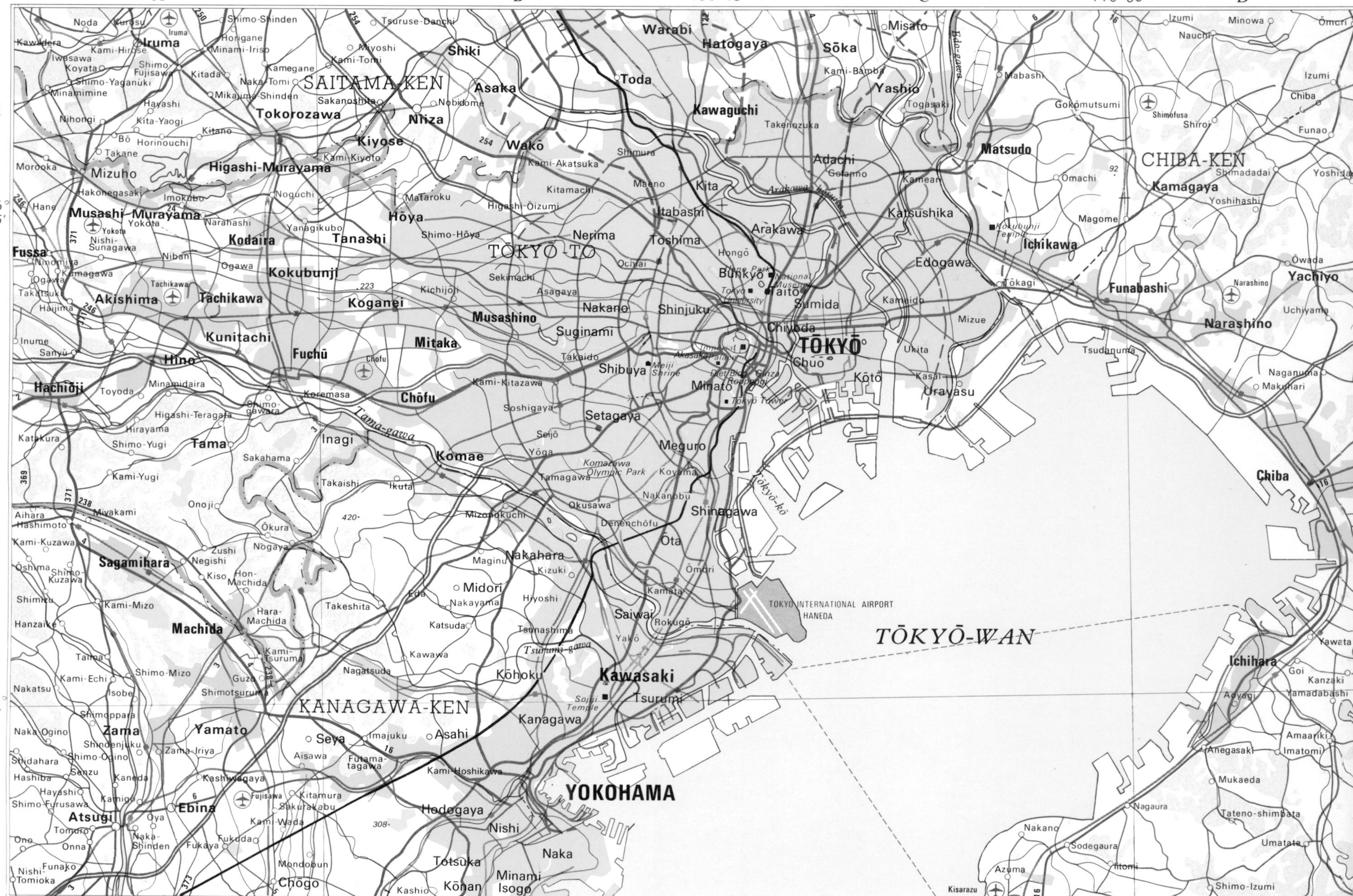

1 : 300 000

0 5 10 15 km

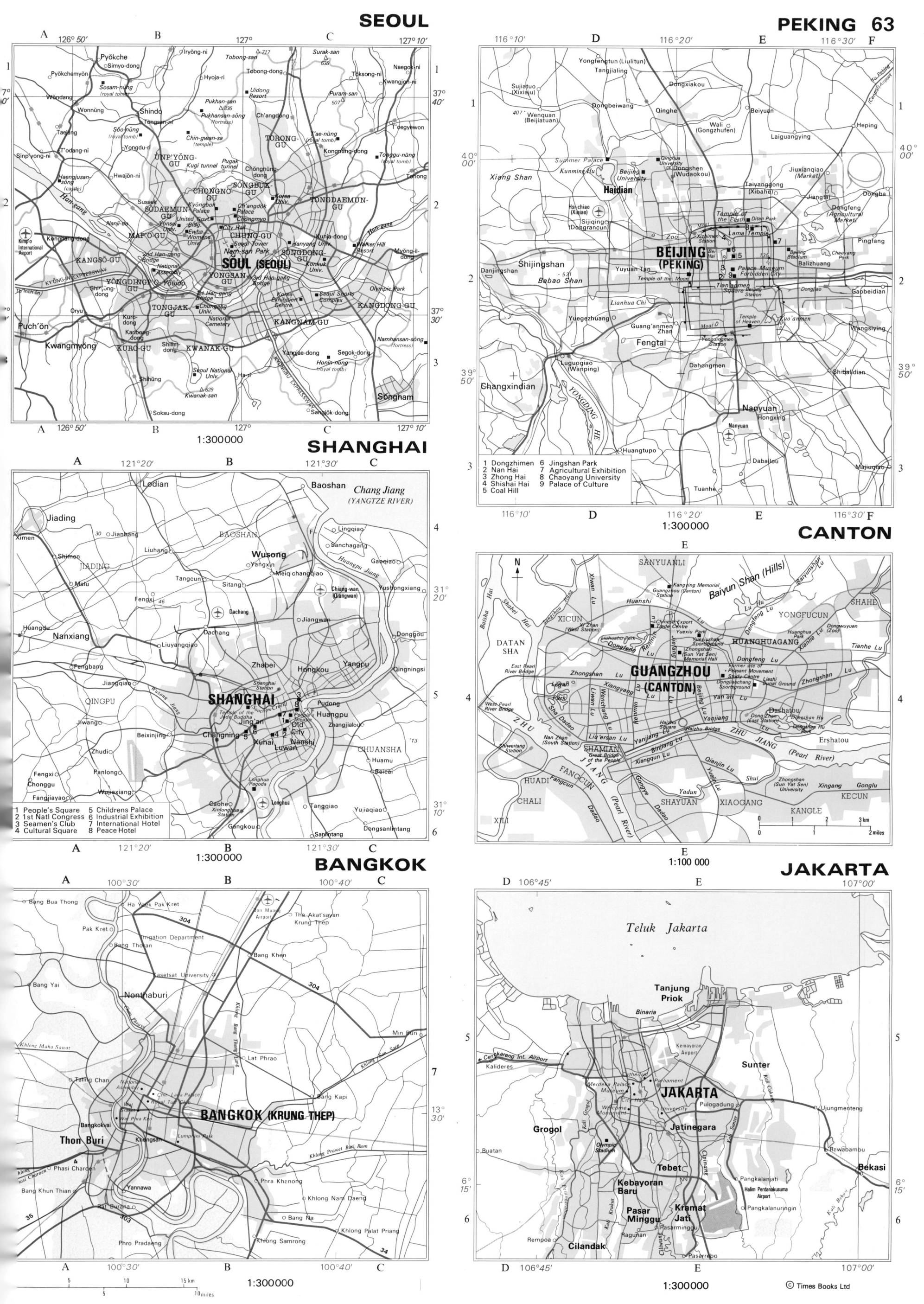

SEOUL

1:300000

PEKING 63

1 Dongzhimen 6 Jingshan Park
2 Nan Hai 7 Agricultural Exhibition
3 Zhong Hai 8 Chaoyang University
4 Shishai Hai 9 Palace of Culture
5 Coal Hill

1:300000

SHANGHAI

1 People's Square 5 Childrens Palace
2 1st Natl Congress 6 Industrial Exhibition
3 Seamen's Club 7 International Hotel
4 Cultural Square 8 Peace Hotel

1:300000

CANTON

1:100 000

BANGKOK

1:300000

JAKARTA

1:300000

© Times Books Ltd

UNION OF SOVIET SOCIALIST REPUBLICS

SIBERIA

MONGOLIA

INNER MONGOLIA

CHINA

SINKIANG

Chinese Turkestan

TIBET

Qing Zang (Chang Tang)

Kunlun Shan

Qilian Shan

Gobi

MANCHURIA

SEA OF OKHOTSK

SAKHALIN

Hokkaido
Sapporo

JAPAN

Honshu
Tokyo
Yokohama
Nagoya
Osaka
Kyoto
Shikoku
Kyushu

NORTH KOREA
SOUTH KOREA
Soul
Inchon
Pusan

Beijing (Peking)
Tianjin
Shenyang
Changchun
Harbin
Dalian
Jinan
Taiyuan
Lanzhou
Xi'an (Sian)
Chengdu
Chongqing
Wuhan
Nanjing (Nanking)
Shanghai
Hangzhou
Hefei
Changsha
Nanchang
Kunming
Guiyang
Guangzhou
HONG KONG (UK)
Macao (Port.)
Wenzhou
Fuzhou (Foochow)

YELLOW SEA
EAST CHINA SEA

TAIWAN (FORMOSA)
T'ai-pei
T'ai-nan

Khabarovsk
Vladivostok

Tropic of Cancer

AFGHANISTAN

PAKISTAN
Peshawar
Islamabad
Lahore
Amritsar
KASHMIR

INDIA
Delhi
Jaipur
Agra
Lucknow
Kanpur
Allahabad
Varanasi
Patna
Jabalpur
Nagpur
Hyderabad
Bangalore
Madras
Pondicherry

NEPAL
Kathmandu
Mt Everest 8848
BHUTAN

BANGLADESH
Dhaka
Calcutta

BURMA
Mandalay
Rangoon
Moulmein

Mouths of the Ganga (Ganges)

BAY OF BENGAL

Andaman Is. (India)
Little Andaman
Nicobar Islands (India)

SRI LANKA (CEYLON)
Colombo

INDIAN OCEAN

THAILAND (SIAM)
Bangkok (Krung Thep)
Chieng-Mai

LAOS
Viangchan

Hanoi
Haiphong
Gulf of Tongking

INDO-CHINA
VIETNAM
Hue
Da Nang (Tourane)
Quy Nhon
Nha Trang

CAMBODIA
Phnom Penh
Tonle Sap

Saigon (Ho Chi Minh)
Mouths of the Mekong

Gulf of Thailand

SOUTH CHINA SEA

PHILIPPINES
Luzon
Manila
Quezon City
Mindoro
Panay
Iloilo
Negros
Cebu
Samar
Leyte
Palawan
Mindanao
Davao

SULU SEA

MALAYSIA
PENINSULAR MALAYSIA
Kuala Lumpur
Singapore

SARAWAK
Kuching
BORNEO
Kota Baharu
George Town (Pinang)

SUMATRA
Medan
Padang
Palembang

CELEBES SEA

SULAWESI (CELEBES)

INDONESIA

JAVA SEA
Jakarta
Surabaya
Bandung
Yogyakarta

Equator

BANDA SEA

LAMBERT AZIMUTHAL EQUAL-AREA PROJECTION   1:24 M

© John Bartholomew & Son Ltd Edinbur[gh]

U.S.S.R.

MONGOLIA

HEILONGJIANG

JILIN

LIAONING

NEI MONGOL ZIZHIQU (MONGOLIAN AUT. REGION)

HEBEI

SHANXI

SHANDONG

SHAANXI

NORTH KOREA

SOUTH KOREA

JAPAN

SEA OF JAPAN

YELLOW SEA (HUANG HAI)

BO HAI (GULF OF CHIHLI)

KOREA BAY

Harbin · Changchun · Jilin · Shenyang · Liaoyang · Benxi · Fushun · Fuxin · Jinzhou · Dalian · Dandong · Chengde · Chifeng (Ulanhad) · Zhangjiakou · BEIJING · Tianjin · Tangshan · Baoding · Shijiazhuang · Hohhot · Baotou · Datong · Taiyuan · Handan · Xingtai · Anyang · Zhengzhou (Chengchow) · Kaifeng · Jinan · Zibo · Weifang · Yantai · Weihai · Qingdao (Tsingtao) · Lianyungang · Xuzhou · Yan'an · Xi'an (Sian)

Vladivostok · Ussuriysk · Spassk-Dal'niy · Nakhodka

Chongjin · Najin · Unggi · Kimchaek · Hungnam · Hamhung · Wonsan · PYONGYANG · Haeju · Kaesong · SEOUL · Inchon · Suwon · Taejon · Chonju · Kwangju · Taegu · Pusan · Mokpo

Cheju-do

TSUSHIMA · KITA-KYUSHU · Shimonoseki

CONIC PROJECTION

1:6 M

Heights and Depths in metres

John Bartholomew & Son Ltd Edinburgh
Times Books Ltd

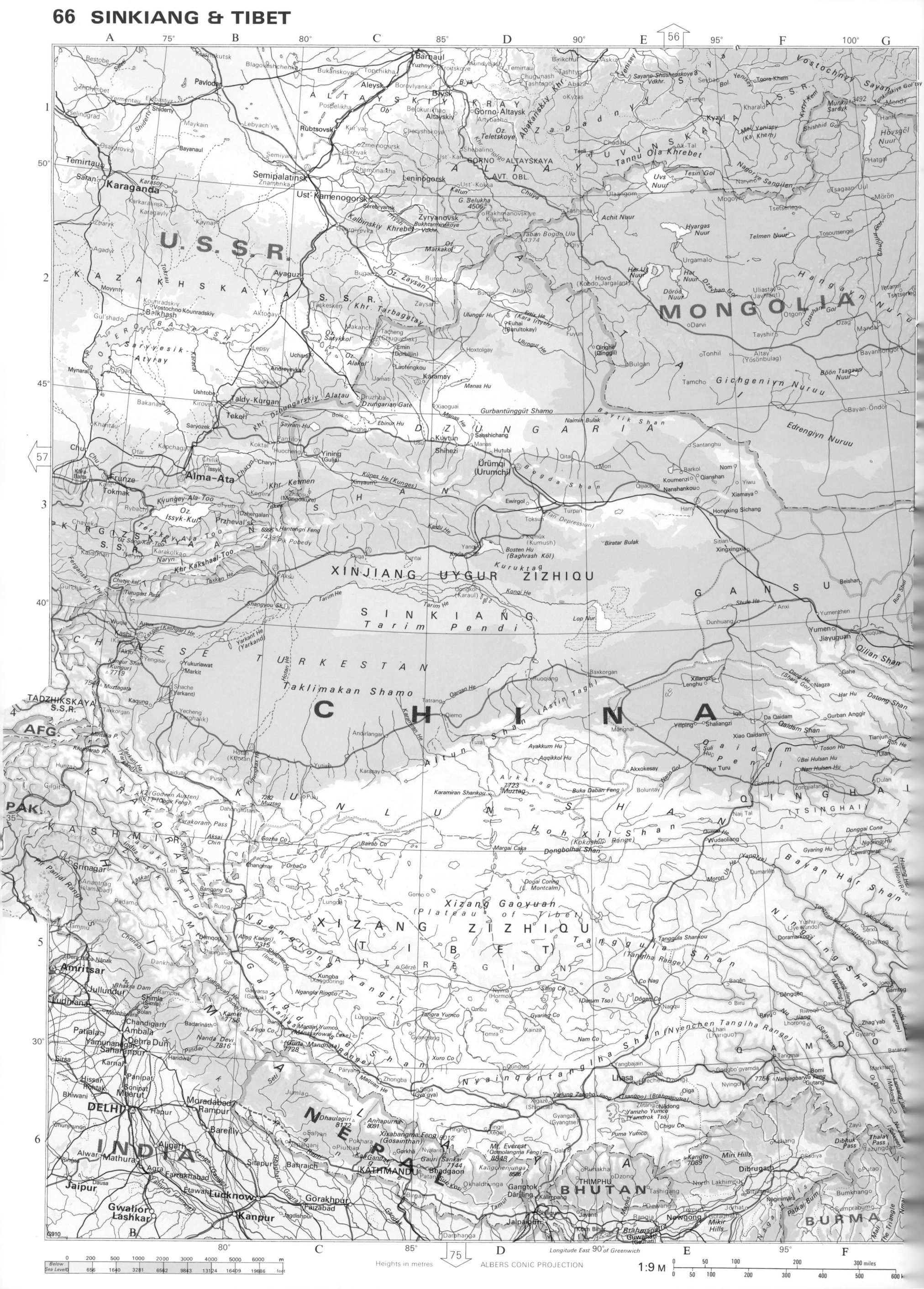

U.S.S.R.
KAZAKHSKAYA S.S.R.
KIRGIZSKAYA S.S.R.
TADZHIKSKAYA S.S.R.
AFG.
PAK.
MONGOLIA
CHINA
XINJIANG UYGUR ZIZHIQU
SINKIANG
Tarim Pendi
CHINESE TURKESTAN
Taklimakan Shamo
DZUNGARIA
TIAN SHAN
KUNLUN SHAN
XIZANG ZIZHIQU (TIBET AUTONOMOUS REGION)
Xizang Gaoyuan (Plateau of Tibet)
Tanggula Shan
Nyainqentanglha Shan
QINGHAI (TSINGHAI)
GANSU
KASHMIR
KARAKORAM RANGE
NEPAL
BHUTAN
INDIA
BURMA
Qaidam Pendi
ALTAY
Altun Shan
Gobi Altai
Semipalatinsk
Ust'-Kamenogorsk
Karaganda
Pavlodar
Barnaul
Biysk
Rubtsovsk
Alma-Ata
Frunze
Tokmak
Balkhash
Taldy-Kurgan
Ayaguz
Kashi
Yining
Ürümqi (Urumchi)
Shihezi
Karamay
Hami
Turpan
Korla
Aksu
Hotan
Yarkant
Lop Nur
Dunhuang
Yumen
Jiayuguan
Lhasa
Xigazê
Gyangzê
Srinagar
Leh
Amritsar
Jullundur
Ludhiana
Shimla
Chandigarh
Ambala
Dehra Dun
Meerut
DELHI
Moradabad
Rampur
Bareilly
Agra
Mathura
Aligarh
Jaipur
Gwalior
Lashkar
Kanpur
Lucknow
Gorakhpur
KATHMANDU
THIMPHU
Darjiling
Gangtok
Dibrugarh
Mt. Everest (Qomolangma Feng) 8848
Kangchenjunga 8586
Dhaulagiri 8172
Annapurna 8091
Xixabangma Feng (Gosainthan) 8012
Nanda Devi 7816
K2 (Godwin Austen) 8611
Pik Pobedy 7439
Khan Tengri 6995
Muztag 7723
Muztag 7282
Gurla Mandhata 7728
Namjagbarwa Feng 7756
Kamet 7756
Kungur Shan 7719
Muztagata 7546
G. Belukha 4506
Taban Bogdo Ula 4374
Munku-Sardyk 3492
Uvs Nuur
Hövsgöl Nuur
Hyargas Nuur
Oz. Zaysan
Ozero Balkhash
Oz. Issyk-Kul'
Oz. Alakol'
Bosten Hu (Baghrash Köl)
Nam Co
Tarim He
Yarlung Zangbo Jiang (Tsangpo) (Brahmaputra)
Ganges
Irtysh
Ob'
Longitude East 90° of Greenwich
Heights in metres
ALBERS CONIC PROJECTION
1:9 M
0 200 500 1000 2000 3000 4000 5000 6000 m
Below Sea Level 0 656 1640 3281 6562 9843 13124 16409 19686 feet
0 50 100 200 300 miles
0 50 100 200 300 400 500 600 km
56
57
75
G910

HONG KONG
1:300,000

S O U T H   C H I N A   S E A

GULF OF TONGKING

HAINAN DAO

TAIWAN (FORMOSA)

TAIWAN STRAIT

Heights and Depths in metres

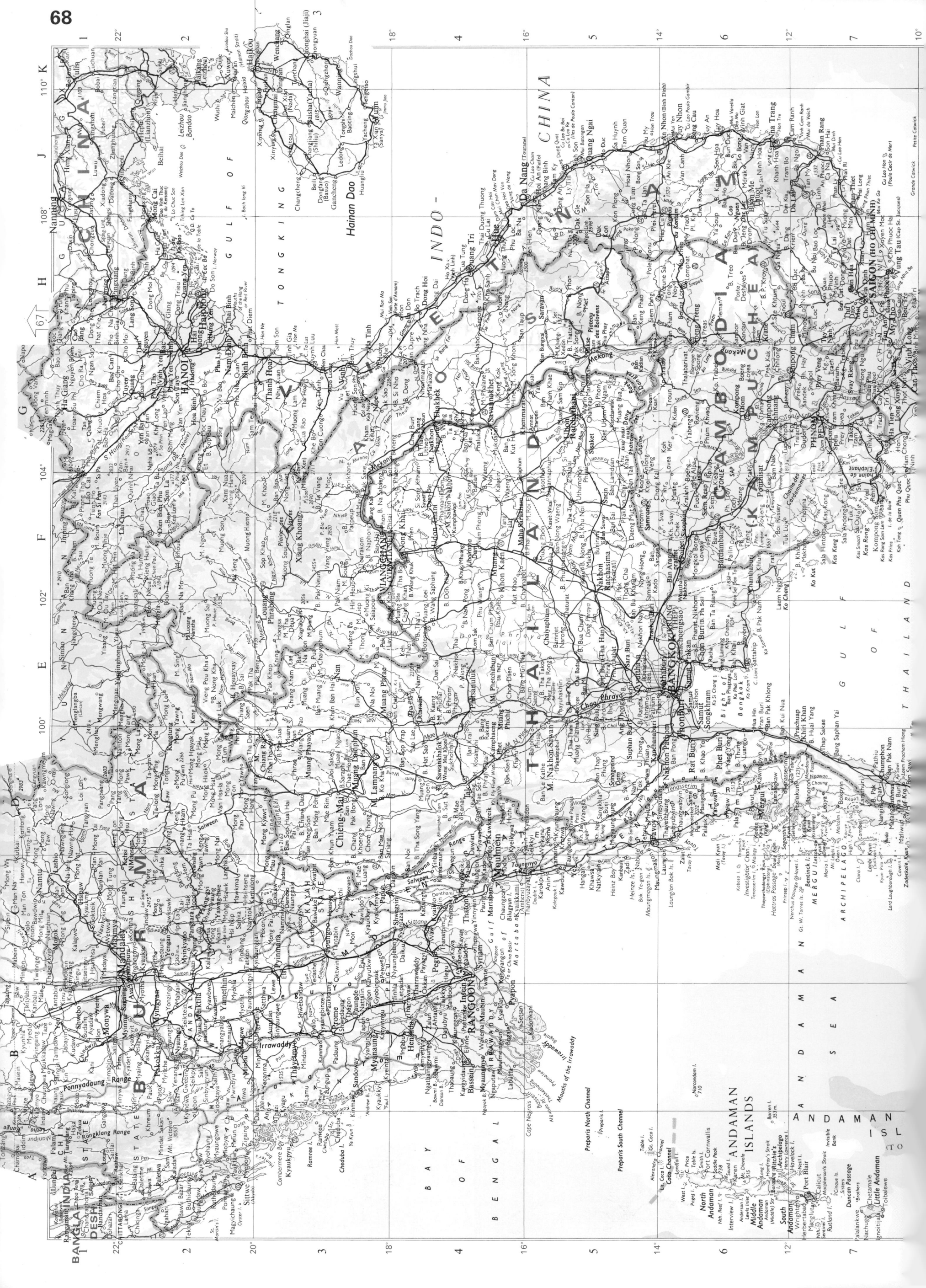
CHINA
BURMA
THAILAND
KAMPUCHEA
INDO-CHINA
Hainan Dao
GULF OF TONGKING
BAY OF BENGAL
ANDAMAN SEA
GULF OF THAILAND
ANDAMAN ISLANDS
MERGUI ARCHIPELAGO
HANOI
RANGOON
BANGKOK
Mandalay
Moulmein
Da Nang
Haiphong
Vientiane
Louang Phrabang
Chieng-Mai
Mekong
Irrawaddy
Mouths of the Irrawaddy
Gulf of Martaban
Preparis North Channel
Preparis South Channel
Coco Channel
Duncan Passage
North Andaman
Middle Andaman
South Andaman
Little Andaman
Port Blair
SAIGON (HO CHI MINH)

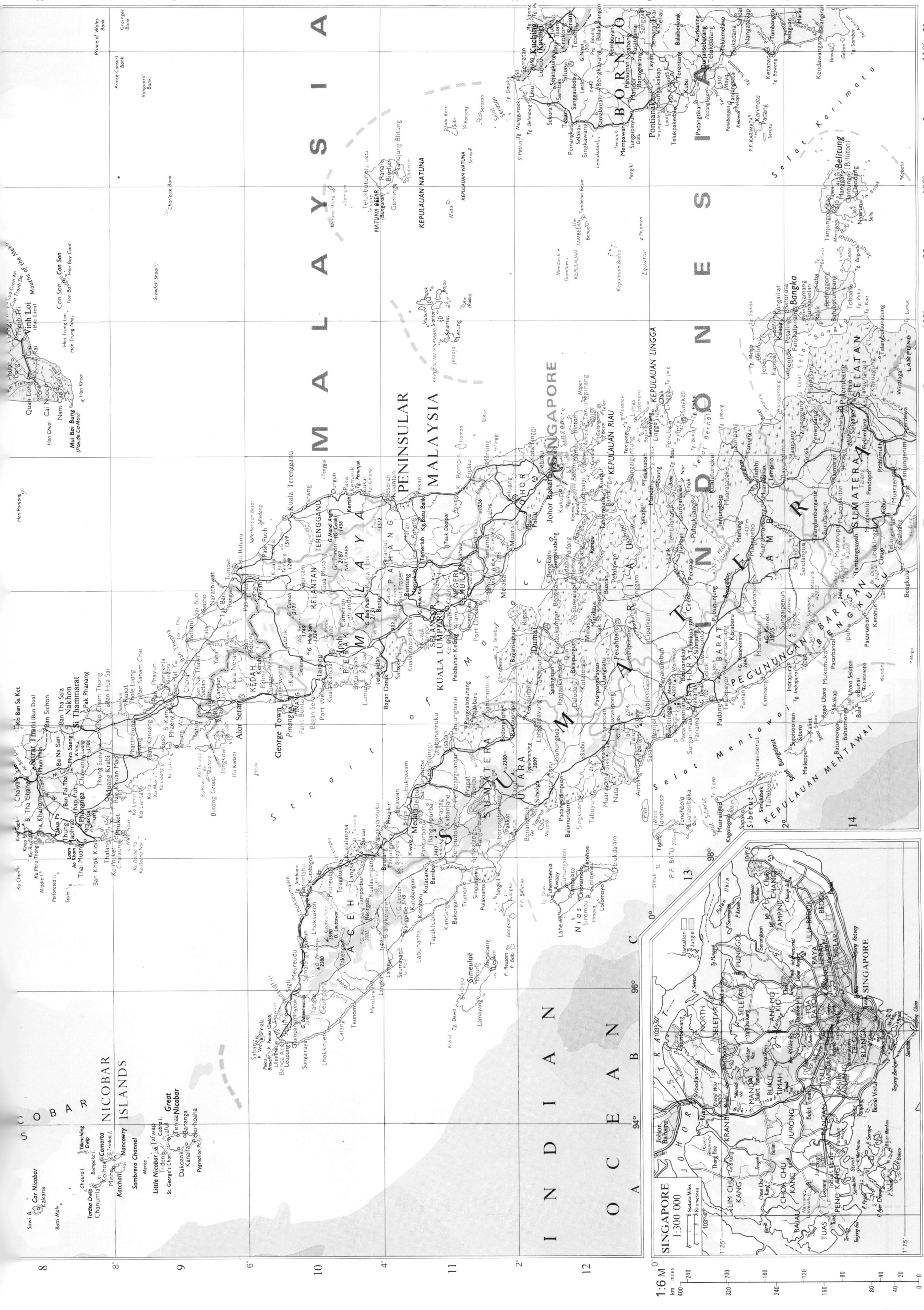

MALAYSIA

BORNEO

INDONESIA

PENINSULAR MALAYSIA

SINGAPORE

MALAYA

KELANTAN
TERENGGANU
PAHANG
PERAK
KEDAH
SELANGOR
NEGERI SEMBILAN
KUALA LUMPUR
PINANG
George Town

SUMATERA UTARA
SUMATERA BARAT
SUMATERA SELATAN
ACEH
JAMBI
BENGKULU
LAMPUNG
RIAU

KEPULAUAN RIAU
KEPULAUAN LINGGA
KEPULAUAN NATUNA
KEPULAUAN ANAMBAS
KEPULAUAN MENTAWAI

Bangka
Belitung (Billiton)
Simeulue
Nias
Siberut

PEGUNUNGAN BARISAN

Selat Karimata
Selat Mentawai
Selat Malaka

NICOBAR ISLANDS
Car Nicobar
Great Nicobar
Little Nicobar
Nancowry
Camorta
Sombrero Channel

INDIAN OCEAN

Kuala Terengganu
Kota Bharu
Kuantan
Pekan
Melaka
Muar
Johor Bahru
Kuching
Pontianak
Palembang
Bengkulu
Padang
Medan
Banda Aceh
Sabang

Alor Setar
Ipoh
Thammarat
Nakhon
Phuket
Thalang

MERCATOR PROJECTION

Heights and Depths in metres

SINGAPORE
1:300 000

JURONG
TUAS
BEDOK
CHANGI
SELETAR
TAMPINES
BUKIT TIMAH
WOODLANDS
PUNGGOL

Johor Bahru
JOHOR STRAIT

1·6 M

BORNEO & CELEBES

PHILIPPINES

M A L A Y S I A

BRUNEI

SABAH

SARAWAK

KALIMANTAN TIMUR

KALIMANTAN BARAT

B O R N E O

KALIMANTAN TENGAH

KALIMANTAN SELATAN

SULAWESI (CELEBES)

Kuching

Pontianak

Balikpapan

Samarinda

Banjarmasin

Palangkaraya

Palu

Parepare

Ujung Pandang (Makassar)

Sunggiminasa

CELEBES SEA

SULU SEA

Teluk Tomini

Selat Makasar

Selat Karimata

J A V A   S E A

I N D O N E S I A

KEPULAUAN LAUT KECIL

Longitude East 116° of Greenwich

KEPULAUAN NATUNA

NATUNA BESAR (Bunguran)

JAVA (JAWA)
(To Indonesia)

SUMATERA SELATAN

Palembang

LAMPUNG

Tanjungkarang Telukbetung

JAKARTA (BATAVIA)

Bogor

Bandung

Cirebon

JAWA BARAT

JAWA TENGAH

JAWA TIMUR

Semarang

Surakarta

Yogyakarta

Surabaya

Madiun

Kediri

Malang

Madura

Pamekasan

BALI

Denpasar

Lombok

J A V A   S E A

Longitude East 110° of Greenwich

KEPULAUAN LAUT KECIL

Heights and Depths in metres

MERCATOR PROJECTION

Feet: 22967 16404 9843 3281 656 0 328 656 1640 3281 6562

m: 7000 5000 3000 1000 200 0 100 200 500 1000 2000

NORTH
MOLUCCAS
(To Indonesia)

HALMAHERA
(JAILOLO GILOLO)

LUZON

PHILIPPINES

MANILA

MINDORO

PALAWAN

SULU SEA

PANAY

SAMAR

LEYTE

CEBU

NEGROS

BOHOL

MINDANAO

SULU ARCHIPELAGO

SABAH

SULAWESI

FLORES SEA

FLORES

SUMBAWA

SUMBA

TIMOR

TIMOR SEA

LESSER SUNDA IS.
(To Indonesia)

John Bartholomew & Son Ltd

Equatorial Scale 1:6 M

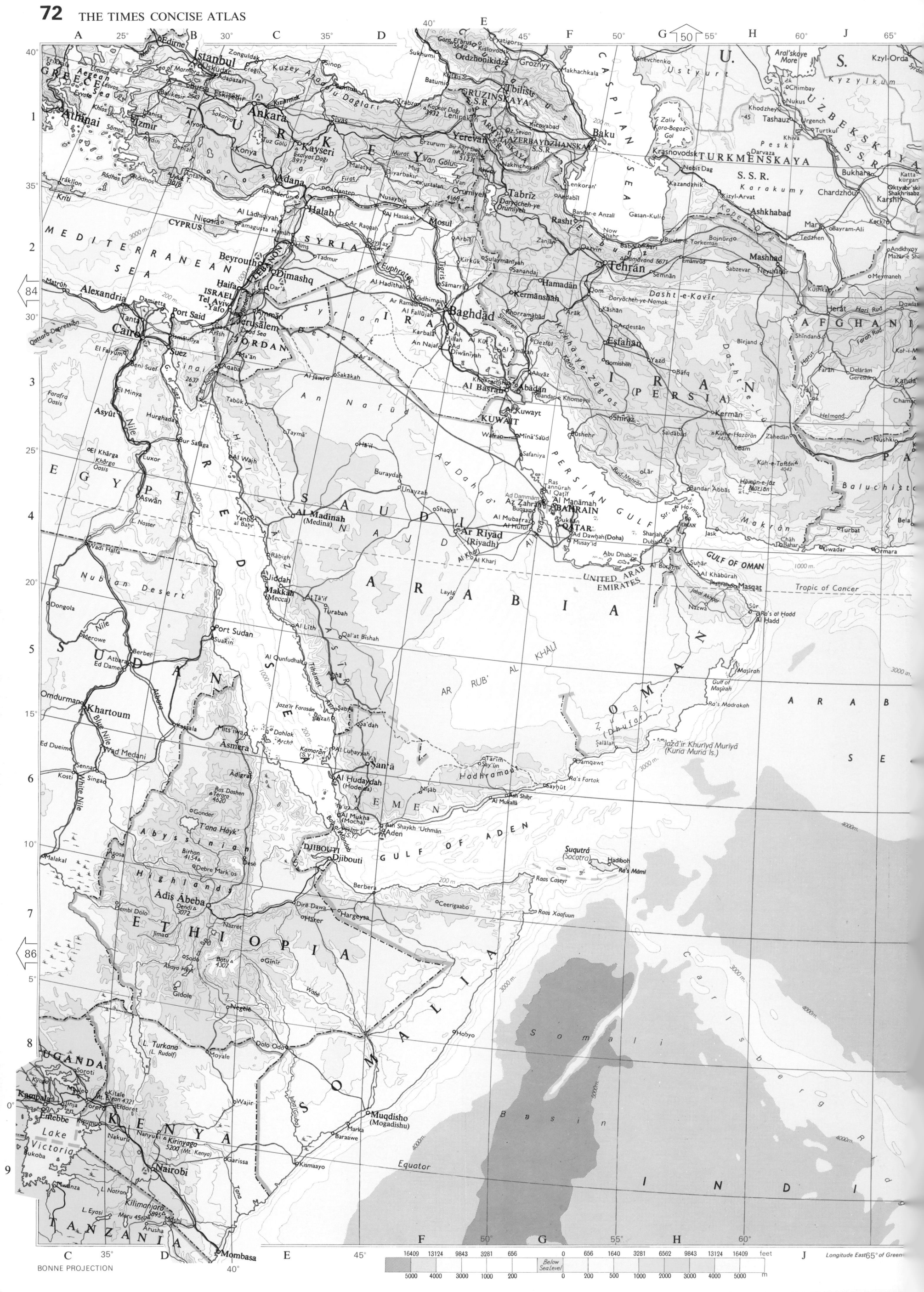

MEDITERRANEAN SEA
CASPIAN SEA
PERSIAN GULF
GULF OF OMAN
GULF OF ADEN
RED SEA
ARABIAN SEA
INDIAN
Tropic of Cancer
Equator
Somali Basin
Carlsberg Ridge
GREECE
TURKEY
CYPRUS
SYRIA
LEBANON
ISRAEL
JORDAN
IRAQ
KUWAIT
BAHRAIN
QATAR
UNITED ARAB EMIRATES
SAUDI ARABIA
OMAN
YEMEN
DJIBOUTI
IRAN (PERSIA)
AFGHANISTAN
U.S.S.R.
GRUZINSKAYA S.S.R.
ARMYANSKAYA S.S.R.
AZERBAYDZHANSKAYA S.S.R.
TURKMENSKAYA S.S.R.
UZBEKSKAYA S.S.R.
EGYPT
SUDAN
ETHIOPIA
SOMALIA
KENYA
UGANDA
TANZANIA
Athinai
İstanbul
Ankara
İzmir
Edirne
Bursa
Konya
Kayseri
Adana
Sivas
Erzurum
Van Gölü
Tbilisi
Yerevan
Baku
Groznyy
Ordzhonikidze
Krasnovodsk
Ashkhabad
Mashhad
Bukhara
Chardzhou
Nicosia
Halab
Beyrouth
Dimashq
Haifa
Tel Aviv-Yafo
Jerusalem
'Ammān
Al 'Aqabah
Mosul
Baghdād
Al Başrah
Ābādān
Al Kuwayt
Tabrīz
Rasht
Tehrān
Hamadān
Kermānshāh
Eşfahan
Shīrāz
Kermān
Zāhedān
Herāt
Bandar 'Abbās
Str. of Hormuz
Tabūk
Al Madīnah (Medina)
Makkah (Mecca)
Jiddah
Aṭ Ṭā'if
Ar Riyāḍ (Riyadh)
Al Manāmah
Ad Dawḥah (Doha)
Abu Dhabi
Dubai
Masqaṭ
Ra's al Hadd
An Nafūd
Ad Dahnā'
AR RUB' AL KHĀLĪ
Ḥaḍramawt
Ṣan'ā
Al Ḥudaydah (Hodeida)
Aden
Djibouti
Suquṭrā (Socotra)
Alexandria
Port Said
Cairo
Suez
Sinai
Asyût
Luxor
Aswān
Wadi Halfa
Nubian Desert
Port Sudan
Khartoum
Omdurman
Kassala
Asmera
Gonder
T'ana Hāyk'
Ādīs Ābeba
Abyssinian Highlands
Harer
Hargeysa
Berbera
Muqdisho (Mogadishu)
Kismaayo
L. Turkana (L. Rudolf)
Kampala
Nairobi
Lake Victoria
Kilimanjaro 5895
Mombasa
BONNE PROJECTION
feet
Below Sea Level
Longitude East 65° of Greenwich

1:15M

Heights and Depths in metres

© John Bartholomew & Son Ltd Edinburgh

AFGHANISTAN
PAKISTAN
BALUCHISTAN
INDIA
IRAN
AFGHAN.
CHINA
U.S.S.R.
KASHMIR
JAMMU AND KASHMIR
NORTHERN AREAS
KARAKORAM RANGE
HIMACHAL PRADESH
PUNJAB
HARYANA
RAJASTHAN
THAR OR INDIAN DESERT
SIND
GUJARAT
MADHYA PRADESH
MAHARASHTRA
UTTAR PRADESH
ANDHRA
N.W. FRONTIER PROV.
DELHI
ISLAMABAD
Rawalpindi
Peshawar
Lahore
Multan
Faisalabad (Lyallpur)
Quetta
Kandahār
Karachi
Hyderabad
Sukkur
Srinagar
Amritsar
Ludhiana
Chandigarh
Shimla (Simla)
Jaipur
Jodhpur
Bikaner
Ajmer
Agra
Gwalior
Ahmadabad
Vadodara (Baroda)
Surat
Bombay
Pune (Poona)
Nasik
Indore
Bhopal
Nagpur
Jabalpur
Udaipur
Kota
Solapur
Secunderabad
Tropic of Cancer
Rann of Kachchh
Gulf of Kachchh
Gulf of Khambhat (Cambay)
Mouths of the Indus
Continued on the same scale
Continued on the same scale
77
76
ALBERS CONIC PROJECTION
1000 200 0 200 500 1000 1500 3000 4500 6000 m
3281 656 0 656 1640 3281 4921 9843 14763 19686 feet

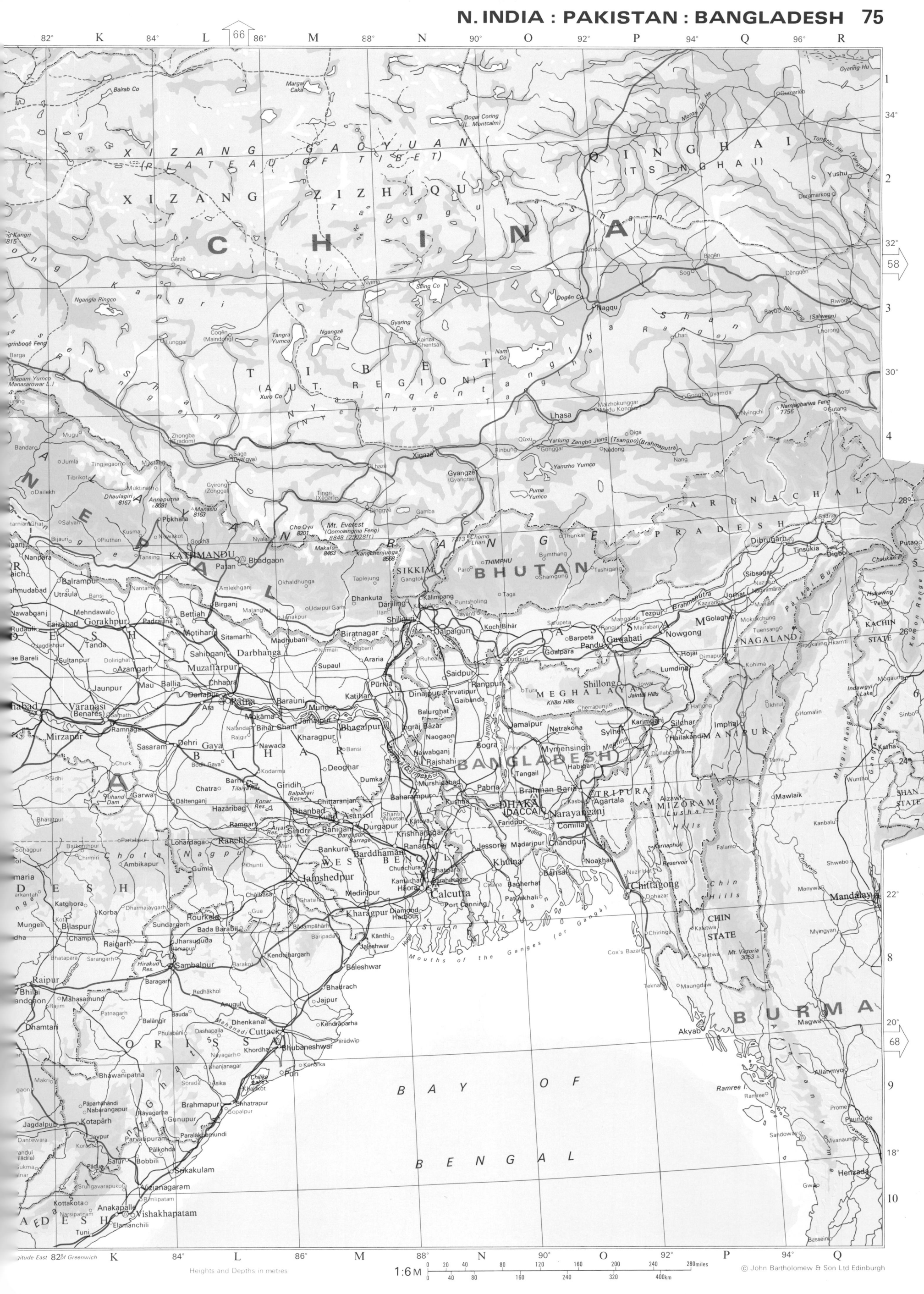

82° K 84° L 66 86° M 88° N 90° O 92° P 94° Q 96° R

1

34°

XIZANG GAOYUAN

2
58

(PLATEAU OF TIBET)

XIZANG ZIZHIQU

CHINA

QINGHAI
(TSINGHAI)

32°

3

Nagqu

Yushu

T I B E T

Lhasa

30°
4

Xigaze

Yarlung Zangbo Jiang (Tsangpo) (Brahmaputra)

Gyangze
(Gyangtse)

ARUNACHAL

28°

Dhaulagiri
8167
Annapurna
8091
Manaslu
8163

Cho Oyu
8201
Mt. Everest
(Qomolangma Feng)
8848 (29028ft)
Makalu
8463
Kangchenjunga
8568

Chomo
Lhari

PRADESH

Dibrugarh

Tinsukia
Digboi

5

KATHMANDU
Patan
Bhadgaon

N E P A L

SIKKIM
Darjiling
Gangtok

THIMPHU
Paro

BHUTAN

Sibsagar

Jorhat

KACHIN
STATE

NAGALAND

Shillong

MEGHALAYA

A S S A M
Guwahati
Nowgong
Golaghat

26°
6

Gorakhpur

Darbhanga

B I H A R

Biratnagar

BANGLADESH

Sylhet

Silchar

M A N I P U R

Imphal

24°

Varanasi
(Benares)

Mirzapur

Patna

Gaya

Rajshahi

DHAKA
(DACCA)
Narayanganj

Comilla

TRIPURA
Agartala

MIZORAM

SHAN
STATE

22°

B I H A R

W E S T   B E N G A L

Durgapur
Asansol

Khulna

Barisal

Chittagong

Chin
Hills

CHIN
STATE

Mandalay

O R I S S A

Jamshedpur

Calcutta

Cox's Bazar

8

Raipur

Bhilai

Cuttack
Bhubaneshwar

Mouths of the Ganges (or Ganga)

Akyab

B U R M A

20°
68

9

B A Y   O F

Puri

Vishakhapatam

B E N G A L

18°

10

Heights and Depths in metres

1:6 M

© John Bartholomew & Son Ltd Edinburgh

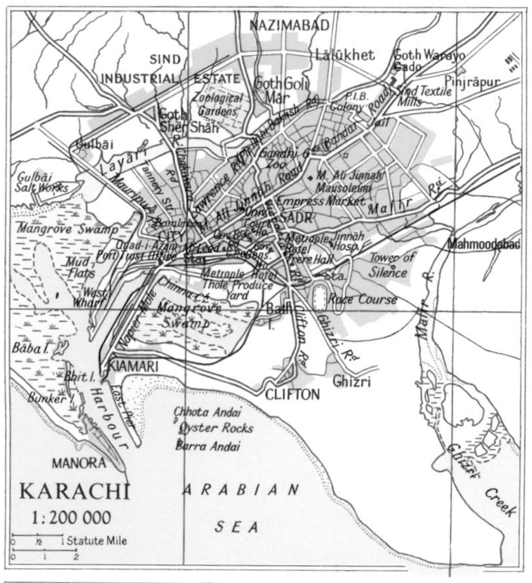

Inset maps

KARACHI 1:200 000
SIND INDUSTRIAL ESTATE
ARABIAN SEA
MANORA
CLIFTON
KIAMARI

BOMBAY 1:240 000
ARABIAN SEA
Bombay Harbour
Butcher I.
Back Bay
Malabar Hill
Gateway of India
COLABA

DELHI 1:240 000
NEW DELHI
OLD DELHI
Palam International Airport

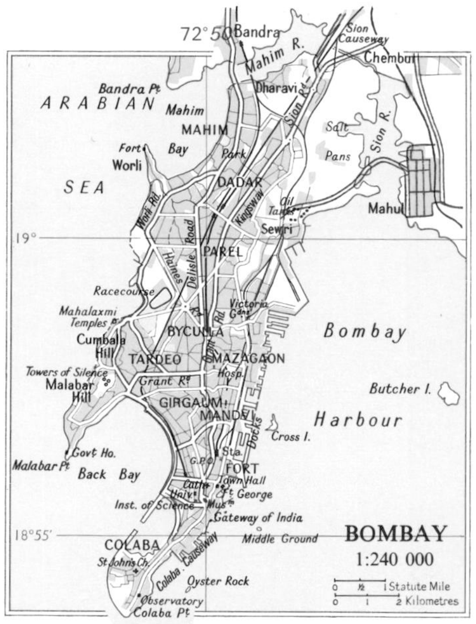

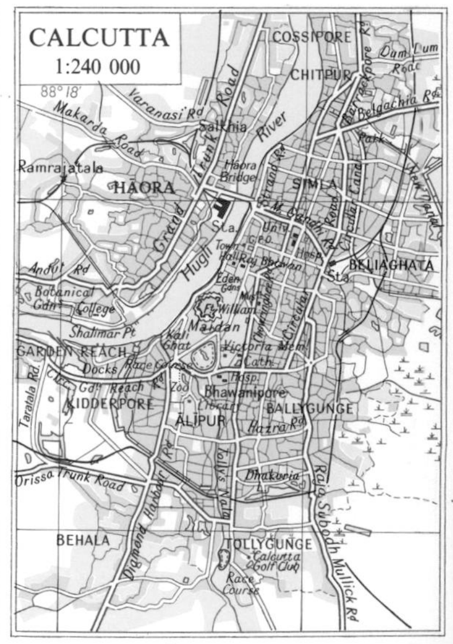

CALCUTTA 1:240 000
COSSIPORE
HAORA
ALIPUR
TOLLYGUNGE
BEHALA

Main map — South India

MADHYA PRADESH
MAHARASHTRA
KARNATAKA
ANDHRA PRADESH
TAMIL NADU
ORISSA
GOA
DAMAN
DIU

Malegaon · Nasik · Manmad · Chalisgaon · Buldana · Karanja · Yeotmal · Hinganghat · Warora · Chandrapur
Bombay · Thāne · Kalyan · Ulhasnagar · Pune (Poona) · Ahmadnagar · Aurangabad · Jalna · Parbhani · Nanded · Nizamabad · Karimnagar · Warangal
Solapur · Gulbarga · Bidar · Secunderabad · Hyderabad · Nalgonda · Khammam · Eluru · Vijayawada · Guntur · Tenali · Machilipatnam (Masulipatnam)
Kolhapur · Sangli · Miraj · Bijapur · Raichur · Kurnool · Nandyal · Ongole · Chirala · Bapatla
Panaji · Belgaum · Dharwad · Hubli · Gadag · Bellary · Anantapur · Cuddapah · Nellore
Karwar · Sirsi · Shimoga · Chitradurga · Davangere · Hindupur · Tirupati · Gudur
Mangalore · Udipi · Chikmagalur · Tumkur · Bangalore · Kolar Gold Fields · Madras · Kanchipuram
Mysore · Hosur · Krishnagiri · Vellore · Chittoor · Arani · Tiruvannamalai · Pondicherry
Calicut · Coimbatore · Erode · Salem · Cuddalore · Chidambaram
Cochin · Ernakulam · Trichur · Palghat · Tiruchchirappalli · Thanjavur · Nagappattinam
Alleppey · Kottayam · Dindigul · Madurai · Pudukkottai
Quilon · Tenkasi · Tirunelveli · Tuticorin · Ramanathapuram
Trivandrum · Nagercoil · Cape Comorin · Palayankottai

LAKSHADWEEP (Laccadive Islands)
Laccadive, Minicoy and Amindivi Islands (India)
Minicoy
Nine Degree Channel
Eight Degree Channel
MALDIVES
Thiladunmathi Atoll
Makunudu Atoll
Miladunmadulu Atoll

ANDAMAN ISLANDS
North Andaman · Middle Andaman · South Andaman · Port Blair
Duncan Passage
Little Andaman
Ten Degree Channel
NICOBAR ISLANDS
Car Nicobar · Little Nicobar · Great Nicobar

SRI LANKA (CEYLON)
Jaffna · Trincomalee · Anuradhapura · Batticaloa · Kandy · Nuwara Eliya · COLOMBO · Moratuwa · Ratnapura · Galle · Matara
Mt Pidurutalagala 2243
Palk Strait · Adam's Bridge · Gulf of Manaar

Coromandel Coast · Malabar Coast · Bay of Bengal · ARABIAN SEA

1:6 M
miles km
Heights and Depths in metres
ALBERS CONIC PROJECTION
© John Bartholomew & Son Ltd Edinburgh

m: 6000 4500 3000 1500 500 200 0 200 1000
feet: 19686 14763 9843 4921 1640 656 0 656 3281

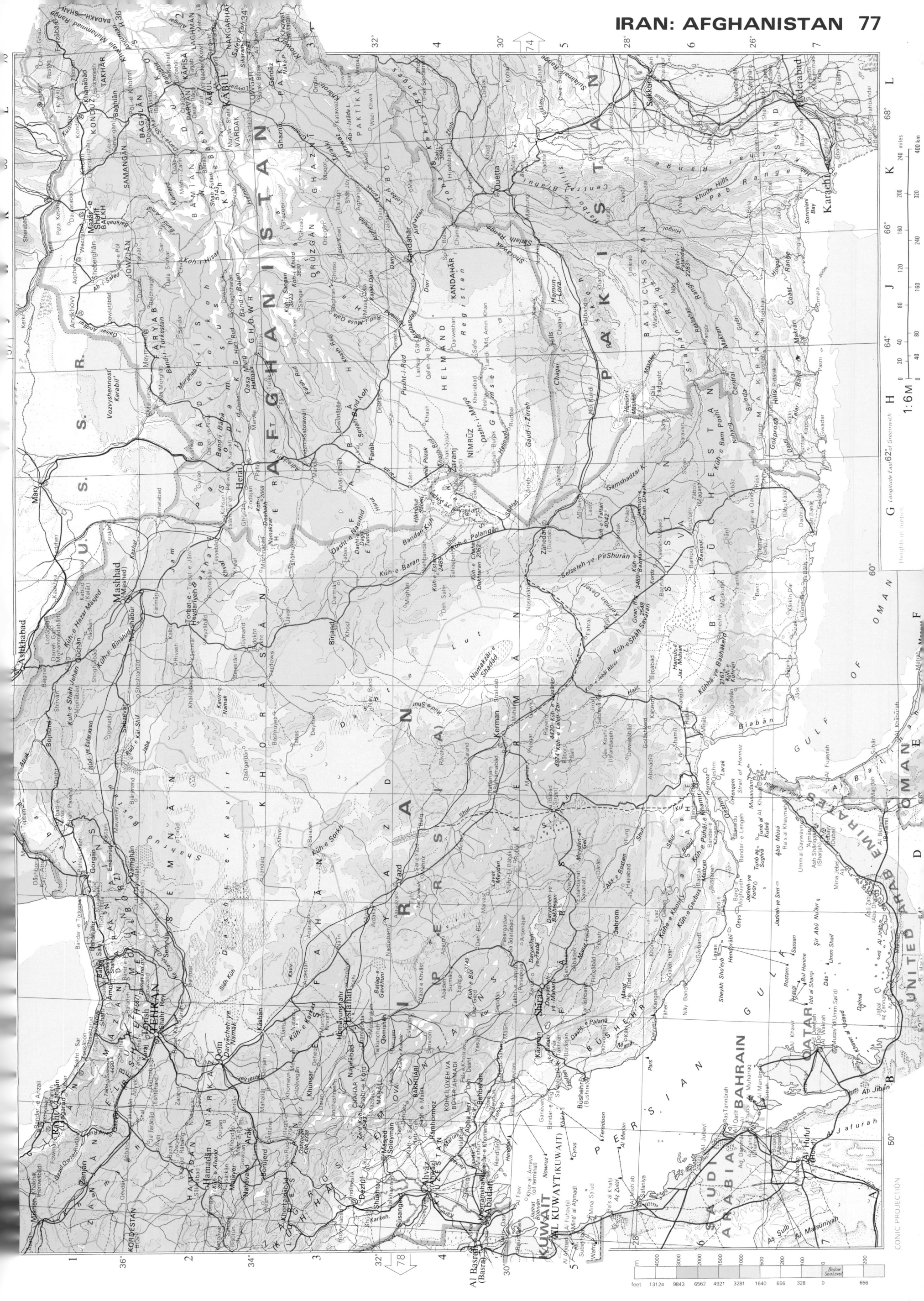
I R A N
A F G H A N I S T A N
P A K I S T A N
U. S. S. R.
TEHRAN
KABUL
Mashhad (Meshed)
Herat
Kandahar
Quetta
Karachi
Hyderabad
Sukkur
Shiraz
Esfahan
Yazd
Kerman
Zahedan
Qom
Hamadan
Bushehr
Ahvaz
Abadan
Mary
Ashkhabad
GULF OF OMAN
PERSIAN GULF
BAHRAIN
QATAR
KUWAIT
SAUDI ARABIA
UNITED ARAB EMIRATES
OMAN
D a s h t - e   K a v i r
D a s h t - e   L u t
B A L U C H I S T A N
1:6M
CONIC PROJECTION

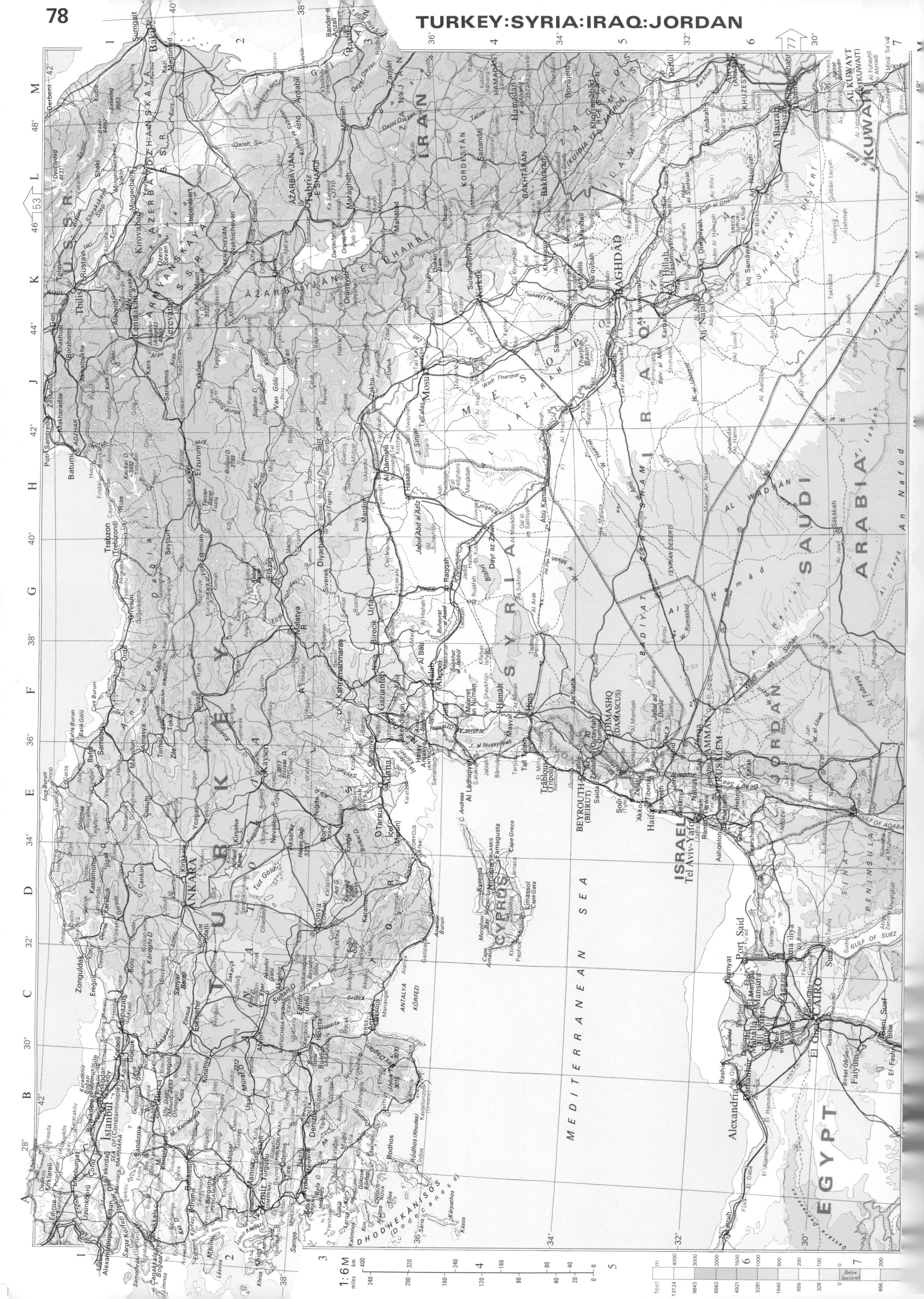
U. S. S. R.
TURKEY
SYRIA
IRAQ
IRAN
JORDAN
SAUDI ARABIA
KUWAIT
ISRAEL
EGYPT
CYPRUS
MEDITERRANEAN SEA
ANKARA
İstanbul
BAGHDĀD
DIMASHQ (DAMASCUS)
BEYROUTH (BEIRUT)
AMMAN
JERUSALEM
CAIRO
Alexandria
Port Said
1:6M

TURKEY

Antalya
(Adalia)

Antalya
Körfezi

Adana
Tarsus
İçel
(Mersin)

İskenderun
(Alexandretta)

Gaziantep
Nizip

Kilis

Halab
(Aleppo)

As Safirah

Al Bâb

Idlib

Hatay
(Antakya)
(Antioch)

Samandağ

Al Ladhiqīyah
(Latakia)
Jablah

Baniyās

Jisr ash Shughūr
Maárrat
an Numân

Khān Shaykhūn

Hamāh

Masyaf

CYPRUS

Kyrenia
Morphou
Bay
Nicosia
Famagusta
Varosha
Famagusta Bay

Larnaca

Limassol

Tartūs
Burj
Safitā

Tall Kalakh
Hims

Halba

Trâblous
(Tripoli)

Hermel
Baalbek

An Nabk

LEBANON

BEYROUTH
(BEIRUT)

Zahlé

Az Zabadāni

DIMASHQ
(DAMASCUS, ESH SHEM, DAMAS)

SYRIA

Saida
(Sidon)

Soûr
(Tyre)

Nahariya
(Acre) Akko
Haifa

Tiberias
Zefat

As Suwaydā'

Nazareth

Irbid
Dar'ā

Jenin

Ajlūn
Mafraq

MEDITERRANEAN SEA

Netanya
Tulkarm
ISRAEL
Herzliyya
Tel Aviv
Yafo
(Jaffa)
Rishon le Zion
Holon

Nablus

Salt
AMMAN
Zarqa

Ramallah
Jericho

Ashdod
JERUSALEM
(EL QUDS ESH SHERIF)
Bethlehem
Madaba

Gaza
Hebron

JORDAN

Khān Yūnis
Rafah
Beersheba

Kerak

Rashid
Rosetta
Alexandria
(Iskandariya)

Damanhûr
Port Said
Dumyât
(Damietta)

El Mansûra
Tanta

Ismâ'iliya
Zagazig

Tafila

CAIRO (EL QÂHIRA)
Heliopolis
El Gîza
Suez
Port Taufiq

Ma'ān

EGYPT

Helwan

Beni Suef

SINAI

Elat
Aqaba

El Minya

SAHARA ESH SHARQIYA

SAUDI ARABIA

El Tûr

MEDITERRANEAN SEA

Longitude East of Greenwich

Heights and Depths in metres

© John Bartholomew & Son
Ltd Edinburgh

CONIC PROJECTION

1:3M

6562 3281 656 0 328 656 1640 3281 4921 6562 9843 13124 feet
2000 1000 200 0 100 200 500 1000 2000 3000 4000 m

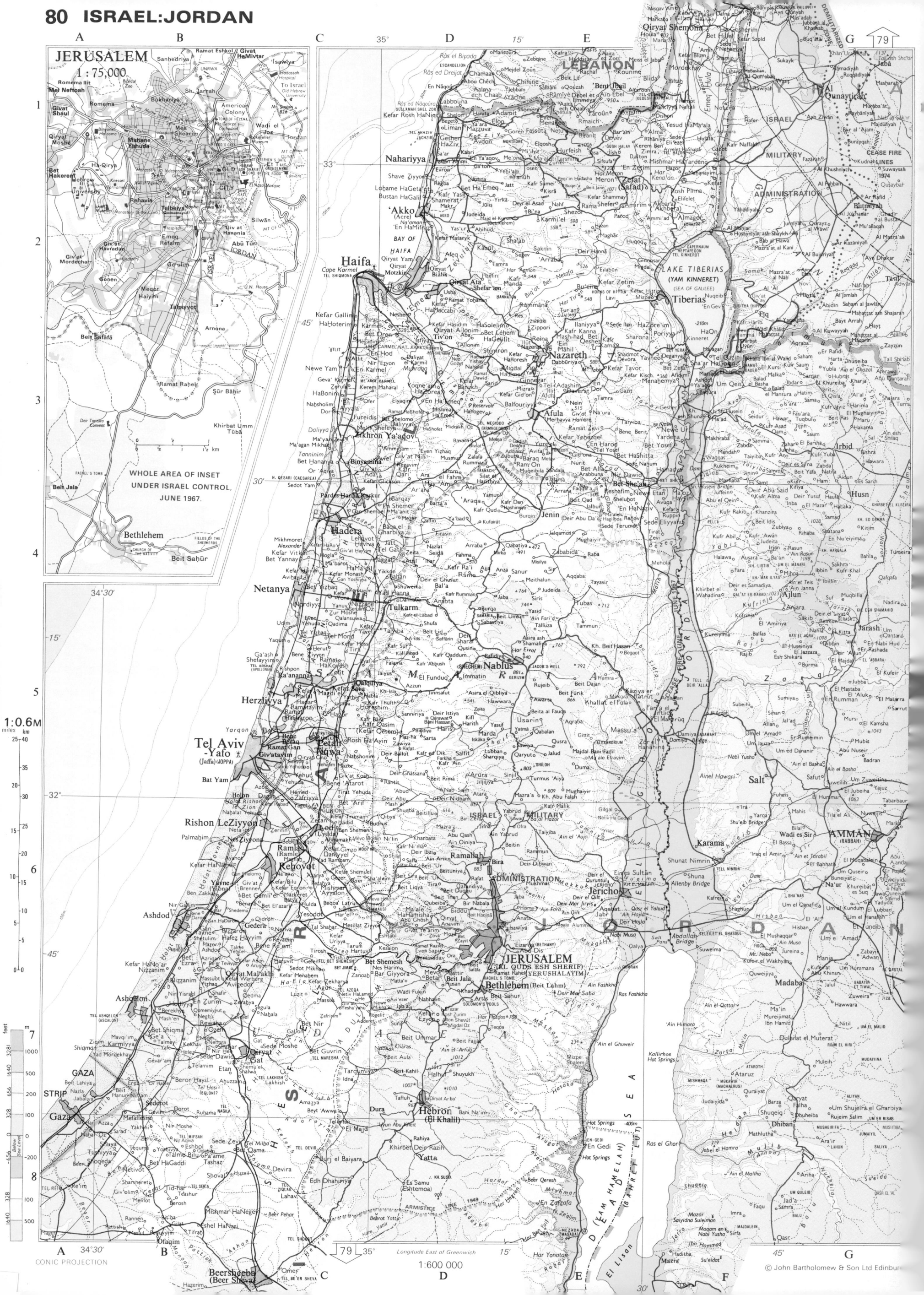
JERUSALEM
1 : 75,000
WHOLE AREA OF INSET UNDER ISRAEL CONTROL, JUNE 1967.
Bethlehem
Beit Jala
Beit Sahur
LEBANON
SYRIA
ISRAEL MILITARY ADMINISTRATION
CEASE FIRE LINES 1974
LAKE TIBERIAS
(YAM KINNERET)
(SEA OF GALILEE)
Tiberias
Haifa
'Akko
Nahariyya
Nazareth
Afula
Hadera
Netanya
Tulkarm
Nablus
Jenin
Herzliyya
Tel Aviv -Yafo
(Jaffa) (JOPPA)
Bat Yam
Rishon LeZiyyon
Ramla
Lod
Rehovot
Ashdod
Ashqelon
Ramallah
Jericho
JERUSALEM
(EL QUDS ESH SHERIF)
(YERUSHALAYIM)
Bethlehem
Hebron
(El Khalil)
GAZA STRIP
Gaza
Beersheba
(Beer Sheva)
Irbid
Ajlun
Jarash
Salt
AMMAN
(RABBAH)
Madaba
Dhiban
Karama
Allenby Bridge
Abdallah Bridge
Ein Gedi
DEAD SEA
JORDAN
1:0.6M
CONIC PROJECTION
Longitude East of Greenwich
1:600 000
© John Bartholomew & Son Ltd Edinburgh

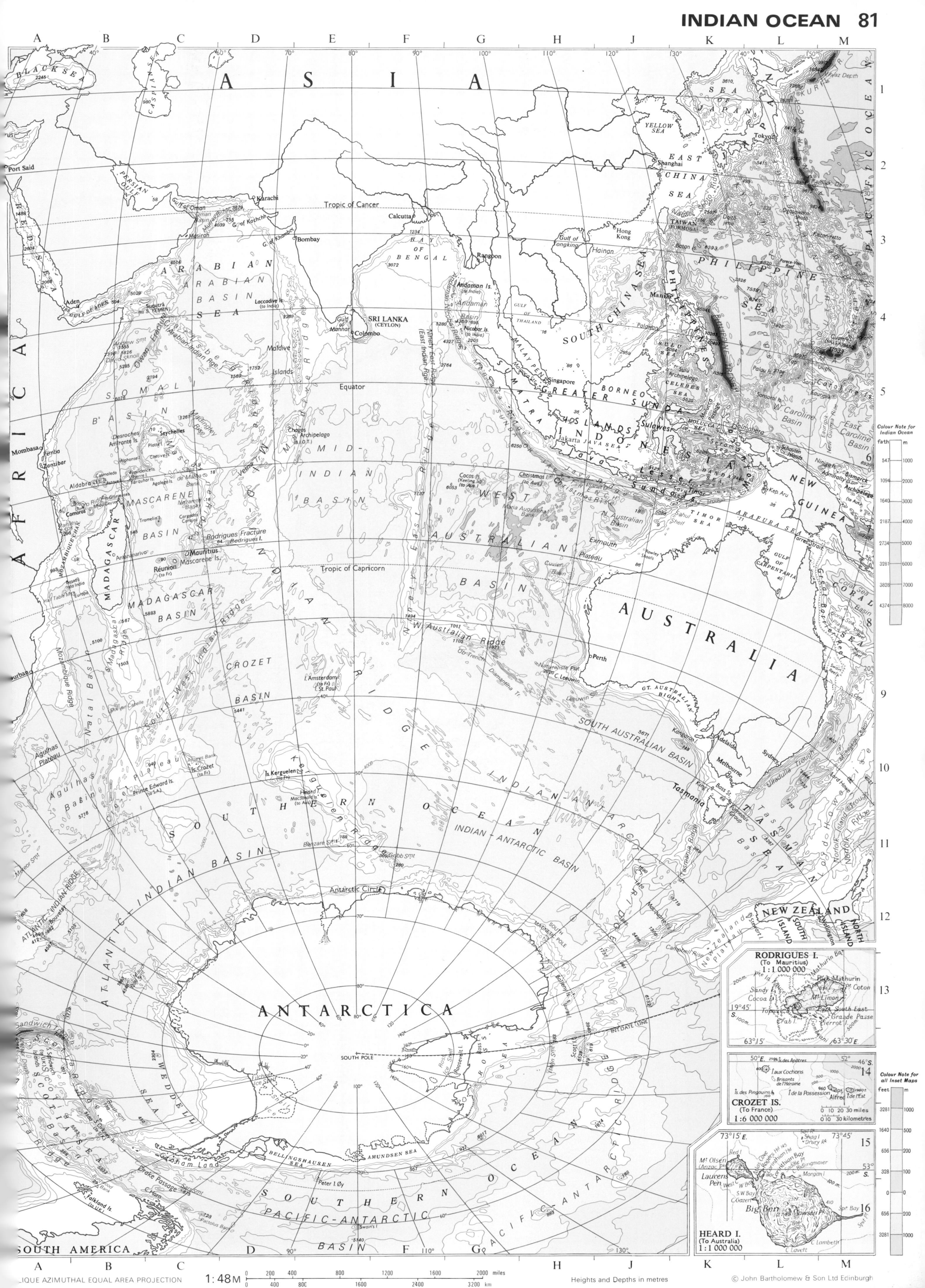

OBLIQUE AZIMUTHAL EQUAL AREA PROJECTION   1:48M

Heights and Depths in metres

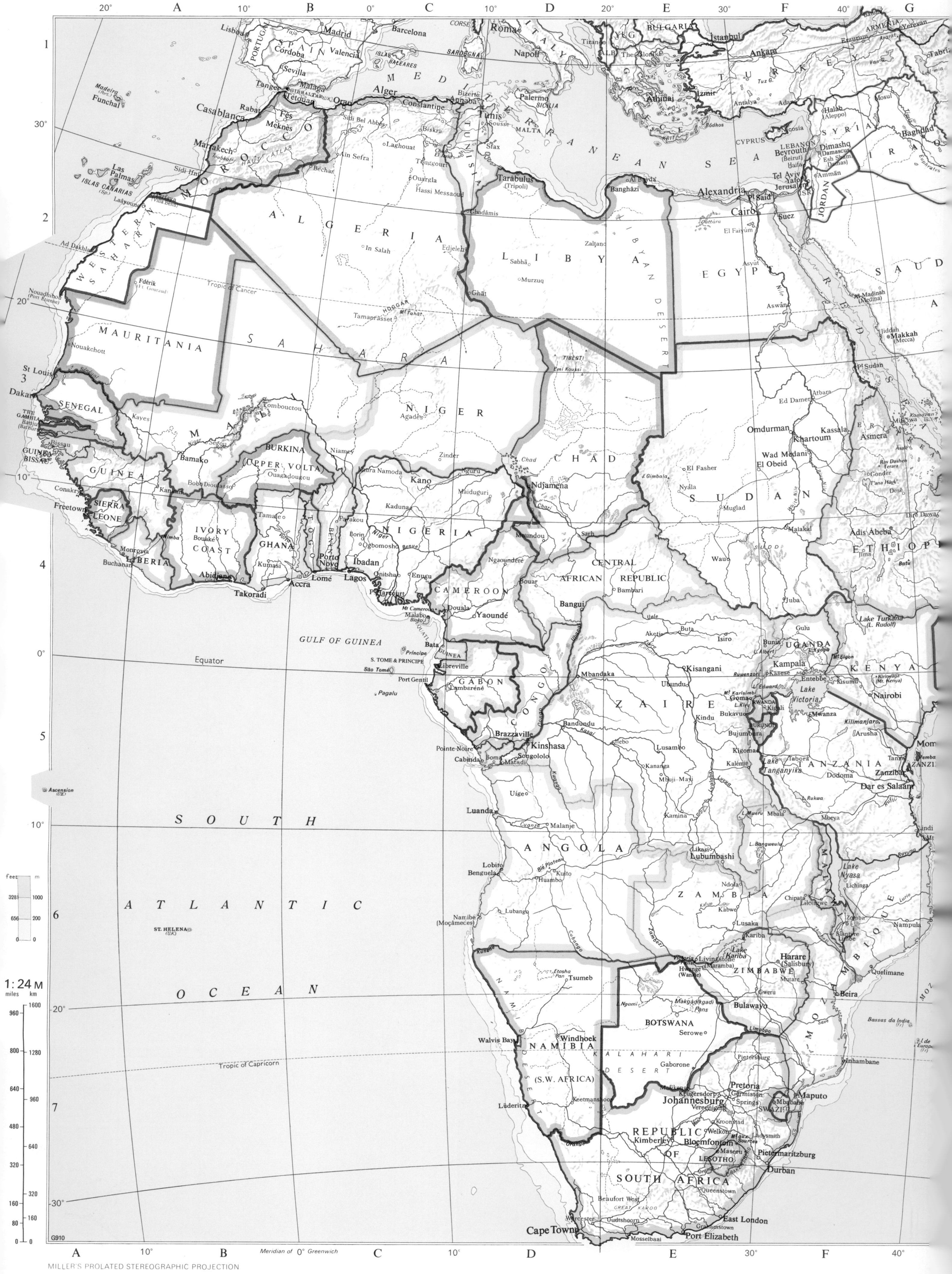

1 : 24 M

MILLER'S PROLATED STEREOGRAPHIC PROJECTION

G910

Meridian of 0° Greenwich

SRI LANKA (CEYLON)
1 : 2 400 000

Statute Miles
0   10   20   30
0 10 20 30 40 50 Kilometres

COCOS IS. (KEELING IS.)
(To Australia)
1 : 1 000 000

Nth Keeling I.

Horsburgh (Luar)   Direction I.   Refuge
Bantam   Home I.
West (Panjang)   Rambling I.
South I. (Atas)

96°50′ E.

CHRISTMAS I.
(To Australia)

105°30′ E.

N.W Point   Flying Fish Cove   N.E. Point
Torn's Ridge   Headridge Hill   Low Pt.
Murray Hill   Allan Pt.
Ross Hill
Jones I.   Middle Pt   McMicken Pt
Stubbings Pt.   Phosphate Works   Aldwin Pt
Medwin Pt

1 : 1 000 000

LAMBERT CONFORMAL CONIC PROJECTION

INDIAN OCEAN

SEYCHELLES
1 : 3 000 000

Bird I.
Denis I.
Arida I.
Booby I.   Curieuse I.
The Sisters
Praslin I.   Marie Anne I.
Cousin Is.   Félicité I.
Silhouette I.   La Digue I.
North I.   Chimney Rocks
Trever Pt.   Haddon Pt.   Frigate I.
Victoria   Anse I.   Recif I.
C. Ternay   Cascade
Thérèse I.   Mahé I.
Conception   Anse Royal
Takamaka   Capucin Pt.

SEYCHELLES BANK

MAHÉ
North Pt
North Hb.
North West
Victoria   4°35′
Anne I.
Ternay   Moyenne I.
Morne   Cerf I.
Seychelles   East I.
Conception   Anse aux Pins
Thérèse   Anse Boileau
L'Espérance   Sel Pt
Anse Royal   4°45′
Point Lazare   Takamaka
Cap Malheureux
Capucin Rock
1 : 1 000 000

MAURITIUS
1 : 1 000 000

Statute Miles
0   10
0   10   20 Kilometres

Quoin Channel
Gunners Quoin
Coin de Mire Malheureux
Cannoniers Pt   Grande Baie
Isle d'Ambre
Fond du sac
Saint-André   Rivière du Rempart
Tombeau Bay
Pamplemousses
Port Louis   Lafayette
Roche Bois   St. Nicolère   Centre de Flacq
Quatre Cocos
Beau Bassin   Quatre Bornes   Rose Hill
St Pierre   Quartier Militaire
Vacoas   Mt Blanche   Ile aux Cerfs
Bambous   Moka   Grande Riv S.E.
Medine   Curepipe   Flamand
Tamarin   Mt Cocotte   Danish Entrance
Grande Riv Noire B.   Rose Belle
Piton de la Petite R. Noire   Mahebourg
Ile aux Bénitiers   Rivière des Anguilles
Pte Sud Ouest   Mt Fourneau   Escalier
Le Morne   Chemin de Grenier
Baie du Cap   Souillac
Benares
57°15′ E.   57°30′   57°45′

feet   metres
6562   2000
4921   1500
3281   1000
1640   500
656   200
0   0
656   200
3281   1000

RÉUNION
(To France)
1 : 1 000 000

St Denis   Ste Marie
La Possession   Ste Suzanne
Le Port   Le Brûlé   Quartier Français
B. de St Paul   St André
St Paul   Cirque   St Benoit
Pl. des Chicots   Pl. des fougères
Salazie   Hell-Bourg
Grand Bénard   Morne
St Leu   des Neiges   Ste Anne
Cilaos   Gt Etang   Rose
La Fontaine   La Plaine   Forêt
St Louis   des Palmistes   Pointe des
St Pierre   Grand   Bassin   Cascades
Les Avirons   Plaine des Cafres   Bois Blanc
Etang-Salé   Piton de la Fournaise
Ste Rose
La Rivière   Le Tampon
Rivière St Etienne   Terre Sainte
Rivière d'Abord   Pointe de la Table
St Joseph   St Philippe

KERGUELEN
(To France)
1 : 3 000 000

Statute Miles
0   20
0   20   40 Kilometres

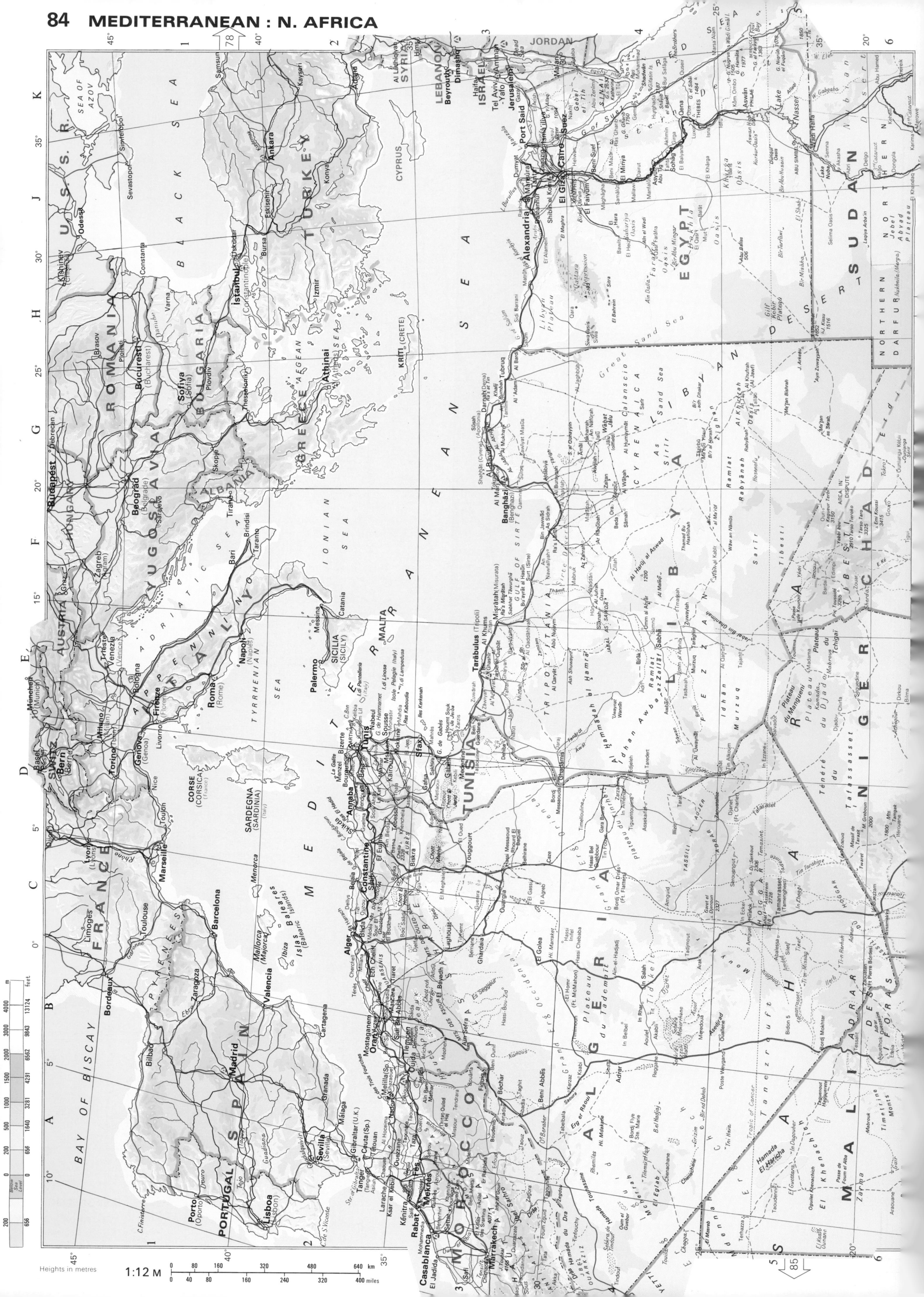

FRANCE
SPAIN
PORTUGAL
ITALY
SWITZ.
AUSTRIA
HUNGARY
YUGOSLAVIA
ROMANIA
BULGARIA
ALBANIA
GREECE
TURKEY
U. S. S. R.
CYPRUS
SYRIA
LEBANON
ISRAEL
JORDAN
EGYPT
SUDAN
LIBYA
TUNISIA
ALGERIA
MOROCCO
MALI
NIGER
CHAD
MALTA
BAY OF BISCAY
BLACK SEA
SEA OF AZOV
AEGEAN SEA
IONIAN SEA
TYRRHENIAN SEA
ADRIATIC SEA
MEDITERRANEAN SEA
RED SEA
GULF OF SIRTE
SAHARA
CORSE (CORSICA)
SARDEGNA (SARDINIA)
SICILIA (SICILY)
KRITI (CRETE)
Islas Baleares (Balearic Islands)
Tropic of Cancer
Heights in metres
1:12 M
0 80 160 320 480 640 km
0 40 80 160 240 320 400 miles

16

84

86

PORT. SPAIN

MEDITERRANEAN SEA

SARDEGNA (SARDINIA) (Italy)

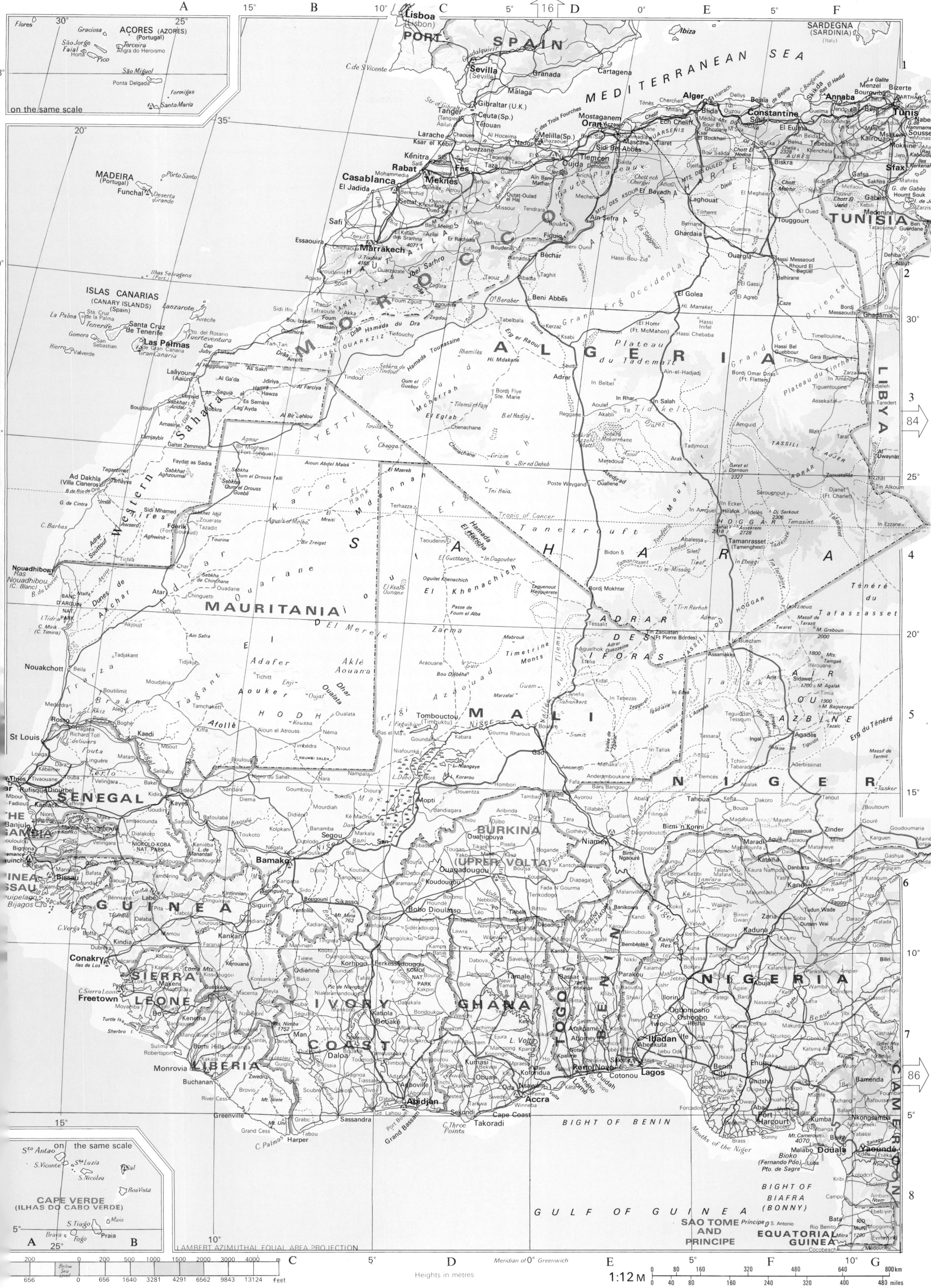

AÇORES (AZORES) (Portugal)
Flores *Graciosa*
Terceira Angra do Heroísmo
São Jorge *Faial* *Pico*
Horta
São Miguel
Ponta Delgada *Formigas*
Santa Maria

on the same scale

MADEIRA (Portugal)
Funchal
Pôrto Santo
Desertas Grande
Ilhas Selvagens (Port.)

ISLAS CANARIAS (CANARY ISLANDS) (Spain)
Lanzarote
La Palma *Tenerife*
Santa Cruz de Tenerife
Gomera *San Sebastián*
Hierro *Valverde*
Las Palmas
Gran Canaria
Fuerteventura

Lisboa (Lisbon)
Sevilla (Seville)
Granada
Cartagena
Gibraltar (U.K.)
Tánger (Tangier)
Tetouan
Málaga
Alger
Oran
Constantine
Annaba
Tunis
TUNISIA

MOROCCO
Rabat
Casablanca
Meknès
Fès
Marrakech

ALGERIA

LIBYA

Western Sahara
Ad Dakhla (Villa Cisneros)
Nouâdhibou

MAURITANIA
Nouakchott
Atar

S A H A R A

Tropic of Cancer

HOGGAR

MALI
Tombouctou (Timbuktu)
Gao

NIGER

SENEGAL
THE GAMBIA
Banjul
GUINEA-BISSAU
Bissau
GUINEA
Conakry
SIERRA LEONE
Freetown
LIBERIA
Monrovia

BURKINA (UPPER VOLTA)
Ouagadougou
Bobo Dioulasso

Bamako

Niamey

NIGERIA
Kano
Kaduna
Abuja
Ibadan
Lagos

IVORY COAST
Abidjan
GHANA
Accra
Kumasi
TOGO
Lomé
BENIN
Porto Novo
Cotonou

BIGHT OF BENIN

GULF OF GUINEA

BIGHT OF BIAFRA (BONNY)

CAMEROON
Yaoundé
Douala

EQUATORIAL GUINEA
Malabo

SAO TOME AND PRINCIPE

CAPE VERDE (ILHAS DO CABO VERDE)
Sto Antão *S. Vicente* *S. Nicolau* *Sal*
S. Luzia *Boa Vista*
Praia
S. Tiago *Fogo* *Brava* *Maio*
on the same scale

LAMBERT AZIMUTHAL EQUAL AREA PROJECTION
Heights in metres
Meridian of 0° Greenwich

1:12 M

Below Sea Level
656 0 656 1640 3281 4291 6562 9843 13124 feet
200 0 200 500 1000 1500 2000 3000 4000 m

0 80 160 240 320 400 480 640 800 km
0 40 80 120 160 240 320 480 miles

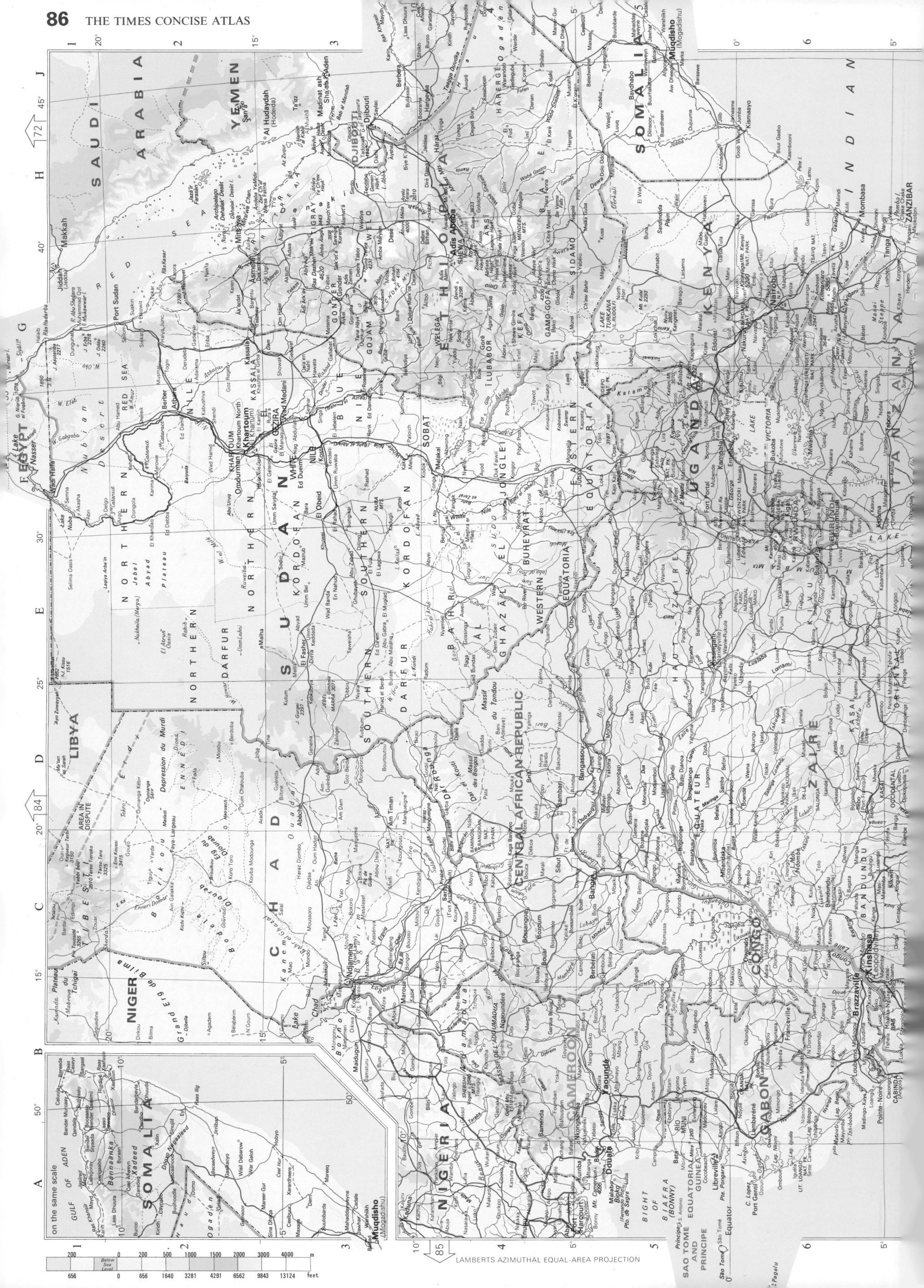
SAUDI ARABIA
YEMEN
EGYPT
LIBYA
NIGER
CHAD
SUDAN
ETHIOPIA
DJIBOUTI
SOMALIA
KENYA
UGANDA
RWANDA
BURUNDI
TANZANIA
ZAIRE
CONGO
GABON
CAMEROON
NIGERIA
CENTRAL AFRICAN REPUBLIC
EQUATORIAL GUINEA
SAO TOME AND PRINCIPE
RED SEA
GULF OF ADEN
BIGHT OF BIAFRA (BONNY)
Khartoum
Addis Ababa
Nairobi
Kinshasa (Léopoldville)
Brazzaville
Kampala
Muqdisho (Mogadishu)
Ndjamena
Bangui
Yaoundé
Libreville
on the same scale
72
84
85
200 0 200 500 1000 1500 2000 3000 4000 m
656 Below Sea Level 0 656 1640 3281 4291 6562 9843 13124 feet
LAMBERTS AZIMUTHAL EQUAL-AREA PROJECTION

Heights in metres

1:12 M

© John Bartholomew & Son Ltd Edinburgh

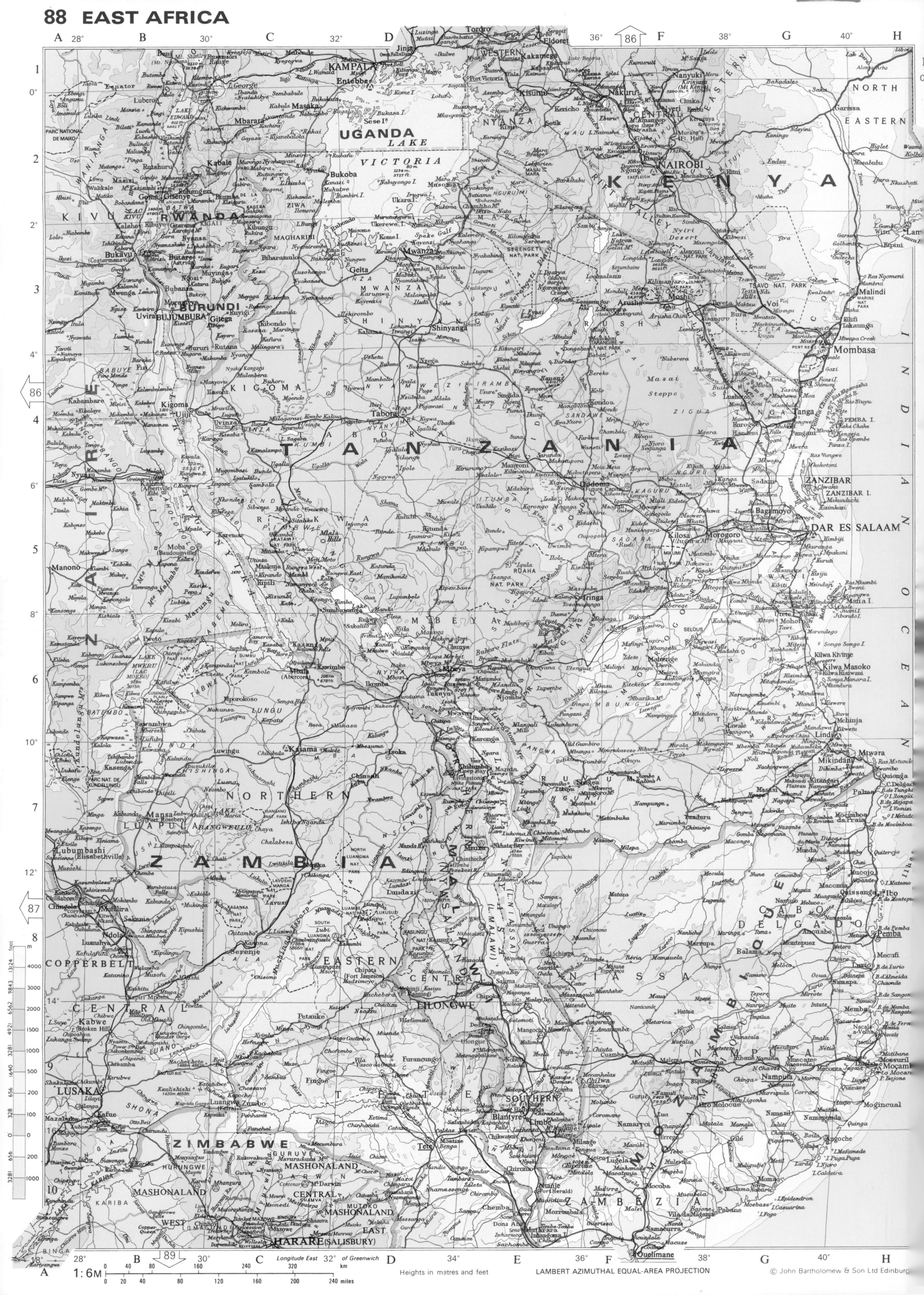

1:6M

Heights in metres and feet

LAMBERT AZIMUTHAL EQUAL-AREA PROJECTION

© John Bartholomew & Son Ltd Edinburgh

Longitude East of Greenwich

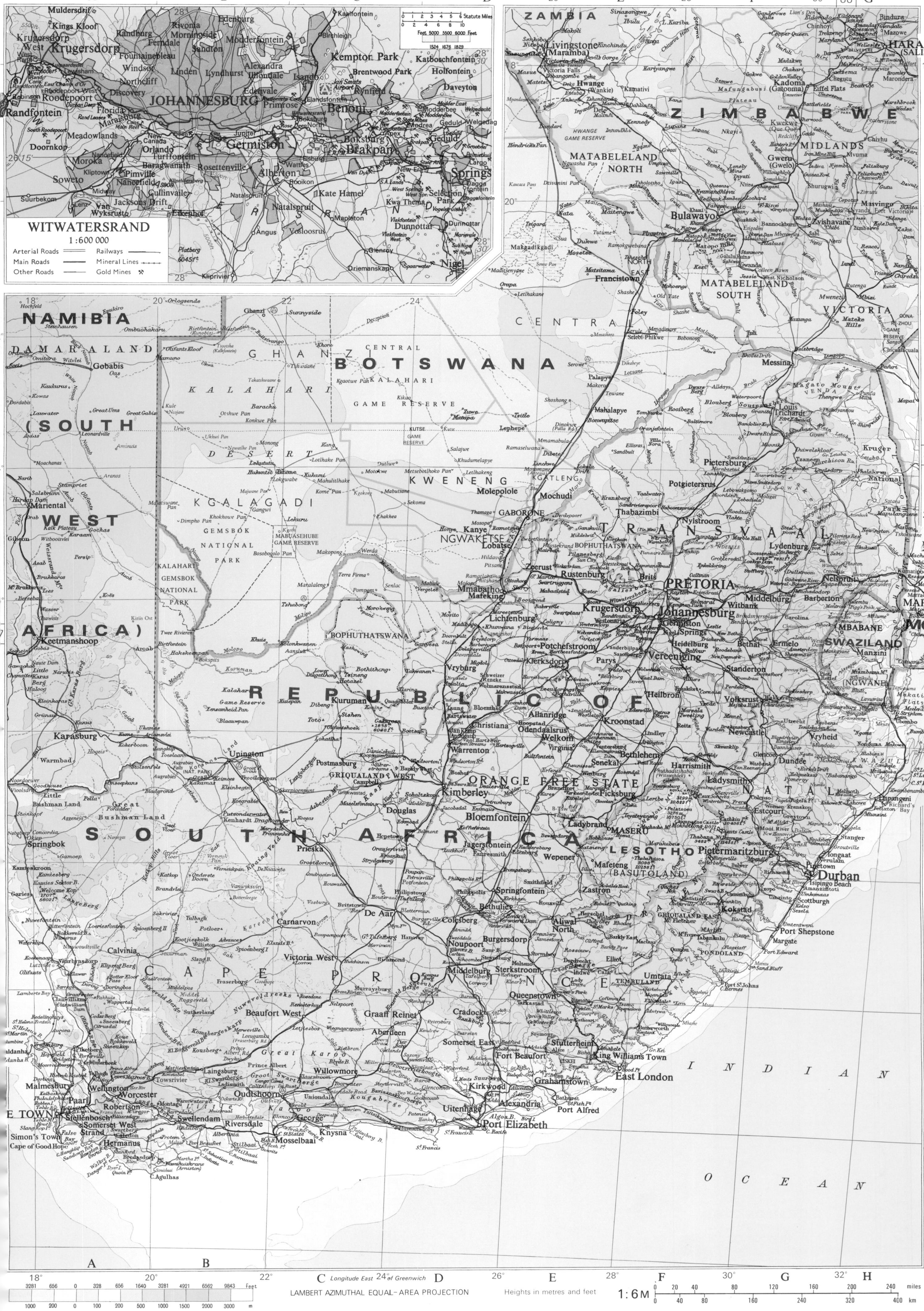

WITWATERSRAND
1:600 000

Arterial Roads	Railways
Main Roads	Mineral Lines
Other Roads	Gold Mines

ZAMBIA

ZIMBABWE

MATABELELAND NORTH

MATABELELAND SOUTH

MIDLANDS

VICTORIA

HARARE (SALISBURY)

NAMIBIA

DAMARALAND

(SOUTH WEST AFRICA)

BOTSWANA

CENTRAL

KALAHARI

GHANZI

KWENENG

NGWAKETSE

KGALAGADI

KALAHARI GEMSBOK NATIONAL PARK

GEMSBOK NATIONAL PARK

GABORONE

REPUBLIC OF

SOUTH AFRICA

BOPHUTHATSWANA

TRANSVAAL

PRETORIA

JOHANNESBURG

ORANGE FREE STATE

NATAL

KWAZULU

CAPE PROVINCE

GRIQUALAND WEST

GRIQUALAND EAST

PONDOLAND

TEMBULAND

GREAT KAROO

LESOTHO (BASUTOLAND)

MASERU

SWAZILAND

MBABANE

MOZ

MAPUTO

Bloemfontein

Kimberley

Durban

Pietermaritzburg

East London

Port Elizabeth

Cape Town

INDIAN OCEAN

LAMBERT AZIMUTHAL EQUAL-AREA PROJECTION

Heights in metres and feet

1:6 M

Longitude East of Greenwich

BERMUDA
(To U.K.)
1 : 450 000

ASCENSION
(To U.K.)
1 : 450 000

ST HELENA
(To U.K.)
1 : 450 000

TRISTAN DA CUNHA
(To U.K.)
1 : 1 000 000

LAMBERT AZIMUTHAL EQUAL-AREA PROJECTION

Heights and Depths in metres

1 : 48 000 000

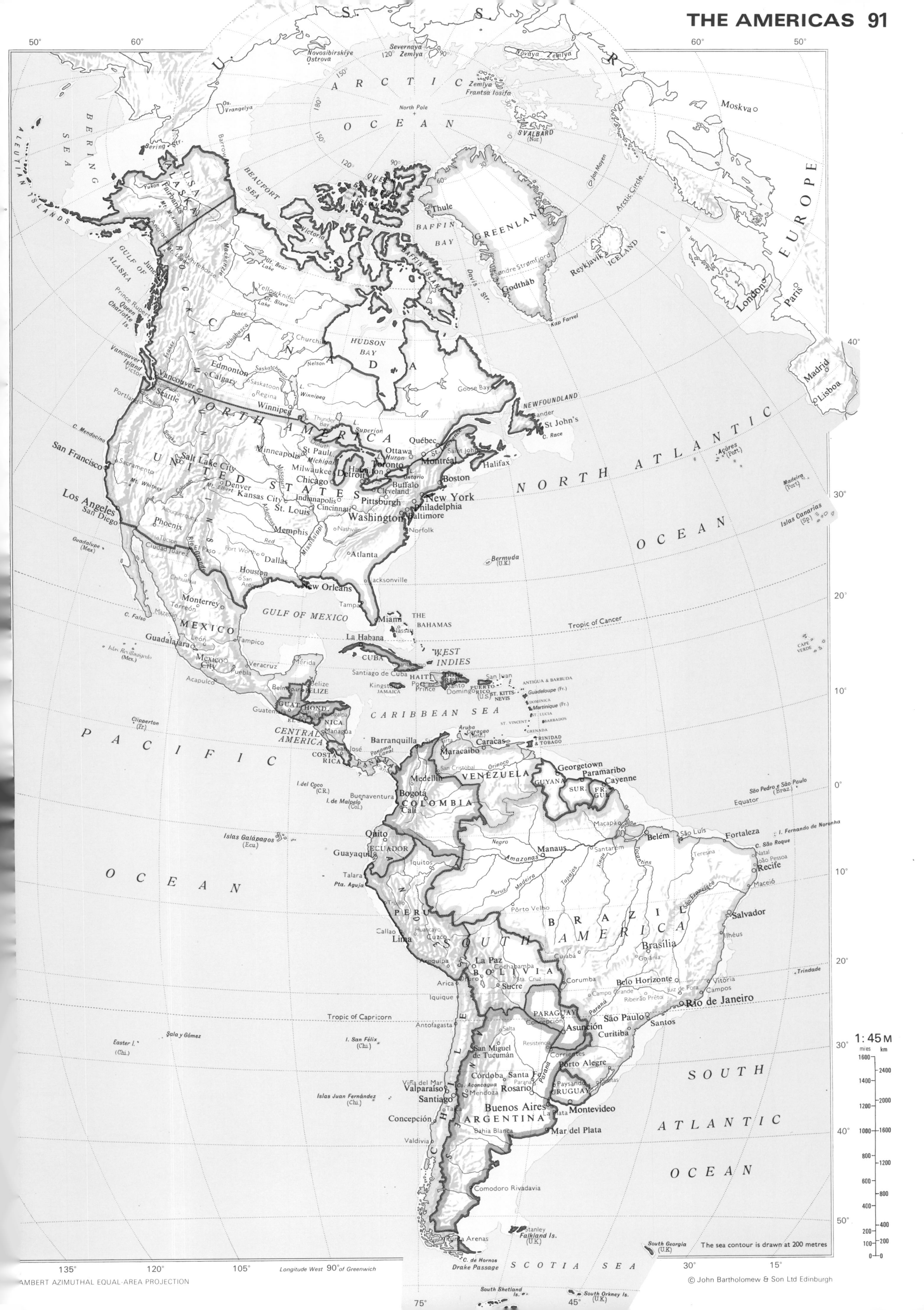

1:45M

The sea contour is drawn at 200 metres

LAMBERT AZIMUTHAL EQUAL-AREA PROJECTION

Longitude West 90° of Greenwich

© John Bartholomew & Son Ltd Edinburgh

© John Bartholomew & Son Ltd Edinburgh

Longitude West 100° of Greenwich

Projection by courtesy of the
National Geographic Society, Washington, D.C.

ATLANTIC OCEAN
WEST INDIES
CARIBBEAN SEA
GREATER ANTILLES
LESSER ANTILLES
LEEWARD ISLANDS
WINDWARD ISLANDS
THE BAHAMAS
BERMUDA (To U.K.)
Hamilton
CUBA
LA HABANA (HAVANA)
HISPANIOLA
HAITI
DOMINICAN REPUBLIC
Santo Domingo
Port au Prince
JAMAICA
Kingston
PUERTO RICO (To U.S.A.)
San Juan
BELIZE
HONDURAS
NIC.
VEN.
Caracas
NETHERLANDS ANTILLES
TRINIDAD AND TOBAGO
Port of Spain
BARBADOS
GRENADA
ST. LUCIA
DOMINICA
Tropic of Cancer
Straits of Florida
Yucatan Channel
Gulf of Saint Lawrence
Cabot Str.
NEW YORK
PENNSYLVANIA
OHIO
INDIANA
KENTUCKY
WEST VIRGINIA
VIRGINIA
NORTH CAROLINA
SOUTH CAROLINA
GEORGIA
ALABAMA
FLORIDA
WASHINGTON
New York
Philadelphia
Boston
Baltimore
Pittsburgh
Cleveland
Detroit
Chicago
Toronto
Montreal
Québec
OTTAWA
Halifax
Buffalo
Atlanta
Jacksonville
Miami
Charleston
Wilmington
Norfolk
Richmond
Louisville
Cincinnati
Indianapolis
Birmingham
Tampa
Orlando
Cape Canaveral
C. Hatteras
C. Cod
Long Island
Cape Breton I.
PRINCE EDWARD I.
NEW BRUNSWICK
1:12.5M
miles
km
Heights in feet
Depths in metres
115
126
128

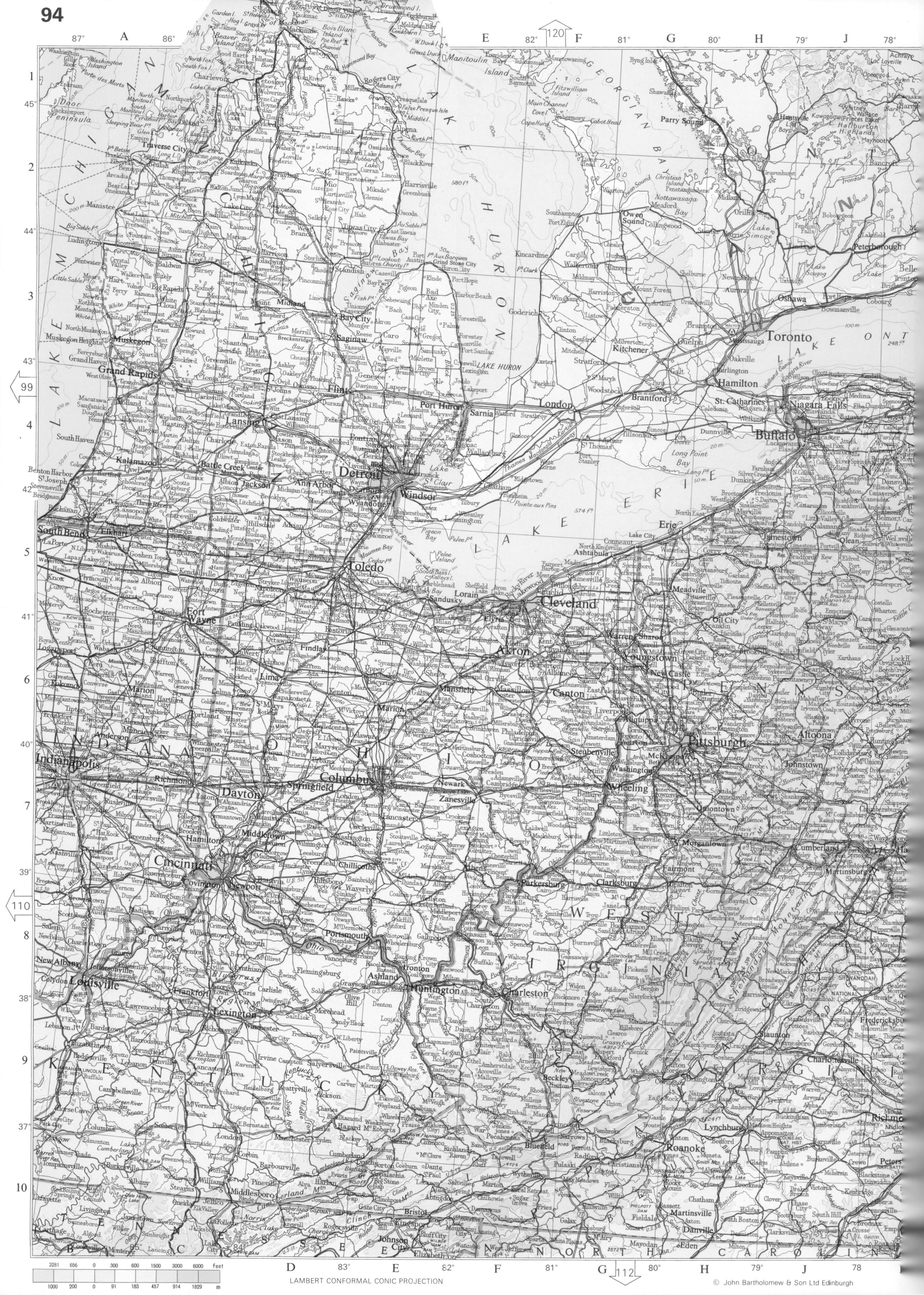
120
99
110
112
LAKE MICHIGAN
LAKE HURON
GEORGIAN BAY
LAKE ERIE
LAKE ONTARIO
MICHIGAN
INDIANA
OHIO
PENNSYLVANIA
WEST VIRGINIA
VIRGINIA
KENTUCKY
TENNESSEE
NORTH CAROLINA
Detroit
Windsor
Toledo
Cleveland
Akron
Youngstown
Pittsburgh
Columbus
Dayton
Cincinnati
Louisville
Lexington
Charleston
Huntington
Toronto
Hamilton
Buffalo
Niagara Falls
London
Kitchener
Lansing
Grand Rapids
Fort Wayne
Indianapolis
Flint
Saginaw
Erie
Wheeling
Roanoke
Lynchburg
Altoona
Johnstown
Cumberland
Staunton
Peterborough
Parry Sound
Traverse City
Muskegon
Kalamazoo
Battle Creek
Jackson
Ann Arbor
South Bend
Port Huron
Sarnia
Canton
Mansfield
Lima
Springfield
Zanesville
Parkersburg
Clarksburg
Morgantown
Fairmont
Portsmouth
Ashland
Frankfort
Bluefield
Beckley
Bristol
Kingsport
Johnson City
Danville
Martinsville
LAMBERT CONFORMAL CONIC PROJECTION
3281 656 0 300 600 1500 3000 6000 feet
1000 200 0 91 183 457 914 1829 m

Continued on Inset
121
CANADA
MAINE
NEW YORK
Montréal
OTTAWA
Portland
Boston
Springfield
Hartford
Providence
New Haven
New York
Philadelphia
Baltimore
WASHINGTON D.C.
Trenton
Atlantic City
Norfolk
Albany
Syracuse
Binghamton
Scranton
Burlington
Augusta
Bangor
Manchester
Worcester
Long Island Sound
LONG ISLAND
Cape Cod
Martha's Vineyard
Nantucket Island
ATLANTIC
OCEAN
Longitude West 76° of Greenwich
Heights in feet Depths in metres
1:3M
miles
km

ATLANTIC OCEAN

Long Island Sound

NEW HAVEN

FAIRFIELD

SUFFOLK

NASSAU

WESTCHESTER

PUTNAM

ORANGE

ROCKLAND

BERGEN

PASSAIC

MORRIS

SOMERSET

MIDDLESEX

MONMOUTH

ESSEX

UNION

HUDSON

NEW YORK

BRONX

QUEENS

BROOKLYN (KINGS)

STATEN ISLAND (RICHMOND)

MANHATTAN

SUSSEX

CONNECTICUT / NEW YORK

NEW JERSEY / NEW YORK

Long Island

Hudson River

Housatonic River

RAMAPO MOUNTAINS

BEARFORT MOUNTAIN

New Haven Harbor

Jones Beach State Park

Fire Island Nat. Seashore

Robert Moses State Park

1:500 000

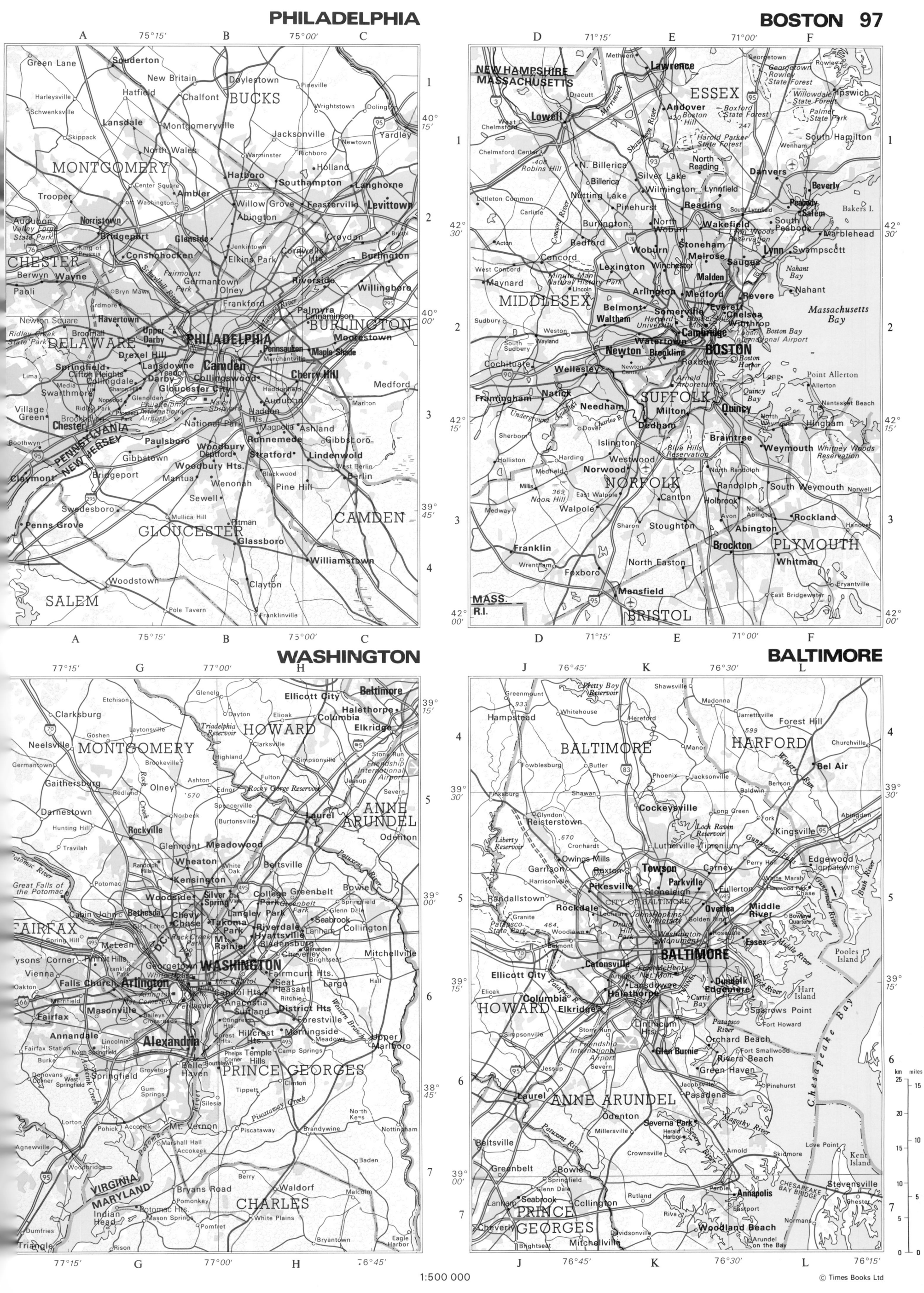

PHILADELPHIA

Green Lane
Souderton
New Britain
Doylestown
Pineville
Harleysville
Hatfield
Chalfont
BUCKS
Wrightstown
Dolington
Schwenksville
Lansdale
Montgomeryville
Jacksonville
Newtown
Yardley
Skippack
North Wales
Warminster
Richboro
Holland
MONTGOMERY
Center Square
Hatboro
Southampton
Langhorne
Trooper
Ambler
Willow Grove
Feasterville
Levittown
Fort Washington
Abington
Audubon
Norristown
Jenkintown
Cornwells Hts.
Valley Forge State Park
Bridgeport
Glenside
Elkins Park
Croydon
Burlington
CHESTER
Conshohocken
Germantown
Riverside
Berwyn
Wayne
Bryn Mawr
Olney
Frankford
Palmyra
Willingboro
Paoli
Ardmore
Havertown
Cinnaminson
BURLINGTON
Newton Square
Upper Darby
PHILADELPHIA
Pennsauken
Moorestown
Broomall
Drexel Hill
Camden
Maple Shade
DELAWARE
Springfield
Lansdowne
Cherry Hill
Medford
Lima
Clifton Heights
Darby
Collingswood
Swarthmore
Sharon Hill
Gloucester City
Haddonfield
Audubon
Village Green
Brookhaven
National Park
Hadden Hts.
Marlton
Chester
PENNSYLVANIA
Paulsboro
Runnemede
Gibbstown
Boothwyn
NEW JERSEY
Woodbury
Ashland
Claymont
Gibbstown
Deptford
Stratford
Lindenwold
Bridgeport
Mantua
Blackwood
West Berlin
Swedesboro
Wenonah
Pine Hill
Berlin
Penns Grove
Sewell
GLOUCESTER
Mullica Hill
Pitman
CAMDEN
Woodstown
Glassboro
SALEM
Clayton
Williamstown
Pole Tavern
Franklinville

WASHINGTON

Etchison
Glenelg
Ellicott City
Baltimore
Clarksburg
Dayton
Elioak
Halethorpe
Neelsville
Laytonsville
Triadelphia Reservoir
HOWARD
Columbia
Elkridge
MONTGOMERY
Brookeville
Clarksville
Germantown
Ashton
Highland
Simpsonville
Friendship International Airport
Gaithersburg
Olney
Fulton
Jessup
Redland
Ednor
Rocky Gorge Reservoir
Severn
Darnestown
Norbeck
Spencerville
Laurel
Hunting Hill
Rockville
Burtonsville
ANNE ARUNDEL
Travilah
Glenmont
Meadowood
Odenton
Wheaton
White Oak
Beltsville
FAIRFAX
Kensington
College Park
Greenbelt
Bowie
Great Falls of the Potomac
Woodside
Silver Spring
Greenbelt Park
Springfield
Cabin John
Bethesda
Cheverly Chase
Langley Park
Seabrook
Glenn Dale
McLean
Takoma Park
Riverdale
Lanham
Collington
Tysons Corner
Mt. Rainier
Hyattsville
Bladensburg
Cheverly
Mitchellville
Vienna
Georgetown
WASHINGTON
Fairmount Hts.
Oakton
DC
The Capitol
Hall
Falls Church
Arlington
Seat Pleasant
Largo
Fairfax
Masonville
Baileys Crossroads
District Hts.
Annandale
Forestville
Burke
Hillcrest Hts.
Morningside
Upper Marlboro
Alexandria
Temple Hills
Camp Springs
Springfield
Clinton
PRINCE GEORGES
Lorton
Pohick
Accotink
Mt. Vernon
Piscataway
Brandywine
Nottingham
Woodbridge
Marshall Hall
Accokeek
Baden
VIRGINIA
MARYLAND
Potomac Hts.
Waldorf
Malcolm
Dumfries
Indian Head
Mason Springs
White Plains
CHARLES
Triangle
Rison
Bryantown
Eagle Harbor

BALTIMORE

Greenmount
Pretty Boy Reservoir
Shawsville
Hampstead
Whitehouse
Hereford
Madonna
Jarrettsville
Forest Hill
BALTIMORE
Manor
HARFORD
Churchville
Fowblesburg
Butler
Jacksonville
Bel Air
Finksburg
Shawan
Baldwin
Benson
Reisterstown
Cockeysville
Long Green
Kingsville
Glyndon
Loch Raven Reservoir
Fork
Liberty Reservoir
Cronhardt
Lutherville
Timonium
Perry Hall
Edgewood
Owings Mills
Garrison
Towson
Carney
White Marsh
Joppatowne
Randallstown
Paxton
Parkville
Fullerton
Harewood Park
Pikesville
Stoneleigh
Overlea
Chase
Rockdale
CITY OF BALTIMORE
Golden Ring
Middle River
Granite
Johns Hopkins University
Rosedale
Essex
Patapsco State Park
Woodlawn
Catonsville
BALTIMORE
Dundalk
Pooles Island
Ellicott City
Lansdowne
Edgemere
Hart Island
HOWARD
Columbia
Halethorpe
Curtis Bay
Sparrows Point
Elkridge
Linthicum Hts.
Fort Howard
Simpsonville
Glen Burnie
Orchard Beach
Fort Smallwood
Friendship International Airport
Riviera Beach
Green Haven
Laurel
ANNE ARUNDEL
Severna Park
Odenton
Pasadena
Beltsville
Bowie
Crownsville
Pinehurst
Greenbelt
Springfield
Riva
Annapolis
Seabrook
Glenn Dale
PRINCE GEORGES
Cheverly
Davidsonville
Woodland Beach
Mitchellville
Eastport

1:500 000

© Times Books Ltd

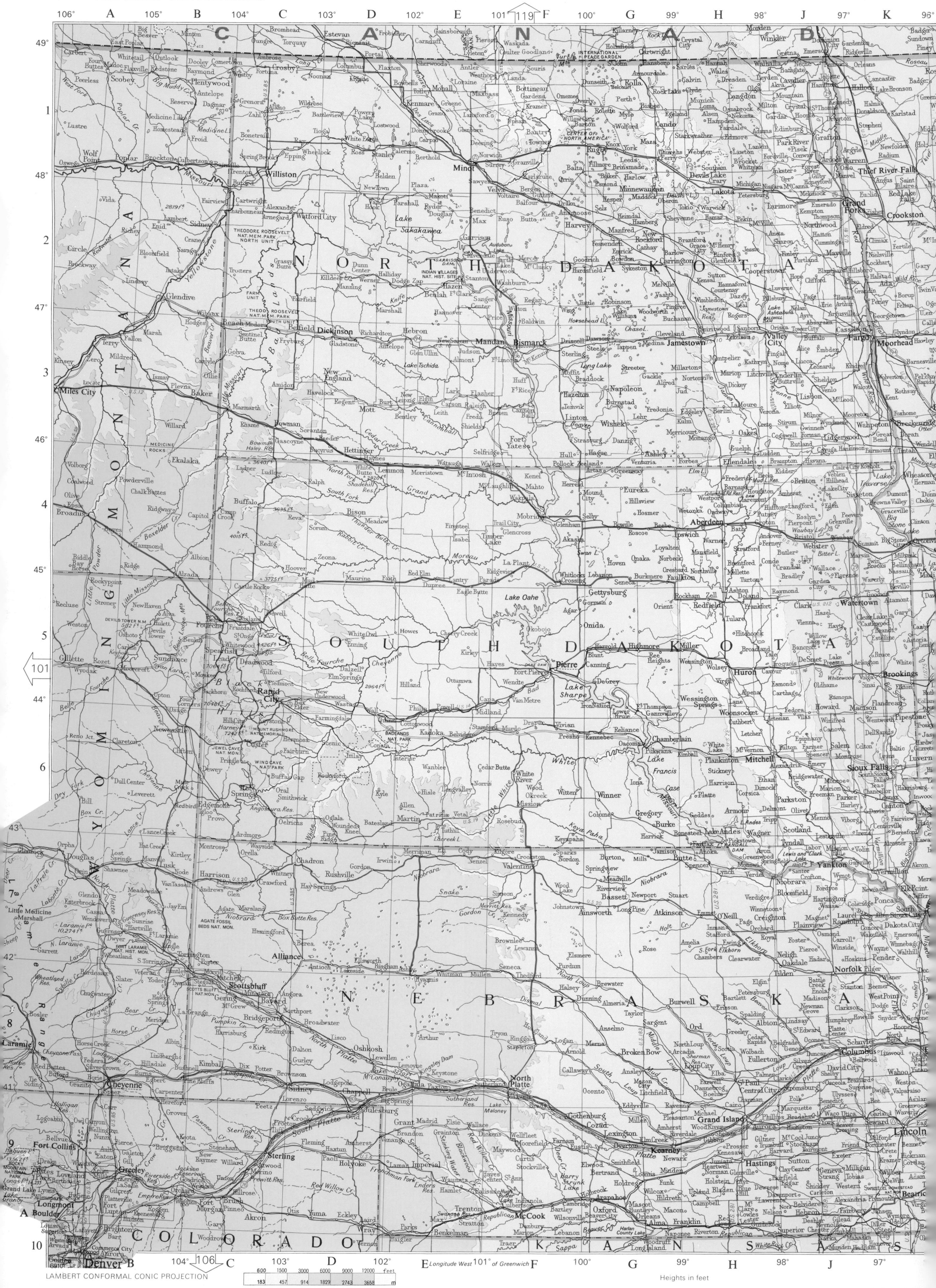

CANADA

MONTANA

NORTH DAKOTA

SOUTH DAKOTA

WYOMING

NEBRASKA

COLORADO KANSAS

Minot · Williston · Dickinson · Mandan · Bismarck · Jamestown · Fargo · Moorhead · Grand Forks · Crookston · Thief River Falls

Miles City · Baker

Rapid City · Pierre · Huron · Brookings · Watertown · Aberdeen · Sioux Falls · Mitchell · Yankton

Denver · Cheyenne · Fort Collins · Greeley · Longmont · Boulder · Laramie

Scottsbluff · Alliance · North Platte · Grand Island · Lincoln · Columbus · Norfolk · Kearney · Hastings · McCook

LAMBERT CONFORMAL CONIC PROJECTION

Longitude West of Greenwich

Heights in feet

600 1500 3000 6000 9000 12000 feet
183 457 914 1829 2743 3658 m

1 : 3 M

© John Bartholomew & Son Ltd Edinburgh

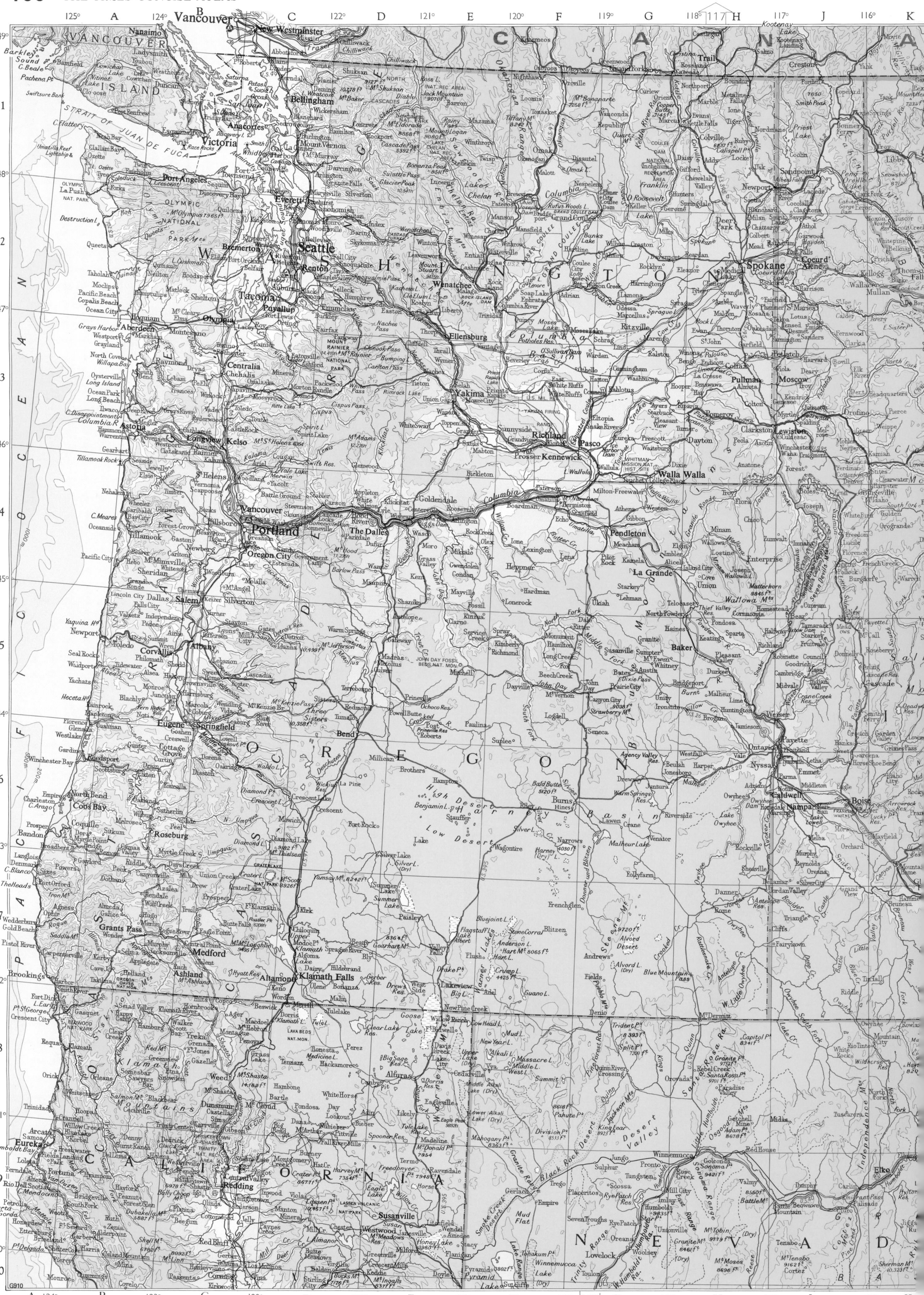

A 124° B 123° C 122° D 121° E 120° F 119° G 118° H 117° J 116° K

3281	656	0	300	600	1500	3000	6000	9000	12000	feet
1000	200	0	91	183	457	914	1829	2743	3658	m

LAMBERT CONFORMAL CONIC PROJECTION

MONTANA

IDAHO

WYOMING

UTAH

COLORADO

Kalispell
Missoula
Helena
Anaconda
Butte
Bozeman
Livingston
Great Falls
Havre
Lewistown
Billings
Miles City
Sheridan
Idaho Falls
Pocatello
Twin Falls
Logan
Brigham City
Ogden
Salt Lake City
Murray
Tooele
Provo
Rock Springs
Casper
Laramie
Rawlins

YELLOWSTONE NATIONAL PARK

GRAND TETON NAT. PARK

GLACIER NATIONAL PARK

GREAT SALT LAKE

GREAT SALT LAKE DESERT

Fort Peck Lake

Flaming Gorge Res.

Heights in feet
Depths in metres

© John Bartholomew & Son Ltd Edinburgh

1:3M

L Long West 114° of Greenwich M 113° N 112° O 103 111° P 110° Q 109° R 108° S 107° T

miles 0 10 20 40 60 80 100 120
km 0 20 40 80 120 160 200

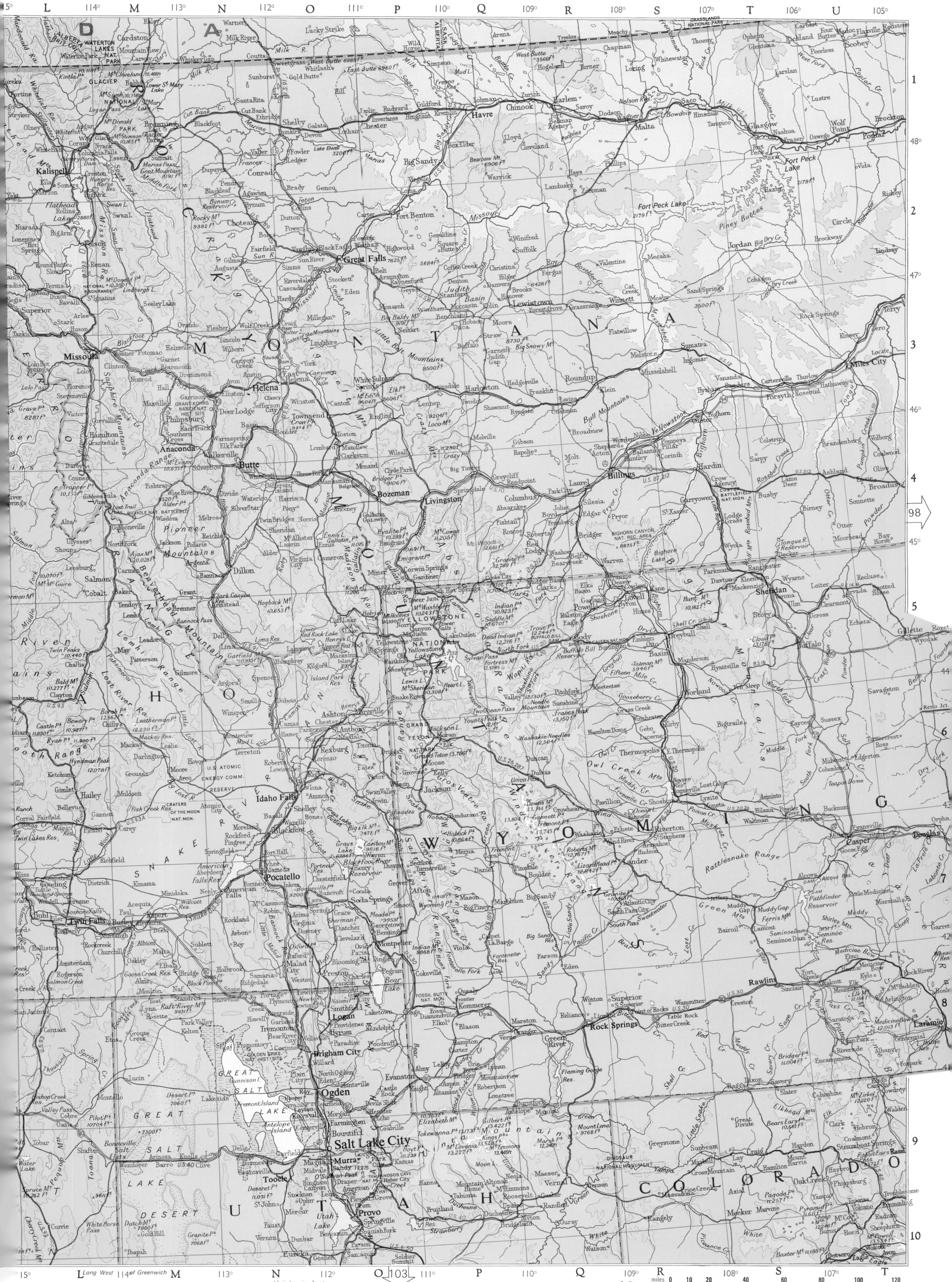

PACIFIC OCEAN

OAHU
(HONOLULU COUNTY)

1:1M

HAWAIIAN ISLANDS
(To U.S.A.)

1:9 000 000

also on page 135

LAMBERT CONFORMAL CONIC PROJECTION

Longitude West of Greenwich

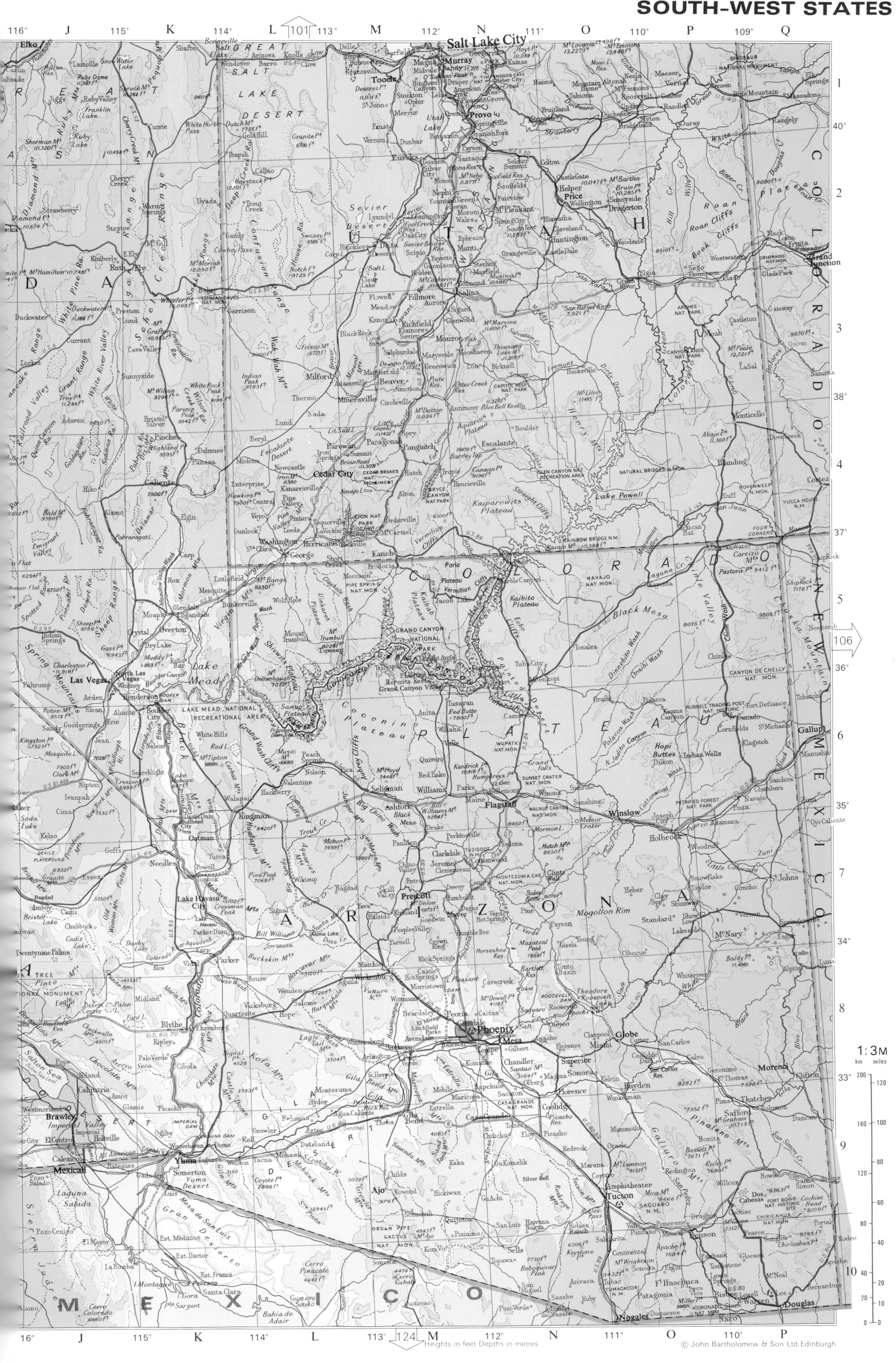

Salt Lake City
Murray
Tooele
Provo
Price
Helper
Green River
Moab
Grand Junction
Ely
Pioche
Caliente
Cedar City
St George
Las Vegas
Henderson
Boulder City
Kingman
Needles
Flagstaff
Winslow
Holbrook
Gallup
Prescott
Phoenix
Mesa
Tempe
Glendale
Chandler
Globe
Yuma
Tucson
Nogales
Douglas
Bisbee
Mexicali
Calexico
El Centro
Brawley
GREAT SALT LAKE DESERT
U T A H
A R I Z O N A
C O L O R A D O P L A T E A U
Lake Mead
Lake Powell
GRAND CANYON NATIONAL PARK
Mogollon Rim
Salton Sea
M E X I C O
NEW MEXICO
COLORADO
101
106
124
1:3M
km miles
Heights in feet Depths in metres

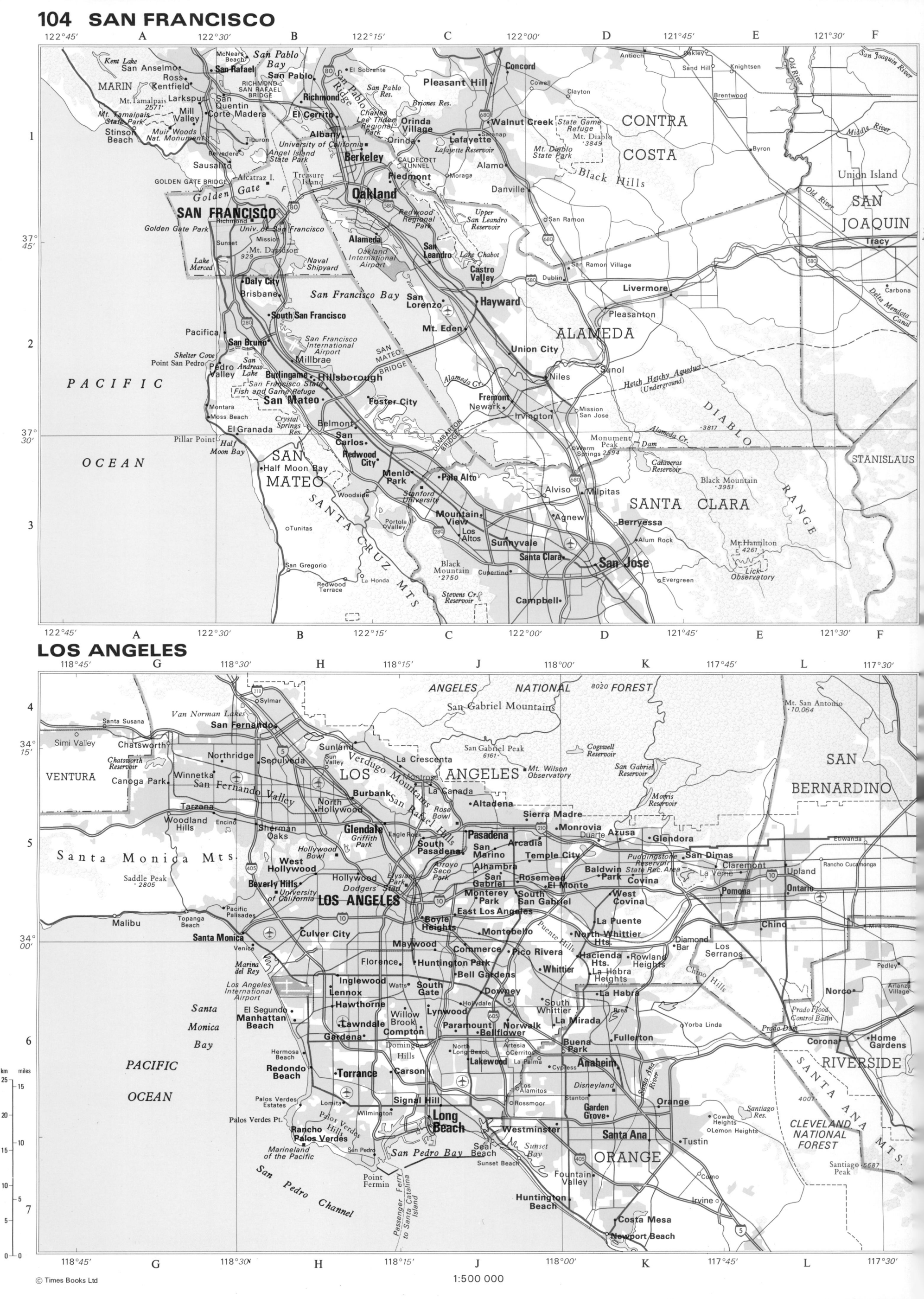

LOS ANGELES

© Times Books Ltd

1:500 000

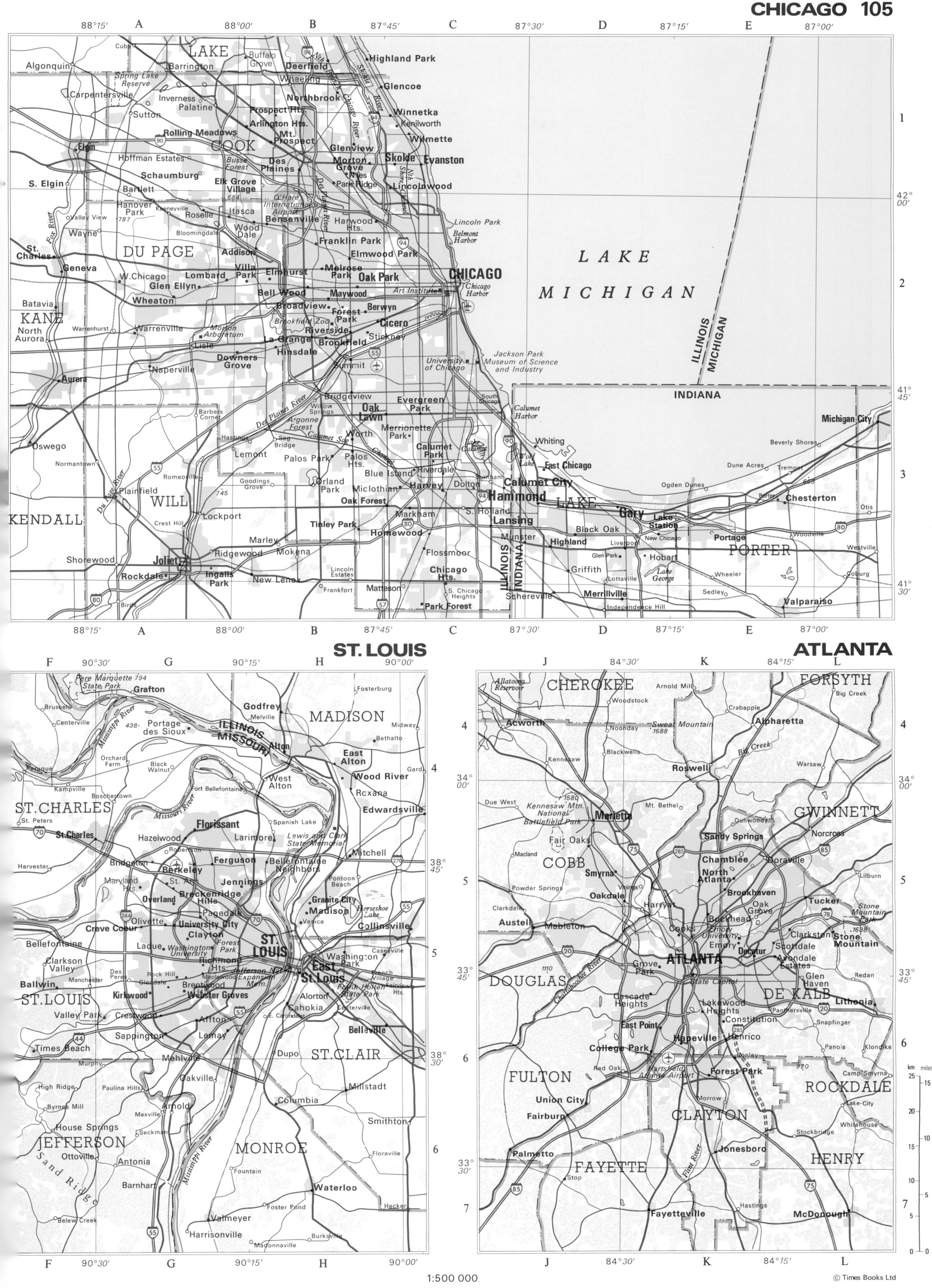

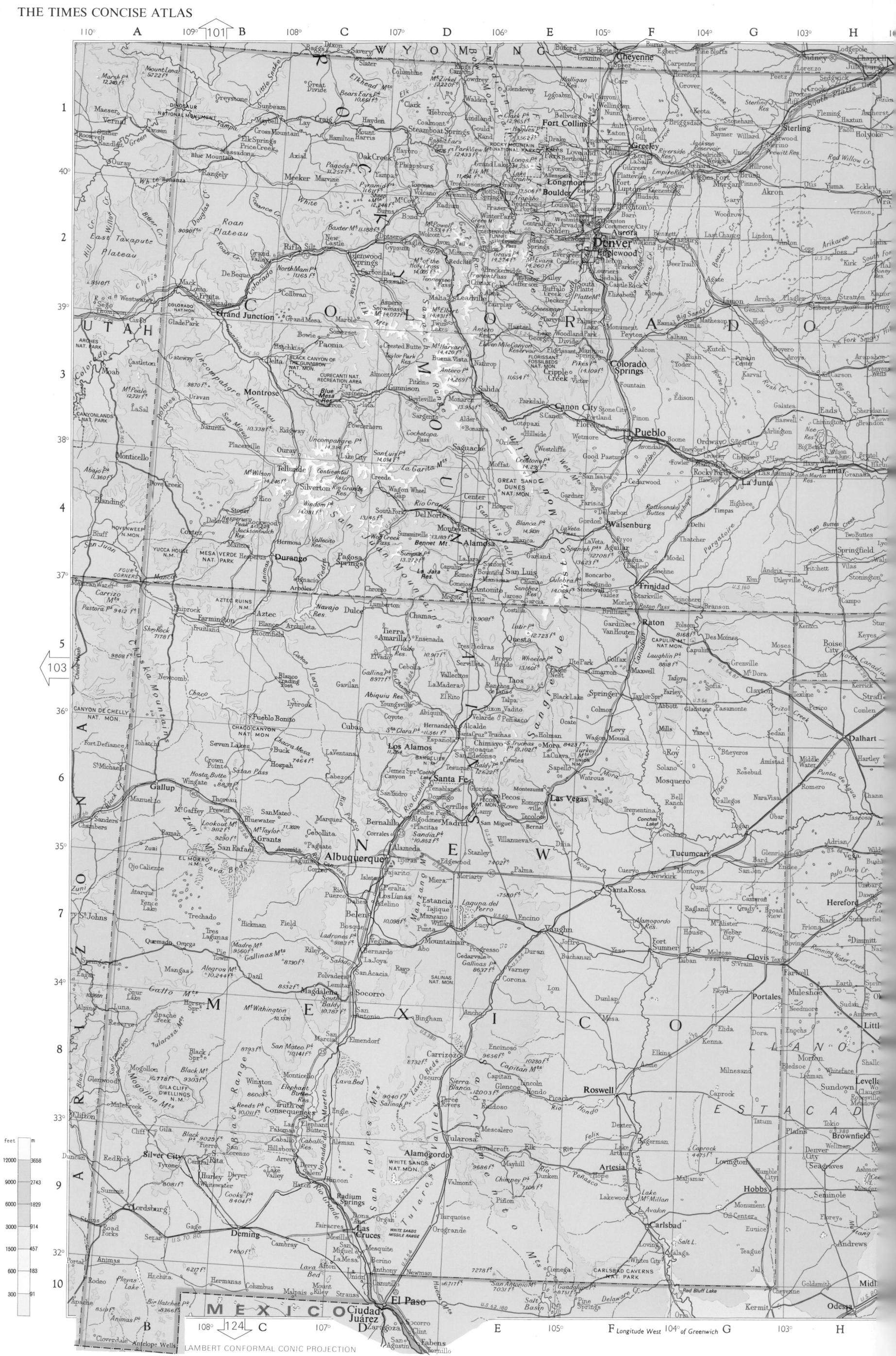

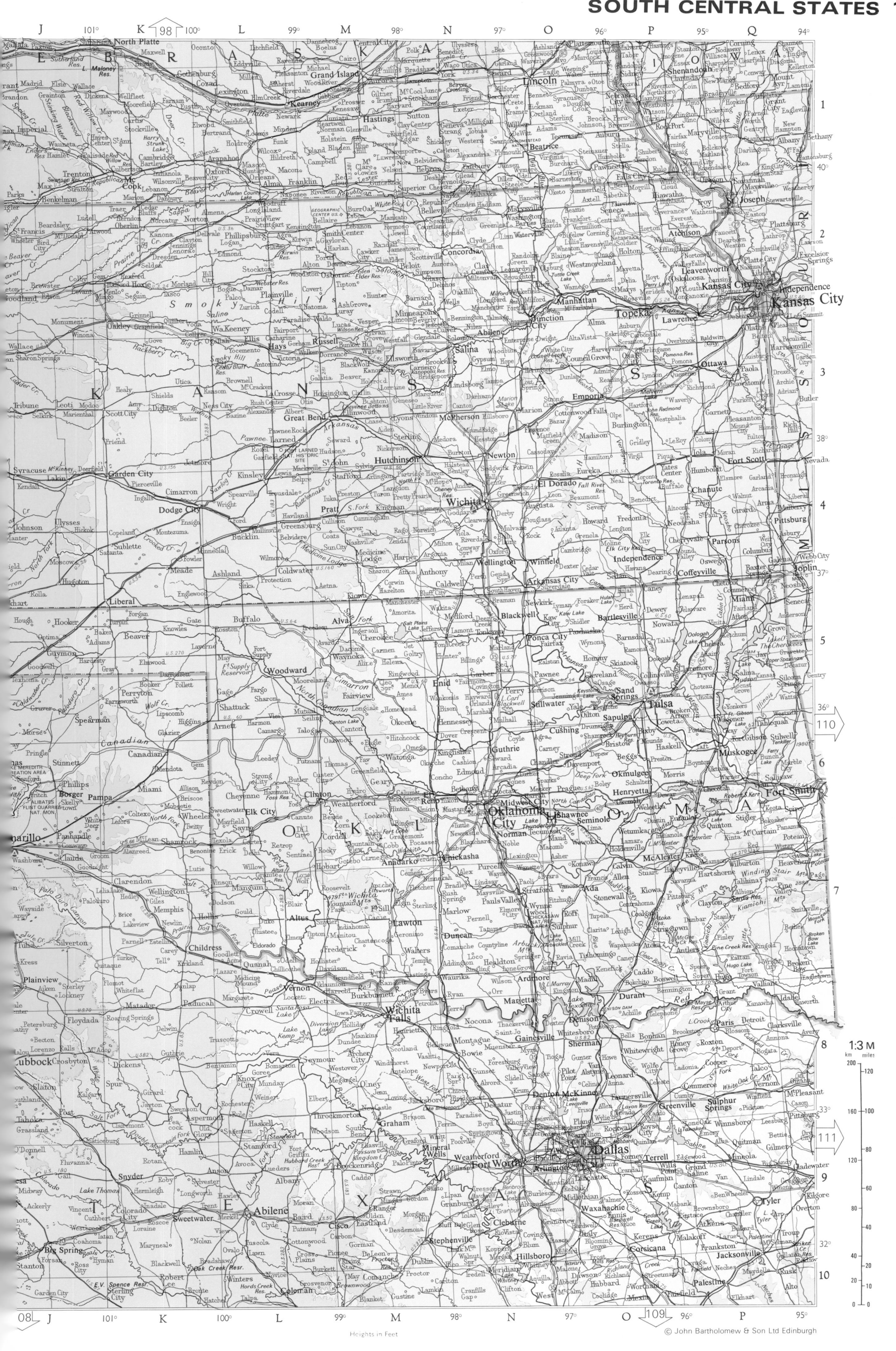
N E B R A S K A
K A N S A S
O K L A H O M A
T E X A S
I O W A
M I S S O U R I
Kansas City
Oklahoma City
Tulsa
Wichita
Dallas
Fort Worth
Lincoln
Topeka
1:3 M
km
miles
Heights in Feet
© John Bartholomew & Son Ltd Edinburgh

106
NEW MEXICO
LLANO ESTACADO
MEXICO
EDWARDS PLATEAU
Santa Rosa
Vaughn
Fort Sumner
Clovis
Portales
Roswell
Artesia
Carlsbad
Hobbs
Alamogordo
Tularosa
Las Cruces
Socorro
El Paso
Ciudad Juárez
Hereford
Canyon
Plainview
Littlefield
Lubbock
Levelland
Brownfield
Lamesa
Snyder
Sweetwater
Big Spring
Midland
Odessa
Monahans
Pecos
Fort Stockton
Alpine
Marfa
Presidio
Ojinaga
San Angelo
Ozona
Sonora
Del Rio
Ciudad Acuña
Eagle Pass
Piedras Negras
Crystal City
Childress
Rio Grande
Rio Bravo del Norte
Pecos
CARLSBAD CAVERNS NAT. PARK
GUADALUPE MTS NAT. PARK
BIG BEND NAT. PARK
WHITE SANDS NAT. MON.
WHITE SANDS MISSILE RANGE
AMISTAD NAT. REC. AREA
Northward continuation of TEXAS on same scale
Amarillo
Dalhart
Dumas
Borger
Pampa
Perryton
Spearman
Guymon
Woodward
Elk City
Clinton
Altus
Vernon
Quanah
OKLAHOMA
NEW MEXICO
LAKE MEREDITH RECREATION AREA
ALIBATES FLINT QUARRIES NAT. MON.
HOUSTON
1: 600 000
feet
m
9000
2743
6000
1829
3000
914
1500
457
600
183
300
91
0
0
656
200
3281
1000

FORT WORTH-DALLAS
1: 720 000

1: 3M

Longitude West 99° of Greenwich

Heights in feet
Depths in metres

© John Bartholomew & Son Ltd Edinburgh

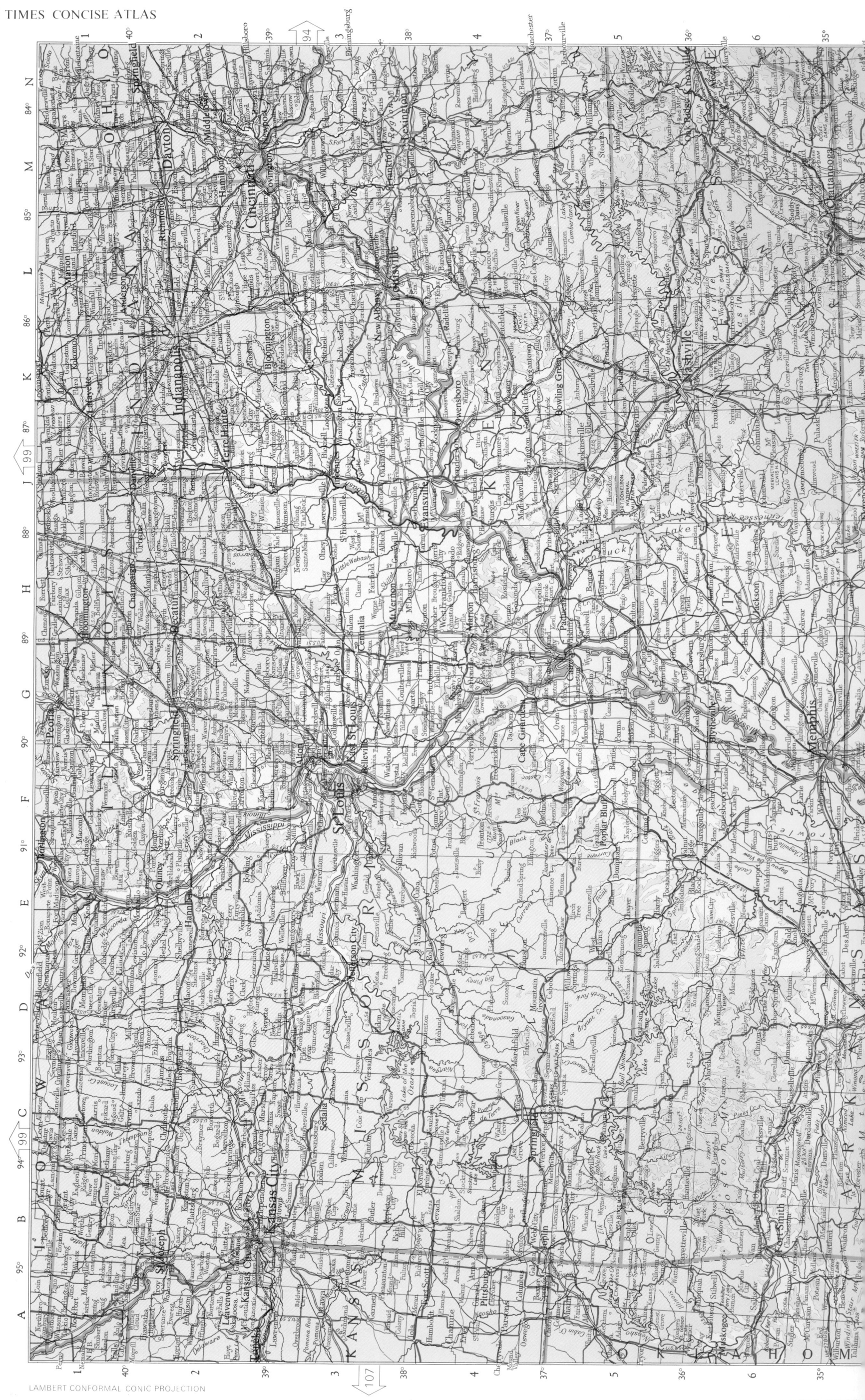

LAMBERT CONFORMAL CONIC PROJECTION

1:3M

ST LOUIS
1:300 000

NEW ORLEANS
1:300 000

Heights in feet Depths in metres

© John Bartholomew & Son Ltd Edinburgh

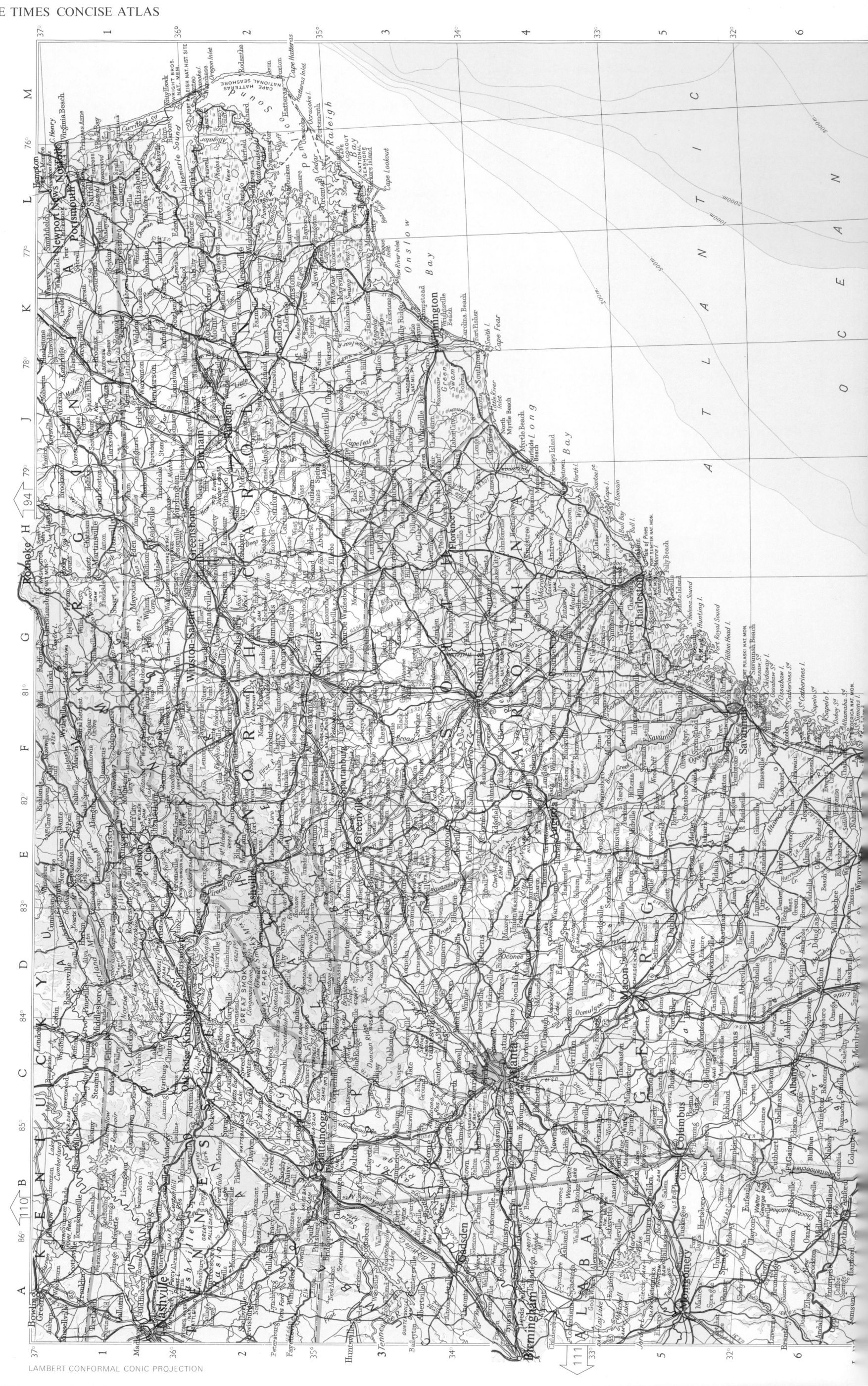

LAMBERT CONFORMAL CONIC PROJECTION

A T L A N T I C
O C E A N
Onslow Bay
Long Bay
Cape Hatteras
Cape Lookout
Cape Fear
Nashville
Chattanooga
Knoxville
Asheville
Charlotte
Greensboro
Winston-Salem
Durham
Raleigh
Wilmington
Columbia
Charleston
Savannah
Augusta
Atlanta
Macon
Columbus
Montgomery
Birmingham
Gadsden
Greenville
Spartanburg
Roanoke
Portsmouth
Newport News
Norfolk
Albany

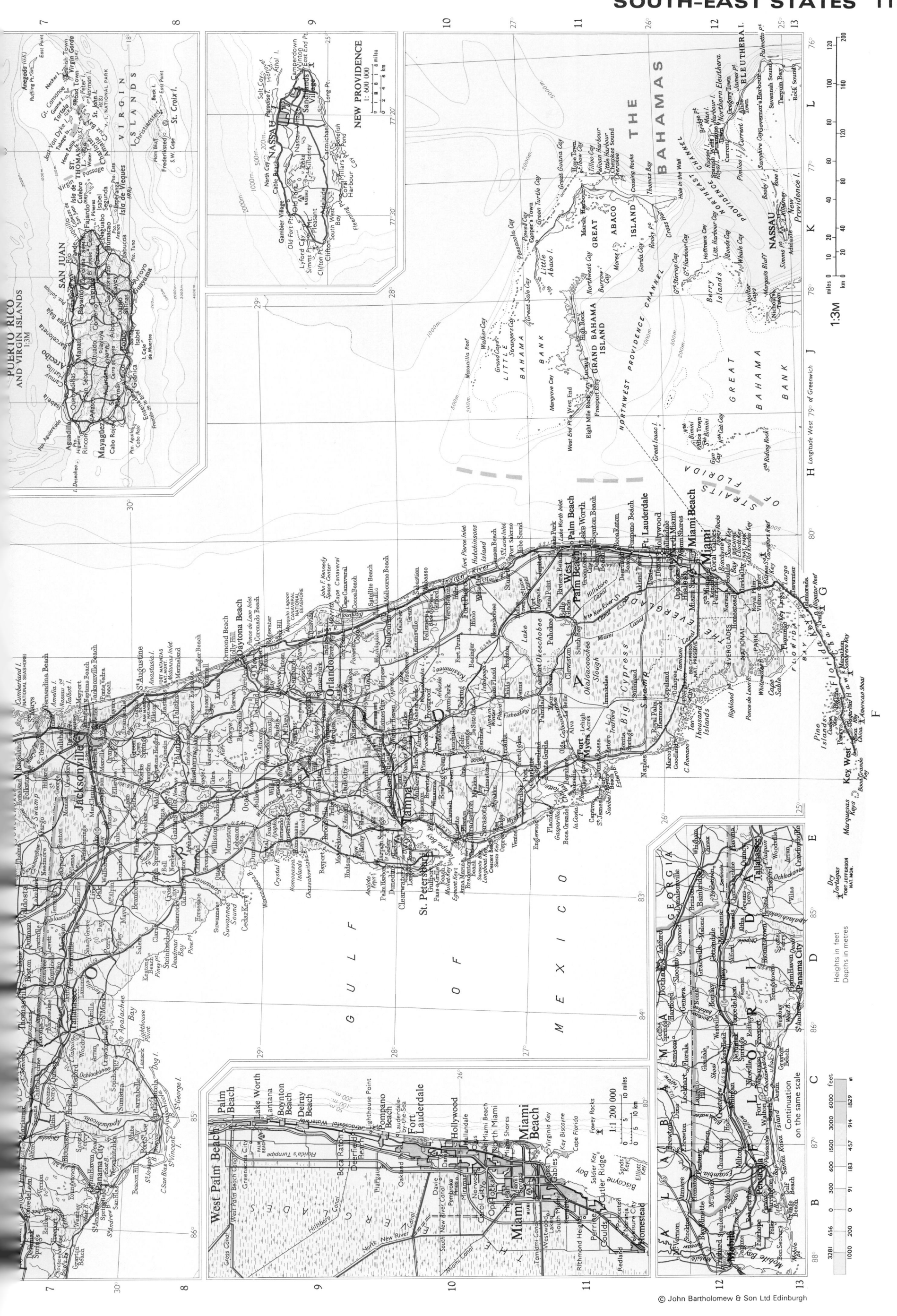
PUERTO RICO AND VIRGIN ISLANDS
1:3M
SAN JUAN
VIRGIN ISLANDS
NEW PROVIDENCE
1: 600 000
NASSAU
THE BAHAMAS
GRAND BAHAMA ISLAND
GREAT ABACO ISLAND
NORTHWEST PROVIDENCE CHANNEL
GREAT BAHAMA BANK
STRAITS OF FLORIDA
GULF OF MEXICO
Jacksonville
St. Augustine
Daytona Beach
Orlando
Tampa
St. Petersburg
Lake Okeechobee
West Palm Beach
Fort Lauderdale
Miami
Miami Beach
Key West
Tallahassee
Pensacola
Panama City
GEORGIA
ALABAMA
1:1 200 000
1:3M
Heights in feet
Depths in metres
Continuation on the same scale
Longitude West 79° of Greenwich

BERING SEA

ALEUTIAN ISLANDS (To U.S.A.)

On the same scale

Near Islands

Andreanof Islands

BEAUFORT SEA

U.S.S.R.

Chukchi Sea

A L A S K A

U.S.A.

Brooks Range

Kuskokwim Mountains

Bristol Bay

Gulf of Alaska

Kodiak Island

PACIFIC OCEAN

YUKON TERRITORY

NORTH WEST TERRITORIES

Great Bear Lake

Great Slave Lake

Yellowknife

Mackenzie Mountains

BRITISH COLUMBIA

ALBERTA

SASKATCHEWAN

Edmonton

Calgary

Saskatoon

Regina

Vancouver Island

Victoria

Vancouver

Queen Charlotte Islands

Prince Rupert

Alexander Archipelago

Juneau

Sitka

WASHINGTON

Seattle

Tacoma

Spokane

Portland

OREGON

IDAHO

MONTANA

NORTH

Helena

Butte

Great Falls

Billings

Projection by courtesy of the National Geographic Society, Washington, D.C.

Heights in feet
Depths in metres

G910

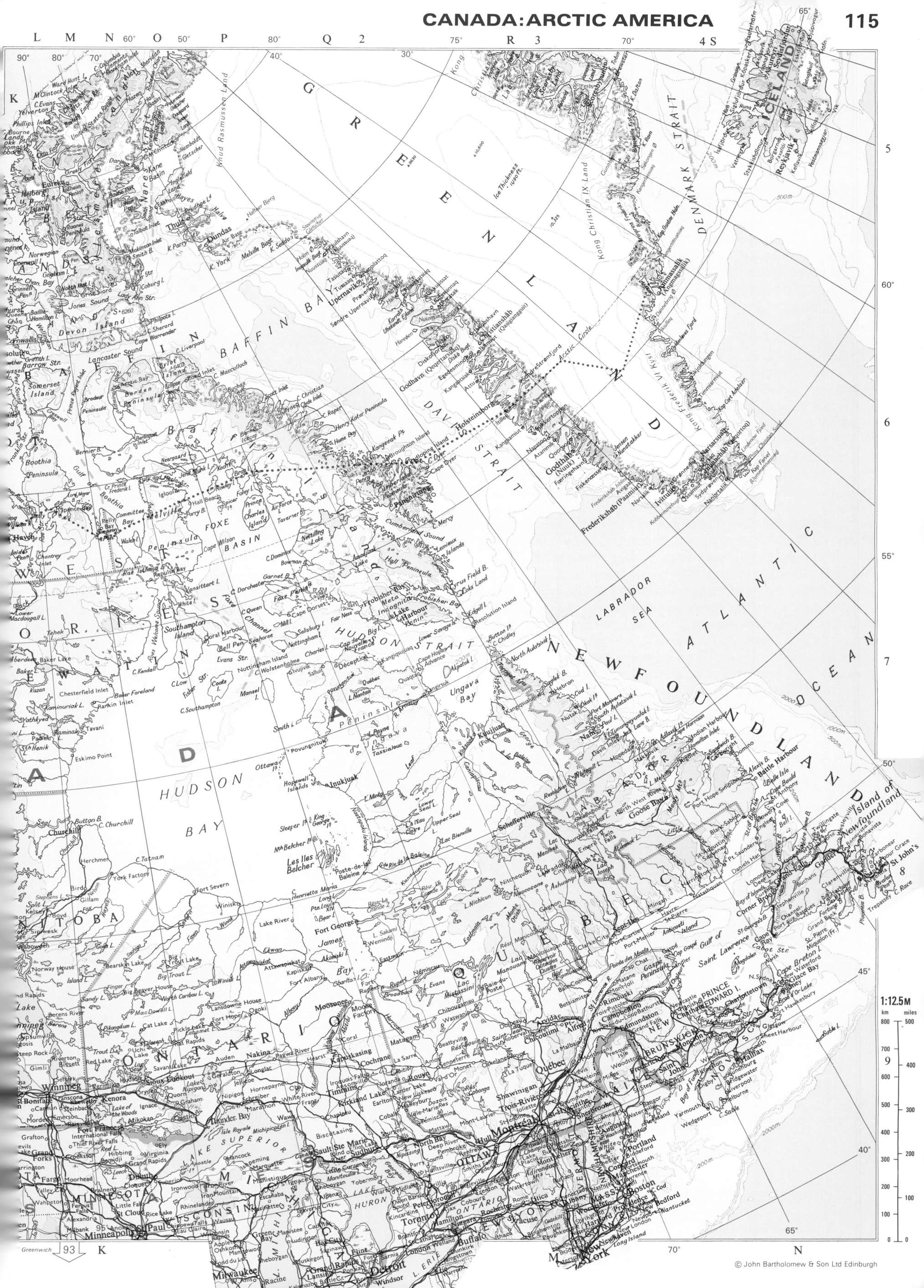
GREENLAND
ICELAND
Reykjavík
DENMARK STRAIT
Ice Thickness 11,190 ft.
Kong Christian IX Land
Kong Frederik VI Kyst
Arctic Circle
BAFFIN BAY
DAVIS STRAIT
Baffin Island
Devon Island
Lancaster Sound
Thule
Dundas
Upernavik
Godthåb (Nuuk)
Holsteinsborg
Frederikshåb (Paamiut)
Angmagssalik
Ellesmere Island
Kane Basin
Jones Sound
Somerset Island
Boothia Peninsula
Gulf of Boothia
Melville Peninsula
FOXE BASIN
Foxe Channel
Prince Charles Island
Cumberland Sound
Pangnirtung
Frobisher Bay
Hall Peninsula
Resolution Island
HUDSON STRAIT
Ungava Bay
Ungava Peninsula
Southampton Island
Coats I.
Mansel I.
Nottingham Island
Chesterfield Inlet
Baker Lake
Rankin Inlet
Eskimo Point
HUDSON BAY
Belcher
Churchill
York Factory
James Bay
Moosonee
LABRADOR SEA
NEWFOUNDLAND
ATLANTIC OCEAN
LABRADOR
Goose Bay
Schefferville
Churchill Falls
Island of Newfoundland
St John's
Corner Brook
Gander
Gulf of Saint Lawrence
Anticosti Island
Cabot Str.
Cape Breton I.
Sydney
Halifax
NOVA SCOTIA
PRINCE EDWARD I.
Charlottetown
NEW BRUNSWICK
Saint John
Fredericton
Moncton
QUEBEC
Québec
Montréal
Chicoutimi
Sept-Îles
Rimouski
Trois-Rivières
Sherbrooke
Hull
Ottawa
ONTARIO
Toronto
Hamilton
Kingston
Sudbury
North Bay
Timmins
Kapuskasing
Cochrane
Sault Ste Marie
Thunder Bay
Kenora
LAKE SUPERIOR
LAKE HURON
LAKE ONTARIO
L. ERIE
Winnipeg
MANITOBA
MINNESOTA
Duluth
Minneapolis
St Paul
WISCONSIN
MICHIGAN
Detroit
Flint
Lansing
Grand Rapids
Milwaukee
Buffalo
Rochester
Syracuse
Albany
Boston
Portland
Concord
New York
MAINE
VERMONT
NEW HAMPSHIRE
MASS.
Providence
Hartford
New Haven
C. Race
C. Sable
Sable I.
1:12.5M
km
miles
Greenwich
93

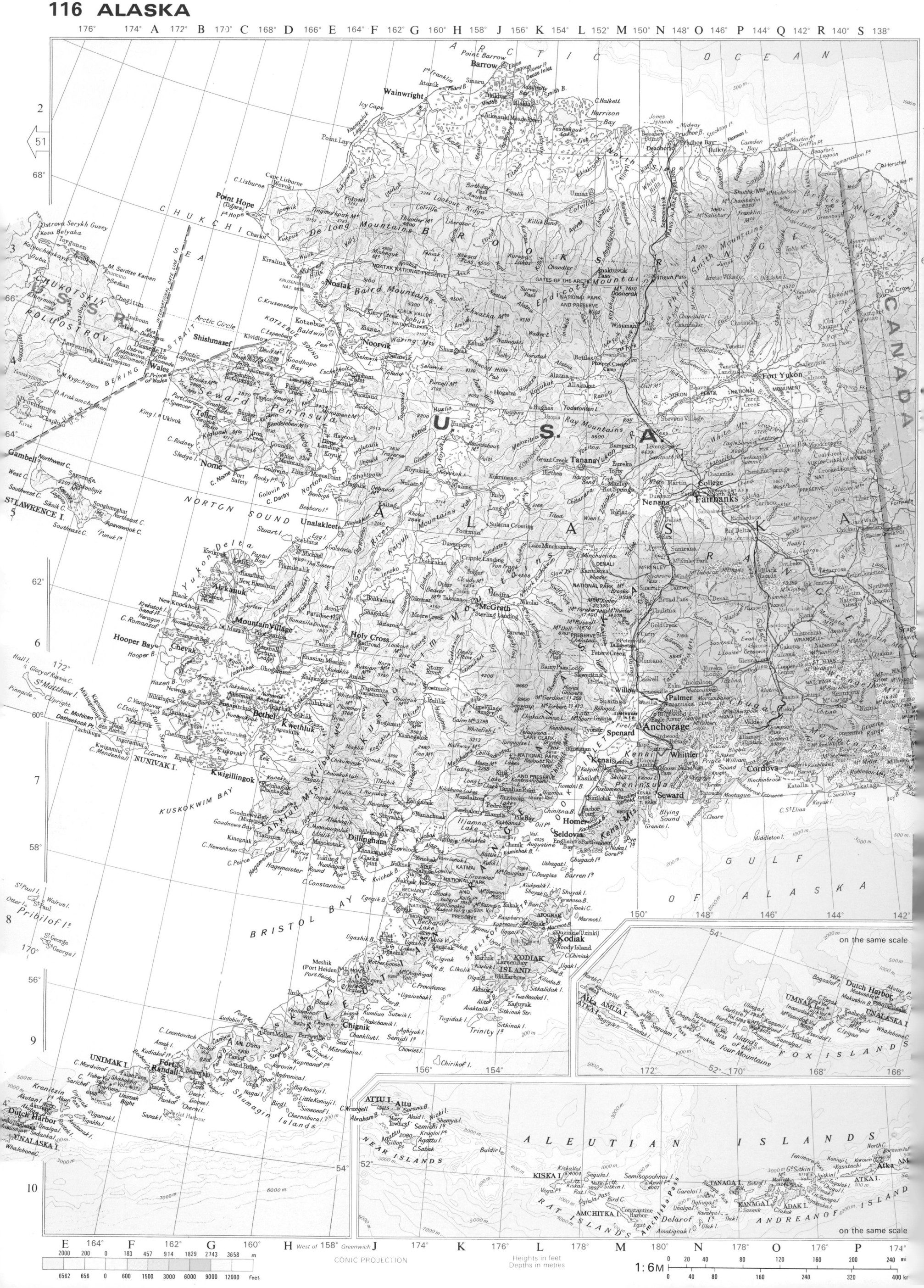

Heights in feet
Depths in metres

CONIC PROJECTION

West of 158° Greenwich

1 : 6 M

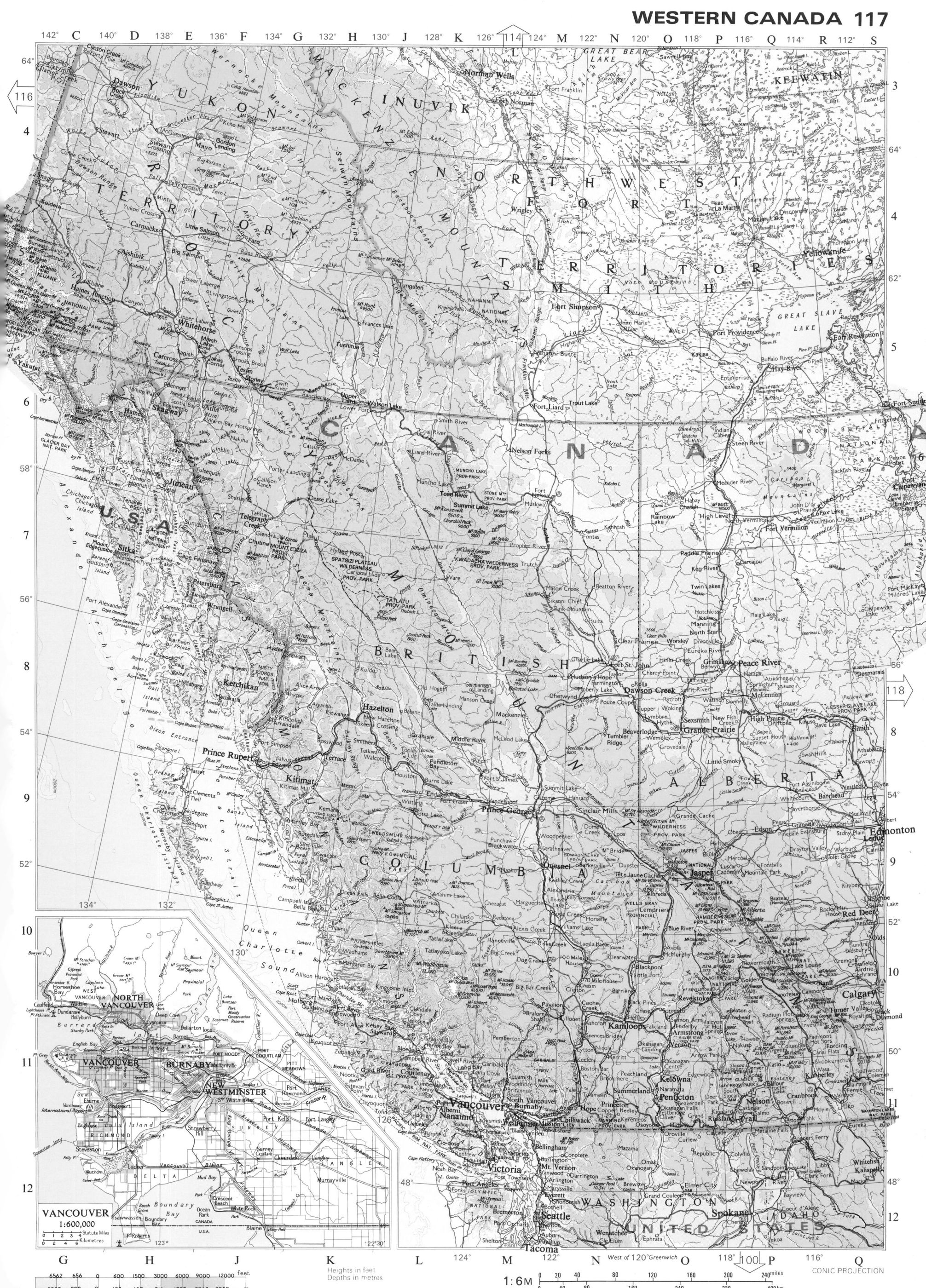

VANCOUVER
1:600,000

Heights in feet
Depths in metres

1:6M

CONIC PROJECTION

West of 120°Greenwich

WINNIPEG
1:300 000
Continuation on the same scale
ALBERTA
SASKA
BRITISH COLUMBIA
ROCKY MOUNTAINS
SWAN HILLS
CYPRESS HILLS
Edmonton
Calgary
Saskatoon
Medicine Hat
Lethbridge
Red Deer
Winnipeg
CANADA
U.S.A.
115
117
101
CONIC PROJECTION
Longitude W
feet
m
9000
2743
6000
1829
3000
914
1500
457
600
183
0
0

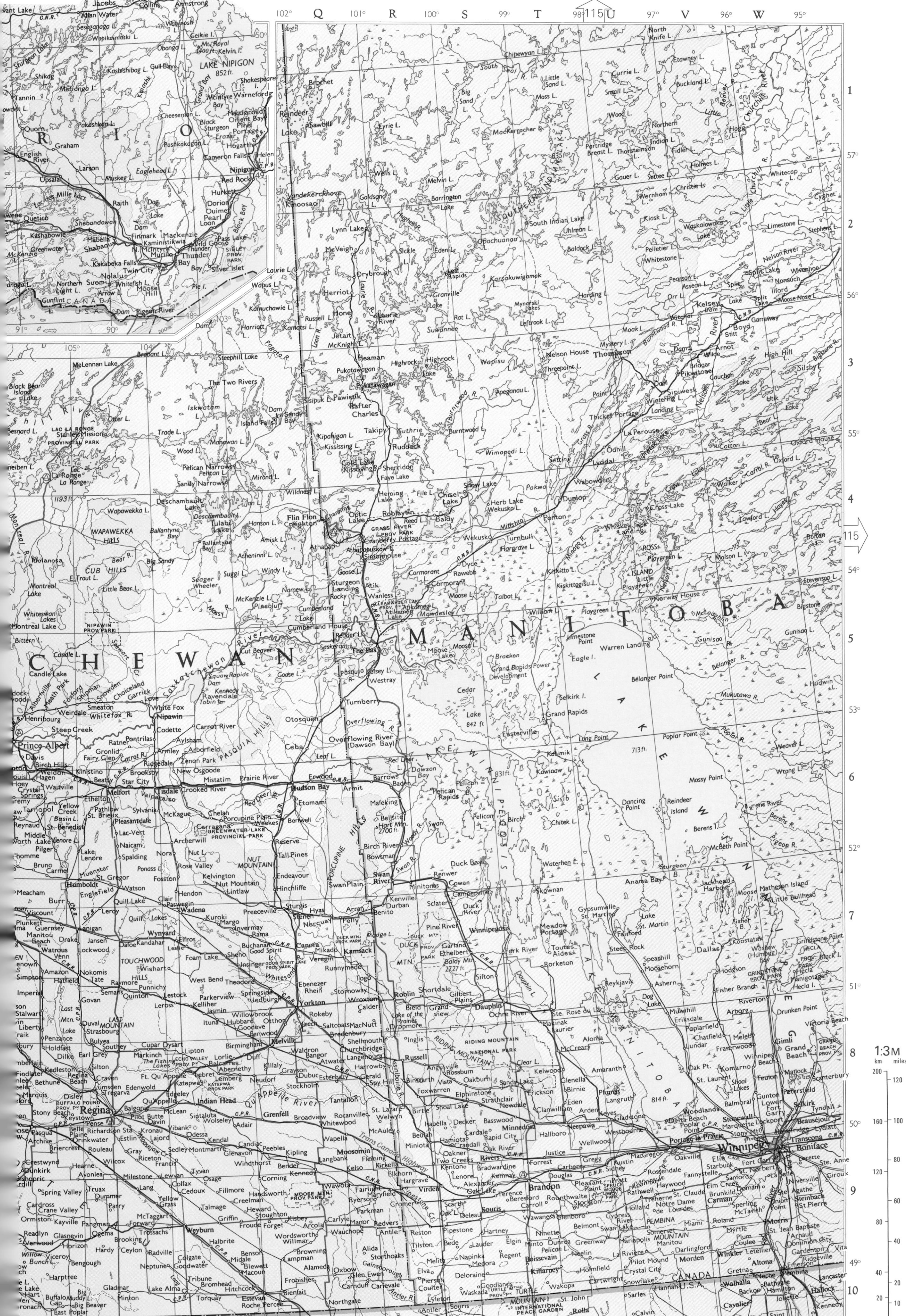

LAKE NIPIGON 852 ft.

CHEWAN

MANITOBA

1:3M

LAKE WINNIPEG
LAKE WINNIPEGOSIS
LAKE MANITOBA
Cedar Lake
Winnipeg
Brandon
Regina
Prince Albert
The Pas
Flin Flon
Thompson
Dauphin
Portage la Prairie
Selkirk
Yorkton
Melville
Weyburn
Moose Jaw
Thunder Bay
Churchill River
Nelson River
Saskatchewan River
Qu'Appelle River
RIDING MOUNTAIN NATIONAL PARK
PORCUPINE HILLS
PASQUIA HILLS
TURTLE MOUNTAIN
PEMBINA MOUNTAIN
CANADA
U.S.A.
115
98

LAKE SUPERIOR
LAKE MICHIGAN
LAKE HURON
GEORGIAN BAY
LAKE NIPIGON
ONTARIO
MICHIGAN
Thunder Bay
Sault Ste. Marie
Sudbury
Timmins
Detroit
Windsor
London
Flint
Lansing
Saginaw
Bay City
Marquette
Geraldton
Nipigon
Wawa
Chapleau
Kapuskasing
Hearst
Cochrane
Moosonee
Owen Sound
Sarnia
Port Huron
Kitchener
Isle Royale NATIONAL PARK
OTTAWA
1:240 000
HULL
VANIER
TORONTO
1:300 000
NORTH YORK
EAST YORK
SCARBOROUGH
LAKE ONTARIO
Feet
Metres
3000
914
1500
457
600
183
300
91
0
0
CONIC PROJECTION
Longitude West 81° of Greenwich

122 →

ST. LAWRENCE SEAWAY
INTERNATIONAL RAPIDS SECTION
1:600 000

Old River Course
Flood Dykes
International Boundary

GREAT LAKES &
ST. LAWRENCE WATERWAY
PROFILE

MONTREAL
1:300 000

1:3 M

Heights in feet   Depths in metres   © John Bartholomew & Son Ltd Edinburgh

L A B R A D O R
NEWFOUNDLAND
N E W F O U N D L A N D
A T L A N T I C
O C E A N
CABOT STRAIT
CAPE BRETON ISLAND
SAINT-PIERRE & MIQUELON
(To France)
ILES DE LA MADELEINE
(Magdalen Islands)
(To Quebec)
SABLE ISLAND BANK
Sable Island
LONG RANGE MOUNTAINS
Strait of Belle Isle
Belle Isle
Gander
Grand Falls
Corner Brook
Stephenville
Channel-Port aux Basques
St. John's
Bonavista
Trinity
Placentia
Burin
Marystown
Grand Bank
Fortune
Harbour Breton
Burgeo
Deer Lake
Botwood
Lewisporte
Twillingate
Fogo
St. Anthony
Port Hope Simpson
Battle Harbour
Cape Race
Sydney
North Sydney
Glace Bay
Louisbourg
Canso
Havre Aubert
Cape North
Inverness
Mulgrave
QUEBEC
1:120 000
Statute Miles
Kilometres
QUÉBEC
LÉVIS
Lauzon
Beauport
Giffard
Charlesbourg
Duberger
Vanier
Sillery
Ste.-Foy
Bergerville
Neilsonville
St. Romuald d'Etchemin
New Liverpool
Chaudière Bassin
Pont Etchemin
St. David-de-Levis
Auberivière
Notre Dame-de-Levis
Villemay
Bienville
Ste.-Petronille
Everell
Ile d'Orléans
St. Laurent
Fleuve
1:3 M
km
miles
West 62° of Greenwich
L
M
N
O
P
Q
R
S
T
© John Bartholomew & Son Ltd Edinburgh

PACIFIC OCEAN

BAJA CALIFORNIA

BAJA CALIFORNIA SUR

SONORA

CHIHUAHUA

COAHUILA

DURANGO

ZACATECAS

SINALOA

NAYARIT

JALISCO

MICHOACÁN

ARIZONA

NEW MEXICO

TEXAS

MEXICO

Gulf of California

Tropic of Cancer

San Diego · Tijuana · Mexicali · Yuma · El Centro · Ensenada

Tucson · Nogales · Douglas · Agua Prieta · Cananea

El Paso · Ciudad Juárez · Las Cruces · Deming

Carlsbad · Hobbs · Odessa · Midland · Big Spring · Lamesa

Hermosillo · Guaymas · Empalme · Ciudad Obregón · Navojoa · Alamos

Los Mochis · Culiacán · Mazatlán · Rosario · Escuinapa

Chihuahua · Delicias · Ciudad Camargo · Hidalgo del Parral · Santa Bárbara

Gómez Palacio · Ciudad Lerdos · Torreón · Matamoros · Parras · Monclova

Durango · Fresnillo · Zacatecas · Aguascalientes · León · Guanajuato

Tepic · Guadalajara · Chapala · Ocotlán · La Piedad · Morelia · Uruapan

Manzanillo · Colima · Tecomán

La Paz · El Triunfo · Todos Santos · Santiago · San José del Cabo · C. Falso · C. San Lucas

Tiburón · Angel de la Guarda · Vizcaíno · Guerrero Negro

Puerto Vallarta · Bahía de Banderas

MEXICO CITY
Naucalpan de Juárez · Azcapotzalco · Tacuba · Tacubaya · Coyoacán · Iztacalco · Iztapalapa · Xochimilco · Tlalpan · Villa Obregón · Mixcoac · Lomas Chapultepec
Aeropuerto Internacional · Ciudad Universitaria · Estadio Azteca
Distrito Federal · Villa Gustavo A. Madero · Juan González Romero
1:250 000
0 1 2 3 4 5 km

PANAMA CANAL
1:900 000
CARIBBEAN SEA
Colón · Cristóbal · Gatún · Gamboa · Balboa · PANAMÁ · Río Abajo
Gatún L. · Madden L.
PACIFIC OCEAN
0 2 4 6 8 10 Statute Miles
0 2 4 6 8 10 12 14 16 Kilometres
feet 164 65 0 328 656 1640 feet
m 50 20 0 100 200 500 m

feet / m
13124 / 4000
9843 / 3000
6562 / 2000
3281 / 1000
1640 / 500
656 / 200
0 / Below sea level
656 / 200
6562 / 2000

CONIC PROJECTION

Golfo de Honduras

CARIBBEAN SEA

HONDURAS

TEGUCIGALPA

NICARAGUA

MANAGUA
Masaya
Granada
Chinandega
León

Bluefields

COSTA RICA

S. JOSÉ
Cartago
Puntarenas
Limón

PANAMÁ
Colón
Cristóbal
Balboa
David
Santiago
Penonomé

Golfo de Panamá
Golfo de Chiriquí

Pto. Armuelles

GULF OF MEXICO

Arrecife Alacrán

Progreso
Mérida
YUCATÁN
Tizimín
Valladolid
Cancún
Ticul

QUINTANA ROO

Campeche
CAMPECHE
Ciudad del Carmen
Frontera
Chetumal

Bahía de Campeche

Veracruz
Córdoba
Orizaba
Puebla
MÉXICO
Toluca
Cuernavaca

Tampico
Ciudad Madero
Ciudad Mante
San Luis Potosí
Querétaro
Pachuca
Poza Rica
Papantla
Tuxpan

Monterrey
Nuevo Laredo
Laredo
Reynosa
Matamoros
Brownsville
San Benito
Harlingen
McAllen
Edinburg

San Antonio
Del Rio

Ciudad Victoria

Laguna Madre

BELIZE
BELMOPAN

Villahermosa
Tenosique

Tuxtla Gutiérrez
CHIAPAS
S. Cristóbal de las Casas
Comitán de Domínguez

GUATEMALA

Minatitlán
Coatzacoalcos

Salina Cruz
Tehuantepec
Juchitán
OAXACA
Oaxaca
Golfo de Tehuantepec

Acapulco
GUERRERO
Chilpancingo

Sierra Madre del Sur

Quezaltenango
Mazatenango
Tapachula
Antigua
GUATEMALA

HONDURAS
TEGUCIGALPA
San Pedro Sula
Pto. Barrios

Golfo de Honduras

EL SALVADOR
S. SALVADOR
Sta. Ana

OCEAN

1 : 6 M

Heights and Depths in metres

© John Bartholomew & Son Ltd Edinburgh

CURAÇAO
1:1 500 000
ARUBA
1:1 500 000
BONAIRE
1:1.5m
Oranjestad
Willemstad
Kralendijk
FLORIDA
U.S.A.
Miami
Key West
Ft Lauderdale
Palm Beach
GRAND BAHAMA
GREAT ABACO
ELEUTHERA
NEW PROVIDENCE
Nassau
ANDROS
CAT I.
SAN SALVADOR
GREAT EXUMA
LONG I.
Straits of Florida
Tropic of Cancer
HABANA
(HAVANA)
Matanzas
Pinar del Río
Cienfuegos
Trinidad
Sancti Spíritus
Camagüey
Holguín
Bayamo
Santiago de Cuba
Guantánamo
CUBA
Isla de la Juventud
Yucatan Channel
MEXICO
Cancún
I. de Cozumel
Grand Cayman
CAYMAN TRENCH
Montego Bay
KINGSTON
Spanish Town
JAMAICA
Swan Is (To Hond.)
Pedro Bank
Rosalind Bank
CARIBBEAN
Islas de la Bahía
La Ceiba
HONDURAS
Mosquitia
Cabo Gracias a Dios
NICARAGUA
MANAGUA
León
Granada
L. de Nicaragua
Bluefields
San Juan del Norte
COSTA RICA
SAN JOSÉ
Limón
Puntarenas
PANAMÁ
Colón
PANAMÁ CANAL
Golfo de Panamá
Golfo de los Mosquitos
Golfo del Darién
PACIFIC OCEAN
Barranquilla
Cartagena
Santa Marta
COLOMBIA
feet
m
13124
4000
9843
3000
6562
2000
3281
1000
1640
500
656
200
0
Below Sea Level
CONIC PROJECTION
Longitude West 74° of Greenwich
113
125
128

TOBAGO
1:1 500 000

JAMAICA
1:1 500 000

TRINIDAD
1:1 500 000

MARTINIQUE
1:1 500 000

GUADELOUPE
1:1 500 000

ST. KITTS
(ST. CHRISTOPHER)
ST. KITTS - NEVIS
NEVIS

ANTIGUA
1:1.5m.

GRENADA
1:1.5m.

BARBADOS
1:1.5m.

HISPANIOLA

DOMINICAN REPUBLIC

SANTO DOMINGO (Ciudad Trujillo)

PUERTO RICO (U.S.)

SAN JUAN

PUERTO RICO TRENCH

Milwaukee Depth 9200m

VIRGIN IS.

ST. CROIX (U.S.)

LEEWARD ISLANDS

ANTILLES

ANTIGUA & BARBUDA

MONTSERRAT (U.K.)

GUADELOUPE (To France)

DOMINICA

MARTINIQUE (To France)

ST. LUCIA

ST. VINCENT

The Grenadines

GRENADA

BARBADOS

CARIBBEAN SEA

GREATER ANTILLES

LESSER ANTILLES

WINDWARD ISLANDS

LESSER ANTILLES

ARUBA (Neth)

CURAÇAO (Neth)

BONAIRE (Neth)

Los Roques (Ven.)

Isla de Margarita

TOBAGO

TRINIDAD AND TOBAGO

TRINIDAD

Port of Spain

San Fernando

VENEZUELA

Maracaibo

Lago de Maracaibo

Golfo de Venezuela

CARACAS

Barquisimeto

Valencia

Maracay

Barcelona

Cumaná

Ciudad Bolívar

Río Orinoco

GUY.

TURKS & CAICOS ISLANDS (U.K.)

Silver Bank

PART OF MAINLAND VENEZUELA

GULF OF PARIA

1:6M

Heights and Depths in metres

© John Bartholomew & Son Ltd Edinburgh

LAMBERT AZIMUTHAL EQUAL AREA PROJECTION   Heights in metres

G 55° H Longitude West 50° of Greenwich J 45° K 40° L 35° M

N O R T H   A T L A N T I C

O C E A N

SURINAME

FRENCH GUIANA

Paramaribo

Cayenne

Serra Tumucumaque

AMAPÁ

Macapá

Mouths of the Amazon

I. de Marajó

Belém (Pará)

São Luis

Fortaleza (Ceará)

Sobral

Teresina

Parnaíba

Natal

B R A Z I L

P A R Á

M A R A N H Ã O

P I A U Í

C E A R Á

RIO GRANDE DO NORTE

P A R A Í B A

João Pessoa

Campina Grande

Olinda

Recife (Pernambuco)

Jaboatão

Caruaru

P E R N A M B U C O

Maceió

Aracaju

A L A G O A S

S E R G I P E

Santarém

Óbidos

Amazonas

Altamira

Marabá

Imperatriz

Carolina

M A T O   G R O S S O

Planalto de Mato Grosso

Cuiabá

Corumbá

Campo Grande

G O I Á S

Goiás

Brasília

Anápolis

Goiânia

B A H I A

Salvador (Bahia)

Ilhéus

Itabuna

Jequié

Vitória da Conquista

Montes Claros

Diamantina

Governador Valadares

M I N A S   G E R A I S

E S P Í R I T O   S A N T O

Vitória

Belo Horizonte

Uberlândia

Uberaba

Araguari

Poços de Caldas

Ribeirão Prêto

Campos

Volta Redonda

Petrópolis

RIO DE JANEIRO

Rio de Janeiro

Niterói

São Paulo

Santos

Sorocaba

Campinas

Presidente Prudente

Londrina

P A R A N Á

U R U G U A Y

Fernando de Noronha (To Brazil)

Equator

1:12 M

km   miles
800 — 480
640 — 400
480 — 320
320 — 200
160 — 80
0 — 0

I. Martin Vaz

I. Trindade (To Brazil)

© John Bartholomew & Son Ltd Edinburgh

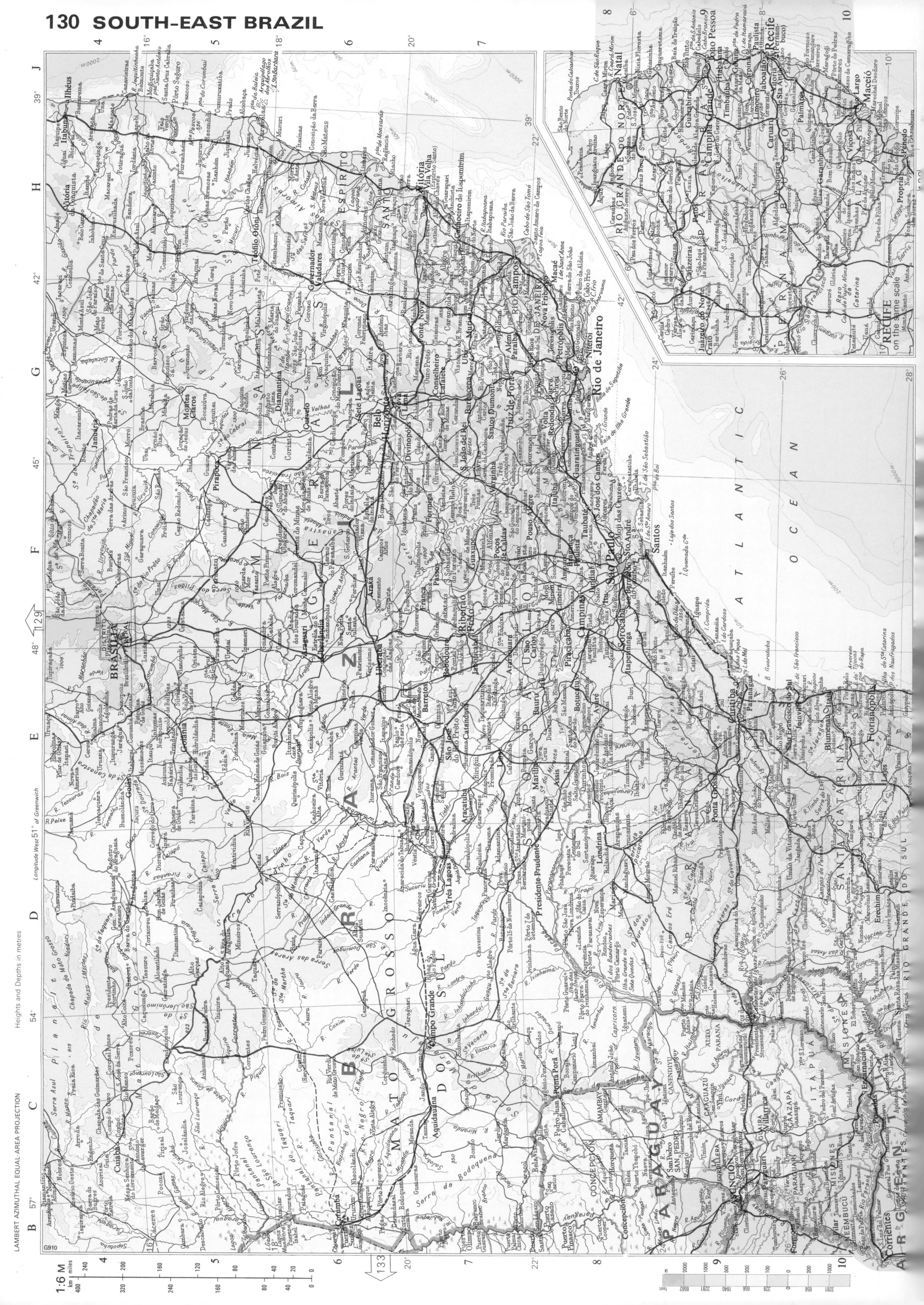
LAMBERT AZIMUTHAL EQUAL-AREA PROJECTION
Heights and Depths in metres
Longitude West 51° of Greenwich
1:6 M
129
133
BRASÍLIA
DISTRITO FEDERAL
Goiânia
Belo Horizonte
Rio de Janeiro
Niterói
São Paulo
Santos
Campinas
Curitiba
Florianópolis
Vitória
Campo Grande
Asunción
Corrientes
Recife
Natal
João Pessoa
Maceió
RECIFE on the same scale
MATO GROSSO DO SUL
MINAS GERAIS
SÃO PAULO
PARANÁ
SANTA CATARINA
RIO GRANDE DO SUL
ESPÍRITO SANTO
RIO DE JANEIRO
PARAGUAY
ARGENTINA
BRAZIL
ATLANTIC OCEAN
G910

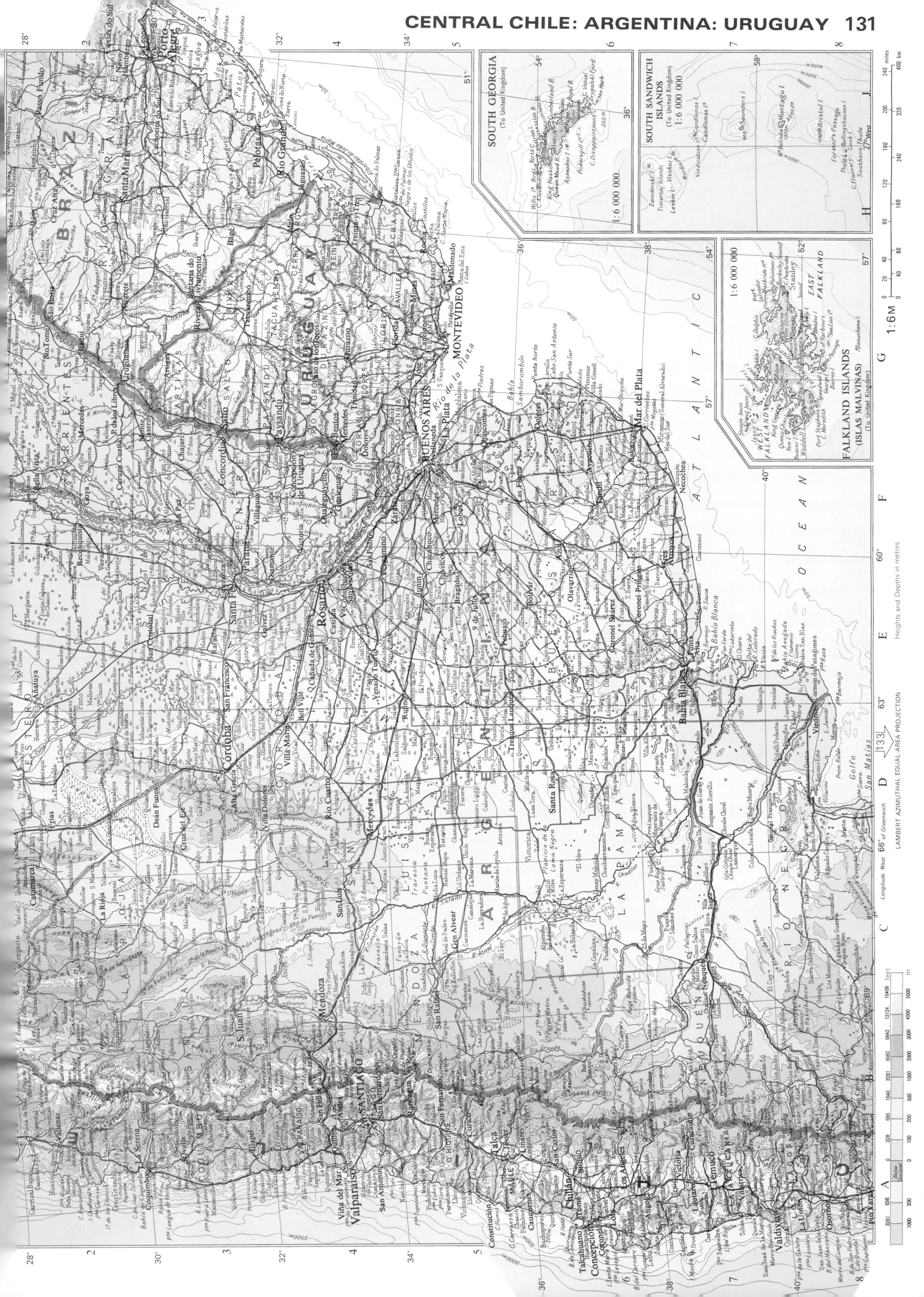

SOUTH GEORGIA
(To United Kingdom)
1:6 000 000

SOUTH SANDWICH
ISLANDS
(To United Kingdom)
1:6 000 000

FALKLAND ISLANDS
(ISLAS MALVINAS)
(To United Kingdom)
1:6 000 000

1:6M

LAMBERT AZIMUTHAL EQUAL-AREA PROJECTION

Heights and Depths in metres

RIO DE JANEIRO

A 43°30' B 43°15' C 43°00' D

RIO DE JANEIRO
NOVA IGUAÇU
DUQUE DE CAXIAS
MAGÉ
ITABORAÍ

Nova Iguaçu
Belford Roxo
Coelho da Rocha
Mesquita
Duque de Caxias
São João de Meriti
Nilópolis
Olinda
São Mateus

GUANABARA

BAÍA DE GUANABARA

ILHA DO GOVERNADOR

São Gonçalo
Sete Pontes
Neves

RIO DE JANEIRO

Niterói

NITERÓI

MARICÁ

SÃO GONÇALO

Copacabana
Ipanema
Leblon
Gávea
Pedra da Gávea

Praia dos Bandeirantes
Lagoa de Marapendi

ATLANTIC OCEAN

A 43°30' B 43°15' C 43°00' D

BUENOS AIRES

A 58°45' B 58°30' C 58°15' D

ESCOBAR
Pilar
PILAR
Tigre
TIGRE
San Fernando
SAN FERNANDO
San Isidro
SAN ISIDRO
Olivos
Vicente López
VICENTE LÓPEZ

RÍO DE LA PLATA

General Sarmiento
José C Paz
Villa de Mayo
GENERAL SARMIENTO

GENERAL SAN MARTÍN
General San Martín

BUENOS

Hurlingham
Caseros
TRES DE FEBRERO

DISTRITO FEDERAL

BUENOS AIRES

General Rodríguez
GENERAL RODRÍGUEZ

Moreno
MORENO
Merlo
MORÓN
Morón
San Justo
Avellaneda
AVELLANEDA
Lanús

AIRES
MERLO

Marcos Paz
MARCOS PAZ

Rafael Castillo
MATANZA

Laferrere
Lomas de Zamora
LOMAS DE ZAMORA

Quilmes
QUILMES

Berazategui
BERAZATEGUI

ESTEBAN ECHEVERRIA
Esteban Echeverría
EZEIZA

ALMIRANTE BROWN
Almirante Brown
Burzaco

Florencio Varela
FLORENCIO VARELA

A 58°45' B 58°30' C 58°15' D

1:300 000

© Times Books Ltd

G910

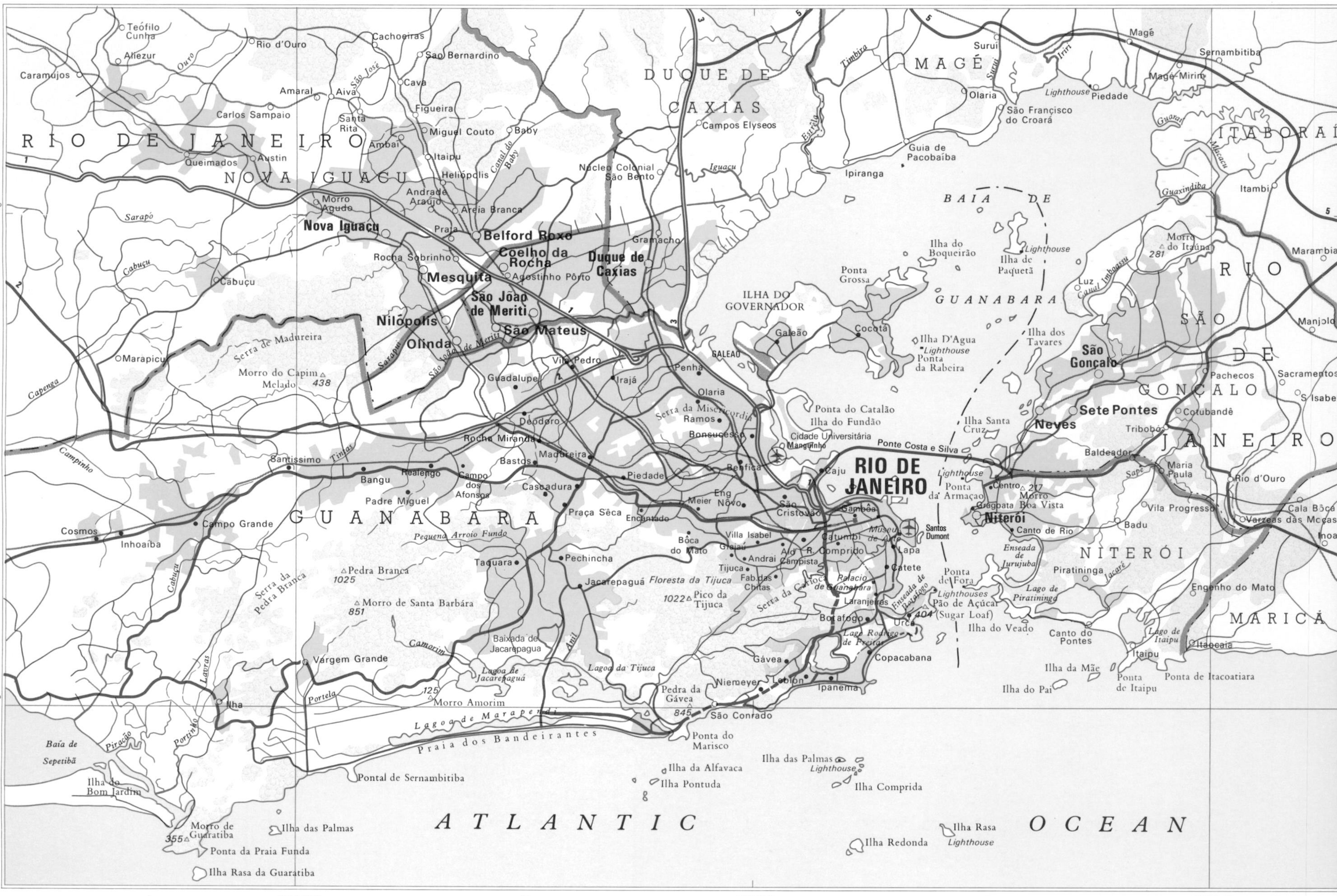

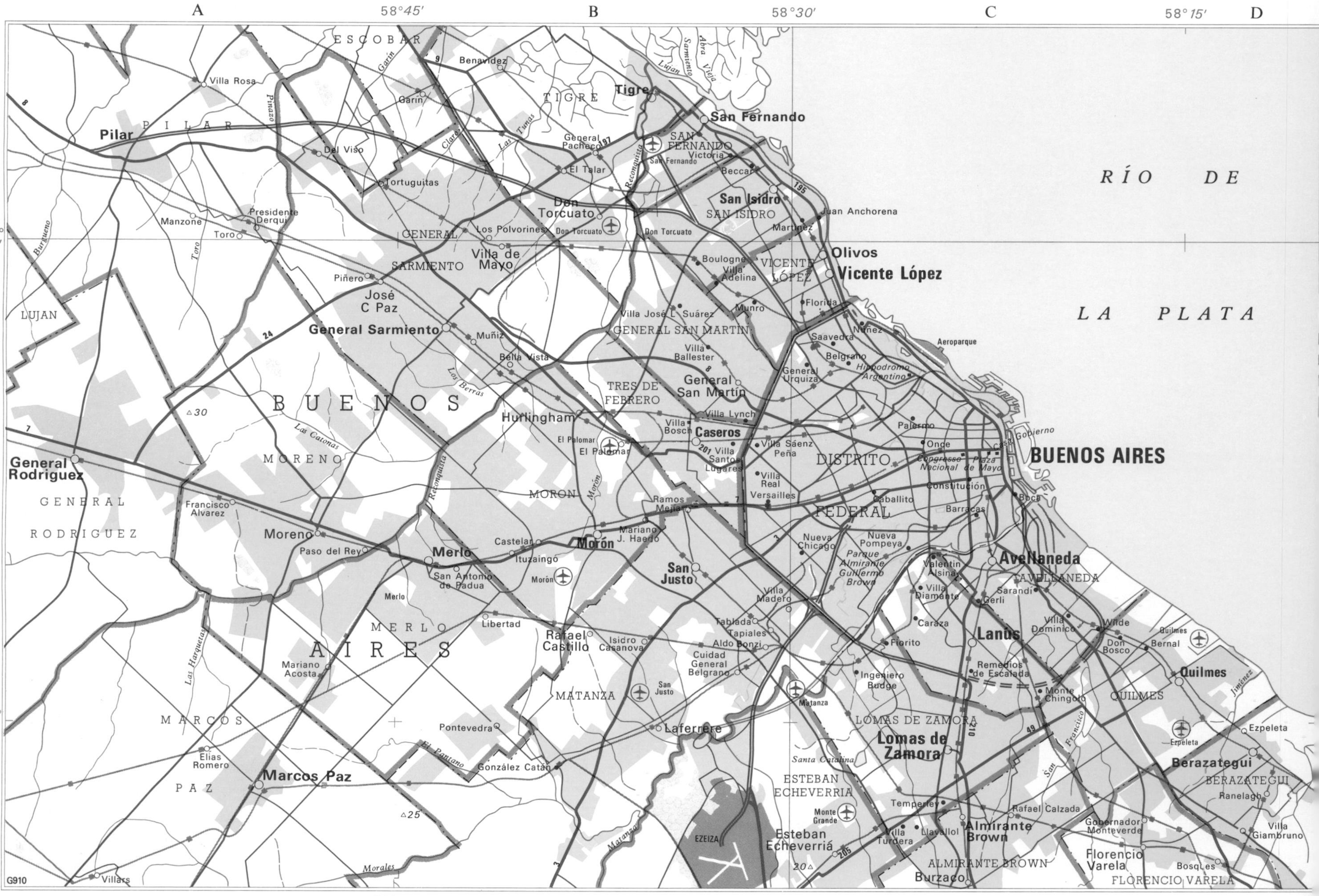

on the same scale
San Félix
San Ambrosio
(To Chile)
Tropic of Capricorn
SOUTH PACIFIC OCEAN
SOUTH ATLANTIC OCEAN
BOLIVIA
PARAGUAY
BRAZIL
URUGUAY
ARGENTINA
CHILE
Antofagasta
Asunción
Córdoba
Rosario
Mendoza
Valparaíso
Santiago
Buenos Aires
Montevideo
La Plata
Mar del Plata
Bahía Blanca
Porto Alegre
Curitiba
São Paulo
Santos
Concepción
Valdivia
Puerto Montt
Comodoro Rivadavia
Río Gallegos
Punta Arenas
Tierra del Fuego
Golfo San Matías
Golfo San Jorge
FALKLAND ISLANDS
(ISLAS MALVINAS)
(To U.K.)
West Falkland
East Falkland
South Georgia
(To U.K.)
Shag Rocks
(To U.K.)
Islas Juan Fernández
(To Chile)
Alejandro Selkirk
(Mas Afuera)
Robinson Crusoe
(Mas Atierra)
Sta. Clara
C. de Hornos
(C. Horn)
I. Diego Ramírez
LAMBERT AZIMUTHAL EQUAL AREA PROJECTION
Heights in metres
1:12M
miles
km
feet
m
Below Sea Level

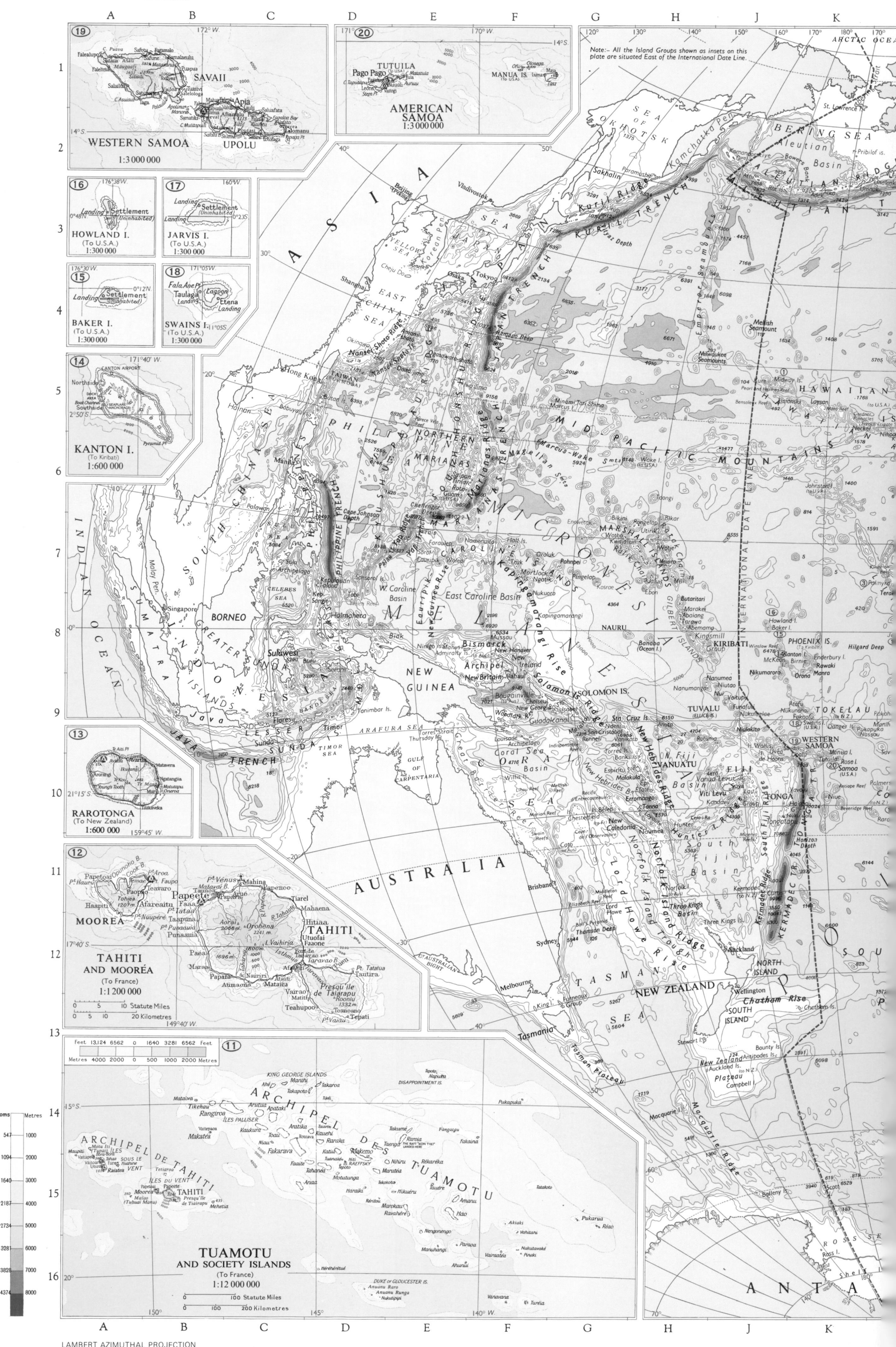

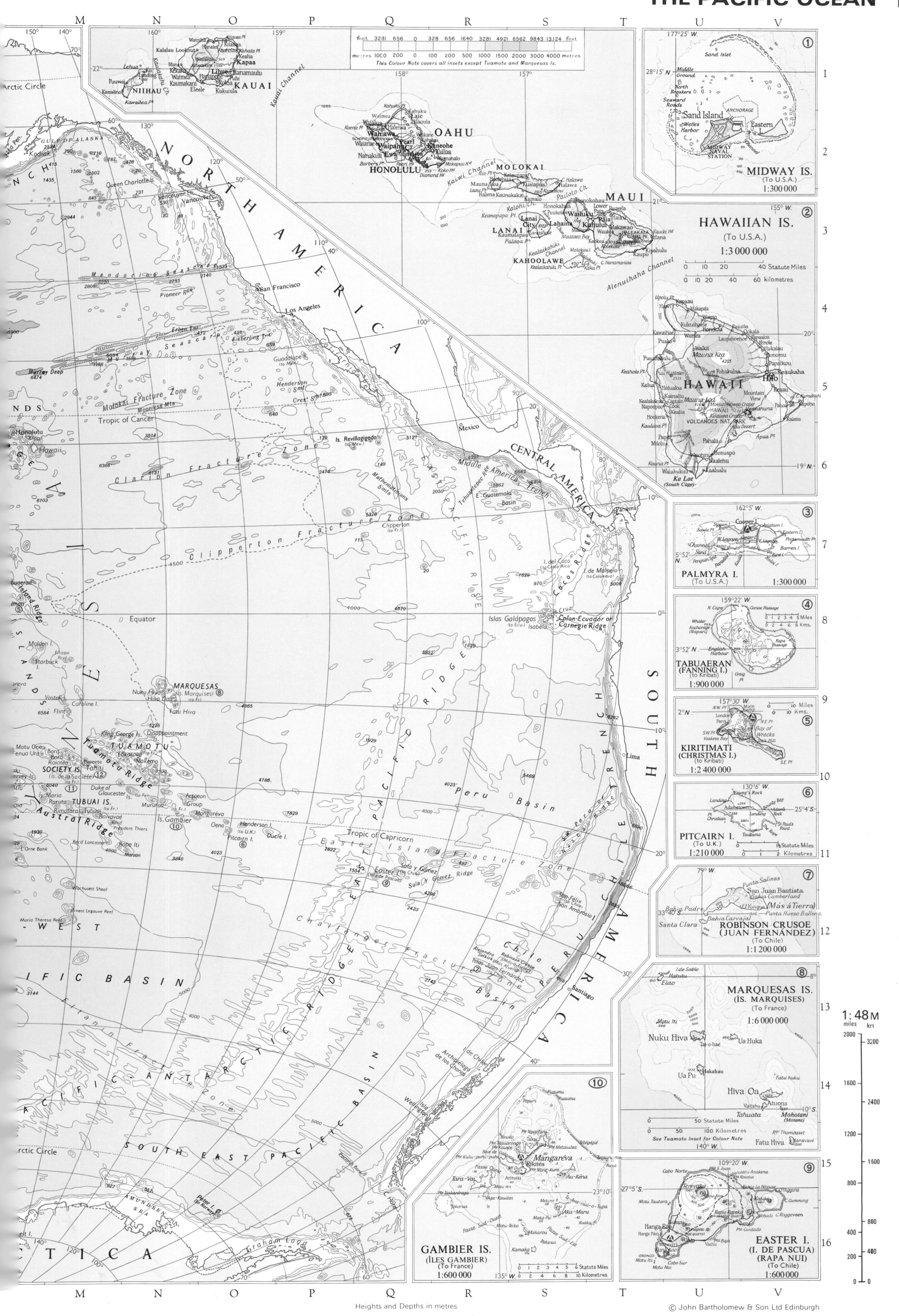

MIDWAY IS.
(To U.S.A.)
1:300 000

HAWAIIAN IS.
(To U.S.A.)
1:3 000 000

0   10   20   40 Statute Miles
0 10 20   40   60 kilometres

PALMYRA I.
(To U.S.A.)   1:300 000

TABUAERAN
(FANNING I.)
(To Kiribati)
1:900 000

KIRITIMATI
(CHRISTMAS I.)
(To Kiribati)
1:2 400 000

PITCAIRN I.
(To U.K.)
1:210 000

ROBINSON CRUSOE
(JUAN FERNÁNDEZ)
(To Chile)
1:1 200 000

MARQUESAS IS.
(IS. MARQUISES)
(To France)
1:6 000 000

0   50 Statute Miles
0   50   100 Kilometres
See Tuamotu Inset for Colour Note

GAMBIER IS.
(ÎLES GAMBIER)
(To France)
1:600 000

0 1 2 3 4 5 Statute Miles
0 1 2 3 4 5 6 7 8 Kms.

EASTER I.
(I. DE PASCUA)
(RAPA NUI)
(To Chile)
1:600 000

1:48 M
miles   km

Heights and Depths in metres

© John Bartholomew & Son Ltd Edinburgh

INDONESIA

MOLUCCAS

SERAM SEA

BANDA SEA

SULAWESI (Celebes)

FLORES SEA

TIMOR SEA

NEW GUINEA

IRIAN JAYA

PAPUA NEW GUINEA

BISMARCK SEA

BISMARCK ARCHIPELAGO

ARAFURA SEA

INDIAN OCEAN

Java Trench

Timor Trough

Darwin

Arnhem Land

Gulf of Carpentaria

Cape York Peninsula

Coral Sea

CORAL SEA ISLANDS

Coral Sea Plateau

NORTHERN TERRITORY

Great Sandy Desert

Gibson Desert

Great Victoria Desert

WESTERN AUSTRALIA

A U S T R A L I A

QUEENSLAND

SOUTH AUSTRALIA

Simpson Desert

Macdonnell Ranges

Alice Springs

Ayers Rock 867

NEW SOUTH WALES

Nullarbor Plain

Great Australian Bight

Perth

Fremantle

Geraldton

Kalgoorlie

Adelaide

Broken Hill

Sydney

Canberra

Wollongong

Newcastle

VICTORIA

Melbourne

Geelong

Ballarat

Bendigo

Bass Strait

TASMANIA

Hobart

Launceston

SOUTH AUSTRALIAN BASIN

Leeuwin Sill

Torres Strait

Gulf of Papua

Port Moresby

BONNE PROJECTION

East of 140° Greenwich

PACIFIC OCEAN

NAURU

GILBERT ISLANDS
(To Kiribati)

KIRIBATI

Kingsmill
Group

TUVALU
(ELLICE IS.)

SOLOMON
ISLANDS

Bougainville
Kieta
Honiara
Guadalcanal
San Cristobal

New
Georgia
Malaita
Maramasike

Santa Cruz Is.

Santa Cruz
Basin

Duff Is.
Swallow Is.

Ontong Java Rise

Rennell Ridge
Louisiade Rise

New
Hebrides
Basin

VANUATU
(NEW
HEBRIDES)

Espiritu Santo
Malakula
Port-Vila
Erromanga
Tanna

Banks
Islands

NTH. FIJI
(PANDORA)
BASIN

Rotuma

WESTERN
SAMOA

Savaii
Upolu
Apia
Tutuila

Iles Wallis
Futuna

FIJI

Vanua Levu
Viti Levu
Nadi
Suva
Lau
Group

Mellish Rise

Iles
Chesterfield
(To Fr.)

Bellona Plateau

NEW
CALEDONIA
(NOUVELLE
CALÉDONIE)
(To France)

Nouméa
Ile des Pins

Is. Loyaute

Hunter
Ridge

Matthew
Hunter
Walpole

SOUTH
FIJI
BASIN

TONGA

Vava'u Group

Ha'apai Group

Nuku'alofa
TONGA
Tongatapu
Group

Niue
(To N.Z.)

Lau (Lau) Ridge

South Fiji (Lau) Ridge

TONGA TRENCH

Minerva Reefs

CORAL
SEA

Brisbane
Ipswich
Lismore
Casino
Grafton

Lord Howe Rise

Norfolk Ridge

Norfolk I.
(To Aust.)
Philip

Middleton Reef
Elizabeth Reef

Lord Howe I.
(To Aust.)
Ball's Pyramid

TASMAN
SEA

North Cape Rise

Three
Kings
Basin

Three King's Is.

C. Maria van Diemen
North Cape
Kaitaia

Whangarei
Dargaville

AUCKLAND
Manukau
Hamilton

NORTH ISLAND

New Plymouth
Hawera
Wanganui

Great Barrier I.
Thames
Bay of Plenty
East Cape
Whakatane
Rotorua
Gisborne
Taupo
Mahia Peninsula
Napier
Hawke Bay

Palmerston
North
Masterton
WELLINGTON

NEW
ZEALAND

Chatham Rise

SOUTH ISLAND

Westport
Nelson
Blenheim
Greymouth
Hokitika
Kaikoura

Christchurch
Lyttelton
Ashburton
Timaru
Oamaru

Kermadec Ridge

Raoul

Kermadec Is.
(To N.Z.)
Macauley I.
Curtis I.
L'Esperance Rock

KERMADEC TRENCH

INTERNATIONAL DATE LINE

Tropic of Capricorn

Chatham Is.
(To N.Z.)
Pitt I.

Queenstown
Alexandra
Gore
Dunedin
Invercargill
Stewart I.

1:15 M
km   miles

Heights and Depths in metres

© John Bartholomew & Son Ltd Edinburgh

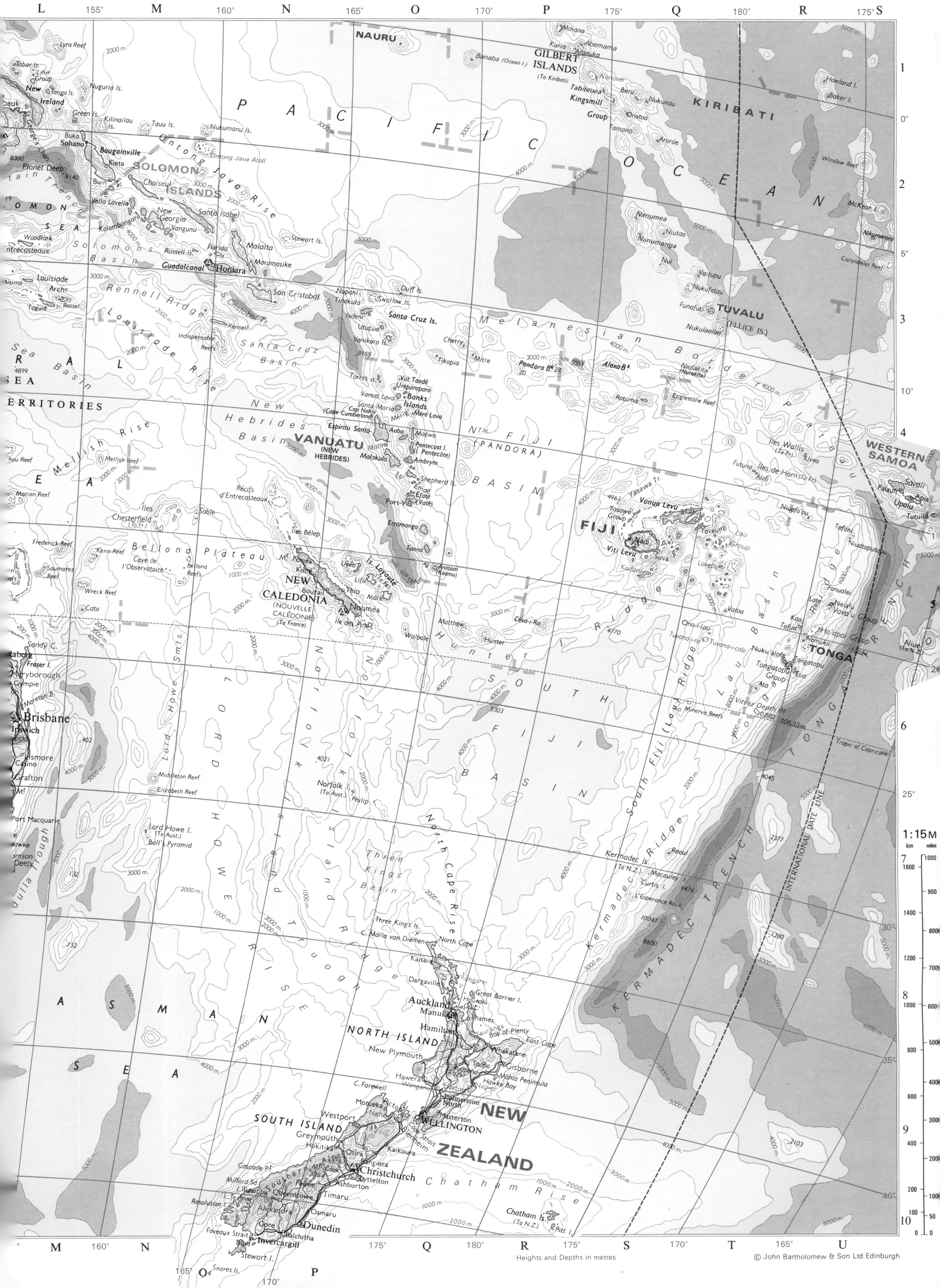

LAMBERT AZIMUTHAL EQUAL-AREA PROJECTION

Heights and Depths in metres

QUEENSLAND

NEW SOUTH WALES

VICTORIA

TASMANIA

SOUTH PACIFIC OCEAN

BASS STRAIT

FURNEAUX GROUP

1:6 M

SYDNEY
AND ENVIRONS
1:300 000

1 Government House
2 Public Offices
3 Observatory
4 General Post Office
5 Town Hall
6 Opera House
7 Anzac Mem. (Hyde Pk.)
8 Central Railway Sta.
9 Sydney University
10 Cricket Ground
11 Macquarie University
12 University of N.S. Wales

Underground

Longitude East 145° of Greenwich

© John Bartholomew & Son Ltd, Edinburgh

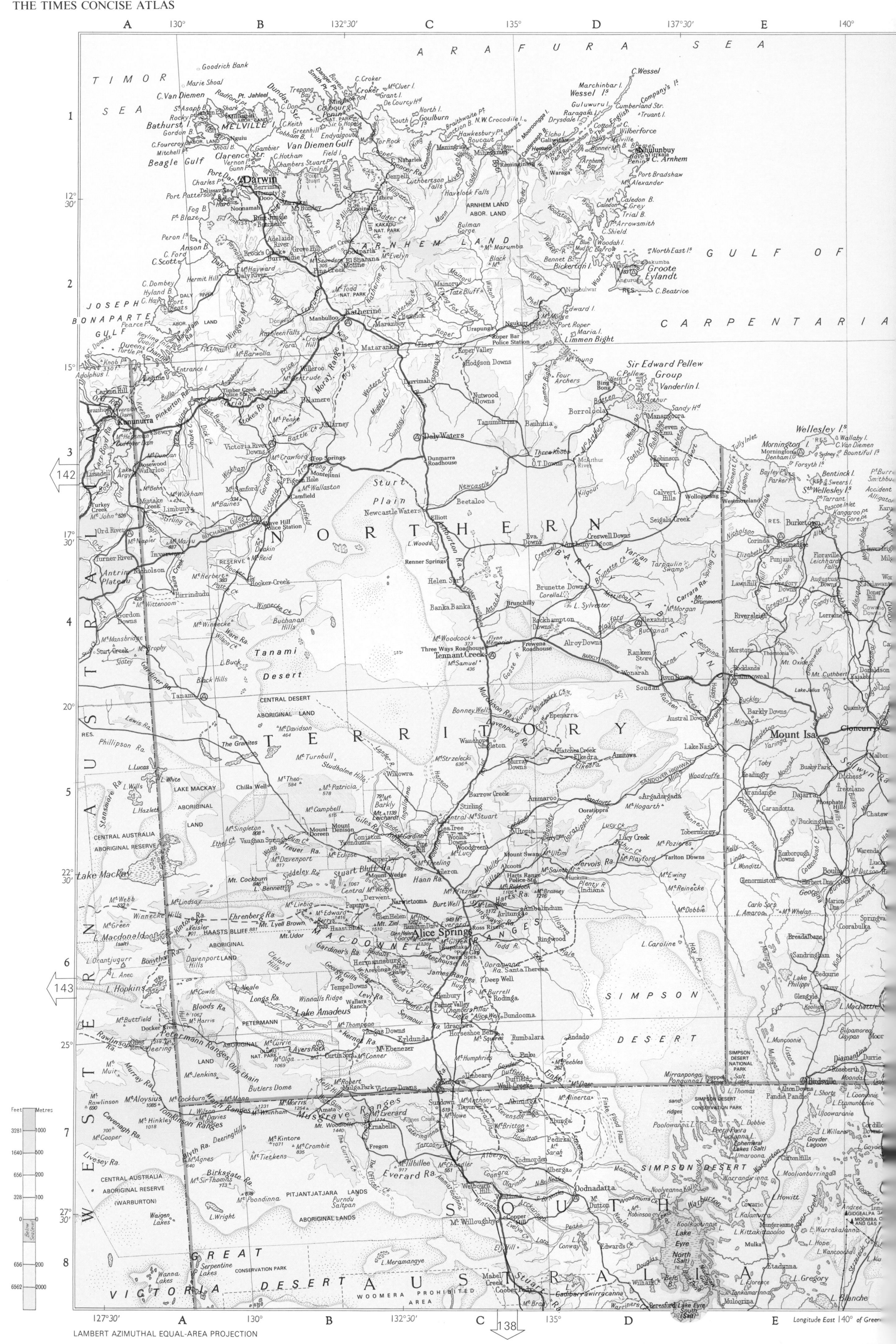

LAMBERT AZIMUTHAL EQUAL-AREA PROJECTION

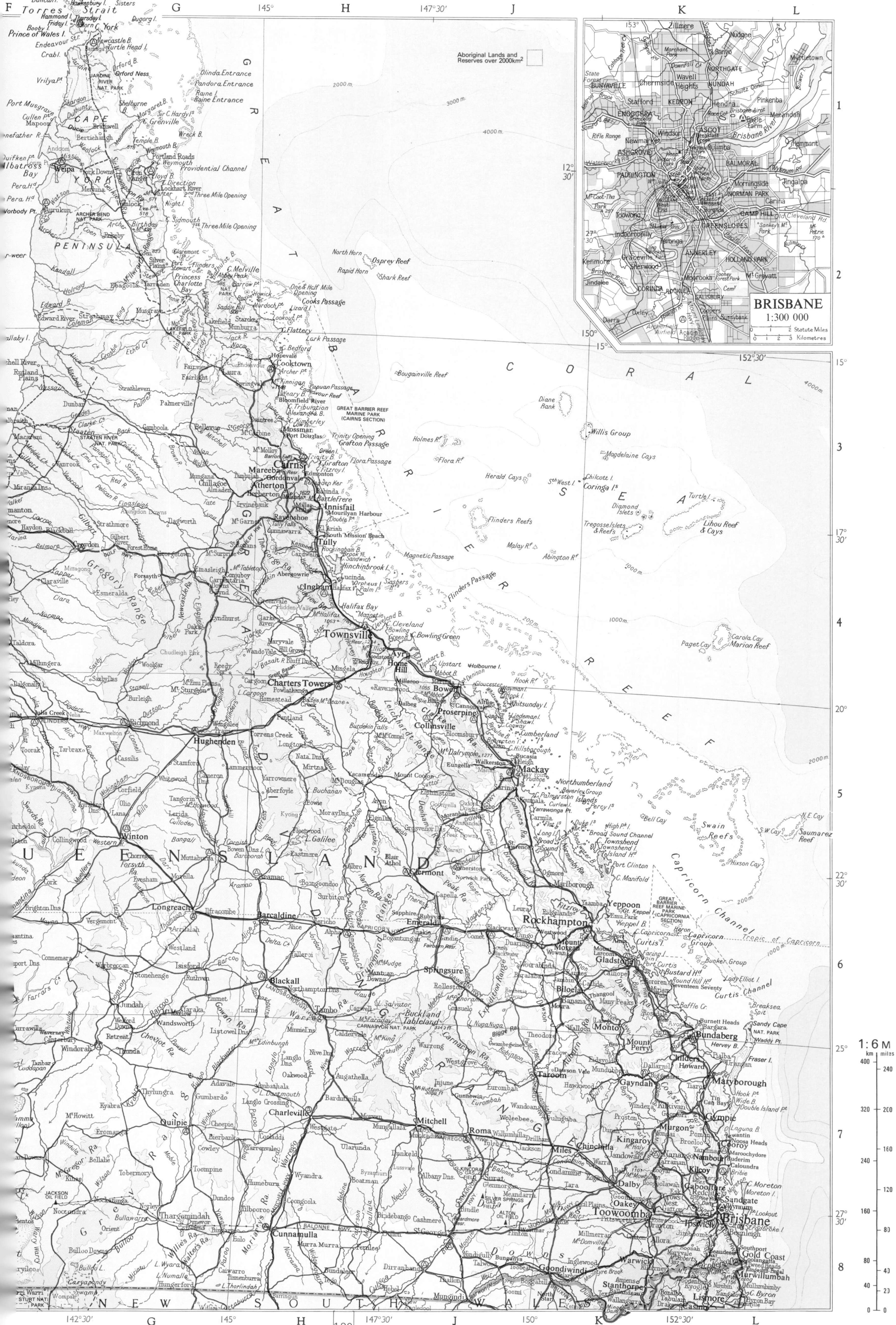

BRISBANE
1:300 000

Statute Miles
Kilometres

Aboriginal Lands and
Reserves over 2000km²

GREAT BARRIER REEF
MARINE PARK
(CAIRNS SECTION)

GREAT BARRIER REEF MARINE PARK
(CAPRICORNIA SECTION)

CORAL SEA

GREAT BARRIER REEF

Torres Strait

CAPE YORK PENINSULA

QUEENSLAND

NEW SOUTH WALES

Tropic of Capricorn

Capricorn Channel
Curtis Channel

Cooktown
Laura
Cairns
Mareeba
Atherton
Innisfail
Ravenshoe
Tully
Ingham
Halifax Bay
Townsville
Ayr
Home Hill
Charters Towers
Bowen
Proserpine
Collinsville
Hughenden
Richmond
Julia Creek
Winton
Mackay
Longreach
Barcaldine
Emerald
Rockhampton
Yeppoon
Gladstone
Blackall
Springsure
Biloela
Monto
Bundaberg
Tambo
Taroom
Gayndah
Maryborough
Charleville
Mitchell
Roma
Gympie
Murgon
Kingaroy
Quilpie
Chinchilla
Dalby
Nambour
Toowoomba
Ipswich
Brisbane
Gold Coast
Cunnamulla
Goondiwindi
Warwick
Stanthorpe
Murwillumbah
Casino

1:6 M
km miles

Heights and Depths in metres

© John Bartholomew & Son Ltd, Edinburgh

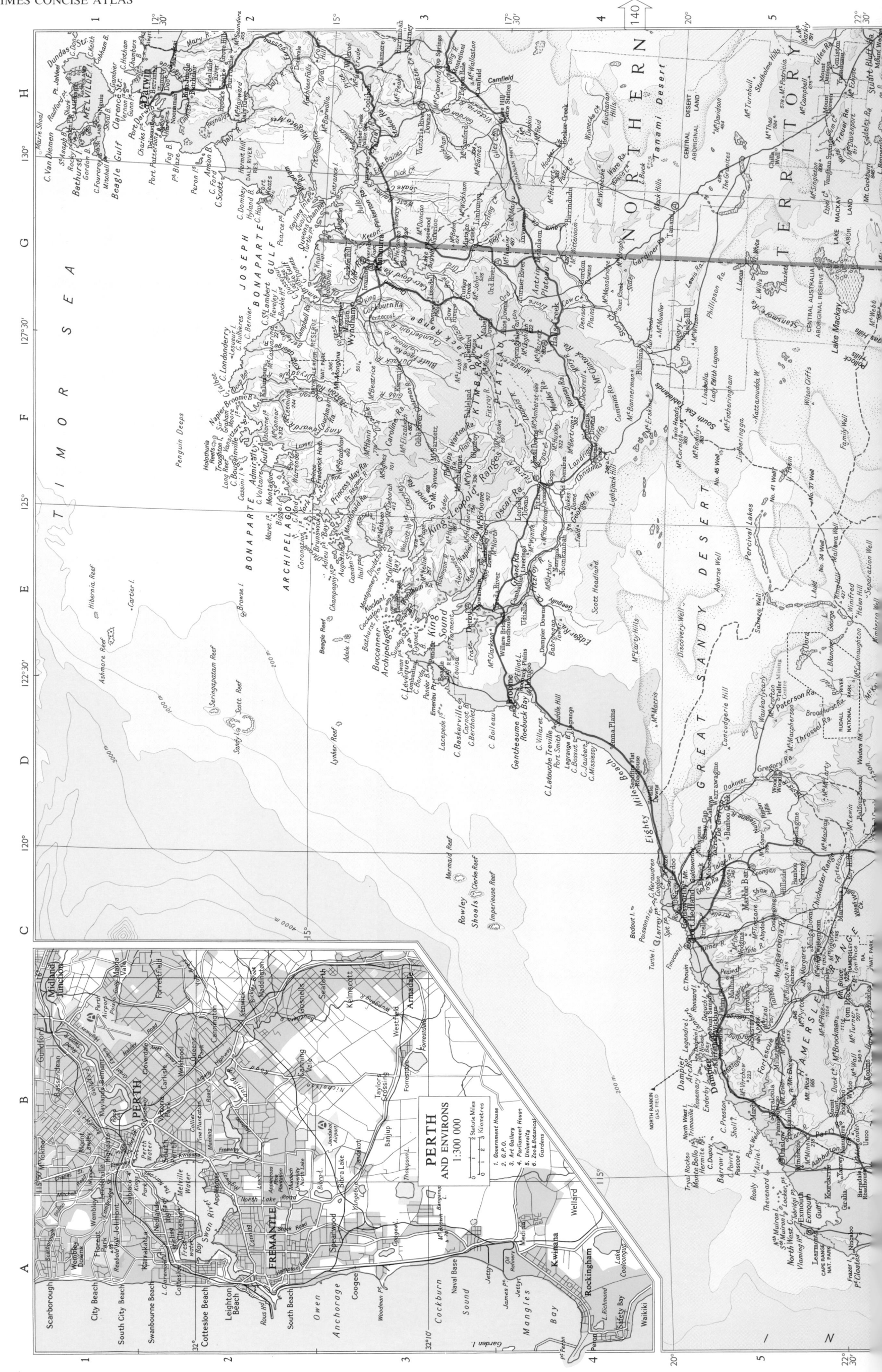

LAMBERT AZIMUTHAL EQUAL-AREA PROJECTION

TIMOR SEA
JOSEPH BONAPARTE GULF
BONAPARTE ARCHIPELAGO
KIMBERLEY PLATEAU
GREAT SANDY DESERT
Tanami Desert
NORTHERN TERRITORY
Darwin
Wyndham
Derby
Broome
Port Hedland
Eighty Mile Beach
King Sound
HAMERSLEY RANGE
PERTH AND ENVIRONS 1:300 000
1. Government House
2. G.P.O.
3. Art Gallery
4. Parliament House
5. University
6. Zoo & Botanical Gardens
PERTH
FREMANTLE
Kwinana
Rockingham
Cockburn Sound
140

1:6 M

Aboriginal Lands and
Reserves over 2000 km²

Heights and Depths in metres

SOUTH AUSTRALIA

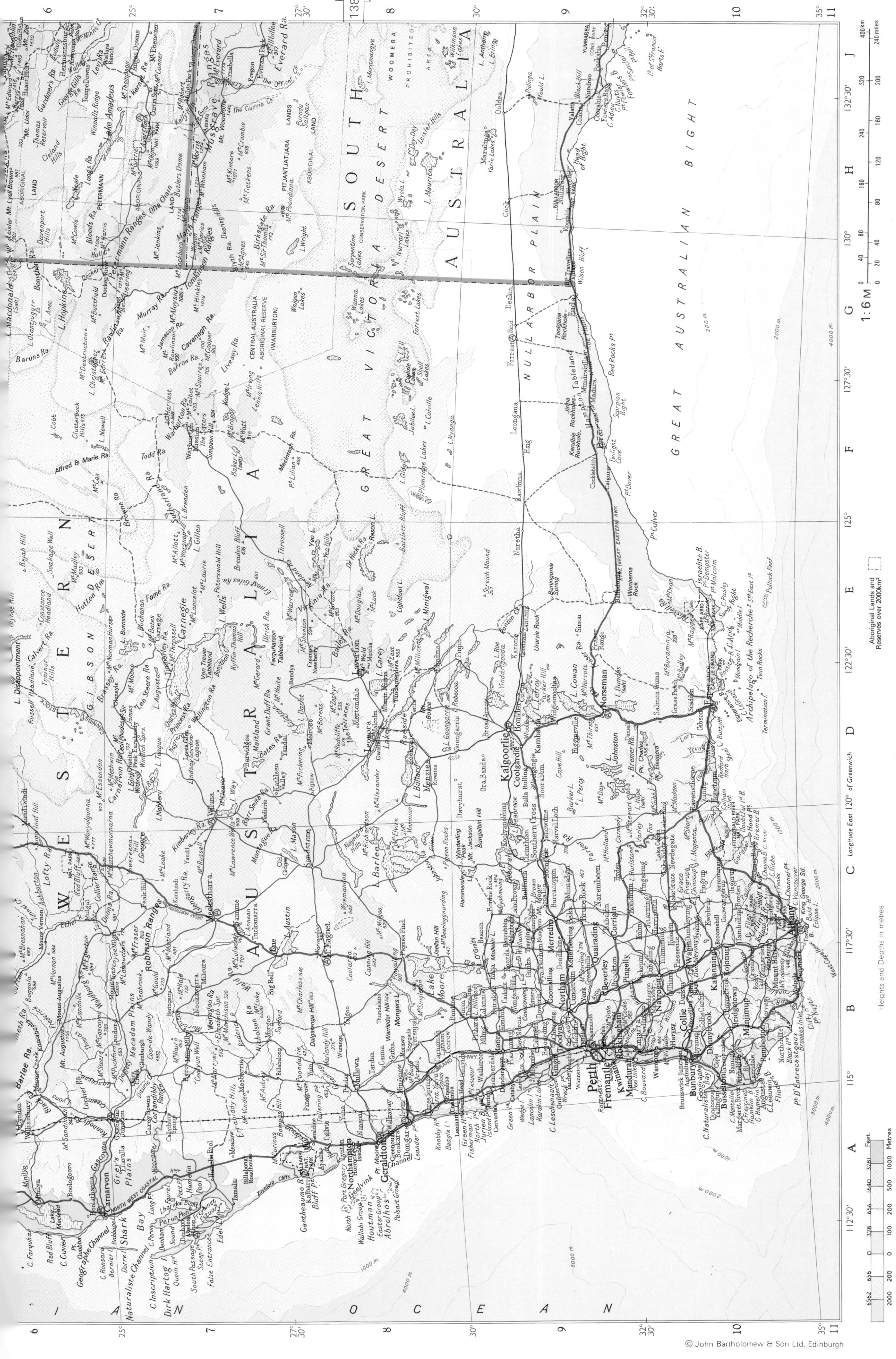

WESTERN AUSTRALIA

GIBSON DESERT

GREAT VICTORIA DESERT

GREAT SANDY DESERT

NULLARBOR PLAIN

Nullarbor Tableland

GREAT AUSTRALIAN BIGHT

WOOMERA PROHIBITED AREA

CENTRAL AUSTRALIA ABORIGINAL RESERVE (WARBURTON)

PITJANTJATJARA ABORIGINAL LAND

INDIAN OCEAN

Perth
Fremantle
Kwinana
Mandurah
Bunbury
Busselton
Geraldton
Northampton
Carnavon
Shark Bay
Kalgoorlie
Coolgardie
Kambalda
Norseman
Esperance
Meekatharra
Wiluna
Leonora
Laverton
Menzies
Southern Cross
Merredin
Narrogin
Katanning
Albany
Collie
Bridgetown
Manjimup
York
Beverley
Pingelly
Corrigin

Naturaliste Channel
Dirk Hartog I.
Dorre I.
Bernier I.
Peron Pen.
Edel Land
Steep Pt.
South Passage
Shark Bay
Cape Leeuwin
C. Naturaliste
Geographe Bay
Houtman Abrolhos
Archipelago of the Recherche

Robinson Ranges
Barlee Ra.
Carnarvon Ra.
Ernest Giles Ra.
Petermann Ranges
Rawlinson Ranges
Musgrave Ranges

Lake Moore
Lake Barlee
L. Carey
L. Wells
L. Disappointment
L. Macdonald
L. Amadeus
L. Cowan
L. Johnston
L. Lefroy

Longitude East 120° of Greenwich

© John Bartholomew & Son Ltd, Edinburgh

Feet / Metres scale:
6552 / 2000
3281 / 1000
1640 / 500
656 / 200
328 / 100
0
656 / 200
2000

400 km / 240 miles

CHRISTCHURCH
AND ENVIRONS
1:300 000

DUNEDIN
AND ENVIRONS
1:300 000

CONIC PROJECTION

© John Bartholomew & Son Ltd Edinburgh

AUCKLAND
AND ENVIRONS
1:300 000

WELLINGTON
AND ENVIRONS
1:300 000

NORTH ISLAND

TASMAN SEA

PACIFIC OCEAN

NORTHLAND

CENTRAL AUCKLAND

SOUTH AUCKLAND–BAY OF PLENTY

EAST COAST

TARANAKI

HAWKE'S BAY

WELLINGTON

NELSON

MARLBOROUGH

COOK STRAIT

Heights in feet
Depths in metres

Longitude East 174° of Greenwich

© John Bartholomew & Son Ltd, Edinburgh

1:2.5 M

0   10   20   40   60   80   100 miles

0   20   40   60   80   100   120   140   160 km

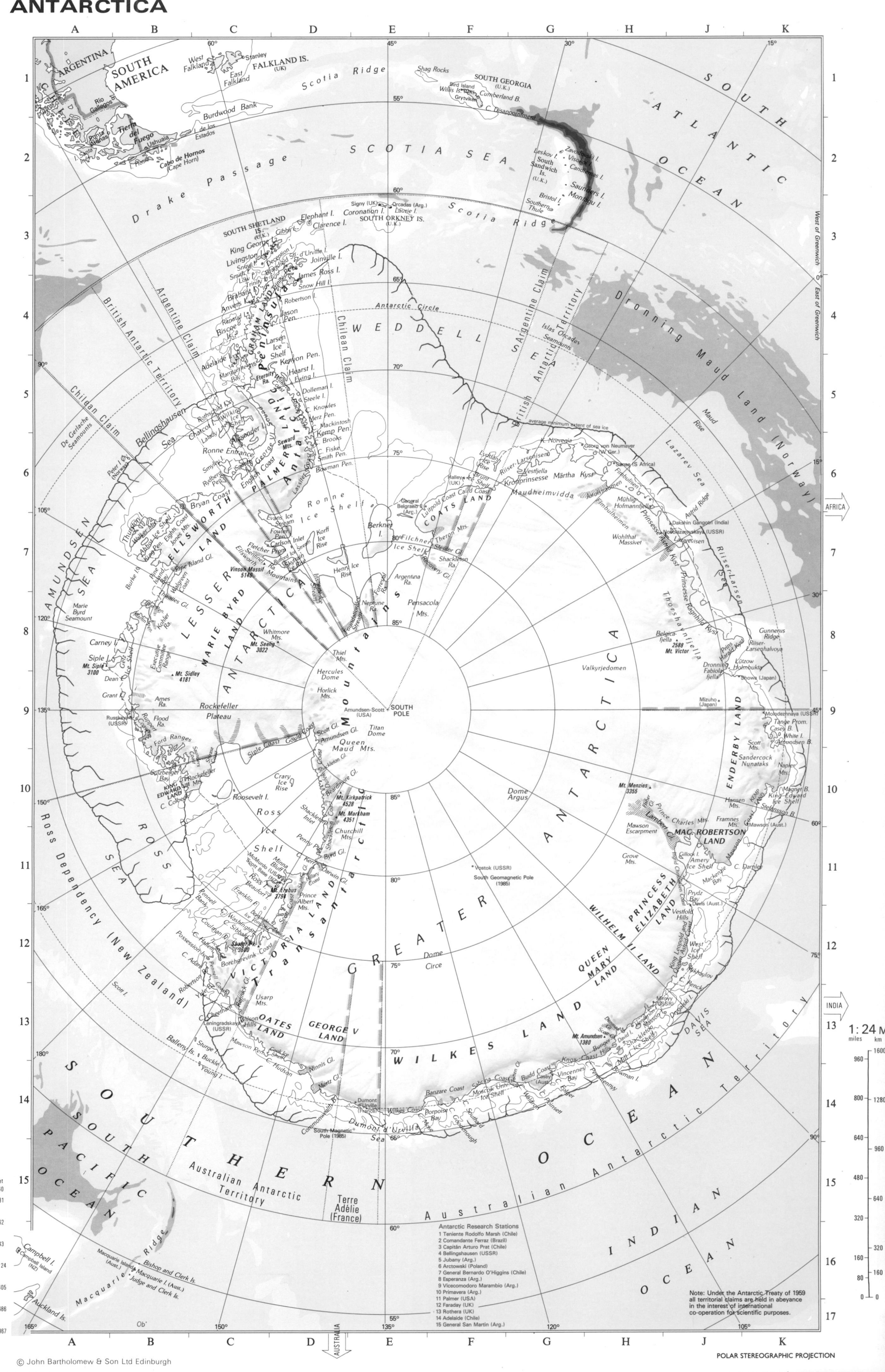

Antarctic Research Stations
1 Teniente Rodolfo Marsh (Chile)
2 Comandante Ferraz (Brazil)
3 Capitán Arturo Prat (Chile)
4 Bellingshausen (USSR)
5 Jubany (Arg.)
6 Arctowski (Poland)
7 General Bernardo O'Higgins (Chile)
8 Esperanza (Arg.)
9 Vicecomodoro Marambio (Arg.)
10 Primavera (Arg.)
11 Palmer (USA)
12 Faraday (UK)
13 Rothera (UK)
14 Adelaide (Chile)
15 General San Martin (Arg.)

Note: Under the Antarctic Treaty of 1959
all territorial claims are held in abeyance
in the interest of international
co-operation for scientific purposes.

1 : 24 M
miles   km

© John Bartholomew & Son Ltd Edinburgh

POLAR STEREOGRAPHIC PROJECTION

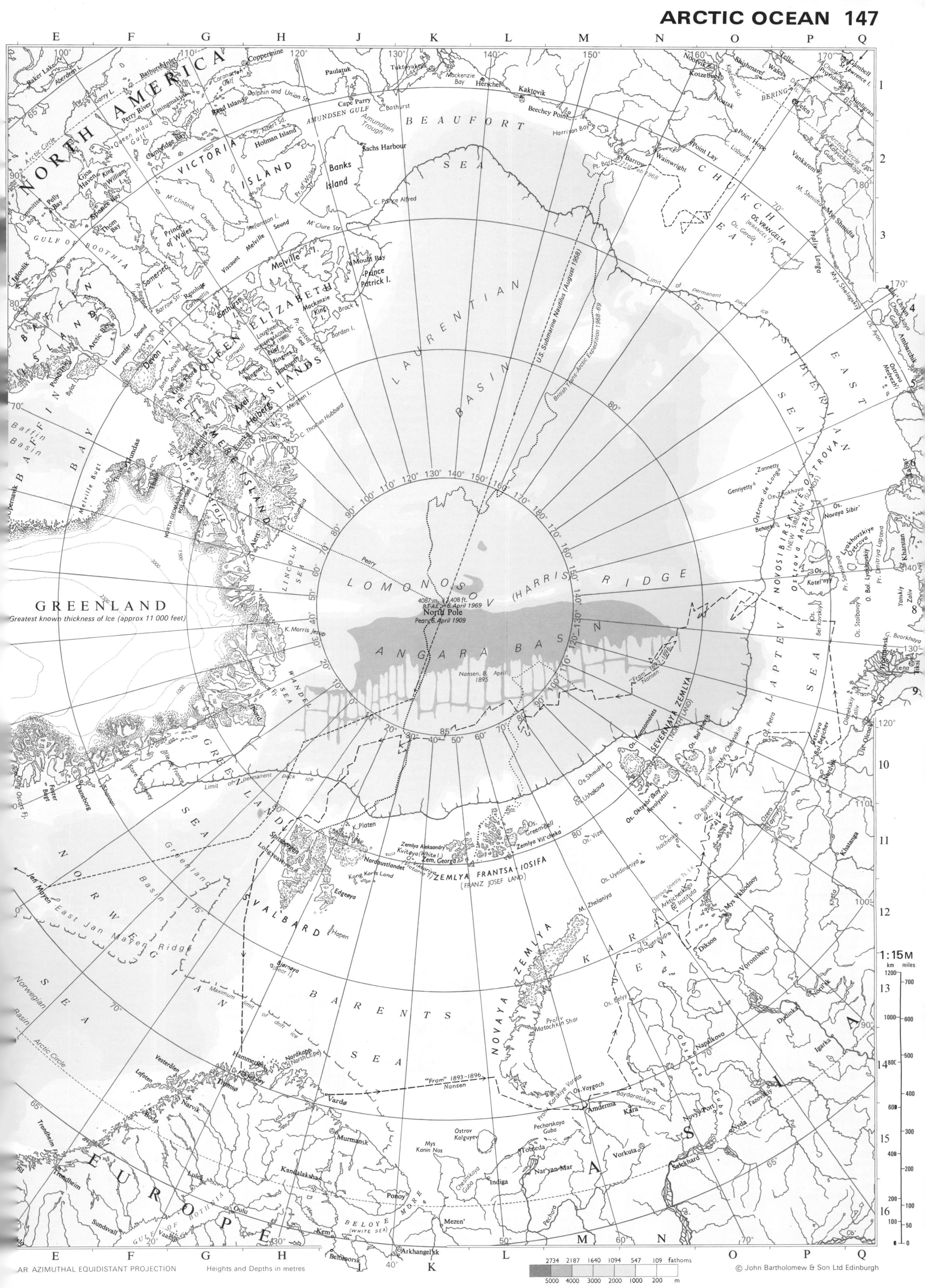
NORTH AMERICA
VICTORIA ISLAND
Banks Island
QUEEN ELIZABETH ISLANDS
BAFFIN BAY
BAFFIN ISLAND
GREENLAND
Greatest known thickness of Ice (approx 11 000 feet)
BEAUFORT SEA
LAURENTIAN BASIN
LOMONOSOV (HARRIS) RIDGE
ANGARA BASIN
North Pole
Peary 6 April 1909
CHUKCHI SEA
EAST SIBERIAN SEA
LAPTEV SEA
NOVOSIBIRSKIYE OSTROVA
(NEW SIBERIAN ISLANDS)
SEVERNAYA ZEMLYA
(NORTH LAND)
ZEMLYA FRANTSA-IOSIFA
(FRANZ JOSEF LAND)
SVALBARD
NOVAYA ZEMLYA
KARA SEA
BARENTS SEA
GREENLAND SEA
NORWEGIAN SEA
WANDEL SEA
LINCOLN SEA
Limit of permanent pack ice
"Fram" 1893-1896 Nansen
US Submarine Nautilus (August 1958)
British Trans Arctic Expedition 1968-69
EUROPE
ASIA
Arctic Circle
1:15M

STATES AND TERRITORIES OF THE WORLD

Country	*Capital or main town*	*Sq. km*	*Sq. miles*	*Population*	*Date*
Afghanistan	Kābul	636,265	245,600	15,510,000	1988
Albania	Tiranë (Tirana)	28,750	11,100	3,140,000	1988
Algeria	El-Djezaïr (Algiers)	2,381,745	919,355	23,840,000	1988
American Samoa	Pago Pago	197	76	37,000	1988
Andorra	Andorra la Vella	465	180	51,400	1988
Angola	Luanda	1,246,700	481,225	9,387,000	1988
Anguilla	The Valley	91	35	6,700	1988
Antigua and Barbuda	St. John's	442	171	76,296	1986
Argentina	Buenos Aires	2,766,889	1,068,302	31,960,000	1988
Aruba	Oranjestad	193	75	60,000	1988
Ascension	Georgetown	88	34	1,007	1988
Australia	Canberra	7,682,300	2,965,370	16,532,000	1989
Austria	Wien (Vienna)	83,855	32,370	7,605,000	1988
Azores	Ponta Delgada	2,335	901	253,500	1986
Bahamas	Nassau	13,865	5,350	245,000	1988
Bahrain	Al Manāmah (Manama)	661	255	421,040	1988
Bangladesh	Dhaka (Dacca)	144,000	55,585	104,530,000	1988
Barbados	Bridgetown	430	166	253,881	1987
Belgium	Bruxelles/(Brussels)	30,520	11,780	9,920,000	1988
Belize	Belmopan	22,965	8,865	176,000	1987
Benin	Porto Novo	112,620	43,470	4,440,000	1988
Bermuda	Hamilton	54	21	58,080	1987
Bhutan	Thimphu	46,620	17,995	1,400,000	1988
Bolivia	La Paz	1,098,575	424,050	7,000,000	1988
Botswana	Gaborone	575,000	221,950	1,211,816	1988
Brazil	Brasília	8,511,965	3,285,620	144,428,000	1988
Brunei	Bandar Seri Begawan	5,765	2,225	241,000	1988
Bulgaria	Sofiya (Sofia)	110,910	42,810	8,973,600	1988
Burkina	Ouagadougou	274,122	105,811	8,530,000	1988
Burma	Rangoon	678,030	261,720	39,840,000	1988
Burundi	Bujumbura	27,835	10,745	5,130,000	1988
Cambodia	Phnom Penh	181,000	69,865	7,870,000	1988
Cameroon	Yaoundé	475,500	183,545	11,082,000	1988
Canada	Ottawa	9,922,385	3,830,840	26,028,000	1988
Canary Islands	Las Palmas (on Gran Canaria) and Santa Cruz (on Tenerife)	7,275	2,810	1,614,882	1986
Cape Verde	Praia	4,035	1,560	359,000	1988
Cayman Islands	George Town	259	100	23,700	1988
Central African Republic	Bangui	624,975	241,240	2,860,000	1988
Chad	Ndjamena	1,284,000	495,625	5,396,000	1988
Channel Islands	St Helier (on Jersey) St Peter Port (on Guernsey)	194	75	138,668	1988
Chile	Santiago	751,625	290,125	12,907,000	1989
China	Beijing (Peking)	9,597,000	3,704,440	1,072,200,000	1988
Colombia	Bogotá	1,138,915	439,620	30,240,000	1988
Comoros	Moroni	1,860	718	422,500	1987
Congo	Brazzaville	342,000	132,010	2,266,000	1988
Corsica (Corse)	Ajaccio	8,680	3,350	248,700	1986
Costa Rica	San José	50,900	19,650	2,816,558	1988
Côte d'Ivoire	Yamoussoukro	322,465	124,470	11,630,000	1988
Crete (Kríti)	Iráklion	8,330	3,215	501,082	1981
Cuba	Habana (Havana)	114,525	44,205	10,487,000	1989
Cyprus	Nicosia	9,250	3,570	686,400	1988
Czechoslovakia	Praha (Prague)	127,870	49,360	15,620,000	1988
Denmark	København (Copenhagen)	43,075	16,625	5,129,254	1988
Djibouti	Djibouti	23,000	8,800	484,000	1988
Dominica	Roseau	751	290	80,000	1988
Dominican Republic	Santo Domingo	48,440	18,700	6,867,000	1988
Ecuador	Quito	461,475	178,130	10,200,000	1988
Egypt	Cairo (El Qâ'hira)	1,000,250	386,095	51,900,000	1988
El Salvador	San Salvador	21,395	8,260	5,110,000	1988
Equatorial Guinea	Malabo	28,050	10,825	420,000	1988
Ethiopia	Ādīs Ābeba (Addis Ababa)	1,023,050	394,895	48,500,000	1989
Faeroes (Føroyar)	Tórshavn	1,399	540	47,000	1987
Falkland Islands	Port Stanley	12,175	4,700	1,916	1986
Fiji	Suva	18,330	7,075	715,375	1986
Finland	Helsinki	337,030	130,095	4,955,000	1988
France	Paris	543,965	209,970	55,854,000	1988
French Guiana	Cayenne	91,000	35,125	90,500	1988
French Polynesia	Papeete	3,940	1,520	191,400	1988
Gabon	Libreville	267,665	103,320	1,226,000	1988
Galapagos Islands		7,845	3,030	7,954	1986
Gambia, The	Banjul	10,690	4,125	788,163	1988
German Democratic Republic (East)	Berlin (East)	108,175	41,755	16,666,000	1988
German Federal Republic (West)	Bonn	248,665	95,985	61,320,000	1989
Ghana	Accra	238,305	91,985	13,812,000	1988
Gibraltar		6.5	2.5	30,000	1988
Greece	Athínai (Athens)	131,985	50,954	9,990,000	1987
Greenland	Godthåb (Nuuk)	2,175,600	839,780	53,406	1986
Grenada	St George's	345	133	98,000	1987
Guadeloupe	Basse-Terre	1,702	657	336,300	1988
Guam	Agaña	450	174	130,400	1987
Guatemala	Guatemala	108,890	42,030	8,990,000	1988
Guinea	Conakry	245,855	94,900	6,533,000	1988
Guinea-Bissau	Bissau	36,125	13,945	932,000	1988
Guyana	Georgetown	214,970	82,980	812,000	1987
Haiti	Port-au-Prince	27,750	10,710	5,523,000	1988
Honduras	Tegucigalpa	112,085	43,265	4,802,000	1988
Hong Kong	Victoria	1,067	412	5,680,000	1988
Hungary	Budapest	93,030	35,910	10,584,000	1989
Iceland	Reykjavík	102,820	39,690	247,357	1987
India	New Delhi	3,166,830	1,222,395	824,000,000	1989
Indonesia	Jakarta	1,919,445	740,905	174,950,000	1988
Iran	Tehrān	1,648,000	636,130	53,920,000	1988
Iraq	Baghdad	438,445	169,240	17,064,000	1988
Ireland, the Republic of (Eire)	Dublin (Baile Átha Cliath)	68,895	26,595	3,540,000	1988
Israel	Jerusalem	20,770	8,015	4,478,000	1989
Italy	Roma (Rome)	301,245	116,280	57,440,000	1988
Jamaica	Kingston	11,425	4,410	2,358,000	1988
Japan	Tokyo	396,700	142,705	122,610,000	1988
Jordan	Amman	90,650	35,000	2,970,000	1988
Kampuchea *see* **Cambodia**					
Kenya	Nairobi	582,645	224,900	22,800,000	1988
Kiribati	Bairiki	684	264	66,250	1987
Korea, North	Pyŏngyang	122,310	47,210	21,890,000	1988
Korea, South	Sŏul (Seoul)	98,445	38,000	41,970,000	1988
Kuwait	Al Kuwayt (Kuwait)	24,280	9,370	1,958,000	1988
Laos	Viangchan (Vientiane)	236,725	91,375	3,830,000	1987
Lebanon	Beyrouth (Beirut)	10,400	4,015	2,762,000	1987
Lesotho	Maseru	30,345	11,715	1,670,000	1988
Liberia	Monrovia	111,370	42,990	2,436,000	1988
Libya	Tarabulus (Tripoli)	1,759,540	679,180	4,083,000	1987
Liechtenstein	Vaduz	160	62	28,000	1988
Luxembourg	Luxembourg	2,585	998	377,000	1989
Macau (Macao)	Macau	16	6	444,000	1988
Madagascar	Antananarivo	594,180	229,345	10,919,000	1988
Madeira	Funchal	796	307	269,500	1986
Malawi	Lilongwe	94,080	36,315	7,755,000	1988
Malaysia	Kuala Lumpur	332,965	128,525	16,968,000	1988
Maldives	Malé	298	115	200,000	1988
Mali	Bamako	1,240,140	478,695	7,784,000	1988
Malta	Valletta	316	122	345,636	1987
Man, Isle of	Douglas	572	221	67,000	1988
Marshall Islands	Majuro	605	234	40,609	1988
Martinique	Fort-de-France	1,079	417	336,000	1988
Mauritania	Nouakchott	1,030,700	397,850	1,894,000	1988
Mauritius	Port Louis	1,865	720	1,056,867	1987
Mexico	Mexico City	1,972,545	761,400	82,734,454	1988
Micronesia	Kolonia	702	271	86,094	1988
Monaco	Monaco	1.6	0.6	27,000	1987
Mongolia	Ulaanbaatar (Ulan Bator)	1,565,000	604,090	2,090,000	1988
Montserrat	Plymouth	106	41	12,000	1987
Morocco (inc. W. Sahara)	Rabat	710,850	274,460	23,910,000	1988
Mozambique	Maputo	784,755	302,915	14,907,000	1988
Namibia (S. W. Africa)	Windhoek	824,295	318,180	1,288,000	1988
Nauru	Yaren	21	8	8,000	1987
Nepal	Kathmandu	141,415	54,585	18,300,000	1988
Netherlands	Amsterdam (seat of government The Hague)	41,160	15,891	14,714,948	1988
Netherlands Antilles	Willemstad	800	308	188,501	1986
New Caledonia	Nouméa	19,105	7,375	153,700	1988
New Zealand	Wellington	265,150	102,350	3,300,000	1988
Nicaragua	Managua	148,000	57,130	3,620,000	1988
Niger	Niamey	1,186,410	457,955	7,249,596	1988
Nigeria	Lagos	923,850	356,605	101,907,000	1987
Northern Mariana Islands	Saipan	471	182	20,591	1988
Norway	Oslo	323,895	125,025	4,198,300	1988
Oman	Masqat (Muscat)	271,950	104,970	1,200,000	1987
Pakistan	Islamabad	803,940	310,320	105,409,000	1988
Palau	Koror	367	142	14,106	1988
Panama	Panama	78,515	30,305	2,322,000	1988
Papua New Guinea	Port Moresby	462,840	178,655	3,561,000	1988
Paraguay	Asunción	406,750	157,005	4,010,000	1988
Peru	Lima	1,285,215	496,095	21,255,900	1988
Philippines	Manila	300,000	115,800	58,721,307	1988
Pitcairn Island	Adamstown	45	17.25	59	1987
Poland	Warszawa (Warsaw)	312,685	120,695	37,811,000	1989
Portugal	Lisboa (Lisbon)	91,630	35,370	10,410,000	1988
Puerto Rico	San Juan	8,960	3,460	3,292,000	1987
Qatar	Ad Dawḥah (Doha)	11,435	4,415	371,863	1987
Réunion	Saint-Denis	2,510	969	574,800	1988
Romania	Bucureşti (Bucharest)	237,500	91,675	23,050,000	1988
Rwanda	Kigali	26,330	10,165	6,710,000	1988
St Kitts and Nevis	Basseterre	262	101	48,000	1987
St Helena	Jamestown	122	47	5,564	1988
St Lucia	Castries	616	238	146,000	1988
St Pierre and Miquelon	St Pierre	241	93	6,400	1988
St Vincent	Kingstown	389	150	113,000	1988
San Marino	San Marino	61	24	22,746	1988
São Tomé and Príncipe	São Tomé	964	372	115,600	1988
Sardinia (Sardegna)	Cagliari	24,090	9,300	1,651,218	1987
Saudi Arabia	Ar Riyāḍ (Riyadh)	2,400,900	926,745	11,520,000	1988
Senegal	Dakar	196,720	75,935	6,982,000	1988
Seychelles	Victoria	404	156	67,000	1988
Sierra Leone	Freetown	72,325	27,920	3,875,000	1988
Singapore	Singapore	616	238	2,647,000	1988
Solomon Islands	Honiara	29,790	11,500	299,000	1988
Somalia	Muqdisho (Mogadiscio)	630,000	243,180	6,220,000	1988
South Africa	Pretoria (administrative) Cape Town (legislative)	1,184,825	457,345	29,600,000	1988
Spain	Madrid	504,880	194,885	39,085,000	1989
Sri Lanka	Colombo	65,610	25,325	16,600,000	1988
Sudan	Khartoum	2,505,815	967,245	25,560,000	1987
Suriname	Paramaribo	163,820	63,235	415,000	1987
Svalbard	Longyearbyen	62,000	23,930	3,942	1986
Swaziland	Mbabane	17,365	6,705	740,000	1988
Sweden	Stockholm	449,790	173,620	8,469,000	1989
Switzerland	Bern	41,285	15,935	6,510,000	1988
Syria	Dimashq (Damascus)	185,680	71,675	11,338,000	1988
Taiwan	T'ai-pei (Taipei)	35,990	13,890	19,700,000	1987
Tanzania	Dodoma	939,760	362,750	24,000,000	1988
Thailand	Bangkok (Krung Thep)	514,000	198,405	54,536,000	1988
Togo	Lomé	56,785	21,920	3,246,000	1988
Tonga	Nuku'alofa	699	270	95,200	1988
Trinidad and Tobago	Port of Spain	5,130	1,980	1,243,000	1988
Tristan da Cunha		98	38	313	1988
Tunisia	Tunis	164,150	63,360	7,810,000	1988
Turkey	Ankara	779,450	300,870	52,420,000	1988
Turks and Caicos Islands	Cockburn Town	430	166	10,800	1988
Tuvalu	Funafuti	24.6	9.5	8,000	1987

Country	Capital or main town	Sq. km	Sq. miles	Population	Date
Uganda	Kampala	236,580	91,320	15,500,000	1987
Union of Soviet Socialist Republics (U.S.S.R.)	Moskva (Moscow)	22,400,000	8,646,000	286,717,000	1989
United Arab Emirates (U.A.E.)	Abū Ẓabī (Abu Dhabi)	75,150	29,010	1,600,000	1988
United Kingdom of Great Britain and Northern Ireland (U.K.)	London	244,755	94,475	57,065,000	1988
United States of America (U.S.A.)	Washington D.C.	9,363,130	3,614,170	245,815,000	1988
Uruguay	Montevideo	186,925	72,155	3,080,000	1988
Vanuatu	Port Vila	14,765	5,700	149,400	1988
Vatican City	Vatican City	0.44	0.17	766	1988
Venezuela	Caracas	912,045	352,050	18,770,000	1988
Vietnam	Hanoi	329,566	127,246	61,400,000	1989
Virgin Islands (U.K.)	Road Town	153	59	13,000	1987
Virgin Islands (U.S.A.)	Charlotte Amalie	345	133	106,000	1987
Wallis and Futuna Islands	Mata-Utu	274	106	15,400	1988
Western Sahara		266,000	102,675	180,000	1986
Western Samoa	Apia	2,840	1,095	165,000	1987
Yemen	Ṣan'ā	189,850	73,280	8,595,000	1988
Yemen (South)	Aden	287,680	111,045	2,345,266	1988
Yugoslavia	Beograd (Belgrade)	255,805	98,740	23,657,000	1989
Zaire	Kinshasa	2,345,410	905,330	32,564,000	1988
Zambia	Lusaka	752,615	290,510	7,531,000	1988
Zimbabwe	Harare	390,310	150,660	8,870,000	1988

METROPOLITAN AREAS

A metropolitan area is a continuous built-up area containing a number of cities and towns. The total combined population is given either as an estimate or from census returns.

Metropolitan areas with populations greater than 7 million.

Metropolitan Area	Country	Population
MEXICO CITY	Mexico	18,748,000
NEW YORK	USA	18,054,000
SÃO PAULO	Brazil	16,710,013
LOS ANGELES	USA	13,471,000
CAIRO	Egypt	13,300,000
BUENOS AIRES	Argentina	12,600,000
SHANGHAI	China	12,050,000
TOKYO	Japan	11,680,282
RIO DE JANEIRO	Brazil	10,980,015
SEOUL	South Korea	9,645,824
BEIJING (PEKING)	China	9,470,000
CALCUTTA	India	9,194,018
LONDON	UK	9,021,683
MOSCOW	USSR	8,967,000
OSAKA-KOBE	Japan	8,594,000
PARIS	France	8,510,000
BOMBAY	India	8,243,405
TIANJIN	China	7,990,000
JAKARTA	Indonesia	7,347,800

The following selection of Metropolitan Areas are listed alphabetically under each continent.

ASIA

Population	Metropolitan Area	Country
2,548,057	**Ahmadabad**	India
1,128,000	**Alma-Ata**	USSR
777,500	**Amman**	Jordan
2,251,533	**Ankara**	Turkey
2,517,080	**Anshan**	China
3,844,608	**Baghdād**	Iraq
1,566,700	**Bandung**	Indonesia
2,921,751	**Bangalore**	India
5,670,692	**Bangkok**	Thailand
1,592,940	**Baotou**	China
915,000	**Basra**	Iraq
9,470,000	**Beijing (Peking)**	China
702,000	**Beirut**	Lebanon
8,243,405	**Bombay**	India
9,194,018	**Calcutta**	India
5,705,230	**Changchun**	China
2,459,920	**Changsha**	China
1,143,000	**Chelyabinsk**	USSR
4,025,180	**Chengdu**	China
1,391,877	**Chittagong**	Bangladesh
6,511,130	**Chongqing**	China
683,000	**Colombo**	Sri Lanka
3,430,312	**Dhaka**	Bangladesh
4,619,060	**Dalian**	China
2,500,000	**Damascus**	Syria
5,729,283	**Delhi**	India
1,104,209	**Faisalabad**	Pakistan
1,157,111	**Fukuoka**	Japan
2,045,150	**Fushun**	China
1,651,500	**Fuzhou**	China
5,669,640	**Guangzhou (Canton)**	China
1,400,000	**Guiyang**	China
1,397,000	**Haiphong**	Vietnam
5,234,150	**Hangzhou**	China
2,878,000	**Hanoi**	Vietnam
2,670,000	**Harbin**	China
1,042,000	**Hiroshima**	Japan
5,613,400	**Hong Kong**	UK colony
1,519,420	**Huainan**	China
2,545,836	**Hyderabad**	India
1,387,475	**Inchon**	South Korea
986,753	**Isfahan**	Iran
379,000	**Islamabad**	Pakistan
1,015,160	**Jaipur**	India
7,347,800	**Jakarta**	Indonesia
482,700	**Jerusalem**	Israel
3,974,260	**Jilin**	China
3,375,830	**Jinan**	China
2,000,000	**Kābul**	Afghanistan
1,639,064	**Kanpur**	India
1,300,000	**Kaohsiung**	Taiwan
5,180,562	**Karachi**	Pakistan
1,114,173	**Kawasaki**	Japan
1,035,053	**Kitakyushu**	Japan
937,875	**Kuala Lumpur**	Malaysia
1,975,820	**Kunming**	China
454,052	**Kuwait**	Kuwait
1,419,390	**Kyoto**	Japan
2,952,689	**Lahore**	Pakistan
2,339,750	**Lanzhou**	China
1,007,604	**Lucknow**	India
1,060,000	**Luoyang**	China
4,289,347	**Madras**	India
6,720,050	**Manila – Quezon City**	Philippines
1,463,508	**Mashhad**	Iran
1,805,500	**Medan**	Indonesia
900,000	**Mosul**	Iraq
2,099,564	**Nagoya**	Japan
1,302,066	**Nagpur**	India
2,471,070	**Nanchang**	China
3,682,270	**Nanjing**	China
1,436,000	**Novosibirsk**	USSR
1,148,000	**Omsk**	USSR
8,594,000	**Osaka-Kobe**	Japan
1,686,109	**Pune (Poona)**	India
3,516,768	**Pusan**	South Korea
2,639,448	**Pyŏngyang**	North Korea
4,204,840	**Qingdao**	China
1,300,000	**Qiqihar**	China
2,458,712	**Rangoon**	Burma
794,843	**Rawalpindi**	Pakistan
1,500,000	**Riyadh**	Saudi Arabia
4,000,000	**Saigon (Ho Chi Minh)**	Vietnam
1,582,073	**Sapporo**	Japan
1,205,800	**Semarang**	Indonesia
9,645,824	**Seoul**	South Korea
2,050,000	**Shanghai**	China
5,054,640	**Shenyang**	China
1,160,000	**Shijiazhuang**	China
2,647,100	**Singapore**	Singapore
2,223,600	**Surabaya**	Indonesia
1,367,000	**Sverdlovsk**	USSR
2,030,649	**Taegu**	South Korea
7,990,000	**Tianjin**	China
2,640,000	**Taipei**	Taiwan
2,176,880	**Taiyuan**	China
1,390,000	**Tangshan**	China
2,073,000	**Tashkent**	USSR
6,042,584	**Tehrān**	Iran
1,555,427	**Tel Aviv**	Israel
1,680,282	**Tokyo**	Japan
4,273,080	**Wuhan**	China
2,911,580	**Xian**	China
1,942,970	**Zhengzhou**	China
2,300,000	**Zibo**	China

EUROPE

Population	Metropolitan Area	Country
1,030,743	**Amsterdam**	Netherlands
476,044	**Antwerp**	Belgium
3,027,331	**Athens**	Greece
1,757,000	**Baku**	USSR
1,703,744	**Barcelona**	Spain
1,407,073	**Belgrade**	Yugoslavia
3,236,009	**Berlin**	Germany
2,311,000	**Birmingham**	UK
291,400	**Bonn**	Germany
545,100	**Bremen**	Germany
970,346	**Brussels**	Belgium
2,272,526	**Bucharest**	Romania
3,962,000	**Budapest**	Hungary
927,500	**Cologne**	Germany
1,343,916	**Copenhagen**	Denmark
1,179,000	**Dnepropetrovsk**	USSR
1,110,000	**Donetsk**	USSR
920,956	**Dublin**	Rep. of Ireland
541,800	**Duisburg**	Germany
579,800	**Düsseldorf**	Germany
2,745,700	**Essen – Dortmund**	Germany
614,700	**Frankfurt**	Germany
384,507	**Geneva**	Switzerland
894,034	**Glasgow**	UK
1,438,000	**Gorkiy**	USSR
680,391	**The Hague**	Netherlands
1,593,600	**Hamburg**	Germany
524,300	**Hannover**	Germany
5,494,916	**Istanbul**	Turkey
1,094,000	**Kazan**	USSR
1,611,000	**Kharkov**	USSR
2,587,000	**Kiev**	USSR
1,257,000	**Kuybyshev**	USSR
5,020,000	**Leningrad**	USSR
1,611,887	**Lisbon**	Portugal
9,021,683	**London**	UK
3,100,507	**Madrid**	Spain
2,577,700	**Manchester**	UK
1,080,000	**Marseilles**	France
1,478,505	**Milan**	Italy
1,589,000	**Minsk**	USSR
8,967,000	**Moscow**	USSR
1,188,800	**Munich**	Germany
1,200,958	**Naples**	Italy
1,115,000	**Odessa**	USSR
1,314,794	**Oporto**	Portugal
453,730	**Oslo**	Norway
8,510,000	**Paris**	France
1,091,000	**Perm**	USSR
1,200,266	**Prague**	Czechoslovakia
915,000	**Riga**	USSR
2,817,227	**Rome**	Italy
1,020,000	**Rostov-on-Don**	USSR
1,035,530	**Rotterdam**	Netherlands
1,128,859	**Sofia**	Bulgaria
1,617,038	**Stockholm**	Sweden
571,100	**Stuttgart**	Germany
482,000	**Tallinn**	USSR
1,260,000	**Tbilisi**	USSR
1,025,390	**Turin**	Italy
1,083,000	**Ufa**	USSR
1,531,000	**Vienna**	Austria
582,000	**Vilnius**	USSR
999,000	**Volgograd**	USSR
1,671,400	**Warsaw**	Poland
1,119,000	**Yerevan**	USSR
1,174,512	**Zagreb**	Yugoslavia

AFRICA

Population	Metropolitan Area	Country
2,000,000	**Abidjan**	Côte d'Ivoire
1,464,901	**Addis Ababa**	Ethiopia
4,000,000	**Alexandria**	Egypt
2,600,000	**Algiers**	Algeria
13,300,000	**Cairo**	Egypt
1,911,521	**Cape Town**	South Africa
2,904,000	**Casablanca**	Morocco
1,400,000	**Dakar**	Senegal
1,096,000	**Dar-es-Salaam**	Tanzania
982,075	**Durban**	South Africa
1,670,800	**El Giza**	Egypt
1,609,408	**Johannesburg**	South Africa
1,343,651	**Khartoum**	Sudan
2,653,558	**Kinshasa**	Zaire
4,200,000	**Lagos**	Nigeria
1,200,000	**Luanda**	Angola
1,288,700	**Nairobi**	Kenya

NORTH & CENTRAL AMERICA

Population	Metropolitan Area	Country
2,657,000	**Atlanta**	USA
2,303,000	**Baltimore**	USA
2,842,000	**Boston**	USA
958,000	**Buffalo**	USA
1,091,000	**Charlotte – Gastonia – Rock Hill**	USA
6,199,000	**Chicago**	USA
1,438,000	**Cincinnati**	USA
1,851,000	**Cleveland**	USA
1,320,000	**Columbus**	USA
3,725,000	**Dallas – Fort Worth**	USA
1,633,000	**Denver**	USA
4,362,000	**Detroit**	USA
3,044,000	**Guadalajara**	Mexico
2,025,700	**Havana**	Cuba
3,228,000	**Houston**	USA
1,546,000	**Kansas City**	USA
13,471,000	**Los Angeles**	USA
18,748,000	**Mexico City**	Mexico
2,954,000	**Miami – Fort Lauderdale**	USA
1,389,000	**Milwaukee**	USA
2,336,000	**Minneapolis – St Paul**	USA
2,335,000	**Monterrey**	Mexico
2,921,357	**Montreal**	Canada
1,321,000	**New Orleans**	USA
1,891,000	**Newark**	USA
18,054,000	**New York**	USA
1,346,000	**Norfolk – Virginia Beach – Newport News**	USA
975,000	**Oklahoma City**	USA
819,263	**Ottawa**	Canada
4,866,000	**Philadelphia**	USA
1,960,000	**Phoenix**	USA
2,105,000	**Pittsburg**	USA
1,168,000	**Portland**	USA
1,217,600	**Puebla de Zaragoza**	Mexico
603,267	**Quebec**	Canada
979,000	**Rochester**	USA
1,336,000	**Sacramento**	USA
1,055,000	**Salt Lake City – Ogden**	USA
1,307,000	**San Antonio**	USA
2,286,000	**San Diego**	USA
3,558,000	**San Francisco – Oakland**	USA
1,415,000	**San Jose**	USA
1,816,300	**San Juan**	Puerto Rico
1,550,739	**Santo Domingo**	Dominican Republic
1,796,000	**Seattle**	USA
2,458,000	**St Louis**	USA
1,965,000	**Tampa – St Petersburg**	USA
3,427,168	**Toronto**	Canada
1,380,729	**Vancouver**	Canada
3,646,000	**Washington DC**	USA
600,700	**Winnipeg**	Canada

SOUTH AMERICA

Population	Metropolitan Area	Country
1,137,150	**Barranquilla**	Colombia
3,475,541	**Belo Horizonte**	Brazil
4,486,000	**Bogotá**	Colombia
1,683,700	**Brasília**	Brazil
12,600,000	**Buenos Aires**	Argentina
1,400,828	**Cali**	Colombia
3,247,698	**Caracas**	Venezuela
1,000,000	**Córdoba**	Argentina
1,600,000	**Guayaquil**	Ecuador
4,605,043	**Lima**	Peru
2,200,000	**Medellín**	Colombia
1,309,100	**Montevideo**	Uruguay
2,886,101	**Pôrto Alegre**	Brazil
1,093,278	**Quito**	Ecuador
2,912,016	**Recife**	Brazil
10,980,015	**Rio de Janeiro**	Brazil
1,000,000	**Rosario**	Argentina
2,329,604	**Salvador**	Brazil
4,858,342	**Santiago**	Chile
16,710,013	**São Paulo**	Brazil

AUSTRALASIA

Population	Metropolitan Area	Country
1,024,000	**Adelaide**	Australia
842,000	**Auckland**	New Zealand
1,240,000	**Brisbane**	Australia
297,000	**Canberra**	Australia
301,000	**Christchurch**	New Zealand
3,001,000	**Melbourne**	Australia
1,118,000	**Perth**	Australia
3,594,000	**Sydney**	Australia
325,200	**Wellington**	New Zealand

GLOSSARY

Language Abbreviations

The entries in this short glossary have been restricted to the less widely-known geographical terms. It also omits terms which are visually similar eg. banc, banco, bank.

Afr	Afrikaans	*Kor*	Korean
Alb	Albanian	*Lao*	Laotian
Ar	Arabic	*Lap*	Lappish
Ben	Bengali	*Lat*	Latvian
Ber	Berber	*Mal*	Malay
Bul	Bulgarian	*Mlg*	Malagasy
Bur	Burmese	*Mon*	Mongolian
Cam	Cambodian	*Nor*	Norwegian
Ch	Chinese	*Per*	Persian
Cz	Czech	*Pol*	Polish
Dan	Danish	*Por*	Portuguese
Dut	Dutch	*Rom*	Romanian
Est	Estonian	*Rus*	Russian
Fae	Faeroese	*Sca*	Scandinavian
Fin	Finnish	*S-C*	Serbo-Croat
Fr	French	*Sla*	Slavonic
Gae	Gaelic	*Som*	Somali
Ger	German	*Sp*	Spanish
Gr	Greek	*Swe*	Swedish
Heb	Hebrew	*Th*	Thai (Siamese)
Hin	Hindi	*Tib*	Tibetan
Hun	Hungarian	*Tu*	Turkish
Ice	Icelandic	*Ur*	Urdu
Ind	Indonesian	*Vt*	Vietnamese
It	Italian	*Wel*	Welsh
Jpn	Japanese		

Name	Language	Meaning
A, –å, –á	*Sca, Ice*	stream
Adası	*Tu*	island
Adrar	*Ber*	mountains
Aiguille	*Fr*	peak, needle
Ain, 'Aīn, 'Ayn	*Ar*	spring, well
Akrotírion	*Gr*	cape, point
Ala–	*Fin*	lower
Alt–a, –o	*It, Por, Sp*	upper
Ao	*Ch, Th*	bay
Arro-io, yo	*Por, Sp*	watercourse
Au	*Cam*	river
Aust–	*Nor*	east(ern)
Ayia, Áyios	*Gr*	saint
Ba	*Vt*	mountain
Bāb	*Ar*	strait
Bādiyah, Bādiet	*Ar*	desert steppe
Baelt	*Dan*	strait
Bahia	*Sp*	bay
Baḩr, Baḩrah	*Ar*	sea, channel
Baixo	*Por*	lower
Baj–a, –o	*Sp*	lower
Ban	*Cam, Lao, Th*	village
–bana	*Jpn*	point, cape
Bandao	*Ch*	peninsula
Bandar	*Ar, Mal, Per,*	port, harbour
Bas, –se	*Fr*	lower
Batin, Batn	*Ar*	depression
Be'er(ot)	*Heb*	well(s)
Bei	*Ch*	north(ern)
Bereg	*Rus*	bank, shore
–berg, Berg(e)	*Sca, Ger*	mountain(s)
Bid	*Ar*	waterhole
Bir, Bīr, B'ir	*Ar*	well
Birk–at, –et	*Ar*	well, pool
–bjerg	*Dan*	hill
Boca	*Por, Sp*	mouth
Bocche	*It*	mouths, estuary
Boğazi	*Tu*	strait
Bol'sh–e, –aya, –oy	*Rus*	big
Bonom	*Vt*	mountain
–botn, –botten	*Nor, Swe*	valley floor
Bouche	*Fr*	mouth, estuary
–bre(en)	*Nor*	glacier
Bredning	*Dan*	bay
Bucht	*Ger*	bay
Bugt	*Dan*	bay
Bukhta	*Rus*	bay
Bukt(en)	*Nor, Swe*	bay
Bur–un, –nu	*Tu*	point, cape
Cabo	*Por, Sp*	cape, highland
Caka	*Tib*	salt lake
cañad–a, –ón	*Sp*	ravine, gorge
Cañon	*Sp*	canyon
Cap, Capo	*Fr, It*	cape, headland
Cerro	*Sp*	hill, peak
Chaco	*Sp*	jungle region
Chaîne	*Fr*	mountain chain
Chiang	*Th*	town
Chott	*Ar*	salt lake, marsh
Cima, Cime	*It, Sp, Fr*	summit
Città	*It*	town, city
Ciudad	*Sp*	town, city
Co	*Tib*	lake
Col	*Fr*	high pass
Cordillera	*Sp*	mountain chain
Corn–e, –o	*Fr, It*	peak
Côte	*Fr*	coast, slope
Cu Lao	*Vt*	island
Cua	*Vt*	estuary inlet
Cun	*Ch*	village
Đa	*Vt*	river
Da	*Ch*	big
Dağ–ı	*Tu*	mountain
Dagh	*Per*	mountain
Dağlar–ı	*Tu*	mountains
–dal, –ur	*Sca, Afr*	valley
–dalur	*Ice*	valley
Dao	*Ch*	island
Darreh	*Per*	valley
Daryācheh	*Per*	lake
Dasht	*Per, Ur*	desert
Denizi	*Tu*	sea
–diep	*Dut*	channel
Djebel, Djibâl	*Ar*	mountain
–djup	*Ice*	fjord
Do, –do	*Vt, Kor*	island
Dolina	*Rus*	valley
Dong	*Ch*	east(ern)
Dorf, –dorf	*Ger, Afr*	village
–dwip	*Hin*	island
Eiland(en)	*Afr, Dut*	island(s)
–elv(a)	*Nor*	river
Embalse	*Sp*	reservoir
Embouchure	*Fr*	estuary
'Emeq	*Heb*	plain
Erg	*Ar*	desert with dunes
Eski	*Tu*	old
Espigão	*Por*	upland
Estero	*Sp*	inlet, estuary; swamp
Estrecho	*Sp*	strait
Estreito	*Por*	strait
Etang	*Fr*	lake, lagoon
–ye(jar)	*Ice*	island(s)
Ezers	*Lat*	lake
Fels	*Ger*	rock
Feng	*Ch*	peak
Fiume	*It*	river
–fjäll, fjell	*Swe, Nor*	mountain
–fjord(en)	*Dan, Nor*	fjord; lagoon
–fjördhur	*Ice*	fjord
–flói	*Ice*	bay
Foce, Foci	*It*	river-mouth(s)
–fonn	*Nor*	glacier
Fuente	*Sp*	source, well
Gang	*Ch*	harbour
–gata	*Jpn*	inlet, lagoon
–gawa	*Jpn*	river
Gebel	*Ar*	mountain
Gebirge	*Ger*	mountains
Gezīret	*Ar*	island
Gipfel	*Ger*	peak
Gji	*Alb*	inlet, bay
Gletscher	*Ger*	glacier
Gobi	*Mon*	desert
Gol	*Mon*	river
Göl(u)	*Tu*	lake
Gonglu	*Ch*	highway
Gor–a, –y	*Sla*	mountain(s)
–got	*Kor*	point, cape
Greben'	*Rus*	ridge
Gryada	*Rus*	ridge
Guan	*Ch*	pass
Guba	*Rus*	bay
–gunto	*Jpn*	island, group
Gunung	*Ind, Mal*	mountain
–haehyop	*Kor*	strait
Haff	*Ger*	bay
Hai	*Ch*	sea
Halbinsel	*Ger*	peninsula
halvöya	*Nor*	peninsula
Ham(m)ād–a	*Ar*	plateau
Hamakhtesh	*Heb*	depression
Hassi	*Ar*	well
–haug	*Nor*	hill
–havn	*Dan, Fae, Nor*	harbour
He	*Ch*	river
–hede, hei	*Dan, Nor*	heath
–hegyseg	*Hun*	mountains
Heide	*Ger*	heath, moor
Hka	*Bur*	river
–ho	*Nor*	peak
Hon	*Vt*	island
Hory	*Cz*	mountains
Hot	*Mon*	town
Hu	*Ch*	lake
Ia	*Vt*	stream, river
imeni	*Rus*	in the name of
Ipsoma	*Gr*	high ground
Irhzer	*Ber*	watercourse
Irmak	*Tu*	large river
'Irq	*Ar*	sand dunes
Iso–	*Fin*	big
Jabal	*Ar*	mountain
–järv, –i	*Est, Fin*	lake
–jaure, javrre	*Lap*	lake
Jazīrah	*Ar*	island
Jezioro	*Pol*	lake
Jiang	*Ch*	river
–jima	*Jpn*	island
–jok–i, –ka	*Fin, Lap*	river
–jökull	*Ice*	glacier
–kai	*Jpn*	bay, inlet, sea
–kaikyo	*Jpn*	strait
Kamen'	*Rus*	stone
–kawa	*Jpn*	river
Kefar	*Heb*	village
Kënet	*Alb*	inlet
Kep	*Alb*	point, cape
Kepulauan	*Ind*	archipelago, islands
Khalig, Khalij	*Ar*	bay, gulf
Khawr	*Ar*	inlet
Khersonisos	*Gr*	peninsula
Khrebet	*Rus*	mountain range
Klit	*Dan*	dunes
Klong	*Th*	canal, creek
–ko	*Jpn*	lake, inlet
Ko	*Th*	island
Kofel, Koge(e)l	*Ger*	dome-shaped hill
Kólpos	*Gr*	gulf
Kopf	*Ger*	hill
Körfezi(i)	*Tu*	bay, gulf
Kosa	*Rus*	spit of land
Kray	*Rus*	region
Kryazh	*Rus*	ridge
Kūh(ha)	*Per*	mountains(s)
Kum	*Rus*	sandy desert
–kundo	*Kor*	island group
Laem	*Th*	point
Lago	*It, Por, Sp*	lake
laht	*Est*	bay
Lam	*Th*	stream
Lande	*Ger*	sandy moor, heath
Laut	*Ind*	sea
Lednik	*Rus*	glacier
Les	*Cz, Rus*	woods, forest
lès, lez	*Fr*	near, beside
Lieh-tao	*Ch*	group of islands
Liman	*Rus*	bay, gulf
Liman–ı	*Tu*	harbour, port
Limni	*Gr*	lake, lagoon
Ling	*Ch*	mountain range
Llano	*Sp*	plain, prairie
Llyn	*Wel*	lake
Lohatanjona	*Mlg*	point
Loma	*Sp*	hill
Lu	*Ch*	street, road
Madīnat	*Ar*	town, city
Mae Nam	*Th*	river
Mal	*Alb*	mountain(s)
Mal–a, –o, –yy	*Sla*	small
Malé	*Cz*	small
Marsa, Mersa	*Ar*	anchorage, inlet
Masabb	*Ar*	canal, estuary
Mega, Megál–a, –o	*Gr*	big
Mesto	*Sla*	place, town
Mikr–í, ón	*Gr*	small
Mīnā'	*Ar*	port, harbour
Moni	*Gr*	monastery
More	*Rus*	sea
Muntii	*Rom*	mountains
Mynydd	*Wel*	mountain
–myr	*Nor, Swe*	moor, swamp
Mys	*Rus*	cape
na	*Sla*	on
nad	*Sla*	above, over
Nafūd	*Ar*	desert, dune
Nagor'ye	*Rus*	highland, uplands
Nagy–	*Hun*	big, great
Nahr	*Ar*	river
Nakhon	*Th*	town
Nam	*Bur, Th, Vt*	river
Nan	*Ch*	south(ern)
Né–a, –on, –os	*Gr*	new
Nei	*Ch*	inner
–nes	*Ice, Nor*	point, cape
Ngoc	*Vt*	mountain, peak
–ni	*Kor*	village
Nizhn–eye, –iy	*Rus*	lower
Nizina	*Cz, Rus*	lowland
Nizmennost'	*Rus*	lowlands
Nos	*Bul, Rus*	ness, point
Nosy	*Mlg*	island
Nov–a, –o	*Sla*	new
Nuur	*Mon*	lake
Ny–	*Sca*	new
ø, øy, ö, öy	*Sca*	island
Okrug	*Rus*	district
–oog	*Ger*	island
Órmos	*Gr*	bay
Óros (Óri)	*Ger*	mountain(s)
Ostrov(a)	*Rus*	island(s)
Otok(i)	*S–C*	island(s)
Oued	*Ar*	dry river-bed
Ozero (Ozera)	*Rus*	lake(s)
pää	*Fin*	hill
Pal–á, –ai, –ó, –ió	*Gr*	old
Parbat	*Ur*	mountain
Pegunungan	*Ind*	mountain range
Pelabohan	*Mal*	harbour
Pellg	*Alb*	bay
Pendi	*Ch*	basin
Pereval	*Rus*	pass
Pertuis	*Fr*	opening, strait
Perv–o, –yy	*Rus*	first
Peski	*Rus*	sands, desert
Pingyuan	*Ch*	plain
Ploskogor'ye	*Rus*	plateau
Pod	*Sla*	under, sub–
Poluostrov	*Rus*	peninsula
Polwysep	*Pol*	peninsula
Porogi	*Rus*	rapids
Poselok	*Rus*	settlement
Pradesh	*Hin*	state
presqu'île	*Fr*	peninsula
Pri	*Rus*	near, cis–
Proliv	*Rus*	strait
Protok–a	*Rus*	channel
Pulau, –pulau	*Ind, Mal*	island(s)
Puy	*Fr*	peak
Qi	*Ch*	admin. div.
Qiao	*Ch*	bridge
Qiryat	*Heb*	town
Qu	*Tib*	stream
Quan	*Ch*	spring
Qundao	*Ch*	archipelago
Rade	*Fr*	roadstead
rags	*Lat*	point, cape
Ramlat	*Ar*	sands
–rani	*Ice*	spur
Ra's	*Ar, Per*	point, cape
Ravnina	*Rus*	plain
Rayon	*Rus*	district
Represa	*Por*	dam
Reshteh	*Per*	mountain range
–retsugan	*Jpn*	chain of rocks
–retto	*Jpn*	chain of islands
–rev	*Nor*	reef, cliff
Ri	*Tib*	mountain
–ri	*Kor*	village
Rosh	*Heb*	point, cape
Rt	*S–C*	point, cape
Rubha	*Gae*	point, cape
Rūd (khāneh)	*Per*	river
Rudohorie	*Cz*	mountains
–saar(i)	*Est, Fin*	island
Sabkhat	*Ar*	salt-flat
Saghīr	*Ar*	small
saḩrā', saḩārā	*Ar*	desert(s)
–saki, –misaki	*Jpn*	point, cape
San, –san	*Lao, Jpn, Kor*	mountain
Sebkra	*Ar*	salt-flat
Selat	*Ind*	strait, channel
Selatan	*Ind, Mal*	south(ern)
selka	*Fin*	ridge; open water
Selo	*Rus, S–C*	village
Selva	*Sp*	forest
–sen	*Jpn*	mountain
–seto	*Jpn*	strait, channel
Sever–o, –naya	*Rus*	north(ern)
Shamo	*Ch*	desert
Shan	*Ch*	mountain(s)
Shandi	*Ch*	mountainous area
Shang	*Ch*	upper
Shankou	*Ch*	pass
Shanmai	*Ch*	mountain range
Shaṭṭ	*Ar*	river (–mouth)
–shima	*Jpn*	island
–shoto	*Jpn*	group of islands
Shuiku	*Ch*	reservoir
–sjo	*Nor*	lake
So	*Dan, Nor*	lake
Song	*Vt*	river
Spitze	*Ger*	peak
Sredn–e, –e, –aya	*Sla*	middle
Sredn–e, –eye, –iy, –yaya	*Rus*	middle
Star–a, –e	*Cz*	old
Star–a, –i	*S–C*	old
Star–aya, –oye, –yy, –yye	*Rus*	old
Step'	*Rus*	steppe
Stor–, Stora	*Swe*	big
–suido	*Jpn*	strait, channel
Sungai	*Ind, Mal*	river
–suo	*Fin*	swamp, marsh
Sveti	*S–C*	saint
Szenti–	*Hun*	saint
–take	*Jpn*	peak
Tanjong	*Ind, Mal*	cape, point
Tao	*Ch*	island
Tasek	*Mal*	lake
Tassili	*Ber*	plateau
Tau	*Rus*	mountain(s)
Tekojarvi	*Fin*	reservoir
Teluk	*Ind*	bay
Tengah	*Ind*	middle
Tepe–si	*Tu*	hill, peak
Thale	*Th*	lake
Timur	*Ind*	east(ern)
–tjakka	*Lap*	mountain
–to	*Jpn*	island
–tong	*Kor*	village
Tonle	*Cam*	lake
–udden	*Swe*	point, cape
Uj–	*Hun*	new
Ujung	*Ind*	point, cape
Urayq	*Ar*	area of dunes
Ust'ye	*Rus*	estuary
Utara, Uttar	*Ind, Hin*	north(ern)
Uul	*Mon*	mountains
Uyun	*Ar*	springs
v	*Sla*	in
–vaara(t)	*Fin*	hill(s)
–vag	*Nor*	bay
–vann, Vatn	*Nor*	lake
–varos	*Hun*	town
–varre	*Nor*	mountain
Vast–er, –ra	*Swe*	western
Vaux	*Fr*	valleys
Velik–a, –o, –aya	*Sla*	big
Verkhn–e, –aya, –iy	*Rus*	upper
–vesi	*Fin*	water, lake
V –ig–ik	*Dan, Nor*	bay
Vinh	*Vt*	bay
Vodokhranil-ishche	*Rus*	reservoir
Vorota	*Rus*	gate, strait
Vostochn–aya, –yy	*Rus*	eastern
Vozvyshennost'	*Rus*	uplands
Vpadina	*Rus*	depression
Vrch(y)	*Cz*	mountain(s)
Vung	*Vt*	bay, gulf
Vysok–aya, –o, –iy	*Rus*	high
Vyssh–aya, –e, –iy	*Rus*	higher
Wad	*Dut*	sand-flat
Wādī	*Ar*	watercourse
Wai	*Ch*	outer
Wan	*Ch*	bay
–wan	*Jpn*	bay
Wielk–a, –i, –o	*Pol*	big
Wysok–a, –i, –o	*Pol*	high
Xi	*Ch*	west; stream
Xia	*Ch*	lower; gorge
Xian	*Ch*	county
Xiao	*Ch*	small
Xu	*Ch*	islet
Yam	*Heb*	lake, sea
–yama	*Jpn*	mountain(s)
Ye	*Bur*	island
Yli–	*Fin*	upper
Yoma	*Bur*	mountain range
You	*Ch*	right
Yuzhn–o, –yy	*Rus*	southern
Za	*Rus*	behind, trans–
–zaki	*Jpn*	point, cape
Zalew, Zaliv	*Pol, Rus*	bay
–zan	*Jpn*	mountain
Zapadn–aya, –o	*Rus*	western
Zapovednik	*Rus*	reserve
Zemlya	*Rus*	land
–zhen	*Ch*	town
Zhong	*Ch*	middle
Zhou	*Ch*	islet
Zui	*Ch*	point, spit
Zuid	*Dut*	south
Zuidelijk	*Dut*	southern

Abbreviations used in the Index

Abbr	Meaning	Abbr	Meaning	Abbr	Meaning
Afghan	Afghanistan	Colo	Colorado	Herts	Hertfordshire
Afr	Africa, African	Conn	Connecticut	Hist reg	Historic region
Ala	Alabama	Czech	Czechoslovakia	Hist site	Historic site
Amer	America, American	Den	Denmark	I, Isld	Island
Anc mon	Ancient monument	Dept	Department, Département	Ind	Indian
Anc site	Ancient site	Des	Desert	Is, Islds	Islands
Arch	Archipel, archipelago, archipiélago	Dist	District	Isld king	Island kingdom
Arg	Argentina	Div	Division	Isth	Isthmus
Ariz	Arizona	Dom Rep	Dominican Republic	Jct, junc, junct	Junction
Ark	Arkansas	E	East, Eastern	L	Lake
A.S.S.R.	Autonomous Soviet Socialist Republic	Eng	England, English	Lancs	Lancashire
Aust	Australia	Eq, Equat	Equatorial	Lincs	Lincolnshire
Aut	Autonomous	Est	Estuary	Lt Ho	Lighthouse
B	Bay	Fed	Federation	Madhya Prad	Madhya Pradesh
Berks	Berkshire	Fj	Fjord	Man	Manitoba
Br	British	Fr	French	Mass	Massachusetts
Br Col	British Columbia	G	Gulf	Med	Mediterranean
Bucks	Buckinghamshire	Ger	Germany	Mich	Michigan
C	Cape	Gla	Glacier	Minn	Minnesota
Cal, Calif	California	Gloucs	Gloucestershire	Miss	Mississippi
Can	Canal	Grp	Group	Mon	Monument
Cat(s)	Cataract(s)	Gt	Great	Mont	Montana
Cent	Central	Hants	Hampshire	Moz	Mozambique
Chan	Channel	Hbr	Harbour	Mt, Mte	Mountain
Co	County, Coast	Hd	Head	Mth(s)	Mouth(s)
		H.E.	Hydro Electric	Mt ra	Mountain range

Abbr	Meaning	Abbr	Meaning	Abbr	Meaning
Mts	Mountains	Plat	Plateau	Staffs	Staffordshire
N	North, Northern, New	Port	Portugal, Portuguese	Stat Area	Statistical Area
Nat Park	National Park	Pr	Prince	Str	Strait
Neth, Nether,	Netherlands	Prefect	Prefecture	Switz	Switzerland
Neths	Netherlands	Princ	Principality	Tenn	Tennessee
Nev	Nevada	Prom	Promontory	Terr	Territory
New Bruns	New Brunswick	Prot	Protectorate	Tex	Texas
New Hamps	New Hampshire	Prov	Province	Tribal dist	Tribal district
New Mex	New Mexico	Pt, Pta, Pto	Point	U.A.E.	United Arab Emirates
Nfld	Newfoundland	Qnsld	Queensland	U.K.	United Kingdom
Notts	Nottinghamshire	R	Rio, river	Union Terr	Union Territory
N Scotia	Nova Scotia	Ra	Range	U.S.A.	United States of America
N S W	New South Wales	Rdg	Ridge	U.S.S.R.	Union of Soviet Socialist Republics
N W Terr	Northwest Territories	Reg	Region	V	Valley
N Y	New York	Rep	Republic	Ven	Venezuela
Oc	Ocean	Res	Reservoir	Vict	Victoria
Okla	Oklahoma	S	South, Southern	Virg	Virginia
Old prov	Old province	Sa	Serra, Sierra	Vol	Volcano
Oxon	Oxford, Oxfordshire	Sask	Saskatchewan	W	West, Western
Pac	Pacific	Sd	Sound	Wash	Washington
Pass	Passage	Sk	Shuiku (reservoir)	W I	West Indies
Pen	Peninsula	Span	Spanish	Wilts	Wiltshire
Penn	Pennsylvania	Spr	Spring	Wyo	Wyoming
People's Rep	People's Republic	S.S.R.	Soviet Socialist Republic	Yorks	Yorkshire
Physical reg	Physical region	St, Ste	Saint, Sainte		
Pk	Peak	Sta	Station		

Germany and Yemen
Although the maps in this edition have been revised to take account of the unification of East and West Germany and of North and South Yemen, the index reflects the previous divisions.

Aa — Ahaura

32 F8 Ahaus W Germany
145 F3 Ahimanawa Range New Zealand
145 D1 Ahipara New Zealand
76 E1 Ahiri India
145 E3 Ahititi New Zealand
116 G7 Ahklun Mts Alaska U.S.A.
29 J10 Ahlainen Finland
32 L7 Ahlden W Germany
32 G9 Ahlen W Germany
32 K6 Ahlerstedt W Germany
32 H7 Ahlhorn W Germany
74 E7 Ahmadabad India
77 E6 Ahmadī Iran
77 A5 Aḥmadi, Al Kuwait
80 G1 Ahmadīyah Syria
74 F9 Ahmadnagar India
74 G9 Ahmadpur India
74 D4 Ahmadpur Pakistan
74 D3 Ahmadpur Pakistan
86 H4 Ahmar Mts Ethiopia
47 J6 Ahmetli Turkey
124 E5 Ahome Mexico
37 L4 Ahorntal W Germany
112 K1 Ahoskie North Carolina U.S.A.
Ah-pa see Aba
36 B3 Ahr R W Germany
36 B3 Ahrdorf W Germany
33 S6 Ahrensberg East Germany
33 N4 Ahrensbök W Germany
32 M5 Ahrensburg W Germany
33 T7 Ahrensfelde East Germany
32 K6 Ahrenswohlde W Germany
Ahrweiler see Bad Neuenahr-Ahrweiler
32 H9 Ahse R W Germany
29 L9 Ähtäri Finland
29 L9 Ähtärinjärvi L Finland
68 B4 Ahtaung Burma
29 K8 Ähtävä Finland
124 G7 Ahuacatlán Mexico
125 P11 Ahuachapán El Salvador
124 H7 Ahualulco de Mercado Mexico
145 F3 Ahuriri Pt New Zealand
144 B6 Ahuriri R New Zealand
27 G16 Åhus Sweden
77 A4 Ahvāz Iran
116 K8 Aiaktalik I Alaska U.S.A.
128 F4 Aiapua,L Brazil
128 E3 Aiari R Brazil
65 A3 Aibag Gol R China
60 Q2 Aibetsu Japan
38 J7 Aich R Austria
37 N7 Aich W Germany
37 L7 Aichach W Germany
61 L10 Aichi prefect Japan
116 Q2 Aichilik R Alaska U.S.A.
26 N3 Aiddejavrre Norway
37 P6 Aidenbach W Germany
46 F6 Aidhipsoú Greece
80 G3 Aidun Jordan
102 S12 Aiea Hawaiian Is
40 E5 Aigle Switzerland
21 M4 Aigle, l' France
122 G2 Aigle, L. à l' Quebec Canada
18 H8 Aigoual,Mt France
18 E7 Aigre France
18 E6 Aigrefeuille d'Aunis France
20 H7 Aigrefeuille-sur-Maine France
19 Q14 Aigu France
19 Q13 Aiguebelle France
121 M4 Aiguebelle, Parc de Quebec Canada
18 H9 Aigues-Mortes France
40 E6 Aiguille du Midi mt France
19 Q14 Aiguilles d'Arves mts France
40 E6 Aiguille Verte mt France
18 F8 Aiguillon France
83 L13 Aiguillon,C d' Kerguelen Indian Oc
18 G6 Aigurande France
Aihui see Heihe
47 O12 Aikaterini, Akra Ayios C Greece
61 M7 Aikawa Japan
112 F4 Aiken South Carolina U.S.A.
45 Q7 Ailano Italy
140 C6 Aileron N Terr Australia
22 E5 Ailette R France
71 M9 Aileu Timor
29 M2 Ailigas mt Finland
19 Q18 Aille R France
40 D2 Aillevillers France
21 P1 Ailly-le-Haut-Clocher France
21 M2 Ailly, Pte, d' France
21 P2 Ailly-sur-Noye France
120 J9 Ailsa Craig Ontario Canada
12 C3 Ailsa Craig isld Scotland
51 N3 Aim U.S.S.R.
71 L9 Aimaro Indonesia
71 K9 Aimere Indonesia
129 K7 Aimores Brazil
129 K7 Aimores,Serra dos mts Brazil
40 B6 Ain R France
40 B5 Ain dept France
52 B5 Ainaži U.S.S.R.
43 A13 Aïn Beïda Algeria
85 D2 Aïn Beni Mathar Morocco
21 O3 Aincourt France
84 H4 'Ain Dalla Egypt
37 K7 Aindling W Germany
43 B12 Aïn Draham Tunisia
80 E1 Aïn Ebel Lebanon
80 G3 Ain el Ghazal Jordan
80 E7 'Ain el Ghuweir Jordan
85 E3 Aïn-el-Hadjadj Algeria
17 H10 Ain el Hadjar Algeria
84 H4 Aîn el Wadi Egypt
80 G3 Ain esh Shilaq Jordan
86 C2 Aïn Galakka Chad
68 B2 Ainggyi Burma
80 G4 Ain Janna Jordan
43 B12 Aïn Kerma Algeria
80 E6 Ain Qilt Jordan
17 H2 Ainsa Spain
85 B5 Ain Safra Mauritania
Ain Salah see In Salah
13 E6 Ainsdale England
85 D2 Aïn Sefra Algeria
123 L7 Ainslie,L C Breton I, Nova Scotia
79 C9 'Ain Sukhna Egypt
98 G7 Ainsworth Nebraska U.S.A.
17 H9 Aïn Tédèles Algeria
17 G9 Aïn Témouchent Algeria
Aïn Touta see El Homr
60 R2 Aioi Japan
60 H11 Aioi Japan
85 C4 Aïoun Abdel Malek Mauritania
85 C5 Aïoun el Atrouss Mauritania
128 E7 Aiquile Bolivia
69 H11 Air isld Indonesia
21 O2 Airaines France
128 F4 Airao Brazil
69 D12 Airbangis Sumatra
118 C7 Airdrie Alberta Canada
12 D2 Airdrie Scotland
22 C2 Aire France
17 K5 Aire,I.del Balearic Is
21 H3 Airel France
13 G6 Aire,R England
18 E9 Airè sur L'Adour France
115 M4 Air Force I Northwest Territories Canada
65 B3 Airgin Sum China
141 J5 Airlie Queensland Australia
100 B5 Airlie Oregon U.S.A.
142 B5 Airlie I Western Australia Australia
45 R7 Airola Italy
85 F5 Aïr ou Azbine mt reg Niger
71 M8 Airpanas Indonesia
8 C1 Air,Pt of Wales
12 E1 Airth Scotland
21 K8 Airvault France
37 K4 Aisch R W Germany
133 C7 Aisén prov Chile
117 E5 Aishihik Yukon Territory Canada
22 F5 Aisne dept France
22 H5 Aisne R France
40 D3 Aissey France
80 E1 Aïta ech Chaab Lebanon
136 J2 Aitape Papua New Guinea
80 E1 Aitaroun Lebanon
37 O6 Aiterhofen W Germany
144 A7 Aitken, Mt New Zealand
99 N3 Aitkin Minnesota U.S.A.
46 E6 Aitolikón Greece
55 B4 Aitova U.S.S.R.
16 E9 Aït Youssef ou Ali Morocco
48 H4 Aiud Romania
18 E6 Aix isld France
18 G5 Aix d'Angillon,les France
19 O18 Aix-en-Provence France
18 F7 Aixe-sur-Vienne France
Aix-la-Chapelle see Aachen
117 J8 Aiyansh British Columbia Canada
79 B9 'Aiyat,El Egypt
46 F7 Aiyina isld Greece
46 F4 Aiyinion Greece
46 E6 Aiyion Greece
46 F7 Áiyos Andréas Greece
47 H9 Áiyos Ioánnis, Akr C Crete Greece
75 P7 Aizawl India
87 C10 Aizeb R Namibia
20 G8 Aizenay France
27 M15 Aizpute U.S.S.R.
61 N8 Aizu-Takada Japan
61 N8 Aizu-Wakamatsu Japan
78 L3 Ajab Shir Iran
18 L11 Ajaccio Corsica
74 J6 Ajaigarh India
128 D3 Ajaju R Colombia
80 G3 'Ajamī Syria
143 A8 Ajana Western Australia Australia
121 M9 Ajax Ontario Canada
144 D5 Ajax, Mt New Zealand
101 M4 Ajax Mt Idaho/Montana U.S.A.
84 G3 Ajdābiyā Libya
42 F3 Ajdovščina Yugoslavia
61 O5 Ajigasawa Japan
61 N10 Ajiro Japan
61 P7 Aji-shima isld Japan
48 D3 Ajka Hungary
80 G4 Ajlun Jordan
77 D7 'Ajmān U.A.E.
74 F5 Ajmer India
103 M9 Ajo Arizona U.S.A.
16 E1 Ajo,C Spain
129 G3 Ajoewa Suriname
103 M9 Ajo,Mt Arizona U.S.A.
71 C2 Aju isld W Irian
128 E4 Ajuana R Brazil
125 J8 Ajuchitlán Mexico
71 F5 Ajuy Philippines
60 Q2 Akabira Japan
85 E3 Akabli Algeria
59 L1 Akademii, Zaliv B U.S.S.R.
71 M9 Akadirunsikun Indonesia
61 M8 Akadomari Japan
61 M10 Akaishi-dake pk Japan
74 G10 Akalkot India
60 S2 Akan Japan
79 D3 Akanthou Cyprus
60 G12 Akaoka Japan
47 L6 Akar R Turkey
61 P12 Akarie-Ue Okinawa
144 D5 Akaroa New Zealand
27 G15 Åkarp, N Sweden
78 H3 Akarsu Turkey
60 G10 Akasaki Japan
86 F1 Akasha Sudan
60 H11 Akashi Japan
29 K4 Äkäsjoki R Finland
29 K4 Äkäsjokisuu Finland
98 F4 Akaska South Dakota U.S.A.
61 N8 Akatani Japan
26 J4 Akavare mt Sweden
80 F2 'Akbara Israel
57 B2 Akbasty U.S.S.R.
57 G1 Akbaur U.S.S.R.
55 F5 Akbeit U.S.S.R.
55 C5 Akbulak U.S.S.R.
78 F2 Akçadağ Turkey
78 G3 Akçakale Turkey
47 N10 Akçaova Turkey
47 K8 Akçay Turkey
85 A4 Akchar,Dunes de l' Mauritania
57 G1 Akchatau U.S.S.R.
57 H3 Akchi U.S.S.R.
47 J7 Akçoava Turkey
47 K6 Ak Dağ mt Turkey
47 K5 Akdağ mt Turkey
78 E2 Akdağmadeni Turkey
56 D5 Ak Dovurak U.S.S.R.
61 L10 Akechi Japan
71 B2 Akelamo Halmahera Indonesia
9 F3 Akeley England
99 M2 Akeley Minnesota U.S.A.
27 B13 Åkernes Norway
27 K12 Akersberga Sweden
27 E12 Akershus county Norway
26 G8 Åkersjön Sweden
27 J12 Akers-styckebruk Sweden
71 B2 Akeselaka Halmahera Indonesia
57 B2 Akespe U.S.S.R.
53 F12 Akhalkalaki U.S.S.R.
53 F12 Akhaltsikhe U.S.S.R.
57 E4 Akhangaran U.S.S.R.
46 F6 Akharnai Greece
80 F2 'Akhbera Israel
84 G3 Akhdar, Jabal al mts Libya
79 G10 Akhḍar, Wādī al watercourse Saudi Arabia
46 E5 Akhelóös R Greece
116 K8 Akhiok Alaska U.S.A.
78 A2 Akhisar Turkey
84 J4 Akhmim Egypt
Akhna see Athna
79 H2 Akhterīn Syria
53 C12 Akhtopol Bulgaria
53 G9 Akhtubinsk U.S.S.R.
53 G12 Akhty U.S.S.R.
53 D8 Akhtyrka U.S.S.R.
57 K6 Akhunbabayev U.S.S.R.
60 G12 Aki Japan
116 G6 Akiak Alaska U.S.A.
52 H3 Akim U.S.S.R.
58 G1 Akima U.S.S.R.
115 L7 Akimiski I Northwest Territories Canada
53 E10 Akimovka U.S.S.R.
60 F11 Aki-nada sea Japan
79 F2 Akıncı Burun C Turkey
47 J7 Akıncılar Turkey
27 G16 Akirkeby Denmark
61 O6 Akita Japan
145 F4 Akitio New Zealand
56 G3 Akitkan, Khrebet mts U.S.S.R.
85 B5 Akjoujt Mauritania
80 G4 'Akka Jordan
85 C3 Akka Morocco
55 D6 Akkabak U.S.S.R.
26 J4 Akkajaure L Sweden
57 A3 Akkala, Mys C U.S.S.R.
116 B4 Akkani U.S.S.R.
55 D5 Akkarga U.S.S.R.
57 E2 Akkense U.S.S.R.
60 S2 Akkeshi Japan
80 D2 'Akko Israel
57 F3 Akkol' U.S.S.R.
57 H2 Akkol' U.S.S.R.
47 J7 Akköy Turkey
55 B6 Akkozinskiy U.S.S.R.
25 E2 Akkrum Netherlands
53 G10 Akkystau U.S.S.R.
46 F7 Akladhókambos Greece
114 F4 Aklavik Northwest Territories Canada
85 C5 Aklé Aouana reg Mauritania
52 B6 Akmene U.S.S.R.
52 C6 Akniste U.S.S.R.
86 F4 Akobo R Ethiopia/Sudan
74 G8 Akola India
116 F6 Akolmiut Alaska U.S.A.
86 G2 Āk'ordat Ethiopia
47 N11 Akören Turkey
74 G8 Akot India
56 C5 Ak-Oyuk, Gora mt U.S.S.R.
115 N5 Akpatok I Northwest Territories Canada
79 D1 Akpınar Turkey
57 J4 Akqi China
98 J1 Akra North Dakota U.S.A.
79 G2 Akrād, Jabal al mt Syria
27 B12 Åkrafjorden inlet Norway
28 R9 Akranes Iceland
46 E6 Akráta Greece
46 E8 Akritas, Akra C Greece
28 D6 Åkrog Bugt B Denmark
120 F4 Akron Ontario Canada
111 J9 Akron Alabama U.S.A.
98 C9 Akron Colorado U.S.A.
94 A5 Akron Indiana U.S.A.
98 K7 Akron Iowa U.S.A.
94 D3 Akron Michigan U.S.A.
94 J3 Akron New York U.S.A.
94 F5 Akron Ohio U.S.A.
95 L6 Akron Pennsylvania U.S.A.
46 G9 Akrotiri Crete Greece
79 D4 Akrotiri B Cyprus
74 H1 Aksai Chin L Kashmir
55 B4 Aksakovo U.S.S.R.
78 E2 Aksaray Turkey
57 H4 Aksay R U.S.S.R.
78 C2 Akşehir Turkey
78 C2 Aksehir Gölü L Turkey
55 B4 Aksenovo U.S.S.R.
58 G1 Aksenovo-Zilovskoye U.S.S.R.
77 D5 Aks-e Rostam R Iran
51 L3 Aksha U.S.S.R.
55 B6 Akshatau U.S.S.R.
57 J1 Akshatau, Khrebet mts U.S.S.R.
57 C1 Akshyganak U.S.S.R.
53 G12 Akstata U.S.S.R.
66 C3 Aksu China
47 L8 Aksu Turkey
47 L7 Aksu R Turkey
57 J2 Aksu R U.S.S.R.
55 D5 Aksuat U.S.S.R.
52 H7 Aksubayevo U.S.S.R.
57 J4 Aksu He R China
86 G3 Aksum Ethiopia
57 E3 Aksumbe U.S.S.R.
Aksu Yangi Shahr see Aksu China
52 H6 Aktanysh U.S.S.R.
57 D1 Aktas U.S.S.R.
56 C5 Aktash U.S.S.R.
57 D5 Aktash U.S.S.R.
55 D5 Aktasty U.S.S.R.
55 F5 Aktau U.S.S.R.
46 G4 Akti Greece
66 B4 Akto China
57 B1 Aktogay U.S.S.R.
57 J2 Aktogay U.S.S.R.
57 H5 Aktu China
57 A3 Aktumsyk, Mys C U.S.S.R.
55 C5 Aktyubinsk U.S.S.R.
53 D7 Akulichi U.S.S.R.
60 D13 Akune Japan
116 E9 Akun I Aleutian Is
85 F7 Akure Nigeria
28 S9 Akureyri Iceland
116 D9 Akutan I Aleutian Is
116 D9 Akutan Pass Aleutian Is
56 B5 Akutikha U.S.S.R.
Akyab see Sittwe
55 C5 Ak'yar U.S.S.R.
79 F2 Akyatan Göl L Turkey
47 L4 Akyazı Turkey
56 B6 Akzhal U.S.S.R.
57 L1 Akzhar U.S.S.R.
57 E3 Akzhaykin, Ozero L U.S.S.R.
27 C11 Ål Norway
41 O6 Ala Italy
111 K8 Alabama state U.S.A.
111 J10 Alabama R Alabama U.S.A.
94 D2 Alabaster Michigan U.S.A.
144 B6 Alabaster, L New Zealand
71 F3 Alabat isld Luzon Philippines
55 E4 Alabota, Oz L U.S.S.R.
78 E1 Alaca Turkey
47 N10 Alaçah Turkey
47 N10 Alaçali Turkey
47 H6 Alaçatı Turkey
113 E8 Alachua Florida U.S.A.
16 D3 Alaejos Spain
47 Q14 Alaérma Rhodes Greece
86 G3 Ālagē mt Ethiopia
53 F11 Alagir U.S.S.R.
40 G6 Alagna Valsesia Italy
18 H7 Alagnon R France
130 J9 Alagoa Grande Brazil
130 H10 Alagoas state Brazil
129 L6 Alagoinhas Brazil
16 C4 Alagón R Spain
17 G3 Alagón Spain
71 G7 Alah Mindanao Philippines
69 E13 Alahanpanjang Sumatra
29 K8 Alahärmä Finland
79 F3 Ālāja Syria
29 K8 Alajärvi Finland
79 G3 'Alā,Jebel al mts Syria
125 M4 Alajuela Costa Rica
47 L8 Alakır R Turkey
57 K2 Alakol', Ozero L U.S.S.R.
29 P5 Alakurtti U.S.S.R.
29 L4 Alakylä Finland
80 G3 'Al'al Jordan
135 T3 Alalakeiki Channel Hawaiian Is
128 F4 Alalaú R Brazil
119 P9 Alameda Saskatchewan Canada
124 H3 Alameda Mexico
102 B4 Alameda California U.S.A.
101 N7 Alameda Idaho U.S.A.
106 D6 Alameda New Mexico U.S.A.
71 D2 Alaminos Luzon Philippines
124 D3 Alamito Mexico
108 C6 Alamito Creek Texas U.S.A.
124 H4 Alamitos, Sa. de los ra Mexico
103 J9 Alamo R California U.S.A.
112 E5 Alamo Georgia U.S.A.
103 J4 Alamo Nevada U.S.A.
98 C1 Alamo North Dakota U.S.A.
110 G6 Alamo Tennessee U.S.A.
109 J9 Alamo Texas U.S.A.
106 E9 Alamogordo New Mexico U.S.A.
106 F7 Alamogordo Res New Mexico U.S.A.
103 L7 Alamo Lake res Arizona U.S.A.
43 C8 Ala, Monti di Sardinia
124 E4 Alamos Mexico
106 E4 Alamosa Colorado U.S.A.
124 F2 Alamos de Peña Mexico
76 D3 Alampor India
26 H7 Alanäs Sweden
33 P7 Aland R East Germany
29 H11 Åland isld Finland
74 G10 Aland India
27 J12 Åland Sweden
26 J9 Ålandsbro Sweden
29 H11 Ålands Hav Finland/Sweden
70 E2 Alang Kalimantan
88 H1 Alanga Bay Kenya
70 E6 Alangalang Tg Kalimantan
69 G13 Alangangtang isld Sumatra
29 L6 Alaniemi Finland
108 D8 Alanreed Texas U.S.A.
87 H11 Alaotra, Farihy L Madagascar
112 D6 Alapaha R Georgia U.S.A.
55 D2 Alapayevsk U.S.S.R.
80 G2 'Alaq R Syria
79 F9 'Alāqān Saudi Arabia
17 F5 Alarcón, Embalse de Spain
71 H9 Alas Indonesia
78 B2 Alaşehir Turkey
56 C5 Alash R U.S.S.R.
116 Alaska state U.S.A.
116 O7 Alaska,G.of Alaska U.S.A.
135 L2 Alaska Pen Alaska U.S.A.
70 Q10 Alas,Selat Indonesia
44 D3 Alassio Italy
29 K11 Alastaro Finland
57 C5 Alat U.S.S.R.
116 L3 Alatna Alaska U.S.A.
45 O6 Alatri Italy
52 G7 Alatyr' U.S.S.R.
17 F2 Alava prov Spain
78 K1 Alaverdi U.S.S.R.
29 O7 Alavuokki Finland
29 K9 Alavus Finland
138 F5 Alawoona South Australia Australia
8 B1 Alaw Res Wales
57 G4 Alay-Ku U.S.S.R.
17 K5 Alayor Menorca
57 F5 Alayskiy Khrebet mts U.S.S.R.
47 L5 Alayunt Turkey
78 L1 Alazan R U.S.S.R.
109 K8 Alazan Bay Texas U.S.A.
53 G12 Alazani R U.S.S.R.
51 P2 Alazeya R U.S.S.R.
40 H2 Alb R W Germany
44 D2 Alba Italy
48 H4 Alba reg Romania
94 C2 Alba Michigan U.S.A.
109 M3 Alba Texas U.S.A.
17 F6 Albacete prov Spain
17 F5 Albacete Spain
138 F6 Albacutya,L Victoria Australia
16 D4 Alba de Tormes Spain
28 E1 Albæk Denmark
56 C5 Albagan, Gora mt U.S.S.R.
79 F3 Al Bahlūlīyeh Syria
17 G6 Albaida Spain
48 H4 Alba Iulia Romania
28 E1 Albæk Bugt B Denmark
144 B6 Alba, Mt New Zealand
121 S4 Albanel Quebec Canada
46 D2 Albania rep S Europe
42 E7 Albani,Colli hills Italy
45 N6 Albano L Italy
45 N6 Albano Laziale Italy
45 J4 Albano, Mte Italy
143 C10 Albany Western Australia Australia
127 L2 Albany Jamaica
111 M10 Albany Georgia U.S.A.
99 Q8 Albany Illinois U.S.A.
110 L1 Albany Indiana U.S.A.
110 L5 Albany Kentucky U.S.A.
111 F11 Albany Louisiana U.S.A.
110 B1 Albany Missouri U.S.A.
95 O4 Albany New York U.S.A.
94 E7 Albany Ohio U.S.A.
100 B5 Albany Oregon U.S.A.
109 H3 Albany Texas U.S.A.
95 P2 Albany Vermont U.S.A.
101 T8 Albany Wyoming U.S.A.
141 J7 Albany Downs Queensland Australia
133 D4 Albardón Argentina
45 K1 Albaredo d'Adige Italy
40 B6 Albarine R France
17 F4 Albarracin, Sa. de mt Spain
141 F2 Albatross B Queensland Australia
126 G6 Albatross Bank Caribbean
32 K9 Albaxen W Germany
71 F4 Albay Gulf Luzon Philippines
40 H2 Albbruck W Germany
112 G2 Albemarle North Carolina U.S.A.
112 L1 Albemarle Sound North Carolina U.S.A.
44 D3 Albenga Italy
100 J1 Albeni Falls Dam Idaho U.S.A.
16 E4 Alberche R Spain
130 B10 Alberdi Paraguay
18 G10 Albéres mts France
138 D2 Alberga South Australia Australia
16 B4 Albergaria a Valha Portugal
17 G5 Alberique Spain
117 L11 Alberni British Columbia Canada
32 K4 Albersdorf W Germany
140 E4 Albert R Queensland Australia
122 H8 Albert New Brunswick Canada
22 D3 Albert France
107 L3 Albert Kansas U.S.A.
118 D5 Alberta Canada
114 H7 Alberta prov Canada
111 J9 Alberta Alabama U.S.A.
94 K10 Alberta Virginia U.S.A.
117 P9 Alberta,Mt Alberta Canada
48 F3 Albertirsa Hungary
22 J1 Albert Kanaal Belgium
138 E6 Albert, L South Australia Australia
86 F5 Albert, L Uganda/Zaire
100 E7 Albert, L Oregon U.S.A.
86 F5 Albert Nile R Uganda
122 H7 Alberton Prince Edward I Canada
126 G3 Albert Town Long Cay Bahamas
127 K2 Albert Town Jamaica
144 B6 Albert Town New Zealand
Albertville see Kalémié
119 M5 Albertville Saskatchewan Canada
40 D6 Albertville France
48 L6 Albeşti Romania
36 B6 Albestroff France
45 L1 Albettone Italy
18 G9 Albi France
99 O8 Albia Iowa U.S.A.
45 L1 Albignásego Italy
98 B8 Albin Wyoming U.S.A.
129 H2 Albina Suriname
45 J2 Albinea Italy
102 A2 Albion California U.S.A.
101 M7 Albion Idaho U.S.A.
110 H3 Albion Illinois U.S.A.
94 B5 Albion Indiana U.S.A.
99 O7 Albion Iowa U.S.A.
94 C4 Albion Michigan U.S.A.
98 B4 Albion Montana U.S.A.
98 H8 Albion Nebraska U.S.A.
94 J3 Albion New York U.S.A.
110 A7 Albion Oklahoma U.S.A.
94 G5 Albion Pennsylvania U.S.A.
44 E3 Albisola Marina Italy
44 D3 Albisola Superior Italy
44 D3 Albissola-Marina Italy
25 C5 Alblasserdam Netherlands
17 H4 Albocácer Spain
27 J15 Alböke Sweden
43 C8 Albo,M Sardinia
17 G5 Alboraya Spain
Ålborg co see Nordjylland co
28 D2 Ålborg Denmark
99 O3 Alborn Minnesota U.S.A.
17 F7 Albox Spain
117 O9 Albreda British Columbia Canada
8 D2 Albrighton England
141 H6 Albro Queensland Australia
16 B7 Albufeira Portugal
17 G5 Albufera L Spain
41 L4 Albula Pass Switzerland
37 J1 Albungen W Germany
16 E8 Albuñol Spain
130 B6 Albuquerque Brazil
106 D6 Albuquerque New Mexico U.S.A.
84 F3 Al Burayqah Libya
95 O2 Alburg Vermont U.S.A.
43 G8 Alburno, Monte Italy
16 C5 Alburquerque Spain
139 H6 Albury Victoria Australia
144 C6 Albury New Zealand
6 M6 Albuskjell oil rig North Sea
19 Q13 Alby France
26 H9 Alby Sweden
16 B6 Alcacer do Sal Portugal
17 H4 Alcalá de Chisvert Spain
16 D7 Alcalá de Guadaira Spain
17 G5 Alcalá del Júcar Spain
16 D8 Alcalá de los Gazules Spain
16 E7 Alcala la Real Spain
131 B2 Alcalde, Pta C Chile
43 E11 Alcamo Sicily
17 G3 Alcanadre R Spain
17 H4 Alcanar Spain
16 C3 Alcañices Spain
17 G3 Alcañiz Spain
16 C5 Alcántara Spain
16 C5 Alcántara, Embalse de res Spain
17 G7 Alcantarilla Spain
130 D5 Alcantilado Brazil
17 F6 Alcaraz Spain
17 F6 Alcaraz, Sa. de mts Spain
16 E7 Alcaudete Spain
16 E5 Alcázar de San Juan Spain
9 E3 Alcester England
98 K6 Alcester South Dakota U.S.A.
17 G5 Alcira Spain
111 C10 Alco Louisiana U.S.A.
112 D2 Alcoa Tennessee U.S.A.
129 L7 Alcobaça Brazil
16 B5 Alcobaca Portugal
17 F3 Alcolea del Pinar Spain
112 G4 Alcolu South Carolina U.S.A.
118 D5 Alcomdale Alberta Canada
118 L1 Alcona Ontario Canada
9 F3 Alconbury Hill England
140 C6 Alcoota N Terr Australia
17 G4 Alcora Spain
17 G4 Alcorisa Spain
101 T7 Alcova Wyoming U.S.A.
17 G6 Alcoy Spain
17 G3 Alcubbiere, Sa. de mt Spain
81 B6 Aldabra Is Indian Oc
124 G3 Aldama Mexico
51 M3 Aldan U.S.S.R.
51 M3 Aldanskoye Nagorye U.S.S.R.
9 E5 Aldbourne England
13 H6 Aldbrough England
16 C3 Aldeadávila de la Ribera Spain
9 H3 Aldeburgh England
107 M3 Alden Kansas U.S.A.
94 B2 Alden Michigan U.S.A.
94 J4 Alden New York U.S.A.
25 F7 Aldenhoven W Germany
9 H3 Alde,R England
106 D3 Alder Colorado U.S.A.
101 N4 Alder Montana U.S.A.
14 E2 Aldergrove N Ireland
100 C3 Alder L Washington U.S.A.
9 E5 Aldermaston England
145 F2 Aldermen Is, The New Zealand
20 F2 Alderney isld Channel Is
102 C6 Alder Pk California U.S.A.
101 M4 Alder Pk Montana U.S.A.
102 A1 Alderpoint California U.S.A.
9 F5 Aldershot England
28 D4 Alderslyst Denmark
118 F8 Alderson Alberta Canada
94 G9 Alderson West Virginia U.S.A.
118 D8 Aldersyde Alberta Canada
8 D1 Aldford England
9 E4 Aldsworth England
28 D5 Åle Denmark
99 Q8 Aledo Illinois U.S.A.
85 B5 Aleg Mauritania
130 B5 Alegra R Brazil
130 F6 Alegre Brazil
133 F3 Alegrete Brazil
106 B7 Alegros Mt New Mexico U.S.A.
133 A9 Alejandro Selkirk isld Juan Fernández Is Pacific Oc
116 H7 Aleknagik Alaska U.S.A.
54 E8 Aleksandriya U.S.S.R.
54 M3 Aleksandro-Nevskiy U.S.S.R.
52 E6 Aleksandrov U.S.S.R.
48 G6 Aleksandrovac Yugoslavia
53 G8 Aleksandrov Gay U.S.S.R.
52 J5 Aleksandrovsk U.S.S.R.
58 G1 Aleksandrovskiy Zavod U.S.S.R.
53 F11 Aleksandrovskoye U.S.S.R.
59 M1 Aleksandrovsk Sakhalinskiy U.S.S.R.
31 L4 Aleksandrów Poland
31 L3 Aleksandrów Kujawski Poland
147 K11 Aleksandry, Zemlya U.S.S.R.
55 E4 Alekseyevka U.S.S.R.
56 G2 Alekseyevsk U.S.S.R.
53 F8 Alekseyevskaya U.S.S.R.
54 F1 Alekseyevskoye U.S.S.R.
53 F8 Aleksikovskiy U.S.S.R.
54 J2 Aleksin U.S.S.R.
46 E1 Aleksinac Yugoslavia
27 F14 Älekulla Sweden
27 H15 Ålem Sweden
106 C9 Aleman New Mexico U.S.A.
133 D3 Alemania Argentina
47 N10 Alemdağ Turkey
47 N10 Alemdağ Ormanı forest Turkey
129 K8 Alem Paraíba Brazil
21 L5 Alençon France
21 L5 Alençon, Campagne d' plain France
129 H4 Alenquer Brazil
16 A5 Alenquer Portugal
102 V13 Alenuihaha Chan Hawaiian Is
76 C6 Aleppey India
Aleppo see Halab
115 N1 Alert Northwest Territories Canada
128 D6 Alerta Peru
117 K10 Alert Bay British Columbia Canada
18 H8 Alès France
43 B9 Ales Sardinia
48 G3 Aleşd Romania
52 G2 Alëshki U.S.S.R.
26 K3 Alesjaure L Sweden
44 E2 Alessándria Italy
44 D1 Alessandria prov Italy
Alessio see Lezhë
28 C3 Ålestrup Denmark
26 B9 Ålesund Norway
18 G10 Alet France
116 L10 Aleutian Is Alaska U.S.A.
116 H8 Aleutian Ra Alaska U.S.A.
107 N7 Alex Oklahoma U.S.A.
137 Q4 Alexa Bank Pacific Oc
21 J5 Alexain France
119 R9 Alexander Manitoba Canada
80 C4 Alexander Israel
107 L3 Alexander Kansas U.S.A.
98 C2 Alexander North Dakota U.S.A.
117 E7 Alexander Archipelago Alaska U.S.A.
87 C11 Alexander B S Africa
111 L9 Alexander City Alabama U.S.A.
146 C5 Alexander Island Antarctica
140 D2 Alexander, Mt N Terr Australia
143 D8 Alexander, Mt Western Australia Australia
142 B6 Alexander, Mt Western Australia Australia
140 F4 Alexandra R Queensland Australia
144 B6 Alexandra New Zealand
131 H6 Alexandra,C S Georgia
117 P5 Alexandra Falls Northwest Territories Canada
147 G6 Alexandra Fiord Northwest Territories Canada
140 D4 Alexandria N Terr Australia
117 M9 Alexandria British Columbia Canada
121 Q7 Alexandria Ontario Canada
79 A7 Alexandria Egypt
84 H3 Alexandria Egypt
127 K2 Alexandria Jamaica
46 G1 Alexandria Romania
89 E9 Alexandria S Africa
12 D2 Alexandria Scotland
110 L1 Alexandria Indiana U.S.A.
110 M3 Alexandria Kentucky U.S.A.
111 D10 Alexandria Louisiana U.S.A.
99 L4 Alexandria Minnesota U.S.A.
110 E1 Alexandria Missouri U.S.A.
98 J9 Alexandria Nebraska U.S.A.
98 J6 Alexandria South Dakota U.S.A.
110 K5 Alexandria Tennessee U.S.A.
95 K8 Alexandria Virginia U.S.A.
95 M2 Alexandria Bay New York U.S.A.
138 E6 Alexandrina, L South Australia Australia
144 C5 Alexandrina, L New Zealand
80 E5 Alexandrium Jordan
78 A1 Alexandroúpolis Greece
99 Q8 Alexis Illinois U.S.A.
115 O7 Alexis B Labrador, Nfld Canada
33 O9 Alexisbad East Germany
117 M9 Alexis Creek British Columbia Canada
123 P1 Alexis R Labrador, Nfld Canada
118 B6 Alexo Alberta Canada
79 F5 'Aley Lebanon
56 B4 Aley R U.S.S.R.
56 B5 Aleysk U.S.S.R.
36 C3 Alf W Germany
36 B3 Alf R W Germany
17 G4 Alfambra R Spain
128 C4 Alfaro Ecuador
17 F2 Alfaro Spain
47 J1 Alfatar Bulgaria
37 M5 Alfeld W Germany
32 L9 Alfeld W Germany
130 F7 Alfenas Brazil
55 G4 Alferovka U.S.S.R.
32 G8 Alfhausen W Germany
45 M3 Alfonsine Italy
9 G1 Alford England
15 F3 Alford Scotland
111 L11 Alford Florida U.S.A.
26 A10 Ålfotbreen gla Norway
95 R3 Alfred Maine U.S.A.
98 G3 Alfred North Dakota U.S.A.
143 F6 Alfred and Marie Ra Western Australia Australia
130 H7 Alfredo Chaves Brazil
145 E4 Alfredton New Zealand
9 E1 Alfreton England
9 G6 Alfriston England
27 H10 Alfta Sweden
36 C2 Alfter W Germany
55 C6 Alga U.S.S.R.
27 A13 Algård Norway
133 D5 Algarrobo del Aguila Argentina
16 B7 Algarve prov Portugal
53 F7 Algasovo U.S.S.R.
57 F3 Algatart U.S.S.R.
16 D8 Algeciras Spain
85 E1 Alger Algeria
94 C2 Alger Michigan U.S.A.
94 D6 Alger Ohio U.S.A.
84 B4 Algeria rep N Africa
43 B8 Alghero Sardinia
27 H14 Älghult Sweden
Algiers see Alger
111 J12 Algiers New Orleans, Louisiana U.S.A.
17 G5 Alginet Spain
89 D9 Algoa B S Africa
130 H10 Algodões Brazil
106 D6 Algodones New Mexico U.S.A.
16 E5 Algodor R Spain
120 H6 Algoma Ontario Canada
100 D7 Algoma Oregon U.S.A.
99 T5 Algoma Wisconsin U.S.A.
99 M6 Algona Iowa U.S.A.
121 M7 Algonquin Park Ontario Canada
110 L5 Algood Tennessee U.S.A.
22 L5 Algrange France
26 J7 Älgsjön Sweden
68 B5 Alguada Reef Burma
17 F2 Alhama R Spain
78 G5 Al Ḥamād reg Jordan/Saudi Arabia
17 F3 Alhama de Aragón Spain
16 E7 Alhama de Granada Spain
17 F7 Alhama de Murcia Spain
17 F8 Alhamilla, Sa mt Spain
84 E4 Al Ḥammādah al Ḥamrā' plateau Libya
78 G3 Al Hīshah Syria
16 E9 Al Hoceima Morocco
16 E9 Al Hoceima, B d' Morocco
86 H3 Al Hudaydah N Yemen
79 E9 Al Ḥumayḍah Egypt
84 G4 Al Ḥumaymāt Libya
26 B10 Ålhus Norway
57 E6 'Alīābād Afghanistan
17 G4 Aliaga Spain
47 H6 Aliağa Turkey
46 E4 Aliákmon R Greece
71 N9 Aliambata Indonesia
74 E9 Alibagh India
47 M10 Alibey R Turkey
48 M5 Alibey,Oz L U.S.S.R.
71 F4 Alibijaban Luzon Philippines
86 G4 Ālībo Ethiopia
48 F5 Alibunar Yugoslavia
46 F3 Ali Butús mt Greece
124 F5 Alicama Mexico
17 G6 Alicante prov Spain
17 G6 Alicante Spain
141 H6 Alice Queensland Australia
141 F3 Alice R Queensland Australia
98 J3 Alice North Dakota U.S.A.
109 J8 Alice Texas U.S.A.
117 J8 Alice Arm British Columbia Canada
142 G4 Alice Downs Western Australia Australia
100 H4 Alicel Oregon U.S.A.
43 H9 Alice,Pta Italy
126 E6 Alice Shoal Caribbean
140 C6 Alice Springs N Terr Australia
113 H12 Alice Town Bahamas
126 E2 Alice Town Bimini Is Bahamas
111 H8 Aliceville Alabama U.S.A.
140 C6 Alice Well N Terr Australia
71 F7 Alicia Mindanao Philippines
110 E6 Alicia Arkansas U.S.A.
141 F5 Alick R Queensland Australia
43 F10 Alicudi, I Italy
119 Q9 Alida Saskatchewan Canada
45 Q7 Alife Italy
74 H5 Aligarh India
77 A3 Alīgudarz Iran
Alihe see Oroqen Zizhiqi
59 H1 A-li-ho China
77 L3 Alī Kheyl Afghanistan
52 G6 Alikovo U.S.S.R.
86 B6 Alima R Congo
125 M3 Alimicamba Nicaragua
47 U17 Alimniá isld Greece
71 F5 Alimodian Philippines
71 E7 Alimpaya Pt Mindanao Philippines
86 D4 Alindao Cent Afr Republic
70 F5 Alindau Sulawesi Indonesia
107 M5 Aline Oklahoma U.S.A.
138 D2 Alinerta,Mt South Australia Australia
77 L2 Alingar R Afghanistan
66 C5 Aling Kangri mt China
27 F14 Alingsås Sweden
94 G6 Aliquippa Pennsylvania U.S.A.
124 D2 Alisos R Mexico
46 F3 Alistáti Greece
116 K8 Alitak B Alaska U.S.A.
46 G6 Alivérion Greece
89 E8 Aliwal North S Africa
118 D6 Alix Alberta Canada
80 G7 Aliyan Jordan
Al Jawf see Al Khufrah
16 B7 Aljezur Portugal
80 G2 Al Jukhadar Syria
16 B7 Aljustrel Portugal
100 F8 Alkali L Nevada U.S.A.
22 J2 Alken Belgium
84 G5 Al Khufrah Libya
25 C3 Alkmaar Netherlands
95 R6 Allagash Maine U.S.A.
95 R7 Allagash L Maine U.S.A.
75 J6 Allahabad India
21 O5 Allaines-Mervilliers France
21 O5 Allainville France
20 F6 Allaire France
83 L9 Allai Tank L Sri Lanka
103 J9 All American Can California U.S.A.
108 C4 Allamoore Texas U.S.A.
118 L7 Allan Saskatchewan Canada
19 N16 Allan France
80 G2 'Allan R Syria
83 M9 Allan Pt Christmas I Indian Oc
89 E6 Allanridge S Africa
84 J5 Allaqi,Radi Egypt
121 N3 Allard R Quebec Canada
122 G6 Allardville New Brunswick Canada
16 B2 Allariz Spain
36 C7 Allarmont France
112 C3 Allatoona Res Georgia U.S.A.
22 H4 Alle Belgium
94 B4 Allegan Michigan U.S.A.
94 J4 Allegany New York U.S.A.
94 H5 Allegheny R Pennsylvania U.S.A.
94 E10 Allegheny Mts U.S.A.
94 H5 Allegheny Res Pennsylvania U.S.A.
127 M4 Allègre, Pte Guadeloupe W Indies
19 O17 Alleins France
111 F12 Allemands Louisiana U.S.A.
89 E7 Allemanskraal Dam res S Africa
19 Q14 Allemont France
71 G4 Allen Philippines
94 E9 Allen Kentucky U.S.A.
98 K7 Allen Nebraska U.S.A.
109 L1 Allen Oklahoma U.S.A.
98 E6 Allen South Dakota U.S.A.
109 L2 Allen Texas U.S.A.
14 D3 Allen, Bog of Ireland
112 F4 Allendale South Carolina U.S.A.
13 F4 Allendale Town England
125 J3 Allende Mexico
32 G10 Allendorf W Germany
32 L10 Allendorf W Germany
36 F1 Allendorf W Germany
36 F2 Allendorf W Germany
120 J8 Allenford Ontario Canada
13 F4 Allenheads England
119 M7 Allen Hills Saskatchewan Canada
14 C2 Allen,L Ireland
144 A7 Allen, Mt New Zealand
116 Q5 Allen,Mt Alaska U.S.A.
106 E1 Allenspark Colorado U.S.A.
31 J7 Allensteig Austria
Allenstein see Olsztyn
95 Q3 Allenstown New Hampshire U.S.A.
110 J5 Allensville Kentucky U.S.A.
95 M6 Allentown Pennsylvania U.S.A.
33 M7 Aller R W Germany
22 K3 Allerborn Luxembourg
36 E6 Allerheiligen W Germany
37 L5 Allersberg W Germany
28 J6 Allerslev Denmark
110 C1 Allerton Iowa U.S.A.
29 K4 Allerum Sweden
21 O2 Allery France
40 D7 Allevard France
127 K3 Alley,The Jamaica
109 L6 Alleyton Texas U.S.A.
41 M3 Allgäuer Alpen mts W Germany/Austria
8 D1 Allgreave England
9 G5 Allhallows England
118 F6 Alliance Alberta Canada
98 D7 Alliance Nebraska U.S.A.
94 F6 Alliance Ohio U.S.A.
18 H6 Allier R France
18 H6 Allier dept France
145 E4 Alligator Headland New Zealand
127 J3 Alligator Pond Jamaica
112 L2 Alligator R North Carolina U.S.A.
140 C2 Alligator R., E N Terr Australia
113 G13 Alligator Reef Florida U.S.A.
28 D4 Alling Denmark
37 M6 Alling W Germany
28 E4 Alling Å R Denmark
28 E4 Allingåbro Denmark
99 O7 Allison Iowa U.S.A.
117 K10 Allison Harbour British Columbia Canada
12 E1 Alloa Scotland
21 P7 Allogny France
13 E4 Allonby England
80 D3 Allonim Israel
21 K8 Allonne Deux Sèvres France
21 P3 Allonne Oise France
21 O5 Allonnes Eure-et-Loir France
21 L7 Allonnes Maine-et-Loire France
80 D7 Allon Shevut Jordan
141 K8 Allora Queensland Australia
143 E7 Allott, Mt Western Australia Australia
99 S2 Allouez Michigan U.S.A.
12 D3 Alloway Scotland
33 O10 Allstedt East Germany
70 F7 Allu Sulawesi Indonesia
121 N7 Allumette I Quebec Canada
121 R4 Ally Quebec Canada
38 G7 Alm Austria
38 J6 Alm R Austria
122 H8 Alma New Brunswick Canada
121 T4 Alma Quebec Canada
110 B6 Alma Arkansas U.S.A.
106 D2 Alma Colorado U.S.A.
112 E6 Alma Georgia U.S.A.
107 O2 Alma Kansas U.S.A.
94 C3 Alma Michigan U.S.A.
110 C2 Alma Missouri U.S.A.
98 G9 Alma Nebraska U.S.A.
99 P5 Alma Wisconsin U.S.A.
57 H3 Alma-Ata U.S.S.R.
16 A6 Almada Portugal
141 G3 Almaden Queensland Australia
16 D6 Almadén Spain
16 D6 Almadén, Sa. de mts Spain
80 F2 Almagor Israel
71 G5 Almagro isld Philippines
48 G6 Almăjului Muntii mts Romania
84 F4 Al Malāqī well Libya
57 E4 Almalyk U.S.S.R.
102 C1 Almanor, L California U.S.A.
17 G6 Almansa Spain
16 D2 Almanza Spain
117 K7 Alma Peak British Columbia Canada
17 F3 Almarza Spain
48 H3 Almaş R Romania
130 E4 Almas, R das Brazil
17 F3 Almazán Spain
57 E4 Almazar U.S.S.R.
54 K8 Almaznaya U.S.S.R.
56 H1 Almaznyy U.S.S.R.
27 H12 Almby Sweden
32 J9 Alme R W Germany
27 H15 Älmeboda Sweden
100 B7 Almeda Oregon U.S.A.
129 H4 Almeirim Brazil
16 B5 Almeirim Portugal
25 G4 Almelo Netherlands
107 L2 Almena Kansas U.S.A.
129 K7 Almenara Brazil
17 F7 Almenara, Sa. de mt Spain
17 F3 Almenar de Soria Spain
16 C3 Almendra, Embalse de res Spain
16 C6 Almendralejo Spain
21 L4 Alménêches France
55 D4 Al'menevo U.S.S.R.
8 D6 Almer England
25 D4 Almere Netherlands
25 D4 Almere-Haven Netherlands
17 F7 Almeria prov Spain
17 F8 Almeria Spain

Almeria — Annerley 5

98 G8 **Almeria** Nebraska U.S.A.
17 F8 **Almeria,G.de** Spain
52 H7 **Al'met'yevsk** U.S.S.R.
27 G15 **Älmhult** Sweden
16 E8 **Almijara, Sierra de** *mts* Spain
28 C5 **Almind** Vejle Denmark
28 C4 **Almind** Viborg Denmark
100 G2 **Almira** Washington U.S.A.
130 E9 **Almirante Tamandaré** Brazil
46 G6 **Almiropótamos** Greece
46 F5 **Almirós** Greece
46 G9 **Almiroú Kólpos** *G* Crete Greece
101 M7 **Almo** Idaho U.S.A.
16 B7 **Almodôvar** Portugal
16 E6 **Almodóvar del Campo** Spain
17 F5 **Almodóvar del Pinar** Spain
133 D3 **Almogasta** Argentina
94 K4 **Almond** New York U.S.A.
99 R5 **Almond** Wisconsin U.S.A.
15 E4 **Almond,R** Scotland
8 D4 **Almondsbury** England
106 D3 **Almont** Colorado U.S.A.
94 D4 **Almont** Michigan U.S.A.
98 E3 **Almont** North Dakota U.S.A.
121 O7 **Almonte** Ontario Canada
16 C5 **Almonte** *R* Spain
74 H4 **Almora** India
16 E4 **Almorox** Spain
100 H3 **Almota** Washington U.S.A.
79 F9 **Al Mudawwara** Jordan
86 H3 **Al Mukhā** Yemen
27 G15 **Almundsryd** Sweden
16 E8 **Almuñécar** Spain
27 H14 **Almvik** Sweden
101 P8 **Almy** Wyoming U.S.A.
111 E7 **Almyra** Arkansas U.S.A.
13 G3 **Aln Br** England
15 D3 **Alness** Scotland
13 G3 **Alnmouth** England
26 J9 **Alnö** Sweden
13 G3 **Alnwick** England
137 R4 **Alofi** *isld* Îles de Horn Pacific Oc
94 C1 **Aloha** Michigan U.S.A.
68 B1 **Alon** Burma
139 H9 **Alonnah** Tasmania Australia
71 E5 **Alonon Pt** Philippines
119 T8 **Alonsa** Manitoba Canada
71 M9 **Alor** *isld* Indonesia
16 D8 **Alora** Spain
71 M8 **Alor,Kep** *isld* Indonesia
71 L9 **Alor,Selat** Indonesia
69 E9 **Alor Setar** Malaysia
16 C7 **Alosno** Spain
Alost *see* **Aalst**
143 G7 **Aloysius, Mt** Western Australia Australia
52 D2 **Alozero** U.S.S.R.
133 E5 **Alpachiri** Argentina
38 E7 **Alpbach** Austria
19 Q14 **Alpe d'Huez** *mt* France
110 C5 **Alpena** Arkansas U.S.A.
94 D1 **Alpena** Michigan U.S.A.
98 H5 **Alpena** South Dakota U.S.A.
94 H8 **Alpena** West Virginia U.S.A.
17 G6 **Alpera** Spain
129 J5 **Alpercatas, Serra das** *mts* Brazil
19 K8 **Alpes-de-Haute-Provence** *dept* France
19 O15 **Alpes du Dauphiné** *mts* France
19 K9 **Alpes-Maritime** *dept* France
46 D2 **Alpet** *mt* Albania
44 C3 **Alpet** *mt* Italy
141 H6 **Alpha** Queensland Australia
99 Q8 **Alpha** Illinois U.S.A.
95 M6 **Alpha** New Jersey U.S.A.
94 J9 **Alpha** Virginia U.S.A.
25 C4 **Alphen** Netherlands
81 C6 **Alphonse I** Indian Oc
16 B5 **Alpiarça** Portugal
44 B1 **Alpignano** Italy
103 P8 **Alpine** Arizona U.S.A.
108 D5 **Alpine** Texas U.S.A.
36 E7 **Alpirsbach** W Germany
16 B7 **Alportel,S Braz de** Portugal
4 F7 **Alps, The** *mt ra* Europe
47 L5 **Alpu** Turkey
79 G3 **Al Qadmūs** Syria
22 B2 **Alquines** France
79 G4 **Al Quşayr** Syria
84 E3 **Al Quşbāt** Libya
79 G5 **Al Quţayfah** Syria
123 L6 **Alright I** Madeleine Is, Quebec Canada
28 E5 **Alrø** *isld* Denmark
140 D4 **Alroy Downs** N Terr Australia
28 D7 **Als** *isld* Denmark
28 E3 **Als** Denmark
19 K4 **Alsace** *prov* France
118 H7 **Alsask** Saskatchewan Canada
17 F2 **Alsasua** Spain
25 F7 **Alsdorf** W Germany
100 B5 **Alsea** Oregon U.S.A.
117 E6 **Alsek** *R* British Columbia Canada
98 H1 **Alsen** North Dakota U.S.A.
36 D4 **Alsenz** W Germany
110 F2 **Alsey** Illinois U.S.A.
36 G2 **Alsfeld** W Germany
28 D6 **Als Fjord** *inlet* Denmark
36 E4 **Alsheim** W Germany
26 J5 **Alsjaur** *L* Sweden
33 P9 **Alsleben** East Germany
28 A5 **Alslev** Denmark
28 C6 **Alslev Kro** Denmark
28 F4 **Ålsø** Denmark
26 F6 **Alstahaug** Norway
32 E8 **Alstätte** W Germany
95 P3 **Alstead** New Hampshire U.S.A.
26 F6 **Alsten** *isld* Norway
32 M5 **Alster** *R* W Germany
13 F4 **Alston** England
27 M15 **Alsunga** U.S.S.R.
26 N2 **Alta** Norway
101 L4 **Alta** Montana U.S.A.
26 N2 **Altaelv** *R* Norway
26 N1 **Altafjord** *inlet* Norway
131 D3 **Alta Gracia** Argentina
127 J9 **Altagracia** Venezuela
128 E2 **Altagracia de Orituco** Venezuela
109 L6 **Altair** Texas U.S.A.
128 E7 **Altamachi** Bolivia
112 E6 **Altamaha** *R* Georgia U.S.A.
133 E4 **Alta Melincué** Argentina
129 H4 **Altamira** Brazil
125 N9 **Altamirano** Mexico
102 C4 **Altamont** California U.S.A.
110 H2 **Altamont** Illinois U.S.A.
100 D7 **Altamont** Oregon U.S.A.
98 K5 **Altamont** South Dakota U.S.A.
110 L6 **Altamont** Tennessee U.S.A.
101 P8 **Altamont** Wyoming U.S.A.
144 B6 **Alta, Mt** New Zealand
43 H8 **Altamura** Italy
65 B2 **Altan Bulag** China
124 D2 **Altar** Mexico
118 G7 **Altario** Alberta Canada
124 F5 **Altata** Mexico
45 R7 **Altavilla Irpina** Italy
99 O6 **Alta Vista** Iowa U.S.A.
107 O3 **Alta Vista** Kansas U.S.A.
94 H9 **Altavista** Virginia U.S.A.
66 D2 **Altay** China
58 C2 **Altay** Mongolia
56 C5 **Altay** *mts* U.S.S.R.
56 C5 **Altayskiy** U.S.S.R.
56 B5 **Altayskiy Kray** *terr* U.S.S.R.
41 J4 **Altdorf** Switzerland
37 L5 **Altdorf** W Germany
37 N6 **Altdorf** Niederbayern W Germany
17 G6 **Altea** Spain
33 O6 **Alte Elde** *R* East Germany
32 H5 **Alte Mellum** W Germany
36 B3 **Altenahr** W Germany
33 M9 **Altenau** W Germany
32 J9 **Altenbeken** W Germany
32 F8 **Altenberge** W Germany
32 J5 **Altenbruch** W Germany
37 N2 **Altenburg** East Germany
37 M7 **Altenerding** W Germany
36 C4 **Altenglan** W Germany
36 E1 **Altenhundem** W Germany
36 D2 **Altenkirchen** W Germany
38 L6 **Altenmarkt** Ober Österreich Austria
38 H7 **Altenmarkt** Salzburg Austria
37 P6 **Altenmarkt** W Germany
33 N6 **Alten Medingen** W Germany
36 H6 **Altenstadt** Baden-Württemberg W Germany
36 F3 **Altenstadt** Hessen W Germany
36 F6 **Altensteig** W Germany
33 S5 **Altentreptow** East Germany
32 J5 **Altenwalde** W Germany
16 B5 **Alter do Chão** Portugal
33 R8 **Altes Lager** East Germany
26 K3 **Altevatn** *L* Norway
111 L11 **Altha** Florida U.S.A.
37 J6 **Altheim** W Germany
111 E7 **Altheimer** Arkansas U.S.A.
38 K8 **Althofen** Austria
9 G4 **Althorne** England
13 H6 **Althorpe** England
138 D6 **Althorpe Is** South Australia Australia
139 G3 **Altiboullin, L** New South Wales Australia
45 M1 **Altino** Italy
47 H5 **Altinoluk** Turkey
47 L5 **Altıntaş** Turkey
47 K8 **Altınyala** Turkey
33 O6 **Alt-Jabel** East Germany
19 K5 **Altkirch** France
33 T7 **Altlandsberg** East Germany
36 E5 **Altleiningen** W Germany
37 M6 **Altmannstein** W Germany
95 L3 **Altmar** New York U.S.A.
33 O7 **Altmark** *reg* East Germany
36 H1 **Altmorschen** W Germany
37 K5 **Altmühl** *R* W Germany
32 K7 **Altmühlen** W Germany
15 D2 **Altnaharra** Scotland
111 A10 **Alto** Texas U.S.A.
16 B6 **Alto Alentejo** *prov* Portugal
130 D5 **Alto Araguaia** Brazil
126 G4 **Alto Cedro** Cuba
130 C4 **Alto Coité** Brazil
130 D5 **Alto Garças** Brazil
87 G9 **Alto Molocue** Mozambique
44 D3 **Alto,Monte** Italy
37 L7 **Altomünster** W Germany
9 F5 **Alton** England
102 A1 **Alton** California U.S.A.
110 F3 **Alton** Illinois U.S.A.
95 L3 **Alton** New York U.S.A.
103 M4 **Alton** Utah U.S.A.
118 D1 **Altona** Manitoba Canada
99 Q8 **Altona** Illinois U.S.A.
101 P9 **Altonah** Utah U.S.A.
138 E2 **Alton Downs** South Australia Australia
141 J8 **Alton Oilfield** Queensland Australia
111 K7 **Altoona** Alabama U.S.A.
113 F9 **Altoona** Florida U.S.A.
107 P4 **Altoona** Kansas U.S.A.
94 J6 **Altoona** Pennsylvania U.S.A.
128 G8 **Alto Paraguay** *dept* Paraguay
130 C9 **Alto Paraná** *dept* Paraguay
129 J5 **Alto Parnaiba** Brazil
45 J4 **Altopascio** Italy
129 H7 **Alto Sucuriú** Brazil
38 G5 **Altötting** W Germany
129 J4 **Alto Turi** Brazil
130 C10 **Alto Uruguai** Brazil
126 A1 **Alto Vista** *hill* Aruba W Indies
13 F6 **Altrincham** England
33 R7 **Altruppin** East Germany
33 T8 **Alt-Schadow** East Germany
54 F4 **Altukhovo** U.S.S.R.
78 K4 **Altun Köprü** Iraq
66 C4 **Altun Shan** *mts* China
99 O5 **Altura** Minnesota U.S.A.
100 E8 **Alturas** California U.S.A.
113 F10 **Alturas** Florida U.S.A.
107 L7 **Altus** Oklahoma U.S.A.
107 L6 **Altus Res** Oklahoma U.S.A.
41 M2 **Altusried** W Germany
36 B6 **Altwiller** France
57 C2 **Altynasar** U.S.S.R.
55 D3 **Altynay** U.S.S.R.
53 G10 **Altyn-Khutsan, Ozero** U.S.S.R.
52 C6 **Alūksne** U.S.S.R.
28 D4 **Alum** Denmark
9 E6 **Alum Bay** England
133 C5 **Aluminé** Argentina
26 M6 **Ålund** Sweden
27 K11 **Alunda** Sweden
103 K6 **Alunite** Nevada U.S.A.
76 C3 **Alur** India
53 D11 **Alushta** U.S.S.R.
17 F4 **Alustante** Spain
83 J11 **Alutgama** Sri Lanka
83 K9 **Alut Oya** Sri Lanka
84 E4 **Al 'Uwaynāt** Libya
16 B4 **Alva** *R* Portugal
12 E1 **Alva** Scotland
113 F11 **Alva** Florida U.S.A.
94 D10 **Alva** Kentucky U.S.A.
107 M5 **Alva** Oklahoma U.S.A.
98 B5 **Alva** Wyoming U.S.A.
16 B7 **Alvalade** Portugal
125 M8 **Alvarado** Mexico
109 K3 **Alvarado** Texas U.S.A.
128 F4 **Alvaraes** Brazil
26 E9 **Alvdal** Norway
118 L6 **Alvena** Saskatchewan Canada
33 O8 **Alvensleben** East Germany
32 K8 **Alverdissen** W Germany
117 D5 **Alverstone Mt** Alaska/Yukon Terr U.S.A./Canada
27 A11 **Alversund** Norway
27 G15 **Alvesta** Sweden
8 D4 **Alveston** England
27 G10 **Älvho** Sweden
110 J1 **Alvin** Illinois U.S.A.
109 M6 **Alvin** Texas U.S.A.
99 S4 **Alvin** Wisconsin U.S.A.
45 P6 **Alvito** Italy
16 B6 **Alvito** Portugal
27 J11 **Älvkarleby** Sweden
98 K9 **Alvo** Nebraska U.S.A.
109 K2 **Alvord** Texas U.S.A.
100 G7 **Alvord L** Oregon U.S.A.
26 F10 **Älvros** Sweden
27 F14 **Älvsborg** *reg* Sweden
26 M6 **Älvsbyn** Sweden
27 F14 **Älvsered** Sweden
99 M2 **Alvwood** Minnesota U.S.A.
78 H6 **Al Wadyān** *reg* Iraq/Saudi Arabia
84 G4 **Al Wāḩah** Libya
87 E12 **Alwal Nth** S Africa
74 G5 **Alwar** India
76 C5 **Alwaye** India
13 F3 **Alwinton** England
6 M2 **Alwyn** *oil rig* North Sea
110 C7 **Aly** Arkansas U.S.A.
140 D2 **Alyangula** N Terr Australia
51 N2 **Alyaskitovyy** U.S.S.R.
55 E2 **Alymka** *R* U.S.S.R.
15 E4 **Alyth** Scotland
31 P1 **Alytus** U.S.S.R.
38 G5 **Alz** *R* W Germany
98 B4 **Alzada** Montana U.S.A.
36 G3 **Alzenau** W Germany
22 L4 **Alzette** *R* Luxembourg
36 E4 **Alzey** W Germany
128 F2 **Amacuro Delta** Venezuela
140 B6 **Amadeus,L** N Terr Australia
86 F4 **Amadi** Sudan
115 M4 **Amadjuak L** Northwest Territories Canada
60 J11 **Amagasaki** Japan
29 K5 **Amager** *isld* Denmark
60 D12 **Amagi** Japan
61 N11 **Amagi-san** *mt* Japan
22 G5 **Amagne** France
21 L4 **Amain, Mt. d'** France
116 F9 **Amak I** Alaska U.S.A.
60 C13 **Amakusa-nada** *sea* Japan
60 D13 **Amakusa-Shimo-shima** *isld* Japan
60 D13 **Amakusa-shotō** *islds* Japan
84 G4 **Āmāl** Libya
27 F12 **Åmål** Sweden
76 F2 **Amalapuram** India
43 F8 **Amalfi** Italy
46 E7 **Amaliás** Greece
16 C5 **Amalia,Sta** Spain
74 F8 **Amalner** India
129 G8 **Amambai** Brazil
130 C8 **Amambai, Serra de** *mts* Brazil/Paraguay
130 C8 **Amambay** *dept* Paraguay
133 F2 **Amambay, Sa. de** *mts* Brazil/Paraguay
128 F4 **Amaná,L** Brazil
40 D2 **Amance** France
40 D3 **Amancey** France
94 E7 **Amanda** Ohio U.S.A.
42 E6 **Amandola** Italy
55 E6 **Amangel'dy** U.S.S.R.
55 D4 **Amankaragay** U.S.S.R.
60 J10 **Amano-hashidate** *inlet* Japan
43 G9 **Amantea** Italy
55 E5 **Amantogay** U.S.S.R.
87 F12 **Amanzimtoti** S Africa
129 H3 **Amapa** Brazil
78 L6 **Amārah, Al** Iraq
88 F9 **Amaramba,L** Mozambique
129 K5 **Amarante** Brazil
119 T8 **Amaranth** Manitoba Canada
68 C2 **Amarapura** Burma
102 H5 **Amargosa Ra** California U.S.A.
106 D5 **Amarilla** New Mexico U.S.A.
108 C8 **Amarillo** Texas U.S.A.
131 B4 **Amarillo,Cerro** *pk* Argentina
75 J7 **Amarkantah** India
129 J6 **Amaro Leite** Brazil
140 E6 **Amaroo,L** Queensland Australia
61 N7 **Amarume** Japan
99 S3 **Amasa** Michigan U.S.A.
45 O7 **Amaseno** Italy
85 B3 **Amasine** Western Sahara
78 D1 **Amasra** Turkey
78 F1 **Amasya** Turkey
138 B2 **Amata** South Australia Australia
128 E4 **Amataura** Brazil
125 N9 **Amatenango** Mexico
87 F11 **Amatikulu** S Africa
124 H7 **Amatitán** Mexico
125 L8 **Amatlan** Mexico
124 G7 **Amatlán de Cañas** Mexico
61 O10 **Amatsu-Kominato** Japan
22 J2 **Amay** Belgium
Amazon *R* *see* **Amazonas** *R*
119 M7 **Amazon** Saskatchewan Canada
128 E4 **Amazonas** *state* Brazil
128 D4 **Amazonas** *div* Colombia
128 C5 **Amazonas** *dept* Peru
129 H4 **Amazonas** *R* S America
128 E3 **Amazonas** *state* Venezuela
110 B2 **Amazonia** Missouri U.S.A.
129 J3 **Amazon,Mouths of the** Brazil
80 C7 **Amazya** Israel
74 E1 **Amb** Pakistan
74 G9 **Ambajogai** India
74 G3 **Ambala** India
83 J11 **Ambalangodo** Sri Lanka
87 H12 **Ambalavao** Madagascar
140 C6 **Ambalindum** N Terr Australia
85 G8 **Ambam** Cameroon
86 G3 **Āmba Maryam** Ethiopia
83 K10 **Amban Ganga** *R* Sri Lanka
87 H10 **Ambanje** Madagascar
70 N9 **Ambarawa** Java
51 Q2 **Ambarchik** U.S.S.R.
18 E8 **Ambarès et Lagrave** France
52 D2 **Ambarnyy** U.S.S.R.
141 H7 **Ambathala** Queensland Australia
128 C4 **Ambato** Ecuador
87 H11 **Ambato-Boeny** Madagascar
87 H11 **Ambatolampy** Madagascar
131 C2 **Ambato,Sa** *ra* Argentina
18 F7 **Ambazac** France
107 N6 **Amber** Oklahoma U.S.A.
100 H2 **Amber** Washington U.S.A.
116 J8 **Amber B** Alaska U.S.A.
99 T4 **Amberg** Wisconsin U.S.A.
37 M5 **Amberg** W Germany
9 E1 **Ambergate** England
127 H4 **Ambergris Cays** *islds* Turks & Caicos Is
19 O13 **Ambérieu-en-Bugey** France
120 J8 **Amberley** Ontario Canada
144 D5 **Amberley** New Zealand
22 K3 **Amberloup** Belgium
21 L8 **Amberre** France
18 H7 **Ambert** France
18 G9 **Ambialet** France
85 B6 **Ambidédi** Mali
75 K7 **Ambikapur** India
71 E4 **Ambil** *isld* Philippines
21 L7 **Ambillou** France
21 K7 **Ambillou-Château** France
87 H10 **Ambilobe** Madagascar
117 H7 **Ambition,Mt** British Columbia Canada
21 P3 **Amblainville** France
13 G3 **Amble** England
116 J3 **Ambler** *R* Alaska U.S.A.
13 F5 **Ambleside** England
22 B2 **Ambleteuse** France
22 L3 **Amblève** Belgium
87 H12 **Amboasary** Madagascar
87 H11 **Ambodifototra** Madagascar
87 H12 **Ambohimahasoa** Madagascar
21 N7 **Amboise** France
20 E6 **Ambon** France
136 F2 **Ambon** Moluccas Indonesia
87 H12 **Amborompotsy** Madagascar
86 G6 **Amboseli, L** Kenya
87 H12 **Ambositra** Madagascar
87 H13 **Ambovombe** Madagascar
103 J7 **Amboy** California U.S.A.
99 R8 **Amboy** Illinois U.S.A.
95 N6 **Amboy,S** New Jersey U.S.A.
21 O8 **Ambrault** France
94 G6 **Ambridge** Pennsylvania U.S.A.
21 J5 **Ambrières-les-Vallées** France
87 B7 **Ambriz** Angola
19 O12 **Ambronay** France
112 D6 **Ambrose** Georgia U.S.A.
98 C1 **Ambrose** North Dakota U.S.A.
137 O5 **Ambrym** *isld* Vanuatu
71 E2 **Ambuklao Dam** Luzon Philippines
71 K9 **Ambulombo Vol** Indonesia
70 O10 **Ambulu** Java
70 O9 **Ambunten** Java
76 D4 **Ambur** India
141 J7 **Amby** Queensland Australia
27 C12 **Åmdal** Norway
86 D3 **Am Dam** Chad
85 E4 **Amded** *watercourse* Algeria
50 F2 **Amderma** U.S.S.R.
75 O2 **Amdo** China
86 G3 **Amedamit** *mt* Ethiopia
102 D1 **Amedee** California U.S.A.
25 E2 **Ameland** *isld* Netherlands
42 E6 **Amelia** Italy
98 H7 **Amelia** Nebraska U.S.A.
94 K9 **Amelia** Virginia U.S.A.
113 F7 **Amelia I** Florida U.S.A.
32 M6 **Amelinghausen** W Germany
43 H9 **Amendolara** Italy
67 A5 **Ameng** China
17 J2 **Amer** Spain
102 D2 **American** *R* California U.S.A.
130 F8 **Americana** Brazil
101 N7 **American Falls** Idaho U.S.A.
103 N1 **American Fork** Utah U.S.A.
138 E6 **American River** South Australia Australia
134 E1 **American Samoa** *islds* Pacific Oc
113 F13 **American Shoal** *lighthouse* Florida U.S.A.
112 C5 **Americus** Georgia U.S.A.
25 D4 **Amerongen** Netherlands
25 D4 **Amersfoort** Netherlands
9 F4 **Amersham** England
143 B9 **Amery** Western Australia Australia
99 O4 **Amery** Wisconsin U.S.A.
146 J11 **Amery Ice Shelf** Antarctica
99 N7 **Ames** Iowa U.S.A.
98 K8 **Ames** Nebraska U.S.A.
107 M5 **Ames** Oklahoma U.S.A.
118 E3 **Amesbury** Alberta Canada
9 E5 **Amesbury** England
95 R4 **Amesbury** Massachusetts U.S.A.
118 J1 **Amesdale** Ontario Canada
120 F3 **Ameson** Ontario Canada
146 B9 **Ames Range** *mts* Antarctica
94 F7 **Amesville** Ohio U.S.A.
7 L9 **Amethyst** *oil rig* North Sea
122 J8 **Amet Sound** Nova Scotia Canada
46 F6 **Amfiklia** Greece
46 E6 **Amfilokhia** Greece
46 F4 **Amfipolis** Greece
46 E6 **Ámfissa** Greece
20 H3 **Amfreville** France
21 M3 **Amfreville-la-Campagne** France
51 N2 **Amga** U.S.S.R.
51 M3 **Amga** *R* U.S.S.R.
58 G2 **Amgalang Bulag** China
51 N4 **Amgu** U.S.S.R.
59 L2 **Amgu** U.S.S.R.
86 D3 **Am Guéréda** Chad
85 F3 **Amguid** Algeria
59 K1 **Amgun'** *R* U.S.S.R.
86 G3 **Amhara** *reg* Ethiopia
Amherst *see* **Kyaikkami**
122 H8 **Amherst** Nova Scotia Canada
106 H1 **Amherst** Colorado U.S.A.
95 T2 **Amherst** Maine U.S.A.
95 P4 **Amherst** Massachusetts U.S.A.
98 G9 **Amherst** Nebraska U.S.A.
95 Q4 **Amherst** New Hampshire U.S.A.
94 E5 **Amherst** Ohio U.S.A.
98 J4 **Amherst** South Dakota U.S.A.
94 H9 **Amherst** Virginia U.S.A.
120 G10 **Amherstburg** Ontario Canada
94 F9 **Amherstdale** West Virginia U.S.A.
123 K6 **Amherst I** Madeleine Is, Quebec Canada
121 O8 **Amherst I** Ontario Canada
99 R5 **Amherst Junction** Wisconsin U.S.A.
142 F4 **Amherst, Mt** Western Australia Australia
42 D6 **Amiata,Monte** Italy
98 C3 **Amidon** North Dakota U.S.A.
141 K8 **Amiens** Queensland Australia
21 P2 **Amiens** France
78 H5 **Amij,Wadi** Iraq
46 E4 **Amindaion** Greece
73 L6 **Amindivi Is** Lakshadweep Indian Oc
60 H10 **Amino** Japan
87 C10 **Aminuis** Namibia
79 F4 **Amioun** Lebanon
80 F1 **'Amir** Israel
83 H5 **Amirante Is** Indian Oc
118 F6 **Amisk** Alberta Canada
119 P4 **Amisk L** Saskatchewan Canada
106 G6 **Amistad** New Mexico U.S.A.
108 G106 **Amistad Nat. Recreation Area** Texas U.S.A.
108 F6 **Amistad Res** Mexico
111 F11 **Amite** Louisiana U.S.A.
111 C7 **Amity** Arkansas U.S.A.
95 O6 **Amityville** Long I, New York U.S.A.
75 L5 **Amlekhganj** Nepal
27 C13 **Amli** Norway
8 B1 **Amlwch** Wales
80 G6 **'Ammān** Jordan
8 C4 **Ammanford** Wales
26 H5 **Ammarfjallet** *mt* Sweden
26 H6 **Ammarnäs** Sweden
140 D5 **Ammaroo** N Terr Australia
115 Q4 **Ammassalik** Greenland
28 E4 **Ammelhede** Denmark
33 P10 **Ammendorf** East Germany
32 L9 **Ammensen** W Germany
41 O2 **Ammer** *R* W Germany
41 N2 **Ammer Gebirge** *mt* W Germany
41 O2 **Ammerland** W Germany
32 G6 **Ammerland** *reg* W Germany
116 R2 **Ammerman Mt** Yukon Territory Canada
37 K5 **Ammerndorf** W Germany
41 O1 **Ammer See** *L* W Germany
80 F2 **'Ammi 'ad** Israel
101 O6 **Ammon** Idaho U.S.A.
68 G5 **Amnat Charoen** Thailand
Amne Machin *see* **A'nyêmaqên Shan**
77 C1 **Āmol** Iran
130 B6 **Amolar** Brazil
36 F2 **Amöneburg** W Germany
36 G4 **Amorbach** W Germany
131 F2 **Amores** *R* Argentina
47 H8 **Amorgós** *isld* Greece
107 M5 **Amorita** Oklahoma U.S.A.
111 H8 **Amory** Mississippi U.S.A.
121 M4 **Amos** Quebec Canada
103 J8 **Amos** California U.S.A.
28 G5 **Åmose Å** *R* Denmark
27 H11 **Åmot** Sweden
27 D12 **Åmot Akershus** Norway
27 C12 **Åmotsdal** Norway
85 B3 **Amott** Morocco
Amoy *see* **Xiamen**
70 D5 **Ampah** Kalimantan
70 G5 **Ampana** Sulawesi Indonesia
87 G12 **Ampanihy** Madagascar
130 F8 **Amparo** Brazil
87 H11 **Ampasimanolotra** Madagascar
128 D7 **Ampato, Cord. de** *mts* Peru
70 Q10 **Ampenan** Indonesia
37 M7 **Amper** *R* W Germany
37 N7 **Ampfing** W Germany
103 O9 **Amphitheater** Arizona U.S.A.
70 G5 **Ampibaku** Sulawesi
85 F7 **Ampier** Nigeria
13 G5 **Ampleforth** England
70 G5 **Ampoa** Sulawesi Indonesia
17 H4 **Amposta** Spain
9 F3 **Ampthill** England
19 N14 **Ampuis** France
17 J2 **Ampurdán** *dist* Spain
80 D2 **'Amqa** Israel
122 E5 **Amqui** Quebec Canada
74 G8 **Amravati** India
74 D8 **Amreli** India
74 F3 **Amritsar** India
30 D1 **Amrum** *isld* W Germany
26 K7 **Åmsele** Sweden
38 J7 **Am Stein** *mt* Austria
25 C4 **Amstelveen** Netherlands
25 C4 **Amsterdam** Netherlands
24 **Amsterdam** *conurbation* Netherlands
113 C7 **Amsterdam** Georgia U.S.A.
101 L7 **Amsterdam** Idaho U.S.A.
95 N4 **Amsterdam** New York U.S.A.
94 G6 **Amsterdam** Ohio U.S.A.
81 E9 **Amsterdam, I** Indian Oc
38 L5 **Amstetten** Austria
27 F12 **Åmtervik, V** Sweden
86 D3 **Am Timan** Chad
28 B2 **Amtoft** Denmark
41 L2 **Amtzell** W Germany
127 J9 **Amuay** Venezuela
57 B4 **Amudar'ya** *R* U.S.S.R.
57 D5 **Amu-Dar'ya** U.S.S.R.
147 H5 **Amund Ringness I** Northwest Territories Canada
146 K9 **Amundsen B** Antarctica
146 D9 **Amundsen Glacier** Antarctica
147 J1 **Amundsen Gulf** Northwest Territories Canada
146 H13 **Amundsen, Mt** Antarctica
146 E9 **Amundsen-Scott** *U.S.A. Base* Antarctica
146 A8 **Amundsen Sea** Antarctica
147 J2 **Amundsen Trough** Arctic Oc
27 H10 **Amungen** *L* Sweden
70 D6 **Amuntai** Kalimantan
59 L1 **Amur** *R* U.S.S.R.
71 J4 **Amurang** Sulawesi Indonesia
71 J4 **Amurang Teluk** *B* Sulawesi Indonesia
144 D5 **Amuri Pass** New Zealand
17 F1 **Amurrio** Spain
59 L1 **Amursk** U.S.S.R.
59 J1 **Amurskaya Oblast'** *prov* U.S.S.R.
55 C4 **Amurskiy** U.S.S.R.
46 E6 **Amvrakia, L** Greece
46 D6 **Amvrakikós Kólpos** *G* Greece
54 K9 **Amvrosiyevka** U.S.S.R.
107 K3 **Amy** Kansas U.S.A.
56 D4 **Amyl** *R* U.S.S.R.
120 F4 **Amyot** Ontario Canada
68 B3 **An** Burma
70 G6 **Anabanua** Sulawesi
138 F5 **Ana Branch** *R* New South Wales Australia
80 D4 **Anabta** Jordan
102 E7 **Anacapa Is** California U.S.A.
45 Q8 **Anacapri** Italy
127 M10 **Anaco** Venezuela
111 C10 **Anacoco** Louisiana U.S.A.
101 N3 **Anaconda** Montana U.S.A.
101 M4 **Anaconda Range** Montana U.S.A.
100 C1 **Anacortes** Washington U.S.A.
107 M6 **Anadarko** Oklahoma U.S.A.
130 H10 **Anadia** Brazil
16 B4 **Anadia** Portugal
78 F1 **Anadolu Dağlari** *mt* Turkey
47 N10 **Anadolufeneri** Turkey
47 N10 **Anadoluhisari** Turkey
51 R2 **Anadyr** U.S.S.R.
51 R2 **Anadyrskoye Ploskogor'ye** *tableland* U.S.S.R.
47 H8 **Anáfi** *isld* Greece
26 F9 **Anafjället** *mt* Sweden
47 H8 **Anafópoulo** *isld* Greece
130 H4 **Anagé** Brazil
45 O6 **Anagni** Italy
102 F8 **Anaheim** California U.S.A.
117 L9 **Anahim Lake** British Columbia Canada
135 O1 **Anahola** Hawaiian Is
125 J4 **Anáhuac** Mexico
111 B12 **Anahuac** Texas U.S.A.
102 R11 **Anahulu** *R* Hawaiian Is
76 C5 **Anaimalai Hills** India
75 K10 **Anakapalle** India
141 J6 **Anakie** Queensland Australia
116 M2 **Anaktuvuk Pass** Alaska U.S.A.
87 H10 **Analalava** Madagascar
128 F4 **Anama** Brazil
119 T7 **Anama Bay** Manitoba Canada
126 E4 **Ana Maria, Cayos de** *islds* Cuba
69 G11 **Anambas, Kepulauan** *isld* Indonesia
61 L8 **Anamizu** Japan
98 F2 **Anamoose** North Dakota U.S.A.
129 G3 **Anamu** *R* Brazil
78 D3 **Anamur** Turkey
60 H12 **Anan** Japan
46 G8 **Anánes** *isld* Greece
71 J7 **Anano** *isld* Indonesia
76 C3 **Anantapur** India
74 F2 **Anantnag** Kashmir
48 M3 **Anan'yev** U.S.S.R.
53 E11 **Anapa** U.S.S.R.
43 G11 **Anapo** *R* Sicily
129 J7 **Anápolis** Brazil
129 H4 **Anapú** *R* Brazil
77 D4 **Anār** Iran
77 C3 **Anārak** Iran
77 G3 **Anār Darrah** Afghanistan
26 F8 **Anaris Fjällen** *mt* Sweden
26 O3 **Anarjokka** *R* Norway/Finland
127 L5 **Añasco** Puerto Rico
26 M7 **Ånåset** Sweden
113 F8 **Anastasia I** Florida U.S.A.
78 D2 **Anatolia** *reg* Turkey
137 O6 **Anatom** *isld* Vanuatu
100 H3 **Anatone** Washington U.S.A.
29 O7 **Änättijärvi** *L* Finland
131 E2 **Añatuya** Argentina
128 F3 **Anauá** *R* Brazil
69 G8 **An Bien** Vietnam
128 C5 **Ancash** *dept* Peru
9 F2 **Ancaster** England
101 O4 **Anceney** Montana U.S.A.
21 H7 **Ancenis** France
21 L7 **Anché** France
130 H7 **Anchieta** Brazil
106 E8 **Ancho** New Mexico U.S.A.
116 N6 **Anchorage** Alaska U.S.A.
94 B8 **Anchorage** Kentucky U.S.A.
94 E4 **Anchor Bay** Michigan U.S.A.
144 A6 **Anchor I** New Zealand
116 M7 **Anchor Point** Alaska U.S.A.
127 J2 **Anchovy** Jamaica
65 C5 **Anci** China
121 T6 **Ancienne Lorette** *airport* Quebec Canada
113 E9 **Anclote Keys** *islds* Florida U.S.A.
128 E7 **Ancohuma** *mt* Bolivia
128 C6 **Ancón** Peru
45 O4 **Ancona** Italy
128 C3 **Ancon de Sardinas B.de** Ecuador
95 O4 **Ancram** New York U.S.A.
22 D4 **Ancre** *R* France
13 F2 **Ancroft** England
13 F3 **Ancrum** Scotland
88 G8 **Ancuabe** Mozambique
133 C6 **Ancud** Chile
133 C5 **Andacollo** Argentina
140 D7 **Andado** N Terr Australia
128 D6 **Andahuaylas** Peru
107 N4 **Andale** Kansas U.S.A.
133 D3 **Andalgala** Argentina
26 C9 **Åndalsnes** Norway
16 D7 **Andalucia** *reg* Spain
111 K10 **Andalusia** Alabama U.S.A.
68 A6 **Andaman Islands** Bay of Bengal
138 D4 **Andamooka** South Australia Australia
52 G5 **Andanga** U.S.S.R.
77 L2 **Andarāb** Afghanistan
129 K6 **Andaria** Brazil
79 H3 **Andarīn, Al** Syria
67 B5 **Ande** China
86 H2 **Andeba Ye Midir Zerf Ch'af** *C* Ethiopia
41 K4 **Andeer** Switzerland
52 H1 **Andeg** U.S.S.R.
21 N3 **Andelle** *R* France
19 J4 **Andelot** France
21 N3 **Andelys,les** France
22 J3 **Andenne** Belgium
85 E5 **Anderamboukane** Mali
26 J2 **Ånderdalen Nat. Park** Norway
41 J4 **Andermatt** Switzerland
36 C3 **Andernach** W Germany
36 C3 **Andernach-Land** W Germany
57 F6 **Anderov** U.S.S.R.
26 L7 **Andersfors** Sweden
114 G4 **Anderson** *R* Northwest Territories Canada
100 C9 **Anderson** California U.S.A.
94 B6 **Anderson** Indiana U.S.A.
110 B5 **Anderson** Missouri U.S.A.
112 E3 **Anderson** South Carolina U.S.A.
139 H8 **Anderson Bay** Tasmania Australia
68 A6 **Anderson I** Andaman Is
100 F7 **Anderson L** Oregon U.S.A.
101 K6 **Anderson Ranch Res** Idaho U.S.A.
112 C5 **Andersonville** Georgia U.S.A.
110 L2 **Andersonville** Indiana U.S.A.
27 G14 **Anderstorp** Sweden
95 N4 **Andes** New York U.S.A.
133 D3 **Andes, Cordillera de los** *mts* S America
98 H6 **Andes,L** South Dakota U.S.A.
87 H11 **Andevoranto** Madagascar
26 H2 **Andfjord** *inlet* Norway
76 D2 **Andhra Pradesh** *prov* India
17 F2 **Andia,Sierra de** *mt* Spain
83 J10 **Andigama** Sri Lanka
46 F9 **Andikithira** *isld* Greece
87 H11 **Andilamena** Madagascar
46 G8 **Andimilos** *isld* Greece
46 G7 **Andipáros** *isld* Greece
47 P13 **Andipaxoi** *isld* Greece
47 H6 **Andipsara** *isld* Greece
78 F3 **Andirin** Turkey
66 C4 **Andirlangar** China
47 H5 **Ándissa** Greece
53 G12 **Andiyskoye Koysu** *R* U.S.S.R.
57 F4 **Andizhan** U.S.S.R.
77 J1 **Andkhvoy** Afghanistan
36 C7 **Andlau** France
87 H10 **Andoany** Madagascar
40 F1 **Andolsheim** France
52 E4 **Andomskiy Pogost** U.S.S.R.
65 G6 **Andong** S Korea
65 D7 **Andongwei** China
141 F1 **Andoom** Queensland Australia
44 D4 **Andora** Italy
26 J3 **Andörja** *isld* Norway
17 J2 **Andorra** *princ* Pyrenees
17 H2 **Andorra la Vella** Andorra
21 J5 **Andouille** France
9 E5 **Andover** England
95 R2 **Andover** Maine U.S.A.
95 Q3 **Andover** New Hampshire U.S.A.
95 N6 **Andover** New Jersey U.S.A.
94 K4 **Andover** New York U.S.A.
94 G5 **Andover** Ohio U.S.A.
98 J4 **Andover** South Dakota U.S.A.
9 E4 **Andoversford** England
26 H2 **Andöya** *isld* Norway
130 D7 **Andradina** Brazil
17 J5 **Andraix** Majorca
116 O10 **Andreanof Is** Aleutian Is
52 D6 **Andreapol'** U.S.S.R.
12 D5 **Andreas** I of Man U.K.
79 E3 **Andreas,C** Cyprus
87 H11 **Andreba** Madagascar
138 F2 **Andree,L** South Australia Australia
115 R3 **Andrée Land** Greenland
130 G7 **Andrel lândia** Brazil
118 E5 **Andrew** Alberta Canada
6 L4 **Andrew** *oil rig* North Sea
99 Q7 **Andrew** Iowa U.S.A.
68 B3 **Andrew B** Burma
143 E10 **Andrew, Mt** Western Australia Australia
94 B6 **Andrews** Indiana U.S.A.
98 C7 **Andrews** Nebraska U.S.A.
112 D2 **Andrews** North Carolina U.S.A.
100 G7 **Andrews** Oregon U.S.A.
112 H4 **Andrews** South Carolina U.S.A.
108 E3 **Andrews** Texas U.S.A.
53 H8 **Andreyevka** U.S.S.R.
54 N1 **Andreyevo** U.S.S.R.
53 D9 **Andreyevo-Ivanovka** U.S.S.R.
55 E2 **Andreyevskoye, Oz** *L* U.S.S.R.
53 D8 **Andreykovichi** U.S.S.R.
43 G7 **Andria** Italy
46 D2 **Andrijevica** Yugoslavia
46 E7 **Andritsaina** Greece
106 G4 **Andrix** Colorado U.S.A.
87 G12 **Androka** Madagascar
116 G9 **Andronica I** Alaska U.S.A.
52 E5 **Andropov** U.S.S.R.
126 E2 **Andros** *isld* Bahamas
46 G7 **Ándros** *isld* Greece
95 R2 **Androscogg** *R* New Hamps/Maine U.S.A.
53 G7 **Androsovka** U.S.S.R.
126 F2 **Andros Town** Andros Bahamas
73 L6 **Androth I** Lakshadweep Indian Oc
53 C8 **Andrushevka** U.S.S.R.
31 L6 **Andrychów** Poland
55 D2 **Andryushino** U.S.S.R.
26 K2 **Andselv** Norway
16 E6 **Andújar** Spain
87 C8 **Andulo** Angola
18 H8 **Anduze** France
27 G14 **Aneby** Sweden
143 G6 **Anec, L** Western Australia Australia
131 B8 **Anecón Grande** *pk* Argentina
85 E5 **Anefis** Mali
113 L7 **Anegada** *isld* Virgin Is
133 E6 **Anegado, B** Argentina
85 E7 **Aného** Togo
118 K7 **Anerley** Saskatchewan Canada
118 K9 **Aneroid** Saskatchewan Canada
21 N4 **Anet** France
98 J2 **Aneta** North Dakota U.S.A.
67 E3 **Anfu** China
140 B3 **Angalarri** *R* N Terr Australia
133 C2 **Angamos, Pta** *C* Chile
125 J8 **Angangue** Mexico
59 H2 **Ang'angxi** China
56 D2 **Angara** *R* U.S.S.R.
147 K8 **Angara Basin** Arctic Oc
56 F4 **Angarsk** U.S.S.R.
140 B7 **Angas Downs** N Terr Australia
142 G6 **Angas Ra** Western Australia Australia
138 E5 **Angaston** South Australia Australia
71 E3 **Angat** Luzon Philippines
130 E8 **Angatuba** Brazil
26 H9 **Ånge** Sweden
26 H10 **Ängebo** Sweden
124 C3 **Angel de la Guarda** *isld* Mexico
71 E3 **Angeles** Luzon Philippines
128 F2 **Angel Falls** *waterfall* Venezuela
27 F15 **Ängelholm** Sweden
94 J4 **Angelica** New York U.S.A.
111 B10 **Angelina** *R* Texas U.S.A.
28 D7 **Angeln** *reg* W Germany
43 G8 **Angelo de Lom,S** Italy
27 H12 **Ängelsberg** Sweden
102 D3 **Angels Camp** California U.S.A.
38 N7 **Anger** Austria
41 J6 **Angera** Italy
26 K9 **Ångermanälven** *isld* Sweden
26 J8 **Ångermanälven** *R* Sweden
32 E10 **Angermund** W Germany
21 J7 **Angers** France
26 G10 **Ängersjö** Sweden
21 O5 **Angerville** France
26 M5 **Ängesä** Sweden
26 N5 **Ängesan** *R* Sweden
26 L8 **Ängesön** *isld* Sweden
70 E5 **Anggana** Kalimantan
70 G7 **Anggowala, Bk** *mt* Sulawesi Indonesia
45 M4 **Anghiari** Italy
112 J2 **Angier** North Carolina U.S.A.
115 K5 **Angikuni L** Northwest Territories Canada
8 A4 **Angle** Wales
144 A7 **Anglem, Mt** New Zealand
120 D4 **Angler** Ontario Canada
139 G7 **Anglesea** Victoria Australia
Anglesey *co see* **Gwynedd**
8 B1 **Anglesey** *isld* Wales
21 M8 **Angles sur-l'Anglin** France
18 D9 **Anglet** France
109 M6 **Angleton** Texas U.S.A.
118 J7 **Anglia** Saskatchewan Canada
21 L8 **Angliers** France
21 N8 **Anglin** *R* France
Angmagssalik *see* **Ammassalik**
88 G10 **Angoche** Mozambique
77 E6 **Angohrān** Iran
131 A6 **Angol** Chile
87 C8 **Angola** *rep* Africa
94 B5 **Angola** Indiana U.S.A.
94 H4 **Angola** New York U.S.A.
90 K11 **Angola Basin** Atlantic Oc
112 K3 **Angola Swamp** North Carolina U.S.A.
117 F7 **Angoon** Alaska U.S.A.
98 C8 **Angora** Nebraska U.S.A.
125 J6 **Angostura** Mexico
124 E5 **Angostura** Mexico
128 D3 **Angostura I, Salto** *cataract* Colombia
124 E2 **Angostura, Presa de la** *res* Mexico
125 N9 **Angostura, Psa. de la** *res* Mexico
98 C6 **Angostura Reserve** South Dakota U.S.A.
18 F7 **Angoulême** France
18 F7 **Angoumois** *prov* France
129 K8 **Angra dos Reis** Brazil
45 R8 **Angri** Italy
21 J6 **Angrie** France
37 L2 **Angstedt-Gräfinau** East Germany
68 E5 **Ang Thong** Thailand
17 G2 **Angués** Spain
126 E3 **Anguila Isles** Bahamas
127 N5 **Anguilla** *isld* Lesser Antilles
45 L1 **Anguillara Ven** Italy
123 N6 **Anguille, C** Newfoundland Canada
86 E6 **Angumu** Zaire
65 C5 **Anguo** China
140 D2 **Angurugu** Northern Territory Australia
Angus *co see* **Tayside** *reg*
98 K1 **Angus** Minnesota U.S.A.
119 Q8 **Angusville** Manitoba Canada
88 C10 **Angwa** *R* Zimbabwe
129 H8 **Anhandui** *R* Brazil
28 H3 **Anholt** *isld* Denmark
28 H3 **Anholt** Denmark
67 D2 **Anhua** China
58 G5 **Anhui** *prov* China
130 C5 **Anhumas** Brazil
Anhwei *prov see* **Anhui** *prov*
61 O5 **Aniai** Japan
116 H6 **Aniak** Alaska U.S.A.
116 H8 **Aniakchak Nat Mon and Preserve** Alaska U.S.A.
116 H8 **Aniakchak Vol. Crater** Alaska U.S.A.
22 E3 **Aniche** France
130 E5 **Anicuns** Brazil
47 H8 **Ánidhros** *isld* Greece
85 E7 **Anié** Togo
45 N6 **Aniene** *R* Italy
18 E10 **Anie, Pic d'** *mt* Spain/France
55 D5 **Anikhovka** U.S.S.R.
52 F5 **Anikovo** U.S.S.R.
106 C4 **Animas** *R* Colorado U.S.A.
106 B10 **Animas** New Mexico U.S.A.
124 C3 **Animas,Pta Las** *C* Mexico
68 C5 **Anin** Burma
48 G5 **Anina** Romania
103 M6 **Anita** Arizona U.S.A.
99 M8 **Anita** Iowa U.S.A.
71 G5 **Anitaguipan Pt** Philippines
130 E10 **Anitápolis** Brazil
116 J2 **Aniuk** *R* Alaska U.S.A.
59 M2 **Aniva, Zaliv** *B* U.S.S.R.
99 R4 **Aniwa** Wisconsin U.S.A.
22 E4 **Anizy-le-Chât** France
29 M11 **Anjalankoski** Finland
74 D7 **Anjar** India
80 G4 **'Anjara** Jordan
67 F1 **Anji** China
65 G2 **Anjia** China
Anjiang *see* **Qianyang**
Anjiangying *see* **Luanping**
61 L11 **Anjō** Japan
21 H7 **Anjou** *reg* France
87 G10 **Anjouan** *isld* Comoros
87 H11 **Anjozorobe** Madagascar
59 J4 **Anjū** N Korea
77 L2 **Anjuman** *reg* Afghanistan
87 G12 **Ankaboa, Tanjona** *C* Madagascar
58 E5 **Ankang** China
78 D2 **Ankara** Turkey
87 H11 **Ankaratra** *mt* Madagascar
27 H14 **Ankarsrum** Sweden
26 J6 **Ankarsund** Sweden
87 G12 **Ankazoabo** Madagascar
99 N8 **Ankeny** Iowa U.S.A.
68 J6 **An Khe** Vietnam
33 T5 **Anklam** East Germany
74 E8 **Ankleshwar** India
86 G4 **Ānkober** Ethiopia
16 D10 **Ankod** Morocco
38 H7 **Ankogel** *mt* Austria
87 E7 **Ankoro** Zaire
52 E6 **An'kovo** U.S.S.R.
32 G7 **Ankum** W Germany
13 H6 **Anlaby** England
67 E3 **Anle** China
22 K4 **Anlier** Belgium
68 H7 **An Loc** Vietnam
67 B4 **Anlong** China
68 G5 **Anlong Veng** Cambodia
58 F5 **Anlu** China
26 F8 **Ånn** Sweden
25 C3 **Anna** Netherlands
110 G4 **Anna** Illinois U.S.A.
94 C6 **Anna** Ohio U.S.A.
109 L2 **Anna** Texas U.S.A.
53 F8 **Anna** U.S.S.R.
85 F1 **Annaba** Algeria
38 H7 **Annaberg** Austria
37 P2 **Annaberg-Buchholz** East Germany
79 G4 **An Nabk** Syria
33 S9 **Annaburg** East Germany
84 G4 **An Nāfūrah** Libya
128 G3 **Annai** Guyana
25 B5 **Anna Jacobapolder** Netherlands
61 M9 **Annaka** Japan
94 K8 **Anna, L** Virginia U.S.A.
68 G3 **Annam** *reg* Vietnam
113 E10 **Anna Maria** Florida U.S.A.
13 E4 **Annan** Scotland
141 J5 **Annandale** Queensland Australia
15 E5 **Annandale** Scotland
99 M4 **Annandale** Minnesota U.S.A.
13 E3 **Annan Water** Scotland
133 C7 **Anna Pink, B** Chile
142 D4 **Anna Plains** Western Australia Australia
95 L8 **Annapolis** Maryland U.S.A.
122 G9 **Annapolis R** Nova Scotia Canada
75 K4 **Annapurna** *mt* Nepal
94 D4 **Ann Arbor** Michigan U.S.A.
33 O9 **Annarode** East Germany
78 L7 **An Nāsirīyah** Iraq
99 R8 **Annawan** Illinois U.S.A.
143 C7 **Annean, L** Western Australia Australia
21 L3 **Annebault** France
19 Q13 **Annecy** France
40 D6 **Annecy,L.d'** France
131 H6 **Annenkov Is** S Georgia
141 K2 **Annerley** *dist* Brisbane, Qnsld Australia

117 H8 **Annette I** Alaska U.S.A.
20 G3 **Anneville-sur-Mer** France
19 N14 **Anneyron** France
68 J6 **An Nhon** Vietnam
141 G2 **Annie** *R* Queensland Australia
123 P5 **Annieopsquotch Mts** Newfoundland Canada
58 D6 **Anning He** *R* China
28 J5 **Annisse** Denmark
111 L8 **Anniston** Alabama U.S.A.
140 D5 **Annitowa** N Terr Australia
40 G5 **Anniviers Val d'** Switzerland
Annobón *isld see* **Pagalu** *isld*
109 N2 **Annona** Texas U.S.A.
19 N14 **Annonay** France
127 L2 **Annotto Bay** Jamaica
22 D2 **Annœulin** France
36 D5 **Annweiler** W Germany
46 G9 **Áno Arkhánai** Crete Greece
99 N4 **Anoka** Minnesota U.S.A.
98 H7 **Anoka** Nebraska U.S.A.
47 P13 **Ano Lefkimmi** Greece
54 M1 **Anopino** U.S.S.R.
22 G4 **Anor** France
87 H10 **Anorontany, Tanjona** *C* Madagascar
36 B7 **Anould** France
46 G9 **Áno Viánnos** Crete Greece
47 O12 **Ano Virón** Greece
68 J7 **An Phuoc** Vietnam
65 C5 **Anping** China
67 C6 **Anpu** China
67 C6 **Anpu Gang** *B* China
58 G5 **Anqing** China
65 D6 **Anqiu** China
25 F6 **Anrath** W Germany
67 D3 **Anren** China
32 H9 **Anröchte** W Germany
22 K2 **Ans** Belgium
28 B5 **Ansager** Denmark
65 A6 **Ansai** China
37 K5 **Ansbach** W Germany
40 A6 **Anse** France
127 H5 **Anse-à-Galets** Haiti
127 J5 **Anse-à-Pitre** Haiti
122 H5 **Anse-au-Griffon** Quebec Canada
126 H5 **Anse-à-Veau** Haiti
127 N4 **Anse Bertrand** Guadeloupe W Indies
126 G5 **Anse d'Hainault** Haiti
98 G8 **Anselmo** Nebraska U.S.A.
22 H3 **Anseremme** Belgium
139 H7 **Anser Gr** *islds* Tasmania Australia
122 B5 **Anse St.Jean,L'** Quebec Canada
127 L4 **Anses d'Arlets, Les** Martinique W Indies
59 H3 **Anshan** China
67 B3 **Anshun** China
131 B3 **Ansilta** *pk* Argentina
131 B3 **Ansilta, Cord. de** *ra* Argentina
109 P3 **Ansley** Louisiana U.S.A.
98 G8 **Ansley** Nebraska U.S.A.
140 B2 **Anson B** N Terr Australia
85 E5 **Ansongo** Mali
94 C6 **Ansonia** Ohio U.S.A.
120 K4 **Ansonville** Ontario Canada
112 G2 **Ansonville** North Carolina U.S.A.
28 C6 **Anst** Denmark
94 F8 **Ansted** West Virginia U.S.A.
15 F4 **Anstruther** Scotland
128 D6 **Anta** Peru
Antakya *see* **Hatay**
78 C3 **Antalya** Turkey
87 H11 **Antananarivo** Madagascar
87 H11 **Antanifotsy** Madagascar
87 H12 **Antanimora** Madagascar
146 **Antarctica**
90 D16 **Antarctic Circle**
146 D6 **Antarctic Pen** Antarctica
81 C10 **Antares Bank** Indian Oc
130 H11 **Antas** Brazil
130 D10 **Antas,R das** Brazil
15 C3 **An Teallach** *mt* Scotland
118 J8 **Antelope** Saskatchewan Canada
98 B1 **Antelope** Montana U.S.A.
98 D3 **Antelope** North Dakota U.S.A.
109 J2 **Antelope** Texas U.S.A.
101 Q9 **Antelope** Utah U.S.A.
87 E10 **Antelope** Zimbabwe
100 H7 **Antelope Cr** Oregon U.S.A.
130 H9 **Antenor Navarro** Brazil
16 D7 **Antequera** Spain
130 B9 **Antequera,Pto** Paraguay
106 D3 **Antero Pk** Colorado U.S.A.
106 E3 **Antero Res** Colorado U.S.A.
38 F8 **Anterselva di Mezzo** Italy
107 N4 **Anthony** Kansas U.S.A.
106 D9 **Anthony** New Mexico U.S.A.
108 A3 **Anthony** New Mex/Tex U.S.A.
138 C4 **Anthony, L** South Australia Australia
140 D4 **Anthony Lagoon** N Terr Australia
138 C2 **Anthony,Mt** South Australia Australia
85 C3 **Anti Atlas** *mts* Morocco
44 B4 **Antibes** France
44 B4 **Antibes,C.d'** France
127 N9 **Antica, I** Venezuela
45 N5 **Anticoli Corrado** Italy
122 J4 **Anticosti I** Quebec Canada
21 L2 **Antifer,C.d'** France
21 M8 **Antigny** France
123 K8 **Antigonish** Nova Scotia Canada
125 O10 **Antigua** Guatemala
127 P4 **Antigua** *isld* Lesser Antilles
127 O6 **Antigua and Barbuda** *islds* West Indies
127 N4 **Antigues Pte. d'** Guadeloupe W Indies
118 B3 **Antikameg** Alberta Canada
133 C5 **Antilhue** Chile
126 G4 **Antilla** Cuba
103 N3 **Antimony** Utah U.S.A.
Antioch *see* **Hatay**
102 C3 **Antioch** California U.S.A.
99 S7 **Antioch** Illinois U.S.A.
98 D7 **Antioch** Nebraska U.S.A.
18 E6 **Antioche, Pertuis d'** *B* France
128 C2 **Antioquia** *div* Colombia
80 C5 **Antipatris** Israel
52 D6 **Antipovo** U.S.S.R.
128 C4 **Antisana** *mt* Ecuador
119 Q9 **Antler** Saskatchewan Canada
98 E1 **Antler** North Dakota U.S.A.
107 P7 **Antlers** Oklahoma U.S.A.
133 C2 **Antofagasta** Chile
133 D3 **Antofagasta de la Sierra** Argentina
133 D3 **Antofalla** *vol* Argentina
109 O1 **Antoine** Arkansas U.S.A.
22 E2 **Antoing** Belgium
44 F2 **Antola,Monte** Italy
106 G2 **Anton** Colorado U.S.A.
108 E2 **Anton** Texas U.S.A.
87 J11 **Antongila, Helodrano** *B* Madagascar
87 G12 **Antongo** Madagascar
130 E9 **Antonina** Brazil
107 L3 **Antonino** Kansas U.S.A.
48 K1 **Antoniny** U.S.S.R.
129 K7 **Antônio** *R* Brazil
130 G7 **Antônio Carlos** Brazil
130 G6 **Antônio Dias** Brazil
Antonio Enes *see* **Angoche**
130 C8 **Antônio João** Brazil
106 D4 **Antonito** Colorado U.S.A.
54 D10 **Antonovka** U.S.S.R.
47 H1 **Antonovo** Bulgaria
126 D3 **Antón Recio** Cuba
21 P4 **Antony** France
140 D4 **Antony Lagoon** N Terr Australia
20 H5 **Antrain** France
52 C4 **Antrea** U.S.S.R.
36 G5 **Antrefftal** W Germany
14 E2 **Antrim** *co* N Ireland
14 E2 **Antrim** N Ireland
95 P3 **Antrim** New Hampshire U.S.A.
95 K5 **Antrim** Pennsylvania U.S.A.
14 E2 **Antrim Hills** N Ireland
142 G4 **Antrim Plat** Western Australia Australia
87 G11 **Antsalova** Madagascar
52 D5 **Antsiferovo** U.S.S.R.
87 H11 **Antsirabe** Madagascar
87 J11 **Antsirakosy, Tanjona** *C* Madagascar
87 H10 **Antsirañana** Madagascar
52 C5 **Antsla** U.S.S.R.
87 H10 **Antsohihy** Madagascar
29 N10 **Anttola** Finland
65 G3 **Antu** China
Antwerp *see* **Antwerpen**
95 M2 **Antwerp** New York U.S.A.
94 C5 **Antwerp** Ohio U.S.A.
22 H1 **Antwerpen** Belgium
14 E3 **An Uaimh** Ireland
75 L8 **Anugul** India
116 F6 **Anukslak L** Alaska U.S.A.
26 K8 **Anundsjö** Sweden
74 E4 **Anupgarh** India
83 K9 **Anuradhapura** Sri Lanka
Anvers *see* **Antwerpen**
45 P6 **Anversa degli Abruzzi** Italy
146 C4 **Anvers Island** Antarctica
116 G5 **Anvik** Alaska U.S.A.
121 P3 **Anvilla** Quebec Canada
117 G4 **Anvil Range** Yukon Territory Canada
22 C3 **Anvin** France
67 F4 **Anxi** China
58 C3 **Anxi** China
67 A1 **An Xian** China
67 D2 **Anxiang** China
65 C5 **Anxin** China
138 C5 **Anxious B** South Australia Australia
58 F4 **Anyang** China
70 K9 **Anyar** Java
58 C5 **A'nyêmaqên Shan** *mts* China
65 B7 **Anyi** China
67 E2 **Anyi** China
67 D7 **Anyou** China
117 J8 **Anyox** British Columbia Canada
67 E4 **Anyuan** China
52 J3 **An'yudin** U.S.S.R.
67 B1 **Anyue** China
51 Q2 **Anyuy** *R* U.S.S.R.
42 B3 **Anza** *R* Italy
118 F2 **Anzac** Alberta Canada
17 G2 **Anzánigo** Spain
40 H6 **Anzasca, Valle** Italy
18 F10 **Anzat** France
65 B6 **Anze** China
22 E2 **Anzegem** Belgium
56 C3 **Anzhero-Sudzhensk** U.S.S.R.
147 P7 **Anzhu Os** *isld* U.S.S.R.
22 E3 **Anzin** France
38 E5 **Anzing** W Germany
45 N7 **Anzio** Italy
128 F2 **Anzoátegui** *state* Venezuela
45 K2 **Anzola dell'Emilia** Italy
137 O5 **Aoba** *isld* Vanuatu
59 L5 **Aoga-shima** *isld* Japan
65 D3 **Aohan Qi** China
18 E10 **Aoiz** Spain
61 O5 **Aomori** Japan
60 N3 **Aonae** Japan
145 E4 **Aorangi Mts** New Zealand
145 D4 **Aorere R** New Zealand
68 D7 **Ao Sawi** *B* Thailand
40 F6 **Aosta** Italy
145 E3 **Aotea Harbour** New Zealand
85 C5 **Aouker** *reg* Mauritania
85 E3 **Aoulef** Algeria
67 B3 **Aoxi** China
60 G10 **Aoya** Japan
86 C1 **Aozou** Chad
103 P10 **Apache** Arizona U.S.A.
109 J1 **Apache** Oklahoma U.S.A.
106 B8 **Apache Creek** New Mexico U.S.A.
103 N8 **Apache Junct** Arizona U.S.A.
103 O10 **Apache Pk** Arizona U.S.A.
113 C7 **Apalachee B** Florida U.S.A.
112 C2 **Apalachia Dam** North Carolina U.S.A.
113 C8 **Apalachicola** Florida U.S.A.
128 D3 **Apaporis** *R* Colombia
130 B8 **Apa.R** Brazil/Paraguay
130 D7 **Aparecida do Tabuado** Brazil
144 B7 **Aparima R** New Zealand
71 E1 **Aparri** Luzon Philippines
70 E6 **Apar, Teluk** *B* Kalimantan
145 D2 **Apata** New Zealand
48 E5 **Apatin** Yugoslavia
52 D1 **Apatity** U.S.S.R.
124 H8 **Apatzingán** Mexico
116 C5 **Apavawook C** St Lawrence I, Alaska U.S.A.
52 C5 **Ape** U.S.S.R.
45 M4 **Apecchio** Italy
119 S3 **Apeganau L** Manitoba Canada
25 E4 **Apeldoorn** Netherlands
32 G6 **Apen** W Germany
33 O7 **Apenburg** East Germany
32 L6 **Apensen** W Germany
128 E6 **Apere** *R* Bolivia
112 J2 **Apex** North Carolina U.S.A.
41 L1 **Apfingen** W Germany
101 L1 **Apgar** Montana U.S.A.
80 C5 **Aphek** Israel
116 E6 **Aphrewn** *R* Alaska U.S.A.
86 E5 **Api** Zaire
134 C1 **Apia** Western Samoa
129 G5 **Apiacás,Serra dos** *mts* Brazil
130 E9 **Apiai** Brazil
45 R7 **Apice** Italy
71 J9 **Api,Gunung** *vol* Indonesia
70 E2 **Apin-Apin** Sabah
130 B10 **Apipe Grande** *isld* Argentina
106 F4 **Apishapa** *R* Colorado U.S.A.
70 G5 **Api,Tg** *C* Sulawesi Indonesia
145 E3 **Apiti** New Zealand
125 K8 **Apizaco** Mexico
124 H5 **Apizolaya** Mexico
56 F2 **Aplinskiy Porog** *falls* U.S.S.R.
129 L5 **Apodi** *R* Brazil
71 E4 **Apo East Pass** Philippines
47 Q14 **Apolakkiá** Rhodes Greece
37 M1 **Apolda** East Germany
Apollonia *see* **Sūsah**
46 G8 **Apollonia** Greece
128 E6 **Apolo** Bolivia
113 F9 **Apopka** Florida U.S.A.
113 F9 **Apopka,L** Florida U.S.A.
133 G1 **Aporé** *R* Brazil
129 H3 **Aporema** Brazil
99 Q2 **Apostle Is** Michigan U.S.A.
133 F3 **Apostoles** Argentina
54 E9 **Apostolovo** U.S.S.R.
128 G3 **Apoteri** Guyana
71 E4 **Apo West Pass** Philippines
94 E10 **Appalachia** Virginia U.S.A.
94 F10 **Appalachian Mts** U.S.A.
27 G11 **Äppelbo** Sweden
32 F9 **Appelhülsen** W Germany
44 D3 **Appennino Liguro,** *mts* Italy
42 C4 **Appennino Tosco-Emiliano** *mts* Italy
42 E5 **Appennino Umbro-Marchigiano** *mts* Italy
36 D6 **Appenweier** W Germany
41 K3 **Appenzell** *canton* Switzerland
13 G6 **Apperley Br** England
21 M3 **Appeville** France
41 O5 **Appiano sulla Strada del Vino** Italy
25 G2 **Appingedam** Netherlands
109 N4 **Appleby** Texas U.S.A.
13 F4 **Appleby-in-Westmorland** England
142 A2 **Applecross** *dist* Perth, W Aust Australia
8 B5 **Appledore** England
102 D3 **Applegate** California U.S.A.
100 B7 **Applegate** Oregon U.S.A.
122 H8 **Apple River** Nova Scotia Canada
109 N4 **Apple Springs** Texas U.S.A.
95 S2 **Appleton** Maine U.S.A.
100 D4 **Appleton** Washington U.S.A.
99 S5 **Appleton** Wisconsin U.S.A.
110 B3 **Appleton City** Missouri U.S.A.
94 J9 **Appomattox** Virginia U.S.A.
54 J1 **Aprelevka** U.S.S.R.
22 J5 **Apremont** France
20 G8 **Apremont** Vendée France
27 M15 **Apriki** U.S.S.R.
43 E7 **Aprilia** Italy
46 G2 **Apriltsi** Bulgaria
53 E11 **Apsheronsk** U.S.S.R.
138 F6 **Apsley** Victoria Australia
121 M8 **Apsley** Ontario Canada
140 B1 **Apsley Str** N Terr Australia
19 O17 **Apt** France
45 H3 **Apuane** Italy
135 V6 **Apua Pt** Hawaiian Is
130 D8 **Apucarana** Brazil
130 D8 **Apucarana, Serra Da** *mts* Brazil
71 D6 **Apurauan** Philippines
128 E2 **Apure** *state* Venezuela
128 D6 **Apurímac** *dept* Peru
48 H4 **Apuseni Muntii** *mt* Romania
88 D6 **Apwa** Tanzania
79 F9 **'Aqaba** Jordan
84 J4 **Aqaba,G.of** Red Sea
77 J1 **Aqchah** Afghanistan
78 K2 **Aq Chai** Iran
66 D4 **Aqqikkol Hu** *L* China
80 G3 **'Aqraba** Jordan
103 L7 **Aquarius Mts** Arizona U.S.A.
103 N4 **Aquarius Plat** Utah U.S.A.
130 B8 **Aquidabán,R** Paraguay
130 C7 **Aquidauana** Brazil
130 C6 **Aquidauana,R** Brazil
124 G3 **Aquiles Serdán** Mexico
109 K4 **Aquilla** Texas U.S.A.
126 H5 **Aquin** Haiti
45 P7 **Aquino** Italy
75 L6 **Ara** India
17 G2 **Ara** *R* Spain
80 F3 **Arab** *R* Jordan
79 F3 **'Arab al Mulk** Syria
38 E8 **Arabba** Italy
112 D6 **Arabi** Georgia U.S.A.
111 K12 **Arabi** New Orleans, Louisiana U.S.A.
123 N3 **Arabian L** Quebec Canada
84 H3 **Arabs Gulf** Egypt
78 D1 **Araç** Turkey
128 F3 **Araçá** *R* Brazil
129 L6 **Aracaju** Brazil
130 C9 **Aracanguy, Mt de** Paraguay
126 G9 **Aracataca** Colombia
129 L4 **Aracati** Brazil
130 E7 **Araçatuba** Brazil
16 C7 **Aracena** Spain
16 C7 **Aracena, Sa. de** *mts* Spain
130 G5 **Araçuai** Brazil
48 G4 **Arad** Romania
86 D2 **Arada** Chad
56 D5 **Aradanskiy Khrebet** *mts* U.S.S.R.
81 L7 **Arafura Sea** Aust/New Guinea
129 H7 **Aragarças** Brazil
78 J1 **Aragats** *mt* U.S.S.R.
61 M9 **Ara-gawa** *R* Japan
100 A6 **Arago,Cape** Oregon U.S.A.
17 G2 **Aragón** *R* Spain
17 G4 **Aragon** *reg* Spain
43 F11 **Aragona** Sicily
17 F4 **Aragoncillo** *mt* Spain
128 E2 **Aragua** *state* Venezuela
129 J6 **Araguaçu** Brazil
128 F2 **Aragua de Barcelona** Venezuela
129 J7 **Araguari** Brazil
129 H3 **Araguari** *R* Brazil
133 H1 **Araguari** *R* Brazil
129 J5 **Araguatins** Brazil
53 F12 **Aragvi** *R* U.S.S.R.
144 C5 **Arahura** New Zealand
61 M8 **Arai** Japan
79 E8 **Araif el Naqa** *mt* Egypt
80 G8 **Ara'ir** Jordan
85 E3 **Arak** Algeria
77 A2 **Arāk** Iran
61 N8 **Arakai-yama** *mt* Japan
128 G2 **Arakaka** Guyana
78 G4 **Arak, Al** Syria
116 A4 **Arakamchechen, Ostrov** *isld* U.S.S.R.
68 A2 **Arakan** *prov* Burma
68 B2 **Arakan Yoma** *ra* Burma
46 F6 **Arákhova** Greece
46 D5 **Árakhthos** *R* Greece
76 D4 **Arakkanam** India
120 C2 **Ara L** Ontario Canada
57 B2 **Aral'sk** U.S.S.R.
57 A3 **Aral'skoye More** *sea* U.S.S.R.
55 B6 **Aralsor, Oz** *L* U.S.S.R.
26 A9 **Åram** Norway
141 H6 **Aramac** Queensland Australia
141 G6 **Aramac** *R* Queensland Australia
125 K5 **Aramberri** Mexico
19 N17 **Aramon** France
43 C7 **Aranci, G** Sardinia
16 E3 **Aranda de Duero** Spain
17 F3 **Aranda de Moncayo** Spain
87 B10 **Arandis** Namibia
145 D1 **Aranga** New Zealand
128 E7 **Arani** Bolivia
76 D4 **Arani** India
14 C1 **Aran I** Ireland
16 E4 **Aranjuez** Spain
8 C2 **Aran Mawddwy** *mt* Wales
89 A5 **Aranos** Namibia
109 L7 **Aransas B** Texas U.S.A.
109 K8 **Aransas Pass** Texas U.S.A.
130 E6 **Arantes,R** Brazil
137 P1 **Aranuka** *isld* Kiribati
85 D5 **Araouane** Mali
106 E1 **Arapaho** *mt* Colorado U.S.A.
106 H3 **Arapahoe** Colorado U.S.A.
98 G9 **Arapahoe** Nebraska U.S.A.
101 R7 **Arapahoe** Wyoming U.S.A.
128 E7 **Arapa,L** Peru
145 E4 **Arapawa I** New Zealand
133 F4 **Arapey** Uruguay
131 G3 **Arapey Grande** *R* Uruguay
130 H10 **Arapiraca** Brazil
78 G2 **Arapkir** Turkey
130 D8 **Arapongas** Brazil
145 E3 **Arapuni** New Zealand
130 E10 **Araquari** Brazil
78 H6 **'Ar'ar** Saudi Arabia
80 D4 **'Ar'Ara** Israel
133 H3 **Araranguá** Brazil
129 J8 **Araraquara** Brazil
130 F8 **Araras** São Paulo Brazil
130 D6 **Araras,Serra das** Mato Grosso Brazil
130 D9 **Araras, Serra das** *mts* Paraná Brazil
139 G6 **Ararat** Victoria Australia
Ararat,Mt *see* **Bügük Ağri**
129 K4 **Arari** Brazil
75 M5 **Araria** India
130 G8 **Araruama L.de** Brazil
78 H6 **Arar,Wadi** Saudi Arabia
80 D5 **A-ras** Jordan
78 J1 **Aras** *R* Turkey
17 G5 **Aras de Alpuente** Spain
126 A1 **Arasji** Aruba W Indies
145 D2 **Aratapu** New Zealand
145 F3 **Aratiatia** New Zealand
61 O7 **Arato** Japan
128 F5 **Araua** *R* Brazil
128 D2 **Arauca** Colombia
133 C5 **Arauco** Chile
127 K10 **Araure** Venezuela
80 E2 **'Arav** Israel
74 E6 **Aravalli Range** India
144 B6 **Arawata R** New Zealand
129 J7 **Araxá** Brazil
128 F1 **Araya,P.de** Venezuela
61 P14 **Ara-zaki** *C* Okinawa
17 G3 **Arba** *R* Spain
86 G4 **Ārba Minch'** Ethiopia
43 C9 **Arbatax** Sardinia
52 G5 **Arbazh** U.S.S.R.
40 C2 **Arbecey** France
37 K5 **Arberg** W Germany
27 H12 **Arboga** Sweden
27 H12 **Arbogaån** *R* Sweden
40 C4 **Arbois** France
41 K2 **Arbon** Switzerland
101 N7 **Arbon** Idaho U.S.A.
119 O5 **Arborfield** Saskatchewan Canada
9 F5 **Arborfield Cross** England
119 U8 **Arborg** Manitoba Canada
99 R4 **Arbor Vitae** Wisconsin U.S.A.
27 H10 **Arbrå** Sweden
13 F1 **Arbroath** Scotland
102 B2 **Arbuckle** California U.S.A.
113 F10 **Arbuckle,L** Florida U.S.A.
109 K1 **Arbuckle Mts** Oklahoma U.S.A.
107 O7 **Arbuckles, Lake of the** Oklahoma U.S.A.
110 F5 **Arbyrd** Missouri U.S.A.
19 J5 **Arc** France
19 O18 **Arc** *R* France
18 E8 **Arcachon** France
94 J4 **Arcade** New York U.S.A.
118 A3 **Arcadia** Alberta Canada
113 F10 **Arcadia** Florida U.S.A.
94 A6 **Arcadia** Indiana U.S.A.
107 Q4 **Arcadia** Kansas U.S.A.
111 D9 **Arcadia** Louisiana U.S.A.
99 U5 **Arcadia** Michigan U.S.A.
110 F4 **Arcadia** Missouri U.S.A.
98 G8 **Arcadia** Nebraska U.S.A.
94 D5 **Arcadia** Ohio U.S.A.
107 N6 **Arcadia** Oklahoma U.S.A.
99 P5 **Arcadia** Wisconsin U.S.A.
95 T2 **Arcadia Nat. Park** Maine U.S.A.
43 G8 **Arcangelo,S** Italy
94 C7 **Arcanum** Ohio U.S.A.
21 L8 **Arçay** France
102 G3 **Arc Dome** *mt* Nevada U.S.A.
45 P6 **Arce** Italy
125 J8 **Arcelia** Mexico
25 F6 **Arcen** Netherlands
45 N4 **Arcévia** Italy
46 F1 **Archar** Bulgaria
95 M5 **Archbald** Pennsylvania U.S.A.
94 C5 **Archbold** Ohio U.S.A.
112 H2 **Archdale** North Carolina U.S.A.
141 F2 **Archer** *R* Queensland Australia
113 E8 **Archer** Florida U.S.A.
141 F2 **Archer Bend Nat. Park** Queensland Australia
109 J2 **Archer City** Texas U.S.A.
141 K2 **Archerfield Airfield** Brisbane, Qnsld Australia
141 H3 **Archer Pt** Queensland Australia
119 O6 **Archerwill** Saskatchewan Canada
40 E1 **Arches** France
103 P3 **Arches Nat. Park** Utah U.S.A.
110 B3 **Archie** Missouri U.S.A.
21 M8 **Archigny** France
119 M8 **Archive** Saskatchewan Canada
106 C5 **Archuleta** New Mexico U.S.A.
18 H4 **Arcis sur Aube** France
138 C2 **Arckaringa** *R* South Australia Australia
101 M6 **Arco** Idaho U.S.A.
98 K5 **Arco** Minnesota U.S.A.
119 P9 **Arcola** Saskatchewan Canada
99 S10 **Arcola** Illinois U.S.A.
111 F8 **Arcola** Mississippi U.S.A.
45 K1 **Árcole** Italy
18 H6 **Arconce** *R* France
138 D4 **Arcoona** South Australia Australia
131 B7 **Arco, Paso de** Arg/Chile
130 F7 **Arcos** Brazil
16 D8 **Arcos de la Frontera** Spain
16 B3 **Arcos de Vale de Vez** Portugal
17 G3 **Arcos,Sierra de** *mt* Spain
76 D4 **Arcot** India
20 D4 **Arcouest,l'** France
130 H10 **Arcoverde** Brazil
19 J5 **Arc-Senans** France
147 F4 **Arctic Bay** Northwest Territories Canada
90 J2 **Arctic Circle**
116 D4 **Arctic Lagoon** Alaska U.S.A.
147 **Arctic Ocean**
114 F4 **Arctic Red River** Northwest Territories Canada
116 P2 **Arctic Village** Alaska U.S.A.
146 D3 **Arctowski, Henryk** *Pol Base* Antarctica
45 L1 **Arcugnano** Italy
22 E5 **Arcy-Ste. Restitue** France
44 G2 **Arda** *R* Italy
78 M2 **Ardabīl** Iran
38 L5 **Ardagger** Austria
78 J1 **Ardahan** Turkey
77 C3 **Ardakan** Esfahān Iran
77 B4 **Ardal** Iran
27 C10 **Årdal** Opland Norway
27 B12 **Årdal** Rogaland Norway
14 C2 **Ardara** Ireland
118 K7 **Ardath** Saskatchewan Canada
52 F6 **Ardatov** U.S.S.R.
120 K7 **Ardbeg** Ontario Canada
12 B2 **Ardbeg** Scotland
45 N6 **Ardea** Italy
18 H8 **Ardèche** *dept* France
14 E3 **Ardee** Ireland
119 S8 **Arden** Manitoba Canada
121 O8 **Arden** Ontario Canada
103 J5 **Arden** Nevada U.S.A.
138 E4 **Arden Mt** South Australia Australia
18 H3 **Ardennes** *dept* France
22 H4 **Ardennes** France
21 O8 **Ardentes** France
12 D1 **Ardentinny** Scotland
77 C3 **Ardestān** Iran
15 D3 **Ardgay** Scotland
14 F2 **Ardglass** N Ireland
46 E4 **Ardhéa** Greece
16 C6 **Ardila,R** Spain
119 M9 **Ardill** Saskatchewan Canada
124 H6 **Ardilla, Cerro La** *pk* Mexico
46 G3 **Ardino** Bulgaria
18 E10 **Ardisa** Spain
70 P9 **Ardjasa** Java
70 O9 **Ardjuna,G** *mt* Java
145 F3 **Ardkeen** New Zealand
118 D6 **Ardley** Alberta Canada
15 D4 **Ardlui** Scotland
12 C2 **Ardminish** Scotland
139 H6 **Ardmona** Victoria Australia
118 G4 **Ardmore** Alberta Canada
107 N7 **Ardmore** Oklahoma U.S.A.
98 C6 **Ardmore** South Dakota U.S.A.
110 K6 **Ardmore** Tennessee U.S.A.
14 D5 **Ardmore B** Ireland
15 B4 **Ardnamurchan Pt** Scotland
15 B5 **Ardnave Pt** Scotland
98 J1 **Ardoch** North Dakota U.S.A.
22 B2 **Ardres** France
12 C1 **Ardrishaig** Scotland
138 E5 **Ardrossan** South Australia Australia
118 D5 **Ardrossan** Alberta Canada
15 D5 **Ardrossan** Scotland
14 F2 **Ards Pen** N Ireland
12 B2 **Ardtalla** Scotland
48 H3 **Ardud** Romania
15 C3 **Ardvasar** Scotland
53 F7 **Ardym** U.S.S.R.
26 F8 **Åre** Sweden
26 N4 **Areavaara** Sweden
127 L5 **Arecibo** Puerto Rico
131 F5 **Areco** *R* Argentina
48 J5 **Areful** Romania
129 L4 **Areia Branca** Brazil
45 Q7 **Areinzo** Italy
118 K6 **Arelee** Saskatchewan Canada
27 E12 **Aremark** Norway
36 B3 **Aremberg** W Germany
118 H9 **Arena** Saskatchewan Canada
71 E6 **Arena** Philippines
95 N4 **Arena** New York U.S.A.
133 C7 **Arenales** *mt* Chile
130 C4 **Arenápolis** Brazil
71 F4 **Arena Pt** Luzon Philippines
124 E6 **Arena, Pta** *C* Mexico
16 D4 **Arenas de S.Pedro** Spain
128 D8 **Arenas,Pta** *C* Chile
32 F7 **Arenberg** *reg* W Germany
27 C13 **Arendal** Norway
22 J1 **Arendonk** Belgium
33 O7 **Arendsee** East Germany
32 L10 **Arenshausen** East Germany
19 Q12 **Arenthon** France
28 D2 **Arentsminde** Denmark
17 J3 **Arenys de Mar** Spain
46 E8 **Areópolis** Greece
128 D7 **Arequipa** Peru
129 H4 **Arere** Brazil
18 E8 **Arès** France
16 D3 **Arévalo** Spain
140 B6 **Areyonga** N Terr Australia
42 D5 **Arezzo** Italy
46 E7 **Arfará** Greece
17 F2 **Arga** *R* Spain
140 D5 **Argadargada** N Terr Australia
16 E5 **Argamasilla de Alba** Spain
16 E4 **Arganda** Spain
16 B4 **Arganil** Portugal
71 F6 **Argao** Philippines
45 P6 **Argatone, M** *mt* Italy
55 D3 **Argayash** U.S.S.R.
55 D3 **Argazi, Oz** U.S.S.R.
18 H10 **Argelès sur Mer** France
41 L2 **Argen** *R* W Germany
21 K3 **Argences** France
19 Q18 **Argens** *R* France
117 P10 **Argenta** British Columbia Canada
45 L2 **Argenta** Italy
101 N4 **Argenta** Montana U.S.A.
21 K4 **Argentan** France
42 D6 **Argentario,Monte** Italy
18 G7 **Argentat** France
44 B3 **Argentera Mt** Italy
21 P4 **Argenteuil** Seine-et-Oise France
123 S6 **Argentia** Newfoundland Canada
40 E6 **Argentières** France
44 C4 **Argentina** *R* Italy
131 D5 **Argentina** *rep* S America
146 E7 **Argentina Range** *mts* Antarctica
90 E13 **Argentine Basin** Atlantic Oc
133 C8 **Argentino,L** Argentina
21 K7 **Argenton** *R* France
20 A4 **Argenton** France
21 K8 **Argenton-Château** France
21 O8 **Argenton-sur-Creuse** France
122 C3 **Argent,R à l'** Quebec Canada
21 J5 **Argentre** France
21 H5 **Argentré-du-Plessis** France
18 G5 **Argent sur Sauldre** France
48 J5 **Argeş** *R* Romania
48 J5 **Argeş** *reg* Romania
48 J6 **Argeşel** *R* Romania
77 J4 **Arghandab** *R* Afghanistan
77 K4 **Arghastan** *R* Afghanistan
84 J6 **Argo** Sudan
20 B5 **Argol** France
46 F7 **Argolikós Kólpos** *B* Greece
107 N4 **Argonia** Kansas U.S.A.
22 J5 **Argonne** *reg* France
99 S4 **Argonne** Wisconsin U.S.A.
70 O9 **Argopura G** *mt* Java
101 N5 **Argora** Idaho U.S.A.
46 F7 **Argos** Greece
94 A5 **Argos** Indiana U.S.A.
46 E4 **Árgos Orestikón** Greece
20 H4 **Argouges** France
18 D10 **Arguedas** Spain
21 O2 **Argueil** France
20 F5 **Arguenon** *R* France
59 H1 **Argun** *R* China/U.S.S.R.
85 E6 **Argungu** Nigeria
146 G10 **Argus, Dome** *ice dome* Antarctica
102 G6 **Argus Ra** California U.S.A.
98 J2 **Argusville** North Dakota U.S.A.
21 N8 **Argy** France
122 G10 **Argyle** Nova Scotia Canada
112 E6 **Argyle** Georgia U.S.A.
94 E3 **Argyle** Michigan U.S.A.
98 K1 **Argyle** Minnesota U.S.A.
99 R7 **Argyle** Wisconsin U.S.A.
142 G3 **Argyle, L** Western Australia Australia
Argyll *co see* **Strathclyde and Highland** *regions*
6 M6 **Argyll** *oil rig* North Sea
Argyrokastron *see* **Gjirokastër**
65 E3 **Ar Horquin Qi** China
28 E4 **Århus** Denmark
28 E4 **Århus** *co* Denmark
145 E3 **Aria** New Zealand
139 H5 **Ariah Pk** New South Wales Australia
60 D13 **Ariake-kai** *G* Japan
87 C11 **Ariamsvlei** Namibia
43 G7 **Ariano Irpino** Italy
45 M2 **Ariano Nel Polésine** Italy
128 D3 **Ariari** *R* Colombia
73 L8 **Ari Atoll** Maldives
85 D6 **Aribinda** Burkina
128 D7 **Arica** Chile
128 D4 **Arica** Colombia
45 N6 **Ariccia** Italy
123 M8 **Arichat** C Breton I, Nova Scotia
60 J11 **Arida** Japan
60 J11 **Arida-gawa** *R* Japan
85 B3 **Aridal, Sabkhat** *Salt lake* Western Sahara
143 E10 **Arid, C** Western Australia Australia
83 J12 **Aride I** Seychelles
Arid I *see* **Rakitu I**
18 G10 **Ariège** *R* France
18 G9 **Ariège** *dept* France
100 C4 **Ariel** Washington U.S.A.
48 H4 **Arieş** *R* Romania
80 G8 **Ariha** Jordan
79 G3 **Arīḩā** Syria
106 H2 **Arikaree** *R* Colorado U.S.A.
60 C13 **Arikawa** Japan
29 K4 **Arild** Sweden
48 F7 **Arilje** Yugoslavia
128 F5 **Arima** Brazil
60 J11 **Arima** Japan
127 O2 **Arima** Trinidad
101 N7 **Arimo** Idaho U.S.A.
128 G3 **Arinda** Guyana
129 J7 **Arinos** Brazil
129 G6 **Arinos** *R* Brazil
101 M9 **Arinosa** Utah U.S.A.
99 L8 **Arion** Iowa U.S.A.
127 P1 **Aripo, Mt** Trinidad
128 D2 **Ariporo** *R* Colombia
128 F5 **Aripuana** *R* Brazil
128 F5 **Ariquemes** Brazil
130 D5 **Ariranha** *R* Brazil
15 C4 **Arisaig** Scotland
79 D7 **'Arīsh, El** Egypt
117 J9 **Aristazabal I** British Columbia Canada
133 D7 **Aristizábal, C** Argentina
111 L10 **Ariton** Alabama U.S.A.
43 C9 **Aritzo** Sardinia
103 N10 **Arivaca** Arizona U.S.A.
87 H11 **Arivonimamo** Madagascar
17 F3 **Ariza** Spain
18 F9 **Arize** *R* France
133 D5 **Arizona** Argentina
103 L7 **Arizona** *state* U.S.A.
124 D2 **Arizpe** Mexico
27 F12 **Årjäng** Sweden
26 J5 **Arjeplog** Sweden
128 D1 **Arjona** Colombia
16 E7 **Arjona** Spain
51 O2 **Arka** U.S.S.R.
110 F7 **Arkabutla Res** Mississippi U.S.A.
53 F8 **Arkadak** U.S.S.R.
109 O1 **Arkadelphia** Arkansas U.S.A.
55 E5 **Arkalyk** U.S.S.R.
109 O1 **Arkansas** *state* U.S.A.
110 C6 **Arkansas** *R* Arkansas U.S.A.
111 E8 **Arkansas City** Arkansas U.S.A.
107 O4 **Arkansas City** Kansas U.S.A.
111 E7 **Arkansas Post Nat. Mem** Arkansas U.S.A.
84 G5 **Arkanu Jebel** *mt* Libya
138 E4 **Arkaroola** South Australia Australia
47 J9 **Arkása** Kárpathos I Greece
66 D4 **Arkatag** *mts* China
117 F5 **Arkell,Mt** Yukon Territory Canada
27 G15 **Arkelstorp** Sweden
47 V14 **Arkhángelos** Rhodes Greece
52 F3 **Arkhangel'sk** U.S.S.R.
53 F11 **Arkhangel'skoye** U.S.S.R.
59 K2 **Arkhara** U.S.S.R.
53 D7 **Arkhipovka** U.S.S.R.
53 D8 **Arkino** U.S.S.R.
14 E4 **Arklow** Ireland
47 H7 **Árkoi** *isld* Greece
120 J9 **Arkona** Ontario Canada
30 H1 **Arkona** East Germany
27 J13 **Arkösund** Sweden
94 K4 **Arkport** New York U.S.A.
52 H6 **Arkul'** U.S.S.R.
95 N4 **Arkville** New York U.S.A.
27 J12 **Ärla** Sweden
18 H7 **Arlanc** France
16 E2 **Arlanza** *R* Spain
41 M3 **Arlberg** *pass* Austria
101 L2 **Arlee** Montana U.S.A.
19 N17 **Arles** Bouches du Rhône France
18 G10 **Arles** Pyrénées-Orientales France
22 E3 **Arleux** France
100 J5 **Arling** Idaho U.S.A.
8 D4 **Arlingham** England
103 M8 **Arlington** Arizona U.S.A.
102 G8 **Arlington** California U.S.A.
106 G3 **Arlington** Colorado U.S.A.
113 F7 **Arlington** Florida U.S.A.
112 C6 **Arlington** Georgia U.S.A.
99 P7 **Arlington** Iowa U.S.A.
107 M4 **Arlington** Kansas U.S.A.
110 G5 **Arlington** Kentucky U.S.A.
99 M5 **Arlington** Minnesota U.S.A.
98 K8 **Arlington** Nebraska U.S.A.
94 D6 **Arlington** Ohio U.S.A.
100 E4 **Arlington** Oregon U.S.A.
98 J5 **Arlington** South Dakota U.S.A.
110 G6 **Arlington** Tennessee U.S.A.
109 N9 **Arlington** Texas U.S.A.
95 O3 **Arlington** Vermont U.S.A.
95 K8 **Arlington** Virginia U.S.A.
117 M11 **Arlington** Washington U.S.A.
101 T8 **Arlington** Wyoming U.S.A.
99 S7 **Arlington Heights** Illinois U.S.A.
110 E4 **Arlington Res** Missouri U.S.A.
85 F5 **Arlit** Niger
22 K4 **Arlon** Belgium
140 C6 **Arltunga** N Terr Australia
107 Q4 **Arma** Kansas U.S.A.
118 E8 **Armada** Alberta Canada
143 B9 **Armadale** Western Australia Australia
12 E2 **Armadale** Scotland
122 B7 **Armagh** Quebec Canada
14 E2 **Armagh** *co* N Ireland
14 E2 **Armagh** N Ireland
18 F9 **Armagnac** *reg* France
18 H5 **Armançon** *R* France
47 H9 **Armathia** *isld* Greece
13 F4 **Armathwaite** England
53 F10 **Armavir** U.S.S.R.
128 C3 **Armenia** Colombia
Armenia *see* **Armyanskaya** *S.S.R.*
48 G5 **Armeniş** Romania
22 D2 **Armentières** France
21 M4 **Armentières** Eure France
101 P2 **Armington** Montana U.S.A.
101 S6 **Arminto** Wyoming U.S.A.
119 Q6 **Armit** Saskatchewan Canada
9 E2 **Armitage** England
55 E3 **Armizonskoye** U.S.S.R.
119 N5 **Armley** Sask Canada
98 H6 **Armour** South Dakota U.S.A.
98 G1 **Armourdale** N Dakota U.S.A.
120 D3 **Arms** Ontario Canada
36 E4 **Armsheim** W Germany
101 N5 **Armstead** Montana U.S.A.
140 B3 **Armstrong** *R* N Terr Australia
117 O10 **Armstrong** British Columbia Canada
99 T9 **Armstrong** Illinois U.S.A.
99 M6 **Armstrong** Iowa U.S.A.
110 D2 **Armstrong** Missouri U.S.A.
109 K9 **Armstrong** Texas U.S.A.
59 L2 **Armu** *R* U.S.S.R.
74 H9 **Armur** India
47 J4 **Armutcuk Dağ** *mt* Turkey
47 K4 **Armutlu** Turkey
53 D10 **Armyansk** U.S.S.R.
78 K1 **Armyanskaya S.S.R.** U.S.S.R.
28 B7 **Arnå** *R* Denmark
21 L6 **Arnage** France
46 F4 **Arnaia** Greece
28 R9 **Arnarstapi** Iceland
118 D1 **Arnaud** Manitoba Canada
115 M6 **Arnaud,R** Quebec Canada
79 C3 **Arnauti, C** Cyprus
18 J5 **Arnay le Duc** France
28 B4 **Arnborg** Denmark
37 P5 **Arnbruck** W Germany
33 Q7 **Arneburg** East Germany
18 D10 **Arnedo** Spain
98 C2 **Arnegard** North Dakota U.S.A.
22 C2 **Arneke** France
26 M6 **Arnemark** Sweden
25 A6 **Arnemuiden** Netherlands
27 E11 **Årnes** Norway
107 L5 **Arnett** Oklahoma U.S.A.
94 F9 **Arnett** West Virginia U.S.A.
28 R9 **Arngerdhareyri** Iceland
25 E5 **Arnhem** Netherlands
140 D1 **Arnhem,C** N Terr Australia
140 C2 **Arnhem Land** *reg* N Terr Australia
140 C2 **Arnhem Land Aboriginal Land** N Terr Australia
21 N4 **Arnières** France
45 H4 **Arno** *R* Italy
138 D5 **Arno Bay** South Australia Australia
102 D3 **Arnold** California U.S.A.
110 F3 **Arnold** Missouri U.S.A.
98 F8 **Arnold** Nebraska U.S.A.
94 H6 **Arnold** Pennsylvania U.S.A.
99 L6 **Arnolds Park** Iowa U.S.A.
38 J8 **Arnoldstein** Austria
21 P7 **Arnon** *R* France
119 V3 **Arnot** Manitoba Canada
26 L1 **Arnöy** Norway
16 B2 **Arnoya** *R* Spain
12 D1 **Arnprior** Scotland
32 G10 **Arnsberg** W Germany
13 F5 **Arnside** England
37 K2 **Arnstadt** East Germany
37 L3 **Arnstein** W Germany
37 O6 **Arnstorf** W Germany
Arnswalde *see* **Choszczno**
121 L4 **Arntfield** Quebec Canada
28 B6 **Arnum** Denmark
128 F2 **Aro** *R* Venezuela
127 K9 **Aroa** Venezuela
87 C11 **Aroab** Namibia
46 E7 **Aroánia** *mt* Greece
124 H4 **Arocha** Mexico
130 C7 **Aroeira** Brazil
32 K10 **Arolsen** W Germany
55 E3 **Aromashevo** U.S.S.R.
21 J5 **Aron** France
21 J5 **Aron** *R* Mayenne France
42 B3 **Arona** Italy
122 E7 **Aroostook** New Brunswick Canada
95 S7 **Aroostook** *R* Maine U.S.A.
116 E6 **Aropuk L** Alaska U.S.A.
137 Q2 **Arorae** *isld* Kiribati
71 F4 **Aroroy** Philippines
28 D6 **Arøsund** Denmark
127 O2 **Arouca** Trinidad
17 F9 **Aroui, Mt** Morocco
145 F3 **Arowhana** *mt* New Zealand
106 G3 **Aroya** Colorado U.S.A.
109 M3 **Arp** Texas U.S.A.
57 G4 **Arpa** U.S.S.R.
18 G8 **Arpajon** France
21 P4 **Arpajon** France
48 J5 **Arpasu de Jos** Romania
55 D1 **Arpavla** U.S.S.R.
120 K4 **Arpin** Ontario Canada
45 P6 **Arpino** Italy
45 L1 **Arquà Petrarca** Italy
45 L1 **Arquà Polesine** Italy
21 N2 **Arques** *R* France
22 C2 **Arques** Pas-de-Calais France
21 N2 **Arques-la-Bataille** France
80 E2 **'Arraba** Israel
141 F7 **Arrabury** Queensland Australia
36 B6 **Arracourt** France
20 E6 **Arradon** France
131 D2 **Arraga** Argentina
16 C4 **Arrago** *R* Spain
129 J6 **Arraias** Brazil
16 B6 **Arraiolos** Portugal
14 C4 **Arra Mts** Ireland
119 Q7 **Arran** Saskatchewan Canada
15 C5 **Arran** *isld* Scotland
111 M11 **Arran** Florida U.S.A.
80 E4 **'Arrana** Jordan
117 H8 **Arrandale** British Columbia Canada
78 G4 **Ar Raqqah** Syria
84 F4 **Ar Rāqūbah** Libya
22 D3 **Arras** Pas-de-Calais France
79 G4 **Ar Rastan** Syria
18 F9 **Arrats** *R* France
28 B5 **Arre** Denmark
18 F10 **Arreau** France
128 E3 **Arrecifal** Colombia
85 B3 **Arrecife** Canary Is
20 C5 **Arrée,Mtgne.d'** France
28 J5 **Arresø** *L* Denmark
106 C9 **Arrey** New Mexico U.S.A.
45 L4 **Arrezzo** *reg* Italy
38 J8 **Arriach** Austria
125 N9 **Arriaga** Mexico
106 G2 **Arriba** Colorado U.S.A.
141 G6 **Arrilalah** Queensland Australia
28 B6 **Arrild** Denmark
9 F3 **Arrington** England
143 B8 **Arrino** Western Australia Australia
12 D1 **Arrochar** Scotland
133 G4 **Arroio Grande** Brazil
21 J3 **Arromanches** France
16 C5 **Arronches** Portugal
44 M6 **Arrone** *R* Italy
18 F9 **Arros** *R* France
21 N5 **Arrou** France
18 H6 **Arroux** *R* France
101 Q2 **Arrow Cr** Montana U.S.A.
117 P10 **Arrowhead** British Columbia Canada
119 O2 **Arrow L** Ontario Canada
14 C2 **Arrow,L** Ireland
117 O10 **Arrow Park** British Columbia Canada
110 D2 **Arrow Rock** Missouri U.S.A.
100 K6 **Arrowrock Res** Idaho U.S.A.
138 F4 **Arrowsmith Mt** New South Wales Australia
144 C5 **Arrowsmith, Mt** New Zealand
140 D2 **Arrowsmith Pt** N Terr Australia
144 B6 **Arrowtown** New Zealand
118 D8 **Arrow Wood** Alberta Canada
16 C5 **Arroyo de la Luz** Spain
108 F6 **Arroyo de la Zorra** *R* Mexico
131 F6 **Arroyo Grande** *R* Argentina
102 D6 **Arroyo Grande** California U.S.A.
106 E5 **Arroyo Hondo** New Mexico U.S.A.
131 F4 **Arroyo Negro** *R* Uruguay
103 J8 **Arroyo Seco** *R* California U.S.A.
128 F6 **Arroyos,L de Los** Bolivia
130 B9 **Arroyos-y-Esteros** Paraguay
130 C4 **Arruda** Brazil
78 G4 **Ar Ruṣāfah** Syria
79 H3 **Ar Ruwayḑah** Syria
28 D3 **Års** Denmark
77 C5 **Arsenajan** Iran
118 J3 **Arsenault L** Saskatchewan Canada
117 Q3 **Arseno L** Northwest Territories Canada
59 K3 **Arsen'yev** U.S.S.R.
55 C3 **Arshinka** U.S.S.R.
86 G4 **Ārsī** *prov* Ethiopia
41 O6 **Arsiero** Italy
76 C4 **Arsikere** India
52 G6 **Arsk** U.S.S.R.
26 J9 **Årskogen** Sweden
57 G4 **Arslanbal** U.S.S.R.
45 O5 **Arsoli** Italy
19 K3 **Ars-sur-Moselle** France
27 J11 **Årsunda** Sweden
22 D5 **Arsy** France
46 D5 **Árta** Greece
17 K5 **Artá** Majorca
80 D7 **Artas** Jordan
98 G4 **Artas** South Dakota U.S.A.
17 K5 **Artá,Sierra de,Mt** Majorca
124 H8 **Arteaga** Mexico
59 K3 **Artem** U.S.S.R.
19 P13 **Artemare** France
126 C3 **Artemisa** Cuba
51 J3 **Artemovak** U.S.S.R.
54 G7 **Artemovka** U.S.S.R.
56 D4 **Artemovsk** U.S.S.R.
53 F9 **Artemovskiy** U.S.S.R.
45 N6 **Artena** Italy
21 O5 **Artenay** France
33 O10 **Artern** East Germany
17 H3 **Artesa de Segre** Spain
Artesia *see* **Mosomane**
111 H8 **Artesia** Mississippi U.S.A.
98 J5 **Artesian** South Dakota U.S.A.
109 H7 **Artesia Wells** Texas U.S.A.
26 G6 **Artfjallet** *mt* Sweden
121 T6 **Arthabaska** Quebec Canada
18 E9 **Arthez** France
21 O3 **Arthies** France
21 O8 **Arthon** France
20 G7 **Arthon-en-Retz** France
139 H8 **Arthur** *R* Tasmania Australia
110 H2 **Arthur** Illinois U.S.A.
98 E8 **Arthur** Nebraska U.S.A.
98 J2 **Arthur** North Dakota U.S.A.
109 M2 **Arthur City** Texas U.S.A.
138 E4 **Arthur,L** South Australia Australia
139 H8 **Arthur,L** Tasmania Australia

Arthur, Mt — Aysarinskoye 7

142 E4 **Arthur, Mt** Western Australia Australia
145 D4 **Arthur, Mt** New Zealand
141 K5 **Arthur Pt** Queensland Australia
143 B10 **Arthur River** Western Australia Australia
144 C5 **Arthur's Pass** New Zealand
126 G2 **Arthur's Town** Cat I Bahamas
55 C3 **Arti** U.S.S.R.
133 F4 **Artigas** Uruguay
114 J5 **Artillery L** Northwest Territories Canada
29 M11 **Artjärvi** Finland
118 H6 **Artland** Saskatchewan Canada
33 M6 **Artlenburg** W Germany
22 C3 **Artois** *prov* France
102 B2 **Artois** California U.S.A.
22 D3 **Artois Collines d'** France
46 E6 **Artotina** Greece
78 F1 **Artova** Turkey
Artsakan Nor *see* **Qagan Nur** *L*
48 M5 **Artsiz** U.S.S.R.
66 B4 **Artux** China
71 B1 **Aru** Halmahera Indonesia
86 F5 **Aru** Zaire
129 H6 **Aruanã** Brazil
126 A2 **Aruba** *isld* W Indies
18 E9 **Arudy** France
80 E8 **Arugot** *R* Jordan
136 G3 **Aru,Kep** *islds* Moluccas Indonesia
25 D2 **Arum** Netherlands
128 F4 **Arumá** Brazil
61 Q12 **Arume** *B* Okinawa
75 Q4 **Arunachal Pradesh** *prov* India
9 F6 **Arundel** England
144 C5 **Arundel** New Zealand
9 F5 **Arun,R** England
28 E6 **Årup** Denmark
76 D6 **Aruppukkottai** India
80 D5 **'Arūra** Jordan
88 F3 **Arusha** Tanzania
70 G4 **Arus,Tg** *C* Sulawesi Indonesia
70 B5 **Arut** *R* Kalimantan
70 E6 **Aru,Tg** *C* Kalimantan
83 K9 **Aruvi Aru** *R* Sri Lanka
86 D5 **Aruwimi** *R* Zaire
106 E2 **Arvada** Colorado U.S.A.
101 T5 **Arvada** Wyoming U.S.A.
26 K7 **Arvån** Sweden
58 D2 **Arvayheer** Mongolia
40 D5 **Arve** *R* France
26 K5 **Arvestuottar** *mt* Sweden
74 H8 **Arvi** India
121 T4 **Arvida** Quebec Canada
26 K6 **Arvidsjaur** Sweden
27 F12 **Arvika** Sweden
102 F6 **Arvin** California U.S.A.
94 J9 **Arvonia** Virginia U.S.A.
65 E1 **Arxan** China
147 Q9 **Ary** U.S.S.R.
55 C3 **Aryazh** U.S.S.R.
47 O13 **Aryirádhes** Greece
46 G9 **Aryiroúpolis** Crete Greece
55 E4 **Aryk-Balyk** U.S.S.R.
57 E4 **Arys'** *R* U.S.S.R.
57 E4 **Arys'** U.S.S.R.
57 D2 **Arys,Ozero** *L* U.S.S.R.
20 E6 **Arz** *R* France
20 F6 **Arzal, Barrage d'** *dam* France
52 F6 **Arzamas** U.S.S.R.
20 D6 **Arzano** France
37 N3 **Arzberg** W Germany
37 L5 **Arzberg** *mt* W Germany
32 K8 **Ärzen** W Germany
85 D1 **Arzew** Algeria
36 B3 **Arzfeld** W Germany
53 F10 **Arzgir** U.S.S.R.
41 O6 **Arzignano** Italy
41 N3 **Arzl** Austria
20 E6 **Arzon** France
16 B2 **Arzúa** Spain
22 K1 **As** Belgium
37 N3 **Aš** Czechoslovakia
26 E8 **Ås** Norway
28 E2 **Aså** Denmark
27 F14 **Åsa** Sweden
87 C11 **Asab** Namibia
74 D1 **Asadābād** Afghanistan
69 D11 **Asahan** *R* Sumatra
60 G10 **Asahi** *R* Japan
61 O10 **Asahi** Chiba Japan
61 N7 **Asahi-dake** *mt* Japan
60 Q2 **Asahi-dake** *mt* Japan
60 Q2 **Asahikawa** Japan
86 H3 **Āsalē** *L* Ethiopia
61 M9 **Asama yama** *vol* Japan
65 G6 **Asan Man** *B* S Korea
75 M7 **Asansol** India
26 G9 **Åsarna** Sweden
84 F5 **Asawanwah** Libya
36 C2 **Asbach** W Germany
71 C3 **Asbakin** W Irian
55 D3 **Asbest** U.S.S.R.
121 T7 **Asbestos** Quebec Canada
89 C7 **Asbestos Mts** S Africa
107 Q4 **Asbury** Kansas U.S.A.
110 B4 **Asbury** Missouri U.S.A.
Ascalon *see* **Tel Ashqelon**
90 B12 **Ascension** *isld* Atlantic Oc
128 F7 **Ascensión** Bolivia
124 E2 **Ascensión** Chihuahua Mexico
126 A1 **Ascension** Curaçao W Indies
37 O6 **Ascha** W Germany
38 L5 **Aschbach** Austria
33 M4 **Ascheberg** W Germany
32 G9 **Ascheberg** Nordrhein-Westfalen W Germany
32 F6 **Aschendorf** W Germany
21 O5 **Aschères-le-Marché** France
33 O9 **Aschersleben** East Germany
17 H3 **Asco** Spain
12 C2 **Ascog** Scotland
42 F6 **Ascoli Piceno** Italy
141 K1 **Ascot** *dist* Brisbane, Qnsld Australia
9 F5 **Ascot** England
133 D2 **Ascotán** Chile
86 H3 **Āseb** Ethiopia
27 H14 **Åseda** Sweden
85 E4 **Asedjrad** *hills* Algeria
53 H7 **Asekeyevoye** U.S.S.R.
86 G4 **Āsela** Ethiopia
26 J7 **Åsele** Sweden
26 E8 **Åsen** Norway
27 G10 **Åsen** Sweden
32 K7 **Asendorf** W Germany
46 G3 **Asenovgrad** Bulgaria
27 B13 **Åseral** Norway
79 G5 **Aşfar, Tall al** *mt* Syria
22 G5 **Asfeld-la-ville** France
27 D12 **Asgårdstr** Norway
55 C3 **Asha** U.S.S.R.
80 C8 **Ashan** *R* Israel
52 J5 **Ashan** U.S.S.R.
55 C3 **Ashap** U.S.S.R.
77 A4 **Ashar** Iran
9 E1 **Ashbourne** England
112 D6 **Ashburn** Georgia U.S.A.
142 B6 **Ashburton** *R* Western Australia Australia
8 C6 **Ashburton** England
144 C5 **Ashburton** New Zealand
140 C4 **Ashburton Ra** N Terr Australia
9 E4 **Ashbury** England
95 N6 **Ashbury Park** New Jersey U.S.A.
99 L3 **Ashby** Minnesota U.S.A.
9 E2 **Ashby de la Zouch** England
57 D2 **Ashchikol', Ozero** *L* U.S.S.R.
57 C1 **Ashchitastysor, Ozero** *L* U.S.S.R.
117 N10 **Ashcroft** British Columbia Canada
80 B6 **Ashdod** Israel
109 N2 **Ash Down** Arkansas U.S.A.
9 G5 **Ashdown Forest** England
112 H2 **Asheboro** North Carolina U.S.A.
107 O7 **Asher** Oklahoma U.S.A.
119 T7 **Ashern** Manitoba Canada
108 H7 **Asherton** Texas U.S.A.
112 E2 **Asheville** North Carolina U.S.A.
110 E5 **Ash Flat** Arkansas U.S.A.
9 G5 **Ashford** England
113 D11 **Ashford** Alabama U.S.A.
100 C3 **Ashford** Washington U.S.A.
9 E5 **Ashford Hill** England
103 M6 **Ashfork** Arizona U.S.A.
141 K1 **Ashgrove** *dist* Brisbane, Qnsld Australia
107 M2 **Ash Grove** Kansas U.S.A.
110 C4 **Ash Grove** Missouri U.S.A.
145 E4 **Ashhurst** New Zealand
60 Q2 **Ashibetsu** Japan
61 N9 **Ashikaga** Japan
9 F6 **Ashington** England
61 N9 **Ashio** Japan
52 G6 **Ashit** *R* U.S.S.R.
60 J11 **Ashiya** Japan
60 G13 **Ashizuri-misaki** *C* Japan
77 D4 **Ashkazar** Iran
77 F1 **Ashkhabad** Iran
77 F1 **Ashkhabad** U.S.S.R.
13 F3 **Ashkirk** Scotland
99 T9 **Ashkum** Illinois U.S.A.
111 L8 **Ashland** Alabama U.S.A.
110 F2 **Ashland** Illinois U.S.A.
107 L4 **Ashland** Kansas U.S.A.
94 E8 **Ashland** Kentucky U.S.A.
95 S7 **Ashland** Maine U.S.A.
101 T4 **Ashland** Montana U.S.A.
98 K8 **Ashland** Nebraska U.S.A.
95 Q3 **Ashland** New Hampshire U.S.A.
94 E6 **Ashland** Ohio U.S.A.
100 C7 **Ashland** Oregon U.S.A.
95 L6 **Ashland** Pennsylvania U.S.A.
94 K9 **Ashland** Virginia U.S.A.
99 Q3 **Ashland** Wisconsin U.S.A.
110 J5 **Ashland City** Tennessee U.S.A.
144 D5 **Ashley** New Zealand
110 G3 **Ashley** Illinois U.S.A.
94 C3 **Ashley** Michigan U.S.A.
98 G3 **Ashley** North Dakota U.S.A.
120 K4 **Ashley Mine** Ontario Canada
55 E3 **Ashlyk** *R* U.S.S.R.
118 F4 **Ashmont** Alberta Canada
108 E3 **Ashmore** Texas U.S.A.
142 E1 **Ashmore Reef** Timor Sea
79 A8 **Ashmûn** Egypt
80 F1 **Ashmura** Syria
95 N5 **Ashokan Res** New York U.S.A.
60 R2 **Ashoro** Japan
80 B7 **Ashqelon** Israel
78 J4 **Ash Sharqat** Iraq
72 F6 **Ash Shaykh' Uthmān** S Yemen
72 F6 **Ash Shihr** S Yemen
84 E4 **Ash Shuwayrif** Libya
94 G5 **Ashtabula** Ohio U.S.A.
98 J2 **Ashtabula,L** North Dakota U.S.A.
74 F9 **Ashti** India
77 A2 **Ashtiān** Iran
121 O7 **Ashton** Ontario Canada
101 O5 **Ashton** Idaho U.S.A.
99 R8 **Ashton** Illinois U.S.A.
94 B3 **Ashton** Michigan U.S.A.
98 H5 **Ashton** South Dakota U.S.A.
13 F6 **Ashton-in-Makerfield** England
142 F3 **Ashton Ra** Western Australia Australia
13 F6 **Ashton-under-Lyne** England
115 N7 **Ashuanipi,L** Labrador, Nfld Canada
121 R3 **Ashuapmuchuan** *R* Quebec Canada
78 J4 **Ashur** Iraq
78 J6 **Ashuriyah, Al** Iraq
111 K8 **Ashville** Alabama U.S.A.
79 G3 **'Āsi** *R* Syria/Lebanon
42 D3 **Asiago** Italy
71 C2 **Asia Pulau Pulau** *islds* Indonesia
71 F4 **Asid Gulf** Philippines
124 H6 **Asientos** Mexico
45 K1 **Asigliano Ven** Italy
75 L9 **Āsika** India
85 C1 **Asilah** Morocco
71 A1 **Asimiro** Halmahera Indonesia
43 B7 **Asinara, Golfo dell'** Sardinia
43 B7 **Asinara, I** Sardinia
56 C3 **Asino** U.S.S.R.
53 D10 **Askaniya Nova** U.S.S.R.
55 C4 **Askarovo** U.S.S.R.
14 C4 **Askeaton Adare** Ireland
27 D12 **Asker** Norway
13 G6 **Askern** England
27 G13 **Askersund** Sweden
72 H1 **Askhabad** U.S.S.R.
26 J7 **Åskilje** Sweden
27 E12 **Askim** Norway
112 K2 **Askin** North Carolina U.S.A.
55 C3 **Askino** U.S.S.R.
28 G7 **Askø** Denmark
29 M11 **Askola** Finland
65 J3 **Askol'd, O** *isld* U.S.S.R.
28 C6 **Askov** Denmark
99 O3 **Askov** Minnesota U.S.A.
13 F5 **Askrigg** England
27 A10 **Askvoll** Norway
79 C9 **Asl** Egypt
47 K5 **Aslanapa** Turkey
79 E2 **Aslanköy Dere** *str* Turkey
74 D1 **Asmar** Afghanistan
Asmara *see* **Āsmera**
86 G2 **Āsmera** Ethiopia
29 K5 **Asminderød** Denmark
28 G5 **Asnæs** Denmark
28 F5 **Asnæs** *pen* Denmark
21 J3 **Asnelles** France
27 G15 **Åsnen** Sweden
27 E11 **Åsnes** Norway
129 G3 **Asoenangka** Brazil
45 J1 **Asola** Italy
28 S9 **Asólfsstadhir** Iceland
60 E13 **Aso Nat. Park** Japan
86 F3 **Āsosa** Ethiopia
86 G1 **Asoteriba, Jebel** *mt* Sudan
100 H3 **Asotin** Washington U.S.A.
85 E3 **Asouf** *watercourse* Algeria
60 C11 **Asō-wan** *B* Japan
60 E13 **Aso zan** *vol* Japan
36 G6 **Aspach** W Germany
48 C3 **Aspang** Austria
26 G8 **Aspås** Sweden
13 E4 **Aspatria** England
17 G6 **Aspe** Spain
26 J8 **Aspeå** Sweden
106 D2 **Aspen** Colorado U.S.A.
101 P8 **Aspen** Wyoming U.S.A.
118 D6 **Aspen Beach Prov. Park** Alberta Canada
36 G6 **Asperg** W Germany
28 D6 **Asperup** Denmark
19 P16 **Aspremont** France
46 D5 **Asprókavos, Akr** *C* Greece
47 P13 **Asprókavos, Akra** *C* Greece
43 G10 **Aspromonte** *mts* Italy
123 M7 **Aspy B** C Breton I, Nova Scotia
118 K6 **Asquith** Saskatchewan Canada
79 H3 **Aş Şā'ān** Syria
74 D1 **Assad-Abad** Afghanistan
79 H2 **As Safirah** Syria
21 K8 **Assais-les-Jumeaux** France
75 O5 **Assam** *prov* India
85 F5 **Assamakka** Niger
95 M8 **Assateague I** Maryland U.S.A.
22 G2 **Asse** Belgium
19 Q17 **Asse** *R* France
119 V2 **Assean L** Manitoba Canada
89 G6 **Assegai** *R* Swaziland
85 F3 **Assekaifaf** Algeria
85 F4 **Assekreme** *mt* Algeria
32 K5 **Assel** W Germany
21 K5 **Asse la Boisne** France
22 K3 **Asselborn** Luxembourg
25 G3 **Assen** Netherlands
36 F3 **Assenheim** W Germany
28 E3 **Assens** Århus Denmark
28 D6 **Assens** Fyn Denmark
20 F7 **Asserac** France
22 J3 **Assesse** Belgium
122 G2 **Assigny,L** Quebec Canada
118 L9 **Assinboia** Saskatchewan Canada
28 B4 **Assing** Denmark
118 L9 **Assiniboia** Saskatchewan Canada
117 Q10 **Assiniboine,Mt** Br Col/Alberta Canada
119 Q8 **Assiniboine R** Manitoba/Sask Canada
84 G4 **As Sirīr** *sands* Libya
46 F4 **Ássiros** Greece
129 H8 **Assis** Brazil
42 E5 **Assisi** Italy
36 D3 **Assmannshausen** W Germany
41 K6 **Asso** Italy
78 G4 **As Sukhnah** Syria
87 H9 **Assumption** *isld* Seychelles
110 G2 **Assumption** Illinois U.S.A.
78 K5 **Aş Suwayrah** Iraq
36 C5 **Assweiler** W Germany
37 N7 **Ast** W Germany
27 E10 **Asta** *R* Norway
18 F8 **Astaffort** France
47 H9 **Astakidha** *isld* Greece
46 E6 **Astakós** Greece
77 A1 **Astaneh** Iran
28 E2 **Åsted** Nordjylland Denmark
28 B3 **Åsted** Viborg Denmark
25 E6 **Asten** Netherlands
77 C1 **Asterabad** Iran
44 D2 **Asti** Italy
16 E1 **Astillero** Spain
Astin Tagh *mt ra see* **Altun Shan**
47 H8 **Astipálaia** *isld* Greece
9 E1 **Aston** England
8 D3 **Aston Cross** England
74 F1 **Astor** Kashmir
16 C2 **Astorga** Spain
99 Q9 **Astoria** Illinois U.S.A.
100 B3 **Astoria** Oregon U.S.A.
98 K5 **Astoria** South Dakota U.S.A.
27 F15 **Åstorp** Sweden
121 L6 **Astorville** Ontario Canada
87 H10 **Astove** *isld* Br Indian Oc Terr
53 G10 **Astrakhan'** U.S.S.R.
55 E5 **Astrakhanka** U.S.S.R.
26 L7 **Åsträsk** Sweden
146 J6 **Astrid Ridge** *ridge* Antarctica
46 F7 **Astros** Greece
28 E6 **Astrup** Fyn Denmark
28 B5 **Åstrup** Ribe Denmark
28 D6 **Åstrup** Sønderjylland Denmark
28 J7 **Åstrup** *isld* Storstrøm Denmark
28 D5 **Åstrup** Vejle Denmark
16 E2 **Astudillo** Spain
45 N7 **Astura** *R* Italy
16 C1 **Asturias** *reg* Spain
9 F3 **Astwood** England
28 E6 **Åsum** Denmark
133 F3 **Asunción** Paraguay
27 H14 **Asunden** *L* Sweden
28 E5 **As Vig** *B* Denmark
84 J5 **Aswân** Egypt
84 J5 **Aswan High Dam** Egypt
84 J4 **Asyût** Egypt
48 E3 **Aszód** Hungary
137 R6 **Ata** *isld* Pacific Oc
57 E3 **Atabay** U.S.S.R.
47 L7 **Atabey** Turkey
133 C3 **Atacama** *reg* Chile
128 E8 **Atacama, Des de** Chile
133 D3 **Atacama, Puna de** *plateau* Argentina
48 L2 **Ataki** U.S.S.R.
85 E7 **Atakpamé** Togo
130 J10 **Atalaia** Brazil
46 F6 **Atalándi** Greece
128 D6 **Atalaya** Peru
130 H6 **Ataléia** Brazil
71 M9 **Atambua** Timor Indonesia
61 N10 **Atami** Japan
115 O5 **Atammik** Greenland
55 F4 **Atansor, Oz** *L* U.S.S.R.
79 C9 **'Ataqa, G** *mt* Egypt
85 B4 **Atar** Mauritania
80 D5 **'Atara** Jordan
80 F7 **Ataroth** Jordan
106 B7 **Atarque** New Mexico U.S.A.
80 F7 **Ataruz** Jordan
Atas *isld see* **South I** Cocos Is
102 D6 **Atascadero** California U.S.A.
109 J6 **Atascosa** *R* Texas U.S.A.
57 F1 **Atasu** U.S.S.R.
68 C4 **Atatano** *R* Burma
17 F2 **Atauri** Spain
71 M9 **Atauro** *isld* Indonesia
86 F2 **Atbara** Sudan
86 G2 **Atbara** *R* Sudan
55 E5 **Atbasar** Kazakhskaya S.S.R. U.S.S.R.
57 H4 **At-Bash** U.S.S.R.
111 E12 **Atchafalaya Bay** Louisiana U.S.A.
107 P2 **Atchison** Kansas U.S.A.
116 G5 **Atchueelinguk** *R* Alaska U.S.A.
112 C3 **Atco** Georgia U.S.A.
95 N7 **Atco** New Jersey U.S.A.
17 F3 **Ateca** Spain
58 E4 **A-t'eng-hsi-lien** China
124 G7 **Atenguillo** Mexico
61 O7 **Aterazawa** Japan
42 F6 **Aterno** *R* Italy
42 D2 **Atesine,Alpi** Italy
42 F6 **Atessa** Italy
22 F2 **Ath** Belgium
117 D4 **Athabasca** Alberta Canada
114 J6 **Athabasca, L** Alberta/Sask Canada
119 C4 **Athapap** Manitoba Canada
119 C4 **Athapapuskow L** Manitoba Canada
28 C4 **Atheden** *reg* Denmark
110 B1 **Athelstan** Iowa U.S.A.
100 G4 **Athena** Oregon U.S.A.
14 C3 **Athenry** Ireland
121 F8 **Athens** Ontario Canada
Athens Greece *see* **Athínai**
110 K7 **Athens** Alabama U.S.A.
112 D4 **Athens** Georgia U.S.A.
99 R10 **Athens** Illinois U.S.A.
109 O3 **Athens** Louisiana U.S.A.
95 S2 **Athens** Maine U.S.A.
94 B4 **Athens** Michigan U.S.A.
94 E7 **Athens** Ohio U.S.A.
95 L5 **Athens** Pennsylvania U.S.A.
112 C2 **Athens** Tennessee U.S.A.
109 M3 **Athens** Texas U.S.A.
99 Q4 **Athens** Wisconsin U.S.A.
121 L8 **Atherley** Ontario Canada
9 E2 **Atherstone** England
141 H3 **Atherton** Queensland Australia
13 F6 **Atherton** England
85 E7 **Athiémé** Benin
22 F4 **Athies** Aisne France
22 D4 **Athies** Somme France
46 F7 **Athínai** Greece
21 K4 **Athis-de-l'Orne** France
14 C3 **Athleague** Ireland
14 D3 **Athlone** Ireland
79 D3 **Athna** Cyprus
76 B2 **Athni** India
144 B6 **Athol** New Zealand
100 J2 **Athol** Idaho U.S.A.
95 P4 **Athol** Massachusetts U.S.A.
113 L9 **Athol I** New Providence I Bahamas
122 F6 **Atholville** New Brunswick Canada
46 G4 **Áthos** *mt* Greece
Athos, Mt *reg see* **Áyion Óros**
79 G9 **Ath Thāyat** *mt* Saudi Arabia
22 K4 **Athus** Belgium
14 E4 **Athy** Ireland
86 C3 **Ati** Chad
145 F3 **Atiamuri** New Zealand
130 F8 **Atibaia** Brazil
128 D7 **Atico** Peru
123 N2 **Aticonipi L** Quebec Canada
17 F3 **Atienza** Spain
119 Q4 **Atik** Manitoba Canada
117 Q8 **Atikameg** Alberta Canada
119 R4 **Atikameg Lake** Manitoba Canada
99 P1 **Atikokan** Ontario Canada
115 N7 **Atikonak, L** Labrador, Nfld Canada
122 H1 **Atikonal L** Labrador, Nfld Canada
118 J1 **Atikwa L** Ontario Canada
71 E3 **Atimonan** Philippines
45 P6 **Atina** Italy
76 D5 **Atirampattinam** India
116 P9 **Atka** Aleutian Is
51 P2 **Atka** U.S.S.R.
53 F8 **Atkarsk** U.S.S.R.
116 J1 **Atkasuk** Alaska U.S.A.
110 D6 **Atkins** Arkansas U.S.A.
99 Q8 **Atkinson** Illinois U.S.A.
98 G7 **Atkinson** Nebraska U.S.A.
112 J3 **Atkinson** North Carolina U.S.A.
71 B3 **Atkri** W Irian
111 M8 **Atlanta** Georgia U.S.A.
105 **Atlanta** *conurbation* Georgia U.S.A.
101 K6 **Atlanta** Idaho U.S.A.
110 G1 **Atlanta** Illinois U.S.A.
94 A6 **Atlanta** Indiana U.S.A.
107 O4 **Atlanta** Kansas U.S.A.
110 D2 **Atlanta** Missouri U.S.A.
95 K4 **Atlanta** New York U.S.A.
109 N2 **Atlanta** Texas U.S.A.
99 L8 **Atlantic** Iowa U.S.A.
112 L3 **Atlantic** North Carolina U.S.A.
95 N7 **Atlantic City** New Jersey U.S.A.
101 R7 **Atlantic City** Wyoming U.S.A.
95 N6 **Atlantic Highlands** New Jersey U.S.A.
90 J15 **Atlantic-Indian Basin** Southern Oc
90 J14 **Atlantic-Indian Ridge** S Atlantic Oc
128 D1 **Atlántico** *div* Colombia
90 **Atlantic Oc**
90 E5 **Atlantis Fracture** Atlantic Oc
94 D4 **Atlas** Michigan U.S.A.
85 C2 **Atlas, Haut** *mts* Morocco
85 C2 **Atlas, Moyen** *mts* Morocco
85 E2 **Atlas Saharien** *mts* Algeria
118 G8 **Atlee** Alberta Canada
117 G6 **Atlin** British Columbia Canada
80 C3 **'Atlit** Israel
125 K8 **Atlixco** Mexico
26 A10 **Atlöy** *isld* Norway
76 D3 **Atmakur** India
113 B11 **Atmore** Alabama U.S.A.
117 L9 **Atnarko** British Columbia Canada
26 D10 **Atnasjö** *L* Norway
55 E2 **Atnis** U.S.S.R.
60 E11 **Atō** Japan
87 H12 **Atofinandrahana** Madagascar
107 O7 **Atoka** Oklahoma U.S.A.
102 G6 **Atolia** California U.S.A.
101 N6 **Atomic City** Idaho U.S.A.
124 H7 **Atotonilco el Alto** Mexico
77 E1 **Atrak** *R* Iran
27 F14 **Atran** Sweden
26 L7 **Åträsk** Sweden
128 C2 **Atrato** *R* Colombia
42 F6 **Atri** Italy
45 R8 **Atripaida** Italy
56 G4 **Atsikyak** U.S.S.R.
61 N10 **Atsugi** Japan
61 N7 **Atsumi** Japan
61 L11 **Atsumi-hantō** *pen* Japan
140 C4 **Attack Cr** N Terr Australia
111 K7 **Attalla** Alabama U.S.A.
68 H5 **Attapu** Laos
47 U14 **Attaviros** *mt* Rhodes Greece
115 L7 **Attawapiskat** Ontario Canada
80 G1 **Aţ Ţayḩah** Syria
36 D1 **Attendorn** W Germany
38 J6 **Attersee** Austria
110 J1 **Attica** Indiana U.S.A.
107 M4 **Attica** Kansas U.S.A.
94 D3 **Attica** Michigan U.S.A.
94 J4 **Attica** New York U.S.A.
94 E5 **Attica** Ohio U.S.A.
22 E5 **Attichy** France
40 B5 **Attignat** France
22 H5 **Attigny** France
95 Q5 **Attleboro** Massachusetts U.S.A.
9 H2 **Attleborough** England
9 H2 **Attlebridge** England
26 J9 **Attmar** Sweden
109 N4 **Attoyac Bayou** *R* Texas U.S.A.
116 J9 **Attu** Aleutian Is
115 O4 **Attu** Greenland
76 D5 **Attur** India
133 D5 **Atuel** *R* Argentina
131 C6 **Atuel, Banados del** *swamps* Argentina
27 H13 **Åtvid** Sweden
27 H13 **Åtvidaberg** Sweden
119 P8 **Atwater** Saskatchewan Canada
102 D4 **Atwater** California U.S.A.
99 M4 **Atwater** Minnesota U.S.A.
13 H6 **Atwick** England
106 G1 **Atwood** Colorado U.S.A.
110 H2 **Atwood** Illinois U.S.A.
107 J2 **Atwood** Kansas U.S.A.
94 F6 **Atwood Res** Ohio U.S.A.
53 G7 **Atyashevo** U.S.S.R.
38 N5 **Atzenbrugg** Austria
33 P9 **Atzendorf** East Germany
36 D2 **Au** Rheinland-Pfalz W Germany
128 E4 **Auati-Paraná** *R* Brazil
135 S3 **Auau Chan** Hawaiian Is
37 J4 **Aub** W Germany
19 P18 **Aubagne** France
22 K4 **Aubange** Belgium
71 F2 **Aubarede Pt** Luzon Philippines
18 H4 **Aube** *R* France
18 H4 **Aube** *dept* France
22 K2 **Aubel** Belgium
22 E3 **Aubencheul-Au-Bac** France
22 G4 **Aubenton** France
21 O4 **Aubergenville** France
83 L13 **Aubert,C** Kerguelen Indian Oc
21 M4 **Aube-sur-Rille** France
18 F7 **Aubeterre** France
21 J8 **Aubiers, les** France
21 L6 **Aubigné** Sarthe France
22 D3 **Aubigny** Pas-de-Calais France
20 H8 **Aubigny** Vendée France
18 G5 **Aubigny sur Nère** France
18 G8 **Aubin** France
18 H8 **Aubrac, Mts d'** France
103 M6 **Aubrey Cliffs** Arizona U.S.A.
143 B7 **Aubrey, Mt** Western Australia Australia
114 G4 **Aubry L** Northwest Territories Canada
141 K7 **Auburn** *R* Queensland Australia
111 L9 **Auburn** Alabama U.S.A.
102 C3 **Auburn** California U.S.A.
110 G2 **Auburn** Illinois U.S.A.
94 B5 **Auburn** Indiana U.S.A.
107 P3 **Auburn** Kansas U.S.A.
110 K5 **Auburn** Kentucky U.S.A.
95 R2 **Auburn** Maine U.S.A.
94 C3 **Auburn** Michigan U.S.A.
99 L9 **Auburn** Nebraska U.S.A.
95 L4 **Auburn** New York U.S.A.
117 M12 **Auburn** Washington U.S.A.
113 F9 **Auburndale** Florida U.S.A.
99 R5 **Auburndale** Wisconsin U.S.A.
141 K7 **Auburn Ra** Queensland Australia
18 G7 **Aubusson** France
133 D5 **Auca Mahuida,Sa** *mt* Argentina
52 B6 **Auce** U.S.S.R.
18 F9 **Auch** France
22 C3 **Auchel** France
12 E4 **Auchencairn** Scotland
12 D4 **Auchenmalg** Scotland
85 F7 **Auchi** Nigeria
12 D3 **Auchinleck** Scotland
12 E1 **Auchterarder** Scotland
13 E1 **Auchterderran** Scotland
13 E1 **Auchtermuchty** Scotland
22 C2 **Auchy-au-Bois** France
113 D7 **Aucilla** *R* Florida U.S.A.
145 F1 **Auckland** New Zealand
68 D6 **Auckland B** Burma
18 G9 **Aude** *R* France
18 G9 **Aude** *dept* France
120 C2 **Auden** Ontario Canada
Audenarde *see* **Oudenaarde**
18 E8 **Audenge** France
20 G2 **Auderville** France
20 A5 **Audierne** France
20 B6 **Audierne, B. d'** France
83 L14 **Audierne, Bd'** Kerguelen Indian Oc
40 E3 **Audincourt** France
22 B2 **Audinghen** France
45 N4 **Auditore** Italy
8 D2 **Audlem** England
22 B2 **Audresselles** France
7 M9 **Audrey** *oil rig* North Sea
22 C2 **Audruicq** France
99 M8 **Audubon** Iowa U.S.A.
98 E2 **Audubon Lake** *res* North Dakota U.S.A.
19 J3 **Audun le Roman** France
37 O2 **Aue** East Germany
32 G6 **Aue** *R* W Germany
84 E4 **Auenat Uennin** Libya
36 G5 **Auenstein** W Germany
37 N2 **Auerbach** East Germany
36 F4 **Auerbach** Hessen W Germany
41 N2 **Auer Berg** *mt* W Germany
37 O2 **Auerswalde** East Germany
111 E12 **Au Far, Point** Louisiana U.S.A.
21 N2 **Auffay** France
20 F6 **Augan** France
141 H7 **Augathella** Queensland Australia
14 E2 **Aughnacloy** N Ireland
14 E4 **Aughrim** Ireland
89 B7 **Augrabies** S Africa
89 B7 **Augrabies Falls** Orange R S Africa
94 D2 **Au Gres** Michigan U.S.A.
37 K7 **Augsburg** W Germany
143 B10 **Augusta** Western Australia Australia
43 G11 **Augusta** Sicily
110 E6 **Augusta** Arkansas U.S.A.
112 E4 **Augusta** Georgia U.S.A.
110 F1 **Augusta** Illinois U.S.A.
107 O4 **Augusta** Kansas U.S.A.
94 C8 **Augusta** Kentucky U.S.A.
95 S2 **Augusta** Maine U.S.A.
94 B4 **Augusta** Michigan U.S.A.
101 N2 **Augusta** Montana U.S.A.
99 P5 **Augusta** Wisconsin U.S.A.
143 E7 **Augusta, L** Western Australia Australia
116 R6 **Augusta,Mt** Yukon Territory Canada
94 H8 **Augusta Springs** Virginia U.S.A.
116 L7 **Augustine I** Alaska U.S.A.
130 G6 **Augusto de Lima** Brazil
130 H8 **Augusto Severo** Brazil
31 O2 **Augustów** Poland
140 E4 **Augustus Downs** Queensland Australia
142 E3 **Augustus Island** Western Australia Australia
143 B6 **Augustus, Mt** Western Australia Australia
37 M6 **Au in der Hallertau** W Germany
40 B2 **Aujon** *R* France
6 M6 **Auk** *oil rig* North Sea
32 L4 **Aukrug** W Germany
26 K6 **Auktsjaur** Sweden
112 K1 **Aulander** North Carolina U.S.A.
142 E5 **Auld, L** Western Australia Australia
18 E6 **Aulnay de Saintonge** France
21 P5 **Aulnay-la-Rivière** France
20 B5 **Aulne** *R* France
118 H1 **Aulneau Pen** Ontario Canada
22 F3 **Aulnoye** France
106 F1 **Ault** Colorado U.S.A.
15 C3 **Aultbea** Scotland
54 F8 **Auly** U.S.S.R.
37 M2 **Auma** *R* East Germany
37 M2 **Auma** East Germany
21 O2 **Aumale** France
18 G6 **Aumance** *R* France
22 K5 **Aumetz** France
57 C4 **Auminzatau,Gory** *mt* U.S.S.R.
40 C4 **Aumont** France
18 H8 **Aumont** Lozère France
33 M5 **Aumühle** W Germany
21 J3 **Aunay-sur-Odon** France
74 F10 **Aundh** India
21 L6 **Aune** *R* France
21 O5 **Auneau** France
21 P3 **Auneuil** France
68 B3 **Aunglan** Burma
28 E4 **Auning** Denmark
18 E6 **Aunis** *prov* France
87 C11 **Auob** *R* Namibia
71 J5 **Auponhia** Moluccas Indonesia
19 Q17 **Aups** France
69 G11 **Aur** *isld* Malaysia
29 K11 **Aura** Finland
26 C9 **Aura** *R* Norway
37 K4 **Aurach** *R* W Germany
74 H5 **Auraiya** India
29 K11 **Aurajoki** *R* Finland
74 F9 **Aurangabad** India
20 E6 **Auray** France
21 J3 **Aure** *R* France
26 C8 **Aure** Norway
19 O16 **Aurel** France
99 L7 **Aurelia** Iowa U.S.A.
85 F1 **Aurès** *mts* Algeria
32 F6 **Aurich** W Germany
130 E5 **Aurilândia** Brazil
18 G8 **Aurillac** France
19 P18 **Auriol** France
70 B5 **Aurkuning** Kalimantan
27 B11 **Aurland** Norway
130 H9 **Aurora** Brazil
121 L9 **Aurora** Ontario Canada
106 F2 **Aurora** Colorado U.S.A.
99 S8 **Aurora** Illinois U.S.A.
94 C7 **Aurora** Indiana U.S.A.
107 N2 **Aurora** Kansas U.S.A.
110 C5 **Aurora** Missouri U.S.A.
98 H9 **Aurora** Nebraska U.S.A.
112 L2 **Aurora** North Carolina U.S.A.
103 N3 **Aurora** Utah U.S.A.
19 P15 **Aurouze, Mt d'** France
76 D4 **Auroville** India
26 C9 **Aursjöen** *L* Norway
27 E12 **Aurskog** Norway
26 E9 **Aursunden** *L* Norway
141 F2 **Aurukun** Queensland Australia
45 P7 **Aurunci Monti** Italy
87 C11 **Aus** Namibia
94 C2 **Au Sable** *R* Michigan U.S.A.
95 O2 **Ausable Forks** New York U.S.A.
94 D2 **Au Sable Pt** Michigan U.S.A.
128 D6 **Ausangate** *mt* Peru
80 F4 **Ausara** Jordan
88 B7 **Aushi** Zambia
15 F1 **Auskerry** Scotland
45 O7 **Ausoni, Monti** *mt* Italy
41 K3 **Ausser-Rhoden** *dist* Switzerland
8 D4 **Aust** England
27 C13 **Austad** Norway
27 C13 **Aust Agder Fylker** Norway
112 C4 **Austell** Georgia U.S.A.
Austerlitz *see* **Slavkov**
119 T9 **Austin** Manitoba Canada
99 O6 **Austin** Minnesota U.S.A.
101 N3 **Austin** Montana U.S.A.
100 G5 **Austin** Oregon U.S.A.
94 J5 **Austin** Pennsylvania U.S.A.
109 K5 **Austin** Texas U.S.A.
143 C8 **Austin, L** Western Australia Australia
109 M4 **Austonio** Texas U.S.A.
140 E5 **Austral Downs** N Terr Australia
136 **Australia** *dominion* Australia
146 F15 **Australian Antarctic Territory** Antarctica
143 B10 **Australind** Western Australia Australia
135 M11 **Austral Ridge** Pacific Oc
26 D8 **Austråt** Norway
27 A11 **Austrheim** Norway
38 E7 **Austria** *rep* Cent Europe
26 G3 **Austvågöy** *isld* Norway
109 L7 **Austwell** Texas U.S.A.
21 N6 **Autainville** France
128 G4 **Autazes** Brazil
22 K4 **Autelbas** Belgium
18 G9 **Auterive** France
123 L3 **Auteuil, L. d'** Quebec Canada
22 C3 **Authie** *R* France
121 M4 **Authier** Quebec Canada
21 K7 **Authion** *R* France
21 M6 **Authon** Loir-et-Cher France
21 M5 **Authon-du-Perche** France
21 O5 **Authon-la-Plaine** France
124 G8 **Autlán de Navarro** Mexico
45 O6 **Autore, M** *mt* Italy
99 U3 **Au Train** Michigan U.S.A.
19 P14 **Autrans** France
21 P5 **Autruy-sur-Juine** France
22 H5 **Autry** France
18 H6 **Autun** France
140 B3 **Auvergne** N Terr Australia
18 H7 **Auvergne** *prov* France
21 K6 **Auvers-le-Hamon** France
21 P3 **Auvers-sur-Oise** France
18 F7 **Auvezère** *R* France
22 G4 **Auvillers-les-Forges** France
21 L8 **Auxances** *R* France
94 E2 **Aux Barques, Pt** Michigan U.S.A.
18 H5 **Auxerre** France
21 P1 **Auxi-le-Château** France
40 B3 **Auxonne** France
110 E2 **Auxvasse** Missouri U.S.A.
128 F2 **Auyán Tepui** *mt* Venezuela
115 M4 **Auyuittuq Nat Park** NW Terr
20 G8 **Auzance** *R* France
18 G6 **Auzances** France
68 B2 **Ava** Burma
110 G4 **Ava** Illinois U.S.A.
110 D5 **Ava** Missouri U.S.A.
26 M5 **Avafors** Sweden
18 F6 **Availles-Limouzine** France
116 H1 **Avalik** *R* Alaska U.S.A.
18 H5 **Avallon** France
102 F8 **Avalon** California U.S.A.
111 F8 **Avalon** Mississippi U.S.A.
95 N7 **Avalon** New Jersey U.S.A.
108 C3 **Avalon, L** New Mexico U.S.A.
123 T6 **Avalon Pen** Newfoundland Canada
131 F2 **Avalos** *R* Argentina
124 J5 **Avalos** Mexico
19 Q15 **Avançon** France
107 M5 **Avard** Oklahoma U.S.A.
129 J8 **Avaré** Brazil
53 G12 **Avarskoye Koysu** *R* U.S.S.R.
47 H4 **Ávas** Greece
116 E9 **Avatanak I** Aleutian Is
26 H7 **Avaträsk** Sweden
26 L5 **Avaudden** Sweden
26 K6 **Avaviken** Sweden
102 H6 **Avawatz Mts** California U.S.A.
47 N10 **Avci Koru** *forest* Turkey
54 J8 **Avdeyevka** U.S.S.R.
9 E5 **Avebury** England
16 D4 **Aveinte** Spain
129 G4 **Aveiro** Brazil
16 B4 **Aveiro** Portugal
77 A2 **Avej** Iran
22 E2 **Avelgem** Belgium
94 G6 **Avella** Pennsylvania U.S.A.
133 F4 **Avellaneda** Argentina
45 R8 **Avellino** Italy
102 D6 **Avenal** California U.S.A.
40 F4 **Avenches** Switzerland
95 Q4 **Aver** Massachusetts U.S.A.
28 E6 **Avernak By** *B* Denmark
26 B8 **Averöy** *isld* Norway
45 Q8 **Aversa** Italy
100 K2 **Avery** Idaho U.S.A.
99 O8 **Avery** Iowa U.S.A.
109 N2 **Avery** Texas U.S.A.
111 E12 **Avery Island** Louisiana U.S.A.
22 F3 **Avesnes** France
22 D3 **Avesnes le Comte** France
22 E3 **Avesnes-les-Aubert** France
90 C7 **Aves Ridge** Atlantic Oc
20 G6 **Avessac** France
27 H11 **Avesta** Sweden
18 G8 **Aveyron** *dept* France
18 F8 **Aveyron** *R* France
45 O5 **Avezzano** Italy
46 F8 **Avgó** *isld* Greece
46 E5 **Avgó** *mt* Greece
47 H9 **Avgó** *isld* Greece
133 E3 **Aviá Terai** Argentina
15 E3 **Aviemore** Scotland
144 C6 **Aviemore, L** New Zealand
115 P5 **Avigaat** Greenland
80 B7 **Avigedor** Israel
43 G8 **Avigliano** Italy
19 N17 **Avignon** France
16 D4 **Avila** *prov* Spain
16 D4 **Ávila, Sa. de** *mts* Spain
16 D1 **Avilés** Spain
40 D3 **Avilley** France
109 N3 **Avinger** Texas U.S.A.
22 D3 **Avion** France
47 O12 **Avlótes** Greece
95 K5 **Avis** Pennsylvania U.S.A.
41 O5 **Avisio** *R* Italy
80 E1 **Avivim** Israel
16 B5 **Aviz** Portugal
47 K8 **Avlan Gölü** *L* Turkey
46 F6 **Avlón** Greece
28 B4 **Avlum** Denmark
80 G2 **Avne Etan** Syria
28 H6 **Avnø Fjord** *inlet* Denmark
28 F6 **Avnslev** Denmark
139 G6 **Avoca** Victoria Australia
14 E4 **Avoca** Ireland
144 C5 **Avoca** New Zealand
94 E3 **Avoca** Michigan U.S.A.
95 K4 **Avoca** New York U.S.A.
108 H3 **Avoca** Texas U.S.A.
14 E4 **Avoca,Vale of** Ireland
138 D5 **Avoid B** South Australia Australia
117 O10 **Avola** British Columbia Canada
43 G12 **Avola** Sicily
8 D5 **Avon** *co* England
15 E3 **Avon** *R* Scotland
106 D2 **Avon** Colorado U.S.A.
95 P5 **Avon** Connecticut U.S.A.
110 F1 **Avon** Illinois U.S.A.
99 M4 **Avon** Minnesota U.S.A.
101 N3 **Avon** Montana U.S.A.
94 K4 **Avon** New York U.S.A.
112 M2 **Avon** North Carolina U.S.A.
94 E5 **Avon** Ohio U.S.A.
98 H6 **Avon** South Dakota U.S.A.
141 K6 **Avondale** Queensland Australia
103 M8 **Avondale** Arizona U.S.A.
106 F3 **Avondale** Colorado U.S.A.
110 B2 **Avondale** Missouri U.S.A.
109 L8 **Avondale** Texas U.S.A.
140 D4 **Avon Downs** N Terr Australia
141 H5 **Avon Downs** Queensland Australia
94 E5 **Avon Lake** Ohio U.S.A.
119 M8 **Avonlea** Saskatchewan Canada
21 L7 **Avon-les-Roches** France
94 H6 **Avonmore** Pennsylvania U.S.A.
8 D4 **Avonmouth** England
113 F10 **Avon Park** Florida U.S.A.
143 B9 **Avon, R** Western Australia Australia
9 E5 **Avon, R** England
9 E3 **Avon, R** England
130 E10 **Avoredo** *lighthouse* Brazil
40 D3 **Avoudrey** France
20 H4 **Avranches** France
22 D4 **Avre** *R* France
21 N4 **Avre** *R* Eure France
36 B6 **Avricourt** France
48 J5 **Avrig** Romania
22 K5 **Avril** France
48 E7 **Avtovac** Yugoslavia
80 F4 **Avuqa** Israel
61 P12 **Awa** Okinawa
69 C12 **Awaay** Indonesia
60 H11 **Awaji-shima** *isld* Japan
145 E3 **Awakino** New Zealand
84 E4 **Awāl** *watercourse* Libya
70 Q10 **Awang** Indonesia
145 D1 **Awanui** New Zealand
86 H4 **Āwarē** Ethiopia
144 B7 **Awarua** New Zealand
86 G4 **Āwasa Hāyk'** *L* Ethiopia
86 H4 **Āwash** Ethiopia
61 N7 **Awa-shima** *isld* Japan
85 D7 **Awaso** Ghana
57 K4 **Awat** China
86 G4 **Āwat'a** *R* Ethiopia
145 E4 **Awatere R** New Zealand
84 E4 **Awbārī** Libya
86 H5 **Aw Dheegle** Somalia
12 C1 **Awe,L** Scotland
112 H4 **Awendaw** South Carolina U.S.A.
84 G4 **Awjilah** Libya
70 G6 **Awo** *R* Sulawesi Indonesia
117 Q4 **Awry L** Northwest Territories Canada
85 B4 **Awserd** Mauritania
116 J2 **Awuna** *R* Alaska U.S.A.
8 D5 **Axbridge** England
25 A6 **Axel** Netherlands
27 F14 **Axelfors** Sweden
147 H5 **Axel Heiberg I** Northwest Territories Canada
106 C1 **Axial** Colorado U.S.A.
128 G4 **Axinim** Brazil
18 G10 **Ax-les-Thermes** France
8 D6 **Axminster** England
112 E6 **Axson** Georgia U.S.A.
107 O2 **Axtell** Kansas U.S.A.
27 G13 **Axvall** Sweden
18 H3 **Ay** France
20 H3 **Ay** *R* France
128 C4 **Ayabaca** Peru
60 J10 **Ayabe** Japan
78 D1 **Ayaç** Turkey
133 F5 **Ayacucho** Argentina
128 D6 **Ayacucho** Peru
68 B1 **Ayadaw** Burma
57 K1 **Ayaguz** U.S.S.R
57 D4 **Ayakkuduk** U.S.S.R.
66 D4 **Ayakkum Hu** *L* China
16 C7 **Ayamonte** Spain
78 E1 **Ayancık** Turkey
80 C6 **Ayanot** Israel
126 G10 **Ayapel** Colombia
128 D6 **Ayaviri** Peru
77 L1 **Āybak** Afghanistan
13 G4 **Aycliffe** England
55 E4 **Aydabul'** U.S.S.R.
54 L8 **Aydar** *R* U.S.S.R.
57 D4 **Aydarkul', Ozero** *L* U.S.S.R.
112 K2 **Ayden** North Carolina U.S.A.
78 A3 **Aydin** Turkey
47 J7 **Aydın** Turkey
79 D2 **Aydıncık** Turkey
47 J7 **Aydin Dağlar** *mts* Turkey
79 B1 **Aydınkent** Turkey
47 N11 **Aydınlı** Turkey
55 C5 **Aydrlinskiy** U.S.S.R.
86 H3 **Ayelu Terara** *mt* Ethiopia
40 G5 **Ayer** Switzerland
17 G2 **Ayerbe** Spain
100 G3 **Ayers** Washington U.S.A.
140 C7 **Ayers Ra** N Terr Australia
140 B7 **Ayers Rock** *mt* N Terr Australia
55 F3 **Ayev** *R* U.S.S.R.
19 O16 **Aygues** *R* France
56 C5 **Aygulaskiy Khrebet** *mts* U.S.S.R.
46 F5 **Ayiá** Greece
46 F6 **Ayía Ánna** Greece
46 G5 **Ayia Irini Akra** *C* Greece
47 H5 **Ayiássos** Greece
46 G4 **Áyion Óros** *reg* Greece
46 F7 **Áyios** *isld* Greece
46 G5 **Áyios Evstrátios** *isld* Greece
47 O12 **Ayios Matthaios** Greece
46 G9 **Áyios Míron** Crete Greece
47 H9 **Ayios Nikólaos** Crete Greece
46 D6 **Ayios Pétros** Greece
79 D3 **Ayios Seryios** Cyprus
79 E3 **Ayios Theodhoros** Cyprus
116 L2 **Ayiyak** *R* Alaska U.S.A.
47 H7 **Aykathonisi** *isld* Greece
86 G3 **Āykel** Ethiopia
47 H7 **Ay Kirikos** Greece
36 B4 **Ayl** W Germany
121 N7 **Aylen,L** Ontario Canada
119 M8 **Aylesbury** Saskatchewan Canada
9 F4 **Aylesbury** England
144 D5 **Aylesbury** New Zealand
122 H8 **Aylesford** Nova Scotia Canada
9 H5 **Aylesham** England
117 D6 **Aylesworth, Mt** Br Col/Alaska Canada/U.S.A.
16 E3 **Ayllón** Spain
16 E3 **Ayllón, Sa. de** *mts* Spain
121 P7 **Aylmer** Quebec Canada
114 J5 **Aylmer L** Northwest Territories Canada
118 B7 **Aylmer,Mt** Alberta Canada
119 O5 **Aylsham** Saskatchewan Canada
9 H2 **Aylsham** England
121 O7 **Aylwin** Quebec Canada
17 F6 **Ayna** Spain
79 H4 **'Ayn al Bayḑā'** Syria
78 J3 **Ayn Diwār** Syria
9 E3 **Aynho** England
112 H4 **Aynor** South Carolina U.S.A.
80 G1 **Ayn Ziwān** Syria
84 G5 **'Ayn Zuwayyah** *well* Libya
147 Q4 **Ayon,Ostrov** *isld* U.S.S.R.
17 G5 **Ayora** Spain
85 E6 **Ayorou** Niger
55 G2 **Aypolovo** U.S.S.R.
Ayr *co see* **Strathclyde** *reg*
141 H4 **Ayr** Queensland Australia
12 D3 **Ayr** Scotland
98 H9 **Ayr** Nebraska U.S.A.
98 J2 **Ayr** North Dakota U.S.A.
21 L8 **Ayron** France
99 M6 **Ayrshire** Iowa U.S.A.
141 G5 **Ayrshire Downs** Queensland Australia
55 F4 **Aysarinskoye** U.S.S.R.

13 G5 Aysgarth England
86 H3 Āysha Ethiopia
57 F1 Ayshirak U.S.S.R.
57 G3 Aytau mts U.S.S.R.
13 H5 Ayton N Yorks England
13 F2 Ayton Scotland
47 J2 Aytos Bulgaria
57 C4 Aytym U.S.S.R.
61 P7 Ayukawahama Japan
65 C2 Ayulhai China
124 G7 Ayutla Mexico
68 E5 Ayutthaya Thailand
78 A2 Ayvacik Turkey
78 A2 Ayvalik Turkey
47 H5 Ayvalık Turkey
22 K3 Aywaille Belgium
80 E1 Ayyelet Ha Shahar Israel
100 B7 Azalea Oregon U.S.A.
61 P13 Azama Okinawa
79 G7 Azamān, Qā' depression Saudi Arabia
75 K5 Azamgarh India
55 C3 Azangulovo U.S.S.R.
55 D2 Azanka U.S.S.R.
22 J5 Azannes-et-Soumazannes France
77 A1 Āzarān Iran
78 K2 Āzārbāyjān-e Gharbī Iran
78 L2 Āzarbāyjān-e Sharqī Iran
85 G6 Azare Nigeria
52 E5 Azatskoye, Oz L U.S.S.R.
21 N8 Azay-le-Ferron France
21 L7 Azay-le-Rideau France
21 M7 Azay-sur-Cher France
21 K8 Azay-sur-Thouet France
79 H2 A'zāz Syria
Azbine reg Niger see Aïr ou Azbine
21 N6 Azé Loire France
40 G7 Azeglio Italy
Azerbaijan see Azerbaydzhanskaya S.S.R.
78 L1 Azerbaydzhanskaya S.S.R. U.S.S.R.
19 N13 Azergues R France
53 F7 Azeyevo U.S.S.R.
55 G4 Azhbulat, Oz L U.S.S.R.
56 C5 Azho-Tayga, Gora mt U.S.S.R.
85 C2 Azilal Morocco
22 C3 Azincourt France
86 A6 Azingo, L Gabon
95 R1 Aziscoos L Maine U.S.A.
84 E3 'Azīzīyan, Al Libya
16 C7 Aznàlcóllar Spain
128 C4 Azogues Ecuador
52 G2 Azopol'ye U.S.S.R.
Azores islds see Açores
90 G5 Azores-Cape St Vincent Ridge Atlantic Oc
86 D3 Azoum R Chad
54 L9 Azov U.S.S.R.
Azov,Sea of see Azovskoye More
54 L9 Azovskiy Kanal U.S.S.R.
53 E10 Azovskoye More U.S.S.R.
17 F1 Azpeitia Spain
85 C2 Azrou Morocco
103 L9 Aztec Arizona U.S.A.
106 C5 Aztec New Mexico U.S.A.
106 B5 Aztec Ruins Nat.Mon New Mexico U.S.A.
127 J5 Azua Dominican Rep
16 D6 Azuaga Spain
17 G3 Azuara Spain
128 C4 Azuay prov Ecuador
60 C12 Azuch-Ō-shima isld Japan
17 F6 Azuer R Spain
125 O6 Azuero,Pen.de Panama
131 B3 Azufre, P. del Chile
48 K5 Azuga Romania
133 F5 Azul Argentina
131 B5 Azul pk Chile
125 P9 Azul R Mexico
131 B8 Azul, Cerro pk Neuquén Argentina
130 E7 Azul Paulista, Mte Brazil
130 C4 Azul,Serra mts Mato Grosso Brazil
61 O8 Azuma-yama mt Japan
80 B8 Azza Israel
79 G5 Az Zabadānī Syria
84 F4 Az Zahrah Libya

B

71 L10 Baa Indonesia
41 M3 Baad Austria
70 E4 Baai R Kalimantan
25 F6 Baal W Germany
79 G4 Baalbek Lebanon
86 H5 Baardheere Somalia
25 C6 Baarle-Hertog Belgium
25 C6 Baarle Nassau Netherlands
25 D4 Baarn Netherlands
60 D14 Baba Japan
46 E4 Baba mt Yugoslavia
47 H5 Baba Burun C Turkey
48 M6 Babadag Romania
47 J3 Babaeski Turkey
128 C4 Babahoyo Ecuador
71 G7 Babak Philippines
143 C9 Babakin Western Australia Australia
77 K2 Bābā, Koh-i- mts Afghanistan
79 H2 Bāb, Al Syria
72 E6 Bab al Mandab str Arabia/Djibouti
79 G3 Bābannā Syria
67 B5 Babao China
71 O8 Babar isld Indonesia
71 O9 Babar,Kep islds Indonesia
70 O9 Babat Java
57 E5 Babatag, Khr mts U.S.S.R.
88 E4 Babati Tanzania
71 L10 Babau Timor Indonesia
80 G7 Babayir et Tiwal Jordan
101 M1 Babb Montana U.S.A.
116 S2 Babbage R Yukon Territory Canada
143 A6 Babbage I Western Australia Australia
99 P2 Babbitt Minnesota U.S.A.
99 Q5 Babcock Wisconsin U.S.A.
33 P5 Bäbelin East Germany
88 C5 Babemba tribe Zaire
88 C7 Babemba tribe Zambia
36 F4 Babenhausen Hessen W Germany
31 M6 Babia Góra mts Czech/Poland
124 E3 Babícora Mexico
124 F3 Babícora, L. de Mexico
141 H3 Babinda Queensland Australia
117 L8 Babine L British Columbia Canada
117 K8 Babine Ra British Columbia Canada
69 C11 Babi, Pulau isld Indonesia
136 G2 Babo W Irian
48 D4 Babócsa Hungary
77 C1 Bābol Iran
103 N10 Baboquivari Pk Arizona U.S.A.
142 E4 Babrongan Tower mt Western Australia Australia
113 F10 Babson Park Florida U.S.A.
36 G5 Babstadt W Germany
16 D9 Bab Taza Morocco
67 B3 Babu China
46 E3 Babuna mt Yugoslavia
56 G5 Babushkin U.S.S.R.
71 E1 Babuyan islds Philippines
71 D6 Babuyan Philippines
71 E1 Babuyan Ch Philippines
124 E4 Baca Mexico
86 A2 Bacaadweyn Somalia
124 E4 Bacabáche Mexico
129 G5 Bacabal Brazil
129 H4 Bacaja R Brazil
71 A3 Bacan isld Indonesia
124 E3 Bacanora Mexico
71 E1 Bacarra Philippines
48 K4 Bacău Romania
68 G1 Bac Can Vietnam
19 K4 Baccarat France
122 G10 Baccaro Pt Nova Scotia Canada
45 L1 Bacchiglione R Italy
41 H5 Baceno Italy
48 L4 Băceşti Romania
68 H2 Bac Giang Vietnam
94 D3 Bach Michigan U.S.A.
37 N5 Bach W Germany
127 J10 Bachaquero Venezuela
36 D3 Bacharach W Germany
115 M2 Bache Pen Northwest Territories Canada
124 F3 Bachiniva Mexico
68 J2 Bach Long Vi isld Vietnam
69 E9 Bacho Thailand
37 L1 Bachra East Germany
57 J5 Bachu China
115 K4 Back R Northwest Territories Canada
48 E5 Backa reg Yugoslavia
27 G14 Bäckaby Sweden
48 E5 Bačka Palanka Yugoslavia
48 F5 Bačka Topola Yugoslavia
95 L10 Back Bay Virginia U.S.A.
117 J4 Backbone Ranges Northwest Territories Canada
26 H8 Backe Sweden
27 F13 Bäckefors Sweden
27 G12 Bäckhammar Sweden
36 G6 Backnang W Germany
119 U10 Backoo North Dakota U.S.A.
48 F5 Bačko Petrovo Selo Yugoslavia
138 E6 Backstaiys Pass South Australia Australia
26 H6 Bäckstrand Sweden
99 M3 Backus Minnesota U.S.A.
8 D5 Backwell England
Bac Lieu see Vinh Loi
71 E2 Bacnotan Luzon Philippines
127 P5 Bacolet Grenada
45 Q8 Bacoli Italy
71 F5 Bacolod Philippines
71 E4 Baco, Mt Philippines
112 C6 Baconton Georgia U.S.A.
21 N2 Bacqueville-en-Caux France
48 E4 Bácsalmás Hungary
48 E4 Bács-Kiskun co Hungary
9 H2 Bacton England
124 F5 Bacubirito Mexico
71 G7 Baculin Bay Mindanao Philippines
13 F6 Bacup England
129 J4 Bacuri,I de Brazil
98 F5 Bad R South Dakota U.S.A.
Bada see Xilin
75 L7 Bada Barabil India
37 N6 Bad Abbach W Germany
76 B5 Badagara India
38 E6 Bad Aibling W Germany
129 J4 Badajós Brazil
16 C6 Badajoz prov Spain
16 C6 Badajoz Spain
128 F4 Badajoz, L Brazil
77 L1 Badakhshān prov Afghanistan
17 J3 Badalona Spain
76 B3 Badami India
75 M7 Bādāmpāhārh India
56 E3 Badan, Khrebet mts U.S.S.R.
65 H3 Badaohe China
Badaojiang see Hunjiang
124 F5 Badariguato Mexico
74 H3 Badarīnaāth India
70 D2 Badas Brunei
69 H12 Badas,Kep isld Indonesia
38 J6 Bad Aussee Austria
94 E3 Bad Axe Michigan U.S.A.
32 G7 Badbergen W Germany
36 D5 Bad Bergzabern W Germany
37 L2 Bad Berka East Germany
36 E1 Bad Berleburg W Germany
37 M3 Bad Berneck W Germany
36 B3 Bad Bertrich W Germany
37 M1 Bad Bibra Halle East Germany
37 L2 Bad Blankenburg East Germany
37 J3 Bad Bocklet W Germany
32 L5 Bad Bramstedt W Germany
123 M7 Baddeck C Breton I, Nova Scotia
32 M8 Baddeckenstedt W Germany
26 M2 Badderen Norway
33 P4 Bad Doberan East Germany
32 K9 Bad Driburg W Germany
33 R9 Bad Düben East Germany
36 E5 Bad Dürkheim W Germany
33 Q10 Bad Dürrenberg East Germany
37 N3 Bad Elster East Germany
36 D3 Bad Ems W Germany
48 C2 Baden Austria
119 Q6 Baden Manitoba Canada
20 E6 Baden France
41 H3 Baden Switzerland
94 G6 Baden Pennsylvania U.S.A.
36 E6 Baden-Baden W Germany
15 D4 Badenoch Scotland
19 K4 Badenviller France
36 G6 Baden-Württemberg W Germany
45 P1 Baderna Yugoslavia
33 U7 Bad Freienwalde East Germany
36 G5 Bad Friedrichshall W Germany
32 M9 Bad Gandersheim W Germany
118 F1 Badger Manitoba Canada
123 Q5 Badger Newfoundland Canada
102 E5 Badger California U.S.A.
98 K1 Badger Minnesota U.S.A.
101 Q5 Badger Basin Wyoming U.S.A.
77 H2 Bādghīs Afghanistan
38 N8 Bad Gleichenberg Austria
36 C2 Bad Godesberg W Germany
30 H5 Bad Gottleuba East Germany
32 M9 Bad Grund W Germany
38 K5 Bad Hall Austria
33 N9 Bad Harzburg W Germany
36 E6 Bad Herrenalb W Germany
36 H2 Bad Hersfeld W Germany
38 H7 Bad Hofgastein Austria
36 F3 Bad Homburg W Germany
36 C2 Bad Honnef W Germany
45 K1 Badia Polesine Italy
45 M4 Badia Tedalda Italy
32 H8 Bad Iburg W Germany
79 H6 Badiet esh Sham desert Jordan/Syria
74 C6 Badin Pakistan
112 G2 Badin North Carolina U.S.A.
112 G2 Badin L North Carolina U.S.A.
38 J6 Bad Ischi Austria
37 J3 Bad Kissingen W Germany
33 O5 Bad Kleinen East Germany
37 M2 Bad Klosterlausnitz East Germany
37 M1 Bad Kösen East Germany
36 D4 Bad Kreuznach W Germany
98 C2 Bad Lands reg North Dakota U.S.A.
98 E6 Badlands Nat.Park South Dakota U.S.A.
37 K1 Bad Langensalza East Germany
33 P10 Bad Lauchstädt East Germany
37 O1 Bad Lausik East Germany
33 M9 Bad Lauterberg W Germany
38 K8 Bad Leonhard Austria
37 K2 Bad Liebenstein East Germany
36 F6 Bad Liebenzell W Germany
32 J9 Bad Lippspringe W Germany
32 J9 Bad Meinberg W Germany
36 H5 Bad Mergentheim W Germany
32 K8 Bad Münder am Deister W Germany
36 D4 Bad Münster W Germany
36 B2 Bad Münstereifel W Germany
36 F3 Bad Nauheim W Germany
32 K8 Bad Nenndorf W Germany
36 C2 Bad Neuenahr W Germany
36 C2 Bad Neuenahr-Ahrweiler W Germany
37 J3 Bad Neustadt W Germany
32 J8 Bad Oeynhausen W Germany
33 M5 Bad Oldersloe W Germany
68 H4 Ba Don Vietnam
67 C1 Badong China
69 H8 Ba Dong Vietnam
36 B6 Badonviller France
36 G3 Bad Orb W Germany
65 D6 Badou China
36 E7 Bad Peterstal W Germany
32 K9 Bad Pyrmont W Germany
36 G5 Bad Rappenau W Germany
38 G6 Bad Reichenhall W Germany
36 E7 Bad Rippoldsau W Germany
32 M8 Bad Salzdetfurth W Germany
33 P8 Bad Salzelmen East Germany
36 H2 Bad Salzschlirf W Germany
32 J8 Bad Salzuflen W Germany
37 J2 Bad Salzungen East Germany
32 H9 Bad Sassendorf W Germany
33 R9 Bad Schmiedeberg East Germany
36 F5 Bad Schönborn W Germany
36 E3 Bad Schwalbach W Germany
33 N5 Bad Schwartau W Germany
33 M5 Bad Segeberg W Germany
36 E3 Bad Soden W Germany
32 L10 Bad Sooden W Germany
37 M3 Bad Steben W Germany
33 Q6 Bad Stuer East Germany
33 O9 Bad Suderode East Germany
37 M1 Bad Sulza East Germany
33 R4 Bad Sülze East Germany
36 F6 Bad Teinach-Zavelstein W Germany
37 K1 Bad Tennstedt East Germany
41 P2 Bad Tölz W Germany
141 F1 Badu I Queensland Australia
83 L10 Badulla Sri Lanka
36 F3 Bad Vilbel W Germany
38 O6 Bad Voslau Austria
102 H5 Badwater L California U.S.A.
36 G1 Bad Wildungen W Germany
33 P7 Bad Wilsnack East Germany
36 G5 Bad Wimpfen W Germany
37 J5 Bad Windsheim W Germany
59 K1 Badzhal'skiy Khrebet mt U.S.S.R.
26 O2 Baeivašgiedde Norway
28 C5 Bække Denmark
28 A4 Bækmarksbro Denmark
28 E3 Bælum Denmark
16 E7 Baena Spain
36 D6 Baerenthal France
128 C4 Baeza Ecuador
16 E7 Baeza Spain
47 J7 Bafa Gölü L Turkey
86 B4 Bafang Cameroon
85 B6 Bafata Guinea-Bissau
115 K3 Baffin dist Northwest Territories Canada
109 K8 Baffin B Texas U.S.A.
147 E6 Baffin Basin Arctic Oc
115 N3 Baffin Bay Greenland/Canada
90 E2 Baffin-Greenland Rise Atlantic Oc
115 M3 Baffin I Northwest Territories Canada
141 K6 Baffle Creek Queensland Australia
86 B5 Bafia Cameroon
85 B6 Bafing R Guinea/Mali
79 H2 Bafliyun Syria
85 B6 Bafoulabé Mali
86 B4 Bafoussam Cameroon
77 D4 Bāfq Iran
78 E1 Bafra Turkey
86 E5 Bafwasende Zaire
58 D3 Baga Bogd Uul mt Mongolia
71 E3 Bagac Bay Luzon Philippines
76 B2 Bagalkot India
88 G5 Bagamoyo Tanzania
69 E11 Bagan Datuk Malaysia
71 G7 Baganga Mindanao Philippines
71 F7 Baganian Peninsula Mindanao Philippines
69 E10 Bagan Serai Malaysia
69 E11 Bagansiapiapi Sumatra
142 A3 Baganup L Western Australia Australia
44 H2 Baganza R Italy
55 D3 Bagaryak U.S.S.R.
32 G6 Bagband W Germany
109 K10 Bagdad Mexico
103 L7 Bagdad Arizona U.S.A.
103 J7 Bagdad California U.S.A.
110 L3 Bagdad Kentucky U.S.A.
58 F1 Bagdarin U.S.S.R.
131 G3 Bagé Brazil
28 F7 Bagenkop Denmark
101 S8 Baggs Wyoming U.S.A.
78 K5 Baghdād Iraq
77 A4 Bāgh-e Malek Iran
75 N7 Bagherhat Bangladesh
43 F10 Bagheria Sicily
77 E4 Baghīn Iran
77 L1 Baghlān Afghanistan
77 J3 Baghran Afghanistan
Baghrash Köl L see Bosten Hu L
14 E4 Baginbun Hd Ireland
69 H14 Baginda, Tanjong C Indonesia
99 L2 Bagley Minnesota U.S.A.
99 P7 Bagley Wisconsin U.S.A.
116 Q6 Bagley Icefield Alaska U.S.A.
45 L3 Bagnacavallo Italy
43 G10 Bagnara Cálabra Italy
110 D3 Bagnell Dam Missouri U.S.A.
18 F9 Bagnères de Bigorre France
18 F10 Bagnères de Luchon France
40 F6 Bagnes,Val De Switzerland
21 K7 Bagneux Maine-et-Loire France
45 J3 Bagni di Lucca Italy
41 L5 Bagni di Masino Italy
44 B3 Bagni di Vinádio Italy
45 K4 Bagno A Ripoli Italy
45 L4 Bagno di Romagna Italy
21 K4 Bagnoles-de-l'Orne France
45 L1 Bagnoli di Sopra Italy
45 L1 Bagnolo di Po Italy
45 J2 Bagnolo in Piano Italy
44 H1 Bagnolo Mella Italy
45 J1 Bagnolo San Vito Italy
19 N16 Bagnols-sur-Cèze France
28 D6 Bågø isld Denmark
85 C6 Bagoe R Ivory Co/Mali
Bagong see Sansui
77 L2 Bagrāmī Afghanistan
31 M1 Bagrationovsk U.S.S.R.
9 F5 Bagshot England
65 E3 Bag Tal China
128 C5 Bagua Peru
85 F5 Baguezane, Mt Niger
71 N9 Baguia Timor Indonesia
71 E2 Baguio Luzon Philippines
71 G7 Baguio Mindanao Philippines
71 F2 Baguio Pt Luzon Philippines
86 C3 Baguirmi dist Chad
126 E2 Bahama Bank,Great Bahamas
126 F1 Bahama Bank, Little Bahamas
126 F2 Bahamas, The W Indies
127 M4 Baham, Pte Martinique W Indies
75 N6 Baharampur India
84 H4 Baharîya Oasis Egypt
69 E14 Bahatmonga Indonesia
70 D3 Bahau R Sarawak
70 D6 Bahaur Kalimantan
74 E4 Bahawalnagar Pakistan
74 D4 Bahawalpur Pakistan
79 F2 Bahçe Turkey
88 E4 Bahi Tanzania
129 K6 Bahia state Brazil
131 E7 Bahia Blanca Argentina
125 L1 Bahia, Islas de la Honduras
124 C3 Bahia Kino Mexico
133 D7 Bahia Laura Argentina
133 C6 Bahia Pargua Chile
124 B4 Bahia Tortugas Mexico
86 G3 Bahir Dar Ethiopia
48 L3 Bahluiul R Romania
48 J4 Bahnea Romania
88 B5 Baholoholo tribe Zaire
70 G6 Bahombelu Sulawesi Indonesia
70 G6 Bahomonte Sulawesi
69 H8 Ba,Hon isld Vietnam
79 A7 Bahra el Burullus lagoon Egypt
79 B7 Bahra el Manzala lagoon Egypt
75 J5 Bahraich India
77 B6 Bahrain sheikhdom Persian Gulf
86 D3 Bahr Aouk R Chad
86 C4 Bahr Aoukale R Cent Afr Republic
86 F3 Bahr el Abiad R Sudan
86 E4 Bahr el Arab watercourse Sudan
86 F3 Bahr el Azraq R Sudan
86 E4 Bahr el Ghazal R Sudan
86 E4 Bahr el Ghazal prov Sudan
86 F4 Bahr ez Zeraf R Sudan
79 H5 Bahr Şaygal Sab 'Ābār L Syria
71 H6 Bahubulu isld Sulawesi Indonesia
77 G7 Bāhu Kālat Iran
129 J4 Baiā Brazil
48 H6 Baia de Aramă Romania
48 H4 Baia de Cris Romania
16 B6 Baia de Setúbal Portugal
87 B9 Baia doz Tigres Angola
128 F7 Baia Grande,L Brazil
48 H3 Baia Mare Romania
45 R8 Baiano Italy
48 H3 Baia Sprie Romania
77 D3 Baiazeh Iran
86 C4 Baïbokoum Chad
65 H3 Baicaogou China
57 K4 Baicheng China
65 F2 Baicheng China
48 K5 Băicoi Romania
121 N5 Baie Carrière Quebec Canada
122 D4 Baie-Comeau Quebec Canada
126 H5 Baie de Henne Haiti
122 E5 Baie de Sables Quebec Canada
123 P2 Baie-du-Milieu Quebec Canada
115 M7 Baie-du-Poste Quebec Canada
122 G6 Baie du Vin New Brunswick Canada
68 F7 Baie,I.de la Cambodia
122 K3 Baie Johan Beetz Quebec Canada
127 N4 Baie Mahault Guadeloupe W Indies
36 E7 Baiersbronn W Germany
122 C5 Baie Ste.Catherine Quebec Canada
122 H4 Baie Ste.Clair Quebec Canada
122 B6 Baie St.Paul Quebec Canada
122 E4 Baie Trinité Quebec Canada
122 J7 Baie Verte New Brunswick Canada
123 Q4 Baie Verte Newfoundland Canada
67 D3 Baifang China
Baiguan see Shangyu
74 J7 Baihar India
58 F5 Baihe China
65 B6 Baijiazhuang China
Baikal L see Baykal,Ozero L
75 K7 Baikunthpur India
Bailādila see Kirandul
65 E1 Bailang China
Baile Átha see Dublin
48 J6 Băile Govora Romania
48 G6 Băile Herculane Romania
16 E6 Bailén Spain
48 J5 Băile Olăneşti Romania
48 H6 Băileşti Romania
48 K4 Băile Tuşnad Romania
22 G3 Baileux Belgium
106 E2 Bailey Colorado U.S.A.
112 J2 Bailey North Carolina U.S.A.
143 D8 Bailey Ra Western Australia Australia
111 K7 Baileyton Alabama U.S.A.
95 U1 Baileyville Maine U.S.A.
14 D3 Bailieborough Ireland
67 D3 Bailin China
129 H3 Bailique, I Brazil
21 N5 Bailleau-le-Pin France
22 D2 Bailleul France
21 K4 Bailleul Orne France
22 D3 Bailleul-Sire-Berthoult France
115 K2 Baillie Hamilton I Northwest Territories Canada
114 G3 Baillie Is Northwest Territories Canada
127 M4 Baillif Guadeloupe W Indies
77 K3 Bailugh Afghanistan
87 C8 Bailundo Angola
111 M11 Bainbridge Georgia U.S.A.
95 M4 Bainbridge New York U.S.A.
94 D7 Bainbridge Ohio U.S.A.
20 G6 Bain-de-Bretagne France
140 B3 Baines, Mt N Terr Australia
127 H5 Bainet Haiti
Baini see Yuqing
19 K4 Bains-les-Bains France
13 H6 Bainton England
98 B1 Bainville Montana U.S.A.
59 J2 Baiquan China
66 C4 Bairab Co L China
109 H3 Baird Texas U.S.A.
116 E6 Baird Inlet Alaska U.S.A.
116 G3 Baird Mts Alaska U.S.A.
65 D3 Bairin Youqi China
58 G3 Bairin Zuoqi China
139 J7 Bairnsdale Victoria Australia
101 S7 Bairoil Wyoming U.S.A.
79 H7 Bā'ir, Wādī watercourse Jordan
20 H6 Bais Ille-et-Vilaine France
21 K5 Bais Mayenne France
18 F8 Baïse R France
Baisha see Jiande
65 B7 Baisha China
67 B2 Baisha China
67 C7 Baisha China
65 B7 Baisha Shuiku res China
67 E3 Baishi Feng mt China
65 A7 Baishui China
58 D5 Baishui Jiang R China
22 E2 Baisieux France
45 J3 Baiso Italy
52 B6 Baisogala U.S.S.R.
74 J4 Baitadi Nepal
68 G3 Bai Thoung Vietnam
19 N15 Baix France
65 C6 Baixiang China
65 A3 Baixingt China
65 E3 Baixingt China
16 B6 Baixo Alentejo prov Portugal
130 H6 Baixo Guandu Brazil
87 C9 Baixo Longa Angola
65 C5 Baiyang Dian L China
67 C1 Baiyangping China
Baiyashi see Dong'an
58 D4 Baiyin China
86 F2 Baiyuda Sudan
67 E3 Baiyun Shan mt China
58 E4 Baiyu Shan mts China
67 B1 Baizi China
48 E4 Baja Hungary
124 B3 Baja California state Mexico
70 Q10 Bajan Indonesia
124 J4 Baján Mexico
124 B3 Baja, Pta C Mexico
69 H11 Bajau isld Indonesia
71 K9 Bajawa Flores Indonesia
48 F7 Bajina Bašta Yugoslavia
48 E5 Bajmok Yugoslavia
128 C2 Bajo Baudo Colombia
70 N9 Bajonegoro Java
126 E7 Bajo Nuevo Caribbean
141 K6 Bajool Queensland Australia
28 C7 Bajstrup Denmark
48 D4 Bak Hungary
70 E3 Bakajan, G mt Kalimantan
55 C4 Bakal U.S.S.R.
86 D4 Bakala Cent Afr Republic
57 H3 Bakanas U.S.S.R.
57 J2 Bakanas R U.S.S.R.
70 E6 Bakaucengal Kalimantan
56 B3 Bakchar R U.S.S.R.
85 B6 Bakel Senegal
133 C7 Baker R Chile
103 H6 Baker California U.S.A.
101 M4 Baker Idaho U.S.A.
98 B3 Baker Montana U.S.A.
103 K2 Baker Nevada U.S.A.
98 G1 Baker North Dakota U.S.A.
100 H5 Baker Oregon U.S.A.
94 J7 Baker West Virginia U.S.A.
103 N7 Baker Butte mt Arizona U.S.A.
137 R1 Baker I Pacific Oc
117 G8 Baker I Alaska U.S.A.
95 R7 Baker L Maine U.S.A.
143 F7 Baker Lake Western Australia Australia
115 K5 Baker Lake Northwest Territories Canada
100 D1 Baker,Mt Washington U.S.A.
125 P9 Bakers Belize
102 F6 Bakersfield California U.S.A.
112 E1 Bakersfield North Carolina U.S.A.
108 E5 Bakersfield Texas U.S.A.
95 P2 Bakersfield Vermont U.S.A.
9 E1 Bakewell England
77 G2 Bakharz reg Iran
53 D11 Bakhchisaray U.S.S.R.
54 D5 Bakhmach U.S.S.R.
78 L4 Bakhtārān Iran
77 B4 Bakhtiyāri Iran
47 J5 Bakır R Turkey
47 M11 Bakırköy Turkey
29 T9 Bakkagerdhi Iceland
25 F2 Bakkeveen Netherlands
47 K7 Baklan Turkey
86 G4 Bako Ethiopia
85 C7 Bako Ivory Coast
69 C11 Bakongan Sumatra
48 D4 Bakony mts Hungary
86 D4 Bakouma Cent Afr Republic
85 C6 Bakoye R Guinea/Mali
54 L1 Baksheyevo U.S.S.R.
26 K6 Baktsjaure Sweden
78 M1 Baku U.S.S.R.
71 G6 Bakulin Pt Mindanao Philippines
32 H7 Bakum W Germany
69 G12 Bakung isld Indonesia
121 L7 Bala Ontario Canada
80 D4 Bal'a Jordan
78 D2 Bâlâ Turkey
8 C2 Bala Wales
71 C7 Balabac Str Borneo/Philippines
70 E6 Balabalangan, Kep islds Indonesia
71 H8 Balabalangan Pulau Pulau islds Indonesia
54 H1 Balabanovo U.S.S.R.
71 C7 Balabec isld Palawan Philippines
54 G9 Balabino U.S.S.R.
128 E6 Bala,Cerros de mts Bolivia
48 H6 Bălăciţa Romania
127 J2 Balaclava Jamaica
77 B1 Baladeh Iran
80 F3 Balad el Basha Jordan
80 F3 Balad el Mansura Jordan
56 F4 Balagansk U.S.S.R.
74 J8 Balaghat India
17 H3 Balaguer Spain
70 B5 Balaiberkuak Kalimantan
70 B4 Balaikarangan Kalimantan
68 A2 Balaing Burma
69 D12 Balaipungut Sumatra
70 B6 Balairiam Kalimantan
70 B4 Balaisepuac Kalimantan
70 K8 Balak, Gunung Sumatra
138 E5 Balaklava South Australia Australia
54 H7 Balakleya U.S.S.R.
8 C2 Bala L Wales
87 G8 Balama Mozambique
70 E1 Balambangan isld Indonesia
77 H2 Balā Morghāb Afghanistan
40 B6 Balan France
48 K4 Bălan Romania
125 O9 Balancán Mexico
71 E3 Balanga Luzon Philippines
75 K8 Balāngīr India
71 H5 Balantak Sulawesi
70 M9 Balapulang Java
71 F5 Balaring Negros Philippines
70 G6 Balase R Sulawesi
48 E2 Balassagyarmat Hungary
84 H4 Balât Egypt
48 D4 Balaton L Hungary
99 L5 Balaton Minnesota U.S.A.
48 D4 Balatonfüred Hungary
48 D4 Balatonszentgyörgy Hungary
71 L9 Balauring Flores Indonesia
124 F10 Balboa Panama
14 E3 Balbriggan Ireland
141 H8 Balbuna Queensland Australia
13 G6 Balby England
86 J5 Balcad Somalia
144 D5 Balcairn New Zealand
138 E4 Balcanoona South Australia Australia
131 F6 Balcarce Argentina
119 O8 Balcarres Saskatchewan Canada
48 H6 Bălceşti Romania
47 J1 Balchik Bulgaria
109 O9 Balch Springs Texas U.S.A.
144 B7 Balclutha New Zealand
9 F5 Balcombe England
100 F6 Bald Butte mt Oregon U.S.A.
94 K6 Bald Eagle Mt Pennsylvania U.S.A.
41 H3 Baldegg See L Switzerland
6 M3 Balder oil rig North Sea
143 C11 Bald Hd Western Australia Australia
44 D2 Baldichieri d'Asti Italy
110 E6 Bald Knob Arkansas U.S.A.
94 F9 Bald Knob West Virginia U.S.A.
101 L5 Bald Mt Idaho U.S.A.
103 J4 Bald Mt Nevada U.S.A.
9 F4 Baldock England
119 T2 Baldock L Manitoba Canada
42 D3 Baldo,Monte Italy
113 F7 Baldwin Florida U.S.A.
110 A3 Baldwin Kansas U.S.A.
94 B3 Baldwin Michigan U.S.A.
98 F2 Baldwin North Dakota U.S.A.
99 O5 Baldwin Wisconsin U.S.A.
102 H7 Baldwin L California U.S.A.
116 F3 Baldwin Pen Alaska U.S.A.
118 H6 Baldwinton Saskatchewan Canada
95 P4 Baldwinville Massachusetts U.S.A.
95 R3 Baldwin, W Maine U.S.A.
111 H7 Baldwyn Mississippi U.S.A.
119 R7 Baldy Mt Manitoba Canada
103 P8 Baldy Pk Arizona U.S.A.
106 E6 Baldy Pk New Mexico U.S.A.
57 E5 Bal'dzhuvon U.S.S.R.
86 H4 Balē prov Ethiopia
69 E14 Bale Indonesia
17 J5 Baleares, Islas arch Spain
Balearic Is see Baleares, Islas arch
70 C4 Baleh R Sarawak
130 H5 Baleia, Pta da C Brazil
115 N6 Baleine,à la R Quebec Canada
83 L14 Baleiniers, Golfe des Kerguelen Indian Oc
71 C7 Balembangan isld Sabah
22 J1 Balen Belgium
48 K6 Băleni Romania
71 E3 Baler Luzon Philippines
71 E3 Baler Bay Luzon Philippines
15 E5 Balerno Scotland
75 M8 Bāleshwar India
58 G1 Baley U.S.S.R.
141 H5 Balfe's Creek Queensland Australia
48 D4 Bal Földvár Hungary
26 K7 Bålforsen Sweden
117 P11 Balfour British Columbia Canada
144 B6 Balfour New Zealand
98 F2 Balfour North Dakota U.S.A.
142 D6 Balfour Downs Western Australia Australia
12 D1 Balfron Scotland
77 F1 Bālgirān Iran
142 G5 Balgo Hill Western Australia Australia
119 N8 Balgonie Saskatchewan Canada
32 K10 Balhorn W Germany
86 B4 Bali Cameroon
70 P10 Bali isld Indonesia
71 F6 Baliangao Mindanao Philippines
69 D11 Balige Sumatra
31 N6 Baligród Poland
65 D4 Balihan China
47 J5 Balıkesir Turkey
78 G4 Balīkh R Syria
86 C3 Bal Illi R Chad
70 G2 Balimbing Tawitaw isld Philippines
69 E10 Baling Malaysia
70 C3 Balingian R Sarawak
70 C3 Balingian Sarawak
65 D3 Balinqiao China
48 G5 Balint Romania
70 P9 Bali Sea Indonesia
70 P10 Bali,Selat Bali/Java
70 G2 Baliungan Tawitawi Philippines
130 D5 Baliza Brazil
32 K5 Balje W Germany
118 K6 Baljennie Saskatchewan Canada
25 E3 Balk Netherlands
48 G3 Balkány Hungary
55 C4 Balkany U.S.S.R.
55 E4 Balkashino U.S.S.R.
25 F3 Balkbrug Netherlands
77 K1 Balkh prov Afghanistan
77 K1 Balkhab R Afghanistan
57 G2 Balkhash U.S.S.R.
57 G2 Balkhash, Ozero L U.S.S.R.
74 H9 Balkonda India
15 C4 Ballachulish Scotland
143 E9 Balladonia Western Australia Australia
14 C3 Ballaghaderreen Ireland
21 P4 Ballancourt-sur-Essonne France
141 K8 Ballandean Queensland Australia
26 J3 Ballangen Norway
101 R4 Ballantine Montana U.S.A.
15 C5 Ballantrae Scotland
119 O4 Ballantyne Bay Saskatchewan Canada
114 H2 Ballantyne Str Northwest Territories Canada
43 C9 Ballao Sardinia
139 G6 Ballarat Victoria Australia
102 G5 Ballarat California U.S.A.
143 D8 Ballard, L Western Australia Australia
80 F4 Ballas Jordan
15 E3 Ballater Scotland
12 D5 Ballaugh I of Man U.K.
28 F4 Balle Denmark
21 K6 Ballée France
28 F5 Ballen Denmark
133 C3 Ballena,Pta C Chile
33 O9 Ballenstedt East Germany
146 C13 Balleny Islands Antarctica
21 J3 Balleroy France
29 K5 Ballerup Denmark
112 C3 Ball Ground Georgia U.S.A.
75 L6 Ballia India
14 B2 Ballina Ireland
14 C3 Ballinasloe Ireland
14 C3 Ballindine Ireland
28 B3 Balling Denmark
14 C4 Ballingarry Ireland
108 H4 Ballinger Texas U.S.A.
15 E4 Ballinluig Scotland
14 B3 Ballinrobe Ireland
14 A5 Ballinskelligs B Ireland
37 J6 Ballmertshofen W Germany
118 B7 Ball,Mt Alberta Canada
12 D1 Balloch Scotland
21 L5 Ballon France
19 K5 Ballon d'Alsace mt France
21 H6 Ballots France
46 D4 Ballsh Albania
137 M8 Ball's Pyramid isld Pacific Oc
37 K1 Ballstädt East Germany
95 O4 Ballston Spa New York U.S.A.
28 B6 Ballum Denmark
14 E2 Ballybay Ireland
14 D2 Ballybofey Ireland
14 B4 Ballybunnion Ireland
14 B2 Ballycastle Ireland
14 E1 Ballycastle N Ireland
14 E2 Ballyclare N Ireland
14 D2 Ballyconnell Ireland
14 D5 Ballycotton B Ireland
14 C4 Ballyduff Ireland
14 C3 Ballygar Ireland
14 D2 Ballygawley N Ireland
12 B2 Ballygrant Scotland
14 D2 Ballyhaise Ireland
14 C3 Ballyhaunis Ireland
14 C4 Ballyhoura Hills Ireland
14 D3 Ballyjamesduff Ireland
14 D3 Ballymahon Ireland
14 E2 Ballymena N Ireland
14 E1 Ballymoney N Ireland
14 C2 Ballymote Ireland
14 F2 Ballynahinch N Ireland
14 F2 Ballyquintin Pt N Ireland
14 D4 Ballyragget Ireland
14 C2 Ballyshannon Ireland
14 E3 Ballytore Ireland
14 B3 Ballyvaghan Ireland
12 D3 Balmaclellan Scotland
12 D1 Balmaha Scotland
95 M2 Balmat New York U.S.A.
48 G3 Balmazújváros Hungary
40 F7 Balme Italy
40 G5 Balmhorn mt Switzerland
141 K1 Balmoral dist Brisbane, Qnsld Australia
138 F6 Balmoral Victoria Australia
119 U8 Balmoral Manitoba Canada
144 D5 Balmoral New Zealand
6 L4 Balmoral oil rig North Sea
15 E3 Balmoral Castle Scotland
108 D5 Balmorhea Texas U.S.A.
13 F1 Balmullo Scotland
87 B8 Balombo Angola
141 J7 Balonne R Queensland Australia
141 J8 Balonne R Queensland Australia
55 D2 Balotovskoye U.S.S.R.
74 E6 Balotra India
33 P6 Balow East Germany
12 D1 Balquhidder Scotland
75 K5 Balrampur India
48 J6 Balş Romania
99 O4 Balsam L Wisconsin U.S.A.
121 M8 Balsam Lake Ontario Canada
129 J5 Balsas Brazil
124 H8 Balsas R Mexico
26 K2 Balsfjord inlet Norway
26 K2 Balsfjord Norway
45 P6 Balsorano Italy
27 J12 Bålsta Sweden
26 G3 Balstad Norway
98 F1 Balta North Dakota U.S.A.
48 M3 Balta U.S.S.R.
16 E3 Baltanás Spain
16 B3 Baltar Spain
133 F4 Baltasar Brum Uruguay
98 K6 Baltic South Dakota U.S.A.
27 H16 Baltic Sea N Europe
79 B7 Balṭîm Egypt
14 B5 Baltimore Ireland
87 E10 Baltimore S Africa
97 Baltimore conurbation Maryland U.S.A.
95 L7 Baltimore Maryland U.S.A.
14 E4 Baltinglass Ireland
Baltit see Hunza
31 M1 Baltiysk U.S.S.R.
32 F5 Baltrum W Germany
80 G8 Balu R Jordan
80 G8 Balu Jordan
77 G6 Balūchestān va Sīstān Iran
74 A4 Baluchistan reg Pakistan
70 C3 Balui R Sarawak
71 E7 Balukbaluk isld Philippines
69 D12 Balumundan Sumatra
70 C5 Baluran, Gunung mt Kalimantan
75 N6 Balurghat India
71 G8 Balut isld Philippines
32 G10 Balve W Germany
52 C6 Balvi U.S.S.R.
47 J5 Balya Turkey
84 J4 Balyana,El Egypt
56 H4 Bal Yeravnoye, Oz L U.S.S.R.
56 C4 Balyksa U.S.S.R.
56 E5 Balyktyg Khem R U.S.S.R.
118 C7 Balzac Alberta Canada
77 F5 Bam Iran
67 B4 Bama China
86 B3 Bama Nigeria
141 F1 Bamaga Queensland Australia
85 C6 Bamako Mali
128 C5 Bambamarca Peru
71 E3 Bamban Luzon Philippines
71 E2 Bambang Luzon Philippines
71 E8 Bambannan isld Philippines
86 D4 Bambari Cent Afr Republic
141 H4 Bambaroo Queensland Australia
13 F6 Bamber Br England
112 F4 Bamberg South Carolina U.S.A.
37 K4 Bamberg W Germany
86 E5 Bambesa Zaire
86 E5 Bambili Zaire
86 C5 Bambio Cent Afr Republic
27 D13 Bamble Norway
142 D5 Bamboo Creek Western Australia Australia
142 C5 Bamboo Springs Western Australia Australia
83 M13 Bambou Mts Mauritius
130 F7 Bambui Brazil
70 D5 Bambulung Kalimantan
13 G2 Bamburgh England
86 B4 Bamenda Cameroon
117 L11 Bamfield British Columbia Canada
77 K2 Bāmīān Afghanistan
67 C4 Bamian China
65 F3 Bamiancheng China
Bamiantong see Muling
86 C4 Bamingui R Cent Afr Republic
86 C4 Bamingui-Bangoran Nat. Park Cent Afr Republic
68 G6 Bam Nak Cambodia
68 E5 Bamnet Narong Thailand
124 E5 Bamoa Mexico
69 A8 Bampoka I Nicobar Is
77 H6 Bam Posht, Kūh-e mts Iran
8 C6 Bampton England
9 E4 Bampton England
77 G6 Bampur R Iran
77 G6 Bampūr Iran
68 H4 Ba Na Vietnam
137 O1 Banaba isld Pacific Oc
129 L5 Banabuiu Açude res Brazil
14 D3 Banagher Ireland
71 E4 Banahao, Mt Luzon Philippines
86 E5 Banalia Zaire
68 G7 Banam Cambodia
85 C6 Banamba Mali
124 D2 Banámichi Mexico
141 K6 Banana Queensland Australia
129 H6 Bananal, Ilha do Brazil
113 G9 Banana R Florida U.S.A.
130 J9 Bananeiras Brazil
76 G7 Bananga Nicobar Is
68 F6 Ban Aranyaprathet Thailand
47 J3 Banarlı Turkey
69 D8 Ba Na San Thailand
48 F6 Banatsko Novo Selo Yugoslavia
15 C4 Banavie Scotland
71 J8 Banawaja isld Indonesia
78 B2 Banaz Turkey
68 E4 Ban Bang Mun Nak Thailand
68 E4 Ban Bang Rakam Thailand
71 G6 Banbayan Pt Mindanao Philippines
69 E10 Ban Betong Thailand
68 J6 Ban Bik Vietnam
14 E2 Banbridge N Ireland
68 E5 Ban Bua Chum Thailand
68 F5 Ban Bua Yai Thailand
68 E5 Ban Bu Khanum Thailand
68 H5 Ban Bungxai Laos
68 G5 Ban Bungxai Laos
9 E3 Banbury England
71 C6 Bancalan Palawan Philippines
138 F4 Bancannia, L New South Wales Australia
85 A4 Banc d'Arguin Nat. Park Mauritania
68 D3 Ban Chang Khoeng Thailand
68 F4 Ban Channabot Thailand
68 D3 Ban Chiang Dao Thailand
15 F3 Banchory Scotland
68 E4 Ban Chum Phae Thailand
125 Q8 Banco Chinchorro isld Mexico
71 D7 Bancoron isld Philippines
121 N7 Bancroft Ontario Canada
101 O7 Bancroft Idaho U.S.A.
99 M6 Bancroft Iowa U.S.A.
98 J5 Bancroft South Dakota U.S.A.
48 J4 Band Romania
74 J6 Banda India
69 B10 Banda Aceh Sumatra
69 C11 Bandahara, Gunung mt Sumatra
61 N7 Bandai-Asahi Nat.Pk Japan
61 O8 Bandai-san mt Japan
85 B7 Bandajuma Sierra Leone
27 C12 Bandak L Norway
85 C7 Bandama R Ivory Coast
68 G5 Ban Dan Thailand
77 G4 Bandan Kuh mt Iran
Bandar see Machilipatnam
77 J2 Bandar Afghanistan
87 F9 Bandar Mozambique

Coord	Name	Coord	Name
75 J4	**Bandar** Nepal	111 J8	**Bankhead L** Alabama U.S.A.
77 E4	**Bandar 'Abbās** Iran	68 G4	**Ban Khing** Laos
70 K8	**Bandaragung** Sumatra	68 F6	**Ban Khling** Thailand
86 B2	**Bandarbeyla** Somalia	69 D8	**Ban Khok Kloi** Thailand
77 A1	**Bandar-e Anzali** Iran	69 D9	**Ban Khuan Mao** Thailand
77 B4	**Bandar-e Deylam** Iran	26 F4	**Ban Khuk Muang** Thailand
77 D6	**Bandar-e Khoemir** Iran	68 F5	**Ban Khun Ban Hai** Thailand
77 A4	**Bandar-e Khomeyni** Iran	68 C3	**Ban Khun Yuam** Thailand
77 A4	**Bandar-e Lengeh** Iran	68 J6	**Ban Kniet** Vietnam
77 A4	**Bandar-e Ma'shūr** Iran	70 E7	**Bankobankoang** isld Indonesia
77 B5	**Bandar-e Rīg** Iran	68 D4	**Ban Krai** Thailand
77 D1	**Bandar-e Torkeman** Iran	111 J7	**Banks** Idaho U.S.A.
86 B1	**Bandar Murcaay** Somalia	110 F7	**Banks** Mississippi U.S.A.
70 D2	**Bandar Seri Begawan** Brunei	100 B4	**Banks** Oregon U.S.A.
136 F3	**Banda Sea** Indonesia	138 F7	**Banks,C** South Australia Australia
88 E7	**Bandawe** Malawi	117 H9	**Banks I** British Columbia Canada
22 J3	**Bande** Belgium	147 J2	**Banks I** Northwest Territories Canada
16 B2	**Bande** Spain	100 F2	**Banks L** Washington U.S.A.
130 H1	**Bandeira** mt Brazil	144 D5	**Banks Peninsula** New Zealand
129 K8	**Bandeira** mt Brazil	139 K7	**Bankstown Airfield** Sydney, New S Wales Australia
130 E8	**Bandeirantes** Brazil	67 D1	**Ban Kui Nua** Thailand
130 D8	**Bandeirantes, I. dos** Brazil	75 M7	**Bankura** India
106 D6	**Bandelier Nat.Mon** New Mexico U.S.A.	68 G1	**Ban Kut Mak** Thailand
77 D6	**Bande-e Moghūyeh** Iran	46 F2	**Bankya** Bulgaria
109 H6	**Bandera** Texas U.S.A.	68 H7	**Bao Loc** Vietnam
108 B4	**Banderas** Mexico	65 J1	**Baoqing** China
124 G7	**Banderas,B de** Mexico	67 G1	**Baoshan** China
28 G7	**Bandholm** Denmark	68 J3	**Baoting** China
85 D6	**Bandiagara** Mali	58 E3	**Baotou** China
77 K2	**Band-i-Amur** R Afghanistan	85 C6	**Boulé** R Mali
77 J2	**Band-i-Balan** mts Afghanistan	59 G5	**Baoying** China
78 B1	**Bandirma** Turkey	56 H3	**Baoyou** see Ledong
47 J4	**Bandirma Körfezi** G Turkey	76 E3	**Bapatla** India
77 J2	**Band-i-Turkestan** mts Afghanistan	22 D3	**Bapaume** France
70 M9	**Bandjar** Java	103 N8	**Bapchule** Arizona U.S.A.
70 M9	**Bandjarmasin** Kalimantan	121 M7	**Baptiste** Ontario Canada
70 M9	**Bandjarnegara** Java	78 K6	**Bāqa el Gharbiya** Israel
19 P18	**Bandol** France	66 E5	**Baqên** China
	Ban Don see Surat Thani	79 F9	**Baqir, J** mt Jordan
14 C5	**Bandon** Ireland	78 K5	**Ba'Qūbah** Iraq
14 C5	**Bandon** Ireland	80 F3	**Baqura** Jordan
100 A6	**Bandon** Oregon U.S.A.	14 E4	**Bann** R Ireland
68 G4	**Ban Dong** Laos	14 E2	**Bann** R N Ireland
68 F4	**Ban Don Khi** Thailand	22 H4	**Bar** R France
74 E9	**Bandra** India	48 L1	**Bar** U.S.S.R.
86 C6	**Bandundu** Zaire	43 H7	**Bar** U.S.S.R.
69 F12	**Bandung** Java	128 E3	**Bara** R Yugoslavia
69 F12	**Bandung** Sumatra	86 F3	**Bara** Sudan
68 G4	**Ban Dupre** Laos	86 H7	**Bara Ba** Vietnam
94 F9	**Bandy** Virginia U.S.A.	44 B2	**Barge** Italy
143 D7	**Bandya** Western Australia Australia	123 Q2	**Barge B** Labrador, Nfld Canada
48 L5	**Băneasa** Romania	45 H3	**Barga** Italy
78 K4	**Baneh** Iran	87 H7	**Bargaal** Somalia
71 B2	**Banema** Halmahera Indonesia	141 K6	**Bargara** Queensland Australia
17 G6	**Bañeras** Spain	17 F5	**Bargas** Spain
126 G4	**Banes** Cuba	40 G3	**Barge** Ethiopia
69 D8	**Ban Fai Tha** Thailand	44 B2	**Barge** Italy
	Banff co see Grampian reg	123 Q2	**Barge B** Labrador, Nfld Canada
118 B7	**Banff** Alberta Canada	16 B5	**Barrage de Maranhão** res Portugal
15 F3	**Banff** Scotland	118 E6	**Barrage d'Oroville** res U.S.S.R.
85 D6	**Banfora** Burkina	16 B5	**Barragem de Montargil Res** Portugal
86 D7	**Banga** Zaire	16 B5	**Barragem do Castello do Bode** Portugal
102 H8	**Banning** California U.S.A.	138 E6	**Barrages** Australia
	Banningville see Bandundu	57 D6	**Basaga** U.S.S.R.
40 H6	**Bannio** Italy	55 D3	**Basai** Iran
121 N8	**Bannockburn** Ontario Canada	69 D11	**Batang** R Indonesia
144 B6	**Bannockburn** New Zealand	69 D12	**Batangtoru** Sumatra
12 E1	**Bannockburn** Scotland	73 C1	**Batanta** isld W Irian
55 E5	**Bannock Pass** Idaho/ Montana U.S.A.	48 E4	**Bátaszek** Hungary
80 E1	**Bar'am** Israel	130 F7	**Batatais** Brazil
70 D3	**Baram** R Sarawak	69 J3	**Batavia** see Jakarta

(Index continues across eight columns; entries read alphabetically from Bandar to Baugé)

| 73 | **Banya** Bulgaria | 13 E5 | **Bardsea** England | 118 D9 | **Barons** Alberta Canada | 143 E8 | **Bartlett Soak** L Western Australia Australia | 69 J12 | **Batangtarang** Indonesia |
| 69 C11 | **Banyak, Kep.** isld Indonesia | 8 B2 | **Bardsey** isld Wales | 143 F6 | **Baron's Ra** Western Australia | 98 F9 | **Bartley** Nebraska U.S.A. | 71 C3 | **Batanta** isld W Irian |

19 Q13	Bauges *dist* France	71 D5	Bay Pt Philippines	21 L5	Beaufay France	9 E5	Beckhampton England
140 D3	Bauhinia N Terr Australia	47 H5	Bayramiç Turkey	40 E6	Beaufort France	36 B5	Beckingen W Germany
141 J6	Bauhinia Downs Queensland	37 M4	Bayreuth W Germany	22 L4	Beaufort Luxembourg	8 D5	Beckington England
	Australia	37 N5	Bayrischer Wald *mts* W	70 D2	Beaufort Sabah	94 F9	Beckley West Virginia U.S.A.
71 N9	Baukau Timor		Germany	112 L3	Beaufort North Carolina	144 B6	Becks New Zealand
70 G7	Baula Sulawesi Indonesia	123 T6	Bay Roberts Newfoundland		U.S.A.	32 H9	Beckum W Germany
123 R2	Bauld,C Newfoundland		Canada	112 G5	Beaufort South Carolina	109 N3	Beckville Texas U.S.A.
	Canada	58 F1	Baysa U.S.S.R.		U.S.A.	102 D2	Beckwourth California U.S.A.
20 F7	Baule,la France	111 G11	Bay St.Louis Mississippi	79 F5	Beaufort Castle *hist site*	48 J3	Beclean Romania
20 G6	Baulon France		U.S.A.		Lebanon	21 J6	Bêcon France
41 J3	Bauma Switzerland	113 F11	Bayshore Florida U.S.A.	21 K7	Beaufort-en-Vallée France	80 D7	Beit Kahil Jordan
9 F1	Baumber England	95 O6	Bay Shore Long I. New York	146 C11	Beaufort I Antarctica	80 D7	Beit Lahiya Israel
19 K5	Baume-les-Dames France		U.S.A.	112 L3	Beaufort Inlet North Carolina	9 G4	Beit Lahiya Israel
33 T6	Baumgarten East Germany	21 K7	Bays Mt Tennessee U.S.A.		U.S.A.	37 O3	Beit Lahm Jordan
37 O7	Baumgarten W Germany	56 E5	Bay-Soot U.S.S.R.	116 R2	Beaufort Lag Alaska U.S.A.	80 E1	Beit Ras Jordan
36 C4	Baumholder W Germany	111 G10	Bay Springs Mississippi	147 K2	Beaufort Sea Arctic Oc	80 G3	Beit Sahur Jordan
70 G6	Bauna Sulawesi		U.S.A.	89 B9	Beaufort West S Africa	80 E6	Beit Sahur Jordan
37 K4	Baunach W Germany		Baytag Bogdo *see* Baytik	21 O6	Beaugency France	26 E7	Beitstad Norway
37 K3	Baunach *R* W Germany		Shan	121 R7	Beauharnois Quebec	70 D10	Bedadung *R* Java
70 C6	Baung Kalimantan	9 G3	Baython End England		Canada	48 G3	Bedale England
58 F1	Baunt U.S.S.R.	66 E2	Baytik Shan *mt ra* China/	121 R7	Beauharnois Power Canal	18 H9	Bedarieux France
128 F6	Baures Bolivia		Mongolia		Quebec Canada	36 B1	Bedburg W Germany
130 E8	Bauru Brazil	109 N6	Baytown Texas U.S.A.	21 Q16	Beaujeu France	8 B1	Beddgelert Wales
130 D6	Baús Brazil	145 F9	Bay View New Zealand	19 N12	Beaujeu France	18 H6	Beddingham England
52 B6	Bauska U.S.S.R.	117 P12	Bayview Idaho U.S.A.	19 H9	Beaujolais, Mts du France	143 E6	Bedajan North Carolina U.S.A.

17 G6 **Benidorm** Spain
17 F10 **Beni Iznassèn** *mts* Morocco
79 A10 **Beni Mazâr** Egypt
85 C2 **Beni Mellal** Morocco
85 E8 **Benin,Bight of** W Africa
85 F7 **Benin City** Nigeria
36 B5 **Bening** France
9 G1 **Benington** England
85 E7 **Benin, Rep. of** W Africa
85 D2 **Beni Ounif** Algeria
17 G9 **Beni Saf** Algeria
79 B9 **Beni Suef** Egypt
47 O12 **Benitses** Greece
103 N1 **Benjamin** Utah U.S.A.
128 D4 **Benjamin Constant** Brazil
124 D2 **Benjamin Hill** Mexico
100 E6 **Benjamin L** Oregon U.S.A.
60 O3 **Benkei Misaki** *C* Japan
98 E9 **Benkelman** Nebraska U.S.A.
15 D2 **Ben Klibreck** *mt* Scotland
42 G4 **Benkovac** Yugoslavia
15 D4 **Ben Lawers** *mt* Scotland
15 D4 **Ben Ledi** *mt* Scotland
15 D4 **Ben Lomond** *mt* Scotland
15 D2 **Ben Loyal** *mt* Scotland
15 D4 **Ben Lui** *mt* Scotland
15 E3 **Ben Macdhui** *mt* Scotland
43 B12 **Ben Mehidi** Algeria
15 D4 **Ben More** *mt* Central Scotland
15 B4 **Ben More** *mt* Highland Scotland
15 D2 **Ben More Assynt** *mt* Scotland
144 C6 **Benmore, L** New Zealand
144 C6 **Benmore Pk** *mt* New Zealand
33 N9 **Benneckenstein** East Germany
98 K9 **Bennet** Nebraska U.S.A.
140 D2 **Bennet B** N Terr Australia
117 F6 **Bennett** British Columbia Canada
99 P8 **Bennett** Iowa U.S.A.
99 P3 **Bennett** Wisconsin U.S.A.
51 P1 **Bennetta, Ostrov** *isld* U.S.S.R.
140 B6 **Bennett, L** N Terr Australia
117 F6 **Bennett L** British Columbia Canada
112 H3 **Bennettsville** South Carolina U.S.A.
15 D4 **Ben Nevis** *mt* Scotland
145 E3 **Benneydale** New Zealand
101 O7 **Bennington** Idaho U.S.A.
107 N2 **Bennington** Kansas U.S.A.
95 Q3 **Bennington** New Hampshire U.S.A.
107 O7 **Bennington** Oklahoma U.S.A.
95 O4 **Bennington** Vermont U.S.A.
85 B6 **Bénnsané** Guinea
120 J6 **Benny** Ontario Canada
20 B6 **Bénodet** France
20 B6 **Benodet,Anse de** *B* France
144 C6 **Ben Ohau Range** New Zealand
99 P3 **Benoit** Wisconsin U.S.A.
87 E11 **Benoni** S Africa
107 K6 **Benonine** Oklahoma U.S.A.
86 B4 **Bénoué** *R* Cameroon
21 K3 **Bénouville** France
36 B1 **Benrath** W Germany
36 C2 **Bensberg** W Germany
32 G5 **Bensersiel** W Germany
37 K2 **Benshausen** East Germany
36 F4 **Bensheim** W Germany
119 O9 **Benson** Saskatchewan Canada
9 E4 **Benson** England
103 O10 **Benson** Arizona U.S.A.
99 R9 **Benson** Illinois U.S.A.
111 C10 **Benson** Louisiana U.S.A.
99 L4 **Benson** Minnesota U.S.A.
112 J2 **Benson** North Carolina U.S.A.
68 H7 **Ben Suc** Vietnam
77 F6 **Bent** Iran
69 E10 **Benta** Malaysia
71 K8 **Benteng** Indonesia
32 F8 **Bentheim** W Germany
68 G3 **Ben Thuy** Vietnam
16 E9 **Ben Tieb** Morocco
140 E3 **Bentinck I** Queensland Australia
68 C7 **Bentinck I** Burma
86 E4 **Bentiu** Sudan
80 E1 **Bent Jbail** Lebanon
118 C6 **Bentley** Alberta Canada
13 G6 **Bentley** S Yorks England
107 N4 **Bentley** Kansas U.S.A.
98 D3 **Bentley** North Dakota U.S.A.
94 G6 **Bentleyville** Pennsylvania U.S.A.
130 B5 **Bento Gomes,R** Brazil
133 G3 **Bento Gonçalves** Brazil
118 G7 **Benton** Alberta Canada
122 E8 **Benton** New Brunswick Canada
111 K9 **Benton** Alabama U.S.A.
111 D7 **Benton** Arkansas U.S.A.
102 F4 **Benton** California U.S.A.
113 E7 **Benton** Florida U.S.A.
110 H3 **Benton** Illinois U.S.A.
110 H5 **Benton** Kentucky U.S.A.
109 O3 **Benton** Louisiana U.S.A.
110 G4 **Benton** Missouri U.S.A.
95 L5 **Benton** Pennsylvania U.S.A.
99 Q7 **Benton** Wisconsin U.S.A.
99 U7 **Benton Harbor** Michigan U.S.A.
111 F9 **Bentonia** Mississippi U.S.A.
110 B5 **Bentonville** Arkansas U.S.A.
68 H7 **Ben Tre** Vietnam
69 E11 **Bentung** Malaysia
33 Q4 **Bentwisch** East Germany
69 H12 **Benua** *isld* Indonesia
70 P10 **Benua** Bali Indonesia
70 C4 **Benuamartinus** Kalimantan
86 A4 **Benue** *R* Nigeria
12 D1 **Ben Venue** *mt* Scotland
15 D4 **Ben Vorlich** *mt* Scotland
14 B2 **Benwee Hd** Ireland
109 M3 **Ben Wheeler** Texas U.S.A.
15 D3 **Ben Wyvis** *mt* Scotland
65 F4 **Benxi** China
21 J4 **Bény Bocage,le** France
33 U5 **Benz** East Germany
80 B6 **Ben Zakkay** Israel
99 U5 **Benzonia** Michigan U.S.A.
48 F5 **Beočin** Yugoslavia
48 F6 **Beograd** Yugoslavia
70 K8 **Bepagut, G** *mt* Sumatra Indonesia
60 E12 **Beppu** Japan
80 E5 **Beqaot** Jordan
80 C6 **Beqoa' Latrun** Israel
70 E6 **Berangas** Kalimantan
37 M5 **Beratzhausen** W Germany
70 E3 **Berau** *R* Kalimantan
86 F2 **Berber** Sudan
86 J3 **Berbera** Somalia
86 C5 **Berbérati** Cent Afr Republic
17 H6 **Berberia, C** Balearic Is
37 L5 **Berching** W Germany
57 A1 **Berchogur** U.S.S.R.
38 G6 **Berchtesgaden** W Germany
22 B3 **Berck** France
22 B3 **Berck Plage** France
109 K7 **Berclair** Texas U.S.A.
56 B4 **Berd'** *R* U.S.S.R.
21 M5 **Berd'huis** France
48 M1 **Berdichev** U.S.S.R.
51 M2 **Berdigestyakh** U.S.S.R.
86 D2 **Berdoba** Chad
56 B4 **Berdsk** U.S.S.R.
55 C3 **Berdyaush** U.S.S.R.
55 E3 **Berdyuzh'ye** U.S.S.R.
98 D7 **Berea** Nebraska U.S.A.
94 F5 **Berea** Ohio U.S.A.
71 B1 **Berebere** Halmahera Indonesia
86 B1 **Bereeda** Somalia
48 J2 **Beregomet** U.S.S.R.
48 H2 **Beregovo** U.S.S.R.
85 D7 **Berekum** Ghana
32 L8 **Berenbostel** W Germany
102 D4 **Berenda** California U.S.A.
84 J5 **Berenice** Egypt
119 U6 **Berens I** Manitoba Canada
119 V6 **Berens River** Manitoba Canada
8 D6 **Bere Regis** England
138 D3 **Beresford** South Australia Australia
119 R9 **Beresford** Manitoba Canada
122 G6 **Beresford** New Brunswick Canada
98 K6 **Beresford** South Dakota U.S.A.
48 L4 **Beresti** Romania
48 G3 **Berettyo** *R* Hungary
48 G3 **Berettyóújfalu** Hungary
48 J1 **Berezhany** U.S.S.R.
54 C5 **Berezna** U.S.S.R.
52 J5 **Berezniki** U.S.S.R.
55 C2 **Berezovka** U.S.S.R.
50 F2 **Berezovo** U.S.S.R.
56 C3 **Berezovskiy** U.S.S.R.
29 N11 **Berezovyy,Ostrov** *isld* U.S.S.R.
26 J2 **Berg** Norway
26 G9 **Berg** Sweden
37 N2 **Berga** East Germany
17 J2 **Berga** Spain
27 G15 **Berga** Sweden
27 H14 **Berga** Sweden
78 A2 **Bergama** Turkey
42 C3 **Bergamo** Italy
45 K1 **Bergantino** Italy
32 G7 **Berge** W Germany
32 M6 **Bergedorf** W Germany
27 A11 **Bergen** Norway
121 N9 **Bergen** New York U.S.A.
98 F1 **Bergen** North Dakota U.S.A.
32 L7 **Bergen** W Germany
25 C3 **Bergen aan Zee** Netherlands
6 M2 **Bergen Bank** North Sea
25 E5 **Berg-en-Dal** Netherlands
25 B6 **Bergen op Zoom** Netherlands
18 F8 **Bergerac** France
25 D6 **Bergeyk** Netherlands
26 L3 **Bergfors** Sweden
36 C1 **Berg. Gladbach** W Germany
145 D1 **Berghan Pt** New Zealand
36 C7 **Bergheim** France
36 B2 **Bergheim** W Germany
94 G6 **Bergholz** Ohio U.S.A.
32 G9 **Bergkamen** W Germany
27 H15 **Bergkvara** Sweden
99 M1 **Bergland** Ontario Canada
99 R3 **Bergland** Michigan U.S.A.
37 M7 **Berglern** W Germany
26 K5 **Bergnäs, N** Sweden
36 D1 **Bergneustadt** W Germany
29 J9 **Bergö** Finland
94 G8 **Bergoo** West Virginia U.S.A.
37 J3 **Bergrheinfeld** W Germany
25 C5 **Bergse Maas** *R* Netherlands
27 K12 **Bergshamra** Sweden
26 J10 **Bergsjö** Sweden
37 N6 **Bergstorf** W Germany
37 J4 **Bergtheim** W Germany
22 C2 **Bergues** France
25 F2 **Bergumer Meer** *L* Netherlands
41 L4 **Bergün** Switzerland
45 L1 **Berici,Monti** Italy
143 B7 **Beringarra** Western Australia Australia
22 J1 **Beringen** Belgium
25 E6 **Beringen** Netherlands
116 Q6 **Bering Glacier** Alaska U.S.A.
116 P6 **Bering L** Alaska U.S.A.
116 E3 **Bering Land Bridge Nat Preserve** Alaska U.S.A.
114 B5 **Bering Sea**
116 C4 **Bering Strait** U.S.S.R./Alaska
106 D9 **Berino** New Mexico U.S.A.
54 E10 **Berislav** U.S.S.R.
17 F8 **Berja** Spain
21 K4 **Berjou** France
26 D9 **Berkåk** Norway
25 F4 **Berkel** *R* Netherlands
32 F9 **Berkel** *R* W Germany
8 D4 **Berkeley** England
102 B4 **Berkeley** California U.S.A.
114 J3 **Berkeley,C** Northwest Territories Canada
142 G2 **Berkeley, R** Western Australia Australia
133 F8 **Berkeley Sd** Falkland Is
9 F4 **Berkhamsted** England
146 E7 **Berkner I** Antarctica
46 F1 **Berkovitsa** Bulgaria
9 E5 **Berkshire** *co* England
95 O4 **Berkshire Hills** Massachusetts U.S.A.
22 F3 **Berlaimont** France
117 P8 **Berland** *R* Alberta Canada
110 K6 **Berland Plateau** Tennessee U.S.A.
17 F3 **Berlanga de Duero** Spain
16 A5 **Berlenga** *isld* Portugal
26 R1 **Berlevåg** Norway
30 G3 **Berlin** Germany
34 **Berlin** *conurbation* Germany
89 E9 **Berlin** S Africa
95 M8 **Berlin** Maryland U.S.A.
95 Q2 **Berlin** New Hampshire U.S.A.
98 H3 **Berlin** North Dakota U.S.A.
94 J7 **Berlin** Pennsylvania U.S.A.
99 S6 **Berlin** Wisconsin U.S.A.
115 L3 **Berlinguet Inlet** Northwest Territories Canada
94 G6 **Berlin Res** Ohio U.S.A.
144 C4 **Berlins** New Zealand
133 E6 **Bermeja,Pta** Argentina
16 D8 **Bermeja, Sa** *mt* Spain
124 H5 **Bermejillo** Mexico
133 D4 **Bermejo** *R* Argentina
128 F8 **Bermejo** *R* Argentina
131 E7 **Bermejo, I** Argentina
17 F1 **Bermeo** Spain
16 C3 **Bermillo de Sayago** Spain
20 G8 **Berm-sur-Mer** France
90 A1 **Bermuda** *isld* Atlantic Oc
90 D5 **Bermuda Rise** Atlantic Oc
40 G4 **Bern** Switzerland
99 L10 **Bern** Kansas U.S.A.
43 H8 **Bernalda** Italy
106 D6 **Bernalillo** New Mexico U.S.A.
118 K8 **Bernard** Saskatchewan Canada
99 Q7 **Bernard** Iowa U.S.A.
103 P10 **Bernardino** Arizona U.S.A.
130 E8 **Bernardino de Campos** Brazil
114 G3 **Bernard Is** Northwest Territories Canada
122 J3 **Bernard,L** Quebec Canada
119 M3 **Bernard L** Saskatchewan Canada
130 D10 **Bernardo de Irigoyen** Argentina
133 E5 **Bernasconi** Argentina
33 T7 **Bernau** East Germany
21 P1 **Bernaville** France
21 M3 **Bernay** Eure France
21 K5 **Bernay** Sarthe France
33 P9 **Bernburg** East Germany
38 O6 **Berndorf** Austria
Berne *see* **Bern**
110 M1 **Berne** Indiana U.S.A.
32 H6 **Berne** W Germany
22 K2 **Berneau** Belgium
36 F6 **Berneck** W Germany
15 A3 **Berneray** *isld* Scotland
20 F7 **Bernerie la** France
40 G4 **Berner Oberland** *reg* Switzerland
16 D2 **Bernesga** *R* Spain
21 N2 **Berneval** France
111 D9 **Bernice** Louisiana U.S.A.
110 G5 **Bernie** Missouri U.S.A.
115 L3 **Bernier B** Northwest Territories Canada
143 A6 **Bernier I** Western Australia Australia
41 L5 **Bernina, Passo del** Switzerland
22 F3 **Bernissart** Belgium
33 P5 **Bernitt** East Germany
36 C4 **Bernkastel-Kues** W Germany
33 S9 **Bernsdorf** East Germany
95 L6 **Bernville** Pennsylvania U.S.A.
37 K5 **Berolzheim** W Germany
80 B7 **Beror Hayil** Israel
87 H12 **Beroroha** Madagascar
80 B8 **Berosh** Israel
85 E6 **Béroubouay** Benin
30 H6 **Beroun** Czechoslovakia
30 H6 **Berounka** *R* Czechoslovakia
46 F3 **Berovo** Yugoslavia
45 L2 **Berra** Italy
40 F4 **Berra** *mt* Switzerland
43 A12 **Berrahal** Algeria
19 O18 **Berre** France
85 C2 **Berrechid** Morocco
19 O18 **Berre, Etang de** France
36 B2 **Berrenrath** W Germany
138 F5 **Berri** South Australia Australia
85 E2 **Berriane** Algeria
15 E2 **Berriedale** Scotland
20 C5 **Berrien** France
99 U8 **Berrien Springs** Michigan U.S.A.
139 H6 **Berrigan** New South Wales Australia
140 B1 **Berrimah** N Terr Australia
22 G5 **Berru** France
21 N7 **Berry** *reg* France
111 J8 **Berry** Alabama U.S.A.
110 M3 **Berry** Kentucky U.S.A.
22 F5 **Berry-au-Bac** France
127 M2 **Berrydale** Jamaica
102 B3 **Berryessa,L** California U.S.A.
8 C7 **Berry Head** England
113 K12 **Berry Is** Bahamas
140 B6 **Berrys Pass** N Terr Australia
110 C5 **Berryville** Arkansas U.S.A.
94 K7 **Berryville** Virginia U.S.A.
87 C11 **Berseba** Namibia
22 E3 **Bersée** France
32 G7 **Bersenbrück** W Germany
48 M2 **Bershad'** U.S.S.R.
22 G3 **Bersillies** Belgium
122 B5 **Bersimis, Les Lacs** Quebec Canada
55 D4 **Bersuat** U.S.S.R.
69 F10 **Bertam** Malaysia
122 D3 **Berté,L** Quebec Canada
21 P8 **Berthenoux,la** France
121 R6 **Berthierville** Quebec Canada
98 E1 **Berthold** North Dakota U.S.A.
98 A9 **Berthoud** Colorado U.S.A.
141 F1 **Bertiehaugh** Queensland Australia
22 D3 **Bertincourt** France
45 M3 **Bertinoro** Italy
22 K3 **Bertogne** Belgium
86 B5 **Bertoua** Cameroon
14 B3 **Bertraghboy B** Ireland
120 F3 **Bertram** Ontario Canada
109 J5 **Bertram** Texas U.S.A.
142 F4 **Bertram,Mt** Western Australia Australia
98 G9 **Bertrand** Nebraska U.S.A.
36 B7 **Bertrichamps** France
22 H4 **Bertrix** Belgium
22 E3 **Bertry** France
119 P6 **Bertwell** Saskatchewan Canada
57 B4 **Beruni** U.S.S.R.
128 F4 **Beruri** Brazil
83 J11 **Beruwala** Sri Lanka
137 Q2 **Berv** *isld* Kiribati
21 L3 **Berville-sur-Mer** France
Berwick *co see* **Borders** *reg*
139 H6 **Berwick** Victoria Australia
122 H8 **Berwick** Nova Scotia Canada
95 F3 **Berwick** Maine U.S.A.
95 L5 **Berwick** Pennsylvania U.S.A.
13 G2 **Berwick-upon-Tweed** England
117 P7 **Berwyn** Alberta Canada
7 H10 **Berwyn Mts** Wales
6 M3 **Beryl** *oil rig* North Sea
103 L4 **Beryl** Utah U.S.A.
22 G3 **Berzee** Belgium
48 D4 **Berzence** Hungary
70 E3 **Besah** Kalimantan
87 G11 **Besalampy** Madagascar
19 K5 **Besançon** France
71 L9 **Besar** Flores Indonesia
70 O8 **Besar, G** *mt* Java
70 D6 **Besar, G** *mt* Kalimantan
69 E10 **Besar,Gunung** Malaysia
69 E11 **Besar Hantu** *mt* Malaysia
19 O15 **Besayes** France
43 B12 **Besbes** Algeria
116 G4 **Besboro I** Alaska U.S.A.
18 H6 **Besbre** *R* France
69 F11 **Beserah** Malaysia
57 H6 **Besharyk** U.S.S.R.
54 A1 **Beshenkovichi** U.S.S.R.
36 G5 **Besigheim** W Germany
71 M9 **Besikama** Timor Indonesia
47 N10 **Beşiktas** Turkey
78 H3 **Beşiri** Turkey
69 C11 **Besitang** Sumatra
31 L6 **Beskidy Zachodnie** *reg* Poland
53 F11 **Beslan** U.S.S.R.
46 E2 **Besna Kobila** *mt* Yugoslavia
57 G1 **Besoba** U.S.S.R.
47 J7 **Beşparmak Dağ** *mt* Turkey
26 D7 **Bessaker** Norway
48 L2 **Bessarabia** *old prov* U.S.S.R.
48 M4 **Bessarabka** U.S.S.R.
19 Q14 **Besse** Isère France
19 Q18 **Besse** Var France
18 H8 **Bessèges** France
121 N7 **Bessemer** Ontario Canada
111 K8 **Bessemer** Alabama U.S.A.
99 Q3 **Bessemer** Michigan U.S.A.
94 G6 **Bessemer** Pennsylvania U.S.A.
112 F2 **Bessemer City** North Carolina U.S.A.
19 N13 **Bessenay** France
36 G4 **Bessenbach** W Germany
23 F5 **Besser** Denmark
21 M6 **Bessé-sur-Braye** France
107 M6 **Bessie** Oklahoma U.S.A.
21 J3 **Bessin** *reg* France
18 F6 **Bessines sur Gartempe** France
25 D5 **Best** Netherlands
57 J1 **Bestamak** U.S.S.R.
28 A3 **Bested** Denmark
55 F4 **Bestobe** U.S.S.R.
140 C2 **Beswick** N Terr Australia
100 C8 **Beswick** California U.S.A.
87 H11 **Betafo** Madagascar
71 M9 **Betano** Timor
87 H13 **Betanty** Madagascar
16 B1 **Betanzos** Spain
16 B1 **Betanzos, Ria de** Spain
17 G5 **Bétara** Spain
86 B4 **Bétaré Oya** Cameroon
80 C6 **Bet 'Arif** Israel
122 C4 **Betchie L** Quebec Canada
99 T2 **Bete Grise Bay** Michigan U.S.A.
69 G13 **Betet** *isld* Sumatra
80 C7 **Bet Guvrin** Israel
80 D2 **Bet Ha'Emeq** Israel
80 B8 **Bet Ha Gaddi** Israel
87 E11 **Bethal** S Africa
89 F6 **Bethal** S Africa
80 C3 **Bet Hananya** Israel
87 C11 **Bethanien** Namibia
110 B1 **Bethany** Missouri U.S.A.
107 N6 **Bethany** Oklahoma U.S.A.
95 M8 **Bethany Beach** Delaware U.S.A.
116 G6 **Bethel** Alaska U.S.A.
95 O5 **Bethel** Connecticut U.S.A.
95 M8 **Bethel** Delaware U.S.A.
95 R2 **Bethel** Maine U.S.A.
99 N4 **Bethel** Minnesota U.S.A.
99 O10 **Bethel** Missouri U.S.A.
112 K2 **Bethel** North Carolina U.S.A.
110 M3 **Bethel** Ohio U.S.A.
95 P3 **Bethel** Vermont U.S.A.
94 G6 **Bethel Park** Pennsylvania U.S.A.
127 J2 **Bethel Town** Jamaica
22 G5 **Bétheniville** France
95 K7 **Bethesda** Maryland U.S.A.
94 F6 **Bethesda** Ohio U.S.A.
8 B1 **Bethesda** Wales
80 F1 **Bet Hillel** Israel
21 M8 **Béthines** France
22 D5 **Béthisy-St.Pierre** France
80 D7 **Bethlehem** Jordan
89 F7 **Bethlehem** S Africa
95 Q2 **Bethlehem** New Hampshire U.S.A.
95 M6 **Bethlehem** Pennsylvania U.S.A.
122 A2 **Béthoulet, L** Quebec Canada
110 K5 **Bethpage** Tennessee U.S.A.
89 D8 **Bethulie** S Africa
119 M8 **Bethune** Saskatchewan Canada
22 D2 **Béthune** France
21 N2 **Béthune** *R* France
106 H2 **Bethune** Colorado U.S.A.
112 G3 **Bethune** South Carolina U.S.A.
130 G6 **Betim** Brazil
87 G12 **Betioky** Madagascar
70 O10 **Betiri, G** Java
80 D2 **Bet Ke'rem** Israel
80 D3 **Bet Lehem** Israel
8 D1 **Betley** England
80 C7 **Bet Nir** Israel
70 B4 **Betong** Sarawak
140 F7 **Betoota** Queensland Australia
80 D3 **Bet Oren** Israel
86 C5 **Bétou** Congo
57 E3 **Betpak-Dala** *reg* U.S.S.R.
80 C8 **Bet Qama** Israel
87 H12 **Betroka** Madagascar
80 E3 **Bet She'an** Israel
80 B7 **Bet Shiqma** Israel
122 D5 **Betsiamites** Quebec Canada
122 C4 **Betsiamites, R** Quebec Canada
87 H11 **Betsiboka** *R* Madagascar
99 U5 **Betsie, Pt** Michigan U.S.A.
99 V3 **Betsy L** Michigan U.S.A.
22 K4 **Bettembourg** Luxembourg
75 L5 **Bettiah** India
109 N3 **Bettie** Texas U.S.A.
116 M3 **Bettles** Alaska U.S.A.
27 J13 **Bettna** Sweden
20 G5 **Betton** France
74 G8 **Betul** India
71 M9 **Betun** Timor Indonesia
70 C4 **Betung, G** *mt* Kalimantan
73 M3 **Betwa** *R* India
8 C1 **Betws-y-Coed** Wales
80 C4 **Bet Yannay** Israel
80 C4 **Bet Yizhaq** Israel
80 F3 **Bet Yosef** Israel
36 D2 **Betzdorf** W Germany
37 L4 **Betzenstein** W Germany
41 O2 **Beuerberg** W Germany
25 E5 **Beugen** Netherlands
119 Q8 **Beulah** Manitoba Canada
99 V5 **Beulah** Michigan U.S.A.
98 E2 **Beulah** North Dakota U.S.A.
100 G6 **Beulah** Oregon U.S.A.
98 B5 **Beulah** Wyoming U.S.A.
8 C3 **Beulah** Wales
112 K3 **Beulaville** North Carolina U.S.A.
9 G5 **Beult,R** England
36 B4 **Beurig** W Germany
22 D4 **Beuvraignes** France
21 O6 **Beuvron** *R* France
21 K3 **Beuvron-en-Auge** France
20 A5 **Beuzec-Cap-Sizun** France
21 L3 **Beuzeville** France
21 L2 **Beuzeville-la-Grenier** France
33 N6 **Bevensen** W Germany
32 G8 **Bever** *R* W Germany
22 G1 **Beveren** Oost Vlaanderen Belgium
112 H2 **B. Everett Jordan Lake** North Carolina U.S.A.
32 G8 **Bevergern** W Germany
41 K4 **Beverin,Piz** *mt* Switzerland
143 B9 **Beverley** Western Australia Australia
118 K8 **Beverley** Saskatchewan Canada
13 H6 **Beverley** England
100 F3 **Beverley** Washington U.S.A.
141 J5 **Beverley Grp** *islds* Queensland Australia
116 H7 **Beverley,L** Alaska U.S.A.
22 J1 **Beverlo** Belgium
118 D5 **Beverly** Alberta Canada
107 N2 **Beverly** Kansas U.S.A.
95 R4 **Beverly** Massachusetts U.S.A.
94 F7 **Beverly** Ohio U.S.A.
94 H8 **Beverly** West Virginia U.S.A.
102 F7 **Beverly Hills** California U.S.A.
114 J5 **Beverly L** Northwest Territories Canada
100 C2 **Beverly Park** Washington U.S.A.
32 L9 **Bevern** W Germany
22 J2 **Beverst** Belgium
32 J6 **Beverstedt** W Germany
32 K9 **Beverungen** W Germany
25 C4 **Beverwijk** Netherlands
99 O10 **Bevier** Missouri U.S.A.
45 K1 **Bevilacqua Boschi** Italy
21 O5 **Béville-le-Comte** France
28 C6 **Bevtoft** Denmark
128 C7 **Beware,Pta** *C* Peru
8 D3 **Bewdley** England
40 F5 **Bex** Switzerland
9 G6 **Bexhill** England
144 D5 **Bexley** New Zealand
47 H4 **Beyçayırı** Turkey
78 C3 **Bey Daglari** Turkey
47 L4 **Beydili** Turkey
47 N10 **Beykoz** Turkey
85 C7 **Beyla** Guinea
47 N10 **Beylerbeyi** Turkey
86 H3 **Beylul** Ethiopia
21 O4 **Beynes** France
78 B1 **Beyoglu** Turkey
78 C1 **Beypazari** Turkey
76 B5 **Beypore** India
79 F5 **Beyrouth** Lebanon
78 C3 **Beyşehir** Turkey
80 C7 **Beyt 'Awwa** Jordan
48 E5 **Bezdan** Yugoslavia
37 O4 **Bezdružice** Czechoslovakia
19 J5 **Bèze** France
80 F4 **Bezeq** *R* Israel
52 C6 **Bezhanitsy** U.S.S.R.
46 G1 **Bezhanovo** Bulgaria
18 H9 **Béziers** France
46 F3 **Bezlet** *mt* Bulgaria
21 O3 **Bezu-la-Forêt** France
75 L5 **Bhadgaon** Nepal
75 M8 **Bhadrach** India
76 E2 **Bhadrachalam** India
76 B4 **Bhadravati** India
74 B4 **Bhag** Pakistan
75 M6 **Bhagalpur** India
74 G9 **Bhainsa** India
76 E1 **Bhairamgarh** India
74 D3 **Bhakkar** Pakistan
74 G9 **Bhalki** India
76 E1 **Bhamragarh** India
74 H8 **Bhandara** India
75 L9 **Bhanjanagar** India
75 J7 **Bharatpur** India
74 E8 **Bharuch** India
74 F3 **Bhatinda** India
76 B4 **Bhatkal** India
75 N7 **Bhatpara** India
74 E2 **Bhaun** Pakistan
76 C5 **Bhavani** India
74 E8 **Bhavnagar** India
75 K9 **Bhawanipatna** India
74 E2 **Bhera** Pakistan
75 J8 **Bhilai** India
74 F6 **Bhilwara** India
73 M5 **Bhima** *R* India
76 E2 **Bhimavaram** India
74 H5 **Bhind** India
74 G4 **Bhiwani** India
74 H10 **Bhongir** India
74 G7 **Bhopal** India
76 E1 **Bhopalpatnam** India
74 E9 **Bhor** India
75 L8 **Bhubaneshwar** India
74 C7 **Bhuj** India
68 D4 **Bhumiphol Dam** Thailand
74 F8 **Bhusawal** India
75 N5 **Bhutan** *kingdom* S Asia
77 E6 **Bīābān** *coastal reg* Iran
85 F8 **Biafra,Bight of** W Africa
71 H5 **Biak** Sulawesi Indonesia
136 H2 **Biak** *isld* W Irian
31 N2 **Biała Piska** Poland
31 O3 **Biała Podlaska** Poland
31 M4 **Białobrzegi** Poland
31 J1 **Białogard** Poland
31 K2 **Biały Bór** Poland
31 O2 **Białystok** Poland
44 G3 **Bianca,P** *C* Italy
43 G10 **Bianco** Italy
45 L2 **Bianco, Canale** Italy
65 F4 **Bianmen** China
Bianzhuang *see* **Cangshan**
71 G7 **Biao** Mindanao Philippines
68 F3 **Bia,Pou** *mt* Laos
77 D1 **Biārjmand** Iran
71 J4 **Biaro** *isld* Indonesia
18 D9 **Biarritz** France
55 G3 **Biaza** U.S.S.R.
79 A10 **Biba** Egypt
87 B8 **Bibala** Angola
42 D5 **Bibbiena** Italy
41 L1 **Biberach** W Germany
37 K5 **Bibert** *R* W Germany
16 C2 **Bibey,R** Spain
85 D7 **Bibiania** Ghana
36 E4 **Biblis** W Germany
Biblos *see* **Jbail**
37 J3 **Bibra** Suhl East Germany
142 A3 **Bibra Lake** *dist* Perth, W Aust Australia
9 E4 **Bibury** England
122 D5 **Bic** Quebec Canada
46 D3 **Bicaj** Albania
130 G7 **Bicas** Brazil
48 K4 **Bicaz** Romania
9 E4 **Bicester** England
41 O2 **Bichl** W Germany
41 N3 **Bichlbach** Austria
122 D5 **Bic, I. du** Quebec Canada
140 D2 **Bickerton I** N Terr Australia
8 C6 **Bickington** England
8 C6 **Bickleigh** England
100 E3 **Bickleton** Washington U.S.A.
142 B2 **Bickley Brook** Perth, W Aust Australia
94 F8 **Bickmore** West Virginia U.S.A.
110 J3 **Bicknell** Indiana U.S.A.
103 N3 **Bicknell** Utah U.S.A.
48 E3 **Bicske** Hungary
85 F7 **Bida** Nigeria
70 F2 **Bidadari, Tanjong** *C* Sabah
76 C2 **Bidar** India
95 R3 **Biddeford** Maine U.S.A
80 D6 **Biddu** Jordan
8 D1 **Biddulph** England
8 B5 **Bideford** England
85 E4 **Bidon 5** Algeria
94 E8 **Bidwell** Ohio U.S.A.
100 D8 **Bieber** California U.S.A
36 G3 **Bieber** W Germany
36 G3 **Biebergemünd** W Germany
36 D5 **Biebermühle** W Germany
36 F2 **Biebertal** W Germany
36 E3 **Biebrich** W Germany
31 O2 **Biebrza** *R* Poland
31 N6 **Biecz** Poland
36 F2 **Biedenkopf** W Germany
33 P8 **Biederitz** East Germany
70 O9 **Biega** Java
40 G1 **Biegel** W Germany
60 Q2 **Biei** Japan
40 F3 **Biel** Switzerland
119 Q7 **Bield** Manitoba Canada
32 J8 **Bielefeld** W Germany
41 M4 **Bielerhöhe** *pass* Austria
40 F3 **Bieler See** *L* Switzerland
42 B3 **Biella** Italy
17 H2 **Bielsa** Spain
31 L6 **Bielsko-Biała** Poland
31 O3 **Bielsk Podlaski** Poland
36 C2 **Bielstein** W Germany
33 M6 **Bienenbüttel** W Germany
119 P9 **Bienfait** Saskatchewan Canada
68 H7 **Bien Hoa** Vietnam
Bienne *see* **Biel**
45 J4 **Bientina** Italy
67 C2 **Bi'er** China
141 H7 **Bierbank** Queensland Australia
36 F7 **Bieringen** W Germany
21 J6 **Bierne** France
28 D2 **Biersted** Denmark
25 A6 **Biervliet** Netherlands
33 P7 **Biese** *R* East Germany
33 T7 **Biesenthal** W Germany
40 B1 **Biesles** France
36 G6 **Bietigheim** W Germany
36 E6 **Bietigheim** W Germany
33 T6 **Bietikow** East Germany
22 J4 **Bièvre** Belgium
21 P4 **Bièvres** France
31 M3 **Bieżun** Poland
43 F7 **Biferno** *R* Italy
86 B6 **Bifoun** Gabon
116 K5 **Big** *R* Alaska U.S.A.
78 A1 **Biga** Turkey
47 J5 **Bigadiç** Turkey
101 L2 **Big Arm** Montana U.S.A.
101 P2 **Big Baldy Mt** Montana U.S.A.
117 M10 **Big Bar Creek** British Columbia Canada
144 B6 **Big Bay** New Zealand
99 T3 **Big Bay** Michigan U.S.A.
102 H7 **Big Bear City** California U.S.A.
109 N8 **Big Bear Cr** Texas U.S.A.
102 G7 **Big Bear L** California U.S.A.
119 M9 **Big Beaver** Saskatchewan Canada
120 H3 **Big Beaver Falls** Ontario Canada
115 L7 **Big Beaver House** Ontario Canada
143 C7 **Big Bell** Western Australia Australia
101 O3 **Big Belt Mts** Montana U.S.A.
100 D8 **Big Bend** California U.S.A.
106 H3 **Big Bend** Colorado U.S.A.
108 D6 **Big Bend Nat.Pk** Texas U.S.A.
111 G8 **Big Black** *R* Mississippi U.S.A.
112 G3 **Big Black Cr** South Carolina U.S.A.
94 E10 **Big Black Mt** Kentucky/Virg U.S.A.
8 C7 **Bigbury B** England
8 C7 **Bigbury-on-Sea** England
108 E5 **Big Canyon** *R* Texas U.S.A.
122 E3 **Big Caotibi L** Quebec Canada
103 M6 **Big Chino Wash** Arizona U.S.A.
110 K4 **Big Clifty** Kentucky U.S.A.
107 K3 **Big Cr** Kansas U.S.A.
117 M10 **Big Creek** British Columbia Canada
94 F8 **Big Creek** West Virginia U.S.A.
113 F12 **Big Cypress Nat Preserve** Florida U.S.A.
113 F11 **Big Cypress Swamp** Florida U.S.A.
116 O4 **Big Delta** Alaska U.S.A.
138 F6 **Big Desert** Victoria Australia
101 T2 **Big Dry Cr** Montana U.S.A.
99 Q5 **Big Eau Pleine Res** Wisconsin U.S.A
101 O6 **Big Elk Mt** Idaho U.S.A.
107 O2 **Bigelow** Kansas U.S.A.
99 N1 **Big Falls** Minnesota U.S.A.
99 N2 **Bigfork** Minnesota U.S.A.
101 L1 **Bigfork** Montana U.S.A.
109 M9 **Big Fossil Cr** Texas U.S.A.
118 K6 **Biggar** Saskatchewan Canada
12 E2 **Biggar** Scotland
36 D1 **Bigge** *R* W Germany
142 F2 **Bigge I** W Australia
26 N2 **Biggeluobbal** Norway
141 K7 **Biggenden** Queensland Australia
32 H10 **Bigge-Olsberg** W Germany
141 J7 **Bigge Range** *mts* Queensland Australia
117 E6 **Bigger,Mt** British Columbia Canada
110 F5 **Biggers** Arkansas U.S.A.
9 F3 **Biggleswade** England
102 C2 **Biggs** California U.S.A.
100 E4 **Biggs** Oregon U.S.A.
99 Q9 **Biggsville** Illinois U.S.A.
106 B10 **Big Hatchet Pk** New Mexico U.S.A.
118 C7 **Big Hill Sp.Prov.Pk** Alberta Canada
101 N4 **Big Hole** *R* Montana U.S.A.
101 M4 **Bighole Nat. Battlefield** Montana U.S.A.
101 S4 **Bighorn** *R* Montana U.S.A.
101 S4 **Bighorn** *R* Wyo/Mont U.S.A.
101 R4 **Bighorn Canyon Nat. Recreation Area** Montana U.S.A.
101 S5 **Bighorn Mts** Wyo/Mont U.S.A.
126 G3 **Bight of Acklins** Bahamas
126 G2 **Bight,The** Cat I Bahamas
115 M5 **Big I** Northwest Territories Canada
118 H1 **Big I** Ontario Canada
111 E8 **Big I** Arkansas U.S.A.
94 H9 **Big Island** Virginia U.S.A.
117 F4 **Big Kalzas L** Yukon Territory Canada
116 H9 **Big Koniuji I** Alaska U.S.A.
117 R3 **Big L** Northwest Territories Canada
95 U1 **Big L** Maine U.S.A.
100 E7 **Big L** Oregon U.S.A.
116 N3 **Big Lake** Alaska U.S.A.
108 F4 **Big Lake** Texas U.S.A.
95 K7 **Biglerville** Pennsylvania U.S.A.
144 A7 **Big Moggy I** New Zealand
95 N3 **Big Moose** New York U.S.A.
110 G4 **Big Muddy** *R* Illinois U.S.A.
98 B1 **Big Muddy Cr** Montana U.S.A.
119 N9 **Big Muddy L** Saskatchewan Canada
20 E6 **Bignan** France
44 C4 **Bignone,Monte** Italy
20 G7 **Bignon,le** France
94 H9 **Big Otter** *R* Virginia U.S.A.
102 F4 **Big Pine** California U.S.A.
99 L3 **Big Pine L** Minnesota U.S.A.
102 E7 **Big Pine Peak** California U.S.A.
110 D4 **Big Piney** *R* Missouri U.S.A.
101 P7 **Big Piney** Wyoming U.S.A.
123 M8 **Big Pond** C Breton I, Nova Scotia
94 B3 **Big Rapids** Michigan U.S.A.
99 Q4 **Big Rib** *R* Wisconsin U.S.A.
118 K5 **Big River** Saskatchewan Canada
99 U5 **Big Sable Pt** Michigan U.S.A.
100 E8 **Big Sage Res** California U.S.A.
117 F5 **Big Salmon** *R* Yukon Territory Canada
119 S1 **Big Sand L** Manitoba Canada
103 L7 **Big Sandy** *R* Arizona U.S.A.
101 P1 **Big Sandy** Montana U.S.A.
109 M3 **Big Sandy** Texas U.S.A.
101 Q7 **Big Sandy** Wyoming U.S.A.
106 H3 **Big Sandy Cr** Colorado U.S.A.
119 N4 **Big Sandy L** Saskatchewan Canada
99 N3 **Big Sandy L** Minnesota U.S.A.
118 H1 **Bigsby I** Ontario Canada
98 K5 **Big Sioux** *R* South Dakota U.S.A.
102 G3 **Big Smoky Valley** Nevada U.S.A.
101 Q3 **Big Snowy Mt** Montana U.S.A.
144 A7 **Big South Cape I** New Zealand
108 F3 **Big Spring** Texas U.S.A.
101 O5 **Big Springs** Idaho U.S.A.
98 D8 **Big Springs** Nebraska U.S.A.
118 H8 **Bigstick L** Saskatchewan Canada
98 K4 **Big Stone City** South Dakota U.S.A.
94 E10 **Big Stone Gap** Virginia U.S.A.
119 W5 **Bigstone L** Manitoba Canada
98 K4 **Big Stone L** Minnesota U.S.A.
119 W3 **Bigstone R** Manitoba Canada
102 C5 **Big Sur** California U.S.A.
109 M5 **Big Thicket L** Texas U.S.A.
109 N5 **Big Thicket Nat. Preserve** Texas U.S.A.
101 Q4 **Bigtimber** Montana U.S.A.
101 S6 **Bigtrails** Wyoming U.S.A.
115 L7 **Big Trout Lake** Ontario Canada
130 E10 **Biguacú** Brazil
118 E6 **Big Valley** Alberta Canada
109 H7 **Big Wells** Texas U.S.A.
111 L7 **Big Wills Cr** Alabama U.S.A.
120 K6 **Bigwood** Ontario Canada
101 L6 **Big Wood** *R* Idaho U.S.A.
42 G4 **Bihac** Yugoslavia
75 L6 **Bihar** *prov* India
75 L6 **Bihār Sharīf** India
48 G4 **Bihor** *reg* Romania
48 G4 **Bihorului Muntii** *mts* Romania
67 F2 **Bihu** China
85 A6 **Bijagós, Arquipélago dos** Guinea-Bissau
74 G5 **Bijaipur** India
76 B2 **Bijapur** India
77 A2 **Bijar** Iran
75 K4 **Bijauri** Nepal
48 E6 **Bijeljina** Yugoslavia
46 D1 **Bijelo Polje** Yugoslavia
67 B3 **Bijie** China
76 E1 **Bijji** India
77 F6 **Bijnābād** Iran
74 H4 **Bijnor** India
74 E4 **Bikaner** India
79 F5 **Bikfaiya** Lebanon
59 K2 **Bikin** U.S.S.R.
59 L2 **Bikin** *R* U.S.S.R.
134 G7 **Bikini** *atoll* Marshall Is Pacific Oc
31 L6 **Bilá** Czechoslovakia
71 G6 **Bilaa Pt** Mindanao Philippines
85 E6 **Bilanga** Burkina
70 F3 **Bilangbilangen** Kalimantan
74 E5 **Bilara** India
79 H4 **Bil'as, Jabal** *mt* Syria
74 G3 **Bilaspur** India
70 F2 **Bilatan** *isld* Philippines
71 H4 **Bilato** Sulawesi Indonesia
68 D5 **Bilauktaung Range** Burma/Thailand
17 F1 **Bilbao** Spain
79 B8 **Bilbeis** Egypt
42 J6 **Bileća** Yugoslavia
78 B1 **Bilecik** Turkey
48 F5 **Biled** Romania
48 D2 **Bilé Karpaty** Czechoslovakia
31 O5 **Biłgoraj** Poland
86 E5 **Bili** Zaire
55 A3 **Bilimbay** U.S.S.R.
68 C4 **Bilin** Burma
30 H5 **Bílina** *R* Czechoslovakia
85 G7 **Biliri** Nigeria
71 D8 **Bilit** Sabah
65 E5 **Biliu He** *R* China
98 A6 **Bill** Wyoming U.S.A.
143 B7 **Billabalong** Western Australia Australia
143 A7 **Billabong Roadhouse** Western Australia Australia
6 D2 **Bill Baileys Bank** N Atlantic Oc
20 H5 **Billé** France
33 M5 **Bille** *R* W Germany
32 F9 **Billerbeck** W Germany
9 G4 **Billericay** England
9 F2 **Billesdon** England
19 P12 **Billiat** France
36 G5 **Billigheim** W Germany
142 G4 **Billiluna** Western Australia Australia
9 F2 **Billingborough** England
27 F16 **Billinge** Sweden
9 F1 **Billinghay** England
101 R4 **Billings** Montana U.S.A.
107 N5 **Billings** Oklahoma U.S.A.
9 F5 **Billingshurst** England
8 D3 **Billingsley** England
Billiton *see* **Belitung** *isld*
18 H7 **Billom** France
28 A5 **Billum** Denmark
28 C5 **Billund** Denmark
103 M6 **Bill Williams Mt** Arizona U.S.A.
56 G1 **Billyakh Porog** *falls* U.S.S.R.
22 K5 **Billy-sous-Mangiennes** France
86 B2 **Bilma** Niger
141 K6 **Biloela** Queensland Australia
42 H3 **Bilo Gora** *dist* Yugoslavia
111 H11 **Biloxi** Mississippi U.S.A.
140 E7 **Bilpamorea Claypan** Queensland Australia
142 C5 **Bilroth,Mt** Western Australia Australia
25 D4 **Bilthoven** Netherlands
86 D3 **Biltine** Chad
26 M2 **Bilto** Norway
68 C4 **Bilugyun** *isld* Burma
71 H4 **Bilungala** Sulawesi Indonesia
125 N2 **Bilwascarma** Nicaragua
22 K2 **Bilzen** Belgium
71 J9 **Bima,Teluk** *B* Sumbawa Indonesia
126 E2 **Bimini Is** Bahamas
75 K10 **Bimlipatam** India
71 F5 **Binalbagan** Negros Philippines
77 F1 **Bīnālūd, Kūh-e-** *mts* Iran
21 N6 **Binas** France
70 B3 **Binatang** Sarawak
141 J5 **Binbee** Queensland Australia
13 H6 **Binbrook** England
22 G3 **Binche** Belgium
28 C5 **Bindeballe** Denmark
141 H8 **Bindebango** Queensland Australia
28 D3 **Binderup** Denmark
69 J11 **Bindjai** Indonesia
141 J8 **Bindle** Queensland Australia
118 G8 **Bindloss** Alberta Canada
89 G1 **Bindura** Zimbabwe
17 H3 **Binéfar** Spain
98 H2 **Binford** North Dakota U.S.A.
87 E9 **Binga** Zimbabwe
87 F9 **Binga,Mt** Mozambique/Zimbabwe
141 G8 **Bingara** Queensland Australia
140 B3 **Bing Bong** N Terr Australia
36 D4 **Bingen** W Germany
107 M6 **Binger** Oklahoma U.S.A.
9 F2 **Bingham** England
95 S1 **Bingham** Maine U.S.A.
99 V5 **Bingham** Michigan U.S.A.
108 A2 **Bingham** New Mexico U.S.A.
101 N9 **Bingham Canyon** Utah U.S.A.
95 M4 **Binghamton** New York U.S.A.
84 E3 **Bin Ghashīr** Libya
120 K4 **Bingle** Ontario Canada
13 G6 **Bingley** England
Bingmei *see* **Congjiang**
78 H2 **Bingol** Turkey
78 H2 **Bingol D** Turkey
9 G2 **Binham** England
Binh Dinh *see* **An Nhon**
68 G7 **Binh Minh** Vietnam
68 J5 **Binh Son** Vietnam
20 E4 **Binic** France
69 J11 **Binjai** Indonesia
69 D11 **Binjai** Sumatra
84 F3 **Bin Jawwād** Libya
71 J7 **Binongka** *isld* Indonesia
119 Q8 **Binscarth** Manitoba Canada
144 C5 **Binser, Mt** New Zealand
36 B4 **Binsfeld** W Germany
69 G12 **Bintan** *isld* Indonesia
71 H4 **Bintauna** Sulawesi Indonesia
71 E4 **Bintuan** Philippines
70 C3 **Bintulu** Sarawak
71 E4 **Binubusan** Philippines
65 G2 **Bin Xian** China
58 G4 **Bin Xian** China
80 C3 **Binyamina** Israel
67 C5 **Binyang** China
Binzhou *see* **Bin Xian**
131 A6 **Biobio** *prov* Chile
46 D2 **Bioča** Yugoslavia
42 G5 **Biograd** Yugoslavia
85 F8 **Bioko** *isld* Equat Guinea
19 O14 **Biol** France
40 E5 **Biot, le** France
32 G7 **Bippen** W Germany
94 B6 **Bippus** Indiana U.S.A.
80 E2 **Biq'at Bet Netofa** Israel
74 F9 **Bir** India
80 D6 **Bira** Jordan
48 L3 **Bîra** Romania
59 K2 **Bira** U.S.S.R.
84 J5 **Bir Abu Husein** Egypt
84 H4 **Bir Abu Minqar** Egypt
71 E2 **Birac** Philippines
84 G4 **Bi'r adh Dhakar** *well* Libya
84 E4 **Birāk** Libya
59 K2 **Birakan** U.S.S.R.
80 G1 **Bi'r al 'Ajam** Syria
84 G4 **Bi'r al Harash** *well* Libya
86 D3 **Birao** Cent Afr Republic
66 E3 **Biratar Bulak** *spring* China
75 M5 **Biratnagar** Nepal
77 F7 **Bīr Bālo** Iran
78 G3 **Bi'r Butaymān** Syria
46 F1 **Birca Gingiova** Romania
116 P3 **Birch Cr** Alaska U.S.A.
116 L4 **Birches** Alaska U.S.A.
145 D4 **Birch Hill** New Zealand
119 M5 **Birch Hills** Saskatchewan Canada
119 S6 **Birch I** Manitoba Canada
9 H5 **Birchington** England
48 G5 **Birchiș** Romania
118 F5 **Birch L** Alberta Canada
117 P4 **Birch L** Northwest Territories Canada
118 J5 **Birch L** Saskatchewan Canada
99 P2 **Birch L** Minnesota U.S.A.
117 R7 **Birch Mts** Alberta Canada
117 R6 **Birch R** Alberta Canada
119 Q6 **Birch River** Manitoba Canada
110 E5 **Birch Tree** Missouri U.S.A.
144 A6 **Birchwood** New Zealand
116 N6 **Birchwood** Alaska U.S.A.
99 P4 **Birchwood** Wisconsin U.S.A.
31 N6 **Bircza** Poland
115 K6 **Bird** Manitoba Canada
107 J2 **Bird City** Kansas U.S.A.
89 E9 **Bird I** *lighthouse* S Africa
83 J12 **Bird I** Seychelles
116 H9 **Bird I** Alaska U.S.A.
146 F1 **Bird Island** *U.K. Base* S Georgia S Atlantic Oc
8 D4 **Birdlip** England

12
Bird Rocks — Bol'shoy Tyuters, Os.

123 L6 **Bird Rocks** *lighthouse* Madeleine Is, Quebec Canada
110 K3 **Birdseye** Indiana U.S.A.
140 E7 **Birdsville** Queensland Australia
140 C3 **Birdum** *R* N Terr Australia
85 D3 **Bir ed Deheb** Algeria
85 D3 **Bir el Hadjaj** Algeria
69 C10 **Bireun** Sumatra
79 H10 **Bi'r Fajr** Saudi Arabia
75 L5 **Birganj** Nepal
37 M5 **Birgland** W Germany
27 E11 **Biri** Norway
71 G4 **Biri** *isld* Philippines
89 G1 **Biri** *R* Zimbabwe
130 E7 **Birigüi** Brazil
56 D4 **Birikchul'** U.S.S.R.
79 G3 **Bīrīn** Syria
86 D4 **Birini** Cent Afr Republic
77 F3 **Bīrjand** Iran
28 B6 **Birkelev** Denmark
28 D2 **Birkelse** Denmark
36 F4 **Birkenau** W Germany
41 H2 **Birkendorf** W Germany
27 C13 **Birkenes** Norway
36 C4 **Birkenfeld** W Germany
13 E6 **Birkenhead** England
33 S7 **Birkenwerder** East Germany
29 K5 **Birkerød** Denmark
36 B2 **Birkesdorf** W Germany
28 G7 **Birket** Denmark
79 A9 **Birket Qârûn** *L* Egypt
38 N7 **Birkfeld** Austria
41 O3 **Birkkar Sp** Austria
28 D7 **Birknack** *C* W Germany
138 A2 **Birksgate Ra** South Australia Australia
48 L4 **Bîrlad** *R* Romania
48 L4 **Bîrlad** Romania
79 D7 **Bîr Lahfân** Egypt
85 C3 **Bir Lahlú, Al** Morocco
78 H5 **Bir Meloza** Iraq
119 P8 **Birmingham** Saskatchewan Canada
9 E3 **Birmingham** England
11 C5 **Birmingham** *conurbation* England
111 K8 **Birmingham** Alabama U.S.A.
99 P9 **Birmingham** Iowa U.S.A.
94 D4 **Birmingham** Michigan U.S.A.
84 H5 **Bir Misâha** Egypt
85 B3 **Bir Moghrein** Mauritania
15 E4 **Birnam** Scotland
37 P7 **Birnbach** W Germany
101 T4 **Birney** Montana U.S.A.
134 K8 **Birnie I** Phoenix Is Pacific Oc
85 E6 **Birni Ngaouré** Niger
85 F6 **Birnin Gwari** Nigeria
85 E6 **Birnin-Kebbi** Nigeria
85 F6 **Birni n'Konni** Niger
71 D6 **Birong** Palawan Philippines
79 H3 **Bi'r Qutnah** *well* Syria
14 D3 **Birr** Ireland
140 A4 **Birrindudu** N Terr Australia
118 K7 **Birsay** Saskatchewan Canada
55 C3 **Birsk** U.S.S.R.
13 G6 **Birstal** W Yorks England
36 G3 **Birstein** W Germany
55 D5 **Birsuat** U.S.S.R.
26 L2 **Birtavarre** Norway
141 G2 **Birthday Mt** Queensland Australia
116 J2 **Birthday Pass** Alaska U.S.A.
13 G4 **Birtley** England
66 E5 **Biru** China
56 E3 **Biryusa** *R* U.S.S.R.
56 E3 **Biryusinsk** U.S.S.R.
52 B6 **Biržai** U.S.S.R.
85 C4 **Bir Zreigat** Mauritania
88 C8 **Bisa** Zambia
61 K10 **Bisai** Japan
74 H4 **Bisalpur** India
103 P10 **Bisbee** Arizona U.S.A.
18 C7 **Biscay,B of** France/Spain
113 G12 **Biscayne Nat. Park** Florida U.S.A.
43 G7 **Bisceglie** Italy
37 K4 **Bischberg** W Germany
36 H1 **Bischhausen** W Germany
36 D6 **Bischheim** France
37 M3 **Bischofsgrün** W Germany
37 J3 **Bischofsheim** W Germany
38 H7 **Bischofshofen** Austria
31 H4 **Bischofswerda** East Germany
19 L4 **Bischwiller** France
112 H2 **Biscoe** North Carolina U.S.A.
146 C4 **Biscoe Is** Antarctica
120 H5 **Biscotasing** Ontario Canada
61 P12 **Bise** Okinawa
45 K4 **Bisenzio** *R* Italy
47 H3 **Biser** Bulgaria
55 C2 **Biser** U.S.S.R.
52 H5 **Biserovo** U.S.S.R.
55 C3 **Bisert'** U.S.S.R.
42 G6 **Biševo** *isld* Yugoslavia
61 P12 **Bise-zaki** *C* Okinawa
67 A5 **Bisezhai** China
67 B2 **Bishan** China
89 E9 **Bisho** S Africa
102 F4 **Bishop** California U.S.A.
112 D4 **Bishop** Georgia U.S.A.
95 M8 **Bishop** Maryland U.S.A.
109 K8 **Bishop** Texas U.S.A.
146 B16 **Bishop and Clerk Is** *islds* S Pacific Oc
144 A7 **Bishop and Clerks Is** New Zealand
13 G4 **Bishop Auckland** England
12 D2 **Bishopbriggs** Scotland
101 L8 **Bishop Creek Res** Nevada U.S.A.
117 P3 **Bishop L** Northwest Territories Canada
119 M8 **Bishopric** Saskatchewan Canada
9 E7 **Bishop Rock** Isles of Scilly England
8 C3 **Bishops Castle** England
123 R4 **Bishop's Falls** Newfoundland Canada
8 C5 **Bishop's Lydeard** England
9 G4 **Bishop's Stortford** England
9 E3 **Bishops Tachbrook** England
9 E6 **Bishops Waltham** England
112 G3 **Bishopville** South Carolina U.S.A.
80 G3 **Bishra** Jordan
78 G4 **Bishrī, Jabal** *mts* Syria
85 F2 **Biskra** Algeria
31 M2 **Biskupiec** Poland
28 D3 **Bislev** Denmark
9 F5 **Bisley** England
71 G6 **Bislig** Mindanao Philippines
71 G6 **Bislig Bay** Mindanao Philippines
111 C7 **Bismarck** Arkansas U.S.A.
99 T9 **Bismarck** Illinois U.S.A.
110 F4 **Bismarck** Missouri U.S.A.
98 F3 **Bismarck** North Dakota U.S.A.
136 K2 **Bismarck Archipelago** Papua New Guinea
136 J3 **Bismarck Range** Papua New Guinea
136 K2 **Bismarck Sea** Papua New Guinea
33 P7 **Bismark** East Germany
78 H3 **Bismil** Turkey
107 N5 **Bison** Oklahoma U.S.A.
98 D4 **Bison** South Dakota U.S.A.
117 P7 **Bison L** Alberta Canada
77 A2 **Bīsotūn** Iran
36 B6 **Bisping** France
32 L6 **Bispingen** W Germany
85 A6 **Bissau** Guinea-Bissau
115 K7 **Bissett** Manitoba Canada
37 K6 **Bissingen** W Germany
117 O6 **Bistcho L** Alberta Canada
46 F1 **Bistretu** Romania
48 K4 **Bistriţa** *R* Romania
48 J3 **Bistriţa** Romania
48 J3 **Bistriţa Năsăud** *reg* Romania
48 K3 **Bistriţei, Muntii** *mt* Romania
71 E5 **Bisucay** *isld* Philippines
31 M1 **Bisztynek** Poland
86 B5 **Bitam** Gabon
36 B4 **Bitburg** W Germany
19 K3 **Bitche** France
80 B8 **Bit'ha** Israel
47 L4 **Bithynia** Turkey
71 B2 **Bitjoli** Halmahera Indonesia
86 C3 **Bitkine** Chad
78 H2 **Bitlis** Turkey
46 E3 **Bitola** Yugoslavia
43 H7 **Bitonto** Italy
42 H5 **Bitovnja** *mt* Yugoslavia
8 B5 **Bittadon** England
103 P2 **Bitter Cr** Utah U.S.A.
101 R8 **Bitter Creek** Wyoming U.S.A.
33 Q9 **Bitterfeld** East Germany
87 C12 **Bitterfontein** S Africa
84 J3 **Bitter L** Egypt
98 J4 **Bitter L** South Dakota U.S.A.
9 E6 **Bitterne** England
144 C6 **Bitterness, Mt** New Zealand
119 M5 **Bittern L** Saskatchewan Canada
118 D5 **Bittern Lake** Alberta Canada
101 L3 **Bitterroot** *R* Montana U.S.A.
100 K2 **Bitterroot Ra** Mont/Idaho U.S.A.
43 C8 **Bitti** Sardinia
33 P8 **Bittkau** East Germany
85 D6 **Bittou** Burkina
71 J4 **Bitung** Sulawesi Indonesia
86 B3 **Biu** Nigeria
48 L3 **Bivolari** Romania
48 K3 **Bivolu** *mt* Romania
59 L4 **Biwa Ko** *L* Japan
110 E4 **Bixby** Missouri U.S.A.
107 P6 **Bixby** Oklahoma U.S.A.
56 C5 **Biya** *R* U.S.S.R.
86 H3 **Bīye K'obē** Ethiopia
56 C4 **Biysk** U.S.S.R.
18 G9 **Bize** France
60 H11 **Bizen** Japan
85 G1 **Bizerte** Tunisia
43 C11 **Bizerte, Lac de** Tunisia
80 B6 **Bizzaron** Israel
28 J6 **Bjæverskov** Denmark
27 H13 **BJärka-Säby** Sweden
26 J3 **Bjarköy** Norway
26 K8 **Bjästa** Sweden
48 E7 **Bjelašnica** *mt* Yugoslavia
27 C13 **Bjelland** Norway
42 F3 **Bjelo-lasica** *mt* Yugoslavia
42 H3 **Bjelovar** Yugoslavia
28 E1 **Bjergby** Denmark
28 G6 **Bjergby** Denmark
28 G5 **Bjerge** Denmark
28 G5 **Bjergsted** Denmark
27 G11 **Björbo** Sweden
27 A10 **Bjordal** Norway
27 B11 **Bjoreia** *R* Norway
26 D9 **Björgan** Norway
27 E12 **Björkelangen** Norway
26 H5 **Björkfjall** *mt* Sweden
26 N6 **Björkfors** Sweden
26 K3 **Björkliden** Sweden
27 J11 **Björklinge** Sweden
27 K12 **Björkö** Sweden
29 J8 **Björköby** Finland
26 J8 **Björksele** Sweden
26 K7 **Björksele** Sweden
26 K8 **Björna** Sweden
27 M10 **Björneborg** Finland
27 G12 **Björneborg** Sweden
115 L2 **Bjorne Pen** Northwest Territories Canada
27 C11 **Bjornesford** *L* Norway
27 J12 **Björnlunda** Sweden
28 E6 **Bjørnø** *isld* Denmark
147 H13 **Bjørnøya** *isld* Arctic Oc
28 C3 **Bjornsholm Å** *R* Denmark
26 H3 **Björnskinn** Norway
28 E5 **Bjørnsknude** *C* Denmark
27 H13 **Björsäter** Sweden
26 J10 **Bjuråker** Sweden
26 K8 **Bjurholm** Sweden
27 H11 **Bjursås** Sweden
27 G12 **Bjurtjärn** Sweden
26 K7 **Bjurträsk** Sweden
85 C6 **Bla** Mali
28 A5 **Blåbjerg** *hill* Denmark
9 E2 **Blaby** England
19 N12 **Blace** France
42 H5 **Blace** Yugoslavia
122 C3 **Blache,L.de la** Quebec Canada
100 B5 **Blachly** Oregon U.S.A.
111 J8 **Black** *R* Alabama U.S.A.
103 P8 **Black** *R* Arizona U.S.A.
110 F5 **Black** *R* Arkansas U.S.A.
111 E10 **Black** *R* Louisiana U.S.A.
94 E3 **Black** *R* Michigan U.S.A.
111 H11 **Black** *R* Mississippi U.S.A.
110 F4 **Black** *R* Missouri U.S.A.
112 J3 **Black** *R* North Carolina U.S.A.
112 H4 **Black** *R* South Carolina U.S.A.
99 Q5 **Black** *R* Wisconsin U.S.A.
116 R3 **Black** *R* Alaska/Yukon Terr U.S.A./Canada
141 H6 **Blackall** Queensland Australia
144 C5 **Blackball** New Zealand
119 P2 **Black Bay** Ontario Canada
100 B8 **Blackbear** California U.S.A.
119 M3 **Black Bear Island L** Saskatchewan Canada
111 H8 **Black Belt** Miss/Ala U.S.A.
8 D2 **Blackbrook** England
141 F4 **Blackbull** Queensland Australia
13 F6 **Blackburn** England
12 E2 **Blackburn** Scotland
116 Q6 **Blackburn,Mt** Alaska U.S.A.
103 K6 **Black Canyon** Nevada U.S.A.
106 C3 **Black Canyon of the Gunnison Nat.Mon** Colorado U.S.A.
146 D5 **Black Coast** Antarctica
103 P6 **Black Creek** Arizona U.S.A.
99 S5 **Black Creek** Wisconsin U.S.A.
118 C8 **Black Diamond** Alberta Canada
100 C2 **Black Diamond** Washington U.S.A.
117 K9 **Black Dome** *mt* British Columbia Canada
121 O7 **Black Donald Mines** Ontario Canada
141 G3 **Blackdown** Queensland Australia
8 C6 **Blackdown Hills** England
99 M2 **Blackduck** Minnesota U.S.A.
101 O2 **Black Eagle** Montana U.S.A.
94 E9 **Blackey** Kentucky U.S.A.
13 F4 **Black Fell** England
118 G5 **Blackfoot** Alberta Canada
101 O6 **Blackfoot** *R* Idaho U.S.A.
101 N6 **Blackfoot** Idaho U.S.A.
101 N1 **Blackfoot** Montana U.S.A.
12 E1 **Blackford** Scotland
118 J2 **Black Hawk** Ontario Canada
14 B3 **Black Head** Ireland
145 F4 **Black Head** New Zealand
123 T5 **Blackhead B** Newfoundland Canada
139 K5 **Blackheath** New South Wales Australia
138 B4 **Black Hill** South Australia Australia
140 A4 **Black Hills** N Terr Australia
98 C5 **Black Hills** South Dakota U.S.A.
119 V7 **Black I** Manitoba Canada
15 D3 **Black I** Scotland
118 D8 **Blackie** Alberta Canada
116 H8 **Black L** Alaska U.S.A.
111 C9 **Black L** Louisiana U.S.A.
94 C1 **Black L** Michigan U.S.A.
95 M2 **Black L** New York U.S.A.
112 J3 **Black L** North Carolina U.S.A.
121 T6 **Black Lake** Quebec Canada
106 E5 **Black Lake** New Mexico U.S.A.
101 N1 **Blackleaf** Montana U.S.A.
127 P6 **Blackman's** Barbados
103 M6 **Black Mesa** *plateau* Arizona U.S.A.
112 E2 **Black Mountain** North Carolina U.S.A.
140 C2 **Black Mt** N Terr Australia
102 G6 **Black Mt** California U.S.A.
106 B8 **Black Mt** New Mexico U.S.A.
122 E6 **Black Mts** Quebec Canada
103 K6 **Black Mts** Arizona U.S.A.
8 C3 **Black Mts** Wales/England
89 A4 **Black Nossob** *R* Namibia
101 M7 **Black Pine Pk** Idaho U.S.A.
117 N10 **Black Pines** British Columbia Canada
106 B9 **Black Pk** New Mexico U.S.A.
117 N10 **Black Pool** British Columbia Canada
13 E6 **Blackpool** England
83 L13 **Black R** Mauritius
143 B6 **Black Ra** Western Australia Australia
106 C8 **Black Range** New Mexico U.S.A.
94 D2 **Black River** Michigan U.S.A.
99 Q5 **Black River Falls** Wisconsin U.S.A.
14 E3 **Blackrock** Ireland
110 E5 **Black Rock** Arkansas U.S.A.
103 M3 **Black Rock** Utah U.S.A.
100 F9 **Black Rock Desert** Nevada U.S.A.
112 F2 **Blacksburg** South Carolina U.S.A.
94 G9 **Blacksburg** Virginia U.S.A.
53 D11 **Black Sea** S E Europe
101 P8 **Blacks Fork** *R* Utah/Wyoming U.S.A.
122 F8 **Blacks Hbr** New Brunswick Canada
112 E6 **Blackshear** Georgia U.S.A.
112 D6 **Blackshear, L** Georgia U.S.A.
14 A2 **Blacksod B** Ireland
106 B8 **Black Springs** New Mexico U.S.A.
27 H14 **Blackstad** Sweden
14 E4 **Blackstairs Mts** Ireland
112 F3 **Blackstock** South Carolina U.S.A.
94 J9 **Blackstone** Virginia U.S.A.
120 B3 **Black Sturgeon L** Ontario Canada
94 G7 **Blacksville** West Virginia U.S.A.
94 H6 **Blackuck** Pennsylvania U.S.A.
122 G7 **Blackville** New Brunswick Canada
112 F4 **Blackville** South Carolina U.S.A.
141 J6 **Blackwater** Queensland Australia
141 G7 **Blackwater** *R* Queensland Australia
14 E4 **Blackwater** Ireland
14 E3 **Blackwater** *R* Ireland
113 C12 **Blackwater** *R* Florida U.S.A.
110 D3 **Blackwater** Missouri U.S.A.
110 C3 **Blackwater** *R* Missouri U.S.A.
12 C3 **Blackwaterfoot** Scotland
117 M3 **Blackwater L** Northwest Territories Canada
9 G4 **Blackwater,R** England
15 D4 **Blackwater Reservoir** Scotland
107 N5 **Blackwell** Oklahoma U.S.A.
108 G3 **Blackwell** Texas U.S.A.
107 M3 **Black Wolf** Kansas U.S.A.
98 E9 **Blackwood Cr** Nebraska U.S.A.
143 B10 **Blackwood, R** Western Australia Australia
112 F6 **Bladen** Georgia U.S.A.
98 H9 **Bladen** Nebraska U.S.A.
112 J3 **Bladenboro** North Carolina U.S.A.
118 L7 **Bladworth** Saskatchewan Canada
8 C2 **Blaenau-Ffestiniog** Wales
8 C4 **Blaenavon** Wales
8 B3 **Blaenporth** Wales
8 C4 **Blaen Rhondda** Wales
28 C3 **Blære** Denmark
8 C6 **Blagdon** England
18 F9 **Blagnac** France
53 F10 **Blagodarnyy** U.S.S.R.
46 F2 **Blagoevgrad** Bulgaria
57 G3 **Blagoveshchenka** U.S.S.R.
59 J1 **Blagoveshchensk** U.S.S.R.
55 C3 **Blagoveshchensk** Bashkirskaya A.S.S.R. U.S.S.R.
52 G3 **Blagoyevo** U.S.S.R.
28 B5 **Blåhøj** Denmark
20 G7 **Blain** France
94 K6 **Blain** Pennsylvania U.S.A.
107 O2 **Blaine** Kansas U.S.A.
117 M11 **Blaine** Washington U.S.A.
94 H7 **Blaine** West Virginia U.S.A.
118 L6 **Blaine Lake** Saskatchewan Canada
20 G3 **Blainville** France
98 K8 **Blair** Nebraska U.S.A.
107 L7 **Blair** Oklahoma U.S.A.
94 F9 **Blair** West Virginia U.S.A.
99 P5 **Blair** Wisconsin U.S.A.
141 H6 **Blair Athol** Queensland Australia
15 E4 **Blair Atholl** Scotland
15 E4 **Blairgowrie** Scotland
102 G3 **Blair Junction** Nevada U.S.A.
12 D1 **Blairmore** Scotland
102 D2 **Blairsden** California U.S.A.
112 D3 **Blairsville** Georgia U.S.A.
94 H6 **Blairsville** Pennsylvania U.S.A.
21 N4 **Blaise** *R* Eure France
48 H4 **Blaj** Romania
112 C6 **Blakely** Georgia U.S.A.
9 H2 **Blakeney** England
99 S1 **Blake Pt** Michigan U.S.A.
99 O9 **Blakesburg** Iowa U.S.A.
26 K2 **Blåmannen** *mt* Norway
26 H4 **Blåmannsisen** *mt* Norway
36 B6 **Blâmont** France
43 C11 **Blanc** *C* Tunisia
131 E7 **Blanca,B** Argentina
106 G7 **Blanca Cr** New Mex/Tex U.S.A.
131 D7 **Blanca Grande,L** Argentina
133 C8 **Blanca,L** Chile
106 E4 **Blanca Pk** Colorado U.S.A.
106 E8 **Blanca, Sa** *mt* New Mexico U.S.A.
100 J1 **Blanchard** Idaho U.S.A.
94 B3 **Blanchard** Michigan U.S.A.
98 J2 **Blanchard** North Dakota U.S.A.
107 N6 **Blanchard** Oklahoma U.S.A.
120 E2 **Blanche** Ontario Canada
121 P7 **Blanche** Quebec Canada
138 C5 **Blanche,C** South Australia Australia
138 F3 **Blanche,L** South Australia Australia
142 E5 **Blanche, L** Western Australia Australia
94 D7 **Blanchester** Ohio U.S.A.
138 E5 **Blanchetown** South Australia Australia
127 O1 **Blanchisseuse** Trinidad
13 F4 **Blanchland** England
21 N8 **Blanc,Le** France
128 F7 **Blanco** *R* Bolivia
128 D5 **Blanco** *R* Peru
106 C5 **Blanco** New Mexico U.S.A.
109 J5 **Blanco** Texas U.S.A.
128 B4 **Blanco,C** Peru
100 A7 **Blanco,C** Oregon U.S.A.
123 P2 **Blanc-Sablon** Quebec Canada
94 F9 **Bland** Virginia U.S.A.
28 S9 **Blanda** *R* Iceland
8 D6 **Blandford** England
103 P4 **Blanding** Utah U.S.A.
99 Q9 **Blandinsville** Illinois U.S.A.
17 J3 **Blanes** Spain
112 G3 **Blaney** South Carolina U.S.A.
99 V3 **Blaney Park** Michigan U.S.A.
69 C11 **Blangkejeren** Sumatra
69 C11 **Blangpidie** Sumatra
21 L3 **Blangy-le-Château** France
21 O2 **Blangy-sur-Bresle** France
22 C3 **Blangy-sur-Ternoise** France
30 H6 **Blanice** *R* Czechoslovakia
33 P5 **Blankenberg** East Germany
22 E1 **Blankenberge** Belgium
33 N9 **Blankenburg** East Germany
37 L2 **Blankenhain** Erfurt East Germany
37 N2 **Blankenhain** Karl-Marx-Stadt East Germany
33 O9 **Blankenheim** East Germany
36 B3 **Blankenheim** W Germany
36 C3 **Blankenrath** W Germany
33 S6 **Blankensee** East Germany
109 J4 **Blanket** Texas U.S.A.
9 F1 **Blankney** England
31 K6 **Blansko** Czechoslovakia
87 G9 **Blantyre** Malawi
12 D2 **Blantyre** Scotland
22 F3 **Blaregnies** Belgium
94 J4 **Blasdell** New York U.S.A.
26 G7 **Båsjön** *L* Sweden
31 L4 **Błaszki** Poland
37 P3 **Blatno** Czechoslovakia
22 F3 **Blaton** Belgium
26 J6 **Blattnicksele** Sweden
71 H4 **Blau** Sulawesi Indonesia
36 H7 **Blaubeuren** W Germany
36 H5 **Blaufelden** W Germany
32 J4 **Blauort** *isld* W Germany
20 D5 **Blavet** *R* France
13 H6 **Blaxton** England
13 G4 **Blaydon** England
18 E7 **Blaye** France
142 C5 **Blaze,Mt** Western Australia Australia
140 B2 **Blaze Pt** N Terr Australia
31 N6 **Błazowa** Poland
33 N6 **Bleckede** W Germany
42 F2 **Bled** Yugoslavia
8 C3 **Bleddfa** Wales
31 J3 **Bledzew** Poland
27 D12 **Blefjell** *mt* Norway
22 E3 **Bleharies** Belgium
36 B3 **Bleialf** W Germany
38 L8 **Bleiburg** Austria
33 N10 **Bleicherode** East Germany
37 M3 **Bleilochsperre** *res* East Germany
27 H15 **Blekinge** *reg* Sweden
99 L8 **Blencoe** Iowa U.S.A.
120 J10 **Blenheim** Ontario Canada
145 D4 **Blenheim** New Zealand
21 M7 **Bléré** France
25 F6 **Blerick** Netherlands
19 J4 **Blesmes** France
109 L7 **Blessing** Texas U.S.A.
14 E3 **Blessington** Ireland
9 E4 **Bletchingdon** England
9 F3 **Bletchley** England
40 B4 **Bletterans** France
121 M6 **Bleu,L** Quebec Canada
111 C8 **Blevins** Arkansas U.S.A.
21 N4 **Blévy** France
119 O9 **Blewett** Saskatchewan Canada
108 G6 **Blewett** Texas U.S.A.
112 H2 **Blewett Falls L** North Carolina U.S.A.
32 J5 **Blexen** W Germany
85 E1 **Blida** Algeria
80 F1 **Blida** Lebanon
27 K12 **Blidö** Sweden
27 F14 **Blidsberg** Sweden
36 C5 **Blies** *R* W Germany
36 C5 **Blieskastel** W Germany
116 O6 **Bligh I** Alaska U.S.A.
38 L5 **Blindenmarkt** Austria
33 T6 **Blindow** East Germany
120 G6 **Blind River** Ontario Canada
46 D3 **Blinisht** Albania
138 E4 **Blinman** South Australia Australia
101 L7 **Bliss** Idaho U.S.A.
94 D5 **Blissfield** Michigan U.S.A.
9 F3 **Blisworth** England
70 O10 **Blitar** Java
85 E7 **Blitta** Togo
100 F7 **Blitzen** Oregon U.S.A.
37 O5 **Blížejov** Czechoslovakia
54 H8 **Bliznyuki** U.S.S.R.
95 Q5 **Block I** Rhode I U.S.A.
117 L10 **Bloedel** British Columbia Canada
25 C4 **Bloemendaal** Netherlands
89 E7 **Bloemfontein** S Africa
87 E11 **Bloemhof** S Africa
21 N6 **Blois** France
28 D2 **Blokhus** Denmark
25 E3 **Blokzijl** Netherlands
32 K9 **Blomberg** W Germany
99 L5 **Blomkest** Minnesota U.S.A.
70 Q10 **Blongas** Indonesia
31 M3 **Błonie** Poland
33 R9 **Blönsdorf** East Germany
21 L3 **Blonville** France
140 A6 **Bloods Ra** N Terr Australia
95 L8 **Bloodsworth I** Maryland U.S.A.
14 C1 **Bloody Foreland** Ireland
106 G4 **Bloom** Colorado U.S.A.
99 P4 **Bloomer** Wisconsin U.S.A.
121 N9 **Bloomfield** Ontario Canada
110 K2 **Bloomfield** Indiana U.S.A.
110 D1 **Bloomfield** Iowa U.S.A.
94 B9 **Bloomfield** Kentucky U.S.A.
110 G5 **Bloomfield** Missouri U.S.A.
98 B2 **Bloomfield** Montana U.S.A.
98 J7 **Bloomfield** Nebraska U.S.A.
106 C5 **Bloomfield** New Mexico U.S.A.
95 Q2 **Bloomfield** Vermont U.S.A.
141 H3 **Bloomfield River** Queensland Australia
109 L3 **Blooming Grove** Texas U.S.A.
99 N6 **Blooming Prairie** Minnesota U.S.A.
101 O7 **Bloomington** Idaho U.S.A.
99 S9 **Bloomington** Illinois U.S.A.
110 K2 **Bloomington** Indiana U.S.A.
99 N5 **Bloomington** Minnesota U.S.A.
109 L7 **Bloomington** Texas U.S.A.
99 Q7 **Bloomington** Wisconsin U.S.A.
95 L5 **Bloomsburg** Pennsylvania U.S.A.
141 J5 **Bloomsbury** Queensland Australia
110 F3 **Bloomsdale** Missouri U.S.A.
95 N4 **Bloomville** New York U.S.A.
94 D5 **Bloomville** Ohio U.S.A.
70 N9 **Blora** Java
37 K6 **Blosenau** W Germany
95 K5 **Blossburg** Pennsylvania U.S.A.
115 R4 **Blosseville Kyst** *coast* Greenland
109 M2 **Blossom** Texas U.S.A.
51 R2 **Blossom, Mys** *C* U.S.S.R.
111 L11 **Blountstown** Florida U.S.A.
126 F6 **Blower Rock** Caribbean
112 F1 **Blowing Rock** North Carolina U.S.A.
9 E3 **Bloxham** England
95 M9 **Bloxom** Virginia U.S.A.
13 G6 **Blubberhouses** England
41 L3 **Bludenz** Austria
103 P8 **Blue** *R* Arizona U.S.A.
106 D2 **Blue** *R* Colorado U.S.A.
107 O7 **Blue** *R* Oklahoma U.S.A.
103 N3 **Blue Bell Knoll** *pk* Utah U.S.A.
117 N7 **Blueberry** *R* British Columbia Canada
144 C6 **Blue Cliffs** New Zealand
101 N8 **Blue Creek** Utah U.S.A.
113 G10 **Blue Cypress L** Florida U.S.A.
94 D9 **Blue Diamond** Kentucky U.S.A.
99 M6 **Blue Earth** *R* Minnesota U.S.A.
99 M6 **Blue Earth** Minnesota U.S.A.
110 C5 **Blue Eye** Missouri U.S.A.
94 F9 **Bluefield** W Virginia/Virginia U.S.A.
125 N3 **Bluefields** Nicaragua
110 M3 **Bluegrass Reg** Kentucky U.S.A.
95 T2 **Blue Hill** Maine U.S.A.
98 H9 **Blue Hill** Nebraska U.S.A.
127 H4 **Blue Hills** Turks & Caicos Is
123 O6 **Blue Hills of Couteau** Newfoundland Canada
100 F7 **Bluejoint L** Oregon U.S.A.
94 J6 **Blue Knob** *mt* Pennsylvania U.S.A.
100 B9 **Blue Lake** California U.S.A.
94 K7 **Bluemont** Virginia U.S.A.
110 G2 **Blue Mound** Illinois U.S.A.
106 B1 **Blue Mountain** Colorado U.S.A.
110 G7 **Blue Mountain** Mississippi U.S.A.
110 B7 **Blue Mt** Arkansas U.S.A.
94 K6 **Blue Mt** Pennsylvania U.S.A.
95 L6 **Blue Mt** Pennsylvania U.S.A.
110 C6 **Blue Mt,L** Arkansas U.S.A.
95 N3 **Blue Mt. Lake** New York U.S.A.
100 H7 **Blue Mt. Pass** Oregon U.S.A.
127 M2 **Blue Mt.Pk** Jamaica
144 B6 **Blue Mts** New Zealand
100 G5 **Blue Mts** Oregon/Wash U.S.A.
139 J5 **Blue Mts Nat Park** New South Wales Australia
127 L2 **Blue Mts, The** Jamaica
140 D2 **Blue Mud B** N Terr Australia
Blue Nile *R see* **Bahr el Azraq**
86 F3 **Blue Nile** *prov* Sudan
114 H4 **Bluenose L** Northwest Territories Canada
117 J6 **Blue R** British Columbia Canada
107 O2 **Blue Rapids** Kansas U.S.A.
118 B4 **Blue Ridge** Alberta Canada
112 C3 **Blue Ridge** Georgia U.S.A.
94 G10 **Blue Ridge** *mts* Virginia U.S.A.
112 C3 **Blue Ridge L** Georgia U.S.A.
117 O9 **Blue River** British Columbia Canada
100 C5 **Blue River** Oregon U.S.A.
121 O6 **Blue Sea Lake** Quebec Canada
14 C2 **Blue Stack Mt** Ireland
106 C6 **Bluewater** New Mexico U.S.A.
144 B7 **Bluff** New Zealand
103 P4 **Bluff** Utah U.S.A.
107 N4 **Bluff City** Kansas U.S.A.
112 E1 **Bluff City** Tennessee U.S.A.
109 J3 **Bluffdale** Texas U.S.A.
141 H4 **Bluff Downs** Queensland Australia
142 F3 **Bluff Face Ra** Western Australia Australia
143 C10 **Bluff Knoll** *mt* Western Australia Australia
143 A8 **Bluff Pt** Western Australia Australia
71 D6 **Bluff Pt** Palawan Philippines
110 F2 **Bluffs** Illinois U.S.A.
126 F2 **Bluff, The** Eleuthera Bahamas
118 C6 **Bluffton** Alberta Canada
110 C7 **Bluffton** Arkansas U.S.A.
112 C6 **Bluffton** Georgia U.S.A.
94 B6 **Bluffton** Indiana U.S.A.
99 L3 **Bluffton** Minnesota U.S.A.
94 D6 **Bluffton** Ohio U.S.A.
112 G5 **Bluffton** South Carolina U.S.A.
109 K3 **Blum** Texas U.S.A.
130 E10 **Blumenau** Brazil
33 O8 **Blumenberg** East Germany
33 T5 **Blumenhagen** East Germany
118 K8 **Blumenhof** Saskatchewan Canada
32 J6 **Blumenthal** W Germany
36 B3 **Blumenthal** W Germany
40 G4 **Blümlisalp** *mt* Switzerland
98 G5 **Blunt** South Dakota U.S.A.
100 D7 **Bly** Oregon U.S.A.
89 C9 **Blyde Berg** *mt* S Africa
116 N7 **Blying Sound** Alaska U.S.A.
140 C1 **Blyth** *R* N Terr Australia
120 J9 **Blyth** Ontario Canada
13 G3 **Blyth** England
13 E2 **Blyth Br** Scotland
9 H3 **Blythburgh** England
110 C1 **Blythedale** Missouri U.S.A.
138 A2 **Blythe Ra** Western Australia Australia
110 G6 **Blytheville** Arkansas U.S.A.
138 A2 **Blyth Ra** South Australia Australia
13 H6 **Blyton** England
55 G3 **Blyudtsy** U.S.S.R.
26 G3 **Bø** Norway
27 D12 **Bø** Norway
85 B7 **Bo** Sierra Leone
27 H13 **Bo** Sweden
71 E4 **Boac** *isld* Philippines
125 M3 **Boaco** Nicaragua
130 F7 **Bôa Esperança** Brazil
67 B5 **Bo'ai** China
65 B7 **Bo'ai** China
120 K7 **Boakview** Ontario Canada
86 C4 **Boali** Cent Afr Republic
67 D7 **Bo'ao** China
79 F5 **Boaqline** Lebanon
45 L1 **Boara Polesine** Italy
94 B2 **Boardman** *R* Michigan U.S.A.
141 H7 **Boatman** Queensland Australia
15 E3 **Boat of Garten** Scotland
128 F3 **Boa Vista** Brazil
71 D5 **Boayan** *isld* Palawan Philippines
111 K7 **Boaz** Alabama U.S.A.
68 J1 **Bobai** China
87 H10 **Bobaomby, Tanjona** *C* Madagascar
75 K9 **Bobbili** India
44 F2 **Bobbio** Italy
121 M8 **Bobcaygeon** Ontario Canada
36 E4 **Bobenheim-Roxheim** W Germany
37 K7 **Bobingen** W Germany
33 O5 **Bobitz** East Germany
36 F6 **Böblingen** W Germany
85 D6 **Bobo Dioulasso** Burkina
31 K2 **Bobolice** Poland
71 G4 **Bobon** Philippines
128 C4 **Bobonaza** Ecuador
46 F2 **Boboshevo** Bulgaria
46 F2 **Bobov Dol** Bulgaria
31 J4 **Bóbr** *R* Poland
54 D8 **Bobrinets** U.S.S.R.
48 J1 **Bobrka** U.S.S.R.
54 M5 **Bobrov** U.S.S.R.
54 C6 **Bobrovitsa** U.S.S.R.
31 H4 **Bobrowice** Poland
94 H7 **Bobtown** Pennsylvania U.S.A.
113 F13 **Boca Chica** *isld* Florida U.S.A.
109 K10 **Boca Chica** Texas U.S.A.
127 M10 **Boca del Pao** Venezuela
128 E5 **Bôca do Acre** Brazil
128 E5 **Bôca do Curuquetê** Brazil
129 H4 **Bôca do Jari** Brazil
128 E5 **Bôca do Moaca** Brazil
21 J6 **Bocages** *reg* France
127 N1 **Boca Grande** *chan* Trinidad/Ven
113 E11 **Boca Grande** Florida U.S.A.
113 F13 **Boca Grande Key** *isld* Florida U.S.A.
129 K7 **Bocaiúva** Brazil
130 E9 **Bocaiúva do Sul** Brazil
130 C8 **Bocajá** Brazil
113 G11 **Boca Raton** Florida U.S.A.
127 N1 **Bocas del Dragon** *chan* Trinidad
125 M2 **Bocay** Nicaragua
45 M2 **Bocche del Po Della Pila** Italy
45 M2 **Bocche del Po Delle Tolle** Italy
45 M2 **Bocche del Po di Goro e di Gnocca** Italy
16 E3 **Boceguillas** Spain
19 P16 **Bochaine** *reg* France
121 R3 **Bochart** Quebec Canada
31 M6 **Bochnia** Poland
22 K1 **Bocholt** Belgium
32 E9 **Bocholt** W Germany
37 P3 **Bochov** Czechoslovakia
32 F10 **Bochum** W Germany
37 O3 **Bockau** East Germany
32 M8 **Bockenem** W Germany
32 H6 **Bockhorn** W Germany
31 O3 **Boćki** Poland
38 H7 **Böckstein** Austria
33 T10 **Bockwitz** East Germany
87 B8 **Bocoio** Angola
127 J10 **Boconó** Venezuela
124 F4 **Bocoyna** Mexico
48 G5 **Bocşa** Romania
86 C5 **Boda** Cent Afr Republic
27 J14 **Böda** Sweden
27 H10 **Boda** Sweden
27 G14 **Bodafors** Sweden
143 C9 **Bodallin** Western Australia Australia
51 L3 **Bodaybo** U.S.S.R.
15 G3 **Boddam** Scotland
99 M7 **Bode** Iowa U.S.A.
102 A3 **Bodega Head** California U.S.A.
86 C2 **Bodele** *dist* Chad
36 F7 **Bodelhausen** W Germany
26 M6 **Boden** Sweden
32 L8 **Bodenburg** W Germany
36 E4 **Bodenheim** W Germany
37 J3 **Bodenlaube** W Germany
37 P5 **Bodenmais** W Germany
41 K2 **Bodensee** *L* Switzerland
33 N7 **Bodenteich** W Germany
32 L9 **Bodenwerder** W Germany
38 L6 **Bodenwies** *mt* Austria
37 N5 **Bodenwöhr** W Germany
14 C3 **Boderg,L** Ireland
102 F6 **Bodfish** California U.S.A.
74 G9 **Bodhan** India
75 L6 **Bodh Gaya** India
36 G5 **Bödigheim** W Germany
20 B4 **Bodilis** France
76 C5 **Bodinayakkanur** India
8 B7 **Bodinnick** England
70 O9 **Bodjonegoro** Java
8 B7 **Bodmin** England
8 B6 **Bodmin Moor** England
118 G6 **Bodo** Alberta Canada
26 G4 **Bodö** Norway
25 C4 **Bodograven** Netherlands
130 C6 **Bodoquena** Brazil
78 A3 **Bodrum** Turkey
26 G9 **Bodsjö** Sweden
68 H7 **Bo Duc** Vietnam
48 F2 **Bodva** *R* Hungary
31 M3 **Bodzanów** Poland
40 D5 **Boëge** France
25 G4 **Boekelo** Netherlands
22 F1 **Boekhoute** Belgium
98 H8 **Boelus** Nebraska U.S.A.
18 H7 **Boën** France
86 D6 **Boende** Zaire
68 G6 **Boeng Lovea** Cambodia
68 G6 **Boeng Me Alpa** Cambodia
70 G7 **Bo Epinang** Sulawesi Indonesia
109 J6 **Boerne** Texas U.S.A.
25 H2 **Boertange** Netherlands
28 G6 **Boeslunde** Denmark
111 E8 **Boeuf** *R* Arkansas U.S.A.
85 B6 **Boffa** Guinea
14 D3 **Bofin,L** Ireland
68 B4 **Bogale** Burma
68 B5 **Bogale** *R* Burma
111 F11 **Bogalusa** Louisiana U.S.A.
85 D6 **Bogande** Burkina
86 C4 **Bogangolo** Cent Afr Republic
141 H6 **Bogantungan** Queensland Australia
17 F6 **Bogarra** Spain
118 B8 **Bogart,Mt** Alberta Canada
109 M2 **Bogata** Texas U.S.A.
53 H7 **Bogatoye** U.S.S.R.
31 H5 **Bogatynia** Poland
86 C5 **Bogbonga** Zaire
55 D3 **Bogdanovich** U.S.S.R.
66 D3 **Bogda Shan** *mts* China
27 K14 **Boge** *isld* Gotland Sweden
55 F4 **Bogembay** U.S.S.R.
37 O6 **Bogen** W Germany
87 C11 **Bogenfels** Namibia
28 E5 **Bogense** Denmark
14 C4 **Boggeragh Mts** Ireland
143 C6 **Boggola** *mt* Western Australia Australia
26 H8 **Boggsjö** Sweden
85 B5 **Boghé** Mauritania
141 J5 **Bogie** *R* Queensland Australia
9 F6 **Bognor Regis** England
22 H4 **Bogny-sur-Meuse** France
28 J7 **Bogø** Denmark
71 F5 **Bogo** Cebu Philippines
54 G6 **Bogodukhov** U.S.S.R.
70 L9 **Bogor** Java
48 J2 **Bogorodchany** U.S.S.R.
59 M1 **Bogorodskoy** U.S.S.R.
128 D3 **Bogotá** Colombia
111 A8 **Bogota** Texas U.S.A.
56 C3 **Bogotol** U.S.S.R.
56 F5 **Bogotol** U.S.S.R.
75 N6 **Bogra** Bangladesh
27 L12 **Bogskär** *lighthouse* Finland
56 E2 **Boguchany** U.S.S.R.
54 M7 **Boguchar** U.S.S.R.
107 L2 **Bogue** Kansas U.S.A.
111 F10 **Bogue Chitto** Mississippi U.S.A.
112 K3 **Bogue Inlet** North Carolina U.S.A.
54 B2 **Bogushevsk** U.S.S.R.
54 B7 **Boguslav** U.S.S.R.
31 J5 **Boguszów** Poland
127 L2 **Bog Walk** Jamaica
70 D4 **Boh** *R* Kalimantan
65 D5 **Bo Hai** *G* China
22 E4 **Bohain** France
65 D5 **Bohai Wan** *B* China
119 M8 **Boharm** Saskatchewan Canada
38 N5 **Böheimkirchen** Austria
30 H6 **Bohemia** *old region* Czechoslovakia
142 F4 **Bohemia Downs** Western Australia Australia
85 E7 **Bohicon** Benin
42 F2 **Bohiniska Bistrica** Yugoslavia
37 N1 **Böhlen** W Germany
32 K7 **Böhme** W Germany
37 N4 **Böhmer Wald** *mts* W Germany
32 H8 **Bohmte** W Germany
33 Q7 **Böhne** East Germany
71 G6 **Bohol** *isld* Philippines
71 F6 **Bohol Str** Philippines
16 D5 **Bohonal de Ibor** Spain
48 D4 **Böhönye** Hungary
80 B8 **Bohu** Israel
128 F4 **Boiaçu** Brazil
43 F7 **Boiano** Italy
122 F7 **Boiestown** New Brunswick Canada
21 P5 **Boigneville** France
122 B5 **Boileau** Quebec Canada
130 C9 **Boi Preto,Serra de** *mts* Brazil
130 F8 **Boi, Pta. do** *C* Brazil
129 J7 **Bois** *R* Brazil
94 C1 **Bois Blanc I** Michigan U.S.A.
123 M7 **Boisdale** C Breton I, Nova Scotia
40 D4 **Bois d' Amont** France
20 G8 **Bois-de-Cené** France
18 H5 **Bois du Roi** *mt* France
100 J6 **Boise** Idaho U.S.A.
106 H5 **Boise City** Oklahoma U.S.A.
20 F5 **Boisgervilly** France
21 N3 **Bois Guillaume** France
114 G4 **Bois, Lac Des** *L* Northwest Territories Canada
Bois-le-Duc *see* **'s-Hertogenbosch**
21 K8 **Boismé** France
18 H7 **Bois Noirs** *hills* France
22 H1 **Boisschot** Belgium
119 R9 **Boissevain** Manitoba Canada
21 M4 **Boissy-les-Perche** France
21 M5 **Boissy-Maugis** France
38 F9 **Boite** *R* Italy
130 F8 **Boituva** Brazil
33 T6 **Boitzenburg** East Germany
33 N6 **Boize** *R* East Germany
33 N6 **Boizenburg** East Germany
46 C3 **Bojana** *R* Albania
28 E6 **Bøjden** Denmark
71 E1 **Bojeador,C** Luzon Philippines
77 E1 **Bojnūrd** Iran
69 D13 **Bojo** *isld* Indonesia
70 K9 **Bojong** Java
48 F5 **Boka** Yugoslavia
42 J6 **Boka Kotorska** *B* Yugoslavia
85 F7 **Bokani** Nigeria
70 G4 **Bokat** Sulawesi
85 B6 **Boké** Guinea
113 E11 **Bokeelia** Florida U.S.A.
32 J6 **Bokel** W Germany
32 K8 **Bokeloh** W Germany
56 F4 **Bokhan** U.S.S.R.
68 H6 **Bo Kheo** Cambodia
89 A8 **Bokkeveld Berg** *mt* S Africa
27 A12 **Boknfjorden** *inlet* Norway
56 B6 **Boko** Kazakhskaya S.S.R. U.S.S.R.
57 H4 **Bokonbayevskoye** U.S.S.R.
86 C3 **Bokoro** Chad
107 Q6 **Bokoshe** Oklahoma U.S.A.
86 D6 **Bokote** Zaire
59 H2 **Bo-ko-tu** China
68 D7 **Bokpyin** Burma
86 D6 **Bokungu** Zaire
68 C5 **Bok Ye-gan** *isld* Burma
70 G5 **Bolaäng** Sulawesi Indonesia
86 D6 **Bolaiti** Zaire
85 A6 **Bolama** Guinea-Bissau
124 H7 **Bolaños** Mexico
67 C5 **Bolao** China
21 L2 **Bolbec** France
55 E2 **Bolchary** U.S.S.R.
99 M9 **Bolckow** Missouri U.S.A.
48 E4 **Bölcske** Hungary
33 T5 **Boldekow** East Germany
28 C6 **Bolderslev** Denmark
48 K5 **Boldeşti-Scăeni** Romania
66 C3 **Bole** China
85 D7 **Bole** Ghana
101 N2 **Bole** Montana U.S.A.
48 H1 **Bolekhov** U.S.S.R.
86 D6 **Boleko** Zaire
100 J4 **Boles** Idaho U.S.A.
31 J4 **Bolesławiec** Poland
107 O6 **Boley** Oklahoma U.S.A.
85 D6 **Bolgatanga** Ghana
121 O4 **Bolger** Quebec Canada
48 M5 **Bolgrad** U.S.S.R.
59 K2 **Boli** China
86 C6 **Bolia** Zaire
26 L7 **Boliden** Sweden
111 H9 **Boligee** Alabama U.S.A.
71 D2 **Bolinao,C** Luzon Philippines
48 K6 **Bolintin Vale** Romania
71 H4 **Boliohutu,Gunung** *mt* Sulawesi Indonesia
131 E6 **Bolivár** Argentina
128 C3 **Bolivar** Colombia
128 D2 **Bolivar** *div* Colombia
128 C4 **Bolivar** *prov* Ecuador
110 C4 **Bolivar** Missouri U.S.A.
94 J4 **Bolivar** New York U.S.A.
110 H6 **Bolivar** Tennessee U.S.A.
128 E2 **Bolivar** *state* Venezuela
128 F2 **Bolivar,Cerro** *mt* Venezuela
109 N6 **Bolivar Pen** Texas U.S.A.
127 J10 **Bolivar, Pico** *mt* Venezuela
128 E7 **Bolivia** *rep* S America
112 J3 **Bolivia** North Carolina U.S.A.
46 E1 **Boljevac** Yugoslavia
78 E3 **Bolkar Dağları** *mts* Turkey
27 D12 **Bolkesjö** Norway
120 G4 **Bolkow** Ontario Canada
31 J5 **Bolków** Poland
41 H2 **Boll** W Germany
36 H6 **Boll** W Germany
27 F14 **Bollebygd** Sweden
45 K4 **Bolle,Le** Italy
36 B4 **Bollendorf** W Germany
19 N16 **Bollène** France
40 G4 **Bolligen** Switzerland
28 B5 **Bølling** Denmark
8 D1 **Bollington** England
27 H10 **Bollnäs** Sweden
141 H8 **Bollon** Queensland Australia
27 G15 **Bolmen** *L* Sweden
9 F6 **Bolney** England
71 F5 **Bolo** Panay Philippines
86 C6 **Bolobo** Zaire
71 E7 **Bolod Islands** Philippines
42 D4 **Bologna** Italy
19 J4 **Bologne** France
52 D6 **Bologovo** U.S.S.R.
54 J2 **Bolokhovo** U.S.S.R.
86 C5 **Bolomba** Zaire
86 D6 **Bolombo** Zaire
59 L2 **Bolon'** U.S.S.R.
125 P7 **Bolonchén de Rejón** Mexico
71 F7 **Bolong** Mindanao Philippines
59 L2 **Bolon,Oz** *L* U.S.S.R.
71 F1 **Bolos Pt** Luzon Philippines
43 B8 **Bolotana** Sardinia
56 B3 **Bolotnoye** U.S.S.R.
68 H5 **Bolovens, Plateau des** Laos
131 C2 **Bolsa,Cerro** *pk* Argentina
42 D6 **Bolsena,L.di** Italy
31 N1 **Bol'shakovo** U.S.S.R.
54 F9 **Bolshaya Belozerka** U.S.S.R.
55 F3 **Bol'shaya Tava** *R* U.S.S.R.
52 F3 **Bol'shaya Tavra** U.S.S.R.
56 G1 **Bol'shaya Yerema** *R* U.S.S.R.
55 F3 **Bol'sherech'ye** U.S.S.R.
51 P3 **Bol'sheretsk** U.S.S.R.
55 C3 **Bolshe-ustikinskoye** U.S.S.R.
54 B4 **Bol'shevik** U.S.S.R.
51 K1 **Bol'shevik, Ostrov** *isld* U.S.S.R.
55 F3 **Bolshiye Uki** U.S.S.R.
56 B1 **Bolshoi Megtyg'yegan** *R* U.S.S.R.
48 J1 **Bol'shovtsy** U.S.S.R.
55 E1 **Bol'shoy Atlym** U.S.S.R.
55 F1 **Bol'shoy Balyk** *R* U.S.S.R.
147 P10 **Bol'shoy Begichev,Os** *isld* U.S.S.R.
56 H2 **Bol'shoy Chuya** *R* U.S.S.R.
55 E3 **Bol'shoye Sorokino** U.S.S.R.
55 G4 **Bol'shoye Topol'noye, Oz** *L* U.S.S.R.
55 G4 **Bol'shoye Yaravoye, Oz** *L* U.S.S.R.
55 E1 **Bol'shoy Kamen'** U.S.S.R.
55 F2 **Bol'shoy Kun'yak** U.S.S.R.
55 D3 **Bol'shoy Kuyash** U.S.S.R.
51 O1 **Bolshoy Lyakhovskiy,Ostrov** *isld* U.S.S.R.
56 D2 **Bol'shoy Pit** *R* U.S.S.R.
55 F1 **Bolshoy Salym** *R* U.S.S.R.
59 L1 **Bol'shoy Shantar,Oz** *isld* U.S.S.R.
55 E1 **Bol'shoy Tap** *R* U.S.S.R.
52 C5 **Bol'shoy Tyuters, Os.** *isld* U.S.S.R.

Bol'shoy Uvat, Oz — Bray-sur-Somme 13

55 F3 **Bol'shoy Uvat, Oz** *L* U.S.S.R.
56 D5 **Bolshoy Yenisey** *R* U.S.S.R.
48 N3 **Bol'shoyy Kuyal'nik** *R* U.S.S.R.
55 F2 **Bol'shoy Yugan** *R* U.S.S.R.
124 G4 **Bolsón de Mapimí** *desert* Mexico
25 E2 **Bolsward** Netherlands
17 H2 **Boltaña** Spain
8 C7 **Bolt Head** England
121 L9 **Bolton** Ontario Canada
13 F6 **Bolton** England
112 J3 **Bolton** North Carolina U.S.A.
13 G6 **Bolton Br** England
119 W4 **Bolton L** Manitoba Canada
13 F5 **Bolton le-Sands** England
78 C1 **Bolu** Turkey
66 E4 **Boluntay** China
14 A5 **Bolus Hd** Ireland
54 F3 **Bolva** *R* U.S.S.R.
78 C2 **Bolvadin** Turkey
47 L6 **Bolvadin** Turkey
8 B6 **Bolventor** England
48 E5 **Bóly** Hungary
47 H2 **Bolyarovo** Bulgaria
42 D2 **Bolzano** Italy
86 B7 **Boma** Zaire
22 K3 **Bomal** Luxembourg/Belgium
86 B5 **Bomandjokou** Congo
109 H2 **Bomarton** Texas U.S.A.
86 C5 **Bomassa** Congo
74 E9 **Bombay** India
145 E2 **Bombay** New Zealand
87 H11 **Bombetoka,B.de** Madagascar
86 F5 **Bombo** Uganda
86 C5 **Bomboma** Zaire
130 H10 **Bom Conselho** Brazil
129 J7 **Bom Despacho** Brazil
66 E6 **Bomi** China
85 B7 **Bomi Hills** Liberia
130 J9 **Bom Jardim** Brazil
130 D5 **Bom Jardim de Goiás** Brazil
128 E5 **Bom Jardin** Brazil
129 K5 **Bom Jesus** Brazil
129 K5 **Bom Jesus da Gurgueia, Serra** *mts* Brazil
129 K6 **Bom Jesus da Lapa** Brazil
130 H7 **Bom Jesus do Itabapoana** Brazil
130 H7 **Bom Jesus do Norte** Brazil
27 A12 **Bömlafjorden** *inlet* Norway
27 A12 **Bömlo** Norway
86 E5 **Bomokandi** *R* Zaire
86 C5 **Bomongo** Zaire
143 B7 **Bompas Hill** Western Australia Australia
130 E10 **Bom Retiro** Brazil
130 G7 **Bom Sucesso** Brazil
118 D5 **Bon Accord** Alberta Canada
94 K9 **Bon Air** Virginia U.S.A.
127 K8 **Bonaire** *isld* Lesser Antilles
127 K9 **Bonaire Trench** Caribbean
116 R6 **Bona,Mt** Alaska U.S.A.
69 D12 **Bonandolok** Sumatra
139 J6 **Bonang** Victoria Australia
125 M3 **Bonanza** Nicaragua
106 D3 **Bonanza** Colorado U.S.A.
100 D7 **Bonanza** Oregon U.S.A.
127 J5 **Bonao** Dominican Rep
99 P9 **Bonaparte** Iowa U.S.A.
142 E2 **Bonaparte Arch** Western Australia Australia
100 F1 **Bonaparte,Mt** Washington U.S.A.
15 D3 **Bonar Bridge** Scotland
121 N8 **Bonarlaw** Ontario Canada
116 G5 **Bonasila Dome** *mt* Alaska U.S.A.
127 N3 **Bonasse** Trinidad
44 G3 **Bonassola** Italy
122 G5 **Bonaventure** Quebec Canada
122 H5 **Bonaventure I** Quebec Canada
123 T5 **Bonavista** Newfoundland Canada
40 C3 **Bonboillon** France
138 D4 **Bon Bon** South Australia Australia
85 G1 **Bon,C** Tunisia
106 F4 **Boncarbo** Colorado U.S.A.
21 O5 **Bonce** France
13 F3 **Bonchester Br** Scotland
9 E6 **Bonchurch** England
101 T10 **Bond** Colorado U.S.A.
86 B6 **Bonda** Gabon
28 C7 **Bonden Au** *R* W Germany
45 K2 **Bondeno** Italy
86 D5 **Bondo** Zaire
71 F4 **Bondoc Penin** Luzon Philippines
71 F4 **Bondoc Pt** Luzon Philippines
71 H9 **Bondokodi** Sumbawa Indonesia
36 F6 **Bondorf** W Germany
85 D7 **Bondoukou** Ivory Coast
70 O9 **Bondowoso** Java
126 F2 **Bonds Cay** *isld* Bahamas
144 C5 **Bonds Peak** *mt* New Zealand
99 S5 **Bonduel** Wisconsin U.S.A.
101 P6 **Bondurant** Wyoming U.S.A.
101 O6 **Bone** Idaho U.S.A.
70 G6 **Bonebone** Sulawesi
113 L9 **Bonefish Pond** New Providence I Bahamas
71 H7 **Bonelipu** Indonesia
70 G7 **Bonelowe** Indonesia
68 G4 **Boneng** Laos
71 K8 **Boneogeh** Indonesia
71 K8 **Bonerate** *isld* Indonesia
71 K8 **Bonerate** Indonesia
26 K3 **Bones** Norway
15 E5 **Boness** Scotland
98 H6 **Bonesteel** South Dakota U.S.A.
131 C2 **Bonete,Cerro** *pk* Argentina
70 G7 **Bone, Teluk** *B* Sulawesi Indonesia
98 C1 **Bonetraill** North Dakota U.S.A.
121 L6 **Bonfield** Ontario Canada
71 E4 **Bongabong** Philippines
86 D5 **Bongandanga** Zaire
70 F2 **Bongao** Philippines
70 M9 **Bongkok** *mt* Java
71 G7 **Bongo** *isld* Mindanao Philippines
86 C3 **Bongor** Chad
68 J5 **Bong Son** Vietnam
109 L2 **Bonham** Texas U.S.A.
118 L1 **Bonheur** Ontario Canada
12 D2 **Bonhill** Scotland
36 C7 **Bonhomme, Col du** *pass* France
43 B7 **Bonifacio,Str.of** Corsica/Sardinia
111 L11 **Bonifay** Florida U.S.A.
Bonin Is *see* **Ogasawara-shoto**
103 P9 **Bonita** Arizona U.S.A.
111 E9 **Bonita** Louisiana U.S.A.
113 F11 **Bonita Springs** Florida U.S.A.
130 C7 **Bonito** Brazil
69 E13 **Bonjol** Sumatra
36 C2 **Bonn** W Germany
18 G6 **Bonnat** France
19 P15 **Bonne** *R* France
19 Q12 **Bonne** France
123 P4 **Bonne Bay** Newfoundland Canada
21 L3 **Bonnebosq** France
22 G3 **Bonne Esperance** Belgium
123 P2 **Bonne Espérance** Quebec Canada
21 P4 **Bonnelles** France
20 G5 **Bonnemain** France
101 M3 **Bonner** Montana U.S.A.
140 D1 **Bonner Mt** N Terr Australia
100 J1 **Bonners Ferry** Idaho U.S.A.
110 B2 **Bonner Springs** Kansas U.S.A.
28 A3 **Bonnet** Denmark
21 L5 **Bonnétable** France
110 F4 **Bonne Terre** Missouri U.S.A.
21 P2 **Bonneuil-les-Eaux** France
21 M8 **Bonneuil-Matours** France
21 N5 **Bonneval** Eure-et-Loir France
40 F7 **Bonneval-sur-Arc** France
40 D4 **Bonnevaux** France
19 Q12 **Bonneville** France
100 D4 **Bonneville** Oregon U.S.A.
101 R6 **Bonneville** Wyoming U.S.A.
21 N3 **Bonneville,la** France
101 N7 **Bonneville Pk** Idaho U.S.A.
101 L9 **Bonneville Salt Flats** Utah/Nev U.S.A.
138 F6 **Bonney,L** South Australia Australia
140 C5 **Bonney Well** N Terr Australia
21 P1 **Bonnières** Pas-de-Calais France
21 O3 **Bonnières** Seine-et-Oise France
143 C9 **Bonnie Rock** Western Australia Australia
19 O17 **Bonnieux** France
36 G5 **Bönnigheim** W Germany
36 H3 **Bonnland** W Germany
18 G5 **Bonny** France
85 F8 **Bonny** Nigeria
Bonny, Bight Of *see* **Biafra, Bight Of**
106 H2 **Bonny Res** Colorado U.S.A.
122 F8 **Bonny River** New Brunswick Canada
118 G4 **Bonnyville** Alberta Canada
20 E6 **Bono** France
43 C8 **Bono** Sardinia
110 F6 **Bono** Arkansas U.S.A.
71 C6 **Bonobond** Palawan Philippines
60 D14 **Bōno-misaki** *C* Japan
68 H7 **Bonom Mhai** *mt* Vietnam
43 B8 **Bonorva** Sardinia
21 M8 **Bonres** France
111 J11 **Bon Secour** Alabama U.S.A.
70 E4 **Bontang** Kalimantan
89 A9 **Bonteberg** *mts* S Africa
85 B7 **Bonthe** Sierra Leone
71 E2 **Bontoc** Luzon Philippines
71 K8 **Bontomatane** Indonesia
70 G7 **Bontosunggu** Sulawesi
109 O5 **Bon Wier** Texas U.S.A.
48 E4 **Bonyhád** Hungary
143 G6 **Bonython Ra** N Terr/W Aust Australia
141 F1 **Booby I** Queensland Australia
113 K12 **Booby I** Bahamas
127 M3 **Booby South Pt** Jamaica
36 D7 **Boofzheim** France
138 C4 **Bookabie** South Australia Australia
143 A8 **Bookara** Western Australia Australia
103 P2 **Book Cliffs** Utah U.S.A.
108 D7 **Booker** Texas U.S.A.
94 H9 **Booker T. Washington Nat Mon** Virginia U.S.A.
85 C7 **Boola** Guinea
142 B6 **Boolaloo** Western Australia Australia
143 A6 **Boolathanna** Western Australia Australia
138 E5 **Booleroo Centre** South Australia Australia
143 A6 **Boologooro** Western Australia Australia
22 G1 **Boom** Belgium
94 B2 **Boon** Michigan U.S.A.
141 L8 **Boonah** Queensland Australia
106 F3 **Boone** Colorado U.S.A.
99 N7 **Boone** Iowa U.S.A.
112 F1 **Boone** North Carolina U.S.A.
94 H9 **Boones Mill** Virginia U.S.A.
110 C6 **Booneville** Arkansas U.S.A.
110 N4 **Booneville** Kentucky U.S.A.
110 H7 **Booneville** Mississippi U.S.A.
94 D9 **Booneville Res** Kentucky U.S.A.
141 H6 **Boongoondoo** Queensland Australia
127 P4 **Boon Pt** Antigua W Indies
94 K7 **Boonsboro** Maryland U.S.A.
58 C2 **Bööntsagaan Nuur** *L* Mongolia
102 A2 **Boonville** California U.S.A.
110 J3 **Boonville** Indiana U.S.A.
110 D3 **Boonville** Missouri U.S.A.
95 M3 **Boonville** New York U.S.A.
71 B3 **Boo,Pulau Pulau** *islds* W Irian
143 D9 **Boorabbin** Western Australia Australia
86 H4 **Boorama** Somalia
21 N3 **Boos** France
86 A1 **Boosaaso** Somalia
13 E5 **Boot** England
147 E3 **Boothia, Gulf of** Northwest Territories Canada
115 K3 **Boothia Pen** Northwest Territories Canada
111 J8 **Boothton** Alabama U.S.A.
13 E5 **Bootle** England
13 F6 **Bootle** England
37 J6 **Bopfingen** W Germany
89 C6 **Bophuthatswana** *homeland* S Africa
65 C6 **Boping** China
36 D3 **Boppard** W Germany
20 E5 **Boqueho** France
129 K6 **Boqueirão, Serra do** *mts* Brazil
128 F8 **Boquerón** *dept* Paraguay
108 E6 **Boquillas** Texas U.S.A.
108 E6 **Boquillas del Carmen** Mexico
37 O4 **Bor** Czechoslovakia
86 E4 **Bo R** Sudan
27 G14 **Bor** Sweden
78 E3 **Bor** Turkey
48 G6 **Bor** Yugoslavia
135 M10 **Bora-Bora** *isld* Society Is Pacific Oc
101 M5 **Borah Pk** Idaho U.S.A.
27 F14 **Borås** Sweden
77 B5 **Borāzjān** Iran
128 G4 **Borba** Brazil
28 B4 **Borbjerg** Denmark
71 G5 **Borbon** Cebu Philippines
130 H9 **Borborema, Planalto da** *plateau* Brazil
48 K3 **Borca** Romania
48 L6 **Borcea** *R* Romania
146 C12 **Borchgrevink Coast** *coast* Antarctica
78 H1 **Borçka** Turkey
138 D6 **Borda,C** South Australia Australia
47 K7 **Bor Dağı** *mt* Turkey
18 E8 **Bordeaux** France
98 B8 **Bordeaux** Wyoming U.S.A.
57 G5 **Bordëbë** U.S.S.R.
143 C10 **Borden** Western Australia Australia
122 J7 **Borden** Prince Edward I Canada
118 K6 **Borden** Saskatchewan Canada
114 H2 **Borden I** Northwest Territories Canada
115 L3 **Borden Pen** Northwest Territories Canada
95 N6 **Bordentown** New Jersey U.S.A.
15 F5 **Borders** *reg* Scotland
138 F6 **Bordertown** South Australia Australia
32 M4 **Bordesholm** W Germany
28 S9 **Bordheyri** Iceland
44 C4 **Bordighera** Italy
85 D3 **Bordj Flye Ste Marie** Algeria
85 F2 **Bordj Messaouda** Algeria
85 E4 **Bordj Mokhtar** Algeria
85 F3 **Bordj Omar Driss** Algeria
6 F1 **Borðoy** *isld* Faeroes
57 H4 **Bordunskiy** U.S.S.R.
85 D5 **Boré** Mali
143 D8 **Boreas,Mt** Western Australia Australia
31 K4 **Borek** Poland
Borgå *see* **Porvoo**
28 S9 **Borgarnes** Iceland
44 C1 **Bórgaro Torinese** Italy
26 G3 **Borge** Norway
26 G6 **Börgefjell** *mt* Norway
32 K9 **Borgentreich** W Germany
25 G3 **Borger** Netherlands
108 C8 **Borger** Texas U.S.A.
32 G7 **Börger** W Germany
32 K9 **Borgholz** W Germany
32 H8 **Borgholzhausen** W Germany
32 F8 **Borghorst** W Germany
43 H10 **Borgia** Italy
22 J2 **Borgloon** Belgium
28 D2 **Børglum** Denmark
40 G5 **Borgne** *R* Switzerland
41 O5 **Borgo** Italy
45 J4 **Borgo a Mozzano** Italy
45 J1 **Borgoforte** Italy
44 E1 **Borgolavezzaro** Italy
45 N6 **Borgo Montello** Italy
44 F1 **Borgonovo Val Tidone** Italy
45 M4 **Borgo Pace** Italy
45 K2 **Borgo Panigale** Italy
45 O5 **Borgorose** Italy
42 D5 **Borgo S. Lorenzo** Italy
41 J6 **Borgoticino** Italy
44 G3 **Borgo Val di Taro** Italy
42 D2 **Borgo Valsugana** Italy
41 H7 **Borgo Vercelli** Italy
26 H9 **Borgsjö** Sweden
27 F14 **Borgstena** Sweden
12 D4 **Borgue** Scotland
26 B9 **Borgund** Norway
27 C10 **Borgund** Norway
26 H8 **Borgvattnet** Sweden
98 B8 **Borie** Wyoming U.S.A.
68 F3 **Borikhane** Laos
31 O6 **Borinya** U.S.S.R.
26 S2 **Boris Gleb** U.S.S.R.
31 O6 **Borislav** U.S.S.R.
57 E3 **Borisovka** U.S.S.R.
55 F4 **Borisovskoye** U.S.S.R.
54 B6 **Borispol** U.S.S.R.
87 H11 **Boriziny** Madagascar
130 C9 **Borja** Paraguay
17 F3 **Borja** Spain
42 H4 **Borja Planina** Yugoslavia
17 H3 **Borjas Blancas** Spain
26 M6 **Börjelslandet** Sweden
32 F9 **Bork** W Germany
32 E9 **Borken** W Germany
36 G1 **Borken** W Germany
54 H7 **Borki** U.S.S.R.
28 D5 **Børkop** Denmark
86 C2 **Borkou** *dist* Chad
52 C6 **Borkovichi** U.S.S.R.
25 G4 **Borkulo** Netherlands
32 E5 **Borkum** W Germany
27 H11 **Borlänge** Sweden
47 J6 **Borlu** Turkey
44 D3 **Bormida di Millésimo** *R* Italy
44 D3 **Bormida di Spigno** *R* Italy
42 C2 **Bormio** Italy
37 O1 **Borna** East Germany
25 E2 **Borndiep** Netherlands
25 G4 **Borne** Netherlands
70 B4 **Borneo** *isld* E Indies
16 C3 **Bornes** *mt* Portugal
36 B2 **Bornheim** W Germany
27 H16 **Bornholm** *isld* Denmark
27 G16 **Bornholmsgattet** *str* Sweden/Denmark
32 M4 **Bornhöved** W Germany
33 R7 **Börnicke** East Germany
33 R8 **Bornim** East Germany
86 B3 **Borno** *prov* Nigeria
16 D8 **Bornos, Embalse de** *res* Spain
86 E4 **Boro** *R* Sudan
48 K3 **Boroaia** Romania
70 M9 **Borobudur** *ruins* Java
71 E5 **Borocay** *isld* Panay Philippines
51 N2 **Borogontsy** U.S.S.R.
57 L3 **Borohoro Shan** *mt ra* China
71 H4 **Boroko** Sulawesi Indonesia
85 D6 **Boromo** Burkina
102 G6 **Boron** California U.S.A.
141 K6 **Bororen** Queensland Australia
13 G5 **Boroughbridge** England
56 B5 **Borovlyanka** U.S.S.R.
55 F4 **Borovoye** U.S.S.R.
54 H1 **Borovsk** U.S.S.R.
55 E3 **Borovskiy** U.S.S.R.
55 D4 **Borovskoy** U.S.S.R.
27 G16 **Borrby** Sweden
29 K6 **Borre** Denmark
33 R5 **Borrenthin** East Germany
138 E5 **Borrika** South Australia Australia
28 B5 **Borris** Denmark
14 E4 **Borris** Ireland
14 D4 **Borrisoleigh** Ireland
140 D3 **Borroloola** N Terr Australia
27 J13 **Börrum** Sweden
48 J3 **Borşa** Romania
58 G1 **Borsch Chovochnyy Khrebet** *mt* U.S.S.R.
33 R10 **Borsdorf** East Germany
48 K4 **Borsec** Romania
26 P1 **Börselv** Norway
48 H2 **Borshava** *R* U.S.S.R.
48 K2 **Borshchev** U.S.S.R.
48 F2 **Borsod-Abaúj Zemplén** Hungary
25 A6 **Borssele** Netherlands
33 N8 **Börssum** W Germany
29 K5 **Borstahusen** Sweden
32 J7 **Borstel** W Germany
57 K3 **Bortala He** *R* China
8 B3 **Borth** Wales
18 G7 **Bort-les-Orgues** France
26 G9 **Börtnan** Sweden
58 F1 **Borto** U.S.S.R.
77 B4 **Borūjen** Iran
77 A3 **Borūjerd** Iran
28 E4 **Borum** Denmark
28 H5 **Borup** Denmark
98 K2 **Borup** Minnesota U.S.A.
56 D4 **Borus,Khrebet** *mts* U.S.S.R.
31 K2 **Bory Tucholskie** *forest* Poland
31 M5 **Borzęcin** Poland
78 J1 **Borzhomi** U.S.S.R.
54 D5 **Borzna** U.S.S.R.
58 G1 **Borzya** *R* U.S.S.R.
58 G1 **Borzya** U.S.S.R.
57 G1 **Bosaginskiy** U.S.S.R.
48 E5 **Bosanski Brod** Yugoslavia
42 G4 **Bosanski Petrovac** Yugoslavia
33 M4 **Bosau** W Germany
8 B6 **Boscastle** England
95 Q3 **Boscawen** New Hampshire U.S.A.
45 K1 **Boschi Santa Anna** Italy
21 N2 **Bosc-le-Hard** France
99 Q6 **Boscobel** Wisconsin U.S.A.
9 E6 **Boscombe** England
45 Q8 **Boscotrecase** Italy
67 B5 **Bose** China
38 K7 **Bosenstein,Gross** *mt* Austria
65 D6 **Boshan** China
89 D7 **Boshof** S Africa
77 E3 **Boshruyeh** Iran
46 E2 **Bosilegrad** Yugoslavia
27 G12 **Bosjön** Sweden
25 C4 **Boskoop** Netherlands
98 A8 **Bosler** Wyoming U.S.A.
8 D1 **Bosley** England
42 H4 **Bosna** *R* Yugoslavia
86 C5 **Bosobolo** Zaire
61 O10 **Bōsō-hantō** *pen* Japan
32 G10 **Bösperde** W Germany
Bosporus *str* *see* **Karadeniz Boğazı** *str*
106 D7 **Bosque** New Mexico U.S.A.
124 G2 **Bosque Bonito** Mexico
86 C4 **Bossambélé** Cent Afr Republic
86 C4 **Bossangoa** Cent Afr Republic
86 C4 **Bossemtele** Cent Afr Republic
111 C9 **Bossier City** Louisiana U.S.A.
87 C9 **Bossiesvlei** Namibia
86 B3 **Bosso** Niger
66 D3 **Bosten Hu** *L* China
9 F2 **Boston** England
113 D7 **Boston** Georgia U.S.A.
95 Q4 **Boston** Massachusetts U.S.A.
97 **Boston** *conurbation* Massachusetts U.S.A.
117 N11 **Boston Bar** British Columbia Canada
127 M2 **Boston Bay** Jamaica
138 D5 **Boston I** South Australia Australia
110 C6 **Boston Mts** Arkansas U.S.A.
13 G6 **Boston Spa** England
28 F6 **Bøstrup** Fyn Denmark
28 D4 **Bøstrup** Viborg Denmark
48 E5 **Bosut** *R* Yugoslavia
123 O5 **Boswarlos** Newfoundland Canada
117 P11 **Boswell** British Columbia Canada
99 T9 **Boswell** Indiana U.S.A.
107 P7 **Boswell** Oklahoma U.S.A.
94 H6 **Boswell** Pennsylvania U.S.A.
110 C2 **Bosworth** Missouri U.S.A.
74 D7 **Botad** India
139 K5 **Botany B** New South Wales Australia
26 J8 **Boteå** Sweden
46 G2 **Botev** *mt* Bulgaria
46 F2 **Botevgrad** Bulgaria
118 E6 **Botha** Alberta Canada
9 F1 **Bothamsall** England
87 E11 **Bothaville** S Africa
13 E4 **Bothel** England
117 M12 **Bothell** Washington U.S.A.
26 L8 **Bothnia,Gulf of** Sweden/Finland
139 H8 **Bothwell** Tasmania Australia
120 J10 **Bothwell** Ontario Canada
12 D2 **Bothwell** Scotland
16 B3 **Boticas** Portugal
87 D10 **Botletle** *R* Botswana
9 E6 **Botley** England
48 M4 **Botna** *R* U.S.S.R.
28 H7 **Bøtø** Denmark
71 D3 **Botolan Pt** Luzon Philippines
48 K3 **Botoşani** Romania
65 C5 **Botou** China
68 H4 **Bo Trach** Vietnam
22 L3 **Botrange** *mt* Belgium
26 L7 **Botsmark** Sweden
89 C4 **Botswana** *rep* Africa
43 G9 **Botte Donato** *mt* Italy
89 A8 **Botter Kloof Pass** S Africa
89 B8 **Bottersleegte** S Africa
9 F2 **Bottesford** England
98 F1 **Bottineau** North Dakota U.S.A.
9 G3 **Bottisham** England
127 N6 **Bottom** Saba W Indies
9 E1 **Bottom House** England
45 M1 **Bottrighe** Italy
32 E9 **Bottrop** W Germany
46 F1 **Botunya** *R* Bulgaria
123 R4 **Botwood** Newfoundland Canada
85 C7 **Bouaflé** Ivory Coast
21 N3 **Bouafles** France
16 D9 **Bou Ahmed** Morocco
85 D7 **Bouaké** Ivory Coast
86 C4 **Bouala** Cent Afr Republic
86 C4 **Bouar** Cent Afr Republic
85 D2 **Bouârfa** Morocco
43 A12 **Bouati Mahmoud** Algeria
20 G7 **Bouaye** France
30 H6 **Boubín** *mt* Czechoslovakia
86 C4 **Bouca** Cent Afr Republic
18 D9 **Boucau** France
140 C1 **Boucaut B** N Terr Australia
21 K4 **Boucé** Orne France
22 E3 **Bouchain** France
21 L7 **Bouchard, l'Île** France
22 D4 **Bouchavesnes** France
43 B12 **Bouchegouf** Algeria
123 N2 **Boucher,L** Quebec Canada
19 N17 **Bouches-du-Rhône** *dept* France
121 P6 **Bouchette** Quebec Canada
22 D4 **Bouchoir** France
85 D2 **Boudenib** Morocco
16 E9 **Boudinar** Morocco
85 D5 **Bou Djébéha** Mali
40 A2 **Boudreville** France
40 E4 **Boudry** Switzerland
20 G7 **Bouée** France
21 O8 **Bouesse** France
20 H5 **Bouexière, la** France
122 E3 **Bouffard,L** Quebec Canada
83 K14 **Bœuf, Nez de** *pk* Réunion
137 M3 **Bougainville** *isld* Papua New Guinea
142 F2 **Bougainville, C** Western Australia Australia
141 H3 **Bougainville Reef** Gt Barrier Reef Aust
71 C2 **Bougainville,Selat** W Irian
85 F1 **Bougaroun,C** Algeria
21 O7 **Bouges le-Château** France
Bougie *see* **Bejaïa**
85 C6 **Bougouni** Mali
43 C11 **Bouhairet Benzart** *G* Tunisia
17 G9 **Bou Hanifa** Algeria
17 G9 **Bou Hanifa, Barrage de** Algeria
127 M4 **Bouillante** Guadeloupe W Indies
21 M3 **Bouille,la** France
21 K7 **Bouillé Loretz** France
21 J6 **Bouillé-Ménard** France
22 J4 **Bouillon** Belgium
20 G8 **Bouin** France
85 C3 **Bou Izakam** Morocco
85 B3 **Boujdour** Western Sahara
85 B3 **Boukra** Western Sahara
123 L3 **Boulain,L** Quebec Canada
19 K3 **Boulay** France
143 D9 **Boulder** Western Australia Australia
98 A9 **Boulder** Colorado U.S.A.
101 N3 **Boulder** Montana U.S.A.
103 N4 **Boulder** Utah U.S.A.
101 Q7 **Boulder** Wyoming U.S.A.
103 K5 **Boulder Can** Nevada U.S.A.
103 K6 **Boulder City** Nevada U.S.A.
102 B4 **Boulder Cr** California U.S.A.
100 J7 **Boulder Cr** Idaho U.S.A.
121 N5 **Bouleau, L. au** Quebec Canada
102 H9 **Boulevard** California U.S.A.
140 E6 **Boulia** Queensland Australia
20 H8 **Boulogne** *R* France
22 B2 **Boulogne** France
21 P4 **Boulogne-Billancourt** France
21 M6 **Bouloire** France
85 C5 **Boulouli** Mali
85 D6 **Boulsa** Burkina
22 H5 **Boult-aux-Bois** France
85 G6 **Boultoum** Niger
22 H4 **Boulzicourt** France
86 C5 **Boumba** *R* Cameroon
85 D7 **Bouna** Ivory Coast
117 C3 **Boundary** Alaska U.S.A.
102 F4 **Boundary Pk** Nevada U.S.A.
118 J9 **Boundary Plateau** Mont/Sask U.S.A./Canada
85 C7 **Boundiali** Ivory Coast
68 H6 **Boung Long** Cambodia
68 E2 **Boun Neua** Laos
106 E4 **Bountiful** Colorado U.S.A.
140 E3 **Bountiful Is** Queensland Australia
118 K7 **Bounty** Saskatchewan Canada
21 J8 **Boupère, le** France
21 P1 **Bouquemaison** France
110 E3 **Bourbeuse** *R* Missouri U.S.A.
94 A5 **Bourbon** Indiana U.S.A.
110 E3 **Bourbon** Missouri U.S.A.
83 L14 **Bourbon,C** Kerguelen Indian Oc
18 H6 **Bourbon-Lancy** France
18 H6 **Bourbon l'Archambault** France
18 H6 **Bourbonnais** *prov* France
40 C2 **Bourbonne les Bains** France
18 G7 **Bourboule,la** France
19 J5 **Bourboune les Bassigny** France
22 C2 **Bourbourg** France
19 O13 **Bourbre** *R* France
20 D5 **Bourbriac** France
19 O15 **Bourdeaux** France
36 B6 **Bourdonnay** France
16 E10 **Boured** Morocco
85 D5 **Bourem** Mali
18 E7 **Bourg** Gironde France
18 G7 **Bourganeuf** France
21 M3 **Bourg-Archard** France
18 H7 **Bourg Argental** France
19 Q15 **Bourg d'Arud** France
19 O14 **Bourg-de-Péage** France
20 G6 **Bourg-des-Comptes** France
21 M2 **Bourg Dun** France
19 O12 **Bourg-en-Bresse** France
21 P7 **Bourges** France
22 F5 **Bourg et Comin** France
40 C6 **Bourget,L.du** France
21 P4 **Bourget,le** Paris France
18 G10 **Bourg-Madame** France
21 K6 **Bourg-Neuf** France
20 F7 **Bourgneuf,B.de** France
21 J7 **Bourgneuf-en-Mauges** France
20 G7 **Bourgneuf-en-Retz** France
21 J5 **Bourgneuf,le** France
22 G5 **Bourgogne** France
19 O13 **Bourgoin** France
40 E6 **Bourg-St-Maurice** France
21 M3 **Bourgtheroulde-Infreville** France
21 K3 **Bourguébus** France
21 L7 **Bourgueil** France
120 K4 **Bourkes** Ontario Canada
121 N4 **Bourlamaque** Quebec Canada
22 E3 **Bourlon** France
121 P4 **Bourmont** Quebec Canada
40 C1 **Bourmont** France
21 M7 **Bournan** France
21 L7 **Bournand** France
9 F2 **Bourne** England
115 K1 **Bourne,C** Northwest Territories Canada
9 F4 **Bourne End** England
9 E6 **Bournemouth** England
21 M3 **Bourneville** France
21 H8 **Bournezeau** France
18 E8 **Bourriot Bergonce** France
32 F7 **Bourtanger Moor** W Germany
21 M4 **Bourth** France
22 B2 **Bourthes** France
86 D3 **Bourtoutou** Chad
22 L4 **Bous** Luxembourg
85 E1 **Bou Saâda** Algeria
43 B12 **Bou Salem** Tunisia
103 K8 **Bouse** Arizona U.S.A.
103 K8 **Bouse Wash** *R* Arizona U.S.A.
36 B5 **Bous/Saar** W Germany
18 G6 **Boussac** France
20 G4 **Boussac,la** France
21 H7 **Boussay** France
22 L5 **Bousse** France
86 C3 **Bousso** Chad
43 B12 **Bouteldja** Algeria
21 P5 **Boutigny** France
85 B5 **Boutilimit** Mauritania
18 E6 **Boutonne** *R* France
143 B10 **Bouvard,C** Western Australia Australia
19 O13 **Bouvesse** France
90 J14 **Bouvet I** S Atlantic Oc
81 A12 **Bouvetøy** *isld* S Atlantic Oc
20 G7 **Bouvron** France
36 C6 **Bouxwiller** France
85 F6 **Bouza** Niger
21 O8 **Bouzanne** *R* France
36 B5 **Bouzonville** France
28 C7 **Bov** Denmark
43 G11 **Bova** Italy
32 L9 **Bovenden** W Germany
70 C4 **Boven Kapuas** *mts* Sarawak
28 F6 **Bovense** Denmark
26 C10 **Böverdal** Norway
21 P2 **Boves** France
44 C3 **Boves** Italy
8 C6 **Bovey Tracey** England
22 K3 **Bovigny** Belgium
100 J3 **Bovill** Idaho U.S.A.
43 G7 **Bovino** Italy
28 A4 **Bøvlingbjerg** Denmark
45 L1 **Bovolenta** Italy
45 K1 **Bovolone** Italy
8 C6 **Bow** England
98 D1 **Bowbells** North Dakota U.S.A.
127 M3 **Bowden** Jamaica
113 F7 **Bowden** Florida U.S.A.
98 G4 **Bowdle** South Dakota U.S.A.
101 S1 **Bowdoin,L** Montana U.S.A.
112 B4 **Bowdon** Georgia U.S.A.
98 G2 **Bowdon** North Dakota U.S.A.
143 B10 **Bowelling** Western Australia Australia
141 J5 **Bowen** *R* Queensland Australia
141 J5 **Bowen** Queensland Australia
110 E1 **Bowen** Illinois U.S.A.
141 H5 **Bowen Downs** Queensland Australia
117 M11 **Bowen I** British Columbia Canada
140 B1 **Bowen Str** N Terr Australia
95 M7 **Bowers** Delaware U.S.A.
94 D7 **Bowersville** Ohio U.S.A.
101 L5 **Bowery Pk** Idaho U.S.A.
13 F5 **Bowes** England
143 B8 **Bowgada** Western Australia Australia
141 H5 **Bowie** Queensland Australia
103 P9 **Bowie** Arizona U.S.A.
106 C3 **Bowie** Colorado U.S.A.
109 K2 **Bowie** Texas U.S.A.
118 F9 **Bow Island** Alberta Canada
78 L3 **Bowkan** Iran
12 D2 **Bowling** Scotland
113 F10 **Bowling Green** Florida U.S.A.
110 J2 **Bowling Green** Indiana U.S.A.
110 K4 **Bowling Green** Kentucky U.S.A.
110 E2 **Bowling Green** Missouri U.S.A.
94 D5 **Bowling Green** Ohio U.S.A.
95 K8 **Bowling Green** Virginia U.S.A.
141 H4 **Bowling Green,C** Queensland Australia
112 D3 **Bowman** Georgia U.S.A.
98 C3 **Bowman** North Dakota U.S.A.
146 H14 **Bowman I** Antarctica
146 D6 **Bowman Peninsula** *pen* Antarctica
121 M9 **Bowmanville** Ontario Canada
15 B5 **Bowmore** Scotland
118 C7 **Bowness** Alberta Canada
13 F5 **Bowness** England
118 C7 **Bow R** Alberta Canada
142 G3 **Bow River** Western Australia Australia
117 N9 **Bowron Lake Prov. Park** British Columbia Canada
117 J7 **Bowser L** British Columbia Canada
119 Q6 **Bowsman** Manitoba Canada
118 B7 **Bow Valley Prov. Park** Alberta Canada
36 H5 **Boxberg** W Germany
98 C7 **Box Butte Res** Nebraska U.S.A.
98 A6 **Box Cr** Wyoming U.S.A.
101 P1 **Box Elder** Montana U.S.A.
98 C5 **Box Elder** South Dakota U.S.A.
106 F2 **Box Elder Cr** Colorado U.S.A.
101 R2 **Boxelder Cr** Montana U.S.A.
98 B4 **Boxelder Cr** Montana U.S.A.
9 F5 **Box Hill** England
27 H13 **Boxholm** Sweden
58 G5 **Bo Xian** China
65 D6 **Boxing** China
25 E5 **Boxmeer** Netherlands
25 D5 **Boxtel** Netherlands
78 E1 **Boyabat** Turkey
128 D2 **Boyacá** *div* Colombia
47 K3 **Boyalık** Turkey
58 G6 **Boyang** China
143 B10 **Boyanup** Western Australia Australia
111 D10 **Boyce** Louisiana U.S.A.
94 J7 **Boyce** Virginia U.S.A.
143 D8 **Boyce,Mt** Western Australia Australia
46 F1 **Boychinovtsi** Bulgaria
119 V3 **Boyd** Manitoba Canada
101 Q4 **Boyd** Montana U.S.A.
109 K2 **Boyd** Texas U.S.A.
123 S4 **Boyd's Cove** Newfoundland Canada
94 J10 **Boydton** Virginia U.S.A.
65 C5 **Boye** China
99 L7 **Boyer** *R* Iowa U.S.A.
99 L7 **Boyer** Iowa U.S.A.
106 G3 **Boyero** Colorado U.S.A.
95 M6 **Boyertown** Pennsylvania U.S.A.
98 A4 **Boyes** Montana U.S.A.
95 K10 **Boykins** Virginia U.S.A.
118 E4 **Boyle** Alberta Canada
14 C3 **Boyle** Ireland
111 F8 **Boyle** Mississippi U.S.A.
123 L8 **Boylston** Nova Scotia Canada
141 K6 **Boyne** *R* Queensland Australia
14 E3 **Boyne** *R* Ireland
94 C1 **Boyne City** Michigan U.S.A.
94 C1 **Boyne Falls** Michigan U.S.A.
21 P5 **Boynes** France
110 C1 **Boynton** Missouri U.S.A.
107 P6 **Boynton** Oklahoma U.S.A.
113 G11 **Boynton Beach** Florida U.S.A.
86 E5 **Boyoma Falls** Zaire
101 R6 **Boysen Res** Wyoming U.S.A.
143 B10 **Boyup Brook** Western Australia Australia
47 J8 **Bozburun** Turkey
47 H5 **Bozca Ada** *isld* Turkey
47 L5 **Boz Dağ** *mt* Turkey
79 G2 **Bozdağ** *mt* Turkey
47 J6 **Boz Dağlar** *mts* Turkey
47 J7 **Bozdoğan** Turkey
101 P4 **Bozeman** Montana U.S.A.
Bozen *see* **Bolzano**
86 C5 **Bozene** Zaire
31 K1 **Boże Pole** Poland
65 C5 **Bozhen** China
37 O3 **Boží Dar** Czechoslovakia
78 D3 **Bozkir** Turkey
54 F1 **Boznya** U.S.S.R.
78 G3 **Bozova** Turkey
48 G6 **Bozovici** Romania
55 F5 **Bozshakol'** U.S.S.R.
45 J1 **Bozzolo** Italy
138 A4 **BP Travellers Village** South Australia Australia
44 C2 **Bra** Italy
22 G2 **Brabançonne** *prov* Belgium
22 G2 **Brabant** *prov* Belgium
146 C4 **Brabant I** Antarctica
119 O2 **Brabant L** Saskatchewan Canada
28 E4 **Brabrand** Denmark
28 H6 **Bråby** Denmark
42 H5 **Brač** *isld* Yugoslavia
15 B3 **Bracadale** Scotland
129 H6 **Braça Menor** *R* Brazil
44 M5 **Bracciano** Italy
44 M5 **Bracciano, Lago di** Italy
42 E6 **Bracciano,Lago di** Italy
121 L7 **Bracebridge** Ontario Canada
21 O6 **Bracieux** France
26 H9 **Bräcke** Sweden
118 J9 **Bracken** Saskatchewan Canada
109 J6 **Bracken** Texas U.S.A.
36 G5 **Brackenheim** W Germany
13 G6 **Brackenhill** England
119 S5 **Bracken L** Manitoba Canada
108 G6 **Brackettville** Texas U.S.A.
9 E3 **Brackley** England
9 F5 **Bracknell** England
32 J9 **Brackwede** W Germany
12 E1 **Braco** Scotland
43 G8 **Bradano** *R* Italy
98 F3 **Braddock** North Dakota U.S.A.
94 H6 **Braddock** Pennsylvania U.S.A.
99 L9 **Braddyville** Iowa U.S.A.
113 E10 **Bradenton** Florida U.S.A.
113 E10 **Bradenton Beach** Florida U.S.A.
28 B7 **Braderup** W Germany
121 L8 **Bradford** Ontario Canada
13 G6 **Bradford** England
8 D5 **Bradford** England
110 E6 **Bradford** Arkansas U.S.A.
99 R8 **Bradford** Illinois U.S.A.
99 N7 **Bradford** Iowa U.S.A.
95 T1 **Bradford** Maine U.S.A.
95 P3 **Bradford** New Hampshire U.S.A.
94 C6 **Bradford** Ohio U.S.A.
94 J5 **Bradford** Pennsylvania U.S.A.
95 Q5 **Bradford** Rhode I U.S.A.
94 B9 **Bradfordsville** Kentucky U.S.A.
111 C8 **Bradley** Arkansas U.S.A.
102 D6 **Bradley** California U.S.A.
99 T8 **Bradley** Illinois U.S.A.
107 N7 **Bradley** Oklahoma U.S.A.
110 D5 **Bradleyville** Missouri U.S.A.
94 D5 **Bradner** Ohio U.S.A.
123 P2 **Bradore Bay** Quebec Canada
123 P2 **Bradore Hills** Quebec Canada
140 B3 **Bradshaw** N Terr Australia
98 J9 **Bradshaw** Nebraska U.S.A.
142 F3 **Bradshaw,Mt** Western Australia Australia
119 R9 **Bradwardine** Manitoba Canada
118 L7 **Bradwell** Saskatchewan Canada
9 G4 **Bradwell** England
98 F8 **Brady** Nebraska U.S.A.
109 H4 **Brady** Texas U.S.A.
117 E6 **Brady Glacier** Alaska U.S.A.
138 C3 **Brady,Mt** South Australia Australia
28 D5 **Brædstrup** Denmark
138 E5 **Braemar** South Australia Australia
15 E3 **Braemar** Scotland
15 E3 **Braeriach** *mt* Scotland
16 B3 **Braga** Portugal
131 E5 **Bragado** Argentina
129 J4 **Bragança** Brazil
16 C3 **Bragança** Portugal
130 F8 **Bragança Paulista** Brazil
112 E6 **Braganza** Georgia U.S.A.
110 G5 **Bragg City** Missouri U.S.A.
118 C7 **Bragg Creek Prov. Park** Alberta Canada
54 B5 **Bragin** U.S.S.R.
99 N4 **Braham** Minnesota U.S.A.
33 N6 **Brahlstorf** Schwerin East Germany
75 O7 **Brahmanbaria** Bangladesh
75 L9 **Brahmapur** India
75 P5 **Brahmaputra** *R* S Asia
32 L4 **Brahmsee** *L* W Germany
77 K5 **Brahui,Cen** *reg* Pakistan
99 S8 **Braidwood** Illinois U.S.A.
48 L5 **Brăila** Romania
9 E2 **Brailsford** England
98 J8 **Brainard** Nebraska U.S.A.
22 F5 **Braine** France
22 G2 **Braine L'Alleud** Belgium
22 G2 **Braine-le Château** Belgium
22 G2 **Braine-le Comte** Belgium
99 M3 **Brainerd** Minnesota U.S.A.
21 L7 **Brain-sur-Allonnes** France
9 G4 **Braintree** England
13 E4 **Braithwaite** England
111 G12 **Braithwaite** Louisiana U.S.A.
140 C1 **Braithwaite Pt** N Terr Australia
22 J2 **Braives** Belgium
89 F4 **Brak** *R* S Africa
32 H6 **Brake** W Germany
22 F2 **Brakel** Belgium
32 K9 **Brakel** W Germany
85 B5 **Brakna** *reg* Mauritania
57 D1 **Brali** U.S.S.R.
117 M10 **Bralorne** British Columbia Canada
107 N5 **Braman** Oklahoma U.S.A.
Brambach *see* **Radiumbad-Brambach**
38 F7 **Bramberg** Austria
13 G6 **Bramham** England
32 H6 **Bramloge** W Germany
28 B6 **Bramming** Denmark
44 B3 **Bram,Monte** Italy
26 J9 **Brämö** *isld* Sweden
9 H3 **Brampton** England
98 J3 **Brampton** North Dakota U.S.A.
141 J5 **Brampton I** Queensland Australia
32 G8 **Bramsche** W Germany
141 G1 **Bramwell** Queensland Australia
94 F9 **Bramwell** West Virginia U.S.A.
9 G2 **Brancaster** England
13 G4 **Brancepeth** England
123 T7 **Branch** Newfoundland Canada
99 U6 **Branch** Michigan U.S.A.
95 K4 **Branchport** New York U.S.A.
112 G4 **Branchville** South Carolina U.S.A.
130 B7 **Branco** *R* Mato Grosso Brazil
128 F3 **Branco** *R* Roraima Brazil
130 J9 **Branco,Cabo** Brazil
131 B2 **Branco,R** Argentina
41 L3 **Brand** Austria
37 O3 **Brand** Czechoslovakia
87 B10 **Brandberg** *mt* Namibia
26 H9 **Brändbo** Sweden
28 C5 **Brande** Denmark
32 L5 **Brande-Hörnerkirchen** W Germany
101 T4 **Brandenberg** Montana U.S.A.
33 R8 **Brandenburg** East Germany
110 K4 **Brandenburg** Kentucky U.S.A.
37 P2 **Brand-Erbisdorf** East Germany
28 C6 **Branderup** Denmark
13 H6 **Brandesburton** England
89 E7 **Brandfort** S Africa
33 R10 **Brandis** East Germany
29 J11 **Brändö** Finland
119 S9 **Brandon** Manitoba Canada
9 G3 **Brandon** England
106 H3 **Brandon** Colorado U.S.A.
98 E9 **Brandon** Nebraska U.S.A.
95 O3 **Brandon** Vermont U.S.A.
99 S6 **Brandon** Wisconsin U.S.A.
14 A4 **Brandon B** Ireland
14 A4 **Brandon Hd** Ireland
14 E4 **Brandon Hill** *mt* Ireland
14 A4 **Brandon Mt** Ireland
95 N3 **Brandreth** New York U.S.A.
13 G5 **Brandsby** England
133 F5 **Brandsen** Argentina
28 D6 **Brandsø** *isld* Denmark
110 E5 **Brandsville** Missouri U.S.A.
98 K5 **Brandt** South Dakota U.S.A.
27 F11 **Brandval** Norway
87 D12 **Brandvlei** S Africa
94 K8 **Brandy** Virginia U.S.A.
95 L8 **Brandywine** Maryland U.S.A.
48 K6 **Brăneşti** Romania
95 P5 **Branford** Connecticut U.S.A.
113 E8 **Branford** Florida U.S.A.
31 M1 **Braniewo** Poland
27 L17 **Braniewo** U.S.S.R.
31 M6 **Branisko** *mts* Czechoslovakia
18 E8 **Branne** France
102 A2 **Branscomb** California U.S.A.
146 C3 **Bransfield Str** Antarctica
106 G4 **Branson** Colorado U.S.A.
110 C5 **Branson** Missouri U.S.A.
9 F1 **Branston** England
118 D8 **Brant** Alberta Canada
70 O10 **Brantas** *R* Java
70 O9 **Brantas** Java
120 K9 **Brantford** Ontario Canada
98 H2 **Brantford** North Dakota U.S.A.
111 K10 **Brantley** Alabama U.S.A.
18 F7 **Brantôme** France
138 F7 **Branxholme** Victoria Australia
123 M8 **Bras d'or L** Nova Scotia Canada
99 O9 **Brashear** Missouri U.S.A.
128 E6 **Brasiléia** Brazil
129 J7 **Brasilia** Brazil
129 G4 **Brasilia Legal** Brazil
52 C6 **Braslav** U.S.S.R.
48 K5 **Brasov** Romania
20 C5 **Brasparts** France
85 F8 **Brass** Nigeria
22 G1 **Brasschaat** Belgium
140 C6 **Brassey Mt** N Terr Australia
143 D6 **Brassey Ra** Western Australia Australia
70 E2 **Brassey Ra** *mts* Sabah
139 G5 **Brassi** New South Wales Australia
28 D4 **Brassø** *L* Denmark
95 R1 **Brassua L** Maine U.S.A.
48 H4 **Bratca** Romania
48 L5 **Brates, L** Romania
46 G1 **Brateş, Lacul** *L* Romania
31 K7 **Bratislava** Czechoslovakia
46 G3 **Bratsigovo** Bulgaria
56 F3 **Bratsk** U.S.S.R.
56 F3 **Bratskoye Vodokhranilishche** *res* U.S.S.R.
48 M2 **Bratslav** U.S.S.R.
26 K7 **Bratten** Sweden
95 P4 **Brattleboro** Vermont U.S.A.
32 M8 **Brau** W Germany
36 D3 **Braubach** W Germany
36 G2 **Brauerschwend** W Germany
38 H5 **Braunau** Austria
36 E3 **Braunfels** W Germany
33 N9 **Braunlage** W Germany
33 P10 **Braunsbedra** East Germany
Braunsberg *see* **Braniewo** Poland
33 N8 **Braunschweig** W Germany
8 B5 **Braunton** England
36 B2 **Brauweiler** W Germany
131 D4 **Brava, L. la** Argentina
94 G7 **Brave** Pennsylvania U.S.A.
27 H13 **Bråviken** *L* Sweden
131 D2 **Bravo,Sa** *mt* Argentina
14 E3 **Bray** Ireland
22 D1 **Bray-Dunes** France
22 E5 **Braye** France
21 M6 **Braye,R** France
21 O3 **Bray-et-Lû** France
8 C5 **Brayford** England
14 A5 **Bray Hd** Ireland
115 M4 **Bray I** Northwest Territories Canada
110 C2 **Braymer** Missouri U.S.A.
18 H4 **Bray sur Seine** France
22 D4 **Bray-sur-Somme** France

14

Brazeau — Bukeye

118 A6 **Brazeau** Alberta Canada
118 B6 **Brazeau Dam** Alberta Canada
128 F6 **Brazil** *rep* S America
110 J2 **Brazil** Indiana U.S.A.
90 G11 **Brazil Basin** Atlantic Oc
109 M6 **Brazoria** Texas U.S.A.
109 L4 **Brazos** *R* Texas U.S.A.
86 C6 **Brazzaville** Congo
48 E6 **Brčko** Yugoslavia
31 K2 **Brda** *R* Poland
48 D1 **Brdo** *mt* Czechoslovakia
140 E6 **Breadalbane** Queensland Australia
143 E7 **Breaden Bluff** *hill* Western Australia Australia
143 F7 **Breaden,L** Western Australia Australia
141 K1 **Breakfast Creek** *dist* Brisbane, Qnsld Australia
144 A6 **Breaksea I** New Zealand
144 B7 **Breaksea Is** New Zealand
141 L6 **Breaksea Spit** Queensland Australia
20 G5 **Bréal-sous-Montfort** France
8 D4 **Bream** England
6 N4 **Bream** *oil rig* North Sea
145 E1 **Bream Bay** New Zealand
27 F15 **Breared** Sweden
21 L2 **Bréaute** France
111 E11 **Breaux Bridge** Louisiana U.S.A.
48 K5 **Breaza** Romania
70 M9 **Brebes** Java
70 M9 **Brebes,Tg** *C* Java
122 B5 **Brébeuf,L** Quebec Canada
121 U4 **Brébeuf, L** Quebec Canada
21 H4 **Brécey** France
20 E6 **Brech** France
36 E3 **Brechen** W Germany
121 L8 **Brechin** Ontario Canada
15 F4 **Brechin** Scotland
20 F3 **Brechou** *isld* Channel Is English Chan
22 H1 **Brecht** Belgium
106 D2 **Breckenridge** Colorado U.S.A.
98 K3 **Breckenridge** Minnesota U.S.A.
110 C2 **Breckenridge** Missouri U.S.A.
109 J3 **Breckenridge** Texas U.S.A.
133 C8 **Brecknock, Pen** Chile
31 K7 **Břeclav** Czechoslovakia
8 C4 **Brecon** Wales
8 C4 **Brecon Beacons** *mts* Wales
Breconshire *co see* **Powys, Gwent, Mid Glamorgan** *counties*
25 C5 **Breda** Netherlands
99 M7 **Breda** Iowa U.S.A.
26 M6 **Bredåker** Sweden
27 H15 **Bredåkra** Sweden
27 G14 **Bredaryd** Sweden
87 D12 **Bredasdorp** S Africa
33 Q7 **Breddin** East Germany
32 K6 **Breddorf** W Germany
28 B6 **Brede** Denmark
9 G6 **Brede** England
28 B6 **Brede Å** *R* Denmark
28 B6 **Bredebro** Denmark
32 J10 **Bredelar** W Germany
22 E1 **Bredene** Belgium
33 R5 **Bredenfelde** East Germany
119 P8 **Bredenyur** Saskatchewan Canada
33 S6 **Bredereiche** East Germany
28 C7 **Bredevad** Denmark
26 L6 **Bredsel** Sweden
27 G12 **Bredsjö** Sweden
30 E1 **Bredstedt** W Germany
28 C5 **Bredsten** Denmark
26 K8 **Bredträsk** Sweden
55 D4 **Bredy** U.S.S.R.
22 K1 **Bree** Belgium
89 A9 **Breede** *R* S Africa
110 G3 **Breese** Illinois U.S.A.
33 Q5 **Breesen** East Germany
46 E3 **Bregalnica** *R* Yugoslavia
41 H2 **Brege** *R* W Germany
41 L2 **Bregenz** Austria
41 L3 **Bregenzer Ache** *R* Austria
41 L3 **Bregenzer Wald** *mt* Austria
28 G5 **Bregninge** Denmark
48 H6 **Bregovo** Bulgaria
20 G4 **Bréhal** France
20 E4 **Bréhat** *isld* France
122 B1 **Bréhat, L** Quebec Canada
33 Q9 **Brehna** East Germany
33 T9 **Brehnitz** East Germany
36 E2 **Breidenbach** W Germany
28 R9 **Breidhafjördhur** *B* Iceland
29 T9 **Breidhdalsvik** Iceland
98 E3 **Breien** North Dakota U.S.A.
21 L5 **Breil-sur-Mérize,le** France
26 B10 **Breim** Norway
40 G1 **Breisach** W Germany
37 M5 **Breitenbrunn** W Germany
33 Q10 **Breitenfeld** East Germany
37 K4 **Breitengüssbach** W Germany
33 P9 **Breitenhagen** East Germany
33 M7 **Breitenhees** W Germany
37 O3 **Breitenhof** East Germany
33 S6 **Breiter Luzinsee** *L* East Germany
40 G5 **Breithorn** *mt* Switzerland
33 Q4 **Breitling** East Germany
37 J2 **Breitungen** W Germany
26 M1 **Breivikbotn** Norway
28 A4 **Brejning** Denmark
129 K4 **Brejo** Brazil
94 C3 **Brekenridge** Michigan U.S.A.
26 E9 **Brekken** Norway
26 D8 **Brekstad** Norway
26 A10 **Bremangerland** *isld* Norway
41 L6 **Brembana, Val** Italy
41 L6 **Brembo** *R* Italy
112 B4 **Bremen** Georgia U.S.A.
94 A5 **Bremen** Indiana U.S.A.
94 E7 **Bremen** Ohio U.S.A.
32 J6 **Bremen** W Germany
140 D1 **Bremer** *isld* N Terr Australia
143 C10 **Bremer Bay** Western Australia Australia
32 J5 **Bremerhaven** W Germany
143 D10 **Bremer Ra** Western Australia Australia
117 M12 **Bremerton** Washington U.S.A.
32 K6 **Bremervörde** W Germany
41 H3 **Bremgarten** Switzerland
116 Q6 **Bremner** *R* Alaska U.S.A.
109 L4 **Bremond** Texas U.S.A.
26 E6 **Bremsteinen** *lighthouse* Norway
139 H3 **Brenda** New South Wales Australia
28 D6 **Brenderup** Denmark
45 K1 **Brendola** Italy
8 C5 **Brendon Hills** England
109 L5 **Brenham** Texas U.S.A.
21 N8 **Brenne** *reg* France
21 M6 **Brenne** *R* Indre-et-Loire France
41 O3 **Brenner** Austria
101 M5 **Brenner** Montana U.S.A.
41 O4 **Brennero** Italy
41 O3 **Brenner Pass** Austria/Italy
41 M6 **Breno** Italy
42 C3 **Breno** Italy
19 P12 **Brénod** France
36 C5 **Brenschelbach** W Germany
121 M6 **Brent** Ontario Canada
6 M1 **Brent** *oil rig* North Sea
111 J9 **Brent** Alabama U.S.A.
42 D3 **Brenta** *R* Italy
41 N5 **Brenta, Gruppa di** *mt* Italy
9 F5 **Brentford** England
98 H4 **Brentford** South Dakota U.S.A.
123 T4 **Brenton Rock** Newfoundland Canada
9 G4 **Brentwood** England
102 C4 **Brentwood** California U.S.A.
37 J6 **Brenz** *R* W Germany
9 G5 **Brenzett** England
89 G6 **Brereton Park** S Africa
45 J2 **Brescello** Italy
41 M6 **Brescia** Italy
25 A6 **Breskens** Netherlands
Breslau *see* **Wrocław**
21 O2 **Bresle** *R* France
21 P3 **Bresles** France
143 C6 **Bresnahan,Mt** Western Australia Australia
41 P4 **Bressanone** Italy
21 K8 **Bressuire** France
20 B5 **Brest** France
31 O3 **Brest** U.S.S.R.
20 D5 **Brest à Nantes, Canal de** France
46 E1 **Brestovac** Yugoslavia
20 A5 **Brest,Rade de** *B* France
83 J14 **Bretagne, Pnte de** Réunion Indian Oc
21 N4 **Bretagnolles** France
48 K4 **Breţcu** Romania
18 G8 **Bretenoux** France
21 M4 **Breteuil-sur-Iton** France
21 P2 **Breteuil-sur-Noye** France
20 G8 **Brétignolles-sur-Mer** France
21 P4 **Brétigny** France
118 C5 **Breton** Alberta Canada
21 M5 **Bretoncelles** France
111 G12 **Breton I** Louisiana U.S.A.
18 E6 **Breton, Pertuis d'** *B* France
95 N6 **Breton Woods** New Jersey U.S.A.
38 K7 **Bretstein** Austria
145 E1 **Brett, C** New Zealand
36 F5 **Bretten** W Germany
21 K3 **Bretteville** France
21 K3 **Bretteville-l'Orgueilleuse** France
37 J5 **Brettheim** W Germany
36 G5 **Bretzfeld** W Germany
36 G4 **Breuberg** W Germany
69 B10 **Breueh, Pulau** *isld* Sumatra
21 L3 **Breuil-en-Auge,le** France
21 N4 **Breuilpont** France
25 D4 **Breukelen** Netherlands
40 C1 **Breuvannes** France
21 O4 **Bréval** France
112 E2 **Brevard** North Carolina U.S.A.
129 H4 **Breves** Brazil
27 D12 **Brevik** Norway
95 T2 **Brewer** Maine U.S.A.
95 L3 **Brewerton** New York U.S.A.
113 E10 **Brewster** Florida U.S.A.
107 J2 **Brewster** Kansas U.S.A.
98 G8 **Brewster** Nebraska U.S.A.
95 O5 **Brewster** New York U.S.A.
94 F6 **Brewster** Ohio U.S.A.
117 O11 **Brewster** Washington U.S.A.
144 B6 **Brewster, Mt** New Zealand
111 J10 **Brewton** Alabama U.S.A.
25 F6 **Breyell** W Germany
52 H6 **Brezhnev** U.S.S.R.
19 O14 **Brezins** France
46 F2 **Breznik** Bulgaria
48 F2 **Brezno** Czechoslovakia
38 M8 **Brezno** Yugoslavia
48 J5 **Brezoi** Romania
21 N4 **Brezolles** France
16 D2 **Brezo, Sa. del** *mts* Spain
46 G2 **Brezovo** Bulgaria
86 D4 **Bria** Cent Afr Republic
103 M4 **Brian Head** Utah U.S.A.
18 G5 **Briare** France
141 L7 **Bribie I** Queensland Australia
108 G1 **Brice** Texas U.S.A.
99 N6 **Bricelyn** Minnesota U.S.A.
48 L2 **Brichany** U.S.S.R.
110 F7 **Brickeys** Arkansas U.S.A.
19 J4 **Bricon** France
123 M2 **Briconnet,L** Quebec Canada
20 G3 **Bricquebec** France
20 G4 **Bricqueville-sur-Mer** France
14 C4 **Bride** *R* Ireland
12 D5 **Bride** I of Man U.K.
8 B3 **Bridell** Wales
8 B6 **Bridestowe** England
119 U3 **Bridgar** Manitoba Canada
117 M10 **Bridge** *R* British Columbia Canada
101 M7 **Bridge** Idaho U.S.A.
112 D6 **Bridgeboro** Georgia U.S.A.
12 B2 **Bridgend** Islay Scotland
13 E1 **Bridgend** Tayside Scotland
8 C5 **Bridgend** Wales
12 E1 **Bridge of Allan** Scotland
12 D3 **Bridge of Doon** Scotland
12 D2 **Bridge of Weir** Scotland
110 L7 **Bridgeport** Alabama U.S.A.
102 E3 **Bridgeport** California U.S.A.
95 O5 **Bridgeport** Connecticut U.S.A.
107 N3 **Bridgeport** Kansas U.S.A.
98 C8 **Bridgeport** Nebraska U.S.A.
100 H5 **Bridgeport** Oregon U.S.A.
100 F2 **Bridgeport** Washington U.S.A.
109 K2 **Bridgeport, L** Texas U.S.A.
102 E3 **Bridgeport Res** California U.S.A.
113 L12 **Bridge Pt** Bahamas
101 R4 **Bridger** Montana U.S.A.
101 P4 **Bridger Pk** Montana U.S.A.
101 S8 **Bridger Pk** Wyoming U.S.A.
95 M7 **Bridgeton** New Jersey U.S.A.
112 K2 **Bridgeton** North Carolina U.S.A.
143 B10 **Bridgetown** Western Australia Australia
127 P6 **Bridgetown** Barbados
122 G9 **Bridgetown** Nova Scotia Canada
122 K8 **Bridgeville** Nova Scotia Canada
100 B9 **Bridgeville** California U.S.A.
122 H9 **Bridgewater** Nova Scotia Canada
95 S7 **Bridgewater** Maine U.S.A.
95 R5 **Bridgewater** Massachusetts U.S.A.
98 J6 **Bridgewater** South Dakota U.S.A.
94 J8 **Bridgewater** Virginia U.S.A.
138 F7 **Bridgewater,C** Victoria Australia
94 A5 **Bridgman** Michigan U.S.A.
8 D2 **Bridgnorth** England
95 R2 **Bridgton** Maine U.S.A.
8 C5 **Bridgwater** England
13 H5 **Bridlington** England
139 H8 **Bridport** Tasmania Australia
8 D6 **Bridport** England
18 G4 **Brie** *reg* France
20 B5 **Briec** France
Brieg *see* **Brzeg**
25 B5 **Brielle** Netherlands
112 F4 **Brier Creek** Georgia U.S.A.
119 M8 **Briercrest** Saskatchewan Canada
118 F4 **Brierville** Alberta Canada
122 F9 **Brier I** Nova Scotia Canada
22 H5 **Brieulles-sur-Bar** France
21 O4 **Brieval** France
22 K5 **Briey** France
40 G5 **Brig** Switzerland
41 H1 **Brigach** *R* W Germany
120 H10 **Brigden** Ontario Canada
13 H6 **Brigg** England
109 K5 **Briggs** Texas U.S.A.
98 B9 **Briggsdale** Colorado U.S.A.
101 N8 **Brigham City** Utah U.S.A.
13 G6 **Brighouse** England
9 E6 **Brighstone** England
103 M5 **Bright Angel Pt** Arizona U.S.A.
9 H4 **Brightlingsea** England
138 E6 **Brighton** South Australia Australia
121 N8 **Brighton** Ontario Canada
9 F6 **Brighton** England
98 B10 **Brighton** Colorado U.S.A.
113 F10 **Brighton** Florida U.S.A.
110 F2 **Brighton** Illinois U.S.A.
99 P8 **Brighton** Iowa U.S.A.
94 D4 **Brighton** Michigan U.S.A.
141 F6 **Brighton Downs** Queensland Australia
145 D4 **Brightwater** New Zealand
20 B4 **Brignogan-Plage** France
123 T6 **Brigus** Newfoundland Canada
17 F4 **Brihuega** Spain
42 F4 **Brijuni** *isld* Yugoslavia
26 G4 **Briksvoer** *isld* Norway
130 C7 **Brilhante,R** Brazil
106 F5 **Brilliant** New Mexico U.S.A.
99 S5 **Brillion** Wisconsin U.S.A.
32 J10 **Brilon** W Germany
99 R9 **Brimfield** Illinois U.S.A.
43 H8 **Brindisi** Italy
138 C4 **Bring,L** South Australia Australia
94 E6 **Brinkhaven** Ohio U.S.A.
9 G3 **Brinkley** England
110 E7 **Brinkley** Arkansas U.S.A.
9 E3 **Brinklow** England
53 E10 **Brin'kovskaya** U.S.S.R.
32 J6 **Brinkum** W Germany
138 E5 **Brinkworth** South Australia Australia
21 P6 **Brinon-sur-Sauldre** France
98 G1 **Brinsmade** North Dakota U.S.A.
113 C7 **Brinson** Georgia U.S.A.
21 J6 **Briollay** France
21 O8 **Brion** Indre France
123 L6 **Brion, I** Madeleine Is, Quebec Canada
21 M3 **Brionne** France
21 K7 **Brion-près-Thouet** France
18 H7 **Brioude** France
21 K4 **Briouze** France
141 L8 **Brisbane** Queensland Australia
141 L7 **Brisbane R** Queensland Australia
108 D8 **Briscoe** Texas U.S.A.
45 L3 **Brisighella** Italy
6 N4 **Brisling** *oil rig* North Sea
21 K7 **Brissac-Quincé** France
41 J4 **Bristenstock** *mt* Switzerland
122 E7 **Bristol** New Brunswick Canada
121 O7 **Bristol** Quebec Canada
8 D5 **Bristol** England
106 H3 **Bristol** Colorado U.S.A.
95 P5 **Bristol** Connecticut U.S.A.
113 C7 **Bristol** Florida U.S.A.
112 E6 **Bristol** Georgia U.S.A.
94 B5 **Bristol** Indiana U.S.A.
95 Q3 **Bristol** New Hampshire U.S.A.
95 M6 **Bristol** Pennsylvania U.S.A.
95 Q5 **Bristol** Rhode I U.S.A.
98 J4 **Bristol** South Dakota U.S.A.
95 O2 **Bristol** Vermont U.S.A.
94 E10 **Bristol** Virginia/Tenn U.S.A.
116 G8 **Bristol B** Alaska U.S.A.
8 C5 **Bristol Chan** England/Wales
146 G3 **Bristol I** S Sandwich Is Atl Oc
103 J7 **Bristol L** California U.S.A.
103 J7 **Bristol Mts** California U.S.A.
103 K3 **Bristol Silver** Nevada U.S.A.
107 O6 **Bristow** Oklahoma U.S.A.
117 M11 **Britannia Beach** British Columbia Canada
146 A3 **British Antarctic Terr** Antarctica
117 K7 **British Columbia** *prov* Canada
115 L1 **British Empire Ra** Northwest Territories Canada
British Guiana *see* **Guyana**
British Honduras *see* **Belize**
81 E6 **British Ind.Oc.Terr** *colony* Indian Oc
116 Q2 **British Mts** Alaska/Yukon Terr U.S.A./Canada
British N. Borneo *see* **Sabah**
British Solomon Is *see* **Solomon Is.**
123 M7 **Briton Cove** C Breton I, Nova Scotia
8 C4 **Briton Ferry** Wales
87 E11 **Brits** S Africa
87 D12 **Britstown** S Africa
120 K7 **Britt** Ontario Canada
99 N6 **Britt** Iowa U.S.A.
27 G14 **Brittatorp** Sweden
107 N6 **Britton** Oklahoma U.S.A.
98 J4 **Britton** South Dakota U.S.A.
138 C2 **Britton,Mt** South Australia Australia
33 T7 **Britz** East Germany
18 G7 **Brive-la-Gaillarde** France
16 E2 **Briviesca** Spain
20 G2 **Brix** France
38 F7 **Brixental** *V* Austria
8 C7 **Brixham** England
48 D1 **Brno** Czechoslovakia
27 F12 **Bro** Sweden
112 D3 **Broad** *R* Georgia U.S.A.
112 F3 **Broad** *R* South Carolina U.S.A.
118 J6 **Broadacres** Saskatchewan Canada
95 N3 **Broadalbin** New York U.S.A.
143 D9 **Broad Arrow** Western Australia Australia
121 M1 **Broadback** *R* Quebec Canada
15 B2 **Broad Bay** Scotland
100 A6 **Broadbent** Oregon U.S.A.
109 N4 **Broaddus** Texas U.S.A.
15 C3 **Broadford** Scotland
14 B2 **Broad Haven** Ireland
8 A4 **Broad Haven** Wales
9 E5 **Broad Hinton** England
142 D5 **Broadhurst Ra** Western Australia Australia
98 H5 **Broadland** South Dakota U.S.A.
15 E5 **Broad Law** Scotland
116 N5 **Broad Pass** Alaska U.S.A.
141 J5 **Broad Sound** Queensland Australia
141 K5 **Broad Sound Chan** Queensland Australia
141 J6 **Broadsound Ra** Queensland Australia
9 H5 **Broadstairs** England
98 A4 **Broadus** Montana U.S.A.
119 P8 **Broadview** Saskatchewan Canada
101 R3 **Broadview** Montana U.S.A.
108 A9 **Broadview** New Mexico U.S.A.
9 F6 **Broadwater** England
98 D8 **Broadwater** Nebraska U.S.A.
9 E3 **Broadway** England
8 D6 **Broadwey** England
8 D6 **Broadwindsor** England
145 D1 **Broadwood** New Zealand
126 C3 **Broa, Ensenada de la** *B* Cuba
28 D7 **Broager** Denmark
28 E6 **Broby** Denmark
27 G15 **Broby** Sweden
119 Q1 **Brochet** Manitoba Canada
122 C4 **Brochet,L.au** Quebec Canada
32 G8 **Brochterbeck** W Germany
121 Q4 **Brochu,L** Quebec Canada
118 J7 **Brock** Saskatchewan Canada
99 L9 **Brock** Nebraska U.S.A.
32 L6 **Brockel** W Germany
33 N9 **Brocken** *mt* East Germany
9 E6 **Brockenhurst** England
118 D9 **Brocket** Alberta Canada
98 H1 **Brocket** North Dakota U.S.A.
114 H2 **Brock I** Northwest Territories Canada
13 H6 **Brocklesby** England
142 B5 **Brockman,Mt** Western Australia Australia
94 K3 **Brockport** New York U.S.A.
98 G7 **Brocksburg** Nebraska U.S.A.
140 B2 **Brock's Creek** N Terr Australia
95 Q4 **Brockton** Massachusetts U.S.A.
98 B1 **Brockton** Montana U.S.A.
121 P8 **Brockville** Ontario Canada
98 A2 **Brockway** Montana U.S.A.
94 J5 **Brockway** Pennsylvania U.S.A.
110 J2 **Brocton** Illinois U.S.A.
94 H4 **Brocton** New York U.S.A.
48 F7 **Brodarevo** Yugoslavia
118 L7 **Broderick** Saskatchewan Canada
115 L3 **Brodeur Pen** Northwest Territories Canada
99 R7 **Brodhead** Wisconsin U.S.A.
48 G6 **Brodica** Yugoslavia
12 C2 **Brodick** Scotland
94 K10 **Brodnax** Virginia U.S.A.
31 L2 **Brodnica** Poland
55 D3 **Brodokalmak** U.S.S.R.
25 C3 **Broek op Langedijk** Netherlands
100 H5 **Brogan** Oregon U.S.A.
21 M3 **Broglie** France
20 F5 **Brohinière,la** France
36 C3 **Brohl-Lützing** W Germany
33 T5 **Brohm-Cosa** East Germany
33 M8 **Broistedt** W Germany
31 N3 **Brok** Poland
99 R4 **Brokaw** Wisconsin U.S.A.
32 K5 **Brokdorf** W Germany
107 P5 **Broken Arrow** Oklahoma U.S.A.
7 M9 **Broken Bank** *oil rig* North Sea
139 K5 **Broken Bay** New South Wales Australia
98 G8 **Broken Bow** Nebraska U.S.A.
107 Q7 **Broken Bow** Oklahoma U.S.A.
107 Q7 **Broken Bow L** Oklahoma U.S.A.
138 F4 **Broken Hill** New South Wales Australia
Broken Hill Zambia *see* **Kabwe**
129 G3 **Brokopondomeer** *L* Suriname
29 K12 **Bromarv** Finland
Bromberg *see* **Bydgoszcz**
33 N7 **Brome** W Germany
8 D3 **Bromfield** England
98 C1 **Bromhead** Saskatchewan Canada
9 G5 **Bromley** England
27 D11 **Bromma** Norway
28 G5 **Bromme** Denmark
70 O9 **Bromo** *mt* Java
13 H5 **Brompton** England
99 O9 **Brompton** Iowa U.S.A.
8 D3 **Bromsgrove** England
8 D3 **Bromyard** England
19 N13 **Bron** France
40 A6 **Bron** France
110 B4 **Bronaugh** Missouri U.S.A.
28 D2 **Brønderslev** Denmark
28 A5 **Brøndum** Denmark
8 C3 **Bronllys** Wales
37 L4 **Bronn** W Germany
27 G15 **Brönnestad** Sweden
55 E2 **Bronnikovo** U.S.S.R.
26 F6 **Brönnöysund** Norway
36 H2 **Bronnzell** W Germany
28 B6 **Brøns** Denmark
113 E8 **Bronson** Florida U.S.A.
94 B5 **Bronson** Michigan U.S.A.
109 N4 **Bronson** Texas U.S.A.
121 L9 **Bronte** Ontario Canada
43 F11 **Bronte** Sicily
108 G4 **Bronte** Texas U.S.A.
139 H8 **Bronte Park** Tasmania Australia
95 O6 **Bronx** New York U.S.A.
41 O5 **Bronzolo** Italy
122 E3 **Brooch L** Quebec Canada
99 T9 **Brook** Indiana U.S.A.
94 K8 **Brooke** Virginia U.S.A.
109 O4 **Brookeland** Texas U.S.A.
113 E8 **Brooker** Florida U.S.A.
71 C6 **Brooke's Pt** Palawan Philippines
122 J8 **Brookfield** Nova Scotia Canada
110 C2 **Brookfield** Missouri U.S.A.
111 F10 **Brookhaven** Mississippi U.S.A.
119 N9 **Brooking** Saskatchewan Canada
100 A7 **Brookings** Oregon U.S.A.
98 K5 **Brookings** South Dakota U.S.A.
141 H4 **Brook Is.Lt.Ho** Queensland Australia
9 G6 **Brookland** England
94 K5 **Brookland** Pennsylvania U.S.A.
112 F5 **Brooklet** Georgia U.S.A.
121 M9 **Brooklin** Ontario Canada
95 Q4 **Brookline** Massachusetts U.S.A.
110 K2 **Brooklyn** Indiana U.S.A.
99 O8 **Brooklyn** Iowa U.S.A.
94 C4 **Brooklyn** Michigan U.S.A.
111 G10 **Brooklyn** Mississippi U.S.A.
95 O6 **Brooklyn** New York U.S.A.
95 M5 **Brooklyn** Pennsylvania U.S.A.
117 N11 **Brookmere** British Columbia Canada
94 H10 **Brookneal** Virginia U.S.A.
99 N4 **Brook Park** Minnesota U.S.A.
110 H4 **Brookport** Illinois U.S.A.
118 F8 **Brooks** Alberta Canada
95 S2 **Brooks** Maine U.S.A.
101 Q2 **Brooks** Montana U.S.A.
117 G5 **Brooks Brook** Yukon Territory Canada
119 N5 **Brooksby** Saskatchewan Canada
146 D6 **Brooks, Cape** *C* Antarctica
109 M6 **Brookshire** Texas U.S.A.
116 M5 **Brooks,Mt** Alaska U.S.A.
116 D4 **Brooks Mt** Alaska U.S.A.
116 H2 **Brooks Range** Alaska U.S.A.
99 O3 **Brookston** Minnesota U.S.A.
109 M2 **Brookston** Texas U.S.A.
113 E9 **Brooksville** Florida U.S.A.
111 H8 **Brooksville** Mississippi U.S.A.
143 B9 **Brookton** Western Australia Australia
95 U1 **Brookton** Maine U.S.A.
95 L4 **Brooktondale** New York U.S.A.
110 M2 **Brookville** Indiana U.S.A.
107 N3 **Brookville** Kansas U.S.A.
94 H5 **Brookville** Pennsylvania U.S.A.
111 J8 **Brookwood** Alabama U.S.A.
141 L7 **Brooloo** Queensland Australia
123 K4 **Broom B** Anticosti I, Quebec
142 D4 **Broome** Western Australia Australia
143 C10 **Broomehill** Western Australia Australia
142 F3 **Broome, Mt** Western Australia Australia
20 F5 **Broons** France
99 L4 **Brooten** Minnesota U.S.A.
142 G4 **Brophy,Mt** Western Australia Australia
143 F7 **Brophy,Mt** Western Australia Australia
15 E2 **Brora** Scotland
28 B5 **Brørup** Denmark
27 G16 **Brösarp** Sweden
14 D3 **Brosna** *R* Ireland
48 K3 **Brosteni** Romania
68 A7 **Brothers** *islds* Andaman Is
100 E6 **Brothers** Oregon U.S.A.
145 E4 **Brothers, The** New Zealand
84 K4 **Brothers,The** *islds* Red Sea
37 J2 **Brotterode** East Germany
21 N5 **Brou** France
13 F4 **Brough** England
15 E1 **Brough Hd** Orkney Scotland
15 F2 **Brough Ness** Scotland
9 F3 **Broughton** England
13 E5 **Broughton** Cumbria England
13 E2 **Broughton** Scotland
110 H4 **Broughton** Illinois U.S.A.
107 N2 **Broughton** Kansas U.S.A.
121 T6 **Broughton Station** Quebec Canada
15 F4 **Broughty Ferry** Scotland
86 C2 **Broulkou** Chad
36 B7 **Brouvelieures** France
25 A5 **Brouwershaven** Netherlands
20 H8 **Brouzils,les** France
40 E4 **Brove** *R* Switzerland
85 C7 **Brovio** Liberia
28 D2 **Brovst** Denmark
99 L3 **Browerville** Minnesota U.S.A.
71 C5 **Brown Bank** Palawan Philippines
94 E3 **Brown City** Michigan U.S.A.
107 L3 **Brownell** Kansas U.S.A.
143 E7 **Browne Ra** Western Australia Australia
108 E2 **Brownfield** Texas U.S.A.
119 P9 **Browning** Saskatchewan Canada
110 C1 **Browning** Missouri U.S.A.
101 M1 **Browning** Montana U.S.A.
144 C5 **Browning Pass** New Zealand
143 C9 **Brown,L** Western Australia Australia
119 M8 **Brownlee** Saskatchewan Canada
98 F7 **Brownlee** Nebraska U.S.A.
138 E4 **Brown,Mt** South Australia Australia
138 F3 **Brown,Mt** South Australia Australia
142 A3 **Brown,Mt** Western Australia Australia
138 C4 **Brown Pt** South Australia Australia
141 G3 **Brown R** Queensland Australia
120 J3 **Brownrigg** Ontario Canada
144 B7 **Browns** New Zealand
110 J3 **Browns** Illinois U.S.A.
109 M3 **Brownsboro** Texas U.S.A.
121 Q7 **Brownsburg** Quebec Canada
110 K2 **Brownsburg** Indiana U.S.A.
126 E2 **Browns Cay** *isld* Bahamas
145 G1 **Browns I** New Zealand
98 C8 **Brownson** Nebraska U.S.A.
127 K2 **Brown's Town** Jamaica
94 A8 **Brownstown** Indiana U.S.A.
98 K4 **Browns Valley** Minnesota U.S.A.
110 L2 **Brownsville** Indiana U.S.A.
110 K4 **Brownsville** Kentucky U.S.A.
100 C5 **Brownsville** Oregon U.S.A.
94 H6 **Brownsville** Pennsylvania U.S.A.
110 G6 **Brownsville** Tennessee U.S.A.
109 K10 **Brownsville** Texas U.S.A.
99 M5 **Brownton** Minnesota U.S.A.
99 R7 **Browntown** Wisconsin U.S.A.
111 J8 **Brownville** Alabama U.S.A.
99 L9 **Brownville** Nebraska U.S.A.
95 M2 **Brownville** New York U.S.A.
95 S1 **Brownville Junc** Maine U.S.A.
109 J4 **Brownwood, L** Texas U.S.A.
142 E2 **Browse I** Australia
142 E2 **Browse I** Indian Oc
15 E5 **Broxburn** Scotland
112 E6 **Broxton** Georgia U.S.A.
16 C5 **Brozas** Spain
45 K4 **Brozzi** Italy
45 P1 **Brtonigla** Yugoslavia
22 D3 **Bruay** France
22 F3 **Bruay-sur-l'Escaut** France
127 P6 **Bruce** Barbados
118 E5 **Bruce** Alberta Canada
145 E4 **Bruce** New Zealand
6 L3 **Bruce** *oil rig* North Sea
111 G7 **Bruce** Mississippi U.S.A.
99 P4 **Bruce** Wisconsin U.S.A.
144 B5 **Bruce Bay** New Zealand
99 R3 **Bruce Crossing** Michigan U.S.A.
120 J9 **Brucefield** Ontario Canada
142 C5 **Bruce,Mt** Western Australia Australia
120 J7 **Bruce Pen** Ontario Canada
143 C9 **Bruce Rock** Western Australia Australia
110 H5 **Bruceton** Tennessee U.S.A.
109 K4 **Bruceville** Texas U.S.A.
19 K4 **Bruche** *R* France
32 K7 **Bruchhausen-Vilsen** W Germany
36 F3 **Bruchköbel** W Germany
36 F5 **Bruchsal** W Germany
31 K7 **Bruck** Austria
33 R8 **Brück** East Germany
37 L4 **Bruck** Bayern W Germany
38 M7 **Bruck-an-der-Mur** Austria
37 M6 **Bruckberg** W Germany
38 L8 **Brückl** Austria
21 K3 **Brucourt** France
19 P18 **Brue-Auriac** France
118 E5 **Bruederheim** Alberta Canada
33 P5 **Brüel** East Germany
14 C4 **Bruff** Ireland
20 H7 **Bruffière,la** France
Bruges *see* **Brugge**
40 H3 **Brugg** Switzerland
22 E1 **Brugge** Belgium
36 D1 **Brügge** W Germany
25 F6 **Brüggen** W Germany
45 L1 **Brùgine** Italy
44 F2 **Brugneto, L. di** Italy
36 B2 **Brühl** W Germany
94 H5 **Bruin** Pennsylvania U.S.A.
103 O2 **Bruin Pt** Utah U.S.A.
117 P9 **Brûlé** Alberta Canada
98 E8 **Brule** Nebraska U.S.A.
99 P3 **Brule** Wisconsin U.S.A.
121 N6 **Brûlé, L** Quebec Canada
121 M7 **Brûlé Lake** Ontario Canada
21 K6 **Brûlon** France
22 J4 **Brûly** Belgium
129 K6 **Brumado** Brazil
25 F4 **Brummen** Netherlands
140 C4 **Brunchilly** N Terr Australia
43 C8 **Bruncu Spina** *mt* Sardinia
108 H7 **Brundage** Texas U.S.A.
111 L10 **Brundidge** Alabama U.S.A.
100 K7 **Bruneau** Idaho U.S.A.
22 G4 **Brunehamel** France
70 D2 **Brunei** *state* Borneo
70 D2 **Brunei B** Brunei
Brunei Town *see* **Bandar Seri Begawan**
140 D4 **Brunette Downs** N Terr Australia
123 Q6 **Brunette I** Newfoundland Canada
21 L2 **Bruneval** France
26 G8 **Brunflo** Sweden
109 J8 **Bruni** Texas U.S.A.
42 D2 **Brunico** Italy
118 D1 **Brunkild** Manitoba Canada
Brünn *see* **Brno**
37 N2 **Brunn** East Germany
29 K4 **Brunnby** Sweden
41 J3 **Brunnen** Switzerland
119 M6 **Bruno** Saskatchewan Canada
99 O3 **Bruno** Minnesota U.S.A.
32 K5 **Brunsbüttelkoog** W Germany
32 L5 **Brunshausen** W Germany
25 E7 **Brunssum** Netherlands
Brunswick *see* **Braunschweig**
112 F6 **Brunswick** Georgia U.S.A.
95 S3 **Brunswick** Maine U.S.A.
94 K7 **Brunswick** Maryland U.S.A.
94 F5 **Brunswick** Ohio U.S.A.
142 E3 **Brunswick B** Western Australia Australia
143 B10 **Brunswick Junction** Western Australia Australia
120 G3 **Brunswick L** Ontario Canada
133 C8 **Brunswick, Pen. de** Chile
31 K6 **Bruntál** Czechoslovakia
146 F6 **Brunt Ice Shelf** *ice shelf* Antarctica
139 H9 **Bruny I** Tasmania Australia
26 G6 **Brurskanken** *mt* Norway
46 F1 **Brusartsi** Bulgaria
106 G1 **Brush** Colorado U.S.A.
95 N2 **Brushton** New York U.S.A.
112 F1 **Brushy Mts** North Carolina U.S.A.
130 E10 **Brusque** Brazil
Brussels *see* **Bruxelles**
120 J9 **Brussels** Ontario Canada
99 T5 **Brussels** Wisconsin U.S.A.
8 D5 **Bruton** England
24 **Bruxelles** *conurbation* Belgium
22 G2 **Bruxelles** Belgium
19 K4 **Bruyères** France
20 G5 **Bruz** France
128 E2 **Bruzual** Venezuela
22 F3 **Bry** France
94 C5 **Bryan** Ohio U.S.A.
109 L5 **Bryan** Texas U.S.A.
146 C6 **Bryan Coast** Antarctica
54 K8 **Bryanka** U.S.S.R.
138 E5 **Bryan,Mt** South Australia Australia
53 G11 **Bryansk** U.S.S.R.
54 F3 **Bryansk** U.S.S.R.
53 D8 **Bryanskaya Oblast'** *prov* U.S.S.R.
109 P1 **Bryant** Arkansas U.S.A.
110 M1 **Bryant** Indiana U.S.A.
110 D5 **Bryant Cr** Missouri U.S.A.
95 R2 **Bryant Pond** Maine U.S.A.
22 C3 **Bryas** France
103 M4 **Bryce Canyon Nat. Park** Utah U.S.A.
144 B7 **Brydone** New Zealand
9 F7 **Bryher** *isld* Isles of Scilly England
8 C4 **Bryn-amman** Wales
8 B2 **Bryn-crug** Wales
8 C1 **Bryneglwys** Wales
26 M1 **Brynilen** Norway
8 C4 **Bryn Mawr** Wales
48 L2 **Brynzeny** U.S.S.R.
28 C4 **Bryrup** Denmark
112 D2 **Bryson City** North Carolina U.S.A.
121 N6 **Bryson,L** Quebec Canada
48 G6 **Brza Palanka** Yugoslavia
31 K5 **Brzeg** Poland
31 M6 **Brzesko** Poland
31 M4 **Brzeziny** Poland
31 L4 **Brzeźnica** Poland
31 N6 **Brzozów** Poland
21 O4 **Bû** France
88 E8 **Bua** *R* Malawi
71 H5 **Buabuang** Sulawesi
71 H7 **Buagi** Indonesia
21 J4 **Buais** France
69 D12 **Buatan** Sumatra
84 F3 **Bu'ayrāt al Hasūn** Libya
33 S7 **Buberow** East Germany
89 F2 **Bubi** *R* Zimbabwe
77 A5 **Būbiyān, Jazīrat** *isld* Kuwait
20 D6 **Bubry** France
71 F7 **Bubuan** *isld* Mindanao Philippines
13 H6 **Bubwith** England
87 F10 **Bubye** *R* Zimbabwe
47 L7 **Bucak** Turkey
128 D2 **Bucaramanga** Colombia
71 G6 **Bucas Grande** Philippines
141 J5 **Bucasia** Queensland Australia
111 H10 **Bucatunda** Mississippi U.S.A.
142 E3 **Buccaneer Arch** Western Australia Australia
43 G8 **Buccino** Italy
48 K3 **Bucecea** Romania
47 K3 **Bü Çekmece** Turkey
48 J1 **Buchach** U.S.S.R.
6 L5 **Buchan** *oil rig* North Sea
15 F3 **Buchan** *dist* Scotland
140 D4 **Buchanan** *R* N Terr Australia
119 P7 **Buchanan** Saskatchewan Canada
85 B7 **Buchanan** Liberia
112 B4 **Buchanan** Georgia U.S.A.
99 U8 **Buchanan** Michigan U.S.A.
106 F7 **Buchanan** New Mexico U.S.A.
98 G2 **Buchanan** North Dakota U.S.A.
94 H9 **Buchanan** Virginia U.S.A.
109 J5 **Buchanan Dam** Texas U.S.A.
140 B4 **Buchanan Hills** N Terr Australia
141 H5 **Buchanan,L** Queensland Australia
143 E7 **Buchanan,L** Western Australia Australia
109 J5 **Buchanan, L** Texas U.S.A.
115 M3 **Buchan Gulf** Northwest Territories Canada
15 G3 **Buchan Ness** Scotland
123 Q5 **Buchans** Newfoundland Canada
123 Q5 **Buchans Jnct** Newfoundland Canada
133 E4 **Buchardo** Argentina
Bucharest *see* **Bucureşti**
37 N7 **Buchbach** W Germany
36 G4 **Buchen** W Germany
36 C4 **Büchenbeuren** W Germany
37 L1 **Buchenwald** East Germany
33 R8 **Buchholz** East Germany
32 L6 **Buchholz** W Germany
41 N2 **Buching** W Germany
41 N1 **Buchloe** W Germany
15 D4 **Buchlyvie** Scotland
41 K3 **Buchs** Switzerland
21 N2 **Buchy** France
106 C6 **Buck** New Mexico U.S.A.
9 F3 **Buckden** England
32 K8 **Bückeburg** W Germany
32 K7 **Bücken** W Germany
103 M8 **Buckeye** Arizona U.S.A.
94 E7 **Buckeye Lake** Ohio U.S.A.
95 K7 **Buckeystown** Maryland U.S.A.
8 C7 **Buckfastleigh** England
94 G8 **Buckhannon** West Virginia U.S.A.
15 E4 **Buckhaven & Methil** Scotland
98 C5 **Buckhorn** Wyoming U.S.A.
15 E3 **Buckie** Scotland
121 P7 **Buckingham** Quebec Canada
9 E3 **Buckingham** England
94 J9 **Buckingham** Virginia U.S.A.
140 D1 **Buckingham B** N Terr Australia
140 E5 **Buckingham Downs** Queensland Australia
140 B4 **Buck,L** N Terr Australia
118 C5 **Buck L** Alberta Canada
116 G4 **Buckland** Alaska U.S.A.
119 V1 **Buckland L** Manitoba Canada
145 G1 **Bucklands Beach** New Zealand
141 J6 **Buckland Tableland** Queensland Australia
146 C13 **Buckle I** Antarctica
140 E5 **Buckley** *R* Queensland Australia
110 H1 **Buckley** Illinois U.S.A.
94 B2 **Buckley** Michigan U.S.A.
100 C2 **Buckley** Washington U.S.A.
38 O6 **Bucklige Welt** *reg* Austria
107 L4 **Bucklin** Kansas U.S.A.
110 D2 **Bucklin** Missouri U.S.A.
Buckner Bay *see* **Nakagusuku-wan**
102 C2 **Bucks** California U.S.A.
103 L7 **Buckskin Mts** Arizona U.S.A.
102 C2 **Bucks Mt** California U.S.A.
95 T2 **Bucksport** Maine U.S.A.
33 Q7 **Bückwitz** East Germany
31 K6 **Bučovice** Czechoslovakia
86 B6 **Buco Zau** Angola
22 D3 **Bucquoy** France
122 H7 **Buctouche** New Brunswick Canada
48 K6 **Bucureşti** Romania
71 E7 **Bucutua** *isld* Philippines
22 F4 **Bucy-les-Pierrepont** France
98 D3 **Bucyrus** North Dakota U.S.A.
26 B9 **Bud** Norway
68 D7 **Buda** *isld* Burma
109 K5 **Buda** Texas U.S.A.
48 E3 **Budafok** Hungary
54 B4 **Buda-Koshelevo** U.S.S.R.
68 B1 **Budalin** Burma
48 E3 **Budapest** Hungary
74 H4 **Budaun** India
9 E1 **Budby** England
146 G14 **Budd Coast** Antarctica
53 F10 **Buddenovsk** U.S.S.R.
143 B8 **Budd,Mt** Western Australia Australia
15 F4 **Buddon Ness** Scotland
8 B6 **Bude** England
32 L4 **Büdelsdorf** W Germany
32 G9 **Büderich** W Germany
141 L7 **Buderim** Queensland Australia
22 K4 **Buderscheid** Luxembourg
48 K6 **Budeşti** Romania
139 K5 **Budgewoi** New South Wales Australia
28 S9 **Budhardalur** Iceland
29 T9 **Budhareyri** Iceland
28 R9 **Budhir** Iceland
29 T9 **Búdhir** Iceland
131 A7 **Budi,L.del** Chile
36 G3 **Büdingen** W Germany
86 C5 **Budjala** Zaire
8 C6 **Budleigh Salterton** England
45 L2 **Budrio** Italy
70 F6 **Budungbudung** Sulawesi
42 J6 **Budva** Yugoslavia
54 H7 **Budy** U.S.S.R.
86 A5 **Buéa** Cameroon
19 P16 **Buech** *R* France
21 N4 **Buéil** France
102 D7 **Buellton** California U.S.A.
128 C3 **Buenaventura** Colombia
71 E4 **Buenavista** Philippines
71 G6 **Buenavista** Mindanao Philippines
106 D3 **Buena Vista** Colorado U.S.A.
112 C5 **Buena Vista** Georgia U.S.A.
94 H9 **Buena Vista** Virginia U.S.A.
126 E3 **Buenavista, B. de** Cuba
17 F4 **Buendia, Embalse de** Spain
Buene *R see* **Bojana**
131 A8 **Bueno** *R* Chile
130 E4 **Buenolândia** Brazil
129 K7 **Buenópolis** Brazil
132 **Buenos Aires** *conurbation* Argentina
131 E6 **Buenos Aires** *prov* Argentina
128 D4 **Buenos Aires** Colombia
133 C7 **Buenos Aires,L** Chile/Arg
127 N3 **Buenos Ayres** Trinidad
133 D7 **Buen Pasto** Argentina
133 D8 **Buen Tiempo,C** Argentina
130 H4 **Buerarema** Brazil
40 E5 **Buet,Mt** France
117 Q6 **Buffalo** *R* Alberta/N W Terr Canada
89 G6 **Buffalo** *R* S Africa
110 C5 **Buffalo** *R* Arkansas U.S.A.
107 P4 **Buffalo** Kansas U.S.A.
110 L4 **Buffalo** Kentucky U.S.A.
98 K3 **Buffalo** *R* Minnesota U.S.A.
99 N4 **Buffalo** Minnesota U.S.A.
110 C4 **Buffalo** Missouri U.S.A.
101 Q3 **Buffalo** Montana U.S.A.
94 J4 **Buffalo** New York U.S.A.
107 L5 **Buffalo** Oklahoma U.S.A.
112 F3 **Buffalo** South Carolina U.S.A.
98 C4 **Buffalo** South Dakota U.S.A.
110 J6 **Buffalo** *R* Tennessee U.S.A.
99 P5 **Buffalo** *R* Wisconsin U.S.A.
101 T5 **Buffalo** Wyoming U.S.A.
101 Q5 **Buffalo Bill Dam** Wyoming U.S.A.
101 Q5 **Buffalo Bill Res** Wyoming U.S.A.
99 N6 **Buffalo Center** Iowa U.S.A.
106 E2 **Buffalo Creek** Colorado U.S.A.
119 M9 **Buffalo Gap** Saskatchewan Canada
98 C6 **Buffalo Gap** South Dakota U.S.A.
118 E6 **Buffalo, L** Alberta Canada
117 Q5 **Buffalo L** Northwest Territories Canada
108 E1 **Buffalo L** Texas U.S.A.
139 H6 **Buffalo,Mt** Victoria Australia
118 J3 **Buffalo Narrows** Saskatchewan Canada
119 M8 **Buffalo Pound Prov Park** Saskatchewan Canada
127 L2 **Buff Bay** Jamaica
112 C3 **Buford** Georgia U.S.A.
98 C1 **Buford** North Dakota U.S.A.
98 A8 **Buford** Wyoming U.S.A.
48 K6 **Buftea** Romania
31 O4 **Bug** *R* Poland/U.S.S.R.
128 C3 **Buga** Colombia
18 G10 **Bugarach, Pic de** *mt* France
58 G1 **Bugarikhta** U.S.S.R.
47 J4 **Buğdaylı** Turkey
70 N9 **Bugel,Tg** Java
40 B6 **Bugey** *dist* France
Buggs Island Lake *see* **John H. Kerr Res.** N Carolina/Virginia
88 D1 **Bugiri** Uganda
26 R2 **Bugöynes** Norway
54 C10 **Bugskiy Liman** *lagoon* U.S.S.R.
71 C6 **Bugsuk** *isld* Palawan Philippines
59 H2 **Bugt** China
18 F8 **Bugue,Le** France
71 E1 **Buguey** Luzon Philippines
78 K2 **Bügük Ağri** *mt* Turkey
57 F3 **Bugun'** U.S.S.R.
57 E3 **Bugun'skoye Vodokhranilishche** *res* U.S.S.R.
78 G4 **Buhayrat al Asad** *L* Syria
87 F9 **Buhera** Zimbabwe
58 C4 **Buh He** *R* China
71 F4 **Buhi** Luzon Philippines
101 L7 **Buhl** Idaho U.S.A.
99 O2 **Buhl** Minnesota U.S.A.
36 E6 **Bühl** W Germany
36 E6 **Bühlerhöhe** W Germany
36 E6 **Bühlertal** W Germany
36 H5 **Bühlertann** W Germany
88 E6 **Buhoro Flats** Tanzania
48 K4 **Buhuşi** Romania
117 N7 **Buick** British Columbia Canada
25 C4 **Buiksloot** Netherlands
8 C3 **Builth Wells** Wales
137 M3 **Buin** Bougainville I Papua New Guinea
41 M4 **Buin,Piz** *mt* Switz/Austria
130 H10 **Buique** Brazil
36 B2 **Buir** W Germany
22 B3 **Buire-le-Sec** France
22 F4 **Buironfosse** France
19 O16 **Buis-les-Baronnies** France
25 F2 **Buitenpost** Netherlands
67 B7 **Bui Thon** Vietnam
122 J2 **Buit,L** Quebec Canada
16 E7 **Bujalance** Spain
46 E2 **Bujanovac** Yugoslavia
17 G3 **Bujaraloz** Spain
42 F3 **Buje** Yugoslavia
88 B3 **Bujumbura** Burundi
48 D3 **Bük** Hungary
137 L3 **Buka** *isld* Papua New Guinea
66 E4 **Buka Daban Feng** *mt* China
88 D2 **Bukakata** Uganda
87 E7 **Bukama** Zaire
88 D2 **Bukasa I** Uganda
88 B3 **Bukavu** Zaire
88 C2 **Bukene** Tanzania
88 B3 **Bukeye** Burundi

57 C5 **Bukhara** U.S.S.R.
46 F2 **Bukhovo** Bulgaria
56 B6 **Bukhtarminskoye Vodokhranilishche** *res* U.S.S.R.
70 C6 **Bukitlidi** Kalimantan
69 E13 **Bukittinggi** Sumatra
48 F2 **Bükk** *mt* Hungary
79 F8 **Bukka, J. el** *mt* Jordan
48 D4 **Bükkösd** Hungary
33 Q9 **Buko** East Germany
88 C2 **Bukoba** Tanzania
48 J2 **Bukovina** *old prov* U.S.S.R.
31 J1 **Bukowo,Jezioro** *L* Poland
136 G2 **Bula** Moluccas Indonesia
71 H4 **Bula anguki** Sulawesi
41 J2 **Bülach** Switzerland
56 H5 **Bulagansk** U.S.S.R.
65 D2 **Bulag Sum** China
139 K4 **Bulahdelah** New South Wales Australia
71 E4 **Bulalacao** Philippines
71 E5 **Bulalacao** Calamian Group Philippines
71 F4 **Bulan** Philippines
71 E7 **Bulan** *isld* Philippines
55 D3 **Bulanash** U.S.S.R.
55 C4 **Bulanavo** U.S.S.R.
89 F3 **Bulawayo** Zimbabwe
55 F3 **Bulayevo** U.S.S.R.
28 C2 **Bulbjerg** *hill* Denmark
47 K6 **Buldan** Turkey
74 G8 **Buldana** India
77 H6 **Buleda** *reg* Pakistan
70 P10 **Buleleng** Bali Indonesia
89 G5 **Bulembu** Swaziland
9 E5 **Bulford** England
58 B2 **Bulgan** Mongolia
58 D2 **Bulgan** Mongolia
46 F2 **Bulgaria** *rep* E Europe
47 J2 **Bŭlgarovo** Bulgaria
40 C1 **Bulgnéville** France
77 C7 **Bul Hanine** *oil well* Persian Gulf
71 B2 **Buli** Halmahera Indonesia
71 C6 **Buliluyan,C** Palawan Philippines
141 K1 **Bulimba** *dist* Brisbane, Qnsld Australia
141 L2 **Bulimba Cr** Brisbane, Qnsld Australia
67 B4 **Buliu He** *R* China
117 K8 **Bulkley** *R* British Columbia Canada
143 D9 **Bulla Bulling** Western Australia Australia
22 L3 **Bullange** Belgium
16 E5 **Bullaque** *R* Spain
109 M3 **Bullard** Texas U.S.A.
27 E13 **Bullaren S** *L* Sweden
17 F6 **Bullas** Spain
141 G8 **Bullawarra,L** Queensland Australia
86 H3 **Bullaxaar** Somalia
36 C3 **Bullay** W Germany
127 L3 **Bull Bay** Jamaica
112 H5 **Bull Bay** South Carolina U.S.A.
40 F4 **Bulle** Switzerland
138 F4 **Bullea,L** New South Wales Australia
116 O1 **Bullen** Alaska U.S.A.
126 A1 **Bullen Baai** *B* Curaçao
139 H6 **Buller, Mt** Victoria Australia
145 D4 **Buller R** New Zealand
143 C9 **Bullfinch** Western Australia Australia
103 K6 **Bullhead City** Nevada U.S.A.
112 H5 **Bull I** South Carolina U.S.A.
102 H7 **Bullion Mts** California U.S.A.
101 R3 **Bull Mts** Montana U.S.A.
141 G5 **Bullock** *R* Queensland Australia
141 G8 **Bulloo** *R* Queensland Australia
141 G8 **Bulloo Downs** Queensland Australia
141 F8 **Bulloo, L** Queensland Australia
133 F8 **Bull Pt** Falkland Is
118 B9 **Bull R** British Columbia Canada
145 E4 **Bulls** New Zealand
127 J3 **Bull Savannah** Jamaica
110 D5 **Bull Shoals Lake** Missouri U.S.A.
22 D3 **Bully** France
100 C9 **Bully Choop Mt** California U.S.A.
140 C2 **Bulman Gorge** N Terr Australia
139 G6 **Buloke,L** Victoria Australia
77 L2 **Bulola** Afghanistan
136 K3 **Bulolo** Papua New Guinea
138 F5 **Bulpunga** New South Wales Australia
87 E11 **Bultfontein** S Africa
71 G7 **Buluan** Mindanao Philippines
70 G7 **Bulubulu** Sulawesi
70 E3 **Bulu, G** *mt* Kalimantan
70 G7 **Bulukumba** Sulawesi
51 M1 **Bulun** U.S.S.R.
86 D7 **Bulungu** Zaire
71 G4 **Bulusan** Luzon Philippines
118 F6 **Bulwark** Alberta Canada
9 E2 **Bulwell** England
141 L1 **Bulwer I** Brisbane, Qnsld Australia
9 F2 **Bulwick** England
119 N8 **Bulyea** Saskatchewan Canada
86 D5 **Bumba** Zaire
84 G3 **Bumbah, Khalīj** Libya
48 H5 **Bumbeşti-Jiu** Romania
103 M7 **Bumble Bee** Arizona U.S.A.
70 G4 **Bumbulan** Sulawesi Indonesia
70 F2 **Bum-Bum** Sabah
70 M9 **Bumiaju** Java
66 F6 **Bumkhang** Burma
100 D3 **Bumping L** Washington U.S.A.
40 F4 **Bümpliz** Switzerland
75 O5 **Bumthang** Bhutan
109 O5 **Buna** Texas U.S.A.
71 G7 **Bunawan** Mindanao Philippines
143 B10 **Bunbury** Western Australia Australia
110 B6 **Bunch** Oklahoma U.S.A.
14 E4 **Bunclody** Ireland
14 D1 **Buncrana** Ireland
141 K6 **Bundaberg** Queensland Australia
141 H8 **Bundaleer** Queensland Australia
32 J8 **Bünde** W Germany
32 F6 **Bunde** W Germany
140 D5 **Bundey** *R* N Terr Australia
74 F6 **Bundi** India
111 C11 **Bundick L** Louisiana U.S.A.
111 C11 **Bundicks Cr** Louisiana U.S.A.
140 C6 **Bundooma** N Terr Australia
14 C2 **Bundoran** Ireland
68 J6 **Bun Duc** Vietnam
12 B1 **Bunessan** Scotland
71 G7 **Bunga** *R* Mindanao Philippines
143 C9 **Bungalbin Hill** Western Australia Australia
9 H3 **Bungay** England
68 E5 **Bung Boraphet** *L* Thailand
146 H13 **Bunger Hills** Antarctica
141 J7 **Bungil** *R* Queensland Australia
71 H6 **Bunginkela** *isld* Sulawesi Indonesia
68 F3 **Bung Kan** Thailand
70 G6 **Bungku** Sulawesi Indonesia
87 C7 **Bungo** Angola
60 G2 **Bungo-suidō** *str* Japan
141 J8 **Bungunya** Queensland Australia
Bunguran *see* **Natuna Besar**
Bunguran Utara, Kepulauan *see* **Natuna Besar**
86 B3 **Buni** Nigeria
86 F5 **Bunia** Zaire
143 E9 **Buningonia Spring** *spring* Western Australia Australia
70 E3 **Bunju** *isld* Kalimantan
110 E4 **Bunker** Missouri U.S.A.
141 K6 **Bunker Grp** *islds* Gt Barrier Reef Aust
116 E4 **Bunker Hill** Alaska U.S.A.
110 G2 **Bunker Hill** Illinois U.S.A.
110 K1 **Bunker Hill** Indiana U.S.A.
107 M3 **Bunker Hill** Kansas U.S.A.
103 K5 **Bunkerville** Nevada U.S.A.
87 E8 **Bunkeya** Zaïre
111 D11 **Bunkie** Louisiana U.S.A.
113 F8 **Bunnell** Florida U.S.A.
9 E2 **Bunny** England
145 E4 **Bunnythorpe** New Zealand
70 G4 **Bunobagu** Sulawesi
68 H7 **Bu Noi** Vietnam
17 G5 **Buñol** Spain
25 D4 **Bunschoten** Netherlands
143 B8 **Buntine** Western Australia Australia
9 F4 **Buntingford** England
70 D5 **Buntok** Kalimantan
70 D5 **Buntokecil** Kalimantan
141 K1 **Bunyaville** *dist* Brisbane, Qnsld Australia
68 E3 **Bun Yun** Thailand
51 L1 **Buolkalakh** U.S.S.R.
68 J6 **Buon Me Thuot** Vietnam
51 N1 **Buor-khaya, Guba** *G* U.S.S.R.
80 G1 **Buq'ātā** Syria
77 A7 **Buqayq** Saudi Arabia
28 A4 **Bur** Denmark
88 G3 **Bura** Kenya
86 A1 **Buraan** Somalia
71 L10 **Buraen** Timor Indonesia
Buraimi *see* **Buraymī, Al**
143 B9 **Burakin** Western Australia Australia
86 E3 **Buram** Sudan
143 E10 **Buraminya,Mt** Western Australia Australia
141 K2 **Buranda** *dist* Brisbane, Qnsld Australia
75 J3 **Burang** China
130 H5 **Buranhaém** Brazil
45 M1 **Burano** Italy
111 G12 **Buras** Louisiana U.S.A.
71 G5 **Burauen** Leyte Philippines
72 E3 **Buraydah** Saudi Arabia
55 C3 **Burayevo** U.S.S.R.
79 G4 **Burayj, Al** Syria
77 D7 **Buraymī, Al** U.A.E.
80 G1 **Burayqah** Syria
36 E2 **Burbach** W Germany
9 E5 **Burbage** England
102 F7 **Burbank** California U.S.A.
98 K9 **Burchard** Nebraska U.S.A.
139 H5 **Burcher** New South Wales Australia
99 N6 **Burchinal** Iowa U.S.A.
86 J4 **Burco** Somalia
57 C5 **Burdalyk** U.S.S.R.
141 H5 **Burdekin** *R* Queensland Australia
141 H5 **Burdekin Falls** Queensland Australia
117 M7 **Burden,Mt** British Columbia Canada
118 F9 **Burdett** Alberta Canada
95 L4 **Burdett** New York U.S.A.
48 K3 **Burdujeni** Romania
78 C3 **Burdur** Turkey
47 L7 **Burdur Gölü** *L* Turkey
90 E14 **Burdwood Bank** Atlantic Oc
86 G4 **Burē** Ethiopia
86 G3 **Burē** Ethiopia
26 M7 **Bureå** Sweden
121 P4 **Bureau, L** Quebec Canada
59 K1 **Bureinskiy, Khrebet** *mts* U.S.S.R.
25 D5 **Buren** Netherlands
32 J9 **Büren** W Germany
59 J2 **Bureya** U.S.S.R.
59 K1 **Bureya** *R* U.S.S.R.
9 E4 **Burford** England
33 P8 **Burg** East Germany
32 K5 **Burg** W Germany
36 D5 **Burgalben** W Germany
47 J2 **Burgas** Bulgaria
38 O7 **Burgau** Austria
37 J7 **Burgau** W Germany
112 J3 **Burgaw** North Carolina U.S.A.
47 N11 **Burgaz** Turkey
47 N11 **Burgaz** *isld* Turkey
47 K6 **Burgaz Dağ** *mt* Turkey
37 J5 **Burgbernheim** W Germany
40 G3 **Burgdorf** Switzerland
100 K4 **Burgdorf** Idaho U.S.A.
32 M8 **Burgdorf** W Germany
37 K4 **Burgebrach** W Germany
37 M2 **Bürgel** East Germany
48 C3 **Burgenland** *prov* Austria
123 P6 **Burgeo** Newfoundland Canada
87 E12 **Burgersdorp** S Africa
9 F6 **Burgess Hill** England
95 L9 **Burgess Store** Virginia U.S.A.
13 E4 **Burgh** England
25 A5 **Burgh** Netherlands
36 H2 **Burghaun** W Germany
38 G5 **Burghausen** W Germany
37 L6 **Burgheim** W Germany
9 G1 **Burgh-le-Marsh** England
43 E11 **Burgio** Sicily
36 H3 **Burgjoss** W Germany
37 L3 **Burgkunstadt** W Germany
37 N5 **Burglengenfeld** W Germany
16 E2 **Burgos** *prov* Spain
16 E2 **Burgos** Spain
37 K3 **Burgpreppach** W Germany
36 H3 **Burgsinn** W Germany
37 O2 **Burgstädt** East Germany
36 G4 **Bürgstadt** W Germany
33 S6 **Burg Stargard** East Germany
32 F8 **Burgsteinfurt** W Germany
27 K14 **Burgsvik** Sweden
17 G2 **Burguete** Spain
36 F2 **Burgwald** W Germany
32 L7 **Burgwedel** W Germany
37 K4 **Burgwindheim** W Germany
47 H5 **Burhaniye** Turkey
32 H5 **Burhave** W Germany
130 E8 **Buri** Brazil
69 E14 **Buriai** Indonesia
71 F4 **Burias** *isld* Philippines
71 F4 **Burias Pass** Luzon Philippines
123 R6 **Burin** Newfoundland Canada
68 F5 **Buriram** Thailand
130 E7 **Buritama** Brazil
128 G6 **Buriti** *R* Brazil
130 E6 **Buriti Alegre** Brazil
129 K5 **Buriti Bravo** Brazil
130 F4 **Buritis** Brazil
80 C8 **Burj el Baiyara** Jordan
79 G4 **Burj Sāfita** Syria
28 C7 **Burkal** Denmark
109 J1 **Burkburnett** Texas U.S.A.
140 E6 **Burke** *R* Queensland Australia
140 F5 **Burke** *R* Queensland Australia
100 K2 **Burke** Idaho U.S.A.
98 G6 **Burke** South Dakota U.S.A.
109 N4 **Burke** Texas U.S.A.
117 K9 **Burke Chan** British Columbia Canada
146 B7 **Burke I** Antarctica
144 C6 **Burke Pass** New Zealand
110 L5 **Burkesville** Kentucky U.S.A.
140 E4 **Burketown** Queensland Australia
109 H4 **Burkett** Texas U.S.A.
94 J9 **Burkeville** Virginia U.S.A.
37 O2 **Burkhardtsdorf** East Germany
85 D6 **Burkina** *rep* W Africa
98 G4 **Burkmere** South Dakota U.S.A.
121 L7 **Burk's Falls** Ontario Canada
55 G4 **Burla** U.S.S.R.
36 G7 **Burladingen** W Germany
141 G5 **Burleigh** Queensland Australia
109 K3 **Burleson** Texas U.S.A.
13 G6 **Burley** England
101 M7 **Burley** Idaho U.S.A.
8 D3 **Burley Gate** England
55 D4 **Burli** U.S.S.R.
55 B5 **Burlin** U.S.S.R.
107 P3 **Burlingame** Kansas U.S.A.
123 Q4 **Burlington** Newfoundland Canada
121 L9 **Burlington** Ontario Canada
106 H2 **Burlington** Colorado U.S.A.
99 P9 **Burlington** Iowa U.S.A.
107 P3 **Burlington** Kansas U.S.A.
95 N6 **Burlington** New Jersey U.S.A.
112 H1 **Burlington** North Carolina U.S.A.
95 O2 **Burlington** Vermont U.S.A.
117 M11 **Burlington** Washington U.S.A.
101 R5 **Burlington** Wyoming U.S.A.
110 A1 **Burlington Junction** Missouri U.S.A.
8 D2 **Burlton** England
57 J2 **Burlyu-Tobe** U.S.S.R.
80 G5 **Burma** Jordan
68 B2 **Burma** *rep* S E Asia
139 H6 **Burmah Forest** Victoria Australia
55 D1 **Burmantovo** U.S.S.R.
101 N9 **Burmester** Utah U.S.A.
118 C9 **Burmis** Alberta Canada
144 D5 **Burnbrae** New Zealand
109 J5 **Burnet** Texas U.S.A.
141 K7 **Burnett** *R* Queensland Australia
141 K6 **Burnett Heads** Queensland Australia
100 D9 **Burney** California U.S.A.
8 C5 **Burnham** England
144 D5 **Burnham** New Zealand
95 S2 **Burnham** Maine U.S.A.
94 K6 **Burnham** Pennsylvania U.S.A.
9 G2 **Burnham Deepdale** England
9 G2 **Burnham Market** England
9 G4 **Burnham-on-Crouch** Essex England
40 F2 **Burnhaupt** France
139 H8 **Burnie** Tasmania Australia
13 H5 **Burniston** England
13 F6 **Burnley** England
13 G4 **Burnopfield** England
57 F3 **Burnoye** U.S.S.R.
101 T10 **Burns** Colorado U.S.A.
100 F6 **Burns** Oregon U.S.A.
98 B8 **Burns** Wyoming U.S.A.
13 G5 **Burnsall** England
110 M5 **Burnside** Kentucky U.S.A.
94 J6 **Burnside** Pennsylvania U.S.A.
143 E7 **Burnside,L** Western Australia Australia
117 L8 **Burns Lake** British Columbia Canada
98 G3 **Burnstad** North Dakota U.S.A.
122 G6 **Burnsville** New Brunswick Canada
110 H7 **Burnsville** Mississippi U.S.A.
112 E2 **Burnsville** North Carolina U.S.A.
94 G8 **Burnsville** West Virginia U.S.A.
101 P8 **Burntfork** Wyoming U.S.A.
126 G3 **Burnt Ground** Long I Bahamas
13 E1 **Burntisland** Scotland
122 J1 **Burnt L** Labrador, Nfld Canada
116 Q3 **Burnt Paw** Alaska U.S.A.
100 H5 **Burnt R** Oregon U.S.A.
100 B9 **Burnt Ranch** California U.S.A.
121 M8 **Burnt River** Ontario Canada
119 R3 **Burntwood L** Manitoba Canada
33 S5 **Burow** East Germany
66 D2 **Burqin** China
119 M6 **Burr** Saskatchewan Canada
138 E5 **Burra** South Australia Australia
143 C9 **Burracoppin** Western Australia Australia
139 K5 **Burragorang L** New South Wales Australia
99 P6 **Burr Oak** Iowa U.S.A.
107 M2 **Burr Oak** Kansas U.S.A.
94 E5 **Burr Oak** Michigan U.S.A.
94 E7 **Burr Oak Res** Ohio U.S.A.
15 F2 **Burray** Scotland
46 D3 **Burrel** Albania
140 C6 **Burrell,Mt** N Terr Australia
13 E1 **Burrelton** Scotland
139 J5 **Burrendong Res.** New South Wales Australia
17 G5 **Burriana** Spain
13 H6 **Burringham** England
124 J3 **Burro** Mexico
103 L7 **Burro Cr** Arizona U.S.A.
108 E6 **Burro, Serranias del** *mts* Mexico
113 K11 **Burrow Cay** Bahamas
140 F3 **Burrowes, Pt** Queensland Australia
15 D6 **Burrow Head** Scotland
107 N3 **Burrton** Kansas U.S.A.
140 B2 **Burrundie** N Terr Australia
133 E3 **Burruyacú** Argentina
111 G13 **Burrwood** Louisiana U.S.A.
8 B4 **Burry Port** Wales
78 B1 **Bursa** Turkey
84 J4 **Bur Safâga** Egypt
36 C1 **Burscheid** W Germany
13 F6 **Burscough** England
32 L9 **Bursfelde** W Germany
8 D1 **Burslem** England
28 G7 **Bursø** Denmark
22 F2 **Burst** Belgium
118 H8 **Burstall** Saskatchewan Canada
99 M6 **Burt** Iowa U.S.A.
98 D3 **Burt** North Dakota U.S.A.
138 F4 **Burta** New South Wales Australia
94 C1 **Burt L** Michigan U.S.A.
9 E6 **Burton** England
98 G7 **Burton** Nebraska U.S.A.
109 L5 **Burton** Texas U.S.A.
8 B4 **Burton** Wales
13 H5 **Burton Agnes** England
13 F5 **Burton-in-Kendal** England
112 D3 **Burton L** Georgia U.S.A.
14 C2 **Burtonport** Ireland
9 E2 **Burton upon Trent** England
26 L7 **Burträsk** Sweden
122 F7 **Burtts Corner** New Brunswick Canada
138 F5 **Burtundy** New South Wales Australia
140 C6 **Burt Well** N Terr Australia
136 F2 **Buru** *isld* Moluccas Indonesia
84 J3 **Burullus** *L* Egypt
Burultokay *see* **Fuhai**
88 B3 **Burundi** *rep* Cent Africa
88 B3 **Bururi** Burundi
85 F7 **Burutu** Nigeria
8 D3 **Burwarton** England
9 G6 **Burwash** England
9 G1 **Burwell** England
98 G8 **Burwell** Nebraska U.S.A.
33 S10 **Burxdorf** East Germany
121 T7 **Bury** Quebec Canada
9 F6 **Bury** England
13 F6 **Bury** Greater Manchester England
56 F5 **Buryatskaya** U.S.S.R.
9 G3 **Bury St.Edmunds** England
43 E11 **Busambra, Rca** *mt* Sicily
71 F7 **Busan B** Mindanao Philippines
87 D7 **Busango** Zaire
118 D5 **Busby** Alberta Canada
101 T4 **Busby** Montana U.S.A.
44 B2 **Busca** Italy
33 R7 **Buschow** East Germany
32 J4 **Buschsand** *isld* W Germany
46 E3 **Buševa Planina** *mt* Yugoslavia
46 D3 **Bushat** Albania
77 B5 **Būshehr** Iran
88 C2 **Bushenyi** Uganda
95 M5 **Bushkill** Pennsylvania U.S.A.
108 B8 **Bushland** Texas U.S.A.
121 L6 **Bushnell** Ontario Canada
113 E9 **Bushnell** Florida U.S.A.
110 F1 **Bushnell** Illinois U.S.A.
98 C8 **Bushnell** Nebraska U.S.A.
107 M3 **Bushton** Kansas U.S.A.
140 E5 **Bushy Park** Queensland Australia
89 F1 **Busi** *R* Zimbabwe
88 E1 **Busia** Uganda
22 E3 **Busigny** France
86 D5 **Businga** Zaire
86 C6 **Busira** *R* Zaire
48 J1 **Busk** U.S.S.R.
27 C11 **Buskerud** *reg* Norway
31 M5 **Busko** Poland
37 P3 **Buškovice** Czechoslovakia
55 D4 **Buskul'** U.S.S.R.
71 B1 **Busobuso** Halmahera Indonesia
79 G6 **Buşrá ash Shām** Syria
19 K5 **Bussang** France
40 E2 **Bussang,Col.de** *pass* France
21 J8 **Busseau,le** France
143 B10 **Busselton** Western Australia Australia
44 H2 **Busseto** Italy
99 O8 **Bussey** Iowa U.S.A.
41 N7 **Bussolengo** Italy
25 D4 **Bussum** Netherlands
77 D6 **Bustaneh** Iran
80 D2 **Bustan Ha Galil** Israel
141 K6 **Bustard Hd** Queensland Australia
48 K5 **Buşteni** Romania
42 B3 **Busto Arsizio** Italy
57 C4 **Buston** U.S.S.R.
71 D4 **Busuanga** Philippines
86 D5 **Busu Djanoa** Zaire
32 J4 **Büsum** W Germany
86 D5 **Buta** Zaire
131 G2 **Butai** *R* Brazil
70 O9 **Butak, G** *mt* Java
69 D9 **Butang Group** *isld* Thailand
133 D5 **Buta Ranquil** Argentina
88 B3 **Butare** Rwanda
71 F3 **Butaunan** *isld* Philippines
Bute *co see* **Strathclyde** *reg*
138 E5 **Bute** South Australia Australia
15 C5 **Bute** *isld* Scotland
117 J9 **Butedale** British Columbia Canada
117 L10 **Bute Inlet** British Columbia Canada
88 B1 **Butembo** Zaire
22 L3 **Bütgenbach** Belgium
Butha Qi *see* **Zalantun**
68 A2 **Buthidaung** Burma
47 P12 **Buthrotum** *hist site* Albania
86 F5 **Butiaba** Uganda
86 B1 **Butiyaalo** Somalia
32 H5 **Butjadingen** *reg* W Germany
55 D3 **Butka** U.S.S.R.
68 B3 **Butle** *R* Burma
111 H9 **Butler** Alabama U.S.A.
112 C5 **Butler** Georgia U.S.A.
94 C5 **Butler** Indiana U.S.A.
110 M3 **Butler** Kentucky U.S.A.
110 B3 **Butler** Missouri U.S.A.
95 N6 **Butler** New Jersey U.S.A.
94 E6 **Butler** Ohio U.S.A.
107 L6 **Butler** Oklahoma U.S.A.
94 H6 **Butler** Pennsylvania U.S.A.
98 J4 **Butler** South Dakota U.S.A.
138 B2 **Butlers Dome** *mt* N Terr Australia
80 G2 **Butmiye** Syria
71 H7 **Buton** *isld* Sulawesi Indonesia
71 H7 **Buton, Selat** *str* Indonesia
46 D5 **Butrintit, Liqen i** *L* Albania
41 K3 **Bütschwil** Switzerland
45 K1 **Buttapietra** Italy
101 N4 **Butte** Montana U.S.A.
98 H7 **Butte** Nebraska U.S.A.
98 F2 **Butte** North Dakota U.S.A.
100 C7 **Butte Falls** Oregon U.S.A.
37 L1 **Buttelstedt** East Germany
102 C1 **Butte Meadows** California U.S.A.
36 G7 **Buttenhausen** W Germany
37 L4 **Buttenheim** W Germany
37 K6 **Buttenwiesen** W Germany
100 F4 **Butter Cr** Oregon U.S.A.
99 M6 **Butterfield** Minnesota U.S.A.
13 E5 **Buttermere** England
9 G2 **Butterwick** England
87 E12 **Butterworth** S Africa
14 C4 **Buttevant** Ireland
143 G6 **Buttfield, Mt** Western Australia Australia
27 K14 **Buttle** Sweden
117 L11 **Buttle L** British Columbia Canada
15 B2 **Butt of Lewis** Scotland
115 K6 **Button B** Manitoba Canada
115 N5 **Button Is** Northwest Territories Canada
102 E6 **Buttonwillow** California U.S.A.
37 L1 **Buttstädt** East Germany
98 J3 **Buttzville** North Dakota U.S.A.
71 G6 **Butuan** Mindanao Philippines
71 G6 **Butuan B** Mindanao Philippines
Butung *isld see* **Buton**
54 M6 **Buturlinovka** U.S.S.R.
68 H6 **Bu Tu Suay** Vietnam
36 F3 **Butzbach** W Germany
33 P5 **Bützow** East Germany
86 J4 **Buuhoodle** Somalia
86 J5 **Buulobarde** Somalia
86 H6 **Buur Gaabo** Somalia
84 H5 **Buurhakaba** Somalia
26 E9 **Buvika** Norway
79 E10 **Buwārah, J** *mt* Saudi Arabia
21 L8 **Buxerolles** France
21 O7 **Buxeuil** France
32 L6 **Buxtehude** W Germany
9 E1 **Buxton** England
112 M2 **Buxton** North Carolina U.S.A.
19 J6 **Buxy** France
55 C3 **Buy** *R* U.S.S.R.
58 G2 **Buyr Nuur** *L* Mongolia
47 N11 **Büyük** *isld* Turkey
47 N11 **Büyükada** Turkey
47 N10 **Büyükdere** Turkey
47 H4 **Büyük Kemikli Br** *C* Turkey
47 J7 **Büyük Menderes** *R* Turkey
21 N8 **Buzançais** France
22 H5 **Buzancy** France
48 K5 **Buzău** *R* Romania
48 K5 **Buzău** Romania
48 K5 **Buzăului Muntii** *mt* Romania
55 B4 **Buzdyak** U.S.S.R.
60 E12 **Buzen** Japan
87 F9 **Buzi** Mozambique
48 G5 **Buziaş** Romania
55 C4 **Buzov'yazy** U.S.S.R.
95 R5 **Buzzards B** Mass U.S.A.
8 C4 **Bwlch** Wales
27 H11 **By** Sweden
47 H1 **Byala** Bulgaria
46 F1 **Byala Slatina** Bulgaria
114 J2 **Byam Martin I** N W Terr Can
109 K1 **Byars** Oklahoma U.S.A.
31 O4 **Bychawa** Poland
31 L4 **Byczyna** Poland
31 K2 **Bydgoszcz** Poland
Byelorussia *see* **Belorusskaya**
106 F2 **Byers** Colorado U.S.A.
109 J1 **Byers** Texas U.S.A.
94 F7 **Byesville** Ohio U.S.A.
9 E3 **Byfield** England
9 F5 **Byfleet** England
26 L7 **Bygdeå** Sweden
26 L7 **Bygdeträsk** Sweden
27 C10 **Bygdin** *L* Norway
26 L7 **Bygdsiljum** Sweden
28 D5 **Bygholm Å** *R* Denmark
27 C13 **Bygland** Norway
27 C13 **Byglandsfj** Norway
110 G7 **Byhalia** Mississippi U.S.A.
54 B3 **Bykhov** U.S.S.R.
27 B12 **Bykle** Norway
27 B12 **Bykleheiane** Norway
59 M2 **Bykov** U.S.S.R.
28 C7 **Bylderup** Denmark
57 H1 **Bylkyldak** U.S.S.R.
115 M3 **Bylot I** Northwest Territories Canada
140 F4 **Bynoe** *R* Queensland Australia
140 B2 **Bynoe Harbour** N Terr Australia
101 N2 **Bynum Res** Montana U.S.A.
111 F9 **Byram** Mississippi U.S.A.
146 D11 **Byrd Glacier** Antarctica
121 O5 **Byrd,L** Quebec Canada
13 F3 **Byrness** England
143 B7 **Byro** Western Australia Australia
112 D5 **Byromville** Georgia U.S.A.
102 C4 **Byron** California U.S.A.
99 R7 **Byron** Illinois U.S.A.
95 R2 **Byron** Maine U.S.A.
101 R5 **Byron** Wyoming U.S.A.
139 L3 **Byron Bay** New South Wales Australia
51 J1 **Byrranga,Gory** *mt* U.S.S.R.
109 J2 **Byrson** Texas U.S.A.
28 F2 **Byrum** Denmark
26 M7 **Byske** Sweden
26 L6 **Byske älv** *R* Sweden
48 F1 **Bystra** *mt* Czechoslovakia
55 F2 **Bystryy** U.S.S.R.
31 K5 **Bystrzyca Kłodzka** Poland
51 N2 **Bytantay** *R* U.S.S.R.
31 L6 **Bytča** Czechoslovakia
31 L5 **Bytom** Poland
54 F3 **Bytosh** U.S.S.R.
31 K1 **Bytów** Poland
Byzantium *see* **Istanbul**
141 J7 **Byzantium** Queensland Australia
31 M3 **Bzura** *R* Poland

C

130 B9 **Caacupé** Paraguay
130 C9 **Caaguazú** *dept* Paraguay
133 F3 **Caaguazu** Paraguay
130 C9 **Caaguazú, Cord de** *mts* Paraguay
87 C8 **Caála** Angola
130 B10 **Caapucú** Paraguay
130 C8 **Caarapó** Brazil
130 F5 **Caatinga** Brazil
130 C10 **Caazapá** Paraguay
129 G7 **Cabacal** *R* Brazil
130 H9 **Cabaceiras** Brazil
126 E3 **Cabaiguán** Cuba
71 E3 **Cabalantian** Luzon Philippines
71 G5 **Cabalian** Leyte Philippines
106 C9 **Caballo** New Mexico U.S.A.
128 D4 **Caballococha** Peru
106 C9 **Caballo Res** New Mexico U.S.A.
124 G3 **Caballos Mesteños, Llano de los** Mexico
71 E3 **Cabanatuan** Luzon Philippines
122 D6 **Cabano** Quebec Canada
71 E2 **Cabarruyan** *isld* Luzon Philippines
19 Q18 **Cabasse** France
141 K1 **Cabbage Tree Cr** Brisbane, Qnsld Australia
16 B2 **Cabe** *R* Spain
130 F4 **Cabeceiras** Brazil
130 J9 **Cabedelo** Brazil
99 S8 **Cabery** Illinois U.S.A.
16 D6 **Cabeza del Buey** Spain
128 F7 **Cabezas** Bolivia
106 C6 **Cabezon** New Mexico U.S.A.
71 F6 **Cabilao** *isld* Philippines
127 J9 **Cabimas** Venezuela
107 P5 **Cabin Creek** Oklahoma U.S.A.
86 B7 **Cabinda** Angola
100 J1 **Cabinet Gorge Dam** Idaho U.S.A.
100 J1 **Cabinet Mts** Idaho U.S.A.
71 E8 **Cabingan** *isld* Philippines
99 P3 **Cable** Wisconsin U.S.A.
113 L9 **Cable Beach** New Providence I Bahamas
133 D7 **Cabo Blanco** Argentina
17 F8 **Cabo de Gata,Sierra del** Spain
88 G8 **Cabo Delgado** *dist* Mozambique
130 G8 **Cabo Frio** Brazil
121 O5 **Cabonga, Rés** Quebec Canada
110 D4 **Cabool** Missouri U.S.A.
141 L7 **Caboolture** Queensland Australia
133 D6 **Cabo Raso** Argentina
113 H7 **Cabo Rojo** Puerto Rico
110 E6 **Cabot** Arkansas U.S.A.
120 J7 **Cabot Head** *C* Ontario Canada
123 M6 **Cabot Str** Nfld/Nova Scotia Canada
21 K3 **Cabourg** France
85 A8 **Cabo Verde, Ilhas do** *islds* Atlantic Oc
71 E4 **Cabra** *isld* Philippines
16 E7 **Cabra del Santo Cristo** Spain
69 A9 **Cabra I** Nicobar Is
127 J5 **Cabral** Dominican Rep
130 G5 **Cabral,Serra do** *mts* Brazil
43 B9 **Cabras** Sardinia
19 P15 **Cabre, Col de** *pass* France
16 B3 **Cabreira** *mt* Portugal
17 J5 **Cabrera** *isld* Balearic Is
127 K5 **Cabrera** Dominican Rep
16 C2 **Cabrera** *R* Spain
126 F4 **Cabreras** *R* Cuba
16 C2 **Cabrera,Sierra** *mt* Spain
118 J8 **Cabri** Saskatchewan Canada
17 F5 **Cabriel** *R* Spain
19 O18 **Cabriès** France
102 G9 **Cabrillo Nat Mon** California U.S.A.
127 M4 **Cabrits, I** Martinique W Indies
130 G10 **Cabrobó** Brazil
128 E2 **Cabruta** Venezuela
71 E7 **Cabucan** *isld* Philippines
71 E2 **Cabugao** Luzon Philippines
71 E5 **Cabulauan** *isld* Philippines
124 E2 **Cabullona** Mexico
71 G8 **Caburan** Mindanao Philippines
128 E1 **Cabure** Venezuela
71 F1 **Cabutunan Pt** Luzon Philippines
133 G3 **Caçador** Brazil
46 D1 **Čačak** Yugoslavia
122 F3 **Cacaoui L** Quebec Canada
130 F8 **Cacapava** Brazil
133 G4 **Caçapava do Sul** Brazil
94 J7 **Cacapon** *R* West Virginia U.S.A.
68 H2 **Cac Ba** *isld* Vietnam
43 B8 **Caccia,C** Sardinia
133 G3 **Cacequi** Brazil
129 G7 **Cáceraes** Brazil
130 B5 **Cáceres** Brazil
16 C5 **Cáceres** *prov* Spain
16 C5 **Cáceres** Spain
110 E6 **Cache** *R* Arkansas U.S.A.
110 G4 **Cache** *R* Illinois U.S.A.
107 M7 **Cache** Oklahoma U.S.A.
120 K6 **Cache Bay** Ontario Canada
102 B3 **Cache Cr** California U.S.A.
85 A6 **Cacheu** Guinea-Bissau
129 G5 **Cachimbo, Serra do** *mts* Brazil
133 D2 **Cachinal** Chile
87 C8 **Cachingues** Angola
129 L6 **Cachoeira** Brazil
130 E6 **Cachoeira Alta** Brazil
130 E5 **Cachoeira de Goiás** Brazil
131 H3 **Cachoeira do Sul** Brazil
130 F8 **Cachoeira Paulista** Brazil
130 H7 **Cachoeiro de Itapemirim** Brazil
102 E7 **Cachuma, L** California U.S.A.
16 E7 **Cacin** *R* Spain
42 H3 **Čačinci** Yugoslavia
71 D5 **Cacnipa** *isld* Philippines
87 C8 **Cacolo** Angola
87 C8 **Caconda** Angola
86 B7 **Cacongo** Angola
122 C6 **Cacouna** Quebec Canada
103 M8 **Cactus** Arizona U.S.A.
109 H8 **Cactus** Texas U.S.A.
118 H6 **Cactus Lake** Saskatchewan Canada
102 H4 **Cactus Ra** Nevada U.S.A.
130 D6 **Caçu** Brazil
87 B9 **Caculavar** *R* Angola
129 K6 **Caculé** Brazil
130 D5 **Caçununga** Brazil
86 J5 **Cadale** Somalia
31 L6 **Čadca** Czechoslovakia
111 C7 **Caddo** *R* Arkansas U.S.A.
107 O7 **Caddo** Oklahoma U.S.A.
109 J3 **Caddo** Texas U.S.A.
111 B9 **Caddo L** Texas U.S.A.
109 L2 **Caddo Mills** Texas U.S.A.
45 J2 **Cadelbosco di Sopra** Italy
111 F12 **Cade,L.de** Louisiana U.S.A.
140 C1 **Cadell** *R* N Terr Australia
141 F5 **Cadell** *R* Queensland Australia
128 D6 **Cadena del Pantiacolla** Peru
32 K5 **Cadenberge** W Germany
19 O17 **Cadenet** France
125 K5 **Cadereyta** Mexico
8 C2 **Cader Idris** *mt* Wales
112 H4 **Cades** South Carolina U.S.A.
138 D3 **Cadibarrawirracanna,L** South Australia Australia
19 P18 **Cadière-d'Azur** France
71 F3 **Cadig Mts** Philippines
121 M4 **Cadillac** Quebec Canada
118 K9 **Cadillac** Saskatchewan Canada
18 E8 **Cadillac** France
94 B2 **Cadillac** Michigan U.S.A.
18 G10 **Cadi, Sierra del** *mts* Spain
71 F5 **Cadiz** Negros Philippines
16 D8 **Cádiz** *prov* Spain
16 C8 **Cádiz** Spain
103 J7 **Cadiz** California U.S.A.
110 J5 **Cadiz** Kentucky U.S.A.
94 G6 **Cadiz** Ohio U.S.A.
16 C8 **Cádiz, B. de** Spain
103 J7 **Cadiz L** California U.S.A.
118 G6 **Cadogan** Alberta Canada
117 P9 **Cadomin** Alberta Canada
38 F9 **Cadore** *reg* Italy
99 P5 **Cadott** Wisconsin U.S.A.
117 P7 **Cadotte** *R* Alberta Canada
143 B9 **Cadoux** Western Australia Australia
8 C5 **Cadoxton** Wales
41 N6 **Cadria,Monte** Italy
45 L1 **Ca Emo** Italy
21 K3 **Caen** France
13 H6 **Caenby Corner** England
8 C1 **Caergwrle** Wales
Caergybi *see* **Holyhead**
8 D4 **Caerleon** Wales
8 B1 **Caernarfon** Wales
8 B1 **Caernarfon B** Wales
Caernarvon *co see* **Gwynedd**
8 C4 **Caerphilly** Wales
8 C3 **Caersws** Wales
8 D4 **Caerwent** Wales
80 C3 **Caesarea** Israel
80 F1 **Caesarea Philippi** Syria
112 E2 **Caesars Head** South Carolina U.S.A.
130 G6 **Caete** Brazil
129 K6 **Caetite** Brazil
130 E7 **Cafelândia** Brazil
83 K14 **Cafres,Pl.des** Réunion Indian Oc
129 G3 **Cafuini** *R* Brazil
71 D7 **Cagayan** Philippines
71 E1 **Cagayan** *R* Luzon Philippines
71 G6 **Cagayan de Oro** Mindanao Philippines
71 E6 **Cagayan Is** Philippines
47 J5 **Çağiş** Turkey
42 E5 **Cagli** Italy
43 C9 **Cagliari** Sardinia
43 C9 **Cagliari,G.di** Sardinia
44 B4 **Cagnes** France
71 F4 **Cagraray** *isld* Philippines
127 L5 **Caguas** Puerto Rico
111 J9 **Cahaba** *R* Alabama U.S.A.
21 J3 **Cahagnes** France
14 B5 **Caha Mts** Ireland
14 D4 **Caher** Ireland
14 A5 **Cahirsiveen** Ireland
88 D9 **Cabora Bassa Dam** Mozambique
14 E4 **Cahore Pt** Ireland
18 G8 **Cahors** France
87 G9 **Caia** Mozambique
129 G6 **Caiabis, Serra dos** Brazil
87 D8 **Caianda** Angola
45 Q7 **Caianello** Italy
129 H7 **Caiapó** *R* Brazil
130 D5 **Caiapónia** Brazil
130 D5 **Caiapo, Serra do** *mts* Brazil
45 Q7 **Caiazzo** Italy
126 E3 **Caibarién** Cuba
68 H7 **Cai Be** Vietnam
130 J9 **Caicará** Brazil
128 E2 **Caicara** Bolivar Venezuela
128 F2 **Caicara** Monagas Venezuela
129 L5 **Caico** Brazil
127 H4 **Caicos Is** W Indies
Caidian *see* **Hanyang**
143 F9 **Caiguna** Western Australia Australia
21 J8 **Caillère, la** France
122 E1 **Cailleteau,L** Quebec Canada
128 D7 **Cailloma** Peru
111 E12 **Caillou B** Louisiana U.S.A.
126 G5 **Caimanera** Cuba
71 D3 **Caiman Pt** Luzon Philippines
109 J5 **Cain City** Texas U.S.A.
87 B9 **Cainde** Angola
133 D1 **Caine** *R* Bolivia
122 G7 **Cains R** New Brunswick Canada
99 N9 **Cainsville** Missouri U.S.A.
69 G8 **Cai Nuoc** Vietnam
45 P6 **Caira, M** *mt* Italy
146 F6 **Caird Coast** Antarctica
12 C1 **Cairnbaan** Scotland
94 J6 **Cairnbrook** Pennsylvania U.S.A.
139 G6 **Cairn Curran Dam** Victoria Australia
15 E3 **Cairn Gorm** *mt* Scotland
116 K6 **Cairn Mt** Alaska U.S.A.
12 C4 **Cairnryan** Scotland
141 H3 **Cairns** Queensland Australia
15 E3 **Cairn Toul** *mt* Scotland
79 B8 **Cairo** Egypt
44 D3 **Cairo** Italy
113 C7 **Cairo** Georgia U.S.A.
110 G4 **Cairo** Illinois U.S.A.
110 D2 **Cairo** Missouri U.S.A.
98 H8 **Cairo** Nebraska U.S.A.
95 N4 **Cairo** New York U.S.A.
94 C6 **Cairo** Ohio U.S.A.
94 F7 **Cairo** West Virginia U.S.A.
67 A3 **Caishentang** China
67 F1 **Caishi** China
9 H2 **Caister** England
13 H6 **Caistor** England
15 E2 **Caithness** *dist* Scotland
87 B8 **Caitou** Angola
87 C9 **Caiundo** Angola
48 K4 **Căiuţi** Romania
45 Q8 **Caivano** Italy
141 G8 **Caiwarro** Queensland Australia
22 D4 **Caix** France
Caiyuanzhen *see* **Shengsi**
67 F1 **Caizi Hu** China
128 C5 **Cajamarca** *dept* Peru
128 C5 **Cajamarca** Peru
18 G8 **Cajarc** France
130 H9 **Cajàzeiras** Brazil
48 F7 **Čajetina** Yugoslavia
71 F4 **Cajidiocan** Philippines
48 E7 **Čajniče** Yugoslavia
130 F7 **Cajuru** Brazil
47 L8 **Çakırlar** Turkey
47 N11 **Çakmakmlar** Turkey
47 K6 **Çal** Turkey
16 C7 **Cala** Spain
85 F7 **Calabar** Nigeria
121 O7 **Calabogie** Ontario Canada
127 L10 **Calabozo** Venezuela
43 G9 **Calabria** *prov* Italy
71 D5 **Calabugdong** Philippines
16 D8 **Calaburras, Pta. de** Spain
128 E7 **Calacoto** Bolivia
46 F1 **Calafat** Romania
133 C8 **Calafate** Argentina
71 F5 **Calagnaan** *isld* Philippines
71 F3 **Calagua** *islds* Philippines
17 F2 **Calahorra** Spain
122 E8 **Calais** New Brunswick Canada
22 B2 **Calais** France
95 T8 **Calais** Maine U.S.A.
Calais,Pas de *see* **Dover,Str.of**
128 F5 **Calama** Brazil
133 D2 **Calama** Chile
126 G9 **Calamar** Colombia
71 D4 **Calamian Group** *islds* Philippines
99 Q7 **Calamine** Wisconsin U.S.A.
22 L2 **Calamine,la** Belgium
48 H5 **Călan** Romania
128 F4 **Calanaque** Brazil
17 G4 **Calanda** Spain
41 K4 **Calanda** *mt* Switzerland
71 E5 **Calandagan** *isld* Philippines
87 C7 **Calandula** Angola
69 B10 **Calang** Sumatra
20 D5 **Calanhel** France
84 G4 **Calanscio Sand Sea** Libya
71 E4 **Calapan** Philippines
100 C5 **Calapooia** *R* Oregon U.S.A.
48 L6 **Călăraşi** Romania
48 K6 **Călăraşi** *reg* Romania
20 D5 **Calarhel** France
43 B9 **Calasetta** Sardinia
17 F6 **Calasparra** Spain
43 E11 **Calatafimi** Sicily
17 F3 **Calatayud** Spain
48 H4 **Călăţele** Romania
33 T9 **Calau** East Germany
71 F4 **Calauag** Philippines
43 F10 **Calavà, C** Sicily
102 C4 **Calaveras Res** California U.S.A.
71 E4 **Calavite,Cape** Philippines
71 E1 **Calayan** *isld* Luzon Philippines
71 G4 **Calbayog** Philippines
33 P9 **Calbe** East Germany
71 G5 **Calbiga** Samar Philippines
131 A8 **Calbuco** *pk* Chile
129 L5 **Calcanhar, Pta. do** *C* Brazil
111 C12 **Calcasieu L** Louisiana U.S.A.
128 B4 **Calceta** Ecuador
133 E3 **Calchaqui** Argentina
45 J4 **Calci** Italy
45 J1 **Calcinato** Italy
129 H3 **Calcoene** Brazil
75 N7 **Calcutta** India
48 J6 **Căldăraru** Romania
128 C2 **Caldas** *div* Colombia
16 A5 **Caldas da Rainha** Portugal
17 J3 **Caldas de Montbuy** Spain
16 B2 **Caldas de Reyes** Spain
16 B3 **Caldas do Gerês** Portugal
130 E5 **Caldas Novas** Brazil
13 E4 **Caldbeck** England
88 G10 **Caldeira** *isld* Mozambique
32 K10 **Calden** W Germany
117 G7 **Calder** Alaska U.S.A.
100 J2 **Calder** Idaho U.S.A.
133 C3 **Caldera** Chile
125 M5 **Caldera** Costa Rica
45 K2 **Calderara di Reno** Italy
12 E2 **Caldercruix** Scotland
12 E5 **Calder Hall** England
16 E5 **Calderina** *mt* Spain
141 H7 **Caldervale** Queensland Australia
8 D4 **Caldicot** Wales
100 J6 **Caldwell** Idaho U.S.A.
107 N4 **Caldwell** Kansas U.S.A.
94 F7 **Caldwell** Ohio U.S.A.
109 L5 **Caldwell** Texas U.S.A.
8 B4 **Caldy I** Wales
89 A10 **Caledon** S Africa
89 E8 **Caledon** *R* S Africa
122 G9 **Caledonia** Nova Scotia Canada
94 B4 **Caledonia** Michigan U.S.A.
99 P6 **Caledonia** Minnesota U.S.A.
94 K4 **Caledonia** New York U.S.A.
94 E6 **Caledonia** Ohio U.S.A.
15 D3 **Caledonian Canal** Scotland
140 D2 **Caledon,Mt** N Terr Australia
17 J3 **Calella** Spain
141 J5 **Calen** Queensland Australia
124 G3 **Calera** Mexico
111 K8 **Calera** Alabama U.S.A.
124 H6 **Calera Victor Rosales** Mexico
128 D7 **Caleta Buena** Chile
133 D8 **Caleta Coig** *est* Argentina
133 D7 **Caleta Olivia** Argentina
131 B8 **Caleufu** *R* Argentina
103 J9 **Calexico** California U.S.A.
12 D5 **Calf of Man** *isld* I of Man U.K.
118 C7 **Calgary** Alberta Canada
106 F2 **Calhan** Colorado U.S.A.
111 M7 **Calhoun** Georgia U.S.A.
110 J4 **Calhoun** Kentucky U.S.A.
111 G8 **Calhoun City** Mississippi U.S.A.
112 E3 **Calhoun Falls** South Carolina U.S.A.
128 C3 **Cali** Colombia
47 K4 **Çalı** Turkey
71 G5 **Calicoan** *isld* Samar Philippines
110 D5 **Calico Rock** Arkansas U.S.A.
68 A7 **Calicut** Andaman Is
76 B5 **Calicut** India
102 F6 **Caliente** California U.S.A.
103 K4 **Caliente** Nevada U.S.A.
127 O2 **California** Trinidad
102 C1 **California** *state* U.S.A.
110 D3 **California** Missouri U.S.A.
94 H6 **California** Pennsylvania U.S.A.
124 D4 **California,G.de** Mexico
102 F6 **California Hot Springs** California U.S.A.
48 J5 **Călimăneşti** Romania
48 J3 **Călimani, Muntii** *mts* Romania
76 D5 **Calimere,Pt** India
133 D4 **Calingasta** Argentina
143 B9 **Calingiri** Western Australia Australia
Calino *isld see* **Kálimnos** *isld*
111 D8 **Calion** Arkansas U.S.A.
103 J8 **Calipatria** California U.S.A.
100 H1 **Calispell Peak** Washington U.S.A.
71 E5 **Calis Pt** Philippines
102 B3 **Calistoga** California U.S.A.
87 D12 **Calitzdorp** S Africa

71 E4 **Calivite Passage** Philippines
109 O5 **Call** Texas U.S.A.
138 F3 **Callabonna** *R* South Australia Australia
113 F7 **Callahan** Florida U.S.A.
14 D4 **Callan** Ireland
121 L6 **Callander** Ontario Canada
12 D1 **Callander** Scotland
71 E2 **Callang** Luzon Philippines
25 C3 **Callantsoog** Netherlands
128 C6 **Callao** Peru
99 O10 **Callao** Missouri U.S.A.
103 L2 **Callao** Utah U.S.A.
95 L9 **Callao** Virginia U.S.A.
142 D5 **Callawa** Western Australia Australia
98 G8 **Callaway** Nebraska U.S.A.
43 B12 **Calle, la** Algeria
125 K6 **Calles** Mexico
141 K6 **Callide** Queensland Australia
109 J7 **Calliham** Texas U.S.A.
118 D3 **Calling L** Alberta Canada
118 E3 **Calling River** Alberta Canada
8 B7 **Callington** England
141 K6 **Calliope** Queensland Australia
117 H6 **Callison Ranch** British Columbia Canada
17 G6 **Callosa de Ensarriá** Spain
143 B7 **Callytharra Springs** Western Australia Australia
118 D5 **Calmar** Alberta Canada
99 P6 **Calmar** Iowa U.S.A.
36 F6 **Calmbach** W Germany
118 L2 **Calm L** Ontario Canada
9 E5 **Calne** England
71 G4 **Calolbon** Philippines
71 F6 **Calolot** Mindanao Philippines
113 F11 **Caloosahatchee** *R* Florida U.S.A.
43 G8 **Calore** *R* Italy
141 L7 **Caloundra** Queensland Australia
17 H6 **Calpe** Spain
101 P7 **Calpet** Wyoming U.S.A.
79 A2 **Çalpınar** Turkey
102 D2 **Calpine** California U.S.A.
125 K8 **Calpulálpam** Mexico
120 F3 **Calstock** Ontario Canada
43 F11 **Caltagirone** Sicily
43 F11 **Caltanissetta** Sicily
47 K7 **Çaltepe** *mt* Turkey
87 C7 **Caluango** Angola
87 C8 **Calucinga** Angola
87 B8 **Calulo** Angola
121 Q7 **Calumet** Quebec Canada
99 S2 **Calumet** Michigan U.S.A.
107 M6 **Calumet** Oklahoma U.S.A.
87 B8 **Caluquembe** Angola
71 E6 **Calusa** *isld* Philippines
40 G7 **Caluso** Italy
86 B1 **Caluula** Somalia
71 E5 **Caluya** *isld* Philippines
103 O8 **Calva** Arizona U.S.A.
18 E3 **Calvados** *dept* France
45 K4 **Calvana,Monte Della** Italy
9 E1 **Calver** England
140 D3 **Calvert** *R* N Terr Australia
111 H10 **Calvert** Alabama U.S.A.
109 L5 **Calvert** Texas U.S.A.
110 H4 **Calvert City** Kentucky U.S.A.
140 D3 **Calvert Hills** N Terr Australia
117 J10 **Calvert I** British Columbia Canada
94 K8 **Calverton** Virginia U.S.A.
143 E6 **Calvert Ra** Western Australia Australia
124 H7 **Calvillo** Mexico
119 T10 **Calvin** North Dakota U.S.A.
107 O7 **Calvin** Oklahoma U.S.A.
89 A8 **Calvinia** S Africa
45 Q7 **Calvi Risorta** Italy
45 J1 **Calvisano** Italy
16 D4 **Calvitero** *mt* Spain
33 O8 **Calvörde** East Germany
36 F6 **Calw-Hirsau** W Germany
112 J2 **Calypso** North Carolina U.S.A.
87 C7 **Camabatela** Angola
129 L7 **Camacá** Brazil
87 B8 **Camacaio** Angola
124 H5 **Camache** Mexico
121 O5 **Camachigama,L** Quebec Canada
87 C8 **Camacupa** Angola
127 L10 **Camaguán** Venezuela
126 F4 **Camagüey** Cuba
126 E3 **Camagüey, Arch. de** *islds* Cuba
69 E10 **Camah, Gunung** Malaysia
128 G5 **Camaitu** *R* Brazil
126 E3 **Camajuani** Cuba
128 D7 **Camaña** Peru
71 G5 **Camandag** Samar Philippines
100 C1 **Camano I** Washington U.S.A.
87 D8 **Camanongue** Angola
130 C6 **Camapuã** Mato Grosso Brazil
133 G4 **Camaquã** Rio Grande do Sul Brazil
131 H3 **Camaquã,R** Brazil
128 F4 **Camara** Brazil
128 G6 **Camarare** *R* Brazil
17 H3 **Camarasa,Embalse de** Spain
18 G9 **Camarès** France
19 N16 **Camaret** France
20 A5 **Camaret** Finistère France
107 L5 **Camargo** Oklahoma U.S.A.
19 N17 **Camargue, La** *reg* France
102 E7 **Camarillo** California U.S.A.
16 A1 **Camariñas** Spain
124 F6 **Camaronero, L. del** Mexico
133 D6 **Camarones** Argentina
101 N5 **Camas** Idaho U.S.A.
100 C4 **Camas** Washington U.S.A.
101 L6 **Camas Cr** Idaho U.S.A.
100 B6 **Camas Valley** Oregon U.S.A.
Ca Mau, Pte De *see* **Mui Bai Bung**
87 C7 **Camaxilo** Angola
16 B2 **Cambados** Spain
142 E4 **Camballin** Western Australia Australia
130 B5 **Cambara** Brazil
Cambay, G. of *see* **Khambhat, G. of**
8 B6 **Cambeak** England
21 H3 **Cambe, la** France
36 E3 **Camberg** W Germany
20 H3 **Cambernon** France
68 F6 **Cambodia** *rep* S E Asia
13 G3 **Cambois** England
18 E9 **Cambo les B** France
130 E10 **Camboriú** Brazil
8 A7 **Camborne** England
22 E3 **Cambrai** France
16 B1 **Cambre** Spain
21 L3 **Cambremer** France
102 C6 **Cambria** California U.S.A.
99 R6 **Cambria** Wisconsin U.S.A.
7 H10 **Cambrian Mts** Wales
144 B6 **Cambrians** New Zealand
120 K9 **Cambridge** Ontario Canada
9 G3 **Cambridge** England
127 J2 **Cambridge** Jamaica
145 E2 **Cambridge** New Zealand
100 J5 **Cambridge** Idaho U.S.A.
99 Q8 **Cambridge** Illinois U.S.A.
99 N8 **Cambridge** Iowa U.S.A.
107 O4 **Cambridge** Kansas U.S.A.
95 L8 **Cambridge** Maryland U.S.A.
95 Q4 **Cambridge** Massachusetts U.S.A.
99 N4 **Cambridge** Minnesota U.S.A.
98 F9 **Cambridge** Nebraska U.S.A.
95 O3 **Cambridge** New York U.S.A.
94 F6 **Cambridge** Ohio U.S.A.
Cambridge and I of Ely *co* *see* **Cambridgeshire**
114 J4 **Cambridge Bay** Northwest Territories Canada
142 G2 **Cambridge G** Western Australia Australia
9 F3 **Cambridgeshire** *co* England
94 G5 **Cambridge Springs** Pennsylvania U.S.A.
17 H3 **Cambrils** Spain
22 D3 **Cambrin** France
21 O1 **Cambron** France
87 C8 **Cambundi-Catembo** Angola
130 F7 **Cambuquira** Brazil
37 M1 **Camburg** East Germany
12 D2 **Cambuslang** Scotland
139 K5 **Camden** New South Wales Australia
111 J10 **Camden** Alabama U.S.A.
111 D8 **Camden** Arkansas U.S.A.
95 M7 **Camden** Delaware U.S.A.
95 S2 **Camden** Maine U.S.A.
94 C5 **Camden** Michigan U.S.A.
95 N7 **Camden** New Jersey U.S.A.
95 M3 **Camden** New York U.S.A.
112 G3 **Camden** South Carolina U.S.A.
110 H5 **Camden** Tennessee U.S.A.
111 B11 **Camden** Texas U.S.A.
116 P1 **Camden B** Alaska U.S.A.
94 G8 **Camden on Gauley** West Virginia U.S.A.
142 E3 **Camden Sd** Western Australia Australia
110 D3 **Camdenton** Missouri U.S.A.
68 F1 **Cam Đuỏng** Vietnam
87 D8 **Cameia,Parque Nacional da** Angola
8 B6 **Camelford** England
8 B7 **Camel,R** England
87 B7 **Camembe** Angola
21 L4 **Camembert** France
45 O4 **Camerano** Italy
45 O4 **Camerata Picena** Italy
42 E5 **Camerino** Italy
103 N6 **Cameron** Arizona U.S.A.
99 Q9 **Cameron** Illinois U.S.A.
111 C12 **Cameron** Louisiana U.S.A.
110 B2 **Cameron** Missouri U.S.A.
101 O4 **Cameron** Montana U.S.A.
106 G7 **Cameron** New Mexico U.S.A.
95 K4 **Cameron** New York U.S.A.
112 H2 **Cameron** North Carolina U.S.A.
94 J5 **Cameron** Pennsylvania U.S.A.
109 L5 **Cameron** Texas U.S.A.
94 G7 **Cameron** West Virginia U.S.A.
99 P4 **Cameron** Wisconsin U.S.A.
88 C6 **Cameron B** Zambia
141 F8 **Cameron Corner** Queensland Australia
141 G5 **Cameron Downs** Queensland Australia
120 B3 **Cameron Falls** Ontario Canada
69 E10 **Cameron Highlands** Malaysia
117 O6 **Cameron Hills** Alberta Canada
114 J2 **Cameron I** Northwest Territories Canada
144 A7 **Cameron Mts** New Zealand
86 B4 **Cameroon** *rep* Africa
85 F8 **Cameroun, Mt** Cameroon
129 J4 **Cameta** Brazil
140 B3 **Camfield** N Terr Australia
140 B3 **Camfield** *R* N Terr Australia
71 G6 **Camiguin** *isld* Philippines
71 E1 **Camiguin** *isld* Luzon Philippines
71 E3 **Camiling** Luzon Philippines
111 M10 **Camilla** Georgia U.S.A.
133 D1 **Camiña** Chile
16 B3 **Caminha** Portugal
102 D3 **Camino** California U.S.A.
129 J4 **Camiranga** Brazil
133 E2 **Camiri** Bolivia
128 D6 **Camisea** *R* Peru
87 D7 **Camissombo** Angola
117 R4 **Camlaren** Northwest Territories Canada
79 E1 **Camlıyayla** Turkey
95 K5 **Cammal** Pennsylvania U.S.A.
43 F11 **Cammarata, Monte** *mt* Sicily
33 R8 **Cammer** East Germany
124 E4 **Camoa** Mexico
125 M3 **Camoapa** Nicaragua
129 K4 **Camocim** Brazil
41 K5 **Camoghe** *mt* Switzerland
44 F3 **Camogli** Italy
41 M6 **Camonica,Val** Italy
140 E4 **Camooweal** Queensland Australia
129 H3 **Camopi** Fr Guiana
20 E6 **Camors** France
69 A8 **Camorta** Nicobar Is
71 G5 **Camotes Islands** Philippines
71 G5 **Camotes Sea** Philippines
124 G8 **Camotlán de Miraflores** Mexico
41 M6 **Camowiche,Alpi** *mt* Italy
42 E7 **Campagna** *reg* Italy
45 M1 **Campagna Lupia** Italy
45 M5 **Campagnano di Roma** Italy
22 B3 **Campagne-lès-Hesdin** France
125 L2 **Campamento** Honduras
133 F4 **Campana** Argentina
124 H4 **Campana** Mexico
133 B7 **Campana, I** Chile
130 C8 **Campanario** Mato Grosso Brazil
130 H6 **Campanário** Minas Gerais Brazil
133 C5 **Campanario** *mt* Chile/Arg
16 D6 **Campanario** Spain
45 Q8 **Campanella, Pta** *C* Italy
130 F7 **Campanha** Brazil
45 R7 **Campania** *reg* Italy
117 J9 **Campania I** British Columbia Canada
141 H5 **Campaspe** *R* Queensland Australia
102 C2 **Camp Beale** California U.S.A.
141 J6 **Campbell** *R* Queensland Australia
102 C4 **Campbell** California U.S.A.
110 F5 **Campbell** Missouri U.S.A.
98 H9 **Campbell** Nebraska U.S.A.
95 K4 **Campbell** New York U.S.A.
94 G5 **Campbell** Ohio U.S.A.
145 E4 **Campbell, C** New Zealand
121 N8 **Campbellford** Ontario Canada
68 D7 **Campbell I** Burma
102 R12 **Campbell Industrial Pk** Hawaiian Is
146 A16 **Campbell Island** *N Z Base* Antarctica
117 J9 **Campbell Island** British Columbia Canada
140 B5 **Campbell, Mt** N Terr Australia
117 D3 **Campbell, Mt** Yukon Territory Canada
74 E2 **Campbellpore** Pakistan
142 G2 **Campbell Ra** Western Australia Australia
117 L10 **Campbell River** British Columbia Canada
121 O7 **Campbell's Bay** Quebec Canada
99 S6 **Campbellsport** Wisconsin U.S.A.
110 L4 **Campbellsville** Kentucky U.S.A.
122 F6 **Campbellton** New Brunswick Canada
123 S4 **Campbellton** Newfoundland Canada
109 J7 **Campbellton** Texas U.S.A.
139 K5 **Campbelltown** New South Wales Australia
139 J8 **Campbell Town** Tasmania Australia
12 C3 **Campbeltown** Scotland
20 G7 **Campbon** France
98 C4 **Camp Crook** South Dakota U.S.A.
99 Q6 **Camp Douglas** Wisconsin U.S.A.
21 O2 **Campeaux** France
125 O8 **Campeche** Mexico
90 A6 **Campeche Bank** Atlantic Oc
125 N8 **Campeche, B.de** Mexico
126 F4 **Campechuela** Cuba
20 F6 **Campénéac** France
139 G7 **Camperdown** Victoria Australia
113 L9 **Camperdown** New Providence I Bahamas
119 R7 **Camperville** Manitoba Canada
141 K2 **Camphill** *dist* Brisbane, Qnsld Australia
111 L9 **Camp Hill** Alabama U.S.A.
45 K4 **Campi Bisenzio** Italy
45 Q8 **Campi Flegrei** Italy
16 D6 **Campillo de Llerena** Spain
16 D7 **Campillos** Spain
130 H9 **Campina Grande** Brazil
130 F8 **Campinas** Brazil
130 E6 **Campina Verde** Brazil
102 F5 **Camp Nelson** California U.S.A.
86 A5 **Campo** Cameroon
18 F10 **Campo** Spain
106 H4 **Campo** Colorado U.S.A.
43 F7 **Campobasso** Italy
122 F9 **Campobello I** New Brunswick Canada
130 F7 **Campo Belo** Brazil
130 E10 **Campo Belo do Sul** Brazil
45 L1 **Campodarsego** Italy
16 E6 **Campo de Calatrava** *physical reg* Spain
16 E5 **Campo de Criptana** Spain
129 H6 **Campo de Diauarum** Brazil
126 G9 **Campo de la Cruz** Colombia
130 D10 **Campo Erê** Brazil
130 E6 **Campo Florido** Brazil
129 K6 **Campo Formoso** Brazil
45 J2 **Campogalliano** Italy
133 E3 **Campo Gallo** Argentina
133 G2 **Campo Grande** Brazil
130 C7 **Campo Grande** Mato Grosso Brazil
130 B9 **Campo Grande** *airport* Paraguay
130 E9 **Campo Largo** Brazil
45 L1 **Campolongo Maggiore** Italy
129 K4 **Campo Maior** Brazil
130 D9 **Campo Mourão** Brazil
130 D10 **Campo Novo** Brazil
45 H3 **Camporgiano** Italy
130 H7 **Campos** Brazil
130 F6 **Campos Altos** Brazil
45 K2 **Camposanto** Italy
45 R7 **Camposauro** *mt* Italy
130 D10 **Campos de Palmas** *plains* Brazil
130 F8 **Campos do Jordão** Brazil
130 D9 **Campos Eré** Brazil
133 G3 **Campos Novos** Brazil
41 J5 **Campo Tencia** *mt* Switzerland
128 E3 **Campo Troco** Colombia
42 D2 **Campo Tures** Italy
99 P9 **Camp Point** Illinois U.S.A.
102 D6 **Camp Roberts** California U.S.A.
109 H5 **Camp San Saba** Texas U.S.A.
12 D1 **Campsie Fells** Scotland
111 C10 **Campti** Louisiana U.S.A.
94 D9 **Campton** Kentucky U.S.A.
95 Q3 **Campton** New Hampshire U.S.A.
102 C2 **Camptonville** California U.S.A.
103 N7 **Camp Verde** Arizona U.S.A.
68 J7 **Cam Ranh** Vietnam
118 E5 **Camrose** Alberta Canada
45 L1 **Camsano Vicentino** Italy
117 M4 **Camsell Range** Northwest Territories Canada
45 K3 **Camugnano** Italy
47 J4 **Çan** Turkey
122 G7 **Canaan** New Brunswick Canada
127 M2 **Canaan** Tobago
95 O4 **Canaan** Connecticut U.S.A.
121 T8 **Canaan** Vermont U.S.A.
103 N4 **Canaan Pk** Utah U.S.A.
122 G8 **Canaan R** New Brunswick Canada
130 F5 **Canabrava** Brazil
129 J6 **Cana Brava** *R* Brazil
71 C6 **Canabungan** *isld* Philippines
114 **Canada** *dominion* N America
123 Q3 **Canada B** Newfoundland Canada
131 E4 **Cañada de Gómez** Argentina
95 R8 **Canada Falls** Maine U.S.A.
95 M5 **Canadensis** Pennsylvania U.S.A.
106 F5 **Canadian** *R* New Mexico U.S.A.
108 D8 **Canadian** *R* Texas U.S.A.
108 D8 **Canadian** Texas U.S.A.
133 D8 **Cañadón de las Vacas** Argentina
133 D6 **Cañadón Grande, Sa** *ra* Argentina
112 G4 **Canadys** South Carolina U.S.A.
47 N10 **Çanak** *R* Turkey
42 G4 **Čanak** Yugoslavia
47 H4 **Canakkale** Turkey
47 H4 **Çanakkale Boğazi** *str* Turkey
43 B11 **Canal de la Galite** *str* Tunisia
127 H5 **Canal de St. Marc** Haiti
129 H3 **Canal do Norte** Brazil
129 J4 **Canal do Sul** Brazil
117 Q10 **Canal Flats** British Columbia Canada
110 G5 **Canalou** Missouri U.S.A.
113 G11 **Canal Point** Florida U.S.A.
94 E7 **Canal Winchester** Ohio U.S.A.
128 D5 **Canama** Brazil
95 K4 **Canandaigua L** New York U.S.A.
124 D2 **Cananea** Mexico
130 F9 **Cananéia** Brazil
128 E3 **Canapiari,Co** *mt* Colombia
21 P1 **Canaples** France
130 E6 **Canápolis** Brazil
128 C4 **Cañar** *prov* Ecuador
126 C4 **Canarreos,Arch.de los** Cuba
90 F6 **Canary Basin** Atlantic Oc
85 A3 **Canary Is** Atlantic Oc
94 K4 **Canaseraga** New York U.S.A.
130 E4 **Canastra, Serra da** *mts* Goiás Brazil
130 F7 **Canastra, Serra da** *mts* Minas Gerais Brazil
124 G5 **Canatlán** Mexico
44 B1 **Canave** Italy
16 C5 **Cañaveral** Spain
113 G9 **Canaveral, C** Florida U.S.A.
113 G9 **Canaveral National Seashore** Florida U.S.A.
17 F4 **Cañaveras** Spain
129 L7 **Canavieiras** Brazil
38 E9 **Canazei** Italy
139 H4 **Canbelego** New South Wales Australia
139 J6 **Canberra** Aust Capital Terr Australia
138 A6 **Canberra & Environs** Australia
100 E8 **Canby** California U.S.A.
98 K5 **Canby** Minnesota U.S.A.
100 C4 **Canby** Oregon U.S.A.
20 G4 **Cancale** France
41 M4 **Cancano, Lago di** Italy
45 Q8 **Cancello** Italy
45 Q7 **Cancello ed Arnone** Italy
22 B3 **Canche** *R* France
21 O1 **Canchy** France
18 F8 **Cancon** France
125 Q7 **Cancún** Mexico
45 K3 **Canda, M** *mt* Italy
47 H6 **Çandarlı** Turkey
47 H6 **Çandarlı Körfezi** *G* Turkey
21 P1 **Candas** France
21 H6 **Candé** France
16 B5 **Candeeiros,Sa.de** Portugal
130 F7 **Candeias** Brazil
128 F5 **Candeias** *R* Brazil
43 G7 **Candela** Italy
45 N4 **Candelara** Italy
130 C10 **Candelaria** Argentina
124 F2 **Candelaria** Mexico
108 C5 **Candelaria** Texas U.S.A.
139 J6 **Candelo** New South Wales Australia
Candia *see* **Iráklion**
119 O8 **Candiac** Saskatchewan Canada
45 L1 **Candiana** Italy
130 D9 **Cândido de Abreu** Brazil
130 E8 **Cândido Mota** Brazil
116 F4 **Candle** Alaska U.S.A.
119 M5 **Candle L** Saskatchewan Canada
146 G2 **Candlemas I** S Sandwich Is S Atlantic Oc
95 O5 **Candlewood,L** Connecticut U.S.A.
118 J6 **Cando** Saskatchewan Canada
98 G1 **Cando** North Dakota U.S.A.
133 G3 **Candói** Brazil
143 B6 **Candolle, Mt** Western Australia Australia
71 E2 **Candon** Luzon Philippines
95 L4 **Candor** New York U.S.A.
112 H2 **Candor** North Carolina U.S.A.
120 K5 **Cane** Ontario Canada
Canea *see* **Khaniá**
94 J4 **Caneadea** New York U.S.A.
129 J6 **Canéia** Brazil
133 G3 **Canela** Brazil
133 F4 **Canelones** Uruguay
130 C9 **Canendiyu** *dept* Paraguay
133 C5 **Cañete** Chile
128 C6 **Cañete** *R* Peru
17 F4 **Cañete** Spain
107 P4 **Caney** Kansas U.S.A.
107 O7 **Caney** Oklahoma U.S.A.
110 L6 **Caney Fork** *R* Tennessee U.S.A.
110 K4 **Caneyville** Kentucky U.S.A.
111 C8 **Canfield** Arkansas U.S.A.
94 G5 **Canfield** Ohio U.S.A.
18 E10 **Canfranc** Spain
87 C8 **Cangamba** Angola
87 C7 **Cangandala** Angola
16 C1 **Cangas de Narcea** Spain
16 D1 **Cangas de Onis** Spain
21 N7 **Cangey** France
69 E9 **Canglun** Malaysia
87 C8 **Cangoa** Angola
89 B9 **Cango Caves** S Africa
87 D8 **Cangombe** Angola
59 H1 **Cangshan** China
65 D7 **Cangshan** China
130 J9 **Canguaretama** Brazil
133 G4 **Canguçu** Brazil
131 H3 **Canguçu,Sa.do** *mt* Brazil
87 C8 **Cangumbe** Angola
67 D5 **Cangwu** China
67 B1 **Cangxi** China
65 C5 **Cang Xian** China
68 D1 **Cangyuan** China
65 C5 **Cangzhou** China
130 H10 **Canhotinho** Brazil
115 N6 **Caniapiscau** *R* Quebec Canada
115 N7 **Caniapiscau,Lac** Quebec Canada
121 N3 **Canica I** Quebec Canada
43 F11 **Canicatti** Sicily
71 G5 **Canigao Ch** Philippines
18 G10 **Canigou** *mt* France
17 F7 **Caniles** Spain
117 N10 **Canim L** British Columbia Canada
129 K5 **Caninde** *R* Brazil
71 E5 **Canipo** *isld* Philippines
15 C2 **Canisp Mt** Scotland
94 K4 **Canisteo** New York U.S.A.
95 K4 **Canisteo** *R* New York U.S.A.
21 H3 **Canisy** France
124 H6 **Cañitas** Mexico
17 F7 **Canjáyar** Spain
78 D1 **Çankiri** Turkey
71 E3 **Canlubang** Luzon Philippines
118 B7 **Canmore** Alberta Canada
143 B8 **Canna** Western Australia Australia
15 B3 **Canna** *isld* Scotland
76 B5 **Cannanore** India
110 K4 **Cannelton** Indiana U.S.A.
41 J5 **Cannero Riviera** Italy
44 B4 **Cannes** France
45 J1 **Canneto s. Oglio** Italy
122 H8 **Canning** Nova Scotia Canada
116 O2 **Canning** *R* Alaska U.S.A.
98 G5 **Canning** South Dakota U.S.A.
143 C8 **Canning Hill** Western Australia Australia
142 B2 **Canning River** Western Australia Australia
142 B2 **Cannington** *dist* Perth, W Aust Australia
121 L8 **Cannington** Ontario Canada
142 B2 **Canning Vale** Western Australia Australia
41 J5 **Cannobio** Italy
99 O5 **Cannon** *R* Minnesota U.S.A.
98 F3 **Cannon Ball** North Dakota U.S.A.
98 E3 **Cannonball** *R* North Dakota U.S.A.
99 O5 **Cannon Falls** Minnesota U.S.A.
139 J7 **Cann R** Victoria Australia
133 G3 **Canoas** Brazil
130 D10 **Canôas, R. das** Brazil
140 F4 **Canobie** Queensland Australia
130 F6 **Canoeiros** Brazil
118 J3 **Canoe L** Saskatchewan Canada
117 O9 **Canoe R** British Columbia Canada
130 E10 **Canoinhas** Brazil
15 F5 **Canonbie** Scotland
106 E3 **Canon City** Colorado U.S.A.
106 C5 **Cañon Largo** *R* New Mexico U.S.A.
94 G6 **Canonsburg** Pennsylvania U.S.A.
112 F6 **Canoochia** *R* Georgia U.S.A.
138 F5 **Canopus** South Australia Australia
119 P7 **Canora** Saskatchewan Canada
43 G7 **Canosa di Puglia** Italy
127 O8 **Canouan** *isld* Lesser Antilles
98 J6 **Canova** South Dakota U.S.A.
139 J5 **Canowindra** New South Wales Australia
47 K6 **Çanşa** Turkey
71 F6 **Cansilan Pt** Negros Philippines
123 M8 **Canso** Nova Scotia Canada
123 L8 **Canso,Str.of** Nova Scotia Canada
16 E1 **Cantabria** *prov* Spain
18 D10 **Cantabria,Sierra de** *mts* Spain
Cantábrica, Mar *see* **Biscay, Bay of**
45 K3 **Cantagallo** Italy
18 G7 **Cantal** *dept* France
45 Q6 **Cantalupo nel Sánnio** Italy
127 O2 **Cantaro** Trinidad
127 M10 **Cantaura** Venezuela
21 N3 **Canteleu** France
122 E8 **Canterbury** New Brunswick Canada
9 H5 **Canterbury** England
144 C5 **Canterbury** *stat area* New Zealand
144 D6 **Canterbury Bight** New Zealand
144 C6 **Canterbury Plains** New Zealand
45 O6 **Canterna, L. di** Italy
68 G7 **Can Tho** Vietnam
102 G6 **Cantil** California U.S.A.
71 G6 **Cantilan** Mindanao Philippines
16 D7 **Cantillana** Spain
129 K5 **Canto do Buriti** Brazil
Canton China *see* **Guangzhou**
63 **Canton** *conurbation* China
112 C3 **Canton** Georgia U.S.A.
110 F1 **Canton** Illinois U.S.A.
107 N3 **Canton** Kansas U.S.A.
95 R2 **Canton** Maine U.S.A.
111 F9 **Canton** Mississippi U.S.A.
110 E1 **Canton** Missouri U.S.A.
101 O3 **Canton** Montana U.S.A.
121 P8 **Canton** New York U.S.A.
112 E2 **Canton** North Carolina U.S.A.
94 F6 **Canton** Ohio U.S.A.
107 M5 **Canton** Oklahoma U.S.A.
95 L5 **Canton** Pennsylvania U.S.A.
98 K6 **Canton** South Dakota U.S.A.
109 M3 **Canton** Texas U.S.A.
121 T4 **Canton-Bégin** Quebec Canada
134 A5 **Canton I** Pacific Oc
107 M5 **Canton L** Oklahoma U.S.A.
110 D1 **Cantril** Iowa U.S.A.
41 K6 **Cantù** Italy
118 J8 **Cantuar** Saskatchewan Canada
130 D9 **Cantú,R** Brazil
130 D9 **Cantú, Serra do** *mt* Brazil
130 G10 **Canudos** Brazil
133 F5 **Cañuelas** Argentina
128 G4 **Canuma** Brazil
128 F5 **Canutama** Brazil
107 L6 **Canute** Oklahoma U.S.A.
124 G4 **Canutillo** Mexico
108 A4 **Canutillo** Texas U.S.A.
145 D4 **Canvastown** New Zealand
9 G5 **Canvey I** England
118 L5 **Canwood** Saskatchewan Canada
21 M2 **Cany-Barville** France
120 F5 **Canyon** Ontario Canada
117 E5 **Canyon** Yukon Territory Canada
108 F1 **Canyon** Texas U.S.A.
101 P5 **Canyon** Wyoming U.S.A.
100 G5 **Canyon City** Oregon U.S.A.
100 K6 **Canyon Cr** Idaho U.S.A.
118 C3 **Canyon Creek** Alberta Canada
101 N3 **Canyon Creek** Montana U.S.A.
103 P5 **Canyon de Chelly Nat.Mon** Arizona U.S.A.
101 O3 **Canyon Ferry Dam** Montana U.S.A.
103 N8 **Canyon L** Arizona U.S.A.
109 J6 **Canyon L** Texas U.S.A.
103 P3 **Canyonlands Nat. Park** Utah U.S.A.
103 O3 **Canyonlands Nat. Park** Utah U.S.A.
117 K4 **Canyon Ranges** Northwest Territories Canada
100 B7 **Canyonville** Oregon U.S.A.
87 D7 **Canzar** Angola
33 T6 **Canzow** East Germany
67 B5 **Cao Bang** Vietnam
65 C5 **Caogoubu** China
67 A3 **Cao Hai** *L* China
65 F4 **Cao He** *R* China
65 F4 **Caohekou** China
Caojiahe *see* **Qichun**
12 C2 **Caolisport, L** Scotland
87 C7 **Caombo** Angola
68 J6 **Cao Nguen Dar Lac** *plateau* Vietnam
122 F1 **Caopacho L** Quebec Canada
122 F2 **Caopacho R** Quebec Canada
121 Q3 **Caopatina, L** Quebec Canada
65 F3 **Caoshi** China
67 D3 **Caoshi** China
65 C7 **Cao Xian** China
98 F5 **Capa** South Dakota U.S.A.
87 D7 **Capaia** Angola
128 E2 **Capanaparo** *R* Venezuela
129 J4 **Capanema** Brazil
130 D9 **Capanema, R** Brazil
45 J4 **Capannoli** Italy
45 J4 **Capannori** Italy
130 F5 **Capão Redondo** Brazil
130 H7 **Caparaó,Sa do** *mts* Brazil
128 E3 **Caparro, Co** *mt* Colombia
71 E3 **Capas** Luzon Philippines
127 J9 **Capatárida** Venezuela
48 H5 **Căpăţînei, Muntii** *mt* Romania
71 D7 **Capayan Sulu** *isld* Philippines
18 D9 **Capbreton** France
122 F4 **Cap Chat** Quebec Canada
121 S6 **Cap de la Madeleine** Quebec Canada
18 G8 **Capdenac** France
122 H4 **Cap de Rabast** Quebec Canada
122 H5 **Cap-d'Espoir** Quebec Canada
95 R4 **Cape Ann** Massachusetts U.S.A.
143 E10 **Cape Arid Nat Park** Western Australia Australia
139 J8 **Cape Barren I** Tasmania Australia
90 K12 **Cape Basin** Atlantic Oc
Cape Bastion *see* **Jinmu Jido**
123 M7 **Cape Breton Highlands Nat Pk** C Breton I, Nova Scotia
123 N7 **Cape Breton I** Nova Scotia Canada
123 U6 **Cape Broyle** Newfoundland Canada
113 G9 **Cape Canaveral** Florida U.S.A.
123 R1 **Cape Charles** Labrador, Nfld Canada
95 L9 **Cape Charles** Virginia U.S.A.
85 D7 **Cape Coast** Ghana
95 S5 **Cape Cod** Massachusetts U.S.A.
95 R5 **Cape Cod B** Massachusetts U.S.A.
95 R5 **Cape Cod Canal** Massachusetts U.S.A.
95 R5 **Cape Cod Nat.Seashore** Massachusetts U.S.A.
113 F11 **Cape Coral** Florida U.S.A.
115 M5 **Cape Dorset** Northwest Territories Canada
115 N4 **Cape Dyer** Northwest Territories Canada
112 K4 **Cape Fear** North Carolina U.S.A.
110 G4 **Cape Girardeau** Missouri U.S.A.
112 M2 **Cape Hatteras** North Carolina U.S.A.
115 N5 **Cape Hopes Advance** Quebec Canada
Cape Horn *see* **Hornos, C. de**
112 H4 **Cape I** South Carolina U.S.A.
116 F3 **Cape Krusenstern Nat Mon** Alaska U.S.A.
143 B10 **Capel** Western Australia Australia
129 L6 **Capela** Brazil
123 P6 **Cape la Hune** Newfoundland Canada
8 C1 **Capel Curig** Wales
143 D10 **Cape Le Grand Nat Park** Western Australia Australia
130 G5 **Capelinha** Brazil
116 E2 **Cape Lisburne** Alaska U.S.A.
141 J6 **Capella** Queensland Australia
22 F4 **Capelle-en-Thierache, la** France
22 K4 **Capellen** Luxembourg
87 C9 **Capelongo** Angola
95 N8 **Cape May** New Jersey U.S.A.
87 C7 **Capenda-Camulemba** Angola
89 A10 **Cape of Good Hope** S Africa
114 G3 **Cape Parry** Northwest Territories Canada
89 B8 **Cape Province** S Africa
89 A10 **Cape Pt** S Africa
141 H5 **Cape R** Queensland Australia
123 T7 **Cape Race** Newfoundland Canada
142 A5 **Cape Range Nat Park** Western Australia Australia
123 N6 **Cape Ray** Newfoundland Canada
80 F2 **Capernaum** Israel
112 H5 **Cape Romain** South Carolina U.S.A.
103 N5 **Cape Royal** Arizona U.S.A.
113 F12 **Cape Sable** *pen* Florida U.S.A.
122 G10 **Cape Sable I** Nova Scotia Canada
122 F9 **Cape St.Mary** Nova Scotia Canada
123 S7 **Cape St. Mary's** *lighthouse* Newfoundland Canada
127 O5 **Capesterre** Marie Galante W Indies
127 N4 **Capesterre-Belle-Eau** Guadeloupe W Indies
45 P5 **Capestrallo** Italy
89 A9 **Cape Town** S Africa
90 E7 **Cape Verde Fracture** Atlantic Oc
90 G7 **Cape Verde Is** *rep* Atlantic Oc
90 G7 **Cape Verde Plateau** Atlantic Oc
95 M9 **Capeville** Virginia U.S.A.
95 L2 **Cape Vincent** New York U.S.A.
15 C2 **Cape Wrath** Scotland
141 F1 **Cape York Pen** Queensland Australia
127 H5 **Cap-Haïtien** Haiti
130 B9 **Capiatá** Paraguay
128 E3 **Capibara** Venezuela
130 J9 **Capiberibe** *R* Brazil
133 F4 **Capilla** Argentina
133 E4 **Capilla del Monte** Argentina
129 J4 **Capim** *R* Brazil
128 E7 **Capinota** Bolivia
41 H6 **Capio, Monte** Italy
45 O6 **Capistrello** Italy
121 O5 **Capitachouane** *R* Quebec Canada
106 E8 **Capitan** New Mexico U.S.A.
146 C3 **Capitan Arturo Prat** *Chile Base* Antarctica
130 C8 **Capitán Bado** Paraguay
131 A8 **Capitanes, Pta** *C* Chile
106 E8 **Capitan Mts** New Mexico U.S.A.
42 E6 **Capitignano** Italy
98 B4 **Capitol** Montana U.S.A.
100 H8 **Capitol Peak** *mt* Nevada U.S.A.
103 N3 **Capitol Reef Nat. Park** Utah U.S.A.
122 G5 **Caplan** Quebec Canada
20 A5 **Cap, Le** *pen* France
71 E5 **Capnoyan** *isld* Philippines
88 D9 **Capoche** *R* Mozambique
129 G5 **Capoeiras, Cachoeira das** *waterfall* Brazil
44 D4 **Capo Mele** Italy
139 K3 **Capoompeta** *mt* New South Wales Australia
45 O5 **Cappadocia** Italy
36 F2 **Cappel** W Germany
14 D4 **Cappoquin** Ireland
127 O7 **Cap Pt** St Lucia
42 C5 **Capraia, I.di** Italy
43 B7 **Caprara o dello Scorno, Pta** *pt* Sardinia
120 K6 **Capreol** Ontario Canada
43 C7 **Caprera, I** Sardinia
45 L4 **Caprese Michelangelo** Italy
45 Q8 **Capri** Italy
45 Q7 **Capriati a Volturno** Italy
141 K5 **Capricorn Chan** Gt Barrier Reef Aust
141 K6 **Capricorn Grp** *islds* Gt Barrier Reef Aust
143 B6 **Capricorn Ra** Western Australia Australia
42 D3 **Caprino Veronese** Italy
87 D9 **Caprivi Strip** Namibia
108 D2 **Caprock** New Mexico U.S.A.
123 M7 **Capstick** C Breton I, Nova Scotia
135 U5 **Captain Cook** Hawaiian Is
139 J6 **Captain's Flat** New South Wales Australia
18 E8 **Captieux** France
113 E11 **Captiva** Florida U.S.A.
45 Q7 **Capua** Italy
71 E7 **Capual** *isld* Philippines
83 K12 **Capucin Pt** Mahé I Indian Oc
71 G4 **Capul** Philippines
106 D4 **Capulin** Colorado U.S.A.
106 G5 **Capulin** New Mexico U.S.A.
128 D4 **Caquetá** *R* Colombia
128 D3 **Caqueta** *div* Colombia
71 E4 **Carabao** *isld* Philippines
128 D6 **Carabaya, Cord.de** *mts* Peru
128 F4 **Carabinani** *R* Brazil
128 E1 **Carabobo** *state* Venezuela
48 J6 **Caracal** Romania
127 L9 **Caracas** Venezuela
129 K5 **Caracol** Brazil
130 C7 **Caracol** Brazil
125 J8 **Caracuaro** Mexico
71 G7 **Caraga** Mindanao Philippines
14 B4 **Caragh,L** Ireland
131 G4 **Caraguatá** *R* Uruguay
130 F8 **Caraguata-tuba** Brazil
130 C9 **Caraĝuatay** Paraguay
133 C5 **Carahue** Chile
130 H5 **Caraí** Brazil
12 C2 **Cara I** Scotland
129 H5 **Carajás, Serra dos** *mts* Brazil
18 G9 **Caraman** France
120 D3 **Caramat** Ontario Canada
71 F4 **Caramoan Pen** Philippines
128 F5 **Caranapatuba** Brazil
130 G7 **Carandaí** Brazil
130 B6 **Carandazal** Brazil
140 E5 **Carandotta** Queensland Australia
129 K8 **Carangola** Brazil
128 F3 **Caransaca,Co** *mt* Venezuela
48 G5 **Caransebeş** Romania
20 C4 **Carantec** France
130 B9 **Carapeguá** Paraguay
138 D5 **Carappee Hill** South Australia Australia
122 H6 **Caraquet** New Brunswick Canada
122 H6 **Caraquet Bay** New Brunswick Canada
128 B4 **Caráquez,B.de** Ecuador
48 G5 **Caraşova** Romania
48 G5 **Caraş-Severin** *reg* Romania
125 N2 **Caratasca** Honduras
130 G6 **Caratinga** Brazil
69 G14 **Carat, Tanjung** *C* Indonesia
128 E4 **Carauari** Brazil
130 H8 **Caraúbas** Brazil
17 F6 **Caravaca de la Cruz** Spain
41 L7 **Caravaggio** Italy
130 H5 **Caravelas** Brazil
128 D7 **Caraveli** Peru
43 B9 **Caravius, M. is** *mt* Sardinia
128 C5 **Caraz** Peru
131 H2 **Carazinho** Brazil
16 B2 **Carballiño** Spain
16 B1 **Carballo** Spain
16 B1 **Carba, Sa. de la** *mts* Spain
119 S9 **Carberry** Manitoba Canada
101 U1 **Carbert** Montana U.S.A.
118 D7 **Carbon** Alberta Canada
43 C9 **Carbonara,C** Sardinia
45 K1 **Carbonara di Po** Italy
118 D5 **Carbondale** Alberta Canada
106 C2 **Carbondale** Colorado U.S.A.
107 P3 **Carbondale** Kansas U.S.A.
95 M5 **Carbondale** Pennsylvania U.S.A.
123 T6 **Carbonear** Newfoundland Canada
17 F8 **Carboneras** Spain
111 J8 **Carbon Hill** Alabama U.S.A.
43 B9 **Carbonia** Sardinia
38 F8 **Carbonin** Italy
130 G5 **Carbonita** Brazil
18 F9 **Carbonne** France
17 G5 **Carcagente** Spain
117 P7 **Carcajou** Alberta Canada
18 E7 **Carcans, Etang de** *L* France
71 F5 **Carcar** Cebu Philippines
131 E4 **Carcaraña** *R* Argentina
18 G9 **Carcassonne** France
128 C3 **Carchi** *prov* Ecuador
139 J5 **Carcoan** New South Wales Australia
117 F5 **Carcross** Yukon Territory Canada
142 A6 **Cardabia** Western Australia Australia
47 K7 **Cardak** Turkey
119 R8 **Cardale** Manitoba Canada
68 F7 **Cardamomes,Chaine des** *mts* Cambodia
125 K6 **Cárdenas** Mexico
139 G3 **Cardenyabba** *R* New South Wales Australia
133 C7 **Cardiel,L** Argentina
8 C5 **Cardiff** Wales
Cardigan *co* *see* **Dyfed**
8 B3 **Cardigan** Wales
123 K7 **Cardigan B** Prince Edward I Canada
8 B2 **Cardigan B** Wales
121 P8 **Cardinal** Ontario Canada
94 E6 **Cardington** Ohio U.S.A.
17 J3 **Cardona** Spain
17 J3 **Cardoner,R** Spain
127 J9 **Cardón,Pta** Venezuela
130 E7 **Cardoso** Brazil
130 F9 **Cardoso,I.do** Brazil
144 B6 **Cardrona** New Zealand
144 B6 **Cardrona, Mt** New Zealand
119 M9 **Cardross** Saskatchewan Canada
12 D2 **Cardross** Scotland
118 D9 **Cardston** Alberta Canada
141 H4 **Cardwell** Queensland Australia
41 O6 **Carega, Cima** *mt* Italy
48 G3 **Carei** Romania
127 O2 **Carenage** Trinidad
22 D3 **Carency** France
20 H3 **Carentan** France
20 F6 **Carentoir** France
8 B4 **Carew** Wales
101 M6 **Carey** Idaho U.S.A.
94 D6 **Carey** Ohio U.S.A.
108 G1 **Carey** Texas U.S.A.
143 B7 **Carey Downs** Western Australia Australia
143 D8 **Carey, L** Western Australia Australia
81 C7 **Cargados Carajos** *islds* Indian Oc
18 L10 **Cargèse** Corsica
120 J8 **Cargill** Ontario Canada
13 E1 **Cargill** Scotland
141 G5 **Cargoon** Queensland Australia
20 C5 **Carhaix-Plouguer** France
122 E1 **Carheil,L** Quebec Canada
47 J7 **Caria** *hist reg* Turkey
130 H7 **Cariacica** Brazil
127 N9 **Cariaco** Venezuela
126 F10 **Caribana,Pta** Colombia
126 C5 **Caribbean Sea** Central America
117 N9 **Cariboo Mts** British Columbia Canada
117 K5 **Caribou** *R* Northwest Territories Canada
122 K8 **Caribou** Nova Scotia Canada
116 G9 **Caribou** *R* Alaska U.S.A.
95 S7 **Caribou** Maine U.S.A.
117 K7 **Caribou Hide** British Columbia Canada
122 K8 **Caribou I** Nova Scotia Canada
120 E5 **Caribou I** Ontario Canada
117 R5 **Caribou Is** Northwest Territories Canada
101 O6 **Caribou Mt** Idaho U.S.A.
117 Q6 **Caribou Mts** Alberta Canada
124 F4 **Carichic** Mexico
119 Q9 **Carievale** Saskatchewan Canada
71 G5 **Carigara** Leyte Philippines
22 J4 **Carignan** France
44 C2 **Carignano** Italy
121 Q7 **Carillon** Quebec Canada
139 J4 **Carinda** New South Wales Australia
17 G3 **Cariñena** Spain
129 K6 **Carinhanha** Brazil
45 P7 **Carinola** Italy
129 J6 **Caripare** Brazil
127 N9 **Caripe** Venezuela
127 N9 **Caripito** Venezuela
130 G9 **Caririaçu** Brazil
128 F5 **Caritianas** Brazil
130 G9 **Cariús** Brazil
107 N5 **Carl Blackwell, L** Oklahoma U.S.A.
22 E4 **Carlepont** France
17 G5 **Carlet** Spain
122 F5 **Carleton** Quebec Canada
94 D4 **Carleton** Michigan U.S.A.
98 J9 **Carleton** Nebraska U.S.A.
122 F6 **Carleton,Mt** New Brunswick Canada
121 O7 **Carleton Place** Ontario Canada
122 K4 **Carleton Pt** Quebec Canada
98 B5 **Carlile** Wyoming U.S.A.
103 H1 **Carlin** Nevada U.S.A.
36 B5 **Carling** France
14 E2 **Carlingford** Ireland
110 G2 **Carlinville** Illinois U.S.A.
142 B2 **Carlisle** *dist* Perth, W Aust Australia
13 F4 **Carlisle** England
110 E7 **Carlisle** Arkansas U.S.A.
110 J3 **Carlisle** Indiana U.S.A.
94 C8 **Carlisle** Kentucky U.S.A.
95 K6 **Carlisle** Pennsylvania U.S.A.
112 F3 **Carlisle** South Carolina U.S.A.
127 P6 **Carlisle B** Barbados
143 F8 **Carlisle Lakes** Western Australia Australia
18 G10 **Carlitte** *mt* France
43 B9 **Carloforte** Sardinia
13 E2 **Carlops** Scotland
133 E6 **Carlos Ameghino, Istmo** Argentina
133 E5 **Carlos Casares** Argentina
130 H5 **Carlos Chagas** Brazil
131 G4 **Carlos Reyles** Uruguay
14 E4 **Carlow** *co* Ireland
14 E4 **Carlow** Ireland
15 B2 **Carloway** Scotland
Carlsbad Czechoslovakia *see* **Karlovy Vary**
102 G8 **Carlsbad** California U.S.A.
108 C3 **Carlsbad** New Mexico U.S.A.
108 C3 **Carlsbad Caverns Nat. Park** New Mexico U.S.A.
72 H7 **Carlsberg Ridge** Indian Oc
37 O3 **Carlsfeld** East Germany
99 T3 **Carlshend** Michigan U.S.A.
118 L6 **Carlton** Saskatchewan Canada
99 O3 **Carlton** Minnesota U.S.A.
100 B4 **Carlton** Oregon U.S.A.
109 J4 **Carlton** Texas U.S.A.
142 G3 **Carlton Hill** Western Australia Australia
9 F1 **Carlton-on-Trent** England
100 D3 **Carlton Pass** Washington U.S.A.
12 E2 **Carluke** Scotland
119 P9 **Carlyle** Saskatchewan Canada

Carlyle — Cerro Prieto

17

110 G3 **Carlyle** Illinois U.S.A.
98 B3 **Carlyle** Montana U.S.A.
118 D1 **Carman** Manitoba Canada
118 D8 **Carmangay** Alberta Canada
123 S4 **Carmanville** Newfoundland Canada
Carmarthen *co see* **Dyfed**
8 B4 **Carmarthen** Wales
8 C4 **Carmarthen Van** *mt* Wales
18 G8 **Carmaux** France
119 M6 **Carmel** Saskatchewan Canada
102 C5 **Carmel** California U.S.A.
110 K2 **Carmel** indiana U.S.A.
94 A7 **Carmel** Indiana U.S.A.
95 O5 **Carmel** New York U.S.A.
95 S2 **Carmell** Maine U.S.A.
80 D3 **Carmel,Mt** Israel
112 E3 **Carmel, Mt** South Carolina U.S.A.
80 D3 **Carmel National Park, Mt** Israel
133 F4 **Carmelo** Uruguay
127 J9 **Carmelo** Venezuela
102 C5 **Carmel Valley** California U.S.A.
126 G10 **Carmen** Colombia
124 D5 **Carmen** *isld* Mexico
124 F2 **Carmen** *R* Mexico
71 G6 **Carmen** Philippines
101 M4 **Carmen** Idaho U.S.A.
107 M5 **Carmen** Oklahoma U.S.A.
133 D2 **Carmen Alto** Chile
130 C10 **Carmen del Paraná** Paraguay
133 E6 **Carmen de Patagones** Argentina
131 B2 **Carmen,R.del** Chile
133 D5 **Carmensa** Argentina
108 E7 **Carmen, Sa del** *mts* Mexico
110 H3 **Carmi** Illinois U.S.A.
113 L9 **Carmichael** New Providence I Bahamas
118 J8 **Carmichael** Saskatchewan Canada
141 J5 **Carmila** Queensland Australia
109 L5 **Carmine** Texas U.S.A.
130 G7 **Carmo** Brazil
44 D3 **Carmo** *mt* Italy
130 F7 **Carmo da Cachoeira** Brazil
130 F6 **Carmo do Paranaiba** Brazil
143 C9 **Carmody, L** Western Australia Australia
16 D7 **Carmona** Spain
13 H5 **Carnaby** England
20 D6 **Carnac** France
143 B8 **Carnamah** Western Australia Australia
138 F4 **Carnanto,L** South Australia Australia
143 A6 **Carnarvon** Western Australia Australia
89 C8 **Carnarvon** S Africa
141 H7 **Carnarvon Nat. Park** Queensland Australia
141 J7 **Carnarvon Ra** Queensland Australia
143 D7 **Carnarvon Ra** Western Australia Australia
71 C5 **Carnatic Shoal** S China Sea
14 D1 **Carndonagh** Ireland
119 Q9 **Carnduff** Saskatchewan Canada
8 C1 **Carnedd Llewelyn** *mt* Wales
143 E7 **Carnegie** Western Australia Australia
107 M6 **Carnegie** Oklahoma U.S.A.
94 G6 **Carnegie** Pennsylvania U.S.A.
143 E7 **Carnegie, L** Western Australia Australia
90 A9 **Carnegie Ridge** Pacific Oc
21 K4 **Carneille, la** France
107 N3 **Carneiro** Kansas U.S.A.
131 A6 **Carnero,B.del** Chile
112 D3 **Carnesville** Georgia U.S.A.
146 B8 **Carney** *isld* Antarctica
99 T4 **Carney** Michigan U.S.A.
107 O6 **Carney** Oklahoma U.S.A.
13 F5 **Carnforth** England
42 E2 **Carniche, Alpi** *mts* Italy
69 A8 **Car Nicobar** *isld* Nicobar Is
22 E3 **Carnieres** France
20 C5 **Carnoët** France
86 C5 **Carnot** Cent Afr Republic
138 D5 **Carnot,C** South Australia Australia
19 Q18 **Carnoules** France
13 F1 **Carnoustie** Scotland
14 E4 **Carnsore Pt** Ireland
12 E2 **Carnwath** Scotland
116 N3 **Caro** Alaska U.S.A.
94 D3 **Caro** Michigan U.S.A.
141 K4 **Carola Cay** *isld* Gt Barrier Reef Australia
112 F2 **Caroleen** North Carolina U.S.A.
129 J5 **Carolina** Brazil
128 C3 **Carolina** Ecuador
87 F11 **Carolina** S Africa
112 K3 **Carolina Beach** North Carolina U.S.A.
118 C6 **Caroline** Alberta Canada
144 B6 **Caroline** New Zealand
135 M9 **Caroline I** Pacific Oc
134 E7 **Caroline Is** Pacific Oc
140 D6 **Caroline, L** N Terr Australia
32 G5 **Carolinensiel** W Germany
144 A6 **Caroline Pk** New Zealand
142 F3 **Caroline Ra** Western Australia Australia
20 G4 **Carolles** France
119 M8 **Caron** Saskatchewan Canada
137 S3 **Carondelet Reef** Phoenix Is Pacific Oc
127 O2 **Caroni** Trinidad
128 F2 **Caroni** *R* Venezuela
127 O2 **Caroni Swamp** Trinidad
127 J9 **Carora** Venezuela
121 O7 **Carp** Ontario Canada
103 K4 **Carp** Nevada U.S.A.
53 B9 **Carpathian Mts** E Europe
48 H5 **Carpații Meridionali** *mts* Romania
41 M7 **Carpenèdolo** Italy
141 G4 **Carpentaria Downs** Queensland Australia
140 E2 **Carpentaria,Gulf of** Australia
98 B8 **Carpenter** Wyoming U.S.A.
99 S7 **Carpentersville** Illinois U.S.A.
100 A7 **Carpenterville** Oregon U.S.A.
19 O16 **Carpentras** France
45 J2 **Carpi** Italy
19 P18 **Carpiâgne** *mt* France
130 J9 **Carpina** Brazil
45 J3 **Carpineti** Italy
45 O6 **Carpineto Romano** Italy
48 F5 **Cărpinis** Romania
102 E7 **Carpinteria** California U.S.A.
98 E1 **Carpio** North Dakota U.S.A.
117 M8 **Carp L** British Columbia Canada
103 M2 **Carp L** Utah U.S.A.
94 C1 **Carp Lake** Michigan U.S.A.
138 F6 **Carpolac** Victoria Australia
20 H7 **Carquefou** France
19 Q18 **Carqueiranne** France
106 F1 **Carr** Colorado U.S.A.
113 C8 **Carrabelle** Florida U.S.A.
119 O6 **Carragana** Saskatchewan Canada
14 B3 **Carra,L** Ireland
16 B4 **Carramulo, Sa. do** *mts* Portugal
131 A5 **Carranza,C** Chile
125 J4 **Carranza, Presa V.** *res* Mexico
128 F2 **Carrao** *R* Venezuela
44 H3 **Carrara** Italy
102 H5 **Carrara** Nevada U.S.A.
140 D4 **Carrara Range** N Terr Australia
17 F4 **Carrascosa del Campo** Spain
17 G7 **Carrascoy,Sierra de** *mts* Spain
139 H5 **Carrathool** New South Wales Australia
14 B5 **Carrauntoohil** *mt* Ireland
142 G3 **Carr Boyd Ra** Western Australia Australia
15 E3 **Carrbridge** Scotland
133 F2 **Carreria** Paraguay
131 B6 **Carrero,Cerro** *pk* Argentina
127 O8 **Carriacou** *isld* Lesser Antilles
15 D5 **Carrick** Scotland
14 F2 **Carrickfergus** N Ireland
14 E3 **Carrickmacross** Ireland
14 C3 **Carrick on Shannon** Ireland
14 D4 **Carrick-on-Suir** Ireland
111 G11 **Carriere** Mississippi U.S.A.
121 N5 **Carrière,L** Quebec Canada
110 H4 **Carriers Mills** Illinois U.S.A.
138 E4 **Carrieton** South Australia Australia
131 B8 **Carri Lafquén, L** Argentina
98 G2 **Carrington** North Dakota U.S.A.
16 D2 **Carrion** *R* Spain
16 D2 **Carrión de los Condes** Spain
127 H8 **Carrizal** Colombia
124 F2 **Carrizal** Mexico
133 C3 **Carrizal Bajo** Chile
131 B2 **Carrizal, Pta** *C* Chile
103 H9 **Carrizo Cr** California U.S.A.
106 G5 **Carrizo Cr** New Mex/Tex U.S.A.
103 P5 **Carrizo Mts** Arizona U.S.A.
108 H7 **Carrizo Springs** Texas U.S.A.
106 E8 **Carrizozo** New Mexico U.S.A.
119 R9 **Carroll** Manitoba Canada
99 M7 **Carroll** Iowa U.S.A.
98 J7 **Carroll** Nebraska U.S.A.
111 H8 **Carrollton** Alabama U.S.A.
112 B4 **Carrollton** Georgia U.S.A.
110 F2 **Carrollton** Illinois U.S.A.
94 B8 **Carrollton** Kentucky U.S.A.
111 G8 **Carrollton** Mississippi U.S.A.
110 C2 **Carrollton** Missouri U.S.A.
94 F6 **Carrollton** Ohio U.S.A.
109 O8 **Carrollton** Texas U.S.A.
94 J6 **Carrolltown** Pennsylvania U.S.A.
99 T7 **Carrollville** Wisconsin U.S.A.
141 F4 **Carron** *R* Queensland Australia
12 E3 **Carronbridge** Scotland
119 V4 **Carrot R** Manitoba Canada
119 O5 **Carrot River** Saskatchewan Canada
21 K4 **Carrouges** France
14 B2 **Carrowmore L** Ireland
118 H6 **Carruthers** Saskatchewan Canada
100 C8 **Carrville** California U.S.A.
95 N2 **Carry Falls Res** New York U.S.A.
19 O18 **Carry-le-Rouet** France
78 F1 **Çarşamba** Turkey
118 D8 **Carseland** Alberta Canada
13 E1 **Carse of Gowrie** *dist* Scotland
45 O5 **Carseolani, Mti** Italy
45 O5 **Carsoli** Italy
99 L8 **Carson** Iowa U.S.A.
102 E2 **Carson** *R* Nevada U.S.A.
98 E3 **Carson** North Dakota U.S.A.
100 D4 **Carson** Washington U.S.A.
94 C3 **Carson City** Michigan U.S.A.
102 E2 **Carson City** Nevada U.S.A.
146 D7 **Carson Inlet** *inlet* Antarctica
102 F2 **Carson L** Nevada U.S.A.
142 F3 **Carson, R** Western Australia Australia
102 F2 **Carson Sink** *dry lake* Nevada U.S.A.
94 E3 **Carsonville** Michigan U.S.A.
12 D3 **Carsphairn** Scotland
118 C7 **Carstairs** Alberta Canada
12 E2 **Carstairs** Scotland
Carstensz, G *see* **Jaya Pk**
128 C1 **Cartagena** Colombia
17 G7 **Cartagena** Spain
128 C3 **Cartago** Colombia
125 N5 **Cartago** Costa Rica
102 F5 **Cartago** California U.S.A.
108 G6 **Carta Valley** Texas U.S.A.
101 P2 **Carter** Montana U.S.A.
107 L6 **Carter** Oklahoma U.S.A.
101 P8 **Carter** Wyoming U.S.A.
13 F3 **Carter Bar** England
20 G3 **Carteret** France
141 G2 **Carter, Mt** Queensland Australia
9 G3 **Carters Bridge** England
111 M7 **Cartersville** Georgia U.S.A.
101 T3 **Cartersville** Montana U.S.A.
145 E4 **Carterton** New Zealand
43 C12 **Carthage** Tunisia
85 G1 **Carthage** *ruins* Tunisia
109 P1 **Carthage** Arkansas U.S.A.
99 P9 **Carthage** Illinois U.S.A.
94 B7 **Carthage** Indiana U.S.A.
111 G9 **Carthage** Mississippi U.S.A.
110 B4 **Carthage** Missouri U.S.A.
95 M3 **Carthage** New York U.S.A.
112 H2 **Carthage** North Carolina U.S.A.
98 J5 **Carthage** South Dakota U.S.A.
94 B10 **Carthage** Tennessee U.S.A.
109 N3 **Carthage** Texas U.S.A.
120 J6 **Cartier** Ontario Canada
142 E1 **Cartier I** Timor Sea
22 F3 **Cartignies** France
13 F5 **Cartmel** England
45 N4 **Cartoceto** Italy
48 J6 **Cartojani** Romania
115 O7 **Cartwright** Labrador, Nfld Canada
119 S9 **Cartwright** Manitoba Canada
98 C2 **Cartwright** North Dakota U.S.A.
130 H10 **Caruarú** Brazil
129 L5 **Caruaru** Brazil
128 F1 **Carúpano** Venezuela
129 J4 **Carutapera** Brazil
110 G5 **Caruthersville** Missouri U.S.A.
94 D9 **Carver** Kentucky U.S.A.
22 D3 **Carvin** France
16 A5 **Carvoeira,C** Portugal
128 F4 **Carvoeiro** Brazil
101 M1 **Carway** Alberta Canada
141 H6 **Carwell** Queensland Australia
33 S6 **Carwitz** East Germany
111 F9 **Cary** Mississippi U.S.A.
112 J2 **Cary** North Carolina U.S.A.
139 G3 **Caryapundy Swamp** New S Wales/Queensland
113 G12 **Carysfort Reef** Florida U.S.A.
45 K3 **Carzolano,Mt** Italy
133 C4 **Casablanca** Chile
85 C2 **Casablanca** Morocco
130 F7 **Casa Branca** Brazil
16 B6 **Casa Branca** Portugal
42 F7 **Casacalenda** Italy
41 L5 **Casaccia** Switzerland
127 P3 **Casa Cruz, C** Trinidad
124 E2 **Casa de János** Mexico
129 G8 **Casado** Paraguay
103 N9 **Casa Grande** Arizona U.S.A.
103 N9 **Casa Grande Nat. Mon** Arizona U.S.A.
17 G5 **Casa Ibáñez** Spain
41 L7 **Casalbuttano** Italy
45 Q7 **Casal di Principe** Italy
44 D1 **Casale** Italy
45 K3 **Casalecchio di Reno** Italy
45 J2 **Casalgrande** Italy
45 H2 **Casalmaggiore** Italy
45 J1 **Casaloldo** Italy
44 G1 **Casalpusterlengo** Italy
45 P6 **Casalvieri** Italy
45 P8 **Casamicciola Terme** Italy
116 E4 **Casapedaga** Alaska U.S.A.
108 C6 **Casa Piedra** Texas U.S.A.
43 J8 **Casarano** Italy
124 F2 **Casas Grandes** Mexico
109 O9 **Casa View** Texas U.S.A.
100 J5 **Cascade** Idaho U.S.A.
101 O2 **Cascade** Montana U.S.A.
95 Q2 **Cascade** New Hampshire U.S.A.
100 D4 **Cascade Locks** Oregon U.S.A.
117 N11 **Cascade Mts** Br Col/Wash Canada
100 D1 **Cascade Pass** Washington U.S.A.
100 C7 **Cascade Ra** U.S.A.
100 K5 **Cascade Res** Idaho U.S.A.
100 D2 **Cascade Tunnel** Washington U.S.A.
100 C5 **Cascadia** Oregon U.S.A.
16 A6 **Cascais** Portugal
122 G5 **Cascapedia** Quebec Canada
122 F5 **Cascapedia R** Quebec Canada
130 D9 **Cascavel** Brazil
45 J4 **Cascina** Italy
95 R2 **Casco** Maine U.S.A.
99 T5 **Casco** Wisconsin U.S.A.
95 R3 **Casco B** Maine U.S.A.
45 M3 **Casemurate** Italy
45 L4 **Casentina** Italy
133 E5 **Caseros** Argentina
45 Q7 **Caserta** Italy
94 D3 **Caseville** Michigan U.S.A.
146 G14 **Casey** *Aust Base* Antarctica
121 Q5 **Casey** Quebec Canada
99 T10 **Casey** Illinois U.S.A.
146 K9 **Casey B** Antarctica
86 B1 **Caseyr, Raas** *C* Somalia
14 D4 **Cashel** Ireland
87 F9 **Cashel** Zimbabwe
107 N6 **Cashion** Oklahoma U.S.A.
141 J8 **Cashmere** Queensland Australia
100 E2 **Cashmere** Washington U.S.A.
99 Q6 **Cashton** Wisconsin U.S.A.
71 F2 **Casiguran** Luzon Philippines
71 F2 **Casiguran B** Luzon Philippines
71 E3 **Casiguran Sound** Luzon Philippines
133 E4 **Casilda** Argentina
48 L6 **Casimcea** Romania
130 G8 **Casimiro de Abreu** Brazil
45 H2 **Casina** Italy
139 L3 **Casino** New South Wales Australia
128 E3 **Casiquiare** *R* Venezuela
124 D2 **Casita** Mexico
31 J6 **Čáslav** Czechoslovakia
128 C5 **Casma** Peru
71 G5 **Casogoran B** Philippines
45 L3 **Casola Valsenio** Italy
109 N2 **Cason** Texas U.S.A.
45 Q8 **Casória** Italy
102 A2 **Caspar** California U.S.A.
17 G3 **Caspe** Spain
101 T7 **Casper** Wyoming U.S.A.
111 C9 **Caspiana** Louisiana U.S.A.
53 G10 **Caspian Sea**
20 F2 **Casquets Lt.Ho** English Chan
144 C5 **Cass** *R* New Zealand
144 C5 **Cass** New Zealand
110 C6 **Cass** Arkansas U.S.A.
94 D3 **Cass** *R* Michigan U.S.A.
94 H8 **Cass** West Virginia U.S.A.
98 B7 **Cassa** Wyoming U.S.A.
18 G8 **Cassagnes-Bégonhès** France
87 D8 **Cassai** Angola
130 F7 **Cássai** Brazil
Cassaigne *see* **Sidi Ali**
87 D8 **Cassamba** Angola
43 G9 **Cassano allo Ionio** Italy
94 D3 **Cass City** Michigan U.S.A.
121 P7 **Casselman** Ontario Canada
98 J3 **Casselton** North Dakota U.S.A.
19 Q14 **Casse Massion** *mt* France
117 J6 **Cassiar** British Columbia Canada
117 H6 **Cassiar Mts** British Columbia Canada
130 D6 **Cassilândia** Brazil
139 J4 **Cassilis** New South Wales Australia
141 G5 **Cassilis** Queensland Australia
87 C9 **Cassinga** Angola
142 F2 **Cassini I** Western Australia Australia
133 G4 **Cassino** Brazil
43 F7 **Cassino** Italy
129 H3 **Cassiporé** *R* Brazil
19 P18 **Cassis** France
99 M2 **Cass L** Minnesota U.S.A.
107 O3 **Cassoday** Kansas U.S.A.
94 B5 **Cassopolis** Michigan U.S.A.
110 C5 **Cassville** Missouri U.S.A.
99 Q7 **Cassville** Wisconsin U.S.A.
20 B5 **Cast** France
45 K1 **Castagnaro** Italy
102 F7 **Castaic** California U.S.A.
129 J4 **Castanhal** Brazil
133 D4 **Castaño** Argentina
131 B3 **Castaño** *R* Argentina
124 J4 **Castaños** Mexico
127 M1 **Castara** Tobago
17 G3 **Castejón,Mt.de** Spain
45 J1 **Castelbelforte** Italy
45 L3 **Castel Bolognese** Italy
45 J1 **Castel d'Ario** Italy
42 D4 **Castel del Rio** Italy
42 F7 **Castel di Sangro** Italy
45 L4 **Castel Focognano** Italy
45 P7 **Castelforte** Italy
45 L4 **Castelfranco di Sopra** Italy
45 K2 **Castelfranco Emilia** Italy
42 D3 **Castelfranco Veneto** Veneto Italy
45 J1 **Castel Goffredo** Italy
18 F8 **Casteljaloux** France
109 J5 **Castell** Texas U.S.A.
37 J4 **Castell** W Germany
100 C8 **Castella** California U.S.A.
43 F8 **Castellabate** Italy
43 E10 **Castellammare del Golfo** Sicily
45 Q8 **Castellammare di Stabia** Italy
40 G7 **Castellamònte** Italy
45 J2 **Castellarano** Italy
133 F5 **Castelli** Argentina
45 K3 **Castello di Serravalle** Italy
17 G4 **Castellón** *prov* Spain
17 G5 **Castellón de la Plana** Spain
17 G4 **Castellote** Spain
45 J1 **Castellucchio** Italy
45 N6 **Castel Madama** Italy
45 K2 **Castel Maggiore** Italy
45 K1 **Castelmassa** Italy
18 G9 **Castelnaudary** France
18 E7 **Castelnau de Médoc** France
18 F8 **Castelnau de Montratier** France
18 F9 **Castelnau-Magnoac** France
45 J2 **Castelnovo di Sotto** Italy
45 H3 **Castel novo ne'Monti** Italy
45 H3 **Castelnuovo di Garfagnana** Italy
45 N5 **Castelnuovo di Porto** Italy
45 J1 **Castelnuovo di Verona** Italy
130 H7 **Castelo** Brazil
16 C5 **Castelo de Vide** Portugal
45 O4 **Castelplanio** Italy
45 M6 **Castel Porziano** Italy
45 R8 **Castel San Giorgio** Italy
45 L4 **Castel San Niccolo** Italy
45 L3 **Castel San Pietro Terme** Italy
18 F8 **Castelsarrasin** France
44 F1 **Castel S.Giov** Italy
43 F11 **Casteltermini** Sicily
45 P5 **Castelvecchio Subequo** Italy
43 E11 **Castelvetrano** Sicily
45 P7 **Castel Volturno** Italy
45 K3 **Castenaso** Italy
41 M7 **Castenedolo** Italy
138 F6 **Casterton** Victoria Australia
18 E9 **Castets** France
122 F7 **Castigan Mts** New Brunswick Canada
45 K3 **Castiglione dei Pepoli** Italy
45 J1 **Castiglione delle Stiviere** Italy
45 H3 **Castiglione di Garfagnana** Italy
45 L4 **Castiglion Fibocchi** Italy
42 D5 **Castiglion Fiorentino** Italy
94 K4 **Castile** New York U.S.A.
133 C3 **Castilla** Chile
16 D4 **Castilla La Vieja** *reg* Spain
71 E3 **Castillejos** Luzon Philippines
16 D6 **Castillejo, Sa. de** *mts* Spain
127 J9 **Castilletes** Venezuela
133 C7 **Castillo** *mt* Chile
131 B4 **Castillo,Cerro del** *pk* Argentina
113 F8 **Castillo de San Marcos Nat. Mon** Florida U.S.A.
124 H3 **Castillón** Mexico
18 F8 **Castillon et Capitourlan** France
18 F8 **Castillonnés** France
133 D7 **Castillo,Pampa del** *plain* Argentina
133 G4 **Castillos** Uruguay
95 T2 **Castine** Maine U.S.A.
9 G2 **Castle Acre** England
14 B3 **Castlebar** Ireland
15 A4 **Castlebay** Scotland
14 E3 **Castlebellingham** Ireland
111 J10 **Castleberry** Alabama U.S.A.
14 E2 **Castleblayney** Ireland
9 E3 **Castle Bromwich** England
13 F4 **Castle Carrock** England
8 D5 **Castle Cary** England
14 D4 **Castlecomer** Ireland
100 J7 **Castle Cr** Idaho U.S.A.
103 N2 **Castle Dale** Utah U.S.A.
14 D2 **Castlederg** N Ireland
14 E4 **Castledermot** Ireland
103 K8 **Castle Dome Mts** Arizona U.S.A.
9 E2 **Castle Donington** England
12 E4 **Castle Douglas** Scotland
12 E3 **Castlefern** Scotland
13 G6 **Castleford** England
101 L7 **Castleford** Idaho U.S.A.
100 H1 **Castlegar** British Columbia Canada
103 O2 **Castle Gate** Utah U.S.A.
90 C1 **Castle Harbour** Bermuda
112 K3 **Castle Hayne** North Carolina U.S.A.
103 M8 **Castle Hot Sp** Arizona U.S.A.
126 G3 **Castle I** Bahamas
14 B4 **Castleisland** Ireland
139 G6 **Castlemaine** Victoria Australia
14 B4 **Castlemaine** Ireland
14 C5 **Castlemartyr** Ireland
118 B7 **Castle, Mt** Alberta Canada
117 F3 **Castle Mt** Yukon Territory Canada
102 D6 **Castle Mt** California U.S.A.
101 L5 **Castle Peak** Idaho U.S.A.
145 F4 **Castlepoint** New Zealand
14 D3 **Castlepollard** Ireland
14 C3 **Castlerea** Ireland
139 J4 **Castlereagh** *R* New South Wales Australia
140 D1 **Castlereagh B** N Terr Australia
9 G2 **Castle Rising** England
106 F2 **Castle Rock** Colorado U.S.A.
98 C5 **Castle Rock** South Dakota U.S.A.
101 O8 **Castle Rock** Utah U.S.A.
100 C3 **Castle Rock** Washington U.S.A.
99 R6 **Castle Rock Res** Wisconsin U.S.A.
13 G4 **Castleside** England
9 E1 **Castleton** England
127 L2 **Castleton** Jamaica
103 P3 **Castleton** Utah U.S.A.
95 O3 **Castleton** Vermont U.S.A.
95 O4 **Castleton on Hudson** New York U.S.A.
12 D5 **Castletown** I of Man U.K.
14 B5 **Castletown Bere** Ireland
14 F2 **Castlewellan** N Ireland
98 J5 **Castlewood** South Dakota U.S.A.
108 D6 **Castolon** Texas U.S.A.
118 F6 **Castor** Alberta Canada
111 D9 **Castor** *R* Louisiana U.S.A.
111 C9 **Castor** Louisiana U.S.A.
95 M3 **Castorland** New York U.S.A.
20 H3 **Castre, Mt** France
18 G9 **Castres** France
25 C3 **Castricum** Netherlands
127 O7 **Castries** St Lucia
133 C6 **Castro** Chile
16 D2 **Castrocalbón** Spain
45 L3 **Castrocaro** Italy
45 O6 **Castro dei Volsci** Italy
16 E2 **Castrogeriz** Spain
16 C1 **Castropol** Spain
32 F9 **Castrop-Rauxel** W Germany
16 E1 **Castro Urdiales** Spain
16 B7 **Castro Verde** Portugal
43 G9 **Castrovillari** Italy
102 C5 **Castroville** California U.S.A.
109 J6 **Castroville** Texas U.S.A.
16 D6 **Castuera** Spain
88 G10 **Casuarina** *isld* Mozambique
142 G2 **Casuarina, Mt** Western Australia Australia
116 N6 **Caswell** Alaska U.S.A.
144 A6 **Caswell Sd** New Zealand
48 E3 **Čata** Czechoslovakia
87 C8 **Catabola** Angola
143 B9 **Cataby** Western Australia Australia
127 J2 **Catadupa** Jamaica
130 G7 **Cataguases** Brazil
111 D10 **Catahoula L** Louisiana U.S.A.
71 F4 **Cataiñgan** Philippines
78 J2 **Çatak** Turkey
78 J3 **Çatak** *R* Turkey
130 F6 **Catalão** Brazil
47 J3 **Çatalca** Turkey
47 J5 **Çatal Dağı** *mt* Turkey
127 K5 **Catalina, I** Dominican Rep
139 H9 **Catamaran** Tasmania Australia
133 D3 **Catamarca** *prov* Argentina
131 D2 **Catamarca** Argentina
71 F4 **Catanauan** Philippines
87 F9 **Catandica** Mozambique
71 G4 **Catanduanes** *isld* Philippines
130 E7 **Catanduva** Brazil
130 D9 **Catanduvas** Brazil
43 G11 **Catania** Sicily
43 G11 **Catania,Golfo di** Sicily
43 H10 **Catanzaro** Italy
113 K7 **Cataõ** Puerto Rico
111 F12 **Cataouatche,L** Louisiana U.S.A.
110 K2 **Cataract L** Indiana U.S.A.
130 C9 **Cataratas del Iguazú** *waterfalls* Argentina/Brazil
71 G4 **Catarman** Philippines
71 G7 **Catarman Pt** Mindanao Philippines
17 G5 **Catarroja** Spain
95 M6 **Catasauqua** Pennsylvania U.S.A.
128 D2 **Catatumbo** *R* Venezuela/Colombia
111 M9 **Cataula** Georgia U.S.A.
129 G4 **Catavara** Brazil
99 Q4 **Catawba** Wisconsin U.S.A.
112 F2 **Catawba L** South Carolina U.S.A.
95 L6 **Catawissa** Pennsylvania U.S.A.
87 F9 **Cataxa** Mozambique
71 G5 **Catbalogan** Samar Philippines
126 E2 **Cat Cays** *islds* Bahamas
101 R2 **Cat Creek** Montana U.S.A.
22 F3 **Cateau,Le** France
71 G7 **Cateel** Mindanao Philippines
20 E3 **Catel** Channel Is
22 E3 **Catelet, le** France
125 M8 **Catemaco** Mexico
45 P5 **Catena di Monte Sirente** Italy
130 J10 **Catende** Brazil
118 J5 **Cater** Saskatchewan Canada
9 F5 **Caterham** England
87 B7 **Catete** Angola
107 L3 **Catharine** Kansas U.S.A.
98 G2 **Cathay** North Dakota U.S.A.
139 J6 **Cathcart** New South Wales Australia
87 E12 **Cathcart** S Africa
108 D5 **Cathedral Mt** Texas U.S.A.
109 P1 **Catherine,L** Arkansas U.S.A.
103 M2 **Catherine, Mt** Utah U.S.A.
127 L2 **Catherine's Peak** Jamaica
89 F7 **Cathkin Pk** *mt* Lesotho
100 B3 **Cathlamet** Washington U.S.A.
94 D1 **Cathro** Michigan U.S.A.
126 G2 **Cat I** Bahamas
111 G11 **Cat I** Mississippi U.S.A.
22 F3 **Catillon-sur-Sambre** France
85 A6 **Catio** Guinea-Bissau
128 F3 **Catisimiña** Venezuela
79 F1 **Çatkıt Suyu** *R* Turkey
115 K7 **Cat Lake** Ontario Canada
94 E8 **Catlettsburg** Kentucky U.S.A.
99 T9 **Catlin** Illinois U.S.A.
144 B7 **Catlins** *R* New Zealand
137 M6 **Cato** *isld* Coral Sea
95 L3 **Cato** New York U.S.A.
94 K7 **Catoctin Mt** Maryland/Virg U.S.A.
130 H9 **Catolé do Rocha** Brazil
42 E5 **Catria,Monte** Italy
133 E5 **Catrilo** Argentina
128 F3 **Catrimani** Brazil
95 O4 **Catskill** New York U.S.A.
95 N4 **Catskill Mts** New York U.S.A.
94 J4 **Cattaraugus** New York U.S.A.
22 L5 **Cattenom** France
13 F6 **Catterall** England
13 G5 **Catterick** England
45 N4 **Cattolica** Italy
87 F11 **Catuane** Mozambique
133 D4 **Catuna** Argentina
128 E3 **Cauaburi** *R* Brazil
45 M1 **Cauárzera** Italy
129 J4 **Cauaxi** *R* Brazil
71 F6 **Cauayan** Negros Philippines
128 C3 **Cauca** *div* Colombia
126 G10 **Cauca,R** Colombia
72 E1 **Caucasus** *mt ra* U.S.S.R.
119 V3 **Cauchon L** Manitoba Canada
95 R7 **Caucomgomoc L** Maine U.S.A.
21 M2 **Caudebec** France
21 N3 **Caudebec-les-Elbeuf** France
17 G6 **Caudete** Spain
22 E3 **Caudry** France
88 C9 **Cauese Mts** Mozambique
121 R7 **Caughnawaga** Quebec Canada
71 G6 **Cauit Pt** Philippines
20 F5 **Caulnes** France
43 G10 **Caulonia** Italy
19 N17 **Caumont** France
21 J3 **Caumont-l'Eventé** France
126 E4 **Caunao** *R* Cuba
18 G9 **Caunes** France
87 C7 **Caungulu** Angola
131 A5 **Cauquenes** Chile
133 C5 **Cauquenes** Chile
128 F2 **Caura** *R* Venezuela
20 D5 **Caurel** France
122 E5 **Causapscal** Quebec Canada
18 G8 **Caussade** France
128 F6 **Cautário** *R* Brazil
18 E10 **Cauterets** France
131 A7 **Cautin** *prov* Chile
126 F4 **Cauto** Cuba
21 L2 **Cauville** France
21 L2 **Caux** *reg* France
45 R8 **Cava** Italy
16 B3 **Cavado** *R* Portugal
40 H7 **Cavaglia** Italy
19 O17 **Cavaillon** France
19 Q18 **Cavalaire** France
129 J6 **Cavalcante** Brazil
41 O5 **Cavalese** Italy
98 J1 **Cavalier** North Dakota U.S.A.
119 U10 **Cavalier** North Dakota U.S.A.
145 D1 **Cavalli Is** New Zealand
109 L7 **Cavallo, Pass** Texas U.S.A.
85 C7 **Cavally** *R* Ivory Co/Liberia
14 D3 **Cavan** *co* Ireland
14 D3 **Cavan** Ireland
47 K7 **Çavdır** Turkey
45 N6 **Cave** Italy
144 C6 **Cave** New Zealand
110 E6 **Cave City** Arkansas U.S.A.
94 B9 **Cave City** Kentucky U.S.A.
103 N8 **Cavecreek** Arizona U.S.A.
143 D9 **Cave Hill** Western Australia Australia
110 H4 **Cave in Rock** Illinois U.S.A.
130 E10 **Caveiras,R** Brazil
100 B7 **Cave Junction** Oregon U.S.A.
120 C2 **Cavell** Ontario Canada
118 J6 **Cavell** Saskatchewan Canada
143 G7 **Cavenagh Ra** Western Australia Australia
138 F6 **Cavendish** Victoria Australia
118 G8 **Cavendish** Alberta Canada
9 G3 **Cavendish** England
45 M2 **Ca Venier** Italy
131 G3 **Cavera** *R* Brazil
131 G3 **Cavera, Serra do** *mts* Brazil
68 C7 **Cavern I** Burma
130 D9 **Cavernoso, Serra do** *mts* Brazil
120 C4 **Cavers** Ontario Canada
9 F5 **Caversham** England
111 L7 **Cave Spring** Georgia U.S.A.
103 K3 **Cave Valley** Nevada U.S.A.
129 H3 **Caviana** *isld* Brazil
18 E7 **Cavignac** France
71 E6 **Cavili** Philippines
71 E3 **Cavite** Luzon Philippines
48 H3 **Cavnic** Romania
45 N6 **Cavo, M** *mt* Italy
44 B2 **Cavour** Italy
98 H5 **Cavour** South Dakota U.S.A.
45 J2 **Cavriago** Italy
42 J6 **Cavtat** Yugoslavia
15 E3 **Cawdor** Scotland
107 M2 **Cawker City** Kansas U.S.A.
138 F4 **Cawndilla L** New South Wales Australia
Cawnpore *see* **Kanpur**
13 G6 **Cawood** England
121 P7 **Cawood Low** Quebec Canada
9 H2 **Cawston** England
130 G7 **Caxambu** Brazil
129 K4 **Caxias** Brazil
128 D4 **Caxias** Amazonas Brazil
131 H2 **Caxias do Sul** Brazil
87 B7 **Caxito** Angola
9 F3 **Caxton** England
9 F3 **Caxton Gibbet** England
47 L6 **Çay** Turkey
47 K3 **Cayağzı** Turkey
128 C3 **Cayambe** *vol* Ecuador
112 F4 **Cayce** South Carolina U.S.A.
68 F8 **Cay Dua** *B* Vietnam
78 H1 **Çayeli** Turkey
129 H3 **Cayenne** Fr Guiana
21 O1 **Cayeux-sur-Mer** France
127 L5 **Cayey** Puerto Rico
18 H9 **Caylar, le** France
118 D8 **Cayley** Alberta Canada
18 G8 **Caylus** France
126 E5 **Cayman Brac** *isld* W Indies
126 D5 **Cayman, Grand** *isld* W Indies
126 D5 **Cayman, Little** *isld* W Indies
90 A6 **Cayman Trench** Caribbean
68 G7 **Cay Mit** Vietnam
86 A2 **Caynabo** Somalia
125 P9 **Cayo** Belize
127 P4 **Cayon** St Kitts W Indies
126 D3 **Cay Sal Bank** Bahamas
102 D6 **Cayucos** California U.S.A.
99 T10 **Cayuga** Indiana U.S.A.
98 J3 **Cayuga** North Dakota U.S.A.
109 M4 **Cayuga** Texas U.S.A.
95 L4 **Cayuga L** New York U.S.A.
16 D7 **Cazalla de la Sierra** Spain
48 L6 **Căzănești** Romania
18 E9 **Cazaubon** France
18 E8 **Cazaux, Etang de** *L* France
85 F2 **Caze** Algeria
95 M4 **Cazenovia** New York U.S.A.
18 F9 **Cazères** France
42 G4 **Cazin** Yugoslavia
42 H3 **Čazma** Yugoslavia
87 D8 **Cazombo** Angola
16 E7 **Cazorla** Spain
87 F9 **Cazula** Mozambique
16 D2 **Cea** *R* Spain
48 K3 **Ceahlău** Romania
48 K4 **Ceahlău** *mt* Romania
Ceanannus Mór *see* **Kells**
130 J8 **Ceará Mirim** Brazil
21 J5 **Ceauce** France
48 H6 **Ceauru, Lacu** *L* Romania
21 L7 **Ceaux-en-Loudun** France
119 P5 **Ceba** Saskatchewan Canada
125 O6 **Cebaco,I** Panama
124 G4 **Ceballos** Mexico
106 D5 **Cebolla** New Mexico U.S.A.
133 D3 **Cebollar** Argentina
133 G4 **Cebollati** *R* Uruguay
17 F3 **Cebollera** *mt* Spain
106 C6 **Cebollita** New Mexico U.S.A.
16 E4 **Cebreros** Spain
71 F5 **Cebu** Philippines
71 F7 **Cebuano Barracks** Mindanao Philippines
43 E7 **Ceccano** Italy
48 E4 **Cece** Hungary
94 C5 **Cecil** Ohio U.S.A.
99 S5 **Cecil** Wisconsin U.S.A.
141 K8 **Cecil Plains** Queensland Australia
143 D7 **Cecil Rhodes, Mt** *mt* Western Australia Australia
95 M7 **Cecilton** Maryland U.S.A.
100 B8 **Cecilville** California U.S.A.
42 D5 **Cecina** Italy
16 C5 **Ceclavin** Spain
99 O7 **Cedar** *R* Iowa U.S.A.
107 M2 **Cedar** Kansas U.S.A.
94 C2 **Cedar** *R* Michigan U.S.A.
98 H8 **Cedar** *R* Nebraska U.S.A.
111 H8 **Cedarbluff** Mississippi U.S.A.
94 F9 **Cedar Bluff** Virginia U.S.A.
107 L3 **Cedar Bluff Res** Kansas U.S.A.
107 K2 **Cedar Bluffs** Kansas U.S.A.
98 K8 **Cedar Bluffs** Nebraska U.S.A.
103 M4 **Cedar Breaks Nat.Mon** Utah U.S.A.
99 T6 **Cedarburg** Wisconsin U.S.A.
98 E6 **Cedar Butte** South Dakota U.S.A.
110 D3 **Cedar City** Missouri U.S.A.
103 L4 **Cedar City** Utah U.S.A.
98 D3 **Cedar Cr** North Dakota U.S.A.
109 K5 **Cedar Creek** Texas U.S.A.
109 O9 **Cedar Crest** Texas U.S.A.
109 L3 **Cedar Cr. L** Texas U.S.A.
101 L7 **Cedar Cr.Res** Idaho U.S.A.
99 O7 **Cedar Falls** Iowa U.S.A.
94 F8 **Cedar Grove** West Virginia U.S.A.
99 T6 **Cedar Grove** Wisconsin U.S.A.
127 P4 **Cedar Grove** Antigua W Indies
112 L2 **Cedar I** North Carolina U.S.A.
95 M9 **Cedar I** Virginia U.S.A.
113 D8 **Cedar Key** Florida U.S.A.
119 R5 **Cedar L** Manitoba Canada
108 E3 **Cedar L** Texas U.S.A.
99 T8 **Cedar Lake** Indiana U.S.A.
109 M7 **Cedar Lane** Texas U.S.A.
102 G3 **Cedar Mts** Nevada U.S.A.
94 D5 **Cedar Pt** Ohio U.S.A.
99 P8 **Cedar Rapids** Iowa U.S.A.
98 H8 **Cedar Rapids** Nebraska U.S.A.
95 K5 **Cedar Run** Pennsylvania U.S.A.
120 H10 **Cedar Springs** Ontario Canada
94 B3 **Cedar Springs** Michigan U.S.A.
111 L7 **Cedartown** Georgia U.S.A.
107 O4 **Cedar Vale** Kansas U.S.A.
106 E7 **Cedarvale** New Mexico U.S.A.
127 L2 **Cedar Valley** Jamaica
100 E8 **Cedarville** California U.S.A.
95 M7 **Cedarville** New Jersey U.S.A.
110 N2 **Cedarville** Ohio U.S.A.
106 F4 **Cedarwood** Colorado U.S.A.
94 K8 **Cedon** Virginia U.S.A.
119 O9 **Cedoux** Saskatchewan Canada
43 C8 **Cedrino** *R* Sardinia
130 G9 **Cedro** Brazil
124 E4 **Cedros** Mexico
124 B3 **Cedros** *isld* Mexico
127 N3 **Cedros Pt** Trinidad
138 C4 **Ceduna** South Australia Australia
86 J4 **Ceel Afweyn** Somalia
86 A3 **Ceelbuur** Somalia
86 A2 **Ceel Hur** Somalia
86 A1 **Ceerigaabo** Somalia
43 F10 **Cefalù** Sicily
16 E3 **Cega** *R* Spain
48 F3 **Cegléd** Hungary
43 H8 **Ceglie Messapico** Italy
17 F6 **Cehegin** Spain
67 B4 **Ceheng** China
48 H3 **Cehu Silvaniei** Romania
48 G4 **Ceica** Romania
128 E3 **Cejal** Colombia
87 C8 **Cela** Angola
Celah, Gunung *see* **Mandi Angin, Gunung**
45 P5 **Celano** Italy
16 B2 **Celanova** Spain
125 J7 **Celaya** Mexico
Celebes *isld see* **Sulawesi**
70 G3 **Celebes Sea** Indonesia
109 L2 **Celeste** Texas U.S.A.
110 M1 **Celina** Ohio U.S.A.
94 C6 **Celina** Ohio U.S.A.
94 B10 **Celina** Tennessee U.S.A.
109 L2 **Celina** Texas U.S.A.
17 G4 **Cella** Spain
48 D3 **Celldömölk** Hungary
32 M7 **Celle** W Germany
22 E2 **Celles** Belgium
21 M7 **Celle-St.Avant,la** France
21 N6 **Cellettes** France
21 N8 **Celon** France
16 B3 **Celorico de Basto** Portugal
7 E12 **Celtic Sea** British Isles/France
47 L7 **Çeltikçi** Turkey
47 H4 **Çeltik Gölü** *L* Turkey
41 O5 **Cembra** Italy
107 M7 **Cement** Oklahoma U.S.A.
94 C4 **Cement City** Michigan U.S.A.
46 D1 **Čemerna Planina** *mt* Yugoslavia
42 H4 **Čemernica** *mt* Yugoslavia
48 E7 **Čemerno** Yugoslavia
8 B1 **Cemlyn B** Wales
8 B1 **Cemmaes** Wales
17 F6 **Cenajo, Embalse del** *res* Spain
8 B3 **Cenarth** Wales
136 H2 **Cenderawasih, Teluk** *B* W Irian
71 A3 **Cenga** Indonesia
44 G2 **Ceno** *R* Italy
133 C6 **Cenoa** *R* Argentina
86 C4 **Cent.Afr.Rep** Equat Africa
130 D8 **Centenario do Sul** Brazil
112 H3 **Centenary** South Carolina U.S.A.
101 T8 **Centennial** Wyoming U.S.A.
103 L8 **Centennial Wash** *R* Arizona U.S.A.
106 D4 **Center** Colorado U.S.A.
110 E2 **Center** Missouri U.S.A.
98 E2 **Center** North Dakota U.S.A.
111 B10 **Center** Texas U.S.A.
94 E6 **Centerburg** Ohio U.S.A.
99 O4 **Center City** Minnesota U.S.A.
95 L9 **Center Cross** Virginia U.S.A.
113 F9 **Center Hill** Florida U.S.A.
110 L5 **Center Hill L** Tennessee U.S.A.
95 P6 **Center Moriches** Long I, New York U.S.A.
95 Q3 **Center Ossipee** New Hampshire U.S.A.
109 H6 **Center Point** Texas U.S.A.
110 D1 **Centerville** Iowa U.S.A.
111 E12 **Centerville** Louisiana U.S.A.
94 H6 **Centerville** Pennsylvania U.S.A.
98 K6 **Centerville** South Dakota U.S.A.
110 J6 **Centerville** Tennessee U.S.A.
109 M4 **Centerville** Texas U.S.A.
101 O9 **Centerville** Utah U.S.A.
100 E4 **Centerville** Washington U.S.A.
124 H3 **Centinela, Pico del** *mt* Mexico
42 D4 **Cento** Italy
44 G3 **Cento Croci, Passo di** Italy
109 L1 **Centrahoma** Oklahoma U.S.A.
107 O7 **Centrahoma** Oklahoma U.S.A.
89 D3 **Central** *dist* Botswana
130 B9 **Central** *dept* Paraguay
15 D4 **Central** *reg* Scotland
116 P4 **Central** Alaska U.S.A.
106 B9 **Central** New Mexico U.S.A.
112 E3 **Central** South Carolina U.S.A.
103 L4 **Central** Utah U.S.A.
86 C4 **Central African Republic** Africa
145 E2 **Central Auckland** *stat area* New Zealand
118 L8 **Central Butt** Saskatchewan Canada
106 E2 **Central City** Colorado U.S.A.
99 P7 **Central City** Iowa U.S.A.
110 J4 **Central City** Kentucky U.S.A.
98 H8 **Central City** Nebraska U.S.A.
94 J6 **Central City** Pennsylvania U.S.A.
140 B5 **Central Desert Aboriginal Land** N Terr Australia
95 Q5 **Central Falls** Rhode I U.S.A.
110 G3 **Centralia** Illinois U.S.A.
107 O2 **Centralia** Kansas U.S.A.
110 D2 **Centralia** Missouri U.S.A.
100 C3 **Centralia** Washington U.S.A.
94 G8 **Centralia** West Virginia U.S.A.
94 B1 **Central Lake** Michigan U.S.A.
140 C5 **Central Mt. Stewart** N Terr Australia
100 C7 **Central Point** Oregon U.S.A.
136 J2 **Central Ra** Papua New Guinea
56 **Central Siberia**
95 L3 **Central Square** New York U.S.A.
102 B1 **Central Valley** California U.S.A.
111 L7 **Centre** Alabama U.S.A.
144 A7 **Centre I** New Zealand
122 E7 **Centreville** New Brunswick Canada
122 F9 **Centreville** Nova Scotia Canada
111 J9 **Centreville** Alabama U.S.A.
95 L7 **Centreville** Maryland U.S.A.
94 B5 **Centreville** Michigan U.S.A.
111 E10 **Centreville** Mississippi U.S.A.
111 J11 **Century** Florida U.S.A.
94 G7 **Century** West Virginia U.S.A.
67 B4 **Cenwanglao Shan** *mt* China
67 C5 **Cenxi** China
48 E7 **Čeotina** *R* Yugoslavia
19 P18 **Cépet,C** France
Cephalonia *isld* Greece *see* **Kefallinia** *isld*
41 M5 **Cepina** Italy
44 C4 **Ceppo Monte** *mt* Italy
45 O6 **Ceprano** Italy
21 L6 **Cérans-Foulletourte** France
128 E2 **Cerbatana, Sa. de la** *mts* Venezuela
103 K6 **Cerbat Mts** Arizona U.S.A.
18 H10 **Cerbère, C** France
16 B7 **Cercal** Portugal
16 E4 **Cercedilla** Spain
37 O5 **Čerchov** *mt* Czechoslovakia
21 O6 **Cercottes** France
18 H6 **Cercy la Tour** France
18 G10 **Cerdaña** *dist* Spain
21 P6 **Cerdon** France
18 G8 **Cère** *R* France
45 K1 **Cerea** Italy
118 G7 **Cereal** Alberta Canada
45 L1 **Ceregnano** Italy
21 N7 **Ceré-la-Ronde** France
20 H4 **Cérences** France
130 E4 **Ceres** Brazil
40 F7 **Ceres** Italy
87 C12 **Ceres** S Africa
13 F1 **Ceres** Scotland
102 C4 **Ceres** California U.S.A.
45 J1 **Ceresara** Italy
40 F7 **Ceresole Reale** Italy
18 G10 **Céret** France
126 G10 **Cereté** Colombia
87 J9 **Cerf** *isld* Br Indian Oc Terr
83 J12 **Cerf I** Mahe I Indian Oc
121 P6 **Cerf. L du** Quebec Canada
22 G3 **Cerfontaine** Belgium
21 P3 **Cergy-Pontoise** France
44 D3 **Ceriale** Italy
43 G7 **Cerignola** Italy
Cerigo *isld* Greece *see* **Kithira** *isld*
18 G6 **Cerilly** France
21 J3 **Cerisy-la Forêt** France
20 H3 **Cerisy-la-Salle** France
21 J8 **Cérizay** France
47 J3 **Çerkesköy** Turkey
42 F3 **Cerknica** Yugoslavia
48 G4 **Cermei** Romania
48 H5 **Cerna** *R* Romania
48 L5 **Cerna** Romania
48 L6 **Cernavodă** Romania
19 K5 **Cernay** France
8 D6 **Cerne Abbas** England
42 H3 **Cernik** Yugoslavia
37 O4 **Černošin** Czechoslovakia
124 E5 **Cerralvo** *isld* Mexico
109 H9 **Cerralvo** Mexico
45 J4 **Cerreto Guidi** Italy
44 H3 **Cerreto, Passo di** Italy
45 R7 **Cerreto Sannita** Italy
8 C1 **Cerrigydrudion** Wales
46 D3 **Cerrik** Albania
106 D6 **Cerrillos** New Mexico U.S.A.
125 J6 **Cerritos** Mexico
130 E9 **Cêrro Azul** Brazil
128 C6 **Cerro de Pasco** Peru
127 L5 **Cerro de Punta** *pk* Puerto Rico
110 H2 **Cerro Gordo** Illinois U.S.A.
131 G4 **Cerro Largo** *dept* Uruguay
127 J9 **Cerrón** *mt* Venezuela
124 F4 **Cerro Prieto** Mexico

18
Cersay — Cheviot

21 K7 Cersay France
45 K4 Certaldo Italy
143 B9 Cervantes Western Australia Australia
45 P7 Cervaro Italy
43 G7 Cervaro R Italy
43 G8 Cervati, M mt Italy
44 H2 Cervellino mt Italy
17 H3 Cervera Spain
17 F2 Cervera del Rio Alhama Spain
16 D2 Cervera de P Spain
42 E4 Cervia Italy
43 G8 Cervialto, M mt Italy
45 R7 Cervinara Italy
41 H7 Cervo R Italy
44 D4 Cervo Italy
128 D2 César div Colombia
126 H10 César,R Colombia
42 E4 Cesena Italy
45 M3 Cesenatico Italy
52 C6 Cēsis U.S.S.R.
37 O5 Česká Kubice Czechoslovakia
31 H5 Česká Lipa Czechoslovakia
31 H7 Ceské Budějovice Czechoslovakia
31 H6 Českézemé reg Czechoslovakia
31 J6 Českomoravská Vysočina mts Czechoslovakia
31 H5 Český Brod Czechoslovakia
31 H7 Český Krumlov Czechoslovakia
37 O4 Český les Sumava mts Czechoslovakia
48 E1 Český Těšin Czechoslovakia
78 A2 Çesme Turkey
47 H6 Ceşnıe Turkey
139 K5 Cessnock New South Wales Australia
48 H6 Cetate Romania
42 H5 Cetina R Yugoslavia
42 J6 Cetinje Yugoslavia
21 M5 Ceton France
43 G9 Cetraro Italy
19 P15 Ceuse, Pic de mt France
85 C1 Ceuta Spanish exclave Morocco
16 D9 Ceuta Spain
137 P6 Ceva-i-Ra reef Pacific Oc
41 N5 Cevedale mt Italy
18 H8 Cevennes mts France
78 G3 Ceylânpinar Turkey
Ceylon rep see Sri Lanka rep
119 N9 Ceylon Saskatchewan Canada
99 M6 Ceylon Minnesota U.S.A.
19 P18 Ceyreste France
57 B6 Chaacha U.S.S.R.
19 P16 Chabestan France
19 O15 Chabeuil France
142 A6 Chabjuwardoo B Western Australia Australia
18 H5 Chablis France
19 P16 Chabre, Mt de France
19 Q16 Chabrières France
21 O7 Chabris France
133 C1 Chaca Chile
131 E5 Chacabuco Argentina
127 N1 Chacachacare I Trinidad
133 D2 Chacance Chile
133 C6 Chacao, Canal de Chile
133 D6 Chacays, Sa. de los mts Argentina
131 C6 Chachahuen,Sa mt Argentina
128 D7 Chachani mt Peru
128 C5 Chachapoyas Peru
68 E6 Chachoengsao Thailand
74 D6 Chachro Pakistan
133 E3 Chaco prov Argentina
128 F8 Chaco dept Paraguay
133 E3 Chaco Austral reg Argentina
133 E2 Chaco Boreal reg Paraguay
106 B5 Chaco Canyon Nat. Mon New Mexico U.S.A.
133 E2 Chaco Central reg Argentina
117 H8 Chacon,C Prince of Wales I, Alaska
129 G5 Chacorâco, Cachoeira do waterfall Brazil
106 C6 Chacra Mesa mt New Mexico U.S.A.
86 C3 Chad rep Equat Africa
56 D5 Chadan U.S.S.R.
112 J3 Chadbourn North Carolina U.S.A.
131 C6 Chadileo,R Argentina
133 D5 Chadileuvú R Argentina
86 B3 Chad,L Equat Africa
56 F2 Chadobets R U.S.S.R.
98 D7 Chadron Nebraska U.S.A.
99 R7 Chadwick Illinois U.S.A.
48 M4 Chadyr Lunga U.S.S.R.
110 G4 Chaffee Missouri U.S.A.
94 J4 Chaffee New York U.S.A.
74 A4 Chagai Pakistan
77 H5 Chagai Hills Pakistan
53 H8 Chagan R U.S.S.R.
51 N3 Chagda U.S.S.R.
8 C6 Chagford England
77 J2 Chaghcharān Afghanistan
55 E4 Chaglinka R U.S.S.R.
40 A4 Chagny France
52 E5 Chagoda U.S.S.R.
52 E5 Chagodoshcha R U.S.S.R.
81 E6 Chagos Arch Indian Oc
94 F5 Chagrin Falls Ohio U.S.A.
127 O2 Chaguanas Trinidad
127 N1 Chaguaramas Trinidad
127 L10 Chaguaramas Venezuela
77 H4 Chahah Burjak Afghanistan
77 B3 Chahār Mahāll va Bakhtīārī prov Iran
77 G7 Chāh Bahār Iran
77 G5 Chah Ghevhī, Hamún-e L Iran
77 L1 Chāh-i-Ghab Afghanistan
78 K4 Chah-I-Surkh Iraq
68 E5 Chai Badan Thailand
75 L7 Chāībāssa India
Chaigoubu see Huai'an
21 J5 Chailland France
19 P14 Chaine de Belledonne mts France
85 E6 Chaîne de l'Atakora mts Benin
19 N17 Chaine des Alpilles mts France
18 H7 Chaise Dieu, la France
69 D8 Chaiya Thailand
68 E5 Chaiyaphum Thailand
20 H8 Chaize-le-Vicomte,la France
131 F3 Chajari Argentina
116 L6 Chakachamna L Alaska U.S.A.
74 F2 Chak Amru Pakistan
88 G4 Chake Chake Tanzania
77 H4 Chakhānsūr Afghanistan
74 E2 Chakwal Pakistan
128 D7 Chala Peru
87 F8 Chalabesa Zambia
40 C4 Chalain,L.de France
18 F7 Chalais France
59 H2 Cha-lan-t'un China
128 D7 Chala,Pta Peru
125 P10 Chalatenango Honduras
69 D9 Chalaung Thailand
124 H6 Chalchihuites Mexico
125 P11 Chalchuapa El Salvador
Chalcis see Khalkis
9 E6 Chale England
122 G6 Chaleurs, Baie des Quebec/New Bruns Canada
128 D6 Chalhuanca Peru
133 C7 Chalia R Argentina
88 B7 Chali,L Zambia
19 J5 Chalindrey France
67 D3 Chaling China
74 F8 Chalisgaon India
9 G5 Chalk England
98 B4 Chalk Buttes Montana U.S.A.
109 K3 Chalk Mountain Texas U.S.A.
121 N6 Chalk River Ontario Canada
144 A7 Chalky Inlet New Zealand
116 Q3 Chalkyitsik Alaska U.S.A.
21 H6 Challain-la-Potherie France
20 G8 Challans France
133 D1 Challapata Bolivia
115 M1 Challenger Mts Northwest Territories Canada
22 H5 Challerange France
101 L5 Challis Idaho U.S.A.
52 E2 Chal'mny Varre U.S.S.R.
75 N7 Chalna Bangladesh
52 D4 Chalna U.S.S.R.
21 J7 Chalonnes France
18 H4 Chalons-sur-Marne France
19 J6 Chalon-sur-Saône France
65 J3 Chaluhe China
18 F7 Châlus France
57 B4 Chalysh U.S.S.R.
37 O5 Cham W Germany
37 O5 Cham R W Germany
106 E4 Chama Colorado U.S.A.
106 D5 Chama New Mexico U.S.A.
74 B3 Chaman Pakistan
68 E6 Chamao,Khao mt Thailand
106 D5 Chama, R New Mexico U.S.A.
128 C5 Chamaya R Peru
74 G2 Chamba India
73 M3 Chambal R Madhya Prad/Rajasthan India
40 B7 Chambaran, Plat. de France
126 E3 Chambas Cuba
119 M8 Chamberlain Saskatchewan Canada
98 G6 Chamberlain South Dakota U.S.A.
95 R7 Chamberlain L Maine U.S.A.
142 G3 Chamberlain R Western Australia Australia
116 P2 Chamberlin,Mt Alaska U.S.A.
103 P6 Chambers Arizona U.S.A.
98 H7 Chambers Nebraska U.S.A.
140 B1 Chambers B N Terr Australia
94 K7 Chambersburg Pennsylvania U.S.A.
99 T4 Chambers I Wisconsin U.S.A.
138 C1 Chambers Pillar pk N Terr Australia
19 P13 Chambéry France
88 C7 Chambeshi R Zambia
128 C4 Chambira R Peru
21 P3 Chambly France
21 L4 Chambois France
18 H7 Chambon, le Loire France
121 S4 Chambord Quebec Canada
21 O6 Chambord France
21 M7 Chambourg-sur-Indre France
66 E5 Chamdo prov China
124 G8 Chamela Mexico
77 B4 Cham-e Zeydun Iran
77 B3 Chamgordan Iran
133 D4 Chamical Argentina
106 D5 Chamita New Mexico U.S.A.
86 G4 Chamo Hāyk' L Ethiopia
110 E3 Chamois Missouri U.S.A.
74 H3 Chamoli India
40 E6 Chamonix France
19 P16 Chamouse,Mt.de France
75 K7 Champa India
89 F7 Champagne Castle mt Lesotho
40 C4 Champagnole France
142 E3 Champagny Is Western Australia Australia
99 S9 Champaign Illinois U.S.A.
131 D3 Champaqui pk Argentina
68 G5 Cham Pasak Laos
121 N4 Champcoeur Quebec Canada
36 C7 Champ du Feu mt France
21 O8 Champenoise,la France
21 K5 Champgeneteux France
19 O14 Champier France
21 J6 Champigné France
21 N6 Champigny France
21 L8 Champigny le Sec France
21 L7 Champigny-sur-Veude France
21 P8 Champillet France
22 J3 Champion Belgium
118 D8 Champion Alberta Canada
99 T3 Champion Michigan U.S.A.
94 G5 Champion Heights Ohio U.S.A.
121 S6 Champlain Quebec Canada
121 R8 Champlain New York U.S.A.
95 O2 Champlain New York U.S.A.
95 O3 Champlain Canal New York U.S.A.
19 J5 Champlitte France
40 B2 Champlitte France
121 N4 Champneuf Quebec Canada
19 Q15 Champoléon France
40 G6 Champorcher Italy
21 N5 Champrond France
21 J4 Champsecret France
21 J7 Champtocé France
20 H7 Champtoceaux France
76 C5 Chamrajnagar India
19 P14 Chamrousse France
16 B5 Chamusca Portugal
69 E9 Chana Thailand
18 H8 Chanac France
133 C3 Chañaral Chile
131 B2 Chañaral R Chile
131 B2 Chañaral, I Chile
98 K6 Chancellor South Dakota U.S.A.
133 C5 Chanco Chile
21 M4 Chandai France
116 P2 Chandalar R Alaska U.S.A.
116 N3 Chandalar Alaska U.S.A.
111 G11 Chandeleur Sound Louisiana U.S.A.
122 H5 Chandler Quebec Canada
116 M2 Chandler R Alaska U.S.A.
103 N8 Chandler Arizona U.S.A.
107 O6 Chandler Oklahoma U.S.A.
109 M3 Chandler Texas U.S.A.
116 L2 Chandler L Alaska U.S.A.
138 C2 Chandler,Mt South Australia Australia
99 Q9 Chandlerville Illinois U.S.A.
128 D6 Chandless R Peru/Brazil
75 O7 Chandpur Bangladesh
74 H9 Chandrapur India
77 G6 Chānf Iran
Chang'an see Rong'an
65 A7 Chang'an China
87 F9 Changara Mozambique
65 G4 Changbai China
65 G4 Changbai Shan mt ra China
68 J3 Changcheng China
67 B1 Changchi China
65 F3 Changchun China
65 F2 Changchunling China
67 F1 Changdang Hu L China
67 D2 Changde China
123 S4 Change I Newfoundland Canada
65 B7 Changge China
65 E5 Changhai China
58 F5 Chang Hu L China
67 F1 Changhua China
67 G4 Chang-hua Taiwan
67 C7 Changhua Jiang R China
67 C1 Chang Jiang R China
67 C7 Changjiang China
67 E2 Chang Jiang R Jiangxi China
65 G4 Changjin Res N Korea
68 F6 Chang,Ko isld Thailand
65 D6 Changle China
67 G2 Changle China
67 F4 Changle China
65 D5 Changli China
59 H3 Changling China
66 B5 Changmar China
67 D3 Changning China
67 A2 Changning China
65 C4 Changping China
Changpuzhen see Suining
65 C6 Changqing China
65 F5 Changsan-got C N Korea
67 D2 Changsha China
67 F2 Changshan China
65 E5 Changshan Qundao islds China
65 D4 Changshanyu China
67 B2 Changshou China
67 G1 Changshu China
67 B3 Changshun China
67 F4 Changtai China
67 E4 Changting China
65 G2 Changting China
65 F3 Changtu China
65 G2 Changwu China
67 F1 Changxing China
65 E5 Changxing Dao isld China
67 D1 Changyang China
65 D6 Changyi China
59 H4 Changyon N Korea
65 C7 Changyuan China
Changzhai see Changshun
65 B6 Changzhi China
67 G1 Changzhou Jiangsu China
67 E1 Changzhuyuan China
83 J8 Chankanai Sri Lanka
116 H8 Chankluit I Alaska U.S.A.
69 C8 Chan,Ko isld Thailand
21 L7 Channay-sur-Lathan France
145 E2 Channel I New Zealand
102 E8 Channel Is California U.S.A.
20 E3 Channel Islands English Chan
123 N6 Channel-Port aux Basques Newfoundland Canada
143 C10 Channel Pt Western Australia Australia
126 F3 Channel Rock Bahamas
76 C4 Channiapatna India
119 P4 Channing airfield Manitoba Canada
99 S3 Channing Michigan U.S.A.
108 B8 Channing Texas U.S.A.
16 B2 Chantada Spain
21 K6 Chantenay Sarthe France
68 F6 Chanthaburi Thailand
21 P3 Chantilly France
21 H8 Chantonnay France
115 K4 Chantrey Inlet Northwest Territories Canada
21 J4 Chanu France
69 A8 Chanumla Nicobar Is
107 P4 Chanute Kansas U.S.A.
110 A4 Chanute Kansas U.S.A.
55 G3 Chany U.S.S.R.
21 J7 Chanzeaux France
17 G10 Chanzy Algeria
Chao'an see Chaozhou
65 C6 Chaocheng China
16 D9 Chaoen Morocco
58 G5 Chao Hu L China
128 C5 Chao, I Peru
68 E5 Chao Phraya Ra Thailand
65 E1 Chaor He R China
58 E5 Chaotianyi China
67 F1 Chao Xian China
Chaoyang see Huinan
59 K2 Ch'ao-Yang China
67 E5 Chaoyang Guangdong China
65 E4 Chaoyang Liaoning China
65 A7 Chaoyi China
67 E5 Chaozhou China
129 J5 Chapada das Mangabeiras mts Brazil
129 K6 Chapada Diamantina mts Brazil
129 K5 Chapada do Araripe mts Brazil
130 C4 Chapada dos Guimarães Brazil
129 K4 Chapadinha Brazil
121 Q3 Chapais Quebec Canada
124 H7 Chapala,L.de Mexico
129 K8 Chaparao,Serra do mts Brazil
53 H8 Chapayev U.S.S.R.
57 C6 Chapayeva, Imeni U.S.S.R.
53 G7 Chapayevsk U.S.S.R.
121 N7 Chapeau Quebec Canada
130 D10 Chapecó Brazil
130 D10 Chapecózinho R Brazil
9 E1 Chapel en le Frith England
112 H2 Chapel Hill North Carolina U.S.A.
110 K6 Chapel Hill Tennessee U.S.A.
21 K5 Chapelle-au-Riboul,la France
20 H7 Chapelle Basse Mer, la France
21 M7 Chapelle, Blanche-St. Martin, la France
20 G6 Chapelle-Bouexic,la France
21 K6 Chapelle d'Aligné, la France
18 G5 Chapelle d' Angillon,la France
20 F7 Chapelle-des-Marais,la France
21 H6 Chapelle-Glain,la France
20 H7 Chapelle-Heulin,la France
22 J4 Chapelle, la France
20 F6 Chapelle,La Morbihan France
123 L3 Chapelle,L. de la Quebec Canada
21 K4 Chapelle-Moche,la France
21 J5 Chapelle-Rainsouin,la France
21 N5 Chapelle Royale France
21 K8 Chapelle St. Laurent, la France
21 O6 Chapelle-st.Mesmin,la France
20 G7 Chapelle-sur-Erdre, La France
9 G1 Chapel St Leonards England
127 K2 Chapelton Jamaica
13 G6 Chapeltown England
110 F2 Chapin Illinois U.S.A.
99 Q10 Chapin Illinois U.S.A.
120 G5 Chapleau Ontario Canada
120 G4 Chapleau R Ontario Canada
120 H4 Chapleau-Nemecosenda Wild R. Prov. Pk Ontario Canada
118 L8 Chaplin Saskatchewan Canada
147 P1 Chaplina,Mys C U.S.S.R.
54 H8 Chaplino U.S.S.R.
54 L3 Chaplygin U.S.S.R.
111 K10 Chapman Alabama U.S.A.
107 N3 Chapman Kansas U.S.A.
101 R1 Chapman Montana U.S.A.
98 H8 Chapman Nebraska U.S.A.
117 O10 Chapman,Mt British Columbia Canada
142 F3 Chapman R Western Australia Australia
109 K8 Chapman Ranch Texas U.S.A.
94 E9 Chapmanville West Virginia U.S.A.
52 E2 Chapoma U.S.S.R.
98 D8 Chappell Nebraska U.S.A.
109 L5 Chappell Hill Texas U.S.A.
139 J8 Chappell Is Tasmania Australia
95 L8 Chaptico Maryland U.S.A.
18 E7 Chapus, le France
120 K4 Chaput Ontario Canada
133 D1 Chaqui Bolivia
128 E7 Chaqui Bolivia
74 G2 Char Kashmir
85 B4 Char Mauritania
51 L3 Chara U.S.S.R.
133 E1 Charagua Bolivia
124 E4 Charay Mexico
98 C2 Charbonneau North Dakota U.S.A.
40 C3 Charcenne France
21 K5 Charchigné France
109 K7 Charco Texas U.S.A.
146 C5 Charcot I Antarctica
118 G3 Chard Alberta Canada
8 D6 Chard England
57 E4 Chardara U.S.S.R.
57 E4 Chardarinskoye Vdkhr res U.S.S.R.
94 F5 Chardon Ohio U.S.A.
126 G5 Chardonnière Haiti
57 C5 Chardzhou U.S.S.R.
18 E7 Charente R France
18 E7 Charente dept France
18 E7 Charente-Maritime dept France
21 M3 Charentonne R France
18 G6 Charenton-sur-Cher France
86 C3 Chari R Chad
77 L2 Chārīkār Afghanistan
9 G5 Charing England
116 D2 Chariot Alaska U.S.A.
18 H5 Charité, la France
99 N8 Chariton Iowa U.S.A.
99 N9 Chariton R Iowa U.S.A.
110 D2 Chariton R Missouri U.S.A.
128 G2 Charity Guyana
52 H2 Charkayuvom U.S.S.R.
74 H6 Charkhari India
57 F5 Charku U.S.S.R.
9 E4 Charlbury England
22 H3 Charleroi Belgium
94 H6 Charleroi Pennsylvania U.S.A.
119 Q3 Charles Manitoba Canada
121 T6 Charlesbourg Quebec Canada
95 M9 Charles,C Virginia U.S.A.
99 O6 Charles City Iowa U.S.A.
115 M5 Charles I Northwest Territories Canada
143 B8 Charles,Mt Western Australia Australia
143 D10 Charles Pk Western Australia Australia
140 B1 Charles Pt N Terr Australia
144 A6 Charles Sd New Zealand
144 C4 Charleston New Zealand
110 B6 Charleston Arkansas U.S.A.
99 S10 Charleston Illinois U.S.A.
111 F7 Charleston Mississippi U.S.A.
110 G5 Charleston Missouri U.S.A.
100 A6 Charleston Oregon U.S.A.
112 H5 Charleston South Carolina U.S.A.
112 C2 Charleston Tennessee U.S.A.
94 F8 Charleston West Virginia U.S.A.
103 J5 Charleston Pk Nevada U.S.A.
14 C3 Charlestown Ireland
94 B8 Charlestown Indiana U.S.A.
95 P3 Charlestown New Hampshire U.S.A.
94 K7 Charles Town West Virginia U.S.A.
127 P4 Charlestown Nevis W Indies
118 A1 Charles Wood Manitoba Canada
Charlet,Ft see Djanet
21 N3 Charleval France
141 H7 Charleville Queensland Australia
22 H4 Charleville-Mézières France
94 B1 Charlevoix Michigan U.S.A.
94 B1 Charlevoix,L Michigan U.S.A.
116 Q4 Charley R Alaska U.S.A.
117 N7 Charlie Lake British Columbia Canada
18 H6 Charlieu France
94 C4 Charlotte Michigan U.S.A.
112 G2 Charlotte North Carolina U.S.A.
109 J7 Charlotte Texas U.S.A.
127 M5 Charlotte Amalie Virgin Is
117 L9 Charlotte L British Columbia Canada
27 F12 Charlottenberg Sweden
33 S7 Charlottenburg W Berlin
33 S9 Charlottenfelde East Germany
94 J8 Charlottesville Virginia U.S.A.
122 J7 Charlottetown Prince Edward I Canada
Charlotte Town Grenada see Gouyave
127 N1 Charlotteville Tobago
139 G6 Charlton Victoria Australia
120 K5 Charlton Ontario Canada
115 M7 Charlton I Northwest Territories Canada
19 K4 Charmes France
40 F4 Charmey Switzerland
40 F3 Chärmoille Switzerland
8 D6 Charmouth England
21 M8 Charnizay France
142 F3 Charnley,R Western Australia Australia
121 T6 Charny Quebec Canada
60 R2 Charo-gawa R Japan
18 H6 Charolles France
21 P8 Charost France
52 E4 Charozero U.S.S.R.
122 J2 Charpeney,L Quebec Canada
21 O3 Chars France
74 D1 Charsadda Pakistan
57 D5 Charshanga U.S.S.R.
56 B6 Charsk U.S.S.R.
99 L7 Charter Oak Iowa U.S.A.
141 H5 Charters Towers Queensland Australia
122 A8 Chartierville Quebec Canada
21 M6 Chartre,la France
21 N5 Chartres France
57 F4 Charvakskoye Vdkhr. U.S.S.R.
19 Q13 Charvin, Mt France
19 Q13 Charvonnex France
56 B5 Charysh R U.S.S.R.
131 F5 Chascomas Argentina
117 O10 Chase British Columbia Canada
107 M3 Chase Kansas U.S.A.
99 P6 Chaseburg Wisconsin U.S.A.
94 J10 Chase City Virginia U.S.A.
98 G3 Chase L North Dakota U.S.A.
55 D3 Chashi U.S.S.R.
57 B5 Chashkent U.S.S.R.
99 N5 Chaska Minnesota U.S.A.
144 B7 Chaslands Mistake New Zealand
117 N10 Chasm British Columbia Canada
52 D1 Chasnachorr, Gora mt U.S.S.R.
52 E3 Chasovenskaya U.S.S.R.
52 H4 Chasovo U.S.S.R.
54 J8 Chasov Yar U.S.S.R.
113 E9 Chassahowitzka B Florida U.S.A.
99 S2 Chassell Michigan U.S.A.
18 F7 Chasseneuil France
18 H8 Chassezac R France
21 O8 Chassignoles France
21 K5 Chassille France
55 E3 Chastoozer'ye U.S.S.R.
52 H6 Chastyye U.S.S.R.
21 J8 Châtaigneraie,la France
116 O4 Chatanika Alaska U.S.A.
121 L10 Chatauqua L New York U.S.A.
127 O8 Chateaubelair St Vincent
20 G7 Chateau Bougon airport France
20 H5 Châteaubourg France
20 H6 Châteaubriant France
18 H5 Château Chinon France
19 O18 Château d'If isld France
18 E7 Château d'Oléron, le France
21 L6 Château-du-Loir France
21 N5 Châteaudun France
21 P4 Châteaufort France
95 N2 Chateaugay New York U.S.A.
20 H5 Châteaugiron France
21 J6 Château-Gontier France
21 L6 Château-la-Vallière France
20 B5 Châteaulin France
21 P8 Châteaumeillant France
19 N14 Châteauneuf-de-Galaure France
20 G4 Châteauneuf-d'Ille-et-Vilaine France
20 C5 Châteauneuf-du-Faou France
21 N4 Châteauneuf-en-Thymerais France
18 E7 Châteauneuf-sur-Charente France
21 P8 Châteauneuf-sur-Cher France
21 P6 Châteauneuf-sur-Loire France
21 J6 Châteauneuf-sur-Sarthe France
22 G4 Château-Porcien France
20 D4 Château,Pte.du France
19 Q16 Châteauredon France
19 N17 Châteaurenard France
21 M6 Château-Renault France
122 A7 Chateau Richer Quebec Canada
21 O8 Châteauroux Indre France
19 K4 Château Salins France
18 H3 Château-Thierry France
121 R5 Chateauvert, L Quebec Canada
127 O4 Châteaux, Pte. des Guadeloupe W Indies
117 O6 Chateh Alberta Canada
20 E4 Châtelaudren France
22 H3 Châtelet Belgium
21 P8 Châtelet,le France
21 N5 Châtelets,les France
18 H7 Chatelguyon France
40 A2 Chatellenot France
21 M8 Châtellerault France
36 C7 Chatenois France
99 O6 Chatfield Minnesota U.S.A.
122 G6 Chatham New Brunswick Canada
120 H10 Chatham Ontario Canada
9 G5 Chatham England
117 F7 Chatham Alaska U.S.A.
99 R10 Chatham Illinois U.S.A.
110 G2 Chatham Illinois U.S.A.
111 D9 Chatham Louisiana U.S.A.
95 S5 Chatham Massachusetts U.S.A.
95 O4 Chatham New York U.S.A.
94 H10 Chatham Virginia U.S.A.
137 R10 Chatham Is Pacific Oc
117 H8 Chatham Sd British Columbia Canada
133 C8 Chatham Stokes mt Chile
22 K4 Châtillon Belgium
40 G6 Châtillon Italy
18 G5 Châtillon-Coligny France
19 P12 Châtillon de Michaille France
21 H5 Châtillon-en-Vendelais France
19 O13 Chatillon-la-Palud France
21 N8 Châtillon-sur-Indre France
18 G5 Châtillon-sur-Loire France
57 F4 Chatkal R U.S.S.R.
57 F4 Chatkal'skiy Khr mts U.S.S.R.
111 H10 Chatom Alabama U.S.A.
75 L6 Chatra India
21 O8 Châtre, la France
140 F5 Chatsworth Queensland Australia
120 K8 Chatsworth Ontario Canada
112 C3 Chatsworth Georgia U.S.A.
110 H1 Chatsworth Illinois U.S.A.
95 N7 Chatsworth New Jersey U.S.A.
89 G2 Chatsworth Zimbabwe
111 L8 Chattahoochee R Alabama/Georgia
111 M11 Chattahoochee Florida U.S.A.
112 B2 Chattanooga Tennessee U.S.A.
100 H2 Chattaroy Washington U.S.A.
94 E9 Chattaroy West Virginia U.S.A.
9 G3 Chatteris England
144 B6 Chatto Cr New Zealand
13 G2 Chatton England
111 L7 Chattooga R Georgia/Alabama U.S.A.
112 D3 Chattooga R S Carolina/Georgia U.S.A.
112 D2 Chatuge L North Carolina U.S.A.
68 E5 Chaturat Thailand
57 H4 Chatyr-Kël' Ozero L U.S.S.R.
20 H8 Chauché France
18 H8 Chaudes-Aigues France
22 K2 Chaudfontaine Belgium
Chau Doc see Chau Phu
21 J7 Chaudron-en-Mauges France
22 E5 Chaudun France
116 H6 Chauekuktuli L Alaska U.S.A.
19 Q15 Chauffayer France
68 B2 Chauk Burma
75 R5 Chaukan Pass Burma/India
22 D4 Chaulnes France
40 B4 Chaumergy France
40 D3 Chaumont mt France
19 J4 Chaumont Haute-Marne France
21 O3 Chaumont-en-Vexin France
22 G4 Chaumont-Porcien France
21 N7 Chaumont-sur-Loire France
21 O6 Chaumont-sur-Tharonne France
94 E7 Chauncey Ohio U.S.A.
68 D6 Chaungwabyin Burma
68 C4 Chaungzon Burma
51 Q2 Chaunskaya Guba G U.S.S.R.
22 E4 Chauny France
68 G7 Chau Phu Vietnam
69 A8 Chaura I Nicobar Is
20 G4 Chausey Is France
21 P2 Chaussée-Tirancourt,la France
19 J6 Chaussin France
54 B3 Chausy U.S.S.R.
94 H4 Chautauqua New York U.S.A.
94 H4 Chautauqua L New York U.S.A.
57 F4 Chauvay U.S.S.R.
20 G7 Chauvé France
21 N6 Chauvigny Loir-et-Cher France
21 M8 Chauvigny Vienne France
118 G6 Chauvin Alberta Canada
19 K5 Chaux de Fonds, la France
40 E3 Chaux de Fonds, La Switzerland
20 H8 Chavagnes-en-Paillers France
19 N14 Chavanay France
52 E2 Chavan'ga U.S.S.R.
130 D4 Chavantina Brazil
130 D7 Chavantina Brazil
16 C3 Chaves Portugal
94 D9 Chavies Kentucky U.S.A.
22 F5 Chavignon France
87 D8 Chavuma Zambia
69 D8 Chawang Thailand
9 F5 Chawton England
56 G2 Chaya R U.S.S.R.
88 C7 Chaya, L Zambia
57 E3 Chayan U.S.S.R.
57 G4 Chayek U.S.S.R.
52 H6 Chaykovskiy U.S.S.R.
78 K2 Chāypareh Iran
66 F6 Ch'a-yü China
21 J6 Chazé-sur-Argos France
52 H4 Chazhegovo U.S.S.R.
133 E4 Chazon Argentina
95 O2 Chazy New York U.S.A.
118 D7 Cheadle Alberta Canada
9 E2 Cheadle England
111 L8 Cheaha Mt Alabama U.S.A.
94 H7 Cheat R West Virginia U.S.A.
110 J5 Cheatham L Tennessee U.S.A.
37 N3 Cheb Czechoslovakia
55 D4 Chebarkul' U.S.S.R.
52 G6 Cheboksary U.S.S.R.
94 C1 Cheboygan Michigan U.S.A.
52 E5 Chebsara U.S.S.R.
53 G11 Chechen-Ingush U.S.S.R.
54 B4 Chechersk U.S.S.R.
31 M5 Chęciny Poland
107 P6 Checotah Oklahoma U.S.A.
21 P6 Chécy France
123 L8 Chedabucto B Nova Scotia Canada
8 D5 Cheddar England
83 K9 Cheddikulam Sri Lanka
68 A3 Cheduba isld Burma
68 A3 Cheduba Burma
68 A3 Cheduba Str Burma
118 G2 Cheecham Alberta Canada
120 J2 Cheepash R Ontario Canada
120 G1 Cheepay R Ontario Canada
141 G7 Cheepie Queensland Australia
119 O1 Cheeseman L Ontario Canada
106 E2 Cheesman,L Colorado U.S.A.
146 C13 Cheetham,C Antarctica
18 E6 Chef-Boutonne France
111 G11 Chef Menteur Louisiana U.S.A.
Chefoo see Yantai
116 E6 Chefornak Alaska U.S.A.
121 R3 Chef,R.du Quebec Canada
59 K1 Chegdomyn U.S.S.R.
85 C3 Chegga Mauritania
116 A3 Chegitun R U.S.S.R.
89 G2 Chegutu Zimbabwe
100 C3 Chehalis Washington U.S.A.
100 B3 Chehalis R Washington U.S.A.
67 B4 Chehe China
87 F8 Cheif Serenje Zambia
21 L7 Cheillé France
59 J5 Cheju S Korea
65 G8 Cheju do isld S Korea
65 G8 Cheju haehyŏp str S Korea
54 H2 Chekalin U.S.S.R.
52 H7 Chekan U.S.S.R.
54 J1 Chekhov U.S.S.R.
Chekiang prov see Zhejiang
55 G2 Chekino U.S.S.R.
51 N3 Chekunda U.S.S.R.
52 E3 Chekuyevo U.S.S.R.
119 O6 Chelan Saskatchewan Canada
100 F2 Chelan Washington U.S.A.
100 E1 Chelan,L Washington U.S.A.
100 E1 Chelan Range Washington U.S.A.
116 M5 Chelatna L Alaska U.S.A.
133 D5 Chelforó Argentina
85 F1 Chelia mt Algeria
85 E1 Chélif R Algeria
55 C3 Chelkakovo U.S.S.R.
57 A1 Chelkar U.S.S.R.
31 O4 Chełm Poland
31 L2 Chełmno Poland
120 J6 Chelmsford Ontario Canada
9 G4 Chelmsford England
52 E3 Chelmuzhi U.S.S.R.
31 L2 Chełmża Poland
99 O8 Chelsea Iowa U.S.A.
94 C4 Chelsea Michigan U.S.A.
107 P5 Chelsea Oklahoma U.S.A.
95 P3 Chelsea Vermont U.S.A.
8 D4 Cheltenham England
20 H6 Chelun France
17 G5 Chelva Spain
55 D3 Chelyabinsk U.S.S.R.
55 D4 Chelyabinskaya Oblast' prov U.S.S.R.
94 F8 Chelyan West Virginia U.S.A.
56 C5 Chelyush U.S.S.R.
51 K1 Chelyuskin,Mys C U.S.S.R.
117 M11 Chemainus British Columbia Canada
100 C4 Chemawa Oregon U.S.A.
21 J6 Chemaze France
87 F9 Chemba Mozambique
57 B6 Chemen-i-Bit U.S.S.R.
21 N7 Chemery France
22 H4 Chémery-sur-Bar France
21 J7 Chemillé France
21 M6 Chemillé-sur-Dême France
40 B4 Chemin France
21 K6 Chemiré-le-Gaudin France
Chemnitz see Karl-Marx-Stadt
95 R7 Chemquasabamticook L Maine U.S.A.
56 B4 Chemskiy U.S.S.R.
95 K4 Chemung R New York U.S.A.
116 O4 Chena R Alaska U.S.A.
74 D3 Chenab R Pakistan
85 D3 Chenachane watercourse Algeria
85 D3 Chenachane Algeria
116 O4 Chena Hot Springs Alaska U.S.A.
95 M4 Chenango R New York U.S.A.
86 G4 Ch'ench'a Ethiopia
22 K2 Chênée Belgium
18 G6 Chénérailles France
121 P7 Chénéville Quebec Canada
107 N4 Cheney Kansas U.S.A.
100 H2 Cheney Washington U.S.A.
111 D10 Cheneyville Louisiana U.S.A.
76 E4 Chengalpattu India
65 C6 Cheng'an China
67 B4 Chengbihe Shuiku res China
67 C3 Chengbu China
65 A7 Chengcheng China
Chengchow see Zhengzhou
65 D4 Chengde China
67 E1 Chengdong Hu L China
67 A1 Chengdu China
67 A4 Chenggong China
67 E5 Chenghai China
67 A4 Chengjiang China
67 C1 Chengkou China
65 D5 Chengkou China
67 C7 Chengmai China
65 E6 Chengshan Jiao pen China
Chengtu see Chengdu
65 C7 Chengwu China
65 E6 Chengyang China
67 F2 Chengyang China
65 E5 Chengzitan China
121 O6 Chenier Quebec Canada
123 N2 Chenil,L Quebec Canada
36 B7 Cheniménil France
65 D7 Cheniu Shan isld China
65 D7 Chenjiagang China
65 C7 Chenliu China
110 H1 Chenoa Illinois U.S.A.
21 N7 Chenonceaux France
40 B3 Chenôve France
67 G1 Chenqian Shan isld China
21 L6 Chenu France
67 C2 Chenxi China
67 D4 Chen Xian China
Chenying see Wannian
68 J6 Cheo Reo Vietnam
67 F3 Chepan China
46 G3 Chepelare Bulgaria
128 C5 Chepén Peru
133 D4 Chepes Argentina
8 D4 Chepstow Wales
99 Q3 Chequamegon B Wisconsin U.S.A.
21 M7 Cher R France
22 K3 Cherain Belgium
44 C2 Cherasco Italy
106 G3 Cheraw Colorado U.S.A.
111 G10 Cheraw Mississippi U.S.A.
112 H3 Cheraw South Carolina U.S.A.
20 G2 Cherbourg France
85 E1 Cherchell Algeria
52 J4 Cherdyn' U.S.S.R.
20 G6 Chère R France
52 B2 Cheremisskoye U.S.S.R.
56 F4 Cheremkhovo U.S.S.R.
55 D3 Cheremshanka U.S.S.R.
55 D1 Cheremukhovo U.S.S.R.
56 D4 Cheremushki U.S.S.R.
56 B4 Cherepanovo U.S.S.R.
54 H2 Cherepet' U.S.S.R.
52 E5 Cherepovets U.S.S.R.
52 D5 Chereptsovo U.S.S.R.
118 C5 Cherhill Alberta Canada
54 C3 Cherikov U.S.S.R.
21 N4 Cherisy France
54 J8 Cherkasskoye U.S.S.R.
53 F11 Cherkessk U.S.S.R.
46 G1 Cherkovitsa Bulgaria
55 F4 Cherlak U.S.S.R.
52 J5 Chermoz U.S.S.R.
141 K1 Chermside dist Brisbane, Qnsld Australia
116 H9 Chernabura I Alaska U.S.A.
46 G3 Chernatitsa hills Bulgaria
55 D2 Chernaya R U.S.S.R.
52 H5 Chernaya Kholunitsa U.S.S.R.
48 J2 Chernaya Tisa R Ukrainskaya S.S.R. U.S.S.R.
56 C3 Chernenko U.S.S.R.
47 J1 Chernevo Bulgaria
54 C5 Chernigov U.S.S.R.
59 K3 Chernigovka U.S.S.R.
116 F9 Cherni I Alaska U.S.A.
55 C4 Chernikovsk U.S.S.R.
47 H1 Cherni Lom R Bulgaria
46 F2 Cherni Vrŭkh mt Bulgaria
53 D8 Chernobyl' U.S.S.R.
56 D4 Chernogorsk U.S.S.R.
55 C2 Chernoistochinsk U.S.S.R.
55 G4 Chernoretskoye U.S.S.R.
55 F4 Chernousovka U.S.S.R.
52 G6 Chernovskoye U.S.S.R.
48 K2 Chernovtsy U.S.S.R.
55 E2 Chernoye U.S.S.R.
55 E3 Chernoye, Oz L U.S.S.R.
55 C3 Chernushka U.S.S.R.
52 G3 Chernut'yevo U.S.S.R.
31 N1 Chernyakhovsk U.S.S.R.
52 J2 Chernysheva, Gryada ridge U.S.S.R.
58 G1 Chernyshevsk U.S.S.R.
31 O1 Chernyshevskoye U.S.S.R.
53 G10 Chernyye Zemli U.S.S.R.
55 C5 Chernyy Otrog U.S.S.R.
53 G9 Chernyy Yar U.S.S.R.
110 J7 Cherokee Alabama U.S.A.
99 L7 Cherokee Iowa U.S.A.
107 Q4 Cherokee Kansas U.S.A.
107 M5 Cherokee Oklahoma U.S.A.
109 J5 Cherokee Texas U.S.A.
112 D1 Cherokee Dam Tennessee U.S.A.
94 D10 Cherokee L Tennessee U.S.A.
111 B9 Cherokee,L Texas U.S.A.
113 K11 Cherokee Pt Bahamas
110 B5 Cherokees, L O'The Oklahoma U.S.A.
126 F1 Cherokee Sound Great Abaco I Bahamas
55 E2 Cherpiya U.S.S.R.
75 O6 Cherrapunji India
20 G4 Cherrueix France
137 O4 Cherry isld Santa Cruz Is
103 K2 Cherry Cr Nevada U.S.A.
98 E5 Cherry Cr South Dakota U.S.A.
94 H4 Cherry Creek New York U.S.A.
103 K1 Cherry Cr.Mt Nevada U.S.A.
95 U2 Cherryfield Maine U.S.A.
117 O7 Cherry Point Alberta Canada
107 P4 Cherryvale Kansas U.S.A.
95 N4 Cherry Valley New York U.S.A.
112 F2 Cherryville North Carolina U.S.A.
56 G3 Cherskogo,Gora mt U.S.S.R.
51 O2 Cherskogo,Khrebet mts U.S.S.R.
17 H4 Cherta Spain
54 M7 Chertkovo U.S.S.R.
54 E1 Chertolino U.S.S.R.
9 F5 Chertsey England
144 C5 Chertsey New Zealand
52 F6 Cherusti U.S.S.R.
19 O13 Cheruy,Pt.de France
52 G4 Cherva U.S.S.R.
48 N3 Chervonoz-namenka U.S.S.R.
9 E3 Cherwell,R England
94 C3 Chesaning Michigan U.S.A.
94 E8 Chesapeake Ohio U.S.A.
95 L10 Chesapeake Virginia U.S.A.
95 L8 Chesapeake B U.S.A.
95 L8 Chesapeake Beach Maryland U.S.A.
95 M7 Chesapeake City Maryland U.S.A.
9 F4 Chesham England
8 D1 Cheshire co England
95 O4 Cheshire Massachusetts U.S.A.
52 G2 Chëshskaya Guba B U.S.S.R.
57 G5 Cheshtebe U.S.S.R.
88 B6 Chesi,L Zambia
8 D6 Chesil Bank England
120 J8 Chesley Ontario Canada
55 D4 Chesma U.S.S.R.
112 F2 Chesnee South Carolina U.S.A.
22 H5 Chesne, le Ardennes France
21 M4 Chesne,le Eure France
122 H9 Chester Nova Scotia Canada
8 D1 Chester England
110 B6 Chester Arkansas U.S.A.
100 D9 Chester California U.S.A.
95 P5 Chester Connecticut U.S.A.
101 O5 Chester Idaho U.S.A.
110 G4 Chester Illinois U.S.A.
95 L7 Chester R Maryland U.S.A.
95 P4 Chester Massachusetts U.S.A.
101 P1 Chester Montana U.S.A.
98 J9 Chester Nebraska U.S.A.
95 M6 Chester Pennsylvania U.S.A.
112 F3 Chester South Carolina U.S.A.
109 N5 Chester Texas U.S.A.
95 P3 Chester Vermont U.S.A.
94 K9 Chester Virginia U.S.A.
122 H9 Chester Basin Nova Scotia Canada
9 E1 Chesterfield England
101 O7 Chesterfield Idaho U.S.A.
110 F2 Chesterfield Illinois U.S.A.
112 G3 Chesterfield South Carolina U.S.A.
94 K9 Chesterfield Virginia U.S.A.
137 M5 Chesterfield, Îles Coral Sea
115 K5 Chesterfield Inlet Northwest Territories Canada
94 F7 Chesterhill Ohio U.S.A.
9 F2 Chesterton England
99 T8 Chesterton Indiana U.S.A.
95 L7 Chestertown Maryland U.S.A.
95 O3 Chestertown New York U.S.A.
121 P7 Chesterville Ontario Canada
109 O3 Chestnut Louisiana U.S.A.
94 H6 Chestnut Ridge Pennsylvania U.S.A.
144 D5 Chest Pk New Zealand
95 R7 Chesuncook L Maine U.S.A.
95 M7 Cheswold Delaware U.S.A.
56 C3 Chet' R U.S.S.R.
68 A7 Chetamale Andaman Is
99 P4 Chetek Wisconsin U.S.A.
123 L7 Cheticamp C Breton I, Nova Scotia
73 L6 Chetlat isld Lakshadweep Indian Oc
107 P4 Chetopa Kansas U.S.A.
125 P8 Chetumal Mexico
145 E4 Chetwode Is New Zealand
117 N8 Chetwynd British Columbia Canada
116 E6 Chevak Alaska U.S.A.
19 O17 Cheval-Blanc France
20 G7 Chevallerais, La Loire-Atlantique France
21 O5 Chevilly France
118 L6 Cheviot Saskatchewan Canada
144 D5 Cheviot New Zealand

13 F3 **Cheviot Hills** England/ Scotland
141 G7 **Cheviot Ra** Queensland Australia
21 K6 **Chevíré-le-Rouge** France
20 A5 **Chèvre, C. de la** France
111 E12 **Chevreuil, Point** Louisiana U.S.A.
21 P4 **Chevreuse** France
40 E7 **Chevril,L** France
20 G7 **Chevrolière, la** France
88 D9 **Chewa** Mozambique
86 G5 **Ch'ew Bahir** *L* Ethiopia
100 H1 **Chewelah** Washington U.S.A.
8 D5 **Chew valley L** England
107 L6 **Cheyenne** Oklahoma U.S.A.
98 D5 **Cheyenne** *R* South Dakota U.S.A.
108 D4 **Cheyenne** Texas U.S.A.
98 B8 **Cheyenne** Wyoming U.S.A.
107 M3 **Cheyenne Bottoms** Kansas U.S.A.
98 A8 **Cheyenne Pass** Wyoming U.S.A.
106 H3 **Cheyenne Wells** Colorado U.S.A.
18 H8 **Cheylard, le** France
143 C10 **Cheyne B** Western Australia Australia
117 M9 **Chezacut** British Columbia Canada
21 P8 **Chezal-Benoit** France
20 E5 **Chèze,la** France
75 L6 **Chhapra** India
74 H6 **Chhatarpur** India
75 L9 **Chhatrapur** India
68 H6 **Chhlong** *R* Cambodia
68 G6 **Chhlong** Cambodia
74 F7 **Chhota Udepur** India
68 G7 **Chhuk** Cambodia
116 H9 **Chiachi I** Alaska U.S.A.
67 G5 **Chia-i** Taiwan
66 D5 **Chia-jen Ts'o** *L* China
40 F7 **Chialamberto** Italy
66 D5 **Chia-man-t'e-k'a-mu Hu** *L* China
87 B9 **Chiange** Angola
68 E2 **Chiang Saen** Thailand
42 E6 **Chiani** *R* Italy
125 N9 **Chiapa del Corzo** Mexico
45 O4 **Chiaravalle** Italy
43 G10 **Chiaravalle Centrale** Italy
41 L5 **Chiareggio** Italy
41 L6 **Chiari** Italy
125 K8 **Chiautla** Mexico
44 F3 **Chiavari** Italy
41 K5 **Chiavenna** Italy
61 O10 **Chiba** *prefect* Japan
61 O10 **Chiba** Japan
61 P13 **Chibana** Okinawa
87 B9 **Chibia** Angola
68 E5 **Chi Bon Dam** Thailand
121 Q3 **Chibougamau** Quebec Canada
121 P3 **Chibougamau** *R* Quebec Canada
121 R3 **Chibougamau,Parc de** Quebec Canada
88 B8 **Chibuluma** Zambia
60 G9 **Chiburi-shima** *isld* Japan
87 F10 **Chibuto** Mozambique
87 E8 **Chibwe** Zambia
99 T8 **Chicago** Illinois U.S.A.
105 **Chicago** *conurbation* Illinois U.S.A.
99 T8 **Chicago Heights** Illinois U.S.A.
122 F5 **Chic-Chocs,Parc des** Quebec Canada
117 E7 **Chichagof I** Alaska U.S.A.
85 C2 **Chichaoua** Morocco
21 K8 **Chiché** France
65 C4 **Chicheng** China
125 P7 **Chichén Itza** *ruins* Mexico
9 F6 **Chichester** England
142 C5 **Chichester Ra** Western Australia Australia
142 B5 **Chichester Ra Nat Park** Western Australia Australia
61 N10 **Chichibu** Japan
61 M9 **Chichibu Tama Nat. Park** Japan
56 C3 **Chichka-Yul** *R* U.S.S.R.
95 K9 **Chickahominy** *R* Virginia U.S.A.
112 B3 **Chickamauga** Georgia U.S.A.
112 B2 **Chickamauga Dam** Tennessee U.S.A.
111 H10 **Chickasawhay** *R* Mississippi U.S.A.
107 O7 **Chickasaw Nat. Recreation Area** Oklahoma U.S.A.
107 N6 **Chickasha** Oklahoma U.S.A.
116 R4 **Chicken** Alaska U.S.A.
8 D5 **Chicklade** England
16 C8 **Chiclana de la Frontera** Spain
128 C5 **Chiclayo** Peru
133 D6 **Chico** *R* Argentina
71 E2 **Chico** *R* Luzon Philippines
102 C2 **Chico** California U.S.A.
100 H4 **Chico** Oregon U.S.A.
109 K2 **Chico** Texas U.S.A.
133 D3 **Chicoana** Argentina
121 M4 **Chicobi,L** Quebec Canada
87 F10 **Chicomo** Mozambique
125 K7 **Chicontepec** Mexico
87 D7 **Chicopa** *R* Angola
95 P4 **Chicopee** Massachusetts U.S.A.
121 T5 **Chicoutimi** *R* Quebec Canada
121 T4 **Chicoutimi** Quebec Canada
122 B5 **Chicoutimi, Parc des** Quebec Canada
89 G4 **Chicualacuala** Mozambique
76 D5 **Chidambaram** India
9 F5 **Chiddingford** England
109 O2 **Chidester** Arkansas U.S.A.
115 N5 **Chidley,C** Quebec Canada
100 F1 **Chief Joseph Dam** Washington U.S.A.
113 E8 **Chiefland** Florida U.S.A.
120 J8 **Chiefs Pt** Ontario Canada
67 B5 **Chiem Hoa** Vietnam
87 E7 **Chiengi** Zambia
68 D3 **Chieng-Mai** Thailand
42 F5 **Chienti** *R* Italy
57 L2 **Chierh Shan** *mts* U.S.S.R.
44 C1 **Chieri** Italy
22 K5 **Chiers** *R* France
41 L5 **Chiesa** Italy
41 M5 **Chiese** *R* Italy
42 F6 **Chieti** Italy
22 F2 **Chièvres** Belgium
130 H5 **Chifre,Serra do** *mts* Brazil
57 G2 **Chiganak** U.S.S.R.
61 N10 **Chigasaki** Japan
116 J8 **Chiginigak Vol., Mt** Alaska U.S.A.
54 D7 **Chigirin** U.S.S.R.
116 L6 **Chigmit Mts** Alaska U.S.A.
122 H8 **Chignecto B** Nova Scotia/ New Bruns Canada
116 H8 **Chignik** Alaska U.S.A.
19 Q13 **Chignin** France
121 R3 **Chigoubiche, L** Quebec Canada
87 F10 **Chigubo** Mozambique
66 E6 **Chigu Co** *L* China
9 G4 **Chigwell** England
Chihli,G. of *see* **Bo Hai**
124 F3 **Chihuahua** Mexico
131 B7 **Chihuido Medio** *pk* Argentina
57 D3 **Chiili** U.S.S.R.
67 C6 **Chikan** China
107 N5 **Chikaskia** *R* Okla/Kansas U.S.A.
76 C4 **Chik Ballapur** India
52 C6 **Chikhachevo** U.S.S.R.
60 O3 **Chikiu-misaki** *C* Japan
76 C3 **Chikjaju** India
76 B4 **Chikmagalur** India
56 G5 **Chikoy** *R* U.S.S.R.
68 G6 **Chikreng** *R* Cambodia
60 D12 **Chikugo** *R* Japan
60 D12 **Chikugo** Japan
61 M9 **Chikuma** *R* Japan
116 H6 **Chikuminuk L** Alaska U.S.A.
61 N11 **Chikura** Japan
88 E10 **Chikwawa** Malawi
68 A2 **Chi-kyaw** Burma
117 L9 **Chilanko Forks** British Columbia Canada
74 F1 **Chilas** Kashmir
83 J10 **Chilaw** Sri Lanka
128 C6 **Chilca, Pta. de** *pt* Peru
102 D2 **Chilcoot** California U.S.A.
117 M10 **Chilcotin** *R* British Columbia Canada
141 K3 **Chilcott I** Gt Barrier Reef Aust
141 K7 **Childers** Queensland Australia
111 K8 **Childersburg** Alabama U.S.A.
108 G1 **Childress** Texas U.S.A.
103 M9 **Childs** Arizona U.S.A.
113 F10 **Childs** Florida U.S.A.
133 C6 **Chile** *rep* S America
128 C5 **Chilete** Peru
9 G5 **Chilham** England
110 C3 **Chilhowee** Missouri U.S.A.
94 F10 **Chilhowie** Virginia U.S.A.
116 K6 **Chilikadrotna** *R* Alaska U.S.A.
75 L9 **Chilika Lake** India
87 E8 **Chililabombwe** Zambia
89 G2 **Chilimanzi** Zimbabwe
59 H1 **Chi-liu Ho** *R* China
117 F6 **Chilkat** *R* Alaska U.S.A.
117 M10 **Chilko** *R* British Columbia Canada
117 F6 **Chilkoot** Alaska U.S.A.
141 G3 **Chillagoe** Queensland Australia
131 A6 **Chillán** Chile
140 B5 **Chilla Well** N Terr Australia
21 P5 **Chilleurs-aux-Bois** France
99 R9 **Chillicothe** Illinois U.S.A.
110 C2 **Chillicothe** Missouri U.S.A.
94 D7 **Chillicothe** Ohio U.S.A.
109 H1 **Chillicothe** Texas U.S.A.
139 G6 **Chillingollah** Victoria Australia
100 D1 **Chilliwack** British Columbia Canada
19 P13 **Chilly** France
101 M5 **Chilly** Idaho U.S.A.
116 J6 **Chilnuk Mts** Alaska U.S.A.
133 C6 **Chiloé** *prov* Chile
135 R14 **Chiloe, I. de** Chile
88 C8 **Chilonga** Zambia
87 F8 **Chilongazi** Zambia
100 D7 **Chiloquin** Oregon U.S.A.
125 K9 **Chilpancingo** Mexico
139 H6 **Chiltern** Victoria Australia
9 F4 **Chiltern Hills** England
99 S5 **Chilton** Wisconsin U.S.A.
88 E7 **Chilumba** Malawi
67 G4 **Chi-lung** Taiwan
88 F9 **Chilwa,L** Malawi
9 E6 **Chilworth** England
125 M9 **Chimalapa** Mexico
87 F9 **Chimanimani** Zimbabwe
87 F10 **Chimanimani Nat. Park** Zimbabwe
22 G3 **Chimay** Belgium
106 E6 **Chimayo** New Mexico U.S.A.
57 A3 **Chimbay** U.S.S.R.
128 C4 **Chimborazo** *mt* Ecuador
128 C5 **Chimbote** Peru
88 C8 **Chimbwin-gombi** *mt* Zambia
55 E3 **Chimeyevo** U.S.S.R.
57 F4 **Chimion** U.S.S.R.
48 M4 **Chimishliya** Moldavskaya S.S.R. U.S.S.R.
57 E4 **Chimkent** U.S.S.R.
123 P4 **Chimney Cove** Newfoundland Canada
108 B3 **Chimney Peak** New Mexico U.S.A.
106 E9 **Chimney Pk** New Mexico U.S.A.
83 J12 **Chimney Rocks** Seychelles
87 F9 **Chimoio** Mozambique
118 E9 **Chin** Alberta Canada
65 F7 **Chin** *isld* S Korea
58 D4 **China** *rep* E Asia
95 S2 **China** Maine U.S.A.
68 C4 **China Bakir** *R* Burma
124 G5 **Chinacates** Mexico
112 G2 **China Grove** North Carolina U.S.A.
125 L3 **Chinandega** Nicaragua
102 F9 **China Pt** California U.S.A.
109 K4 **China Spring** Texas U.S.A.
108 C6 **Chinati Mts** Texas U.S.A.
57 E4 **Chinaz** U.S.S.R.
120 J7 **Chin, Cape** Ontario Canada
128 C6 **Chincha Alta** Peru
117 O6 **Chinchaga** *R* Alberta Canada
128 C6 **Chincha, Is** Peru
141 K7 **Chinchilla** Queensland Australia
17 F6 **Chinchilla de Monte Aragón** Spain
128 C4 **Chinchipe** *R* Ecuador/Peru
16 E4 **Chinchón** Spain
95 M9 **Chincoteague** Virginia U.S.A.
95 M8 **Chincoteague B** Maryland U.S.A.
87 G9 **Chinde** Mozambique
73 P4 **Chindwin** *R* Burma
61 P14 **Chinen** Okinawa
88 E8 **Chinengue** Mozambique
66 B4 **Chinese Turkestan** *reg* Xinjiang Uygur Zizhiqu China
67 D1 **Ching-Chiang Res** China
Chinghai *prov see* **Qinghai** *prov*
55 B5 **Chingirlau** U.S.S.R.
88 A8 **Chingola** Zambia
87 B8 **Chingoroi** Angola
87 C8 **Chinguai** Angola
73 P4 **Chin Hills** Burma
88 C10 **Chinhoyi** Zimbabwe
116 L8 **Chiniak,C** Alaska U.S.A.
Chining *see* **Jining**
74 E3 **Chiniot** Pakistan
124 E4 **Chinipas** Mexico
116 L7 **Chinitna B** Alaska U.S.A.
65 G7 **Chinju** S Korea
86 D4 **Chinko** *R* Cent Afr Republic
103 P5 **Chinle** Arizona U.S.A.
103 P5 **Chinle V** Arizona U.S.A.
103 P5 **Chinle Wash** Arizona U.S.A.
67 F4 **Chin-men** Taiwan
143 C10 **Chinocup, L** Western Australia Australia
21 L7 **Chinon** France
118 G7 **Chinook** Alberta Canada
101 Q1 **Chinook** Montana U.S.A.
100 D3 **Chinook Pass** Washington U.S.A.
103 M7 **Chino Valley** Arizona U.S.A.
87 F8 **Chinsali** Zambia
88 D7 **Chinsali** Zambia
68 A1 **Chin State** Burma
75 P8 **Chin State** *prov* Burma
76 E1 **Chintalnar** India
88 E7 **Chintheche** Malawi
126 G10 **Chinú** Colombia
22 J4 **Chiny** Belgium
55 G3 **Chinyavino** U.S.S.R.
42 E3 **Chioggia** Italy
Chios *isld see* **Khios** *isld*
88 D8 **Chipata** Zambia
87 E9 **Chipepo** Zambia
88 D9 **Chipera** Mozambique
88 E10 **Chiperone** *mt* Mozambique
119 T1 **Chipewyan,L** Manitoba Canada
117 R7 **Chipewyan Lake** Alberta Canada
87 E8 **Chipili** Zambia
65 C6 **Chiping** China
87 F10 **Chipinge** Zimbabwe
117 Q9 **Chip Lake** Alberta Canada
111 L11 **Chipley** Florida U.S.A.
111 M9 **Chipley** Georgia U.S.A.
74 E10 **Chiplun** India
122 G7 **Chipman** New Brunswick Canada
120 D3 **Chipman L** Ontario Canada
88 E8 **Chipoka** Malawi
111 L11 **Chipola** *R* Florida U.S.A.
88 A9 **Chiposhya, L** Zambia
68 G7 **Chi Pou** Cambodia
121 L9 **Chippawa** Ontario Canada
8 D5 **Chippenham** England
99 L4 **Chippewa** *R* Minnesota U.S.A.
99 P5 **Chippewa Falls** Wisconsin U.S.A.
99 P4 **Chippewa Lake** Wisconsin U.S.A.
13 F6 **Chipping** England
9 E3 **Chipping Campden** England
9 E4 **Chipping Norton** England
8 D4 **Chipping Sodbury** England
46 F1 **Chiprovtsi** Bulgaria
128 C6 **Chiquian** Peru
128 D2 **Chiquinquirá** Colombia
131 F6 **Chiquita, L. Mar** Buenos Aires Argentina
128 F7 **Chiquitos, Llanos de** Bolivia
128 B4 **Chira** *R* Peru
76 E3 **Chirala** India
87 F9 **Chiramba** Mozambique
128 C3 **Chirambirá, Pta** *pt* Colombia
77 J2 **Chiras** Afghanistan
57 E4 **Chirchik** U.S.S.R.
87 F10 **Chiredzi** Zimbabwe
89 G3 **Chiredzi** *R* Zimbabwe
111 B10 **Chireno** Texas U.S.A.
109 N4 **Chireno** Texas U.S.A.
84 E5 **Chirfa** Niger
103 P9 **Chirica Hua Nat.Mon** Arizona U.S.A.
103 P10 **Chiricahua Pk** Arizona U.S.A.
126 H10 **Chiriguaná** Colombia
116 K9 **Chirikof I** Alaska U.S.A.
75 P8 **Chiringa** Bangladesh
125 N5 **Chiriqui,G.de** Panama
75 K7 **Chirmiri** India
47 J1 **Chirnogeni** Romania
13 F2 **Chirnside** Scotland
15 F5 **Chirnside** Borders Scotland
88 E10 **Chiromo** Malawi
46 G2 **Chirpan** Bulgaria
Chirua, L *see* **Chilwa, L**
87 E9 **Chirundu** Zimbabwe
22 D4 **Chiry-Ourscamps** France
88 B9 **Chisamba** Zambia
116 R5 **Chisana** Alaska U.S.A.
116 Q6 **Chisana Glacier** Alaska U.S.A.
44 B2 **Chisane** *R* Italy
119 R4 **Chisel Lake** Manitoba Canada
88 D6 **Chisenga** Malawi
55 C4 **Chishmy** U.S.S.R.
118 C4 **Chisholm** Alberta Canada
95 R2 **Chisholm** Maine U.S.A.
99 O2 **Chisholm** Minnesota U.S.A.
74 E4 **Chishtian Mandi** Pakistan
67 F4 **Chishui** China
67 B2 **Chishui** China
67 B3 **Chishui He** *R* China
88 B7 **Chisi** *isld* Zambia
Chisimaio *see* **Kismaayo**
87 F8 **Chisimba Falls** Zambia
Chişinău *see* **Kishinev**
48 G4 **Chişineu-Criş** Romania
108 D6 **Chisos Mts** Texas U.S.A.
108 C5 **Chispa Cr** Texas U.S.A.
116 P5 **Chistochina** Alaska U.S.A.
55 G4 **Chisto-ozernoye** U.S.S.R.
52 H6 **Chistopol** U.S.S.R.
55 E4 **Chistopol'ye** U.S.S.R.
55 G4 **Chistovo** U.S.S.R.
55 F4 **Chistyakovskoye** U.S.S.R.
88 E8 **Chisumulu** *isld* Mozambique
58 F1 **Chita** U.S.S.R.
87 B9 **Chitado** Angola
116 L4 **Chitanana** *R* Alaska U.S.A.
58 C5 **Chi-t'ang** China
61 K11 **Chita wan** *G* Japan
52 G4 **Chitayevo** U.S.S.R.
118 K5 **Chitek** Saskatchewan Canada
119 S6 **Chitek L** Manitoba Canada
87 C8 **Chitembo** Angola
45 L4 **Chitignano** Italy
116 Q6 **Chitina** *R* Alaska U.S.A.
116 P6 **Chitina** Alaska U.S.A.
56 G5 **Chitinskaya Oblast'** *prov* U.S.S.R.
60 P3 **Chitose** Japan
76 C3 **Chitradurga** India
74 J6 **Chitrakut** India
74 D1 **Chitral** Pakistan
125 O5 **Chitré** Panama
75 O7 **Chittagong** Bangladesh
75 M7 **Chittaranjan** India
74 F6 **Chittaurgarh** India
143 B9 **Chittering** Western Australia Australia
76 D4 **Chittoor** India
76 C5 **Chittur** India
89 G1 **Chitungwiza** Zimbabwe
88 F8 **Chiulézi** *R* Mozambique
87 D9 **Chiume** Angola
42 D2 **Chiusa** Italy
42 D5 **Chiusi** Italy
45 L4 **Chiusi di Verna** Italy
87 G8 **Chiuta, L** Malawi
88 E9 **Chiuta,L** Mozambique
17 G5 **Chiva** Spain
40 G7 **Chivasso** Italy
124 C4 **Chivato,Pta** *C* Mexico
128 D7 **Chivay** Peru
87 E9 **Chivemba** Angola
89 G2 **Chivhu** Zimbabwe
131 E5 **Chivilcoy** Argentina
106 H3 **Chivington** Colorado U.S.A.
22 F4 **Chivy** France
67 D6 **Chixi** China
125 O10 **Chixoy** *R* Guatemala
89 E1 **Chizarira Hills** Zimbabwe
52 F2 **Chizha** U.S.S.R.
Chizhou *see* **Guichi**
60 H10 **Chizu** Japan
55 F4 **Chkalovo** U.S.S.R.
57 H6 **Chkalovsk** U.S.S.R.
52 D2 **Chkalovskiy** U.S.S.R.
31 J5 **Chlumec nad Cidlinou** Czechoslovakia
31 M5 **Chmielnik** Poland
65 F5 **Cho** *isld* N Korea
65 G7 **Ch'o** *isld* S Korea
68 G5 **Choam Ksan** Cambodia
131 B3 **Choapo,R** Chile
87 D9 **Chobe Nat. Park** Botswana
9 F5 **Chobham** England
68 G2 **Cho Bo** Vietnam
31 J5 **Choceň** Czechoslovakia
121 O5 **Chochocouane** *R* Quebec Canada
67 B6 **Cho Chu** Vietnam
31 J4 **Chocianów** Poland
128 C2 **Chocó** *div* Colombia
103 K8 **Chocolate Mts** Arizona U.S.A.
103 J8 **Chocolate Mts** California U.S.A.
95 Q3 **Chocorua** New Hampshire U.S.A.
112 K2 **Chocowinity** North Carolina U.S.A.
107 N6 **Choctaw** Oklahoma U.S.A.
111 K11 **Choctawhatchee B** Florida U.S.A.
37 O3 **Chodov** Czechoslovakia
31 K3 **Chodziez** Poland
133 D5 **Choele Choel** Argentina
88 C9 **Chofombo** Mozambique
68 H7 **Cho Giua** Vietnam
119 N5 **Choiceland** Saskatchewan Canada
137 M3 **Choiseul** *isld* Solomon Is
133 F8 **Choiseul Sd** Falkland Is
19 Q12 **Choisy** France
22 D5 **Choisy-au-Bac** France
124 E4 **Choix** Mexico
31 H3 **Chojna** Poland
31 K2 **Chojnice** Poland
31 J4 **Chojnów** Poland
61 O6 **Chōkai-san** *mt* Japan
86 G3 **Ch'ok'ē Mts** Ethiopia
98 K4 **Chokio** Minnesota U.S.A.
57 G3 **Choknar** U.S.S.R.
57 H4 **Choktal** U.S.S.R.
51 O1 **Chokurdakh** U.S.S.R.
87 F10 **Chókwè** Mozambique
102 D6 **Cholame** California U.S.A.
102 D6 **Cholame Cr** California U.S.A.
133 C4 **Cholchagua** *prov* Chile
21 J7 **Cholet** France
13 F3 **Chollerford** England
68 H7 **Cho Lon** Vietnam
57 H4 **Cholpon** U.S.S.R.
57 H4 **Cholpon-Ata** U.S.S.R.
125 K8 **Cholula** Mexico
125 L3 **Choluleca** Honduras
87 E9 **Choma** Zambia
68 F7 **Chomna** Cambodia
68 G2 **Cho Moi** Vietnam
75 N5 **Chomo Lhari** *mt* Bhutan/ China
68 D3 **Chom Thong** Thailand
37 P3 **Chomutov** Czechoslovakia
56 H1 **Chona** *R* U.S.S.R.
68 E6 **Chon Buri** Thailand
68 E4 **Chon Daen** Thailand
128 B4 **Chone** Ecuador
67 F3 **Chong'an** China
67 G1 **Chongde** China
65 H4 **Ch'ŏngjin** N Korea
65 F5 **Chŏngju** N Korea
65 G6 **Ch'ŏngju** S Korea
68 F6 **Chong Kal** Cambodia
65 C4 **Chongli** China
67 G1 **Chongming** China
67 G1 **Chongming Dao** *isld* China
67 B2 **Chongqing** China
67 A1 **Chongqing** China
67 E3 **Chongren** China
67 E4 **Chongshi** China
88 B9 **Chongwe** *R* Zambia
67 E2 **Chongyang** China
67 F3 **Chongyang Xi** *R* China
67 E4 **Chongyi** China
56 D5 **Chongyz-Tayga, Gora** *mt* U.S.S.R.
68 H1 **Chongzuo** China
65 G7 **Chŏnju** S Korea
133 C6 **Chonos,Arch.de los** *islds* Chile
125 N9 **Chontalpa** Mexico
68 H7 **Chon Thanh** Vietnam
75 M4 **Cho Oyu** *pk* China/Nepal
48 G2 **Chop** U.S.S.R.
13 G5 **Chop Gate** England
68 H7 **Cho Phuoc Hai** Vietnam
130 D9 **Chopim, R** Brazil
130 D9 **Chopimzinho** Brazil
95 M8 **Choptank** *R* Maryland U.S.A.
56 F3 **Chora** *R* U.S.S.R.
68 G1 **Cho Ra** Vietnam
33 T7 **Chorin** East Germany
16 E5 **Chorito, Sa. del** *mts* Spain
13 F6 **Chorley** England
131 B2 **Choros** *R* Chile
131 B2 **Choros,I.de los** Chile
31 O2 **Choroszcz** Poland
141 G6 **Chorregon** Queensland Australia
128 C6 **Chorrillos** Peru
130 G10 **Chorrochó** Brazil
48 K1 **Chortkov** U.S.S.R.
31 M2 **Chorzele** Poland
31 L5 **Chorzów** Poland
Chōsen-kaikyō *see* **Nishi-suido**
61 O10 **Chōshi** Japan
133 C5 **Chos Malal** Argentina
65 G5 **Choson-Man** *B* N Korea
31 J2 **Choszczno** Poland
128 C5 **Chota** Peru
75 K7 **Chota Nagpur** *reg* India
101 N2 **Choteau** Montana U.S.A.
107 P5 **Choteau** Oklahoma U.S.A.
31 J6 **Chotěbor** Czechoslovakia
37 P4 **Chotěšov** Czechoslovakia
85 E2 **Chott ech Chergui** *salt lake* Algeria
85 E1 **Chott El Hodna** *marsh* Algeria
85 F2 **Chott El Jerid** *salt flats* Tunisia
85 F2 **Chott Melrhir** *salt flats* Algeria
21 L7 **Chouzé-sur-Loire** France
21 N6 **Chouzy-sur-Cisse** France
112 L1 **Chowan** *R* North Carolina U.S.A.
102 D4 **Chowchilla** California U.S.A.
138 F5 **Chowilla Dam** South Australia Australia
117 O9 **Chown,Mt** Alberta Canada
58 F2 **Choybalsan** Mongolia
40 C3 **Choye** France
48 D1 **Chřiby** Czechoslovakia
31 K6 **Chřiby** *dist* Czechoslovakia
109 L5 **Chriesman** Texas U.S.A.
99 T10 **Chrisman** Illinois U.S.A.
89 G6 **Chrissiesmeer** S Africa
144 D5 **Christabel, L** New Zealand
127 P6 **Christchurch** *parish* Barbados
9 E6 **Christchurch** England
144 B4 **Christchurch** New Zealand
116 P3 **Christian** Alaska U.S.A.
127 K2 **Christiana** Jamaica
89 D6 **Christiana** S Africa
95 L7 **Christiana** Pennsylvania U.S.A.
115 N3 **Christian,C** Northwest Territories Canada
120 K8 **Christian I** Ontario Canada
94 C6 **Christiansburg** Ohio U.S.A.
110 M1 **Christiansburg** Ohio U.S.A.
94 G9 **Christiansburg** Virginia U.S.A.
28 C6 **Christiansfeld** Denmark
115 O4 **Christianshåb** Greenland
28 C4 **Christianshede** Denmark
27 H16 **Christiansø** *isld* Denmark
127 M6 **Christiansted** Virgin Is
69 C8 **Christie I** Burma
119 V2 **Christie L** Manitoba Canada
101 Q2 **Christina** Montana U.S.A.
118 G3 **Christina,L** Alberta Canada
100 G1 **Christina L** British Columbia Canada
144 B6 **Christina, Mt** New Zealand
118 G2 **Christina R** Alberta Canada
109 J7 **Christine** Texas U.S.A.
142 F4 **Christmas Creek** Western Australia Australia
Christmas I *see* **Kiritimati**
83 M9 **Christmas I** Indian Oc
120 H2 **Christopher Falls** Ontario Canada
143 G6 **Christopher, L** W Australia
108 G4 **Christoval** Texas U.S.A.
131 H3 **Christovão Pereira,Pte** Brazil
106 D4 **Chromo** Colorado U.S.A.
31 J6 **Chrudim** Czechoslovakia
31 L5 **Chrzanow** Poland
57 G3 **Chu** U.S.S.R.
57 F3 **Chu** *R* U.S.S.R.
125 O10 **Chuacús,Sa.de** *ra* Guatemala
67 F2 **Chuankeng** China
67 G1 **Chuansha** China
57 J1 **Chubartau** U.S.S.R.
103 J7 **Chubbuck** California U.S.A.
61 L9 **Chubu-Sangaku Nat. Park** Japan
133 D6 **Chubut** *R* Argentina
133 D6 **Chubut** *prov* Argentina
Chuchow *see* **Zhuzhou**
103 J8 **Chuckwalla Mts** California U.S.A.
133 E4 **Chucul** Argentina
37 P5 **Chudenice** Czechoslovakia
55 D4 **Chudinovo** U.S.S.R.
8 C6 **Chudleigh** England
141 G4 **Chudleigh Park** Queensland Australia
120 K6 **Chudleigh River Valley** Ontario Canada
52 D5 **Chudovo** U.S.S.R.
52 C5 **Chudskoye, Ozero** *L* U.S.S.R.
116 M7 **Chugach Is** Alaska U.S.A.
116 O6 **Chugach Mts** Alaska U.S.A.
60 F11 **Chūgoku sanchi** *mts* Japan
Chuguchak *see* **Tacheng**
56 C4 **Chugunash** U.S.S.R.
55 F3 **Chugunly** U.S.S.R.
54 H7 **Chuguyev** U.S.S.R.
98 B8 **Chugwater** Wyoming U.S.A.
98 B8 **Chugwater Cr** Wyoming U.S.A.
103 N9 **Chuichu** Arizona U.S.A.
59 L1 **Chukchagirskoye, Oz** *L* U.S.S.R.
147 O3 **Chukchi Sea** Arctic Oc
52 F5 **Chukhloma** U.S.S.R.
52 F5 **Chukhlomskoye, Oz** *L* U.S.S.R.
116 A3 **Chukotskiy Poluostrov** U.S.S.R.
112 D6 **Chula** Georgia U.S.A.
99 N10 **Chula** Missouri U.S.A.
94 K9 **Chula** Virginia U.S.A.
56 G2 **Chula** *R* U.S.S.R.
57 E3 **Chulak-Kurgan** U.S.S.R.
52 G3 **Chulasa** U.S.S.R.
102 G9 **Chula Vista** California U.S.A.
116 N5 **Chulitna** *R* Alaska U.S.A.
51 M3 **Chul'man** U.S.S.R.
8 C6 **Chulmleigh** England
128 B5 **Chulucanas** Peru
58 D2 **Chuluut Gol** *R* Mongolia
56 D3 **Chulym** *R* U.S.S.R.
56 B3 **Chulym** U.S.S.R.
56 C5 **Chulyshman** *R* U.S.S.R.
56 C5 **Chulyshmunskiy Khrebet** *mts* U.S.S.R.
74 H2 **Chumar** Kashmir
133 D3 **Chumbicha** Argentina
47 H2 **Chumerna** *mt* Bulgaria
59 L1 **Chumikan** U.S.S.R.
68 D7 **Chumphon** Thailand
68 E5 **Chum Saeng** Thailand
111 J11 **Chumuckla** Florida U.S.A.
56 B4 **Chumysh** *R* U.S.S.R.
56 E2 **Chuna** *R* U.S.S.R.
67 F2 **Chun'an** China
65 G6 **Ch'unch'ŏn** S Korea
111 H11 **Chunchula** Alabama U.S.A.
75 N7 **Chunchura** India
Chungking *see* **Chongqing**
66 C6 **Chung-pa** China
68 K3 **Chung-yüan** China
65 H3 **Chunhua** China
56 E1 **Chunku** *R* U.S.S.R.
58 D6 **Chün-lien** China
67 C1 **Chunmuying** China
83 K8 **Chunnakam** Sri Lanka
56 E2 **Chunoyar** U.S.S.R.
88 D6 **Chunya** Tanzania
56 E1 **Chunya** *R* U.S.S.R.
59 J3 **Chunyang** China
69 G8 **Chuoi,Hon** *isld* Vietnam
52 D2 **Chupa** U.S.S.R.
127 O1 **Chupara Pt** Trinidad
128 D6 **Chuquibambilla** Peru
133 D2 **Chuquicamata** Chile
133 E2 **Chuquisaca** *dept* Bolivia
41 L4 **Chur** Switzerland
52 H6 **Chur** U.S.S.R.
52 J5 **Churaki** U.S.S.R.
51 N2 **Churapcha** U.S.S.R.
55 C3 **Churayevo** U.S.S.R.
119 Q8 **Churchbridge** Saskatchewan Canada
95 L8 **Church Creek** Maryland U.S.A.
94 E10 **Church Hill** Tennessee U.S.A.
115 N7 **Churchill** *R* Labrador, Nfld Canada
115 K6 **Churchill** Manitoba Canada
118 L3 **Churchill** *R* Saskatchewan Canada
8 D5 **Churchill** England
101 M7 **Churchill** Idaho U.S.A.
118 J2 **Churchill L** Saskatchewan Canada
95 R7 **Churchill L** Maine U.S.A.
146 D11 **Churchill Mts** Antarctica
117 L6 **Churchill Pk** British Columbia Canada
119 W1 **Churchill R** Manitoba Canada
8 C6 **Churchingford** England
111 D11 **Church Point** Louisiana U.S.A.
122 F9 **Church Pt** Nova Scotia Canada
98 G1 **Churchs Ferry** North Dakota U.S.A.
8 D2 **Church Stretton** England
94 K3 **Churchville** New York U.S.A.
94 H8 **Churchville** Virginia U.S.A.
99 M7 **Churdan** Iowa U.S.A.
56 D5 **Chureg-Tag,Gora** *mt* U.S.S.R.
41 K3 **Churfirsten** *mt* Switzerland
75 K6 **Churk** India
52 F3 **Churkino** U.S.S.R.
74 F4 **Churu** India
94 B5 **Churubusco** Indiana U.S.A.
128 E1 **Churuguara** Venezuela
52 F4 **Chushevitsy** U.S.S.R.
106 B5 **Chuska Mts** Ariz/New Mex U.S.A.
55 C2 **Chusovaya** *R* U.S.S.R.
55 C2 **Chusovoy** U.S.S.R.
52 J4 **Chusovskoy** U.S.S.R.
57 F4 **Chust** U.S.S.R.
122 D4 **Chute-aux-Outardes** Quebec Canada
122 A4 **Chute-des-Passes** Quebec Canada
52 J4 **Chuval** U.S.S.R.
67 F1 **Chu Xian** China
61 N9 **Chūzenji-ko** *L* Japan
37 P3 **Chyše** Czechoslovakia
88 F3 **Chyulu Ra** Kenya
70 M9 **Ciamis** Java
45 N6 **Ciampino** Italy
70 L9 **Cianjur** Java
42 C4 **Ciano d'Enza** Italy
103 O7 **Cibecue** Arizona U.S.A.
70 L9 **Cibinong** Java
48 H5 **Cibinului,Munţii** *mts* Romania
103 K8 **Cibola** Arizona U.S.A.
70 L9 **Ci Buni** *R* Java
124 D2 **Cibuta** Mexico
42 F3 **Čičarija** *mt* Yugoslavia
45 R8 **Cicciano** Italy
47 K7 **Çiçekbaba Tepe** *mt* Turkey
94 A6 **Cicero** Indiana U.S.A.
95 L3 **Cicero** New York U.S.A.
129 L6 **Cicero Dantas** Brazil
46 E1 **Čicevac** Yugoslavia
67 G1 **Cicheng** China
17 F2 **Cidacos** *R* Spain
70 L9 **Cidaun** Java
78 D1 **Cide** Turkey
31 J5 **Cidlina** *R* Czechoslovakia
31 M3 **Ciéchanow** Poland
31 N3 **Ciechanowiec** Poland
31 L3 **Ciechocinek** Poland
126 E4 **Ciego de Avila** Cuba
70 L9 **Ciemas** Java
128 D1 **Ciénaga** Colombia
126 G10 **Ciénaga de Oro** Colombia
126 G10 **Ciénaga Grande** *marshy lake* Colombia
106 E9 **Cienega** New Mexico U.S.A.
124 H5 **Ciénega del Carmen** Mexico
124 H5 **Cieneguilla** Mexico
124 D3 **Cieneguita** Mexico
126 D3 **Cienfuegos** Cuba
22 J3 **Ciergnon** Belgium
31 O5 **Cieszanow** Poland
31 L6 **Cieszyn** Poland
17 G6 **Cieza** Spain
31 M6 **Ciężkowice** Poland
47 M10 **Çiftalan** Turkey
47 L5 **Çifteler** Turkey
17 F4 **Cifuentes** Spain
70 K9 **Cigeulis** Java
40 H7 **Cigliano** Italy
17 F5 **Cigüela** *R* Spain
78 D2 **Cihanbeyli** Turkey
124 G8 **Cihuatlán** Mexico
16 D5 **Cijara, Embalse de** *res* Spain
70 M9 **Cikalong** Java
46 D4 **Çikës, Mal i** *mt* Albania
70 M9 **Cilacap** Java
70 L9 **Cilangkahan** Java
78 J1 **Cildir G** *L* Turkey
67 D2 **Cili** China
8 C3 **Cilycwm** Wales
103 J6 **Cima** California U.S.A.
70 L9 **Cimahi** Java
70 M9 **Ci Manuk** *R* Java
106 C3 **Cimarron** Colorado U.S.A.
107 K4 **Cimarron** Kansas U.S.A.
106 F5 **Cimarron** New Mexico U.S.A.
107 M5 **Cimarron** *R* Okla/Kansas U.S.A.
31 O2 **Cimochy** Poland
42 D4 **Cimone, M** *mt* Italy
48 H4 **Cîmpeni** Romania
48 H4 **Cîmpia Turzii** Romania
48 K5 **Cîmpina** Romania
48 J5 **Cîmpulung** Romania
48 K3 **Cîmpulung Moldovenesc** Romania
48 K4 **Cîmpuri** Romania
128 E2 **Cinaruco** *R* Venezuela
18 F10 **Cinca** *R* Spain
42 H5 **Cincer** *mt* Yugoslavia
99 O9 **Cincinnati** Iowa U.S.A.
94 C7 **Cincinnati** Ohio U.S.A.
95 M4 **Cincinnatus** New York U.S.A.
126 E4 **Cinco-Balas, Cayo** *islds* Cuba
116 H8 **Cinder** *R* Alaska U.S.A.
8 D4 **Cinderford** England
48 K5 **Cîndeşti** Romania
48 H5 **Cîndrelu** *mt* Romania
47 J7 **Çine** *R* Turkey
47 J7 **Çine** Turkey
22 J3 **Ciney** Belgium
16 B3 **Cinfães** Portugal
70 F5 **Cinoko, Tanjong** *C* Sulawesi
21 L7 **Cinq Mars** France
68 A7 **Cinque I** Andaman Is
129 J5 **Cinta,Serra da** *mts* Brazil
85 A4 **Cintra, G.de** Western Sahara
45 O6 **Ciociaria** Italy
48 J6 **Ciolăneşti** Romania
70 M9 **Cipatuja** Java
67 E3 **Ciping** China
21 K5 **Ciral** France
17 G4 **Cirat** Spain
146 E12 **Circe, Dome** *ice dome* Antarctica
43 E7 **Circeo, M** *mt* Italy
43 E7 **Circeo, M** *lighthouse* Italy
116 P4 **Circle** Alaska U.S.A.
98 A2 **Circle** Montana U.S.A.
94 E7 **Circleville** Ohio U.S.A.
103 M3 **Circleville** Utah U.S.A.
70 M9 **Cirebon** Java
9 E4 **Cirencester** England
69 E13 **Cirenti** Sumatra
21 P3 **Cires-les-Mello** France
19 K4 **Cirey** France
36 B6 **Cirey-sur-Vezouse** France
44 C1 **Ciriè** Italy
18 E8 **Ciron** *R* France
21 N8 **Ciron** France
44 G3 **Cisa, Passo di** Italy
99 S9 **Cisco** Illinois U.S.A.
109 J3 **Cisco** Texas U.S.A.
103 P3 **Cisco** Utah U.S.A.
89 E9 **Ciskei** *homeland* S Africa
48 K5 **Cislău** Romania
33 N4 **Cismar** W Germany
31 N6 **Cisna** Poland
48 J5 **Cisnadie** Romania
110 H3 **Cisne** Illinois U.S.A.
128 C2 **Cisneros** Colombia
133 C6 **Cisnes** *R* Chile
70 L9 **Cisompet** Java
100 D3 **Cispus** *R* Washington U.S.A.
100 D3 **Cispus Pass** Washington U.S.A.
21 N6 **Cisse** *R* France
37 O3 **Čistá** Czechoslovakia
109 K6 **Cistern** Texas U.S.A.
45 N6 **Cisterna di Latina** Italy
16 D2 **Cistierna** Spain
129 G3 **Citare** *R* Brazil
125 L8 **Citlaltépetl** Mexico
113 E8 **Citra** Florida U.S.A.
111 H10 **Citronelle** Alabama U.S.A.
87 C12 **Citrusdal** S Africa
42 D3 **Cittadella** Italy
42 E6 **Citta della Pieve** Italy
42 E5 **Città di Castello** Italy
43 G10 **Cittanova** Italy
142 A1 **City Beach** *dist* Perth, W Aust Australia
113 G9 **City Point** Florida U.S.A.
48 K5 **Ciucaşu** *mt* Romania
48 H4 **Ciucea** Romania
48 K4 **Ciucului Muntii** *mt* Romania
108 G6 **Ciudad Acuña** Mexico
125 J8 **Ciudad Altamirano** Mexico
128 F2 **Ciudad Bolivar** Venezuela
124 G4 **Ciudad Camargo** Mexico
109 J9 **Ciudad Camargo** Mexico
125 O8 **Ciudad del Carmen** Mexico
124 G3 **Ciudad Delicias** Mexico
17 K4 **Ciudadela** Spain
127 N10 **Ciudad Guayana** Venezuela
124 F3 **Ciudad Guerrero** Mexico
124 H8 **Ciudad Guzmán** Mexico
125 N10 **Ciudad Hidalgo** Mexico
106 D10 **Ciudad Juárez** Mexico
124 H5 **Ciudad Lerdo** Mexico
125 L6 **Ciudad Madero** Mexico
125 K6 **Ciudad Mante** Mexico
124 E4 **Ciudad Obregón** Mexico
128 F2 **Ciudad Piar** Venezuela
16 E6 **Ciudad Real** *prov* Spain
16 E6 **Ciudad Real** Spain
16 C4 **Ciudad Rodrigo** Spain
125 N10 **Ciudad Tecún Umán** Mexico
Ciudad Trujillo *see* **Santo Domingo** Dominican Rep.
125 K6 **Ciudad Victoria** Mexico
48 G4 **Ciumeghiu** Romania
48 L5 **Ciuşlea** Romania
42 E2 **Cividale del F** Italy
42 E6 **Civita Castellana** Italy
42 F5 **Civitanova Marche** Italy
44 L5 **Civitavecchia** *lighthouse* Italy
45 L3 **Civitella di Romagna** Italy
45 O6 **Civitella Roveto** Italy
44 B1 **Civrari Monte** Italy
18 F6 **Civray** France
21 P8 **Civray** Cher France
47 K6 **Çivril** Turkey
67 G1 **Cixi** China
65 C6 **Ci Xian** China
78 J3 **Cizre** Turkey
12 C2 **Clachan** Scotland
100 C4 **Clackamas** *R* Oregon U.S.A.
143 B9 **Clackline** Western Australia Australia
Clackmannon *co see* **Central** *reg*
9 H4 **Clacton-on-Sea** England
12 C1 **Cladich** Scotland
107 M3 **Claflin** Kansas U.S.A.
100 J1 **Clagstone** Idaho U.S.A.
20 E6 **Claie,R** France
21 L8 **Clain** *R* France
119 N6 **Clair** Saskatchewan Canada
6 J2 **Clair** *oil rig* North Sea
68 G1 **Claire** *R* Vietnam
98 J4 **Claire City** South Dakota U.S.A.
117 R6 **Claire, L** Alberta Canada
108 G2 **Clairemont** Texas U.S.A.
94 H6 **Clairton** Pennsylvania U.S.A.
19 J6 **Clairvaux** France
21 N8 **Claise** *R* France
100 A1 **Clallam Bay** Washington U.S.A.
18 H5 **Clamecy** France
102 G2 **Clan Alpine Mts** Nevada U.S.A.
101 N3 **Clancy** Montana U.S.A.
144 C6 **Clandeboye** New Zealand
118 F5 **Clandonald** Alberta Canada
9 E4 **Clanfield** England
111 K9 **Clanton** Alabama U.S.A.
119 S8 **Clanwilliam** Manitoba Canada
87 C12 **Clanwilliam** S Africa
12 C2 **Claonaig** Scotland
9 F5 **Clapham** England
13 F5 **Clapham** N Yorks England
44 B3 **Clapier, Mt** France
141 F4 **Clara** *R* Queensland Australia
14 D3 **Clara** Ireland
113 D8 **Clara** Florida U.S.A.
99 L5 **Clara City** Minnesota U.S.A.
68 C7 **Clara I** Burma
141 F4 **Claraville** Queensland Australia
138 E5 **Clare** South Australia Australia
9 G3 **Clare** England
14 C3 **Clare** *R* Ireland
14 C4 **Clare** *co* Ireland
99 M7 **Clare** Iowa U.S.A.
94 C3 **Clare** Michigan U.S.A.
14 C4 **Clarecastle** Ireland
139 G5 **Clare Corner** New South Wales Australia
14 A3 **Clare I** Ireland
142 A2 **Claremont** *dist* Perth, W Aust Australia
127 K2 **Claremont** Jamaica
95 P3 **Claremont** New Hampshire U.S.A.
98 H4 **Claremont** South Dakota U.S.A.
141 G2 **Claremont Is** Gt Barrier Reef Australia
14 C3 **Claremorris** Ireland
139 L3 **Clarence** *R* New South Wales Australia
144 D5 **Clarence** New Zealand
99 P8 **Clarence** Iowa U.S.A.
99 O10 **Clarence** Missouri U.S.A.
110 D2 **Clarence Cannon Res** Missouri U.S.A.
146 D3 **Clarence I** South Shetland Is Antarctica
133 C8 **Clarence,I** Chile
140 B1 **Clarence Str** N Terr Australia
117 G8 **Clarence Str** Alaska U.S.A.
126 G3 **Clarence Town** Long I Bahamas
121 O8 **Clarendon** Ontario Canada
127 K3 **Clarendon** *parish* Jamaica
110 E7 **Clarendon** Arkansas U.S.A.
94 H5 **Clarendon** Pennsylvania U.S.A.
108 G1 **Clarendon** Texas U.S.A.
123 S5 **Clarenville** Newfoundland Canada
118 D8 **Claresholm** Alberta Canada
19 P16 **Claret** France
98 B6 **Clareton** Wyoming U.S.A.
32 H9 **Clarholz** W Germany
141 F4 **Clarina** *R* Queensland Australia
99 L9 **Clarinda** Iowa U.S.A.
127 M10 **Clarines** Venezuela
94 H5 **Clarington** Pennsylvania U.S.A.
99 N7 **Clarion** Iowa U.S.A.
94 H5 **Clarion** *R* Pennsylvania U.S.A.
94 H5 **Clarion** Pennsylvania U.S.A.
126 H4 **Clarion Bank** Bahamas
145 E2 **Claris** New Zealand
107 O7 **Clarita** Oklahoma U.S.A.
102 H8 **Clark** *L* California U.S.A.
101 T9 **Clark** Colorado U.S.A.
110 D2 **Clark** Missouri U.S.A.
98 J5 **Clark** South Dakota U.S.A.
101 N4 **Clark Canyon Res** Montana U.S.A.
103 M7 **Clarkdale** Arizona U.S.A.
141 G4 **Clarke** *R* Queensland Australia
122 F3 **Clarke City** Quebec Canada
139 J8 **Clarke I** Tasmania Australia
118 K4 **Clarke L** Saskatchewan Canada
141 J5 **Clarke Ra** Queensland Australia
141 H4 **Clarke River** Queensland Australia
112 D3 **Clarkesville** Georgia U.S.A.
98 L5 **Clarkfield** Minnesota U.S.A.
117 Q12 **Clark Fork** *R* Idaho U.S.A.
100 J1 **Clark Fork** Idaho U.S.A.
112 E4 **Clark Hill Dam** Georgia U.S.A.
112 E4 **Clark Hill L** *res* Georgia U.S.A.
100 J2 **Clarkia** Idaho U.S.A.
116 K6 **Clark,L** Alaska U.S.A.
117 M3 **Clark,Mt** Northwest Territories Canada
103 J6 **Clark Mt** California U.S.A.
106 E1 **Clark Pk** Colorado U.S.A.
120 J8 **Clark Pt** Ontario Canada
111 D9 **Clarks** Louisiana U.S.A.
98 J8 **Clarks** Nebraska U.S.A.
101 Q5 **Clarks** *R* Wyoming U.S.A.
110 H6 **Clarksburg** Tennessee U.S.A.
94 G7 **Clarksburg** West Virginia U.S.A.
111 F7 **Clarksdale** Mississippi U.S.A.
99 N6 **Clarks Grove** Minnesota U.S.A.
122 G10 **Clark's Harbour** Nova Scotia Canada
110 K1 **Clarks Hill** Indiana U.S.A.
144 C6 **Clarks Junction** New Zealand
121 L9 **Clarkson** Ontario Canada
98 J8 **Clarkson** Nebraska U.S.A.
142 E4 **Clarkson, Mt** Western Australia Australia
116 H7 **Clarks Point** Alaska U.S.A.
94 D4 **Clarkston** Michigan U.S.A.
101 O3 **Clarkston** Montana U.S.A.
100 H3 **Clarkston** Washington U.S.A.
127 K2 **Clark's Town** Jamaica
144 B7 **Clarksville** New Zealand
110 C6 **Clarksville** Arkansas U.S.A.
110 F2 **Clarksville** Illinois U.S.A.
99 O7 **Clarksville** Iowa U.S.A.
94 B4 **Clarksville** Michigan U.S.A.
110 J5 **Clarksville** Tennessee U.S.A.
109 M2 **Clarksville** Texas U.S.A.
94 J10 **Clarksville** Virginia U.S.A.
112 J3 **Clarkton** North Carolina U.S.A.
109 K8 **Clarkwood** Texas U.S.A.
100 E5 **Clarno** Oregon U.S.A.
129 H7 **Claro** *R* Brazil
22 E3 **Clary** France
141 H6 **Claude** *R* Queensland Australia
108 C8 **Claude** Texas U.S.A.
130 G7 **Cláudio** Brazil
32 M8 **Clauen** W Germany
37 O2 **Claussnitz** East Germany
33 M9 **Clausthal-Zellerfeld** W Germany
71 E1 **Claveria** Luzon Philippines
118 L8 **Clavet** Saskatchewan Canada
19 N14 **Claveyson** France
112 F5 **Claxton** Georgia U.S.A.
102 C3 **Clay** California U.S.A.
110 J4 **Clay** Kentucky U.S.A.
109 L5 **Clay** Texas U.S.A.
94 F8 **Clay** West Virginia U.S.A.
107 N2 **Clay Center** Kansas U.S.A.
98 H9 **Clay Center** Nebraska U.S.A.
110 H3 **Clay City** Illinois U.S.A.
110 J2 **Clay City** Indiana U.S.A.
110 N4 **Clay City** Kentucky U.S.A.
9 E1 **Clay Cross** England
118 J9 **Claydon** Saskatchewan Canada

20
Claydon — Cónico

9 H3 Claydon England
18 H6 Clayette, la France
103 L5 Clayhole Wash creek Arizona U.S.A.
118 J1 Clay L Ontario Canada
6 K4 Claymore oil rig North Sea
107 P5 Claymore Oklahoma U.S.A.
117 L11 Clayoquot British Columbia Canada
103 O8 Claypool Arizona U.S.A.
103 O7 Clay Springs Arizona U.S.A.
94 G6 Claysville Pennsylvania U.S.A.
138 E3 Clayton R South Australia Australia
9 F6 Clayton England
111 L10 Clayton Alabama U.S.A.
112 D3 Clayton Georgia U.S.A.
101 L5 Clayton Idaho U.S.A.
99 Q9 Clayton Illinois U.S.A.
110 K2 Clayton Indiana U.S.A.
107 K2 Clayton Kansas U.S.A.
106 G5 Clayton New Mexico U.S.A.
95 L2 Clayton New York U.S.A.
112 J2 Clayton North Carolina U.S.A.
107 P7 Clayton Oklahoma U.S.A.
95 R7 Clayton Lake Maine U.S.A.
13 F6 Clayton-le-Moors England
94 G9 Claytor Lake Virginia U.S.A.
95 M4 Clayville New York U.S.A.
131 F4 Clé R Argentina
107 O7 Clear Boggy Cr Oklahoma U.S.A.
99 L2 Clearbrook Minnesota U.S.A.
144 C6 Clearburn New Zealand
14 B5 Clear,C Ireland
94 G8 Clearco West Virginia U.S.A.
103 O7 Clear Cr R Arizona U.S.A.
101 T5 Clear Cr Wyoming U.S.A.
100 B8 Clear Creek California U.S.A.
116 O7 Cleare,C Alaska U.S.A.
99 M9 Clearfield Iowa U.S.A.
94 J5 Clearfield Pennsylvania U.S.A.
101 N8 Clearfield Utah U.S.A.
108 G3 Clear Fork R Texas U.S.A.
117 O7 Clear Hills Alberta Canada
14 B5 Clear I Ireland
119 S8 Clear L Manitoba Canada
121 N7 Clear, L Ontario Canada
102 B2 Clear L California U.S.A.
99 N6 Clear L Iowa U.S.A.
109 P4 Clear L Louisiana U.S.A.
99 N4 Clear L Minnesota U.S.A.
98 K5 Clear L South Dakota U.S.A.
103 M2 Clear L Utah U.S.A.
99 O4 Clear L Wisconsin U.S.A.
100 D8 Clear L. Res California U.S.A.
101 T5 Clearmont Wyoming U.S.A.
117 O7 Clear Prairie Alberta Canada
117 N10 Clearwater British Columbia Canada
113 E10 Clearwater Florida U.S.A.
100 K3 Clearwater Idaho U.S.A.
100 J3 Clearwater R Idaho U.S.A.
107 N4 Clearwater Kansas U.S.A.
98 H7 Clearwater Nebraska U.S.A.
119 Q4 Clearwater L. Prov. Park Manitoba Canada
100 K3 Clearwater Mts Idaho U.S.A.
118 B6 Clearwater R Alberta Canada
110 F4 Clearwater Res Missouri U.S.A.
99 L2 Clearwter R Minnesota U.S.A.
143 D7 Cleaver, Mt Western Australia Australia
107 O2 Cleburne Kansas U.S.A.
109 K3 Cleburne Texas U.S.A.
21 K4 Clécy France
8 B4 Cleddau, R Wales
20 B4 Cléder France
8 D3 Clee Hill England
100 D2 Cle Elum L Washington U.S.A.
13 H6 Cleethorpes England
118 H5 Cleeves Saskatchewan Canada
40 B1 Clefmont France
21 K6 Clefs France
109 J7 Clegg Texas U.S.A.
20 D5 Cléguérec France
140 B6 Cleland Hills N Terr Australia
22 K4 Clemency Luxembourg
102 C3 Clements California U.S.A.
115 N1 Clements Markham Inlet Northwest Territories Canada
122 G9 Clementsport Nova Scotia Canada
122 G9 Clementsvale Nova Scotia Canada
94 F8 Clendenin West Virginia U.S.A.
94 F6 Clendening Res Ohio U.S.A.
8 D3 Cleobury Mortimer England
71 D5 Cleopatra Needle mt Philippines
107 M5 Cleo Springs Oklahoma U.S.A.
21 L7 Cléré France
21 N2 Clères France
121 M4 Cléricy Quebec Canada
142 C3 Clerke Reef Indian Oc
133 J9 Clerke Rocks S Georgia
141 J6 Clermont Queensland Australia
122 B6 Clermont Quebec Canada
21 P3 Clermont Oise France
113 F9 Clermont Florida U.S.A.
99 P6 Clermont Iowa U.S.A.
94 J5 Clermont Pennsylvania U.S.A.
21 K6 Clermont-Créans France
19 J3 Clermont en Argonne France
18 H7 Clermont Ferrand France
18 H9 Clermont l'Herault France
121 L4 Clerval Quebec Canada
40 D3 Clerval France
22 L3 Clervaux Luxembourg
21 O3 Cléry-en-Vexin France
21 O6 Cléry-St. André France
22 D4 Clery-sur-Somme France
42 D2 Cles Italy
21 K8 Clessé France
138 D5 Cleve South Australia Australia
8 D5 Clevedon England
13 G4 Cleveland co England
110 D6 Cleveland Arkansas U.S.A.
113 F11 Cleveland Florida U.S.A.
112 D3 Cleveland Georgia U.S.A.
101 O7 Cleveland Idaho U.S.A.
99 N5 Cleveland Minnesota U.S.A.
111 F8 Cleveland Mississippi U.S.A.
101 Q1 Cleveland Montana U.S.A.
95 M3 Cleveland New York U.S.A.
112 G2 Cleveland North Carolina U.S.A.
98 G3 Cleveland North Dakota U.S.A.
94 F5 Cleveland Ohio U.S.A.
107 O5 Cleveland Oklahoma U.S.A.
112 E2 Cleveland South Carolina U.S.A.
112 C2 Cleveland Tennessee U.S.A.
109 M5 Cleveland Texas U.S.A.
103 O2 Cleveland Utah U.S.A.
99 T6 Cleveland Wisconsin U.S.A.
141 H4 Cleveland, C Queensland Australia
13 G4 Cleveland Hills England
130 D10 Clevelândia Brazil
101 M1 Cleveland,Mt Montana U.S.A.
113 G11 Clewiston Florida U.S.A.
9 H2 Cley England
14 A3 Clifden Ireland
144 A7 Clifden New Zealand
106 B9 Cliff New Mexico U.S.A.
100 D3 Cliffdell Washington U.S.A.
71 D5 Cliff Head Philippines
101 O5 Cliff Lake Montana U.S.A.
94 D3 Clifford Michigan U.S.A.
98 J2 Clifford North Dakota U.S.A.
94 H9 Clifford Virginia U.S.A.
99 Q4 Clifford Wisconsin U.S.A.
100 H7 Cliffs Idaho U.S.A.
112 F2 Cliffside North Carolina U.S.A.
141 K8 Clifton Queensland Australia
113 K9 Clifton New Providence I Bahamas
8 D5 Clifton England
103 P8 Clifton Arizona U.S.A.
99 T9 Clifton Illinois U.S.A.
107 N2 Clifton Kansas U.S.A.
95 N6 Clifton New Jersey U.S.A.
98 B6 Clifton Wyoming U.S.A.
94 H9 Clifton Forge Virginia U.S.A.
138 E2 Clifton Hills South Australia Australia
113 K9 Clifton Pt New Providence I Bahamas
118 J9 Climax Saskatchewan Canada
106 D2 Climax Colorado U.S.A.
111 M11 Climax Georgia U.S.A.
94 B4 Climax Michigan U.S.A.
98 K2 Climax Minnesota U.S.A.
112 C2 Clinch R Tennessee U.S.A.
94 E9 Clinchco Virginia U.S.A.
94 E10 Clinch Mt Tenn/Virg U.S.A.
94 E10 Clinchport Virginia U.S.A.
117 P9 Cline, Mt Alberta Canada
37 K1 Clingen East Germany
112 D2 Clingmans Dome Tennessee U.S.A.
108 A4 Clint Texas U.S.A.
117 N10 Clinton British Columbia Canada
120 J9 Clinton Ontario Canada
144 B7 Clinton New Zealand
110 D6 Clinton Arkansas U.S.A.
95 P5 Clinton Connecticut U.S.A.
99 S9 Clinton Illinois U.S.A.
99 T10 Clinton Indiana U.S.A.
99 Q8 Clinton Iowa U.S.A.
110 H5 Clinton Kentucky U.S.A.
111 E11 Clinton Louisiana U.S.A.
95 S2 Clinton Maine U.S.A.
95 Q4 Clinton Massachusetts U.S.A.
94 D4 Clinton Michigan U.S.A.
98 K4 Clinton Minnesota U.S.A.
111 F9 Clinton Mississippi U.S.A.
110 C3 Clinton Missouri U.S.A.
101 M3 Clinton Montana U.S.A.
95 M3 Clinton New York U.S.A.
107 M6 Clinton Oklahoma U.S.A.
112 F3 Clinton South Carolina U.S.A.
112 C1 Clinton Tennessee U.S.A.
99 S7 Clinton Wisconsin U.S.A.
114 J5 Clinton-Colden L Northwest Territories Canada
114 E5 Clinton Creek Yukon Territory Canada
99 S5 Clintonville Wisconsin U.S.A.
103 N7 Clints Well Arizona U.S.A.
110 C1 Clio Iowa U.S.A.
94 D3 Clio Michigan U.S.A.
112 H3 Clio South Carolina U.S.A.
21 N8 Clion France
135 Q7 Clipperton atoll Pacific Oc
15 B3 Clisham Mt Lewis Scotland
20 H7 Clisson France
13 F6 Clitheroe England
118 D6 Clive Alberta Canada
145 F3 Clive New Zealand
101 M9 Clive Utah U.S.A.
117 O4 Clive L Northwest Territories Canada
118 J6 Cloan Saskatchewan Canada
14 D3 Cloghan Ireland
14 D2 Clogher N Ireland
14 E3 Clogher Hd Ireland
20 C6 Clohars France
140 F5 Clonagh Queensland Australia
14 C5 Clonakilty Ireland
14 C5 Clonakilty B Ireland
140 F5 Cloncurry Queensland Australia
140 F4 Cloncurry R Queensland Australia
14 E3 Clondalkin Ireland
14 E4 Clonegal Ireland
14 D2 Clones Ireland
59 J3 Clŏngjin N Korea
14 D4 Clonmel Ireland
99 L4 Clontarf Minnesota U.S.A.
117 L11 Clo-oose British Columbia Canada
9 F3 Clophill England
32 H7 Cloppenburg W Germany
99 O3 Cloquet Minnesota U.S.A.
130 B9 Clorinda Argentina
12 E3 Closeburn Scotland
123 L3 Cloudberry Pt Quebec Canada
106 E9 Cloudcroft New Mexico U.S.A.
101 S5 Cloud Pk Wyoming U.S.A.
145 E4 Cloudy Bay New Zealand
116 J5 Cloudy Mt Alaska U.S.A.
121 L4 Cloutier Quebec Canada
20 H8 Clouzeaux, les France
121 P4 Clova Quebec Canada
15 E4 Clova Scotland
8 B5 Clovelly England
13 F2 Clovenfords Scotland
112 F2 Clover South Carolina U.S.A.
94 J10 Clover Virginia U.S.A.
102 A3 Cloverdale California U.S.A.
110 K2 Cloverdale Indiana U.S.A.
106 B10 Cloverdale New Mexico U.S.A.
110 K4 Cloverport Kentucky U.S.A.
106 G7 Clovis New Mexico U.S.A.
8 D3 Clows Top England
21 N6 Cloyes France
14 C5 Cloyne Ireland
21 O8 Cluis France
48 H4 Cluj reg Romania
48 H4 Cluj-Napoca Romania
8 C3 Clun England
139 G7 Clunes Victoria Australia
140 E6 Cluny Queensland Australia
118 E8 Cluny Alberta Canada
102 H1 Cluro Nevada U.S.A.
40 E5 Cluses France
41 L6 Clusone Italy
120 J3 Clute Ontario Canada
144 B6 Clutha R New Zealand
144 B7 Clutha R New Zealand
99 O7 Clutier Iowa U.S.A.
117 P3 Clut L Northwest Territories Canada
143 F6 Clutterbuck Hills Western Australia Australia
8 C1 Clwyd R Wales
8 C1 Clwyd co Wales
113 D7 Clyattville Georgia U.S.A.
8 C4 Clydach Wales
118 D4 Clyde Alberta Canada
115 N3 Clyde Northwest Territories Canada
144 B6 Clyde New Zealand
6 M6 Clyde oil rig North Sea
107 N2 Clyde Kansas U.S.A.
95 L3 Clyde New York U.S.A.
98 H1 Clyde North Dakota U.S.A.
94 E5 Clyde Ohio U.S.A.
109 H3 Clyde Texas U.S.A.
12 D2 Clydebank Scotland
12 D3 Clyde,Firth of Scotland
121 O7 Clyde Forks Ontario Canada
101 P4 Clyde Park Montana U.S.A.
122 G10 Clyde R Nova Scotia Canada
12 D2 Clyde,R Scotland
144 B7 Clydevale New Zealand
99 S6 Clyman Wisconsin U.S.A.
94 H6 Clymer Pennsylvania U.S.A.
8 B1 Clynnog-fawr Wales
8 C3 Clyro Wales
8 C6 Clyst Honiton England
16 C4 Coa R Portugal
103 H8 Coachella California U.S.A.
123 M3 Coacoachou L Quebec Canada
108 F3 Coahoma Texas U.S.A.
124 H4 Coahuila state Mexico
117 K5 Coal R Br Col/Yukon Terr Canada
94 F8 Coal R West Virginia U.S.A.
99 S8 Coal City Illinois U.S.A.
124 H8 Coalcomán de Matamoros Mexico
116 Q4 Coal Creek Alaska U.S.A.
118 E9 Coaldale Alberta Canada
102 G3 Coaldale Nevada U.S.A.
144 C5 Coalgate New Zealand
107 O7 Coalgate Oklahoma U.S.A.
94 E8 Coal Grove Ohio U.S.A.
110 C6 Coal Hill Arkansas U.S.A.
144 A7 Coal I New Zealand
102 D5 Coalinga California U.S.A.
101 T9 Coalmont Colorado U.S.A.
94 J6 Coalport Pennsylvania U.S.A.
117 K6 Coal River British Columbia Canada
94 E7 Coalton Ohio U.S.A.
9 E2 Coalville England
101 O9 Coalville Utah U.S.A.
98 A4 Coalwood Montana U.S.A.
127 L5 Coamo Puerto Rico
128 F4 Coari Brazil
117 G7 Coast Mts British Columbia Canada
141 K7 Coast Ra mts Queensland Australia
141 K7 Coast Ra Queensland Australia
100 B9 Coast Range mts U.S.A.
102 A1 Coast Rge California U.S.A.
12 E2 Coatbridge Scotland
125 L8 Coatepec Mexico
95 M6 Coatesville Pennsylvania U.S.A.
121 T7 Coaticook Quebec Canada
107 M4 Coats Kansas U.S.A.
112 J2 Coats North Carolina U.S.A.
115 L5 Coats I Northwest Territories Canada
146 E7 Coats Land Antarctica
110 D1 Coatsville Iowa U.S.A.
125 M8 Coatzacoalcos Mexico
121 L5 Cobalt Ontario Canada
101 L4 Cobalt Idaho U.S.A.
125 O10 Cobán Guatemala
139 H4 Cobar New South Wales Australia
139 J6 Cobargo New South Wales Australia
99 Q7 Cobb Wisconsin U.S.A.
139 J6 Cobberas,Mt Victoria Australia
143 F6 Cobb, L Western Australia Australia
9 E6 Cobblers Corner England
145 D4 Cobb Res New Zealand
139 G7 Cobden Victoria Australia
121 O7 Cobden Ontario Canada
110 G4 Cobden Illinois U.S.A.
122 J8 Cobequid B Nova Scotia Canada
122 J8 Cobequid Mts Nova Scotia Canada
14 C5 Cóbh Ireland
140 B1 Cobham B N Terr Australia
128 E6 Cobija Bolivia
95 N4 Cobleskill New York U.S.A.
121 M8 Coboconk Ontario Canada
121 M9 Cobourg Ontario Canada
140 B1 Cobourg Pen N Terr Australia
143 B6 Cobra Western Australia Australia
139 H6 Cobram New South Wales Australia
101 L8 Cobre Nevada U.S.A.
127 L2 Cobre, R Jamaica
87 F8 Cobue Mozambique
100 B5 Coburg Oregon U.S.A.
37 K3 Coburg W Germany
115 M2 Coburg I Northwest Territories Canada
16 D3 Coca Spain
128 D7 Cocachacra Peru
128 D6 Cocamá Peru
42 C2 Coca, Pzo. di Italy
45 M3 Coccolia Italy
17 G6 Cocentaina Spain
128 E7 Cochabamba Bolivia
128 C3 Cocha, L Colombia
127 N9 Coche, I Venezuela
106 D3 Cochetopa Pass Colorado U.S.A.
76 C6 Cochin India
68 G7 Cochin reg Vietnam
128 E8 Cochinoca Argentina
126 D3 Cochinos, B. de Cuba
103 P9 Cochise Arizona U.S.A.
103 P9 Cochise Head mt Arizona U.S.A.
106 D6 Cochiti L New Mexico U.S.A.
112 D5 Cochran Georgia U.S.A.
118 C7 Cochrane Alberta Canada
120 J3 Cochrane Ontario Canada
133 C7 Cochrane, L Chile/Arg
94 G5 Cochranton Pennsylvania U.S.A.
33 O9 Cochstedt East Germany
142 E3 Cockatoo I Western Australia Australia
15 E3 Cock Bridge Scotland
141 G3 Cockburn R Queensland Australia
138 F4 Cockburn South Australia Australia
133 C8 Cockburn, Canal str Chile
127 J4 Cockburn Harbour Turks & Caicos Is
120 G7 Cockburn I Ontario Canada
140 A7 Cockburn, Mt N Terr Australia
140 B6 Cockburn, Mt N Terr Australia
142 G3 Cockburn Ra Western Australia Australia
142 A3 Cockburn Sd Western Australia Australia
13 F2 Cockburnspath Scotland
126 G2 Cockburn Town San Salvador Bahamas
13 F2 Cockenzie Scotland
13 F6 Cockerham England
13 E4 Cockermouth England
95 L7 Cockeysville Maryland U.S.A.
143 F9 Cocklebiddy Western Australia Australia
127 J2 Cockpit pk Jamaica
127 J2 Cockpit Country, The reg Jamaica
109 N9 Cockrell Hill Texas U.S.A.
15 F5 Cocksburnpath Scotland
89 D9 Cockscomb mt S Africa
129 J5 Côco R Brazil
125 M2 Coco R Honduras/Nicaragua
113 G9 Cocoa Florida U.S.A.
113 G9 Cocoa Beach Florida U.S.A.
126 E3 Coco, Cayo isld Cuba
111 F12 Cocodrie Louisiana U.S.A.
100 J1 Cocolalla Idaho U.S.A.
103 M6 Coconino Plat Arizona U.S.A.
139 H5 Cocoparra Rge New South Wales Australia
71 E5 Cocoro isld Philippines
127 P2 Cocos B Trinidad
81 G6 Cocos I Indian Oc
90 A8 Cocos I Pacific Oc
90 A8 Cocos Ridge Pacific Oc
83 L13 Cocotte, Mt Mauritius
124 H7 Cocula Mexico
6 M5 Cod oil rig North Sea
43 C8 Coda Cavallo, C Sardinia
48 L4 Codăeşti Romania
128 F4 Codajas Brazil
107 L2 Codell Kansas U.S.A.
118 L8 Coderre Saskatchewan Canada
119 N5 Codette Saskatchewan Canada
144 A7 Codfish I New Zealand
115 N6 Cod I Labrador, Nfld Canada
9 F4 Codicote England
42 E4 Codigoro Italy
48 J5 Codlea Romania
129 K4 Codó Brazil
44 G1 Codogno Italy
127 N6 Codrington Barbuda W Indies
123 N6 Codroy Newfoundland Canada
123 O5 Codroy Pond Newfoundland Canada
48 G4 Codrului Muntii mts Romania
122 G8 Cody New Brunswick Canada
98 E7 Cody Nebraska U.S.A.
101 Q5 Cody Wyoming U.S.A.
94 E10 Coeburn Virginia U.S.A.
121 N8 Coe Hill Ontario Canada
141 G2 Coen Queensland Australia
141 F2 Coen R Queensland Australia
32 F9 Coesfeld W Germany
81 C6 Coëtivy Is Indian Oc
100 J2 Coeur d'Alene Idaho U.S.A.
22 E5 Coeuvres et Valsery France
25 G3 Coevorden Netherlands
21 K5 Coevrons, les mts France
20 G8 Coëx France
112 E6 Coffee Georgia U.S.A.
117 D4 Coffee Creek Yukon Territory Canada
101 P2 Coffee Creek Montana U.S.A.
110 G2 Coffeen Illinois U.S.A.
111 L10 Coffee Springs Alabama U.S.A.
111 G8 Coffeeville Mississippi U.S.A.
107 P4 Coffeyville Kansas U.S.A.
138 D5 Coffin B South Australia Australia
123 L6 Coffin I Madeleine Is, Quebec Canada
139 L4 Coffs Harbour New South Wales Australia
17 G5 Cofrentes Spain
48 M6 Cogealac Romania
9 G4 Coggeshall England
42 B3 Coggiola Italy
99 P7 Coggon Iowa U.S.A.
43 B8 Coghinas R Sardinia
43 C8 Coghinas, L.d Sardinia
142 G4 Coghlan, Mt Western Australia Australia
18 E7 Cognac France
40 F6 Cogne, V.de Italy
44 E3 Cogoleto Italy
16 E4 Cogolludo Spain
41 N5 Cógolo Italy
98 J3 Cogswell North Dakota U.S.A.
101 T2 Cohagen Montana U.S.A.
20 E5 Cohiniac France
95 K4 Cohocton R New York U.S.A.
94 K4 Cohocton New York U.S.A.
95 O4 Cohoes New York U.S.A.
139 G6 Cohuna Victoria Australia
112 C3 Cohutta Georgia U.S.A.
125 O6 Coiba, I Panama
133 C8 Coig R Argentina
21 O4 Coignières France
133 C7 Coihaique Chile
76 C5 Coimbatore India
129 G7 Coimbra Brazil
16 B4 Coimbra Portugal
16 D8 Coin Spain
110 A1 Coin Iowa U.S.A.
128 E7 Coipasa, L Bolivia
Coire see Chur Switzerland
19 N15 Coiron, Mts du France
128 E2 Cojedes state Venezuela
128 B3 Cojimies Ecuador
48 H4 Cojocna Romania
127 J9 Cojoro Venezuela
133 D7 Cojudo Blanco mt Argentina
47 N10 Cok R Turkey
99 M4 Cokato Minnesota U.S.A.
94 G6 Cokeburg Pennsylvania U.S.A.
101 P7 Cokeville Wyoming U.S.A.
26 O2 Cokkarassa mt Norway
139 G7 Colac Victoria Australia
144 A7 Colac New Zealand
131 B2 Colanguil, Cerro de mt Argentina
130 H6 Colatina Brazil
36 F2 Cölbe W Germany
146 B10 Colbeck, C Antarctica
100 H2 Colbert Washington U.S.A.
33 P8 Colbitz East Germany
33 P8 Colbitz-Letzlinger Heide East Germany
121 N8 Colborne Ontario Canada
107 J2 Colby Kansas U.S.A.
99 Q5 Colby Wisconsin U.S.A.
128 D7 Colca R Peru
9 G4 Colchester England
95 P5 Colchester Connecticut U.S.A.
99 Q9 Colchester Illinois U.S.A.
8 D5 Cold Ashton England
116 F9 Cold B Alaska U.S.A.
44 B2 Col de Longet France
94 J4 Colden New York U.S.A.
13 F4 Cold Fell mt England
13 F2 Coldingham Scotland
37 O1 Colditz East Germany
118 G4 Cold L Alberta Canada
119 Q3 Cold L Manitoba Canada
99 M4 Cold Spring Minnesota U.S.A.
109 M5 Coldspring Texas U.S.A.
13 F2 Coldstream Scotland
121 L8 Coldwater Ontario Canada
107 L4 Coldwater Kansas U.S.A.
94 C5 Coldwater Michigan U.S.A.
111 F7 Coldwater R Mississippi U.S.A.
110 M1 Coldwater Ohio U.S.A.
108 C7 Coldwater Cr Texas/Okla U.S.A.
120 D4 Coldwell Ontario Canada
139 H8 Colebrook Tasmania Australia
121 T8 Colebrook New Hampshire U.S.A.
110 C3 Cole Camp Missouri U.S.A.
116 Q2 Coleen R Alaska U.S.A.
8 D4 Coleford England
94 J5 Colegrove Pennsylvania U.S.A.
141 F2 Coleman R Queensland Australia
118 C9 Coleman Alberta Canada
113 E9 Coleman Florida U.S.A.
94 C3 Coleman Michigan U.S.A.
109 H4 Coleman Texas U.S.A.
22 B2 Colembert France
138 F6 Coleraine Victoria Australia
121 T7 Coleraine Quebec Canada
14 E1 Coleraine N Ireland
99 N2 Coleraine Minnesota U.S.A.
118 G9 Coleridge Alberta Canada
98 J7 Coleridge Nebraska U.S.A.
139 J8 Coles B Tasmania Australia
89 D8 Colesberg S Africa
8 E4 Colesborne England
9 E2 Coleshill England
128 D7 Coles, Pta C Peru
118 H7 Coleville Saskatchewan Canada
102 E3 Coleville California U.S.A.
119 O9 Colfax Saskatchewan Canada
102 D2 Colfax California U.S.A.
110 H1 Colfax Illinois U.S.A.
110 K1 Colfax Indiana U.S.A.
99 N8 Colfax Iowa U.S.A.
111 D10 Colfax Louisiana U.S.A.
106 F5 Colfax New Mexico U.S.A.
100 H3 Colfax Washington U.S.A.
99 P4 Colfax Wisconsin U.S.A.
119 O9 Colgate Saskatchewan Canada
133 D7 Colhué Huapi, L Argentina
131 B5 Coliauco Argentina
131 B7 Colico, L Chile
25 A5 Colijnsplaat Netherlands
124 H8 Colima Mexico
129 K5 Colinas Brazil
13 F1 Colinsburgh Scotland
118 D4 Colinton Alberta Canada
13 E2 Colinton Scotland
12 C2 Colintraive Scotland
15 B4 Coll isld Scotland
139 H4 Collabah New South Wales Australia
139 J3 Collarenebri New South Wales Australia
106 C2 Collbran Colorado U.S.A.
42 D5 Colle di Val d'Elsa Italy
89 F3 Colleen Bawn Zimbabwe
116 O4 College Alaska U.S.A.
110 M2 College Corner Indiana U.S.A.
110 K6 College Grove Tennessee U.S.A.
111 M8 College Park Georgia U.S.A.
95 L7 College Park Maryland U.S.A.
100 G3 College Place Washington U.S.A.
109 L5 College Station Texas U.S.A.
45 P6 Collelongo Italy
139 H3 Collerina New South Wales Australia
42 C5 Collesalvetti Italy
45 J4 Collesalvetti Italy
45 R7 Colle Sannita Italy
109 N9 Colleyville Texas U.S.A.
45 N6 Colli Albani Italy
139 J4 Collie New South Wales Australia
143 B10 Collie Western Australia Australia
143 B10 Collie Cardiff Western Australia Australia
142 E3 Collier B Western Australia Australia
113 F12 Collier City Florida U.S.A.
143 C6 Collier Ra mts Western Australia Australia
110 G6 Collierville Tennessee U.S.A.
8 B6 Colliford L England
12 E3 Collin Scotland
45 J3 Collina, Passo di Italy
20 E5 Collinée France
21 O3 Collines-du-Vexin, Plaine et France
9 E5 Collingbourne Kingston England
9 F1 Collingham England
13 G6 Collingham England
95 N7 Collingswood New Jersey U.S.A.
141 F5 Collingwood Queensland Australia
120 K8 Collingwood Ontario Canada
145 D4 Collingwood New Zealand
112 E5 Collins Georgia U.S.A.
111 G10 Collins Mississippi U.S.A.
110 C4 Collins Missouri U.S.A.
101 O2 Collins Montana U.S.A.
94 J4 Collins New York U.S.A.
114 J3 Collinson Pen Northwest Territories Canada
111 E9 Collinston Louisiana U.S.A.
14 E3 Collinstown Ireland
141 J5 Collinsville Queensland Australia
111 L7 Collinsville Alabama U.S.A.
110 G3 Collinsville Illinois U.S.A.
107 P5 Collinsville Oklahoma U.S.A.
110 J6 Collinwood Tennessee U.S.A.
41 M6 Collio Italy
120 J1 Collis Ontario Canada
37 Q1 Cölln East Germany
19 Q18 Collobrières France
131 B8 Collon Cura R Argentina
14 C2 Collooney Ireland
107 K2 Collyer Kansas U.S.A.
40 F1 Colmar France
37 J5 Colmberg W Germany
133 E3 Colmena Argentina
16 E8 Colmenar Spain
16 E4 Colmenar de Oreja Spain
16 E4 Colmenar Vieja Spain
109 N5 Colmesneil Texas U.S.A.
12 D3 Colmonell Scotland
21 J5 Colmont R France
106 F5 Colmor New Mexico U.S.A.
13 F6 Colne England
9 G4 Colne, R England
124 A2 Colnett, C Mexico
139 K5 Colo R New South Wales Australia
99 N7 Colo Iowa U.S.A.
41 O7 Cologna Italy
45 K1 Cologna Veneta Italy
Cologne see Köln
99 N5 Cologne Minnesota U.S.A.
94 A4 Coloma Michigan U.S.A.
99 R5 Coloma Wisconsin U.S.A.
21 K3 Colombelles France
40 A1 Colombey les Deux Églises France
129 J8 Colombia Brazil
108 H8 Colombia Mexico
128 C3 Colombia rep S America
90 B7 Colombian Basin Atlantic Oc
121 N4 Colombiere Quebec Canada
83 J11 Colombo Sri Lanka
20 G3 Colomby France
98 G6 Colome South Dakota U.S.A.
133 E4 Colón Argentina
126 D3 Colón Cuba
125 P5 Colón Panama
94 B5 Colon Michigan U.S.A.
138 B4 Colona South Australia Australia
126 G3 Colonel Hill Crooked I Bahamas
131 F5 Colonia Uruguay
133 D5 Colonia Catriel Argentina
131 D7 Colonia Choele Choel isld Argentina
133 F4 Colonia del Sac Uruguay
124 E2 Colonia Díaz Mexico
133 D7 Colonia las Heras Argentina
95 K8 Colonial Beach Virginia U.S.A.
94 K9 Colonial Heights Virginia U.S.A.
95 L9 Colonial Nat. Hist. Park Virginia U.S.A.
130 H4 Colônia, R Brazil
125 M2 Colón, Montañas de ra Honduras
43 H9 Colonna, C Italy
119 M7 Colonsay Saskatchewan Canada
15 B4 Colonsay isld Scotland
107 P3 Colony Kansas U.S.A.
131 D7 Colorada Grande, L Argentina
127 N10 Coloradito Venezuela
131 B5 Colorado R Chile
106 B2 Colorado state U.S.A.
103 L5 Colorado R Arizona U.S.A.
106 B2 Colorado R Colorado U.S.A.
109 J4 Colorado R Texas U.S.A.
103 J10 Colorado, Cerro pk Mexico
108 G3 Colorado City Texas U.S.A.
131 E7 Colorado, Delta del R Argentina
106 B2 Colorado Nat.Mon Colorado U.S.A.
103 N5 Colorado Plat Arizona U.S.A.
103 K7 Colorado R.Aqueduct California U.S.A.
106 F3 Colorado Springs Colorado U.S.A.
16 C4 Colorico da Beira Portugal
45 H2 Colorno Italy
19 Q17 Colostre R France
125 L10 Colotepec Mexico
124 H6 Colotlán Mexico
20 E6 Colpo France
120 K8 Colpoys B Ontario Canada
133 D1 Colquechaca Bolivia
111 M10 Colquitt Georgia U.S.A.
9 F2 Colsterworth England
101 T4 Colstrip Montana U.S.A.
108 D8 Coltexo Texas U.S.A.
9 H2 Coltishall England
102 G7 Colton California U.S.A.
95 L8 Colton Maryland U.S.A.
95 N2 Colton New York U.S.A.
98 K6 Colton South Dakota U.S.A.
103 O2 Colton Utah U.S.A.
100 H3 Colton Washington U.S.A.
117 O10 Columbia R British Columbia Canada
111 L10 Columbia Alabama U.S.A.
113 E7 Columbia Florida U.S.A.
110 F3 Columbia Illinois U.S.A.
94 B9 Columbia Kentucky U.S.A.
111 D9 Columbia Louisiana U.S.A.
95 L7 Columbia Maryland U.S.A.
111 G10 Columbia Mississippi U.S.A.
110 D3 Columbia Missouri U.S.A.
112 L2 Columbia North Carolina U.S.A.
95 L6 Columbia Pennsylvania U.S.A.
112 F3 Columbia South Carolina U.S.A.
98 H4 Columbia South Dakota U.S.A.
110 J6 Columbia Tennessee U.S.A.
94 J9 Columbia Virginia U.S.A.
100 E4 Columbia R Wash/Oregon U.S.A.
117 O11 Columbia R Wash/Br Col U.S.A./Canada
100 F2 Columbia Basin reg Washington U.S.A.
115 N1 Columbia, C Northwest Territories Canada
94 B5 Columbia City Indiana U.S.A.
95 L8 Columbia, Dist. of (D.C.) U.S.A.
101 L1 Columbia Falls Montana U.S.A.
116 O6 Columbia Glacier Alaska U.S.A.
117 Q10 Columbia Lake British Columbia Canada
117 P9 Columbia, Mt Br Col/Alberta Canada
114 G7 Columbia Mts British Columbia Canada
111 K8 Columbiana Alabama U.S.A.
94 G6 Columbiana Ohio U.S.A.
100 E2 Columbia River Washington U.S.A.
98 H4 Columbia Road Res South Dakota U.S.A.
95 O4 Columbiaville New York U.S.A.
106 D1 Columbine Colorado U.S.A.
101 T6 Columbine Wyoming U.S.A.
89 A9 Columbine, C S Africa
17 H5 Columbretes, I Spain
111 M9 Columbus Georgia U.S.A.
110 L2 Columbus Indiana U.S.A.
107 Q4 Columbus Kansas U.S.A.
111 H8 Columbus Mississippi U.S.A.
101 Q4 Columbus Montana U.S.A.
98 J8 Columbus Nebraska U.S.A.
106 C10 Columbus New Mexico U.S.A.
98 D1 Columbus North Dakota U.S.A.
94 D7 Columbus Ohio U.S.A.
109 L6 Columbus Texas U.S.A.
99 R6 Columbus Wisconsin U.S.A.
126 G3 Columbus Bank Bahamas
99 P8 Columbus City Iowa U.S.A.
126 G2 Columbus Mon San Salvador Bahamas
126 G2 Columbus Pt Cat I Bahamas
127 M2 Columbus Pt Tobago
102 B2 Colusa California U.S.A.
12 E4 Colvend Scotland
94 J6 Colver Pennsylvania U.S.A.
145 E2 Colville New Zealand
116 L2 Colville R Alaska U.S.A.
100 H1 Colville Washington U.S.A.
114 G4 Colville L Northwest Territories Canada
143 F8 Colville, Lake Western Australia Australia
137 Q8 Colville Ridge sea feature Pacific Oc
13 F3 Colwell England
99 O6 Colwell Iowa U.S.A.
8 C1 Colwyn Bay Wales
8 C6 Colyford England
45 M2 Comacchio Italy
125 O10 Comalapa Guatemala
125 N8 Comalcalco Mexico
131 B8 Comallo R Argentina
48 K6 Comana Romania
107 N7 Comanche Oklahoma U.S.A.
109 J4 Comanche Texas U.S.A.
146 D3 Comandante Ferraz Brazil Base Antarctica
133 D7 Comandante Luis Piedrabuena Argentina
133 D4 Comandante Salas Argentina
48 K4 Comăneşti Romania
48 K5 Comarnic Romania
125 L2 Comayagua Honduras
16 B4 Comba Dão Portugal
112 G5 Combahee R South Carolina U.S.A.
133 C4 Combarbala Chile
40 C2 Combeaufontaine France
8 B5 Combe Martin England
120 H10 Comber Ontario Canada
14 F2 Comber N Ireland
121 N7 Combermere Ontario Canada
68 A3 Combermere B Burma
109 K9 Combes Texas U.S.A.
22 D3 Combles France
69 F12 Combol isld Indonesia
20 G5 Combourg France
139 L4 Comboyne New South Wales Australia
21 N5 Combres France
20 B6 Combrit France
94 D9 Combs Kentucky U.S.A.
131 D4 Comechingones, Sa. de ra Argentina
38 G8 Comeglians Italy
38 G8 Comelico Italy
130 E6 Comendador Gomes Brazil
111 L9 Comer Alabama U.S.A.
112 D3 Comer Georgia U.S.A.
14 D4 Comeragh Mts Ireland
130 H5 Comercinho Brazil
98 B1 Comertown Montana U.S.A.
141 J6 Comet R Queensland Australia
141 J6 Comet Queensland Australia
109 J6 Comfort Texas U.S.A.
99 M5 Comfrey Minnesota U.S.A.
75 O7 Comilla Bangladesh
22 E2 Comines France
43 F12 Comino isld Malta
43 C8 Comino, C Sardinia
94 C2 Comins Michigan U.S.A.
43 F12 Comiso Sicily
125 N9 Comitán de Dominguez Mexico
20 C5 Commana France
121 L7 Commanda Ontario Canada
18 G6 Commentry France
20 G8 Commequiers France
21 J5 Commer France
112 D3 Commerce Georgia U.S.A.
107 Q5 Commerce Oklahoma U.S.A.
109 M2 Commerce Texas U.S.A.
106 F2 Commerce City Colorado U.S.A.
19 J4 Commercy France
45 J1 Commessaggio Italy
121 S4 Commissaires, Lac des Quebec Canada
115 L4 Committee B Northwest Territories Canada
146 D14 Commonwealth B Antarctica
138 C3 Commonwealth Hill South Australia Australia
139 K6 Commonwealth Terr New South Wales Australia
41 K6 Como Italy
106 E2 Como Colorado U.S.A.
111 G7 Como Mississippi U.S.A.
133 D7 Comodoro Rivadavia Argentina
41 K5 Como, Lago di Italy
124 D4 Comondú Mexico
125 J7 Comonfort Mexico
76 C6 Comorin, C India
81 B7 Comoro Ridge Indian Oc
87 G10 Comoros islds, rep Indian Oc
118 G7 Compeer Alberta Canada
22 D5 Compiègne France
22 D5 Compiègne, Forêt de France
124 G7 Compostela Mexico
71 G7 Compostela Mindanao Philippines
130 F9 Comprida, I São Paulo Brazil
102 A2 Comptche California U.S.A.
102 F8 Compton California U.S.A.
99 R8 Compton Illinois U.S.A.
12 E1 Comrie Scotland
95 O3 Comstock New York U.S.A.
108 F6 Comstock Texas U.S.A.
45 O4 Cona Italy
66 E5 Co Nag L China
85 B7 Conakry Guinea
133 D6 Cona Niyeo Argentina
112 C3 Conasauga R Georgia U.S.A.
98 D6 Conata South Dakota U.S.A.
45 N4 Conca R Italy
108 H6 Concan Texas U.S.A.
20 C6 Concarneau France
130 H9 Conceição Paraíba Brazil
130 H6 Conceição da Barra Brazil
130 E6 Conceiçao das Alagoas Brazil
129 J5 Conceiçao do Araguaia Brazil
130 G6 Conceição do Mato Dentro Brazil
133 D3 Concepción Argentina
128 E6 Concepcíon Beni Bolivia
128 F7 Concepción Santa Cruz Bolivia
131 A6 Concepcion Chile
124 C2 Concepcion R Mexico
130 B8 Concepción dept Paraguay
130 B8 Concepción Paraguay
131 A6 Concepción, B. del Chile
133 B8 Concepción, Can str Chile
130 C10 Concepción de la Sierra Argentina
124 J5 Concepción del Oro Mexico
131 F4 Concepción del Uruguay Argentina
128 F7 Concepción, L Bolivia
124 D4 Concepción, Pta C Mexico
99 M9 Conception Missouri U.S.A.
123 U6 Conception B Newfoundland Canada
87 B10 Conception B Namibia
123 T6 Conception Harb Newfoundland Canada
126 G3 Conception I Bahamas
83 K12 Conception I Mahé I Indian Oc
124 G6 Concha Mexico
130 E8 Conchas Brazil
106 F6 Conchas New Mexico U.S.A.
106 F6 Conchas Lake New Mexico U.S.A.
21 M4 Conches France
133 D2 Conchi Chile
124 G4 Concho Mexico
103 P7 Concho Arizona U.S.A.
107 N6 Concho Oklahoma U.S.A.
108 G4 Concho R Texas U.S.A.
108 B7 Conchos, Rio Mexico
102 B4 Concord California U.S.A.
111 M8 Concord Georgia U.S.A.
94 C4 Concord Michigan U.S.A.
98 K7 Concord Nebraska U.S.A.
95 Q3 Concord New Hampshire U.S.A.
112 G2 Concord North Carolina U.S.A.
95 Q2 Concord Vermont U.S.A.
131 F3 Concordia Argentina
130 D10 Concórdia Brazil
124 F6 Concordia Mexico
107 N2 Concordia Kansas U.S.A.
110 C3 Concordia Missouri U.S.A.
45 J2 Concórdia sulla Secchia Italy
100 D1 Concrete Washington U.S.A.
68 G3 Con Cuong Vietnam
101 O7 Conda Idaho U.S.A.
141 K7 Condamine R Queensland Australia
141 K7 Condamine Queensland Australia
18 G7 Condat France
129 L6 Cónde Brazil
98 H4 Conde South Dakota U.S.A.
88 E9 Condédzi R Mozambique
125 L3 Condega Nicaragua
21 M5 Condé-sur-Huîsne France
22 F3 Condé-sur-l'Escaut France
21 J4 Condé-sur-Noireau France
21 O4 Condé-sur-Vesgres France
21 H3 Condé-sur-Vire France
130 H4 Condeúba Brazil
139 H5 Condobolin New South Wales Australia
18 F9 Condom France
100 E4 Condon Oregon U.S.A.
142 C5 Condon Creek B Western Australia Australia
128 C4 Condor, Cord. del mts Ecuador/Peru
12 D2 Condorrat Scotland
19 N14 Condrieu France
22 J3 Condroz Belgium
142 E3 Cone B Western Australia Australia
111 K10 Conecuh R Alabama U.S.A.
42 E3 Conegliano Italy
17 J5 Conejera isld Balearic Is
106 D4 Conejos Colorado U.S.A.
94 H6 Conemaugh R Pennsylvania U.S.A.
45 O4 Cónero, M mt Italy
133 E6 Conesa Argentina
94 K4 Conesus L New York U.S.A.
99 P8 Conesville Iowa U.S.A.
94 F6 Conesville Ohio U.S.A.
123 Q4 Coney Arm Newfoundland Canada
90 C1 Coney I Bermuda
95 O6 Coney Island New York U.S.A.
40 D2 Conflans France
19 J3 Conflans-Jarny France
21 P4 Conflans-Ste. Honorine France
21 P2 Conflans-Ste. Honorine Villers-Bretonneux France
94 H7 Confluence Pennsylvania U.S.A.
18 F6 Confolens France
103 L2 Confusion Range Utah U.S.A.
130 B9 Confuso, R Paraguay
14 B3 Cong Ireland
112 G4 Congaree R South Carolina U.S.A.
112 G4 Congaree Swamp Nat. Mon South Carolina U.S.A.
67 D5 Conghua China
67 C4 Congjiang China
8 D1 Congleton England
85 C6 Congo R West Africa
86 C6 Congo rep W Africa
Congo (Brazzaville) rep see Congo rep
Congo (Kinshasa) rep see Zaïre rep
130 G7 Congonhas Brazil
8 D5 Congresbury England
118 L9 Congress Saskatchewan Canada
21 H6 Congrier France
68 J5 Cong Tum Vietnam
20 D7 Conguel, Pte. de France
133 C6 Cónico mt Chile/Arg

21 N5 **Conie** *R* France
106 E2 **Conifer** Colorado U.S.A.
9 F1 **Coningsby** England
13 G6 **Conisbrough** England
140 B5 **Coniston** N Terr Australia
120 K6 **Coniston** Ontario Canada
13 E5 **Coniston** England
141 G4 **Conjuboy** Queensland Australia
118 F3 **Conklin** Alberta Canada
108 B7 **Conlen** Texas U.S.A.
21 K5 **Conlie** France
40 C4 **Conliège** France
120 K4 **Connaught** Ontario Canada
14 B3 **Connaught** *prov* Ireland
142 E6 **Connaughton, Mt** Western Australia **Australia**
19 N16 **Connaux** France
94 G5 **Conneaut** Ohio U.S.A.
94 G5 **Conneautville** Pennsylvania U.S.A.
95 O5 **Connecticut** *state* U.S.A.
95 P3 **Connecticut** *R* U.S.A.
15 C4 **Connel Ferry** Scotland
100 G3 **Connell** Washington U.S.A.
94 H6 **Connellsville** Pennsylvania U.S.A.
141 F6 **Connemara** Queensland Australia
14 B3 **Connemara** *dist* Ireland
101 L4 **Conner** Montana U.S.A.
140 B7 **Conner, Mt** N Terr Australia
138 B2 **Conner, Mt** N Terr Australia
21 M5 **Connerre** France
94 B7 **Connersville** Indiana U.S.A.
14 B2 **Conn, L** Ireland
142 F2 **Connor, Mt** Western Australia Australia
122 D6 **Connors** New Brunswick Canada
141 J5 **Connors Ra** *mts* Queensland Australia
128 C4 **Cononaco** *R* Ecuador
112 F2 **Conover** North Carolina U.S.A.
99 R3 **Conover** Wisconsin U.S.A.
33 S6 **Conow** East Germany
20 G6 **Conquereuil** France
118 K7 **Conquest** Saskatchewan Canada
20 A5 **Conquet, le** France
130 F6 **Conquista** Brazil
101 O1 **Conrad** Montana U.S.A.
139 J7 **Conran, C** Victoria Australia
99 Q4 **Conrath** Wisconsin U.S.A.
109 M5 **Conroe** Texas U.S.A.
109 M5 **Conroe, L** Texas U.S.A.
45 L2 **Consandolo** Italy
121 N9 **Consecon** Ontario Canada
130 G7 **Conselheiro Lafaiete** Brazil
45 L3 **Conselice** Italy
45 L1 **Conselve** Italy
22 J5 **Consenvoye** France
13 G4 **Consett** England
95 M6 **Conshohocken** Pennsylvania U.S.A.
22 H4 **Cons-la-Grandville** France
126 C3 **Consolación del Sur** Cuba
69 H8 **Con Son** *isld* Vietnam
69 H8 **Con Son** Vietnam
118 G6 **Consort** Alberta Canada
95 M3 **Constableville** New York U.S.A.
Constance *see* **Konstanz**
143 E6 **Constance Headland** *hill* Western Australia Australia
Constance, L *see* **Bodensee**
128 F5 **Constância dos Baetas** Brazil
48 M6 **Constanța** Romania
16 D7 **Constantina** Spain
85 F1 **Constantine** Algeria
94 B5 **Constantine** Michigan U.S.A.
116 H7 **Constantine, C** Alaska U.S.A.
117 C5 **Constantine, Mt** Yukon Territory Canada
Constantinople *see* **İstanbul**
127 N4 **Constant, Morne** *hill* Guadeloupe W Indies
127 L2 **Constant Spring** Jamaica
131 A5 **Constitución** Chile
141 J6 **Consuelo** Queensland Australia
118 H9 **Consul** Saskatchewan Canada
101 L8 **Contact** Nevada U.S.A.
130 G7 **Contagalo** Brazil
128 D5 **Contamana** Peru
128 F3 **Contão** Brazil
131 D4 **Contara** *R* Argentina
45 M1 **Contarina** Italy
129 K6 **Côntas** *R* Brazil
21 O2 **Conteville** France
40 F5 **Conthey** Switzerland
21 J6 **Contigné** France
103 O10 **Continental** Arizona U.S.A.
94 C5 **Continental** Ohio U.S.A.
106 C4 **Continental Res** Colorado U.S.A.
95 Q3 **Contoocook** New Hampshire U.S.A.
125 Q7 **Contoy, I** Mexico
16 E8 **Contraviesa, Sa** *mts* Spain
121 R7 **Contrecoeur** Quebec Canada
133 C8 **Contreras, I** Chile
21 N7 **Contres** Loir-et-Cher France
22 H5 **Contreuve** France
40 C1 **Contrexéville** France
130 G6 **Contria** Brazil
118 F7 **Control** Alberta Canada
36 C5 **Contwig** W Germany
114 J4 **Contwoyto L** Northwest Territories Canada
21 P2 **Conty** France
126 H10 **Convención** Colombia
43 H8 **Conversano** Italy
94 B6 **Converse** Indiana U.S.A.
111 C10 **Converse** Louisiana U.S.A.
94 C6 **Convoy** Ohio U.S.A.
110 D6 **Conway** Arkansas U.S.A.
99 M9 **Conway** Iowa U.S.A.
110 D4 **Conway** Missouri U.S.A.
95 Q3 **Conway** New Hampshire U.S.A.
112 K1 **Conway** North Carolina U.S.A.
98 J1 **Conway** North Dakota U.S.A.
112 H4 **Conway** South Carolina U.S.A.
8 C1 **Conway B** Wales
141 J5 **Conway, C** Queensland Australia
138 D3 **Conway, L** South Australia Australia
110 D6 **Conway, L** Arkansas U.S.A.
140 C6 **Conway, Mt** N Terr Australia
95 Q2 **Conway, N** New Hampshire U.S.A.
144 D5 **Conway R** New Zealand
107 N4 **Conway Springs** Kansas U.S.A.
8 B4 **Conwil Elvet** Wales
8 C1 **Conwy** Wales
8 C1 **Conwy R** Wales
112 C4 **Conyers** Georgia U.S.A.
22 K3 **Coo** Belgium
138 C3 **Coober Pedy** South Australia Australia
9 G6 **Cooden** England
142 A3 **Coogee** *dist* Perth, W Aust Australia
142 A3 **Coogee L** Western Australia Australia
142 C5 **Cooglegong** Western Australia Australia
141 J7 **Coogoon** *R* Queensland Australia
140 C2 **Cooinda** N Terr Australia
138 B4 **Cook** South Australia Australia
99 O2 **Cook** Minnesota U.S.A.
99 K9 **Cook** Nebraska U.S.A.
133 C9 **Cook, B.de** Chile
117 K10 **Cook, C** British Columbia Canada
101 Q4 **Cooke City** Montana U.S.A.
143 B9 **Cooke, Mt** Western Australia Australia
94 B10 **Cookeville** Tennessee U.S.A.
9 F4 **Cookham** England
146 D13 **Cook Ice Shelf** Antarctica
118 D5 **Cooking L** Alberta Canada
116 L7 **Cook Inlet** Alaska U.S.A.
134 L10 **Cook Is** Pacific Oc
144 C5 **Cook, Mt** New Zealand
117 D5 **Cook, Mt** Alaska/Yukon Terr U.S.A./Canada
99 U4 **Cooks** Michigan U.S.A.
123 Q2 **Cook's Hbr** Newfoundland Canada
121 T7 **Cookshire** Quebec **Canada**
141 H2 **Cook's Passage** Queensland Australia
106 C9 **Cooks Pk** New Mexico U.S.A.
121 L8 **Cookstown** Ontario Canada
14 E2 **Cookstown** N Ireland
145 E4 **Cook Strait** New Zealand
141 H3 **Cooktown** Queensland Australia
141 H7 **Cooladdi** Queensland Australia
139 J4 **Coolah** New South Wales Australia
139 H5 **Coolamon** New South Wales Australia
139 L3 **Coolangatta** New South Wales **Australia**
141 L8 **Coolangatta** Queensland Australia
143 C8 **Coolarda** *hill* Western Australia **Australia**
142 A2 **Coolbellup, L** Western Australia **Australia**
112 G2 **Cooleemee** North Carolina U.S.A.
143 D9 **Coolgardie** Western Australia Australia
140 B3 **Coolibah** N Terr **Australia**
103 N9 **Coolidge** Arizona U.S.A.
112 D6 **Coolidge** Georgia U.S.A.
109 L4 **Coolidge** Texas U.S.A.
127 P4 **Coolidge** *airport* Antigua W Indies
103 O8 **Coolidge Dam** Arizona U.S.A.
143 B8 **Coolimba** Western Australia Australia
100 J1 **Coolin** Idaho U.S.A.
141 K8 **Coolmunda Dam** Queensland **Australia**
142 A4 **Cooloongup, L** Western Australia **Australia**
94 F7 **Coolville** Ohio U.S.A.
143 B7 **Coolyun Well** Western Australia **Australia**
139 J6 **Cooma** New South Wales Australia
14 A5 **Coomacarrea** *mt* Ireland
9 E5 **Coombe Bissett** England
8 D4 **Coombe Hill** England
143 B9 **Coomberdale** Western Australia **Australia**
139 J4 **Coonabarabran** New South Wales **Australia**
138 F6 **Coonalpyn** South Australia Australia
139 J4 **Coonamble** New South Wales **Australia**
143 E9 **Coonana** Western Australia Australia
138 F6 **Coonawarra** South Australia Australia
138 F5 **Coonbah Roadhouse** New South Wales **Australia**
138 D4 **Coondambo** South Australia Australia
76 B4 **Coondapoor** India
142 C5 **Coongan, R** Western Australia **Australia**
141 H8 **Coongoola** Queensland Australia
138 C2 **Coongra** *R* South Australia Australia
138 F2 **Cooninnie, L** South Australia Australia
76 C5 **Coonoor** India
99 M8 **Coon Rapids** Iowa U.S.A.
99 N4 **Coon Rapids** Minnesota U.S.A.
140 C1 **Cooper** *R* N Terr **Australia**
129 G8 **Cooper** Paraguay
109 M2 **Cooper** Texas U.S.A.
141 F7 **Cooper Cr** Qnsld/S Aust Australia
144 A6 **Cooper I** New Zealand
143 G7 **Cooper, Mt** Western Australia Australia
139 L4 **Coopernook** New South Wales **Australia**
141 K2 **Coopers Plains** *dist* Brisbane, Qnsld **Australia**
113 K11 **Cooper's Town** Bahamas
126 F1 **Coopers Town** Great Abaco I **Bahamas**
95 M4 **Cooperstown** New York U.S.A.
98 H2 **Cooperstown** North Dakota U.S.A.
94 B3 -**Coopersville** Michigan U.S.A.
127 O3 **Coora** Trinidad
138 B4 **Coorabie** South Australia Australia
140 F6 **Coorabulka** Queensland Australia
143 B7 **Coor-de-Wandy** *mt* Western Australia **Australia**
138 E6 **Coorong, The** *L* South Australia **Australia**
143 B8 **Coorow** Western Australia Australia
141 L7 **Cooroy** Queensland **Australia**
111 L7 **Coosa** *R* Alabama U.S.A.
112 C3 **Coosawattee** *R* Georgia U.S.A.
112 F5 **Coosawhatchie** *R* South Carolina U.S.A.
100 A6 **Coos Bay** Oregon U.S.A.
139 J5 **Cootamundra** New South Wales **Australia**
14 E2 **Cootehill** Ireland
141 K7 **Cooyar** Queensland **Australia**
131 B6 **Copahué** *pk* Chile
133 C5 **Copahue** *mt* Chile/Arg
100 A2 **Copalis Beach** Washington U.S.A.
109 K7 **Copano B** Texas U.S.A.
100 C8 **Copco** California U.S.A.
106 H2 **Cope** Colorado U.S.A.
128 F4 **Copea, Paraná** *R* Brazil
113 F12 **Copeland** Florida U.S.A.
100 J1 **Copeland** Idaho U.S.A.
107 K4 **Copeland** Kansas U.S.A.
94 B2 **Copemish** Michigan U.S.A.
Copenhagen *see* **København**
95 M3 **Copenhagen** New York U.S.A.
133 E5 **Copetonas** Argentina
139 K3 **Copeton Res.** New South Wales **Australia**
133 D3 **Copiapo** *vol* Chile
133 C3 **Copiapó** Chile
15 F2 **Copinsay** Scotland
138 E4 **Copley** South Australia Australia
128 D6 **Coporaque** Peru
45 L2 **Copparo** Italy
120 G3 **Coppell** Ontario Canada
109 N8 **Coppell** Texas U.S.A.
129 G2 **Coppename** *R* Suriname
32 L8 **Coppenbrügge** W Germany
116 P5 **Copper** *R* Alaska U.S.A.
109 K4 **Copperas Cove** Texas U.S.A.
100 G1 **Copper Butte** *mt* Washington U.S.A.
116 P6 **Copper Center** Alaska U.S.A.
120 J6 **Copper Cliff** Ontario Canada
99 T2 **Copper Hbr** Michigan U.S.A.
138 C3 **Copper Hill** South Australia Australia
114 H4 **Coppermine** Northwest Territories **Canada**
120 F6 **Coppermine Pt** *C* Ontario Canada
117 N11 **Copper Mt** British Columbia Canada
100 K8 **Copper Mt** Nevada U.S.A.
117 Q5 **Copp L** Northwest Territories Canada
48 J4 **Copșa Mică** Romania
131 B6 **Copulhue, Paso del** Arg/Chile
75 L3 **Coqên** China
22 B2 **Coquelles** France
13 G3 **Coquet I** England
13 G3 **Coquet, R** England
Coquilhatville *see* **Mbandaka**
100 A6 **Coquille** Oregon U.S.A.
131 B2 **Coquimbo** Chile
101 P7 **Cora** Wyoming U.S.A.
46 G1 **Corabia** Romania
130 G5 **Coração de Jesus** Brazil
139 L3 **Coraki** New South Wales Australia
120 J2 **Coral** Ontario **Canada**
71 C6 **Coral B** Palawan Philippines
113 L9 **Coral Harbour** New Providence I **Bahamas**
115 L5 **Coral Harbour** Northwest Territories **Canada**
137 K4 **Coral Sea Islands Terr** Australasia
99 P8 **Coralville Lake** *res* Iowa U.S.A.
101 L1 **Coram** Montana U.S.A.
139 G7 **Corangamite, L** Victoria Australia
129 G3 **Corantijn** *R* Suriname
94 G6 **Coraopolis** Pennsylvania U.S.A.
43 G7 **Corato** Italy
20 C5 **Coray** France
21 P4 **Corbeil-Essonnes** France
19 P13 **Corbelin** France
22 F5 **Corbény** France
120 K8 **Corbetton** Ontario Canada
21 P2 **Corbie** France
20 F3 **Corbiere** Channel Is
18 G10 **Corbières** *reg* France
18 H5 **Corbigny** France
94 C10 **Corbin** Kentucky U.S.A.
123 R7 **Corbin Hd** Newfoundland Canada
45 M1 **Córbola** Italy
16 D7 **Corbones** *R* Spain
13 F4 **Corbridge** England
9 F2 **Corby** Lincs England
9 F2 **Corby** Northants England
Corcaigh *see* **Cork**
36 B7 **Corcieux** France
102 E5 **Corcoran** California U.S.A.
20 G8 **Corcoué-sur-Logne** France
133 C6 **Corcovado** *mt* Chile
133 C6 **Corcovado, Golfo** Chile
16 A2 **Corcubion** Spain
112 D6 **Cordele** Georgia U.S.A.
107 M6 **Cordell** Oklahoma U.S.A.
20 G7 **Cordemais** France
18 G8 **Cordes** France
129 J5 **Cordilheiras, Serra das** *mts* Brazil
16 D1 **Cordillera Cantábrica** *mts* Spain
128 C3 **Cordillera Central** *mts* Colombia
127 J5 **Cordillera Central** *mts* Dominican Rep
125 O5 **Cordillera Central** *mts* Panama
128 C5 **Cordillera Central** *mts* Peru
71 E2 **Cordillera Central** *mts* Luzon Philippines
127 J10 **Cordillera de Mérida** *mts* Venezuela
128 C3 **Cordillera Occidental** *mts* Colombia
128 D2 **Cordillera Oriental** *mts* Colombia
71 F5 **Cordilleras Ra** Panay Philippines
138 F2 **Cordillo Downs** South Australia Australia
130 G6 **Cordisburgo** Brazil
131 D4 **Cordoba** *prov* Argentina
131 D3 **Córdoba** Argentina
128 C2 **Córdoba** *div* Colombia
125 L8 **Cordoba** Mexico
16 D7 **Córdoba** *prov* Spain
16 D7 **Córdoba** Spain
131 D3 **Cordoba, Sierra de** *ra* Argentina
128 C6 **Córdova** Peru
111 J8 **Cordova** Alabama U.S.A.
116 P6 **Cordova** Alaska U.S.A.
99 Q8 **Cordova** Illinois U.S.A.
121 N8 **Cordova Mines** Ontario Canada
116 P6 **Cordova Pk** Alaska U.S.A.
45 J3 **Coreglia Antelminelli** Italy
140 F4 **Corella** *R* Queensland Australia
140 D4 **Corella L** N Terr Australia
141 G5 **Corfield** Queensland Australia
45 P5 **Corfinio** Italy
Corfu *isld* Greece *see* **Kérkira** *isld*
94 J4 **Corfu** New York U.S.A.
100 F3 **Corfu** Washington U.S.A.
16 C2 **Corgo** Spain
130 C6 **Corguinho** Brazil
45 N6 **Cori** Italy
16 C5 **Coria** Spain
16 C7 **Coria del R** Spain
45 N4 **Coriano** Italy
121 O3 **Coribelle** Quebec Canada
139 K5 **Coricudgy** *mt* New South Wales Australia
43 H9 **Corigliano Calabro** Italy
45 O4 **Corinaldo** Italy
141 K2 **Corinda** *dist* Brisbane, Qnsld Australia
140 E4 **Corinda** Queensland Australia
141 K3 **Coringa Is** Gt Barrier Reef Aust
141 K3 **Coringa Is** Coral Sea
139 H8 **Corinna** Tasmania Australia
101 N8 **Corinne** Utah U.S.A.
Corinth *see* **Kórinthos**
101 S4 **Corinth** Montana U.S.A.
95 O3 **Corinth** New York U.S.A.
Corinth, Gulf of *see* **Korinthiakós Kólpos**
143 C9 **Corinthian** Western Australia Australia
130 G6 **Corinto** Brazil
130 C6 **Corixinha, R** Brazil
14 C5 **Cork** *co* Ireland
14 C5 **Cork** Ireland
20 D5 **Corlay** France
43 E11 **Corleone** Sicily
47 J3 **Çorlu** Turkey
123 P4 **Cormack** Newfoundland Canada
123 Q5 **Cormack** *mt* Newfoundland Canada
21 O5 **Cormainville** France
21 L3 **Cormeilles** France
21 M7 **Cormery** France
22 F5 **Cormicy** France
123 L2 **Cormier, L** Quebec Canada
21 J3 **Cormolain** France
119 R4 **Cormorant** Manitoba Canada
6 L1 **Cormorant** *oil rig* North Sea
123 L4 **Cormorant Pt** Anticosti I, Quebec
107 M6 **Corn** Oklahoma U.S.A.
41 M6 **Corna** Italy
45 P6 **Còrnacchia, Monte** Italy
32 H7 **Cornau** W Germany
21 K7 **Corne** France
112 D3 **Cornelia** Georgia U.S.A.
133 G2 **Cornélio Procópio** Brazil
99 S9 **Cornell** Illinois U.S.A.
99 P4 **Cornell** Wisconsin U.S.A.
123 P5 **Corner Brook** Newfoundland Canada
139 H7 **Corner Inlet** Victoria Australia
110 K6 **Cornersville** Tennessee U.S.A.
111 D9 **Corney L** Louisiana U.S.A.
103 P6 **Cornfields** Arizona U.S.A.
13 F2 **Cornhill-on-Tweed** England
20 H5 **Cornille** France
40 E2 **Cornimont** France
119 P9 **Corning** Saskatchewan Canada
110 F5 **Corning** Arkansas U.S.A.
99 M9 **Corning** Iowa U.S.A.
107 O2 **Corning** Kansas U.S.A.
99 L9 **Corning** Missouri U.S.A.
95 K4 **Corning** New York U.S.A.
94 E7 **Corning** Ohio U.S.A.
Corn Is *see* **Maiz, Is. del**
141 G5 **Cornish** *R* Queensland Australia
95 P3 **Cornish Flat** New Hampshire U.S.A.
142 F5 **Cornish, Mt** Western Australia **Australia**
45 J3 **Corno alle Scale** *mt* Italy
42 F6 **Corno, M** *mt* Italy
20 B5 **Cornouaille** *reg* France
21 J6 **Cornuaille, la** France
100 H4 **Cornucopia** Oregon U.S.A.
99 P3 **Cornucopia** Wisconsin U.S.A.
18 H9 **Cornus** France
121 Q7 **Cornwall** Ontario Canada
8 B7 **Cornwall** *co* England
115 K2 **Cornwallis I** Northwest Territories Canada
138 D5 **Corny Pt** South Australia Australia
127 K9 **Coro** Venezuela
130 G6 **Coroaci** Brazil
129 K4 **Coroatá** Brazil
87 B9 **Coroca** *R* Angola
128 E7 **Corocoro** Bolivia
128 E7 **Coroico** Bolivia
130 F6 **Coromandel** Brazil
145 E2 **Coromandel** New Zealand
76 E5 **Coromandel Coast** India
145 E2 **Coromandel Peninsula** New Zealand
21 J7 **Coron** France
71 E4 **Coron** Philippines
138 F4 **Corona** New South Wales Australia
102 G8 **Corona** California U.S.A.
106 E7 **Corona** New Mexico U.S.A.
119 M9 **Coronach** Saskatchewan Canada
102 G9 **Coronado** California U.S.A.
71 F7 **Coronado B** Mindanao Philippines
125 N5 **Coronado, B.de** Costa Rica
113 G8 **Coronado Beach** Florida U.S.A.
103 O10 **Coronado Nat. Mem** Arizona U.S.A.
118 F6 **Coronation** Alberta Canada
114 H4 **Coronation G** Northwest Territories Canada
146 E3 **Coronation I** S Orkney Is Antarctica
142 E2 **Coronation Is** Western Australia **Australia**
71 E5 **Coron B** Philippines
71 E5 **Coron Delian** *isld* Philippines
131 A6 **Coronel** Chile
133 E5 **Coronel Dorrego** Argentina
130 G6 **Coronel Fabriciano** Brazil
130 C9 **Coronel Oviedo** Paraguay
130 C4 **Coronel Ponce** Brazil
131 E6 **Coronel Pringles** Argentina
131 E6 **Coronel Suárez** Argentina
133 F5 **Coronel Vidal** Argentina
144 B6 **Coronet Pk** New Zealand
128 D7 **Coropuna** *mt* Peru
46 D4 **Çorovodë** Albania
139 H6 **Corowa** New South Wales Australia
126 G10 **Corozal** Colombia
127 O1 **Corozal Pt** Trinidad
20 G6 **Corps-Nuds** France
130 C10 **Corpus** Argentina
109 K8 **Corpus Christi** Texas U.S.A.
133 D1 **Corque** Bolivia
101 L6 **Corral** Idaho U.S.A.
16 E5 **Corralde Almaguer** Spain
124 G5 **Corrales** Mexico
16 D3 **Corrales** Spain
133 F4 **Corrales** Uruguay
126 D3 **Corralillo** Cuba
124 F2 **Corralitos** Mexico
143 B7 **Corrandibby Ra** *mts* Western Australia **Australia**
14 B3 **Corraun** Ireland
14 B3 **Corraun Pen** Ireland
99 L7 **Correctionville** Iowa U.S.A.
71 E3 **Corregidor** Luzon Philippines
130 E5 **Córrego do Ouro** Brazil
129 J6 **Corrente** Brazil
130 D6 **Corrente, R** Goiás Brazil
43 F12 **Correnti, C.I. de** Sicily
129 K6 **Correntina** Brazil
106 C7 **Correo** New Mexico U.S.A.
18 G7 **Corrèze** *dept* France
18 G7 **Corrèze** *R* France
45 K1 **Correzzo** Italy
45 M1 **Corrèzzola** Italy
14 B3 **Corrib, L** Ireland
12 C2 **Corrie** Scotland
130 B10 **Corrientes** Argentina
131 F2 **Corrientes** *prov* Argentina
133 F3 **Corrientes** *R* Argentina
128 C4 **Corrientes** *R* Peru
133 F5 **Corrientes, C** Argentina
126 B4 **Corrientes, C** Cuba
124 G7 **Corrientes, C** Mexico
109 N5 **Corrigan** Texas U.S.A.
143 C9 **Corrigin** Western Australia Australia
139 K5 **Corrimal** New South Wales Australia
13 H6 **Corringham** England
14 B4 **Corrofin** Ireland
94 H5 **Corry** Pennsylvania U.S.A.
139 J6 **Corryong** Victoria Australia
12 C1 **Corryvreckan, Str.of** Scotland
18 L11 **Corse-du-Sud** *dept* Corsica
20 F5 **Corseul** France
12 C3 **Corsewall Pt** Scotland
8 D5 **Corsham** England
18 L10 **Corsica** *isld* France
98 H6 **Corsica** South Dakota U.S.A.
109 L3 **Corsicana** Texas U.S.A.
12 E3 **Corsock Br** Scotland
8 D5 **Corston** England
13 E2 **Corstorphine** Scotland
115 P5 **Cort Adelaer, Kap** *C* Greenland
103 N9 **Cortaro** Arizona U.S.A.
16 C7 **Cortegana** Spain
130 J10 **Cortès** Brazil
106 B4 **Cortez** Colorado U.S.A.
102 H1 **Cortez** Nevada U.S.A.
38 F8 **Cortina d'Ampezzo** Italy
98 K9 **Cortland** Nebraska U.S.A.
95 L4 **Cortland** New York U.S.A.
94 G5 **Cortland** Ohio U.S.A.
9 H2 **Corton** England
42 D5 **Cortona** Italy
85 B6 **Corubal** *R* Guinea/Guinea-Bissau
16 B6 **Coruche** Portugal
78 H1 **Çoruh** *R* Turkey
15 B3 **Coruisk, L** Scotland
78 E1 **Çorum** Turkey
130 B6 **Corumbá** Brazil
130 E4 **Corumbá de Goiás** Brazil
130 E6 **Corumbaíba** Brazil
130 E5 **Corumbá, R** Brazil
130 H5 **Corumbaú, Pta. do** *C* Brazil
128 F6 **Corumbiara** *R* Brazil
128 F2 **Corumo** *R* Venezuela
16 B1 **Coruña** *prov* Spain
Corunna *see* **Lá Coruña**
94 C4 **Corunna** Michigan U.S.A.
130 H11 **Coruripe** Brazil
101 L3 **Corvallis** Montana U.S.A.
100 B5 **Corvallis** Oregon U.S.A.
38 E8 **Corvara in Badia** Italy
32 K9 **Corvey** W Germany
8 C2 **Corwen** Wales
107 M4 **Corwin** Kansas U.S.A.
116 E7 **Corwin, C** Alaska U.S.A.
101 P4 **Corwin Springs** Montana U.S.A.
94 A8 **Corydon** Indiana U.S.A.
99 N9 **Corydon** Iowa U.S.A.
110 J4 **Corydon** Kentucky U.S.A.
94 J5 **Corydon** Pennsylvania U.S.A.
9 G5 **Coryton** England
21 K6 **Corzé** France
Cos *isld* *see* **Kos** *isld*
124 F5 **Cosalá** Mexico
125 M8 **Cosamaloapan** Mexico
43 G9 **Cosenza** Italy
9 E6 **Cosham** England
94 F6 **Coshocton** Ohio U.S.A.
81 B6 **Cosmoledo Is** Indian Oc
143 E8 **Cosmo Newberry** Western Australia Australia
99 M5 **Cosmos** Minnesota U.S.A.
18 G5 **Cosne** France
18 G6 **Cosne-d'Allier** France
102 G5 **Coso Junction** California U.S.A.
133 E4 **Cosquin** Argentina
21 J6 **Cossé-le-Vivien** France
21 O6 **Cosson** *R* France
109 K6 **Cost** Texas U.S.A.
17 G7 **Costa Blanca** *reg* Spain
17 K3 **Costa Brava** *reg* Spain
16 C7 **Costa de la Luz** *reg* Spain
17 F8 **Costa del Sol** Spain
45 L1 **Costa di Rovigo** Italy
113 E11 **Costa I, La** Florida U.S.A.
102 G8 **Costa Mesa** California U.S.A.
125 M4 **Costa Rica** *rep* Central America
124 C2 **Costa Rica** Mexico
123 K3 **Costebelle, L** Quebec Canada
94 J5 **Costello** Pennsylvania U.S.A.
Costermansville *see* **Bukavu**
48 J6 **Costeşhi** Romania
95 T1 **Costigan** Maine U.S.A.
106 E5 **Costilla** New Mexico U.S.A.
33 Q9 **Coswig** East Germany
71 G7 **Cotabato** Mindanao Philippines
128 E8 **Cotagaita** Bolivia
128 D7 **Cotahuasi** Peru
102 B3 **Cotati** California U.S.A.
130 H6 **Cotaxé, R** Brazil
121 Q7 **Côteau Station** Quebec Canada
118 K7 **Coteau, The** Saskatchewan Canada
126 G5 **Coteaux** Haiti
111 E12 **Cote Blanche B** Louisiana U.S.A.
44 B4 **Côte d'Azur** France
19 J5 **Côte d'Or** *dept* France
19 J5 **Côte d'Or** France
20 G3 **Cotentin** *pen* France
18 C4 **Côtes-du-Nord** *dept* France
141 J6 **Cotherstone** Queensland Australia
13 F4 **Cotherstone** England
19 Q18 **Cotignac** France
45 L3 **Cotignola** Italy
128 F3 **Cotinga** *R* Brazil
85 E7 **Cotonou** Benin
128 C4 **Cotopaxi** *vol* Ecuador
106 E3 **Cotopaxi** Colorado U.S.A.
9 E4 **Cotswold Hills** England
100 B6 **Cottage Grove** Oregon U.S.A.
112 G5 **Cottageville** South Carolina U.S.A.
94 F8 **Cottageville** West Virginia U.S.A.
33 S9 **Cottbus** *reg* East Germany
31 H4 **Cottbus** East Germany
123 T5 **Cottel I** Newfoundland Canada
9 G3 **Cottenham** England
110 D5 **Cotter** Arkansas U.S.A.
83 M14 **Cotter, C** Mauritius
142 A2 **Cottesloe Beach** *dist* Perth, W Aust Australia
9 F2 **Cottesmore** England
129 H3 **Cottica** Suriname
13 H6 **Cottingham** England
99 O2 **Cotton** Minnesota U.S.A.
140 E6 **Cottonbush Cr** Queensland Australia
111 J8 **Cottondale** Alabama U.S.A.
111 L11 **Cottondale** Florida U.S.A.
140 D1 **Cotton I** N Terr Australia
119 V3 **Cotton L** Manitoba Canada
110 E6 **Cotton Plant** Arkansas U.S.A.
111 D11 **Cottonport** Louisiana U.S.A.
109 O3 **Cotton Valley** Louisiana U.S.A.
111 L10 **Cottonwood** Alabama U.S.A.
103 N7 **Cottonwood** Arizona U.S.A.
100 C9 **Cottonwood** California U.S.A.
100 J3 **Cottonwood** Idaho U.S.A.
99 M5 **Cottonwood** *R* Minnesota U.S.A.
98 E6 **Cottonwood** South Dakota U.S.A.
109 H3 **Cottonwood** Texas U.S.A.
103 L6 **Cottonwood Cliffs** Arizona U.S.A.
107 O3 **Cottonwood Falls** Kansas U.S.A.
103 O6 **Cottonwood Wash** *R* Arizona U.S.A.
127 J5 **Cotui** Dominican Rep
109 H7 **Cotulla** Texas U.S.A.
18 E7 **Coubre, Pointe de la** *pt* France
142 F3 **Couchman Ra** Western Australia **Australia**
22 E4 **Coucy-le-Château Auffrique** France
21 N7 **Couddes** France
22 C1 **Coudekerque-Branche** France
99 P4 **Couderay** Wisconsin U.S.A.
94 J5 **Coudersport** Pennsylvania U.S.A.
21 O3 **Coudray-St. Germer, le** France
21 M6 **Coudrecieux** France
21 N4 **Coudres** France
122 B6 **Coudres, I.aux** Quebec Canada
138 D6 **Coüedic, C.de** South Australia **Australia**
20 G7 **Couëron** France
21 J5 **Couesmes-Vaucé** France
20 H5 **Couesnon** *R* France
20 H7 **Couffé** France
100 C3 **Cougar** Washington U.S.A.
18 F6 **Couhé** France
14 A5 **Coulagh B** Ireland
21 L5 **Coulans** France
15 C2 **Coulbeag Mt** Scotland
100 F2 **Coulee City** Washington U.S.A.
100 G1 **Coulee Dam** Washington U.S.A.
100 G1 **Coulee Dam Nat. Recreation Area** Washington U.S.A.
21 L5 **Coulimer** France
146 C12 **Coulman I** Antarctica
21 O6 **Coulmiers** France
22 B2 **Coulogne** France
21 C4 **Coulombs** Eure France
121 O6 **Coulonge** *R* Quebec Canada
18 E6 **Coulonges-Sur-l'Autize** France
21 K8 **Coulonges Thouarsais** France
21 H4 **Coulouvray-Boisbenâtre** France
119 R9 **Coulter** Manitoba **Canada**
102 D4 **Coulterville** California U.S.A.
110 G3 **Coulterville** Illinois U.S.A.
116 F4 **Council** Alaska U.S.A.
100 J5 **Council** Idaho U.S.A.
99 L8 **Council Bluffs** Iowa U.S.A.
107 O3 **Council Grove** Kansas U.S.A.
8 D2 **Cound** England
107 N7 **Countyline** Oklahoma U.S.A.
15 E4 **Coupar Angus** Scotland
123 Q7 **Coupe, C** Langlade I **Atlantic** Oc
100 C1 **Coupeville** Washington U.S.A.
109 K5 **Coupland** Texas U.S.A.
22 B2 **Couple, Mt** France
21 K5 **Couptrain** France
117 S3 **Courageous L** Northwest Territories **Canada**
21 P5 **Courances** France
122 B8 **Courcelles** Quebec **Canada**
21 L5 **Courcemont** France
21 N6 **Cour Cheverny** France
21 K5 **Courcité** France
21 L5 **Courgains** France
21 J8 **Courlay** France
18 H7 **Courpière** France
22 D3 **Courrières** France
18 H9 **Coursan** France
21 K3 **Courseulles** France
18 H5 **Courson les Carrières** France
21 N5 **Courtalain** France
40 F3 **Courtelary** Switzerland
117 L11 **Courtenay** British Columbia Canada
98 H2 **Courtenay** North Dakota U.S.A.
18 G7 **Courtine, la** France
110 J7 **Courtland** Alabama U.S.A.
107 N2 **Courtland** Kansas U.S.A.
99 M5 **Courtland** Minnesota U.S.A.
95 K10 **Courtland** Virginia U.S.A.
14 C5 **Courtmacsherry** Ireland
109 L5 **Courtney** Texas U.S.A.
21 L4 **Courtomer** France
Courtrai *see* **Kortrijk**
22 H2 **Court Saint-Etienne** Belgium
118 L8 **Courval** Saskatchewan Canada
21 N5 **Courville** France
109 O3 **Coushatta** Louisiana U.S.A.
83 J12 **Cousin I** Seychelles
22 G3 **Cousolre** France
21 M8 **Coussay-les-Bois** France
19 O17 **Coustellet** France
87 D9 **Coutada do Mucusso** Angola
20 H3 **Coutances** France
21 K4 **Couterne** France
22 J2 **Couthuin** Belgium
18 E7 **Coutras** France
101 N1 **Coutts** Alberta Canada
21 K7 **Coutures** France
127 O2 **Couva** Trinidad
20 G2 **Couville** France
22 H3 **Couvin** Belgium
22 F4 **Couvron-et-Aumencourt** France
48 K5 **Covasna** Romania
48 K5 **Covasna** *reg* Romania
109 N1 **Cove** Arkansas U.S.A.
100 H4 **Cove** Oregon U.S.A.
112 K2 **Cove City** North Carolina U.S.A.
103 M3 **Cove Fort** Utah U.S.A.
100 B10 **Covelo** California U.S.A.
94 K7 **Cove Mt** Pennsylvania U.S.A.
126 G10 **Coveñas** Colombia
9 E3 **Coventry** England
95 L8 **Cove Point** Maryland U.S.A.
107 M2 **Covert** Kansas U.S.A.
94 A4 **Covert** Michigan U.S.A.
94 J9 **Covesville** Virginia U.S.A.
16 B4 **Covilhã** Portugal
116 K7 **Coville, L** Alaska U.S.A.
112 D4 **Covington** Georgia U.S.A.
99 T9 **Covington** Indiana U.S.A.
94 C7 **Covington** Kentucky U.S.A.
111 F11 **Covington** Louisiana U.S.A.
99 S3 **Covington** Michigan U.S.A.
94 C6 **Covington** Ohio U.S.A.
107 N5 **Covington** Oklahoma U.S.A.
110 G6 **Covington** Tennessee U.S.A.
109 K3 **Covington** Texas U.S.A.
94 G9 **Covington** Virginia U.S.A.
120 G5 **Cow** *R* Ontario **Canada**
15 C4 **Cowal** Scotland
139 J5 **Cowal, L** New South Wales Australia
119 R6 **Cowan** Manitoba Canada
110 K6 **Cowan** Tennessee U.S.A.
140 E4 **Cowan Downs** Queensland Australia
138 F6 **Cowangie** Victoria **Australia**
118 K4 **Cowan L** Saskatchewan Canada
143 D9 **Cowan, Lake** Western Australia **Australia**
101 P4 **Cowan, Mt** Montana U.S.A.
121 S7 **Cowansville** Quebec **Canada**
138 D3 **Coward Springs** South Australia **Australia**
58 C5 **Cowargarzê** China
138 E2 **Cowarie** South Australia Australia
9 F2 **Cowbit** England
103 L2 **Cowboy Pass** Utah U.S.A.
8 C5 **Cowbridge** Wales
143 B9 **Cowcowing L** Western Australia **Australia**
100 G2 **Cow Cr** Washington U.S.A.
110 H2 **Cowden** Illinois U.S.A.
13 E1 **Cowdenbeath** Scotland
101 T9 **Cowdrey** Colorado U.S.A.
138 D5 **Cowell** South Australia Australia
94 G8 **Cowen** West Virginia U.S.A.
139 H7 **Cowes** Victoria **Australia**
9 E6 **Cowes** England
107 P6 **Coweta** Oklahoma U.S.A.
9 F6 **Cowfold** England
123 P4 **Cow Head** Newfoundland Canada
100 E8 **Cow Head L** California U.S.A.
100 A1 **Cowichan, L** British Columbia **Canada**
140 A6 **Cowle, Mt** N Terr **Australia**
98 H9 **Cowles** Nebraska U.S.A.
106 E6 **Cowles** New Mexico U.S.A.
141 G7 **Cowley** Queensland **Australia**
118 D9 **Cowley** Alberta **Canada**
101 R5 **Cowley** Wyoming U.S.A.
100 C3 **Cowlitz** *R* Washington U.S.A.
100 D3 **Cowlitz Pass** Washington U.S.A.
94 H8 **Cowpasture** *R* Virginia U.S.A.
112 F2 **Cowpens** South Carolina U.S.A.
112 F2 **Cowpens Nat.Bat.Site** South Carolina U.S.A.
139 J5 **Cowra** New South Wales Australia
130 G4 **Coxa, R** Brazil
139 H9 **Cox Bight** Tasmania Australia
13 G4 **Coxhoe** England
130 C4 **Coxibó do Ouro** Brazil
130 C6 **Coxim** Brazil
123 O2 **Coxipi L** Quebec Canada
130 C4 **Coxipó da Ponté** Brazil
143 F6 **Cox,Mt** Western Australia Australia
140 D3 **Cox R** N Terr Australia
95 O4 **Coxsackie** New York U.S.A.
75 O8 **Cox's Bazar** Bangladesh
123 P4 **Cox's Cove** Newfoundland Canada
108 B6 **Coyame** Mexico
108 D5 **Coyanosa Cr** Texas U.S.A.
21 P3 **Coye-la-Forêt** France
107 N6 **Coyle** Oklahoma U.S.A.
102 C4 **Coyote** California U.S.A.
102 H6 **Coyote L** California U.S.A.
102 F5 **Coyote Peak** California U.S.A.
103 L9 **Coyote Pk** Arizona U.S.A.
124 D5 **Coyote, Pta** *C* Mexico
124 F6 **Coyotitán** Mexico
98 G9 **Cozad** Nebraska U.S.A.
44 B2 **Cozie Alpi** *mt* Italy
124 C2 **Cozón, Cerro** *mt* Mexico
125 Q7 **Cozumel, I.de** Mexico
100 F3 **Crab Cr** Washington U.S.A.
141 F1 **Crab I** Queensland **Australia**
139 J4 **Craboon** New South Wales Australia
94 C9 **Crab Orchard** Kentucky U.S.A.
112 C2 **Crab Orchard** Tennessee U.S.A.
110 G4 **Crab Orchard L** Illinois U.S.A.
127 H2 **Crab Pond Pt** Jamaica
139 H7 **Crab Pt** Victoria Australia
8 B6 **Crackington Haven** England
8 D2 **Crackleybank** England
Cracow *see* **Kraków**
141 K7 **Cracow** Queensland Australia
139 H8 **Cradle, Mt** Tasmania Australia
138 E4 **Cradock** South Australia Australia
89 D9 **Cradock** S Africa
117 G8 **Craig** Alaska U.S.A.
101 S9 **Craig** Colorado U.S.A.
113 G13 **Craig** Florida U.S.A.
99 L9 **Craig** Missouri U.S.A.
101 O2 **Craig** Montana U.S.A.
98 K8 **Craig** Nebraska U.S.A.
15 E3 **Craigellachie** Scotland
13 E1 **Craigend** Scotland
15 C5 **Craighouse** Scotland
12 D2 **Craigie** Scotland
144 C5 **Craigieburn** New Zealand
100 J3 **Craigmont** Idaho U.S.A.
116 R6 **Craig, Mt** Alaska U.S.A.
118 E7 **Craigmyle** Alberta Canada
13 E1 **Craigrothie** Scotland
94 H8 **Craigsville** Virginia U.S.A.
14 D4 **Craiguenamanagh** Ireland
119 M7 **Craik** Saskatchewan **Canada**
13 F1 **Crail** Scotland
37 J5 **Crailsheim** W Germany
48 H6 **Craiova** Romania
13 E2 **Cramond** Scotland
121 Q8 **Cranberry, L** New York U.S.A.
119 Q4 **Cranberry Portage** Manitoba Canada
9 E6 **Cranborne** England
143 C10 **Cranbrook** Western Australia Australia
117 Q11 **Cranbrook** British Columbia Canada
9 G5 **Cranbrook** England
119 R8 **Crandall** Manitoba Canada
98 J4 **Crandall** South Dakota U.S.A.
109 L3 **Crandall** Texas U.S.A.
99 S4 **Crandon** Wisconsin U.S.A.
127 P6 **Crane** Barbados
110 C5 **Crane** Missouri U.S.A.
98 B2 **Crane** Montana U.S.A.
100 G6 **Crane** Oregon U.S.A.
108 E4 **Crane** Texas U.S.A.
100 J5 **Crane Cr.Res** Idaho U.S.A.
118 H8 **Crane L** Saskatchewan Canada
119 M9 **Crane Valley** Saskatchewan Canada
109 K4 **Cranfills Gap** Texas U.S.A.
9 F5 **Cranleigh** England
100 A8 **Crannell** California U.S.A.
13 F2 **Cranshaws** Scotland
95 Q5 **Cranston** Rhode I U.S.A.
13 H6 **Cranswick** England
21 J6 **Craon** France
22 F5 **Craonne** France
18 H7 **Craponne-sur-Arzon** France
98 H1 **Crary** North Dakota U.S.A.
146 D10 **Crary Ice Rise** *ice rise* Antarctica
48 L4 **Crasna** Romania
48 H3 **Crasna** *R* Romania
48 H3 **Crasnei, Muntii** *mt* Romania
100 C7 **Crater L** Oregon U.S.A.
100 C7 **Crater Lake Nat. Park** Oregon U.S.A.
100 D9 **Crater Peak** *mt* California U.S.A.
101 M6 **Craters of the Moon Nat.Mon** Idaho U.S.A.
43 G9 **Crati** *R* Italy
130 G9 **Crato** Brazil
21 L7 **Cravant-les Coteaux** Indre-et-Loire France
119 N8 **Craven** Saskatchewan Canada
130 F7 **Cravinhos** Brazil
128 D2 **Cravo Norte** *R* Colombia
6 L3 **Crawford** *oil rig* North Sea
12 E3 **Crawford** Scotland
112 D4 **Crawford** Georgia U.S.A.
111 H8 **Crawford** Mississippi U.S.A.
98 C7 **Crawford** Nebraska U.S.A.
109 K4 **Crawford** Texas U.S.A.
12 E3 **Crawfordjohn** Scotland
140 B3 **Crawford,Mt** N Terr Australia
95 Q2 **Crawford Notch** New Hampshire U.S.A.
71 D5 **Crawford Pt** Philippines
110 K1 **Crawfordsville** Indiana U.S.A.
111 M11 **Crawfordville** Florida U.S.A.
112 E4 **Crawfordville** Georgia U.S.A.
9 F5 **Crawley** England
8 C4 **Cray** Wales
9 G5 **Crayford** England
116 P4 **Crazy Mts** Alaska U.S.A.
101 P3 **Crazy Mts** Montana U.S.A.
101 P4 **Crazy Pk** Montana U.S.A.
101 T5 **Crazy Woman Cr** Wyoming U.S.A.
15 D4 **Creag Meagaidh** *mt* Scotland
143 B6 **Cream, R** Western Australia Australia
20 G3 **Créances** France
118 L4 **Crean L** Saskatchewan Canada
40 A5 **Crêches** France
22 B3 **Crécy-en-Pontieu** France
22 F4 **Crécy-sur-Serre** France
8 C6 **Crediton** England
12 D4 **Cree Bridge** Scotland
106 D4 **Creede** Colorado U.S.A.
112 J1 **Creedmoor** North Carolina U.S.A.
101 R9 **Creek** Colorado U.S.A.
94 H6 **Creekside** Pennsylvania U.S.A.
113 L9 **Creek Village** New Providence I **Bahamas**
114 J6 **Cree L** Saskatchewan Canada
124 F4 **Creel** Mexico
119 O9 **Creelman** Saskatchewan Canada
120 K8 **Creemore** Ontario **Canada**
114 J6 **Cree River** Saskatchewan Canada
12 D4 **Creetown** Scotland
37 J5 **Creglingen** W Germany
119 P4 **Creighton** Saskatchewan Canada
98 H7 **Creighton** Nebraska U.S.A.
120 J6 **Creighton Mine** Ontario Canada
21 P3 **Creil** France
44 G1 **Crema** Italy
47 R14 **Cremasti** Rhodes Greece
19 O13 **Crémieu** France
118 C7 **Cremona** Alberta Canada
44 G1 **Crémona** Italy
111 F7 **Crenshaw** Mississippi U.S.A.
18 E8 **Créon** France
48 F5 **Crepaja** Yugoslavia
129 G5 **Crepori** *R* Brazil

22 Crépy-en-Valois — Dampicourt

22 D5 **Crépy-en-Valois** France
120 K6 **Crerar** Ontario Canada
42 F4 **Cres** Yugoslavia
98 G4 **Cresbard** South Dakota U.S.A.
107 N6 **Crescent** Oklahoma U.S.A.
113 G10 **Crescent Beach** Florida U.S.A.
112 J4 **Crescent Beach** South Carolina U.S.A.
100 A8 **Crescent City** California U.S.A.
139 K4 **Crescent Head** New South Wales Australia
113 F8 **Crescent L** Florida U.S.A.
100 D6 **Crescent L** Oregon U.S.A.
100 B1 **Crescent, L** Washington U.S.A.
100 E9 **Crescent Mills** California U.S.A.
103 J6 **Crescent Pk** Nevada U.S.A.
99 O6 **Cresco** Iowa U.S.A.
45 L2 **Crespino** Italy
8 B4 **Cresselly** Wales
109 K3 **Cresson** Texas U.S.A.
139 H8 **Cressy** Tasmania Australia
139 G7 **Cressy** Victoria Australia
19 O15 **Crest** France
94 E6 **Crestline** Ohio U.S.A.
100 J1 **Creston** British Columbia Canada
123 R6 **Creston** Newfoundland Canada
99 M8 **Creston** Iowa U.S.A.
101 L1 **Creston** Montana U.S.A.
100 G2 **Creston** Washington U.S.A.
101 S8 **Creston** Wyoming U.S.A.
106 E3 **Crestone Pk** Colorado U.S.A.
111 K11 **Crestview** Florida U.S.A.
110 J6 **Crestview** Tennessee U.S.A.
119 M8 **Crestwynd** Saskatchewan Canada
112 L2 **Creswell** North Carolina U.S.A.
100 B6 **Creswell** Oregon U.S.A.
115 K3 **Creswell B** Northwest Territories Canada
140 D4 **Creswell Downs** N Terr Australia
139 G7 **Creswick** Victoria Australia
19 J6 **Crêt de la Neige** *mt* France
Crete *isld see* **Kriti** *isld*
99 T8 **Crete** Illinois U.S.A.
98 K9 **Crete** Nebraska U.S.A.
98 H3 **Crete** North Dakota U.S.A.
46 G9 **Crete, Sea of** Greece
21 J3 **Creully** France
17 K2 **Creus, C** Spain
18 G6 **Creuse** *dept* France
21 N8 **Creuse** *R* France
37 M4 **Creussen** W Germany
37 J1 **Creuzburg** East Germany
45 K2 **Crevalcore** Italy
21 P2 **Crèvecoeur-le-Grand** France
21 L3 **Crèvecœur** France
17 G6 **Crevillente** Spain
41 H5 **Crevola** Italy
8 D1 **Crewe** England
94 J9 **Crewe** Virginia U.S.A.
8 D6 **Crewkerne** England
12 D1 **Crianlarich** Scotland
8 B2 **Criccieth** Wales
9 E1 **Crich** England
118 K9 **Crichton** Saskatchewan Canada
133 H3 **Criciuma** Brazil
9 E3 **Crick** England
8 C4 **Crickhowell** Wales
9 E4 **Cricklade** England
94 C6 **Cridersville** Ohio U.S.A.
12 E1 **Crieff** Scotland
21 N1 **Criel-sur-Mer** France
15 E6 **Criffell** *mt* Scotland
42 F3 **Crikvenica** Yugoslavia
117 E6 **Crillon, Mt** Alaska U.S.A.
99 O1 **Crilly** Ontario Canada
Crimea *see* **Krym**
37 N2 **Crimmitschau** East Germany
12 C1 **Crinan** Scotland
15 C4 **Crinan Canal** Scotland
106 E3 **Cripple Creek** Colorado U.S.A.
116 J5 **Cripple Landing** Alaska U.S.A.
9 G6 **Cripps's Corner** England
21 L2 **Criquetot-l'Esneval** France
48 G4 **Crişana** Romania
130 F5 **Cristalina** Brazil
129 H6 **Cristalino** *R* Brazil
38 F8 **Cristallo** *mt* Italy
126 H10 **Cristóbal Colón, Pico** *mt* Colombia
48 J4 **Cristuru Secuiesc** Romania
48 G4 **Crişul Alb** *R* Romania
48 G4 **Crişul Negru** *R* Romania
48 H4 **Crişul Repede** *R* Romania
94 C8 **Crittenden** Kentucky U.S.A.
33 P5 **Crivitz** East Germany
99 S4 **Crivitz** Wisconsin U.S.A.
38 L9 **Črna** Yugoslavia
46 E3 **Crna** *R* Yugoslavia
46 E2 **Crna Gora** *mt* Yugoslavia
46 E2 **Crna Trava** Yugoslavia
46 D3 **Crni Drim** *R* Yugoslavia
38 M9 **Črni-vrh** *mt* Yugoslavia
14 B3 **Croagh Patrick Mt** Ireland
139 J7 **Croajingolong Nat. Park** Victoria Australia
Croatia *see* **Hrvatska**
41 O5 **Croce, C** *mt* Italy
43 G11 **Croce, S., C** Sicily
110 D4 **Crocker** Missouri U.S.A.
70 D2 **Crocker Ra** Borneo
12 E3 **Crocketford** Scotland
109 M4 **Crockett** Texas U.S.A.
9 G5 **Crockham Hill** England
21 K4 **Crocy** France
38 F8 **Croda Rossa** *mt* Italy
110 J4 **Crofton** Kentucky U.S.A.
98 J7 **Crofton** Nebraska U.S.A.
142 D5 **Crofton,Mt** Western Australia Australia
95 M3 **Croghan** New York U.S.A.
19 O18 **Croisette, C** France
20 E7 **Croisic,le** France
22 D3 **Croisilles** France
145 D4 **Croisilles Harbour** New Zealand
127 H5 **Croix des Bouquets** Haiti
19 P15 **Croix Haute, Col de la** *pass* France
21 H5 **Croixille,la** France
21 M7 **Croix,la** France
122 B2 **Croix, L.à la** Quebec Canada
122 E8 **Croix R** New Brunswick Canada
22 D5 **Croix-St.Ouen, la** France
21 N3 **Croix-st.Leufroy,la** France
120 K8 **Croker, Cape** Ontario Canada
140 B2 **Croker Hill** N Terr Australia
140 C1 **Croker I** N Terr Australia
15 D3 **Cromarty** Scotland
15 D3 **Cromarty Firth** Scotland
138 B2 **Crombie, Mt** South Australia Australia
119 Q9 **Cromer** Manitoba Canada
9 H2 **Cromer** England
144 B6 **Cromwell** New Zealand
99 O3 **Cromwell** Minnesota U.S.A.
144 C5 **Cronadun** New Zealand
37 K5 **Cronheim** W Germany
13 F5 **Crook** Cumbria England
13 G4 **Crook** Durham England
98 D9 **Crook** Colorado U.S.A.
107 K4 **Crooked Cr** Kansas U.S.A.
100 G7 **Crooked Cr** Oregon U.S.A.
126 G3 **Crooked I** Bahamas
126 G3 **Crooked I.Passage** Bahamas
123 Q5 **Crooked L** Newfoundland Canada
113 F10 **Crooked L** Florida U.S.A.
117 M8 **Crooked R** British Columbia Canada
100 E5 **Crooked R** Oregon U.S.A.
119 O6 **Crooked River** Saskatchewan Canada
13 F2 **Crookham** England
14 B5 **Crookhaven** Ireland
109 M2 **Crook, L** Texas U.S.A.
13 F5 **Crooklands** England
12 E1 **Crook of Devon** Scotland
98 K2 **Crookston** Minnesota U.S.A.
98 F7 **Crookston** Nebraska U.S.A.
94 E7 **Crooksville** Ohio U.S.A.
139 J5 **Crookwell** New South Wales Australia
14 C4 **Croom** Ireland
113 E9 **Croom** Florida U.S.A.
139 K3 **Croppa Cr** New South Wales Australia
9 E3 **Cropredy** England
123 R2 **Croque** Newfoundland Canada
141 G3 **Crosbie** *R* Queensland Australia
99 N3 **Crosby** Minnesota U.S.A.
111 E10 **Crosby** Mississippi U.S.A.
98 C1 **Crosby** North Dakota U.S.A.
109 M6 **Crosby** Texas U.S.A.
108 F2 **Crosbyton** Texas U.S.A.
8 D5 **Cross** England
85 F7 **Cross** *R* Nigeria
20 F7 **Crossac** France
12 C2 **Crossaig** Scotland
87 B10 **Cross, C** Namibia
113 D8 **Cross City** Florida U.S.A.
111 E8 **Crossett** Arkansas U.S.A.
13 F4 **Cross Fell** England
118 C7 **Crossfield** Alberta Canada
13 E1 **Crossgates** Scotland
8 C3 **Cross Gates** Wales
8 B4 **Cross Hands** Wales
113 K12 **Cross Harbour** Bahamas
14 C5 **Crosshaven** Ireland
12 D3 **Crosshill** Scotland
112 F3 **Cross Hill** South Carolina U.S.A.
113 K11 **Crossing Rocks** Bahamas
121 O8 **Cross, L** Ontario Canada
111 C9 **Cross L** Louisiana U.S.A.
119 U4 **Cross Lake** Manitoba Canada
144 D5 **Crossley, Mt** New Zealand
118 D4 **Cross L. Prov. Park** Alberta Canada
12 B5 **Crossmaglen** N Ireland
103 K7 **Crossman Pk** Arizona U.S.A.
12 E4 **Crossmichael** Scotland
14 B2 **Crossmolina** Ireland
106 B1 **Cross Mountain** Colorado U.S.A.
109 H3 **Cross Plains** Texas U.S.A.
94 B1 **Cross Village** Michigan U.S.A.
110 L6 **Crossville** Tennessee U.S.A.
116 P5 **Crosswind L** Alaska U.S.A.
45 J2 **Crostolo** *R* Italy
94 E3 **Croswell** Michigan U.S.A.
110 L3 **Crothersville** Indiana U.S.A.
43 H9 **Crotone** Italy
21 O1 **Crotoy,le** France
37 O3 **Crottendorf** East Germany
100 K5 **Crouch** Idaho U.S.A.
9 G4 **Crouch, R** England
22 E5 **Crouy** France
21 L7 **Crouzilles** France
101 S4 **Crow Agency** Montana U.S.A.
139 H4 **Crowal** *R* New South Wales Australia
9 G5 **Crowborough** England
8 C5 **Crowcombe** England
106 F1 **Crow Cr** Colorado U.S.A.
111 F7 **Crowder** Mississippi U.S.A.
107 P6 **Crowder** Oklahoma U.S.A.
118 F1 **Crowduck L.** Manitoba Canada
139 L4 **Crowdy Hd** New South Wales Australia
108 H2 **Crowell** Texas U.S.A.
139 G7 **Crowes** Victoria Australia
101 Q6 **Crowheart** Wyoming U.S.A.
139 H4 **Crowl** *R* New South Wales Australia
9 F2 **Crowland** England
13 H6 **Crowle** England
106 G3 **Crowley** Colorado U.S.A.
111 D11 **Crowley** Louisiana U.S.A.
102 F4 **Crowley, L** California U.S.A.
94 E8 **Crown City** Ohio U.S.A.
103 M7 **Crown King** Arizona U.S.A.
106 B6 **Crown Point** New Mexico U.S.A.
95 O3 **Crown Point** New York U.S.A.
115 L4 **Crown Prince Frederick I** Northwest Territories Canada
127 M2 **Crown Pt** Tobago
99 T8 **Crown Pt** Indiana U.S.A.
101 O3 **Crow Peak** Montana U.S.A.
141 K7 **Crow's Nest** Queensland Australia
118 C9 **Crowsnest Pass** Alberta/Br Col Canada
99 M3 **Crow Wing** *R* Minnesota U.S.A.
13 G4 **Croxdale** England
8 B5 **Croyde** England
141 F4 **Croydon** Queensland Australia
142 C5 **Croydon** Western Australia Australia
9 F5 **Croydon** England
144 B7 **Croydon** New Zealand
83 L13 **Croy, Î de** Kerguelen Indian Oc
94 J8 **Crozet** Virginia U.S.A.
81 D9 **Crozet Basin** Indian Oc
81 C10 **Crozet, Îs** Indian Oc
81 B10 **Crozet Plateau** Indian Oc
114 G2 **Crozier Chan** Northwest Territories Canada
20 B5 **Crozon** France
19 N15 **Cruas** France
126 D3 **Cruces** Cuba
128 C2 **Cruces, Pta** *pt* Colombia
22 L4 **Cruchten** Luxembourg
94 H7 **Crucible** Pennsylvania U.S.A.
15 G3 **Cruden B** Scotland
8 D2 **Crudgington** England
8 D4 **Crudwell** England
111 F8 **Cruger** Mississippi U.S.A.
21 M4 **Crûlai** France
14 E2 **Crumlin** N Ireland
100 F7 **Crump L** Oregon U.S.A.
19 Q12 **Cruseilles** France
22 K5 **Crusnes** France
133 E4 **Cruz** Argentina
133 G3 **Cruz Alta** Brazil
131 D3 **Cruz del Eje** Argentina
130 G8 **Cruzeiro** Brazil
133 G2 **Cruzeiro do Oeste** Brazil
128 D5 **Cruzeiro do Sul** Brazil
133 C3 **Cruz Grande** Chile
128 C3 **Cruz, La** Colombia
18 G9 **Cruzy** France
117 M8 **Crysdale, Mt** British Columbia Canada
106 C2 **Crystal** *R* Colorado U.S.A.
103 K5 **Crystal** Nevada U.S.A.
98 J1 **Crystal** North Dakota U.S.A.
113 E9 **Crystal B** Florida U.S.A.
138 E5 **Crystal Brook** South Australia Australia
119 T9 **Crystal City** Manitoba Canada
108 H7 **Crystal City** Texas U.S.A.
99 S3 **Crystal Falls** Michigan U.S.A.
99 S7 **Crystal L** Illinois U.S.A.
99 U5 **Crystal L** Michigan U.S.A.
99 N6 **Crystal Lake** Iowa U.S.A.
113 E9 **Crystal River** Florida U.S.A.
119 M6 **Crystal Springs** Saskatchewan Canada
111 F9 **Crystal Springs** Mississippi U.S.A.
99 U6 **Crystal Valley** Michigan U.S.A.
48 F4 **Csanytelek** Hungary
48 E3 **Csepel Sziget** *R* Hungary
48 F4 **Csongrád** *co* Hungary
48 F4 **Csongrád** Hungary
48 D3 **Csorna** Hungary
48 F4 **Csorvas** Hungary
48 E3 **Csóványos** *mt* Hungary
48 D4 **Csurgó** Hungary
127 L9 **Cúa** Venezuela
88 F9 **Cuambo** Mozambique
87 D9 **Cuando** *R* Angola
87 C9 **Cuangar** Angola
87 C7 **Cuango** Angola
86 C7 **Cuango** Zaire
87 B7 **Cuanza** *R* Angola
67 A7 **Cua Rao** Vietnam
133 F4 **Cuareim** Brazil
131 F3 **Cuaro** *R* Uruguay
133 E4 **Cuarto** *R* Argentina
124 H4 **Cuatro Ciénegas de Carranza** Mexico
68 H4 **Cua Tung** Vietnam
124 F3 **Cuauhtémoc** Mexico
124 G8 **Cuautitlán** Mexico
125 K8 **Cuautla** Mexico
16 B6 **Cuba** Portugal
110 F1 **Cuba** Illinois U.S.A.
107 N2 **Cuba** Kansas U.S.A.
110 E3 **Cuba** Missouri U.S.A.
106 D5 **Cuba** New Mexico U.S.A.
94 J4 **Cuba** New York U.S.A.
126 D4 **Cuba** *rep* W Indies
103 M10 **Cubabi, Cerro** *pk* Mexico
99 Q7 **Cuba City** Wisconsin U.S.A.
127 M9 **Cubagua, I** Venezuela
143 B10 **Cuballing** Western Australia Australia
87 C9 **Cubango** *R* Angola
130 F8 **Cubatão** Brazil
119 N4 **Cub Hills** Saskatchewan Canada
127 K10 **Cubiro** Venezuela
48 J6 **Cuca** Romania
133 C6 **Cucao, B.de** Chile
133 F4 **Cuchilla de Haedo** *hills* Uruguay
9 F5 **Cuckfield** England
9 E1 **Cuckney** England
94 K9 **Cuckoo** Virginia U.S.A.
87 C8 **Cucumbi** Angola
124 D2 **Cucurpe** Mexico
128 D2 **Cúcuta** Colombia
99 T7 **Cudahy** Wisconsin U.S.A.
76 D5 **Cuddalore** India
76 D3 **Cuddapah** India
141 F7 **Cuddapan,L** Queensland Australia
102 G6 **Cuddeback L** California U.S.A.
113 F13 **Cudjoe Key** *isld* Florida U.S.A.
119 M6 **Cudworth** Saskatchewan Canada
143 C7 **Cue** Western Australia Australia
16 E3 **Cuéllar** Spain
128 C4 **Cuenca** Ecuador
71 E4 **Cuenca** Philippines
17 F4 **Cuenca** Spain
17 F5 **Cuenca** *prov* Spain
124 H5 **Cuencamé de Ceniceros** Mexico
17 F4 **Cuenca, Serrania de** *mts* Spain
125 K8 **Cuernavaca** Mexico
109 K6 **Cuero** Texas U.S.A.
19 Q18 **Cuers** France
106 F6 **Cuervo** New Mexico U.S.A.
102 D6 **Cuesta Pass** California U.S.A.
126 G4 **Cueto** Cuba
17 F7 **Cuevas del Almanzora** Spain
133 E2 **Cuevo** Bolivia
22 E5 **Cuffies** France
123 N2 **Cuff L** Quebec Canada
19 P18 **Cuges-les-Pins** France
48 H5 **Cugir** Romania
43 B8 **Cuglieri** Sardinia
20 G5 **Cuguen** France
130 C4 **Cuiabá** Brazil
14 D2 **Cuilcagh** *mt* N Ireland
15 B3 **Cuillin Hills** Scotland
87 C7 **Cuilo** *R* Angola
59 J2 **Cuiluan** China
87 C8 **Cuima** Angola
22 D2 **Cuinchy** France
36 B4 **Cuint** W Germany
22 E5 **Cuise-la-Motte** France
130 H9 **Cuité** Brazil
130 H6 **Cuité, R** Brazil
87 C9 **Cuito** *R* Angola
87 C9 **Cuito Cuanavale** Angola
128 F4 **Cuiuni** *R* Brazil
110 E2 **Cuivre** *R* Missouri U.S.A.
71 E7 **Cujangan** *isld* Philippines
48 H6 **Cujmir** Romania
69 F10 **Cukai** Malaysia
78 J3 **Çukurca** Turkey
68 H4 **Cu Lai** Vietnam
18 G6 **Culan** France
68 J5 **Cu Lao Bo Bai** *isld* Vietnam
68 J5 **Cu Lao Cham** *isld* Vietnam
68 J7 **Cu Lao Hon** *isld* Vietnam
68 J5 **Cu Lao Re** *isld* Vietnam
71 F5 **Culasi** Panay Philippines
98 B1 **Culbertson** Montana U.S.A.
98 F9 **Culbertson** Nebraska U.S.A.
139 H6 **Culcairn** New South Wales Australia
22 G4 **Cul-des-Sarts** Belgium
106 E4 **Culebra Pk** Colorado U.S.A.
16 C3 **Culebra, Sa de la** *mts* Spain
25 D5 **Culemborg** Netherlands
87 C9 **Culevai** Angola
141 H8 **Culgoa** *R* N S W/Qnsld Australia
139 H3 **Culgoa, R** New S Wales/Queensland
124 F5 **Culiacán** Mexico
124 F5 **Culiacancito** Mexico
71 D5 **Culion** Philippines
129 H6 **Culiseu** *R* Brazil
17 F7 **Cúllar de Baza** Spain
139 J5 **Cullarin Rge** New South Wales Australia
15 F3 **Cullen** Scotland
17 G5 **Cullera** Spain
107 M4 **Cullison** Kansas U.S.A.
111 K7 **Cullman** Alabama U.S.A.
141 G5 **Culloden** *R* Queensland Australia
8 C6 **Cullompton** England
125 M2 **Culmi** Honduras
8 D3 **Culmington** England
19 P13 **Culoz** France
94 J8 **Culpeper** Virginia U.S.A.
128 A7 **Culpepper** *isld* Galapagos Is
15 E5 **Culter Fell** Scotland
129 H6 **Culuene** *R* Brazil
99 U8 **Culver** Indiana U.S.A.
107 N3 **Culver** Kansas U.S.A.
100 D5 **Culver** Oregon U.S.A.
144 D5 **Culverden** New Zealand
143 E10 **Culver,Pt** Western Australia Australia
129 K4 **Cuma, B.de** Brazil
47 H4 **Cumalı** Turkey
128 F1 **Cumana** Venezuela
127 N9 **Cumanacoa** Venezuela
47 J6 **Cumaovası** Turkey
130 E6 **Cumari** Brazil
Cumberland *co see* **Cumbria**
117 L11 **Cumberland** British Columbia Canada
99 M8 **Cumberland** Iowa U.S.A.
94 D9 **Cumberland** Kentucky U.S.A.
94 J7 **Cumberland** Maryland U.S.A.
94 F7 **Cumberland** Ohio U.S.A.
110 J5 **Cumberland** *R* Tennessee U.S.A.
94 J9 **Cumberland** Virginia U.S.A.
99 O4 **Cumberland** Wisconsin U.S.A.
Cumberland, C *see* **Nahoï, C**
110 J5 **Cumberland City** Tennessee U.S.A.
94 D10 **Cumberland Gap** Tenn/Virg U.S.A.
119 P5 **Cumberland House** Saskatchewan Canada
113 F7 **Cumberland I** Georgia U.S.A.
141 J5 **Cumberland Is** Queensland Australia
119 P4 **Cumberland L** Saskatchewan Canada
110 L5 **Cumberland, L** Kentucky U.S.A.
94 B10 **Cumberland, L** Kentucky U.S.A.
94 D10 **Cumberland Mt** Tennessee U.S.A.
115 N4 **Cumberland Pen** Northwest Territories Canada
111 K7 **Cumberland Plateau** Alabama U.S.A.
99 R2 **Cumberland Pt** Michigan U.S.A.
94 D10 **Cumberland R** Kentucky U.S.A.
94 J7 **Cumberland Res** Pennsylvania U.S.A.
115 N4 **Cumberland Sound** Northwest Territories Canada
140 D1 **Cumberland Str** N Terr Australia
12 E2 **Cumbernauld** Scotland
139 J3 **Cumborah** New South Wales Australia
133 C7 **Cumbrera** *mt* Chile
13 E4 **Cumbria** *co* England
76 D3 **Cumbum** India
109 M2 **Cumby** Texas U.S.A.
44 B2 **Cumiana** Italy
129 G4 **Cumina** *R* Brazil
129 G3 **Cuminapanema** *R* Brazil
13 E4 **Cummertrees** Scotland
112 C3 **Cumming** Georgia U.S.A.
102 A2 **Cummings** California U.S.A.
98 J2 **Cummings** North Dakota U.S.A.
138 D5 **Cummins** South Australia Australia
142 F4 **Cummins Ra** Western Australia Australia
139 J5 **Cumnock** New South Wales Australia
12 D3 **Cumnock** Scotland
124 E2 **Cumpas** Mexico
78 D3 **Çumra** Turkey
124 E3 **Cumuripa** Mexico
130 H5 **Cumuruxatiba** Brazil
127 O2 **Cumuto** Trinidad
126 E3 **Cunagua** Cuba
129 H3 **Cunani** Brazil
124 D6 **Cuñaño** Mexico
131 G3 **Cuñapiru** *R* Uruguay
133 C5 **Cunco** Chile
142 D5 **Cuncudgerie Hill** Western Australia Australia
143 B9 **Cunderdin** Western Australia Australia
128 D3 **Cundinamarca** *div* Colombia
87 B9 **Cunene** *R* Angola
44 C3 **Cúneo** Italy
138 C4 **Cungena** South Australia Australia
17 H6 **Cunillera** *isld* Balearic Is
18 H7 **Cunlhat** France
141 H8 **Cunnamulla** Queensland Australia
107 M4 **Cunningham** Kansas U.S.A.
100 G3 **Cunningham** Washington U.S.A.
127 O2 **Cunupia** Trinidad
21 K7 **Cuon** France
119 N8 **Cupar** Saskatchewan Canada
13 E1 **Cupar** Scotland
128 C2 **Cupica, G.de** Colombia
46 E1 **Ćuprija** Yugoslavia
100 J4 **Cuprum** Idaho U.S.A.
124 D5 **Cupula, P** Mexico
71 B1 **Cur** Halmahera Indonesia
129 G7 **Curabá** *R* Brazil
129 L5 **Curaçá** Brazil
126 B1 **Curaçao** *isld* W Indies
131 B7 **Curacáutin** Chile
131 D7 **Curaco, R** Argentina
131 E6 **Cura Malal, Cerro** *pk* Argentina
133 C5 **Curanilahue** Chile
128 C4 **Curaray** *R* Peru/Ecuador
131 B4 **Curaumilla, Pta de** *C* Chile
48 K6 **Curcani** Romania
21 K7 **Curçay-sur-Dive** France
138 D4 **Curdlawidny Lagoon** South Australia Australia
9 E2 **Curdworth** England
18 H5 **Cure** *R* France
106 C3 **Curecanti Nat. Recreation Area** Colorado U.S.A.
83 M13 **Curepipe** Mauritius
133 C5 **Curepto** Chile
127 O10 **Curiapo** Venezuela
131 B5 **Curico** Chile
131 D8 **Curico, L** Argentina
128 E4 **Curicuriari** *R* Brazil
83 J12 **Curieuse I** Seychelles
130 J9 **Curimataú** *R* Brazil
143 A7 **Curious,Mt** Western Australia Australia
128 D3 **Curiplaya** Colombia
133 H3 **Curitiba** Brazil
130 E10 **Curitibanos** Brazil
100 G1 **Curlew** Washington U.S.A.
141 J5 **Curlew I** Queensland Australia
139 K4 **Curlewis** New South Wales Australia
111 H12 **Curlew Is** Louisiana U.S.A.
116 F5 **Curlew L** Alaska U.S.A.
123 L3 **Curlew Pt** Quebec Canada
123 O5 **Curling** Newfoundland Canada
138 E4 **Curnamona** South Australia Australia
44 F2 **Curone** *R* Italy
139 K4 **Currabubula** New South Wales Australia
130 H9 **Currais Novas** Brazil
138 C2 **Curralulla** *R* South Australia Australia
121 Q7 **Curran** Ontario Canada
94 D2 **Curran** Michigan U.S.A.
103 J3 **Currant** Nevada U.S.A.
139 G4 **Curranyalpa** New South Wales Australia
141 F7 **Currawilla** Queensland Australia
126 F2 **Current** Eleuthera Bahamas
110 E4 **Current** *R* Missouri U.S.A.
113 L12 **Current I** Bahamas
139 G7 **Currie** Tasmania Australia
13 E2 **Currie** Scotland
99 L5 **Currie** Minnesota U.S.A.
103 K1 **Currie** Nevada U.S.A.
112 J3 **Currie** North Carolina U.S.A.
138 B2 **Currie Cr., The** South Australia Australia
119 U1 **Currie L** Manitoba Canada
140 B7 **Currie,Mt** N Terr Australia
112 L1 **Currituck** North Carolina U.S.A.
112 M1 **Currituck Sound** North Carolina U.S.A.
139 K6 **Currockbilly, Mt** New South Wales Australia
110 E2 **Curryville** Missouri U.S.A.
37 L2 **Cursdorf** East Germany
45 L1 **Curtarolo** Italy
48 J5 **Curtea de Argeş** Romania
48 G4 **Curtici** Romania
143 D9 **Curtin** Western Australia Australia
100 B6 **Curtin** Oregon U.S.A.
140 B7 **Curtin Springs** N Terr Australia
16 B1 **Curtis** Spain
111 C9 **Curtis** Louisiana U.S.A.
99 V3 **Curtis** Michigan U.S.A.
98 F9 **Curtis** Nebraska U.S.A.
141 L6 **Curtis Chan** Gt Barrier Reef Australia
139 H7 **Curtis Group** *islds* Tasmania Australia
141 K6 **Curtis I** Queensland Australia
137 R8 **Curtis I** Kermadec Is Pacific Oc
94 D2 **Curtisville** Michigan U.S.A.
129 G4 **Curuá** Brazil
129 H5 **Curuaés** *R* Brazil
129 H3 **Curuá, I** Brazil
129 G3 **Curuapanema** *R* Brazil
129 J4 **Curuca** Brazil
128 D5 **Curuçá** *R* Brazil
133 F2 **Curuguaty** Paraguay
69 F14 **Curup** Sumatra
129 J4 **Cururupu** Brazil
131 F2 **Curuzú Cuatiá** Argentina
129 K7 **Curvelo** Brazil
94 J6 **Curwensville** Pennsylvania U.S.A.
14 E1 **Cushendall** N Ireland
14 E1 **Cushendun** N Ireland
99 M3 **Cushing** Minnesota U.S.A.
107 O6 **Cushing** Oklahoma U.S.A.
111 B10 **Cushing** Texas U.S.A.
110 E6 **Cushman** Arkansas U.S.A.
101 Q3 **Cushman** Montana U.S.A.
100 A6 **Cushman** Oregon U.S.A.
100 B2 **Cushman, L** Washington U.S.A.
124 F3 **Cusihuiráchic** Mexico
45 H3 **Cusna, Mt** Italy
18 H6 **Cusset** France
112 C5 **Cusseta** Georgia U.S.A.
99 O1 **Cusson** Minnesota U.S.A.
144 D5 **Cust** New Zealand
101 S3 **Custer** Montana U.S.A.
98 C6 **Custer** South Dakota U.S.A.
101 S4 **Custer Battlefield Nat.Mon** Montana U.S.A.
107 M6 **Custer City** Oklahoma U.S.A.
45 J1 **Custoza** Italy
117 O8 **Cutbank** *R* Alberta Canada
101 N1 **Cut Bank** Montana U.S.A.
119 P5 **Cut Beaver L** Saskatchewan Canada
111 A8 **Cuthand Cr** Texas U.S.A.
112 C6 **Cuthbert** Georgia U.S.A.
98 H6 **Cuthbert** South Dakota U.S.A.
108 F3 **Cuthbert** Texas U.S.A.
140 E4 **Cuthbert, Mt** Queensland Australia
45 J3 **Cutigliano** Italy
118 H6 **Cut Knife** Saskatchewan Canada
120 H6 **Cutler** Ontario Canada
116 H3 **Cutler** *R* Alaska U.S.A.
102 E5 **Cutler** California U.S.A.
95 T9 **Cutler** Maine U.S.A.
14 C3 **Cutra, L** Ireland
22 E4 **Cuts** France
139 H3 **Cuttaburra** *R* New South Wales Australia
75 L8 **Cuttack** India
103 O8 **Cutter** Arizona U.S.A.
81 H7 **Cuvier Basin** Indian Oc
143 A6 **Cuvier,C** Western Australia Australia
145 E2 **Cuvier I** New Zealand
87 C8 **Cuvo** *R* Angola
32 J5 **Cuxhaven** W Germany
Cu Xu, I *see* **Quan Dao Co To**
94 F5 **Cuyahoga** *R* Ohio U.S.A.
94 F5 **Cuyahoga Falls** Ohio U.S.A.
102 E6 **Cuyama** *R* California U.S.A.
71 E3 **Cuyapo** Luzon Philippines
71 E5 **Cuyo** *isld* Philippines
71 E5 **Cuyo East Passage** Philippines
71 E5 **Cuyo West Passage** Philippines
99 N3 **Cuyuna** Minnesota U.S.A.
128 G2 **Cuyuni** *R* Guyana
125 N2 **Cuyu Tigni** Nicaragua
128 E8 **Cuzco** *mt* Bolivia
128 D6 **Cuzco** Peru
42 H5 **Čvrsnica** *mt* Yugoslavia
8 C4 **Cwmbran** Wales
88 B3 **Cyangugu** Rwanda
31 H3 **Cybinka** Poland
Cyclades *islds see* **Kikládhes** *islds*
139 H9 **Cygnet** Tasmania Australia
119 W2 **Cygnet L** Manitoba Canada
138 D6 **Cygnet River** South Australia Australia
118 B5 **Cynthia** Alberta Canada
110 M3 **Cynthiana** Kentucky U.S.A.
110 G4 **Cypress** Illinois U.S.A.
111 C10 **Cypress** Louisiana U.S.A.
109 M6 **Cypress** Texas U.S.A.
111 A8 **Cypress Cr** Texas U.S.A.
109 N3 **Cypress Cr., Lit** Texas U.S.A.
118 H9 **Cypress Hills** Saskatchewan Canada
118 G9 **Cypress Hills Prov. Park** Alberta Canada
113 F9 **Cypress L** Florida U.S.A.
119 S9 **Cypress River** Manitoba Canada
79 D4 **Cyprus** *rep* Mediterranean Sea
84 G4 **Cyrenaica** *reg* Libya
Cyrene *see* **Shaḥḥāt**
77 A5 **Cyrus** *oil well* Persian Gulf
115 N5 **Cyrus Field B** Northwest Territories Canada
22 E2 **Cysoing** France
31 J2 **Czaplinek** Poland
118 G6 **Czar** Alberta Canada
31 M4 **Czarna** *R* Poland
31 K2 **Czarne** Poland
31 K3 **Czarnków** Poland
31 M6 **Czarny Dunajec** Poland
31 M6 **Czchów** Poland
31 J6 **Czechoslovakia** *rep* Europe
31 K3 **Czempin** Poland
31 O3 **Czeremcha** Poland
Czernowitz *see* **Chernovtsy**
31 K2 **Czersk** Poland
31 J3 **Czerwiensk** Poland
31 L5 **Czestochowa** Poland
31 J2 **Człopa** Poland
31 K2 **Człuchów** Poland
31 N3 **Czyżew** Poland

D

36 D2 **Daaden** W Germany
65 F2 **Da'an** China
71 F5 **Daanbantayan** Cebu Philippines
122 B7 **Daaquam** Quebec Canada
67 B2 **Daba** China
79 F7 **Dabāb, J. Ed** *mt* Jordan
127 J9 **Dabajuro** Venezuela
85 D7 **Dabakala** Ivory Coast
58 D4 **Daban Shan** *mt* China
48 E3 **Dabas** Hungary
67 C1 **Daba Shan** *mts* China
86 G3 **Dabat** Ethiopia
128 C2 **Dabeiba** Colombia
68 C4 **Dabein** Burma
33 P5 **Dabel** East Germany
74 E7 **Dabhoi** India
31 H2 **Dąbie** Poland
67 E1 **Dabie Shan** *mts* China
79 G10 **Dabl Mushāsh** *well* Saudi Arabia
36 C6 **Dabo** France
85 B6 **Dabola** Guinea
85 D7 **Dabou** Ivory Coast
85 D7 **Daboya** Ghana
36 C1 **Dabringhausen** W Germany
31 O2 **Dąbrowa** Poland
31 M2 **Dąbrówno** Poland
67 E4 **Dabu** China
65 D7 **Dabu** China
65 F2 **Dabusu Pao** *L* China
Dacca *see* **Dhaka**
65 C5 **Dachang** China
37 L7 **Dachau** W Germany
37 L7 **Dachauer Moos** *marshes* W Germany
37 K4 **Dachsbach** W Germany
38 J7 **Dachstein** *mt* Austria
38 J7 **Dachstein-Gebirge** *mts* Austria
31 J6 **Dačice** Czechoslovakia
107 M5 **Dacoma** Oklahoma U.S.A.
128 G3 **Dadanawa** Guyana
79 H2 **Dādāt** Syria
78 D1 **Daday** Turkey
113 E9 **Dade City** Florida U.S.A.
111 L9 **Dadeville** Alabama U.S.A.
74 B4 **Dadhar** Pakistan
65 D7 **Dadian** China
65 G3 **Dadianzi** China
71 C3 **Dadi, Tg** *C* W Irian
68 J1 **Dadong** China
18 G9 **Dadou** *R* France
27 H11 **Dådran** Sweden
74 E8 **Dadra & Nagar Haveli** *Union Terr* India
74 G4 **Dadri** India
74 B5 **Dadu** Pakistan
68 H7 **Da Dung** *R* Vietnam
48 L6 **Dăeni** Romania
65 C4 **Da'erhao** China
140 D7 **Daer,Mt** N Terr Australia
71 F3 **Daet** Philippines
67 B3 **Dafang** China
80 F1 **Dafna** Israel
119 N7 **Dafoe** Saskatchewan Canada
68 B4 **Daga** *R* Burma
27 C11 **Dagali** Norway
85 A5 **Dagana** Senegal
47 K5 **Dagardı** Turkey
71 A1 **Dagasuli** Indonesia
30 D1 **Dagebüll** W Germany
9 G4 **Dagenham** England
53 G11 **Dagestan A.S.S.R** U.S.S.R.
102 H7 **Daggett** California U.S.A.
99 T4 **Daggett** Michigan U.S.A.
78 K5 **Daghgharah, Al** Iraq
27 G12 **Daglösen** Sweden
98 B1 **Dagmar** Montana U.S.A.
65 D5 **Dagu** China
67 A3 **Daguan** China
21 K7 **Daguenière,la** France
71 E2 **Dagupan** Luzon Philippines
94 J5 **Dagus Mines** Pennsylvania U.S.A.
68 C4 **Dagwin** Burma
141 G4 **Dagworth** Queensland Australia
66 E6 **Dagzê** China
79 E10 **Dahab** Egypt
117 L4 **Dahadinni** *R* Northwest Territories Canada
67 D5 **Dahao Dao** *isld* China
65 J1 **Dahezhen** China
59 H2 **Da Hinggan Ling** *mt ra* China
32 G10 **Dahle** W Germany
36 B3 **Dahleim** W Germany
33 R10 **Dahlen** East Germany
33 N6 **Dahlenburg** W Germany
33 S8 **Dahlewitz** East Germany
95 K8 **Dahlgren** Virginia U.S.A.
112 C3 **Dahlonega** Georgia U.S.A.
33 T8 **Dahme** *R* East Germany
33 S9 **Dahme** East Germany
33 O4 **Dahme** W Germany
33 R5 **Dahmen** East Germany
33 O4 **Dahmeshöved** W Germany
36 D5 **Dahn** W Germany
72 F3 **Dahnā, Ad** *reg* Saudi Arabia
74 F7 **Dāhod** India
78 J3 **Dahok** Iraq
Dahomey *rep see* **Benin, Rep. of**
66 B4 **Dahongliutan** China
65 E4 **Dahongqi** China
67 D1 **Dahong Shan** *mts* China
33 N7 **Dähre** East Germany
78 J3 **Dahuk** Iraq
65 E4 **Dahushan** China
139 G5 **Dahwilly** New South Wales Australia
71 O8 **Dai** *isld* Indonesia
48 K7 **Daia** Romania
65 C5 **Daicheng** China
65 B4 **Dai Hai** *L* China
69 G13 **Daik** Indonesia
68 C4 **Daik-U** Burma
75 J4 **Dailekh** Nepal
121 T3 **Dailleboust, L** Quebec Canada
60 G9 **Daimanji-san** *mt* Japan
16 E5 **Daimiel** Spain
109 N2 **Daingerfield** Texas U.S.A.
61 K10 **Dainichiga-take** *pk* Japan
66 F5 **Dainkog** China
141 H3 **Daintree** *R* Queensland Australia
141 H3 **Daintree** Queensland Australia
61 K11 **Daiō** Japan
65 E2 **Daiqin Tal** China
Dairen *see* **Dalian**
84 J4 **Dairût** Egypt
100 D7 **Dairy** Oregon U.S.A.
143 B7 **Dairy Creek** Western Australia Australia
60 G10 **Dai-sen** *mt* Japan
60 G10 **Dai sen-Oki Nat. Park** Japan
109 N5 **Daisetta** Texas U.S.A.
67 G1 **Dai Shan** *isld* China
67 G1 **Daishan** China
129 K5 **Dais Irmaos, Serra** *mts* Brazil
100 G1 **Daisy** Washington U.S.A.
58 F4 **Dai Xian** China
Daiyue *see* **Shanyin**
67 F4 **Daiyun Shan** *mts* China
127 J5 **Dajabón** Dominican Rep
140 E5 **Dajarra** Queensland Australia
58 D5 **Dajin Chuan** *R* China
67 G2 **Dajing** China
45 P1 **Dajla** Yugoslavia
70 D5 **Daju** Kalimantan
85 A6 **Dakar** Senegal
67 D5 **Dakengkou** China
67 D4 **Dakengkou** China
68 H5 **Dak Gle** Vietnam
85 A4 **Dakhla, Ad** Western Sahara
84 H4 **Dakhla Oasis** Egypt
68 H5 **Dak Kon** Vietnam
69 A9 **Dakoank** Nicobar Is
85 F6 **Dakoro** Niger
99 R7 **Dakota** Illinois U.S.A.
99 P6 **Dakota** Minnesota U.S.A.
99 M7 **Dakota City** Iowa U.S.A.
98 K7 **Dakota City** Nebraska U.S.A.
46 D2 **Dakovica** Yugoslavia
48 E5 **Dakovo** Yugoslavia
146 J7 **Dakshin Gangotri** *India Base* Antarctica
28 D3 **Dal** Denmark
27 E11 **Dal** Norway
87 D8 **Dala** Angola
27 J11 **Dalä** *L* Sweden
41 L3 **Dalaas Tal** Austria
85 B6 **Dalaba** Guinea
65 A4 **Dalad Qi** China
Dalai *see* **Da'an**
Dalai Nor *L see* **Hulun Nur** *L*
58 G3 **Dalai Nur** *L* China
27 G11 **Dala-Järna** Sweden
78 B3 **Dalaman** *R* Turkey
58 D3 **Dalandzadgad** Mongolia
71 E5 **Dalanganem** *islds* Philippines
58 E2 **Dalanjargalan** Mongolia
27 K12 **Dalarö** Sweden
70 B3 **Dalat** Sarawak
68 J7 **Da Lat** Vietnam
71 C6 **Dalawan B** Philippines
77 J5 **Dalbandin** Pakistan
15 E6 **Dalbeattie** Scotland
141 H5 **Dalbeg** Queensland Australia
27 F13 **Dalbosjön** *L* Sweden
141 K7 **Dalby** Queensland Australia
28 F5 **Dalby** Denmark
27 F11 **Dalby** Sweden
12 D5 **Dalby** I of Man U.K.
28 E3 **Dalbyneder** Denmark
28 E3 **Dalbyover** Denmark
27 A11 **Dale** Norway
27 A10 **Dale** Norway
110 K3 **Dale** Indiana U.S.A.
100 G5 **Dale** Oregon U.S.A.
94 J6 **Dale** Pennsylvania U.S.A.
109 K6 **Dale** Texas U.S.A.
8 A4 **Dale** Wales
110 L5 **Dale Hollow L** Kentucky/Tennessee
118 D8 **Dalemead** Alberta Canada
143 B9 **Dale,Mt** Western Australia Australia
25 G3 **Dalen** Netherlands
28 B7 **Daler** Denmark
31 M5 **Daleszyce** Poland
68 A2 **Dalet** *R* Burma
68 A3 **Dalet** Burma
68 A2 **Daletme** Burma
110 L1 **Daleville** Indiana U.S.A.
27 H10 **Dalfors** Sweden
25 F4 **Dalfsen** Netherlands
143 B8 **Dalgaranger Hill** Western Australia Australia
139 J6 **Dalgety** New South Wales Australia
12 E1 **Dalginross** Scotland
141 F5 **Dalgonally** Queensland Australia
108 B7 **Dalhart** Texas U.S.A.
114 G3 **Dalhousie, C** Northwest Territories Canada
65 A7 **Dali** China
59 H4 **Dalian** China
58 D6 **Daliang Shan** China
65 E5 **Dalian Wan** *B* China
71 G7 **Daliao** Philippines
106 D7 **Dalies** New Mexico U.S.A.
65 A6 **Dali He** *R* China
Dalinghe *see* **Jin Xian**
80 D3 **Daliyat el Karmil** Israel
65 G4 **Dalizi** China
48 E5 **Dalj** Yugoslavia
15 E5 **Dalkeith** Scotland
14 E3 **Dalkey** Ireland
141 K7 **Dallarnil** Queensland Australia
119 U7 **Dallas** Manitoba Canada
111 M8 **Dallas** Georgia U.S.A.
100 B5 **Dallas** Oregon U.S.A.
109 N10 **Dallas** Texas U.S.A.
99 P4 **Dallas** Wisconsin U.S.A.
99 N8 **Dallas Center** Iowa U.S.A.
99 P9 **Dallas City** Illinois U.S.A.
95 L7 **Dallastown** Pennsylvania U.S.A.
102 D4 **Dallas Warner Res** California U.S.A.
100 D4 **Dalles, The** Oregon U.S.A.
117 G8 **Dall I** Alaska U.S.A.
116 F6 **Dall L** Alaska U.S.A.
116 N3 **Dall Mt** Alaska U.S.A.
85 E6 **Dallol Bosso** *watercourse* Niger
77 C7 **Dalmā** *isld* U.A.E.
133 E4 **Dalmacio Velez Sarsfield** Argentina
12 D1 **Dalmally** Scotland
42 G4 **Dalmatia** *reg* Yugoslavia
55 D3 **Dalmatovo** U.S.S.R.
12 D3 **Dalmellington** Scotland
118 L6 **Dalmeny** Saskatchewan Canada
28 G6 **Dalmose** Denmark
12 D2 **Dalmuir** Scotland
59 L3 **Dal'negorsk** U.S.S.R.
59 K2 **Dal'nerechensk** U.S.S.R.
52 F6 **Dal'neye-Konstantinovo** U.S.S.R.
52 E1 **Dal'niye Zelentsy** U.S.S.R.
85 C7 **Daloa** Ivory Coast
67 C5 **Dalongdong Shuiku** *res* China
67 B3 **Dalou Shan** *mt ra* China
121 M4 **Dalquier** Quebec Canada
118 D7 **Dalroy** Alberta Canada
15 D5 **Dalry** Dumfries & Galloway Scotland
15 D5 **Dalry** Strathclyde Scotland
141 H4 **Dalrymple** Queensland Australia
15 D5 **Dalrymple** Scotland
141 J5 **Dalrymple,Mt** Queensland Australia
29 K11 **Dalsbruk** Finland
28 S9 **Dalsmynni** Iceland
13 F4 **Dalston** England
75 L6 **Dāltenganj** India
120 F4 **Dalton** Ontario Canada
13 E3 **Dalton** Scotland
112 C3 **Dalton** Georgia U.S.A.
95 O4 **Dalton** Massachusetts U.S.A.
98 D8 **Dalton** Nebraska U.S.A.
95 M5 **Dalton** Pennsylvania U.S.A.
115 R4 **Dalton, Kap** *C* Greenland
69 E12 **Daludalu** Sumatra
65 F5 **Dalu Dao** *isld* China
28 E6 **Dalum** Denmark
68 E2 **Daluo** China
65 H2 **Daluolemi** China
65 G1 **Daluozhen** China
71 G4 **Dalupiri** Philippines
71 E1 **Dalupiri** *isld* Philippines
12 E3 **Dalveen P** Scotland
28 S9 **Dalvik** Iceland
143 B9 **Dalwallinu** Western Australia Australia
15 D4 **Dalwhinnie** Scotland
36 F1 **Dalwigksthal** W Germany
109 N9 **Dalworthington Gardens** Texas U.S.A.
140 B2 **Daly** *R* N Terr Australia
102 B4 **Daly City** California U.S.A.
140 B2 **Daly R** N Terr Australia
140 B2 **Daly River** N Terr Australia
140 D1 **Daly River Aboriginal Land** N Terr Australia
140 C3 **Daly Waters** N Terr Australia
98 D5 **Dalzell** South Dakota U.S.A.
79 G10 **'Damaj, Bargā** *hill* Saudi Arabia
74 E8 **Daman** India
79 A7 **Damanhûr** Egypt
65 C4 **Damaqun Shan** *mt ra* China
71 O8 **Damar** *isld* Indonesia
71 B3 **Damar** *isld* Indonesia
107 L2 **Damar** Kansas U.S.A.
86 C5 **Damara** Cent Afr Republic
87 B10 **Damara** *homeland* Namibia
89 A4 **Damaraland** *tribal area* Namibia
95 S2 **Damariscotta L** Maine U.S.A.
Damas *see* **Dimashq**
Damascus *see* **Dimashq**
110 D6 **Damascus** Arkansas U.S.A.
95 K7 **Damascus** Maryland U.S.A.
94 F10 **Damascus** Virginia U.S.A.
131 B5 **Damas, Paso de las** Chile/Arg
86 B3 **Damaturu** Nigeria
77 C2 **Damavand** Iran
87 C7 **Damba** Angola
36 C7 **Dambach** France
83 K10 **Dambulla** Sri Lanka
68 J4 **Dam Cau Hai** Vietnam
126 G5 **Dame Marie** Haiti
20 E6 **Damgan** France
77 D1 **Dāmghān** Iran
28 A4 **Damhus Å** *R* Denmark
65 D3 **Damiao** China
48 L4 **Dămieneşti** Romania
21 L5 **Damigni** France
65 C6 **Daming** China
67 C5 **Daming Shan** *mts* China
80 F5 **Damiya** Jordan
80 F5 **Damiya Br** Jordan
71 E8 **Dammai** *isld* Philippines
77 B6 **Dammām, Ad** Saudi Arabia
21 O5 **Dammarie** France
18 G3 **Dammartin-en-Goële** France
22 E1 **Damme** Belgium
32 H7 **Damme** W Germany
74 H7 **Damoh** India
109 M6 **Damon** Texas U.S.A.
85 D7 **Damongo** Ghana
79 F5 **Damour** Lebanon
70 F4 **Dampelas, Tg** *C* Celebes
22 K4 **Dampicourt** Belgium

24
Desatoya Mts — Dongxiang

102 G2 Desatoya Mts Nevada U.S.A.
9 F3 Desborough England
130 B5 Descalvado Mato Grosso Brazil
130 F7 Descalvado São Paulo Brazil
124 A1 Descanso Mexico
102 H9 Descanso California U.S.A.
21 M8 Descartes France
121 S6 Deschaillons Quebec Canada
100 E4 Deschutes R Oregon U.S.A.
109 J3 Desdemona Texas U.S.A.
86 G3 Desē Ethiopia
45 M1 Dese R Italy
133 P7 Deseado Argentina
41 N7 Desenzano del Garda Italy
103 M2 Deseret Utah U.S.A.
101 N9 Deseret Pk Utah U.S.A.
121 N8 Deseronto Ontario Canada
103 J8 Desert Center California U.S.A.
102 H8 Desert Hot Springs California U.S.A.
121 O6 Desért, L Quebec Canada
101 M8 Desert Pk Utah U.S.A.
103 J5 Desert Ra Nevada U.S.A.
100 G8 Desert Valley Nevada U.S.A.
103 N5 Desert View Arizona U.S.A.
127 M4 Deshaies Guadeloupe W Indies
67 A3 Deshengpo China
98 J9 Deshler Nebraska U.S.A.
94 D5 Deshler Ohio U.S.A.
74 E5 Deshnok India
77 H4 Deshu Afghanistan
124 B1 Desierto de Altar desert Mexico
17 H4 Desierto de las Palmas Spain
98 E1 Des Lacs R North Dakota U.S.A.
118 D3 Desmarais Alberta Canada
121 O3 Desmaraisville Quebec Canada
100 J2 Desmet Idaho U.S.A.
101 L3 De Smet Montana U.S.A.
98 J5 De Smet South Dakota U.S.A.
130 B10 Desmochados Paraguay
99 M7 Des Moines R Iowa U.S.A.
99 N8 Des Moines Iowa U.S.A.
99 L6 Des Moines R Minnesota U.S.A.
106 G5 Des Moines New Mexico U.S.A.
54 B6 Desna R U.S.S.R.
54 E2 Desnogorsk U.S.S.R.
133 C8 Desolación, I Chile
71 G5 Desolation Pt Philippines
110 G4 De Soto Illinois U.S.A.
107 Q3 De Soto Kansas U.S.A.
110 F3 De Soto Missouri U.S.A.
99 P6 De Soto Wisconsin U.S.A.
113 F10 De Soto City Florida U.S.A.
16 E6 Despeñaperros, Pto. de Spain
99 T7 Des Plaines Illinois U.S.A.
48 G6 Despotovac Yugoslavia
83 H5 Desroches isld Seychelles
33 Q9 Dessau East Germany
40 E3 Dessoubre R France
111 K11 Destin Florida U.S.A.
31 K5 Deštná mt Poland
138 E6 D'Estrees, B South Australia Australia
117 D5 Destruction Bay Yukon Territory Canada
100 A2 Destruction I Washington U.S.A.
143 G6 Destruction,Mt Western Australia Australia
22 B2 Desvres France
48 G5 Deta Romania
87 E9 Dete Zimbabwe
32 G6 Detern W Germany
121 N7 Detlor Ontario Canada
32 J9 Detmold W Germany
94 D1 Detour Passage Michigan U.S.A.
99 U4 Detour, Pt Michigan U.S.A.
94 D1 Detour Village Michigan U.S.A.
94 D4 Detroit Michigan U.S.A.
109 M2 Detroit Texas U.S.A.
122 H4 Détroit d'Honguedo Quebec Canada
99 L3 Detroit Lakes Minnesota U.S.A.
94 D4 Detroit R Michigan U.S.A.
100 C5 Detroit Res Oregon U.S.A.
37 J4 Dettelbach W Germany
36 G6 Dettenhausen W Germany
36 H3 Detter W Germany
36 F7 Dettingen Baden-Württemberg W Germany
36 G3 Dettingen Bayern W Germany
36 C6 Dettwiller France
68 G5 Det Udom Thailand
48 E2 Detva Czechoslovakia
74 G8 Deūlgaon Rāja India
25 E6 Deurne Netherlands
37 Q2 Deutsch-Einsiedel East Germany
33 R7 Deutschhof East Germany
48 D3 Deutschkreutz Austria
37 P2 Deutsch-Neudorf East Germany
122 B2 Deux Décharges, L Quebec Canada
121 M6 Deux Rivieres Ontario Canada
18 E6 Deux-Sèvres dept France
48 H5 Deva Romania
16 D1 Deva R Spain
110 E7 De Valls Bluff Arkansas U.S.A.
48 F3 Dévaványa Hungary
47 L8 Devecitaşi Adası isld Turkey
48 D3 Devecser Hungary
78 E2 Develi Turkey
25 F4 Deventer Netherlands
112 D4 Devereux Georgia U.S.A.
86 H4 De Verme Falls Ethiopia
6 L1 Deveron oil rig North Sea
15 F3 Deveron R Scotland
46 E1 Devica mt Yugoslavia
74 D5 Devikot India
21 N3 Deville France
116 E3 Devil Mt Alaska U.S.A.
145 D4 Devil River Pk New Zealand
108 F5 Devils R Texas U.S.A.
14 D4 Devilsbit Mt Ireland
8 C3 Devils Bridge Wales
102 E6 Devils Den California U.S.A.
15 E4 Devil's Elbow Scotland
116 K5 Devils Elbow V Alaska U.S.A.
102 E3 Devils Gate California U.S.A.
89 E1 Devil's Gorge Zambia
6 L6 Devil's Hole North Sea
99 Q2 Devils I Michigan U.S.A.
110 H4 Devil's Kitchen L Illinois U.S.A.
98 H1 Devils Lake North Dakota U.S.A.
100 K8 Devils L. Res Nevada U.S.A.
117 G6 Devils Paw mt Br Col/Alaska Canada/U.S.A.
102 E4 Devils Pk California U.S.A.
103 J7 Devils Playground desert California U.S.A.
126 G2 Devil's Point Cat I Bahamas
102 E4 Devils Postpile Nat.Mon California U.S.A.
101 O8 Devils Slide Utah U.S.A.
139 H7 Devils Tower isld Tasmania Australia
98 B5 Devils Tower Wyoming U.S.A.
46 G3 Devin Bulgaria
109 J6 Devine Texas U.S.A.
80 C8 Devira Israel
9 E5 Devizes England
74 F6 Devli India
107 M7 Devol Oklahoma U.S.A.
46 D4 Devoll R Albania
118 D5 Devon Alberta Canada
120 G5 Devon Ontario Canada
8 C6 Devon co England
101 O1 Devon Montana U.S.A.
115 L2 Devon I Northwest Territories Canada
139 H8 Devonport Tasmania Australia
8 B7 Devonport England
80 E3 Devora Israel
78 D1 Devrek R Turkey
78 D1 Devrez R Turkey
89 G2 Devuli R Zimbabwe
52 H6 Devyaternya U.S.S.R.
52 E4 Devyatiny U.S.S.R.
55 E2 Devyatkova U.S.S.R.
70 F7 Dewakang Besar isld Indonesia
70 F7 Dewakang Ketjil isld Indonesia
107 P6 Dewar Oklahoma U.S.A.
118 H7 Dewar Lake Saskatchewan Canada
74 G7 Dewas India
69 B11 Dewa, Tanjong C Indonesia
118 G5 Dewberry Alberta Canada
98 H9 Deweese Nebraska U.S.A.
103 M7 Dewey Arizona U.S.A.
107 P5 Dewey Oklahoma U.S.A.
98 C6 Dewey South Dakota U.S.A.
94 E9 Dewey Res Kentucky U.S.A.
22 E1 De Wielingen Belgium/Neths
118 C8 De Winton Alberta Canada
111 E7 De Witt Arkansas U.S.A.
94 C4 De Witt Michigan U.S.A.
110 C2 De Witt Missouri U.S.A.
98 K9 De Witt Nebraska U.S.A.
95 L3 De Witt New York U.S.A.
13 G6 Dewsbury England
67 F2 Dexing China
111 D7 Dexter Arkansas U.S.A.
99 M8 Dexter Iowa U.S.A.
107 O4 Dexter Kansas U.S.A.
95 S1 Dexter Maine U.S.A.
94 D4 Dexter Michigan U.S.A.
99 O6 Dexter Minnesota U.S.A.
110 G5 Dexter Missouri U.S.A.
108 C2 Dexter New Mexico U.S.A.
95 L2 Dexter New York U.S.A.
109 L2 Dexter Texas U.S.A.
113 F8 Dexter, L Florida U.S.A.
99 Q5 Dexterville Wisconsin U.S.A.
138 B3 Dey-Dey, L South Australia Australia
22 L3 Deyfeldt Belgium
77 E3 Deyhuk Iran
57 C5 Deynau U.S.S.R.
136 H3 Deyong, Tanjung C W Irian
77 B6 Deyyer Iran
117 E5 Dezadeash L Yukon Territory Canada
77 A3 Dezfūl Iran
77 B4 Dez Gerd Iran
65 C6 Dezhou China
41 M6 Dezzo Italy
46 E7 Dháfni Greece
79 G6 Dhahab, Wādī adh watercourse Syria
Dhahran see Z̧ahrān, Az
75 O7 Dhaka Bangladesh
79 D3 Dhali Cyprus
75 J8 Dhamtari India
75 M7 Dhanbad India
74 J4 Dhangarhi Nepal
109 H6 D'Hanis Texas U.S.A.
75 M5 Dhankuta Nepal
76 D6 Dhanushkodi India
74 F7 Dhar India
76 C5 Dharapuram India
75 K7 Dharmajaygarh India
76 D4 Dharmapuri India
76 C3 Dharmavaram India
74 G2 Dharmsala India
86 A1 Dharoor R Somalia
85 C5 Dhar Oualata plateau Mauritania
76 B3 Dhārwād India
66 C6 Dhaulagiri mt Nepal
74 G5 Dhaulpur India
75 L8 Dhenkanal India
47 H7 Dhenoúsa isld Greece
46 D4 Dhërmi Albania
46 E5 Dheskáti Greece
46 G8 Dhespotikó isld Greece
40 A4 Dheune R France
80 G7 Dhiban Jordan
46 F7 Dhídhimoi Greece
47 H3 Dhidhimótikhon Greece
46 G9 Dhíkti Ori mt Crete Greece
46 G7 Dhílos isld Greece
46 E7 Dhimitsána Greece
80 F8 Dhira Jordan
46 F6 Dhírfis mt Greece
47 H7 Dhodhekánisos islds Greece
74 G5 Dholpur India
46 E5 Dhomokós Greece
76 C3 Dhone India
74 D8 Dhoraji India
46 G3 Dhoxáton Greece
46 G7 Dhragonísi isld Greece
47 O12 Dhráhstis, Akra C Greece
74 D7 Dhrangadhra India
46 F5 Dhrépanon, Ákr C Greece
46 D5 Dhrin R Albania
75 N5 Dhuburi India
Dhufar see Z̧ufār
21 O6 Dhuison France
74 F8 Dhule India
74 E2 Dhulian Pakistan
86 B2 Dhuudo Somalia
46 G9 Dia isld Crete Greece
129 H2 Diable, I.du Fr Guiana
40 F5 Diablerets mt Switzerland
100 D1 Diablo L Washington U.S.A.
127 K2 Diablo, Mt Jamaica
108 C4 Diablo, Sa mts Texas U.S.A.
127 O7 Diablotin, Morne hill Dominica
99 M9 Diagonal Iowa U.S.A.
85 B6 Dialakoto Senegal
133 D4 Diamante R Argentina
131 E4 Diamante Argentina
141 F6 Diamantina R Queensland Australia
129 K7 Diamantina Brazil
130 G6 Diamantina Minas Gerais Brazil
141 F6 Diamantina Lakes Queensland Australia
129 G6 Diamantino Brazil
130 C4 Diamantino Mato Grosso Brazil
130 D5 Diamantino Mato Grosso Brazil
110 B5 Diamond Missouri U.S.A.
118 E9 Diamond City Alberta Canada
75 N7 Diamond Harb India
144 D5 Diamond Harbour New Zealand
102 S12 Diamond Hd Hawaiian Is
141 K3 Diamond Islets Gt Barrier Reef Australia
100 C6 Diamond L Oregon U.S.A.
103 J2 Diamond Mts Nevada U.S.A.
100 C6 Diamond Peak mt Oregon U.S.A.
103 J2 Diamond Pk Nevada U.S.A.
102 D3 Diamond Springs California U.S.A.
101 P8 Diamondville Wyoming U.S.A.
94 G8 Diana West Virginia U.S.A.
141 J3 Diana Bank Gt Barrier Reef Aust
28 G5 Dianaland Denmark
67 C6 Dianbai China
Dianbu see Feidong
67 A4 Dian Chi L China
67 B1 Dianjiang China
44 D4 Diano Marina Italy
129 J6 Dianópolis Brazil
65 H2 Diaoling China
85 E6 Diapaga Burkina
71 F2 Diapitan B Luzon Philippines
46 F4 Diavata Greece
68 A6 Diavolo, Mt Andaman Is
65 A5 Dibabu China
87 D7 Dibaya Zaire
86 D3 Dibbis Sudan
66 F6 Dibhuk Pass India/Burma
86 B4 Dibi Cameroon
109 N4 Diboll Texas U.S.A.
75 Q5 Dibrugarh India
66 E6 Dibrugarh India
71 E3 Dicapanisan Pt Luzon Philippines
Diciosânmârtin see Tîrnăveni
98 E9 Dickens Nebraska U.S.A.
108 G2 Dickens Texas U.S.A.
95 R6 Dickey Maine U.S.A.
98 H3 Dickey North Dakota U.S.A.
98 D3 Dickinson North Dakota U.S.A.
109 M6 Dickinson Texas U.S.A.
9 H3 Dickleburgh England
36 D3 Dickscheid-Geroldstein W Germany
110 J5 Dickson Tennessee U.S.A.
95 M5 Dickson City Pennsylvania U.S.A.
78 H3 Dicle R Turkey
45 L4 Dicomano Italy
71 F1 Didacas isld Luzon Philippines
9 E4 Didcot England
85 C6 Didiéni Mali
109 L8 Dido Texas U.S.A.
118 C7 Didsbury Alberta Canada
74 F5 Didwana India
121 S4 Didyme Quebec Canada
19 O15 Die France
89 G5 Die Berg mt S Africa
36 B5 Diebling France
85 D6 Diébougou Burkina
36 F4 Dieburg W Germany
118 K7 Diefenbaker, L Saskatchewan Canada
33 N6 Die Göhrde reg W Germany
131 F3 Diego Lamas Uruguay
133 D9 Diego Ramirez, Is Chile
Diego Suarez see Antsiranana
30 D1 Die Halligen inlet W Germany
32 L8 Diekholzen W Germany
22 L4 Diekirch Luxembourg
20 G2 Diélette France
32 H8 Dielingen W Germany
85 C6 Diema Mali
32 K9 Diemel R W Germany
36 C6 Diemeringen France
68 F2 Dien Bien Phu Vietnam
68 G3 Dien Chau Vietnam
32 J8 Diepenau W Germany
25 G4 Diepenheim Netherlands
32 H7 Diepholz W Germany
21 N2 Dieppe France
127 P4 Dieppe Bay Town St Kitts W Indies
36 D2 Dierdorf W Germany
25 F4 Dieren Netherlands
33 Q4 Dierhagen East Germany
36 D2 Dieringhausen W Germany
109 N1 Dierks Arkansas U.S.A.
65 F2 Di'er Songhua Jiang R China
33 N7 Diesdorf East Germany
41 J2 Diessenhofen Switzerland
22 J2 Diest Belgium
110 H2 Dieterich Illinois U.S.A.
37 K3 Dietersdorf W Germany
37 M5 Dietfurt W Germany
41 H3 Dietikon Switzerland
101 L7 Dietrich Idaho U.S.A.
36 F3 Dietzenbach W Germany
19 O15 Dieulefit France
19 K4 Dieuze France
25 F3 Dieverbrug Netherlands
36 B2 Die Ville reg W Germany
36 E3 Diez W Germany
65 D7 Difang China
22 K4 Differdange Luxembourg
67 F1 Digang China
75 Q5 Digboi India
122 G9 Digby Nova Scotia Canada
9 F1 Digby England
83 M14 Digby, C Kerguelen Indian Oc
122 F9 Digby Neck Nova Scotia Canada
107 K3 Dighton Kansas U.S.A.
95 Q5 Dighton Massachusetts U.S.A.
94 B2 Dighton Michigan U.S.A.
74 G9 Diglur India
19 Q16 Digne France
21 N4 Digny France
18 H6 Digoin France
71 F2 Digollorin Pt Luzon Philippines
71 G7 Digos Mindanao Philippines
74 G8 Digras India
136 H3 Digul R W Irian
86 H5 Diinsoor Somalia
71 E5 Diit isld Philippines
22 H2 Dijle R Belgium
19 J5 Dijon France
86 C4 Dik Chad
89 E4 Dikabeye Botswana
26 H6 Dikanäs Sweden
86 H3 Dikhil Djibouti
47 H5 Dikili Turkey
79 B7 Dîkirnis Egypt
22 D2 Dikkebus Belgium
67 F3 Dikou China
83 K11 Dikoya Sri Lanka
55 D2 Dikoye, Oz L U.S.S.R.
22 D1 Diksmuide Belgium
50 H1 Dikson U.S.S.R.
50 G1 Dikson, Ostrov isld U.S.S.R.
86 B3 Dikwa Nigeria
47 J7 Dilek Dağ mt Turkey
106 E6 Dilia New Mexico U.S.A.
68 A6 Diligent Str Andaman Is
68 J7 Di Linh Vietnam
47 N11 Diliskelesi Ist lighthouse Turkey
119 M8 Dilke Saskatchewan Canada
103 O6 Dilkon Arizona U.S.A.
36 E2 Dill R W Germany
118 G6 Dillberry L. Prov Park Alberta Canada
107 L6 Dill City Oklahoma U.S.A.
36 E2 Dillenburg W Germany
98 K9 Diller Nebraska U.S.A.
109 H7 Dilley Texas U.S.A.
86 E3 Dilling Sudan
36 B5 Dillingen W Germany
116 H7 Dillingham Alaska U.S.A.
118 H3 Dillon Saskatchewan Canada
106 D2 Dillon Colorado U.S.A.
101 N4 Dillon Montana U.S.A.
112 H3 Dillon South Carolina U.S.A.
144 D5 Dillon Cone mt New Zealand
94 E6 Dillon Res Ohio U.S.A.
95 K6 Dillsburg Pennsylvania U.S.A.
94 J9 Dillwyn Virginia U.S.A.
87 D8 Dilolo Zaire
75 P6 Dimapur India
124 F6 Dimas Mexico
79 G5 Dimashq Syria
86 D7 Dimbelenge Zaire
85 D7 Dimbokro Ivory Coast
138 F6 Dimboola Victoria Australia
48 J5 Dîmbo Viţa R Romania
48 J6 Dîmboviţa reg Romania
141 H3 Dimbulah Queensland Australia
54 J8 Dimitrov U.S.S.R.
54 E8 Dimitrova U.S.S.R.
47 H2 Dimitrovgrad Bulgaria
53 G7 Dimitrovgrad U.S.S.R.
46 F1 Dimitrovgrad Yugoslavia
46 G2 Dimitrov, Yazovir G. res Bulgaria
108 E1 Dimmitt Texas U.S.A.
98 H6 Dimock South Dakota U.S.A.
79 F7 Dimona Israel
46 F1 Dimovo Bulgaria
71 G5 Dinagat isld Philippines
71 G5 Dinagat Sound Philippines
75 N6 Dinajpur Bangladesh
20 F5 Dinan France
22 H3 Dinant Belgium
47 L6 Dinar Turkey
42 G4 Dinara Planina Yugoslavia
20 F4 Dinard-St.Enogat France
86 F3 Dinder R Sudan
76 C5 Dindigul India
109 K7 Dinero Texas U.S.A.
86 C7 Dinga Zaire
71 E3 Dingalan B Luzon Philippines
68 K3 Ding'an China
58 E4 Dingbian China
32 E9 Dingden W Germany
20 G5 Dingé France
33 M10 Dingelstädt East Germany
33 O9 Dingelstedt East Germany
48 K3 Dîngeni Romania
75 M4 Dinggyê China
67 G1 Dinghai China
101 O7 Dingle Idaho U.S.A.
14 A4 Dingle B Ireland
67 E4 Dingnan China
141 J6 Dingo Queensland Australia
37 O6 Dingolfing W Germany
71 E1 Dingras Luzon Philippines
65 C7 Dingtao China
85 B6 Dinguiraye Guinea
123 M7 Dingwall C Breton I, Nova Scotia
15 D3 Dingwall Scotland
58 D4 Dingxi China
65 C5 Ding Xian China
65 B5 Dingxiang China
65 C5 Dingxing China
65 E6 Dingzi Gang B China
69 H8 Dinh An, Cua river mouth Vietnam
67 B6 Dinh Lap Vietnam
25 H4 Dinkel R Netherlands
37 J5 Dinkelsbühl W Germany
37 K7 Dinkelscherben W Germany
32 H7 Dinklage W Germany
103 O5 Dinnebito Wash creek Arizona U.S.A.
13 G3 Dinnington England
87 E10 Dinokwe Botswana
118 K1 Dinorwic L Ontario Canada
101 Q9 Dinosaur Nat.Mon Utah/Colo U.S.A.
32 E9 Dinslaken W Germany
118 K7 Dinsmore Saskatchewan Canada
113 F7 Dinsmore Florida U.S.A.
70 K8 Dintiteladas C Sumatra
102 E5 Dinuba California U.S.A.
94 K9 Dinwiddie Virginia U.S.A.
25 F5 Dinxperlo Netherlands
27 G15 Diö Sweden
85 C6 Dioila Mali
116 C4 Diomede Is Bering Str
51 S2 Diomida, Ostrova islds U.S.S.R.
22 H3 Dion Belgium
86 D2 Diona Chad
130 D10 Dionisio Cerqueira Brazil
130 D5 Diorama Brazil
48 F2 Diósgyőr Hungary
85 A6 Diouloulou Senegal
85 C6 Dioura Mali
85 A6 Diourbel Senegal
74 C6 Diplo Pakistan
71 F6 Dipolog Mindanao Philippines
22 L4 Dippach Luxembourg
12 C2 Dippen Scotland
12 C3 Dippin Scotland
144 B6 Dipton New Zealand
74 D1 Dir Pakistan
27 B13 Dirdal Norway
141 G2 Direction,C Queensland Australia
83 M8 Direction I Cocos Is Indian Oc
86 H4 Dirē Dawa Ethiopia
125 L4 Diriamba Nicaragua
87 D9 Dirico Angola
43 F11 Dirillo R Sicily
143 A7 Dirk Hartog I Western Australia Australia
84 E6 Dirkou Niger
25 B5 Dirksland Netherlands
13 F1 Dirleton Scotland
36 C5 Dirmingen W Germany
86 E3 Dirra Sudan
141 J8 Dirranbandi Queensland Australia
103 O3 Dirty Devil R Utah U.S.A.
102 T13 Disappearing I Hawaiian Is
131 H6 Disappointment, C S Georgia
100 A3 Disappointment, C Washington U.S.A.
135 N9 Disappointment Is Tuamotu Arch Pacific Oc
143 E6 Disappointment,L Western Australia Australia
139 K6 Disaster B New South Wales Australia
100 F1 Disautel Washington U.S.A.
37 J6 Dischingen W Germany
117 Q4 Discovery Northwest Territories Canada
138 F7 Discovery B S Aust/Vict Australia
127 K1 Discovery Bay Jamaica
100 C2 Discovery Bay Washington U.S.A.
100 C1 Discovery I Washington U.S.A.
90 J13 Discovery Tablemount S Atlantic Oc
142 E5 Discovery Well Western Australia Australia
41 J4 Disentis Switzerland
13 G5 Dishforth England
116 J5 Dishkakat Alaska U.S.A.
116 J5 Dishna R Alaska U.S.A.
80 F1 Dishon R Israel
80 F1 Dishon Israel
115 O4 Diskofjord Greenland
119 M8 Disley Saskatchewan Canada
140 F4 Dismal R Queensland Australia
98 F8 Dismal R Nebraska U.S.A.
95 L10 Dismal Swamp Virginia U.S.A.
52 C6 Disna U.S.S.R.
22 K2 Dison Belgium
95 K9 Disputanta Virginia U.S.A.
121 T7 Disraëli Quebec Canada
9 H3 Diss England
21 L8 Dissay France
21 L6 Dissay-sous-Courcillon France
32 H8 Dissen W Germany
122 C4 Dissimieux, L Quebec Canada
100 C6 Disston Oregon U.S.A.
95 L8 District of Columbia (D.C.) U.S.A.
79 A7 Disûq Egypt
9 F6 Ditchling England
33 O9 Ditfurt East Germany
32 K4 Dithmarschen reg W Germany
43 F11 Dittaino R Sicily
36 G6 Ditzingen W Germany
74 D8 Diu India
71 G6 Diuata Mts Mindanao Philippines
21 K7 Dive R France
52 D5 Divenskaya U.S.S.R.
121 L6 Diver Ontario Canada
110 G2 Divernon Illinois U.S.A.
142 G3 Diversion Dam Western Australia Australia
109 H2 Diversion L Texas U.S.A.
21 K3 Dives R France
21 K3 Dives sur Mer France
20 G2 Divette R France
26 L3 Dividal R Norway
106 E3 Divide Colorado U.S.A.
141 H6 Dividing Range Queensland Australia
71 F2 Divilacan B Luzon Philippines
87 F10 Divinhe Mozambique
130 G7 Divinópolis Brazil
22 C3 Divion France
100 F8 Division Peak mt Nevada U.S.A.
53 F10 Divnoye U.S.S.R.
85 C7 Divo Ivory Coast
78 G2 Divrigi Turkey
74 B5 Diwana Pakistan
78 K6 Dīwānīyah, Ad Iraq
121 O4 Dix Quebec Canada
98 C8 Dix Nebraska U.S.A.
95 R2 Dixfield Maine U.S.A.
111 K8 Dixiana Alabama U.S.A.
111 K10 Dixie Alabama U.S.A.
113 D7 Dixie Georgia U.S.A.
100 K4 Dixie Idaho U.S.A.
100 G3 Dixie Washington U.S.A.
100 G5 Dixie Pass Oregon U.S.A.
102 F2 Dixie Valley Nevada U.S.A.
121 Q5 Dix Milles, L.des Quebec Canada
95 S2 Dixmont Maine U.S.A.
95 O2 Dix Mt New York U.S.A.
Dixmude see Diksmuide
102 C3 Dixon California U.S.A.
99 R8 Dixon Illinois U.S.A.
110 D4 Dixon Missouri U.S.A.
101 L2 Dixon Montana U.S.A.
98 K7 Dixon Nebraska U.S.A.
106 E5 Dixon New Mexico U.S.A.
101 S8 Dixon Wyoming U.S.A.
117 G8 Dixon Entrance str Br Col/Alaska Canada/U.S.A.
111 J9 Dixons Mills Alabama U.S.A.
117 P7 Dixonville Alberta Canada
94 H6 Dixonville Pennsylvania U.S.A.
67 A4 Dixu China
121 T7 Dixville Quebec Canada
65 H3 Diyingou China
74 B9 Diz Pakistan
77 H6 Diz Pakistan
67 C2 Dizhuang China
8 B6 Dizzard Pt England
86 B5 Dja R Cameroon
84 E5 Djado Niger
84 E5 Djado, Pl.du Niger
71 A2 Djailolo Halmahera Indonesia
Djailolo Gilolo isld see Halmahera isld
Djajapura see Jayapura
86 B6 Djambala Congo
69 F13 Djambi prov Sumatra
70 L9 Djampang-Kulon Java
85 F4 Djanet Algeria
70 E6 Djangeru Kalimantan
70 E3 Djanlonong Kalimantan
85 E3 Djaret watercourse Algeria
70 L9 Djatinegara Java
70 M9 Djatiwangi Java
86 B2 Djbella Niger
69 G13 Djebus Indonesia
86 C3 Djédaa Chad
85 E2 Djedi watercourse Algeria
85 E2 Djelfa Algeria
86 E4 Djéma Cent Afr Republic
70 F7 Djeneponto Sulawesi
Djerba, I de see Jerba, I de
86 B4 Djérem R Cameroon
Djezair, El see Alger
85 D6 Djibasso Burkina
85 D6 Djibo Burkina
86 H3 Djibouti Djibouti
86 H3 Djibouti rep N E Africa
86 D7 Djokopunda Zaire
86 D5 Djolu Zaire
70 D7 Djorong Kalimantan
86 B6 Djoué R Congo
85 C5 Djouf, El reg Mauritania/Mali
85 E7 Djougou Benin
86 B5 Djoum Cameroon
86 C2 Djourab dist Chad
86 F5 Djugu Zaire
29 T9 Djupivogur Iceland
27 H11 Djura Sweden
27 K12 Djursholm Sweden
28 F4 Djursland reg Denmark
111 G10 D'Lo Mississippi U.S.A.
51 O1 Dmitriya Lapteva, Proliv str U.S.S.R.
55 G3 Dmitriyevka U.S.S.R.
54 G4 Dmitriyev-L'govskiy U.S.S.R.
54 J1 Dmitrov U.S.S.R.
54 D6 Dmitrovka U.S.S.R.
54 G4 Dmitrovsk-Orlovskiy U.S.S.R.
54 B4 Dnepr R U.S.S.R.
54 F8 Dneprodzerzhinsk U.S.S.R.
54 G8 Dnepropetrovsk U.S.S.R.
54 F9 Dneprorudnoye U.S.S.R.
53 C7 Dneprovskaya Nizmennost lowland U.S.S.R.
54 C10 Dneprovskiy Liman lagoon U.S.S.R.
53 C9 Dnestr R Europe
48 M4 Dnestrovsk U.S.S.R.
48 N4 Dnestrovskiy Liman lagoon Ukrainskaya S.S.R. U.S.S.R.
Dnieper R see Dnepr R
Dniester R see Dnestr R
52 C5 Dno U.S.S.R.
77 K2 Doāb Mekh-i-Zarīn Afghanistan
122 F7 Doaktown New Brunswick Canada
70 E7 Doangdoangan Besar isld Indonesia
70 E7 Doangdoangan Ketjil isld Indonesia
67 B6 Doan Hung Vietnam
86 C4 Doba Chad
33 Q5 Dobbertin East Germany
138 E2 Dobbie, L South Australia Australia
140 E6 Dobbie,Mt N Terr Australia
109 M5 Dobbin Texas U.S.A.
31 M6 Dobczyce Poland
52 B6 Dobele U.S.S.R.
37 P1 Döbeln East Germany
33 T9 Doberlug Kirchhain East Germany
31 J3 Dobiegniew Poland
133 E5 Doblas Argentina
136 G3 Dobo Moluccas Indonesia
48 E6 Doboj Yugoslavia
112 F6 Doboy Sd Georgia U.S.A.
31 J2 Dobra Poland
37 M3 Döbraberg mt W Germany
37 P4 Dobřany Czechoslovakia
38 J8 Dobratsch mt Austria
31 M2 Dobre Miasto Poland
48 G4 Dobresti Romania
48 H6 Dobreta-Turnu-Severin Romania
38 J8 Döbriach Austria
Dobrič see Tolbukhin
33 S9 Döbrichau East Germany
46 F3 Dobrinishte Bulgaria
31 H6 Dobříš Czechoslovakia
33 Q8 Dobritz East Germany
31 L5 Dobrodzień Poland
31 O6 Dobromil U.S.S.R.
54 J8 Dobropol'ye U.S.S.R.
48 J6 Dobroteşti Romania
54 F2 Dobroye U.S.S.R.
54 C4 Dobrush U.S.S.R.
54 C4 Dobryanka U.S.S.R.
31 L3 Dobrzyn Poland
48 F2 Dobšiná Czechoslovakia
144 B6 Dobson R New Zealand
144 C5 Dobson New Zealand
112 G1 Dobson North Carolina U.S.A.
8 B7 Dobwalls England
127 N1 Docas del Dragón chan Trinidad/Ven
71 D7 Doc Can isld Sulu Arch Philippines
130 G6 Doce, R Brazil
143 G6 Docker Cr Western Australia Australia
140 A6 Docker River N Terr Australia
9 G2 Docking England
26 H9 Dockmyr Sweden
142 F4 Dockrell, Mt Western Australia Australia
26 K8 Docksta Sweden
36 B3 Dockweiler W Germany
109 H10 Doctor Cos Mexico
143 E8 Doctor Hicks Ra Western Australia Australia
48 G4 Doctor Petru Groza Romania
121 P3 Doda, L Quebec Canada
76 C4 Dod Ballapur India
13 F2 Doddington England
109 O2 Doddridge Arkansas U.S.A.
118 E5 Dodds Alberta Canada
Dodecanese islds see Dhodhekánisos islds
98 K8 Dodge Nebraska U.S.A.
98 D2 Dodge North Dakota U.S.A.
99 O5 Dodge Center Minnesota U.S.A.
107 K4 Dodge City Kansas U.S.A.
99 Q7 Dodgeville Wisconsin U.S.A.
8 B7 Dodman Pt England
88 E5 Dodoma Tanzania
33 O6 Dodow East Germany
118 J7 Dodsland Saskatchewan Canada
109 P3 Dodson Louisiana U.S.A.
101 R1 Dodson Montana U.S.A.
47 K5 Dodurga Turkey
22 G1 Doel Belgium
112 D6 Doerun Georgia U.S.A.
25 F4 Doesburg Netherlands
25 F5 Doetinchem Netherlands
71 J5 Dofa Indonesia
36 F6 Doffingen W Germany
66 D5 Dogai Coring L China
47 H6 Doğanbey Burun C Turkey
79 F2 Doğankent Turkey
78 G1 Doğankent Turkey
117 M10 Dog Creek British Columbia Canada
66 E5 Dogên Co L China
47 L5 Döğer Turkey
7 M8 Dogger Bank North Sea
127 N5 Dog I Lesser Antilles
144 B7 Dog I New Zealand
113 C8 Dog I Florida U.S.A.
119 T7 Dog L Manitoba Canada
99 R1 Dog L Ontario Canada
44 C2 Dogliani Italy
38 H9 Dogna Italy
60 G9 Dōgo isld Japan
85 E6 Dogondoutchi Niger
60 G10 Dōgo-yama mt Japan
118 C7 Dog Pound Alberta Canada
126 E2 Dog Rocks Bahamas
78 K2 Doğubayazit Turkey
127 P4 Dogwood Pt Nevis W Indies
Doha see Dawḥah, Ad
Dohad see Dāhod
75 P7 Dohazar Bangladesh
121 S5 Doheny Quebec Canada
33 N4 Döhnsdorf W Germany
71 A1 Doi Indonesia
68 D3 Doi Saket Thailand
22 H3 Doische Belgium
130 E8 Dois Córregos Brazil
46 F3 Dojran Yugoslavia
46 F3 Dojrawsko ezero L Yugoslavia
27 D11 Dokka Norway
26 M4 Dokkas Sweden
28 E3 Dokkedal Denmark
25 E2 Dokkum Netherlands
55 D5 Dokuchayevka U.S.S.R.
54 J9 Dokuchayevsk U.S.S.R.
136 H3 Dolak isld W Irian
98 H5 Doland South Dakota U.S.A.
121 S4 Dolbeau Quebec Canada
32 G9 Dolberg W Germany
20 G4 Dol-de Bretagne France
19 J5 Dôle France
125 N5 Dolega Panama
42 G3 Dolenjske Toplice Yugoslavia
8 C3 Dolfor Wales
8 C2 Dolgellau Wales
95 N3 Dolgeville New York U.S.A.
116 G9 Dolgoi I Alaska U.S.A.
55 E3 Dolgovskoye U.S.S.R.
48 H2 Dolgoye U.S.S.R.
43 C9 Dolianova Sardinia
48 H2 Dolina U.S.S.R.
59 M2 Dolinsk U.S.S.R.
54 D8 Dolinskaya U.S.S.R.
75 K5 Dolirighat India
71 A3 Dolit Indonesia
46 F1 Dolj Romania
46 E1 Doljevac Yugoslavia
38 G8 Döllach Austria
12 E1 Dollar Scotland
118 J9 Dollard Saskatchewan Canada
122 F3 Dollard, L Quebec Canada
15 E5 Dollar Law mt Scotland
32 F6 Dollart inlet W Germany/Neths
32 M8 Dollbergen W Germany
33 P8 Dolle East Germany
146 D5 Dolleman I Antarctica
28 C4 Dollerup Denmark
37 L6 Dollnstein W Germany
21 M5 Dollon France
37 K1 Döllstädt East Germany
46 G1 Dolna Mitropbliya Bulgaria
46 E3 Dolneni Yugoslavia
46 G1 Dolni Dŭbnik Bulgaria
37 Q2 Dolní Jiřetin Czechoslovakia
31 J6 Dolní Královice Czechoslovakia
37 O3 Dolní Žandov Czechoslovakia
45 M1 Dolo Italy
70 F5 Dolo Sulawesi
19 P13 Dolomieu France
42 D2 Dolomitiche, Alpi Italy
Dolonnur see Duolun
86 H5 Dolo Odo Ethiopia
131 F6 Dolores Argentina
125 P9 Dolores Guatemala
17 G6 Dolores Spain
131 F4 Dolores Uruguay
106 B4 Dolores Colorado U.S.A.
106 B3 Dolores R Colorado U.S.A.
125 J7 Dolores Hidalgo Mexico
133 F8 Dolphin, C Falkland Is
127 H1 Dolphin Hd hill Jamaica
87 B11 Dolphin Hd Namibia
142 B5 Dolphin I Western Australia Australia
13 E2 Dolphinton Scotland
114 H4 Dolphin & Union Str Northwest Territories Canada
38 G8 Dölsach Austria
31 K4 Dolsk Poland
68 G3 Do Luong Vietnam
21 M7 Dolus-le-Sec France
8 C1 Dolwyddelan Wales
136 H2 Dom mt W Irian
122 H2 Domagaya L Labrador, Nfld Canada
119 U9 Domain Manitoba Canada
47 K5 Domaniç Turkey
47 K5 Domaniç Dağı mt Turkey
21 P1 Domart-en-Ponthieu France
37 O5 Domažlice Czechoslovakia
55 C5 Dombarovskiy U.S.S.R.
26 D9 Dombås Norway
19 K4 Dombasle France
87 B8 Dombe Grande Angola
140 A2 Dombey,C N Terr Australia
48 E4 Dombóvár Hungary
48 G2 Dombrád Hungary
37 J5 Dombühl W Germany
25 A5 Domburg Netherlands
103 K9 Dome Arizona U.S.A.
117 N9 Dome Creek British Columbia Canada
40 E7 Dôme-de-Chasseforêt France
103 K8 Dome Rock Mts Arizona U.S.A.
144 D5 Domett New Zealand
145 D4 Domett, Mt New Zealand
36 B6 Domèvre France
21 J4 Domfront France
106 D6 Domingo New Mexico U.S.A.
127 O7 Dominica isld Lesser Antilles
127 J5 Dominican Rep W Indies
123 M7 Dominion C Breton I, Nova Scotia
115 M4 Dominion, C Northwest Territories Canada
119 U9 Dominion City Manitoba Canada
123 L1 Dominion L Labrador, Nfld Canada
115 O7 Domino Labrador, Nfld Canada
33 O6 Dömitz East Germany
21 H4 Domjean France
130 G6 Dom Joaquim Brazil
41 K4 Domleschg R Switzerland
18 F8 Domme France
25 D6 Dommel R Netherlands
33 R9 Dommitzsch East Germany
86 A2 Domo Ethiopia
54 J1 Domodedovo U.S.S.R.
41 H5 Domodossola Italy
21 P3 Domont France
146 E14 Domont d'Urville Sea Antarctica
40 D1 Dompaire France
21 H5 Dompierre-du-Chemin France
22 B3 Dompierre-sur-Authie France
20 H8 Dompierre-sur-Yon France
36 B7 Domptail France
71 J9 Dompu Sumbawa Indonesia
119 M6 Domremy Saskatchewan Canada
26 K8 Domsjö Sweden
88 E9 Domue pk Mozambique
131 B6 Domuyo pk Argentina
141 K8 Domville mt Queensland Australia
141 K8 Domville,Mt Queensland Australia
46 F6 Domvraina Greece
42 F2 Domžale Yugoslavia
141 J5 Don R Queensland Australia
22 D2 Don France
20 G6 Don R France
124 E4 Don Mexico
15 F3 Don R Scotland
54 L5 Don R U.S.S.R.
106 D9 Dona Ana New Mexico U.S.A.
45 M1 Donada Italy
14 F2 Donaghadee N Ireland
139 G6 Donald Victoria Australia
121 M8 Donald Ontario Canada
118 E6 Donalda Alberta Canada
144 A6 Donald, Mt New Zealand
140 F4 Donaldson Queensland Australia
109 P1 Donaldson Arkansas U.S.A.
98 K1 Donaldson Minnesota U.S.A.
111 E11 Donaldsonville Louisiana U.S.A.
112 C6 Donalsonville Georgia U.S.A.
14 E3 Donard Ireland
124 G5 Donato Guerra Mexico
38 L5 Donau R Austria
37 L6 Donau R W Germany
41 J2 Donaueschingen W Germany
37 L6 Donaumoos reg W Germany
37 K6 Donauried reg W Germany
37 N5 Donaustauf W Germany
37 K6 Donauwörth W Germany
118 K7 Donavon Saskatchewan Canada
38 M7 Donawitz Austria
54 J8 Donbass (Donetskiy Ugol'nyy Basseyn) U.S.S.R.
16 D6 Don Benito Spain
140 B1 Don,C N Terr Australia
13 G6 Doncaster England
95 K8 Doncaster Maryland U.S.A.
22 H4 Donchery France
22 K4 Doncols Luxembourg
87 B7 Dondo Angola
87 F9 Dondo Mozambique
71 E6 Dondonay isld Philippines
70 G4 Dondo, Teluk B Sulawesi
70 G4 Dondo, Tg C Sulawesi
73 N7 Dondra Head C Sri Lanka
48 L2 Dondyushany U.S.S.R.
14 D2 Donegal co Ireland
14 C2 Donegal Ireland
14 C2 Donegal Bay B Ireland
14 B4 Donegal Pt Ireland
110 K5 Donelson Tennessee U.S.A.
14 C4 Doneraile Ireland
54 J8 Donetsk U.S.S.R.
53 E9 Donetskiy Kryazh mts U.S.S.R.
127 J2 Don Figuerero Mts Jamaica
86 B4 Donga R Nigeria
59 K2 Dong'an China
67 D3 Dong'an China
68 J5 Dong An Vietnam
143 A8 Dongara W Australia
74 J8 Dongargarh India
66 D4 Dongbolhai Shan mts China
Dongchangshou see Xinle
Dongcun see Haiyang
68 H2 Dong Dang Vietnam
65 C6 Dong'e China
25 C5 Dongen Netherlands
20 F7 Donges France
68 J3 Dongfang China
65 J1 Dongfanghong China
65 F3 Dongfeng China
70 F5 Donggala Sulawesi
58 C4 Donggi Cona L China
67 D1 Donggong China
65 F4 Donggou China
67 E3 Donggu China
67 E5 Dongguan China
65 C6 Dongguang China
68 H4 Dong Ha Vietnam
65 D7 Donghai China
67 C6 Donghai Dao isld China
58 E4 Dong He R China
58 D3 Dong He R China
68 H4 Dong Hoi Vietnam
Donghuang see Xishui Guizhou
67 C4 Dongjiang China
65 H2 Dongjingcheng China
70 F6 Dongkait, Tanjong C Sulawesi
70 G4 Dongkalang Sulawesi
68 H1 Dong Khe Vietnam
67 C3 Dongkou China
67 B4 Donglan China
Dongliao see Liaoyuan
65 F3 Dongliao He R China
67 B5 Dongling China
67 E1 Dongliu China
65 C7 Dongming China
68 H7 Dong Nai R Vietnam
59 K2 Dongning China
87 C8 Dongo Angola
41 K5 Dongo Italy
86 C5 Dongo Zaire
84 J6 Dongola Sudan
86 C5 Dongou Congo
68 E4 Dong Phraya Fai ra Thailand
68 E5 Dong Phraya Yen Thailand
Dongping see Anhua
65 C7 Dongping China
65 C6 Dongping Hu L China
68 H7 Dong Sai Vietnam
67 F5 Dongshan China
67 F5 Dongshan Dao isld China
67 E6 Dongsha Qundao isld China
65 A5 Dongsheng China
67 B2 Dongsheng China
67 D2 Dongting Hu L China
67 G3 Dongtou China
67 B6 Dong Trieu Vietnam
65 D2 Dong Ujimqin Qi China
68 G1 Dong Van Vietnam
87 D8 Dongwe R Zambia
67 B2 Dongxi China
67 E2 Dongxiang China

54 J8 **Dzerzhinsk** U.S.S.R.
57 K2 **Dzerzhinskoye** U.S.S.R.
59 K1 **Dzhagdy,Khrebet** *mts* U.S.S.R.
56 D5 **Dzhakul', Gora** *mt* U.S.S.R.
57 G4 **Dzhalal-Abad** U.S.S.R.
59 H1 **Dzhalinda** U.S.S.R.
55 B5 **Dzhambeyty** U.S.S.R.
57 C4 **Dzhankel'dy** U.S.S.R.
57 J2 **Dzhansugurov** U.S.S.R.
56 D5 **Dzhebashskiy Khrebet** *mts* U.S.S.R.
46 G3 **Dzhebel** Bulgaria
57 J3 **Dzhergalan** U.S.S.R.
55 D5 **Dzhetygara** U.S.S.R.
57 C4 **Dzhetymtau, Gory** *mt* U.S.S.R.
57 E4 **Dzhetysay** U.S.S.R.
57 D1 **Dzhezdy** U.S.S.R.
57 E1 **Dzhezkazgan** U.S.S.R.
56 G5 **Dzhida** *R* U.S.S.R.
56 F5 **Dzhidinskiy,Khrebet** *mts* Mongolia/U.S.S.R.
57 B4 **Dzhigirbent** U.S.S.R.
57 E4 **Dzhizak** U.S.S.R.
56 D4 **Dzhoyskiy Khrebet** *mts* U.S.S.R.
57 D5 **Dzhuma** U.S.S.R.
57 K2 **Dzhungarskiy Alatau, Khrebet** *mts* U.S.S.R.
48 L2 **Dzhurin** U.S.S.R.
57 C2 **Dzhusaly** U.S.S.R.
31 M2 **Działdowo** Poland
31 M5 **Działoszyce** Poland
31 L4 **Działoszyn** Poland
31 L2 **Dzierzgoń** Poland
31 K5 **Dzierżoniów** Poland
125 O7 **Dzitbalché** Mexico
31 H1 **Dziwnów** Poland
52 B6 **Dzūkste** U.S.S.R.
66 C3 **Dzungaria** *reg* China
66 C2 **Dzungarian Gate** *pass* U.S.S.R./China
58 E3 **Dzüünbayan** Mongolia

E

106 H3 **Eads** Colorado U.S.A.
103 P7 **Eagar** Arizona U.S.A.
101 T10 **Eagle** Colorado U.S.A.
100 J6 **Eagle** Idaho U.S.A.
110 M3 **Eagle** *R* Kentucky U.S.A.
98 K9 **Eagle** Nebraska U.S.A.
99 S7 **Eagle** Wisconsin U.S.A.
101 R5 **Eagle** Wyoming U.S.A.
98 E4 **Eagle Butte** South Dakota U.S.A.
107 M6 **Eagle City** Oklahoma U.S.A.
102 G6 **Eagle Crags** California U.S.A.
121 O6 **Eagle Depot** Quebec Canada
141 K1 **Eagle Farm** *dist* Brisbane, Qnsld Australia
99 N7 **Eagle Grove** Iowa U.S.A.
99 S2 **Eagle Harbor** Michigan U.S.A.
139 J9 **Eaglehawk Neck** Tasmania Australia
119 O1 **Eaglehead L** Ontario Canada
119 T5 **Eagle I** Manitoba Canada
118 J1 **Eagle L** Ontario Canada
100 E9 **Eagle L** California U.S.A.
95 S6 **Eagle L** Maine U.S.A.
95 R7 **Eagle L** Maine U.S.A.
113 F10 **Eagle Lake** Florida U.S.A.
109 L6 **Eagle Lake** Texas U.S.A.
103 J8 **Eagle Mts** California U.S.A.
106 E5 **Eagle Nest** New Mexico U.S.A.
108 G7 **Eagle Pass** Texas U.S.A.
100 E8 **Eagle Peak** *mt* California U.S.A.
114 F4 **Eagle Plain** Yukon Territory Canada
100 C7 **Eagle Point** Oregon U.S.A.
99 S2 **Eagle River** Michigan U.S.A.
99 R4 **Eagle River** Wisconsin U.S.A.
94 H9 **Eagle Rock** Virginia U.S.A.
12 D2 **Eaglesham** Scotland
137 Q4 **Eaglestone Reef** Pacific Oc
116 O4 **Eagle Summit** Alaska U.S.A.
103 L8 **Eagle Tail Mts** Arizona U.S.A.
109 N1 **Eagleton** Arkansas U.S.A.
107 Q7 **Eagletown** Oklahoma U.S.A.
100 E8 **Eagleville** California U.S.A.
71 L10 **Eahun** Rcti Indonesia
61 O7 **Eai-gawa** *R* Japan
68 H6 **Ea Kan** *R* Vietnam
9 F4 **Ealing** England
144 C6 **Ealing** New Zealand
143 D7 **Earaheedy** Western Australia Australia
8 D3 **Eardisland** England
117 L11 **Ear Lakes Cove** British Columbia Canada
110 F6 **Earle** Arkansas U.S.A.
99 M8 **Earlham** Iowa U.S.A.
102 E6 **Earlimart** California U.S.A.
99 L8 **Earling** Iowa U.S.A.
110 J4 **Earlington** Kentucky U.S.A.
100 A8 **Earl,L** California U.S.A.
144 A6 **Earl Mts** New Zealand
13 F2 **Earlston** Scotland
121 L5 **Earlton** Ontario Canada
99 S8 **Earlville** Illinois U.S.A.
99 P7 **Earlville** Iowa U.S.A.
13 E1 **Earn,Br.of** Scotland
117 F4 **Earn L** Yukon Territory Canada
12 D1 **Earn,L** Scotland
12 E1 **Earn,R** Scotland
144 B6 **Earnslaw, Mt** New Zealand
103 K7 **Earp** California U.S.A.
13 G3 **Earsdon** England
9 F6 **Easebourne** England
13 G4 **Easington** Durham England
13 J6 **Easington** Humberside England
13 G5 **Easingwold** England
112 E3 **Easley** South Carolina U.S.A.
110 F3 **East Alton** Illinois U.S.A.
121 T7 **East Angus** Quebec Canada
123 M7 **East B** C Breton I, Nova Scotia
113 B7 **East B** Florica U.S.A.
111 G12 **East B** Louisiana U.S.A.
111 B12 **East B** Texas U.S.A.
112 G1 **East Bend** North Carolina U.S.A.
95 L7 **East Berlin** Pennsylvania U.S.A.
109 L6 **East Bernard** Texas U.S.A.
9 G6 **Eastbourne** England
145 G4 **Eastbourne** New Zealand
94 H6 **East Brady** Pennsylvania U.S.A.
8 D5 **East Brent** England
111 J10 **East Brewton** Alabama U.S.A.
71 G6 **East Bucas** Philippines
101 O1 **East Butte** *mt* Montana U.S.A.
127 J4 **East Caicos** *isld* Turks & Caicos Is
145 G2 **East Cape** New Zealand
99 T8 **East Chicago** Indiana U.S.A.
64 G4 **East China Sea**
145 F3 **East Coast** *stat area* New Zealand
145 E2 **East Coast Bays** New Zealand
118 E7 **East Coulee** Alberta Canada
9 G6 **Eastdean** England
9 G2 **East Dereham** England
99 Q7 **East Dubuque** Illinois U.S.A.
103 K2 **East Ely** Nevada U.S.A.
118 J9 **Eastend** Saskatchewan Canada
143 A8 **Easter Grp** *islds* Western Australia Australia
135 U16 **Easter I** Pacific Oc
141 F5 **Eastern Creek** Queensland Australia
84 J4 **Eastern Desert** Egypt
86 F4 **Eastern Equatoria** *prov* Sudan
76 C4 **Eastern Ghats** *mts* India
123 S5 **Eastern Meelpaeg** *L* Newfoundland Canada
119 S5 **Easterville** Manitoba Canada
122 E7 **East Florenceville** New Brunswick Canada
120 J3 **Eastford** Ontario Canada
99 Q9 **East Galesburg** Illinois U.S.A.
102 G2 **Eastgate** Nevada U.S.A.
East Germany *see* **German Democratic Republic**
101 M1 **East Glacier Park** Montana U.S.A.
9 F5 **East Grinstead** England
8 D1 **Eastham** England
95 P6 **East Hampton** Long I, New York U.S.A.
95 P4 **Easthampton** Massachusetts U.S.A.
101 O3 **East Helena** Montana U.S.A.
9 G6 **East Hoathly** England
123 L6 **East I** Madeleine Is, Quebec Canada
9 E4 **East Ilsley** England
95 P4 **East Jaffrey** New Hampshire U.S.A.
147 E12 **East Jan Mayen Rdg** Norwegian Sea
122 J9 **East Jeddore** Nova Scotia Canada
122 G10 **East Jordan** Nova Scotia Canada
94 B1 **East Jordan** Michigan U.S.A.
9 G1 **East Keal** England
122 G9 **East Kemptville** Nova Scotia Canada
12 D2 **East Kilbride** Scotland
95 R6 **East L** Maine U.S.A.
99 U5 **East Lake** Michigan U.S.A.
109 J3 **Eastland** Texas U.S.A.
94 C4 **East Lansing** Michigan U.S.A.
9 E6 **Eastleigh** England
110 N1 **East Liberty** Ohio U.S.A.
13 F2 **East Linton** Scotland
94 G6 **East Liverpool** Ohio U.S.A.
89 E9 **East London** S Africa
East Lothian *co see* **Lothian** *reg*
94 E8 **East Lynn** West Virginia U.S.A.
115 M7 **Eastmain** Quebec Canada
112 D5 **Eastman** Georgia U.S.A.
141 H6 **Eastmere** Queensland Australia
143 E8 **East, Mt** Western Australia Australia
8 D3 **Eastnor** England
99 R9 **Easton** Illinois U.S.A.
95 Q4 **Easton** Massachusetts U.S.A.
99 N6 **Easton** Minnesota U.S.A.
110 B2 **Easton** Missouri U.S.A.
95 M6 **Easton** Pennsylvania U.S.A.
100 D2 **Easton** Washington U.S.A.
112 G4 **Eastover** South Carolina U.S.A.
East Pakistan *see* **Bangladesh**
113 F8 **East Palatka** Florida U.S.A.
94 G6 **East Palestine** Ohio U.S.A.
102 B2 **East Park Res** California U.S.A.
99 N8 **East Peru** Iowa U.S.A.
117 N8 **East Pine** British Columbia Canada
123 L6 **East Point** Madeleine Is, Quebec Canada
121 L1 **East Point** Ontario Canada
123 L7 **East Point** Prince Edward I Canada
123 N10 **East Point** Sable I, Nova Scotia
111 M8 **East Point** Georgia U.S.A.
94 E9 **East Point** Kentucky U.S.A.
119 M9 **East Poplar** Saskatchewan Canada
106 E2 **East Portal** Colorado U.S.A.
110 G5 **East Prairie** Missouri U.S.A.
122 G10 **East Pubnico** Nova Scotia Canada
94 G9 **East Rainelle** West Virginia U.S.A.
100 H9 **East Range** Nevada U.S.A.
9 F1 **East Retford** England
9 H5 **Eastry** England
110 F3 **East St Louis** Illinois U.S.A.
147 P5 **East Siberian Sea** Arctic Oc
139 J7 **East Sister I** Tasmania Australia
100 K2 **East Sister Peak** *mt* Idaho U.S.A.
9 F1 **East Stoke** England
8 D5 **East Stour** England
9 G6 **East Sussex** *co* England
94 D2 **East Tawas** Michigan U.S.A.
139 H4 **East Toorale** New South Wales Australia
119 N4 **East Trout L** Saskatchewan Canada
99 S7 **East Troy** Wisconsin U.S.A.
103 N7 **East Verde** *R* Arizona U.S.A.
95 M9 **Eastville** Virginia U.S.A.
13 E1 **East Wemyss** Scotland
9 E1 **East Wood** England
138 C2 **Eateringinna Cr** South Australia Australia
98 B9 **Eaton** Colorado U.S.A.
110 L1 **Eaton** Indiana U.S.A.
110 M2 **Eaton** Ohio U.S.A.
118 H7 **Eatonia** Saskatchewan Canada
94 C4 **Eaton Rapids** Michigan U.S.A.
9 F3 **Eaton Socon** England
112 D4 **Eatonton** Georgia U.S.A.
100 C3 **Eatonville** Washington U.S.A.
17 F9 **Eau, C. de l'** Morocco
99 U7 **Eau Claire** Michigan U.S.A.
99 P5 **Eau Claire** *R* Wisconsin U.S.A.
99 P5 **Eau Claire** Wisconsin U.S.A.
122 G1 **Eau-Claire, L. à l'** Labrador, Nfld Canada
115 M6 **Eau Claire, L. à l'** Quebec Canada
113 G9 **Eau Gallie** Florida U.S.A.
121 Q3 **Eau-Jaune, L. a l'** Quebec Canada
21 N2 **Eaulne** *R* France
134 E7 **Eauripik - New Guinea Rise** Pacific Oc
18 F9 **Eauze** France
141 G2 **Ebagoola** Queensland Australia
125 K6 **Ebano** Mexico
36 D1 **Ebbe** *mts* W Germany
13 H5 **Ebberston** England
28 D6 **Ebberup** Denmark
8 C4 **Ebbw Vale** Wales
86 B5 **Ebebiyin** Equat Guinea
33 N10 **Ebeleben** East Germany
28 F4 **Ebeltoft** Denmark
28 F4 **Ebeltoft Vig** *B* Denmark
119 P7 **Ebenezer** Saskatchewan Canada
99 U3 **Eben Junction** Michigan U.S.A.
94 J6 **Ebensburg** Pennsylvania U.S.A.
38 J6 **Ebensee** Austria
37 K3 **Ebensfeld** W Germany
36 G5 **Eberbach** W Germany
78 C2 **Eber Gölü** Turkey
32 M9 **Ebergötzen** W Germany
37 L4 **Ebermannstadt** W Germany
37 K3 **Ebern** W Germany
36 D4 **Ebernburg** W Germany
110 M4 **E Bernstadt** Kentucky U.S.A.
36 H6 **Ebersbach** W Germany
36 H3 **Ebersburg** W Germany
37 L3 **Ebersdorf** W Germany
36 F4 **Eberstadt** W Germany
38 L8 **Eberstein** Austria
33 T7 **Eberswalde** East Germany
60 P2 **Ebetsu** Japan
55 F4 **Ebeyty, Oz** *L* U.S.S.R.
67 A2 **Ebian** China
36 G7 **Ebingen** W Germany
60 D13 **Ebino** Japan
66 C3 **Ebinur Hu** *L* China
79 G3 **Ebla** *anc site* Syria
41 K3 **Ebnat** Switzerland
37 J6 **Ebnat** W Germany
86 D5 **Ebola** *R* Zaire
43 G8 **Eboli** Italy
86 B5 **Ebolowa** Cameroon
37 K4 **Ebrach** W Germany
9 F2 **E Bridgford** England
44 F2 **Ebro** *mt* Italy
16 E2 **Ebro** *R* Spain
16 E2 **Ebro, Embalse del** *res* Spain
36 E2 **Ebschloh** *mt* W Germany
36 F2 **Ebsdorfergrund** W Germany
33 M6 **Ebstorf** W Germany
22 G2 **Ecaussines** Belgium
13 E3 **Ecclefechan** Scotland
13 F2 **Eccles** Scotland
94 F9 **Eccles** West Virginia U.S.A.
13 G6 **Ecclesfield** England
8 D2 **Eccleshall** England
127 P2 **Ecclesville** Trinidad
47 H4 **Eceabat** Turkey
40 E4 **Echallens** Switzerland
21 L4 **Échauffour** France
85 E1 **Ech Cheliff** Algeria
67 E1 **Echeng** China
101 U5 **Echeta** Wyoming U.S.A.
19 P14 **Échirolles** France
61 J10 **Echizen-misaki** *C* Japan
99 L5 **Echo** Minnesota U.S.A.
100 F4 **Echo** Oregon U.S.A.
101 O9 **Echo** Utah U.S.A.
103 K5 **Echo B** Nevada U.S.A.
120 G6 **Echo Bay** Ontario Canada
103 N5 **Echo Cliffs** Arizona U.S.A.
139 H8 **Echo,L** Tasmania Australia
121 P5 **Échouani L** Quebec Canada
122 H4 **Echouerie, L'** Quebec Canada
119 O8 **Echo Valley Prov. Park** Saskatchewan Canada
25 E6 **Echt** Netherlands
15 F3 **Echt** Scotland
32 M9 **Echte** W Germany
25 F3 **Echten** Netherlands
36 G6 **Echterdingen** W Germany
22 L4 **Echternach** Luxembourg
139 G6 **Echuca** Victoria Australia
36 F3 **Echzell** W Germany
16 D7 **Écija** Spain
36 H5 **Eckartshausen** W Germany
98 H3 **Eckelson** North Dakota U.S.A.
37 L4 **Eckental** W Germany
30 E1 **Eckernförde** W Germany
109 J5 **Eckert** Texas U.S.A.
13 F3 **Eckford** Scotland
8 D3 **Eckington** England
9 E1 **Eckington** England
12 C1 **Eck,L** Scotland
98 D9 **Eckley** Colorado U.S.A.
94 F9 **Eckman** West Virginia U.S.A.
118 C6 **Eckville** Alberta Canada
32 H5 **Eckwarderhörne** W Germany
111 K9 **Eclectic** Alabama U.S.A.
143 C11 **Eclipse I** Western Australia Australia
140 B5 **Eclipse, Mt** N Terr Australia
115 M3 **Eclipse Sound** Northwest Territories Canada
21 L6 **Écommoy** France
110 L2 **Economy** Indiana U.S.A.
121 O5 **Écorces,L.aux** Quebec Canada
21 O3 **Ecos** France
21 K4 **Écouché** France
21 N3 **Ecouis** France
21 L4 **Écouves, Forêt d'** France
22 J4 **Ecouviez** Belgium
22 C2 **Ecques** France
20 G3 **Ecréhou, les** English Chan
111 G7 **Ecru** Mississippi U.S.A.
128 C4 **Ecuador** *rep* S America
21 N7 **Écueillé** France
123 K9 **Ecum Secum** Nova Scotia Canada
86 H3 **Ēd** Ethiopia
118 J5 **Edam** Saskatchewan Canada
25 D3 **Edam** Netherlands
15 F1 **Eday** Scotland
118 E6 **Edberg** Alberta Canada
109 K9 **Edcouch** Texas U.S.A.
6 N6 **Edda** *oil rig* North Sea
86 E3 **Ed Da'ein** Sudan
86 F3 **Ed Damazin** Sudan
86 F2 **Ed Damer** Sudan
86 F2 **Ed Debba** Sudan
32 K5 **Eddelak** W Germany
123 Q2 **Eddies Cove** Newfoundland Canada
13 E2 **Eddleston** Scotland
15 C2 **Eddrachillis B** Scotland
86 F3 **Ed Dueim** Sudan
100 K2 **Eddy** Montana U.S.A.
109 K4 **Eddy** Texas U.S.A.
8 B7 **Eddystone Lt. Ho** English Chan
139 J8 **Eddystone Pt** Tasmania Australia
99 O8 **Eddyville** Iowa U.S.A.
110 H4 **Eddyville** Kentucky U.S.A.
98 G8 **Eddyville** Nebraska U.S.A.
25 E4 **Ede** Netherlands
85 E7 **Ede** Nigeria
86 B5 **Edéa** Cameroon
27 G11 **Edebäck** Sweden
27 K11 **Edebo** Sweden
130 E5 **Edéia** Brazil
48 F2 **Edelény** Hungary
143 A7 **Edel Land** *pen* Western Australia Australia
139 J6 **Eden** New South Wales Australia
119 S8 **Eden** Manitoba Canada
101 O2 **Eden** Montana U.S.A.
94 J4 **Eden** New York U.S.A.
94 H10 **Eden** North Carolina U.S.A.
112 H1 **Eden** North Carolina U.S.A.
98 J4 **Eden** South Dakota U.S.A.
108 H4 **Eden** Texas U.S.A.
101 O8 **Eden** Utah U.S.A.
99 S6 **Eden** Wisconsin U.S.A.
101 Q7 **Eden** Wyoming U.S.A.
9 G5 **Edenbridge** England
89 D7 **Edenburg** S Africa
144 B7 **Edendale** New Zealand
14 D3 **Edenderry** Ireland
13 F6 **Edenfield** England
138 F6 **Edenhope** Victoria Australia
120 J8 **Edenhurst** Ontario Canada
36 E5 **Edenkoben** W Germany
119 R2 **Eden L** Manitoba Canada
9 G5 **Eden,R** England
71 N9 **Eden,Tg** *C* Indonesia
112 L1 **Edenton** North Carolina U.S.A.
94 C3 **Edenville** Michigan U.S.A.
119 N8 **Edenwold** Saskatchewan Canada
36 E1 **Eder** *R* W Germany
36 G1 **Edermünde** W Germany
33 O10 **Edersleben** East Germany
36 F1 **Ederstausee** *res* W Germany
36 G1 **Edertal** W Germany
27 F13 **Edet, L** Sweden
32 G6 **Edewecht** W Germany
32 G6 **Edewechterdamm** W Germany
101 R4 **Edgar** Montana U.S.A.
98 J9 **Edgar** Nebraska U.S.A.
111 F11 **Edgard** Louisiana U.S.A.
142 D5 **Edgar, Mt** Western Australia Australia
142 E4 **Edgar Ra** Western Australia Australia
110 E4 **Edgar Springs** Missouri U.S.A.
95 R5 **Edgartown** Massachusetts U.S.A.
109 M9 **Edgecliff** Texas U.S.A.
145 F2 **Edgecumbe** New Zealand
112 F4 **Edgefield** South Carolina U.S.A.
119 O8 **Edgeley** Saskatchewan Canada
98 H3 **Edgeley** North Dakota U.S.A.
115 N5 **Edgell I** Northwest Territories Canada
110 D6 **Edgemont** Arkansas U.S.A.
98 C6 **Edgemont** South Dakota U.S.A.
50 B1 **Edgeöya** *isld* Spitzbergen
109 O5 **Edgerly** Louisiana U.S.A.
118 G6 **Edgerton** Alberta Canada
94 C5 **Edgerton** Ohio U.S.A.
99 R7 **Edgerton** Wisconsin U.S.A.
101 T6 **Edgerton** Wyoming U.S.A.
113 G9 **Edgewater** Florida U.S.A.
117 O11 **Edgewood** British Columbia Canada
110 H3 **Edgewood** Illinois U.S.A.
95 L7 **Edgewood** Maryland U.S.A.
106 D6 **Edgewood** New Mexico U.S.A.
109 M3 **Edgewood** Texas U.S.A.
9 F4 **Edgware** England
80 C8 **Edh Dhahiriya** Jordan
46 E4 **Édhessa** Greece
144 B6 **Edievale** New Zealand
36 C3 **Ediger-Eller** W Germany
84 F5 **Edimpi** Chad
99 N5 **Edina** Minnesota U.S.A.
94 G5 **Edinboro** Pennsylvania U.S.A.
99 R10 **Edinburg** Illinois U.S.A.
111 G9 **Edinburg** Mississippi U.S.A.
98 J1 **Edinburg** North Dakota U.S.A.
109 J9 **Edinburg** Texas U.S.A.
94 J8 **Edinburg** Virginia U.S.A.
13 E2 **Edinburgh** Scotland
110 L2 **Edinburgh** Indiana U.S.A.
141 H7 **Edinburgh, Mt** Queensland Australia
22 F2 **Edingen** Belgium
47 H3 **Edirne** Turkey
102 F6 **Edison** California U.S.A.
106 F3 **Edison** Colorado U.S.A.
111 M10 **Edison** Georgia U.S.A.
112 G4 **Edisto** *R* South Carolina U.S.A.
112 G5 **Edisto Island** South Carolina U.S.A.
138 E6 **Edithburgh** South Australia Australia
117 P9 **Edith Cavell,Mt** Alberta Canada
101 O3 **Edith, Mt** Montana U.S.A.
143 D7 **Edith Withnell, L** Western Australia Australia
85 F3 **Edjeleh** Algeria
143 D8 **Edjudina** Western Australia Australia
13 G3 **Edlingham** England
38 O6 **Edlitz** Austria
95 M4 **Edmeston** New York U.S.A.
107 L2 **Edmond** Kansas U.S.A.
107 N6 **Edmond** Oklahoma U.S.A.
100 C2 **Edmonds** Washington U.S.A.
141 H3 **Edmonton** Queensland Australia
118 D5 **Edmonton** Alberta Canada
9 F4 **Edmonton** England
94 C3 **Edmore** Michigan U.S.A.
98 H1 **Edmore** North Dakota U.S.A.
122 D6 **Edmundston** New Brunswick Canada
109 L7 **Edna** Texas U.S.A.
13 F2 **Ednam** Scotland
27 J13 **Ed, O** Sweden
61 N10 **Edo-gawa** *R* Japan
27 M14 **Edole** U.S.S.R.
42 C2 **Edolo** Italy
26 C8 **Edoy** *isld* Norway
47 J5 **Edremit** Turkey
47 H5 **Edremit Körfezi** *B* Turkey
58 C3 **Edrengiyn Nuruu** *mt* Mongolia
109 K8 **Edroy** Texas U.S.A.
27 K12 **Edsbro** Sweden
27 H13 **Edsbruk** Sweden
27 H10 **Edsbyn** Sweden
26 J8 **Edsele** Sweden
58 D3 **Edsin Gol** China
117 P9 **Edson** Alberta Canada
107 J2 **Edson** Kansas U.S.A.
27 J14 **Ed, V** Sweden
118 E4 **Edwand** Alberta Canada
139 G6 **Edward** *R* New South Wales Australia
140 D2 **Edward I** N Terr Australia
120 B4 **Edward I** Ontario Canada
88 B2 **Edward, L** Zaire
140 B6 **Edward, Mt** N Terr Australia
141 F2 **Edward River** Queensland Australia
102 G7 **Edwards** California U.S.A.
99 Q8 **Edwards** *R* Illinois U.S.A.
111 F9 **Edwards** Mississippi U.S.A.
95 M2 **Edwards** New York U.S.A.
94 A5 **Edwardsburg** Michigan U.S.A.
138 D3 **Edwards Creek** South Australia Australia
144 B7 **Edwardson, C** New Zealand
144 A6 **Edwardson Sd** New Zealand
108 G5 **Edwards Plateau** Texas U.S.A.
110 G3 **Edwardsville** Illinois U.S.A.
15 F4 **Edzell** Scotland
117 H7 **Edziza, Mt** British Columbia Canada
22 F1 **Eeklo** Belgium
100 B9 **Eel** *R* California U.S.A.
94 B6 **Eel** *R* Indiana U.S.A.
25 G2 **Eelde** Netherlands
25 D4 **Eem** *R* Netherlands
25 D4 **Eem Meer** Netherlands
89 B6 **Eenzamheid Pan** *salt lake* S Africa
22 E1 **Eernegem** Belgium
137 O5 **Éfaté** *isld* Vanuatu
38 K5 **Eferding** Austria
99 N2 **Effie** Minnesota U.S.A.
99 P6 **Effigy Mounds Nat. Mon.** Iowa U.S.A.
110 H2 **Effingham** Illinois U.S.A.
107 P2 **Effingham** Kansas U.S.A.
48 M6 **Eforie** Romania
71 B3 **Ef Torobi** *isld* W Irian
28 B5 **Eg** Denmark
28 E4 **Egå** Denmark
18 D10 **Ega** *R* Spain
43 E10 **Egadi, I** Sicily
133 F5 **Egaña** Argentina
103 K2 **Egan Range** Nevada U.S.A.
121 N7 **Eganville** Ontario Canada
85 F7 **Egbe** Nigeria
98 B8 **Egbert** Wyoming U.S.A.
28 H5 **Egebjerg** Denmark
115 O4 **Egedesminde** Greenland
116 J7 **Egegik B** Alaska U.S.A.
98 G1 **Egeland** North Dakota U.S.A.
33 O9 **Egeln** East Germany
36 F4 **Egelsbach** W Germany
28 D7 **Egen** Denmark
28 F4 **Egens** Denmark
28 E3 **Egense** Denmark
48 F3 **Eger** Hungary
37 J6 **Eger** *R* W Germany
28 D7 **Egernsund** Denmark
27 A13 **Egersund** Norway
143 C6 **Egerton, Mt** Western Australia Australia
32 M6 **Egestorf** W Germany
41 L3 **Egg** Austria
27 D11 **Eggedal** Norway
31 J7 **Eggenburg** Austria
37 O7 **Eggenfelden** W Germany
33 U5 **Eggesin** East Germany
28 G6 **Eggeslevmagle** Denmark
99 T4 **Egg Harbor** Wisconsin U.S.A.
95 N7 **Egg Harbor City** New Jersey U.S.A.
95 N7 **Egg Harbor, Gt** New Jersey U.S.A.
95 N7 **Egg Harbor, Little** New Jersey U.S.A.
116 G5 **Egg I** Alaska U.S.A.
139 G7 **Egg Lagoon** Tasmania Australia
13 G4 **Eggleston** England
37 N6 **Eggmühl** W Germany
37 L4 **Eggolsheim** W Germany
9 F5 **Egham** England
22 H2 **Eghezee** Belgium
28 G6 **Egholm** *isld* Denmark
28 D2 **Egholm** *isld* Nordjylland Denmark
15 F1 **Egilsay** Scotland
142 C5 **Eginbah** Western Australia Australia
85 D3 **Eglab,El** *reg* Algeria
18 G7 **Egletons** France
36 G1 **Egling** W Germany
13 G3 **Eglingham** England
144 B6 **Eglinton** *R* New Zealand
114 H2 **Eglinton I** Northwest Territories Canada
41 J2 **Eglisau** Switzerland
37 L4 **Egloffstein** W Germany
25 C3 **Egmond aan Zee** Netherlands
122 H7 **Egmont B** Prince Edward I Canada
113 E10 **Egmont Key** *isld* Florida U.S.A.
145 E3 **Egmont, Mt** New Zealand
145 E3 **Egmont Village** New Zealand
28 J6 **Egøje** Denmark
118 D4 **Egremont** Alberta Canada
47 L6 **Eğret** Turkey
47 L7 **Eğridir** Turkey
78 C2 **Egridir Gölü** *L* Turkey
47 K5 **Eğrigöz Daği** *mt* Turkey
47 J5 **Eğri Karaagaç Daği** *mt* Turkey
13 H5 **Egton** England
28 C5 **Egtved** Denmark
71 E7 **Eguet Pt** Philippines
19 O17 **Éguilles** France
18 G6 **Éguzon** France
28 C6 **Egvad** Denmark
48 F3 **Egyek** Hungary
84 H4 **Egypt** *rep* Africa
112 F5 **Egypt** Georgia U.S.A.
111 H8 **Egypt** Mississippi U.S.A.
109 L6 **Egypt** Texas U.S.A.
79 F4 **Ehden** Lebanon
36 H7 **Ehingen** W Germany
33 Q8 **Ehle** *R* East Germany
32 K10 **Ehlen** W Germany
36 F6 **Ehningen** W Germany
33 N7 **Ehra-Lessien** W Germany
113 E9 **Ehren** Florida U.S.A.
103 K8 **Ehrenberg** Arizona U.S.A.
140 B6 **Ehrenberg Ra** N Terr Australia
36 D3 **Ehrenbreitstein** W Germany
32 J7 **Ehrenburg** W Germany
37 O2 **Ehrenfriedersdorf** East Germany
112 F4 **Ehrhardt** South Carolina U.S.A.
36 E2 **Ehringshausen** W Germany
60 D14 **Ei** Japan
36 E2 **Eibach** W Germany
36 E2 **Eibelshausen** W Germany
37 J4 **Eibelstadt** W Germany
37 O3 **Eibenstock** East Germany
25 G4 **Eibergen** Netherlands
38 M8 **Eibiswald** Austria
33 O8 **Eichenbarleben** East Germany
37 O6 **Eichendorf** W Germany
37 M5 **Eichhofen** W Germany
32 M10 **Eichsfeld** *mts* East Germany
37 L6 **Eichstätt** W Germany
40 G1 **Eichstetten** W Germany
36 F5 **Eichtersheim** W Germany
33 T8 **Eichwalde** East Germany
36 H2 **Eichzell** W Germany
32 M7 **Eicklingen** W Germany
27 D12 **Eidanger** Norway
26 B9 **Eide** Norway
32 L4 **Eider** *R* W Germany
32 J4 **Eider** W Germany
6 F1 **Eiði** Faeroes
26 G3 **Eidsfjord** Norway
27 D12 **Eidsfoss** Norway
27 F11 **Eidskog** Norway
26 C9 **Eidsvåg** Norway
141 K7 **Eidsvold** Queensland Australia
27 E11 **Eidsvoll** Norway
25 C2 **Eierlandse Gat** Netherlands
36 B3 **Eifel** *mts* W Germany
89 F2 **Eiffel Flats** Zimbabwe
37 J1 **Eigenrieden** East Germany
40 G4 **Eiger** *mt* Switzerland
15 B4 **Eigg** *isld* Scotland
113 J11 **Eight Mile Rock** Bahamas
146 B7 **Eights Coast** Antarctica
142 D4 **Eighty Mile Beach** Western Australia Australia
26 A10 **Eikefjord** Norway
27 D12 **Eikeren** *R* Norway
26 C9 **Eikesdalsvatn** *L* Norway
139 H6 **Eildon** Victoria Australia
33 R10 **Eilenburg** East Germany
129 G3 **Eilerts de Haan Geb** *mts* Suriname
33 O8 **Eilsleben** East Germany
32 L8 **Eime** W Germany
33 M7 **Eimke** W Germany
27 E11 **Eina** Norway
141 G4 **Einasleigh** Queensland Australia
32 L9 **Einbeck** W Germany
25 D6 **Eindhoven** Netherlands
32 L4 **Einfeld** W Germany
68 B4 **Einme** Burma
36 C5 **Einöd** W Germany
37 P6 **Einödsriegel** *mt* W Germany
Einsiedel *see* **Deutsch-Einsiedel**
79 F8 **Ein Yahav** Israel
Eire *rep see* **Ireland, Rep of**
120 G4 **Eire River** Ontario Canada
128 E5 **Eirunepe** Brazil
22 L4 **Eisch** *R* Luxembourg
22 K2 **Eisden** Belgium
25 E7 **Eisden** Netherlands
36 C4 **Eisen** W Germany
37 J2 **Eisenach** East Germany
37 M2 **Eisenberg** East Germany
36 E4 **Eisenberg** W Germany
38 L6 **Eisenerz** Austria
38 L7 **Eisenerzer-Alpen** *mts* Austria
106 E2 **Eisenhower Tunnel** Colorado U.S.A.
38 J8 **Eisenhut** *mt* Austria
31 H3 **Eisenhüttenstadt** East Germany
38 L8 **Eisenkappel** Austria
48 D3 **Eisenstadt** Austria
38 J8 **Eisentratten** Austria
38 L5 **Eisenwurzen** *reg* Austria
36 D2 **Eiserfeld** W Germany
37 K3 **Eisfeld** East Germany
33 P9 **Eisleben** East Germany
36 H6 **Eislingen** W Germany
37 L6 **Eitensheim** W Germany
36 H2 **Eiterfeld** W Germany
36 C2 **Eitorf** W Germany
17 G2 **Ejea de los Caballeros** Spain
87 G12 **Ejeda** Madagascar
28 D5 **Ejer Bavnehoj** *hill* Denmark
28 B3 **Ejerslev** Denmark
127 J10 **Ejido** Venezuela
65 A5 **Ejin Horo Qi** China
65 C2 **Ej Nur** China
28 B3 **Ejsing** Denmark
28 C5 **Ejstrup** Denmark
85 D7 **Ejura** Ghana
98 B4 **Ekalaka** Montana U.S.A.
27 J15 **Ekby** Sweden
22 F2 **Eke** Belgium
29 K12 **Ekenäs** Finland
22 G1 **Ekeren** Belgium
145 E4 **Eketahuna** New Zealand
26 N5 **Ekfors** Sweden
46 D6 **Ekhinádhes** *isld* Greece
46 G3 **Ekhinos** Greece
55 G5 **Ekibastuz** U.S.S.R.
59 K1 **Ekimchan** U.S.S.R.
116 N6 **Eklutna** Alaska U.S.A.
6 N6 **Ekofisk** *oil rig* North Sea
27 J12 **Ekoln** *L* Sweden
22 F1 **Eksaarde** Belgium
27 G11 **Ekshärad** Sweden
27 G14 **Eksjö** Sweden
26 L7 **Ekträsk** Sweden
115 L7 **Ekwan** *R* Ontario Canada
116 J7 **Ekwok** Alaska U.S.A.
68 C3 **Ela** Burma
El Aaiún *see* **Laâyoune**
46 F8 **Elafónisos** *isld* Greece
111 F7 **Elaine** Arkansas U.S.A.
80 E5 **El 'Ajâjira** Jordan
103 H10 **El Alamo** Mexico
75 K10 **Elamanchili** India
99 R5 **Eland** Wisconsin U.S.A.
89 E5 **Elands** *R* S Africa
89 C8 **Elands Berg** *mt* S Africa
8 C3 **Elan Valley Reservoirs** Wales
43 B13 **El Aouinet** Algeria
41 L4 **Ela, Piz** *mt* Switzerland
16 D7 **El Arahal** Spain
El Arâich *see* **Larache** Morocco
124 C4 **El Arco** Mexico
80 F5 **El Ardah** Jordan
141 H4 **El Arish** Queensland Australia
46 E5 **Elassón** Greece
79 E9 **Elat** Israel
46 F6 **Elátia** Greece
86 E2 **El Atrun Oasis** Sudan
80 D7 **El 'Azar** Jordan
78 G2 **Elâzig** Turkey
111 K10 **Elba** Alabama U.S.A.
101 M7 **Elba** Idaho U.S.A.
98 H8 **Elba** Nebraska U.S.A.
94 J3 **Elba** New York U.S.A.
42 C6 **Elba, I.d'** Italy
126 H10 **El Banco** Colombia
16 D4 **El Barco de Avila** Spain
46 D3 **Elbasan** Albania
127 K10 **El Baúl** Venezuela
32 J5 **Elbe** *est* W Germany
33 M6 **Elbe** *R* W Germany
33 N5 **Elbe-Lübeck Kanal** W Germany
79 G4 **El Beqa'a** *R* Lebanon
110 J3 **Elberfield** Indiana U.S.A.
32 F8 **Elbergen** W Germany
99 O7 **Elberon** Iowa U.S.A.
109 J2 **Elbert** Texas U.S.A.
99 U5 **Elberta** Michigan U.S.A.
106 D2 **Elbert,Mt** Colorado U.S.A.
112 E3 **Elberton** Georgia U.S.A.
21 N3 **Elbeuf** France
Elbing *see* **Elblag**
33 N9 **Elbingerode** East Germany
78 F2 **Elbistan** Turkey
31 L1 **Elblag** Poland
17 F6 **El Bonillo** Spain
124 H6 **El Bordo** Mexico
16 D9 **El Borj** Morocco
118 L7 **Elbow** Saskatchewan Canada
113 L11 **Elbow Cay** *isld* Bahamas
98 K4 **Elbow L** Minnesota U.S.A.
118 C8 **Elbow R** Alberta Canada
124 J6 **El Bozal** Mexico
53 F11 **El'brus** *mt* U.S.S.R.
86 E4 **El Buheyrat** *prov* Sudan
25 E4 **Elburg** Netherlands
16 E3 **El Burgo de Osma** Spain
100 K9 **Elburz** Nevada U.S.A.
77 B1 **Elburz Mountains** Iran
102 H9 **El Cajon** California U.S.A.
128 F2 **El Callao** Venezuela
16 D5 **El Campillo de la Jara** Spain
109 L6 **El Campo** Texas U.S.A.
102 H9 **El Capitan Res** California U.S.A.
128 C2 **El Carmen** Colombia
124 G5 **El Casco** Mexico
17 G3 **El Castellar** Spain
103 J9 **El Centro** California U.S.A.
128 F7 **El Cerro** Bolivia
16 C7 **El Cerro de Andévalo** Spain
124 F3 **El Charco** Mexico
17 G6 **Elche** Spain
17 F6 **Elche de la Sierra** Spain
124 G3 **El Chilicote** Mexico
127 K9 **El Chino** Venezuela
99 R4 **Elcho** Wisconsin U.S.A.
140 D1 **Elcho I** N Terr Australia
133 E2 **El Chorro** Argentina
124 H5 **El Cobre** Mexico
128 D2 **El Cocuy** Colombia
126 C3 **El Cotorro** Cuba
126 G4 **El Cristo** Cuba
108 B5 **El Cuervo** Mexico
32 L8 **Eldagsen** W Germany
124 C2 **El Dátil** Mexico
33 Q6 **Elde** *R* East Germany
33 O6 **Eldena** East Germany
138 F4 **Elder,L** South Australia Australia
99 R5 **Elderon** Wisconsin U.S.A.
6 N6 **Eldfisk** *oil rig* North Sea
126 A4 **El Diaz** Mexico
126 G10 **El Dificil** Colombia
33 M7 **Eldingen** W Germany
124 G8 **El Divisadero** Mexico
128 C3 **El Diviso** Colombia
124 B2 **El Doctor** Mexico
99 O9 **Eldon** Iowa U.S.A.
110 D3 **Eldon** Missouri U.S.A.
100 B2 **Eldon** Washington U.S.A.
99 N7 **Eldora** Iowa U.S.A.
130 C10 **Eldorado** Argentina
130 E9 **Eldorado** Brazil
114 J6 **Eldorado** Saskatchewan Canada
124 F5 **Eldorado** Mexico
109 P2 **El Dorado** Arkansas U.S.A.
110 H4 **Eldorado** Illinois U.S.A.
107 O4 **El Dorado** Kansas U.S.A.
107 L7 **Eldorado** Oklahoma U.S.A.
108 G5 **Eldorado** Texas U.S.A.
128 F2 **El Dorado** Venezuela
89 G1 **Eldorado** Zimbabwe
100 D1 **Eldorado,Mt** Washington U.S.A.
103 K6 **Eldorado Mts** Nevada U.S.A.
110 B4 **El Dorado Springs** Missouri U.S.A.
88 E1 **Eldoret** Kenya
98 K2 **Eldred** Minnesota U.S.A.
95 N5 **Eldred** New York U.S.A.
94 J5 **Eldred** Pennsylvania U.S.A.
27 F15 **Eldsberga** Sweden
100 H2 **Eleanor** Washington U.S.A.
143 D10 **Eleanora Pk** Western Australia Australia
102 E3 **Eleanor, L** California U.S.A.
89 E4 **Elebe** *mt* Botswana
109 J1 **Electra** Texas U.S.A.
101 P5 **Electric Pk** Mont/Wyoming U.S.A.
135 O1 **Eleele** Hawaiian Is
52 B6 **Eleja** U.S.S.R.
48 G4 **Elek** Hungary
54 K1 **Elektrogorsk** U.S.S.R.
54 K1 **Elektrostal'** U.S.S.R.
22 J2 **Elemalle** Belgium
47 H2 **Elena** Bulgaria
128 D4 **El Encanto** Colombia
33 N9 **Elend** East Germany
106 C8 **Elephant Butte** New Mexico U.S.A.
106 C8 **Elephant Butte Res** New Mexico U.S.A.
68 G7 **Elephant, Chaine de l'** *mts* Cambodia
146 D3 **Elephant I** South Shetland Is Antarctica
83 K8 **Elephant Pass** Sri Lanka
116 G3 **Elephant Point** Alaska U.S.A.
46 F3 **Eleshnitsa** Bulgaria
128 E3 **El Esmeralda** Venezuela
128 C3 **El Espinal** Colombia
56 H4 **Elesun** U.S.S.R.
84 J5 **Elet, Wadi** *watercourse* Sudan
85 F1 **El Eulma** Algeria
113 L12 **Eleuthera I** Bahamas
99 P5 **Eleva** Wisconsin U.S.A.
106 E3 **Eleven Mile Canyon Res** Colorado U.S.A.
110 E5 **Eleven Point** *R* Missouri U.S.A.
46 F6 **Elevsis** Greece
22 H2 **Elewijt** Belgium
20 C5 **Elez** *R* France
80 G2 **El Fahham** Syria
43 C12 **El Fahs** Tunisia
86 E3 **El Fasher** Sudan
16 D9 **El Fendek** Morocco
16 B1 **El Ferrol** Spain
117 E6 **Elfin Cove** Alaska U.S.A.
119 O7 **Elfros** Saskatchewan Canada
86 H4 **El Fud** Ethiopia
124 E4 **El Fuerte** Mexico
86 E3 **El Fula** Sudan
80 D5 **El Fundug** Jordan
26 E9 **Elgå** Norway
26 E9 **Elgepiggen** *mt* Norway
37 K2 **Elgersburg** East Germany
86 F3 **El Geteina** Sudan
86 F3 **El Gezira** *prov* Sudan
80 F5 **El Ghor** Jordan
119 R9 **Elgin** Manitoba Canada
122 G8 **Elgin** New Brunswick Canada
15 E3 **Elgin** Scotland
103 O10 **Elgin** Arizona U.S.A.
99 S7 **Elgin** Illinois U.S.A.
99 P7 **Elgin** Iowa U.S.A.
98 H8 **Elgin** Nebraska U.S.A.
103 K4 **Elgin** Nevada U.S.A.
98 E3 **Elgin** North Dakota U.S.A.
107 M7 **Elgin** Oklahoma U.S.A.
100 H4 **Elgin** Oregon U.S.A.
109 K5 **Elgin** Texas U.S.A.
103 O3 **Elgin** Utah U.S.A.
141 H5 **Elgin Downs** Queensland Australia
86 F5 **Elgon, Mt** Uganda
17 H2 **El Grado** Spain
124 G8 **El Grullo** Mexico
128 D3 **El Guamo** Colombia
84 H4 **El Harra** Egypt
86 F3 **El Hawata** Sudan
85 E3 **El Homr** Algeria
87 D7 **Elias Garcia** Angola
127 J5 **Elias Piña** Dominican Rep
109 J3 **Eliasville** Texas U.S.A.
108 D2 **Elida** New Mexico U.S.A.
119 U9 **Elie** Manitoba Canada
13 F1 **Elie** Scotland
46 F6 **Elikón** *mt* Greece
29 M11 **Elimäki** Finland
46 F2 **Elin Pelin** Bulgaria
95 R3 **Eliot** Maine U.S.A.
29 O10 **Elisenvaara** U.S.S.R.
129 K5 **Eliseu Martins** Brazil
53 F10 **Elista** U.S.S.R.
106 F2 **Elizabeth** Colorado U.S.A.
99 Q7 **Elizabeth** Illinois U.S.A.
109 P5 **Elizabeth** Louisiana U.S.A.
95 N6 **Elizabeth** New Jersey U.S.A.
94 F7 **Elizabeth** West Virginia U.S.A.
112 L1 **Elizabeth City** North Carolina U.S.A.
95 R5 **Elizabeth Is** Massachusetts U.S.A.
142 F3 **Elizabeth, Mt** Western Australia Australia
122 F6 **Elizabeth,Mt** New Brunswick Canada
101 P9 **Elizabeth Mt** Utah U.S.A.
137 M7 **Elizabeth Reef** Pacific Oc
143 B7 **Elizabeth Spring** Western Australia Australia
94 E10 **Elizabethton** Tennessee U.S.A.
94 B7 **Elizabethtown** Indiana U.S.A.
94 B9 **Elizabethtown** Kentucky U.S.A.
95 O2 **Elizabethtown** New York U.S.A.
112 J3 **Elizabethtown** North Carolina U.S.A.
95 L6 **Elizabethtown** Pennsylvania U.S.A.
Elizabethville *see* **Lubumbashi**
95 L6 **Elizabethville** Pennsylvania U.S.A.
138 E6 **Eliza,L** South Australia Australia
18 D9 **Elizondo** Spain
124 G4 **El Jaralito** Mexico
86 F3 **El Jebelein** Sudan
126 E4 **El Jibaro** Cuba
31 N2 **Ełk** Poland
102 A2 **Elk** California U.S.A.
110 B5 **Elk** *R* Missouri U.S.A.
108 B3 **Elk** New Mexico U.S.A.
95 M7 **Elk** *R* Penn/Maryland U.S.A.
110 K6 **Elk** *R* Tennessee U.S.A.
94 F8 **Elk** *R* West Virginia U.S.A.
101 P6 **Elk** Wyoming U.S.A.
99 P7 **Elkader** Iowa U.S.A.
86 F2 **El Kamlin** Sudan
101 R5 **Elk Basin** Wyoming U.S.A.
100 K4 **Elk City** Idaho U.S.A.
107 P4 **Elk City** Kansas U.S.A.
107 L6 **Elk City** Oklahoma U.S.A.
102 B2 **Elk Creek** California U.S.A.
140 D5 **Elkedra** N Terr Australia
43 B12 **El Kef** Tunisia
85 C2 **El Kelaâ des Srarhna** Morocco
86 H4 **Ēl Kerē** Ethiopia
102 C3 **Elk Grove** California U.S.A.
86 F2 **El Khandaq** Sudan
79 E7 **El Kharrûba** Egypt
94 B5 **Elkhart** Indiana U.S.A.
107 J4 **Elkhart** Kansas U.S.A.
109 M4 **Elkhart** Texas U.S.A.
99 T6 **Elkhart Lake** Wisconsin U.S.A.
101 S9 **Elkhead Mts** Colorado U.S.A.
119 Q9 **Elkhorn** Manitoba Canada
99 L8 **Elk Horn** Iowa U.S.A.
98 H7 **Elkhorn** *R* Nebraska U.S.A.
99 S7 **Elkhorn** Wisconsin U.S.A.
47 H2 **Elkhovo** Bulgaria
112 G1 **Elkin** North Carolina U.S.A.
118 E5 **Elk I. Nat. Park** Alberta Canada
108 C2 **Elkins** New Mexico U.S.A.
94 H8 **Elkins** West Virginia U.S.A.
94 B2 **Elk L** Michigan U.S.A.
120 K5 **Elk Lake** Ontario Canada
95 K4 **Elkland** Pennsylvania U.S.A.
110 K7 **Elkmont** Alabama U.S.A.
106 D1 **Elk Mt** Colorado U.S.A.
101 T8 **Elk Mt** Wyoming U.S.A.
100 K1 **Elko** British Columbia Canada
100 K9 **Elko** Nevada U.S.A.
101 P8 **Elkol** Wyoming U.S.A.
86 H4 **Ēl K'oran** Ethiopia
101 N3 **Elk Park** Montana U.S.A.
112 F1 **Elk Park** North Carolina U.S.A.
118 G5 **Elk Point** Alberta Canada
98 K7 **Elk Pt** South Dakota U.S.A.
118 C9 **Elk R** British Columbia Canada
99 N4 **Elk R** Minnesota U.S.A.
94 B2 **Elk Rapids** Michigan U.S.A.
43 C12 **El Krib** Tunisia
100 J3 **Elk River** Idaho U.S.A.
43 B13 **El Ksour** Tunisia
106 B1 **Elk Springs** Colorado U.S.A.
113 F8 **Elkton** Florida U.S.A.
110 J5 **Elkton** Kentucky U.S.A.

Elkton — Estagno Pt

27

95 M7 **Elkton** Maryland U.S.A.
99 O6 **Elkton** Minnesota U.S.A.
100 B6 **Elkton** Oregon U.S.A.
98 K5 **Elkton** South Dakota U.S.A.
110 K6 **Elkton** Tennessee U.S.A.
94 J8 **Elkton** Virginia U.S.A.
79 E9 **El Kuntilla** Egypt
94 C10 **Elk Valley** Tennessee U.S.A.
110 G4 **Elkville** Illinois U.S.A.
79 G4 **El Laboue** Lebanon
86 E3 **El Lagowa** Sudan
83 K10 **Ellamulla** Sri Lanka
12 C1 **Ellanbeich** Scotland
13 G6 **Elland** England
143 A7 **Ellavalla** Western Australia Australia
113 D7 **Ellaville** Florida U.S.A.
111 M9 **Ellaville** Georgia U.S.A.
20 D5 **Elle** *R* France
37 N3 **Ellefeld** W Germany
114 J2 **Ellef Ringnes I** Northwest Territories Canada
143 C10 **Elleker** Western Australia Australia
95 O2 **Ellenburg** New York U.S.A.
95 M8 **Ellendale** Delaware U.S.A.
111 F12 **Ellendale** Louisiana U.S.A.
98 H3 **Ellendale** North Dakota U.S.A.
103 O3 **Ellen,Mt** Utah U.S.A.
95 P2 **Ellen,Mt** Vermont U.S.A.
143 C10 **Ellen Pk** Western Australia Australia
13 E4 **Ellen,R** England
100 E2 **Ellensburg** Washington U.S.A.
32 H6 **Ellenserdamm** W Germany
113 E10 **Ellenton** Florida U.S.A.
95 N5 **Ellenville** New York U.S.A.
36 C3 **Ellenz-Poltersdorf** W Germany
112 G2 **Eller** North Carolina U.S.A.
112 H2 **Ellerbe** North Carolina U.S.A.
113 E7 **Ellerbee** Florida U.S.A.
36 D4 **Ellerspring** *mt* W Germany
144 B6 **Ellery, L** New Zealand
139 J6 **Ellery,Mt** Victoria Australia
8 D2 **Ellesmere** England
115 L2 **Ellesmere I** Northwest Territories Canada
144 D5 **Ellesmere, L** New Zealand
8 D1 **Ellesmere Port** England
110 K2 **Ellettsville** Indiana U.S.A.
22 F2 **Ellezelles** Belgium
20 C5 **Elliant** France
Ellice Is. *see* **Tuvalu** *islds state*
95 L7 **Ellicott City** Maryland U.S.A.
94 J4 **Ellicottville** New York U.S.A.
28 D3 **Ellidshøj** Denmark
112 C3 **Ellijay** Georgia U.S.A.
28 E2 **Elling** Denmark
28 F6 **Ellinge** Denmark
37 K5 **Ellingen** W Germany
13 G3 **Ellington** England
110 F4 **Ellington** Missouri U.S.A.
107 M3 **Ellinwood** Kansas U.S.A.
89 E8 **Elliot** S Africa
95 L8 **Elliot** Maryland U.S.A.
112 G3 **Elliot** South Carolina U.S.A.
142 E4 **Elliot Lake** Western Australia Australia
120 H6 **Elliot Lake** Ontario Canada
141 H4 **Elliot, Mt** Queensland Australia
140 C3 **Elliott** N Terr Australia
99 L8 **Elliott** Iowa U.S.A.
98 J3 **Elliott** North Dakota U.S.A.
113 G12 **Elliott Key** *isld* Florida U.S.A.
122 H4 **Ellis B** Quebec Canada
89 E4 **Ellisras** S Africa
138 C5 **Elliston** South Australia Australia
123 T5 **Elliston** Newfoundland Canada
101 N3 **Elliston** Montana U.S.A.
94 G9 **Elliston** Virginia U.S.A.
111 G10 **Ellisville** Mississippi U.S.A.
143 G8 **Ell, L** Western Australia Australia
38 F6 **Ellmau** Austria
36 F6 **Ellmendingen** W Germany
15 F3 **Ellon** Scotland
74 F8 **Ellora** India
112 G4 **Elloree** South Carolina U.S.A.
33 N9 **Ellrich** W Germany
118 E4 **Ellscott** Alberta Canada
110 F5 **Ellsinore** Missouri U.S.A.
107 M3 **Ellsworth** Kansas U.S.A.
95 T2 **Ellsworth** Maine U.S.A.
99 L6 **Ellsworth** Minnesota U.S.A.
98 D7 **Ellsworth** Nebraska U.S.A.
99 O5 **Ellsworth** Wisconsin U.S.A.
109 J1 **Ellsworth,L** Oklahoma U.S.A.
146 B7 **Ellsworth Land** Antarctica
146 C7 **Ellsworth Mts** Antarctica
37 J6 **Ellwangen** W Germany
94 G6 **Ellwood City** Pennsylvania U.S.A.
32 H6 **Ellwürden** W Germany
41 K4 **Elm** Switzerland
32 K5 **Elm** W Germany
99 O6 **Elma** Iowa U.S.A.
100 B2 **Elma** Washington U.S.A.
133 C6 **El Maitén** Argentina
47 K8 **Elmalı** Turkey
86 F3 **El Manaquil** Sudan
124 A2 **El Maneadero** Mexico
124 G5 **El Martinez** Mexico
109 L7 **Elmaton** Texas U.S.A.
103 J9 **El Mayor** Mexico
79 D7 **El Mazâr** Egypt
112 K2 **Elm City** North Carolina U.S.A.
98 G9 **Elm Cr** Nebraska U.S.A.
118 D1 **Elm Creek** Manitoba Canada
107 N6 **Elm Cr.Res.,E** Oklahoma U.S.A.
108 A2 **Elmendorf** New Mexico U.S.A.
127 J9 **El Mene de Mauroa** Venezuela
32 M5 **Elmenhorst** W Germany
99 O10 **Elmer** Missouri U.S.A.
95 M7 **Elmer** New Jersey U.S.A.
109 H1 **Elmer** Oklahoma U.S.A.
100 G1 **Elmer City** Washington U.S.A.
43 B13 **El Meskiana** Algeria
99 T8 **Elmhurst** Illinois U.S.A.
79 F4 **El Mîna** Lebanon
123 K7 **Elmira** Prince Edward I Canada
102 C3 **Elmira** California U.S.A.
94 C1 **Elmira** Michigan U.S.A.
95 L4 **Elmira** New York U.S.A.
103 M8 **El Mirage** Arizona U.S.A.
98 H4 **Elm L** South Dakota U.S.A.
109 K4 **Elm Mott** Texas U.S.A.
107 N3 **Elmo** Kansas U.S.A.
99 L9 **Elmo** Missouri U.S.A.
101 T8 **Elmo** Wyoming U.S.A.
16 E4 **El Molar** Spain
108 G7 **El Moral** Mexico
139 G6 **Elmore** Victoria Australia
111 K9 **Elmore** Alabama U.S.A.
99 M6 **Elmore** Minnesota U.S.A.
94 D5 **Elmore** Ohio U.S.A.
109 K1 **Elmore City** Oklahoma U.S.A.
106 B6 **El Morro Nat.Mon** New Mexico U.S.A.
122 J9 **Elmsdale** Nova Scotia Canada
32 L5 **Elmshorn** W Germany
98 D5 **Elm Springs** South Dakota U.S.A.
36 D5 **Elmstein** W Germany
122 J8 **Elmsvale** Nova Scotia Canada
86 E3 **El Muglad** Sudan
120 J8 **Elmwood** Ontario Canada
110 G1 **Elmwood** Illinois U.S.A.
107 K5 **Elmwood** Oklahoma U.S.A.
99 O5 **Elmwood** Wisconsin U.S.A.
18 G10 **Elne** France
71 D5 **El Nido** Philippines
118 D7 **Elnora** Alberta Canada
110 J3 **Elnora** Indiana U.S.A.
86 F3 **El Obeid** Sudan
111 G12 **Eloi Bay** Louisiana U.S.A.
80 D1 **Elon** Israel
110 K6 **Elora** Tennessee U.S.A.
20 B5 **Elorn** *R* France
128 C4 **El Oro** *prov* Ecuador
125 J8 **El Oro** Mexico
124 F6 **Elota** Mexico
103 N9 **Eloy** Arizona U.S.A.
124 G5 **El Palmito** Mexico
128 F2 **El Pao** Venezuela
16 E4 **El Pardo** Spain
99 R9 **El Paso** Illinois U.S.A.
108 A4 **El Paso** Texas U.S.A.
131 B4 **El Peñón** *pk* Chile
14 C3 **Elphin** Ireland
141 J5 **Elphinstone** Queensland Australia
119 R8 **Elphinstone** Manitoba Canada
127 N9 **El Pilar** Venezuela
133 E2 **El Pintado** Argentina
83 K11 **Elpitiya** Sri Lanka
102 E4 **El Portal** California U.S.A.
128 C5 **El Portugues** Peru
108 B4 **El Porvenir** Mexico
16 D5 **El Puente del Arzobispo** Spain
16 C8 **El Puerto de Sta. Maria** Spain
80 E1 **El Qouzah** Lebanon
131 B2 **Elqui** *R* Chile
79 E8 **El Quşeima** Egypt
79 F9 **El Quweira** Jordan
124 G6 **El Regocijo** Mexico
108 F7 **El Remolino** Mexico
125 J6 **El Retorno** Mexico
116 N5 **Elridge Glacier** Alaska U.S.A.
106 D5 **El Rito** New Mexico U.S.A.
16 C7 **El Ronquillo** Spain
99 M4 **Elrosa** Minnesota U.S.A.
118 J7 **Elrose** Saskatchewan Canada
99 Q6 **Elroy** Wisconsin U.S.A.
124 H6 **El Rucio** Mexico
117 F4 **Elsa** Yukon Territory Canada
42 D5 **Elsa** *R* Italy
109 K9 **Elsa** Texas U.S.A.
124 G6 **El Salto** Mexico
125 P11 **El Salvador** *rep* Central America
71 G6 **El Salvador** Mindanao Philippines
120 H4 **Elsas** Ontario Canada
108 A6 **El Sauz** Mexico
109 J9 **El Sauz** Texas U.S.A.
25 E4 **Elsberg** *hill* Netherlands
110 F2 **Elsberry** Missouri U.S.A.
32 K6 **Elsdorf** W Germany
32 H8 **Else** *R* W Germany
22 L3 **Elsenborn** Belgium
36 F5 **Elsenz** *R* W Germany
140 C2 **Elsey** N Terr Australia
26 G5 **Elsfjord** Norway
32 H6 **Elsfleth** W Germany
98 E9 **Elsie** Nebraska U.S.A.
100 B4 **Elsie** Oregon U.S.A.
103 M3 **Elsinore** Utah U.S.A.
102 G8 **Elsinore L** California U.S.A.
25 E7 **Elsloo** Netherlands
98 F7 **Elsmere** Nebraska U.S.A.
107 P4 **Elsmore** Kansas U.S.A.
33 Q9 **Elsnigk** East Germany
130 C10 **El Soberbio** Argentina
127 M10 **El Socorro** Venezuela
127 L10 **El Sombrero** Venezuela
116 K1 **Elson Lagoon** Alaska U.S.A.
25 E4 **Elspeet** Netherlands
25 E5 **Elst** Netherlands
9 F5 **Elstead** England
33 Q10 **Elster** *R* East Germany
33 R9 **Elster** East Germany
37 N2 **Elsterberg** East Germany
33 T10 **Elsterwerda** East Germany
145 F3 **Elsthorpe** New Zealand
9 F4 **Elstree** England
108 A6 **El Sueco** Mexico
124 G8 **El Tabaco** Mexico
16 C2 **El Teleno** *mt* Spain
25 F5 **Elten** W Germany
37 O2 **Elterlein** East Germany
9 G5 **Eltham** England
145 E3 **Eltham** New Zealand
79 E9 **El Thamad** Egypt
128 F2 **El Tigre** Venezuela
9 F3 **Eltisley** England
37 K4 **Eltmann** W Germany
128 E2 **El Tocuyo** Venezuela
109 P5 **Elton** Louisiana U.S.A.
100 G3 **Eltopia** Washington U.S.A.
133 C3 **El toro** Chile
102 G8 **El Toro** California U.S.A.
133 C3 **El Tránsito** Chile
124 C2 **El Tren** Mexico
124 D6 **El Triunfo** Mexico
118 K1 **Eltrut L** Ontario Canada
127 O2 **El Tucuche** *mt* Trinidad
133 C8 **El Turbio** Argentina
36 E3 **Eltville** W Germany
76 E2 **Eluru** India
119 Q9 **Elva** Manitoba Canada
52 C5 **Elva** U.S.S.R.
106 D5 **El Vado** New Mexico U.S.A.
128 C2 **El Valle** Colombia
127 L9 **El Valle** Venezuela
12 E3 **Elvanfoot** Scotland
27 E10 **Elvdal** Norway
26 N2 **Elvebakken** Norway
20 E6 **Elven** France
27 E11 **Elverum** Norway
125 L3 **El Viejo** Nicaragua
128 D2 **El Vigia** Venezuela
128 D5 **Elvira** Brazil
114 J3 **Elvira,C** Northwest Territories Canada
143 C8 **Elvire, Mt** Western Australia Australia
142 B5 **Elvire, Mt** Western Australia Australia
142 G4 **Elvire, R** Western Australia Australia
44 D1 **Elvo** *R* Italy
133 C4 **El Volcán** Chile
86 H5 **El Wak** Kenya
101 O1 **Elwell, L** *res* Montana U.S.A.
99 S8 **Elwood** Illinois U.S.A.
94 B6 **Elwood** Indiana U.S.A.
110 B2 **Elwood** Missouri U.S.A.
98 G9 **Elwood** Nebraska U.S.A.
9 G3 **Ely** England
99 P8 **Ely** Iowa U.S.A.
99 P2 **Ely** Minnesota U.S.A.
103 K2 **Ely** Nevada U.S.A.
80 D3 **Elyaqim** Israel
138 C3 **Ely Hill** South Australia Australia
99 N5 **Elysian** Minnesota U.S.A.
36 E3 **Elz** W Germany
40 H1 **Elz** *R* W Germany
36 E7 **Elzach** W Germany
124 G5 **El Zape** Mexico
32 L7 **Elze** W Germany
27 G10 **Emådalen** Sweden
137 O5 **Émaé** *isld* Vanuatu
77 D1 **Emāmrūd** Iran
27 H14 **Emån** *R* Sweden
57 A1 **Emba** U.S.S.R.
50 E4 **Emba** *R* U.S.S.R.
122 G1 **Embar** Labrador, Nfld Canada
133 E2 **Embarcación** Argentina
110 H2 **Embarras** *R* Illinois U.S.A.
117 R6 **Embarras Portage** Alberta Canada
99 O2 **Embarrass** Minnesota U.S.A.
98 J3 **Embden** North Dakota U.S.A.
60 P1 **Embetsu** Japan
128 D5 **Embira** *R* Brazil
101 R5 **Emblem** Wyoming U.S.A.
13 G3 **Embleton** England
47 U14 **Embóna** Rhodes Greece
121 P7 **Embrun** Ontario Canada
88 F2 **Embu** Kenya
99 R9 **Emden** Illinois U.S.A.
32 F6 **Emden** W Germany
67 A2 **Emei** China
67 A2 **Emei Shan** *mt* China
80 F1 **Emeq Hula** Israel
80 D2 **'Emeq Zevulun** Israel
98 J2 **Emerado** North Dakota U.S.A.
141 J6 **Emerald** Queensland Australia
114 H2 **Emerald I** Northwest Territories Canada
71 D5 **Emergency Pt** Philippines
142 E3 **Emeriau Pt** Western Australia Australia
115 N7 **Emeril** Labrador, Nfld Canada
119 U9 **Emerson** Manitoba Canada
99 L8 **Emerson** Iowa U.S.A.
98 K7 **Emerson** Nebraska U.S.A.
98 J6 **Emery** South Dakota U.S.A.
47 K5 **Emet** Turkey
101 P4 **Emigrant** Montana U.S.A.
102 D2 **Emigrant Gap** California U.S.A.
100 J9 **Emigrant Pass** Nevada U.S.A.
101 P4 **Emigrant Pk** Montana U.S.A.
103 J4 **Emigrant Valley** Nevada U.S.A.
86 C2 **Emi Koussi** *mt* Chad
42 D4 **Emilia-Romagna** *prov* Italy
40 F6 **Emilius, M** Italy
57 L2 **Emin** China
66 C2 **Emin** China
47 J2 **Emine,N** Bulgaria
94 B8 **Eminence** Kentucky U.S.A.
110 E4 **Eminence** Missouri U.S.A.
47 J2 **Eminska Planina** *plateau* Bulgaria
47 K7 **Emir** *R* Turkey
78 C2 **Emirdag** Turkey
139 J7 **Emita** Flinders I, Tasmania Australia
94 H5 **Emlenton** Pennsylvania U.S.A.
32 E7 **Emlichheim** W Germany
27 H15 **Emmaboda** Sweden
126 B1 **Emmastad** Curaçao
27 N13 **Emmaste** U.S.S.R.
95 M6 **Emmaus** Pennsylvania U.S.A.
139 K3 **Emmaville** New South Wales Australia
40 G4 **Emme** *R* Switzerland
118 L3 **Emmeline L** Saskatchewan Canada
25 E3 **Emmeloord** Netherlands
25 G3 **Emmen** Netherlands
41 H3 **Emmen** Switzerland
40 G4 **Emmen Tal** Switzerland
25 F5 **Emmerich** W Germany
28 B7 **Emmerlev** Denmark
32 K8 **Emmern** W Germany
38 M5 **Emmersdorf** Austria
28 E7 **Emmerske** Denmark
32 K9 **Emmerthal** W Germany
141 G6 **Emmet** Queensland Australia
100 J6 **Emmet** Idaho U.S.A.
98 H7 **Emmet** Nebraska U.S.A.
99 M6 **Emmetsburg** Iowa U.S.A.
107 O2 **Emmett** Kansas U.S.A.
76 C3 **Emmiganuru** India
95 K7 **Emmitsburg** Maryland U.S.A.
103 O1 **Emmons,Mt** Utah U.S.A.
99 N1 **Emo** Ontario Canada
48 F3 **Emöd** Hungary
109 M3 **Emory** Texas U.S.A.
108 D6 **Emory Pk** Texas U.S.A.
124 D4 **Empalme** Mexico
89 G7 **Empangeni** S Africa
32 K7 **Empede** W Germany
133 F3 **Empedrado** Argentina
25 F5 **Empel** W Germany
112 D5 **Empire** Georgia U.S.A.
99 U5 **Empire** Michigan U.S.A.
100 F9 **Empire** Nevada U.S.A.
100 A6 **Empire** Oregon U.S.A.
106 F1 **Empire Res** Colorado U.S.A.
42 D5 **Empoli** Italy
107 O3 **Emporia** Kansas U.S.A.
94 K10 **Emporia** Virginia U.S.A.
94 J5 **Emporium** Pennsylvania U.S.A.
118 G8 **Empress** Alberta Canada
22 J3 **Emptinne** Belgium
19 N14 **Empurany** France
98 G2 **Emrick** North Dakota U.S.A.
32 F6 **Ems** *R* W Germany
32 F8 **Emsbüren** W Germany
32 F9 **Emscher** *R* W Germany
121 L7 **Emsdale** Ontario Canada
32 G8 **Emsdetten** W Germany
32 G6 **Ems-Jade Kanal** W Germany
37 K4 **Emskirchen** W Germany
32 F7 **Emslage** W Germany
36 G1 **Emstal** W Germany
32 H7 **Emstek** W Germany
9 F6 **Emsworth** England
65 G3 **Emu** China
141 F3 **Emu Ck** Queensland Australia
61 L10 **Ena** Japan
27 J10 **Enånger** Sweden
80 C3 **'En Ayyala** Israel
101 T8 **Encampment** Wyoming U.S.A.
17 H4 **Encanade** *mt* Spain
108 B6 **Encantada** Mexico
124 B2 **Encantada, Cerro de la** Mexico
131 H3 **Encantadas,Sa** *mts* Brazil
124 C4 **Encantado, Cerro** *mt* Mexico
71 E3 **Encanto,C** Luzon Philippines
124 H7 **Encarnación** Mexico
130 C10 **Encarnación** Paraguay
118 E8 **Enchant** Alberta Canada
85 D7 **Enchi** Ghana
109 H7 **Encinal** Texas U.S.A.
108 A6 **Encinillas** Mexico
102 G8 **Encinitas** California U.S.A.
108 B1 **Encino** New Mexico U.S.A.
108 B2 **Encinoso** New Mexico U.S.A.
128 D2 **Encontrados** Venezuela
138 E6 **Encounter B** South Australia Australia
133 G4 **Encruzilhada do Sul** Brazil
48 G2 **Encs** Hungary
117 L8 **Endako** British Columbia Canada
69 F11 **Endau** *R* Malaysia
69 F11 **Endau** Malaysia
71 K9 **Ende** *isld* Flores Indonesia
99 R6 **Endeavor** Wisconsin U.S.A.
141 H3 **Endeavour** Queensland Australia
119 P6 **Endeavour** Saskatchewan Canada
141 F1 **Endeavour Str** Queensland Australia
108 A8 **Endee** New Mexico U.S.A.
71 K9 **Endeh** Indonesia
28 E5 **Endelave** Denmark
134 K8 **Enderbury I** Phoenix Is Pacific Oc
117 O10 **Enderby** British Columbia Canada
142 B5 **Enderby I** Western Australia Australia
146 J10 **Enderby Land** Antarctica
98 J3 **Enderlin** North Dakota U.S.A.
98 E9 **Enders Res** Nebraska U.S.A.
118 E7 **Endiang** Alberta Canada
95 L4 **Endicott** New York U.S.A.
100 H3 **Endicott** Washington U.S.A.
117 G7 **Endicott Arm** *pen* Alaska U.S.A.
116 L3 **Endicott Mts** Alaska U.S.A.
117 G4 **End,Mt** Yukon Territory Canada
8 D1 **Endon** England
80 E3 **'En Dor** Israel
140 C1 **Endyalgout I** N Terr Australia
128 D6 **Ene** *R* Peru
143 B8 **Eneabba** Western Australia Australia
55 C5 **Energetik** U.S.S.R.
54 F9 **Energodar** U.S.S.R.
134 G7 **Enewetak** *atoll* Marshall Is Pacific Oc
78 A1 **Enez** Turkey
47 H4 **Enez** Turkey
79 F4 **Enfe** Lebanon
43 C12 **Enfida** Tunisia
122 J9 **Enfield** Nova Scotia Canada
9 F4 **Enfield** England
110 H3 **Enfield** Illinois U.S.A.
95 P3 **Enfield** New Hampshire U.S.A.
112 K1 **Enfield** North Carolina U.S.A.
127 K5 **Engaño, C** Dominican Rep
71 E1 **Engaño,C** Luzon Philippines
60 R1 **Engaru** Japan
28 B7 **Enge** W Germany
80 E8 **En Gedi** Israel
41 H4 **Engelberg** Switzerland
112 M2 **Engelhard** North Carolina U.S.A.
38 J5 **Engelhartszell** Austria
53 G8 **Engel's** U.S.S.R.
36 C2 **Engelskirchen** W Germany
41 J2 **Engen** W Germany
130 C4 **Engenho** Brazil
138 D3 **Engenina** *R* South Australia Australia
32 J8 **Enger** W Germany
26 E10 **Engerdal** Norway
27 F10 **Engeren,L** Norway
36 D3 **Engers** W Germany
28 C4 **Engesvang** Denmark
80 F2 **'En Gev** Israel
Enghien *see* **Edingen**
21 P4 **Enghien-les-Bains** France
117 F6 **Engineer** British Columbia Canada
22 J2 **Engis** Belgium
70 B4 **Engkilili** Sarawak
8 D3 **England** U.K.
111 E7 **England** Arkansas U.S.A.
106 C8 **Engle** New Mexico U.S.A.
123 Q3 **Englee** Newfoundland Canada
119 N6 **Englefield** Saskatchewan Canada
117 K10 **Englewood** British Columbia Canada
106 F2 **Englewood** Colorado U.S.A.
113 E11 **Englewood** Florida U.S.A.
107 L4 **Englewood** Kansas U.S.A.
112 C2 **Englewood** Tennessee U.S.A.
110 K3 **English** Indiana U.S.A.
122 E4 **English Bay** Quebec Canada
116 L7 **English Bay** Alaska U.S.A.
7 H13 **English Channel** England/France
146 C6 **English Coast** Antarctica
140 D1 **English Company's Is** N Terr Australia
127 P4 **English Harbour Town** Antigua W Indies
123 R6 **English Harbour W** Newfoundland Canada
119 N1 **English River** Ontario Canada
52 D2 **Engozero** U.S.S.R.
36 G7 **Engstingen** W Germany
17 G6 **Énguera** Spain
52 B6 **Engure** U.S.S.R.
80 D3 **'En Ha'Emeq** Israel
80 D2 **'En HaMifraz** Israel
80 E3 **'En Harod** Israel
79 F8 **'En Hazeva** Israel
80 C3 **'En Hod** Israel
98 B2 **Enid** Montana U.S.A.
107 N5 **Enid** Oklahoma U.S.A.
111 G7 **Enid L** Mississippi U.S.A.
142 B5 **Enid, Mt** Western Australia Australia
118 A3 **Enilda** Alberta Canada
36 G7 **Eningen** W Germany
60 P3 **Eniwa** Japan
60 P3 **Eniwa dake** *mt* Japan
85 C5 **Enji** Mauritania
80 C3 **'En Karmel** Israel
36 D5 **Enkenbach-Alsenborn** W Germany
25 D3 **Enkhuizen** Netherlands
36 C4 **Enkirch** W Germany
27 J12 **Enköping** Sweden
128 G8 **En Madrejón** Paraguay
114 J5 **Ennadai** Northwest Territories Canada
86 E3 **En Nahud** Sudan
86 D2 **Ennedi** *plateau* Chad
14 D3 **Ennell,L** Ireland
32 F10 **Ennepetal** W Germany
127 H5 **Ennery** Haiti
139 H3 **Enngonia** New South Wales Australia
32 H9 **Ennigerloh** W Germany
98 D5 **Enning** South Dakota U.S.A.
27 E13 **Enningdal** Norway
14 C4 **Ennis** Ireland
101 O4 **Ennis** Montana U.S.A.
109 L3 **Ennis** Texas U.S.A.
14 E4 **Enniscorthy** Ireland
14 D2 **Enniskillen** N Ireland
14 B4 **Ennistimon** Ireland
80 D1 **Enn Nâqoûra** Lebanon
38 K6 **Ennstaler Alpen** *mts* Austria
80 G4 **En Nu'eiyima** Jordan
29 P9 **Eno** Finland
108 E2 **Enochs** Texas U.S.A.
141 K1 **Enoggera** *dist* Brisbane, Qnsld Australia
69 F13 **Enok** Sumatra
98 J8 **Enola** Nebraska U.S.A.
29 O9 **Enonkoski** Finland
29 K3 **Enontekiö** Finland
112 F3 **Enoree** *R* South Carolina U.S.A.
112 F3 **Enoree** South Carolina U.S.A.
95 P2 **Enosburg Falls** Vermont U.S.A.
67 D5 **Enping** China
70 F6 **Enrekang** Sulawesi
71 E2 **Enrile** Luzon Philippines
127 J5 **Enriquillo, Lago de** Dominican Rep
25 E3 **Ens** Netherlands
139 J6 **Ensay** Victoria Australia
25 G4 **Enschede** Netherlands
36 B5 **Ensdorf** W Germany
32 H10 **Ense** W Germany
133 F4 **Ensenada** Argentina
124 A2 **Ensenada** Mexico
106 D5 **Ensenada** New Mexico U.S.A.
126 B3 **Ensenada de Guadiana** *B* Cuba
36 C5 **Ensheim** W Germany
80 D4 **'En Shemer** Israel
67 C1 **Enshi** China
118 D8 **Ensign** Alberta Canada
107 K4 **Ensign** Kansas U.S.A.
99 U4 **Ensign** Michigan U.S.A.
19 K5 **Ensisheim** France
28 F4 **Enslev** Denmark
9 E4 **Enstone** England
86 F5 **Entebbe** Uganda
37 N4 **Entenbühl** *mt* W Germany
12 E3 **Enterkinfoot** Scotland
117 P5 **Enterprise** Northwest Territories Canada
121 O8 **Enterprise** Ontario Canada
111 L10 **Enterprise** Alabama U.S.A.
107 N3 **Enterprise** Kansas U.S.A.
111 H9 **Enterprise** Mississippi U.S.A.
100 H4 **Enterprise** Oregon U.S.A.
103 L4 **Enterprise** Utah U.S.A.
71 D5 **Enterprise Pt** Philippines
100 E2 **Entiat Mts** Washington U.S.A.
70 C4 **Entimau, Bt** *mt* Sarawak
17 F8 **Entinas,Pta. De Las** Spain
133 D8 **Entrada,Pta** Argentina
18 H5 **Entrains** France
21 J6 **Entrammes** France
140 A3 **Entrance I** N Terr Australia
18 G8 **Entraygues** France
143 B10 **Entrecasteaux, Pt.d'** Western Australia Australia
137 N5 **Entrecasteaux, Récifs D'** *reefs* New Caledonia
83 J14 **Entre-Deux** Réunion Indian Oc
123 L6 **Entré, I. d'** Madeleine Is, Quebec Canada
129 H5 **Entre Rios** Brazil
130 G7 **Entre Rios de Minas** Brazil
36 F6 **Entringen** W Germany
103 M7 **Entro** Arizona U.S.A.
89 E2 **Entuba** Zimbabwe
118 C5 **Entwistle** Alberta Canada
85 F7 **Enugu** Nigeria
100 D2 **Enumclaw** Washington U.S.A.
21 N2 **Envermeu** France
27 H11 **Enviken** Sweden
8 D3 **Enville** England
128 D5 **Envira** Brazil
67 B1 **Enyang** China
48 E4 **Enying** Hungary
144 C5 **Enys, Mt** New Zealand
36 F6 **Enz** *R* W Germany
45 H2 **Enza** *R* Italy
80 E8 **'En Zafzafa** Israel
61 M10 **Enzan** Japan
37 M6 **Enzelhausen** W Germany
36 E6 **Enzklösterle** W Germany
80 B7 **En Zurim** Israel
36 F6 **Enzweihingen** W Germany
111 D11 **Eola** Louisiana U.S.A.
110 E2 **Eolia** Missouri U.S.A.
21 L3 **Epaignes** France
45 P8 **Epameo, M** *mt* Italy
21 K4 **Epaney** France
46 F4 **Epanomi** Greece
25 E4 **Epe** Netherlands
32 F8 **Epe** W Germany
133 E5 **Epecuén,L** Argentina
22 E3 **Epéhy** France
140 D5 **Epenarra** N Terr Australia
22 C2 **Éperlecques** France
18 H3 **Épernay** France
87 B9 **Epernbe** Namibia
21 O4 **Épernon** France
111 H9 **Epes** Alabama U.S.A.
21 J8 **Epesses, les** France
36 C7 **Epfig** France
138 E2 **Ephemeral Lakes** South Australia Australia
103 N2 **Ephraim** Utah U.S.A.
95 L6 **Ephrata** Pennsylvania U.S.A.
100 F2 **Ephrata** Washington U.S.A.
137 O5 **Épi** *isld* Vanuatu
88 G10 **Epidendron** *isld* Mozambique
46 F7 **Epidhavros** Greece
21 O6 **Epieds** France
17 G3 **Épila** Spain
19 K4 **Epinal** France
20 F8 **Epine, l'** Vendée France
20 G5 **Epiniac** France
98 J6 **Epiphany** South Dakota U.S.A.
79 C4 **Episkopi** Cyprus
21 O4 **Epône** France
36 B5 **Eppelborn** W Germany
37 P2 **Eppendorf** East Germany
22 F4 **Eppes** France
22 G3 **Eppe-Sauvage** France
9 G4 **Epping** England
95 Q3 **Epping** New Hampshire U.S.A.
98 C1 **Epping** North Dakota U.S.A.
36 F5 **Eppingen** W Germany
36 E3 **Eppstein** W Germany
98 A4 **Epsie** Montana U.S.A.
9 F5 **Epsom** England
21 M6 **Epuisay** France
87 C10 **Epukiro** Namibia
13 H6 **Epworth** England
99 Q7 **Epworth** Iowa U.S.A.
77 C4 **Eqlīd** Iran
110 H4 **Equality** Illinois U.S.A.
86 D5 **Equateur** *prov* Zaire
86 E4 **Equatoria** *prov* Sudan
73 L9 **Equatorial Chan** Maldives
85 F8 **Equatorial Guinea** *rep* W Africa
20 G2 **Equeurdreville** France
95 M5 **Equmunk** Pennsylvania U.S.A.
60 O4 **Era** Japan
86 E4 **Era** *watercourse* Sudan
141 H7 **Erac** *R* Queensland Australia
71 C6 **Eran** Palawan Philippines
71 C6 **Eran Bay** Palawan Philippines
111 D12 **Erath** Louisiana U.S.A.
78 F1 **Erbaa** Turkey
36 D5 **Erbach** *R* W Germany
36 H7 **Erbach** Baden-Wurttemberg W Germany
36 G4 **Erbach** Hessen W Germany
86 G1 **Erba, Jebel** *mt* Sudan
37 N4 **Erbendorf** W Germany
135 N4 **Erben Tablemount** Pacific Oc
36 C4 **Erbes Kopf** *mt* W Germany
20 H6 **Erbray** France
22 D4 **Ercheu** France
78 E2 **Erciyas Dag** Turkey
45 Q8 **Ercolana** Italy
48 E3 **Ercsi** Hungary
48 E3 **Erd** Hungary
65 H2 **Erdaohezi** China
65 G3 **Erdao Jiang** *R* China
47 J4 **Erdek** Turkey
47 J4 **Erdek Körfezi** *B* Turkey
79 E2 **Erdemh** Turkey
56 F6 **Erdenet** Mongolia
20 D6 **Erdeven** France
86 D2 **Erdi** *dist* Chad
37 M7 **Erding** W Germany
37 M7 **Erdinger Moos** *marsh* W Germany
9 E2 **Erdington** England
37 P2 **Erdmansdorf** East Germany
36 B3 **Erdorf** W Germany
20 H6 **Erdre** *R* France
20 F5 **Éréac** France
128 F2 **Erebato** *R* Venezuela
146 D11 **Erebus, Mt** *vol* Ross I Antarctica
78 K6 **Erech** Iraq
130 D10 **Erechim** Brazil
58 G2 **Ereentsav** Mongolia
Ereğli *see* **Marmaraereğlisi**
78 C1 **Ereğli** Turkey
71 H7 **Ereke** Indonesia
47 L7 **Eren** *R* Turkey
47 K8 **Eren Dağ** *mt* Turkey
65 D2 **Eren Gobi** China
65 B3 **Erenhot** China
Erenköy *see* **Intepe**
47 N11 **Erenköy** Turkey
129 G4 **Erepecu, L** Brazil
16 D3 **Eresma** *R* Spain
47 H5 **Eressós** Greece
80 B7 **Erez** Israel
22 K3 **Erezée** Belgium
32 K4 **Erfde** W Germany
89 E7 **Erfenis Dam** *res* S Africa
65 A4 **Erfenzi** China
85 D2 **Erfoud** Morocco
36 B2 **Erft** *R* W Germany
36 B2 **Erftstadt** W Germany
37 L2 **Erfurt** East Germany
56 D4 **Ergak-Targak-Tayga, Khrebet** *mts* U.S.S.R.
78 G2 **Ergani** Turkey
85 D4 **Erg Chech** *desert region* Mali/Algeria
86 C2 **Erg du Djourab** *dist* Chad
47 H3 **Ergene** *R* Turkey
85 D3 **Erg er Raoui** *desert region* Algeria
85 C3 **Erg Iguid** *sand desert* Algeria/Mauritania
55 E1 **Erginskiy Sor, Oz** *L* U.S.S.R.
52 C6 **Ērgli** U.S.S.R.
37 N6 **Ergolding** W Germany
37 N6 **Ergoldsbach** W Germany
65 G1 **Ergu** China
20 B6 **Ergué-Armel** France
86 C3 **Erguig** *R* Chad
Ergun He *R* China/USSR *see* **Argun** *R*
59 H1 **Ergun Youqi** China
59 H1 **Ergun Zuoqi** China
37 O7 **Erharting** W Germany
16 D2 **Eria** *R* Spain
86 G2 **Eriba** Sudan
16 A6 **Ericeira** Portugal
32 K7 **Erichshagen** W Germany
107 L6 **Erick** Oklahoma U.S.A.
119 S8 **Erickson** Manitoba Canada
122 G2 **Eric L** Quebec Canada
99 N1 **Ericsburg** Minnesota U.S.A.
98 H8 **Ericson** Nebraska U.S.A.
98 A9 **Erie** Colorado U.S.A.
99 Q8 **Erie** Illinois U.S.A.
107 P4 **Erie** Kansas U.S.A.
94 D5 **Erie** Michigan U.S.A.
103 J6 **Erie** Nevada U.S.A.
98 J2 **Erie** North Dakota U.S.A.
94 G4 **Erie** Pennsylvania U.S.A.
120 J10 **Erieau** Ontario Canada
94 G4 **Erie,L** U.S.A./Canada
79 H1 **Erikli** Turkey
47 O12 **Erikoúsa** *isld* Greece
119 T8 **Eriksdale** Manitoba Canada
46 E7 **Erimanthos** *mt* Greece
60 R4 **Erimo-misaki** *C* Japan
22 C3 **Erin** France
37 P7 **Ering** W Germany
27 H15 **Eringsboda** Sweden
127 N3 **Erin Pt** Trinidad
15 A3 **Eriskay** *isld* Scotland
9 G5 **Erith** England
46 F6 **Erithrai** Greece
Eritrea *see* **Ertra**
25 F6 **Erkelenz** W Germany
27 K12 **Erken** Sweden
33 T8 **Erkner** East Germany
86 G2 **Erkowit** Sudan
32 E10 **Erkrath** W Germany
38 F6 **Erl** Austria
Erlangdiang *see* **Dawu**
37 L4 **Erlangen** W Germany
94 C7 **Erlanger** Kentucky U.S.A.
38 M5 **Erlauf** *R* Austria
37 N3 **Erlbach** East Germany
140 C7 **Erldunda** N Terr Australia
36 F3 **Erlensee** W Germany
111 C8 **Erling,L** Arkansas U.S.A.
65 G3 **Erlong Shan** *mt* China
38 F8 **Erlsbach** Austria
25 E4 **Ermelo** Netherlands
89 F6 **Ermelo** S Africa
79 D2 **Ermenek** *R* Turkey
78 D3 **Ermenek** Turkey
71 M9 **Ermera** Indonesia
Ermoúpolis *see* **Siros**
33 O9 **Ermsleben** East Germany
138 B2 **Ernabella** South Australia Australia
138 B2 **Ernabella** *R* South Australia Australia
76 C6 **Ernakulam** India
36 E1 **Erndtebrück** W Germany
14 C2 **Erne** *R* Ireland
21 J5 **Ernée** France
21 J5 **Ernée** *R* France
14 D2 **Erne,L.Lower** N Ireland
14 D2 **Erne,L.Upper** N Ireland
143 E7 **Ernest Giles Ra** Western Australia Australia
144 A7 **Ernest Is** New Zealand
135 M12 **Ernest Legouve Reef** Pacific Oc
117 G8 **Ernest Sd** Alaska U.S.A.
118 L8 **Ernfold** Saskatchewan Canada
45 O6 **Ernici, Monti** *mt* Italy
36 G4 **Ernstthal** W Germany
76 C5 **Erode** India
78 J2 **Erois** Turkey
141 G7 **Eromanga** Queensland Australia
111 D9 **Eros** Louisiana U.S.A.
36 B2 **Erp** W Germany
22 G3 **Erquelinnes** Belgium
20 F4 **Erquy** France
20 F4 **Erquy, C.d'** France
143 B7 **Errabiddy Hills** Western Australia Australia
85 D2 **Er Rachidia** Morocco
86 F3 **Er Rahad** Sudan
80 G6 **Er Rajib** Jordan
88 F10 **Errego** Mozambique
14 C1 **Errigal** *mt* Ireland
28 G7 **Errindlev** Denmark
14 A2 **Erris Hd** Ireland
28 D5 **Erritsø** Denmark
111 G12 **Errol I** Louisiana U.S.A.
137 O5 **Erromango** *isld* Vanuatu
86 F3 **Er Roseires** Sudan
46 D4 **Ersekë** Albania
118 E6 **Erskine** Alberta Canada
142 F4 **Erskine, Mount** Western Australia Australia
26 M6 **Ersnäs** Sweden
36 D7 **Erstein** France
19 L4 **Ersteir** France
36 H3 **Erthal** W Germany
54 M5 **Ertil'** U.S.S.R.
66 D2 **Ertix He** *R* China
86 G2 **Ertra** *prov* Ethiopia
47 J5 **Ertugrul** Turkey
22 F1 **Ertvelde** Belgium
145 E3 **Erua** New Zealand
138 E4 **Erudina** South Australia Australia
27 H12 **Ervalla** Sweden
21 K6 **Erve** *R* France
37 Q2 **Ervěnice** Czechoslovakia
22 D3 **Ervillers** France
112 J2 **Erwin** North Carolina U.S.A.
112 E1 **Erwin** Tennessee U.S.A.
32 H9 **Erwitte** W Germany
119 P6 **Erwood** Saskatchewan Canada
8 C3 **Erwood** Wales
33 O8 **Erxleben** East Germany
46 D3 **Erzen** *R* Albania
37 N3 **Erzgebirge** East Germany
56 E5 **Erzin** U.S.S.R.
78 G2 **Erzincan** Turkey
78 H2 **Erzurum** Turkey
52 B7 **Erzvilkas** U.S.S.R.
60 P4 **Esan-misaki** *C* Japan
21 J3 **Esaue** *R* France
28 A6 **Esbjerg** Denmark
107 M2 **Esbon** Kansas U.S.A.
17 G2 **Esca** *R* Spain
18 E10 **Esca** *R* Spain
130 J10 **Escada** Brazil
103 N4 **Escalante** *R* Utah U.S.A.
103 N4 **Escalante** Utah U.S.A.
103 L4 **Escalante Des** Utah U.S.A.
131 A8 **Escalera,Pta** Chile
124 G4 **Escalón** Mexico
16 E4 **Escalona** Spain
111 J11 **Escambia** *R* Florida U.S.A.
99 T4 **Escanaba** Michigan U.S.A.
99 T3 **Escanaba** *R* Michigan U.S.A.
125 O8 **Escárcega** Mexico
21 H7 **Escarpière, l'** France
22 E3 **Escaut** *R* France
22 L5 **Esch** Luxembourg
36 E3 **Esch** W Germany
36 G4 **Eschau** W Germany
36 F3 **Eschborn** W Germany
22 K4 **Eschdorf** Luxembourg
32 E7 **Eschebrügge** W Germany
32 M7 **Eschede** W Germany
37 L4 **Eschenau** W Germany
37 M4 **Eschenbach** W Germany
36 E2 **Eschenberg** W Germany
32 L9 **Eschershausen** W Germany
40 G4 **Escholzmatt** Switzerland
116 G3 **Eschscholtz B** Alaska U.S.A.
22 K4 **Esch-sur-la-Sûre** Luxembourg
37 J1 **Eschwege** W Germany
25 F7 **Eschweiler** W Germany
127 K5 **Escocesa, B** Dominican Rep
130 H5 **Escondido** Brazil
102 G8 **Escondido** California U.S.A.
20 F7 **Escoublac** France
122 C5 **Escoumins,R** Quebec Canada
21 P5 **Escrennes** France
13 G6 **Escrick** England
124 G6 **Escuinapa de Hidalgo** Mexico
122 F5 **Escuminac** Quebec Canada
122 H6 **Escuminac, Pt** New Brunswick Canada
86 B5 **Eséka** Cameroon
47 K8 **Eşen** Turkey
47 N10 **Esenceli** Turkey
32 G5 **Esens** W Germany
17 H2 **Esera** *R* Spain
77 B3 **Eşfahān** Iran
16 E3 **Esgueva** *R* Spain
80 B8 **Eshbol** Israel
80 B8 **Eshel Ha Nasi** Israel
9 F5 **Esher** England
77 L1 **Eshkamesh** Afghanistan
57 F6 **Eshkāshem** Afghanistan
87 F11 **Eshowe** S Africa
Esh Sham *see* **Dimashq**
77 B2 **Eshtehard** Iran
80 D8 **Eshtemoa** Jordan
87 E10 **Esigodini** Zimbabwe
42 E5 **Esino** *R* Italy
141 K7 **Esk** Queensland Australia
139 H8 **Esk** *R* Tasmania Australia
116 N6 **Eska** Alaska U.S.A.
118 L8 **Eskbank** Saskatchewan Canada
145 F3 **Eskdale** New Zealand
13 E5 **Eskdale Green** England
14 C2 **Eske, L** Ireland
47 K7 **Eskere** Turkey
29 T9 **Eskifjordhur** Iceland
28 H5 **Eskildstrup** Denmark
28 H7 **Eskilstrup** Denmark
27 H12 **Eskilstuna** Sweden
122 J3 **Eskimo I** Quebec Canada
114 F4 **Eskimo Lakes** Northwest Territories Canada
115 K5 **Eskimo Point** Northwest Territories Canada
78 D1 **Eskipazar** Turkey
47 L5 **Eskişehir** Turkey
13 H5 **Esk,R** England
15 E5 **Esk,R** Scotland
107 O3 **Eskridge** Kansas U.S.A.
16 D2 **Esla** *R* Spain
16 D3 **Esla, Embalse del** *res* Spain
78 L4 **Eslamabad-e Gharb** Iran
77 G2 **Eslām Qal'eh** Afghanistan
37 O4 **Eslarn** W Germany
47 K7 **Eşler Dağı** *mt* Turkey
32 H10 **Eslohe** W Germany
27 F16 **Eslöv** Sweden
47 K6 **Eşme** Turkey
141 G4 **Esmeralda** Queensland Australia
126 E4 **Esmeralda** Cuba
133 B7 **Esmeralda, I** Chile
128 C3 **Esmeraldas** Ecuador
98 G1 **Esmond** North Dakota U.S.A.
98 J5 **Esmond** South Dakota U.S.A.
120 D2 **Esnagami L** Ontario Canada
120 F4 **Esnagi L** Ontario Canada
22 J2 **Esnaux** Belgium
27 E11 **Espa** Norway
127 J8 **Espada,Pta** Colombia
18 G8 **Espalion** France
17 H6 **Espalmador** *isld* Balearic Is
120 J6 **Espanola** Ontario Canada
128 B8 **Española** *isld* Galapagos Is
113 F8 **Espanola** Florida U.S.A.
106 D6 **Espanola** New Mexico U.S.A.
19 P17 **Esparron** France
102 B3 **Esparto** California U.S.A.
125 M5 **Esparza** Costa Rica
28 E6 **Espe** Denmark
27 D10 **Espedals-vatn** *L* Norway
32 J8 **Espelkamp** W Germany
116 E3 **Espenberg,C** Alaska U.S.A.
37 N1 **Espenhain** East Germany
88 F8 **Esperança** Mozambique
143 D10 **Esperance** Western Australia Australia
143 D10 **Esperance B** Western Australia Australia
146 D3 **Esperanza** *Arg Base* Graham Land Antarctica
131 E3 **Esperanza** Argentina
124 E4 **Esperanza** Mexico
113 K7 **Esperanza** Puerto Rico
108 B4 **Esperanza** Texas U.S.A.
125 M2 **Esperanza, Sa. de la** *ra* Honduras
29 K5 **Espergærde** Denmark
45 P7 **Esperia** Italy
16 A6 **Espichel,C** Portugal
16 D6 **Espiel** Spain
130 E10 **Espigão,Serra do** *mts* Brazil
16 D2 **Espigüete** *mt* Spain
128 D6 **Espinar** Peru
19 Q16 **Espinasses** France
124 J4 **Espinazo** Mexico
130 G6 **Espinhaço,Serra,do** *mt* Brazil
16 B4 **Espinho** Portugal
131 G2 **Espinilho, Serra do** *ra* Brazil
130 G4 **Espinosa** Brazil
130 H6 **Espirito Santo** *state* Brazil
124 D5 **Espíritu Santo** *isld* Mexico
137 O5 **Espiritu Santo** *isld* Vanuatu
125 Q8 **Espiritu Santo, B. del** Mexico
133 D8 **Espiritu Santo,C** Chile/Arg
71 G4 **Espiritu Santo,C** Philippines
125 P7 **Espita** Mexico
123 R6 **Espoir, B. d'** Newfoundland Canada
16 B3 **Esposende** Portugal
40 D2 **Esprels** France
87 F10 **Espungabera** Mozambique
100 F3 **Esquatzel Coulee** *R* Washington U.S.A.
124 E2 **Esqueda** Mexico
133 C6 **Esquel** Argentina
22 C2 **Esquelbecq** France
100 B1 **Esquimalt** British Columbia Canada
117 M11 **Esquimalt** British Columbia Canada
133 F3 **Esquina** Argentina
29 K4 **Esrum Sø** *L* Denmark
55 D1 **Ess** *R* U.S.S.R.
80 F3 **Es Samt** Jordan
80 D8 **Es Samu** Jordan
85 C2 **Essaouira** Morocco
80 G3 **Es Sarih** Jordan
21 O4 **Essarts-le-Roi, les** France
20 H8 **Essarts, les** Vendée France
21 L4 **Essay** France
85 E2 **Es Seggeur** *watercourse* Algeria
32 L7 **Essel** W Germany
22 G1 **Essen** Belgium
32 G7 **Essen** Niedersachsen W Germany
32 E10 **Essen** Nordrhein-Westfalen W Germany
37 N6 **Essenbach** W Germany
143 D6 **Essendon, Mt** Western Australia Australia
120 H10 **Essex** Ontario Canada
9 G4 **Essex** *co* England
103 J7 **Essex** California U.S.A.
95 P5 **Essex** Connecticut U.S.A.
99 L9 **Essex** Iowa U.S.A.
101 M1 **Essex** Montana U.S.A.
95 O2 **Essex** New York U.S.A.
95 O2 **Essex Junct** Vermont U.S.A.
94 D3 **Essexville** Michigan U.S.A.
37 M6 **Essing** W Germany
37 J6 **Essingen** W Germany
36 G6 **Esslingen** W Germany
21 P4 **Essonne** *dept* France
21 P5 **Essonne** *R* France
52 D4 **Essoyla** U.S.S.R.
100 C4 **Estacada** Oregon U.S.A.
16 B1 **Estaca de Bares, Pta. de la** Spain
106 G8 **Estacado, Llano** *plain* New Mex/Tex U.S.A.
103 K10 **Estacion Doctor** Mexico
103 K10 **Estacion France** Mexico
103 K9 **Estación Mèdanos** Mexico
133 E8 **Estados, I. de los** Argentina
18 G10 **Estagel** France
71 F2 **Estagno Pt** Luzon Philippines

Fermoselle — Fort McMahon
29

16 C3 **Fermoselle** Spain
14 C4 **Fermoy** Ireland
128 A8 **Fernandina** *isld* Galapagos Is
113 F7 **Fernandina Beach** Florida U.S.A.
90 G9 **Fernando de Noronha** *isld* Atlantic Oc
130 E7 **Fernandópolis** Brazil
Fernando Póo *isld see* **Bioko**
16 D7 **Fernán Núñez** Spain
130 G5 **Fernão Dias** Brazil
100 C1 **Ferndale** Washington U.S.A.
98 H4 **Ferney** South Dakota U.S.A.
9 F5 **Fernhurst** England
118 B9 **Fernie** British Columbia Canada
141 H8 **Fernlee** Queensland Australia
102 E2 **Fernley** Nevada U.S.A.
41 N3 **Fern Pass** Austria
100 B5 **Fern Ridge Res** Oregon U.S.A.
14 E4 **Ferns** Ireland
144 D5 **Fernside** New Zealand
36 F2 **Fernwald** W Germany
100 J2 **Fernwood** Idaho U.S.A.
111 F10 **Fernwood** Mississippi U.S.A.
123 P2 **Ferolle Pt** Newfoundland Canada
47 H4 **Férrai** Greece
42 D4 **Ferrara** Italy
17 G9 **Ferrat,C** Algeria
44 B4 **Ferrat,Cape** France
43 C9 **Ferrato,C** Sardinia
16 B6 **Ferreira do Alentejo** Portugal
129 H3 **Ferreira Gomes** Brazil
130 D7 **Ferreiros** Brazil
20 H5 **Ferré, le** France
128 C5 **Ferreñafe** Peru
18 E8 **Ferret,C** France
40 F6 **Ferret,Col** *pass* Switz/Italy
19 K5 **Ferreue** France
111 E10 **Ferriday** Louisiana U.S.A.
118 C6 **Ferrier** Alberta Canada
21 K4 **Ferrière-aux-Étangs,la** France
21 K8 **Ferriere,la** Deux Sèvres France
20 H8 **Ferrière,la** Vendée France
21 M7 **Ferrière-Larçon** France
18 G4 **Ferrières** France
21 O2 **Ferrières-en-Bray** France
21 M4 **Ferrière-sur-Risle,la** France
28 A3 **Ferring** Denmark
28 A3 **Ferring Sø** Denmark
99 P9 **Ferris** Illinois U.S.A.
95 O2 **Ferrisburg** Vermont U.S.A.
101 S7 **Ferris Mts** Wyoming U.S.A.
28 F6 **Ferritslev** Denmark
43 C7 **Ferro,C** Sardinia
130 G6 **Ferros** Brazil
123 N2 **Ferru,L** Quebec Canada
43 B8 **Ferru, M** *mt* Sardinia
94 G10 **Ferrum** Virginia U.S.A.
116 N5 **Ferry** Alaska U.S.A.
99 U6 **Ferry** Michigan U.S.A.
13 G6 **Ferrybridge** England
123 U6 **Ferryland** Newfoundland Canada
107 P5 **Ferry Res** Oklahoma U.S.A.
99 U6 **Ferrysburg** Michigan U.S.A.
8 B4 **Ferryside** Wales
99 P6 **Ferryville** Wisconsin U.S.A.
55 C4 **Fershampenuaz** U.S.S.R.
28 H5 **Ferslev** Denmark
21 P5 **Ferté-Alais,la** France
21 M5 **Ferté-Bernard,la** France
21 M4 **Ferté-Fresnel, la** France
18 H4 **Ferté Gaucher,La** France
21 O7 **Ferté-Imbault,la** France
22 F4 **Ferté, la** France
21 K4 **Ferté-Macé,la** France
21 O6 **Ferté-St.Aubin,la** France
21 O6 **Ferté-St. Cyr,la** France
18 H4 **Ferté sur Jouarre, la** France
21 M4 **Ferté-Vidame,la** France
98 K2 **Fertile** Minnesota U.S.A.
48 D3 **Fertöszentmiklos** Hungary
Fertö Tór *see* **Neusiedler See**
21 L3 **Fervaques** France
41 M3 **Ferwall Gruppe** *mt* Austria
25 E2 **Ferwerd** Netherlands
85 C2 **Fès** Morocco
86 C7 **Feshi** Zaire
98 G2 **Fessenden** North Dakota U.S.A.
19 P15 **Festre, Col du** *pass* France
22 D2 **Festubert** France
110 F3 **Festus** Missouri U.S.A.
48 L6 **Feteşti** Romania
14 D4 **Fethard** Ireland
47 K8 **Fethiye** Turkey
47 K8 **Fethiye Körfezi** *B* Turkey
43 A12 **Fetzara, L** Algeria
37 L5 **Feucht** W Germany
41 N3 **Feuchten** Austria
37 J5 **Feuchtwangen** W Germany
118 K7 **Feudal** Saskatchewan Canada
21 O3 **Feuillie, la** France
123 M3 **Feu, L. du** Quebec Canada
21 O2 **Feuquières** France
21 O1 **Feuquières-en-Vimeu** France
18 H7 **Feurs** France
77 L1 **Feyzābād** Afghanistan
77 F2 **Feyzābād** Iran
84 E4 **Fezzan** *reg* Libya
8 C2 **Ffestiniog** Wales
8 C4 **Fforest Fawr** *mts* Wales
133 D3 **Fiambalá** Argentina
45 O5 **Fiamignano** Italy
87 H11 **Fianarantsoa** Madagascar
86 C4 **Fianga** Chad
40 F7 **Fiano** Italy
48 G5 **Fibiş** Romania
45 K2 **Ficarolo** Italy
86 G4 **Fichē** Ethiopia
123 R2 **Fichot I** Newfoundland Canada
37 O3 **Fichtelberg** *mt* East Germany
37 M3 **Fichtelberg** W Germany
37 M3 **Fichtelfebirge** *mts* W Germany
37 J5 **Fichtenau** W Germany
89 E7 **Ficksburg** S Africa
44 H2 **Fidenza** Italy
119 V1 **Fidler L** Manitoba Canada
135 O4 **Fieberling Table Mt** Pacific Oc
106 C7 **Field** New Mexico U.S.A.
94 G10 **Fieldale** Virginia U.S.A.
140 B1 **Field I** N Terr Australia
118 K6 **Fielding** Saskatchewan Canada
100 G7 **Fields** Oregon U.S.A.
100 A9 **Fields Landing** California U.S.A.
139 H8 **Field West Mt** Tasmania Australia
48 J5 **Fieni** Romania
22 B2 **Fiennes** France
46 D4 **Fier** Albania
19 P13 **Fier** *R* France
42 D2 **Fiera di Primiero** Italy
106 B9 **Fierro** New Mexico U.S.A.
13 E1 **Fife** *reg* Scotland
109 H4 **Fife** Texas U.S.A.
119 M9 **Fife L** Saskatchewan Canada
13 F1 **Fife Ness** Scotland
139 J5 **Fifield** New South Wales Australia
99 Q4 **Fifield** Wisconsin U.S.A.
101 R5 **Fifteen Mile Cr** Wyoming U.S.A.
17 G9 **Figalo,C** Algeria
43 C8 **Figari,C** Sardinia
18 G8 **Figeac** France
27 J14 **Figeholm** Sweden
45 K4 **Figline Valdarno** Italy
127 P4 **Fig Tree** Nevis W Indies
16 B4 **Figuera da Foz** Portugal
16 B5 **Figuera dos Vinhos** Portugal
18 G10 **Figueras** Spain
85 D2 **Figuig** Morocco
137 Q5 **Fiji** *islds* Pacific Oc
17 F7 **Filabres, Sierra de los** *mts* Spain
129 J5 **Filadélfia** Brazil
128 F8 **Filadelfia** Paraguay
48 F2 **Filakovo** Czechoslovakia
146 E7 **Filchner Ice Shelf** Antarctica
27 C10 **Filefj** *mt* Norway
119 R4 **File L** Manitoba Canada
101 L7 **Filer** Idaho U.S.A.
45 O6 **Filettino** Italy
13 H5 **Filey** England
46 D5 **Filiátes** Greece
46 E7 **Filiatrá** Greece
43 F10 **Filicudi, I** Italy
85 E6 **Filingué** Niger
31 O1 **Filipów** Poland
27 G12 **Filipstad** Sweden
41 L4 **Filisur** Switzerland
48 H6 **Fillaşi** Romania
22 C3 **Fillièvres** France
119 O9 **Fillmore** Saskatchewan Canada
102 F7 **Fillmore** California U.S.A.
94 J4 **Fillmore** New York U.S.A.
98 G1 **Fillmore** North Dakota U.S.A.
103 M3 **Fillmore** Utah U.S.A.
36 H6 **Fils** *R* W Germany
28 C5 **Filskov** Denmark
28 A5 **Filsø** Denmark
8 D4 **Filton** England
86 H4 **Filtu** Ethiopia
146 H6 **Fimbulheimen** *ra* Antarctica
146 H6 **Fimbulisen** *ice shelf* Antarctica
42 D4 **Finale Emilia** Italy
44 D3 **Finale Ligure** Italy
17 F7 **Fiñana** Spain
94 H9 **Fincastle** Virginia U.S.A.
121 P7 **Finch** Ontario Canada
9 F4 **Finchley** England
28 C4 **Finderup** Denmark
15 E3 **Findhorn** *R* Scotland
15 E3 **Findhorn** Scotland
78 H1 **Fındıklı** Turkey
79 E2 **Fındıkpınarı** Turkey
119 M8 **Findlater** Saskatchewan Canada
99 S10 **Findlay** Illinois U.S.A.
94 D5 **Findlay** Ohio U.S.A.
117 P10 **Findlay,Mt** British Columbia Canada
9 F6 **Findon** England
9 F3 **Finedon** England
139 J8 **Fingal** Tasmania Australia
98 J3 **Fingal** North Dakota U.S.A.
110 H6 **Finger** Tennessee U.S.A.
115 K7 **Finger L** Ontario Canada
95 L4 **Finger Lakes** New York U.S.A.
14 E3 **Finglas** Ireland
88 C9 **Fingoe** *mt* Mozambique
88 C9 **Fingoe** Mozambique
47 L8 **Finike** Turkey
47 P12 **Finiq** Albania
16 A2 **Finisterre,C** Spain
138 D2 **Finke** *R* N Terr Australia
140 C7 **Finke** N Terr Australia
138 D2 **Finke Flood Flats** South Australia Australia
140 C6 **Finke Gorge** N Terr Australia
138 C4 **Finke,Mt** South Australia Australia
140 D7 **Finke, R** N Terr Australia
29 L8 **Finland** *rep* N Europe
99 P2 **Finland** Minnesota U.S.A.
52 C5 **Finland, Gulf of** Finland/U.S.S.R.
114 G6 **Finlay** *R* British Columbia Canada
99 O3 **Finlayson** Minnesota U.S.A.
98 J2 **Finley** North Dakota U.S.A.
109 M1 **Finley** Oklahoma U.S.A.
119 O2 **Finmark** Ontario Canada
14 D2 **Finn** *R* Ireland
12 D1 **Finnart** Scotland
118 E7 **Finnegan** Alberta Canada
26 H4 **Finneid** Norway
36 D1 **Finnentrop** W Germany
26 L7 **Finnforsfallet** Sweden
141 H3 **Finnigan, Mt** Queensland Australia
140 B2 **Finniss** *R* N Terr Australia
138 C5 **Finniss,C** South Australia Australia
26 O1 **Finnmark** *county* Norway
26 N2 **Finnmarksvidda** *reg* Norway
116 J6 **Finn Mt** Alaska U.S.A.
27 F11 **Finnskog** Norway
27 F11 **Finnskoga,S** Sweden
26 K2 **Finnsnes** Norway
26 M6 **Finnträsk** Sweden
33 T7 **Finow** East Germany
33 T7 **Finowfurt** East Germany
33 T7 **Finow Kanal** East Germany
27 H13 **Finspång** Sweden
40 H4 **Finsteraarhorn** *mt* Switzerland
33 T9 **Finsterwalde** East Germany
15 E1 **Finstown** Scotland
29 H11 **Finström** Finland
36 E4 **Finthen** W Germany
14 D2 **Fintona** N Ireland
12 D1 **Fintry** Scotland
142 C5 **Finucane I** Western Australia Australia
141 F5 **Finucane Ra** Queensland Australia
40 F5 **Fionnay** Switzerland
15 C3 **Fionn Loch** *L* Scotland
12 B1 **Fionphort** Scotland
45 J2 **Fiorano Modenese** Italy
144 A6 **Fiordland Nat. Park** New Zealand
44 G2 **Fiorenzuola d'Arda** Italy
45 N4 **Fiorenzuola di Focara** Italy
88 C5 **Fip** Tanzania
78 G2 **Firat** *R* Turkey
102 D5 **Firebaugh** California U.S.A.
116 M6 **Fire I** Alaska U.S.A.
42 D5 **Firenze** Italy
42 D4 **Firenzuola** Italy
98 E4 **Firesteel** South Dakota U.S.A.
48 H3 **Firiza** Romania
133 E4 **Firmat** Argentina
18 H7 **Firminy** France
118 L9 **Fir Mt** Saskatchewan Canada
74 H5 **Firozabad** India
77 H2 **Firozkoh** *reg* Afghanistan
74 F3 **Firozpur** India
112 F2 **First R** North Carolina U.S.A.
116 R2 **Firth** *R* Alaska/Yukon Terr U.S.A./Canada
77 C5 **Fīrūzābād** Iran
37 K7 **Fischach** W Germany
36 C4 **Fischbach** W Germany
38 M7 **Fischbacher Alpen** *mts* Austria
33 Q7 **Fischbeck** East Germany
36 E2 **Fischelbach** W Germany
41 M3 **Fischen** W Germany
109 J6 **Fischer** Texas U.S.A.
32 K6 **Fischerhude** W Germany
33 S6 **Fischerwall** East Germany
89 A5 **Fish** *watercourse* Namibia
9 E6 **Fishbourne** England
102 E4 **Fish Camp** California U.S.A.
116 L1 **Fish Cr** Alaska U.S.A.
101 M6 **Fish Cr.Res** Idaho U.S.A.
113 F10 **Fisheating Cr** Florida U.S.A.
121 N4 **Fisher** Quebec Canada
111 C10 **Fisher** Louisiana U.S.A.
98 K2 **Fisher** Minnesota U.S.A.
119 U7 **Fisher Branch** Manitoba Canada
146 H10 **Fisher Glacier** Antarctica
143 A9 **Fisherman I** Western Australia Australia
95 M9 **Fishermans I** Virginia U.S.A.
115 L5 **Fisher Str** Northwest Territories Canada
116 E9 **Fisher Vol** Aleutian Is
8 B4 **Fishguard** Wales
8 A3 **Fishguard B** England
95 L8 **Fishing Creek** Maryland U.S.A.
117 M4 **Fish L** Northwest Territories Canada
116 M4 **Fish L** Alaska U.S.A.
103 N3 **Fish L** Utah U.S.A.
94 D3 **Fish Pt** Michigan U.S.A.
102 A3 **Fish Rock** California U.S.A.
101 Q4 **Fishtail** Montana U.S.A.
101 M4 **Fishtrap** Montana U.S.A.
94 E9 **Fishtrap L** Kentucky U.S.A.
46 D6 **Fiskárdho** Greece
28 C3 **Fiskbæk** Denmark
95 P4 **Fiskdale** Massachusetts U.S.A.
118 J7 **Fiske** Saskatchewan Canada
146 D6 **Fiske, C** Antarctica
115 O5 **Fiskenæsset** Greenland
28 S9 **Fiskivötn** *lakes* Iceland
22 F5 **Fismes** France
95 Q4 **Fitchburg** Massachusetts U.S.A.
86 C3 **Fitri, L** Chad
28 C5 **Fitting** Denmark
9 F6 **Fittleworth** England
128 D6 **Fitzcarrald** Peru
143 C10 **Fitzgerald** *R* Western Australia Australia
117 R6 **Fitzgerald** Alberta Canada
112 D6 **Fitzgerald** Georgia U.S.A.
143 C10 **Fitzgerald River Nat Park** Western Australia Australia
109 L1 **Fitzhugh** Oklahoma U.S.A.
117 K10 **Fitzhugh Sd** British Columbia Canada
22 C5 **Fitz James** France
140 B2 **Fitzmaurice** *R* N Terr Australia
121 S5 **Fitzpatrick** Quebec Canada
133 D7 **Fitz Roy** Argentina
141 K6 **Fitzroy** *R* Queensland Australia
133 C7 **Fitz Roy** *mt* Chile/Arg
142 F4 **Fitzroy Crossing** Western Australia Australia
121 O7 **Fitzroy Harbour** Ontario Canada
141 H3 **Fitzroy I** Queensland Australia
142 E4 **Fitzroy R** Western Australia Australia
120 J7 **Fitzwilliam I** Ontario Canada
42 E7 **Fiuggi** Italy
45 J3 **Fiumalbo** Italy
Fiume *see* **Rijeka**
42 E7 **Fiumicino** Italy
45 M3 **Fiumi Uniti** *R* Italy
144 A6 **Five Fingers Pen** New Zealand
122 H8 **Five Islands** Nova Scotia Canada
101 R6 **Fivemile Cr** Wyoming U.S.A.
14 D2 **Fivemiletown** N Ireland
144 B6 **Five Rivers** New Zealand
88 B4 **Fizi** Zaire
26 L4 **Fjällåsen** Sweden
26 G6 **Fjällfjällen** *mt* Sweden
26 F9 **Fjällnäs** Sweden
28 H7 **Fjelde** Denmark
28 F3 **Fjellerup** Denmark
28 E6 **Fjelsted** Denmark
28 D6 **Fjelstrup** Denmark
28 C2 **Fjerritslev** Denmark
27 B10 **Fjordane** *reg* Norway
27 B13 **Fjotland** Norway
27 D11 **Flå** Norway
37 K5 **Flachslanden** W Germany
28 A3 **Flade Sø** Denmark
28 B6 **Fladså** *R* Denmark
37 J2 **Fladungen** W Germany
106 G2 **Flagler** Colorado U.S.A.
113 F8 **Flagler Beach** Florida U.S.A.
103 N6 **Flagstaff** Arizona U.S.A.
95 R1 **Flagstaff L** Maine U.S.A.
100 E7 **Flagstaff L** Oregon U.S.A.
100 K1 **Flagstone** British Columbia Canada
28 G6 **Flakkebjerg** Denmark
26 F3 **Flakstad** Norway
27 B11 **Flåm** Norway
20 G2 **Flamanville** France
99 Q4 **Flambeau** *R* Wisconsin U.S.A.
99 Q3 **Flambeau Res** Wisconsin U.S.A.
13 H5 **Flamborough Hd** England
133 C3 **Flamenco** Chile
131 E8 **Flamenco, I** Argentina
33 R9 **Fläming** *reg* East Germany
101 Q8 **Flaming Gorge Res** Utah/Wyoming U.S.A.
113 G12 **Flamingo** Florida U.S.A.
18 F10 **Flamisell** *R* Spain
36 C2 **Flammersfeld** W Germany
127 O2 **Flanagin Town** Trinidad
99 O1 **Flanders** Ontario Canada
22 D2 **Flandre** *prov* France
22 E3 **Flandre** France
98 K5 **Flandreau** South Dakota U.S.A.
102 E1 **Flanigan** Nevada U.S.A.
38 H6 **Flankenmarkt** Austria
26 K8 **Flärke** Sweden
98 E3 **Flasher** North Dakota U.S.A.
26 H7 **Flåsjön** *L* Sweden
117 K5 **Flat** *R* Northwest Territories Canada
94 B3 **Flat** *R* Michigan U.S.A.
109 K4 **Flat** Texas U.S.A.
123 O5 **Flat Bay** Newfoundland Canada
118 C4 **Flatbush** Alberta Canada
111 J8 **Flat Creek** Alabama U.S.A.
101 L2 **Flathead L** Montana U.S.A.
101 L1 **Flathead Mts** Montana U.S.A.
117 Q11 **Flathead R** Idaho U.S.A.
5 C5 **Flat Holm** *isld* Bristol Channel England
141 J5 **Flat I** Queensland Australia
118 E4 **Flat L** Alberta Canada
144 A6 **Flat Mt** New Zealand
109 K6 **Flatonia** Texas U.S.A.
110 F4 **Flat River** Missouri U.S.A.
110 J3 **Flat Rock** Illinois U.S.A.
94 B7 **Flat Rock** Indiana U.S.A.
141 H2 **Flattery, C** Queensland Australia
100 A1 **Flattery,C** Washington U.S.A.
38 K8 **Flattnitz** Austria
94 F9 **Flat Top** West Virginia U.S.A.
101 R3 **Flatwillow** Montana U.S.A.
94 G8 **Flatwoods** West Virginia U.S.A.
41 O3 **Flaurling** Austria
27 C12 **Flåv** *L* Norway
28 E2 **Flavenskjold** Denmark
22 F4 **Flavigny le Grd. et Beaurain** France
22 E4 **Flavy le Martel** France
8 D5 **Flax Bourton** England
118 H7 **Flaxcombe** Saskatchewan Canada
116 P1 **Flaxman I** Alaska U.S.A.
98 D1 **Flaxton** North Dakota U.S.A.
98 A1 **Flaxville** Montana U.S.A.
20 B4 **Flèche** *R* France
21 K6 **Flèche, La** France
33 O8 **Flechtingen** East Germany
113 K9 **Fleeming Pt** New Providence I Bahamas
118 F6 **Fleet** Alberta Canada
9 G2 **Fleet Hargate** England
141 H5 **Fleetwood** Queensland Australia
13 E6 **Fleetwood** England
95 M6 **Fleetwood** Pennsylvania U.S.A.
36 G5 **Flein** W Germany
95 N4 **Fleischmanns** New York U.S.A.
27 B13 **Flekkefjord** Norway
27 C13 **Flekkeröy** *isld* Norway
Flemhude *see* **Quarnbek**
119 Q8 **Fleming** Saskatchewan Canada
98 D9 **Fleming** Colorado U.S.A.
94 D8 **Flemingsburg** Kentucky U.S.A.
95 N6 **Flemington** New Jersey U.S.A.
90 F4 **Flemish Cap** Atlantic Oc
28 E6 **Flemløse** Denmark
27 J12 **Flen** Sweden
29 K4 **Fleninge** Sweden
28 D7 **Flensborg Fjord** *inlet* Denmark/W Germany
28 C7 **Flensburg** W Germany
21 N7 **Fléré-la-Rivière** France
22 D3 **Flers** France
21 J4 **Flers** France
101 N2 **Flesher** Montana U.S.A.
120 K8 **Flesherton** Ontario Canada
112 E2 **Fletcher** North Carolina U.S.A.
107 M7 **Fletcher** Oklahoma U.S.A.
94 D2 **Fletcher Pond** Michigan U.S.A.
146 C7 **Fletcher Promontory** *pen* Antarctica
9 F2 **Fletton** England
18 F9 **Fleurance** France
123 Q3 **Fleur de Lys** Newfoundland Canada
122 H2 **Fleur-de-May,L** Labrador, Nfld Canada
40 E4 **Fleurier** Switzerland
22 H3 **Fleurus** Belgium
21 N3 **Fleury-sur-Andelle** France
68 G1 **Fleuve Rouge** *R* Vietnam
36 H3 **Flieden** W Germany
41 K4 **Flims** Switzerland
9 G5 **Flimwell** England
140 F4 **Flinders** *R* Queensland Australia
143 B10 **Flinders B** Western Australia Australia
141 G2 **Flinders Group** *islds* Gt Barrier Reef Aust
139 J7 **Flinders I** Tasmania Australia
141 J4 **Flinder's Passage** Australia
141 J4 **Flinders Reefs** Gt Barrier Reef Aust
138 E4 **Flinders Rge** South Australia Australia
22 E3 **Flines-le-Râches** France
119 Q4 **Flin Flon** Manitoba Canada
Flint *co see* **Clwyd**
110 K7 **Flint** *R* Alabama U.S.A.
111 M10 **Flint** *R* Georgia U.S.A.
94 D3 **Flint** Michigan U.S.A.
8 C1 **Flint** Wales
107 O4 **Flint Hills** Kansas U.S.A.
135 M9 **Flint I** Pacific Oc
120 E3 **Flint L** Ontario Canada
118 L9 **Flintoft** Saskatchewan Canada
141 J8 **Flinton** Queensland Australia
110 D5 **Flippin** Arkansas U.S.A.
112 C4 **Flirt** *R* Georgia U.S.A.
27 F11 **Flisa** Norway
27 H14 **Fliseryd** Sweden
17 H3 **Flix** Spain
13 H6 **Flixborough** England
21 P1 **Flixecourt** France
22 H4 **Flize** France
13 G6 **Flockton Moor** England
111 J11 **Flomaton** Florida U.S.A.
108 G1 **Flomot** Texas U.S.A.
36 E4 **Flonheim** W Germany
67 D1 **Flood Basin** *L* Hubei China
146 B9 **Flood Ra** Antarctica
99 O3 **Floodwood** Minnesota U.S.A.
110 H3 **Flora** Illinois U.S.A.
94 A6 **Flora** Indiana U.S.A.
111 F9 **Flora** Mississippi U.S.A.
100 H4 **Flora** Oregon U.S.A.
18 H8 **Florac** France
111 K10 **Florala** Alabama U.S.A.
113 E9 **Floral City** Florida U.S.A.
142 B5 **Flora, Mt** Western Australia Australia
141 H3 **Flora Pass** Gt Barrier Reef Aust
140 E4 **Floraville** Queensland Australia
142 A1 **Floreat Park** *dist* Perth, W Aust Australia
22 H3 **Floreffe** Belgium
Florence *see* **Firenze**
110 J7 **Florence** Alabama U.S.A.
103 N8 **Florence** Arizona U.S.A.
106 E3 **Florence** Colorado U.S.A.
100 J4 **Florence** Idaho U.S.A.
107 O3 **Florence** Kansas U.S.A.
94 C8 **Florence** Kentucky U.S.A.
111 F9 **Florence** Mississippi U.S.A.
101 L3 **Florence** Montana U.S.A.
95 N6 **Florence** New Jersey U.S.A.
100 A6 **Florence** Oregon U.S.A.
112 H3 **Florence** South Carolina U.S.A.
98 J4 **Florence** South Dakota U.S.A.
109 K5 **Florence** Texas U.S.A.
99 S4 **Florence** Wisconsin U.S.A.
103 N8 **Florence Junc** Arizona U.S.A.
102 F4 **Florence L** California U.S.A.
128 F8 **Florencia** Argentina
128 C3 **Florencia** Colombia
22 H3 **Florennes** Belgium
22 J4 **Florenville** Belgium
131 F5 **Flores** *R* Argentina
85 A1 **Flores** *isld* Azores Atlantic Oc
130 H9 **Flores** Brazil
125 P9 **Flores** Guatemala
71 K9 **Flores** *isld* Indonesia
131 F4 **Flores** *dept* Uruguay
48 L3 **Floreshty** U.S.S.R.
117 K11 **Flores I** British Columbia Canada
71 J8 **Flores Sea** Indonesia
130 H10 **Floresta** Brazil
109 J6 **Floresville** Texas U.S.A.
108 E3 **Florey** Texas U.S.A.
129 K5 **Floriano** Brazil
128 E5 **Floriano Peixoto** Brazil
130 E10 **Florianopólis** Brazil
126 E4 **Florida** Cuba
137 N3 **Florida** *isld* Solomon Is
131 G5 **Florida** Uruguay
113 B12 **Florida** *state* U.S.A.
94 C5 **Florida** Ohio U.S.A.
113 G12 **Florida B** Florida U.S.A.
113 F13 **Florida Keys** *islds* Florida U.S.A.
113 H12 **Florida,Str.of** U.S.A./Bahamas
130 B10 **Florida,V** Paraguay
43 G11 **Floridia** Sicily
109 O4 **Florien** Louisiana U.S.A.
46 E4 **Flórina** Greece
99 O9 **Floris** Iowa U.S.A.
106 E3 **Florissant** Colorado U.S.A.
106 E3 **Florissant Fossilbeds Nat. Mon.** Colorado U.S.A.
26 A10 **Flörö** Norway
36 G3 **Flörsbach** W Germany
47 M11 **Florya** Turkey
37 N4 **Floss** W Germany
37 N4 **Flossenbürg** W Germany
15 F2 **Flotta** Scotland
118 J4 **Flotten L** Saskatchewan Canada
103 M3 **Flowell** Utah U.S.A.
120 J7 **Flowerpot I. Nat. Park** Ontario Canada
123 Q2 **Flower's Cove** Newfoundland Canada
98 K7 **Floyd** *R* Iowa U.S.A.
108 D1 **Floyd** New Mexico U.S.A.
108 F2 **Floydada** Texas U.S.A.
103 M6 **Floyd,Mt** Arizona U.S.A.
27 D11 **Fluberg** Norway
41 L4 **Flüela Pass** Switzerland
21 O6 **Fluery les Aubrais** France
25 E3 **Fluessen** *R* Netherlands
71 A3 **Fluk** Indonesia
111 F11 **Fluker** Louisiana U.S.A.
20 G5 **Flume** *R* France
17 G3 **Flumen** *R* Spain
43 B9 **Fluminimaggiore** Sardinia
36 F7 **Fluorn** W Germany
Flushing Netherlands *see* **Vlissingen**
94 D3 **Flushing** Michigan U.S.A.
94 F6 **Flushing** Ohio U.S.A.
108 F3 **Fluvanna** Texas U.S.A.
18 G10 **Fluvia** *R* Spain
28 C4 **Fly** Denmark
136 J3 **Fly** *R* Papua/W Irian
83 M9 **Flying Fish Cove** Christmas I Indian Oc
140 C2 **Flying Fox Cr** N Terr Australia
28 A4 **Flynder Kirke** Denmark
28 B3 **Flynder Sø** *L* Denmark
6 M6 **Flyndre** *oil rig* North Sea
109 L4 **Flynn** Texas U.S.A.
140 C4 **Flynn Mem** N Terr Australia
119 O7 **Foam Lake** Saskatchewan Canada
73 L9 **Foa Mulaku I** Maldives
47 H6 **Foça** Turkey
22 J3 **Focant** Belgium
45 H3 **Foce d. Radici** *mt* Italy
15 E3 **Fochabers** Scotland
42 E4 **Foci del Po** Italy
48 L5 **Focşani** Romania
28 H6 **Fodby** Denmark
21 P7 **Foëcy** France
140 D3 **Foelsche** *R* N Terr Australia
67 D5 **Fogang** China
140 B2 **Fog B** N Terr Australia
57 E4 **Fogelevo** U.S.S.R.
43 G7 **Foggia** Italy
42 E5 **Foglia** *R* Italy
45 N7 **Fogliano** *L* Italy
29 H11 **Föglö** Finland
123 S4 **Fogo** Newfoundland Canada
88 G10 **Fogo** *isld* Mozambique
123 S4 **Fogo,C** Newfoundland Canada
28 C4 **Fogstrup** Denmark
38 L7 **Fohnsdorf** Austria
28 A7 **Föhr** *isld* W Germany
45 R7 **Foiana in Val Fortore** Italy
14 A5 **Foilclogh** *mt* Ireland
15 D2 **Foinaven,Mt** Scotland
18 G10 **Foix** France
52 H6 **Foki** U.S.S.R.
54 F3 **Fokina, imeni** U.S.S.R.
54 F3 **Fokino** U.S.S.R.
26 D9 **Fokstua** Norway
26 G4 **Folda** *inlet* Norway
48 F4 **Földeák** Hungary
26 F7 **Foldereid** Norway
28 B6 **Foldingbro** Denmark
28 C6 **Folding Kirke** Denmark
28 B6 **Fole** Denmark
46 G8 **Folégandros** *isld* Greece
89 E3 **Foley** Botswana
111 J11 **Foley** Alabama U.S.A.
113 D7 **Foley** Florida U.S.A.
99 N4 **Foley** Minnesota U.S.A.
120 H4 **Foleyet** Ontario Canada
115 M4 **Foley I** Northwest Territories Canada
27 B11 **Folgefonna** *gla* Norway
116 J5 **Folger** Alaska U.S.A.
146 G14 **Folger, Cape** *C* Antarctica
20 B4 **Folgoët, le** France
42 E6 **Foligno** Italy
9 H5 **Folkestone** England
9 F2 **Folkingham** England
113 E7 **Folkston** Georgia U.S.A.
112 K3 **Folkstone** North Carolina U.S.A.
26 D9 **Folla** *R* Norway
26 D9 **Folldal** Norway
28 E4 **Følle** Denmark
25 E3 **Follega** Netherlands
28 G5 **Føllenslev** Denmark
20 H4 **Folligny** France
26 G8 **Föllinge** Sweden
27 E12 **Follo** Norway
42 D6 **Follonica** Italy
112 H5 **Folly Beach** South Carolina U.S.A.
100 G6 **Follyfarm** Oregon U.S.A.
102 C3 **Folsom** California U.S.A.
111 F11 **Folsom** Louisiana U.S.A.
106 G5 **Folsom** New Mexico U.S.A.
102 C3 **Folsom L** California U.S.A.
48 L5 **Folteşti** Romania
126 E3 **Fómento** Cuba
52 F6 **Fominki** U.S.S.R.
52 G2 **Fominskaya** U.S.S.R.
52 F5 **Fominskoye** U.S.S.R.
99 M7 **Fonda** Iowa U.S.A.
95 N4 **Fonda** New York U.S.A.
98 F1 **Fonda** North Dakota U.S.A.
114 J6 **Fond-du-Lac** Saskatchewan Canada
99 S6 **Fond du Lac** Wisconsin U.S.A.
94 D10 **Fonde** Kentucky U.S.A.
21 M7 **Fondettes** France
43 E7 **Fondi** Italy
45 O7 **Fondi, L. di** Italy
26 E8 **Fongen** *mt* Norway
43 C8 **Fonni** Sardinia
16 C1 **Fonsagrada** Spain
28 D6 **Fønsskov** Denmark
22 G3 **Fontaine** Belgium
21 N6 **Fontaine** Loir-et-Cher France
18 G4 **Fontainebleau** France
19 O17 **Fontaine-de-Vaucluse** France
40 B2 **Fontaine-Française** France
21 M3 **Fontaine-l'Abbé** France
21 N2 **Fontaine-le-Bourg** France
21 M2 **Fontaine-le-Dun** France
40 B3 **Fontaine-lès-Dijon** France
21 K6 **Fontaine-Milon** France
21 L6 **Fontaine-St. Martin,la** France
133 C6 **Fontana,L** Argentina
112 D2 **Fontana L** North Carolina U.S.A.
45 P6 **Fontana Liri** Italy
45 L3 **Fontanelice** Italy
117 N6 **Fontas** British Columbia Canada
40 D7 **Fontcouvert** France
38 F7 **Fonte** Italy
128 E4 **Fonte Boa** Brazil
128 G6 **Fonte do Pau d'Água** Brazil
18 E6 **Fontenay-le-Comte** France
21 O3 **Fontenay-St.Père** France
123 L2 **Fonteneau,L** Quebec Canada
122 H5 **Fontenelle** Quebec Canada
101 P7 **Fontenelle Fork** *R* Wyoming U.S.A.
101 P7 **Fontenelle Res** Wyoming U.S.A.
22 E2 **Fontenoy** Belgium
21 L7 **Fontevrault l'Abbaye** France
8 D6 **Fontmell Magna** England
22 L5 **Fontoy** France
137 S5 **Fonualei** *isld* Tonga
48 D4 **Fonyód** Hungary
Foochow *see* **Fuzhou** Fujian
103 M2 **Fool Cr.Res** Utah U.S.A.
117 P9 **Foothills** Alberta Canada
99 R7 **Footville** Wisconsin U.S.A.
41 H5 **Foppiano** Italy
27 J14 **Föra** Sweden
107 O5 **Foraker** Oklahoma U.S.A.
116 M5 **Foraker,Mt** Alaska U.S.A.
19 K3 **Forbach** France
36 E6 **Forbach** W Germany
139 J5 **Forbes** New South Wales Australia
99 O2 **Forbes** Minnesota U.S.A.
98 H4 **Forbes** North Dakota U.S.A.
117 P10 **Forbes, Mt** Alberta Canada
85 F7 **Forcados** Nigeria
19 Q18 **Forcalqueiret** France
19 P17 **Forcalquier** France
38 E8 **Forchetta** *mt* Italy
37 L4 **Forchheim** W Germany
36 H5 **Forchtenberg** W Germany
13 F2 **Ford** England
107 L4 **Ford** Kansas U.S.A.
94 C9 **Ford** Kentucky U.S.A.
99 T3 **Ford** *R* Michigan U.S.A.
140 A2 **Ford, C** N Terr Australia
102 E6 **Ford City** California U.S.A.
94 H6 **Ford City** Pennsylvania U.S.A.
26 A10 **Förde** Norway
145 E3 **Fordell** New Zealand
33 P9 **Förderstedt** East Germany
9 G3 **Fordham** England
9 E6 **Fordingbridge** England
103 J8 **Ford L** California U.S.A.
110 D4 **Fordland** Missouri U.S.A.
31 L2 **Fordon** Poland
146 B9 **Ford Ranges** Antarctica
139 H3 **Ford's Br** New South Wales Australia
110 K4 **Fordsville** Kentucky U.S.A.
109 K6 **Fordtran** Texas U.S.A.
98 J1 **Fordville** North Dakota U.S.A.
111 D8 **Fordyce** Arkansas U.S.A.
98 J7 **Fordyce** Nebraska U.S.A.
26 G5 **Fore** Norway
85 B7 **Forécariah** Guinea
8 C5 **Foreland,The** England
115 Q4 **Forel, Mont** *mt* Greenland
109 N2 **Foreman** Arkansas U.S.A.
118 F9 **Foremost** Alberta Canada
22 G2 **Forest** Belgium
120 H9 **Forest** Ontario Canada
100 J3 **Forest** Idaho U.S.A.
111 G9 **Forest** Mississippi U.S.A.
94 D6 **Forest** Ohio U.S.A.
118 E6 **Forestburg** Alberta Canada
109 K2 **Forestburg** Texas U.S.A.
110 F6 **Forest City** Arkansas U.S.A.
99 N6 **Forest City** Iowa U.S.A.
112 F2 **Forest City** North Carolina U.S.A.
95 M5 **Forest City** Pennsylvania U.S.A.
142 B3 **Forestdale** *dist* Perth, W Aust Australia
95 O3 **Forest Dale** Vermont U.S.A.
109 O1 **Forester** Arkansas U.S.A.
94 E3 **Forester** Michigan U.S.A.
100 B9 **Forest Glen** California U.S.A.
101 Q3 **Forestgrove** Montana U.S.A.
100 B4 **Forest Grove** Oregon U.S.A.
102 D2 **Foresthill** California U.S.A.
111 D10 **Forest Hill** Louisiana U.S.A.
109 M9 **Forest Hill** Texas U.S.A.
141 G4 **Forest Home** Queensland Australia
139 J8 **Forestier, C** Tasmania Australia
139 J9 **Forestier Pen** Tasmania Australia
99 O4 **Forest Lake** Minnesota U.S.A.
15 D4 **Forest of Atholl** Scotland
99 N4 **Foreston** Minnesota U.S.A.
95 M3 **Forestport** New York U.S.A.
98 J1 **Forest River** North Dakota U.S.A.
9 G5 **Forest Row** England
122 C5 **Forestville** Quebec Canada
102 B3 **Forestville** California U.S.A.
94 E3 **Forestville** Michigan U.S.A.
94 H4 **Forestville** New York U.S.A.
122 C5 **Forestville, Parc de** Quebec Canada
20 C6 **Forêt, B.de la** *B* France
19 J3 **Forêt d'Argonne** France
20 C6 **Forêt, la** France
21 P5 **Forêt-Ste Croix, la** France
18 H7 **Forez, Mts du** France
15 F4 **Forfar** Scotland
118 K7 **Forgan** Saskatchewan Canada
107 K5 **Forgan** Oklahoma U.S.A.
20 E5 **Forges, les** France
21 O2 **Forges-les-Eaux** France
121 O4 **Forget** Quebec Canada
119 P9 **Forget** Saskatchewan Canada
41 N2 **Forggen See** *L* W Germany
45 P8 **Forio** Italy
110 G6 **Forked Deer** *R* Tennessee U.S.A.
119 R7 **Fork River** *R* Manitoba Canada
100 A2 **Forks** Washington U.S.A.
144 C5 **Forks, The** New Zealand
94 J9 **Fork Union** Virginia U.S.A.
42 E4 **Forli** Italy
45 M3 **Forlimpopoli** Italy
14 E4 **Forlorn Pt** Ireland
98 J3 **Forman** North Dakota U.S.A.
13 E6 **Formby** England
138 D6 **Formby B** South Australia Australia
13 E6 **Formby Pt** England
45 M5 **Formello** Italy
17 H6 **Formentera** *isld* Balearic Is
21 O2 **Formerie** France
43 F7 **Formia** Italy
130 F7 **Formiga** Brazil
126 G5 **Formigas Bank** Caribbean
45 J2 **Formigine** Italy
45 L2 **Formignana** Italy
21 J3 **Formigny** France
26 F7 **Formofoss** Norway
Formosa *see* **Taiwan**
133 F3 **Formosa** Argentina
129 J7 **Formosa** Brazil
129 J6 **Formosa** *R* Brazil
129 J6 **Formosa do Rio Prêto** Brazil
129 G6 **Formosa, Serra** *mts* Brazil
Formosa Strait *see* **Taiwan Str**
130 F4 **Formoso** Brazil
107 M2 **Formoso** Kansas U.S.A.
28 F4 **Fornæs** *C* Denmark
17 K4 **Fornells** Menorca
38 G8 **Forni Avoltri** Italy
6 F1 **Føroyar** *islds* N Atlantic Oc
15 E3 **Forres** Scotland
143 G9 **Forrest** Western Australia Australia
119 S9 **Forrest** Manitoba Canada
99 S9 **Forrest** Illinois U.S.A.
146 E7 **Forrestal Ra** Antarctica
117 G8 **Forrester I** Alaska U.S.A.
142 C2 **Forrestfield** *dist* Perth, W Aust Australia
143 G8 **Forrest Lakes** Western Australia Australia
143 G6 **Forrest, Mt** Western Australia Australia
99 R7 **Forreston** Illinois U.S.A.
142 G3 **Forrest River Mission** Western Australia Australia
26 J9 **Fors** Sweden
26 J3 **Forsa** Norway
26 J10 **Forsa** Sweden
108 F3 **Forsan** Texas U.S.A.
27 B13 **Forsand** Norway
141 G4 **Forsayth** Queensland Australia
27 J11 **Forsbacka** Sweden
27 F12 **Forshaga** Sweden
27 F13 **Forshem** Sweden
27 F15 **Förslöv** Sweden
27 K11 **Forsmark** Sweden
26 J8 **Forsmo** Sweden
26 K5 **Forsnäs** Sweden
26 C8 **Forsnes** Norway
29 K11 **Forssa** Finland
31 H4 **Forst** East Germany
139 L4 **Forster** New South Wales Australia
112 D4 **Forsyth** Georgia U.S.A.
99 S10 **Forsyth** Illinois U.S.A.
101 T3 **Forsyth** Montana U.S.A.
121 O4 **Forsythe** Quebec Canada
145 E4 **Forsyth I** New Zealand
140 E3 **Forsyth Is** Queensland Australia
141 G6 **Forsyth Ra** Queensland Australia
74 E4 **Fort Abbas** Pakistan
111 E10 **Fort Adams** Mississippi U.S.A.
115 L7 **Fort Albany** Ontario Canada
129 L4 **Fortaleza** Brazil
128 E5 **Fortaleza de Ituxi** Brazil
122 G9 **Fort Anne Nat. Hist. Park** Nova Scotia Canada
Fort Archambault *see* **Sarh**
94 J7 **Fort Ashby** West Virginia U.S.A.
118 C4 **Fort Assiniboine** Alberta Canada
99 S7 **Fort Atkinson** Wisconsin U.S.A.
15 D3 **Fort Augustus** Scotland
87 E12 **Fort Beaufort** S Africa
122 H8 **Fort Beau Sejour Nat. Hist. Park** New Brunswick Canada
101 R1 **Fort Belknap Agency** Montana U.S.A.
111 M9 **Fort Benning** Georgia U.S.A.
101 P2 **Fort Benton** Montana U.S.A.
100 E8 **Fort Bidwell** California U.S.A.
118 K3 **Fort Black** Saskatchewan Canada
103 P9 **Fort Bowie Nat. Hist. Site** Arizona U.S.A.
102 A2 **Fort Bragg** California U.S.A.
110 J3 **Fort Branch** Indiana U.S.A.
101 P8 **Fort Bridger** Wyoming U.S.A.
99 K8 **Fort Calhoun** Nebraska U.S.A.
Fort Carnot *see* **Ikongo**
Fort Charlet *see* **Djanet**
Fort Chimo *see* **Kuujjuaq**
117 R6 **Fort Chipewyan** Alberta Canada
98 E2 **Fort Clark** North Dakota U.S.A.
107 M6 **Fort Cobb** Oklahoma U.S.A.
98 A9 **Fort Collins** Colorado U.S.A.
140 F5 **Fort Constantine** Queensland Australia
121 O7 **Fort Coulonge** Quebec Canada
95 N2 **Fort Covington** New York U.S.A.
Fort Dauphin *see* **Tôlañaro**
111 L9 **Fort Davis** Alabama U.S.A.
108 D5 **Fort Davis** Texas U.S.A.
108 D5 **Fort Davis Nat. Hist. Site** Texas U.S.A.
103 P6 **Fort Defiance** Arizona U.S.A.
127 L4 **Fort de France** Martinique W Indies
111 K10 **Fort Deposit** Alabama U.S.A.
100 A8 **Fort Dick** California U.S.A.
99 M7 **Fort Dodge** Iowa U.S.A.
110 J5 **Fort Donelson Nat Mil Park** Tennessee U.S.A.
113 G10 **Fort Drum** Florida U.S.A.
9 E3 **Fort Dunlop** England
123 P2 **Forteau** Labrador, Nfld Canada
130 B6 **Forte Coimbra** Brazil
44 H4 **Forte dei Marmi** Italy
121 L10 **Fort Erie** Ontario Canada
142 B5 **Fortescue R** Western Australia Australia
142 C5 **Fortescue, R** Western Australia Australia
95 L9 **Fort Eustis** Virginia U.S.A.
95 T7 **Fort Fairfield** Maine U.S.A.
112 K4 **Fort Fisher** North Carolina U.S.A.
Fort Flatters *see* **Bordj Omar Driss**
99 N1 **Fort Frances** Ontario Canada
117 M3 **Fort Franklin** Northwest Territories Canada
117 L8 **Fort Fraser** British Columbia Canada
112 F6 **Fort Frederica Nat. Mon** Georgia U.S.A.
111 L10 **Fort Gaines** Georgia U.S.A.
Fort Garaud *see* **Fdérik**
106 E4 **Fort Garland** Colorado U.S.A.
118 B1 **Fort Garry** Manitoba Canada
94 E8 **Fort Gay** West Virginia U.S.A.
115 M7 **Fort George** Quebec Canada
15 D3 **Fort George** Scotland
107 P6 **Fort Gibson** Oklahoma U.S.A.
107 P5 **Fort Gibson L** Oklahoma U.S.A.
114 G4 **Fort Good Hope** Northwest Territories Canada
113 F10 **Fort Green** Florida U.S.A.
138 F3 **Fort Grey** New South Wales Australia
109 H3 **Fort Griffin** Texas U.S.A.
12 E2 **Forth** Scotland
Fort Hall *see* **Murang'a** Kenya
101 N6 **Fort Hall** Idaho U.S.A.
13 F1 **Forth, Firth of** Scotland
115 L7 **Fort Hope** Ontario Canada
12 D1 **Forth, R** Scotland
103 O10 **Fort Huachuca** Arizona U.S.A.
121 S6 **Fortierville** Quebec Canada
6 L5 **Forties** *oil rig* North Sea
122 H9 **Forties Settlement** Nova Scotia Canada
103 K3 **Fortification Ra** Nevada U.S.A.
128 F8 **Fortin Carlos Antonio López** Paraguay
101 L1 **Fortine** Montana U.S.A.
128 G8 **Fortin Falcón** Paraguay
133 F2 **Fortin Gen. Caballero** Paraguay
128 F8 **Fortin General Eugenio Garay** Paraguay
128 F8 **Fortin Infante Rivarola** Paraguay
122 E3 **Fortin, L** Quebec Canada
133 E3 **Fortin Lavalle** Argentina
128 F8 **Fortin Linares** Paraguay
133 F2 **Fortin Madrejón** Paraguay
128 F7 **Fortin Ravelo** Bolivia
128 G8 **Fortin Rojas Silva** Paraguay
128 F7 **Fortin Suárez Arana** Bolivia
128 G7 **Fortin Teniente Américo Picco** Paraguay
Fort Jameson Zambia *see* **Chipata**
113 E13 **Fort Jefferson Nat.Mon** Florida U.S.A.
Fort Johnston *see* **Mangochi**
100 C8 **Fort Jones** California U.S.A.
118 G4 **Fort Kent** Alberta Canada
95 S6 **Fort Kent** Maine U.S.A.
100 C7 **Fort Klamath** Oregon U.S.A.
94 B9 **Fort Knox** Kentucky U.S.A.
Fort Lallemande *see* **Belhirane**
Fort Lamy *see* **N'djamena**
98 B7 **Fort Laramie** Wyoming U.S.A.
98 B7 **Fort Laramie Nat. Hist. Mon.** Wyoming U.S.A.
107 L3 **Fort Larned Nat. Hist. Site** Kansas U.S.A.
113 G11 **Fort Lauderdale** Florida U.S.A.
112 G3 **Fort Lawn** South Carolina U.S.A.
100 C2 **Fort Lewis** Washington U.S.A.
117 M5 **Fort Liard** Northwest Territories Canada
127 J5 **Fort Liberté** Haiti
98 F3 **Fort Lincoln** North Dakota U.S.A.
112 C2 **Fort Loudon Lake** Tennessee U.S.A.
98 B9 **Fort Lupton** Colorado U.S.A.
106 G3 **Fort Lyon** Colorado U.S.A.
108 G5 **Fort McKavett** Texas U.S.A.
117 S7 **Fort MacKay** Alberta Canada
101 S5 **Fort Mackenzie** Wyoming U.S.A.
118 D9 **Fort Macleod** Alberta Canada
Fort McMahon *see* **El Homr**

118 F2 **Fort McMurray** Alberta Canada
114 F4 **Fort McPherson** Northwest Territories Canada
99 P9 **Fort Madison** Iowa U.S.A.
22 B3 **Fort Mahon Plage** France
Fort Manning *see* **Mchinji**
113 F8 **Fort Matanzas Nat.Mon** Florida U.S.A.
113 F10 **Fort Meade** Florida U.S.A.
112 G2 **Fort Mill** South Carolina U.S.A.
106 G1 **Fort Morgan** Colorado U.S.A.
98 C9 **Fort Morgan** Colorado U.S.A.
113 F11 **Fort Myers** Florida U.S.A.
113 E11 **Fort Myers Beach** Florida U.S.A.
117 M6 **Fort Nelson** British Columbia Canada
117 L3 **Fort Norman** Northwest Territories Canada
113 F10 **Fort Ogden** Florida U.S.A.
43 G7 **Fortore** *R* Italy
111 L7 **Fort Payne** Alabama U.S.A.
101 T2 **Fort Peck L** *res* Montana U.S.A.
113 G10 **Fort Pierce** Florida U.S.A.
98 F5 **Fort Pierre** South Dakota U.S.A.
Fort Pierre Bordes *see* **Tin Zaouaten**
95 N4 **Fort Plain** New York U.S.A.
86 F5 **Fort Portal** Uganda
117 P5 **Fort Providence** Northwest Territories Canada
112 G5 **Fort Pulaski Nat. Mon** Georgia U.S.A.
119 O8 **Fort Qu' Appelle** Saskatchewan Canada
112 M2 **Fort Raleigh Nat.Hist.Site** North Carolina U.S.A.
116 F9 **Fort Randall** Alaska U.S.A.
98 H6 **Fort Randall Dam** South Dakota U.S.A.
94 C6 **Fort Recovery** Ohio U.S.A.
114 J5 **Fort Reliance** Northwest Territories Canada
117 R5 **Fort Resolution** Northwest Territories Canada
101 Q5 **Fortress Mt** Wyoming U.S.A.
123 M8 **Fortress of Louisburg Nat. Hist. Park** C Breton I, Nova Scotia
98 F3 **Fort Rice** North Dakota U.S.A.
107 O2 **Fort Riley** Kansas U.S.A.
99 M3 **Fort Ripley** Minnesota U.S.A.
87 E10 **Fort Rixon** Zimbabwe
98 C7 **Fort Robinson** Nebraska U.S.A.
100 D6 **Fort Rock** Oregon U.S.A.
144 B7 **Fortrose** New Zealand
Fort Rosebery Zambia *see* **Mansa**
102 A3 **Fort Ross** California U.S.A.
Fort Rousset *see* **Owando**
121 M1 **Fort Rupert** Quebec Canada
117 L8 **Fort St. James** British Columbia Canada
117 N7 **Fort St. John** British Columbia Canada
Fort Sandeman *see* **Zhob**
118 D5 **Fort Saskatchewan** Alberta Canada
107 Q4 **Fort Scott** Kansas U.S.A.
115 L6 **Fort Severn** Ontario Canada
100 B9 **Fort Seward** California U.S.A.
107 M7 **Fort Sill** Oklahoma U.S.A.
117 N5 **Fort Simpson** Northwest Territories Canada
114 G5 **Fort Smith** *dist* Northwest Territories Canada
117 R5 **Fort Smith** Northwest Territories Canada
107 Q6 **Fort Smith** Arkansas U.S.A.
101 T8 **Fort Steele** Wyoming U.S.A.
108 E5 **Fort Stockton** Texas U.S.A.
108 C1 **Fort Sumner** New Mexico U.S.A.
112 H5 **Fort Sumter Nat.Mon** South Carolina U.S.A.
107 L5 **Fort Supply** Oklahoma U.S.A.
108 E7 **Fort Supply Res** Oklahoma U.S.A.
103 P8 **Fort Thomas** Arizona U.S.A.
98 G5 **Fort Thompson** South Dakota U.S.A.
107 P7 **Fort Towson** Oklahoma U.S.A.
27 C10 **Fortun** Norway
17 G6 **Fortuna** Spain
100 A9 **Fortuna** California U.S.A.
98 C1 **Fortuna** North Dakota U.S.A.
116 F6 **Fortuna Ledge** Alaska U.S.A.
123 R6 **Fortune** Newfoundland Canada
106 E6 **Fort Union Nat.Mon** New Mexico U.S.A.
112 D5 **Fort Valley** Georgia U.S.A.
117 Q6 **Fort Vermilion** Alberta Canada
Fort Victoria *see* **Masvingo**
94 B7 **Fortville** Indiana U.S.A.
111 K11 **Fort Walton Beach** Florida U.S.A.
101 R6 **Fort Washakie** Wyoming U.S.A.
94 B5 **Fort Wayne** Indiana U.S.A.
113 E8 **Fort White** Florida U.S.A.
118 A2 **Fort Whyte** Manitoba Canada
15 C4 **Fort William** Scotland
109 M10 **Fort Worth** Texas U.S.A.
98 F3 **Fort Yates** North Dakota U.S.A.
116 R5 **Fortymile** *R* Alaska U.S.A.
116 P3 **Fort Yukon** Alaska U.S.A.
77 D6 **Forūr, Jazīreh-ye** *isld* Iran
22 J2 **Forville** Belgium
119 N9 **Forward** Saskatchewan Canada
52 H5 **Fosforitnaya** U.S.S.R.
67 D5 **Foshan** China
115 L2 **Fosheim Pen** Northwest Territories Canada
26 D8 **Fosna** Norway
26 E7 **Fosnes** Norway
107 L6 **Foss** Oklahoma U.S.A.
44 C2 **Fossano** Italy
22 H3 **Fosse** Belgium
100 E4 **Fossil** Oregon U.S.A.
101 P8 **Fossil** Wyoming U.S.A.
101 P8 **Fossil Butte Nat. Mon.** Wyoming U.S.A.
142 F4 **Fossil Downs** Western Australia Australia
121 L6 **Fossmill** Ontario Canada
42 E5 **Fossombrone** Italy
119 O6 **Fosston** Saskatchewan Canada
99 L2 **Fosston** Minnesota U.S.A.
139 H7 **Foster** Victoria Australia
121 S7 **Foster** Quebec Canada
98 J7 **Foster** Nebraska U.S.A.
100 C5 **Foster** Oregon U.S.A.
147 E10 **Foster Bugt** Greenland
99 T4 **Foster City** Michigan U.S.A.
118 J8 **Fosterton** Saskatchewan Canada
110 K6 **Fosterville** Tennessee U.S.A.
94 D5 **Fostoria** Ohio U.S.A.
109 M5 **Fostoria** Texas U.S.A.
67 F4 **Fotan** China
142 F5 **Fotheringham, Mt** Western Australia Australia
21 O2 **Foucarmont** France
36 C7 **Foucday** France
20 B6 **Fouesnant** France
86 B6 **Fougamou** Gabon
20 H5 **Fougères** France
83 K13 **Fougères,Pl.des** Réunion Indian Oc
21 J5 **Fougerolles-du-Plessis** France
21 P2 **Fouilloy** France
109 O2 **Fouke** Arkansas U.S.A.
68 B3 **Foul** *isld* Burma
84 K5 **Foul Bay** Egypt
9 G4 **Foulness Pt** England
13 E5 **Foulney** *isld* England
144 C4 **Foulwind, C** New Zealand
86 B4 **Foumban** Cameroon
85 C3 **Foum el Hassan** Morocco
85 C2 **Foum Zguid** Morocco
146 D8 **Foundation Ice Stream** *ice stream* Antarctica
106 F3 **Fountain** Colorado U.S.A.
99 U5 **Fountain** Michigan U.S.A.
99 O6 **Fountain** Minnesota U.S.A.
112 K2 **Fountain** North Carolina U.S.A.
103 N2 **Fountain Grn** Utah U.S.A.
111 E8 **Fountain Hill** Arkansas U.S.A.
112 E3 **Fountain Inn** South Carolina U.S.A.
16 B7 **Foupana** *R* Portugal
140 D3 **Four Archers** *mt* N Terr Australia
18 E7 **Fouras** France
101 U1 **Four Buttes** Montana U.S.A.
21 M5 **Fourche, la** France
110 B7 **Fourche la Fave** *R* Arkansas U.S.A.
19 J4 **Fourchies, Mts des** France
123 M8 **Fourchu** C Breton I, Nova Scotia
103 P4 **Four Corners** Utah U.S.A.
98 B5 **Four Corners** Wyoming U.S.A.
140 A1 **Fourcroy, C** N Terr Australia
20 E7 **Four, le** *isld* France
22 G3 **Fourmies** France
83 K14 **Fournaise, Piton de la** *vol* Réunion Indian Oc
46 E5 **Fournás** Greece
83 L13 **Fourneau** *isld* Mauritius
123 P2 **Fournel, L** Quebec Canada
22 D2 **Fournes-en-Weppes** France
122 G2 **Fournier, L** Quebec Canada
47 H7 **Foúrnoi** *isld* Greece
127 K3 **Four Paths** Jamaica
19 N17 **Fourques** France
13 F3 **Fourstones** England
99 R3 **Fourteenmile Pt** Michigan U.S.A.
85 B6 **Fouta Djalon** *mt reg* Guinea
85 B5 **Fouta Ferlo** *reg* Senegal
8 D5 **Fovant** England
144 A7 **Foveaux Strait** New Zealand
28 C3 **Fovlum** Denmark
8 B7 **Fowey** England
113 G12 **Fowey Rocks** Florida U.S.A.
126 F2 **Fowl Cay** *isld* Bahamas
106 F2 **Fowler** Colorado U.S.A.
99 T9 **Fowler** Indiana U.S.A.
107 K4 **Fowler** Kansas U.S.A.
94 C3 **Fowler** Michigan U.S.A.
101 O1 **Fowler** Montana U.S.A.
146 C7 **Fowler Peninsula** *pen* Antarctica
138 B4 **Fowler Pt** South Australia Australia
138 B4 **Fowlers B** South Australia Australia
139 F4 **Fowlers Gap** New South Wales Australia
109 J7 **Fowlerton** Texas U.S.A.
94 C4 **Fowlerville** Michigan U.S.A.
110 G6 **Fowlkes** Tennessee U.S.A.
111 M11 **Fowlstown** Georgia U.S.A.
77 A1 **Fowman** Iran
115 K6 **Fox** *R* Manitoba Canada
99 S8 **Fox** *R* Illinois U.S.A.
99 T4 **Fox** Michigan U.S.A.
99 U3 **Fox** *R* Michigan U.S.A.
99 P9 **Fox** *R* Missouri U.S.A.
100 F5 **Fox** Oregon U.S.A.
99 S5 **Fox** *R* Wisconsin U.S.A.
123 L4 **Fox B** Anticosti I, Quebec
95 M5 **Foxburg** Pennsylvania U.S.A.
117 P8 **Fox Creek** Alberta Canada
115 M4 **Foxe Basin** Northwest Territories Canada
115 L4 **Foxe Chan** Northwest Territories Canada
115 M5 **Foxe Pen** Northwest Territories Canada
119 M5 **Foxford** Saskatchewan Canada
14 B3 **Foxford** Ireland
123 R1 **Fox Harbour** Labrador, Nfld Canada
13 H5 **Foxholes** England
98 K3 **Foxhome** Minnesota U.S.A.
116 P8 **Fox Islands** *isld* Aleutian Is
143 C10 **Fox, L** Western Australia Australia
99 S7 **Fox Lake** Illinois U.S.A.
99 S6 **Fox Lake** Wisconsin U.S.A.
101 T8 **Foxpark** Wyoming U.S.A.
144 C5 **Fox Peak** *mt* New Zealand
123 L4 **Fox Pt** Anticosti I, Quebec
117 L7 **Fox R** British Columbia Canada
145 E4 **Foxton** New Zealand
118 H8 **Fox Valley** Saskatchewan Canada
119 Q8 **Foxwarren** Manitoba Canada
111 G10 **Foxworth** Mississippi U.S.A.
15 D3 **Foyers** Scotland
14 C2 **Foyle** *R* N Ireland
14 D1 **Foyle, L** Ireland
14 B4 **Foynes** Ireland
16 C1 **Foz** Spain
87 B9 **Foz do Cunene** Angola
128 D5 **Foz do Gregório** Brazil
129 G8 **Foz do Iguaçú** Brazil
128 F5 **Foz do Jamari** Brazil
128 E4 **Foz do Jordao** Brazil
128 E4 **Foz do Jutai** Brazil
128 E4 **Foz do Mamoriá** Brazil
128 D5 **Foz do Riozinho** Brazil
67 E1 **Foziling Shuiku** *res* China
128 F8 **Foz Tarauacá** Brazil
95 L6 **Frackville** Pennsylvania U.S.A.
8 B7 **Fraddon** England
17 H3 **Fraga** Spain
36 B7 **Fraize** France
95 Q4 **Framingham** Massachusetts U.S.A.
9 H3 **Framlingham** England
36 G3 **Frammersbach** W Germany
146 J10 **Framnes Mts** Antarctica
31 O5 **Frampol** Poland
130 F7 **Franca** Brazil
43 H8 **Francavilla Fontana** Italy
18 H9 **France** *rep* W Europe
147 F10 **France, Ile de** Greenland
138 F6 **Frances** South Australia Australia
117 J5 **Frances** *R* Yukon Territory Canada
100 B3 **Frances** Washington U.S.A.
117 J5 **Frances Creek** N Terr Australia
117 J5 **Frances L** Yukon Territory Canada
101 N1 **Frances, L** Montana U.S.A.
127 K5 **Frances Viejo, C** Dominican Rep
99 U9 **Francesville** Indiana U.S.A.
86 B6 **Franceville** Gabon
19 J6 **Franche Comté** *prov* France
119 O8 **Francis** Saskatchewan Canada
107 O7 **Francis** Oklahoma U.S.A.
98 G6 **Francis Case, L** South Dakota U.S.A.
128 D4 **Francisco de Orellana** Peru
124 H5 **Francisco I. Madero** Coahuila Mexico
124 G5 **Francisco I. Madero** Durango Mexico
130 C9 **Francisco, S** *R* Brazil
130 G5 **Francisco Sá** Brazil
123 R1 **Francis Harbour** Labrador, Nfld Canada
95 Q1 **Francis, L** New Hampshire U.S.A.
89 E3 **Francistown** Botswana
123 Q6 **François** Newfoundland Canada
117 K8 **François L** British Columbia Canada
127 M4 **François, Le** Martinique W Indies
45 L2 **Francolino** Italy
22 K2 **Francorchamps** Belgium
101 Q6 **Francs Pk** Wyoming U.S.A.
21 N7 **Francueil** France
25 E2 **Franeker** Netherlands
118 C9 **Frank** Alberta Canada
36 F1 **Frankenau** W Germany
36 F2 **Frankenbach** W Germany
37 P2 **Frankenberg** East Germany
36 F1 **Frankenberg/Eder** W Germany
37 J5 **Frankenhardt** W Germany
37 J5 **Frankenhöhe** *mts* W Germany
94 D3 **Frankenmuth** Michigan U.S.A.
36 D5 **Frankenstein** W Germany
36 E4 **Frankenthal** W Germany
37 M3 **Frankenwald** *mts* E & W Germany
127 K2 **Frankfield** Jamaica
121 N8 **Frankford** Ontario Canada
110 E2 **Frankford** Missouri U.S.A.
94 G9 **Frankford** West Virginia U.S.A.
94 A6 **Frankfort** Indiana U.S.A.
107 O2 **Frankfort** Kansas U.S.A.
94 C8 **Frankfort** Kentucky U.S.A.
99 U5 **Frankfort** Michigan U.S.A.
95 M3 **Frankfort** New York U.S.A.
94 D7 **Frankfort** Ohio U.S.A.
98 H5 **Frankfort** South Dakota U.S.A.
33 T7 **Frankfurt** East Germany
36 F3 **Frankfurt am Main** W Germany
31 H3 **Frankfurt an der Oder** East Germany
37 K6 **Fränkische Alb** *mts* W Germany
37 L4 **Fränkische Schweiz** *reg* W Germany
139 J7 **Frankland, C** Tasmania Australia
111 L8 **Franklin** Georgia U.S.A.
101 O7 **Franklin** Idaho U.S.A.
94 A7 **Franklin** Indiana U.S.A.
110 K5 **Franklin** Kentucky U.S.A.
111 E12 **Franklin** Louisiana U.S.A.
95 T2 **Franklin** Maine U.S.A.
95 Q4 **Franklin** Massachusetts U.S.A.
101 Q3 **Franklin** Montana U.S.A.
98 H9 **Franklin** Nebraska U.S.A.
95 Q3 **Franklin** New Hampshire U.S.A.
95 N5 **Franklin** New Jersey U.S.A.
95 M4 **Franklin** New York U.S.A.
112 D2 **Franklin** North Carolina U.S.A.
94 C7 **Franklin** Ohio U.S.A.
94 H5 **Franklin** Pennsylvania U.S.A.
110 K6 **Franklin** Tennessee U.S.A.
109 L4 **Franklin** Texas U.S.A.
95 L10 **Franklin** Virginia U.S.A.
94 H8 **Franklin** West Virginia U.S.A.
114 G3 **Franklin B** Northwest Territories Canada
100 G1 **Franklin D. Roosevelt L** Washington U.S.A.
99 R8 **Franklin Grove** Illinois U.S.A.
138 D5 **Franklin Harb** South Australia Australia
146 C11 **Franklin I** Antarctica
120 K7 **Franklin I** Ontario Canada
103 J1 **Franklin L** Nevada U.S.A.
117 L3 **Franklin Mts** Northwest Territories Canada
144 A6 **Franklin Mts** New Zealand
116 P2 **Franklin Mts** Alaska U.S.A.
116 H1 **Franklin, Pt** Alaska U.S.A.
139 J8 **Franklin Snd** Tasmania Australia
115 K3 **Franklin Str** Northwest Territories Canada
111 F11 **Franklinton** Louisiana U.S.A.
112 J1 **Franklinton** North Carolina U.S.A.
94 J4 **Franklinville** New York U.S.A.
112 H2 **Franklinville** North Carolina U.S.A.
100 J6 **Franklin Whitney** *airport* Idaho U.S.A.
144 D5 **Franklyn, Mt** New Zealand
37 J3 **Fränk Saale** *R* W Germany
139 H7 **Frankston** Victoria Australia
109 M3 **Frankston** Texas U.S.A.
99 Q4 **Franksville** Wisconsin U.S.A.
144 B6 **Frankton** New Zealand
101 R5 **Frannie** Wyoming U.S.A.
87 B10 **Franschhoek** Namibia
26 H9 **Fränsta** Sweden
9 G5 **Frant** England
37 N3 **Františkovy Lázně** Czechoslovakia
147 L11 **Frantsa-losifa, Zemlya** Arctic Oc
120 F4 **Franz** Ontario Canada
33 R4 **Franzburg** East Germany
144 C5 **Franz Josef Gla** New Zealand
Franz Josef Land *see* **Frantsa-losifa, Zemlya**
38 G7 **Franz-Josefs Höhe** *mt* Austria
43 B9 **Frasca, C. d** Sardinia
42 E7 **Frascati** Italy
100 C1 **Fraser** *R* British Columbia Canada
106 E2 **Fraser** Colorado U.S.A.
87 D12 **Fraserburg** S Africa
15 F3 **Fraserburgh** Scotland
120 J3 **Fraserdale** Ontario Canada
141 L7 **Fraser I** Queensland Australia
143 C7 **Fraser, Mt** Western Australia Australia
143 E9 **Fraser Range** Western Australia Australia
69 E11 **Fraser's Hill** Malaysia
145 F3 **Frasertown** New Zealand
119 U8 **Fraserwood** Manitoba Canada
46 D4 **Frashër** Albania
48 K6 **Frăsinet** Romania
19 K6 **Frasne** France
22 F2 **Frasnes-les-Buissenal** Belgium
25 F5 **Frasselt** W Germany
45 J3 **Frassinoro** Italy
120 E5 **Frater** Ontario Canada
45 L1 **Fratta Polesine** Italy
41 J2 **Frauenfeld** Switzerland
33 S10 **Frauenhain** East Germany
37 O5 **Frauenstein** *mt* W Germany
37 K2 **Frauenwald** East Germany
28 E6 **Fraugde** Denmark
131 F4 **Fray Bentos** Uruguay
21 N5 **Frazé** France
99 M3 **Frazee** Minnesota U.S.A.
101 T1 **Frazer** Montana U.S.A.
139 G7 **Frazer I** Western Australia Australia
120 B3 **Frazer L** Ontario Canada
36 D2 **Frechen** W Germany
16 D2 **Frechilla** Spain
32 G9 **Freckenhorst** W Germany
13 F6 **Freckleton** England
99 Q4 **Freda** Michigan U.S.A.
98 E3 **Freda** North Dakota U.S.A.
36 E1 **Fredeburg** W Germany
29 K5 **Fredensborg** Denmark
94 C2 **Frederic** Michigan U.S.A.
99 O4 **Frederic** Wisconsin U.S.A.
95 M7 **Frederica** Delaware U.S.A.
28 D5 **Fredericia** Denmark
99 Q9 **Frederick** Illinois U.S.A.
95 K7 **Frederick** Maryland U.S.A.
107 L7 **Frederick** Oklahoma U.S.A.
98 H4 **Frederick** South Dakota U.S.A.
120 J3 **Frederick House** *R* Ontario Canada
137 L6 **Frederick Reef** Coral Sea
99 O7 **Fredericksburg** Iowa U.S.A.
95 L6 **Fredericksburg** Pennsylvania U.S.A.
94 K8 **Fredericksburg** Virginia U.S.A.
117 F7 **Frederick Sd** Alaska U.S.A.
110 F4 **Fredericktown** Missouri U.S.A.
94 E6 **Fredericktown** Ohio U.S.A.
122 F8 **Fredericton** New Brunswick Canada
122 F8 **Fredericton Junct** New Brunswick Canada
28 C4 **Frederiks** Denmark
29 K5 **Frederiksberg** Denmark
28 C5 **Frederikshåb** Denmark
115 P5 **Frederikshåb** Greenland
115 O5 **Frederikshåb Isblink** Greenland
28 F2 **Frederikshavn** Denmark
28 H5 **Frederikssund** Denmark
113 L8 **Frederiksted** Virgin Is
28 J5 **Frederiksværk** Denmark
128 C2 **Fredonia** Colombia
103 M5 **Fredonia** Arizona U.S.A.
107 P4 **Fredonia** Kansas U.S.A.
110 H4 **Fredonia** Kentucky U.S.A.
110 H4 **Fredonia** New York U.S.A.
98 G3 **Fredonia** North Dakota U.S.A.
109 J5 **Fredricksburg** Texas U.S.A.
26 K7 **Fredrika** Sweden
27 E12 **Fredrikstad** Norway
110 E3 **Freeburg** Missouri U.S.A.
95 K6 **Freeburg** Pennsylvania U.S.A.
100 J4 **Freedom** Idaho U.S.A.
110 K2 **Freedom** Indiana U.S.A.
107 L5 **Freedom** Oklahoma U.S.A.
100 E9 **Freedonyer Peak** *mt* California U.S.A.
95 N6 **Freehold** New Jersey U.S.A.
94 C3 **Freeland** Michigan U.S.A.
95 M5 **Freeland** Pennsylvania U.S.A.
138 E4 **Freeling Heights** *mt* South Australia Australia
140 C6 **Freeling Mt** N Terr Australia
102 E3 **Freel Peak** California U.S.A.
123 T4 **Freels, C** Newfoundland Canada
118 B4 **Freeman** *R* Alberta Canada
98 J6 **Freeman** South Dakota U.S.A.
110 K1 **Freeman, L** Indiana U.S.A.
111 G12 **Freemason I** Louisiana U.S.A.
122 F9 **Freeport** Nova Scotia Canada
111 K11 **Freeport** Florida U.S.A.
99 R7 **Freeport** Illinois U.S.A.
95 R3 **Freeport** Maine U.S.A.
94 F6 **Freeport** Ohio U.S.A.
94 H6 **Freeport** Pennsylvania U.S.A.
109 M7 **Freeport** Texas U.S.A.
113 J11 **Freeport City** Grand Bahama I
109 J8 **Freer** Texas U.S.A.
99 U5 **Freesoil** Michigan U.S.A.
126 F2 **Freetown** Eleuthera Bahamas
122 J7 **Freetown** Prince Edward I Canada
85 B7 **Freetown** Sierra Leone
94 A8 **Freetown** Indiana U.S.A.
127 P4 **Freetown** Antigua W Indies
95 L4 **Freeville** New York U.S.A.
16 C6 **Fregenal de la Sierra** Spain
138 B2 **Fregon** South Australia Australia
20 F4 **Fréhel** France
20 F4 **Fréhel, C** France
26 C8 **Frei** Norway
37 P2 **Freiberg** East Germany
36 G6 **Freiberg** W Germany
37 O1 **Freiberger Mulde** *R* East Germany
40 G1 **Freiburg** W Germany
32 K10 **Freienhagen** W Germany
32 H10 **Freienohl** W Germany
36 G3 **Freiensteinau** W Germany
37 M4 **Freihung** W Germany
36 D2 **Freilingen** W Germany
133 C3 **Freirina** Chile
36 C4 **Freisen** W Germany
37 M7 **Freising** W Germany
38 L4 **Freistadt** Austria
16 C3 **Freixo de Espada à Cinta** Portugal
28 D2 **Frejlev** Denmark
143 B9 **Fremantle** Western Australia Australia
94 C5 **Fremont** Indiana U.S.A.
99 V6 **Fremont** Michigan U.S.A.
98 K8 **Fremont** Nebraska U.S.A.
112 K2 **Fremont** North Carolina U.S.A.
94 D5 **Fremont** Ohio U.S.A.
103 O3 **Fremont** *R* Utah U.S.A.
101 N8 **Fremont I** Utah U.S.A.
101 O7 **Fremont, L** Wyoming U.S.A.
106 D2 **Fremont Pass** Colorado U.S.A.
101 Q6 **Fremont Pk** Wyoming U.S.A.
20 F4 **Frênaye, B.de la** France
112 D2 **French Broad** *R* Tennessee U.S.A.
94 D9 **Frenchburg** Kentucky U.S.A.
94 G5 **French Cr** Pennsylvania U.S.A.
100 J4 **French Creek** Idaho U.S.A.
102 T13 **French Frigate Shoals** Hawaiian Is
100 G7 **Frenchglen** Oregon U.S.A.
129 H3 **French Guiana** *French dept* S America
100 C9 **French Gulch** California U.S.A.
139 H7 **French I** Victoria Australia
110 K3 **French Lick** Indiana U.S.A.
102 F2 **Frenchman** Nevada U.S.A.
95 T2 **Frenchman Bay** Maine U.S.A.
118 H5 **Frenchman Butte** Saskatchewan Canada
139 H8 **Frenchman Cap** Tasmania Australia
101 S1 **Frenchman Cr** Mont/Sask U.S.A./Canada
103 J5 **Frenchman Flat** *dry lake* Nevada U.S.A.
98 E9 **Frenchman Fork** *R* Nebraska U.S.A.
118 J9 **Frenchman** *R* Saskatchewan Canada
123 O4 **Frenchman's Cove** Newfoundland Canada
14 C3 **Frenchpark** Ireland
145 D4 **French Pass** New Zealand
French Terr. of the Afars and the Issas (FTAI) *see* **Djibouti** *rep*
95 M6 **Frenchtown** New Jersey U.S.A.
22 B2 **Frencq** France
19 Q14 **Frêne, Pic du** *mt* France
21 M3 **Freneuse-sur-Risle** France
37 K4 **Frensdorf** W Germany
31 L6 **Frenštát** Czechoslovakia
32 G8 **Freren** W Germany
143 D7 **Frere Ra** Western Australia Australia
129 H5 **Fresco** *R* Brazil
14 D4 **Freshford** Ireland
144 B6 **Freshford Plain** New Zealand
9 E6 **Freshwater** England
100 A9 **Freshwater** California U.S.A.
21 L5 **Fresnay** France
21 L5 **Fresnay-sur-Chédouet, la** France
40 C2 **Fresnes** France
22 F3 **Fresnes-sur-L'Escaut** France
124 H6 **Fresnillo de Gonzâlez Echeverria** Mexico
102 E4 **Fresno** *R* California U.S.A.
102 E5 **Fresno** California U.S.A.
101 P1 **Fresno Res** Montana U.S.A.
21 N2 **Fresnoy-Folny** France
22 E4 **Fresnoy-le-Grand** France
40 C4 **Fresse, Mt.de** France
21 O1 **Fressenneville** France
27 B10 **Fresvik** Norway
21 N6 **Fréteval** France
27 B11 **Fretheim** Norway
19 J5 **Frétigney** France
20 A5 **Fret,le** France
13 E1 **Freuchie** Scotland
36 G4 **Freudenberg** Baden-Württemberg W Germany
36 D2 **Freudenberg** Nordrhein-Westfalen W Germany
36 E7 **Freudenstadt** W Germany
22 C3 **Frévent** France
140 D4 **Frewena Roadhouse** N Terr Australia
94 H4 **Frewsburg** New York U.S.A.
37 M1 **Freyburg** East Germany
143 A10 **Freycinet, C** Western Australia Australia
143 A7 **Freycinet Estuary** *inlet* Western Australia Australia
139 J8 **Freycinet Pen** Tasmania Australia
33 Q6 **Freyenstein** East Germany
36 B5 **Freyming** France
37 L5 **Freystadt** W Germany
30 H7 **Freyung** W Germany
85 B6 **Fria** Guinea
87 B9 **Fria, C** Namibia
102 E5 **Friant** California U.S.A.
102 E4 **Friant Dam** California U.S.A.
127 P4 **Friar's B.**, **North** St Kitts W Indies
83 L10 **Friar's Hood** *mt* Sri Lanka
111 F7 **Friars Point** Mississippi U.S.A.
131 D2 **Frías** Argentina
40 F4 **Fribourg** Switzerland
36 E3 **Frickhofen** W Germany
22 D3 **Fricourt** France
100 B1 **Friday Harbour** Washington U.S.A.
141 F1 **Friday I** Queensland Australia
13 H5 **Fridaythorpe** England
38 O7 **Friedberg** Austria
37 K7 **Friedberg** Bayern W Germany
36 F3 **Friedberg** Hessen W Germany
33 P9 **Friedeburg** East Germany
38 M4 **Friedersbach** Austria
33 T8 **Friedersdorf** East Germany
33 T5 **Friedland** East Germany
32 L10 **Friedland** W Germany
37 K2 **Friedrichroda** East Germany
33 P7 **Friedrichsdorf** W Germany
33 T7 **Friedrichsfelde** East Germany
41 K2 **Friedrichshafen** W Germany
33 T8 **Friedrichshagen** East Germany
32 J4 **Friedrichskoog** W Germany
33 P5 **Friedrichsruhe** East Germany
30 E1 **Friedrichstadt** W Germany
33 T6 **Friedrichswalde** East Germany
37 K2 **Friedrichswerth** East Germany
36 G2 **Frielendorf** W Germany
107 K3 **Friend** Kansas U.S.A.
98 J9 **Friend** Nebraska U.S.A.
Friendly Is *see* **Tonga**
127 K2 **Friendship** *pk* Jamaica
95 S3 **Friendship** Maine U.S.A.
94 J4 **Friendship** New York U.S.A.
94 D8 **Friendship** Ohio U.S.A.
99 R6 **Friendship** Wisconsin U.S.A.
70 C2 **Friendship Shoal** S China Sea
94 H7 **Friendsville** Maryland U.S.A.
27 D12 **Frierfjord** *inlet* Norway
94 F10 **Fries** Virginia U.S.A.
38 K8 **Friesach** Austria
33 R7 **Friesack** East Germany
25 F2 **Friesche Gat** Netherlands
36 D7 **Friesenheim** W Germany
28 A7 **Friesische Inseln** *islds* W Germany
25 E2 **Friesland** Netherlands
32 G6 **Friesoythe** W Germany
83 J12 **Frigate** *isld* Seychelles
6 M3 **Frigg** *oil rig* North Sea
27 G12 **Frignano** Italy
9 H4 **Frinton-on-Sea** England
124 H6 **Frio** Mexico
109 J7 **Frio** *R* Texas U.S.A.
130 H8 **Frio, C** Brazil
15 F4 **Friockheim** Scotland
108 E1 **Frio Draw** *R* New Mex/Tex U.S.A.
36 F6 **Friolzheim** W Germany
22 L4 **Frisange** Luxembourg
12 O3 **Frisco** Texas U.S.A.
111 J10 **Frisco City** Alabama U.S.A.
103 L3 **Frisco Mt** Utah U.S.A.
108 C8 **Fritch** Texas U.S.A.
8 B6 **Frithelstock Stone** England
36 G1 **Fritzlar** W Germany
42 E2 **Friuli-Venezia-Giulia** *prov* Italy
21 O1 **Friville-Escarbotin** France
12 E5 **Frizington** England
26 D8 **Froan** *isld* Norway
119 P9 **Frobisher** Saskatchewan Canada
115 N5 **Frobisher Bay** Northwest Territories Canada
114 J6 **Frobisher L** Saskatchewan Canada
8 D1 **Frodsham** England
19 P14 **Froges** France
118 G5 **Frog L** *L* Alberta Canada
26 D8 **Frohavet** *inlet* Norway
37 O1 **Frohburg** East Germany
33 T9 **Frohnau** East Germany
33 P8 **Frohse** East Germany
98 B1 **Froid** Montana U.S.A.
22 G3 **Froid-Chapelle** Belgium
130 F5 **Frois** Brazil
21 O1 **Froissy** France
36 B2 **Frölzheim** W Germany
52 J5 **Frolovskaya** U.S.S.R.
55 E1 **Froly** U.S.S.R.
101 R4 **Fromberg** Montana U.S.A.
31 M1 **Frombork** Poland
138 E3 **Frome** *R* South Australia Australia
8 D5 **Frome** England
127 H1 **Frome** Jamaica
138 E4 **Frome Downs** South Australia Australia
138 E4 **Frome, L** South Australia Australia
22 D2 **Fromelles** France
21 K4 **Fromentel** France
20 F8 **Fromentine** France
32 G10 **Fröndenberg** W Germany
36 F2 **Fronhausen** W Germany
16 B5 **Fronteira** Portugal
37 K4 **Frontenay Rohan-Rohan** France
37 O6 **Frontenhausen** W Germany
125 N8 **Frontera** Mexico
124 E2 **Fronteras** Mexico
118 J9 **Frontier** Saskatchewan Canada
101 P8 **Frontier** Wyoming U.S.A.
18 H9 **Frontignan** France
106 E1 **Front Range** Colorado U.S.A.
94 J8 **Front Royal** Virginia U.S.A.
28 F6 **Frørup** Denmark
33 O9 **Frose** East Germany
43 E7 **Frosinone** Italy
28 B3 **Frøslev** Denmark
20 G7 **Frossay** France
109 L3 **Frost** Texas U.S.A.
26 E8 **Frosta** Norway
94 J7 **Frostburg** Maryland U.S.A.
113 F10 **Frostproof** Florida U.S.A.
28 B2 **Frøstrup** Denmark
26 G7 **Frostviken** Sweden
37 K2 **Fröttstädt** East Germany
19 K4 **Frouard** France
119 O9 **Froude** Saskatchewan Canada
27 H12 **Frövi** Sweden
9 E5 **Froxfield** England
26 C8 **Frøya** *isld* Norway
26 B8 **Frøyabanken** Norway
22 C3 **Fruges** France
106 B2 **Fruita** Colorado U.S.A.
111 H10 **Fruitdale** Alabama U.S.A.
98 C5 **Fruitdale** South Dakota U.S.A.
100 J5 **Fruitland** Idaho U.S.A.
106 B5 **Fruitland** New Mexico U.S.A.
101 P9 **Fruitland** Utah U.S.A.
144 B6 **Fruitlands** New Zealand
100 J5 **Fruitvale** Idaho U.S.A.
48 K3 **Frumușica** Romania
57 G3 **Frunze** U.S.S.R.
54 F8 **Frunzenskiy** U.S.S.R.
48 M3 **Frunzovka** U.S.S.R.
46 F5 **Fruška Gora** *mt* Yugoslavia
130 E7 **Frutal** Brazil
40 G4 **Frutigen** Switzerland
102 B2 **Fruto** California U.S.A.
54 K1 **Fryanovo** U.S.S.R.
98 C3 **Fryburg** North Dakota U.S.A.
48 E1 **Frýdek Místek** Czechoslovakia
95 R2 **Fryeburg** Maine U.S.A.
27 F11 **Fryksände** Sweden
46 E5 **Ftéri** *mt* Greece
67 F3 **Fu'an** China
45 J4 **Fucecchio** Italy
65 B7 **Fucheng** China
65 C6 **Fucheng** China
36 E2 **Fuchskauten** *mt* W Germany
60 G11 **Fuchū** Japan
67 D4 **Fuchuan** China
59 G6 **Fuchun Jiang** *R* China
42 F7 **Fucino, Piana del** Italy
61 P5 **Fudai** Japan
67 G3 **Fuding** China
16 D8 **Fuengirola** Spain
108 G7 **Fuente** Mexico
17 G7 **Fuente Alamo de Murcia** Spain
16 C6 **Fuente de Cantos** Spain
16 C4 **Fuenteguinaldo** Spain
16 D6 **Fuenteobejuna** Spain
16 D3 **Fuentesaúco** Spain
17 G3 **Fuentes de Ebro** Spain
16 C4 **Fuentes de Oñoro** Spain
130 B7 **Fuerte Olimpo** Paraguay
85 B3 **Fuerteventura** *isld* Canary Is
71 E1 **Fuga** *isld* Luzon Philippines
38 E7 **Fügen** Austria
28 H6 **Fuglebjerg** Denmark
6 F1 **Fugloy** *isld* Faeroes
26 L1 **Fugløy** *isld* Norway
28 F7 **Fuglsbølle** Denmark
65 C7 **Fugou** China
65 B5 **Fugu** China
Fuguo *see* **Zhanhua**
66 D2 **Fuhai** China
77 A5 **Fuhayhil, Al** Kuwait
33 Q9 **Fuhne** *R* East Germany
32 L7 **Fuhrberg** W Germany
21 H7 **Fuilet, le** France
77 E7 **Fujayrah, Al** U.A.E.
67 F3 **Fujian** *prov* China
67 B1 **Fu Jiang** *R* China
61 M11 **Fujieda** Japan
61 M10 **Fuji Hakone Izu Nat. Park** Japan
61 M10 **Fuji-kawa** *R* Japan
59 K2 **Fujin** China
61 M10 **Fujinomiya** Japan
61 H5 **Fujioka** Japan
61 O5 **Fujisaki** Japan
61 M10 **Fuji-san** *vol* Japan
61 N10 **Fujisawa** Japan
61 M10 **Fujiyoshida** Japan
61 N5 **Fukaura** Japan
61 N9 **Fukaya** Japan
Fukien *prov* *see* **Fujian**
60 J10 **Fukuchiyama** Japan
60 B13 **Fukue** Japan
60 B13 **Fukue-jima** *isld* Japan
61 K9 **Fukui** Japan
60 D12 **Fukuma** Japan
61 K9 **Fukuno** Japan
60 D12 **Fukuoka** Japan
60 H11 **Fukura** Japan
61 L11 **Fukuroi** Japan
61 O8 **Fukushima** *prefect* Japan
60 O4 **Fukushima** Hokkaido Japan
61 O8 **Fukushima** Honshu Japan
60 G11 **Fukuyama** Honshu Japan
60 D14 **Fukuyama** Kyūshū Japan
60 H10 **Fukuzaki** Japan
85 B6 **Fulacunda** Guinea-Bissau
77 C1 **Fulād Mahalleh** Iran
99 L6 **Fulda** Minnesota U.S.A.
36 H2 **Fulda** *R* W Germany
36 H2 **Fulda** W Germany
36 G1 **Fuldabrück** W Germany
13 G6 **Fulford** England
58 D6 **Fulin** China
67 B3 **Fuling** China
67 B2 **Fuling** China
141 K5 **Fullarton** *R* Queensland Australia
127 N3 **Fullarton** Trinidad
102 G8 **Fullerton** California U.S.A.
94 E8 **Fullerton** Kentucky U.S.A.
109 P4 **Fullerton** Louisiana U.S.A.
98 H8 **Fullerton** Nebraska U.S.A.
6 M6 **Fulmar** *oil rig* North Sea
65 F2 **Fulongquan** China
48 E4 **Fülöpszállás** Hungary
38 K7 **Fulpmes** Austria
111 J10 **Fulton** Alabama U.S.A.
111 C8 **Fulton** Arkansas U.S.A.
99 Q8 **Fulton** Illinois U.S.A.
94 A6 **Fulton** Indiana U.S.A.
107 Q3 **Fulton** Kansas U.S.A.
110 H5 **Fulton** Kentucky U.S.A.
111 C11 **Fulton** Louisiana U.S.A.
111 H7 **Fulton** Mississippi U.S.A.
110 E3 **Fulton** Missouri U.S.A.
95 L3 **Fulton** New York U.S.A.
94 E6 **Fulton** Ohio U.S.A.
98 J6 **Fulton** South Dakota U.S.A.
95 N4 **Fultonham** New York U.S.A.
95 N4 **Fultonville** New York U.S.A.
27 F10 **Fuluälven** *R* Sweden
27 F10 **Fulufj** *mt* Sweden
27 F10 **Fulunäs** Sweden
22 H4 **Fumay** France
18 F8 **Fumel** France
41 N5 **Fumo, Mt** Italy
19 N4 **Funabashi** Japan
137 Q3 **Funafuti** *atoll* Tuvalu
60 E14 **Funahiki** Japan
Funan *see* **Fusui**
65 F4 **Funan** China
26 G10 **Funäsdalen** Sweden
85 A2 **Funchal** Madeira
16 B7 **Funcheira** Portugal
126 G9 **Fundación** Colombia
130 H6 **Fundão** Brazil
124 E4 **Fundición** Mexico
38 E8 **Fundres** Italy
48 K4 **Fundulea** Romania
41 N3 **Fundus Feiler** *mt* Austria
122 G8 **Fundy, B. of** Nova Scotia/New Bruns Canada
122 G8 **Fundy Nat. Park** New Brunswick Canada
Funen *isld see* **Fyn** *isld*
102 H5 **Funeral Peak** California U.S.A.
87 F10 **Funhalouro** Mozambique
65 D5 **Funing** China
65 F5 **Funing** China
98 G9 **Funk** Nebraska U.S.A.
123 T4 **Funk I** Newfoundland Canada
141 J5 **Funnel** *R* Queensland Australia
117 F6 **Funter** Alaska U.S.A.
85 F6 **Funtua** Nigeria
65 C5 **Fuping** China
65 A7 **Fuping** China
67 F4 **Fuqing** China
112 J2 **Fuquay Springs** North Carolina U.S.A.
88 D9 **Furancungo** Mozambique
60 Q2 **Furano** Japan
60 J2 **Furao** China
46 G1 **Furculești** Romania
80 C3 **Fureidis** Israel
60 Q3 **Furenai** Japan
60 T2 **Füren ko** *L* Japan
29 K5 **Furesø** *L* Denmark
36 G5 **Fürfeld** Baden-Württemberg W Germany
36 D4 **Fürfeld** Rheinland-Pfalz W Germany
77 D5 **Furg** Iran
112 F5 **Furman** South Carolina U.S.A.
52 F6 **Furmanov** U.S.S.R.
57 G3 **Furmanovka** U.S.S.R.
12 E1 **Furnace** Scotland
130 F7 **Furnas Dam** Brazil
139 J8 **Furneaux Group** *islds* Tasmania Australia
138 F6 **Furner** South Australia Australia
Furnes *see* **Veurne**
27 E11 **Furnes** Norway
118 H5 **Furness** Saskatchewan Canada
67 B2 **Furong Jiang** *R* China
67 E3 **Furong Shan** *mt* China
32 G7 **Fürstenau** W Germany
33 S6 **Fürstenberg** East Germany
36 F1 **Fürstenberg** W Germany
38 O7 **Fürstenfeld** Austria
37 L7 **Fürstenfeldbrück** W Germany
30 H3 **Fürstenwalde** East Germany
33 T6 **Fürstenwerder** East Germany
37 P6 **Fürstenzell** W Germany
36 F4 **Fürth** W Germany
37 O5 **Furth im Wald** W Germany
41 H1 **Furtwangen** W Germany
60 O2 **Furuhira** Japan
61 L9 **Furukawa** Japan
61 O7 **Furukawa** Japan
115 L4 **Fury & Hecla Str** Northwest Territories Canada
27 A11 **Fusa** Norway
128 D3 **Fusagasuga** Colombia
45 Q8 **Fusaro** *L* Italy
43 G9 **Fuscaldo** Italy
38 G7 **Fusch** Austria
32 M8 **Fuse** *R* W Germany
65 E6 **Fushan** China
65 B6 **Fushan** China
68 J3 **Fushan** China
13 E2 **Fushiebridge** Scotland
61 K9 **Fushiki** Japan
59 H3 **Fushun** China
65 D6 **Fushun** China
67 A2 **Fushun** China
45 L3 **Fusignano** Italy
118 H7 **Fusilier** Saskatchewan Canada
Fusin *see* **Fuxin**
45 M1 **Fusina** Italy
41 J5 **Fusio** Switzerland
59 J3 **Fusong** China
41 N2 **Füssen** W Germany
28 D4 **Fussing Sø** *L* Denmark
67 B5 **Fusui** China
61 L11 **Futagawa** Japan
60 E12 **Futago-san** *mt* Japan
60 D11 **Futaoi-jima** *isld* Japan
45 K3 **Futa, Passo di** Italy
61 O5 **Futatsui** Japan
61 N13 **Futatsu-ne** *rocks* Japan
61 P13 **Futenma** Okinawa
61 N10 **Futtsu** Japan
137 R4 **Futuna** *isld* Îles de Horn Pacific Oc
67 F3 **Futun Xi** *R* China
79 A7 **Fuwa** Egypt
65 E5 **Fu Xian** China
65 E3 **Fuxian Hu** *L* China
65 E3 **Fuxin** China
Fuxing *see* **Wangmo**
67 F5 **Fuyang** China
67 F1 **Fuyang** China
58 G5 **Fuyang** China
67 G3 **Fuying Dao** *isld* China
59 H2 **Fuyu** China
59 K2 **Fuyuan** China
67 A4 **Fuyuan** China
66 D2 **Fuyun** China
48 F3 **Füzesabony** Hungary
48 G3 **Füzesgyarmat** Hungary
67 F3 **Fuzhou** Fujian China
67 E2 **Fuzhou** Jiangxi China
65 E5 **Fuzhoucheng** China
9 E4 **Fyfield** England
9 G4 **Fyfield** Essex England
28 E6 **Fyn** *isld* Denmark
28 E6 **Fyn** *co* Denmark
12 C1 **Fyne, L** Scotland
28 D7 **Fynshav** Denmark
28 F5 **Fynshoved** *C* Denmark
27 C12 **Fyresv** *L* Norway
127 O3 **Fyzabad** Trinidad

G

86 A2 **Gaalkacyo** Somalia
70 C4 **Gaat** *R* Sarawak
52 D4 **Gabanova** U.S.S.R.
123 M8 **Gabarouse** C Breton I, Nova Scotia
17 J3 **Gabarras, Mts** Spain
18 F9 **Gabarret** France
102 G3 **Gabbs** Nevada U.S.A.
102 F3 **Gabbs Valley Ra** Nevada U.S.A.
87 B8 **Gabela** Angola
Gaberones *see* **Gaborone**
85 F2 **Gabès** Tunisia
85 G2 **Gabès, Golfe de** Tunisia
84 J5 **Gabgaba, Wadi** *watercourse* Sudan
102 C5 **Gabilan Ra** California U.S.A.
31 M3 **Gabin** Poland
145 G3 **Gable End Foreland** New Zealand
117 K9 **Gable Mt** British Columbia Canada
139 J7 **Gabo** *isld* Victoria Australia
28 C6 **Gabøl** Denmark
86 B6 **Gabon** *rep* Equat Africa
89 D5 **Gaborone** Botswana
95 N2 **Gabriels** New York U.S.A.
16 C4 **Gabriel y Galán, Embalse** *res* Spain
77 F7 **Gābrik** Iran
46 G2 **Gabrovo** Bulgaria
85 B6 **Gabú** Guinea-Bissau
83 L14 **Gaby** *isld* Kerguelen Indian Oc
21 L4 **Gacé** France
77 B4 **Gach Sārān** Iran
20 F6 **Gacilly, la** France
98 G5 **Gackle** North Dakota U.S.A.
42 H5 **Gacko** Yugoslavia
85 B3 **Ga'da, Al** Western Sahara
76 B3 **Gadag** India
86 G2 **Gadamai** Sudan
28 C5 **Gadbjerg** Denmark
26 G7 **Gäddede** Sweden
32 J8 **Gadderbaum** W Germany
33 O5 **Gadebusch** East Germany
80 D3 **Gadish** Israel
17 F8 **Gador, Sierra de** Spain
80 F1 **Gadot** Israel
118 E6 **Gadsby** Alberta Canada
111 L8 **Gadsden** Alabama U.S.A.

Gadsden — Gesten

31

103 K9 **Gadsden** Arizona U.S.A.
28 J5 **Gadstrup** Denmark
76 C2 **Gadwal** India
54 F6 **Gadyach** U.S.S.R.
89 G2 **Gadzema** Zimbabwe
86 C5 **Gadzi** Cent Afr Republic
20 F5 **Gaël** France
48 J6 **Găeşti** Romania
43 F7 **Gaeta** Italy
45 P8 **Gaeta, Gulf of** Italy
112 F2 **Gaffney** South Carolina U.S.A.
71 A2 **Gafi** *isld* Indonesia
38 L6 **Gaflenz** Austria
85 F2 **Gafsa** Tunisia
57 H6 **Gafurov** U.S.S.R.
57 E4 **Gafurov** U.S.S.R.
71 B3 **Gag** *isld* Indonesia
54 F1 **Gagarin** U.S.S.R.
106 B9 **Gage** New Mexico U.S.A.
107 L5 **Gage** Oklahoma U.S.A.
122 H7 **Gage, C** Prince Edward I Canada
99 R4 **Gagen** Wisconsin U.S.A.
19 O15 **Gagère, P. de la** *mt* France
122 F8 **Gagetown** New Brunswick Canada
36 E6 **Gaggenau** W Germany
52 F6 **Gagino** U.S.S.R.
27 H11 **Gagnef** Sweden
85 C7 **Gagnoa** Ivory Coast
122 D2 **Gagnon** Quebec Canada
121 P6 **Gagnon, L** Quebec Canada
52 H4 **Gagshor** U.S.S.R.
66 F4 **Gahe** China
38 N6 **Gahns** *mt* Austria
89 A6 **Gaiab** *watercourse* Namibia
130 B5 **Gaiba** *L* Bolivia/Brazil
75 N6 **Gaibanda** Bangladesh
48 L4 **Găiceana** Romania
47 H10 **Gaïdhouronísi** *isld* Crete Greece
38 J8 **Gail** *R* Austria
36 H6 **Gaildorf** W Germany
18 G9 **Gaillac** France
122 E1 **Gaillarbois, L** Quebec Canada
21 O2 **Gaillefontaine** France
21 N3 **Gaillon** France
38 G8 **Gailtaler Alpen** *mts* Austria
133 D6 **Gaiman** Argentina
37 L6 **Gaimersheim** W Germany
94 B10 **Gainesboro** Tennessee U.S.A.
111 H9 **Gainesville** Alabama U.S.A.
113 E8 **Gainesville** Florida U.S.A.
109 K2 **Gainesville** Texas U.S.A.
13 G4 **Gainford** England
119 Q9 **Gainsborough** Saskatchewan Canada
13 H6 **Gainsborough** England
47 P13 **Gáïos** Greece
138 D4 **Gairdner Lake** South Australia Australia
15 C3 **Gairloch** Scotland
15 C4 **Gairlochy** Scotland
15 E3 **Gairn** *R* Scotland
38 L7 **Gaishorn** Austria
95 K7 **Gaithersburg** Maryland U.S.A.
65 E4 **Gai Xian** China
70 P9 **Gajam** Indonesia
76 B3 **Gajendragara** India
89 C6 **Gakarosa** *mt* S Africa
116 P5 **Gakona** Alaska U.S.A.
52 E4 **Gakugsa** U.S.S.R.
66 D6 **Gala** China
15 F5 **Gala** *R* Scotland
57 C5 **Galaasiya** U.S.S.R.
77 H2 **GāLā, Band-i-** *mts* Afghanistan
83 K10 **Galagedera** Sri Lanka
118 F6 **Galahad** Alberta Canada
79 B9 **Galâla el Baharîya, G. el** *mts* Egypt
79 C10 **Galâla el Qiblîya, G. el** *mts* Egypt
17 G4 **Galamocha** Spain
88 G3 **Galana** *R* Kenya
69 G12 **Galang Besar** *isld* Indonesia
26 N3 **Galanito** Norway
48 D2 **Galanta** Czechoslovakia
128 A7 **Galapagos Is** Pacific Oc
13 F2 **Galashiels** Scotland
101 O1 **Galata** Montana U.S.A.
46 F7 **Galatás** Greece
145 F3 **Galatea** New Zealand
106 G3 **Galatea** Colorado U.S.A.
137 R8 **Galathea Depth** Pacific Oc
48 L5 **Galati** Romania
110 H4 **Galatia** Illinois U.S.A.
107 M3 **Galatia** Kansas U.S.A.
43 J8 **Galatina** Italy
Galatz *see* **Galati**
19 O14 **Galaure** *R* France
94 G10 **Galax** Virginia U.S.A.
46 E6 **Galaxidhion** Greece
47 N10 **Galaza Burun** *C* Turkey
141 F3 **Galbraith** Queensland Australia
124 J5 **Gal. Cepeda** Mexico
26 C10 **Galdhöpiggen** *mt* Norway
124 F2 **Galeana** Mexico
130 G8 **Galeào** Brazil
45 L4 **Galeata** Italy
77 C6 **Galeh Dār** Iran
71 A2 **Galela** Indonesia
116 J4 **Galena** Alaska U.S.A.
99 Q7 **Galena** Illinois U.S.A.
107 Q4 **Galena** Kansas U.S.A.
95 M7 **Galena** Maryland U.S.A.
110 C5 **Galena** Missouri U.S.A.
109 G9 **Galena Park** Texas U.S.A.
33 T5 **Galenbecker See** *L* East Germany
127 P3 **Galeota Pt** Trinidad
17 F7 **Galera** Spain
128 B3 **Galera, Pta** *pt* Ecuador
131 A8 **Galera, Pta. de la** Chile
99 Q9 **Galesburg** Illinois U.S.A.
94 B4 **Galesburg** Michigan U.S.A.
99 P5 **Galesville** Wisconsin U.S.A.
120 K1 **Galeton** Ontario Canada
98 B9 **Galeton** Colorado U.S.A.
94 K5 **Galeton** Pennsylvania U.S.A.
83 J13 **Galets, Pte des** Réunion Indian Oc
13 F6 **Galgate** England
83 K10 **Galgiriya** *mt* Sri Lanka
117 M11 **Galiano I** British Columbia Canada
19 Q14 **Galibier, Col du** *pass* France
100 B7 **Galice** Oregon U.S.A.
48 J1 **Galich** U.S.S.R.
46 F1 **Galiche** Bulgaria
52 F5 **Galichskoye, Oz** *L* U.S.S.R.
16 B2 **Galicia** Spain
99 U8 **Galien** Michigan U.S.A.
141 H5 **Galilee, L** Queensland Australia
80 F2 **Galilee, Sea of** Israel
127 L2 **Galina Pt** Jamaica
94 E6 **Galion** Ohio U.S.A.
127 M4 **Galion, Baie du** Martinique W Indies
123 O2 **Galissonnière, L.la** Quebec Canada
43 C11 **Galite, La** Tunisia
103 O9 **Galiurov Mts** Arizona U.S.A.
140 D1 **Galiwinku** N Terr Australia
55 D3 **Galkino** U.S.S.R.
86 G3 **Gallabat** Sudan
42 B3 **Gallarate** Italy
21 O4 **Gallardon** France
99 N10 **Gallatin** Missouri U.S.A.
101 O4 **Gallatin** *R* Montana U.S.A.
110 K5 **Gallatin** Tennessee U.S.A.
109 M4 **Gallatin** Texas U.S.A.
101 O4 **Gallatin Gateway** Montana U.S.A.
101 O4 **Gallatin Pk** Montana U.S.A.
101 P4 **Gallatin Ra** Mont/Wyoming U.S.A.
83 K11 **Galle** Sri Lanka
17 G3 **Gállego** *R* Spain
133 C8 **Gallegos** *R* Argentina
106 G6 **Gallegos** New Mexico U.S.A.
45 J4 **Galleno** Italy
123 O2 **Gallet** *L* Quebec Canada
14 C5 **Galley Hd** Ireland
45 J3 **Gallicano** Italy
45 N6 **Gallicano nel Lazio** Italy
46 F4 **Gallikós** *R* Greece
33 Q5 **Gallin** East Germany
106 D5 **Gallina Pk** New Mexico U.S.A.
44 D3 **Gallinara** *isld* Italy
108 B1 **Gallinas Peak** New Mexico U.S.A.
128 D1 **Gallinas, Pta** *C* Colombia
43 H8 **Gallipoli** Italy
Gallipoli Turkey *see* **Gelibolu**
94 E8 **Gallipolis** Ohio U.S.A.
94 J6 **Gallitzin** Pennsylvania U.S.A.
26 L4 **Gällivare** Sweden
45 Q7 **Gallo** Italy
17 F4 **Gallo** *R* Spain
26 H9 **Gällö** Sweden
43 E10 **Gallo, C** Sicily
17 F4 **Gallocanta, L.de** Spain
41 M5 **Gallo, Lago di** Italy
106 B8 **Gallo Mts** New Mexico U.S.A.
95 L3 **Galloo I** New York U.S.A.
7 M11 **Galloper Lightship** North Sea
15 D6 **Galloway** Scotland
27 F14 **Gällstad** Sweden
106 B6 **Gallup** New Mexico U.S.A.
17 G3 **Gallur** Spain
45 K4 **Galluzzo** Italy
85 F6 **Galmi** Niger
139 J5 **Galong** New South Wales Australia
83 L10 **Gal Oya** *R* Sri Lanka
83 K9 **Galoya** Sri Lanka
83 L10 **Gal Oya Nat. Park** Sri Lanka
124 H5 **Gal. Simon Bolivar** Mexico
28 C6 **Galsted** Denmark
12 D2 **Galston** Scotland
26 J9 **Galström** Sweden
102 C3 **Galt** California U.S.A.
99 N9 **Galt** Missouri U.S.A.
85 B3 **Galtat Zemmour** Western Sahara
28 D4 **Galten** Denmark
26 N1 **Galten** Norway
124 F3 **Gal. Trias** Mexico
41 M4 **Galtür** Austria
14 C4 **Galtymore** *mt* Ireland
99 R8 **Galva** Illinois U.S.A.
94 A6 **Galveston** Indiana U.S.A.
111 B12 **Galveston** Texas U.S.A.
131 E4 **Galvez** Argentina
14 B3 **Galway** *co* Ireland
14 B3 **Galway** Ireland
14 B3 **Galway Bay** Ireland
71 B3 **Gam** *isld* Indonesia
71 C3 **Gam** *isld* W Irian
21 O2 **Gamaches** France
61 L11 **Gamagōri** Japan
131 E8 **Gama, I** Argentina
94 B10 **Gamaliel** Kentucky U.S.A.
71 G4 **Gamay Bay** Philippines
75 N4 **Gamba** China
85 D6 **Gambaga** Ghana
21 O4 **Gambais** France
45 J4 **Gambassi Terme** Italy
45 R6 **Gambatesa** Italy
86 F4 **Gambēla** Ethiopia
116 B5 **Gambell** St Lawrence I, Alaska U.S.A.
45 M3 **Gambettola** Italy
85 A6 **Gambia** *R* The Gambia/Senegal
85 A6 **Gambia, The** *rep* W Africa
94 E6 **Gambier** Ohio U.S.A.
140 B1 **Gambier, C** N Terr Australia
138 D6 **Gambier Is** South Australia Australia
135 R15 **Gambier Is** Pacific Oc
113 L9 **Gambier Village** New Providence I Bahamas
124 F9 **Gamboa** Panama
86 C6 **Gamboma** Congo
141 G3 **Gamboola** Queensland Australia
86 C5 **Gamboula** Cent Afr Republic
71 H4 **Gambuta** *mt* Sulawesi
Gamcaka *see* **Lelai**
130 J10 **Gameleira** Brazil
71 A2 **Gamkunoro Gunung** *mt* Indonesia
71 A2 **Gamlaba** Indonesia
27 H14 **Gamleby** Sweden
26 M6 **Gammelstad** Sweden
36 G7 **Gammertingen** W Germany
16 D4 **Gamo** *R* Spain
86 G4 **Gamo-Gofa** *prov* Ethiopia
83 K10 **Gampola** Sri Lanka
77 G5 **Gamshadzai K** *mts* Iran
66 F5 **Gamtog** China
26 Q1 **Gamvik** Norway
18 E9 **Gan** France
73 L9 **Gan** Maldives
37 O6 **Ganacker** W Germany
103 P6 **Ganado** Arizona U.S.A.
109 L6 **Ganado** Texas U.S.A.
121 O8 **Gananoque** Ontario Canada
67 C7 **Gancheng** China
Gand *see* **Gent**
87 B8 **Ganda** Angola
70 F6 **Gandadiwata G** *mt* Sulawesi
87 D7 **Gandajika** Zaire
74 B4 **Gandava** Pakistan
123 S5 **Gander** Newfoundland Canada
123 S4 **Gander Bay** Newfoundland Canada
32 J6 **Ganderkesee** W Germany
123 R5 **Gander R** Newfoundland Canada
17 H3 **Gandesa** Spain
74 D7 **Gāndhīdhām** India
74 F6 **Gāndhi Sāgar** *L* India
17 G6 **Gandia** Spain
28 E2 **Gandrup** Denmark
103 L2 **Gandy** Utah U.S.A.
77 B5 **Ganēveh** Iran
83 K10 **Ganewatta** Sri Lanka
74 H5 **Gangā** *R* India
74 G9 **Gangakher** India
Gangā, Mouths of the *see* **Ganges, Mouths of the**
133 D6 **Gan Gan** Argentina
74 E4 **Ganganagar** India
68 B1 **Gangaw** Burma
76 C3 **Gangawati** India
75 R6 **Gangaw Range** Burma
66 C5 **Gangdisê Shan** *mt ra* China
25 F7 **Gangelt** W Germany
Ganges *R* *see* **Gangā** *R*
18 H9 **Ganges** France
75 N8 **Ganges, Mouths of the** Bangladesh/India
27 F14 **Gånghester** Sweden
37 O7 **Gangkofen** W Germany
65 F4 **Gangou** China
75 N5 **Gangtok** India
65 A6 **Ganguyi** China
67 E3 **Gan Jiang** *R* China
Ganjig *see* **Horqin Zuoyi Houqi**
139 H5 **Ganmam** New South Wales Australia
18 H6 **Gannat** France
6 L5 **Gannet** *oil rig* North Sea
145 E2 **Gannet I** New Zealand
101 L6 **Gannett** Idaho U.S.A.
101 Q6 **Gannett Pk** Wyoming U.S.A.
80 C5 **Ganne Yehuda** Israel
98 G5 **Gannvalley** South Dakota U.S.A.
80 C6 **Gan Shelomo** Israel
58 C3 **Gansu** *prov* China
85 C7 **Ganta** Liberia
Gantang *see* **Taiping**
143 A8 **Gantheaume B** Western Australia Australia
138 E6 **Gantheaume, C** South Australia Australia
142 D4 **Gantheaume Pt** Western Australia Australia
69 J14 **Gantung** Indonesia
67 E4 **Gan Xian** China
58 E4 **Ganyanchi** China
80 B6 **Gan Yavne** Israel
87 D11 **Ganyesa** S Africa
65 D7 **Ganyu** China
65 D4 **Ganzhao** China
Ganzhe *see* **Minhou**
67 E4 **Ganzhou** China
33 Q6 **Ganzlin** East Germany
85 D5 **Gao** Mali
67 E2 **Gao'an** China
Gaobeidian *see* **Xincheng**
65 C5 **Gaocheng** China
67 F1 **Gaochun** China
Gaocun *see* **Mayang**
65 B5 **Gaocun** China
67 D5 **Gaohe** China
67 E1 **Gaohebu** China
65 A5 **Gaojiabu** China
65 A7 **Gaoling** China
67 B4 **Gaolou Ling** *mt* China
65 D6 **Gaomi** China
67 E4 **Gaopi** China
65 B7 **Gaoping** China
65 D6 **Gaoqing** China
67 C3 **Gaosha** China
65 B4 **Gaoshan** China
65 E3 **Gaotaishan** China
65 C6 **Gaotang** China
85 D6 **Gaoua** Burkina
85 B6 **Gaoual** Guinea
67 A2 **Gao Xian** China
65 C7 **Gaoxianji** China
Gaoya *see* **Zhaoqing**
58 G4 **Gaoyang** China
65 C6 **Gaoyi** China
59 G5 **Gaoyou** China
59 G5 **Gaoyou Hu** *L* China
67 C6 **Gaozhou** China
19 Q15 **Gap** France
71 E3 **Gapan** Luzon Philippines
19 P18 **Gapeau** *R* France
66 C5 **Gar** China
85 F3 **Gara Brune** Algeria
86 A2 **Garadag** Somalia
43 C11 **Garaet Ichkeul** *L* Tunisia
139 J3 **Garah** New South Wales Australia
47 H1 **Gara Khitrino** Bulgaria
14 C3 **Gara, L** Ireland
130 H10 **Garanhuns** Brazil
71 H9 **Garantah** Indonesia
130 F5 **Garapuava** Brazil
86 D4 **Garba** Cent Afr Republic
107 N5 **Garber** Oklahoma U.S.A.
100 B9 **Garberville** California U.S.A.
9 G3 **Garboldisham** England
130 E8 **Garça** Brazil
130 D4 **Garças** *R* Brazil
37 M7 **Garching** W Germany
106 E4 **Garcia** Colorado U.S.A.
16 D5 **Garcia de Sola, Embalse de** *res* Spain
130 D7 **Garcias** Brazil
18 H9 **Gard** *R* France
18 H8 **Gard** *dept* France
41 N6 **Garda, Lago di** Italy
19 O18 **Gardanne** France
98 J1 **Gardar** North Dakota U.S.A.
27 J15 **Gårdby** Sweden
33 O7 **Gardelegen** East Germany
99 U4 **Garden** Michigan U.S.A.
100 J6 **Gardena** Idaho U.S.A.
98 F1 **Gardena** North Dakota U.S.A.
111 K7 **Garden City** Alabama U.S.A.
107 K4 **Garden City** Kansas U.S.A.
110 B3 **Garden City** Missouri U.S.A.
112 F5 **Garden City** South Carolina U.S.A.
98 J5 **Garden City** South Dakota U.S.A.
108 F4 **Garden City** Texas U.S.A.
101 O8 **Garden City** Utah U.S.A.
109 H7 **Gardendale** Texas U.S.A.
102 G8 **Garden Grove** California U.S.A.
99 N9 **Garden Grove** Iowa U.S.A.
142 A3 **Garden I** Western Australia Australia
143 B9 **Garden I** Western Australia Australia
99 V4 **Garden I** Michigan U.S.A.
111 G12 **Garden I Bay** Louisiana U.S.A.
140 B1 **Garden Point** N Terr Australia
119 V9 **Gardenton** Manitoba Canada
100 K5 **Garden Valley** Idaho U.S.A.
77 L3 **Gardēz** Afghanistan
120 J3 **Gardiner** Ontario Canada
95 S2 **Gardiner** Maine U.S.A.
101 P4 **Gardiner** Montana U.S.A.
106 F5 **Gardiner** New Mexico U.S.A.
100 A6 **Gardiner** Oregon U.S.A.
118 L7 **Gardiner Dam** Saskatchewan Canada
140 C5 **Gardiner, Mt** N Terr Australia
142 G4 **Gardiner Ra** Australia
95 P5 **Gardiners I** New York U.S.A.
140 B6 **Gardiner's Range** N Terr Australia
32 J4 **Garding** W Germany
106 E4 **Gardner** Colorado U.S.A.
113 F10 **Gardner** Florida U.S.A.
99 S8 **Gardner** Illinois U.S.A.
95 P4 **Gardner** Massachusetts U.S.A.
95 U2 **Gardner L** Maine U.S.A.
102 E3 **Gardnerville** Nevada U.S.A.
31 K1 **Gardno, Jezioro** *L* Poland
27 G13 **Gårdsjö** Sweden
26 H6 **Gardsjönas** Sweden
27 J15 **Gärdslösa** Sweden
Gardula *see* **Gīdolē**
12 D1 **Gare L** Scotland
12 D1 **Garelochhead** Scotland
42 H3 **Garešnica** Yugoslavia
44 D3 **Garessio** Italy
85 F3 **Garet el Djenoun** *mt* Algeria
45 H3 **Garfagnane** *R* Italy
110 C5 **Garfield** Arkansas U.S.A.
112 E5 **Garfield** Georgia U.S.A.
107 L3 **Garfield** Kansas U.S.A.
101 N9 **Garfield** Utah U.S.A.
100 H2 **Garfield** Washington U.S.A.
101 N5 **Garfield Mt** Idaho/Montana U.S.A.
46 E7 **Gargaliánoi** Greece
16 D5 **Gargáligas** *R* Spain
42 G7 **Gargano, Promontorio del** *prom* Italy
120 E5 **Gargantua, C** Ontario Canada
26 N2 **Gargia** Norway
41 N6 **Gargnano** Italy
26 J6 **Gargnäs** Sweden
13 F6 **Gargrave** England
12 D1 **Gargunnock** Scotland
52 B6 **Gargždai** U.S.S.R.
74 H7 **Garhakota** India
55 D2 **Gari** U.S.S.R.
100 B4 **Garibaldi** Oregon U.S.A.
117 M11 **Garibaldi Prov. Park** British Columbia Canada
43 F7 **Garigliano** *R* Italy
15 F3 **Garioch** Scotland
88 G2 **Garissa** Kenya
119 R7 **Garland** Manitoba Canada
107 Q4 **Garland** Kansas U.S.A.
98 K9 **Garland** Nebraska U.S.A.
112 J3 **Garland** North Carolina U.S.A.
94 H5 **Garland** Pennsylvania U.S.A.
109 O9 **Garland** Texas U.S.A.
101 N8 **Garland** Utah U.S.A.
101 R5 **Garland** Wyoming U.S.A.
44 E1 **Garlasco** Italy
12 D4 **Garlieston** Scotland
18 E9 **Garlin** France
111 K10 **Garlrand** Alabama U.S.A.
32 M6 **Garlstorf** W Germany
57 F5 **Garm** U.S.S.R.
41 O3 **Garmisch-Partenkirchen** W Germany
77 H4 **Garmsel** *reg* Afghanistan
20 G8 **Garnache, la** France
99 P7 **Garnavillo** Iowa U.S.A.
122 J2 **Garneau, R** Quebec Canada
101 Q3 **Garneill** Montana U.S.A.
99 N6 **Garner** Iowa U.S.A.
112 J2 **Garner** North Carolina U.S.A.
118 E4 **Garner Lake Prov. Park** *pk* Alberta Canada
101 M3 **Garnet** Montana U.S.A.
115 M4 **Garnet Bay** Northwest Territories Canada
107 P3 **Garnett** Kansas U.S.A.
18 F9 **Garonne** *R* France
130 E11 **Garopaba** Brazil
74 F6 **Garoth** India
86 B4 **Garoua** Cameroon
86 B4 **Garoua Boulai** Cameroon
119 V3 **Garraway** Manitoba Canada
32 H7 **Garrel** W Germany
98 K6 **Garretson** South Dakota U.S.A.
94 B5 **Garrett** Indiana U.S.A.
94 H7 **Garrett** Pennsylvania U.S.A.
101 U7 **Garrett** Wyoming U.S.A.
94 F5 **Garrettsville** Ohio U.S.A.
119 N5 **Garrick** Saskatchewan Canada
99 O7 **Garrison** Iowa U.S.A.
94 D8 **Garrison** Kentucky U.S.A.
99 N3 **Garrison** Minnesota U.S.A.
101 N3 **Garrison** Montana U.S.A.
95 O5 **Garrison** New York U.S.A.
98 E2 **Garrison** North Dakota U.S.A.
109 N4 **Garrison** Texas U.S.A.
103 L3 **Garrison** Utah U.S.A.
98 E2 **Garrison Dam** North Dakota U.S.A.
16 C5 **Garrovillas** Spain
15 D4 **Garry** *L* Scotland
115 K4 **Garry L** Northwest Territories Canada
101 S4 **Garryowen** Montana U.S.A.
88 H3 **Garsen** Kenya
28 D5 **Gårslev** Denmark
27 G16 **Gärsnäs** Sweden
118 G2 **Garson L** Alberta Canada
32 M7 **Garssen** W Germany
38 F7 **Garsstein** *mt* Austria
13 F6 **Garstang** England
13 F6 **Garston** England
144 B6 **Garston** New Zealand
18 F6 **Gartempe** *R* France
8 C3 **Garth** Wales
8 C2 **Garthmyl** Wales
Gartok *see* **Garyarsa**
33 O6 **Gartow** W Germany
31 H2 **Gartz** East Germany
70 M9 **Garut** Java
13 F2 **Garvald** Scotland
15 D3 **Garve** Scotland
144 B6 **Garvie Mts** New Zealand
31 N4 **Garwolin** Poland
100 J2 **Garwood** Idaho U.S.A.
109 L6 **Garwood** Texas U.S.A.
98 C9 **Gary** Colorado U.S.A.
99 T8 **Gary** Indiana U.S.A.
98 K2 **Gary** Minnesota U.S.A.
98 K5 **Gary** South Dakota U.S.A.
109 N3 **Gary** Texas U.S.A.
94 F9 **Gary** West Virginia U.S.A.
66 C5 **Garyarsa** China
60 F11 **Garyū zan** *mt* Japan
33 Q6 **Garz** East Germany
58 C5 **Garzê** China
128 C3 **Garzón** Colombia
50 E5 **Gasan-Kuli** U.S.S.R.
33 Q10 **Gaschwitz** East Germany
45 J4 **Gasciana Terme** Italy
94 B6 **Gas City** Indiana U.S.A.
18 E9 **Gascogne** *prov* France
18 D8 **Gascogne, G. de** France/Spain
110 E3 **Gasconade** *R* Missouri U.S.A.
122 H5 **Gascons** Quebec Canada
98 C3 **Gascoyne** North Dakota U.S.A.
143 B7 **Gascoyne Junction** Western Australia Australia
143 B6 **Gascoyne, Mt** Western Australia Australia
143 A6 **Gascoyne, R** Western Australia Australia
Gascuña, Golfo de *see* **Gascogne, G.de**
86 G2 **Gash** *R* Ethiopia
85 G7 **Gashaka** Nigeria
74 G1 **Gasherbrum** *mt* Kashmir
85 G6 **Gashua** Nigeria
Gashuun Nuur *L* *see* **Gaxun Nur**
26 H4 **Gaskacok** *mt* Norway
21 O3 **Gasny** France
126 E4 **Gaspar** Cuba
127 J5 **Gaspar Hernández** Dominican Rep
113 E11 **Gasparilla** *isld* Florida U.S.A.
69 H14 **Gaspar, Selat** *str* Indonesia
122 H5 **Gaspé** Quebec Canada
122 H5 **Gaspé, B. de** Quebec Canada
122 H5 **Gaspé, C** Quebec Canada
122 F5 **Gaspé Pen** Quebec Canada
122 H9 **Gaspereau** *L* Nova Scotia Canada
122 G7 **Gaspereau Forks** New Brunswick Canada
122 F5 **Gaspesie, Parc de la** Quebec Canada
100 B8 **Gasquet** California U.S.A.
61 O7 **Gassan** *mt* Japan
94 G8 **Gassaway** West Virginia U.S.A.
25 G3 **Gasselte** Netherlands
85 F2 **Gassi, El** Algeria
40 G7 **Gassino Tor** Italy
44 C1 **Gassino Torinese** Italy
85 G7 **Gassol** Nigeria
103 J5 **Gass Pk** Nevada U.S.A.
28 E3 **Gassum** Denmark
38 H7 **Gasteiner Tal** Austria
100 B4 **Gaston** Oregon U.S.A.
112 F2 **Gastonia** North Carolina U.S.A.
94 J10 **Gaston, L** Virginia U.S.A.
47 O12 **Gastoúri** Greece
133 D6 **Gastre** Argentina
17 F8 **Gata, C.de** Spain
117 K6 **Gataga** *R* British Columbia Canada
48 G5 **Gătaia** Romania
16 C4 **Gata, Sa. de** *mts* Spain
52 D5 **Gatchina** U.S.S.R.
108 D7 **Gate** Oklahoma U.S.A.
94 E10 **Gate City** Virginia U.S.A.
12 D4 **Gatehouse of Fleet** Scotland
100 C5 **Gates** Oregon U.S.A.
13 G4 **Gateshead** England
116 L3 **Gates of the Arctic Nat Park and Preserve** Alaska U.S.A.
101 O3 **Gates of the Mts** *pass* Montana U.S.A.
112 L1 **Gatesville** North Carolina U.S.A.
109 K4 **Gatesville** Texas U.S.A.
106 B3 **Gateway** Colorado U.S.A.
100 K1 **Gateway** Montana U.S.A.
100 D5 **Gateway** Oregon U.S.A.
21 L7 **Gâtine** *reg* France
121 P7 **Gatineau** Quebec Canada
121 P5 **Gatineau** *R* Quebec Canada
21 J8 **Gâtine Hauteurs de** *hills* France
112 D2 **Gatlinburg** Tennessee U.S.A.
80 D1 **Ga'ton** Israel
Gatooma *see* **Kadoma**
33 S8 **Gatow** East Germany
61 N7 **Gatsugi** Japan
20 H2 **Gatteville** France
41 H6 **Gattinara** Italy
141 K8 **Gatton** Queensland Australia
124 E9 **Gatun** Panama
125 O5 **Gatún L** Panama
9 F5 **Gatwick Airport** England
36 E4 **Gau-Algesheim** W Germany
21 H8 **Gaubretière, la** France
16 D8 **Gaucin** Spain
16 D6 **Gaudalmellato** *R* Spain
77 H5 **Gaud-I-Zirreh** *salt desert* Afghanistan
123 K3 **Gaudreault, L** Quebec Canada
119 U1 **Gauer** *L* Manitoba Canada
Gauhati *see* **Guwahati**
26 E9 **Gauldalen** *R* Norway
94 F8 **Gauley Bridge** West Virginia U.S.A.
21 M5 **Gault, le** France
123 R6 **Gaultois** Newfoundland Canada
21 N5 **Gault-St.Denis, le** France
69 F13 **Gaung** Sumatra
36 E4 **Gau-Odernheim** W Germany
66 D6 **Gaur Sankar** *mt* Nepal/China
27 D10 **Gausdal, Ö** Norway
27 D10 **Gausdal, V** Norway
27 C12 **Gausta** *mt* Norway
77 G7 **Gavater** Iran
77 C6 **Gavbandi** Iran
77 C6 **Gavbus Kūh-e** *mt* Iran
46 F10 **Gavdhopoúla** *isld* Greece
46 G10 **Gávdhos** *isld* Crete Greece
18 E9 **Gave de Pau** *R* France
130 H4 **Gavião, R** Brazil
106 C5 **Gavilan** New Mexico U.S.A.
102 D7 **Gaviota** California U.S.A.
77 E5 **Gāv Koshī** Iran
27 J11 **Gävle** Sweden
27 J11 **Gävlebukten** *B* Sweden
20 H4 **Gavray** France
20 G6 **Gavre, le** France
52 E6 **Gavrilov Yam** U.S.S.R.
52 F5 **Gavrino** U.S.S.R.
46 G7 **Gávrion** Greece
74 G8 **Gawilgarh** India
138 E5 **Gawler** South Australia Australia
138 D4 **Gawler Ranges** South Australia Australia
26 H8 **Gåxsjö** Sweden
58 D3 **Gaxun Nur** *L* China
99 S2 **Gay** Michigan U.S.A.
75 L6 **Gaya** India
85 E6 **Gaya** Niger
85 F6 **Gaya** Nigeria
17 H3 **Gaya** *R* Spain
65 H3 **Gaya He** *R* China
70 F2 **Gaya, Pulau** *isld* Sabah
9 E3 **Gaydon** England
107 M2 **Gaylord** Kansas U.S.A.
94 C1 **Gaylord** Michigan U.S.A.
99 M5 **Gaylord** Minnesota U.S.A.
100 A7 **Gaylord** Oregon U.S.A.
141 K7 **Gayndah** Queensland Australia
52 H4 **Gayny** U.S.S.R.
48 M2 **Gaysin** U.S.S.R.
99 Q6 **Gays Mills** Wisconsin U.S.A.
52 E5 **Gayutino** U.S.S.R.
98 J7 **Gayville** South Dakota U.S.A.
48 M2 **Gayvoron** U.S.S.R.
79 E7 **Gaza** Egypt
85 F6 **Gazaoua** Niger
80 A7 **Gaza Strip** Israel
100 C8 **Gazelle** California U.S.A.
21 O4 **Gazeran** France
57 D4 **Gazgan** U.S.S.R.
78 F3 **Gaziantep** Turkey
78 D3 **Gazipaşa** Turkey
57 C4 **Gazli** U.S.S.R.
45 J1 **Gazoldo degli Ippoliti** Italy
45 K1 **Gazzo Veronese** Italy
45 J1 **Gazzuolo** Italy
85 C7 **Gbanga** Liberia
85 F7 **Gboko** Nigeria
31 L1 **Gdańsk** Poland
52 C5 **Gdov** U.S.S.R.
31 L1 **Gdynia** Poland
80 B7 **Ge'a** Israel
100 B3 **Gearhart** Oregon U.S.A.
100 E7 **Gearhart Mt** Oregon U.S.A.
107 M6 **Geary** Oklahoma U.S.A.
71 B3 **Gebe** *isld* Indonesia
37 K1 **Gebesee** East Germany
47 N11 **Gebze** Turkey
86 G3 **Gedaref** Sudan
141 F3 **Geddes** *R* Queensland Australia
98 H6 **Geddes** South Dakota U.S.A.
9 F3 **Geddington** England
36 G3 **Gedern** W Germany
28 H7 **Gedesby** Denmark
70 L9 **Gede, Tg** *C* Java
28 C4 **Gedhus** Denmark
22 H4 **Gedinne** Belgium
47 J6 **Gediz** *R* Turkey
47 K5 **Gediz** Turkey
86 H4 **Gedlegubē** Ethiopia
Gedong *see* **Fangshan**
70 B4 **Gedong** Sarawak
28 H7 **Gedser** Denmark
28 C3 **Gedsted** Denmark
70 K8 **Gedungpakuan** Sumatra
142 E4 **Geegully Ck** Western Australia Australia
22 H1 **Geel** Belgium
139 G7 **Geelong** Victoria Australia
143 A8 **Geelvink Chan** Western Australia Australia
89 A7 **Geel Vloer** S Africa
110 D6 **Geers Ferry L** Arkansas U.S.A.
25 C5 **Geertruidenberg** Netherlands
32 J5 **Geestekanal** W Germany
32 J5 **Geestenseth** W Germany
33 M6 **Geesthacht** W Germany
22 J2 **Geetbets** Belgium
139 H9 **Geeveston** Tasmania Australia
37 M3 **Gefell** East Germany
80 C7 **Gefen** Israel
37 M3 **Gefrees** W Germany
65 E2 **Gegenmiao** China
65 D5 **Gegu** China
65 G7 **Gehaku** *lighthouse* S Korea
36 G2 **Gehau** W Germany
21 N7 **Gehée** France
32 L8 **Gehrden** W Germany
67 F1 **Ge Hu** *L* China
85 G6 **Geidam** Nigeria
41 P3 **Geierspitze** *mt* Austria
120 B2 **Geikie I** Ontario Canada
141 G2 **Geikie Ra** Queensland Australia
25 F7 **Geilenkirchen** W Germany
27 C11 **Geilo** Norway
33 R5 **Geilow** East Germany
36 E5 **Geinsheim** W Germany
26 B9 **Geiranger** Norway
37 N6 **Geiselhöring** W Germany
37 J4 **Geiselwind** W Germany
37 M6 **Geisenfeld** W Germany
37 N7 **Geisenhausen** W Germany
36 D3 **Geisenheim** W Germany
41 J2 **Geisingen** W Germany
36 F7 **Geislingen** W Germany
36 H6 **Geislingen an der Steige** W Germany
37 J1 **Geismar** East Germany
36 D6 **Geispolsheim** France
88 D3 **Geita** Tanzania
37 O1 **Geithain** East Germany
27 D12 **Geithus** Norway
73 R5 **Gejiu** China
43 F11 **Gela** *R* Sicily
43 F11 **Gela** Sicily
86 J4 **Geladī** Ethiopia
88 F3 **Gelai** *mt* Tanzania
33 Q4 **Gelbensande** East Germany
37 J4 **Gelchsheim** W Germany
25 F3 **Gelderingen** Netherlands
25 F4 **Gelderland** Netherlands
25 D5 **Geldermalsen** Netherlands
25 F5 **Geldern** W Germany
25 E6 **Geldrop** Netherlands
47 J5 **Gelembe** Turkey
37 O2 **Gelenau** East Germany
121 M8 **Gelert** Ontario Canada
47 H4 **Gelibolu** Turkey
78 D1 **Gelicek** Turkey
79 H1 **Gelinbuğday** Turkey
22 J2 **Gelinden** Belgium
67 F4 **Geling** China
86 J4 **Gelinsoor** Somalia
71 L9 **Gelinting** Flores Indonesia
36 G3 **Gelnhausen** W Germany
28 C6 **Gelså** *R* Denmark
Gelsdorf *see* **Grafschaft**
32 F9 **Gelsenkirchen** W Germany
28 D6 **Gelsted** Denmark
28 D7 **Gelting** W Germany
69 G14 **Gelumbang** Sumatra
118 E8 **Gem** Alberta Canada
107 K2 **Gem** Kansas U.S.A.
69 F11 **Gemas** Malaysia
22 H2 **Gembloux** Belgium
32 E9 **Gemen** W Germany
86 C5 **Gemena** Zaire
19 P18 **Gémenos** France
78 F2 **Gemerek** Turkey
86 H3 **Gemerī Hāyk'** *L* Ethiopia
25 E5 **Gemert** Netherlands
47 K4 **Gemlik Körfezi** *B* Turkey
22 K2 **Gemmenich** Belgium
36 F5 **Gemmingen** W Germany
42 E2 **Gemona del Friuli** Italy
18 E7 **Gémozac** France
84 J4 **Gemsa** Egypt
89 B5 **Gemsbok Nat. Park** Botswana
36 B2 **Gemünd** W Germany
36 H3 **Gemünden** Bayern W Germany
36 F2 **Gemünden** Hessen W Germany
36 D4 **Gemünden** Rheinland-Pfalz W Germany
70 E7 **Gemuru** Kalimantan
86 H4 **Genalē** *R* Ethiopia
22 G2 **Genappe** Belgium
27 F16 **Genarp** Sweden
45 N6 **Genazzano** Italy
78 H2 **Genç** Turkey
18 F6 **Gençay** France
25 F5 **Gendringen** Netherlands
107 N7 **Gene Autry** Oklahoma U.S.A.
86 D3 **Geneina** Sudan
25 F3 **Genemuiden** Netherlands
133 E5 **General Acha** Argentina
133 E5 **General Alvear** Argentina
131 C5 **General Alvear** Mendoza Argentina
130 C9 **General Aquvino** Paraguay
133 E4 **General Arenales** Argentina
130 C10 **General Artigas** Paraguay
146 E6 **General Belgrano** *Arg Base* Antarctica
146 D3 **General Bernardo O'Higgins** *Chile Base* Graham Land Antarctica
130 D4 **General Caneiro** Brazil
133 E3 **General Capdevila** Argentina
102 F5 **General Grant Grove Sctn** California U.S.A.
133 F5 **General Guido** Argentina
17 G5 **Generalisimo, Emb. de** Spain
133 F3 **General José de San Martin** Argentina
133 E5 **General La Madrid** Argentina
133 F5 **General Lavalle** Argentina
71 G6 **General Luna** Philippines
71 G5 **General MacArthur** Philippines
133 F5 **General Madariaga** Argentina
128 E8 **General Martin M. de Güemes** Argentina
130 B10 **General Paz** Argentina
133 C6 **General Paz, L** Argentina
146 C5 **General San Martin** *Arg Base* Antarctica
71 G7 **General Santos** Philippines
47 J1 **General Toshevo** Bulgaria
109 H9 **General Treviño** Mexico
133 E5 **General Viamonte** Argentina
100 J3 **Genesee** Idaho U.S.A.
94 D3 **Genesee** Michigan U.S.A.
94 K4 **Genesee** *R* New York U.S.A.
99 Q8 **Geneseo** Illinois U.S.A.
107 M3 **Geneseo** Kansas U.S.A.
94 K4 **Geneseo** New York U.S.A.
20 G7 **Geneston** France
20 H4 **Genêts** France
Geneva *see* **Genève**
111 L10 **Geneva** Alabama U.S.A.
111 M9 **Geneva** Georgia U.S.A.
94 C6 **Geneva** Indiana U.S.A.
98 J9 **Geneva** Nebraska U.S.A.
94 G5 **Geneva** Ohio U.S.A.
109 O4 **Geneva** Texas U.S.A.
Geneva, L *see* **Léman, Lac**
99 S7 **Geneva, L** Wisconsin U.S.A.
120 J6 **Geneva Lake Mine** Ontario Canada
40 D5 **Genève** Switzerland
36 E7 **Gengenbach** W Germany
68 D1 **Gengma** China
Genhe *see* **Ergun Zuoqi**
59 H1 **Gen He** *R* China
120 J3 **Genier** Ontario Canada
16 E7 **Genil** *R* Spain
21 N7 **Génillé** France
58 E4 **Genjiawan** China
22 K2 **Genk** Belgium
60 D12 **Genkai-nada** *sea* Japan
40 B3 **Genlis** France
25 E5 **Gennep** Netherlands
28 C6 **Genner** Denmark
21 K7 **Gennes** Maine-et-Loire France
21 J6 **Gennes** Mayenne France
21 H6 **Gennes-sur-Seiche** France
21 L6 **Genneteil** France
21 P4 **Gennevilliers** France
Genoa *see* **Genova**
139 J6 **Genoa** Victoria Australia
106 G2 **Genoa** Colorado U.S.A.
113 E7 **Genoa** Florida U.S.A.
99 S7 **Genoa** Illinois U.S.A.
98 J8 **Genoa** Nebraska U.S.A.
102 E2 **Genoa** Nevada U.S.A.
94 D5 **Genoa** Ohio U.S.A.
99 P6 **Genoa** Wisconsin U.S.A.
99 S7 **Genoa City** Wisconsin U.S.A.
101 O1 **Genou** Montana U.S.A.
21 O7 **Genouilly** Cher France
44 E3 **Genova** Italy
128 B7 **Genovesa** *isld* Galapagos Is
51 P1 **Genriyetty, Ostrov** *isld* U.S.S.R.
22 F1 **Gent** Belgium
70 P9 **Genteng** Indonesia
70 L9 **Genteng** Java
33 Q8 **Genthin** East Germany
111 K12 **Gentilly** New Orleans, Louisiana U.S.A.
69 H11 **Genting** *isld* Indonesia
118 B1 **Gent Lon** Manitoba Canada
29 K5 **Gentofte** Denmark
110 B5 **Gentry** Arkansas U.S.A.
99 M9 **Gentry** Missouri U.S.A.
45 N6 **Genzano di Roma** Italy
48 H5 **Geoagiu** Romania
143 B10 **Geographe B** Western Australia Australia
143 A6 **Geographe Chan** Western Australia Australia
107 M2 **Geographic Center of US** Kansas U.S.A.
22 H3 **Geopinnes** Belgium
138 D3 **George** *R* South Australia Australia
115 N6 **George** *R* Quebec Canada
83 M14 **George** *C* Kerguelen Indian Oc
89 C9 **George** S Africa
116 J5 **George** *R* Alaska U.S.A.
99 L6 **George** Iowa U.S.A.
123 L8 **George B** Nova Scotia Canada
140 B6 **George Gills Ra** N Terr Australia
139 J6 **George, L** New South Wales Australia
138 F6 **George, L** South Australia Australia
142 E5 **George, L** Western Australia Australia
99 W3 **George, L** Ontario Canada
88 C1 **George, L** Uganda
116 N6 **George, L** Alaska U.S.A.
113 F8 **George, L** Florida U.S.A.
37 L5 **Georgensgmünd** W Germany
37 K2 **Georgenthal** East Germany
90 C4 **Georges Bank** Atlantic Oc
144 A6 **George Sd** New Zealand
90 A11 **Georgetown** Ascension I
141 G4 **Georgetown** Queensland Australia
138 E5 **Georgetown** South Australia Australia
139 H8 **George Town** Tasmania Australia
122 K7 **Georgetown** Prince Edward I Canada
129 G2 **Georgetown** Guyana
69 E10 **Georgetown** Malaysia
144 C6 **Georgetown** New Zealand
127 O8 **Georgetown** St Vincent
85 B6 **Georgetown** The Gambia
110 E6 **Georgetown** Arkansas U.S.A.
102 D3 **Georgetown** California U.S.A.
95 M8 **Georgetown** Delaware U.S.A.
113 F8 **Georgetown** Florida U.S.A.
111 L10 **Georgetown** Georgia U.S.A.
101 O7 **Georgetown** Idaho U.S.A.
99 T10 **Georgetown** Illinois U.S.A.
94 C8 **Georgetown** Kentucky U.S.A.
111 F10 **Georgetown** Mississippi U.S.A.
94 D8 **Georgetown** Ohio U.S.A.
112 H4 **Georgetown** South Carolina U.S.A.
109 K5 **Georgetown** Texas U.S.A.
121 S7 **Georgeville** Quebec Canada
146 C6 **George VI Sound** Antarctica
146 D13 **George V Land** Antarctica
109 J7 **George West** Texas U.S.A.
112 C5 **Georgia** *state* U.S.A.
Georgia *S.S.R.* U.S.S.R. *see* **Gruzinskaya** *S.S.R.*
111 K10 **Georgiana** Alabama U.S.A.
120 J7 **Georgian B** Ontario Canada
117 L11 **Georgia, St. of** British Columbia Canada
140 E5 **Georgina** *R* N Terr Australia
140 E5 **Georgina** *R* N Terr/Queensland Australia
140 E5 **Georgina** *R* Queensland Australia
140 E4 **Georgina Cr** N Terr Australia
47 J2 **Georgi Traykov** Bulgaria
54 L6 **Georgiu-Dezh** U.S.S.R.
53 F11 **Georgiyevsk** U.S.S.R.
32 F7 **Georgsdorf** W Germany
32 F6 **Georgsheil** W Germany
32 H8 **Georgsmarienhütte** W Germany
146 G6 **Georg von Neumayer** *W Germany Base* Antarctica
41 N4 **Gepatschhaus** Austria
21 J4 **Ger** France
28 E2 **Gerå** *R* Denmark
37 K2 **Gera** *R* East Germany
37 N2 **Gera** East Germany
22 F2 **Geraardsbergen** Belgium
36 H5 **Gerabronn** W Germany
119 Q8 **Gerald** Saskatchewan Canada
110 E3 **Gerald** Missouri U.S.A.
143 A8 **Geraldine** Western Australia Australia
144 C6 **Geraldine** New Zealand
101 P2 **Geraldine** Montana U.S.A.
51 S2 **Geral'd, Ostrov** *islds* U.S.S.R.
143 A8 **Geraldton** Western Australia Australia
120 D3 **Geraldton** Ontario Canada
120 C3 **Geraldton** Ontario Canada
130 E10 **Geral, Serra** *mts* Brazil
80 B8 **Gerar** *R* Israel
19 K4 **Gérardmer** France
143 E7 **Gerard, Mt** Western Australia Australia
80 G4 **Gerasa** Jordan
55 F2 **Gerasimovka** U.S.S.R.
100 C9 **Gerber** California U.S.A.
100 D7 **Gerber Res** Oregon U.S.A.
33 P9 **Gerbstedt** East Germany
36 H4 **Gerchsheim** W Germany
78 H3 **Gercuş** Turkey
116 L6 **Gerdine, Mt** Alaska U.S.A.
78 D1 **Gerede** Turkey
77 J4 **Gereshk** Afghanistan
17 F7 **Gérgal** Spain
40 A4 **Gergy** France
37 K3 **Gerhardtsgereuth** East Germany
69 E10 **Gerik** Malaysia
98 C8 **Gering** Nebraska U.S.A.
37 O1 **Geringswalde** East Germany
100 F9 **Gerlach** Nevada U.S.A.
48 F1 **Gerlachovsky** *mt* Czechoslovakia
36 H4 **Gerlachsheim** W Germany
28 H5 **Gerlev** Denmark
28 G6 **Gerlev** Denmark
36 G6 **Gerlingen** W Germany
38 E7 **Gerlostal** *R* Austria
30 G2 **German Democratic Republic** Cent Europe
30 **German Federal Republic** W Europe
133 E4 **Germania** Argentina
117 L8 **Germansen Landing** British Columbia Canada
110 G3 **Germantown** Illinois U.S.A.
95 K7 **Germantown** Maryland U.S.A.
95 O4 **Germantown** New York U.S.A.
94 C7 **Germantown** Ohio U.S.A.
110 G6 **Germantown** Tennessee U.S.A.
47 J7 **Germencik** Turkey
37 L7 **Germering** W Germany
36 E5 **Germersheim** W Germany
89 F6 **Germiston** S Africa
28 C5 **Gerndrup** Denmark
36 E6 **Gernsbach** W Germany
36 F4 **Gernsheim** W Germany
61 L10 **Gero** Japan
70 P10 **Gerokgak** Bali Indonesia
36 B3 **Gerolstein** W Germany
37 J4 **Gerolzhofen** W Germany
100 G1 **Gerome** Washington U.S.A.
17 J3 **Gerona** Spain
17 J2 **Gerona** *prov* Spain
103 O8 **Geronimo** Arizona U.S.A.
107 M7 **Geronimo** Oklahoma U.S.A.
139 K5 **Gerringong** New South Wales Australia
18 F9 **Gers** *dept* France
18 F9 **Gers** *R* France
36 H3 **Gersfeld** W Germany
36 F4 **Gersprenz** *R* W Germany
37 J6 **Gerstetten Herbrechtingen** W Germany
37 K7 **Gersthofen** W Germany
37 J2 **Gerstingen** East Germany
116 P5 **Gerstle** *R* Alaska U.S.A.
33 T6 **Gerswalde** East Germany
140 B3 **Gertrude, Mt** N Terr Australia
48 K2 **Gertsa** U.S.S.R.
80 C4 **Gerulim** Israel
19 O15 **Gervanne** *R* France
66 C5 **Gêrzê** China
78 E1 **Gerze** Turkey
37 N7 **Gerzen** W Germany
32 E9 **Gescher** W Germany
32 J9 **Geseke** W Germany
80 D1 **Gesher HaZiv** Israel
22 H4 **Gespunsart** France
37 K7 **Gessertshausen** W Germany
44 B3 **Gesso** *R* Italy
21 H7 **Gesté** France
28 C5 **Gesten** Denmark

86 H4 **Gestro, Wabē** *R* Ethiopia
26 H8 **Gesunden** *L* Sweden
29 H11 **Geta** Finland
16 E4 **Getafe** Spain
100 H8 **Getchell Mine** Nevada U.S.A.
22 J2 **Gete** *R* Belgium
123 M3 **Gethsémani** Quebec Canada
28 A3 **Gettrup** Denmark
95 K7 **Gettysburg** Pennsylvania U.S.A.
98 G5 **Gettysburg** South Dakota U.S.A.
67 B4 **Getu He** *R* China
130 D10 **Getúlio Vargas** Brazil
146 B8 **Getz Ice Shelf** Antarctica
107 N4 **Geuda Springs** Kansas U.S.A.
69 C11 **Geumapang** *R* Sumatra
69 C10 **Geumpang** Sumatra
69 C10 **Geureudong, Gunung** *mt* Sumatra
139 J4 **Geurie** New South Wales Australia
80 C3 **Geva' Karmel** Israel
32 F10 **Gevelsberg** W Germany
80 B7 **Gever'am** Israel
20 G5 **Geveze** France
33 S5 **Gevezin** East Germany
46 E3 **Gevgelija** Yugoslavia
19 K6 **Gex** France
79 C2 **Geydik Dağ** *mt* Turkey
37 O2 **Geyer** East Germany
36 G4 **Geyersberg** *mt* W Germany
47 H5 **Geyikli** Turkey
79 C2 **Geyne Çayı** *str* Turkey
101 P2 **Geyser** Montana U.S.A.
81 B7 **Geyser, Banc du** Madagascar
28 S9 **Geysir** Iceland
47 L4 **Geyve** Turkey
84 D3 **Ghadāmis** Libya
80 G2 **Ghadir al Bustan** Syria
77 C1 **Ghaem Shahr** Iran
73 N3 **Ghaghara** *R* India
85 D7 **Ghana** *rep* W Africa
84 E5 **Ghanīmah, Jabal Bin** *mts* Libya
89 C4 **Ghanzi** *dist* Botswana
89 B3 **Ghanzi** Botswana
80 E7 **Ghar** *R* Jordan
78 K6 **Gharab** Iraq
85 E2 **Ghardaia** Algeria
43 B12 **Ghardimaou** Tunisia
43 C11 **Ghar El Melh** Tunisia
84 J4 **Gharib, Gebel** Egypt
84 E3 **Gharyan** Libya
84 E5 **Ghāt** Libya
75 M7 **Ghatsila** India
86 E4 **Ghazāl, Al** *prov* Sudan
17 F9 **Ghazaouet** Algeria
74 G4 **Ghaziabad** India
77 L3 **Ghaznī** Afghanistan
77 K3 **Ghazoor** Afghanistan
99 O2 **Gheen** Minnesota U.S.A.
Ghent *see* **Gent**
94 B8 **Ghent** Kentucky U.S.A.
99 L5 **Ghent** Minnesota U.S.A.
48 K4 **Gheorghe Gheorghiu-Dej** Romania
48 K4 **Gheorgheni** Romania
48 H3 **Gherla** Romania
43 B8 **Ghilarza** Sardinia
48 K4 **Ghimeş Făget** Romania
133 C7 **Ghio, L** Argentina
22 F2 **Ghislenghien** Belgium
77 J3 **Ghizao** Afghanistan
118 L1 **Ghost** *R* Ontario Canada
117 Q4 **Ghost L** Northwest Territories Canada
117 P9 **Ghost Mt** British Columbia Canada
77 J2 **Ghowr** *prov* Afghanistan
86 E3 **Ghubaysh** Sudan
Ghudamis *see* **Ghadāmis**
79 H4 **Ghunthur** Syria
77 G2 **Ghūriān** Afghanistan
22 D1 **Ghyvelde** France
68 H7 **Gia Dinh** Vietnam
68 H6 **Gia Nghia** Vietnam
42 D6 **Giannutri, I.di** Italy
89 F7 **Giants Castle** *mt* S Africa
14 E1 **Giant's Causeway** N Ireland
83 K9 **Giants Tank** *L* Sri Lanka
70 P10 **Gianyar** Indonesia
69 G8 **Gia Rai** Vietnam
43 G11 **Giarre** Sicily
18 G7 **Giat** France
44 B1 **Giaveno** Italy
126 F4 **Gibara** Cuba
98 H9 **Gibbon** Nebraska U.S.A.
100 G4 **Gibbon** Oregon U.S.A.
101 M4 **Gibbons Pass** Montana U.S.A.
101 M4 **Gibbonsville** Idaho U.S.A.
142 F3 **Gibb River** Western Australia Australia
99 S3 **Gibbs City** Michigan U.S.A.
146 D3 **Gibbs I** S Shetland Is Antarctica
143 C10 **Gibbs, Mt** Western Australia Australia
87 C11 **Gibeon** Namibia
26 K2 **Gibostad** Norway
16 C7 **Gibraleón** Spain
16 D8 **Gibraltar** *colony* S W Europe
127 J10 **Gibraltar** Venezuela
16 D9 **Gibraltar, Str of** Spain/ Africa
111 C9 **Gibsland** Louisiana U.S.A.
100 C8 **Gibson** California U.S.A.
112 E4 **Gibson** Georgia U.S.A.
101 Q3 **Gibson** Montana U.S.A.
94 D5 **Gibsonburg** Ohio U.S.A.
99 S9 **Gibson City** Illinois U.S.A.
143 D6 **Gibson Des** Western Australia Australia
117 M11 **Gibsons** British Columbia Canada
143 D10 **Gibson Soak** Western Australia Australia
113 E10 **Gibsonton** Florida U.S.A.
112 H1 **Gibsonville** North Carolina U.S.A.
58 B2 **Gichgeniyn Nuruu** *mt* Mongolia
52 H5 **Gidayevo** U.S.S.R.
79 D8 **Giddi, G el** Egypt
109 L5 **Giddings** Texas U.S.A.
26 K8 **Gideå** *R* Sweden
26 K8 **Gideå** Sweden
110 G5 **Gideon** Missouri U.S.A.
141 F6 **Gideon, Mt** Queensland Australia
138 F3 **Gidgealpa Gas Field** South Australia Australia
143 F8 **Gidgi, L** Western Australia Australia
31 L5 **Gidle** Poland
86 G4 **Gīdolē** Ethiopia
36 H4 **Giebelstadt** W Germany
32 M9 **Gieboldehausen** W Germany
18 G5 **Gien** France
37 J6 **Giengen** W Germany
19 Q18 **Giens** France
19 N13 **Gier** *R* France
33 P7 **Giesenslage** East Germany
36 F2 **Giessen** W Germany
25 G2 **Gieten** Netherlands
25 F3 **Giethoorn** Netherlands
84 J4 **Gifatin I** Egypt
13 F2 **Gifford** Scotland
113 G10 **Gifford** Florida U.S.A.
99 N7 **Gifford** Iowa U.S.A.
100 G1 **Gifford** Washington U.S.A.
33 N8 **Gifhorn** W Germany
61 K10 **Gifu** Japan
124 D5 **Giganta, Sa de la** Mexico
124 E9 **Gigante** Panama
124 G3 **Gigantes, Llanos de los** Mexico
15 C5 **Gigha** *isld* Scotland
42 D6 **Giglio, I. del** Italy
19 O18 **Gignac** France
19 P17 **Gignac** France
18 H9 **Gignac** France
40 F6 **Gignod** Italy
16 D1 **Gijón** Spain
103 P9 **Gila** *R* Arizona U.S.A.
106 B9 **Gila** New Mexico U.S.A.
103 M9 **Gila Bend** Arizona U.S.A.
103 L8 **Gila Bend Mts** Arizona U.S.A.
106 B8 **Gila Cliff Dwellings Nat.Mon** New Mexico U.S.A.
103 K9 **Gila Mts** Arizona U.S.A.
77 A1 **Gīlān** Iran
78 K4 **Gilan Garb** Iran
121 R5 **Gilardo Dam** Quebec Canada
71 B2 **Gila, Tanjong** *C* Indonesia
48 H4 **Gilău** Romania
141 F3 **Gilbert** *R* Queensland Australia
103 N8 **Gilbert** Arizona U.S.A.
99 O2 **Gilbert** Minnesota U.S.A.
102 G3 **Gilbert** Nevada U.S.A.
94 F9 **Gilbert** West Virginia U.S.A.
137 P2 **Gilbert Is** Pacific Oc
117 L10 **Gilbert, Mt** British Columbia Canada
116 O6 **Gilbert, Mt** Alaska U.S.A.
111 H10 **Gilbertown** Alabama U.S.A.
101 P9 **Gilbert Pk** Utah U.S.A.
119 R7 **Gilbert Plains** Manitoba Canada
141 G4 **Gilbert River** Queensland Australia
28 J4 **Gilbjerghoved** *C* Denmark
129 J5 **Gilbués** Brazil
98 J1 **Gilby** North Dakota U.S.A.
98 B9 **Gilcrest** Colorado U.S.A.
13 G6 **Gildersome** England
26 G4 **Gildeskal** Norway
101 P1 **Gildford** Montana U.S.A.
88 G10 **Gilé** Mozambique
95 R2 **Gilead** Maine U.S.A.
98 J9 **Gilead** Nebraska U.S.A.
143 G6 **Giles** Western Australia Australia
143 G7 **Giles** Western Australia Australia
108 G1 **Giles** Texas U.S.A.
143 C8 **Giles, L** Western Australia Australia
140 B5 **Giles Ra** N Terr Australia
84 H5 **Gilf Kebir Plateau** Egypt
139 K3 **Gilgai** New South Wales Australia
139 J4 **Gilgandra** New South Wales Australia
80 E6 **Gilgat** Jordan
139 J3 **Gil Gil** *R* New South Wales Australia
88 F2 **Gilgil** Kenya
74 F1 **Gilgit** Kashmir
139 H4 **Gilgunnia** New South Wales Australia
117 J9 **Gil I** British Columbia Canada
70 P10 **Gilimanuk** Bali Indonesia
46 D1 **Giljeva Planina** *mt* Yugoslavia
98 B9 **Gill** Colorado U.S.A.
115 K6 **Gillam** Manitoba Canada
28 J4 **Gilleleje** Denmark
143 E7 **Gillen, L** Western Australia Australia
140 C6 **Gillen, Mt** N Terr Australia
138 D4 **Gilles, L** South Australia Australia
103 M8 **Gillespie** Arizona U.S.A.
110 G2 **Gillespie** Illinois U.S.A.
144 B5 **Gillespies Pt** New Zealand
111 E7 **Gillett** Arkansas U.S.A.
95 L5 **Gillett** Pennsylvania U.S.A.
109 K6 **Gillett** Texas U.S.A.
99 S5 **Gillett** Wisconsin U.S.A.
98 A5 **Gillette** Wyoming U.S.A.
109 N1 **Gillham** Arkansas U.S.A.
26 G9 **Gillhov** Sweden
110 C2 **Gilliam** Missouri U.S.A.
141 F5 **Gilliat** *R* Queensland Australia
141 F5 **Gilliat** Queensland Australia
13 G5 **Gilling** England
9 G5 **Gillingham** England
8 D5 **Gillingham** England
109 O5 **Gillis** Louisiana U.S.A.
14 C2 **Gill, L** Ireland
146 J11 **Gillock I** *isld* Antarctica
99 T4 **Gills Rock** Wisconsin U.S.A.
22 G3 **Gilly** Belgium
99 S9 **Gilman** Illinois U.S.A.
99 O8 **Gilman** Iowa U.S.A.
101 N2 **Gilman** Montana U.S.A.
99 Q4 **Gilman** Wisconsin U.S.A.
110 C1 **Gilman City** Missouri U.S.A.
109 N3 **Gilmer** Texas U.S.A.
101 M5 **Gilmore** Idaho U.S.A.
99 M7 **Gilmore City** Iowa U.S.A.
121 N8 **Gilmour** Ontario Canada
86 F4 **Gilo** *R* Ethiopia
48 H6 **Gilort** *R* Romania
117 N9 **Gilpin** British Columbia Canada
118 L8 **Gilroy** Saskatchewan Canada
102 C4 **Gilroy** California U.S.A.
28 R9 **Gilsfjördhur** *inlet* Iceland
13 F3 **Gilsland** England
98 H9 **Giltner** Nebraska U.S.A.
8 C4 **Gilwern** Wales
51 M3 **Gilyuy** *R* U.S.S.R.
86 D3 **Gimbala** *mt* Sudan
127 O8 **Gimie** *mt* St Lucia
101 L6 **Gimlet** Idaho U.S.A.
119 V8 **Gimli** Manitoba Canada
27 K11 **Gimo** Sweden
52 D3 **Gimoly** U.S.S.R.
18 F9 **Gimone** *R* France
18 F9 **Gimont** France
26 G3 **Gimsöy** Norway
80 C6 **Gimzo** Israel
19 P17 **Ginasservis** France
141 J6 **Gindie** Queensland Australia
76 D4 **Gingee** India
36 H6 **Gingen** W Germany
127 J2 **Ginger Hill** Jamaica
141 K6 **Gin Gin** Queensland Australia
143 B9 **Gingin** Western Australia Australia
71 G6 **Gingoog B** Philippines
86 H4 **Gīnīr** Ethiopia
80 E3 **Ginnegar** Israel
28 F4 **Ginnerup** Denmark
80 F2 **Ginnosar** Israel
43 H8 **Ginosa** Italy
61 P13 **Ginowan** Okinawa
16 B2 **Ginzo de Limia** Spain
45 K3 **Giogo di Casaglia** Italy
45 K3 **Giogo di Scarperia** Italy
45 P6 **Gioia dei Marsi** Italy
43 G10 **Gioia,G.di** Italy
45 Q7 **Gioia Sannitica** Italy
46 E6 **Gióna** *mt* Greece
41 J5 **Giornico** Switzerland
43 H9 **Giovanni in Fiore, S** Italy
45 K4 **Giovi** *mt* Italy
139 H7 **Gippsland** Victoria Australia
139 J7 **Gippsland Basin Oil & Gas Fields** Victoria Australia
142 A6 **Giralia** Western Australia Australia
31 N6 **Giraltovce** Czechoslovakia
40 D1 **Girancourt** France
77 F5 **Giran Rig** *mt* Iran
99 R10 **Girard** Illinois U.S.A.
107 Q4 **Girard** Kansas U.S.A.
94 G5 **Girard** Ohio U.S.A.
94 G4 **Girard** Pennsylvania U.S.A.
108 G2 **Girard** Texas U.S.A.
128 D3 **Girardot** Colombia
15 F3 **Girdle Ness** Scotland
78 G1 **Giresun** Turkey
84 J4 **Girga** Egypt
74 D8 **Gir Hills** India
86 C5 **Giri** *R* Zaire
75 M6 **Giridih** India
139 H4 **Girilambone** New South Wales Australia
83 K10 **Giriulla** Sri Lanka
19 K5 **Giromagny** France
18 E7 **Gironde** *R* France
18 E8 **Gironde** *dept* France
17 J2 **Gironella** Spain
18 G9 **Girou** *R* France
119 V9 **Giroux** Manitoba Canada
130 C11 **Giruá** Brazil
15 D5 **Girvan** *R* Scotland
15 D5 **Girvan** Scotland
119 M7 **Girvin** Saskatchewan Canada
108 E4 **Girvin** Texas U.S.A.
116 H4 **Gisasa** *R* Alaska U.S.A.
145 G3 **Gisborne** New Zealand
13 F6 **Gisburn** England
123 S6 **Gisburn L** Newfoundland Canada
117 M8 **Giscome** British Columbia Canada
103 N7 **Gisela** Arizona U.S.A.
88 B2 **Gisenye** Rwanda
26 A9 **Giske** *isld* Norway
28 F6 **Gislev** Denmark
28 H5 **Gislinge** Denmark
21 O3 **Gisors** France
37 K1 **Gispersleben** East Germany
57 E5 **Gissar** U.S.S.R.
57 E5 **Gissarskiy Khrebet** *mts* U.S.S.R.
22 D1 **Gistel** Belgium
88 B3 **Gitega** Burundi
32 M9 **Gittelde** W Germany
Giuba *R* *see* **Jubba** *R*
41 N6 **Giudicarie Val** Italy
45 Q8 **Giugliano in Campo** Italy
45 O6 **Giuliano di Roma** Italy
42 F6 **Giulianova** Italy
48 J3 **Giumalău** *mt* Romania
48 L6 **Giurgeni** Romania
48 K4 **Giurgeului, Muntii** *mts* Romania
47 H1 **Giurgiu** Romania
48 K6 **Giurgiu** *reg* Romania
80 C3 **Giv'at 'Ada** Israel
80 C5 **Giv'atayim** Israel
28 C5 **Give** Denmark
22 D3 **Givenchy-en-Gohelle** France
22 H3 **Givet** Belgium
19 N13 **Givors** France
22 G3 **Givry** Belgium
19 J6 **Givry** France
40 A4 **Givry** France
28 C5 **Givskud** Denmark
89 F4 **Giyani** S Africa
79 B8 **Gîza, El** Egypt
21 L7 **Gizeux** France
57 C5 **Gizhduvan** U.S.S.R.
51 Q2 **Gizhiga** U.S.S.R.
22 F4 **Gizy** France
31 N1 **Gizycko** Poland
27 C10 **Gjende** *L* Norway
27 C10 **Gjendesheim** Norway
28 E3 **Gjerlev** Denmark
28 D4 **Gjern** Denmark
28 F3 **Gjerrild** Denmark
27 C13 **Gjerstad** Norway
26 F7 **Gjersvik** Norway
26 D9 **Gjevil-vatn** *L* Norway
46 D4 **Gjirokastër** Albania
115 K4 **Gjoa Haven** Northwest Territories Canada
28 D2 **Gjøl** Denmark
28 C3 **Gjørup** Denmark
27 C13 **Gjovdal** Norway
27 E11 **Gjövik** Norway
46 C4 **Gjuhëzës, Kep I** *C* Albania
78 E1 **Gkirmak** *R* Turkey
22 H2 **Glabbeek Zuurbemde** Belgium
123 N7 **Glace Bay** Nova Scotia Canada
20 G2 **Glacerie, la** France
117 P10 **Glacier** British Columbia Canada
117 E6 **Glacier B** Alaska U.S.A.
117 E6 **Glacier Bay Nat. Park** Alaska U.S.A.
117 E6 **Glacier Bay Nat Park and Preserve** Alaska U.S.A.
116 O6 **Glacier I** Alaska U.S.A.
116 Q4 **Glacier Mt** Alaska U.S.A.
117 O10 **Glacier Nat. Park** British Columbia Canada
101 M1 **Glacier Nat. Park** Montana U.S.A.
100 D1 **Glacier Peak** Washington U.S.A.
115 M2 **Glacier Str** Northwest Territories Canada
36 B2 **Gladbach** W Germany
32 E9 **Gladbeck** W Germany
99 O7 **Gladbrook** Iowa U.S.A.
107 L2 **Glade** Kansas U.S.A.
36 F2 **Gladenbach** W Germany
106 B3 **Glade Park** Colorado U.S.A.
94 F10 **Glade Spring** Virginia U.S.A.
109 N3 **Gladewater** Texas U.S.A.
119 N9 **Gladmar** Saskatchewan Canada
26 E6 **Gladstad** Norway
141 K6 **Gladstone** Queensland Australia
138 E5 **Gladstone** South Australia Australia
139 J8 **Gladstone** Tasmania Australia
119 T8 **Gladstone** Manitoba Canada
145 E4 **Gladstone** New Zealand
99 T4 **Gladstone** Michigan U.S.A.
110 B2 **Gladstone** Missouri U.S.A.
98 D3 **Gladstone** North Dakota U.S.A.
94 C3 **Gladwin** Michigan U.S.A.
94 H8 **Glady** West Virginia U.S.A.
94 H9 **Gladys** Virginia U.S.A.
117 G6 **Gladys L** British Columbia Canada
28 G6 **Glænø** *isld* Denmark
27 F12 **Glafsfj** *L* Sweden
118 K7 **Glamis** Saskatchewan Canada
15 F4 **Glamis** Scotland
103 J8 **Glamis** California U.S.A.
42 H4 **Glamoe** Yugoslavia
Glamorgan *co see* **W., Mid & S.Glam.** *counties*
28 E6 **Glamsbjerg** Denmark
38 K8 **Glan** *R* Austria
71 G8 **Glan** Mindanao Philippines
27 H13 **Glan** *L* Sweden
36 D4 **Glan** *R* W Germany
14 B4 **Glanaruddery Mts** Ireland
19 P15 **Glandage** France
19 Q14 **Glandon, Col du** *pass* France
32 G8 **Glandorf** W Germany
32 G8 **Glane** *R* W Germany
38 K8 **Glanegg** Austria
41 J4 **Glärnisch** *mt* Switzerland
41 K3 **Glarus** Switzerland
107 N2 **Glasco** Kansas U.S.A.
95 O4 **Glasco** New York U.S.A.
99 R9 **Glasford** Illinois U.S.A.
127 H1 **Glasgow** Jamaica
12 D2 **Glasgow** Scotland
94 B10 **Glasgow** Kentucky U.S.A.
110 D2 **Glasgow** Missouri U.S.A.
101 T1 **Glasgow** Montana U.S.A.
94 H9 **Glasgow** Virginia U.S.A.
38 M8 **Glashutten** Austria
133 D6 **Glasier** Argentina
118 J5 **Glaslyn** Saskatchewan Canada
15 E4 **Glas Maol** *mt* Scotland
119 M9 **Glasnevin** Saskatchewan Canada
95 M7 **Glassboro** New Jersey U.S.A.
108 D5 **Glass Mts** Texas U.S.A.
8 D5 **Glastonbury** England
41 J3 **Glatt** *R* Switzerland
Glatz *see* **Kłodzko**
37 N2 **Glauchau** East Germany
47 H1 **Glavinitsa** Bulgaria
108 D7 **Glazier** Texas U.S.A.
52 H5 **Glazov** U.S.S.R.
31 K2 **Głda** *R* Poland
110 H5 **Gleason** Tennessee U.S.A.
99 R4 **Gleason** Wisconsin U.S.A.
94 K5 **Gleasonton** Pennsylvania U.S.A.
103 P10 **Gleeson** Arizona U.S.A.
37 K3 **Gleichberg** *mt* East Germany
118 D8 **Gleichen** Alberta Canada
33 P10 **Gleina** East Germany
38 L7 **Glein Alpe** *mts* Austria
38 N7 **Gleisdorf** Austria
Gleiwitz *see* **Gliwice**
28 B5 **Glejbjerg** Denmark
98 C7 **Glen** Nebraska U.S.A.
95 Q2 **Glen** New Hampshire U.S.A.
100 A6 **Glenada** Oregon U.S.A.
15 D3 **Glen Affric** Scotland
145 E2 **Glen Afton** New Zealand
121 P7 **Glen Almond** Quebec Canada
112 F2 **Glen Alpine** North Carolina U.S.A.
20 C6 **Glénans, Iles de** France
15 D5 **Glen App** Scotland
144 B6 **Glenaray** New Zealand
14 F2 **Glenarm** N Ireland
12 D1 **Glen Artney** Scotland
119 O8 **Glenavon** Saskatchewan Canada
144 C6 **Glenavy** New Zealand
143 D7 **Glenayle** Western Australia Australia
118 K9 **Glenbain** Saskatchewan Canada
12 C2 **Glenbarr** Scotland
139 K4 **Glenbawn Reservoir** New South Wales Australia
119 S9 **Glenboro** Manitoba Canada
145 E2 **Glenbrook** New Zealand
143 B7 **Glenburgh** Western Australia Australia
98 E1 **Glenburn** North Dakota U.S.A.
138 F6 **Glenburnie** South Australia Australia
123 P4 **Glenburnie** Newfoundland Canada
95 L7 **Glen Burnie** Maryland U.S.A.
118 K5 **Glenbush** Saskatchewan Canada
15 D3 **Glen Cannich** Scotland
103 N5 **Glen Canyon** Arizona U.S.A.
103 N4 **Glen Canyon Nat. Recreation Area** Utah U.S.A.
15 C3 **Glen Carron** *R* Scotland
13 E1 **Glencarse** Scotland
15 E4 **Glen Clova** Scotland
138 F6 **Glencoe** South Australia Australia
120 J10 **Glencoe** Ontario Canada
89 G7 **Glencoe** S Africa
111 L8 **Glencoe** Alabama U.S.A.
99 M5 **Glencoe** Minnesota U.S.A.
106 E8 **Glencoe** New Mexico U.S.A.
98 F4 **Glencross** South Dakota U.S.A.
103 M8 **Glendale** Arizona U.S.A.
102 F7 **Glendale** California U.S.A.
111 K11 **Glendale** Florida U.S.A.
107 N3 **Glendale** Kansas U.S.A.
103 K5 **Glendale** Nevada U.S.A.
94 C7 **Glendale** Ohio U.S.A.
100 B7 **Glendale** Oregon U.S.A.
94 G7 **Glendale** West Virginia U.S.A.
117 L10 **Glendale Cove** British Columbia Canada
12 C1 **Glendaruel** Scotland
139 K5 **Glen Davis** New South Wales Australia
106 E1 **Glendevey** Colorado U.S.A.
12 E1 **Glendevon** Scotland
98 B2 **Glendive** Montana U.S.A.
98 A7 **Glendo** Wyoming U.S.A.
118 F4 **Glendon** Alberta Canada
111 F8 **Glendora** Mississippi U.S.A.
14 C2 **Glendowan Mts** Ireland
141 H4 **Gleneagle** Queensland Australia
15 E4 **Gleneagles** Scotland
107 M2 **Glen Elder** Kansas U.S.A.
138 E5 **Glenelg** South Australia Australia
138 F6 **Glenelg** *R* Victoria Australia
15 C3 **Glenelg** Scotland
119 S8 **Glenella** Manitoba Canada
119 P9 **Glen Ewen** Saskatchewan Canada
12 D1 **Glen Falloch** Scotland
13 E1 **Glenfarg** Scotland
95 M3 **Glenfield** New York U.S.A.
98 H2 **Glenfield** North Dakota U.S.A.
15 C4 **Glenfinnan** Scotland
109 L6 **Glen Flora** Texas U.S.A.
14 D1 **Glengad Hd** Ireland
14 B5 **Glengariff** Ireland
15 C3 **Glen Garry** *R* Scotland
15 D4 **Glen Garry** Scotland
143 C7 **Glengarry Ra** Western Australia Australia
127 L2 **Glengoffe** Jamaica
140 E6 **Glengyle** Queensland Australia
144 B7 **Glenham** New Zealand
98 F4 **Glenham** South Dakota U.S.A.
140 C6 **Glen Helen** N Terr Australia
140 C6 **Glen Helen Gorge** N Terr Australia
145 D4 **Glenhope** New Zealand
139 K3 **Glen Innes** New South Wales Australia
118 K8 **Glen Kerr** Saskatchewan Canada
99 V5 **Glen L** Michigan U.S.A.
12 D4 **Glenluce** Scotland
139 G4 **Glen Lyon** New South Wales Australia
15 D4 **Glen Lyon** Scotland
95 L5 **Glen Lyon** Pennsylvania U.S.A.
145 E2 **Glen Massey** New Zealand
109 P5 **Glenmora** Louisiana U.S.A.
15 D3 **Glen More** Scotland
141 J7 **Glenmorgan** Queensland Australia
15 D3 **Glen Moriston** Scotland
102 B2 **Glenn** California U.S.A.
116 P5 **Glennallen** Alaska U.S.A.
14 C3 **Glennamaddy** Ireland
139 H7 **Glennie** *isld* Victoria Australia
94 D2 **Glennie** Michigan U.S.A.
103 P9 **Glenn, Mt** Arizona U.S.A.
100 K7 **Glenns Ferry** Idaho U.S.A.
102 F6 **Glennville** California U.S.A.
112 F6 **Glennville** Georgia U.S.A.
12 D1 **Glen Ogle** Scotland
144 B7 **Glenomaru** New Zealand
117 H7 **Glenora** British Columbia Canada
139 H8 **Glenorchy** Tasmania Australia
144 B6 **Glenorchy** New Zealand
15 D4 **Glen Orchy** Scotland
141 F4 **Glenore** Queensland Australia
144 B7 **Glenore** New Zealand
140 E6 **Glenormiston** Queensland Australia
139 L4 **Glenreagh** New South Wales Australia
108 A8 **Glenrio** New Mex/Tex U.S.A.
121 Q7 **Glen Robertson** Ontario Canada
98 A7 **Glenrock** Wyoming U.S.A.
109 K3 **Glen Rose** Texas U.S.A.
13 E1 **Glenrothes** Scotland
142 F3 **Glenroy** Western Australia Australia
95 O3 **Glens Falls** New York U.S.A.
15 E4 **Glen Shee** Scotland
118 L7 **Glenside** Saskatchewan Canada
15 D4 **Glen Spean** Scotland
28 D3 **Glenstrup Sø** *L* Denmark
101 T1 **Glentana** Montana U.S.A.
14 C2 **Glenties** Ireland
144 C5 **Glentunnel** New Zealand
118 L9 **Glentworth** Saskatchewan Canada
98 E3 **Glen Ullin** North Dakota U.S.A.
15 D3 **Glen Urquhart** Scotland
120 K5 **Glenvale** Ontario Canada
99 T7 **Glenview** Illinois U.S.A.
99 N6 **Glenville** Minnesota U.S.A.
98 H9 **Glenville** Nebraska U.S.A.
94 G8 **Glenville** West Virginia U.S.A.
112 D2 **Glenville L** North Carolina U.S.A.
123 S5 **Glenwood** Newfoundland Canada
111 K10 **Glenwood** Alabama U.S.A.
111 C7 **Glenwood** Arkansas U.S.A.
112 E5 **Glenwood** Georgia U.S.A.
94 B7 **Glenwood** Indiana U.S.A.
99 L8 **Glenwood** Iowa U.S.A.
99 L4 **Glenwood** Minnesota U.S.A.
99 O9 **Glenwood** Missouri U.S.A.
106 B8 **Glenwood** New Mexico U.S.A.
112 F2 **Glenwood** North Carolina U.S.A.
100 B4 **Glenwood** Oregon U.S.A.
103 N3 **Glenwood** Utah U.S.A.
100 D3 **Glenwood** Washington U.S.A.
94 E8 **Glenwood** West Virginia U.S.A.
99 O4 **Glenwood** Wisconsin U.S.A.
106 C2 **Glenwood Springs** Colorado U.S.A.
118 D9 **Glenwoodville** Alberta Canada
28 F4 **Glesborg** Denmark
33 N4 **Gleschendorf** W Germany
41 H4 **Gletsch** Switzerland
118 H7 **Glidden** Saskatchewan Canada
99 Q3 **Glidden** Wisconsin U.S.A.
100 B6 **Glide** Oregon U.S.A.
33 S8 **Glienick** East Germany
33 S7 **Glienicke** East Germany
14 B4 **Glin** Ireland
32 M5 **Glinde** W Germany
31 M3 **Glinojeck** Poland
48 J1 **Glinyany** U.S.S.R.
26 G9 **Glissjöberg** Sweden
26 C10 **Glittertind** *mt* Norway
31 L5 **Gliwice** Poland
46 D4 **Gllavë** Albania
103 O8 **Globe** Arizona U.S.A.
Glogau *see* **Głogów**
48 C3 **Gloggnitz** Austria
31 J4 **Głogów** Poland
31 K5 **Glogówek** Poland
33 Q8 **Gloine** East Germany
20 D5 **Glomel** France
26 G5 **Glomfjord** Norway
26 E9 **Glomma** *R* Norway
26 L6 **Glommerstrask** Sweden
27 J15 **Glönminge** Sweden
130 H10 **Glória** Brazil
106 E6 **Glorieta** New Mexico U.S.A.
87 H10 **Glorieuses, Is** Indian Oc
116 C6 **Glory of Russia C** Alaska U.S.A.
21 L3 **Glos** France
21 M4 **Glos-la-Ferrière** France
13 G6 **Glossop** England
21 M3 **Glos-sur-Risle** France
111 E10 **Gloster** Mississippi U.S.A.
29 K5 **Glostrup** Denmark
52 G3 **Glotovo** U.S.S.R.
139 K4 **Gloucester** New South Wales Australia
8 D4 **Gloucester** England
95 R4 **Gloucester** Massachusetts U.S.A.
95 L9 **Gloucester** Virginia U.S.A.
95 M7 **Gloucester City** New Jersey U.S.A.
141 J4 **Gloucester I** Queensland Australia
94 E7 **Glouster** Ohio U.S.A.
123 P5 **Glover I** Newfoundland Canada
95 N3 **Gloversville** New York U.S.A.
33 Q7 **Glöwen** East Germany
31 M4 **Głowno** Poland
54 M8 **Glubokiy** U.S.S.R.
56 B5 **Glubokoye** U.S.S.R.
31 K5 **Głuchołazy** Poland
28 D7 **Glucksburg** W Germany
32 K5 **Glückstadt** W Germany
28 D5 **Glud** Denmark
28 C4 **Gludsted** Denmark
54 E5 **Glukhov** U.S.S.R.
52 F6 **Glukhovo** U.S.S.R.
69 B10 **Glumpangminyeuk** Sumatra
29 K5 **Glumslöv** Sweden
28 H6 **Glumsø** Denmark
13 F6 **Glusburn** England
55 E4 **Glyadyanskoye** U.S.S.R.
48 K2 **Glyboka** U.S.S.R.
8 B1 **Glyder Fawr** *mt* Wales
143 E6 **Glynde Hill** Western Australia Australia
95 L7 **Glyndon** Maryland U.S.A.
98 K3 **Glyndon** Minnesota U.S.A.
28 B3 **Glyngøre** Denmark
8 C4 **Glynneath** Wales
8 C4 **Glyntawe** Wales
31 J7 **Gmünd** Austria
38 J6 **Gmunden** Austria
33 P9 **Gnadau** East Germany
94 F6 **Gnadenhutten** Ohio U.S.A.
26 J9 **Gnarp** Sweden
32 K6 **Gnarrenburg** W Germany
38 N8 **Gnas** Austria
28 G4 **Gniben** *C* Denmark
31 L2 **Gniew** Poland
31 K3 **Gniezno** Poland
33 M4 **Gnissau** W Germany
46 E2 **Gnjilane** Yugoslavia
33 R5 **Gnoien** East Germany
8 D2 **Gnosall** England
37 K5 **Gnotzheim** W Germany
143 C10 **Gnowangerup** W Australia
143 B9 **Gnuka** W Australia
32 L4 **Gnutz** W Germany
76 A3 **Goa, Daman & Diu** *terr* India
139 K6 **Goalen Head** New South Wales Australia
75 O5 **Goalpara** India
71 H9 **Goang** Indonesia
12 C2 **Goat Fell** *mt* Scotland
13 H5 **Goathland** England
101 M1 **Goat Mt** Montana U.S.A.
87 F11 **Goba** Mozambique
89 A4 **Gobabis** Namibia
58 D3 **Gobi Desert** Mongolia
60 J12 **Gobō** Japan
8 C2 **Gobowen** England
25 F5 **Goch** W Germany
87 C10 **Gochas** Namibia
86 G4 **Gocho** Ethiopia
36 F5 **Gochsheim** W Germany
79 C2 **Göçuk** Turkey
9 F5 **Godalming** England
74 J9 **Godavari** *R* India
76 F2 **Godavari, Mouths of the** India
122 E4 **Godbout** Quebec Canada
122 E4 **Godbout, R** Quebec Canada
117 E7 **Goddard** Alaska U.S.A.
107 N4 **Goddard** Kansas U.S.A.
36 F4 **Goddelau-Wolfskehlen** W Germany
46 F1 **Godech** Bulgaria
27 H13 **Godegård** Sweden
32 K9 **Godelheim** W Germany
47 L8 **Gödene** Turkey
120 J9 **Goderich** Ontario Canada
21 L2 **Goderville** France
22 D2 **Godewaersvelde** France
121 O8 **Godfrey** Ontario Canada
110 F3 **Godfrey** Illinois U.S.A.
115 O4 **Godhavn** Greenland
74 E7 **Godhra** India
109 K3 **Godley** Texas U.S.A.
144 C5 **Godley Gl** New Zealand
144 C5 **Godley R** New Zealand
9 F3 **Godmanchester** England
71 J5 **Godo** *mt* Indonesia
48 E3 **Gödöllö** Hungary
9 E6 **Godshill** England
115 K7 **Gods L** Manitoba Canada
9 F5 **Godstone** England
115 O5 **Godthåb** Greenland
112 J2 **Godwin** North Carolina U.S.A.
Godwin Austen *mt see* **K2** *mt*
25 A5 **Goedereede** Netherlands
121 O3 **Goeland** Quebec Canada
25 A5 **Goeree** Netherlands
25 A6 **Goes** Netherlands
107 P2 **Goff** Kansas U.S.A.
103 J7 **Goffs** Carolina U.S.A.
95 Q3 **Goffstown** New Hampshire U.S.A.
120 J5 **Gogama** Ontario Canada
60 F10 **Gō-gawa** *R* Japan
99 R3 **Gogebic** Michigan U.S.A.
99 R3 **Gogebic Range** *mts* Michigan U.S.A.
37 K7 **Goggingen** W Germany
41 H5 **Goglio** Italy
7 L10 **Gog Magog Hills** England
36 B6 **Gogney** France
22 F3 **Gognies-Chaussée** Belgium
142 F4 **Gogo** Western Australia Australia
31 K5 **Gogolin** Poland
86 E4 **Gogrial** Sudan
33 Q9 **Gohrau** East Germany
33 N6 **Göhrde** W Germany
130 J9 **Goiana** Brazil
130 E6 **Goiandira** Brazil
130 E4 **Goianésia** Brazil
130 E5 **Goiânia** Brazil
130 J9 **Goianinha** *lighthouse* Brazil
130 E4 **Goiás** Brazil
130 E6 **Goiatuba** Brazil
12 D1 **Goil, L** Scotland
130 D9 **Goio Erê** Brazil
25 D5 **Goirle** Netherlands
45 J1 **Goito** Italy
86 G3 **Gojam** *prov* Ethiopia
86 G4 **Gojeb** *R* Ethiopia
61 J11 **Gojō** Japan
61 O6 **Gojōme** Japan
47 K5 **Gök** *R* Turkey
76 B2 **Gokak** India
47 K7 **Gökbel** *mt* Turkey
47 H4 **Gökçeada** *isld* Turkey
47 K5 **Gökçedağ** Turkey
32 K4 **Gokels** W Germany
78 A3 **Gökova Körfezi** Turkey
77 H7 **Gokprosh Hills** Pakistan
78 D3 **Göksu** *R* Turkey
78 F2 **Göksun** Turkey
68 C1 **Gokteik** Burma
79 C2 **Göktepe** Turkey
47 K7 **Göktepe** Turkey
47 K8 **Gök Tepe** *mt* Turkey
87 E9 **Gokwe** Zimbabwe
27 C11 **Gol** Norway
75 P5 **Golaghat** India
80 G2 **Golan** Syria
31 K3 **Gołańcz** Poland
77 E6 **Golāshkerd** Iran
54 D10 **Golaya Pristan'** U.S.S.R.
77 L2 **Golbahār** Afghanistan
38 G8 **Gölbnerjoch** *mt* Austria
74 H10 **Golconda** India
110 H4 **Golconda** Illinois U.S.A.
100 H9 **Golconda** Nevada U.S.A.
Gölcük *see* **Etili**
47 N11 **Gölcük** Turkey
94 K5 **Gold** Pennsylvania U.S.A.
31 N1 **Gołdap** Poland
100 A7 **Gold Beach** Oregon U.S.A.
33 P7 **Goldbeck** East Germany
33 Q5 **Goldberg** East Germany
123 L8 **Goldboro** Nova Scotia Canada
101 O1 **Gold Butte** Montana U.S.A.
141 L8 **Gold Coast** Queensland Australia
28 C7 **Goldelund** W Germany
117 P10 **Golden** British Columbia Canada
98 A10 **Golden** Colorado U.S.A.
100 K4 **Golden** Idaho U.S.A.
110 E1 **Golden** Illinois U.S.A.
145 D4 **Golden Bay** New Zealand
110 B4 **Golden City** Missouri U.S.A.
100 E4 **Goldendale** Washington U.S.A.
144 D4 **Golden Downs** New Zealand
33 N10 **Goldene Aue** East Germany
102 B4 **Golden Gate** California U.S.A.
102 B4 **Golden Gate Nat. Recreation Area** California U.S.A.
103 J4 **Golden Gate Ra** Nevada U.S.A.
127 M3 **Golden Grove** Jamaica
121 N7 **Golden Lake** Ontario Canada
111 F12 **Golden Meadow** Louisiana U.S.A.
110 H5 **Golden Pond** Kentucky U.S.A.
118 H8 **Golden Prairie** Saskatchewan Canada
127 P4 **Golden Rock** *airport* St Kitts W Indies
101 N8 **Golden Spike Nat. Hist. Site** Utah U.S.A.
32 H7 **Goldenstedt** W Germany
14 C4 **Golden Vale** Ireland
123 K8 **Goldenville** Nova Scotia Canada
99 N7 **Goldfield** Iowa U.S.A.
102 G4 **Goldfield** Nevada U.S.A.
109 J7 **Goldfinch** Texas U.S.A.
101 M9 **Gold Hill** Utah U.S.A.
102 G4 **Gold Point** Nevada U.S.A.
118 K1 **Gold Rock** Ontario Canada
119 R1 **Goldsand L** Manitoba Canada
95 M7 **Goldsboro** Maryland U.S.A.
112 K2 **Goldsboro** North Carolina U.S.A.
108 E4 **Goldsmith** Texas U.S.A.
102 H6 **Goldstone L** California U.S.A.
142 C5 **Goldsworthy** Western Australia Australia
142 C5 **Goldsworthy, Mt** Western Australia Australia
109 J4 **Goldthwaite** Texas U.S.A.
112 F3 **Goldville** South Carolina U.S.A.
78 J1 **Göle** Turkey
85 E2 **Golea, El** Algeria
89 G6 **Golela** S Africa
31 H2 **Goleniów** Poland
102 E7 **Goleta** California U.S.A.
16 C7 **Golfo de Cádiz** Spain
43 E10 **Golfo di Castellammare** Sicily
43 E7 **Golfo di Gaeta** Italy
44 E3 **Golfo di Genova** Italy
45 N1 **Golfo di Venezia** Adriatic Sea
138 F5 **Gol Gol** New South Wales Australia
109 K7 **Goliad** Texas U.S.A.
46 D1 **Golija Planina** *mt* Yugoslavia
65 E2 **Golin Baixing** China
Gollel *see* **Lavumisa**
33 T6 **Gollin** East Germany
38 H6 **Golling** Austria
33 S10 **Gollmberg** *pk* East Germany
33 T9 **Gollmitz** East Germany
47 J6 **Gölmarmara** Turkey
33 S8 **Golmberg** *pk* East Germany
37 M2 **Golmsdorf** East Germany
66 E4 **Golmud** China
71 E4 **Golo** *isld* Philippines
52 H1 **Golodnaya Guba, Oz** *L* U.S.S.R.
57 E4 **Golodnaya Step'** U.S.S.R.
86 H4 **Gololcha** Ethiopia
88 E9 **Golomoti** Malawi
48 N2 **Golovanevsk** U.S.S.R.
116 F4 **Golovin** Alaska U.S.A.
60 T2 **Golovnino** Kuril Is U.S.S.R.
77 B3 **Golpāyegān** Iran
47 L4 **Gölpazarı** Turkey
116 G5 **Golsovia** Alaska U.S.A.
15 E3 **Golspie** Scotland
33 T9 **Golssen** East Germany
28 D2 **Gølstrup** Denmark
107 M5 **Goltry** Oklahoma U.S.A.
31 L2 **Gołub** Poland
55 F4 **Golubovka** U.S.S.R.
89 F3 **Golulu Ruins** Zimbabwe
87 B7 **Golungo Alto** Angola
98 C3 **Golva** North Dakota U.S.A.
46 G3 **Golyam Perelik** *mt* Bulgaria
31 M3 **Gołymin** Poland
54 C2 **Golynki** U.S.S.R.
55 E3 **Golyshmanovo** U.S.S.R.
33 R8 **Golzow** East Germany
88 B2 **Goma** Zaire
85 G6 **Gombe** Nigeria
44 H4 **Gombo** Italy
70 M9 **Gombong** Java
47 H5 **Gömeç** Turkey
54 B4 **Gomel'** U.S.S.R.
85 A3 **Gomera** *isld* Canary Is
124 H5 **Gómez Palacio** Mexico
125 K4 **Gómez, Presa M.R.** *res* Mexico
20 F5 **Gommené** France
33 P8 **Gommern** East Germany
66 C5 **Gomo** China
71 A3 **Gomumu** *isld* Indonesia
127 H5 **Gonaïves** Haiti
51 M3 **Gonam** *R* U.S.S.R.
89 G3 **Gona-re-zhou Game Res.** Zimbabwe
126 H5 **Gonâve, Île de la** Haiti
48 G2 **Gönc** Hungary
19 Q14 **Goncelin** France
74 D8 **Gondal** India
36 F5 **Gondelsheim** W Germany
86 G3 **Gonder** Ethiopia
86 G3 **Gonder** *prov* Ethiopia
74 J8 **Gondia** India
19 J4 **Gondrecourt** France
80 F1 **Gonen** Israel
47 J4 **Gönen** *R* Turkey
47 J4 **Gönen** Turkey
19 Q18 **Gonfaron** France
21 L2 **Gonfreville l'Orcher** France
83 K11 **Gongala** *mt* Sri Lanka
67 D1 **Gong'an** China
66 E5 **Gongbo'gyamda** China
67 C4 **Gongcheng** China
75 O4 **Gonggar** China
58 D6 **Gongga Shan** *mt* China
57 K3 **Gongliu** China
Gonglüe *see* **Donggu**
85 G6 **Gongola** *R* Nigeria
139 H4 **Gongolgon** New South Wales Australia
67 D3 **Gongpingxu** China
67 D2 **Gongtian** China
65 B7 **Gong Xian** China
65 D4 **Gongyingzi** China
Gongzhuling *see* **Huaide**
31 O2 **Goniądz** Poland
88 G4 **Gonja** Tanzania
36 G7 **Gönningen** W Germany
46 E5 **Gónnos** Greece
61 P5 **Gonohe** Japan
60 C12 **Gōnoura** Japan
40 D3 **Gonsans** France
99 L2 **Gonvick** Minnesota U.S.A.
45 J2 **Gonzaga** Italy
102 C5 **Gonzales** California U.S.A.
109 K6 **Gonzales** Texas U.S.A.
36 C4 **Gonzerath** W Germany
86 H6 **Goob Weyn** Somalia
94 K9 **Goochland** Virginia U.S.A.
146 F14 **Goodenough, C** Antarctica
121 M8 **Gooderham** Ontario Canada
119 O7 **Goodeve** Saskatchewan Canada
94 B1 **Good Hart** Michigan U.S.A.
99 V4 **Good Hbr. B** Michigan U.S.A.
89 B8 **Goodhope** S Africa
116 E4 **Goodhope** *R* Alaska U.S.A.
116 F3 **Goodhope B** Alaska U.S.A.
87 C12 **Good Hope, C. of** S Africa
117 L10 **Good Hope, Mt** British Columbia Canada
87 C11 **Goodhouse** S Africa
99 O5 **Goodhue** Minnesota U.S.A.
101 L7 **Gooding** Idaho U.S.A.
107 J2 **Goodland** Kansas U.S.A.
119 R9 **Goodlands** Manitoba Canada
83 M12 **Goodlands** Mauritius
110 K5 **Goodlettsville** Tennessee U.S.A.
99 S4 **Goodman** Wisconsin U.S.A.
116 F7 **Goodnews B** Alaska U.S.A.
108 C8 **Goodnight** Texas U.S.A.
139 H3 **Goodooga** New South Wales Australia
140 B2 **Goodparla** N Terr Australia
116 P4 **Goodpaster** *R* Alaska U.S.A.
106 F3 **Good Pasture** Colorado U.S.A.
98 B9 **Goodrich** Colorado U.S.A.
100 J5 **Goodrich** Idaho U.S.A.
98 F2 **Goodrich** North Dakota U.S.A.
111 B11 **Goodrich** Texas U.S.A.
99 Q4 **Goodrich** Wisconsin U.S.A.
140 B1 **Goodrich Bank** N Terr Australia
117 P10 **Goodsir, Mt** British Columbia Canada
118 H4 **Goodsoil** Saskatchewan Canada
119 P7 **Good Spirit L** Saskatchewan Canada
103 J6 **Goodsprings** Nevada U.S.A.
119 O9 **Goodwater** Saskatchewan Canada
111 K8 **Good Water** Alabama U.S.A.
107 J5 **Goodwell** Oklahoma U.S.A.
8 A3 **Goodwick** Wales
121 L4 **Goodwin** Ontario Canada
103 M7 **Goodwin** Arizona U.S.A.
98 K5 **Goodwin** South Dakota U.S.A.
7 M11 **Goodwin Sands** English Chan
144 C6 **Goodwood** New Zealand
9 F6 **Goodwood Park** England
13 H6 **Goole** England
139 H5 **Goolgowi** New South Wales Australia
139 J4 **Goolma** New South Wales Australia
139 J5 **Gooloogong** New South Wales Australia
138 E6 **Goolwa** South Australia Australia
140 C1 **Goomadeer** *R* N Terr Australia
143 B9 **Goomalling** Western Australia Australia
139 H3 **Goombalie** New South Wales Australia
141 K7 **Goombungee** Queensland Australia
141 K7 **Goomeri** Queensland Australia
141 K8 **Goondiwindi** Queensland Australia
143 D9 **Goongarrie** Western Australia Australia
143 D8 **Goongarrie, L** Western Australia Australia
141 J5 **Goonyella** Queensland Australia
25 G4 **Goor** Netherlands
117 P8 **Goose** *R* Alberta Canada
115 N7 **Goose Bay** Labrador, Nfld Canada
144 D5 **Goose Bay** New Zealand
101 R5 **Gooseberry Cr** Wyoming U.S.A.
118 G6 **Gooseberry L. Prov. Park** Alberta Canada
123 R2 **Goose Cove** Newfoundland Canada
101 M7 **Goose Cr** Idaho U.S.A.
112 G4 **Goose Creek** South Carolina U.S.A.
101 M8 **Goose Cr. Mts** Utah U.S.A.
101 T7 **Goose Egg** Wyoming U.S.A.

106 D2 **Green Mt Res** Colorado U.S.A.
95 O3 **Green Mts** Vermont U.S.A.
101 S7 **Green Mts** Wyoming U.S.A.
12 D2 **Greenock** Scotland
14 E2 **Greenore** Ireland
14 E4 **Greenore Pt** Ireland
143 A8 **Greenough** Western Australia Australia
116 R2 **Greenough, Mt** Alaska U.S.A.
112 G5 **Green Pond** South Carolina U.S.A.
95 P5 **Greenport** Long I. New York U.S.A.
122 D6 **Green R** New Brunswick Canada
101 Q8 **Green River** Wyoming U.S.A.
94 B9 **Green R. Res** Kentucky U.S.A.
111 J9 **Greensboro** Alabama U.S.A.
111 M11 **Greensboro** Florida U.S.A.
112 D4 **Greensboro** Georgia U.S.A.
112 H1 **Greensboro** North Carolina U.S.A.
95 P2 **Greensboro** Vermont U.S.A.
94 B7 **Greensburg** Indiana U.S.A.
107 L4 **Greensburg** Kansas U.S.A.
94 B9 **Greensburg** Kentucky U.S.A.
111 F11 **Greensburg** Louisiana U.S.A.
94 H6 **Greensburg** Pennsylvania U.S.A.
141 K2 **Greenslopes** dist Brisbane, Qnsld Australia
123 T4 **Greenspond** Newfoundland Canada
94 J7 **Green Spring** West Virginia U.S.A.
94 D5 **Green Springs** Ohio U.S.A.
99 O9 **Greentop** Missouri U.S.A.
94 B6 **Greentown** Indiana U.S.A.
113 K11 **Green Turtle Cay** isld Bahamas
110 H2 **Greenup** Illinois U.S.A.
141 H4 **Greenvale** Queensland Australia
85 C8 **Greenville** Liberia
111 K10 **Greenville** Alabama U.S.A.
100 E9 **Greenville** California U.S.A.
113 D7 **Greenville** Florida U.S.A.
110 G3 **Greenville** Illinois U.S.A.
110 J4 **Greenville** Kentucky U.S.A.
95 S1 **Greenville** Maine U.S.A.
94 B3 **Greenville** Michigan U.S.A.
111 E8 **Greenville** Mississippi U.S.A.
110 F4 **Greenville** Missouri U.S.A.
95 Q4 **Greenville** New Hampshire U.S.A.
95 N4 **Greenville** New York U.S.A.
112 K2 **Greenville** North Carolina U.S.A.
94 C6 **Greenville** Ohio U.S.A.
94 G5 **Greenville** Pennsylvania U.S.A.
112 E3 **Greenville** South Carolina U.S.A.
109 L2 **Greenville** Texas U.S.A.
94 H8 **Greenville** Virginia U.S.A.
119 N2 **Greenwater L** Ontario Canada
119 O6 **Greenwater L. Prov. Park** Saskatchewan Canada
119 S9 **Greenway** Manitoba Canada
98 G4 **Greenway** South Dakota U.S.A.
9 G5 **Greenwich** England
107 N4 **Greenwich** Kansas U.S.A.
95 O3 **Greenwich** New York U.S.A.
94 E5 **Greenwich** Ohio U.S.A.
103 N3 **Greenwich** Utah U.S.A.
100 G1 **Greenwood** British Columbia Canada
110 B6 **Greenwood** Arkansas U.S.A.
102 D3 **Greenwood** California U.S.A.
95 M8 **Greenwood** Delaware U.S.A.
94 A7 **Greenwood** Indiana U.S.A.
94 C10 **Greenwood** Kentucky U.S.A.
111 C9 **Greenwood** Louisiana U.S.A.
111 F8 **Greenwood** Mississippi U.S.A.
98 K9 **Greenwood** Nebraska U.S.A.
112 E3 **Greenwood** South Carolina U.S.A.
98 H7 **Greenwood** South Dakota U.S.A.
99 Q5 **Greenwood** Wisconsin U.S.A.
111 H8 **Greenwood Springs** Mississippi U.S.A.
100 J3 **Greer** Idaho U.S.A.
112 E3 **Greer** South Carolina U.S.A.
111 C7 **Greeson, L** Arkansas U.S.A.
32 F5 **Greetsiel** W Germany
21 M5 **Greez** France
25 F6 **Grefrath** W Germany
119 S9 **Gregg** Manitoba Canada
111 B9 **Greggton** Texas U.S.A.
118 F2 **Gregoire L** Alberta Canada
128 D5 **Gregório** R Brazil
98 G6 **Gregory** South Dakota U.S.A.
140 E4 **Gregory Downs** Queensland Australia
143 C7 **Gregory, L** Western Australia Australia
142 G5 **Gregory L** Western Australia Australia
141 G4 **Gregory Ra** Queensland Australia
142 D5 **Gregory Ra** Western Australia Australia
113 L12 **Gregory Town** Bahamas
38 H8 **Greifenburg** Austria
41 J3 **Greifensee** L Switzerland
33 T6 **Greiffenberg** East Germany
33 S4 **Greifswald** East Germany
33 T4 **Greifswalder Bodden** East Germany
33 T4 **Greifswalder Oie** isld East Germany
38 K7 **Greimberg** mt Austria
38 L5 **Grein** Austria
41 J4 **Greina Pass** Switzerland
38 M5 **Greinerwald** woods Austria
37 L5 **Greisselbach** W Germany
37 N2 **Greiz** East Germany
52 E1 **Gremikha** U.S.S.R.
33 N4 **Gremsmühlen** W Germany
28 F4 **Grenå** Denmark
127 P5 **Grenada** isld Lesser Antilles
100 C8 **Grenada** California U.S.A.
111 G8 **Grenada** Mississippi U.S.A.
18 E9 **Grenade** France
18 F9 **Grenade sur Garonne** France
127 O8 **Grenadines, The** islds Lesser Antilles
40 F3 **Grenchen** Switzerland
28 C5 **Grene** Denmark
28 F1 **Grenen** C Denmark
139 J5 **Grenfell** New South Wales Australia
119 P8 **Grenfell** Saskatchewan Canada
19 P14 **Grenoble** France
107 O4 **Grenola** Kansas U.S.A.
98 C1 **Grenora** North Dakota U.S.A.
26 S2 **Grense/Jakobselv** Norway
127 P5 **Grenville** Grenada
106 G5 **Grenville** New Mexico U.S.A.
98 J4 **Grenville** South Dakota U.S.A.
141 G1 **Grenville C** Queensland Australia
117 J9 **Grenville Chan** British Columbia Canada
117 L10 **Grenville, Mt** British Columbia Canada
19 P17 **Gréoux-les-Bains** France
33 Q9 **Greppin** East Germany
33 Q4 **Gresenhorst** East Germany
100 C4 **Gresham** Oregon U.S.A.
70 O9 **Gresik** Java
19 P15 **Gresse** France
19 Q13 **Grésy-sur-Isère** France
139 K5 **Greta** New South Wales Australia
13 G5 **Greta Br** England
119 U9 **Gretna** Manitoba Canada
111 G12 **Gretna** Louisiana U.S.A.
111 J13 **Gretna** New Orleans, Louisiana U.S.A.
94 H10 **Gretna** Virginia U.S.A.
13 E3 **Gretna Green** Scotland
37 K1 **Greussen** East Germany
45 K4 **Greve** Italy
25 A5 **Grevelingen** Netherlands
32 G8 **Greven** W Germany
46 E4 **Grevená** Greece
36 B1 **Grevenbroich** W Germany
32 L5 **Grevenkop** W Germany
33 O5 **Grevesmühlen** East Germany
27 F16 **Grevie** Sweden
29 K4 **Grevie** Sweden
28 H5 **Grevinge** Denmark
101 R5 **Greybull** Wyoming U.S.A.
140 D2 **Grey, C** N Terr Australia
101 Q4 **Greycliff** Montana U.S.A.
99 M4 **Grey Eagle** Minnesota U.S.A.
117 F4 **Grey Hunter Pk** Yukon Territory Canada
123 R3 **Grey I** Newfoundland Canada
123 R3 **Grey Is** Newfoundland Canada
144 C5 **Greymouth** New Zealand
123 Q5 **Grey R** Newfoundland Canada
141 G8 **Grey Ra** Qnsld/N S W
141 G8 **Grey Range** Queensland Australia
101 P6 **Greys** R Wyoming U.S.A.
143 A7 **Grey's Plains** Western Australia Australia
13 F4 **Greystoke** England
101 R9 **Greystone** Colorado U.S.A.
14 E3 **Greystones** Ireland
145 E4 **Greytown** New Zealand
89 G7 **Greytown** S Africa
22 H2 **Grez-Doiceau** Belgium
21 J6 **Grez-en-Bouère** France
46 D4 **Griba** mt Albania
81 F11 **Gribb Seamount** Southern Oc
86 C4 **Gribingui** R Cent Afr Republic
52 D2 **Gridino** U.S.S.R.
102 C2 **Gridley** California U.S.A.
99 S9 **Gridley** Illinois U.S.A.
107 P3 **Gridley** Kansas U.S.A.
87 D11 **Griekwastad** S Africa
25 D2 **Griend** Netherlands
37 P7 **Griesbach** W Germany
36 F4 **Griesheim** W Germany
41 O3 **Gries im Sellrain** Austria
Griessen see **Klettgau**
25 F5 **Grieth** W Germany
38 L8 **Griffen** Austria
111 M8 **Griffin** Georgia U.S.A.
113 F9 **Griffin, L** Florida U.S.A.
116 Q1 **Griffin Pt** Alaska U.S.A.
139 H5 **Griffith** New South Wales Australia
115 K3 **Griffith I** Northwest Territories Canada
110 E6 **Griffithville** Arkansas U.S.A.
112 K2 **Grifton** North Carolina U.S.A.
99 Q10 **Griggsville** Illinois U.S.A.
41 K6 **Grigna** mt Italy
19 N16 **Grignan** France
18 E8 **Grignols** France
48 M3 **Grigoriopol'** U.S.S.R.
25 F2 **Grijpskerk** Netherlands
86 C4 **Grimari** Cent Afr Republic
19 Q18 **Grimaud** France
21 L8 **Grimaudière, la** France
48 K1 **Grimaylov** U.S.S.R.
139 G8 **Grim, C** Tasmania Australia
102 C2 **Grimes** California U.S.A.
100 K5 **Grimes Pass** Idaho U.S.A.
33 R10 **Grimma** East Germany
33 S4 **Grimmen** East Germany
Grimmenthal see **Obermassfeld-Grimmenthal**
33 T7 **Grimnitzsee** East Germany
121 L9 **Grimsby** Ontario Canada
13 H6 **Grimsby** England
41 H4 **Grimsel** mt Switzerland
28 S8 **Grimsey** isld Iceland
117 P7 **Grimshaw** Alberta Canada
27 C13 **Grimstad** Norway
28 B5 **Grimstrup** Denmark
28 R10 **Grindavik** Iceland
40 H4 **Grindelwald** Switzerland
28 C3 **Grinderslev** Denmark
28 B5 **Grindsted Å** Denmark
95 S8 **Grindstone** Maine U.S.A.
94 E2 **Grind Stone City** Michigan U.S.A.
123 L6 **Grindstone Island** Quebec Canada
119 U7 **Grindstone Prov. Park** Manitoba Canada
119 V7 **Grindstone Pt** Manitoba Canada
99 O8 **Grinnell** Iowa U.S.A.
107 K2 **Grinnell** Kansas U.S.A.
115 K2 **Grinnell Pen** Northwest Territories Canada
42 F2 **Grintavec** mt Yugoslavia
13 G5 **Grinton** England
26 C8 **Grip** lighthouse Norway
33 O6 **Grippel** W Germany
89 F8 **Griqualand E** reg S Africa
89 C7 **Griqualand W** reg S Africa
40 F6 **Grisanche, Val** Italy
115 L2 **Grise Fiord** Northwest Territories Canada
45 L1 **Grisignano** Italy
69 F14 **Grisik** Sumatra
22 B2 **Gris Nez, C** France
18 F9 **Grisolles** France
27 K11 **Grisslehamn** Sweden
99 L8 **Griswold** Iowa U.S.A.
52 H4 **Griva** U.S.S.R.
21 P2 **Grivesnes** France
40 F6 **Grivola** mt Italy
33 P9 **Grizeline** East Germany
85 D3 **Grizim** Algeria
117 N3 **Grizzly Bear Mt** Northwest Territories Canada
26 C9 **Grjotli** Norway
42 G4 **Grmeč Plan** Yugoslavia
123 R3 **Groais I** Newfoundland Canada
33 S10 **Gröba** East Germany
33 Q10 **Gröbers** East Germany
27 M15 **Grobina** U.S.S.R.
9 E2 **Groby** England
33 P9 **Gröbzig** East Germany
28 B7 **Gröde-Appelland** isld W Germany
31 O2 **Gródek** Poland
31 K5 **Grodków** Poland
33 S10 **Grödlitz** East Germany
31 O2 **Grodno** U.S.S.R.
31 J3 **Grodzisk** Poland
31 M3 **Grodzisk Mazowiecki** Poland
89 C8 **Groen** watercourse S Africa
22 G2 **Groenendaal** Belgium
25 G4 **Groenlo** Netherlands
109 L4 **Groesbeck** Texas U.S.A.
25 E5 **Groesbeek** Netherlands
25 C3 **Groet** Netherlands
32 K8 **Grohnde** W Germany
22 F3 **Groise, la** France
37 N1 **Groitzsch** East Germany
20 D6 **Groix** France
20 D6 **Groix, I de** France
31 M4 **Grójec** Poland
43 C12 **Grombalia** Tunisia
28 C7 **Grønå** R Denmark
32 L8 **Gronau** Niedersachsen W Germany
32 F8 **Gronau** Nordrhein-Westfalen W Germany
28 B4 **Grønbjerg** Denmark
26 F7 **Grong** Norway
28 C4 **Grønhøj** Denmark
33 O9 **Gröningen** East Germany
25 G2 **Groningen** Netherlands
25 F2 **Groningerwad** Netherlands
119 N5 **Gronlid** Saskatchewan Canada
115 P5 **Grønnedal** Greenland
26 F5 **Grönöy** Norway
27 K12 **Grönskär** lighthouse Sweden
27 H14 **Grönskåra** Sweden
28 J7 **Grønsund** chan Denmark
89 D9 **Groot** R S Africa
140 D2 **Groote Eylandt** isld N Terr Australia
25 F2 **Grootegast** Netherlands
89 B9 **Groot Swartberge** mts S Africa
89 C8 **Groot Tafelberg** mt S Africa
89 B7 **Groot Vloer** S Africa
87 D11 **Grootvloer** L S Africa
89 E9 **Groot Winterberg** mt S Africa
22 K4 **Grosbous** Luxembourg
20 G8 **Grosbreuil** France
127 O7 **Gros Islet** St Lucia
27 G14 **Grosjö** Sweden
123 P4 **Gros Morne** pk Newfoundland Canada
122 G4 **Gros Morne** Quebec Canada
127 H5 **Gros Morne** Haiti
127 L4 **Gros Morne** Martinique W Indies
123 P4 **Gros Morne Nat. Park** Newfoundland Canada
19 J6 **Grosne** R France
20 F3 **Grosnez Pt** Channel Is
41 M5 **Grosotto** Italy
123 P3 **Gros Pate** pk Newfoundland Canada
113 F7 **Gross** Florida U.S.A.
37 M4 **Gross Albershof** W Germany
40 H4 **Gross Aletsch Gl** Switzerland
32 L10 **Grossalmerode** W Germany
33 O9 **Gross Alsleben** East Germany
33 P8 **Gross Ammensleben** East Germany
37 P5 **Gross Arber** mt W Germany
33 S8 **Grossbeeren** East Germany
33 T8 **Grossbesten** East Germany
33 M10 **Grossbodungen** East Germany
37 O1 **Gross Bothen** East Germany
36 G5 **Grossbottwar** W Germany
37 L2 **Gross-Breitenbach** East Germany
33 T7 **Gross-Dölln** East Germany
37 M2 **Gross Ebersdorf** East Germany
123 L6 **Grosse I** Madeleine Is, Quebec Canada
36 F2 **Grossenbuseck** W Germany
37 K1 **Grossenehrich** East Germany
33 O7 **Gross Engersen** East Germany
33 T10 **Grossenhain** East Germany
32 H7 **Grossenkneten** W Germany
37 N2 **Grossenstein** East Germany
127 N4 **Grosse Pointe** Guadeloupe W Indies
33 S10 **Grosse Röder** R East Germany
42 D6 **Grosseto** Italy
51 N4 **Grossevichi** U.S.S.R.
36 D5 **Gross Eyberg** mt W Germany
36 E3 **Gross Feldberg** mt W Germany
33 T6 **Gross Fredenwalde** East Germany
36 E4 **Gross-Gerau** W Germany
33 M8 **Gross Gleidingen** W Germany
38 G7 **Gross-Glockner** Austria
33 P6 **Gross-Godems** East Germany
37 N1 **Gross Görschen** East Germany
33 N5 **Gross Gronau** W Germany
33 M5 **Gross Hansdorf** W Germany
37 P2 **Gross Hartmannsdorf** East Germany
32 F5 **Grossheide** W Germany
37 M1 **Gross Heringen** East Germany
33 M7 **Gross-Kain** W Germany
36 E4 **Gross Karlbach** W Germany
33 O4 **Gross Klützhöved** East Germany
37 L2 **Gross Kochberg** East Germany
33 Q10 **Gross Korbetha** East Germany
33 T8 **Gross Köris** East Germany
33 R8 **Gross Kreutz** East Germany
37 N6 **Gross Laaber** R W Germany
37 J4 **Gross-Langheim** W Germany
36 H2 **Grosslüder** W Germany
33 S8 **Gross-Machnow** East Germany
37 M6 **Grossmehring** W Germany
33 M7 **Gross-Oesingen** W Germany
36 G4 **Grossostheim** W Germany
33 M4 **Gross Plöner See** L W Germany
37 P6 **Gross Rachel** mt W Germany
38 L6 **Grossraming** Austria
32 M9 **Gross Rhüden** W Germany
36 B5 **Grossrosseln** W Germany
37 L1 **Gross Rudestedt** East Germany
33 T7 **Gross Schönebeck** East Germany
33 P7 **Gross Schwechten** East Germany
33 T8 **Gross Selchower See** L East Germany
33 N8 **Gross-Sisbeck** W Germany
33 S6 **Gross Stechlinsee** L East Germany
36 H6 **Gross Süssen** W Germany
36 F4 **Gross-Umstadt** W Germany
37 P2 **Gross Waltersdorf** East Germany
33 P6 **Gross-Warnow** East Germany
33 Q6 **Gross Welle** East Germany
33 Q7 **Gross Wudicke** East Germany
33 R5 **Gross Wüstenfelde** East Germany
33 Q8 **Gross Wusterwitz** East Germany
33 T7 **Gross Ziethen** East Germany
36 F4 **Gross-Zimmern** W Germany
36 B6 **Gros Tenquin** France
21 M3 **Gros Theil, le** France
42 F3 **Grosuplje** Yugoslavia
141 J5 **Grosvenor Downs** Queensland Australia
116 K7 **Grosvenor, L** Alaska U.S.A.
101 P6 **Gros Ventre Ra** Wyoming U.S.A.
32 J9 **Grotenberg** mt W Germany
22 F2 **Grotenberge** Belgium
22 H1 **Grote Nete** R Belgium
95 Q5 **Groton** Connecticut U.S.A.
95 Q4 **Groton** Massachusetts U.S.A.
95 L4 **Groton** New York U.S.A.
98 H4 **Groton** South Dakota U.S.A.
95 P2 **Groton** Vermont U.S.A.
26 G4 **Grötöy** Norway
45 Q8 **Grotta Azzurra** Italy
45 O7 **Grotta delle Capre** Italy
22 J3 **Grotte-de-Han** Belgium
19 N16 **Grottes de St. Marcel** France
94 J8 **Grottoes** Virginia U.S.A.
36 F5 **Grotzingen** W Germany
117 P8 **Grouard** Alberta Canada
20 G4 **Grouin, Pte.du** France
120 H4 **Groundhog** R Ontario Canada
101 M6 **Grouse** Idaho U.S.A.
101 M8 **Grouse Creek** Utah U.S.A.
25 E2 **Grouw** Netherlands
27 C13 **Grovane** Norway
107 Q5 **Grove** Oklahoma U.S.A.
94 E7 **Grove City** Ohio U.S.A.
94 G5 **Grove City** Pennsylvania U.S.A.
117 O8 **Grovedale** Alberta Canada
140 B2 **Grove Hill** N Terr Australia
111 J10 **Grove Hill** Alabama U.S.A.
28 C4 **Grove Kirke** Denmark
102 D4 **Groveland** California U.S.A.
26 F9 **Grövelsjön** Sweden
146 H11 **Grove Mts** Antarctica
98 B9 **Grover** Colorado U.S.A.
101 P7 **Grover** Wyoming U.S.A.
111 C12 **Groves** Texas U.S.A.
109 M4 **Groveton** Texas U.S.A.
95 Q2 **Groveton** Vermont U.S.A.
145 D4 **Grovetown** New Zealand
112 E4 **Grovetown** Georgia U.S.A.
101 P6 **Grovont** Wyoming U.S.A.
103 L9 **Growler** Arizona U.S.A.
103 L9 **Growler Mts** Arizona U.S.A.
47 J1 **Grozd'ovo** Bulgaria
45 P1 **Groznjan** Yugoslavia
57 F3 **Groznoye** U.S.S.R.
53 G11 **Groznyy** U.S.S.R.
41 J4 **Gr. Scheerh** mt Switzerland
33 O4 **Grube** W Germany
32 L9 **Grubenhagen** W Germany
42 H3 **Grubišno Polje** Yugoslavia
37 P6 **Grubweg** W Germany
21 M2 **Gruchet-le-Valasse** France
42 J6 **Gruda** Yugoslavia
47 J2 **Grudovo** Bulgaria
31 M2 **Grudusk** Poland
31 L2 **Grudziadz** Poland
128 D8 **Gruesa, Pta** C Chile
122 B6 **Grues, I. aux** Quebec Canada
44 C1 **Grugliasco** Italy
12 B2 **Gruinart** Scotland
109 J9 **Grulla** Texas U.S.A.
36 D4 **Grumbach** W Germany
43 H7 **Grumo Appula** Italy
27 F12 **Grums** Sweden
37 O2 **Gruna** East Germany
15 C3 **Grunard Bay** Scotland
33 T8 **Grunau** East Germany
87 C11 **Grünau** Namibia
36 G6 **Grunbach** W Germany
36 F2 **Grünberg** W Germany
36 G3 **Gründau** W Germany
Gründelhardt see **Frankenhardt**
26 K8 **Grundsunda** Sweden
26 J8 **Grundtjärn** Sweden
99 O7 **Grundy Center** Iowa U.S.A.
120 K7 **Grundy Lake Prov. Park** Ontario Canada
28 D7 **Grünholz** W Germany
124 J5 **Gruñidora** Mexico
33 Q8 **Grüningen** East Germany
36 F2 **Grüningen** W Germany
36 H4 **Grünsfeld** W Germany
36 E4 **Grünstadt** W Germany
38 E8 **Gruppo** mt Italy
41 L4 **Grüsch** Switzerland
108 C7 **Gruver** Texas U.S.A.
40 F4 **Gruyère, L. de la** Switzerland
52 B6 **Gruzdžiai** U.S.S.R.
53 F12 **Gruzinskaya S.S.R.** U.S.S.R.
54 L4 **Gryazi** U.S.S.R.
52 F5 **Gryazovets** U.S.S.R.
31 M6 **Grybów** Poland
27 H11 **Grycksbo** Sweden
31 J2 **Gryfice** Poland
31 H2 **Gryfino** Poland
99 L1 **Grygla** Minnesota U.S.A.
27 G12 **Grythyttehed** Sweden
26 H3 **Grytöy** L Norway
26 C9 **Grytten** Norway
131 H6 **Grytviken** S Georgia
31 J2 **Grzmiaca** Poland
41 O3 **Gschnitz** Austria
36 H6 **Gschwend** W Germany
40 F5 **Gstaad** Switzerland
40 F5 **Gsteig** Switzerland
19 P15 **Guâ** France
75 L7 **Gua** India
41 O7 **Gua** R Italy
128 D3 **Guacamayas** Colombia
126 F4 **Guacanayabo, G.de** Cuba
127 L9 **Guacara** Venezuela
103 M9 **Gu Achi** Arizona U.S.A.
128 D2 **Guachiria** R Colombia
130 C8 **Guaçu** Brazil
124 H7 **Guadalajara** Mexico
16 E4 **Guadalajara** Spain
17 F4 **Guadalajara** prov Spain
137 M3 **Guadalcanal** isld Solomon Is
16 D6 **Guadalcanal** Spain
16 E6 **Guadalén** R Spain
17 F7 **Guadalentin** R Spain
16 D8 **Guadalete** R Spain
16 E8 **Guadalfeo** R Spain
16 E8 **Guadalhorce** R Spain
16 E6 **Guadalimar** R Spain
17 F6 **Guadalmena** R Spain
16 D6 **Guadalmez** R Spain
16 D7 **Guadalquivir** R Spain
131 C5 **Guadal, Sa. de** Argentina
124 H6 **Guadalupe** Mexico
108 A4 **Guadalupe** Mexico
71 F5 **Guadalupe** Cebu Philippines
102 D7 **Guadalupe** California U.S.A.
109 J6 **Guadalupe** R Texas U.S.A.
108 C4 **Guadalupe Pk** Texas U.S.A.
16 D5 **Guadalupe, Sa de** mts Spain
124 G5 **Guadalupe Victoria** Durango Mexico
124 F4 **Guadalupe y Calvo** Mexico
16 E4 **Guadarrama, Sa. de** mts Spain
17 F5 **Guadazaón** R Spain
127 N4 **Guadeloupe** islds Lesser Antilles
16 E6 **Guadiana** R Portugal/Spain
16 E7 **Guadiano Menor** R Spain
16 D6 **Guadiato** R Spain
17 F4 **Guadiela** R Spain
16 E7 **Guadix** Spain
133 C6 **Guafo** isld Chile
127 P2 **Guaico** Trinidad
130 C7 **Guaicuras** Brazil
128 F2 **Guaina** Venezuela
128 E3 **Guainia** R Colombia
130 C9 **Guaira** Brazil
130 C9 **Guaira** Paraguay
133 C6 **Guaitecas, Is** Chile
126 F4 **Guajaba, Cayo** isld Cuba
128 E6 **Guajará Mirim** Brazil
128 E5 **Guajarraã** Brazil
128 F5 **Guajaturaba** Brazil
124 H4 **Guaje, Llano de** reg Mexico
125 L2 **Guajiniquil** Honduras
128 D1 **Guajira** div Colombia
128 D1 **Guajira, Pena de** pen Colombia
102 A3 **Gualala** California U.S.A.
42 E5 **Gualdo Tadino** Italy
131 F4 **Gualeguay** R Argentina
131 F4 **Gualeguay** Argentina
133 F4 **Gualeguaychu** Argentina
131 D8 **Gualicho Salina** salt pan Argentina
128 E7 **Guallatiri** mt Chile
45 J2 **Gualtieri** Italy
134 E6 **Guam** isld Mariana Is Pacific Oc
129 J4 **Guamá** R Brazil
129 J4 **Guamá** Brazil
127 K9 **Guama** Venezuela
133 B6 **Guamblin, I** Chile
133 E5 **Guamini** Argentina
124 E5 **Guamúchil** Mexico
69 E10 **Gua Musang** Malaysia
65 C5 **Gu'an** China
126 C3 **Guanabacoa** Cuba
130 G8 **Guanabara** Brazil
125 M4 **Guanacaste, Cord. de** ra Costa Rica
124 G5 **Guanacevi** Mexico
126 B3 **Guanahacabibes, Pen. de** Cuba
126 C3 **Guanajay** Cuba
124 J7 **Guanajuato** Mexico
129 K6 **Guanambi** Brazil
128 C5 **Guañape, I** Peru
127 O2 **Guanapo** Trinidad
128 E2 **Guanarito** Venezuela
65 B5 **Guancen Shan** mt ra China
67 C6 **Guanchang** China
133 D3 **Guandacol** Argentina
65 G3 **Guandi** China
67 C1 **Guandiankou** China
126 B3 **Guane** Cuba
67 B1 **Guang'an** China
67 E3 **Guangchang** China
67 F1 **Guangde** China
65 D3 **Guangdegong** China
67 D5 **Guangdong** prov China
67 F2 **Guangfeng** China
67 A1 **Guangfu** China
67 A1 **Guanghan** China
65 B6 **Guanghua** China
58 F5 **Guanghua** China
67 E2 **Guangji** China
58 F4 **Guangling** China
65 E5 **Guanglu Dao** isld China
67 F1 **Guangming Ding** mt China
67 B4 **Guangnan** China
67 D5 **Guangning** China
65 C6 **Guangping** China
65 D6 **Guangrao** China
67 E1 **Guangshan** China
58 F5 **Guangshui** China
67 B5 **Guangxi** prov China
67 F1 **Guangyang** China
58 E5 **Guangyuan** China
67 F3 **Guangze** China
67 D5 **Guangzhou** China
65 C6 **Guangzong** China
130 G6 **Guanhães** Brazil
65 D7 **Guanhu** China
127 L5 **Guánica** Puerto Rico
128 F2 **Guanipa** R Venezuela
67 D3 **Guanjiazui** China
67 B4 **Guanling** China
67 C1 **Guanmian Shan** mts China
65 D7 **Guannan** China
100 F7 **Guano L** Oregon U.S.A.
65 G1 **Guansongzhen** China
Guansuo see **Guanling**
128 F1 **Guanta** Venezuela
126 G4 **Guantánamo** Cuba
126 G5 **Guantánamo, B. de** Cuba
65 C6 **Guantao** China
65 C4 **Guanting Shuiku** res China
65 C6 **Guan Xian** China
67 A1 **Guan Xian** China
67 D4 **Guanyang** China
65 D7 **Guanyun** China
130 F7 **Guapé** Brazil
128 C3 **Guapi** Colombia
133 G3 **Guaporé** Brazil
130 J9 **Guarabira** Brazil
130 D10 **Guarama** Brazil
130 F8 **Guarantinguetá** Brazil
130 H7 **Guarapari** Brazil
130 D9 **Guarapuava** Brazil
130 E9 **Guaraqueçaba** Brazil
130 E7 **Guararapes** Brazil
130 J10 **Guararapes** Brazil
17 G2 **Guara, Sa. de** Spain
18 E10 **Guara, Sierra de** mts Spain
130 E9 **Guaratuba** Brazil
45 O6 **Guarcino** Italy
16 C4 **Guarda** Portugal
17 F7 **Guardal** R Spain
130 F5 **Guarda Mor** Brazil
127 L10 **Guardatinajas** Venezuela
13 F1 **Guardbridge** Scotland
133 E6 **Guardia Mitre** Argentina
133 D7 **Guardián, C** Argentina
45 R7 **Guardia Sanframondi** Italy
16 D2 **Guardo** Spain
16 B4 **Guardunha Sa.da** mts Portugal
128 F5 **Guariba** R Amazonas Brazil
127 L10 **Guárico** R Venezuela
128 E2 **Guárico** state Venezuela
130 D10 **Guarita** R Brazil
124 E5 **Guasave** Mexico
128 C3 **Guascama, Pta** pt Colombia
125 K7 **Guasima** Mexico
130 C9 **Guassú, R** Brazil
42 D4 **Guastalla** Italy
125 O10 **Guatemala** rep Central America
126 G4 **Guatemala** Cuba
125 O10 **Guatemala** Guatemala
127 L9 **Guatire** Venezuela
128 E3 **Guaviare** R Colombia
126 F4 **Guayabal** Cuba
128 E2 **Guayabal** Venezuela
128 D3 **Guayabero** R Colombia
131 C3 **Guayaguas, Sa. da** ra Argentina
127 P3 **Guayaguayare** Trinidad
127 L5 **Guayama** Puerto Rico
128 C4 **Guayaquil** Ecuador
128 B4 **Guayaquil, Golfo de** Ecuador
128 E6 **Guayaramerin** Bolivia
128 B4 **Guayas** prov Ecuador
133 B7 **Guayeco Arch** islds Chile
124 D4 **Guaymas** Mexico
131 F3 **Guayquiraró, R** Argentina
130 F7 **Guazupé** Brazil
86 G3 **Guba** Ethiopia
87 E8 **Guba** Zaire
67 A2 **Gubai** China
52 J5 **Gubakha** U.S.S.R.
71 G4 **Gubat** Philippines
42 E5 **Gubbio** Italy
52 J4 **Gubdor** U.S.S.R.
65 D4 **Gubeikou** China
Guben see **Wilhelm Pieck Stadt**
31 H4 **Gubin** East Germany
54 J5 **Gubkin** U.S.S.R.
47 H2 **Gübübovo** Bulgaria
65 C6 **Gucheng** China
67 D1 **Gucheng** China
17 G4 **Gudar, Sa. de** mts Spain
28 F6 **Gudbjerg** Denmark
26 C9 **Gudbrandsdalen** Norway
28 D5 **Gudenå** R Denmark
36 G1 **Gudensberg** W Germany
36 F4 **Gudernheim** W Germany
28 D6 **Guderup** Denmark
27 G16 **Gudhjem** Denmark
28 F6 **Gudme** Denmark
77 J6 **Gudri** R Pakistan
65 B7 **Gudui** China
28 G6 **Gudum** Denmark
28 E3 **Gudumholm** Denmark
28 A3 **Gudum Kirke** Denmark
76 D3 **Gudur** India
27 B11 **Gudvangen** Norway
19 K5 **Guebwiller** France
133 C6 **Guechucuicui, Pta** Chile
85 B7 **Guéckédou** Guinea
21 M5 **Gué-de-la-Chaîne** France
21 O4 **Gue-de-Longroi, le** France
20 E6 **Guegon** France
121 N4 **Guéguen** L Quebec Canada
20 E6 **Guéhenno** France
16 E7 **Güéjar Sierra** Spain
86 C3 **Guelengdeng** Chad
85 F1 **Guelma** Algeria
85 B3 **Guelmine** Western Sahara
98 H3 **Guelph** North Dakota U.S.A.
85 D5 **Guem** Mali
36 C7 **Guémar** France
20 G6 **Guémene-Penfao** France
20 D5 **Guéméné-sur-Scorff** France
121 P6 **Guenette** Quebec Canada
133 C7 **Guenguel** R Argentina
20 G6 **Guenroue** France
20 F6 **Guer** France
16 C6 **Gueraña** Spain
20 F7 **Guérande** France
86 C3 **Guéra, Pic de** mt Chad
85 E2 **Guerara** Algeria
20 H6 **Guerche-de-Bretagne, la** France
18 G6 **Guerche-sur-l'Aubois, la** France
86 D3 **Guéréda** Chad
18 G6 **Guéret** France
121 L5 **Guerin** Quebec Canada
20 F8 **Guérinière, la** France
20 D5 **Guerlédan, L.de** France
20 D5 **Guern** France
18 D9 **Guernica** Spain
119 M7 **Guernsey** Saskatchewan Canada
98 B7 **Guernsey** Wyoming U.S.A.
20 E3 **Guernsey I** Channel Is
98 B7 **Guernsey Res** Wyoming U.S.A.
21 M4 **Gueroulde, la** France
109 J9 **Guerra** Texas U.S.A.
21 O2 **Guerville** France
85 D4 **Guettara, El** Mali
18 H6 **Gueugnon** France
111 D12 **Gueydan** Louisiana U.S.A.
41 K4 **Güferhorn** mt Switzerland
38 E6 **Güffert-Spitze** mt Austria
86 G4 **Guga** mt Ethiopia
86 G4 **Gugā** mt Ethiopia
42 F7 **Guglionesi** Italy
48 H5 **Gugu** mt Romania
70 K9 **Guhakolak, Tanjong** C Java
33 R6 **Gühlen-Glienecke** East Germany
130 C4 **Guia** Brazil
20 G6 **Guichen** France
67 F1 **Guichi** China
125 M9 **Guichicovi** Mexico
20 C4 **Guiclan** France
20 D6 **Guidel** France
86 B4 **Guider** Cameroon
98 H9 **Guide Rock** Nebraska U.S.A.
67 B3 **Guiding** China
45 J1 **Guidizzolo** Italy
67 D3 **Guidong** China
19 P13 **Guiers** R France
85 A5 **Guiers, L. de** Senegal
45 J3 **Guiglia** Italy
85 C7 **Guiglo** Ivory Coast
20 G6 **Guignen** France
22 J2 **Guigoven** Belgium
127 L9 **Güigüi** Venezuela
Guihua see **Mingxi**
87 F10 **Guija** Mozambique
67 C4 **Gui Jiang** R China
67 G2 **Guiji Shan** mts China
143 B9 **Guilderton** Western Australia Australia
143 B9 **Guildford** Western Australia Australia
9 F5 **Guildford** England
95 Q2 **Guildhall** Vermont U.S.A.
65 E1 **Guiler Gol** R China
95 P5 **Guilford** Connecticut U.S.A.
95 S1 **Guilford** Maine U.S.A.
112 H1 **Guilford Ct. Ho. Nat. Mil. Park** North Carolina U.S.A.
67 C4 **Guilin** China
20 F6 **Guillac** France
20 F5 **Guilliers** France
20 B6 **Guilvinec, le** France
16 B3 **Guimaraes** Portugal
71 F5 **Guimaras** isld Philippines
71 F5 **Guimaras Str** Philippines
20 B5 **Guimiliau** France
111 J8 **Guin** Alabama U.S.A.
125 M3 **Güina** Nicaragua
71 F5 **Guinauayan** isld Philippines
126 E3 **Guinchos Cay** isld Cuba
102 B3 **Guinda** California U.S.A.
71 G6 **Guindulman** Philippines
85 B6 **Guinea** rep W Africa
90 J8 **Guinea Basin** Atlantic Oc
85 A6 **Guinea-Bissau** rep W Africa
85 E8 **Guinea, Gulf of** W Africa
122 C3 **Guinecourt, L** Quebec Canada
126 D3 **Güines** Cuba
22 B2 **Guines** France
20 D4 **Guingamp** France
71 F5 **Guintacan** isld Philippines
71 F3 **Guintinua** isld Philippines
110 E6 **Guion** Arkansas U.S.A.
20 B5 **Guipavas** France
67 C5 **Guiping** China
17 F1 **Guipúzcoa** prov Spain
85 D5 **Guir** Mali
126 C3 **Güira de Melena** Cuba
130 D5 **Guiratinga** Brazil
129 H3 **Guisanbourg** Fr Guiana
13 G5 **Guisborough** England
22 E4 **Guiscard** France
20 C5 **Guiscriff** France
22 F4 **Guise** France
13 G6 **Guiseley** England
20 B4 **Guisseny** France
9 G2 **Guist** England
71 G5 **Guiuan** Philippines
22 E4 **Guivry** France
67 F2 **Guixi** China
67 C5 **Gui Xian** China
67 B3 **Guiyang** Guizhou China
67 B3 **Guizhou** prov China
74 D7 **Gujarat** prov India
74 F2 **Gujranwala** Pakistan
74 F2 **Gujrat** Pakistan
67 C1 **Gujunba** China
103 N9 **Gu Komelik** Arizona U.S.A.
54 L8 **Gukovo** U.S.S.R.
58 D4 **Gulang** China
139 J4 **Gulargambone** New South Wales Australia
74 G10 **Gulbarga** India
52 C6 **Gulbene** U.S.S.R.
57 G4 **Gul'cha** U.S.S.R.
28 A5 **Guldager** Denmark
28 E5 **Guldbjerg** Denmark
28 H7 **Guldborg** Denmark
36 D4 **Guldental** W Germany
27 H12 **Guldsmedshyttan** Sweden
76 B2 **Guledgarh** India
79 E1 **Gülek** Turkey
27 A10 **Gulen** Norway
112 H2 **Gulf** North Carolina U.S.A.
111 J11 **Gulf Beach** Florida U.S.A.
141 G4 **Gulf Highway** Queensland Australia
111 H11 **Gulf Islands Nat Seashore** Mississippi U.S.A.
113 E10 **Gulfport** Florida U.S.A.
111 G11 **Gulfport** Mississippi U.S.A.
26 R1 **Gulgofjorden** Norway
139 J4 **Gulgong** New South Wales Australia
67 B2 **Gulin** China
57 E4 **Gulistan** U.S.S.R.
33 P6 **Gülitz** East Germany
Gulja see **Yining**
116 P5 **Gulkana** Alaska U.S.A.
118 D6 **Gull** L Alberta Canada
27 H15 **Gullabo** Sweden
13 F1 **Gullane** Scotland
119 O1 **Gull Bay** Ontario Canada
28 D4 **Gullev** Denmark
6 L1 **Gullfaks** oil rig North Sea
28 S9 **Gullfoss** waterfall Iceland
99 V4 **Gull I** Michigan U.S.A.
99 V3 **Gulliver** Michigan U.S.A.
99 M3 **Gull L** Minnesota U.S.A.
118 J8 **Gull Lake** Saskatchewan Canada
26 K6 **Gullön** Sweden
27 G13 **Gullspång** Sweden
26 M5 **Gullträsk** Sweden
47 J7 **Güllük** Turkey
47 J7 **Güllük Körfezi** B Turkey
65 F2 **Gulong** China
25 E7 **Gulpen** Netherlands
33 Q7 **Gülper See** L East Germany
47 H5 **Gülpinar** Turkey
77 G2 **Gulran** Afghanistan
78 E2 **Gülşehir** Turkey
26 J8 **Gulsele** Sweden
57 G2 **Gul'shad** U.S.S.R.
33 S5 **Gültz** East Germany
86 F5 **Gulu** Uganda
141 J7 **Guluguba** Queensland Australia
140 D1 **Guluwuru I** N Terr Australia
59 H1 **Gulya** U.S.S.R.
46 G1 **Gulyantsi** Bulgaria
54 H9 **Gulyaypole** U.S.S.R.
33 S4 **Gülzow** East Germany
141 G7 **Gumbardo** Queensland Australia
26 M7 **Gumboda** Sweden
140 B5 **Gum Cr** N Terr Australia
85 F6 **Gumel** Nigeria
125 K6 **Gümez** Mexico
16 E3 **Gumiel de Hizán** Spain
75 L7 **Gumla** India
61 M9 **Gumma** prefect Japan
36 D1 **Gummersbach** W Germany
85 F6 **Gummi** Nigeria
71 E2 **Gumotgong** Luzon Philippines
69 C10 **Gumpang** R Sumatra
94 K9 **Gum Spring** Virginia U.S.A.
33 Q7 **Gumtow** East Germany
67 A5 **Gumu** China
47 L7 **Gümüşgün** Turkey
78 G1 **Gümüşhane** Turkey
74 G6 **Guna** India
86 G3 **Guna, Terara** mt Ethiopia
139 H5 **Gunbar** New South Wales Australia
113 H12 **Gun Cay** Bahamas
58 F1 **Gunda** U.S.S.R.
139 J6 **Gundagai** New South Wales Australia
37 J6 **Gundelfingen** W Germany
36 G5 **Gundelsheim** W Germany
28 C3 **Gundersted** Denmark
36 E4 **Gundheim** W Germany
70 N9 **Gundik** Java
86 D5 **Gundji** Zaire
28 H7 **Gundslev** Denmark
71 B3 **Gunedidalem** Indonesia
47 K6 **Güney** Turkey
119 N2 **Gunflint** Ontario Canada
86 C7 **Gungu** Zaire
119 V5 **Gunisao** L Manitoba Canada
119 U5 **Gunisao** R Manitoba Canada
103 L4 **Gunlock** Utah U.S.A.
114 J6 **Gunnar** Saskatchewan Canada
26 J6 **Gunnarn** Sweden
26 M5 **Gunnarsbyn** Sweden
141 H4 **Gunnawarra** Queensland Australia
115 R4 **Gunnbjørn Fjeld** mt Greenland
27 J14 **Gunnebo** Sweden
139 K4 **Gunnedah** New South Wales Australia
146 K8 **Gunnerus Ridge** Antarctica
141 J7 **Gunnewin** Queensland Australia
139 J5 **Gunning** New South Wales Australia
8 B7 **Gunnislake** England
106 B3 **Gunnison** R Colorado U.S.A.
106 D3 **Gunnison** Colorado U.S.A.
101 N8 **Gunnison I** Utah U.S.A.
140 B1 **Gunn Pt** N Terr Australia
140 E4 **Gunpowder** R Queensland Australia
101 N1 **Gunsight** Montana U.S.A.
76 C3 **Guntakal** India
100 B6 **Gunter** Oregon U.S.A.
109 L2 **Gunter** Texas U.S.A.
33 N9 **Güntersberge** East Germany
36 E4 **Guntersblum** W Germany
111 K7 **Guntersville** Alabama U.S.A.
119 U8 **Gunton** Manitoba Canada
111 H7 **Guntown** Mississippi U.S.A.
76 E2 **Guntur** India
71 N8 **Gunungapi** isld Indonesia
70 B3 **Gunung Ayer** Sarawak
70 E6 **Gunungbatubesar** Kalimantan
69 C12 **Gunungsitoli** Indonesia
70 K8 **Gunungsugih** Sumatra
69 D12 **Gunungtua** Sumatra
75 K9 **Gunupur** India
118 J7 **Gunworth** Saskatchewan Canada
143 B9 **Gunyidi** Western Australia Australia
37 J7 **Günz** R W Germany
37 J7 **Günzburg** W Germany
37 K5 **Gunzenhausen** W Germany
33 N9 **Günzerode** East Germany
67 B5 **Guohua** China
65 C4 **Guojiatun** China
Guoluezhen see **Lingbao**
58 G5 **Guoyang** China
65 B5 **Guoyangzhen** China
65 D7 **Gupei** China
48 K3 **Gura Humorului** Romania
66 F4 **Gurban Anggir** China
65 B3 **Gurban Obo** China
66 D2 **Gurbantünggüt Shamo** desert China
138 E6 **Gurchen B** South Australia Australia
74 F2 **Gurdaspur** India
111 C8 **Gurdon** Arkansas U.S.A.
47 K6 **Güre** Turkey
74 G4 **Gurgaon** India
86 D3 **Gurgei, Jebel** mt Sudan
129 K5 **Gurgueia** R Brazil
127 N11 **Guri** Venezuela
128 F2 **Guri, Embalse de** res Venezuela
130 E6 **Gurinhatã** Brazil
46 D4 **Gur-i-Topit** mt Albania
38 J8 **Gurk** R Austria
47 H2 **Gurkovo** Bulgaria
38 K8 **Gurktal** V Austria
38 J8 **Gurktaler Alpen** mts Austria
66 C5 **Gurla Mandhata** mt China
57 B4 **Gurlen** U.S.S.R.
110 K7 **Gurley** Alabama U.S.A.
98 D8 **Gurley** Nebraska U.S.A.
88 D10 **Guro** Mozambique
59 L1 **Gurskoye** U.S.S.R.
88 F9 **Gurué** Mozambique
78 F2 **Gürün** Turkey
129 H4 **Gurupá** Brazil
129 J4 **Gurupi** R Brazil
129 J6 **Gurupi** Brazil
129 J4 **Gurupi, C** Brazil
87 F9 **Guruve** Zimbabwe
76 D2 **Guruzala** India
58 D3 **Gurvan Sayhan Uul** mt Mongolia
50 E4 **Gur'yev** U.S.S.R.
56 C4 **Gur'yevsk** U.S.S.R.
85 F6 **Gusau** Nigeria
33 P8 **Güsen** East Germany
31 N1 **Gusev** U.S.S.R.
59 H4 **Gushan** China
101 Q9 **Gusher** Utah U.S.A.
67 E1 **Gushi** China
61 P14 **Gushikami** Okinawa
61 P13 **Gushikawa** Okinawa
70 E1 **Gusi** Sabah
52 G7 **Gusikha** U.S.S.R.
46 D2 **Gusinje** Yugoslavia
56 G5 **Gusinoozersk** U.S.S.R.
56 G5 **Gusinoye, Oz** L U.S.S.R.
52 F6 **Gus'Khrustal'nyy** U.S.S.R.
46 D4 **Gusmar** Albania
67 B2 **Gusong** China
43 B9 **Guspini** Sardinia
48 C3 **Güssing** Austria
45 J1 **Gussola** Italy
27 G11 **Gustav Adolf** Sweden
115 Q4 **Gustav Holm, Kap** C Greenland
127 N6 **Gustavia** Lesser Antilles
124 C2 **Gustavo Sotelo** Mexico
117 F6 **Gustavus** Alaska U.S.A.
33 P9 **Güsten** East Germany
36 E2 **Gusternhain** W Germany
102 C4 **Gustine** California U.S.A.
109 J4 **Gustine** Texas U.S.A.
33 S4 **Gustow** East Germany
33 Q5 **Güstrow** East Germany
27 H13 **Gusum** Sweden
48 K1 **Gusyatin** U.S.S.R.
36 E7 **Gutach** W Germany
66 E6 **Gutarg** China
56 E4 **Gutarskiy Khrebet** mts U.S.S.R.
38 L5 **Gutau** Austria
37 M3 **Gutenfürst** East Germany
38 N6 **Gutenstein** Austria
33 P9 **Gütergltick** East Germany
32 H9 **Gütersloh** W Germany
143 B8 **Gutha** Western Australia Australia
110 J5 **Guthrie** Kentucky U.S.A.
99 M2 **Guthrie** Minnesota U.S.A.

98 F1 **Guthrie** North Dakota U.S.A.
107 N6 **Guthrie** Oklahoma U.S.A.
108 G2 **Guthrie** Texas U.S.A.
99 M8 **Guthrie Center** Iowa U.S.A.
119 R3 **Guthrie L** Manitoba Canada
67 F3 **Gutian** China
125 L7 **Gutiérrez Zamora** Mexico
Guting see **Yutai**
33 S8 **Gut-Neuhof** East Germany
33 Q5 **Gutow** East Germany
38 L8 **Guttaring** Austria
99 P7 **Guttenberg** Iowa U.S.A.
87 F9 **Gutu** Zimbabwe
54 G6 **Guty** U.S.S.R.
33 S5 **Gützkow** East Germany
80 C7 **Guvrin** R Israel
75 O5 **Guwahati** India
36 G1 **Guxhagen** W Germany
65 B6 **Gu Xian** China
65 C4 **Guyan** China
128 G3 **Guyana** rep S America
94 E8 **Guyandotte** R West Virginia U.S.A.
65 A4 **Guyang** China
58 F3 **Guyang** China
121 M4 **Guyenne** Quebec Canada
18 E8 **Guyenne** prov France
9 G2 **Guyhirn** England
Guyi see **Sanjiang** Guangxi
107 J5 **Guymon** Oklahoma U.S.A.
116 R6 **Guyot Glacier** Alaska U.S.A.
139 K4 **Guyra** New South Wales Australia
123 L8 **Guysborough** Nova Scotia Canada
112 F5 **Guyton** Georgia U.S.A.
79 B2 **Güzelbağ** Turkey
67 C2 **Guzhang** China
58 G5 **Guzhen** China
Guzhou see **Rongjiang**
124 F2 **Guzmán, L. de** Mexico
31 N1 **Gvardeysk** U.S.S.R.
53 D10 **Gvardeyskoye** U.S.S.R.
48 K1 **Gvardeyskoye** U.S.S.R.
48 J2 **Gvozdets** U.S.S.R.
68 B4 **Gwa** Burma
89 E2 **Gwaai** Zimbabwe
139 J4 **Gwabegar** New South Wales Australia
38 G8 **Gwabl** Austria
74 B10 **Gwadar** Pakistan
89 E2 **Gwai** R Zimbabwe
8 B1 **Gwalchmai** Wales
143 D8 **Gwalia** Western Australia Australia
74 H5 **Gwalior** India
141 J7 **Gwambegwine** Queensland Australia
89 F3 **Gwanda** Zimbabwe
86 E5 **Gwane** Zaire
8 B3 **Gwbert-on-Sea** Wales
68 B2 **Gwebin** Burma
14 C2 **Gweebarra B** Ireland
Gwelo see **Gweru**
100 E4 **Gwendolen** Oregon U.S.A.
8 D4 **Gwent** co Wales
89 F2 **Gweru** R Zimbabwe
89 F2 **Gweru** Zimbabwe
99 T3 **Gwinn** Michigan U.S.A.
98 J3 **Gwinner** North Dakota U.S.A.
139 J3 **Gwydir** R New South Wales Australia
8 B1 **Gwynedd** co Wales
118 D6 **Gwynne** Alberta Canada
19 J5 **Gy** France
Gya'gya see **Saga**
66 C5 **Gyangrang** China
Gyangtse see **Gyangzê**
66 D6 **Gyangzê** China
66 D5 **Gyaring Co** L China
58 C5 **Gyaring Hu** L China
50 G1 **Gydanskiy Poluostrov** pen U.S.S.R.
75 L4 **Gyirong** China
66 F5 **Gyitang** China
8 C2 **Gylchedd** mt Wales
115 P5 **Gyldenløves Fjord** Greenland
28 H5 **Gyldenløves Høj** hill Denmark
26 N5 **Gyljen** Sweden
28 E5 **Gylling** Denmark
28 E5 **Gylling Næs** Denmark
141 L7 **Gympie** Queensland Australia
68 B3 **Gyobingauk** Burma
61 N9 **Gyōda** Japan
48 F4 **Gyomaendrőd** Hungary
48 F3 **Gyöngyös** R Hungary
48 F3 **Gyöngyös** Hungary
48 E4 **Gyönk** Hungary
48 D3 **Győr** Hungary
48 D3 **Győr-Sopron** Hungary
106 D2 **Gypsum** Colorado U.S.A.
107 N3 **Gypsum** Kansas U.S.A.
117 Q5 **Gypsum Pt** Northwest Territories Canada
119 T7 **Gypsumville** Manitoba Canada
28 H5 **Gyrstinge** Denmark
27 J11 **Gysinge** Sweden
46 F2 **Gyueshevo** Bulgaria
48 G4 **Gyula** Hungary
52 D6 **Gzhat'** R U.S.S.R.
Gzhatsk see **Gagarin**

H

22 H2 **Haacht** Belgium
37 M4 **Haag** W Germany
25 G4 **Haaksbergen** Netherlands
137 S5 **Ha'apai Group** islds Tonga
29 L8 **Haapajärvi** Finland
29 L9 **Haapamäki** Finland
29 L7 **Haapavesi** Finland
52 B5 **Haapsalu** U.S.S.R.
25 C4 **Haarlem** Netherlands
32 G9 **Haarstrang** W Germany
144 B5 **Haast** New Zealand
140 B6 **Haast Bluff** N Terr Australia
25 C5 **Haastrecht** Netherlands
140 A6 **Haasts Bluff Aboriginal Land** N Terr Australia
80 G4 **Habaka** Jordan
126 C3 **Habana** Cuba
83 K9 **Habarane** Sri Lanka
86 G5 **Habaswein** Kenya
117 O6 **Habay** Alberta Canada
22 K4 **Habay-la-Neuve** Belgium
78 J5 **Habbamyah** Iraq
32 K10 **Habichtswald** wood W Germany
75 O6 **Habiganj** Bangladesh
65 C3 **Habirag** China
80 G7 **Habis** R Jordan
80 C5 **Habla** Israel
27 K14 **Hablingo** Sweden
27 G14 **Habo** Sweden
80 C3 **Ha Bonim** Israel
60 P1 **Haboro** Japan
22 L3 **Habscheid** W Germany
61 N11 **Habuminato** Japan
131 B7 **Hachado, Paso de** Arg/Chile
32 G10 **Hachen** W Germany
36 D2 **Hachenburg** W Germany
59 L5 **Hachijō Jima** isld Japan
61 N5 **Hachimori** Japan
60 O2 **Hachinai dake** mt Japan
59 M3 **Hachinohe** Japan
59 L4 **Hachiōjio** Japan
106 B10 **Hachita** New Mexico U.S.A.
100 D8 **Hackamore** California U.S.A.
26 G9 **Hackås** Sweden
103 L6 **Hackberry** Arizona U.S.A.
111 C12 **Hackberry** Louisiana U.S.A.
107 K3 **Hackberry Cr** Kansas U.S.A.
118 E6 **Hackett** Alberta Canada
110 B6 **Hackett** Arkansas U.S.A.
95 N6 **Hackettstown** New Jersey U.S.A.
111 J7 **Hackleburg** Alabama U.S.A.
138 E4 **Hack, Mt** South Australia Australia
13 H5 **Hackness** England
87 C8 **Haco** Angola
68 H2 **Ha Coi** Vietnam
36 E3 **Hadamar** W Germany
80 C5 **Hadar** Israel
98 J7 **Hadar** Nebraska U.S.A.
72 H4 **Hadd, Al** Oman
107 N2 **Haddam** Kansas U.S.A.
9 G3 **Haddenham** England
13 F2 **Haddington** Scotland
9 H2 **Haddiscoe** England
112 D4 **Haddock** Georgia U.S.A.
73 L8 **Haddunmahti Atoll** Maldives
85 F6 **Hadejia** R Nigeria
27 D11 **Hadeland** Norway
32 J5 **Hadelner Kanal** W Germany
32 K4 **Hademarschen** W Germany
80 C4 **Hadera** R Israel
80 C4 **Hadera** Israel
38 N5 **Hadersdorf** Austria
Haderslev co see **Sønderjylland** co
28 C6 **Haderslev** Denmark
28 B4 **Haderup** Denmark
72 F5 **Hadhramaut** reg S Yemen
72 G6 **Hadīboh** Socotra
79 G3 **Ḩadīdīyah** Syria
85 F1 **Hadid, Ras El** C Algeria
43 A11 **Hadid, Ras El** C Algeria
78 J4 **Hadithah, Al** Iraq
9 G3 **Hadleigh** England
9 G4 **Hadleigh** England
114 J3 **Hadley B** Northwest Territories Canada
144 C6 **Hadlow** New Zealand
33 O9 **Hadmersleben** East Germany
26 G3 **Hadsel** Norway
26 G3 **Hädselöy** isld Norway
28 E4 **Hadsten** Denmark
28 E3 **Hadsund** Denmark
116 O3 **Hadweenzic** R Alaska U.S.A.
131 G3 **Haedo, Cuchilla de** ra Uruguay
65 F5 **Haeju** N Korea
80 C7 **Ha-Ela** Israel
28 E6 **Hæsinge** Denmark
41 O3 **Hafelekar Sp** mt Austria
80 C6 **Hafez Ḩayyim** Israel
28 R9 **Haffjördhur** B Iceland
33 N4 **Haffkrug-Scharbeutz** W Germany
115 N2 **Haffner Bjerg** mt Greenland
118 K6 **Hafford** Saskatchewan Canada
43 C13 **Haffouz** Tunisia
78 F2 **Hafik** Turkey
74 E2 **Hafizabad** Pakistan
75 P6 **Haflong** India
28 S9 **Hafnarfjördhur** Iceland
38 H7 **Hafner** mt Austria
77 A4 **Haft Gel** Iran
77 H2 **Haftqala** R Afghanistan
Hafun see **Xaafuun** Somalia
86 F3 **Hag Abdullah** Sudan
112 F5 **Hagan** Georgia U.S.A.
27 J11 **Hagaström** Sweden
32 F5 **Hage** W Germany
80 D3 **Ha Gelilit** Israel
33 R8 **Hagelsberg** mt East Germany
116 G7 **Hagemeister I** Alaska U.S.A.
119 M6 **Hagen** Saskatchewan Canada
32 F10 **Hagen** W Germany
32 K8 **Hagenburg** W Germany
38 H6 **Hagen-Gebirge** mts Austria
33 O6 **Hagenow** East Germany
101 L7 **Hagerman** Idaho U.S.A.
106 F8 **Hagerman** New Mexico U.S.A.
27 H13 **Hägerstad** Sweden
94 B7 **Hagerstown** Indiana U.S.A.
94 K7 **Hagerstown** Maryland U.S.A.
120 K10 **Hagersville** Ontario Canada
27 G11 **Hagfors** Sweden
26 G8 **Häggenås** Sweden
13 G2 **Haggerston** England
85 B3 **Haggounia, Al** Western Sahara
26 G8 **Häggsjön** Sweden
68 G1 **Ha Giang** Vietnam
48 K4 **Hăgimaş** mt Romania
61 L10 **Hagiwara** Japan
8 D3 **Hagley** England
19 K3 **Hagondage** France
112 G3 **Hagood** South Carolina U.S.A.
80 C5 **Ḩagor** Israel
80 F1 **Ha Gosherim** Israel
14 B4 **Hags Hd** Ireland
118 L6 **Hague** Saskatchewan Canada
95 O3 **Hague** New York U.S.A.
98 F3 **Hague** North Dakota U.S.A.
20 G2 **Hague, C. de la** France
19 L4 **Haguenau** France
98 A9 **Hagues Pk** Colorado U.S.A.
Hague, The see **Den Haag**
18 E9 **Haguetmau** France
123 O3 **Haha Bay** Quebec Canada
122 B5 **Ha Ha, L** Quebec Canada
80 D6 **Ha Hamisha** Jordan
113 D7 **Hahira** Georgia U.S.A.
37 M4 **Hahnbach** W Germany
36 D2 **Hahnbei** W Germany
33 M9 **Hahnenklee-Bockswiese** W Germany
80 C3 **Ha Hoterim** Israel
67 C6 **Hai'an** China
67 G1 **Hai'an** China
67 F4 **Haicheng** China
65 E4 **Haicheng** China
37 N5 **Haidhof** W Germany
43 B13 **Haïdra** Tunisia
37 O5 **Haidstein** mt W Germany
68 H2 **Hai Duong** Vietnam
22 J2 **Haien** Belgium
80 C2 **Haifa** Israel
80 D2 **Ḩaifa, Bay of** Israel
67 E5 **Haifeng** China
143 F9 **Haig** Western Australia Australia
36 E2 **Haiger** W Germany
36 F7 **Haigerloch** W Germany
117 P7 **Haig Lake** Alberta Canada
98 E10 **Haigler** Nebraska U.S.A.
65 D5 **Hai He** R China
67 C6 **Haikang** China
60 C12 **Haiki** Japan
69 D9 **Hai,Ko** isld Thailand
68 K2 **Haikou** China
135 T3 **Haiku** Hawaiian Is
75 P6 **Hailakandi** India
59 G2 **Hailar** China
101 L6 **Hailey** Idaho U.S.A.
121 L5 **Haileybury** Ontario Canada
107 P7 **Haileyville** Oklahoma U.S.A.
59 J3 **Hailin** China
67 D6 **Hailing Dao** isld China
65 J3 **Hailong** China
68 J7 **Hai Long** Vietnam
9 G6 **Hailsham** England
59 J2 **Hailun** China
29 L6 **Hailuoto** isld Finland
29 L6 **Hailuoto** Finland
32 M8 **Haimar** W Germany
67 G1 **Haimen** China
67 G2 **Haimen** China
67 D7 **Hainan Dao** isld China
68 D2 **Hai-nang** Burma
Hainan Strait see **Qiongzhou Haixia**
22 F2 **Hainaut** Belgium
22 F3 **Hainaut** France
31 K7 **Hainburg** Austria
117 F6 **Haines** Alaska U.S.A.
100 H5 **Haines** Oregon U.S.A.
113 F9 **Haines City** Florida U.S.A.
117 E5 **Haines Junction** Yukon Territory Canada
22 G3 **Haine-St-Paul** Belgium
38 N5 **Hainfeld** Austria
68 B4 **Haing** R Burma
37 P2 **Hainichen** East Germany
67 G1 **Haining** China
33 N10 **Hainleite** East Germany
37 Q2 **Hainsberg** East Germany
94 D4 **Haintramck** Michigan U.S.A.
68 H2 **Haiphong** Vietnam
118 F5 **Hairy Hill** Alberta Canada
65 E3 **Haisgai** China
127 H5 **Haiti** rep W Indies
68 J3 **Haitou** China
65 F2 **Haituo** China
103 N9 **Haivana Nakya** Arizona U.S.A.
102 G5 **Haiwee Res** California U.S.A.
65 D5 **Haixing** China
86 G2 **Haiya Junct** Sudan
67 G1 **Haiyan** China
65 E6 **Haiyang** China
65 F5 **Haiyang Dao** isld China
Haiyou see **Sanmen**
67 B5 **Haiyuan** China
68 H1 **Haiyuan** China
48 G3 **Hajdú-Bihar** co Hungary
48 G3 **Hajdúböszörmény** Hungary
48 G3 **Hajdúdorog** Hungary
48 G3 **Hajdúhadház** Hungary
48 G3 **Hajdúnánás** Hungary
48 G3 **Hajdúszoboszló** Hungary
61 M7 **Hajiki-saki** C Japan
79 G9 **Ḩājj** Saudi Arabia
31 O3 **Hajnówka** Poland
65 F7 **Hajo** isld S Korea
68 A1 **Haka** Burma
135 V5 **Hakalou** Hawaiian Is
80 G3 **Hakama** Jordan
87 E7 **Hakansson** mts Zaire
27 F13 **Håkantorp** Sweden
144 A7 **Hakapoua, L** New Zealand
61 N8 **Hakase-yama** mt Japan
144 C6 **Hakataramea** New Zealand
60 G11 **Hakata shima** isld Japan
131 B8 **Hakelhuincul, Altiplanicie de** plateau Argentina
78 J3 **Hakkari** Turkey
26 M5 **Hakkas** Sweden
61 J11 **Hakken-zan** mt Japan
61 O5 **Hakkōda san** Japan
60 Q1 **Hako dake** mt Japan
59 M3 **Hakodate** Japan
60 O4 **Hakodate wan** B Japan
61 K9 **Haku-san** mt Japan
61 K9 **Hakusan Nat. Park** Japan
Hal see **Halle** Belgium
79 H2 **Ḩalab** Syria
78 G4 **Halabiye** Syria
78 K4 **Halabja** Iraq
65 F2 **Halahai** China
86 G1 **Halaib** Sudan
79 D8 **Halâl, G** mt Egypt
48 G3 **Halasto** L Hungary
79 G9 **Ḩālat 'Ammār** Saudi Arabia
48 K3 **Hălăuceşti** Romania
135 S2 **Halawa** Hawaiian Is
80 F4 **Halawa** Jordan
135 S2 **Halawa, C** Hawaiian Is
79 G4 **Halba** Lebanon
86 H3 **Halba Desēt** isld Red Sea
33 T8 **Halbe** East Germany
33 O9 **Halberstadt** East Germany
8 C6 **Halberton** England
119 O9 **Halbrite** Saskatchewan Canada
145 E4 **Halcombe** New Zealand
71 E4 **Halcon, Mt** Philippines
117 P10 **Halcyon Hot Springs** British Columbia Canada
28 E3 **Hald** Århus Denmark
28 C3 **Hald** Viborg Denmark
28 H6 **Haldagerlille** Denmark
27 E12 **Halden** Norway
33 O8 **Haldensleben** East Germany
28 C4 **Hald Sø** L Denmark
28 E4 **Haldum** Denmark
74 H4 **Haldwani** India
140 D6 **Hale** R N Terr Australia
106 H2 **Hale** Colorado U.S.A.
94 D2 **Hale** Michigan U.S.A.
110 C2 **Hale** Missouri U.S.A.
135 T3 **Haleakala Crater** Hawaiian Is
108 F1 **Hale Center** Texas U.S.A.
135 Q2 **Haleiwa** Hawaiian Is
143 B7 **Hale, Mt** Western Australia Australia
135 R2 **Halena** Hawaiian Is
112 B2 **Hales Bar Dam** Tennessee U.S.A.
9 D3 **Halesowen** England
9 G5 **Hale Street** England
9 H3 **Halesworth** England
111 J7 **Haleyville** Alabama U.S.A.
144 B7 **Halfmoon Bay** New Zealand
9 E3 **Halford** England
107 K2 **Halford** Kansas U.S.A.
117 M7 **Halfway** R British Columbia Canada
94 K7 **Halfway** Maryland U.S.A.
100 H5 **Halfway** Oregon U.S.A.
108 F1 **Halfway** Texas U.S.A.
116 K6 **Halfway Mt** Alaska U.S.A.
25 C4 **Halfweg** Netherlands
80 B7 **Halib** Israel
121 M7 **Haliburton** Ontario Canada
141 H4 **Halifax** Queensland Australia
123 J9 **Halifax** Nova Scotia Canada
13 G6 **Halifax** England
112 K1 **Halifax** North Carolina U.S.A.
95 L6 **Halifax** Pennsylvania U.S.A.
94 H10 **Halifax** Virginia U.S.A.
141 H4 **Halifax B** Queensland Australia
141 H4 **Halifax, Mt** Queensland Australia
29 K11 **Halikko** Finland
77 E5 **Halil** R Iran
79 G4 **Halimah** mt Lebanon
70 L9 **Halimun, G** mt Java
Haliut see **Urad Zhongqi**
76 B3 **Haliyal** India
26 N4 **Halju** mt Sweden
28 D6 **Halk** Denmark
116 L1 **Halkett, C** Alaska U.S.A.
118 E6 **Halkirk** Alberta Canada
15 E2 **Halkirk** Scotland
26 O2 **Halkkavarre** mt Norway
101 M3 **Hall** Montana U.S.A.
26 J8 **Hälla** Sweden
9 G6 **Halland** England
26 F8 **Hålland** Sweden
27 F15 **Halland** county Sweden
113 G12 **Hallandale** Florida U.S.A.
27 F15 **Hallandsås** hills Sweden
29 K4 **Hallands Väderö** isld Sweden
138 D5 **Hall B** South Australia Australia
115 N1 **Hall Basin** Canada/Greenland
119 S8 **Hallboro** Manitoba Canada
22 G2 **Halle** Belgium
33 O9 **Halle** reg East Germany
33 P10 **Halle** East Germany
32 H8 **Halle** W Germany
27 H15 **Hälleberga** Sweden
120 G3 **Hallebourg** Ontario Canada
28 G5 **Halleby Å** R Denmark
100 K9 **Halleck** Nevada U.S.A.
27 G12 **Hällefors** Sweden
38 H6 **Hallein** Austria
26 G8 **Hallen** Sweden
36 F1 **Hallenberg** W Germany
21 O2 **Hallencourt** France
28 F4 **Hallendrup** Denmark
26 H9 **Hällesjö** Sweden
146 C12 **Hallett, Cape** C Antarctica
109 L6 **Hallettsville** Texas U.S.A.
146 F6 **Halley** U.K. Base Antarctica
111 E8 **Halley** Arkansas U.S.A.
116 B6 **Hall I** Bering Sea
98 D2 **Halliday** North Dakota U.S.A.
98 A9 **Halligan Res** Colorado U.S.A.
27 D11 **Hallingdalselv** R Norway
27 C11 **Hallingskarvet** mt Norway
27 B11 **Hallingskeid** Norway
115 L4 **Hall Lake** L Northwest Territories Canada
27 J11 **Hållnäs** Sweden
119 V10 **Hallock** Minnesota U.S.A.
118 K8 **Hallonquist** Saskatchewan Canada
115 N5 **Hall Pen** Northwest Territories Canada
110 G6 **Halls** Tennessee U.S.A.
8 C7 **Hallsands** England
27 H12 **Hallsberg** Sweden
142 G4 **Halls Creek** Western Australia Australia
138 F6 **Halls Gap** Victoria Australia
37 K4 **Hallstadt** W Germany
27 H12 **Hallstahammar** Sweden
106 G3 **Hall Station** Colorado U.S.A.
38 J6 **Hallstatt** Austria
27 K11 **Hallstavik** Sweden
95 M5 **Hallstead** Pennsylvania U.S.A.
111 C9 **Hall Summit** Louisiana U.S.A.
110 D2 **Hallsville** Missouri U.S.A.
109 N3 **Hallsville** Texas U.S.A.
81 A8 **Hall Table Mt** Indian Oc
41 O3 **Halltal** Austria
94 J5 **Hallton** Pennsylvania U.S.A.
22 E2 **Halluin** France
25 E2 **Hallum** Netherlands
28 E2 **Hallund** Denmark
28 C5 **Hallundbæk** Denmark
26 H8 **Hallviken** Sweden
98 K1 **Halma** Minnesota U.S.A.
71 B2 **Halmahera** isld Indonesia
71 B3 **Halmahera** sea Indonesia
48 H3 **Halmeu** Romania
27 F15 **Halmstad** Sweden
43 C12 **Halq el Oued** Tunisia
28 E2 **Hals** Denmark
26 C8 **Halsa** Norway
37 P2 **Halsbrucke** East Germany
36 F2 **Halsdorf** W Germany
98 F8 **Halsey** Nebraska U.S.A.
100 B5 **Halsey** Oregon U.S.A.
71 D5 **Halsey Harbour** Philippines
28 H5 **Halsnæs** pen Denmark
28 G6 **Halsskov** Denmark
98 K2 **Halstad** Minnesota U.S.A.
9 G4 **Halstead** England
107 N4 **Halstead** Kansas U.S.A.
36 B5 **Halstroff** France
29 L8 **Halsua** Finland
26 E9 **Haltdalen** Norway
26 D7 **Halten** Norway
32 F9 **Haltern** W Germany
29 J2 **Halti** mt Finland
109 M9 **Haltom City** Texas U.S.A.
13 F4 **Haltwhistle** England
77 C7 **Ḩālūl** isld Qatar
71 K10 **Halura** isld Indonesia
36 C1 **Halver** W Germany
118 L8 **Halvorgate** Saskatchewan Canada
28 D2 **Halvrimmen** Denmark
141 K7 **Haly, Mt** Queensland Australia
22 E4 **Ham** France
80 G3 **Ham** Jordan
60 F12 **Hama** Japan
60 F11 **Hamada** Japan
85 F3 **Hamada de Tinrhert** stony desert Algeria
85 D4 **Hamada El Haricha** reg Mali
77 A2 **Hamadān** Iran
85 C3 **Hamada Tounassine** stony desert Algeria
80 F3 **Ḩamadya** Israel
79 G3 **Ḩamāh** Syria
61 P13 **Hamahika-jima** isld Okinawa
61 L11 **Hamakita** Japan
60 P2 **Hamamasu** Japan
59 L5 **Hamamatsu** Japan
60 T2 **Hamanaka** Japan
61 L11 **Hamana ko** L Japan
80 C4 **Ha Ma 'Pil** Israel
27 E11 **Hamar** Norway
98 H2 **Hamar** North Dakota U.S.A.
26 H3 **Hamaröy** Norway
60 H10 **Hamasaka** Japan
84 J5 **Hamâta, Gebel** mt Egypt
80 F3 **Hamat Gader** Jordan
60 Q1 **Hama-Tombetsu** Japan
36 C5 **Hambach** France
83 L11 **Hambantota** Sri Lanka
98 G2 **Hamberg** North Dakota U.S.A.
32 J6 **Hambergen** W Germany
117 O9 **Hamber Prov. Park** British Columbia Canada
9 F5 **Hambledon** England
13 G6 **Hambleton** England
13 G5 **Hambleton Hills** England
100 D8 **Hambone** California U.S.A.
32 L7 **Hambühren** W Germany
111 E8 **Hamburg** Arkansas U.S.A.
100 B8 **Hamburg** California U.S.A.
99 L9 **Hamburg** Iowa U.S.A.
95 N5 **Hamburg** New Jersey U.S.A.
94 J4 **Hamburg** New York U.S.A.
95 M6 **Hamburg** Pennsylvania U.S.A.
34 **Hamburg** conurbation W Germany
20 H4 **Hambye** France
95 M4 **Hamden** New York U.S.A.
94 E7 **Hamden** Ohio U.S.A.
29 L10 **Hame** prov Finland
29 K10 **Hämeenkyrö** Finland
29 L11 **Hämeenlinna** Finland
143 A10 **Hamelin B** Western Australia Australia
143 A7 **Hamelin Pool** Western Australia Australia
32 K8 **Hameln** W Germany
101 N6 **Hamer** Idaho U.S.A.
33 O8 **Hamersleben** East Germany
142 C5 **Hamersley** Western Australia Australia
142 B5 **Hamersley Ra** W Australia
142 B6 **Hamersley Ra. Nat Park** Western Australia Australia
33 P7 **Hamerten** East Germany
65 G5 **Hamhŭng** N Korea
66 E3 **Hami** China
140 F6 **Hamilton** R Queensland Australia
140 F6 **Hamilton** Queensland Australia
138 C2 **Hamilton** R South Australia Australia
139 H8 **Hamilton** Tasmania Australia
138 F6 **Hamilton** Victoria Australia
90 B2 **Hamilton** Bermuda
121 L9 **Hamilton** Ontario Canada
145 E2 **Hamilton** New Zealand
12 D2 **Hamilton** Scotland
111 J7 **Hamilton** Alabama U.S.A.
101 S9 **Hamilton** Colorado U.S.A.
111 M9 **Hamilton** Georgia U.S.A.
99 P9 **Hamilton** Illinois U.S.A.
94 C5 **Hamilton** Indiana U.S.A.
107 O4 **Hamilton** Kansas U.S.A.
94 A4 **Hamilton** Michigan U.S.A.
101 L3 **Hamilton** Montana U.S.A.
95 M4 **Hamilton** New York U.S.A.
119 U10 **Hamilton** North Dakota U.S.A.
94 C7 **Hamilton** Ohio U.S.A.
100 F5 **Hamilton** Oregon U.S.A.
109 J4 **Hamilton** Texas U.S.A.
100 D1 **Hamilton** Washington U.S.A.
102 C2 **Hamilton City** California U.S.A.
101 R6 **Hamilton Dome** Wyoming U.S.A.
140 C6 **Hamilton Downs** N Terr Australia
115 O7 **Hamilton Inlet** Labrador, Nfld Canada
111 C7 **Hamilton,L** Arkansas U.S.A.
103 J2 **Hamilton, Mt** Nevada U.S.A.
29 N11 **Hamina** Finland
74 J6 **Hamirpur** India
Hamitabat see **İsparta**
94 C5 **Hamler** Ohio U.S.A.
94 A5 **Hamlet** Indiana U.S.A.
98 E9 **Hamlet** Nebraska U.S.A.
112 H3 **Hamlet** North Carolina U.S.A.
138 E5 **Hamley Bridge** South Australia Australia
94 K3 **Hamlin** New York U.S.A.
108 G3 **Hamlin** Texas U.S.A.
94 E8 **Hamlin** West Virginia U.S.A.
94 A2 **Hamlin L** Michigan U.S.A.
32 G9 **Hamm** W Germany
17 G9 **Hammam Bou Hadjar** Algeria
43 D12 **Hammamet** Tunisia
85 G1 **Hammamet, G de** Tunisia
85 G1 **Hammam Lif** Tunisia
29 H11 **Hammarland** Finland
27 F11 **Hammarsbyn** Sweden
29 M3 **Hammastunturi** mt Finland
22 G1 **Hamme** Belgium
32 J6 **Hamme** R W Germany
28 D4 **Hammel** Denmark
36 H3 **Hammelburg** W Germany
28 F4 **Hammelev** Denmark
28 C6 **Hammelev** Denmark
33 S6 **Hammelspring** East Germany
22 H2 **Hamme-Mille** Belgium
26 H8 **Hammerdal** Sweden
147 H14 **Hammerfest** Norway
28 D3 **Hammershøj** Denmark
143 C9 **Hammersley L** Western Australia Australia
36 C3 **Hammerstein** W Germany
13 G6 **Hammerton** England
28 C4 **Hammerum** Denmark
100 K7 **Hammett** Idaho U.S.A.
32 E9 **Hamminkeln** W Germany
107 L6 **Hammon** Oklahoma U.S.A.
138 E4 **Hammond** South Australia Australia
99 T8 **Hammond** Illinois U.S.A.
110 H2 **Hammond** Illinois U.S.A.
111 F11 **Hammond** Louisiana U.S.A.
98 B4 **Hammond** Montana U.S.A.
95 M2 **Hammond** New York U.S.A.
100 B3 **Hammond** Oregon U.S.A.
99 O5 **Hammond** Wisconsin U.S.A.
94 D1 **Hammond B** Michigan U.S.A.
141 F1 **Hammond I** Queensland Australia
95 K4 **Hammondsport** New York U.S.A.
122 G8 **Hammond Vale** New Brunswick Canada
102 C2 **Hammonton** California U.S.A.
95 N7 **Hammonton** New Jersey U.S.A.
26 O1 **Hamnbukt** Norway
26 L2 **Hamneidet** Norway
26 S1 **Hamningberg** Norway
68 G7 **Ham Ninh** Vietnam
121 T7 **Ham Nord** Quebec Canada
26 L4 **Håmojokk** Sweden
22 K1 **Hamont** Belgium
86 G2 **Hamoyet, Jebel** mt Sudan
123 Q4 **Hampden** Newfoundland Canada
144 C6 **Hampden** New Zealand
98 H1 **Hampden** North Dakota U.S.A.
95 T2 **Hampden Highlands** Maine U.S.A.
28 C4 **Hampen** Denmark
36 B6 **Hampont** France
9 E5 **Hampshire** co England
122 F8 **Hampstead** New Brunswick Canada
95 K7 **Hampstead** Maryland U.S.A.
112 K3 **Hampstead** North Carolina U.S.A.
122 G8 **Hampton** New Brunswick Canada
9 F5 **Hampton** England
111 D8 **Hampton** Arkansas U.S.A.
113 E8 **Hampton** Florida U.S.A.
111 M8 **Hampton** Georgia U.S.A.
99 N7 **Hampton** Iowa U.S.A.
98 J9 **Hampton** Nebraska U.S.A.
95 R4 **Hampton** New Hampshire U.S.A.
100 E6 **Hampton** Oregon U.S.A.
112 F5 **Hampton** South Carolina U.S.A.
95 L9 **Hampton** Virginia U.S.A.
101 P8 **Hampton** Wyoming U.S.A.
95 P6 **Hampton Bays** Long I, New York U.S.A.
143 F9 **Hampton Tableland** Western Australia Australia
27 H10 **Hamra** Sweden
27 J11 **Hamrånge** Sweden
79 G4 **Ḩamrāt, Al** Syria
101 P7 **Hams Fork** R Wyoming U.S.A.
9 G5 **Hamstreet** England
68 H7 **Ham Tan** Vietnam
135 T3 **Hana** Hawaiian Is
126 D3 **Hanábana** R Cuba
135 O1 **Hanalei** Hawaiian Is
135 T3 **Hanamanioa, C** Hawaiian Is
135 O1 **Hanamaulu** Hawaiian Is
135 O1 **Hanapepe** Hawaiian Is
61 N13 **Hanare-iwa** islds Japan
36 F3 **Hanau** W Germany
102 S12 **Hanauma B** Hawaiian Is
121 L5 **Hanbury** Ontario Canada
117 M10 **Hanceville** British Columbia Canada
111 K7 **Hanceville** Alabama U.S.A.
58 F4 **Hancheng** China
67 D1 **Hanchuan** China
95 T2 **Hancock** Maine U.S.A.
94 J7 **Hancock** Maryland U.S.A.
99 S2 **Hancock** Michigan U.S.A.
99 L4 **Hancock** Minnesota U.S.A.
95 P4 **Hancock** New Hampshire U.S.A.
95 M5 **Hancock** New York U.S.A.
99 R5 **Hancock** Wisconsin U.S.A.
113 F10 **Hancock, L** Florida U.S.A.
61 K11 **Handa** Japan
58 F4 **Handan** China
28 B4 **Handbjerg** Denmark
9 F5 **Handcross** England
118 J6 **Handel** Saskatchewan Canada
27 K12 **Handen** Sweden
88 G4 **Handeni** Tanzania
28 D3 **Handest** Denmark
65 D1 **Handgai** China
109 K3 **Handley** Texas U.S.A.
119 P9 **Handsworth** Saskatchewan Canada
32 K4 **Hanerau** W Germany
102 E5 **Hanford** California U.S.A.
76 B3 **Hangal** India
68 C5 **Hangan** Burma
65 G6 **Hangang** R S Korea
145 F3 **Hangaroa** New Zealand
27 C11 **Hangastöl** Norway
145 E3 **Hangatiki** New Zealand
58 C2 **Hangayn Nuruu** mt Mongolia
Hangchow see **Hangzhou**
33 T8 **Hangelsberg** East Germany
27 G14 **Hånger** Sweden
58 E3 **Hanggin Houqi** China
94 E8 **Hanging Rock** Ohio U.S.A.
89 A10 **Hangklip, C** S Africa
100 H2 **Hangman Cr** Washington U.S.A.
29 K12 **Hango** Finland
65 D5 **Hangu** China
67 D4 **Hanguang** China
59 H5 **Hangzhou** China
59 H5 **Hangzhou Wan** B China
79 F4 **Hanidiyah, Al** Syria
32 M7 **Hänigsen** W Germany
86 H3 **Hanish al Kabir** islds Red Sea
80 D1 **Hanita** Israel
Hanjiang see **Yangzhou**
67 F4 **Hanjiang** China
29 M9 **Hankasalmi** Finland
85 C4 **Hank, El** Mauritania
98 J3 **Hankinson** North Dakota U.S.A.
58 F5 **Hankou** China
103 O3 **Hanksville** Utah U.S.A.
118 L7 **Hanley** Saskatchewan Canada
8 D1 **Hanley** England
99 L5 **Hanley Falls** Minnesota U.S.A.
144 D5 **Hanmer Springs** New Zealand
118 F7 **Hanna** Alberta Canada
101 P9 **Hanna** Utah U.S.A.
101 T8 **Hanna** Wyoming U.S.A.
98 H2 **Hannaford** North Dakota U.S.A.
119 T10 **Hannah** North Dakota U.S.A.
120 K1 **Hannah B** Ontario Canada
99 P10 **Hannibal** Missouri U.S.A.
99 Q4 **Hannibal** Wisconsin U.S.A.
28 A4 **Hanning Kirke** Denmark
142 F3 **Hann, Mt** Western Australia Australia
98 E2 **Hannover** North Dakota U.S.A.
32 L8 **Hannover** W Germany
140 C6 **Hann Ra** N Terr Australia
22 J2 **Hannut** Belgium
27 H16 **Hanöbukten** B Sweden
68 G2 **Hanoi** Vietnam
48 D4 **Hanót** Hungary
120 J8 **Hanover** Ontario Canada
127 H1 **Hanover** parish Jamaica
89 D8 **Hanover** S Africa
107 O2 **Hanover** Kansas U.S.A.
99 N4 **Hanover** Minnesota U.S.A.
101 Q2 **Hanover** Montana U.S.A.
95 P3 **Hanover** New Hampshire U.S.A.
133 C8 **Hanover, I** Chile
48 E6 **Han Pijesak** Yugoslavia
48 D3 **Hanság** Hungary
117 N8 **Hansard** British Columbia Canada
98 G1 **Hansboro** North Dakota U.S.A.
120 F3 **Hansen** Ontario Canada
146 J10 **Hansen mts** Antarctica
67 F1 **Hanshan** China
67 D2 **Hanshou** China
67 D1 **Han Shui** R China
58 E5 **Han Shui** R China
74 F4 **Hansi** India
27 G10 **Hansjö** Sweden
140 C5 **Hanson** R N Terr Australia
138 D4 **Hanson, L** South Australia Australia
119 P4 **Hanson L** Saskatchewan Canada
28 D5 **Hansted** Vejle Denmark
28 B2 **Hanstholm** Denmark
28 B2 **Hanstholm Havn** C Denmark
65 D2 **Han Sum** China
22 J3 **Han-sur-Lesse** Belgium
25 B6 **Hansweert** Netherlands
Hantan see **Handan**
66 C3 **Hantengri Feng** mt U.S.S.R.
Hanting see **Wei Xian**
Hants co see **Hampshire**
122 H8 **Hantsport** Nova Scotia Canada
36 C7 **Hantz, Col du** pass France
79 H3 **Hānūbah, Al** Syria
65 D2 **Han Ul** China
20 B5 **Hanvec** France
67 A1 **Hanwang** China
83 K11 **Hanwella** Sri Lanka
58 F5 **Hanyang** China
57 K4 **Hanyaylak** China
61 N9 **Hanyū** Japan
58 D6 **Hanyuan** China
58 E5 **Hanzhong** China
65 D7 **Hanzhuang** China
135 N10 **Hao** atoll Tuamotu Arch Pacific Oc
65 H1 **Haolianghe** China
80 F3 **Ha On** Israel
75 N7 **Hāora** India
26 N6 **Haparanda** Sweden
71 B1 **Hapo** Halmahera Indonesia
9 H2 **Happisburgh** England
100 B8 **Happy Camp** California U.S.A.
140 E5 **Happy Cr** N Terr Australia
144 D5 **Hapuku** New Zealand
83 L11 **Haputale** Sri Lanka
79 E9 **Ḩaql** Saudi Arabia
58 E2 **Hara** Mongolia
26 M5 **Harads** Sweden
86 H4 **Hara Fanna** Ethiopia
111 H12 **Harahan** New Orleans, Louisiana U.S.A.
26 B9 **Haram** Norway
59 M4 **Haramachi** Japan
86 H4 **Hārar** Ethiopia
88 C10 **Harare** Zimbabwe
58 E2 **Har-ayrag** Mongolia
86 C3 **Haraz Djombo** Chad
86 D3 **Haraz-Mangueigne** Chad
80 E8 **Har Ben Yai'r** Israel
65 G2 **Harbin** China
27 J11 **Harbo** Sweden
77 K5 **Harboi Hills** Pakistan
28 J7 **Hårbølle** Denmark
22 D4 **Harbonnières** France
28 A3 **Harboør** Denmark
28 A3 **Harboør Tange** pen Denmark
100 A7 **Harbor** Oregon U.S.A.
94 E3 **Harbor Beach** Michigan U.S.A.
117 E6 **Harbor Pt** Alaska U.S.A.
94 B1 **Harbor Springs** Michigan U.S.A.
13 F3 **Harbottle** England
123 R6 **Harbour Breton** Newfoundland Canada
123 S6 **Harbour Buffett** Newfoundland Canada
113 K12 **Harbour Cay, Little** isld Bahamas
123 Q3 **Harbour Deep** Newfoundland Canada
123 T6 **Harbour Grace** Newfoundland Canada
113 L12 **Harbour I** Bahamas
123 S6 **Harbour Mille** Newfoundland Canada
122 H8 **Harbourville** Nova Scotia Canada
37 K6 **Harburg** Bayern W Germany
32 L6 **Harburg** Niedersachsen W Germany
28 E6 **Hårby** Denmark
122 G7 **Harcourt** New Brunswick Canada
103 L7 **Harcuvar Mts** Arizona U.S.A.
74 G7 **Harda Khās** India
27 B11 **Hardanger** Norway
27 B11 **Hardanger-fjorden** inlet Norway
27 C11 **Hardangervidda** plateau Norway
27 B11 **Hardangervidda Nat. Park** Norway
89 A5 **Hardap Dam** Namibia
111 F9 **Hardee** Mississippi U.S.A.
112 F5 **Hardeeville** South Carolina U.S.A.
25 E2 **Hardegarijp** Netherlands
32 L9 **Hardegsen** W Germany
22 B2 **Hardelot-Plage** France
25 G3 **Hardenberg** Netherlands
70 D2 **Harden, Bt** mt Kalimantan
25 E4 **Harderwijk** Netherlands
107 J5 **Hardesty** Oklahoma U.S.A.
142 B6 **Hardey, R** Western Australia Australia
36 H4 **Hardheim** W Germany
110 F2 **Hardin** Illinois U.S.A.
110 C2 **Hardin** Missouri U.S.A.
101 S4 **Hardin** Montana U.S.A.
87 E12 **Harding** S Africa
99 M3 **Harding** Minnesota U.S.A.
116 M6 **Harding Icefield** Alaska U.S.A.
119 T2 **Harding L** Manitoba Canada
111 L9 **Harding, L** Georgia U.S.A.
110 K4 **Hardinsburg** Kentucky U.S.A.
118 F6 **Hardisty** Alberta Canada
117 P3 **Hardisty L** Northwest Territories Canada
21 P2 **Hardivillers** France
100 F4 **Hardman** Oregon U.S.A.
142 E4 **Hardman, Mt** Western Australia Australia
80 D8 **Hardof** R Jordan
98 K6 **Hardwick** Minnesota U.S.A.
95 P2 **Hardwick** Vermont U.S.A.
8 D4 **Hardwicke** England
138 D5 **Hardwicke B** South Australia Australia
119 N9 **Hardy** Saskatchewan Canada
110 E5 **Hardy** Arkansas U.S.A.
101 O2 **Hardy** Montana U.S.A.
Hardy, Mt see **Rangipova**
133 D9 **Hardy, Pen** Chile
94 B3 **Hardy Res** Michigan U.S.A.
123 S5 **Hare B** Newfoundland Canada
80 E4 **Hare Gilboa** Israel
26 B9 **Hareid** Norway
22 E2 **Harelbeke** Belgium
32 F7 **Haren** W Germany
115 O3 **Hareøen** isld Greenland
9 F1 **Hare Park** England
86 H4 **Hārergē** prov Ethiopia
13 G6 **Harewood** England
79 F5 **Harf el Mreffi** mt Lebanon
21 L2 **Harfleur** France
27 K11 **Harg** Sweden
36 B5 **Hargarten aux Mines** France
86 H4 **Hargele** Ethiopia
86 H4 **Hargeysa** Somalia
48 K4 **Harghita, Muntii** mt Romania
22 E4 **Hargicourt** France
109 J9 **Hargill** Texas U.S.A.
22 J3 **Hargimont** Belgium
22 H3 **Hargnies** France
119 Q9 **Hargrave** Manitoba Canada
119 S4 **Hargrave L** Manitoba Canada
79 E8 **Har Hakippa** mt Israel
79 E8 **Har Harif** Israel
80 D8 **Har Ḩezron** Israel
66 F4 **Har Hu** L China
61 M9 **Hari** Japan
74 H4 **Haridwār** India
76 B3 **Harihar** India
144 C5 **Harihari** New Zealand
79 G2 **Ḩārim** Syria
60 H11 **Harima-nada** sea Japan
25 B5 **Haringvliet** Netherlands
74 E1 **Haripur** Pakistan
77 J2 **Hari Rud** R Afghanistan/Iran
79 G6 **Ḩarīr, Wādī adh** watercourse Syria
87 C10 **Haris** Namibia
26 G10 **Härjån** R Sweden
29 J10 **Harjavalta** Finland
26 F10 **Härjehågna** mt Sweden
80 F2 **Har Kena'an** pk Israel
112 L3 **Harkers I** North Carolina U.S.A.
99 L8 **Harlan** Iowa U.S.A.
107 M2 **Harlan** Kansas U.S.A.
94 D10 **Harlan** Kentucky U.S.A.
98 G9 **Harlan County Lake** res Nebraska U.S.A.
22 K4 **Harlange** Luxembourg
32 G5 **Harle** W Germany
8 B2 **Harlech** Wales
112 E4 **Harlem** Georgia U.S.A.
101 R1 **Harlem** Montana U.S.A.
32 L5 **Harlesiel** W Germany
9 H3 **Harleston** England
28 D4 **Harlev** Denmark
28 J6 **Hårlev** Denmark
112 G4 **Harleyville** South Carolina U.S.A.
25 D2 **Harlingen** Netherlands
109 K9 **Harlingen** Texas U.S.A.
32 G5 **Harlinger Land** W Germany
33 M9 **Harlingerode** W Germany
9 G4 **Harlow** England
98 G1 **Harlow** North Dakota U.S.A.
101 Q3 **Harlowton** Montana U.S.A.
94 H8 **Harman** West Virginia U.S.A.
47 K5 **Harmancık** Turkey
26 J10 **Harmånger** Sweden
25 C4 **Harmelen** Netherlands
80 E2 **Har Meron** pk Israel
107 L5 **Harmon** Oklahoma U.S.A.
118 A2 **Harmon R** Alberta Canada
95 S2 **Harmony** Maine U.S.A.
99 O6 **Harmony** Minnesota U.S.A.
79 E8 **Har Natha** mt Israel
100 F6 **Harney Basin** reg Oregon U.S.A.
113 F9 **Harney, L** Florida U.S.A.
100 F6 **Harney L** Oregon U.S.A.
98 C6 **Harney Pk** South Dakota U.S.A.
28 E6 **Harnorup** Denmark
26 J9 **Härnösand** Sweden
65 E2 **Har Nur** China
58 B2 **Har Nuur** L Mongolia
80 E3 **Harod** R Israel
26 B9 **Haröy** isld Norway
9 F4 **Harpenden** England
85 C8 **Harper** Liberia
107 M4 **Harper** Kansas U.S.A.
100 H6 **Harper** Oregon U.S.A.
109 H5 **Harper** Texas U.S.A.
116 L4 **Harper Bend** Alaska U.S.A.
117 Q6 **Harper Cr** Alberta Canada
102 G6 **Harper L** California U.S.A.
116 Q4 **Harper, Mt** Alaska U.S.A.
144 C5 **Harper Pass** New Zealand
94 K7 **Harpers Ferry** West Virginia U.S.A.
110 J5 **Harpeth** R Tennessee U.S.A.
8 C6 **Harpford** England
9 G2 **Harpley** England
27 F15 **Harplinge** Sweden
32 J7 **Harpstedt** W Germany
119 M9 **Harptree** Saskatchewan Canada
65 D4 **Harqin** China
65 D4 **Harqin Qi** China
103 L8 **Harquahala Mts** Arizona U.S.A.
85 E1 **Harrach, El** Algeria
107 N6 **Harrah** Oklahoma U.S.A.
26 F7 **Harran** Norway
37 K3 **Harras** East Germany
28 B3 **Harre** Denmark
111 D8 **Harrell** Arkansas U.S.A.
144 D5 **Harrelville** New Zealand
121 L2 **Harricana** R Quebec Canada
28 E3 **Harridslev** Denmark
94 B2 **Harrietta** Michigan U.S.A.
112 C2 **Harriman** Tennessee U.S.A.
95 M8 **Harrington** Delaware U.S.A.
95 U2 **Harrington** Maine U.S.A.
100 G2 **Harrington** Washington U.S.A.
123 N3 **Harrington-Harbour** Quebec Canada
119 P2 **Harriot L** Saskatchewan Canada
118 K7 **Harris** Saskatchewan Canada
15 B3 **Harris** div Scotland
100 B9 **Harris** California U.S.A.
99 N9 **Harris** Missouri U.S.A.
110 F6 **Harrisburg** Arkansas U.S.A.
110 H4 **Harrisburg** Illinois U.S.A.
98 C8 **Harrisburg** Nebraska U.S.A.
94 D7 **Harrisburg** Ohio U.S.A.
100 B5 **Harrisburg** Oregon U.S.A.
95 L6 **Harrisburg** Pennsylvania U.S.A.
98 K6 **Harrisburg** South Dakota U.S.A.
118 H2 **Harris Hill** Ontario Canada
138 D4 **Harris, L** South Australia Australia
113 F9 **Harris, L** Florida U.S.A.
143 C10 **Harrismith** Western Australia Australia
89 F7 **Harrismith** S Africa
140 A6 **Harris, Mt** N Terr Australia
144 B6 **Harris Mts** New Zealand
110 C5 **Harrison** Arkansas U.S.A.
112 E5 **Harrison** Georgia U.S.A.
100 J2 **Harrison** Idaho U.S.A.
94 C2 **Harrison** Michigan U.S.A.
101 O4 **Harrison** Montana U.S.A.
98 C7 **Harrison** Nebraska U.S.A.

98 H6 **Harrison** South Dakota U.S.A.
116 L1 **Harrison B** Alaska U.S.A.
111 E10 **Harrisonburg** Louisiana U.S.A.
94 J8 **Harrisonburg** Virginia U.S.A.
115 O7 **Harrison, C** Labrador, Nfld Canada
117 M11 **Harrison L** British Columbia Canada
83 K12 **Harrison, Mt** Mahé I Indian Oc
110 B3 **Harrisonville** Missouri U.S.A.
94 D2 **Harrisville** Michigan U.S.A.
95 M2 **Harrisville** New York U.S.A.
94 F7 **Harrisville** West Virginia U.S.A.
110 K2 **Harrodsburg** Indiana U.S.A.
94 C9 **Harrodsburg** Kentucky U.S.A.
13 G6 **Harrogate** England
98 G5 **Harrold** South Dakota U.S.A.
109 H1 **Harrold** Texas U.S.A.
120 H10 **Harrow** Ontario Canada
9 F4 **Harrow** England
119 Q8 **Harrowby** Manitoba Canada
26 H7 **Harrsjön** Sweden
27 F14 **Härryda** Sweden
110 C3 **Harry S. Truman Res** Missouri U.S.A.
98 F9 **Harry Strunk L** Nebraska U.S.A.
79 E8 **Har Saggi** *mt* Israel
32 K6 **Harsefeld** W Germany
32 H9 **Harsewinkel** W Germany
26 L5 **Harsprånget** Sweden
26 J3 **Harstad** Norway
32 L8 **Harsum** W Germany
28 A4 **Harsyssel** *reg* Denmark
119 M9 **Hart** Saskatchewan Canada
13 G4 **Hart** England
99 U6 **Hart** Michigan U.S.A.
65 E3 **Hartao** China
89 B7 **Hartbees** *watercourse* S Africa
89 E5 **Hartbeespoortdam** S Africa
38 N7 **Hartberg** Austria
27 B11 **Hårteigen** *mt* Norway
118 C8 **Hartell** Alberta Canada
22 E5 **Hartennes-et-Taux** France
36 E2 **Hartenrod** W Germany
37 O2 **Hartenstein** East Germany
37 J5 **Hartershofen** W Germany
15 E5 **Hart Fell** Scotland
9 G5 **Hartfield** England
111 L10 **Hartford** Alabama U.S.A.
109 N1 **Hartford** Arkansas U.S.A.
95 P5 **Hartford** Connecticut U.S.A.
107 P3 **Hartford** Kansas U.S.A.
110 K4 **Hartford** Kentucky U.S.A.
94 A4 **Hartford** Michigan U.S.A.
94 E6 **Hartford** Ohio U.S.A.
112 D2 **Hartford** Tennessee U.S.A.
99 S6 **Hartford** Wisconsin U.S.A.
94 B6 **Hartford City** Indiana U.S.A.
95 P5 **Hartford, E** Connecticut U.S.A.
37 O1 **Hartha** East Germany
37 O2 **Harthau** East Germany
12 E2 **Harthill** Scotland
9 E1 **Hartington** England
98 J7 **Hartington** Nebraska U.S.A.
80 E2 **Har Tir'an** Israel
122 D2 **Hart-jaune, R** Quebec Canada
138 D4 **Hart, L** South Australia Australia
122 E7 **Hartland** New Brunswick Canada
8 B6 **Hartland** England
95 S2 **Hartland** Maine U.S.A.
8 B5 **Hartland Pt** England
8 D3 **Hartlebury** England
13 G4 **Hartlepool** England
13 G3 **Hartley** England
99 L6 **Hartley** Iowa U.S.A.
108 B8 **Hartley** Texas U.S.A.
117 J9 **Hartley Bay** British Columbia Canada
9 F5 **Hartley Wintney** England
100 F2 **Hartline** Washington U.S.A.
106 H3 **Hartman** Colorado U.S.A.
37 P5 **Hartmanice** Czechoslovakia
37 O2 **Hartmannsdorf** East Germany
36 G3 **Hartmannshain** W Germany
142 E3 **Hart, Mt** Western Australia Australia
119 Q6 **Hart Mt** Manitoba Canada
100 F7 **Hart Mt** Oregon U.S.A.
119 R9 **Hartney** Manitoba Canada
29 M10 **Hartola** Finland
13 G4 **Harton** England
106 E2 **Hartsel** Colorado U.S.A.
111 K7 **Hartselle** Alabama U.S.A.
37 J6 **Härtsfeld** *mts* W Germany
107 P7 **Hartshorne** Oklahoma U.S.A.
138 C4 **Harts I** South Australia Australia
140 C6 **Harts Range Police Station** N Terr Australia
112 G3 **Hartsville** South Carolina U.S.A.
110 K5 **Hartsville** Tennessee U.S.A.
89 D6 **Hartswater** S Africa
80 C6 **Hartuv** Israel
110 D4 **Hartville** Missouri U.S.A.
98 B7 **Hartville** Wyoming U.S.A.
112 E3 **Hartwell** Georgia U.S.A.
112 E3 **Hartwell L** *res* South Carolina U.S.A.
120 H3 **Harty** Ontario Canada
89 D6 **Hartz** *R* S Africa
84 F4 **Harūj al Aswad, Al** Libya
79 G1 **Haruniye** Turkey
58 B2 **Har Us Nuur** *L* Mongolia
80 C7 **Haruvit** Israel
102 H7 **Harvard** California U.S.A.
100 J3 **Harvard** Idaho U.S.A.
99 S7 **Harvard** Illinois U.S.A.
98 H9 **Harvard** Nebraska U.S.A.
116 O6 **Harvard Gl** Alaska U.S.A.
106 D3 **Harvard, Mt** Colorado U.S.A.
143 F7 **Harvest, Mt** Western Australia Australia
143 B10 **Harvey** Western Australia Australia
99 T8 **Harvey** Illinois U.S.A.
99 O8 **Harvey** Iowa U.S.A.
111 J13 **Harvey** New Orleans, Louisiana U.S.A.
98 F2 **Harvey** North Dakota U.S.A.
102 C1 **Harvey Mt** California U.S.A.
122 F8 **Harvey Stn** New Brunswick Canada
107 P3 **Harveyville** Kansas U.S.A.
110 F5 **Harviell** Missouri U.S.A.
9 E4 **Harwell** England
9 H4 **Harwich** England
109 K6 **Harwood** Texas U.S.A.
36 E4 **Harxheim** W Germany
74 F4 **Haryana** *prov* India
80 E8 **Har Yonatan** Israel
33 N9 **Harz** *mts* Germany
33 O9 **Harzegerode** East Germany
79 F8 **Hāsā** Jordan
72 F4 **Hasā, Al** *reg* Saudi Arabia
78 H3 **Hasakah, Al** Syria
78 E2 **Hasan Daği** *mt* Turkey
74 H9 **Hasanparti** India
80 E7 **Hasasa** *R* Jordan
79 F5 **Hâsbaiya** Lebanon
32 G8 **Hasbergen** W Germany
36 B5 **Hasborn-Dautweiler** W Germany
32 G7 **Hase** *R* W Germany
37 K2 **Hasel** *R* East Germany
32 L5 **Haseldorf** W Germany
32 F7 **Haselünne** W Germany
80 D4 **Hashimiye** Jordan
61 J11 **Hashimoto** Japan
26 H8 **Håsjö** Sweden
111 D7 **Haskell** Arkansas U.S.A.
107 P6 **Haskell** Oklahoma U.S.A.
108 H2 **Haskell** Texas U.S.A.
38 K4 **Haslach** Austria
36 E7 **Haslach** W Germany
27 G16 **Hasle** Denmark
109 M8 **Haslet** Texas U.S.A.
28 H6 **Haslev** Denmark
13 F6 **Haslingden** England
41 H4 **Hasli Tal** Switzerland
28 E4 **Haslund** Denmark
28 E5 **Hasmark** Denmark
22 E3 **Hasnon** France
80 D3 **Ha Solelim** Israel
18 E9 **Hasparren** France
32 F10 **Haspe** W Germany
22 E3 **Haspres** France
76 C4 **Hassan** India
103 M8 **Hassayampa** *R* Arizona U.S.A.
37 K3 **Hassberge** *mts* W Germany
26 J9 **Hassela** Sweden
33 N9 **Hasselfelde** East Germany
115 K2 **Hassel Sd** Northwest Territories Canada
22 J2 **Hasselt** Belgium
25 F3 **Hasselt** Netherlands
28 F4 **Hassensør** *C* Denmark
33 N9 **Hasserode** East Germany
37 K3 **Hassfurt** W Germany
17 F10 **Hassi Berkane** Morocco
85 E2 **Hassi-Bou-Zid** Algeria
85 E3 **Hassi Chebaba** Algeria
28 A3 **Hassing** Denmark
37 L3 **Hasslach** W Germany
33 T6 **Hassleben** East Germany
37 K1 **Hassleben** Erfurt East Germany
27 G15 **Hässleholm** Sweden
27 G13 **Hasslerör** Sweden
36 E5 **Hassloch** W Germany
22 H3 **Hastière-Lavaux** Belgium
139 L4 **Hastings** *R* New South Wales Australia
139 H9 **Hastings** Tasmania Australia
127 P6 **Hastings** Barbados
121 N8 **Hastings** Ontario Canada
9 G6 **Hastings** England
145 F3 **Hastings** New Zealand
113 F8 **Hastings** Florida U.S.A.
99 L9 **Hastings** Iowa U.S.A.
94 B4 **Hastings** Michigan U.S.A.
99 O5 **Hastings** Minnesota U.S.A.
98 H9 **Hastings** Nebraska U.S.A.
107 M7 **Hastings** Oklahoma U.S.A.
94 J6 **Hastings** Pennsylvania U.S.A.
28 E6 **Håstrup** Denmark
27 G15 **Hästveda** Sweden
106 H3 **Hasty** Colorado U.S.A.
26 M1 **Hasvik** Norway
106 G3 **Haswell** Colorado U.S.A.
58 E3 **Hatanbulag** Mongolia
79 G2 **Hatay** Turkey
95 M6 **Hatboro** Pennsylvania U.S.A.
106 C9 **Hatch** New Mexico U.S.A.
103 M4 **Hatch** Utah U.S.A.
140 D5 **Hatches Cr** N Terr Australia
126 F2 **Hatchet Bay** Eleuthera Bahamas
110 G6 **Hatchie** *R* Tennessee U.S.A.
98 B7 **Hat Cr** Wyoming U.S.A.
100 D9 **Hat Creek** California U.S.A.
48 H5 **Haţeg** Romania
145 F3 **Hatepe** New Zealand
67 H4 **Haterumashima** Japan
139 G5 **Hatfield** New South Wales Australia
119 M7 **Hatfield** Saskatchewan Canada
9 F4 **Hatfield** England
111 B7 **Hatfield** Arkansas U.S.A.
98 K6 **Hatfield** Minnesota U.S.A.
9 G4 **Hatfield Peverel** England
101 T3 **Hathaway** Montana U.S.A.
138 F6 **Hatherleigh** South Australia Australia
8 B6 **Hatherleigh** England
9 E1 **Hathersage** England
74 H5 **Hathras** India
68 G7 **Ha Tien** Vietnam
80 G3 **Hatim** Jordan
68 G3 **Ha Tinh** Vietnam
71 M9 **Hatohudo** Indonesia
127 K5 **Hato Mayor** Dominican Rep
56 C3 **Hatskiy** U.S.S.R.
60 F11 **Hatsukaichi** Japan
138 F5 **Hattah** Victoria Australia
70 F2 **Hattan, Mt** Sabah
25 F4 **Hattem** Netherlands
36 D6 **Hatten** France
112 M2 **Hatteras** North Carolina U.S.A.
112 M2 **Hatteras Inlet** North Carolina U.S.A.
36 E3 **Hattersheim** W Germany
26 G6 **Hattfjelldal** Norway
111 G10 **Hattiesburg** Mississippi U.S.A.
36 B6 **Hattigny** France
28 D5 **Hatting** Denmark
32 F10 **Hattingen** W Germany
118 H8 **Hatton** Saskatchewan Canada
21 P3 **Hatton** France
98 J2 **Hatton** North Dakota U.S.A.
100 G3 **Hatton** Washington U.S.A.
68 C6 **Hattras Passage** Burma
40 F1 **Hattstatt** France
29 L10 **Hattula** Finland
126 F4 **Hatuey** Cuba
145 F4 **Hatuma** New Zealand
48 F3 **Hatvan** Hungary
38 O8 **Hatzendorf** Austria
36 C3 **Hatzenport** W Germany
36 F2 **Hatzfeld** W Germany
22 D2 **Haubourdin** France
86 A2 **Haud** *reg* Ethiopia
80 G4 **Haufa** Jordan
28 C4 **Hauge** Denmark
27 C10 **Hauge** Norway
99 P4 **Haugen** Wisconsin U.S.A.
27 A12 **Haugesund** Norway
111 C9 **Haughton** Louisiana U.S.A.
31 J7 **Haugsdorf** Austria
29 L10 **Hauho** Finland
145 E3 **Hauhungaroa Ra** New Zealand
27 B12 **Haukeliseter** Norway
29 L6 **Haukipudas** Finland
29 N9 **Haukivesi** *L* Finland
29 N9 **Haukivuori** Finland
145 F3 **Haumoana** New Zealand
36 H2 **Haune** *R* W Germany
36 H2 **Hauneck** W Germany
36 H2 **Haunetal** Hessen W Germany
37 K7 **Haunstetten** W Germany
144 C5 **Haupiri, L** New Zealand
37 O5 **Hauptenberg** *mt* W Germany
145 E2 **Hauraki Gulf** New Zealand
144 A6 **Hauroko, L** New Zealand
27 A11 **Haus** Norway
36 E7 **Hausach** W Germany
32 J8 **Hausberge** W Germany
101 O3 **Hauser L. Dam** Montana U.S.A.
38 H5 **Hausruck** *mts* Austria
Haussez Iles d' *see* **Mercury Is**
41 K4 **Hausstock** *mt* Switzerland
29 O5 **Hautajarvi** Finland
22 B3 **Haut Banc, Pte du** France
40 B2 **Haut du Sec** *mt* France
18 L10 **Haute-Corse** *dept* Corsica
19 O12 **Hautecourt** France
18 F7 **Hautefort** France
18 F9 **Haute-Garonne** *dept* France
18 H7 **Haute-Loire** *dept* France
40 E6 **Hauteluce** France
19 J4 **Haute-Marne** *dept* France
121 Q4 **Haute Mauricie, Parc de** Quebec Canada
122 D4 **Hauterive** Quebec Canada
19 Q15 **Hautes Alpes** *dept* France
19 J5 **Haute-Saône** *dept* France
40 D6 **Haute-Savoie** *dept* France
22 L2 **Hautes Fagnes** Belgium
18 E9 **Hautes-Pyrénées** *dept* France
22 H4 **Hautes Rivières** France
18 F7 **Haute-Vienne** *dept* France
20 G4 **Hauteville-sur-Mer** France
36 B5 **Haut-Hombourg** France
95 T2 **Haut, I. au** Maine U.S.A.
22 F3 **Hautmont** France
19 K5 **Haut-Rhin** *dept* France
85 D2 **Hauts Plateaux** Morocco/Algeria
86 E5 **Haut-Zaire** *prov* Zaire
135 Q2 **Hauula** Hawaiian Is
145 E4 **Hauwai** New Zealand
Havana Cuba *see* **Habana**
110 C6 **Havana** Arkansas U.S.A.
111 M11 **Havana** Florida U.S.A.
99 R9 **Havana** Illinois U.S.A.
107 P4 **Havana** Kansas U.S.A.
98 J4 **Havana** North Dakota U.S.A.
9 F6 **Havant** England
103 K7 **Havasu, L** Cal/Ariz U.S.A.
28 C3 **Havbro** Denmark
28 J5 **Havdrup** Denmark
33 R6 **Havel** East Germany
22 J3 **Havelange** Belgium
33 Q7 **Havelberg** East Germany
33 R7 **Havelland** *reg* East Germany
33 R7 **Havelland Grosse Haupt-kanal** East Germany
122 G8 **Havelock** New Brunswick Canada
121 N8 **Havelock** Ontario Canada
145 D4 **Havelock** New Zealand
112 L3 **Havelock** North Carolina U.S.A.
98 D3 **Havelock** North Dakota U.S.A.
140 C2 **Havelock Falls** N Terr Australia
68 A7 **Havelock I** Andaman Is
145 F3 **Havelock North** New Zealand
107 N4 **Haven** Kansas U.S.A.
107 O2 **Havensville** Kansas U.S.A.
8 B4 **Haverfordwest** Wales
9 G3 **Haverhill** England
95 Q4 **Haverhill** Massachusetts U.S.A.
95 Q3 **Haverhill** New Hampshire U.S.A.
76 B3 **Haveri** India
26 H9 **Haverö** Sweden
22 J3 **Haversin** Belgium
28 C2 **Haverslev** Denmark
28 D3 **Haverslev** Nordjylland Denmark
95 N5 **Haverstraw** New York U.S.A.
107 L4 **Haviland** Kansas U.S.A.
94 C5 **Haviland** Ohio U.S.A.
120 F6 **Haviland Bay** Ontario Canada
48 K2 **Havirna** Romania
31 J6 **Havlíčkův Brod** Czechoslovakia
28 D6 **Havnbjerg** Denmark
28 E3 **Havndal** Denmark
28 B6 **Havneby** Denmark
28 G5 **Havnsø** Denmark
28 B4 **Havnstrup** Denmark
26 O1 **Havoysund** Norway
47 J5 **Havran** Turkey
22 G3 **Havre** Belgium
101 Q1 **Havre** Montana U.S.A.
21 L2 **Havre Antifer, Pont du** France
123 L6 **Havre Aubert** Madeleine Is, Quebec Canada
28 G6 **Havrebjerg** Denmark
123 L8 **Havre Boucher** Nova Scotia Canada
95 L7 **Havre de Grace** Maryland U.S.A.
122 J3 **Havre-St-Pierre** Quebec Canada
137 Q8 **Havre Trench** *sea feature* Pacific Oc
28 A5 **Havrvig** Denmark
26 H7 **Havsnäs** Sweden
78 E1 **Havza** Turkey
135 U5 **Hawaii** *isld* Hawaiian Is
135 **Hawaiian Is** Pacific Oc
86 B3 **Hawal** *R* Nigeria
118 L7 **Hawarden** Saskatchewan Canada
144 D5 **Hawarden** New Zealand
98 K0 **Hawarden** Iowa U.S.A.
8 C1 **Hawarden** Wales
138 F6 **Hawdon, L** South Australia Australia
144 B6 **Hawea** New Zealand
144 B6 **Hawea Flat** New Zealand
145 E3 **Hawera** New Zealand
102 G7 **Hawes** California U.S.A.
110 K4 **Hawesville** Kentucky U.S.A.
13 F5 **Hawes Water** England
135 U4 **Hawi** Hawaiian Is
13 F3 **Hawick** Scotland
144 B6 **Hawkdun Range** New Zealand
145 F3 **Hawke Bay** New Zealand
139 L4 **Hawke, C** New South Wales Australia
138 E4 **Hawker** South Australia Australia
138 F3 **Hawker Gate** New South Wales Australia
145 F3 **Hawke's Bay** *stat area* New Zealand
141 F1 **Hawkesbury I** Queensland Australia
140 C1 **Hawkesbury Pt** N Terr Australia
139 K5 **Hawkesbury R** New South Wales Australia
9 G5 **Hawkhurst** England
103 L4 **Hawkins Pk** Utah U.S.A.
112 D5 **Hawkinsville** Georgia U.S.A.
120 F4 **Hawk Junct** Ontario Canada
118 J1 **Hawk Lake** Ontario Canada
110 E3 **Hawk Point** Missouri U.S.A.
94 D1 **Hawks** Michigan U.S.A.
126 F2 **Hawksbill Cay** *isld* Bahamas
13 E5 **Hawkshead** England
126 G2 **Hawks Nest Pt** Cat I Bahamas
98 B8 **Hawk Springs** Wyoming U.S.A.
141 K7 **Hawkwood** Queensland Australia
106 G4 **Hawley** Colorado U.S.A.
98 K3 **Hawley** Minnesota U.S.A.
95 M5 **Hawley** Pennsylvania U.S.A.
108 H3 **Hawley** Texas U.S.A.
68 D2 **Hawng Luk** Burma
13 G6 **Haworth** England
107 Q8 **Haworth** Oklahoma U.S.A.
112 H2 **Haw R** North Carolina U.S.A.
78 H5 **Hawran, Wadi** Iraq
78 L5 **Hawr as S'adiyah** *L* Iraq
13 H5 **Hawsker** England
113 E8 **Hawthorn** Florida U.S.A.
102 F3 **Hawthorne** Nevada U.S.A.
99 P3 **Hawthorne** Wisconsin U.S.A.
80 D5 **Hawwara** Jordan
85 B3 **Hawza** Western Sahara
65 F2 **Haxat** China
65 B2 **Haxat Hudag** China
101 T2 **Haxby** Montana U.S.A.
98 D9 **Haxtun** Colorado U.S.A.
139 G5 **Hay** New South Wales Australia
117 N6 **Hay** *R* British Columbia Canada
100 H3 **Hay** Washington U.S.A.
99 P4 **Hay** *R* Wisconsin U.S.A.
61 P6 **Hayachine-san** *mt* Japan
60 P3 **Hayakita** Japan
19 K3 **Hayange** France
60 E12 **Hayasui-seto** *str* Japan
101 T9 **Haybro** Colorado U.S.A.
47 N10 **Haydarpaşa** Turkey
103 O8 **Hayden** Arizona U.S.A.
101 S9 **Hayden** Colorado U.S.A.
100 J2 **Hayden L** Idaho U.S.A.
141 F4 **Haydon** Queensland Australia
13 F4 **Haydon Br** England
20 G3 **Haye-du-Puits, la** France
21 N3 **Haye, la** France
20 H4 **Haye-Pesnel, la** France
115 K6 **Hayes** *R* Manitoba Canada
111 D11 **Hayes** Louisiana U.S.A.
98 E5 **Hayes** South Dakota U.S.A.
21 M4 **Haye-St.Sylvestre, la** France
98 E9 **Hayes Center** Nebraska U.S.A.
116 L6 **Hayes Glaciers** Alaska U.S.A.
115 N2 **Hayes Halvø** *pen* Greenland
68 C7 **Hayes I** Burma
116 O5 **Hayes, Mt** Alaska U.S.A.
112 D2 **Hayesville** North Carolina U.S.A.
13 G6 **Hayfield** England
99 O6 **Hayfield** Minnesota U.S.A.
103 J8 **Hayfield Res** Carolina U.S.A.
102 A1 **Hayfork** California U.S.A.
13 F5 **Haygarth** England
36 G7 **Hayingen** W Germany
117 O6 **Hay L** Alberta Canada
118 D5 **Hay Lakes** Alberta Canada
8 A7 **Hayle** England
9 F6 **Hayling** England
113 E7 **Haylow** Georgia U.S.A.
141 J5 **Hayman I** Queensland Australia
94 K8 **Haymarket** Virginia U.S.A.
140 C6 **Hay, Mt** N Terr Australia
109 O3 **Haynesville** Louisiana U.S.A.
95 T8 **Haynesville** Maine U.S.A.
111 K9 **Hayneville** Alabama U.S.A.
21 N2 **Hayons, les** France
8 C3 **Hay-on-Wye** England
141 J5 **Hay Point** Queensland Australia
140 D6 **Hay R** N Terr Australia
47 J3 **Hayrabolu** *R* Turkey
47 J3 **Hayrabolu** Turkey
117 Q5 **Hay River** Northwest Territories Canada
118 F8 **Hays** Alberta Canada
107 L3 **Hays** Kansas U.S.A.
101 R1 **Hays** Montana U.S.A.
98 D7 **Hay Springs** Nebraska U.S.A.
100 K8 **Haystack Mt** Nevada U.S.A.
103 L2 **Haystack Pk** Utah U.S.A.
118 G6 **Hayter** Alberta Canada
110 G5 **Hayti** Missouri U.S.A.
98 J5 **Hayti** South Dakota U.S.A.
13 H6 **Hayton** England
102 B4 **Hayward** California U.S.A.
99 N6 **Hayward** Minnesota U.S.A.
107 N5 **Hayward** Oklahoma U.S.A.
99 P4 **Hayward** Wisconsin U.S.A.
140 B2 **Hayward, Mt** N Terr Australia
9 F6 **Haywards Heath** England
119 T9 **Haywood** Manitoba Canada
80 E2 **Hazan** Israel
77 J3 **Hazarajat** *reg* Afghanistan
94 D9 **Hazard** Kentucky U.S.A.
95 P4 **Hazardville** Connecticut U.S.A.
75 L7 **Hazāribag** India
77 F1 **Hazar Masjed, Kūh-e** *mts* Iran
22 D2 **Hazebrouck** France
98 K1 **Hazel** Minnesota U.S.A.
98 J5 **Hazel** South Dakota U.S.A.
119 V9 **Hazelridge** Manitoba Canada
117 K8 **Hazelton** British Columbia Canada
107 M4 **Hazelton** Kansas U.S.A.
98 F3 **Hazelton** North Dakota U.S.A.
110 E7 **Hazen** Arkansas U.S.A.
102 E2 **Hazen** Nevada U.S.A.
98 E2 **Hazen** North Dakota U.S.A.
116 E6 **Hazen B** Alaska U.S.A.
115 N1 **Hazen, L** Northwest Territories Canada
118 K9 **Hazenmore** Saskatchewan Canada
114 H2 **Hazen Str** Northwest Territories Canada
80 B8 **Hazerim** Israel
25 C4 **Hazerswoude** Netherlands
112 E2 **Hazewood** North Carolina U.S.A.
112 E6 **Hazlehurst** Georgia U.S.A.
111 F10 **Hazlehurst** Mississippi U.S.A.
95 M6 **Hazleton** Pennsylvania U.S.A.
142 G5 **Hazlett, L** Western Australia Australia
37 N3 **Hazlov** Czechoslovakia
80 F2 **Hazor** Israel
80 F3 **HaZore'im** Israel
80 C7 **He** Israel
9 G2 **Heacham** England
9 G5 **Headcorn** England
14 B3 **Headford** Ireland
122 E9 **Head Harbor I** Maine U.S.A.
140 E5 **Headingly** Queensland Australia
111 L10 **Headland** Alabama U.S.A.
144 B6 **Headlong Pk** New Zealand
138 B4 **Head of Bight** *B* South Australia Australia
100 K3 **Headquarters** Idaho U.S.A.
83 M9 **Headridge Hill** Christmas I Indian Oc
100 A7 **Heads, The** *C* Oregon U.S.A.
99 R4 **Heafford Junct** Wisconsin U.S.A.
102 B3 **Healdsburg** California U.S.A.
109 K1 **Healdton** Oklahoma U.S.A.
139 H7 **Healesville** Victoria Australia
116 N5 **Healy** Alaska U.S.A.
116 P4 **Healy** *R* Alaska U.S.A.
107 K3 **Healy** Kansas U.S.A.
116 P5 **Healy L** Alaska U.S.A.
119 Q3 **Heaman** Manitoba Canada
9 E1 **Heanor** England
81 K16 **Heard I** Southern Oc
119 M8 **Hearne** Saskatchewan Canada
109 L5 **Hearne** Texas U.S.A.
117 R4 **Hearne L** Northwest Territories Canada
120 G3 **Hearst** Ontario Canada
102 A2 **Hearst** California U.S.A.
146 D5 **Hearst I** Antarctica
98 D3 **Heart** *R* North Dakota U.S.A.
118 F3 **Heart L** Alberta Canada
101 P5 **Heart L** Wyoming U.S.A.
118 A3 **Heart R** Alberta Canada
123 T6 **Heart's Content** Newfoundland Canada
123 T6 **Heart's Delight** Newfoundland Canada
98 H9 **Heartwell** Nebraska U.S.A.
128 E6 **Heath** *R* Bolivia/Peru
139 G6 **Heathcote** Victoria Australia
6 L2 **Heather** *oil rig* North Sea
123 O5 **Heatherton** Newfoundland Canada
9 G6 **Heathfield** England
123 L4 **Heath Pt** Anticosti I, Quebec
9 F5 **Heathrow Airport** England
112 G3 **Heath Springs** South Carolina U.S.A.
122 F6 **Heath Steel Mines** New Brunswick Canada
95 L9 **Heathsville** Virginia U.S.A.
107 Q7 **Heavener** Oklahoma U.S.A.
109 J8 **Hebbronville** Texas U.S.A.
13 F6 **Hebden Br** England
65 C5 **Hebei** *prov* China
141 J8 **Hebel** Queensland Australia
103 O7 **Heber** Arizona U.S.A.
32 L6 **Heber** W Germany
101 O9 **Heber City** Utah U.S.A.
110 D6 **Heber Springs** Arkansas U.S.A.
121 P3 **Hébert, L** Quebec Canada
121 T4 **Hébertville Station** Quebec Canada
101 O5 **Hebgen L** Montana U.S.A.
65 C7 **Hebi** China
100 B4 **Hebo** Oregon U.S.A.
115 N6 **Hebron** Labrador, Nfld Canada
122 F10 **Hebron** Nova Scotia Canada
80 D7 **Hebron** Jordan
101 T9 **Hebron** Colorado U.S.A.
99 S7 **Hebron** Illinois U.S.A.
99 T8 **Hebron** Indiana U.S.A.
98 J9 **Hebron** Nebraska U.S.A.
98 E3 **Hebron** North Dakota U.S.A.
94 E7 **Hebron** Ohio U.S.A.
27 J12 **Heby** Sweden
117 H9 **Hecate Str** British Columbia Canada
100 A5 **Heceta Head** Oregon U.S.A.
117 G8 **Heceta I** Alaska U.S.A.
67 C4 **Hechi** China
36 F7 **Hechingen** W Germany
22 J1 **Hechtel** Belgium
32 K5 **Hechthausen** W Germany
36 E4 **Hechtsheim** W Germany
67 B1 **Hechuan** China
33 T7 **Heckelberg** East Germany
9 F2 **Heckington** England
33 P9 **Hecklingen** East Germany
98 H4 **Hecla** South Dakota U.S.A.
114 H2 **Hecla & Griper B** Northwest Territories Canada
119 V7 **Hecla I** Manitoba Canada
119 V7 **Hecla Prov. Park** Manitoba Canada
122 F9 **Hectanooga** Nova Scotia Canada
144 C4 **Hector** New Zealand
99 M5 **Hector** Minnesota U.S.A.
117 P10 **Hector, Mt** Alberta Canada
145 E4 **Hector, Mt** New Zealand
144 B6 **Hector Mts** New Zealand
127 M2 **Hector's River** Jamaica
27 H12 **Hed** Sweden
61 M11 **Heda** Japan
27 D11 **Hedal** Norway
21 P1 **Hédauville** France
26 K6 **Hedberg** Sweden
27 D12 **Heddal** Norway
36 F4 **Heddesheim** W Germany
13 G3 **Heddon on-the-Wall** England
20 G5 **Hédé** France
26 G9 **Hede** Sweden
25 D5 **Hedel** Netherlands
27 H11 **Hedemora** Sweden
32 L10 **Hedemunden** W Germany
28 E6 **Heden** Denmark
26 M6 **Heden** Sweden
26 N5 **Hedenäset** Sweden
28 D5 **Hedensted** Denmark
33 O9 **Hedersleben** East Germany
27 J11 **Hedesunda** Sweden
26 G9 **Hedeviken** Sweden
144 B7 **Hedgehope** New Zealand
101 Q3 **Hedgesville** Montana U.S.A.
94 J7 **Hedgesville** West Virginia U.S.A.
67 C6 **Hedi Shuiku** *res* China
117 N11 **Hedley** British Columbia Canada
27 E11 **Hedmark** Norway
27 E10 **Hedmark** *county* Norway
61 Q12 **Hedo** Okinawa
61 Q12 **Hedo-misaki** *C* Okinawa
13 H6 **Hedon** England
83 L11 **Hedo Oya** *R* Sri Lanka
99 O8 **Hedrick** Iowa U.S.A.
28 A4 **Hee** Denmark
32 F7 **Heede** W Germany
33 T7 **Heegermühle** East Germany
32 F8 **Heek** W Germany
25 C4 **Heemstede** Netherlands
32 J8 **Heepen** W Germany
22 H3 **Heer** Belgium
25 E7 **Heer** Netherlands
25 F4 **Heerde** Netherlands
25 E3 **Heerenveen** Netherlands
25 C3 **Heerhugo-waard** Netherlands
25 E7 **Heerlen** Netherlands
25 E5 **Heesch** Netherlands
25 E6 **Heeze** Netherlands
67 F1 **Hefei** China
67 C2 **Hefeng** China
117 N10 **Heffley** British Columbia Canada
111 L8 **Heflin** Alabama U.S.A.
65 H1 **Hegang** China
61 K8 **Hegura-jima** *isld* Japan
88 E5 **Hehe** Tanzania
26 D10 **Heidal** Norway
80 F8 **Heidan** *R* Jordan
32 K4 **Heide** W Germany
37 L5 **Heideck** W Germany
111 H10 **Heidelberg** Mississippi U.S.A.
36 F5 **Heidelberg** W Germany
87 E11 **Heidelburg** S Africa
110 N4 **Heidelburg** Kentucky U.S.A.
36 F5 **Heidelsheim** W Germany
37 M4 **Heide Naab** *R* W Germany
37 J6 **Heidenheim** W Germany
36 D3 **Heidenrod** W Germany
94 B2 **Heights, The** Michigan U.S.A.
60 F12 **Heigun-tō** *isld* Japan
59 J1 **Heihe** China
59 J1 **Hei-ho** China
25 E6 **Heijthuizsen** Netherlands
87 E11 **Heilbron** S Africa
36 G5 **Heilbronn** W Germany
38 G7 **Heiligenblut** Austria
33 P4 **Heiligendamm** East Germany
30 F1 **Heiligenhafen** W Germany
32 M10 **Heiligenstadt** East Germany
37 L4 **Heiligenstadt** W Germany
65 D7 **Heilin** China
59 J1 **Heilong Jiang** *R* China
59 H1 **Heilongjiang** *prov* China
37 K5 **Heilsbronn** W Germany
Heilungkiang *prov see* **Heilongjiang** *prov*
36 B2 **Heimbach** W Germany
36 G4 **Heimbuchenthal** W Germany
33 N9 **Heimburg** East Germany
6 M3 **Heimdal** *oil rig* North Sea
26 D8 **Heimdal** Norway
98 G2 **Heimdal** North Dakota U.S.A.
36 F6 **Heimsheim** W Germany
29 O9 **Heinävesi** Finland
36 H1 **Heinebach** W Germany
22 L3 **Heinerscheid** Luxembourg
37 L3 **Heinersdorf** East Germany
36 C5 **Heinitz** W Germany
25 F4 **Heino** Netherlands
29 M10 **Heinola** Finland
33 P8 **Heinrichsburg** East Germany
25 F6 **Heinsberg** W Germany
118 G5 **Heinsburg** Alberta Canada
33 S9 **Heinsdorf** East Germany
68 C5 **Heinz B** Burma
68 C5 **Heinze I** Burma
65 E4 **Heishan** China
65 C3 **Heishantou** China
67 C2 **Heishui** China
118 E6 **Heisler** Alberta Canada
22 E1 **Heist** Belgium
22 H1 **Heist-op-den-Berg** Belgium
80 G3 **Heit** Syria
80 G2 **Heital** Syria
79 D8 **Heitân, G** *mt* Egypt
40 G2 **Heitersheim** W Germany
65 F2 **Heiyupao** China
84 H4 **Heiz, El** Egypt
65 A5 **Hejialiang** China
67 B2 **Hejiang** China
67 C6 **Hejiang** China
67 D5 **He Jiang** *R* China
67 D4 **Hejie** China
65 A7 **Hejin** China
28 D6 **Hejls** Denmark
28 C6 **Hejlsminde** Denmark
28 B5 **Hejnsvig** Denmark
28 D6 **Hejsager** Denmark
28 S10 **Hekla** *mt* Iceland
Hekou *see* **Yanshan**
65 B4 **Hekou** China
67 D5 **Hekou** Guangdong China
67 A5 **Hekou** Yunnan China
31 L1 **Hel** Poland
80 E2 **Hela** Israel
26 F9 **Helagsfjället** *mt* Sweden
58 E4 **Helan Shan** *mt ra* China
37 K1 **Helbe** *R* East Germany
28 E3 **Helberskov** Denmark
33 O9 **Helbra** East Germany
22 J1 **Helchteren** Belgium
37 K3 **Heldburg** East Germany
36 F3 **Heldenbergen** W Germany
127 P3 **Helden's Pt** St Kitts W Indies
33 O10 **Heldrungen** East Germany
112 D3 **Helen** Georgia U.S.A.
111 K8 **Helena** Alabama U.S.A.
111 F7 **Helena** Arkansas U.S.A.
100 B9 **Helena** California U.S.A.
112 E5 **Helena** Georgia U.S.A.
101 N3 **Helena** Montana U.S.A.
107 M5 **Helena** Oklahoma U.S.A.
102 G7 **Helendale** California U.S.A.
118 J5 **Heléne L** Saskatchewan Canada
142 E6 **Helen Hill** Western Australia Australia
71 C1 **Helen I** Pacific Oc
119 P1 **Helen L** Ontario Canada
141 F5 **Helen, Mt** Queensland Australia
15 D4 **Helensburgh** Scotland
140 C4 **Helen Springs** N Terr Australia
145 E2 **Helensville** New Zealand
33 P10 **Helfta** East Germany
26 F6 **Helgeland** *reg* Norway
27 D12 **Helgen** Norway
32 G4 **Helgoländ** *isld* W Germany
32 H4 **Helgoländer Bucht** W Germany
26 K1 **Helgöy** Norway
65 H1 **Heli** China
79 B8 **Heliopolis** Egypt
26 E8 **Hell** Norway
28 S10 **Hella** Iceland
33 O7 **Hellberg** *hills* East Germany
29 K4 **Hellebæk** Denmark
77 B5 **Helleh** *R* Iran
26 J4 **Hellemobotn** Norway
25 F4 **Hellendoorn** Netherlands
36 B3 **Hellenthal** W Germany
29 K5 **Hellerup** Denmark
28 J6 **Hellested** Denmark
26 B9 **Hellesylt** Norway
28 E2 **Hellevad** Nordjylland Denmark
28 C6 **Hellevad** Sønderjylland Denmark
26 L2 **Helligskogen** Norway
26 G4 **Helligvoer** *isld* Norway
17 F6 **Hellin** Spain
Hell's Canyon *see* **Snake River Canyon**
127 L3 **Hellshire Hills** Jamaica
28 E2 **Hellum** Denmark
32 K6 **Hellwege** W Germany
102 D5 **Helm** California U.S.A.
77 H4 **Helmand** *R* Afghanistan
32 K9 **Helmarshausen** W Germany
37 M3 **Helmbrechts** W Germany
33 N10 **Helme** *R* East Germany
87 C11 **Helmeringhausen** Namibia
37 J2 **Helmershausen** East Germany
9 H3 **Helmingham** England
25 E6 **Helmond** Netherlands
32 J4 **Helmsand** *sandbank* W Germany
15 E2 **Helmsdale** *R* Scotland
15 E2 **Helmsdale** Scotland
13 G5 **Helmsley** England
36 F5 **Helmstadt** W Germany
33 O8 **Helmstedt** W Germany
101 N3 **Helmville** Montana U.S.A.
28 D6 **Helnæs** Denmark
28 E6 **Helnæs Bugt** *B* Denmark
26 P1 **Helnes** Norway
65 F2 **Helong** China
59 J3 **Helong** China
109 J6 **Helotes** Texas U.S.A.
103 O2 **Helper** Utah U.S.A.
33 T6 **Helpter Berge** *pk* East Germany
32 L10 **Helsa-Wickenrode** W Germany
29 K4 **Helsingborg** Sweden
28 J4 **Helsinge** Denmark
Helsingfors *see* **Helsinki**
29 K4 **Helsingør** Denmark
29 L11 **Helsinki** Finland
9 G6 **Helston** England
32 L7 **Helstorf** W Germany
110 K3 **Heltonville** Indiana U.S.A.
130 H5 **Helvécia** Brazil
14 D4 **Helvick Hd** Ireland
84 J4 **Helwan** Egypt
28 D4 **Hem** Vejle Denmark
28 B3 **Hem** Viborg Denmark
118 F7 **Hemaruka** Alberta Canada
37 M5 **Hemau** W Germany
32 E9 **Hemden** W Germany
9 F4 **Hemel Hempstead** England
25 D3 **Hemelum** Netherlands
32 G10 **Hemer** W Germany
102 H8 **Hemet** California U.S.A.
36 B6 **Héming** France
98 C7 **Hemingford** Nebraska U.S.A.
119 Q4 **Heming Lake** Manitoba Canada
112 H4 **Hemingway** South Carolina U.S.A.
141 L1 **Hemmant** *dist* Brisbane, Qnsld Australia
32 J4 **Hemme** W Germany
28 F3 **Hemmed** Denmark
32 L8 **Hemmendorf** W Germany
28 A5 **Hemmet** Denmark
32 L8 **Hemmingen** W Germany
121 R7 **Hemmingford** Quebec Canada
32 K5 **Hemmoor** W Germany
26 G5 **Hemnesberget** Norway
111 C10 **Hemphill** Texas U.S.A.
95 O6 **Hempstead** Long I, New York U.S.A.
109 L5 **Hempstead** Texas U.S.A.
9 H2 **Hemsby** England
27 K14 **Hemse** *isld* Gotland Sweden
27 C11 **Hemsedal** Norway
27 C11 **Hemsil** *R* Norway
27 G15 **Hemsjö** Sweden
32 L6 **Hemslingen** W Germany
26 K9 **Hemsö** Sweden
13 G6 **Hemsworth** England
65 B7 **Henan** *prov* China
20 F4 **Hénanbihen** France
145 E1 **Hen and Chicken Is** New Zealand
20 F4 **Hénansal** France
16 E4 **Henares** *R* Spain
61 N5 **Henashi-zaki** *C* Japan
140 C6 **Henbury** N Terr Australia
18 D9 **Hendaye** France
22 D3 **Hendecourt-lès Cagnicourt** France
47 L4 **Hendek** Turkey
103 K5 **Henderson** Nevada U.S.A.
95 L3 **Henderson** New York U.S.A.
112 J1 **Henderson** North Carolina U.S.A.
110 H6 **Henderson** Tennessee U.S.A.
109 N3 **Henderson** Texas U.S.A.
94 E8 **Henderson** West Virginia U.S.A.
146 H13 **Henderson I** *isld* Antarctica
135 O11 **Henderson I** Pacific Oc
112 E2 **Hendersonville** North Carolina U.S.A.
77 A4 **Hendījān** Iran
77 A4 **Hendījān** *oil well* Persian Gulf
119 O6 **Hendon** Saskatchewan Canada
9 F4 **Hendon** England
77 C6 **Hendorābī** *isld* Iran
48 J4 **Hendorf** Romania
141 K1 **Hendra** *dist* Brisbane, Qnsld Australia
98 K5 **Hendricks** Minnesota U.S.A.
94 H7 **Hendricks** West Virginia U.S.A.
129 G3 **Hendrik Top** *mt* Suriname
89 D8 **Hendrik Verwoerd Dam** S Africa
8 B4 **Hendy** Wales
101 O8 **Henefer** Utah U.S.A.
65 H2 **Hengdaohezi** China
65 G3 **Hengdaozi** China
67 D3 **Hengdong** China
58 C6 **Hengduan Shan** *mts* China
25 G4 **Hengelo** Netherlands
37 P6 **Hengersberg** W Germany
67 F2 **Hengfeng** China
67 A2 **Heng Jiang** *R* China
67 D2 **Henglongqiao** China
67 D3 **Hengnan** China
67 D3 **Hengshan** China
67 D3 **Heng Shan** *mt* China
58 G4 **Hengshui** China
37 J5 **Hengstfeld** W Germany
67 C5 **Heng Xian** China
69 A9 **Henhoaha** Nicobar Is
22 D3 **Hénin-Beaumont** France
144 C6 **Henley** New Zealand
123 R2 **Henley Hbr** Labrador, Nfld Canada
9 E3 **Henley-in-Arden** England
9 F4 **Henley-on-Thames** England
100 C10 **Henleyville** California U.S.A.
9 F3 **Henlow** England
109 J5 **Henly** Texas U.S.A.
27 E12 **Henmes** Norway
61 P13 **Henna** Okinawa
26 H9 **Hennan** Sweden
28 A5 **Henne** Denmark
37 J3 **Henneberg** East Germany
20 D6 **Hennebont** France
36 C2 **Hennef** W Germany
37 K5 **Hennenbach** W Germany
99 R8 **Hennepin** Illinois U.S.A.
21 L3 **Hennequeville** France
107 N5 **Hennessey** Oklahoma U.S.A.
33 S8 **Hennickendorf** East Germany
33 S7 **Hennigsdorf** East Germany
95 Q3 **Henniker** New Hampshire U.S.A.
110 J1 **Henning** Illinois U.S.A.
99 L3 **Henning** Minnesota U.S.A.
110 G6 **Henning** Tennessee U.S.A.
26 G3 **Henningsvaer** Norway
32 K4 **Hennstedt** W Germany
21 P3 **Hénonville** France
77 D6 **Henqam** *isld* Iran
119 M5 **Henribourg** Saskatchewan Canada
22 K2 **Henri-Chapelle** Belgium
109 J2 **Henrietta** Texas U.S.A.
115 L6 **Henrietta Maria, C** Ontario Canada
103 N4 **Henrieville** Utah U.S.A.
117 L7 **Henri, Mt** British Columbia Canada
Henrique de Carvalho *see* **Saurimo**
101 O7 **Henry** Idaho U.S.A.
99 R8 **Henry** Illinois U.S.A.
95 M10 **Henry, C** Virginia U.S.A.
146 D7 **Henry Ice Rise** *ice rise* Antarctica
115 N4 **Henry Kater Pen** Northwest Territories Canada
111 K8 **Henry L** Alabama U.S.A.
68 A6 **Henry Lawrence I** Andaman Is
100 K1 **Henry, Mt** Montana U.S.A.
103 O4 **Henry Mts** Utah U.S.A.
142 B6 **Henry, R** Western Australia Australia
101 O5 **Henrys Fork** *R* Idaho U.S.A.
110 L3 **Henryville** Indiana U.S.A.
120 J9 **Hensall** Ontario Canada
110 H4 **Henshaw** Kentucky U.S.A.
102 H8 **Henshaw, L** California U.S.A.
12 E5 **Hensingham** England
142 G3 **Hensman, Mt** Western Australia Australia
32 L5 **Henstedt-Ulzburg** W Germany
8 D6 **Henstridge** England
58 E2 **Hentiy** Mongolia
58 E2 **Hentiyn Nuruu** *mt* Mongolia
139 H6 **Henty** New South Wales Australia
68 B4 **Henzada** Burma
61 P13 **Henza-jima** *isld* Okinawa
118 L6 **Hepburn** Saskatchewan Canada
67 E1 **Hepeng** China
112 E4 **Hephzibah** Georgia U.S.A.
Heping *see* **Yanhe**
67 E4 **Heping** China
Hepo *see* **Jiexi**
36 B2 **Heppendorf** W Germany
36 F4 **Heppenheim** W Germany
100 F4 **Heppner** Oregon U.S.A.
80 F2 **Heptapegon** Israel
68 J2 **Hepu** China
120 J8 **Hepworth** Ontario Canada
65 B5 **Hequ** China
27 E11 **Heradsbygd** Norway
141 J3 **Herald Cays** *islds* Gt Barrier Reef Aust
77 H2 **Herāt** Afghanistan
18 H9 **Hérault** *R* France
18 H9 **Hérault** *dept* France
19 O14 **Herbasse** *R* France
20 F7 **Herbaudiere, Pte,de l'** France
21 N6 **Herbault** France
32 F10 **Herbede** W Germany
36 D3 **Herberge, K** *mt* W Germany
32 G9 **Herbern** W Germany
141 H4 **Herbert** *R* Queensland Australia
118 K8 **Herbert** Saskatchewan Canada
144 C6 **Herbert** New Zealand
68 A7 **Herbertabad** Andaman Is
140 E6 **Herbert Downs** Queensland Australia
140 B4 **Herbert, Mt** N Terr Australia
142 F3 **Herbert, Mt** Western Australia Australia
141 H3 **Herberton** Queensland Australia
145 F4 **Herbertville** New Zealand
22 K2 **Herbesthal** Belgium
22 J4 **Herbeumont** Belgium
21 H8 **Herbiers, les** France
20 F7 **Herbignac** France
36 C5 **Herbitzheim** France
119 S4 **Herb L** Manitoba Canada
36 D7 **Herbolzheim** W Germany
36 E2 **Herborn** W Germany
36 G2 **Herbstein** W Germany
31 L5 **Herby** Poland
42 J6 **Herceg Novi** Yugoslavia
42 H5 **Hercegovina** *reg* Yugoslavia
115 K6 **Herchmer** Manitoba Canada
36 H4 **Herchsheim** W Germany
146 D9 **Hercules Dome** *ice dome* Antarctica
107 O5 **Herd** Oklahoma U.S.A.
32 F10 **Herdecke** W Germany
125 M4 **Heredia** Costa Rica
Hereford *co see* **Hereford and Worcester** *co*
8 D3 **Hereford** England
98 B9 **Hereford** Colorado U.S.A.
108 E1 **Hereford** Texas U.S.A.
8 D3 **Hereford and Worcester** *co* England
47 N11 **Hereke** Turkey
145 D1 **Herekino** New Zealand
16 E5 **Herencia** Spain
40 F5 **Herens, Val. d'** Switzerland
22 H1 **Herentals** Belgium
87 C10 **Herero** *homeland* Namibia
144 B5 **Heretaniwha Pt** New Zealand
28 J6 **Herfølge** Denmark
32 J8 **Herford** W Germany
22 L2 **Hergenrath** Belgium
20 G7 **Heric** France
19 K5 **Hericourt** France
33 N10 **Heringen** East Germany
107 O3 **Herington** Kansas U.S.A.
22 G2 **Herinnes** Belgium
144 B6 **Heriot** New Zealand
13 F2 **Heriot** Scotland
117 L10 **Heriot Bay** British Columbia Canada

41 K3 Herisau Switzerland
22 J2 Herk-de-Stad Belgium
95 N3 Herkimer New York U.S.A.
121 Q9 Herkimer New York U.S.A.
37 N2 Herlasgrün East Germany
58 F2 Herlen Gol R Mongolia
58 G2 Herlen He R China
37 J1 Herleshausen W Germany
29 K5 Herlev Denmark
28 H6 Herlufmagle Denmark
20 F3 Herm isld Channel Is
38 H8 Hermagor Austria
99 S3 Herman Michigan U.S.A.
98 K4 Herman Minnesota U.S.A.
98 K8 Herman Nebraska U.S.A.
71 D3 Hermana Mayor isld Philippines
124 J4 Hermanas Mexico
106 C10 Hermanas New Mexico U.S.A.
110 E3 Hermann Missouri U.S.A.
32 M7 Hermannsberg W Germany
140 C6 Hermannsburg N Terr Australia
37 P4 Hermanova Hut' Czechoslovakia
99 T4 Hermansville Michigan U.S.A.
89 A10 Hermanus S Africa
111 F10 Hermanville Mississippi U.S.A.
79 G4 Hermel Lebanon
21 P3 Hermes France
36 B4 Hermeskeil W Germany
22 H3 Hermeton-sur-Meuse Belgium
139 H4 Hermidale New South Wales Australia
22 E3 Hermies France
100 F4 Hermiston Oregon U.S.A.
123 R6 Hermitage Newfoundland Canada
111 D8 Hermitage Arkansas U.S.A.
123 Q3 Hermitage B Newfoundland Canada
20 E5 Hermitage, l' France
142 B5 Hermite I Western Australia Australia
133 D9 Hermite, Is Chile
21 M6 Hermites, les France
140 B2 Hermit Hill N Terr Australia
136 K2 Hermit Is Bismarck Arch
105 M5 Hermits Rest Arizona U.S.A.
108 G3 Hermleigh Texas U.S.A.
Hermön, Mt see Sheikh, J. esh
22 F5 Hermonville France
98 C6 Hermosa South Dakota U.S.A.
124 D3 Hermosillo Mexico
Hermsdorf see Ottendorf-Okrilla
130 C9 Hernandarias Paraguay
113 E9 Hernando Florida U.S.A.
110 G7 Hernando Mississippi U.S.A.
102 E5 Herndon California U.S.A.
99 M8 Herndon Iowa U.S.A.
107 K2 Herndon Kansas U.S.A.
110 J5 Herndon Kentucky U.S.A.
95 L6 Herndon Pennsylvania U.S.A.
94 F9 Herndon West Virginia U.S.A.
32 F9 Herne W Germany
9 H5 Herne Bay England
28 B4 Herning Denmark
124 C2 Heroica Caborca Mexico
37 L4 Heroldsberg W Germany
22 J2 Héron Belgium
100 K1 Heron Montana U.S.A.
120 D4 Heron Bay Ontario Canada
25 F6 Herongen W Germany
141 K6 Heron I Gt Barrier Reef Aust
144 C5 Heron, L New Zealand
99 L6 Heron L Minnesota U.S.A.
Herowābād see Khalkhāl
26 A9 Heroy Norway
130 B10 Herradura Argentina
16 D5 Herrara del Duque Spain
98 F4 Herreid South Dakota U.S.A.
36 F6 Herrenberg W Germany
36 E6 Herrenwies W Germany
133 E3 Herrera Argentina
17 G3 Herrera mt Spain
16 C5 Herrera de Alcántara Spain
17 G3 Herrera de los Navarros Spain
124 G5 Herreras Mexico
28 F6 Herrested Denmark
139 J8 Herrick Tasmania Australia
98 G6 Herrick South Dakota U.S.A.
110 G4 Herrin Illinois U.S.A.
123 S4 Herring Neck Newfoundland Canada
94 C9 Herrington L Kentucky U.S.A.
119 Q2 Herriot Manitoba Canada
28 H7 Herritslev Denmark
36 H7 Herrlingen W Germany
27 F13 Herrljunga Sweden
36 E4 Herrnsheim W Germany
36 C4 Herrstein W Germany
18 G9 Hers R France
37 L5 Hersbruck W Germany
36 D1 Herscheid W Germany
118 J7 Herschel Saskatchewan Canada
116 S2 Herschel Yukon Territory Canada
99 S8 Herscher Illinois U.S.A.
37 J3 Herschfeld W Germany
22 H1 Herselt Belgium
94 B3 Hersey Michigan U.S.A.
95 L6 Hershey Pennsylvania U.S.A.
28 D5 Herslev Denmark
28 D3 Hersom Denmark
22 K2 Herstal Belgium
9 G6 Herstmonceux England
22 E2 Hertain Belgium
32 F9 Herten W Germany
9 F4 Hertford England
112 L1 Hertford North Carolina U.S.A.
9 F4 Hertfordshire co England
80 C5 Herut Israel
16 D4 Hervas Spain
22 K2 Herve Belgium
141 L7 Hervey B Queensland Australia
121 S6 Hervey Junction Quebec Canada
141 H4 Hervey Ra Queensland Australia
36 E5 Herxheim W Germany
33 S9 Herzberg East Germany
33 M9 Herzberg W Germany
33 T8 Herzfelde East Germany
32 G7 Herzlake W Germany
80 C5 Herzliyya Israel
37 K4 Herzogenaurach W Germany
38 N5 Herzogenburg Austria
25 F7 Herzogenrath W Germany
33 Q6 Herzsprung East Germany
22 B2 Hesdigneul-lès-Boulogne France
22 C3 Hesdin France
32 G6 Hesel W Germany
67 D5 Heshui China
67 E3 He Shui R China
65 B6 Heshun China
27 B13 Heskestad Norway
98 G2 Hesper North Dakota U.S.A.
22 L4 Hesperange Luxembourg
102 G7 Hesperia California U.S.A.
94 A3 Hesperia Michigan U.S.A.
106 B4 Hesperus Colorado U.S.A.
106 B4 Hesperus Pk Colorado U.S.A.
117 G4 Hess R Yukon Territory Canada
116 N4 Hess Cr Alaska U.S.A.
28 F6 Hesselager Denmark
37 K5 Hesselberg mt W Germany
28 H4 Hesselø isld Denmark
33 N8 Hessen East Germany
36 F2 Hessen land W Germany
36 F1 Hessenstein W Germany
36 H5 Hessenthal W Germany
36 H1 Hessisch Lichtenau W Germany
117 H4 Hess Mts Yukon Territory Canada
107 N3 Hesston Kansas U.S.A.
28 J7 Hesteholved C Denmark
28 R8 Hesteyri Iceland
26 F5 Hestmannen isld Norway
27 G14 Hestra, N Sweden
22 G3 Hestrud France
102 C5 Hetch Hetchy California U.S.A.
94 C2 Hetherton Michigan U.S.A.
25 E4 Het Loo Netherlands
68 J2 Hetou China
22 L5 Hettange Gde France
Hettenhausen see Ebersburg
36 E4 Hettenleidelheim W Germany
98 D3 Hettinger North Dakota U.S.A.
13 G4 Hetton-le-Hole England
33 P9 Hettstedt East Germany
36 F4 Hetzbach W Germany
36 B4 Hetzerath W Germany
22 E1 Het Zoute Belgium
36 H6 Heubach W Germany
41 J1 Heuberg dist W Germany
22 C3 Heuchin France
33 N9 Heudeber East Germany
36 C2 Heumar W Germany
21 N3 Heuqueville France
25 D5 Heusden Netherlands
37 J3 Heustreu W Germany
95 M2 Heuvelton New York U.S.A.
21 L2 Hève, C.de la France
80 E8 Hever R Jordan
13 F5 Heversham England
48 F3 Heves Hungary
28 E3 Hevring Å R Denmark
80 C8 Hevron R Israel
119 O9 Heward Saskatchewan Canada
7 M9 Hewett oil rig North Sea
13 F4 Hexham England
67 F4 Hexi China
67 D4 He Xian China
67 F1 He Xian China
65 D3 Hexigten Qi China
109 H5 Hext Texas U.S.A.
65 A7 Heyang China
47 N11 Heybeli isld Turkey
47 N11 Heybeli Turkey
101 M7 Heyburn Idaho U.S.A.
107 O6 Heyburn Res Oklahoma U.S.A.
139 H7 Heyfield Victoria Australia
13 F5 Heysham England
8 D5 Heytesbury England
67 E5 Heyuan China
138 F7 Heywood Victoria Australia
13 F6 Heywood England
65 C7 Heze China
113 G12 Hialeah Florida U.S.A.
79 G5 Hiānah, Buhayrat al L Syria
112 D3 Hiawassee Georgia U.S.A.
107 P2 Hiawatha Kansas U.S.A.
103 O2 Hiawatha Utah U.S.A.
121 O5 Hibbard Quebec Canada
99 O2 Hibbing Minnesota U.S.A.
142 F1 Hibernia Reef Timor Sea
60 D11 Hibiki-nada sea Japan
71 G5 Hibuson isld Philippines
103 M9 Hickiwan Arizona U.S.A.
13 G6 Hickleton England
110 G5 Hickman Kentucky U.S.A.
98 K9 Hickman Nebraska U.S.A.
106 C7 Hickman New Mexico U.S.A.
123 T5 Hickman's Hbr Newfoundland Canada
107 J4 Hickok Kansas U.S.A.
111 G9 Hickory Mississippi U.S.A.
112 F2 Hickory North Carolina U.S.A.
112 F2 Hickory, L North Carolina U.S.A.
110 G6 Hickory Valley Tennessee U.S.A.
109 M8 Hicks Texas U.S.A.
145 G2 Hicks Bay New Zealand
125 P9 Hicks Cays islds Belize
139 J7 Hicks, Pt Victoria Australia
94 C5 Hicksville Ohio U.S.A.
109 J4 Hico Texas U.S.A.
48 H3 Hida Romania
60 G3 Hidaka Japan
60 J12 Hidaka R Japan
60 R3 Hidaka-sammyaku mts Japan
124 G4 Hidalgo de Parral Mexico
32 J8 Hiddenhausen W Germany
30 G1 Hiddensee isld East Germany
141 H4 Hidden Valley Queensland Australia
32 J9 Hiddesen W Germany
130 E5 Hidrolândia Brazil
130 E4 Hidrolina Brazil
20 C5 Hière R France
21 P1 Hiermont France
28 S9 Hierodhsvótn R Iceland
85 A3 Hierro isld Canary Is
127 N9 Hierro, Pto. de Venezuela
60 F11 Higashi-Hiroshima isld Japan
61 O13 Higashi-iwa islds Japan
61 N9 Higashi-Matsuyama Japan
61 O7 Higashine Japan
61 P13 Higashi-Onna Okinawa
61 J11 Higashi-Ōsaka Japan
60 C12 Higashi-suidō str Japan
110 D2 Higbee Missouri U.S.A.
94 C2 Higgins L Michigan U.S.A.
143 D9 Higginsville Western Australia Australia
110 C2 Higginsville Missouri U.S.A.
9 E1 Higham England
9 F3 Higham Ferrers England
8 B6 Highampton England
106 G4 Highbee Colorado U.S.A.
8 D5 Highbridge England
95 N6 High Bridge New Jersey U.S.A.
12 D3 High Br. of Ken Scotland
9 E5 Highclere England
99 S5 High Cliff Wisconsin U.S.A.
100 E6 High Desert Oregon U.S.A.
99 S4 High Falls Reservoir Wisconsin U.S.A.
142 B1 Highgate dist Perth, W Aust Australia
9 G5 Highgate England
127 L2 Highgate Jamaica
13 F4 High Hesket England
119 W3 High Hill L Manitoba Canada
99 V4 High I Michigan U.S.A.
109 N6 High Island Texas U.S.A.
15 C3 Highland reg Scotland
102 G7 Highland California U.S.A.
99 Q9 Highland Illinois U.S.A.
107 P2 Highland Kansas U.S.A.
99 Q6 Highland Wisconsin U.S.A.
99 T7 Highland Park Illinois U.S.A.
94 D4 Highland Park Michigan U.S.A.
109 O9 Highland Park Texas U.S.A.
102 E3 Highland Peak California U.S.A.
103 K4 Highland Pk Nevada U.S.A.
112 D2 Highlands North Carolina U.S.A.
109 M6 Highlands Texas U.S.A.
95 K9 Highland Springs Virginia U.S.A.
117 P6 High Level Alberta Canada
98 G5 Highmore South Dakota U.S.A.
141 K5 High Peak I Queensland Australia
118 K8 High Point Saskatchewan Canada
112 H2 High Point North Carolina U.S.A.
117 P8 High Prairie Alberta Canada
118 D8 High River Alberta Canada
119 R3 Highrock Manitoba Canada
113 J11 High Rock Grand Bahama I
112 G2 High Rock L North Carolina U.S.A.
139 H9 High Rocky Pt Tasmania Australia
113 E8 High Springs Florida U.S.A.
95 N6 Hightstown New Jersey U.S.A.
99 S7 Highwood Illinois U.S.A.
101 P2 Highwood Montana U.S.A.
9 E4 Highworth England
9 F4 High Wycombe England
124 E5 Higuera de Zaragoza Mexico
17 F1 Higuer, C Spain
127 L9 Higuerote Venezuela
127 K5 Higüey Dominican Rep
145 E3 Hihitahi New Zealand
27 N13 Hiiumaa isld U.S.S.R.
79 G5 Hijānah, Al Syria
17 G3 Hijar Spain
69 F14 Hijau, Gunung mt Sumatra
60 E12 Hiji Japan
71 G7 Hijo Philippines
60 E12 Hikari Japan
60 H11 Hiketa Japan
60 J12 Hiki R Japan
83 J11 Hikkaduwa Sri Lanka
103 J4 Hiko Nevada U.S.A.
61 K10 Hikone Japan
60 D12 Hiko-san mt Japan
145 E2 Hikuai New Zealand
145 G2 Hikurangi mt New Zealand
145 E1 Hikurangi New Zealand
145 E2 Hikutaia New Zealand
71 N8 Hila Indonesia
70 G7 Hilahila Sulawesi
101 S6 Hiland Wyoming U.S.A.
36 E1 Hilchenbach W Germany
118 G8 Hilda Alberta Canada
33 O10 Hildburghausen East Germany
100 D7 Hildebrand Oregon U.S.A.
36 B1 Hilden W Germany
37 J2 Hilders W Germany
32 L8 Hildesheim W Germany
98 G9 Hildreth Nebraska U.S.A.
101 Q2 Hilger Montana U.S.A.
143 B9 Hill R Western Australia Australia
101 O1 Hill Montana U.S.A.
95 Q3 Hill New Hampshire U.S.A.
127 P6 Hillaby, Mt Barbados
78 K5 Hillah, Al Iraq
98 E5 Hilland South Dakota U.S.A.
27 F14 Hillared Sweden
146 D11 Hillary Coast Antarctica
125 P9 Hill Bank Belize
101 K6 Hill City Idaho U.S.A.
107 L2 Hill City Kansas U.S.A.
99 N3 Hill City Minnesota U.S.A.
98 C6 Hill City South Dakota U.S.A.
103 P2 Hill Cr Utah U.S.A.
118 C9 Hillcrest Alberta Canada
117 C11 Hillcrest Creek Alberta Canada
25 C4 Hillegom Netherlands
32 J8 Hillegossen W Germany
28 J5 Hillerød Denmark
28 E6 Hillerslev Denmark
28 B2 Hillerslev Denmark
28 C7 Hillerup W Germany
36 B3 Hillesheim W Germany
26 K2 Hillesöy Norway
139 K4 Hillgrove New South Wales Australia
141 H4 Hill Grove Queensland Australia
144 C6 Hillgrove New Zealand
98 J4 Hillhead South Dakota U.S.A.
118 E5 Hilliard Alberta Canada
113 F7 Hilliard Florida U.S.A.
9 G2 Hillington England
20 E4 Hillion France
94 D1 Hillman Michigan U.S.A.
99 N3 Hillman Minnesota U.S.A.
143 B9 Hillman, L Western Australia Australia
118 H5 Hillmond Saskatchewan Canada
15 E3 Hill of Fearn Scotland
15 D5 Hill of Stake mt Scotland
98 C9 Hillrose Colorado U.S.A.
99 P8 Hills Iowa U.S.A.
98 K6 Hills Minnesota U.S.A.
112 D4 Hillsboro Georgia U.S.A.
110 G2 Hillsboro Illinois U.S.A.
99 P9 Hillsboro Iowa U.S.A.
107 N3 Hillsboro Kansas U.S.A.
110 F3 Hillsboro Missouri U.S.A.
95 Q3 Hillsboro New Hampshire U.S.A.
106 C9 Hillsboro New Mexico U.S.A.
98 J2 Hillsboro North Dakota U.S.A.
110 N2 Hillsboro Ohio U.S.A.
100 C4 Hillsboro Oregon U.S.A.
109 K3 Hillsboro Texas U.S.A.
94 G8 Hillsboro West Virginia U.S.A.
113 G11 Hillsboro Can Florida U.S.A.
122 H8 Hillsborough New Brunswick Canada
112 H1 Hillsborough North Carolina U.S.A.
122 J7 Hillsborough B Prince Edward I Canada
141 J5 Hillsborough, C Queensland Australia
36 D3 Hillscheid W Germany
121 L8 Hillsdale Ontario Canada
94 C5 Hillsdale Michigan U.S.A.
98 B8 Hillsdale Wyoming U.S.A.
142 C5 Hillside Western Australia Australia
103 M7 Hillside Arizona U.S.A.
106 E3 Hillside Colorado U.S.A.
120 E3 Hillsport Ontario Canada
139 H5 Hillston New South Wales Australia
98 G4 Hillsview South Dakota U.S.A.
94 G10 Hillsville Virginia U.S.A.
112 F5 Hilltonia Georgia U.S.A.
110 F2 Hillview Illinois U.S.A.
102 V14 Hilo Hawaiian Is
113 G10 Hilolo Florida U.S.A.
37 L5 Hilpoltstein W Germany
36 F5 Hilsbach W Germany
8 B7 Hilsea Pt England
36 D7 Hilsenheim France
94 K3 Hilton New York U.S.A.
112 G5 Hilton Head I South Carolina U.S.A.
37 L4 Hiltpoltstein W Germany
32 G9 Hiltrup W Germany
100 G8 Hilts California U.S.A.
29 N10 Hiltula Finland
25 D6 Hilvarenbeek Netherlands
25 D4 Hilversum Netherlands
74 G2 Himachal Pradesh prov India
74 F1 Himalayan Mt.Ra.,Great Asia
29 K7 Himanka Finland
46 D4 Himarë Albania
145 E4 Himatangi New Zealand
33 N6 Himbergen W Germany
60 H11 Himeji Japan
61 P6 Himekami dake mt Japan
101 R5 Himes Wyoming U.S.A.
60 E12 Hime-shima isld Japan
61 K9 Himi Japan
32 K5 Himmelpforten W Germany
32 K9 Himmighausen W Germany
79 G3 Ḥimṣ Syria
79 G4 Hims, Bahrat L Syria
71 F5 Himugaan Philippines
30 D13 Hinagu Japan
39 D11 Hinaikiri Sumatra
39 C12 Hinako isld Indonesia
145 E4 Hinakura New Zealand
71 G6 Hinatuan Philippines
127 J5 Hinche Haiti
116 O6 Hinchinbrook Entrance str Alaska U.S.A.
141 H4 Hinchinbrook I Queensland Australia
116 O6 Hinchinbrook I Alaska U.S.A.
119 P6 Hincliffe Saskatchewan Canada
9 E2 Hinckley England
99 O3 Hinckley Minnesota U.S.A.
103 M2 Hinckley Utah U.S.A.
95 N3 Hinckley Res New York U.S.A.
74 G5 Hindaun India
41 M2 Hindelang W Germany
25 D3 Hindeloopen Netherlands
Hindenburg see Lindenhagen
28 A7 Hindenburg Damm causeway W Germany
26 N6 Hindersön isld Sweden
109 J7 Hindes Texas U.S.A.
9 F5 Hindhead England
13 F6 Hindley England
138 F6 Hindmarsh, L Victoria Australia
8 D5 Hindon England
144 C6 Hindon New Zealand
144 C6 Hinds New Zealand
123 Q4 Hinds Hill pk Newfoundland Canada
28 F5 Hindsholm Denmark
123 P5 Hinds L Newfoundland Canada
74 B3 Hindubagh Pakistan
72 K1 Hindu Kush mts Afghanistan
76 C4 Hindupur India
118 G5 Hindville Alberta Canada
68 G4 Hine Laos
95 O2 Hinesburg Vermont U.S.A.
117 O7 Hines Creek Alberta Canada
112 F6 Hinesville Georgia U.S.A.
74 H8 Hinganghat India
28 D4 Hinge Denmark
101 P1 Hingham Montana U.S.A.
77 J7 Hinglaj Pakistan
20 F5 Hinglé, le France
77 K6 Hingol R Pakistan
74 G9 Hingoli India
102 G7 Hinkley California U.S.A.
143 G7 Hinkley, Mt Western Australia Australia
29 J11 Hinnerjoki Finland
28 E4 Hinnerup Denmark
26 H3 Hinnöy isld Norway
61 K9 Hino R Japan
71 F6 Hinoba-an Philippines
16 D6 Hinojosa del Duque Spain
60 E13 Hinokage Japan
60 F10 Hinomi saki C Japan
99 S8 Hinsdale Illinois U.S.A.
95 O4 Hinsdale Massachusetts U.S.A.
101 S1 Hinsdale Montana U.S.A.
94 J4 Hinsdale New York U.S.A.
9 D2 Hinstock England
28 D7 Hinterbichl Austria
36 E3 Hintermeilingen W Germany
41 K4 Hinterrhein Switzerland
41 O3 Hinter Riss Austria
38 K6 Hinterstoder Austria
41 P3 Hinter Tux Austria
36 D5 Hinter Weidenthal W Germany
9 H3 Hintlesham England
117 P9 Hinton Alberta Canada
107 M6 Hinton Oklahoma U.S.A.
61 O9 Hi-numa Japan
129 J7 Hiocolândia Brazil
135 R2 Hio Pt Hawaiian Is
124 H5 Hipólito Mexico
25 C3 Hippolytushoef Netherlands
80 F2 Hippos Syria
60 C12 Hirado Japan
60 C12 Hirado-shima isld Japan
85 F4 Hirafok Algeria
145 E2 Hirakimata New Zealand
75 K8 Hirakud Res India
95 R3 Hiram Maine U.S.A.
60 C12 Hira shima isld Japan
60 F10 Hirata Japan
61 N10 Hiratsuka Japan
125 O5 Hiray Mexico
78 D2 Hirfanli Baraji dam Turkey
48 K3 Hîrlău Romania
61 O8 Hirono Japan
60 R3 Hiroo Japan
61 O5 Hirosaki Japan
60 G10 Hirose Japan
60 F11 Hiroshima Japan
61 P7 Hirota-wan B Japan
36 F6 Hirsau W Germany
37 M4 Hirschau W Germany
Hirschberg see Jelenia Góra
37 M3 Hirschberg East Germany
38 L7 Hirschegg Austria
37 O6 Hirschenstein mt W Germany
36 F5 Hirschhorn W Germany
48 J6 Hirşeşti Romania
28 F2 Hirsholmene isld Denmark
22 H3 Hirson France
48 L6 Hirşova Romania
28 D1 Hirtshals Denmark
29 M10 Hirvensalmi Finland
29 L7 Hirvineva Finland
8 C4 Hirwaun Wales
61 K11 Hisai Japan
60 B13 Hisaka-jima isld Japan
74 F4 Hisar India
77 J2 Hisar, Koh-i- mts Afghanistan
80 F6 Hisban R Jordan
27 F15 Hishult Sweden
98 E6 Hisle South Dakota U.S.A.
80 E6 Hisma Jordan
127 J5 Hispaniola isld W Indies
80 G1 Hispin Syria
79 G4 Hisyah Syria
78 J5 Hit Iraq
60 D12 Hita Japan
61 O9 Hitachi Japan
61 O9 Hitachi-Ōta Japan
60 C11 Hitakatsu Japan
9 G3 Hitcham England
119 O9 Hitchcock Saskatchewan Canada
107 M6 Hitchcock Oklahoma U.S.A.
98 H5 Hitchcock South Dakota U.S.A.
109 M6 Hitchcock Texas U.S.A.
9 F4 Hitchin England
107 P6 Hitchita Oklahoma U.S.A.
103 O4 Hite Utah U.S.A.
60 D13 Hitoyoshi Japan
26 C8 Hitra Norway
32 L6 Hittfeld W Germany
33 O6 Hitzacker W Germany
61 N9 Hiuchiga-take mt Japan
60 G11 Hiuchi-nada sea Japan
135 N9 Hiva Oa isld Pacific Oc
60 H12 Hiwasa Japan
112 C2 Hiwassee R N Carolina/Tenn U.S.A.
112 C2 Hiwassee Lake North Carolina U.S.A.
141 L5 Hixson Cay isld Gt Barrier Reef Aust
60 O3 Hiyama prefect Japan
78 J2 Hizan Turkey
28 E2 Hjallerup Denmark
27 H12 Hjälmaren L Sweden
28 C3 Hjarbæk Denmark
28 B2 Hjardemål Denmark
26 G6 Hjarfjell mt Norway
28 E5 Hjarnø isld Denmark
27 C12 Hjartdal Norway
28 C6 Hjarup Denmark
26 B10 Hjelle Norway
28 F4 Hjelm isld Denmark
29 K7 Hjelm Bugt B Denmark
27 B12 Hjelmeland Norway
26 O1 Hjelmsöy isld Norway
28 G5 Hjembæk Denmark
26 D9 Hjerkinn Norway
28 B4 Hjerm Denmark
28 C6 Hjerndrup Denmark
28 B6 Hjerpsted Denmark
28 A5 Hjerting Denmark
27 G13 Hjo Sweden
28 C4 Hjøllund Denmark
28 C6 Hjordkær Denmark
Hjørring co see Nordjylland co
28 D2 Hjørring Denmark
28 E7 Hjortø Denmark
28 G1 Hjortshøj Denmark
28 C5 Hjortsvang Denmark
26 B9 Hjörundfjord Norway
27 D12 Hjuksebö Norway
68 D2 Hka R Burma
68 D2 Hkok R Burma
68 C4 Hlegu Burma
28 S10 Hlidharendi Iceland
28 P3 Hlinec R Czechoslovakia
31 K7 Hlohovec Czechoslovakia
28 A5 Ho Denmark
86 G4 Ho Ghana
67 B6 Hoa Binh Vietnam
89 A4 Hoachanas Namibia
118 C6 Hoadley Alberta Canada
98 F8 Hoagland Nebraska U.S.A.
68 J5 Hoai Nhon Vietnam
68 G1 Hoang Su Phi Vietnam
87 B9 Hoanib R Namibia
60 E12 Hoashi Japan
101 P6 Hoback R Wyoming U.S.A.
101 P6 Hoback Pk Wyoming U.S.A.
139 H8 Hobart Tasmania Australia
99 T8 Hobart Indiana U.S.A.
107 L6 Hobart Oklahoma U.S.A.
108 D3 Hobbs New Mexico U.S.A.
111 K7 Hobbs Island Alabama U.S.A.
113 G10 Hobe Sound Florida U.S.A.
112 K1 Hobgood North Carolina U.S.A.
22 G1 Hoboken Belgium
112 E6 Hoboken Georgia U.S.A.
Hobot Xar see Xianghuang Qi
28 D3 Hobro Denmark
101 Q3 Hobson Montana U.S.A.
112 L2 Hobucken North Carolina U.S.A.
28 A5 Ho Bugt B Denmark
27 K15 Hoburgen lighthouse Sweden
86 A2 Hobyo Somalia
71 D5 Hoc isld Philippines
47 K6 Hocalar Turkey
111 B7 Hochatown Oklahoma U.S.A.
38 N8 Hocheck mt Austria
87 C10 Hochfeld Namibia
36 D6 Hochfelden France
38 G7 Hochfilzen Austria
41 N4 Hochfinstermünz Austria
38 F8 Hochgall mt Italy
37 K2 Hochheim East Germany
109 K6 Hochheim Texas U.S.A.
36 E3 Hochheim W Germany
Ho Chi Minh see Saigon
38 K8 Hochobir mt Austria
38 F7 Hoch Platte mt W Germany
38 M6 Hochschwab mt Austria
36 D5 Hochspeyer W Germany
37 K6 Höchstädt W Germany
37 K4 Höchstadt W Germany
36 D2 Höchstenbach W Germany
144 C5 Hochstetter, L New Zealand
38 K9 Hochstuhl mt Yugoslavia
36 F5 Hockenheim W Germany
94 E7 Hocking R Ohio U.S.A.
94 E7 Hockingport Ohio U.S.A.
109 M5 Hockley Texas U.S.A.
9 E3 Hockley Heath England
9 F4 Hockliffe England
6 N6 Hod oil rig North Sea
28 B5 Hodde Denmark
13 F6 Hodder, R England
9 F4 Hoddesdon England
Hodeida see Hudaydah, Al
111 D9 Hodge Louisiana U.S.A.
110 L4 Hodgenville Kentucky U.S.A.
98 B3 Hodges Montana U.S.A.
112 E3 Hodges South Carolina U.S.A.
123 Q4 Hodges Hill pk Newfoundland Canada
118 L8 Hodgeville Saskatchewan Canada
119 U7 Hodgson Manitoba Canada
140 C3 Hodgson Downs N Terr Australia
85 C5 Hodh reg Mauritania
80 B7 Hodiyya Israel
48 F4 Hódmezővásárhely Hungary
85 E1 Hodna, Mts. du Algeria
8 D2 Hodnet England
31 K7 Hodonin Czechoslovakia
48 C4 Hodoš Yugoslavia
28 B4 Hodsager Denmark
116 N3 Hodzana, R Alaska U.S.A.
28 F4 Hoed Denmark
25 A6 Hoedekenskerke Netherlands
20 E7 Hoëdic isld France
106 F4 Hoehne Colorado U.S.A.
25 B5 Hoeksche Waard Netherlands
25 B5 Hoek van Holland Netherlands
119 M6 Hoey Saskatchewan Canada
37 M3 Hof W Germany
36 H2 Hofbieber W Germany
Hofei see Hefei
36 F6 Höfen W Germany
37 J6 Hofen W Germany
98 L4 Hoffman Minnesota U.S.A.
112 H2 Hoffman North Carolina U.S.A.
113 K12 Hoffmans Cay isld Bahamas
32 K10 Hofgeismar W Germany
36 E3 Hofheim W Germany
37 K3 Hofheim W Germany
37 P6 Hofkirchen W Germany
29 T9 Hofn Iceland
28 S9 Hofsjökull ice cap Iceland
28 S9 Hofsos Iceland
60 E11 Hōfu Japan
29 K4 Höganäs Sweden
139 H7 Hogan Group islds Tasmania Australia
102 D3 Hogan Res California U.S.A.
111 M8 Hogansville Georgia U.S.A.
141 H7 Hoganthulla R Queensland Australia
119 P1 Hogarth Ontario Canada
140 D5 Hogarth, Mt N Terr Australia
116 K3 Hogatza Alaska U.S.A.
116 K3 Hogatza R R Alaska U.S.A.
101 N5 Hogback Mt Montana U.S.A.
27 F12 Hogboda Sweden
27 J14 Högby Sweden
28 C7 Högel W Germany
101 R1 Hogeland Montana U.S.A.
27 H12 Högfors Sweden
85 F4 Hoggar mt reg Algeria
119 V1 Hogg L Manitoba Canada
48 J5 Hoghiz Romania
94 B1 Hog I Michigan U.S.A.
95 M9 Hog I Virginia U.S.A.
28 B4 Høgild Denmark
80 C4 Hogla Israel
27 H14 Högsby Sweden
126 H4 Hogsty Reef Bahamas
26 G5 Högtuvbre mt Norway
100 A2 Hoh R Washington U.S.A.
33 R10 Hohburg East Germany
36 C3 Hohe Acht mt W Germany
41 N3 Hohe Geige mt Austria
37 K6 Hohen-Altheim W Germany
38 N6 Hohenberg Austria
37 M3 Hohenberg W Germany
33 S9 Hohenbucke East Germany
37 M5 Hohenburg W Germany
33 N10 Hohenebra East Germany
32 M8 Hoheneggelsen W Germany
36 H1 Hoheneiche W Germany
41 L3 Hohenems Austria
37 M5 Hohenfels W Germany
33 Q7 Hohengöhren East Germany
36 G6 Hohenheim W Germany
37 M7 Hohenkammer W Germany
33 Q10 Hohenleina East Germany
37 N2 Hohenleuben East Germany
32 G10 Hohenlimburg W Germany
32 L5 Hohenlockstedt W Germany
33 S5 Hohenmocker East Germany
37 N1 Hohenmölsen East Germany
33 Q7 Hohennauen East Germany
36 H2 Hohenroda W Germany
33 Q8 Hohenseeden East Germany
33 S9 Hohenseefeld East Germany
36 E2 Hohensolms W Germany
36 H6 Hohenstaufen W Germany
36 G7 Hohenstein W Germany
37 O2 Hohenstein-Ernstthal East Germany
110 J6 Hohenwald Tennessee U.S.A.
37 L6 Hohenwart W Germany
32 K9 Hohenwepel W Germany
32 L4 Hohenwestedt W Germany
33 N6 Hohenzethen W Germany
36 F7 Hohenzollern W Germany
41 M3 Hoher Ifen mt Austria
41 M3 Hohes Licht mt Austria
37 J5 Hohe Steig mt W Germany
38 F7 Hohe Tauern Austria
58 F3 Hohhot China
36 E6 Hohloh mt W Germany
33 M7 Hohne W Germany
19 K4 Hohneck mt France
33 N6 Hohnstorf W Germany
116 J6 Hoholitna R Alaska U.S.A.
32 K4 Hohrr W Germany
66 E4 Hoh Sai Hu L China
33 N4 Hohwacht W Germany
36 C7 Hohwald France
66 D4 Hoh Xil Shan ra China
68 J5 Hoi An Vietnam
107 M3 Hoisington Kansas U.S.A.
66 F4 Hoit Taria China
67 B6 Hoi-Xuan Vietnam
75 P6 Hojai India
28 E6 Højby Denmark
28 C5 Højen Denmark
28 B7 Højer Denmark
29 K6 Højerup Denmark
60 F12 Hōjō Japan
28 B6 Højrup Denmark
28 C3 Højslev Denmark
68 D2 Hok R Burma
99 P6 Hokah Minnesota U.S.A.
Hokang see Hegang
27 K11 Hökhuvud Sweden
61 N9 Hōki R Japan
145 D1 Hokianga Harbour New Zealand
144 C5 Hokitika New Zealand
60 Q2 Hokkaidō isld Japan
27 D12 Hokksund Norway
61 O9 Hokota Japan
61 K10 Hokunō Japan
61 K10 Hokuriku Tunnel Japan
27 C11 Hol Norway
27 E12 Höland Norway
Holbæk co see Vestjælland co
28 E3 Holbæk Denmark
28 H5 Holbæk Denmark
9 G2 Holbeach England
117 K10 Holberg British Columbia Canada
28 C7 Holbøl Denmark
141 J4 Holbourne I Queensland Australia
139 H6 Holbrook New South Wales Australia
103 O7 Holbrook Arizona U.S.A.
101 N7 Holbrook Idaho U.S.A.
98 F9 Holbrook Nebraska U.S.A.
13 F6 Holcombe England
99 P4 Holcombe Wisconsin U.S.A.
118 E5 Holden Alberta Canada
95 Q4 Holden Massachusetts U.S.A.
110 C3 Holden Missouri U.S.A.
103 M2 Holden Utah U.S.A.
94 E9 Holden West Virginia U.S.A.
107 O6 Holdenville Oklahoma U.S.A.
119 M8 Holdfast Saskatchewan Canada
99 M4 Holdingford Minnesota U.S.A.
32 H7 Holdorf W Germany
98 G9 Holdrege Nebraska U.S.A.
28 G7 Holeby Denmark
113 K12 Hole in the Wall pt Bahamas
27 E12 Hølen Norway
76 C4 Hole Narsipur India
31 K6 Holešov Czechoslovakia
127 P6 Holetown Barbados
94 C5 Holgate Ohio U.S.A.
126 F4 Holguín Cuba
48 D2 Holič Czechoslovakia
116 H5 Holikachuk Alaska U.S.A.
116 H5 Holitna R Alaska U.S.A.
27 F11 Höljes Sweden
119 T9 Holland Manitoba Canada
9 F2 Holland div England
99 U7 Holland Michigan U.S.A.
98 K5 Holland Minnesota U.S.A.
94 J4 Holland New York U.S.A.
100 B7 Holland Oregon U.S.A.
109 K5 Holland Texas U.S.A.
111 F8 Hollandale Mississippi U.S.A.
127 M3 Holland B Jamaica
120 K8 Holland Centre Ontario Canada
143 C9 Holland,Mt Western Australia Australia
141 K2 Holland Park dist Brisbane, Qnsld Australia
25 C5 Hollandsch Diep Netherlands
22 K4 Hollange Belgium
32 M8 Holle W Germany
33 N5 Hollenbek W Germany
32 H6 Hollenstedt W Germany
38 N6 Hollen-Tal V Austria
38 F7 Hollersbach Austria
9 G6 Hollesley B England
94 K3 Holley New York U.S.A.
37 L4 Hollfeld W Germany
109 J2 Holliday Texas U.S.A.
94 J6 Hollidaysburg Pennsylvania U.S.A.
107 L7 Hollis Oklahoma U.S.A.
102 C5 Hollister California U.S.A.
101 L7 Hollister Idaho U.S.A.
110 C5 Hollister Missouri U.S.A.
107 M7 Hollister Oklahoma U.S.A.
22 J2 Hollogne-sur-Geer Belgium
111 D10 Holloway Louisiana U.S.A.
29 K6 Höllviken C Sweden
106 H3 Holly Colorado U.S.A.
94 D4 Holly Michigan U.S.A.
111 F9 Holly Bluff Mississippi U.S.A.
144 B6 Hollyford R New Zealand
111 E7 Holly Grove Arkansas U.S.A.
113 F8 Holly Hill Florida U.S.A.
112 G4 Holly Hill South Carolina U.S.A.
112 K3 Holly Ridge North Carolina U.S.A.
110 G7 Holly Springs Mississippi U.S.A.
113 G11 Hollywood Florida U.S.A.
95 L8 Hollywood Maryland U.S.A.
28 D6 Holm Denmark
26 F6 Holm Norway
26 J9 Holm Sweden
106 E5 Holman New Mexico U.S.A.
114 H3 Holman Island Northwest Territories Canada
28 S9 Holmavik Iceland
28 B5 Holme Å R Denmark
99 P6 Holmen Wisconsin U.S.A.
8 D1 Holmes Chapel England
119 V1 Holmes L Manitoba Canada
101 P5 Holmes, Mt Wyoming U.S.A.
141 J3 Holmes Reef Great Barrier Reef Aust
27 D12 Holmestr Norway
119 S9 Holmfield Manitoba Canada
13 G6 Holmfirth England
26 K6 Holmfors Sweden
115 O3 Holm Ø isld Greenland
26 L8 Holmögadd lighthouse Sweden
26 L8 Holmön Sweden
13 J6 Holmpton England
27 D12 Holmsbu Norway
26 J8 Holmsjö Sweden
26 H9 Holmsjön L Sweden
28 A4 Holmsland Klit sand spit Denmark
28 E6 Holmstrup Fyn Denmark
28 G5 Holmstrup Vestjælland Denmark
26 L8 Holmsund Sweden
27 K14 Holmudden lighthouse Gotland Sweden
111 C11 Holmwood Louisiana U.S.A.
37 M5 Holnstein W Germany
27 J12 Hölö Sweden
88 C5 Holoholo Tanzania
80 C5 Holon Israel
87 C11 Holoog Namibia
113 F9 Holopaw Florida U.S.A.
80 B6 Holot Ashdod Israel
142 F2 Holothuria Reefs Western Australia Australia
80 B6 Holot Yavne Israel
26 E9 Holöydal Norway
141 F2 Holroyd R Queensland Australia
28 B4 Holstebro Denmark
28 B5 Holsted Denmark
120 K8 Holstein Ontario Canada
99 L7 Holstein Iowa U.S.A.
98 H9 Holstein Nebraska U.S.A.
28 G6 Holsteinborg Denmark
115 O4 Holsteinsborg Greenland
112 E1 Holston R Tennessee U.S.A.
94 F10 Holston R Virginia U.S.A.
33 N4 Holst Schweiz W Germany
8 B6 Holsworthy England
9 H2 Holt England
111 J8 Holt Alabama U.S.A.
111 K11 Holt Florida U.S.A.
94 C4 Holt Michigan U.S.A.
98 K1 Holt Minnesota U.S.A.
8 D1 Holt Wales
98 G7 Holt Cr Nebraska U.S.A.
29 K5 Holte Denmark
33 O9 Holtemme R East Germany
25 F4 Holten Netherlands
101 O3 Holter L. Dam Montana U.S.A.
33 O5 Holthusen East Germany
94 B7 Holton Indiana U.S.A.
107 P2 Holton Kansas U.S.A.
94 B3 Holton Michigan U.S.A.
65 D2 Holt Sum China
28 C4 Holtum Å R Denmark
103 J9 Holtville California U.S.A.
120 K4 Holtyre Ontario Canada
135 U5 Holualoa Hawaiian Is
27 C13 Holum Norway
25 E2 Holwerd Netherlands
116 H5 Holy Cross Alaska U.S.A.
8 B1 Holyhead Wales
8 B1 Holyhead B Wales
Holy I see Lindisfarne
12 C3 Holy I Scotland
8 B1 Holy I Wales
118 G4 Holyoke Alberta Canada
106 H1 Holyoke Colorado U.S.A.
95 P4 Holyoke Massachusetts U.S.A.
123 T6 Holyrood Newfoundland Canada
107 M3 Holyrood Kansas U.S.A.
37 P4 Holýšov Czechoslovakia
8 D6 Holywell England
8 C1 Holywell Wales
14 F2 Holywood N Ireland
36 D3 Holzappel W Germany
33 S9 Holzdorf East Germany
33 P5 Holzendorf East Germany
32 H8 Holzhausen W Germany
36 D3 Holzhausen W Germany
37 K6 Holzheim W Germany
32 K9 Holzminden W Germany
32 G10 Holzwickede W Germany
28 H6 Høm Denmark
86 G6 Homa Bay Kenya
75 Q6 Homalin Burma
36 G1 Homberg W Germany
60 R2 Hombetsu Japan
22 E4 Hombliėres France
85 D5 Hombori Mali
Homburg see Nümbrecht
36 H4 Homburg Bayern W Germany
36 C5 Homburg Rheinland-Pfalz W Germany
115 N4 Home B Northwest Territories Canada
100 J6 Homedale Idaho U.S.A.
141 H4 Home Hill Queensland Australia
83 M8 Home I Cocos Is Indian Oc
116 M7 Homer Alaska U.S.A.
99 T9 Homer Illinois U.S.A.
111 C9 Homer Louisiana U.S.A.
94 C4 Homer Michigan U.S.A.
94 H6 Homer City Pennsylvania U.S.A.
9 H3 Homersfield England
144 A6 Homer Tun New Zealand
112 E6 Homerville Georgia U.S.A.
141 H5 Homestead Queensland Australia
113 G12 Homestead Florida U.S.A.
99 P8 Homestead Iowa U.S.A.
98 B1 Homestead Montana U.S.A.
107 M5 Homestead Oklahoma U.S.A.
100 J4 Homestead Oregon U.S.A.
98 K9 Homestead Nat Mon Nebraska U.S.A.
145 E4 Homewood New Zealand
111 K8 Homewood Alabama U.S.A.
68 A6 Homfray's Str Andaman Is
107 O5 Hominy Oklahoma U.S.A.
26 E9 Hommelfjell mt Norway
26 E8 Hommelvik Norway
25 E3 Hommerts Netherlands
21 L7 Hommes France
74 G10 Homnabad India
89 H5 Homoine Mozambique
48 G6 Homoljske Planina mt Yugoslavia
71 G5 Homonhon Philippines
48 J4 Homorod Romania
113 E9 Homosassa Florida U.S.A.
Homs Libya see Khums, Al
60 F12 Honai Japan
Honan prov see Henan
76 B3 Honavar India
47 K7 Honaz Dag mt Turkey
68 G7 Hon Chong Vietnam
102 C2 Honcut California U.S.A.
128 D2 Honda Colombia
71 D6 Honda B Palawan Philippines
125 P8 Hondo R Belize
118 D3 Hondo Alberta Canada
60 D13 Hondo Japan
106 E8 Hondo New Mexico U.S.A.
109 H6 Hondo Texas U.S.A.
22 D2 Hondschoote France
125 L2 Honduras rep Central America
119 Q2 Hone Manitoba Canada
112 E3 Honea Path South Carolina U.S.A.
36 H2 Hönebach W Germany
27 D11 Hönefoss Norway
95 M5 Honesdale Pennsylvania U.S.A.
102 A1 Honeydew California U.S.A.
98 J1 Honeyford North Dakota U.S.A.
109 M2 Honey Grove Texas U.S.A.
109 N5 Honey Island Texas U.S.A.
100 E9 Honey L California U.S.A.
120 K8 Honeywood Ontario Canada
21 L3 Honfleur France
28 G5 Høng Denmark
65 G2 Hongai China
68 H2 Hon Gai Vietnam
67 E1 Hong'an China
67 B6 Hon Gay Vietnam
65 B2 Honggor China

67 E5 **Honghai Wan** *B* China
58 F5 **Hong He** *R* China
67 D2 **Honghu** China
67 C3 **Hongjiang** China
67 G6 **Hong Kong** *colony* E Asia
67 F4 **Honglai** China
68 G7 **Hong Ngu** Vietnam
Hongning *see* **Wulian**
58 F2 **Hongor** Mongolia
67 D7 **Hongqizhen** China
68 E3 **Hongsa** Laos
67 B4 **Hongshui He** *R* China
65 B6 **Hongtong** China
61 J12 **Hongū** Japan
122 H4 **Honguedo Passage** Canada
66 E3 **Hongxing Sichang** China
67 A2 **Hongya** China
58 G5 **Hongze Hu** *L* China
137 N3 **Honiara** Guadalcanal I Solomon Is
9 H2 **Honingham** England
8 C6 **Honiton** England
61 O6 **Honjō** Japan
29 J10 **Honkajoki** Finland
68 H3 **Hon Matt** *isld* Vietnam
68 G3 **Hon Me** *isld* Vietnam
76 B3 **Honnali** India
26 P1 **Honningsvåg** Norway
102 V13 **Honokaa** Hawaiian Is
135 S3 **Honokahua** Hawaiian Is
145 F2 **Honokawa** New Zealand
135 S3 **Honokohau** Hawaiian Is
102 S12 **Honolulu** Hawaiian Is
135 V5 **Honomu** Hawaiian Is
102 R12 **Honouliuli** Hawaiian Is
68 H7 **Hon Quan** Vietnam
17 F5 **Honrubia** Spain
59 K4 **Honshū** *isld* Japan
28 H5 **Hønsinge** Denmark
135 U6 **Honuapo** Hawaiian Is
100 D4 **Hood, Mt** Oregon U.S.A.
143 C10 **Hood Pt** Western Australia Australia
100 D4 **Hood River** Oregon U.S.A.
100 B2 **Hoodsport** Washington U.S.A.
32 K10 **Hoof** W Germany
25 C4 **Hoofddorp** Netherlands
25 A6 **Hoofdplaat** Netherlands
25 F3 **Hooger Smilde** Netherlands
25 G3 **Hoogeveen** Netherlands
25 G2 **Hoogezand** Netherlands
25 G3 **Hooghalen** Netherlands
22 D2 **Hoogstade** Belgium
22 H1 **Hoogstraten** Belgium
41 K2 **Höohster** *mt* W Germany
9 F5 **Hook** England
144 C6 **Hook** New Zealand
135 U5 **Hookena** Hawaiian Is
107 J5 **Hooker** Oklahoma U.S.A.
140 B4 **Hooker Creek** N Terr Australia
14 E4 **Hook Hd** Ireland
141 J5 **Hook I** Queensland Australia
141 L7 **Hook Pt** Queensland Australia
141 J4 **Hook Reef** Gt Barrier Reef Aust
109 N2 **Hooks** Texas U.S.A.
95 Q3 **Hooksett** New Hampshire U.S.A.
32 H5 **Hooksiel** W Germany
102 V13 **Hoolehua** Hawaiian Is
117 F6 **Hoonah** Alaska U.S.A.
100 B8 **Hoopa** California U.S.A.
106 E4 **Hooper** Colorado U.S.A.
98 K8 **Hooper** Nebraska U.S.A.
101 N8 **Hooper** Utah U.S.A.
100 G3 **Hooper** Washington U.S.A.
116 D6 **Hooper Bay** Alaska U.S.A.
95 L8 **Hooper I** Maryland U.S.A.
99 T9 **Hoopeston** Illinois U.S.A.
123 Q3 **Hooping Hbr** Newfoundland Canada
98 J1 **Hoople** North Dakota U.S.A.
89 D6 **Hoopstad** S Africa
27 G16 **Höör** Sweden
25 D3 **Hoorn** Noord Netherlands
25 C2 **Hoorn** Texel Netherlands
95 O4 **Hoosick Falls** New York U.S.A.
118 H7 **Hoosier** Saskatchewan Canada
98 C4 **Hoover** South Dakota U.S.A.
103 K5 **Hoover Dam** Arizona U.S.A.
94 E6 **Hoover Res** Ohio U.S.A.
94 J6 **Hooversville** Pennsylvania U.S.A.
78 H1 **Hopa** Turkey
95 M5 **Hop Bottom** Pennsylvania U.S.A.
9 E4 **Hopcrofts Holt** England
117 N11 **Hope** British Columbia Canada
103 L8 **Hope** Arizona U.S.A.
111 C8 **Hope** Arkansas U.S.A.
94 B7 **Hope** Indiana U.S.A.
107 N3 **Hope** Kansas U.S.A.
98 J2 **Hope** North Dakota U.S.A.
127 M2 **Hope Bay** Jamaica
115 N6 **Hopedale** Labrador, Nfld Canada
Hopeh *prov see* **Hebei**
138 E3 **Hope, L** South Australia Australia
143 D9 **Hope,L** Western Australia Australia
138 E3 **Hopeless, Mt** South Australia Australia
112 J3 **Hope Mills** North Carolina U.S.A.
147 J12 **Hopen** *isld* Arctic Oc
144 D5 **Hope Pass** New Zealand
116 D2 **Hope, Pt** Alaska U.S.A.
138 F6 **Hopetoun** Victoria Australia
143 D10 **Hopetoun** Western Australia Australia
113 L11 **Hope Town** Bahamas
89 D7 **Hopetown** S Africa
141 H3 **Hopevale** Queensland Australia
122 K8 **Hopewell** Nova Scotia Canada
94 J6 **Hopewell** Pennsylvania U.S.A.
95 K9 **Hopewell** Virginia U.S.A.
115 M6 **Hopewell Is** Northwest Territories Canada
103 O6 **Hopi Buttes** *mt* Arizona U.S.A.
67 E4 **Ho-p'ing** China
139 G7 **Hopkins** *R* Victoria Australia
94 B4 **Hopkins** Michigan U.S.A.
99 M9 **Hopkins** Missouri U.S.A.
143 G6 **Hopkins,L** Western Australia Australia
144 B5 **Hopkins, Mt** New Zealand
110 J5 **Hopkinsville** Kentucky U.S.A.
102 A3 **Hopland** California U.S.A.
68 C2 **Hopong** Burma
33 T7 **Hoppegarten** East Germany
26 Q1 **Hopseidet** Norway
32 G8 **Hopsten** W Germany
9 H2 **Hopton** England
28 C6 **Hoptrup** Denmark
94 H7 **Hopwood** Pennsylvania U.S.A.
141 G5 **Hopwood,Mt** Queensland Australia
100 B2 **Hoquiam** Washington U.S.A.
107 J3 **Horace** Kansas U.S.A.
37 P2 **Hora Svatého Šebastiána** Czechoslovakia
37 P2 **Hora Svaté Katering** Czechoslovakia
111 B8 **Horatio** Arkansas U.S.A.
30 H6 **Horaždovice** Czechoslovakia
36 F7 **Horb** W Germany
28 J7 **Horbelev** Denmark
37 O7 **Horbering** W Germany
118 B6 **Horburg** Alberta Canada
13 G6 **Horbury** England
28 D3 **Hørby** Nordjylland Denmark
28 E2 **Hørby** Nordjylland Denmark
27 G16 **Hörby** Sweden
16 D5 **Horcajo de los Montes** Spain
16 E5 **Horcajo de Santiago** Spain
124 G3 **Horcasitas** Mexico
36 E4 **Horchheim** W Germany
27 A11 **Hordaland** *reg* Norway
109 H4 **Hords Cr. Res** Texas U.S.A.
28 A3 **Hørdum** Denmark
8 B3 **Horeb** Wales
88 C6 **Hore B** Zambia
48 H5 **Horezu** Romania
48 F4 **Horgoš** Yugoslavia
31 J5 **Hořice** Czechoslovakia
99 S6 **Horicon** Wisconsin U.S.A.
58 F3 **Horinger** China
22 J2 **Horion Hozémont** Belgium
119 M9 **Horizon** Saskatchewan Canada
137 S6 **Horizon Depth** Pacific Oc
31 H4 **Horka** East Germany
9 F5 **Horley** England
146 D9 **Horlick Mts** Antarctica
28 E2 **Hørmested** Denmark
Hormo *see* **Nyima**
77 E6 **Hormoz** *isld* Iran
77 E6 **Hormuz, Strait of** Iran
31 J7 **Horn** Austria
28 R8 **Horn** *C* Iceland
25 E6 **Horn** Netherlands
27 H14 **Horn** Sweden
48 F2 **Hornad** *R* Czechoslovakia
26 J5 **Hornavan** *L* Sweden
36 C5 **Hornbach** W Germany
32 J9 **Horn-Bad Meinog** W Germany
29 K4 **Hornbæk** Denmark
111 C10 **Hornbeck** Louisiana U.S.A.
36 E7 **Hornberg** W Germany
27 G13 **Hornborgasjön** *L* Sweden
100 C8 **Hornbrook** California U.S.A.
33 N8 **Hornburg** W Germany
9 F1 **Horncastle** England
27 H11 **Horndal** Sweden
33 N6 **Horndorf** W Germany
28 E1 **Horne** Denmark
28 B5 **Horne** Ribe Denmark
32 L5 **Horneburg** W Germany
26 L8 **Hörnefors** Sweden
28 E6 **Horneland** Denmark
94 K4 **Hornell** New York U.S.A.
120 F3 **Hornepayne** Ontario Canada
110 F5 **Hornersville** Missouri U.S.A.
27 C13 **Hornesund** Norway
28 G2 **Hornfiskrøn** *isld* Denmark
14 C1 **Horn Hd** Ireland
33 O8 **Hornhsleben** East Germany
141 F1 **Horn I** Queensland Australia
111 H11 **Horn I** Mississippi U.S.A.
31 K6 **Horni Benešov** Czechoslovakia
137 R4 **Horn, Îles de** Îles Wallis Pacific Oc
124 E4 **Hornillos** Mexico
26 B10 **Hornindal** Norway
26 B10 **Hornindalsvatn** *L* Norway
36 E6 **Hornisgrinde** *mt* W Germany
37 O3 **Horni Slavkov** Czechoslovakia
41 J3 **Hörnli** *mt* Switzerland
117 N4 **Horn Mts** Northwest Territories Canada
116 H6 **Horn Mts** Alaska U.S.A.
27 C13 **Hornnes** Norway
133 C6 **Hornopiren** *mt* Chile
124 H5 **Hornos** Mexico
133 D9 **Hornos, C. de** Chile
21 O2 **Hornoy-le Bourg** France
117 O4 **Horn R** Northwest Territories Canada
139 K5 **Hornsby** New South Wales Australia
110 H6 **Hornsby** Tennessee U.S.A.
8 B6 **Horns Cross** England
13 H6 **Hornsea** England
26 L8 **Hörnsjö** Sweden
28 E4 **Hornslet** Denmark
80 E2 **Horns of Hittin** Israel
37 K1 **Hornsömmern** East Germany
33 P5 **Hornstorf** East Germany
28 D5 **Hornstrup** Denmark
28 D5 **Hornum** Vejle Denmark
28 A7 **Hørnum** W Germany
33 S6 **Horn Zieritz** East Germany
60 T1 **Horobetsu** Japan
60 R3 **Horoizumi** Japan
60 Q1 **Horonai** Japan
145 E3 **Horopito** New Zealand
144 C5 **Hororata** New Zealand
60 Q3 **Horoshiri-dake** *mt* Japan
65 A5 **Horo Sum** China
30 H6 **Hořovice** Czechoslovakia
83 K9 **Horowupotana** Sri Lanka
21 K5 **Horps,le** France
59 H2 **Horqin Youyi Qianqi** China
65 E2 **Horqin Youyi Zhongqi** China
65 F2 **Horqin Zouyi Zhongqi** China
65 E3 **Horqin Zuoyi Houqi** China
129 G8 **Horqueta** Paraguay
133 F2 **Horqueta** Paraguay
28 H7 **Horreby** Denmark
27 F14 **Horred** Sweden
36 B2 **Horrem** W Germany
143 A8 **Horrocks** Western Australia Australia
83 M8 **Horsburgh I** Cocos Is Indian Oc
37 J1 **Hörschel** East Germany
110 K4 **Horse Branch** Kentucky U.S.A.
9 G6 **Horsebridge** E Sussex England
94 B9 **Horse Cave** Kentucky U.S.A.
106 G3 **Horse Cr** Colorado U.S.A.
110 B4 **Horse Cr** Missouri U.S.A.
98 A8 **Horse Cr** Wyoming U.S.A.
117 N9 **Horsefly** British Columbia Canada
98 F2 **Horsehead L** North Dakota U.S.A.
95 L4 **Horseheads** New York U.S.A.
123 R3 **Horse Is** Newfoundland Canada
37 J2 **Hörsel** *R* East Germany
102 D1 **Horse L** California U.S.A.
37 J2 **Hörsel Berge** *mt* East Germany
28 D5 **Horsens** Vejle Denmark
28 E5 **Horsens Fjord** *inlet* Denmark
118 F2 **Horse, R** Alberta Canada
113 D8 **Horseshoe** Florida U.S.A.
111 L9 **Horseshoe Band Nat. Mil. Park** Alabama U.S.A.
138 C2 **Horseshoe Bend** N Terr Australia
140 C7 **Horseshoe Bend** N Terr Australia
100 J6 **Horse Shoe Bend** Idaho U.S.A.
127 P4 **Horse Shoe Pt** St Kitts W Indies
103 N7 **Horseshoe Res** Arizona U.S.A.
106 B8 **Horse Springs** New Mexico U.S.A.
138 F6 **Horsham** Victoria Australia
118 H8 **Horsham** Saskatchewan Canada
9 F5 **Horsham** England
29 K5 **Hørsholm** Denmark
13 G4 **Horsley** England
28 G7 **Horslunde** Denmark
37 O4 **Horšovský Týn** Czechoslovakia
33 S4 **Horst** East Germany
25 F6 **Horst** Netherlands
32 L5 **Horst** W Germany
32 G8 **Hörstel** W Germany
25 F6 **Hörstgen** W Germany
32 F8 **Horstmar** W Germany
48 E2 **Hor Stubňa** Czechoslovakia
27 D12 **Horten** Norway
112 F6 **Hortense** Georgia U.S.A.
26 M6 **Hortlax** Sweden
114 G4 **Horton** *R* Northwest Territories Canada
107 P2 **Horton** Kansas U.S.A.
27 C10 **Horungane** Norway
28 C7 **Hörup** W Germany
28 G5 **Hørve** Denmark
27 G15 **Hörvik** Sweden
13 F6 **Horwich** England
120 H5 **Horwood L** Ontario Canada
37 P5 **Hory Matky Boží** Czechoslovakia
31 J5 **Hory Orlické** *mts* Czechoslovakia
47 K7 **Horzom** *R* Turkey
86 G4 **Hosa'ina** Ethiopia
36 G3 **Hösbach** W Germany
76 C4 **Hosdurga** India
70 C3 **Hose Mts** Sarawak
84 G5 **Hosenofu** Libya
77 A3 **Hoseynābad** Iran
111 M11 **Hosford** Florida U.S.A.
74 C10 **Hoshab** Pakistan
77 H6 **Hoshāb** Pakistan
74 G7 **Hoshangabad** India
74 F3 **Hoshiarpur** India
98 J7 **Hoskins** Nebraska U.S.A.
98 G4 **Hosmer** South Dakota U.S.A.
60 E13 **Hososhima** Japan
106 C6 **Hospah** New Mexico U.S.A.
76 C3 **Hospet** India
14 C4 **Hospital** Ireland
131 G3 **Hospital, Cuchilla del** *mt* Uruguay
29 O6 **Hossa** Finland
106 B6 **Hosta Butte** *mt* New Mexico U.S.A.
133 D9 **Hoste, I** Chile
18 E8 **Hostens** France
27 G13 **Höstholmen** Sweden
37 O4 **Hostouň** Czechoslovakia
28 A5 **Hostrup** Ribe Denmark
28 B7 **Hostrup** Sønderjylland Denmark
28 D7 **Hostrup** W Germany
28 C7 **Hostrup Sø** *L* Denmark
76 C4 **Hosur** India
26 G8 **Hotagen** Sweden
61 L9 **Hotaka** Japan
66 B4 **Hotan** China
66 C4 **Hotan He** *R* China
87 D11 **Hotazel** S Africa
117 P7 **Hotchkiss** Alberta Canada
106 C3 **Hotchkiss** Colorado U.S.A.
102 H3 **Hot Creek Ra** Nevada U.S.A.
33 O8 **Hötensleben** East Germany
140 B1 **Hotham,C** N Terr Australia
116 F3 **Hotham Inlet** Alaska U.S.A.
139 H6 **Hotham, Mt** Victoria Australia
26 H7 **Hoting** Sweden
80 E8 **Hot Springs** Israel
111 C7 **Hot Springs** Arkansas U.S.A.
109 O1 **Hot Springs** *nat park* Arkansas U.S.A.
101 L2 **Hot Springs** Montana U.S.A.
112 E2 **Hot Springs** North Carolina U.S.A.
98 C6 **Hot Springs** South Dakota U.S.A.
108 D6 **Hot Springs** Texas U.S.A.
94 H9 **Hot Springs** Virginia U.S.A.
106 D1 **Hot Sulphur Springs** Colorado U.S.A.
117 O3 **Hottah L** Northwest Territories Canada
22 J3 **Hotton** Belgium
108 B5 **Hot Wells** Texas U.S.A.
32 L6 **Hötzingen** W Germany
28 E2 **Hou** Denmark
20 E7 **Houat** *isld* France
22 D3 **Houdain** France
21 O4 **Houdan** France
22 G3 **Houdeng** Belgium
18 E8 **Houeillès** France
22 K3 **Houffalize** Belgium
107 J5 **Hough** Oklahoma U.S.A.
141 H4 **Houghton** *R* Queensland Australia
99 S2 **Houghton** Michigan U.S.A.
94 J4 **Houghton** New York U.S.A.
98 H4 **Houghton** South Dakota U.S.A.
94 C2 **Houghton L** Michigan U.S.A.
13 G4 **Houghton-le-Spring** England
145 D1 **Houhora** New Zealand
80 F1 **Houla** Lebanon
21 K3 **Houlgate** France
111 G7 **Houlka** Mississippi U.S.A.
21 N2 **Houlme,le** France
95 T7 **Houlton** Maine U.S.A.
65 B7 **Houma** China
111 F12 **Houma** Louisiana U.S.A.
85 G2 **Houmt Souk** Tunisia
85 D6 **Houndé** Burkina
9 F5 **Hounslow** England
18 E7 **Hourtin** France
95 O5 **Housatonic** *R* Connecticut U.S.A.
108 D1 **House** New Mexico U.S.A.
123 L6 **House Hbr** Madeleine Is. Quebec Canada
12 D3 **House o'-Hill** Scotland
118 E3 **House R** Alberta Canada
103 L2 **House Ra** Utah U.S.A.
117 K8 **Houston** British Columbia Canada
99 P6 **Houston** Minnesota U.S.A.
111 H8 **Houston** Mississippi U.S.A.
110 E4 **Houston** Missouri U.S.A.
109 F9 **Houston** Texas U.S.A.
110 C3 **Houstonia** Missouri U.S.A.
109 M5 **Houston, L** Texas U.S.A.
111 C11 **Houston R** Louisiana U.S.A.
89 F4 **Hout** *R* S Africa
89 A10 **Hout B** S Africa
25 D4 **Houten** Netherlands
22 J1 **Houthalen** Belgium
143 A8 **Houtman Abrolhos** *arch* Western Australia Australia
94 J6 **Houtzdale** Pennsylvania U.S.A.
22 J3 **Houyet** Belgium
28 E5 **Hov** Denmark
29 K4 **Hov** Sweden
27 G13 **Hova** Sweden
28 B5 **Hovborg** Denmark
58 B2 **Hovd** Mongolia
27 B12 **Hovden** Norway
26 H9 **Hovdsjö** Sweden
28 A3 **Hove** Denmark
28 G5 **Høve** Vestjælland Denmark
9 F6 **Hove** England
28 D5 **Hovedgård** Denmark
32 J9 **Hövelhof** W Germany
28 B5 **Hoven** Denmark
98 G4 **Hoven** South Dakota U.S.A.
103 P4 **Hovenweep Nat. Mon** Utah U.S.A.
28 A4 **Hover** Denmark
28 A4 **Hover Å** *R* Denmark
77 A4 **Hoveyzeh** Iran
99 R2 **Hovland** Minnesota U.S.A.
28 C6 **Hovslund** Denmark
141 L7 **Howard** Queensland Australia
107 O4 **Howard** Kansas U.S.A.
94 E6 **Howard** Ohio U.S.A.
94 K5 **Howard** Pennsylvania U.S.A.
98 J5 **Howard** South Dakota U.S.A.
99 S5 **Howard** Wisconsin U.S.A.
94 B3 **Howard City** Michigan U.S.A.
108 F5 **Howard Cr** Texas U.S.A.
140 D1 **Howard I** N Terr Australia
99 M4 **Howard L** Minnesota U.S.A.
116 J2 **Howard Pass** Alaska U.S.A.
99 T6 **Howards Grove** Wisconsin U.S.A.
86 D2 **Howar, Wadi** *watercourse* Sudan
13 H6 **Howden** England
101 M6 **Howe** Idaho U.S.A.
94 B5 **Howe** Indiana U.S.A.
109 N1 **Howe** Oklahoma U.S.A.
109 L2 **Howe** Texas U.S.A.
139 J6 **Howe, C** New South Wales Australia
83 L13 **Howe, Î** Kerguelen Indian Oc
94 D4 **Howell** Michigan U.S.A.
101 N8 **Howell** Utah U.S.A.
98 J8 **Howells** Nebraska U.S.A.
138 C2 **Howe, Mt** South Australia Australia
15 F4 **Howe of Mearns** Scotland
98 D5 **Howes** South Dakota U.S.A.
117 M11 **Howe Sound** British Columbia Canada
121 R7 **Howick** Quebec Canada
145 E2 **Howick** New Zealand
141 H2 **Howick Group** *islds* Gt Barrier Reef Aust
138 E2 **Howitt, L** South Australia Australia
139 H6 **Howitt, Mt** Victoria Australia
95 T1 **Howland** Maine U.S.A.
137 R1 **Howland I** Pacific Oc
123 P4 **Howley** Newfoundland Canada
117 P10 **Howser** British Columbia Canada
14 E3 **Howth** Ireland
68 H4 **Ho Xa** Vietnam
110 F5 **Hoxie** Arkansas U.S.A.
107 K2 **Hoxie** Kansas U.S.A.
32 K9 **Höxter** W Germany
66 D2 **Hoxtolgay** China
15 E2 **Hoy** Scotland
32 K7 **Hoya** W Germany
31 H4 **Hoyerswerda** East Germany
8 C1 **Hoylake** England
26 F7 **Höylandet** Norway
120 J4 **Hoyle** Ontario Canada
110 G3 **Hoyleton** Illinois U.S.A.
33 O9 **Hoym** East Germany
16 C4 **Hoyos** Spain
15 E2 **Hoy Snd** Scotland
122 F8 **Hoyt** New Brunswick Canada
107 P2 **Hoyt** Kansas U.S.A.
29 O9 **Höytiäinen** *L* Finland
101 O9 **Hoyt Pk** Utah U.S.A.
68 C2 **Hpa Lai** Burma
68 C3 **Hpasawg** Burma
37 P4 **Hracholuská Nádrž** *res* Czechoslovakia
31 J5 **Hradec Králové** Czechoslovakia
37 P3 **Hradiště** *mt* Czechoslovakia
31 K6 **Hranice** Czechoslovakia
Hranice Czechoslovakia *see* **Rossbach**
48 F2 **Hriňová** Czechoslovakia
31 L7 **Hron** *R* Czechoslovakia
37 O3 **Hroznetín** Czechoslovakia
31 O5 **Hrubieszów** Poland
31 J7 **Hrušovany** Czechoslovakia
42 G4 **Hrvatska** *reg* Yugoslavia
68 C2 **Hsa Mong Hkam** Burma
66 D5 **Hsia-ju Ts'o** *L* China
67 G6 **Hsiao-lan Hsü** *isld* Taiwan
58 G5 **Hsieh-chia-chi** China
68 C2 **Hsi Hkip** Burma
68 C2 **Hsi-hseng** Burma
58 G4 **Hsin-chi** China
58 F4 **Hsin-ch'iang** China
67 G4 **Hsin-chu** Taiwan
68 J3 **Hsing-ying** China
59 H3 **Hsin-min** China
68 C1 **Hsipaw** Burma
66 D5 **Hsi-tsang Kao-yüan** *reg* China
68 C1 **Hsumhsai** Burma
68 K2 **Hsü-wen** China
67 F4 **Hua'an** China
128 C6 **Huacho** Peru
65 H1 **Huachuan** China
128 C5 **Huacrachuco** Peru
65 C4 **Huade** China
59 J3 **Huadian** China
67 G2 **Huading Shan** *mt* China
68 D6 **Hua Hin** Thailand
68 F5 **Huai** *R* Thailand
65 C4 **Huai'an** China
58 G5 **Huaibei** China
65 F3 **Huaice** China
65 F3 **Huaidezhen** China
58 F5 **Huai He** *R* China
67 C3 **Huaihua** China
67 D5 **Huaiji** China
65 C4 **Huailai** China
68 F4 **Huai Luang** *R* Thailand
58 G5 **Huainan** China
67 E1 **Huaining** China
58 F4 **Huairen** China
65 C4 **Huairou** China
68 F4 **Huai Yang Res** Thailand
59 G5 **Huaiyin** China
67 C4 **Huaiyuan** China
125 L9 **Huajuápan de León** Mexico
71 N8 **Huaki** Indonesia
103 L6 **Hualapai Mts** Arizona U.S.A.
67 E2 **Hualin** China
128 C5 **Huallaga** *R* Peru
128 C5 **Huallanca** Peru
65 H1 **Huama** China
65 H1 **Huanan** China
128 E7 **Huanay** Bolivia
128 C6 **Huancabamba** Pasco Peru
128 C5 **Huancabamba** Piura Peru
128 E7 **Huancane** Peru
128 C6 **Huancavelica** Peru
128 C6 **Huancayo** Peru
128 E8 **Huanchaca** Bolivia
128 F6 **Huanchaca, Sa. de** *mts* Bolivia
128 C5 **Huanchaco** Peru
Huang'an *see* **Hong'an**
67 G1 **Huangang** China
Huangcaoba *see* **Qianxinan**
58 G5 **Huangchuan** China
67 E1 **Huanggang** China
65 D3 **Huanggangliang** *mt* China
67 F3 **Huanggang Shan** *mt* China
Huang Hai *see* **Yellow Sea**
58 D4 **Huang He** *R* China
65 D5 **Huanghua** China
65 C7 **Huangkou** China
67 E2 **Huanglaomen** China
65 A7 **Huangling** China
68 J3 **Huangliu** China
65 A7 **Huanglong** China
65 C7 **Huanglongsi** China
67 E1 **Huangmei** China
67 C4 **Huangmian** China
65 G3 **Huangnihe** China
67 E1 **Huangpi** China
67 B3 **Huangpin** China
67 C6 **Huangpo** China
67 D5 **Huangpu** China
67 E2 **Huangshagang** China
67 F1 **Huang Shan** *mts* China
65 E6 **Huangshanguan** China
58 D4 **Huang Shui** *R* China
65 G3 **Huangsongdian** China
65 D4 **Huangtuliangzi** China
65 E6 **Huang Xian** China
67 G2 **Huangyan** China
67 D3 **Huangyangsi** China
Huangzhou *see* **Huanggang**
67 C7 **Huangzhu** China
67 G1 **Huaniao Shan** *isld* China
67 A4 **Huaning** China
67 C4 **Huanjiang** China
58 E4 **Huan Jiang** *R* China
65 F4 **Huanren** China
Huanshan *see* **Yuhuan**
58 G5 **Huanshi** China
128 D6 **Huanta** Peru
65 D6 **Huantai** China
128 C5 **Huánuco** Peru
128 D6 **Huanzo, Cord. de** *mts* Peru
125 N3 **Huaonta** Nicaragua
67 G4 **Hua-p'ing Hsü** *isld* Taiwan
128 E7 **Huara** Chile
128 C5 **Huaraz** Peru
128 C6 **Huariaca** Peru
128 C6 **Huarmey** Peru
67 D2 **Huarong** China
128 C5 **Huascarán** *mt* Peru
133 C3 **Huasco** Chile
131 B2 **Huasco, R** Chile
67 D3 **Huashi** China
125 M2 **Huaspuc** Honduras
124 E4 **Huatabampo** Mexico
58 E4 **Huating** China
65 E3 **Hua Tugal** China
125 L8 **Huatusco** Mexico
125 K7 **Huauchinango** Mexico
65 A7 **Hua Xian** China
65 C7 **Hua Xian** China
67 D5 **Hua Xian** China
65 A7 **Huayin** China
67 B1 **Huaying Shan** *mts* China
67 E1 **Huayuan** China
67 C2 **Huayuan** China
67 C6 **Huazhou** China
65 F4 **Huazi** China
119 O7 **Hubbard** Saskatchewan Canada
99 N7 **Hubbard** Iowa U.S.A.
109 L4 **Hubbard** Texas U.S.A.
109 H3 **Hubbard Cr. Res** Texas U.S.A.
94 D2 **Hubbard L** Michigan U.S.A.
117 D5 **Hubbard, Mt** Alaska/Yukon Terr U.S.A./Canada
122 H9 **Hubbards** Nova Scotia Canada
98 J9 **Hubbell** Nebraska U.S.A.
103 P6 **Hubbell Trading Post Nat. Hist. Site** Arizona U.S.A.
58 F5 **Hubei** *prov* China
41 N3 **Huben** Austria
121 Q7 **Huberdeau** Quebec Canada
33 T7 **Hubertusstock** East Germany
76 B3 **Hubli** India
32 J6 **Huchting** W Germany
25 F6 **Hückelhoven-Ratheim** W Germany
36 C1 **Hückeswagen** W Germany
140 D6 **Huckitta** N Terr Australia
9 E1 **Hucknall** England
22 B2 **Hucqueliers** France
72 E6 **Hudaydah, Al** N Yemen
13 G6 **Huddersfield** England
27 J12 **Huddinge** Sweden
32 H6 **Hude** W Germany
32 L7 **Hudemühlen** W Germany
26 J10 **Hudiksvall** Sweden
20 H4 **Hudimesnil** France
115 K7 **Hudson** Ontario Canada
133 C7 **Hudson** *mt* Chile
106 F1 **Hudson** Colorado U.S.A.
113 E9 **Hudson** Florida U.S.A.
110 G1 **Hudson** Illinois U.S.A.
94 B5 **Hudson** Indiana U.S.A.
99 O7 **Hudson** Iowa U.S.A.
107 M3 **Hudson** Kansas U.S.A.
94 C5 **Hudson** Michigan U.S.A.
95 O4 **Hudson** New York U.S.A.
95 O3 **Hudson** *R* New York U.S.A.
94 F5 **Hudson** Ohio U.S.A.
101 R7 **Hudson** Wyoming U.S.A.
115 L6 **Hudson Bay** Canada
119 P6 **Hudson Bay** Saskatchewan Canada
146 C13 **Hudson, Cape** *C* Antarctica
95 O3 **Hudson Falls** New York U.S.A.
107 P5 **Hudson, L.** Oklahoma U.S.A.
117 N7 **Hudson's Hope** British Columbia Canada
115 M5 **Hudson Str** Canada
94 B4 **Hudsonville** Michigan U.S.A.
119 W5 **Hudwin L** Manitoba Canada
68 H4 **Hue** Vietnam
16 C4 **Huebra** *R* Spain
131 B7 **Huechulafquén, L** Argentina
108 B4 **Hueco Mts** Texas U.S.A.
48 H4 **Huedin** Romania
124 G5 **Huehueto, Cerro** *mt* Mexico
125 K7 **Huejutla** Mexico
20 C5 **Huelgoat** France
16 E7 **Huelma** Spain
16 C7 **Huelva** *R* Spain
16 C7 **Huelva** *prov* Spain
16 C7 **Huelva** Spain
68 G4 **Huen** Laos
131 B3 **Huentelauquén** Chile
124 D3 **Huépac** Mexico
133 C6 **Huequi, Pen** Chile
17 F7 **Huércal Overa** Spain
106 F3 **Huerfano** *R* Colorado U.S.A.
131 C3 **Huerta, Sa. de la** *ra* Argentina
17 G6 **Huertas, C. de las** Spain
124 J5 **Huertecillas** Mexico
17 G3 **Huerva** *R* Spain
17 G2 **Huesca** *prov* Spain
17 G2 **Huesca** Spain
17 F7 **Huéscar** Spain
16 D7 **Huesna** *R* Spain
108 B5 **Hueso, Sierra del** *mts* Mexico
125 J8 **Huétamo** Mexico
17 F4 **Huete** Spain
98 F3 **Huff** North Dakota U.S.A.
36 G5 **Hüffenhardt** W Germany
98 H4 **Huffton** South Dakota U.S.A.
77 A7 **Hufuf, Al** Saudi Arabia
116 K4 **Huggins I** Alaska U.S.A.
98 F9 **Hugh Butler L** Nebraska U.S.A.
141 G5 **Hughenden** Queensland Australia
118 F6 **Hughenden** Alberta Canada
121 L4 **Hughes** Ontario Canada
110 F7 **Hughes** Arkansas U.S.A.
119 R2 **Hughes R** Manitoba Canada
109 N3 **Hughes Springs** Texas U.S.A.
110 C3 **Hughesville** Missouri U.S.A.
140 C6 **Hugh R** N Terr Australia
118 K7 **Hughton** Saskatchewan Canada
9 F7 **Hugh Town** Isles of Scilly England
75 M8 **Hugli** *R* India
106 G2 **Hugo** Colorado U.S.A.
99 N4 **Hugo** Minnesota U.S.A.
107 P7 **Hugo** Oklahoma U.S.A.
100 B7 **Hugo** Oregon U.S.A.
107 P7 **Hugo L** Oklahoma U.S.A.
107 J4 **Hugoton** Kansas U.S.A.
36 D7 **Hugsweier** W Germany
65 B6 **Huguan** China
Huhehot *see* **Hohhot**
58 F3 **Huhehot** China
67 F4 **Hui'an** China
145 F3 **Huiarau Range** New Zealand
67 E4 **Huichang** China
Huicheng *see* **She Xian**
124 H7 **Huicholes, Sa. de los** *mts* Mexico
59 J3 **Hŭich'ŏn** N Korea
67 E5 **Huidong** China
65 G2 **Huifaheng** China
128 C3 **Huila** *div* Colombia
58 G4 **Huimin** China
65 G3 **Huinan** China
67 B3 **Huishui** China
21 L7 **Huismes** France
21 M5 **Huîsne** *R* France
21 N6 **Huisseau-sur-Cosson** France
65 C7 **Huiting** China
67 C3 **Huitong** China
29 K10 **Huittinen** Finland
125 K8 **Huitzuco** Mexico
65 B7 **Hui Xian** China
125 N10 **Huixtla** Mexico
Huiyang *see* **Huizhou**
25 D4 **Huizen** Netherlands
67 E5 **Huizhou** China
145 F3 **Huka Falls** New Zealand
145 E4 **Hukanui** New Zealand
144 C5 **Hukarere** New Zealand
75 R5 **Hukawng Valley** Burma
145 E1 **Hukerenui** New Zealand
67 E2 **Hukou** China
87 D10 **Hukuntsi** Botswana
107 O5 **Hulah** Oklahoma U.S.A.
107 O5 **Hulah L** Oklahoma U.S.A.
59 J2 **Hulan** China
65 F1 **Hulan Ergi** China
65 G1 **Hulan He** *R* China
80 F1 **Hulata** Israel
98 B5 **Hulett** Wyoming U.S.A.
Huliao *see* **Dabu**
65 J2 **Hulin** China
65 E2 **Hulin He** *R* China
121 P7 **Hull** Quebec Canada
99 P10 **Hull** Illinois U.S.A.
98 K6 **Hull** Iowa U.S.A.
98 F3 **Hull** North Dakota U.S.A.
109 N5 **Hull** Texas U.S.A.
140 A6 **Hull Cr** N Terr Australia
138 A1 **Hull Cr** N Terr Australia
22 G2 **Hulpe, la** Belgium
28 E1 **Hulsig** Denmark
25 B6 **Hulst** Netherlands
27 H14 **Hultsfred** Sweden
65 E4 **Huludao** China
69 E11 **HUlu Kali, Gunung** Malaysia
58 G2 **Hulun Nur** *L* China
69 E10 **Hulu Soh, Gunung** *mt* Malaysia
59 J1 **Huma** China
127 M5 **Humacao** Puerto Rico
59 H1 **Huma He** *R* China
128 F5 **Humaitá** Brazil
130 B10 **Humaitá** Paraguay
87 D12 **Humansdorp** S Africa
110 C4 **Humansville** Missouri U.S.A.
128 C6 **Humay** Peru
87 C9 **Humbe** Angola
123 P5 **Humbermouth** Newfoundland Canada
13 H6 **Humber, R** England
13 H6 **Humberside** *co* England
99 Q5 **Humbird** Wisconsin U.S.A.
28 F7 **Humble** Denmark
109 M6 **Humble** Texas U.S.A.
106 G9 **Humble City** New Mexico U.S.A.
119 M6 **Humboldt** Saskatchewan Canada
103 M7 **Humboldt** Arizona U.S.A.
99 S10 **Humboldt** Illinois U.S.A.
99 M7 **Humboldt** Iowa U.S.A.
107 P4 **Humboldt** Kansas U.S.A.
102 F1 **Humboldt** *R* Nevada U.S.A.
102 F1 **Humboldt** Nevada U.S.A.
110 H6 **Humboldt** Tennessee U.S.A.
100 A9 **Humboldt B** California U.S.A.
115 N2 **Humboldt Gletscher** *gla* Greenland
102 F2 **Humboldt L** Nevada U.S.A.
144 B6 **Humboldt Mts** New Zealand
100 G9 **Humboldt Range** Nevada U.S.A.
102 F1 **Humboldt Rge** Nevada U.S.A.
102 G2 **Humboldt Salt Marsh** Nevada U.S.A.
94 J8 **Hume** Virginia U.S.A.
141 H7 **Humeburn** Queensland Australia
77 F7 **Hūmedān** Iran
48 G2 **Humenné** Czechoslovakia
139 H6 **Hume Res** New South Wales Australia
99 N9 **Humeston** Iowa U.S.A.
29 K5 **Humlebæk** Denmark
28 B3 **Humlum** Denmark
32 K9 **Humme** W Germany
95 L6 **Hummelstown** Pennsylvania U.S.A.
32 G7 **Hümmling** *hills* W Germany
144 C6 **Hummock** *mt* New Zealand
127 K10 **Humocaro Bajo** Venezuela
131 A5 **Humos, C** Chile
87 B9 **Humpata** Angola
111 E7 **Humphrey** Arkansas U.S.A.
101 N5 **Humphrey** Idaho U.S.A.
98 J8 **Humphrey** Nebraska U.S.A.
100 D2 **Humphrey** Washington U.S.A.
102 E5 **Humphreys** California U.S.A.
110 C1 **Humphreys** Missouri U.S.A.
103 N6 **Humphreys Pk** Arizona U.S.A.
140 C7 **Humphries, Mt** N Terr Australia
31 J6 **Humpolec** Czechoslovakia
29 K11 **Humppila** Finland
100 B2 **Humptulips** Washington U.S.A.
140 B2 **Humpty Doo** N Terr Australia
84 F4 **Hūn** Libya
28 S9 **Húna-flói** *B* Iceland
67 C3 **Hunan** *prov* China
65 H3 **Hunchun** China
144 D5 **Hundalee** New Zealand
28 A3 **Hundborg** Denmark
28 B6 **Hunderup** Denmark
28 H5 **Hundested** Denmark
117 N10 **Hundred Mile House** British Columbia Canada
26 M6 **Hundsjö** Sweden
28 E5 **Hundslund** Denmark
38 G7 **Hundstein** *mt* Austria
28 D2 **Hune** Denmark
48 H5 **Hunedoara** *reg* Romania
48 H5 **Hunedoara** Romania
36 H2 **Hünfeld** W Germany
36 E3 **Hünfelden** W Germany
48 D3 **Hungary** *rep* Europe
26 H9 **Hunge** Sweden
36 F3 **Hungen** W Germany
141 G8 **Hungerford** Queensland Australia
9 E5 **Hungerford** England
65 G5 **Hŭngnam** N Korea
101 L1 **Hungry Horse Dam** Montana U.S.A.
101 M1 **Hungry Horse Res** Montana U.S.A.
68 H2 **Hung Yen** Vietnam
65 E4 **Hun He** *R* China
65 B4 **Hun He** *R* China
65 G4 **Hunjiang** China
65 F4 **Hun Jiang** *R* China
13 H5 **Hunmanby** England
99 P10 **Hunnewell** Missouri U.S.A.
25 F7 **Hünshoven** W Germany
9 G2 **Hunstanton** England
28 B2 **Hunstrup** Denmark
76 C4 **Hunsur** India
65 E2 **Hunt** China
109 H5 **Hunt** Texas U.S.A.
120 J3 **Hunta** Ontario Canada
32 H8 **Hunte** *R* W Germany
32 H8 **Hunteburg** W Germany
139 K4 **Hunter** *R* New South Wales Australia
144 C6 **Hunter** New Zealand
137 P6 **Hunter** *isld* Pacific Oc
110 E6 **Hunter** Arkansas U.S.A.
107 M2 **Hunter** Kansas U.S.A.
98 J2 **Hunter** North Dakota U.S.A.
107 N5 **Hunter** Oklahoma U.S.A.
109 J6 **Hunter** Texas U.S.A.
139 G8 **Hunter I** Tasmania Australia
117 J10 **Hunter I** British Columbia Canada
99 P1 **Hunter I** Ontario Canada
116 M5 **Hunter, Mt** Alaska U.S.A.
144 A6 **Hunter Mts** New Zealand
144 B6 **Hunter R** New Zealand
122 J7 **Hunter River** Prince Edward I Canada
100 G1 **Hunters** Washington U.S.A.
68 A3 **Hunter's B** Burma
144 C6 **Hunter's Hills, The** New Zealand
12 D2 **Hunterston** Scotland
112 G2 **Huntersville** North Carolina U.S.A.
94 G8 **Huntersville** West Virginia U.S.A.
94 B5 **Huntertown** Indiana U.S.A.
145 E3 **Hunterville** New Zealand
110 K3 **Huntingburg** Indiana U.S.A.
121 Q7 **Huntingdon** Quebec Canada
9 F3 **Huntingdon** England
94 J6 **Huntingdon** Pennsylvania U.S.A.
110 H6 **Huntingdon** Tennessee U.S.A.
Huntingdon and Peterborough *co see* **Cambridgeshire**
122 J3 **Hunting I** Quebec Canada
112 G5 **Hunting I** South Carolina U.S.A.
94 B6 **Huntington** Indiana U.S.A.
95 O6 **Huntington** Long I, New York U.S.A.
100 H5 **Huntington** Oregon U.S.A.
111 B10 **Huntington** Texas U.S.A.
103 O2 **Huntington** Utah U.S.A.
94 E8 **Huntington** West Virginia U.S.A.
102 F8 **Huntington Beach** California U.S.A.
102 E4 **Huntington L** California U.S.A.
8 D4 **Huntley** England
101 R4 **Huntley** Montana U.S.A.
98 G9 **Huntley** Nebraska U.S.A.
98 B8 **Huntley** Wyoming U.S.A.
32 H7 **Huntlosen** W Germany
145 E2 **Huntly** New Zealand
15 F3 **Huntly** Scotland
117 J5 **Hunt, Mt** Yukon Territory Canada
138 D3 **Hunt Pen** South Australia Australia
101 S5 **Hunts Mt** Wyoming U.S.A.
122 H10 **Hunts Pt** Nova Scotia Canada
121 L7 **Huntsville** Ontario Canada
110 K7 **Huntsville** Alabama U.S.A.
110 C5 **Huntsville** Arkansas U.S.A.
110 D2 **Huntsville** Missouri U.S.A.
109 M5 **Huntsville** Texas U.S.A.
101 O8 **Huntsville** Utah U.S.A.
32 E9 **Hünxe** W Germany
88 C10 **Hunyani Rge** *mts* Zimbabwe
65 B5 **Hunyuan** China
66 A4 **Hunza** Kashmir
25 G2 **Hunze** *R* Netherlands
66 C3 **Huocheng** China
65 F1 **Huodifangzi** China
65 B7 **Huojia** China
139 H9 **Huon** *R* Tasmania Australia
68 H4 **Huong Hoa** Vietnam
68 G3 **Huong Khe** Vietnam
68 H8 **Huong My** Vietnam
68 G3 **Huong Son** Vietnam
68 H4 **Huong Thuy** Vietnam
139 H9 **Huonville** Tasmania Australia
65 B6 **Huo Shan** *mt* China
67 E1 **Huoshan** China
67 G5 **Huo-shao Tao** *isld* Taiwan
65 B6 **Huo Xian** China
Hupeh *prov see* **Hubei** *prov*
21 O1 **Huppy** France
33 M10 **Hüpstedt** East Germany
48 E3 **Hurbanovo** Czechoslovakia
27 E11 **Hurdals** *L* Norway
120 J7 **Hurd, Cape** Ontario Canada
86 B1 **Hurdiyo** Somalia
110 D1 **Hurdland** Missouri U.S.A.
98 F2 **Hurdsfield** North Dakota U.S.A.
65 E3 **Hure Qi** China
80 E1 **Hurfeish** Israel
84 J4 **Hurghada** Egypt
18 G6 **Huriel** France
119 P2 **Hurkett** Ontario Canada
9 F4 **Hurley** England
111 H11 **Hurley** Mississippi U.S.A.
106 B9 **Hurley** New Mexico U.S.A.
98 J6 **Hurley** South Dakota U.S.A.
99 Q3 **Hurley** Wisconsin U.S.A.
12 D2 **Hurlford** Scotland
15 E2 **Hurliness** Scotland
95 M8 **Hurlock** Maryland U.S.A.
143 C10 **Hurlstone, L** Western Australia Australia
102 D5 **Huron** California U.S.A.
94 E5 **Huron** Ohio U.S.A.
98 H5 **Huron** South Dakota U.S.A.
99 S3 **Huron B** Michigan U.S.A.
94 E2 **Huron City** Michigan U.S.A.
94 E2 **Huron, L** U.S.A./Canada
99 T3 **Huron Mts** Michigan U.S.A.
103 L4 **Hurricane** Utah U.S.A.
94 E8 **Hurricane** West Virginia U.S.A.
112 E6 **Hurricane Cr** Georgia U.S.A.
126 E3 **Hurricane Flats** Bahamas
110 J6 **Hurricane Mills** Tennessee U.S.A.
9 E5 **Hursley** England
109 M9 **Hurst** Texas U.S.A.
9 E5 **Hurstbourne Tarrant** England
9 G5 **Hurst Green** England
9 F6 **Hurstpierpoint** England
131 B3 **Hurtado** *R* Chile
36 B2 **Hürtgen** W Germany
36 B2 **Hürth** W Germany
111 L9 **Hurtsboro** Alabama U.S.A.
70 C4 **Hurung, Gunung** *mt* Kalimantan
88 B10 **Hurungwe** *dist* Zimbabwe
144 D5 **Hurunui R** New Zealand
28 E3 **Hurup** Denmark
28 D7 **Hurup** W Germany
28 S9 **Husavik** Iceland
9 E3 **Husbands Bosworth** England
28 A4 **Husby** Denmark
71 L10 **Husdale** Indonesia
80 F3 **Husein Br** Jordan
Hushan *see* **Cixi**
65 H2 **Hushan** China
48 L4 **Huşi** Romania
80 D3 **Husifa** Israel
139 K6 **Huskisson** New South Wales Australia
27 G14 **Huskvarna** Sweden
116 J4 **Huslia** Alaska U.S.A.
80 G4 **Husn** Jordan
101 L2 **Huson** Montana U.S.A.
27 A10 **Husöy** Norway
118 E7 **Hussar** Alberta Canada
26 B9 **Hustadvika** Norway
28 B6 **Husum** Denmark
30 E1 **Husum** W Germany
131 H6 **Husvik** S Georgia
58 D2 **Hutag** Mongolia
69 D12 **Hutanopan** Sumatra
109 O10 **Hutchins** Texas U.S.A.
107 N3 **Hutchinson** Kansas U.S.A.
99 M5 **Hutchinson** Minnesota U.S.A.
113 G10 **Hutchinsons I** Florida U.S.A.
103 N7 **Hutch Mt** Arizona U.S.A.
68 D4 **Huthi** Burma
59 K2 **Hutou** China
110 J2 **Hutsonville** Illinois U.S.A.
38 H7 **Hüttau** Austria
21 L5 **Hutte, la** France
37 L4 **Hüttenbach** W Germany
38 L8 **Hüttenberg** Austria
36 G3 **Hüttengesäss** W Germany
37 P6 **Hutthurm** W Germany
111 D8 **Huttig** Arkansas U.S.A.
109 K5 **Hutto** Texas U.S.A.
6 L1 **Hutton** *oil rig* North Sea
141 J7 **Hutton, Mt** Queensland Australia
143 E6 **Hutton Ra** Western Australia Australia
94 G8 **Huttonsville** West Virginia U.S.A.
40 G3 **Huttwil** Switzerland
66 D3 **Hutubi** China
58 F4 **Hutuo He** *R* China
73 L8 **Huvadu Atoll** Maldives
79 G3 **Huwayz, Al** Syria
118 D7 **Huxley** Alberta Canada
142 F4 **Huxley, Mt** Western Australia Australia
144 B6 **Huxley, Mt** New Zealand
116 R6 **Huxley, Mt** Alaska U.S.A.
22 J3 **Huy** Belgium
67 G1 **Huzhou** China
27 E12 **Hvaler** *isld* Norway
28 C3 **Hvalpsund** Denmark
115 M2 **Hvalsund** *Sd* Greenland
28 C3 **Hvam** Denmark
42 H5 **Hvar** *isld* Yugoslavia
42 G5 **Hvar** Yugoslavia
28 S10 **Hveragerdhi** Iceland
28 S9 **Hveravellir** Iceland
28 B3 **Hvidbjerg** Denmark
28 B6 **Hviding** Denmark
28 E4 **Hvilsager** Denmark
28 D3 **Hvilsom** Denmark
28 E4 **Hvilsted** Denmark
28 S9 **Hvita** *R* Iceland
27 E12 **Hvitsten** Norway
27 D12 **Hvittingfoss** Norway
Hwainan *see* **Huainan**
89 E2 **Hwange** Zimbabwe

Jiamusi — Kalibek, Oz

41

65 H1 **Jiamusi** China
67 E3 **Ji'an** China
65 G4 **Ji'an** China
65 F4 **Jianchang** China
65 D4 **Jianchang** China
67 F2 **Jiande** China
67 B2 **Jiang'an** China
67 B2 **Jiangbei** China
68 E1 **Jiangcheng** China
67 C3 **Jiangdong** China
67 F1 **Jiangdu** China
67 C6 **Jianghong** China
67 D4 **Jianghua** China
67 B2 **Jiangjin** China
Jiangkou *see* **Fengkai**
67 C3 **Jiangkou** China
67 D1 **Jiangkou** China
67 F3 **Jiangle** China
67 D1 **Jiangling** China
67 D5 **Jiangmen** China
67 F1 **Jiangpu** China
67 F2 **Jiangshan** China
58 G5 **Jiangsu** *prov* China
67 E3 **Jiangxi** *prov* China
65 B7 **Jiang Xian** China
67 F1 **Jiangxiang** China
67 G1 **Jiangyin** China
67 D4 **Jiangyong** China
67 A1 **Jiangyou** China
67 C3 **Jianhe** China
67 D2 **Jianli** China
67 E3 **Jianning** China
67 F3 **Jian'ou** China
65 D4 **Jianping** China
65 D5 **Jianping** China
67 C1 **Jianshi** China
67 A5 **Jianshui** China
67 F3 **Jianyang** China
58 D5 **Jianyang** China
65 B6 **Jiaocheng** China
59 J3 **Jiaohe** China
65 B6 **Jiaokou** China
67 E4 **Jiaoling** China
65 E7 **Jiaonan** China
65 D6 **Jiao Xian** China
58 F4 **Jiaozuo** China
65 G3 **Jiapigou** China
58 G5 **Jiashan** China
67 G1 **Jiashan** China
57 H5 **Jiashi** China
65 D7 **Jiawang** China
65 B7 **Jia Xian** China
65 A5 **Jia Xian** China
59 H5 **Jiaxing** China
67 C4 **Jiaya** China
59 K2 **Jiayin** China
67 D2 **Jiayu** China
58 C4 **Jiayuguan** China
65 E7 **Jiazohou Wan** *B* China
77 B7 **Jiban, Al** Saudi Arabia
129 J7 **Jibao, Serra do** *mts* Brazil
88 G6 **Jibondo** *isld* Tanzania
48 H3 **Jibou** Romania
67 B3 **Jichang** China
31 J5 **Jičin** Czechoslovakia
86 G1 **Jiddah** Saudi Arabia
65 H2 **Jidong** China
Jiehu *see* **Yinan**
26 L2 **Jiekkevarre** *mt* Norway
67 E5 **Jieshi** China
67 E5 **Jieshi Wan** *B* China
26 O2 **Jiesjavrre** *L* Norway
67 E5 **Jiexi** China
65 B6 **Jiexiu** China
143 D6 **Jiggalong** Western Australia Australia
100 K9 **Jiggs** Nevada U.S.A.
67 E1 **Jigong Shan** *mt* China
79 H4 **Jihar, Wādī el** *watercourse* Syria
31 J6 **Jihlava** Czechoslovakia
31 H6 **Jihočesky** *reg* Czechoslovakia
31 J6 **Jihomoravský** *reg* Czechoslovakia
85 F1 **Jijel** Algeria
48 L3 **Jijia** *R* Romania
86 H4 **Jijiga** Ethiopia
80 G3 **Jijjin** Jordan
17 G6 **Jijona** Spain
48 K6 **Jilava** Romania
86 H5 **Jilib** Somalia
65 G3 **Jilin** China
59 H2 **Jilin** *prov* China
65 F3 **Jilin Hada Ling** *mt ra* China
59 H1 **Jiliu He** *R* China
17 G4 **Jiloca** *R* Spain
116 M3 **Jim** *R* Alaska U.S.A.
86 G4 **Jima** Ethiopia
69 G14 **Jimar** Sumatra
142 F5 **Jimberingga** Western Australia Australia
48 F5 **Jimbolia** Romania
141 L8 **Jimboomba** Queensland Australia
16 D8 **Jimena de la Frontera** Spain
124 G4 **Jiménez** Mexico
140 C2 **Jim Jim Cr** N Terr Australia
65 E6 **Jimo** China
65 C6 **Jinan** China
65 B7 **Jincheng** China
139 J6 **Jindabyne** New South Wales Australia
37 O3 **Jindřichovice** Czechoslovakia
31 J6 **Jindřichův Hradec** Czechoslovakia
67 E2 **Jing'an** China
67 F1 **Jingde** China
67 F2 **Jingdezhen** China
Jingfeng *see* **Hexigten Qi**
65 D5 **Jinghai** China
65 E6 **Jinghaiwei** China
66 C3 **Jinghe** China
58 E5 **Jing He** *R* China
68 E2 **Jinghong** China
67 G1 **Jingjiang** China
65 B5 **Jingle** China
67 D1 **Jingmen** China
Jingping *see* **Pinglu**
65 G2 **Jingpo** China
65 G3 **Jingpo Hu** *L* China
67 D1 **Jingshan** China
58 F5 **Jing Shan** *mt ra* China
58 D4 **Jingtai** China
67 F1 **Jing Xian** China
65 C6 **Jing Xian** China
59 H2 **Jingxing** China
67 A2 **Jingyan** China
65 A7 **Jingyang** China
65 G3 **Jingyu** China
58 D4 **Jingyuan** China
Jingzhou *see* **Jiangling**
67 F2 **Jinhua** China
65 C7 **Jining** China
65 B4 **Jining** Nei Monggol Zizhiqu China
88 D1 **Jinja-Bugembe** Uganda
67 E2 **Jin Jiang** *R* China
67 C3 **Jin Jiang** *R* China
67 F4 **Jinjiang** China
67 D2 **Jinjing** China
67 E1 **Jinkou** China
65 E6 **Jinkou** China
67 F4 **Jinlong Jiang** *R* China
67 C7 **Jinmu Jiao** China
68 J3 **Jinmu Jiao** *C* China
125 M3 **Jinotega** Nicaragua
125 L4 **Jinotepe** Nicaragua
68 F1 **Jinping** China
67 C3 **Jinping** China
Jinsha *see* **Nantong**
67 B3 **Jinsha** China
58 C6 **Jinsha Jiang** *R* China
Jinshan *see* **Harqin Qi**
67 G1 **Jinshan** China
67 D2 **Jinshi** China
67 F1 **Jintan** China
67 A1 **Jintang** China
67 C5 **Jintian Shuiku** *res* China
71 F5 **Jintotolo** *isld* Philippines
71 F5 **Jintotolo Ch** Philippines
67 B5 **Jinxi** China
67 F3 **Jin Xi** China
67 E3 **Jinxi** China
59 H3 **Jinxi** China
67 E2 **Jinxian** China
65 C5 **Jin Xian** China
65 E5 **Jin Xian** China
65 E4 **Jin Xian** China
65 C7 **Jinxiang** China
67 G3 **Jinxiang** China
67 C4 **Jinxiu** China
67 G2 **Jinyun** China
67 E1 **Jinzhai** China
65 E4 **Jinzhou** China
65 E5 **Jinzhou Wan** *B* China
128 B4 **Jipijapa** Ecuador
126 F4 **Jiquaní** Cuba
130 H5 **Jiquitaia** Brazil
77 C7 **Jirāb, Al** *isld* U.A.E.
143 F9 **Jirina Rockholes** *rockhole* Western Australia Australia
65 D2 **Jirin Gol** China
37 P3 **Jirkov** Czechoslovakia
48 L5 **Jirlău** Romania
86 A2 **Jirriiban** Somalia
65 A7 **Jishan** China
67 C2 **Jishou** China
67 E3 **Jishui** China
79 G3 **Jisr ash Shughūr** Syria
16 C2 **Jistredo, Sa. de** *mts* Spain
143 C10 **Jitarning** Western Australia Australia
Jitian *see* **Lianshan**
69 E9 **Jitra** Malaysia
48 H6 **Jiu** *R* Romania
Jiucheng *see* **Wucheng**
67 A1 **Jiuding Shan** *mt* China
67 E2 **Jiujiang** China
58 G6 **Jiujiang** China
67 D1 **Jiukou** China
67 E4 **Jiulian Shan** *mts* China
67 E2 **Jiuling Shan** *mt ra* China
58 C4 **Jiuquan** China
65 E6 **Jiurongcheng** China
59 J3 **Jiutai** China
67 C4 **Jiuwan Dashan** *mts* China
65 C5 **Jiuwuqing** China
65 C5 **Jiuxincheng** China
67 B4 **Jiuxu** China
67 F1 **Jiuyuhang** China
67 B4 **Jiuzhou** China
77 G7 **Jiwani** Iran
74 B10 **Jiwani** Pakistan
67 F1 **Jixi** China
65 H2 **Jixi** China
65 A6 **Ji Xian** China
65 C7 **Ji Xian** China
65 D4 **Ji Xian** China
65 C6 **Ji Xian** China
59 K2 **Jixian** China
65 D6 **Jiyang** China
65 B7 **Jiyuan** China
79 F7 **Jiza** Jordan
80 G7 **Jiza** Jordan
65 C6 **Jize** China
31 H5 **Jizera** *R* Czechoslovakia
60 G10 **Jizō zaki** *C* Japan
86 E1 **J. Kissu** *mt* Sudan
120 G1 **Joab L** Ontario Canada
130 D10 **Joaçaba** Brazil
33 T7 **Joachimsthal** East Germany
130 H5 **Joaíma** Brazil
85 A6 **Joal-Fadiout** Senegal
129 L5 **Joao Camara** Brazil
129 J4 **João Coelho** Brazil
131 H4 **João Maria, Albardão do** Brazil
130 E10 **João Paulo** *R* Brazil
130 J9 **João Pessoa** Brazil
130 F5 **João Pinheiro** Brazil
111 B10 **Joaquin** Texas U.S.A.
126 F4 **Jobabo** Cuba
61 O9 **Jōban** Japan
71 G6 **Jobo Pt** Mindanao Philippines
20 G2 **Jobourg** France
102 F2 **Job Pk** Nevada U.S.A.
120 D2 **Jobrin** Ontario Canada
38 F7 **Jochberg** Austria
16 E7 **Jódar** Spain
74 E5 **Jodhpur** India
74 D7 **Jodiya Bandar** India
22 H2 **Jodoigne** Belgium
123 S4 **Joe Batt's Arm** Newfoundland Canada
29 O9 **Joensuu** Finland
106 H2 **Joes** Colorado U.S.A.
26 G6 **Joeström** Sweden
61 M8 **Jōetsu** Japan
87 F10 **Jofane** Mozambique
106 E7 **Joffre** New Mexico U.S.A.
117 Q10 **Joffre, Mt** British Columbia Canada
61 L9 **Joganji** *R* Japan
75 M5 **Jogbani** India
65 C3 **Jogdor** China
52 C5 **Jõgeva** U.S.S.R.
122 H8 **Joggins** Nova Scotia Canada
74 G3 **Jogindarnagar** India
120 E2 **Jog L** Ontario Canada
38 N7 **Joglland** Austria
61 K9 **Jōhana** Japan
32 J9 **Johannaberg** W Germany
89 A1 **Johannesburg** S Africa
102 G6 **Johannesburg** California U.S.A.
37 O3 **Johanngeorgenstadt** East Germany
115 M2 **Johan Pen** Northwest Territories Canada
60 F13 **Jōhen** Japan
116 L3 **John** *R* Alaska U.S.A.
122 J8 **John, C** Nova Scotia Canada
127 M2 **John Crow Mts** Jamaica
100 G5 **John Day** Oregon U.S.A.
100 E4 **John Day** *R* Oregon U.S.A.
100 E5 **John Day Fossil Beds Nat. Mon.** Oregon U.S.A.
117 Q6 **John d'Or Prairie** Alberta Canada
113 G9 **John F. Kennedy Space Center** Florida U.S.A.
94 J10 **John H. Kerr Res** N Carolina/Virg U.S.A.
106 H3 **John Martin Res** Colorado U.S.A.
142 G3 **John,Mt** Western Australia Australia
15 E2 **John O'Groats** Scotland
107 P3 **John Redmond Res** Kansas U.S.A.
107 J4 **Johnson** Kansas U.S.A.
99 K9 **Johnson** Nebraska U.S.A.
94 J5 **Johnsonburg** Pennsylvania U.S.A.
95 M4 **Johnson City** New York U.S.A.
94 E10 **Johnson City** Tennessee U.S.A.
109 J5 **Johnson City** Texas U.S.A.
99 S6 **Johnson Cr** Wisconsin U.S.A.
117 G5 **Johnsons Crossing** Yukon Territory Canada
127 P4 **Johnsons Pt** Antigua W Indies
112 H4 **Johnsonville** South Carolina U.S.A.
112 F4 **Johnston** South Carolina U.S.A.
8 A4 **Johnston** Wales
110 H4 **Johnston City** Illinois U.S.A.
15 D5 **Johnstone** Scotland
117 K10 **Johnstone Str** British Columbia Canada
88 B7 **Johnston Falls** Zambia
143 D9 **Johnston,L** Western Australia Australia
143 C8 **Johnston Ra** Western Australia Australia
14 E3 **Johnstown** Ireland
98 F7 **Johnstown** Nebraska U.S.A.
95 N4 **Johnstown** New York U.S.A.
94 E6 **Johnstown** Ohio U.S.A.
94 J6 **Johnstown** Pennsylvania U.S.A.
94 E9 **John W Flannagan Res** Virginia U.S.A.
61 P5 **Jōhōji** Japan
69 F12 **Johor** Malaysia
69 F12 **Johor Baharo** Malaysia
37 P2 **Jöhstadt** East Germany
52 C5 **Jõhvi** U.S.S.R.
18 H5 **Joigny** France
110 F6 **Joiner** Arkansas U.S.A.
130 E10 **Joinville** Brazil
19 J4 **Joinville** France
146 D3 **Joinville I** Antarctica
125 K8 **Jojutla** Mexico
26 N5 **Jokk** Sweden
26 L5 **Jokkmokk** Sweden
27 C10 **Jokuleggi** *mt* Norway
29 T9 **Jökulsa á Fjöllum** *R* Iceland
29 T9 **Jökulsa o Bru** *R* Iceland
78 K2 **Jolfā** Iran
99 S8 **Joliet** Illinois U.S.A.
101 Q4 **Joliet** Montana U.S.A.
121 R6 **Joliette** Quebec Canada
119 U10 **Joliette** North Dakota U.S.A.
142 A1 **Jolimont** *dist* Perth, W Aust Australia
99 M7 **Jolley** Iowa U.S.A.
117 S3 **Jolly L** Northwest Territories Canada
71 E7 **Jolo** Philippines
102 C6 **Jolon** California U.S.A.
26 B10 **Jölstervatn** *L* Norway
26 G7 **Joma** *mt* Norway
29 H11 **Jomala** Finland
71 F3 **Jomalig** *isld* Luzon Philippines
70 O9 **Jombang** Java
66 F5 **Jomda** China
71 A3 **Jome** Indonesia
27 D13 **Jomfruland** *isld* Norway
52 B6 **Jonava** U.S.S.R.
22 F5 **Jonchery-sur-Vesle** France
7 E13 **Jones Bank** Atlantic Oc
110 F6 **Jonesboro** Arkansas U.S.A.
111 M8 **Jonesboro** Georgia U.S.A.
110 G4 **Jonesboro** Illinois U.S.A.
109 P3 **Jonesboro** Louisiana U.S.A.
95 U2 **Jonesboro** Maine U.S.A.
112 H2 **Jonesboro** North Carolina U.S.A.
100 H6 **Jonesboro** Oregon U.S.A.
112 E1 **Jonesboro** Tennessee U.S.A.
109 K4 **Jonesboro** Texas U.S.A.
116 N1 **Jones Is** Alaska U.S.A.
146 B7 **Jones Mts** Antarctica
95 U2 **Jonesport** Maine U.S.A.
83 M9 **Jones Pt** Christmas I Indian Oc
115 L2 **Jones Sound** Northwest Territories Canada
111 F7 **Jonestown** Mississippi U.S.A.
94 B7 **Jonesville** Indiana U.S.A.
111 E10 **Jonesville** Louisiana U.S.A.
94 C5 **Jonesville** Michigan U.S.A.
112 F3 **Jonesville** South Carolina U.S.A.
94 D10 **Jonesville** Virginia U.S.A.
86 F4 **Jonglei** *prov* Sudan
52 B6 **Joniskis** U.S.S.R.
27 G14 **Jönköping** Sweden
27 G14 **Jönköping** *county* Sweden
121 T4 **Jonquière** Quebec Canada
29 K4 **Jönstorp** Sweden
18 E7 **Jonzac** France
110 B4 **Joplin** Missouri U.S.A.
101 P1 **Joplin** Montana U.S.A.
80 B5 **Joppa** Israel
110 F4 **Joppa** Illinois U.S.A.
141 H6 **Jordan** *R* Queensland Australia
80 F1 **Jordan** *R* Israel/Jordan
80 **Jordan** *kingdom* S W Asia
99 N5 **Jordan** Minnesota U.S.A.
101 T2 **Jordan** Montana U.S.A.
95 L3 **Jordan** New York U.S.A.
100 H7 **Jordan** *R* Oregon U.S.A.
129 K7 **Jordânia** Brazil
122 G9 **Jordan L** Nova Scotia Canada
111 K9 **Jordan L** Alabama U.S.A.
48 F1 **Jordanow** Poland
100 H7 **Jordan Valley** Oregon U.S.A.
130 D9 **Jordão, R** Brazil
28 C3 **Jordbro Å** *R* Denmark
33 R5 **Jördenstorf** East Germany
27 F10 **Jordet** Norway
28 E6 **Jordløse** Denmark
28 C5 **Jordrup** Denmark
28 B6 **Jordsand** *isld* Denmark
26 P2 **Jorgastak** Norway
133 B8 **Jorge Montt, I** Chile
75 Q5 **Jorhat** India
32 L5 **Jork** W Germany
57 F6 **Jorm** Afghanistan
26 G7 **Jormlien** Sweden
26 L6 **Jörn** Sweden
106 C9 **Jornada del Muerto** *reg* New Mexico U.S.A.
27 B12 **Jörpeland** Norway
21 K4 **Jort** France
85 F7 **Jos** Nigeria
71 G8 **Jose Abad Santos** Mindanao Philippines
133 C6 **José de San Martin** Argentina
129 J8 **José dos Campos** Brazil
130 C5 **Joselândia** Brazil
133 E5 **José Maria Blanco** Argentina
27 B12 **Josenfjord** *inlet* Norway
71 F3 **Jose Pañganiban** Philippines
100 J4 **Joseph** Idaho U.S.A.
100 H4 **Joseph** Oregon U.S.A.
142 G2 **Joseph Bonaparte G** Australia
142 G2 **Joseph Bonaparte Gulf** Australia
103 O7 **Joseph City** Arizona U.S.A.
6 M6 **Josephine** *oil rig* North Sea
115 N7 **Joseph L** Labrador, Nfld Canada
123 K4 **Joseph Pt** Anticosti I, Quebec
144 B6 **Josephville** New Zealand
61 M9 **Jō-Shin-Etsu Nat. Park** Japan
109 K3 **Joshua** Texas U.S.A.
102 H7 **Joshua Tree** California U.S.A.
21 O6 **Josnes** France
36 H3 **Jossatal** W Germany
20 E6 **Josselin** France
26 E7 **Jössund** Nord-Tröndelag Norway
26 D8 **Jössund** Sör-Tröndelag Norway
26 B10 **Jostedal** Norway
26 B10 **Jostedalsbreen** *gla* Norway
48 F2 **Josvafö** Hungary
26 N2 **Jotkajavrre** Norway
27 C10 **Jotunheimen** *mt* Norway
79 F5 **Jouaiya** Lebanon
21 C4 **Jouars** France
21 K4 **Joué-du-Bois** France
21 M7 **Joué-lès-Tours** France
20 H7 **Joué-sur-Erdre** France
19 K3 **Jœuf** France
29 N6 **Joukokylä** Finland
113 J12 **Joulters Cays** *islds* Bahamas
79 F5 **Jôunié** Lebanon
109 J7 **Jourdanton** Texas U.S.A.
25 E3 **Joure** Netherlands
118 B3 **Joussard** Alberta Canada
121 M3 **Joutel** Quebec Canada
29 M10 **Joutsa** Finland
29 N5 **Joutsijärvi** Finland
40 D4 **Joux, L.de** Switzerland
21 O4 **Jouy** France
21 O6 **Jouy-le-Potier** France
126 D3 **Jovellanos** Cuba
75 P6 **Jowai** India
77 J **Jowzjān** *prov* Afghanistan
14 B3 **Joyce's Country** Ireland
117 G4 **Joy, Mt** Yukon Territory Canada
60 C3 **Jōzankei** Japan
31 N4 **Józefów** Poland
110 K5 **J. Percy Priest L** Tennessee U.S.A.
71 E3 **Ju** *isld* Indonesia
124 H5 **Juan Aldama** Mexico
65 C7 **Juancheng** China
141 J7 **Juandah** *R* Queensland Australia
127 K2 **Juan de Bolas** *pk* Jamaica
100 A1 **Juan de Fuca, Str. of** Canada/U.S.A.
87 G11 **Juan de Nova** *isld* Madagascar
133 A9 **Juan Fernández, Is** Pacific Oc
127 N9 **Juangriego** Venezuela
88 G6 **Juani** *isld* Tanzania
128 C5 **Juanjui** Peru
29 N8 **Juankoski** Finland
44 B4 **Juan les Pins** France
124 E2 **Juan M. Ortíz** Mexico
131 B2 **Juan Soldado, C.de** Chile
133 B7 **Juan Stuven, I** Chile
133 F5 **Juárez** Argentina
103 J9 **Juárez, Sa** *ra* Mexico
129 K5 **Juazeiro** Brazil
130 G9 **Juàzeiro do Norte** Brazil
86 F5 **Juba** Sudan
146 D3 **Jubany** *Argentina Base* Antarctica
77 A6 **Jubayl, Al** Saudi Arabia
80 G5 **Jubba** Jordan
86 H5 **Jubba** *R* Somalia
80 G1 **Jubbāta el Khashab** Syria
123 R5 **Jubilee L** Newfoundland Canada
143 F8 **Jubilee Lake** Western Australia Australia
102 H6 **Jubilee Peak** California U.S.A.
21 K5 **Jublains** France
85 B3 **Juby, Cap** *C* Morocco
17 F5 **Júcar** *R* Spain
36 B1 **Jüchen** W Germany
124 H7 **Juchipila** Mexico
125 M9 **Juchitán** Mexico
124 H7 **Juchitlán** Mexico
129 K7 **Jucurucú** *R* Brazil
98 H3 **Jud** North Dakota U.S.A.
99 R7 **Juda** Wisconsin U.S.A.
80 B7 **Judaea** Israel
79 G5 **Judaydat al Wadī** Syria
123 S6 **Jude I** Newfoundland Canada
80 D2 **Judeida** Israel
37 L3 **Judenbach** East Germany
38 L7 **Judenburg** Austria
146 B16 **Judge and Clerk Is** *islds* S Pacific Oc
123 L8 **Judique** C Breton I, Nova Scotia
101 Q2 **Judith** *R* Montana U.S.A.
101 Q2 **Judith Basin** *reg* Montana U.S.A.
101 Q3 **Judith Gap** Montana U.S.A.
98 E3 **Judson** North Dakota U.S.A.
Juegang *see* **Rudong**
28 E5 **Juelsminde** Denmark
130 H5 **Juerana** Brazil
128 F4 **Jufari** *R* Brazil
84 F4 **Jufrah Oasis, Al** Libya
20 F5 **Jugon-les-Lacs** France
65 E4 **Juhua Dao** *isld* China
21 H6 **Juigné-des-Moutiers** France
18 F7 **Juillac** France
21 P4 **Juine** *R* France
32 E5 **Juist** *isld* W Germany
32 F5 **Juist** W Germany
129 K8 **Juiz de Fora** Brazil
65 D3 **Jujinchang** China
69 E13 **Jujuhan** *R* Sumatra
19 O12 **Jujurieux** France
128 E8 **Jujuy** *prov* Argentina
26 L7 **Juken** Sweden
26 L4 **Jukkasjärvi** Sweden
67 D3 **Jukoupu** China
26 H6 **Juktån** *R* Sweden
128 E8 **Julaca** Bolivia
98 D9 **Julesburg** Colorado U.S.A.
128 E7 **Juli** Peru
141 F5 **Julia** *R* Queensland Australia
128 D7 **Juliaca** Peru
141 F5 **Julia Creek** Queensland Australia
100 J3 **Juliaetta** Idaho U.S.A.
102 H8 **Julian** California U.S.A.
115 P5 **Julianehåb** Greenland
14 E3 **Julianstown** Ireland
36 B2 **Jülich** W Germany
42 E2 **Julijske A** *mts* Yugoslavia
124 G3 **Julimes** Mexico
80 D2 **Jūlis** Israel
27 H12 **Julita** Sweden
140 E5 **Julius L.** Queensland Australia
20 G4 **Jullouville** France
28 D4 **Julsø** *L* Denmark
65 C6 **Julu** China
80 G8 **Jumaiyil** Jordan
86 H6 **Jumba** Somalia
117 P10 **Jumbo Mt** British Columbia Canada
21 K7 **Jumelles** France
21 J7 **Jumellière,la** France
22 G3 **Jumet** Belgium
21 M3 **Jumièges** France
17 G6 **Jumilla** Spain
75 K4 **Jumla** Nepal
74 D8 **Junagadh** India
65 D7 **Junan** China
65 D2 **Jun Bulen** China
124 D5 **Juncal** Mexico
131 D8 **Juncal, L** Argentina
108 H5 **Junction** Texas U.S.A.
103 M3 **Junction** Utah U.S.A.
140 C1 **Junction B** N Terr Australia
111 D8 **Junction City** Arkansas U.S.A.
111 M9 **Junction City** Georgia U.S.A.
107 O2 **Junction City** Kansas U.S.A.
110 M4 **Junction City** Kentucky U.S.A.
94 C9 **Junction City** Kentucky U.S.A.
100 B5 **Junction City** Oregon U.S.A.
99 R5 **Junction City** Wisconsin U.S.A.
141 G6 **Jundah** Queensland Australia
65 C4 **Jundu Shan** *mt ra* China
117 F6 **Juneau** Alaska U.S.A.
99 S6 **Juneau** Wisconsin U.S.A.
139 J5 **Junee** New South Wales Australia
113 F10 **June in Winter, L** Florida U.S.A.
102 E4 **June Lake** California U.S.A.
65 A5 **Jungar Qi** China
40 G4 **Jungfrau** *mt* Switzerland
40 G4 **Jungfraujoch** Switzerland
22 L4 **Junglinster** Luxembourg
100 G9 **Jungo** Nevada U.S.A.
98 H9 **Juniata** Nebraska U.S.A.
95 K6 **Juniata** *R* Pennsylvania U.S.A.
131 E5 **Junin** Argentina
128 D7 **Junin** Chile
128 C6 **Junin** Peru
133 C5 **Junin de los Andes** Argentina
94 H8 **Junior** West Virginia U.S.A.
95 T1 **Junior L** Maine U.S.A.
122 E7 **Juniper** New Brunswick Canada
103 L6 **Juniper Mts** Arizona U.S.A.
102 C5 **Junipero Sierra Pk** California U.S.A.
61 O5 **Jūni sho** Japan
22 G5 **Juniville** France
116 O2 **Junjik** *R* Alaska U.S.A.
36 B3 **Jünkerath** W Germany
26 H5 **Junkerdal** Norway
67 A2 **Junlian** China
108 F5 **Juno** Texas U.S.A.
118 K5 **Junor** Saskatchewan Canada
26 M4 **Junosuando** Sweden
26 J8 **Junsele** Sweden
67 E2 **Junshan Hu** *L* China
16 A5 **Junto** *mt* Portugal
65 A5 **Juntuliang** China
100 G6 **Juntura** Oregon U.S.A.
29 O6 **Juntusranta** Finland
29 O9 **Juojärvi** *L* Finland
26 N5 **Juoksengi** Sweden
130 H6 **Juparaña, Lagoa** *L* Brazil
130 D7 **Jupia** Brazil
130 D7 **Jupia Dam** Brazil
22 K2 **Jupille** Belgium
21 L6 **Jupilles** France
113 G11 **Jupiter** Florida U.S.A.
122 J4 **Jupiter R** Quebec Canada
129 J8 **Juquiá** Brazil
86 E4 **Jur** *R* Sudan
40 C4 **Jura** *dept* France
15 C4 **Jura** Scotland
40 F3 **Jura** *canton* Switzerland
128 C2 **Jurado** Colombia
31 L5 **Jura Krakowska** *reg* Poland
130 G5 **Juramento** Brazil
52 B6 **Jurbarkas** U.S.S.R.
12 D5 **Jurby** I of Man U.K.
79 F8 **Jurf ed Darāwīsh** Jordan
65 E2 **Jurh** China
143 B9 **Jurien** Western Australia Australia
143 B9 **Jurien B** Western Australia Australia
48 M6 **Jurilovca** Romania
52 B6 **Jurmala** U.S.S.R.
67 F1 **Jurong** China
38 N9 **Juršinci** Yugoslavia
128 E4 **Juruá** Brazil
128 D5 **Juruá** *R* Brazil
128 G6 **Juruena** Brazil
129 G4 **Juruti** Brazil
29 J9 **Jurva** Finland
61 O5 **Jūsan-ko** *L* Japan
127 N10 **Jusepin** Venezuela
79 G4 **Jūsīyah** Syria
19 J5 **Jussey** France
119 S8 **Justice** Manitoba Canada
108 F2 **Justiceburg** Texas U.S.A.
109 K2 **Justin** Texas U.S.A.
133 D4 **Justo Daract** Argentina
128 E5 **Jutaí** Brazil
33 S9 **Jüterbog** East Germany
130 C8 **Juti** Brazil
125 L2 **Juticalpa** Honduras
26 J5 **Jutis** Sweden
Jutland *see* **Jylland**
26 E10 **Jutulhugget** *pass* Norway
146 H6 **Jutulstraumen** *ice stream* Antarctica
29 O8 **Juuka** Finland
29 N10 **Juva** Finland
126 C4 **Juventud, Isla de la** Cuba
21 H5 **Juvigné** France
21 H4 **Juvigny-le-Tertre** France
21 J4 **Juvigny-sous-Andaine** France
21 P4 **Juvisy** France
28 B6 **Juvre** Denmark
70 N9 **Juwana** Java
79 H5 **Juwayf, Al** Syria
65 D7 **Ju Xian** China
65 C7 **Juye** China
77 F2 **Jūymand** Iran
40 A1 **Juzennecourt** France
Jye Kundo *see* **Yushu**
28 B4 **Jylland** *reg* Denmark
29 M9 **Jyväskylä** Finland

K

66 B4 **K2** *mt* Kashmir/China
85 E6 **Ka** *R* Nigeria
102 S11 **Kaaawa** Hawaiian Is
89 B7 **Kaaing Veld** *plateau* S Africa
57 A5 **Kaakhka** U.S.S.R.
102 R11 **Kaala** *pk* Hawaiian Is
26 L4 **Kaalasjarvi** *L* Sweden
135 U6 **Kaalualu** Hawaiian Is
29 N2 **Kaamanen** Finland
86 H6 **Kaambooni** Somalia
89 C7 **Kaap Plato** S Africa
33 O6 **Kaarssen** East Germany
29 N9 **Kaavi** Finland
48 G3 **Kaba** Hungary
70 G7 **Kabaena** *isld* Sulawesi
85 B7 **Kabala** Sierra Leone
86 F5 **Kabalega Falls** Uganda
86 E7 **Kabalo** Zaire
88 A4 **Kabambare** Zaire
69 D11 **Kabanjahe** Sumatra
85 D5 **Kabara** Mali
53 F11 **Kabardino Balkarskaya** U.S.S.R.
88 B3 **Kabare** Zaire
71 F7 **Kabasalang** Philippines
60 C13 **Kaba shima** *isld* Japan
68 C3 **Kabaung** *R* Burma
85 F7 **Kabba** Nigeria
26 G3 **Kabelvåg** *lighthouse* Norway
120 E4 **Kabenung L** Ontario Canada
70 G4 **Kabetan. I** Sulawesi
99 O1 **Kabetogama** Minnesota U.S.A.
99 N1 **Kabetogama L** Minnesota U.S.A.
120 F3 **Kabinakagami** *R* Ontario Canada
86 C7 **Kabinda** Zaire
71 M9 **Kabir** Indonesia
79 F3 **Kabīr** *R* Syria/Lebanon
57 E5 **Kabla** U.S.S.R.
47 J2 **Kableshkovo** Bulgaria
86 C4 **Kabo** Cent Afr Republic
87 D8 **Kabompo** *R* Zambia
70 B4 **Kabong** Sarawak
87 E7 **Kabongo** Zaire
68 C6 **Kabosa I.** Burma
85 G1 **Kaboudia, Rass** *C* Tunisia
52 E5 **Kabozha** U.S.S.R.
80 D1 **Kabri** Israel
77 F1 **Kabūd Gonbad** Iran
71 E2 **Kabugao** Philippines
77 L2 **Kābul** Afghanistan
80 D2 **Kābūl** Israel
88 C2 **Kabula** Uganda
87 E8 **Kabunda** Zaire
88 B7 **Kabunda** Zambia
71 H9 **Kabunduk** Indonesia
86 F2 **Kabushiya** Sudan
88 B9 **Kabwe** Zambia
55 F3 **Kabyrdak** U.S.S.R.
55 D5 **Kabyrga** *R* U.S.S.R.
46 E2 **Kačanik** Yugoslavia
71 B3 **Kacepi** Indonesia
87 F8 **Kachalola** Zambia
74 C7 **Kachchh, Gulf of** India
74 C6 **Kachchh, Rann of** India
116 M7 **Kachemak B** Alaska U.S.A.
100 D2 **Kachess L** Washington U.S.A.
85 F7 **Kachia** Nigeria
75 R5 **Kachin State** *prov* Burma
55 G4 **Kachiry** U.S.S.R.
55 C2 **Kachkanar** U.S.S.R.
56 G4 **Kachug** U.S.S.R.
78 H1 **Kaçkar Dağlar** *mt* Turkey
60 J11 **Kada** Japan
68 C4 **Kadaingti** Burma
86 F5 **Kadam Mt** Uganda
37 P3 **Kadaň** Czechoslovakia
68 D6 **Kadan Kyun** *isld* Burma
70 D7 **Kadapongan** *isld* Indonesia
43 D4 **Kadarkút** Hungary
71 H7 **Kadatung** *isld* Indonesia
41 H2 **Kadelburg** W Germany
61 P13 **Kadena** Okinawa
71 K9 **Kadesa** Indonesia
143 F7 **Kadgo L** Western Australia Australia
78 K5 **Kādhimain** Iraq
74 E7 **Kadi** India
85 C6 **Kadiana** Mali
46 F3 **Kadijica** *mt* Yugoslavia
47 N11 **Kadıköy** Turkey
138 E5 **Kadina** South Australia Australia
74 F9 **Kadirabad** India
47 J8 **Kadirga Burun** *C* Turkey
76 D3 **Kadiri** India
78 F3 **Kadirli** Turkey
70 G7 **Kadjang** Sulawesi
73 L6 **Kadmat** *isld* Lakshadweep Indian Oc
52 F5 **Kadnikov** U.S.S.R.
68 C4 **Kado** Burma
60 E13 **Kadogawa** Japan
98 E6 **Kadoka** South Dakota U.S.A.
89 F2 **Kadoma** Zimbabwe
68 B5 **Kadonkani** Burma
46 E3 **Kadrifakovo** Yugoslavia
86 E3 **Kadugli** Sudan
86 A3 **Kaduna** Nigeria
76 C4 **Kadur** India
52 E5 **Kaduy** U.S.S.R.
56 E5 **Kadyr-Egi-Tayga, Khrebet** *mts* U.S.S.R.
52 F5 **Kadyy** U.S.S.R.
57 H4 **Kadzhi-Say** U.S.S.R.
85 B5 **Kaedi** Mauritania
123 R5 **Kaegudeck L** Newfoundland Canada
86 B3 **Kaélé** Cameroon
145 D1 **Kaeo** New Zealand
28 D6 **Kærum** Denmark
65 G5 **Kaesŏng** N Korea
87 D7 **Kāfakumba** Zaire
85 F7 **Kafanchan** Nigeria
85 A6 **Kaffrine** Senegal
71 C3 **Kafiau** *isld* W Irian
46 G7 **Kafiréos, Porthmós** *str* Greece
46 G6 **Kafirévs, Akr** *C* Greece
26 N2 **Kåfjord** Norway
26 L2 **Kåfjord** *inlet* Norway
80 E1 **Kafra** Lebanon
80 D5 **Kafr 'Abbush** Jordan
80 D5 **Kafr 'Ain** Jordan
79 G3 **Kafr Buhum** Syria
80 F6 **Kafrein** *R* Jordan
79 A7 **Kafr el Dauwâr** Egypt
80 D4 **Kafr-el-Labad** Jordan
79 A7 **Kafr el Sheik** Egypt
79 A8 **Kafr el Zaiyât** Egypt
80 D2 **Kafr Mañdā** Israel
80 D4 **Kafr Qud** Jordan
80 D4 **Kafr Ra'i** Jordan
80 D4 **Kafr Rumman** Jordan
79 G4 **Kafrūn Bashūr** Syria
80 D5 **Kafr Zibad** Jordan
88 B9 **Kafue** Zambia
87 E8 **Kafue Nat. Park** Zambia
87 E7 **Kafulwe** Zambia
55 C4 **Kaga** U.S.S.R.
86 C4 **Kaga Bandoro** Cent Afr Republic
60 G10 **Kagami** Japan
57 C5 **Kagan** U.S.S.R.
116 G7 **Kagati L** Alaska U.S.A.
60 G11 **Kagawa** *prefect* Japan
120 H7 **Kagawong** Ontario Canada
26 M7 **Kåge** Sweden
88 C2 **Kagera National Park** Rwanda
28 J5 **Kagerup** Denmark
120 C2 **Kagianagami L** Ontario Canada
120 D3 **Kagiano L** Ontario Canada
47 M10 **Kâğithane** Turkey
78 J1 **Kagizman** Turkey
69 D13 **Kagologolo** Indonesia
60 D14 **Kagoshima** Japan
48 L5 **Kagul** Moldavskaya S.S.R. U.S.S.R.
48 L5 **Kagul, Ozero** *L* U.S.S.R.
116 L8 **Kaguyak** Alaska U.S.A.
70 D6 **Kahajan** *R* Kalimantan
70 E5 **Kahala** Kalimantan
135 O1 **Kahala Pt** Hawaiian Is
102 S12 **Kahaluu** Hawaiian Is
88 D3 **Kahama** Tanzania
74 C4 **Kahan** Pakistan
102 S11 **Kahana** Hawaiian Is
145 F3 **Kaharoa** *mt* New Zealand
71 A2 **Kahatola** *isld* Halmahera Indonesia
87 C7 **Kahemba** Zaire
102 R12 **Kahe Pt** Hawaiian Is
144 A6 **Kaherekoau Mts** New Zealand
116 M5 **Kahiltna Gl** Alaska U.S.A.
36 G3 **Kahl** *R* W Germany
37 M2 **Kahla** East Germany
36 F1 **Kahler-Asten** *mt* W Germany
100 G3 **Kahlotus** Washington U.S.A.
117 N6 **Kahntah** British Columbia Canada
77 E6 **Kahnuj** Iran
110 E1 **Kahoka** Missouri U.S.A.
61 K9 **Kahoku-gata** *L* Japan
102 V13 **Kahoolawe** *isld* Hawaiian Is
29 J2 **Kahperusvaara** *mt* Finland
78 F3 **Kahramanmaraş** Turkey
135 Q1 **Kahuku** Hawaiian Is
102 S11 **Kahuku Pt** Hawaiian Is
135 T3 **Kahului** Hawaiian Is
Kahutara Pt *see* **Table Cape**
85 E7 **Kaiama** Nigeria
144 D5 **Kaiapoi** New Zealand
119 O1 **Kaiashk** *R* Ontario Canada
103 M5 **Kaibab Plat** Arizona U.S.A.
60 J10 **Kaibara** Japan
103 N5 **Kaibito Plat** Arizona U.S.A.
66 D3 **Kaidu He** *R* China
128 G2 **Kaieteur Falls** Guyana
65 C7 **Kaifeng** China
145 D1 **Kaihu** New Zealand
67 F2 **Kaihua** China
145 E3 **Kai-Iwi** New Zealand
67 B1 **Kaijiang** China
136 G3 **Kai, Kep** *islds* Moluccas Indonesia
145 D1 **Kaikohe** New Zealand
67 B3 **Kaikou** China
144 D5 **Kaikoura** New Zealand
144 D5 **Kaikoura Range** New Zealand
Kailas Range *see* **Gangdisê Shan**
36 G4 **Kailbach** W Germany
67 B3 **Kaili** China
65 E3 **Kailu** China
135 T5 **Kailua** Hawaiian Is
102 S12 **Kailua** Hawaiian Is
145 E2 **Kaimai Ra** New Zealand
46 E4 **Kaïmakchalán** *mt* Greece
136 G2 **Kaimana** W Irian
145 E3 **Kaimanawa Mts** New Zealand
144 C5 **Kaimata** New Zealand
60 D14 **Kaimon-dake** *pk* Japan
135 V5 **Kaimu** Hawaiian Is
27 N13 **Käina** U.S.S.R.
38 M7 **Kainach** *R* Austria
135 U5 **Kainaliu** Hawaiian Is
60 J11 **Kainan** Japan
46 G3 **Kainchal** *mt* Greece
57 G3 **Kainda** U.S.S.R.
68 B2 **Kaing** Burma
145 F3 **Kaingaroa Forest** New Zealand
145 F3 **Kaingaroa Plat.** New Zealand
38 J6 **Kainisch** Austria
85 E6 **Kainji Res** Nigeria
71 H7 **Kaioba** Indonesia
145 E2 **Kaipara Flats** New Zealand
103 N4 **Kaiparowits Plat** Utah U.S.A.
67 D5 **Kaiping** China
65 D5 **Kaiping** China
29 N4 **Kairala** Finland
43 C13 **Kairouan** Tunisia
38 F6 **Kaiser-Gebirge** *mts* Austria
102 E4 **Kaiser Pk** California U.S.A.
36 C3 **Kaisersesch** W Germany
36 D5 **Kaiserslautern** W Germany
40 G1 **Kaiserstuhl** *mt* W Germany
32 E10 **Kaiserswerth** W Germany
60 F11 **Kaita** Japan
145 D1 **Kaitaia** New Zealand
144 B7 **Kaitangata** New Zealand
145 F3 **Kaitawa** New Zealand
145 D4 **Kaiteriteri** New Zealand
74 G4 **Kaithal** India
145 E4 **Kaitoki** New Zealand
Kaitong *see* **Tongyu**
26 L4 **Kaitum** Sweden
26 K4 **Kaitumälven** *R* Sweden
26 K4 **Kaitumj** Sweden
26 L3 **Kaivare** *mt* Sweden
145 E2 **Kaiwaka** New Zealand
71 N9 **Kaiwatu** Indonesia
102 V13 **Kaiwi Ch** Hawaiian Is
67 C1 **Kai Xian** China
67 B3 **Kaiyang** China
59 H3 **Kaiyuan** China
67 A5 **Kaiyuan** China
116 H5 **Kaiyuh Mts** Alaska U.S.A.
60 J11 **Kaizuka** Japan
70 E3 **Kaja** Kalimantan
29 N7 **Kajaani** Finland
141 F5 **Kajabbi** Queensland Australia
77 J3 **Kajaki Dam** Afghanistan
71 L9 **Kajan** *isld* Indonesia
69 E11 **Kajang** Malaysia
88 F2 **Kajiado** Kenya
61 M10 **Kajikazawa** Japan
60 D14 **Kajiki** Japan
71 A2 **Kajoa** *isld* Halmahera Indonesia
86 F5 **Kajo Kaji** Sudan
71 K8 **Kajuadi** *isld* Indonesia
85 F6 **Kajuru** Nigeria
86 F3 **Kaka** Sudan
103 M9 **Kaka** Arizona U.S.A.
70 F3 **Kakaban** *isld* Kalimantan
119 O2 **Kakabeka Falls** Ontario Canada
71 L8 **Kakabia** *isld* Indonesia
140 C2 **Kakadu Nat Park** N Terr Australia
118 J1 **Kakagi L** Ontario Canada
145 E3 **Kakahi** New Zealand
71 G7 **Kakal** *R* Mindanao Philippines
70 F5 **Kakali** Sulawesi
87 D11 **Kakamas** S Africa
88 E1 **Kakamega** Kenya
69 A8 **Kakana** Nicobar Is
144 C6 **Kakanui** New Zealand
135 T3 **Kaka Pt** Hawaiian Is
145 E3 **Kakaramea** New Zealand
85 B7 **Kakata** Liberia
145 E3 **Kakatahi** New Zealand
57 D5 **Kakaydy** U.S.S.R.
60 F11 **Kake** Japan
117 G7 **Kake** Alaska U.S.A.
61 M11 **Kakegawa** Japan
56 E5 **Ka-Khem** *R* U.S.S.R.
116 K7 **Kakhonak** Alaska U.S.A.
54 E10 **Kakhovka** U.S.S.R.
54 E10 **Kakhovskoye Vdkhr** *res* U.S.S.R.
77 F2 **Kakht** Iran
77 B5 **Kākī** Iran
76 F2 **Kākināda** India
117 P5 **Kakisa L** Northwest Territories Canada
61 M8 **Kakizaki** Japan
60 H11 **Kakogawa** Japan
55 E4 **Kak, Oz** *L* U.S.S.R.
85 D7 **Kakpin** Ivory Coast
66 B3 **Kak Shaal Too, Khrebet** *mts* U.S.S.R.
116 Q1 **Kaktovik** Alaska U.S.A.
61 O8 **Kakuda** Japan
61 O6 **Kakumagawa** Japan
61 O6 **Kakunodate** Japan
70 C3 **Kakus** *R* Sarawak
86 E7 **Kakuyu** Zaire
117 O8 **Kakwa** *R* Alberta Canada
48 F3 **Kál** Hungary
43 D13 **Kalaâ Kebira** Tunisia
43 B13 **Kalaat Es Senam** *mt* Tunisia
71 M9 **Kalabahi** Indonesia
46 E5 **Kalabáka** Greece
70 E2 **Kalaban** Sabah
138 F4 **Kalabity** South Australia Australia
87 D8 **Kalabo** Zambia
54 N6 **Kalach** U.S.S.R.
55 F3 **Kalachinsk** U.S.S.R.
53 F9 **Kalach-na-donu** U.S.S.R.
54 N6 **Kalachskaya Vozvyshennost'** *uplands* U.S.S.R.
68 A2 **Kaladan** Burma
121 N8 **Kaladar** Ontario Canada
102 V14 **Kalae** Hawaiian Is
70 G6 **Kalaena** *R* Sulawesi
47 R14 **Kaláfou** Rhodes Greece
68 C1 **Kalagwe** Burma
89 B4 **Kalahari Desert** Botswana
89 B6 **Kalahari Game Res** S Africa
89 B5 **Kalahari Gemsbok Nat. Park** S Africa
57 F5 **Kalai-Khumb** U.S.S.R.
57 B6 **Kala-I-Mor** U.S.S.R.
29 K7 **Kalajoki** Finland
29 L8 **Kalajoki** *R* Finland
58 G1 **Kalakan** U.S.S.R.
135 O1 **Kalalau Lookout** Hawaiian Is
70 G5 **Kalaliok** Sulawesi
74 E1 **Kalam** Pakistan
100 C3 **Kalama** Washington U.S.A.
46 E7 **Kalámai** Greece
Kalamata Greece *see* **Kalámai**
94 B4 **Kalamazoo** Michigan U.S.A.
70 D7 **Kalambau** *isld* Indonesia
87 F7 **Kalambo Falls** Tanzania
46 D6 **Kálamos** *isld* Greece
46 F6 **Kálamos** Greece
143 B9 **Kalamunda** Western Australia Australia
138 E3 **Kalamurra, L** South Australia Australia
143 B9 **Kalannie** Western Australia Australia
29 J11 **Kalanti** Finland
71 K8 **Kalao** *isld* Indonesia
71 G7 **Kalaong** Mindanao Philippines
71 K8 **Kalaotoa** *isld* Indonesia
83 K9 **Kala Oya** *R* Sri Lanka
69 G13 **Kalapa** Indonesia
58 G1 **Kalar** *R* U.S.S.R.
48 L3 **Kalarash** U.S.S.R.
26 H9 **Kälarne** Sweden
83 L9 **Kal Aru** *R* Sri Lanka
74 B4 **Kalat** Pakistan
77 G6 **Kalateh-Masjed** Iran
135 S2 **Kalaupapa** Hawaiian Is
53 F10 **Kalaus** *R* U.S.S.R.
47 R14 **Kalavardha** Rhodes Greece
46 E6 **Kalávrita** Greece
68 C2 **Kalaw** Burma
83 K9 **Kalawewa** Sri Lanka
36 H3 **Kalbach** W Germany
143 A8 **Kalbarri** Western Australia Australia
143 A8 **Kalbarri Nat Park** Western Australia Australia
33 O7 **Kalbe** East Germany
56 B6 **Kalbinskiy Khrebet** *mts* U.S.S.R.
77 F2 **Kalbū** Iran
42 F3 **Kalce** Yugoslavia
55 B5 **Kaldygayty** *R* U.S.S.R.
47 K7 **Kale** Turkey
78 D1 **Kalecik** Turkey
71 H7 **Kaledupa** *isld* Indonesia
68 C5 **Kalegauk I** Burma
88 E6 **Kalehe** Zaire
68 B3 **Kaleindaung** *inlet* Burma
86 D6 **Kalema** Zaire
88 B4 **Kalémié** Zaire
32 K7 **Kalenberg** *reg* W Germany
31 L5 **Kalety** Poland
94 B2 **Kaleva** Michigan U.S.A.
29 P6 **Kalevala** U.S.S.R.
28 S10 **Kalfafell** Iceland
52 E3 **Kalgachikha** U.S.S.R.
Kalgan *see* **Zhangjiakou**
58 G3 **Kalgan** China
143 C10 **Kalgan,R** Western Australia Australia
108 F2 **Kalgary** Texas U.S.A.
116 M6 **Kalgin I** Alaska U.S.A.
143 D9 **Kalgoorlie** Western Australia Australia
46 E4 **Kali** Greece
47 L6 **Kalı** *R* Turkey
46 E6 **Kaliakoúdha** *mt* Greece
47 J1 **Kaliakra, N** Bulgaria
70 K8 **Kalianda** Sumatra
70 O9 **Kalianget** Indonesia
55 F4 **Kalibek, Oz** *L* U.S.S.R.

71 F5 **Kalibo** Philippines
94 C6 **Kalida** Ohio U.S.A.
69 D14 **Kaliet** Indonesia
86 E6 **Kalima** Zaire
70 **Kalimantan** Borneo
70 B4 **Kalimantan Barat** Borneo
70 D6 **Kalimantan Selatan** Kalimantan
70 C5 **Kalimantan Tengah** Kalimantan
70 E3 **Kalimantan Timur** Kalimantan
47 H8 **Kalimnos** *isld* Greece
75 N5 **Kālimpang** India
71 H7 **Kalingsusuh Tk** *B* Indonesia
52 E6 **Kalinin** U.S.S.R.
57 E5 **Kalininabad** U.S.S.R.
27 L17 **Kaliningrad** U.S.S.R.
55 C3 **Kalinino** U.S.S.R.
53 F8 **Kalininsk** U.S.S.R.
52 D6 **Kalininskaya Oblast'** *prov* U.S.S.R.
48 E7 **Kalinovik** Yugoslavia
55 C6 **Kalinovka** U.S.S.R.
48 M1 **Kalinovka** U.S.S.R.
55 D3 **Kalinovo** U.S.S.R.
70 O10 **Kalisat** Java
101 L1 **Kalispell** Montana U.S.A.
31 L4 **Kalisz** Poland
53 F9 **Kalitva** *R* U.S.S.R.
88 C4 **Kaliua** Tanzania
26 N6 **Kalix** Sweden
26 N5 **Kalix älv** *R* Sweden
26 L4 **Kalixfors** Sweden
74 G3 **Kalka** India
55 G5 **Kalkaman** U.S.S.R.
47 K8 **Kalkan** Turkey
25 F5 **Kalkar** W Germany
94 B2 **Kalkaska** Michigan U.S.A.
33 T8 **Kalkberge** East Germany
87 C10 **Kalkfeld** Namibia
Kalkfontein *see* **Tsootsha**
33 O5 **Kalkhorst** East Germany
47 J5 **Kalkım** Turkey
89 A5 **Kalk Plateau** Namibia
87 C10 **Kalkrand** Namibia
83 L10 **Kalkudah** Sri Lanka
138 D2 **Kallakoopah** *R* South Australia Australia
52 C5 **Kallaste** U.S.S.R.
29 N9 **Kallavesi** *L* Finland
33 O7 **Kallehne** East Germany
32 H10 **Kallenhardt** W Germany
32 J8 **Kalletal** W Germany
37 P2 **Kallich** Czechoslovakia
47 V16 **Kallidhiés** Rhodes Greece
80 F7 **Kallirhoe Hot Sp** Jordan
46 D3 **Kallmet** Albania
37 M5 **Kallmünz** W Germany
47 H5 **Kalloni** Greece
47 H5 **Kallonis Kólpos** Greece
26 F8 **Kallsjön** Sweden
29 O5 **Kallunki** Finland
57 D2 **Kalmakkyrgan** *R* U.S.S.R.
27 H14 **Kalmar** *county* Sweden
27 H15 **Kalmar** Sweden
27 H15 **Kalmarsund** *chan* Sweden
36 E5 **Kalmit** *mt* W Germany
53 E10 **Kal'mius** U.S.S.R.
22 H1 **Kalmthout** Belgium
83 L10 **Kalmunai** Sri Lanka
55 B6 **Kalmykovo** U.S.S.R.
53 G9 **Kalmytskaya A.S.S.R** U.S.S.R.
48 E4 **Kalocsa** Hungary
46 G2 **Kalofer** Bulgaria
135 S3 **Kalohi Ch** Hawaiian Is
79 C3 **Kalokhorio** Cyprus
74 E7 **Kalol** India
87 E9 **Kalomo** Zambia
46 F4 **Kalón** Greece
99 P8 **Kalona** Iowa U.S.A.
117 K9 **Kalone Peak** British Columbia Canada
71 F3 **Kalongkooan** *isld* Luzon Philippines
71 F3 **Kalotkot** *isld* Luzon Philippines
28 E4 **Kalø Vig** *B* Denmark
46 G2 **Kaloyanovc** Bulgaria
73 L6 **Kalpeni I** Lakshadweep Indian Oc
74 H5 **Kalpi** India
57 J4 **Kalpin** China
83 J9 **Kalpitiya** Sri Lanka
28 E5 **Kalsenakke** Denmark
77 E1 **Kāl-Shūr, Rūd-e** *R* Iran
6 F1 **Kalsoy** *isld* Faeroes
116 H4 **Kaltag** Alaska U.S.A.
56 C4 **Kaltan** U.S.S.R.
41 M3 **Kalte Berg** *mt* Austria
37 M4 **Kaltenbrunn** W Germany
32 L5 **Kaltenkirchen** W Germany
37 J2 **Kaltennordheim** East Germany
37 J2 **Kaltensundheim** East Germany
54 H2 **Kaluga** U.S.S.R.
83 K11 **Kalu Ganga** *R* Sri Lanka
70 E7 **Kalukalukuang** *isld* Indonesia
70 F6 **Kaluku** Sulawesi
70 D3 **Kalulong, Bt** *mt* Sarawak
87 E8 **Kalulushi** Zambia
142 F2 **Kalumburu** Western Australia Australia
70 F6 **Kalumpang** Sulawesi
28 G5 **Kalundborg** Denmark
28 F5 **Kalundborg Fjord** *inlet* Denmark
88 D6 **Kalungu** *R* Zambia
88 B6 **Kalungwishi** *R* Zambia
70 E1 **Kalupis Falls** Sabah
48 J1 **Kalush** U.S.S.R.
31 N3 **Kałuszyn** Poland
83 J11 **Kalutara** Sri Lanka
53 D7 **Kaluzhskaya Oblast'** *prov* U.S.S.R.
31 O1 **Kalvarija** U.S.S.R.
28 J6 **Kalvehave** Denmark
29 K8 **Kälviä** Finland
29 N10 **Kalvitsa** Finland
29 L10 **Kalvola** Finland
28 B6 **Kalvslund** Denmark
38 L7 **Kalwang** Austria
55 C1 **Kal'ya** U.S.S.R.
74 E9 **Kalyan** India
76 C3 **Kalyāndurg** India
74 G10 **Kalyani** India
52 H5 **Kama** *R* U.S.S.R.
55 G3 **Kama** Novosibirskaya obl U.S.S.R.
55 D1 **Kama** Sverdlovskaya obl U.S.S.R.
86 B1 **Kamada** Niger
60 E13 **Kamae** Japan
61 P6 **Kamaishi** Japan
61 N13 **Kama iwa** *islds* Iwo Jima Japan
135 S2 **Kamakou** *pk* Hawaiian Is
61 N10 **Kamakura** Japan
70 O9 **Kamal** Indonesia
74 E3 **Kamalia** Pakistan
135 S3 **Kamalo** Hawaiian Is
85 B7 **Kamalu** Sierra Leone
68 C4 **Kamamaung** Burma
78 D2 **Kaman** Turkey
87 D8 **Kamapanda** Zambia
72 E5 **Kamarān** *isld* S Yemen
77 K2 **Kamard** *reg* Afghanistan
74 H9 **Kamareddi** India
75 N7 **Kamarhati** India
74 B9 **Kamarod** Pakistan
101 O9 **Kamas** Utah U.S.A.
87 E9 **Kamativi** Zimbabwe
119 P2 **Kamatsi L** Saskatchewan Canada
60 H11 **Kamatsushima** Japan
143 D9 **Kambalda** Western Australia Australia
52 G1 **Kambal'nitskiye Koshki, Ova** *islds* U.S.S.R.
76 C6 **Kambam** India
69 E13 **Kambang** Sumatra
70 M9 **Kambangan** *isld* Java
71 H7 **Kambara** Indonesia
52 H6 **Kambarka** U.S.S.R.
85 B7 **Kambia** Sierra Leone
83 M8 **Kambling** *isld* Cocos Is Indian Oc
65 H4 **Kambo Ho** *mt* N Korea
70 F6 **Kambuno** *mt* Sulawesi
51 Q3 **Kamchatka** *pen* U.S.S.R.
51 Q3 **Kamchatskaya Oblast'** *prov* U.S.S.R.
47 J1 **Kamchiya** *R* Bulgaria
47 H2 **Kamchiya, Yazovir** *res* Bulgaria
52 F4 **Kamchuga** U.S.S.R.
61 N8 **Kameda** Japan
100 G4 **Kamela** Oregon U.S.A.
32 G9 **Kamen** W Germany
52 D6 **Kamenets** U.S.S.R.
48 K2 **Kamenets-Podol'skiy** U.S.S.R.
46 D4 **Kamenicë** Albania
42 F4 **Kamenjak. Rt** *C* Yugoslavia
52 F2 **Kamenka** U.S.S.R.
52 H1 **Kamenka** U.S.S.R.
56 E2 **Kamenka** *R* U.S.S.R.
53 B8 **Kamenka-Bugskaya** U.S.S.R.
54 F9 **Kamenka-Dneprovskaya** U.S.S.R.
56 B4 **Kamen'na-Obi** U.S.S.R.
29 O11 **Kamennogorsk** U.S.S.R.
52 D3 **Kamennoye, Oz** *L* U.S.S.R.
47 J2 **Kameno** Bulgaria
54 M9 **Kamenolomni** U.S.S.R.
59 K3 **Kamen Rybolov** U.S.S.R.
56 G5 **Kamensk** U.S.S.R.
55 E3 **Kamenskoye** U.S.S.R.
53 F9 **Kamensk-Shakhtinskiy** U.S.S.R.
55 D3 **Kamensk-Ural'skiy** U.S.S.R.
31 O3 **Kamenyuki** U.S.S.R.
30 H4 **Kamenz** East Germany
61 J10 **Kameoka** Japan
12 C2 **Kames** Scotland
54 N1 **Kameshkovo** U.S.S.R.
74 H3 **Kamet** *mt* India/Xizang Zizhiqu
61 K11 **Kameyama** Japan
100 J3 **Kamiah** Idaho U.S.A.
31 K2 **Kamien** Poland
31 J5 **Kamienna Góra** Poland
31 H2 **Kamień Pomorski** Poland
31 L4 **Kamieńsk** Poland
87 C12 **Kamieskroon** S Africa
89 A8 **Kamies Sektor Berg** *mt* S Africa
60 Q2 **Kami-Furano** Japan
60 Q2 **Kamikawa** *prefect* Japan
60 C14 **Kami-Koshiki-jima** *isld* Japan
140 F4 **Kamileroi** Queensland Australia
114 J5 **Kamilukuak L** Northwest Territories Canada
87 D7 **Kamina** Zaire
115 K5 **Kaminak L** Northwest Territories Canada
99 R1 **Kaministikwia** Ontario Canada
60 C11 **Kami no-shima** *isld* Japan
115 K5 **Kaminuriak L** Northwest Territories Canada
61 L9 **Kamioka** Japan
47 Q14 **Kamiros** *hist site* Rhodes Greece
116 L7 **Kamishak B** Alaska U.S.A.
60 R2 **Kami-Shihoro** Japan
Kamishli *see* **Qāmishlī, Al**
88 B3 **Kamituga** Zaire
61 O13 **Kamiyama-jima** *isld* Okinawa
60 R1 **Kami-Yūbetsu** Japan
57 F3 **Kamkaly** U.S.S.R.
56 C5 **Kamlak** U.S.S.R.
117 N10 **Kamloops** British Columbia Canada
68 B3 **Kamma** Burma
29 P7 **Kammenoye, Oz** *L* U.S.S.R.
60 E12 **Kammon Kaikyō** *str* Japan
60 D12 **Kammon Tunnels** Japan
60 J10 **Kammuri shima** *isld* Japan
60 F11 **Kammuri-yama** *mt* Japan
42 F2 **Kamnik** Yugoslavia
56 H3 **Kamniokan** U.S.S.R.
61 M8 **Kamo** Japan
145 E1 **Kamo** New Zealand
56 E1 **Kamo** *R* U.S.S.R.
78 K1 **Kamo** U.S.S.R.
128 G3 **Kamoa Mts** Guyana
60 O2 **Kamoenai** Japan
61 O10 **Kamogawa** Japan
60 H11 **Kamojima** Japan
122 C6 **Kamouraska** Quebec Canada
38 N4 **Kamp** *R* Austria
69 G13 **Kampa** Indonesia
86 F5 **Kampala** Uganda
69 E12 **Kamparkiri** *R* Sumatra
36 D3 **Kamp-Bornhofen** W Germany
25 E3 **Kampen** Netherlands
28 A7 **Kampen** W Germany
86 E6 **Kampene** Zaire
22 H2 **Kampenhout** Belgium
38 M5 **Kamp, Gr** *R* Austria
68 D4 **Kamphaeng Phet** Thailand
88 B6 **Kampinda** Zambia
88 B7 **Kampolombo, L** Zambia
68 G7 **Kampong Cham** Cambodia
68 G6 **Kampong Chhnang** Cambodia
68 G7 **Kampot** Cambodia
85 D6 **Kampti** Burkina
Kampuchea *rep see* **Cambodia**
99 N7 **Kamrar** Iowa U.S.A.
119 Q7 **Kamsack** Saskatchewan Canada
52 G6 **Kamskoye Ust'ye** U.S.S.R.
74 H8 **Kāmthi** India
119 P2 **Kamuchawie L** Saskatchewan Canada
60 Q3 **Kamui-dake** *mt* Japan
46 E4 **Kamvoúnia, Óri** *mts* Greece
53 G8 **Kamyshin** U.S.S.R.
55 D3 **Kamyshlov** U.S.S.R.
57 B2 **Kamyshlybash** U.S.S.R.
55 D5 **Kamyshnoye** U.S.S.R.
54 F6 **Kamyshnya** U.S.S.R.
54 H9 **Kamysh-Zarya** U.S.S.R.
68 B1 **Kan** Burma
85 G6 **Kan** Nigeria
56 D3 **Kan** *R* U.S.S.R.
89 E2 **Kana** *R* Zimbabwe
103 M4 **Kanab** Utah U.S.A.
103 M5 **Kanab Cr** Arizona U.S.A.
70 C3 **Kana, Bt** *mt* Sarawak
61 O5 **Kanagi** Japan
42 F2 **Kanal** Yugoslavia
46 F5 **Kanália** Greece
69 A9 **Kanalla** Nicobar Is
118 C8 **Kananaskis L** Alberta Canada
86 D7 **Kananga** Zaire
55 C4 **Kananikol'skoye** U.S.S.R.
103 L4 **Kanarraville** Utah U.S.A.
52 G6 **Kanash** U.S.S.R.
46 F5 **Kanastraion, Ákr** *C* Greece
116 K8 **Kanatak** Alaska U.S.A.
52 H4 **Kanava** U.S.S.R.
99 N7 **Kanawha** Iowa U.S.A.
109 M2 **Kanawha** Texas U.S.A.
94 E8 **Kanawha** *R* West Virginia U.S.A.
94 F7 **Kanawha, Little** *R* West Virginia U.S.A.
61 M11 **Kanaya** Japan
61 K9 **Kanazawa** Japan
61 K9 **Kanazu** Japan
75 Q7 **Kanbalu** Burma
68 C5 **Kanbauk** Burma
68 D5 **Kanchanaburi** Thailand
57 J1 **Kanchingiz, Khrebet** *mt* U.S.S.R.
76 D4 **Kanchipuram** India
60 D12 **Kanda** Japan
74 B4 **Kanda** Pakistan
77 J4 **Kandahār** Afghanistan
119 N7 **Kandahar** Saskatchewan Canada
52 D2 **Kandalaksha** U.S.S.R.
52 D2 **Kandalalakshskaya Guba** *B* U.S.S.R.
69 C11 **Kandang** Sumatra
70 D6 **Kandangan** Kalimantan
46 F9 **Kándanos** Crete Greece
52 B6 **Kandava** U.S.S.R.
137 Q5 **Kandavu** *isld* Fiji
36 E5 **Kandel** W Germany
40 G2 **Kandern** W Germany
28 E1 **Kandestederne** Denmark
74 C4 **Kandhkot** Pakistan
85 E6 **Kandi** Benin
76 D2 **Kandi** India
77 K5 **Kandi** Pakistan
116 R4 **Kandik** *R* Alaska U.S.A.
47 L3 **Kandıra** Turkey
70 G4 **Kandi, Tg** *C* Sulawesi
139 J5 **Kandos** New South Wales Australia
87 H11 **Kandreho** Madagascar
55 B4 **Kandry** U.S.S.R.
76 D3 **Kandukur** India
83 K10 **Kandy** Sri Lanka
110 F2 **Kane** Illinois U.S.A.
94 J5 **Kane** Pennsylvania U.S.A.
101 R5 **Kane** Wyoming U.S.A.
115 M2 **Kane Basin** Canada/Greenland
116 G7 **Kanektok** *R* Alaska U.S.A.
86 C3 **Kanem** *dist* Chad
102 S12 **Kaneohe** Hawaiian Is
102 S12 **Kaneohe Bay** Hawaiian Is
54 C7 **Kanev** U.S.S.R.
52 E2 **Kanevka** U.S.S.R.
54 C7 **Kanevskoye Vodokhranilishche** *res* U.S.S.R.
61 O7 **Kaneyama** Japan
42 F3 **Kanfanar** Yugoslavia
87 D10 **Kang** Botswana
115 O4 **Kangaamiut** Greenland
115 O4 **Kangaatsiak** Greenland
85 C6 **Kangaba** Mali
78 F2 **Kangal** Turkey
77 C6 **Kangan** Iran
69 E9 **Kangar** Malaysia
138 D6 **Kangaroo I** South Australia Australia
140 E4 **Kangaroo Pt** Queensland Australia
29 L7 **Kangas** Finland
29 N9 **Kangaslampi** Finland
29 M9 **Kangasniemi** Finland
77 A2 **Kangāvar** Iran
48 M4 **Kangaz** U.S.S.R.
65 C4 **Kangbao** China
75 N5 **Kangchenjunga** *mt* Nepal/India
58 D5 **Kangding** China
70 P9 **Kangean** *isld* Indonesia
115 N4 **Kangeeak Pt** Northwest Territories Canada
115 Q4 **Kangerlussuaq** *inlet* Greenland
115 Q4 **Kangertittivatsiaq** *inlet* Greenland
86 G5 **Kangetet** Kenya
59 J3 **Kanggye** N Korea
115 M5 **Kangiqsujuaq** Quebec Canada
65 B5 **Kangjiahui** China
65 G1 **Kangjinjing** China
59 J4 **Kangnŭng** S Korea
86 B5 **Kango** Gabon
61 N13 **Kangoku-iwa** *islds* Iwo Jima Japan
26 N4 **Kangosfors** Sweden
65 F3 **Kangping** China
75 J3 **Kangrinboqê Feng** *mt* Xizang Zizhiqu
71 E8 **Kang Tipayan Dakula** *isld* Philippines
57 E5 **Kangurt** U.S.S.R.
Kan-hsien *see* **Ganzhou**
68 B1 **Kani** Burma
87 D7 **Kaniama** Zaire
57 F4 **Kanibadam** U.S.S.R.
144 C5 **Kaniere** New Zealand
144 C5 **Kaniere, L** New Zealand
76 D3 **Kanigiri** India
57 D4 **Kanimekh** U.S.S.R.
52 F1 **Kanin Nos, Mys** *C* U.S.S.R.
52 F1 **Kanin, Poluostrov** *pen* U.S.S.R.
52 F1 **Kaninskiy Bereg** *coast* U.S.S.R.
61 O5 **Kanita** Japan
26 N5 **Kaniulasjärvi** Sweden
138 F6 **Kaniva** Victoria Australia
48 F4 **Kanjiža** Yugoslavia
29 J10 **Kankaanpää** Finland
99 S8 **Kankakee** *R* Illinois U.S.A.
85 C6 **Kankan** Guinea
75 J8 **Kanker** India
83 J8 **Kankesanturai** Sri Lanka
29 L4 **Kankonen** Finland
74 E6 **Kankroli** India
68 D7 **Kanmaw Kyun** *isld* Burma
56 D5 **Kanmegirskiy Khrebet** *mts* U.S.S.R.
27 G15 **Kånna** Sweden
112 G2 **Kannapolis** North Carolina U.S.A.
22 K2 **Kanne** Belgium
74 G7 **Kannod** India
29 L9 **Kannonkoski** Finland
29 K8 **Kannus** Finland
71 J6 **Kano** *isld* Indonesia
60 E11 **Kano** Japan
85 F6 **Kano** Nigeria
107 K2 **Kanona** Kansas U.S.A.
55 G5 **Kanonerka** U.S.S.R.
60 G11 **Kanonji** Japan
126 B2 **Kanon, Pt** Curaçao
107 M3 **Kanopolis** Kansas U.S.A.
103 M3 **Kanosh** Utah U.S.A.
70 C3 **Kanowit** Sarawak
60 D14 **Kanoya** Japan
74 J5 **Kanpur** India
107 K3 **Kansas** *state* U.S.A.
99 T10 **Kansas** Illinois U.S.A.
107 P2 **Kansas** *R* Kansas U.S.A.
107 Q5 **Kansas** Oklahoma U.S.A.
107 Q2 **Kansas City** Kansas U.S.A.
110 B2 **Kansas City** Missouri U.S.A.
67 E4 **Kanshi** China
56 E3 **Kansk** U.S.S.R.
56 E4 **Kanskoye Belogor'ye** *mts* U.S.S.R.
88 A5 **Kansonge** Zaire
Kansu *prov see* **Gansu**
57 G3 **Kant** U.S.S.R.
29 N9 **Kantala** Finland
85 E6 **Kantchari** Burkina
85 E6 **Kanté** Togo
68 G5 **Kantharalak** Thailand
75 M8 **Kānthi** India
116 M4 **Kantishna** *R* Alaska U.S.A.
61 M10 **Kanto sanchi** *mts* Japan
68 C2 **Kantulong** Burma
14 C4 **Kanturk** Ireland
77 J5 **Kanuk** Afghanistan
102 S11 **Kanuku** Hawaiian Is
128 G3 **Kanuku Mts** Guyana
61 N9 **Kanuma** Japan
87 C11 **Kanus** Namibia
116 M3 **Kanuti** *R* Alaska U.S.A.
89 D5 **Kanye** Botswana
68 B3 **Kanyinngu** Burma
68 C3 **Kanyutkwin** Burma
38 J8 **Kanzel** *mt* Austria
87 E8 **Kanzenze** Zaire
137 R5 **Kao** *isld* Tonga
87 B9 **Kaoko Veld** *reg* Namibia
85 A6 **Kaolack** Senegal
47 J1 **Kaolinovo** Bulgaria
87 D8 **Kaoma** Zambia
65 F2 **Kaoshan** China
102 V13 **Kapaa** Hawaiian Is
102 V13 **Kapaau** Hawaiian Is
74 E7 **Kapadvanj** India
57 J2 **Kapal** U.S.S.R.
71 O9 **Kapala** *isld* Indonesia
71 A3 **Kapalabuaya** Indonesia
71 M9 **Kapan** Timor Indonesia
87 D7 **Kapanga** Zaire
87 F7 **Kapatu** Zambia
66 B3 **Kapchagay** U.S.S.R.
57 H3 **Kapchagayskoye Vdkhr.** *res* U.S.S.R.
22 G1 **Kapellen** Belgium
25 F5 **Kapellen** W Germany
86 G5 **Kapenguria** Kenya
38 M7 **Kapfenberg** Austria
47 J4 **Kapıdaği Yar** *pen* Turkey
70 G5 **Kapinyu, Tanjong** *C* Sulawesi
87 E8 **Kapiri Mposhi** Zambia
77 L2 **Kāpīsā** Afghanistan
115 L7 **Kapiskau** Ontario Canada
70 C4 **Kapit** Sarawak
54 C8 **Kapitanovka** U.S.S.R.
145 E4 **Kapiti I** New Zealand
111 D11 **Kaplan** Louisiana U.S.A.
31 H7 **Kaplice** Czechoslovakia
69 D8 **Kapoe** Thailand
86 F5 **Kapoeta** Sudan
135 V5 **Kapoho** Hawaiian Is
71 L9 **Kapondai, Tanjong** Indonesia
145 E3 **Kaponga** New Zealand
70 F7 **Kapoposang** *isld* Indonesia
48 E4 **Kapos** *R* Hungary
48 D4 **Kaposvár** Hungary
71 C3 **Kapotjol** W Irian
74 B10 **Kappar** Pakistan
28 G7 **Kappel** Denmark
36 C3 **Kappel** W Germany
28 D7 **Kappeln** W Germany
36 E6 **Kappelrodeck** W Germany
27 K14 **Kappelshamn** *isld* Gotland Sweden
41 M3 **Kappl** Austria
38 G7 **Kaprun** Austria
31 O1 **Kapsukas** U.S.S.R.
88 C9 **Kapsuku** *mt* Zimbabwe
70 D5 **Kapuas** *R* Kalimantan
70 B4 **Kapuas** *R* Kalimantan
70 C4 **Kapuas Hulu, Peg** Kalimantan
138 E5 **Kapunda** South Australia Australia
145 E3 **Kapuni** New Zealand
74 F3 **Kapurthala** India
120 H4 **Kapuskasing** *R* Ontario Canada
120 H3 **Kapuskasing** Ontario Canada
139 K4 **Kaputar** *mt* New South Wales Australia
48 D3 **Kapuvár** Hungary
56 H4 **Kapylyushi, Oz** *L* U.S.S.R.
66 B4 **Kaqung** China
85 E7 **Kara** Togo
78 G2 **Kara** *R* Turkey
79 G6 **Karā', Arḑ al** Syria
57 G5 **Karaart** U.S.S.R.
57 G3 **Kara Balta** U.S.S.R.
54 K1 **Karabanovo** U.S.S.R.
57 H2 **Karabas** U.S.S.R.
57 C5 **Karabekaul** U.S.S.R.
47 J4 **Karabiga** Turkey
57 C6 **Karabil', Vozvyshennost'** *uplands* U.S.S.R.
78 D1 **Karabuk** Turkey
57 J4 **Karabulak** China
46 C4 **Karaburun** Albania
47 J8 **Kara Burun** *C* Turkey
47 H6 **Karaburun** Turkey
47 H6 **Kara Burun** *C* Turkey
55 D6 **Karabutak** U.S.S.R.
47 J4 **Karacabey** Turkey
47 J3 **Karacaköy** Turkey
79 C2 **Karaçal Tepe** *mt* Turkey
47 J3 **Karacaoğlan** Turkey
47 K7 **Karacasu** Turkey
53 F11 **Karachayevo-Cherkesskaya Aut. Obl.** U.S.S.R.
54 F3 **Karachev** U.S.S.R.
74 B6 **Karachi** Pakistan
76 B2 **Karad** India
78 D3 **Karadağ** *mt* Turkey
57 G4 **Karadar'ya** *R* U.S.S.R.
47 M11 **Karadeniz Boğazı** *str* Turkey
55 F2 **Karagach** U.S.S.R.
55 F6 **Karaganda** U.S.S.R.
57 H1 **Karagayly** U.S.S.R.
51 Q4 **Karaginskiy, Ostrova** *islds* U.S.S.R.
47 K8 **Kara Göl** *l* Turkey
56 B5 **Karaguzhikha** U.S.S.R.
47 K6 **Karahalh** Turkey
47 J7 **Karahayıt** Turkey
55 C3 **Karaidel'** U.S.S.R.
76 D5 **Kāraikāl** India
Kara Irtysh *R see* **Ertix He**
70 E4 **Karaitan** Kalimantan
83 J9 **Karaitivu** Sri Lanka
77 B2 **Karaj** Iran
79 F7 **Karak** Jordan
47 H6 **Karaka Burun** *C* Turkey
57 A3 **Karakalpakskaya A.S.S.R** *prov* U.S.S.R.
57 C2 **Karaketken** U.S.S.R.
143 B9 **Karakin Ls** Western Australia Australia
57 E2 **Karakoin, Ozero** *L* U.S.S.R.
57 H4 **Karakolka** U.S.S.R.
74 F1 **Karakoram** *ra* Kashmir
74 G1 **Karakoram Pass** Kashmir
85 B5 **Karakoro** *R* Mauritania/Mali
58 D2 **Karakorum** Mongolia
78 J2 **Karaköse** Turkey
55 G5 **Karakuduk** U.S.S.R.
55 F4 **Kara-Kuga** U.S.S.R.
57 G4 **Kara Kul'** U.S.S.R.
57 C5 **Karakul'** U.S.S.R.
52 H6 **Karakulino** U.S.S.R.
57 G5 **Kara-Kul', Ozero** *L* U.S.S.R.
55 D4 **Karakul'skoye** U.S.S.R.
57 C5 **Karakumskiy Kanal** U.S.S.R.
50 E5 **Karakumy** U.S.S.R.
57 A5 **Karakumy, Peski** *desert* U.S.S.R.
60 D14 **Karakuni-dake** *mt* Japan
38 M8 **Karalpe** *mts* Austria
143 C7 **Karalundi** Western Australia Australia
70 F6 **Karam** *R* Sulawesi
80 F6 **Karama** Jordan
47 K7 **Karaman** Turkey
47 K7 **Karamanlı** Turkey
66 C2 **Karamay** China
145 D4 **Karamea** New Zealand
70 D7 **Karamian** *isld* Indonesia
47 L6 **Karamık Gölü** *l* Turkey
66 C4 **Karamiran He** *R* China
66 D4 **Karamiran Shankou** *pass* China
86 F5 **Karamoja** *dist* Uganda
47 K4 **Karamürsel** Turkey
78 L4 **Karand** Iran
69 G14 **Karangagung** Sumatra
70 K8 **Karangan** Sumatra
144 B5 **Karangarua R** New Zealand
70 P10 **Karangasem** Indonesia
70 M9 **Karangbolong Tanjong** *C* Java
70 F7 **Karang Bril** Indonesia
70 F5 **Karang, Tg** *C* Sulawesi
74 G8 **Karanja** India
47 J7 **Karaova** Turkey
57 G2 **Karaoy** U.S.S.R.
57 D3 **Karaozek** U.S.S.R.
47 J1 **Karapelit** Bulgaria
78 D3 **Karapinar** Turkey
145 E2 **Karapiro** New Zealand
66 C4 **Karasay** China
57 J4 **Karasay** U.S.S.R.
89 A7 **Karasburg** Namibia
147 M12 **Kara Sea** Arctic Oc
55 G5 **Karashoky** U.S.S.R.
26 O2 **Karasjok** Norway
26 O2 **Karasjokka** *R* Norway
55 G5 **Karasor** U.S.S.R.
78 H1 **Karasu** *R* Turkey
47 L3 **Karasu** Turkey
55 F4 **Karasu** Kokchetavskaya obl U.S.S.R.
55 D5 **Karasu** Kustanayskaya U.S.S.R.
55 G4 **Karasuk** U.S.S.R.
56 B4 **Karasuk** *R* U.S.S.R.
61 O9 **Karasuyama** Japan
55 E2 **Karas'ye, Oz** *L* U.S.S.R.
57 H2 **Karatal** *R* U.S.S.R.
57 L1 **Karatal** U.S.S.R.
78 E3 **Karatas** Turkey
57 F3 **Kara Tau** U.S.S.R.
68 D7 **Karathuri** Burma
83 J9 **Karativu** *isld* Sri Lanka
26 K5 **Karatjaur** *L* Sweden
55 B6 **Karatobe** U.S.S.R.
57 B2 **Karatobe, Mys** *C* U.S.S.R.
55 D5 **Karatomarskoye Vodokhranilishche** *res* U.S.S.R.
60 C12 **Karatsu** Japan
57 A2 **Karatup, Poluostrov** *pen* U.S.S.R.
55 E6 **Karaturgay** *R* U.S.S.R.
Karaul *see* **Qongkol**
57 J1 **Karaul** U.S.S.R.
50 H1 **Karaul** U.S.S.R.
57 A3 **Kara-uzyak** U.S.S.R.
46 E5 **Karáva** *mt* Greece
57 F4 **Karavan** U.S.S.R.
46 C4 **Karavastas, Kënet'e** Albania
79 C4 **Karavostasi** Cyprus
70 L9 **Karawang** Java
70 L8 **Karawang Tg.** *C* Java
38 K8 **Karawanken** *mt* Austria
57 F1 **Karazhal** U.S.S.R.
57 G2 **Karazhingil** U.S.S.R.
78 J5 **Karbala** Iraq
36 F3 **Karben** W Germany
26 H10 **Kårböle** Sweden
33 Q6 **Karbow-Vietlübbe** East Germany
55 G6 **Karbushevka** U.S.S.R.
28 B3 **Karby** Denmark
48 F3 **Karcag** Hungary
46 E8 **Kardhamila** Greece
47 H6 **Kardhámila** Greece
46 E5 **Kardhitsa** Greece
26 N5 **Kardis** Sweden
52 B5 **Kärdla** U.S.S.R.
138 B2 **Karee** N Terr Australia
52 D3 **Karelskaya** *A.S.S.R.* U.S.S.R.
52 D3 **Karel'skaya Masel'ga** U.S.S.R.
87 F7 **Karema** Tanzania
68 C3 **Karen State** Burma
85 C4 **Karet** Mauritania
145 F2 **Karewa I** New Zealand
55 C5 **Kargala** U.S.S.R.
57 G1 **Kargaly** U.S.S.R.
55 D3 **Kargapolye** U.S.S.R.
56 B3 **Kargat** *R* U.S.S.R.
Karghalik *see* **Yecheng**
78 E1 **Kargı** Turkey
52 E4 **Kargopol'** U.S.S.R.
33 R6 **Kargow** East Germany
31 J3 **Kargowa** Poland
85 G6 **Kargueri** Niger
117 G8 **Karheen** Alaska U.S.A.
29 M11 **Karhula** Finland
88 B10 **Kariba** Zimbabwe
88 B10 **Kariba Dam** Zimbabwe/Zambia
88 B10 **Kariba,L** Zimbabwe/Zambia
60 N3 **Kariba yama** *mt* Japan
87 C10 **Karibib** Namibia
89 C9 **Kariega** *watercourse* S Africa
29 M2 **Karigasniemi** Finland
29 J9 **Karijoki** Finland
145 D1 **Karikari, C** New Zealand
86 F2 **Karima** Sudan
75 P6 **Karimganj** India
74 H9 **Karimnagar** India
69 F12 **Karimun Besar** *isld* Indonesia
70 N8 **Karimundjawa** *isld* Indonesia
70 N8 **Karimundjawa, Pulau Pulau** *islds* Indonesia
86 A1 **Karin** Somalia
145 E2 **Karioi** *mt* New Zealand
145 E3 **Karioi** New Zealand
29 K11 **Karis** Finland
28 J6 **Karise** Denmark
88 E6 **Karisimbi. Mt** Zaire
46 G6 **Káristos** Greece
144 C6 **Karitane** New Zealand
76 B4 **Karkal** India
79 H2 **Karkamiş** Turkey
136 K2 **Karkar** *isld* Papua New Guinea
57 H1 **Karkaralinsk** U.S.S.R.
77 F7 **Kārkīn Dar** Iran
29 L11 **Karkkila** Finland
29 L11 **Kärkölä** Finland
138 D5 **Karkoo** South Australia Australia
Karlá *l see* **Voïvi4is** *l*
54 G5 **Karla Libknekhta** U.S.S.R.
57 G6 **Karla Marksa, Pik** *mt* U.S.S.R.
28 F4 **Karlby** Denmark
26 R1 **Karlebotn** Norway
28 J7 **Karleby** Denmark
31 J1 **Karlino** Poland
37 O2 **Karl-Marx-Stadt** East Germany
42 G4 **Karlobag** Yugoslavia
54 G7 **Karlovka** U.S.S.R.
46 G2 **Karlovo** Bulgaria
37 O3 **Karlovy Vary** Czechoslovakia
26 K8 **Karlsbäck** Sweden
36 E6 **Karlsbad** W Germany
29 K6 **Karlsberg** Sweden
27 G13 **Karlsborg** Sweden
37 L7 **Karlsfeld** W Germany
32 K9 **Karlshafen** W Germany
27 G15 **Karlshamn** Sweden
27 G12 **Karlskoga** Sweden
27 H15 **Karlskrona** Sweden
26 L1 **Karlsöy** Norway
98 F1 **Karlsruhe** North Dakota U.S.A.
36 E5 **Karlsruhe** W Germany
27 F12 **Karlstad** Sweden
98 K1 **Karlstad** Minnesota U.S.A.
36 H4 **Karlstadt** W Germany
116 K8 **Karluk L** Alaska U.S.A.
57 D5 **Karlyuk** U.S.S.R.
76 B1 **Karmala** India
52 E6 **Karmanovo** U.S.S.R.
80 C2 **Karmel, Cape** Israel
80 E2 **Karmi'el** Israel
80 B7 **Karmiyya** Israel
27 A12 **Karmöy** *isld* Norway
109 N3 **Karnack** Texas U.S.A.
110 H4 **Karnak** Illinois U.S.A.
74 G4 **Karnal** India
76 B3 **Karnataka** *prov* India
109 K7 **Karnes City** Texas U.S.A.
38 G8 **Karnische Alpen** *mts* Austria
47 H2 **Karnobat** Bulgaria
27 E13 **Kärnsj** *L* Sweden
38 H8 **Kärnten** Austria
87 E9 **Karoi** Zimbabwe
77 H2 **Karokh** Afghanistan
68 C5 **Karokpi** Burma
71 K8 **Karompalompo** *isld* Indonesia
128 G3 **Karona Fall** Guyana
88 D6 **Karonga** Malawi
143 D9 **Karonie** Western Australia Australia
57 H4 **Karool-Dëbë** U.S.S.R.
138 E6 **Karoonda** South Australia Australia
47 H8 **Káros** *isld* Greece
70 F5 **Karossa** Sulawesi Indonesia
71 J9 **Karossa, Tg** *C* Indonesia
47 O12 **Karousádhes** Greece
33 Q5 **Karow** East Germany
47 J9 **Kárpathos** *isld* Greece
47 J9 **Kárpathos** Kárpathos I Greece
47 J9 **Karpathos Str** Greece
46 E6 **Karpenision** Greece
41 K4 **Kärpf** *mt* Switzerland
37 P7 **Karpfham** W Germany
55 C2 **Karpinsk** U.S.S.R.
52 F3 **Karpogory** U.S.S.R.
55 D2 **Karpuniskiy** U.S.S.R.
55 C2 **Karpushikha** U.S.S.R.
79 C2 **Karpuz** *R* Turkey
47 J7 **Karpuzlu** Turkey
142 A1 **Karrakatta** *dist* Perth, W Aust Australia
142 B5 **Karratha** Western Australia Australia
115 O3 **Karrats Fjord** Greenland
28 H6 **Karrebæk** Denmark
28 H6 **Karrebæksminde** Denmark
28 G6 **Karrebæksminde Bugt** *B* Denmark
89 B8 **Karreeberge** *mts* S Africa
143 B10 **Karridale** Western Australia Australia
78 J1 **Kars** Turkey
57 D1 **Karsakpay** U.S.S.R.
119 S2 **Karsakuwigamak L** Manitoba Canada
29 M8 **Kärsämäki** Finland
52 C6 **Kārsava** U.S.S.R.
57 D5 **Karshi** U.S.S.R.
57 D5 **Karshinskaya Step'** U.S.S.R.
75 N5 **Kārsiyāng** India
50 E1 **Karskiye Vorota, Proliv** *str* U.S.S.R.
33 P6 **Karstädt** East Germany
28 B5 **Karstoft** Denmark
29 L9 **Karstula** Finland
26 H10 **Karsvall** Sweden
46 G3 **Kartál** *mt* Greece
47 N11 **Kartal** Turkey
55 D4 **Kartaly** U.S.S.R.
52 H3 **Kartayël** U.S.S.R.
94 J5 **Karthaus** Pennsylvania U.S.A.
36 B4 **Karthaus** W Germany
29 N9 **Karttula** Finland
31 L1 **Kartuzy** Poland
87 E9 **Karubwe** Zambia
61 M9 **Karuizawa** Japan
143 F9 **Karulbie Rockhole** *rockhole* Western Australia Australia
140 F3 **Karumba** Queensland Australia
77 A4 **Karun** *R* Iran
26 N5 **Karungi** Sweden
71 J9 **Karuni** Indonesia
142 G3 **Karunjie** Western Australia Australia
106 G3 **Karval** Colorado U.S.A.
29 K9 **Karvia** Finland
26 K2 **Kårvik** Norway
31 L6 **Karviná** Czechoslovakia
48 E1 **Karvina** Czechoslovakia
76 B3 **Karwar** India
41 O3 **Karwendel Geb** *mts* Austria
55 E1 **Karym** U.S.S.R.
28 D2 **Kås** Denmark
47 K8 **Kaş** Turkey
56 C2 **Kas** *R* U.S.S.R.
88 C6 **Kasaba B** Zambia
87 D7 **Kasai** *R* Zaire
86 D6 **Kasai** *prov* Zaire
87 D8 **Kasaji** Zaire
61 O9 **Kasama** Japan
88 C7 **Kasama** Zambia
57 D5 **Kasan** U.S.S.R.
88 C6 **Kasanga** Tanzania
57 F4 **Kasansay** U.S.S.R.
76 B4 **Kasaragod** India
75 O7 **Kasba** Bangladesh
114 J5 **Kasba L** Northwest Territories Canada
27 G16 **Kåseberga** Sweden
60 D14 **Kaseda** Japan
116 F1 **Kasegaluk Lag** Alaska U.S.A.
87 E8 **Kasempa** Zambia
37 L3 **Kasendorf** W Germany
88 B7 **Kasenga** Zaire
86 F5 **Kasenyi** Zaire
77 B5 **Kāserūn** Iran
88 C1 **Kasese** Uganda
86 E6 **Kasese** Zaire
68 F5 **Kaset Wisai** Thailand
119 N2 **Kashabowie** Ontario Canada
77 B2 **Kāshān** Iran
Kashgar *see* **Kashi**
66 B4 **Kashi** China
61 J11 **Kashihara** Japan
60 D12 **Kashima** Japan
52 E6 **Kashin** U.S.S.R.
74 H4 **Kashipur** India
54 K2 **Kashira** U.S.S.R.
119 O1 **Kashishibog L** Ontario Canada
61 M8 **Kashiwazaki** Japan
57 D5 **Kashkadar'in-skaya Oblast** U.S.S.R.
57 G2 **Kashkanteniz** U.S.S.R.
52 D4 **Kashkany** U.S.S.R.
52 E2 **Kashkarantsy** U.S.S.R.
57 H4 **Kashkasu** U.S.S.R.
77 F2 **Kāshmar** Iran
66 B5 **Kashmir** *prov* India/Pakistan
74 C4 **Kashmor** Pakistan
88 G3 **Kasigao** *mt* Kenya
70 G5 **Kasimbar** Sulawesi
71 A3 **Kasiruta** *isld* Indonesia
110 G2 **Kaskaskia** *R* Illinois U.S.A.
26 K6 **Kasker** Sweden
29 J9 **Kaskinen** Finland
Kaskö *see* **Kaskinen**
68 F7 **Kas Kong** Cambodia
55 D3 **Kasli** U.S.S.R.
117 P11 **Kaslo** British Columbia Canada
69 F14 **Kasmaran** Sumatra
70 C5 **Kasongan** Kalimantan
86 E6 **Kasongo** Zaire
87 C7 **Kasongo-Lunda** Zaire
47 H9 **Kásos** *isld* Greece
47 H9 **Kásos Str** Greece
47 J1 **Kaspichan** Bulgaria
54 C1 **Kasplya** *R* U.S.S.R.
68 H6 **Kas Preas** Cambodia
68 F7 **Kas Prins** *isld* Cambodia
68 F7 **Kas Rong** *isld* Cambodia
68 F7 **Kas Rong Sam Lem** *isld* Cambodia
86 G2 **Kassala** Sudan
46 F4 **Kassándra** Greece
32 L10 **Kassel** W Germany
85 F1 **Kasserine** Tunisia
47 O12 **Kassiópi** Greece
68 F7 **Kas Smach** *isld* Cambodia
99 O5 **Kasson** Minnesota U.S.A.
78 D1 **Kastamonu** Turkey
47 H3 **Kastanéai** Greece
28 E3 **Kastbjerg** Denmark
36 E3 **Kastel** W Germany
36 C3 **Kastellaun** W Germany
46 F9 **Kastélli** Crete Greece
46 G9 **Kastéllion** Crete Greece
47 K8 **Kastellórizon** *isld* Greece
36 B1 **Kaster** W Germany
22 H1 **Kasterlee** Belgium
37 M5 **Kastl** W Germany
27 H15 **Kastlösa** Sweden
33 N5 **Kastorf** W Germany
46 E4 **Kastoria** Greece
46 E4 **Kastorias, L** Greece
46 G5 **Kástron** Limnos I Greece
46 F4 **Kástron Nigrita** Greece
46 D5 **Kastrosikiá** Greece
29 K5 **Kastrup** Denmark
60 F10 **Kasubuchi** Japan
60 D12 **Kasuga** Japan
61 K10 **Kasugai** Japan
61 O9 **Kasumiga-ura** *L* Japan
70 C6 **Kasungan** Kalimantan
87 F8 **Kasungu** Malawi
88 E9 **Kasupe** Malawi
74 F3 **Kasur** Pakistan
85 G6 **Katagum** Nigeria
95 S8 **Katahdin, Mt** Maine U.S.A.
86 D6 **Katako-Kombe** Zaire
46 E7 **Katákolon** Greece
116 P2 **Katakturuk** *R* Alaska U.S.A.
116 P6 **Katalla** Alaska U.S.A.
86 D7 **Katanda** Zaire
56 F2 **Katanga** *R* U.S.S.R.
74 H8 **Katangi** India
59 M1 **Katangli** U.S.S.R.
143 C10 **Katanning** Western Australia Australia
75 J4 **Katarnian Ghat** India
46 D7 **Katastári** Greece
61 J10 **Katata** Japan
88 C5 **Katavi Nat. Park** Tanzania
77 L3 **Katāwāz-Urgan** Afghanistan
55 D3 **Kataysk** U.S.S.R.
69 A9 **Katchall** *isld* Nicobar Is
38 J7 **Katchberg** Austria
87 C8 **Katchiungo** Angola
116 H4 **Kateel** *R* Alaska U.S.A.
119 O8 **Katepwa** Saskatchewan Canada
46 F4 **Katerini** Greece
25 F4 **Katerveer** Netherlands
117 G7 **Kates Needle** *mt* British Columbia Canada
75 K7 **Katghora** India
75 R6 **Katha** Burma
84 J4 **Katherina, Gebel** *hill* Egypt
140 B2 **Katherine** N Terr Australia
140 C2 **Katherine R** N Terr Australia
74 H4 **Kathgodam** India
74 D8 **Kathiawar** *reg* India
83 L9 **Kathiraveli** Sri Lanka
113 E9 **Kathleen** Florida U.S.A.
140 B2 **Kathleen Falls** N Terr Australia
143 D7 **Kathleen Valley** Western Australia Australia
75 L5 **Kathmandu** Nepal
118 D7 **Kathryn** Alberta Canada
98 H3 **Kathryn** North Dakota U.S.A.
74 F2 **Kathwa** Kashmir
85 C6 **Kati** Mali
70 C4 **Katibas** *R* Sarawak
75 M6 **Katihar** India
145 E2 **Katikati** New Zealand
87 D9 **Katima Mulilo** Namibia
119 S6 **Katimik L** Manitoba Canada
85 C7 **Katiola** Ivory Coast
29 L3 **Kätkätunturi** *mt* Finland
89 A8 **Katkop Hills** S Africa
48 M5 **Katlabuk, Oz** *L* U.S.S.R.
32 M9 **Katlenburg** W Germany
116 K8 **Katmai B** Alaska U.S.A.
116 K7 **Katmai Nat Park and Preserve** Alaska U.S.A.
116 K7 **Katmai Vol., Mt** Alaska U.S.A.
74 J7 **Katni** India
46 E6 **Káto Akhaïa** Greece
46 E6 **Katokhi** Greece
88 C9 **Katondwe** Zambia
46 F3 **Káto Nevrokópion** Greece
139 K5 **Katoomba** New South Wales Australia
70 G5 **Katoposa, Gunung** *mt* Sulawesi
46 F4 **Káto Stavrós** Greece
55 C4 **Katov-Ivanovsk** U.S.S.R.
31 L5 **Katowice** Poland
75 N7 **Kātoya** India
47 L7 **Katrancı Dag** *mt* Turkey
27 H10 **Katrineberg** Sweden
27 H13 **Katrineholm** Sweden
12 D1 **Katrine, L** Scotland
85 F6 **Katsina** Nigeria
61 P13 **Katsuren-zaki** *C* Okinawa
61 O9 **Katsuta** Japan
61 O10 **Katsuura** Japan
61 N10 **Katsuyama** Japan
61 K9 **Katsuyama** Fukui Japan
60 G10 **Katsuyama** Okayama Japan
57 D5 **Kattakurgan** U.S.S.R.
142 F5 **Kattamudda Well** Western Australia Australia
29 K4 **Kattarp** Sweden
47 Q15 **Kattaviá** Rhodes Greece
47 J9 **Kattavia** Rhodes Greece
120 K3 **Kattawagami L** Ontario Canada
28 E3 **Kattegat** *str* Denmark
32 G8 **Kattenvenne** W Germany
27 K14 **Katthammarsvik** *isld* Gotland Sweden
28 D5 **Kattrup** Denmark
88 A8 **Katue** *R* Zambia
87 E7 **Katumba** Zaire
88 D7 **Katumbi** Malawi
56 C5 **Katun'** *R* U.S.S.R.
83 J10 **Katunayaka** Sri Lanka
56 C6 **Katunskiy Khr** *mts* U.S.S.R.
88 B2 **Katwe** Uganda
25 B4 **Katwijk aan Zee** Netherlands
31 K4 **Katy Wrocł** Poland
36 G5 **Katzenbuckel** *mt* W Germany
36 D3 **Katzenelnbogen** W Germany
37 L2 **Katzhütte** East Germany
71 A2 **Kau** Halmahera Indonesia
102 V13 **Kauai** *isld* Hawaiian Is
102 V13 **Kauai Ch** Hawaiian Is
144 B7 **Kauana** New Zealand
36 D3 **Kaub** W Germany
89 D2 **Kaucaca Pans** Botswana
135 U6 **Kau Desert** Hawaiian Is
41 N2 **Kaufbeuren** W Germany
41 N1 **Kaufering** W Germany
109 L3 **Kaufman** Texas U.S.A.
32 L10 **Kaufungen** W Germany
29 K8 **Kauhava** Finland
135 T3 **Kauiki Hd** Hawaiian Is
145 E2 **Kaukapakapa** New Zealand
99 S5 **Kaukauna** Wisconsin U.S.A.
102 U13 **Kaula** *isld* Hawaiian Is
102 U13 **Kaulakahi Ch** Hawaiian Is
135 U5 **Kauluoa Pt** Hawaiian Is
135 O1 **Kaumakani** Hawaiian Is
38 N5 **Kaumberg** Austria
135 R2 **Kaunakakai** Hawaiian Is
135 U6 **Kauna Pt** Hawaiian Is
53 B7 **Kaunas** U.S.S.R.
29 L11 **Kauniainen** Finland
145 E3 **Kaupokonui Stream** New Zealand
85 F6 **Kaura Namoda** Nigeria
48 M4 **Kaushany** U.S.S.R.
29 K8 **Kaustinen** Finland
22 L4 **Kautenbach** Luxembourg
71 A2 **Kau, Tk** *B* Halmahera Indonesia
26 N3 **Kautokeino** Norway
68 D7 **Kau-ye Kyun** *isld* Burma
47 K5 **Kavacık** Turkey
46 E3 **Kavadarci** Yugoslavia
46 D3 **Kavajë** Albania
47 J7 **Kavaklıdere** Turkey
59 K3 **Kavalerovo** U.S.S.R.
76 E3 **Kavali** India
46 G4 **Kaválla** Greece
87 C9 **Kavango** *R* Namibia
87 C9 **Kavango** *homeland* Namibia
73 L6 **Kavaratti** *isld* Lakshadweep Indian Oc
47 J1 **Kavarna** Bulgaria
33 Q4 **Kavelstorf** East Germany
136 L2 **Kavieng** New Ireland
116 O2 **Kavik** *R* Alaska U.S.A.
27 F16 **Kävlinge** Sweden
47 P13 **Kavos** Greece
47 H9 **Kavoúsi** Crete Greece
88 C5 **Kavu** *R* Tanzania
80 D2 **Kavul** Israel
87 D8 **Kavungo** Angola
129 H3 **Kaw** Fr Guiana
121 M7 **Kawagama L** Ontario Canada
61 N10 **Kawagoe** Japan
61 N10 **Kawaguchi** Japan
60 H10 **Kawahara** Japan
61 M7 **Kawaharada** Japan
135 U4 **Kawaihae** Hawaiian Is
135 N1 **Kawaihoa Pt** Hawaiian Is
135 O1 **Kawaikini** *pk* Hawaiian Is
102 R11 **Kawailoa Bch** Hawaiian Is
61 M10 **Kawakami** Japan
145 E1 **Kawakawa** New Zealand
145 E2 **Kawakawa B** New Zealand
60 E13 **Kawakita** Japan
61 O8 **Kawamata** Japan
88 B6 **Kawambwa** Zambia
61 N11 **Kawana** Japan
71 J4 **Kawangkoan** Sulawesi
60 G11 **Kawanoe** Japan
144 B6 **Kawarau R** New Zealand
75 J7 **Kawardha** India

8 B6 **Kilkhampton** England
14 B3 **Kilkieran B** Ireland
46 F4 **Kilkis** Greece
141 K7 **Kilkivan** Queensland Australia
14 E3 **Kill** Ireland
14 B2 **Killala** Ireland
14 B2 **Killala B** Ireland
120 D3 **Killala L** Ontario Canada
121 N7 **Killaloe** Ontario Canada
14 C4 **Killaloe** Ireland
119 P8 **Killaly** Saskatchewan Canada
118 F6 **Killam** Alberta Canada
140 B3 **Killarney** N Terr Australia
141 K8 **Killarney** Queensland Australia
119 S9 **Killarney** Manitoba Canada
120 J7 **Killarney** Ontario Canada
14 B4 **Killarney** Ireland
120 J6 **Killarney Prov. Park** Ontario Canada
14 A3 **Killary Hbr** Ireland
14 D2 **Killashandra** Ireland
118 L9 **Killdeer** Saskatchewan Canada
98 D2 **Killdeer** North Dakota U.S.A.
99 O8 **Killduff** Iowa U.S.A.
12 D1 **Killearn** Scotland
109 K4 **Killeen** Texas U.S.A.
47 J5 **Killer** *R* Turkey
15 E4 **Killiecrankie, Pass of** Scotland
116 K2 **Killik Bend** Alaska U.S.A.
14 C3 **Killimor** Ireland
15 D4 **Killin** Scotland
26 E9 **Killingdal** Norway
46 E7 **Killini** *mt* Greece
46 E7 **Killini** Greece
14 B4 **Killorglin** Ireland
14 C2 **Killybegs** Ireland
14 F2 **Killyleagh** N Ireland
14 C4 **Kilmallock** Ireland
15 B3 **Kilmaluag** Scotland
13 F1 **Kilmany** Scotland
12 D2 **Kilmarnock** Scotland
95 L9 **Kilmarnock** Virginia U.S.A.
12 C1 **Kilmartin** Scotland
52 H6 **Kil'mez** U.S.S.R.
111 G8 **Kilmichael** Mississippi U.S.A.
12 C1 **Kilmichael Glassary** Scotland
139 G6 **Kilmore** Victoria Australia
12 C2 **Kilmory** Scotland
12 D1 **Kilmun** Scotland
13 E4 **Kilnhill** England
12 C1 **Kilninver** Scotland
13 J6 **Kilnsea** England
88 F6 **Kilombero** *R* Tanzania
88 F5 **Kilosa** Tanzania
29 H2 **Kilpisjärvi** Finland
29 L7 **Kilpua** Finland
29 Q2 **Kilp'yavr** U.S.S.R.
14 E2 **Kilrea** N Ireland
14 B4 **Kilrush** Ireland
9 E3 **Kilsby** England
12 D2 **Kilsyth** Scotland
73 L6 **Kiltan** *isld* Lakshadweep Indian Oc
14 C3 **Kiltimagh** Ireland
26 M5 **Kilvo** Sweden
87 E7 **Kilwa** Zaire
88 B6 **Kilwa** *isld* Zambia
88 G6 **Kilwa Kisiwani** Tanzania
88 G6 **Kilwa Kivinje** Tanzania
88 G6 **Kilwa Masoko** Tanzania
12 D2 **Kilwinning** Scotland
106 G4 **Kim** Colorado U.S.A.
101 M7 **Kimama** Idaho U.S.A.
70 D2 **Kimanis B** Sabah
138 D5 **Kimba** South Australia Australia
98 C8 **Kimball** Nebraska U.S.A.
98 H6 **Kimball** South Dakota U.S.A.
94 F9 **Kimball** West Virginia U.S.A.
116 P5 **Kimball, Mt** Alaska U.S.A.
99 L8 **Kimballton** Iowa U.S.A.
86 C7 **Kimbao** Zaire
117 Q11 **Kimberley** British Columbia Canada
120 K8 **Kimberley** Ontario Canada
89 D7 **Kimberley** S Africa
141 H3 **Kimberley,C** Queensland Australia
142 E3 **Kimberley Downs** Western Australia Australia
142 F3 **Kimberley Plateau** Western Australia Australia
143 C7 **Kimberley Ra** Western Australia Australia
101 L7 **Kimberly** Idaho U.S.A.
103 J2 **Kimberly** Nevada U.S.A.
99 S5 **Kimberly** Wisconsin U.S.A.
9 F3 **Kimbolton** England
145 E4 **Kimbolton** New Zealand
88 D5 **Kimbu** Tanzania
46 G6 **Kimi** Greece
29 K11 **Kimito** Finland
118 A3 **Kimiwan Lake** Alberta Canada
110 F3 **Kimmswick** Missouri U.S.A.
46 G8 **Kimolos** *isld* Greece
61 M7 **Kimpoku-san** *mt* Japan
52 E6 **Kimry** U.S.S.R.
27 H13 **Kimstad** Sweden
71 H5 **Kimtom** Sulawesi
52 F2 **Kimzha** U.S.S.R.
68 B1 **Kin** Burma
61 P13 **Kin** Okinawa
61 P13 **Kina** Okinawa
70 E1 **Kinabalu** *mt* Sabah
70 E2 **Kinabatangan** *R* Sabah
70 F2 **Kinabatangan, Kualu** *est* Sabah
47 N11 **Kinali** *isld* Turkey
88 F2 **Kinangop, Mt** Kenya
47 H8 **Kinaros** *isld* Greece
70 D2 **Kinarut** Sabah
117 O10 **Kinbasket** British Columbia Canada
117 O9 **Kinbasket L** Canada
118 F8 **Kinbrook I. Prov. Pk** Alberta Canada
118 K9 **Kincaid** Saskatchewan Canada
107 P3 **Kincaid** Kansas U.S.A.
Kincardine *co see* **Grampian** *reg*
120 J8 **Kincardine** Ontario Canada
12 E1 **Kincardine** Scotland
117 J8 **Kincolith** British Columbia Canada
141 J7 **Kincora Gas Field** Queensland Australia
15 E3 **Kincraig** Scotland
87 E7 **Kinda** Zaire
94 E3 **Kinde** Michigan U.S.A.
33 O10 **Kindelbrück** East Germany
109 P5 **Kinder** Louisiana U.S.A.
36 C3 **Kinderbeuern** W Germany
118 J7 **Kindersley** Saskatchewan Canada
85 B6 **Kindia** Guinea
57 G3 **Kindiktas, Gory** *mts* U.S.S.R.
98 J3 **Kindred** North Dakota U.S.A.
86 E6 **Kindu** Zaire
116 G7 **Kinegnak** Alaska U.S.A.
53 H7 **Kinel'** *R* U.S.S.R.
53 H7 **Kinel'-Cherkasy** U.S.S.R.
52 F6 **Kineshma** U.S.S.R.
140 C1 **King** *R* N Terr Australia
140 E6 **King** *R* Queensland Australia
141 G2 **King** *R* Queensland Australia
141 K7 **Kingaroy** Queensland Australia
133 C6 **King, Canal** *str* Chile
114 J2 **King Christian I** Northwest Territories Canada
102 C5 **King City** California U.S.A.
99 M9 **King City** Missouri U.S.A.
117 K10 **Kingcome Inlet** British Columbia Canada
116 F9 **King Cove** Alaska U.S.A.
146 K10 **King Edward Ice Shelf** Antarctica
142 F3 **King Edward R** Western Australia Australia
146 B10 **King Edward VII Land** Antarctica
95 R2 **Kingfield** Maine U.S.A.
107 N6 **Kingfisher** Oklahoma U.S.A.
146 D3 **King George I** South Shetland Is Antarctica
115 M6 **King George Is** Northwest Territories Canada
135 N10 **King George Is** Tuamotu Arch Pacific Oc
118 B8 **King George, Mt** British Columbia Canada
117 D5 **King George, Mt** Yukon Territory Canada
142 F2 **King George R** Western Australia Australia
143 C11 **King George Sd** Western Australia Australia
131 H6 **King Haakon B** S Georgia
142 E5 **King Hill** Western Australia Australia
120 C3 **Kinghorn** Ontario Canada
13 E1 **Kinghorn** Scotland
King I *see* **Kaydan Kyun**
139 G7 **King I** Tasmania Australia
117 K9 **King I** British Columbia Canada
52 C5 **Kingisepp** U.S.S.R.
52 B5 **Kingissepa** U.S.S.R.
100 G8 **King Lear** *mt* Nevada U.S.A.
146 J12 **King Leopold & Queen Astrid Coast** Antarctica
142 E3 **King Leopold Ra** Western Australia Australia
118 E5 **Kingman** Alberta Canada
103 K6 **Kingman** Arizona U.S.A.
107 M4 **Kingman** Kansas U.S.A.
95 T1 **Kingman** Maine U.S.A.
141 H7 **King, Mt** Queensland Australia
142 C5 **King, Mt** Western Australia Australia
108 E4 **King Mt** Texas U.S.A.
86 E6 **Kingombe** Zaire
138 D4 **Kingoonya** South Australia Australia
146 B7 **King Pen** Antarctica
139 H8 **King, R** Tasmania Australia
142 G3 **King, R** Western Australia Australia
102 D5 **Kings** *R* California U.S.A.
100 G8 **Kings** *R* Nevada U.S.A.
116 J7 **King Salmon** Alaska U.S.A.
13 F1 **Kingsbarns** Scotland
8 C7 **Kingsbridge** England
102 E5 **Kingsburg** California U.S.A.
109 K6 **Kingsbury** Texas U.S.A.
106 D1 **Kings Canyon** Colorado U.S.A.
102 F4 **Kings Canyon Nat Park** California U.S.A.
9 E5 **Kingsclere** England
139 L3 **Kingscliff-Fingal** New South Wales Australia
138 D6 **Kingscote** South Australia Australia
14 E3 **Kingscourt** Ireland
145 E2 **Kingseat** New Zealand
9 G5 **Kingsferry Bridge** England
9 F5 **Kingsfold** England
109 P2 **Kingsland** Arkansas U.S.A.
113 F7 **Kingsland** Georgia U.S.A.
9 F4 **Kings Langley** England
99 L7 **Kingsley** Iowa U.S.A.
94 B2 **Kingsley** Michigan U.S.A.
98 E8 **Kingsley Dam** Nebraska U.S.A.
9 G2 **King's Lynn** England
137 P2 **Kingsmill Group** *islds* Kiribati
112 F2 **Kings Mt** North Carolina U.S.A.
95 O6 **Kings Park** Long I, New York U.S.A.
101 P9 **Kings Pks** Utah U.S.A.
122 H8 **Kingsport** Nova Scotia Canada
94 E10 **Kingsport** Tennessee U.S.A.
142 E3 **Kings Sd** Western Australia Australia
8 C6 **Kingsteignton** England
138 E6 **Kingston** South Australia Australia
139 H9 **Kingston** Tasmania Australia
121 O8 **Kingston** Ontario Canada
9 F5 **Kingston** England
127 L3 **Kingston** Jamaica
144 B6 **Kingston** New Zealand
110 C5 **Kingston** Arkansas U.S.A.
110 B2 **Kingston** Missouri U.S.A.
95 R4 **Kingston** New Hampshire U.S.A.
95 N5 **Kingston** New York U.S.A.
94 E7 **Kingston** Ohio U.S.A.
107 O7 **Kingston** Oklahoma U.S.A.
95 M5 **Kingston** Pennsylvania U.S.A.
100 C2 **Kingston** Washington U.S.A.
94 F9 **Kingston** West Virginia U.S.A.
9 E4 **Kingston Lisle** England
103 J6 **Kingston Pk** California U.S.A.
13 H6 **Kingston upon Hull** England
13 F4 **Kingstown** England
127 O8 **Kingstown** St Vincent
112 H4 **Kingstree** South Carolina U.S.A.
120 H10 **Kingsville** Ontario Canada
94 G5 **Kingsville** Ohio U.S.A.
109 K8 **Kingsville** Texas U.S.A.
8 C7 **Kingswear** England
8 C3 **Kington** England
86 C7 **Kinguji** Zaire
15 D3 **Kingussie** Scotland
115 K4 **King William I** Northwest Territories Canada
89 E9 **King William's Town** S Africa
94 H7 **Kingwood** West Virginia U.S.A.
87 E8 **Kiniama** Zaire
47 J5 **Kınık** Turkey
119 M6 **Kinistino** Saskatchewan Canada
61 P7 **Kinka-san** *C* Japan
87 H11 **Kinkony, Farihy** *L* Madagascar
122 J7 **Kinkora** Prince Edward I Canada
145 E3 **Kinleith** New Zealand
118 K6 **Kinley** Saskatchewan Canada
144 B6 **Kinloch** New Zealand
15 C3 **Kinlochewe** Scotland
15 D4 **Kinlochleven** Scotland
15 D4 **Kinloch Rannoch** Scotland
68 B3 **Kinmaw** Burma
61 P13 **Kin-misaki** *C* Okinawa
121 M8 **Kinmount** Ontario Canada
110 H3 **Kinmundy** Illinois U.S.A.
27 F14 **Kinna** Sweden
117 P11 **Kinnaird** British Columbia Canada
15 F3 **Kinnairds Hd** Scotland
101 R6 **Kinnear** Wyoming U.S.A.
80 F3 **Kinneret** Israel
80 B8 **Kinneret-Negev-Conduit** Israel
83 L9 **Kinniyai** Sri Lanka
29 L8 **Kinnula** Finland
60 J11 **Kino** *R* Japan
61 K10 **Kinomoto** Japan
119 Q1 **Kinoosa** Manitoba Canada
60 H10 **Kinosaki** Japan
13 E1 **Kinqlassie** Scotland
Kinross *co see* **Tayside** *reg*
13 E1 **Kinross** Scotland
7 E11 **Kinsale** *oil rig* Celtic Sea
14 C5 **Kinsale** Ireland
95 L8 **Kinsale** Virginia U.S.A.
14 C5 **Kinsale, Old Hd of** *C* Ireland
118 F5 **Kinsella** Alberta Canada
101 U3 **Kinsey** Montana U.S.A.
86 C6 **Kinshasa** Zaire
60 C11 **Kin Shimo no-shima** Japan
107 L4 **Kinsley** Kansas U.S.A.
94 G5 **Kinsman** Ohio U.S.A.
112 K2 **Kinston** North Carolina U.S.A.
107 P6 **Kinta** Oklahoma U.S.A.
70 P10 **Kintamani, G** *mt* Indonesia
85 C6 **Kintinnian** Guinea
101 L1 **Kintla Pk** Montana U.S.A.
70 D6 **Kintop** Kalimantan
15 F3 **Kintore** Scotland
138 B2 **Kintore, Mt** South Australia Australia
140 A6 **Kintore Ra** N Terr Australia
12 C2 **Kintyre** *pen* Scotland
68 B1 **Kinu** Burma
61 N9 **Kinu** *R* Japan
118 B3 **Kinuso** Alberta Canada
14 C3 **Kinvarra** Ireland
61 P13 **Kin wan** *B* Okinawa
86 F5 **Kinyeti** *mt* Sudan
55 C6 **Kinzhaly** U.S.S.R.
36 D7 **Kinzig** *R* Baden-Württemberg W Germany
36 G3 **Kinzig** *R* Hessen W Germany
100 E5 **Kinzua** Oregon U.S.A.
71 N9 **Kio** Indonesia
100 F3 **Kiona** Washington U.S.A.
121 M6 **Kiosk** Ontario Canada
106 F2 **Kiowa** Colorado U.S.A.
107 M4 **Kiowa** Kansas U.S.A.
107 P7 **Kiowa** Oklahoma U.S.A.
119 Q3 **Kipahigan L** Manitoba Canada
135 T3 **Kipahulu** Hawaiian Is
46 E7 **Kiparissia** Greece
46 E7 **Kiparissiakós Kolpos** *B* Greece
121 M6 **Kipawa** Quebec Canada
88 C5 **Kipili** Tanzania
86 H6 **Kipini** Kenya
119 P8 **Kipling** Saskatchewan Canada
116 E7 **Kipnuk** Alaska U.S.A.
118 E9 **Kipp** Alberta Canada
12 D1 **Kippen** Scotland
36 D7 **Kippenheim** W Germany
123 O5 **Kippens** Newfoundland Canada
95 M9 **Kiptopeke** Virginia U.S.A.
87 E8 **Kipushi** Zaire
47 M10 **Kıraçköy** Turkey
60 H12 **Kiragawa** Japan
79 D1 **Kıraman** Turkey
75 J8 **Kirandul** India
76 E1 **Kirandul** India
47 H4 **Kirazh** Turkey
Kirberg *see* **Hünfelden**
120 F6 **Kirby** Ontario Canada
9 H4 **Kirby** England
111 C7 **Kirby** Arkansas U.S.A.
101 R6 **Kirby** Wyoming U.S.A.
111 C11 **Kirbyville** Texas U.S.A.
38 N8 **Kirchbach** Austria
38 M5 **Kirchberg** Austria
37 O2 **Kirchberg** East Germany
36 H5 **Kirchberg** Baden-Württemberg W Germany
36 C4 **Kirchberg** Rheinland-Pfalz W Germany
33 O5 **Kirchdorf** East Germany
37 P6 **Kirchdorf** W Germany
37 M4 **Kirchenlaibach** W Germany
37 M3 **Kirchenlamitz** W Germany
36 D2 **Kirchen-Sieg** W Germany
36 G6 **Kirchentellinsfurt** W Germany
37 M4 **Kirchenthumbach** W Germany
33 T9 **Kirchhain** East Germany
36 F2 **Kirchhain** W Germany
37 K1 **Kirchheilingen** E Ger
36 G5 **Kirchheim** W Germany
36 D4 **Kirchheim Bolanden** W Germany
32 E9 **Kirchhellen** W Germany
36 E1 **Kirchhundem** W Germany
33 O6 **Kirch Jesar** East Germany
32 H6 **Kirchkimmen** W Germany
37 K3 **Kirchlauter** W Germany
32 J8 **Kirchlengern** W Germany
32 K7 **Kirchlinteln** W Germany
38 K5 **Kirchschlag** Austria
32 J7 **Kirchweyhe** W Germany
32 J6 **Kirchwistedt** W Germany
47 J5 **Kireç** Turkey
33 Q5 **Kireh Grubenhagen** E Ger
56 G3 **Kirenga** *R* U.S.S.R.
47 K7 **Kirenis** *R* Turkey
56 G2 **Kirensk** U.S.S.R.
55 E6 **Kirey** *R* U.S.S.R.
54 J3 **Kireyevsk** U.S.S.R.
83 K11 **Kirgalpotta** *mt* Sri Lanka
Kirghizstan *see* **Kirgizskaya** *S.S.R.*
55 G6 **Kirgiziya** U.S.S.R.
55 B4 **Kirgiz-Miyaki** U.S.S.R.
57 F4 **Kirgizskaya S.S.R.** U.S.S.R.
86 C6 **Kiri** Zaire
137 Q2 **Kiribati** *rep* Pacific Oc
86 A2 **Kiridh** Somalia
89 A6 **Kiriis Ost** Namibia
78 F3 **Kirikhan** Turkey
78 D2 **Kirikkale** Turkey
145 E1 **Kirikopuni** New Zealand
29 O11 **Kirillovskoye** U.S.S.R.
Kirin *see* **Jilin**
83 L11 **Kirindi Oya** *R* Sri Lanka
88 F2 **Kirinyaga** Kenya
145 E1 **Kiripa** New Zealand
52 D5 **Kirishi** U.S.S.R.
60 D14 **Kirishima-Ōmuta Nat. Park** Japan
135 U10 **Kiritimati** *isld* Pacific Oc
136 L3 **Kiriwina Is** Papua New Guinea
106 H2 **Kirk** Colorado U.S.A.
98 C8 **Kirk** Nebraska U.S.A.
100 D7 **Kirk** Oregon U.S.A.
47 L5 **Kırka** Turkey
47 J5 **Kırkağaç** Turkey
12 E4 **Kirkbean** Scotland
13 E4 **Kirkbride** England
13 F5 **Kirkby Lonsdale** England
13 H5 **Kirkbymoorside** England
13 F5 **Kirkby Stephen** England
118 D8 **Kirkcaldy** Alberta Canada
13 E1 **Kirkcaldy** Scotland
12 C4 **Kirkcolm** Scotland
12 D4 **Kirkcowan** Scotland
Kirkcudbright *co see* **Dumfries and Galloway** *reg*
12 D4 **Kirkcudbright** Scotland
12 D4 **Kirkcudbright B** Scotland
13 G6 **Kirk Deighton** England
28 F6 **Kirkeby** Fyn Denmark
28 B6 **Kirkeby** Sønderjylland Denmark
28 G5 **Kirke Helsinge** Denmark
28 H5 **Kirke Hvalsø** Denmark
28 H5 **Kirke Hyllinge** Denmark
119 Q8 **Kirkella** Manitoba Canada
36 C5 **Kirkel-Neuhausel** W Germany
26 R2 **Kirkenes** Norway
28 H5 **Kirke Såby** Denmark
28 G6 **Kirke Stillinge** Denmark
26 K3 **Kirkestind** *mt* Norway
12 E2 **Kirkfieldbank** Scotland
13 F6 **Kirkham** England
12 D4 **Kirkinner** Scotland
12 D2 **Kirkintilloch** Scotland
29 L11 **Kirkkonummi** Finland
12 E3 **Kirkland** Scotland
103 M7 **Kirkland** Arizona U.S.A.
99 S7 **Kirkland** Illinois U.S.A.
120 K4 **Kirkland Lake** Ontario Canada
47 J3 **Kirklareli** Turkey
94 A6 **Kirklin** Indiana U.S.A.
9 F1 **Kirklington** England
13 G5 **Kirklington** N Yorks England
12 E2 **Kirkliston** Scotland
144 C6 **Kirkliston Range** New Zealand
99 L8 **Kirkman** Iowa U.S.A.
12 D3 **Kirkmichael** Scotland
13 F4 **Kirkoswald** England
12 D3 **Kirkoswald** Scotland
13 E3 **Kirkpatrick-Fleming** Scotland
146 D10 **Kirkpatrick,Mt** Antarctica
13 F5 **Kirkstone Pass** England
110 D1 **Kirksville** Missouri U.S.A.
78 K4 **Kirkūk** Iraq
15 F2 **Kirkwall** Scotland
89 D9 **Kirkwood** S Africa
102 B2 **Kirkwood** California U.S.A.
95 M4 **Kirkwood** New York U.S.A.
98 E5 **Kirley** South Dakota U.S.A.
79 G1 **Kirmith** Turkey
12 D2 **Kirn** Scotland
36 C4 **Kirn** W Germany
54 F2 **Kirov** Kaluga U.S.S.R.
52 G5 **Kirov** Kirovskaya obl U.S.S.R.
78 L1 **Kirovabad** Azerbaydzhanskaya S.S.R. U.S.S.R.
78 K1 **Kirovakan** U.S.S.R.
55 D3 **Kirovo** U.S.S.R.
54 D8 **Kirovograd** U.S.S.R.
52 D1 **Kirovsk** U.S.S.R.
52 G5 **Kirovskaya Oblast'** *prov* U.S.S.R.
57 E5 **Kirovskiy** U.S.S.R.
118 G7 **Kirriemuir** Alberta Canada
15 E4 **Kirriemuir** Scotland
52 H5 **Kirs** U.S.S.R.
78 E2 **Kirşehir** Turkey
87 D11 **Kirstonia** S Africa
98 B7 **Kirtley** Wyoming U.S.A.
13 H6 **Kirton** England
9 F2 **Kirton Holme** England
36 G2 **Kirtorf** W Germany
26 L4 **Kiruna** Sweden
86 E6 **Kirundu** Zaire
144 D5 **Kirwee** New Zealand
107 M2 **Kirwin** Kansas U.S.A.
61 N9 **Kiryū** Japan
54 K1 **Kirzhach** U.S.S.R.
27 H14 **Kisa** Sweden
61 N6 **Kisakata** Japan
87 G7 **Kisaki** Tanzania
46 F9 **Kisámou, K** *B* Crete Greece
86 E5 **Kisangani** Zaire
71 N9 **Kisar** *isld* Indonesia
116 G6 **Kisaralik** *R* Alaska U.S.A.
69 D11 **Kisaran** Sumatra
61 N10 **Kisarazu** Japan
48 D3 **Kisbér** Hungary
119 P9 **Kisbey** Saskatchewan Canada
56 C4 **Kiselevsk** U.S.S.R.
74 F5 **Kishangarh** India
85 E7 **Kishi** Nigeria
55 F4 **Kishikaroy, Oz** *L* U.S.S.R.
48 M3 **Kishinev** U.S.S.R.
60 J11 **Kishiwada** Japan
74 F2 **Kishtwar** Kashmir
Kisi *see* **Jixi**
88 G3 **Kisigau Mt** Kenya
88 E5 **Kisigo** *R* Tanzania
88 E2 **Kisii** Kenya
119 T4 **Kiskittogisu L** Manitoba Canada
119 T4 **Kiskitto L** Manitoba Canada
48 D4 **Kiskomárom** Hungary
48 E4 **Kiskörei-viztárole** *L* Hungary
48 F3 **Kisköreiviztároló** *L* Hungary
48 F4 **Kiskundorozsma** Hungary
48 F4 **Kiskunfélegyháza** Hungary
48 E4 **Kiskunhalas** Hungary
48 F4 **Kiskunmajsa** Hungary
53 F11 **Kislovodsk** U.S.S.R.
86 H6 **Kismaayo** Somalia
61 L10 **Kiso** Japan
61 L10 **Kiso-Fukushima** Nagano Japan
61 L10 **Kiso-sammyaku** *mts* Japan
48 E3 **Kispest** Hungary
117 J8 **Kispiox** *R* British Columbia Canada
28 H5 **Kisserup** Denmark
85 B7 **Kissidougou** Guinea
113 F9 **Kissimmee** Florida U.S.A.
113 F10 **Kissimmee** *R* Florida U.S.A.
119 Q3 **Kississing L** Manitoba Canada
41 L2 **Kisslegg** W Germany
84 H5 **Kissu, Jebel** *mt* Sudan
26 L3 **Kistefjell** *mt* Norway
48 F4 **Kistelek** Hungary
48 F2 **Kisterenye** Hungary
26 O1 **Kistrand** Norway
48 F3 **Kisújszallás** Hungary
88 E2 **Kisumu** Kenya
48 G2 **Kisvárda** Hungary
79 G5 **Kiswah, Al** Syria
85 C6 **Kita** Mali
57 D5 **Kitab** U.S.S.R.
60 H12 **Kitagawa** Japan
61 O9 **Kita-Ibaraki** Japan
26 L5 **Kitajaur** Sweden
61 P6 **Kitakami** Japan
61 N8 **Kitakata** Japan
60 D12 **Kita-Kyūshū** Japan
86 G5 **Kitale** Kenya
60 R2 **Kitami** Japan
60 Q1 **Kitami-sanchi** *mts* Japan
61 N9 **Kitamoto** Japan
88 G7 **Kitangari** Tanzania
61 N13 **Kitano-hana** *C* Japan
61 O9 **Kita-ura** *L* Japan
61 J12 **Kitayama** *R* Japan
48 M5 **Kitay, Ozero** *L* U.S.S.R.
106 H3 **Kit Carson** Colorado U.S.A.
120 K9 **Kitchener** Ontario Canada
112 E5 **Kite** Georgia U.S.A.
29 P9 **Kitee** Finland
86 F5 **Kitgum** Uganda
46 F6 **Kithairón** *mt* Greece
46 F8 **Kithira** *isld* Greece
46 G7 **Kíthnos** *isld* Greece
120 H3 **Kitigan** Ontario Canada
114 H3 **Kitikmeot** *dist* Northwest Territories Canada
80 G4 **Kitim** Jordan
117 J8 **Kitimat** British Columbia Canada
117 J9 **Kitimat Mill** Alberta Canada
29 M3 **Kitinen** *R* Finland
29 M4 **Kitinen** *R* Finland
52 C1 **Kitinen** *R* Finland
46 E2 **Kitka** *mt* Yugoslavia
46 F4 **Kitros** Greece
118 G5 **Kitscoty** Alberta Canada
48 K2 **Kitsman'** U.S.S.R.
60 E12 **Kitsuki** Japan
61 O9 **Kitsuregawa** Japan
138 E3 **Kittakittaooloo, L** South Australia Australia
94 H6 **Kittanning** Pennsylvania U.S.A.
95 N5 **Kittatinny Mts** New Jersey U.S.A.
33 R5 **Kittendorf** East Germany
95 R3 **Kittery** Maine U.S.A.
29 L4 **Kittilä** Finland
112 M1 **Kitty Hawk** North Carolina U.S.A.
88 G2 **Kitui** Kenya
88 D5 **Kitunda** Tanzania
117 J8 **Kitwanga** British Columbia Canada
88 B8 **Kitwe-Nkana** Zambia
38 F7 **Kitzbüheler Alpen** *mts* Austria
37 J4 **Kitzingen** W Germany
27 M10 **Kiukainen** Finland
116 L7 **Kiukpalik I** Alaska U.S.A.
68 D3 **Kiu Lom Dam** Thailand
86 E7 **Kiumbi** Zaire
29 M8 **Kiuruvesi** Finland
116 A4 **Kivak** U.S.S.R.
116 E3 **Kivalina** Alaska U.S.A.
53 C8 **Kivertsy** U.S.S.R.
116 E3 **Kividlo** Alaska U.S.A.
29 L8 **Kivijärvi** Finland
27 G17 **Kivik** Sweden
52 C5 **Kiviõli** U.S.S.R.
46 E4 **Kivotós** Greece
88 B2 **Kivu, Lac** Zaire/Rwanda
145 D4 **Kiwi** New Zealand
56 C3 **Kiya** *R* U.S.S.R.
55 E6 **Kiyakty, Oz** *L* U.S.S.R.
61 O14 **Kiyan** Okinawa
61 O14 **Kiyan-zaki** *C* Okinawa
54 B6 **Kiyev** U.S.S.R.
55 F5 **Kiyevka** U.S.S.R.
54 B5 **Kiyevskoy Vdkr** *res* U.S.S.R.
47 J3 **Kiyiköy** Turkey
47 L5 **Kıyır** *R* Turkey
118 H7 **Kiyiu L** Saskatchewan Canada
55 E5 **Kiyma** U.S.S.R.
52 J5 **Kizel** U.S.S.R.
52 F4 **Kizema** U.S.S.R.
47 M11 **Kızıl Adalar** *islds* Turkey
79 D2 **Kızılca** Turkey
47 K7 **Kızılcabölük** Turkey
47 K7 **Kızılcadağ** Turkey
47 K8 **Kızılca Dağ** *mt* Turkey
78 D1 **Kizilcahamam** Turkey
47 K7 **Kızılhişar** Turkey
78 E1 **Kızılırmak** *R* Turkey
47 L7 **Kızılkaya** Turkey
79 D2 **Kızılman Burun** *C* Turkey
55 C5 **Kizil'skoye** U.S.S.R.
47 N11 **Kiziltoprak** Turkey
79 C1 **Kızılyaka** Turkey
56 D4 **Kizir** *R* U.S.S.R.
53 G11 **Kizlyar** U.S.S.R.
50 E5 **Kizyl-Arvat** U.S.S.R.
26 M2 **Kjaekan** Norway
28 C4 **Kjellerup** Denmark
26 P1 **Kjelvik** Norway
26 G4 **Kjerringöy** Norway
26 Q1 **Kjöllefjord** Norway
71 J4 **Klabat** *mt* Sulawesi
48 E6 **Kladanj** Yugoslavia
30 H5 **Kladno** Czechoslovakia
48 H6 **Kladovo** Yugoslavia
37 O4 **Kladruby** Czechoslovakia
70 E2 **Klagan** Sabah
38 K8 **Klagenfurt** Austria
103 P6 **Klagetoh** Arizona U.S.A.
52 B6 **Klaipeda** U.S.S.R.
28 D5 **Klakring** Denmark
6 F1 **Klaksvik** Faeroes
100 B8 **Klamath** *R* California U.S.A.
100 A8 **Klamath** California U.S.A.
100 D7 **Klamath Falls** Oregon U.S.A.
100 B8 **Klamath Mts** California U.S.A.
100 C8 **Klamath River** California U.S.A.
71 C3 **Klamono** W Irian
70 D4 **Klampo** Kalimantan
117 J7 **Klappan** *R* British Columbia Canada
27 F12 **Klarä** *R* Sweden
27 F11 **Klarabro** Sweden
27 F11 **Klarälven** *R* Sweden
37 P3 **Klášterec** Czechoslovakia
70 N9 **Klaten** Java
37 P5 **Klatovy** Czechoslovakia
38 O5 **Klausen-Leopoldsdorf** Austria
41 J4 **Klausen P** *mt* Switzerland
117 G8 **Klawock** Alaska U.S.A.
31 K3 **Kłecko** Poland
31 L3 **Kleczew** Poland
122 J3 **Kleczkowski L** Quebec Canada
117 L10 **Kleena Kleene** British Columbia Canada
101 S5 **Kleenburn** Wyoming U.S.A.
33 S5 **Kleeth** East Germany
25 F5 **Klefe** W Germany
28 S9 **Kleifar** Iceland
101 R3 **Klein** Montana U.S.A.
33 P6 **Kleinberge** East Germany
22 J1 **Kleine-Brogel** Belgium
33 S9 **Kleine Elster** *R* East Germany
32 J9 **Kleinenberg** W Germany
22 H1 **Kleine Nete** *R* Belgium
33 R8 **Klein Kreutz** East Germany
37 N6 **Klein Laaber** *R* W Germany
36 F2 **Klein Linden** W Germany
89 B9 **Klein Roggeveld Berge** *mts* S Africa
89 B9 **Klein Swartberge** *mts* S Africa
33 N5 **Klein Thurow** East Germany
33 Q8 **Klein Wusterwitz** East Germany
38 N6 **Klein Zell** Austria
28 D3 **Klejtrup** Denmark
42 H4 **Klekovača** *mt* Yugoslavia
99 N6 **Klemme** Iowa U.S.A.
22 E1 **Klemskerke** Belgium
117 J9 **Klemtu** British Columbia Canada
48 F6 **Klenak** Yugoslavia
33 N7 **Klenze** W Germany
89 E6 **Klerksdorp** S Africa
116 G3 **Klery Creek** Alaska U.S.A.
54 E3 **Kletnya** U.S.S.R.
53 F9 **Kletskiy** U.S.S.R.
41 H2 **Klettgau** *R* W Germany
33 T9 **Klettwitz** East Germany
100 D3 **Klickitat** *R* Washington U.S.A.
79 E3 **Klidhes Is** Cyprus
33 Q7 **Klietz** East Germany
28 C2 **Klim** Denmark
31 N5 **Klimontów** Poland
54 C3 **Klimovichi** U.S.S.R.
52 H5 **Klimovka** U.S.S.R.
54 D4 **Klimovo** U.S.S.R.
54 J1 **Klimovsk** U.S.S.R.
26 G6 **Klimpfjäll** Sweden
54 H1 **Klin** U.S.S.R.
117 L10 **Klinaklini** *R* British Columbia Canada
112 F4 **Kline** South Carolina U.S.A.
71 G8 **Kling** Mindanao Philippines
37 Q2 **Klingenberg** East Germany
36 G4 **Klingenberg** W Germany
36 D5 **Klingenmünster** W Germany
37 N3 **Klingenthal** East Germany
70 B4 **Klingkang Ra** Sarawak
41 H2 **Klingnau** W Germany
33 R6 **Klink** East Germany
37 O3 **Klinovec** *mt* Czechoslovakia
28 E5 **Klinte** Denmark
27 K14 **Klintehamn** Sweden
54 D4 **Klintsy** U.S.S.R.
47 H5 **Klió** Greece
27 F15 **Klippan** Sweden
89 A8 **Kliprug Berg** *mt* S Africa
46 G2 **Klisura** Bulgaria
28 B2 **Klitmøller** Denmark
28 B7 **Klixbüll** W Germany
42 H4 **Ključ** Yugoslavia
31 L5 **Kłobuck** Poland
121 M6 **Klock** Ontario Canada
33 U6 **Klockow** East Germany
31 L3 **Kłodawa** Poland
31 K5 **Kłodzko** Poland
27 E11 **Klöfta** Norway
25 B6 **Kloosterzande** Netherlands
46 D3 **Klos** Albania
41 L3 **Kloster** *R* Austria
33 S7 **Klosterfelde** East Germany
28 A4 **Klosterhede Plantage** Denmark
41 M3 **Klösterle** Austria
33 Q6 **Kloster Malchow** East Germany
33 O9 **Kloster Mansfeld** East Germany
31 J7 **Klosterneuburg** Austria
36 E6 **Klosterreichenbach** W Germany
41 L4 **Klosters** Switzerland
33 S8 **Kloster Zinna** East Germany
27 H12 **Kloten** Sweden
36 C3 **Klotten** W Germany
33 O7 **Klötze** East Germany
28 C5 **Klovborg** Denmark
26 G9 **Klövsjö** Sweden
117 D5 **Kluane** Yukon Territory Canada
117 D5 **Kluane Nat. Park** Yukon Territory Canada
31 L5 **Kluczbork** Poland
70 E6 **Klumpang, Teluk** *B* Kalimantan
25 C5 **Klundert** Netherlands
70 P10 **Klungkung** Indonesia
36 C1 **Kluppelberg** W Germany
116 P6 **Klutina L** Alaska U.S.A.
26 L7 **Klutmark** Sweden
33 O5 **Klütz** East Germany
52 H7 **Klyavlino** U.S.S.R.
52 F6 **Klyazma** *R* U.S.S.R.
52 F2 **Klyuchevaya** U.S.S.R.
51 Q3 **Klyuchevskaya Sopka** *mt* U.S.S.R.
55 G4 **Klyuchi** U.S.S.R.
55 D2 **Klyuchi** U.S.S.R.
56 C2 **Klyuvinka** U.S.S.R.
27 B13 **Knabengruber** Norway
38 J7 **Knallstein, Gross** *mt* Austria
99 O5 **Knapp** Wisconsin U.S.A.
13 G5 **Knaresborough** England
13 F4 **Knarsdale** England
37 M2 **Knau** East Germany
9 F4 **Knebworth** England
32 H5 **Knechtsand** *sandbank* W Germany
118 K3 **Knee L** Saskatchewan Canada
33 N7 **Knesebeck** W Germany
22 E1 **Knesselare** Belgium
37 K4 **Knetsgau** W Germany
117 L9 **Knewstubb L** British Columbia Canada
46 G1 **Knezha** Bulgaria
98 D2 **Knife** *R* North Dakota U.S.A.
116 K7 **Knife Pk** Alaska U.S.A.
99 P3 **Knife River** Minnesota U.S.A.
101 P8 **Knight** Wyoming U.S.A.
116 O6 **Knight I** Alaska U.S.A.
117 K10 **Knight Inlet** British Columbia Canada
8 C3 **Knighton** Wales
94 B7 **Knightstown** Indiana U.S.A.
110 J2 **Knightsville** Indiana U.S.A.
42 G4 **Knin** Yugoslavia
32 H5 **Kniphausen** W Germany
109 H6 **Knippa** Texas U.S.A.
38 L7 **Knittelfeld** Austria
27 J12 **Knivsta** Sweden
46 E1 **Knjaževac** Yugoslavia
110 F5 **Knobel** Arkansas U.S.A.
142 G2 **Knob Pk** Western Australia Australia
14 C3 **Knock** Ireland
14 B5 **Knockboy** *mt* Ireland
14 B5 **Knockbrack** *mt* Ireland
14 E1 **Knocklayd** *mt* N Ireland
14 D4 **Knockmealdown Mts** Ireland
14 B5 **Knockowen** *mt* Ireland
22 E1 **Knokke** Belgium
29 O5 **Knolayarvi** U.S.S.R.
101 M9 **Knolls** Utah U.S.A.
29 L10 **Knorevesi** Finland
28 E2 **Knøsen** *hill* Denmark
46 G9 **Knossos** Crete Greece
108 F3 **Knott** Texas U.S.A.
9 E3 **Knowle** England
107 K5 **Knowles** Oklahoma U.S.A.
146 D5 **Knowles, Cape** *C* Antarctica
121 S7 **Knowlton** Quebec Canada
99 R5 **Knowlton** Wisconsin U.S.A.
99 U8 **Knox** Indiana U.S.A.
98 G1 **Knox** North Dakota U.S.A.
94 H5 **Knox** Pennsylvania U.S.A.
117 G8 **Knox, C** Graham I, Br Col Canada
110 E1 **Knox City** Missouri U.S.A.
108 H2 **Knox City** Texas U.S.A.
146 G13 **Knox Coast** Antarctica
102 B3 **Knoxville** California U.S.A.
99 Q9 **Knoxville** Illinois U.S.A.
99 N8 **Knoxville** Iowa U.S.A.
111 E10 **Knoxville** Mississippi U.S.A.
94 K5 **Knoxville** Pennsylvania U.S.A.
112 C1 **Knoxville** Tennessee U.S.A.
83 K10 **Knuckles** *mt* Sri Lanka
115 N2 **Knud Rasmussen Land** Greenland
28 H6 **Knudshoved** *C* Denmark
36 G2 **Knüllwald** W Germany
8 D1 **Knutsford** England
52 D2 **Knyazhaya Guba** U.S.S.R.
52 F5 **Knyazhevo** U.S.S.R.
87 D12 **Knysna** S Africa
31 O2 **Knyszyn** Poland
29 M2 **Koarvikods** *mt* Finland
69 H14 **Koba** Indonesia
60 D14 **Koba** Japan
28 H6 **Kobanke** *hill* Denmark
69 D8 **Ko Ban Sa Ket** Thailand
42 F2 **Kobarid** Yugoslavia
60 D13 **Kobayashi** Japan
115 P5 **Kobberminebugt** *B* Greenland
28 C3 **Kobberup** Denmark
Kobdo Jargalant *see* **Hovd**
71 A2 **Kobe** Halmahera Indonesia
60 J11 **Kōbe** Japan
28 G7 **Købelev** Denmark
54 F7 **Kobelyaki** U.S.S.R.
89 A8 **Kobe Mts** S Africa
29 K5 **København** Denmark
38 H5 **Kobernausser Wald** *reg* Austria
36 C3 **Kobern-Gondorf** W Germany
67 H4 **Kōbi-sho** *isld* Japan
36 D3 **Koblenz** W Germany
86 F4 **Kobowem Swamp** Sudan
52 E5 **Kobozha** *R* U.S.S.R.
52 H5 **Kobra** *R* U.S.S.R.
52 H4 **Kobra** U.S.S.R.
61 M10 **Kobuchizawa** Japan
116 J3 **Kobuk** Alaska U.S.A.
116 H3 **Kobuk** *R* Alaska U.S.A.
116 H3 **Kobuk Valley Nat Park** Alaska U.S.A.
31 K4 **Kobylin** Poland
47 K8 **Koca** *R* Turkey
47 J4 **Kocabaş** *R* Turkey
78 C1 **Kocaeli** Turkey
46 E3 **Kočani** Yugoslavia
47 J7 **Koçarlı** Turkey
47 L6 **Koca Tepe** *mt* Turkey
48 F6 **Koceljevo** Yugoslavia
42 F3 **Kočevje** Yugoslavia
75 N5 **Koch Bihār** India
52 F4 **Kochen'ga** U.S.S.R.
36 H5 **Kocher** *R* W Germany
46 F2 **Kocherinovo** Bulgaria
54 M4 **Kochetovka** U.S.S.R.
52 H5 **Kochevo** U.S.S.R.
115 M4 **Koch I** Northwest Territories Canada
60 G12 **Kōchi** *prefect* Japan
60 G12 **Kōchi** Japan
60 F11 **Kōchi** Japan
61 P14 **Kochinada** Okinawa
52 D3 **Kochkoma** U.S.S.R.
57 H4 **Kochkorka** U.S.S.R.
52 K2 **Kochmes** U.S.S.R.
101 O4 **Koch Mt** Montana U.S.A.
53 G11 **Kochubey** U.S.S.R.
31 K4 **Kocie Góry** *mts* Poland
31 N4 **Kock** Poland
33 O7 **Köckte** East Germany
48 E4 **Kocsola** Hungary
52 J3 **Kodachdikost** U.S.S.R.
76 C5 **Kodaikanal** India
60 O4 **Kodamari misaki** *C* Japan
75 L6 **Kodarma** India
83 L9 **Koddiyar B** Sri Lanka
31 O4 **Kodeń** Poland
116 L8 **Kodiak** Alaska U.S.A.
116 L8 **Kodiak I** Alaska U.S.A.
83 K8 **Kodikamam** Sri Lanka
76 D5 **Kodikkarai** India
52 F4 **Kodima** U.S.S.R.
74 D8 **Kodinar** India
52 E3 **Kodino** U.S.S.R.
86 F4 **Kodok** Sudan
60 O4 **Kodomari** Japan
48 M2 **Kodyma** U.S.S.R.
102 G6 **Koehn L** California U.S.A.
22 D1 **Koekelare** Belgium
22 J1 **Koersel** Belgium
87 C11 **Koës** Namibia
60 P1 **Koetoi** Japan
103 L8 **Kofa Mts** Arizona U.S.A.
37 N6 **Köfering** W Germany
87 E11 **Koffiefontein** S Africa
85 D7 **Koforidua** Ghana
61 M10 **Kōfu** Japan
61 N9 **Koga** Japan
141 K7 **Kogan** Queensland Australia
28 J6 **Køge** Denmark
29 K6 **Køge Bugt** *B* Denmark
52 J3 **Kogel'** *R* U.S.S.R.
48 M4 **Kogil'nik** *R* U.S.S.R.
116 H6 **Kogrukluk** *R* Alaska U.S.A.
60 D11 **Kogushi** Japan
74 D2 **Kohat** Pakistan
52 B5 **Kohila** U.S.S.R.
75 Q6 **Kohima** India
68 G6 **Koh Ker** Cambodia
77 B4 **Kohkīlūyeh va Būyer Aḥmadi** *prov* Iran
146 B8 **Kohler Ra** Antarctica
74 C4 **Kohlu** Pakistan
37 O1 **Kohren Sahlis** East Germany
77 G2 **Kohsun** Afghanistan
68 F7 **Koh Tang** *isld* Cambodia
52 C5 **Kohtla-Järve** U.S.S.R.
145 E3 **Kohuratahi** New Zealand
61 M8 **Koide** Japan
116 R6 **Koidern** Yukon Territory Canada
69 A8 **Koihoa** Nicobar Is
52 H3 **Koin** *R* U.S.S.R.
78 K3 **Koi Sanjaq** Iraq
29 P8 **Koitere** *L* Finland
29 L5 **Koivu** Finland
65 G7 **Kōje** *isld* S Korea
31 K6 **Kojetin** Czechoslovakia
60 N4 **Ko jima** *isld* Japan
143 B10 **Kojonup** Western Australia Australia
95 S1 **Kokadjo** Maine U.S.A.
83 L10 **Kokagala** *mt* Sri Lanka
86 G4 **K'ok'a Häyk'** *L* Ethiopia
55 D6 **Kokalaat** U.S.S.R.
57 F4 **Kokand** U.S.S.R.
117 P11 **Kokanee Glacier Nat. Park** British Columbia Canada
57 B2 **Kokaral** U.S.S.R.
48 F2 **Kokava** Czechoslovakia
60 J11 **Kokawa** Japan
56 C5 **Kokbesh** U.S.S.R.
57 F6 **Kokcha** *R* Afghanistan
55 E4 **Kokchetav** U.S.S.R.
29 K10 **Kokemäenjoki** *R* Finland
29 J10 **Kokemäki** Finland
136 H2 **Kokenau** W Irian
54 A2 **Kokhanovo** U.S.S.R.
80 B7 **Kokhav** Israel
29 K8 **Kokkola** Finland
85 E6 **Koko** Nigeria
136 K3 **Kokoda** Papua New Guinea
102 S12 **Koko Head** Hawaiian Is
116 F2 **Kokolik** *R* Alaska U.S.A.
94 A6 **Kokomo** Indiana U.S.A.
144 C6 **Kokonga** New Zealand
Koko Nor *L see* **Qinghai Hu** *L*
52 C4 **Kokonselka** *L* Finland
54 F4 **Kokorevka** U.S.S.R.
69 B11 **Kokos** *isld* Indonesia
116 K4 **Kokrines Hills** Alaska U.S.A.
57 E4 **Koksaray** U.S.S.R.
52 G6 **Kokshaga** *R* U.S.S.R.
52 F4 **Kokshen'ga** *R* U.S.S.R.
22 D1 **Koksijde** Belgium
115 N6 **Koksoak** *R* Quebec Canada
54 M8 **Koksovyy** U.S.S.R.
89 F8 **Kokstad** S Africa
60 D14 **Kokubu** Japan
60 D12 **Kokura** Japan
70 G7 **Koku, Tg** *C* Sulawesi
116 H7 **Kokwok** *R* Alaska U.S.A.
57 G4 **Kok-Yangak** U.S.S.R.
52 D1 **Kola** U.S.S.R.
70 G7 **Kolaka** Sulawesi
71 F6 **Kolambugan** Mindanao Philippines
76 D4 **Kolar** India
76 D4 **Kolar Gold Fields** India
29 K4 **Kolari** Finland
Kolarovgrad *see* **Shumen**
48 D3 **Kolárovo** Czechoslovakia
26 F8 **Kolåsen** Sweden
46 D2 **Kolašin** Yugoslavia
27 H12 **Kolbäck** Sweden
71 M10 **Kolbano** Timor
Kolberg *see* **Kołobrzeg**
38 H8 **Kölbnitz** Austria
26 D9 **Kolbotn** Norway
31 N5 **Kolbuszowa** Poland
28 F5 **Kolby** Denmark
52 E6 **Kol'chugino** U.S.S.R.
85 A6 **Kolda** Senegal
28 B3 **Koldby** Denmark
28 C6 **Kolding** Denmark
86 E5 **Kole** Zaire
135 T3 **Kolekole** *pk* Hawaiian Is
48 M4 **Kolesnoye** U.S.S.R.
37 P5 **Koleveč** Czechoslovakia
52 B5 **Kolga laht** *G* U.S.S.R.
50 D2 **Kolguyev Ostrov** *isld* U.S.S.R.
76 B2 **Kolhapur** India
29 O8 **Koli** Finland
48 L5 **Kolibash** U.S.S.R.
116 J7 **Koliganek** Alaska U.S.A.
47 R14 **Kolimbia** Rhodes Greece
31 J5 **Kolin** Czechoslovakia
101 Q2 **Kolin** Montana U.S.A.
28 F4 **Kolind** Denmark
37 P5 **Kolinec** Czechoslovakia
28 C4 **Kølkær** Denmark
121 N7 **Kol. Kienitz** Ontario Canada
33 T7 **Kol Kienitz** East Germany
37 L1 **Kölleda** East Germany
76 C4 **Kollegal** India
76 D5 **Kollidam** *R* India
46 E7 **Kollinai** Greece
25 F2 **Kollum** Netherlands
28 C4 **Kollund** Ringkøbing Denmark
28 C7 **Kollund** Sønderjylland Denmark
36 B2 **Köln** W Germany
31 N2 **Kolno** Poland
31 L3 **Koło** Poland
135 O1 **Koloa** Hawaiian Is
31 J1 **Kołobrzeg** Poland
33 S9 **Kolochau** East Germany
54 D2 **Kolodnya** U.S.S.R
52 F5 **Kologriv** U.S.S.R.
71 B3 **Kolok** Indonesia
85 C6 **Kolokani** Mali
137 M3 **Kolombangara** *isld* Solomon Is
56 B2 **Kolominskiye Grivy** U.S.S.R.
54 K1 **Kolomna** U.S.S.R.
48 J2 **Kolomyya** U.S.S.R.
70 G6 **Kolonedale** Sulawesi
71 B2 **Kolorai** *isld* Halmahera Indonesia
55 F3 **Kolosovka** U.S.S.R.
Kolozsvar *see* **Cluj-Napoca**
52 E5 **Kolp'** *R* U.S.S.R.
42 G3 **Kolpa** *R* Yugoslavia
56 B2 **Kolpashevo** U.S.S.R.
33 R6 **Kölpin-See** *L* East Germany
33 Q10 **Kölsa** East Germany
26 G9 **Kolsätt** Sweden
52 D1 **Kol'skiy Poluostrov** *pen* U.S.S.R.
52 D1 **Kol'skiy Zaliv** *G* U.S.S.R.
28 F6 **Kølstrup** Denmark
27 H12 **Kolsva** Sweden
52 A3 **Kol'tsovo** U.S.S.R.
48 F6 **Kolubara** *R* Yugoslavia
145 D1 **Koluikohu** New Zealand
73 L8 **Kolumadulu Atoll** Maldives
31 M4 **Koluszki** Poland
55 E5 **Koluton** U.S.S.R.
52 J1 **Kolva** *R* Komi A.S.S.R. U.S.S.R.
52 J4 **Kolva** *R* Permskaya obl U.S.S.R.
26 E7 **Kolvereid** Norway
26 O1 **Kolvik** Norway
52 D2 **Kolvitsa** U.S.S.R.
87 E8 **Kolwezi** Zaire
54 K1 **Kolyberovo** U.S.S.R.

Kolyma — Kuramoto 45

51 P2 **Kolyma** *R* U.S.S.R.
54 H1 **Kolyubakino** U.S.S.R.
147 P2 **Kolyuchinskaya** U.S.S.R.
116 A3 **Kolyuchinskaya Guba** *G* U.S.S.R.
56 B5 **Kolyvan'** U.S.S.R.
27 G14 **Kölzby** Sweden
46 F1 **Kom** *mt* Bulgaria
68 D5 **Koma** Burma
86 G4 **Koma** Ethiopia
61 P6 **Kōma** Japan
85 G6 **Komadugu Gana** *R* Nigeria
61 L10 **Komagane** Japan
60 O3 **Komaga-take** *mt* Hokkaido Japan
61 N8 **Komaga-take** *mt* Honshu Japan
26 N1 **Komagfjord** Norway
26 S1 **Komagvaer** Norway
55 C2 **Komarikhinskiy** U.S.S.R.
119 U8 **Komarno** Manitoba Canada
48 E3 **Komárno** Czechoslovakia
48 E3 **Komárom** *co* Hungary
48 E3 **Komárom** Hungary
89 G6 **Komati** *R* Swaziland
89 G5 **Komatipoort** S Africa
103 M8 **Komatke** Arizona U.S.A.
61 K9 **Komatsu** Ishikawa Japan
61 O7 **Komatsu** Yamagata Japan
71 L8 **Komba** *isld* Indonesia
71 J4 **Kombot** Sulawesi
46 E5 **Kombóti** Greece
28 E3 **Komdrup** Denmark
88 D2 **Kome I** Uganda
89 E9 **Komga** S Africa
61 O5 **Kominato** Japan
52 H5 **Komi-Permyatskiy Avtonomnyy Okrug** *dist* U.S.S.R.
48 E2 **Komjatice** Czechoslovakia
48 E4 **Komló** Hungary
53 E9 **Kommunarsk** U.S.S.R.
57 F5 **Kommunizma, Pik** *mt* U.S.S.R.
71 J9 **Komodo** *isld* Indonesia
85 D7 **Komoé** *R* Ivory Coast
85 D7 **Komoé Nat. Park** Ivory Coast
84 J5 **Kôm Ombo** Egypt
61 M9 **Komoro** Japan
46 G3 **Komotini** Greece
46 D2 **Komovi** *mt* Yugoslavia
89 D8 **Kompas Berg** *mt* S Africa
68 G6 **Kompong Kleang** Cambodia
68 F7 **Kompong Som** Cambodia
68 G7 **Kompong Speu** Cambodia
68 G6 **Kompong Sralao** Cambodia
68 G6 **Kompong Thom** Cambodia
68 G6 **Kompong Trabek** Cambodia
68 G7 **Kompong Trach** Cambodia
68 G7 **Kompong Tralach** Cambodia
48 M4 **Komrat** U.S.S.R.
89 B9 **Komsbergeskarp** *mts* S Africa
55 D4 **Komsomolets** U.S.S.R.
51 J1 **Komsomolets, Ostrov** *isld* U.S.S.R.
52 F6 **Komsomol'sk** U.S.S.R.
54 E8 **Komsomol'sk** Ukrainskaya S.S.R. U.S.S.R.
55 D1 **Komsomol'skiy** U.S.S.R.
54 K9 **Komsomol'skoye** U.S.S.R.
59 L1 **Komsomol'skoye-na-Amure** U.S.S.R.
103 M10 **Kom Vo** Arizona U.S.A.
53 G12 **Konagkend** U.S.S.R.
52 E6 **Konakovo** U.S.S.R.
75 M9 **Konārka** India
77 B5 **Konār Takhteh** Iran
109 L1 **Konawa** Oklahoma U.S.A.
42 H3 **Končanica** Yugoslavia
55 E2 **Konda** *R* U.S.S.R.
71 C3 **Konda** W Irian
76 E1 **Kondagaon** India
121 O6 **Kondiaronk, L** Quebec Canada
143 C10 **Kondinin** Western Australia Australia
88 E4 **Kondoa** Tanzania
52 D4 **Kondopoga** U.S.S.R.
48 F4 **Kondoros** Hungary
54 G2 **Kondrovo** U.S.S.R.
86 B3 **Konduga** Nigeria
143 B9 **Kondut** Western Australia Australia
56 D2 **Konduyak** U.S.S.R.
77 L1 **Kondūz** Afghanistan
52 J3 **Konetsbor** U.S.S.R.
52 E4 **Konevo** U.S.S.R.
28 H6 **Køng** Denmark
85 D7 **Kong** Ivory Coast
116 R2 **Kongakut** *R* Alaska U.S.A.
115 Q4 **Kong Christian IX Land** Greenland
115 R3 **Kong Christian X Land** Greenland
28 B6 **Kongeå** *R* Denmark
29 K5 **Kongens Lyngby** Denmark
115 P5 **Kong Frederik VI Kyst** *coast* Greenland
29 M9 **Konginkangas** Finland
68 F7 **Kong Kaôh Kong** Cambodia
50 B1 **Kong Karls Land** *isld* Spitzbergen
70 E4 **Kong Kat** *mt* Kalimantan
70 E4 **Kongkemul** *mt* Kalimantan
87 D9 **Kongola** Namibia
86 E7 **Kongolo** Zaire
86 F4 **Kongor** Sudan
147 E10 **Kong Oscars Fj** Greenland
26 J3 **Kongsbakktind** *mt* Norway
27 D12 **Kongsberg** Norway
26 R1 **Kongsfjord** *inlet* Norway
26 R1 **Kongsfjord** Norway
28 B6 **Kongsmark** Denmark
26 F7 **Kongsmoen** Norway
28 J6 **Kongsted** Denmark
27 E11 **Kongsvinger** Norway
66 B4 **Kongur Shan** *mt* China
88 F5 **Kongwa** Tanzania
31 M5 **Koniecpol** Poland
36 H4 **Königheim** W Germany
36 F6 **Königsbach** W Germany
Königsberg *see* **Kaliningrad**
36 D4 **Königsberg** *mt* W Germany
37 J6 **Königsbronn** W Germany
33 T10 **Königsbrück** East Germany
37 K7 **Königsbrunn** W Germany
41 O2 **Königsdorf** W Germany
37 L2 **Königsee** East Germany
37 L4 **Königsfeld** W Germany
Königshofen *see* **Lauda-Königshofen**
36 H4 **Königshofen** W Germany
33 N8 **Königslutter** W Germany
36 F5 **Königsstuhl** *mt* W Germany
36 E3 **Königstein** W Germany
38 L5 **Königswiesen** Austria
36 C2 **Königswinter** W Germany
33 T8 **Königs Wusterhausen** East Germany
31 L3 **Konin** Poland
145 E4 **Konini** New Zealand
46 D5 **Konispol** Albania
42 H5 **Konjic** Yugoslavia
88 B1 **Konjo** *tribal dist* Zaire
48 E6 **Konjuh** *mt* Yugoslavia
26 M3 **Konkämä Älv** *R* Sweden/Finland
88 A8 **Konkola** Zambia
85 B6 **Konkouré** *R* Guinea
33 P9 **Könnern** East Germany
37 N3 **Konnersreuth** W Germany
29 M9 **Konnevesi** Finland
85 D7 **Konongo** Ghana
88 C5 **Konongo** Tanzania
61 N9 **Kōnosu** Japan
54 E5 **Konotop** U.S.S.R.
66 D3 **Konqi He** *R* China
85 C7 **Konsankoro** Guinea
31 M4 **Końskie** Poland
53 F10 **Konstantinovsk** U.S.S.R.
41 K2 **Konstanz** W Germany
85 F6 **Kontagora** Nigeria
86 B4 **Kontcha** Cameroon
22 G1 **Kontich** Belgium
29 N7 **Kontiomäki** Finland
47 O12 **Kontókali** Greece
116 L6 **Kontrashibuna L** Alaska U.S.A.
68 J6 **Kontum, Plat. du** Vietnam
52 F2 **Konushin, Mys** *C* U.S.S.R.
78 D3 **Konya** Turkey
36 B4 **Konz** W Germany
88 F2 **Konza** Kenya
37 O5 **Konzell** W Germany
55 C2 **Konzhakovskiy Kamen', G** *mt* U.S.S.R.
25 C4 **Koog** Netherlands
116 C5 **Kookooligit Mts** St Lawrence I, Alaska U.S.A.
143 D8 **Kookynie** Western Australia Australia
140 D2 **Koolatong** *R* N Terr Australia
102 S11 **Koolauloa** Hawaiian Is
102 S12 **Koolaupoko** Hawaiian Is
142 B6 **Kooline** W Australia
140 E6 **Koolivoo,L** Queensland Australia
143 C9 **Koolyanobbing** Western Australia Australia
143 G9 **Koonalda** South Australia Australia
142 B6 **Koorabooka** *R* Western Australia Australia
143 B6 **Koorabooka** Western Australia Australia
143 B9 **Koorda** Western Australia Australia
142 B5 **Koordarrie** Western Australia Australia
29 T8 **Kópasker** Iceland
48 L2 **Kopaygorod** U.S.S.R.
144 A7 **Kopeka B** New Zealand
33 T8 **Kopenick** East Germany
26 K8 **Köpmanholmen** Sweden
27 F10 **Kopparberg** *county* Sweden
79 C2 **Köprülü** Turkey
145 E2 **Kopu** New Zealand
145 E4 **Kopuaranga** New Zealand
77 C4 **Kor** *R* Iran
86 H4 **K'orahē** Ethiopia
47 O12 **Korakiána** Greece
75 K7 **Korba** India
32 J10 **Korbach** W Germany
100 B9 **Korbel** California U.S.A.
69 E10 **Korbu, G.** *mt* Malaysia
46 D4 **Korcë** Albania
42 H6 **Korčula** Yugoslavia
36 B4 **Kordel** W Germany
77 A2 **Kordestān** Iran
77 D1 **Kord Kūv** Iran
Kordofan *prov* Sudan *see* **Northern and Southern Kordofan** *provs*
77 G6 **Kords** *reg* Iran
59 H4 **Korea Bay** China/Korea
65 G4 **Korea, North** *rep* E Asia
65 H6 **Korea, South** *rep* E Asia
52 D2 **Korelaksha** U.S.S.R.
52 J4 **Korelino** U.S.S.R.
54 F5 **Korenevo** U.S.S.R.
146 D7 **Korff Ice Rise** *ice rise* Antarctica
26 G5 **Korgen** Norway
85 C7 **Korhogo** Ivory Coast
60 D14 **Kori** Japan
46 F4 **Korinós** Greece
28 E6 **Korinth** Denmark
46 E6 **Korinthiakós Kólpos** *G* Greece
46 F7 **Kórinthos** Greece
46 D2 **Koritnik** *mt* Yugoslavia
Koritsa *see* **Korcë**
61 O8 **Kōriyama** Japan
55 D4 **Korkino** U.S.S.R.
47 L7 **Korkuteli** Turkey
66 D3 **Korla** China
54 B3 **Korma** U.S.S.R.
120 G5 **Kormak** Ontario Canada
48 D3 **Körmend** Hungary
55 F3 **Kormilovka** U.S.S.R.
42 G5 **Kornat** *isld* Yugoslavia
37 L5 **Kornburg** W Germany
25 F7 **Kornelimünster** W Germany
37 K1 **Körner** East Germany
48 L3 **Korneshty** U.S.S.R.
55 F5 **Korneyevka** U.S.S.R.
55 E4 **Korneyevka** U.S.S.R.
27 E13 **Kornsjö** Norway
28 C3 **Kornum** Denmark
36 G6 **Kornwestheim** W Germany
70 G5 **Koro** *R* Sulawesi
54 J6 **Korocha** U.S.S.R.
78 C1 **Köroglu D** Turkey
88 G4 **Korogwe** Tanzania
138 F7 **Koroit** Victoria Australia
144 D4 **Koromiko** New Zealand
113 F8 **Korona** Florida U.S.A.
85 E7 **Koronga** *mt* Togo
139 G6 **Korong Vale** Victoria Australia
46 E8 **Koróni** Greece
46 F4 **Korónia, L** Greece
31 K2 **Koronowo** Poland
54 D5 **Korop** U.S.S.R.
48 J2 **Koropets** U.S.S.R.
46 F7 **Koropí** Greece
48 F4 **Körös** *R* Hungary
53 C8 **Korosten** U.S.S.R.
53 C8 **Korostyshev** U.S.S.R.
86 C2 **Koro Toro** Chad
54 L6 **Korotoyak** U.S.S.R.
116 G9 **Korovin I** Alaska U.S.A.
29 M9 **Korpilahti** Finland
26 N5 **Korpilombolo** Sweden
29 J11 **Korpo** Finland
59 M2 **Korsakov** U.S.S.R.
27 H14 **Korsberga** Sweden
36 B1 **Korschenbroich** W Germany
28 H5 **Korshage** *C* Denmark
48 J2 **Korshev** U.S.S.R.
28 E3 **Korsholm** *isld* Denmark
27 H11 **Korsnäs** Sweden
26 H3 **Korsnes** Norway
28 G6 **Korsør** Denmark
54 C7 **Korsun' Shevchenkovskiy** U.S.S.R.
22 E1 **Kortemark** Belgium
29 K8 **Kortesjärvi** Finland
22 J2 **Kortessem** Belgium
27 G12 **Kortfors** Sweden
25 A5 **Kortgene** Netherlands
52 H4 **Kortkeros** U.S.S.R.
22 E2 **Kortrijk** Belgium
52 F5 **Kortsovo** U.S.S.R.
47 J5 **Korucu** Turkey
139 H7 **Korumburra** Victoria Australia
29 O3 **Korvatunturi** *mt* Finland
29 O4 **Korya** U.S.S.R.
52 G4 **Koryazhma** U.S.S.R.
54 D5 **Koryukovka** U.S.S.R.
47 J8 **Kos** *isld* Greece
52 H5 **Kosa** U.S.S.R.
53 E10 **Kosa Arabatskaya Strelka** *spit* U.S.S.R.
55 D5 **Kosagal** U.S.S.R.
61 L11 **Kosai** Japan
61 O5 **Kosaka** Japan
69 E8 **Ko Samui** *isld* Thailand
57 D1 **Kosay** U.S.S.R.
54 J2 **Kosaya Gora** U.S.S.R.
56 E2 **Kosaya, Shiv** U.S.S.R.
57 C4 **Kosboget** U.S.S.R.
37 M6 **Kösching** W Germany
31 K3 **Kościan** Poland
31 K1 **Kościerzyna** Poland
111 G8 **Kosciusko** Mississippi U.S.A.
117 G7 **Kosciusko I** Alaska U.S.A.
139 J6 **Kosciusko, Mt** New South Wales Australia
139 J6 **Kosciusko Nat Park** New South Wales Australia
33 S10 **Koselitz** East Germany
33 U4 **Koserow** East Germany
56 B1 **Koses** *R* U.S.S.R.
76 C2 **Kosgi** India
56 C6 **Kosh Agach** U.S.S.R.
55 D2 **Koshay** U.S.S.R.
57 G4 **Kosh-Dëbë** U.S.S.R.
60 S2 **Koshikawa** Japan
60 C14 **Koshiki-kaikyō** *str* Japan
60 C14 **Koshiki-rettō** *islds* Japan
110 E5 **Koshkonong** Missouri U.S.A.
57 K2 **Koshkorkol', Ozero** *L* U.S.S.R.
57 B4 **Kosh-Kupyr** U.S.S.R.
61 M9 **Kōshoku** Japan
57 D4 **Koshrabad** U.S.S.R.
48 G2 **Košice** Czechoslovakia
68 E6 **Ko Si Chang** *isld* Thailand
76 C3 **Kosigi** India
89 H6 **Kosi L** S Africa
55 C5 **Kos-Istek** U.S.S.R.
48 E5 **Koška** Yugoslavia
123 R6 **Koskaecodde L** Newfoundland Canada
29 K11 **Koski** Finland
26 M5 **Koskivaara** Sweden
57 D1 **Koskol'** U.S.S.R.
57 H3 **Koskuduk** U.S.S.R.
26 L4 **Koskullskulle** Sweden
52 G3 **Koslan** U.S.S.R.
Köslin *see* **Koszalin**
52 G2 **Kosma** *R* U.S.S.R.
48 J2 **Kosmach** U.S.S.R.
100 C3 **Kosmos** Washington U.S.A.
59 J4 **Kosŏng** N Korea
48 J2 **Kosov** U.S.S.R.
46 D2 **Kosovo** *reg* Yugoslavia
46 E2 **Kosovo Polje** Yugoslavia
33 S10 **Kossdorf** East Germany
109 L4 **Kosse** Texas U.S.A.
33 P9 **Kösseln** East Germany
37 O1 **Kössern** East Germany
37 P7 **Kösslarn** W Germany
31 N3 **Kossów** Poland
27 H15 **Kosta** Sweden
33 T9 **Kostebrau** East Germany
46 F2 **Kostenets** Bulgaria
28 J7 **Koster** Denmark
54 L1 **Kosterevo** U.S.S.R.
48 L2 **Kosteshty-Synka, Vodokhranilishche** *res* U.S.S.R.
48 L3 **Kostesty** U.S.S.R.
86 F3 **Kosti** Sudan
46 F2 **Kostinbrod** Bulgaria
50 H2 **Kostino** U.S.S.R.
52 D3 **Kostomuksha** U.S.S.R.
52 F5 **Kostroma** U.S.S.R.
52 F5 **Kostromskaya Oblast'** *prov* U.S.S.R.
54 D3 **Kostyukovichi** U.S.S.R.
54 B4 **Kostyukovka** U.S.S.R.
61 L9 **Kosugi** Japan
52 J2 **Kos'yu** U.S.S.R.
52 J2 **Kos'yuvom** U.S.S.R.
31 J1 **Koszalin** Poland
48 D3 **Köszeg** Hungary
75 K7 **Kota** India
70 K8 **Kotaagung** Sumatra
69 F9 **Kota Baharu** Malaysia
70 E6 **Kotabaru** Kalimantan
70 B5 **Kotabaru** Kalimantan
69 C11 **Kotabaru** Sumatra
69 E13 **Kotabaru** Sumatra
70 E1 **Kota Belud** Sabah
70 C6 **Kotabesi** Kalimantan
70 K8 **Kotabumi** Sumatra
70 E2 **Kota Kinabalu** Sabah
29 O4 **Kotala** Finland
71 J4 **Kotamubagu** Sulawesi
76 F1 **Kotapārh** India
69 E12 **Kotapinang** Sumatra
69 E12 **Kotatengah** Sumatra
69 F12 **Kota Tinggi** Malaysia
70 B6 **Kotawaringin** Kalimantan
117 N6 **Kotcho** *R* British Columbia Canada
47 H2 **Kotel** Bulgaria
53 F9 **Kotel'nikovo** U.S.S.R.
51 N1 **Kotel'nyy, Ostrov** *isld* U.S.S.R.
145 F3 **Kotemaori** New Zealand
33 P9 **Köthen** East Germany
74 F3 **Kot Kapura** India
52 H2 **Kotkino** U.S.S.R.
55 G2 **Kotkino** U.S.S.R.
52 G4 **Kotlas** U.S.S.R.
29 O11 **Kotlin, O** *isld* U.S.S.R.
28 S10 **Kötlutangi** *C* Iceland
52 C5 **Kotly** U.S.S.R.
60 G11 **Kotohira** Japan
60 P2 **Kotoni** Japan
42 J6 **Kotor** Yugoslavia
42 H4 **Kotor Varoš** Yugoslavia
53 C10 **Kotovsk** U.S.S.R.
74 C6 **Kotri** Pakistan
57 A1 **Kotr-Tas** U.S.S.R.
38 H8 **Kötschach** Austria
74 J10 **Kottagudem** India
75 K10 **Kottakota** India
76 C6 **Kottayam** India
83 J11 **Kotte** Sri Lanka
86 D4 **Kotto** *R* Cent Afr Republic
26 H8 **Köttsjön** Sweden
76 C3 **Kotturu** India
51 K1 **Kotuy** *R* U.S.S.R.
48 M3 **Kotyuzhany** U.S.S.R.
116 F3 **Kotzebue** Alaska U.S.A.
116 E3 **Kotzebue Sd** Alaska U.S.A.
37 Q1 **Kötzschenbroda** East Germany
37 O5 **Kötzting** W Germany
85 E6 **Kouandé** Benin
86 D4 **Kouango** Cent Afr Republic
86 C2 **Kouba Modounga** Chad
85 D6 **Koudougou** Burkina
89 A9 **Koue Bokkeveld** *reg* S Africa
89 D8 **Koueveld Berge** *mts* S Africa
47 H10 **Koufonisi** *isld* Crete Greece
47 H8 **Koufonisia** *isld* Greece
89 C9 **Kougaberge** *mts* S Africa
86 B6 **Koulamoutou** Gabon
85 C6 **Koulikoro** Mali
141 J5 **Koumala** Queensland Australia
66 E3 **Koumenzi** China
86 C4 **Koumra** Chad
86 C3 **Koungouri** Chad
48 C1 **Kounice** Czechoslovakia
47 H8 **Kounoupói** *isld* Greece
57 G2 **Kounradskiy** U.S.S.R.
111 B11 **Kountze** Texas U.S.A.
85 D6 **Koupela** Burkina
Kouqian *see* **Yongji**
61 Q12 **Kouri-jima** *isld* Okinawa
84 F5 **Kourizo, Passe de** Chad
129 H2 **Kourou** Fr Guiana
85 C6 **Kouroussa** Guinea
89 B9 **Kousberg** *mt* S Africa
85 C5 **Koussa** Mauritania
86 B3 **Kousséri** Cameroon
85 C6 **Koutiala** Mali
85 C7 **Kouto** Ivory Coast
46 F7 **Koutsopódhi** Greece
29 M11 **Kouvola** Finland
86 C6 **Kouyou** *R* Congo
56 F2 **Kova** *R* U.S.S.R.
47 H2 **Kovachevo** Bulgaria
48 F5 **Kovačica** Yugoslavia
46 C1 **Kovač Planina** *mt* Yugoslavia
52 D2 **Kovda** U.S.S.R.
52 D2 **Kovdozero, Oz** *L* U.S.S.R.
55 E1 **Kovenskaya** *R* U.S.S.R.
52 F6 **Kovernino** U.S.S.R.
29 P9 **Kovero** Finland
48 F6 **Kovin** Yugoslavia
46 D1 **Kovren** Yugoslavia
52 G1 **Kovriga, Gora** *mt* U.S.S.R.
54 N1 **Kovrov** U.S.S.R.
52 E5 **Kovzha** *R* U.S.S.R.
52 E4 **Kovzhskoye, Oz** *L* U.S.S.R.
144 C5 **Kowai Bush** New Zealand
31 L3 **Kowal** Poland
31 L2 **Kowalewo** Poland
71 J9 **Kowangge** Sumbawa Indonesia
144 C5 **Kowhitirangi** New Zealand
120 C2 **Kowkash** Ontario Canada
67 G6 **Kowloon** Hong Kong
55 G6 **Koyandy** U.S.S.R.
61 J11 **Kōyasan** Japan
47 K8 **Koyceğiz** Turkey
47 J8 **Köyceğiz Gölü** *L* Turkey
52 F2 **Koyda** U.S.S.R.
52 H4 **Koygorodok** U.S.S.R.
46 G1 **Koynare** Bulgaria
52 G3 **Koynas** U.S.S.R.
61 O6 **Koyoshi-gawa** *R* Japan
52 J4 **Koyp, Gora** *mt* U.S.S.R.
54 L9 **Koysug** U.S.S.R.
57 D4 **Koytash** U.S.S.R.
116 G4 **Koyuk** Alaska U.S.A.
116 L3 **Koyukuk** *R* Alaska U.S.A.
116 J4 **Koyukuk I** Alaska U.S.A.
78 F1 **Koyulhisar** Turkey
55 C2 **Koyva** *R* U.S.S.R.
29 P7 **Koyvayarvi** U.S.S.R.
61 J12 **Koza** *R* Japan
60 C11 **Kō-zaki** *C* Japan
60 G11 **Kōzan** Japan
78 E3 **Kozan** Turkey
46 E4 **Kozáni** Greece
42 H3 **Kozara Plan** Yugoslavia
48 E2 **Kozárovce** Czechoslovakia
54 C6 **Kozelets** U.S.S.R.
54 E7 **Kozel'shchina** U.S.S.R.
54 G2 **Kozel'sk** U.S.S.R.
55 E5 **Kozhakol', Oz** *L* U.S.S.R.
55 G3 **Kozhevnikovo** U.S.S.R.
52 J2 **Kozhim** U.S.S.R.
52 J2 **Kozhimvom** U.S.S.R.
52 E3 **Kozhozero, Oz** *L* U.S.S.R.
52 E3 **Kozhposelok** U.S.S.R.
55 G3 **Kozhurla** U.S.S.R.
52 J2 **Kozhva** U.S.S.R.
52 J3 **Kozhymiz, Gora** *mt* U.S.S.R.
31 N4 **Kozienice** Poland
42 F3 **Kozina** Yugoslavia
46 E3 **Kozjak** *mt* Yugoslavia
31 L5 **Koźle** Poland
46 F1 **Kozloduy** Bulgaria
46 G1 **Kozlovets** Bulgaria
54 M6 **Kozlovka** U.S.S.R.
78 C1 **Kozlu** Turkey
31 K4 **Koźmin** Poland
57 E3 **Kozmoldak** U.S.S.R.
48 J1 **Kozova** U.S.S.R.
31 J4 **Kozuchów** Poland
61 N11 **Kōzu-shima** *isld* Japan
85 E7 **Kpalime** Togo
85 D7 **Kpandu** Ghana
89 E8 **Kraai** *R* S Africa
33 O6 **Kraak** East Germany
25 B6 **Krabbendijke** Netherlands
68 D7 **Kra Buri** Thailand
37 M2 **Kraftsdorf** East Germany
70 N9 **Kragan** Java
28 C4 **Kragelund** Denmark
28 G7 **Kragenæs** Denmark
27 D13 **Kragerö** Norway
48 F6 **Kragujevac** Yugoslavia
36 G4 **Krahenberg** W Germany
37 K2 **Krahnberg** *mt* East Germany
36 F5 **Kraich** *R* W Germany
36 F5 **Kraichtal** W Germany
73 Q7 **Kra, Isthmus of** Thailand
70 K9 **Krakatau** *isld* Sumatra
26 A9 **Kråkenes** Norway
68 F6 **Krakor** Cambodia
48 H1 **Krakovets** U.S.S.R.
33 Q5 **Krakow** East Germany
31 M5 **Kraków** Poland
68 F6 **Kralanh** Cambodia
48 G2 **Král Chlmec** Czechoslovakia
31 K5 **Králiky** Czechoslovakia
46 D1 **Kraljevo Vrnjacka** Yugoslavia
48 E1 **Kralovany** Czechoslovakia
37 Q4 **Kralovice** Czechoslovakia
37 P3 **Kralupy** Czechoslovakia
69 G11 **Kramat** Indonesia
98 F1 **Kramer** North Dakota U.S.A.
26 J9 **Kramfors** Sweden
68 E6 **Kram, Ko** *isld* Thailand
26 S1 **Krampenes** Norway
25 F5 **Kranenburg** W Germany
26 H8 **Krångede** Sweden
46 E5 **Kraniá** Greece
37 L2 **Kranichfeld** East Germany
46 F7 **Kranidhion** Greece
42 F2 **Kranj** Yugoslavia
38 J9 **Kranjska-Gord** Yugoslavia
31 K5 **Krapkowice** Poland
29 K4 **Krapperup** Sweden
52 G4 **Krasavino** U.S.S.R.
54 K1 **Krashy Oktyabr'** U.S.S.R.
48 K1 **Krasilov** U.S.S.R.
50 E1 **Krasino** U.S.S.R.
59 K3 **Kraskino** U.S.S.R.
52 C6 **Krāslava** U.S.S.R.
37 O3 **Kraslice** Czechoslovakia
31 N5 **Krasnik** Poland
37 O3 **Krásno** Czechoslovakia
55 E4 **Krasnoarmeyesk** U.S.S.R.
54 K1 **Krasnoarmeysk** U.S.S.R.
54 J8 **Krasnoarmeysk** U.S.S.R.
58 G1 **Krasnoarmeysk** U.S.S.R.
55 D4 **Krasnoarmeyskiy** Kustanayskaya U.S.S.R.
52 G4 **Krasnoborsk** U.S.S.R.
31 O5 **Krasnobród** Poland
53 E11 **Krasnodar** U.S.S.R.
53 E10 **Krasnodarskiy Kray** *reg* U.S.S.R.
54 L8 **Krasnodon** U.S.S.R.
52 D5 **Krasnofarfornyy** U.S.S.R.
52 C6 **Krasnogorodskoye** U.S.S.R.
59 M2 **Krasnogorsk** U.S.S.R.
55 D4 **Krasnogorskiy** Chelyabinskaya obl U.S.S.R.
52 H5 **Krasnogorskoye** U.S.S.R.
54 G7 **Krasnograd** U.S.S.R.
55 D3 **Krasnogvardeyskiy** U.S.S.R.
55 B5 **Krasnokholm** Orenburgskaya obl U.S.S.R.
54 G6 **Krasnokutsk** U.S.S.R.
55 G4 **Krasnokutsk** Pavlodarskaya obl U.S.S.R.
55 E1 **Krasnoleninskiy** U.S.S.R.
54 L5 **Krasnolesniyy** U.S.S.R.
31 N1 **Krasnoles'ye** U.S.S.R.
54 J7 **Krasnooskol'skoye Vodokhranilishche** *res* U.S.S.R.
52 C4 **Krasnoostrovskiy** U.S.S.R.
54 H7 **Krasnopavlovka** U.S.S.R.
54 C3 **Krasnopol'ye** U.S.S.R.
54 K7 **Krasnorechenskoye** U.S.S.R.
53 F9 **Krasnoslobodsk** U.S.S.R.
55 D2 **Krasnotur'insk** U.S.S.R.
55 C3 **Krasnoufimsk** U.S.S.R.
55 D2 **Krasnoural'sk** U.S.S.R.
55 C4 **Krasnousol'skiy** U.S.S.R.
52 J4 **Krasnovishersk** U.S.S.R.
50 E4 **Krasnovodsk** U.S.S.R.
55 F3 **Krasnoyarka** Omskaya obl U.S.S.R.
55 D2 **Krasnoyarka** Sverdlovskaya obl U.S.S.R.
56 D3 **Krasnoyarsk** U.S.S.R.
54 K4 **Krasnoye** U.S.S.R.
48 J1 **Krasnoye** U.S.S.R.
54 M1 **Krasnoye Ekho** U.S.S.R.
57 B6 **Krasnoye Znamya** U.S.S.R.
52 H4 **Krasnozatonskiy** U.S.S.R.
55 G4 **Krasnozerskoye** U.S.S.R.
55 C4 **Krasnoznamenskiy** Bashkirskaya A.S.S.R. U.S.S.R.
55 E5 **Krasnoznamenskoye** Tselinogradskaya obl U.S.S.R.
52 H6 **Krasny Bor** U.S.S.R.
54 J8 **Krasny Liman** U.S.S.R.
54 K8 **Krasny Luch** U.S.S.R.
54 N1 **Krasny Mayak** U.S.S.R.
31 O5 **Krasnystaw** Poland
54 L1 **Krasny Tkach** U.S.S.R.
54 C2 **Krasnyy** U.S.S.R.
52 G6 **Krasnyye-Baki** U.S.S.R.
48 M3 **Krasnyye Okna** U.S.S.R.
52 E5 **Krasnyye Tkachi** U.S.S.R.
52 E5 **Krasnyy Kholm** Kalininskaya obl U.S.S.R.
55 C3 **Krasnyy-Klyuch** U.S.S.R.
55 D3 **Krasnyy Oktyabr** U.S.S.R.
52 E5 **Krasnyy Pereval** U.S.S.R.
55 F3 **Krasnyy Yar** Omskaya obl U.S.S.R.
55 D2 **Krasnyy Yar** Sverdlovskaya obl U.S.S.R.
68 H6 **Kratie** Cambodia
38 L7 **Kraubath** Austria
41 K1 **Krauchenwies** W Germany
115 O3 **Kraulshavn** Greenland
36 H5 **Krautheim** W Germany
32 K5 **Krautsand** W Germany
107 P7 **Krebs** Oklahoma U.S.A.
25 G6 **Krefeld** W Germany
28 J5 **Kregme** Denmark
36 F4 **Krehberg** *mt* W Germany
32 L9 **Kreiensen** W Germany
116 D5 **Krekatok I** Alaska U.S.A.
46 F1 **Kremena** Bulgaria
54 E7 **Kremenchug** U.S.S.R.
54 D7 **Kremenchugskoye Vdkhr** *res* U.S.S.R.
54 K7 **Kremennaya** U.S.S.R.
46 F2 **Kremikovtsi** Bulgaria
101 P1 **Kremlin** Montana U.S.A.
33 N8 **Kremlingen** W Germany
33 S7 **Kremmen** East Germany
106 D1 **Kremmling** Colorado U.S.A.
32 K5 **Krempe** W Germany
38 N5 **Krems** Austria
38 M5 **Krems** *R* Austria
116 D9 **Krenitzin Is** Aleutian Is
33 Q10 **Krensitz** East Germany
48 E7 **Kreševo** Yugoslavia
56 B3 **Kreshchenskoye** U.S.S.R.
46 F3 **Kresna** Bulgaria
108 F1 **Kress** Texas U.S.A.
52 D6 **Kresti** U.S.S.R.
54 G7 **Krestische** U.S.S.R.
52 H2 **Krestovka** U.S.S.R.
51 H1 **Kresty** U.S.S.R.
27 M16 **Kretinga** U.S.S.R.
41 P2 **Kreuth** W Germany
36 B2 **Kreuzau** W Germany
41 O3 **Kreuzeck** *mt* W Germany
38 H8 **Kreuzeck-Gruppe** *mts* Austria
38 L5 **Kreuzen** Austria
38 E7 **Kreuzjoch** *mt* Austria
41 K2 **Kreuzlingen** Switzerland
36 E2 **Kreuztal** W Germany
86 A5 **Kribi** Cameroon
54 C3 **Krichev** U.S.S.R.
46 G2 **Krichim** Bulgaria
28 A3 **Krik** Denmark
28 A3 **Krik Vig** *B* Denmark
38 F7 **Krimml** Austria
38 F7 **Krimmler Fälle** Austria
38 F7 **Krimmler Tal** *R* Austria
26 D10 **Kringen** Norway
46 E6 **Krionéri** Greece
46 F9 **Kriós, Akr** *C* Crete Greece
76 C2 **Krishna** *R* India
76 D4 **Krishnagiri** India
75 N7 **Krishnanagar** India
27 H14 **Kristdala** Sweden
17 G9 **Kristel** Algeria
27 H15 **Kristianopel** Sweden
27 C13 **Kristiansand** Norway
27 G15 **Kristianstad** Sweden
27 F15 **Kristianstad** *county* Sweden
26 C8 **Kristiansund** Norway
29 J9 **Kristiinankaupunki** Finland
27 G12 **Kristinehamn** Sweden
28 E4 **Kristrup** Denmark
46 G9 **Kriti** *isld* Greece
48 M3 **Kriulyany** U.S.S.R.
46 E2 **Kriva** *R* Yugoslavia
48 E6 **Krivaja** *R* Yugoslavia
46 E2 **Kriva Palanka** Yugoslavia
46 F1 **Krivodol** Bulgaria
48 N3 **Krivoye Ozero** U.S.S.R.
54 E9 **Krivoy Rog** U.S.S.R.
52 G5 **Krivyachka** U.S.S.R.
42 F3 **Krk** Yugoslavia
42 G5 **Krka** *R* Yugoslavia
31 J5 **Krkonoše** *mts* Czechoslovakia
31 K5 **Krnov** Czechoslovakia
31 K4 **Krobia** Poland
27 D11 **Kröderen** Norway
28 B5 **Krogager** Denmark
37 P1 **Krögis** East Germany
28 E5 **Krogsbølle** Denmark
37 O6 **Kröhstorf** W Germany
70 M9 **Kroja** Java
27 H13 **Krokek** Sweden
26 G6 **Kroken** Norway
89 E5 **Krokodil** *R* S Africa
26 G8 **Krokom** Sweden
31 L1 **Krokowa** Poland
26 J7 **Kroksjö** Sweden
54 E5 **Krolevets** U.S.S.R.
36 D2 **Krombach** W Germany
48 D1 **Kroměříž** Czechoslovakia
25 D5 **Kromme Rijn** *R* Netherlands
37 L3 **Kronach** W Germany
119 N8 **Kronau** Saskatchewan Canada
36 E3 **Kronberg** W Germany
37 P3 **Krondorf** Czechoslovakia
36 B3 **Kronenberg** W Germany
68 H5 **Krong Poko** *R* Vietnam
27 G15 **Kronoberg** *county* Sweden
29 K8 **Kronoby** Finland
146 F6 **Kronprinsess Märtha Kyst** *coast* Antarctica
115 Q4 **Kronprins Frederiks Bjerge** *mts* Greenland
29 O12 **Kronshtadt** U.S.S.R.
68 D5 **Kronwa** Burma
37 N7 **Kronwinkl** W Germany
89 E6 **Kroonstad** S Africa
55 C3 **Kropachevo** U.S.S.R.
33 P4 **Kröpelin** East Germany
53 F10 **Kropotkin** U.S.S.R.
29 K4 **Kropp** Sweden
33 O9 **Kroppenstedt** East Germany
33 R9 **Kropstädt** East Germany
33 T4 **Kröslin** East Germany
31 L3 **Krośniewice** Poland
37 M2 **Krossen** East Germany
31 K4 **Krotoszyn** Poland
41 O2 **Krotten Kopf** *mt* W Germany
111 E11 **Krotz Springs** Louisiana U.S.A.
46 F3 **Kroúsia** *mt* Greece
46 D2 **Krrab** *mt* Albania
36 C3 **Kruft-Mendig** W Germany
89 G4 **Kruger Nat. Park** S Africa
89 E6 **Krugersdorp** S Africa
70 K8 **Krui** Sumatra
22 F2 **Kruishoutem** Belgium
46 D3 **Krujë** Albania
109 K2 **Krum** Texas U.S.A.
38 O6 **Krumbach** Austria
37 J7 **Krumbach** W Germany
46 D2 **Krume** Albania
36 D1 **Krummenerl** W Germany
32 F6 **Krummhörn** W Germany
33 T4 **Krummin** East Germany
47 H3 **Krumovgrad** Bulgaria
41 O2 **Krün** W Germany
Krungkao *see* **Ayutthaya**
Krung Thep *see* **Bangkok**
68 E6 **Krung Thep** Thailand
48 E6 **Krupanj** Yugoslavia
48 E2 **Krupina** Czechoslovakia
116 F3 **Krusenstern, C** Alaska U.S.A.
46 E1 **Kruševac** Yugoslavia
46 E3 **Kruševo** Yugoslavia
Krušné Hory *mts see* **Erzgebirge**
52 C6 **Krustpils** U.S.S.R.
52 H3 **Krutaya** U.S.S.R.
19 K5 **Kruth** France
55 D4 **Krutoyarskiy** U.S.S.R.
117 F7 **Kruzof I** Alaska U.S.A.
118 K6 **Krydor** Saskatchewan Canada
27 H11 **Krylbo** Sweden
31 P5 **Krylów** Poland
53 D10 **Krymskaya Oblast'** *prov* U.S.S.R.
48 F1 **Krynica** Poland
31 O2 **Krynki** Poland
37 P3 **Kryry** Czechoslovakia
54 J1 **Kryukovo** U.S.S.R.
56 E4 **Kryzhina, Khr** *mts* U.S.S.R.
48 M2 **Kryzhopol'** U.S.S.R.
31 L5 **Krzepice** Poland
31 N5 **Krzeszów** Poland
31 M5 **Krzeszowice** Poland
31 K4 **Krzywin** Poland
31 J3 **Krzyż** Poland
85 D3 **Ksabi** Algeria
85 C4 **Ksalb Ounane, El** Mali
85 E1 **Ksar el Boukhari** Algeria
16 D9 **Ksar el Kebir** Morocco
16 D9 **Ksar Sghir** Morocco
16 D9 **Ksar Sghir Oued Laou** Morocco
52 J4 **Ksenofontova** U.S.S.R.
85 E2 **Ksour, Mts. des** Algeria
52 F6 **Kstovo** U.S.S.R.
79 C4 **Ktima** Cyprus
69 D9 **Kuah** Malaysia
67 A4 **Kuaize He** *R* China
70 B6 **Kualajelai** Kalimantan
69 E10 **Kuala Kangsar** Malaysia
70 D6 **Kualakapuas** Kalimantan
69 F10 **Kuala Kerai** Malaysia
70 C6 **Kualakuagan** Kalimantan
70 C5 **Kualakurun** Kalimantan
69 C10 **Kualalangsa** Sumatra
69 F10 **Kuala Lipis** Malaysia
69 E11 **Kuala Lumpur** Malaysia
69 E9 **Kuala Nerang** Malaysia
70 C6 **Kualapembuang** Kalimantan
70 D2 **Kuala Penyu** Sabah
69 F11 **Kuala Pilah** Malaysia
135 S2 **Kualapuu** Hawaiian Is
70 C6 **Kualasampit** Kalimantan
69 E11 **Kuala Selangor** Malaysia
69 F10 **Kuala Terengganu** Malaysia
69 F13 **Kualatungkal** Sumatra
70 E2 **Kuamut** *R* Sabah
70 E2 **Kuamut** Sabah
65 D4 **Kuancheng** China
71 H4 **Kuandang, Tk** *B* Sulawesi Indonesia
59 H3 **Kuandian** China
Kuang-chou *see* **Guangzhou**
69 F11 **Kuantan** Malaysia
145 E2 **Kuaotunu** New Zealand
53 G12 **Kuba** U.S.S.R.
53 F11 **Kuban'** *R* U.S.S.R.
78 G4 **Kubar, el** Syria
79 H3 **Kubaybāt** Syria
26 K8 **Kubbe** Sweden
86 D3 **Kubbum** Sudan
52 F4 **Kubena** *R* U.S.S.R.
52 E5 **Kubenskoye, Oz** *L* U.S.S.R.
52 G6 **Kubnya** *R* U.S.S.R.
60 G12 **Kubokawa** Japan
79 A8 **Kubra, El** Egypt
47 H1 **Kubrat** Bulgaria
69 J13 **Kubu** Indonesia
70 P10 **Kubu** Indonesia
70 D3 **Kubuang** Kalimantan
58 F1 **Kubukhay** U.S.S.R.
70 D4 **Kubumesaäi** Kalimantan
48 G6 **Kučevo** Yugoslavia
52 F2 **Kuchema** U.S.S.R.
36 H6 **Kuchen** W Germany
41 M3 **Kuchen Spitze** *mt* Austria
70 B4 **Kuching** Sarawak
60 D13 **Kuchinotsu** Japan
60 F10 **Kuchitagi** Japan
55 G4 **Kuchukskoye, Oz** *L* U.S.S.R.
48 M3 **Kuchurgan** *R* U.S.S.R.
Kucing *see* **Kuching**
33 N5 **Kücknitz** W Germany
47 M10 **Küçükçekmece** Turkey
47 M10 **Küçükçekmece Gölu** Turkey
47 M11 **Küçükçekmece Koya** *crater* Turkey
47 J6 **Küçük Menderes** *R* Turkey
83 K11 **Kuda** *R* Sri Lanka
61 P14 **Kudaka-jima** *isld* Okinawa
60 E11 **Kudamatsu** Japan
70 B5 **Kudangan** Kalimantan
69 F12 **Kudap** Sumatra
70 E1 **Kudat** Sabah
68 B1 **Kudaw** Burma
55 C4 **Kudeyevskiy** U.S.S.R.
116 F9 **Kudiakof Is** Alaska U.S.A.
31 O1 **Kudirkos Naumiestis** U.S.S.R.
80 G1 **Kudnah** Syria
116 G8 **Kudobin Is** Alaska U.S.A.
57 E5 **Kuduk** U.S.S.R.
70 N9 **Kudus** Java
52 H5 **Kudymkar** U.S.S.R.
80 D4 **Kufairāt** Jordan
47 K6 **Kûfi** *R* Turkey
80 F4 **Kufr Alma** Jordan
80 F4 **Kufrinja** *R* Jordan
80 F4 **Kufrinja** Jordan
80 G3 **Kufr Jayiz** Jordan
80 G4 **Kufr Khal** Jordan
80 G3 **Kufr Kifiya** Jordan
80 F4 **Kufr Rakib** Jordan
80 G3 **Kufr Saum** Jordan
38 F6 **Kufstein** Austria
60 F11 **Kuga** Japan
57 D5 **Kugitangtau, Khr** *mts* U.S.S.R.
116 F4 **Kugruk** *R* Alaska U.S.A.
37 L7 **Kühbach** W Germany
33 Q6 **Kuhbier** East Germany
77 A2 **Kūh-e Alvand** Iran
77 K2 **Kūh-e-Bābā** *mts* Afghanistan
77 C4 **Kūh-e Būl** *mt* Iran
77 B3 **Kūh-e Karkas** Iran
78 L2 **Kuhha-ye Sabalan** *mt* Iran
33 T4 **Kühlenhagen** East Germany
29 L10 **Kuhmalahti** Finland
29 O7 **Kuhmo** Finland
77 F6 **Kūhrān, Kūh-e** *mt* Iran
33 Q5 **Kuhs** East Germany
32 J6 **Kuhstedt** W Germany
47 K8 **Kuhu Dağ** *mt* Turkey
87 C11 **Kuibis** Namibia
87 C10 **Kuiseb** *R* Namibia
87 C8 **Kuito** Angola
117 F7 **Kuiu I** Alaska U.S.A.
29 L6 **Kuivajoki** *R* Finland
29 L6 **Kuivaniemi** Finland
59 J4 **Kujang-dong** N Korea
61 O9 **Kuji-gawa** Japan
60 E12 **Kujū-san** *mt* Japan
116 G1 **Kuk** *R* Alaska U.S.A.
116 M7 **Kukak** Alaska U.S.A.
116 K7 **Kukaklek L** Alaska U.S.A.
116 G6 **Kukaklik L** Alaska U.S.A.
120 H4 **Kukatush** Ontario Canada
143 C10 **Kukerin** Western Australia Australia
46 D2 **Kukës** Albania
29 L5 **Kukkola** Finland
52 H6 **Kukmor** U.S.S.R.
52 E5 **Kukoboy** U.S.S.R.
116 F2 **Kukpowruk** *R* Alaska U.S.A.
116 E2 **Kukpuk** *R* Alaska U.S.A.
135 U4 **Kukuihaele** Hawaiian Is
135 O1 **Kukuiula** Hawaiian Is
118 K1 **Kukukus L** Ontario Canada
83 K11 **Kukulugala** *mt* Sri Lanka
69 F12 **Kukup** Malaysia
70 D6 **Kukusan, G** *mt* Kalimantan
55 C2 **Kukushtan** U.S.S.R.
89 B4 **Kul** Botswana
46 F1 **Kula** Bulgaria
47 K6 **Kula** Turkey
48 F5 **Kula** Yugoslavia
69 D12 **Kulabu, Gunung** *mt* Sumatra
74 D3 **Kulachi** Pakistan
57 A2 **Kulandy** U.S.S.R.
57 A2 **Kulandy, Poluostrov** *pen* U.S.S.R.
55 F6 **Kulanutpes** *R* U.S.S.R.
71 E7 **Kulassein** *isld* Philippines
46 F3 **Kulata** Bulgaria
70 F5 **Kulawi** Sulawesi Indonesia
27 M15 **Kuldiga** U.S.S.R.
117 K8 **Kuldo** British Columbia Canada
57 C4 **Kul'dzhuktau, Gory** *mt* U.S.S.R.
52 F6 **Kulebaki** U.S.S.R.
54 G8 **Kulebovka** U.S.S.R.
42 G4 **Kulen Vakuf** Yugoslavia
55 D4 **Kulevchi** U.S.S.R.
140 C7 **Kulgera** N Terr Australia
52 H5 **Kuligi** U.S.S.R.
48 J1 **Kulikov** U.S.S.R.
69 E10 **Kulim** Malaysia
143 C10 **Kulin** Western Australia Australia
56 G1 **Kulingda** U.S.S.R.
143 B9 **Kulja** Western Australia Australia
139 G4 **Kulkyne** *R* New South Wales Australia
29 K4 **Kulla Gunnarstorp** Sweden
29 K4 **Kullen** *mt* Sweden
32 M10 **Küllstedt** East Germany
98 H3 **Kulm** North Dakota U.S.A.
37 M4 **Kulmain** W Germany
37 L3 **Kulmbach** W Germany
52 F4 **Kuloy** *R* U.S.S.R.
52 F3 **Kuloy** U.S.S.R.
138 E5 **Kulpara** South Australia Australia
95 L6 **Kulpmont** Pennsylvania U.S.A.
38 G7 **Kuls** Austria
50 E4 **Kul'sary** U.S.S.R.
36 H4 **Külsheim** W Germany
56 G5 **Kul'skiy Stanok** U.S.S.R.
29 M3 **Kultala** Finland
75 M7 **Kulti** India
26 H7 **Kultsjöluspen** Sweden
26 G6 **Kultsjön** *L* Sweden
33 R10 **Kültzschau** East Germany
78 D2 **Kulu** Turkey
56 B4 **Kulunda** *R* U.S.S.R.
55 G4 **Kulunda** U.S.S.R.
57 E5 **Kulyab** U.S.S.R.
47 J6 **Kum** *R* Turkey
60 F12 **Kuma** Japan
53 G11 **Kuma** *R* U.S.S.R.
60 D13 **Kuma-gawa** *R* Japan
61 N9 **Kumagaya** Japan
70 B6 **Kumai** Kalimantan
70 B6 **Kumai, Teluk** *B* Kalimantan
55 C5 **Kumak** *R* U.S.S.R.
55 D5 **Kumak** U.S.S.R.
60 D13 **Kumamoto** Japan
83 L11 **Kumana** Sri Lanka
48 F7 **Kumanica** Yugoslavia
61 K12 **Kumano** Japan
46 E2 **Kumanovo** Yugoslavia
70 D6 **Kumap** *R* Kalimantan
144 C5 **Kumara** New Zealand
51 M3 **Kumara** U.S.S.R.
144 C5 **Kumara Junction** New Zealand
85 D7 **Kumasi** Ghana
74 H3 **Kumaun** *reg* India
86 A5 **Kumba** Cameroon
76 D5 **Kumbakonam** India
47 L5 **Kümbet** Turkey
83 L11 **Kumbukkan Oya** *R* Sri Lanka
59 J4 **Kŭmch'ŏn** S Korea
47 L6 **Kumdanlı** Turkey
47 N10 **Kumdere** Turkey
55 C4 **Kumertau** U.S.S.R.
86 F5 **Kumi** Uganda
60 H10 **Kumihama** Japan
55 E2 **Kuminskiy** U.S.S.R.
47 H5 **Kumkale** Turkey
27 H12 **Kumla** Sweden
29 H11 **Kumlinge** Finland
116 J8 **Kumliun, C** Alaska U.S.A.
79 G2 **Kumlu** Turkey
47 L8 **Kumluca** Turkey
33 R5 **Kummerow** East Germany
33 R4 **Kummerow** Rostock East Germany
33 R5 **Kummerower See** *L* East Germany
37 M5 **Kümmersbruck** W Germany
33 S8 **Kummersdorf** East Germany
65 G7 **Kŭmo** *isld* S Korea
57 D2 **Kumola** *R* U.S.S.R.
75 R5 **Kumon Range** Burma
68 F4 **Kumphawapi** Thailand
76 B3 **Kumta** India
135 V5 **Kumukahi, C** Hawaiian Is
Kumush *see* **Kümüx**
66 D3 **Kümüx** China
68 C3 **Kun** *R* Burma
116 J2 **Kuna** *R* Alaska U.S.A.
143 E6 **Kunanaggi Well** Western Australia Australia
74 D1 **Kunar** Afghanistan
55 D3 **Kunashak** U.S.S.R.
60 T1 **Kunashir Ostrov** *isld* U.S.S.R.
52 C5 **Kunda** U.S.S.R.
88 A6 **Kundelungu** *mt* Zaire
86 E3 **Kundi, L** Sudan
143 D10 **Kundip** Western Australia Australia
74 D7 **Kundla** India
55 D4 **Kundravy** U.S.S.R.
Kunduk *see* **Kogil'nik**
69 F12 **Kundur** *isld* Indonesia
66 C3 **Künes He** *R* China
27 E14 **Kungälv** Sweden
Kunges *R see* **Künes He**
117 H9 **Kunghit I** British Columbia Canada
57 K3 **Kung-liu** China
57 A3 **Kungrad** U.S.S.R.
27 F14 **Kungsbacka** Sweden
27 J11 **Kungsgården** Sweden
27 H12 **Kungsör** Sweden
86 C5 **Kungu** Zaire
Kungur *mt see* **Kongur Shan** *mt*
55 C2 **Kungur** U.S.S.R.
68 C4 **Kungyangon** Burma
48 F3 **Kunhegyes** Hungary
68 D2 **Kunhing** Burma
61 Q12 **Kunigami** Okinawa
60 E13 **Kunimi-dake** *mt* Japan
70 M9 **Kuningan** Java
67 C5 **Kunlun Guan** *pass* China
48 F3 **Kunmadaras** Hungary
67 A4 **Kunming** China
60 R2 **Kunneppu** Japan
25 E3 **Kunnre** Netherlands
60 O3 **Kunnui** *R* Japan
6 F1 **Kunoy** *isld* Faeroes
65 G7 **Kunsan** S Korea
67 G1 **Kunshan** China
48 F4 **Kunszentmárton** Hungary
48 E3 **Kunszentmiklós** Hungary
52 E6 **Kuntsevo** U.S.S.R.
143 C9 **Kununoppin** Western Australia Australia
142 G3 **Kununurra** Western Australia Australia
52 D6 **Kunya** U.S.S.R.
57 A4 **Kunya Urgench** U.S.S.R.
65 E6 **Kunyu Shan** *mts* China
36 H5 **Künzelsau** W Germany
67 G2 **Kuocang Shan** *mts* China
52 C2 **Kuolayarvi** U.S.S.R.
29 N9 **Kuopio** Finland
29 N2 **Kuorboaivi** *mt* Finland
29 K9 **Kuortane** Finland
29 M10 **Kuortti** Finland
26 L5 **Kuouka** Sweden
26 L3 **Kuoutatjärro** *mt* Sweden
71 L10 **Kupang** Timor Indonesia
71 L10 **Kupang, Tk** *B* Timor Indonesia
116 N1 **Kuparuk** *R* Alaska U.S.A.
37 M3 **Kupferberg** W Germany
36 H5 **Kupferzell** W Germany
55 G4 **Kupino** U.S.S.R.
52 B6 **Kupiškis** U.S.S.R.
36 E6 **Kuppenheim** W Germany
117 G7 **Kupreanof I** Alaska U.S.A.
116 H9 **Kupreanof Pt** Alaska U.S.A.
116 L7 **Kupreanof St** Alaska U.S.A.
37 L3 **Küps** W Germany
54 J7 **Kupyansk** U.S.S.R.
54 J7 **Kupyansk-Uzlovoy** U.S.S.R.
66 C3 **Kuqa** China
59 L1 **Kur** *R* U.S.S.R.
78 J1 **Kura** *R* Turkey
57 G3 **Kuragaty** U.S.S.R.
60 F11 **Kurahashi-jima** *isld* Japan
70 E6 **Kurambu** Kalimantan
57 E4 **Kuramins'kiy Khr** *mts* U.S.S.R.
60 C12 **Kuramoto** Japan

Grid	Name	Grid	Name
107 N5	Lamont Oklahoma U.S.A.	29 K5	Landskrona Sweden
101 S7	Lamont Wyoming U.S.A.	36 D5	Landstuhl W Germany
124 G3	La Morita Mexico	20 C5	Landudal France
19 P14	La Morte France	20 B6	Landudec France
22 J4	Lamorteau Belgium	101 R2	Landusky Montana U.S.A.
121 M4	La Motte Quebec Canada	32 L10	Landwehrhagen W Germany
21 P6	Lamotte-Beuvron France	37 N3	Landwüst East Germany
19 P15	La Motte d'Aveillans France	12 H4	Lane South Carolina U.S.A.
19 P13	La Motte-Servolans France	98 H5	Lane South Dakota U.S.A.
98 H3	La Moure North Dakota U.S.A.	109 L6	Lane City Texas U.S.A.
68 F4	Lam Pao Res Thailand	22 G3	Laneffe Belgium
109 J4	Lampasas Texas U.S.A.	99 P6	Lanesboro Minnesota U.S.A.
109 K5	Lampasas R Texas U.S.A.	111 L9	Lanett Alabama U.S.A.
109 K4	Lampaul-Plouarzel France	22 D5	Laneuvilleroy France
125 K4	Lampazos Mexico	22 J5	Laneuville-sur-Meuse France
43 E13	Lampedusa, I. di Italy	18 G7	Lanfains France
36 E4	Lampertheim W Germany		Lanfeng see Lankao
33 T10	Lampërtswalde East Germany	118 G7	Lanfine Alberta Canada
8 B3	Lampeter Wales	119 N9	Lang Saskatchewan Canada
8 B3	Lamphey Wales	28 F6	Langå Denmark
46 F5	Lampinoú Greece	99 S3	Langa de Duero Spain
43 E13	Lampione, I. di Italy	123 Q2	Langadhás Greece
68 F5	Lam Plai Thailand	46 F4	Langadhás Greece
119 P9	Lampman Saskatchewan Canada	46 F6	Langades Greece
45 J4	Lamporecchio Italy	77 A1	Langarüd Iran
9 F3	Lamport England	119 P8	Langbank Saskatchewan Canada
52 F2	Lampozhnya U.S.S.R.	67 B6	Lang Chanh Vietnam
29 O6	Lämpsä Finland		Lang-ch'u Ho see Sutlej
70 K8	Lampung prov Sumatra	67 D4	Langdon Beck England
70 K8	Lampung Teluk B Sumatra	99 P6	Langsing Iowa U.S.A.
68 G5	Lam Si Bai R Thailand	107 Q2	Lansing Kansas U.S.A.
32 M9	Lamspringe W Germany	94 C4	Lansing Michigan U.S.A.
32 K5	Lamstedt W Germany	112 F1	Lansing North Carolina U.S.A.
86 B3	Lamu Kenya	31 K6	Lanskroun Czechoslovakia
86 H6	Lamu Kenya	19 P14	Lans, Mts de France
19 P15	La Mure France	68 G4	Lan, Ko isld Thailand
19 N12	Lamure-sur-Azergues France	21 O7	Lar'thenay France
106 E6	Lamy New Mexico U.S.A.	65 A7	Lartian see Lianyuan
141 G5	Lana Queensland Australia	98 E4	Lantry South Dakota U.S.A.
42 D2	Lana Italy	43 G9	Lanusei Sardinia
135 S3	Lanai isld Hawaiian Is	71 G6	Laoag Luzon Philippines
135 S3	Lanai City Hawaiian Is	20 E6	Lanvaux, Landes de reg France
135 S3	Lanaihale pk Hawaiian Is	74 C5	Lanxana Pakistan
22 K2	Lanaken Belgium	12 E2	Larkhall Scotland
74 H1	Lanak Pass Kashmir/Xizang Zizhiqu	123 O4	Lark Harb Newfoundland
71 G7	Lanao L Mindanao Philippines	111 C2	La Troya, R Argentina
	Lanark co see Strathclyde reg	110 K7	Larkinsville Alabama U.S.A.
121 F5	Lanark Ontario Canada	141 H3	Lark Pass Gt Barrier Reef Aust
12 E2	Lanark Scotland		
113 C8	Lanark Florida U.S.A.	9 G3	Lark, R England
99 R7	Lanark Illinois U.S.A.	106 F2	Larkspur Colorado U.S.A.
70 E2	Lanas Sabah	74 Q9	Larkspur Colorado U.S.A.
68 C7	Lanbi Kyun isld Burma		
71 F6	Lanboyan Pt Mindanao Philippines	26 H2	Langeness lighthouse Norway
68 D1	Lancang China	71 E1	Langay Luzon Philippines
	Lancang Jiang R see Mekong	71 G4	Lanaang Philippines
13 F6	Lancashire co England	65 A5	Lao Cai Vietnam
121 O7	Lancaster Ontario Canada	67 A4	Laochang China
13 F5	Lancaster England	65 S9	Laohe He R China
102 F7	Lancaster California U.S.A.	58 F5	Lao-ho-k'ou China
110 M4	Lancaster Kentucky U.S.A.	14 D4	Laois co Ireland
98 K1	Lancaster Minnesota U.S.A.	65 G4	Laoxing China
110 D1	Lancaster Missouri U.S.A.	20 F4	Léon France
95 Q2	Lancaster New Hampshire U.S.A.	17 F5	La Roda Spain
94 J4	Lancaster New York U.S.A.	16 C9	La Roda de A Spain
94 E7	Lancaster Ohio U.S.A.	127 K5	La Romana Dominican Rep
95 L6	Lancaster Pennsylvania U.S.A.	70 G6	Larompong Sulawesi
112 G3	Lancaster South Carolina U.S.A.	119 M3	La Ronge Saskatchewan Canada
109 L3	Lancaster Texas U.S.A.		
95 L5	Lancaster Virginia U.S.A.	72 J25	La Rosa Mexico
99 Q7	Lancaster Wisconsin U.S.A.	111 F12	La Rose Louisiana U.S.A.
115 L3	Lancaster Sd Northwest Territories Canada	124 J3	La Rosita Mexico
		142 C5	Larrey Pt Western Australia
98 B6	Lance Cr Wyoming U.S.A.		Australia
143 B9	Lancelin Western Australia	139 J9	Larrimah N Terr Australia
143 B9	Lancelin I Western Australia		Australia
143 E7	Lancelot, Mt Western Australia	140 C3	Larrs R Nova Scotia
9 O16	Lance, Mt. de la France	123 L8	Larry's R Nova Scotia
118 J8	Lancer Saskatchewan Canada		
21 O1	Lanchester England	146 D4	Larsen Ice Shelf Antarctica
13 G4	Lanchester England	101 T1	Larslan Montana U.S.A.
66 C5	Lan-chia Ts'o L China	29 K8	Larsmo Finland
48 J2	Lanchin U.S.S.R.	121 O2	Larson Ontario Canada
	Lanchow see Lanzhou	109 M3	La Rue Texas U.S.A.
42 F6	Lanciano Italy	18 E10	Laruns France
20 F4	Lancieux France	123 A4	Larvik Norway
94 D3	Lancing Tennessee U.S.A.	27 D11	Larvik Norway
19 O17	Lançon France	36 F2	Lasauch W Germany
21 N5	Lancut Poland	40 B4	Lasauf Switzerland
27 D11	Land reg Norway	35 G5	Laufen Switzerland
98 F1	Land North Dakota U.S.A.	41 J4	Lauffen W Germany
32 K10	Landau Hessen W Germany	8 B4	Laugharne Wales
36 E5	Landau Rheinland-Pfalz W Germany	70 D2	Laulara Sulawesi
		70 G6	Laulara Sulawesi
21 H5	Landéan France	79 R8	Laun, P Michigan
41 N3	Landeck Austria		
26 G4	Landegode isld Norway	106 F5	Laughlin Pk New Mexico U.S.A.
20 C5	Landeleau France	119 V4	Laurent L Manitoba Canada
21 H4	Landelles-et-Coupigny France	141 K6	Laurieton New South Wales
22 J2	Landen Belgium	81 B3	Lauwin mt Sarawak
140 C5	Lander R N Terr Australia	70 C4	Lawit, C mt Sarawak
101 R7	Lander Wyoming U.S.A.	70 C4	Lawit, G mt Sarawak
20 B5	Landerneau France	81 B3	Lawn reg S W Asia
140 B5	Lander R N Terr Australia		

118 H5 Lone Rock Saskatchewan Canada
100 F4 Lonerock Oregon U.S.A.
99 Q6 Lone Rock Wisconsin U.S.A.
101 P8 Lonetree Wyoming U.S.A.
98 F2 Lonetree Res North Dakota U.S.A.
107 L7 Lone Wolf Oklahoma U.S.A.
87 C8 Longa Angola
129 K4 Longa R Brazil
46 E8 Longa Greece
70 D3 Longagung Kalimantan
70 D3 Long Akah Sarawak
67 B5 Long'an China
141 F5 Longara Queensland Australia
45 L1 Longara Italy
45 L1 Longare Italy
42 E2 Longarone Italy
133 C5 Longavi mt Chile
127 K3 Long B Jamaica
70 D3 Longbawan Kalimantan
127 M2 Long Bay Jamaica
112 J4 Long Bay South Carolina
144 C6 Longbeach New Zealand
102 F8 Long Beach California U.S.A.
95 O6 Long Beach Long I, New York U.S.A.
111 G11 Long Beach Mississippi U.S.A.
100 A3 Long Beach Washington U.S.A.
9 F2 Long Bennington England
70 D3 Longberini Kalimantan
70 E3 Longbia Kalimantan
113 E10 Longboat Key isld Florida U.S.A.
70 D4 Longboh Kalimantan
95 N6 Long Branch New Jersey U.S.A.
8 D5 Longbridge Deverill England
145 E4 Longburn New Zealand
8 D6 Long Burton England
22 K3 Longchamps Belgium
67 B2 Longchang China
67 E4 Longchuan China
9 E3 Long Compton England
138 C3 Long Cr South Australia Australia
119 O9 Long Cr Saskatchewan Canada
98 C1 Long Cr North Dakota U.S.A.
100 F5 Long Creek Oregon U.S.A.
66 D3 Long Dai Vietnam
107 M5 Longdale Oklahoma U.S.A.
58 E4 Longde China
9 E2 Longdon England
9 E2 Longdon England
40 B3 Longecourt France
95 M5 Long Eddy New York U.S.A.
36 B1 Longerich W Germany
95 R1 Long Falls Dam Maine U.S.A.
108 E5 Longfellow Texas U.S.A.
144 D5 Longfellow, Mt New Zealand
65 G2 Longfengshan Shuiku res China
139 H8 Longford Tasmania Australia
14 D3 Longford co Ireland
14 D3 Longford Ireland
145 D4 Longford New Zealand
107 N2 Longford Kansas U.S.A.
13 F2 Longformacus Scotland
6 K5 Long Forties bank North Sea
13 G3 Longframlington England
65 G3 Longgang Shan mt ra China
65 H2 Longguan China
70 D4 Longguan Arkansas U.S.A.
26 H5 Lönsdal Norway
99 N5 Lonsdale Minnesota U.S.A.
139 G6 Lonsdale L Victoria Australia
36 H6 Lonsee W Germany
26 D9 Lønset Norway
28 D2 Lønstrup Denmark
22 L3 Lonsheim Belgium
36 E5 Lontra, R Brazil
36 E5 Lontra R Brazil
71 F4 Looc Philippines
9 B7 Looe, E England
110 K3 Loogootee Indiana U.S.A.
107 M6 Lookeba Oklahoma U.S.A.
94 C4 Lookingglass R Michigan U.S.A.
85 B7 Los, Îles de Guinea
42 F4 Lošinj isld Yugoslavia
89 F5 Loskop Dam S Africa
106 B6 Lookout Mt New Mexico U.S.A.
108 A4 Los Médanos Mexico
100 C9 Los Molinos California U.S.A.
106 F2 Los Mochis Mexico
21 N3 Los Muros France
131 B3 Los Molles, R Chile
27 D10 Løsna Norway
16 D5 Los Navalmorales Spain
26 M7 Løsning Denmark
48 E3 Los Olivos Spain
48 D3 Los Palacios Cuba

[Index page — Lone Rock to Luoqing Jiang. Dense multi-column gazetteer of place names with map grid references. Full verbatim transcription of every entry is not reliably legible at this resolution.]

67 C4 **Luorong** China
67 D2 **Luoshan** China
67 E1 **Luoshan** China
67 E1 **Luotian** China
65 E1 **Luotuobozi** China
67 B1 **Luowenba** China
65 B7 **Luoyang** China
67 F3 **Luoyuan** China
86 B6 **Luozi** Zaire
88 D6 **Lupa** *R* Tanzania
88 D8 **Lupachi** *R* Malawi
89 E2 **Lupane** Zimbabwe
89 F2 **Lupani** *R* Zimbabwe
70 B4 **Lupar** *R* Sarawak
31 K1 **Łupawa** *R* Poland
37 M5 **Lupburg** W Germany
48 H5 **Lupeni** Romania
127 J5 **Luperón** Dominican Rep
41 J1 **Lupfen** *mt* W Germany
87 G8 **Lupilichi** Mozambique
67 B3 **Luping** China
87 C8 **Lupire** Angola
42 F3 **Lupoglav** Yugoslavia
54 B3 **Lupolovo** U.S.S.R.
71 G7 **Lupon** Mindanao Philippines
33 R10 **Luppa** East Germany
110 D3 **Lupus** Missouri U.S.A.
87 D7 **Luputa** Zaire
52 H4 **Lup'ya** *R* U.S.S.R.
130 B9 **Luque** Paraguay
107 M2 **Luray** Kansas U.S.A.
94 J8 **Luray** Virginia U.S.A.
112 E2 **Lure, L** North Carolina U.S.A.
19 P16 **Lure, Mt de** France
14 E2 **Lurgan** N Ireland
128 E7 **Luribay** Bolivia
128 C6 **Lurin** Peru
87 H8 **Lurio** Mozambique
26 F5 **Luröy** Norway
19 P17 **Lurs** France
110 C6 **Lurton** Arkansas U.S.A.
21 P7 **Lury sur-Arnon** France
88 B9 **Lusaka** Zambia
86 D6 **Lusambo** Zaire
86 C6 **Lusanga** Zaire
88 C8 **Lusangazi** Zambia
20 G6 **Lusanger** France
117 P9 **Luscar** Alberta Canada
118 H6 **Luseland** Saskatchewan Canada
88 C6 **Lusenga Plain Nat. Park** Zambia
75 P7 **Lushai Hills** India
65 D6 **Lu Shan** *mt* China
58 F5 **Lushi** China
142 F3 **Lush, Mt** Western Australia Australia
88 G4 **Lushoto** Tanzania
65 E5 **Lüshun** China
67 G1 **Lüsi** China
70 N9 **Lusi** *R* Java
18 F6 **Lusignan** France
98 B7 **Lusk** Wyoming U.S.A.
19 P15 **Lus-la-Croix Haute** France
38 E8 **Luson** Italy
26 L4 **Luspebryggan** Sweden
15 D4 **Luss** Scotland
18 F6 **Lussac les Châteaux** France
12 C3 **Lussa, L** Scotland
129 H8 **Lussanvira** Brazil
78 J6 **Lussuf, Al** Iraq
141 J7 **Lussvale** Queensland Australia
36 E5 **Lustadt** W Germany
41 L3 **Lustenau** Austria
37 J5 **Lustenau** W Germany
27 B10 **Luster** Norway
22 H3 **Lustin** Belgium
101 U1 **Lustre** Montana U.S.A.
Lutai *see* **Ninghe**
77 E3 **Lut, Dasht-e** *desert* Iran
87 D8 **Lutembo** Angola
110 G4 **Lutesville** Missouri U.S.A.
99 N8 **Luther** Iowa U.S.A.
107 N6 **Luther** Oklahoma U.S.A.
108 G1 **Lutie** Texas U.S.A.
33 N4 **Lütjenburg** W Germany
9 F4 **Luton** England
40 E4 **Lutry** Switzerland
87 C7 **Lutshima** *R* Zaire
32 M9 **Lutter am Barenberge** W Germany
32 M7 **Lutterloh** W Germany
9 E3 **Lutterworth** England
22 G3 **Luttre** Belgium
112 D1 **Luttrell** Tennessee U.S.A.
36 C1 **Lüttringhausen** W Germany
54 L8 **Lutugino** U.S.S.R.
113 E9 **Lutz** Florida U.S.A.
36 C6 **Lutzelbourg** France
36 C6 **Lutzelhouse** France
33 Q10 **Lützen** East Germany
36 B3 **Lutzerath** W Germany
33 O5 **Lützow** East Germany
146 J8 **Lützow-Holmbukta** *B* Antarctica
29 N11 **Luumäki** Finland
86 H5 **Luuq** Somalia
29 N5 **Luusua** Finland
111 K10 **Luverne** Alabama U.S.A.
99 M7 **Luverne** Iowa U.S.A.
98 K6 **Luverne** Minnesota U.S.A.
98 J2 **Luverne** North Dakota U.S.A.
29 J10 **Luvia** Finland
26 K5 **Luvos** Sweden
29 P7 **Luvozero** U.S.S.R.
87 E7 **Luvua** *R* Zaire
87 D8 **Luvuei** Angola
88 F6 **Luwegu** *R* Tanzania
87 F8 **Luwingu** Zambia
71 B2 **Luwo** *isld* Halmahera Indonesia
68 J1 **Luwu** China
70 B5 **Luwuhuyu** Kalimantan
71 H5 **Luwuk** Sulawesi
88 D7 **Luwumbu** *R* Zambia
111 J8 **Luxapalila** *R* Alabama U.S.A.
22 L4 **Luxembourg** *Grand Duchy* Europe
22 L4 **Luxembourg** Luxembourg
99 P7 **Luxemburg** Iowa U.S.A.
40 D2 **Luxeuil-les-Bains** France
67 A4 **Luxi** China
67 C2 **Luxi** China
67 B2 **Lu Xian** China
84 J4 **Luxor** Egypt
18 E9 **Luy** *R* France
21 M7 **Luynes** France
18 E10 **Luz** France
52 G4 **Luza** U.S.S.R.
52 J2 **Luza** *R* Komi A.S.S.R. U.S.S.R.
21 P3 **Luzarches** France
18 F8 **Luzech** France
21 N8 **Luzeret** France
41 H3 **Luzern** Switzerland
94 C2 **Luzerne** Michigan U.S.A.
95 O3 **Luzerne** New York U.S.A.
67 C4 **Luzhai** China
67 B3 **Luzhi** China
67 B2 **Luzhou** China
130 F5 **Luziânia** Brazil
21 N7 **Luzillé** France
31 H6 **Lužnice** *R* Czechoslovakia
71 E2 **Luzon** Philippines
18 H6 **Luzy** France
45 J2 **Luzzara** Italy
48 J1 **L'vov** U.S.S.R.
88 B7 **Lwela** *R* Zambia
88 C7 **Lwitikila** *R* Zambia
31 J3 **Lwówek** Poland
31 J4 **Lwówek Śląski** Poland
52 E4 **Lyadiny** U.S.S.R.
48 L2 **Lyadova** *R* U.S.S.R.
147 Q7 **Lyakhovskiye 0s** *isld* U.S.S.R.
144 A6 **Lyall, Mt** New Zealand
Lyallpur *see* **Faisalabad**
57 E5 **Lyal'-Mikar** U.S.S.R.
55 D2 **Lyalya** *R* U.S.S.R.
55 F1 **Lyamin** *R* U.S.S.R.
57 D4 **Lyangar** U.S.S.R.
52 D4 **Lyaskelya** U.S.S.R.
47 H1 **Lyaskovets** Bulgaria
106 C5 **Lybrook** New Mexico U.S.A.
15 E2 **Lybster** Scotland
28 C3 **Lyby** Denmark
106 H4 **Lycan** Colorado U.S.A.
33 S6 **Lychen** East Germany
52 D5 **Lychkovo** U.S.S.R.
47 K8 **Lycia** Turkey
Lyck *see* **Ełk**
26 K7 **Lycksele** Sweden
9 G6 **Lydd** England
Lydda *see* **Lod**
119 T3 **Lyddal** Manitoba Canada
146 F6 **Lyddan Ice Rise** *ice rise* Antarctica
89 G5 **Lydenburg** S Africa
8 B6 **Lydford** England
8 D2 **Lydham** England
47 J6 **Lydia** *hist reg* Turkey
112 G3 **Lydia** South Carolina U.S.A.
119 V8 **Lydiatt** Manitoba Canada
8 D4 **Lydney** England
8 B6 **Lyd, R** England
28 A5 **Lydum** Denmark
21 N7 **Lye** France
145 D4 **Lyell** New Zealand
140 B6 **Lyell Brown, Mt** N Terr Australia
117 H9 **Lyell I** British Columbia Canada
139 H8 **Lyell, Mt** Tasmania Australia
111 L7 **Lyerly** Georgia U.S.A.
26 K2 **Lyfjord** Norway
109 K9 **Lyford** Texas U.S.A.
113 K9 **Lyford Cay** *isld* New Providence I Bahamas
27 B13 **Lygna** *R* Norway
95 L6 **Lykens** Pennsylvania U.S.A.
52 D5 **Lykoshino** U.S.S.R.
99 O6 **Lyle** Minnesota U.S.A.
100 D4 **Lyle** Washington U.S.A.
110 J6 **Lyles** Tennessee U.S.A.
119 Q9 **Lyleton** Manitoba Canada
111 G11 **Lyman** Mississippi U.S.A.
107 O5 **Lyman** Oklahoma U.S.A.
112 E3 **Lyman** South Carolina U.S.A.
101 P8 **Lyman** Wyoming U.S.A.
117 O8 **Lymburn** Alberta Canada
95 P3 **Lyme** New Hampshire U.S.A.
8 D6 **Lyme B** England
8 D6 **Lyme Regis** England
9 H5 **Lyminge** England
9 E6 **Lymington** England
31 M1 **Łyna** *R* Poland
28 H5 **Lynæs** Denmark
98 H7 **Lynch** Nebraska U.S.A.
94 D7 **Lynchburg** Ohio U.S.A.
110 K6 **Lynchburg** Tennessee U.S.A.
94 H9 **Lynchburg** Virginia U.S.A.
112 G3 **Lynches** *R* South Carolina U.S.A.
95 R2 **Lynchville** Maine U.S.A.
141 G4 **Lynd** Queensland Australia
141 G3 **Lynd** *R* Queensland Australia
28 H5 **Lyndby** Denmark
100 C1 **Lynden** Washington U.S.A.
141 G4 **Lyndhurst** Queensland Australia
138 E4 **Lyndhurst** South Australia Australia
9 E6 **Lyndhurst** England
144 C5 **Lyndhurst** New Zealand
143 B6 **Lyndon** Western Australia Australia
107 P3 **Lyndon** Kansas U.S.A.
95 P2 **Lyndon** Vermont U.S.A.
109 J5 **Lyndon B. Johnson, L** Texas U.S.A.
143 A6 **Lyndon, R** Western Australia Australia
94 J3 **Lyndonville** New York U.S.A.
95 P2 **Lyndonville** Vermont U.S.A.
28 A5 **Lyne** Denmark
13 E2 **Lyne** Scotland
28 F4 **Lyngby** Denmark
28 D4 **Lyngbygd Å** *R* Denmark
27 B13 **Lyngdal** Norway
28 H6 **Lynge** Denmark
26 L2 **Lyngen** Norway
27 D13 **Lyngör** Norway
28 A3 **Lyngs** Denmark
28 F2 **Lyngså** Denmark
26 L2 **Lyngseidet** Norway
26 L2 **Lyngsfjord** *inlet* Norway
142 D3 **Lynher Reef** Western Australia Australia
8 C5 **Lynmouth** England
111 J7 **Lynn** Alabama U.S.A.
94 C6 **Lynn** Indiana U.S.A.
95 R4 **Lynn** Massachusetts U.S.A.
101 M8 **Lynn** Utah U.S.A.
117 F6 **Lynn Canal** Alaska U.S.A.
103 M2 **Lynndyl** Utah U.S.A.
111 L11 **Lynn Haven** Florida U.S.A.
119 Q2 **Lynn Lake** Manitoba Canada
99 O8 **Lynnville** Iowa U.S.A.
110 J6 **Lynnville** Tennessee U.S.A.
143 A8 **Lynton** Western Australia Australia
8 C5 **Lynton** England
28 E6 **Lyø** Denmark
18 N13 **Lyon** France
40 A6 **Lyon** France
94 C2 **Lyon Manor** Michigan U.S.A.
95 O2 **Lyon Mountain** New York U.S.A.
18 H7 **Lyonnais, Mts.du** France
Lyons *see* **Lyon**
138 C4 **Lyons** South Australia Australia
98 A9 **Lyons** Colorado U.S.A.
112 E5 **Lyons** Georgia U.S.A.
110 J3 **Lyons** Indiana U.S.A.
107 M3 **Lyons** Kansas U.S.A.
94 C4 **Lyons** Michigan U.S.A.
98 K8 **Lyons** Nebraska U.S.A.
95 L3 **Lyons** New York U.S.A.
94 C5 **Lyons** Ohio U.S.A.
100 C5 **Lyons** Oregon U.S.A.
98 K6 **Lyons** South Dakota U.S.A.
109 L5 **Lyons** Texas U.S.A.
99 S7 **Lyons** Wisconsin U.S.A.
95 M3 **Lyons Falls** New York U.S.A.
21 N3 **Lyons-la-Forêt** France
143 B6 **Lyons, R** Western Australia Australia
137 L2 **Lyra Reef** Bismarck Arch
22 D2 **Lys** *R* France
42 B3 **Lys** *R* Italy
31 H5 **Lysá** Czechoslovakia
27 B12 **Lyse** Norway
27 B13 **Lysefjorden** *inlet* Norway
27 E13 **Lysekil** Sweden
79 D3 **Lysi** Cyprus
101 S6 **Lysite** Wyoming U.S.A.
40 F3 **Lyss** Switzerland
121 T6 **Lyster** Quebec Canada
55 C2 **Lys'va** U.S.S.R.
27 F11 **Lysvik** Sweden
53 F8 **Lysyye Gory** U.S.S.R.
8 D6 **Lytchett** England
13 E6 **Lytham St.Anne's** England
68 J5 **Ly Tin** Vietnam
109 J6 **Lytle** Texas U.S.A.
144 B4 **Lyttleton** New Zealand
117 N10 **Lytton** British Columbia Canada
121 O6 **Lytton** Quebec Canada
102 B3 **Lytton** California U.S.A.
52 D5 **Lyuban'** U.S.S.R.
48 N3 **Lyubashevka** U.S.S.R.
52 E6 **Lyubertsu** U.S.S.R.
54 J1 **Lyubertsy** U.S.S.R.
52 F5 **Lyubim** U.S.S.R.
47 H3 **Lyubimets** Bulgaria
55 C2 **Lyubimova** U.S.S.R.
55 F3 **Lyubinskiy** U.S.S.R.
52 D5 **Lyublino** U.S.S.R.
54 F3 **Lyubokhna** U.S.S.R.
54 G7 **Lyubotin** U.S.S.R.
54 F3 **Lyudinovo** U.S.S.R.
52 H6 **Lyuk** U.S.S.R.
52 G6 **Lyunda** *R* U.S.S.R.
52 J2 **Lyzha** *R* U.S.S.R.

M

68 D1 **Ma** *R* Burma
80 F3 **Ma'ad** Jordan
79 B9 **Ma'âdi** Egypt
80 F3 **Ma'agan** Israel
80 C3 **Ma'agan Mikha'el** Israel
87 H8 **Maaia** Mozambique
135 T3 **Maalaea** Hawaiian Is
80 E6 **Maale Alummin** Jordan
73 L7 **Maalosmadulu Atoll** Maldives
79 F8 **Ma'ān** Jordan
29 N8 **Maaninka** Finland
29 O8 **Maanselkä** Finland
58 G5 **Ma'anshan** China
71 F5 **Ma-ao** Negros Philippines
25 E6 **Maarheeze** Netherlands
79 G2 **Ma'arrat al Ikhwān** Syria
79 G3 **Ma'arrat an Nu'mān** Syria
25 D4 **Maarsbergen** Netherlands
25 D5 **Maarsser** Netherlands
25 D4 **Maartensdijk** Netherlands
25 D5 **Maas** *R* Netherlands
25 E6 **Maasbracht** Netherlands
22 K1 **Maaseik** Belgium
22 K2 **Maasmechelen** Belgium
25 B5 **Maassluis** Netherlands
22 K2 **Maastricht** Belgium
25 E7 **Maastricht** Netherlands
139 H9 **Maatsuyker Is** Tasmania Australia
Maba *see* **Qujiang**
71 B2 **Maba** Halmahera Indonesia
87 F10 **Mabalane** Mozambique
109 L3 **Mabank** Texas U.S.A.
80 C4 **Ma'barot** Israel
71 F4 **Mabatobato** Philippines
6 M4 **Mabel** *oil rig* North Sea
99 P6 **Mabel** Minnesota U.S.A.
138 C3 **Mabel Creek** South Australia Australia
142 G3 **Mabel Downs** Western Australia Australia
119 O2 **Mabella** Ontario Canada
94 F9 **Maben** West Virginia U.S.A.
121 O8 **Maberly** Ontario Canada
122 K2 **Mabille, L** Quebec Canada
28 B4 **Måbjerg** Denmark
9 G1 **Mablethorpe** England
123 L7 **Mabou** C Breton I, Nova Scotia
85 D5 **Mabrouk** Mali
84 E5 **Mabrous** Niger
84 F4 **Mabruk** Libya
100 E3 **Mabton** Washington U.S.A.
89 D5 **Mabule** Botswana
61 P14 **Mabuni** Okinawa
84 G4 **Ma'būs Yūsuf** *well* Libya
89 C5 **Mabutsane** Botswana
133 C7 **Maca** *mt* Chile
122 E8 **McAdam** New Brunswick Canada
143 B7 **Macadam Plains** Western Australia Australia
140 A2 **Macadam Ra** N Terr Australia
130 H3 **Macaé** Brazil
130 J8 **Macaiba** Brazil
71 G6 **Macajalar B** Philippines
109 M1 **McAlester** Oklahoma U.S.A.
139 J5 **Macalister, Mt** New South Wales Australia
109 J9 **McAllen** Texas U.S.A.
101 O4 **McAllister** Montana U.S.A.
113 E7 **McAlpin** Florida U.S.A.
114 J4 **MacAlpine L** Northwest Territories Canada
121 L4 **Macamic** Quebec Canada
Macan, Kepulauan *isld see* **Taka' Bonerate, Kepulauan**
67 D5 **Macao** *terr* E Asia
16 B5 **Macão** Portugal
128 E5 **Macapá** Amazonas Brazil
130 H4 **Macarani** Brazil
127 O10 **Macareo** *R* Venezuela
141 F3 **Macaroni** Queensland Australia
138 F7 **Macarthur** Victoria Australia
100 D8 **McArthur** California U.S.A.
94 E7 **McArthur** Ohio U.S.A.
140 D3 **McArthur R** N Terr Australia
140 D3 **McArthur River** N Terr Australia
94 A4 **Macatawa** Michigan U.S.A.
Macau *see* **Macao**
129 L5 **Macau** Brazil
119 Q8 **McAuley** Manitoba Canada
137 R8 **Macauley I** Kermadec Is Pacific Oc
94 B2 **McBain** Michigan U.S.A.
110 D3 **McBaine** Missouri U.S.A.
112 F4 **McBean** Georgia U.S.A.
112 G3 **McBee** South Carolina U.S.A.
119 U6 **McBeth Pt** Manitoba Canada
117 N9 **McBride** British Columbia Canada
133 F8 **Macbride Hd** Falkland Is
100 J5 **McCall** Idaho U.S.A.
108 E4 **McCamey** Texas U.S.A.
101 N7 **McCammon** Idaho U.S.A.
122 H8 **Maccan** Nova Scotia Canada
98 J1 **McCanna** North Dakota U.S.A.
44 M6 **Maccarese** Italy
117 H9 **McCauley I** British Columbia Canada
100 B2 **McCleary** Washington U.S.A.
112 H4 **McClellanville** South Carolina U.S.A.
113 E7 **MacClenny** Florida U.S.A.
8 D1 **Macclesfield** England
123 S5 **Maccles L** Newfoundland Canada
114 J3 **McClintock Ch** Northwest Territories Canada
142 F4 **McClintock Ra** Western Australia Australia
100 C8 **McCloud** California U.S.A.
140 C1 **McCluer I** N Terr Australia
94 D5 **McClure** Ohio U.S.A.
95 K6 **McClure** Pennsylvania U.S.A.
102 D4 **McClure, L** California U.S.A.
114 H3 **McClure Str** Northwest Territories Canada
113 H3 **McClusker R** Saskatchewan Canada
98 F2 **McClusky** North Dakota U.S.A.
111 F10 **McComb** Mississippi U.S.A.
94 D5 **McComb** Ohio U.S.A.
98 D8 **McConaughy, L** Nebraska U.S.A.
117 M3 **McConnell Range** Northwest Territories Canada
94 J7 **McConnellsburg** Pennsylvania U.S.A.
98 F9 **McCook** Nebraska U.S.A.
111 G8 **McCool** Mississippi U.S.A.
98 J9 **McCool Junct** Nebraska U.S.A.
118 L9 **McCord** Saskatchewan Canada
112 E4 **McCormick** South Carolina U.S.A.
106 D2 **McCoy** Colorado U.S.A.
107 L3 **McCracken** Kansas U.S.A.
119 S8 **McCreary** Manitoba Canada
110 E3 **McCredie** Missouri U.S.A.
110 E6 **McCrory** Arkansas U.S.A.
115 M3 **Macculloch, C** Northwest Territories Canada
103 J6 **McCullough Ridge** Nevada U.S.A.
110 B6 **McCurtain** Oklahoma U.S.A.
109 K5 **McDade** Texas U.S.A.
117 J6 **McDame** British Columbia Canada
100 H8 **McDermitt** Nevada U.S.A.
94 D8 **McDermott** Ohio U.S.A.
120 B3 **Macdiarmid** Ontario Canada
100 C8 **Macdoel** California U.S.A.
107 J2 **McDonald** Kansas U.S.A.
81 E11 **Macdonald Is** Southern Oc
143 G6 **Macdonald, L** Western Australia Australia
101 M1 **McDonald, L** Montana U.S.A.
100 E9 **McDonald Peak** *mt* California U.S.A.
101 M2 **McDonald Pk** Montana U.S.A.
142 E3 **Macdonald Ra** Western Australia Australia
101 L1 **Macdonald Range** British Columbia Canada
138 E3 **McDonnell** *R* South Australia Australia
140 B6 **MacDonnell Ranges** N Terr Australia
112 C4 **McDonough** Georgia U.S.A.
138 D3 **McDouall Peak** South Australia Australia
115 K7 **MacDowell L** Ontario Canada
103 N8 **McDowell Pk** Arizona U.S.A.
15 F3 **MacDuff** Scotland
16 C3 **Macedo de Chavaleiros** Portugal
95 K3 **Macedon** New York U.S.A.
Macedonia *see* **Makedhonia**
99 L8 **Macedonia** Iowa U.S.A.
139 G7 **Macedon, Mt** Victoria Australia
130 J10 **Maceió** Alagoas Brazil
87 G8 **Maceloge** Mozambique
85 C7 **Macenta** Guinea
42 E5 **Macerata** Italy
100 G5 **McEwen** Oregon U.S.A.
110 J5 **McEwen** Tennessee U.S.A.
101 T8 **McFadden** Wyoming U.S.A.
99 M9 **McFall** Missouri U.S.A.
107 O2 **McFarland** Kansas U.S.A.
138 D4 **Macfarlane, L** South Australia Australia
144 B5 **Macfarlane, Mt** New Zealand
106 B6 **McGaffey** New Mexico U.S.A.
118 J7 **McGee** Saskatchewan Canada
107 P7 **McGee Creek Res** Oklahoma U.S.A.
111 E8 **McGehee** Arkansas U.S.A.
103 K2 **McGill** Nevada U.S.A.
100 K1 **McGillvray Range** *mts* British Columbia Canada
14 B5 **Macgillycuddy's Reeks** *mts* Ireland
116 K5 **McGrath** Alaska U.S.A.
95 L4 **McGraw** New York U.S.A.
119 T9 **MacGregor** Manitoba Canada
94 E3 **McGregor** Michigan U.S.A.
99 N3 **McGregor** Minnesota U.S.A.
109 K4 **McGregor** Texas U.S.A.
118 E8 **McGregor L** Alberta Canada
117 N8 **McGregor R** British Columbia Canada
141 F7 **McGregor Ra** Queensland Australia
98 C8 **McGrew** Nebraska U.S.A.
101 L4 **McGuire, Mt** Idaho U.S.A.
77 K5 **Mach** Pakistan
89 F7 **Machache Mt** Lesotho
128 C4 **Machachi** Ecuador
130 F7 **Machado** Brazil
80 F7 **Machaerus** Jordan
87 F10 **Machaila** Mozambique
88 F2 **Machakos** Kenya
128 C4 **Machala** Ecuador
70 C4 **Machan** Sarawak
67 B3 **Machangping** China
133 E2 **Machareti** Bolivia
140 E6 **Machattie L** Queensland Australia
22 G5 **Machault** France
87 F10 **Machaze** Mozambique
20 G8 **Machecoul** France
112 D4 **Machen** Georgia U.S.A.
67 E1 **Macheng** China
99 S7 **McHenry** Illinois U.S.A.
111 G11 **McHenry** Mississippi U.S.A.
76 D2 **Macherla** India
33 R10 **Machern** East Germany
95 U2 **Machias** Maine U.S.A.
95 S7 **Machias** *R* Maine U.S.A.
17 F1 **Machichaco, C** Spain
76 E2 **Machilipatnam** India
88 G6 **Mchinja** Tanzania
88 D8 **Mchinji** Malawi
127 H9 **Machiques** Venezuela
12 C2 **Machrie** Scotland
12 C3 **Machrihanish** Scotland
8 C2 **Machynlleth** Wales
87 F10 **Macia** Mozambique
Macias Nguema Biyogo *see* **Bioko**
141 G2 **McIlwraith Ra** Queensland Australia
48 L5 **Măcin** Romania
85 C6 **Macina** *reg* Mali
120 J3 **Mc. Innes** Ontario Canada
99 O6 **McIntire** Iowa U.S.A.
118 J1 **McIntosh** Ontario Canada
98 E4 **McIntosh** South Dakota U.S.A.
143 F7 **Macintosh Ra** Western Australia Australia
120 B3 **McIntyre B** Ontario Canada
141 K8 **Macintyre Brook** Queensland Australia
106 B2 **Mack** Colorado U.S.A.
119 O6 **McKague** Saskatchewan Canada
141 J5 **Mackay** Queensland Australia
101 M6 **Mackay** Idaho U.S.A.
114 H5 **MacKay L** Northwest Territories Canada
120 D3 **McKay L** Ontario Canada
142 G5 **Mackay, L** N Terr /W Aust
142 D5 **Mackay, Mt** Western Australia Australia
117 R7 **McKay R** Alberta Canada
143 D6 **McKay Ra** Western Australia Australia
137 S2 **McKean I** Phoenix Is Pacific Oc
94 H6 **McKeesport** Pennsylvania U.S.A.
94 G6 **McKees Rocks** Pennsylvania U.S.A.
33 T10 **Mäckenberg** East Germany
133 E4 **Mackenna** Argentina
33 N9 **Mackenrode** East Germany
141 J6 **Mackenzie** *R* Queensland Australia
114 G5 **Mackenzie** *R* Northwest Territories Canada
111 K10 **McKenzie** Alabama U.S.A.
98 F3 **McKenzie** North Dakota U.S.A.
110 H5 **McKenzie** Tennessee U.S.A.
146 J11 **Mackenzie B** Antarctica
114 F4 **Mackenzie B** Yukon Territory Canada
100 C5 **McKenzie Bridge** Oregon U.S.A.
114 H2 **Mackenzie King I** Northwest Territories Canada
119 N2 **McKenzie L** Ontario Canada
119 P4 **McKenzie L** Saskatchewan Canada
117 H3 **Mackenzie Mts** Yukon Terr/N W Terr Canada
100 D5 **McKenzie Pass** Oregon U.S.A.
119 S1 **MacKerracher L** Manitoba Canada
144 B6 **McKerrow, L** New Zealand
94 C1 **Mackinac** Michigan U.S.A.
94 C1 **Mackinac, Str. of** Michigan U.S.A.
99 R9 **Mackinaw** *R* Illinois U.S.A.
99 R9 **Mackinaw** Illinois U.S.A.
94 C1 **Mackinaw City** Michigan U.S.A.
141 F5 **McKinlay** *R* Queensland Australia
141 F5 **McKinlay** Queensland Australia
116 M5 **McKinley, Mt** Alaska U.S.A.
110 M4 **McKinney** Kentucky U.S.A.
109 L2 **McKinney** Texas U.S.A.
107 J3 **McKinney, L** Kansas U.S.A.
144 A6 **McKinnon Pass** New Zealand
146 D5 **Mackintosh, Cape** *C* Antarctica
139 H8 **Mackintosh L.** Tasmania Australia
120 B3 **McKirdy** Ontario Canada
102 E6 **McKittrick** California U.S.A.
118 H6 **Macklin** Saskatchewan Canada
119 Q2 **McKnight L** Manitoba Canada
38 O8 **Mačkovci** Yugoslavia
94 F7 **Macksburg** Ohio U.S.A.
101 O5 **Macks Inn** Idaho U.S.A.
139 L4 **Macksville** New South Wales Australia
107 M4 **Macksville** Kansas U.S.A.
141 F6 **Mackunda** *R* Queensland Australia
111 H10 **McLain** Mississippi U.S.A.
116 O5 **Maclaren** *R* Alaska U.S.A.
138 E6 **McLaren Vale** South Australia Australia
142 E4 **McLarty Hills** Western Australia Australia
142 D5 **McLarty, Mt** Western Australia Australia
118 G6 **McLaughlin** Alberta Canada
98 F4 **McLaughlin** South Dakota U.S.A.
119 U5 **McLaughlin R** Manitoba Canada
139 L3 **Maclean** New South Wales Australia
119 N8 **McLean** Saskatchewan Canada
99 R9 **McLean** Illinois U.S.A.
118 H2 **McLean L** Saskatchewan Canada
110 H3 **McLeansboro** Illinois U.S.A.
87 E12 **Maclear** S Africa
88 E8 **Maclear, C** Malawi
139 L4 **Macleay** *R* New South Wales Australia
118 A3 **McLennan** Alberta Canada
119 N3 **McLennan Lake** Saskatchewan Canada
98 J3 **McLeod** North Dakota U.S.A.
114 J5 **McLeod B** Northwest Territories Canada
143 A6 **Macleod, L** Western Australia Australia
117 M8 **McLeod Lake** British Columbia Canada
118 B5 **McLeod R** Alberta Canada
68 C7 **McLeods I** Burma
110 A2 **McLouth** Kansas U.S.A.
118 K8 **McMahon** Saskatchewan Canada
94 G7 **McMechen** West Virginia U.S.A.
83 M9 **McMicken Pt** Christmas I Indian Oc
141 G1 **Macmillan** *R* Queensland Australia
117 F4 **Macmillan** *R* Yukon Territory Canada
99 V3 **McMillan** Michigan U.S.A.
106 F9 **McMillan, L** New Mexico U.S.A.
140 C6 **McMinns Cr** N Terr Australia
100 B4 **McMinnville** Oregon U.S.A.
110 L6 **McMinnville** Tennessee U.S.A.
118 J7 **McMorran** Saskatchewan Canada
118 F1 **McMunn** Manitoba Canada
146 D11 **McMurdo** *U.S.A. Base* Antarctica
117 O10 **McMurphy** British Columbia Canada
100 C1 **McMurray** Washington U.S.A.
111 E10 **McNair** Mississippi U.S.A.
103 P7 **McNary** Arizona U.S.A.
108 B4 **McNary** Texas U.S.A.
100 F4 **McNary Dam** Oregon U.S.A.
103 P10 **McNeal** Arizona U.S.A.
111 C8 **McNeil** Arkansas U.S.A.
109 K5 **McNeil** Texas U.S.A.
111 G11 **McNeill** Mississippi U.S.A.
119 Q7 **MacNutt** Saskatchewan Canada
122 G10 **McNutt I** Nova Scotia Canada
128 D1 **Macollo, Pta** *C* Venezuela
110 F1 **Macomb** Illinois U.S.A.
107 O6 **Macomb** Oklahoma U.S.A.
43 B8 **Macomer** Sardinia
88 H8 **Macomia** Mozambique
22 G3 **Maçon** Belgium
19 J6 **Mâcon** France
112 D5 **Macon** Georgia U.S.A.
99 S10 **Macon** Illinois U.S.A.
111 H8 **Macon** Mississippi U.S.A.
99 O10 **Macon** Missouri U.S.A.
98 G9 **Macon** Nebraska U.S.A.
87 D8 **Macondo** Angola
119 O9 **Macoun** Saskatchewan Canada
107 N3 **McPherson** Kansas U.S.A.
142 D5 **Macpherson, Mt** Western Australia Australia
141 L8 **Macpherson Ra** N S W/Qnsld Australia
68 A7 **Macpherson's Str** Andaman Is
139 J4 **MacQuarie** *R* New South Wales Australia
139 H8 **Macquarie** *R* Tasmania Australia
139 H8 **Macquarie Harbour** Tasmania Australia
81 J12 **Macquarie I** S Pacific Oc
146 B16 **Macquarie Island** *Australia Base* Antarctica
139 K5 **Macquarie, L** New South Wales Australia
139 J4 **Macquarie Marshes** New South Wales Australia
139 J5 **Macquarie, Mt** New South Wales Australia
81 J12 **Macquarie Ridge** S Pacific Oc
22 G4 **Macquenoise** Belgium
117 E4 **McQuesten** *R* Yukon Territory Canada
117 E4 **McQuesten** Yukon Territory Canada
112 E5 **McRae** Georgia U.S.A.
144 D5 **McRae, L** New Zealand
142 C5 **McRae, Mt** Western Australia Australia
144 C6 **Macraes Flat** New Zealand
94 E9 **McRoberts** Kentucky U.S.A.
146 J11 **MacRobertson Land** Antarctica
14 C5 **Macroom** Ireland
118 K7 **Macrorie** Saskatchewan Canada
119 N9 **McTaggart** Saskatchewan Canada
71 G5 **Mactan** *isld* Philippines
118 D1 **McTavish** Manitoba Canada
128 D3 **Macujer** Colombia
71 G4 **Maculiv** Philippines
138 D2 **Macumba** *R* South Australia Australia
95 M6 **Macungie** Pennsylvania U.S.A.
128 D6 **Macusani** Peru
87 G9 **Macuse** Mozambique
125 N9 **Macuspana** Mexico
124 E4 **Macuzari, Presa** *res* Mexico
119 Q2 **McVeigh** Manitoba Canada
94 E9 **McVeigh** Kentucky U.S.A.
117 N3 **McVicar Arm** *inlet* Northwest Territories Canada
98 H2 **McVille** North Dakota U.S.A.
121 M4 **McWatters** Quebec Canada
111 J10 **McWilliams** Alabama U.S.A.
86 A4 **Mada** *R* Nigeria
80 G7 **Madaba** Jordan
86 D2 **Madadi** Chad
87 H11 **Madagascar** *rep* Indian Oc
81 C8 **Madagascar Basin** Indian Oc
76 C4 **Madakasira** India
70 E1 **Madalon** *mt* Sabah
84 E5 **Madama** Niger
46 G3 **Madan** Bulgaria
76 D4 **Madanapalle** India
136 K3 **Madang** Papua New Guinea
85 F6 **Madaoua** Niger
75 O7 **Madaripur** Bangladesh
85 F6 **Madarounfa** Niger
121 N7 **Madawaska** *R* Ontario Canada
121 M7 **Madawaska** Ontario Canada
95 S6 **Madawaska** Maine U.S.A.
122 D6 **Madawaska R** Quebec Canada
68 C1 **Madaya** Burma
43 C7 **Maddalena, la** Sardinia
45 Q7 **Maddaloni** Italy
143 C10 **Madden, Mt** Western Australia Australia
142 C2 **Maddington** *dist* Perth, W Aust Australia
98 G2 **Maddock** North Dakota U.S.A.
85 A2 **Madeira** *isld* Atlantic Oc
128 F5 **Madeira** *R* Brazil
128 F5 **Madeirinho** *R* Brazil
41 M3 **Madelegabel** *mt* Austria
21 M5 **Madeleine-Bouvet, la** France
123 L6 **Madeleine, Iles de la** Quebec Canada
18 H6 **Madeleine, Mts.de la** France
99 M5 **Madelia** Minnesota U.S.A.
100 E8 **Madeline** California U.S.A.
99 Q3 **Madeline I** Wisconsin U.S.A.
78 G2 **Maden** Turkey
57 J1 **Madeniyet** U.S.S.R.
124 E3 **Madera** Mexico
102 D5 **Madera** California U.S.A.
94 J6 **Madera** Pennsylvania U.S.A.
108 E5 **Madera Mt** Texas U.S.A.
29 M4 **Madetkoski** Finland
32 J10 **Madfeld** W Germany
76 A3 **Madgaon** India
119 Q7 **Madge L** Saskatchewan Canada
83 J12 **Madge Rocks** Seychelles
75 M5 **Madhubani** India
74 G7 **Madhya Pradesh** *prov* India
65 H3 **Madida** China
128 E6 **Madidi** *R* Bolivia
70 C4 **Madi, Dtt** Kalimantan
138 E3 **Madigan Gulf** South Australia Australia
76 B4 **Madikeri** India
109 L1 **Madill** Oklahoma U.S.A.
86 C6 **Madimba** Zaire
72 D4 **Madinah, Al** Saudi Arabia
86 H3 **Madinat ash Sha'ab** S Yemen
81 C5 **Madingley Rise** Indian Oc
86 B6 **Madingo-Kayes** Congo
86 B6 **Madingou** Congo
78 G4 **Ma'din Jadid** Syria
118 J7 **Madison** Saskatchewan Canada
111 M12 **Madison** St Louis
110 K7 **Madison** Alabama U.S.A.
110 F6 **Madison** Arkansas U.S.A.
113 D7 **Madison** Florida U.S.A.
112 D4 **Madison** Georgia U.S.A.
107 O3 **Madison** Kansas U.S.A.
98 K4 **Madison** Minnesota U.S.A.
110 D2 **Madison** Missouri U.S.A.
101 O4 **Madison** *R* Montana U.S.A.
98 J8 **Madison** Nebraska U.S.A.
112 H1 **Madison** North Carolina U.S.A.
94 F5 **Madison** Ohio U.S.A.
98 J5 **Madison** South Dakota U.S.A.
110 K5 **Madison** Tennessee U.S.A.
94 J8 **Madison** Virginia U.S.A.
94 F8 **Madison** West Virginia U.S.A.
99 R6 **Madison** Wisconsin U.S.A.
94 H9 **Madison Heights** Virginia U.S.A.
101 P5 **Madison Junct** Wyoming U.S.A.
101 O4 **Madison Ra** Montana U.S.A.
110 J4 **Madisonville** Kentucky U.S.A.
111 F11 **Madisonville** Louisiana U.S.A.
112 C2 **Madisonville** Tennessee U.S.A.
109 M5 **Madisonville** Texas U.S.A.
71 K10 **Madita** Sumba Indonesia
70 N9 **Madiun** Java
8 D3 **Madley** England
143 E6 **Madley, Mt** Western Australia Australia
121 N8 **Madoc** Ontario Canada
98 A1 **Madoc** Montana U.S.A.
86 G5 **Mado Gashi** Kenya
52 C6 **Madona** U.S.S.R.
100 B9 **Mad R** California U.S.A.
47 J5 **Madra Dağı** *mt* Turkey
76 E4 **Madras** India
100 D5 **Madras** Oregon U.S.A.
128 E6 **Madre de Dios** *R* Bolivia/Peru
128 D6 **Madre de Dios** *dept* Peru
133 B8 **Madre de Dios, I** Chile
125 L5 **Madre. Laguna** Mexico
109 K9 **Madre, Laguna** Texas U.S.A.
124 F4 **Madre Occidental, Sierra** *mts* Mexico
18 G10 **Madrès** *mt* France
71 F2 **Madre, Sierra** *mts* Luzon Philippines
71 G6 **Madrid** Mindanao Philippines
16 E4 **Madrid** *prov* Spain
16 E4 **Madrid** Spain
99 N8 **Madrid** Iowa U.S.A.
98 E9 **Madrid** Nebraska U.S.A.
106 D6 **Madrid** New Mexico U.S.A.
95 M2 **Madrid** New York U.S.A.
71 F5 **Madridejos** Philippines
16 E5 **Madridejos** Spain
16 D3 **Madrigal de las Atlas Torres** Spain
16 E6 **Madrona, Sa** *mts* Spain
128 G4 **Madruba, L** Brazil
126 D3 **Madruga** Cuba
79 E11 **Madsûs, G** *mt* Egypt
71 K8 **Madu** *isld* Indonesia
71 E5 **Maducang** *isld* Philippines
28 A4 **Madum** Denmark
28 D3 **Madum Sø** Denmark
143 F9 **Madura** Western Australia Australia
70 O9 **Madura** *isld* Indonesia
76 D6 **Madurai** India
70 O9 **Madura, Selat** *str* Java
83 L10 **Maduru Oya** *R* Sri Lanka
52 H4 **Madzha** U.S.S.R.
47 H3 **Madzharovo** Bulgaria
60 D12 **Maebaru** Japan
61 N9 **Maebashi** Japan
68 C3 **Mae Hong Son** Thailand
61 O13 **Mae-jima** *isld* Okinawa
68 D5 **Mae Khlong** *R* Thailand
69 D8 **Mae Kirirath** *R* Thailand
27 C12 **Mael** Norway
68 D3 **Mae Lao** *R* Thailand
20 D5 **Maël-Carhaix** France
68 D3 **Mae Li** *R* Thailand
17 H3 **Maella** Spain
20 D5 **Maël-Pestivien** France
69 D8 **Mae Luang** *R* Thailand
68 F4 **Mae Nam** *R* Thailand
68 E3 **Mae Nam Ing** *R* Thailand
68 F5 **Mae Nam Mun** *R* Thailand
68 E3 **Mae Nam Nan** *R* Thailand
68 D3 **Mae Nam Ping** *R* Thailand
68 E3 **Mae Nam Yom** *R* Thailand
68 D3 **Mae Rim** Thailand
48 K5 **Măeruş** Romania
103 P1 **Maeser** Utah U.S.A.
8 C4 **Maesteg** Wales
45 M2 **Maestra, Pta** Italy
126 F4 **Maestra, Sierra** *mts* Cuba
71 E4 **Maestre de Campo** *isld* Philippines
137 O5 **Maéwo** *isld* Vanuatu
71 A2 **Mafa** Halmahera Indonesia
88 H10 **Mafameda** *isld* Mozambique
119 Q6 **Mafeking** Manitoba Canada
89 E7 **Mafeteng** Lesotho
139 H7 **Maffra** Victoria Australia
88 G5 **Mafia Channel** Tanzania
88 G5 **Mafia,I** Tanzania
89 D5 **Mafikeng** S Africa
88 E8 **Mafinto** Mozambique
67 E1 **Ma-fou** China
130 E10 **Mafra** Brazil
16 A6 **Mafra** Portugal
89 F2 **Mafungabusi Plateau** Zimbabwe
51 P3 **Magadan** U.S.S.R.
51 P2 **Magadanskaya Oblast'** U.S.S.R.
88 F2 **Magadi** *L* Kenya
88 F2 **Magadi** Kenya
122 E8 **Magaguadavic L** New Brunswick Canada
133 C8 **Magallanes** *prov* Chile
71 F4 **Magallanes** Philippines
133 C8 **Magallanes, Estrecho de** *chan* Chile
71 F5 **Magallon** Negros Philippines
71 C3 **Magamo** W Irian
126 G10 **Magangué** Colombia
128 C2 **Magangue** Colombia
85 F6 **Magaria** Niger
61 Q12 **Magari-zaki** *C* Okinawa
71 E2 **Magat** *R* Luzon Philippines
89 G4 **Magato Mts** S Africa
110 C6 **Magazine Mt** Arkansas U.S.A.
85 B7 **Magburaka** Sierra Leone
59 J1 **Magdagachi** U.S.S.R.
37 L2 **Magdala** East Germany
128 F6 **Magdalena** Bolivia
128 D2 **Magdalena** *div* Colombia
128 C3 **Magdalena** *R* Colombia
124 D2 **Magdalena** Sonora Mexico
106 C7 **Magdalena** New Mexico U.S.A.
133 C6 **Magdalena, I** Chile
124 C5 **Magdalena, I** Mexico
70 E2 **Magdalena, Mt** Sabah
Magdalen Is *see* **Madeleine, Iles de la**
33 P8 **Magdeburg** *reg* East Germany
33 P8 **Magdeburg** East Germany
33 Q8 **Magdeburgerforth** East Germany
141 K3 **Magdelaine Cays** *islds* Gt Barrier Reef Aust
33 O9 **Mägdesprung** East Germany
80 C5 **Magdi'el** Israel
111 G10 **Magee** Mississippi U.S.A.
14 F2 **Magee, I** N Ireland
116 K7 **Mageik Vol** Alaska U.S.A.
70 N9 **Magelang** Java
133 D8 **Magellan, Str. of** Chile
80 A8 **Magen** Israel
80 E3 **Magen Shaul** Israel
41 J7 **Magenta** Italy
143 C10 **Magenta, L** Western Australia Australia
41 K3 **Magereu** *mt* Switzerland
26 P1 **Mageröya** *isld* Norway
80 D4 **Maggal** Israel
41 J5 **Maggia, Val** Switzerland
44 F2 **Maggiorasca** *mt* Italy
41 J6 **Maggiore, Lago** Italy
43 F7 **Maggiore, M** *mt* Italy
127 J2 **Maggotty** Jamaica
79 A10 **Maghâgha** Egypt
79 D8 **Maghâra, G** *mt* Egypt
14 A4 **Magharee Is** Ireland
14 E2 **Maghera** N Ireland
14 E2 **Magherafelt** N Ireland
17 F10 **Maghnia** Algeria
84 H3 **Maghra, El** Egypt
13 F6 **Maghull** England
101 L6 **Magic Res** Idaho U.S.A.
14 E1 **Magilligan Pt** N Ireland
16 E7 **Mágina** *mt* Spain
56 G3 **Magistral'nyy** U.S.S.R.
48 E6 **Maglaj** Yugoslavia
40 E5 **Magland** France
29 K6 **Magleby** Denmark
29 K7 **Magleby** *isld* Denmark
28 G7 **Maglehöjstrand** Denmark
45 M6 **Magliana** Italy
45 O5 **Magliano de Marsi** Italy
48 E7 **Maglić** *mt* Yugoslavia
43 J8 **Maglie** Italy
103 N8 **Magma** Arizona U.S.A.
18 F6 **Magnac-Laval** France
98 J7 **Magnet** Nebraska U.S.A.
121 L7 **Magnetawan** Ontario Canada
146 K10 **Magnet B** Antarctica
141 H4 **Magnetic I** Queensland Australia
55 C3 **Magnitka** U.S.S.R.
55 C4 **Magnitogorsk** U.S.S.R.
109 O2 **Magnolia** Arkansas U.S.A.
111 F10 **Magnolia** Mississippi U.S.A.
112 J3 **Magnolia** North Carolina U.S.A.
109 M5 **Magnolia** Texas U.S.A.
27 F12 **Magnor** Norway
6 L1 **Magnus** *oil rig* North Sea
21 O3 **Magny-en-Vexin** France
21 K3 **Magny-la-Campagne** France
88 C9 **Magoe** Mozambique
121 S7 **Magog** Quebec Canada
8 D4 **Magor** Wales
47 O12 **Magouládhes** Greece
120 F4 **Magpie** Ontario Canada
122 H3 **Magpie** Quebec Canada
122 H2 **Magpie L** Quebec Canada
120 F4 **Magpie Mine** Ontario Canada
122 H2 **Magpie R** Quebec Canada
44 G3 **Magra, R** Italy
118 E9 **Magrath** Alberta Canada
41 O5 **Magrè sulla Strada del Vino** Italy
17 G5 **Magro** *R* Spain
102 G4 **Magruder Mt** Nevada U.S.A.
71 E2 **Magsingal** Luzon Philippines
28 C6 **Magstrup** Denmark
67 A5 **Maguan** China
129 J4 **Maguari, C** Brazil
89 H5 **Magude** Mozambique
67 D5 **Magui** China
86 B3 **Magumeri** Nigeria
68 B2 **Magwe** Burma
68 A2 **Magyichaung** Burma
78 K3 **Mahābād** Iran
74 E10 **Mahabaleshwar** India
87 G12 **Mahabo** Madagascar
74 E9 **Mahad** India
86 A3 **Mahaddayweyne** Somalia
74 H7 **Mahadeo Hills** India
94 J6 **Mahaffey** Pennsylvania U.S.A.
86 F5 **Mahagi** Zaire
87 H11 **Mahajamba, Helodrano** *B* Madagascar
87 H11 **Mahajanga** Madagascar
70 D4 **Mahakam** *R* Kalimantan
89 E4 **Mahalapye** Botswana
46 E6 **Mahalás** Greece
79 B8 **Mahalla, El** Egypt
77 B3 **Mahallāt** Iran
70 O10 **Mahameru, G** *mt* Java
77 E4 **Mahān** Iran
75 K8 **Mahanadi** *R* India
71 G5 **Mahanay** *isld* Philippines
95 L6 **Mahanoy City** Pennsylvania U.S.A.
65 G3 **Mahao** China
83 J10 **Maha Oya** *R* Sri Lanka
74 E9 **Maharashtra** *prov* India
75 K8 **Mahasamund** India
68 F4 **Maha Sarakham** Thailand
98 J10 **Mahaska** Kansas U.S.A.
87 H11 **Mahavavy** *R* Madagascar
87 H11 **Mahavelona** Madagascar
83 K10 **Mahaweli Ganga** *R* Sri Lanka
68 G4 **Mahaxay** Laos
74 H10 **Mahbubabad** India
76 C2 **Mahbubnagar** India
77 D7 **Mahḍah** Oman
85 G1 **Mahdia** Tunisia
76 B5 **Mahe** India

83 J12 **Mahé** *isld* Seychelles
83 M13 **Mahebourg** Mauritius
88 F6 **Mahenge** Tanzania
144 C6 **Maheno** New Zealand
120 J3 **Maher** Ontario Canada
74 E7 **Mahesāna** India
74 F7 **Maheshwar** India
145 F3 **Mahia** New Zealand
74 E9 **Mahim** India
144 C5 **Mahinapua, L** New Zealand
144 B6 **Mahinerangi, L** New Zealand
80 G6 **Mahis** Jordan
87 F11 **Mahlabatini** S Africa
68 B2 **Mahlaing** Burma
33 S8 **Mahlow** East Germany
33 P8 **Mahlwinkel** East Germany
75 J5 **Mahmudabad** India
48 M5 **Mahmudia** Romania
47 M10 **Mahmutbe** Turkey
79 C2 **Mahmutlar** Turkey
47 N10 **Mahmutşevketpaşa** Turkey
83 K10 **Maho** Sri Lanka
74 H6 **Mahoba** India
145 E3 **Mahoenui** New Zealand
100 F8 **Mahogany Peak** *mt* Nevada U.S.A.
99 S9 **Mahomet** Illinois U.S.A.
17 K5 **Mahón** Menorca
122 H9 **Mahone Bay** Nova Scotia Canada
117 L3 **Mahony L** Northwest Territories Canada
17 F5 **Mahora** Spain
85 G2 **Mahrès** Tunisia
98 F4 **Mahto** South Dakota U.S.A.
145 E4 **Mahuri** New Zealand
74 D8 **Mahuva** India
137 P1 **Maiana** *atoll* Kiribati
71 M9 **Maibang** Indonesia
61 K10 **Maibara** Japan
48 L5 **Măicăneşti** Romania
19 K5 **Maich** France
40 E3 **Maiche** France
68 J2 **Maichen** China
68 J2 **Mai-ch'u** China
129 H3 **Maicuru** *R* Brazil
142 C1 **Maida Vale** Western Australia Australia
112 F2 **Maiden** North Carolina U.S.A.
8 D5 **Maiden Bradley** England
9 F4 **Maidenhead** England
8 D6 **Maiden Newton** England
99 O5 **Maiden Rock** Wisconsin U.S.A.
12 D3 **Maidens** Scotland
71 A2 **Maidi** Halmahera Indonesia
118 H5 **Maidstone** Saskatchewan Canada
9 G5 **Maidstone** England
86 B3 **Maidugun** Nigeria
42 F6 **Maiella, M.della** Italy
41 L3 **Maienfeld** Switzerland
21 P2 **Maignelay** France
128 E2 **Maigualida, Sierra** *mts* Venezuela
14 C4 **Maigue** *R* Ireland
74 J8 **Maikala Range** India
36 E5 **Maikammer** W Germany
86 E6 **Maiko, Parc Nacional de** *nat. park* Zaire
69 D14 **Maileppe** Indonesia
102 R12 **Maili** Hawaiian Is
21 N4 **Maillebois** France
21 M3 **Mailleraye-sur-Seine, la** France
22 D3 **Mailly Maillet** France
74 E4 **Mailsi** Pakistan
144 C5 **Maimai** New Zealand
127 J5 **Maimon, B.de** Dominican Rep
80 F7 **Ma'in** Jordan
14 E2 **Main** *R* N Ireland
37 K3 **Main** *R* W Germany
123 N8 **Main-à-Dieu** C Breton I, Nova Scotia
37 J4 **Mainbernheim** W Germany
123 Q2 **Main Brook** Newfoundland Canada
37 M6 **Mainburg** W Germany
118 K8 **Main Centre** Saskatchewan Canada
120 J7 **Main Channel Cave I** Ontario Canada
86 C6 **Mai Ndombe, L** Zaire
Maindong *see* **Coqên**
121 O9 **Main Duck I** Ontario Canada
20 H8 **Maine** *R* France
21 J5 **Maine** *reg* France
21 J7 **Maine** *R* France
20 H4 **Maine** *R* France
95 R1 **Maine** *state* U.S.A.
103 N6 **Maine** Arizona U.S.A.
95 L4 **Maine** New York U.S.A.
18 E5 **Maine-et-Loire** *dept* France
85 G6 **Mainé-Soroa** Niger
110 M2 **Maineville** Ohio U.S.A.
68 D6 **Maingy** *isld* Burma
36 H5 **Mainhardt** W Germany
71 G6 **Mainit, L** Mindanao Philippines
15 G2 **Mainland** Shetland Scotland
140 C2 **Mainoru** N Terr Australia
74 H5 **Mainpuri** India
138 F4 **Main Range Barrier** New South Wales Australia
122 F7 **Main S.W. Miramichi R** New Brunswick Canada
36 F3 **Maintal** W Germany
21 O4 **Maintenon** France
87 G11 **Maintirano** Madagascar
123 Q4 **Main Topsail** *pk* Newfoundland Canada
29 N7 **Mainua** Finland
74 D2 **Mainwali** Pakistan
36 E3 **Mainz** W Germany
45 R8 **Maiori** Italy
133 C4 **Maipo** *R* Chile
133 D4 **Maipo** *mt* Chile/Arg
131 B5 **Maipo, Vol** *pk* Arg/Chile
133 F5 **Maipu** Argentina
127 L9 **Maiquetia** Venezuela
44 B3 **Maira** *R* Italy
75 P5 **Mairabari** India
37 L7 **Maisach** W Germany
20 H7 **Maisdon-sur-Sèvre** France
126 G4 **Maisi** Cuba
126 G4 **Maisi, Pta. de** Cuba
122 G6 **Maisonnette** New Brunswick Canada
21 P4 **Maisons-Laffitte** France
38 N4 **Maissau** Austria
21 P5 **Maisse** France
22 J4 **Maissin** Belgium
139 K5 **Maitland** New South Wales Australia
138 D5 **Maitland** South Australia Australia
122 J8 **Maitland** Nova Scotia Canada
99 L9 **Maitland** Missouri U.S.A.
122 G9 **Maitland Br** Nova Scotia Canada
143 D7 **Maitland, L** Western Australia Australia
143 C7 **Maitland, Mt** Western Australia Australia
142 B5 **Maitland, R** Western Australia Australia
70 E2 **Maitland Ra** Sabah
140 C2 **Maiwok** *R* N Terr Australia
61 P7 **Maiya** Japan
140 A4 **Maiyu, Mt** N Terr Australia
75 O4 **Maizhokunggar** China
36 B6 **Maizières-les-Vic** France
125 N3 **Maiz, Is. del** Nicaragua
60 J10 **Maizuru** Japan
128 D2 **Majagual** Colombia
70 M9 **Majalengka** Java
74 G9 **Mājalgaon** India
128 F3 **Majari** *R* Brazil
26 F6 **Majavatn** *L* Norway
28 H7 **Majbølle** Denmark
80 E5 **Majdal Bani Fadil** Jordan
80 F8 **Majdalein** Jordan
31 N5 **Majdan** Poland
48 G6 **Majdanpek** Yugoslavia
80 D2 **Majd el Kurum** Israel
80 G1 **Majdūliyah** Syria
130 G8 **Majé** Brazil
70 F6 **Majene** Sulawesi
48 E6 **Majevica** *mts* Yugoslavia
86 G4 **Maji** Ethiopia
67 D5 **Majiang** China
67 B3 **Majiang** China
67 A4 **Majie** China
67 F2 **Majin** China
67 D2 **Majitang** China
118 H7 **Major** Saskatchewan Canada
Majorca *isld* *see* **Mallorca**
89 F6 **Majuba Hill** S Africa
Majunga *see* **Mahajanga**
89 B5 **Majwane Pan** Botswana
85 B6 **Maka** Senegal
61 P14 **Makabe** Okinawa
102 R12 **Makaha** Hawaiian Is
70 F6 **Makale** Sulawesi
69 E14 **Makalo** Indonesia
75 M5 **Makalu** *mt* China/Nepal
87 F7 **Makambako** Tanzania
86 C5 **Makanza** Zaire
135 U4 **Makapala** Hawaiian Is
102 S12 **Makapuu Hd** Hawaiian Is
145 E2 **Makarau** New Zealand
144 B7 **Makarewa** New Zealand
52 J2 **Makarikha** U.S.S.R.
144 B6 **Makarora** *R* New Zealand
59 M2 **Makarov** U.S.S.R.
42 H5 **Makarska** Yugoslavia
52 G3 **Makar-Yb** U.S.S.R.
52 G5 **Makar'ye** U.S.S.R.
Makassar *see* **Ujung Pandang**
70 F5 **Makassar Str** Indonesia
89 H6 **Makatini Flats** *reg* S Africa
135 T3 **Makawao** Hawaiian Is
71 C3 **Makbon** W Irian
46 E4 **Makedhonia** Greece
46 E3 **Makedonija** Yugoslavia
135 N10 **Makemo** *atoll* Pacific Oc
85 B7 **Makeni** Sierra Leone
145 F2 **Maketu** New Zealand
54 K8 **Makeyevka** U.S.S.R.
89 D3 **Makgadikgadi** *salt pans* Botswana
78 J1 **Makharadze** U.S.S.R.
16 D9 **Makhazen, Oued** *R* Morocco
55 D2 **Makhnevo** U.S.S.R.
55 E4 **Makhorovka** U.S.S.R.
80 F3 **Makhraba** Jordan
61 M8 **Maki** Japan
71 A2 **Makian** Halmahera Indonesia
144 C6 **Makikihi** New Zealand
119 S8 **Makinak** Manitoba Canada
55 F4 **Makinsk** U.S.S.R.
115 M2 **Makinson Inlet** Northwest Territories Canada
26 S1 **Makkaur** Norway
25 F3 **Makkinga** Netherlands
115 O6 **Makkovik** Labrador, Nfld Canada
25 D2 **Makkum** Netherlands
48 F4 **Makó** Hungary
120 C1 **Makokibatan L** Ontario Canada
87 F7 **Makongolosi** Tanzania
145 F3 **Makorako** *mt* New Zealand
98 E2 **Makoti** North Dakota U.S.A.
145 F4 **Makotuku** New Zealand
86 C5 **Makoua** Congo
31 L6 **Makov** Czechoslovakia
31 M6 **Maków** Poland
31 N3 **Maków Mazowiecki** Poland
80 D2 **Makr** Israel
47 H8 **Makrá** *isld* Greece
74 F5 **Makrana** India
77 J7 **Makran Coast Range** Pakistan
47 H4 **Mákri** Greece
76 E1 **Makri** India
46 G7 **Makronísi** *isld* Greece
52 J3 **Maksim** U.S.S.R.
56 C2 **Maksimkin Yar** U.S.S.R.
85 F1 **Makthar** Tunisia
78 K2 **Maku** Iran
70 C4 **Makup, Bt** *mt* Kalimantan
60 D14 **Makurazaki** Japan
86 A4 **Makurdi** Nigeria
55 E3 **Makushino** U.S.S.R.
116 D10 **Makushin Vol** Aleutian Is
88 D7 **Makutu Mts** Zambia
118 H4 **Makwa L** Saskatchewan Canada
89 G1 **Makwiro** Zimbabwe
128 C6 **Mala** Peru
71 G7 **Malabang** Mindanao Philippines
113 G9 **Malabar** Florida U.S.A.
76 B5 **Malabar Coast** India
70 L9 **Malabar, G** *mt* Java
85 F8 **Malabo** Bioko Equat Guinea
71 C6 **Malabuñgan** Palawan Philippines
69 E11 **Malacca, Str. of** Malaysia
118 H1 **Malachi** Ontario Canada
31 K7 **Malacky** Czechoslovakia
101 N7 **Malad City** Idaho U.S.A.
17 H2 **Maladeta** Spain
31 L6 **Malá Fatra** *mts* Czechoslovakia
16 E8 **Málaga** Spain
16 D8 **Málaga** *prov* Spain
100 E2 **Malaga** Washington U.S.A.
88 C4 **Malagarasi** Tanzania
Malagasy Rep *see* **Madagascar**
16 E5 **Malagón** Spain
71 K9 **Malahar** Indonesia
14 E3 **Malahide** Ireland
87 G12 **Malaimbandy** Madagascar
137 N3 **Malaita** *isld* Solomon Is
71 J9 **Malaka** *mt* Sumbawa Indonesia
86 F4 **Malakal** Sudan
42 G4 **Mala Kapela** Yugoslavia
109 L3 **Malakoff** Texas U.S.A.
71 B2 **Malaku** *islds* Indonesia
137 O5 **Malakula** *isld* Vanuatu
45 L2 **Malalbergo** Italy
71 A3 **Malamala** *isld* Indonesia
70 G6 **Malamala** Sulawesi
71 E7 **Malamaui** *isld* Philippines
45 M1 **Malamocco** Italy
71 D5 **Malampaya Snd** Philippines
141 H3 **Malanda** Queensland Australia
70 O10 **Malang** Java
88 E6 **Malangali** Tanzania
70 M9 **Malangbong** Java
26 K2 **Malangen** *inlet* Norway
26 K2 **Malangen** Norway
26 J2 **Malangsgrunnen** *shoal* Norway
75 L5 **Malangwa** Nepal
71 F7 **Malanipa** *isld* Philippines
87 C7 **Malanje** Angola
20 F6 **Malansac** France
71 D6 **Malanut B** Philippines
85 E6 **Malanville** Benin
65 D4 **Malanyu** China
131 C3 **Malanzaán, Sa. de** *mts* Argentina
76 C5 **Malappuram** India
27 J12 **Mälaren** *L* Sweden
131 B5 **Malargue** *R* Argentina
133 D5 **Malargue** Argentina
129 H3 **Malaripo** Brazil
121 M4 **Malartic** Quebec Canada
70 F7 **Malasoro, Tk** *B* Sulawesi
117 C6 **Malaspina Gl** Alaska U.S.A.
144 A6 **Malaspina Reach** New Zealand
117 L11 **Malaspina Str** British Columbia Canada
26 K6 **Malåtrask** Sweden
78 G2 **Malatya** Turkey
19 O16 **Malaucène** France
21 N2 **Malaunay** France
70 E1 **Malawali** *isld* Sabah
88 D8 **Malawi** *rep* Africa
Malawi, L *see* **Nyasa, L**
29 J9 **Malax** Finland
55 D1 **Malaya Sos'va** *R* U.S.S.R.
52 D5 **Malaya Vishera** U.S.S.R.
77 A2 **Malāyer** Iran
141 J4 **Malay Reef** Gt Barrier Reef Aust
69 **Malaysia** S E Asia
69 E10 **Malaysia, Peninsular** S E Asia
14 B4 **Mal B** Ireland
122 B6 **Malbaie** *R* Quebec Canada
122 H5 **Mal Baie** Quebec Canada
131 B6 **Malbarco, L** Argentina
140 F5 **Malbon** Queensland Australia
38 J9 **Malborghetto** Italy
31 L1 **Malbork** Poland
41 N6 **Malcesine** Italy
33 R5 **Malchin** East Germany
33 Q6 **Malchow** East Germany
143 D8 **Malcolm** Western Australia Australia
116 R2 **Malcolm** *R* Yukon Territory Canada
68 D7 **Malcolm I** Burma
143 E10 **Malcolm,Pt** Western Australia Australia
99 O8 **Malcom** Iowa U.S.A.
22 E1 **Maldegem** Belgium
95 Q4 **Malden** Massachusetts U.S.A.
110 G5 **Malden** Missouri U.S.A.
100 H2 **Malden** Washington U.S.A.
94 F8 **Malden** West Virginia U.S.A.
135 M8 **Malden I** Pacific Oc
73 L8 **Maldive Is** *rep* Indian Oc
43 B9 **Mal di Ventre, I. di** Sardinia
73 L9 **Maldive Ridge** Indian Oc
9 G4 **Maldon** England
131 G5 **Maldonado** *dept* Uruguay
131 G5 **Maldonado** Uruguay
41 N5 **Male** Italy
73 L8 **Male** Maldives
46 F8 **Maléa, Akr** *C* Greece
47 H5 **Maléa, Akr** Turkey
74 F8 **Malegaon** India
70 G6 **Malehu** Sulawesi
48 D2 **Malé Karpaty** Czechoslovakia
121 P4 **Mâle, L.du** Quebec Canada
88 F9 **Malema** Mozambique
87 E7 **Malemba Nkulu** Zaire
46 F9 **Máleme** Crete
52 E3 **Malen'ga** U.S.S.R.
33 N4 **Malente** W Germany
74 F3 **Maler Kotla** India
47 H9 **Máles** Crete Greece
21 P5 **Malesherbes** France
20 F6 **Malestroit** France
54 K3 **Malevka** U.S.S.R.
89 B10 **Malgas** S Africa
37 O6 **Malgersdorf** W Germany
86 E2 **Malha** Sudan
13 F5 **Malham** England
100 H5 **Malheur** Oregon U.S.A.
100 H6 **Malheur** *R* Oregon U.S.A.
83 K12 **Malheureu, Cap** Mahé I Indian Oc
100 G6 **Malheur L** Oregon U.S.A.
66 F6 **Mali** *R* Burma
85 D5 **Mali** *rep* W Africa
71 M9 **Maliana** Indonesia
21 K6 **Malicorne-sur-Sarthe** France
71 F7 **Maligoy B** Mindanao Philippines
80 F4 **Malih** *R* Jordan
19 Q16 **Malijai** France
70 D6 **Maliku** Kalimantan
71 H5 **Maliku** Sulawesi
68 D6 **Mali Kyun** *isld* Burma
70 G6 **Malili** Sulawesi
27 H14 **Målilla** Sweden
88 B5 **Malimba** *mts* Zaire
70 K9 **Malimping** Java
100 D7 **Malin** Oregon U.S.A.
71 G5 **Malinao Inlet** Philippines
71 F6 **Malindang, Mt** Mindanao Philippines
88 H3 **Malindi** Kenya
48 F2 **Malinec** Czechoslovakia
Malines *see* **Mechelen**
70 G4 **Maling, G** *mt* Sulawesi
27 H12 **Malingsbo** Sweden
14 D1 **Malin Hd** Ireland
48 K3 **Mălini** Romania
14 C2 **Malin More** Ireland
70 F7 **Malino** Sulawesi
54 H7 **Malinovka** U.S.S.R.
55 G5 **Malinovoye Ozero** *L* U.S.S.R.
68 G1 **Malipo** China
71 G7 **Malita** Mindanao Philippines
71 G5 **Malitbog** Leyte Philippines
68 D7 **Maliwun** Burma
106 G9 **Maljamar** New Mexico U.S.A.
48 F6 **Maljen** *mt* Yugoslavia
80 F3 **Malka** Jordan
53 F11 **Malka** *R* U.S.S.R.
47 J2 **Malkapapiye** Bulgaria
74 G8 **Malkapur** India
47 H4 **Malkara** Turkey
56 G5 **Malkhanskiy Khr** *mts* U.S.S.R.
31 N3 **Małkinia** Poland
80 F1 **Malkiyya** Israel
139 J7 **Mallacoota** Victoria Australia
118 F4 **Mallaig** Alberta Canada
15 C3 **Mallaig** Scotland
99 M7 **Mallard** Iowa U.S.A.
84 J4 **Mallawi** Egypt
131 A7 **Malleco** *prov* Chile
19 O17 **Mallemort** France
37 N6 **Mallersdorf** W Germany
41 N4 **Malles Venosta** Italy
130 E9 **Mallét** Brazil
142 C5 **Mallina** Western Australia Australia
28 E4 **Malling** Denmark
38 H8 **Mallnitz** Austria
17 J5 **Mallorca** *isld* Balearic Is
94 F9 **Mallory** West Virginia U.S.A.
121 P8 **Mallorytown** Ontario Canada
14 C4 **Mallow** Ireland
142 E5 **Mallowa Well** Western Australia Australia
8 B1 **Malltraeth B** Wales
8 C2 **Mallwyd** Wales
22 F5 **Malmaison, la** France
27 G14 **Malmbäck** Sweden
26 L4 **Malmberget** Sweden
22 L3 **Malmédy** Belgium
8 D4 **Malmesbury** England
89 A9 **Malmesbury** S Africa
26 K6 **Malmesjaure** *L* Sweden
27 J12 **Malmköping** Sweden
29 K5 **Malmö** Sweden
27 F16 **Malmöhus** *county* Sweden
126 A2 **Malmok** *pt* Bonaire W Indies
52 H6 **Malmyzh** U.S.S.R.
26 G3 **Malnes** Norway
137 O5 **Malo** *isld* Vanuatu
54 H4 **Maloarkhangel'sk** U.S.S.R.
129 G3 **Maloca** Amapá Brazil
129 H5 **Maloca** Pará Brazil
41 L5 **Maloggia** Switzerland
71 E3 **Malolos** Luzon Philippines
55 C2 **Malomal'sk** U.S.S.R.
88 E9 **Malombe,L** Malawi
47 H2 **Malomir** Bulgaria
47 R14 **Malóna** Rhodes Greece
121 N8 **Malone** Ontario Canada
113 B7 **Malone** Florida U.S.A.
95 N2 **Malone** New York U.S.A.
109 L4 **Malone** Texas U.S.A.
98 F8 **Maloney Res** Nebraska U.S.A.
67 A4 **Malong** China
87 D8 **Malonga** Zaire
26 N6 **Malören** Sweden
31 P4 **Malorita** U.S.S.R.
52 E3 **Maloshuyka** U.S.S.R.
89 F7 **Maloti Mts** Lesotho
100 F1 **Malott** Washington U.S.A.
26 A10 **Måløy** Norway
54 H1 **Maloyaroslavets** U.S.S.R.
55 E2 **Maloye Gorodishche** U.S.S.R.
52 H1 **Malozemel'skaya Tundra** *plain* U.S.S.R.
106 C10 **Malpais** New Mexico U.S.A.
138 F5 **Malpas** South Australia Australia
8 D1 **Malpas** England
124 H6 **Malpaso** Mexico
90 A8 **Malpelo I** Pacific Oc
122 J7 **Malpeque B** Prince Edward I Canada
16 D5 **Malpica** Spain
16 B1 **Malpica de Bergantiños** Spain
131 B4 **Malpo** *R* Chile
73 L5 **Malprabha** *R* India
74 F5 **Malpura** India
36 E6 **Malsch** W Germany
31 H7 **Malše** *R* Czechoslovakia
26 K2 **Målselv** *R* Norway
26 K2 **Målselv** Norway
36 H1 **Malsfeld** W Germany
77 A7 **Malsūnīyah, Al** Saudi Arabia
38 J8 **Malta** Austria
43 F13 **Malta** *rep* Mediterranean Sea
106 D2 **Malta** Colorado U.S.A.
101 M7 **Malta** Idaho U.S.A.
101 S1 **Malta** Montana U.S.A.
94 F7 **Malta** Ohio U.S.A.
43 F12 **Malta Ch** Mediterranean Sea
87 C10 **Maltahöhe** Namibia
38 H7 **Maltatel** *V* Austria
9 G1 **Maltby** England
13 G6 **Maltby** S Yorks England
144 C5 **Malte Brun** *mt* New Zealand
47 N11 **Maltepe** Turkey
121 L9 **Malton** *airport* Ontario Canada
13 H5 **Malton** England
48 K6 **Malu** Romania
71 D5 **Malubutglubut** *isld* Philippines
85 F6 **Malumfashi** Nigeria
70 F6 **Malunda** Sulawesi
27 G11 **Malung** Sweden
41 K5 **Malvaglia** Switzerland
76 A2 **Malvan** India
127 J2 **Malvern** Jamaica
127 J3 **Malvern** *pk* Jamaica
109 P1 **Malvern** Arkansas U.S.A.
99 L9 **Malvern** Iowa U.S.A.
94 F6 **Malvern** Ohio U.S.A.
8 D3 **Malvern Wells** England
20 G7 **Malville** France
Malvinas, Is *see* **Falkland Is.**
74 F7 **Malwa Plateau** India
83 K9 **Malwatu Oya** *R* Sri Lanka
78 K1 **Maly Kavkaz** *mt* U.S.S.R.
55 E1 **Malyy Atlym** U.S.S.R.
55 F1 **Malyy Balyk** *R* U.S.S.R.
55 G4 **Malyye Chany, Oz** *L* U.S.S.R.
52 G6 **Malyy Kundysh** *R* U.S.S.R.
51 O1 **Malyy Lyakhovski,Ostrov** *isld* U.S.S.R.
51 K1 **Malyy Taymyr, Ostrov** *isld* U.S.S.R.
55 G2 **Malyy Yugan** *R* U.S.S.R.
56 H2 **Mama** *R* U.S.S.R.
56 H2 **Mama** U.S.S.R.
52 H6 **Mamadysh** U.S.S.R.
48 M6 **Mamaia** Romania
120 F5 **Mamainse Point** Ontario Canada
145 F3 **Mamaku** New Zealand
145 D1 **Mamaranui** New Zealand
70 F6 **Mamasa** Sulawesi
71 D7 **Mambahenauhan** *isld* Philippines
71 G6 **Mambajao** Philippines
89 F3 **Mambala Cave** Zimbabwe
86 E5 **Mambasa** Zaire
136 H2 **Mamberamo** *R* W Irian
86 C4 **Mambéré** *R* Cent Afr Republic
70 F6 **Mambi** Sulawesi
79 H2 **Mambij** Syria
71 E4 **Mamburao** Philippines
118 K1 **Mameigwess L** Ontario Canada
83 J12 **Mamelle** *isld* Seychelles
118 D6 **Ma-Me-O Beach** Alberta Canada
118 D5 **Ma-Me-O Beach Prov. Park** Alberta Canada
22 K4 **Mamer** Luxembourg
21 L5 **Mamers** France
86 A4 **Mamfé** Cameroon
128 F4 **Mamia, L** Brazil
40 D3 **Mamirolle** France
55 E4 **Mamlyutka** U.S.S.R.
120 F2 **Mammamattawa** Ontario Canada
28 D4 **Mammen** Denmark
37 L7 **Mammendorf** W Germany
37 O6 **Mamming** W Germany
43 G10 **Mammola** Italy
94 F8 **Mammoth** West Virginia U.S.A.
110 K4 **Mammoth Cave** Kentucky U.S.A.
101 P5 **Mammoth Hot Springs** Wyoming U.S.A.
110 E5 **Mammoth Spring** Arkansas U.S.A.
126 G9 **Mamonal** Colombia
130 G4 **Mamonas** Brazil
31 M1 **Mamo-novo** U.S.S.R.
128 E6 **Mamore** *R* Bolivia/Brazil
128 F4 **Mamoré, L** Brazil
85 B6 **Mamou** Guinea
111 D11 **Mamou** Louisiana U.S.A.
87 H11 **Mampikohy** Madagascar
16 D1 **Mampodre** *mt* Spain
85 D7 **Mampong** Ghana
83 J9 **Mampuri** Sri Lanka
31 N1 **Mamry,Jezioro** *L* Poland
15 C3 **Mam Soul** *mt* Scotland
Mamuji *see* **Yucheng**
70 F6 **Mamuji** Sulawesi
87 D10 **Mamuno** Botswana
55 C5 **Mamyt** U.S.S.R.
85 C7 **Man** Ivory Coast
94 F9 **Man** West Virginia U.S.A.
129 H3 **Mana** *R* Fr Guiana
135 N1 **Mana** Hawaiian Is
56 D3 **Mana** *R* U.S.S.R.
128 B4 **Manabi** Ecuador
128 F4 **Manacapuru** Brazil
128 F4 **Manacapuru,L.Grande de** Brazil
17 K5 **Manacor** Majorca
71 J4 **Manado** Sulawesi
71 J4 **Manadotua** *isld* Sulawesi
22 G3 **Manage** Belgium
140 D3 **Managoora** N Terr Australia
125 L3 **Managua** Nicaragua
145 E4 **Mana I** New Zealand
145 E3 **Manaia** New Zealand
87 H12 **Manakara** Madagascar
145 E4 **Manakau** New Zealand
144 D5 **Manakau** *mt* New Zealand
136 K2 **Manam** *isld* Papua New Guinea
76 D6 **Manamadurai** India
77 B6 **Manamah,Al** Bahrain
87 G11 **Manambaho** *R* Madagascar
127 N10 **Mánamo** *R* Venezuela
71 E5 **Manamoc** *isld* Philippines
102 S12 **Manana** Hawaiian Is
87 H11 **Mananara** Madagascar
139 G6 **Manangatang** Victoria Australia
87 H12 **Mananjary** Madagascar
128 F2 **Manano,Caño** *creek* Venezuela
85 B6 **Manantali, Lac de** *res* Mali
76 C5 **Mānantavādi** India
87 H12 **Manantenina** Madagascar
144 A6 **Manapouri** New Zealand
66 D3 **Manas** China
Manasarowar Lake *see* **Mapam Yumco**
74 H3 **Mana Shankou** *pass* India/China
66 D3 **Manas He** *R* China
66 D2 **Manas Hu** *L* China
75 L4 **Manaslu** *mt* Nepal
95 N6 **Manasquan** New Jersey U.S.A.
106 E4 **Manassa** Colorado U.S.A.
94 K8 **Manassas** Virginia U.S.A.
71 M9 **Manatang** Indonesia
127 L5 **Manati** Puerto Rico
128 G4 **Manaus** Brazil
78 C3 **Manavgat** Turkey
99 S5 **Manawa** Wisconsin U.S.A.
119 P3 **Manawan L** Saskatchewan Canada
145 E2 **Manawaru** New Zealand
145 E4 **Manawatu R** New Zealand
71 G7 **Manay** Mindanao Philippines
140 B2 **Manbulloo** N Terr Australia
94 C2 **Mancelona** Michigan U.S.A.
16 E7 **Mancha Real** Spain
18 E3 **Manche** *dept* France
21 P5 **Manchecourt** France
Manche,la *see* **English Channel**
74 H9 **Mancheral** India
11 E2 **Manchester** *conurbation* England
127 K3 **Manchester** *parish* Jamaica
102 A3 **Manchester** California U.S.A.
95 P5 **Manchester** Connecticut U.S.A.
112 C5 **Manchester** Georgia U.S.A.
110 F2 **Manchester** Illinois U.S.A.
99 P7 **Manchester** Iowa U.S.A.
107 N2 **Manchester** Kansas U.S.A.
110 N4 **Manchester** Kentucky U.S.A.
94 C4 **Manchester** Michigan U.S.A.
95 Q4 **Manchester** New Hampshire U.S.A.
95 K4 **Manchester** New York U.S.A.
94 D8 **Manchester** Ohio U.S.A.
107 M5 **Manchester** Oklahoma U.S.A.
95 L6 **Manchester** Pennsylvania U.S.A.
110 K6 **Manchester** Tennessee U.S.A.
95 O3 **Manchester** Vermont U.S.A.
37 M6 **Manching** W Germany
127 M2 **Manchioneal** Jamaica
65 E1 **Manchuria** *reg* China
42 D6 **Manciano** Italy
128 B4 **Máncora** Peru
106 B4 **Mancos** Colorado U.S.A.
77 B5 **Mand** *R* Iran
87 F8 **Manda** Tanzania
130 D8 **Mandaguari** Brazil
80 F3 **Mandah** Jordan
69 F13 **Mandah** Sumatra
88 D7 **Manda Hd** Zambia
77 G3 **Mandal** Afghanistan
58 D2 **Mandal** Mongolia
27 B13 **Mandal** Norway
68 C2 **Mandalay** Burma
78 A3 **Mandalaya** *isld* Turkey
58 E2 **Mandalgovĭ** Mongolia
78 K5 **Mandalī** Iraq
58 D3 **Mandal-Ovoo** Mongolia
27 B13 **Mandalsåni** *R* Norway
Mandalt *see* **Sonid Zuoqi**
98 F3 **Mandan** North Dakota U.S.A.
69 E12 **Mandau** Sumatra
36 C5 **Mandelbachtal** W Germany
127 K2 **Mandeville** Jamaica
144 B7 **Mandeville** New Zealand
111 F11 **Mandeville** Louisiana U.S.A.
69 F10 **Mandi Angin, Gunung** *mt* Malaysia
130 B6 **Mandioré, Lagoa** *L* Bolivia/Brazil
74 J7 **Mandla** India
69 J12 **Mandor** Indonesia
46 F6 **Mandoúdhion** Greece
74 F6 **Mandsaur** India
143 B10 **Mandurah** Western Australia Australia
48 K5 **Maneciu** Romania
41 N6 **Manerba del Garda** Italy
17 G7 **Manga del Mar Menor** Spain
145 E3 **Mangakino** New Zealand
76 E2 **Mangalagiri** India
76 B4 **Mangalore** India
145 E4 **Mangamahoe** New Zealand
145 E3 **Mangamahu** New Zealand
144 D5 **Mangamaunu** New Zealand
145 D1 **Mangamuka** New Zealand
145 E3 **Mangapehi** New Zealand
145 E4 **Mangatainoka** New Zealand
145 E3 **Mangaweka** New Zealand
145 E2 **Mangawhai** New Zealand
142 A4 **Mangles B** Western Australia Australia
66 E4 **Mangnai** China
85 E6 **Mango** Togo
88 E9 **Mangochi** Malawi
87 G12 **Mangoky** *R* Madagascar
145 D1 **Mangonui** New Zealand
87 H12 **Mangoro** Madagascar
74 D8 **Māngral** India
113 J11 **Mangrove Cay** *isld* Bahamas
126 F2 **Mangrove Cay** Andros Bahamas
71 E4 **Mangsoagui Pt** Philippines
130 H10 **Manguaba,L** Brazil
16 B4 **Mangualde** Portugal
86 D3 **Mangueigne** Chad
131 H4 **Mangueira, L** Brazil
130 D9 **Mangueirinha** Brazil
84 E5 **Mangueni,Pl.du** Niger
59 H1 **Mangui** China
87 G7 **Mangula** Tanzania
108 E9 **Mangum** Oklahoma U.S.A.
67 A5 **Manhao** China
99 T8 **Manhattan** Illinois U.S.A.
107 O2 **Manhattan** Kansas U.S.A.
101 O4 **Manhattan** Montana U.S.A.
102 G3 **Manhattan** Nevada U.S.A.
22 K3 **Manhay** Belgium
130 H7 **Manhuaçu** Brazil
130 H6 **Manhuaçu,R** Brazil
113 L12 **Man I** Bahamas
87 E7 **Mani** Zaire
87 H11 **Mania** *R* Madagascar
42 E2 **Maniago** Italy
88 E8 **Maniamba** Mozambique
87 F9 **Manica** Mozambique
71 G5 **Manicani** *isld* Philippines
122 D4 **Manic Deux Dam** Quebec Canada
128 F5 **Manicoré** *R* Brazil
122 D3 **Manicouagan** Quebec Canada
122 D4 **Manicouagan Pen** Quebec Canada
122 D4 **Manicouagan R** Quebec Canada
122 D2 **Manicouagan, Res** Quebec Canada
141 K6 **Manifold, C** Queensland Australia
119 V7 **Manigotagan** Manitoba Canada
71 E3 **Manila** Luzon Philippines
110 F6 **Manila** Arkansas U.S.A.
101 Q9 **Manila** Utah U.S.A.
71 E3 **Manila B** Luzon Philippines
139 J5 **Manildra** New South Wales Australia
139 K4 **Manilla** New South Wales Australia
99 L8 **Manilla** Iowa U.S.A.
70 F5 **Manimbaja,Tg** *C* Sulawesi
69 E13 **Manindjan,Danau** *L* Sumatra
87 H11 **Maningory** Madagascar
140 C1 **Maningrida** N Terr Australia
85 C6 **Maninian** Ivory Coast
69 E13 **Maninjau Danau** *L* Sumatra
73 P4 **Manipur** *R* Burma
75 P6 **Manipur** *prov* India
47 J6 **Manisa** Turkey
17 G5 **Manises** Spain
12 D5 **Man,Isle of** U.K.
70 B6 **Manismata** Kalimantan
94 B2 **Manistee** *R* Michigan U.S.A.
99 U5 **Manistee** Michigan U.S.A.
99 U4 **Manistique** Michigan U.S.A.
99 U3 **Manistique** *R* Michigan U.S.A.
99 V3 **Manistique L** Michigan U.S.A.
99 R9 **Manito** Illinois U.S.A.
114 J6 **Manitoba** Canada
119 S7 **Manitoba, L** Manitoba Canada
118 H6 **Manito L** Saskatchewan Canada
119 T9 **Manitou** Manitoba Canada
109 J1 **Manitou** Oklahoma U.S.A.
119 M7 **Manitou Bch** Saskatchewan Canada
99 T2 **Manitou I** Michigan U.S.A.
120 J7 **Manitou L** Ontario Canada
122 G3 **Manitou,L** Quebec Canada
120 H7 **Manitoulin I** Ontario Canada
122 G2 **Manitou R** Quebec Canada
106 F3 **Manitou Springs** Colorado U.S.A.
120 E3 **Manitouwadge** Ontario Canada
120 J7 **Manitowaning** Ontario Canada
120 F4 **Manitowik L** Ontario Canada
99 T5 **Manitowoc** Wisconsin U.S.A.
121 P6 **Maniwaki** Quebec Canada
128 C2 **Manizales** Colombia
80 G6 **Manja** Jordan
87 G12 **Manja** Madagascar
143 B10 **Manjimup** Western Australia Australia
38 M5 **Mank** Austria
107 M2 **Mankato** Kansas U.S.A.
99 N5 **Mankato** Minnesota U.S.A.
89 G6 **Mankayane** Swaziland
86 B5 **Mankim** Cameroon
109 J2 **Mankins** Texas U.S.A.
85 C7 **Mankono** Ivory Coast
118 K9 **Mankota** Saskatchewan Canada
48 N2 **Man'kovka** U.S.S.R.
83 K8 **Mankulam** Sri Lanka
95 M3 **Manlius** New York U.S.A.
17 J2 **Manlleu** Spain
139 K5 **Manly** New South Wales Australia
145 E2 **Manly** New Zealand
99 N6 **Manly** Iowa U.S.A.
74 F8 **Manmad** India
139 K3 **Mann** *R* New South Wales Australia
140 C2 **Mann** *R* N Terr Australia
138 F4 **Mannahill** South Australia Australia
83 J9 **Mannar** Sri Lanka
73 M7 **Mannar,G.of** India/Sri Lanka
76 D5 **Mannargudi** India
83 J8 **Mannar I** Sri Lanka
36 F5 **Mannheim** W Germany
14 A3 **Mannin B** Ireland
139 K4 **Manning** *R* New South Wales Australia
117 P7 **Manning** Alberta Canada
109 P1 **Manning** Arkansas U.S.A.
99 L8 **Manning** Iowa U.S.A.
98 D2 **Manning** North Dakota U.S.A.
112 G4 **Manning** South Carolina U.S.A.
109 N4 **Manning** Texas U.S.A.
117 N11 **Manning Prov. Park** British Columbia Canada
94 G7 **Mannington** West Virginia U.S.A.
9 H4 **Manningtree** England
140 A7 **Mann, Mt** N Terr Australia
140 A7 **Mann Ranges** N Terr/S Aust Australia
112 M2 **Manns Harbor** North Carolina U.S.A.
95 L3 **Mannsville** New York U.S.A.
43 C9 **Mannu** *R* Sardinia
43 B8 **Mannu,C** Sardinia
138 E5 **Mannum** South Australia Australia
118 F5 **Mannville** Alberta Canada
85 B7 **Mano** Sierra Leone
128 E5 **Manoa** Bolivia
80 B8 **Manoah** *R* Israel
127 N1 **Man of War B** Tobago
116 H7 **Manokotak** Alaska U.S.A.
136 G2 **Manokwari** W Irian
46 E6 **Manolás** Greece
87 G12 **Manombo** Madagascar
88 A5 **Manono** Zaire
119 Q9 **Manor** Saskatchewan Canada
112 E6 **Manor** Georgia U.S.A.
109 K5 **Manor** Texas U.S.A.
8 B4 **Manorbier** Wales
144 B6 **Manorburn Res** New Zealand
14 C2 **Manorhamilton** Ireland
85 B7 **Mano River** Liberia
68 D7 **Manoron** Burma
19 P17 **Manosque** France
21 M4 **Manou** France
121 Q5 **Manouane** Quebec Canada
122 B3 **Manouane L** Quebec Canada
61 M8 **Mano-wan** *B* Japan
68 C1 **Man Pan** Burma
134 K9 **Manra** *isld* Phoenix Is Pacific Oc
17 J3 **Manresa** Spain
88 B7 **Mansa** Zambia
85 A6 **Mansaba** Guinea-Bissau
85 A6 **Mansa Konko** The Gambia
71 E4 **Mansalay B** Philippines
71 H5 **Mansalean** Indonesia
68 C1 **Man Sam** Burma
142 G4 **Mansbridge, Mt** Western Australia Australia
115 L5 **Mansel I** Northwest Territories Canada
33 O9 **Mansfeld** East Germany
139 H6 **Mansfield** Victoria Australia
9 E1 **Mansfield** England
110 B6 **Mansfield** Arkansas U.S.A.
112 D4 **Mansfield** Georgia U.S.A.
99 S9 **Mansfield** Illinois U.S.A.
109 O3 **Mansfield** Louisiana U.S.A.
95 Q4 **Mansfield** Massachusetts U.S.A.
110 D4 **Mansfield** Missouri U.S.A.
94 E6 **Mansfield** Ohio U.S.A.
98 H4 **Mansfield** South Dakota U.S.A.
109 K3 **Mansfield** Texas U.S.A.
100 F2 **Mansfield** Washington U.S.A.
95 P2 **Mansfield,Mt** Vermont U.S.A.
21 L6 **Mansigne** France
56 D4 **Manskoye Belogor'ye** *mts* U.S.S.R.
18 F7 **Mansle** France
99 M7 **Manson** Iowa U.S.A.
100 E2 **Manson** Washington U.S.A.
117 L8 **Manson Creek** British Columbia Canada
130 C4 **Manso,R** Brazil
80 D1 **Mansoyra** Israel
8 D6 **Manston** England
111 D10 **Mansura** Louisiana U.S.A.
79 B7 **Mansûra,El** Egypt
128 B4 **Manta** Ecuador
71 C6 **Mantalingajan, Mt** Palawan Philippines
70 E1 **Mantanani Besar** *isld* Sabah
86 D6 **Mantantale** Zaire
65 H4 **Mantap-san** *mt* N Korea
71 J5 **Mantarara** Indonesia
118 H7 **Mantario** Saskatchewan Canada
128 C6 **Mantaro** *R* Peru
102 C4 **Manteca** California U.S.A.
111 G8 **Mantee** Mississippi U.S.A.
71 J4 **Mantehase** *isld* Sulawesi
37 N4 **Mantel** W Germany
130 H6 **Mantena** Brazil
99 T8 **Manteno** Illinois U.S.A.
112 M2 **Manteo** North Carolina U.S.A.
107 J4 **Manter** Kansas U.S.A.
21 O4 **Mantes-la-Jolie** France
25 E2 **Mantgum** Netherlands
74 H9 **Manthani** India
21 M7 **Manthelan** France
103 N2 **Manti** Utah U.S.A.
130 F8 **Mantiqueira,Serra da** *mts* Brazil
100 D9 **Manton** California U.S.A.
94 B2 **Manton** Michigan U.S.A.
65 B5 **Mantou Shan** *mt ra* China
45 J1 **Mantova** Italy
29 L11 **Mäntsälä** Finland
29 L10 **Mänttä** Finland
126 B3 **Mantua** Cuba
Mantua Italy *see* **Mantova**
94 F5 **Mantua** Ohio U.S.A.
141 H6 **Mantuan Downs** Queensland Australia
52 F5 **Manturovo** U.S.S.R.
29 J10 **Mäntyluoto** Finland
128 D6 **Manú** Peru
Manuan *see* **Manouane**
122 B3 **Manuanis,L** Quebec Canada
71 F6 **Manucan** Mindanao Philippines
129 J5 **Manuel Alves** *R* Brazil
106 B6 **Manuelito** New Mexico U.S.A.
130 D9 **Manuel Ribas** Brazil
133 C8 **Manuel Rodríguez, I** Chile
128 E5 **Manuel Urbano** Brazil
129 H5 **Manuelzinho** Brazil
71 H6 **Manui** *isld* Indonesia
77 E6 **Manūjān** Iran
145 G2 **Manukau** New Zealand
145 E2 **Manukau Hbr** New Zealand
70 F2 **Manuk Manka** Philippines
138 E4 **Manunda** *R* South Australia Australia
145 E3 **Manunui** New Zealand
71 C3 **Manuran** *isld* W Irian
128 E6 **Manuripe** *R* Bolivia/Peru
136 K2 **Manus** *isld* Bismarck Arch
145 E3 **Manutahi** New Zealand
138 E3 **Manuwalkaninna** South Australia Australia
98 J1 **Manvel** North Dakota U.S.A.
76 C3 **Manvi** India
98 B7 **Manville** Wyoming U.S.A.
109 O4 **Many** Louisiana U.S.A.
52 K4 **Man'ya** U.S.S.R.
88 B10 **Manyangau** *mt* Zimbabwe
88 G3 **Manyara,L** Tanzania
47 J4 **Manyas** Turkey
118 G9 **Manyberries** Alberta Canada
54 M9 **Manych** *R* U.S.S.R.
118 G8 **Many Island I** Alberta Canada
88 E4 **Manyoni** Tanzania
141 K6 **Many Peaks** Queensland Australia
143 C10 **Many Peaks, Mt** Western Australia Australia
79 B7 **Manzala,El** Egypt
84 J3 **Manzala, L** Egypt
89 E2 **Manzamnyama** *R* Zimbabwe
16 E5 **Manzanares** Spain
127 P2 **Manzanilla B** Trinidad
126 F4 **Manzanillo** Cuba
124 G8 **Manzanillo** Mexico
106 D7 **Manzano** New Mexico U.S.A.
131 A8 **Manzano,B del** Chile
106 G3 **Manzanola** Colorado U.S.A.
106 D7 **Manzano Mts** New Mexico U.S.A.
58 G2 **Manzhouli** China
79 G7 **Manzil** Jordan
89 G6 **Manzini** Swaziland
Manzovka *see* **Sibirtsevo**
86 C3 **Mao** Chad
65 G2 **Mao'ershan** China
136 H2 **Maoke, Pegunungan** *ra* W Irian
65 F4 **Maokui Shan** *mt* China
65 G3 **Maolin** China
67 C6 **Maoming** China
67 C1 **Maoping** China
67 G6 **Mao-pi T'ou** *C* Taiwan
67 B3 **Maotai** China
67 A1 **Maowen** China
65 F2 **Maoxing** China
80 F4 **Ma'oz** Israel
87 F10 **Mapai** Mozambique
66 C5 **Mapam Yumco** *L* China
70 G5 **Mapane** Sulawesi
67 D1 **Maping** China
128 F2 **Mapire** Venezuela
129 H3 **Mapireme** Brazil
128 E7 **Mapiri** *R* La Paz Bolivia
128 F4 **Mapixari, L** Brazil
99 L7 **Maple** *R* Iowa U.S.A.
94 C3 **Maple** *R* Michigan U.S.A.
118 H9 **Maple Creek** Saskatchewan Canada
99 N6 **Maple Island** Minnesota U.S.A.
111 K9 **Maplesville** Alabama U.S.A.
122 H8 **Mapleton** Nova Scotia Canada
99 L7 **Mapleton** Iowa U.S.A.
95 S7 **Mapleton** Maine U.S.A.
99 N6 **Mapleton** Minnesota U.S.A.
100 B5 **Mapleton** Oregon U.S.A.
100 C2 **Maple Valley** Washington U.S.A.
95 L3 **Maple View** New York U.S.A.
141 F1 **Mapoon** Queensland Australia
69 G12 **Mapor** *isld* Indonesia
144 C5 **Mapourika, L** New Zealand
13 H6 **Mappleton** England
129 G4 **Mapuera** *R* Brazil
89 H6 **Maputo** *R* Mozambique
87 F11 **Maputo** Mozambique
80 F8 **Maqam en Nabi Yusha** Jordan
78 H6 **Maqar an Naam** Iraq
46 D3 **Maqellarë** Albania
58 C5 **Maqên Gangri** *mt* China
65 H2 **Maqiaohe** China
79 E10 **Maqnā** Saudi Arabia
66 C6 **Maquan He** *R* China
71 G4 **Maqueda Chan** Philippines
122 H5 **Maquereau Pte.au** Quebec Canada
133 D6 **Maquinchao** Argentina
131 B8 **Maquinchao, R** Argentina
99 Q7 **Maquoketa** Iowa U.S.A.
99 Q9 **Maquon** Illinois U.S.A.
70 G7 **Mara** Sulawesi
127 J9 **Mara** Venezuela
128 E4 **Maraa** Brazil
129 J5 **Marabá** Brazil
70 D6 **Marabahan** Kalimantan
40 B2 **Marac** France
127 J9 **Maracaibo** Venezuela
127 J9 **Maracaibo, L. de** Venezuela
129 H3 **Maracá, Ilha de** Amapá Brazil
128 F3 **Maracá, Ilha de** Roraima Brazil
133 F2 **Maracaju** Brazil
130 C7 **Maracaju,Serra de** *mts* Brazil
129 J4 **Maracana** Brazil
127 O2 **Maracas B** Trinidad
127 L9 **Maracay** Venezuela
84 F4 **Marādah** Libya
85 F6 **Maradi** Niger
145 E3 **Maraetai** New Zealand
78 L3 **Marāgheh** Iran
130 J10 **Maragogi** Brazil
144 D4 **Marahau** New Zealand
128 E3 **Marahuaca,Co** *mt* Venezuela
65 E2 **Marain Sum** China
110 A3 **Marais des Cygnes** *R* Kansas/Missouri U.S.A.
21 L3 **Marais-Vernier** France
129 J4 **Marajó,I.de** Brazil
86 G5 **Maralal** Kenya
55 G4 **Maraldy** U.S.S.R.
86 C4 **Marali** Cent Afr Republic
137 N3 **Maramasike** *isld* Solomon Is
Maramba *see* **Livingstone** Zambia
48 H3 **Maramures** *old prov* Romania
69 F11 **Maran** Malaysia
103 N9 **Marana** Arizona U.S.A.
140 C2 **Maranboy** N Terr Australia
17 F3 **Maranchón** Spain
78 K2 **Marand** Iran
45 J2 **Maranello** Italy
68 D7 **Marang** Burma
69 F10 **Marang** Malaysia
129 L4 **Maranguape** Brazil
129 J4 **Maranhão** *state* Brazil
130 E4 **Maranhão** *R* Brazil

Mertzon — Misawa 55

108 G4 **Mertzon** Texas U.S.A.
21 P3 **Méru** France
88 F1 **Meru** Kenya
88 F3 **Meru** *mt* Tanzania
74 C8 **Merui** Pakistan
70 G4 **Merunu** Sulawesi
70 E2 **Merutai** Sabah
22 D2 **Merville** France
118 J5 **Mervin** Saskatchewan Canada
100 C4 **Merwin, L** Washington U.S.A.
18 H4 **Méry-sur-Seine** France
78 E1 **Merzifon** Turkey
36 B5 **Merzig** W Germany
146 D5 **Merz Peninsula** *pen* Antarctica
71 B2 **Mesa** Halmahera Indonesia
17 F3 **Mesa** *R* Spain
103 N8 **Mesa** Arizona U.S.A.
100 J5 **Mesa** Idaho U.S.A.
106 F8 **Mesa** New Mexico U.S.A.
99 N2 **Mesabi Ra** *mts* Minnesota U.S.A.
43 H8 **Mesagne** Italy
117 Q3 **Mesa L** Northwest Territories Canada
116 K6 **Mesa Mt** Alaska U.S.A.
47 Q14 **Mesanagrós** Rhodes Greece
69 G12 **Mesanak** *isld* Indonesia
20 H7 **Mésanger** France
70 D2 **Mesapo** Sabah
46 G10 **Mesarás, Kólpos** *B* Crete Greece
106 B4 **Mesa Verde Nat. Park** Colorado U.S.A.
103 O10 **Mescal** Arizona U.S.A.
106 E8 **Mescalero** New Mexico U.S.A.
32 H10 **Meschede** W Germany
26 J7 **Meselefors** Sweden
68 C3 **Mesenan** Burma
48 H3 **Meseşului, Muntii** *mts* Romania
128 F2 **Meseta del Cerro Jaua** *mts* Venezuela
52 G6 **Mesha** *R* U.S.S.R.
54 L1 **Meshcherskaya Nizina** *lowland* U.S.S.R.
54 G2 **Meshchovsk** U.S.S.R.
52 H3 **Meshchura** U.S.S.R.
Meshed *see* **Mashhad**
57 B4 **Meshekli** U.S.S.R.
116 H8 **Meshik** Alaska U.S.A.
86 E4 **Meshra er Req** Sudan
94 B2 **Mesick** Michigan U.S.A.
117 L7 **Mesilinka** *R* British Columbia Canada
106 D9 **Mesilla** New Mexico U.S.A.
80 C6 **Mesillat Ziyyon** Israel
28 F5 **Mesinge** Denmark
21 J6 **Meslay-du-Maine** France
27 E10 **Mesna** *L* Norway
21 N2 **Mesnières-en-Béthune** France
21 J4 **Mesnil-Auzouf,le** France
21 P2 **Mesnil-St.Firmin,le** France
20 H3 **Mesnil-Vigot,le** France
21 K4 **Mesnil-Villement,le** France
41 K5 **Mesocco** Switzerland
45 M2 **Mésola** Italy
41 K5 **Mesolcina, Valle** Switzerland
46 E6 **Mesolóngion** Greece
78 J4 **Mesopotamia** Iraq
20 F7 **Mesquer** France
130 G6 **Mesquita** Brazil
103 K5 **Mesquite** Nevada U.S.A.
106 D9 **Mesquite** New Mexico U.S.A.
109 O9 **Mesquite** Texas U.S.A.
103 J6 **Mesquite L** California U.S.A.
20 G6 **Messac** France
Messalo *R see* **Mualo** *R*
87 G8 **Messalo** *R* Mozambique
22 K4 **Messancy** Belgium
85 F2 **Messaoud, Hassi** Algeria
33 P7 **Messdorf** East Germany
21 J4 **Messei** France
Messick *see* **Poquoson**
133 C7 **Messie, Can** *str* Chile
89 F4 **Messina** S Africa
43 G10 **Messina** Sicily
22 J4 **Messincourt** France
121 O6 **Messines** Quebec Canada
13 H6 **Messingham** England
46 E7 **Messini** Greece
46 E8 **Messiniakós Kólpos** *B* Greece
41 K2 **Messkirch** W Germany
47 O12 **Messongi** Greece
Mesta *R see* **Néstos** *R*
46 F3 **Mesta** *R* Bulgaria
16 E6 **Mestanza** Spain
33 P5 **Mestlin** East Germany
42 G3 **Mesto, N** Yugoslavia
37 P4 **Město-Touškov** Czechoslovakia
42 E3 **Mestre** Italy
45 L1 **Mestrino** Italy
128 D3 **Meta** *div* Colombia
45 Q8 **Meta** Italy
110 D3 **Meta** Missouri U.S.A.
128 E2 **Meta** *R* Venezuela/Colombia
115 N5 **Meta Incognita Pen** Northwest Territories Canada
111 F11 **Metairie** Louisiana U.S.A.
111 H12 **Metairie** New Orleans, Louisiana U.S.A.
120 C2 **Meta L** Ontario Canada
48 H4 **Metalici, Muntii** *mts* Romania
117 P11 **Metaline Falls** Washington U.S.A.
42 D5 **Metallifere, Colline** *hills* Italy
99 R9 **Metamora** Illinois U.S.A.
133 E3 **Metán** Argentina
70 D6 **Metangai** Kalimantan
87 F8 **Metangula** Mozambique
43 H8 **Metaponto** Italy
42 E5 **Metauro** *R* Italy
80 E3 **Metav** Israel
122 F9 **Meteghan** Nova Scotia Canada
32 F8 **Metelen** W Germany
86 G3 **Metema** Ethiopia
141 J6 **Meteor** *R* Queensland Australia
90 G14 **Meteor Depth** S Atlantic Oc
90 K14 **Meteor Seamount** S Atlantic Oc
22 D2 **Méteren** France
46 F7 **Méthana** Greece
119 S7 **Methley** Manitoba Canada
46 E8 **Methóni** Greece
100 E1 **Methow** *R* Washington U.S.A.
95 Q4 **Methuen** Massachusetts U.S.A.
142 E3 **Methuen,Mt** Western Australia Australia
144 C5 **Methven** New Zealand
12 E1 **Methven** Scotland
143 D7 **Methwin,Mt** Western Australia Australia
9 G2 **Methwold** England
119 N1 **Metionga L** Ontario Canada
118 G6 **Metiskow** Alberta Canada
122 E5 **Metis L** Quebec Canada
42 H5 **Metković** Yugoslavia
117 H8 **Metlakatla** Alaska U.S.A.
85 F2 **Metlaoui** Tunisia
38 K8 **Metnitz** Austria
46 D2 **Metohija** *mts* Yugoslavia
46 D2 **Metohija** Yugoslavia
100 D5 **Metolius** Oregon U.S.A.
46 E1 **Metovnica** Yugoslavia
70 K8 **Metro** Sumatra
110 H4 **Metropolis** Illinois U.S.A.
29 N6 **Metsäkylä** Finland
25 F2 **Metslawier** Netherlands
46 E5 **Métsovon** Greece
37 O6 **Metten** W Germany
36 B4 **Mettendorf** W Germany
112 E5 **Metter** Georgia U.S.A.
22 H3 **Mettet** Belgium
32 G8 **Mettingen** W Germany
36 B4 **Mettlach** W Germany
32 E10 **Mettmann** W Germany
36 B4 **Mettnich** W Germany
21 M7 **Mettray** France
76 C5 **Mettuppalaiyam** India
76 C5 **Mettur** India
88 H7 **Metudo** *isld* Mozambique
79 F5 **Metulla** Israel
19 K3 **Metz** France
40 F1 **Metzeral** France
22 L5 **Metzervisse** France
36 G6 **Metzingen** W Germany
20 F5 **Meu** *R* France
88 G9 **Meucate** Mozambique
36 D3 **Meudt** W Germany
69 C10 **Meulaboh** Sumatra
21 O3 **Meulan** France
22 E2 **Meulebeke** Belgium
21 L4 **Meulles** France
21 O6 **Meung-sur-Loire** France
69 C10 **Meureudu** Sumatra
40 A4 **Meursault** France
19 K4 **Meurthe** *R* France
36 B6 **Meurthe et Moselle** *dept* France
22 H3 **Meuse** *R* Belgium
19 J4 **Meuse** *dept* France
19 J3 **Meuse** *R* France
37 N1 **Meuselwitz** East Germany
21 O7 **Meusnes** France
8 B7 **Mevagissey** England
80 D6 **Meva Horon** Jordan
80 C6 **Meva Modiin** Jordan
13 G6 **Mexborough** England
109 L4 **Mexia** Texas U.S.A.
129 J3 **Mexiana** *isld* Brazil
103 J9 **Mexicali** Mexico
103 P4 **Mexican Hat** Utah U.S.A.
124 F3 **Mexicanos, Lago de los** Mexico
103 P5 **Mexican Water** Arizona U.S.A.
124 G6 **Mexico** *rep* N America
94 A6 **Mexico** Indiana U.S.A.
95 R2 **Mexico** Maine U.S.A.
110 E2 **Mexico** Missouri U.S.A.
95 L3 **Mexico** New York U.S.A.
125 K8 **Mexico City** Mexico
125 M6 **Mexico, G. of** Mexico
40 B6 **Meximieux** France
71 E3 **Meycawayan** Luzon Philippines
77 D5 **Meydān-e-Gel** *salt lake* Iran
33 Q6 **Meyenburg** East Germany
117 G8 **Meyers Chuck** Alaska U.S.A.
94 H7 **Meyersdale** Pennsylvania U.S.A.
18 G7 **Meymac** France
77 J2 **Meymaneh** Afghanistan
77 B3 **Meymeh** Iran
118 L8 **Meyronne** Saskatchewan Canada
18 H8 **Meyrueis** France
18 G7 **Meyssac** France
80 E8 **Mezada** Israel
125 N9 **Mezcalapa** *R* Mexico
46 F1 **Mezdra** Bulgaria
18 H9 **Mèze** France
19 Q17 **Mézel** France
52 G3 **Mezen'** *R* U.S.S.R.
52 F2 **Mezen'** Arkhangel'skaya obl U.S.S.R.
52 F2 **Mezenskaya Guba** *B* U.S.S.R.
80 D4 **Mezer** Israel
54 C1 **Mezha** *R* U.S.S.R.
52 G3 **Mezhdurechensk** U.S.S.R.
56 C4 **Mezhdurechensk** U.S.S.R.
55 E2 **Mezhdurechenskiy** U.S.S.R.
31 N1 **Mezhdurech'ye** U.S.S.R.
50 D1 **Mezhdusharskiy Ostrov** *isld* U.S.S.R.
48 H2 **Mezhgor'ye** U.S.S.R.
42 F2 **Mežica** Yugoslavia
21 K3 **Mézidon-Canon** France
21 N8 **Mézières-en-Brenne** France
21 O4 **Mézières-sur-Seine** France
31 H6 **Mezimosti** Czechoslovakia
18 F8 **Mézin** France
54 M1 **Mezinovskiy** U.S.S.R.
48 G4 **Mezöberény** Hungary
48 F3 **Mezöcsát** Hungary
48 F4 **Mezöhegyes** Hungary
48 F4 **Mezökovacsháza** Hungary
48 F3 **Mezökövesd** Hungary
18 E8 **Mézos** France
48 F3 **Mezötúr** Hungary
124 G6 **Mezquital** *R* Mexico
124 G6 **Mezquital** Mexico
124 H6 **Mezquitic** Mexico
41 N5 **Mezzana** Italy
45 M3 **Mezzano** Italy
41 O4 **Mezzaselva** Italy
45 M2 **Mezzogoro** Italy
41 K5 **Mezzola, Lago di** Italy
41 L5 **Mezzoldo** Italy
42 D2 **Mezzolombardo** Italy
89 G7 **Mfolozi** *R* S Africa
52 D5 **Mga** U.S.S.R.
74 F10 **Mhasvad** India
89 G6 **Mhlume** Swaziland
125 L9 **Miahuatián de Porfirio Diaz** Mexico
16 D5 **Miajadas** Spain
119 T9 **Miami** Manitoba Canada
103 O8 **Miami** Arizona U.S.A.
113 G12 **Miami** Florida U.S.A.
94 C7 **Miami** *R* Ohio U.S.A.
107 Q5 **Miami** Oklahoma U.S.A.
108 D8 **Miami** Texas U.S.A.
113 G12 **Miami Beach** Florida U.S.A.
113 G11 **Miami Canal** Florida U.S.A.
94 C6 **Miami, Great** *R* Ohio U.S.A.
94 C7 **Miami, Little** *R* Ohio U.S.A.
94 C7 **Miamisburg** Ohio U.S.A.
113 G12 **Miami Shores** Florida U.S.A.
113 G12 **Miami Springs** Florida U.S.A.
65 B7 **Mianchi** China
78 L3 **Miandowab** Iran
87 H11 **Miandrivazo** Madagascar
77 A1 **Mianeh** Iran
67 E4 **Mian Shui** *R* China
58 E5 **Mian Xian** China
67 D1 **Mianyang** China
67 A1 **Mianzhu** China
65 E6 **Miao Dao** *isld* China
65 E5 **Miaodao Qundao** *islds* China
65 H3 **Miaoling** China
67 B3 **Miao Ling** *mt ra* China
67 C4 **Miaoping** China
87 H11 **Miarinarivo** Madagascar
55 D3 **Miass** *R* U.S.S.R.
31 K1 **Miastko** Poland
103 O9 **Mica Mt** Arizona U.S.A.
58 E5 **Micang Shan** *mt ra* China
113 E8 **Micanopy** Florida U.S.A.
128 C3 **Micay** Colombia
113 C7 **Miccosukee** Florida U.S.A.
52 H3 **Michaichmon'** U.S.S.R.
48 G2 **Michal'any** Czechoslovakia
48 G2 **Michalovce** Czechoslovakia
118 C9 **Michel** British Columbia Canada
118 H3 **Michel** Saskatchewan Canada
38 N5 **Michelbach** Austria
36 E3 **Michelbach** W Germany
116 Q2 **Michelson, Mt** Alaska U.S.A.
36 G4 **Michelstadt** W Germany
33 S8 **Michendorf** East Germany
127 K5 **Miches** Dominican Rep
118 E7 **Michichi** Alberta Canada
112 J1 **Michie, L** North Carolina U.S.A.
99 S3 **Michigamme** Michigan U.S.A.
99 S3 **Michigamme L** Michigan U.S.A.
99 S3 **Michigamme Res** Michigan U.S.A.
94 A1 **Michigan** *state* U.S.A.
98 H1 **Michigan** North Dakota U.S.A.
94 C4 **Michigan Center** Michigan U.S.A.
99 U8 **Michigan City** Indiana U.S.A.
94 A4 **Michigan, L** U.S.A.
110 K1 **Michigantown** Indiana U.S.A.
120 F5 **Michipicoten** Ontario Canada
31 N4 **Michów** Poland
47 J2 **Michurin** Bulgaria
54 M4 **Michurinsk** U.S.S.R.
13 F4 **Mickle Fell** *mt* England
9 E3 **Mickleton** England
127 O8 **Micoud** St Lucia
134 F7 **Micronesia** Pacific Oc
69 H11 **Midai** *isld* Indonesia
119 O9 **Midale** Saskatchewan Canada
100 J8 **Midas** Nevada U.S.A.
90 E6 **Mid-Atlantic Ridge** Atlantic Oc
12 E2 **Mid Calder** Scotland
25 A6 **Middelburg** Netherlands
87 D12 **Middelburg** S Africa
89 D8 **Middelburg** Cape Prov S Africa
89 F5 **Middelburg** Transvaal S Africa
25 B5 **Middelharnis** Netherlands
22 D1 **Middelkerke** Belgium
89 B9 **Middel Roggeveld** *reg* S Africa
87 E10 **Middelwit** S Africa
25 C3 **Middenbeemster** Netherlands
90 A7 **Middle America Trench** Pacific Oc
68 A6 **Middle Andaman** *isld* Andaman Is
138 D5 **Middleback, Mt** South Australia Australia
95 R5 **Middleboro** Massachusetts U.S.A.
94 G7 **Middlebourne** West Virginia U.S.A.
118 F1 **Middlebro** Manitoba Canada
95 K6 **Middleburg** Pennsylvania U.S.A.
94 K8 **Middleburg** Virginia U.S.A.
95 N4 **Middleburgh** New York U.S.A.
94 B5 **Middlebury** Indiana U.S.A.
95 O2 **Middlebury** Vermont U.S.A.
108 G4 **Middle Concho** *R* Texas U.S.A.
28 D5 **Middlefart** Denmark
144 A6 **Middle Fiord** New Zealand
13 G5 **Middleham** England
143 E10 **Middle I** Western Australia Australia
69 C8 **Middle I** Thailand
90 B16 **Middle I** Tristan da Cunha
94 D1 **Middle I** Michigan U.S.A.
100 F8 **Middle L** Nevada U.S.A.
119 M6 **Middle Lake** Saskatchewan Canada
98 G8 **Middle Loup** *R* Nebraska U.S.A.
144 C6 **Middlemarch** New Zealand
8 D6 **Middlemarsh** England
94 J3 **Middleport** New York U.S.A.
94 E8 **Middleport** Ohio U.S.A.
83 M9 **Middle Pt** Christmas I Indian Oc
94 C6 **Middle Pt** Ohio U.S.A.
98 K1 **Middle R** Minnesota U.S.A.
123 R5 **Middle Rge** Newfoundland Canada
95 L7 **Middle River** Maryland U.S.A.
118 G8 **Middle Sand Hills, The** Alberta Canada
94 D10 **Middlesboro** Kentucky U.S.A.
13 G4 **Middlesbrough** England
125 P9 **Middlesex** Belize
95 K4 **Middlesex** New York U.S.A.
141 F5 **Middleton** Queensland Australia
122 G9 **Middleton** Nova Scotia Canada
13 F5 **Middleton** Cumbria England
13 F6 **Middleton** Greater Manchester England
13 H6 **Middleton** Humberside England
100 J6 **Middleton** Idaho U.S.A.
94 C3 **Middleton** Michigan U.S.A.
110 H6 **Middleton** Tennessee U.S.A.
99 R6 **Middleton** Wisconsin U.S.A.
116 P7 **Middleton I** Alaska U.S.A.
13 F4 **Middleton in Teesdale** England
8 C2 **Middletown** England
95 P5 **Middletown** Connecticut U.S.A.
95 M7 **Middletown** Delaware U.S.A.
94 B6 **Middletown** Indiana U.S.A.
94 K7 **Middletown** Maryland U.S.A.
95 N5 **Middletown** New York U.S.A.
110 M2 **Middletown** Ohio U.S.A.
95 L6 **Middletown** Pennsylvania U.S.A.
8 D2 **Middletown** Wales
94 B4 **Middleville** Michigan U.S.A.
95 N3 **Middleville** New York U.S.A.
108 B8 **Middle Water** Texas U.S.A.
8 D1 **Middlewich** England
122 H9 **Middlewood** Nova Scotia Canada
85 D2 **Midelt** Morocco
109 L7 **Midfield** Texas U.S.A.
8 C4 **Mid Glamorgan** *co* Wales
145 E3 **Midhirst** New Zealand
121 L8 **Midhurst** Ontario Canada
9 F6 **Midhurst** England
18 G9 **Midi, Canal du** France
18 E10 **Midi d'Ossau, Pic du** *mt* France
18 F10 **Midi du Bigorre, Pic du** *mt* France
143 B9 **Midland** Western Australia Australia
110 B6 **Midland** Arkansas U.S.A.
103 K8 **Midland** California U.S.A.
94 J7 **Midland** Maryland U.S.A.
94 C3 **Midland** Michigan U.S.A.
98 E5 **Midland** South Dakota U.S.A.
108 E4 **Midland** Texas U.S.A.
111 L10 **Midland City** Alabama U.S.A.
89 F2 **Midlands** *prov* Zimbabwe
14 C5 **Midleton** Ireland
Midlothian *co see* **Lothian and Borders** *regions*
109 K3 **Midlothian** Texas U.S.A.
94 K9 **Midlothian** Virginia U.S.A.
32 J5 **Midlum** W Germany
111 F8 **Midnight** Mississippi U.S.A.
87 H12 **Midongy Atsimo** Madagascar
60 D13 **Midori-kawa** *R* Japan
18 E9 **Midouze** *R* France
134 G5 **Mid-Pacific Mountains** Pacific Oc
71 G7 **Midsayap** Philippines
100 J5 **Midvale** Idaho U.S.A.
101 O9 **Midvale** Utah U.S.A.
112 E5 **Midville** Georgia U.S.A.
117 O11 **Midway** British Columbia Canada
111 L9 **Midway** Alabama U.S.A.
112 F6 **Midway** Georgia U.S.A.
94 C8 **Midway** Kentucky U.S.A.
109 M4 **Midway** Texas U.S.A.
135 U2 **Midway Is** *atoll* Hawaiian Is
116 O1 **Midway Is** Alaska U.S.A.
122 E1 **Midway L** Quebec Canada
143 E6 **Midway Well** Western Australia Australia
101 T6 **Midwest** Wyoming U.S.A.
107 N6 **Midwest City** Oklahoma U.S.A.
25 F2 **Midwolde** Netherlands
78 H3 **Midyat** Turkey
15 G1 **Mid Yell** Scotland
46 F1 **Midžor** *mt* Yugoslavia
61 K11 **Mie** *prefect* Japan
31 M5 **Miechów** Poland
40 F3 **Miécourt** Switzerland
31 J3 **Międzychód** Poland
31 K5 **Międzylesie** Poland
31 O4 **Międzyrzec** Poland
31 J3 **Międzyrzecz** Poland
31 K4 **Miejska Gorka** Poland
29 L5 **Miekojärvi** *L* Finland
18 F9 **Miélan** France
31 N5 **Mielec** Poland
41 N3 **Mieminger Kette** *mt* Austria
27 G15 **Mien** *L* Sweden
139 H8 **Miena** Tasmania Australia
67 G4 **Mien-hua Hsü** *isld* Taiwan
109 H9 **Mier** Mexico
106 D7 **Miera** New Mexico U.S.A.
48 K4 **Miercurea-Ciuc** Romania
16 D1 **Mieres** Spain
26 N2 **Mieron** Norway
38 E6 **Miesbach** W Germany
86 H4 **Mī 'ēso** Ethiopia
33 O8 **Mieste** East Germany
31 H3 **Mieszkowice** Poland
94 K6 **Mifflin** Pennsylvania U.S.A.
95 K6 **Mifflinburg** Pennsylvania U.S.A.
95 K6 **Mifflintown** Pennsylvania U.S.A.
83 L9 **Migaswewa** Sri Lanka
80 F2 **Migdal** Israel
80 D7 **Migdal Oz** Jordan
77 F4 **Mighān** Iran
45 L2 **Migliarino** Italy
21 L8 **Mignaloux Beauvoir** France
45 P7 **Mignano** Italy
44 G2 **Mignano, L. di** Italy
21 N8 **Migné** Indre France
21 L8 **Migné-Auxances** Vienne France
44 L5 **Mignone** *R* Italy
122 F5 **Miguasha-Ouest** Quebec Canada
124 H5 **Miguel Auza** Mexico
88 H2 **Migwani** Kenya
68 B3 **Migyaunye** Burma
48 K3 **Mihăileni** Romania
60 G11 **Mihara** Japan
61 N11 **Mihara-yama** *vol* Japan
61 O8 **Miharu** Japan
37 J1 **Mihla** East Germany
60 G10 **Miho wan** *B* Japan
40 D5 **Mijoux** France
119 P7 **Mikado** Saskatchewan Canada
94 D2 **Mikado** Michigan U.S.A.
60 P2 **Mikasa** Japan
61 K9 **Mikawa** Japan
61 L11 **Mikawa-wan** *B* Japan
54 L2 **Mikhaylov** U.S.S.R.
46 F1 **Mikhaylovgrad** Bulgaria
146 J12 **Mikhaylov I** Antarctica
48 L1 **Mikhaylovka** U.S.S.R.
47 H2 **Mikhaylovo** Bulgaria
55 C3 **Mikhaylovsk** U.S.S.R.
55 G4 **Mikhaylovskiy** Altayskiy Kray U.S.S.R.
80 C4 **Mikhmoret** Israel
79 E9 **Mikhrot Timna** Israel
88 H7 **Mikindani** Tanzania
100 E4 **Mikkalo** Oregon U.S.A.
29 N10 **Mikkeli** Finland
117 Q7 **Mikkwa** *R* Alberta Canada
31 N2 **Mikołajki** Poland
31 L5 **Mikołow** Poland
46 G1 **Mikre** Bulgaria
46 E4 **Mikrí Préspa L** Greece
47 H3 **Mikrón Dhérion** Greece
52 G1 **Mikulkin, Mys** *C* U.S.S.R.
48 D2 **Mikulov** Czechoslovakia
87 G7 **Mikumi** Tanzania
88 F5 **Mikumi Nat. Park** Tanzania
61 N8 **Mikuni sammyaku** *mts* Japan
61 N12 **Mikura-jima** *isld* Japan
99 N4 **Milaca** Minnesota U.S.A.
73 L7 **Miladunmadulu Atoll** Maldives
130 H9 **Milagres** Brazil
Milan *see* **Milano**
122 A8 **Milan** Quebec Canada
94 B7 **Milan** Indiana U.S.A.
107 N4 **Milan** Kansas U.S.A.
94 D4 **Milan** Michigan U.S.A.
99 L4 **Milan** Minnesota U.S.A.
99 N9 **Milan** Missouri U.S.A.
94 E5 **Milan** Ohio U.S.A.
110 H6 **Milan** Tennessee U.S.A.
100 H2 **Milan** Washington U.S.A.
138 E6 **Milang** South Australia Australia
88 E10 **Milange** Mozambique
39 **Milano** *conurbation* Italy
109 L5 **Milano** Texas U.S.A.
17 G4 **Milares** *R* Spain
47 J7 **Milas** Turkey
43 G10 **Milazzo** Sicily
98 K4 **Milbank** South Dakota U.S.A.
95 U2 **Milbridge** Maine U.S.A.
94 A4 **Milburg** Michigan U.S.A.
144 B7 **Milburn** New Zealand
9 G3 **Mildenhall** England
120 J8 **Mildmay** Ontario Canada
118 K5 **Mildred** Saskatchewan Canada
98 A3 **Mildred** Montana U.S.A.
95 L5 **Mildred** Pennsylvania U.S.A.
117 R7 **Mildred Lake** Alberta Canada
138 F5 **Mildura** Victoria Australia
67 A4 **Mile** China
46 F5 **Miléai** Greece
127 J2 **Mile Gully** Jamaica
141 K7 **Miles** Queensland Australia
100 G2 **Miles** Washington U.S.A.
101 U3 **Miles City** Montana U.S.A.
21 L5 **Milesse,la** France
119 N9 **Milestone** Saskatchewan Canada
43 G10 **Mileto** Italy
45 Q7 **Miletto, M** *mt* Italy
143 B7 **Mileura** Western Australia Australia
31 H6 **Milevsko** Czechoslovakia
9 F5 **Milford** Surrey England
102 D1 **Milford** California U.S.A.
95 O5 **Milford** Connecticut U.S.A.
95 M8 **Milford** Delaware U.S.A.
99 T9 **Milford** Illinois U.S.A.
94 B5 **Milford** Indiana U.S.A.
99 L6 **Milford** Iowa U.S.A.
107 O2 **Milford** Kansas U.S.A.
95 T2 **Milford** Maine U.S.A.
95 Q4 **Milford** Massachusetts U.S.A.
94 D4 **Milford** Michigan U.S.A.
98 J9 **Milford** Nebraska U.S.A.
95 Q4 **Milford** New Hampshire U.S.A.
95 N4 **Milford** New York U.S.A.
109 L3 **Milford** Texas U.S.A.
103 L3 **Milford** Utah U.S.A.
94 K8 **Milford** Virginia U.S.A.
94 D6 **Milford Center** Ohio U.S.A.
8 A4 **Milford Haven** Wales
9 E6 **Milford on Sea** England
144 A6 **Milford Sound** New Zealand
140 F4 **Milgarra** Queensland Australia
143 C8 **Milgoo, Mt** Western Australia Australia
143 C7 **Milgun** Western Australia Australia
85 E1 **Miliana** Algeria
43 C12 **Miliane** *R* Tunisia
31 K4 **Milicz** Poland
140 B1 **Milikapiti** N Terr Australia
143 B9 **Miling** Western Australia Australia
140 C1 **Milingimbi** N Terr Australia
20 A5 **Milizac** France
51 P3 **Milkovo** U.S.S.R.
118 F9 **Milk R** Alberta/Montana Canada/U.S.A.
127 K3 **Milk River Bath** Jamaica
86 E2 **Milk, Wadi el** *watercourse* Sudan
25 E5 **Mill** Netherlands
141 H4 **Millaa Millaa** Queensland Australia
21 O7 **Millançay** France
99 O9 **Millard** Missouri U.S.A.
141 H5 **Millaroo** Queensland Australia
98 H3 **Millarton** North Dakota U.S.A.
94 H9 **Millboro** Virginia U.S.A.
121 M8 **Millbrook** Ontario Canada
95 O5 **Millbrook** New York U.S.A.
102 F1 **Mill City** Nevada U.S.A.
100 C5 **Mill City** Oregon U.S.A.
102 C1 **Mill Creek** California U.S.A.
109 L1 **Mill Creek** Oklahoma U.S.A.
94 H8 **Mill Creek** West Virginia U.S.A.
112 D4 **Milledgeville** Georgia U.S.A.
99 R8 **Milledgeville** Illinois U.S.A.
101 O2 **Millegan** Montana U.S.A.
99 N3 **Mille Lacs** *L* Minnesota U.S.A.
119 N2 **Mille Lacs, Lac des** Ontario Canada
112 F5 **Millen** Georgia U.S.A.
138 D3 **Miller** *R* South Australia Australia
110 C4 **Miller** Missouri U.S.A.
98 G9 **Miller** Nebraska U.S.A.
98 H5 **Miller** South Dakota U.S.A.
124 B3 **Miller, Desembarcadero de** Mexico
116 Q6 **Miller, Mt** Alaska U.S.A.
54 M8 **Millerovo** U.S.S.R.
103 O10 **Miller Pk** Arizona U.S.A.
102 G3 **Millers** Nevada U.S.A.
94 B5 **Millersburg** Indiana U.S.A.
110 M3 **Millersburg** Kentucky U.S.A.
94 D1 **Millersburg** Michigan U.S.A.
94 F6 **Millersburg** Ohio U.S.A.
95 L6 **Millersburg** Pennsylvania U.S.A.
138 D4 **Millers Creek** South Australia Australia
95 P4 **Millers Falls** Massachusetts U.S.A.
111 J9 **Millers Ferry** Alabama U.S.A.
144 B6 **Miller's Flat** New Zealand
12 D2 **Millerston** Scotland
94 H6 **Millerstown** Pennsylvania U.S.A.
108 H4 **Millersview** Texas U.S.A.
122 G7 **Millerton** New Brunswick Canada
144 C4 **Millerton** New Zealand
95 O5 **Millerton** New York U.S.A.
102 E4 **Millerton L** California U.S.A.
123 Q5 **Millertown** Newfoundland Canada
123 Q4 **Millertown Junct** Newfoundland Canada
118 D5 **Millet** Alberta Canada
94 E9 **Millet** West Virginia U.S.A.
102 G2 **Millett** Nevada U.S.A.
109 H7 **Millett** Texas U.S.A.
18 G7 **Millevaches, Plateau de** France
14 D1 **Millford** Ireland
94 K5 **Mill Hall** Pennsylvania U.S.A.
146 H13 **Mill I** Antarctica
115 M5 **Mill I** Northwest Territories Canada
100 E6 **Millican** Oregon U.S.A.
109 L5 **Millican** Texas U.S.A.
138 F6 **Millicent** South Australia Australia
118 F8 **Millicent** Alberta Canada
143 D8 **Millicent,Mt** Western Australia Australia
111 K11 **Milligan** Florida U.S.A.
98 J9 **Milligan** Nebraska U.S.A.
106 F1 **Milliken** Colorado U.S.A.
95 M7 **Millington** Maryland U.S.A.
94 D3 **Millington** Michigan U.S.A.
110 G6 **Millington** Tennessee U.S.A.
95 S8 **Millinocket** Maine U.S.A.
141 K8 **Millmerran** Queensland Australia
13 E5 **Millom** England
12 D2 **Millport** Scotland
111 H8 **Millport** Alabama U.S.A.
95 L4 **Millport** New York U.S.A.
111 H10 **Millry** Alabama U.S.A.
141 G5 **Mills** *R* Queensland Australia
106 F5 **Mills** New Mexico U.S.A.
101 T7 **Mills** Wyoming U.S.A.
109 J3 **Millsap** Texas U.S.A.
102 B2 **Millsaps** California U.S.A.
95 M8 **Millsboro** Delaware U.S.A.
94 G7 **Millsboro** Pennsylvania U.S.A.
117 O5 **Mills L** Northwest Territories Canada
99 Q5 **Millston** Wisconsin U.S.A.
142 B5 **Millstream** Western Australia Australia
14 B4 **Millstreet** Ireland
8 C2 **Milltir Cerig** *mt* Wales
122 E8 **Milltown** New Brunswick Canada
123 R6 **Milltown** Newfoundland Canada
14 B4 **Milltown Malbay** Ireland
141 F4 **Millungera** Queensland Australia
102 E4 **Mill Valley** California U.S.A.
122 H9 **Mill Village** Nova Scotia Canada
122 E7 **Millville** New Brunswick Canada
94 C7 **Millville** Ohio U.S.A.
95 L5 **Millville** Pennsylvania U.S.A.
109 N2 **Millwood Res** Arkansas U.S.A.
21 P5 **Milly-la-Forêt** France
143 B7 **Milly Milly** Western Australia Australia
21 P3 **Milly-sur Thérain** France
33 T6 **Milmersdorf** East Germany
13 E1 **Milnathort** Scotland
115 R3 **Milne Land** Greenland
112 C4 **Milner** Georgia U.S.A.
101 L7 **Milner** Idaho U.S.A.
118 E1 **Milner Ridge** Manitoba Canada
120 K6 **Milnet** Ontario Canada
12 D2 **Milngavie** Scotland
98 J3 **Milnor** North Dakota U.S.A.
13 F5 **Milnthorpe** England
118 E8 **Milo** Alberta Canada
88 E6 **Milo** Tanzania
99 N8 **Milo** Iowa U.S.A.
95 S1 **Milo** Maine U.S.A.
100 B7 **Milo** Oregon U.S.A.
135 U6 **Milolii** Hawaiian Is
31 M2 **Miłomłyn** Poland
46 G8 **Milos** *isld* Greece
31 K3 **Miłosław** Poland
33 Q7 **Milow** East Germany
31 L6 **Milówka** Poland
138 F3 **Milparinka** New South Wales Australia
102 C4 **Milpitas** California U.S.A.
110 L2 **Milroy** Indiana U.S.A.
94 K6 **Milroy** Pennsylvania U.S.A.
37 O5 **Miltach** W Germany
36 G4 **Miltenberg** W Germany
139 K6 **Milton** New South Wales Australia
122 H9 **Milton** Nova Scotia Canada
144 B7 **Milton** New Zealand
12 D2 **Milton** Scotland
95 M8 **Milton** Delaware U.S.A.
111 J11 **Milton** Florida U.S.A.
99 Q10 **Milton** Illinois U.S.A.
110 D1 **Milton** Iowa U.S.A.
107 N4 **Milton** Kansas U.S.A.
95 R3 **Milton** Maine U.S.A.
94 H10 **Milton** North Carolina U.S.A.
98 J1 **Milton** North Dakota U.S.A.
95 L5 **Milton** Pennsylvania U.S.A.
95 O2 **Milton** Vermont U.S.A.
94 E8 **Milton** West Virginia U.S.A.
99 S7 **Milton** Wisconsin U.S.A.
8 B6 **Milton Abbot** England
139 J3 **Milton Downs** New South Wales Australia
100 G4 **Milton Freewater** Oregon U.S.A.
12 D3 **Miltonish** Scotland
9 F3 **Milton Keynes** England
107 N2 **Miltonvale** Kansas U.S.A.
86 C3 **Miltou** Chad
33 S4 **Miltzow** East Germany
67 D2 **Miluo** China
8 C5 **Milverton** England
99 T6 **Milwaukee** Wisconsin U.S.A.
127 K5 **Milwaukee Depth** Caribbean
60 E13 **Mimitsu** Japan
18 E8 **Mimizan** France
60 O4 **Mimmaya** Japan
31 H5 **Mimoň** Czechoslovakia
86 B6 **Mimongo** Gabon
60 H10 **Mimuro yama** *mt* Japan
102 A2 **Mina** California U.S.A.
102 F3 **Mina** Nevada U.S.A.
77 A5 **Mina' al Ahmadi** Iran
77 E6 **Mīnāb** Iran
60 J12 **Minabe** Japan
124 F3 **Miñaca** Mexico
119 T4 **Minago R** Manitoba Canada
71 H4 **Minahassa Peninsula** Sulawesi Indonesia
77 D7 **Mina Jebel Ali** U.A.E.
79 H2 **Mīnakh** Syria
118 H1 **Minaki** Ontario Canada
100 H4 **Minam** Oregon U.S.A.
60 D13 **Minamata** Japan
61 L10 **Minami Alps Nat. Park** Japan
85 C6 **Mina, Mt** Mali
126 F4 **Minas** Cuba
69 E12 **Minas** Sumatra
131 G5 **Minas** Uruguay
77 A5 **Mina' Sa'ud** Kuwait
122 H8 **Minas Basin** Nova Scotia Canada
126 C3 **Minas de Matahambre** Cuba
16 C7 **Minas de Riotinto** Spain
16 C7 **Minas de Tharsis** Spain
130 F5 **Minas Gerais** *state* Brazil
130 G5 **Minas Novas** Brazil
129 K7 **Minas Novas** Brazil
125 P10 **Minas, Sa. de las** *mts* Guatemala
98 C8 **Minatare** Nebraska U.S.A.
120 B2 **Minataree** Ontario Canada
125 M9 **Minatitlán** Mexico
68 B2 **Minbu** Burma
118 F5 **Minburn** Alberta Canada
99 M8 **Minburn** Iowa U.S.A.
68 A2 **Minbya** Burma
116 M5 **Minchumina, L** Alaska U.S.A.
45 J1 **Mincio** *R* Italy
107 N6 **Minco** Oklahoma U.S.A.
31 M6 **Minčol** *mt* Czechoslovakia
71 G7 **Mindanao** Philippines
71 G6 **Mindanao Sea** Philippines
138 F5 **Mindarie** South Australia Australia
68 A2 **Mindat Sakan** Burma
37 J7 **Mindel** *R* W Germany
41 M1 **Mindelheim** W Germany
121 M8 **Minden** Ontario Canada
111 C9 **Minden** Louisiana U.S.A.
98 G9 **Minden** Nebraska U.S.A.
102 E3 **Minden** Nevada U.S.A.
94 F9 **Minden** West Virginia U.S.A.
32 J8 **Minden** W Germany
94 E3 **Minden City** Michigan U.S.A.
142 B5 **Minderoo** Western Australia Australia
68 B3 **Mindon** Burma
138 F5 **Mindona L** New South Wales Australia
71 E4 **Mindoro** *isld* Philippines
71 E4 **Mindoro Str** Philippines
48 H5 **Mîndra** Romania
48 F4 **Mindszent** Hungary
55 C4 **Mindyak** U.S.S.R.
60 E11 **Mine** Japan
99 O1 **Mine Centre** Ontario Canada
14 D5 **Mine Hd** Ireland
8 C5 **Minehead** England
130 D5 **Mineiros** Brazil
21 J3 **Mine,la** France
99 L8 **Mineola** Iowa U.S.A.
109 M3 **Mineola** Texas U.S.A.
101 P4 **Miner** Montana U.S.A.
102 C1 **Mineral** California U.S.A.
109 K7 **Mineral** Texas U.S.A.
94 K8 **Mineral** Virginia U.S.A.
100 C3 **Mineral** Washington U.S.A.
125 K7 **Mineral del Monte** Mexico
103 M3 **Mineral Mts** Utah U.S.A.
99 Q7 **Mineral Pt** Wisconsin U.S.A.
109 O2 **Mineral Springs** Arkansas U.S.A.
109 J3 **Mineral Wells** Texas U.S.A.
45 K2 **Minerbio** Italy
103 M3 **Minersville** Utah U.S.A.
94 F6 **Minerva** Ohio U.S.A.
137 R6 **Minerva Rfs** Pacific Oc
43 G7 **Minervino Murge** Italy
95 L3 **Minetto** New York U.S.A.
94 E8 **Minford** Ohio U.S.A.
68 C4 **Mingaladon** Burma
122 H3 **Mingan** Quebec Canada
122 J3 **Mingan Chan** Quebec Canada
122 J3 **Mingan Is** Quebec Canada
138 F4 **Mingary** South Australia Australia
67 D5 **Mingcheng** China
78 L1 **Mingechaur** U.S.S.R.
78 L1 **Mingechaurskoye Vdkhr** *res* U.S.S.R.
141 H4 **Mingela** Queensland Australia
143 B8 **Mingenew** Western Australia Australia
140 E5 **Mingera** *R* Queensland Australia
68 B1 **Mingin** Burma
75 Q6 **Mingin Range** Burma
67 B5 **Mingjiang** China
58 G5 **Ming-kuang** China
17 G5 **Minglanilla** Spain
67 C4 **Minglun** China
99 N8 **Mingo** Iowa U.S.A.
107 K2 **Mingo** Kansas U.S.A.
94 G6 **Mingo Junct** Ohio U.S.A.
87 G8 **Mingoyo** Tanzania
67 A1 **Mingshan** China
Mingshui *see* **Zhangqiu**
65 F1 **Mingshui** China
109 J3 **Mingus** Texas U.S.A.
67 F3 **Mingxi** China
68 G8 **Minh Hoa, Hon** *isld* Vietnam
68 B4 **Minhla** Burma
16 B3 **Minho** *prov* Portugal
16 B2 **Minho** *R* Spain/Portugal
127 K2 **Minho, R** Jamaica
67 F3 **Minhou** China
20 G4 **Miniac Morvan** France
46 E1 **Minićevo** Yugoslavia
73 L7 **Minicoy I** Lakshadweep Indian Oc
101 M7 **Minidoka** Idaho U.S.A.
99 R9 **Minier** Illinois U.S.A.
143 E8 **Minigwal,L** Western Australia Australia
143 A6 **Minilya** Western Australia Australia
143 A6 **Minilya R** Western Australia Australia
110 K4 **Mining City Res** Kentucky U.S.A.
119 Q8 **Miniota** Manitoba Canada
83 K10 **Minipe** Sri Lanka
123 L1 **Minipi L** Labrador, Nfld Canada
118 H4 **Ministikwan L** Saskatchewan Canada
17 F3 **Ministra, Sierra** Spain
119 Q6 **Minitonas** Manitoba Canada
67 F3 **Min Jiang** *R* China
58 D5 **Min Jiang** *R* China
140 C1 **Minjilang** N Terr Australia
102 E5 **Minkler** California U.S.A.
48 L2 **Min'kovtsy** U.S.S.R.
57 G4 **Min-Kush** U.S.S.R.
138 D5 **Minlaton** South Australia Australia
85 F7 **Minna** Nigeria
146 D11 **Minna Bluff** *pt* Antarctica
61 P12 **Minna-jima** *isld* Okinawa
107 N2 **Minneapolis** Kansas U.S.A.
99 N4 **Minneapolis** Minnesota U.S.A.
119 S8 **Minnedosa** Manitoba Canada
107 L4 **Minneola** Kansas U.S.A.
99 N3 **Minnesota** *state* U.S.A.
99 M5 **Minnesota** *R* Minnesota U.S.A.
99 P5 **Minnesota City** Minnesota U.S.A.
99 N6 **Minnesota Lake** Minnesota U.S.A.
27 E11 **Minnesund** Norway
99 N5 **Minnetonka** Minnesota U.S.A.
118 B7 **Minnewanka, L** Alberta Canada
99 L4 **Minnewaska L** Minnesota U.S.A.
98 G1 **Minnewaukan** North Dakota U.S.A.
143 B6 **Minnie Creek** Western Australia Australia
141 H7 **Minnie Downs** Queensland Australia
142 B5 **Minnie,Mt** Western Australia Australia
138 D5 **Minnipa** South Australia Australia
120 G4 **Minnipuka** Ontario Canada
118 K1 **Minnitaki L** Ontario Canada
61 K10 **Mino** Japan
16 B2 **Miño** *R* Spain
61 M10 **Minobu** Japan
99 R4 **Minocqua** Wisconsin U.S.A.
61 K10 **Minokamo** Japan
61 K11 **Minokuchi** Japan
99 P3 **Minong** Wisconsin U.S.A.
99 R9 **Minonk** Illinois U.S.A.
99 S8 **Minooka** Illinois U.S.A.
40 A2 **Minot** France
98 E1 **Minot** North Dakota U.S.A.
67 F3 **Minqing** China
65 C7 **Minquan** China
20 F4 **Minquiers,les** English Chan
32 G5 **Minsen** W Germany
65 A4 **Minsheng Canal** China
53 C7 **Minsk** U.S.S.R.
31 N3 **Mińsk Mazowiecki** Poland
9 H5 **Minster** England
94 C6 **Minster** Ohio U.S.A.
74 F1 **Mintaka Pass** China/Kashmir
111 J9 **Minter** Alabama U.S.A.
111 F8 **Minter City** Mississippi U.S.A.
119 S9 **Minto** Manitoba Canada
122 F7 **Minto** New Brunswick Canada
117 E4 **Minto** Yukon Territory Canada
114 J3 **Minto Hd** Northwest Territories Canada
114 H3 **Minto Inlet** Northwest Territories Canada
115 M6 **Minto, L** Quebec Canada
98 B1 **Minton** Saskatchewan Canada
106 D2 **Minturn** Colorado U.S.A.
45 P7 **Minturno** Italy
79 A8 **Minûf** Egypt
56 D4 **Minusinsk** U.S.S.R.
58 D5 **Min Xian** China
79 A10 **Minya, El** Egypt
79 B8 **Minya el Qamn** Egypt
Minya Konka *mt see* **Gongga Shan** *mt*
55 C3 **Min'yar** U.S.S.R.
138 F6 **Minyip** Victoria Australia
68 B1 **Minywa** Burma
94 C2 **Mio** Michigan U.S.A.
83 J10 **Mi Oya** *R* Sri Lanka
78 K5 **Miqdādiyah** Iraq
123 Q6 **Miquelon** *isld* Atlantic Oc
123 Q6 **Miquelon** Miquelon I Atlantic Oc
121 O3 **Miquelon** Quebec Canada
123 Q6 **Miquelon, C** Miquelon I Atlantic Oc
118 E5 **Miquelon Prov. Park** Alberta Canada
123 N7 **Mira** C Breton I, Nova Scotia
45 M1 **Mira** Italy
16 B7 **Mira** *R* Portugal
17 G5 **Mira** Spain
19 P17 **Mirabeau** France
130 G5 **Mirabela** Brazil
45 R7 **Mirabella Eclano** Italy
130 G7 **Miracema** Brazil
128 D2 **Miraflores** Boyaca Colombia
124 E6 **Miraflores** Mexico
102 G7 **Mirage L** California U.S.A.
130 G7 **Mirai** Brazil
76 B2 **Miraj** India
130 G5 **Miralta** Brazil
19 O17 **Miràmas** France
18 E7 **Mirambeau** France
122 G6 **Miramichi B** New Brunswick Canada
18 F8 **Miramont de Guyenne** France
133 F5 **Miranda** Argentina
145 E2 **Miranda** New Zealand
128 E1 **Miranda** *state* Venezuela
17 F2 **Miranda de E.Haro** Spain
16 C3 **Miranda do D** Portugal
141 F3 **Miranda Downs** Queensland Australia
130 C6 **Miranda, R** Brazil
18 F9 **Mirande** France
16 C3 **Mirandela** Portugal
109 J8 **Mirando City** Texas U.S.A.
45 K2 **Mirandola** Italy
130 D7 **Mirandópolis** Brazil
45 M1 **Mirano** Italy
130 E8 **Mirante Serra do** *mts* Brazil
60 F11 **Mirasaka** Japan
17 G5 **Mira, Sierra de** *mts* Spain
130 E7 **Mirassol** Brazil
16 C2 **Miravalles** *mt* Spain
46 E3 **Miravci** Yugoslavia
77 L2 **Mīr Bacheh Kowt** Afghanistan
25 E3 **Mirdum** Netherlands
21 K6 **Miré** France
86 G1 **Mirear I** Egypt
127 H5 **Mirebalais** Haiti
19 J5 **Mirebeau** Côte-d'Or France
21 L8 **Mirebeau** Vienne France
18 G9 **Mirepoix** France
54 E7 **Mirgorod** U.S.S.R.
70 D2 **Miri** Sarawak
141 K6 **Miriam Vale** Queensland Australia
85 A5 **Mirik, C** Mauritania
127 K9 **Mirimire** Venezuela
131 H4 **Mirim, L** Brazil/Uruguay
131 F2 **Miriñay, R** Argentina
141 G8 **Mirintu** *R* Queensland Australia
128 D4 **Miriti-Paraná** *R* Colombia
77 G5 **Mīrjāveh** Iran
80 D4 **Mirka** Jordan
45 P1 **Mirna** *R* Yugoslavia
146 H13 **Mirnyy** *U.S.S.R. Base* Antarctica
56 H1 **Mirnyy** U.S.S.R.
40 E3 **Miroir, Mt** France
144 D5 **Miromiro** *mt* New Zealand
119 P3 **Mirond L** Saskatchewan Canada
54 B7 **Mironovka** U.S.S.R.
31 J2 **Mirosławiec** Poland
33 R6 **Mirow** East Germany
77 L7 **Mirpur Khas** Pakistan
140 D7 **Mirranponga Pongunna L** N Terr Australia
85 F6 **Mirria** Niger
118 D6 **Mirror** Alberta Canada
48 J6 **Mîrşani** Romania
56 D5 **Mirskoy Khrebet** *mts* U.S.S.R.
141 H5 **Mirtna** Queensland Australia
46 F7 **Mirtoan Sea** Greece
59 J4 **Miryang** S Korea
56 E1 **Miryuginskiy Porog** *falls* U.S.S.R.
57 B5 **Mirzachiria** U.S.S.R.
75 K6 **Mirzapur** India
45 O4 **Misa** *R* Italy
60 G11 **Mi-saki** *C* Japan
60 F12 **Misaki** Japan
61 L10 **Misakubo** Japan
45 N4 **Misano Monte** Italy
61 P13 **Misato** Okinawa
61 P5 **Misawa** Japan

56 Misburg — Montsoreau

32 L8 **Misburg** W Germany
40 G5 **Mischabel** *mt* Switzerland
122 J7 **Miscouche** Prince Edward I Canada
122 H6 **Miscou I** New Brunswick Canada
122 H5 **Miscou, Pt** New Brunswick Canada
127 P4 **Misery, Mt** St Kitts W Indies
80 F1 **Misgav 'Am** Israel
69 A9 **Misha** Nicobar Is
77 A5 **Mish'ab, Al** U.A.E.
128 D6 **Mishahua** *R* Peru
65 H2 **Mishan** China
94 A5 **Mishawaka** Indiana U.S.A.
116 G2 **Misheguk Mt** Alaska U.S.A.
56 F4 **Mishelevka** U.S.S.R.
120 E4 **Mishibishu L** Ontario Canada
99 T5 **Mishicot** Wisconsin U.S.A.
61 M10 **Mishima** Japan
60 E11 **Mi shima** *isld* Japan
55 C3 **Mishkino** Bashkirskaya A.S.S.R. U.S.S.R.
55 D3 **Mishkino** Sverdlovskaya obl U.S.S.R.
80 F7 **Mishmaqa** Jordan
80 C6 **Mishmar 'Ayyalon** Israel
80 B8 **Mishmar Ha Negev** Israel
80 F1 **Mishmar Ha Yarden** Israel
121 P5 **Mishomis** Quebec Canada
52 J2 **Mishvan'** U.S.S.R.
80 E4 **Misilya** Jordan
137 L4 **Misima** *isld* Louisiade Arch
128 E6 **Misión Cavinas** Bolivia
130 C10 **Misiones** *prov* Argentina
130 B10 **Misiones** *dept* Paraguay
130 C10 **Misiones, Sa.de** *ra* Argentina
88 B4 **Misisi** Zaire
125 N2 **Miskito, Cayos** *islds* Nicaragua
48 F2 **Miskolc** Hungary
38 M9 **Mislinja** Yugoslavia
79 G5 **Mismīyah, Al** Syria
60 G10 **Misogu chi** Japan
71 C3 **Misoöl** *isld* W Irian
99 Q2 **Misquah Hills** Minnesota U.S.A.
84 F3 **Miṣrātah** Libya
84 F3 **Miṣrātah, Ra's** *C* Libya
120 F4 **Missanabie** Ontario Canada
130 G9 **Missão Velhá** Brazil
20 F7 **Missillac** France
120 G4 **Missinaibi L** Ontario Canada
120 H2 **Missinaibi R** Ontario Canada
100 C1 **Mission** British Columbia Canada
98 F6 **Mission** South Dakota U.S.A.
109 J9 **Mission** Texas U.S.A.
117 M11 **Mission City** British Columbia Canada
98 J7 **Mission Hill** South Dakota U.S.A.
101 M2 **Mission Range** Montana U.S.A.
121 L1 **Missisicabi** *R* Quebec Canada
120 G6 **Mississagi** *R* Ontario Canada
121 L9 **Mississauga** Ontario Canada
110 L1 **Mississinewa L** Indiana U.S.A.
94 B6 **Mississinewa L** Indiana U.S.A.
111 F9 **Mississippi** *state* U.S.A.
111 E10 **Mississippi** *R* U.S.A.
111 G12 **Mississippi Delta** Louisiana U.S.A.
121 O7 **Mississippi, L** Ontario Canada
111 H11 **Mississippi Sound** Mississippi U.S.A.
Missolonghi Greece *see* **Mesolóngion**
120 H4 **Missonga** Ontario Canada
101 L3 **Missoula** Montana U.S.A.
110 C3 **Missouri** *state* U.S.A.
110 C2 **Missouri** *R* Missouri U.S.A.
109 O2 **Missouri, Lit** *R* Arkansas U.S.A.
98 F3 **Missouri Res** North Dakota U.S.A.
99 L8 **Missouri Valley** Iowa U.S.A.
141 H5 **Mistake Cr** Queensland Australia
140 A3 **Mistake Creek** N Terr Australia
123 K2 **Mistanipisipou R** Quebec Canada
121 S4 **Mistassini** Quebec Canada
115 M7 **Mistassini, Lac** Quebec Canada
119 O6 **Mistatim** Saskatchewan Canada
121 M3 **Mistawak L** Quebec Canada
31 K7 **Mistelbach** Austria
27 J14 **Misterhult** Sweden
126 C5 **Misteriosa Bank** Caribbean
8 D6 **Misterton** England
128 D7 **Misti** *mt* Peru
122 E5 **Mistigougèche L** Quebec Canada
37 P3 **Misto** Czechoslovakia
131 D3 **Mistolar, L** Argentina
26 E10 **Mistra** *R* Norway
43 F11 **Mistretta** Sicily
117 H8 **Misty Fjords Nat Mon** Alaska U.S.A.
60 E11 **Misumi** Japan
60 D13 **Misumi** Japan
60 E13 **Mitai** Japan
127 P2 **Mitan** Trinidad
124 G7 **Mita, Pta.de** *C* Mexico
8 D4 **Mitcheldean** England
141 J7 **Mitchell** Queensland Australia
120 J9 **Mitchell** Ontario Canada
8 A7 **Mitchell** England
110 K3 **Mitchell** Indiana U.S.A.
98 C8 **Mitchell** Nebraska U.S.A.
100 E5 **Mitchell** Oregon U.S.A.
98 H6 **Mitchell** South Dakota U.S.A.
111 K9 **Mitchell L** Alabama U.S.A.
94 B2 **Mitchell, L** Michigan U.S.A.
112 E2 **Mitchell, Mt** North Carolina U.S.A.
140 A1 **Mitchell Pt** N Terr Australia
141 F3 **Mitchell River** Queensland Australia
14 C4 **Mitchelstown** Ireland
121 Q5 **Mitchinamecus, L** Quebec Canada
74 C6 **Mithi** Pakistan
47 H5 **Mithimna** Greece
71 B2 **Miti** *isld* Halmahera Indonesia
47 H5 **Mitilíni** Greece
52 G2 **Mitina** U.S.S.R.
119 S4 **Mitishto R** Manitoba Canada
117 G7 **Mitkof I** Alaska U.S.A.
79 C8 **Mitla Pass** Egypt
61 O9 **Mito** Japan
86 A5 **Mitra** *mt* Equat Guinea
137 P4 **Mitre** *isld* Santa Cruz Is
145 E4 **Mitre, Mt** New Zealand
144 A6 **Mitre Pk** New Zealand
52 J3 **Mitrofan-Dikost** U.S.S.R.
116 H9 **Mitrofania I** Alaska U.S.A.
46 D5 **Mitsikéli** *R* Greece
86 H2 **Mits'iwa** Ethiopia
86 G2 **Mits'iwa** Ethiopia
60 F11 **Mitsu** Japan
60 F12 **Mitsuhama** Japan
60 H11 **Mitsuishi** Japan
60 Q3 **Mitsuishi** Japan
61 N9 **Mitsukaidō** Japan
61 M8 **Mitsuke** Japan
60 R2 **Mitsumata** Japan
139 K5 **Mittagong** New South Wales Australia
141 F4 **Mittagong** Queensland Australia
41 L3 **Mittagspitze** *mt* Austria
139 J6 **Mitta Mitta** Victoria Australia
41 N4 **Mittelberg** Austria
37 J5 **Mittelfranken** *dist* Bayern W Germany
40 F4 **Mittelland** *dist* Switzerland
32 H8 **Mittellandkanal** W Germany
33 R8 **Mittelmark** *reg* East Germany
36 H3 **Mittelsinn** W Germany
41 O3 **Mittenwald** W Germany
33 T8 **Mittenwalde** East Germany
38 M6 **Mitterbach** Austria
37 O6 **Mitterfels** W Germany
38 G7 **Mitter Pinzgau** *V* Austria
36 B6 **Mittersheim** France
37 N4 **Mitterteich** W Germany
140 D4 **Mittiebah** *R* N Terr Australia
37 O2 **Mittweida** East Germany
128 D3 **Mitú** Colombia
88 B3 **Mitumba** *mts* Zaire
87 E7 **Mitwaba** Zaire
55 D1 **Mityayevo** U.S.S.R.
86 B5 **Mitzic** Gabon
61 N10 **Miura** Japan
54 K9 **Mius** *R* U.S.S.R.
54 K9 **Miusskiy Liman** *lagoon* U.S.S.R.
65 B7 **Mi Xian** China
38 M7 **Mixnitz** Austria
61 K11 **Miya-gawa** *R* Japan
61 O7 **Miyagi** *prefect* Japan
61 Q12 **Miyagi** Okinawa
61 P13 **Miyagusuku-jima** *isld* Okinawa
78 G4 **Miyāh, Wadi Al** Syria
61 N11 **Miyake-jima** *isld* Japan
61 P6 **Miyako** Japan
60 E14 **Miyakonojō** Japan
55 B6 **Miyaly** U.S.S.R.
60 E14 **Miyazaki** Japan
60 E13 **Miyazaki** *prefect* Japan
60 J10 **Miyazu** Japan
60 F11 **Miyoshi** Japan
65 C4 **Miyun** China
65 D4 **Miyun Shuiku** *res* China
86 G4 **Mīzan Teferī** Ethiopia
84 E3 **Mizdah** Libya
111 G10 **Mize** Mississippi U.S.A.
14 B5 **Mizen Hd** Cork Ireland
14 E4 **Mizen Hd** Wicklow Ireland
65 A6 **Mizhi** China
48 K6 **Mizil** Romania
46 F1 **Miziya** Bulgaria
75 P7 **Mizoram** *prov* India
99 M2 **Mizpah** Minnesota U.S.A.
79 E7 **Mizpe Ramon** Israel
146 J9 **Mizuho** *Japanese Base* Antarctica
61 P6 **Mizusawa** Japan
26 K9 **Mjällom** Sweden
88 C1 **Mjanji** Uganda
27 F14 **Mjöbäck** Sweden
27 H13 **Mjölby** Sweden
28 B6 **Mjolden** Denmark
27 D12 **Mjöndalen** Norway
27 F14 **Mjörn** *L* Sweden
27 E11 **Mjösa** *L* Norway
88 C9 **Mkokomo** *mt* Zambia
88 G4 **Mkokotoni** Tanzania
88 B8 **Mkuku** Zambia
88 B8 **Mkushi** *R* Zambia
87 E8 **Mkushi** Zambia
89 H6 **Mkuze** S Africa
31 H5 **Mladá Boleslav** Czechoslovakia
48 F6 **Mladenovac** Yugoslavia
37 P4 **Mladotice** Czechoslovakia
88 C5 **Mlala Hills** Tanzania
48 G6 **Mlava** *R* Yugoslavia
31 M2 **Mława** Poland
88 G10 **M'lela** *R* Mozambique
87 G7 **Mlimba** Tanzania
42 H6 **Mljet** *isld* Yugoslavia
88 E7 **Mlowe** Malawi
89 D5 **Mmabatho** S Africa
89 E3 **Mmashoro** Botswana
37 O3 **Mnichov** Czechoslovakia
31 H5 **Mnichovo Hradiště** Czechoslovakia
48 F2 **Mnišek** Czechoslovakia
26 K8 **Mo** Sweden
128 D5 **Moa** *R* Brazil
71 N9 **Moa** *isld* Indonesia
85 B7 **Moa** *R* Sierra Leone/Guinea
103 P3 **Moab** Utah U.S.A.
126 G4 **Moa Grande, Cayo** *isld* Cuba
141 F1 **Moa I** Queensland Australia
119 U3 **Moak L** Manitoba Canada
139 G6 **Moama** New South Wales Australia
89 H5 **Moamba** Mozambique
144 C5 **Moana** New Zealand
138 F3 **Moanba, L** South Australia Australia
86 B6 **Moanda** Gabon
86 B7 **Moanda** Zaire
103 K5 **Moapa** Nevada U.S.A.
71 N8 **Moapora** *isld* Indonesia
14 D3 **Moate** Ireland
88 D10 **Moatize** Mozambique
145 E3 **Moawhango** New Zealand
87 E7 **Moba** Zaire
61 O10 **Mobara** Japan
77 B3 **Mobārakeh** Iran
86 D5 **Mobaye** Cent Afr Republic
86 D5 **Mobayi-Mbongo** Zaire
110 D2 **Moberly** Missouri U.S.A.
117 N8 **Moberly Lake** British Columbia Canada
120 E4 **Mobert** Ontario Canada
111 H11 **Mobile** Alabama U.S.A.
103 M8 **Mobile** Arizona U.S.A.
111 J11 **Mobile Pt** Alabama U.S.A.
141 G7 **Moble** *R* Queensland Australia
71 F4 **Mobo** Philippines
28 A4 **Møborg** Denmark
98 F4 **Mobridge** South Dakota U.S.A.
Mobutu, L *see* **Albert, L**
127 J5 **Moca** Dominican Rep
129 J4 **Mocajuba** Brazil
Moçambique *see* **Mozambique**
88 H9 **Moçambique** *dist* Mozambique
Moçâmedes *see* **Namibe**
95 L5 **Mocanaqua** Pennsylvania U.S.A.
103 M5 **Moccasin** Arizona U.S.A.
101 Q2 **Moccasin** Montana U.S.A.
68 G2 **Moc Chau** Vietnam
125 Q7 **Mocche** Mexico
Mocha *see* **Mukha, Al**
131 A7 **Mocha** *isld* Chile
124 E5 **Mochicahui** Mexico
127 K2 **Mocho Mts** Jamaica
89 E5 **Mochudi** Botswana
88 H7 **Mocimboa da Praia** Mozambique
48 H4 **Mociu** Romania
27 G15 **Möckeln** *L* Sweden
33 P8 **Möckern** East Germany
95 M9 **Mockhorn** *isld* Virginia U.S.A.
27 J15 **Möckleby, N** Sweden
27 H15 **Möckleby, S** Sweden
36 G5 **Mockmühl** W Germany
33 R9 **Mockrehna** East Germany
112 G2 **Mocksville** North Carolina U.S.A.
100 A2 **Moclips** Washington U.S.A.
128 C3 **Mocoa** Colombia
130 F7 **Mococa** Brazil
131 F3 **Mocoretá** *R* Argentina
124 F5 **Mocorito** Mexico
124 F2 **Moctezuma** Chihuahua Mexico
124 E3 **Moctezuma** Sonora Mexico
88 F10 **Mocuba** Mozambique
40 E7 **Modane** France
83 K9 **Modaragam Aru** *R* Sri Lanka
74 E7 **Modasa** India
22 J3 **Modave** Belgium
8 C7 **Modbury** England
89 D7 **Modder** *R* S Africa
106 F4 **Model** Colorado U.S.A.
45 J2 **Modena** Italy
45 J3 **Modena** *prov* Italy
103 L4 **Modena** Utah U.S.A.
19 L4 **Moder** *R* France
38 K7 **Moderbrugg** Austria
102 C4 **Modesto** California U.S.A.
43 F12 **Modica** Sicily
45 L3 **Modigliana** Italy
80 C6 **Modi'im** Israel
86 D5 **Modjamboli** Zaire
94 B6 **Modoc** Indiana U.S.A.
107 J3 **Modoc** Kansas U.S.A.
112 E4 **Modoc** South Carolina U.S.A.
100 D7 **Modoc Point** Oregon U.S.A.
36 B2 **Mödrath** W Germany
48 E6 **Modriča** Yugoslavia
48 E2 **Modrý Kameň** Czechoslovakia
68 J5 **Mo Đuc** Vietnam
139 H7 **Moe** Victoria Australia
145 E2 **Moehau** *mt* New Zealand
20 C6 **Moelan** France
8 B1 **Moelfre** Wales
8 C2 **Moel Sych** *mt* Wales
27 E11 **Moelv** Norway
129 H2 **Moengo** Suriname
103 N5 **Moenkopi** Arizona U.S.A.
144 B5 **Moeraki, L** New Zealand
22 F1 **Moerbeke** Belgium
25 C5 **Moerdijk** Netherlands
22 D1 **Moere** Belgium
20 G7 **Moëre,la** France
145 E1 **Moerewa** New Zealand
145 E3 **Moeroa** New Zealand
Moero, Lac *see* **Mweru, L**
13 E3 **Moffat** Scotland
106 E3 **Moffat** Colorado U.S.A.
144 B6 **Moffat Pk** New Zealand
98 F3 **Moffit** North Dakota U.S.A.
48 H3 **Moftin** Romania
74 F3 **Moga** India
Mogadiscio *see* **Muqdisho**
Mogadishu *see* **Muqdisho**
94 F5 **Mogadore** Ohio U.S.A.
16 C3 **Mogadouro** Portugal
89 F4 **Mogalakwena** *R* S Africa
61 N7 **Mogami-gawa** *R* Japan
67 F1 **Mogan Shan** *mt* China
75 R6 **Mogaung** Burma
28 B7 **Møgeltønder** Denmark
17 G6 **Mogente** Spain
36 H6 **Mögglingen** W Germany
60 C13 **Mogi** Japan
129 J8 **Mogi das Cruzes** Brazil
31 M4 **Mogielnica** Poland
130 F7 **Mogi Guaçu** *R* Brazil
54 H9 **Mogila-Bel'mak Gora** *mt* U.S.S.R.
54 B3 **Mogilëv** U.S.S.R.
48 L2 **Mogilev-Podol'skiy** U.S.S.R.
139 J3 **Mogil-Mogil** New South Wales Australia
31 K3 **Mogilno** Poland
130 F8 **Mogi Mirim** Brazil
88 H9 **Mogincual** Mozambique
45 J2 **Móglia** Italy
45 M1 **Mogliano Veneto** Italy
42 E3 **Mogliano Veneto** Italy
46 D4 **Moglicë** Albania
19 N12 **Mogneneins** France
59 G1 **Mogocha** U.S.S.R.
68 C1 **Mogok** Burma
89 E4 **Mogol** *R* S Africa
106 B8 **Mogollon** New Mexico U.S.A.
106 B8 **Mogollon Mts** New Mexico U.S.A.
103 O7 **Mogollon Rim** *tableland* Arizona U.S.A.
106 D4 **Mogote** Colorado U.S.A.
58 C2 **Mogoyn** Mongolia
56 F5 **Mogoyty** U.S.S.R.
16 C7 **Moguer** Spain
143 B9 **Mogumber** Western Australia Australia
48 E5 **Mohács** Hungary
145 F3 **Mohaka** New Zealand
98 E1 **Mohall** North Dakota U.S.A.
17 H9 **Mohammadia** Algeria
85 C2 **Mohammedia** Morocco
103 K6 **Mohave, L** Nev/Ariz U.S.A.
103 K7 **Mohave Mts** Cal/Ariz U.S.A.
103 L9 **Mohawk** Arizona U.S.A.
99 S2 **Mohawk** Michigan U.S.A.
95 N4 **Mohawk** *R* New York U.S.A.
103 L9 **Mohawk Mts** Arizona U.S.A.
59 H1 **Mohe** China
27 G14 **Moheda** Sweden
87 G10 **Mohéli** *isld* Comoros
87 D9 **Mohembo** Botswana
74 C5 **Mohenjo Daro** *anc site* Pakistan
14 B4 **Moher, Cliffs of** Ireland
116 D6 **Mohican, C** Alaska U.S.A.
14 D3 **Mohill** Ireland
100 J3 **Mohler** Idaho U.S.A.
32 H10 **Möhne** *R* W Germany
32 H10 **Möhnesee** W Germany
32 H10 **Möhnestausee** *L* W Germany
27 G13 **Moholm** Sweden
20 E5 **Mohon** France
103 L7 **Mohon Pk** Arizona U.S.A.
88 G6 **Mohoro** Tanzania
124 H4 **Mohovano Ranch** Mexico
37 J2 **Möhra** East Germany
36 G6 **Möhringen** W Germany
28 D7 **Mohrkirch** W Germany
27 B13 **Moi** Norway
16 B4 **Moimenta da Beira** Portugal
66 C5 **Moincêr** China
21 H7 **Moine** *R* France
95 N2 **Moira** New York U.S.A.
26 G5 **Mo i Rana** Norway
19 P14 **Moirans** France
46 G9 **Moires** Crete Greece
52 C5 **Mõisaküla** U.S.S.R.
20 H6 **Moisdon** France
55 G2 **Moiseyevka** U.S.S.R.
122 F3 **Moisie** Quebec Canada
19 Q17 **Moissac** France
86 C4 **Moissala** Chad
21 O3 **Moisson** France
21 N6 **Moisy** France
27 K12 **Möja** Sweden
17 F7 **Mojácar** Spain
102 F6 **Mojave** California U.S.A.
102 G7 **Mojave** *R* California U.S.A.
102 G6 **Mojave Desert** California U.S.A.
60 E12 **Moji** Japan
130 F8 **Moji das Cruzes** Brazil
120 B2 **Mojikit L** Ontario Canada
86 G4 **Mojo** Ethiopia
71 H9 **Mojo** *isld* Indonesia
86 F5 **Mojo** Uganda
70 O9 **Mojokerto** Java
128 E7 **Mojos, Llanos de** *plain* Bolivia
129 J4 **Moju** *R* Brazil
61 O9 **Mōka** Japan
145 E3 **Mokai** New Zealand
75 L6 **Mokāma** India
110 E3 **Mokane** Missouri U.S.A.
102 S12 **Mokapu Pen** Hawaiian Is
145 E3 **Mokau** New Zealand
102 D3 **Mokelumne** *R* California U.S.A.
89 F7 **Mokhotlong** *mt* Lesotho
55 F3 **Mokhovoy Prival** U.S.S.R.
27 J11 **Möklinta** Sweden
85 G1 **Moknine** Tunisia
145 E1 **Mokohinau Is** New Zealand
145 E3 **Mokoia** New Zealand
75 Q5 **Mokokchung** India
86 B3 **Mokolo** Cameroon
144 B7 **Mokoreta** New Zealand
144 B7 **Mokotua** New Zealand
65 G7 **Mokp'o** S Korea
46 D2 **Mokra Gora** *mt* Yugoslavia
48 F5 **Mokrin** Yugoslavia
55 E3 **Mokrousovo** U.S.S.R.
29 L8 **Möksy** Finland
102 S11 **Mokuauia I** Hawaiian Is
135 U5 **Mokuaweoweo Crater** Hawaiian Is
102 R11 **Mokuleia** Hawaiian Is
102 S12 **Mokulua Is** Hawaiian Is
22 J1 **Mol** Belgium
20 F6 **Molac** France
100 C4 **Molalla** Oregon U.S.A.
125 K7 **Molango** Mexico
46 F8 **Moláoi** Greece
42 F4 **Molat** *isld* Yugoslavia
70 G6 **Molawe** Sulawesi
21 J3 **Molay-Littry, le** France
32 G7 **Molbergen** W Germany
28 B5 **Mølby** Denmark
8 C1 **Mold** Wales
48 G2 **Moldava nad Bodvon** Czech
Moldavia *see* **Moldavskaya** *S.S.R.*
53 C10 **Moldavskaya** *SSR rep* U.S.S.R
26 B9 **Molde** Norway
48 K3 **Moldova** *R* Romania
48 J5 **Moldoveanu** *mt* Romania
48 K3 **Moldoviṭa** Romania
28 D3 **Møldrup** Denmark
40 D5 **Môle** *mt* France
20 A5 **Molène** *isld* France
89 D5 **Molepolole** Botswana
8 C6 **Mole, R** England
9 F5 **Mole, R** England
144 D5 **Molesworth** New Zealand
43 H7 **Molfetta** Italy
133 C5 **Molina** Chile
17 F4 **Molina de Aragón** Spain
17 G6 **Molina de Segura** Spain
99 Q8 **Moline** Illinois U.S.A.
107 O4 **Moline** Kansas U.S.A.
94 B4 **Moline** Michigan U.S.A.
45 L2 **Molinella** Italy
38 E8 **Molini** Italy
124 D3 **Molino** Mexico
111 J11 **Molino** Florida U.S.A.
42 F7 **Molise** *prov* Italy
40 D2 **Mollans** France
29 K4 **Mölle** Sweden
28 C5 **Møllebjerg** *hill* Denmark
33 S6 **Möllenbeck** East Germany
128 D7 **Mollendo** Peru
33 R5 **Möllenhagen** East Germany
143 C9 **Mollerin L** Western Australia
28 D4 **Mollerup** Denmark
17 H3 **Mollerusa** Spain
26 O2 **Mollesjok** Norway
21 P2 **Molliens-Dreuil** France
12 D2 **Mollinsburn** Scotland
26 M2 **Mollius** *mt* Norway
33 S5 **Mölln** East Germany
33 N5 **Mölln** W Germany
38 G8 **Molltal** *V* Austria
27 F14 **Mölndal** Sweden
54 G9 **Molochansk** U.S.S.R.
53 E10 **Molochnyy, Liman** U.S.S.R.
88 G10 **Molocue** *R* Mozambique
146 K9 **Molodezhnaya** *U.S.S.R. Base* Antarctica
54 D8 **Molodezhnoye** U.S.S.R.
55 F5 **Molodezhnyy** U.S.S.R.
56 B2 **Molodezhnyy** U.S.S.R.
55 F4 **Molodogvardeyskoye** U.S.S.R.
52 D6 **Molodoy-Tud** U.S.S.R.
52 E5 **Mologa** *R* U.S.S.R.
102 V13 **Molokai** *isld* Hawaiian Is
135 S3 **Molokini** *isld* Hawaiian Is
52 E5 **Molokovo** U.S.S.R.
52 G5 **Moloma** *R* U.S.S.R.
139 J5 **Molong** New South Wales Australia
89 B6 **Molopo** *R* S Africa
46 F6 **Mólos** Greece
86 C5 **Moloundou** Cameroon
28 F4 **Mols B** *hill* Denmark
89 F5 **Molsgat** S Africa
36 D6 **Molsheim** France
118 E1 **Molson** Manitoba Canada
119 V4 **Molson L** Manitoba Canada
101 R4 **Molt** Montana U.S.A.
87 E12 **Molteno** S Africa
Moluccas *see* **Malaku** *islds*
88 G10 **Moma** Mozambique
51 O2 **Moma** *R* U.S.S.R.
86 D6 **Moma** Zaire
139 G4 **Momba** New South Wales Australia
88 D6 **Momba** *R* Tanzania
45 N4 **Mombaroccio** Italy
88 G4 **Mombasa** Kenya
60 Q3 **Mombetsu** Japan
60 R1 **Mombetsu** Japan
130 D6 **Mombuca, Serra da** *mts* Brazil
46 G3 **Momchilgrad** Bulgaria
99 T8 **Momence** Illinois U.S.A.
22 G3 **Momignies** Belgium
36 D6 **Mommenheim** France
70 G5 **Momo** Sulawesi
71 F4 **Mompog Passage** Philippines
86 D5 **Mompono** Zaire
126 G10 **Mompós** Colombia
Môn *isld see* **Anglesey**
68 C3 **Mon** Burma
68 B2 **Mon** *R* Burma
29 K7 **Møn** *isld* Denmark
127 L2 **Mona** Jamaica
103 N2 **Mona** Utah U.S.A.
94 G6 **Monaca** Pennsylvania U.S.A.
15 A3 **Monach I** Outer Hebrides Scotland
44 B4 **Monaco** *princ* W Europe
15 D3 **Monadhliath Mts** Scotland
29 J8 **Monå Fjärd** *inlet* Finland
128 F2 **Monagas** *state* Venezuela
14 E2 **Monaghan** *co* Ireland
14 E2 **Monaghan** Ireland
108 E4 **Monahans** Texas U.S.A.
127 L5 **Mona, I** Puerto Rico
98 H3 **Monango** North Dakota U.S.A.
87 C7 **Mona Quimbundo** Angola
118 D9 **Monarch** Alberta Canada
106 D3 **Monarch** Colorado U.S.A.
101 P2 **Monarch** Montana U.S.A.
117 L10 **Monarch Mt** British Columbia Canada
103 N2 **Mona Res** Utah U.S.A.
117 O10 **Monashee Mts** British Columbia Canada
14 D3 **Monasterevin** Ireland
18 H8 **Monastier, le** France
43 D13 **Monastir** Tunisia
48 J1 **Monastyriska** U.S.S.R.
55 D2 **Monastyrskoye** U.S.S.R.
44 C2 **Moncalieri** Italy
16 B2 **Monção** Portugal
17 F3 **Moncayo, Sierra del** Spain
22 F4 **Monceau-le-Neuf** France
38 L5 **Mönchdorf** Austria
52 D1 **Monchegorsk** U.S.S.R.
36 B1 **Mönchengladbach** W Germany
30 H1 **Mönchgut** *pen* East Germany
16 B7 **Monchique** Portugal
101 R1 **Monchy** Saskatchewan Canada
112 G4 **Moncks Corner** South Carolina U.S.A.
124 J4 **Monclova** Mexico
20 E5 **Moncontour** Côtes-du-Nord France
21 K8 **Moncontour** Vienne France
122 A5 **Moncouche, L** Quebec Canada
21 J8 **Moncoutant** France
122 H7 **Moncton** New Brunswick Canada
130 D10 **Mondai** Brazil
99 L8 **Mondamin** Iowa U.S.A.
45 N4 **Mondavio** Italy
130 C9 **Monday, R** Paraguay
16 B4 **Mondego** *R* Portugal
16 B4 **Mondego, C** Portugal
16 E4 **Mondéjar** Spain
21 K3 **Mondeville** France
89 G3 **Mondi** *R* Zimbabwe
89 G6 **Mondlo** S Africa
86 C3 **Mondo** Chad
45 O4 **Mondolfo** Italy
16 C1 **Mondoñedo** Spain
22 L4 **Mondorf-les-Bains** Luxembourg
21 M6 **Mondoubleau** France
44 C3 **Mondovi** Italy
99 P5 **Mondovi** Wisconsin U.S.A.
19 N16 **Mondragon** France
45 P7 **Mondragone** Italy
143 E10 **Mondrain I** Western Australia Australia
41 P3 **Mondschein Spitze** *mt* Austria
38 H6 **Mondsee** Austria
127 K2 **Moneague** Jamaica
44 F3 **Moneglia** Italy
18 E9 **Monein** France
46 F8 **Monemvasia** Greece
94 H9 **Moneta** Virginia U.S.A.
101 S6 **Moneta** Wyoming U.S.A.
110 C5 **Monett** Missouri U.S.A.
110 F6 **Monette** Arkansas U.S.A.
42 F3 **Monfalcone** Italy
68 D3 **Mon Fang** Thailand
44 C2 **Monferrato** *dist* Italy
86 D5 **Monga** Zaire
95 N5 **Mongaup Vall** New York U.S.A.
68 H2 **Mong Cai** Vietnam
142 A1 **Monger L** Perth, W Aust Australia
143 B8 **Monger, L** Western Australia Australia
68 D2 **Mong Hai** Burma
68 D2 **Mong Hang** Burma
45 K3 **Monghidoro** Italy
68 E2 **Mong Hkan** Burma
68 D2 **Mong Hkok** Burma
68 D2 **Mong Hpayak** Burma
68 D2 **Mong Hsat** Burma
68 C2 **Mong Hsawk** Burma
68 D2 **Mong Hsu** Burma
44 C3 **Mongioie** *mt* Italy
68 F6 **Mongkol Borey** Cambodia
68 D3 **Mong Kyawt** Burma
68 D2 **Mong La** Burma
68 E2 **Mong Lin** Burma
68 E2 **Mong Loi** Burma
68 C2 **Mong Long** Burma
68 C1 **Mong Long** Burma
68 C3 **Mong Mau** Burma
68 C2 **Mong Nai** Burma
68 D2 **Mong Nawng** Burma
17 H6 **Mongo** *mt* Spain
94 B5 **Mongo** Indiana U.S.A.
58 C2 **Mongolia** *rep* Asia
Mongolküre *see* **Zhaosu**
85 G8 **Mongomo** Mbini Equat Guinea
142 F3 **Mongona,Mt** Western Australia Australia
86 B3 **Mongonu** Nigeria
68 C3 **Mong Pai** Burma
68 D2 **Mong Pan** Burma
68 D1 **Mong Pat** Burma
68 D1 **Mong Pawk** Burma
68 C2 **Mong Pawn** Burma
68 D2 **Mong Ping** Burma
68 D2 **Mong Pu** Burma
68 D2 **Mong Pu-awn** Burma
124 H9 **Mongrove, Pta** *C* Mexico
68 D2 **Mong Ton** Burma
68 D2 **Mong Tum** Burma
68 C1 **Mong Tung** Burma
87 D9 **Mongu** Zambia
38 F8 **Monguelfo** Italy
68 E2 **Mong Un** Burma
68 D1 **Mong Yai** Burma
68 D2 **Mong Yang** Burma
68 D2 **Mong Yawn** Burma
68 E2 **Mong Yawng** Burma
95 S3 **Monhegan I** Maine U.S.A.
37 K6 **Monheim** Bayern W Germany
36 B1 **Monheim** Nordrhein-Westfalen W Germany
113 E7 **Moniac** Georgia U.S.A.
12 E3 **Moniaive** Scotland
19 O16 **Monieux** France
13 F1 **Monifieth** Scotland
18 H7 **Monistrol-sur-Loire** France
118 G7 **Monitor** Alberta Canada
102 H3 **Monitor** *pk* Nevada U.S.A.
14 C3 **Monivea** Ireland
28 B7 **Mönkebüll** W Germany
140 F6 **Monkira** Queensland Australia
86 D6 **Monkoto** Zaire
120 J9 **Monkton** Ontario Canada
12 D3 **Monkton** Scotland
Monmouth *co see* **Gwent**
99 Q9 **Monmouth** Illinois U.S.A.
95 R2 **Monmouth** Maine U.S.A.
8 D4 **Monmouth** Wales
117 M10 **Monmouth, Mt** British Columbia Canada
21 L4 **Monnai** France
21 M7 **Monnaie** France
25 D3 **Monnickendam** Netherlands
85 E7 **Mono** *R* Togo
102 F3 **Mono L** California U.S.A.
47 U17 **Monólithos** Rhodes Greece
95 S5 **Monomoy Pt** Massachusetts U.S.A.
99 U9 **Monon** Indiana U.S.A.
99 P6 **Monona** Iowa U.S.A.
94 G7 **Monongah** West Virginia U.S.A.
94 H6 **Monongahela** Pennsylvania U.S.A.
43 H8 **Monopoli** Italy
48 E3 **Monor** Hungary
127 N1 **Monos I** Trinidad
86 D2 **Monou** Chad
17 G6 **Monóvar** Spain
144 A6 **Monowai** New Zealand
98 H7 **Monowi** Nebraska U.S.A.
18 F8 **Monpont** France
36 C3 **Monreal** W Germany
17 G4 **Monreal del Campo** Spain
43 E10 **Monreale** Sicily
102 A2 **Monroe** California U.S.A.
112 D4 **Monroe** Georgia U.S.A.
94 C6 **Monroe** Indiana U.S.A.
99 N8 **Monroe** Iowa U.S.A.
111 D9 **Monroe** Louisiana U.S.A.
94 D5 **Monroe** Michigan U.S.A.
95 N5 **Monroe** New York U.S.A.
112 G3 **Monroe** North Carolina U.S.A.
100 B5 **Monroe** Oregon U.S.A.
95 L5 **Monroe** Pennsylvania U.S.A.
98 J6 **Monroe** South Dakota U.S.A.
103 M3 **Monroe** Utah U.S.A.
94 H9 **Monroe** Virginia U.S.A.
100 D2 **Monroe** Washington U.S.A.
99 R7 **Monroe** Wisconsin U.S.A.
99 P10 **Monroe City** Missouri U.S.A.
113 F9 **Monroe, L** Florida U.S.A.
110 K2 **Monroe L** Indiana U.S.A.
111 J10 **Monroeville** Alabama U.S.A.
94 C6 **Monroeville** Indiana U.S.A.
94 E5 **Monroeville** Ohio U.S.A.
85 B7 **Monrovia** Liberia
102 G7 **Monrovia** California U.S.A.
17 G4 **Monroyo** Spain
22 F3 **Mons** Belgium
16 C4 **Monsanto** Portugal
130 H6 **Monsarás, Pta. de** Brazil
22 L2 **Monschau** W Germany
71 H7 **Monse** Indonesia
42 D3 **Monselice** Italy
36 E4 **Monsheim** W Germany
29 K7 **Møns Klint** *cliffs* Denmark
95 P4 **Monson** Massachusetts U.S.A.
68 C3 **Mon State** Burma
28 C4 **Mønsted** Denmark
25 B4 **Monster** Netherlands
27 H14 **Mönsterås** Sweden
45 J4 **Monsummano Terme** Italy
22 K3 **Mont** Belgium
36 D3 **Montabaur** W Germany
41 L3 **Montafon** *V* Austria
45 K1 **Montagnana** Italy
89 B9 **Montagu** S Africa
122 K7 **Montague** Prince Edward I Canada
100 C8 **Montague** California U.S.A.
94 A3 **Montague** Michigan U.S.A.
109 K2 **Montague** Texas U.S.A.
139 K6 **Montague I** New South Wales Australia
103 K10 **Montague, I** Mexico
116 O6 **Montague I** Alaska U.S.A.
143 C7 **Montague Ra** Western Australia Australia
142 F2 **Montague Sd** Western Australia Australia
116 N7 **Montague Str** Alaska U.S.A.
146 G3 **Montagu I** S Sandwich Is S Atlantic Oc
20 H8 **Montaigu** France
18 F8 **Montaigu-de-Quercy** France
40 D7 **Montaimont** France
45 J4 **Montaione** Italy
70 D5 **Montalat** *R* Kalimantan
17 G4 **Montalbán** Spain
127 K9 **Montalbán** Venezuela
45 K4 **Montale** Italy
16 B3 **Montalegre** Portugal
40 B6 **Montalieu** France
19 O13 **Montalieu Vercieu** France
43 G10 **Montalto** *mt* Italy
21 L8 **Montamise** France
101 P3 **Montana** *state* U.S.A.
116 N5 **Montana** Alaska U.S.A.
40 G7 **Montanaro** Italy
16 C5 **Montánchez** Spain
121 T5 **Mont-Apica** Quebec Canada
18 G5 **Montargis** France
21 P3 **Montataire** France
18 F9 **Montauban** France
20 F5 **Montauban-de-Bretagne** France
21 J5 **Montaudin** France
18 H5 **Montbard** France
40 C3 **Montbarrey** France
21 M7 **Montbazon** France
40 E2 **Montbéliard** France
109 N6 **Mont Belvieu** Texas U.S.A.
40 D4 **Montbenoit** France
20 H7 **Montbert** France
40 E6 **Mont Blanc** *mt* France
17 H3 **Montblanch** Spain
40 D3 **Montbozon** France
21 H4 **Montbray** France
18 H7 **Montbrison** France
Montcalm, L *see* **Dogai Coring**
18 F10 **Montcalm, Pic** *mt* France
21 J4 **Montchamp** France
22 G4 **Montcornet** France
18 E9 **Mont de Marsan** France
22 D4 **Montdidier** France
43 G9 **Montea** *mt* Italy
110 L6 **Monteagle** Tennessee U.S.A.
129 H4 **Monte Alegre** Brazil
17 G6 **Montealegre del Castillo** Spain
130 E6 **Monte Alegre de Minas** Brazil
130 G4 **Monte Azul** Brazil
121 Q7 **Montebello** Quebec Canada
142 B5 **Monte Bello Is** Western Australia Australia
45 K1 **Montebello Vic** Italy
42 E3 **Montebelluna** Italy
20 H3 **Montebourg** France
45 N4 **Montecalvo in Foglia** Italy
45 S7 **Montecalvo Irpino** Italy
133 G3 **Montecarlo** Argentina
44 B4 **Monte-Carlo** Monaco
129 J7 **Monte Carmelo** Brazil
45 O4 **Montecarotto** Italy
131 F3 **Monte Caseros** Argentina
45 J4 **Montecatini Terme** Italy
45 J2 **Montécchio Emilia** Italy
45 K1 **Montecchio Maggiore** Italy
45 H2 **Montecchio nell'Emilia** Italy
45 N5 **Montecélio** Italy
18 F9 **Montech** France
112 H3 **Monte Clare** South Carolina U.S.A.
45 R8 **Montecorvino Rovella** Italy
45 J3 **Montecreto** Italy
127 J5 **Montecristi** Dominican Rep
128 F6 **Monte Cristo** Bolivia
42 C6 **Montecristo, I.di** Italy
41 O4 **Montecroce, Pta di** *mt* Italy
124 H6 **Monte Escobedo** Mexico
45 M4 **Montefeltro** Italy
45 J3 **Montefiorino** Italy
45 R8 **Monteforte Irpina** Italy
16 E7 **Montefrio** Spain
127 J1 **Montego Bay** Jamaica
45 M4 **Monte Grimano** Italy
130 H9 **Monteiro** Brazil
140 B3 **Montejinnie** N Terr Australia
45 O6 **Montelanico** Italy
131 E6 **Monte, L.del** Argentina
19 N15 **Montélimar** France
129 G8 **Monte Lindo** Paraguay
108 G6 **Montell** Texas U.S.A.
45 S8 **Montella** Italy
16 D8 **Montellanto** Spain
101 L8 **Montello** Nevada U.S.A.
99 R6 **Montello** Wisconsin U.S.A.
45 K4 **Montelupo Fiorentino** Italy
45 R8 **Montemárano** Italy
45 O4 **Montemarciano** Italy
133 D6 **Montemayor, Meseta de** *hills* Argentina
45 L4 **Montemignaio** Italy
45 R7 **Montemiletto** Italy
125 K5 **Montemorelos** Mexico
45 K4 **Montemurio** Italy
21 J5 **Montenay** France
18 E7 **Montendre** France
46 C2 **Montenegro** *hist reg* Yugoslavia
20 F6 **Monteneuf** France
42 D6 **Montepescali** Italy
127 K5 **Monte Plata** Dominican Rep
45 O4 **Monteporzio** Italy
88 G8 **Montepuez** Mozambique
42 D5 **Montepulciano** Italy
18 G4 **Montereau** France
45 K3 **Monterenzio** Italy
102 C5 **Monterey** California U.S.A.
99 U8 **Monterey** Indiana U.S.A.
110 L5 **Monterey** Tennessee U.S.A.
94 H8 **Monterey** Virginia U.S.A.
102 B5 **Monterey B** California U.S.A.
126 G10 **Montería** Colombia
128 F7 **Montero** Bolivia
21 N2 **Montérolier** France
45 M5 **Monterosi** Italy
44 M5 **Monterosi, L** Italy
45 N5 **Monterotondo** Italy
125 J5 **Monterrey** Mexico
42 G7 **Monte S. Angelo** Italy
100 B3 **Montesano** Washington U.S.A.
130 G11 **Monte Santo** Brazil
130 F7 **Monte Santo de Minas** Brazil
45 R7 **Montesarchio** Italy
45 O7 **Monte S. Biágio** Italy
129 K7 **Montes Claros** Brazil
45 J3 **Montese** Italy
45 O4 **Montesicuro** Italy
45 K4 **Montespértoli** Italy
18 F9 **Montesquieu-Volvestre** France
18 H6 **Montet, le** France
19 N16 **Monteux** France
111 K8 **Montevallo** Alabama U.S.A.
42 D5 **Montevarchi** Italy
45 K3 **Monteveglio** Italy
45 O5 **Monte Velino** Italy
131 G5 **Montevideo** Uruguay
99 L5 **Montevideo** Minnesota U.S.A.
101 N6 **Monteview** Idaho U.S.A.
106 D4 **Monte Vista** Colorado U.S.A.
103 L8 **Montezuma** Arizona U.S.A.
112 C5 **Montezuma** Georgia U.S.A.
99 T10 **Montezuma** Indiana U.S.A.
99 O8 **Montezuma** Iowa U.S.A.
107 K4 **Montezuma** Kansas U.S.A.
106 E6 **Montezuma** New Mexico U.S.A.
103 N7 **Montezuma Castle Nat.Mon** Arizona U.S.A.
102 G4 **Montezuma Pk** Nevada U.S.A.
20 H2 **Montfarville** France
21 H7 **Montfaucon** Maine-et-Loire France
22 J5 **Montfaucon** Meuse France
19 P14 **Montferrat** France
21 O4 **Montfort-l'Amaury** France
21 L5 **Montfort-le-Rotrou** France
20 G5 **Montfort-sur-Meu** France
21 M3 **Montfort-sur-Risle** France
19 N17 **Montfrin** France
Montgomery *co see* **Powys**
111 K9 **Montgomery** Alabama U.S.A.
111 D10 **Montgomery** Louisiana U.S.A.
94 C5 **Montgomery** Michigan U.S.A.
99 N5 **Montgomery** Minnesota U.S.A.
109 M5 **Montgomery** Texas U.S.A.
94 F8 **Montgomery** West Virginia U.S.A.
8 C2 **Montgomery** Wales
110 E3 **Montgomery City** Missouri U.S.A.
100 D9 **Montgomery Creek** California U.S.A.
142 E3 **Montgomery I** Western Australia Australia
18 E7 **Montguyon** France
22 H4 **Monthermé** France
40 E5 **Monthey** Switzerland
22 H5 **Monthois** France
40 C1 **Monthureux-sur-Saône** France
43 C8 **Monti** Sardinia
111 E8 **Monticello** Arkansas U.S.A.
113 D7 **Monticello** Florida U.S.A.
112 D4 **Monticello** Georgia U.S.A.
110 H1 **Monticello** Illinois U.S.A.
110 K1 **Monticello** Indiana U.S.A.
99 P7 **Monticello** Iowa U.S.A.
110 M5 **Monticello** Kentucky U.S.A.
95 T7 **Monticello** Maine U.S.A.
99 N4 **Monticello** Minnesota U.S.A.
111 F10 **Monticello** Mississippi U.S.A.
110 E1 **Monticello** Missouri U.S.A.
106 C8 **Monticello** New Mexico U.S.A.
95 N5 **Monticello** New York U.S.A.
103 P4 **Monticello** Utah U.S.A.
99 R7 **Monticello** Wisconsin U.S.A.
45 J1 **Montichiari** Italy
43 C8 **Monti del Gennargentu** Sardinia
131 F3 **Montiel, Cuchilla de** *mts* Argentina
21 O8 **Montierchaume** France
19 J4 **Montier en Der** France
22 D5 **Montiers** France
18 F7 **Montignac** France
18 F7 **Montignac-Charente** France
21 H4 **Montigny** Manche France
36 B6 **Montigny** Meurthe-et-Moselle France
40 B2 **Montigny-le-Roi** France
16 B6 **Montijo** Portugal
16 C6 **Montijo** Spain
125 O6 **Montijo, G.de** Panama
16 D7 **Montilla** Spain
21 O8 **Montipouret** France
45 N5 **Monti Sabini** Italy
130 D5 **Montividiu** Brazil
21 L2 **Montivilliers** France
21 J7 **Montjean** Maine-et-Loire France
21 J5 **Montjean** Mayenne France
21 H4 **Montjoie** France
122 D5 **Mont-Joli** Quebec Canada
138 F2 **Montkeleary** *R* South Australia Australia
21 N5 **Montlandon** France
121 P6 **Mont-Laurier** Quebec Canada
40 E3 **Montlebon** France
21 P4 **Montlhéry** France
18 E7 **Montlieu** France
122 G4 **Mont Louis** Quebec Canada
18 G10 **Mont Louis** France
18 G6 **Montluçon** France
19 O13 **Montluel** France
122 B7 **Montmagny** Quebec Canada
20 G4 **Montmartin-sur-Mer** France
119 O8 **Montmartre** Saskatchewan Canada
22 J4 **Montmédy** France
19 Q14 **Montmélian** France
40 A5 **Montmerle** France
19 Q17 **Montmeyan** France
19 N15 **Montmeyran** France
18 H4 **Montmirail** Marne France
21 M5 **Montmirail** Sarthe France
18 F7 **Montmoreau St Cybard** France
21 P4 **Montmorency** France
122 A6 **Montmorency, R** Quebec Canada
18 F6 **Montmorillon** France
19 P16 **Montmorin** France
141 K6 **Monto** Queensland Australia
20 F7 **Montoir-de-Bretagne** France
21 M6 **Montoire-sur-le-Loir** France
45 M3 **Montone** *R* Italy
16 E6 **Montoro** Spain
99 O8 **Montour** Iowa U.S.A.
95 L4 **Montour Falls** New York U.S.A.
21 J8 **Montournais** France
95 L5 **Montoursville** Pennsylvania U.S.A.
106 F6 **Montoya** New Mexico U.S.A.
127 J2 **Montpelier** Jamaica
101 O7 **Montpelier** Idaho U.S.A.
110 L1 **Montpelier** Indiana U.S.A.
98 H3 **Montpelier** North Dakota U.S.A.
94 C5 **Montpelier** Ohio U.S.A.
95 P2 **Montpelier** Vermont U.S.A.
121 P7 **Montpellier** Quebec Canada
18 H9 **Montpellier** France
40 B4 **Montpont** France
120 K5 **Montreal** *R* Ontario Canada
121 R7 **Montréal** Quebec Canada
18 G9 **Montréal** France
99 Q3 **Montreal** Wisconsin U.S.A.
120 F5 **Montreal I** Ontario Canada
119 M4 **Montreal Lake** Saskatchewan Canada
119 M4 **Montreal R** Saskatchewan Canada
120 F5 **Montreal River** Ontario Canada
18 G9 **Montredon Labessonié** France
18 F9 **Montrejeau** France
21 N7 **Montrésor** France
22 B3 **Montreuil** France
21 K7 **Montreuil Bellay** France
21 K5 **Montreuil-le-Chetif** France
20 G5 **Montreuil-sur-Ille** France
40 E5 **Montreux** Switzerland
21 H7 **Montrevault** France
21 N7 **Montrichard** France
19 P18 **Montrieux le Vieux** France
6 L5 **Montrose** *oil rig* North Sea
15 F4 **Montrose** Scotland
111 E8 **Montrose** Arkansas U.S.A.
106 C3 **Montrose** Colorado U.S.A.
110 H2 **Montrose** Illinois U.S.A.
99 P9 **Montrose** Iowa U.S.A.
98 C7 **Montrose** Nebraska U.S.A.
95 L5 **Montrose** Pennsylvania U.S.A.
98 J6 **Montrose** South Dakota U.S.A.
95 L8 **Montross** Virginia U.S.A.
22 G3 **Mont. St.Christophe** Belgium
22 H2 **Mont.St.Guibert** Belgium
22 G2 **Mont-St.Jean** Belgium
22 K4 **Mont St.Martin** France
20 G4 **Mont-St. Michel, B. du** France
20 G4 **Mont-St.Michel, le** France
21 J4 **Montsecret** France
17 H2 **Montseny** *mt* Spain
17 J3 **Montseny, Sierra de** *mts* Spain
127 N6 **Montserrat** *isld* Lesser Antilles
17 J3 **Montserrat** *dist* Spain
129 H3 **Montsinery** Fr Guiana
21 L7 **Montsoreau** France

69 D13 Muarasigep Indonesia
69 D12 Muarasipongi Sumatra
69 D12 Muarasoma Sumatra
70 F4 Muaras Rf Indonesia
69 F13 Muaratebo Sumatra
69 F13 Muaratembesi Sumatra
70 D5 Muarateweh Kalimantan
70 E4 Muarawahau Kalimantan
71 A3 Muari Halmahera Indonesia
57 D5 Mubarek U.S.S.R.
77 A7 Mubarraz,Al Saudi Arabia
38 C1 Mubende Uganda
80 G5 Mubis Jordan
79 F8 Mubrak, J mt Jordan
69 H11 Mubur isld Indonesia
142 C5 Muccan Western Australia Australia
36 C2 Much W Germany
117 K11 Muchalat British Columbia Canada
15 F3 Muchalls Scotland
143 B9 Muchea Western Australia Australia
33 P10 Mücheln East Germany
88 C8 Muchinga Escarpment Zambia
52 G3 Muchkas U.S.S.R.
67 A2 Muchuan China
8 D2 Much Wenlock England
15 B4 Muck isld Inner Hebrides Scotland
141 J7 Muckadilla Queensland Australia
14 D1 Muckish Mt Ireland
15 G1 Muckle Flugga isld Shetland Scotland
15 G2 Muckle Roe isld Shetland Scotland
9 E2 Muckley Corner England
14 C2 Muckros Hd Ireland
88 H8 Mucojo Mozambique
87 D8 Muconda Angola
130 H6 Mucuri Brazil
130 H5 Mucuri,R Brazil
87 D9 Mucusso Angola
69 E10 Muda R Malaysia
80 G7 Mudaiyina Jordan
65 H2 Mudanjiang China
65 H2 Mudan Jiang R China
47 K4 Mudanya Turkey
47 N10 Mudarlı Turkey
36 G4 Mudau W Germany
98 D4 Mud Butte South Dakota U.S.A.
98 G8 Mud Cr Nebraska U.S.A.
76 C2 Muddebinal India
26 L5 Muddus Nat. Park Sweden
107 O7 Muddy Boggy Cr Oklahoma U.S.A.
103 N3 Muddy Cr Utah U.S.A.
101 S8 Muddy Cr Wyoming U.S.A.
101 P8 Muddy Cr Wyoming U.S.A.
101 T7 Muddy Cr Wyoming U.S.A.
101 S7 Muddy Gap pass Wyoming U.S.A.
118 H6 Muddy L Saskatchewan Canada
103 K5 Muddy Pk Nevada U.S.A.
33 M7 Müden W Germany
139 J4 Mudgee New South Wales Australia
141 H6 Mudge, Mt Queensland Australia
76 B2 Mudhol India
74 G9 Mudhol Andhra Pradesh India
101 N6 Mud L Idaho U.S.A.
101 Q1 Mud L Montana U.S.A.
102 G4 Mud L Nevada U.S.A.
98 H4 Mud L.Res South Dakota U.S.A.
68 C4 Mudon Burma
47 L4 Mudurnu R Turkey
52 E3 Mud'yuga U.S.S.R.
88 D10 Mudzi R Zimbabwe
21 K3 Mue R France
88 G7 Mueda Mozambique
20 F5 Muel France
17 G4 Muela de Ares mt Spain
17 G3 Muela,Sierra de la Spain
142 G4 Mueller, Mt Western Australia Australia
142 F4 Mueller Ra Western Australia Australia
141 F6 Muellers Ra Queensland Australia
119 N5 Muenster Saskatchewan Canada
109 K2 Muenster Texas U.S.A.
125 N2 Muerto,Cayo isld Nicaragua
126 D2 Muertos Cays reefs Bahamas
52 G3 Muftyuga U.S.S.R.
88 B8 Mufulira Zambia
67 E2 Mufu Shan mts Jiangxi/Hubei China
67 B5 Mugang China
16 B5 Muge Portugal
87 G9 Mugeba Mozambique
45 K4 Mugello Italy
33 S10 Mügeln East Germany
37 L4 Muggendorf W Germany
79 H9 Mughayrā', Al Saudi Arabia
59 K5 Mugi Japan
16 A1 Mugia Spain
88 B5 Mugila mts Zaire
47 J7 Muğla Turkey
47 H2 Müglizh Bulgaria
57 A1 Mugodzhary mts U.S.S.R.
18 E9 Mugron France
75 K4 Mugu Nepal
86 G1 Muhammad Qol Sudan
77 B6 Muharraq,Al Bahrain
36 F6 Mühlacker W Germany
36 H2 Mühlbach W Germany
33 S10 Mühlberg Cottbus East Germany
37 K2 Mühlberg Erfurt East Germany
38 G5 Mühldorf W Germany
41 K3 Mühlehorn Switzerland
33 S7 Mühlenbeck East Germany
33 O5 Mühlen Eichsen East Germany
37 J1 Mühlhausen East Germany
37 K4 Mühlhausen W Germany
36 C4 Mühlheim W Germany
146 H6 Mühlig-Hofmannfjella mts Antarctica
37 M2 Mühltroff East Germany
29 M7 Muhos Finland
38 H7 Muhr Austria
80 D3 Muhraqa Israel
36 F7 Mühringen W Germany
52 B5 Muhu U.S.S.R.
88 C2 Muhutwe Tanzania
88 F7 Muhuwesi R Tanzania
69 G8 Mui Bai Bung Vietnam
68 J4 Mui Chon May Dong C Vietnam
68 J7 Mui da Vaich C Vietnam
25 D4 Muiden Netherlands
21 O6 Muides-sur-Loire France
68 J7 Mui Dinh C Vietnam
21 N3 Muids France
61 M8 Muikamachi Japan
71 B3 Muilijk isld Indonesia
14 E4 Muine Bheag Ireland
94 C3 Muir Michigan U.S.A.
88 D10 Muira R Mozambique
13 F1 Muirdrum Scotland
117 E6 Muir Gl Alaska U.S.A.
13 E1 Muirhead Scotland
12 D3 Muirkirk Scotland
143 B10 Muir, L Western Australia Australia
143 G7 Muir, Mt Western Australia Australia
142 A5 Muiron I., N Western Australia Australia
102 B4 Muir Woods Nat.Mon California U.S.A.
87 G8 Muite Mozambique
68 J6 Mui Yen C Vietnam
125 Q7 Mujeres, I Mexico
80 F8 Mujib R Jordan
87 D8 Mujimbeji Zambia
70 C3 Mujong R Sarawak
48 H2 Mukachevo U.S.S.R.
70 C3 Mukah Sarawak
72 F6 Mukallā, Al S Yemen
80 E6 Mukallik R Jordan
60 Q3 Mu-kawa R Japan
60 P3 Mukawa Japan
80 F7 Mukawir Jordan
86 G1 Mukawwar I Sudan
68 G4 Mukdahan Thailand
Mukden see Shenyang
13 F5 Muker England
72 E6 Mukha, Al N Yemen
84 G3 Mukhaylī, Al Libya
74 G9 Mukher India
80 E6 Mukhmas Jordan
58 F1 Mukhor-Konduy U.S.S.R.
143 C9 Mukinbudin Western Australia Australia
69 D9 Muk,Ko isld Thailand
69 E14 Mukomuko Sumatra
33 P9 Mukrena East Germany
57 D5 Mukry U.S.S.R.
75 K4 Muktinath Nepal
86 D7 Mukumbi Zaire
86 G5 Mukutan Kenya
119 U5 Mukutawa R Manitoba Canada
87 D9 Mukwe Namibia
99 S7 Mukwonago Wisconsin U.S.A.
17 G6 Mula Spain
73 L8 Mulaku Atoll Maldives
57 J2 Mulaly U.S.S.R.
65 G2 Mulan China
71 F4 Mulanay Philippines
88 E9 Mulanje mt Malawi
88 E10 Mulanje Malawi
129 H4 Mulata Brazil
124 E3 Mulatos Mexico
125 Q5 Mulatupo Sasardi Panama
110 C6 Mulberry R Arkansas U.S.A.
110 B6 Mulberry Arkansas U.S.A.
113 F10 Mulberry Florida U.S.A.
110 K1 Mulberry Indiana U.S.A.
107 Q4 Mulberry Kansas U.S.A.
110 B4 Mulberry Missouri U.S.A.
111 K8 Mulberry Fork R Alabama U.S.A.
110 G3 Mulberry Grove Illinois U.S.A.
116 K6 Mulchatna R Alaska U.S.A.
133 C5 Mulchen Chile
37 P2 Mulda East Germany
28 E3 Muldbjerge hill Denmark
33 Q9 Mulde R East Germany
101 M6 Muldoon Idaho U.S.A.
108 E5 Mule Cr Texas U.S.A.
98 B6 Mule Cr Wyoming U.S.A.
106 B8 Mule Creek New Mexico U.S.A.
124 C4 Mulegé Mexico
80 G7 Muleih Jordan
88 C8 Mulembo R Zambia
86 D6 Mulenda Zaire
71 K9 Mules isld Flores Indonesia
108 E1 Muleshoe Texas U.S.A.
87 G9 Mulevala Mozambique
36 H5 Mulfingen W Germany
142 C5 Mulga Downs Western Australia Australia
140 B7 Mulga Park N Terr Australia
138 C4 Mulgathing South Australia Australia
138 C4 Mulgathing Rocks mt South Australia Australia
123 L8 Mulgrave Nova Scotia Canada
116 F3 Mulgrave Hills Alaska U.S.A.
143 C6 Mulgul Western Australia Australia
16 E7 Mulhacén mt Spain
107 N5 Mulhall Oklahoma U.S.A.
32 E10 Mülheim W Germany
40 F2 Mulhouse France
65 H2 Muling China
65 D6 Muling Guan pass China
65 J2 Muling He R China
138 E3 Mulka South Australia Australia
76 B4 Mulki India
15 C4 Mull isld Scotland
14 B4 Mullaghareirk Mts Ireland
83 K8 Mullaittivu Sri Lanka
139 J4 Mullaley New South Wales Australia
100 K2 Mullan Idaho U.S.A.
98 E7 Mullen Nebraska U.S.A.
109 J4 Mullen Texas U.S.A.
139 H4 Mullengudgery New South Wales Australia
94 F9 Mullens West Virginia U.S.A.
140 C6 Muller R N Terr Australia
70 C4 Muller,Peg mts Kalimantan
113 E10 Mullet Key isld Florida U.S.A.
94 C1 Mullett L Michigan U.S.A.
143 B8 Mullewa Western Australia Australia
15 F1 Mull Head Orkney Scotland
40 G2 Müllheim W Germany
95 N7 Mullica R New Jersey U.S.A.
140 E6 Mulligan R Queensland Australia
14 D3 Mullingar Ireland
112 H3 Mullins South Carolina U.S.A.
107 L4 Mullinville Kansas U.S.A.
139 J5 Mullion Creek New South Wales Australia
83 K8 Mulliyavalai Sri Lanka
15 D6 Mull of Galloway Scotland
15 C5 Mull of Kintyre Scotland
12 B2 Mull of Oa Scotland
27 G14 Mullsjö Sweden
15 C4 Mull, Sound of Scotland
139 L3 Mullumbimby New South Wales Australia
87 E9 Mulobezi Zambia
87 C9 Mulondo Angola
87 E7 Mulongo Zaire
138 E3 Muloorina South Australia Australia
14 D1 Mulroy B Ireland
21 L6 Mulsanne France
33 P5 Mulsow East Germany
74 D3 Multan Pakistan
55 F1 Multanovy U.S.S.R.
29 L9 Multia Finland
26 J8 Multrå Sweden
70 D2 Mulu, G mt Sarawak
130 J9 Mulungu Brazil
107 N4 Mulvane Kansas U.S.A.
119 T8 Mulvihill Manitoba Canada
139 G4 Mulyah,Mt New South Wales Australia
55 E1 Mulym'ya R U.S.S.R.
138 F4 Mulyungarie South Australia Australia
8 C4 Mumbles Wales
87 B8 Mumbondo Angola
87 C8 Mumbué Angola
87 E8 Mumbwa Zambia
87 E8 Mumena Zaire
109 L5 Mumford Texas U.S.A.
69 D9 Mum Nauk,Laem C Thailand
71 H7 Muna isld Indonesia
125 P7 Muna Mexico
67 B5 Munankwan Lin pass Vietnam/China
141 G2 Munburra Queensland Australia
37 M3 Münchberg W Germany
30 H3 Müncheberg East Germany
39 München conurbation W Germany
37 M2 Münchenbernsdorf East Germany
36 F2 Münchhausen W Germany
117 L6 Muncho Lake British Columbia Canada
37 N5 Münchshofen W Germany
37 O6 Münchshofen W Germany
37 M6 Münchsmünster W Germany
110 L1 Muncie Indiana U.S.A.
140 E7 Muncoonie, L Queensland Australia
95 L5 Muncy Pennsylvania U.S.A.
118 E5 Mundare Alberta Canada
109 H2 Munday Texas U.S.A.
99 S7 Mundelein Illinois U.S.A.
83 J10 Mundel L Sri Lanka
98 J10 Munden Kansas U.S.A.
32 L10 Münden W Germany
36 H7 Munderkingen W Germany
9 H2 Mundesley England
9 G2 Mundford England
143 D6 Mundiwindi Western Australia Australia
141 F4 Mundjuro R Queensland Australia
17 F6 Mundo R Spain
129 K6 Mundo Nôvo Brazil
143 G9 Mundrabilla Western Australia Australia
141 K7 Mundubbera Queensland Australia
56 C4 Mundybash U.S.S.R.
46 D3 Munella mt Albania
17 F5 Munera Spain
110 L4 Munfordville Kentucky U.S.A.
141 J7 Mungallala Queensland Australia
141 H8 Mungallala R Queensland Australia
141 G3 Mungana Queensland Australia
87 F9 Mungari Mozambique
142 C5 Mungaroona Ra Western Australia Australia
56 D5 Mungash-Kul', Gora mt U.S.S.R.
86 E5 Mungbere Zaire
75 J7 Mungeli India
75 M6 Munger India
94 D3 Munger Michigan U.S.A.
138 E3 Mungerannie South Australia Australia
69 J12 Munggures ak, Tanjong C Indonesia
141 J8 Mungindi Queensland Australia
87 C8 Munhango Angola
98 H1 Munich North Dakota U.S.A.
Munich W Germany see München
88 B8 Muniengashi R Zaire
17 G3 Muniesa Spain
130 H7 Muniz Freire Brazil
28 H5 Munke Bjergby Denmark
28 F6 Munkebo Denmark
27 E13 Munkedal Sweden
26 G8 Munkflohögen Sweden
27 G12 Munkfors Sweden
28 A7 Munkmarsch W Germany
26 M6 Munksund Sweden
56 F5 Munku-Sardyk,Gora mt Mongolia/U.S.S.R.
37 J3 Münnerstadt W Germany
22 J4 Muno Belgium
71 E3 Muñoz Luzon Philippines
133 C8 Muñoz Gamero, Pen Chile
139 J8 Munro,Mt Tasmania Australia
36 H7 Münsingen W Germany
118 E7 Munson Alberta Canada
111 K11 Munson Florida U.S.A.
40 F1 Munster France
14 B4 Munster prov Ireland
41 H5 Münster Switzerland
32 M7 Münster Niedersachsen W Germany
32 G9 Münster Nordrhein-Westfalen W Germany
36 C3 Münstermaifeld W Germany
143 C9 Muntadgin Western Australia Australia
70 F4 Munte Sulawesi
48 H4 Muntelui Mare mt Romania
70 P10 Muntjar Java
87 E9 Munyati R Zimbabwe
36 F3 Münzenberg W Germany
26 N4 Muodoslompolo Sweden
29 O6 Muojärvi L Finland
68 F1 Muong Boum Vietnam
68 F2 Muong Hiem Laos
68 F2 Muong Hun Xieng Hung Laos
68 F3 Muong Khao Laos
68 F2 Muong Khoua Laos
68 G1 Muong Khuong Vietnam
68 E3 Muong Ki Laos
68 G3 Muong Lam Vietnam
68 E3 Muong Liep Laos
68 E2 Muong Louang Namtha Laos
68 H7 Muong Man Vietnam
68 F3 Muong May Laos
68 F3 Muong Moc Laos
68 F2 Muong Ngoi Laos
68 F1 Muong Nhie Vietnam
68 H4 Muong Nong Laos
68 E3 Muong Oua Laos
68 E1 Muong ou Neua Laos
68 E1 Muong ou Tay Laos
68 E3 Muong Pa Laos
68 G4 Muong Phalane Laos
68 E3 Muong Phiang Laos
68 E2 Muong Sai Laos
68 E3 Muong Saiapoun Laos
68 E2 Muong Sing Laos
68 F2 Muong Son Laos
68 G4 Muong Song Khone Laos
68 F3 Muong Soui Laos
68 F3 Muong Soum Laos
68 F1 Muong Te Vietnam
68 E3 Muong Tha Deua Laos
68 E3 Muong Thong Laos
68 F2 Muong Va Laos
Muong Xen see Ky Son
29 K4 Muonio Finland
26 N3 Muonio älv R Sweden/Finland
29 K4 Muoniojoki R Finland
26 N4 Muonionalusta Sweden
71 B2 Muor isld Halmahera Indonesia
41 J4 Muotathal Switzerland
88 B9 Mupata Gorge Zambia
65 E6 Muping China
80 G4 Muqbilla Jordan
86 J5 Muqdisho Somalia
130 H7 Muqui Brazil
38 J7 Mur R Austria
56 E2 Mura R U.S.S.R.
48 C4 Mura R Yugoslavia
80 G1 Murāba 'āt Syria
47 J6 Muradiye Turkey
45 L4 Muraglione,Pso.di pass Italy
61 N7 Murakami Japan
48 D4 Murakeresztúr Hungary
133 C7 Murallón mt Chile/Arg
61 N8 Muramatsu Japan
88 F2 Murang'a Kenya
45 M1 Murano Italy
52 G5 Murashi U.S.S.R.
18 G7 Murat France
78 H2 Murat R Turkey
47 K6 Murat Dağı Turkey
47 J3 Muratlı Turkey
78 J2 Murat Suyu R Turkey
38 K7 Murau Austria
77 C7 Murban U.A.E.
16 C3 Murça Portugal
77 B3 Murcheh Khvort Iran
33 T5 Murchin East Germany
139 H6 Murchison Victoria Australia
145 D4 Murchison New Zealand
6 M1 Murchison oil rig North Sea
Murchison Falls Uganda see Kabalega Falls
143 B7 Murchison, Mt Western Australia Australia
145 D4 Murchison, Mt New Zealand
144 C5 Murchison, Mt New Zealand
144 A6 Murchison Mts New Zealand
143 A8 Murchison, R Western Australia Australia
140 C5 Murchison Ra N Terr Australia
89 G4 Murchison Ra S Africa
88 E9 Murchison Rapids Malawi
17 G7 Murcia Spain
17 F7 Murcia prov Spain
17 F6 Murcia reg Spain
71 F6 Murcielagos B Mindanao Philippines
18 G8 Mur-de-Barrez France
20 E5 Mur-de-Bretagne France
21 O7 Mur-de-Sologne France
98 F6 Murdo South Dakota U.S.A.
141 G2 Murdoch Pt Queensland Australia
122 G5 Murdochville Quebec Canada
113 E10 Murdock Florida U.S.A.
61 M9 Mure Japan
21 O4 Mureaux, Les France
38 N8 Mureck Austria
47 J4 Mürefte Turkey
86 G4 Murel Ethiopia
48 J4 Mureş R Romania
48 J4 Mureş reg Romania
18 F9 Muret France
111 C7 Murfreesboro Arkansas U.S.A.
95 K10 Murfreesboro North Carolina U.S.A.
110 K6 Murfreesboro Tennessee U.S.A.
36 E6 Murg R W Germany
57 G5 Murgab R U.S.S.R.
57 G5 Murgab U.S.S.R.
46 D5 Murgána mt Greece
46 F2 Murgash mt Bulgaria
140 C1 Murgenella Cr N Terr Australia
48 L4 Murgeni Romania
77 H2 Murghab R Afghanistan
74 C3 Murgha Kibzai Pakistan
48 K4 Murgoci mt Romania
141 K7 Murgon Queensland Australia
143 B7 Murgoo Western Australia Australia
58 D4 Muri China
75 L7 Muri India
130 G7 Muriaé Brazil
70 N9 Muria, Gunung mt Java
16 C2 Murias de Paredes Spain
87 D7 Muriege Angola
118 G4 Muriel L Alberta Canada
60 R2 Murii-dake mt Japan
119 O2 Murill Ontario Canada
17 G2 Murillo de Gállego Spain
20 G6 Murin, L. de France
33 R6 Müritz L East Germany
145 F3 Muriwai New Zealand
26 L5 Murjek Sweden
36 B3 Mürlenbach W Germany
52 D1 Murmansk U.S.S.R.
52 D1 Murmanskaya Oblast' prov U.S.S.R.
52 D1 Murmashi U.S.S.R.
54 M2 Murmino U.S.S.R.
41 O2 Murnau W Germany
18 L11 Muro, Cap di C Corsica
102 G7 Muroc L California U.S.A.
52 F6 Murom U.S.S.R.
55 G3 Muromtsevo U.S.S.R.
60 O3 Muroran Japan
16 A2 Muros Spain
60 H12 Muroto Japan
60 H12 Muroto-zaki Japan
60 N3 Murotsu-shima isld Japan
48 L2 Murovanyye Kurilovtsy U.S.S.R.
31 K3 Murowana Goslina Poland
60 E12 Murozumi Japan
100 J6 Murphy Idaho U.S.A.
112 C2 Murphy North Carolina U.S.A.
100 B7 Murphy Oregon U.S.A.
102 D3 Murphys California U.S.A.
110 G4 Murphysboro Illinois U.S.A.
141 H8 Murra Murra Queensland Australia
139 G6 Murray R New South Wales Australia
99 N8 Murray Iowa U.S.A.
110 H5 Murray Kentucky U.S.A.
99 K9 Murray Nebraska U.S.A.
103 N1 Murray Utah U.S.A.
138 E6 Murray Bridge South Australia Australia
94 E7 Murray City Ohio U.S.A.
135 L5 Murray Deep Pacific Oc
140 C5 Murray Downs N Terr Australia
122 K7 Murray Hbr Prince Edward I Canada
123 K8 Murray Hd Prince Edward I Canada
83 M9 Murray Hill pk Christmas I Indian Oc
107 N7 Murray,L Oklahoma U.S.A.
112 F3 Murray, L South Carolina U.S.A.
143 B10 Murray, R Western Australia Australia
117 N8 Murray R British Columbia Canada
143 G7 Murray Ra Western Australia Australia
122 K7 Murray River Prince Edward I Canada
89 C8 Murraysburg S Africa
135 M5 Murray Seascarp Pacific Oc
138 E5 Murray Town South Australia Australia
138 F6 Murrayville Victoria Australia
99 Q10 Murrayville Illinois U.S.A.
112 H4 Murrells Inlet South Carolina U.S.A.
40 G4 Mürren Switzerland
36 H6 Murrhardt W Germany
139 J5 Murringo New South Wales Australia
143 D8 Murrin Murrin Western Australia Australia
14 B3 Murrisk mts Ireland
139 G5 Murrumbidgee R New South Wales Australia
139 J5 Murrumburrah & Harden New South Wales Australia
139 K4 Murrurundi New South Wales Australia
19 O17 Murs France
38 O8 Murska Sobota Yugoslavia
74 G8 Murtajāpur India
38 K7 Mur Tal V Austria
41 M4 Murtarol,Piz mt Italy
101 L7 Murtaugh Idaho U.S.A.
139 G4 Murtee New South Wales Australia
40 F4 Murten See L Switzerland
42 G5 Murter isld Yugoslavia
138 F3 Murteree,L South Australia Australia
117 O9 Murtle L British Columbia Canada
138 F6 Murtoa Victoria Australia
29 O6 Murtovaara Finland
74 E9 Murud India
70 D3 Murud mt Kalimantan
65 E3 Muruin Sum Shuiku res China
70 D5 Murui, R Kalimantan
70 D4 Murung,R Kalimantan
145 F3 Murupara New Zealand
128 F3 Murupu Brazil
109 N3 Murvaul Res Texas U.S.A.
22 K5 Murville France
74 J7 Murwara India
139 L3 Murwillumbah New South Wales Australia
52 G5 Murygino U.S.S.R.
38 M6 Mürzsteg Austria
38 M7 Murz Tal V Austria
84 E4 Murzuq Libya
38 N6 Mürzzuchlag Austria
78 H2 Muş Turkey
86 D6 Musadi Zaire
79 D10 Mûsa, G mt Egypt
74 C3 Musa Khel Bazar Pakistan
47 N10 Musaköyalçağı Burun C Turkey
46 F2 Musala mt Bulgaria
69 D12 Musala isld Sumatra
59 J3 Musan N Korea
77 E6 Musandam pen Oman
77 J3 Musa Qala Afghanistan
77 B7 Musay'īd Qatar
Muscat see Masqat
99 P8 Muscatine Iowa U.S.A.
Muscat & Oman sultanate see Oman
110 J7 Muscle Shoals Alabama U.S.A.
99 Q6 Muscoda Wisconsin U.S.A.
95 S3 Muscongus B Maine U.S.A.
88 C9 Muse R Mozambique
80 G8 Museitiba Jordan
141 G2 Musgrave Queensland Australia
138 B2 Musgrave Ranges South Australia Australia
123 S5 Musgravetown Newfoundland Canada
89 G3 Mushandike Dam Zimbabwe
80 G8 Musheirifa Jordan
14 C5 Musheramore mt Ireland
86 C6 Mushie Zaire
28 G6 Musholm isld Denmark
103 L6 Music Mt Arizona U.S.A.
103 N2 Musinia Pk Utah U.S.A.
117 M5 Muskeg R Northwest Territories Canada
99 L1 Muskeg B Minnesota U.S.A.
95 R5 Muskeget Chan Massachusetts U.S.A.
119 O1 Muskeg L Ontario Canada
94 A3 Muskegon R Michigan U.S.A.
94 A3 Muskegon Michigan U.S.A.
94 A3 Muskegon Heights Michigan U.S.A.
26 H4 Musken Norway
94 F7 Muskingum R Ohio U.S.A.
27 K13 Muskö Sweden
110 A6 Muskogee Oklahoma U.S.A.
121 L7 Muskoka,L Ontario Canada
101 S6 Muskrat Cr Wyoming U.S.A.
77 F6 Mūskutān Iran
118 C2 Muskwa R Alberta Canada
79 H2 Muslimīyah Syria
52 H6 Muslyumovo U.S.S.R.
86 G2 Musmar Sudan
80 D3 Musmus Israel
88 D2 Musoma Tanzania
45 M1 Musone R Italy
45 O4 Musone Italy
123 L3 Musquanus L Quebec Canada
123 L3 Musquaro Quebec Canada
122 F8 Musquash New Brunswick Canada
122 J8 Musquodoboit Nova Scotia Canada
122 J9 Musquodoboit Hbr Nova Scotia Canada
28 H7 Musse Denmark
25 H3 Mussel Aa R Netherlands
13 E2 Musselburgh Scotland
101 S3 Musselshell R Montana U.S.A.
101 R3 Musselshell Montana U.S.A.
87 C8 Mussende Angola
18 F7 Mussidan France
43 F11 Mussomeli Sicily
47 K4 Mustafa Kemalpaşa Turkey
47 K5 Mustafa Kemalpşa R Turkey
86 H4 Mustahīl Ethiopia
75 K4 Mustang Nepal
107 N6 Mustang Oklahoma U.S.A.
108 E3 Mustang Cr Texas U.S.A.
109 K8 Mustang I Texas U.S.A.
55 B5 Mustayevo U.S.S.R.
133 D7 Muster,L Argentina
98 K4 Mustinka R Minnesota U.S.A.
127 O8 Mustique isld Lesser Antilles
27 M13 Mustjala Estonskaya S.S.R. U.S.S.R.
52 C5 Mustla U.S.S.R.
29 N3 Mustola Finland
13 H5 Muston England
52 C5 Mustvee U.S.S.R.
65 H4 Musu-dan C N Korea
139 K4 Muswellbrook New South Wales Australia
48 F1 Muszyna Poland
84 H4 Mut Egypt
78 D3 Mut Turkey
38 M8 Muta Yugoslavia
88 C1 Mutai Uganda
89 G4 Mutale R S Africa
87 E8 Mutanda Zambia
Mutankiang see Mudanjiang
88 E10 Mutarara Mozambique
87 F9 Mutare Zimbabwe
37 O4 Mutěnin Czechoslovakia
88 C10 Mutepatepa Zimbabwe
12 E1 Muthill Scotland
71 M9 Mutis mt Timor Indonesia
52 J2 Mutnyy-Materik U.S.S.R.
88 D10 Mutoko Zimbabwe
87 D7 Mutombo Mukulu Zaire
138 F4 Mutooroo South Australia Australia
88 C10 Mutorashanga Zimbabwe
65 D4 Mutoudeng China
65 D3 Mutougou China
45 R7 Mutria, M mt Italy
87 G10 Mutsamudu Comoros
87 D8 Mutshatsha Zaire
60 P4 Mutsu Japan
61 O5 Mutsu-wan B Japan
141 G6 Muttaburra Queensland Australia
40 G1 Muttersholtz France
36 E5 Mutterstadt W Germany
41 M4 Muttler mt Switzerland
123 O3 Mutton Bay Quebec Canada
144 B7 Muttonbird Is. New Zealand
14 B4 Mutton I Ireland
107 L5 Mutual Oklahoma U.S.A.
87 G8 Mutuala Mozambique
129 H7 Mutum Mato Grosso Brazil
130 H6 Mutum Minas Gerais Brazil
128 F5 Mutumparaná Brazil
83 L9 Mutur Sri Lanka
36 C6 Mutzig France
33 R10 Mutzschen East Germany
29 M9 Muurame Finland
29 L5 Muurola Finland
65 A5 Mu Us Shamo desert China
58 F1 Muya R U.S.S.R.
88 C3 Muyinga Burundi
125 M3 Muy Muy Nicaragua
57 A3 Muynak U.S.S.R.
87 E7 Muyumba Zaire
67 C1 Muyuping China
74 E1 Muzaffarabad Kashmir
74 D3 Muzaffargarh Pakistan
74 G4 Muzaffarnagar India
75 L5 Muzaffarpur India
130 F7 Muzambinho Brazil
57 K4 Muzat He R China
50 F2 Muzhi U.S.S.R.
20 F6 Muzillac France
40 A3 Muzin R France
117 G8 Muzon, C Alaska U.S.A.
108 F8 Múzquiz Mexico
66 D4 Muztag mt China
66 C4 Muztag mt China
66 B4 Muztagata mt China
88 E8 Mvera Malawi
86 E4 Mvolo Sudan
87 G7 Mvomero Tanzania
86 B6 M'Vouti Congo
89 G2 Mvuma Zimbabwe
88 C10 Mvurwi Ra mts Zimbabwe
88 D7 Mwambwa R Zambia
88 D3 Mwanza Tanzania
88 D6 Mwaya Tanzania
14 B3 Mweelrea mts Ireland
86 D6 Mweka Zaire
87 D7 Mwene Ditu Zaire
87 F10 Mwenezi Zimbabwe
89 G3 Mwenezi R Zimbabwe
89 G3 Mwenezi Zimbabwe
88 B3 Mwenga Zaire
88 G6 Mwera Tanzania
89 G2 Mwerihari R Zimbabwe
88 B6 Mweru, L Zaire/Zambia
88 B6 Mweru Wantipa Zambia
89 F3 Mwewe R Zimbabwe
87 D7 Mwimba Zaire
87 D8 Mwinilunga Zambia
68 B2 Myaing Burma
113 E10 Myakka Florida U.S.A.
113 E10 Myakka City Florida U.S.A.
52 E5 Myaksa U.S.S.R.
31 H3 Myálibórz Poland
139 K4 Myall L New South Wales Australia
68 B3 Myanaung Burma
52 D3 Myanduselga U.S.S.R.
54 G2 Myatlevo U.S.S.R.
68 A2 Myaungbwe Burma
68 B4 Myaungmya Burma
68 D4 Myawadi Burma
46 F7 Mycenae Greece
68 A2 Myebon Burma
95 L6 Myerstown Pennsylvania U.S.A.
68 B2 Myingyan Burma
68 C2 Myinkyado Burma
68 D6 Myinmoletkat mt Burma
68 B2 Myinmu Burma
68 B2 Myitche Burma
68 D5 Myitta Burma
68 C2 Myittha Burma
48 D2 Myjava Czechoslovakia
26 F5 Myken lighthouse Norway
6 E1 Mykines isld Faeroes
52 H2 Myla U.S.S.R.
37 N2 Mylau East Germany
29 M11 Myllykoski Finland
98 G1 Mylo North Dakota U.S.A.
75 O6 Mymensingh Bangladesh
29 J11 Mynämäki Finland
57 G2 Mynaral U.S.S.R.
57 C4 Mynbulak U.S.S.R.
8 B3 Mynydd Bach mts Wales
8 C3 Mynydd Eppynt mts Wales
68 A2 Myohaung Burma
68 B2 Myohla Burma
68 B2 Myotha Burma
68 B2 Myothit Burma
47 K8 Myra Turkey
109 K2 Myra Texas U.S.A.
141 F3 Myra Vale Queensland Australia
27 B11 Myrdal Norway
28 S10 Myrdalsjökull ice cap Iceland
26 H3 Myre Norway
27 G14 Myresjö Sweden
26 L6 Myrheden Sweden
118 F5 Myrnam Alberta Canada
119 U9 Myrtle Manitoba Canada
121 M8 Myrtle Ontario Canada
100 J3 Myrtle Idaho U.S.A.
111 G7 Myrtle Mississippi U.S.A.
112 J4 Myrtle Beach South Carolina U.S.A.
100 B6 Myrtle Cr Oregon U.S.A.
139 H6 Myrtleford Victoria Australia
100 A6 Myrtle Point Oregon U.S.A.
138 E4 Myrtle Springs South Australia Australia
141 L1 Myrtletown Queensland Australia
65 H3 Mys Gamova lighthouse U.S.S.R.
52 E5 Myshkino U.S.S.R.
47 J5 Mysia hist reg Turkey
56 C4 Myski U.S.S.R.
31 M6 Myślenice Poland
76 C4 Mysore India
147 P3 Mys Shmidta U.S.S.R.
26 G9 Myssjo Sweden
119 U3 Mystery L Manitoba Canada
112 D6 Mystic Georgia U.S.A.
99 O9 Mystic Iowa U.S.A.
52 H4 Mysy Permskaya obl U.S.S.R.
31 N2 Myszyniec Poland
52 F6 Myt U.S.S.R.
68 H7 My Tho Vietnam
54 J1 Mytishchi U.S.S.R.
101 P9 Myton Utah U.S.A.
68 J6 My Trach Vietnam
29 T9 Myvatn L Iceland
57 H1 Myylybulak U.S.S.R.
37 O4 Mže R Czechoslovakia
85 C4 Mzereb,El Mali
88 D7 Mzimba Malawi
89 F8 Mzimvubu R S Africa
88 E7 Mzuzu Malawi

N

37 M5 Naab R W Germany
25 B5 Naaldwijk Netherlands
135 U6 Naalehu Hawaiian Is
80 C6 Na'an Israel
86 E4 Naandi Sudan
29 J11 Naantali Finland
25 D4 Naarden Netherlands
14 E3 Naas Ireland
29 N2 Näätämönjoki R Finland
89 A7 Nababeep S Africa
16 B5 Nabaõ R Portugal
75 K9 Nabarangapur India
61 K11 Nabari Japan
140 C1 Nabarlek N Terr Australia
71 F5 Nabas Panay Philippines
80 G1 Nab'as Şakhr Syria
79 F5 Nabatīyet Ett Tahta Lebanon
143 D7 Nabberu, L Western Australia Australia
71 E2 Nabbuan Luzon Philippines
37 N5 Nabburg W Germany
Naberezhnyy Chelny see Brezhnev
116 Q5 Nabesna Gl Alaska U.S.A.
43 D12 Nabeul Tunisia
139 K4 Nabiac New South Wales Australia
130 B7 Nabileque,R Brazil
136 H2 Nabire W Irian
123 K3 Nabisipi R Quebec Canada
79 F5 Nabi Younés, Ras en C Lebanon
80 E5 Nablus Jordan
79 E10 Nabq Egypt
71 F6 Nabulao B Negros Philippines
68 D5 Nabule Burma
88 H9 Nacala Mozambique
88 H9 Nacala-a-Velha Mozambique
125 L3 Nacaome Honduras
67 B5 Nacham Vietnam
100 E3 Naches Washington U.S.A.
100 D2 Naches Pass Washington U.S.A.
87 G8 Nachingwea Tanzania
74 D5 Nāchna India
66 E5 Na Ch'u R China
68 A7 Nachuge Andaman Is
102 C6 Nacimiento R California U.S.A.
102 C6 Nacimiento Res California U.S.A.
33 R7 Nackel East Germany
103 P10 Naco Mexico
111 B10 Nacogdoches Texas U.S.A.
68 B6 Nacondam I Andaman Is
124 E2 Nacozari de García Mexico
Nada see Dan Xian
103 L3 Nada Utah U.S.A.
61 M8 Nadachi Japan
124 J4 Nadadores Mexico
67 B6 Nadang China
99 T4 Nadeau Michigan U.S.A.
Nådendal see Naantali
55 D4 Nadezhdinka U.S.S.R.
137 Q5 Nadi Viti Levu Fiji
74 E7 Nadiad India
48 F4 Nădlac Romania
85 D1 Nador Morocco
48 G3 Nádudvar Hungary
77 C3 Nadūshan Iran
52 D3 Nadvoitsy U.S.S.R.
48 J2 Nadvornaya U.S.S.R.
50 G2 Nadym U.S.S.R.
27 A13 Naerbö Norway
26 E7 Naeröy Norway
29 K5 Nærum Denmark
28 B5 Næsbjerg Denmark
28 C3 Næsborg Denmark
28 H6 Næsby Denmark
28 E6 Næsbyhoved Denmark
28 A3 Næs Sund inlet Denmark
28 H6 Næstelsø Denmark
28 H6 Næstved Denmark
68 A2 Naf R Burma
101 M7 Naf Idaho U.S.A.
85 G6 Nafada Nigeria
77 A4 Naft-e Safīd Iran
78 K4 Naft-e Shāh Iran
77 J6 Nāg Pakistan
71 F4 Naga Philippines
120 F3 Nagagami Ontario Canada
120 F3 Nagagamisis L Ontario Canada
60 F12 Nagahama Japan
75 Q5 Nagaland prov India
139 H6 Nagambie Victoria Australia
61 O13 Nagannu-jima isld Okinawa
61 M9 Nagano Japan
61 L9 Nagano prefect Japan
61 M9 Naganohara Japan
61 M8 Nagaoka Japan
76 D5 Nagappattinam India
76 E1 Nāgāram India
76 D2 Nāgārjuna Sāgar res India
76 D2 Nagar Karnul India
74 D6 Nagar Parkar Pakistan
60 C13 Nagasaki Japan
60 C12 Nagasaki prefect Japan
60 D14 Nagasaki-bana Japan
60 D13 Naga shima isld Japan
60 F12 Naga-shima isld Japan
60 E12 Nagasu Japan
60 E11 Nagato Japan
74 E5 Nagaur India
Nagchu Dzong see Nagqu
76 C6 Nagercoil India
26 H9 Naggen Sweden
74 H4 Nagina India
75 Q5 Nāginimāra India
61 P12 Nago Okinawa
74 J6 Nagod India
36 F6 Nagold R W Germany
36 F6 Nagold W Germany
52 H5 Nagorsk U.S.S.R.
61 P13 Nago-wan B Okinawa
61 K10 Nagoya Japan
74 H8 Nagpur India
66 E5 Nagqu China
29 J11 Nagu Finland
127 K5 Nagua Dominican Rep
71 E2 Naguilian Luzon Philippines
71 G4 Nagumbuaya Pt Philippines
48 D4 Nagyatád Hungary
48 D4 Nagybajom Hungary
48 G3 Nagyecsed Hungary
48 G3 Nagykálló Hungary
48 D4 Nagykanizsa Hungary
48 F3 Nagykáta Hungary
48 F3 Nagykörös Hungary
48 G3 Nagyléta Hungary
48 E3 Nagymaros Hungary
Nagyvárad see Oradea
66 F4 Nagza China
61 P13 Naha Okinawa
70 D4 Nahabuan Kalimantan
80 D3 Nahalal Israel
80 C7 Nahalat Israel
74 G3 Nahan India
117 M5 Nahanni Butte Northwest Territories Canada
117 L5 Nahanni Nat. Park Northwest Territories Canada
80 D1 Nahariyya Israel
77 A2 Nahāvand Iran
36 C4 Nahbollenbach W Germany
36 C4 Nahe R W Germany
80 G4 Nahla Jordan
137 O4 Nahoï, C Vanuatu
21 O7 Nahon R France
79 H2 Nahr Sājūr R Syria
80 C3 Nahsholim Israel
131 B8 Nahuel Huapi, L Argentina
133 D6 Nahuel Niyeu Argentina
112 E6 Nahunta Georgia U.S.A.
71 E3 Naic Luzon Philippines
124 G4 Naica Mexico
119 N6 Naicam Saskatchewan Canada
66 E4 Naij Tal China
71 L9 Naikliu Timor Indonesia
37 M3 Naila W Germany
65 D4 Nailin China
8 D5 Nailsea England
8 D4 Nailsworth England
65 E3 Naiman Qi China
66 E3 Naimin Bulak spring China
115 N6 Nain Labrador, Nfld Canada
77 C3 Nā'īn Iran
74 J7 Nainpur India
21 L8 Naintré France
Nairn co see Highland reg
120 J6 Nairn Ontario Canada
15 E3 Nairn Scotland
143 B7 Nairn, Mt Western Australia Australia
15 D3 Nairn,R Scotland
88 F2 Nairobi Kenya
52 B5 Naissaar isld U.S.S.R.
88 F2 Naivasha Kenya
20 E6 Naizin France
77 B3 Najafābād Iran
78 K6 Najaf, An Iraq
126 F4 Najasa R Cuba
17 F2 Nājera Spain
17 F2 Najerilla R Spain
65 H3 Najin N Korea
77 B2 Najmabad Iran
60 H12 Naka R Japan
60 C13 Nakadōri shima isld Japan
60 C12 Nakagumi Japan
61 P13 Nakagusuku-wan B Okinawa
61 N7 Nakajō Japan
60 C14 Naka koshiki jima isld Japan
60 D12 Nakama Japan
61 O9 Nakaminato Japan
60 E14 Nakamura Japan
60 F13 Nakamura Japan
61 M9 Nakano Japan
61 M9 Nakanojō Japan
60 G9 Nakano-shima isld Japan
67 H4 Nakanougan-jima isld Japan
61 Q12 Nakaoshi Okinawa
77 L3 Naka Pass Afghanistan
61 O5 Nakasato Japan
60 R3 Nakasatsunai Japan
60 T2 Naka-shibetsu Japan
55 D2 Nakatay U.S.S.R.
60 Q1 Naka-Tombetsu Japan
60 E12 Nakatsu Japan
61 L10 Nakatsugawa Japan
60 G10 Naka-umi Japan
116 J8 Nakchamik I Alaska U.S.A.
116 O6 Naked I Alaska U.S.A.
86 G2 Nak'fa Ethiopia
78 K2 Nakhichevan U.S.S.R.
84 J4 Nakhl Egypt
65 J3 Nakhodka U.S.S.R.
68 E5 Nakhon Nayok Thailand
68 D6 Nakhon Pathom Thailand
68 F5 Nakhon Ratchasima Thailand
69 E8 Nakhon Si Thammarat Thailand
68 E4 Nakhon Thai Thailand
59 L2 Nakhtakhe U.S.S.R.
61 P12 Nakijin Okinawa
117 G6 Nakina British Columbia Canada
120 D2 Nakina Ontario Canada
29 K3 Näkkälä Finland
29 J10 Nakkila Finland
31 K2 Nakło Poland
116 J7 Naknek Alaska U.S.A.
61 O9 Nakoso Japan
67 F3 Nakou China
Naksho Biru see Biru
28 G7 Nakskov Denmark
26 G9 Näkten L Sweden
65 G7 Naktong R S Korea
88 F2 Nakuru Kenya
88 E2 Nakuru, L Kenya
117 P10 Nakusp British Columbia Canada

Na-lang — Neunkirchen
59

68 C1 **Na-lang** Burma
58 E2 **Nalayh** Mongolia
53 F11 **Nal'chik** U.S.S.R.
74 G10 **Naldurg** India
76 D2 **Nalgonda** India
22 G3 **Nalinnes** Belgium
76 D3 **Nallamala Hills** India
94 G8 **Nallen** West Virginia U.S.A.
21 M8 **Nalliers** Vienne France
78 C1 **Nallihan** Turkey
87 D9 **Nalolo** Zambia
6 M2 **N Alwyn** *oil rig* North Sea
68 C1 **Nam** *R* Burma
68 F3 **Nam** *R* Laos
65 G5 **Nam** *R* N Korea
60 C12 **Nama** Japan
87 C9 **Namacunde** Angola
88 F10 **Namacurra** Mozambique
118 D8 **Namaka** Alberta Canada
118 K2 **Namakan L** Minnesota/Ontario U.S.A./Canada
77 F4 **Namakiār-e Shadād** *salt lake* Iran
77 E2 **Namak, Kavīr-e** *salt waste* Iran
69 H14 **Namang** Indonesia
57 F4 **Namangan** U.S.S.R.
88 G8 **Namapa** Mozambique
88 G9 **Namaponda** Mozambique
87 C11 **Namaqualand** *tribal area* Namibia
87 C12 **Namaqualand** *dist* S Africa
88 F9 **Namarroi** Mozambique
86 F5 **Namasagali** Uganda
87 E9 **Nambala** Zambia
68 E2 **Nam Beng** *R* Laos
141 L7 **Nambour** Queensland Australia
139 L4 **Nambucca Heads** New South Wales Australia
68 G3 **Nam Ca Dinh** *R* Laos
69 G8 **Nam Can** Vietnam
66 E5 **Nam Co** *L* China
26 F7 **Namdalen** *V* Norway
26 E7 **Namdalseid** Norway
68 G2 **Nam Đing** Vietnam
88 G8 **Namecala** Mozambique
99 P3 **Namekagon** *R* Wisconsin U.S.A.
61 L9 **Namerikawa** Japan
48 E1 **Námestovo** Czechoslovakia
88 G9 **Nametil** Mozambique
119 P4 **Namew L** Saskatchewan Canada
68 F2 **Nam Het** *R* Laos
68 D2 **Nam Hsin** *R* Burma
87 B10 **Namib Des** Namibia
87 B9 **Namibe** Angola
87 B10 **Namib Game Res.** Namibia
87 C10 **Namibia** *terr* Africa
88 F9 **Namicunde** Mozambique
61 O8 **Namie** Japan
61 O5 **Namioka** Japan
87 C11 **Namisis** *mt* Namibia
66 F6 **Namjagbarwa Feng** *mt* China
68 F3 **Nam Khan** *R* Laos
68 D2 **Nam Kok** *R* Thailand
68 C1 **Namlan** Burma
68 C2 **Namlang** *R* Burma
68 E2 **Nam Loi** *R* Burma
68 E2 **Nam Ma** *R* Laos
68 C3 **Nammekon** Burma
68 G3 **Nam Muone** *R* Laos
68 F1 **Nam Na** *R* Vietnam
68 G4 **Nam One** *R* Laos
68 E2 **Nam Ngaou** *R* Laos
68 F2 **Nam Noud** *R* Vietnam
139 J4 **Namoi** *R* New South Wales Australia
68 E1 **Nam Ou** *R* Laos
85 D2 **Namous** *watercourse* Algeria
118 A2 **Nampa** Alberta Canada
29 M5 **Nampa** Finland
100 J6 **Nampa** Idaho U.S.A.
85 C5 **Nampala** Mali
68 E4 **Nam Pa Sak** *R* Thailand
68 E4 **Nam Pat** Thailand
68 F4 **Nam Phong** Thailand
65 F5 **Namp'o** N Korea
22 B3 **Nampont** France
88 G9 **Nampula** Mozambique
68 G4 **Nam Pung Res** Thailand
26 F7 **Namsen** *R* Norway
68 F2 **Nam Seng** *R* Laos
26 E7 **Namsos** Norway
68 F2 **Nam Suong** *R* Laos
26 G7 **Namsvatn** *L* Norway
68 C2 **Nam Teng** Burma
68 E2 **Nam Tha** Laos
68 G4 **Nam Theun** *R* Laos
68 C2 **Namtok** Burma
68 D5 **Nam Tok** Thailand
68 D1 **Namton** Burma
51 M2 **Namtsy** U.S.S.R.
88 F9 **Namuli** *mt* Mozambique
87 G8 **Namuno** Mozambique
83 L11 **Namunukula** *mt* Sri Lanka
22 H3 **Namur** Belgium
121 Q7 **Namur** Quebec Canada
117 R7 **Namur L** Alberta Canada
87 C9 **Namutoni** Namibia
87 E9 **Namwala** Zambia
68 D4 **Nam Wang** *R* Thailand
88 E9 **Namwera** Malawi
31 L4 **Namysłaki** Poland
31 K4 **Namysłów** Poland
68 E3 **Nan** Thailand
100 B1 **Nanaimo** British Columbia Canada
102 R12 **Nanakuli** Hawaiian Is
65 H4 **Nanam** N Korea
67 F4 **Nan'an** China
67 B6 **Nanan** China
141 K7 **Nanango** Queensland Australia
67 F5 **Nan'ao** China
61 K8 **Nanao** Japan
67 F5 **Nan'ao Dao** *isld* China
61 L8 **Nanao wan** *B* Japan
61 K8 **Nanatsu-jima** *isld* Japan
67 B3 **Nanbai** China
67 B1 **Nanbazhen** China
67 B1 **Nanbu** China
21 P7 **Nançay** France
59 J2 **Nancha** China
67 E2 **Nanchang** China
65 E6 **Nanchangshan Dao** *isld* China
67 E3 **Nancheng** China
67 B1 **Nanchong** China
69 A9 **Nancowry** *isld* Nicobar Is
19 K4 **Nancy** France
144 A6 **Nancy Sd** New Zealand
74 H3 **Nanda Devi** *mt* India
67 B4 **Nandan** China
74 G9 **Nānded** India
139 K4 **Nandewar Ra** *mts* New South Wales Australia
37 M6 **Nandlstadt** W Germany
22 J3 **Nandrin** Belgium
67 C7 **Nandu Jiang** *R* China
74 F8 **Nandurbar** India
76 D3 **Nandyal** India
36 D4 **Nane** *R* W Germany
65 F4 **Nanfen** China
67 D5 **Nanfeng** China
67 E3 **Nanfeng** China
75 P4 **Nang** China
70 C4 **Nangabadau** Kalimantan
70 B6 **Nangabulik** Kalimantan
86 B5 **Nanga Eboko** Cameroon
70 C4 **Nangahbunut** Kalimantan
70 C4 **Nangahdangkan** Kalimantan
70 B5 **Nangah Dedai** Kalimantan
70 C4 **Nangahembaloh** Kalimantan
70 B4 **Nangahkantuk** Kalimantan
70 B4 **Nangahketungau** Kalimantan
70 B5 **Nangahmau** Kalimantan
70 B4 **Nangah Merakai** Kalimantan
70 B5 **Nangahpinoh** Kalimantan
70 C5 **Nangahserawai** Kalimantan
70 C4 **Nangahsuruk** Kalimantan
70 C4 **Nangahtempuai** Kalimantan
74 G3 **Nangal** India
71 E5 **Nangalao** *isld* Philippines
74 F1 **Nanga Parbat** *mt* Kashmir
71 K9 **Nangarendi** Indonesia
77 L2 **Nangarhār** *prov* Afghanistan
70 B5 **Nangataman** Kalimantan
69 K13 **Nangatayap** Indonesia
68 D7 **Nangin** Burma
18 G4 **Nangis** France
65 G5 **Nangnim Sanmaek** *mts* N Korea
65 C6 **Nangong** China
76 C6 **Nanguneri** India
87 D9 **Nangweshi** Zambia
Nanhai *see* **Foshan**
Nanhaoqian *see* **Shangyi**
65 C6 **Nanhe** China
67 D1 **Nan He** *R* China
67 G1 **Nanhui** China
66 F4 **Nan Hulsan Hu** *L* China
76 C4 **Nanjangud** India
58 E5 **Nanjiang** China
67 D2 **Nanjiangqiao** China
Nanjie *see* **Guangning**
67 F1 **Nanjing** China
67 F4 **Nanjing** China
67 C6 **Nankang** China
67 E4 **Nankang** China
Nanking *see* **Nanjing**
65 C4 **Nankouzhen** China
65 C6 **Nanle** China
67 D4 **Nan Ling** *mts* China
67 F1 **Nanling** China
Nanma *see* **Yiyuan**
67 G2 **Nanma** China
67 E3 **Nanmiao** Jiangxi China
37 L7 **Nannhofen** W Germany
143 C7 **Nannine** Western Australia Australia
67 C5 **Nanning** China
143 B10 **Nannup** Western Australia Australia
127 M2 **Nanny Town** *hist site* Jamaica
115 P5 **Nanortalik** Greenland
67 A4 **Nanpan Jiang** *R* China
75 J5 **Nanpara** India
67 F5 **Nanpeng Liedao** *islds* China
65 C5 **Nanpi** China
65 H3 **Nanping** China
68 E3 **Nan Poui** *R* Laos
65 D5 **Nanpu** China
67 F3 **Nanpu Xi** *R* China
Nanqiao *see* **Fengxian**
67 F4 **Nanri Dao** *isld* China
68 C2 **Nansang** Burma
134 D4 **Nansei Shoto Ridge** Pacific Oc
134 D5 **Nansei Shoto Tr** Pacific Oc
51 J5 **Nan Shan** *mt ra* China
66 E3 **Nanshankou** China
88 D3 **Nansio** Tanzania
143 A8 **Nanson** Western Australia Australia
18 H8 **Nant** France
112 D2 **Nantahala L** North Carolina U.S.A.
115 M5 **Nantais,L** Quebec Canada
75 K5 **Nantanwa** India
21 P4 **Nanterre** France
122 A8 **Nantes** Quebec Canada
20 G7 **Nantes** France
8 C4 **Nant-garw** Wales
70 K8 **Nanti** *mt* Sumatra
67 G2 **Nantian** China
18 F6 **Nantiat** France
120 K10 **Nanticoke** Ontario Canada
95 M8 **Nanticoke** *R* Delaware/Maryland U.S.A.
95 L5 **Nanticoke** Pennsylvania U.S.A.
8 C4 **Nant Moel** Wales
118 D8 **Nanton** Alberta Canada
67 G1 **Nantong** China
40 C5 **Nantua** France
95 R5 **Nantucket I** Massachusetts U.S.A.
88 G8 **Nantulo** Mozambique
8 D1 **Nantwich** England
94 J6 **Nanty Glo** Pennsylvania U.S.A.
137 Q3 **Nanumanga** *isld* Tuvalu
137 Q3 **Nanumea** *isld* Tuvalu
130 H5 **Nanuque** Brazil
116 M2 **Nanushuk** *R* Alaska U.S.A.
142 B5 **Nanutarra** Western Australia Australia
65 B6 **Nanweiquan** China
67 A2 **Nanxi** China
67 D2 **Nan Xian** China
67 C5 **Nanxiang** China
67 E4 **Nanxiong** China
58 F5 **Nanyang** China
67 C2 **Nanyaojie** China
65 C7 **Nanyi** China
67 F1 **Nanyi Hu** China
61 O7 **Nan'yō** Japan
65 C5 **Nanyuan** China
88 F1 **Nanyuki** Kenya
65 F4 **Nanzamu** China
67 D1 **Nanzhang** China
67 G3 **Nanzhen** China
17 H6 **Nao,C.de la** Spain
115 M7 **Naococane,L** Quebec Canada
61 M8 **Naoetsu** Japan
75 N6 **Naogaon** Bangladesh
74 C6 **Naokot** Pakistan
59 K2 **Naol He** *R* China
77 G3 **Naomid, Dasht-e** *desert* Iran
101 O8 **Naomi Pk** Utah U.S.A.
46 E4 **Náousa** Greece
67 C6 **Naozhou Dao** *isld* China
102 B3 **Napa** California U.S.A.
71 H7 **Napabalana** Indonesia
122 F7 **Napadogan** New Brunswick Canada
121 O8 **Napanee** Ontario Canada
116 G6 **Napaskiak** Alaska U.S.A.
115 O4 **Napasoq** Greenland
100 C3 **Napavine** Washington U.S.A.
71 F4 **Napayauan** Philippines
68 G3 **Nape** Laos
99 S8 **Naperville** Illinois U.S.A.
123 O2 **Napetipi R** Quebec Canada
40 G4 **Napf** *mt* Switzerland
145 F3 **Napier** New Zealand
99 L9 **Napier** Missouri U.S.A.
142 F2 **Napier Broome B** Western Australia Australia
140 A4 **Napier, Mt** N Terr Australia
146 K10 **Napier Mts** Antarctica
140 D1 **Napier Pen** N Terr Australia
142 E3 **Napier Ra** Western Australia Australia
121 R7 **Napierville** Quebec Canada
119 R9 **Napinka** Manitoba Canada
Naples *see* **Napoli** Italy
113 F11 **Naples** Florida U.S.A.
95 K4 **Naples** New York U.S.A.
109 N2 **Naples** Texas U.S.A.
67 B5 **Napo** China
68 G1 **Napo** China
128 C4 **Napo** *R* Peru/Ecuador
94 B7 **Napoleon** Indiana U.S.A.
98 G3 **Napoleon** North Dakota U.S.A.
94 C5 **Napoleon** Ohio U.S.A.
111 E12 **Napoleonville** Louisiana U.S.A.
43 G7 **Napoletano, Appennino** *mts* Italy
45 Q8 **Napoli** Italy
98 G9 **Naponee** Nebraska U.S.A.
135 U5 **Napoopoo** Hawaiian Is
131 E7 **Naposta** *R* Argentina
141 F8 **Nappamerry** Queensland Australia
94 A5 **Nappanee** Indiana U.S.A.
140 C6 **Napperby** N Terr Australia
110 C2 **Napton** Missouri U.S.A.
78 K3 **Naqadeh** Iran
79 F8 **Naqb Ishtar** Jordan
79 C9 **Naqb Malba** *mt* Egypt
61 J11 **Nara** Japan
85 C5 **Nara** Mali
139 G7 **Naracoopa** Tasmania Australia
138 F6 **Naracoorte** South Australia Australia
139 H5 **Naradhan** New South Wales Australia
117 O11 **Naramata** British Columbia Canada
83 K10 **Narammala** Sri Lanka
65 C2 **Naran Bulag** China
113 G12 **Naranja** Florida U.S.A.
124 E5 **Naranjo** Mexico
76 E2 **Naraspur** India
69 E9 **Narathiwat** Thailand
106 G6 **Nara Visa** New Mexico U.S.A.
75 O7 **Narayanganj** Bangladesh
76 C2 **Narayanpet** India
Narbada *R see* **Narmada** *R*
18 H9 **Narbonne** France
9 G2 **Narborough** England
16 C1 **Narcea** *R* Spain
43 J8 **Nardò** Italy
8 B7 **Nare Head** England
143 C9 **Narembeen** Western Australia Australia
74 H3 **Narendranagar** India
90 D6 **Nares Deep** Atlantic Oc
115 M2 **Nares Str** Canada/Greenland
143 E9 **Naretha** Western Australia Australia
31 O3 **Narew** Poland
65 G3 **Narhong** China
65 A5 **Narin** China
66 E4 **Narin Gol** *R* China
128 C3 **Nariño** *div* Colombia
61 O10 **Narita** Japan
127 P2 **Nariva** *co* Trinidad
127 P2 **Nariva Swamp** Trinidad
60 G11 **Nariwa** Japan
124 D4 **Narizon** *pt* Mexico
107 N2 **Narka** Kansas U.S.A.
29 M5 **Narkaus** Finland
26 N5 **Narken** Sweden
74 F7 **Narmada** *R* India
42 E6 **Narni** Italy
71 F5 **Naro** *isld* Philippines
52 K2 **Narodnaya, Gora** *mt* U.S.S.R.
89 A7 **Naroegas** S Africa
54 H1 **Naro-Fominsk** U.S.S.R.
88 E2 **Narok** Kenya
16 B1 **Naron** Spain
139 K6 **Narooma** New South Wales Australia
74 F2 **Narowal** Pakistan
29 J9 **Närpes** Finland
139 K4 **Narrabri** New South Wales Australia
139 J4 **Narrabri West** New South Wales Australia
95 Q5 **Narragansett** Rhode I U.S.A.
139 J3 **Narran** *R* New South Wales Australia
139 H5 **Narrandera** New South Wales Australia
139 H3 **Narran,L** New South Wales Australia
117 N8 **Narraway** *R* British Columbia Canada
141 H6 **Narrien Ra** Queensland Australia
143 E10 **Narrogin** Western Australia Australia
139 J4 **Narromine** New South Wales Australia
100 G6 **Narrows** Oregon U.S.A.
94 G9 **Narrows** Virginia U.S.A.
95 M5 **Narrowsburg** New York U.S.A.
142 B1 **Narrows, The** *str* Perth, W Aust Australia
127 P4 **Narrows,The** *chan* St Kitts W Indies
143 B7 **Narryer, Mt** Western Australia Australia
115 P5 **Narsalik** Greenland
115 P5 **Narsaq** Greenland
115 P5 **Narsarsuaq** Greenland
37 O1 **Narsdorf** East Germany
74 G7 **Narsinghgarh** India
75 K10 **Narsipatnam** India
65 C3 **Nart** China
46 C4 **Nartës,Gjol i** *isld* Albania
61 O7 **Naruko** Japan
131 F2 **Narunjito, L** Argentina
60 B13 **Naru-shima** *isld* Japan
61 O10 **Narutō** Japan
60 H11 **Naruto-kaikyō** *str* Japan
52 C5 **Narva** U.S.S.R.
71 E2 **Narvacan** Luzon Philippines
26 J3 **Narvik** Norway
52 C5 **Narvskiy Zaliv** *G* U.S.S.R.
74 G4 **Narwana** India
74 G6 **Narwar** India
140 C6 **Narwietooma** N Terr Australia
52 H1 **Nar'yan-Mar** U.S.S.R.
141 F8 **Naryilco** Queensland Australia
56 B6 **Narymskiy Khrebet** *mts* U.S.S.R.
57 H4 **Naryn** U.S.S.R.
57 G4 **Naryn Ugyut** *R* U.S.S.R.
54 G4 **Naryshkino** U.S.S.R.
27 G11 **Nås** Sweden
85 F7 **Nasarawa** Nigeria
48 J3 **Năsăud** Romania
26 M5 **Näsberg** Sweden
18 H8 **Nasbinals** France
144 C6 **Naseby** New Zealand
107 M5 **Nash** Oklahoma U.S.A.
8 C5 **Nash** Wales
122 F6 **Nash Cr** New Brunswick Canada
116 D6 **Nash Harbor** Alaska U.S.A.
140 E5 **Nash, L** Queensland Australia
8 C5 **Nash Pt** Wales
99 O7 **Nashua** Iowa U.S.A.
101 T1 **Nashua** Montana U.S.A.
95 Q4 **Nashua** New Hampshire U.S.A.
111 C8 **Nashville** Arkansas U.S.A.
112 D6 **Nashville** Georgia U.S.A.
110 G3 **Nashville** Illinois U.S.A.
94 A7 **Nashville** Indiana U.S.A.
107 M4 **Nashville** Kansas U.S.A.
94 B4 **Nashville** Michigan U.S.A.
112 J2 **Nashville** North Carolina U.S.A.
94 E6 **Nashville** Ohio U.S.A.
110 K5 **Nashville** Tennessee U.S.A.
99 N2 **Nashwauk** Minnesota U.S.A.
48 E5 **Našice** Yugoslavia
29 K10 **Näsijärvi** *L* Finland
74 E8 **Nasik** India
70 B4 **Nasilat** Kalimantan
86 F4 **Nasir** Sudan
79 A8 **Nasr** Egypt
79 H4 **Naşrānī, Jebel an** *mts* Syria
117 J8 **Nass** *R* British Columbia Canada
141 F3 **Nassau** *R* Queensland Australia
113 L9 **Nassau** New Providence I Bahamas
98 K4 **Nassau** Minnesota U.S.A.
95 O4 **Nassau** New York U.S.A.
36 D3 **Nassau** W Germany
133 D9 **Nassau,B.de** Chile
113 F7 **Nassau Sd** Florida U.S.A.
95 M9 **Nassawadox** Virginia U.S.A.
33 T10 **Nassebõhla** East Germany
37 L6 **Nassenfels** W Germany
33 S7 **Nassenheide** East Germany
84 J5 **Nasser, L** Egypt
27 G14 **Nässjö** Sweden
22 J3 **Nassogne** Belgium
38 N6 **Nasswald** Austria
115 M6 **Nastapoka Is** Northwest Territories Canada
36 D3 **Nastätten** W Germany
71 E3 **Nasugbu** Luzon Philippines
61 N8 **Nasu-Yumoto** Japan
52 D6 **Nasva** U.S.S.R.
26 J10 **Näsviken** Sweden
87 E10 **Nata** Botswana
89 E3 **Nata** *R* Botswana
141 H5 **Natal** *R* Queensland Australia
128 F5 **Natal** Brazil
118 C9 **Natal** British Columbia Canada
89 F7 **Natal** *prov* S Africa
69 D12 **Natal** Sumatra
90 M13 **Natal Basin** Indian Oc
141 H5 **Natal Downs** Queensland Australia
109 J6 **Natalia** Texas U.S.A.
55 C3 **Natalinsk** U.S.S.R.
77 B3 **Naṭanz** Iran
123 L3 **Natashquan** Quebec Canada
123 L3 **Natashquan R** Quebec/Labrador Canada
116 K3 **Natavukti L** Alaska U.S.A.
116 R6 **Natazhat Mt** Alaska U.S.A.
111 E10 **Natchez** Mississippi U.S.A.
111 C10 **Natchitoches** Louisiana U.S.A.
139 H6 **Nathalia** Victoria Australia
115 R3 **Nathorsts Land** Greenland
106 D3 **Nathrop** Colorado U.S.A.
124 J5 **Natillas** Mexico
138 F6 **Natimuk** Victoria Australia
116 R4 **Nation** Alaska U.S.A.
101 L2 **National Bison Ra** Montana U.S.A.
102 G9 **National City** California U.S.A.
86 C3 **National Park** Chad
117 L8 **Nation R** British Columbia Canada
123 K4 **Natiskotek B** Anticosti I, Quebec
141 H6 **Native Companion Cr** Queensland Australia
124 B4 **Natividad** *isld* Mexico
129 J6 **Natividade** Brazil
68 C5 **Natkyizin** Burma
107 M2 **Natoma** Kansas U.S.A.
124 E3 **Nátora** Mexico
61 O7 **Natori** Japan
22 J3 **Natoye** Belgium
101 T6 **Natrona** Wyoming U.S.A.
88 F3 **Natron L** Tanzania
61 O8 **Natsui-gawa** *R* Japan
68 B3 **Nattalin** Burma
83 J10 **Nattandiya** Sri Lanka
29 N3 **Nattaset** *mt* Finland
68 C3 **Nattaung** *mt* Burma
26 L5 **Nattavaara** Sweden
37 O6 **Natternberg** W Germany
37 J6 **Nattheim** W Germany
27 H15 **Nättraby** Sweden
69 H10 **Natuna Besar** *isld* Indonesia
69 H11 **Natuna, Kepulauan** *islds* Indonesia
69 H10 **Natuna Utara** *isld* Indonesia
95 M2 **Natural Bridge** New York U.S.A.
94 H9 **Natural Bridge** Virginia U.S.A.
103 O4 **Natural Br.Nat.Mon** Utah U.S.A.
108 F3 **Natural Dam L** Texas U.S.A.
143 B10 **Naturaliste, C** Western Australia Australia
143 A7 **Naturaliste Chan** Western Australia Australia
81 H9 **Naturaliste Plateau** Indian Oc
106 B3 **Naturita** Colorado U.S.A.
99 V3 **Naubinway** Michigan U.S.A.
87 C10 **Nauchas** Namibia
121 T4 **Naudville** Quebec Canada
33 R7 **Nauen** East Germany
130 E10 **Naufragados, Pta Dos** *C* Brazil
95 O5 **Naugatuck** Connecticut U.S.A.
71 E4 **Naujan** Philippines
29 N8 **Naulavaara** *mt* Finland
87 B9 **Naulila** Angola
37 M1 **Naumburg** East Germany
36 G1 **Naumburg** W Germany
68 C4 **Naunglon** Burma
68 C3 **Naungpale** Burma
33 R10 **Naunhof** East Germany
80 G6 **Na'ur** Jordan
36 D2 **Nauroth** W Germany
137 O2 **Nauru** *rep* Pacific Oc
55 D5 **Naurzum** U.S.S.R.
26 A10 **Naustdal** Norway
26 C9 **Nauste** Norway
128 D4 **Nauta** Peru
89 A6 **Naute Dam** Namibia
111 J8 **Nauvoo** Alabama U.S.A.
99 P9 **Nauvoo** Illinois U.S.A.
108 G7 **Nava** Mexico
57 F5 **Navabad** U.S.S.R.
57 E5 **Navabadskiy** U.S.S.R.
16 D3 **Nava de Rey** Spain
16 E5 **Navahermosa** Spain
103 P6 **Navajo** Arizona U.S.A.
103 M4 **Navajo L** Utah U.S.A.
103 O4 **Navajo Mt** Utah U.S.A.
103 O5 **Navajo Nat.Mon** Arizona U.S.A.
103 N5 **Navajo Pt** Arizona U.S.A.
106 C5 **Navajo Res** Colo/New Mex U.S.A.
16 E4 **Navalcarnero** Spain
16 D5 **Navalmoral de la Mata** Spain
86 E5 **Nava R** Zaire
133 D9 **Navarino, I** Chile
17 F2 **Navarra** *prov* Spain
139 G6 **Navarre** Victoria Australia
94 F6 **Navarre** Ohio U.S.A.
102 A2 **Navarro** *R* California U.S.A.
102 A2 **Navarro** California U.S.A.
109 L4 **Navarro Mills Res** Texas U.S.A.
109 L5 **Navasota** Texas U.S.A.
126 G5 **Navassa I** Caribbean
45 P5 **Navelli** Italy
9 F1 **Navenby** England
16 C1 **Navia** *R* Spain
16 C1 **Navia** Spain
109 L6 **Navidad** *R* Texas U.S.A.
127 K4 **Navidad Bank** Caribbean
130 H10 **Navio** *R* Brazil
54 F4 **Navlya** *R* U.S.S.R.
54 F4 **Navlya** U.S.S.R.
48 M6 **Năvodari** Romania
57 D4 **Navoi** U.S.S.R.
124 E4 **Navojoa** Mexico
124 F5 **Navolato** Mexico
52 F5 **Navoloki** U.S.S.R.
46 E6 **Návpaktos** Greece
46 F7 **Návplion** Greece
28 B4 **Navr** Denmark
85 D6 **Navrongo** Ghana
74 E8 **Navsari** India
75 N6 **Nawabganj** Bangladesh
75 J5 **Nawabganj** India
74 C5 **Nawabshah** Pakistan
75 L6 **Nawada** India
77 K3 **Nāwah** Afghanistan
83 K10 **Nawalapitiya** Sri Lanka
84 F3 **Nawfalīyah,an** Libya
68 D1 **Nawng-Hpa** Burma
68 C1 **Nawngkio** Burma
68 D1 **Nawngleng** Burma
67 B2 **Naxi** China
47 H7 **Náxos** *isld* Greece
46 G7 **Náxos** Greece
18 E9 **Nay** France
16 E4 **Nayacerrada, Pto. de** *pk* Spain
75 L8 **Nayagarh** India
124 G6 **Nayar** Mexico
124 G7 **Nayarit** *state* Mexico
77 E3 **Nay Band** Iran
9 G4 **Nayland** England
113 D7 **Naylor** Georgia U.S.A.
110 F5 **Naylor** Missouri U.S.A.
67 B3 **Nayong** China
59 M3 **Nayoro** Japan
76 D4 **Nāyudupeta** India
129 L6 **Nazaré** Brazil
16 A5 **Nazaré** Portugal
130 J9 **Nazaré da Mata** Brazil
22 F2 **Nazareth** Belgium
76 C6 **Nazareth** India
80 E3 **Nazareth** Israel
95 M6 **Nazareth** Pennsylvania U.S.A.
130 E5 **Nazário** Brazil
54 N2 **Nazarovka** U.S.S.R.
56 D3 **Nazarovo** Krasnoyarskiy Kray U.S.S.R.
55 F3 **Nazarovo** Tyumenskaya obl U.S.S.R.
124 G5 **Nazas** Mexico
128 D6 **Nazca** Peru
59 J6 **Naze** Japan
9 H4 **Naze,The** *C* England
47 J7 **Nazilli** Turkey
56 A1 **Nazinskaya** *R* U.S.S.R.
75 Q5 **Nazira** India
75 O7 **Nazir Hat** Bangladesh
117 M9 **Nazko** British Columbia Canada
80 A7 **Nazla** Israel
80 D4 **Nazlat** Jordan
86 G4 **Nazrēt** Ethiopia
67 B4 **Nazuo** China
72 H4 **Nazwá** Oman
55 E1 **Nazym** *R* U.S.S.R.
55 F3 **Nazyvayevsk** U.S.S.R.
37 J1 **Nazza** East Germany
6 L4 **N Brae** *oil rig* North Sea
89 F3 **Ncema Dam** Zimbabwe
88 A8 **Nchanga** Zambia
88 E9 **Ncheu** Malawi
89 B4 **Ncojane** Botswana
87 B7 **N'dalatando** Angola
85 E6 **Ndali** Benin
71 L10 **Ndao** *isld* Indonesia
86 D4 **Ndéle** Cent Afr Republic
86 B6 **Ndendé** Gabon
137 O4 **Ndeni** *isld* Santa Cruz Is
86 B5 **Ndikiniméki** Cameroon
86 B6 **Ndindi** Gabon
86 C3 **Ndjamena** Chad
86 B6 **Ndjolé** Gabon
86 B6 **Ndogo, Lagune** *lagoon* Gabon
88 B8 **Ndola** Zambia
71 K9 **Ndona** Flores Indonesia
86 B6 **N'Dongo** Congo
26 E8 **Nea** Norway
141 J7 **Neabul** *R* Queensland Australia
46 D5 **Néa Filippías** Greece
14 E2 **Neagh,L** N Ireland
107 O4 **Neal** Kansas U.S.A.
140 B6 **Neale,L** N Terr Australia
138 D3 **Neales** *R* South Australia Australia
46 F4 **Neá Moudhaniá** Greece
48 K4 **Neamţ** *reg* Romania
20 F5 **Néant** France
21 O6 **Néant** *R* France
15 G2 **Neap** Shetland Scotland
47 H9 **Neápolis** Crete Greece
46 E4 **Neápolis** Makedhonia Greece
46 F8 **Neápolis** Pelopónnisos Greece
46 F6 **Néa Psará** Greece
116 J9 **Near Is** Aleutian Is
8 C4 **Neath** Wales
21 O4 **Neauphle-le-Château** France
47 H3 **Néa Víssi** Greece
85 D6 **Nebbou** Burkina
52 G3 **Nebdino** U.S.S.R.
33 Q5 **Nebel** *R* East Germany
28 A7 **Nebel** W Germany
41 M3 **Nebelhorn** *mt* W Germany
43 B12 **Nebeur** Tunisia
43 C12 **Nebhana** *R* Tunisia
141 H8 **Nebine** *R* Queensland Australia
50 E5 **Nebit-Dag** U.S.S.R.
141 J5 **Nebo** Queensland Australia
52 D5 **Nebolchi** U.S.S.R.
80 F5 **Nebo, Mt** Jordan
103 N2 **Nebo,Mt** Utah U.S.A.
33 P10 **Nebra** East Germany
98 G8 **Nebraska** *state* U.S.A.
99 L9 **Nebraska City** Nebraska U.S.A.
43 F11 **Nebrodi,Monti** Sicily
99 Q5 **Necedah** Wisconsin U.S.A.
117 L9 **Nechako R** British Columbia Canada
98 J1 **Neche** North Dakota U.S.A.
109 M4 **Neches** *R* Texas U.S.A.
128 D2 **Nechi** *R* Colombia
33 T6 **Nechlin** East Germany
36 F7 **Neckar** *R* W Germany
36 F5 **Neckarbischofsheim** W Germany
36 G5 **Neckarelz** W Germany
36 F5 **Neckargemünd** W Germany
36 F5 **Neckarsteinach** W Germany
36 G5 **Neckarsulm** W Germany
102 J13 **Necker I** Hawaiian Is
144 B7 **Neck, The** New Zealand
131 F7 **Necochea** Argentina
37 P4 **Nečtiny** Czechoslovakia
86 B6 **Necuto** Angola
21 K4 **Nécy** France
16 B1 **Neda** Spain
33 S5 **Neddemin** East Germany
121 L5 **Nedelec** Quebec Canada
46 G3 **Nedelino** Bulgaria
106 E2 **Nederland** Colorado U.S.A.
109 N6 **Nederland** Texas U.S.A.
25 E5 **Neder Rijn** *R* Netherlands
25 E6 **Nederweert** Netherlands
142 A2 **Nedlands** *dist* Perth, W Aust Australia
33 Q8 **Nedlitz** East Germany
66 E6 **Nêdong** China
17 F9 **Nedroma** Algeria
31 L5 **Nedza** Poland
25 G4 **Neede** Netherlands
9 H3 **Needham Market** England
101 Q5 **Needle Mt** Wyoming U.S.A.
103 K7 **Needles** California U.S.A.
145 E2 **Needles Pt** New Zealand
9 E6 **Needles, The** *rocks* England
109 M6 **Needville** Texas U.S.A.
119 S9 **Neelin** Manitoba Canada
101 N7 **Neely** Idaho U.S.A.
110 F5 **Neelyville** Missouri U.S.A.
130 B10 **Neembucú** *dept* Paraguay
99 S5 **Neenah** Wisconsin U.S.A.
119 S8 **Neepawa** Manitoba Canada
25 E6 **Neer** Netherlands
106 H3 **Nee Res** Colorado U.S.A.
115 M3 **Neergaard L** Northwest Territories Canada
22 J1 **Neerpelt** Belgium
22 J2 **Neerwinden** Belgium
28 A4 **Nees** Denmark
112 F4 **Neeses** South Carolina U.S.A.
55 F2 **Nefedovo** U.S.S.R.
85 F2 **Nefta** Tunisia
57 F4 **Nefteabad** U.S.S.R.
53 H7 **Neftegorsk** U.S.S.R.
52 H6 **Neftekamsk** U.S.S.R.
8 B2 **Nefyn** Wales
43 C12 **Nefza** Tunisia
87 C7 **Negage** Angola
85 C6 **Negala** Mali
83 K10 **Negama** Sri Lanka
70 P10 **Negara** Bali Indonesia
70 D6 **Negara** *R* Kalimantan
70 D6 **Negara** Kalimantan
99 T3 **Negaunee** Michigan U.S.A.
80 B7 **Negba** Israel
86 G4 **Negelē** Ethiopia
69 F11 **Negeri Sembilan** Malaysia
79 E8 **Negev** *mt reg* Israel
130 C8 **Negla** *R* Paraguay
48 J5 **Negoiu** *mt* Romania
87 G8 **Negomano** Mozambique
83 J10 **Negombo** Sri Lanka
48 H6 **Negotin** Yugoslavia
46 E3 **Negotino** Yugoslavia
73 P5 **Negrais,C** Burma
131 H5 **Negra o de los Difuntos, L** Uruguay
143 D7 **Negrara,R** Western Australia Australia
130 G6 **Negra,Serra** *mts* Brazil
16 B2 **Negreira** Spain
48 J6 **Negreni** Romania
18 G3 **Nègrepelisse** France
48 L4 **Negreşti** Romania
48 H3 **Negreşti-Oaş** Romania
127 H1 **Negril Pt.N** Jamaica
128 F4 **Negro** *R* Brazil
16 D9 **Negro,C** Morocco
94 H7 **Negro Mt** Penn/Maryland U.S.A.
131 C7 **Negro,R** Argentina
130 B9 **Negro,R** Paraguay
131 F4 **Negro,R** Uruguay
71 F5 **Negros** *isld* Philippines
47 J1 **Negru Vodă** Romania
100 B4 **Nehalem** Oregon U.S.A.
80 C5 **Nehalim** Israel
77 G4 **Nehbandān** Iran
59 H2 **Nehe** China
32 G10 **Neheim-Hüsten** W Germany
48 K5 **Nehoiaşu** Romania
20 G3 **Néhou** France
33 R4 **Nehringen** East Germany
137 S5 **Neiafu** Tonga
127 J5 **Neiba** Dominican Rep
33 R10 **Neichen** East Germany
52 C1 **Neiden** Norway
118 K8 **Neidpath** Saskatchewan Canada
101 P3 **Neihart** Montana U.S.A.
58 F4 **Neihuang** China
65 C7 **Neihuang** China
67 B2 **Neijiang** China
Neikiang *see* **Neijiang**
16 E2 **Neila,Sa.de** *mts* Spain
118 H6 **Neilburg** Saskatchewan Canada
68 A7 **Neill I** Andaman Is
99 Q5 **Neillsville** Wisconsin U.S.A.
123 M7 **Neil's Harbour** C Breton I, Nova Scotia
100 B2 **Neilton** Washington U.S.A.
58 E3 **Nei Mongol Zizhiqu** *aut reg* China
33 N8 **Neindorf** W Germany
36 G5 **Neipperg** W Germany
65 C6 **Neiqiu** China
Neisse *see* **Nysa**
31 H4 **Neisse** *R* E Germany/Poland
128 C3 **Neiva** Colombia
37 O3 **Nejdek** Czechoslovakia
86 G4 **Nejo** Ethiopia
86 G4 **Nek'emtē** Ethiopia
53 F8 **Nekhayevskiy** U.S.S.R.
98 H1 **Nekoma** North Dakota U.S.A.
99 R5 **Nekoosa** Wisconsin U.S.A.
28 G5 **Nekselø** *isld* Denmark
27 H16 **Neksø** Denmark
27 C13 **Nelaug** Norway
141 F5 **Nelia** Queensland Australia
54 D1 **Nelidovo** U.S.S.R.
52 D6 **Nelidovo** U.S.S.R.
98 J7 **Neligh** Nebraska U.S.A.
142 E3 **Nellie,Mt** Western Australia Australia
139 K6 **Nelligen** New South Wales Australia
76 D3 **Nellore** India
59 L2 **Nel'ma** U.S.S.R.
52 F5 **Nel'sha** U.S.S.R.
138 F7 **Nelson** Victoria Australia
117 P11 **Nelson** British Columbia Canada
13 F6 **Nelson** England
145 D4 **Nelson** New Zealand
144 C4 **Nelson** *stat area* New Zealand
103 L6 **Nelson** Arizona U.S.A.
102 C2 **Nelson** California U.S.A.
98 H9 **Nelson** Nebraska U.S.A.
103 K6 **Nelson** Nevada U.S.A.
112 J2 **Nelson** North Carolina U.S.A.
95 K5 **Nelson** Pennsylvania U.S.A.
99 P5 **Nelson** Wisconsin U.S.A.
8 C4 **Nelson** Wales
138 F7 **Nelson,C** Victoria Australia
144 C5 **Nelson Creek** New Zealand
133 C8 **Nelson,Estrecho** *chan* Chile
117 M6 **Nelson Forks** British Columbia Canada
119 T3 **Nelson House** Manitoba Canada
116 E6 **Nelson I** Alaska U.S.A.
145 D4 **Nelson Lakes Nat. Park** New Zealand
119 V3 **Nelson R** Manitoba Canada
101 S1 **Nelson Res** Montana U.S.A.
94 E7 **Nelsonville** Ohio U.S.A.
89 G5 **Nelspruit** S Africa
52 J4 **Nem** *R* U.S.S.R.
85 C5 **Néma** Mauritania
52 H5 **Nema** U.S.S.R.
99 O3 **Nemadji** *R* Minnesota U.S.A.
99 L9 **Nemaha** Nebraska U.S.A.
76 C6 **Nemam** India
52 A6 **Neman** U.S.S.R.
31 O2 **Neman** *R* U.S.S.R.
52 F5 **Nemda** *R* U.S.S.R.
52 H3 **Nemed** U.S.S.R.
120 G5 **Nemegos** Ontario Canada
120 G4 **Nemegosenda L** Ontario Canada
119 M3 **Nemeiban** Saskatchewan Canada
46 D4 **Nëmerçkë** Albania
52 D1 **Nemetskiy, Mys** *C* U.S.S.R.
45 N6 **Nemi** *L* Italy
48 K4 **Nemira** *mt* Romania
48 M2 **Nemirov** U.S.S.R.
115 M7 **Nemiscau** Quebec Canada
18 G4 **Nemours** France
71 L10 **Nemperola** Indonesia
60 T2 **Nemuro** Japan
60 S2 **Nemuro** *prefect* Japan
60 T1 **Nemuro-kaikyō** *str* Japan/U.S.S.R.
14 C4 **Nenagh** Ireland
116 N4 **Nenana** Alaska U.S.A.
41 L3 **Nendeln** Liechtenstein
9 F2 **Nene, R** England
59 J2 **Nenjiang** China
59 H2 **Nen Jiang** *R* China
36 B4 **Nennig** W Germany
36 H1 **Nentershausen** W Germany
13 F4 **Nenthead** England
98 E7 **Nenzel** Nebraska U.S.A.
41 L3 **Nenzing** Austria
107 P4 **Neodesha** Kansas U.S.A.
99 S10 **Neoga** Illinois U.S.A.
99 L8 **Neola** Iowa U.S.A.
103 O1 **Neola** Utah U.S.A.
47 H7 **Néon Karlóvasi** Greece
99 S5 **Neopit** Wisconsin U.S.A.
130 H11 **Neópolis** Brazil
107 P4 **Neosho** *R* Kansas/Okla U.S.A.
99 S6 **Neosho** Wisconsin U.S.A.
80 D3 **Neot Golan** Israel
80 F1 **Ne'ot Mordekhay** Israel
56 G2 **Nepa** *R* U.S.S.R.
75 K4 **Nepal** *kingdom* S Asia
75 J5 **Nepalganj** India
103 N2 **Nephi** Utah U.S.A.
14 B2 **Nephin** *mt* Ireland
14 B2 **Nephin Beg** *mt* Ireland
121 N8 **Nephton** Ontario Canada
45 M5 **Nepi** Italy
37 P3 **Nepomyšl** Czechoslovakia
119 N9 **Neptune** Saskatchewan Canada
113 F7 **Neptune Beach** Florida U.S.A.
138 D6 **Neptune Is** South Australia Australia
146 E8 **Neptune Ra** Antarctica
31 L4 **Ner** *R* Poland
42 E6 **Nera** *R* Italy
48 G6 **Nera** *R* Romania
18 F8 **Nérac** France
116 D6 **Neragon I** Alaska U.S.A.
58 G1 **Nercha** *R* U.S.S.R.
33 R10 **Nerchau** East Germany
58 G1 **Nerchinsk** U.S.S.R.
59 G1 **Nerchinsky Zavod** U.S.S.R.
68 C7 **Nerchus Passage** Burma
52 J5 **Nerdva** U.S.S.R.
52 F5 **Nerekhta** U.S.S.R.
37 J6 **Neresheim** W Germany
42 H5 **Neretva** *R* Yugoslavia
87 D9 **Neriquinha** Angola
116 H7 **Nerka,L** Alaska U.S.A.
52 F6 **Nerl'** U.S.S.R.
52 E6 **Nerl'** U.S.S.R.
45 N5 **Nerola** Italy
18 G5 **Nerondes** France
45 N4 **Nerone, M** *mt* Italy
130 E5 **Nerópolis** Brazil
52 J3 **Neroyka, Gora** *mt* U.S.S.R.
17 F6 **Nerpio** Spain
142 E4 **Nerrima** Western Australia Australia
54 E4 **Nerussa** *R* U.S.S.R.
16 C7 **Nerva** Spain
44 F3 **Nervi** Italy
52 K2 **Ner'yuvom** U.S.S.R.
25 E2 **Nes** Netherlands
27 D11 **Nesbyen** Norway
95 L5 **Nescopeck** Pennsylvania U.S.A.
47 J2 **Nesebŭr** Bulgaria
52 C6 **Neshcherdo Oz** *L* U.S.S.R.
80 D2 **Nesher** Israel
116 A3 **Neshkan** Alaska U.S.A.
99 R6 **Neshkoro** Wisconsin U.S.A.
111 G9 **Neshoba** Mississippi U.S.A.
29 T9 **Neskaupsstadhur** Iceland
27 D13 **Neslandsvatn** Norway
22 D4 **Nesle** France
123 N3 **Nesle,L** Quebec Canada
26 F5 **Nesna** Norway
26 F5 **Nesöy** *isld* Norway
100 G1 **Nespelem** Washington U.S.A.
45 O5 **Nespolo** Italy
19 O16 **Nesque** *R* France
107 L3 **Ness City** Kansas U.S.A.
37 K1 **Nesse** *R* East Germany
26 R1 **Nesseby** Norway
117 F6 **Nesselrode,Mt** Br Col/Alaska Canada/U.S.A.
18 F10 **Neste** *R* France
31 O1 **Nesterov** U.S.S.R.
120 G6 **Nesterville** Ontario Canada
52 G6 **Nestiary** U.S.S.R.
127 P2 **Nestor** Trinidad
118 J1 **Nestor Falls** Ontario Canada
99 S3 **Nestoria** Michigan U.S.A.
46 E4 **Nestórion** Greece
46 G3 **Néstos** *R* Greece
27 A11 **Nesttun** Norway
80 C6 **Nes Ziyyona** Israel
80 C4 **Netanya** Israel
107 P2 **Netawaka** Kansas U.S.A.
95 N6 **Netcong** New Jersey U.S.A.
32 K9 **Nethe** *R* W Germany
118 H7 **Netherhill** Saskatchewan Canada
25 **Netherlands** *kingdom* Europe
8 C5 **Nether Stowey** England
145 E2 **Netherton** New Zealand
15 E3 **Nethy Bridge** Scotland
80 C6 **Netiva** Israel
80 C7 **Netiv HaLamed** Israel
80 B8 **Netivot** Israel
43 H9 **Neto** *R* Italy
36 E2 **Netphen** W Germany
37 J1 **Netra** W Germany
75 O6 **Netrakona** Bangladesh
36 C3 **Nette** *R* W Germany
36 B3 **Nettersheim** W Germany
25 F6 **Nettetal** W Germany
115 M4 **Nettilling L** Northwest Territories Canada
99 N1 **Nett L** Minnesota U.S.A.
9 F4 **Nettlebed** England
120 K4 **Nettle Lakes Prov. Park** Ontario Canada
110 F6 **Nettleton** Arkansas U.S.A.
111 H7 **Nettleton** Mississippi U.S.A.
45 N7 **Nettuno** Italy
125 N9 **Netzahaulcoyotl, Presa** *res* Mexico
37 N2 **Netzschkau** East Germany
36 H1 **Neu** W Germany
32 G7 **Neu Arenberg** W Germany
37 N5 **Neubäu** W Germany
32 H9 **Neubeckum** W Germany
21 M3 **Neuborg,le** France
33 S5 **Neubrandenburg** East Germany
33 R5 **Neubrandenburg** *reg* East Germany
32 J7 **Neubruchhausen** W Germany
36 H4 **Neubrunn** W Germany
33 P4 **Neubukow** East Germany
33 P5 **Neuburg** East Germany
37 L6 **Neuburg** W Germany
40 E3 **Neuchâtel** *canton* Switzerland
40 E4 **Neuchâtel, Lac de** Switzerland
32 M9 **Neuckrug** W Germany
119 P8 **Neudorf** Saskatchewan Canada
37 M3 **Neudrossenfeld** W Germany
32 L10 **Neu-Eichenberg** W Germany
36 F6 **Neuenburg** Baden-Württemberg W Germany
32 G6 **Neuenburg** Niedersachsen W Germany
32 E7 **Neuenhaus** W Germany
32 J6 **Neuenkirchen** Niedersachsen W Germany
32 F8 **Neuenkirchen** Nordrhein-Westfalen W Germany
32 G10 **Neuenrade** W Germany
36 G5 **Neuenstadt** W Germany
36 H5 **Neuenstein** W Germany
36 G2 **Neuental** W Germany
32 J5 **Neuenwalde** W Germany
37 M7 **Neufahrn** W Germany
40 G1 **Neuf Brisach** France
22 J4 **Neufchateau** Belgium
19 J4 **Neufchâteau** France
21 L5 **Neufchâtel** Sarthe France
21 N2 **Neufchâtel-en-Bray** France
22 B2 **Neufchâtel-Hardelot** France
22 F5 **Neufchâtel-sur-Aisne** France
38 K5 **Neufelden** Austria
36 G6 **Neuffen** W Germany
21 O3 **Neuf-Marché** France
36 G7 **Neufra** W Germany
41 N2 **Neugablonz** W Germany
33 S6 **Neuglobsow** East Germany
32 G5 **Neuharlingersiel** W Germany
33 N6 **Neuhaus** East Germany
37 M4 **Neuhaus** Bayern W Germany
32 K5 **Neuhaus** Niedersachsen W Germany
37 P2 **Neuhausen** East Germany
36 G6 **Neuhausen** W Germany
33 S8 **Neuhof** East Germany
38 K5 **Neuhofen** Austria
36 G5 **Neuhütten** W Germany
21 N8 **Neuillay-les-Bois** France
21 M4 **Neuilly** Orne France
21 P3 **Neuilly-en-Thelle** France
21 H3 **Neuilly-la-Forêt** France
36 F3 **Neu-Isenburg** W Germany
33 R5 **Neukalen** East Germany
33 O6 **Neu Kaliss** East Germany
38 F7 **Neukirchen** Austria
37 O2 **Neukirchen** East Germany
33 O4 **Neukirchen** Schleswig-Holstein W Germany
37 N5 **Neukirchen Balbini** W Germany
33 P5 **Neukloster** East Germany
32 L6 **Neukloster** W Germany
21 M6 **Neullé-Pont-Pierre** France
20 E5 **Neulliac** France
37 N2 **Neumark** East Germany
38 H6 **Neumarkt** Salzburg Austria
38 K7 **Neumarkt** Steiermark Austria
37 L5 **Neumarkt** W Germany
37 O7 **Neumarkt-St Veit** W Germany
32 L4 **Neumünster** W Germany
37 N5 **Neunburg** W Germany
21 O6 **Neung-sur-Beuvron** France
38 O6 **Neunkirchen** Austria
36 C2 **Neunkirchen** W Germany
36 D2 **Neunkirchen** Nordrhein-Westfalen W Germany

60 Neunkirchen — Nižm Medzev

36 E2 **Neunkirchen** Rheinland-Pfalz W Germany
36 C5 **Neunkirchen** Saarland W Germany
37 O7 **Neuötting** W Germany
131 C7 **Neuquén** Argentina
131 B7 **Neuquén** *terr* Argentina
131 B7 **Neuquén, R** Argentina
33 R7 **Neuruppin** East Germany
37 K7 **Neusäss** W Germany
112 L3 **Neuse R** North Carolina U.S.A.
48 D3 **Neusiedla** Austria
48 D3 **Neusiedler See** Austria
36 B1 **Neuss** W Germany
18 H7 **Neussargues** France
48 C3 **Neustadt** Austria
37 M2 **Neustadt** Gera East Germany
33 Q7 **Neustadt** Potsdam East Germany
37 K2 **Neustadt** Suhl East Germany
36 G2 **Neustadt** Hessen W Germany
36 H3 **Neustadt** Hessen W Germany
36 G4 **Neustadt** Hessen W Germany
36 E5 **Neustadt** Rheinland-Pfalz W Germany
37 K4 **Neustadt an der Aisch** W Germany
37 N4 **Neustadt an der Waldnaab** W Germany
37 L3 **Neustadt bei Coburg** W Germany
33 P6 **Neustadt-Glewe** East Germany
32 G6 **Neustadt-gödens** W Germany
Neustettin *see* **Szczecinek**
37 M7 **Neustift** W Germany
33 S6 **Neustrelitz** East Germany
37 J7 **Neu Ulm** W Germany
22 D2 **Neuve Chapelle** France
21 M4 **Neuve-Lyre,la** France
40 F3 **Neuveville** Switzerland
18 G7 **Neuvic** France
109 N4 **Neuville** Texas U.S.A.
21 P5 **Neuville-aux-Bois** France
21 L8 **Neuville-de-Poitou** Vienne France
22 G5 **Neuville-en-Tourne-à-Fuy** France
19 O12 **Neuville-les-Dames** France
21 N2 **Neuville-les-Dieppe** France
21 K8 **Neuvy Bouin** France
21 M6 **Neuvy-le-Roi** France
21 O8 **Neuvy Pailloux** France
21 O8 **Neuvy St. Sépulchre** France
21 P7 **Neuvy-sur-Barangeon** France
33 O8 **Neuwegersleben** East Germany
36 E6 **Neuweier** W Germany
32 H5 **Neuwerk** *isld* W Germany
36 C3 **Neuwied** W Germany
36 C6 **Neuwiller** France
32 L6 **Neu-Wulmstorf** W Germany
27 G11 **Neva** Sweden
99 R4 **Neva** Wisconsin U.S.A.
52 D5 **Neva** *R* U.S.S.R.
102 F2 **Nevada** *state* U.S.A.
99 N7 **Nevada** Iowa U.S.A.
110 B4 **Nevada** Missouri U.S.A.
109 L2 **Nevada** Texas U.S.A.
102 C2 **Nevada City** California U.S.A.
128 D2 **Nevada de Cocuy,Sa** *mts* Colombia
124 H8 **Nevada de Colima** Mexico
16 E7 **Nevada, Sierra** *mts* Spain
131 C5 **Nevado, Cerro** *pk* Argentina
131 E6 **Nevados Chillán** *mt* Chile
131 C5 **Nevado, Sierra del** *ra* Argentina
54 A1 **Nevel'** U.S.S.R.
59 M2 **Nevel'sk** U.S.S.R.
59 H1 **Never** U.S.S.R.
8 B3 **Nevern** Wales
26 F6 **Nevernes** Norway
18 H5 **Nevers** France
139 J4 **Nevertire** New South Wales Australia
48 E7 **Nevesinje** Yugoslavia
20 C6 **Névez** France
45 H2 **Neviano d'Arduini** Italy
32 F10 **Neviges** W Germany
118 K9 **Neville** Saskatchewan Canada
21 M2 **Neville** France
112 F5 **Nevils** Georgia U.S.A.
53 F11 **Nevinnomyssk** U.S.S.R.
79 E9 **Neviot** Egypt
118 D6 **Nevis** Alberta Canada
127 P4 **Nevis** *isld* Lesser Antilles
99 M3 **Nevis** Minnesota U.S.A.
127 P4 **Nevis Pk** Nevis W Indies
80 E6 **Nevit HaGedud** Jordan
78 E2 **Nevşehir** Turkey
65 J2 **Nevskoye** U.S.S.R.
55 D2 **Nev'yansk** U.S.S.R.
103 J9 **New** *R* California U.S.A.
112 F1 **New** *R* North Carolina U.S.A.
94 F9 **New** *R* Virginia/W Virginia U.S.A.
12 E4 **New Abbey** Scotland
95 S3 **Newagen** Maine U.S.A.
87 G8 **Newala** Tanzania
94 B8 **New Albany** Indiana U.S.A.
111 G7 **New Albany** Mississippi U.S.A.
95 L5 **New Albany** Pennsylvania U.S.A.
99 P6 **New Albin** Iowa U.S.A.
99 S4 **Newald** Wisconsin U.S.A.
9 E5 **New Alresford** England
141 J8 **New Angledool** New South Wales Australia
9 F1 **Newark** England
110 E6 **Newark** Arkansas U.S.A.
102 B4 **Newark** California U.S.A.
95 M7 **Newark** Delaware U.S.A.
99 S8 **Newark** Illinois U.S.A.
98 G9 **Newark** Nebraska U.S.A.
95 N6 **Newark** New Jersey U.S.A.
95 K3 **Newark** New York U.S.A.
94 E6 **Newark** Ohio U.S.A.
95 L4 **Newark Valley** New York U.S.A.
110 G3 **New Athens** Illinois U.S.A.
99 P4 **New Auburn** Wisconsin U.S.A.
111 G10 **New Augusta** Mississippi U.S.A.
94 E4 **New Baltimore** Michigan U.S.A.
94 J7 **New Baltimore** Pennsylvania U.S.A.
95 R5 **New Bedford** Massachusetts U.S.A.
100 C4 **Newberg** Oregon U.S.A.
99 Q10 **New Berlin** Illinois U.S.A.
95 M4 **New Berlin** New York U.S.A.
111 J9 **Newbern** Alabama U.S.A.
112 K2 **New Bern** North Carolina U.S.A.
110 G5 **Newbern** Tennessee U.S.A.
102 H7 **Newberry** California U.S.A.
113 E8 **Newberry** Florida U.S.A.
110 J3 **Newberry** Indiana U.S.A.
99 V3 **Newberry** Michigan U.S.A.
112 F3 **Newberry** South Carolina U.S.A.
94 H5 **New Bethlehem** Pennsylvania U.S.A.
13 G3 **Newbiggin by-the-Sea** England
13 E3 **Newbigging** Scotland
110 D3 **New Bloomfield** Missouri U.S.A.
99 R4 **Newbold** Wisconsin U.S.A.
121 O8 **Newboro** Ontario Canada
8 B1 **Newborough** Wales
99 Q8 **New Boston** Illinois U.S.A.
109 N2 **New Boston** Texas U.S.A.
109 J6 **New Braunfels** Texas U.S.A.
94 C6 **New Bremen** Ohio U.S.A.
12 E3 **New Bridge** Scotland
8 C3 **Newbridge** Wales
118 G7 **New Brigden** Alberta Canada
95 P5 **New Britain** Connecticut U.S.A.
136 K3 **New Britain** Papua New Guinea
111 L10 **New Brockton** Alabama U.S.A.
122 F7 **New Brunswick** *prov* Canada
95 N6 **New Brunswick** New Jersey U.S.A.
9 H3 **New Buckenham** England
99 U8 **New Buffalo** Michigan U.S.A.
99 O8 **Newburg** Iowa U.S.A.
110 E4 **Newburg** Missouri U.S.A.
94 K6 **Newburg** Pennsylvania U.S.A.
94 H7 **Newburg** West Virginia U.S.A.
121 O8 **Newburgh** Ontario Canada
15 F3 **Newburgh** Scotland
15 E4 **Newburgh** Fife Scotland
110 J4 **Newburgh** Indiana U.S.A.
95 N5 **Newburgh** New York U.S.A.
123 T5 **New Burnt Cove** Newfoundland Canada
9 E5 **Newbury** England
95 R4 **Newburyport** Massachusetts U.S.A.
85 E6 **New Bussa** Nigeria
137 N6 **New Caledonia** *isld* Pacific Oc
95 O5 **New Canaan** Connecticut U.S.A.
99 P10 **New Canton** Illinois U.S.A.
122 G5 **New Carlisle** Quebec Canada
94 C7 **New Carlisle** Ohio U.S.A.
139 K5 **Newcastle** New South Wales Australia
122 G6 **Newcastle** New Brunswick Canada
121 M9 **Newcastle** Ontario Canada
14 E3 **Newcastle** Ireland
127 L2 **Newcastle** Jamaica
14 F2 **Newcastle** N Ireland
89 F6 **Newcastle** S Africa
102 C3 **Newcastle** California U.S.A.
106 C2 **New Castle** Colorado U.S.A.
94 B7 **New Castle** Indiana U.S.A.
110 L3 **New Castle** Kentucky U.S.A.
98 K7 **Newcastle** Nebraska U.S.A.
95 M7 **New Castle** New Jersey U.S.A.
107 N6 **Newcastle** Oklahoma U.S.A.
94 G6 **New Castle** Pennsylvania U.S.A.
109 J2 **Newcastle** Texas U.S.A.
103 L4 **Newcastle** Utah U.S.A.
94 G9 **New Castle** Virginia U.S.A.
98 B6 **Newcastle** Wyoming U.S.A.
127 P4 **Newcastle** Nevis W Indies
141 G1 **Newcastle B** Queensland Australia
122 F7 **Newcastle Br** New Brunswick Canada
8 B3 **Newcastle Emlyn** Wales
118 E7 **Newcastle Mine** Alberta Canada
141 G4 **Newcastle Ra** Queensland Australia
15 F5 **Newcastleton** Scotland
8 D1 **Newcastle Under Lyme** England
13 G4 **Newcastle-upon-Tyne** England
140 C3 **Newcastle Waters** N Terr Australia
14 B4 **Newcastle West** Ireland
9 F5 **New Chapel** England
106 B5 **Newcomb** New Mexico U.S.A.
94 F6 **Newcomerstown** Ohio U.S.A.
94 F7 **New Concord** Ohio U.S.A.
12 D3 **New Cumnock** Scotland
12 D3 **New Dailly** Scotland
119 R8 **Newdale** Manitoba Canada
101 O6 **Newdale** Idaho U.S.A.
118 E9 **New Dayton** Alberta Canada
15 F3 **New Deer** Scotland
143 C10 **Newdegate** Western Australia Australia
76 **New Delhi** India
117 P11 **New Denver** British Columbia Canada
111 M7 **New Echota Nat.Mon** Georgia U.S.A.
111 D8 **New Edinburg** Arkansas U.S.A.
113 E7 **Newell** Georgia U.S.A.
99 L7 **Newell** Iowa U.S.A.
112 G2 **Newell** North Carolina U.S.A.
98 C5 **Newell** South Dakota U.S.A.
112 F4 **New Ellenton** South Carolina U.S.A.
143 F6 **Newell,L** Western Australia Australia
118 E8 **Newell L** Alberta Canada
111 E9 **Newellton** Louisiana U.S.A.
98 D3 **New England** North Dakota U.S.A.
139 K4 **New England Ra** *mts* New South Wales Australia
90 D4 **New England Seamount Chain** Atlantic Oc
116 F7 **Newenham,C** Alaska U.S.A.
8 D4 **Newent** England
94 A3 **New Era** Michigan U.S.A.
80 F3 **Newe Ur** Israel
80 C3 **Newe Yam** Israel
94 J3 **Newfane** New York U.S.A.
95 P3 **Newfane** Vermont U.S.A.
141 K1 **New Farm** *dist* Brisbane, Qnsld Australia
95 R3 **Newfield** Maine U.S.A.
95 M7 **Newfield** New Jersey U.S.A.
117 P8 **New Fish Creek** Alberta Canada
110 E3 **New Florence** Missouri U.S.A.
98 K1 **Newfolden** Minnesota U.S.A.
9 E6 **New Forest** England
95 Q3 **Newfound L** New Hampshire U.S.A.
115 N6 **Newfoundland** *prov* Canada
123 P5 **Newfoundland** *isld* Newfoundland Canada
95 M5 **Newfoundland** Pennsylvania U.S.A.
90 F4 **Newfoundland Basin** Atlantic Oc
90 E4 **Newfoundland Rise** Atlantic Oc
110 D2 **New Franklin** Missouri U.S.A.
95 L7 **New Freedom** Pennsylvania U.S.A.
8 A4 **Newgale** Wales
12 D3 **New Galloway** Scotland
118 B9 **Newgate** British Columbia Canada
137 M3 **New Georgia** *isld* Solomon Is
122 H9 **New Germany** Nova Scotia Canada
99 R7 **New Glarus** Wisconsin U.S.A.
122 K8 **New Glasgow** Nova Scotia Canada
95 R3 **New Gloucester** Maine U.S.A.
127 O3 **New Grant** Trinidad
136 J3 **New Guinea** *isld* S E Asia
109 M6 **Newgulf** Texas U.S.A.
100 D1 **Newhalem** Washington U.S.A.
116 K7 **Newhalen** Alaska U.S.A.
102 F7 **Newhall** California U.S.A.
116 F5 **New Hamilton** Alaska U.S.A.
95 Q4 **New Hampshire** *state* U.S.A.
99 O6 **New Hampton** Iowa U.S.A.
99 M9 **New Hampton** Missouri U.S.A.
95 S3 **New Harbor** Maine U.S.A.
110 J3 **New Harmony** Indiana U.S.A.
95 O5 **New Hartford** Connecticut U.S.A.
9 G6 **Newhaven** England
95 P5 **New Haven** Connecticut U.S.A.
94 B5 **New Haven** Indiana U.S.A.
110 E3 **New Haven** Missouri U.S.A.
94 F8 **New Haven** West Virginia U.S.A.
98 B5 **New Haven** Wyoming U.S.A.
117 K8 **New Hazelton** British Columbia Canada
New Hebrides *see* **Vanuatu**
13 F6 **New Hey** England
13 H6 **New Holland** England
99 R9 **New Holland** Illinois U.S.A.
99 S6 **New Holstein** Wisconsin U.S.A.
109 O1 **Newhope** Arkansas U.S.A.
12 E2 **Newhouse** Scotland
111 E12 **New Iberia** Louisiana U.S.A.
9 H5 **Newington** England
112 F5 **Newington** Georgia U.S.A.
137 L2 **New Ireland** *isld* Bismarck Arch
95 N7 **New Jersey** *state* U.S.A.
94 H6 **New Kensington** Pennsylvania U.S.A.
95 L9 **New Kent** Virginia U.S.A.
106 F6 **Newkirk** New Mexico U.S.A.
107 N5 **Newkirk** Oklahoma U.S.A.
143 E8 **Newland Ra** Western Australia Australia
98 E3 **New Leipzig** North Dakota U.S.A.
94 E7 **New Lexington** Ohio U.S.A.
99 Q6 **New Lisbon** Wisconsin U.S.A.
121 L5 **New Liskeard** Ontario Canada
99 P9 **New London** Iowa U.S.A.
99 M4 **New London** Minnesota U.S.A.
99 P10 **New London** Missouri U.S.A.
95 P3 **New London** New Hampshire U.S.A.
94 E5 **New London** Ohio U.S.A.
99 S5 **New London** Wisconsin U.S.A.
12 D4 **New Luce** Scotland
110 G5 **New Madrid** Missouri U.S.A.
12 E2 **Newmains** Scotland
143 C6 **Newman** Western Australia Australia
145 E4 **Newman** New Zealand
102 C4 **Newman** California U.S.A.
99 T10 **Newman** Illinois U.S.A.
106 D9 **Newman** New Mexico U.S.A.
98 J8 **Newman Gr** Nebraska U.S.A.
142 C6 **Newman,Mt** Western Australia Australia
123 T5 **Newman's Cove** Newfoundland Canada
141 K1 **Newmarket** *dist* Brisbane, Qnsld Australia
121 L8 **Newmarket** Ontario Canada
9 G3 **Newmarket** England
14 B4 **Newmarket** Ireland
127 J2 **Newmarket** Jamaica
110 K7 **New Market** Alabama U.S.A.
99 M9 **New Market** Iowa U.S.A.
95 Q3 **Newmarket** New Hampshire U.S.A.
94 J8 **New Market** Virginia U.S.A.
94 E7 **New Marshfield** Ohio U.S.A.
94 G7 **New Martinsville** West Virginia U.S.A.
94 F7 **New Matamoras** Ohio U.S.A.
100 J5 **New Meadows** Idaho U.S.A.
102 D4 **New Melones Res** California U.S.A.
106 D6 **New Mexico** *state* U.S.A.
94 C7 **New Miami** Ohio U.S.A.
95 O5 **New Milford** Connecticut U.S.A.
95 M5 **New Milford** Pennsylvania U.S.A.
12 D2 **Newmilns** Scotland
108 E2 **New Moore** Texas U.S.A.
111 M8 **Newnan** Georgia U.S.A.
113 E8 **Newnan L** Florida U.S.A.
139 K5 **Newnes** New South Wales Australia
8 D4 **Newnham** England
143 B9 **New Norcia** Western Australia Australia
139 H8 **New Norfolk** Tasmania Australia
118 E6 **New Norway** Alberta Canada
111 F11 **New Orleans** Louisiana U.S.A.
119 O6 **New Osgoode** Saskatchewan Canada
95 K7 **New Oxford** Pennsylvania U.S.A.
95 N5 **New Paltz** New York U.S.A.
94 C7 **New Paris** Ohio U.S.A.
94 A8 **New Pekin** Indiana U.S.A.
94 F6 **New Philadelphia** Ohio U.S.A.
100 E7 **New Pine Creek** Oregon U.S.A.
15 F3 **New Pitsligo** Scotland
145 E3 **New Plymouth** New Zealand
100 J6 **New Plymouth** Idaho U.S.A.
122 H5 **Newport** Quebec Canada
126 B2 **New Port** Curaçao
8 D2 **Newport** England
9 E6 **Newport** England
9 G4 **Newport** England
14 B3 **Newport** Ireland
127 K3 **Newport** Jamaica
110 E6 **Newport** Arkansas U.S.A.
99 T10 **Newport** Indiana U.S.A.
110 M2 **Newport** Kentucky U.S.A.
94 D5 **Newport** Michigan U.S.A.
99 O5 **Newport** Minnesota U.S.A.
98 G7 **Newport** Nebraska U.S.A.
95 P3 **Newport** New Hampshire U.S.A.
95 M7 **Newport** New Jersey U.S.A.
112 L3 **Newport** North Carolina U.S.A.
100 A5 **Newport** Oregon U.S.A.
95 K6 **Newport** Pennsylvania U.S.A.
95 Q5 **Newport** Rhode I U.S.A.
112 D2 **Newport** Tennessee U.S.A.
109 J2 **Newport** Texas U.S.A.
95 P2 **Newport** Vermont U.S.A.
100 H1 **Newport** Washington U.S.A.
8 B3 **Newport** Wales
8 D4 **Newport** Wales
8 B3 **Newport B** Wales
102 G8 **Newport Beach** California U.S.A.
95 L10 **Newport News** Virginia U.S.A.
13 F1 **Newport-on-Tay** Scotland
9 F3 **Newport Pagnell** England
113 E9 **New Port Richey** Florida U.S.A.
112 D1 **New Powell** Tennessee U.S.A.
99 N5 **New Prague** Minnesota U.S.A.
113 L9 **New Providence** *isld* Bahamas
8 A7 **Newquay** England
8 B3 **New Quay** Wales
113 E8 **New R** Florida U.S.A.
8 C3 **New Radnor** Wales
106 G1 **New Raymer** Colorado U.S.A.
99 N6 **New Richland** Minnesota U.S.A.
122 G5 **New Richmond** Quebec Canada
94 C8 **New Richmond** Ohio U.S.A.
99 O4 **New Richmond** Wisconsin U.S.A.
110 M5 **New River** Tennessee U.S.A.
112 K3 **New River Inlet** North Carolina U.S.A.
111 E11 **New Roads** Louisiana U.S.A.
98 G2 **New Rockford** North Dakota U.S.A.
9 G6 **New Romney** England
14 E4 **New Ross** Ireland
110 K2 **New Ross** Indiana U.S.A.
140 A3 **Newry** N Terr Australia
14 E2 **Newry** N Ireland
95 R2 **Newry** Maine U.S.A.
94 J6 **Newry** Pennsylvania U.S.A.
14 E2 **Newry Canal** N Ireland
98 E3 **New Salem** North Dakota U.S.A.
94 H7 **New Salem** Pennsylvania U.S.A.
13 E1 **New Scone** Scotland
99 O8 **New Sharon** Iowa U.S.A.
New Siberian Is *see* **Novosibirskiye Ostrova**
113 G8 **New Smyrna Beach** Florida U.S.A.
139 G5 **New South Wales** *state* Australia
94 E7 **New Straitsville** Ohio U.S.A.
85 D7 **New Tamale** Ghana
94 D10 **New Tazewell** Tennessee U.S.A.
116 E6 **Newtok** Alaska U.S.A.
9 G2 **Newton** England
13 E3 **Newton** Scotland
111 L10 **Newton** Alabama U.S.A.
110 H3 **Newton** Illinois U.S.A.
99 N8 **Newton** Iowa U.S.A.
107 N3 **Newton** Kansas U.S.A.
95 Q4 **Newton** Massachusetts U.S.A.
111 G9 **Newton** Mississippi U.S.A.
112 F2 **Newton** North Carolina U.S.A.
109 O5 **Newton** Texas U.S.A.
8 C6 **Newton Abbot** England
13 E4 **Newton Arlosh** England
95 M2 **Newton Falls** New York U.S.A.
94 G5 **Newton Falls** Ohio U.S.A.
8 B7 **Newton Ferrers** England
112 J2 **Newton Grove** North Carolina U.S.A.
94 K6 **Newton Hamilton** Pennsylvania U.S.A.
13 F6 **Newton-le-Willows** England
12 D2 **Newton Mearns** Scotland
15 D3 **Newtonmore** Scotland
101 O8 **Newton Res** Utah U.S.A.
12 D4 **Newton Stewart** Scotland
123 T4 **Newtown** Newfoundland Canada
110 C1 **Newtown** Missouri U.S.A.
95 K9 **Newtown** Virginia U.S.A.
8 C3 **Newtown** Wales
14 E2 **Newtownabbey** N Ireland
14 F2 **Newtownards** N Ireland
14 D2 **Newtown Butler** N Ireland
14 E2 **Newtownhamilton** N Ireland
14 E3 **Newtown Mt.Kennedy** Ireland
98 D2 **New Town Sanish** North Dakota U.S.A.
14 D2 **Newtown Stewart** N Ireland
99 M5 **New Ulm** Minnesota U.S.A.
109 L6 **New Ulm** Texas U.S.A.
98 D5 **New Underwood** South Dakota U.S.A.
111 L10 **Newville** Alabama U.S.A.
102 B2 **Newville** California U.S.A.
94 K6 **Newville** Pennsylvania U.S.A.
99 N8 **New Virginia** Iowa U.S.A.
94 E6 **New Washington** Ohio U.S.A.
123 M7 **New Waterford** C Breton I, Nova Scotia
109 M5 **New Waverly** Texas U.S.A.
117 J11 **New Westminster** British Columbia Canada
95 K7 **New Windsor** Maryland U.S.A.
123 S4 **New World I** Newfoundland Canada
100 F8 **New Year L** Nevada U.S.A.
96 **New York** *conurbation*
95 K4 **New York** *state* U.S.A.
103 J6 **New York Mts** California U.S.A.
144 **New Zealand** *dominion* S W Pacific
94 C5 **Ney** Ohio U.S.A.
52 F5 **Neya** U.S.S.R.
8 B4 **Neyland** Wales
77 D5 **Neyrīz** Iran
77 F1 **Neyshābūr** Iran
76 D5 **Neyveli** India
55 D2 **Neyvo Shaytanskiy** U.S.S.R.
31 H6 **Nežárka** *R* Czechoslovakia
54 C5 **Nezhin** U.S.S.R.
100 J3 **Nezperce** Idaho U.S.A.
61 N7 **Nezugaseki** Japan
86 C6 **N'Gabé** Congo
68 D5 **Nga Chong,Khao** *mt* Burma/Thailand
68 H5 **Ngac Linh** *mt* Vietnam
71 J9 **Ngadubolu** Sumba Indonesia
68 A2 **Ngahan** Burma
144 C5 **Ngahere** New Zealand
71 K10 **Ngalu** Indonesia
145 E3 **Ngamatapouri** New Zealand
145 F3 **Ngamatea Swamp** New Zealand
66 F5 **Ngamda** China
87 D10 **Ngami, L** Botswana
66 C5 **Ngangla Ringco** *L* China
66 C5 **Nganglong Kangri** China
74 J2 **Nganglong Kangri** *mt ra* China
75 M3 **Ngangzê Co** *L* China
70 N9 **Nganjuk** Java
68 G3 **Ngan Pha** *R* Vietnam
68 G3 **Ngan Sau** *R* Vietnam
68 G1 **Ngan Son** Vietnam
86 C6 **N'Gao** Congo
86 B4 **Ngaoundéré** Cameroon
144 C6 **Ngapara** New Zealand
68 B2 **Ngape** Burma
144 C6 **Ngapuna** New Zealand
70 K8 **Ngaras** Sumatra
145 E3 **Ngaroma** New Zealand
145 E2 **Ngaruawahia** New Zealand
145 F3 **Ngaruroro R** New Zealand
145 D1 **Ngataki** New Zealand
145 F3 **Ngatapo** New Zealand
145 E2 **Ngatea** New Zealand
68 B4 **Ngathainggyaung** Burma
145 E3 **Ngatira** New Zealand
145 E3 **Ngauruhoe** *vol* New Zealand
68 D7 **Ngawan Chaung** *R* Burma
145 F2 **Ngawaro** New Zealand
70 N9 **Ngawi** Java
68 B4 **Ngayok B** Burma
Ngemda *see* **Ngamda**
89 G3 **Ngezi** *R* Zimbabwe
89 G3 **Ngezi** Zimbabwe
89 G2 **Ngezi** *R* Zimbabwe
89 G2 **Ngezi Dam** Zimbabwe
Nghia Hung *see* **Thai Hoa**
68 G2 **Nghia Lô** Vietnam
71 M9 **Ngilmina** Indonesia
70 O9 **Ngimbang** Java
88 F6 **Ngindo** Tanzania
86 C5 **Ngoko** *R* Congo
87 E9 **Ngoma** Zambia
88 F2 **Ngong** Kenya
145 F3 **Ngongotaha** New Zealand
88 D7 **Ngoni** Malawi
66 F5 **Ngoring Hu** *L* China
88 E3 **Ngorongoro Crater** Tanzania
71 A2 **Ngotakiaha** Halmahera Indonesia
86 B6 **Ngounié** *R* Gabon
86 B2 **N'Gourti** Niger
88 B3 **Ngozi** Burundi
86 B3 **N'Guigmi** Niger
140 B1 **Nguiu** N Terr Australia
140 C2 **Ngukurr** N Terr Australia
68 F3 **Ngum** *R* Laos
71 K10 **Ngundju,Tg** *C* Sumba Indonesia
145 E1 **Ngunguru** New Zealand
88 E7 **Nguni** Tanzania
70 O10 **Ngunut** Java
85 G6 **Nguru** Nigeria
67 B5 **Nguyen Binh** Vietnam
89 D5 **Ngwaketse** *dist* Botswana
89 B4 **Ngwatlhe Pan** Botswana
87 G10 **Nhachengue** Mozambique
128 G6 **Nhambiquara** Brazil
129 G4 **Nhamunda** Brazil
67 A6 **Nhan Nghia** Vietnam
68 J6 **Nha Trang** Vietnam
130 C6 **Nhecolândia** Brazil
68 F3 **Nhiep** *R* Laos
138 F6 **Nhill** Victoria Australia
68 G4 **Nhommarath** Laos
140 D1 **Nhulunbuy** N Terr Australia
68 G3 **Nhu Xuan** Vietnam
144 B7 **Niagara** New Zealand
98 H1 **Niagara** North Dakota U.S.A.
99 S4 **Niagara** Wisconsin U.S.A.
121 L9 **Niagara Falls** Ontario Canada
94 J3 **Niagara Falls** New York U.S.A.
121 L9 **Niagara-on-the-Lake** Ontario Canada
70 C3 **Niah** Sarawak
85 C7 **Niakaramandougou** Ivory Coast
85 E6 **Niamey** Niger
86 E5 **Niangara** Zaire
85 D5 **Niangaye,L** Mali
85 C7 **Niangbo,Pic de** *mt* Ivory Coast
85 D6 **Niangoloko** Burkina
110 D4 **Niangua** *R* Missouri U.S.A.
Niangxi *see* **Xinshao**
86 E5 **Nia Nia** Zaire
95 P5 **Niantic** Connecticut U.S.A.
65 E1 **Nianzishan** China
101 L2 **Niarada** Montana U.S.A.
86 B6 **Niari** *R* Congo
69 C12 **Nias** *isld* Indonesia
88 F8 **Niassa** Mozambique
46 F8 **Niata** Greece
101 R4 **Nibbe** Montana U.S.A.
28 D3 **Nibe** Denmark
28 D2 **Nibe Bredning** *B* Denmark
121 R3 **Nicabau** Quebec Canada
125 L3 **Nicaragua** *rep* Central America
125 M4 **Nicaragua, Lac de** Nicaragua
95 T1 **Nicatous L**
44 B4 **Nice** France
102 B2 **Nice** California U.S.A.
111 K11 **Niceville** Florida U.S.A.
115 M7 **Nichicun, L** Quebec Canada
60 E11 **Nichihara** Japan
112 E6 **Nicholls** Georgia U.S.A.
99 P8 **Nichols** Iowa U.S.A.
95 L4 **Nichols** New York U.S.A.
140 E4 **Nicholson** *R* Queensland Australia
142 G4 **Nicholson** Western Australia Australia
143 B7 **Nicholson Ra** Western Australia Australia
95 N2 **Nicholville** New York U.S.A.
99 O1 **Nickel L** Ontario Canada
129 G2 **Nickerie** *R* Suriname
107 M3 **Nickerson** Kansas U.S.A.
142 B5 **Nickol B** Western Australia Australia
122 F3 **Nicman** Quebec Canada
69 A8 **Nicobar Is** Bay of Bengal
117 N10 **Nicola** British Columbia Canada
121 S6 **Nicolet** Quebec Canada
99 M5 **Nicollet** Minnesota U.S.A.
Nicomedia *see* **Kocaeli**
78 D4 **Nicosia** Cyprus
43 F11 **Nicosia** Sicily
43 G10 **Nicotera** Italy
125 M4 **Nicoya** Costa Rica
125 M5 **Nicoya,Pen.de** Costa Rica
122 E6 **Nictau** New Brunswick Canada
31 M5 **Nida** *R* Poland
76 E2 **Nidadavole** India
40 F3 **Nidau** Switzerland
36 G3 **Nidda** W Germany
36 F3 **Nidda** *R* W Germany
36 F3 **Niddatal** W Germany
36 B2 **Nideggen** W Germany
27 C13 **Nidelv** *R* Norway
41 H4 **Nidwalden** *canton* Switzerland
31 M2 **Nidzica** Poland
30 D1 **Niebüll** W Germany
36 G1 **Niedenstein** W Germany
37 N6 **Niederaichbach** W Germany
37 L6 **Niederarnbach** W Germany
36 H2 **Nieder Aula** W Germany
37 N6 **Niederbayern** *dist* W Germany
36 C3 **Niederbieber** Germany
19 L4 **Niederbronn** France
33 O6 **Nieder Elde** *R* East Germany
36 G2 **Nieder Gemünden** W Germany
33 R9 **Niedergörsdorf** East Germany
36 C2 **Niederkassel** W Germany
25 F6 **Niederkrüchten** W Germany
36 D3 **Nieder Lahnstein** W Germany
32 J10 **Nieder Marsberg** W Germany
33 M6 **Nieder Marschacht** W Germany
36 H5 **Niedernhall** W Germany
36 E3 **Niedernhausen** W Germany
36 E4 **Nieder Olm** W Germany
36 E3 **Nieder Ouembach** W Germany
32 J7 **Niedersachsen** *land* W Germany
36 D2 **Nieder Schelden** W Germany
36 E3 **Niederselters** W Germany
32 J10 **Niedersfeld** W Germany
36 H5 **Niederstetten** W Germany
37 J6 **Niederstotzingen** W Germany
36 D4 **Niederwald** W Germany
36 E2 **Nieder Weidbach** W Germany
36 F2 **Nieder Weimar** W Germany
37 P2 **Niederwiesa** East Germany
36 F3 **Nieder Wöllstadt** W Germany
36 C3 **Nieder Zissen** W Germany
33 T8 **Nieder Zittau** East Germany
32 K9 **Nieheim** W Germany
98 K2 **Nielsville** Minnesota U.S.A.
88 B5 **Niemba** *R* Zaire
88 B4 **Niemba** Zaire
33 Q9 **Niemberg** East Germany
31 K5 **Niemcza** Poland
33 R8 **Niemegk** East Germany
26 N5 **Niemis** Sweden
26 M5 **Niemisel** Sweden
31 K5 **Niemodlin** Poland
33 N7 **Nienbergen** W Germany
32 F8 **Nienborg** W Germany
33 P9 **Nienburg** East Germany
32 K7 **Nienburg** W Germany
33 N5 **Niendorf** W Germany
31 M5 **Niepołomice** Poland
22 D2 **Nieppe** France
25 F5 **Niers** *R* W Germany
36 E4 **Nierstein** W Germany
31 L3 **Nieszawa** Poland
85 C7 **Niete, Mt** Liberia
33 P10 **Nietleben** East Germany
20 H8 **Nieul le Dolent** France
129 G2 **Nieuw Amsterdam** Suriname
25 D4 **Nieuwegein** Netherlands
25 B5 **Nieuwe Maas** Netherlands
25 C5 **Nieuwendijk** Netherlands
25 D4 **Nieuwersluis** Netherlands
25 H2 **Nieuweschans** Netherlands
32 F6 **Nieuweschans** W Germany
22 D2 **Nieuwkerke** Belgium
25 C4 **Nieuwkoop** Netherlands
129 G2 **Nieuw Nickerie** Suriname
25 G2 **Nieuwolda** Netherlands
22 D1 **Nieuwpoort** Belgium
25 C5 **Nieuwpoort** Netherlands
25 E6 **Nieuwstadt** Netherlands
25 C4 **Nieuw-Vennep** Netherlands
18 H5 **Nièvre** *dept* France
122 G6 **Nigadoo** New Brunswick Canada
78 E3 **Niğde** Turkey
85 B6 **Niger** *R* W Africa
85 F5 **Niger** *rep* W Africa
85 F7 **Nigeria** *rep* W Africa
85 F8 **Niger,Mouths of the** Nigeria
144 B6 **Nightcaps** New Zealand
100 F1 **Nighthawk** Washington U.S.A.
141 G2 **Night I** Great Barrier Reef Aust
Nightingale I *see* **Bach Long Vi,I.**
90 B16 **Nightingale I** Tristan da Cunha
116 K2 **Nigu** *R* Alaska U.S.A.
21 O8 **Niherne** France
102 U13 **Nihoa** Hawaiian Is
131 C5 **Nihuili, Embalse del** *res* Argentina
61 N8 **Niigata** Japan
60 G12 **Niihama** Japan
135 N1 **Niihau** *isld* Hawaiian Is
61 N11 **Nii-jima** *isld* Japan
60 Q3 **Niikappu** *R* Japan
60 G10 **Niimi** Japan
60 D4 **Niitomi** Japan
61 N8 **Niitsu** Japan
17 F8 **Níjar** Spain
25 F2 **Nijega** Netherlands
60 S2 **Nijibetsu** Japan
79 F8 **Nijil** Jordan
25 D4 **Nijkerk** Netherlands
25 E5 **Nijmegen** Netherlands
25 F4 **Nijverdal** Netherlands
116 K6 **Nikabuna Lakes** Alaska U.S.A.
Nikaria *isld* *see* **Ikaria** *isld*
26 S2 **Nikel'** U.S.S.R.
55 C5 **Nikel'tau** U.S.S.R.
71 M9 **Nikiniki** Timor Indonesia
46 F4 **Nikitas** Greece
52 D6 **Nikitinka** U.S.S.R.
54 K8 **Nikitovka** U.S.S.R.
85 E7 **Nikki** Benin
61 N9 **Nikkō** Japan
61 N9 **Nikkō Nat. Park** Japan
40 G5 **Niklaus** Switzerland
116 K5 **Nikolai** Alaska U.S.A.
48 H1 **Nikolayev** U.S.S.R.
54 D10 **Nikolayev** U.S.S.R.
55 E4 **Nikolayevka** U.S.S.R.
53 G8 **Nikolayevsk** U.S.S.R.
55 D4 **Nikolayevskiy** U.S.S.R.
59 M1 **Nikolayevsk-na-Amure** U.S.S.R.
52 G5 **Nikol'sk** U.S.S.R.
52 F5 **Nikolskoye** U.S.S.R.
55 C5 **Nikol'skoye** U.S.S.R.
88 C3 **Nikonga** *R* Tanzania
46 G1 **Nikopol** Bulgaria
54 F9 **Nikopol'** U.S.S.R.
77 G6 **Nīkshahr** Iran
42 J6 **Nikšić** Yugoslavia
78 F1 **Niksir** Turkey
137 S2 **Nikumaroro** *isld* Phoenix Is Pacific Oc
71 O8 **Nila** *isld* Indonesia
103 J8 **Niland** California U.S.A.
73 L8 **Nilande Atoll** Maldives
83 L9 **Nilaveli** Sri Lanka
84 J4 **Nile** *R* N E Africa
86 F2 **Nile** *prov* Sudan
102 B4 **Niles** California U.S.A.
107 N3 **Niles** Kansas U.S.A.
94 A5 **Niles** Michigan U.S.A.
94 G5 **Niles** Ohio U.S.A.
121 N6 **Nilgaut, L** Quebec Canada
76 C5 **Nilgiri Hills** India
116 E6 **Nilikluguk** Alaska U.S.A.
57 K3 **Nilka** China
29 N8 **Nilsiä** Finland
47 K4 **Nilüfer** *R* Turkey
57 F5 **Nil'van** U.S.S.R.
83 K11 **Nilwala** *R* Sri Lanka
28 D5 **Nim** Denmark
74 F6 **Nimach** India
85 C7 **Nimba, Mts** Guinea/Liberia/Ivory Co
142 E6 **Nimberra Well** Western Australia Australia
139 L3 **Nimbin** New South Wales Australia
18 H9 **Nîmes** France
47 O12 **Nimfai** Greece
74 F5 **Nimka Thana** India
139 J6 **Nimmitabel** New South Wales Australia
101 M3 **Nimrod** Montana U.S.A.
Nimrod Bay *see* **Xiangshan Gang**
110 C7 **Nimrod L** Arkansas U.S.A.
144 C6 **Nimrod, Mt** New Zealand
109 O1 **Nimrod Res** Arkansas U.S.A.
77 H4 **Nīmrūz** *reg* Afghanistan
28 F4 **Nimtofte** Denmark
42 G4 **Nin** Yugoslavia
71 F4 **Nin Bay** Philippines
87 D8 **Ninda** Angola
141 J8 **Nindigully** Queensland Australia
73 L7 **Nine Degree Chan** Lakshadweep Indian Oc
13 E2 **Nine Mile Burn** Scotland
139 G4 **Nine Mile L** New South Wales Australia
103 H2 **Ninemile Pk** Nevada U.S.A.
108 D6 **Nine Point Mesa** *mt* Texas U.S.A.
119 S9 **Ninette** Manitoba Canada
139 J7 **Ninety Mile Beach** Victoria Australia
145 D1 **Ninety Mile Beach** New Zealand
112 E3 **Ninety Six** South Carolina U.S.A.
94 G7 **Ninevah** Pennsylvania U.S.A.
133 E6 **Ninfas,Pta** Argentina
9 G6 **Ninfield** England
143 A6 **Ningaloo** Western Australia Australia
59 J3 **Ning'an** China
67 G2 **Ningbo** China
65 D4 **Ningcheng** China
67 F3 **Ningde** China
67 E3 **Ningdu** China
67 D3 **Ninggang** China
67 F1 **Ningguo** China
67 G2 **Ninghai** China
65 D5 **Ninghe** China
Ning-hsia *see* **Yinchuan**
67 E3 **Ninghua** China
65 C6 **Ningjin** China
58 F4 **Ningjin** China
66 F5 **Ningjing Shan** *ra* China
65 C7 **Ningling** China
67 B5 **Ningming** China
Ningpo *see* **Ningbo**
Ningsia *aut reg* *see* **Ningxia**
65 B5 **Ningwu** China
58 E4 **Ningxia** *aut reg* China
67 D2 **Ningxiang** China
65 C7 **Ningyang** China
67 D4 **Ningyuan** China
67 B6 **Ninh Binh** Vietnam
68 J6 **Ninh Hoa** Vietnam
6 L2 **Ninian** *oil rig* North Sea
116 M6 **Ninilchik** Alaska U.S.A.
142 C5 **Niningarra** Western Australia Australia
107 N7 **Ninnekah** Oklahoma U.S.A.
107 N4 **Ninnescah** *R* Kansas U.S.A.
146 D14 **Ninnis Glacier** Antarctica
111 C9 **Ninock** Louisiana U.S.A.
61 P5 **Ninohe** Japan
60 E14 **Ninokata** Japan
22 G2 **Ninove** Belgium
130 C7 **Nioaque** Brazil
94 H4 **Niobe** New York U.S.A.
98 E7 **Niobrara** *R* Nebraska U.S.A.
98 J7 **Niobrara** Nebraska U.S.A.
86 C6 **Nioki** Zaire
85 B6 **Niokolo-koba,Parc Nat.du** Senegal
85 A6 **Nioro du Rip** Senegal
85 C5 **Nioro du Sahel** Mali
18 E6 **Niort** France
Nios *isld* *see* **Íos** *isld*
99 P9 **Niota** Illinois U.S.A.
112 C2 **Niota** Tennessee U.S.A.
85 C5 **Niout** Mauritania
76 B2 **Nipani** India
71 H6 **Nipanipa,Tg** *C* Sulawesi
119 N5 **Nipawin** Saskatchewan Canada
119 N4 **Nipawin Prov.Park** Saskatchewan Canada
120 B3 **Nipigon** Ontario Canada
120 C4 **Nipigon B** Ontario Canada
120 B3 **Nipigon, Lake** Ontario Canada
118 H3 **Nipin R** Saskatchewan Canada
118 C3 **Nipisi R** Alberta Canada
122 G6 **Nipisquit,B** New Brunswick Canada
121 L6 **Nipissing Junc** Ontario Canada
120 K6 **Nipissing,L** Ontario Canada
122 F3 **Nipissis L** Quebec Canada
122 F3 **Nipissis R** Quebec Canada
122 G3 **Nipisso L** Quebec Canada
102 D6 **Nipomo** California U.S.A.
103 J6 **Nipton** California U.S.A.
84 J5 **Niqrûb el Fuqâni, Gebel** *mt* Egypt
126 F4 **Niquero** Cuba
61 M10 **Nirasaki** Japan
80 C3 **Nir 'Ezyon** Israel
80 B6 **Nir Gallim** Israel
80 B7 **Nir Hen** Israel
74 H9 **Nirmal** India
75 M5 **Nirmali** India
80 B8 **Nir Moshe** Israel
94 B3 **Nirvana** Michigan U.S.A.
80 C6 **Nir Zevi** Israel
46 E1 **Niš** Yugoslavia
16 B5 **Nisa** Portugal
72 F6 **Nişāb** S Yemen
46 F1 **Nisava** *R* Yugoslavia
95 K5 **Nisbet** Pennsylvania U.S.A.
60 O3 **Niseko** Japan
67 C2 **Nishi** China
61 P5 **Nishi-Hōji** Japan
60 J11 **Nishinomiya** Japan
60 F9 **Nishino-shima** *isld* Japan
61 L11 **Nishio** Japan
60 C13 **Nishi-Sonogi-hantō** *pen* Japan
60 C11 **Nishi-suidō** *str* Japan
60 H10 **Nishiwaki** Japan
116 H6 **Nishlik L** Alaska U.S.A.
99 L8 **Nishnabotna, E** *R* Iowa U.S.A.
99 L8 **Nishnabotna, W** *R* Iowa U.S.A.
130 J9 **Nísia Floresta** Brazil
48 J3 **Nisipitul** Romania
47 J8 **Nísiros** *isld* Greece
31 N5 **Nisko** Poland
98 C5 **Nisland** South Dakota U.S.A.
117 D4 **Nisling** *R* Yukon Territory Canada
48 L3 **Nisporeny** U.S.S.R.
100 C3 **Nisqually** *R* Washington U.S.A.
27 F15 **Nissan** *R* Sweden
27 C12 **Nissedal** Norway
27 C12 **Nisserv** *L* Norway
28 A3 **Nissum Bredning** *B* Denmark
28 A4 **Nissum Fjord** *inlet* Denmark
117 G5 **Nisutlin** *R* Yukon Territory Canada
115 M7 **Nitchequon** Quebec Canada
130 G8 **Niterói** Brazil
15 E5 **Nith,R** Scotland
15 E5 **Nithsdale** Scotland
71 M9 **Nitibe** Timor
80 G7 **Nitil** Jordan
100 A1 **Nitinat L** British Columbia Canada
9 E6 **Niton** England
31 L7 **Nitra** *R* Czechoslovakia
48 E2 **Nitra** Czechoslovakia
94 F8 **Nitro** West Virginia U.S.A.
55 D2 **Nitsa** *R* U.S.S.R.
29 N2 **Nitsjärvi** *L* Finland
37 N5 **Nittenau** W Germany
37 M5 **Nittendorf** W Germany
29 P11 **Nityuyarvi** U.S.S.R.
137 R5 **Niuafo'ou** *isld* Pacific Oc
137 S5 **Niuatoputapu** *isld* Pacific Oc
137 T5 **Niue** *isld* Pacific Oc
137 Q4 **Niulakita** *isld* Tuvalu
65 F4 **Niumaowu** China
69 F13 **Niur, Pulau** *isld* Sumatra
Niushan *see* **Donghai**
137 Q3 **Niutao** *isld* Tuvalu
65 E4 **Niuzhuang** China
29 K5 **Nivå** Denmark
29 L8 **Nivala** Finland
141 H7 **Nive** *R* Queensland Australia
18 E9 **Nive** *R* France
141 H7 **Nive Downs** Queensland Australia
22 G2 **Nivelles** Belgium
18 H5 **Nivernais** *prov* France
118 D1 **Niverville** Manitoba Canada
21 P3 **Nivillers** France
102 G4 **Nivloc** Nevada U.S.A.
40 B6 **Nivolas-Vermelle** France
52 D2 **Nivskiy** U.S.S.R.
74 J7 **Niwas** India
102 E2 **Nixon** Nevada U.S.A.
109 K6 **Nixon** Texas U.S.A.
47 N11 **Niyandros** *isld* Turkey
70 B4 **Niyat, Gunung** *mt* Kalimantan
74 H9 **Nizamabad** India
52 E3 **Nizhmozero** U.S.S.R.
56 G3 **Nizhneangarsk** U.S.S.R.
52 H2 **Nizhne Bugayevo** U.S.S.R.
54 L9 **Nizhne Gnilovskoy** U.S.S.R.
52 H6 **Nizhnekamsk** U.S.S.R.
52 H6 **Nizhnekamskoye Vodokhranilishche** *res* U.S.S.R.
55 B4 **Nizhne-troitskiy** U.S.S.R.
56 E4 **Nizhneudinsk** U.S.S.R.
55 G1 **Nizhnevartovsk** U.S.S.R.
55 B4 **Nizhneye Il'yasovo** U.S.S.R.
52 D2 **Nizhneye Kuyto, Oz** *L* U.S.S.R.
Nizhniy Novgorod *see* **Gor'kiy**
55 C2 **Nizhniy Tagil** U.S.S.R.
52 H6 **Nizhniy Takanysh** U.S.S.R.
56 F5 **Nizhniy Torey** U.S.S.R.
52 E2 **Nizhniy Vyalozerskiy** U.S.S.R.
52 G4 **Nizhniy Yenangsk** U.S.S.R.
55 E2 **Nizhnyaya Aremzyan** U.S.S.R.
55 C3 **Nizhnyaya Irga** U.S.S.R.
55 F3 **Nizhnyaya Omka** U.S.S.R.
52 J3 **Nizhnyaya-Omra** U.S.S.R.
52 G2 **Nizhnyaya Pesha** U.S.S.R.
56 E3 **Nizhnyaya Pomya** U.S.S.R.
55 D2 **Nizhnyaya Salda** U.S.S.R.
55 G4 **Nizhnyaya Suyetka** U.S.S.R.
55 E2 **Nizhnyaya Tavda** U.S.S.R.
52 F3 **Nizhnyaya Toyma** *R* U.S.S.R.
56 G1 **Nizhnyaya Tunguska** *R* U.S.S.R.
55 C2 **Nizhnyaya Tura** U.S.S.R.
52 H4 **Nizhnyaya Voch'** U.S.S.R.
52 F2 **Nizhnyaya Zolotitsa** U.S.S.R.
29 Q4 **Nizh Pirengskoye Ozero** *L* U.S.S.R.
56 G2 **Nizh Tunguska** *R* U.S.S.R.
116 Q6 **Nizina** Alaska U.S.A.
78 F3 **Nizip** Turkey
31 L7 **Nízké Tatry** *mts* Czechoslovakia
48 F2 **Nižm Medzev** Czechoslovakia

Olpe — Oudler
63

107 O3 Olpe Kansas U.S.A.
36 D1 Olpe W Germany
41 P3 Olperer mt Austria
107 O2 Olsburg Kansas U.S.A.
31 L6 Olše R Czechoslovakia
54 G6 Ol'shany U.S.S.R.
25 F4 Olst Netherlands
31 M2 Olsztyn Poland
31 M2 Olsztynek Poland
48 K4 Olt R Romania
40 G3 Olten Switzerland
48 K6 Olteniţa Romania
133 D6 Olte,Sa.de mts Argentina
48 H6 Olteţ R Romania
108 E1 Olton Texas U.S.A.
78 H1 Oltu Turkey
67 G6 O-luan-pi C Taiwan
113 E7 Olustee Florida U.S.A.
107 L7 Olustee Oklahoma U.S.A.
71 F7 Olutanga isld Philippines
33 P8 Olvenstedt East Germany
16 D8 Olvera Spain
46 E7 Olympia Greece
100 C2 Olympia Washington U.S.A.
100 B2 Olympic Mts Washington U.S.A.
100 B2 Olympic Nat. Park Washington U.S.A.
100 A2 Olympic Nat. Park Washington U.S.A.
Olympus mt Cyprus see Troödos Mt
Olympus mt Greece see Ólimbos mt
100 B2 Olympus,Mt Washington U.S.A.
95 M5 Olyphant Pennsylvania U.S.A.
51 Q2 Olyutorskiy U.S.S.R.
36 B3 Olzheim W Germany
56 B3 Om' R U.S.S.R.
60 O4 Ōma Japan
111 F10 Oma Mississippi U.S.A.
52 G2 Oma U.S.S.R.
61 L9 Ōmachi Japan
61 M11 Omae zaki C Japan
14 D2 Omagh N Ireland
128 D4 Omaguas Peru
110 C5 Omaha Arkansas U.S.A.
99 L8 Omaha Nebraska U.S.A.
109 N2 Omaha Texas U.S.A.
126 F4 Omaja Cuba
100 F1 Omak Washington U.S.A.
144 B6 Omakau New Zealand
145 F4 Omakere New Zealand
72 H5 Oman sultanate Arabian Pen
77 F7 Oman, Gulf of Iran/Oman
145 D1 Omapere, L New Zealand
94 E9 Omar West Virginia U.S.A.
144 B6 Omarama New Zealand
87 C10 Omaruru Namibia
128 D7 Omate Peru
71 J9 Omatema Indonesia
60 O4 Ōma-zaki C Japan
120 C2 Ombabika Ontario Canada
120 B2 Ombabika B Ontario Canada
71 M9 Ombai,Selat str Indonesia
61 N11 Ombase-jima isld Japan
8 D3 Ombersley England
69 C12 Ombolata Indonesia
86 A6 Omboue Gabon
45 J4 Ombrone R Italy
66 D5 Ombu China
86 F2 Omdurman Sudan
61 N10 Ōme Japan
111 L10 Omega Alabama U.S.A.
112 D6 Omega Georgia U.S.A.
107 M6 Omega Oklahoma U.S.A.
121 M8 Omemee Ontario Canada
98 F1 Omemee North Dakota U.S.A.
94 B1 Omena Michigan U.S.A.
80 C8 'Omer Israel
94 D2 Omer Michigan U.S.A.
47 J5 Ömerköy Turkey
47 N10 Ömerli Baraji dam Turkey
14 A3 Omey I Ireland
86 G3 Om Hājer Ethiopia
61 L8 Ōmi Japan
22 D4 Omiecourt France
144 D5 Omihi New Zealand
57 L2 O-min U.S.S.R.
60 P4 Ōminato Japan
117 L8 Omineca R British Columbia Canada
117 K7 Omineca Mts British Columbia Canada
42 H5 Omis Yugoslavia
60 F11 Ōmi-shima isld Japan
60 E11 Ōmi-shima isld Japan
61 N10 Ōmiya Japan
117 F7 Ommaney,C Alaska U.S.A.
114 J3 Ommanney B Northwest Territories Canada
28 B5 Omme Å R Denmark
25 F3 Ommen Netherlands
28 G6 Omø Denmark
86 G4 Omo R Ethiopia
43 B8 Omodeo, L Sardinia
51 P2 Omolon R U.S.S.R.
51 N2 Omoloy R U.S.S.R.
61 O6 Omono-gawa R Japan
22 H4 Omont France
20 G2 Omonville-la Rogue France
61 O6 Ōmori Japan
61 P6 Omoto Japan
61 P6 Omoto-gawa R Japan
99 S5 Omro Wisconsin U.S.A.
55 F3 Omsk U.S.S.R.
55 G3 Omskaya Oblast' prov U.S.S.R.
68 D1 O-mu Burma
60 Q1 Ōmu Japan
31 N2 Omulew R Poland
83 L10 Omuna Sri Lanka
60 C13 Ōmura Japan
60 C13 Ōmura wan B Japan
47 H1 Omurtag Bulgaria
60 D12 Ōmuta Japan
55 E3 Omutinskiy U.S.S.R.
52 H5 Omutninsk U.S.S.R.
26 B9 Ona Norway
16 E2 Oña Spain
113 F10 Ona Florida U.S.A.
56 C5 Ona R U.S.S.R.
107 O2 Onaga Kansas U.S.A.
61 P7 Onagawahama Japan
61 P7 Onagawa-wan B Japan
61 O9 Onahama Japan
98 G4 Onaka South Dakota U.S.A.
120 J2 Onakawana Ontario Canada
120 J1 Onakwehegan R Ontario Canada
100 C3 Onalaska Washington U.S.A.
99 P6 Onalaska Wisconsin U.S.A.
120 C2 Onaman L Ontario Canada
99 N3 Onamia Minnesota U.S.A.
95 M9 Onancock Virginia U.S.A.
70 F6 Onang Sulawesi
86 B6 Onangue, L Gabon
120 J5 Onaping L Ontario Canada
110 H1 Onarga Illinois U.S.A.
121 U3 Onatchiway,L Quebec Canada
124 F2 Oñate Mexico
124 E3 Onavas Mexico
98 K7 Onawa Iowa U.S.A.
94 C1 Onaway Michigan U.S.A.
87 B9 Oncocua Angola
17 G5 Onda Spain
87 C9 Ondangwa Namibia
31 N6 Ondava R Czechoslovakia
25 G2 Onderdendam Netherlands
87 C9 Ondjiva Angola
85 E7 Ondo Nigeria
58 F2 Öndörhaan Mongolia
65 E2 Ondor Had China
73 L8 One and Half Degree Chan Indian Oc
113 E10 Oneco Florida U.S.A.
Onega L see Onezhskoye, Oz
52 E3 Onega U.S.S.R.
52 E4 Onega R U.S.S.R.
44 D4 Oneglia Italy
141 H2 One & Half Mile Opening str Gt Barrier Reef Aust
99 Q8 Oneida Illinois U.S.A.
99 P7 Oneida Iowa U.S.A.
94 D9 Oneida Kentucky U.S.A.
95 M3 Oneida New York U.S.A.
110 M5 Oneida Tennessee U.S.A.
95 L3 Oneida L New York U.S.A.
98 H7 O'Neill Nebraska U.S.A.
145 D4 Onekaka New Zealand
94 A2 Onekama Michigan U.S.A.
86 D6 Onema Zaire
111 K8 Oneonta Alabama U.S.A.
95 M4 Oneonta New York U.S.A.
145 E1 Onerahi New Zealand
145 E2 Oneroa I New Zealand
118 J1 One Sided Lake Ontario Canada
52 E4 Onezhskoye,Oz L U.S.S.R.
145 F3 Ongaonga New Zealand
9 G4 Ongar England
145 E3 Ongarue New Zealand
89 C8 Ongers watercourse S Africa
143 C10 Ongerup Western Australia Australia
65 B3 Onggon Ul China
19 P16 Ongles France
65 D3 Ongniud Qi China
76 E3 Ongole India
56 G4 Onguren U.S.S.R.
15 C4 Onich Scotland
98 G5 Onida South Dakota U.S.A.
87 G12 Onilahy R Madagascar
118 H5 Onion Lake Saskatchewan Canada
60 P1 Onishika Japan
122 A3 Onistagan L Quebec Canada
85 F7 Onitsha Nigeria
21 N1 Onival France
29 N8 Onkivesi L Finland
95 M9 Onley Virginia U.S.A.
61 P13 Onna Okinawa
61 P13 Onna-dake mt Okinawa
22 F3 Onnaing France
60 O4 Ōno Japan
60 E11 Onoda Japan
61 N11 Ōnohara-jima isld Japan
137 R6 Ono-i-lau isld Pacific Oc
145 E4 Onoke, L New Zealand
60 G11 Onomichi Japan
58 G1 Onon R U.S.S.R.
69 C12 Ononamolo Indonesia
94 C4 Onondaga Michigan U.S.A.
58 F2 Onon Gol R Mongolia
61 O8 Ono-Niimachi Japan
59 M1 Onor U.S.S.R.
128 E2 Onoto Venezuela
137 Q2 Onotoa atoll Kiribati
118 C5 Onoway Alberta Canada
28 F5 Onsbjerg Denmark
16 B2 Ons., I.de Spain
28 H7 Ønslev Denmark
142 B5 Onslow Western Australia Australia
112 K3 Onslow B North Carolina U.S.A.
144 B6 Onslow, L New Zealand
94 C4 Onsted Michigan U.S.A.
36 G7 Onstmettingen W Germany
25 H2 Onstwedde Netherlands
61 L10 Ontake-san mt Japan
115 K7 Ontario prov Canada
102 G7 Ontario California U.S.A.
100 J5 Ontario Oregon U.S.A.
99 Q6 Ontario Wisconsin U.S.A.
94 J3 Ontario,L U.S.A./Canada
17 G6 Onteniente Spain
99 R3 Ontonagon Michigan U.S.A.
137 M3 Ontong Java Is Solomon Is
17 G6 Ontur Spain
60 O4 Onuma Japan
111 F9 Onward Mississippi U.S.A.
102 F6 Onyx California U.S.A.
21 N6 Onzain France
138 E5 Oodla Wirra South Australia Australia
138 D2 Oodnadatta South Australia Australia
135 V4 Ookala Hawaiian Is
138 B4 Ooldea South Australia Australia
138 B4 Ooldea Ra South Australia Australia
110 K3 Oolitic Indiana U.S.A.
107 P5 Oologah Oklahoma U.S.A.
107 P5 Oologah L Oklahoma U.S.A.
25 B5 Ooltgensplaat Netherlands
140 C6 Ooraminna Ra N Terr Australia
140 D5 Ooratippra R N Terr Australia
140 D5 Ooratippra N Terr Australia
141 F5 Oorindi Queensland Australia
111 L7 Oostanaula R Georgia U.S.A.
25 A6 Oostburg Netherlands
22 D2 Oost Cappel France
22 D1 Oostduinkerke Belgium
22 D1 Oostende Belgium
25 E5 Oosterbeër Netherlands
25 D2 Oosterend Netherlands
25 C5 Oosterhout Netherlands
25 A5 Oosterschelde Netherlands
25 F3 Oosterwolde Netherlands
22 F2 Oosterzele Belgium
25 D3 Oosthuizen Netherlands
25 E4 Oostlijk-Flevoland prov Netherlands
25 F2 Oostmahoorn Netherlands
22 H1 Oostmalle Belgium
22 F1 Oost Vlaanderen Belgium
25 D2 Oost Vlieland Netherlands
25 B5 Oostvoorne Netherlands
25 G4 Ootmarsum Netherlands
117 L9 Ootsa Lake British Columbia Canada
119 S2 Opachuanau L Manitoba Canada
102 R11 Opaeula R Hawaiian Is
47 H1 Opaka Bulgaria
145 E4 Opaki New Zealand
118 D5 Opal Alberta Canada
124 H5 Opal Mexico
101 P8 Opal Wyoming U.S.A.
51 P3 Opala U.S.S.R.
86 D6 Opala Zaire
31 J3 Opalenica Poland
113 G12 Opa-Locka Florida U.S.A.
83 K11 Opanake Sri Lanka
86 F5 Opari Sudan
52 G5 Oparino U.S.S.R.
120 H3 Opasatika Ontario Canada
120 G3 Opasatika L Ontario Canada
42 F3 Opatija Yugoslavia
31 N5 Opatów Poland
31 L4 Opatówek Poland
31 K5 Opava R Czechoslovakia
31 K6 Opava Czechoslovakia
121 P3 Opawica, L Quebec Canada
111 L9 Opelika Alabama U.S.A.
111 D11 Opelousas Louisiana U.S.A.
120 D2 Opemisha Ontario Canada
144 B5 Open Bay Is New Zealand
121 M7 Opeongo L Ontario Canada
22 F2 Ophasselt Belgium
101 T1 Opheim Montana U.S.A.
100 A7 Ophir Oregon U.S.A.
101 N9 Ophir Utah U.S.A.
69 E12 Ophir, Gunung mt Sumatra
22 K1 Ophoven Belgium
142 C6 Ophthalmia Ra Western Australia Australia
45 P6 Opi Italy
86 E5 Opienge Zaire
144 C6 Opihi R New Zealand
36 B1 Opladen W Germany
85 F8 Opobo Nigeria
52 C6 Opochka U.S.S.R.
122 F1 Opocopa L Quebec Canada
31 M4 Opoczno Poland
124 D3 Opodepe Mexico
31 K5 Opole Poland
145 F3 Oponae New Zealand
145 D1 Opononi New Zealand
Oporto see Porto
54 F7 Oposhnya U.S.S.R.
145 F3 Opotiki New Zealand
145 E2 Opoutere New Zealand
111 K10 Opp Alabama U.S.A.
61 P7 Oppa-gawa R Japan
61 P7 Oppa-wan B Japan
26 D9 Oppdal Norway
45 K1 Oppeano Italy
33 T9 Oppelhaun East Germany
Oppeln see Opole
36 E7 Oppenau W Germany
36 E4 Oppenheim W Germany
36 G6 Oppenweiler W Germany
28 J5 Oppe Sundby Denmark
27 D10 Oppland county Norway
119 Q4 Optic Lake Manitoba Canada
107 J5 Optima Oklahoma U.S.A.
145 E1 Opua New Zealand
145 E1 Opuawhanga New Zealand
145 D3 Opunake New Zealand
124 E2 Oputo Mexico
87 B9 Opuwo Namibia
22 G2 Opwijk Belgium
99 Q9 Oquawka Illinois U.S.A.
124 D2 Oquitoa Mexico
95 R2 Oquossoc Maine U.S.A.
27 G15 Ör Sweden
55 C5 Or' R U.S.S.R.
41 O5 Ora Italy
84 F4 Ora Libya
143 D9 Ora Banda Western Australia Australia
127 L2 Oracabessa Jamaica
103 O9 Oracle Arizona U.S.A.
48 G3 Oradea Romania
18 F7 Oradour-sur-Vayres France
29 T9 Oræfajökull ice cap Iceland
74 H6 Orai India
103 O6 Oraibi Arizona U.S.A.
103 O5 Oraibi Wash creek Arizona U.S.A.
29 L5 Orajärvi Finland
29 M4 Orajärvi L Finland
98 C6 Oral South Dakota U.S.A.
85 D1 Oran Algeria
110 G4 Oran Missouri U.S.A.
139 J5 Orange New South Wales Australia
19 N16 Orange France
87 C11 Orange R S Africa/Namibia
102 G8 Orange California U.S.A.
95 P4 Orange Massachusetts U.S.A.
109 O5 Orange Texas U.S.A.
94 J8 Orange Virginia U.S.A.
111 J11 Orange Beach Alabama U.S.A.
112 G4 Orangeburg South Carolina U.S.A.
129 H3 Orange,C Brazil
126 E2 Orange Cay isld Bahamas
113 F9 Orange City Florida U.S.A.
116 Q3 Orange Cr Alaska U.S.A.
123 L8 Orangedale C Breton I, Nova Scotia
113 F7 Orangedale Florida U.S.A.
95 N6 Orange, E New Jersey U.S.A.
89 D7 Orange Free State prov S Africa
129 G3 Orange Gebergte mts Suriname
109 K8 Orange Grove Texas U.S.A.
113 E8 Orange L Florida U.S.A.
113 F7 Orange Park Florida U.S.A.
99 R7 Orangeville Illinois U.S.A.
103 N2 Orangeville Utah U.S.A.
145 E3 Orangimea New Zealand
71 E3 Orani Luzon Philippines
43 C8 Orani Sardinia
33 Q9 Oranienbaum East Germany
33 S7 Oranienburg East Germany
80 D3 Oranim Israel
87 C11 Oranjemund Namibia
126 A1 Oranjestad Aruba W Indies
127 N6 Oranjestad St Eustatius W Indies
14 C3 Oranmore Ireland
133 E2 Orán, N Argentina
Orantes R see 'Āsi R
143 G6 Orantjugurr,L Western Australia Australia
80 C3 Or'Aqiva Israel
144 C6 Orari New Zealand
71 G4 Oras Philippines
71 G4 Oras B Philippines
48 E5 Orašje Yugoslavia
48 H5 Orăştie Romania
48 H3 Oraşu Nou Romania
124 H5 Oratario Mexico
48 M1 Oratov U.S.S.R.
31 L6 Orava R Czechoslovakia
29 J8 Oravais Finland
48 G5 Oraviţa Romania
31 L6 Oravská Magura mts Czechoslovakia
144 A7 Orawia New Zealand
18 H9 Orb R France
44 E2 Orba R Italy
66 C5 Orba Co L China
21 L3 Orbec France
42 D6 Orbetello Italy
21 N7 Orbigny France
16 D2 Orbigo R Spain
94 K6 Orbisonia Pennsylvania U.S.A.
139 J7 Orbost Victoria Australia
28 F5 Ørby Denmark
27 F14 Örby Sweden
27 J11 Örbyhus Sweden
116 O6 Orca B Alaska U.S.A.
146 E3 Orcadas Arg Base S Orkney Is S Atlantic Oc
146 G4 Orcadas Seamounts, Islas seamounts Antarctica
21 L8 Orches France
128 E1 Orchila, La isld Venezuela
16 B1 Ordenes Spain
103 M4 Orderville Utah U.S.A.
28 B3 Ørding Denmark
142 F3 Ord,Mt Western Australia Australia
102 H7 Ord Mt California U.S.A.
52 D3 Ordozero U.S.S.R.
142 G3 Ord River Western Australia Australia
78 F1 Ordu Turkey
78 K2 Ordubail U.S.S.R.
16 E2 Orduña Spain
106 G3 Ordway Colorado U.S.A.
98 H4 Ordway South Dakota U.S.A.
53 F11 Ordzhonikidze U.S.S.R.
55 D4 Ordzhonikidze Kazakhskaya S.S.R. U.S.S.R.
56 C4 Ordzhonikidzevskiy U.S.S.R.
28 E5 Ore Denmark
26 C9 Öre Norway
26 K7 Oreälv R Sweden
100 J6 Oreana Idaho U.S.A.
102 F1 Oreana Nevada U.S.A.
27 H12 Örebro Sweden
27 G12 Örebro county Sweden
109 N3 Ore City Texas U.S.A.
100 E6 Oregon state U.S.A.
99 R7 Oregon Illinois U.S.A.
110 A2 Oregon Missouri U.S.A.
99 R7 Oregon Wisconsin U.S.A.
100 B7 Oregon Caves Nat. Mon Oregon U.S.A.
100 C4 Oregon City Oregon U.S.A.
112 M2 Oregon Inlet North Carolina U.S.A.
27 K11 Öregrund Sweden
54 G9 Orekhov U.S.S.R.
46 G1 Orekhovitsa Bulgaria
55 F3 Orekhovo U.S.S.R.
52 E6 Orekhovo Zuyevo U.S.S.R.
54 B2 Orekhovsk U.S.S.R.
54 F8 Orel' R U.S.S.R.
54 H4 Orël Orlovskaya obl U.S.S.R.
52 J5 Orël Permskaya obl U.S.S.R.
98 C7 Orella Nebraska U.S.A.
128 C5 Orellana Peru
16 D5 Orellana, Embalse de res Spain
53 E7 Orel Oblast' prov U.S.S.R.
59 L1 Orel', Oz L U.S.S.R.
103 N1 Orem Utah U.S.A.
47 J7 Ören Turkey
55 C5 Orenburg U.S.S.R.
50 E3 Orenburgskaya Oblast' prov U.S.S.R.
16 B2 Orense prov Spain
16 B2 Orense Spain
46 F6 Oreoí Greece
144 A7 Orepuki New Zealand
47 H3 Orestiás Greece
29 K5 Öresund str Sweden/Denmark
144 B7 Oreti R New Zealand
145 E2 Orewa New Zealand
22 J2 Oreye Belgium
139 J8 Orford Tasmania Australia
9 H3 Orford England
95 P3 Orford New Hampshire U.S.A.
141 G1 Orford Ness Queensland Australia
9 H3 Orford Ness England
106 D9 Organ New Mexico U.S.A.
126 C3 Organos, Sa. de los hills Cuba
103 M9 Organ Pipe Cactus Nat. Mon Arizona U.S.A.
16 E5 Orgaz Spain
21 P4 Orge R France
40 C4 Orgelet France
21 O5 Orgères-en-Beauce France
21 O4 Orgeval France
48 M3 Orgeyev U.S.S.R.
45 K1 Orgiano Italy
16 E8 Órgiva Spain
47 N10 Örgök Burun C Turkey
65 B3 Orgon Tal China
52 F6 Orgtrud U.S.S.R.
77 L3 Orgūn Afghanistan
47 K5 Orhaneli R Turkey
47 K5 Orhaneli Turkey
47 K4 Orhangazi Turkey
Orhanie see Botevgrad
47 J5 Orhanlar Turkey
58 D2 Orhon Gol R Mongolia
17 F1 Oria R Spain
17 F7 Oria Spain
52 G5 Orichi U.S.S.R.
100 A8 Orick California U.S.A.
141 G8 Orient Queensland Australia
106 E3 Orient Colorado U.S.A.
99 M8 Orient Iowa U.S.A.
98 G5 Orient South Dakota U.S.A.
108 G4 Orient Texas U.S.A.
100 G1 Orient Washington U.S.A.
112 L2 Oriental North Carolina U.S.A.
120 B3 Orient Bay Ontario Canada
95 P5 Orient I New York U.S.A.
138 F3 Orientos New South Wales Australia
141 F8 Orientos Queensland Australia
22 G4 Origny-en-Thiérache France
22 E4 Origny-St.-Benoîte France
17 G6 Orihuela Spain
121 L8 Orillia Ontario Canada
29 M11 Orimattila Finland
98 A7 Orin Wyoming U.S.A.
48 K2 Orinin U.S.S.R.
128 F2 Orinoco R Venezuela
128 F2 Orinoco, Mouths of the Venezuela
43 G8 Oriolo Italy
118 G9 Orion Alberta Canada
99 Q8 Orion Illinois U.S.A.
98 J3 Oriska North Dakota U.S.A.
95 M4 Oriskany Falls New York U.S.A.
75 K8 Orissa prov India
43 B9 Oristano Sardinia
43 B9 Oristano, G. di Sardinia
128 E2 Orituco R Venezuela
29 O9 Orivesi L Finland
129 G4 Oriximiná Brazil
125 L8 Orizaba Mexico
47 J2 Orizare Bulgaria
42 J6 Orjen mt Yugoslavia
26 D8 Orkdalen V Norway
27 F15 Örkelljunga Sweden
27 G15 Örkened Sweden
26 D9 Orkla R Norway
118 K9 Orkney Saskatchewan Canada
87 E11 Orkney S Africa
15 F1 Orkney isld Scotland
37 M2 Orla R East Germany
31 K4 Orla R Poland
108 D4 Orla Texas U.S.A.
37 M2 Orlamünde East Germany
102 B2 Orland California U.S.A.
94 B5 Orland Indiana U.S.A.
95 T2 Orland Maine U.S.A.
113 F9 Orlando Florida U.S.A.
107 N5 Orlando Oklahoma U.S.A.
43 F10 Orlando, C.d' Sicily
21 N5 Orléanais reg France
21 O6 Orléans France
100 B8 Orleans California U.S.A.
110 K3 Orleans Indiana U.S.A.
95 S5 Orleans Massachusetts U.S.A.
98 K1 Orleans Minnesota U.S.A.
98 G9 Orleans Nebraska U.S.A.
95 P2 Orleans Vermont U.S.A.
121 U6 Orleans, Île d' Quebec Canada
Orléansville see Ech Cheliff
31 J5 Orlice R Czechoslovakia
56 E5 Orlik U.S.S.R.
31 L6 Orlová Czechoslovakia
56 C2 Orlovka U.S.S.R.
55 F3 Orlovo U.S.S.R.
53 E7 Orlovskaya Oblast' prov U.S.S.R.
52 F2 Orlovskiy, Mys C U.S.S.R.
21 P4 Orly airport France
74 C10 Ormara Pakistan
13 G4 Ormesby England
36 C5 Ormesheim W Germany
21 M8 Ormes,les France
119 M9 Ormiston Saskatchewan Canada
71 G5 Ormoc Philippines
145 F3 Ormond New Zealand
113 F8 Ormond Florida U.S.A.
113 F8 Ormond Beach Florida U.S.A.
145 F4 Ormondville New Zealand
38 O9 Ormož Yugoslavia
99 M6 Ormsby Minnesota U.S.A.
99 R4 Ormsby Wisconsin U.S.A.
26 H7 Ormsjö Sweden
13 F6 Ormskirk England
121 R7 Ormstown Quebec Canada
19 J4 Ornain R France
19 K5 Ornans France
41 H6 Ornavasso Italy
37 K5 Ornbau W Germany
18 E4 Orne dept France
21 L5 Orne R France
31 M1 Orneta Poland
27 K12 Orno Sweden
26 K8 Örnsköldsvik Sweden
28 H5 Orø Denmark
42 C2 Orobie, Alpi mts Italy
41 L5 Orobie, Alpi mt Italy
51 M3 Orochen U.S.S.R.
128 D3 Orocué Colombia
85 D6 Orodara Burkina
100 J3 Orofino Idaho U.S.A.
102 G7 Oro Grande California U.S.A.
100 K4 Orogrande Idaho U.S.A.
106 D9 Orogrande New Mexico U.S.A.
61 P13 Oroku Okinawa
122 F8 Oromocto New Brunswick Canada
122 F8 Oromocto L New Brunswick Canada
79 F8 Oron Israel
134 K9 Orona isld Phoenix Is Pacific Oc
121 M9 Orono Ontario Canada
95 T2 Orono Maine U.S.A.
110 B4 Oronogo Missouri U.S.A.
12 B1 Oronsay isld Scotland
16 D5 Oropesa Spain
127 P2 Oropuche R Trinidad
59 H1 Oroqen Zizhiqi China
71 F6 Oroquieta Mindanao
129 L5 Orós, Açude res Brazil
43 C8 Orosei Sardinia
43 C8 Orosei, G.di Sardinia
48 F4 Orosháza Hungary
48 E3 Oroszlany Hungary
51 P2 Orotukan U.S.S.R.
145 E4 Oroua R New Zealand
100 H8 Orovada Nevada U.S.A.
102 C2 Oroville California U.S.A.
100 F1 Oroville Washington U.S.A.
101 U7 Orpha Wyoming U.S.A.
141 H4 Orpheus I Queensland Australia
21 O4 Orphin France
19 P16 Orpierre France
98 J1 Orr North Dakota U.S.A.
107 N7 Orr Oklahoma U.S.A.
28 B4 Ørre Denmark
27 H15 Orrefors Sweden
15 D3 Orrin R Scotland
98 F1 Orrin North Dakota U.S.A.
119 U2 Orr L Manitoba Canada
26 G10 Orrmosjön L Sweden
138 E4 Orroroo South Australia Australia
27 J11 Orrskog Sweden
94 K6 Orrstown Pennsylvania U.S.A.
94 F6 Orrville Ohio U.S.A.
27 G10 Orsa Sweden
44 H3 Orsaro mt Italy
21 P4 Orsay France
9 G5 Orsett England
54 B2 Orsha U.S.S.R.
52 G6 Orshanka U.S.S.R.
27 H15 Örsjö Sweden
55 C5 Orsk U.S.S.R.
27 F13 Örslösa Sweden
28 E2 Ørsø Denmark
48 G6 Orşova Romania
32 E9 Orsoy W Germany
26 B9 Örsta Norway
27 J12 Örsundsbro Sweden
47 K8 Ortaca Turkey
47 J7 Ortaklar Turkey
80 G1 Or Tal Syria
41 H6 Orta, L. d' Italy
26 K7 Örtäsk Sweden
42 E6 Orte Italy
16 B1 Ortegal, C Spain
Ortelsburg see Szczytno
36 G3 Ortenberg W Germany
37 P6 Ortenburg W Germany
30 F1 Orth W Germany
18 E9 Orthez France
45 L4 Ortignano Raggiolo Italy
16 B1 Ortigueira Spain
28 E5 Ørting Denmark
100 C2 Orting Washington U.S.A.
124 D3 Ortiz Mexico
106 D4 Ortiz Colorado U.S.A.
128 E2 Ortiz Venezuela
41 N4 Ortles mt Italy
37 O2 Ortmannsdorf East Germany
127 P3 Ortoire R Trinidad
128 E6 Orton R Bolivia
13 F5 Orton England
42 F6 Ortona Italy
98 K4 Ortonville Minnesota U.S.A.
57 H4 Orto-Tokoy U.S.S.R.
33 T10 Ortrand East Germany
32 M7 Ortze R W Germany
51 M2 Orulgan, Khrebet mt U.S.S.R.
28 D4 Ørum Denmark
28 E2 Ørum Denmark
78 K3 Orūmīyeh Iran
78 K3 Orūmīyeh, Daryācheh-ye L Iran
133 D1 Oruro Bolivia
145 D1 Oruru New Zealand
27 E13 Orust isld Sweden
77 J3 Orūzgān Afghanistan
20 G7 Orvault France
42 E6 Orvieto Italy
21 O4 Orvilliers France
45 N5 Orvinio Italy
94 K5 Orviston Pennsylvania U.S.A.
95 L3 Orwell New York U.S.A.
94 G5 Orwell Ohio U.S.A.
95 O3 Orwell Vermont U.S.A.
58 G2 Orxon Gol R China
46 F1 Oryakhovo Bulgaria
41 L7 Orzinuovi Italy
31 M2 Orzyc R Poland
31 N2 Orzysz Poland
26 E9 Os Norway
27 G14 Os Sweden
27 E10 Osa R Norway
119 O9 Osage Saskatchewan Canada
99 O6 Osage Iowa U.S.A.
107 O5 Osage Oklahoma U.S.A.
98 B6 Osage Wyoming U.S.A.
107 P3 Osage City Kansas U.S.A.
110 D4 Osage Fork R Missouri U.S.A.
62 Ōsaka conurbation Japan
55 F5 Osakarovka U.S.S.R.
99 L4 Osakis Minnesota U.S.A.
99 L4 Osakis L Minnesota U.S.A.
107 Q3 Osawatomie Kansas U.S.A.
120 E3 Osawin R Ontario Canada
142 F2 Osborne Is Western Australia Australia
27 G15 Osby Sweden
142 F4 Oscar Ra Western Australia Australia
110 G6 Osceola Arkansas U.S.A.
99 N8 Osceola Iowa U.S.A.
110 C3 Osceola Missouri U.S.A.
98 J8 Osceola Nebraska U.S.A.
94 J6 Osceola Pennsylvania U.S.A.
99 O4 Osceola Wisconsin U.S.A.
33 S10 Oschatz East Germany
33 O8 Oschersleben East Germany
94 D2 Oscoda Michigan U.S.A.
106 D8 Oscura New Mexico U.S.A.
26 E7 Osen Norway
54 K2 Osetr R U.S.S.R.
60 B13 Ōse-zaki C Japan
94 B7 Osgood Indiana U.S.A.
110 C1 Osgood Missouri U.S.A.
121 P7 Osgoode Station Ontario Canada
100 H8 Osgood Mts Nevada U.S.A.
57 G4 Osh U.S.S.R.
55 F3 Osha R U.S.S.R.
87 C9 Oshakati Namibia
60 O3 Oshamambe Japan
121 M9 Oshawa Ontario Canada
60 P1 Oshidomari Japan
61 P7 Oshika-Hantō pen Japan
61 N11 Ō-shima isld Japan
59 J6 O-shima isld Japan
98 D8 Oshkosh Nebraska U.S.A.
99 S6 Oshkosh Wisconsin U.S.A.
52 J2 Oshkur'ya U.S.S.R.
55 D1 Oshmar'ye U.S.S.R.
73 K3 Oshnoviyeh Iran
85 E7 Oshogbo Nigeria
98 B5 Oshoto Wyoming U.S.A.
77 A3 Oshtorān Kūh mt Iran
52 K2 Oshvor U.S.S.R.
86 C6 Oshwe Zaire
46 G1 Osica Romania
48 J6 Osica de Jos Romania
48 E5 Osijek Yugoslavia
45 O4 Osimo Italy
56 C4 Osinniki U.S.S.R.
54 B2 Osintorf U.S.S.R.
74 E5 Osiyān India
26 N3 Oskal Norway
99 O8 Oskaloosa Iowa U.S.A.
107 P2 Oskaloosa Kansas U.S.A.
27 H14 Oskarshamn Sweden
27 F15 Oskarström Sweden
121 P4 Oskelaneo Quebec Canada
54 J7 Oskol R U.S.S.R.
31 J6 Oslava R Czechoslovakia
118 L6 Osler Saskatchewan Canada
27 E12 Oslo Norway
98 J1 Oslo Minnesota U.S.A.
71 F6 Oslob Cebu Philippines
27 E13 Oslofjord inlet Norway
28 C2 Øsløs Denmark
54 E2 Os'ma R U.S.S.R.
74 G9 Osmanabad India
78 E1 Osmancik Turkey
47 K4 Osmaneli Turkey
52 C5 Osmino U.S.S.R.
27 J13 Ösmo Sweden
98 J7 Osmond Nebraska U.S.A.
98 H1 Osnabrock North Dakota U.S.A.
32 H8 Osnabrück W Germany
31 H3 Ośno Poland
46 E2 Osogovske Planina mt Yugoslavia
41 N7 Osone R Italy
60 O4 Osore yama mt Japan
131 A8 Osorno prov Chile
131 A8 Osorno Chile
16 E2 Osorno Spain
131 A8 Osorno, Vol pk Chile
133 C6 Osorro mt Chile
100 F1 Osoyoos British Columbia Canada
44 C4 Ospedaletti Italy
117 M7 Ospika R British Columbia Canada
113 E10 Osprey Florida U.S.A.
141 H2 Osprey Reef Gt Barrier Reef Aust
9 G5 Ospringe England
25 E5 Oss Netherlands
46 F5 Óssa mt Greece
112 F6 Ossabaw I Georgia U.S.A.
139 H8 Ossa, Mt Tasmania Australia
16 B6 Ossa, Sa. d' mts Portugal
85 F7 Osse R Nigeria
99 P5 Osseo Wisconsin U.S.A.
38 J8 Ossiach Austria
99 P6 Ossian Iowa U.S.A.
94 D2 Ossineke Michigan U.S.A.
95 O5 Ossining New York U.S.A.
95 Q3 Ossipee L New Hampshire U.S.A.
27 E10 Os-sjöen L Norway
32 J8 Ossning hills W Germany
41 H5 Ossola, Val d' Italy
51 Q3 Ossora U.S.S.R.
71 N9 Ossu Timor
121 M5 Ostaboningue, L Quebec Canada
77 A2 Ostan-e Markazi Iran
52 E6 Ostashevo U.S.S.R.
52 D6 Ostashkov U.S.S.R.
26 H9 Östavell Sweden
32 G8 Ostbevern W Germany
32 K5 Oste R W Germany
113 F9 Osteen Florida U.S.A.
45 L2 Ostellato Italy
32 K5 Osten W Germany
Ostend see Oostende
32 L7 Ostenholz W Germany
41 K6 Osteno Italy
54 D3 Oster R U.S.S.R.
33 P7 Osterburg East Germany
94 J6 Osterburg Pennsylvania U.S.A.
36 G5 Osterburken W Germany
27 J11 Österby Sweden
27 H14 Österbymo Sweden
32 H8 Ostercappeln W Germany
27 G10 Österdalälven R Sweden
32 E5 Osterems est W Germany
27 H13 Östergotland county Sweden
37 P6 Osterhofen W Germany
32 J6 Osterholz-Scharmbeck W Germany
38 H6 Osterhorn Gruppe mts Austria
28 D3 Øster Hornum Nordjylland Denmark
27 J11 Österlövsta Sweden
26 J7 Österноret Sweden
Osterode Poland see Ostróda
32 M9 Osterode W Germany
27 A11 Osteröy isld Norway
38 H5 Osterreich dist Austria
26 G8 Östersund Sweden
28 H7 Øster Ulslev Denmark
27 J11 Östervåla Sweden
33 N9 Osterwieck East Germany
36 G6 Ostfildern W Germany
27 E12 Östfold reg Norway
32 F5 Ostfriesische Inseln islds W Germany
32 F6 Ostfriesland reg W Germany
32 G6 Ostgrossefehn W Germany
27 K11 Östhammar Sweden
36 C7 Ostheim France
37 J3 Ostheim W Germany
45 M6 Ostia Italy
45 K1 Ostiglia Italy
27 F11 Östmark Sweden
33 R5 Ost Peene R East Germany
45 O4 Ostra Italy
94 D6 Ostrander Ohio U.S.A.
37 P1 Ostrau East Germany
31 L6 Ostrava Czechoslovakia
45 O4 Ostra Vetere Italy
31 M2 Ostróda Poland
31 N2 Ostrołęka Poland
120 J5 Ostrom Ontario Canada
37 O3 Ostrov Czechoslovakia
48 L6 Ostrov Romania
52 C6 Ostrov U.S.S.R.
55 F3 Ostrovnaya U.S.S.R.
51 Q2 Ostrovnoye U.S.S.R.
65 J3 Ostrov Russkiy isld U.S.S.R.
31 K4 Ostrów Poland
31 N5 Ostrowiec Poland
31 O4 Ostrów Lubelski Poland
31 N3 Ostrów Mazowiecka Poland
28 C3 Østrup Denmark
37 P5 Ostrý mt Czechoslovakia
31 K4 Ostrzeszów Poland
33 O5 Ostseebad Boltenhagen East Germany
33 Q4 Ostseebad Graal-Müritz East Germany
33 P4 Ostseebad Kühlungsborn East Germany
33 P4 Ostseebad Nienhagen East Germany
33 P4 Ostseebad Rerik East Germany
43 H8 Ostuni Italy
52 D6 Osuga R U.S.S.R.
100 F3 O'Sullivan Dam Washington U.S.A.
120 D2 O'Sullivan, L Ontario Canada
121 P5 O'Sullivan, L Quebec Canada
46 D4 Osum R Albania
46 G1 Osūm R Bulgaria
60 D14 Ōsumi-hantō pen Japan
16 D7 Osuna Spain
52 C6 Osveya U.S.S.R.
13 G5 Oswaldkirk England
94 J5 Oswayo Pennsylvania U.S.A.
95 M2 Oswegalchie R New York U.S.A.
99 S8 Oswego Illinois U.S.A.
107 P4 Oswego Kansas U.S.A.
101 U1 Oswego Montana U.S.A.
95 L3 Oswego New York U.S.A.
8 C2 Oswestry England
31 L5 Oświęcim Poland
111 F10 Osyka Mississippi U.S.A.
61 N9 Ōta Japan
60 F11 Ōta R Japan
144 B6 Otago stat area New Zealand
144 D7 Otago Peninsula New Zealand
144 C6 Otaio New Zealand
60 F11 Ōtake Japan
145 E3 Otakeho New Zealand
61 M10 Ōtaki Japan
145 E4 Otaki New Zealand
61 O8 Ōtakine-yama mt Japan
145 F3 Otane New Zealand
145 F2 Otanewainuku New Zealand
29 N7 Otanmäki Finland
83 K9 Otappuwa Sri Lanka
57 H3 Otar U.S.S.R.
60 O2 Otaru Japan
144 B7 Otatara New Zealand
144 B7 Otautau New Zealand
30 H6 Otava R Czechoslovakia
128 C3 Otavalo Ecuador
87 C9 Otavi Namibia
87 B9 Otchinjau Angola
95 M4 Otego New York U.S.A.
144 C6 Otekaieke New Zealand
48 F5 Otelec Romania
48 G5 Oţelu Roşu Romania
144 C6 Otematata New Zealand
52 C5 Otepää U.S.S.R.
58 C2 Otgon Mongolia
22 K5 Othain R France
22 J2 Othée Belgium
18 H4 Othe, Forêt d' France
100 F3 Othello Washington U.S.A.
27 K14 Othem Sweden
8 D5 Othery England
46 C5 Othonoi isld Greece
46 F5 Óthris mt Greece
70 F5 Oti Sulawesi
85 E7 Oti R W Africa
124 G5 Otinapa Mexico
144 C5 Otira New Zealand
106 H1 Otis Colorado U.S.A.
107 L3 Otis Kansas U.S.A.
95 O4 Otis Massachusetts U.S.A.
95 L4 Otisco L New York U.S.A.
122 B1 Otish Mts Quebec Canada
95 N5 Otisville New York U.S.A.
87 C10 Otjiwarongo Namibia
60 O3 Otobe-dake mt Japan
42 G4 Otočac Yugoslavia
99 K9 Otoe Nebraska U.S.A.
60 R2 Otofuke Japan
60 Q1 Otoineppu Japan
145 F3 Otoko New Zealand
145 E3 Otorohanga New Zealand
119 P5 Otosquen Saskatchewan Canada
27 C13 Otra R Norway
126 B1 Otrabanda Curaçao
54 H3 Otradinskiy U.S.S.R.
43 J8 Otranto Italy
43 J8 Otranto, C.d' Italy
46 C4 Otranto, Str of Adriatic Sea
94 C2 Otsego Michigan U.S.A.
95 N4 Otsego I New York U.S.A.
94 C2 Otsego Lake Michigan U.S.A.
95 M4 Otselic, South New York U.S.A.
60 R3 Ōtsu Hokkaido Japan
61 J10 Ōtsu Honshu Japan
61 P6 Ōtsuchi-wan B Japan
61 M10 Ōtsuki Japan
26 C10 Otta R Norway
26 D10 Otta Norway
22 L5 Ottange France
27 F16 Ottarp Sweden
45 Q8 Ottaviano Italy
120 D9 Ottawa Ontario Canada
99 S8 Ottawa Illinois U.S.A.
107 P3 Ottawa Kansas U.S.A.
94 C5 Ottawa Ohio U.S.A.
115 L6 Ottawa Is Northwest Territories Canada
121 L6 Ottawa R Ontario/Quebec
32 K9 Ottbergen W Germany
27 H15 Ottenby Sweden
36 H5 Ottendorf W Germany
37 M2 Ottendorf-Okrilla East Germany
36 E6 Ottenhöfen W Germany
38 M5 Ottenshlag Austria
32 K9 Ottenstein Niedersachsen W Germany
32 E8 Ottenstein Nordrhein-Westfalen W Germany
101 T4 Otter Montana U.S.A.
110 J1 Otterbein Indiana U.S.A.
36 D4 Otterberg W Germany
13 F3 Otterburn England
118 D1 Otterburne Manitoba Canada
113 E8 Otter Creek Florida U.S.A.
103 N3 Otter Cr Res Utah U.S.A.
38 E6 Otterfing W Germany
116 D8 Otter I Pribilof Is Bering Sea
120 D4 Otter I Ontario Canada
119 N3 Otter L Saskatchewan Canada
94 D3 Otter Lake Michigan U.S.A.
25 E4 Otterlo Netherlands
32 J5 Otterndorf W Germany
26 B9 Otteröy isld Norway
26 E7 Otteröy Norway
32 K6 Ottersberg W Germany
9 F5 Ottershaw England
33 P8 Ottersleben East Germany
15 G1 Otterswick Scotland
98 K3 Otter Tail R Minnesota U.S.A.
99 L3 Otter Tail L Minnesota U.S.A.
28 E5 Otterup Denmark
8 B6 Ottery, R England
8 C6 Ottery St. Mary England
119 P7 Otthon Saskatchewan Canada
22 H2 Ottignies Belgium
57 H4 Ottik U.S.S.R.
109 L4 Otto Texas U.S.A.
101 R5 Otto Wyoming U.S.A.
37 M7 Ottobrunn W Germany
115 L1 Otto Fiord Northwest Territories Canada
94 C6 Ottoville Ohio U.S.A.
36 C7 Ottrott France
99 O8 Ottumwa Iowa U.S.A.
98 E5 Ottumwa South Dakota U.S.A.
36 C5 Ottweiler W Germany
118 K2 Otukamanoan L Ontario Canada
144 B6 Oturehua New Zealand
85 F7 Oturkpo Nigeria
94 D8 Otway Ohio U.S.A.
133 C8 Otway, B Chile
139 G7 Otway, C Victoria Australia
31 N3 Otwock Poland
48 J2 Otynya U.S.S.R.
41 N3 Ötz Austria
36 B1 Otzenrath W Germany
41 N3 Ötztal Austria
41 N4 Ötztaler Alpen mt Austria
111 D8 Ouachita R Arkansas U.S.A.
110 C7 Ouachita, L Arkansas U.S.A.
109 N1 Ouachita Mts Ark/Okla U.S.A.
86 D3 Ouadai dist Chad
85 B4 Ouadane Mauritania
86 D4 Ouadda Cent Afr Republic
85 D6 Ouagadougou Burkina
85 D6 Ouahigouya Burkina
86 D4 Ouaka R Cent Afr Republic
85 C5 Oualata Mauritania
85 E4 Ouallene Algeria
86 D4 Ouanda Djallé Cent Afr Republic
86 D5 Ouango Cent Afr Republic
85 C7 Ouangolodougou Ivory Coast
18 H5 Ouanne R France
85 F3 Ouan Taredert Algeria
129 H3 Ouaqui Fr Guiana
85 C4 Ouarane reg Mauritania
121 Q6 Ouareau, L Quebec Canada
85 F2 Ouargla Algeria
85 C3 Ouarkziz, Jbel mt reg Morocco/Algeria
21 O5 Ouarville France
85 C2 Ouarzazate Morocco
86 D5 Oubangui R Cent Afr Republic/Zaire
40 B3 Ouche R France
21 N6 Oucques France
25 A5 Ouddorp Netherlands
25 B5 Oude R Netherlands
25 F5 Oude Ijssel R Netherlands
22 D1 Oudekapelle Belgium
22 F2 Oudenaarde Belgium
25 C5 Oudenbosch Netherlands
25 H2 Oude Pekela Netherlands
25 C4 Oude Rijn Netherlands
25 C2 Oudeschild Netherlands
25 F3 Oude Smildervaart R Netherlands
25 C4 Oudewater Netherlands
22 L3 Oudler Belgium

21 L6 **Parigné-l'Eveque** France
128 G2 **Parika** Guyana
144 D5 **Parikawa** New Zealand
145 E3 **Parikino** New Zealand
29 O10 **Parikkala** Finland
128 F3 **Parima, Sa** *mts* Brazil/Venezuela
128 D7 **Parinacocha, L** Peru
128 D4 **Parinari** Peru
128 B4 **Pariñas, Pta** Peru
48 L4 **Parincea** Romania
138 F5 **Paringa** South Australia Australia
129 G4 **Parintins** Brazil
23 **Paris** *conurbation* France
110 C6 **Paris** Arkansas U.S.A.
101 O7 **Paris** Idaho U.S.A.
99 T10 **Paris** Illinois U.S.A.
110 M3 **Paris** Kentucky U.S.A.
110 E2 **Paris** Missouri U.S.A.
110 H5 **Paris** Tennessee U.S.A.
109 M2 **Paris** Texas U.S.A.
95 L3 **Parish** New York U.S.A.
99 W3 **Parisienne, Ile** Ontario Canada
69 E10 **Parit Buntar** Malaysia
71 L10 **Pariti** Timor Indonesia
55 D4 **Parizh** U.S.S.R.
26 N4 **Parkajoki** Sweden
29 K9 **Parkano** Finland
118 L8 **Parkbeg** Saskatchewan Canada
110 K4 **Park City** Kentucky U.S.A.
101 R4 **Park City** Montana U.S.A.
103 N1 **Park City** Utah U.S.A.
106 E3 **Parkdale** Colorado U.S.A.
100 D4 **Parkdale** Oregon U.S.A.
103 K7 **Parker** Arizona U.S.A.
106 F2 **Parker** Colorado U.S.A.
101 O6 **Parker** Idaho U.S.A.
107 Q3 **Parker** Kansas U.S.A.
98 J6 **Parker** South Dakota U.S.A.
110 L1 **Parker City** Indiana U.S.A.
94 H5 **Parker City** Pennsylvania U.S.A.
103 K7 **Parker Dam** California U.S.A.
143 D9 **Parker Hill** Western Australia Australia
140 E3 **Parker Pt** Queensland Australia
143 C9 **Parker Range** Western Australia Australia
99 O7 **Parkersburg** Iowa U.S.A.
94 F7 **Parkersburg** West Virginia U.S.A.
99 L3 **Parkers Prairie** Minnesota U.S.A.
119 O7 **Parkerview** Saskatchewan Canada
139 J5 **Parkes** New South Wales Australia
95 M6 **Parkesburg** Pennsylvania U.S.A.
99 Q4 **Park Falls** Wisconsin U.S.A.
102 D6 **Parkfield** California U.S.A.
12 E3 **Parkgate** Scotland
95 L8 **Park Hall** Maryland U.S.A.
57 E5 **Parkhar** U.S.S.R.
120 J9 **Parkhill** Ontario Canada
26 K5 **Parkijaur** *L* Sweden
110 F6 **Parkin** Arkansas U.S.A.
118 E9 **Park Lake Prov. Park** Alberta Canada
118 D8 **Parkland** Alberta Canada
119 Q9 **Parkman** Saskatchewan Canada
101 S5 **Parkman** Wyoming U.S.A.
99 L3 **Park Rapids** Minnesota U.S.A.
99 T8 **Park Ridge** Illinois U.S.A.
98 J1 **Park River** North Dakota U.S.A.
103 N6 **Parks** Arizona U.S.A.
98 E9 **Parks** Nebraska U.S.A.
111 L13 **Parks Airport** St Louis
118 L5 **Parkside** Saskatchewan Canada
95 M9 **Parksley** Virginia U.S.A.
140 C6 **Parks, Mt** N Terr Australia
109 K2 **Park Springs** Texas U.S.A.
37 N4 **Parkstein** W Germany
98 J6 **Parkston** South Dakota U.S.A.
95 L7 **Parkton** Maryland U.S.A.
112 H3 **Parkton** North Carolina U.S.A.
101 M8 **Park Valley** Utah U.S.A.
106 D1 **Park View Mt** Colorado U.S.A.
100 D3 **Parkway** Washington U.S.A.
26 K5 **Pärlälven** *R* Sweden
127 M1 **Parlatuvier** Tobago
74 G9 **Parli Vaijnāth** India
45 H2 **Parma** *R* Italy
45 H2 **Parma** Italy
100 J6 **Parma** Idaho U.S.A.
94 C4 **Parma** Michigan U.S.A.
110 G5 **Parma** Missouri U.S.A.
94 F5 **Parma** Ohio U.S.A.
129 K6 **Parnaguá** Brazil
129 J5 **Parnaiba** *R* Brazil
129 K4 **Parnaiba** Brazil
46 F6 **Parnassós** *mt* Greece
144 D5 **Parnassus** New Zealand
99 O8 **Parnell** Iowa U.S.A.
99 M9 **Parnell** Missouri U.S.A.
108 G1 **Parnell** Texas U.S.A.
46 F6 **Párnis** *mt* Greece
46 F7 **Párnon Óros** *mts* Greece
52 B5 **Pärnu** U.S.S.R.
52 B5 **Pärnu laht** *G* U.S.S.R.
144 C5 **Paroa** New Zealand
59 M1 **Paromay** U.S.S.R.
110 D7 **Paron** Arkansas U.S.A.
141 G8 **Paroo** *R* Queensland Australia
139 G4 **Paroo Chan** New South Wales Australia
77 G2 **Paropamisus** *mts* Afghanistan
70 F6 **Paroreang, Bk** *mt* Sulawesi
46 G7 **Páros** *isld* Greece
127 J3. **Parottee Pt** Jamaica
103 M4 **Parowan** Utah U.S.A.
99 T8 **Parr** Indiana U.S.A.
112 F3 **Parr** South Carolina U.S.A.
8 C5 **Parracombe** England
133 C5 **Parral** Chile
139 K5 **Parramatta** New South Wales Australia
95 M9 **Parramore I** Virginia U.S.A.
124 H5 **Parras de la Fuente** Mexico
8 D5 **Parrett, R** England
111 J8 **Parrish** Alabama U.S.A.
113 E10 **Parrish** Florida U.S.A.
112 G5 **Parris I** South Carolina U.S.A.
111 M10 **Parrott** Georgia U.S.A.
94 G9 **Parrott** Virginia U.S.A.
122 H8 **Parrsboro** Nova Scotia Canada
119 N9 **Parry** Saskatchewan Canada
115 L4 **Parry B** Northwest Territories Canada
120 K7 **Parry I** Ontario Canada
114 H2 **Parry Is** Northwest Territories Canada
115 M2 **Parry, Kap** Greenland
127 N3 **Parrylands** Trinidad
142 B5 **Parry Ra** Western Australia Australia
77 B6 **Pars** *oil well* Persian Gulf
33 N7 **Parsau** W Germany
37 M5 **Parsberg** W Germany
41 M3 **Parseier Spitze** *mt* Austria
98 D2 **Parshall** North Dakota U.S.A.
103 K3 **Parsnip Pk** Nevada U.S.A.
107 P4 **Parsons** Kansas U.S.A.
110 H6 **Parsons** Tennessee U.S.A.
94 H7 **Parsons** West Virginia U.S.A.
123 P3 **Parson's Pond** Newfoundland Canada
43 E11 **Partanna** Sicily
26 J4 **Pårtefjället** *mt* Sweden
36 E4 **Partenheim** W Germany
21 K8 **Parthenay** France
46 F7 **Parthénion** Greece
124 D5 **Partida** *isld* Mexico
43 E10 **Partinico** Sicily
59 K3 **Partizansk** U.S.S.R.
56 D2 **Partizansk** U.S.S.R.
120 K2 **Partridge** *R* Ontario Canada
107 M4 **Partridge** Kansas U.S.A.
123 R5 **Partridgeberry Hills** Newfoundland Canada
119 U1 **Partridge Breast L** Manitoba Canada
123 Q3 **Partridge Pt** Newfoundland Canada
129 H4 **Paru** *R* Brazil
145 E1 **Parua Bay** New Zealand
77 L2 **Parvan** *prov* Afghanistan
66 C6 **Paryang** China
27 H15 **Påryd** Sweden
89 E6 **Parys** S Africa
102 G7 **Pasadena** California U.S.A.
109 G9 **Pasadena** Texas U.S.A.
128 B4 **Pasado, C** Ecuador
133 E3 **Pasaje** *R* Argentina
124 H5 **Pasaje** Mexico
106 G5 **Pasamonte** New Mexico U.S.A.
70 F5 **Pasangkaiu** Sulawesi
69 E14 **Pasarbantal** Sumatra
77 C4 **Pasargadae** Iran
69 E14 **Pasarseblat** Sumatra
71 H7 **Pasarwadjo** Indonesia
111 H11 **Pascagoula** *R* Mississippi U.S.A.
121 N4 **Pascalis** Quebec Canada
48 K3 **Paşcani** Romania
128 C6 **Pasco** *dept* Peru
100 F3 **Pasco** Washington U.S.A.
95 Q5 **Pascoag** Rhode I U.S.A.
130 H5 **Pascoal, Mte** Brazil
142 B5 **Pascoe I** Western Australia Australia
140 E3 **Pascoe Inlet** Queensland Australia
141 G2 **Pascoe, R** Queensland Australia
120 A2 **Pascopee** Ontario Canada
133 C7 **Pascua** *R* Chile
18 G2 **Pas-de-Calais** *dept* France
22 C3 **Pas en Artois** France
33 T5 **Pasewalk** East Germany
52 D4 **Pasha** U.S.S.R.
52 J3 **Pashnya** U.S.S.R.
71 E3 **Pasig** Luzon Philippines
71 J4 **Pasige** *isld* Indonesia
78 H1 **Pasinler** Turkey
70 O10 **Pasirian** Java
69 E12 **Pasirpangarayan** Sumatra
69 F10 **Pasir Putih** Malaysia
71 K8 **Pasitelu, Pulau Pulau** *islds* Indonesia
27 H14 **Påskallavik** Sweden
102 B2 **Paskenta** California U.S.A.
31 M1 **Pasłęk** Poland
143 E10 **Pasley, C** Western Australia Australia
29 L4 **Pasmajärvi** Finland
42 G5 **Pasman** *isld* Yugoslavia
138 E4 **Pasmore** *R* South Australia Australia
77 H7 **Pasni** Pakistan
133 D6 **Paso de Indios** Argentina
125 M4 **Paso del Cascal** *mt* Nicaragua
133 F3 **Paso de los Libres** Argentina
133 F4 **Paso de los Toros** Uruguay
130 B10 **Paso de Patria** Paraguay
68 B2 **Pasok** Burma
133 C6 **Paso Limay** Argentina
125 M2 **Paso Reál** Honduras
133 C7 **Paso Rio Mayo** Argentina
102 D6 **Paso Robles** California U.S.A.
122 G5 **Paspébiac** Quebec Canada
119 M8 **Pasqua** Saskatchewan Canada
119 O5 **Pasquia Hills** Saskatchewan Canada
119 Q5 **Pasquia R** Manitoba Canada
112 L1 **Pasquotank R** North Carolina U.S.A.
77 C5 **Pas Rūdak** Iran
95 T1 **Passadumkeag** Maine U.S.A.
20 F8 **Passage du Gois** France
120 B4 **Passage I** Ontario Canada
99 S1 **Passage I** Michigan U.S.A.
113 E10 **Pass-a-Grille Beach** Florida U.S.A.
95 N6 **Passaic** New Jersey U.S.A.
21 J4 **Passais** France
38 H4 **Passau** W Germany
40 D2 **Passavant** France
111 G11 **Pass Christian** Mississippi U.S.A.
101 T8 **Pass Cr** Wyoming U.S.A.
22 E2 **Passendale** Belgium
43 G12 **Passero, C** Sicily
123 Q6 **Pass I** Newfoundland Canada
71 F5 **Passi** Philippines
41 O4 **Passiria, Val** Italy
99 S1 **Pass L** Ontario Canada
120 B4 **Pass Lake** Ontario Canada
15 C4 **Pass of Brander** Scotland
133 H2 **Passos** Brazil
128 C4 **Pastaza** *prov* Ecuador
122 F3 **Pasteur, L** Quebec Canada
128 C3 **Pasto** Colombia
116 F5 **Pastol B** Alaska U.S.A.
9 H2 **Paston** England
103 P5 **Pastora Pk** Arizona U.S.A.
129 K5 **Pastos Bons** Brazil
71 E1 **Pasuquin** Luzon Philippines
70 O9 **Pasuruan** Java
52 B6 **Pasvalys** U.S.S.R.
52 C1 **Pasvikelv** *R* Norway
119 O6 **Paswegin** Saskatchewan Canada
31 M2 **Pasym** Poland
48 F3 **Pásztó** Hungary
86 D4 **Pata** Cent Afr Republic
71 E8 **Pata** *isld* Philippines
133 C7 **Patagonia** *terr* Chile/Arg
103 O10 **Patagonia** Arizona U.S.A.
100 H3 **Pataha** *R* Washington U.S.A.
77 K1 **Pata Kesar** Afghanistan
130 G10 **Patamuté** Brazil
75 L5 **Patan** Nepal
71 B2 **Patani** Indonesia
95 L7 **Patapsco** *R* Maryland U.S.A.
21 O5 **Patay** France
138 F6 **Patchewollock** Victoria Australia
95 P6 **Patchogue** Long I, New York U.S.A.
88 H3 **Pate** *isld* Kenya
145 E3 **Patea** New Zealand
144 C6 **Patearoa** New Zealand
85 F7 **Pategi** Nigeria
43 F11 **Paternò** Sicily
45 R8 **Paternopoli** Italy
100 F1 **Pateros** Washington U.S.A.
141 H8 **Paterson** *R* Queensland Australia
95 N6 **Paterson** New Jersey U.S.A.
100 F4 **Paterson** Washington U.S.A.
144 B7 **Paterson Inlet** New Zealand
142 D5 **Paterson Ra** Western Australia Australia
25 G2 **Paterswolde** Netherlands
74 F2 **Pathankot** India
74 F9 **Pathardi** India
101 T7 **Pathfinder Res** Wyoming U.S.A.
13 F2 **Pathhead** Lothian Scotland
12 D3 **Pathhead** Strathclyde Scotland
68 D7 **Pathiu** Thailand
119 N6 **Pathlow** Saskatchewan Canada
74 G9 **Pathri** India
68 E5 **Pathum Thani** Thailand
70 N9 **Pati** Java
128 C3 **Patia** *R* Colombia
74 G3 **Patiala** India
143 F6 **Patience Well** Western Australia Australia
70 G7 **Patiro Tg** *C* Sulawesi
128 C6 **Pativilca** Peru
70 N10 **Patjitan** Java
75 Q5 **Pātkai Bum** *reg* India
109 M2 **Pat Mayse Res** Texas U.S.A.
47 H7 **Pátmos** *isld* Greece
111 C8 **Patmos** Arkansas U.S.A.
75 L6 **Patna** India
12 D3 **Patna** Scotland
75 K8 **Patnagarh** India
71 F3 **Patnanongan** *isld* Luzon Philippines
78 J2 **Patnos** Turkey
145 F3 **Patoka** New Zealand
110 G3 **Patoka** Illinois U.S.A.
110 K3 **Patoka** *R* Indiana U.S.A.
99 M7 **Paton** Iowa U.S.A.
130 H9 **Patos** Brazil
129 J7 **Patos de Minas** Brazil
127 N1 **Patos, I** Trinidad
100 C1 **Patos I** Washington U.S.A.
131 H3 **Patos, Lagoa dos** Brazil
108 A5 **Patos, Laguna de** Mexico
131 E3 **Patos, L. de los** Santa Fé Argentina
131 B3 **Patos, R. de los** Argentina
133 D4 **Patquia** Argentina
46 E6 **Pátrai** Greece
Patras Greece *see* **Pátrai**
28 R9 **Patreksfjördhur** *inlet* Iceland
118 F8 **Patricia** Alberta Canada
98 E6 **Patricia** South Dakota U.S.A.
140 B5 **Patricia, Mt** N Terr Australia
133 B7 **Patricio Lynch, I** Chile
13 G5 **Patrick Brompton** England
121 T7 **Patrie, La** Quebec Canada
110 M3 **Patriot** Indiana U.S.A.
133 H1 **Patrocinio** Brazil
111 K10 **Patsaliga** *R* Alabama U.S.A.
41 O3 **Patscherkofel** *mt* Austria
52 C1 **Patsoyoki** *R* U.S.S.R.
43 C8 **Pattada** Sardinia
57 D6 **Pattakesar** U.S.S.R.
70 F7 **Pattalasa** Sulawesi Indonesia
76 C6 **Pattanapuram** India
69 E9 **Pattani** *R* Thailand
69 E9 **Pattani** Thailand
95 S7 **Patten** Maine U.S.A.
32 L8 **Pattensen** W Germany
13 F5 **Patterdale** England
102 C4 **Patterson** California U.S.A.
112 E6 **Patterson** Georgia U.S.A.
101 M5 **Patterson** Idaho U.S.A.
111 E12 **Patterson** Louisiana U.S.A.
94 H7 **Patterson Cr** West Virginia U.S.A.
117 F3 **Patterson, Mt** Yukon Territory Canada
102 E5 **Patterson Mt** California U.S.A.
99 V4 **Patterson, Pt** Michigan U.S.A.
71 N9 **Patti** Indonesia
43 F10 **Patti** Sicily
140 B4 **Pattie Cr** N Terr Australia
43 G10 **Patti, G. di** Sicily
80 B8 **Pattish** *R* Israel
111 F10 **Pattison** Mississippi U.S.A.
94 J6 **Patton** Pennsylvania U.S.A.
99 M9 **Pattonsburg** Missouri U.S.A.
130 H9 **Patu** Brazil
78 H2 **Patu** Turkey
75 O7 **Patuakhali** Bangladesh
118 K3 **Patuanak** Saskatchewan Canada
48 H6 **Pătuele** Romania
70 L9 **Patuha, G** *mt* Java
117 J7 **Patullo, Mt** British Columbia Canada
144 D4 **Paturau River** New Zealand
145 F3 **Patutahi** New Zealand
145 E3 **Patutu** *mt* New Zealand
95 L8 **Patuxent** *R* Maryland U.S.A.
18 E9 **Pau** France
145 D1 **Paua** New Zealand
129 J5 **Pau D'Arco** Brazil
21 C7 **Paudy** France
121 C7 **Paugan Falls** Quebec Canada
18 E7 **Pauillac** France
128 E5 **Pauini** Brazil
68 E2 **Pauk** Burma
68 A2 **Pauktaw** Burma
101 M7 **Paul** Idaho U.S.A.
38 H8 **Paularo** Italy
114 G4 **Paulatuk** Northwest Territories Canada
103 M7 **Paulden** Arizona U.S.A.
94 C5 **Paulding** Ohio U.S.A.
18 H9 **Paulhan** France
115 N6 **Paul I** Labrador, Nfld Canada
116 H9 **Paul I** Alaska U.S.A.
100 F5 **Paulina** Oregon U.S.A.
33 R7 **Paulinenaue** East Germany
Paulis *see* **Isiro**
130 J9 **Paulista** Brazil
129 K5 **Paulistana** Brazil
99 L7 **Paullina** Iowa U.S.A.
41 K7 **Paullo** Italy
21 N8 **Paulnay** France
130 H10 **Paulo Alfonso, Cachoeira de** *falls* Brazil
25 C3 **Paulowna** Netherlands
107 N7 **Pauls Valley** Oklahoma U.S.A.
37 M5 **Paulushofen** W Germany
20 G8 **Paulx** France
68 C4 **Paung** Burma
68 B3 **Paungde** Burma
74 H8 **Pauni** India
74 H3 **Pauri** India
37 M2 **Pausa** East Germany
128 D7 **Pausa** Peru
33 S7 **Pausin** East Germany
128 D2 **Pauto** *R* Colombia
26 J7 **Pauträsk** Sweden
22 G5 **Pauvres** France
135 T3 **Pauwela** Hawaiian Is
103 M3 **Pavant Ra** Utah U.S.A.
55 C2 **Pavda** U.S.S.R.
46 G2 **Pavel Banya** Bulgaria
54 L3 **Pavelets** U.S.S.R.
44 F1 **Pavia** Italy
117 N10 **Pavilion** British Columbia Canada
94 K4 **Pavilion** New York U.S.A.
101 R6 **Pavillion** Wyoming U.S.A.
21 M2 **Pavilly** France
27 M15 **Pāvilosta** U.S.S.R.
52 G5 **Pavino** U.S.S.R.
46 G1 **Pavlikeni** Bulgaria
55 G4 **Pavlodar** U.S.S.R.
116 G9 **Pavlof** Alaska U.S.A.
116 F9 **Pavlof Harbour** Aleutian Is
116 G9 **Pavlof Vol** Alaska U.S.A.
54 G8 **Pavlograd** U.S.S.R.
55 F4 **Pavlogradka** U.S.S.R.
55 C3 **Pavlovka** Bashkirskaya A.S.S.R. U.S.S.R.
55 F5 **Pavlovka** Kazakhskaya S.S.R. U.S.S.R.
52 F6 **Pavlovo** U.S.S.R.
56 B4 **Pavlovsk** Altayskiy Kray U.S.S.R.
52 D5 **Pavlovsk** Leningradskaya obl U.S.S.R.
55 D4 **Pavlovskiy** Kazakhskaya S.S.R. U.S.S.R.
52 H5 **Pavlovskiy** Permskaya obl U.S.S.R.
113 D7 **Pavo** Georgia U.S.A.
45 J3 **Pavullo nel Frignano** Italy
107 O5 **Pawhuska** Oklahoma U.S.A.
119 Q3 **Pawistik** Manitoba Canada
95 O3 **Pawlet** Vermont U.S.A.
8 D5 **Pawlett** England
112 H4 **Pawleys Island** South Carolina U.S.A.
68 C3 **Pawn** *R* Burma
99 R10 **Pawnee** Illinois U.S.A.
107 O5 **Pawnee** Oklahoma U.S.A.
109 K7 **Pawnee** Texas U.S.A.
99 L9 **Pawnee City** Nebraska U.S.A.
98 C9 **Pawnee Cr** Colorado U.S.A.
107 L3 **Pawnee Rock** Kansas U.S.A.
94 B4 **Paw Paw** Michigan U.S.A.
94 J7 **Paw Paw** West Virginia U.S.A.
95 Q5 **Pawtucket** Rhode I U.S.A.
46 G9 **Paximádhia** *isld* Crete Greece
Paxoi *see* **Paxos**
47 P13 **Paxos** *isld* Greece
116 P5 **Paxson** Alaska U.S.A.
116 P5 **Paxson L** Alaska U.S.A.
99 S9 **Paxton** Illinois U.S.A.
98 E8 **Paxton** Nebraska U.S.A.
68 C4 **Payagyi** Burma
71 A2 **Payahe** Halmahera Indonesia
58 E3 **Pa-yen-kao-le** China
40 E4 **Payerne** Switzerland
100 J5 **Payette** *R* Idaho U.S.A.
100 J5 **Payette** Idaho U.S.A.
109 L3 **Pay Hubbard, L** Texas U.S.A.
50 F2 **Pay-Khoy, Khrebet** *mt* U.S.S.R.
112 D5 **Payne** Georgia U.S.A.
94 C5 **Payne** Ohio U.S.A.
115 M6 **Payne, L** Quebec Canada
102 C1 **Paynes Cr** California U.S.A.
143 C8 **Payne's Find** Western Australia Australia
99 M4 **Paynesville** Minnesota U.S.A.
118 J5 **Paynton** Saskatchewan Canada
131 F4 **Paysandu** Uruguay
21 K3 **Pays-d'Auge** *reg* France
21 O2 **Pays-de-Bray** *reg* France
19 N13 **Pays de Dombes** *reg* France
40 F5 **Pays d'Enhaut** Switzerland
103 N7 **Payson** Arizona U.S.A.
103 N1 **Payson** Utah U.S.A.
57 K6 **Paytug** U.S.S.R.
131 B6 **Payún** *vol* Argentina
70 C3 **Payung Tanjong** *C* Sarawak
131 B6 **Payún Matru, Cerros** *hills* Argentina
77 A4 **Pāzanūn** Iran
46 G2 **Pazardzhik** Bulgaria
47 J5 **Pazarköy** Turkey
47 J6 **Pazaryeri** Turkey
124 D5 **Paz, B. de la** Mexico
128 D2 **Paz de Rio** Colombia
42 F3 **Pazin** Yugoslavia
41 M3 **Paznauntal** Austria
52 D5 **Pchevzha** U.S.S.R.
31 M6 **Pcim** Poland
46 E2 **Pčinja** *R* Yugoslavia
68 D6 **Pe** Burma
111 L10 **Pea** *R* Alabama U.S.A.
117 R6 **Peace Point** Alberta Canada
118 A2 **Peace R** Alberta Canada
117 M7 **Peace R** Br Col/Alberta Canada
113 F10 **Peace R** Florida U.S.A.
117 P7 **Peace River** Alberta Canada
117 O11 **Peachland** British Columbia Canada
103 L6 **Peach Sp** Arizona U.S.A.
94 B2 **Peacock** Michigan U.S.A.
141 J5 **Peak Downs** Queensland Australia
138 D3 **Peake** *R* South Australia Australia
71 D5 **Peaked Pt** Philippines
140 B3 **Peake, Mt** N Terr Australia
143 C7 **Peak Hill** Western Australia Australia
102 E7 **Peak Mt** California U.S.A.
141 J6 **Peak Ra** Queensland Australia
103 P3 **Peale, Mt** Utah U.S.A.
100 B9 **Peanut** California U.S.A.
118 D9 **Pearce** Alberta Canada
103 P10 **Pearce** Arizona U.S.A.
140 A2 **Pearce Pt** N Terr Australia
111 C7 **Pearcy** Arkansas U.S.A.
116 H1 **Peard B** Alaska U.S.A.
110 C5 **Pea Ridge Nat. Mil. Park** Arkansas U.S.A.
119 P2 **Pearl** Ontario Canada
110 F2 **Pearl** Illinois U.S.A.
111 F9 **Pearl** Mississippi U.S.A.
111 G11 **Pearl** *R* Miss/Louisiana U.S.A.
109 G10 **Pearland** Texas U.S.A.
102 S12 **Pearl City** Hawaiian Is
99 R7 **Pearl City** Illinois U.S.A.
102 S12 **Pearl Hbr** Hawaiian Is
144 A7 **Pearl I** New Zealand
109 H7 **Pearsall** Texas U.S.A.
112 E6 **Pearson** Georgia U.S.A.
138 C5 **Pearson Is** South Australia Australia
119 V2 **Pearson L** Manitoba Canada
114 J2 **Peary Ch** Northwest Territories Canada
109 H1 **Pease** *R* Texas U.S.A.
20 F6 **Péaule** France
99 S3 **Peavy Falls Res** Michigan U.S.A.
142 C5 **Peawah, R** Western Australia Australia
88 G10 **Pebane** Mozambique
128 D4 **Pebas** Peru
133 F8 **Pebble I** Falkland Is
70 G5 **Pebengko** Sulawesi
46 D2 **Peć** Yugoslavia
111 D12 **Pecan Island** Louisiana U.S.A.
130 E9 **Peças, I. das** Brazil
99 R7 **Pecatonica** *R* Illinois U.S.A.
99 R7 **Pecatonica** Illinois U.S.A.
45 J4 **Péccioli** Italy
48 L5 **Pechea** Romania
48 J2 **Pechenezhin** U.S.S.R.
54 H6 **Pechenezhskoye Vodokhranilishche** *res* U.S.S.R.
29 P2 **Pechenga** U.S.S.R.
55 D1 **Pecherakh** U.S.S.R.
52 J2 **Pechora** U.S.S.R.
52 J3 **Pechora** *R* U.S.S.R.
50 E2 **Pechorskaya Guba** *sea* U.S.S.R.
52 C5 **Pechory** U.S.S.R.
48 G4 **Pecica** Romania
100 B7 **Peck** Oregon U.S.A.
33 S5 **Peckatel** East Germany
32 K9 **Peckelsheim** W Germany
43 B9 **Pecora, C** Sardinia
43 G10 **Pecoraro, M** *mt* Italy
106 F6 **Pecos** *R* New Mexico U.S.A.
106 E6 **Pecos** New Mexico U.S.A.
108 D4 **Pecos** Texas U.S.A.
108 F5 **Pecos** *R* Texas/Mexico U.S.A./Mexico
106 E6 **Pecos Nat. Mon** New Mexico U.S.A.
48 E4 **Pécs** Hungary
48 E4 **Pécsvárad** Hungary
110 B3 **Peculiar** Missouri U.S.A.
125 O6 **Pedasí** Panama
139 H9 **Pedder, L** Tasmania Australia
100 B5 **Pedee** Oregon U.S.A.
127 J5 **Pedernales** Dominican Rep
124 F3 **Pedernales** Mexico
127 N10 **Pedernales** Venezuela
28 H6 **Pedersborg** Denmark
70 L9 **Pedes** Java
79 C4 **Pedhoulas** Cyprus
138 D2 **Pedirka** South Australia Australia
71 A2 **Pediwang** Indonesia
129 K7 **Pedra Azul** Brazil
130 J9 **Pedra, Pta. de** *C* Brazil
128 F6 **Pedras Negras** Brazil
124 H5 **Pedriceña** Mexico
129 J5 **Pedro Afonso** Brazil
126 E6 **Pedro Bank** Caribbean
116 K7 **Pedro Bay** Alaska U.S.A.
126 D3 **Pedro Betancourt** Cuba
126 F6 **Pedro Cays** *reefs* Caribbean
Peebles *co see* **Borders** *reg*
140 D7 **Peebles, Mt** N Terr Australia
142 B5 **Peedamulla** Western Australia Australia
12 D5 **Peel** I of Man U.K.
144 C5 **Peel, Mt** New Zealand
103 M7 **Peeples Valley** Arizona U.S.A.
117 Q7 **Peerless L** Alberta Canada
118 A5 **Peers** Alberta Canada
139 G4 **Peery, L** New South Wales Australia
106 G1 **Peetz** Colorado U.S.A.
98 K4 **Peever** South Dakota U.S.A.
144 D5 **Pegasus Bay** New Zealand
37 N1 **Pegau** East Germany
38 M7 **Peggau** Austria
44 E3 **Pegli** Italy
37 M4 **Pegnitz** W Germany
17 G6 **Pego** Spain
45 J2 **Pegognaga** Italy
101 O7 **Pegram** Idaho U.S.A.
13 G3 **Pegswood** England
69 F13 **Peg Tigabuluh** *mt* Sumatra
68 C4 **Pegu** Burma
69 E13 **Pegunungan Barisan** *mt* Sumatra
69 K12 **Pegunungan Bayang** *mt* Indonesia
68 B3 **Pegu Yoma** *ra* Burma
9 H5 **Pegwell B** England
52 H3 **Pegysh** U.S.S.R.
46 F3 **Pehčevo** Yugoslavia
67 B1 **Peijiangchang** China
67 G3 **Pei-Kan-t'ang Tao** *isld* Taiwan
20 F6 **Peillac** France
38 M5 **Peilstein** *mt* Austria
32 M8 **Peine** W Germany
133 C8 **Peineta** *mt* Chile
68 B2 **Peinwa** Burma
19 P16 **Peipin** France
Peipus, L *see* **Chudskoye, Ozero**
41 N2 **Peiting** W Germany
133 G2 **Peixe** *R* Brazil
130 C5 **Peixe de Couro, R** Brazil
65 D7 **Pei Xian** China
65 C7 **Pei Xian** China
69 H12 **Pejantan** *isld* Indonesia
48 G6 **Pek** *R* Yugoslavia
70 F6 **Pekabata** Sulawesi
70 M9 **Pekalongan** Java
69 F11 **Pekan** Malaysia
69 E12 **Pekanbaru** Sumatra
110 G1 **Pekin** Illinois U.S.A.
99 R9 **Pekin** Illinois U.S.A.
98 H2 **Pekin** North Dakota U.S.A.
Peking *see* **Beijing**
117 Q10 **Pekisko** Alberta Canada
29 M5 **Pekkala** Finland
68 C3 **Pekon** Burma
69 E11 **Pelabuhan Kelang** Malaysia
43 E13 **Pelagie, Isole** Italy
45 L4 **Pelago** Italy
46 G5 **Pélagos** *isld* Greece
111 G9 **Pelahatchee** Mississippi U.S.A.
69 F12 **Pelalawan** Sumatra
17 G4 **Pelarda, Sa** *mts* Spain
46 F6 **Pelasyia** Greece
89 F7 **Pelatsoeu** *mt* Lesotho
70 F4 **Pelawanbesar** Kalimantan
31 J2 **Pełczyce** Poland
48 H5 **Peleaga** *mt* Romania
56 H2 **Peleduy** *R* U.S.S.R.
120 H10 **Pelee Island** Ontario Canada
127 L4 **Pelée, Mt** Martinique W Indies
47 O12 **Pélekas** Greece
71 H5 **Peleng** *isld* Indonesia
71 H5 **Peleng, Selat** *str* Sulawesi
71 H5 **Peleng, Tk** *B* Indonesia
112 C6 **Pelham** Georgia U.S.A.
31 J6 **Pelhřimov** Czechoslovakia
119 R6 **Pelican B** Manitoba Canada
113 L11 **Pelican Harbour** Bahamas
118 D3 **Pelican L** Alberta Canada
119 S9 **Pelican L** Manitoba Canada
119 O3 **Pelican L** Saskatchewan Canada
99 O1 **Pelican L** Minnesota U.S.A.
99 R4 **Pelican L** Wisconsin U.S.A.
118 E3 **Pelican Portage** Alberta Canada
141 G3 **Pelican R** Queensland Australia
119 R6 **Pelican Rapids** Manitoba Canada
98 K3 **Pelican Rapids** Minnesota U.S.A.
48 L3 **Peliniya** U.S.S.R.
59 L1 **Peliny Osipenko, imeni** U.S.S.R.
112 F4 **Pelion** South Carolina U.S.A.
26 J5 **Peljekaise Nat. Park** Sweden
42 H6 **Pelješac** *pen* Yugoslavia
29 N4 **Pelkosenniemi** Finland
52 D3 **Pelkula** U.S.S.R.
32 G9 **Pelkum** W Germany
43 G8 **Pella** Italy
80 F4 **Pella** Jordan
99 O8 **Pella** Iowa U.S.A.
111 K8 **Pell City** Alabama U.S.A.
133 E5 **Pellegrini** Argentina
133 D5 **Pellegrini, L** Argentina
21 H5 **Pellerine, la** France
20 G7 **Pellerin, le** France
45 M1 **Pellestrina** Italy
119 U2 **Pelletier L** Manitoba Canada
21 N8 **Pellevoisin** France
140 D3 **Pellew C** N Terr Australia
36 B4 **Pellingen** W Germany
29 L5 **Pello** Finland
21 K6 **Pellouailles** France
94 C1 **Pellston** Michigan U.S.A.
30 D1 **Pellworm** *isld* W Germany
119 Q7 **Pelly** Saskatchewan Canada
117 E4 **Pelly** *R* Yukon Territory Canada
115 L4 **Pelly Bay** Northwest Territories Canada
117 E4 **Pelly Crossing** Yukon Territory Canada
114 J4 **Pelly L** Northwest Territories Canada
117 G5 **Pelly Mts** Yukon Territory Canada
71 J8 **Pelokang** *isld* Indonesia
46 E7 **Pelopónnisos** Greece
43 G11 **Peloritani, Mi** *mts* Sicily
145 D4 **Pelorus Sound** New Zealand
131 H3 **Pelotas** Brazil
130 D10 **Pelotas, R.das** Brazil
46 G1 **Pelovo** Bulgaria
31 L2 **Pelplin** Poland
143 A8 **Pelsart Group** *islds* Western Australia Australia
33 T5 **Pelsin** East Germany
110 C6 **Pelsor** Arkansas U.S.A.
29 L3 **Peltovuoma** Finland
44 B2 **Pelvo d'Elva** *mt* Italy
19 Q15 **Pelvoux, Mt** France
55 D2 **Pelym** U.S.S.R.
55 D1 **Pelym** *R* U.S.S.R.
55 D1 **Pelymskiy Tuman, Oz** *L* U.S.S.R.
8 B7 **Pelynt** England
112 E3 **Pelzer** South Carolina U.S.A.
33 N4 **Pelzerhaken** W Germany
120 G5 **Pemache, R** Ontario Canada
95 S1 **Pemadumcook L** Maine U.S.A.
70 M9 **Pemalang** Java
70 M9 **Pemalang, Ujung** *C* Java
71 H5 **Pemali, Tg** *C* Sulawesi
69 J12 **Pemangkat** Indonesia
70 E5 **Pemarung, P** Kalimantan
69 D11 **Pematangsiantar** Sumatra
88 H8 **Pemba** Mozambique
87 E9 **Pemba** Zambia
87 H8 **Pemba, B.de** Mozambique
88 G4 **Pemba I** Tanzania
143 B10 **Pemberton** Western Australia Australia
117 M10 **Pemberton** British Columbia Canada
98 H1 **Pembina** *R* Manitoba Canada
119 U10 **Pembina** North Dakota U.S.A.
118 B5 **Pembina Oil Fields** Alberta Canada
119 T9 **Pembina Mt** Manitoba Canada
118 C5 **Pembina Prov. Park** Alberta Canada
118 C4 **Pembina R** Alberta Canada
99 T4 **Pembine** Wisconsin U.S.A.
Pembroke *co see* **Dyfed**
121 N7 **Pembroke** Ontario Canada
112 F5 **Pembroke** Georgia U.S.A.
110 J5 **Pembroke** Kentucky U.S.A.
112 H3 **Pembroke** North Carolina U.S.A.
94 G9 **Pembroke** Virginia U.S.A.
8 B4 **Pembroke** Wales
133 F8 **Pembroke, C** Falkland Is
144 A6 **Pembroke, Mt** New Zealand
9 G5 **Pembury** England
70 B5 **Pemuar** Kalimantan
127 J5 **Peña** Dominican Rep
106 D6 **Penablanca** New Mexico U.S.A.
95 Q3 **Penacook** New Hampshire U.S.A.
17 G2 **Peña de Oroel** *mt ra* Spain
16 B3 **Penafiel** Portugal
16 E3 **Peñafiel** Spain
17 G4 **Peñagolosa** *mt* Spain
127 O3 **Penal** Trinidad
8 B4 **Penally** Wales
70 D3 **Penambo Ra** Kalimantan
16 C3 **Peña Mira** *mt* Spain
70 E2 **Penampang** Sabah
131 B2 **Peña Negra, Pasco de** Arg/Chile
125 K6 **Peña Nevada, Cerro** *mt* Mexico
Penang *see* **Pinang** *isld*
130 E7 **Penápolis** Brazil
16 D1 **Peña Prieta** *mt* Spain
16 D4 **Peñaranda de Bracamonte** Spain
95 M6 **Pen Argyl** Pennsylvania U.S.A.
139 G5 **Penarie** New South Wales Australia
17 G4 **Peñarroya** *mt* Spain
16 D6 **Peñarroya-Pueblonuevo** Spain
8 C5 **Penarth** Wales
16 C1 **Peña Rubia** *mt* Spain
17 G2 **Peña, Sa. de la** *mts* Spain
124 M4 **Peñas Blancas** Nicaragua
16 D1 **Peñas, C. de** Spain
106 E5 **Penasco** New Mexico U.S.A.
108 C3 **Penasco, Rio** *R* New Mexico U.S.A.
16 E3 **Peñas de Cervera** Spain
17 F6 **Peñas de San Pedro** Spain
133 C7 **Penas, G.de** Chile
69 B10 **Penasi, Pulau** *isld* Sumatra
127 N9 **Peñas, Pta** Venezuela
16 C2 **Peña Trevinca** *mt* Spain
16 D1 **Peña Vieja** *mt* Spain
100 H3 **Penawawa** Washington U.S.A.
65 F4 **Pen-ch'i** China
146 J12 **Penck, C** Antarctica
131 C4 **Pencoso, Alto de** *mt* Argentina
70 C5 **Pendadahian** Kalimantan
46 E4 **Pendálofon** Greece
118 F9 **Pendant d'Oreille** Alberta Canada
86 C4 **Pende** *R* Cent Afr Republic
46 F6 **Pendelikón** *mt* Greece
85 B7 **Pendembu** Sierra Leone
130 H8 **Pendencia** Brazil
142 E3 **Pender** Western Australia Australia
98 K7 **Pender** Nebraska U.S.A.
142 E3 **Pender Bay** Western Australia Australia
144 A6 **Pender, Mt** New Zealand
47 N11 **Pendik** Turkey
8 B4 **Pendine** Wales
13 F6 **Pendlebury** England
13 F6 **Pendle Hill** England
94 B7 **Pendleton** Indiana U.S.A.
100 G4 **Pendleton** Oregon U.S.A.
112 E3 **Pendleton** South Carolina U.S.A.
117 J6 **Pendleton, Mt** British Columbia Canada
69 F14 **Pendopo** Sumatra
100 H1 **Pend Oreille** *R* Washington U.S.A.
117 P11 **Pend Oreille, L** Idaho U.S.A.
101 N1 **Pendroy** Montana U.S.A.
69 J13 **Penebangan** *isld* Indonesia
16 B3 **Peneda** *mt* Portugal
129 L6 **Penedo** Brazil
20 F7 **Penestin** France
94 J5 **Penfield** Pennsylvania U.S.A.
70 L9 **Pengalengan** Java
67 B1 **Peng'an** China
67 G4 **P'eng-chia Hsü** *isld* Taiwan
86 D7 **Penge** Zaire
67 F5 **P'eng-hu Lieh-tao** *isld* Taiwan
67 F5 **P'eng-hu Tao** *isld* Taiwan
69 J12 **Pengiki** *isld* Indonesia
67 E4 **Pengkou** China
65 E6 **Penglai** China
58 G5 **Peng-pu** China
67 A1 **Pengshan** China
67 C2 **Pengshui** China
139 H8 **Penguin** Tasmania Australia
142 F2 **Penguin Deeps** Timor Sea
67 B1 **Pengxi** China
67 A1 **Peng Xian** China
67 E2 **Pengze** China
130 E10 **Penha** Brazil
20 A5 **Penhir, Pte de** France
118 D6 **Penhold** Alberta Canada
8 D4 **Penhow** Wales
120 F3 **Penhurst** Ontario Canada
44 F2 **Penice** *mt* Italy
16 A5 **Peniche** Portugal
13 E2 **Penicuik** Scotland
70 P10 **Penida** *isld* Indonesia
37 O2 **Penig** East Germany
71 G5 **Peninsula Pt** Philippines
69 E10 **Peninsular Malaysia** S E Asia
17 H4 **Peñiscola** Spain
13 G6 **Penistone** England
70 M9 **Penju, Teluk** *B* Java
78 K4 **Penjwin** Iran
38 H8 **Penk** Austria
56 B3 **Pen'ki** U.S.S.R.
8 D2 **Penkridge** England
8 C1 **Penmaenmawr** Wales
20 B6 **Penmarc'h** France
20 B6 **Penmarc'h, Pte de** France
118 K5 **Penn** Saskatchewan Canada
45 M4 **Pennabilli** Italy
45 L4 **Penna, M** *mt* Italy
118 J8 **Pennant** Saskatchewan Canada
122 J9 **Pennant Pt** Nova Scotia Canada
42 F6 **Penna, Pta. della** Italy
42 F6 **Penne** Italy
18 F8 **Penne d'Agenais** France
146 C11 **Pennell Bank** *sea feature* Antarctica
146 C12 **Pennell Coast** *coast* Antarctica
138 E6 **Penneshaw** South Australia Australia
122 F8 **Pennfield** New Brunswick Canada
40 G5 **Pennine, Alpi** *mts* Switzerland
7 J8 **Pennine Chain** *mts* England
26 G7 **Penningkejsen** *mt* Norway/Sweden
95 N6 **Pennington** New Jersey U.S.A.
109 M4 **Pennington** Texas U.S.A.
94 D10 **Pennington Gap** Virginia U.S.A.
42 E5 **Pennino, M** *mt* Italy
95 M6 **Pennsburg** Pennsylvania U.S.A.
95 M7 **Penns Grove** New Jersey U.S.A.
94 H6 **Pennsylvania** *state* U.S.A.
95 K4 **Penn Yan** New York U.S.A.
12 B1 **Pennyghael** Scotland
115 N4 **Penny Ice Cap** Northwest Territories Canada
146 D11 **Penny Point** *pt* Antarctica
115 K2 **Penny Str** Northwest Territories Canada
52 D6 **Peno** U.S.S.R.
95 T1 **Penobscot** *R* Maine U.S.A.
95 T2 **Penobscot B** Maine U.S.A.
122 G8 **Penobsquis** New Brunswick Canada
138 F6 **Penola** South Australia Australia
124 G5 **Peñón Blanco** Mexico
138 C4 **Penong** South Australia Australia
125 O5 **Penonomé** Panama
100 C8 **Penoyar** California U.S.A.
8 B2 **Penrhyndeudraeth** Wales
139 K5 **Penrith** New South Wales Australia
13 F4 **Penrith** England
8 A7 **Penryn** England
111 J11 **Pensacola** Florida U.S.A.
113 K10 **Pensacola Cay** Bahamas
146 E8 **Pensacola Mts** Antarctica
119 N8 **Pense** Saskatchewan Canada
8 D5 **Pensford** England
138 F7 **Penshurst** Victoria Australia
9 G5 **Penshurst** England
70 E2 **Pensiangan** Sabah
137 O5 **Pentecost I** Vanuatu
142 G3 **Pentecost, R** Western Australia Australia
Pentecôte, Î *see* **Pentecost I**
122 E4 **Pentecôte, L** Quebec Canada
48 K5 **Penteleu** *mt* Romania
117 O11 **Penticton** British Columbia Canada
141 H5 **Pentland** Queensland Australia
15 E2 **Pentland Firth** Scotland
13 E2 **Pentland Hills** Scotland
15 F2 **Pentland Skerries** Orkney Scotland
8 B1 **Pentraeth** Wales
8 C1 **Pentre-Foelas** Wales
94 A3 **Pentwater** Michigan U.S.A.
131 E5 **Penuajo** Argentina
69 G13 **Penuba** Indonesia
69 G14 **Penuguan** Sumatra
69 F10 **Penunjuk, Tanjong** *C* Malaysia
20 D4 **Penvénan** France
68 C3 **Penwegon** Burma
8 C1 **Pen-y-benclog** Wales
8 C3 **Penybont** Wales
8 B1 **Pen-y-groes** Wales
53 F7 **Penza** U.S.S.R.
119 M7 **Penzance** Saskatchewan Canada
9 F6 **Penzance** England
41 O2 **Penzberg** W Germany
51 Q2 **Penzhinskaya Guba** *G* U.S.S.R.
33 S6 **Penzlin** East Germany
100 H3 **Peola** Washington U.S.A.
101 R1 **Peoples Cr** Montana U.S.A.
103 M8 **Peoria** Arizona U.S.A.
99 R9 **Peoria** Illinois U.S.A.
99 T8 **Peotone** Illinois U.S.A.
89 C6 **Pepani** *watercourse* S Africa
85 B7 **Pepel** Sierra Leone
25 F3 **Peperga** Netherlands
145 D4 **Pepin I** New Zealand
99 O5 **Pepin, L** Wisconsin U.S.A.
22 K2 **Pepinster** Belgium
130 D10 **Pepiri Guaçu. R** Brazil
44 B3 **Pépoiri, Mt** France
46 D3 **Peqin** Albania
131 H3 **Pequena, L** Brazil
124 C4 **Pequeña, Pta** *C* Mexico
103 K1 **Pequop Mts** Nevada U.S.A.
99 M3 **Pequot Lakes** Minnesota U.S.A.
37 O7 **Perach** W Germany
141 F2 **Pera Hd** Queensland Australia
70 M9 **Perahu, Gunung** *mt* Java
69 E10 **Perai** Malaysia
69 E10 **Perak** *prov* Malaysia
69 D10 **Perak** *isld* Malaysia
46 F6 **Perakhóra** Greece
38 G8 **Peralba** *mt* Italy
106 D7 **Peralta** New Mexico U.S.A.
46 G9 **Pérama** Crete Greece
69 F13 **Peranap** Sumatra
29 M5 **Perä-Posio** Finland
29 K9 **Peräseinäjoki** Finland
80 E3 **Perazon** Israel
122 H5 **Percé** Quebec Canada
21 J3 **Percée, Pte. de la** France
18 G10 **Perche, Col de la** *pass* France
21 M4 **Perche, Coteaux du** *hills* France
8 B2 **Percilan Hd** Wales
45 N5 **Percile** Italy
99 L9 **Percival** Iowa U.S.A.
142 E5 **Percival Ls** Western Australia Australia
21 H4 **Percy** France
110 G3 **Percy** Illinois U.S.A.
99 N8 **Percy** Iowa U.S.A.
141 K5 **Percy Is** Queensland Australia
143 D9 **Percy, L** Western Australia Australia
133 D6 **Perdido** *R* Argentina
17 H2 **Perdido** *mt* Spain
111 J11 **Perdido** *R* Alabama/Florida U.S.A.
18 F10 **Perdido, M** *mt* Spain
130 B7 **Perdido, R** Brazil
118 K6 **Perdue** Saskatchewan Canada
122 B3 **Perdu, L** Quebec Canada
99 U6 **Pere** *R* Michigan U.S.A.
48 G2 **Perechin** U.S.S.R.
48 J2 **Pereginskoye** U.S.S.R.
50 F2 **Peregrebnoye** U.S.S.R.
128 C3 **Pereira** Colombia
130 D7 **Pereira Barreto** Brazil
Pereira de Eça *see* **Ondjiva**
129 G5 **Pereirinha** Brazil
17 H4 **Perello** Spain
94 A3 **Pere Marquette** *R* Michigan U.S.A.
146 G13 **Peremennyy, C** Antarctica
48 J1 **Peremyshlyany** U.S.S.R.
143 B8 **Perenjori** Western Australia Australia
116 L7 **Perenosa B** Alaska U.S.A.
52 E6 **Pereslavl' Zalesskiy** U.S.S.R.
45 O5 **Pereto** Italy
48 H2 **Pereval Veretski** *mt* U.S.S.R.
55 B5 **Perevolotskiy** U.S.S.R.
54 C6 **Pereyaslav Khmel'nitskiy** U.S.S.R.
133 D3 **Pérez** Chile
100 D8 **Perez** California U.S.A.
69 C8 **Perforated I** Thailand
131 E4 **Pergamino** Argentina
Pergamum *see* **Bergama**
45 N4 **Pergola** Italy
52 E4 **Perguba** U.S.S.R.
99 L3 **Perham** Minnesota U.S.A.
69 F10 **Perhentian Besar** *isld* Malaysia
29 L8 **Perho** Finland
29 L8 **Perhojoki** *R* Finland
48 F4 **Periam** Romania
121 S4 **Péribonca** Quebec Canada
121 T3 **Péribonca** *R* Quebec Canada
122 A3 **Peribonca L** Quebec Canada
133 D2 **Perico** Argentina
124 F5 **Pericos** Mexico
20 H3 **Périers** France
129 J3 **Perigoso, Can** Brazil
18 F7 **Périgueux** France
127 H9 **Perijá, Sa. de** *mts* Colombia/Venezuela
123 P2 **Peril Rock** Quebec Canada
117 F7 **Peril Str** Alaska U.S.A.

66 Perim — Pisuerga

72 E6 Perim isld S Yemen
118 C2 Perimeter Highway Manitoba Canada
130 H10 Periquito, Sa do mts Brazil
48 K6 Periş Romania
46 E5 Peristéri mt Greece
133 C7 Perito Moreno Argentina
47 P13 Perivóli Greece
76 C5 Periyakulam India
95 M6 Perkasie Pennsylvania U.S.A.
69 G13 Perkat, Tanjong C Indonesia
112 F5 Perkins Georgia U.S.A.
111 C11 Perkins Louisiana U.S.A.
99 T4 Perkins Michigan U.S.A.
111 G11 Perkinston Mississippi U.S.A.
103 M7 Perkinsville Arizona U.S.A.
53 F11 Per Klukhorskiy mt U.S.S.R.
42 G5 Perković Yugoslavia
22 L5 Perl W Germany
41 P1 Perlach W Germany
125 P5 Perlas, Arch. de las islds Panama
33 P6 Perleberg East Germany
37 P6 Perlesreut W Germany
54 K5 Perlevka U.S.S.R.
98 K2 Perley Minnesota U.S.A.
48 F5 Perlez Yugoslavia
69 E9 Perlis prov Malaysia
52 J5 Perm' U.S.S.R.
101 L2 Perma Montana U.S.A.
53 F11 Per Mamisonskiy mt U.S.S.R.
53 F11 Per Marukhskiy mt U.S.S.R.
52 G5 Permas U.S.S.R.
46 D4 Përmet Albania
55 C2 Permskaya Oblast' prov U.S.S.R.
Pernambuco see Recife
130 H9 Pernambuco state Brazil
138 D4 Pernatty Lagoon South Australia Australia
107 N7 Pernell Oklahoma U.S.A.
22 C3 Pernes France
46 F2 Pernik Bulgaria
29 K11 Perniö Finland
25 B5 Pernis Netherlands
40 C5 Peron France
143 A7 Peron, C Western Australia Australia
140 B2 Peron Is N Terr Australia
22 D4 Péronne France
22 G3 Peronnes Belgium
143 A7 Peron Pen Western Australia Australia
21 O5 Péronville France
18 G10 Perpignan France
112 L1 Perquimans R North Carolina U.S.A.
8 A7 Perranporth England
21 O4 Perray-en-Yvelines, le France
20 D5 Perret France
21 N3 Perriers-sur-Andelle France
109 J2 Perrin Texas U.S.A.
113 G12 Perrine Florida U.S.A.
102 G8 Perris California U.S.A.
40 B2 Perrogney France
108 B1 Perro, Laguna del New Mexico U.S.A.
121 N4 Perron Quebec Canada
20 D4 Perros-Guirec France
120 F5 Perry Ontario Canada
110 D6 Perry Arkansas U.S.A.
113 D7 Perry Florida U.S.A.
112 D5 Perry Georgia U.S.A.
110 F2 Perry Illinois U.S.A.
99 M8 Perry Iowa U.S.A.
94 C4 Perry Michigan U.S.A.
110 E2 Perry Missouri U.S.A.
94 K4 Perry New York U.S.A.
107 N5 Perry Oklahoma U.S.A.
116 O6 Perry I Alaska U.S.A.
120 D2 Perry L Ontario Canada
110 A2 Perry L Kansas U.S.A.
107 P2 Perry L Kansas U.S.A.
95 L7 Perryman Maryland U.S.A.
94 D5 Perrysburg Ohio U.S.A.
108 D7 Perryton Texas U.S.A.
118 D4 Perryvale Alberta Canada
110 D6 Perryville Arkansas U.S.A.
110 G4 Perryville Missouri U.S.A.
21 P3 Persan France
Persepolis see Takht-e Jamshid
128 F6 Perseverancia Bolivia
121 O4 Pershing Quebec Canada
8 D3 Pershore England
54 H8 Pershotravensk U.S.S.R.
Persia see Iran
99 L8 Persia Iowa U.S.A.
77 A5 Persian Gulf S W Asia
27 J14 Persnäs Sweden
Perth co see Central and Tayside regions
139 H8 Perth Tasmania Australia
143 E9 Perth Western Australia Australia
121 O8 Perth Ontario Canada
12 E1 Perth Scotland
107 N4 Perth Kansas U.S.A.
98 G1 Perth North Dakota U.S.A.
95 N6 Perth Amboy New Jersey U.S.A.
122 E7 Perth-Andover New Brunswick Canada
38 L4 Pertholz Austria
41 P3 Pertisau Austria
52 E3 Pertominsk U.S.S.R.
42 J6 Pertovac Yugoslavia
21 H5 Pertre, le France
29 M10 Pertunmaa Finland
52 G5 Pertyugskiy U.S.S.R.
128 D6 Peru rep S America
99 R8 Peru Illinois U.S.A.
94 A6 Peru Indiana U.S.A.
99 L9 Peru Nebraska U.S.A.
95 O2 Peru New York U.S.A.
135 S12 Peru-Chile Trench Pacific Oc
42 E5 Perugia Italy
129 J8 Peruibe Brazil
46 G2 Perushtitsa Bulgaria
42 G4 Perušić Yugoslavia
22 F3 Peruwelz Belgium
78 J3 Pervari Turkey
21 L5 Pervenchères France
54 G4 Pervoavgustovskiy U.S.S.R.
55 F5 Pervomayka U.S.S.R.
54 K8 Pervomaysk U.S.S.R.
52 H4 Pervomayskaya U.S.S.R.
58 G1 Pervomayskiy U.S.S.R.
56 B5 Pervomayskiy U.S.S.R.
55 C4 Pervomayskiy Bashkirskaya A.S.S.R. U.S.S.R.
55 B5 Pervomayskiy Orenburgskaya obl U.S.S.R.
55 D2 Pervomayskiy Sverdlovskaya obl U.S.S.R.
56 C3 Pervomayskoye U.S.S.R.
51 Q2 Pervorechenskiy U.S.S.R.
55 C3 Pervoural'sk U.S.S.R.
22 H2 Perwez Belgium
52 D5 Pes' R U.S.S.R.
45 K4 Pesa R Italy
70 B6 Pesaguan Kalimantan
45 N4 Pesaro Italy
102 B4 Pescadero California U.S.A.
Pescadores islds see P'eng-hu Lieh-tao
128 D7 Pescadores, Pta C Peru
45 H4 Pescaglia Italy
42 F6 Pescara R Italy
42 F6 Pescara Italy
45 P6 Pescasseroli Italy
42 G7 Peschici Italy
45 J1 Peschiera del Garda Italy
45 J4 Pescia Italy
45 P5 Pescina Italy
45 R7 Pesco Sannita Italy
45 P6 Pescosolido Italy
52 G2 Pesha R U.S.S.R.
74 D1 Peshawar Pakistan
46 D3 Peshkopi Albania
46 G2 Peshtera Bulgaria
99 T4 Peshtigo Wisconsin U.S.A.
99 S4 Peshtigo R Wisconsin U.S.A.
26 J5 Peskehaure Sweden
55 E4 Peski U.S.S.R.
57 B2 Peski Priaral'skiye Karkumy U.S.S.R.
57 C5 Peski Sundukli U.S.S.R.
52 H5 Peskovka U.S.S.R.
38 N8 Pesnica R Yugoslavia
16 B3 Péso de Regua Portugal
110 H2 Pesotum Illinois U.S.A.
129 L5 Pesqueira Brazil
18 E8 Pessac France
33 R7 Pessin East Germany
48 E3 Pest co Hungary
48 H6 Peşteana Jiu Romania
52 E5 Pestovo U.S.S.R.
52 F6 Pestyaki U.S.S.R.
46 E5 Péta Greece
80 C5 Petah Tiqwa Israel
29 L9 Petäjävesi Finland
71 B2 Petak, Tg C Halmahera Indonesia
111 G10 Petal Mississippi U.S.A.
29 J9 Petalax Finland
69 G14 Petaling Sumatra
46 G7 Petalioi isld Greece
46 G7 Petalión Kólpos G Greece
102 B3 Petaluma California U.S.A.
22 K4 Petange Luxembourg
70 E6 Petangis Kalimantan
127 L9 Petare Venezuela
88 C9 Petauke Zambia
121 P6 Petawaga, L Quebec Canada
121 N7 Petawawa Ontario Canada
125 P9 Petén Itzá, L Guatemala
99 R5 Petenwell Lake res Wisconsin U.S.A.
120 G4 Peterbell Ontario Canada
138 E5 Peterborough South Australia Australia
121 M8 Peterborough Ontario Canada
9 F2 Peterborough England
95 Q4 Peterborough New Hampshire U.S.A.
15 F3 Peterculter Scotland
15 G3 Peterhead Scotland
146 B6 Peter I Øy isld Antarctica
13 G4 Peterlee England
140 B6 Petermann Aboriginal Land N Terr Australia
115 O1 Petermann Gletscher gla Greenland
143 G6 Petermann Ra N Terr/W Aust Australia
131 B5 Peteroa, Vol pk Arg/Chile
118 H2 Peter Pond L Saskatchewan Canada
36 H2 Petersberg W Germany
117 G7 Petersburg Alaska U.S.A.
110 G1 Petersburg Illinois U.S.A.
110 J3 Petersburg Indiana U.S.A.
94 D5 Petersburg Michigan U.S.A.
98 H8 Petersburg Nebraska U.S.A.
98 H1 Petersburg North Dakota U.S.A.
94 J6 Petersburg Pennsylvania U.S.A.
110 K6 Petersburg Tennessee U.S.A.
108 F2 Petersburg Texas U.S.A.
94 K9 Petersburg Virginia U.S.A.
94 H7 Petersburg West Virginia U.S.A.
116 M5 Peters Creek Alaska U.S.A.
119 V8 Petersfield Manitoba Canada
9 F5 Petersfield England
33 T7 Petershagen East Germany
32 J8 Petershagen W Germany
37 L7 Petershausen W Germany
99 L7 Peterson Iowa U.S.A.
90 D16 Peter 1st I Antarctica
116 M5 Petersville Alaska U.S.A.
143 E7 Peterswald Hill Western Australia Australia
123 R4 Peterview Newfoundland Canada
43 H9 Petilia Policastro Italy
17 G2 Petilla de Aragón Spain
111 H11 Petit Bois I Mississippi U.S.A.
127 N4 Petit Bourg Guadeloupe W Indies
127 N4 Petit Canal Guadeloupe W Indies
122 G8 Petitcodiac New Brunswick Canada
127 N4 Petit Cul de Sac Marin B Guadeloupe W Indies
122 G5 Petite Cascapedia, Parc de la Quebec Canada
122 E5 Petite Matane Quebec Canada
121 Q7 Petite-Nation, Parc Quebec Canada
122 B6 Petite Rivière Quebec Canada
122 H9 Petite Rivière Bridge Nova Scotia Canada
127 H5 Petite Rivière de l'Artibonite Haiti
21 M2 Petites Dalles, les France
123 M7 Petit Etang C Breton I, Nova Scotia
127 O4 Petite Terre, Îles de la Guadeloupe W Indies
122 G4 Petite Vallée Quebec Canada
127 H5 Petit Goâve Haiti
123 N5 Petit Jardin Newfoundland Canada
110 C6 Petit Jean R Arkansas U.S.A.
95 U2 Petit Manan Pt Maine U.S.A.
20 H7 Petit Mars France
36 B6 Petitmont France
117 N6 Petitot R British Columbia Canada
122 G6 Petit Rocher New Brunswick Canada
29 P9 Petkeljärvi Nat. Park Finland
29 M4 Petkula Finland
74 E7 Petlad India
125 P7 Peto Mexico
145 G4 Petone New Zealand
133 C4 Petorca Chile
94 C1 Petoskey Michigan U.S.A.
52 G4 Petrakovo U.S.S.R.
43 F11 Petralia Sicily
51 L1 Petra, Ostrov isld U.S.S.R.
65 H3 Petra Velikogo, Zaliv B U.S.S.R.
45 P7 Petrella, M mt Italy
121 N9 Petre, Pt Ontario Canada
52 J4 Petretsovo U.S.S.R.
45 N4 Petriano Italy
46 F3 Petricn Bulgaria
141 L2 Petrie, Mt Brisbane, Qnsld Australia
103 P6 Petrified Forest Nat. Park Arizona U.S.A.
54 F8 Petrikovka U.S.S.R.
48 H5 Petrila Romania
8 B6 Petrockstow England
52 C5 Petrodvorets U.S.S.R.
46 F1 Petrokhanski P Bulgaria
52 D5 Petrokrepost' U.S.S.R.
129 L5 Petrolândia Brazil
109 J8 Petroleum Texas U.S.A.
120 H10 Petrolia Ontario Canada
100 A9 Petrolia California U.S.A.
109 J2 Petrolia Texas U.S.A.
129 K5 Petrolina Brazil
46 F6 Petromagoúla Greece
52 A4 Petropavlovka U.S.S.R.
56 G5 Petropavlovka U.S.S.R.
56 G2 Petropavlovsk U.S.S.R.
55 E4 Petropavlovsk U.S.S.R.
51 P3 Petropavlovsk-Kamchatskiy U.S.S.R.
129 K8 Petrópolis Brazil
112 C1 Petros Tennessee U.S.A.
48 H5 Petroşani Romania
48 G6 Petrovac Yugoslavia
48 F5 Petrovaradin Yugoslavia
55 E4 Petrovka U.S.S.R.
52 E3 Petrovskiy Yam U.S.S.R.
55 C4 Petrovskoye Bashkirskaya A.S.S.R. U.S.S.R.
52 E6 Petrovskoye Yaroslavskaya obl U.S.S.R.
56 G5 Petrovsk-Zabaykal'skiy U.S.S.R.
52 D4 Petrozavodsk U.S.S.R.
52 K2 Petrun' U.S.S.R.
48 J3 Petru Rareş Romania
Petsamo see Pechenga
29 N2 Petsikko mt Finland
25 C3 Petten Netherlands
38 K6 Pettenbach Austria
14 D2 Pettigoe Ireland
110 C6 Pettigrew Arkansas U.S.A.
109 K7 Pettus Texas U.S.A.
123 U6 Petty Hbr Newfoundland Canada
55 E3 Petukhovo U.S.S.R.
9 F6 Petworth England
38 L8 Petzen mt Austria
38 J5 Peuerbach Austria
69 C10 Peuetsagu, Gunung mt Sumatra
116 J8 Peulik, Mt Alaska U.S.A.
29 M4 Peurasuvanto Finland
26 J5 Peuraure Sweden
69 C10 Peureula Sumatra
9 G6 Pevensey England
94 C3 Pewamo Michigan U.S.A.
99 S6 Pewaukee Wisconsin U.S.A.
9 E5 Pewsey England
32 F6 Pewsum W Germany
36 B7 Pexonne France
19 P18 Peynier France
19 P18 Peypin France
18 E9 Peyrehorade France
18 H8 Peyreleau France
19 P13 Peyrieu France
19 P17 Peyrolles-en-Provence France
19 P16 Peyruis France
106 F2 Peyton Colorado U.S.A.
52 G2 Peza R U.S.S.R.
18 H9 Pézenas France
31 K7 Pezinok Czechoslovakia
52 H4 Pezmog U.S.S.R.
37 N6 Pfaffenberg W Germany
37 L6 Pfaffenhofen an der Ilm W Germany
36 D6 Pfaffenhoffen France
41 J3 Pfäffikon Switzerland
37 P2 Pfaffroda East Germany
36 C4 Pfälzer Bergland reg W Germany
36 D5 Pfalzer Wald mts W Germany
36 D3 Pfalzfeld W Germany
36 F6 Pfalzgrafenweiler W Germany
37 L6 Pfalzpaint W Germany
37 O7 Pfarrkirchen W Germany
37 K3 Pfarrweisach W Germany
37 N6 Pfatter W Germany
36 E4 Pfeddersheim W Germany
37 M6 Pfeffenhausen W Germany
36 F6 Pfinztal W Germany
140 C6 Pfitzner, Mt N Terr Australia
41 N2 Pflach Austria
37 M6 Pförring W Germany
36 F6 Pforzheim W Germany
37 N5 Pfreimd W Germany
36 D4 Pfrimm R W Germany
41 K2 Pfullendorf W Germany
36 G7 Pfullingen W Germany
41 N4 Pfunds Austria
36 F4 Pfungstadt W Germany
37 L6 Pfünz W Germany
74 F3 Phagwara India
68 E6 Phai, Ko isld Thailand
95 T7 Phair Maine U.S.A.
74 E5 Phalodi India
88 E9 Phalombe Malawi
36 C6 Phalsbourg France
76 B2 Phaltan India
69 D8 Pha Luai, Ko isld Thailand
69 E8 Pha Ngan, Ko isld Thailand
69 D8 Phangnga Thailand
68 J7 Phan Ly Vietnam
68 G5 Phanom Dang Raek mt Thailand
68 D5 Phanom Thuan Thailand
68 J7 Phan Rang Vietnam
68 J7 Phan Ri Vietnam
68 J7 Phan Thiet Vietnam
103 M5 Phantom Ranch Arizona U.S.A.
109 J9 Pharr Texas U.S.A.
68 H2 Phat Diem Vietnam
69 D9 Phatthalung Thailand
69 D8 Phayam, Ko isld Thailand
68 E5 Phayuhakhiri Thailand
140 D2 Phelp R N Terr Australia
94 E9 Phelps Kentucky U.S.A.
95 K4 Phelps New York U.S.A.
109 M5 Phelps Texas U.S.A.
99 R3 Phelps Wisconsin U.S.A.
112 L2 Phelps L North Carolina U.S.A.
68 F4 Phen Thailand
94 J9 Phenix Virginia U.S.A.
111 L9 Phenix City Alabama U.S.A.
68 D6 Phet Buri Thailand
68 H5 Phia Phay Laos
111 G9 Philadelphia Mississippi U.S.A.
99 P10 Philadelphia Missouri U.S.A.
95 M2 Philadelphia New York U.S.A.
97 Philadelphia conurbation Pennsylvania U.S.A.
84 J5 Philae ruins Egypt
111 J7 Phil Campbell Alabama U.S.A.
98 E5 Philip South Dakota U.S.A.
137 O7 Philip I Pacific Oc
111 F8 Philipp Mississippi U.S.A.
Philippeville see Skikda
22 G3 Philippeville Belgium
94 G7 Philippi West Virginia U.S.A.
140 E6 Philippi, L Queensland Australia
25 A6 Philippine Netherlands
71 Philippines rep E Indies
89 D8 Philippolis S Africa
Philippopolis Bulgaria see Plovdiv
36 E5 Philippsburg W Germany
121 R7 Philipsburg Quebec Canada
101 M3 Philipsburg Montana U.S.A.
94 J6 Philipsburg Pennsylvania U.S.A.
116 O2 Philip Smith Mts Alaska U.S.A.
139 H7 Phillip I Victoria Australia
95 R2 Phillips Maine U.S.A.
101 R1 Phillips Montana U.S.A.
98 H9 Phillips Nebraska U.S.A.
108 C8 Phillips Texas U.S.A.
99 Q4 Phillips Wisconsin U.S.A.
107 L2 Phillipsburg Kansas U.S.A.
115 L1 Phillips Inlet Northwest Territories Canada
138 C3 Phillipson, L South Australia Australia
142 G5 Phillipson Ra Western Australia Australia
142 F3 Phillips Ra Western Australia Australia
95 O4 Philmont New York U.S.A.
102 A2 Philo California U.S.A.
100 B5 Philomath Oregon U.S.A.
118 F3 Philomena Alberta Canada
115 M3 Philpots Island Northwest Territories Canada
94 G10 Philpott Dam Virginia U.S.A.
68 G5 Phimun Mangsahan Thailand
118 J6 Phippen Saskatchewan Canada
106 D1 Phippsburg Colorado U.S.A.
68 E4 Phitsanulok Thailand
68 G7 Phnom Penh Cambodia
67 B6 Pho Binh Gia Vietnam
144 D5 Phoebe New Zealand
95 N4 Phoenicia New York U.S.A.
103 M8 Phoenix Arizona U.S.A.
111 G12 Phoenix Louisiana U.S.A.
95 L3 Phoenix New York U.S.A.
134 K8 Phoenix Is Pacific Oc
95 M6 Phoenixville Pennsylvania U.S.A.
68 G1 Pho Lu Vietnam
68 H4 Phong Nha Vietnam
68 F2 Phongsali Laos
68 F1 Phong Tho Vietnam
68 F3 Phon Phisai Thailand
139 G7 Phoques B Tasmania Australia
140 E5 Phosphate Hill Queensland Australia
68 H7 Phouc Le Vietnam
68 D3 Phrao Thailand
68 E5 Phra Phutthabat Thailand
69 D8 Phra Saeng Thailand
69 C8 Phra Thong, Ko isld Thailand
68 E5 Phrom Buri Thailand
47 L6 Phrygia Turkey
68 G2 Phuc Yen Vietnam
67 B7 Phu Dien Vietnam
69 D9 Phuket, Ko isld Thailand
68 F4 Phu Khieo Thailand
75 L8 Phulabāni India
67 B6 Phulang Thuong Vietnam
68 H4 Phu Loc Vietnam
68 G2 Phu Ly Vietnam
68 F6 Phum Bavel Cambodia
68 G7 Phum Hay Cambodia
68 G6 Phum Khvao Cambodia
68 G6 Phum Koulen Cambodia
68 F6 Phum Siem Cambodia
68 F6 Phum Svai Cambodia
68 F6 Phum Treng Cambodia
68 F6 Phum Troy Toch Cambodia
68 J5 Phu My Vietnam
68 G2 Phu Nho Quan Vietnam
69 D8 Phun Phin Thailand
75 N5 Phuntsholing Bhutan
69 G8 Phuoc Long Vietnam
Phu Qui see Thai Hoa
68 F7 Phu Quoc Vietnam
68 G2 Phu Tho Vietnam
129 J5 Piaca Brazil
44 F2 Piacenza prov Italy
44 G1 Piacenza Italy
45 L1 Piacenza d'Adige Italy
45 J1 Piadena Italy
122 B2 Piakoudie L Quebec Canada
141 L7 Pialba Queensland Australia
139 J4 Pian R New South Wales Australia
45 P5 Piana del Fucino Italy
41 K5 Pianazzo Italy
130 H9 Piancó R Brazil
45 K3 Pian del Vóglio Italy
45 L4 Pian de Sco Italy
45 M4 Pian di Meleto Italy
45 N4 Pianello Italy
139 G6 Piangil Victoria Australia
45 M1 Pianiga Italy
42 G6 Pianosa isld Adriatic Sea
42 C6 Pianosa, I Italy
65 B5 Pianquan China
118 H9 Piapot Saskatchewan Canada
127 O2 Piarco airport Trinidad
31 M3 Piaseczno Poland
122 K3 Piashti, L Quebec Canada
31 O4 Piaski Poland
31 L3 Piątek Poland
48 K4 Piatra Neamt Romania
129 K5 Piauí state Brazil
129 K5 Piauí, Sa. do mts Brazil
42 E2 Piave R Italy
143 B9 Piawaning Western Australia Australia
45 H3 Piazza al Serchio Italy
43 F11 Piazza Armerina Sicily
133 C8 Piazzi isld Chile
45 L1 Piazzolas B Italy
86 F4 Pibor Post Sudan
118 D4 Pibroch Alberta Canada
103 L6 Pica Arizona U.S.A.
101 L6 Picabo Idaho U.S.A.
103 N9 Picacho Arizona U.S.A.
103 K8 Picacho California U.S.A.
106 E8 Picacho New Mexico U.S.A.
103 N9 Picacho Res Arizona U.S.A.
124 B3 Picachos, Cerro dos mt Mexico
22 D4 Picardie France
20 H3 Picauville France
111 G11 Picayune Mississippi U.S.A.
123 O5 Piccadilly Newfoundland Canada
106 B2 Piceance Cr Colorado U.S.A.
45 R8 Picentini, Mti mt Italy
124 F3 Picháchic Mexico
133 E2 Pichanal Argentina
131 B4 Pichidangul, B Chile
133 C4 Pichilemu Chile
128 C4 Pichincha prov Ecuador
52 G6 Pichkasy U.S.S.R.
118 D4 Pickardville Alberta Canada
111 F9 Pickens Mississippi U.S.A.
112 E3 Pickens South Carolina U.S.A.
94 G8 Pickens West Virginia U.S.A.
120 K7 Pickerel Ontario Canada
99 P1 Pickerel L Ontario Canada
13 H5 Pickering England
110 B1 Pickering Missouri U.S.A.
143 D8 Pickering, Mt Western Australia Australia
126 D4 Pickle Bank Caribbean
115 K7 Pickle Lake Ontario Canada
98 H6 Pickstown South Dakota U.S.A.
109 M2 Pickton Texas U.S.A.
110 H6 Pickwick L Tennessee U.S.A.
45 P7 Pico Italy
16 D4 Pico de Almanzor mt Spain
16 E4 Pico Penalara mt Spain
129 K5 Picos Brazil
16 C2 Picos de Ancares, Sa. de mts Spain
16 C6 Picos de Aroche mt Spain
21 P2 Picquigny France
120 D4 Pic R Ontario Canada
139 K5 Picton New South Wales Australia
121 N8 Picton Ontario Canada
145 E4 Picton New Zealand
139 H9 Picton, Mt Tasmania Australia
122 K8 Pictou Nova Scotia Canada
122 K8 Pictou I Nova Scotia Canada
118 E9 Picture Butte Alberta Canada
99 U3 Pictured Rocks Nat. Lakeshore Michigan U.S.A.
95 L5 Picture Rocks Pennsylvania U.S.A.
130 H9 Picuí Brazil
131 B7 Picún Leufú Argentina
138 B4 Pidinga South Australia Australia
45 Q7 Piedimonte d'Alife Italy
111 L8 Piedmont Alabama U.S.A.
110 F4 Piedmont Missouri U.S.A.
112 E3 Piedmont South Carolina U.S.A.
98 C5 Piedmont South Dakota U.S.A.
94 F6 Piedmont Res Ohio U.S.A.
17 F3 Piedra R Spain
102 E5 Piedra California U.S.A.
106 C4 Piedra R Colorado U.S.A.
16 E5 Piedrabuena Spain
16 C2 Piedrafita, Pto. de pass Spain
16 D4 Piedrahita Spain
131 B3 Piedra Lobos, Pta Chile
102 C6 Piedras Blancas Pt California U.S.A.
125 J3 Piedras Negras Mexico
71 D5 Piedras Point Philippines
133 F5 Piedras, Pta Argentina
128 D6 Piedras, R.de las R Peru
99 R1 Pie I Ontario Canada
29 N9 Pieksämäki Finland
38 M5 Pielach R Austria
29 M8 Pielavesi L Finlan
29 O8 Pielinen L Finlan
29 O9 Pielisjoki R Finlan
139 H8 Pieman R Tasmania Australia
44 C3 Piemonte reg Italy
31 M1 Pieniężno Poland
22 K5 Piennes France
36 B2 Pier W Germany
106 F1 Pierce Colorado U.S.A.
113 F10 Pierce Florida U.S.A.
100 K3 Pierce Idaho U.S.A.
98 J7 Pierce Nebraska U.S.A.
13 G4 Piercebridge England
110 B5 Pierce City Missouri U.S.A.
94 B5 Pierceton Indiana U.S.A.
107 K4 Pierceville Kansas U.S.A.
102 A2 Piercy California U.S.A.
46 E4 Piéria Óri Greece
15 F1 Pierowall Orkney Scotland
98 J4 Pierpont South Dakota U.S.A.
19 J6 Pierre France
98 F5 Pierre South Dakota U.S.A.
18 F7 Pierre-Buffière France
19 P15 Pierre-Châtel France
21 P6 Pierrefitte-sur-Sauldre France
22 D5 Pierrefonds France
120 K3 Pierre L Ontario Canada
19 N16 Pierrelatte France
22 K5 Pierrepont France
121 S6 Pierreville Quebec Canada
127 P3 Pierreville Trinidad
119 Q9 Pierson Manitoba Canada
113 F8 Pierson Florida U.S.A.
36 B4 Piesport W Germany
143 B10 Piesseville Western Australia Australia
31 K7 Piešťany Czechoslovakia
Pietarsaari see Jakobstad
89 G7 Pietermaritzburg S Africa
89 F4 Pietersburg S Africa
22 G3 Piéton Belgium
106 B7 Pie Town New Mexico U.S.A.
44 D3 Pietra Ligure Italy
45 Q7 Pietramelara Italy
44 B3 Pietraporzio Italy
44 H4 Pietrasanta Italy
45 Q7 Pietravairano Italy
87 F11 Piet Retief S Africa
48 J3 Pietroşu mt Romania
29 P2 Piets'yarvi, Oz L U.S.S.R.
20 G2 Pieux, les France
38 F9 Pieve Italy
42 E2 Pieve di Cadore Italy
45 K2 Pieve di Cento Italy
45 J3 Pievepelago Italy
45 M4 Pieve S. Stefano Italy
Pigádhia see Kárpathos
94 C1 Pigeon R Michigan U.S.A.
94 D3 Pigeon Michigan U.S.A.
120 H10 Pigeon B Ontario Canada
111 K10 Pigeon Cr Alabama U.S.A.
140 B3 Pigeon Hole N Terr Australia
127 K3 Pigeon I Jamaica
118 C5 Pigeon L Alberta Canada
121 M8 Pigeon L Ontario Canada
127 M2 Pigeon Pt Tobago
102 B4 Pigeon Pt California U.S.A.
119 V6 Pigeon R Manitoba Canada
119 O2 Pigeon River Ontario Canada
143 C8 Pigeon Rocks Western Australia Australia
94 H10 Pigg R Virginia U.S.A.
110 F5 Piggott Arkansas U.S.A.
89 G8 Pigg's Peak Swaziland
19 Q18 Pignans France
45 P7 Pignataro Interamna Italy
45 Q7 Pignatoro Maggiore Italy
133 E5 Pigüe Argentina
145 D3 Pihaina New Zealand
67 E1 Pi He R China
29 L9 Pihlajavesi Finland
29 M8 Pihtipudas Finland
56 E4 Pik Grandioznyy mt U.S.S.R.
115 P5 Pikiulleq isld Greenland
31 K2 Piła Poland
19 N14 Pilat, Mt France
48 F3 Pilis Hungary
48 E3 Pilisvörösvár Hungary
98 J2 Pillsbury North Dakota U.S.A.
102 B2 Pillsbury, L California U.S.A.
52 G6 Pil'na U.S.S.R.
8 D4 Pilning England
130 F5 Pilões, Sa. dos mts Brazil
126 F5 Pilón Cuba
46 E8 Pilos Greece
119 N8 Pilot Butte Saskatchewan Canada
110 D3 Pilot Grove Missouri U.S.A.
119 T9 Pilot Mound Manitoba Canada
112 G1 Pilot Mountain North Carolina U.S.A.
102 G3 Pilot Pk Nevada U.S.A.
101 Q5 Pilot Pk Wyoming U.S.A.
116 J8 Pilot Point Alaska U.S.A.
109 L2 Pilot Point Texas U.S.A.
100 G4 Pilot Rock Oregon U.S.A.
116 F5 Pilot Station Alaska U.S.A.
139 J6 Pilot, The mt New South Wales Australia
133 E2 Piloya R Bolivia
37 M5 Pilsach W Germany
Pilsen see Plzeň
99 T5 Pilsen Wisconsin U.S.A.
41 O1 Pilsen See L W Germany
37 O6 Pilsting W Germany
55 F1 Pil'tan-Lor, Oz L U.S.S.R.
27 M14 Piltene U.S.S.R.
8 D5 Pilton England
52 J4 Pil'va R U.S.S.R.
31 N6 Pilzno Poland
55 F1 Pim U.S.S.R.
103 P9 Pima Arizona U.S.A.
138 D4 Pimba South Australia Australia
129 G4 Pimenta Brazil
128 F6 Pimenta Bueno Brazil
127 J5 Pimental Dominican Rep
128 C5 Pimentel Peru
113 L12 Pimlico I Bahamas
71 H4 Pimpi Sulawesi
86 D5 Pimu Zaire
17 G3 Pina Spain
103 L10 Pinacate, Cerro pk Mexico
124 G2 Pinacate, Sa. del mt Mexico
103 O9 Pinaleno Mts Arizona U.S.A.
71 E4 Pinamalayan Philippines
131 G6 Pinamar Argentina
69 E10 Pinang isld Malaysia
70 E2 Pinangah Sabah
78 F2 Pinarbaşi Turkey
126 C3 Pinar del Rio Cuba
47 J3 Pinarhisar Turkey
138 F3 Pinaroo, L New South Wales Australia
133 D4 Piñas Argentina
21 L4 Pin-au-Haras, le France
45 L2 Pincara Italy
9 F2 Pinchbeck England
118 D9 Pincher Creek Alberta Canada
117 L8 Pinchi British Columbia Canada
128 C4 Pinchincha mt Ecuador
94 D4 Pinckney Michigan U.S.A.
110 G3 Pinckneyville Illinois U.S.A.
21 J4 Pinçon, Mt France
94 C3 Pinconning Michigan U.S.A.
48 G4 Pîncota Romania
31 M5 Pińczów Poland
129 H6 Pindaiba Brazil
110 D5 Pindall Arkansas U.S.A.
143 B8 Pindar Western Australia Australia
129 J4 Pindaré R Brazil
70 G6 Pindolo Sulawesi
28 E4 Pindstrup Denmark
138 F4 Pine R New South Wales Australia
103 N7 Pine Arizona U.S.A.
100 K6 Pine Idaho U.S.A.
94 B2 Pine R Michigan U.S.A.
99 Q6 Pine R Wisconsin U.S.A.
111 K10 Pine Apple Alabama U.S.A.
111 D7 Pine Bluff Arkansas U.S.A.
119 P4 Pinebluff L Saskatchewan Canada
98 B8 Pine Bluffs Wyoming U.S.A.
123 T7 Pine, C Newfoundland Canada
113 F9 Pinecastle Florida U.S.A.
111 E7 Pine City Arkansas U.S.A.
99 O4 Pine City Minnesota U.S.A.
103 H1 Pine Cr Nevada U.S.A.
94 K5 Pine Cr Pennsylvania U.S.A.
140 B2 Pine Creek N Terr Australia
102 E3 Pinecrest California U.S.A.
107 P7 Pine Cr. Res Oklahoma U.S.A.
16 E2 Pineda de la S Spain
117 P9 Pinedale Alberta Canada
102 E5 Pinedale California U.S.A.
101 Q7 Pinedale Wyoming U.S.A.
102 E5 Pine Flat Res California U.S.A.
100 G8 Pine Forest Range Nevada U.S.A.
52 G3 Pinega R U.S.S.R.
52 F3 Pinega U.S.S.R.
140 C6 Pine Gap N Terr Australia
143 B8 Pinegrove Western Australia Australia
95 L6 Pine Grove Pennsylvania U.S.A.
140 C5 Pine Hill N Terr Australia
118 K3 Pine House Saskatchewan Canada
118 L3 Pine House L Saskatchewan Canada
112 H2 Pinehurst North Carolina U.S.A.
100 C2 Pinehurst Washington U.S.A.
118 F4 Pinehurst L Alberta Canada
113 E11 Pine I Florida U.S.A.
99 O5 Pine Island Minnesota U.S.A.
146 B7 Pine Island B Antarctica
146 B7 Pine Island Glacier glacier Antarctica
99 S4 Pine L Wisconsin U.S.A.
109 O4 Pineland Texas U.S.A.
71 J4 Pineleng Sulawesi
144 B6 Pinelheugh mt New Zealand
113 E10 Pinellas airport Florida U.S.A.
102 C6 Pine Mt California U.S.A.
107 P7 Pine Mt Oklahoma U.S.A.
103 L7 Pine Pk Arizona U.S.A.
117 Q5 Pine Point Northwest Territories Canada
119 P1 Pine Portage Ontario Canada
117 Q5 Pine Pt Northwest Territories Canada
113 D8 Pine Pt Florida U.S.A.
118 D4 Pine R Alberta Canada
117 M8 Pine R British Columbia Canada
98 D6 Pine Ridge South Dakota U.S.A.
119 R7 Pine River Manitoba Canada
118 K3 Pine River Saskatchewan Canada
99 M3 Pine River Minnesota U.S.A.
44 B2 Pinerolo Italy
120 J9 Pinery Prov. Park Ontario Canada
112 H5 Pines, I of South Carolina U.S.A.
111 B9 Pines, L. O'The Texas U.S.A.
108 C4 Pine Springs Texas U.S.A.
89 G7 Pinetown S Africa
110 B7 Pine Valley Oklahoma U.S.A.
103 L4 Pine Valley Utah U.S.A.
103 L4 Pine Valley Mts Utah U.S.A.
94 D10 Pineville Kentucky U.S.A.
111 D10 Pineville Louisiana U.S.A.
110 B5 Pineville Missouri U.S.A.
112 G2 Pineville North Carolina U.S.A.
94 F9 Pineville West Virginia U.S.A.
99 M1 Pinewood Ontario Canada
99 L2 Pinewood Minnesota U.S.A.
112 G4 Pinewood South Carolina U.S.A.
98 K1 Piney Manitoba Canada
101 T2 Piney Buttes hills Montana U.S.A.
110 C6 Piney Cr Arkansas U.S.A.
113 D8 Piney Pt Florida U.S.A.
58 D4 Ping'an China
65 F2 Ping'an China
143 C10 Pingaring Western Australia Australia
67 A5 Pingbian China
67 B1 Pingchang China
65 D7 Ping Dao isld China
67 C3 Pingdeng China
65 B6 Pingding China
Pingdingbu see Guyan
65 F4 Pingdingshan China
65 G1 Pingding Shan mt China
58 F5 Pingdingshan China
65 D6 Pingdu China
143 B10 Pingelly Western Australia Australia
65 F3 Pinggang China
65 C7 Pinggang China
65 D4 Pinggu China
67 B5 Pingguo China
67 F4 Pinghai China
67 F4 Pinghe China
Pinghu see Pingtang
67 G1 Pinghu China
67 D2 Pingjiang China
67 C4 Pingle China
58 E4 Pingliang China
67 D1 Pinglin China
65 B7 Pinglu China
65 B5 Pinglu China
58 E4 Pingluo China
Pingma see Tiandong
75 N6 Pingna Bangladesh
67 F3 Pingnan China
67 C5 Pingnan China
Pingqiao see Xinyang
65 D4 Pingquan China
101 N6 Pingree Idaho U.S.A.
98 G2 Pingree North Dakota U.S.A.
143 C10 Pingrup Western Australia Australia
65 C5 Pingshan China
67 A2 Pingshan China
65 D7 Pingshang China
67 E4 Pingshi China
67 D4 Pingshi China
65 B6 Pingshun China
67 F4 Pingtan China
67 F4 Pingtan Dao isld China
67 B4 Pingtang China
67 G5 P'ing-tung Taiwan
67 B5 Pingxiang China
67 D3 Pingxiang China
67 G3 Pingyang China
65 F1 Pingyang China
65 B6 Pingyao China
65 D7 Pingyi China
65 C6 Pingyin China
67 C3 Pingyong China
65 C6 Pingyuan China
67 E4 Pingyuan China
67 A5 Pingyuanjie China
130 F8 Pinhal Brazil
16 B3 Pinhão Portugal
129 J4 Pinheiro Brazil
16 C4 Pinhel Portugal
69 D12 Pini isld Indonesia
46 E7 Piniós R Greece
46 E5 Piniós R Greece
143 B10 Pinjarra Western Australia Australia
143 E9 Pinjin Western Australia Australia
38 O7 Pinka R Austria
38 O7 Pinkafeld Austria
141 K1 Pinkenba dist Brisbane, Qnsld Australia
140 A3 Pinkerton Ra N Terr Australia
118 H7 Pinkham Saskatchewan Canada
112 K2 Pink Hill North Carolina U.S.A.
117 M7 Pink Mountain British Columbia Canada
21 M5 Pin-la-Garenne, le France
68 C2 Pinlaung Burma
145 D4 Pinnacle mt New Zealand
116 C6 Pinnacle I Bering Sea
102 C5 Pinnacles Nat. Mon California U.S.A.
138 F6 Pinnaroo South Australia Australia
32 L5 Pinn Au R W Germany
32 L5 Pinneberg W Germany
106 G1 Pinneo Colorado U.S.A.
9 F4 Pinner England
33 T5 Pinnow East Germany
70 B5 Pinoh R Kalimantan
111 F10 Pinola Mississippi U.S.A.
106 F3 Pinon Colorado U.S.A.
106 E9 Pinon New Mexico U.S.A.
112 H4 Pinopolis Dam South Carolina U.S.A.
102 E7 Pinos, Mt California U.S.A.
17 G6 Pinoso Spain
125 K9 Pinotepa Nacional Mexico
70 G6 Pinrang Sulawesi Indonesia
70 F6 Pinrang Sulawesi
137 O6 Pins, Île Des New Caledonia
53 C8 Pinsk U.S.S.R.
111 K8 Pinson Alabama U.S.A.
110 H6 Pinson Tennessee U.S.A.
120 J10 Pins, Pte. aux Ontario Canada
128 A7 Pinta isld Galapagos Is
103 P6 Pinta Arizona U.S.A.
133 D2 Pintados Chile
103 L9 Pinta, Sa Arizona U.S.A.
70 E2 Pintasan Sabah
133 E3 Pinto Argentina
118 K9 Pinto Butte pk Saskatchewan Canada
103 J8 Pinto Mts California U.S.A.
103 L4 Pintura Utah U.S.A.
103 J5 Pintwater Ra Nevada U.S.A.
123 Q2 Pinware R Labrador, Nfld Canada
12 D3 Pinwherry Scotland
143 B8 Pinyalling mt Western Australia Australia
52 G4 Pinyug U.S.S.R.
41 N5 Pinzolo Italy
45 M4 Piòbbico Italy
103 K4 Pioche Nevada U.S.A.
19 N16 Piolenc France
42 D6 Piombino Italy
94 C5 Pioneer Ohio U.S.A.
109 H3 Pioneer Texas U.S.A.
101 M4 Pioneer Mts Montana U.S.A.
56 C3 Pioner U.S.S.R.
51 J1 Pioner, Ostrova islds U.S.S.R.
55 D1 Pionerskiy U.S.S.R.
31 M1 Pionerskiy U.S.S.R.
145 E3 Piopio New Zealand
128 F4 Piorini L Brazil
44 B2 Piossasco Italy
31 L3 Piotrków Bydgoszcz Poland
31 M4 Piotrków Trybunalski Łódź Poland
45 M1 Piove di Sacco Italy
65 G3 Pipa Dingzi mt China
74 E5 Pipar India
6 L4 Piper oil rig North Sea
102 G4 Piper Pk Nevada U.S.A.
103 M5 Pipe Spring Nat. Mon Arizona U.S.A.
119 R9 Pipestone Manitoba Canada
98 K6 Pipestone Minnesota U.S.A.
119 Q9 Pipestone Cr Manitoba Canada
98 K5 Pipestone Nat. Mon Minnesota U.S.A.
145 E3 Pipipi mt New Zealand
145 E3 Pipiriki New Zealand
121 U3 Pipmuacan, Rés Quebec Canada
122 B4 Pipmuacan, Res Quebec Canada
60 Q2 Pippu Japan
20 G6 Pipriac France
107 P4 Piqua Kansas U.S.A.
110 M1 Piqua Ohio U.S.A.
17 F2 Piqueras, Pto. de Spain
130 C5 Piquiri, R Mato Grosso Brazil
130 D9 Piquiri, R Paraná Brazil
85 E7 Pira Benin
130 E5 Piracanjuba Brazil
129 J7 Piracanjuba R Brazil
129 J8 Piracicaba Brazil
130 G6 Piracicaba R Brazil
133 F3 Piracuacito Argentina
130 F7 Piraçununga Brazil
129 K4 Piraeuruca Brazil
46 F7 Piraiévs Greece
56 E4 Piramida, G mt U.S.S.R.
42 F3 Piran Yugoslavia
129 L5 Piranhas Alagoas Brazil
130 D5 Piranhas Goiás Brazil
130 D8 Pirapó, R Brazil
129 K7 Pirapora Brazil
122 A3 Piraube, L Quebec Canada
130 C10 Piray R Argentina
128 F7 Piray R Bolivia
9 F5 Pirbright England
20 H5 Piré France
129 J7 Pires do Rio Brazil
46 E7 Pirgos Greece
46 G9 Pirgos Crete Greece
20 E7 Piriac France
130 B9 Piribebuy Paraguay
46 F3 Pirin plateau Bulgaria
17 G2 Pirineos mt Spain
145 E4 Pirinoa New Zealand
145 F3 Piripaua New Zealand
129 K4 Piripiri Brazil
127 M9 Píritu Anzoátegui Venezuela
127 K10 Piritu Miranda Venezuela
37 N3 Pirk East Germany
29 K10 Pirkkala Finland
36 D5 Pirmasens W Germany
30 H5 Pirna East Germany
12 C2 Pirnmill Scotland
145 E2 Pirongia New Zealand
46 F1 Pirot Yugoslavia
20 G3 Pirou France
74 F2 Pir Panjal Rge Kashmir
29 M5 Pirttikoski Finland
136 F2 Piru Moluccas Indonesia
102 F7 Piru California U.S.A.
54 D6 Piryatin U.S.S.R.
47 H6 Piryi Greece
77 J4 Pirzada Afghanistan
45 H4 Pisa Italy
133 C1 Pisagua Chile
71 B3 Pisang isld Indonesia
44 H3 Pisanino mt Italy
144 B6 Pisa Range New Zealand
70 F1 Pisau, Tg C Sabah
43 G8 Pisciotta Italy
128 C6 Pisco Peru
Piscopi isld see Tilos isld
95 N3 Piseco New York U.S.A.
30 H6 Písek Czechoslovakia
98 J1 Pisek North Dakota U.S.A.
80 F6 Pisga Jordan
99 L8 Pisgah Iowa U.S.A.
144 C6 Pisgah, Mt New Zealand
112 E2 Pisgah, Mt North Carolina U.S.A.
77 G6 Pishīn Iran
74 B3 Pishin Pakistan
70 G7 Pising Sulawesi
103 M9 Pisinimo Arizona U.S.A.
102 D6 Pismo Bch California U.S.A.
128 F6 Piso Firme Bolivia
41 M6 Pisogne Italy
85 D6 Pissila Burkina
133 D3 Pissis vol Argentina
29 P6 Pista R U.S.S.R.
29 P6 Pistayarvi L U.S.S.R.
43 H8 Pisticci Italy
45 J4 Pistoia Italy
123 R2 Pistolet B Newfoundland Canada
100 A7 Pistol River Oregon U.S.A.
52 F6 Pistsovo U.S.S.R.
8 C2 Pistyll Rhaeadr mt Wal
6 E3 Pisuerga R Spain

31 N2 **Pisz** Poland
100 D8 **Pit** *R* California U.S.A.
85 B6 **Pita** Guinea
122 G1 **Pitaga** Labrador, Nfld Canada
139 G5 **Pitarpunga L** New South Wales Australia
71 G7 **Pitas Pt** Mindanao Philippines
135 U11 **Pitcairn I** Pacific Oc
101 Q5 **Pitchfork** Wyoming U.S.A.
127 O3 **Pitch L** Trinidad
26 M6 **Piteå** Sweden
26 L6 **Piteälv** *R* Sweden
45 J3 **Piteglio** Italy
48 J6 **Pitești** Romania
143 B9 **Pithara** Western Australia Australia
21 P5 **Pithiviers** France
42 D6 **Pitigliano** Italy
124 C2 **Pitiquito** Mexico
138 B2 **Pitjantjatjara Lands** South Australia Australia
106 D3 **Pitkin** Colorado U.S.A.
111 D11 **Pitkin** Louisiana U.S.A.
52 D1 **Pitkul'** U.S.S.R.
52 D4 **Pitkyaranta** U.S.S.R.
15 E4 **Pitlochry** Scotland
95 M7 **Pitman** New Jersey U.S.A.
87 G12 **Piton des Neiges** *mt* Réunion
111 G11 **Pitre, I. au** Louisiana U.S.A.
13 F1 **Pitscottie** Scotland
9 G4 **Pitsea** England
13 F1 **Pittenweem** Scotland
117 J9 **Pitt I** British Columbia Canada
137 R10 **Pitt I** Chatham Is Pacific Oc
112 H2 **Pittsboro** North Carolina U.S.A.
102 C3 **Pittsburg** California U.S.A.
110 B4 **Pittsburg** Kansas U.S.A.
110 M4 **Pittsburg** Kentucky U.S.A.
121 T7 **Pittsburg** New Hampshire U.S.A.
107 P7 **Pittsburg** Oklahoma U.S.A.
109 N3 **Pittsburg** Texas U.S.A.
94 H6 **Pittsburgh** Pennsylvania U.S.A.
110 E2 **Pittsfield** Illinois U.S.A.
95 S2 **Pittsfield** Maine U.S.A.
95 O4 **Pittsfield** Massachusetts U.S.A.
95 Q3 **Pittsfield** New Hampshire U.S.A.
94 C5 **Pittsford** Michigan U.S.A.
94 K3 **Pittsford** New York U.S.A.
95 O3 **Pittsford** Vermont U.S.A.
95 M5 **Pittston** Pennsylvania U.S.A.
111 L9 **Pittsview** Alabama U.S.A.
95 M8 **Pittsville** Maryland U.S.A.
110 C3 **Pittsville** Missouri U.S.A.
99 Q5 **Pittsville** Wisconsin U.S.A.
141 K8 **Pittsworth** Queensland Australia
100 D8 **Pittville** California U.S.A.
88 E6 **Pitu** *R* Tanzania
140 E6 **Pituri** *R* Queensland Australia
41 N3 **Pitz Tal** Austria
45 J1 **Più bega** Italy
19 Q17 **Piumoisson** France
128 B5 **Piura** Peru
128 B4 **Piura** *dept* Peru
103 J7 **Piute Mts** California U.S.A.
102 F6 **Piute Pk** California U.S.A.
103 M3 **Piute Res** Utah U.S.A.
75 K4 **Piuthan** Nepal
42 J5 **Piva** *R* Yugoslavia
120 G2 **Pivabiska** *R* Ontario Canada
126 G9 **Pivijay** Colombia
31 M6 **Piwniczna** Poland
102 E6 **Pixley** California U.S.A.
46 E5 **Piyai** Greece
60 Q1 **Piyashiri yama** *mt* Japan
128 E7 **Pizacoma** Peru
52 G5 **Pizhanka** U.S.S.R.
52 G5 **Pizhma** U.S.S.R.
41 K4 **Pizol** *mt* Switzerland
43 G10 **Pizzo** Italy
45 O6 **Pizzodeta, M** *mt* Italy
33 Q5 **Plaaz** East Germany
20 B4 **Plabennec** France
109 L7 **Placedo** Texas U.S.A.
123 T6 **Placentia** Newfoundland Canada
71 G6 **Placer** Mindanao Philippines
102 F1 **Placeritos** Nevada U.S.A.
102 D3 **Placerville** California U.S.A.
106 B3 **Placerville** Colorado U.S.A.
126 E3 **Placetas** Cuba
46 G2 **Plachkovitsi** Bulgaria
113 E11 **Placida** Florida U.S.A.
113 F10 **Placid, L** Florida U.S.A.
106 D6 **Placitas** New Mexico U.S.A.
46 E3 **Plačkovica** *mt* Yugoslavia
12 C3 **Pladda I** Scotland
15 C5 **Pladda Lt. Ho** Scotland
41 F4 **Plaffeien** Switzerland
99 Q6 **Plain** Wisconsin U.S.A.
94 D6 **Plain City** Ohio U.S.A.
101 N8 **Plain City** Utah U.S.A.
111 C9 **Plain Dealing** Louisiana U.S.A.
21 J7 **Plaine, la** France
20 F7 **Plaine-sur-Mer, la** France
94 A7 **Plainfield** Indiana U.S.A.
99 O7 **Plainfield** Iowa U.S.A.
95 N6 **Plainfield** New Jersey U.S.A.
99 R5 **Plainfield** Wisconsin U.S.A.
112 C5 **Plains** Georgia U.S.A.
101 L2 **Plains** Montana U.S.A.
108 E2 **Plains** Texas U.S.A.
94 K8 **Plains, The** Virginia U.S.A.
20 E5 **Plaintel** France
110 C6 **Plainview** Arkansas U.S.A.
99 O5 **Plainview** Minnesota U.S.A.
98 J7 **Plainview** Nebraska U.S.A.
108 F1 **Plainview** Texas U.S.A.
95 P5 **Plainville** Connecticut U.S.A.
110 E2 **Plainville** Illinois U.S.A.
107 L2 **Plainville** Kansas U.S.A.
94 B4 **Plainwell** Michigan U.S.A.
18 F9 **Plaisance** France
127 H5 **Plaisance** Haiti
69 G14 **Plaju** Sumatra
46 G4 **Pláka, Akr** *C* Greece
47 H9 **Pláka, Akra** *C* Crete Greece
46 D3 **Plakenska Pl** *mt* Yugoslavia
118 E4 **Plamondon** Alberta Canada
70 P9 **Plampang** Indonesia
37 O4 **Planá** Czechoslovakia
102 D4 **Planada** California U.S.A.
129 L5 **Planalto da Borborema** *plateau* Brazil
129 H7 **Planalto de Mato Grosso** *plateau* Brazil
17 G6 **Plana Ó Nueva Tabarca** *isld* Spain
40 E2 **Plancher les Mines** France
40 D4 **Planches-en-Montagne, Les** France
131 B5 **Planchon, Paso de** Chile/Arg
20 F4 **Plancoët** France
19 O15 **Plan-de-Baix** France
19 N17 **Plan d'Orgon** France
17 G9 **Plane** *isld* Algeria
33 R8 **Plane, R** East Germany
126 O10 **Planeta Rica** Colombia
137 L3 **Planet Deep** Solomon Sea
37 P5 **Plánice** Czechoslovakia
37 L4 **Plankenfels** W Germany
98 H6 **Plankinton** South Dakota U.S.A.
109 L2 **Plano** Texas U.S.A.
127 M3 **Plantain Garden R** Jamaica
113 E9 **Plant City** Florida U.S.A.
111 K9 **Plantersville** Alabama U.S.A.
111 E11 **Plaquemine** Louisiana U.S.A.
16 C4 **Plasencia** Spain
27 F10 **Plassen** Norway
55 D4 **Plast** U.S.S.R.
33 R5 **Plasten** East Germany
103 J9 **Plaster City** California U.S.A.
37 P4 **Plasy** Czechoslovakia
43 E11 **Platani** *R* Sicily
133 C2 **Plata, Puerta** Chile
131 G5 **Plata, Rio de la** Arg/Uruguay
19 O14 **Plateau de Chambarand** France
19 J15 **Plateau de Langres** France
19 P16 **Plateau de St. Etienne** France
86 B1 **Plateau du Tchigaï** Niger
85 C3 **Plateau du Tinrhert** *stony desert* Algeria
Plateau of Tibet *see* **Xizang Gacyuan**
123 T5 **Plate Cove** Newfoundland Canada
124 H6 **Plateros** Mexico
46 F4 **Platí** Greece
46 G4 **Platí Ákra** *C* Greece
46 F5 **Platikambos** Greece
102 B1 **Platina** California U.S.A.
116 G7 **Platinum** Alaska U.S.A.
118 J7 **Plato** Saskatchewan Canada
126 G10 **Plato** Colombia
110 D4 **Plato** Missouri U.S.A.
56 D5 **Plato Alash** U.S.S.R.
79 C4 **Platres** Cyprus
99 M9 **Platte** *R* Missouri U.S.A.
98 G9 **Platte** *R* Nebraska U.S.A.
98 H6 **Platte** South Dakota U.S.A.
37 N4 **Platte** *mt* W Germany
98 J8 **Platte Center** Nebraska U.S.A.
110 B2 **Platte City** Missouri U.S.A.
106 E2 **Platte Mt** Colorado U.S.A.
98 B9 **Platteville** Colorado U.S.A.
99 Q7 **Platteville** Wisconsin U.S.A.
36 E6 **Plättig** W Germany
37 O6 **Plattling** W Germany
110 B2 **Plattsburg** Missouri U.S.A.
95 O2 **Plattsburgh** New York U.S.A.
99 K8 **Plattsmouth** Nebraska U.S.A.
33 Q6 **Plau** East Germany
33 Q8 **Plaue** East Germany
37 K2 **Plaue** Erfurt East Germany
37 N3 **Plauen** East Germany
46 D2 **Plav** Yugoslavia
52 C6 **Plaviņas** U.S.S.R.
42 J6 **Plavnica** Yugoslavia
54 J3 **Plavsk** U.S.S.R.
124 H8 **Playa Azul** Mexico
126 G5 **Playa Daiquirí** Cuba
128 B4 **Playas** Ecuador
106 B10 **Playas L** New Mexico U.S.A.
68 H6 **Play Cu** Vietnam
140 D4 **Playford** *R* N Terr Australia
140 D6 **Playford Mt** N Terr Australia
119 U4 **Playgreen L** Manitoba Canada
124 E5 **Playón** Mexico
98 E1 **Plaza** North Dakota U.S.A.
133 D5 **Plaza Huincul** Argentina
12 E1 **Plean** Scotland
110 M1 **Pleasant** Ohio U.S.A.
95 S5 **Pleasant B** Massachusetts U.S.A.
123 M7 **Pleasant Bay** C Breton I, Nova Scotia
94 F7 **Pleasant City** Ohio U.S.A.
119 N6 **Pleasantdale** Saskatchewan Canada
94 K6 **Pleasant Gap** Pennsylvania U.S.A.
101 O9 **Pleasant Grove** Utah U.S.A.
110 F2 **Pleasant Hill** Illinois U.S.A.
111 C10 **Pleasant Hill** Louisiana U.S.A.
110 B3 **Pleasant Hill** Missouri U.S.A.
94 E6 **Pleasant Hill Res** Ohio U.S.A.
103 M8 **Pleasant, L** Arizona U.S.A.
122 F8 **Pleasant, Mt** New Brunswick Canada
112 H5 **Pleasant, Mt** South Carolina U.S.A.
102 C4 **Pleasanton** California U.S.A.
110 B3 **Pleasanton** Kansas U.S.A.
98 G9 **Pleasanton** Nebraska U.S.A.
109 J7 **Pleasanton** Texas U.S.A.
110 E6 **Pleasant Plains** Arkansas U.S.A.
119 S9 **Pleasant Pt** Manitoba Canada
144 C6 **Pleasant Pt** New Zealand
100 H5 **Pleasant Valley** Oregon U.S.A.
100 G3 **Pleasant View** Washington U.S.A.
99 N8 **Pleasantville** Iowa U.S.A.
95 N7 **Pleasantville** New Jersey U.S.A.
94 H5 **Pleasantville** Pennsylvania U.S.A.
9 E1 **Pleasley** England
110 L3 **Pleasureville** Kentucky U.S.A.
18 G7 **Pleaux** France
37 L4 **Plech** W Germany
18 H5 **Plédéliac** France
120 G2 **Pledger L** Ontario Canada
20 E5 **Plédran** France
133 F4 **Pledra Sola** Uruguay
20 D4 **Pléhédel** France
71 A5 **Pleieran** *R* Sarawak
70 D6 **Pleihari** Kalimantan
68 J5 **Plei Herel** Vietnam
68 J6 **Plei Kly** Vietnam
20 G4 **Pleine Fougères** France
37 L5 **Pleinfeld** W Germany
20 E3 **Pleinmont Pt** Channel Is
37 P6 **Pleinting** W Germany
37 N1 **Pleisse** *R* East Germany
68 H5 **Plei Ta Un** Vietnam
20 E5 **Plélan-le-Grand** France
20 F5 **Plélan-le-Petit** France
20 E5 **Plemet** France
17 F1 **Plencia** Spain
20 F5 **Plénée-Jugon** France
20 F4 **Pléneuf** France
48 H6 **Plenita** Romania
118 J7 **Plenty** Saskatchewan Canada
145 F2 **Plenty, Bay of** New Zealand
140 D6 **Plenty** *R* N Terr Australia
98 B1 **Plentywood** Montana U.S.A.
20 G4 **Plerguer** France
20 E4 **Plérin** France
20 E6 **Plescop** France
52 F3 **Plesetsk** U.S.S.R.
55 E3 **Pleshkova** U.S.S.R.
20 G5 **Plésidy** France
48 F2 **Plešivec** Czechoslovakia
71 J4 **Plesko, Tanjong** *C* Sulawesi
20 F4 **Pleslin-Trivagou** France
20 G6 **Plessé** France
12' T6 **Plessisville** Quebec Canada
20 F5 **Plestan** France
20 C4 **Plestin-les-Greves** France
122 B2 **Pletipi L** Quebec Canada
36 D1 **Plettenberg** W Germany
83 C10 **Plettenberg B** S Africa
20 G4 **Pleubian** France
20 G4 **Pleudihen-sur-Rance** France
20 G5 **Pleugueneuc** France
21 M8 **Pleumartin** France
20 C4 **Pleumeur** France
20 E4 **Pleurtuit** France
46 G1 **Pleven** Bulgaria
101 Q3 **Plevna** Montana U.S.A.
20 C5 **Pleyben** France
20 C4 **Pleyber-Christ** France
37 N4 **Pleystein** W Germany
145 E4 **Plimmerton** New Zealand
31 M1 **Pliskov** U.S.S.R.
42 G4 **Pljesivica** *dist* Yugoslavia
42 E7 **Pljevlja** Yugoslavia
43 B8 **Ploaghe** Sardinia
36 D7 **Plobsheim** France
42 H5 **Ploča** *lighthouse* Yugoslavia
36 G6 **Plochingen** W Germany
31 M3 **Płock** Poland
30 H7 **Plöckenstein** *mt* Czechoslovakia
22 D2 **Ploegsteert** Belgium
20 D6 **Ploemel** France
20 D6 **Ploemeur** France
20 D5 **Ploërdut** France
20 F6 **Ploërmel** France
20 B6 **Plogastel-St. Germain** France
20 A5 **Plogoff** France
20 B5 **Plogonnec** France
48 K6 **Ploiești** Romania
47 H6 **Plomàrion** Greece
18 G7 **Plomb du Cantal** *mt* France
19 K5 **Plombières-les-Bains** France
40 A3 **Plombières-les-Dijon** France
20 B6 **Plomelin** France
139 L4 **Plomer, Pt** New South Wales Australia
20 B6 **Plomeur** France
22 G4 **Plomion** France
33 M4 **Plön** W Germany
31 J2 **Płona** *R* Poland
20 B5 **Plonéis** France
20 B6 **Plonéour-Lanvern** France
20 C5 **Plonévez-du-Faou** France
20 B5 **Plonévez-Porzay** France
31 M3 **Płońsk** Poland
48 K5 **Plopeni** Romania
48 H6 **Plopi** Romania
52 D6 **Ploskosh'** U.S.S.R.
37 N4 **Plössberg** W Germany
31 J2 **Płoty** Poland
20 D6 **Plouagat** France
20 D4 **Plouaret** France
20 A5 **Plouarzel** France
20 D6 **Plouay** France
20 F4 **Ploubalay** France
20 E5 **Plœuc** France
31 H5 **Ploučnice** *R* Czechoslovakia
20 A4 **Ploudalmézeau** France
20 B4 **Ploudaniel** France
20 B5 **Ploudiry** France
20 B4 **Plouénan** France
20 G4 **Plouër-Langrolay-sur-Rance** France
20 B4 **Plouescat** France
20 E4 **Plouézec** France
20 E4 **Plouézec, Pte.de** France
20 B5 **Plougastel-Daoulas** France
20 E5 **Plougenast** France
20 A5 **Plougonvelin** France
20 C4 **Plougonven** France
20 D5 **Plougonver** France
20 E6 **Plougoumelen** France
20 D4 **Plougrescant** France
20 A4 **Plouguerneau** France
20 D5 **Plouguenevel** France
20 E4 **Plouha** France
20 D6 **Plouharnel** France
20 A5 **Plouhinec** Finistère France
20 D6 **Plouhinec** Morbihan France
20 D4 **Plouigneau** France
20 C4 **Ploujean** France
20 D4 **Ploumanac'h** France
20 C4 **Ploumilliau** France
20 A5 **Ploumoguer** France
20 B5 **Plounéour-Ménez** France
20 B4 **Plounéour-Trez** France
20 C4 **Plounérin** France
20 B4 **Plounévez-Lochrist** France
20 D5 **Plounevez-Quintin** France
20 C5 **Plourach** France
20 D5 **Plouray** France
20 A4 **Plourin** France
20 B4 **Plouvien** France
20 B4 **Plouvorn** France
20 C5 **Plouyé** France
20 B4 **Plouzévéde** France
46 G2 **Plovdiv** Bulgaria
99 M7 **Plover** Iowa U.S.A.
99 R5 **Plover** *R* Wisconsin U.S.A.
99 R5 **Plover** Wisconsin U.S.A.
116 K1 **Plover Is** Alaska U.S.A.
20 B6 **Plozévet** France
36 H6 **Plüderhausen** W Germany
119 S8 **Plumas** Manitoba Canada
20 F5 **Plumaugat** France
99 O5 **Plum City** Wisconsin U.S.A.
118 D1 **Plum Coulee** Manitoba Canada
20 E6 **Plumelec** France
20 E6 **Pluméliau** France
20 E6 **Plumelin** France
20 E6 **Plumergat** France
95 P5 **Plum I** New York U.S.A.
20 E5 **Plumieux** France
100 J2 **Plummer** Idaho U.S.A.
116 H6 **Plummer, Mt** Alaska U.S.A.
110 D6 **Plummerville** Arkansas U.S.A.
13 F4 **Plumpton Hd** England
143 F8 **Plumridge Lakes** Western Australia Australia
87 E10 **Plumtree** Zimbabwe
20 E6 **Pluneret** France
52 B6 **Plunge** U.S.S.R.
119 M7 **Plunkett** Saskatchewan Canada
100 F7 **Plush** Oregon U.S.A.
20 D6 **Pluvigner** France
36 B4 **Pluwig** W Germany
20 C4 **Pluzunet** France
8 B7 **Plymouth** England
127 M2 **Plymouth** Tobago
102 D3 **Plymouth** California U.S.A.
94 A5 **Plymouth** Indiana U.S.A.
99 N6 **Plymouth** Iowa U.S.A.
95 R5 **Plymouth** Massachusetts U.S.A.
98 K9 **Plymouth** Nebraska U.S.A.
95 Q3 **Plymouth** New Hampshire U.S.A.
94 E6 **Plymouth** Ohio U.S.A.
95 M5 **Plymouth** Pennsylvania U.S.A.
101 N8 **Plymouth** Utah U.S.A.
95 P3 **Plymouth** Vermont U.S.A.
99 T6 **Plymouth** Wisconsin U.S.A.
127 O6 **Plymouth** Montserrat W Indies
122 G9 **Plympton** Nova Scotia Canada
8 B7 **Plympton** England
8 C3 **Plynlimon Fawr** *mt* Wales
52 C5 **Plyussa** *R* U.S.S.R.
52 C5 **Plyussa** U.S.S.R.
37 O4 **Plzen** Czechoslovakia
31 J3 **Pniewy** Poland
42 J2 **Po** *R* Italy
85 D6 **Po** Burkina
71 H5 **Poat** *isld* Sulawesi
139 H8 **Poatina** Tasmania Australia
85 E7 **Pobé** Benin
66 C3 **Pobedy, Pik** *mt* U.S.S.R./China
37 O5 **Poběžovice** Czechoslovakia
31 K3 **Pobiedziska** Poland
17 J2 **Pobla de Lilleta, L** Spain
17 H2 **Pobla de Segur** Spain
110 F5 **Pocahontas** Arkansas U.S.A.
99 M7 **Pocahontas** Iowa U.S.A.
94 F9 **Pocahontas** Virginia U.S.A.
107 N6 **Pocasse** Oklahoma U.S.A.
94 F8 **Pocatalico** *R* West Virginia U.S.A.
101 N7 **Pocatello** Idaho U.S.A.
31 J6 **Počátky** Czechoslovakia
131 D3 **Pocha, Sa. de** *mts* Argentina
54 E4 **Pochep** U.S.S.R.
54 D2 **Pochinok** U.S.S.R.
38 M5 **Pochlarn** Austria
125 L10 **Pochutla** Mexico
37 P5 **Pocinovice** Czechoslovakia
37 P2 **Pockau** East Germany
37 P7 **Pocking** W Germany
13 H6 **Pocklington** England
70 F2 **Pock, Mt** Sabah
128 D7 **Pocoma** Peru
95 M8 **Pocomoke City** Maryland U.S.A.
95 M9 **Pocomoke Sd** Virginia U.S.A.
129 G7 **Poconé** Brazil
95 M6 **Pocono Mts** Pennsylvania U.S.A.
95 M5 **Pocono Pines** Pennsylvania U.S.A.
129 J8 **Pocos de Caldas** Brazil
125 O6 **Pocri** Panama
125 P9 **Poctún** Guatemala
103 L5 **Pocum Wash** *creek* Arizona U.S.A.
37 P3 **Podbořany** Czechoslovakia
52 J3 **Podcher'ye** U.S.S.R.
31 L4 **Poddębice** Poland
118 C4 **Poddle R** Alberta Canada
52 D5 **Poddor'ye** U.S.S.R.
31 J5 **Poděbrady** Czechoslovakia
45 M2 **Po delle Tolle** *R* Italy
18 E8 **Podensac** France
48 J1 **Podgaytsy** U.S.S.R.
Podgorica *see* **Titograd**
54 G8 **Podgornoye** U.S.S.R.
45 M2 **Po di Goro** *R* Italy
76 D3 **Podile** India
45 L2 **Po di Volano** *R* Italy
51 Q2 **Podkagernoye** U.S.S.R.
56 D1 **Podkamennay** *R* U.S.S.R.
38 J9 **Podkoren** Yugoslavia
46 G3 **Podkova** Bulgaria
48 F1 **Podolinec** Czechoslovakia
54 J1 **Podol'sk** U.S.S.R.
85 B5 **Podor** Senegal
52 G4 **Podosinovets** U.S.S.R.
42 H4 **Podovi** Yugoslavia
52 D4 **Podporozh'ye** U.S.S.R.
55 E2 **Podrezovo** U.S.S.R.
56 D2 **Podtesovo** U.S.S.R.
48 L3 **Podu Iloaiei** Romania
46 E2 **Podujevo** Yugoslavia
48 L4 **Podu Turcului** Romania
52 F4 **Podyuga** U.S.S.R.
33 O4 **Poel** *isld* East Germany
22 D2 **Poelkapelle** Belgium
140 E7 **Poeppel Corner** N Terr Australia
94 C1 **Poe Reef Lt. Ho** Michigan U.S.A.
144 C5 **Poerua** New Zealand
87 C11 **Pofadder** S Africa
45 O6 **Pofi** Italy
120 J6 **Pogamasing** Ontario Canada
54 E4 **Pogar** U.S.S.R.
33 S4 **Poggendorf** East Germany
42 D5 **Poggibonsi** Italy
45 K4 **Poggio a Caiano** Italy
45 N5 **Poggio Moiano** Italy
45 K2 **Pôggio Renatico** Italy
45 K2 **Póggio Rusco** Italy
59 M1 **Pogibi** U.S.S.R.
48 L6 **Pogoanele** Romania
46 D4 **Pogradec** Albania
45 M2 **Po Grande** *R* Italy
65 H2 **Pogranichnyy** U.S.S.R.
48 M1 **Pogrebishche** U.S.S.R.
116 E9 **Pogromni Vol** Aleutian Is
32 F6 **Pogum** W Germany
71 H5 **Poh** Sulawesi
135 U5 **Pohakuloa** Hawaiian Is
59 J4 **Pohang** S Korea
145 E4 **Pohangina** New Zealand
145 D4 **Pohara** New Zealand
29 K11 **Pohja** Finland
29 O8 **Pohjois-Karjala** *prov* Finland
36 F3 **Pohl-Göns** W Germany
36 F2 **Pohlheim** W Germany
145 F3 **Pohokura** *mt* New Zealand
145 E3 **Pohokura** New Zealand
48 F2 **Pohorelá** Czechoslovakia
31 K7 **Pohořelice** Czechoslovakia
38 M9 **Pohorje** *mt* Yugoslavia
102 V14 **Pohue B** Hawaiian Is
45 K1 **Poiana Magg** Italy
46 F1 **Poiana Mare** Romania
48 K3 **Poiana Teiului** Romania
71 J4 **Poigar** Sulawesi Indonesia
123 O2 **Poincaré, L** Quebec Canada
146 G14 **Poinsett, C** Antarctica
113 G9 **Poinsett, L** Florida U.S.A.
102 D7 **Point Arguello** California U.S.A.
109 M5 **Pointblank** Texas U.S.A.
138 E5 **Point Broughton** South Australia Australia
102 D6 **Point Buchon** California U.S.A.
109 L7 **Point Comfort** Texas U.S.A.
102 D7 **Point Conception** California U.S.A.
123 N3 **Pointe-à Maurier** Quebec Canada
127 O3 **Pointe-á-Pierre** Trinidad
127 N4 **Pointe-á-Pitre** Guadeloupe W Indies
120 K7 **Pointe au Baril Station** Ontario Canada
122 E4 **Pointe aux Anglais** Quebec Canada
121 R7 **Pointe aux Trembles** Quebec Canada
121 S4 **Pointe Bleue** Quebec Canada
122 H7 **Pointe du Chêne** New Brunswick Canada
120 H9 **Point Edward** Ontario Canada
122 D4 **Pointe le Bel** Quebec Canada
86 B6 **Pointe-Noire** Congo
127 M4 **Pointe Noire** Guadeloupe W Indies
22 C1 **Pointe Synthe** France
122 G6 **Pointe Verte** New Brunswick Canada
127 N3 **Point Fortin** Trinidad
123 K8 **Point George, C** Nova Scotia Canada
112 M1 **Point Harbor** North Carolina U.S.A.
139 H8 **Point Hills** Tasmania Australia
116 D2 **Point Hope** Alaska U.S.A.
117 R3 **Point L** Northwest Territories Canada
116 F2 **Point Lay** Alaska U.S.A.
139 L4 **Point Lookout** *mt* New South Wales Australia
95 L8 **Point Lookout** Maryland U.S.A.
94 H7 **Point Marion** Pennsylvania U.S.A.
94 K7 **Point of Rocks** Maryland U.S.A.
101 R8 **Point of Rocks** Wyoming U.S.A.
120 H10 **Point Pelee Nat Park** Ontario Canada
95 N6 **Point Pleasant** New Jersey U.S.A.
94 E8 **Point Pleasant** West Virginia U.S.A.
142 B5 **Point Samson** Western Australia Australia
140 B1 **Point Stuart** N Terr Australia
102 C5 **Point Sur** California U.S.A.
138 D5 **Point Turton** South Australia Australia
145 E2 **Point Waikato** New Zealand
68 F6 **Poipet** Cambodia
20 G8 **Poiré-sur-Vie, le** France
52 H6 **Poisevo** U.S.S.R.
101 S6 **Poison Cr** Wyoming U.S.A.
142 B1 **Poison Gully** *R* Perth, W Aust Australia
121 P6 **Poisson Blanc, L** Quebec Canada
142 C5 **Poissonnier Pt** Western Australia Australia
21 P4 **Poissy** France
21 L8 **Poitiers** France
21 J8 **Poitou** *reg* France
142 B5 **Poivre, C** Western Australia Australia
21 O2 **Poix-de-Picardie** France
22 J3 **Poix St. Hubert** Belgium
22 H4 **Poix-Terron** France
46 D4 **Pojan** Albania
106 D6 **Pojoaque** New Mexico U.S.A.
102 R12 **Pokai Bay** Hawaiian Is
145 E3 **Pokaka** New Zealand
74 D5 **Pokaran** India
139 J3 **Pokataroo** New South Wales Australia
52 J3 **Pokcha** U.S.S.R.
145 E2 **Pokeno** New Zealand
75 L4 **Pokhara** Nepal
29 M3 **Pokka** Finland
86 E5 **Poko** Zaire
31 K5 **Pokój** Poland
116 F2 **Poko Mt** Alaska U.S.A.
52 E6 **Pokrov** U.S.S.R.
55 G3 **Pokrovka** Novosibirskaya obl U.S.S.R.
55 B5 **Pokrovka** Orenburgskaya obl U.S.S.R.
55 E5 **Pokrovka** Tselinogradskaya obl U.S.S.R.
55 E3 **Pokrovskoye** U.S.S.R.
52 F3 **Pokshen'ga** *R* U.S.S.R.
71 E4 **Pola** Philippines
71 E4 **Pola B** Philippines
103 O6 **Polacca** Arizona U.S.A.
103 O6 **Polacca Wasa** *R* Arizona U.S.A.
16 D1 **Pola de Laviana** Spain
16 D1 **Pola de Lena** Spain
16 D1 **Pola de Siero** Spain
31 K4 **Poland** *rep* Europe
95 M3 **Poland** New York U.S.A.
31 K1 **Polanow** Poland
99 S4 **Polar** Wisconsin U.S.A.
101 M4 **Polaris** Montana U.S.A.
78 D2 **Polatli** Turkey
8 B7 **Polbathick** England
36 C3 **Polch** W Germany
133 C5 **Polcura** Chile
31 J2 **Połczyn Zdrój** Poland
52 E3 **Pole** U.S.S.R.
37 P5 **Poledník** *mt* Czechoslovakia
80 C5 **Poleg** *R* Israel
9 G6 **Polegate** England
68 H5 **Polei Monu** Vietnam
57 B6 **Polekhatum** U.S.S.R.
77 L2 **Pol-e-Khomrī** Afghanistan
37 P5 **Poleň** Czechoslovakia
45 L2 **Polesella** Italy
31 N1 **Polessk** U.S.S.R.
53 C8 **Polesye** *marsh* U.S.S.R.
55 D3 **Polevskoy** U.S.S.R.
70 F6 **Polewali** Sulawesi
48 G3 **Polgár** Hungary
48 E3 **Polgárdi** Hungary
86 B4 **Poli** Cameroon
46 G8 **Políaigos** *isld* Greece
43 G8 **Policastro, G. di** Italy
31 H2 **Police** Poland
138 E6 **Policemans Point** South Australia Australia
31 J6 **Polička** Czechoslovakia
19 J6 **Poligny** France
46 F3 **Polikastron** Greece
47 H5 **Políkhnitos** Greece
71 E3 **Polillo** *isld* Luzon Philippines
45 J3 **Polinago** Italy
38 H8 **Polinik** *mt* Austria
127 L3 **Polink Pt** Jamaica
79 C3 **Polis** Cyprus
71 J4 **Polisan, Tanjong** *C* Sulawesi
52 D5 **Polist'** *R* U.S.S.R.
52 G3 **Politovo** U.S.S.R.
98 J8 **Polk** Nebraska U.S.A.
94 H5 **Polk** Pennsylvania U.S.A.
56 D1 **Polkan, Gora** *mt* U.S.S.R.
113 F9 **Polk City** Florida U.S.A.
33 P7 **Polkritz** East Germany
76 C5 **Pollachi** India
37 L5 **Pollanten** W Germany
14 E3 **Pollaphuca Res** Ireland
110 F5 **Pollard** Arkansas U.S.A.
38 N7 **Pöllau** Austria
32 K9 **Polle** W Germany
122 A1 **Pollet, L** Quebec Canada
43 G9 **Pollino, M** *mt* Italy
33 P7 **Pollitz** East Germany
100 J4 **Pollock** Idaho U.S.A.
111 D10 **Pollock** Louisiana U.S.A.
98 F4 **Pollock** South Dakota U.S.A.
142 G6 **Pollock Hills** Western Australia Australia
143 E10 **Pollock Reef** Western Australia Australia
112 K3 **Pollocksville** North Carolina U.S.A.
118 F7 **Pollockville** Alberta Canada
144 B6 **Pollux** *mt* New Zealand
29 N2 **Polmak** Finland
26 Q1 **Polmak** Norway
12 E2 **Polmont** Scotland
31 J6 **Polná** Czechoslovakia
52 C5 **Polna** U.S.S.R.
99 R8 **Polo** Illinois U.S.A.
110 B2 **Polo** Missouri U.S.A.
54 H9 **Pologi** U.S.S.R.
71 G7 **Polomoloc** Mindanao Philippines
54 G2 **Polotnanyy Zavod** U.S.S.R.
52 C6 **Polotsk** U.S.S.R.
55 E4 **Polovinnoye** U.S.S.R.
52 H3 **Polovniki** U.S.S.R.
8 B7 **Polperro** England
83 K10 **Polpitigama** Sri Lanka
38 L7 **Pöls** *R* Austria
47 H2 **Polski Gradets** Bulgaria
47 H1 **Polski Trŭmbesh** Bulgaria
101 L2 **Polson** Montana U.S.A.
38 K7 **Pöls-Tal** *V* Austria
52 F2 **Polta** *R* U.S.S.R.
48 F2 **Poltár** Czechoslovakia
54 F7 **Poltava** U.S.S.R.
55 F4 **Poltavka** U.S.S.R.
121 P7 **Poltimore** Quebec Canada
52 C5 **Põltsamaa** U.S.S.R.
55 E4 **Poludino** U.S.S.R.
55 D1 **Polunochnoye** U.S.S.R.
50 E4 **Poluostrov Buzachi** *pen* U.S.S.R.
106 D7 **Polvadera** New Mexico U.S.A.
29 O9 **Polvijärvi** Finland
118 L5 **Polwarth** Saskatchewan Canada
31 L1 **Półwysep Hel** *pen* Poland
55 E1 **Pol'yanovo** U.S.S.R.
52 D1 **Polyarnyy** U.S.S.R.
116 N5 **Polychrome Pass** Alaska U.S.A.
46 F4 **Políyiros** Greece
134 K12 **Polynesia** *ethnic reg* Pacific Oc
56 C4 **Polysayevo** U.S.S.R.
37 N2 **Pölzig** East Germany
133 D2 **Poma** Argentina
144 B6 **Pomahaka** *R* New Zealand
133 D3 **Poman** Argentina
16 B7 **Pomarão** Portugal
112 F3 **Pomaria** South Carolina U.S.A.
29 J10 **Pomarkku** Finland
130 G7 **Pomba** *R* Brazil
129 L5 **Pombal** Brazil
16 B5 **Pombal** Portugal
130 D7 **Pombo, R** Brazil
19 O18 **Pomègues, Île** France
31 G2 **Pomerania** *reg* E Germany/Poland
99 M7 **Pomercy** Iowa U.S.A.
103 O9 **Pomerene** Arizona U.S.A.
14 E2 **Pomeroy** N Ireland
94 E7 **Pomeroy** Ohio U.S.A.
100 H3 **Pomeroy** Washington U.S.A.
45 M6 **Pomezia** Italy
95 P5 **Pomfret** Connecticut U.S.A.
45 Q8 **Pomigliano d'Arco** Italy
110 C4 **Pomme de Terre** *R* Missouri U.S.A.
37 M5 **Pommelsbrunn** W Germany
20 D4 **Pommerit-Jaudy** France
20 D4 **Pommerit-le-Vicomte** France
21 O8 **Pommiers** France
107 P3 **Pomoma** Kansas U.S.A.
141 L7 **Pomona** Queensland Australia
125 P9 **Pomona** Belize
87 C11 **Pomona** Namibia
110 E5 **Pomona** Missouri U.S.A.
47 J2 **Pomorie** Bulgaria
52 E3 **Pomorskiy Bereg** *coast* U.S.S.R.
48 J1 **Pomoryany** U.S.S.R.
54 C8 **Pomoshnaya** U.S.S.R.
21 K8 **Pompaire** France
113 G11 **Pompano Beach** Florida U.S.A.
45 Q8 **Pompei** Italy
95 L4 **Pompey** New York U.S.A.
142 G3 **Pompeys Pillar** *mt* Western Australia Australia
101 S4 **Pompeys Pillar** Montana U.S.A.
95 N5 **Pompton Lakes** New Jersey U.S.A.
88 D10 **Pompué** *R* Mozambique
123 L8 **Pomquet** Nova Scotia Canada
33 R10 **Pomssen** East Germany
119 N6 **Ponass L** Saskatchewan Canada
98 K7 **Ponca** Nebraska U.S.A.
107 N5 **Ponca City** Oklahoma U.S.A.
127 L5 **Ponce** Puerto Rico
111 L11 **Ponce de Leon** Florida U.S.A.
113 F12 **Ponce de Leon B** Florida U.S.A.
113 F8 **Ponce de Leon Inlet** Florida U.S.A.
111 F11 **Ponchatoula** Louisiana U.S.A.
124 H7 **Poncitlán** Mexico
107 N5 **Pond Creek** Oklahoma U.S.A.
109 K2 **Ponder** Texas U.S.A.
76 D5 **Pondicherry** India
115 M3 **Pond Inlet** Northwest Territories Canada
89 F8 **Pondoland** *reg* S Africa
100 D8 **Pondosa** California U.S.A.
100 H4 **Pondosa** Oregon U.S.A.
99 M1 **Ponemah** Minnesota U.S.A.
44 E3 **Ponente** Italy
94 B6 **Poneto** Indiana U.S.A.
16 C2 **Ponferrada** Spain
86 A5 **Pongara, Pte** Gabon
145 F4 **Pongaroa** New Zealand
38 H7 **Pongau** *reg* Austria
70 G7 **Pongkolaero** Sulawesi
52 D2 **Pon'goma** U.S.S.R.
122 H9 **Ponhook L** Nova Scotia Canada
33 T10 **Ponickau** East Germany
31 K4 **Poniec** Poland
71 H4 **Poniki, Mt** Sulawesi
70 G5 **Ponindilisa, Tg** *C* Sulawesi
68 A2 **Ponnagyun** Burma
68 B1 **Ponnyadaung** *ra* Burma
118 D6 **Ponoka** Alberta Canada
55 B4 **Ponomarevka** U.S.S.R.
70 N9 **Ponorogo** Java
52 F2 **Ponoy** U.S.S.R.
52 E2 **Ponoy** *R* U.S.S.R.
18 E7 **Pons** France
17 H3 **Pons** Spain
45 J4 **Ponsacco** Italy
71 G5 **Ponson** *isld* Philippines
18 E9 **Pontacq** France
130 E9 **Ponta Grossa** Brazil
40 B3 **Pontailler** France
19 J5 **Pontailler-sur-Saône** France
19 O15 **Pontaix** France
22 E3 **Pont-à-Marcq** France
19 J4 **Pont à Mousson** France
129 G8 **Ponta Porá** Brazil
8 C4 **Pontardawe** Wales
8 B4 **Pontarddulais** Wales
19 K6 **Pontarlier** France
45 K4 **Pontassieve** Italy
20 H4 **Pontaubault** France
21 M3 **Pont Audemer** France
18 G7 **Pontaumur** France
20 C6 **Pont-Aven** France
22 F5 **Pontavert** France
121 M1 **Pontax** *R* Quebec Canada
122 K3 **Pontbriand B** Quebec Canada
40 G7 **Pont-Canav** Italy
19 Q14 **Pontcharra** France
111 F11 **Pontchartrain, L** Louisiana U.S.A.
20 F7 **Pont-Château** France
20 B5 **Pont-Croix** France
19 Q17 **Pont-d'Aiguines** France
19 O12 **Pont d'Ain** France
19 O15 **Pont-de-Barret** France
21 M6 **Pont-de-Braye** France
20 B5 **Pont-de-Buis** France
21 N3 **Pont-de-l'Arche** France
40 C4 **Pont-de-Poitte** France
19 J6 **Pont de Vaux** France
19 J6 **Pont de Veyle** France
21 K4 **Pont-d'Ouilly** France
129 J6 **Ponte Alta do Norte** Brazil
42 E2 **Pontebba** Italy
45 R8 **Pontecagnano** Italy
45 P7 **Pontecorvo** Italy
16 B3 **Ponte da Barca** Portugal
129 G6 **Ponte de Pedra** Brazil
45 J4 **Pontedera** Italy
16 B5 **Ponte de Sor** Portugal
16 B3 **Ponte do Lima** Portugal
13 G6 **Pontefract** England
118 K9 **Ponteix** Saskatchewan Canada
45 L2 **Pontelagoscuro** Italy
13 G3 **Ponteland** England
45 R7 **Pontelandolfo** Italy
45 M1 **Pontelongo** Italy
130 G7 **Ponte Nova** Brazil
18 E8 **Pontenx les Forges** France
8 C3 **Ponterwyd** Wales
45 L1 **Ponte San Nicolò** Italy
16 B2 **Pontevedra** *prov* Spain
16 B2 **Pontevedra** Spain
113 F7 **Ponte Vedra Beach** Florida U.S.A.
19 N13 **Pont-Evêque** France
41 M7 **Pontevico** Italy
21 H4 **Pontfarcy** France
22 G5 **Pont Faverger** France
21 N5 **Pontgouin** France
20 E5 **Pont-Hamon** France
21 H3 **Pont-Hébert** France
99 S9 **Pontiac** Illinois U.S.A.
94 D4 **Pontiac** Michigan U.S.A.
70 A5 **Pontianak** Kalimantan
43 E7 **Pontinia** Italy
20 E5 **Pontivy** France
20 B6 **Pont-l'Abbé** France
122 H6 **Pont Lafrance** New Brunswick Canada
40 A1 **Pont la Ville** France
21 L3 **Pont-l'Evêque** France
21 N7 **Pontlevoy** France
20 D5 **Pont-Melvez** France
119 S4 **Ponton** Manitoba Canada
143 E9 **Ponton Ck** Western Australia Australia
20 H4 **Pontorson** France
111 G7 **Pontotoc** Mississippi U.S.A.
109 J5 **Pontotoc** Texas U.S.A.
44 G3 **Pontremoli** Italy
41 L4 **Pontresina** Switzerland
8 C3 **Pontrhydfendigaid** Wales
8 B1 **Pont Rhythallt** Wales
20 D4 **Pontrieux** France
119 N5 **Pontrilas** Saskatchewan Canada
8 D4 **Pontrilas** England
121 T6 **Pont Rouge** Quebec Canada
19 N16 **Pont-St. Esprit** France
22 D5 **Pont-Ste. Maxence** France
20 D6 **Pont-Scorff** France
21 J7 **Ponts-de-Cé, les** France
22 F3 **Pont-sur-Sambre** France
18 H4 **Pont-sur-Yonne** France
20 B4 **Pontusval, Pte.de** France
21 L6 **Pontvallain** France
121 M8 **Pontypool** Ontario Canada
8 C4 **Pontypool** Wales
8 C4 **Pontypridd** Wales
145 E2 **Ponui I** New Zealand
101 O4 **Pony** Montana U.S.A.
43 E8 **Ponza, I di** Italy
43 E8 **Ponziane, Isole** *islds* Italy
138 C4 **Poochera** South Australia Australia
13 G6 **Pool** England
138 D2 **Poolawanna L** South Australia Australia
144 B6 **Poolburn Dam** New Zealand
9 E6 **Poole** England
138 F3 **Poole, Mt** New South Wales Australia
112 F5 **Pooler** Georgia U.S.A.
95 K7 **Poolesville** Maryland U.S.A.
15 C3 **Poolewe** Scotland
12 E1 **Pool of Muckart** Scotland
109 K3 **Poolville** Texas U.S.A.
Poona *see* **Pune**
139 G5 **Pooncarie** New South Wales Australia
143 B8 **Poondarrie,Mt** Western Australia Australia
139 G4 **Poopelloe, L** New South Wales Australia
128 E7 **Poopó** Bolivia
145 E1 **Poor Knights Is** New Zealand
116 K4 **Poorman** Alaska U.S.A.
86 C7 **Popakabaka** Zaire
129 G3 **Popakai** Suriname
54 K8 **Popasnaya** U.S.S.R.
128 C3 **Popayan** Colombia
103 J8 **Pope** California U.S.A.
111 G7 **Pope** Mississippi U.S.A.
27 M14 **Pope** U.S.S.R.
99 N7 **Popejoy** Iowa U.S.A.
58 F1 **Poperechnoye** U.S.S.R.
22 D2 **Poperinge** Belgium
95 L8 **Popes Creek** Maryland U.S.A.
95 S3 **Popham Beach** Maine U.S.A.
51 K1 **Popigay** *R* U.S.S.R.
138 F5 **Popiltah** New South Wales Australia
98 A1 **Poplar** Montana U.S.A.
99 P3 **Poplar** Wisconsin U.S.A.
110 F5 **Poplar Bluff** Missouri U.S.A.
101 U1 **Poplar Cr** Montana U.S.A.
119 U6 **Poplar Pt** Manitoba Canada
111 G11 **Poplarville** Mississippi U.S.A.
125 K8 **Popocatepetl** *vol* Mexico
116 G9 **Popof I** Alaska U.S.A.
70 N10 **Popoh** Java
45 P5 **Popoli** Italy
136 K3 **Popondetta** Papua New Guinea
47 H1 **Popovo** Bulgaria
37 M5 **Poppberg** *mt* W Germany
25 H4 **Poppe** Netherlands
22 J1 **Poppel** Belgium
37 J3 **Poppenhausen** W Germany
45 L4 **Poppi** Italy
48 F1 **Poprad** *R* Czechoslovakia
31 M6 **Poprad** Czechoslovakia
128 E8 **Poquis** *mt* Chile/Arg
95 L9 **Poquoson** Virginia U.S.A.
145 F4 **Porangahau** New Zealand
74 C8 **Porbander** India
117 H9 **Porcher I** British Columbia Canada
54 B1 **Porch'ye** Pskovskaya Oblast' U.S.S.R.
133 D1 **Porco** Bolivia
16 E7 **Porcuna** Spain
141 G5 **Porcupine** *R* Queensland Australia
116 R3 **Porcupine** *R* Alaska/Yukon Terr U.S.A./Canada
90 H3 **Porcupine Bank** Atlantic Oc
101 T1 **Porcupine Cr** Montana U.S.A.
118 C8 **Porcupine Hills** Alberta Canada
119 Q6 **Porcupine Hills** Manitoba/Sask Canada
99 R3 **Porcupine Mts** Michigan U.S.A.
119 O6 **Porcupine Plain** Saskatchewan Canada
42 E3 **Pordenoné** Italy
46 G1 **Pordim** Bulgaria
42 F3 **Poreč** Yugoslavia
130 D8 **Porecatu** Brazil
55 D2 **Porech'ye** U.S.S.R.
52 G6 **Poretskoye** U.S.S.R.
145 E4 **Porewa** New Zealand
85 E6 **Porga** Benin
29 J10 **Pori** Finland
145 F4 **Porirua** New Zealand
80 F3 **Poriyya** Israel
26 L5 **Porjus** Sweden
29 L12 **Porkala** Finland
52 C5 **Porkhov** U.S.S.R.
128 F1 **Porlamar** Venezuela
41 K5 **Porlezza** Italy
8 C5 **Porlock** England
37 L6 **Pörnbach** W Germany
20 F7 **Pornic** France
20 F7 **Pornichet** France
71 G5 **Poro** *isld* Philippines
52 E3 **Porog** Arkhangel'skaya obl U.S.S.R.
52 J4 **Porog** Kom A.S.S.R. U.S.S.R.
59 M2 **Poronaysk** U.S.S.R.
68 G6 **Porong** *R* Cambodia
143 C10 **Porongurup** Western Australia Australia
60 Q1 **Poronupuri yama** *mt* Japan
145 E3 **Porootarao** New Zealand
46 F7 **Póros** *isld* Greece
60 Q1 **Poroshiri yama** *mt* Japan
52 D3 **Porosozero** U.S.S.R.
52 H3 **Porozhsk** U.S.S.R.
56 F3 **Porozhskiy** U.S.S.R.
146 E14 **Porpoise B** Antarctica
19 Q18 **Porquerolles, I. de** France
120 K4 **Porquis Junct** Ontario Canada
40 F3 **Pörrentruy** Switzerland
45 J3 **Porretta Terme** Italy
16 B2 **Porriño** Spain
26 N1 **Porsa** Norway
26 O1 **Pörsangen** *inlet* Norway
27 D12 **Porsgrunn** Norway
20 A4 **Porspoder** France
33 Q9 **Porst** East Germany
47 L5 **Porsük** *R* Turkey
128 F7 **Portachuelo** Bolivia
138 E5 **Port Adelaide** South Australia Australia
14 E2 **Portadown** N Ireland
144 B7 **Port Adventure** New Zealand
14 F2 **Portaferry** N Ireland
122 H7 **Portage** Prince Edward I Canada
116 N6 **Portage** Alaska U.S.A.
95 S7 **Portage** Maine U.S.A.
101 O2 **Portage** Montana U.S.A.
94 D5 **Portage** *R* Ohio U.S.A.
94 J6 **Portage** Pennsylvania U.S.A.
101 N8 **Portage** Utah U.S.A.
110 F3 **Portage des Sioux** Missouri U.S.A.
122 G6 **Portage I** New Brunswick Canada
119 T9 **Portage la Prairie** Manitoba Canada
110 G5 **Portageville** Missouri U.S.A.
94 J4 **Portageville** New York U.S.A.
103 P10 **Portal** Arizona U.S.A.
112 F5 **Portal** Georgia U.S.A.
98 D1 **Portal** North Dakota U.S.A.
14 D3 **Portalaoise** Ireland
117 L11 **Port Alberni** British Columbia Canada
139 H7 **Port Albert** Victoria Australia
120 J9 **Port Albert** Ontario Canada
145 E2 **Port Albert** New Zealand
16 C5 **Portalegre** Portugal
106 G7 **Portales** New Mexico U.S.A.
117 F7 **Port Alexander** Alaska U.S.A.
89 E9 **Port Alfred** S Africa
117 K10 **Port Alice** British Columbia Canada
94 J5 **Port Allegany** Pennsylvania U.S.A.
111 E11 **Port Allen** Louisiana U.S.A.
141 K6 **Port Alma** Queensland Australia
117 M11 **Port Angeles** Washington U.S.A.
109 K8 **Port Aransas** Texas U.S.A.
102 A3 **Port Arena** California U.S.A.

68 **Portarlington — Prudhoe Land**

14 D3 **Portarlington** Ireland
Port Arthur *see* **Lüshun**
139 J9 **Port Arthur** Tasmania Australia
109 N6 **Port Arthur** Texas U.S.A.
12 B2 **Port Askaig** Scotland
138 D4 **Port Augusta** South Australia Australia
123 O5 **Port-au-Port** Newfoundland Canada
123 N5 **Port-au-Port** *pen* Newfoundland Canada
127 H5 **Port-au-Prince** Haiti
94 D2 **Port Austin** Michigan U.S.A.
32 J8 **Porta Westfalica** W Germany
20 G3 **Portbail** France
12 C2 **Port Bannatyne** Scotland
111 E11 **Port Barre** Louisiana U.S.A.
71 D5 **Port Barton** Palawan Philippines
123 L8 **Port Bickerton** Nova Scotia Canada
68 A7 **Port Blair** Andaman Is
109 N6 **Port Bolivar** Texas U.S.A.
17 K2 **Port Bou** Spain/France
85 D8 **Port Bouet** Ivory Coast
140 D2 **Port Bradshaw** *inlet* N Terr Australia
21 J5 **Port Brillet** France
120 J10 **Port Bruce** Ontario Canada
120 K10 **Port Burwell** Ontario Canada
99 Q8 **Port Byron** Illinois U.S.A.
95 L3 **Port Byron** New York U.S.A.
139 G7 **Port Campbell** Victoria Australia
75 N7 **Port Canning** India
121 L7 **Port Carling** Ontario Canada
13 E4 **Port Carlisle** England
122 F3 **Port Cartier** Quebec Canada
144 D7 **Port Chalmers** New Zealand
145 E2 **Port Charles** New Zealand
15 B5 **Port Charlotte** Scotland
95 O6 **Port Chester** New York U.S.A.
111 G12 **Port Chicot I** Louisiana U.S.A.
116 D4 **Port Clarence** *hbr* Alaska U.S.A.
117 G9 **Port Clements** British Columbia Canada
141 K5 **Port Clinton** *inlet* Queensland Australia
94 E5 **Port Clinton** Ohio U.S.A.
95 S3 **Port Clyde** Maine U.S.A.
121 L10 **Port Colborne** Ontario Canada
117 M11 **Port Coquitlam** British Columbia Canada
68 A6 **Port Cornwallis** Andaman Is
121 L9 **Port Credit** Ontario Canada
19 Q18 **Port Cros, I. de** France
141 K6 **Port Curtis** *inlet* Queensland Australia
121 L9 **Port Dalhousie** Ontario Canada
122 H5 **Port Daniel** Quebec Canada
139 H9 **Port Davey** Tasmania Australia
19 N18 **Port de Bouc** France
19 N18 **Port de Fos** *hbr* France
102 A1 **Port Delgada** California U.S.A.
127 H5 **Port-de-Paix** Haiti
21 M7 **Port-de-Piles** France
69 E11 **Port Dickson** Malaysia
8 B1 **Port Dinorwic** Wales
141 H3 **Port Douglas** Queensland Australia
120 K10 **Port Dover** Ontario Canada
123 K9 **Port Dufferin** Nova Scotia Canada
111 G12 **Porte a la Hache** Louisiana U.S.A.
Porte d'Annam *see* **Vinh Son**
99 U4 **Porte des Morts** Wisconsin U.S.A.
117 H8 **Port Edward** British Columbia Canada
89 G8 **Port Edward** S Africa
130 G4 **Porteirinha** Brazil
129 H4 **Portel** Brazil
16 B6 **Portel** Portugal
130 H7 **Portela** Brazil
122 H7 **Port Elgin** New Brunswick Canada
120 J8 **Port Elgin** Ontario Canada
127 O8 **Port Elizabeth** Lesser Antilles
89 D9 **Port Elizabeth** S Africa
22 B2 **Portel, le** France
12 B2 **Port Ellen** Scotland
130 B9 **Porteña** *R* Argentina
21 J3 **Port-en-Bessin-Huppain** France
98 K5 **Porter** Minnesota U.S.A.
98 C7 **Porter** Nebraska U.S.A.
107 P6 **Porter** Oklahoma U.S.A.
110 D4 **Porterdale** Georgia U.S.A.
99 T4 **Porterfield** Wisconsin U.S.A.
12 D5 **Port Erin** I of Man U.K.
117 H6 **Porter Landing** British Columbia Canada
15 G3 **Port Errol** Scotland
87 C12 **Porterville** S Africa
102 E5 **Porterville** California U.S.A.
127 K3 **Port Esquivel** Jamaica
8 B4 **Port Eynon** Wales
138 F7 **Port Fairy** South Australia Australia
123 L8 **Port Felix** Nova Scotia Canada
145 E2 **Port Fitzroy** New Zealand
Port Francqui *see* **Ilebo**
86 A6 **Port Gentil** Gabon
122 G9 **Port George** Nova Scotia Canada
111 E10 **Port Gibson** Mississippi U.S.A.
12 D2 **Port Glasgow** Scotland
14 E2 **Portglenone** N Ireland
15 E3 **Portgordon** Scotland
145 E4 **Port Gore** New Zealand
116 M7 **Port Graham** Alaska U.S.A.
143 A8 **Port Gregory** *B* Western Australia Australia
122 H8 **Port Greville** Nova Scotia Canada
8 C4 **Porth** Wales
85 F8 **Port Harcourt** Nigeria
117 K10 **Port Hardy** British Columbia Canada
145 D4 **Port Hardy** New Zealand
Port Harrison *see* **Inukjuak**
123 L8 **Port Hastings** C Breton I, Nova Scotia
123 L8 **Port Hawkesbury** C Breton I, Nova Scotia
8 C5 **Porthcawl** Wales
8 B2 **Porth Dinlleyn** *B* Wales
142 C5 **Port Hedland** Western Australia Australia
127 L3 **Port Henderson** Jamaica
95 O3 **Port Henry** New York U.S.A.
Port Herald *see* **Nsanje**
100 J1 **Porthill** Idaho U.S.A.
8 B2 **Porthmadog** Wales
8 B2 **Porth Neigwl** *B* Wales
123 L8 **Port Hood** C Breton I, Nova Scotia
121 M9 **Port Hope** Ontario Canada
94 E3 **Port Hope** Michigan U.S.A.
123 Q1 **Port Hope Simpson** Labrador, Nfld Canada
102 E7 **Port Hueneme** California U.S.A.
120 H10 **Port Huron** Ontario Canada
94 E4 **Port Huron** Michigan U.S.A.
45 Q8 **Portici** Italy
16 B7 **Portimão** Portugal
29 M5 **Portimo** Finland
12 C1 **Portinnisherrich** Scotland
107 M2 **Portis** Kansas U.S.A.
8 B6 **Port Isaac** England
109 K9 **Port Isabel** Texas U.S.A.
99 T2 **Port Isabelle** Michigan U.S.A.
8 D5 **Portishead** England
139 K5 **Port Jackson** New South Wales Australia
95 O6 **Port Jefferson** Long I, New York U.S.A.
95 N5 **Port Jervis** New York U.S.A.
20 F8 **Port Joinville** France
127 J3 **Port Kaiser** Jamaica
140 A2 **Port Keats** N Terr Australia
139 K5 **Port Kembla** New South Wales Australia
138 C5 **Port Kenney** South Australia Australia
139 J5 **Portland** New South Wales Australia
138 F7 **Portland** Victoria Australia
127 P6 **Portland** Barbados
121 O8 **Portland** Ontario Canada
127 M2 **Portland** *parish* Jamaica
145 E1 **Portland** New Zealand
106 E3 **Portland** Colorado U.S.A.
94 C6 **Portland** Indiana U.S.A.
95 R3 **Portland** Maine U.S.A.
94 C4 **Portland** Michigan U.S.A.
98 J2 **Portland** North Dakota U.S.A.
100 C4 **Portland** Oregon U.S.A.
110 K5 **Portland** Tennessee U.S.A.
109 K8 **Portland** Texas U.S.A.
127 K3 **Portland Bight** Jamaica
8 D7 **Portland, Bill of** *head* England
139 J8 **Portland, C** Tasmania Australia
117 H8 **Portland Canal** Br Col/Alaska Canada/U.S.A.
123 P3 **Portland Cr. Pond** Newfoundland Canada
8 D6 **Portland Hbr** England
145 F3 **Portland I** New Zealand
117 H8 **Portland Inlet** British Columbia Canada
127 K3 **Portland Ridge** Jamaica
141 G2 **Portland Roads** Queensland Australia
126 F6 **Portland Rock** Caribbean
71 E8 **Port Languyan** Philippines
139 H8 **Port Latta** Tasmania Australia
109 L7 **Port Lavaca** Texas U.S.A.
14 D4 **Portlaw** Ireland
144 B4 **Port Levy** New Zealand
95 M3 **Port Leyden** New York U.S.A.
138 D5 **Port Lincoln** South Australia Australia
12 D4 **Port Logan** Scotland
120 K7 **Port Loring** Ontario Canada
20 D6 **Port-Louis** France
83 L12 **Port Louis** Mauritius
127 N4 **Port Louis** Guadeloupe W Indies
140 D3 **Port McArthur** *B* N Terr Australia
138 F7 **Port MacDonnell** South Australia Australia
121 L8 **Port McNicoll** Ontario Canada
139 L4 **Port Macquarie** New South Wales Australia
122 F10 **Port Maitland** Nova Scotia Canada
121 L10 **Port Maitland** Ontario Canada
109 K9 **Port Mansfield** Texas U.S.A.
115 N6 **Port Manvers** Labrador, Nfld Canada
127 L2 **Port Maria** Jamaica
94 J6 **Port Matilda** Pennsylvania U.S.A.
113 G11 **Port Mayaca** Florida U.S.A.
122 H9 **Port Medway** Nova Scotia Canada
117 M11 **Port Mellon** British Columbia Canada
122 H4 **Port Menier** Quebec Canada
116 G8 **Port Moller** Alaska U.S.A.
117 M11 **Port Moody** British Columbia Canada
127 M3 **Port Morant** Jamaica
136 K3 **Port Moresby** Papua New Guinea
123 N7 **Port Morien** C Breton I, Nova Scotia
21 N3 **Port-Mort** France
122 H10 **Port Mouton** Nova Scotia Canada
122 H10 **Port Mouton I** Nova Scotia Canada
141 F1 **Port Musgrave** *inlet* Queensland Australia
15 C4 **Portnacroish** Scotland
12 B2 **Portnahaven** Scotland
20 E6 **Port Navalo** France
109 O6 **Port Neches** Texas U.S.A.
138 D5 **Port Neill** South Australia Australia
126 G3 **Port Nelson** Bahamas
101 N7 **Portneuf** Idaho U.S.A.
121 S5 **Portneuf, Parc** Quebec Canada
122 C5 **Portneuf, R** Quebec Canada
122 C5 **Portneuf-sur-Mer** Quebec Canada
145 G4 **Port Nicholson** New Zealand
138 E6 **Port Noarlunga** South Australia Australia
87 C11 **Port Nolloth** S Africa
95 M7 **Port Norris** New Jersey U.S.A.
115 N6 **Port-Nouveau Québec** Quebec Canada
129 K4 **Pôrto** Brazil
16 B3 **Porto** Portugal
128 E5 **Pôrto Acre** Brazil
130 D7 **Pôrto Alegre** Mato Grosso Brazil
131 H3 **Pôrto Alegre** Rio Grande do Sul Brazil
Porto Alexandre *see* **Tombua**
87 B8 **Porto Amboim** Angola
Porto Amelia *see* **Pemba** Mozambique
129 G6 **Pôrto Artur** Brazil
144 D7 **Portobello** New Zealand
13 E2 **Portobello** Scotland
130 E10 **Pôrto Belo** Brazil
116 G8 **Port O'Brian** Alaska U.S.A.
130 C9 **Pôrto Britânia** Brazil
43 C7 **Porto Cervo** Sardinia
109 L7 **Port O'Connor** Texas U.S.A.
16 B3 **Pôrto de Leixões** Portugal
129 H4 **Pôrto de Moz** Brazil
129 H6 **Pôrto dos Meinacos** Brazil
43 F11 **Porto Empedocle** Sicily
128 G7 **Pôrto Espiridião** Brazil
42 C6 **Portoferraio** Elba Italy
44 F3 **Portofino** Italy
12 D1 **Port of Menteith** Scotland
15 B2 **Port of Ness** Scotland
127 O2 **Port of Spain** Trinidad
45 M2 **Porto Garibaldi** Italy
129 H3 **Pôrto Grande** Brazil
42 E3 **Portogruaro** Italy
129 G7 **Pôrto Jofre** Brazil
102 D2 **Portola** California U.S.A.
29 J9 **Portom** Finland
45 L2 **Portomaggiore** Italy
45 J1 **Porto Mantovano** Italy
44 D4 **Porto Maurizio** Italy
88 H9 **Porto Mocambo** Mozambique
129 G8 **Pôrto Murtinho** Brazil
129 J6 **Pôrto Nacional** Brazil
85 E7 **Porto Novo** Benin
113 G8 **Port Orange** Florida U.S.A.
117 M12 **Port Orchard** Washington U.S.A.
42 F5 **Porto Recanati** Italy
100 A7 **Port Orford** Oregon U.S.A.
133 G2 **Pôrto San José** Brazil
42 D6 **Porto San Stefano** Italy
43 E8 **Porto Santo** *isld* Madeira
129 H8 **Pôrto São José** Brazil
130 H5 **Pôrto Seguro** Brazil
45 M2 **Porto Tolle** Italy
43 B8 **Porto Torres** Sardinia
133 G3 **Pôrto União** Brazil
128 F5 **Pôrto Velho** Brazil
44 G3 **Portovenere** Italy
128 B4 **Portoviejo** Ecuador
12 C4 **Portpatrick** Scotland
140 B2 **Port Patterson** *inlet* N Terr Australia
144 A7 **Port Pegasus** New Zealand
121 M8 **Port Perry** Ontario Canada
139 G7 **Port Phillip B** Victoria Australia
138 E5 **Port Pirie** South Australia Australia
114 H4 **Port Radium** Northwest Territories Canada
8 A7 **Portreath** England
15 B3 **Portree** Scotland
118 J8 **Portreeve** Saskatchewan Canada
83 M8 **Port Refuge** Cocos Is Indian Oc
100 A1 **Port Renfrew** British Columbia Canada
123 T5 **Port Rexton** Newfoundland Canada
102 A4 **Port Reyes** California U.S.A.
100 B1 **Port Roberts** Washington U.S.A.
144 D5 **Port Robinson** New Zealand
140 D2 **Port Roper** *inlet* N Terr Australia
120 K10 **Port Rowan** Ontario Canada
127 L3 **Port Royal** Jamaica
112 G5 **Port Royal** South Carolina U.S.A.
95 K8 **Port Royal** Virginia U.S.A.
122 G9 **Port Royal Nat. Hist. Park** Ontario Canada
14 E1 **Portrush** N Ireland
79 C7 **Port Said** Egypt
113 B8 **Port St. Joe** Florida U.S.A.
89 F8 **Port St Johns** S Africa
19 N18 **Port St. Louis** France
18 F8 **Port St. Marie** France
20 G7 **Port St.Père** France
20 A4 **Portsall** France
14 D1 **Portsalon** Ireland
94 E3 **Port Sanilac** Michigan U.S.A.
123 P3 **Port Saunders** Newfoundland Canada
Port Say *see* **Marsa Ben Mehdi**
38 K8 **Pörtschach** Austria
89 G8 **Port Shepstone** S Africa
117 H8 **Port Simpson** British Columbia Canada
142 D4 **Port Smith** *B* Western Australia Australia
121 O8 **Portsmouth** Ontario Canada
127 O7 **Portsmouth** Dominica
9 E6 **Portsmouth** England
99 L8 **Portsmouth** Iowa U.S.A.
95 R3 **Portsmouth** New Hampshire U.S.A.
112 L2 **Portsmouth** North Carolina U.S.A.
94 E8 **Portsmouth** Ohio U.S.A.
95 Q5 **Portsmouth** Rhode I U.S.A.
95 L10 **Portsmouth** Virginia U.S.A.
12 C1 **Portsonachan** Scotland
15 F3 **Portsoy** Scotland
120 J10 **Port Stanley** Ontario Canada
139 K5 **Port Stephens** New South Wales Australia
141 G2 **Port Stewart** *inlet* Queensland Australia
14 E1 **Portstewart** N Ireland
86 G2 **Port Sudan** Sudan
8 C4 **Port Talbot** Wales
71 F4 **Port Tambang** Philippines
79 C9 **Port Taufiq** Egypt
127 O2 **Port Tembladora** Trinidad
29 M3 **Porttipahdan tekojärvi** *L* Finland
117 M11 **Port Townsend** Washington U.S.A.
Portugal *rep* W Europe
83 J9 **Portugal B** Sri Lanka
123 U6 **Portugal Cove** Newfoundland Canada
17 F1 **Portugalete** Spain
128 E2 **Portuguesa** *state* Venezuela
Portuguese Guinea *see* **Guinea-Bissau** *rep*
14 C3 **Portumna** Ireland
123 T5 **Port Union** Newfoundland Canada
18 H10 **Port Vendres** France
102 F8 **Port Vicente** California U.S.A.
88 D1 **Port Victoria** Kenya
137 O5 **Port-Vila** Vanuatu
94 J4 **Portville** New York U.S.A.
138 E5 **Port Vincent** South Australia Australia
52 D1 **Port Vladimir** U.S.S.R.
138 E5 **Port Wakefield** South Australia Australia
142 F2 **Port Warrender** *inlet* Western Australia Australia
99 T6 **Port Washington** Wisconsin U.S.A.
142 B5 **Port Weld** *B* Western Australia Australia
116 N6 **Port Wells** *inlet* Alaska U.S.A.
112 F5 **Port Wentworth** Georgia U.S.A.
12 D4 **Port William** Scotland
122 H8 **Port Williams** Nova Scotia Canada
99 P3 **Port Wing** Wisconsin U.S.A.
107 P6 **Porum** Oklahoma U.S.A.
127 K2 **Porus** Jamaica
133 C8 **Porvenir** Chile
108 C5 **Porvenir** Texas U.S.A.
29 M11 **Porvoo** Finland
36 C2 **Porz** W Germany
16 E5 **Porzuna** Spain
16 E5 **Porzuna, Sa. de** *mts* Spain
43 C8 **Posada** *R* Sardinia
133 F3 **Posadas** Argentina
16 D7 **Posadas** Spain
41 M5 **Poschiavo** Switzerland
94 D1 **Posen** Michigan U.S.A.
110 J3 **Poseyville** Indiana U.S.A.
52 E5 **Poshekhonye** U.S.S.R.
119 O1 **Poshkokagan L** Ontario Canada
46 F5 **Posidhion, Ákr** *C* Greece
41 O6 **Posina** *R* Italy
37 J5 **Pösing** W Germany
29 N5 **Posio** Finland
45 Q8 **Positano** Italy
70 G5 **Poso** Sulawesi
78 J1 **Posof** Turkey
129 J6 **Posse** Brazil
33 P9 **Posseck** East Germany
146 C12 **Possession Is** Antarctica
37 M2 **Pössneck** East Germany
21 J7 **Possonnière, la** France
38 M8 **Possruck** Yugoslavia
109 J3 **Possum Kingdom L** Texas U.S.A.
100 E5 **Post** Oregon U.S.A.
108 D3 **Post** Texas U.S.A.
37 N6 **Postau** W Germany
37 L5 **Postbauer-Heng** W Germany
8 C6 **Postbridge** England
115 M6 **Poste-de-la-Baleine** Quebec Canada
68 H6 **Poste Deshayes** Cambodia
Poste Maurice Cortier *see* **Bidon 5**
83 M12 **Poste, R du** Mauritius
85 E4 **Poste Weygand** Algeria
100 J2 **Post Falls** Idaho U.S.A.
71 J8 **Postiljon Pulau** *isld* Indonesia
89 C7 **Postmasburg** S Africa
129 H6 **Pôsto Alto Manissaua** Brazil
128 C4 **Posto Bobonazo** Peru
42 F3 **Postojna** Yugoslavia
99 P6 **Postville** Iowa U.S.A.
42 H5 **Posušje** Yugoslavia
71 K9 **Pota** Indonesia
124 D4 **Potam** Mexico
46 G3 **Potamoi** Greece
46 F8 **Potamós** Greece
47 O12 **Potamós** Greece
50 H2 **Potapovo** U.S.S.R.
128 G2 **Potaro** *R* Guyana
89 E6 **Potchefstroom** S Africa
48 J6 **Potcoava** Romania
130 H5 **Potê** Brazil
107 Q7 **Poteau** *R* Okla/Ark U.S.A.
107 Q6 **Poteau** Oklahoma U.S.A.
109 J6 **Poteet** Texas U.S.A.
130 J8 **Potengi** *R* Brazil
43 G8 **Potenza** Italy
144 A7 **Poteriteri, L** New Zealand
16 D1 **Potes** Spain
89 F5 **Potgietersrus** S Africa
109 J6 **Poth** Texas U.S.A.
100 F2 **Potholes Res** Washington U.S.A.
129 K5 **Poti** *R* Brazil
21 K4 **Potigny** France
85 G6 **Potiskum** Nigeria
71 K9 **Potjo Mandasawu** *mt* Indonesia
100 J3 **Potlatch** Idaho U.S.A.
89 B8 **Potloer** *mt* S Africa
48 K6 **Potlogi** Romania
101 M3 **Potomac** Montana U.S.A.
94 J7 **Potomac S. Branch** *R* West Virginia U.S.A.
133 D2 **Potosí** *dept* Bolivia
133 D1 **Potosí** Bolivia
110 F4 **Potosi** Missouri U.S.A.
103 J6 **Potosi Mt** Nevada U.S.A.
71 F5 **Pototan** Panay Philippines
133 D3 **Potrerillos** Chile
131 B2 **Potro, Cerro de** *pk* Chile
33 R7 **Potsdam** *reg* East Germany
33 S8 **Potsdam** East Germany
95 N2 **Potsdam** New York U.S.A.
37 L4 **Pottenstein** W Germany
120 K4 **Potter** Ontario Canada
98 C8 **Potter** Nebraska U.S.A.
9 E5 **Potterne** England
9 F4 **Potter's Bar** England
102 A2 **Potter Valley** California U.S.A.
94 C4 **Potterville** Michigan U.S.A.
37 L6 **Pöttmes** W Germany
9 F3 **Potton** England
109 L2 **Pottsboro** Texas U.S.A.
111 G7 **Potts Camp** Mississippi U.S.A.
95 M6 **Pottstown** Pennsylvania U.S.A.
95 L6 **Pottsville** Pennsylvania U.S.A.
109 J4 **Pottsville** Texas U.S.A.
83 L11 **Pottuvil** Sri Lanka
107 N4 **Potwin** Kansas U.S.A.
21 H6 **Pouancé** France
68 F3 **Pou Bia** *mt* Laos
117 N8 **Pouce Coupé** British Columbia Canada
123 U6 **Pouch Cove** Newfoundland Canada
21 J6 **Pouëze la** France
95 O5 **Poughkeepsie** New York U.S.A.
18 H5 **Pougues les Eaux** France
21 N7 **Pouillé** France
18 E9 **Pouillon** France
18 J5 **Pouilly en Auxois** France
21 O7 **Poulaines** France
20 B5 **Pouldergat** France
20 B6 **Pouldreuzic** France
20 C6 **Pouldu,le** France
21 N8 **Pouligny St. Pierre** France
20 F7 **Pouliguen,le** France
122 B5 **Poulin de Courval, L** Quebec Canada
20 C5 **Poulaouen** France
68 J5 **Poulo Canton, Is de** Vietnam
69 G8 **Poulo Dama, Iles** Vietnam
68 J6 **Poulo Gambir, Cu Lao** *isld* Vietnam
95 O3 **Poultney** Vermont U.S.A.
13 E6 **Poulton-le-Fylde** England
68 E4 **Pou Miang** *mt* Thailand
99 S4 **Pound** Wisconsin U.S.A.
9 F5 **Pound Hill** England
19 P18 **Pourcieux** France
145 F4 **Pourerere** New Zealand
145 G3 **Poureva I** New Zealand
40 E6 **Pourri, Mont** France
21 N2 **Pourville** France
68 F3 **Pou San** *mt* Laos
68 F3 **Pou Sao** *mt* Laos
68 H5 **Pou Set** *mt* Laos
129 G6 **Pouso Alegre** Mato Grosso Brazil
130 F8 **Pouso Alegre** Minas Gerais Brazil
29 O6 **Poussu** Finland
145 F4 **Poutama I** New Zealand
68 F6 **Pouthisat** Cambodia
145 E2 **Pouto** New Zealand
121 Q3 **Poutrincourt, L** Quebec Canada
40 D1 **Pouxeux** France
21 J8 **Pouzauges** France
21 M7 **Pouzay** France
48 E1 **Pov Bystrica** Czechoslovakia
52 D3 **Povenets** U.S.S.R.
145 F3 **Poverty Bay** New Zealand
9 F5 **Povey Cross** England
42 D4 **Poviglio** Italy
47 H6 **Povlen** *mt* Yugoslavia
16 B3 **Póvoa de Varzim** Portugal
65 J3 **Povorotnyy, Mys** *C* U.S.S.R.
115 M5 **Povungnituk** Quebec Canada
121 L6 **Powassan** Ontario Canada
101 T5 **Powder** *R* Wyo/Mont U.S.A.
106 C3 **Powderhorn** Colorado U.S.A.
100 H5 **Powder R** Oregon U.S.A.
98 A4 **Powderville** Montana U.S.A.
141 G7 **Powell** *R* Queensland Australia
103 K7 **Powell** Arizona U.S.A.
98 E5 **Powell** South Dakota U.S.A.
94 D10 **Powell** *R* Tenn/Virg U.S.A.
99 R3 **Powell** Wisconsin U.S.A.
101 R5 **Powell** Wyoming U.S.A.
100 D5 **Powell Butte** Oregon U.S.A.
113 K11 **Powell Cay** *isld* Bahamas
103 O4 **Powell, L** Ariz/Utah U.S.A.
106 D2 **Powell, Mt** Colorado U.S.A.
102 F3 **Powell Mt** Nevada U.S.A.
126 F2 **Powell Pt** Eleuthera Bahamas
117 L10 **Powell River** British Columbia Canada
94 F8 **Powellton** West Virginia U.S.A.
101 O2 **Power** Montana U.S.A.
99 T4 **Powers** Michigan U.S.A.
100 A7 **Powers** Oregon U.S.A.
98 D1 **Powers L** North Dakota U.S.A.
111 C10 **Powhatan** Louisiana U.S.A.
94 K9 **Powhatan** Virginia U.S.A.
107 P2 **Powhattan** Kansas U.S.A.
8 D3 **Powick** England
141 H5 **Powlathanga** Queensland Australia
95 O4 **Pownal** Vermont U.S.A.
8 C3 **Powys** *co* Wales
130 C5 **Poxoreu** *R* Brazil
67 E2 **Poyang Hu** *L* China
99 S5 **Poygan, L** Wisconsin U.S.A.
31 K7 **Poysdorf** Austria
124 C5 **Poza Grande** Mexico
78 E3 **Pozanti** Turkey
48 G6 **Požarevac** Yugoslavia
125 L7 **Poza Rica** Mexico
48 F7 **Požega** Yugoslavia
59 K2 **Pozharskoye** U.S.S.R.
52 J5 **Pozhva** U.S.S.R.
22 D3 **Pozières** France
140 D5 **Poziers,Mt** N Terr Australia
31 K3 **Poznań** Poland
102 D6 **Pozo** California U.S.A.
17 F7 **Pozo Alcón** Spain
133 D2 **Pozo Almonte** Chile
16 D6 **Pozoblanco** Spain
103 J9 **Pozo Cenizo** Mexico
17 F6 **Pozohondo** Spain
103 J9 **Pozo Salado** Mexico
103 N10 **Pozo Verde** Mexico
52 H4 **Poztykeros** U.S.S.R.
133 D2 **Pozuelos, L. de** Argentina
45 J1 **Pozzolengo** Italy
45 L1 **Pozzonovo** Italy
45 Q8 **Pozzuoli** Italy
68 F2 **P. Phac Mo** *mt* Vietnam
85 D7 **Pra** *R* Ghana
69 G14 **Prabumulih** Sumatra
31 L2 **Prabuty** Poland
45 J3 **Prachia** Italy
68 D7 **Prachan Hiang, Laem** Thailand
30 H7 **Prachatice** Czechoslovakia
68 E5 **Prachin Buri** Thailand
68 D7 **Prachuap Khiri Khan** Thailand
16 C1 **Pradairo** Spain
31 K5 **Praděd** *mt* Czechoslovakia
18 G10 **Prades** France
70 P9 **Pradjekan** Java
28 E2 **Præstbro** Denmark
Præsto *co see* **Storstrøm and Roskilde** *counties*
28 J6 **Præsto** Denmark
38 N9 **Pragersko** Yugoslavia
38 F7 **Prägraten** Austria
Prague *see* **Praha**
107 O6 **Prague** Oklahoma U.S.A.
31 H5 **Praha** Czechoslovakia
48 K6 **Prahova** *R* Romania
48 K5 **Prahova** Romania
48 H6 **Prahovo** Yugoslavia
85 B8 **Praia** Cape Verde
133 G4 **Praia Albardão** *beach* Brazil
48 J4 **Praid** Romania
129 H4 **Prainha** Brazil
122 B3 **Prairies, L. des** Quebec Canada
109 K6 **Prairia Lea** Texas U.S.A.
141 G5 **Prairie** Queensland Australia
100 K6 **Prairie** Idaho U.S.A.
110 F1 **Prairie City** Illinois U.S.A.
100 G5 **Prairie City** Oregon U.S.A.
107 K2 **Prairie Dog Cr** Kansas U.S.A.
108 F1 **Prairie Dog Town Fork** *R* Texas U.S.A.
99 P6 **Prairie du Chien** Wisconsin U.S.A.
99 R6 **Prairie du Sac** Wisconsin U.S.A.
110 B6 **Prairie Grove** Arkansas U.S.A.
109 L4 **Prairie Hill** Texas U.S.A.
119 P6 **Prairie River** Saskatchewan Canada
119 Q7 **Prairies, L of the** Manitoba/Sask Canada
110 J2 **Prairieton** Indiana U.S.A.
107 L2 **Prairie View** Kansas U.S.A.
111 F11 **Prairieville** Louisiana U.S.A.
94 E9 **Praise** Kentucky U.S.A.
68 F5 **Prakhon Chai** Thailand
40 E7 **Pralognan** France
42 E2 **Pramaggiore, Mont** *mt* Italy
70 N9 **Prambanan** Java
37 O3 **Prameny** Czechoslovakia
69 D8 **Pram, Khao** *mt* Thailand
68 D6 **Pran** *R* Thailand
68 D6 **Pran Buri** Thailand
38 K7 **Prankerhöhe** *mt* Austria
69 D11 **Prapat** Sumatra
40 B2 **Praslay** France
83 J12 **Praslin** *isld* Seychelles
47 Q15 **Prasonisi** *isld* Greece
47 J9 **Prasonisi, Akr** *C* Rhodes Greece
31 L4 **Praszka** Poland
129 J7 **Prata** *R* Brazil
Pratas *isld see* **Dongsha Qundao**
33 R9 **Pratau** East Germany
17 J3 **Prat de Llobregat** Spain
41 L4 **Prätigau** *V* Switzerland
45 K4 **Prato** Italy
45 R8 **Pràtola Serra** Italy
45 L4 **Pratomagno** Italy
42 D5 **Pratomagno** *mt* Italy
45 H3 **Prato, Mt** Italy
45 L4 **Pratovecchio** Italy
18 G10 **Prats-de-Mollo** France
119 T9 **Pratt** Manitoba Canada
107 M4 **Pratt** Kansas U.S.A.
95 N4 **Prattsville** New York U.S.A.
111 K9 **Prattville** Alabama U.S.A.
40 B2 **Prauthoy** France
31 N1 **Pravdinsk** U.S.S.R.
54 J1 **Pravdinskiy** U.S.S.R.
46 F2 **Pravets** Bulgaria
16 C1 **Pravia** Spain
8 C7 **Prawle Pt** England
70 Q10 **Praya** Indonesia
21 N7 **Préaux** France
37 O3 **Prebuz** Czechoslovakia
20 H4 **Precey** France
52 D6 **Prechistoye** U.S.S.R.
21 K6 **Précigné** France
21 P3 **Précy-sur-Oise** France
45 L3 **Predappio** Italy
42 D2 **Predazzo** Italy
37 O5 **Predigtstuhl** *mt* W Germany
38 M8 **Preding** Austria
38 J7 **Predlitz** Austria
38 F7 **Predoi** Italy
44 E2 **Predosa** Italy
51 O2 **Predporozhnyy** U.S.S.R.
119 P7 **Preeceville** Saskatchewan Canada
21 K5 **Pré-en-Pail** France
33 M4 **Preetz** W Germany
20 F7 **Préfailles** France
31 M1 **Pregolya** *R* U.S.S.R.
127 J10 **Pregonero** Venezuela
18 E8 **Preignac** France
52 C6 **Preili** U.S.S.R.
121 M4 **Preissac** Quebec Canada
68 G6 **Prek Kak** Cambodia
68 F6 **Prek Preas** *R* Cambodia
68 G7 **Prek Sandek** Cambodia
68 F7 **Prek Taley** *R* Cambodia
8 B3 **Pren-gwyn** Wales
46 D4 **Prenj** Yugoslavia
33 S6 **Prenzlau** East Germany
53 F3 **Preobrazheniye** U.S.S.R.
42 A3 **Pré-St.-Didier** Italy
144 A7 **Preservation Inlet** New Zealand
130 D8 **Presidente Prudente** Brazil
108 C6 **Presidio** Texas U.S.A.
95 T7 **Presque Isle** Maine U.S.A.
18 F6 **Pressac** France
8 C1 **Prestatyn** Wales
8 C3 **Presteigne** Wales
13 F6 **Preston** England
101 O7 **Preston** Idaho U.S.A.
95 M8 **Preston** Maryland U.S.A.
99 O6 **Preston** Minnesota U.S.A.
110 C4 **Preston** Missouri U.S.A.
103 J3 **Preston** Nevada U.S.A.
107 P6 **Preston** Oklahoma U.S.A.
13 F4 **Preston Candover** England
109 O9 **Preston Hollow** Texas U.S.A.
13 F2 **Prestonpans** Scotland
94 E9 **Prestonsburg** Kentucky U.S.A.
13 F6 **Prestwich** England
12 D3 **Prestwick** Scotland
129 K6 **Prêto** *R* Bahia Brazil
129 J7 **Prêto** *R* Minas Gerais Brazil
128 F4 **Prêto do Igapó Açu** *R* Brazil
89 F5 **Pretoria** S Africa
45 R6 **Pretoro** Italy
33 R9 **Prettin** East Germany
95 L8 **Prettyboy Res** Maryland U.S.A.
107 M4 **Pretty Prairie** Kansas U.S.A.
33 O7 **Pretzier** East Germany
33 R9 **Pretzsch** East Germany
21 M8 **Preuilly-sur-Claise** France
38 L8 **Prevalje** Yugoslavia
46 D6 **Préveza** Greece
106 B6 **Prewitt** New Mexico U.S.A.
106 G1 **Prewitt Res** Colorado U.S.A.
21 N4 **Prey** France
68 G7 **Prey Lovea** Cambodia
68 G7 **Prey Veng** Cambodia
45 P5 **Prezza** Italy
69 B10 **Priala** Sumatra
54 H9 **Priazovskaya Vozvyshennost'** *uplands* U.S.S.R.
116 D8 **Pribilof Is** Bering Sea
30 H6 **Příbram** Czechoslovakia
122 D5 **Price** Quebec Canada
95 M7 **Price** Maryland U.S.A.
98 F2 **Price** North Dakota U.S.A.
103 O2 **Price** *R* Utah U.S.A.
103 O2 **Price** Utah U.S.A.
68 A6 **Price, C** Andaman Is
106 B1 **Price Creek** Colorado U.S.A.
117 J9 **Price I** British Columbia Canada
111 H11 **Prichard** Alabama U.S.A.
100 K2 **Prichard** Idaho U.S.A.
54 E9 **Prichernomorskaya Nizmennost'** *lowland* U.S.S.R.
37 J4 **Prichsenstadt** W Germany
127 P5 **Prickly Pt** Grenada
109 J4 **Priddy** Texas U.S.A.
54 D7 **Pridneprovskaya Nizmennost'** *lowland* U.S.S.R.
54 C8 **Pridneprovskaya Vozvyshennost'** *uplands* U.S.S.R.
17 F4 **Priego** Spain
16 E7 **Priego de C** Spain
27 M15 **Priekule** Latviyskaya S.S.R. U.S.S.R.
27 M16 **Priekule** Litovskaya S.S.R. U.S.S.R.
33 Q5 **Priemerburg** East Germany
89 C7 **Prieska** S Africa
37 M1 **Priessnitz** East Germany
33 T10 **Priestewitz** East Germany
100 J1 **Priest L** Idaho U.S.A.
127 M2 **Priestman's River** Jamaica
100 F3 **Priest Rapids** Washington U.S.A.
100 E3 **Priest Rapids Lake** *res* Washington U.S.A.
100 J1 **Priest River** Idaho U.S.A.
117 P11 **Priest River** Idaho U.S.A.
31 L7 **Prievidza** Czechoslovakia
33 Q6 **Prignitz** *reg* East Germany
56 C4 **Priiskovyy** U.S.S.R.
42 H4 **Prijedor** Yugoslavia
53 G9 **Prikaspiyskaya Nizmennost** *lowlands* U.S.S.R.
46 E3 **Prilep** Yugoslavia
54 D6 **Priluki** U.S.S.R.
40 B7 **Primarette** France
118 H6 **Primate** Saskatchewan Canada
37 O4 **Přimda** Czechoslovakia
20 C4 **Primel,Pte.de** France
20 C4 **Primel-Trégastel** France
126 E4 **Primero de Enero** Cuba
131 D3 **Primero, R** Argentina
139 J8 **Prime Seal I** Tasmania Australia
99 L6 **Primghar** Iowa U.S.A.
53 E10 **Primorsk** *B* U.S.S.R.
52 C4 **Primorsk** U.S.S.R.
53 F9 **Primorskiy** U.S.S.R.
56 F5 **Primorskiy Khrebet** *mts* U.S.S.R.
59 K2 **Primorskiy Kray** *reg* U.S.S.R.
47 J2 **Primorsko** Bulgaria
53 E9 **Primorskoye** U.S.S.R.
48 N5 **Primorskoye** *Ukraine* U.S.S.R.
48 M5 **Primorskoye** *Ukraine* U.S.S.R.
122 J7 **Prim, Pt** Prince Edward I Canada
117 F5 **Primrose** *R* Br Col/Yukon Terr Canada
118 H4 **Primrose L** Saskatchewan Canada
36 B5 **Prims** *R* W Germany
36 C4 **Primstal** W Germany
118 J6 **Prince** Saskatchewan Canada
119 M5 **Prince Albert** Saskatchewan Canada
89 C9 **Prince Albert** S Africa
146 D11 **Prince Albert Mts** Antarctica
118 L5 **Prince Albert Nat. Park** Saskatchewan Canada
114 H3 **Prince Albert Pen** Northwest Territories Canada
114 G3 **Prince Alfred, C** Northwest Territories Canada
115 M4 **Prince Charles I** Northwest Territories Canada
146 H10 **Prince Charles Mts** Antarctica
121 O9 **Prince Edward B** Ontario Canada
122 J7 **Prince Edward I** *prov* Canada
90 M14 **Prince Edward I** Indian Oc
122 J7 **Prince Edward I. Nat. Park** Canada
95 L8 **Prince Frederick** Maryland U.S.A.
142 F3 **Prince Frederick Harb** Western Australia Australia
117 M9 **Prince George** British Columbia Canada
114 J2 **Prince Gustaf Adolf Sea** Northwest Territories Canada
116 C4 **Prince of Wales, C** Alaska U.S.A.
141 F1 **Prince of Wales I** Queensland Australia
114 J3 **Prince of Wales I** Northwest Territories Canada
117 G8 **Prince of Wales I** Alaska U.S.A.
114 H3 **Prince of Wales Str** Northwest Territories Canada
114 H2 **Prince Patrick I** Northwest Territories Canada
115 K3 **Prince Regent Inlet** Northwest Territories Canada
142 F3 **Prince Regent R** Western Australia Australia
117 H8 **Prince Rupert** British Columbia Canada
130 H9 **Princesa Isabel** Brazil
Princes Is *see* **Kizil Adalar**
Princess Lake Ontario *see* **Wallace**
9 F4 **Princes Risborough** England
95 M8 **Princess Anne** Maryland U.S.A.
141 G2 **Princess Charlotte B** Queensland Australia
146 H12 **Princess Elizabeth Land** Antarctica
142 F3 **Princess May Ra** Western Australia Australia
144 A6 **Princess Mts** New Zealand
143 D7 **Princess Ra** Western Australia Australia
117 J9 **Princess Royal I** British Columbia Canada
127 O3 **Prince's Town** Trinidad
9 E3 **Princethorpe** England
117 N11 **Princeton** British Columbia Canada
102 B2 **Princeton** California U.S.A.
99 R8 **Princeton** Illinois U.S.A.
110 J3 **Princeton** Indiana U.S.A.
110 J4 **Princeton** Kentucky U.S.A.
95 U1 **Princeton** Maine U.S.A.
99 T3 **Princeton** Michigan U.S.A.
99 N4 **Princeton** Minnesota U.S.A.
99 N9 **Princeton** Missouri U.S.A.
95 N6 **Princeton** New Jersey U.S.A.
112 J2 **Princeton** North Carolina U.S.A.
94 F9 **Princeton** West Virginia U.S.A.
99 R6 **Princeton** Wisconsin U.S.A.
8 C6 **Princetown** England
121 T6 **Princeville** Quebec Canada
99 R9 **Princeville** Illinois U.S.A.
116 O6 **Prince William Sound** Alaska U.S.A.
86 A5 **Principe** *isld* G of Guinea
128 F6 **Principe da Beira** Brazil
100 E5 **Prineville** Oregon U.S.A.
98 C6 **Pringle** South Dakota U.S.A.
108 C8 **Pringle** Texas U.S.A.
19 Q13 **Pringy** France
115 P5 **Prins Christian Sund** Greenland
25 C5 **Prinsenhage** Netherlands
68 C6 **Prinsep I** Burma
146 H7 **Prinsesse Astrid Kyst** *coast* Antarctica
146 J7 **Prinsesse Ragnhild Kyst** *coast* Antarctica
146 J8 **Prins Harald Kyst** *coast* Antarctica
50 A1 **Prins Karls Forland** Spitzbergen
123 L4 **Prinsta B** Anticosti I, Quebec
125 N3 **Prinzapolca** Nicaragua
54 L2 **Priokskiy** U.S.S.R.
16 B1 **Prior, C** Spain
52 D4 **Priozersk** U.S.S.R.
52 K3 **Pripolyarnyy Ural** *mts* U.S.S.R.
53 C8 **Pripyat** *R* U.S.S.R.
29 P3 **Prirechnyy** U.S.S.R.
37 P3 **Přísečnice** Czechoslovakia
48 J3 **Prislop Pass** Romania
46 E4 **Prispansko ezero** *L* Yugoslavia
46 E2 **Priština** Yugoslavia
106 H4 **Pritchett** Colorado U.S.A.
33 Q6 **Pritzerbe** East Germany
33 Q6 **Pritzier** East Germany
33 Q6 **Pritzwalk** East Germany
19 N15 **Privas** France
45 O7 **Priverno** Italy
45 O6 **Privernum** Italy
42 F3 **Privka** Yugoslavia
52 F6 **Privolzhsk** U.S.S.R.
53 G7 **Privolzhskaya Vozvyshennost** *uplands* U.S.S.R.
53 G7 **Privolzh'ye** U.S.S.R.
20 D5 **Priziac** France
46 D2 **Prizren** Yugoslavia
43 E11 **Prizzi** Sicily
48 K1 **Probezhnaya** U.S.S.R.
70 O9 **Probolinggo** Java
37 L2 **Probstzella** East Germany
8 B7 **Probus** England
31 J4 **Prochowice** Poland
43 F8 **Procida** *isld* Italy
45 Q8 **Procida** Italy
106 H1 **Proctor** Colorado U.S.A.
109 J4 **Proctor** Texas U.S.A.
95 O3 **Proctor** Vermont U.S.A.
109 J3 **Proctor Res** Texas U.S.A.
95 P3 **Proctorsville** Vermont U.S.A.
16 B5 **Proênca a Nova** Portugal
37 N1 **Profen** East Germany
22 H3 **Profondeville** Belgium
125 L2 **Progreso** Honduras
125 P7 **Progreso** Mexico
59 J2 **Progress** U.S.S.R.
106 E7 **Progresso** New Mexico U.S.A.
56 B6 **Prokhladnoye** U.S.S.R.
55 G2 **Prokhorkino** U.S.S.R.
54 H5 **Prokhorovka** U.S.S.R.
46 D2 **Prokletije** Yugoslavia
56 C4 **Prokop'yevsk** U.S.S.R.
46 E1 **Prokuplje** Yugoslavia
52 D5 **Proletariy** U.S.S.R.
54 K8 **Proletarsk** U.S.S.R.
53 F10 **Proletarsk** U.S.S.R.
56 G6 **Proletarskiy** U.S.S.R.
54 J1 **Proletarskiy** U.S.S.R.
59 N2 **Proliv Frizi** *str* U.S.S.R.
50 E1 **Proliv Matochkin Shar** U.S.S.R.
37 K4 **Prolsdorf** W Germany
68 B3 **Prome** Burma
99 N9 **Promise City** Iowa U.S.A.
101 N8 **Promontory** Utah U.S.A.
56 C3 **Promyshlennaya** U.S.S.R.
53 G10 **Promyslovka** U.S.S.R.
52 F5 **Pronino** U.S.S.R.
100 G9 **Pronto** Nevada U.S.A.
54 M2 **Pronya** *R* U.S.S.R.
117 M6 **Prophet River** British Columbia Canada
99 R8 **Prophetstown** Illinois U.S.A.
130 H11 **Propriá** Brazil
33 S10 **Prösen** East Germany
141 J5 **Proserpine** Queensland Australia
33 Q9 **Prosigk** East Germany
31 K3 **Prosna** *R* Poland
52 H5 **Prosnitsa** U.S.S.R.
46 F3 **Prosotsáni** Greece
95 M3 **Prospect** New York U.S.A.
94 D6 **Prospect** Ohio U.S.A.
100 C7 **Prospect** Oregon U.S.A.
94 G6 **Prospect** Pennsylvania U.S.A.
127 M3 **Prospect Pt** Jamaica
100 A6 **Prosper** Oregon U.S.A.
112 F3 **Prosperity** South Carolina U.S.A.
98 H9 **Prosser** Nebraska U.S.A.
100 F3 **Prosser** Washington U.S.A.
31 K6 **Prostějov** Czechoslovakia
141 K7 **Proston** Queensland Australia
52 H2 **Prosunduy** U.S.S.R.
54 H8 **Prosyanaya** U.S.S.R.
31 M5 **Proszowice** Poland
107 L4 **Protection** Kansas U.S.A.
99 O6 **Protivin** Iowa U.S.A.
54 J2 **Protva** *R* U.S.S.R.
33 T7 **Prötzel** East Germany
47 H1 **Provadiya** Bulgaria
115 O3 **Prøven** Greenland
111 C10 **Provencal** Louisiana U.S.A.
19 O17 **Provence** *prov* France
36 C7 **Provenchères-sur-Fave** France
127 P5 **Providence** Grenada
110 J4 **Providence** Kentucky U.S.A.
112 J1 **Providence** North Carolina U.S.A.
95 Q5 **Providence** Rhode I U.S.A.
101 O8 **Providence** Utah U.S.A.
120 H7 **Providence Bay** Ontario Canada
144 A7 **Providence, C** New Zealand
116 J8 **Providence, C** Alaska U.S.A.
87 J9 **Providence I** Br Indian Oc Terr
103 J7 **Providence Mts** California U.S.A.
127 H4 **Providenciales** *isld* Turks & Caicos Is
128 F6 **Providencia, Sa. da** *mts* Brazil
116 A4 **Provideniya** U.S.S.R.
141 G2 **Providential Chan** Gt Barrier Reef Aust
95 R4 **Provincetown** Massachusetts U.S.A.
18 H4 **Provins** France
98 C6 **Provo** South Dakota U.S.A.
103 N1 **Provo** Utah U.S.A.
118 G6 **Provost** Alberta Canada
22 D4 **Proyart** France
42 H5 **Prozor** Yugoslavia
130 E9 **Prudentópolis** Brazil
94 C2 **Prudenville** Michigan U.S.A.
116 N1 **Prudhoe Bay** Alaska U.S.A.
141 J5 **Prudhoe I** Queensland Australia
115 N2 **Prudhoe Land** Greenland

Prud'homme — Radevormwald
69

119 M6 Prud'homme Saskatchewan Canada
31 K5 Prudnik Poland
54 H6 Prudyanka U.S.S.R.
36 B3 Prüm W Germany
21 M6 Prunay France
21 O5 Prunay-le-Gillon France
45 J3 Prunetta Italy
19 Q15 Prunières France
21 P8 Pruniers Indre France
21 O7 Pruniers Loir-et-Cher France
52 H4 Prupt R U.S.S.R.
31 K2 Pruszcz Poland
31 M3 Pruszków Poland
48 L4 Prut R U.S.S.R.
48 L3 Prutul R Romania
41 N3 Prutz Austria
52 D4 Pryazha U.S.S.R.
31 L6 Prýdek Místek Czechoslovakia
146 J11 Prydz B Antarctica
101 R4 Pryor Montana U.S.A.
107 P5 Pryor Oklahoma U.S.A.
31 M2 Przasnysz Poland
31 K2 Przechlewo Poland
31 M4 Przedbórz Poland
31 O6 Przemyśl Poland
31 N5 Przeworsk Poland
31 H4 Przewóz Poland
57 J4 Przheval'sk U.S.S.R.
31 M4 Przysucha Poland
46 F6 Psakhná Greece
47 H6 Psará isld Greece
46 G5 Psathoúra isld Greece
31 K4 Psie Pole Poland
47 R14 Psíndhos Rhodes Greece
47 H9 Psira isld Greece
52 C5 Pskov U.S.S.R.
52 C5 Pskovskaya Oblast' prov U.S.S.R.
52 C5 Pskovskoye, Ozero L U.S.S.R.
42 H3 Psunj mt Yugoslavia
31 L1 Pszczółki Poland
31 L6 Pszczyna Poland
53 C7 Ptich' R U.S.S.R.
46 E4 Ptolemais Greece
38 N9 Ptuj Yugoslavia
135 U4 Puako Hawaiian Is
116 K8 Puale B Alaska U.S.A.
133 E5 Puán Argentina
67 C5 Pubei China
122 G10 Pubnico Nova Scotia Canada
128 C5 Pucacaca Peru
128 D5 Pucallpa Peru
21 O3 Puchay France
38 N6 Puchberg Austria
67 F3 Pucheng China
65 C7 Pucheng China
65 A7 Pucheng China
52 F6 Puchezh U.S.S.R.
31 L6 Puchov Czechoslovakia
71 E5 Pucio Pt Panay Philippines
31 L1 Puck Poland
99 R6 Puckaway L Wisconsin U.S.A.
9 G4 Puckeridge England
111 G9 Puckett Mississippi U.S.A.
143 B7 Puckford,Mt Western Australia Australia
29 M6 Pudasjärvi Finland
8 D6 Puddletown England
52 H5 Pudem U.S.S.R.
70 E6 Pudi Kalimantan
67 B3 Puding China
123 Q5 Pudops L Newfoundland Canada
52 E4 Pudozh U.S.S.R.
52 E4 Pudozhgora U.S.S.R.
13 G6 Pudsey England
125 K8 Puebla Mexico
16 D5 Puebla de Alcocer Spain
17 F7 Puebla de Don Fadrique Spain
16 D5 Puebla de Don Rodrigo Spain
16 C2 Puebla de Sanabria Spain
16 C2 Puebla de Trives Spain
106 F3 Pueblo Colorado U.S.A.
106 C5 Pueblo Bonito New Mexico U.S.A.
133 C3 Pueblo Hundido Chile
100 G7 Pueblo Mts Oregon U.S.A.
124 G6 Pueblo Nuevo Mexico
125 N9 Pueblo Viejo Mexico
125 L6 Pueblo Viejo, L. de Mexico
133 D5 Puelches Argentina
133 D5 Puelén Argentina
16 B2 Puenteareas Spain
16 B2 Puente-Caldelas Spain
16 D7 Puente Genil Spain
103 P7 Puerco R Arizona U.S.A.
106 C6 Puerco, R New Mexico U.S.A.
128 C2 Puerta Mutis Colombia
133 C7 Puerto Aisén Chile
125 N5 Puerto Armuelles Panama
128 C3 Puerto Asis Colombia
128 E2 Puerto Ayacucho Venezuela
125 P10 Puerto Barrios Guatemala
128 D6 Puerto Bermúdez Peru
128 D2 Puerto Berrio Colombia
133 C7 Puerto Bertrand Chile
128 C6 Puerto Caballas Peru
128 E1 Puerto Cabello Venezuela
125 N2 Puerto Cabezas Nicaragua
Puerto Capaz Morocco see Jebha
128 E2 Puerto Carreño Colombia
130 B8 Puerto Casado Paraguay
128 C5 Puerto Chicama Peru
133 C6 Puerto Cisnes Chile
133 D8 Puerto Coig Argentina
128 D1 Puerto Colombia Colombia
125 Q10 Puerto Cortés Honduras
128 E1 Puerto Cumarebo Venezuela
125 L10 Puerto Escondido Mexico
127 J8 Puerto Estrella Colombia
128 C5 Puerto Eten Peru
133 C5 Puerto Fuy Chile
128 F7 Puerto Grether Bolivia
133 D8 Puerto Harberton Argentina
128 E6 Puerto Heath Bolivia
128 D3 Puerto Huitoto Colombia
133 E5 Puerto Ingeniero White Argentina
125 Q7 Puerto Juárez Mexico
127 M9 Puerto La Cruz Venezuela
128 D4 Puerto Leguizamo Colombia
125 N2 Puerto Lempira Honduras
16 E6 Puertollano Spain
128 D7 Puerto Lomas Peru
127 J9 Puerto López Colombia
17 F7 Puerto Lumbreras Spain
133 D6 Puerto Madryn Argentina
128 E6 Puerto Maldonado Peru
126 F4 Puerto Manatí Cuba
128 D4 Puerto Miraña Colombia
133 C6 Puerto Montt Chile
133 C8 Puerto Natales Chile
128 E2 Puerto Nuevo Colombia
133 F3 Puerto Ocampo Argentina
128 F2 Puerto Ordaz Venezuela
126 F4 Puerto Padre Cuba
133 C2 Puerto Patillos Chile
124 C2 Puerto Penasco Mexico
133 F2 Puerto Pinasco Paraguay
133 E6 Puerto Pirámides Argentina
128 F1 Puerto Piritu Venezuela
127 J5 Puerto Plata Dominican Rep
128 D5 Puerto Portillo Peru
130 C9 Puerto Presidente Stroessner Paraguay
71 D6 Puerto Princesa Palawan Philippines
125 M5 Puerto Quepos Costa Rica
128 E6 Puerto Rico Bolivia
113 J7 Puerto Rico terr Caribbean
127 L5 Puerto Rico Trench Caribbean
126 G4 Puerto Samá Cuba
125 L3 Puerto Sandino Nicaragua
130 B8 Puerto Sastre Paraguay
128 E6 Puerto Siles Bolivia
130 B6 Puerto Suárez Bolivia
124 G7 Puerto Vallarta Mexico
133 C6 Puerto Varas Chile
128 F7 Puerto Velarde Bolivia
128 D5 Puerto Victoria Peru
128 D2 Puerto Villamizar Colombia
133 D7 Puerto Visser Argentina
128 D2 Puerto Wilches Colombia
133 C7 Pueyrredón, L Chile/Arg
25 F7 Puffendorf W Germany
124 G7 Puga Mexico
52 H6 Pugachevo U.S.S.R.
74 E4 Pugal India
88 G10 Puga Puga isld Mozambique
100 C2 Puget Sound Washington U.S.A.
19 P13 Pugieu France
43 G8 Puglia prov Italy
71 K9 Pugubengo Flores Indonesia
70 K8 Pugung, G mt Sumatra
122 J8 Pugwash Nova Scotia Canada
145 F3 Puha New Zealand
135 O1 Puhi Hawaiian Is
145 E2 Puhoi New Zealand
48 H5 Pui Romania
48 L4 Puiești Romania
17 J2 Puigcerda Spain
71 G7 Pujada B Mindanao Philippines
65 G4 Pujan Res N Korea
19 N16 Pujaut France
67 A1 Pujiang China
67 F2 Pujiang China
119 Q3 Pukatawagan Manitoba Canada
46 D2 Pukë Albania
145 G2 Pukeamaru mt New Zealand
145 E3 Pukearuhe New Zealand
145 F3 Pukehou New Zealand
145 E2 Pukekawa New Zealand
145 E2 Pukekohe New Zealand
144 C5 Pukekura New Zealand
145 E2 Pukemiro New Zealand
145 D1 Pukenui New Zealand
145 F3 Pukeokahu New Zealand
144 C6 Pukerangi New Zealand
144 B7 Pukerau New Zealand
145 E3 Pukeroa New Zealand
145 G3 Puketawai New Zealand
144 D5 Puketeraki Range New Zealand
145 F3 Puketitiri New Zealand
145 F2 Puketoetoe mt New Zealand
145 F4 Puketoi Range New Zealand
145 E3 Puketutu New Zealand
145 F2 Puketutu I New Zealand
144 C6 Pukeuri Junction New Zealand
29 M11 Pukkila Finland
67 F1 Pukou China
52 F3 Puksa U.S.S.R.
52 H5 Puksib U.S.S.R.
52 F3 Puksoozero U.S.S.R.
98 G6 Pukwana South Dakota U.S.A.
42 F4 Pula Yugoslavia
128 E8 Pulacayo Bolivia
43 C9 Pula, C. di Sardinia
69 C11 Pulaksama Sumatra
Pulandian see Xinjin
71 G6 Pulangi R Mindanao Philippines
70 D6 Pulangpisau Kalimantan
70 K8 Pulao Seribu isld Sumatra
70 K9 Pulasari mt Java
71 K8 Pulasi isld Indonesia
99 O9 Pulaski Iowa U.S.A.
95 L3 Pulaski New York U.S.A.
110 J6 Pulaski Tennessee U.S.A.
94 G9 Pulaski Virginia U.S.A.
99 S5 Pulaski Wisconsin U.S.A.
69 F13 Pulaukidjang Sumatra
70 B4 Pulaumadjang Kalimantan
69 E13 Pulaupunjung Sumatra
31 N4 Puławy Poland
9 F6 Pulborough England
76 D3 Pulivendla India
76 C6 Puliyangudi India
83 K9 Puliyankulam Sri Lanka
29 M7 Pulkkila Finland
100 H3 Pullman Washington U.S.A.
71 E2 Pulog, Mt Luzon Philippines
83 K8 Puloli Sri Lanka
52 F2 Pulonga U.S.S.R.
52 D1 Pulozero U.S.S.R.
124 D4 Púlpito, Pta C Mexico
33 T10 Pulsnitz R East Germany
31 M3 Pułtusk Poland
66 C4 Pulu China
70 P10 Pulukan Bali Indonesia
66 E6 Puma Yumco L China
Pumiao see Yongning
98 A4 Pumpkin Cr Montana U.S.A.
98 C8 Pumpkin Cr Nebraska U.S.A.
108 F6 Pumpville Texas U.S.A.
8 C3 Pumsaint Wales
128 B4 Puná isld Ecuador
70 G5 Puna R Sulawesi
144 C5 Punakaiki New Zealand
83 L10 Punani Sri Lanka
74 F2 Punch Kashmir
117 M9 Punchaw British Columbia Canada
52 F4 Punduga U.S.S.R.
76 A1 Pune India
55 D1 Punga R U.S.S.R.
112 L2 Pungo North Carolina U.S.A.
59 J3 Pungsan N Korea
86 E6 Punia Zaire
70 Q10 Punikan, G mt Indonesia
131 B2 Punilla, Sa. de la mts Chile
74 F3 Punjab prov India
74 D3 Punjab, The prov Pakistan
140 E4 Punjaub Queensland Australia
29 O10 Punkaharju Finland
29 K10 Punkalaidun Finland
119 N7 Punnichy Saskatchewan Canada
128 D6 Puno dept Peru
128 D7 Puno Peru
106 D7 Punta New Mexico U.S.A.
131 E7 Punta Alta Argentina
133 C8 Punta Arenas Chile
43 C7 Puntaccia, Monte mt Sardinia
133 C3 Punta Colorada Chile
108 B8 Punta de Agua Cr. R Texas/New Mex U.S.A.
17 H4 Punta de la Baña Spain
125 P9 Punta Gorda Belize
125 N4 Punta Gorda Nicaragua
100 A9 Punta Gorda California U.S.A.
113 E11 Punta Gorda Florida U.S.A.
131 G6 Punta Norte Argentina
127 J5 Punta Palenque Dominican Rep
124 B3 Punta Prieta Mexico
125 M5 Puntarenas Costa Rica
128 G8 Punta Rieles Paraguay
125 N5 Punta San Pedrillo Costa Rica
127 M5 Punta Tuna Puerto Rico
128 D1 Punto Fijo Venezuela
46 G4 Punto Lágo Greece
133 D7 Puntudo, Cerro mt Argentina
116 C5 Punuk Is Bering Sea
94 J6 Punxsutawney Pennsylvania U.S.A.
68 F6 Puok Cambodia
29 N7 Puolanka Finland
26 L5 Puottaure Sweden
128 E6 Puoya mt Bolivia
145 D4 Puponga New Zealand
58 F6 Puqi China
128 D6 Puquio Peru
133 D3 Puquios Chile
50 G2 Pur R U.S.S.R.
128 C3 Puracé vol Colombia
70 M9 Purbalingga Java
107 N7 Purcell Oklahoma U.S.A.
116 J3 Purcell Mt Alaska U.S.A.
117 P10 Purcell Mts British Columbia Canada
100 K1 Purcell Range Montana U.S.A.
94 K7 Purcellville Virginia U.S.A.
17 F7 Purchena Spain
99 N10 Purdin Missouri U.S.A.
98 F7 Purdum Nebraska U.S.A.
110 C5 Purdy Missouri U.S.A.
145 E3 Pureora mt New Zealand
124 H8 Purépero Mexico
145 E1 Purerua New Zealand
9 E6 Purewell England
106 G4 Purgatoire R Colorado U.S.A.
116 N3 Purgatory Alaska U.S.A.
38 M5 Purgstall Austria
75 L9 Puri India
128 D3 Purificación Colombia
145 E2 Puriri New Zealand
9 F5 Purley England
25 C3 Purmerend Netherlands
74 G9 Purna India
138 B2 Purndu Saltpan South Australia Australia
52 E3 Purnema U.S.S.R.
75 M6 Pūrnia India
118 F9 Purple Springs Alberta Canada
128 E4 Purué R Brazil
70 D5 Purukcahu Kalimantan
128 F4 Purus R Brazil
29 O10 Puruvesi L Finland
111 G10 Purvis Mississippi U.S.A.
46 G2 Pŭrvomay Bulgaria
70 L9 Purwakarta Java
70 M9 Purwarejo Java
70 N9 Purwodadi Java
70 M9 Purwokerto Java
110 H5 Puryear Tennessee U.S.A.
66 B4 Pusa China
70 B4 Pusa Sarawak
52 C6 Puša U.S.S.R.
74 G9 Pusad India
52 B6 Pušalotas U.S.S.R.
65 H7 Pusan S Korea
71 G7 Pusan Pt Mindanao Philippines
70 B4 Pusatdamai Kalimantan
79 D2 Pusatlı Dağı mt Turkey
65 D6 Pushang China
95 T2 Pushaw L Maine U.S.A.
52 D5 Pushkin U.S.S.R.
54 J1 Pushkino U.S.S.R.
52 E3 Pushlakhta U.S.S.R.
123 Q6 Pushthrough Newfoundland Canada
77 H4 Pusht-i-Rud reg Afghanistan
120 E4 Puskaskwa Nat. Park Ontario Canada
121 O3 Puskitamika L Quebec Canada
48 G3 Püspökladány Hungary
21 O5 Pussay France
22 H4 Pussemange Belgium
38 K7 Pusterwald Austria
52 C6 Pustoshka U.S.S.R.
102 B3 Putah Cr California U.S.A.
67 G5 Pu-tai Taiwan
71 M9 Putain Timor Indonesia
21 K4 Putanges-Pont-Ecrepin France
75 R5 Putao Burma
145 E3 Putaruru New Zealand
30 G1 Putbus East Germany
70 P9 Puteran isld Indonesia
83 K8 Puthukkudiyiruppu Sri Lanka
67 F4 Putian China
43 H8 Putignano Italy
48 J3 Putila U.S.S.R.
52 F5 Putilovo U.S.S.R.
70 B6 Puting Tg C Kalimantan
54 E5 Putivl' U.S.S.R.
33 Q8 Putlitz East Germany
48 K3 Putna Romania
95 Q5 Putnam Connecticut U.S.A.
108 E3 Putnam Oklahoma U.S.A.
109 H3 Putnam Texas U.S.A.
112 C6 Putney Georgia U.S.A.
98 H4 Putney South Dakota U.S.A.
95 P4 Putney Vermont U.S.A.
51 J2 Putorana, Plato mt U.S.S.R.
145 F3 Putorino New Zealand
83 J9 Puttalam Sri Lanka
83 J9 Puttalam Lag Sri Lanka
22 G1 Putte Belgium
36 B5 Puttelange France
33 O5 Püttelkow East Germany
25 E4 Putten Netherlands
28 G7 Puttgarden W Germany
36 B5 Püttlingen W Germany
128 C3 Putumayo div Colombia
128 D4 Putumayo R Peru/Colombia
67 G2 Putuo China
67 G1 Putuo Shan isld China
70 C4 Putusibau Kalimantan
33 T5 Putzar East Germany
135 U5 Puuanahulu Hawaiian Is
135 U5 Puu Hualalei crater Hawaiian Is
135 S3 Puukoli Hawaiian Is
29 M10 Puulavesi L Finland
29 N10 Puumala Finland
22 G1 Puurs Belgium
135 N1 Puuwai Hawaiian Is
Puxian see Pucheng
65 A6 Pu Xian China
117 M12 Puyallup Washington U.S.A.
65 C7 Puyang China
18 G7 Puy de Dôme dept France
18 G7 Puy-de-Sancy mt France
131 A8 Puyehue, L de Chile
131 B8 Puyehue, P. de Argentina
131 A8 Puyehue, V Chile
21 M8 Puye, La France
19 Q14 Puy Gris mt France
18 G9 Puylaurens France
18 H7 Puy, le France
18 F8 Puy l'Evêque France
18 G7 Puy Mary mt France
21 K7 Puy Notre Dame, le France
21 N2 Puys France
52 H4 Puzla U.S.S.R.
88 G5 Pwani prov Tanzania
88 B6 Pweto Zaire
68 B2 Pwinbyu Burma
8 B2 Pwllheli Wales
52 E2 Pyalitsa U.S.S.R.
52 E4 Pyal'ma U.S.S.R.
68 B3 Pyalo Burma
68 B5 Pyamalaw R Burma
52 F6 Pyana R U.S.S.R.
57 E6 Pyandzh Tadzhikskaya S.S.R. U.S.S.R.
57 E6 Pyandzh R U.S.S.R./Afghanistan
52 J4 Pyanteg U.S.S.R.
52 D2 Pyaozero, Oz L U.S.S.R.
76 C3 Pyapalli India
68 B4 Pyapon Burma
51 H1 Pyasina R U.S.S.R.
53 F11 Pyatigorsk U.S.S.R.
54 E8 Pyatikhatki U.S.S.R.
52 H4 Pyatiqory U.S.S.R.
110 D5 Pyatt Arkansas U.S.A.
52 H6 Pychas U.S.S.R.
116 M7 Pye Is Alaska U.S.A.
29 M9 Pyhä-Häki Nat. Park Finland
29 M8 Pyhäjärvi Finland
27 M11 Pyhajärvi L Finland
29 L7 Pyhäjoki Finland
29 M7 Pyhäntä Finland
29 J11 Pyhäranta Finland
29 O9 Pyhäselkä Finland
29 M4 Pyhätunturi Nat. Park Finland
38 N5 Pyhra Austria
68 C3 Pyinmana Burma
8 C4 Pyle Wales
29 L9 Pylkönmäki Finland
94 G5 Pymatuning Res Ohio/Penn U.S.A.
69 A9 Pymgalion Pt Nicobar Is
59 J3 Pyöktong N Korea
65 F5 Pyöngyang N Korea
100 F9 Pyramid Nevada U.S.A.
103 K6 Pyramid Canyon Ariz/Nev U.S.A.
139 G6 Pyramid Hill Victoria Australia
106 C1 Pyramid Pk Colorado U.S.A.
94 A2 Pyramid Pt Michigan U.S.A.
102 E2 Pyramid Rge Nevada U.S.A.
18 F9 Pyrénées mts France/Spain
18 E9 Pyrénées Atlantiques dept France
18 G10 Pyrénées-Orientales dept France
142 B5 Pyrton,Mt Western Australia Australia
31 H2 Pyrzyce Poland
52 G5 Pyshchug U.S.S.R.
55 D3 Pyshma U.S.S.R.
52 C6 Pytalovo U.S.S.R.
121 O6 Pythonga, L Quebec Canada
68 C3 Pyu R Burma
68 C3 Pyu Burma
68 C4 Pyuntaza Burma
31 K3 Pyzdry Poland

Q

84 E3 Qaddāhiyah, Al Libya
74 F3 Qadian India
80 G4 Qafqafa Jordan
58 G2 Qagan China
Qagan Nur see Zhengxiangbai Qi
65 C3 Qagan Nur L China
65 B3 Qagan Nur China
65 B4 Qagan Nur L China
65 F2 Qagan Nur L China
65 D1 Qagan Qulut China
65 D3 Qagan Us China
65 B4 Qahar Youyi Houqi China
65 B4 Qahar Youyi Qianqi China
65 B4 Qahar Youyi Zhongqi China
Qâhira, El see Cairo
66 E4 Qaidam Pendi reg China
66 F4 Qaidam Shan mts China
77 J4 Qala Bist Afghanistan
86 G3 Qala'en Nahl Sudan
77 J3 Qala-i-Ghor Afghanistan
77 H3 Qala-i-Kāl Afghanistan
77 K3 Qalāt Afghanistan
79 G4 Qal 'at al Hisn Syria
79 F3 Qal'at al Marqab Syria
78 H4 Qal'at as Salihīyah Syria
80 F4 Qal'at er Rabad Jordan
78 L6 Qal'at Sālih Iraq
77 J4 Qal'eh-ye Bost Afghanistan
77 H2 Qal'eh-ye Now Afghanistan
80 C5 Qalqiliya Israel
80 E6 Qalya Jordan
79 B8 Qalyûb Egypt
80 G3 Qam Jordan
74 C5 Qambar Pakistan
66 F5 Qamdo reg China
84 F3 Qaminis Libya
78 H3 Qāmishlī, Al Syria
74 C3 Qamruddin Karez Pakistan
80 D5 Qana Jordan
86 A1 Qandala Somalia
65 C3 Qangdin Gol China
65 C3 Qangdin Sum China
79 C8 Qanṭara, El Egypt
79 G6 Qanwāt, Al Syria
Qaqortoq see Julianehåb
84 H4 Qara Egypt
79 F5 Qaraaoun Lebanon
77 L2 Qarah Bāgh Afghanistan
80 D5 Qarawat Bani Ḥassan Jordan
79 G3 Qardāhah, Al Syria
86 A2 Qardho Somalia
78 L2 Qareh Su R Iran
79 C10 Qarn el Kabsh, G mt Egypt
66 D4 Qarqan He R China
79 F4 Qartaba Lebanon
84 E3 Qaryāt, Al Libya
79 H4 Qaryatayn, Al Syria
80 G7 Qaryat Falha Jordan
77 H2 Qasa Murg Afghanistan
Qasigiannguit see Christianshåb
80 F8 Qasr Jordan
79 H4 Qasr al Ḥayr Syria
79 F8 Qasr ed Deir, J mt Jordan
84 H4 Qasr, El Egypt
78 K4 Qasr-e-Shirin Iran
80 G8 Qasr eth Thuraiya Jordan
84 H4 Qasr Farâfra Egypt
115 P5 Qassimiut Greenland
79 G5 Qatana Syria
77 B7 Qatar state Persian Gulf
77 B6 Qatīf, Al Saudi Arabia
79 G7 Qatrāna Jordan
84 E5 Qaṭrūn, Al Libya
84 H4 Qattara Depression Egypt
77 F3 Qāyen Iran
78 J4 Qayyarah Iraq
77 A1 Qazvīn Iran
84 J4 Qena Egypt
Qeqertarsuaq see Godhavn
77 E6 Qeshm Iran
77 A1 Qeydār Iran
77 C6 Qeys isld Iran
77 A1 Qezel Owzan R Iran
79 E8 Qeẕi'ot Israel
65 D4 Qian'an China
65 F2 Qian'an China
67 C3 Qiancheng China
65 F2 Qian Gorlos China
67 C3 Qiangu'ao China
Qianguozhen see Qian Gorlos
65 D7 Qiangwei He R China
67 C2 Qianjiang R China
67 D1 Qianjiang China
67 C5 Qianjiang China
59 K2 Qianjin China
67 E1 Qianshan China
66 E3 Qianshan China
65 F4 Qian Shan mt ra China
65 E4 Qianwei China
67 A2 Qianwei China
67 B3 Qianxi China
65 D4 Qianxi China
67 A4 Qianxinan China
67 C3 Qianyang China
67 E3 Qiaotou China
65 D3 Qiaotou China
67 E1 Qichun China
67 D3 Qidong China
67 G1 Qidong China
66 D4 Qiemo China
67 C2 Qifeng Guan pass China
65 C6 Qihe China
65 B3 Qihreg China
58 E6 Qijiang China
66 E3 Qijiaojing China
Qike see Xunke
65 D5 Qikou China
77 H6 Qila Lādgasht Pakistan
65 D4 Qilaotu Shan mt ra China
74 A8 Qila Safed Pakistan
74 C3 Qila Saifullah Pakistan
Qili see Shitai
66 F4 Qilian Shan mt ra China
65 E4 Qilihe China
67 F2 Qimen China
65 G1 Qing'an China
65 D6 Qingcheng China
65 E6 Qingdao China
65 E5 Qingduizi China
65 C7 Qingfeng China
67 A2 Qingfu China
65 G1 Qinggang China
Qinggil see Qinghe
65 C7 Qingguji China
66 E4 Qinghai prov China
58 D4 Qinghai Hu L China
65 C6 Qinghe China
66 E2 Qinghe China
65 H1 Qinghe China
65 F4 Qinghecheng China
65 E4 Qinghemen China
65 F3 Qinghe Shuiku res China
67 F2 Qinghu China
65 A6 Qingjian China
67 C1 Qing Jiang R China
67 E2 Qingjiang China
65 A6 Qingjian He R China
Qingkou see Ganyu
67 C7 Qinglan China
67 D7 Qinglan Gang inlet China
67 D4 Qinglian China
67 E3 Qingliu China
67 B4 Qinglong China
65 D4 Qinglong China
65 D4 Qinglong He R China
65 C6 Qingping China
68 J2 Qingping China
67 G1 Qingpu China
67 A2 Qingshen China
65 B5 Qingshuihe China
58 E4 Qingshui He R China
67 C3 Qingshui Jiang R China
67 G2 Qingtian China
65 C5 Qing Xian China
65 B6 Qingxu China
Qingyang see Jinjiang
67 F1 Qingyang China
58 E4 Qingyang China
Qingyuan see Yishan
59 J3 Qingyuan China
67 F3 Qingyuan China
67 D5 Qingyuan China
65 D6 Qingyun China
65 B7 Qin He R China
65 D5 Qinhuangdao China
67 C6 Qin Jiang R China
58 E5 Qin Ling mt ra China
65 B7 Qinshui China
67 C5 Qintang China
58 F4 Qin Xian China
58 F4 Qinyang China
67 G3 Qinyu China
65 B6 Qinyuan China
67 C6 Qinzhou China
68 J2 Qinzhou Wan B China
68 K3 Qionghai China
58 D5 Qionglai China
58 D5 Qionglai Shan mt ra China
68 K3 Qiongshan China
67 C7 Qiongzhong China
Qiongzhou see Qiongshan
68 J2 Qiongzhou Haixia China
67 B1 Qiping China
59 H2 Qiqihar China
77 C5 Qīr Iran
80 D7 Qiryat Arba' Jordan
80 D2 Qiryat Ata Israel
80 D2 Qiryat Bialik Israel
80 C7 Qiryat Gat Israel
80 D2 Qiryat Motmkin Israel
80 F1 Qiryat Shemona Israel
80 D3 Qiryat Tiv'on Israel
80 D2 Qiryat Yam Israel
80 D6 Qiryat Yearim Israel
67 C6 Qisha China
80 D3 Qishon 'Eneq Yizre'el Israel
68 J2 Qishui China
66 D3 Qitai China
65 H2 Qitaihe China
67 A4 Qiubei China
65 C6 Qiu Xian China
65 E6 Qixia China
65 B6 Qi Xian China
65 C7 Qi Xian China
65 B4 Qixiaying China
65 J1 Qixing He R China
65 H1 Qixingpao China
67 D3 Qiyang China
67 E1 Qizhou China
65 C2 Qog Ul China
Qogur Feng mt see K2 mt
77 B2 Qom Iran
77 B3 Qomishēh Iran
Qomolangma Feng mt see Everest, Mt
66 D3 Qongkol China
115 O5 Qoornoq Greenland
77 A2 Qorveh Iran
79 G4 Qoubaiyat Lebanon
95 P4 Quabbin Res Massachusetts U.S.A.
122 G8 Quaco Hd New Brunswick Canada
74 D2 Quaidabad Pakistan
102 H6 Quail Mts California U.S.A.
143 B9 Quairading Western Australia Australia
32 G7 Quakenbrück W Germany
95 M6 Quakertown Pennsylvania U.S.A.
45 Q8 Qualiano Italy
85 E6 Quallam Niger
139 G6 Quambatook Victoria Australia
139 J4 Quambone New South Wales Australia
140 F5 Quamby Queensland Australia
108 H1 Quanah Texas U.S.A.
128 F4 Quanaru, Ilha Brazil
68 H2 Quan Dao Co To isld Vietnam
68 J5 Quang Nam Vietnam
68 J5 Quang Ngai Vietnam
68 H4 Quang Tri Vietnam
67 B6 Quang Yen Vietnam
67 F1 Quanjiao China
69 G8 Quan Long Vietnam
67 E4 Quannan China
68 F7 Quan Phu Quoc isld Vietnam
94 K8 Quantico Virginia U.S.A.
120 E1 Quantz L Ontario Canada
67 C4 Quanzhou China
119 O8 Qu'Appelle Saskatchewan Canada
119 P8 Qu'Appelle R Saskatchewan Canada
118 L7 Qu'Appelle R. Dam Saskatchewan Canada
133 F4 Quarai Brazil
131 G3 Quarai, R Brazil
32 L4 Quarnbek W Germany
122 G7 Quarryville New Brunswick Canada
95 L7 Quarryville Pennsylvania U.S.A.
40 F6 Quart Italy
45 L2 Quartesana Italy
45 N6 Quartière Mt. Sacro Italy
83 M12 Quartier Militaire Mauritius
43 C9 Quartu Sant'Elena Sardinia
102 H4 Quartzite Mt Nevada U.S.A.
102 G2 Quartz Mt Nevada U.S.A.
100 G1 Quartz Mt Washington U.S.A.
103 K8 Quartzsite Arizona U.S.A.
99 P7 Quasqueton Iowa U.S.A.
22 G2 Quatre Bras Belgium
22 H5 Quatre-Champs France
117 K10 Quatsino British Columbia Canada
45 H2 Quattro Castella Italy
106 G7 Quay New Mexico U.S.A.
77 F1 Qūchān Iran
101 P8 Quealy Wyoming U.S.A.
139 J6 Queanbeyan New South Wales Australia
115 M7 Quebec prov Canada
121 T6 Québec Quebec Canada
130 F6 Quebra Anzol R Brazil
88 D9 Quebrabasa Rapids Mozambique
133 E3 Quebracho Coto Argentina
131 A8 Quedal, C. de Chile
33 O9 Quedlinburg East Germany
17 G9 Qued Tlélat Algeria
95 L8 Queen Anne Maryland U.S.A.
117 L10 Queen Bess, Mt British Columbia Canada
9 G5 Queenborough England
115 M5 Queen, C Northwest Territories Canada
133 E8 Queen Charlotte B Falkland Is
117 G9 Queen Charlotte Is British Columbia Canada
117 J10 Queen Charlotte Sd British Columbia Canada
145 E4 Queen Charlotte Sound New Zealand
117 K10 Queen Charlotte Str British Columbia Canada
99 O9 Queen City Missouri U.S.A.
109 N2 Queen City Texas U.S.A.
115 K2 Queen Elizabeth Is Northwest Territories Canada
146 H12 Queen Mary Land Antarctica
117 D5 Queen Mary, Mt Yukon Territory Canada
114 J4 Queen Maud Gulf Northwest Territories Canada
146 D9 Queen Maud Mts Antarctica
13 G6 Queensbury England
140 A2 Queens Chan N Terr Australia
115 K2 Queens Chan Northwest Territories Canada
139 G7 Queenscliff Victoria Australia
13 E2 Queensferry Scotland
140 F6 Queensland state Australia
142 B2 Queens Park dist Perth, W Aust Australia
123 L8 Queensport Nova Scotia Canada
139 H8 Queenstown Tasmania Australia
118 E8 Queenstown Alberta Canada
144 B6 Queenstown New Zealand
89 E8 Queenstown S Africa
95 L8 Queenstown Maryland U.S.A.
100 A2 Queets Washington U.S.A.
131 F4 Queguay Grande R Uruguay
36 E5 Queich R W Germany
16 C2 Queija, S. de mts Spain
129 L6 Queimadas Brazil
87 C7 Quela Angola
21 J6 Quelaines France
87 B7 Quele Angola
88 F10 Quelimane Mozambique
124 F6 Quelite Mexico
133 C6 Quellen Chile
106 B7 Quemado New Mexico U.S.A.
108 G7 Quemado Texas U.S.A.
20 B5 Quéménéven France
Quemoy see Chin-men
133 E5 Quemu Quemu Argentina
22 B3 Quend France
9 G4 Quendon England
22 B3 Quend Plage France
107 P3 Quenemo Kansas U.S.A.
111 F10 Quentin Mississippi U.S.A.
Que Que see Kwekwe
133 F5 Quequén Argentina
22 C2 Quercamps France
130 D8 Querência do Norte Brazil
125 J7 Querétaro Mexico
33 P10 Querfurt East Germany
124 D2 Querobabi Mexico
20 G2 Querqueville France
20 C6 Querrien France
21 P2 Querrieu France
117 M9 Quesnel British Columbia Canada
117 N9 Quesnel L British Columbia Canada
22 D4 Quesnoy France
22 F3 Quesnoy, le France
22 E2 Quesnoy-sur-Deule, le France
20 E5 Quessoy France
106 E5 Questa New Mexico U.S.A.
20 F6 Questembert France
133 D2 Quetena Bolivia
99 Q1 Quetico Ontario Canada
118 L2 Quetico L Ontario Canada
99 P1 Quetico Provincial Park Ontario Canada
74 B3 Quetta Pakistan
20 H2 Quettehou France
21 L3 Quetteville France
20 H4 Quettreville France
111 D11 Queue de Tortue R Louisiana U.S.A.
21 O4 Queue-lèz-Yvelines,la France
21 P2 Quevauvillers France
121 O3 Quévillon Quebec Canada
125 O10 Quezaltenango Guatemala
71 C6 Quezon Palawan Philippines
71 E3 Quezon City Luzon Philippines
65 D7 Qufu China
87 B8 Quibala Angola
87 B7 Quibate Angola
128 C2 Quibdó Colombia
118 J1 Quibell Ontario Canada
20 D7 Quiberon France
20 D6 Quiberon,B.de France
21 M2 Quiberville France
127 K10 Quíbor Venezuela
87 B7 Quicama Nat. Park Angola
68 G3 Qui Chau Vietnam
32 L5 Quickborn W Germany
36 C5 Quierschied W Germany
117 G5 Quiet L Yukon Territory Canada
22 F3 Quievrain Belgium
22 E3 Quiévy France
118 G2 Quigley Alberta Canada
133 F3 Quiindy Paraguay
103 M9 Quijotoa Arizona U.S.A.
124 F5 Quilá Mexico
133 C6 Quilán, C Chile
16 E9 Quilates, C Morocco
128 D7 Quilca Peru
100 C2 Quilcene Washington U.S.A.
87 B8 Quilengues Angola
133 E4 Quilino Argentina
128 D6 Quillabamba Peru
128 E7 Quillacollo Bolivia
18 G10 Quillan France
21 M3 Quillebeuf France
131 B7 Quillén, L Argentina
119 N6 Quill Lake Saskatchewan Canada
131 B4 Quillota Chile
119 N7 Quillsks L Saskatchewan Canada
20 G7 Quilly France
141 G7 Quilpie Queensland Australia
87 C8 Quimbango Angola
20 B5 Quimerch France
20 B6 Quimper France
20 C6 Quimperlé France
71 F3 Quinabucasan Pt Philippines
71 F4 Quinalasag isld Philippines
100 B2 Quinault Washington U.S.A.
100 A2 Quinault R Washington U.S.A.
21 N2 Quincampoix France
21 L8 Quinçay France
128 D6 Quince Mil Peru
102 D2 Quincy California U.S.A.
111 M11 Quincy Florida U.S.A.
99 P10 Quincy Illinois U.S.A.
95 R4 Quincy Massachusetts U.S.A.
110 N1 Quincy Ohio U.S.A.
100 B3 Quincy Oregon U.S.A.
100 F2 Quincy Washington U.S.A.
20 H2 Quineville France
68 F2 Quinh Nhai Vietnam
128 E3 Quinigua, Cerro mts Venezuela
71 E5 Quiniluban isld Philippines
109 L3 Quinlan Texas U.S.A.
98 D6 Quinn South Dakota U.S.A.
103 J4 Quinn Canyon Ra Nevada U.S.A.
100 G8 Quinn River Crossing Nevada U.S.A.
19 Q17 Quinson France
16 E5 Quintanar de la Orden Spain
125 P8 Quintana Roo terr Mexico
107 K2 Quinter Kansas U.S.A.
20 E5 Quintin France
131 D5 Quinto R Argentina
17 G3 Quinto Spain
119 N7 Quinton Saskatchewan Canada
107 P6 Quinton Oklahoma U.S.A.
45 L1 Quinto Vicentino Italy
8 A7 Quintrel Downs England
94 G8 Quinwood West Virginia U.S.A.
88 H7 Quionga Mozambique
130 J10 Quipapá Brazil
87 B8 Quipungo Angola
15 B3 Quirang Scotland
87 C8 Quirima Angola
139 K4 Quirindi New South Wales Australia
131 A6 Quiriquina isld Chile
127 N10 Quiriquire Venezuela
120 H6 Quirke L Ontario Canada
36 C5 Quirnbach W Germany
16 C2 Quiroga Spain
123 R2 Quirpon Newfoundland Canada
123 R2 Quirpon I Newfoundland Canada
88 H8 Quissanga Mozambique
87 F10 Quissico Mozambique
45 J1 Quistello Italy
20 D6 Quistinic France
87 C8 Quitapa Angola
126 D7 Quita Sueño Bank Caribbean
130 D6 Quitéria R Brazil
110 D6 Quitman Arkansas U.S.A.
113 D7 Quitman Georgia U.S.A.
109 P3 Quitman Louisiana U.S.A.
111 H9 Quitman Mississippi U.S.A.
109 M3 Quitman Texas U.S.A.
128 C4 Quito Ecuador
103 M10 Quitovac Mexico
21 N3 Quittebeuf France
103 M6 Quivero Arizona U.S.A.
128 C5 Quivilla Peru
129 L4 Quixadá Brazil
67 D4 Qujiang China
67 B1 Qu Jiang R China
67 C6 Qujie China
67 A4 Qujing China
46 D3 Qukës-Shkumbin Albania
80 G6 Quleib R Jordan
66 E4 Qumar He R China
58 C5 Qumarlêb China
89 F8 Qumbu S Africa
80 G1 Qunayṭirah, El Syria
84 G4 Qunayyin, S. al Libya
72 E5 Qunfudhah, Al Saudi Arabia
66 D5 Qungtag China
143 A6 Quobba,Pt Western Australia Australia
83 M12 Quoin Channel Mauritius
140 A2 Quoin I N Terr Australia
141 K6 Quoin I Queensland Australia
89 A10 Quoin Pt S Africa
138 E4 Quorn South Australia Australia
119 N1 Quorn Ontario Canada
80 G6 Qureiyat Nafi Jordan
80 G6 Qureiyat Salim Jordan
129 J4 Qurem Brazil
84 J4 Qus Egypt
80 G1 Quṣaybah Syria
84 J4 Quseir Egypt
77 G6 Quṣr-e-Qand Iran
67 C1 Qutang Xia Wu Xia China
87 E12 Quthing Lesotho
79 H2 Quwayq R Syria
79 B8 Quweisna Egypt
65 B7 Quwo China
58 E4 Quwu Shan mt ra China
67 A5 Quxi China
Qu Xian see Quzhou
67 B1 Qu Xian China
75 O4 Qüxü China
67 E3 Quyang China
65 C5 Quyang China
67 B7 Quynh Luu Vietnam
68 J6 Quy Nhon Vietnam
121 O7 Quyon Quebec Canada
65 C6 Quzhou China
67 F2 Quzhou China

R

29 K5 Rå Sweden
27 F16 Råå Sweden
Raab see Györ
31 J7 Raabs Austria
38 N7 Raab Tal V Austria
29 L7 Raahe Finland
138 F5 Raak Plain Victoria Australia
29 O9 Rääl-kylä Finland
25 F4 Raalte Netherlands
115 L2 Raanes Pen Northwest Territories Canada
29 L5 Raanujärvi Finland
70 P9 Raas isld Indonesia
77 A5 Ra'as Al Khafji Saudi Arabia
15 B3 Raasay, Sd of Scotland
42 F4 Rab isld Yugoslavia
48 D3 Rába R Hungary
71 J9 Raba Sumbawa Indonesia
80 E4 Raba Jordan
48 F1 Raba R Poland
16 C3 Rabaçal R Portugal
18 F9 Rabastens de Bigorre Hautes-Pyrénées France
85 C2 Rabat Morocco
137 L2 Rabaul New Britain
Rabbah see 'Ammān
117 K6 Rabbit R British Columbia Canada
98 D4 Rabbit Cr South Dakota U.S.A.
106 D1 Rabbit Ears Pass Colorado U.S.A.
145 D4 Rabbit I New Zealand
118 K5 Rabbit Lake Saskatchewan Canada
117 N5 Rabbitskin R Northwest Territories Canada
28 D7 Rabel W Germany
36 F2 Rabenau W Germany
77 E5 Rābor Iran
52 F6 Rabotki U.S.S.R.
37 P3 Rabštejn Czechoslovakia
112 D3 Rabun, L Georgia U.S.A.
84 G5 Rabyānah well Libya
84 G5 Rabyānah, Ramlat sands Libya
46 D1 Rača Yugoslavia
44 C2 Racconigi Italy
99 M8 Raccoon R Iowa U.S.A.
126 G3 Raccoon Cay Bahamas
94 E8 Raccoon Cr Ohio U.S.A.
38 N9 Rače Yugoslavia
123 T7 Race, C Newfoundland Canada
94 E8 Raceland Kentucky U.S.A.
111 F12 Raceland Louisiana U.S.A.
113 E7 Race Pond Florida U.S.A.
95 R4 Race Pt Massachusetts U.S.A.
100 B1 Race Rocks British Columbia Canada
101 N3 Race Track Montana U.S.A.
80 E1 Rachaf Lebanon
79 F5 Rachaiya Lebanon
109 J9 Rachal Texas U.S.A.
69 D9 Racha Noi, Ko isld Thailand
69 D9 Racha Yai, Ko isld Thailand
68 G8 Rach Gia Vietnam
31 L5 Racibórz Poland
37 P3 Račic Czechoslovakia
94 F8 Racine Ohio U.S.A.
99 T7 Racine Wisconsin U.S.A.
122 D1 Racine-de-Bouleau, R Quebec Canada
120 G4 Racine L Ontario Canada
33 Q10 Rackwitz East Germany
37 O4 Racovský mt Czechoslovakia
46 E1 Radan mt Yugoslavia
48 K3 Rădăuți Romania
37 P4 Radbuza R Czechoslovakia
110 L4 Radcliff Kentucky U.S.A.
13 F6 Radcliffe England
99 N7 Radcliffe Iowa U.S.A.
27 E12 Råde Norway
30 H4 Radeberg East Germany
37 Q1 Radebeul East Germany
33 T10 Radeburg East Germany
19 Q18 Rade d'Hyères B France
33 Q9 Radegast East Germany
38 M8 Radel Pass Austria
36 C1 Radevormwald W Germany

94 G9 **Radford** Virginia U.S.A.
140 B1 **Radford Pt** N Terr Australia
74 D7 **Radhanpur** India
118 K6 **Radisson** Saskatchewan Canada
99 P4 **Radisson** Wisconsin U.S.A.
101 T10 **Radium** Colorado U.S.A.
98 K1 **Radium** Minnesota U.S.A.
37 N3 **Radiumbad-Brambach** East Germany
138 F4 **Radium Hill** *pk* South Australia Australia
117 P10 **Radium Hot Springs** British Columbia Canada
106 D9 **Radium Springs** New Mexico U.S.A.
70 O9 **Radja, I** Indonesia
77 F1 **Rādkān** Iran
Radldorf *see* **Bergstorf**
38 L6 **Radmer-an-dem-Hasel** Austria
47 H2 **Radnevo** Bulgaria
30 H6 **Radnice** Czechoslovakia
Radnor *co see* **Powys**
41 J2 **Radolfzell** W Germany
31 N4 **Radom** Poland
86 D4 **Radom** Sudan
46 F2 **Radomir** Bulgaria
31 L4 **Radomsko** Poland
37 P3 **Radonice** Czechoslovakia
31 K7 **Radošina** Czechoslovakia
31 M4 **Radoszyce** Poland
46 E3 **Radoviš** Yugoslavia
54 L1 **Radovitskiy** U.S.S.R.
42 F2 **Radovljica** Yugoslavia
38 H7 **Radstadt** Austria
8 D5 **Radstock** England
38 L9 **Raduha** *mt* Yugoslavia
42 H5 **Radusa** *mt* Yugoslavia
52 B6 **Radviliškis** U.S.S.R.
119 N9 **Radville** Saskatchewan Canada
118 E4 **Radway** Alberta Canada
31 O6 **Radymno** Poland
31 M3 **Radzanów** Poland
31 L3 **Radziejów** Poland
31 N3 **Radzymin** Poland
31 O4 **Radzyń Podlaski** Poland
117 P4 **Rae** Northwest Territories Canada
75 J5 **Rae Bareli** India
112 H3 **Raeford** North Carolina U.S.A.
115 L4 **Rae Isthmus** Northwest Territories Canada
114 H5 **Rae L** Northwest Territories Canada
118 B8 **Rae, Mt** British Columbia Canada
22 L2 **Raeren** Belgium
32 E9 **Raesfeld** W Germany
143 D8 **Raeside, L** Western Australia Australia
115 K4 **Rae Str** Northwest Territories Canada
145 D1 **Raetea** *mt* New Zealand
145 E3 **Raetihi** New Zealand
131 E3 **Rafaela** Argentina
79 E7 **Rafah** Egypt
86 D5 **Rafai** Cent Afr Republic
53 C8 **Rafalovka** U.S.S.R.
80 D5 **Rafat** Jordan
17 G5 **Rafelbûnol** Spain
78 J7 **Rafḥā'** Saudi Arabia
77 E4 **Rafsanjān** Iran
101 M7 **Raft** *R* Idaho U.S.A.
119 Q3 **Rafter** Manitoba Canada
101 M8 **Raft R. Mts** Utah U.S.A.
26 H3 **Raftsund** Norway
86 E4 **Raga** Sudan
71 G7 **Ragang, Mt** Philippines
71 F4 **Ragay G** Philippines
28 J4 **Rågeleje** Denmark
33 R6 **Rägelin** East Germany
126 G3 **Ragged I** Bahamas
143 E10 **Ragged,Mt** Western Australia Australia
127 P6 **Ragged Pt** Barbados
145 E2 **Raglan** New Zealand
8 D4 **Raglan** Wales
111 K8 **Ragland** Alabama U.S.A.
108 D1 **Ragland** New Mexico U.S.A.
145 D4 **Raglan Range** New Zealand
107 M4 **Rago** Kansas U.S.A.
44 G2 **Ragola Monte** Italy
33 R8 **Ragösen** East Germany
28 G7 **Rågø Sund** *chan* Denmark
33 Q9 **Raguhn** East Germany
26 H8 **Ragunda** Sweden
Ragusa *see* **Dubrovnik**
43 F12 **Ragusa** Sicily
71 H7 **Raha** Indonesia
86 G3 **Rahad** *R* Sudan
86 D3 **Rahad el Berdi** Sudan
Rahaeng *see* **Tak**
80 E8 **Rahaf** Israel
27 J11 **Råhällan** Sweden
32 J8 **Rahden** W Germany
86 E2 **Rahib** Sudan
80 D8 **Rahiya** Jordan
145 D3 **Raholu** New Zealand
74 F9 **Rahuri** India
16 B6 **Raia** *R* Portugal
45 P5 **Raiano** Italy
Raibu *see* **Air**
76 C2 **Raichur** India
71 K10 **Raidjua** *isld* Indonesia
75 K8 **Raigarh** India
102 G2 **Railroad Pass** Nevada U.S.A.
103 J3 **Railroad Valley** Nevada U.S.A.
37 N6 **Rain** W Germany
37 K6 **Rain** W Germany
37 J6 **Rainau** W Germany
138 F6 **Rainbow** Victoria Australia
103 O4 **Rainbow Br. Nat. Mon** Utah U.S.A.
124 E9 **Rainbow City** Panama
111 K8 **Rainbow City** Alabama U.S.A.
141 G1 **Raine I** Gt Barrier Reef Aust
9 G4 **Rainham** England
100 C3 **Rainier** Oregon U.S.A.
100 C3 **Rainier** Washington U.S.A.
100 D3 **Rainier, Mt** Washington U.S.A.
100 B5 **Rainrock** Oregon U.S.A.
94 J7 **Rainsburg** Pennsylvania U.S.A.
94 C1 **Rainy** *R* Michigan U.S.A.
99 M1 **Rainy** *R* Minnesota U.S.A.
118 J2 **Rainy L** Minnesota/Ontario U.S.A./Canada
99 N1 **Rainy Lake** Ontario Canada
100 E1 **Rainy Pass** Washington U.S.A.
116 L5 **Rainy Pass Lodge** Alaska U.S.A.
118 H2 **Rainy R** Ontario Canada
99 M1 **Rainy River** Ontario Canada
29 J8 **Raippaluoto** *isld* Finland
75 J8 **Raipur** India
74 G7 **Raisen** India
27 M11 **Raisio** Finland
22 E3 **Raismes** France
29 N5 **Raistakka** Finland
119 O2 **Raith** Ontario Canada
68 A1 **Raithaw** Burma
145 D4 **Rai Valley** New Zealand
70 F4 **Raja** Kalimantan
70 C5 **Raja, Bt** *mt* Kalimantan
70 B5 **Raja, Bt** *mt* Kalimantan
76 E2 **Rajahmundry** India
76 D3 **Rajampet** India
70 B3 **Rajang** Sarawak
74 D4 **Rajanpur** Pakistan
76 C6 **Rajapalaiyam** India
74 D5 **Rajasthan** *prov* India
69 C11 **Raja, Ujung** *C* Sumatra
46 D2 **Rajë** Albania
75 L6 **Rajgir** India
31 O2 **Rajgród** Poland
80 F5 **Rajib** *R* Jordan
80 F5 **Rajib** Jordan
69 G14 **Rajik** Bangka Indonesia
75 J8 **Rajim** India
42 F4 **Rajinac** *mt* Yugoslavia
74 D7 **Rajkot** India
75 J8 **Raj Nandgaon** India
74 E8 **Rajpipla** India
75 N6 **Rajshahi** Bangladesh
76 D1 **Rajura** India
88 C2 **Rakai** Uganda
144 D5 **Rakaia** New Zealand
Rakata *isld see* **Krakatau** *isld*
145 F3 **Rakauroa** New Zealand
99 N6 **Rake** Iowa U.S.A.
144 A7 **Rakeahua** *mt* New Zealand
56 C6 **Rakhmanoviskoye** U.S.S.R.
56 C6 **Rakhmanovskiye Klyuchi** U.S.S.R.
48 J2 **Rakhov** U.S.S.R.
77 J6 **Rakhshan** *R* Pakistan
145 E2 **Rakino I** New Zealand
26 L3 **Rakisvaara** *mt* Sweden
70 M8 **Rakit** *isld* Indonesia
71 C7 **Rakit** Sabah
46 G3 **Rakitovo** Bulgaria
145 E2 **Rakitu I** New Zealand
55 C5 **Rakityanka** U.S.S.R.
Raki-ura *isld see* **Stewart I**
27 E12 **Rakkestad** Norway
69 D8 **Ra, Ko** *isld* Thailand
31 J3 **Rakoniewice** Poland
87 D10 **Rakops** Botswana
30 H5 **Rakovník** Czechoslovakia
46 G2 **Rakovski** Bulgaria
33 S4 **Rakow** East Germany
52 F3 **Rakula** U.S.S.R.
52 G4 **Rakulka** U.S.S.R.
52 B5 **Rakvere** Estonskaya S.S.R. U.S.S.R.
111 G9 **Raleigh** Mississippi U.S.A.
112 J2 **Raleigh** North Carolina U.S.A.
98 E3 **Raleigh** North Dakota U.S.A.
112 L3 **Raleigh B** North Carolina U.S.A.
101 M1 **Raley** Alberta Canada
70 F7 **Ralla** Sulawesi
108 F2 **Ralls** Texas U.S.A.
99 T3 **Ralph** Michigan U.S.A.
98 C4 **Ralph** South Dakota U.S.A.
107 O5 **Ralston** Oklahoma U.S.A.
95 L5 **Ralston** Pennsylvania U.S.A.
100 G3 **Ralston** Washington U.S.A.
101 R5 **Ralston** Wyoming U.S.A.
117 M5 **Ram** *R* Northwest Territories Canada
79 F9 **Ram** Jordan
119 P7 **Rama** Saskatchewan Canada
80 D4 **Rāma** Jordan
125 M3 **Rama** Nicaragua
78 J5 **Ramādi, Ar** Iraq
106 F2 **Ramah** Colorado U.S.A.
106 B6 **Ramah** New Mexico U.S.A.
16 E1 **Ramales de la Victoria** Spain
129 K6 **Ramalho, Sa. do** *mts* Brazil
133 E4 **Ramalio** Argentina
80 D6 **Ramallah** Jordan
76 D6 **Ramanathapuram** India
75 K8 **Rāmapur** India
89 E3 **Ramaquabane** *R* Zimbabwe
54 E4 **Ramasukha** U.S.S.R.
80 C5 **Ramatayim** Israel
80 C5 **Ramat Gan** Israel
80 C5 **Ramat Ha Kovesh** Israel
80 C5 **Ramat Ha Sharon** Israel
80 D3 **Ramat HaShofet** Israel
80 D2 **Ramat Yohanan** Israel
83 K10 **Rambe** Sri Lanka
36 E5 **Ramberg** W Germany
36 B7 **Rambervillers** France
83 K9 **Rambewa** Sri Lanka
127 J2 **Ramble** Jamaica
133 D4 **Ramblon** Argentina
21 O4 **Rambouillet** France
33 P6 **Rambow** East Germany
76 B3 **Ramdurg** India
123 P6 **Ramea** Newfoundland Canada
139 J7 **Rame Hd** Victoria Australia
52 E6 **Ramenskoye** U.S.S.R.
111 K9 **Ramer** Alabama U.S.A.
52 E6 **Rameshki** U.S.S.R.
83 J8 **Rameswaram** India
75 L7 **Ramgarh** India
77 A4 **Rāmhormoz** Iran
44 B2 **Ramière, Punta** *mt* Italy/France
22 H2 **Ramillies-Offus** Belgium
140 D1 **Ramingining** N Terr Australia
109 K10 **Ramírez** Mexico
109 J8 **Ramirez** Texas U.S.A.
109 J9 **Ramirito** Texas U.S.A.
86 H4 **Ramīs** *R* Ethiopia
80 E1 **Râmîye** Lebanon
27 G14 **Ramkvilla** Sweden
80 C6 **Ramla** Israel
80 C6 **Ramle** Israel
28 J4 **Ramløse** Denmark
27 G11 **Rämmen** Sweden
75 K6 **Ramnagar** India
27 H12 **Ramnäs** Sweden
89 E3 **Ramokgwebana** Botswana
80 E3 **Ram On** Israel
54 L5 **Ramon'** U.S.S.R.
102 H8 **Ramona** California U.S.A.
94 B3 **Ramona** Michigan U.S.A.
107 P5 **Ramona** Oklahoma U.S.A.
98 J5 **Ramona** South Dakota U.S.A.
120 K4 **Ramore** Ontario Canada
124 G5 **Ramos** Mexico
71 C6 **Ramos** *isld* Philippines
80 F1 **Ramot Naftali** Israel
87 E10 **Ramotsua** Botswana
116 M4 **Rampart** Alaska U.S.A.
116 R3 **Rampart House** Yukon Territory Canada
13 E5 **Rampside** England
74 H4 **Rampur** India
74 F6 **Rampura** India
68 A3 **Ramree** Burma
142 F4 **Ramsay Ra** Western Australia Australia
32 H10 **Ramsbeck** W Germany
27 H12 **Ramsberg** Sweden
13 F6 **Ramsbottom** England
32 E9 **Ramsdorf** W Germany
32 F7 **Ramsel** W Germany
26 H8 **Ramsele** Sweden
112 H2 **Ramseur** North Carolina U.S.A.
120 H5 **Ramsey** Ontario Canada
9 F3 **Ramsey** England
12 D5 **Ramsey** I of Man U.K.
110 G2 **Ramsey** Illinois U.S.A.
95 N5 **Ramsey** New Jersey U.S.A.
8 A4 **Ramsey I** Wales
9 H5 **Ramsgate** England
13 G5 **Ramsgill** England
28 B3 **Ramsing** Denmark
26 H9 **Ramsjö** Sweden
22 D1 **Ramskapelle** Belgium
74 H8 **Ramtek** India
79 G6 **Ramtha** Jordan
71 J9 **Ramu** *mt* Sumbawa Indonesia
136 K3 **Ramu** *R* Papua New Guinea
26 J9 **Ramvik** Sweden
127 M4 **Ramville, I** Martinique
52 B6 **Ramygala** U.S.S.R.
26 G5 **Rana** *inlet* Norway
16 C1 **Rañadoiro, Sa. de** *mts* Spain
26 F5 **Ranafjord** *inlet* Norway
75 N7 **Ranaghat** India
69 J10 **Ranai** Indonesia
145 E3 **Ranana** New Zealand
27 K12 **Rånäs** Sweden
27 E11 **Rånåsfoss** Norway
70 K8 **Ranau, D** *L* Sumatra
131 B5 **Rancagua** Chile
22 G3 **Rance** Belgium
20 G4 **Rance** *R* Côtes-du-Nord France
133 G2 **Rancharia** Brazil
117 F5 **Rancheria** Yukon Territory Canada
101 S5 **Ranchester** Wyoming U.S.A.
75 L7 **Ranchi** India
129 G6 **Rancho de Caça dos Tapiúnas** Brazil
124 H6 **Rancho Grande** Mexico
106 E5 **Ranchos de Taos** New Mexico U.S.A.
126 D3 **Rancho Veloz** Cuba
131 A8 **Ranco, L. de** Chile
106 D1 **Rand** Colorado U.S.A.
109 J8 **Randado** Texas U.S.A.
99 N7 **Randall** Iowa U.S.A.
107 M2 **Randall** Kansas U.S.A.
99 M3 **Randall** Minnesota U.S.A.
14 E2 **Randalstown** N Ireland
43 F11 **Randazzo** Sicily
89 A1 **Randburg** S Africa
Randers *co see* **Århus** *co*
28 E4 **Randers** Denmark
37 J4 **Randersacker** W Germany
26 L5 **Randijaur** *L* Sweden
100 D3 **Randle** Washington U.S.A.
112 H2 **Randleman** North Carolina U.S.A.
109 J1 **Randlett** Oklahoma U.S.A.
103 P1 **Randlett** Utah U.S.A.
28 E5 **Randlev** Denmark
99 L9 **Randolph** Iowa U.S.A.
107 O2 **Randolph** Kansas U.S.A.
95 S2 **Randolph** Maine U.S.A.
111 G7 **Randolph** Mississippi U.S.A.
98 J7 **Randolph** Nebraska U.S.A.
94 J4 **Randolph** New York U.S.A.
101 O8 **Randolph** Utah U.S.A.
95 P3 **Randolph** Vermont U.S.A.
99 S6 **Randolph** Wisconsin U.S.A.
123 T5 **Random I** Newfoundland Canada
99 T6 **Random Lake** Wisconsin U.S.A.
21 M4 **Randonnai** France
102 G6 **Randsburg** California U.S.A.
27 D11 **Randsfjord** Norway
32 E5 **Randzel** *sandbank* W Germany
26 N6 **Råneå** Norway
21 K4 **Rânes** France
118 F5 **Ranfurly** Alberta Canada
144 C6 **Ranfurly** New Zealand
69 E9 **Rangae** Thailand
70 F6 **Rangasa, Tanjong** *C* Sulawesi
70 F6 **Rangas, Tanjong** *C* Sulawesi
145 E3 **Rangataua** New Zealand
145 D1 **Rangaunu Harbour** New Zealand
111 J10 **Range** Alabama U.S.A.
95 R2 **Rangeley** Maine U.S.A.
101 R9 **Rangely** Colorado U.S.A.
109 J3 **Ranger** Texas U.S.A.
94 E8 **Ranger** West Virginia U.S.A.
120 G6 **Ranger L** Ontario Canada
75 O5 **Rangia** India
144 D5 **Rangiora** New Zealand
145 F2 **Rangipoua** New Zealand
145 F3 **Rangitaiki** New Zealand
145 F3 **Rangitaiki R** New Zealand
144 C6 **Rangitata** New Zealand
145 E4 **Rangitikei R** New Zealand
145 E2 **Rangitoto I** New Zealand
145 E3 **Rangitoto Ra** New Zealand
145 G2 **Rangitukia** New Zealand
69 D10 **Rangkalanberandan** Sumatra
70 L9 **Rangkasbitung** Java
68 C4 **Rangoon** *R* Burma
68 C4 **Rangoon** Burma
75 N6 **Rangpur** Bangladesh
69 F12 **Rangsang** *isld* Sumatra
33 S8 **Rangsdorf** W Germany
28 C6 **Rangstrup** Denmark
76 B3 **Ranibennur** India
99 N1 **Ranier** Minnesota U.S.A.
75 M7 **Raniganj** India
37 M2 **Ranis** East Germany
74 E6 **Raniwara** India
140 D5 **Ranken** *R* N Terr Australia
140 D4 **Ranken Store** N Terr Australia
110 J1 **Rankin** Illinois U.S.A.
108 F4 **Rankin** Texas U.S.A.
115 K5 **Rankin Inlet** Northwest Territories Canada
139 H5 **Rankin's Springs** New South Wales Australia
80 B8 **Rannen** Israel
141 K6 **Rannes** Queensland Australia
55 B5 **Ranneye** U.S.S.R.
15 D4 **Rannoch Moor** Scotland
87 H12 **Ranohira** Madagascar
120 J2 **Ranoke** Ontario Canada
68 D7 **Ranong** Thailand
69 E9 **Ranot** Thailand
26 G6 **Ransarn** *L* Sweden
36 D3 **Ransel** W Germany
99 S8 **Ransom** Illinois U.S.A.
107 L3 **Ransom** Kansas U.S.A.
94 K7 **Ranson** West Virginia U.S.A.
36 G3 **Ranstadt** W Germany
29 N9 **Rantasalmi** Finland
70 D6 **Rantau** Kalimantan
69 F12 **Rantau** *isld* Sumatra
69 E12 **Rantaukampar** Sumatra
70 E3 **Rantaupandjang** Kalimantan
70 C5 **Rantaupanjang** Kalimantan
69 D11 **Rantauprapat** Sumatra
70 C6 **Rantaupulut** Kalimantan
70 F6 **Rantemario, Gunung** *mt* Sulawesi
70 F6 **Rantepao** Sulawesi
21 P3 **Rantigny** France
110 H1 **Rantoul** Illinois U.S.A.
102 H1 **Rant Pass** Nevada U.S.A.
29 M7 **Rantsila** Finland
29 M6 **Ranua** Finland
131 A8 **Ranue, R** Chile
28 C3 **Ranum** Denmark
78 K3 **Ranya** Iraq
68 G3 **Rao Go** *mt* Laos
65 J1 **Raohe** China
36 B7 **Raon-l'Etape** France
36 C6 **Raon-sur-Plaine** France
67 E5 **Raoping** China
41 O6 **Raossi** Italy
137 R7 **Raoul** *isld* Kermadec Is Pacific Oc
65 C5 **Raoyang** China
144 C5 **Rapahoe** New Zealand
44 F3 **Rapallo** Italy
131 B4 **Rapel** *R* Chile
101 Q4 **Rapelje** Montana U.S.A.
115 N4 **Raper, C** Northwest Territories Canada
94 H9 **Raphine** Virginia U.S.A.
14 D2 **Raphoe** Ireland
116 R3 **Rapid** *R* Alaska U.S.A.
99 M1 **Rapid** *R* Minnesota U.S.A.
94 J8 **Rapidan** Virginia U.S.A.
94 K8 **Rapidan** *R* Virginia U.S.A.
138 E6 **Rapid B** South Australia Australia
119 R8 **Rapid City** Manitoba Canada
98 C5 **Rapid City** South Dakota U.S.A.
121 R5 **Rapide Blanc** Quebec Canada
121 N6 **Rapides des Joachims** Quebec Canada
141 H2 **Rapid Horn** *C* Gt Barrier Reef Aust
99 U4 **Rapid River** Michigan U.S.A.
118 H4 **Rapid View** Saskatchewan Canada
52 C5 **Räpina** U.S.S.R.
52 B5 **Rapla** U.S.S.R.
95 K8 **Rappahannock** *R* Virginia U.S.A.
70 F6 **Rappang** Sulawesi
41 J3 **Rapperswil** Switzerland
46 F5 **Rapsáni** Greece
128 E6 **Rapulo** *R* Bolivia
71 G4 **Rapu Rapu** Philippines
80 G1 **Raqqādīyah** Syria
95 N2 **Raquette** *R* New York U.S.A.
95 N3 **Raquette Lake** New York U.S.A.
28 B2 **Rær** Denmark
140 D1 **Raragala I** N Terr Australia
71 K9 **Rarakah** *mt* Flores Indonesia
95 N6 **Raritan B** New Jersey U.S.A.
40 G5 **Raron** Switzerland
134 A10 **Rarotonga** *isld* Pacific Oc
71 D6 **Rasa** *isld* Palawan Philippines
42 F3 **Raša** Yugoslavia
79 F3 **Ra's al Basiţ** *C* Syria
77 D7 **Ra's al Khaymah** U.A.E.
133 E6 **Rasa, Pta** Argentina
131 E8 **Rasa, Pta** *C* Argentina
79 G4 **Ras Baalbek** Lebanon
86 G3 **Ras Dashen** *mt* Ethiopia
52 B6 **Raseiniai** U.S.S.R.
80 G4 **Ras el Aqra** Jordan
80 F8 **Ras el Ghor** Jordan
84 H3 **Râs el Kenâyis** *C* Egypt
85 D5 **Ras el Ma** Mali
72 G5 **Ra's Fartak** *C* S Yemen
79 D10 **Râs Ghârib** Egypt
86 F3 **Rashad** Sudan
86 G1 **Râs Hadarba** *C* Egypt
79 F8 **Rashādīya** Jordan
79 A7 **Rashîd** Egypt
77 A1 **Rasht** Iran
76 D5 **Rasipuram** India
77 G6 **Rāsk** Iran
46 D1 **Raška** Yugoslavia
86 G2 **Râs Kasar** *C* Sudan
28 D5 **Raskmølle** Denmark
77 J5 **Raskoh** *reg* Pakistan
84 F3 **Ra's Lānūf** Libya
31 N6 **Raslavice** Czechoslovakia
72 H5 **Ra's Madrakah** *C* Oman
72 G6 **Ra's Māmī** *C* Socotra
79 C9 **Râs Matarma** Egypt
84 J4 **Ras Muhammad** *C* Egypt
85 A4 **Ras Nouadhibou** Mauritania
133 D6 **Raso, C** Argentina
130 H10 **Raso da Catarina** Brazil
143 E8 **Rason L** Western Australia Australia
46 F1 **Rasovo** Bulgaria
116 L7 **Raspberry I** Alaska U.S.A.
79 D10 **Râs Shukheir** Egypt
53 F7 **Rasskazov** U.S.S.R.
26 P1 **Råsstigáisa** *mt* Norway
77 B6 **Ras Tannurah** Saudi Arabia
Ras Tarf *see* **Quilates,C**
16 D9 **Ras Targa** Morocco
36 E6 **Rastatt** W Germany
28 A4 **Råsted** Denmark
32 H6 **Rastede** W Germany
Rastenburg *see* **Kętrzyn**
38 M4 **Rastenfeld** Austria
38 E7 **Rastkogel** *mt* Austria
26 M3 **Råstoätno** *R* Sweden
43 B8 **Rasu, M** *mt* Sardinia
80 G4 **Rasun** Jordan
145 E3 **Rata** New Zealand
71 J4 **Ratahan** Sulawesi
70 K8 **Ratai, Gunung** *mt* Sumatra Indonesia
31 H6 **Rataje** Czechoslovakia
26 G9 **Rätan** Sweden
26 L8 **Ratan** Sweden
74 F4 **Ratangarh** India
68 D6 **Rat Buri** Thailand
55 B4 **Ratchino** U.S.S.R.
110 C6 **Ratcliff** Arkansas U.S.A.
109 M4 **Ratcliff** Texas U.S.A.
33 N5 **Ratekau** W Germany
74 H6 **Rath** India
99 N9 **Rathburn Lake** *res* Iowa U.S.A.
14 E4 **Rathdrum** Ireland
100 J2 **Rathdrum** Idaho U.S.A.
68 A2 **Rathedaung** Burma
33 Q7 **Rathenow** East Germany
14 E2 **Rathfriland** N Ireland
14 C4 **Ráth Luirc** Ireland
14 D1 **Rathmelton** Ireland
14 E4 **Rathnew** Ireland
119 T9 **Rathwell** Manitoba Canada
Ratibor *see* **Racibórz**
32 E10 **Ratingen** W Germany
116 L10 **Rat Is** Aleutian Is
Ratisbon *see* **Regensburg**
119 S2 **Rat L** Manitoba Canada
74 F7 **Ratlam** India
116 C4 **Ratmanova, Ostrov** *isld* U.S.S.R.
76 A2 **Ratnagiri** India
83 K11 **Ratnapura** Sri Lanka
119 N5 **Ratner** Saskatchewan Canada
106 F5 **Raton** New Mexico U.S.A.
19 O18 **Ratonneau, I** France
106 F4 **Raton Pass** Colorado U.S.A.
115 K7 **Rat Rapids** Ontario Canada
117 R5 **Rat River** Northwest Territories Canada
109 M1 **Rattan** Oklahoma U.S.A.
37 K3 **Rattelsdorf** W Germany
38 N7 **Ratten** Austria
38 E7 **Rattenberg** Austria
106 F4 **Rattlesnake Buttes** *mts* Colorado U.S.A.
107 L4 **Rattlesnake Cr** Kansas U.S.A.
100 H7 **Rattlesnake Cr** Oregon U.S.A.
101 S7 **Rattlesnake Ra** Wyoming U.S.A.
123 Q4 **Rattling Brook** Newfoundland Canada
15 G3 **Rattray Head** Scotland
27 H11 **Rättvik** Sweden
33 N5 **Ratzeburg** W Germany
33 N5 **Ratzeburger See** *L* W Germany
71 B1 **Rau** Halmahera Indonesia
69 E11 **Raub** Malaysia
133 F5 **Rauch** Argentina
22 H4 **Raucourt** France
29 M5 **Raudanjoki** *R* Finland
29 T8 **Raufarhöfn** Iceland
27 E11 **Raufoss** Norway
36 G7 **Rauhe Alb** *mts* W Germany
37 K4 **Rauhe Ebrach** *R* W Germany
37 K4 **Rauhenebrach** W Germany
145 F2 **Raukokore** New Zealand
145 G2 **Raukumara** New Zealand
145 F3 **Raukumara Range** New Zealand
27 C12 **Rauland** Norway
27 M10 **Rauma** Finland
26 C9 **Rauma** *R* Norway
145 E4 **Raumati** New Zealand
36 E6 **Raumünzach** W Germany
52 C6 **Rauna** U.S.S.R.
27 B11 **Raundal** *R* Norway
70 P10 **Raung, G** *mt* Java
145 E3 **Raurimu** New Zealand
29 K4 **Raus** Sweden
36 F2 **Rauschenberg** W Germany
60 T1 **Rausu** Japan
29 M9 **Rautalampi** Finland
26 K3 **Rautasjaure** *L* Sweden
29 N8 **Rautavaara** Finland
29 O10 **Rautjärvi** Finland
101 L2 **Ravalli** Montana U.S.A.
31 O5 **Rava Russkaya** U.S.S.R.
45 R8 **Ravello** Italy
94 F9 **Raven** Virginia U.S.A.
95 O4 **Ravena** New York U.S.A.
119 O5 **Ravendal** Saskatchewan Canada
102 D1 **Ravendale** California U.S.A.
22 C4 **Ravenel** France
13 E5 **Ravenglass** England
45 L3 **Ravenna** *reg* Italy
45 M3 **Ravenna** Italy
102 F7 **Ravenna** California U.S.A.
110 N4 **Ravenna** Kentucky U.S.A.
98 H8 **Ravenna** Nebraska U.S.A.
94 F5 **Ravenna** Ohio U.S.A.
20 H3 **Ravenoville** France
141 H6 **Ravensbourne** *R* Queensland Australia
33 S6 **Ravensbrück** East Germany
41 L2 **Ravensburg** W Germany
13 H5 **Ravenscar** England
118 H9 **Ravenscrag** Saskatchewan Canada
141 H4 **Ravenshoe** Queensland Australia
25 E5 **Ravenstein** Netherlands
143 D10 **Ravensthorpe** Western Australia Australia
141 H5 **Ravenswood** Queensland Australia
94 F8 **Ravenswood** West Virginia U.S.A.
121 L7 **Ravensworth** Ontario Canada
74 E3 **Ravi** *R* Pakistan
109 L1 **Ravia** Oklahoma U.S.A.
18 H5 **Ravières** France
46 E1 **Ravna Reka** Yugoslavia
38 L8 **Ravne Na Koroškem** Yugoslavia
57 C2 **Ravnina Dar'yalytakyr** U.S.S.R.
115 K4 **Ravn, Kap** Greenland
28 D3 **Ravnkilde** Denmark
48 E6 **Ravno** *mt* Yugoslavia
42 H6 **Ravno** Yugoslavia
74 E2 **Rawalpindi** Pakistan
117 Q3 **Rawalpindi L** Northwest Territories Canada
31 M4 **Rawa Mazowiecka** Poland
78 K3 **Rawandiz** Iraq
121 R6 **Rawdon** Quebec Canada
119 R4 **Rawebb** Manitoba Canada
145 D1 **Rawene** New Zealand
98 B7 **Rawhide Cr** Wyoming U.S.A.
31 K4 **Rawicz** Poland
69 D9 **Rawi, Ko** *isld* Thailand
143 F9 **Rawlinna** Western Australia Australia
101 S8 **Rawlins** Wyoming U.S.A.
143 G7 **Rawlinson Mt** Western Australia Australia
143 F7 **Rawlinson, Mt** Western Australia Australia
133 D6 **Rawson** Argentina
94 D6 **Rawson** Ohio U.S.A.
38 N6 **Raxalpe** *mts* Austria
116 M4 **Ray** *R* Alaska U.S.A.
99 N1 **Ray** Minnesota U.S.A.
98 C1 **Ray** North Dakota U.S.A.
76 D3 **Rayachoti** India
76 C3 **Rāyadurg** India
75 K9 **Rāyagarha** India
79 G5 **Rayak** Lebanon
26 R3 **Rayakoski** U.S.S.R.
86 B4 **Ray-Bouba** Cameroon
123 N6 **Ray, C** Newfoundland Canada
59 J2 **Raychikhinsk** U.S.S.R.
112 D6 **Ray City** Georgia U.S.A.
77 E5 **Rāyen** Iran
55 B4 **Rayevskiy** U.S.S.R.
54 J8 **Raygorodok** U.S.S.R.
80 G1 **Rayhānīyah** Syria
9 G4 **Rayleigh** England
118 E9 **Raymond** Alberta Canada
102 E4 **Raymond** California U.S.A.
110 G2 **Raymond** Illinois U.S.A.
111 F9 **Raymond** Mississippi U.S.A.
98 B1 **Raymond** Montana U.S.A.
98 J5 **Raymond** South Dakota U.S.A.
109 N3 **Raymond** Texas U.S.A.
100 B3 **Raymond** Washington U.S.A.
139 K5 **Raymond Terrace** New South Wales Australia
109 K9 **Raymondville** Texas U.S.A.
119 N7 **Raymore** Saskatchewan Canada
116 L4 **Ray Mts** Alaska U.S.A.
111 D11 **Rayne** Louisiana U.S.A.
101 P2 **Raynesford** Montana U.S.A.
108 A1 **Rayo** New Mexico U.S.A.
68 E6 **Rayong** Thailand
110 B3 **Raytown** Missouri U.S.A.
66 E5 **Rayü** China
111 E9 **Rayville** Louisiana U.S.A.
77 A2 **Razan** Iran
48 N4 **Razdel'naya** U.S.S.R.
56 D2 **Razdolinsk** U.S.S.R.
47 H1 **Razgrad** Bulgaria
48 M6 **Razim, Lacul** *L* Romania
46 F3 **Razlog** Bulgaria
20 A5 **Raz, Pte.du** France
110 B1 **Rea** Missouri U.S.A.
142 A1 **Reabold Hill** Western Australia Australia
117 D6 **Reaburn, Mt** Alaska U.S.A.
109 O2 **Reader** Arkansas U.S.A.
119 Q5 **Reader L** Manitoba Canada
9 F5 **Reading** England
127 J2 **Reading** Jamaica
94 C5 **Reading** Michigan U.S.A.
99 L6 **Reading** Minnesota U.S.A.
95 M6 **Reading** Pennsylvania U.S.A.
119 M9 **Readlyn** Saskatchewan Canada
95 P4 **Readsboro** Vermont U.S.A.
99 Q6 **Readstown** Wisconsin U.S.A.
109 L4 **Reagan** Texas U.S.A.
128 E7 **Real, Cord** *mts* Bolivia
128 C4 **Real, Cord** *mts* Ecuador
44 C1 **Reale** Italy
133 E5 **Realico** Argentina
109 J8 **Realitos** Texas U.S.A.
68 F7 **Ream** Cambodia
100 H2 **Reardan** Washington U.S.A.
15 G2 **Reawick** Scotland
112 D6 **Rebecca** Georgia U.S.A.
143 D9 **Rebecca, L** Western Australia Australia
100 H8 **Rebel Creek** Nevada U.S.A.
33 T5 **Rebelow** East Germany
117 P3 **Rebesca L** Northwest Territories Canada
28 D3 **Rebild** Denmark
128 G5 **Reboja, Cachoeira de** Brazil
29 P8 **Reboly** U.S.S.R.
46 F2 **Rebrovo** Bulgaria
60 P1 **Rebun-suidō** *str* Japan
60 P1 **Rebun-tō** *isld* Japan
133 E5 **Recalde** Argentina
48 G5 **Recaş** Romania
44 F3 **Recco** Italy
40 A2 **Recey** France
19 J5 **Recey-sur-Ource** France
143 D10 **Recherche, Arch.of the** Western Australia Australia
36 B6 **Réchicourt le Château** France
54 B4 **Rechitsa** U.S.S.R.
33 R6 **Rechlin** East Germany
22 L3 **Recht** Belgium
130 J10 **Recife** Brazil
89 D10 **Recife, C** S Africa
83 J12 **Recif I** Seychelles
32 G8 **Recke** W Germany
32 F9 **Recklinghausen** W Germany
101 U5 **Recluse** Wyoming U.S.A.
22 J4 **Recogne** Belgium
131 F2 **Reconquista** Argentina
19 O15 **Recoubeau** France
146 E7 **Recovery Glacier** Antarctica
133 D3 **Recreo** Argentina
31 J2 **Recz** Poland
110 E6 **Red** *R* Arkansas U.S.A.
98 K2 **Red** *R* Minnesota U.S.A.
69 F10 **Redang** *isld* Malaysia
22 K4 **Redange** Luxembourg
122 G7 **Red Bank** New Brunswick Canada
95 N6 **Red Bank** New Jersey U.S.A.
Red Basin *see* **Sichuan Pendi**
123 Q2 **Red Bay** Labrador, Nfld Canada
120 J8 **Red Bay** Ontario Canada
111 H7 **Red Bay** Alabama U.S.A.
113 B7 **Redbay** Florida U.S.A.
118 K6 **Redberry L** Saskatchewan Canada
109 N10 **Redbird Airport** Texas U.S.A.
143 C6 **Red Bluff** *mt* Western Australia Australia
102 B1 **Red Bluff** California U.S.A.
108 D4 **Red Bluff L** Texas/New Mex U.S.A.
9 F4 **Redbourn** England
110 G3 **Red Bud** Illinois U.S.A.
103 M6 **Red Butte** *mt* Arizona U.S.A.
98 A8 **Red Buttes** Wyoming U.S.A.
99 M2 **Redby** Minnesota U.S.A.
13 G4 **Redcar** England
106 D2 **Red Cliff** Colorado U.S.A.
141 L7 **Redcliffe** Queensland Australia
89 F2 **Redcliffe** Zimbabwe
143 D8 **Redcliffe, Mt** Western Australia Australia
138 F5 **Red Cliffs** Victoria Australia
111 H11 **Red Cr** Mississippi U.S.A.
101 R8 **Red Cr** Wyoming U.S.A.
95 L3 **Red Creek** New York U.S.A.
118 D6 **Red Deer** Alberta Canada
119 Q6 **Red Deer L** Manitoba Canada
119 P6 **Red Deer R** Saskatchewan Canada
111 D11 **Reddell** Louisiana U.S.A.
13 E4 **Red Dial** England
113 E8 **Reddick** Florida U.S.A.
102 B1 **Redding** California U.S.A.
118 H1 **Reddit** Ontario Canada
9 E3 **Redditch** England
33 O6 **Redefin** East Germany
98 E4 **Red Elm** South Dakota U.S.A.
129 K5 **Redenção** Brazil
20 D6 **Redené** France
85 F2 **Redeyef** Tunisia
111 D7 **Redfield** Arkansas U.S.A.
99 M8 **Redfield** Iowa U.S.A.
98 H5 **Redfield** South Dakota U.S.A.
101 L5 **Redfish L** Idaho U.S.A.
108 C6 **Redford** Texas U.S.A.
99 R5 **Redgranite** Wisconsin U.S.A.
75 L8 **Redhākhol** India
9 F5 **Redhill** England
145 D4 **Red Hill** *mt* New Zealand
111 K10 **Red Hills** Alabama U.S.A.
95 O5 **Red Hook** New York U.S.A.
100 H8 **Red House** Nevada U.S.A.
123 S6 **Red I** Newfoundland Canada
98 C4 **Redig** South Dakota U.S.A.
123 Q5 **Red Indian L** Newfoundland Canada
103 O9 **Redington** Arizona U.S.A.
98 C8 **Redington** Nebraska U.S.A.
85 D2 **Redjem Demouch** Algeria
110 L1 **Red Key** Indiana U.S.A.
52 E6 **Redkino** U.S.S.R.
117 O5 **Redknife** *R* Northwest Territories Canada
103 K6 **Red L** Arizona U.S.A.
115 K7 **Red Lake** Ontario Canada
103 M6 **Red Lake** Arizona U.S.A.
102 G7 **Redlands** California U.S.A.
98 K2 **Red L. Falls** Minnesota U.S.A.
95 L7 **Red Lion** Pennsylvania U.S.A.
101 Q4 **Red Lodge** Montana U.S.A.
118 C7 **Red Lodge Prov. Park** Alberta Canada
145 E2 **Red Mercury I** New Zealand
13 G5 **Redmire** England
110 J2 **Redmon** Illinois U.S.A.
100 D5 **Redmond** Oregon U.S.A.
103 N2 **Redmond** Utah U.S.A.
102 G6 **Red Mt** California U.S.A.
112 C1 **Red Mt** Tennessee U.S.A.
37 L5 **Rednitz** *R* W Germany
99 L8 **Red Oak** Iowa U.S.A.
110 A7 **Red Oak** Oklahoma U.S.A.
109 L3 **Red Oak** Texas U.S.A.
20 F6 **Redon** France
127 N6 **Redonda** *isld* Antigua & Barbuda W Indies
16 B2 **Redondela** Spain
16 B6 **Redondo** Portugal
102 F8 **Redondo Beach** California U.S.A.
128 F3 **Redondo, Pico** *mt* Brazil
116 L6 **Redoubt Vol** Alaska U.S.A.
117 O9 **Red Pass** British Columbia Canada
118 J6 **Red Pheasant** Saskatchewan Canada
141 G2 **Red Pt** Queensland Australia
117 J6 **Red R** British Columbia Canada
119 U9 **Red R** Manitoba Canada
111 D10 **Red R** Louisiana U.S.A.
109 J1 **Red R** Texas U.S.A.
Red R Vietnam *see* **Song-koi** *R*
122 E7 **Red Rapids** New Brunswick Canada
101 K4 **Red R. Hot Springs** Idaho U.S.A.
119 P2 **Red Rock** Ontario Canada
103 N9 **Redrock** Arizona U.S.A.
106 B9 **Red Rock** New Mexico U.S.A.
107 N5 **Red Rock** Oklahoma U.S.A.
109 K6 **Red Rock** Texas U.S.A.
117 Q3 **Redrock L** Northwest Territories Canada
99 N8 **Red Rock Res** Iowa U.S.A.
143 G9 **Red Rocks Pt** Western Australia Australia
8 A7 **Redruth** England
86 G1 **Red Sea** Africa/Arabian Pen
112 H3 **Red Springs** North Carolina U.S.A.
117 M9 **Redstone** British Columbia Canada
117 K4 **Redstone** *R* Northwest Territories Canada
120 J4 **Redstone** *R* Ontario Canada
101 V1 **Redstone** Montana U.S.A.
124 E9 **Red Tank** Panama
22 J4 **Redu** Belgium
119 Q9 **Redvers** Saskatchewan Canada
118 D5 **Redwater** Alberta Canada
121 L6 **Redwater** Ontario Canada
98 A2 **Redwater** *R* Montana U.S.A.
109 N2 **Redwater** Texas U.S.A.
8 B1 **Red Wharf B** Wales
118 E6 **Red Willow** Alberta Canada
98 E9 **Red Willow Cr** Nebraska U.S.A.
99 O5 **Red Wing** Minnesota U.S.A.
102 B4 **Redwood City** California U.S.A.
99 L5 **Redwood Falls** Minnesota U.S.A.
100 A8 **Redwood Nat. Park** California U.S.A.
102 A2 **Redwood Valley** California U.S.A.
71 C5 **Reed Bank** S China Sea
94 B3 **Reed City** Michigan U.S.A.
98 D3 **Reeder** North Dakota U.S.A.
102 E5 **Reedley** California U.S.A.
101 Q4 **Reedpoint** Montana U.S.A.
106 C8 **Reeds Pk** New Mexico U.S.A.
100 A6 **Reedsport** Oregon U.S.A.
112 E3 **Reedy** *R* South Carolina U.S.A.
94 F8 **Reedy** West Virginia U.S.A.
138 D4 **Reedy Lagoon** South Australia Australia
141 G4 **Reedy Springs** Queensland Australia
144 C5 **Reefton** New Zealand
98 G5 **Ree Heights** South Dakota U.S.A.
14 C3 **Ree, L** Ireland
110 G5 **Reelfoot L** Tennessee U.S.A.
32 G6 **Reepsholt** W Germany
28 G5 **Reersø** Denmark
25 F5 **Rees** W Germany
94 D3 **Reese** Michigan U.S.A.
100 H9 **Reese** *R* Nevada U.S.A.
120 G3 **Reesor** Ontario Canada
33 P6 **Reetz** East Germany
78 G2 **Refahiye** Turkey
111 J8 **Reform** Alabama U.S.A.
133 D3 **Refresco** Chile
28 F6 **Refs** Denmark
27 G14 **Reftele** Sweden
109 K7 **Refugio** Texas U.S.A.
31 J2 **Rega** *R* Poland
120 E4 **Regan** Ontario Canada
80 D3 **Regavim** Israel
37 N5 **Regen** *R* W Germany
37 N5 **Regensburg** W Germany
37 N5 **Regenstauf** W Germany
119 R9 **Regent** Manitoba Canada
120 F5 **Regent** Ontario Canada
85 E3 **Reggane** Algeria
45 L4 **Reggello** Italy
43 G10 **Reggio di Calabria** Italy
45 J2 **Reggiolo** Italy
45 J2 **Reggio nell Emilia** Italy
129 H3 **Regina** Brazil
119 N8 **Regina** Saskatchewan Canada
37 N1 **Regis** East Germany
77 J4 **Registan** Afghanistan
20 G3 **Regnéville** France
22 G4 **Régniowez** France
37 K4 **Regnitz** *R* W Germany
16 B6 **Reguengos de Monsaraz** Portugal
20 E6 **Reguiny** France
37 N3 **Rehau** W Germany
36 D5 **Rehberg** *mt* W Germany
32 H7 **Rehden** W Germany
33 Q7 **Rehfeld** East Germany
74 H7 **Rehli** India
32 J8 **Rehme** W Germany
33 O5 **Rehna** East Germany
87 C10 **Rehoboth** Namibia
95 M8 **Rehoboth Beach** Delaware U.S.A.
80 C6 **Rehovot** Israel
36 F3 **Reichelshausen** W Germany
37 N2 **Reichenbach** East Germany
38 L7 **Reichenfels** Austria
37 J1 **Reichensachsen** W Germany
38 F5 **Reichertsheim** W Germany
37 L6 **Reichertshofen** W Germany
101 N4 **Reichle** Montana U.S.A.
36 D2 **Reichshof** W Germany
36 D6 **Reichshoffen** France
143 G9 **Reid** Western Australia Australia
118 J8 **Reid L** Saskatchewan Canada
140 B4 **Reid, Mt** N Terr Australia
141 H4 **Reid R** Queensland Australia
112 E5 **Reidsville** Georgia U.S.A.
112 H1 **Reidsville** North Carolina U.S.A.
9 F5 **Reigate** England
27 N13 **Reigi** U.S.S.R.
21 M7 **Reignac-sur-Indre** Indre-et-Loire France
25 C5 **Reijen** Netherlands
103 O9 **Reiley Pk** Arizona U.S.A.
36 F5 **Reilingen** W Germany
19 P17 **Reillanne** France
22 G5 **Reims** France
18 H3 **Reims, Mt de** France
133 C8 **Reina Adelaida, Arch. de la** *islds* Chile
99 O7 **Reinbeck** Iowa U.S.A.
32 M5 **Reinbek** W Germany
33 S4 **Reinberg** East Germany
119 U6 **Reindeer I** Manitoba Canada
119 Q1 **Reindeer L** Manitoba/Sask Canada
26 F4 **Reine** Norway
140 D6 **Reinecke, Mt** N Terr Australia
27 C11 **Reineskarvet** *mt* Norway
33 M5 **Reinfeld** W Germany
145 D1 **Reinga, C** New Zealand
32 L10 **Reinhausen** W Germany
36 C5 **Reinheim** W Germany
33 S7 **Reinickendorf** W Berlin
16 E1 **Reinosa** Spain
26 L2 **Reinöy** *isld* Norway
37 P1 **Reinsberg** East Germany
36 B4 **Reinsfeld** W Germany
33 P5 **Reinstorf** East Germany
26 M2 **Reisa** *R* Norway
37 O6 **Reisbach** W Germany
29 L8 **Reisjärvi** Finland
38 H8 **Reisseck** *mt* Austria
25 F2 **Reitdiep** *R* Netherlands
38 G6 **Reiter Alpen** *mt* Austria
38 J7 **Reitereck** *mt* Austria
87 E11 **Reitz** S Africa
37 P2 **Reitzenhain** East Germany
27 H13 **Rejmyre** Sweden
31 O4 **Rejowiec** Poland
28 B6 **Rejsby** Denmark
27 H12 **Rekarne** Sweden
32 F9 **Reken** W Germany
60 R3 **Rekifune-gawa** *R* Japan
109 N4 **Reklaw** Texas U.S.A.
46 E1 **Rekovac** Yugoslavia
20 B5 **Relecq-Kerhoun,le** France
112 E6 **Relee** Georgia U.S.A.
98 G6 **Reliance** South Dakota U.S.A.
101 Q8 **Reliance** Wyoming U.S.A.
85 E1 **Relizane** Algeria
124 G4 **Rellano** Mexico
36 C2 **Remagen** W Germany
21 M5 **Rémalard** France
138 E4 **Remarkable, Mt** South Australia Australia
70 N9 **Rembang** Java
36 F6 **Remchingen** W Germany
37 L2 **Remda** East Germany
126 E3 **Remedios** Cuba
124 F5 **Remedios** Mexico
32 G6 **Remels** W Germany
77 F6 **Remeshk** Iran
22 L4 **Remich** Luxembourg
121 L5 **Rémigny** Quebec Canada
120 H3 **Remi L** Ontario Canada
22 J4 **Remilly-Allicourt** France
99 T9 **Remington** Indiana U.S.A.
94 K8 **Remington** Virginia U.S.A.
40 E1 **Remiremont** France
33 N8 **Remlingen** W Germany
100 B6 **Remote** Oregon U.S.A.
22 K3 **Remouchamps** Belgium
19 N17 **Remoulins** France
83 K14 **Remparts, R. des** Réunion Indian Oc
36 H6 **Rems** *R* W Germany
36 C1 **Remscheid** W Germany
99 L7 **Remsen** Iowa U.S.A.
121 P9 **Remsen** New York U.S.A.
20 E6 **Remungol** France
94 B3 **Remus** Michigan U.S.A.
19 O16 **Rémuzat** France
27 E10 **Rena** Norway
120 G4 **Renabie** Ontario Canada
20 G6 **Renac** France
Renaix *see* **Ronse**
71 D2 **Rena Pt** Luzon Philippines
128 E4 **Renascenca** Brazil
146 C4 **Renaud I** *isld* Antarctica
21 H6 **Renazé** France
36 E6 **Renchen** W Germany
26 E10 **Rendal** Norway
28 A5 **Renderne** Denmark
32 L4 **Rendsburg** W Germany
121 L4 **Reneault** Quebec Canada
123 U7 **Renews** Newfoundland Canada
Renfrew *co see* **Strathclyde** *reg*
121 O7 **Renfrew** Ontario Canada
12 D2 **Renfrew** Scotland
70 L9 **Rengasdengklok** Java
69 F13 **Rengat** Sumatra
67 C1 **Ren He** *R* China
67 D4 **Renhua** China
67 B3 **Renhuai** China
48 L5 **Reni** U.S.S.R.
94 G9 **Renick** West Virginia U.S.A.
120 J2 **Renison** Ontario Canada
139 H8 **Renison Bell** Tasmania Australia
86 F3 **Renk** Sudan
29 L11 **Renko** Finland
25 E5 **Renkum** Netherlands
115 R3 **Renland** *reg* Greenland
138 F5 **Renmark** South Australia Australia
65 F1 **Renmin** China
26 D9 **Rennebu** Norway
137 N4 **Rennell** *isld* Solomon Is
36 E2 **Rennerod** W Germany

Renner Springs — Rockcliffe
71

140 C4 Renner Springs N Terr Australia
37 L6 Rennertshafen W Germany
20 G5 Rennes France
27 A12 Rennesöy isld Norway
146 C13 Rennick Glacier glacier Antarctica
118 F1 Rennie Manitoba Canada
38 J7 Rennweq Austria
45 K3 Reno R Italy
102 E2 Reno Nevada U.S.A.
99 L4 Reno, L Minnesota U.S.A.
122 G7 Renous New Brunswick Canada
94 K5 Renovo Pennsylvania U.S.A.
119 M7 Renown Saskatchewan Canada
65 C5 Renqiu China
28 C7 Rens Denmark
67 E5 Renshan China
67 A2 Renshou China
99 T9 Rensselaer Indiana U.S.A.
95 O4 Rensselaer New York U.S.A.
95 N4 Rensselaerville New York U.S.A.
25 E4 Renswoude Netherlands
100 C2 Renton Washington U.S.A.
37 K3 Rentweinsdorf W Germany
37 J3 Rentwertshausen East Germany
99 L5 Renville Minnesota U.S.A.
119 R6 Renwer Manitoba Canada
22 H4 Renwez France
145 D4 Renwick New Zealand
99 N7 Renwick Iowa U.S.A.
65 C6 Ren Xian China
67 D7 Renxing China
18 E8 Réole, la France
76 E2 Repalle India
129 G4 Repartição Brazil
129 G4 Repartimento Brazil
40 E3 Repentis, Mt France
29 J8 Replot Finland
55 E1 Repolovo U.S.S.R.
145 F3 Reporoa New Zealand
40 E6 Reposoir, Chaine de mt France
26 J5 Reppentjåkko mt Sweden
111 J10 Repton Alabama U.S.A.
107 N2 Republic Kansas U.S.A.
94 D5 Republic Ohio U.S.A.
100 G1 Republic Washington U.S.A.
98 H9 Republican R Nebraska/Kansas U.S.A.
141 J5 Repulse Bay Queensland Australia
115 L4 Repulse Bay Northwest Territories Canada
26 P1 Repvåg Norway
54 K5 Rep'yevka U.S.S.R.
98 F2 Reqan North Dakota U.S.A.
130 H6 Reqência Brazil
98 D3 Reqent North Dakota U.S.A.
25 G4 Reqqe R Netherlands
100 A8 Requa California U.S.A.
128 D5 Requena Peru
17 G5 Requena Spain
18 G8 Réquista France
21 P7 Rère R France
145 F3 Rerewhakaaitu L New Zealand
15 G2 Rerwick Scotland
78 F1 Reşadiye Turkey
70 K8 Resag, G mt Sumatra
102 F7 Reseda California U.S.A.
26 J8 Resele Sweden
28 C4 Resen Denmark
28 C3 Resen Denmark
46 E3 Resen Yugoslavia
119 P6 Reserve Saskatchewan Canada
111 F11 Reserve Louisiana U.S.A.
98 B1 Reserve Montana U.S.A.
106 B8 Reserve New Mexico U.S.A.
54 F7 Reshetilovka U.S.S.R.
41 N4 Resia Italy
133 F3 Resistencia Argentina
48 G5 Reşiţa Romania
122 E6 Resitgouche R New Brunswick Canada
115 K3 Resolute Northwest Territories Canada
144 A6 Resolution I New Zealand
115 N5 Resolution Island Northwest Territories Canada
115 N6 Resolution L Quebec Canada
32 L7 Resse W Germany
21 P3 Ressons France
22 D4 Ressons-sur-Matz France
127 K3 Rest Jamaica
12 D1 Rest and be Thankful hill Scotland
122 F5 Restigouche Quebec Canada
119 Q9 Reston Manitoba Canada
13 F2 Reston Scotland
94 K7 Reston Virginia U.S.A.
121 L6 Restoule Ontario Canada
31 N1 Reszel Poland
48 H5 Retezatului, Munti mts Romania
22 G5 Rethel France
32 K7 Rethem W Germany
32 L8 Rethen W Germany
46 G9 Réthimnon Crete Greece
42 C2 Retiche, Alpi mts Italy
22 J1 Retie Belgium
20 H6 Retiers France
118 E8 Retlaw Alberta Canada
141 G7 Retreat Queensland Australia
108 E8 Retrop Oklahoma U.S.A.
48 E3 Rétság Hungary
9 G4 Rettendon England
36 D3 Rettert W Germany
31 J7 Retz Austria
20 F7 Retz reg France
36 H4 Retzbach W Germany
21 M7 Reugny Indre-et-Loire France
21 P7 Reuilly Indre France
22 L3 Reuland Belgium
83 K13 Réunion isld Indian Oc
17 H3 Reus Spain
69 C11 Reusam, Pulau isld Indonesia
25 D6 Reusel Netherlands
41 J4 Reuss R Switzerland
33 Q10 Reussen East Germany
48 L3 Reut R U.S.S.R.
33 R5 Reuterstadt Stavenhagen East Germany
37 M3 Reuth East Germany
37 N4 Reuth W Germany
36 G7 Reutlingen W Germany
41 N3 Reutte Austria
98 C4 Reva South Dakota U.S.A.
80 C6 Revadim Israel
40 C6 Revard mt France
103 H4 Reveille Pk Nevada U.S.A.
18 G9 Revel France
142 G2 Reveley I Western Australia Australia
117 O10 Revelstoke British Columbia Canada
118 J6 Revenue Saskatchewan Canada
45 K1 Revere Italy
9 F1 Revesby England
19 J4 Revigny France
117 H8 Revillagigedo I Alaska U.S.A.
20 H2 Réville France
98 K5 Revillo South Dakota U.S.A.
22 H4 Revin France
79 E7 Revivim Israel
28 F6 Revninge Denmark
26 O1 Revsbotn Norway
26 H9 Revsund Sweden
88 D9 Revubué R Mozambique
94 J5 Rew Pennsylvania U.S.A.
75 J6 Rewa India
145 E4 Rewa mt New Zealand
80 B7 Rewaḥa Israel
118 H6 Reward Saskatchewan Canada
74 G4 Rewari India
99 Q7 Rewey Wisconsin U.S.A.
101 O6 Rexburg Idaho U.S.A.
107 K2 Rexford Kansas U.S.A.
100 K1 Rexford Montana U.S.A.
22 D2 Rexpoede France
122 H7 Rexton New Brunswick Canada
80 D2 Reyba Israel
29 T9 Reydharfjördhur inlet Iceland
107 L6 Reydon Oklahoma U.S.A.
102 E7 Reyes Pk California U.S.A.
28 S9 Reykir Iceland
28 R10 Reykjanesta C Iceland
119 T7 Reykjavik Manitoba Canada
28 R9 Reykjavik Iceland
119 M6 Reynaud Saskatchewan Canada
140 B2 Reynolds R N Terr Australia
112 C5 Reynolds Georgia U.S.A.
100 J6 Reynolds Idaho U.S.A.
99 Q8 Reynolds Illinois U.S.A.
110 K1 Reynolds Indiana U.S.A.
98 J9 Reynolds Nebraska U.S.A.
138 D4 Reynolds, L South Australia Australia
140 C5 Reynolds Ra N Terr Australia
94 J5 Reynoldsville Pennsylvania U.S.A.
109 J9 Reynosa Mexico
40 B5 Reyssouze R France
78 K3 Rezaiyeh Iran
37 K5 Rezat R W Germany
20 G7 Reze France
52 C6 Rēzekne U.S.S.R.
55 D3 Rezh U.S.S.R.
48 M3 Rezina U.S.S.R.
47 J3 Rezvaya R Turkey
41 K5 Rezzonico Italy
32 K6 Rhade W Germany
98 C3 Rhame North Dakota U.S.A.
41 L3 Rhätikon mt Switzerland
36 C4 Rhaunen W Germany
8 C3 Rhayader Wales
32 H9 Rheda-Wiedenbrück W Germany
32 F6 Rhede Niedersachsen W Germany
32 E9 Rhede Nordrhein-Westfalen W Germany
25 F4 Rheden Netherlands
9 F3 Rhee, R England
119 P7 Rhein Saskatchewan Canada
36 E6 Rhein R W Europe
36 D6 Rheinau W Germany
36 B2 Rheinbach W Germany
36 D3 Rheinböllen W Germany
36 C3 Rheinbrohl W Germany
25 F6 Rheindahlen W Germany
32 F8 Rheine W Germany
41 J2 Rheinfall Switzerland
40 G2 Rheinfeldon Switzerland
32 E10 Rheinhausen W Germany
36 B3 Rheinland-Pfalz land W Germany
36 E6 Rheinmünster W Germany
33 R6 Rheinsberg East Germany
36 E6 Rheinstetten W Germany
41 L3 Rhein Tal V Switzerland
36 E5 Rheinzabern W Germany
40 F6 Rhêmes, Val de Italy
85 D3 Rhemilès Algeria
32 J10 Rhena W Germany
25 E5 Rhenen Netherlands
36 D3 Rhens W Germany
36 B1 Rheydt W Germany
33 R6 Rhin R East Germany
40 G2 Rhin R France
36 D7 Rhinau France
Rhine R France see Rhin R
Rhine R Germany/Switzerland see Rhein R
112 D6 Rhine Georgia U.S.A.
95 O5 Rhinebeck New York U.S.A.
99 R4 Rhinelander Wisconsin U.S.A.
33 R7 Rhinkanal East Germany
33 Q7 Rhinow East Germany
16 E9 Rhis, Oued R Morocco
41 K6 Rho Italy
127 K1 Rhoades, Pt Jamaica
95 Q5 Rhode I state U.S.A.
94 F9 Rhodell West Virginia U.S.A.
32 K10 Rhoden W Germany
Rhodes isld see Ródhos isld
83 L13 Rhodes B Kerguelen Indian Oc
94 C3 Rhodes Michigan U.S.A.
Rhodesia see Zimbabwe
112 F2 Rhodhiss L North Carolina U.S.A.
109 K2 Rhome Texas U.S.A.
8 C4 Rhondda Wales
19 J7 Rhône dept France
19 O13 Rhône R France
41 H5 Rhône R Switzerland
19 N18 Rhône, Grand R France
19 Rhône Valley France
8 B4 Rhosili Wales
8 B1 Rhosneigr Wales
8 C1 Rhos-on-Sea Wales
85 F2 Rhourd El Baguel Algeria
8 C1 Rhuddlan Wales
18 G7 Rhue R France
20 E6 Rhuis, Presqu'île de pen France
32 M9 Rhume R W Germany
18 D9 Rhune, la mt France/Spain
8 C3 Rhydd Hywel mt Wales
8 C1 Rhyl Wales
32 G9 Rhynern W Germany
15 F3 Rhynie Scotland
131 E8 Riachos, I de los Argentina
16 B2 Ria de Arosa est Spain
16 A2 Ria de Corcubion est Spain
16 A1 Ria de Lage est Spain
16 A2 Ria de Murosa y Noya est Spain
16 B2 Ria de Pontevedra est Spain
16 B1 Ria de Sta. Marta est Spain
16 B2 Ria de Vigo est Spain
20 H6 Riallé France
70 B5 Riam Kalimantan
45 N5 Riano Italy
16 D2 Riaño Spain
19 P17 Rians France
16 E5 Riansares R Spain
20 D6 Riantec France
74 F2 Riasi Kashmir
69 F12 Riau, Kep islds Indonesia
16 E3 Riaza R Spain
16 B2 Ribadavia Spain
16 C1 Ribadeo Spain
16 D1 Ribadesella Spain
17 H2 Ribagorza dist Spain
129 K4 Ribamar Brazil
17 H3 Ribarroja, Emb. de res Spain
17 J2 Ribas de Fresser Spain
130 D7 Ribas do Rio Pardo Brazil
16 B5 Ribatejo prov Portugal
88 G9 Ribauè Mozambique
26 K1 Ribbenesöy isld Norway
13 F6 Ribble, R England
28 B6 Ribe Denmark
28 B6 Ribe Å R Denmark
40 F1 Ribeauville France
22 D4 Ribécourt France
133 H2 Ribeira R Brazil
133 H2 Ribeirão Prêto Brazil
129 J5 Ribeiro Gonçalves Brazil
22 E4 Ribemont France
43 E11 Ribera Sicily
18 F7 Ribérac France
128 E6 Riberalta Bolivia
19 P16 Ribiers France
121 L5 Rib Lake Ontario Canada
99 Q4 Rib Lake Wisconsin U.S.A.
99 R5 Rib Mt Wisconsin U.S.A.
42 F3 Ribnica Yugoslavia
33 Q4 Ribnitz-Damgarten East Germany
118 G6 Ribstone Alberta Canada
118 F6 Ribstone Cr Alberta Canada
142 B5 Rica,Mt Western Australia Australia
109 K8 Ricardo Texas U.S.A.
45 M3 Riccione Italy
103 K7 Rice California U.S.A.
109 L3 Rice Texas U.S.A.
112 F6 Riceboro Georgia U.S.A.
121 M8 Rice L Ontario Canada
99 N3 Rice L Minnesota U.S.A.
120 H5 Rice Lake Ontario Canada
99 P4 Rice Lake Wisconsin U.S.A.
119 N8 Riceton Saskatchewan Canada
99 O6 Riceville Iowa U.S.A.
18 H5 Riceys, les France
118 K6 Richard Saskatchewan Canada
110 L6 Richard City Tennessee U.S.A.
114 H3 Richard Collinson Inlet Northwest Territories Canada
89 H7 Richard's B S Africa
114 F4 Richards I Northwest Territories Canada
116 N6 Richardson Alaska U.S.A.
109 L3 Richardson Texas U.S.A.
109 O8 Richardson Texas U.S.A.
117 O3 Richardson I Northwest Territories Canada
95 R2 Richardson Lakes Maine U.S.A.
143 C8 Richardson, Mt Western Australia Australia
114 F4 Richardson Mts Yukon Terr/N W Terr Canada
144 B6 Richardson Mts New Zealand
119 N8 Richardson Sta Saskatchewan Canada
85 A5 Richard Toll Senegal
98 D3 Richardton North Dakota U.S.A.
94 J4 Richburg New York U.S.A.
118 F7 Richdale Alberta Canada
143 C10 Riche, C Western Australia Australia
121 R7 Richelieu R Quebec Canada
21 L7 Richelieu France
21 O2 Richemont France
123 P3 Riche Pt Newfoundland Canada
101 U2 Richey Montana U.S.A.
101 L6 Richfield Idaho U.S.A.
107 J4 Richfield Kansas U.S.A.
103 M3 Richfield Utah U.S.A.
95 L4 Richford New York U.S.A.
121 S8 Richford Vermont U.S.A.
102 E6 Richgrove California U.S.A.
110 B3 Rich Hill Missouri U.S.A.
122 H7 Richibucto New Brunswick Canada
118 F4 Rich Lake Alberta Canada
112 C5 Richland Georgia U.S.A.
94 B4 Richland Michigan U.S.A.
110 D4 Richland Missouri U.S.A.
101 T1 Richland Montana U.S.A.
95 N7 Richland New Jersey U.S.A.
100 H5 Richland Oregon U.S.A.
100 F3 Richland Washington U.S.A.
99 Q6 Richland Center Wisconsin U.S.A.
109 L4 Richland Cr Texas U.S.A.
112 K3 Richlands North Carolina U.S.A.
94 F9 Richlands Virginia U.S.A.
109 J4 Richland Springs Texas U.S.A.
118 J7 Richlea Saskatchewan Canada
139 K5 Richmond New South Wales Australia
141 G5 Richmond Queensland Australia
139 H8 Richmond Tasmania Australia
121 P7 Richmond Ontario Canada
122 H7 Richmond Prince Edward I Canada
121 S7 Richmond Quebec Canada
9 F5 Richmond England
13 G5 Richmond North Yorkshire England
127 L2 Richmond Jamaica
145 D4 Richmond New Zealand
89 C8 Richmond S Africa
102 B4 Richmond California U.S.A.
110 M2 Richmond Indiana U.S.A.
110 M4 Richmond Kentucky U.S.A.
95 S2 Richmond Maine U.S.A.
99 M4 Richmond Minnesota U.S.A.
100 F5 Richmond Oregon U.S.A.
109 M6 Richmond Texas U.S.A.
101 O8 Richmond Utah U.S.A.
94 K9 Richmond Virginia U.S.A.
121 L9 Richmond Hill Ontario Canada
112 F6 Richmond Hill Georgia U.S.A.
142 A4 Richmond, L Western Australia Australia
139 L3 Richmond R New South Wales Australia
139 L3 Richmond Ra mts New South Wales Australia
95 N4 Richmondville New York U.S.A.
118 H8 Richmound Saskatchewan Canada
110 B7 Rich Mt Arkansas U.S.A.
33 R4 Richtenberg East Germany
111 H10 Richton Mississippi U.S.A.
99 L3 Richville Minnesota U.S.A.
94 D6 Richwood Ohio U.S.A.
94 G8 Richwood West Virginia U.S.A.
99 S6 Richwood Wisconsin U.S.A.
110 F3 Richwoods Missouri U.S.A.
32 M4 Rickling W Germany
9 F4 Rickmansworth England
17 G3 Ricla Spain
106 B4 Rico Colorado U.S.A.
40 F5 Riddes Switzerland
100 J7 Riddle Idaho U.S.A.
100 B7 Riddle Oregon U.S.A.
140 C6 Riddock, Mt N Terr Australia
121 P7 Rideau R Ontario Canada
121 P8 Rideau Canal Ontario Canada
121 O8 Rideau, L Ontario Canada
120 F2 Ridge R Ontario Canada
98 B4 Ridge Montana U.S.A.
102 G6 Ridgecrest California U.S.A.
119 N5 Ridgedale Saskatchewan Canada
101 N7 Ridgedale Idaho U.S.A.
99 T10 Ridge Farm Illinois U.S.A.
95 O5 Ridgefield Connecticut U.S.A.
111 F9 Ridgeland Mississippi U.S.A.
112 F5 Ridgeland South Carolina U.S.A.
99 P4 Ridgeland Wisconsin U.S.A.
141 K6 Ridgelands Queensland Australia
94 J7 Ridgeley West Virginia U.S.A.
95 M8 Ridgely Maryland U.S.A.
112 F4 Ridge Spring South Carolina U.S.A.
120 J10 Ridgetown Ontario Canada
98 F4 Ridgeview South Dakota U.S.A.
118 E1 Ridgeville Manitoba Canada
110 L1 Ridgeville Indiana U.S.A.
112 G4 Ridgeville South Carolina U.S.A.
110 C1 Ridgeway Missouri U.S.A.
112 G3 Ridgeway South Carolina U.S.A.
99 Q6 Ridgeway Wisconsin U.S.A.
110 G5 Ridgley Tennessee U.S.A.
106 C3 Ridgway Colorado U.S.A.
110 H4 Ridgway Illinois U.S.A.
98 B4 Ridgway Montana U.S.A.
119 R8 Riding Mt Manitoba Canada
143 D10 Ridley,Mt Western Australia Australia
142 C5 Ridley, R Western Australia Australia
118 J7 Ridpath Saskatchewan Canada
13 F3 Ridsdale England
26 J5 Riebnes L Sweden
20 C6 Riec France
38 H5 Ried Austria
37 M5 Rieden W Germany
37 M6 Riedenburg W Germany
36 D5 Riedseltz France
33 T6 Riegenwalde East Germany
40 G2 Riehen Switzerland
118 B2 Riel Manitoba Canada
32 H8 Riemsloh W Germany
36 H3 Rieneck W Germany
110 H7 Rienzi Mississippi U.S.A.
33 S10 Riesa East Germany
133 C8 Riesco, I Chile
43 F11 Riesi Sicily
33 O10 Riestedt East Germany
89 D7 Riet R S Africa
52 B6 Rietavas U.S.S.R.
32 H9 Rietberg W Germany
89 B3 Rietfontein Namibia
42 E6 Rieti Italy
41 O3 Rietzer Grieskogel mt Austria
18 G8 Rieupeyroux France
20 F6 Rieux Morbihan France
19 Q17 Riez France
22 G4 Rièzes Belgium
16 D10 Rif dist Morocco
100 C3 Riffe Lake Washington U.S.A.
106 C2 Rifle Colorado U.S.A.
94 C2 Rifle R Michigan U.S.A.
29 T8 Rifstangi C Iceland
52 B5 Rīga U.S.S.R.
Riga, Gulf of see Rizhskiy Zaliv
142 B5 Riga,Mt Western Australia Australia
77 F5 Rigān Iran
121 Q7 Rigaud Quebec Canada
101 O6 Rigby Idaho U.S.A.
110 F2 Riggston Illinois U.S.A.
37 M4 Riglasreuth W Germany
45 K4 Rignano sull'Arno Italy
21 L7 Rigny-Ussé France
115 O7 Rigolet Labrador, Nfld Canada
80 G4 Rihaba Jordan
29 M4 Riipi Finland
146 K8 Riiser-Larsenhalvøya pen Antarctica
146 J7 Riiser-Larsen Sea Antarctica
42 F3 Rijeka Yugoslavia
25 C5 Rijsbergen Netherlands
25 G4 Rijssen Netherlands
25 B4 Rijswijk Netherlands
48 H2 Rika R U.S.S.R.
69 C10 Rikitgaib Sumatra
60 R2 Rikubetsu Japan
61 Q6 Rikuchū Kaigan Nat. park Japan
61 P6 Rikuzen Takata Japan
46 F2 Rila plateau Bulgaria
46 F2 Rila Bulgaria
110 J2 Riley Indiana U.S.A.
107 O2 Riley Kansas U.S.A.
106 C7 Riley New Mexico U.S.A.
100 F6 Riley Oregon U.S.A.
21 L7 Rillé France
46 F2 Rilski Manastir Bulgaria
128 C4 Rimachi, L Peru
145 E1 Rimariki I New Zealand
40 B1 Rimaucourt France
69 G14 Rimau, Pulau isld Sumatra
48 F2 Rimava R Czechoslovakia
118 C6 Rimbey Alberta Canada
27 K12 Rimbo Sweden
94 H5 Rimersburg Pennsylvania U.S.A.
27 H13 Rimforsa Sweden
45 N3 Rimini Italy
48 L5 Rîmmicu Sărat Romania
80 E2 Rimmon Israel
48 K5 Rimna R Romania
48 J5 Rîmnicu Vîlcea Romania
22 H4 Rimoqne France
122 D5 Rimouski R Quebec Canada
36 H4 Rimpar W Germany
40 G5 Rimpfischhorn mt Switzerland
75 N4 Rinbung China
71 J9 Rinca isld Indonesia
37 P6 Rinchnach W Germany
106 C9 Rincon New Mexico U.S.A.
126 A2 Rincon Bonaire W Indies
133 D2 Rinconada Argentina
124 H6 Rincón de Romos Mexico
28 A6 Rindby Denmark
70 K8 Rindingan, Bukit hill Sumatra
70 Q10 Rindjani, Gunung mt Indonesia
28 B4 Rind Kirke Denmark
139 J8 Ringarooma Tasmania Australia
74 F5 Ringas India
28 E6 Ringe Denmark
27 D10 Ringebu Norway
41 K4 Ringelspitz mt Switzerland
27 D11 Ringerike L Norway
12 D4 Ringford Scotland
37 J1 Ringgau W Germany
109 O3 Ringgold Louisiana U.S.A.
109 K2 Ringgold Texas U.S.A.
28 C5 Ringive Denmark
28 A4 Ringkøbing Denmark
47 P13 Ringládhes Greece
101 P3 Ringling Montana U.S.A.
109 K1 Ringling Oklahoma U.S.A.
9 G6 Ringmer England
109 M1 Ringold Oklahoma U.S.A.
27 E11 Ringsaker Norway
28 H6 Ringsted Denmark
99 M6 Ringsted Iowa U.S.A.
27 H13 Ringstorp Sweden
26 K2 Ringvassöy isld Norway
140 C6 Ringwood N Terr Australia
9 E6 Ringwood England
107 M5 Ringwood Oklahoma U.S.A.
46 G7 Rinia isld Greece
133 C5 Rinihue Chile
131 A7 Riñihue, L Chile
27 H15 Rinkabyholm Sweden
28 D7 Rinkenæs Denmark
41 O3 Rinn Austria
12 B2 Rinns Pt Scotland
27 G16 Rinqsjön L Sweden
32 K8 Rinteln W Germany
22 B2 Rinxent France
99 Q8 Rio Illinois U.S.A.
111 G11 Rio Louisiana U.S.A.
99 R6 Rio Wisconsin U.S.A.
125 P5 Río Abajo Panama
130 C5 Rio Aleqre Brazil
124 G4 Rio Arreola Mexico
128 C4 Riobamba Ecuador
85 F8 Rio Benito Mbini Equat Guinea
128 E5 Rio Branco Brazil
133 G4 Rio Branco Uruguay
130 E9 Rio Branco do Sul Brazil
109 J10 Río Bravo Mexico
108 B5 Rio Bravo del Norte R Mexico
133 C6 Rio Bueno Chile
127 K1 Rio Bueno Jamaica
127 N9 Río Caribe Venezuela
133 D7 Río Chico Argentina
127 M9 Río Chico Venezuela
130 F8 Rio Claro Brazil
127 P3 Rio Claro Trinidad
127 K10 Rio Claro Venezuela
131 D4 Río Cuarto Argentina
132 Rio de Janeiro conurbation Brazil
100 A9 Rio Dell Scotia California U.S.A.
128 D2 Rio de Oro Colombia
85 A4 Rio de Oro, B. de Western Sahara
131 E2 Río Dulce Argentina
133 D8 Río Gallegos Argentina
131 B6 Río Grande R Argentina
131 H4 Rio Grande Brazil
124 H6 Río Grande Mexico
125 M3 Rio Grande R Nicaragua
106 D4 Rio Grande R U.S.A./Mexico
109 J9 Rio Grande City Texas U.S.A.
130 H8 Rio Grande do Norte Brazil
131 G2 Rio Grande do Sul state Brazil
106 C4 Rio Grande Res Colorado U.S.A.
90 F12 Rio Grande Rise Atlantic Oc
109 K10 Rio Grande Valley airport Texas U.S.A.
127 H9 Ríohacha Colombia
108 B2 Rio Hondo R New Mexico U.S.A.
109 K9 Rio Hondo Texas U.S.A.
128 C5 Rioja Peru
102 C3 Rio Landa California U.S.A.
130 J10 Rio Largo Brazil
102 C3 Rio Linda California U.S.A.
45 L3 Riolo Terme Italy
16 B5 Rio Maior Portugal
109 J6 Riomedina Texas U.S.A.
18 G7 Riom ès Montagne France
133 E3 Río Muerto Argentina
133 D1 Río Mulatos Bolivia
85 G8 Río Muni prov Equat Guinea
131 C8 Rio Negro prov Argentina
130 E10 Rio Negro Brazil
131 F4 Rio Negro dept Uruguay
131 G4 Rio Negro, Embalse del res Uruguay
130 C6 Rio Negro, Pantanal do swamp Brazil
43 G8 Rionero in Vulture Italy
124 F3 Rio Palacio Mexico
17 F6 Riópar Spain
133 G4 Rio Pardo Brazil
127 M5 Río Piedras Puerto Rico
130 F5 Rio Prêto, Sa. do mts Brazil
128 E8 Río Quetena R Bolivia
129 L6 Rio Real Brazil
45 J2 Rio Saliceto Italy
130 J9 Rio Tinto Brazil
100 K8 Rio Tinto Nevada U.S.A.
71 C6 Rio Tuba Philippines
133 C8 Río Turbio Mines Argentina
19 O18 Riou, I. de France
128 C3 Rioverde Ecuador
125 J7 Río Verde Mexico
130 C6 Rio Verdi de Mato Grosso Brazil
109 K3 Rio Vista Texas U.S.A.
130 C6 Riozinho, R Brazil
48 F6 Ripanj Yugoslavia
44 B1 Riparia Italy
100 G3 Riparia Washington U.S.A.
26 L5 Ripats Sweden
122 K2 Ripault, L Quebec Canada
45 O4 Ripe Italy
45 O6 Ripi Italy
120 J8 Ripley Ontario Canada
9 F5 Ripley England
9 E1 Ripley England
13 G5 Ripley N Yorks England
103 K8 Ripley California U.S.A.
110 H7 Ripley Mississippi U.S.A.
94 H4 Ripley New York U.S.A.
110 N3 Ripley Ohio U.S.A.
107 O5 Ripley Oklahoma U.S.A.
110 G6 Ripley Tennessee U.S.A.
94 F8 Ripley West Virginia U.S.A.
17 J2 Ripoll Spain
121 P7 Ripon Quebec Canada
13 G5 Ripon England
102 C4 Ripon California U.S.A.
99 S6 Ripon Wisconsin U.S.A.
142 D5 Ripon Hills Western Australia Australia
99 M8 Rippey Iowa U.S.A.
13 G6 Ripponden England
100 J4 Riqgins Idaho U.S.A.
45 N5 Riqnano Flaminio Italy
28 C5 Ris Denmark
42 J6 Risan Yugoslavia
79 D8 Risân 'Aneiza mt Egypt
26 H7 Risbäck Sweden
18 E9 Riscle France
131 B5 Risco Plateado pk Argentina
28 C6 Rise Denmark
26 H7 Risede Sweden
28 C3 Risgårde Bredning B Denmark
47 H2 Rish Bulgaria
60 P1 Rishiri-suidō str Japan
60 P1 Rishiri-tō isld Japan
80 C6 Rishon LeZiyyon Israel
57 J6 Rishtan U.S.S.R.
112 B3 Rising Fawn Georgia U.S.A.
109 J3 Rising Star Texas U.S.A.
95 L7 Rising Sun Maryland U.S.A.
94 D5 Rising Sun Ohio U.S.A.
110 M3 Risinq Sun Indiana U.S.A.
117 M10 Riske Creek British Columbia Canada
21 L3 Risle R France
42 F3 Risnjak mt Yugoslavia
48 J5 Rîsnov Romania
111 D8 Rison Arkansas U.S.A.
27 D13 Risör Norway
21 P4 Ris-Orangis France
40 D4 Risoux, Mont France
36 H7 Riss R W Germany
26 D8 Rissa Norway
145 F3 Rissington New Zealand
52 B5 Rist U.S.S.R.
29 N10 Ristiina Finland
29 N7 Ristijärvi Finland
28 F7 Ristinge Denmark
26 M5 Risträsk Sweden
28 B7 Risum-Lindholm W Germany
108 B8 Rita Blanca Cr R Texas U.S.A.
70 D4 Ritan R Kalimantan
142 B5 Ritchie Reef Western Australia Australia
68 A6 Ritchie's Arch Andaman Is
83 K9 Ritigala mt Sri Lanka
37 J3 Ritschenhausen East Germany
100 F5 Ritter Oregon U.S.A.
32 J6 Ritterhude W Germany
102 E4 Ritter, Mt California U.S.A.
94 F6 Rittman Ohio U.S.A.
32 M10 Rittmarshausen W Germany
100 G2 Ritzville Washington U.S.A.
68 D7 Riu, Laem Thailand
71 K9 Riung Flores Indonesia
41 N6 Riva Italy
47 N10 Riva Turkey
47 N11 Riva R Turkey
21 K3 Riva Bella France
133 E2 Rivadavia Argentina
133 C3 Rivadavia Chile
38 F8 Riva di Tures Italy
22 K3 Rivage Belgium
19 N14 Rival R France
44 B1 Rivalta di Torinese Italy
125 M4 Rivas Nicaragua
133 E5 Rivera Argentina
131 G3 Rivera Uruguay
102 D4 Riverbank California U.S.A.
85 C7 River Cess Liberia
102 E5 Riverdale California U.S.A.
107 N4 Riverdale Kansas U.S.A.
101 O2 Riverdale Montana U.S.A.
98 G9 Riverdale Nebraska U.S.A.
98 E2 Riverdale North Dakota U.S.A.
123 L8 River Denys C Breton I, Nova Scotia
111 K10 River Falls Alabama U.S.A.
99 O5 River Falls Wisconsin U.S.A.
123 T7 Riverhead Newfoundland Canada
95 P6 Riverhead Long I, New York U.S.A.
122 H8 River Hébert Nova Scotia Canada
118 L8 Riverhurst Saskatchewan Canada
139 H5 Riverina reg New Scuth Wales Australia
143 D8 Riverina Western Australia Australia
122 J8 River John Nova Scotia Canada
109 L9 River Oaks Texas U.S.A.
123 P3 River of Ponds Newfoundland Canada
133 C7 Rivero, I Chile
122 H9 Riverport Nova Scotia Canada
119 R8 Rivers Manitoba Canada
145 F4 Riversdale New Zealand
144 B6 Riversdale New Zealand
89 B10 Riversdale S Africa
120 H10 Riverside Ontario Canada
102 G8 Riverside California U.S.A.
95 K8 Riverside Maryland U.S.A.
100 G6 Riverside Oregon U.S.A.
109 M5 Riverside Texas U.S.A.
101 N8 Riverside Utah U.S.A.
101 T8 Riverside Wyoming U.S.A.
98 B9 Riverside Res Colorado U.S.A.
117 K10 Rivers Inlet British Columbia Canada
140 E4 Riversleigh Queensland Australia
119 M9 Rivers, L. of the Saskatchewan Canada
138 E5 Riverton South Australia Australia
119 U8 Riverton Manitoba Canada
144 B7 Riverton New Zealand
110 G2 Riverton Illinois U.S.A.
99 L9 Riverton Iowa U.S.A.
98 H9 Riverton Nebraska U.S.A.
94 J8 Riverton Virginia U.S.A.
101 R6 Riverton Wyoming U.S.A.
100 C2 Riverton Heights Washington U.S.A.
110 F6 Rivervale Arkansas U.S.A.
122 H7 Riverview New Brunswick Canada
98 G7 Riverview Nebraska U.S.A.
19 P14 Rives France
110 G5 Rives Tennessee U.S.A.
94 C4 Rives Junc Michigan U.S.A.
94 G7 Rivesville West Virginia U.S.A.
103 K6 Riviera Nevada U.S.A.
109 K8 Riviera Texas U.S.A.
113 G11 Riviera Beach Florida U.S.A.
44 F3 Riviera di Levante Italy
44 D4 Riviera di Ponente Italy
21 J4 Rivière Orne France
22 D3 Rivière Pas-de-Calais France
122 G4 Rivière à Claude Quebec Canada
122 J4 Rivière-à-la-Loutre Quebec Canada
121 S6 Rivière à Pierre Quebec Canada
122 H5 Rivière-au-Renard Quebec Canada
122 G3 Rivière aux Graines Quebec Canada
121 S5 Rivière-aux-Rats Quebec Canada
122 D6 Rivière Bleue Quebec Canada
122 K4 Rivière-de-la-Chaloupe Quebec Canada
83 M13 Rivière des Anguilles Mauritius
122 C6 Rivière du Loup Quebec Canada
121 S5 Rivière du Milieu Quebec Canada
122 B5 Rivière du Moulin Quebec Canada
121 M4 Rivière Héva Quebec Canada
122 G4 Rivière La Madeleine Quebec Canada
122 B6 Rivière Ouelle Quebec Canada
122 E4 Rivière Pentecôte Quebec Canada
122 G3 Rivière Pigou Quebec Canada
127 M4 Rivière Pilote Martinique W Indies
122 H3 Rivière St. Jean Quebec Canada
21 L3 Rivière-St. Sauveur, la France
127 L4 Rivière Salée Martinique W Indies
122 D6 Rivière-Verte New Brunswick Canada
122 C6 Rivière Verte Quebec Canada
44 C1 Rivoli Italy
138 E6 Rivoli B South Australia Australia
145 D4 Riwaka New Zealand
72 F4 Riyāḍ, Ar Saudi Arabia
Riyadh see Riyāḍ, Ar
71 E3 Rizal Luzon Philippines
78 H1 Rize Turkey
65 D7 Rizhao China
52 B5 Rizhskiy Zaliv U.S.S.R.
79 E3 Rizokarpaso Cyprus
46 E5 Rizoma Greece
43 H10 Rizzuto, C Italy
27 C12 Rjukan Norway
27 B12 Rjuven Norway
85 A5 Rkiz, L Mauritania
80 E1 Rmaich Lebanon
68 H5 Ro Vietnam
27 E11 Roa Norway
16 E3 Roa Spain
110 K2 Roachdale Indiana U.S.A.
9 F3 Roade England
106 B9 Road Forks New Mexico U.S.A.
127 M5 Road Town Virgin Is
28 B6 Roager Denmark
103 P2 Roan Cliffs Utah U.S.A.
106 B2 Roan Cr Colorado U.S.A.
112 E1 Roan Mt North Carolina U.S.A.
18 H6 Roanne France
111 L8 Roanoke Alabama U.S.A.
99 R9 Roanoke Illinois U.S.A.
94 B6 Roanoke Indiana U.S.A.
109 K3 Roanoke Texas U.S.A.
94 H9 Roanoke Virginia U.S.A.
112 M2 Roanoke I North Carolina U.S.A.
112 K1 Roanoke Rapids North Carolina U.S.A.
106 B2 Roan Plateau Colorado U.S.A.
103 P2 Roan Plateau Utah U.S.A.
109 M5 Roans Prairie Texas U.S.A.
95 L5 Roaring Branch Pennsylvania U.S.A.
112 F1 Roaring Gap North Carolina U.S.A.
108 G2 Roaring Springs Texas U.S.A.
14 B5 Roaringwater B Ireland
77 D4 Robāt Iran
77 B2 Robāṭ Karim Iran
109 J9 Robberson Texas U.S.A.
112 H2 Robbins North Carolina U.S.A.
139 G8 Robbins I Tasmania Australia
112 D2 Robbinsville North Carolina U.S.A.
44 E1 Robbio Italy
138 E6 Robe South Australia Australia
14 B3 Robe R Ireland
33 R6 Röbel East Germany
109 O4 Robeline Louisiana U.S.A.
138 F4 Robe, Mt New South Wales Australia
122 K3 Robe Noir, L. de la Quebec Canada
142 B5 Robe R Western Australia Australia
112 K2 Robersonville North Carolina U.S.A.
108 G4 Robert Lee Texas U.S.A.
140 B7 Robert, Mt N Terr Australia
13 F3 Roberton Scotland
101 N6 Roberts Idaho U.S.A.
101 Q4 Roberts Montana U.S.A.
100 E5 Roberts Oregon U.S.A.
123 R4 Robert's Arm Newfoundland Canada
9 G6 Robertsbridge England
102 H2 Roberts Cr. Mt Nevada U.S.A.
111 J11 Robertsdale Alabama U.S.A.
26 L7 Robertsfors Sweden
110 A6 Robert S. Kerr Res Oklahoma U.S.A.
141 K8 Roberts, Mt Queensland Australia
101 Q7 Roberts Mt Wyoming U.S.A.
141 G4 Robertson R Queensland Australia
89 A9 Robertson S Africa
101 P8 Robertson Wyoming U.S.A.
146 C12 Robertson Bay Antarctica
146 D4 Robertson I Antarctica
142 D6 Robertson Ra Western Australia Australia
121 T6 Robertsonville Quebec Canada
85 B7 Robertsport Liberia
138 E5 Robertstown South Australia Australia
14 E3 Robertstown Ireland
122 G6 Robertville New Brunswick Canada
121 S4 Roberval Quebec Canada
115 N1 Robeson Chan Canada/Greenland
8 B4 Robeston Wathen Wales
101 N7 Robin Idaho U.S.A.
100 J5 Robinette Oregon U.S.A.
13 H5 Robin Hoods Bay England
141 J7 Robinson R Queensland Australia
110 J2 Robinson Illinois U.S.A.
98 G2 Robinson North Dakota U.S.A.
133 B9 Robinson Crusoe isld Juan Fernández Is Pacific Oc
138 D2 Robinson, Mt South Australia Australia
142 C6 Robinson, Mt Western Australia Australia
116 Q6 Robinson Mts Alaska U.S.A.
143 C7 Robinson Ras Western Australia Australia
140 D3 Robinson River N Terr Australia
122 F6 Robinsonville New Brunswick Canada
139 G5 Robinvale New South Wales Australia
17 F6 Robledo Spain
103 N9 Robles Pass Arizona U.S.A.
103 N9 Robles Ranch Arizona U.S.A.
118 A1 Roblin Park Manitoba Canada
128 G7 Robore Bolivia
118 H9 Robsart Saskatchewan Canada
117 O9 Robson, Mt Alberta/Br Col Canada
117 O9 Robson, Mt British Columbia Canada
109 K8 Robstown Texas U.S.A.
16 A6 Roca, C. da Portugal
119 Q8 Rocanville Saskatchewan Canada
129 M4 Rocas isld Brazil
124 B5 Rocas Alijos isld Mexico
43 G8 Roccadaspide Italy
45 P5 Rocca di Mezzo Italy
45 N6 Rocca di Papa Italy
45 O6 Roccagorga Italy
43 H8 Rocca Imperiale Italy
Rocca Littorio see Gaalkacyo
45 P7 Roccamonfina Italy
38 E9 Rocca Pietore Italy
45 L3 Rocca San Casciano Italy
45 P6 Roccasecca Italy
45 N5 Rocca Sinibalda Italy
42 D5 Roccastrada Italy
44 B1 Rocciamelone mt Italy
40 E5 Roc d'Enfer mt France
131 G5 Rocha Uruguay
131 G4 Rocha dept Uruguay
21 K5 Rochard, Mt France
13 F6 Rochdale England
121 N4 Rochebaucourt Quebec Canada
20 F6 Roche-Bernard, la France
21 H7 Roche Blanche, la France
18 F7 Rochechouart France
20 D4 Roche-Derrien, la France
22 K3 Roche-en-Ardenne, La Belgium
22 J3 Rochefort Belgium
18 E7 Rochefort France
19 N17 Rochefort-du-Gard France
20 F6 Rochefort-en-Terre France
18 G7 Rochefort-Montagne France
18 F7 Rochefoucauld, la France
21 O3 Roche-Guyon, la France
22 J4 Rochehaut Belgium
113 E8 Rochelle Florida U.S.A.
112 D6 Rochelle Georgia U.S.A.
99 R8 Rochelle Illinois U.S.A.
111 D10 Rochelle Louisiana U.S.A.
109 H4 Rochelle Texas U.S.A.
18 E6 Rochelle, la France
119 P9 Roche Percee Saskatchewan Canada
110 D3 Rocheport Missouri U.S.A.
21 M8 Roche-Posay, la France
127 L4 Rocher du Diamant Martinique W Indies
123 O2 Rocher, L. du Quebec Canada
117 R5 Rocher River Northwest Territories Canada
122 E3 Rochers, R. aux Quebec Canada
20 E3 Roches Douvres islds English Chan
20 H8 Rocheservière France
83 M12 Roches, Plaine des Mauritius
40 E1 Rochesson France
139 G6 Rochester Victoria Australia
118 D4 Rochester Alberta Canada
9 G5 Rochester England
13 F3 Rochester Northumberland England
110 G2 Rochester Illinois U.S.A.
94 A5 Rochester Indiana U.S.A.
94 D4 Rochester Michigan U.S.A.
99 O5 Rochester Minnesota U.S.A.
95 Q3 Rochester New Hampshire U.S.A.
95 K3 Rochester New York U.S.A.
121 N9 Rochester New York U.S.A.
94 E5 Rochester Ohio U.S.A.
94 G6 Rochester Pennsylvania U.S.A.
108 H2 Rochester Texas U.S.A.
100 B3 Rochester Washington U.S.A.
20 H8 Roche-sur-Yon, La France
9 G4 Rochford England
98 C5 Rochford South Dakota U.S.A.
118 B5 Rochfort Br Alberta Canada
37 O1 Rochlitz East Germany
118 E6 Rochon Sands Prov. Park Alberta Canada
21 P3 Rochy-Condé France
117 K5 Rock R Yukon Territory Canada
98 K6 Rock R Iowa/Minnesota U.S.A.
107 O4 Rock Kansas U.S.A.
99 T3 Rock Michigan U.S.A.
99 S6 Rock R Wisconsin U.S.A.
6 B5 Rockall N Atlantic Oc
90 H3 Rockall Bank Atlantic Oc
144 C6 Rock and Pillar Range New Zealand
117 L10 Rock Bay British Columbia Canada
12 E4 Rockcliffe Scotland

72
Rock Cr — Rumbek

101 M3 **Rock Cr** Montana U.S.A.
101 S1 **Rock Cr** Montana U.S.A.
94 G5 **Rock Cr** Ohio U.S.A.
100 E4 **Rock Cr** Oregon U.S.A.
101 T8 **Rock Cr** Wyoming U.S.A.
117 D3 **Rock Creek** Yukon Territory Canada
101 L7 **Rockcreek** Idaho U.S.A.
109 K5 **Rockdale** Texas U.S.A.
146 B10 **Rockefeller Mts** Antarctica
146 C9 **Rockefeller Plat** Antarctica
36 D4 **Rockenhausen** W Germany
99 R8 **Rock Falls** Illinois U.S.A.
94 J9 **Rockfish** Virginia U.S.A.
111 K9 **Rockford** Alabama U.S.A.
101 N6 **Rockford** Idaho U.S.A.
99 R7 **Rockford** Illinois U.S.A.
94 B3 **Rockford** Michigan U.S.A.
99 N4 **Rockford** Minnesota U.S.A.
94 C6 **Rockford** Ohio U.S.A.
100 H2 **Rockford** Washington U.S.A.
119 M9 **Rockglen** Saskatchewan Canada
98 H5 **Rockham** South Dakota U.S.A.
141 K6 **Rockhampton** Queensland Australia
140 D4 **Rockhampton Downs** N Terr Australia
99 S1 **Rock Harbor** Michigan U.S.A.
118 J6 **Rockhaven** Saskatchewan Canada
112 F3 **Rock Hill** South Carolina U.S.A.
99 Q8 **Rock I** Illinois U.S.A.
143 B9 **Rockingham** Western Australia Australia
112 H3 **Rockingham** North Carolina U.S.A.
141 H4 **Rockingham B** Queensland Australia
121 S7 **Rock Island** Quebec Canada
109 L6 **Rock Island** Texas U.S.A.
98 G1 **Rock L** North Dakota U.S.A.
100 H2 **Rock L** Washington U.S.A.
121 P7 **Rockland** Ontario Canada
101 N7 **Rockland** Idaho U.S.A.
95 S2 **Rockland** Maine U.S.A.
99 R3 **Rockland** Michigan U.S.A.
109 N4 **Rockland** Texas U.S.A.
140 E4 **Rocklands** Queensland Australia
138 F6 **Rocklands Res** Victoria Australia
141 K2 **Rocklea** *dist* Brisbane, Qnsld Australia
142 B6 **Rocklea** Western Australia Australia
100 G2 **Rockdyn** Washington U.S.A.
112 B3 **Rockmart** Georgia U.S.A.
117 Q3 **Rocknest L** Northwest Territories Canada
33 R10 **Röcknitz** East Germany
95 L8 **Rock Point** Maryland U.S.A.
102 A2 **Rockport** California U.S.A.
110 E2 **Rockport** Illinois U.S.A.
110 J4 **Rockport** Indiana U.S.A.
95 S2 **Rockport** Maine U.S.A.
95 R4 **Rockport** Massachusetts U.S.A.
110 A1 **Rock Port** Missouri U.S.A.
109 K7 **Rockport** Texas U.S.A.
100 D1 **Rockport** Washington U.S.A.
101 U8 **Rock River** Wyoming U.S.A.
113 L13 **Rock Sound** Bahamas
126 F2 **Rock Sound** Eleuthera Bahamas
103 M7 **Rock Springs** Arizona U.S.A.
101 T3 **Rock Springs** Montana U.S.A.
108 G5 **Rocksprings** Texas U.S.A.
101 Q8 **Rock Springs** Wyoming U.S.A.
144 D4 **Rocks Pt.** New Zealand
128 G2 **Rockstone** Guyana
99 R7 **Rockton** Illinois U.S.A.
98 K6 **Rock Valley** Iowa U.S.A.
145 D4 **Rockville** New Zealand
95 P5 **Rockville** Connecticut U.S.A.
110 J2 **Rockville** Indiana U.S.A.
95 K7 **Rockville** Maryland U.S.A.
100 H6 **Rockville** Oregon U.S.A.
112 G5 **Rockville** South Carolina U.S.A.
103 L4 **Rockville** Utah U.S.A.
109 L3 **Rockwall** Texas U.S.A.
99 N7 **Rockwell** Iowa U.S.A.
112 G2 **Rockwell** North Carolina U.S.A.
99 M7 **Rockwell City** Iowa U.S.A.
106 C4 **Rockwood** Colorado U.S.A.
95 S1 **Rockwood** Maine U.S.A.
94 H7 **Rockwood** Pennsylvania U.S.A.
112 C2 **Rockwood** Tennessee U.S.A.
109 H4 **Rockwood** Texas U.S.A.
112 G2 **Rocky** *R* North Carolina U.S.A.
107 L6 **Rocky** Oklahoma U.S.A.
112 E3 **Rocky** *R* South Carolina U.S.A.
100 K6 **Rocky Bar** Idaho U.S.A.
139 H8 **Rocky C** Tasmania Australia
118 D7 **Rockyford** Alberta Canada
106 G3 **Rocky Ford** Colorado U.S.A.
112 F5 **Rocky Ford** Georgia U.S.A.
98 D6 **Rockyford** South Dakota U.S.A.
94 D7 **Rocky Fork Res** Ohio U.S.A.
94 H5 **Rocky Grove** Pennsylvania U.S.A.
143 B10 **Rocky Gully** Western Australia Australia
120 H5 **Rocky Island L** Ontario Canada
119 Q4 **Rocky L** Manitoba Canada
112 K2 **Rocky Mount** North Carolina U.S.A.
94 H10 **Rocky Mount** Virginia U.S.A.
118 C6 **Rocky Mountain House** Alberta Canada
101 N2 **Rocky Mt** Montana U.S.A.
98 A9 **Rocky Mt Nat. Park** Colorado U.S.A.
118 B8 **Rocky Mts** British Columbia Canada
106 C1 **Rocky Mts** N America
127 K3 **Rocky Point** Jamaica
95 P6 **Rocky Point** Long I, New York U.S.A.
98 A5 **Rockypoint** Wyoming U.S.A.
113 K11 **Rocky Pt** Bahamas
116 F4 **Rocky Pt** Alaska U.S.A.
94 F5 **Rocky River** Ohio U.S.A.
131 D7 **Ró Colorado** Argentina
20 F3 **Rocque Pt. La** Channel Is
22 H4 **Rocroi** France
37 M2 **Roda** *R* East Germany
36 D5 **Rodalben** W Germany
27 C11 **Rödberg** Norway
28 G7 **Rødby** Denmark
28 G7 **Rødbyhavn** Denmark
123 Q3 **Roddickton** Newfoundland Canada
28 B3 **Rødding** Denmark
28 C6 **Rødding** Sønderjylland Denmark
27 H15 **Rödeby** Sweden
25 F2 **Roden** Netherlands
32 K8 **Rodenberg** W Germany
27 E12 **Rödenes** Norway
32 H6 **Rodenkirchen** W Germany
37 L3 **Rödental** W Germany
124 G5 **Rodeo** Mexico
106 B10 **Rodeo** New Mexico U.S.A.
33 S10 **Röderau** East Germany
109 O3 **Rodessa** Louisiana U.S.A.
32 K7 **Rodewald** W Germany
37 N2 **Rodewisch** East Germany
18 G8 **Rodez** France
36 F2 **Rodheim-Bieber** W Germany
46 F4 **Rodholívos** Greece
47 V14 **Ródhos** *isld* Greece
47 V14 **Ródhos** Greece
45 J1 **Rodigo** Italy
37 O5 **Roding** W Germany
140 C6 **Rodinga** N Terr Australia
52 J2 **Rodionovo** U.S.S.R.
28 C4 **Rødkærsbro** Denmark
77 J6 **Rodkhan** Pakistan
48 J3 **Rodnei, Muntii** Romania
120 J10 **Rodney** Ontario Canada
94 B3 **Rodney** Michigan U.S.A.
116 D4 **Rodney, C** Alaska U.S.A.
52 F6 **Rodniki** U.S.S.R.
55 C5 **Rodnikovka** U.S.S.R.
54 D3 **Rodnya** U.S.S.R.
139 H7 **Rodondo** *isld* Victoria Australia
13 E3 **Rodono** Scotland
46 G3 **Rodopi Planina** Bulgaria
Rodosto *see* **Tekirdağ**
26 F5 **Rödöy** Norway
128 D5 **Rodrigues** Brazil
81 D7 **Rodrigues I** Indian Oc
28 H7 **Rødsand** *sandbank* Denmark
28 D3 **Rød Sø** Denmark
29 K6 **Rødvig** Denmark
14 E2 **Roe** *R* N Ireland
111 E7 **Roe** Arkansas U.S.A.
142 B5 **Roebourne** Western Australia Australia
142 D4 **Roebuck B** Western Australia Australia
142 D4 **Roebuck Plains** Western Australia Australia
143 E9 **Roe, L** Western Australia Australia
21 H6 **Roë, la** France
143 G9 **Roe Plains** Western Australia Australia
25 E6 **Roermond** Netherlands
22 D2 **Roesbrugge-Haringe** Belgium
22 E2 **Roeselare** Belgium
115 L5 **Roes Welcome Sound** Northwest Territories Canada
45 L2 **Ro Ferrarese** Italy
109 L1 **Roff** Oklahoma U.S.A.
54 B3 **Rogachev** U.S.S.R.
128 E7 **Rogaguado, L** Bolivia
128 E6 **Rogagua, L** Bolivia
27 A12 **Rogaland** *county* Norway
54 H7 **Rogan'** U.S.S.R.
109 O5 **Roganville** Texas U.S.A.
48 J1 **Rogatin** U.S.S.R.
33 P8 **Rogatz** East Germany
26 F9 **Rogen** *L* Sweden
121 M5 **Roger, Lac** Quebec Canada
110 B5 **Rogers** Arkansas U.S.A.
98 H2 **Rogers** North Dakota U.S.A.
109 K5 **Rogers** Texas U.S.A.
94 D1 **Rogers City** Michigan U.S.A.
102 G7 **Rogers L.** California U.S.A.
117 P10 **Rogers, Mt** British Columbia Canada
101 L7 **Rogerson** Idaho U.S.A.
122 G7 **Rogersville** New Brunswick Canada
110 J7 **Rogersville** Alabama U.S.A.
110 C4 **Rogersville** Missouri U.S.A.
112 D1 **Rogersville** Tennessee U.S.A.
98 B9 **Roggen** Colorado U.S.A.
33 O5 **Roggendorf** East Germany
89 A8 **Roggeveld Berge** *mts* S Africa
8 D4 **Rogiet** Wales
43 G9 **Rogliano** Italy
19 O18 **Rognac** France
26 H4 **Rognan** Norway
19 O17 **Rognes** France
33 O6 **Rögnitz** *R* East Germany
44 B2 **Rognosa, Punta** *mt* Italy
46 D1 **Rogozna** *mt* Yugoslavia
31 K3 **Rogoźno** Poland
100 A7 **Rogue** *R* Oregon U.S.A.
20 E5 **Rohan** France
121 Q3 **Rohault, L** Quebec Canada
33 P6 **Rohlsdorf** East Germany
28 J6 **Roholte** Denmark
37 M6 **Rohr** W Germany
38 J4 **Rohrbach** Austria
36 C5 **Rohrbach** France
37 O7 **Rohrbach** W Germany
33 O7 **Rohrberg** East Germany
36 G4 **Rohrbrunn** W Germany
74 C5 **Rohri** Pakistan
37 L7 **Röhrmoos** W Germany
74 G4 **Rohtak** India
111 E8 **Rohwer** Arkansas U.S.A.
21 L7 **Roiffe** France
22 E4 **Roisel** France
22 F3 **Roisin** Belgium
33 Q9 **Roitzsch** Halle East Germany
33 R9 **Roitzsch** Leipzig East Germany
52 B6 **Roja** U.S.S.R.
26 G9 **Röjan** Sweden
133 E4 **Rojas** Argentina
127 L5 **Rojo, C** Puerto Rico
141 G2 **Rokeby** Queensland Australia
119 P7 **Rokeby** Saskatchewan Canada
29 O5 **Rokhmoyva, G** *mt* U.S.S.R.
52 C6 **Rokiškis** U.S.S.R.
53 C8 **Rokitnoye** U.S.S.R.
77 L2 **Rokkah** Afghanistan
61 P5 **Rokkasho** Japan
26 M6 **Roknäs** Sweden
29 M7 **Rokua Nat. Park** Finland
61 O6 **Rokugō** Japan
61 L8 **Rokugō-saki** *C* Japan
30 H6 **Rokycany** Czechoslovakia
44 C4 **Rola** *R* Italy
40 B2 **Rolampont** France
118 D1 **Roland** Manitoba Canada
83 L13 **Roland** *isld* Kerguelen Indian Oc
110 D7 **Roland** Arkansas U.S.A.
99 N7 **Roland** Iowa U.S.A.
130 D8 **Rolândia** Brazil
28 D3 **Rold** Denmark
27 B12 **Röldal** Norway
25 G3 **Rolde** Netherlands
98 G1 **Rolette** North Dakota U.S.A.
99 M7 **Rolfe** Iowa U.S.A.
94 J5 **Rolfe** Pennsylvania U.S.A.
141 H6 **Rolfes** Queensland Australia
103 L9 **Roll** Arizona U.S.A.
117 N8 **Rolla** British Columbia Canada
107 J4 **Rolla** Kansas U.S.A.
110 E4 **Rolla** Missouri U.S.A.
98 G1 **Rolla** North Dakota U.S.A.
27 D11 **Rollag** Norway
141 J6 **Rolleston** Queensland Australia
144 D5 **Rolleston** New Zealand
144 C5 **Rolleston, Mt** New Zealand
144 C5 **Rolleston Range** New Zealand
121 L5 **Rollet** Quebec Canada
21 L2 **Rolleville** France
110 L4 **Rolling Fork** *R* Kentucky U.S.A.
111 F9 **Rolling Fork** Mississippi U.S.A.
101 L2 **Rollins** Montana U.S.A.
45 J2 **Rolo** Italy
33 R4 **Rolofshagen** East Germany
68 G6 **Rolous** Cambodia
121 N6 **Rolphton** Ontario Canada
28 F6 **Rolsted** Denmark
26 N1 **Rolvsöy** *isld* Norway
28 A3 **Rom** Denmark
141 J7 **Roma** Queensland Australia
71 N8 **Roma** *isld* Indonesia
44 M6 **Roma** Italy
27 K14 **Roma** Sweden
45 H3 **Romagna** *reg* Italy
42 B3 **Romagnano Sesia** Italy
20 H5 **Romagné** France
22 J5 **Romagne-sous-Montfaucon** France
144 B7 **Romahapa** New Zealand
122 J3 **Romaine, R** Quebec Canada
109 H9 **Roma Los Saenz** Texas U.S.A.
46 F1 **Roman** Bulgaria
48 K4 **Roman** Romania
126 F3 **Romana, Cayo** *isld* Cuba
19 P14 **Romanche** *R* France
90 H8 **Romanche Gap** Atlantic Oc
19 N12 **Romanèche-Thorins** France
48 G5 **Romania** *rep* E Europe
113 F12 **Romano, C** Florida U.S.A.
58 F1 **Romanovka** U.S.S.R.
55 D2 **Romanovo** U.S.S.R.
36 C6 **Romanswiller** France
116 D6 **Romanzof, C** Alaska U.S.A.
116 Q2 **Romanzof Mts** Alaska U.S.A.
128 F4 **Romão** Brazil
20 H5 **Romazy** France
71 F4 **Romblon** Philippines
Rome *see* **Roma**
111 L7 **Rome** Georgia U.S.A.
95 M3 **Rome** New York U.S.A.
95 L5 **Rome** Pennsylvania U.S.A.
110 K5 **Rome** Tennessee U.S.A.
106 E4 **Romeo** Colorado U.S.A.
94 D4 **Romeo** Michigan U.S.A.
36 E5 **Römerberg** W Germany
22 H3 **Romerée** Belgium
27 E11 **Romerike** *reg* Norway
125 K8 **Romero** Mexico
106 E6 **Romeroville** New Mexico U.S.A.
36 H7 **Römerstein** W Germany
40 C6 **Romey, Val** France
9 G4 **Romford** England
37 K3 **Römhild** East Germany
20 G5 **Romille** France
18 H4 **Romilly** France
21 M3 **Romilly** Eure France
21 N3 **Romilly-sur-Andelle** France
142 F5 **Romily, Mt** Western Australia Australia
57 E5 **Romit** U.S.S.R.
57 C5 **Romitan** U.S.S.R.
36 B1 **Rommerskirchen** W Germany
94 J7 **Romney** West Virginia U.S.A.
54 E6 **Romny** U.S.S.R.
28 A6 **Rømø** *isld* Denmark
54 E6 **Romodan** U.S.S.R.
21 O7 **Romorantin** France
69 F11 **Rompin** Malaysia
36 G2 **Romrod** W Germany
26 C9 **Romsdal** *V* Norway
26 B9 **Romsdalsfjord** *inlet* Norway
9 E6 **Romsey** England
28 F5 **Romsø** *isld* Denmark
94 D4 **Romulus** Michigan U.S.A.
68 H4 **Ron** Vietnam
15 C3 **Rona** *isld* Scotland
101 L2 **Ronan** Montana U.S.A.
28 B3 **Rønbjerg** Denmark
126 D8 **Roncador Bank** Caribbean
129 H6 **Roncador, Sa. do** *mts* Brazil
94 G9 **Ronceverte** West Virginia U.S.A.
20 H4 **Roncey** France
40 E2 **Ronchamp** France
44 M5 **Ronciglione** Italy
45 M3 **Ronco** *R* Italy
45 J1 **Roncoferraro** Italy
45 M3 **Roncofreddo** Italy
22 E2 **Roncq** France
16 D8 **Ronda** Spain
26 D10 **Rondane** Norway
16 D8 **Ronda, Sa. de** *mts* Spain
128 F7 **Rondas-das-Salinas** Brazil
28 E4 **Rønde** Denmark
120 J10 **Rondeau Prov. Park** Ontario Canada
83 L14 **Ronde I** Kerguelen Indian Oc
26 D10 **Rondeslottet** *mt* Norway
128 D2 **Rondón** Colombia
128 F6 **Rondônia** Brazil
130 C5 **Rondonópolis** Brazil
128 F3 **Rondon, Pico** *mt* Brazil
88 G7 **Rondo Plat** Tanzania
36 B2 **Rondorf** W Germany
95 N5 **Rondout Res** New York U.S.A.
27 K14 **Ronehamn** Sweden
67 C4 **Rong'an** China
67 B2 **Rongchang** China
65 C5 **Rongcheng** China
65 E6 **Rongcheng** China
67 C4 **Rongjiang** China
67 C4 **Rong Jiang** *R* China
68 A1 **Rongklang Ra** Burma
70 G6 **Rongko** *R* Sulawesi
145 E4 **Rongotea** New Zealand
67 C4 **Rongshui** China
88 H7 **Rongüi** *isld* Mozambique
67 C5 **Rong Xian** China
67 A2 **Rong Xian** China
28 A3 **Rønland** *C* Denmark
27 G16 **Rønne** Denmark
27 F15 **Rönnea** *R* Sweden
37 N2 **Ronneburg** East Germany
27 H15 **Ronneby** Sweden
146 C6 **Ronne Entrance** Antarctica
146 D6 **Ronne Ice Shelf** Antarctica
32 L8 **Ronnenberg** W Germany
26 G8 **Rönnöfors** Sweden
142 C5 **Ronsard I** Western Australia Australia
22 F2 **Ronse** Belgium
129 H6 **Ronuro** *R* Brazil
25 G2 **Roodeschool** Netherlands
110 F2 **Roodhouse** Illinois U.S.A.
22 L4 **Roodt** Luxembourg
89 F4 **Rooiberg** *mt* S Africa
25 B5 **Roosendaal** Netherlands
103 N8 **Roosevelt** Arizona U.S.A.
99 L1 **Roosevelt** Minnesota U.S.A.
109 H1 **Roosevelt** Oklahoma U.S.A.
108 G5 **Roosevelt** Texas U.S.A.
101 P9 **Roosevelt** Utah U.S.A.
100 E4 **Roosevelt** Washington U.S.A.
103 N8 **Roosevelt Dam** Arizona U.S.A.
117 O12 **Roosevelt, F.D., L** Washington U.S.A.
135 L16 **Roosevelt I** Antarctica
146 C10 **Roosevelt I** Antarctica
117 L6 **Roosevelt, Mt** British Columbia Canada
14 D3 **Roosky** Ireland
89 F5 **Roossenekal** *mt* S Africa
117 L4 **Root** *R* Northwest Territories Canada
99 P6 **Root** *R* Minnesota U.S.A.
116 E9 **Rootok I** Aleutian Is
52 B6 **Ropaži** U.S.S.R.
52 H3 **Ropcha** U.S.S.R.
31 N5 **Ropczyce** Poland
140 D2 **Roper** *R* N Terr Australia
112 L2 **Roper** North Carolina U.S.A.
140 C2 **Roper Bar Police Station** N Terr Australia
29 J3 **Ropi** *mt* Finland
36 D6 **Roppenheim** France
18 E8 **Roquefort** France
121 L4 **Roquemaure** Quebec Canada
19 N16 **Roquemaure** France
19 P18 **Roquevaire** France
15 E2 **Rora Head** Scotland
128 F3 **Roraima** *state* Brazil
128 F2 **Roraima** *mt* Guyana
27 F10 **Rörbäcksnäs** Sweden
28 D3 **Rørbæk** Denmark
28 G5 **Rørby** Denmark
89 G7 **Rorke's Drift** S Africa
119 S7 **Rorketon** Manitoba Canada
26 E9 **Röros** Norway
41 L3 **Rorschach** Switzerland
26 H4 **Rörstad** Norway
28 H5 **Rørvig** Denmark
26 E7 **Rörvik** Norway
48 N1 **Ros'** *R* U.S.S.R.
26 G6 **Röså** *R* Norway
43 B12 **Rosa, C** Algeria
122 B7 **Rosaire** Quebec Canada
107 O4 **Rosalia** Kansas U.S.A.
100 H2 **Rosalia** Washington U.S.A.
118 E6 **Rosalind** Alberta Canada
126 D6 **Rosalind Bank** Caribbean
102 F7 **Rosamond** California U.S.A.
102 F7 **Rosamond L** California U.S.A.
40 G6 **Rosa, Monte** *mt* Italy
124 G6 **Rosamorada** Mexico
109 K6 **Rosanky** Texas U.S.A.
41 M3 **Rosanna** *R* Austria
19 P16 **Rosans** France
124 E4 **Rosa, Pta** *C* Mexico
131 E4 **Rosario** Argentina
129 K4 **Rosário** Brazil
128 E8 **Rosario** Chile
124 E4 **Rosario** Mexico
124 B2 **Rosario** Baja California Mexico
124 H4 **Rosario** Coahuila Mexico
130 B9 **Rosario** Paraguay
71 E4 **Rosario** Philippines
127 H9 **Rosario** Venezuela
126 B5 **Rosario Bank** Caribbean
126 D4 **Rosario, Cayo del** Cuba
133 E3 **Rosario de la Frontera** Argentina
133 D2 **Rosario de Lerma** Argentina
133 F4 **Rosario del Tala** Argentina
126 C3 **Rosario, Sa. del** *hills* Cuba
124 D4 **Rosarito** Mexico
124 B3 **Rosarito** Mexico
16 D4 **Rosarito Embalse de** *res* Spain
17 K2 **Rosas** Spain
20 A5 **Roscanvel** France
33 N7 **Rosche** W Germany
99 S7 **Roscoe** Illinois U.S.A.
101 Q4 **Roscoe** Montana U.S.A.
95 N5 **Roscoe** New York U.S.A.
98 G4 **Roscoe** South Dakota U.S.A.
108 G3 **Roscoe** Texas U.S.A.
20 C4 **Roscoff** France
14 C3 **Roscommon** *co* Ireland
14 C3 **Roscommon** Ireland
94 C2 **Roscommon** Michigan U.S.A.
14 D4 **Roscrea** Ireland
98 G7 **Rose** Nebraska U.S.A.
127 O7 **Roseau** Dominica
98 K1 **Roseau** *R* Minnesota U.S.A.
139 H8 **Roseberry** Tasmania Australia
100 J5 **Roseberry** Idaho U.S.A.
140 E7 **Roseberth** Queensland Australia
123 O6 **Rose Blanche** Newfoundland Canada
112 J3 **Roseboro** North Carolina U.S.A.
118 D7 **Rosebud** Alberta Canada
110 E3 **Rosebud** Missouri U.S.A.
101 T3 **Rosebud** Montana U.S.A.
108 A8 **Rosebud** New Mexico U.S.A.
98 F6 **Rosebud** South Dakota U.S.A.
109 L4 **Rosebud** Texas U.S.A.
101 T4 **Rosebud Cr** Montana U.S.A.
101 S4 **Rosebud Mts** Montana U.S.A.
100 B6 **Roseburg** Oregon U.S.A.
94 C3 **Rosebush** Michigan U.S.A.
94 C2 **Rose City** Michigan U.S.A.
102 G1 **Rose Creek** Nevada U.S.A.
141 K6 **Rosedale** Queensland Australia
118 E7 **Rosedale** Alberta Canada
110 J2 **Rosedale** Indiana U.S.A.
111 F8 **Rosedale** Mississippi U.S.A.
13 H5 **Rosedale Abbey** England
22 H3 **Rosée** Belgium
38 K8 **Rosegg** Austria
127 J1 **Rose Hall** Jamaica
83 L12 **Rose Hill** Mauritius
99 O8 **Rose Hill** Iowa U.S.A.
112 J3 **Rose Hill** North Carolina U.S.A.
113 K12 **Rose I** Bahamas
111 F11 **Roseland** Louisiana U.S.A.
118 F7 **Rose Lynn** Alberta Canada
118 E8 **Rosemary** Alberta Canada
6 D3 **Rosemary Bank** N Atlantic Oc
142 B5 **Rosemary I** Western Australia Australia
99 N5 **Rosemount** Minnesota U.S.A.
102 E2 **Rose, Mt** Nevada U.S.A.
38 J8 **Rosenbach** *mt* Austria
33 O5 **Rosenberg** East Germany
109 M6 **Rosenberg** Texas U.S.A.
36 G5 **Rosenberg** W Germany
22 C1 **Rosendaël** France
32 F8 **Rosendahl** W Germany
110 B1 **Rosendale** Missouri U.S.A.
121 M8 **Roseneath** Ontario Canada
12 D1 **Roseneath** Scotland
36 F7 **Rosenfeld** W Germany
32 L6 **Rosengarten** W Germany
38 F6 **Rosenheim** W Germany
38 M8 **Rosenkopf** *mt* Austria
38 J8 **Rosennock** *mt* Austria
38 K8 **Rosental** *V* Austria
36 F2 **Rosenthal** W Germany
109 O5 **Rosepine** Louisiana U.S.A.
117 H8 **Rose Pt** British Columbia Canada
140 D2 **Rose R** N Terr Australia
118 J8 **Roseray** Saskatchewan Canada
126 G3 **Roses** Long I Bahamas
118 K7 **Rosetown** Saskatchewan Canada
141 H5 **Rosetta** *R* Queensland Australia
Rosetta Egypt *see* **Rashîd**
101 M8 **Rosette** Utah U.S.A.
119 O6 **Rose Valley** Saskatchewan Canada
110 F1 **Roseville** Illinois U.S.A.
94 E7 **Roseville** Ohio U.S.A.
118 A5 **Rosewear** Alberta Canada
140 B3 **Rosewood** N Terr Australia
141 K8 **Rosewood** Queensland Australia
101 L7 **Roseworth** Idaho U.S.A.
52 E6 **Roshal'** U.S.S.R.
109 M6 **Rosharon** Texas U.S.A.
52 C4 **Roshchino** U.S.S.R.
55 E4 **Roshchinskoye** U.S.S.R.
36 C6 **Rosheim** France
80 C5 **Rosh Ha 'Ayin** Israel
77 F2 **Roshkhvār** Iran
98 K4 **Rosholt** South Dakota U.S.A.
99 R5 **Rosholt** Wisconsin U.S.A.
80 F2 **Rosh Pinna** Israel
57 F6 **Roshtkala** U.S.S.R.
80 D7 **Rosh Zurim** Jordan
31 J6 **Rosice** Czechoslovakia
110 H4 **Rosiclare** Illinois U.S.A.
22 D4 **Rosières-en-Santerre** France
122 H5 **Rosiers, C.des** Quebec Canada
21 K7 **Rosiers, les** France
142 A5 **Rosily I** Western Australia Australia
48 J6 **Roşiori de Vede** Romania
46 G1 **Rositsa** *R* Bulgaria
47 J1 **Rositsa** Bulgaria
37 N1 **Rositz** East Germany
28 J5 **Roskilde** *co* Denmark
28 J5 **Roskilde** Denmark
33 R8 **Roskow** East Germany
103 N9 **Roskruge Mts** Arizona U.S.A.
54 D3 **Roslavl'** U.S.S.R.
14 D2 **Roslea** N Ireland
28 B3 **Roslev** Denmark
52 F5 **Roslyatino** U.S.S.R.
98 J4 **Roslyn** South Dakota U.S.A.
100 D2 **Roslyn** Washington U.S.A.
120 C3 **Roslyn L** Ontario Canada
28 F4 **Rosmus** Denmark
28 F5 **Røsnæs** *C* Denmark
21 N8 **Rosnay** France
20 B5 **Rosnoen** France
45 M1 **Rosolina** Italy
20 C6 **Rosporden** France
22 L4 **Rosport** Luxembourg
36 C2 **Rosrath** W Germany
139 J8 **Ross** Tasmania Australia
83 L14 **Ross** *mt* Kerguelen Indian Oc
144 C5 **Ross** New Zealand
98 D1 **Ross** North Dakota U.S.A.
101 U6 **Ross** Wyoming U.S.A.
41 K5 **Rossa** Switzerland
37 K3 **Rossach** W Germany
Ross and Cromarty *co see* **Highland** *reg*
43 H9 **Rossano** Italy
14 C2 **Rossan Pt** Ireland
37 N3 **Rossbach** Czechoslovakia
33 P10 **Rossbach** East Germany
111 G9 **Ross Barnett Res** Mississippi U.S.A.
119 R8 **Rossburn** Manitoba Canada
14 B5 **Ross Carbery** Ireland
108 F3 **Ross City** Texas U.S.A.
146 A10 **Ross Dependency** Antarctica
37 J2 **Rossdorf** East Germany
121 L7 **Rosseau** Ontario Canada
137 L4 **Rossel** *isld* Louisiade Arch
119 T9 **Rossendale** Manitoba Canada
109 L3 **Rosser** Texas U.S.A.
8 D1 **Rossett** Wales
26 K2 **Rossfjord** Norway
83 M9 **Ross Hill** *mt* Christmas I Indian Oc
146 C11 **Ross I** Antarctica
119 U4 **Ross I** Manitoba Canada
146 C10 **Ross Ice Shelf** Antarctica
22 J4 **Rossignal** Belgium
122 G9 **Rossignol Res** Nova Scotia Canada
94 J6 **Rossiter** Pennsylvania U.S.A.
143 E10 **Rossiter B** Western Australia Australia
52 **Rossiyskaya SFSR** U.S.S.R.
100 D1 **Ross L** Washington U.S.A.
33 O10 **Rossla** East Germany
100 E1 **Ross Lake Nat. Recreation Area** Washington U.S.A.
100 H1 **Rossland** British Columbia Canada
14 E4 **Rosslare** Ireland
33 Q9 **Rosslau** East Germany
33 O10 **Rossleben** East Germany
145 E4 **Ross, Mt** New Zealand
85 A5 **Rosso** Mauritania
26 H8 **Rossön** Sweden
8 D4 **Ross-on-Wye** England
54 L6 **Rossosh'** U.S.S.R.
33 R6 **Rossow** East Germany
120 C4 **Rossport** Ontario Canada
140 C6 **Ross River** N Terr Australia
117 G4 **Ross River** Yukon Territory Canada
146 B11 **Ross Sea** Antarctica
37 K5 **Rosstal** W Germany
108 E7 **Rosston** Oklahoma U.S.A.
33 O9 **Rosstrappe** East Germany
26 G6 **Rössvassbukt** Norway
26 G6 **Rössvatn** *L* Norway
110 J5 **Rossview Res** Tennessee U.S.A.
112 B3 **Rossville** Georgia U.S.A.
110 J1 **Rossville** Illinois U.S.A.
107 P2 **Rossville** Kansas U.S.A.
37 P1 **Rosswein** East Germany
117 J8 **Rosswood** British Columbia Canada
26 F4 **Röst** *isld* Norway
26 L3 **Rosta** Norway
26 L3 **Rostaelv** *R* Norway
26 L2 **Rostafjord** *mt* Norway
77 C7 **Rostam** *oil well* Persian Gulf
27 F16 **Röstånga** Sweden
77 L1 **Rostāq** Afghanistan
118 L6 **Rosthern** Saskatchewan Canada
36 C2 **Rostingen** W Germany
33 Q4 **Rostock** *reg* East Germany
33 Q4 **Rostock** East Germany
26 M3 **Rostonsölkä** *reg* Sweden
52 E6 **Rostov** U.S.S.R.
53 E10 **Rostov-na-Donu** U.S.S.R.
53 F10 **Rostovskaya Oblast'** *prov* U.S.S.R.
20 D5 **Rostrenen** France
28 D3 **Rostrup** Denmark
46 D3 **Rostuša** Yugoslavia
26 D9 **Röstvangen** Norway
52 H2 **Rosvinskoye** U.S.S.R.
112 C3 **Roswell** Georgia U.S.A.
108 C2 **Roswell** New Mexico U.S.A.
27 G10 **Rot** Sweden
41 M1 **Rot** *R* W Germany
26 F5 **Rota** *C* Norway
16 C8 **Rota** Spain
37 J5 **Rot am See** W Germany
108 G3 **Rotan** Texas U.S.A.
37 N5 **Rot Buhl** *mt* W Germany
71 L10 **Rote** *isld* Timor Indonesia
36 H2 **Rotenburg** Hessen W Germany
32 K6 **Rotenburg/Wümme** Niedersachsen W Germany
38 G8 **Roter Kopf** *mt* Austria
37 L3 **Roter Main** *R* W Germany
32 H5 **Roter Sand** W Germany
41 L3 **Rote Wand** *mt* Austria
25 F7 **Rotgen** W Germany
36 D2 **Roth** W Germany
37 N1 **Rötha** East Germany
36 E1 **Rothaargebirge** *mts* W Germany
36 C7 **Rothau** France
13 G3 **Rothbury** England
99 U6 **Rothbury** Michigan U.S.A.
36 D2 **Rothe Mühle** W Germany
37 L5 **Röthenbach** W Germany
41 L2 **Röthenbach** W Germany
33 P9 **Rothenburg** East Germany
37 J5 **Rothenburg ober der Tauber** W Germany
20 G4 **Rothéneuf** France
36 H4 **Rothenfels** W Germany
36 E6 **Rothenfels** Baden-Württemberg W Germany
37 L3 **Rothenkirchen** W Germany
33 O10 **Rothenschirmbach** East Germany
146 C5 **Rothera** *U.K. Base* Antarctica
13 G6 **Rotherham** England
144 D5 **Rotherham** New Zealand
9 G5 **Rother, R** England
15 E3 **Rothes** Scotland
122 G8 **Rothesay** New Brunswick Canada
12 C2 **Rothesay** Scotland
40 H4 **Rothorn** *mt* Switzerland
98 K3 **Rothsay** Minnesota U.S.A.
146 C5 **Rothschild I** Antarctica
Roti *see* **Rote**
71 L10 **Roti** Indonesia
71 L10 **Roti, Selat** Indonesia
139 H5 **Roto** New South Wales Australia
145 E3 **Rotoaira, L** New Zealand
145 F2 **Rotoehu, L** New Zealand
145 D4 **Rotoiti, L** New Zealand
145 F3 **Rotoiti, L** New Zealand
145 F3 **Rotomahana** New Zealand
145 F3 **Rotoma, L** New Zealand
144 C5 **Rotomanu** New Zealand
43 H8 **Rotondella** Italy
45 O5 **Rotondo, M** *mt* Italy
144 D4 **Rotoroa** New Zealand
145 D4 **Rotoroa, L** New Zealand
145 F3 **Rotorua** New Zealand
145 E2 **Rotowaro** New Zealand
21 K3 **Rots** France
41 N2 **Rott** W Germany
37 O7 **Rott** *R* W Germany
33 R9 **Rotta** East Germany
36 F7 **Rottenburg** W Germany
37 J4 **Rottendorf** W Germany
38 K6 **Rottenmann** Austria
38 K7 **Rottenmanner Tauern** *mts* Austria
25 C5 **Rotterdam** Netherlands
37 P7 **Rotthalmünster** W Germany
9 F6 **Rottingdean** England
36 H4 **Rottingen** W Germany
33 N9 **Rottleberode** East Germany
143 B9 **Rottnest I** Western Australia Australia
33 R8 **Rottstock** East Germany
25 G1 **Rottumeroog** *isld* Netherlands
25 F2 **Rottumerplaat** Netherlands
41 J1 **Rottweil** W Germany
137 Q4 **Rotuma** *isld* Pacific Oc
37 O5 **Rötz** W Germany
20 G7 **Rouans** France
22 E2 **Roubaix** France
19 N15 **Roubion** *R* France
31 H5 **Roudnice** Czechoslovakia
20 C5 **Roudouallec** France
21 N3 **Rouen** France
40 F2 **Rouffach** France
20 H6 **Rougé** France
40 D3 **Rougemont** France
7 L9 **Rough** *oil rig* North Sea
8 D2 **Roughclose** England
144 B6 **Rough Ridge** New Zealand
110 K4 **Rough River L** Kentucky U.S.A.
19 P18 **Rougiers** France
18 E7 **Rouillac** France
119 N8 **Rouleau** Saskatchewan Canada
Roulers *see* **Roeselare**
94 J5 **Roulette** Pennsylvania U.S.A.
121 L5 **Roulier** Quebec Canada
22 G3 **Rœulx** Belgium
18 F7 **Roumazières** France
116 J4 **Roundabout Mt** Alaska U.S.A.
101 L2 **Round Butte** Montana U.S.A.
123 R4 **Round Harbour** Newfoundland Canada
118 E5 **Round Hill** Alberta Canada
141 K6 **Round Hill Hd** Queensland Australia
87 G12 **Round I** Mauritius
116 H7 **Round I** Alaska U.S.A.
109 J5 **Round Mountain** Texas U.S.A.
139 K4 **Round Mt** New South Wales Australia
102 G3 **Round Mt** Nevada U.S.A.
123 R5 **Round Pond** Newfoundland Canada
95 S3 **Round Pond** Maine U.S.A.
109 K5 **Round Rock** Texas U.S.A.
117 R3 **Roundrock L** Northwest Territories Canada
110 E4 **Round Spring** Missouri U.S.A.
101 R3 **Roundup** Montana U.S.A.
119 S9 **Rounthwaite** Manitoba Canada
129 H3 **Roura** Fr Guiana
44 B2 **Roure** Italy
75 L7 **Rourkela** India
15 F1 **Rousay** Orkney Scotland
106 F4 **Rouse** Colorado U.S.A.
94 H5 **Rouseville** Pennsylvania U.S.A.
142 A2 **Rous Hd** Perth, W Aust Australia
133 D9 **Rous, Pen** Chile
19 O17 **Roussillon** France
22 L5 **Roussy-le-Village** France
19 P15 **Route Napoléon** France
21 M3 **Routot** France
25 F3 **Rouveen** Netherlands
121 U3 **Rouvray, L** Quebec Canada
40 A2 **Rouvres** France
22 H4 **Rouvroy-sur-Audry** France
22 G3 **Roux** Belgium
89 E8 **Rouxville** S Africa
121 M4 **Rouyn** Quebec Canada
48 L1 **Rov** *R* U.S.S.R.
41 M6 **Rovato** Italy
26 A9 **Rovde** Norway
52 F4 **Rovdino** U.S.S.R.
54 L8 **Roven'ki** U.S.S.R.
45 J1 **Roverbella** Italy
41 O6 **Rovereto** Italy
68 F6 **Rovieng** Cambodia
45 L1 **Rovigo** Italy
45 P1 **Rovinj** Yugoslavia
45 P1 **Rovinjsko Selo** Yugoslavia
53 C8 **Rovno** U.S.S.R.
87 G8 **Rovuma** *R* Mozambique
99 N7 **Rowan** Iowa U.S.A.
118 J1 **Rowan L** Ontario Canada
106 E6 **Rowe** New Mexico U.S.A.
139 J3 **Rowena** New South Wales Australia
108 G4 **Rowena** Texas U.S.A.
112 G4 **Rowesville** South Carolina U.S.A.
100 K8 **Rowland** Nevada U.S.A.
94 H7 **Rowlesburg** West Virginia U.S.A.
118 E7 **Rowley** Alberta Canada
115 M4 **Rowley I** Northwest Territories Canada
142 C3 **Rowley Shoals** Western Australia Australia
103 M9 **Rowood** Arizona U.S.A.
9 E1 **Rowsley** England
103 K5 **Rox** Nevada U.S.A.
71 E2 **Roxas** Luzon Philippines
71 E4 **Roxas** Mindoro Philippines
71 D5 **Roxas** Palawan Philippines
71 F5 **Roxas** Panay Philippines
112 H1 **Roxboro** North Carolina U.S.A.
127 N2 **Roxborough** Tobago
140 E6 **Roxborough Downs** Queensland Australia
Roxburgh *co see* **Borders** *reg*
144 B6 **Roxburgh** New Zealand
144 B6 **Roxburgh,L** New Zealand
95 N4 **Roxbury** New York U.S.A.
95 P2 **Roxbury** Vermont U.S.A.
138 D4 **Roxby Downs** South Australia Australia
27 H13 **Roxen** *L* Sweden
111 E10 **Roxie** Mississippi U.S.A.
109 M2 **Roxton** Texas U.S.A.
121 S7 **Roxton-Sud** Quebec Canada
101 N7 **Roy** Idaho U.S.A.
101 R2 **Roy** Montana U.S.A.
106 F6 **Roy** New Mexico U.S.A.
101 N8 **Roy** Utah U.S.A.
100 C2 **Roy** Washington U.S.A.
98 H7 **Royal** Nebraska U.S.A.
14 E3 **Royal Canal** Ireland
99 U9 **Royal Center** Indiana U.S.A.
70 C1 **Royal Charlotte Reef** S China Sea
113 L12 **Royal I** Bahamas
120 B3 **Royal, Mount** Ontario Canada
119 P1 **Royal, Mt** Ontario Canada
89 F7 **Royal Natal Nat. Park** S Africa
94 D4 **Royal Oak** Michigan U.S.A.
113 F12 **Royal Palm Hammock** Florida U.S.A.
113 G12 **Royal Palm Ranger Sta** Florida U.S.A.
118 C8 **Royalties** Alberta Canada
9 G5 **Royal Tunbridge Wells** England
18 E7 **Royan** France
19 O14 **Roybon** France
22 D4 **Roye** France
95 M6 **Royersford** Pennsylvania U.S.A.
142 C5 **Roy Hill** Western Australia Australia
27 D11 **Röykenvik** Norway
122 C4 **Roy, L** Quebec Canada
26 G7 **Röyrvik** Norway
109 L3 **Royse City** Texas U.S.A.
26 C10 **Röysheim** Norway
9 F3 **Royston** England
112 D3 **Royston** Georgia U.S.A.
29 L6 **Röytta** Finland
31 N3 **Różan** Poland
46 E3 **Rožden** Yugoslavia
20 F3 **Rozel** Channel Is
107 L3 **Rozel** Kansas U.S.A.
20 G3 **Rozel, Pte du** France
98 A5 **Rozet** Wyoming U.S.A.
31 L1 **Rozewie** *C* Poland
55 F5 **Rozhdestvenka** U.S.S.R.
52 G5 **Rozhdestvenskoye** U.S.S.R.
22 G4 **Rozoy** France
31 M4 **Rozprza** Poland
31 N5 **Rozwadów** Poland
46 D3 **Rrësen** Albania
46 E1 **Rtanj** *mt* Yugoslavia
87 B9 **Ruacana** Namibia
87 G7 **Ruaha, Gt** *R* Tanzania
88 E5 **Ruaha Nat. Park** Tanzania
145 F4 **Ruahine Range** New Zealand
145 E1 **Ruakaka** New Zealand
71 J4 **Ruang** *isld* Indonesia
145 E3 **Ruapehu** *vol* New Zealand
144 B7 **Ruapuke I** New Zealand
145 F3 **Ruatahuna** New Zealand
144 C5 **Ruatapu** New Zealand
71 J9 **Rua, Tg** *C* Sumba Indonesia
145 F3 **Ruatoki** New Zealand
145 G2 **Ruatoria** New Zealand
145 E2 **Ruawai** New Zealand
77 C7 **Ru'ays, Ar** U.A.E.
54 B1 **Ruba** U.S.S.R.
72 F5 **Rub al Khālī** *desert* Saudi Arabia
53 G12 **Rubas** *R* U.S.S.R.
33 N9 **Rübeland** East Germany
60 R2 **Rubeshibe** Japan
54 K7 **Rubezhnoye** U.S.S.R.
15 C2 **Rubha Coigeach** Scotland
15 B3 **Rubha Hunish** Scotland
15 C3 **Rubha Reidh** Scotland
86 E5 **Rubi** *R* Zaire
102 D3 **Rubicon** *R* California U.S.A.
45 J2 **Rubiera** Italy
133 G2 **Rubinéia** Brazil
124 F3 **Rubio** Mexico
16 E3 **Rubio** *mt* Spain
28 D2 **Rubjerg Knude** *hill* Denmark
56 B5 **Rubtsovsk** U.S.S.R.
116 K4 **Ruby** Alaska U.S.A.
103 N10 **Ruby** Arizona U.S.A.
101 N4 **Ruby** *R* Montana U.S.A.
100 H1 **Ruby** Washington U.S.A.
103 J1 **Ruby Dome** *pk* Nevada U.S.A.
103 J1 **Ruby L** Nevada U.S.A.
103 J1 **Ruby Mts** Nevada U.S.A.
141 J6 **Rubyvale** Queensland Australia
103 J1 **Ruby Valley** Nevada U.S.A.
100 B7 **Ruch** Oregon U.S.A.
52 H4 **Ruch'** U.S.S.R.
67 D4 **Rucheng** China
52 F2 **Ruch'i** U.S.S.R.
Ruchugi *see* **Uvinza**
27 H14 **Ruda** Sweden
138 D5 **Rudall** South Australia Australia
143 E6 **Rudall, R** Western Australia Australia
142 D5 **Rudall River Nat Park** Western Australia Australia
140 B6 **Rudalls** *R* N Terr Australia
77 E6 **Rudan** Iran
75 J5 **Rudauli** India
77 H4 **Rudbar** Afghanistan
77 A1 **Rudbār** Iran
28 B7 **Rudbøl** Denmark
118 K6 **Ruddell** Saskatchewan Canada
22 E1 **Ruddervoorde** Belgium
119 R3 **Ruddock** Manitoba Canada
116 P6 **Rude** *R* Alaska U.S.A.
38 L8 **Ruden** Austria
33 T4 **Ruden** *isld* East Germany
36 H6 **Rudersberg** W Germany
33 T8 **Rudersdorf** East Germany
36 D4 **Rüdesheim** W Germany
31 O6 **Rudki** U.S.S.R.
28 F7 **Rudkøbing** Denmark
31 J4 **Rudna** Poland
59 L3 **Rudnaya Pristan'** U.S.S.R.
52 H5 **Rudnichnyy** U.S.S.R.
55 D2 **Rudnichnyy** Sverdlovskaya Oblast' U.S.S.R.
31 N5 **Rudnik** Poland
54 C2 **Rudnya** U.S.S.R.
55 D4 **Rudnyy** U.S.S.R.
Rudok *see* **Rutog**
46 D3 **Rudoka Planina** *mt* Yugoslavia
50 E1 **Rudol'fa, O** *isld* U.S.S.R.
Rudolf, L *see* **Turkana, L**
37 L2 **Rudolstadt** East Germany
67 G1 **Rudong** China
46 G3 **Rudozem** Bulgaria
77 B1 **Rūdsar** Iran
28 G5 **Ruds Vedby** Denmark
101 P1 **Rudyard** Montana U.S.A.
22 B3 **Rue** France
120 J5 **Ruel** Ontario Canada
21 P3 **Rue St. Pierre, la** France
86 F3 **Rufa'a** Sudan
18 F6 **Ruffec** France
21 N8 **Ruffec** Indre France
20 F6 **Ruffiac** France
20 H6 **Ruffigne** France
112 G4 **Ruffin** South Carolina U.S.A.
88 F6 **Rufiji** *R* Tanzania
45 K4 **Rufina** Italy
131 E5 **Rufino** Argentina
85 A6 **Rufisque** Senegal
88 C9 **Rufunsa** *R* Zambia
100 F1 **Rufus Woods L** Washington U.S.A.
67 G1 **Rugao** China
9 E3 **Rugby** England
98 G1 **Rugby** North Dakota U.S.A.
9 E2 **Rugeley** England
30 H1 **Rügen** *isld* East Germany
144 A7 **Rugged Is** New Zealand
37 K5 **Rügland** W Germany
21 M4 **Rugles** France
29 P5 **Rug Oz** *L* U.S.S.R.
52 D3 **Rugozero** U.S.S.R.
80 B7 **Ruhama** Israel
75 N5 **Ruhea** Bangladesh
33 N7 **Rühen** W Germany
29 L11 **Ruhimäki** Finland
37 J2 **Ruhla** East Germany
33 T10 **Ruhland** East Germany
33 S7 **Ruhleben** East Germany
37 O6 **Ruhmannsfelden** W Germany
33 P5 **Rühn** East Germany
33 P6 **Ruhner Bge** *mt* East Germany
32 F10 **Ruhr** *R* W Germany
35 **Ruhr, The** *reg* W Germany
88 E6 **Ruhudji** *R* Tanzania
88 E7 **Ruhuhu** *R* Tanzania
67 G3 **Rui'an** China
67 E2 **Ruichang** China
65 A7 **Ruicheng** China
108 C6 **Ruidosa** Texas U.S.A.
108 B2 **Ruidoso** New Mexico U.S.A.
106 E8 **Ruidoso** New Mexico U.S.A.
67 E4 **Ruijin** China
80 G7 **Ruim el Hiri** Jordan
22 E1 **Ruiselede** Belgium
9 F4 **Ruislip** England
25 H3 **Ruiten Aa** *R* Netherlands
124 G7 **Ruiz** Mexico
128 C3 **Ruiz, Nevada del** *vol* Colombia
80 G7 **Rujeim Salim** Jordan
46 E2 **Rujen** *mt* Yugoslavia
52 C5 **Rūjiena** U.S.S.R.
70 D5 **Rujon** Kalimantan
29 O5 **Rukatunturi** *mt* U.S.S.R.
88 C10 **Rukovakuona Mts** Zimbabwe
88 D7 **Rukuru** *R* Malawi
71 H7 **Rukuwa** Indonesia
88 C5 **Rukwa** *reg* Tanzania
88 D5 **Rukwa, L** Tanzania
107 J2 **Ruleton** Kansas U.S.A.
111 F8 **Ruleville** Mississippi U.S.A.
26 G10 **Rullbo** Sweden
99 L9 **Rulo** Nebraska U.S.A.
36 E5 **Rülzheim** W Germany
15 B3 **Rum** *isld* Scotland
48 F5 **Ruma** Yugoslavia
Rumania *see* **Romania**
71 J4 **Rumbai** Sulawesi
140 C7 **Rumbalara** N Terr Australia
86 E4 **Rumbek** Sudan

Rumburk — St Ibb

73

31 H5 **Rumburk** Czechoslovakia
126 G3 **Rum Cay** *isld* Bahamas
22 E3 **Rumegies** France
22 L5 **Rumelange** Luxembourg
47 N10 **Rumelifeneri** Turkey
95 R2 **Rumford** Maine U.S.A.
22 G4 **Rumigny** France
22 E2 **Rumillies** Belgium
140 B2 **Rum Jungle** N Terr Australia
80 E2 **Rummāna** Israel
Rummelsburg *see* **Miastko**
60 P2 **Rumoi** Japan
88 D7 **Rumphi** Malawi
118 E7 **Rumsey** Alberta Canada
95 N6 **Rumson** New Jersey U.S.A.
144 C5 **Rumu** New Zealand
144 C5 **Runanga** New Zealand
127 K1 **Runaway Bay** Jamaica
8 D1 **Runcorn** England
89 G3 **Runde** *R* Zimbabwe
36 C1 **Ründeroth** W Germany
28 D7 **Rundhof** W Germany
26 A9 **Rundöy** Norway
87 C9 **Rundu** Namibia
71 J7 **Runduma** *isld* Indonesia
29 G8 **Rundvik** Sweden
71 M8 **Rung** *isld* Indonesia
70 C6 **Rungan** *R* Kalimantan
109 K7 **Runge** Texas U.S.A.
29 K5 **Rungsted** Denmark
88 D5 **Rungwa** *R* Tanzania
88 D6 **Rungwe** *pk* Tanzania
27 J11 **Runhällen** Sweden
36 E3 **Runkel** W Germany
27 H11 **Runn** *L* Sweden
99 N8 **Runnells** Iowa U.S.A.
108 E1 **Running Water Cr** Texas/Okla U.S.A.
119 Q7 **Runnymede** Saskatchewan Canada
143 E6 **Runton Ra** Western Australia Australia
29 O10 **Ruokolahti** Finland
66 D4 **Ruoqiang** China
58 D3 **Ruo Shui** *R* China
29 L10 **Ruovesi** Finland
131 A8 **Rupanco, L** Chile
139 G6 **Rupanyup** Victoria Australia
69 E12 **Rupat** *isld* Sumatra
48 J4 **Rupea** Romania
141 F5 **Rupert** *R* Queensland Australia
101 M7 **Rupert** Idaho U.S.A.
95 O3 **Rupert** Vermont U.S.A.
94 G9 **Rupert** West Virginia U.S.A.
121 L1 **Rupert B** Quebec Canada
121 N1 **Rupert, R** Quebec Canada
37 L6 **Rupertsbuch** W Germany
146 B9 **Ruppert Coast** Antarctica
36 G2 **Ruppertenrod** W Germany
36 F2 **Ruppertsberg** W Germany
36 C2 **Ruppichteroth** W Germany
33 S7 **Ruppiner Kanal** East Germany
128 G3 **Rupununi** *R* Guyana
80 G2 **Ruqqād** *R* Syria
80 G1 **Ruqqād Sakhr** Syria
25 F6 **Rur** *R* W Germany
112 G1 **Rural Hall** North Carolina U.S.A.
94 F10 **Rural Retreat** Virginia U.S.A.
128 E6 **Rurrenabaque** Bolivia
28 C6 **Rurup** Denmark
17 F5 **Rus** *R* Spain
71 L9 **Rusah** *isld* Indonesia
87 F9 **Rusape** Zimbabwe
Ruschuk *see* **Ruse**
47 H1 **Ruse** Bulgaria
38 M8 **Ruše** Yugoslavia
37 P6 **Rusel** W Germany
146 F6 **Rüser-Larsenisen** *ice shelf* Antarctica
14 E3 **Rush** Ireland
106 F3 **Rush** Colorado U.S.A.
9 E5 **Rushall** England
65 E6 **Rushan** China
57 F5 **Rushanskiy Khrebet** *mts* U.S.S.R.
107 L3 **Rush Center** Kansas U.S.A.
99 O4 **Rush City** Minnesota U.S.A.
106 G3 **Rush Cr** Colorado U.S.A.
9 F3 **Rushden** England
99 P6 **Rushford** Minnesota U.S.A.
94 J4 **Rushford** New York U.S.A.
118 K8 **Rush Lake** Saskatchewan Canada
107 N7 **Rush Springs** Oklahoma U.S.A.
110 F1 **Rushville** Illinois U.S.A.
110 L2 **Rushville** Indiana U.S.A.
98 D7 **Rushville** Nebraska U.S.A.
139 H6 **Rushworth** Victoria Australia
109 M4 **Rusk** Texas U.S.A.
113 E10 **Ruskin** Florida U.S.A.
26 K7 **Rusksele** Sweden
26 K7 **Rusktrask** Sweden
98 F2 **Ruso** North Dakota U.S.A.
129 L4 **Russas** Brazil
38 H6 **Russbachsaag** Austria
113 L12 **Russel I** Bahamas
119 Q8 **Russell** Manitoba Canada
121 P7 **Russell** Ontario Canada
145 E1 **Russell** New Zealand
99 N9 **Russell** Iowa U.S.A.
107 M3 **Russell** Kansas U.S.A.
94 E8 **Russell** Kentucky U.S.A.
99 L5 **Russell** Minnesota U.S.A.
95 M2 **Russell** New York U.S.A.
94 H5 **Russell** Pennsylvania U.S.A.
143 E6 **Russell Headland** *mt* Western Australia Australia
115 K3 **Russell I** Northwest Territories Canada
137 M3 **Russell Is** Solomon Is
119 Q2 **Russell L** Manitoba Canada
117 Q4 **Russell L** Northwest Territories Canada
143 C7 **Russell,Mt** Western Australia Australia
116 M5 **Russell, Mt** Alaska U.S.A.
143 E10 **Russell Ra** Western Australia Australia
110 L4 **Russell Springs** Kentucky U.S.A.
110 N1 **Russells Pt** Ohio U.S.A.
111 J7 **Russellville** Alabama U.S.A.
110 D6 **Russellville** Arkansas U.S.A.
110 K5 **Russellville** Kentucky U.S.A.
110 D3 **Russellville** Missouri U.S.A.
94 D8 **Russellville** Ohio U.S.A.
45 M3 **Russi** Italy
116 G6 **Russian Mission** Alaska U.S.A.
116 H6 **Russian Mts** Alaska U.S.A.
Russian Soviet Federated Socialist Republic *see* **Rossiyskaya SFSR**
146 B9 **Russkaya** *U.S.S.R. Base* Antarctica
50 F1 **Russkaya Gavan'** U.S.S.R.
55 F4 **Russkaya-Polyana** U.S.S.R.
55 D3 **Russkaya-Techa** U.S.S.R.
54 M6 **Russkaya-Zhuravka** U.S.S.R.
52 H6 **Russkiy Aktash** U.S.S.R.
51 J1 **Russkiy, Ostrova** *islds* U.S.S.R.
78 K1 **Rustavi** U.S.S.R.
94 H9 **Rustburg** Virginia U.S.A.
26 Q1 **Rustefjelbma** Norway
89 E5 **Rustenburg** S Africa
32 H5 **Rustersiel** W Germany
100 C7 **Rustler Peak** *mt* Oregon U.S.A.
109 P3 **Ruston** Louisiana U.S.A.
71 A3 **Ruta** Indonesia
88 C3 **Rutana** Burundi
16 E7 **Rute** Spain
27 K14 **Rute** Sweden
33 S6 **Rutenberg** East Germany
32 F7 **Rütenbrock** W Germany
71 K9 **Ruteng** Flores Indonesia
146 D7 **Rutford Ice Stream** *ice stream* Antarctica
102 A1 **Ruth** California U.S.A.
103 K2 **Ruth** Nevada U.S.A.
32 H10 **Rüthen** W Germany
112 F2 **Rutherfordton** North Carolina U.S.A.
121 L6 **Rutherglen** Ontario Canada
12 D2 **Rutherglen** Scotland
94 K9 **Ruther Glen** Virginia U.S.A.
116 M5 **Ruth Glacier** Alaska U.S.A.
118 J7 **Ruthilda** Saskatchewan Canada
8 C1 **Ruthin** Wales
98 K5 **Ruthton** Minnesota U.S.A.
141 G6 **Ruthven** Queensland Australia
99 M6 **Ruthven** Iowa U.S.A.
88 E7 **Rutikira** *R* Tanzania
52 G6 **Rutka** *R* U.S.S.R.
Rutland *co see* **Leicestershire**
99 R9 **Rutland** Illinois U.S.A.
98 J3 **Rutland** North Dakota U.S.A.
94 E7 **Rutland** Ohio U.S.A.
95 P3 **Rutland** Vermont U.S.A.
68 A7 **Rutland I** Andaman Is
141 F3 **Rutland Plains** Queensland Australia
118 H6 **Rutland Station** Saskatchewan Canada
9 F2 **Rutland Water** *L* England
99 O3 **Rutledge** Minnesota U.S.A.
110 D1 **Rutledge** Missouri U.S.A.
66 B5 **Rutog** China
25 E3 **Rutten** Netherlands
120 K6 **Rutter** Ontario Canada
25 F4 **Ruurlo** Netherlands
88 G5 **Ruvu** *R* Tanzania
87 G7 **Ruvu** Tanzania
88 G7 **Ruvuma** *R* Tanzania
88 E7 **Ruvuma** Tanzania
89 G1 **Ruwa** Zimbabwe
86 E2 **Ruweiba** Sudan
88 C1 **Ruwenzori Rge** *mts* Uganda
36 B4 **Ruwer** W Germany
87 F9 **Ruya** *R* Zimbabwe
65 B7 **Ruyang** China
67 D4 **Ruyuan** China
55 E4 **Ruzayevka** U.S.S.R.
48 M1 **Ruzhin** U.S.S.R.
48 E1 **Ružomberok** Czechoslovakia
88 B2 **Rwanda** *rep* Cent Africa
28 D4 **Ry** Denmark
28 D2 **Ryå** Denmark
47 H1 **Ryakhovo** Bulgaria
144 C5 **Ryall,Mt** New Zealand
99 P7 **Ryan** Iowa U.S.A.
109 K1 **Ryan** Oklahoma U.S.A.
12 C4 **Ryan, Loch** Scotland
101 T8 **Ryan Park** Wyoming U.S.A.
101 L6 **Ryan Pk** Idaho U.S.A.
53 E7 **Ryazan'** U.S.S.R.
54 M3 **Ryazhsk** U.S.S.R.
57 H4 **Rybach'ye** U.S.S.R.
37 O3 **Rybáře** Czechoslovakia
Rybinsk *see* **Andropov**
52 E5 **Rybinskoye Vdkhr** *res* U.S.S.R.
31 L5 **Rybnik** Poland
48 M3 **Rybnitsa** U.S.S.R.
54 L2 **Rybnoye** U.S.S.R.
55 D2 **Rychkovo** U.S.S.R.
31 J5 **Rychnov** Czechoslovakia
31 L3 **Rychwał** Poland
33 S4 **Ryckgraben** *R* East Germany
117 O8 **Rycroft** Alberta Canada
120 G6 **Rydal Bank** Ontario Canada
146 C6 **Rydberg Peninsula** *pen* Antarctica
28 B4 **Ryde** Denmark
28 G7 **Ryde** Denmark
9 E6 **Ryde** England
98 E2 **Ryder** North Dakota U.S.A.
100 B3 **Ryderwood** Washington U.S.A.
27 H14 **Ryd, V** Sweden
28 D4 **Rye** Denmark
28 H5 **Rye** Denmark
9 G6 **Rye** England
106 F4 **Rye** Colorado U.S.A.
95 R3 **Rye** New Hampshire U.S.A.
109 N5 **Rye** Texas U.S.A.
77 B5 **R-ye Dalaki** *R* Iran
101 Q3 **Ryegate** Montana U.S.A.
100 G9 **Rye Patch** Nevada U.S.A.
102 F1 **Rye Patch Res** Nevada U.S.A.
119 Q9 **Ryerson** Saskatchewan Canada
21 J3 **Ryes** France
27 A12 **Ryfylke** Norway
13 G4 **Ryhope** England
31 N4 **Ryki** Poland
120 G3 **Ryland** Ontario Canada
118 E5 **Ryley** Alberta Canada
54 F5 **Ryl'sk** U.S.S.R.
139 J5 **Rylstone** New South Wales Australia
31 N6 **Rymanow** Poland
31 K6 **Rýmařov** Czechoslovakia
55 F1 **Rymovy** U.S.S.R.
31 N2 **Ryn** Poland
52 E1 **Rynda** U.S.S.R.
53 G9 **Ryn Peski** *desert* U.S.S.R.
28 F4 **Ryomgard** Denmark
61 P7 **Ryōri-zaki** *C* Japan
61 M7 **Ryōtsu** Japan
31 L2 **Rypin** Poland
48 L3 **Ryshkany** U.S.S.R.
48 F1 **Rysk** *mt* Czech/Poland
28 F6 **Ryslinge** Denmark
32 F6 **Rysum** W Germany
31 M6 **Rysy** *mt* Czech/Poland
61 O10 **Ryūgasaki** Japan
31 H3 **Rzepin** Poland
31 N5 **Rzeszów** Poland
54 E3 **Rzhanitsa** U.S.S.R.
52 D6 **Rzhev** U.S.S.R.

S

77 C4 **Sa'ādatābād** Iran
33 R4 **Saal** East Germany
37 J3 **Saal** W Germany
36 F5 **Saal** *R* W Germany
38 G7 **Saalach** *R* Austria
37 M3 **Saalburg** East Germany
36 F3 **Saalburg** W Germany
33 P9 **Saale** *R* East Germany
37 M3 **Saale** *R* W Germany
36 C7 **Saales** France
37 L2 **Saalfeld** East Germany
40 F5 **Saanen** Switzerland
117 M11 **Saanich** British Columbia Canada
36 B5 **Saar** *R* W Germany
19 K3 **Saarbrücken** France
36 B5 **Saarbrücken** W Germany
36 B4 **Saarburg** W Germany
27 M14 **Sääre** U.S.S.R.
27 M13 **Saaremaa** U.S.S.R.
29 M5 **Saarenkylä** Finland
29 O10 **Saari** Finland
29 L9 **Saarijärvi** Finland
29 N3 **Saariselkä** *mts* Finland
36 B5 **Saarland** *land* W Germany
115 P5 **Saarloq** Greenland
36 B5 **Saarlouis** W Germany
33 S8 **Saarmund** East Germany
36 B5 **Saar-Wellingen** W Germany
36 D7 **Saasenheim** France
40 G5 **Saas Tal** Switzerland
133 E5 **Saavedra** Argentina
131 A7 **Saavedra, Pto** Chile
125 L2 **Sabá** Honduras
127 N6 **Saba** *isld* Lesser Antilles
32 L9 **Sababurg** W Germany
48 F6 **Sabac** Yugoslavia
17 J3 **Sabadell** Spain
70 E2 **Sabah** *state* Borneo
69 E11 **Sabak** Malaysia
71 J8 **Sabalana, Kepulauan** *islds* Indonesia
44 M5 **Saba, Mt** Italy
126 D3 **Sabana, Arch. de** *islds* Cuba
127 K5 **Sabana de la Mar** Dominican Rep
127 J10 **Sabana de Mendoza** Venezuela
128 D1 **Sabanalarga** Colombia
127 K9 **Sabaneta** Venezuela
70 G6 **Sabang** Sulawesi
70 F4 **Sabang** Sulawesi
69 B10 **Sabang** Sumatra
83 K11 **Sabaragamuwa** *reg* Sri Lanka
71 J8 **Sabaru** *isld* Indonesia
80 D4 **Sabastiya** Jordan
45 O7 **Sabaudia** Italy
128 E7 **Sabaya** Bolivia
41 M6 **Sabbia, V** Italy
45 H2 **Sabbioneta** Italy
77 G4 **Şāberi, Hāmūn-e** *L* Iran
107 P2 **Sabetha** Kansas U.S.A.
84 E4 **Sabhā** Libya
87 F10 **Sabi** *R* Zimbabwe
89 G5 **Sabie** *R* S Africa
52 B6 **Sabile** U.S.S.R.
45 N5 **Sabina** Italy
94 D7 **Sabina** Ohio U.S.A.
124 F2 **Sabinal** Mexico
109 H6 **Sabinal** Texas U.S.A.
126 F4 **Sabinal, Pen. de** Cuba
17 G2 **Sabiñánigo** Spain
108 F8 **Sabinas** Mexico
125 J4 **Sabinas Hidalgo** Mexico
111 C11 **Sabine** *R* Louisiana/Texas U.S.A.
111 C12 **Sabine L** Louisiana U.S.A.
111 C12 **Sabine Pass** Louisiana U.S.A.
42 E6 **Sabini, Monti** Italy
79 H2 **Sabkhat al Jabbūl** Syria
79 H3 **Sabkhat al Marāghah** *salt lake* Syria
79 D7 **Sabkhet el Bardawîl** Egypt
71 E4 **Sablayan** Philippines
137 M5 **Sable** *isld* Coral Sea
123 N10 **Sable I** Nova Scotia Canada
122 G10 **Sable River** Nova Scotia Canada
18 D6 **Sables-d'Olonne, les** France
20 F4 **Sables d'Or** France
120 H6 **Sables, L. aux** Ontario Canada
120 H6 **Sables, River Aux** Ontario Canada
21 K6 **Sable-sur-Sarthe** France
19 O16 **Sablet** France
19 N18 **Sablon, Pte. du** France
19 N14 **Sablons** France
16 C3 **Sabor** *R* Portugal
131 G2 **Sā Borja** Brazil
94 H7 **Sabraton** West Virginia U.S.A.
18 E8 **Sabres** France
146 F14 **Sabrina Coast** Antarctica
28 E4 **Sabro** Denmark
16 C4 **Sabugal** Portugal
99 C7 **Sabula** Iowa U.S.A.
70 G5 **Sabulu** Sulawesi
47 L5 **Sabuncu** Turkey
70 F9 **Sabunten** *isld* Indonesia
Sabzawar *see* **Shīndand**
77 E1 **Sabzevār** Iran
110 C4 **Sac** *R* Missouri U.S.A.
128 E7 **Sacaca** Bolivia
103 N8 **Sacaton** Arizona U.S.A.
99 L7 **Sac City** Iowa U.S.A.
43 E7 **Sacco** *R* Italy
45 L1 **Saccolongo** Italy
17 F4 **Sacedón** Spain
115 K7 **Sachigo** *R* Ontario Canada
109 O8 **Sachse** Texas U.S.A.
36 F1 **Sachsenberg** W Germany
38 H8 **Sachsenburg** Austria
33 O10 **Sachsenburg** East Germany
32 K8 **Sachsenhagen** W Germany
32 K10 **Sachsenhausen** W Germany
114 G3 **Sachs Harbour** Northwest Territories Canada
42 E3 **Sacile** Italy
95 L3 **Sackets Harbor** New York U.S.A.
122 H8 **Sackville** New Brunswick Canada
110 B3 **Sac, L** Missouri U.S.A.
21 P5 **Saclas** France
95 R3 **Saco** Maine U.S.A.
101 S1 **Saco** Montana U.S.A.
71 F7 **Sacol** *isld* Philippines
40 B2 **Sacquenay** France
102 B2 **Sacramento** *R* California U.S.A.
102 C3 **Sacramento** California U.S.A.
108 B3 **Sacramento Mts** New Mexico U.S.A.
102 B1 **Sacramento V** California U.S.A.
103 K6 **Sacramento Wash** *R* Arizona U.S.A.
16 E8 **Sacratif, C** Spain
122 D5 **Sacré Coeur** Quebec Canada
122 C5 **Sacré-Coeur Saguenay** Quebec Canada
130 F6 **Sacremento** Brazil
48 G3 **Săcueni** Romania
18 E10 **Sadaba** Spain
77 B5 **Sa'dabad** Iran
72 E5 **Şa'dah** N Yemen
60 F12 **Sada-misaki** Japan
69 E9 **Sadao** Thailand
13 G4 **Sadberge** England
74 D2 **Sadda** Pakistan
141 G2 **Saddle Hill** Queensland Australia
142 D4 **Saddle Hill** Western Australia Australia
100 A7 **Saddle Mt** Oregon U.S.A.
101 Q5 **Saddle Mt** Wyoming U.S.A.
68 A6 **Saddle Pk** Andaman Is
68 G7 **Sa Dec** Vietnam
48 K2 **Sadgora** U.S.S.R.
127 O3 **Sadhoowa** Trinidad
94 C8 **Sadieville** Kentucky U.S.A.
85 B6 **Sadiola** Mali
74 D4 **Sadiqabad** Pakistan
16 B6 **Sado** *R* Portugal
61 M7 **Sado-shima** *isld* Japan
46 G2 **Sadovo** Bulgaria
74 E6 **Sadri** India
26 H5 **Sadvajaur** *L* Sweden
28 F2 **Sæby** Nordjylland Denmark
28 G5 **Sæby** Vestjælland Denmark
28 J6 **Sædder** Denmark
28 B4 **Sædding** Denmark
60 E13 **Saeki** Japan
60 E13 **Saeki-wan** *B* Japan
17 F5 **Saelices** Spain
32 G8 **Saerbeck** W Germany
28 E5 **Særslev** Denmark
28 E2 **Saesing** Denmark
22 K4 **Saeul** Luxembourg
Safad *see* **Zefat**
55 D4 **Safakulevo** U.S.S.R.
48 F2 **Šáfárikovo** Czechoslovakia
57 F5 **Safed Khirs** *reg* Afghanistan
77 L2 **Safed Koh** *mt* Afghanistan
38 O7 **Safen** *R* Austria
77 J4 **Safer** Afghanistan
142 A4 **Safety Bay** *dist* Western Australia Australia
80 D5 **Saffārin** Jordan
79 B9 **Saff, El** Egypt
27 F12 **Säffle** Sweden
111 J9 **Safford** Alabama U.S.A.
103 P9 **Safford** Arizona U.S.A.
20 G7 **Saffré** France
9 G3 **Saffron Walden** England
85 C2 **Safi** Morocco
77 G4 **Safidabeh** Iran
77 A1 **Safid Rud** *R* Iran
41 K4 **Safier Tal** Switzerland
130 H6 **Safiras, Sa. das** *mts* Brazil
54 K3 **Safonovka** U.S.S.R.
52 G2 **Safonovo** U.S.S.R.
78 D1 **Safranbolu** Turkey
27 G11 **Säfsnäs** Sweden
80 G5 **Safut** Jordan
66 D6 **Saga** China
60 D12 **Saga** *prefect* Japan
60 D12 **Saga** Kyūshū Japan
60 G12 **Saga** Shikoku Japan
60 C11 **Saga** Tsushima Japan
57 C1 **Saga** U.S.S.R.
61 O7 **Sagae** Japan
68 B2 **Sagaing** Burma
59 L5 **Sagami-nada** *B* Japan
61 N10 **Sagami-wan** *B* Japan
94 H6 **Sagamore** Pennsylvania U.S.A.
119 N2 **Saganaga L** Ontario Canada
120 H3 **Saganash L** Ontario Canada
60 E12 **Saganoseki** Japan
68 D6 **Saganthit Kyun** *isld* Burma
56 E5 **Sagan-Tologoy** U.S.S.R.
76 C2 **Sagar** India
61 M11 **Sagara** Japan
88 F5 **Sagara** Tanzania
116 N2 **Sagavanirktok** *R* Alaska U.S.A.
101 P8 **Sage** Wyoming U.S.A.
32 H7 **Sage** W Germany
101 P1 **Sage Cr** Montana U.S.A.
101 S8 **Sage Cr** Wyoming U.S.A.
27 G11 **Sågen** Sweden
71 C3 **Sageurin** W Irian
26 H4 **Sagfjord** Norway
26 J5 **Saggat** *L* Sweden
95 P6 **Sag Harbor** Long I, New York U.S.A.
94 D3 **Saginaw** Michigan U.S.A.
109 L9 **Saginaw** Texas U.S.A.
94 D3 **Saginaw Bay** Michigan U.S.A.
88 D2 **Sagitu** *isld* Uganda
115 N6 **Saglek B** Labrador, Nfld Canada
71 H6 **Sago** *isld* Indonesia
99 S3 **Sagola** Michigan U.S.A.
17 F7 **Sagra, La** *mt* Spain
85 F8 **Sagre, Pto.de** Bioko Equat Guinea
16 B8 **Sagres** Portugal
71 L9 **Sagu** Indonesia
106 D3 **Saguache** Colorado U.S.A.
126 G4 **Sagua de Tánamo** Cuba
126 D3 **Sagua la Grande** Cuba
103 N8 **Saguaro L** Arizona U.S.A.
103 O9 **Saguaro Nat.Mon** Arizona U.S.A.
115 M8 **Saguenay** *R* Quebec Canada
85 B3 **Saguia al Hamra, As** *R* Western Sahara
17 G5 **Sagunto** Spain
116 N2 **Sagwan** Alaska U.S.A.
80 G3 **Saham** Jordan
85 C4 **Sahara** *desert* N Africa
79 E10 **Sahara, G** *mt* Egypt
74 G4 **Saharanpur** India
142 E5 **Sahara Well** Western Australia Australia
75 L5 **Sahibganj** India
28 D4 **Sahl** Denmark
124 E3 **Sahuaripa** Mexico
103 O10 **Sahuarita** Arizona U.S.A.
124 H7 **Sahuayo** Mexico
136 F4 **Sahul Shelf** Timor Sea
19 O16 **Sahune** France
68 J5 **Sa Huynh** Vietnam
61 L9 **Sai** *R* Japan
136 J3 **Saibai I** Papua New Guinea
69 E9 **Sai Buri** *R* Thailand
69 E9 **Sai Buri** Thailand
85 E2 **Saïda** Algeria
79 F5 **Saïda** Lebanon
77 D5 **Sa'īdābād** Iran
68 F6 **Sai Dao Tai, Khao** *mt* Thailand
86 D4 **Said Bundas** Sudan
75 N6 **Saidpur** Bangladesh
74 E1 **Saidu** Pakistan
40 E3 **Saignelégier** Switzerland
60 G9 **Saigō** Japan
68 H7 **Saigon** *R* Vietnam
68 H7 **Saigon** Vietnam
29 O4 **Saija** Finland
60 G12 **Saijō** Japan
60 C13 **Saikai Nat. Park** Japan
71 C3 **Saileen** W Irian
19 O15 **Saillans** France
71 C3 **Sailolo** W Irian
100 K7 **Sailor Cr** Idaho U.S.A.
76 C1 **Sailu** India
65 F4 **Saima** China
29 N10 **Saimaa** *L* Finland
29 N11 **Saimaa Canal** Finland/U.S.S.R.
124 H6 **Sain Alto** Mexico
77 G5 **Saindak** Pakistan
78 L3 **Sa'īndezh** Iran
22 D2 **Sainghin-en-Weppes** France
22 G3 **Sains-du-Nord** France
22 F4 **Sains-Richaumont** France
15 F5 **St. Abb's Head** Scotland
122 H5 **Ste. Adelaide** Quebec Canada
121 Q7 **Ste.Adèle** Quebec Canada
21 L2 **Ste.Adresse** France
38 N6 **St.Aegyd** Austria
18 G9 **St.Affrique** France
121 T6 **St.Agapit** Quebec Canada
119 U9 **Ste.Agathe** Manitoba Canada
121 Q6 **Ste.Agathe des Monts** Quebec Canada
21 M5 **St.Agil** France
121 L4 **Ste.Agnes** Quebec Canada
8 A7 **St.Agnes** England
9 F7 **St.Agnes** *isld* Isles of Scilly England
21 N7 **St.Aignan** France
21 H6 **St.Aignan-sur-Roë** France
28 D3 **Ste. Ajstrup** Denmark
20 E4 **St.Alban** France
19 P13 **St.-Alban-Leysee** France
40 C6 **St.-Alban-Leysse** France
123 R6 **St.Alban's** Newfoundland Canada
9 F4 **St.Albans** England
95 P2 **St.Albans** Vermont U.S.A.
94 F8 **St.Albans** West Virginia U.S.A.
118 D5 **St.Albert** Alberta Canada
122 C6 **St.Alexandre** Quebec Canada
121 R6 **St.Alexis des Monts** Quebec Canada
22 E3 **St.Amand-les-Eaux** France
21 N6 **St. Amand-Longpré** France
18 G6 **St. Amand Mont Rond** France
21 J8 **St.Amand-sur-Sèvre** France
40 F2 **St.Amarin** France
121 T4 **St.-Ambroise** Quebec Canada
21 P8 **St.Ambroix** Cher France
122 D5 **St.Anaclet** Quebec Canada
19 N17 **St.-Andiol** France
38 L8 **St. Andra-im-Lavanttal** Austria
83 K13 **St.André** Réunion Indian Oc
83 M12 **Saint-André** Mauritius
33 M9 **St. Andreasberg** W Germany
19 N13 **St.Andre-de-Corcy** France
18 E8 **St.André-de-Cubzac** France
21 N4 **St.André-de-l'Eure** France
20 F7 **St.-André-des-Eaux** France
21 N4 **St.André,Plaine de** France
127 L2 **St.Andrew** *parish* Jamaica
127 P2 **St.Andrew** *co* Trinidad
111 L11 **St.Andrew** Florida U.S.A.
123 N6 **St.Andrew's** Newfoundland Canada
144 C6 **St. Andrews** New Zealand
13 F1 **St.Andrews** Scotland
123 M7 **St.Andrew's Chan** Nova Scotia Canada
113 F7 **St.Andrew Sd** Georgia U.S.A.
127 K2 **St.Ann** *parish* Jamaica
98 F9 **St.Ann** Nebraska U.S.A.
126 B2 **St. Anna-Baai** *B* Curaçao
119 V9 **Ste.Anne** Manitoba Canada
21 M4 **Ste.Anne** France
99 T8 **St.Anne** Illinois U.S.A.
127 N4 **Ste.Anne** Guadeloupe W Indies
127 L4 **Ste.Anne** Martinique W Indies
20 E6 **Ste.Anne-d'Auray** France
121 U5 **Ste.-Anne-de-Beaupré** Quebec Canada
121 S6 **Ste. Anne de la Pérade** Quebec Canada
122 B6 **Ste.Anne de la Pocatière** Quebec Canada
122 F4 **Ste.Anne des Monts** Quebec Canada
121 P6 **Ste.Anne du Lac** Quebec Canada
122 E3 **Ste.Anne, L** Quebec Canada
118 C5 **Ste. Anne, Lac** Alberta Canada
122 B6 **Ste.Anne, R** Quebec Canada
20 F2 **St.Annes** Channel Is
117 Q9 **St.Ann, L** Alberta Canada
123 M7 **St. Anns** Nova Scotia Canada
127 K2 **St. Ann's Bay** Jamaica
12 E3 **St Ann's Bridge** Scotland
99 O6 **St.Ansgar** Iowa U.S.A.
25 E5 **St.Anthonis** Netherlands
123 R2 **St.Anthony** Newfoundland Canada
101 O6 **St.Anthony** Idaho U.S.A.
19 O18 **St.Antoine** France
41 M3 **St.Anton** Austria
122 C6 **St.Antonin** Quebec Canada
18 G8 **St.Antonin** France
21 O8 **St.Août** France
21 N3 **St.Aquilin-de-Pacy** France
139 G6 **St.Arnaud** Victoria Australia
145 D4 **St. Arnaud** New Zealand
21 O4 **St. Arnoult-en-Yvelines** France
122 C6 **St.Arsène** Quebec Canada
8 C1 **St. Asaph** Wales
140 B1 **St.Asaph B** N Terr Australia
18 F7 **St.Astier** France
122 C6 **St.Athanase** Quebec Canada
122 B6 **St.Aubert** Quebec Canada
20 F3 **St.Aubin** Channel Is
21 K3 **St.Aubin** Calvados France
20 G5 **St.Aubin-d'Aubigné** France
21 L3 **St.Aubin-de-Scellon** France
20 H4 **St.Aubin-de-Terregatte** France
20 H5 **St.Aubin-du-Cormier** France
21 N2 **St.Aubin-le-Cauf** France
123 O2 **St.Augustin** Quebec Canada
36 C2 **St. Augustin** W Germany
123 O2 **St.Augustin B** Quebec Canada
87 G12 **St.Augustin, B.de** Madagascar
21 J7 **St.Augustin-des-Bois** France
127 O2 **St.Augustine** Trinidad
113 F8 **St.Augustine** Florida U.S.A.
123 N2 **St.Augustin R** Quebec Canada
18 F7 **St.Aulaye** France
8 B7 **St. Austell** England
21 M7 **St.Avertin** France
19 K3 **St.Avold** France
123 Q2 **St. Barbe** Newfoundland Canada
121 S6 **St.Barnabé Nord** Quebec Canada
121 R6 **St.Barthélémi** Quebec Canada
18 G10 **St.Barthélemy** France
127 N5 **St. Barthélemy** *isld* Lesser Antilles
144 B6 **St. Bathans** New Zealand
21 P8 **St.Baudel** France
19 P18 **Ste.Baume** France
18 F10 **St. Béat** France
12 E5 **St.Bees** England
119 M6 **St.Benedict** Saskatchewan Canada
99 M6 **St.Benedict** Iowa U.S.A.
21 L8 **St.Benoit** Vienne France
18 F6 **St.-Benoît-du-Sault** France
122 B7 **St.Benoit Labre** Quebec Canada
21 P6 **St.Benoît-sur-Loire** France
122 H5 **Ste.Bernadette** Quebec Canada
121 T6 **St.Bernard** Quebec Canada
144 D5 **St. Bernard** *mt* New Zealand
40 F6 **St. Bernard, Col du Gd.** Switz/Italy
42 A3 **St. Bernard, Petit** *pass* Italy/France
110 J2 **St.Bernice** Indiana U.S.A.
19 P13 **St.Beron** France
21 J5 **St.Berthevin** France
36 C7 **St.Blaise** France
122 D5 **Ste.Blandine** Quebec Canada
8 B7 **St.Blazey** England
118 D1 **St.Boniface** Manitoba Canada
118 L8 **St.Boswells** Saskatchewan Canada
13 F2 **St. Boswells** Scotland
21 M7 **St. Branchs** France
123 T5 **St.Brendan's** Newfoundland Canada
20 F7 **St.Brévin-les-Pins** France
20 F4 **St.Briac** France
20 H5 **St.Brice-en-Cogles** France
118 B7 **St.Bride, Mt** Alberta Canada
123 S7 **St.Bride's** Newfoundland Canada
8 A4 **St. Bride's** Wales
20 E4 **St.Brieuc** France
20 E4 **St.Brieuc,B.de** France
119 N6 **St.Brieux** Saskatchewan Canada
20 G4 **St.Broladre** France
121 L5 **St. Bruno de Guiques** Quebec Canada
21 M6 **St.Calais** France
119 T9 **St.Calude** Manitoba Canada
122 B7 **St.Camille** Quebec Canada
20 E5 **St.Caradec** France
20 E5 **St. Carreuc** France
121 S6 **St.Casimir** Quebec Canada
20 F4 **St.Cast** France
121 L9 **St. Catharines** Ontario Canada
127 K2 **St. Catherine** *parish* Jamaica
127 P5 **St.Catherine, Mt** Grenada
112 F6 **St.Catherines I** Georgia U.S.A.
9 E6 **St.Catherines Pt** England
122 B8 **Ste.Cécile** Quebec Canada
18 G8 **St. Céré** France
18 G7 **St.Cernin** France
121 R7 **St.Césaire** Quebec Canada
18 H7 **St.Chamond** France
118 A1 **St.Charles** Manitoba Canada
101 O7 **St.Charles** Idaho U.S.A.
99 S8 **St.Charles** Illinois U.S.A.
94 C3 **St.Charles** Michigan U.S.A.
99 O6 **St.Charles** Minnesota U.S.A.
110 F3 **St.Charles** Missouri U.S.A.
21 O8 **St.Chartier** France
19 O13 **St. Chef** France
18 H8 **St. Chély l'Apcher** France
21 P4 **St.Chéron** France
18 G9 **St.Chinian** France
126 A1 **St.Christoffel Berg** *mt* Curaçao
19 Q15 **St.Christophe d'Oisans** France
20 G8 **St.Christophe-du-Ligneron** France
21 O7 **St. Christophe-en-Bazelle** France
St. Christopher *isld see* **St Kitts**
121 T4 **St.-Cîour-de-Marie** Quebec Canada
21 H3 **St.Clair** France
94 E4 **St.Clair** Michigan U.S.A.
99 N5 **St.Clair** Minnesota U.S.A.
110 F3 **St.Clair** Missouri U.S.A.
94 E4 **St. Clair, L** U.S.A./Canada
120 H9 **St.Clair R** Ontario/Michigan Canada/U.S.A.
21 O3 **St.Clair-sur-Epte** France
19 J6 **St.Claude** France
127 N4 **St.Claude** Guadeloupe W Indies
8 B4 **St.Clears** Wales
122 C6 **St.Clement** Quebec Canada
21 J6 **St. Clement-de-la-Place** France
121 S7 **Ste.Clothilde** Quebec Canada
113 F9 **St.Cloud** Florida U.S.A.
99 M4 **St.Cloud** Minnesota U.S.A.
8 B7 **St.Columb** England
20 G7 **St. Columban** France
121 R6 **St.Côme** Quebec Canada
20 H3 **St.Côme-du-Mont** France
21 L5 **St.Cosme-de-Vair** France
122 E8 **Ste.Croix** New Brunswick Canada
40 D4 **Ste.Croix** Switzerland
99 O4 **St. Croix** *R* Wisconsin U.S.A.
95 T8 **St. Croix** *R* Maine/New Brunswick U.S.A./Canada
36 C7 **Ste.Croix aux Mines** France
113 L8 **St.Croix I** Virgin Is
122 C6 **St.Cyprien** Quebec Canada
18 F8 **St.Cyprien** France
19 P18 **St.Cyr** France
21 K5 **St.Cyr** Mayenne France
21 J4 **St.Cyr-du-Bailleul** France
21 K7 **St.Cyr-en-Bourg** France
21 O6 **St.Cyr-en-Val** France
121 S7 **St.Cyrille** Quebec Canada
121 P4 **St.Cyr, L** Quebec Canada
118 J4 **St. Cyr Lake** Saskatchewan Canada
21 M7 **St.-Cyr-sur-Loire** France
122 B7 **St.Damien** Quebec Canada
127 P1 **St.David** *co* Trinidad
110 F1 **St.David** Illinois U.S.A.
122 A5 **St.David-de-Falardeau** Quebec Canada
123 O5 **St. David's** Newfoundland Canada
8 A4 **St. David's** Wales
90 D1 **St.Davids I** Bermuda
22 G3 **St.Denis** Belgium
121 R7 **St.Denis** Quebec Canada
21 P4 **St. Denis** France
83 J13 **St.Denis** Réunion Indian Oc
21 K6 **St.Denis-d'Anjou** France
21 J5 **St. Denis-de-Gastines** France
21 O8 **St.Denis-de-Jouhet** France
21 K5 **St.Denis-d'Orques** France
20 H8 **St. Denis la Chevasse** France
21 K5 **St.Denis-sur-Sarthon** France
20 F4 **St.Denoual** France
19 O16 **St.Didier** France
36 B7 **St. Dié** France
19 J4 **St.Dizier** France
20 F6 **St.Dolay** France
20 G5 **St Domineuc** France
19 N14 **St.Donat sur l'Herbasse** France
98 J8 **St.Edward** Nebraska U.S.A.
116 P7 **St.Elias, C** Alaska U.S.A.
117 D5 **St. Elias Mts** Alaska/Yukon Terr U.S.A./Canada
121 S4 **Ste.Elisabeth** Quebec Canada
127 J2 **St.Elizabeth** *parish* Jamaica
110 H2 **St.Elmo** Illinois U.S.A.
122 C5 **St.Eloi** Quebec Canada
18 G6 **St Éloy-les-Mines** France
121 R6 **Ste.Emélie** Quebec Canada
18 H8 **Ste.Enimie** France
20 H3 **Sainteny** France
21 M7 **St.Epain** France
122 B7 **St.Ephrem** Quebec Canada
121 L3 **St.Ephrem de Paradis** Quebec Canada
122 C6 **St.-Epiphane** Quebec Canada
20 G5 **St.Erblon** France
22 F5 **St.Erme-Outre-et-Ramecourt** France
18 E7 **Saintes** France
127 L4 **St. Ésprit, Le** Martinique W Indies
22 B2 **St.Étienne-au-Mont** France
18 E9 **St. Étienne de Baïgorry** France
20 G7 **St.Étienne-de-Montluc** France
19 O14 **St.Étienne de St.Geoirs** France
21 N3 **St.Étienne-du-Rouvray** France
121 S4 **St.-Eugène** Quebec Canada
121 M4 **St. Eugène** Quebec Canada
122 D6 **St.Eusèbe** Quebec Canada
121 R7 **St.Eustache** Quebec Canada
127 N6 **Sint Eustatius** *isld* Lesser Antilles
21 L4 **St.Evroult Notre Dame-du-Bois** France
122 D5 **St.Fabien** Quebec Canada
122 B7 **Ste.Familie** Quebec Canada
121 P6 **Ste.Famille d'Aumond** Quebec Canada
18 H5 **St.Fargeau** France
121 S4 **St.Félicien** Quebec Canada
122 E5 **Ste.Félicité** Quebec Canada
121 R6 **St. Félix de Valois** Quebec Canada
12 D1 **St.Fillans** Scotland
14 A5 **St. Finan's B** Ireland
123 O5 **St.Fintan's** Newfoundland Canada
19 Q15 **St. Firmin** France
20 G8 **Ste. Flaive-des-Loups** France
121 T6 **St.Flavien** Quebec Canada
122 E5 **Ste.Florence** Quebec Canada
20 H8 **St.Florent-des-Bois** France
18 H4 **St.Florentin** France
21 H7 **St.Florent-le-Vieil** France
21 P8 **St.Florent-sur-Cher** France
18 H7 **St.Flour** France
21 N8 **St.Flovier** France
121 T7 **St.Fortunat** Quebec Canada
19 N15 **St.Fortunat** France
121 T6 **Ste. Foy** Quebec Canada
18 F8 **Ste.Foy-la-Grande** France
107 J2 **St.Francis** Kansas U.S.A.
110 F5 **St. Francis** *R* Missouri/Ark U.S.A.
95 R6 **St. Francis** *R* Maine/New Brunswick U.S.A./Canada
89 D10 **St. Francis B** S Africa
123 U6 **St.Francis, C** Newfoundland Canada
89 D10 **St. Francis C** S Africa
138 C4 **St.Francis, I.of** South Australia Australia
110 J3 **St. Francisville** Illinois U.S.A.
111 E11 **St.Francisville** Louisiana U.S.A.
121 S7 **St. François** *R* Quebec Canada
127 N4 **St.François** Guadeloupe W Indies
121 T7 **St. François, L** Quebec Canada
110 F4 **St. Francois Mts** Missouri U.S.A.
121 S7 **St.François Xavier** Quebec Canada
95 S7 **St.Froid L** Maine U.S.A.
21 H8 **St.Fulgent** France
111 E11 **St.Gabriel** Louisiana U.S.A.
121 R6 **St.Gabriel de Brandon** Quebec Canada
122 H5 **St.Gabriel de Gaspé** Quebec Canada
41 K3 **St. Gallen** Switzerland
21 L4 **Ste.Gauburge-Ste.Colombe** France
18 F9 **St.Gaudens** France
21 N8 **St.Gaultier** France
122 B8 **St.Gédéon** Quebec Canada
21 N8 **Ste.Gemme** France
21 P3 **Ste. Geneviève** Oise France
110 F4 **Ste.Genevieve** Missouri U.S.A.
123 P2 **St.Genevieve B** Quebec Canada
18 G8 **St.Geniez** France
21 N8 **St.Genou** France
19 P14 **St Geoire-en-Valdaine** France
141 J8 **St.George** Queensland Australia
141 G3 **St. George** *R* Queensland Australia
127 P6 **St.George** *parish* Barbados
90 C1 **St.George** Bermuda
122 F8 **St.George** New Brunswick Canada
127 O2 **St.George** *co* Trinidad
113 E7 **St.George** Georgia U.S.A.
112 G4 **St.George** South Carolina U.S.A.
103 L4 **St.George** Utah U.S.A.
123 N5 **St.George, C** Newfoundland Canada
139 K6 **St.George Hd** New South Wales Australia
116 D8 **St. George I** Pribilof Is Bering Sea
113 C8 **St.George I** Florida U.S.A.
41 H1 **St.Georgen** W Germany
100 A8 **St.George, Pt** California U.S.A.
142 E4 **St.George Ra** Western Australia Australia
123 O5 **St.George's** Newfoundland Canada
122 B7 **St.Georges** Quebec Canada
36 B6 **St.Georges** France
129 H3 **St.Georges** Fr Guiana
127 P5 **St.George's** Grenada
123 N5 **St.George's B** Newfoundland Canada
125 P9 **St. Georges Cay** *isld* Belize
7 F11 **St Georges Chan** U.K.
137 L2 **St.George's Channel** Bismarck Arch
14 E5 **St. Georges Channel** Ireland/U.K.
69 A9 **St.George's Channel** Nicobar Is
20 H8 **St.Georges-de-Montaigu** France
20 H4 **St.Georges-de-Reintembault** France
21 M3 **St.Georges-du-Mesnil** France
21 M3 **St. Georges du-Vièvre** France
90 C1 **St.George's I** Bermuda
21 L8 **St.Georges-les-Baillargeaux** France
21 N4 **St.Georges-Motel** Eure France
21 N5 **St.Georges-sur-Eure** France
21 O7 **St.Georges-sur-la Prée** France
21 J7 **St.Georges-sur-Loire** France
22 H3 **St.Gérard** Belgium
121 M4 **St. Gerard-Centre** Quebec Canada
19 N13 **St. Germain au Mt D'Or** France
21 J5 **St.Germain-d'Anxure** France
19 P12 **St. Germain-de-Joux** France
21 M5 **St.Germain-de-la-Coudre** France
18 H6 **St.Germain-des-Fosses** France
19 J6 **St.Germain du Bois** France
122 B7 **Ste.Germaine** Quebec Canada
21 P4 **St. Germain-en-Laye** France
20 G3 **St. Germain, Hâvre de** France
21 L3 **St.Germain-la-Campagne** France
18 G7 **St.Germain-les-Belles** France
20 G3 **St.Germain-sur-Ay** France
8 B7 **St.Germans** England
21 O3 **St. Germer-de-Fly** France
41 N5 **St. Gertrude** Italy
20 G8 **St.Gervais** Vendée France
40 E6 **St. Gervais-les-Bains** France
21 L8 **St. Gervais-les-Trois-Clochers** France
22 F3 **St.Ghislain** Belgium
20 E6 **St.Gildas-de-Rhuis** France
20 F6 **St.Gildas-des-Bois** France
20 F7 **St.Gildas,Pte.de** France
121 T6 **St.-Giles** Quebec Canada
127 N1 **St. Giles Is** Tobago
20 G8 **St. Gilles-Croix-de-Vie** France
20 D5 **St.Gilles-Pligeaux** France
22 G1 **St. Gillis-bij-Dendermonde** Belgium
22 G1 **St.Gillis-Waas** Belgium
18 F10 **St.Girons** France
27 F12 **St.Gla** *L* Sweden
36 D3 **St.Goar** W Germany
20 C5 **St.Goazec** France
22 E4 **St.Gobain** France
122 G5 **St.Godefroi** Quebec Canada
41 J4 **St.Gotthard** *pass* Switzerland
8 B4 **St.Govan's Hd** Wales
119 N6 **St.Gregor** Saskatchewan Canada
123 O4 **St.Gregory, Mt** Newfoundland Canada
20 B6 **St.Guénolé** France
121 S7 **St. Guillaume** Quebec Canada
19 Q15 **St. Guillaume, Mt** France
94 C2 **St.Helen** Michigan U.S.A.
90 B14 **St. Helena** *isld* Atlantic Oc
102 B3 **St.Helena** California U.S.A.
89 A9 **St.Helena B** S Africa
90 H10 **St Helena Fracture** Atlantic Oc
94 B1 **St.Helena I** Michigan U.S.A.
112 G5 **St.Helena Sd** South Carolina U.S.A.
122 B6 **Ste.Hélène** Quebec Canada
18 E8 **Ste.Hélène** France
139 J8 **St.Helens** Tasmania Australia
13 F6 **St.Helens** England
100 C4 **St.Helens** Oregon U.S.A.
100 C3 **St.Helens, Mt** Washington U.S.A.
139 J8 **St.Helens Pt** Tasmania Australia
122 H4 **St.Helier** Quebec Canada
20 F3 **St Hélier** Channel Is
121 U6 **Ste.Hénédine** Quebec Canada
121 T6 **St.Henri** Quebec Canada
20 G7 **St.-Herblain** France
121 T7 **St.Herménégilde** Quebec Canada
21 H8 **Ste.Hermine** France
18 G9 **St.Hilaire** France
98 K1 **St.Hilaire** Minnesota U.S.A.
20 G7 **St. Hilaire-de-Chaléons** France
20 H7 **St. Hilaire-de-Loulay** France
20 G8 **St. Hilaire-de-Riez** France
21 H4 **St. Hilaire-du-Harcouet** France
21 K7 **St. Hilaire St. Florent** France
21 O6 **St.Hilaire-St.Mesmin** France
140 D6 **Sainthill,Mt** N Terr Australia
19 K5 **St.Hippolyte** Doubs France
21 N7 **St.Hippolyte** Indre-et-Loire France
18 H9 **St.Hippolyte du Fort** France
122 A5 **St.Honoré** Quebec Canada
122 C6 **St.Honoré** Quebec Canada
21 J3 **Ste.Honorine** France
21 K3 **Ste.Honorine-du-Fay** France
22 J3 **St.Hubert** Belgium
25 F6 **St.Hubert** W Germany
29 K5 **St Ibb** Sweden

74
St.Ignace — Salvator, L

94 C1 St.Ignace Michigan U.S.A.
121 R6 St.Ignace du Lac Quebec Canada
120 C4 St. Ignace, Isle Ontario Canada
101 L2 St.Ignatius Montana U.S.A.
40 E3 St.Imier Switzerland
36 C5 St.Ingbert W Germany
122 B6 St.Irénée Quebec Canada
121 T7 St.Isidore Quebec Canada
121 L5 St.Isidore Quebec Canada
26 K3 St.Istind mt Norway
8 A7 St.Ives England
9 F3 St.Ives England
20 C6 St.Ivy France
25 E2 St.Jacobi Parochie Netherlands
122 D6 St.Jacques New Brunswick Canada
20 G5 St.Jacques-de-la-Lande France
38 F8 St.Jakob Austria
118 A1 St.James Manitoba Canada
20 H4 St.James France
127 J2 St.James parish Jamaica
99 V4 St.James Michigan U.S.A.
99 M5 St.James Minnesota U.S.A.
110 E3 St.James Missouri U.S.A.
117 H10 St.James, C British Columbia Canada
113 E11 St.James City Florida U.S.A.
22 D2 Sint Jan Belgium
121 L4 St.Janvier Quebec Canada
121 R7 St.Jean Quebec Canada
21 K5 St.Jean France
119 U9 St.Jean Baptiste Manitoba Canada
121 S5 St.Jean Bosco Quebec Canada
20 E6 St.Jean-Brévelay France
18 E7 St.-Jean-d'Angély France
21 L5 St.Jean-d'Asse France
19 O13 St.Jean-de-Bournay France
21 O6 St.-Jean-de-Braye France
21 H3 St.Jean-de-Daye France
122 C5 St.Jean de Dieu Quebec Canada
21 O6 St.-Jean-de-la-Ruelle France
19 J5 St.Jean de Losne France
18 D9 St.Jean-de-Luz France
121 R6 St. Jean-de-Matha Quebec Canada
19 Q14 St.Jean-de-Maurienne France
20 F8 St.Jean-de-Monts France
21 L8 St.Jean-de-Sauves France
18 H8 St.Jean du Gard France
19 O14 St.Jean-en-Royans France
121 S4 Saint-Jean, Lac Quebec Canada
20 G4 St.Jean-le-Thomas France
18 E9 St.Jean Pied de Port France
122 B6 St.Jean Port Joli Quebec Canada
122 H3 St.Jean, R Quebec Canada
36 B5 St.Jean Rohrbach France
20 H5 St.Jean-sur-Couesnon France
121 Q7 St.Jérôme Quebec Canada
19 N14 St. Jeure D'Ay France
109 K2 St.Jo Texas U.S.A.
122 B6 St.Joachim Quebec Canada
20 F7 St.Joachim France
41 O3 St.Jodok Austria
110 D5 St.Joe Arkansas U.S.A.
100 J2 St.Joe Idaho U.S.A.
94 C5 St.Joe Indiana U.S.A.
36 E4 St.Johann W Germany
38 G8 St. Johann-im-Walde Austria
127 P6 St.John parish Barbados
122 F8 St.John New Brunswick Canada
107 M3 St.John Kansas U.S.A.
95 R7 St. John R Maine U.S.A.
119 S10 St.John North Dakota U.S.A.
103 M1 St.John Utah U.S.A.
100 H2 St.John Washington U.S.A.
123 P3 St John B Newfoundland Canada
123 R3 St.John, C Newfoundland Canada
113 L7 St.John I Virgin Is
123 S5 St.John, L Newfoundland Canada
122 E7 St. John R New Brunswick Canada
122 G5 St. John R Quebec Canada
123 T6 St. John's Newfoundland Canada
103 P7 St.Johns Arizona U.S.A.
94 C3 St.Johns Michigan U.S.A.
127 P4 St.John's Antigua W Indies
95 P2 St.Johnsbury Vermont U.S.A.
13 F4 St.John's Chapel England
14 C2 St.John's Pt Ireland
113 F7 St.Johns R Florida U.S.A.
95 N3 St.Johnsville New York U.S.A.
20 H3 St.Jores France
22 H2 St.Joris-Winge Belgium
127 P6 St.Joseph parish Barbados
121 U6 St.Joseph Quebec Canada
83 K14 St.Joseph Réunion Indian Oc
127 P2 St.Joseph Mayoro Trinidad
127 O2 St.Joseph St George Trinidad
111 E10 St.Joseph Louisiana U.S.A.
94 A5 St. Joseph R Michigan U.S.A.
99 U7 St.Joseph Michigan U.S.A.
99 M10 St.Joseph Missouri U.S.A.
127 L4 St.Joseph Martinique W Indies
113 B8 St. Joseph Bay Florida U.S.A.
120 G6 St. Joseph I Ontario Canada
109 L8 St. Joseph I Texas U.S.A.
115 K7 St. Joseph, L Ontario Canada
123 T6 St.Joseph's Newfoundland Canada
22 B3 St.Josse France
20 F5 St. Jouan-de-l'Isle France
20 G4 St Jouan-des-Guerets France
21 L2 St.Jouin France
21 K8 St.Jouin-de-Marnes France
121 Q6 St. Jovite Quebec Canada
126 A1 St. Jozefsdal Curaçao
19 N14 St.Julian Molin-Molette France
40 D5 St.Julien France
20 E5 St.Julien Côtes-du-Nord France
20 H7 St.Julien-de-Concelles France
20 G8 St. Julien-des-Landes France
20 H6 St.Julien-de-Vouvantes France
19 O15 St.Julien en Quint France
21 L8 St.Julien-l'Ars France
21 L3 St.Julien-le-Faucon France
18 F7 St.Junien France
9 F7 St.Just England
21 P2 St.Just-en-Chaussée France
18 H7 St.Just-en-Chevalet France
38 M7 St.Katherein Austria
15 A1 St. Kilda isld Scotland
127 P4 St.Kitts isld Lesser Antilles
127 P4 St. Kitts-Nevis islds West Indies
126 A1 St.Kruis Curaçao
121 T6 St.Lambert Quebec Canada
121 R7 St.Lambert Quebec Canada
142 G2 St.Lambert,C Western Australia Australia
21 K7 St. Lambert des Levées France
21 J7 St.Lambert-du-Lattay France
111 D11 St.Landry Louisiana U.S.A.
119 U8 St.Laurent Manitoba Canada
121 L4 Saint-Laurent Quebec Canada
19 J6 St. Laurent France
129 H2 St.Laurent Fr Guiana
18 G10 St.Laurent de la Salanque France
19 O13 St.Laurent-de-Mûre France
21 H7 St. Laurent-des-Autels France
21 O6 St.Laurent-des-Eaux France
19 P14 St.Laurent-du-Pont France
21 M2 St.Laurent-en-Caux France
21 M6 St.Laurent-en-Gâtines France
18 E7 St.Laurent-et-Benon France
121 U5 St.Laurent, R Quebec Canada
21 J3 St.Laurent-sur-Mer France
22 K5 St.Laurent-sur-Othain France
21 J8 St. Laurent-sur-Sèvre France
141 J5 St.Lawrence Queensland Australia
123 R7 St.Lawrence Newfoundland Canada
95 M2 St. Lawrence R Canada/U.S.A.
122 K5 St.Lawrence, G.of Canada
116 B5 St.Lawrence I Bering Sea
121 O8 St. Lawrence I Nat. Park Ontario Canada
121 P8 St.Lawrence Seaway Canada/U.S.A.
119 Q8 St.Lazare Manitoba Canada
22 K4 St.Léger Belgium
21 O4 St.Léger-en-Yvelines France
22 H1 St.Lenaarts Belgium
122 E5 St.Léon Quebec Canada
122 E6 St.-Léonard New Brunswick Canada
121 S6 St.Léonard Quebec Canada
36 B7 St. Léonard France
18 G7 St.-Léonard-de-Noblat France
9 G6 St.Leonards England
121 T4 St.-Léon-de-Chicoutimi Quebec Canada
122 B7 St.Léon de Standon Quebec Canada
38 L8 St.Leonhard Kärnten Austria
38 N4 St.Leonhard Nieder Österreich Austria
123 Q1 St.Lewis R Labrador, Nfld Canada
121 S7 St.Liboire Quebec Canada
18 F8 Ste. Livrade France
21 P7 Ste.Lizaigne France
18 F9 St.Lizier France
21 H3 St.Lô France
122 H7 St.Louis Prince Edward I Canada
119 M6 St.Louis Saskatchewan Canada
83 J14 St.Louis Réunion Indian Oc
85 A5 St.Louis Mauritania
94 C3 St.Louis Michigan U.S.A.
99 O2 St. Louis R Minnesota U.S.A.
105 St.Louis conurbation Missouri U.S.A.
127 N4 St.Louis Marie Galante W Indies
122 H7 St.Louis de Kent New Brunswick Canada
122 D6 St.Louis du Ha Ha Quebec Canada
126 H5 St.Louis du Sud Haiti
122 B6 Ste.Louise Quebec Canada
121 R7 St.Louis, L Quebec Canada
36 C5 St. Louis-lès-Bitche France
94 E6 St.Louisville Ohio U.S.A.
21 K8 St. Loup-Lamaire France
40 D2 St. Loup-sur-Semoise France
21 N4 St.Lubin-des-Joncherets France
127 L4 Ste.Luce Martinique W Indies
141 K2 St.Lucia dist Brisbane, Qnsld Australia
127 O8 St. Lucia isld Lesser Antilles
87 F11 St. Lucia, C S Africa
121 Q6 Ste.Lucie Quebec Canada
113 G10 St. Lucie Canal Florida U.S.A.
127 P6 St.Lucy parish Barbados
122 B8 St.Ludger Quebec Canada
127 H5 St.Luis du Nord Haiti
123 R2 St Lunaire Newfoundland Canada
20 F4 St.Lunaire France
20 F7 St.Lyphard France
127 N5 Sint Maarten isld Lesser Antilles
25 B5 St.Maartens-dijk Netherlands
18 E8 St. Macaire Gironde France
21 J7 St. Macaire-en-Mauges France
15 G2 St.Magnus B Scotland
122 B7 St.Malachie Quebec Canada
20 F4 St.Malo France
20 G3 St.Malo-de-la-Lande France
20 F4 St.Malo,G.de France
20 F5 St.Malon-sur-Mel France
19 P18 St.Mandrier France
20 B5 St.Marc Finistère France
20 F7 St.Marc Loire-Inférieure France
127 H5 St.Marc Haiti
121 S6 St.Marc des Carrières Quebec Canada
122 B7 St.Marcel Quebec Canada
21 O8 St.Marcel Indre France
19 O14 St.Marcellin France
21 H3 St.Marcouf,Is France
20 H5 St.Marc-sur-Couesnon France
22 K4 St.Mard Belgium
123 P2 St.Margaret B Newfoundland Canada
122 J9 St.Margaret B Nova Scotia Canada
38 K8 St.Margarethen Austria
32 K5 St.Margarethen W Germany
9 H5 St. Margaret's at Cliffe England
15 F2 St.Margarets Hope Scotland
20 F7 Ste.Marguerite France
122 F3 Ste.Marguerite, R Quebec Canada
122 B5 Ste.Marguerite, R Quebec Canada
121 T6 Ste.Marie Quebec Canada
83 K13 Ste.Marie Réunion Indian Oc
110 H3 Ste.Marie Illinois U.S.A.
127 L4 Ste.Marie Martinique W Indies
19 K4 Ste.Marie aux Mines France
36 C7 Ste. Marie, Col de pass France
20 H3 Ste.Marie-du-Mont France
19 Q17 St Marie Mourre de Chanier mt France
100 J2 St.Maries Idaho U.S.A.
113 C7 St.Marks Florida U.S.A.
21 L6 St. Mars-d'Outille France
20 H7 St.Mars-du-Désert France
21 L5 St.Mars-la-Brière France
21 H6 St.Mars-la-Jaille France
21 H5 St.Mars-sur-la-Futaie France
122 F4 Ste.Marthe de Gaspé Quebec Canada
19 P17 St.-Martin France
18 E6 St.Martin France
20 F6 St.Martin Morbihan France
127 N5 St.Martin isld Lesser Antilles
22 B2 St.Martin-Boulogne France
89 A9 St.Martin, C S Africa
127 L4 St. Martin, C Martinique W Indies
21 O4 St.Martin-de-Bretencourt France
19 N17 St.Martin-de-Crau France
21 H4 St.Martin-de-Landelle France
21 J3 St.Martin-des-Besaces France
21 H8 St.Martin-des-Noyers France
16 E4 St.Martin de Valdeiglesias Spain
19 P14 St.-Martin-d'Heres France
19 P12 St.Martin-du-Fresne France
19 O12 St.Martin-du-Mont France
40 B4 St.Martin en Bresse France
21 N2 St.Martin-en-Campagne France
99 U4 St.Martin I Michigan U.S.A.
119 T7 St. Martin, L Manitoba Canada
21 M7 St. Martin-le-Beau France
122 G8 St. Martin's New Brunswick Canada
9 F7 St. Martin's isld Isles of Scilly England
68 A2 St.Martin's I Burma
20 E3 St.Martin's Pt Channel Is
119 T7 St. Martin Station Manitoba Canada
111 E11 St.Martinville Louisiana U.S.A.
20 F3 St.Mary Channel Is
127 L2 St.Mary parish Jamaica
101 M1 St. Mary R Montana/Alberta U.S.A./Canada
123 N3 St. Mary Is Quebec Canada
101 M1 St.Mary L Montana U.S.A.
117 P11 St. Mary, Mt British Columbia Canada
144 B6 St. Mary, Mt New Zealand
123 N3 St.Mary Reefs Quebec Canada
118 D9 St.Mary Res Alberta Canada
139 J8 St.Marys Tasmania Australia
123 T7 St.Marys Newfoundland Canada
9 F7 St.Mary's isld Isles of Scilly England
15 F2 St. Marys Scotland
127 O3 St. Mary's Trinidad
116 F5 St. Marys Alaska U.S.A.
113 F7 St. Marys Georgia U.S.A.
94 B6 St. Marys R Indiana U.S.A.
107 O2 St Marys Kansas U.S.A.
110 G4 St.Marys Missouri U.S.A.
94 C6 St.Marys Ohio U.S.A.
94 J5 St.Marys Pennsylvania U.S.A.
94 F7 St.Marys West Virginia U.S.A.
123 T7 St.Mary's B Newfoundland Canada
122 F9 St.Mary's B Nova Scotia Canada
95 L8 St. Marys City Maryland U.S.A.
89 H6 St.Mary's Hill S Africa
15 E5 St. Marys Loch Scotland
123 K8 St.Mary's, R Nova Scotia Canada
113 F7 St.Marys R Florida/Georgia U.S.A.
112 G4 St. Mathews South Carolina U.S.A.
121 M4 St.Mathieu Quebec Canada
20 A5 St.Mathieu,Pte de France
20 G8 St.Mathurin France
116 C6 St.Matthew I Bering Sea
136 K2 St. Matthias Group islds Bismarck Arch
21 M7 Ste.Maure-de-Touraine France
40 E2 St.Maurice France
21 K7 St. Maurice la Fougereuse Deux Sèvres France
21 M4 St. Maurice-les-Charencey France
8 A7 St. Mawes England
122 B7 St. Maxime Quebec Canada
19 P18 St.Maximin France
20 D5 St.Mayeux France
22 J4 St. Médard Belgium
18 E8 St Medard en Jalles France
20 F5 St.Meen France
110 K3 St.Meinrad Indiana U.S.A.
8 C4 St.Mellons Wales
20 G4 St.Méloir-des-Ondes France
19 J3 St. Menehould France
22 H4 St.Menges France
20 H3 Ste.Mère-Église France
21 J8 St.Mesmin Vendée France
127 P6 St.Michael parish Barbados
98 H8 St.Michael Nebraska U.S.A.
32 K5 St.Michaelisdonn W Germany
103 P6 St.Michaels Arizona U.S.A.
95 L8 St.Michaels Maryland U.S.A.
22 G4 St.Michel Aisne France
21 H6 St.Michel Maine-et-Loire France
20 F7 St.Michel-Chef-Chef France
127 H5 St.Michel de L'Atalaye Haiti
121 R6 St.Michel des Saints Quebec Canada
21 J8 St.Michel-Mont Mercure France
20 C5 St.Michel,Mt Finistère France
20 C5 St.Michel,Res.de France
36 B7 St.Michel-sur-Meurthe France
126 B1 St.Michiel Curaçao
19 J4 St Mihiel France
22 C2 St.Momelin France
13 F1 St.Monance Scotland
41 L5 St.Moritz Switzerland
20 F7 St.Nazaire Loire-Atlantique France
19 O14 St.Nazaire-en-Royans France
9 F3 St.Neots England
20 B5 St.Nic France
126 A2 Sint Nicolaas Aruba W Indies
St.Nicolas see St.Niklaas
21 N2 St.Nicolas-d'Aliermont France
20 F6 St.Nicolas-de-Redon France
20 D5 St.Nicolas-du-Pélem France
22 G1 St.Niklaas Belgium
21 P4 St.-Nom-la-Bretêche France
119 U9 St.Norbert Manitoba Canada
25 F6 St.Odilienberg Netherlands
25 D5 St.Oedenrode Netherlands
122 F5 St.Omer Quebec Canada
22 C2 St.Omer France
145 D4 St. Omer New Zealand
21 P2 St.-Omer-en-Chaussée France
18 E7 Saintonge prov France
98 C5 St.Onge South Dakota U.S.A.
20 H4 St.Osvin France
21 P4 St.-Ouen France
21 J5 St.Ouen-des-Toits France
21 P3 St.Ouen-l'Aumône France
121 R7 St.Ours Quebec Canada
122 C6 St.Pacôme Quebec Canada
20 G4 St.Pair France
18 E9 St.Palais France
122 C7 St.Pamphile Quebec Canada
18 F7 St.Pardoux la Rivière France
94 D6 St.Paris Ohio U.S.A.
122 C6 St.Pascal Quebec Canada
21 L6 St. Paterne Indre-et-Loire France
21 L5 St. Paterne Sarthe France
121 N6 St.Patrice, L- Quebec Canada
127 O3 St.Patrick co Trinidad
38 L8 St.Paul Austria
118 F4 St.Paul Alberta Canada
18 E9 St.Paul France
85 C7 St. Paul R Guinea/Liberia
83 J13 St.Paul Réunion Indian Oc
110 C6 St.Paul Arkansas U.S.A.
94 B7 St.Paul Indiana U.S.A.
107 P4 St.Paul Kansas U.S.A.
99 N4 St.Paul Minnesota U.S.A.
98 H8 St.Paul Nebraska U.S.A.
112 G4 St.Paul South Carolina U.S.A.
94 E10 St.Paul Virginia U.S.A.
18 G10 St. Paul de Fenouillet France
122 C6 St.-Paul-de-la-Croix Quebec Canada
122 B7 St.Paul de Montriny Quebec Canada
122 C5 St.Paul du Nord Quebec Canada
116 D8 St. Paul I Pribilof Is Bering Sea
123 M6 St.Paul I C Breton I, Nova Scotia
81 E9 St. Paul, Î Indian Oc
18 H7 St.Paulien France
121 R6 St.Paulin Quebec Canada
19 P17 St.Paul-les-Durance France
123 P2 St.Paul R Quebec Canada
90 G8 St.Paul Rocks Atlantic Oc
112 H3 St.Pauls North Carolina U.S.A.
127 P4 St.Pauls St Kitts W Indies
123 P4 St.Paul's Inlet Newfoundland Canada
19 N16 St Paul-Trois-Châteaux France
20 G7 St. Pazanne France
18 E9 St.Pé de B France
21 O5 St. Peravy-la-Colombe France
20 F7 St. Père-en-Retz France
122 C6 Ste.Perpétue Quebec Canada
110 H3 St.Peter Illinois U.S.A.
32 J4 Sankt Peter W Germany
38 K7 St.Peter-am-Kammersberg Austria
123 R1 St.Peter B Labrador, Nfld Canada
32 J4 St Peter-Ording W Germany
20 E3 St. Peter Port Channel Is
122 H5 St.Peter, Pt Quebec Canada
122 K7 St.Peters Prince Edward I Canada
123 M8 St.Peters C Breton I, Nova Scotia
St.Petersburg see Leningrad
113 E10 St.Petersburg Florida U.S.A.
69 J12 St.Petrus isld Indonesia
20 G8 St. Philbert-de-Bouaine France
20 G7 St. Philbert-de-Grandlieu France
122 B7 St.Philémon Quebec Canada
127 P6 St. Philip parish Barbados
25 B5 St.Philipsland Netherlands
121 S7 St.Pie Quebec Canada
123 Q7 St. Pierre St. Pierre I Atlantic Oc
119 V9 St.Pierre Manitoba Canada
20 D6 St. Pierre Morbihan France
83 J14 St.Pierre Réunion Indian Oc
127 L4 St.Pierre Martinique W Indies
123 Q7 St. Pierre and Miquelon islds Atlantic Oc
19 Q13 St Pierre d'Albigny France
21 N3 St. Pierre-d'Autils France
21 M8 St. Pierre-de-Maillé France
20 G5 St. Pierre-de-Plesguen France
21 M7 St.-Pierre-des-Corps France
21 J8 St. Pierre-des-Echaubrognes France
21 K5 St. Pierre-des-Nids France
21 J8 St. Pierre-du-Chemin France
21 N3 St. Pierre-du-Vauvray France
20 H2 St. Pierre-Église France
21 L2 St. Pierre-en-Port France
123 Q7 St. Pierre, I Atlantic Oc
81 C6 St. Pierre I Indian Oc
121 S6 St.Pierre, L Quebec Canada
21 H5 St. Pierre-la-Cour France
20 H4 St. Pierre-Langers France
18 H6 St. Pierre le Môutier France
21 N3 St. Pierre-lès-Elbeuf France
20 A5 St. Pierre-Quilbignon France
21 K3 St. Pierre-sur-Dives France
21 K5 St. Pierre-sur-Orthe France
21 H4 St. Pois France
21 H6 St. Poix France
22 C1 St.Pol France
22 C3 St.Pol France
20 C4 St. Pol-de-Leon France
38 N5 St.Pölten Austria
19 K6 St.Pon, L.de France
18 G9 St Pons France
18 H6 St.Pourcain-sur-Sioule France
121 S4 St.-Prime Quebec Canada
21 J8 St. Prouant France
20 E4 St. Quay-Portrieux France
122 E6 St.Quentin New Brunswick Canada
22 E4 St.Quentin Aisne France
21 J6 St.-Quentin Maine-et-Loire France
21 P4 St. Quentin-en-Yvelines France
22 B3 St.Quentin, Pte.de France
36 C6 St.Quirin France
18 H7 St.Rambert France
122 B7 St.Raphaël Quebec Canada
121 T6 St.Raymond Quebec Canada
101 L2 St.Regis Montana U.S.A.
95 N2 St. Regis Falls New York U.S.A.
121 R7 St.Rémi Quebec Canada
19 N17 St. Rémy Bouches du Rhône France
21 K4 St. Rémy Calvados France
21 L5 St. Rémy-des-Monts France
21 L5 St. Rémy-du-Plain France
20 G5 St Remy du Plain France
21 N4 St. Rémy-sur-Avre France
18 H7 St. Rémy-sur-Durolle France
20 A5 St. Renan France
40 F6 St.Rhémy Italy
19 J6 St. Rigaud, Mt France
21 O1 St. Riquier France
121 R7 St.Robert Quebec Canada
122 A8 St.Romain Quebec Canada
21 L2 St. Romain-de-Colbosc France
21 N7 St. Romain-sur-Cher France
121 T6 St.Romuald Quebec Canada
141 G4 St. Ronans Queensland Australia
121 R7 Ste.Rose Quebec Canada
127 N4 Ste.Rose Guadeloupe W Indies
119 S7 Ste.Rose de Lac Manitoba Canada
122 D6 Ste.Rose du Dégelé Quebec Canada
38 N7 St.Ruprecht-an-der-Raab Austria
21 N2 St. Saëns France
20 E3 St. Sampson Channel Is
20 E5 St. Samson France
21 P8 St. Saturnin France
19 O17 St.Saturnin d'Apt France
19 N17 St Saturnin-lès-Avig-non France
21 P2 St. Sauflieu France
121 Q7 St.Sauveur Quebec Canada
19 O16 St. Sauveur France
20 B5 St. Sauveur Finistère France
21 K4 St. Sauveur Orne France
20 H3 St. Sauveur-Lendelin France
20 G3 St. Sauveur-le-Vicomte France
21 N4 St. Sauveur-Marville Eure France
18 E7 St.Savin France
21 M8 St. Savin Vienne France
21 L4 Ste. Scolasse France
20 B5 St. Segal France
18 G9 St.Sernin-sur-Rance France
20 F4 St. Servan France
18 E9 St.Sever France
21 H4 St. Sever-Calvados France
21 P8 Ste. Sévère-sur-Indre Indre France
123 T7 St.Shott's Newfoundland Canada
122 C5 St.Simon Quebec Canada
22 E4 St.Simon France
112 F6 St. Simons Georgia U.S.A.
26 J4 St. Sjöfallets Nat. Park Sweden
122 E8 St.Stephen New Brunswick Canada
112 H4 St.Stephen South Carolina U.S.A.
101 R7 St.Stephens Wyoming U.S.A.
18 G9 St.Sulpice France
21 M4 St. Sulpice Orne France
20 G6 St. Sulpice-des-Landes France
18 F6 St. Sulpice Laurière France
21 K5 Ste. Suzanne France
83 K13 Ste.Suzanne Réunion Indian Oc
21 K3 St. Sylvain France
121 T6 St.-Sylvestre Quebec Canada
18 E8 St.Symphorien France
117 F6 St. Terese Alaska U.S.A.
122 E5 St.Tharsicius Quebec Canada
121 S6 Ste.Thècle Quebec Canada
20 C4 St. Thégonnec France
122 B8 St. Théophile Quebec Canada
121 R7 Ste.Thérèse Quebec Canada
117 N3 Ste. Thérèse, Lac Northwest Territories Canada
40 C1 St.Thiébault France
127 P6 St.Thomas parish Barbados
120 J10 St.Thomas Ontario Canada
127 M3 St.Thomas parish Jamaica
98 J1 St.Thomas North Dakota U.S.A.
113 K7 St.Thomas I Virgin Is
20 C6 St Thurien France
121 S6 St.Tite Quebec Canada
122 B6 St.Tite des Caps Quebec Canada
40 B5 St.Trivier de Courtes France
19 N12 St. Trivier-Moignans France
St.Trond see St.Truiden
22 J2 St.Truiden Belgium
8 B2 St. Tudwal's Is Wales
27 H11 St.Tuna Sweden
122 E5 St.Ulric Quebec Canada
122 B6 St.Urbain Quebec Canada
21 M2 St. Vaast France
20 H2 St. Vaast-la-Hougue France
21 M2 St. Valéry-en-Caux France
21 O1 St. Valery-sur-Somme France
122 B7 St.Vallier Quebec Canada
21 K8 St. Varent France
38 H7 St.Veit Austria
38 K8 St.Veit-an-der-Glan Austria
22 D2 St.Venant France
20 F5 St. Véran Côtes-du-Nord France
121 Q6 Ste.Véronique Quebec Canada
21 O6 St. Viâtre France
20 F7 St Viaud France
20 G7 St. Viaud France
19 P17 Ste Victoire, Mt France
20 F6 St. Vincent France
127 O8 St. Vincent isld Lesser Antilles
21 L6 St Vincent-de-Larouer France
18 E9 St.Vincent-de-Tyrosse France
138 E5 St.Vincent, G South Australia Australia
113 B8 St. Vincent I Florida U.S.A.
139 H9 St.Vincent, Pt Tasmania Australia
123 T7 St.Vincent's Newfoundland Canada
118 A2 St.Vital Manitoba Canada
94 C1 St. Vital Pt Michigan U.S.A.
22 L3 St.Vith Belgium
18 E7 St.Vivien-de-Médoc France
106 G7 St.Vrain New Mexico U.S.A.
118 H5 St.Walburg Saskatchewan Canada
21 M2 St. Wandrille France
36 C5 St.Wendel W Germany
126 A1 St. Willebrordus Curaçao
120 K10 St.Williams Ontario Canada
101 S4 St.Xavier Montana U.S.A.
18 F7 St. Yrieix France
122 H4 St.Yvon Quebec Canada
19 P18 St.Zacharie France
21 O5 Sainville France
134 E6 Saipan isld Mariana Is Pacific Oc
20 H2 Saire R France
20 H2 Saire, Pte. de France
18 E9 Saison R France
61 M10 Saitama prefect Japan
68 A1 Saitlai Burma
60 E13 Saito Japan
26 N3 Saivomuotka Sweden
77 L2 Saiydabad Afghanistan
77 L1 Saiyid Afghanistan
74 E3 Saiyidwala Pakistan
71 B2 Sajafi isld Indonesia
128 E7 Sajama mt Bolivia
128 E7 Sajama Bolivia
71 B2 Sajang isld Indonesia
48 F2 Sajó R Hungary
89 B7 Sak watercourse S Africa
88 G2 Saka Kenya
Saka Dzong see Saga China
59 L5 Sakai Japan
60 G11 Sakaide Japan
60 G10 Sakai Minato Japan
78 H7 Sākākah Saudi Arabia
98 E2 Sakakawea, L North Dakota U.S.A.
70 Q9 Sakala isld Indonesia
61 N7 Sakamachi Japan
115 M7 Sakami, L Quebec Canada
88 B8 Sakania Zaire
47 H3 Sakar hills Bulgaria
57 C5 Sakar U.S.S.R.
87 G12 Sakaraha Madagascar
57 B5 Sakar-chaga U.S.S.R.
78 C1 Sakarya R Turkey
78 C2 Sakarya R Turkey
59 L4 Sakata Japan
111 H8 Sakatonchee R Mississippi U.S.A.
85 E7 Sakete Benin
59 M1 Sakhalin isld U.S.S.R.
51 O4 Sakhalinskaya Oblast' U.S.S.R.
51 O3 Sakhalinskiy Zaliv B U.S.S.R.
85 F2 Sakhira Tunisia
54 G7 Sakhnovshchina U.S.S.R.
77 B1 Sakht-Sar Iran
52 B7 Šakiai U.S.S.R.
80 G4 Sakib Jordan
60 H12 Sakihama Japan
67 H4 Sakishima-guntō islds Japan
55 C5 Sakmara U.S.S.R.
85 B3 Sakn, As Western Sahara
68 C3 Sa-koi Burma
95 Q5 Sakonnet R Rhode I U.S.A.
87 D12 Sakrivier S Africa
28 E5 Saksild Denmark
28 H7 Sakskøbing Denmark
75 K7 Sakti India
51 M1 Saktyakh U.S.S.R.
61 M9 Saku Japan
61 L10 Sakuma Japan
61 J11 Sakurai Japan
60 D14 Sakura jima isld Japan
27 M10 Säkylä Finland
80 G3 Sal Jordan
53 F9 Sal R U.S.S.R.
48 D2 Šala Czechoslovakia
27 J12 Sala Sweden
68 F7 Sala Andong Tuk Cambodia
71 H6 Salabangka isld Sulawesi
52 B5 Salacgriva U.S.S.R.
43 G8 Sala Consilina Italy
109 K5 Salad Texas U.S.A.
133 C3 Salada, B Chile
131 G6 Salada, L Buenos Aires Argentina
131 F2 Salada, L Corrientes Argentina
124 B1 Salada, L Mexico
103 J9 Salada, Laguna L Mexico
131 E4 Saladillo R Argentina
131 B2 Salado R La Rioja Argentina
131 E2 Salado, R Santa Fé Argentina
106 C7 Salado, R New Mexico U.S.A.
85 D7 Salaga Ghana
68 F7 Sala Hintoun Cambodia
56 C4 Salair U.S.S.R.
56 C4 Salairskiy Kryazh ridge U.S.S.R.
48 H3 Šalaj prov Romania
70 G7 Salajar, Selat str Sulawesi
70 L9 Salak, G mt Java
86 C3 Salal Chad
72 G5 Şalālah Oman
125 O10 Salamá Guatemala
16 D4 Salamanca Spain
16 C4 Salamanca prov Spain
94 J4 Salamanca New York U.S.A.
86 C4 Salamat R Chad
70 D6 Salamban Kalimantan
128 C2 Salamina Colombia
79 D3 Salamis Cyprus
46 F7 Salamís Greece
79 H3 Salamīyah Syria
94 B6 Salamonie R Indiana U.S.A.
26 J3 Salangen Norway
52 B6 Salantai U.S.S.R.
45 K2 Salara Italy
48 G3 Sălard Romania
133 D2 Salar de Arizaro salt pan Argentina
133 D2 Salar de Atacama salt pan Chile
133 D2 Salar de Cauchari salt pan Argentina
133 D1 Salar de Coipasa salt pan Bolivia
133 D3 Salar del Hombre Muerto salt pan Argentina
133 D2 Salar de Uyuni salt pan Bolivia
16 C1 Salas Spain
46 E1 Salaš Yugoslavia
16 E2 Salas de los Infantes Spain
18 F9 Salat R France
70 N9 Salatiga Java
18 F10 Salau, Pont de pass France/Spain
52 H6 Salaushi U.S.S.R.
55 C4 Salavat U.S.S.R.
128 C5 Salaverry Peru
133 E3 Salavina Argentina
71 C3 Salawati isld W Irian
71 G6 Salay Mindanao Philippines
135 Q11 Sala y Gómez isld Pacific Oc
Salazar see N'dalatando
21 P7 Salbris France
126 D3 Sal, Cay isld Bahamas
127 J5 Salcedo Dominican Rep
116 P4 Salcha R Alaska U.S.A.
116 O4 Salchaket Alaska U.S.A.
33 P8 Salchau East Germany
37 O6 Salching W Germany
46 G1 Salcia Romania
8 C7 Salcombe England
47 K7 Salda Gölü L Turkey
16 D2 Saldaña Spain
87 C12 Saldanha S Africa
41 N4 Saldura, Pta mt Italy
52 B6 Saldus U.S.S.R.
139 H7 Sale Victoria Australia
68 B2 Sale Burma
8 D1 Sale England
85 C2 Salé Morocco
70 G5 Salea Sulawesi
112 C6 Sale City Georgia U.S.A.
112 B2 Sale Creek Tennessee U.S.A.
77 A2 Sālehābad Iran
71 H9 Saleh, Teluk B Indonesia
147 N15 Salekhard U.S.S.R.
76 D5 Salem India
111 L9 Salem Alabama U.S.A.
110 E5 Salem Arkansas U.S.A.
113 D8 Salem Florida U.S.A.
110 H3 Salem Illinois U.S.A.
110 K3 Salem Indiana U.S.A.
95 R4 Salem Massachusetts U.S.A.
110 E4 Salem Missouri U.S.A.
95 Q4 Salem New Hampshire U.S.A.
95 M7 Salem New Jersey U.S.A.
106 C9 Salem New Mexico U.S.A.
95 O3 Salem New York U.S.A.
94 G6 Salem Ohio U.S.A.
100 B5 Salem Oregon U.S.A.
112 E3 Salem South Carolina U.S.A.
98 J6 Salem South Dakota U.S.A.
94 G9 Salem Virginia U.S.A.
99 S7 Salem Wisconsin U.S.A.
43 E11 Salemi Sicily
15 C4 Salen Scotland
27 F10 Sälen Sweden
142 E3 Sale, R Western Australia Australia
19 Q17 Salernes France
43 F8 Salerno Italy
113 G10 Salerno Florida U.S.A.
43 F8 Salerno, Golfo di Italy
45 L1 Saletto Italy
21 P2 Saleux France
19 Q12 Salève, Mt France
13 F6 Salford England
130 H9 Salgado R Brazil
131 H2 Salgado Filho airport Brazil
48 F2 Salgótarján Hungary
130 G10 Salgueiro Brazil
80 E1 Sâlhâni Lebanon
79 C8 Sâlhîya, El Egypt
127 P2 Salibea Trinidad
106 D3 Salida Colorado U.S.A.
18 E9 Salies de Béarn France
18 F9 Salies du Salat France
47 J6 Salihli Turkey
87 F8 Salima Malawi
70 E3 Salimbatu Kalimantan
68 B2 Salin R Burma
68 B2 Salin Burma
107 N3 Salina Kansas U.S.A.
110 A5 Salina Oklahoma U.S.A.
103 N3 Salina Utah U.S.A.
125 M9 Salina Cruz Mexico
43 F10 Salina, I Italy
133 D4 Salina La Antigua salt pan Argentina
126 G3 Salina Pt Acklins I Bahamas
129 K7 Salinas Brazil
128 B4 Salinas Ecuador
128 C6 Salinas Peru
102 C5 Salinas R California U.S.A.
102 C5 Salinas California U.S.A.
133 D4 Salinas Grandes Argentina
106 D7 Salinas Nat. Mon New Mexico U.S.A.
108 A1 Salinas Nat.Mon New Mexico U.S.A.
131 C3 Salinas, Pampa de la Argentina
106 D8 Salinas Pk New Mexico U.S.A.
87 B8 Salinas, Pte. das Angola
12 E1 Saline Scotland
111 D8 Saline R Arkansas U.S.A.
110 H4 Saline R Illinois U.S.A.
107 L2 Saline R Kansas U.S.A.
94 D4 Saline Michigan U.S.A.
127 P2 Saline B Trinidad
109 P3 Saline Bayou R Louisiana U.S.A.
109 P4 Saline L Louisiana U.S.A.
127 P5 Salines, Pt Grenada
102 G5 Saline V California U.S.A.
94 G6 Salineville Ohio U.S.A.
68 B1 Salingyi Burma
133 C3 Salinitas Chile
129 J4 Salinópolis Brazil
Salisbury see Harare Zimbabwe
141 K2 Salisbury dist Brisbane, Qnsld Australia
138 E5 Salisbury South Australia Australia
122 G7 Salisbury New Brunswick Canada
9 E5 Salisbury England
95 O4 Salisbury Connecticut U.S.A.
95 M8 Salisbury Maryland U.S.A.
110 D2 Salisbury Missouri U.S.A.
112 G2 Salisbury North Carolina U.S.A.
94 H7 Salisbury Pennsylvania U.S.A.
95 O3 Salisbury Vermont U.S.A.
115 M5 Salisbury I Northwest Territories Canada
86 F5 Salisbury, L Uganda
116 O2 Salisbury, Mt Alaska U.S.A.
9 E5 Salisbury Plain England
48 H5 Săliste Romania
129 K6 Salitre R Brazil
80 G8 Saliya Jordan
45 K1 Salizzole Italy
112 F4 Salkehatchie R South Carolina U.S.A.
79 G6 Şalkhad Syria
28 D4 Sall Denmark
38 L7 Salla Austria
29 O5 Salla Finland
21 J7 Salle-de-Vihiers, la France
17 G2 Sallent de G Spain
19 N16 Salles France
18 G8 Salles-Curan France
112 F4 Salley South Carolina U.S.A.
33 T9 Sallgast East Germany
28 B3 Salling reg Denmark
107 Q6 Sallisaw Oklahoma U.S.A.
86 G2 Sallom Sudan
78 K6 Salman, As Iraq
78 K2 Salmās Iran
17 F4 Salmerón Spain
29 N5 Salmivaara Finland
100 H1 Salmo British Columbia Canada
117 M8 Salmon R British Columbia Canada
116 Q3 Salmon Alaska U.S.A.
101 M4 Salmon Idaho U.S.A.
117 O10 Salmon Arm British Columbia Canada
123 P2 Salmon Bay Quebec Canada
101 L7 Salmon Cr.Res Idaho U.S.A.
142 F3 Salmond R Western Australia Australia
101 L7 Salmon Falls Idaho U.S.A.
116 R4 Salmon Fork R Alaska U.S.A.
143 D10 Salmon Gums Western Australia Australia
123 T6 Salmonier Newfoundland Canada
100 B8 Salmon Mt California U.S.A.
122 G7 Salmon R New Brunswick Canada
122 K4 Salmon, R Quebec Canada
95 M3 Salmon Res New York U.S.A.
100 K5 Salmon River Mts Idaho U.S.A.
36 G3 Salmünster W Germany
52 E2 Sal'nitsa U.S.S.R.
42 D3 Salò Italy
52 G6 Salobelyak U.S.S.R.
130 C7 Salobra, R Brazil
29 L7 Saloinen Finland
99 L1 Salol Minnesota U.S.A.
103 L8 Salome Arizona U.S.A.
127 L4 Salomon, C Martinique W Indies
40 C2 Salon R France
19 O17 Salon-de-Provence France
86 D6 Salonga, Parc Nacional de la nat park Zaire
Salonica see Thessaloniki
48 G4 Salonta Romania
Salop co see Shropshire
17 H3 Salou, C Spain
29 M11 Salpausselkä reg Finland
53 F10 Sal'sk U.S.S.R.
43 F11 Salso R Sicily
44 G2 Salsomaggiore Terme Italy
80 F5 Salt Jordan
103 N8 Salt R Arizona U.S.A.
110 L3 Salt R Kentucky U.S.A.
110 E2 Salt R Missouri U.S.A.
133 D2 Salta Argentina
55 F3 Saltaim, Oz L U.S.S.R.
8 B7 Saltash England
28 G5 Saltbæk Vig lagoon Denmark
108 B4 Salt Basin Texas U.S.A.
13 H4 Saltburn-by-the-Sea England
119 P7 Saltcoats Saskatchewan Canada
12 D2 Saltcoats Scotland
110 G1 Salt Cr Illinois U.S.A.
99 R9 Salt Cr R Illinois U.S.A.
94 E7 Salt Cr Ohio U.S.A.
101 T6 Salt Cr Wyoming U.S.A.
138 E6 Salt Creek South Australia Australia
26 H4 Saltdal Norway
108 C4 Salt Draw R Texas U.S.A.
14 E4 Saltee Is Ireland
26 H5 Saltelv R Norway
26 G4 Salten reg Norway
28 D4 Salten Langsø L Denmark
26 G4 Saltfjord inlet Norway
108 B4 Salt Flat Texas U.S.A.
13 J6 Saltfleet England
107 M5 Salt Fork R Oklahoma U.S.A.
108 F2 Salt Fork R Texas U.S.A.
109 H4 Salt Gap Texas U.S.A.
29 K5 Saltholm isld Denmark
125 J5 Saltillo Mexico
94 J6 Saltillo Pennsylvania U.S.A.
110 H6 Saltillo Tennessee U.S.A.
106 G9 Salt L New Mexico U.S.A.
108 C4 Salt L Texas U.S.A.
101 O9 Salt Lake City Utah U.S.A.
94 D8 Salt Lick Kentucky U.S.A.
133 E4 Salto Argentina
130 F8 Salto Brazil
42 E6 Salto R Italy
131 F3 Salto dept Uruguay
131 F3 Salto Uruguay
130 D7 Salto do Urubupungá falls Brazil
131 F3 Salto Grande, Embalse de res Argentina/Uruguay
45 O5 Salto, L. del Italy
26 K4 Saltoluokta Sweden
103 J8 Salton Sea California U.S.A.
Saltos do Iguaçu see Cataratas del Iguazú waterfalls
107 M5 Salt Plains L Oklahoma U.S.A.
127 L3 Salt Ponds, The Jamaica
74 E2 Salt Range Pakistan
127 K3 Salt River Jamaica
127 H5 Saltrou Haiti
101 P7 Salt R. Ra Wyoming U.S.A.
27 K12 Saltsjöbaden Sweden
27 L11 Saltvik Finland
94 F10 Saltville Virginia U.S.A.
102 F2 Salt Wells Nevada U.S.A.
112 E3 Saluda R South Carolina U.S.A.
112 F3 Saluda South Carolina U.S.A.
71 H5 Salue isld Indonesia
71 H5 Salue Timpaus, Selat str Indonesia
84 H3 Salûm Egypt
45 N4 Saluoecio Italy
71 F7 Saluping isld Philippines
76 F1 Salur India
110 C6 Salus Arkansas U.S.A.
129 H2 Salut, I.du Fr Guiana
44 B2 Saluzzo Italy
129 L6 Salvador Brazil
118 H6 Salvador Saskatchewan Canada
84 E5 Salvador Niger
111 F12 Salvador, L Louisiana U.S.A.
123 T5 Salvage Newfoundland Canada
16 B5 Salvaterra de Magos Portugal
125 J7 Salvatierra Mexico
103 N3 Salvation Cr Utah U.S.A.
141 H6 Salvator, L Queensland Australia

Salvetat, la — Santa Maria, Pta 75

18 G8 Salvetat, la Aveyron France
18 G9 Salvetat, la Hérault France
117 J8 Salvus British Columbia Canada
73 Q5 Salween R Burma/Thailand
75 K4 Salyan Nepal
94 D9 Salyersville Kentucky U.S.A.
55 F1 Salym U.S.S.R.
38 L6 Salza R Austria
32 F8 Salzbergen W Germany
38 H6 Salzburg Austria
38 H7 Salzburg prov Austria
32 L9 Salzderhelden W Germany
33 M8 Salzgitter W Germany
33 M8 Salzgitter-Bad W Germany
38 J6 Salzkammer-gut res Austria
32 J9 Salzkotten W Germany
33 P9 Salzmünde East Germany
33 O7 Salzwedel East Germany
101 O6 Sam Idaho U.S.A.
80 G3 Sama Jordan
80 G4 Samad Jordan
71 J5 Samada isld Indonesia
16 D1 Sama de Langreo Spain
56 E5 Samagaltay U.S.S.R.
84 F4 Samāh Libya
80 F2 Samak Syria
71 G7 Samal isld Mindanao Philippines
69 C10 Samalanga Sumatra
69 J12 Samalantan Indonesia
108 A4 Samalayuca Mexico
71 E7 Samales Group islds Philippines
76 F2 Samalkot India
84 J4 Samâlût Egypt
127 K5 Samaná Dominican Rep
126 H3 Samana Cay isld Bahamas
78 E3 Samandağı Turkey
47 N11 Samandira Turkey
60 Q3 Samani Japan
70 N10 Samanu Java
121 S3 Samaqua R Quebec Canada
80 G3 Samar Jordan
71 G5 Samar isld Philippines
53 H7 Samara R U.S.S.R.
136 L4 Samarai Papua New Guinea
80 D4 Samaria Jordan
101 N7 Samaria Idaho U.S.A.
46 E4 Samarina Greece
70 E5 Samarinda Kalimantan
57 D5 Samarkand U.S.S.R.
78 J4 Sāmarrā' Iraq
71 G5 Samar Sea Philippines
71 C3 Samate W Irian
78 K6 Samāwah, Aq Iraq
70 C5 Samba R Kalimantan
86 D5 Samba Equateur Zaire
86 E6 Samba Kasai Oriental Zaire
87 C7 Samba Caju Angola
71 A3 Sambaki, Selat Indonesia
70 F4 Sambaliung mts Kalimantan
75 L8 Sambalpur India
70 G7 Sambapolulu, G mt Sulawesi
87 J10 Sambava Madagascar
25 E5 Sambeek Netherlands
74 H4 Sambhal India
71 H5 Sambiat Sulawesi
21 N7 Sambin France
70 F4 Sambit isld Kalimantan
129 K5 Sambito R Brazil
70 F6 Sambo Sulawesi
70 E5 Sambodja Kalimantan
68 H6 Sambor Cambodia
48 H1 Sambor U.S.S.R.
131 G6 Samborombón, B Argentina
22 H3 Sambre R Belgium
69 F12 Sambu Indonesia
70 D5 Sambuah Kalimantan
45 J3 Sambuca Pistojese Italy
59 J4 Samchŏk S Korea
68 D6 Same Burma
88 F4 Same Tanzania
22 B2 Samer France
68 E6 Samet, Ko isld Thailand
87 E8 Samfya Zambia
68 A2 Sami Burma
46 D6 Sámi Greece
71 H4 Samia, Tg C Sulawesi Indonesia
128 D5 Samiria R Peru
85 E5 Samit Mali
68 C2 Samka Burma
29 K11 Sammatti Finland
80 F3 Sammu' Jordan
68 F5 Samnak Kado Thailand
41 M3 Samnaun Gruppe mt Austria
80 E6 Samniya Auja R Jordan
84 F4 Samnū Libya
100 A9 Samoa California U.S.A.
Samoa i Sisifo islds see Western Samoa
42 G3 Samobor Yugoslavia
52 F3 Samoded U.S.S.R.
40 E5 Samoëns France
46 F2 Samokov Bulgaria
68 C2 Samon R Burma
47 H7 Sámos isld Greece
Samothrace see Samothráki
46 D5 Samothráki isld Ionian Is Greece
47 H4 Samothráki isld Thraki Greece
133 E4 Sampacho Argentina
70 F6 Sampaga Sulawesi
71 E3 Sampaloc Pt Luzon Philippines
70 O9 Sampang Indonesia
17 G3 Samper de Calanda Spain
113 L12 Samphire Cay isld Bahamas
70 C6 Sampit Kalimantan
70 C6 Sampit, Teluk B Kalimantan
87 E7 Sampwe Zaire
80 F8 Samra Jordan
109 N4 Sam Rayburn L Texas U.S.A.
111 B10 Sam Rayburn Res Texas U.S.A.
22 K3 Samrée Belgium
68 F6 Samrong R Cambodia
78 G3 Samsat Turkey
28 F5 Samsø isld Denmark
111 K10 Samson Alabama U.S.A.
68 G3 Sam Son Vietnam
78 F1 Samsun Turkey
67 A6 Sam Teu Laos
140 C4 Samuel, Mt N Terr Australia
47 H1 Samuil Bulgaria
56 B3 Samus' U.S.S.R.
68 E6 Samut Prakan Thailand
68 E6 Samut Sakhon Thailand
68 E6 Samut Songkhram Thailand
71 J5 Samuya Indonesia
85 D6 San Mali
31 N6 San R Poland
72 E5 Şan'ā' N Yemen
42 H4 Sana R Yugoslavia
106 D7 San Acacia New Mexico U.S.A.
146 H6 Sanae S African Base Antarctica
86 B5 Sanaga R Cameroon
106 D10 San Agustin Mexico
71 G7 San Agustin, C Mindanao Philippines
133 D4 San Agustín de Valle Fértil Argentina
116 F9 Sanak I Aleutian Is
45 M2 San Alberto Italy
79 G5 Şanamayn, Aş Syria
135 S12 San Ambrosio isld Pacific Oc
102 D3 San Andreas California U.S.A.
125 P9 San Andrés Guatemala
106 D9 San Andres Mts New Mexico U.S.A.
125 M8 San Andrés Tuxtla Mexico
41 K7 San Angelo Italy
108 G4 San Angelo Texas U.S.A.
126 C3 San Anton de los Baños Cuba
125 P9 San Antonio Belize
131 B4 San Antonio Chile
125 L2 San Antonio Honduras
124 E6 San Antonio Mexico
71 E2 San Antonio Luzon Philippines
113 E9 San Antonio Florida U.S.A.
106 D8 San Antonio New Mexico U.S.A.
109 K7 San Antonio R Texas U.S.A.
109 J6 San Antonio Texas U.S.A.
128 E3 San Antonio Venezuela
17 H6 San Antonio Abad Ibiza
71 C6 San Antonio B Palawan Philippines
109 L7 San Antonio B Texas U.S.A.
133 F5 San Antonio, C Argentina
126 B4 San Antonio, C Cuba
17 H6 San Antonio, C Spain
133 D2 San Antonio de los Cobres Argentina
124 E3 San Antonio del Rio Mexico
127 N9 San Antonio de Maturín Venezuela
127 L10 San Antonio de Tamanaco Venezuela
102 G7 San Antonio, Mt California U.S.A.
108 B4 San Antonio Mt Texas U.S.A.
133 E6 San Antonio Oeste Argentina
130 J9 San Antonio, Pta. de C Brazil
128 E2 Sanariapo Venezuela
19 P18 Sanary France
111 B10 San Augustine Texas U.S.A.
74 G7 Sanawad India
16 B7 San Bartolómeu de Messines Portugal
45 R7 San Bartolomew in Galdo Italy
42 F6 San Benedetto del Tronto Italy
45 J1 San Benedetto Po Italy
125 P9 San Benito Guatemala
102 C5 San Benito R California U.S.A.
109 K9 San Benito Texas U.S.A.
102 D5 San Benito Mt California U.S.A.
71 G4 San Bernadino Str Philippines
109 M6 San Bernard R Texas U.S.A.
130 B9 San Bernardino Paraguay
102 G7 San Bernardino California U.S.A.
103 J8 San Bernardino Mts California U.S.A.
41 K5 San Bernardino P Switzerland
131 B4 San Bernardo Chile
124 G4 San Bernardo Mexico
128 C2 San Bernardo, I.de Colombia
60 F10 Sanbe-san mt Japan
45 L2 San Biagio Italy
124 G7 San Blas Nayarit Mexico
124 E4 San Blas Sonora Mexico
113 B7 San Blas Florida U.S.A.
125 P5 San Blas, Archipélago de islds Panama
113 B8 San Blas, C Florida U.S.A.
125 P5 San Blas, Serrania de mts Panama
41 O7 San Bonifacio Italy
128 E6 San Borja Bolivia
124 C3 San Borja Mexico
99 L6 Sanborn Iowa U.S.A.
99 L5 Sanborn Minnesota U.S.A.
98 H3 Sanborn North Dakota U.S.A.
95 Q3 Sanbornville New Hampshire U.S.A.
124 J4 San Buenaventura Mexico
68 E5 San Buri Thailand
128 F8 San Camilo Argentina
133 D4 San Carlos Argentina
131 B6 San Carlos Chile
124 C4 San Carlos Baja Cal Sur Mexico
124 H5 San Carlos Coahuila Mexico
71 E3 San Carlos Luzon Philippines
71 F5 San Carlos Negros Philippines
133 G4 San Carlos Uruguay
103 O8 San Carlos Arizona U.S.A.
127 K10 San Carlos Venezuela
131 B8 San Carlos de Bariloche Argentina
17 H4 San Carlos de la Rápita Spain
128 D2 San Carlos del Zulia Venezuela
128 E3 San Carlos de Rio Negro Venezuela
124 B3 San Carlos, Mesa de mt Mexico
103 O8 San Carlos Res Arizona U.S.A.
45 K4 San Casciano in Valdi Pesa Italy
17 J3 San Celoni Spain
18 G5 Sancergues France
18 G5 Sancerre France
45 K2 San Cesario sul Panaro Italy
21 O5 Sancheville France
127 K5 Sànchez Dominican Rep
106 E4 Sanchez Res Colorado U.S.A.
52 G6 Sanchursk U.S.S.R.
125 K7 San Ciro de Acosta Mexico
17 F5 San Clemente Spain
102 G8 San Clemente California U.S.A.
102 F9 San Clemente isld California U.S.A.
18 G6 Sancoins France
71 G6 Sanco Pt Mindanao Philippines
130 B10 San Cosme Argentina
133 F3 San Cosme Paraguay
45 O4 San Costanzo Italy
131 E3 San Cristóbal Argentina
127 J5 San Cristóbal Dominican Rep
128 B8 San Cristóbal isld Galapagos Is
137 N4 San Cristobal Solomon Is
128 D2 San Cristóbal Venezuela
125 N9 San Cristóbal de las Casas Mexico
103 L9 San Cristobal Wash R Arizona U.S.A.
45 J4 San Croce sulee Arno Italy
133 C4 San Cruz Chile
126 E4 Sancti Spiritus Cuba
118 J7 Sanctuary Saskatchewan Canada
22 K5 Sancy France
27 B12 Sand Norway
89 E7 Sand R Orange Free State S Africa
89 F4 Sand R Transvaal S Africa
60 J11 Sanda Japan
15 C5 Sanda isld Scotland
28 D6 Sandager Denmark
70 F2 Sandakan Sabah
70 F2 Sandakan, Pelabuhan hbr Sabah
68 H6 Sandan Cambodia
26 B10 Sandane Norway
46 F3 Sandanski Bulgaria
65 H2 Sandaotong China
65 G1 Sandaozhen China
85 B6 Sandare Mali
27 J10 Sandarne Sweden
106 H4 Sand Arroyo R Colo/Kansas U.S.A.
33 Q7 Sandau East Germany
15 F1 Sanday Scotland
8 D5 Sand B England
8 D1 Sandbach England
37 P6 Sandbach W Germany
27 G15 Sandbäck Sweden
12 D2 Sandbank Scotland
120 H1 Sandbank L Ontario Canada
89 E4 Sandbult S Africa
28 G7 Sandby Denmark
26 F7 Sanddöla R Norway
26 A9 Sande Norway
27 A10 Sande Norway
32 H5 Sande W Germany
27 D12 Sandefj Norway
146 J10 Sandercock Nunataks mt peaks Antarctica
103 P6 Sanders Arizona U.S.A.
100 J2 Sanders Idaho U.S.A.
37 M6 Sandersdorf W Germany
33 P9 Sandersleben East Germany
113 E7 Sanderson Florida U.S.A.
108 E5 Sanderson Texas U.S.A.
112 E5 Sandersville Georgia U.S.A.
111 H10 Sandersville Mississippi U.S.A.
33 M5 Sandesneben W Germany
28 B5 Sandet Denmark
142 D4 Sandfire Flat Roadhouse Western Australia Australia
118 L3 Sandfly L Saskatchewan Canada
94 G8 Sand Fork West Virginia U.S.A.
141 L7 Sandgate Queensland Australia
9 H5 Sandgate England
36 F5 Sandhausen W Germany
12 D4 Sandhead Scotland
26 G4 Sandhornöy isld Norway
99 Q3 Sand I Wisconsin U.S.A.
109 K7 Sandia Texas U.S.A.
106 D6 Sandia Pk New Mexico U.S.A.
124 G3 San Diego Mexico
102 G9 San Diego California U.S.A.
109 J8 San Diego Texas U.S.A.
102 G8 San Diego Aqueduct California U.S.A.
133 D8 San Diego, C Argentina
128 F2 San Diego de Cabrutica Venezuela
47 L6 Sandıklı Turkey
74 J5 Sandila India
118 E1 Sandilands Manitoba Canada
113 M9 Sandilands Village New Providence I Bahamas
21 P6 Sandillon France
143 B6 Sandiman, Mt Western Australia Australia
124 G5 San Dimas Mexico
69 E14 Sanding isld Indonesia
116 D5 Sand Is Alaska U.S.A.
52 J2 Sandivey R U.S.S.R.
32 H6 Sandkrug W Germany
38 L4 Sandl Austria
120 F5 Sand Lake Ontario Canada
110 K7 Sand Mountain Alabama U.S.A.
27 C13 Sandnes Aust Agder Norway
27 A13 Sandnes Rogaland Norway
15 G2 Sandness Scotland
26 F5 Sandnessjöen Norway
Sando see Sandoy
87 D7 Sandoa Zaire
31 N5 Sandomierz Poland
45 P6 San Donato Val di Comino Italy
110 G3 Sandoval Illinois U.S.A.
106 D6 Sandoval New Mexico U.S.A.
140 D5 Sandover R N Terr Australia
52 E5 Sandovo U.S.S.R.
68 B3 Sandoway Burma
9 E6 Sandown England
89 A10 Sandown B S Africa
6 F1 Sandoy isld Faeroes
116 G9 Sand Point Alaska U.S.A.
117 F11 Sandpoint Idaho U.S.A.
118 F4 Sand R Alberta Canada
140 E6 Sandringham Queensland Australia
9 G2 Sandringham England
99 T3 Sands Michigan U.S.A.
27 G14 Sandsjö, N Sweden
113 G12 Sands Key isld Florida U.S.A.
117 H9 Sandspit British Columbia Canada
38 G8 Sandspitze mt Austria
101 S2 Sand Springs Montana U.S.A.
107 O5 Sand Springs Oklahoma U.S.A.
102 F2 Sand Springs Salt Flat Nevada U.S.A.
26 D8 Sandstad Norway
32 J6 Sandstedt W Germany
95 K9 Sandston Virginia U.S.A.
143 C8 Sandstone Western Australia Australia
99 O3 Sandstone Minnesota U.S.A.
103 M9 Sand Tanks Mts Arizona U.S.A.
123 L4 Sandtop, C Anticosti I, Quebec
67 B3 Sandu China
67 B4 Sandu Guizhou China
67 E2 Sandu Jiangxi China
94 E3 Sandusky Michigan U.S.A.
94 D5 Sandusky R Ohio U.S.A.
94 E5 Sandusky Ohio U.S.A.
28 H6 Sandved Denmark
87 C11 Sandverhaar Namibia
27 G16 Sandvig Denmark
27 D12 Sandvika Norway
27 J11 Sandviken Sweden
9 H5 Sandwich England
99 S8 Sandwich Illinois U.S.A.
95 R5 Sandwich Massachusetts U.S.A.
115 O7 Sandwich B Labrador, Nfld Canada
141 H4 Sandwich, C Queensland Australia
15 G2 Sandwick Scotland
118 J5 Sandwith Saskatchewan Canada
95 R2 Sandy R Maine U.S.A.
103 J6 Sandy Nevada U.S.A.
100 C4 Sandy Oregon U.S.A.
103 N1 Sandy Utah U.S.A.
119 P3 Sandy Bay Saskatchewan Canada
127 H1 Sandy Bay Jamaica
118 K1 Sandybeach L Ontario Canada
141 L6 Sandy C Queensland Australia
139 G8 Sandy C Tasmania Australia
101 O9 Sandy City Utah U.S.A.
109 L6 Sandy Cr Texas U.S.A.
101 Q7 Sandy Cr Wyoming U.S.A.
121 O7 Sandy Creek Quebec Canada
95 L3 Sandy Creek New York U.S.A.
95 O5 Sandy Hook Connecticut U.S.A.
94 D8 Sandy Hook Kentucky U.S.A.
111 G10 Sandy Hook Mississippi U.S.A.
95 N6 Sandy Hook pt New Jersey U.S.A.
57 C6 Sandykachi U.S.S.R.
123 Q4 Sandy L Newfoundland Canada
115 K7 Sandy L Ontario Canada
119 R8 Sandy Lake Manitoba Canada
119 O3 Sandy Narrows Saskatchewan Canada
112 L2 Sandy Pt North Carolina U.S.A.
127 P4 Sandy Pt St Kitts W Indies
126 G9 San Estanislao Colombia
129 G8 San Estanislao Paraguay
71 E2 San Fabian Luzon Philippines
45 O7 San Felice Circeo Italy
45 K2 San Felice sul Panaro Italy
131 B4 San Felipe Chile
128 E3 San Felipe Colombia
124 B2 San Felipe Baja California Mexico
124 F4 San Felipe Chihuahua Mexico
127 K9 San Felipe Venezuela
126 C4 San Felipe, Cayos de islds Cuba
17 F4 San Felipe, Cerro de pk Spain
103 H8 San Felipe Cr California U.S.A.
106 D6 San Felipe Pueblo New Mexico U.S.A.
17 K3 San Feliú de Guixols Spain
17 J3 San Feliu de Llobregat Spain
135 S12 San Félix isld Pacific Oc
131 B5 San Fernando Chile
124 B3 San Fernando Mexico
71 E2 San Fernando Luzon Philippines
16 C8 San Fernando Spain
127 O3 San Fernando Trinidad
102 F7 San Fernando California U.S.A.
128 E2 San Fernando de Apure Venezuela
128 E3 San Fernando de Atabape Venezuela
26 G9 Sånfjället mt Sweden
118 D1 Sanford Manitoba Canada
106 E4 Sanford Colorado U.S.A.
113 F9 Sanford Florida U.S.A.
95 R3 Sanford Maine U.S.A.
112 H2 Sanford North Carolina U.S.A.
108 C8 Sanford Texas U.S.A.
94 C3 Sanford L Michigan U.S.A.
116 Q5 Sanford, Mt Alaska U.S.A.
143 B7 Sanford, R Western Australia Australia
127 N3 San Francique Trinidad
131 E3 San Francisco Argentina
106 B8 San Francisco R Ariz/New Mex U.S.A.
104 San Francisco conurbation California U.S.A.
127 J9 San Francisco Venezuela
102 B4 San Francisco Bay California U.S.A.
108 E6 San Francisco Cr Texas U.S.A.
124 G4 San Francisco de Conchos Mexico
133 E3 San Francisco del Chanar Argentina
133 D4 San Francisco del Monte de Oro Argentina
124 G4 San Francisco del Oro Mexico
124 H7 San Francisco del Rincón Mexico
127 J5 San Francisco de Macoris Dominican Rep
133 D7 San Francisco de Paula, C Argentina
133 G4 San Gabriel Brazil
102 G7 San Gabriel Mts California U.S.A.
124 C3 San Gabriel, Pta C Mexico
69 G14 Sangaigerong Sumatra
76 B1 Sangammer India
99 R10 Sangamon R Illinois U.S.A.
77 J3 Sangan, Koh-i mt Afghanistan
51 M2 Sangar U.S.S.R.
76 D2 Sangāreddi India
70 E5 Sangasanga Kalimantan
70 F2 Sanga Sanga isld Philippines
85 C6 Sangasso Mali
22 B2 Sangatte France
43 B9 San Gavino Monreale Sardinia
128 C4 Sangay vol Ecuador
71 E7 Sangboy Island Philippines
71 J9 Sangeang isld Indonesia
102 E5 Sanger California U.S.A.
98 E2 Sanger North Dakota U.S.A.
109 K2 Sanger Texas U.S.A.
33 O10 Sangerhausen East Germany
127 L5 San Germán Puerto Rico
65 C4 Sanggan He R China
71 J9 Sanggar Sumbawa Indonesia
71 J9 Sanggar, Teluk B Indonesia
70 B4 Sanggau Kalimantan
69 J12 Sanggauledo Indonesia
65 E6 Sanggou Wan B China
86 C5 Sangha R Congo
74 C5 Sānghar Pakistan
56 B1 Sangil'ka R U.S.S.R.
45 R7 San Giorgio del Sannio Italy
45 J1 San Giórgio di Màntova Italy
42 E3 San Giorgio di N Italy
45 K2 San Giorgio di Piano Italy
45 R7 San Giorgio la Molara Italy
38 E8 San Giovanni Italy
45 Q8 San Giovanni a Teducio Italy
45 J1 San Giovanni in Croce Italy
45 K2 San Giovanni in Persiceto Italy
45 K1 San Giovanni Lupatoto Italy
43 G10 San Giovanni, V Italy
45 L4 San Giovanni Valdarno Italy
71 E3 Sangitan Luzon Philippines
45 M1 San Giuliano Italy
45 H4 San Giuliano Terme Italy
45 R8 San Giuseppe Vesuviano Italy
45 M4 San Giustino Italy
65 G6 Sangju S Korea
70 F7 Sangkarang, Kep isld Sulawesi
68 D5 Sangkhla Buri Thailand
70 E4 Sangkulirang Kalimantan
70 F4 Sangkulirang, Teluk B Kalimantan
74 E3 Sangla Pakistan
76 B2 Sangli India
86 B5 Sangmélima Cameroon
89 G4 Sango Zimbabwe
45 L4 San Godenzo Italy
17 G7 Sangonera R Spain
102 H7 San Gorgonio Mt California U.S.A.
71 B1 Sangowo Halmahera Indonesia
106 E5 Sangre de Cristo Mts New Mex/Colo U.S.A.
102 F2 San Gregorio California U.S.A.
127 P2 Sangre Grande Trinidad
42 F6 Sangro R Italy
74 F3 Sangrur India
88 E5 Sangu Tanzania
118 C5 Sangudo Alberta Canada
129 G6 Sangue R Brazil
18 E10 Sangüesa Spain
41 O7 Sanguinetto Italy
Sangyuan see Wuqiao
67 C2 Sangzhi China
Sanhe see Sandu Guizhou
65 D4 Sanhe China
59 H1 Sanhe China
67 D1 Sanhedian China
59 J1 Sanhezhan China
124 D5 San Hilario Mexico
59 H1 San-ho China
67 D1 San Hu L China
67 B1 Sanhuizhen China
113 E11 Sanibel I Florida U.S.A.
130 C10 San Ignacio Argentina
128 E6 San Ignacio Beni Bolivia
128 F7 San Ignacio Santa Cruz Bolivia
124 D2 San Ignacio Mexico
124 C4 San Ignacio, Laguna Mexico
16 E4 San Ildefonso Spain
106 D6 San Ildefonso New Mexico U.S.A.
71 F2 San Ildefonso, C Luzon Philippines
79 H3 Saniman, Wādī watercourse Syria
60 H10 San'in Japan
106 E4 San Isabel Colorado U.S.A.
133 F4 San Isidro Argentina
124 H5 San Isidro Mexico
71 G5 San Isidro Leyte Philippines
33 Q4 Sanitz East Germany
126 G10 San Jacinto Colombia
71 F4 San Jacinto Philippines
101 L8 San Jacinto Nevada U.S.A.
102 H8 San Jacinto Mts California U.S.A.
133 F4 San Javier Argentina
124 F4 San Javier Mexico
131 F2 San Javier, R Argentina
125 J9 San Jerónimo Mexico
Sanjiang see Liannan Guangdong
67 C4 Sanjiang China
65 F3 Sanjiangkou China
65 F3 Sanjiazi China
61 M8 Sanjō Japan
128 F6 San Joaquin Bolivia
130 C9 San Joaquin Paraguay
102 D4 San Joaquin R California U.S.A.
102 D5 San Joaquin California U.S.A.
102 D5 San Joaquin Valley California U.S.A.
108 A8 San Jon New Mexico U.S.A.
128 C2 San Jorge R Colombia
133 D7 San Jorge, G Argentina
17 H4 San Jorge, G.de Spain
131 B4 San Jose vol Chile
125 M5 San José Costa Rica
124 D5 San José isld Mexico
71 E4 San Jose Philippines
131 G5 San José dept Uruguay
131 G5 San José Uruguay
102 C4 San Jose California U.S.A.
99 R9 San Jose Illinois U.S.A.
106 E6 San Jose New Mexico U.S.A.
131 F3 San José, Cuchilla de mts Uruguay
128 F2 San José de Amacuro Venezuela
128 F7 San José de Chiquitos Bolivia
124 D3 San José de Dimas Mexico
133 F4 San José de Feliciano Argentina
124 F4 San José de Gracia Sinaloa Mexico
127 M10 San José de Guaribe Venezuela
127 J5 San José de las Matas Dominican Rep
124 E6 San José del Cabo Mexico
128 D3 San José del Gauviare Colombia
127 J5 San José de Ocoa Dominican Rep
128 D3 San José de Ocuné Colombia
106 C6 San Jose, R New Mexico U.S.A.
131 C3 San Juan Argentina
131 B3 San Juan prov Argentina
128 F7 San Juan Bolivia
128 C3 San Juan R Colombia
125 M4 San Juan R Costa Rica
126 D4 San Juan mt Cuba
127 J5 San Juan Dominican Rep
124 F4 San Juan Chihuahua Mexico
124 J4 San Juan Coahuila Mexico
128 D7 San Juan Peru
71 G6 San Juan Mindanao Philippines
127 L5 San Juan Puerto Rico
102 D6 San Juan R California U.S.A.
109 J9 San Juan Texas U.S.A.
103 F4 San Juan R Utah U.S.A.
128 E2 San Juan Venezuela
102 C5 San Juan Bautista California U.S.A.
128 C7 San Juan, B. de B Peru
133 E8 San Juan, C Argentina
102 G8 San Juan Capistrano California U.S.A.
124 H5 San Juan de Guadalupe Mexico
18 G10 San Juan de las Abadesas Spain
124 H8 San Juan de Lima, Pta C Mexico
125 N4 San Juan del Norte Nicaragua
127 K9 San Juan de los Cayos Venezuela
124 H7 San Juan de los Lagos Mexico
127 L10 San Juan de los Morros Venezuela
125 J7 San Juan del Rio Mexico
100 C1 San Juan Is Washington U.S.A.
124 F7 San Juanito, I Mexico
106 C4 San Juan Mts Colo/New Mex U.S.A.
125 L9 San Juan Quiotepec Mexico
131 C3 San Juan, R Argentina
126 C3 San Juan y Martinez Cuba
133 D7 San Julián Argentina
133 E4 San Justo Argentina
17 G4 San Just, Sa. de mts Spain
85 C6 Sankarani R Guinea/Mali
76 C6 Sankarankovil India
76 B2 Sankeshwar India
88 E10 Sankhulani Malawi
86 D6 Sankuru R Zaire
45 H2 San Lazzaro Italy
102 B4 San Leandro California U.S.A.
45 M4 San Leo Italy
124 C3 San Lino, Sa mt Mexico
133 E4 San Lorenzo Argentina
128 E6 San Lorenzo Bolivia
133 C7 San Lorenzo mt Chile/Arg
128 C3 San Lorenzo Ecuador
125 P9 San Lorenzo Guatemala
124 C3 San Lorenzo isld Mexico
124 F3 San Lorenzo Mexico
128 E6 San Lorenzo Peru
106 C9 San Lorenzo New Mexico U.S.A.
127 J10 San Lorenzo Venezuela
44 C4 San Lorenzo al Mare Italy
128 B4 San Lorenzo, C Ecuador
16 E4 San Lorenzo de El Escorial Spain
17 F5 San Lorenzo de la Parrilla Spain
17 J2 San Lorenzo de Morunys Spain
128 C6 San Lorenzo, I Peru
45 N4 San Lorenzo in Campo Italy
16 C8 Sanlúcar de Barrameda Spain
16 C7 Sanlúcar la Mayor Spain
128 E8 San Lucas Bolivia
124 E6 San Lucas Mexico
102 C5 San Lucas California U.S.A.
131 C4 San Luis prov Argentina
131 C4 San Luis Argentina
126 G4 San Luis Cuba
125 P9 San Luis Guatemala
125 J9 San Luis Mexico
124 F4 San Luis Chihuahua Mexico
124 D3 San Luis Sonora Mexico
71 E2 San Luis Luzon Philippines
103 K9 San Luis Arizona U.S.A.
106 E4 San Luis Colorado U.S.A.
127 K9 San Luis Venezuela
124 E4 San Luis Babarocos Mexico
125 J7 San Luis de la Paz Mexico
128 F6 San Luis, L Bolivia
103 K9 San Luis, Mesa de Mexico
102 D6 San Luis Obispo California U.S.A.
109 M6 San Luis Pass Texas U.S.A.
106 D3 San Luis Pk Colorado U.S.A.
125 J6 San Luis Potosí Mexico
102 G8 San Luis Rey R California U.S.A.
124 B1 San Luis Rio Colorado Mexico
131 C4 San Luis, Sa. de mts Argentina
71 E3 San Marcelino Luzon Philippines
124 D3 San Marcial Mexico
106 C8 San Marcial New Mexico U.S.A.
124 D5 San Marcial, Pta C Mexico
43 B9 San Marco, C Sardinia
126 G10 San Marcos Colombia
124 C4 San Marcos isld Mexico
124 G7 San Marcos Mexico
109 K6 San Marcos Texas U.S.A.
42 E5 San Marino rep S Europe
128 F6 San Martin R Bolivia
128 D3 San Martin Colombia
128 C5 San Martin dept Peru
133 C6 San Martin de los Andes Argentina
133 C7 San Martin, L Chile/Arg
45 L2 San Martino in Argine Italy
38 E8 San Martino in Badia Italy
45 J2 San Martino in Rio Italy
45 K2 San Martino in Spino Italy
125 M5 San Mateo Costa Rica
17 H4 San Mateo Spain
102 B4 San Mateo California U.S.A.
106 C6 San Mateo New Mexico U.S.A.
127 M10 San Mateo Venezuela
106 C8 San Mateo Pk New Mexico U.S.A.
128 G7 San Matias Bolivia
131 D8 San Matias, G Argentina
121 R5 Sanmaur Quebec Canada
127 L10 San Mauricio Venezuela
44 C1 San Mauro Torinese Italy
67 G2 Sanmen China
67 G2 Sanmen Wan B China
65 B7 Sanmenxia China
45 K1 San Michele Extra Italy
128 F7 San Miguel Bolivia
128 C3 San Miguel R Ecuador
125 Q11 San Miguel Honduras
124 D3 San Miguel R Mexico
124 J5 San Miguel Mexico
128 D6 San Miguel Peru
71 D6 San Miguel islds Philippines
103 N10 San Miguel Arizona U.S.A.
102 D6 San Miguel California U.S.A.
106 B3 San Miguel R Colorado U.S.A.
71 F4 San Miguel B Philippines
109 J9 San Miguel Camargo Mexico
109 J7 San Miguel Cr Texas U.S.A.
125 J7 San Miguel de Allende Mexico
128 E7 San Miguel de Huachi Bolivia
133 D3 San Miguel de Tucumán Argentina
102 D7 San Miguel I California U.S.A.
67 F3 Sanming China
45 J4 San Miniato Italy
71 E3 San Narciso Luzon Philippines
44 E1 Sannazzaro de 'Burgondi Italy
42 G7 Sannicandro Garganico Italy
131 E4 San Nicolas Argentina
124 G5 San Nicolás Mexico
71 E2 San Nicolas Luzon Philippines
71 E1 San Nicolas Luzon Philippines
102 E8 San Nicolas I California U.S.A.
45 L2 San Nicolo Ferrarese Italy
27 D13 Sannidal Norway
51 O1 Sannikova, Proliv str U.S.S.R.
45 R7 Sannio mts Italy
61 N9 Sano Japan
31 N6 Sanok Poland
133 D8 San Pablo Argentina
133 D2 San Pablo Bolivia
128 F7 San Pablo R Bolivia
71 E3 San Pablo Luzon Philippines
124 F4 San Pablo Balleza Mexico
124 B4 San Pablo, Pta C Mexico
124 H6 San Pascual Mexico
131 F4 San Pedro Buenos Aires Argentina
128 F8 San Pedro Jujuy Argentina
130 C10 San Pedro Misiones Argentina
124 E4 San Pedro Mexico
130 B9 San Pedro Paraguay
103 O9 San Pedro R Arizona U.S.A.
102 F8 San Pedro California U.S.A.
128 F2 San Pedro Venezuela
71 G5 San Pedro B Philippines
131 A8 San Pedro, B.de Chile
102 F8 San Pedro Chan California U.S.A.
128 D3 San Pedro de Arimena Colombia
124 E3 San Pedro de la Cueva Mexico
124 H5 San Pedro de las Colonias Mexico
128 C5 San Pedro de Lloc Peru
17 G7 San Pedro del Pinatar Spain
127 K5 San Pedro de Macoris Dominican Rep
133 C3 San Pedro, Pta C Chile
16 C5 San Pedro, Sa. de mts Spain
125 P10 San Pedro Sula Honduras
41 L6 San Pellegrino Terme Italy
44 E3 San Pier d'Arena Italy
45 K4 San Piero a Sieve Italy
99 U8 San Pierre Indiana U.S.A.
45 K1 San Pietro di Morubio Italy
45 K2 San Pietro di Piano Italy
43 H8 San Pietro, I Italy
43 B9 San Pietro, I. di Sardinia
42 C3 San Pietro, Pte Italy
100 G1 Sanpoil R Washington U.S.A.
45 J2 San Polo d'Enza Italy
45 H2 San Polo d'Enza in Caviano Italy
45 J2 San Possidónio Italy
45 K2 San Prospero Italy
15 E5 Sanquhar Scotland
124 A2 San Quintin Mexico
131 C5 San Rafael Argentina
128 F7 San Rafael Bolivia
102 B4 San Rafael California U.S.A.
106 C6 San Rafael New Mexico U.S.A.
103 O2 San Rafael R Utah U.S.A.
127 K10 San Rafael Venezuela
127 K5 San Rafael, C Dominican Rep
127 K5 San Rafael del Yuma Dominican Rep
103 O3 San Rafael Knob mt Utah U.S.A.
102 E7 San Rafael Mts California U.S.A.
125 M3 San Ramón Nicaragua
128 C6 San Ramón Peru
67 E5 Sanrao China
44 C4 San Remo Italy
108 F7 San Rodrigo R Mexico
127 J8 San Román, C Venezuela
16 D8 San Roque Spain
108 G5 San Saba R Texas U.S.A.
109 J4 San Saba Texas U.S.A.
126 A3 San Salvador isld Bahamas
125 P11 San Salvador El Salvador
128 A8 San Salvador isld Galapagos Is
131 F4 San Salvador R Uruguay
133 D2 San Salvador de Jujuy Argentina
133 D8 San Sebastián Argentina
85 A3 San Sebastian Canary Is
124 C3 San Sebastián isld Mexico
17 F1 San Sebastian Spain
127 L10 San Sebastián Venezuela
129 J8 San Sebastião Brazil
42 E5 Sansepolcro Italy
42 G7 San Severo Italy
67 G3 Sansha China
66 D3 Sanshichang China
67 D5 Sanshui China
128 E6 San Silvestre Bolivia
127 J10 San Silvestre Venezuela
102 C6 San Simeon California U.S.A.
103 P9 San Simon Arizona U.S.A.
103 P9 San Simon Cr Arizona U.S.A.
42 H4 Sanski Most Yugoslavia
145 E4 Sanson New Zealand
108 B6 San Sostenes Mexico
44 C4 San Stefano al Mare Italy
127 N4 Sans Toucher mt Guadeloupe W Indies
67 C3 Sansui China
128 C5 Santa Peru
125 O9 Santa Amelia Guatemala
128 E6 Santa Ana Bolivia
128 B4 Santa Ana Ecuador
125 P11 Santa Ana El Salvador
124 D2 Santa Ana Mexico
102 G8 Santa Ana R California U.S.A.
102 G8 Santa Ana California U.S.A.
127 M10 Santa Ana Venezuela
124 F3 Santa Ana Babicora Mexico
102 G8 Santa Ana Mts California U.S.A.
44 F1 Santa Angelo Italy
109 H4 Santa Anna Texas U.S.A.
130 G6 Santa Bárbara Brazil
124 G4 Santa Bárbara Mexico
102 E7 Santa Barbara California U.S.A.
127 N10 Santa Bárbara Venezuela
102 D7 Santa Barbara Ch California U.S.A.
102 E8 Santa Barbara I California U.S.A.
102 E7 Santa Barbara Res California U.S.A.
130 D7 Santa Barbara, Sa de mts Brazil
128 E8 Santa Catalina Argentina
133 D3 Santa Catalina Chile
124 D5 Santa Catalina isld Mexico
102 G8 Santa Catalina, G.of California U.S.A.
102 F8 Santa Catalina, I California U.S.A.
133 G3 Santa Catarina state Brazil
124 B3 Santa Catarina Mexico
124 G5 Santa Catarina de Tepehuanes Mexico
126 B1 Santa Catharina Curaçao
128 E4 Santa Clara Colombia
126 E3 Santa Clara Cuba
103 K10 Santa Clara Mexico
133 B9 Santa Clara isld Juan Fernández Is Pacific Oc
102 E7 Santa Clara R California U.S.A.
102 B4 Santa Clara California U.S.A.
95 N2 Santa Clara New York U.S.A.
103 L4 Santa Clara Utah U.S.A.
110 K3 Santa Claus Indiana U.S.A.
17 J3 Santa Coloma de Farnés Spain
16 B1 Santa Comba Spain
133 C7 Santa Cruz prov Argentina
128 F7 Santa Cruz Bolivia
128 D5 Santa Cruz Amazonas Brazil
130 J9 Santa Cruz Rio Grande do Norte Brazil
128 A8 Santa Cruz isld Galapagos Is
124 D5 Santa Cruz isld Mexico
128 C5 Santa Cruz Peru
71 E3 Santa Cruz Luzon Philippines
71 D3 Santa Cruz Luzon Philippines
71 E2 Santa Cruz Luzon Philippines
71 F6 Santa Cruz Negros Philippines
102 B5 Santa Cruz California U.S.A.
106 D6 Santa Cruz New Mexico U.S.A.
126 A1 Santa Cruz Aruba W Indies
130 H5 Santa Cruz Cabralia Brazil
85 A3 Santa Cruz de la Palma Canary Is
16 E5 Santa Cruz de la Zarza Spain
126 F4 Santa Cruz del Sur Cuba
16 E6 Santa Cruz de Mudela Spain
85 A3 Santa Cruz de Tenerife Canary Is
133 G3 Santa Cruz do Sul Brazil
137 O4 Santa Cruz Is Solomon Is
127 J2 Santa Cruz Mts Jamaica
102 B4 Santa Cruz Mts California U.S.A.
17 F3 Santa Cruz, Sa. de mts Spain
79 B8 Santa, El Egypt
128 B4 Santa Elena Ecuador
109 J9 Santa Elena Texas U.S.A.
128 F3 Santa Elena Venezuela
128 B4 Santa Elena, B. de Ecuador
125 M4 Santa Elena, C Costa Rica
100 J2 Santa Emida Idaho U.S.A.
16 A2 Santa Eugenia de Ribeira Spain
17 G4 Santa Eulalia Spain
17 J6 Santa Eulalia del Rio Ibiza
133 E4 Santa Fe prov Argentina
131 E3 Santa Fe Argentina
128 A8 Santa Fe isld Galapagos Is
71 F4 Santa Fe Philippines
16 E7 Santafé Spain
113 E8 Santa Fe R Florida U.S.A.
106 E6 Santa Fe New Mexico U.S.A.
129 J5 Santa Filomena Brazil
124 E6 Santa Genovéva mt Mexico
124 G4 Santa Gertrudis Mexico
129 J4 Santa Helena Brazil
58 E5 Santai China
133 C8 Santa Ines, I Chile
133 D5 Santa Isabel Argentina
128 G5 Santa Isabel Brazil
Santa Isabel Fernando Póo see Malabo Bioko
137 M3 Santa Isabel isld Solomon Is
124 B2 Santa Isabel, Sa mts Mexico
129 J5 Santa Isobel do Araguaia Brazil
129 G5 Santa Julia Brazil
130 F6 Santa Juliana Brazil
58 D4 Santala China
126 B3 Santa Lucia Cuba
124 G5 Santa Lucia Mexico
131 F2 Santa Lucia, R Argentina
131 G5 Santa Lucia, R Uruguay
102 C5 Santa Lucia Rge California U.S.A.
130 C6 Santa Luisa, Sa. de mts Brazil
130 H9 Santa Luzia Brazil
124 D5 Santa Margarita isld Mexico
102 G8 Santa Margarita R California U.S.A.
102 D6 Santa Margarita California U.S.A.
44 F3 Santa Margherita Italy
133 D3 Santa Maria Argentina
133 D5 Santa Maria mt Argentina
131 G3 Santa Maria R Brazil
128 G4 Santa Maria Amazonas Brazil
131 H2 Santa Maria Rio Grande do Sul Brazil
128 A8 Santa Maria isld Galapagos Is
124 F2 Santa Maria R Mexico
103 L7 Santa Maria R Arizona U.S.A.
102 D7 Santa Maria California U.S.A.
137 O4 Santa Maria isld Vanuatu
87 E8 Santa Maria Zambia
131 G5 Santa Maria, C Uruguay
43 F7 Santa Maria Capua Vetere Italy
126 E3 Santa Maria, Cayo isld Cuba
16 B8 Santa Maria, C. de Portugal
16 B7 Santa Maria, C. de Portugal
130 F4 Santa Maria, Chapadão de hills Brazil
124 F4 Santa Maria de Cuevas Mexico
127 M10 Santa Maria de Ipire Venezuela
124 G5 Santa Maria del Oro Mexico
43 J9 Santa Maria di Leuca, C Italy
45 M1 Santa Maria di Sala Italy
131 A6 Santa Maria, I Chile
103 M7 Santa Maria Mts Arizona U.S.A.
128 C6 Santa Maria, Pta C Peru

Scotia — Shamrock

77

100 H1 **Scotia** Washington U.S.A.
117 G6 **Scotia Bay** British Columbia Canada
146 F3 **Scotia Ridge** Antarctica
81 A14 **Scotia Ridge** Antarctica
81 A15 **Scotia Sea** Antarctica
146 E2 **Scotia Sea** Antarctica
15 **Scotland** U.K.
98 J6 **Scotland** South Dakota U.S.A.
109 J2 **Scotland** Texas U.S.A.
112 K1 **Scotland Neck** North Carolina U.S.A.
111 E11 **Scotlandville** Louisiana U.S.A.
122 H8 **Scots B** Nova Scotia Canada
122 K8 **Scotsburn** Nova Scotia Canada
118 J9 **Scotsguard** Saskatchewan Canada
121 T7 **Scotstown** Quebec Canada
138 E4 **Scott** *R* South Australia Australia
143 B10 **Scott** *R* Western Australia Australia
118 J6 **Scott** Saskatchewan Canada
100 C8 **Scott** *R* California U.S.A.
112 E5 **Scott** Georgia U.S.A.
111 E8 **Scott** Mississippi U.S.A.
94 C6 **Scott** Ohio U.S.A.
100 C8 **Scott Bar** California U.S.A.
146 D11 **Scott Base** *N Z Base* Antarctica
89 G8 **Scottburgh** S Africa
117 J10 **Scott, C** Vancouver I, Br Col Canada
140 A2 **Scott, Cape** N Terr Australia
107 K3 **Scott City** Kansas U.S.A.
146 D12 **Scott Coast** Antarctica
94 H6 **Scottdale** Pennsylvania U.S.A.
146 H13 **Scott Glacier** Antarctica
146 D9 **Scott Glacier** Antarctica
142 E4 **Scott Headland** *mt* Western Australia Australia
115 M3 **Scott Inlet** Northwest Territories Canada
117 J10 **Scott, Is** British Columbia Canada
100 C7 **Scott, Mt** Oregon U.S.A.
146 K9 **Scott Mts** Antarctica
142 D2 **Scott Reef** Indian Oc
94 B4 **Scotts** Michigan U.S.A.
98 C8 **Scottsbluff** Nebraska U.S.A.
98 C8 **Scotts Bluff Nat. Mon** Nebraska U.S.A.
110 K7 **Scottsboro** Alabama U.S.A.
94 B8 **Scottsburg** Indiana U.S.A.
100 B6 **Scottsburg** Oregon U.S.A.
94 J10 **Scottsburg** Virginia U.S.A.
139 J8 **Scottsdale** Tasmania Australia
103 N8 **Scottsdale** Arizona U.S.A.
111 L11 **Scotts Ferry** Florida U.S.A.
127 O7 **Scotts Head** Dominica
123 L7 **Scottsville** C Breton I, Nova Scotia
107 N2 **Scottsville** Kansas U.S.A.
110 K5 **Scottsville** Kentucky U.S.A.
94 J9 **Scottsville** Virginia U.S.A.
94 A3 **Scottville** Michigan U.S.A.
102 G4 **Scottys Castle** California U.S.A.
102 G4 **Scottys Junct** Nevada U.S.A.
15 C2 **Scourie** Scotland
118 L9 **Scout Lake** Saskatchewan Canada
15 E2 **Scrabster** Scotland
7 M10 **Scram** *oil rig* North Sea
110 C6 **Scranton** Arkansas U.S.A.
107 P3 **Scranton** Kansas U.S.A.
98 C3 **Scranton** North Dakota U.S.A.
95 M5 **Scranton** Pennsylvania U.S.A.
95 L3 **Scriba** New York U.S.A.
98 K8 **Scribner** Nebraska U.S.A.
15 B4 **Scridain, Loch** Scotland
44 E2 **Scrivia R** Italy
120 H10 **Scudder** Ontario Canada
121 M8 **Scugog, L** Ontario Canada
13 H6 **Scunthorpe** England
45 O5 **Scurcola Marsicana** Italy
Scutari *see* **Üsküdar**
Scutari Albania *see* **Shkodër**
112 K1 **Seaboard** North Carolina U.S.A.
109 M6 **Seabrook** Texas U.S.A.
143 C9 **Seabrook, L** Western Australia Australia
143 C7 **Seabrook, Mt** Western Australia Australia
144 C6 **Seacliff** New Zealand
89 D8 **Seacow** *R* S Africa
109 L7 **Seadrift** Texas U.S.A.
139 G7 **Sea Elephant B** Tasmania Australia
9 G6 **Seaford** England
95 M8 **Seaford** Delaware U.S.A.
142 C3 **Seaforth** Western Australia Australia
120 J9 **Seaforth** Ontario Canada
127 M3 **Seaforth** Jamaica
119 O4 **Seager Wheeler L** Saskatchewan Canada
108 E3 **Seagraves** Texas U.S.A.
112 H2 **Seagrove** North Carolina U.S.A.
13 G4 **Seaham** England
122 G1 **Seahorse** Labrador, Nfld Canada
115 L5 **Seahorse Pt** Northwest Territories Canada
70 C2 **Seahorse Shoal** S China Sea
13 G2 **Seahouses** England
112 F6 **Sea Island** Georgia U.S.A.
95 N7 **Sea Isle City** New Jersey U.S.A.
115 K6 **Seal** *R* Manitoba Canada
139 G6 **Sea Lake** Victoria Australia
123 R1 **Seal Bight** Labrador, Nfld Canada
89 C10 **Seal C** S Africa
116 H9 **Seal C** Alaska U.S.A.
127 J4 **Seal Cays** *islds* Turks & Caicos Is
122 F9 **Seal Cove** New Brunswick Canada
123 Q4 **Seal Cove** Newfoundland Canada
111 L9 **Seale** Alabama U.S.A.
144 C5 **Seal I** New Zealand
133 F8 **Sea Lion Is** Falkland Is
139 H7 **Seal Is** Victoria Australia
115 M6 **Seal Lakes** Quebec Canada
144 A7 **Seal Pt** New Zealand
100 A5 **Seal Rock** Oregon U.S.A.
109 L6 **Sealy** Texas U.S.A.
144 C5 **Sealy, Mt** New Zealand
144 C5 **Sealy Pass** New Zealand
103 J4 **Seaman Ra** Nevada U.S.A.
13 H5 **Seamer** England
7 M9 **Sean** *oil rig* North Sea
9 H2 **Sea Palling** England
103 K6 **Searchlight** Nevada U.S.A.
120 F6 **Searchmont** Ontario Canada
110 E6 **Searcy** Arkansas U.S.A.
102 G6 **Searles** California U.S.A.
102 G6 **Searles Lake** California U.S.A.
95 T2 **Searsport** Maine U.S.A.
123 N6 **Searston** Newfoundland Canada
12 E5 **Seascale** England
102 C5 **Seaside** California U.S.A.
100 B4 **Seaside** Oregon U.S.A.
95 N7 **Seaside Heights** New Jersey U.S.A.
8 C6 **Seaton** England
100 C2 **Seattle** Washington U.S.A.
117 D5 **Seattle, Mt** Alaska/Yukon Terr U.S.A./Canada
141 H4 **Seaview Ra** Queensland Australia
95 N7 **Seaville, S** New Jersey U.S.A.
144 D5 **Seaward Kaikoura Range** New Zealand
127 P6 **Seawell** *airport* Barbados
71 K10 **Seba** Indonesia
118 C5 **Seba Beach** Alberta Canada
95 R3 **Sebago L** Maine U.S.A.
70 E5 **Sebakung** Kalimantan
89 G2 **Sebakwe** *R* Zimbabwe
70 C6 **Sebangan, Teluk** *B* Kalimantan
68 G4 **Se Bang Fai** *R* Laos
69 G12 **Sebangka** *isld* Indonesia
113 G10 **Sebastian** Florida U.S.A.
109 K9 **Sebastian** Texas U.S.A.
124 B3 **Sebastián Vizcaino, B** Mexico
95 S2 **Sebasticook L** Maine U.S.A.
102 B3 **Sebastopol** California U.S.A.
111 G9 **Sebastopol** Mississippi U.S.A.
70 E2 **Sebatik** *isld* Borneo
70 C3 **Sebauh** Sarawak
70 B5 **Sebayan, Bukit** *mt* Kalimantan
28 D3 **Sebbersund** Denmark
99 L3 **Sebeka** Minnesota U.S.A.
78 C1 **Seben** Turkey
Sebenico *see* **Sibenik**
124 D4 **Seberi, Cerro** *mt* Mexico
48 H5 **Sebeş** *R* Romania
70 K8 **Sebesi** *isld* Sumatra
48 H5 **Sebeşului, Muntii** *mts* Romania
94 D3 **Sebewaing** Michigan U.S.A.
52 C6 **Sebezh** U.S.S.R.
78 G1 **Şebinkarahisar** Turkey
48 G4 **Sebis** Romania
85 B4 **Sebkha de Chinchane** Mauritania
85 B4 **Sebkha Oum el Drouss Guebli** Mauritania
85 B4 **Sebkha Oum el Drouss Telli** Mauritania
43 C13 **Sebkhat Kelbia** *L* Tunisia
85 B4 **Sebkhet Idjil** Mauritania
85 E3 **Sebkra Azzel Matti** *salt flats* Algeria
85 C3 **Sebkra de Tindouf** *salt flats* Algeria
17 G9 **Sebkra d'Oran** Algeria
85 E3 **Sebkra Mekerrhane** *salt flats* Algeria
31 H5 **Sebnitz** East Germany
95 T1 **Seboeis L** Maine U.S.A.
95 R8 **Seboomook L** Maine U.S.A.
85 C2 **Sebou** *R* Morocco
110 J4 **Sebree** Kentucky U.S.A.
95 K10 **Sebrell** Virginia U.S.A.
113 F10 **Sebring** Florida U.S.A.
94 F6 **Sebring** Ohio U.S.A.
16 D9 **Sebt Beni Zarfet** Morocco
70 K8 **Sebuku** *isld* Indonesia
70 E6 **Sebuku** *isld* Kalimantan
70 B4 **Sebuyau** Sarawak
37 Q4 **Seč** Czechoslovakia
42 C4 **Secchia** *R* Italy
112 E3 **Secession L** South Carolina U.S.A.
68 G4 **Se Cham** *R* Laos
122 C1 **Séchelles, L** Quebec Canada
128 B5 **Sechura, B. de** Peru
128 B5 **Sechura, Des. de** *desert* Peru
38 L7 **Seckau** Austria
38 L7 **Seckauer Alpen** *mts* Austria
22 E2 **Seclin** France
133 D7 **Seco** *R* Argentina
17 H4 **Seco** *R* Spain
21 K8 **Secondigny** France
118 L8 **Secretan** Saskatchewan Canada
144 A6 **Secretary I** New Zealand
76 D2 **Secunderabad** India
128 E7 **Sécure** *R* Bolivia
48 E3 **Séd** *R* Hungary
16 B5 **Seda** *R* Portugal
52 B6 **Seda** U.S.S.R.
71 L10 **Sedah** Indonesia
118 G7 **Sedalia** Alberta Canada
106 F2 **Sedalia** Colorado U.S.A.
94 D7 **Sedalia** Ohio U.S.A.
138 E5 **Sedan** South Australia Australia
19 J3 **Sedan** France
107 O4 **Sedan** Kansas U.S.A.
106 G5 **Sedan** New Mexico U.S.A.
56 F3 **Sedannavskaya, Shiver** *falls* U.S.S.R.
16 E2 **Sedano** Spain
13 F5 **Sedbergh** England
145 E4 **Seddon** New Zealand
115 O2 **Seddon, Kap** *C* Greenland
144 C4 **Seddonville** New Zealand
47 H4 **Seddülbahir** Turkey
79 E8 **Sede Boqer** Israel
80 B7 **Sede Dawid** Israel
80 F1 **Sede Eli'ezer** Israel
80 F4 **Sede Eliyyahu** Israel
47 N11 **Sedef** *isld* Turkey
55 G3 **Sedel'nikovo** U.S.S.R.
80 C7 **Sede Moshe** Israel
80 F1 **Sede Neẹmya** Israel
19 P16 **Séderon** France
80 B7 **Sederot** Israel
80 G2 **Sede Yaaqov** Syria
80 B8 **Sede Zevi** Israel
9 E3 **Sedgeberrow** England
13 G4 **Sedgefield** England
8 D2 **Sedgley** England
106 H1 **Sedgwick** Colorado U.S.A.
107 N4 **Sedgwick** Kansas U.S.A.
95 T2 **Sedgwick** Maine U.S.A.
69 E12 **Sedinginan** Sumatra
70 E6 **Sedjaka** Kalimantan
31 H6 **Sedlčany** Czechoslovakia
9 G6 **Sedlescombe** England
119 O8 **Sedley** Saskatchewan Canada
79 F7 **Sedom** Israel
103 N7 **Sedona** Arizona U.S.A.
68 G5 **Se Done** *R* Laos
80 C7 **Sedot Mikha** Israel
80 C4 **Sedot Yam** Israel
100 C1 **Sedro Woolley** Washington U.S.A.
70 E4 **Sedulang** Kalimantan
52 B6 **Šeduva** U.S.S.R.
20 H4 **See** *R* France
33 O4 **Seebad Heringsdorf** W Germany
118 C7 **Seebe** Alberta Canada
37 K2 **Seebergen** East Germany
33 P10 **Seeburg** East Germany
41 O3 **Seefeld** Austria
33 T7 **Seefeld** East Germany
40 G2 **Seefelden** W Germany
33 O8 **Seehausen** East Germany
87 C11 **Seeheim** Namibia
36 F4 **Seeheim** W Germany
36 D7 **Seelbach** W Germany
101 M2 **Seeley Lake** Montana U.S.A.
121 O8 **Seeleys Bay** Ontario Canada
146 D8 **Seelig, Mt** Antarctica
33 R10 **Seelingstädt** East Germany
36 C2 **Seelscheid** W Germany
28 B6 **Seem** Denmark
70 P10 **Seemanandjung** Java
33 S10 **Seerhausen** East Germany
41 J2 **Seerücken** *mt* Switzerland
21 L4 **Sées** France
32 M9 **Seesen** W Germany
41 O2 **Seeshaupt** W Germany
38 L7 **Seetaler Alpen** *mts* Austria
41 K3 **Seez** *R* Switzerland
47 H6 **Seferihisar** Turkey
17 G9 **Sefioun** *R* Algeria
85 D2 **Sefrou** Morocco
144 D5 **Sefton** New Zealand
144 C5 **Sefton, Mt** New Zealand
70 F2 **Segama** *R* Sabah
69 F11 **Segamat** Malaysia
70 M9 **Segara Anakan** Java
48 H6 **Şegarcea** Romania
71 B2 **Segea** Halmahera Indonesia
86 G4 **Segen** *watercourse* Ethiopia
56 F4 **Segentuy** U.S.S.R.
70 F7 **Segeri** Sulawesi
43 E11 **Segesta** Sicily
71 C3 **Seget** W Irian
52 D3 **Segezha** U.S.S.R.
57 D3 **Segiz, Ozero** *L* U.S.S.R.
20 D5 **Seglien** France
41 K4 **Segnes Pass** Switzerland
45 O6 **Segni** Italy
103 P2 **Sego** Utah U.S.A.
17 G5 **Segorbe** Spain
85 C6 **Segou** Mali
16 E4 **Segovia** Spain
16 E3 **Segovia** *prov* Spain
108 H5 **Segovia** Texas U.S.A.
52 D3 **Segozero, Oz** *L* U.S.S.R.
21 J6 **Segré** France
17 H2 **Segre** *R* Spain
21 L5 **Segrie** France
84 E5 **Séguedine** Niger
85 C7 **Séguéla** Ivory Coast
124 J5 **Seguin** Mexico
107 K2 **Seguin** Kansas U.S.A.
109 K6 **Seguin** Texas U.S.A.
133 E4 **Segundo** *R* Argentina
106 F4 **Segundo** Colorado U.S.A.
17 F6 **Segura** *R* Spain
17 F6 **Segura, Sa de** *mts* Spain
32 L8 **Sehnde** W Germany
71 J5 **Seho** *isld* Indonesia
71 A2 **Sehu** Halmahera Indonesia
74 B5 **Sehwan** Pakistan
100 B8 **Seiad Valley** California U.S.A.
37 L3 **Seibelsdorf** W Germany
106 H2 **Seibert** Colorado U.S.A.
127 K5 **Seibo** Dominican Rep
20 H6 **Seiche** *R* France
21 K6 **Seiches** France
80 D4 **Seidā** Jordan
80 F3 **Seidur** Jordan
140 E4 **Seigals Creek** N Terr Australia
122 C1 **Seignelay, R** Quebec Canada
68 B2 **Seikpyu** Burma
68 B2 **Seiktein** Burma
12 C1 **Seil** *isld* Scotland
26 N1 **Seiland** *isld* Norway
18 G7 **Seilhac** France
107 M5 **Seiling** Oklahoma U.S.A.
19 K4 **Seille** *R* France
29 K9 **Seinäjoki** Finland
21 N3 **Seine** *R* France
21 K2 **Seine, B. de la** France
18 H4 **Seine-et-Marne** *dept* France
18 F3 **Seine-Maritime** *dept* France
21 P4 **Seine-St. Denis** *dept* France
20 A5 **Sein, I. de** France
113 E10 **Seista Key** *isld* Florida U.S.A.
38 L5 **Seitenstetten** Austria
18 F10 **Seix** France
69 J12 **Sejangkung** Indonesia
28 G5 **Sejerø** *isld* Denmark
28 G5 **Sejerø** Denmark
28 B3 **Sejerslev** Denmark
28 E3 **Sejflod** Denmark
31 O1 **Sejny** Poland
28 D4 **Sejs** Denmark
28 B6 **Sejstrup** Denmark
70 B5 **Sekadau** Kalimantan
70 D6 **Sekakajang** Kalimantan
69 G13 **Sekanak, Teluk** *B* Sumatra
69 F12 **Sekapil** Sumatra
70 E3 **Sekatak Bengarao** Kalimantan
69 F14 **Sekayu** Sumatra
88 E4 **Sekenke** Tanzania
61 K10 **Seki** Japan
70 K8 **Sekicau** *mt* Sumatra
89 C5 **Sekoma** Botswana
85 D7 **Sekondi** Ghana
86 G3 **Sek'ota** Ethiopia
77 G4 **Sekuheh** Iran
69 J12 **Sekura** Indonesia
69 E14 **Selagan** *R* Sumatra
100 E3 **Selah** Washington U.S.A.
69 J12 **Selakau** Indonesia
70 B4 **Selalang** Sarawak
69 E10 **Selama** Malaysia
69 E11 **Selangor** Malaysia
68 H4 **Se La Nong** *R* Laos
29 M10 **Selänpää** Finland
68 F4 **Selaphum** Thailand
70 D7 **Selatan, Tg** *C* Kalimantan
69 D13 **Selat Bungalaut** *str* Indonesia
69 D13 **Selat Mentawai** *str* Indonesia
69 F12 **Selatpanjang** Sumatra
69 F12 **Selat Panjang** *R* Sumatra
69 D13 **Selat Siberut** *str* Sumatra
69 D14 **Selat Sipura** *str* Indonesia
116 H3 **Selawik** Alaska U.S.A.
116 G3 **Selawik L** Alaska U.S.A.
37 N3 **Selb** W Germany
37 M3 **Selbitz** W Germany
27 A12 **Selbjörnfj** *inlet* Norway
26 E8 **Selbusjö** *L* Norway
13 G6 **Selby** England
98 F4 **Selby** South Dakota U.S.A.
116 K3 **Selby, L** Alaska U.S.A.
95 M8 **Selbyville** Delaware U.S.A.
28 C3 **Selde** Denmark
107 K2 **Selden** Kansas U.S.A.
123 S4 **Seldom** Newfoundland Canada
116 M7 **Seldovia** Alaska U.S.A.
43 G8 **Sele** *R* Italy
71 C3 **Sele** W Irian
87 E10 **Selebi Phikwe** Botswana
59 K1 **Selemdzha** *R* U.S.S.R.
47 K6 **Selendi** Turkey
56 G5 **Selenga** *R* U.S.S.R.
86 C6 **Selenge** Zaire
58 E2 **Selenge Mörön** *R* Mongolia
56 G5 **Selenginsk** U.S.S.R.
46 D4 **Selenicë** Albania
51 O2 **Selennyakh** *R* U.S.S.R.
33 M4 **Selent** W Germany
33 M4 **Selenter See** *L* W Germany
71 C3 **Sele, Selat** *str* W Irian
40 F1 **Sélestat** France
55 F4 **Seleti** *R* U.S.S.R.
28 S10 **Selfoss** Iceland
98 F3 **Selfridge** North Dakota U.S.A.
85 B5 **Selibaby** Mauritania
54 F4 **Selichnya** U.S.S.R.
36 F3 **Seligenstadt** W Germany
52 D6 **Seliger, Oz** *L* U.S.S.R.
103 M6 **Seligman** Arizona U.S.A.
110 C5 **Seligman** Missouri U.S.A.
84 H5 **Selima Oasis** Sudan
70 C4 **Selimbau** Kalimantan
47 J7 **Selimiye** Turkey
85 C6 **Selingue, Lac de** *res* Mali
46 E7 **Selinoús** Greece
95 L6 **Selinsgrove** Pennsylvania U.S.A.
55 F1 **Seliyarovo** U.S.S.R.
52 D6 **Selizharovo** U.S.S.R.
33 O9 **Selke** *R* East Germany
Selkirk *co see* **Borders** *reg*
119 V8 **Selkirk** Manitoba Canada
13 F2 **Selkirk** Scotland
107 J3 **Selkirk** Kansas U.S.A.
94 C2 **Selkirk** Michigan U.S.A.
117 O10 **Selkirk Mts** Br Col/Idaho Canada/U.S.A.
119 S5 **Selkirk T** Manitoba Canada
20 G6 **Sel, le** France
21 P2 **Selle** *R* France
100 D2 **Selleck** Washington U.S.A.
94 B8 **Sellersburg** Indiana U.S.A.
21 O7 **Selles-St. Denis** France
21 O7 **Selles-sur-Cher** France
141 H5 **Sellheim** *R* Queensland Australia
40 C4 **Sellières** France
9 G5 **Sellindge** England
41 O3 **Sellrain** Austria
103 N10 **Sells** Arizona U.S.A.
32 F9 **Selm** W Germany
111 J9 **Selma** Alabama U.S.A.
111 D10 **Selma** Louisiana U.S.A.
112 J2 **Selma** North Carolina U.S.A.
100 B7 **Selma** Oregon U.S.A.
110 H6 **Selmer** Tennessee U.S.A.
33 N5 **Selmsdorf** East Germany
21 N6 **Selommes** France
70 Q10 **Selong** Indonesia
40 B2 **Selongey** France
19 Q16 **Sélonnet** France
88 F6 **Selous Game Res** Tanzania
117 G4 **Selous, Mt** Yukon Territory Canada
71 C3 **Selpele** Indonesia
83 K12 **Sel Pt** Mahé I Indian Oc
9 F6 **Selsey** England
32 K6 **Selsingen** W Germany
36 D2 **Selters** W Germany
54 F3 **Sel'tso** U.S.S.R.
52 H6 **Selty** U.S.S.R.
33 S5 **Seltz** East Germany
36 E6 **Seltz** France
69 H10 **Seluan** *isld* Indonesia
69 H14 **Selui** *isld* Indonesia
20 H4 **Selune** *R* France
133 E3 **Selva** Argentina
38 E8 **Selva di V. Gardena** Italy
128 D5 **Selvas** *forests* Brazil
45 L1 **Selvazzano Dentro** Italy
117 H4 **Selwyn Mts** Yukon Territory Canada
140 F5 **Selwyn Ra** Queensland Australia
48 J3 **Selyatin** U.S.S.R.
52 G3 **Sel'yb** U.S.S.R.
98 G2 **Selz** North Dakota U.S.A.
36 E4 **Selz** *R* W Germany
40 F3 **Selzach** Switzerland
38 K6 **Selzthal** Austria
70 E5 **Semajang, D** *L* Kalimantan
21 L5 **Semallé** France
46 D4 **Seman** *R* Albania
70 K8 **Semang Ka, Teluk** *B* Sumatra
79 G2 **Sem'ān, Jebel** *mts* Syria
119 N7 **Semans** Saskatchewan Canada
85 B3 **Semara, Es** Western Sahara
70 N9 **Semarang** Java
71 L10 **Semau** *isld* Timor Indonesia
88 C2 **Sembabule** Uganda
70 E3 **Sembakung** *R* Kalimantan
86 B5 **Sembé** Congo
21 M6 **Semblançay** France
52 F6 **Semenov** U.S.S.R.
54 D4 **Semenovka** Chernigovskaya obl U.S.S.R.
54 E7 **Semenovka** Poltavskaya obl U.S.S.R.
52 G6 **Semenovo** U.S.S.R.
52 F5 **Semenovskoye** Kostromskaya obl U.S.S.R.
52 F5 **Sementsovo** U.S.S.R.
70 O10 **Semeru** Java
116 J8 **Semidi Is** Alaska U.S.A.
52 F5 **Semigorodnyaya** U.S.S.R.
54 M9 **Semikarakorsk** U.S.S.R.
31 J5 **Semily** Czechoslovakia
111 G10 **Seminary** Mississippi U.S.A.
101 T7 **Seminoe Dam** Wyoming U.S.A.
101 T7 **Seminoe Res** Wyoming U.S.A.
107 O6 **Seminole** Oklahoma U.S.A.
108 E3 **Seminole** Texas U.S.A.
111 M11 **Seminole, L** Georgia U.S.A.
56 C5 **Seminsky Khrebet** *mts* U.S.S.R.
55 D4 **Semiozernoye** U.S.S.R.
56 B5 **Semipalatinsk** U.S.S.R.
55 E4 **Semipolka** U.S.S.R.
71 E5 **Semirara** *isld* Philippines
77 B4 **Semirom** Iran
70 C4 **Semitau** Kalimantan
69 H10 **Semium** *isld* Indonesia
55 G5 **Semiyarka** U.S.S.R.
55 F5 **Semiz-Bugu** U.S.S.R.
33 R4 **Semlow** East Germany
33 T7 **Semmelberg** *mt* East Germany
38 N6 **Semmering** Austria
86 F1 **Semna** Sudan
77 C2 **Semnān** Iran
20 G6 **Semnon** *R* France
22 J4 **Semois** *R* Belgium
89 F3 **Semokwe** *R* Zimbabwe
70 E1 **Sempang Mangayau, Tg** *C* Sabah
70 F2 **Semporna** Sabah
45 O6 **Semprevisa** *mt* Italy
70 O10 **Sempu** *isld* Java
26 H5 **Semskefjell** *mt* Norway
129 H4 **Sem Tripa** Brazil
88 E3 **Semu** *R* Tanzania
18 H5 **Semur-en-Auxois** France
89 F2 **Semwe** *R* Zimbabwe
52 F2 **Semzha** U.S.S.R.
128 E6 **Sena** Bolivia
88 E10 **Sena** Mozambique
129 L5 **Senador Pompeu** Brazil
70 E1 **Senaja** Sabah
128 E5 **Sena Madureira** Brazil
87 D9 **Senango** Zambia
70 B4 **Senaning** Kalimantan
21 O2 **Sénarpont** France
19 O17 **Sénas** France
118 H9 **Senate** Saskatchewan Canada
110 F5 **Senath** Missouri U.S.A.
111 G7 **Senatobia** Mississippi U.S.A.
69 G13 **Senayang** Indonesia
61 O7 **Sendai** Honshu Japan
60 D14 **Sendai** Kyūshū Japan
60 D14 **Sendai-gawa** *R* Japan
87 C11 **Sendelingsdrif** Namibia
37 J7 **Senden** W Germany
32 G9 **Sendenhorst** W Germany
16 C3 **Sendim** Portugal
70 B5 **Senduruhan** Kalimantan
74 F8 **Sendwha** India
69 E11 **Senebui, Tg** *C* Sumatra
99 S8 **Seneca** Illinois U.S.A.
107 O2 **Seneca** Kansas U.S.A.
110 B5 **Seneca** Missouri U.S.A.
98 F7 **Seneca** Nebraska U.S.A.
100 G5 **Seneca** Oregon U.S.A.
112 E3 **Seneca** South Carolina U.S.A.
98 G4 **Seneca** South Dakota U.S.A.
95 L4 **Seneca L** New York U.S.A.
94 F7 **Seneca Lake** Ohio U.S.A.
94 F7 **Senecaville** Ohio U.S.A.
22 G2 **Seneffe** Belgium
85 B6 **Senegal** *rep* W Africa
85 B5 **Sénégal** *R* W Africa
87 E11 **Senekal** S Africa
99 V3 **Seney** Michigan U.S.A.
30 H4 **Senftenberg** East Germany
87 F7 **Senga Hill** Zambia
70 E4 **Sengata** Kalimantan
52 H1 **Sengeyskiy, Ostrov** *isld* U.S.S.R.
56 E5 **Sengilen, Khrebet** *mts* U.S.S.R.
38 K6 **Sengsengebirge** *mts* Austria
133 C7 **Senguerr** *R* Argentina
88 B10 **Sengwa** *R* Zimbabwe
32 H5 **Sengwärden** W Germany
87 E9 **Sengwe** *R* Zimbabwe
129 K6 **Senhor do Bonfim** Brazil
45 O4 **Senigallia** Italy
45 L3 **Senio** *R* Italy
80 F1 **Senir** Israel
43 G8 **Senise** Italy
42 F4 **Senj** Yugoslavia
26 J2 **Senja** *isld* Norway
67 H4 **Senkaku-shotō** *isld* Japan
52 H2 **Sen'kina** U.S.S.R.
79 G2 **Senköy** Turkey
118 H6 **Senlac** Saskatchewan Canada
65 H3 **Senlin Shan** *mt* China
68 H6 **Senmonorom** Cambodia
86 F3 **Sennar** Sudan
32 J9 **Senne** *reg* W Germany
40 A4 **Sennecey le Grand** France
32 J9 **Sennelager** W Germany
28 B3 **Sennels** Denmark
121 N4 **Senneterre** Quebec Canada
21 L2 **Senneville** France
54 A2 **Senno** U.S.S.R.
8 C4 **Sennybridge** Wales
133 C8 **Seno Almirantazgo** *G* Chile
68 G4 **Se Noi** *R* Laos
111 M8 **Senoia** Georgia U.S.A.
21 N4 **Senonches** France
19 K4 **Senones** France
133 C8 **Seno Otway** *G* Chile
133 C8 **Seno Skyring** *G* Chile
18 H4 **Sens** France
20 G5 **Sens-de-Bretagne** France
40 F4 **Sense R** Switzerland
48 F5 **Senta** Yugoslavia
70 B4 **Sentarum** *L* Kalimantan
18 F10 **Sentem** France
103 L9 **Sentinel** Arizona U.S.A.
109 H1 **Sentinel** Oklahoma U.S.A.
98 C3 **Sentinel Butte** North Dakota U.S.A.
117 N8 **Sentinel Pk** British Columbia Canada
146 C7 **Sentinel Ra** Antarctica
124 G7 **Sentispac** Mexico
22 H5 **Senuc** France
70 E4 **Senyiur** Kalimantan
78 H3 **Şenyurt** Turkey
56 C4 **Senzas** U.S.S.R.
33 R7 **Senzke** East Germany
74 H7 **Seoni** India
Seoul *see* **Sŏul**
63 **Seoul** *conurbation* China
70 E5 **Sepan** Kalimantan
70 P9 **Sepandjang** Indonesia
70 C5 **Sepangsimin** Kalimantan
106 B9 **Separ** New Mexico U.S.A.
142 E6 **Separation Well** Western Australia Australia
70 E4 **Sepasu** Kalimantan
70 B4 **Sepauk** Kalimantan
130 G8 **Sepetiba, B. de** Brazil
77 C4 **Sepidān** Fārs Iran
70 F4 **Sepinang** Kalimantan
70 D3 **Seping** *R* Sarawak
45 R7 **Sepino** Italy
21 M7 **Sepmes** France
31 K2 **Sępolno** Poland
68 H4 **Sepone** Laos
31 N1 **Sępopol** Poland
130 B4 **Sepotuba** *R* Brazil
32 F9 **Seppenrade** W Germany
19 N13 **Septême** France
19 O18 **Septêmes les Valdonne** France
46 G2 **Septemvri** Bulgaria
21 O4 **Septeuil** France
21 J5 **Sept-Forges** France
122 F3 **Sept Îles** Quebec Canada
20 D4 **Sept Isles, les** France
122 B2 **Sept-Milles, L** Quebec Canada
16 E3 **Sepúlveda** Spain
70 K8 **Seputih** *R* Sumatra
112 B2 **Sequatchie** *R* Tennessee U.S.A.
16 D3 **Sequillo** *R* Spain
100 B1 **Sequim** Washington U.S.A.
102 F5 **Sequoia Nat. Park** California U.S.A.
71 O9 **Sera** Indonesia
22 G4 **Seraincourt** France
22 K2 **Seraing** Belgium
71 J9 **Seraja** *isld* Indonesia
70 P10 **Seraja, G** *mt* Indonesia
70 M9 **Seraju** *R* Java
57 B6 **Serakhs** U.S.S.R.
76 C2 **Seram** India
136 F2 **Seram** *isld* Moluccas Indonesia
136 F2 **Seram Sea** Indonesia
70 L9 **Serang** Java
69 J11 **Serasan** *isld* Indonesia
69 J11 **Seraya** Indonesia
46 D1 **Serbia** *hist reg* Yugoslavia
45 H4 **Serchio** *R* Italy
86 H3 **Serdo** Ethiopia
53 F7 **Serdobsk** U.S.S.R.
55 F3 **Serebryanoye** U.S.S.R.
56 B6 **Serebryansk** U.S.S.R.
54 K2 **Serebryanyye Prudy** U.S.S.R.
88 F5 **Serebu** *mt* Tanzania
52 F5 **Sereda** U.S.S.R.
54 G2 **Seredeyskiy** U.S.S.R.
52 C5 **Seredka** U.S.S.R.
78 D2 **Şereflikoçhisar** Turkey
18 H5 **Serein** *R* France
69 E11 **Seremban** Malaysia
71 C3 **Seremuk** *R* W Irian
88 E3 **Serengeti Nat. Park** Tanzania
88 C8 **Serenje** Zambia
20 F6 **Serent** France
48 K1 **Seret** *R* U.S.S.R.
56 D3 **Serezh** *R* U.S.S.R.
52 F6 **Serezha** *R* U.S.S.R.
46 G7 **Serfopoúla** *isld* Greece
52 G6 **Sergach** U.S.S.R.
98 K7 **Sergeant Bluff** Iowa U.S.A.
58 E2 **Sergelen** Mongolia
87 E7 **Serge Tshimbo** Zaire
55 E4 **Sergeyevka** Kokchetavskaya obl U.S.S.R.
55 G3 **Sergeyevka** Novosibirskaya obl U.S.S.R.
55 E1 **Serginskiy** U.S.S.R.
129 L6 **Sergipe** *state* Brazil
52 E2 **Sergozero, Oz** *L* U.S.S.R.
70 D2 **Seria** Brunei
41 L6 **Seriana, Val** Italy
69 D11 **Seribudolok** Sumatra
130 H9 **Seridó** *R* Brazil
21 O3 **Sérifontaine** France
46 G7 **Sérifos** *isld* Greece
20 C5 **Serignac** France
19 N16 **Sérignan** France
68 C5 **Serim** Burma
142 C2 **Seringapatam Reef** Indian Oc
129 H5 **Seringa, Serra da** *mts* Brazil
45 R8 **Serino** Italy
41 L7 **Serio** *R* Italy
85 F4 **Serkout, Dj** *mt* Algeria
138 E4 **Serle, Mt** South Australia Australia
21 P5 **Sermaises** France
71 O9 **Sermata** *isld* Indonesia
45 K1 **Sermide** Italy
45 N6 **Sermoneta** Italy
38 H9 **Sernio** *mt* Italy
33 U6 **Sernitz** *R* East Germany
33 Q8 **Serno** East Germany
60 T2 **Sernovodsk** U.S.S.R.
57 A5 **Sernyy-Zavod** U.S.S.R.
31 N3 **Serock** Poland
126 A2 **Seroe Colorado** Aruba W Indies
17 F7 **Serón** Spain
85 F4 **Serouenout** Algeria
55 D2 **Serov** U.S.S.R.
89 E4 **Serowe** Botswana
16 B7 **Serpa** Portugal
87 C8 **Serpa Pinto** Angola
43 C9 **Serpeddi, Pta** *mt* Sardinia
116 E4 **Serpentine Hot Springs** Alaska U.S.A.
138 A3 **Serpentine Lakes** South Australia Australia
143 B9 **Serpentine, R** Western Australia Australia
122 A3 **Serpent, R. au** Quebec Canada
128 F1 **Serpents Mouth** *str* Venezuela
17 G6 **Serpis** *R* Spain
54 J2 **Serpukhov** U.S.S.R.
21 O2 **Serqueux** Seine-Inférieure France
21 M3 **Serquigny** France
130 H7 **Serra** Brazil
45 L4 **Serra, Alpe di** *mts* Italy
130 E10 **Serra Alta** Brazil
130 F4 **Serra Bonita** Brazil
130 F4 **Serra das Araras** Brazil
129 H3 **Serra do Navio** Brazil
33 Q5 **Serrahn** East Germany
46 F3 **Sérrai** Greece
45 J3 **Serramazzoni** Italy
125 O2 **Serrana Bank** Caribbean
125 P2 **Serranilla Bank** Caribbean
43 G10 **Serra San Bruno** Italy
43 C11 **Serrat, Cape** *C* Tunisia
45 J4 **Serravalle Pistojese** Italy
22 F4 **Serre** *R* France
18 G10 **Serrère, Pic de** *mt* France
19 P16 **Serres** France
133 D4 **Serrezuela** Argentina
19 N14 **Serrières** France
129 L6 **Serrinha** Brazil
45 M4 **Serriola, Bocca** *pass* Italy
43 B12 **Sers** Tunisia
16 B5 **Sertã** Portugal
130 F7 **Sertãozinho** Brazil
70 K9 **Sertung** *isld* Sumatra
69 D10 **Seruai** Sumatra
70 C6 **Serujan** *R* Kalimantan
89 E3 **Serule** Botswana
40 E2 **Servance** France
46 E4 **Sérvia** Greece
100 E5 **Service Creek** Oregon U.S.A.
138 F6 **Serviceton** Victoria Australia
106 E5 **Servilleta** New Mexico U.S.A.
71 N9 **Serwaro** Indonesia
66 F5 **Sêrxü** China
22 G4 **Séry** France
22 E4 **Séry-les-Mezières** France
68 G4 **Se Sang Soi** *R* Laos
70 E3 **Sesatap** Kalimantan
88 D2 **Sese Is** Uganda
120 K4 **Sesekinika** Ontario Canada
71 A3 **Sesepe** Indonesia
87 B9 **Sesfontein** Namibia
87 D9 **Sesheka** Zambia
41 H7 **Sesia R** Italy
16 A6 **Sesimbra** Portugal
26 N6 **Seskarön** *isld* Sweden
47 Q14 **Seskli** *isld* Greece
61 P12 **Sesoko-jima** *isld* Okinawa
43 F7 **Sessa Aurunca** Italy
36 D6 **Sessenheim** France
110 G3 **Sesser** Illinois U.S.A.
37 K3 **Sesslach** W Germany
71 K9 **Sessok** Flores Indonesia
45 M4 **Sestino** Italy
45 K4 **Sesto Fiorentino** Italy
31 O1 **Seštokai** U.S.S.R.
45 J3 **Sestola** Italy
52 E6 **Sestra** *R* U.S.S.R.
44 E3 **Sestri** Italy
44 F3 **Sestri Levante** Italy
29 O11 **Sestroretsk** U.S.S.R.
60 D12 **Setaka** Japan
60 N3 **Setana** Japan
9 G2 **Setchey** England
18 H9 **Sète** France
130 G6 **Sete Lagoas** Brazil
130 D8 **Sete Quedas, Ilha Grande ou** *isld* Brazil
27 B12 **Setesdal** Norway
94 F8 **Seth** West Virginia U.S.A.
85 F1 **Sétif** Algeria
60 C13 **Seto** Japan
60 F12 **Seto Naikai** *sea* Japan
60 G11 **Seto Naikai Nat. Park** Japan
68 B4 **Setsan** Burma
85 C2 **Settat** Morocco
86 A6 **Sette Cama** Gabon
119 U1 **Settee L** Manitoba Canada
119 T3 **Setting L** Manitoba Canada
13 F5 **Settle** England
140 E3 **Settlement Cr** Queensland Australia
90 C15 **Settlement of Edinburgh** Tristan da Cunha
16 B6 **Setúbal** Portugal
37 M5 **Seubersdorf** W Germany
37 K5 **Seukendorf** W Germany
55 E1 **Seul'** *R* U.S.S.R.
99 V4 **Seul Choix Pt** Michigan U.S.A.
69 B10 **Seulimeum** Sumatra
115 K7 **Seul, Lac** Ontario Canada
21 J3 **Seulles** *R* France
69 C11 **Seumayan** Sumatra
40 B3 **Seurre** France
78 K1 **Sevan, Ozero** U.S.S.R.
53 D11 **Sevastopol'** U.S.S.R.
54 H6 **Sev Donets** *R* U.S.S.R.
28 B4 **Sevel** Denmark
100 J4 **Seven Devils Mts** Idaho U.S.A.
140 D3 **Seven Emu** N Terr Australia
14 C5 **Seven Hd** Ireland
122 F3 **Seven Is. Bay** Quebec Canada
106 C6 **Seven Lakes** New Mexico U.S.A.
9 G5 **Sevenoaks** England
118 G9 **Seven Persons** Alberta Canada
109 J7 **Seven Sisters** Texas U.S.A.
112 K2 **Seven Springs** North Carolina U.S.A.
141 K6 **Seventeen Seventy** Queensland Australia
102 F1 **Seven Troughs** Nevada U.S.A.
117 N10 **Seventy Mile House** British Columbia Canada
25 F6 **Sevenum** Netherlands
20 F6 **Sévérac** France
18 H8 **Séverac-le-Château** France
107 P2 **Severance** Kansas U.S.A.
139 K3 **Severn** *R* New South Wales Australia
121 L8 **Severn** *R* Ontario Canada
52 J4 **Severnaya Mylva** *R* U.S.S.R.
51 K1 **Severnaya Zemlya** *arch* Arctic Oc
55 G3 **Severnoye** U.S.S.R.
8 D4 **Severn, R** England
55 D3 **Severnyy** U.S.S.R.
52 J3 **Severnyy Ural** *mts* U.S.S.R.
56 G3 **Severobaykal'sk** U.S.S.R.
51 L3 **Severo-Baykal'skoye Nagor'ye** *uplands* U.S.S.R.
37 P3 **Severocesky Kraj** *reg* Czechoslovakia
52 E3 **Severodvinsk** U.S.S.R.
55 E4 **Severo-Kazakhstanskaya Oblast'** *prov* U.S.S.R.
31 K6 **Severomoravský** *reg* Czechoslovakia
52 D1 **Severomorsk** U.S.S.R.
55 C1 **Severouralsk** U.S.S.R.
54 K2 **Severo Zadonsk** U.S.S.R.
107 O4 **Severy** Kansas U.S.A.
20 H3 **Sèves** *R* France
29 O2 **Sevettijarvi** Finland
56 D5 **Sevi** U.S.S.R.
103 M3 **Sevier** Utah U.S.A.
103 M2 **Sevier** *R* Utah U.S.A.
103 M2 **Sevier Bridge Res** Utah U.S.A.
103 M2 **Sevier Des** Utah U.S.A.
112 D2 **Sevierville** Tennessee U.S.A.
20 F5 **Sévignac** France
22 G4 **Sevigny** France
126 F4 **Sevilla** *R* Cuba
16 D7 **Sevilla** *prov* Spain
16 D7 **Sevilla** Spain
Seville *see* **Sevilla**
46 G2 **Sevlievo** Bulgaria
48 J2 **Sevola** *mt* U.S.S.R.
53 F11 **Sev. Osetinsk. A.S.S.R** U.S.S.R.
21 J8 **Sèvre** *R* France
18 E6 **Sèvre-Niortaise** *R* France
40 B5 **Sevron** *R* France
54 F4 **Sevsk** U.S.S.R.
85 B7 **Sewa** *R* Sierra Leone
110 L6 **Sewanee** Tennessee U.S.A.
116 N6 **Seward** Alaska U.S.A.
107 M3 **Seward** Kansas U.S.A.
98 J9 **Seward** Nebraska U.S.A.
107 N6 **Seward** Oklahoma U.S.A.
94 H6 **Seward** Pennsylvania U.S.A.
116 R6 **Seward Glacier** Yukon Terr/Alaska Canada/U.S.A.
146 D6 **Seward Mts** Antarctica
116 E4 **Seward Pen** Alaska U.S.A.
133 C4 **Sewell** Chile
40 E2 **Sewen** France
94 G6 **Sewickley** Pennsylvania U.S.A.
117 O8 **Sexsmith** Alberta Canada
124 G4 **Sextín** Mexico
77 H3 **Seyah Band Koh** *mts* Afghanistan
43 B12 **Seybouse** *R* Algeria
83 J12 **Seychelles** *rep* Indian Oc
33 R9 **Seyda** East Germany
52 K2 **Seyda** U.S.S.R.
29 T9 **Seydhisfjördhur** Iceland
78 C3 **Seydişehir** Turkey
20 G3 **Seye** *R* France
78 E3 **Seyhan** *R* Turkey
79 F1 **Seyhan Barajı** *res* Turkey
47 L5 **Seyit** *R* Turkey
47 L5 **Seyitgazi** Turkey
54 D5 **Seym** *R* U.S.S.R.
139 H6 **Seymour** Victoria Australia
95 O5 **Seymour** Connecticut U.S.A.
94 B8 **Seymour** Indiana U.S.A.
110 C1 **Seymour** Iowa U.S.A.
110 D4 **Seymour** Missouri U.S.A.
109 H2 **Seymour** Texas U.S.A.
99 S5 **Seymour** Wisconsin U.S.A.
140 C6 **Seymour Ra** N Terr Australia
19 Q16 **Seyne-les-Alpes** France
42 F3 **Sežana** Yugoslavia
18 H4 **Sezanne** France
52 D6 **Sezha** *R* U.S.S.R.
45 O6 **Sezze** Italy
85 G2 **Sfax** Tunisia
46 F9 **Sfinári** Crete Greece
48 K5 **Sfîntu Gheorghe** Romania
48 M6 **Sfîntu Gheorghe** *R* Romania
's-Gravenhage *see* **Den Haag**
25 B5 **'s-Gravenzande** Netherlands
15 D3 **Sgurr Mor** *mt* Scotland
80 D2 **Sha'ab** Israel
58 E4 **Shaanxi** *prov* China
80 F3 **Sha'ar** Israel
87 E7 **Shaba** *reg* Zaire
Shabani *see* **Zvishavane**
119 O2 **Shabaqua** Ontario Canada
99 S8 **Shabbona** Illinois U.S.A.
84 H5 **Shab, El** Egypt
53 E10 **Shabel'skoye** U.S.S.R.
78 K2 **Shabestar** Iran
79 F9 **Shabibī, J. esh** *mt* Jordan
47 J1 **Shabla** Bulgaria
86 E6 **Shabunda** Zaire
55 D2 **Shaburovo** U.S.S.R.
67 B3 **Shachang** China
66 B4 **Shache** China
118 J8 **Shackleton** Saskatchewan Canada
146 D11 **Shackleton Coast** Antarctica
146 D10 **Shackleton Glacier** Antarctica
146 H13 **Shackleton Ice Shelf** Antarctica
146 D10 **Shackleton Inlet** Antarctica
146 F7 **Shackleton Ra** Antarctica
78 H3 **Shadādah, Ash** Syria
74 B5 **Shadadkot** Pakistan
68 C3 **Shadaw** Burma
98 D4 **Shadehill Res** South Dakota U.S.A.
67 E3 **Shadi** China
55 D3 **Shadrinsk** U.S.S.R.
84 J4 **Shadwân** Egypt
111 K10 **Shady Grove** Alabama U.S.A.
113 D7 **Shady Grove** Florida U.S.A.
146 C12 **Shafer Peak** *mt* Antarctica
57 C4 **Shafirkan** U.S.S.R.
55 C4 **Shafranovo** U.S.S.R.
102 E6 **Shafter** California U.S.A.
101 L9 **Shafter** Nevada U.S.A.
108 C6 **Shafter** Texas U.S.A.
8 D5 **Shaftesbury** England
55 G5 **Shagan** *R* U.S.S.R.
65 E4 **Shagang** China
48 M5 **Shagany, Oz** *L* U.S.S.R.
Shagedu *see* **Jungar Qi**
55 F4 **Shaglyteniz, Oz** *L* U.S.S.R.
56 D5 **Shagonar** U.S.S.R.
144 C6 **Shag R** New Zealand
57 A2 **Shagray, Plato** *plateau* U.S.S.R.
146 E1 **Shag Rocks** S Georgia S Atlantic Oc
76 C2 **Shahabad** India
76 B3 **Shahapur** India
80 B7 **Shahar** Israel
74 C6 **Shahbadpur** Pakistan
74 B6 **Shahbandar** Pakistan
75 J7 **Shahdol** India
65 D6 **Shahe** China
65 C6 **Shahe** China
67 E2 **Shahezhen** China
Shahezi *see* **Wan Xian**
77 K2 **Shah Fuladi** *mt* Afghanistan
84 G3 **Shaḥḥāt** Libya
74 H5 **Shahjahanpur** India
77 E1 **Shāh Jehān, Kuh-e** *mts* Iran
77 K3 **Shāh Jūy** Afghanistan
65 E4 **Shahousuo** China
74 G7 **Shahpur** India
74 F6 **Shahpura** India
77 J2 **Shahrak** Afghanistan
77 G3 **Shāhrakht** Iran
77 D4 **Shahr-e Bābak** Iran
77 B3 **Shahr-e Kord** Iran
77 B2 **Shahr Rey** Iran
77 D2 **Shahrud Bustam** Iran
77 F5 **Shāh Savāran, Kūh-e** *mts* Iran
55 D1 **Shaim** U.S.S.R.
79 H4 **Shā'īr, Jabal** *mt* Syria
80 G3 **Shajara** Jordan
65 F4 **Shajianzi** China
52 E6 **Shakhovskaya** U.S.S.R.
57 D5 **Shakhrisabz** U.S.S.R.
54 K8 **Shakhtersk** U.S.S.R.
59 M2 **Shakhtersk** Sakhalin U.S.S.R.
55 F6 **Shakhtinsk** U.S.S.R.
54 M9 **Shakhty** U.S.S.R.
52 G5 **Shakhun'ya** U.S.S.R.
85 E7 **Shaki** Nigeria
99 N5 **Shakopee** Minnesota U.S.A.
59 L3 **Shakotan misaki** *C* Japan
55 C4 **Shaksha** U.S.S.R.
116 G4 **Shaktolik** Alaska U.S.A.
86 G4 **Shala Hāyk'** *L* Ethiopia
52 F4 **Shalakusha** U.S.S.R.
117 M10 **Shalalth** British Columbia Canada
65 G2 **Shalan** China
67 D6 **Shalang** China
55 G4 **Shalday** U.S.S.R.
52 F6 **Shaldezh** U.S.S.R.
9 F5 **Shalford** England
52 E4 **Shalgachëva** U.S.S.R.
57 F2 **Shalgiya** U.S.S.R.
66 E4 **Shaliangzi** China
77 E4 **Shalidab** Iran
55 D5 **Shalkar Karashatau** *L* U.S.S.R.
55 D5 **Shalkar-Yega-Kara** *L* U.S.S.R.
57 J3 **Shalkudysu** U.S.S.R.
80 G3 **Shallala** Jordan
112 J4 **Shallotte** North Carolina U.S.A.
108 E2 **Shallowater** Texas U.S.A.
120 J8 **Shallow Lake** Ontario Canada
80 C7 **Shalwa** Israel
55 C3 **Shalya** U.S.S.R.
56 C4 **Shalym** U.S.S.R.
88 D5 **Shama** *R* Tanzania
56 C5 **Shaman, Khrebet** *mts* U.S.S.R.
55 C3 **Shamary** U.S.S.R.
86 F4 **Shambe** Sudan
80 D2 **Shamerat** Israel
75 O5 **Shamgong** Bhutan
77 E6 **Shamīl** Iran
80 F1 **Shamir** Israel
78 K6 **Shamiya Des** Iraq
95 L6 **Shamokin** Pennsylvania U.S.A.
118 L8 **Shamrock** Saskatchewan Canada

78
Shamrock — Silver Pit

113 D8 **Shamrock** Florida U.S.A.
107 O6 **Shamrock** Oklahoma U.S.A.
108 D8 **Shamrock** Texas U.S.A.
88 C10 **Shamva** Zimbabwe
68 C2 **Shan** *prov* Burma
80 G6 **Sha'nab** Jordan
Shanchengzhen *see* **Nanjing**
77 G5 **Shāndak** Iran
58 D4 **Shandan** China
65 C3 **Shandian He** *R* China
12 D1 **Shandon** Scotland
102 D6 **Shandon** California U.S.A.
65 C6 **Shandong** *prov* China
65 E6 **Shandong Bandao** *pen* China
87 E9 **Shangani** *R* Zimbabwe
65 D4 **Shangbancheng** China
67 E1 **Shangcheng** China
65 F3 **Shangchengzhen** China
67 D6 **Shangchuan Dao** *isld* China
65 B4 **Shangdu** China
Shangdundu *see* **Linchuan**
67 E2 **Shangfu** China
67 E2 **Shanggao** China
67 G1 **Shanghai** China
63 **Shanghai** *conurbation* China
67 E4 **Shanghang** China
65 D6 **Shanghe**
65 C4 **Shanghuangqi** China
67 C1 **Shangkan** China
67 C5 **Shanglin** China
87 D9 **Shangombo** Zambia
Shangpaihe *see* **Feixi**
58 G5 **Shangqiu** China
67 F2 **Shangrao** China
67 B5 **Shangsi** China
58 E5 **Shang Xian** China
65 B5 **Shangyangwu** China
65 C4 **Shangyi** China
67 E4 **Shangyou** China
66 C3 **Shangyou Shuiku** *res* China
67 G1 **Shangyu** China
59 J2 **Shangzhi** China
65 D5 **Shanhaiguan** China
65 G2 **Shanhetun** China
100 E4 **Shaniko** Oregon U.S.A.
9 E6 **Shanklin** England
67 E2 **Shankou** China
94 J6 **Shanksville** Pennsylvania U.S.A.
145 E4 **Shannon** New Zealand
112 B3 **Shannon** Georgia U.S.A.
99 R7 **Shannon** Illinois U.S.A.
111 H7 **Shannon** Mississippi U.S.A.
14 C4 **Shannon Airport** Ireland
99 M9 **Shannon City** Iowa U.S.A.
14 D2 **Shannon Pot** Ireland
14 C2 **Shannon R** Ireland
Shansi *prov see* **Shanxi** *prov*
65 G3 **Shansonggang** China
80 G4 **Shantana** Jordan
51 N3 **Shantarskiye, Ostrova** *islds* U.S.S.R.
67 E5 **Shantou** China
Shantung *prov see* **Shandong** *prov*
Shantung Peninsula *see* **Shandong Bandao**
67 E5 **Shanwei** China
58 F4 **Shanxi** *prov* China
65 C7 **Shan Xian** China
67 F4 **Shanyao** China
58 F4 **Shanyin** China
67 F1 **Shaobo** China
67 D3 **Shaodong** China
67 D3 **Shaoshan** China
67 F3 **Shaowu** China
59 H5 **Shaoxing** China
67 D3 **Shaoyang** China
15 F1 **Shapinsay** Scotland
52 H2 **Shapkina** *R* U.S.S.R.
56 C5 **Shapshal'skiy Khrebet** *mts* U.S.S.R.
Shara Gol *R see* **Dang He** *R*
52 H7 **Sharan** U.S.S.R.
52 G6 **Sharanga** U.S.S.R.
121 O8 **Sharbot Lake** Ontario Canada
48 L2 **Shargorod** U.S.S.R.
60 S2 **Shari** Japan
79 H4 **Sharīfah** Syria
77 D7 **Shāriqah, Ash** U.A.E.
Sharjah *see* **Shāriqah, Ash**
52 H6 **Sharkan** U.S.S.R.
71 D5 **Shark Fin B** Philippines
52 C6 **Sharkovshchina** U.S.S.R.
141 H2 **Shark Reef** Gt Barrier Reef Aust
55 B4 **Sharlyk** U.S.S.R.
79 F10 **Sharmah** Saudi Arabia
95 O5 **Sharon** Connecticut U.S.A.
112 E4 **Sharon** Georgia U.S.A.
107 M4 **Sharon** Kansas U.S.A.
94 B2 **Sharon** Michigan U.S.A.
98 J2 **Sharon** North Dakota U.S.A.
108 E7 **Sharon** Oklahoma U.S.A.
110 H5 **Sharon** Tennessee U.S.A.
95 P3 **Sharon** Vermont U.S.A.
99 S7 **Sharon** Wisconsin U.S.A.
80 C5 **Sharon, Plain of** Israel
107 J3 **Sharon Springs** Kansas U.S.A.
54 G6 **Sharovka** U.S.S.R.
98 F5 **Sharpe, L** South Dakota U.S.A.
95 L9 **Sharps** Virginia U.S.A.
99 M9 **Sharpsburg** Iowa U.S.A.
94 K7 **Sharpsburg** Maryland U.S.A.
94 A6 **Sharpsville** Indiana U.S.A.
79 F5 **Sharqi, Jebel esh** *mts* Lebanon
52 G5 **Shar'ya** U.S.S.R.
Sharypovo *see* **Chernenko**
89 F3 **Shashani** *R* Zimbabwe
89 E3 **Shashe** Botswana
89 G2 **Shashe** *R* Zimbabwe
87 E10 **Shashe** *R* Zimbabwe/Botswana
86 G4 **Shashemenē** Ethiopia
67 D1 **Shashi** China
100 C9 **Shasta L** California U.S.A.
100 C8 **Shasta, Mt** California U.S.A.
67 D4 **Shatian** China
52 F6 **Shatki** U.S.S.R.
55 D3 **Shatrovo** U.S.S.R.
108 E7 **Shattuck** Oklahoma U.S.A.
54 L1 **Shatura** U.S.S.R.
79 F8 **Shaubak** Jordan
57 J2 **Shaukar, Poluostrov** *pen* U.S.S.R.
80 G3 **Shaumar** Jordan
118 J9 **Shaunavon** Saskatchewan Canada
52 D3 **Shaverki** U.S.S.R.
102 E4 **Shaver L** California U.S.A.
94 H8 **Shavers Fork** *R* West Virginia U.S.A.
80 D2 **Shave Ziyyon** Israel
111 F8 **Shaw** Mississippi U.S.A.
120 K7 **Shawanaga** Ontario Canada
95 N5 **Shawangunk Mts** New York U.S.A.
99 S5 **Shawano** Wisconsin U.S.A.
99 S5 **Shawano L** Wisconsin U.S.A.
121 R7 **Shawbridge** Quebec Canada
8 D2 **Shawbury** England
141 J5 **Shaw I** Queensland Australia
121 S6 **Shawinigan** Quebec Canada
79 H4 **Shawmarīyah, Jabal ash** *mt* Syria
101 Q3 **Shawmut** Montana U.S.A.
94 E7 **Shawnee** Ohio U.S.A.
107 O6 **Shawnee** Oklahoma U.S.A.
98 A7 **Shawnee** Wyoming U.S.A.
110 H4 **Shawneetown** Illinois U.S.A.
121 O7 **Shawville** Quebec Canada
67 F3 **Sha Xi** *R* China
67 F3 **Sha Xian** China
67 D1 **Shayang** China
142 D5 **Shay Gap** Western Australia Australia
84 J4 **Shayib el Banât, Gebel** *mt* Egypt
79 G6 **Shaykh Miskīn** Syria
52 J4 **Shaytanovka** U.S.S.R.
67 G1 **Shazhou** China
57 F5 **Shazud** U.S.S.R.
54 J3 **Shchekino** U.S.S.R.
54 K1 **Shchelkovo** U.S.S.R.
52 H2 **Shchel'yayur** U.S.S.R.
55 G4 **Shcherbakty** U.S.S.R.
54 J1 **Shcherbinka** U.S.S.R.
54 H5 **Shchigry** U.S.S.R.
54 C5 **Shchors** U.S.S.R.
54 F8 **Shchorsk** U.S.S.R.
55 F4 **Shchuchinsk** U.S.S.R.
55 D3 **Shchuch'ye** U.S.S.R.
54 M5 **Shchuch'ye** Voronezhskaya Oblast' U.S.S.R.
55 C3 **Shchuch'ye Ozero** U.S.S.R.
54 K1 **Shchurovo** U.S.S.R.
128 G3 **Shea** Guyana
100 H6 **Sheaville** Oregon U.S.A.
119 O2 **Shebandowan L** Ontario Canada
54 H6 **Shebekino** U.S.S.R.
86 H4 **Shebelē, Wabē** *R* Ethiopia
77 J1 **Sheberghān** Afghanistan
99 T6 **Sheboygan** Wisconsin U.S.A.
86 B4 **Shebshi Mts** Nigeria
80 E5 **Shechem** Jordan
100 B5 **Shedd** Oregon U.S.A.
120 J10 **Shedden** Ontario Canada
122 H7 **Shediac** New Brunswick Canada
14 D3 **Sheelin, L** Ireland
121 N7 **Sheenboro** Quebec Canada
116 Q2 **Sheenjek** *R* Alaska U.S.A.
117 O9 **Sheep Cr** Alberta Canada
101 U7 **Sheep Cr** Wyoming U.S.A.
14 D1 **Sheep Haven** Ireland
101 T10 **Sheephorn** Colorado U.S.A.
106 C2 **Sheep Mt** Colorado U.S.A.
103 J5 **Sheep Pk** Nevada U.S.A.
103 J5 **Sheep Ra** Nevada U.S.A.
14 B5 **Sheep's Hd** Ireland
118 F7 **Sheerness** Alberta Canada
9 G5 **Sheerness** England
122 K9 **Sheet Harbour** Nova Scotia Canada
80 D2 **Shefar'am** Israel
80 C7 **Shefela** Israel
139 H8 **Sheffield** Tasmania Australia
13 G6 **Sheffield** England
144 D5 **Sheffield** New Zealand
110 J7 **Sheffield** Alabama U.S.A.
99 R8 **Sheffield** Illinois U.S.A.
99 N7 **Sheffield** Iowa U.S.A.
95 O4 **Sheffield** Massachusetts U.S.A.
94 H5 **Sheffield** Pennsylvania U.S.A.
108 F5 **Sheffield** Texas U.S.A.
94 E5 **Sheffield Lake** Ohio U.S.A.
56 B3 **Shegarka** *R* U.S.S.R.
52 G3 **Shegmas** U.S.S.R.
120 J7 **Sheguiandah** Ontario Canada
119 O7 **Sheho** Saskatchewan Canada
67 B1 **Shehong** China
133 C7 **Shehuén** *R* Argentina
79 F5 **Sheikh, J. esh** *mt* Lebanon/Syria
120 F3 **Shekak** *R* Ontario Canada
Shekar Dzong *see* **Tingri**
54 M4 **Shekhman'** U.S.S.R.
74 F3 **Shekhupura** Pakistan
53 G12 **Sheki** U.S.S.R.
52 E5 **Sheksna** *R* U.S.S.R.
52 E5 **Sheksna** U.S.S.R.
94 E9 **Shelbiana** Kentucky U.S.A.
110 D2 **Shelbina** Missouri U.S.A.
110 J2 **Shelburn** Indiana U.S.A.
122 G10 **Shelburne** Nova Scotia Canada
120 K8 **Shelburne** Ontario Canada
95 O2 **Shelburne** Vermont U.S.A.
141 G1 **Shelburne B** Queensland Australia
95 P4 **Shelburne Falls** Massachusetts U.S.A.
99 T8 **Shelby** Indiana U.S.A.
99 L8 **Shelby** Iowa U.S.A.
99 U6 **Shelby** Michigan U.S.A.
111 F8 **Shelby** Mississippi U.S.A.
101 O1 **Shelby** Montana U.S.A.
98 J8 **Shelby** Nebraska U.S.A.
112 F2 **Shelby** North Carolina U.S.A.
94 E6 **Shelby** Ohio U.S.A.
110 H2 **Shelbyville** Illinois U.S.A.
110 L2 **Shelbyville** Indiana U.S.A.
110 L3 **Shelbyville** Kentucky U.S.A.
110 E2 **Shelbyville** Missouri U.S.A.
110 K6 **Shelbyville** Tennessee U.S.A.
109 N4 **Shelbyville** Texas U.S.A.
99 T9 **Sheldon** Illinois U.S.A.
99 L6 **Sheldon** Iowa U.S.A.
110 B4 **Sheldon** Missouri U.S.A.
98 J3 **Sheldon** North Dakota U.S.A.
117 H4 **Sheldon, Mt** Yukon Territory Canada
95 P2 **Sheldon Springs** Vermont U.S.A.
122 H3 **Sheldrake** Quebec Canada
56 F5 **Shelekhov** U.S.S.R.
51 P3 **Shelikhova, Zaliv** *B* U.S.S.R.
116 K8 **Shelikof Str** Alaska U.S.A.
99 L3 **Shell** *R* Minnesota U.S.A.
101 S5 **Shell** Wyoming U.S.A.
111 G12 **Shell Beach** Louisiana U.S.A.
118 L5 **Shellbrook** Saskatchewan Canada
101 R8 **Shell Cr** Wyoming U.S.A.
101 N6 **Shelley** Idaho U.S.A.
139 K5 **Shellharbour** New South Wales Australia
99 P4 **Shell L** Wisconsin U.S.A.
118 K5 **Shell Lake** Saskatchewan Canada
143 F8 **Shell Lakes** Western Australia Australia
111 M10 **Shellman** Georgia U.S.A.
119 Q8 **Shellmouth** Manitoba Canada
102 A1 **Shell Mt** California U.S.A.
99 O7 **Shellrock** *R* Iowa U.S.A.
99 O7 **Shell Rock** Iowa U.S.A.
99 P7 **Shellsburg** Iowa U.S.A.
80 D1 **Shelomi** Israel
58 G1 **Shelopugino** U.S.S.R.
102 A1 **Shelter Cove** California U.S.A.
95 P5 **Shelter I** Long I, New York U.S.A.
144 B7 **Shelter Pt** New Zealand
95 O5 **Shelton** Connecticut U.S.A.
98 H9 **Shelton** Nebraska U.S.A.
117 M12 **Shelton** Washington U.S.A.
52 E4 **Sheltozero** U.S.S.R.
78 M1 **Shemakha** U.S.S.R.
56 B5 **Shemonaikha** U.S.S.R.
52 H6 **Shemordan** U.S.S.R.
52 G6 **Shemursha** U.S.S.R.
99 L9 **Shenandoah** Iowa U.S.A.
95 L6 **Shenandoah** Pennsylvania U.S.A.
94 J8 **Shenandoah** Virginia U.S.A.
94 H8 **Shenandoah Mts** W Virginia/Virginia U.S.A.
94 J8 **Shenandoah Nat. Park** Virginia U.S.A.
94 G5 **Shenango Res** Ohio/Penn U.S.A.
57 D1 **Shenber** U.S.S.R.
65 B5 **Shenchi** China
86 A4 **Shendam** Nigeria
86 F2 **Shendi** Sudan
65 J1 **Shending Shan** *mt* China
57 J3 **Shengel'dy** U.S.S.R.
46 D3 **Shëngjin** Albania
65 F1 **Shengping** China
67 G1 **Shengsi** China
67 G1 **Shengsi Liedao** *islds* China
67 G2 **Sheng Xian** China
52 F4 **Shenkursk** U.S.S.R.
65 A5 **Shenmu** China
67 C1 **Shennongjia** China
Shensi *prov see* **Shaanxi**
52 H7 **Shentala** U.S.S.R.
143 E8 **Shenton, Mt** Western Australia Australia
Shentza Dzong *see* **Xainza**
65 C5 **Shen Xian** China
65 C6 **Shen Xian** China
59 H3 **Shenyang** China
65 C5 **Shenze** China
Shenzhen *see* **Bao'an**
74 D5 **Sheo** India
74 G6 **Sheopur** India
118 D7 **Shepard** Alberta Canada
94 C3 **Shepherd** Michigan U.S.A.
101 R4 **Shepherd** Montana U.S.A.
109 M5 **Shepherd** Texas U.S.A.
137 O5 **Shepherd Is** Vanuatu
94 K7 **Shepherdstown** West Virginia U.S.A.
94 B9 **Shepherdsville** Kentucky U.S.A.
117 G7 **Sheppard, Mt** British Columbia Canada
139 H6 **Shepparton** Victoria Australia
9 G5 **Sheppey** *isld* England
8 D5 **Shepton Mallet** England
77 K1 **Sherabad** U.S.S.R.
115 M3 **Sherard, C** Northwest Territories Canada
55 F4 **Sherbakul'** U.S.S.R.
8 D6 **Sherborne** England
85 B7 **Sherbro I** Sierra Leone
121 T7 **Sherbrooke** Quebec Canada
122 H9 **Sherbrooke L** Nova Scotia Canada
13 G6 **Sherburn** England
13 H5 **Sherburn** England
99 M6 **Sherburn** Minnesota U.S.A.
95 M4 **Sherburne** New York U.S.A.
86 C1 **Sherda** Chad
9 F5 **Shere** England
84 J6 **Shereik** Sudan
54 J1 **Sheremet'yevo** *airport* U.S.S.R.
74 E5 **Shergarh** India
111 D7 **Sheridan** Arkansas U.S.A.
94 A6 **Sheridan** Indiana U.S.A.
94 B3 **Sheridan** Michigan U.S.A.
101 N4 **Sheridan** Montana U.S.A.
100 B4 **Sheridan** Oregon U.S.A.
101 T5 **Sheridan** Wyoming U.S.A.
115 N1 **Sheridan, C** Northwest Territories Canada
106 H3 **Sheridan L** Colorado U.S.A.
101 P5 **Sheridan, Mt** Wyoming U.S.A.
138 D5 **Sheringa** South Australia Australia
9 H2 **Sheringham** England
111 H7 **Sherman** Mississippi U.S.A.
94 H4 **Sherman** New York U.S.A.
109 L2 **Sherman** Texas U.S.A.
95 S8 **Sherman Mills** Maine U.S.A.
103 J1 **Sherman Mt** Nevada U.S.A.
101 O7 **Sherman Pk** Idaho U.S.A.
98 H8 **Sherman Res** Nebraska U.S.A.
77 L2 **Sherpur** Afghanistan
119 Q3 **Sherridon** Manitoba Canada
95 M3 **Sherrill** New York U.S.A.
25 D5 **'s-Hertogenbosch** Netherlands
141 K2 **Sherwood** *dist* Brisbane, Qnsld Australia
122 J7 **Sherwood** Prince Edward I Canada
98 E1 **Sherwood** North Dakota U.S.A.
108 G4 **Sherwood** Texas U.S.A.
144 C5 **Sherwood Downs** New Zealand
9 E1 **Sherwood Forest** England
52 H6 **Sheshma** *R* U.S.S.R.
77 E1 **Sheshtamad** Iran
67 E1 **She Shui** *R* China
117 H6 **Sheslay** British Columbia Canada
52 H5 **Shestakovo** U.S.S.R.
99 L5 **Shetek, L** Minnesota U.S.A.
15 G2 **Shetland** *reg* Scotland
50 E4 **Shevchenko** U.S.S.R.
48 M5 **Shevchenko, Liman** *B* U.S.S.R.
57 B2 **Shevchenko, Zaliv** *G* U.S.S.R.
99 L2 **Shevlin** Minnesota U.S.A.
86 G4 **Shewa** *prov* Ethiopia
86 G4 **Shewa Gimīra** Ethiopia
67 F2 **She Xian** China
65 B6 **She Xian** China
98 J3 **Sheyenne** *R* North Dakota U.S.A.
98 G2 **Sheyenne** North Dakota U.S.A.
77 C6 **Sheykh Sho'eyb** *isld* Iran
80 E2 **Shezor** Israel
15 B3 **Shiant** *isld* Scotland
94 C3 **Shiawassee** *R* Michigan U.S.A.
61 N8 **Shibata** Japan
65 B4 **Shibatai** China
60 S2 **Shibecha** Japan
60 T2 **Shibetsu** Japan
84 J3 **Shibîn el Kom** Egypt
79 B8 **Shibîn el Qanâtir** Egypt
67 C3 **Shibing** China
61 M9 **Shibukawa** Japan
60 E14 **Shibushi-wan** Japan
65 D6 **Shibuzi** China
67 B3 **Shichang** China
67 E3 **Shicheng** China
61 P5 **Shichinohe** Japan
98 J9 **Shickley** Nebraska U.S.A.
95 L5 **Shickshinny** Pennsylvania U.S.A.
122 F5 **Shickshock Mts** Quebec Canada
Shicun *see* **Xiangfen**
65 E6 **Shidao** China
65 E6 **Shidao Wan** *B* China
55 F5 **Shiderty** U.S.S.R.
55 F5 **Shiderty** *R* U.S.S.R.
107 O5 **Shidler** Oklahoma U.S.A.
60 H11 **Shido** Japan
15 C3 **Shieldaig** Scotland
140 D2 **Shield, C** N Terr Australia
107 K3 **Shields** Kansas U.S.A.
98 E3 **Shields** North Dakota U.S.A.
67 A1 **Shifang** China
8 D2 **Shifnal** England
61 K10 **Shiga** *prefect* Japan
Shigatse *see* **Xigazê**
122 G5 **Shigawake** Quebec Canada
65 A4 **Shiguaigou** China
67 F1 **Shih-chiu Hu** *L* China
58 G5 **Shi He** *R* China
66 D3 **Shihezi** China
Shihkiachwang *see* **Shijiazhuang**
86 J4 **Shiikh** Somalia
61 M8 **Shiiya** Japan
46 D3 **Shijak** Albania
67 A1 **Shijiaba** China
Shijiao *see* **Fogang**
65 C5 **Shijiazhuang** China
65 B5 **Shijiazhuang** China
67 F1 **Shijiu Hu** China
65 D7 **Shijiusuo** China
60 O3 **Shikabe** Japan
119 N1 **Shikag L** Ontario Canada
60 H11 **Shikama** Japan
68 J2 **Shikang** China
77 L2 **Shikar, Darya-i-** *R* Afghanistan
76 B3 **Shikarpur** India
74 C5 **Shikarpur** Pakistan
61 N11 **Shikine-jima** *isld* Japan
60 G12 **Shikoku** *isld* Japan
60 F12 **Shikoku-sanchi** *mts* Japan
59 N3 **Shikotan** *isld* Japan
60 O3 **Shikotsu Toya Nat. Park** Japan
86 H4 **Shilabo** Ethiopia
52 G4 **Shilador** U.S.S.R.
80 D6 **Shilat** Jordan
55 D5 **Shil'da** U.S.S.R.
75 N5 **Shiliguri** India
Shiliu *see* **Changjiang**
59 G1 **Shilka** *R* U.S.S.R.
14 E4 **Shillelagh** Ireland
9 E4 **Shillingford** England
120 K4 **Shillington** Ontario Canada
95 M6 **Shillington** Pennsylvania U.S.A.
75 O6 **Shillong** India
110 H6 **Shiloh Nat. Mil. Park** Tennessee U.S.A.
67 D5 **Shilong** China
67 C5 **Shilong** China
65 A6 **Shilou** China
54 M2 **Shilovo** U.S.S.R.
Shima *see* **Longhai**
67 E3 **Shima** China
60 D13 **Shimabara** Japan
61 M11 **Shimada** Japan
60 F10 **Shimane** *prefect* Japan
59 J1 **Shimanovsk** U.S.S.R.
60 F13 **Shimanto** Japan
67 D2 **Shimen** China
65 D4 **Shimenzhai** China
61 M11 **Shimizu** Japan
74 G3 **Shimla** India
61 L9 **Shimminato** Japan
61 M11 **Shimoda** Japan
61 O9 **Shimodate** Japan
60 P4 **Shimofuro** Japan
76 B4 **Shimoga** India
60 E11 **Shimogo** Japan
60 Q1 **Shimokawa** Japan
61 O8 **Shimo-kitaba** Japan
60 O4 **Shimokita-hantō** *pen* Japan
60 C14 **Shimo koshiki jima** *isld* Japan
61 M9 **Shimonita** Japan
59 K5 **Shimonoseki** Japan
60 D14 **Shimo-Taniguchi** Japan
60 E13 **Shimo-Tashima** Japan
61 N9 **Shimotsuma** Japan
80 D3 **Shimron** Israel
52 D5 **Shimsk** U.S.S.R.
67 C5 **Shinan** China
59 L4 **Shinano** *R* Japan
77 H3 **Shīndand** Afghanistan
61 K11 **Shindō** Japan
109 K6 **Shiner** Texas U.S.A.
94 J5 **Shinglehouse** Pennsylvania U.S.A.
145 D4 **Shingle Pk** New Zealand
99 U3 **Shingleton** Michigan U.S.A.
100 D9 **Shingletown** California U.S.A.
61 J12 **Shingū** Japan
120 J5 **Shining Tree** Ontario Canada
61 O7 **Shinjō** Japan
60 E11 **Shin-Nan'yō** Japan
94 G7 **Shinnston** West Virginia U.S.A.
61 M9 **Shinonoi** Japan
79 G4 **Shinshār** Syria
61 L11 **Shinshiro** Japan
60 Q2 **Shintoku** Japan
88 D3 **Shinyanga** Tanzania
61 P7 **Shiogama** Japan
61 L9 **Shiojiri** Japan
61 J12 **Shiono-misaki** *C* Japan
Shipai *see* **Huaining**
126 F2 **Ship Chan. Cay** *isld* Bahamas
123 S6 **Ship Cove** Newfoundland Canada
9 G2 **Shipdham** England
111 H11 **Ship I** Mississippi U.S.A.
52 G4 **Shipitsino** U.S.S.R.
46 G2 **Shipka P** Bulgaria
74 H3 **Shipki Pass** India/Xizang Zizhiqu
13 G6 **Shipley** England
119 N5 **Shipman** Saskatchewan Canada
94 K6 **Shippensburg** Pennsylvania U.S.A.
106 B5 **Shiprock** New Mexico U.S.A.
121 T4 **Shipshaw Dam** Quebec Canada
111 E13 **Ship Shoal Lt. Hse** Louisiana U.S.A
13 G5 **Shipton** N Yorks England
9 E4 **Shipton under Wychwood** England
Shipu *see* **Huanglong**
67 G2 **Shipu** China
67 C3 **Shiqian** China
Shiqiao *see* **Panyu**
67 D5 **Shiqiao** China
80 A7 **Shiqma** Israel
80 C8 **Shiqma** *R* Israel
58 E5 **Shiquan** China
66 C5 **Shiquan He** *R* China
74 H2 **Shiquanhe** China
60 J12 **Shirahama** Japan
60 O4 **Shirakami-misaki** *C* Japan
61 O8 **Shirakawa** Fukushima, Honshu Japan
61 K9 **Shirakawa** Toyama, Honshu Japan
78 L1 **Shirakskaya Step'** U.S.S.R.
61 N9 **Shirane-san** *mt* Tochigi Japan
61 M10 **Shirane san** *mt* Yamanashi Japan
60 S3 **Shiranuka** Japan
60 P3 **Shiraoi** Japan
146 C10 **Shirase Coast** Antarctica
77 C5 **Shīrāz** Iran
79 B7 **Shirbîn** Egypt
88 E9 **Shire** *R* Malawi
88 E9 **Shire Highlands** Malawi
65 G4 **Shiren** China
60 T1 **Shiretoko misaki** *C* Japan
60 O3 **Shiribeshi** *prefect* Japan
57 C3 **Shirikrabat** U.S.S.R.
60 O4 **Shiriuchi** Japan
60 P4 **Shiriya-zaki** *C* Japan
9 E6 **Shirley** England
9 E3 **Shirley** England
110 D6 **Shirley** Arkansas U.S.A.
101 T7 **Shirley Mts** Wyoming U.S.A.
61 O8 **Shiroishi** Japan
54 E9 **Shirokoye** U.S.S.R.
61 K10 **Shirotori** Japan
61 L9 **Shirouma-dake** *mt* Japan
77 E1 **Shīrvān** Iran
116 E9 **Shishaldin Vol** Aleutian Is
60 H12 **Shishikui** Japan
60 C11 **Shishimi** Japan
116 D3 **Shishmaref** Alaska U.S.A.
116 E3 **Shishmaref Inlet** Alaska U.S.A.
67 D2 **Shishou** China
67 F1 **Shitai** China
61 L10 **Shitara** Japan
74 G6 **Shivpuri** India
103 L5 **Shivwits Plat** Arizona U.S.A.
67 B6 **Shiwan Dashan** *mts* China
87 F8 **Shiwa Ngandu** Zambia
67 E4 **Shixing** China
67 B2 **Shiyangchang** China
67 C2 **Shiye** China
Shizhaihe *see* **Zhenping**
67 C2 **Shizhu** China
Shizilu *see* **Junan**
67 A4 **Shizong** China
61 P7 **Shizugawa** Japan
58 E4 **Shizuishan** China
65 A6 **Shizuiyi** China
61 O6 **Shizukuishi** Japan
60 Q3 **Shizunai** Japan
59 L5 **Shizuoka** Japan
61 M10 **Shizuoka** *prefect* Japan
54 B2 **Shklov** U.S.S.R.
46 D2 **Shkodër** Albania
46 D3 **Shkumbin** *R* Albania
52 D5 **Shlino** *R* U.S.S.R.
51 J1 **Shmidta, Ostrova** *islds* U.S.S.R.
61 L9 **Shō** *R* Japan
113 A7 **Shoal** *R* Florida U.S.A.
140 B1 **Shoal B** N Terr Australia
123 T5 **Shoal Harb** Newfoundland Canada
139 K5 **Shoalhaven R** New South Wales Australia
119 U8 **Shoal L** Manitoba Canada
118 F1 **Shoal L** Ontario Canada
110 K3 **Shoals** Indiana U.S.A.
141 K5 **Shoalwater B** Queensland Australia
60 F11 **Shōbara** Japan
60 H11 **Shōdo-shima** *isld* Japan
9 G4 **Shoeburyness** England
123 R4 **Shoe Cove** Newfoundland Canada
145 E2 **Shoe I** New Zealand
77 F1 **Shoghlābād** Iran
51 K1 **Shokal'skogo, Proliv** *str* U.S.S.R.
60 P2 **Shokambetsu dake** *mt* Japan
57 E6 **Shokh** U.S.S.R.
60 R1 **Shokotsu** Japan
52 E4 **Shola** *R* U.S.S.R.
55 D5 **Sholaksay** U.S.S.R.
55 F5 **Sholakshalkar, Oz** *L* U.S.S.R.
142 B5 **Sholl I** Western Australia Australia
52 D2 **Shomba** U.S.S.R.
80 E1 **Shomera** Israel
52 H3 **Shomvukva** U.S.S.R.
57 A2 **Shomyshkol'** U.S.S.R.
88 B9 **Shona** Zambia
55 G5 **Shoptykul'** U.S.S.R.
52 G6 **Shora** *R* U.S.S.R.
76 C5 **Shoranur** India
76 C2 **Shorapur** India
77 J5 **Shorawak** *reg* Afghanistan
9 F6 **Shoreham-by-Sea** England
99 T6 **Shorewood** Wisconsin U.S.A.
55 F5 **Shortandy** U.S.S.R.
103 M5 **Short Cr** Arizona U.S.A.
119 Q7 **Shortdale** Manitoba Canada
111 L9 **Shorter** Alabama U.S.A.
138 E2 **Short, L** South Australia Australia
143 C10 **Short, Mt** Western Australia Australia
95 K4 **Shortsville** New York U.S.A.
57 A2 **Shoshkakol'** U.S.S.R.
102 H6 **Shoshone** California U.S.A.
101 L7 **Shoshone** Idaho U.S.A.
101 R5 **Shoshone** *R* Wyoming U.S.A.
101 Q5 **Shoshone Cavern Nat. Mon** Wyoming U.S.A.
101 P5 **Shoshone L** Wyoming U.S.A.
102 G2 **Shoshone Mts** Nevada U.S.A.
102 H5 **Shoshone Pk** Nevada U.S.A.
101 R6 **Shoshoni** Wyoming U.S.A.
54 E5 **Shostka** U.S.S.R.
9 H4 **Shotley** England
144 B6 **Shotover R** New Zealand
67 F2 **Shouchang** China
67 C4 **Shoucheng** China
65 D6 **Shouguang** China
116 Q3 **Shoulder Mt** Alaska U.S.A.
118 E8 **Shouldice** Alberta Canada
67 F3 **Shouning** China
101 L4 **Shoup** Idaho U.S.A.
65 B6 **Shouyang** China
80 B8 **Shoval** Israel
99 N3 **Shovel L** Minnesota U.S.A.
146 J9 **Showa** *Japanese Base* Antarctica
86 G3 **Showak** Sudan
60 O3 **Shōwa-Shinzan** *mt* Japan
103 O7 **Show Low** Arizona U.S.A.
52 F1 **Shoyna** U.S.S.R.
52 F4 **Shozhma** U.S.S.R.
54 C7 **Shpola** U.S.S.R.
94 F6 **Shreve** Ohio U.S.A.
111 C9 **Shreveport** Louisiana U.S.A.
8 D2 **Shrewsbury** England
111 H12 **Shrewsbury** New Orleans, Louisiana U.S.A.
9 E5 **Shrewton** England
76 B1 **Shrigonda** India
76 B1 **Shrirampur** India
9 E4 **Shrivenham** England
8 D2 **Shropshire** *co* England
54 K8 **Shterovka** U.S.S.R.
65 G2 **Shuang-ch'eng** China
65 F2 **Shuangchengpu** China
67 D3 **Shuangfeng** China
65 E2 **Shuanggang** China
67 D1 **Shuanggou** China
65 G3 **Shuanghezhen** China
Shuanghuyu *see* **Zizhou**
Shuangjiang *see* **Tongdao**
59 H3 **Shuangliao** China
67 A1 **Shuangliu** China
65 F3 **Shuangshan** China
65 F3 **Shuangyang** China
59 K2 **Shuangyashan** China
55 C6 **Shubar-Kuduk** U.S.S.R.
79 H3 **Shubayt, Jebel ash** *mts* Syria
122 J8 **Shubenacadie** Nova Scotia Canada
122 J9 **Shubenacadie L** Nova Scotia Canada
99 L9 **Shubert** Nebraska U.S.A.
116 P2 **Shublik Mts** Alaska U.S.A.
79 A7 **Shubra Khît** Egypt
111 H10 **Shubuta** Mississippi U.S.A.
67 E1 **Shucheng** China
80 F6 **Shu'eib** *R* Jordan
80 F6 **Shu'eib Br** Jordan
80 D4 **Shufa** Jordan
57 H5 **Shufu** China
55 G4 **Shuga** U.S.S.R.
57 F5 **Shugnan** U.S.S.R.
57 F5 **Shugnanskiy Khrebet** *mts* U.S.S.R.
52 D5 **Shugozero** U.S.S.R.
55 E1 **Shugur** U.S.S.R.
52 H6 **Shugurovo** U.S.S.R.
65 D7 **Shu He** *R* China
67 B2 **Shuibatang** China
67 A3 **Shuicheng** China
Shuiji *see* **Laixi**
67 F3 **Shuiji** China
67 F3 **Shuikou** China
67 C4 **Shuikou** China
67 D5 **Shuikou** China
65 G2 **Shuiquliu** China
65 E5 **Shuishiying** China
74 D4 **Shujaabad** Pakistan
74 G7 **Shujalpur** India
55 D1 **Shukhtungort** U.S.S.R.
100 D1 **Shuksan, Mt** Washington U.S.A.
59 J3 **Shulan** China
57 H5 **Shule** China
58 C3 **Shule He** *R* China
Shulinzhao *see* **Dalad Qi**
99 Q7 **Shullsburg** Wisconsin U.S.A.
65 C6 **Shulu** China
116 G9 **Shumagin Is** Alaska U.S.A.
116 Q3 **Shuman House** Alaska U.S.A.
60 Q1 **Shumarinai** Japan
56 C6 **Shumek** U.S.S.R.
55 D5 **Shumekty** U.S.S.R.
47 H1 **Shumen** Bulgaria
52 G6 **Shumerlya** U.S.S.R.
55 D3 **Shumikha** U.S.S.R.
54 A1 **Shumilino** U.S.S.R.
52 H4 **Shumino** U.S.S.R.
56 E4 **Shumskiy** U.S.S.R.
65 E1 **Shumugou** China
103 O7 **Shumway** Arizona U.S.A.
80 F6 **Shunat Nimrin** Jordan
67 F3 **Shunchang** China
67 D5 **Shunde** China
52 D3 **Shunga** U.S.S.R.
65 C4 **Shunyi** China
67 B5 **Shuolong** China
58 F4 **Shuo Xian** China
80 F8 **Shuqeiq** *R* Jordan
111 H9 **Shuqualak** Mississippi U.S.A.
77 G4 **Shur** *R* Iran
57 F4 **Shurab** U.S.S.R.
52 G6 **Shuran** U.S.S.R.
61 P13 **Shuri** Okinawa
58 F1 **Shurinda** U.S.S.R.
52 H6 **Shurma** U.S.S.R.
87 E9 **Shurugwi** Zimbabwe
77 A3 **Shūsh** Iran
78 L2 **Shusha** U.S.S.R.
46 D4 **Shushicë** *R* Albania
77 A3 **Shūshtar** Iran
117 O10 **Shuswap L** British Columbia Canada
139 H4 **Shuttleton** New South Wales Australia
80 B8 **Shuva** Israel
52 F6 **Shuya** Ivanovskaya obl U.S.S.R.
52 D4 **Shuya** Karel'skaya U.S.S.R.
116 L7 **Shuyak I** Alaska U.S.A.
65 D8 **Shuyang** China
52 D3 **Shuyeretskoye** U.S.S.R.
55 G4 **Shuyreksor, Oz** *L* U.S.S.R.
52 F5 **Shuyskoye** U.S.S.R.
61 M11 **Shuzenji** Japan
68 B3 **Shwebandaw** Burma
68 B1 **Shwebo** Burma
68 B3 **Shwedaung** Burma
68 C4 **Shwegun** Burma
68 C4 **Shwegyin** Burma
68 C2 **Shwenyaung** Burma
74 H1 **Shyok** Kashmir
69 D12 **Siabu** Sumatra
77 H6 **Siahan Range** Pakistan
69 E12 **Siak Sri Inderapura** Sumatra
74 F2 **Sialkot** Pakistan
Siam *see* **Thailand**
Sian *see* **Xi'an**
Siangtan *see* **Xiangtan**
47 Q14 **Siánna** Rhodes Greece
31 J1 **Sianów** Poland
69 H11 **Siantan** *isld* Indonesia
69 D8 **Si Ao Ban Don, Laem** Thailand
128 E3 **Siapa** *R* Venezuela
71 G6 **Siargao** *isld* Philippines
95 S5 **Siasconset** Massachusetts U.S.A.
71 E8 **Siasi** Philippines
71 F6 **Siaton** Negros Philippines
52 B6 **Siauliai** U.S.S.R.
84 J4 **Sibâi, Gebel** *mt* Egypt
126 F4 **Sibanicú** Cuba
71 E5 **Sibay** *isld* Philippines
55 C4 **Sibay** U.S.S.R.
89 H6 **Sibayi** S Africa
118 G7 **Sibbald** Alberta Canada
146 C12 **Sibbald, Cape** *C* Antarctica
29 L11 **Sibbo** Finland
42 G5 **Sibenik** Yugoslavia
69 D13 **Siberut** *isld* Indonesia
74 B4 **Sibi** Pakistan
69 B11 **Sibigo** Indonesia
42 E6 **Sibillini, Monti** Italy
59 K3 **Sibirtsevo** U.S.S.R.
86 B6 **Sibiti** Congo
48 J5 **Sibiu** Romania
9 G4 **Sible Hedingham** England
99 S9 **Sibley** Illinois U.S.A.
99 L6 **Sibley** Iowa U.S.A.
109 O3 **Sibley** Louisiana U.S.A.
120 B4 **Sibley Prov. Park** Ontario Canada
70 G4 **Siboa** Sulawesi
69 D12 **Sibolga, Tel** *B* Sumatra
71 E4 **Sibolon** *isld* Philippines
126 G5 **Siboney** Cuba
69 D11 **Siborongborong** Sumatra
41 M3 **Sibratsgfäll** Austria
75 Q5 **Sibsagar** India
9 G1 **Sibsey** England
70 B3 **Sibu** Sarawak
71 F7 **Sibuco** Mindanao Philippines
71 F7 **Sibuguey Bay** Mindanao Philippines
86 C4 **Sibut** Cent Afr Republic
70 C2 **Sibuti** Sarawak
71 F4 **Sibuyan** *isld* Philippines
48 H4 **Sic** Romania
71 E1 **Sicapoo** *mt* Luzon Philippines
128 E7 **Sicasica** Bolivia
71 F6 **Sicayac** Mindanao Philippines
138 E4 **Siccus** *R* South Australia Australia
68 E6 **Si Chang, Ko** *isld* Thailand
67 A1 **Sichuan** *prov* China
67 B1 **Sichuan Pendi** *basin* China
43 E11 **Sicilia** *isld* Italy
43 D11 **Sicilian Chan** S Europe
Sicily *see* **Sicilia**
111 E10 **Sicily Island** Louisiana U.S.A.
119 R2 **Sickle L** Manitoba Canada
71 F5 **Sicogon** *isld* Philippines
128 D6 **Sicuani** Peru
48 E5 **Šid** Yugoslavia
71 A2 **Sidangoli** Halmahera Indonesia
47 O12 **Sidari** Greece
85 F5 **Sidawet** Niger
8 D5 **Sidcot** England
9 G5 **Sidcup** England
140 B6 **Siddeley Ra** N Terr Australia
74 E7 **Siddhapur** India
76 D3 **Siddhavattam** India
8 D1 **Siddington** England
76 D1 **Siddipet** India
29 J9 **Sideby** Finland
99 T10 **Sidell** Illinois U.S.A.
70 F6 **Sidenreng, D** *L* Sulawesi
26 K8 **Sidensjö** Sweden
85 D6 **Sidéradougou** Burkina
43 H10 **Siderno Marina** Italy
118 H8 **Sidewood** Saskatchewan Canada
46 G4 **Sidheritis** *isld* Greece
47 H9 **Sidheros, Akra** *C* Crete Greece
75 J6 **Sidhi** India
46 F3 **Sidhirókastron** Greece
17 H8 **Sidi Ali** Algeria
84 H3 **Sidi Barrani** Egypt
85 D1 **Sidi Bel Abbès** Algeria
43 C13 **Sidi Bou Ali** Tunisia
85 B3 **Sidi Ifni** Morocco
85 C2 **Sidi Kacem** Morocco
69 D11 **Sidikalang** Sumatra
85 B4 **Sidi Mhamed** Western Sahara
13 E1 **Sidlaw Hills** Scotland
146 B9 **Sidley, Mt** Antarctica
8 C6 **Sidmouth** England
141 G2 **Sidmouth, C** Queensland Australia
99 S3 **Sidnaw** Michigan U.S.A.
117 M11 **Sidney** British Columbia Canada
100 B1 **Sidney** British Columbia Canada
119 S9 **Sidney** Manitoba Canada
99 S9 **Sidney** Illinois U.S.A.
99 L9 **Sidney** Iowa U.S.A.
98 B2 **Sidney** Montana U.S.A.
98 D8 **Sidney** Nebraska U.S.A.
95 M4 **Sidney** New York U.S.A.
110 M1 **Sidney** Ohio U.S.A.
85 C6 **Sido** Mali
70 G4 **Sidoan** Sulawesi
70 O9 **Sidoardjo** Java
68 B2 **Sidoktaya** Burma
Sidon *see* **Saïda**
84 F3 **Sidrah, As** Libya
130 C7 **Sidrolândia** Brazil
36 C2 **Siebengebirge** *mt* W Germany
37 P1 **Siebenlehn** East Germany
32 J7 **Siedenburg** W Germany
31 N3 **Siedlce** Poland
36 D2 **Sieg** *R* W Germany
36 E2 **Siegbach** W Germany
36 C2 **Siegburg** W Germany
Siegelsdorf *see* **Seukendorf**
37 M6 **Siegenburg** W Germany
31 O3 **Siemiatycze** Poland
68 H5 **Siem Pang** Cambodia
68 F6 **Siem Reap** Cambodia
42 D5 **Siena** Italy
31 O5 **Sieniawa** Poland
20 H4 **Sienne** *R* France
29 K4 **Sieppijärvi** Finland
31 L4 **Sieradz** Poland
31 J3 **Sieraków** Poland
22 L5 **Sierck** France
40 F2 **Sierentz** France
31 M3 **Sierpc** Poland
108 B4 **Sierra Blanca** Texas U.S.A.
102 D2 **Sierra Buttes** *pk* California U.S.A.
133 D6 **Sierra Colorada** Argentina
133 D6 **Sierra Grande** Argentina
124 J6 **Sierra Hermosa** Mexico
85 B7 **Sierra Leone** *rep* W Africa
90 H8 **Sierra Leone Basin** Atlantic Oc
90 H8 **Sierra Leone Rise** Atlantic Oc
125 J9 **Sierra Madre del Sur** *mts* Mexico
102 D7 **Sierra Madre Mts** California U.S.A.
125 J5 **Sierra Madre Oriental** *mts* Mexico
124 H4 **Sierra Mojada** Mexico
102 D2 **Sierraville** California U.S.A.
36 D3 **Siershahn** W Germany
130 B8 **Siete Puntas, R** Paraguay
33 R6 **Sietow** East Germany
48 J4 **Şieu** Romania
45 K4 **Sieve** *R* Italy
33 Q7 **Sieversdorf** East Germany
32 M8 **Sievershausen** W Germany
29 L8 **Sievi** Finland
67 C5 **Sifang Ling** *mts* China
65 G1 **Sifangtai** China
80 E1 **Sifsufa** Israel
119 R7 **Sifton** Manitoba Canada
117 K7 **Sifton Pass** British Columbia Canada
17 G9 **Sig** Algeria
28 B5 **Sig** Denmark
52 D2 **Sig** U.S.S.R.
27 D11 **Sigdal** Norway
18 G9 **Sigean** France
110 H2 **Sigel** Illinois U.S.A.
94 H5 **Sigel** Pennsylvania U.S.A.
26 H3 **Sigerfjord** Norway
48 H3 **Sighetu Marmaţiei** Romania
48 J4 **Sighişoara** Romania
47 J4 **Sığırcı** Turkey
69 B10 **Sigli** Sumatra
28 S8 **Siglufjördhur** Iceland
71 F5 **Sigma** Panay Philippines
41 K1 **Sigmaringen** W Germany
45 K4 **Signa** Italy
103 L7 **Signal** Arizona U.S.A.
18 G7 **Signal du Luguet** *mt* France
112 B2 **Signal Mt** Tennessee U.S.A.
103 K8 **Signal Pk** Arizona U.S.A.
19 P18 **Signes** France
146 E3 **Signy** *U.K. Base* S Orkney Is S Atlantic Oc
22 G4 **Signy-l'Abbaye** France
22 G4 **Signy-le-petit** France
69 D14 **Sigoisooinan** Indonesia
99 O8 **Sigourney** Iowa U.S.A.
128 C4 **Sigsig** Ecuador
27 J12 **Sigtuna** Sweden
125 L2 **Siguatepeque** Honduras
17 F3 **Sigüenza** Spain
85 C6 **Siguiri** Guinea
103 N3 **Sigurd** Utah U.S.A.
21 N2 **Sigy-en-Bray** France
68 B1 **Sihaung Myauk** Burma
65 D4 **Siheyong** China
41 J3 **Sihl** *R* Switzerland
41 J3 **Sihl See** *L* Switzerland
74 J7 **Sihora** India
67 D5 **Sihui** China
29 J10 **Siikainen** Finland
52 C3 **Siikajoki** *R* Finland
29 N8 **Siilinjärvi** Finland
78 H3 **Siirt** Turkey
69 E13 **Sijunjung** Sumatra
69 E14 **Sikakap** Indonesia
117 M7 **Sikanni Chief** British Columbia Canada
74 F5 **Sikar** India
77 L2 **Sikaram** *mt* Afghanistan
85 C6 **Sikasso** Mali
70 G7 **Sikeli** Sulawesi
110 G5 **Sikeston** Missouri U.S.A.
59 K3 **Sikhote Alin'** *mts* U.S.S.R.
46 G8 **Sikinos** *isld* Greece
46 F6 **Sikionia** Greece
75 N5 **Sikkim** *prot* India
48 E5 **Siklós** Hungary
116 B5 **Siknik C** Alaska U.S.A.
71 A2 **Siko** *isld* Halmahera Indonesia
70 E1 **Sikuati** Sabah
16 C2 **Sil** *R* Spain
52 B6 **Šilale** U.S.S.R.
41 N4 **Silandro** Italy
70 B4 **Silantek, G** *mt* Sarawak/Kalimantan
71 G4 **Sila Pt** Philippines
111 H10 **Silas** Alabama U.S.A.
69 B10 **Silawaih Agam** *vol* Sumatra
71 F5 **Silay** Negros Philippines
75 P6 **Silchar** India
26 M1 **Silda** *isld* Norway
47 N10 **Şile** Turkey
22 G3 **Silenrieux** Belgium
27 F12 **Silen, V** *L* Sweden
112 H2 **Siler City** North Carolina U.S.A.
31 K4 **Silesia** *reg* Poland/Czech
101 R4 **Silesia** Montana U.S.A.
85 E4 **Silet** Algeria
55 F4 **Siletiteniz, Ozero** *L* U.S.S.R.
20 D5 **Silfiac** France
74 J4 **Silgarhi** Nepal
83 J12 **Silhouette I** Seychelles
67 C4 **Silian** China
43 C12 **Siliana** Tunisia
99 N2 **Silica** Minnesota U.S.A.
66 D5 **Siling Co** *L* China
43 B9 **Siliqua** Sardinia
47 J1 **Silistra** Bulgaria
47 J3 **Silivri** Turkey
27 G11 **Siljan** *L* Sweden
28 C4 **Silkeborg** Denmark
13 G6 **Silkstone** England
128 E7 **Sillajhuay** *mt* Chile/Bolivia
52 C5 **Sillamäe** U.S.S.R.
45 H3 **Sillano** Italy
45 L3 **Sillaro** *R* Italy
21 K5 **Sillé-le-Guillaume** France
38 F8 **Sillian** Austria
21 L4 **Silli-en-Gouffern** France
20 D4 **Sillon-de-Talbert** France
47 H3 **Silo** *mt* Greece
110 B5 **Siloam Springs** Arkansas U.S.A.
109 N5 **Silsbee** Texas U.S.A.
119 W3 **Silsby L** Manitoba Canada
106 C2 **Silt** Colorado U.S.A.
119 N8 **Silton** Saskatchewan Canada
86 C2 **Siltou** Chad
70 Q10 **Silungblanak** Indonesia
111 K8 **Siluria** Alabama U.S.A.
52 B6 **Šilutė** U.S.S.R.
78 H2 **Silvan** Turkey
130 E5 **Silvânia** Brazil
Silva Porto *see* **Kuito**
74 E8 **Silvassa** India
127 K4 **Silver Bank** Caribbean
99 P2 **Silver Bay** Minnesota U.S.A.
103 N9 **Silver Bell** Arizona U.S.A.
101 N3 **Silver Bow** Montana U.S.A.
121 L5 **Silver Centre** Ontario Canada
100 J6 **Silver City** Idaho U.S.A.
111 F8 **Silver City** Mississippi U.S.A.
106 B9 **Silver City** New Mexico U.S.A.
103 M2 **Silver City** Utah U.S.A.
98 J8 **Silver Cr** Nebraska U.S.A.
100 F6 **Silver Cr** Oregon U.S.A.
111 F10 **Silver Creek** Mississippi U.S.A.
94 H4 **Silver Creek** New York U.S.A.
98 A8 **Silver Crown** Wyoming U.S.A.
145 E2 **Silverdale** New Zealand
107 O4 **Silverdale** Kansas U.S.A.
118 F6 **Silver Heights** Alberta Canada
120 B4 **Silver Islet** Ontario Canada
99 T3 **Silver L** Michigan U.S.A.
100 E6 **Silver L** Oregon U.S.A.
100 D6 **Silver Lake** Oregon U.S.A.
123 P4 **Silver Mt** Newfoundland Canada
102 G4 **Silverpeak** Nevada U.S.A.
7 L9 **Silver Pit** North Sea

Silver Plains — Sokur 79

141 G2 **Silver Plains** Queensland Australia
94 J4 **Silver Springs** New York U.S.A.
141 J8 **Silver Springs Gas Field** Queensland Australia
101 N4 **Silver Star** Montana U.S.A.
117 O10 **Silver Star Prov. Park** British Columbia Canada
117 K10 **Silverthrone Mt** British Columbia Canada
106 C4 **Silverton** Colorado U.S.A.
100 C5 **Silverton** Oregon U.S.A.
108 F1 **Silverton** Texas U.S.A.
100 D1 **Silverton** Washington U.S.A.
128 G4 **Silves** Brazil
16 B7 **Silves** Portugal
131 C4 **Silveyra, L** Argentina
100 F6 **Silvies** *R* Oregon U.S.A.
41 M4 **Silvretta Gruppe** *mt* Switzerland
41 M4 **Silvrettahorn** *mt* Switz/Austria
80 D6 **Silwād** Jordan
36 B5 **Silwingen** W Germany
55 C3 **Sim** U.S.S.R.
70 B4 **Simanggang** Sarawak
68 E1 **Simao** China
71 F4 **Simara** *isld* Philippines
121 M5 **Simàrd, Lac** Quebec Canada
70 G4 **Simatang** *isld* Sulawesi
47 J4 **Simav** *R* Turkey
47 K5 **Simav** Turkey
47 K5 **Simav Gölü** *L* Turkey
37 O6 **Simbach** W Germany
71 E7 **Simbahan** Philippines
79 B8 **Simbillâwein, El** Egypt
45 O6 **Simbruini, Monti** *mt* Italy
120 K10 **Simcoe** Ontario Canada
98 F7 **Simeon** Nebraska U.S.A.
116 H9 **Simeonof I** Alaska U.S.A.
47 H2 **Simeonovgrad** Bulgaria
48 H5 **Simeria** Romania
28 D3 **Simested** Denmark
43 F11 **Simeto** *R* Sicily
69 C11 **Simeuluë** *isld* Indonesia
53 D11 **Simferopol'** U.S.S.R.
47 Q14 **Simi** Greece
47 U14 **Simi** *isld* Greece
46 F3 **Simitli** Bulgaria
102 F7 **Simi Valley** California U.S.A.
Simla *see* **Shimla**
106 F2 **Simla** Colorado U.S.A.
48 H3 **Şimleu Silvaniei** Romania
37 L4 **Simmelsdorf** W Germany
40 G4 **Simmental** *R* Switzerland
36 C4 **Simmer** *R* W Germany
22 L2 **Simmerath** W Germany
36 D4 **Simmern** W Germany
111 E11 **Simmesport** Louisiana U.S.A.
118 J9 **Simmie** Saskatchewan Canada
102 E6 **Simmler** California U.S.A.
109 J7 **Simmons** Texas U.S.A.
126 G3 **Simms** Long I Bahamas
101 O2 **Simms** Montana U.S.A.
111 B8 **Simms** Texas U.S.A.
113 K9 **Simms Pt** New Providence I Bahamas
31 O1 **Simnas** U.S.S.R.
29 L6 **Simo** Finland
27 D12 **Simoa** *R* Norway
29 M6 **Simojoki** *R* Finland
29 N11 **Simola** Finland
143 E9 **Simon** Western Australia Australia
102 G3 **Simon** Nevada U.S.A.
117 O8 **Simonette** *R* Alberta Canada
119 Q4 **Simonhouse** Manitoba Canada
121 P7 **Simon, L** Quebec Canada
13 G5 **Simon Seat** *mt* England
27 H13 **Simonstorp** Sweden
89 A10 **Simon's Town** S Africa
117 K10 **Simoom Sd** British Columbia Canada
69 G13 **Simpang** Sumatra
69 C11 **Simpangkiri** Sumatra
29 O10 **Simpele** Finland
25 E7 **Simpelveld** Netherlands
129 K5 **Simplicio Mendes** Brazil
40 H5 **Simplon Tunnel** Italy/Switz
119 M7 **Simpson** Saskatchewan Canada
107 N2 **Simpson** Kansas U.S.A.
99 O6 **Simpson** Minnesota U.S.A.
101 P1 **Simpson** Montana U.S.A.
140 D6 **Simpson Des** N Terr Australia
138 E2 **Simpson Desert Conservation Park** South Australia Australia
140 E7 **Simpson Desert Nat Park** Queensland Australia
143 F7 **Simpson Hill** Western Australia Australia
120 C4 **Simpson I** Ontario Canada
133 C7 **Simpson, I** Chile
117 R5 **Simpson Is** Northwest Territories Canada
115 L4 **Simpson Pen** Northwest Territories Canada
102 H2 **Simpson Pk Mts** Nevada U.S.A.
112 E3 **Simpsonville** South Carolina U.S.A.
27 G16 **Simrishamn** Sweden
100 C8 **Sims** California U.S.A.
100 D5 **Simtustus, L** Oregon U.S.A.
69 C13 **Simuk** *isld* Indonesia
69 D13 **Simulubek** Indonesia
70 B4 **Simunjan** Sarawak
70 F2 **Simunul** *isld* Philippines
69 C11 **Sinabang** Indonesia
69 D11 **Sinabung** *mt* Sumatra
42 G4 **Sinac** Yugoslavia
86 J4 **Sina Dhaqa** Somalia
84 J4 **Sinai** *pen* Egypt
98 J5 **Sinai** South Dakota U.S.A.
48 K5 **Sinaia** Romania
124 F5 **Sinaloa** *state* Mexico
42 D5 **Sinalunga** Italy
127 J9 **Sinamaica** Venezuela
67 C3 **Sinan** China
46 D4 **Sinanaj** Albania
55 D3 **Sinara** *R* U.S.S.R.
47 O12 **Sinarádhes** Greece
68 B3 **Sinbaungwe** Burma
75 R6 **Sinbo** Burma
68 D6 **Sinbyubyin** Burma
68 D6 **Sinbyudaing** Burma
68 B2 **Sinbyugyun** Burma
126 G10 **Sincé** Colombia
126 G10 **Sincelejo** Colombia
22 E4 **Sinceny** France
101 S8 **Sinclair** Wyoming U.S.A.
112 D4 **Sinclair L** Georgia U.S.A.
117 N9 **Sinclair Mills** British Columbia Canada
138 C4 **Sinclair, Pt** South Australia Australia
15 E2 **Sinclairs B** Scotland
94 H4 **Sinclairville** New York U.S.A.
74 C6 **Sind** *reg* Pakistan
28 E2 **Sindal** Denmark
71 F6 **Sindañgan** Mindanao Philippines
70 L9 **Sindangbarang** Java
71 K9 **Sindeh, Tk** *B* Flores Indonesia
47 J1 **Sindel** Bulgaria
36 G6 **Sindelfingen** W Germany
55 D1 **Sindeya** U.S.S.R.
76 C2 **Sindgi** India
76 C3 **Sindhnur** India
52 B5 **Sindi** U.S.S.R.
47 J5 **Sindirği** Turkey
48 K4 **Sîndominic** Romania
52 H3 **Sindor** U.S.S.R.
75 M7 **Sindri** India
36 G5 **Sindringen** W Germany
54 M9 **Sinegorskiy** U.S.S.R.
52 H5 **Sinegor'ye** U.S.S.R.
47 J4 **Sinekçi** Turkey
47 J3 **Sinekli** Turkey
54 G8 **Sinel'nikoyo** U.S.S.R.
16 B7 **Sines** Portugal
29 L5 **Sinettä** Finland
Sinfu *see* **Jianping**
68 D2 **Sing** Burma
86 F3 **Singa** Sudan
68 C2 **Singaingmyo** Burma
69 G12 **Singapore** *rep* S E Asia
69 B14 **Singapore** *city* Singapore
69 F12 **Singapore, Str. of** S E Asia
70 P10 **Singaraja** Indonesia
68 E5 **Sing Buri** Thailand
41 J2 **Singen** W Germany
48 J4 **Sîngeorgiu de Pădure** Romania
48 J3 **Sîngeorz-Bąi** Romania
111 C11 **Singer** Louisiana U.S.A.
88 E4 **Singida** Tanzania
46 F4 **Singitikós, Kólpos** *G* Greece
75 Q5 **Singkaling Hkamti** Burma
70 G7 **Singkang** Sulawesi
69 E13 **Singkarak** Sumatra
69 G13 **Singkep** Indonesia
69 C11 **Singkil** Sumatra
69 D12 **Singkuang** Sumatra
139 K4 **Singleton** New South Wales Australia
140 C5 **Singleton** N Terr Australia
9 F6 **Singleton** England
109 M5 **Singleton** Texas U.S.A.
140 B5 **Singleton, Mt** N Terr Australia
143 B8 **Singleton, Mt** Western Australia Australia
Singora *see* **Songkhla**
68 B1 **Singu** Burma
47 O12 **Siniais** Greece
46 E4 **Siniátsikon** *mt* Greece
71 E3 **Siniloan** Luzon Philippines
Sining *see* **Xining**
Sining Ho *R see* **Huang Shui** *R*
70 F5 **Sinio, Gunung** *mt* Sulawesi
43 C8 **Siniscola** Sardinia
55 D5 **Siniy-Shikhan** U.S.S.R.
70 G7 **Sinjai** Sulawesi
46 C2 **Sinjajevina** *mt* Yugoslavia
86 G2 **Sinkat** Sudan
Sinkiang *aut reg see* **Xinjiang Uygur Zizhiqu**
94 D7 **Sinking Spring** Ohio U.S.A.
65 F5 **Sinmi** *isld* N Korea
36 E2 **Sinn** W Germany
36 H3 **Sinn** *R* W Germany
129 H2 **Sinnamary** Fr Guiana
76 B1 **Sinnar** India
94 J5 **Sinnemahoning** Pennsylvania U.S.A.
43 H8 **Sinni** *R* Italy
13 H5 **Sinnington** England
36 H3 **Sinntal** W Germany
79 A9 **Sinnûris** Egypt
48 M6 **Sinoe, L** Romania
78 E1 **Sinop** Turkey
124 D2 **Sinoquipe** Mexico
131 H2 **Sinos** *R* Brazil
59 J3 **Sinp'o** N Korea
36 F5 **Sinsheim** W Germany
36 B4 **Sinspelt** W Germany
119 O8 **Sintaluta** Saskatchewan Canada
70 B4 **Sintang** Kalimantan
109 K7 **Sinton** Texas U.S.A.
16 A6 **Sintra** Portugal
59 H3 **Sinŭiju** N Korea
86 A2 **Sinujiif** Somalia
126 G10 **Sinú, R** Colombia
52 C6 **Sinyaya** *R* U.S.S.R.
36 E6 **Sinzheim** W Germany
36 C2 **Sinzig** W Germany
28 F7 **Siø** *isld* Denmark
48 E4 **Sió** *R* Hungary
71 F7 **Siocon** Mindanao Philippines
20 G6 **Sion** France
40 F5 **Sion** Switzerland
18 G6 **Sioule** *R* France
98 K6 **Sioux Center** Iowa U.S.A.
98 K7 **Sioux City** Iowa U.S.A.
98 K6 **Sioux Falls** South Dakota U.S.A.
118 L1 **Sioux Lookout** Ontario Canada
99 L7 **Sioux Rapids** Iowa U.S.A.
71 F6 **Sipalay** Negros Philippines
127 O3 **Siparia** Trinidad
Siping *see* **Huangpin**
59 H3 **Siping** China
70 D2 **Sipitang** Sabah
119 U3 **Sipiwesk** Manitoba Canada
146 C10 **Siple Coast** Antarctica
146 A8 **Siple I** *isld* Antarctica
146 A8 **Siple, Mt** Antarctica
29 N11 **Sippola** Finland
111 J8 **Sipsey** *R* Alabama U.S.A.
111 J7 **Sipsey** Alabama U.S.A.
69 D14 **Sipura** *isld* Indonesia
71 F6 **Siquijor** Philippines
128 E1 **Siquisique** Venezuela
80 G6 **Sir** *R* Jordan
76 C4 **Sira** India
27 B13 **Sira** *R* Norway
128 D5 **Sira** *mt* Peru
77 D7 **Şir Abū Nu'āyr** *isld* U.A.E.
19 Q15 **Sirac** *mt* France
68 E6 **Si Racha** Thailand
43 G11 **Siracusa** Sicily
117 N9 **Sir Alexander, Mt** British Columbia Canada
85 E6 **Sirba** *watercourse* Niger/Burkina
123 S4 **Sir Charles Hamilton Sd** Newfoundland Canada
141 G1 **Sir Charles Hardy Is** Gt Barrier Reef Aust
27 B13 **Sirdalsvatn** *L* Norway
118 B8 **Sir Douglas, Mt** Alberta Canada
140 D3 **Sir Edward Pellew Group** *islds* N Terr Australia
99 O4 **Siren** Wisconsin U.S.A.
45 P5 **Sirente, M** *mt* Italy
48 K3 **Siret** *R* Romania
80 F8 **Sirfa** Jordan
140 B1 **Sir George Hope Is** N Terr Australia
142 F2 **Sir Graham Moore Is** Western Australia Australia
79 H7 **Sirhān, Wādī** *watercourse* Saudi Arabia
68 E4 **Siri Kit Dam** Thailand
70 B3 **Sirik, Tg** *C* Sarawak
138 D5 **Sir Isaac Pt** South Australia Australia
117 J4 **Sir James McBrien, Mt** Northwest Territories Canada
143 D7 **Sir James, Mt** Western Australia Australia
138 D5 **Sir Joseph Banks Group** *islds* South Australia Australia
29 L4 **Sirkka** Finland
29 L5 **Sirkkakoski** Finland
74 G5 **Sir Muttra** India
47 H8 **Sirna** *isld* Greece
78 J3 **Sirnak** Turkey
74 E6 **Sirohi** India
42 H5 **Široki Brijeg** Yugoslavia
45 O4 **Sirolo** Italy
69 C12 **Sirombu** Indonesia
76 E1 **Sironcha** India
74 G6 **Sironj** India
46 G7 **Siros** Greece
76 D1 **Sirpur** India
102 F6 **Sirretta Pk** California U.S.A.
77 D7 **Sīrrī, Jazīreh-ye** *isld* Iran
74 F4 **Sirsa** India
117 P10 **Sir Sandford** *mt* British Columbia Canada
117 P10 **Sir Sanford, Mt** British Columbia Canada
76 B3 **Sirsi** India
Sirte *see* **Surt**
84 F3 **Sirte Desert** Libya
84 F3 **Sirte, G. of** Libya
138 A2 **Sir Thomas, Mt** South Australia Australia
71 M9 **Sirung** *isld* Indonesia
117 O9 **Sir Wilfrid Laurier, Mt** British Columbia Canada
141 G2 **Sir William Thompson Ra** Queensland Australia
68 G5 **Sisaket** Thailand
16 B1 **Sisargas** *isld* Spain
87 D11 **Sishen** S Africa
65 D7 **Sishui** China
119 S6 **Sisib L** Manitoba Canada
56 D4 **Sisim** *R* U.S.S.R.
119 Q3 **Sisipuk L** Manitoba Canada
99 S2 **Siskiwit B** Michigan U.S.A.
100 B8 **Siskiyou Mts** Cal/Oregon U.S.A.
124 F4 **Sisogúichic** Mexico
68 F4 **Si Song Khram** Thailand
68 F6 **Sisophon** Cambodia
102 D7 **Sisquoc** California U.S.A.
40 G3 **Sissach** Switzerland
98 J4 **Sisseton** South Dakota U.S.A.
122 E6 **Sisson Branch Res** New Brunswick Canada
22 F4 **Sissonne** France
77 G4 **Sistan, Daryacheh ye** *L* Afghanistan
109 J6 **Sisterdale** Texas U.S.A.
19 P16 **Sisteron** France
68 A7 **Sisters** *islds* Andaman Is
100 D5 **Sisters** Oregon U.S.A.
143 F7 **Sisters, The** *mt* Western Australia Australia
83 J12 **Sisters, The** *isld* Seychelles
116 G5 **Sisters, The** *mt* Alaska U.S.A.
94 G7 **Sistersville** West Virginia U.S.A.
36 B3 **Sistig** W Germany
45 O7 **Sisto** *R* Italy
52 E5 **Sit** *R* U.S.S.R.
75 L5 **Sitamarhi** India
70 F2 **Sitangkai** Philippines
74 J5 **Sitapur** India
26 J3 **Sitasjaure** *L* Sweden
89 G6 **Siteki** Swaziland
17 J3 **Sitges** Spain
46 F4 **Sithoniá** Greece
47 H9 **Sitía** Crete Greece
66 E3 **Sitian** China
130 F4 **Sitio da Abadia** Brazil
129 K6 **Sítio de Mato** Brazil
117 F7 **Sitka** Alaska U.S.A.
107 L4 **Sitka** Kansas U.S.A.
116 L8 **Sitkalidak I** Alaska U.S.A.
117 F7 **Sitka Nat Historical Park** Alaska U.S.A.
116 L8 **Sitkinak I** Alaska U.S.A.
100 B6 **Sitkum** Oregon U.S.A.
46 D2 **Sitnica** *R* Yugoslavia
55 E3 **Sitnikovo** U.S.S.R.
26 K4 **Sitojaure** *L* Sweden
84 H4 **Sitra** *oasis* Egypt
77 B6 **Sitrah** Bahrain
68 C4 **Sittang** *R* Burma
25 E7 **Sittard** Netherlands
Sitten *see* **Sion**
32 K6 **Sittensen** W Germany
9 G5 **Sittingbourne** England
68 A2 **Sittwe** Burma
70 P9 **Situbondo** Java
33 R10 **Sitzenroda** East Germany
71 H7 **Siumpu** *isld* Indonesia
125 M3 **Siuna** Nicaragua
29 M6 **Siuruanjoki** *R* Finland
59 J1 **Sivaki** U.S.S.R.
78 F2 **Sivas** Turkey
53 E10 **Sivash, Zaliv** *B* U.S.S.R.
47 K6 **Sivaslı** Turkey
78 G3 **Siverek** Turkey
52 D5 **Siverskiy** U.S.S.R.
52 K2 **Sivomaskinskiy** U.S.S.R.
47 M11 **Sivri** *isld* Turkey
78 C2 **Sivrihisar** Turkey
22 G3 **Sivry** Belgium
22 J5 **Sivry-sur-Meuse** France
84 H4 **Siwa** Egypt
70 G6 **Siwa** Sulawesi
100 A7 **Sixes** Oregon U.S.A.
19 P18 **Six Fours-la-Plage** France
14 C4 **Sixmilebridge** Ireland
111 E12 **Six Mile L** Louisiana U.S.A.
20 F6 **Sixt** Ille-et-Vilaine France
40 E5 **Sixt Vallorcine** France
52 F3 **Siya** U.S.S.R.
86 G1 **Siyâl I** Egypt
52 G6 **Siyava** U.S.S.R.
101 M1 **Siyeh, Mt** Montana U.S.A.
56 E5 **Sizim** U.S.S.R.
59 M1 **Siziman** U.S.S.R.
65 B4 **Siziwang Qi** China
20 B5 **Sizun** France
52 H2 **Sizyabsk** U.S.S.R.
28 G5 **Sjælland** *isld* Denmark
28 G5 **Sjællands Odde** *C* Denmark
26 K8 **Själevad** Sweden
46 D1 **Sjenica** Yugoslavia
26 D10 **Sjoa** *R* Norway
27 G16 **Sjöbo** Sweden
127 M10 **S. José de Guanipa** Venezuela
26 G7 **Sjoutnäs** Sweden
27 F14 **Sjövik** Sweden
26 G7 **Sjulsåsen** Sweden
26 M6 **Sjulsmark** Sweden
26 O2 **Sjusjavrre** Norway
26 F8 **Skäckerfjällen** *mt* Sweden
42 J6 **Skadarsko Jez** *L* Yugoslavia
28 G6 **Skælskør** Denmark
28 S10 **Skaftárós** *est* Iceland
27 J14 **Skaftet** Sweden
27 K11 **Skäfthammar** Sweden
28 S9 **Skagafjördhur** *inlet* Iceland
27 C10 **Skagastölstindane** *mt* Norway
28 S9 **Skagastrand** Iceland
28 F1 **Skagen** Denmark
27 G13 **Skagern** *L* Sweden
27 C14 **Skagerrak** *chan* Denmark/Norway
27 D10 **Skaget** *mt* Norway
100 D1 **Skagit** *R* Washington U.S.A.
117 F6 **Skagway** Alaska U.S.A.
79 D4 **Skala** Cyprus
46 F8 **Skåla** Greece
48 K2 **Skala-Podol'skaya** U.S.S.R.
27 F15 **Skälderviken** *B* Sweden
26 K5 **Skalka** *L* Sweden
26 S1 **Skallelv** Norway
28 A5 **Skallingen** *pen* Denmark
27 F14 **Skallsjö** Sweden
27 J13 **Skällvik** Sweden
31 K4 **Skalmierzyce** Poland
37 N3 **Skalná** Czechoslovakia
28 G7 **Skalø** *isld* Denmark
28 C3 **Skals Å** *R* Denmark
100 C4 **Skamania** Washington U.S.A.
28 E5 **Skamby** Denmark
28 D6 **Skamlingsbanken** *hill* Denmark
Skanderborg *co see* **Vejle** *co*
99 T3 **Skandia** Michigan U.S.A.
27 F16 **Skåne** *physical reg* Sweden
95 L4 **Skaneateles** New York U.S.A.
99 S3 **Skanee** Michigan U.S.A.
26 J3 **Skånland** Norway
28 D4 **Skannerup** Denmark
27 F16 **Skanör** Sweden
26 H7 **Skansholm** Sweden
26 J6 **Skansnäs** Sweden
46 G5 **Skantzoúra** *isld* Greece
27 F13 **Skara** Sweden
27 F13 **Skaraborg** *reg* Sweden
26 F9 **Skardörfjell** *mt* Norway
74 F1 **Skardu** Kashmir
27 E11 **Skarnes** Norway
28 E6 **Skarø** *isld* Denmark
28 F6 **Skårop** Denmark
28 B5 **Skarrild** Denmark
26 F9 **Skarsfjället** *mt* Sweden
31 L1 **Skarszewy** Poland
25 J7 **Skarvsjö** Sweden
31 N4 **Skaryszew** Poland
31 M4 **Skarżysko-Kamienna** Poland
28 B5 **Skast** Denmark
26 H10 **Skästra** Sweden
27 G15 **Skatelöv** Sweden
13 F2 **Skateraw** Scotland
27 G12 **Skattkärr** Sweden
27 G10 **Skattungen** *L* Sweden
52 B6 **Skaudvilė** U.S.S.R.
28 B4 **Skave** Denmark
31 M6 **Skawina** Poland
120 K6 **Skead** Ontario Canada
117 J8 **Skeena** *R* British Columbia Canada
117 K8 **Skeena Crossing** British Columbia Canada
117 J7 **Skeena Mts** British Columbia Canada
9 G1 **Skegness** England
28 H6 **Skelby** Denmark
28 H7 **Skelby** Storstrøm Denmark
28 D7 **Skelde** Denmark
140 D3 **Skeleton** *R* N Terr Australia
87 B9 **Skeleton Coast Nat. Park** Namibia
28 C4 **Skelhøje** Denmark
26 L7 **Skellefteå** Sweden
26 L6 **Skellefte älv** *R* Sweden
26 M7 **Skelleftehamm** Sweden
13 F6 **Skelmersdale** England
146 D11 **Skelton Glacier** *glacier* Antarctica
28 E3 **Skelund** Denmark
27 F14 **Skene** Sweden
28 J5 **Skensved** Denmark
46 F6 **Skhimatárion** Greece
46 E8 **Skhíza** *isld* Greece
46 G8 **Skhoinoúsa** *isld* Greece
27 E12 **Ski** Norway
46 F5 **Skiathos** *isld* Greece
107 O5 **Skiatook** Oklahoma U.S.A.
14 B5 **Skibbereen** Ireland
28 B4 **Skibbild** Denmark
28 H5 **Skibby** Denmark
28 C5 **Skibet** Denmark
28 J6 **Skibinge** Denmark
26 L2 **Skibotn** Norway
28 A3 **Skibsted Fjord** Denmark
112 F6 **Skidaway I** Georgia U.S.A.
117 H9 **Skidegate** British Columbia Canada
31 P2 **Skidel'** U.S.S.R.
95 L8 **Skidmore** Maryland U.S.A.
109 K7 **Skidmore** Texas U.S.A.
27 D12 **Skien** Norway
31 M4 **Skierniewice** Poland
118 F9 **Skiff** Alberta Canada
29 J11 **Skiftet Kihti** Finland
85 F1 **Skikda** Algeria
116 M6 **Skilak L** Alaska U.S.A.
46 F7 **Skillaion, Akra** *C* Greece
27 G14 **Skillengaryd** Sweden
110 H3 **Skillet** *R* Illinois U.S.A.
46 D7 **Skinári, Akra** *C* Greece
28 B3 **Skinnerup** Denmark
27 H12 **Skinnskatteberg** Sweden
26 Q1 **Skipagurra** Norway
12 C2 **Skipness** Scotland
144 B6 **Skippers** New Zealand
144 B6 **Skippers Range** New Zealand
13 H6 **Skipsea** England
139 G6 **Skipton** Victoria Australia
13 F6 **Skipton** England
46 G6 **Skiros** *isld* Greece
28 C3 **Skive** Denmark
28 C3 **Skive Fj** *inlet* Denmark
26 C10 **Skjåk** Norway
28 S9 **Skjalfandafljot** *R* Iceland
28 S8 **Skjálfandi** *B* Iceland
26 G5 **Skjelåtind** *mt* Norway
28 D3 **Skjellerup** Denmark
28 A5 **Skjern** Ringkøbing Denmark
28 D4 **Skjern** Viborg Denmark
28 C5 **Skjern Å** *R* Denmark
26 H4 **Skjerstad** Norway
26 L1 **Skjervöy** Norway
28 D4 **Skjød** Denmark
27 A12 **Skjold** Norway
28 B3 **Skjoldborg** Denmark
27 C10 **Skjolden** Norway
28 E7 **Skjoldnæs** *C* Denmark
115 P5 **Skjoldungen** Greenland
26 J3 **Skjomen** Norway
26 H4 **Skjönstå** Norway
26 E6 **Sklinna** *lighthouse* Norway
26 D6 **Sklinnabanken** Norway
48 E1 **Skoczow** Poland
28 C6 **Skodborg** Denmark
28 A5 **Skodsbøl** Denmark
29 K5 **Skodsborg** Denmark
28 E4 **Skødstrup** Denmark
42 F2 **Skofja Loka** Yugoslavia
26 K9 **Skog** Sweden
26 O2 **Skoganvarre** Norway
26 R2 **Skogerøy** Norway
27 F12 **Skoghall** Sweden
8 A4 **Skokholm I** Wales
99 T8 **Skokie** Illinois U.S.A.
55 D6 **Skol'** U.S.S.R.
31 O6 **Skole** U.S.S.R.
48 H1 **Skole** U.S.S.R.
27 H12 **Sköllersta** Sweden
8 A4 **Skomer I** Wales
26 F4 **Skomvoer** Norway
117 Q11 **Skookumchuk** British Columbia Canada
46 F5 **Skópelos** *isld* Greece
46 G6 **Skópelos Kaloyeroi** *isld* Greece
54 L3 **Skopin** U.S.S.R.
46 E2 **Skopje** Yugoslavia
31 L2 **Skórcz** Poland
55 F2 **Skorodum** U.S.S.R.
26 F7 **Skorovatn** Norway
26 J8 **Skorped** Sweden
28 D3 **Skørping** Denmark
28 G7 **Skørringe** Denmark
27 D12 **Skotselv** Norway
28 F7 **Skovballe** Denmark
28 D4 **Skovby** Århus Denmark
28 E5 **Skovby** Fyn Denmark
28 D7 **Skovby** Sønderjylland Denmark
27 G13 **Skövde** Sweden
28 B5 **Skovlund** Denmark
59 H1 **Skovorodino** U.S.S.R.
95 S2 **Skowhegan** Maine U.S.A.
119 S7 **Skownan** Manitoba Canada
28 C2 **Skræm** Denmark
27 E11 **Skreia** Norway
28 F7 **Skrøbelev** Denmark
26 M5 **Skröven** Sweden
28 C6 **Skrydstrup** Denmark
27 A12 **Skudeneshavn** Norway
27 E12 **Skulerud** Norway
103 H5 **Skull Pk** Nevada U.S.A.
103 M7 **Skull V** Arizona U.S.A.
48 L3 **Skulyany** U.S.S.R.
111 G8 **Skuna** *R* Mississippi U.S.A.
110 E1 **Skunk** *R* Iowa U.S.A.
27 M15 **Skuodas** U.S.S.R.
27 F16 **Skurup** Sweden
31 J6 **Skuteč** Czechoslovakia
27 J11 **Skutskär** Sweden
26 H3 **Skutvik** Norway
6 F1 **Skúvoy** *isld* Faeroes
48 M1 **Skvira** U.S.S.R.
116 M6 **Skwentna** Alaska U.S.A.
31 J3 **Skwierzyna** Poland
15 B3 **Skye, I. of** Scotland
100 D2 **Skykomish** Washington U.S.A.
146 D7 **Skytrain Ice Rise** *ice rise* Antarctica
55 D2 **Sladkovskoye** U.S.S.R.
28 G6 **Slagelse** Denmark
13 F4 **Slaggyford** England
111 C10 **Slagle** Louisiana U.S.A.
28 H5 **Slaglille** Denmark
26 K6 **Slagnäs** Sweden
70 N9 **Slahung** Java
13 F6 **Slaidburn** England
12 E2 **Slamannan** Scotland
70 M9 **Slamet, G** *mt* Java
48 F2 **Slana** *R* Czechoslovakia
116 P5 **Slana** Alaska U.S.A.
14 E3 **Slane** Ireland
14 E4 **Slaney** *R* Ireland
89 B8 **Slang Berg** *mt* S Africa
28 J5 **Slangerup** Denmark
89 A10 **Slang Kop Pt** S Africa
48 K5 **Slănic** Romania
48 K4 **Slănic-Moldova** Romania
42 H6 **Slano** Yugoslavia
52 C5 **Slantsy** U.S.S.R.
30 H5 **Slaný** Czechoslovakia
37 N3 **Slapany** Czechoslovakia
15 B3 **Slapin, L** Scotland
141 H4 **Slashers Reefs** Gt Barrier Reef Aust
120 D4 **Slate I** Ontario Canada
101 S9 **Slater** Colorado U.S.A.
110 C2 **Slater** Missouri U.S.A.
98 B8 **Slater** Wyoming U.S.A.
102 G6 **Slate Ra** California U.S.A.
111 G8 **Slate Springs** Mississippi U.S.A.
48 J6 **Slatina** Romania
42 H3 **Slatina, P** Yugoslavia
108 F2 **Slaton** Texas U.S.A.
27 H11 **Slättberg** Sweden
26 O1 **Slåtten** Norway
94 G8 **Slatyfork** West Virginia U.S.A.
111 E11 **Slaughter** Louisiana U.S.A.
51 Q2 **Slautnoye** U.S.S.R.
118 C3 **Slave Lake** Alberta Canada
117 Q5 **Slave Pt** Northwest Territories Canada
117 R5 **Slave R** Northwest Territories Canada
54 C3 **Slavgorod** Belorusskaya A.S.S.R. U.S.S.R.
54 G8 **Slavgorod** Dnepropetrovskaya obl U.S.S.R.
31 N1 **Slavinek** U.S.S.R.
48 D1 **Slavkov** Czechoslovakia
52 C5 **Slavkovichi** U.S.S.R.
42 H3 **Slavonia** *reg* Yugoslavia
46 F2 **Slavovvrŭkh** *mt* Bulgaria
42 H3 **Slav Požega** Yugoslavia
48 H2 **Slavskoye** U.S.S.R.
46 G1 **Slavyanovo** Bulgaria
54 J8 **Slavyansk** U.S.S.R.
31 J4 **Sława** Poland
31 O4 **Sławatycze** Poland
31 K1 **Sławno** Poland
31 J2 **Sławoborze** Poland
99 L6 **Slayton** Minnesota U.S.A.
9 F1 **Sleaford** England
138 D6 **Sleaford B** South Australia Australia
116 D4 **Sledge I** Alaska U.S.A.
118 K4 **Sled L** Saskatchewan Canada
13 H5 **Sledmere** England
115 M6 **Sleeper Is** Northwest Territories Canada
94 A2 **Sleeping Bear Pt** Michigan U.S.A.
99 M5 **Sleepy Eye** Minnesota U.S.A.
116 J6 **Sleetmute** Alaska U.S.A.
22 F1 **Sleidinge** Belgium
6 M4 **Sleipner** *oil rig* North Sea
70 N9 **Sleman** Java
52 C5 **Slepino** U.S.S.R.
31 L3 **Slesiń** Poland
146 F7 **Slessor Glacier** Antarctica
28 F4 **Sletterhage** *C* Denmark
28 C2 **Slettestrand** Denmark
26 Q1 **Slettnes** Norway
111 G11 **Slidell** Louisiana U.S.A.
109 K2 **Slidell** Texas U.S.A.
27 D10 **Slidre** Norway
25 C5 **Sliedrecht** Netherlands
14 D2 **Slieve Anierin** *mt* Ireland
14 C3 **Slieve Aughty** *mts* Ireland
14 D2 **Slieve Beagh** *mt* Ireland
14 C4 **Slieve Bernagh** Ireland
14 D3 **Slieve Bloom Mts** Ireland
14 B2 **Slieve Car** *mt* Ireland
14 F2 **Slieve Donard** *mt* N Ireland
14 B3 **Slieve Elva** *mt* Ireland
14 C4 **Slievefelim Cullaun Mts** Ireland
14 B2 **Slieve Gamph** *mt* Ireland
14 E2 **Slieve Gullion** *mt* N Ireland
14 C2 **Slieve League** *mt* Ireland
14 B4 **Slieve Mish** *mts* Ireland
14 B5 **Slieve Miskish** *mt* Ireland
14 A3 **Slievemore** *mt* Ireland
14 D2 **Slievenakilla** *hill* Ireland
14 D4 **Slievenamon** *mt* Ireland
14 D1 **Slieve Snaght** *mt* Ireland
14 C2 **Slieve Tooey** *mt* Ireland
15 B3 **Sligachan** Scotland
14 C2 **Sligo** *co* Ireland
14 C2 **Sligo** Ireland
94 H5 **Sligo** Pennsylvania U.S.A.
28 H6 **Slimminge** Denmark
99 S6 **Slinger** Wisconsin U.S.A.
15 C3 **Slioch Mt** Scotland
145 E2 **Slipper I** New Zealand
94 G5 **Slippery Rock** Pennsylvania U.S.A.
27 K14 **Slite** Sweden
47 H2 **Sliven** Bulgaria
46 F2 **Slivnitsa** Bulgaria
98 K7 **Sloan** Iowa U.S.A.
101 L2 **Sloan** Montana U.S.A.
103 J6 **Sloan** Nevada U.S.A.
102 D2 **Sloat** California U.S.A.
52 H5 **Slobedskoy** U.S.S.R.
54 M5 **Sloboda** U.S.S.R.
52 G4 **Slobodchikovo** U.S.S.R.
48 M3 **Slobodka** U.S.S.R.
48 M4 **Slobodzeya** U.S.S.R.
48 L6 **Slobozia** Ialomita Romania
48 J6 **Slobozia** Teleorman Romania
117 P11 **Slocan** British Columbia Canada
25 G2 **Slochteren** Netherlands
111 L10 **Slocomb** Alabama U.S.A.
117 G6 **Sloko** *R* British Columbia Canada
27 F15 **Slömge** Sweden
31 H3 **Słońsk** Poland
25 E3 **Sloten** Netherlands
25 E3 **Sloter Meer** Netherlands
28 G6 **Slots** Denmark
81 B9 **Slot van Capelle** Indian Oc
9 F4 **Slough** England
48 F2 **Slovakia** Czechoslovakia
42 F3 **Slovenija** *reg* Yugoslavia
38 N8 **Slovenske Gorice** *mts* Yugoslavia
48 E2 **Slovenské Pravno** Czechoslovakia
31 L7 **Slovenské Rudohorie** *mts* Czechoslovakia
48 F2 **Slovensko** *aut reg* Czechoslovakia
116 L5 **Slow Fork** *R* Alaska U.S.A.
12 D1 **Sloy, L** Scotland
31 H3 **Słubice** Poland
53 C8 **Sluch'** *R* U.S.S.R.
52 H4 **Sludka** Komi A.S.S.R. U.S.S.R.
25 A6 **Sluis** Netherlands
25 A6 **Sluiskil** Netherlands
31 H4 **Sluknov** Czechoslovakia
31 K3 **Słupca** Poland
31 K1 **Słupsk** Poland
14 A3 **Slyne Hd** Ireland
111 D8 **Smackover** Arkansas U.S.A.
15 E4 **Sma Glen** Scotland
13 F2 **Smailholm** Scotland
27 G15 **Småland** *physical reg* Sweden
28 G6 **Smålandsfarvandet** Denmark
27 F14 **Småll Burseryd** Sweden
101 N5 **Small** Idaho U.S.A.
119 U1 **Small L** Manitoba Canada
95 S3 **Small Pt** Maine U.S.A.
115 N7 **Smallwood Res** Labrador, Nfld Canada
9 G5 **Smarden** England
119 N5 **Smeaton** Saskatchewan Canada
48 F6 **Smederevo** Yugoslavia
48 F6 **Smederevska Palanka** Yugoslavia
27 H11 **Smedjebacken** Sweden
54 C7 **Smela** U.S.S.R.
26 S1 **Smelror** Norway
94 J5 **Smethport** Pennsylvania U.S.A.
59 K2 **Smidovich** U.S.S.R.
28 J4 **Smidstrup** Denmark
31 K3 **Smigiel** Poland
118 H7 **Smiley** Saskatchewan Canada
109 K6 **Smiley** Texas U.S.A.
52 C6 **Smiltene** U.S.S.R.
46 G3 **Smilyan** Bulgaria
46 G1 **Smirdiasa** Romania
31 J5 **Smiřice** Czechoslovakia
55 E4 **Smirnovo** U.S.S.R.
59 M2 **Smirnykh** U.S.S.R.
117 Q8 **Smith** Alberta Canada
102 E3 **Smith** Nevada U.S.A.
94 H10 **Smith** *R* Virginia/N Carolina U.S.A.
114 G4 **Smith Arm** *B* Northwest Territories Canada
115 M2 **Smith B** Northwest Territories Canada
116 K1 **Smith B** Alaska U.S.A.
110 G3 **Smithboro** Illinois U.S.A.
140 F3 **Smithburne R** Queensland Australia
107 M2 **Smith Center** Kansas U.S.A.
117 K8 **Smithers** British Columbia Canada
89 E8 **Smithfield** S Africa
98 G9 **Smithfield** Nebraska U.S.A.
112 J2 **Smithfield** North Carolina U.S.A.
94 H7 **Smithfield** Pennsylvania U.S.A.
109 M9 **Smithfield** Texas U.S.A.
101 O8 **Smithfield** Utah U.S.A.
95 L9 **Smithfield** Virginia U.S.A.
94 G7 **Smithfield** West Virginia U.S.A.
68 A6 **Smith I** Andaman Is
146 C3 **Smith I** S Shetland Is Antarctica
115 M5 **Smith I** Northwest Territories Canada
95 M8 **Smith I** Maryland U.S.A.
112 K4 **Smith I** North Carolina U.S.A.
95 M9 **Smith I** Virginia U.S.A.
100 C1 **Smith I** Washington U.S.A.
94 H9 **Smith Mountain Lake** Virginia U.S.A.
146 D6 **Smith Peninsula** *pen* Antarctica
100 J1 **Smith Pk** *mt* Idaho U.S.A.
140 B1 **Smith Pt** *inlet* N Terr Australia
122 J8 **Smith Pt** Nova Scotia Canada
101 O2 **Smith R** Montana U.S.A.
117 K6 **Smith River** British Columbia Canada
100 A8 **Smith River** California U.S.A.
121 O8 **Smiths Falls** Ontario Canada
100 J5 **Smiths Ferry** Idaho U.S.A.
110 K4 **Smiths Grove** Kentucky U.S.A.
7 M10 **Smiths Knoll** *oil rig* North Sea
115 M2 **Smith Sound** Northwest Territories Canada
139 H8 **Smithton** Australia
110 C3 **Smithton** Missouri U.S.A.
139 L4 **Smithtown-Gladstone** New South Wales Australia
111 M10 **Smithville** Georgia U.S.A.
110 B2 **Smithville** Missouri U.S.A.
107 Q7 **Smithville** Oklahoma U.S.A.
110 L6 **Smithville** Tennessee U.S.A.
109 K6 **Smithville** Texas U.S.A.
94 F7 **Smithville** West Virginia U.S.A.
98 C6 **Smithwick** South Dakota U.S.A.
46 D4 **Smlikas** *mt* Greece
102 E1 **Smoke Creek Desert** Nevada U.S.A.
94 H8 **Smoke Hole** West Virginia U.S.A.
117 O8 **Smoky** *R* Alberta Canada
138 C4 **Smoky B** South Australia Australia
139 L4 **Smoky C** New South Wales Australia
123 M7 **Smoky C** Nova Scotia Canada
120 H2 **Smoky Falls** Ontario Canada
106 H2 **Smoky Hill** *R* Colo/Kansas U.S.A.
107 L2 **Smoky Hills** Kansas U.S.A.
118 E4 **Smoky Lake** Alberta Canada
26 C8 **Smöla** *isld* Norway
54 D2 **Smolensk** U.S.S.R.
53 D7 **Smolenskaya Oblast'** *prov* U.S.S.R.
54 E2 **Smolensko-Moskovskaya Vozvyshennost'** *upland* U.S.S.R.
46 G3 **Smolyan** Bulgaria
101 P7 **Smoot** Wyoming U.S.A.
120 J3 **Smooth Rock Falls** Ontario Canada
120 A2 **Smooth Rock L** Ontario Canada
118 L3 **Smoothstone R** Saskatchewan Canada
48 K2 **Smotrich** U.S.S.R.
47 J1 **Smyadovo** Bulgaria
54 G1 **Smychka** U.S.S.R.
27 F16 **Smygehamn** Sweden
146 C6 **Smyley** *isld* Antarctica
Smyrna *see* **Izmir**
95 M7 **Smyrna** Delaware U.S.A.
112 C4 **Smyrna** Georgia U.S.A.
95 M4 **Smyrna** New York U.S.A.
110 K6 **Smyrna** Tennessee U.S.A.
95 S7 **Smyrna Mills** Maine U.S.A.
12 D5 **Snaefell** *mt* I of Man U.K.
29 T9 **Snæfell** *mt* Iceland
139 H9 **Snag** Tasmania Australia
68 G7 **Snaipol** Cambodia
13 G6 **Snaith** England
101 O6 **Snake** *R* Idaho/Wyoming U.S.A.
98 E7 **Snake** *R* Nebraska U.S.A.
100 G3 **Snake** *R* Washington U.S.A.
103 K2 **Snake Ra** Nevada U.S.A.
100 J4 **Snake R. Canyon** Idaho/Oregon U.S.A.
101 N6 **Snake R. Plain** Idaho U.S.A.
126 F3 **Snap Pt** Andros Bahamas
28 E5 **Snaptun** Denmark
117 Q3 **Snare L** Northwest Territories Canada
117 P4 **Snare River** Northwest Territories Canada
26 F7 **Snåsa** Norway
26 F8 **Snasahögarna** *mt* Sweden
26 E7 **Snåsavatn** *L* Norway
111 M11 **Sneads** Florida U.S.A.
25 E2 **Sneek** Netherlands
25 E2 **Sneeker Meer** Netherlands
14 B5 **Sneem** Ireland
89 D8 **Sneeuberg** *mts* S Africa
89 A9 **Sneeukop** *mt* S Africa
29 K4 **Snekkersten** Denmark
102 D4 **Snelling** California U.S.A.
28 B5 **Sneum Å** *R* Denmark
54 L8 **Snezhnoye** U.S.S.R.
31 J5 **Sněžka** *mt* Czechoslovakia
42 F3 **Snežnik** *mt* Yugoslavia
31 N2 **Sniadowo** Poland
31 N2 **Sniardwy, Jezioro** *L* Poland
31 N7 **Snina** Czechoslovakia
118 A3 **Snipe L** Alberta Canada
15 B3 **Snizort, Loch** Scotland
28 F6 **Snøde** Denmark
28 D5 **Snoghøj** Denmark
26 D9 **Snöhetta** *mt* Norway
100 C2 **Snohomish** Washington U.S.A.
28 J5 **Snoldelev** Denmark
127 M3 **Snook Pt** Jamaica
100 D2 **Snoqualmie Pass** Washington U.S.A.
26 G10 **Snössvallen** Sweden
68 H6 **Snoul** Cambodia
54 D4 **Snov** *R* U.S.S.R.
94 D3 **Snover** Michigan U.S.A.
116 L6 **Snowcap Mt** Alaska U.S.A.
119 N5 **Snowden** Saskatchewan Canada
100 B8 **Snowden** California U.S.A.
8 B1 **Snowdon** *mt* Wales
114 H5 **Snowdrift** Northwest Territories Canada
119 T9 **Snowflake** Manitoba Canada
103 O7 **Snowflake** Arizona U.S.A.
95 M8 **Snow Hill** Maryland U.S.A.
112 K2 **Snow Hill** North Carolina U.S.A.
146 D4 **Snow Hill I** Antarctica
146 C3 **Snow I** S Shetland Is Antarctica
119 R4 **Snow Lake** Manitoba Canada
111 E7 **Snow Lake** Arkansas U.S.A.
106 C2 **Snowmass Mt** Colorado U.S.A.
121 O8 **Snow Road** Ontario Canada
94 K5 **Snow Shoe** Pennsylvania U.S.A.
100 K1 **Snowshoe Pk** *mt* Montana U.S.A.
138 E5 **Snowtown** South Australia Australia
101 N8 **Snowville** Utah U.S.A.
103 K1 **Snow Water L** Nevada U.S.A.
139 J6 **Snowy Mts** Vict/N S W Australia
48 K2 **Snyatyn** U.S.S.R.
98 K8 **Snyder** Nebraska U.S.A.
107 M7 **Snyder** Oklahoma U.S.A.
108 G3 **Snyder** Texas U.S.A.
27 H12 **Snyten** Sweden
143 E6 **Soakage Well** Western Australia Australia
144 A6 **Soaker, Mt** New Zealand
87 H11 **Soalala** Madagascar
40 G7 **Soana, Val di** Italy
87 H11 **Soanierana Ivongo** Madagascar
65 G7 **Soan kundo** *isld* S Korea
100 F2 **Soap Lake** Washington U.S.A.
48 J5 **Soarş** Romania
71 A2 **Soa-Siu** Halmahera Indonesia
45 K1 **Soave** Italy
15 B3 **Soay** Scotland
41 K5 **Soazza** Switzerland
85 F6 **Soba** Nigeria
86 F4 **Sobat** *prov* Sudan
86 F4 **Sobat** *R* Sudan
36 D4 **Sobernheim** W Germany
31 H6 **Soběslav** Czechoslovakia
54 M1 **Sobinka** U.S.S.R.
53 H8 **Sobolevo** U.S.S.R.
60 E13 **Sobo-san** *mt* Japan
38 M8 **Soboth** Austria
31 K5 **Sobótka** Poland
129 K6 **Sobradinho, Barragem de** *res* Brazil
129 K4 **Sobral** Brazil
48 G2 **Sobrance** Czechoslovakia
18 F10 **Sobrarbe** *dist* Spain
68 H1 **Soc Bang Giang** *R* Vietnam
68 H1 **Soc Giang** Vietnam
31 M3 **Sochaczew** Poland
40 E2 **Sochaux** France
53 E11 **Sochi** U.S.S.R.
112 D4 **Social Circle** Georgia U.S.A.
112 H3 **Society Hill** South Carolina U.S.A.
135 M10 **Society Is** Pacific Oc
Socna *see* **Sūknah**
128 E8 **Socompa** *vol* Chile/Arg
130 F8 **Socorro** Brazil
108 A1 **Socorro** New Mexico U.S.A.
133 B6 **Socorro, I** Chile
Socotra *see* **Suqutrá**
17 F5 **Socuéllamos** Spain
117 M9 **Soda Creek** British Columbia Canada
103 H6 **Soda L** California U.S.A.
29 M4 **Sodankylä** Finland
101 O7 **Soda Springs** Idaho U.S.A.
102 F3 **Sodaville** Nevada U.S.A.
112 B2 **Soddy-Daisy** Tennessee U.S.A.
36 F3 **Södel** W Germany
27 K12 **Söderby-Karl** Sweden
26 J9 **Söderfjärden** Sweden
27 J11 **Söderfors** Sweden
27 J10 **Söderhamn** Sweden
27 H13 **Söderköping** Sweden
27 H12 **Södermanland** *reg* Sweden
27 J12 **Södertälje** Sweden
86 E3 **Sodiri** Sudan
86 G4 **Sodo** Ethiopia
95 K3 **Sodus** New York U.S.A.
89 H6 **Sodwana B** S Africa
71 M9 **Soë** Timor Indonesia
60 D12 **Soeda** Japan
87 E10 **Soekmekaar** S Africa
52 B5 **Soela Väin** *chan* U.S.S.R.
25 D4 **Soest** Netherlands
32 H9 **Soest** W Germany
32 G7 **Soeste** *R* W Germany
46 E5 **Sofádhes** Greece
Sofala *see* **Beira** Mozambique
139 J5 **Sofala** New Scuth Wales Australia
79 F5 **Sofar** Lebanon
Sofia *see* **Sofiya**
87 H11 **Sofia** *R* Madagascar
106 G5 **Sofia** New Mexico U.S.A.
46 F7 **Sofikón** Greece
46 F2 **Sofiya** Bulgaria
36 H7 **Söflingen** W Germany
52 D2 **Sofporog** U.S.S.R.
75 P3 **Sog** China
128 D2 **Sogamoso** Colombia
32 G7 **Sögel** W Germany
45 M3 **Sogliano al Rubicone** Italy
27 B10 **Sogn** *reg* Norway
27 C13 **Søgne** Norway
27 B10 **Sognefjorden** *inlet* Norway
26 B10 **Sogn og Fjordane** Norway
71 G5 **Sogod** Philippines
55 E1 **Sogom** U.S.S.R.
78 C1 **Söğüt** Turkey
47 K7 **Söğüt** Turkey
47 K7 **Söğüt Gölü** *L* Turkey
84 J4 **Sohâg** Egypt
75 J7 **Sohagpur** India
9 G3 **Soham** England
137 L3 **Sohano** Bougainville I Papua New Guinea
68 D5 **Sohng Gwe, Khao** *mt* Burma/Thailand
36 H1 **Söhrewald** W Germany
65 F7 **Sohŭksan** *isld* S Korea
22 G2 **Soignies** Belgium
21 O7 **Soings-en-Sologne** France
29 L9 **Soini** Finland
22 E5 **Soissons** France
60 G11 **Sōja** Japan
74 E6 **Sojat** India
71 F6 **Sojoton Pt** Philippines
53 H7 **Sok** *R* U.S.S.R.
78 A3 **Soke** Turkey
46 F4 **Sokhós** Greece
48 L2 **Sokiryany** U.S.S.R.
46 E1 **Soko Banja** Yugoslavia
85 E7 **Sokodé** Togo
52 F5 **Sokol** U.S.S.R.
31 O2 **Sokółka** Poland
31 L4 **Sokolniki** Poland
85 C6 **Sokolo** Mali
37 O3 **Sokolov** Czechoslovakia
55 E3 **Sokolovka** U.S.S.R.
52 J2 **Sokolovo** U.S.S.R.
31 N5 **Sokołów Małopolski** Poland
31 N3 **Sokołów Podlaski** Poland
52 D2 **Sokolozero** U.S.S.R.
52 F6 **Sokol'skoye** U.S.S.R.
31 O3 **Sokoły** Poland
115 R4 **Søkongen Ø** *isld* Greenland
61 Q12 **Sokoniya** Okinawa
85 F6 **Sokoto** *R* Nigeria
85 F6 **Sokoto** Nigeria
56 C3 **Sokur** U.S.S.R.

Spy Hill — Stuart, Mt

81

119 Q8 Spy Hill Saskatchewan Canada
117 M11 Squamish British Columbia Canada
95 Q3 Squam L New Hampshire U.S.A.
95 S7 Squapan L Maine U.S.A.
101 P2 Square Butte Montana U.S.A.
95 S6 Square L Maine U.S.A.
122 D6 Squattack Quebec Canada
123 L3 Squaw L Quebec Canada
99 M2 Squaw L Minnesota U.S.A.
119 O5 Squaw Rapids Saskatchewan Canada
43 H10 Squillace, Golfo di Italy
43 J8 Squinzano Italy
138 C2 Squires, Mt N Terr Australia
143 G7 Squires,Mt Western Australia Australia
120 F2 Squirrel R Ontario Canada
116 G3 Squirrel R Alaska U.S.A.
70 N9 Sragen Java
46 D2 Srbica Yugoslavia
46 D1 Srbija Yugoslavia
48 F5 Srbobran Yugoslavia
68 F7 Srê Âmbêl Cambodia
46 C1 Srebrenica Yugoslavia
47 J2 Sredetska R Bulgaria
46 G2 Sredna Gora Bulgaria
51 K2 Sredne-Sibirskoye Ploskogor'ye tableland U.S.S.R.
52 D2 Sredneye Kuyto, Oz L U.S.S.R.
58 G1 Sredniy Kalar U.S.S.R.
55 C3 Sredniy Ural ra U.S.S.R.
53 F10 Sredniy Yegorlyk U.S.S.R.
46 G2 Srednogorie Bulgaria
53 F9 Srednyaya Akhtuba U.S.S.R.
55 G2 Sred Vasyugan U.S.S.R.
68 H6 Sre Khtum Cambodia
31 K3 Srem Poland
48 F6 Srem Mitrovica Yugoslavia
48 E6 Srem Raca Yugoslavia
48 F5 Sremski Karlovci Yugoslavia
58 G1 Sretensk U.S.S.R.
74 F4 Sri Düngargarh India
76 F1 Srikakulam India
76 D4 Sri Kālahasti India
83 Sri Lanka rep S Asia
74 F1 Srinagar Kashmir
68 E5 Srinagarind Dam Thailand
76 B4 Sringeri India
76 C6 Srivilliputtur India
42 H4 Srnetica Yugoslavia
31 K3 Sroda Poland
31 K4 Sroda Sląska Poland
76 F1 Srungavarapukota India
141 F3 Staaten R Queensland Australia
141 F3 Staaten River Nat. Park Queensland Australia
26 O1 Stabbursely R Norway
33 Q4 Stäbelow East Germany
100 D4 Stabler Washington U.S.A.
28 A4 Staby Denmark
120 J5 Stackpool Ontario Canada
15 D1 Stack Skerry isld Scotland
14 B4 Stack's Mts Ireland
16 E4 Sta. Cruz del Retamar Spain
100 E9 Stacy California U.S.A.
112 L3 Stacy North Carolina U.S.A.
32 K5 Stade W Germany
22 E2 Staden Belgium
36 F3 Staden W Germany
9 E4 Stadhampton England
28 A4 Stadil Denmark
28 A4 Stadil Fjord inlet Denmark
26 A9 Stadlandet Norway
25 G2 Stadskanaal Netherlands
36 F2 Stadt Allendorf W Germany
37 N5 Stadtamhof W Germany
37 K7 Stadtbergen W Germany
32 K8 Stadthagen W Germany
37 L2 Stadtilm East Germany
36 B3 Stadtkyll W Germany
32 H6 Stadtland W Germany
37 J3 Stadtlauringen W Germany
37 J2 Stadtlengsfeld East Germany
32 E8 Stadtlohn W Germany
32 L9 Stadtoldendorf W Germany
36 G4 Stadtprozelten W Germany
37 M2 Stadtroda East Germany
37 J4 Stadt Schwarzach W Germany
37 M3 Stadtsteinach W Germany
15 B4 Staffa isld Scotland
33 R7 Staffelde East Germany
37 L3 Staffelstein W Germany
44 F2 Staffora R Italy
141 K1 Stafford dist Brisbane, Qnsld Australia
8 D2 Stafford England
107 M4 Stafford Kansas U.S.A.
98 H7 Stafford Nebraska U.S.A.
94 K8 Stafford Virginia U.S.A.
8 D2 Staffordshire co England
95 P5 Stafford Springs Connecticut U.S.A.
70 E6 Stagen Kalimantan
117 Q4 Stagg L Northwest Territories Canada
45 H4 Stagno Italy
9 F3 Stagsden England
33 S4 Stahlbrode East Germany
33 S8 Stahnsdorf East Germany
52 B5 Staicele U.S.S.R.
38 K6 Stainach Austria
9 F5 Staines England
12 D3 Stair Scotland
13 H4 Staithes England
48 G2 Stakčín Czechoslovakia
53 E9 Stakhanov U.S.S.R.
28 B5 Stakroge Denmark
46 E1 Stalać Yugoslavia
27 J12 Stålboga Sweden
8 D6 Stalbridge England
9 H2 Stalham England
27 B11 Stalheim Norway
Stalingrad see Volgograd
117 L6 Stalin, Mt British Columbia Canada
Stalino see Donetsk
38 H8 Stall Austria
37 O5 Stallwang W Germany
119 M7 Stalwart Saskatchewan Canada
13 F6 Stalybridge England
46 G2 Stamboliyski Bulgaria
46 G1 Stamboliyski, Yazovir A. res Bulgaria
141 G5 Stamford Queensland Australia
9 F2 Stamford England
95 O5 Stamford Connecticut U.S.A.
95 N4 Stamford New York U.S.A.
98 E6 Stamford South Dakota U.S.A.
108 H3 Stamford Texas U.S.A.
37 L6 Stammham W Germany
27 A11 Stamnes Norway
Stampalia isld see Astipálaia isld
100 D2 Stampede Washington U.S.A.
94 C8 Stamping Ground Kentucky U.S.A.
87 C10 Stampriet Namibia
25 E6 Stamproij Netherlands
109 O2 Stamps Arkansas U.S.A.
37 O5 Stamsried W Germany
26 G3 Stamsund Norway
94 J8 Stanadsville Virginia U.S.A.
99 M9 Stanberry Missouri U.S.A.
147 Q6 Stanchik U.S.S.R.
118 E7 Standard Alberta Canada
103 O7 Standard Arizona U.S.A.
87 E11 Standerton S Africa
94 D3 Standish Michigan U.S.A.
101 M8 Standrod Utah U.S.A.
100 F4 Stanfield Oregon U.S.A.
110 K2 Stanford Indiana U.S.A.
110 M4 Stanford Kentucky U.S.A.
101 P2 Stanford Montana U.S.A.
9 G4 Stanford-le-Hope England
8 D3 Stanford on Teme England
27 K14 Stånga Sweden
27 E11 Stange Norway
87 F11 Stanger S Africa
45 L1 Stanghella Italy
26 C9 Stangvik Norway
126 F2 Staniard Cr Andros Bahamas
102 D3 Stanislaus R California U.S.A.
Stanislav see Ivano-Frankovsk
46 F2 Stanke Dimitrov Bulgaria
37 P4 Staňkov Czechoslovakia
139 H8 Stanley Tasmania Australia
122 F7 Stanley New Brunswick Canada
131 G8 Stanley Falkland Is
15 E4 Stanley Scotland
101 L5 Stanley Idaho U.S.A.
106 E6 Stanley New Mexico U.S.A.
112 F2 Stanley North Carolina U.S.A.
98 D1 Stanley North Dakota U.S.A.
109 M1 Stanley Oklahoma U.S.A.
94 J8 Stanley Virginia U.S.A.
99 Q5 Stanley Wisconsin U.S.A.
119 M3 Stanley Mission Saskatchewan Canada
139 G8 Stanley, Mt Tasmania Australia
88 B1 Stanley, Mt Uganda/Zaire
86 C6 Stanley Pool Zaire
Stanleyville see Kisangani
118 F7 Stanmore Alberta Canada
145 E2 Stanmore Bay New Zealand
99 T2 Stannard Rock Michigan U.S.A.
13 G3 Stannington England
55 F3 Stanovka U.S.S.R.
55 D2 Stanovoy U.S.S.R.
51 M3 Stanovoy Khrebet mts U.S.S.R.
41 P3 Stans Austria
138 E5 Stansbury South Australia Australia
142 G5 Stansmore Ra Western Australia Australia
9 G4 Stansted England
141 K8 Stanthorpe Queensland Australia
147 J1 Stanton Northwest Territories Canada
99 L9 Stanton Iowa U.S.A.
94 D9 Stanton Kentucky U.S.A.
94 B3 Stanton Michigan U.S.A.
98 J8 Stanton Nebraska U.S.A.
98 E2 Stanton North Dakota U.S.A.
110 G6 Stanton Tennessee U.S.A.
108 F3 Stanton Texas U.S.A.
6 E6 Stanton Banks Atlantic Oc
56 B3 Stantsionno-Oyashinskiy U.S.S.R.
94 B3 Stanwood Michigan U.S.A.
117 M11 Stanwood Washington U.S.A.
41 N3 Stanzach Austria
33 N9 Stapelburg East Germany
25 F3 Staphorst Netherlands
9 E5 Stapleford England
111 J11 Stapleton Alabama U.S.A.
112 E4 Stapleton Georgia U.S.A.
111 F9 Star Mississippi U.S.A.
112 H2 Star North Carolina U.S.A.
109 J4 Star Texas U.S.A.
54 F3 Star' U.S.S.R.
48 F1 Stara L'ubovňa Czechoslovakia
37 O3 Stará-Role Czechoslovakia
53 G7 Staraya Drozhzhanoye U.S.S.R.
53 G8 Staraya Kulatka U.S.S.R.
52 D5 Staraya Russa U.S.S.R.
48 L1 Staraya Sinyava U.S.S.R.
48 L2 Staraya Ushitsa U.S.S.R.
55 E1 Staraya Vorpavla U.S.S.R.
47 H2 Stara Zagora Bulgaria
119 U9 Starbuck Manitoba Canada
99 L4 Starbuck Minnesota U.S.A.
100 G3 Starbuck Washington U.S.A.
135 L9 Starbuck I Pacific Oc
119 N6 Star City Saskatchewan Canada
111 E8 Star City Arkansas U.S.A.
94 A6 Star City Indiana U.S.A.
94 H7 Star City West Virginia U.S.A.
141 G2 Starcke Queensland Australia
8 C6 Starcross England
37 O4 Staré Sedliště Czechoslovakia
31 J2 Stargard Poland
42 H4 Stari Majdan Yugoslavia
31 N6 Starina Czechoslovakia
52 D6 Staritsa U.S.S.R.
103 O10 Stark Arizona U.S.A.
101 L2 Stark Montana U.S.A.
95 Q2 Stark New Hampshire U.S.A.
55 C6 Star Karabutak U.S.S.R.
113 E8 Starke Florida U.S.A.
100 J5 Starkey Idaho U.S.A.
100 G4 Starkey Oregon U.S.A.
109 O5 Starks Louisiana U.S.A.
106 F4 Starkville Colorado U.S.A.
111 H8 Starkville Mississippi U.S.A.
98 H1 Starkweather North Dakota U.S.A.
99 R3 Starlake Wisconsin U.S.A.
41 O1 Starnberg W Germany
56 C4 Starobachati U.S.S.R.
54 K7 Star'obel'sk U.S.S.R.
54 D4 Starodub U.S.S.R.
31 L2 Starogard Poland
48 M4 Starokazach'ye U.S.S.R.
48 L1 Starokonstantinov U.S.S.R.
55 F3 Staromalinovka U.S.S.R.
31 O2 Starosielce Poland
55 F3 Starosoldatskoye U.S.S.R.
55 C4 Starosubkhangulovo U.S.S.R.
55 C3 Staroutkinsk U.S.S.R.
52 G5 Starovercheskaya U.S.S.R.
52 H6 Staroye Baysarovo U.S.S.R.
102 F1 Star Pk Nevada U.S.A.
8 C7 Start Pt England
15 F1 Start Pt Scotland
48 F1 Stary Sącz Poland
52 H6 Staryye Zyattsy U.S.S.R.
52 H6 Staryy Menzelyabash U.S.S.R.
50 G2 Staryy Nadym U.S.S.R.
54 J5 Staryy Oskol U.S.S.R.
52 D5 Staryy Ryad U.S.S.R.
48 H1 Staryy Sambor U.S.S.R.
31 O6 Staryy Sambor U.S.S.R.
33 P9 Stassfurt East Germany
31 N5 Staszów Poland
99 N7 State Center Iowa U.S.A.
94 K6 State College Pennsylvania U.S.A.
111 H10 State Line Mississippi U.S.A.
Staten I Argentina see Estados, I de los
95 N6 Staten I New York U.S.A.
112 F5 Statesboro Georgia U.S.A.
112 G2 Statesville North Carolina U.S.A.
6 M1 Statfjord oil rig North Sea
27 D12 Stathelle Norway
33 S10 Stauchitz East Germany
36 F2 Staufenberg W Germany
100 E6 Stauffer Oregon U.S.A.
8 D4 Staunton England
110 G2 Staunton Illinois U.S.A.
94 H8 Staunton Virginia U.S.A.
27 A13 Stavanger Norway
22 H3 Stave Belgium
117 M11 Stave L British Columbia Canada
9 E1 Staveley England
13 F5 Staveley Cumbria England
22 K3 Stavelot Belgium
118 D8 Stavely Alberta Canada
33 S5 Staven East Germany
25 B5 Stavenisse Netherlands
28 A5 Stavning Denmark
28 F3 Stavnshoved C Denmark
25 D3 Stavoren Netherlands
28 J6 Stavreby Denmark
28 F6 Stavreshoved C Denmark
53 F10 Stavropol' U.S.S.R.
55 E4 Stavropolka U.S.S.R.
53 F10 Stavropol'skaya Vozvyshennost' uplands U.S.S.R.
53 F11 Stavropol'skiy Kray reg U.S.S.R.
46 E5 Stavrós Greece
46 G9 Stavrós, Akra C Crete Greece
46 G3 Stavroúpolis Greece
139 G6 Stawell Victoria Australia
31 N2 Stawiski Poland
31 L4 Stawiszyn Poland
120 K8 Stayner Ontario Canada
100 C5 Stayton Oregon U.S.A.
45 H4 Stazzema Italy
102 E2 Steamboat Nevada U.S.A.
106 D1 Steamboat Springs Colorado U.S.A.
94 C10 Stearns Kentucky U.S.A.
31 M2 Stębark Poland
116 F5 Stebbins Alaska U.S.A.
33 Q7 Stechow East Germany
41 J2 Steckborn Switzerland
28 B7 Stedesand W Germany
116 R4 Steel Creek Alaska U.S.A.
111 K8 Steele Alabama U.S.A.
110 G5 Steele Missouri U.S.A.
98 G3 Steele North Dakota U.S.A.
98 K9 Steele City Nebraska U.S.A.
146 D5 Steele I Antarctica
117 C5 Steele,Mt Yukon Territory Canada
110 G3 Steeleville Illinois U.S.A.
120 D4 Steel R Ontario Canada
95 L6 Steelton Pennsylvania U.S.A.
110 E4 Steelville Missouri U.S.A.
25 B5 Steenbergen Netherlands
89 G5 Steenkamps Berg mts S Africa
22 G2 Steenkerque Belgium
117 P6 Steen River Alberta Canada
25 D6 Steensel Netherlands
100 G7 Steens Mt Oregon U.S.A.
115 O2 Steenstrup Gletscher gla Greenland
22 D2 Steenvoorde France
22 D2 Steenwerck France
25 F3 Steenwijk Netherlands
119 M5 Steep Cr Saskatchewan Canada
119 O3 Steephill L Saskatchewan Canada
131 F7 Steeple Jason isld Falkland Is
71 D6 Steep Pt Philippines
119 T7 Steep Rock Manitoba Canada
118 K2 Steep Rock Ontario Canada
143 B6 Steere, Mt Western Australia Australia
13 G6 Steeton England
48 L3 Ştefăneşti Romania
43 F10 Stefano di Cam., S Sicily
146 K10 Stefansson B Antarctica
147 H3 Stefansson I Northwest Territories Canada
133 C6 Steffen mt Chile/Arg
36 F2 Steffenberg W Germany
98 C8 Stegall Nebraska U.S.A.
28 J7 Stege Denmark
28 J6 Stege Bugt B Denmark
33 P8 Stegelitz East Germany
29 K7 Stege Nor L Denmark
99 T8 Steger Illinois U.S.A.
87 F11 Stegi Swaziland
33 S8 Steglitz W Berlin
100 E1 Stehekin Washington U.S.A.
38 L7 Steiermark prov Austria
37 J4 Steigerwald hil's W Germany
37 L5 Stein W Germany
37 L3 Steinach East Germany
37 J5 Steinach W Germany
36 H3 Steinau W Germany
99 K9 Steinauer Nebraska U.S.A.
118 E1 Steinbach Manitoba Canada
37 J2 Steinbach East Germany
36 E6 Steinbach W Germany
37 K2 Steinbach Hallenberg East Germany
28 D7 Steinberg W Germany
38 G6 Steinberge Austria
36 C6 Steinbourg France
129 H6 Steinen R Brazil
38 G7 Steinernes Meer mts Austria
32 H7 Steinfeld W Germany
22 K4 Steinfort Luxembourg
32 H8 Steinhagen W Germany
113 D8 Steinhatchee Florida U.S.A.
87 C10 Steinhausen Namibia
37 L3 Steinheid East Germany
36 F3 Steinheim W Germany
33 M5 Steinhorst W Germany
32 K8 Steinhuder Meer L W Germany
32 L5 Steinkirchen W Germany
26 E8 Steinkjer Norway
87 C11 Steinkopf S Africa
38 L7 Steinplan mt Austria
106 B9 Steins New Mexico U.S.A.
36 F5 Steinsfurt W Germany
37 L3 Steinwiesen W Germany
22 G1 Stekene Belgium
99 L9 Stella Nebraska U.S.A.
112 K3 Stella North Carolina U.S.A.
122 K8 Stellarton Nova Scotia Canada
45 K2 Stellata Italy
32 M6 Stelle W Germany
87 C12 Stellenbosch S Africa
116 Q6 Steller, Mt Alaska U.S.A.
42 D2 Stelvio, Passo di Italy
112 J1 Stem North Carolina U.S.A.
32 K7 Stemmen W Germany
26 C8 Stemshaug Norway
32 H8 Stemwede W Germany
22 J5 Stenay France
28 A3 Stenbjerg Denmark
33 P7 Stendal East Germany
52 B6 Stende U.S.S.R.
28 D5 Stenderup Denmark
28 D7 Stenderup W Germany
119 P7 Stenen Saskatchewan Canada
28 E2 Stenhöj Denmark
138 D6 Stenhouse B South Australia Australia
28 D3 Stenild Denmark
28 H5 Stenlille Denmark
28 J5 Stenløse Denmark
15 G2 Stenness Shetland Scotland
15 E1 Stenness,L.of Orkney Scotland
47 P13 Stenón Kerkíras, Vório chan Greece/Albania
26 J6 Stensele Sweden
27 G14 Stensjön Sweden
27 G13 Stenstorp Sweden
28 E6 Stenstrup Denmark
26 L5 Stenträsk Sweden
27 E13 Stenungsund Sweden
28 F4 Stenvad Denmark
78 L2 Stepanakert U.S.S.R.
78 K1 Stepanavan U.S.S.R.
55 C5 Stepanovka U.S.S.R.
33 O5 Stepenitz R East Germany
33 P6 Stepenitz R East Germany
37 O6 Stephansposching W Germany
98 K1 Stephen Minnesota U.S.A.
109 O2 Stephens Arkansas U.S.A.
94 J7 Stephens City Virginia U.S.A.
138 F4 Stephens Creek New South Wales Australia
117 H8 Stephens I British Columbia Canada
115 K6 Stephens L Manitoba Canada
119 W2 Stephens L Manitoba Canada
99 T4 Stephenson Michigan U.S.A.
145 D1 Stephenson I New Zealand
117 G7 Stephens Pass Alaska U.S.A.
123 O5 Stephenville Newfoundland Canada
109 J3 Stephenville Texas U.S.A.
123 O5 Stephenville Crossing Newfoundland Canada
57 D5 Step' Karnabchul' U.S.S.R.
55 F5 Stepnogorsk U.S.S.R.
57 G3 Stepnoye U.S.S.R.
55 F4 Stepnyak U.S.S.R.
116 G9 Stepovak B Alaska U.S.A.
28 C6 Stepping Denmark
103 K2 Steptoe Nevada U.S.A.
36 H3 Sterbfritz W Germany
87 E12 Sterkstroom S Africa
108 F1 Sterley Texas U.S.A.
55 C4 Sterlibashevo U.S.S.R.
106 G1 Sterling Colorado U.S.A.
99 R8 Sterling Illinois U.S.A.
107 M3 Sterling Kansas U.S.A.
94 C2 Sterling Michigan U.S.A.
98 K9 Sterling Nebraska U.S.A.
98 F3 Sterling North Dakota U.S.A.
109 J1 Sterling Oklahoma U.S.A.
103 N2 Sterling Utah U.S.A.
108 G4 Sterling City Texas U.S.A.
94 D4 Sterling Heights Michigan U.S.A.
55 C4 Sterlitamak U.S.S.R.
33 P5 Sternberg East Germany
31 K6 Šternberk Czechoslovakia
22 H2 Sterrebeek Belgium
52 E4 Steshevskaya U.S.S.R.
31 K3 Stęszew Poland
46 D1 Stet Yugoslavia
41 K1 Stetten W Germany
Stettin see Szczecin
33 U5 Stettiner Haff East Germany
118 E6 Stettler Alberta Canada
99 U3 Steuben Michigan U.S.A.
99 Q6 Steuben Wisconsin U.S.A.
94 G6 Steubenville Ohio U.S.A.
33 Q9 Steutz East Germany
9 F4 Stevenage England
120 E3 Stevens Ontario Canada
145 D4 Stevens, Mt New Zealand
138 C2 Stevenson R South Australia Australia
119 U9 Stevenson Manitoba Canada
110 L7 Stevenson Alabama U.S.A.
100 D4 Stevenson Washington U.S.A.
119 W5 Stevenson L Manitoba Canada
99 R5 Stevens Pt Wisconsin U.S.A.
12 D2 Stevenston Scotland
116 N4 Stevens Village Alaska U.S.A.
94 A4 Stevensville Michigan U.S.A.
32 F9 Stever R W Germany
118 F8 Steveville Prov.Pk Alberta Canada
29 K6 Stevns pen Denmark
22 J2 Stevoort Belgium
99 S8 Steward Illinois U.S.A.
110 H2 Stewardson Illinois U.S.A.
141 G2 Stewart R Queensland Australia
117 H8 Stewart British Columbia Canada
117 D4 Stewart Yukon Territory Canada
99 M5 Stewart Minnesota U.S.A.
102 E2 Stewart Nevada U.S.A.
140 C1 Stewart, C N Terr Australia
144 A7 Stewart I New Zealand
137 N3 Stewart Is Pacific Oc
143 C10 Stewart, Mt Western Australia Australia
15 D5 Stewarton Scotland
95 L7 Stewartstown Pennsylvania U.S.A.
110 B2 Stewartsville Missouri U.S.A.
127 K2 Stewart Town Jamaica
118 K8 Stewart Valley Saskatchewan Canada
99 O6 Stewartville Minnesota U.S.A.
122 J8 Stewiacke Nova Scotia Canada
32 K7 Steyerberg W Germany
9 F6 Steyning England
8 A4 Steynton Wales
38 K5 Steyr Austria
121 S7 St-Hyacinthe Quebec Canada
45 L4 Stia Italy
8 B6 Stibb Cross England
100 K5 Stibnite Idaho U.S.A.
9 G1 Stickford England
32 G6 Stickhausen W Germany
9 G1 Stickney England
98 H6 Stickney South Dakota U.S.A.
33 N9 Stiege East Germany
25 E2 Stiens Netherlands
45 L2 Stienta Italy
107 P6 Stigler Oklahoma U.S.A.
43 G8 Stigliano Italy
26 J9 Stigsjö Sweden
117 H7 Stikine R Alaska/Br Col U.S.A./Canada
117 H6 Stikine Ranges British Columbia Canada
117 G7 Stikine Str Alaska U.S.A.
108 F4 Stiles Texas U.S.A.
110 K2 Stilesville Indiana U.S.A.
46 F6 Stilís Greece
28 D4 Stilling Denmark
13 G5 Stillington England
99 R7 Stillman Valley Illinois U.S.A.
99 O4 Stillwater Minnesota U.S.A.
101 L1 Stillwater R Montana U.S.A.
102 F2 Stillwater Nevada U.S.A.
107 N5 Stillwater Oklahoma U.S.A.
102 F2 Stillwater Ra Nevada U.S.A.
43 H10 Stilo, Pta Italy
48 J5 Stîlpeni Romania
110 B6 Stilwell Oklahoma U.S.A.
46 E7 Stimfalias, L Greece
101 M1 Stimson,Mt Montana U.S.A.
12 D3 Stinchar,R Scotland
98 E9 Stinking Water Cr Nebraska U.S.A.
46 E3 Štip Yugoslavia
46 G6 Stíra Greece
Stirling co see Strathclyde and Central regions
140 C5 Stirling N Terr Australia
138 E5 Stirling South Australia Australia
118 E9 Stirling Alberta Canada
121 N8 Stirling Ontario Canada
144 B7 Stirling New Zealand
12 E1 Stirling Scotland
100 D10 Stirling City California U.S.A.
143 C9 Stirling, Mt Western Australia Australia
143 C10 Stirling Ra Western Australia Australia
44 H2 Stirone R Italy
98 J3 Stirum North Dakota U.S.A.
100 K3 Stites Idaho U.S.A.
119 V3 Stitt Manitoba Canada
99 Q7 Stitzer Wisconsin U.S.A.
27 K14 Stjärnarve Sweden
26 N1 Stjernöya isld Norway
26 E8 Stjördalselv R Norway
26 E8 Stjördalshalsen Norway
18 E6 St-Maixent-l'École France
121 R5 St-Maurice, Parc Quebec Canada
13 E2 Stobo Scotland
41 K2 Stockach W Germany
27 G14 Stockaryd Sweden
9 E5 Stockbridge England
95 O4 Stockbridge Massachusetts U.S.A.
94 C4 Stockbridge Michigan U.S.A.
94 E8 Stockdale Ohio U.S.A.
109 K6 Stockdale Texas U.S.A.
33 N5 Stockelsdorf W Germany
48 C2 Stockerau Austria
36 B6 Stock,Etang du L France
101 O2 Stockett Montana U.S.A.
98 J9 Stockham Nebraska U.S.A.
37 L3 Stockheim W Germany
119 P8 Stockholm Saskatchewan Canada
27 K12 Stockholm Sweden
27 J12 Stockholm county Sweden
95 S6 Stockholm Maine U.S.A.
40 G4 Stockhorn mt Switzerland
139 J5 Stockinbingal New South Wales Australia
13 F6 Stockport England
94 F7 Stockport Ohio U.S.A.
139 K5 Stockton New South Wales Australia
119 S9 Stockton Manitoba Canada
144 C4 Stockton New Zealand
111 J10 Stockton Alabama U.S.A.
102 C4 Stockton California U.S.A.
99 Q7 Stockton Illinois U.S.A.
107 L2 Stockton Kansas U.S.A.
95 M8 Stockton Maryland U.S.A.
110 C4 Stockton Missouri U.S.A.
101 N9 Stockton Utah U.S.A.
99 Q3 Stockton I Wisconsin U.S.A.
116 O1 Stockton Is Alaska U.S.A.
110 C4 Stockton L Missouri U.S.A.
13 G4 Stockton-on-Tees England
95 T2 Stockton Springs Maine U.S.A.
98 F9 Stockville Nebraska U.S.A.
31 N4 Stoczek Łukowski Poland
37 P4 Stod Czechoslovakia
26 E7 Stod Norway
99 P6 Stoddard Wisconsin U.S.A.
26 J9 Stöde Sweden
68 H6 Stoeng Treng Cambodia
15 C2 Stoer,Pt of Scotland
28 C4 Stoholm Denmark
145 D4 Stoke New Zealand
9 G2 Stoke Ferry England
8 C7 Stoke Fleming England
9 F4 Stokenchurch England
8 D1 Stoke-on-Trent England
120 J7 Stokes Bay Ontario Canada
112 H1 Stokesdale North Carolina U.S.A.
143 D10 Stokes Inlet Western Australia Australia
145 E4 Stokes, Mt New Zealand
139 G8 Stokes Pt Tasmania Australia
140 B3 Stokes Ra N Terr Australia
53 C8 Stokhod R U.S.S.R.
28 G7 Stokkemarke Denmark
28 S10 Stokkseyri Iceland
26 D7 Stokksund Norway
26 G3 Stokmarknes Norway
42 H5 Stolac Yugoslavia
33 N9 Stolberg East Germany
25 F7 Stolberg W Germany
147 Q8 Stolbovoy,Ostrov U.S.S.R.
48 F2 Stolica mt Czechoslovakia
37 O2 Stollberg East Germany
32 H5 Stollhamm W Germany
Stolp see Słupsk
90 A16 Stoltenhoff I Tristan da Cunha
32 K7 Stolzenau W Germany
36 D3 Stolzenfels W Germany
46 F5 Stómion Greece
36 B1 Stommeln W Germany
8 D2 Stone England
94 G5 Stoneboro Pennsylvania U.S.A.
9 E3 Stonebridge England
106 F3 Stone City Colorado U.S.A.
121 N6 Stonecliffe Ontario Canada
100 F7 Stone Corral L Oregon U.S.A.
122 A7 Stoneham Quebec Canada
98 C9 Stoneham Colorado U.S.A.
95 N7 Stone Harbor New Jersey U.S.A.
15 F4 Stonehaven Scotland
141 G6 Stonehenge Queensland Australia
9 E5 Stonehenge anc mon England
8 D4 Stonehouse England
99 P4 Stone L Wisconsin U.S.A.
112 C4 Stone Mt Georgia U.S.A.
117 L6 Stone Mt. Prov. Park British Columbia Canada
110 K6 Stones River Nat. Battlefield Tennessee U.S.A.
118 D1 Stonewall Manitoba Canada
111 H9 Stonewall Mississippi U.S.A.
109 L1 Stonewall Oklahoma U.S.A.
109 J5 Stonewall Texas U.S.A.
121 L9 Stoney Creek Ontario Canada
12 D4 Stoneykirk Scotland
26 J2 Stonglandet Norway
106 H4 Stonington Colorado U.S.A.
95 Q5 Stonington Connecticut U.S.A.
99 R10 Stonington Illinois U.S.A.
95 T2 Stonington Maine U.S.A.
119 M8 Stony Beach Saskatchewan Canada
94 K10 Stony Creek Virginia U.S.A.
8 D3 Stony Cross England
102 B2 Stonyford California U.S.A.
127 L2 Stony Hill Jamaica
118 D1 Stony Mountain Manitoba Canada
118 D5 Stony Plain Alberta Canada
95 N5 Stony Point New York U.S.A.
112 F2 Stony Point North Carolina U.S.A.
144 C6 Stony R New Zealand
114 J6 Stony Rapids Saskatchewan Canada
116 J6 Stony River Alaska U.S.A.
9 F3 Stony Stratford England
120 H1 Stooping R Ontario Canada
32 L4 Stör R W Germany
28 C4 Storå R Denmark
27 H12 Storå Sweden
26 G8 Storåbränna Sweden
6 F1 Stóra Dimun isld Faeroes
27 E12 Stora Le L Sweden
26 L5 Stora Lule älv R Sweden
26 K4 Stora Lulevatten L Sweden
26 F9 Storån R Sweden
26 J4 Stora Sjoffallet L Sweden
26 K6 Storavan L Sweden
26 K6 Storberg Sweden
27 L11 Storby Finland
27 A12 Stord Norway
26 B9 Stordal Möre og Romsdal Norway
26 E8 Stordal Sör-Tröndelag Norway
28 D3 Store Arden Denmark
28 F5 Store Bælt chan Denmark
26 G6 Store Börgefjeld mt Norway
27 H14 Storebro Sweden
28 B6 Store Darum Denmark
28 G5 Store Fuglede Denmark
29 K6 Store Heddinge Denmark
28 C7 Store Jyndevad Denmark
29 K7 Storeklint cliffs Denmark
147 F10 Store Koldewey isld Greenland
26 P1 Storelv R Norway
27 E10 Stor-Elvdal Norway
29 K5 Store Magleby Denmark
28 H5 Store Merløse Denmark
26 R1 Store Molvik Norway
26 D8 Stören Norway
28 E7 Store Rise Denmark
28 J6 Store Spjellerup Denmark
28 J6 Store Tårnby Denmark
28 D2 Store Vildmose Denmark
26 H6 Storfjellet,N mt Sweden
26 G6 Storfjellet,S mt Sweden
26 B9 Storfjord inlet Norway
26 G5 Storfosshei Norway
26 H8 Storhögen Sweden
26 A9 Storholmen Norway
26 G7 Storjorm L Sweden
33 P5 Störkanal East Germany
114 G3 Storkerson B Northwest Territories Canada
26 F8 Storlien Sweden
26 K7 Storlögda Sweden
32 L5 Stormarn reg W Germany
139 J9 Storm B Tasmania Australia
89 E8 Stormberge mts S Africa
99 L7 Storm L Iowa U.S.A.
118 K1 Stormy L Ontario Canada
119 P7 Stornoway Saskatchewan Canada
15 B2 Stornoway Scotland
52 H4 Storozhevsk U.S.S.R.
48 K2 Storozhinets U.S.S.R.
26 F8 Storrensjön L Sweden
9 F6 Storrington England
15 B3 Storr,The mt Scotland
27 E11 Stor-s L Norway
26 L7 Storsävarträsk Sweden
26 F9 Storsjö Sweden
27 E10 Stor-sjöen L Norway
27 F10 Storsjøen Sweden
27 J11 Storsjön L Gävleborg Sweden
26 F9 Storsjön L Jämtland Sweden
28 H6 Storstrøm co Denmark
28 H7 Storstrømmen chan Denmark
119 Q9 Storthoaks Saskatchewan Canada
26 J6 Storuman Sweden
27 G10 Storvarden mt Sweden
26 F9 Storvigelen mt Norway
27 J11 Storvik Sweden
26 J6 Stor-vindein L Sweden
28 E2 Storvorde Denmark
101 T5 Story Wyoming U.S.A.
99 N7 Story City Iowa U.S.A.
133 B7 Stosch, I Chile
37 M1 Stössen East Germany
26 F5 Stött Norway
41 N2 Stotten W Germany
37 L1 Stotternheim East Germany
28 D5 Stouby Denmark
121 L9 Stouffville Ontario Canada
119 O9 Stoughton Saskatchewan Canada
95 Q4 Stoughton Massachusetts U.S.A.
99 R7 Stoughton Wisconsin U.S.A.
22 K3 Stoumont Belgium
46 E4 Stoupi Greece
8 D3 Stourbridge England
8 D3 Stourport England
9 H5 Stour,R England
8 D3 Stourton England
94 E7 Stoutsville Ohio U.S.A.
28 E3 Støvring Denmark
28 D3 Støvring Denmark
13 F2 Stow Scotland
95 P2 Stowe Vermont U.S.A.
109 N6 Stowell Texas U.S.A.
9 G3 Stowmarket England
9 E4 Stow on the Wold England
28 E6 Stoy Denmark
59 K1 Stoyba U.S.S.R.
46 C2 Stožac mt Yugoslavia
45 M1 Stra Italy
33 R9 Straach East Germany
14 D2 Strabane N Ireland
12 C1 Strachur Scotland
14 D3 Stradbally Ireland
44 F1 Stradella Italy
38 N8 Straden Austria
9 G2 Stradsett England
25 F6 Straelen W Germany
110 C4 Strafford Missouri U.S.A.
139 H8 Strahan Tasmania Australia
103 N4 Straight Cliffs Utah U.S.A.
22 J4 Straimont Belgium
12 D3 Straiton Scotland
30 H6 Strakonice Czechoslovakia
47 H2 Straldzha Bulgaria
33 S4 Stralsund East Germany
27 E10 Strand Hedmark Norway
27 A12 Strand Rogaland Norway
89 A10 Strand S Africa
26 B9 Stranda Norway
28 C3 Strandby Nordjylland Denmark
28 F2 Strandby Vendsyssel Denmark
98 J9 Strang Nebraska U.S.A.
113 J10 Strangers Cay isld Bahamas
14 F2 Strangford N Ireland
14 F2 Strangford L N Ireland
27 J12 Strängnäs Sweden
27 H13 Strångsjö Sweden
140 C3 Strangways R N Terr Australia
140 C6 Strangways Ra N Terr Australia
14 D2 Stranorlar Ireland
118 J7 Stranraer Saskatchewan Canada
12 C4 Stranraer Scotland
119 N7 Strasbourg Saskatchewan Canada
36 D6 Strasbourg France
33 T5 Strasburg East Germany
106 F2 Strasburg Colorado U.S.A.
110 H2 Strasburg Illinois U.S.A.
98 F3 Strasburg North Dakota U.S.A.
94 F6 Strasburg Ohio U.S.A.
94 J8 Strasburg Virginia U.S.A.
48 M3 Strasheny U.S.S.R.
38 N8 Strass Steiermark Austria
38 E7 Strass Tirol Austria
27 H12 Stråssa Sweden
38 K8 Strassburg Austria
36 C2 Strassenhaus W Germany
38 M7 Strassgang Austria
37 O6 Strasskirchen W Germany
38 H6 Strasswalchen Austria
139 H7 Stratford Victoria Australia
122 A8 Stratford Quebec Canada
145 E3 Stratford New Zealand
95 O5 Stratford Connecticut U.S.A.
99 N7 Stratford Iowa U.S.A.
95 Q2 Stratford New Hampshire U.S.A.
109 L1 Stratford Oklahoma U.S.A.
98 H4 Stratford South Dakota U.S.A.
108 B7 Stratford Texas U.S.A.
99 Q5 Stratford Wisconsin U.S.A.
9 E3 Stratford-on-Avon England
9 H4 Stratford St. Mary England
138 E6 Strathalbyn South Australia Australia
15 D5 Strathaven Scotland
12 D2 Strathblane Scotland
15 D2 Strath Brora Scotland
15 D3 Strath Carron Scotland
119 R8 Strathclair Manitoba Canada
15 D5 Strathclyde reg Scotland
117 L11 Strathcona Prov. Park British Columbia Canada
15 E3 Strath Dearn Scotland
15 D3 Strath Farrar Scotland
15 E2 Strath Halladale Scotland
141 G3 Strathleven Queensland Australia
123 L7 Strathlorne Nova Scotia Canada
13 E1 Strathmiglo Scotland
141 G4 Strathmore Queensland Australia
118 D7 Strathmore Alberta Canada
15 E4 Strathmore dist Scotland
117 M9 Strathnaver British Columbia Canada
15 D3 Strathpeffer Scotland
120 J10 Strathroy Ontario Canada
15 D2 Strathy Pt Scotland
12 D1 Strathyre Scotland
8 B6 Stratton England
106 H2 Stratton Colorado U.S.A.
95 R1 Stratton Maine U.S.A.
98 E9 Stratton Nebraska U.S.A.
37 O6 Straubing W Germany
26 G4 Straumen Norway
30 H3 Strausberg East Germany
108 A3 Strauss New Mexico U.S.A.
37 K1 Straussfurt East Germany
101 Q3 Straw Montana U.S.A.
110 E5 Strawberry R Arkansas U.S.A.
103 J2 Strawberry Nevada U.S.A.
100 G5 Strawberry Mt Oregon U.S.A.
99 P7 Strawberry Pt Iowa U.S.A.
101 P9 Strawberry Res Utah U.S.A.
121 R5 Strawhat Depot Quebec Canada
99 S9 Strawn Illinois U.S.A.
109 J3 Strawn Texas U.S.A.
37 O4 Stráž Czechoslovakia
47 H1 Strazhitsa Bulgaria
31 K7 Strážnice Czechoslovakia
31 M6 Štrba Czechoslovakia
138 C5 Streaky B South Australia Australia
118 G5 Streamstown Alberta Canada
9 F5 Streatham England
9 E4 Streatley England
99 S8 Streator Illinois U.S.A.
31 H6 Středočeský reg Czechoslovakia
31 L7 Strědoslovenský reg Czechoslovakia
8 D5 Street England
98 G3 Streeter North Dakota U.S.A.
109 H5 Streeter Texas U.S.A.
109 L4 Streetman Texas U.S.A.
48 H6 Strehaia Romania
33 S10 Strehla East Germany
48 H5 Strei R Romania
143 E9 Streich Mound Western Australia Australia
37 L4 Streitberg W Germany
48 J6 Strejeşti Romania
37 P4 Střela R Czechoslovakia
46 G2 Strelcha Bulgaria
54 K5 Strelitsa U.S.S.R.
33 S6 Strelitz-Alt East Germany
56 D2 Strelka U.S.S.R.
28 B5 Strellev Kirke Denmark
142 C5 Strelley Western Australia Australia
142 C5 Strelley R W Australia
52 E2 Strel'na R U.S.S.R.
52 E2 Strel'na U.S.S.R.
52 C5 Strenči U.S.S.R.
41 M3 Strengen Austria
27 C12 Strengen Norway
13 G5 Strensall England
46 E2 Strešer mt Yugoslavia
54 B4 Streshin U.S.S.R.
9 G3 Stretham England
43 G10 Stretto di Messina Sicily
9 E1 Stretton England
9 F2 Stretton England
8 D1 Stretton England
37 J3 Streu R W Germany
37 K3 Streufdorf East Germany
6 F1 Streymoy isld Faeroes
55 G1 Strezhevoy U.S.S.R.
28 D5 Strib Denmark
37 P4 Stříbro Czechoslovakia
15 F3 Strichen Scotland
120 J3 Strickland Ontario Canada
25 C5 Strijen Netherlands
109 N4 Striker Cr.Res Texas U.S.A.
26 G5 Strimasund Sweden
46 F3 Strimón R Greece
46 F4 Strimonikós,Kólpos G Greece
109 L1 Stringtown Oklahoma U.S.A.
12 C2 Striven,L Scotland
48 E5 Striživojna Yugoslavia
38 H6 Strobl Austria
46 D7 Strofádhes isld Greece
32 J7 Ströhen W Germany
54 H6 Stroitel' U.S.S.R.
14 C3 Strokestown Ireland
33 T6 Strom R East Germany
15 E2 Stroma isld Orkney Scotland
32 H9 Stromberg Nordrhein-Westfalen W Germany
36 D4 Stromberg Rheinland-Pfalz W Germany
43 G10 Stromboli, I Italy
118 E6 Strome Alberta Canada
15 C3 Stromeferry Scotland
26 L7 Strömfors Sweden
15 E2 Stromness Orkney Scotland
131 H6 Stromness S Georgia
131 H6 Stromness B S Georgia
26 J10 Strömsbruck Sweden
98 J8 Stromsburg Nebraska U.S.A.
27 E13 Stromstad Sweden
26 H8 Strömsund Sweden
26 H8 Stromsvattudal L Sweden
12 D1 Stronachlachar Scotland
98 A5 Stroner Wyoming U.S.A.
111 D8 Strong Arkansas U.S.A.
95 R2 Strong Maine U.S.A.
111 H8 Strong Mississippi U.S.A.
107 O3 Strong City Kansas U.S.A.
107 L6 Strong City Oklahoma U.S.A.
118 L7 Strongfield Saskatchewan Canada
99 Q9 Stronghurst Illinois U.S.A.
47 O12 Strongili Greece
43 H9 Strongoli Italy
94 F5 Strongsville Ohio U.S.A.
15 F1 Stronsay Scotland
15 F1 Stronsay Firth Scotland
9 G5 Strood England
31 N6 Stropkov Czechoslovakia
112 F3 Strother South Carolina U.S.A.
139 K4 Stroud New South Wales Australia
8 D4 Stroud England
107 O6 Stroud Oklahoma U.S.A.
139 K4 Stroud Road New South Wales Australia
95 M6 Stroudsburg Pennsylvania U.S.A.
138 F6 Struan South Australia Australia
15 E4 Struan Scotland
32 G6 Strücklingen W Germany
38 L5 Strudengau V Austria
28 B3 Struer Denmark
46 D3 Struga Yugoslavia
52 C5 Strugi-Krasnyye U.S.S.R.
89 B10 Struisbaai S Africa
14 D2 Strule R N Ireland
99 P5 Strum Wisconsin U.S.A.
46 F3 Struma R Bulgaria
8 A3 Strumble Head Wales
46 F3 Strumica Yugoslavia
46 F3 Strumitsa R Yugoslavia
54 K1 Strunino U.S.S.R.
120 E4 Struthers Ontario Canada
94 G5 Struthers Ohio U.S.A.
37 P3 Stružná Czechoslovakia
46 G2 Stryama R Bulgaria
101 L1 Stryker Montana U.S.A.
94 C5 Stryker Ohio U.S.A.
31 M4 Stryków Poland
28 F7 Strynø Denmark
26 B10 Strynvatn L Norway
31 O6 Stryy R U.S.S.R.
48 H1 Stryy U.S.S.R.
31 J5 Strzegom Poland
31 J3 Strzelce Poland
31 L5 Strzelce Poland
138 F3 Strzelecki Cr South Australia Australia
140 C5 Strzelecki, Mt N Terr Australia
139 J8 Strzelecki Pk Tasmania Australia
31 K5 Strzelin Poland
31 L3 Strzelno Poland
31 N6 Strzyżów Poland
141 K7 Stuart R Queensland Australia
113 G10 Stuart Florida U.S.A.
99 M8 Stuart Iowa U.S.A.
98 G7 Stuart Nebraska U.S.A.
109 L1 Stuart Oklahoma U.S.A.
94 G10 Stuart Virginia U.S.A.
140 B6 Stuart Bluff Ra N Terr Australia
138 D3 Stuart Creek South Australia Australia
116 F5 Stuart I Alaska U.S.A.
117 L8 Stuart L British Columbia Canada
100 E2 Stuart, Mt Washington U.S.A.

82

Stuart Mts — Tabernes de Valldigna

144 A6 **Stuart Mts** New Zealand
140 B1 **Stuart Pt** N Terr Australia
138 C3 **Stuart Rge** South Australia Australia
139 J5 **Stuart Town** New South Wales Australia
41 O3 **Stubaier Alpen** *mt* Austria
41 O3 **Stubai Tal** Austria
38 L7 **Stub Alpe** *mts* Austria
28 J7 **Stubbekøbing** Denmark
32 J6 **Stubben** W Germany
28 B4 **Stubbergd Sø** *L* Denmark
28 F4 **Stubbe Sø** *L* Denmark
83 M9 **Stubbings Pt** Christmas I Indian Oc
41 M3 **Stuben** Austria
38 N7 **Stubenberg** Austria
38 M6 **Stübming** *R* Austria
47 H3 **Studen Kladenets, Yazovir** *res* Bulgaria
38 N7 **Studenzen** Austria
140 B5 **Studholme Hills** N Terr Australia
144 C6 **Studholme Junction** New Zealand
144 C6 **Studholme, Mt** New Zealand
46 G1 **Studina** Romania
9 E6 **Studland** England
28 B4 **Studsgård** Denmark
26 H8 **Stugun** Sweden
32 J6 **Stuhr** W Germany
32 J9 **Stukenbrock** W Germany
9 G3 **Stump Cross** England
112 M2 **Stumpy Point** North Carolina U.S.A.
33 Q9 **Stumsdorf** East Germany
68 G6 **Stung Chinle** *R* Cambodia
68 G6 **Stung Sen** *R* Cambodia
26 N2 **Stuorajavrre** *L* Norway
117 L9 **Stupendous Mt** British Columbia Canada
54 K2 **Stupino** U.S.S.R.
40 G7 **Stura** *R* Italy
44 B1 **Stura di Ala** *R* Italy
44 B3 **Stura di Demonte** *R* Italy
44 B1 **Stura di V,Grande** *R* Italy
44 B1 **Stura di Viu** *R* Italy
146 C13 **Sturge I** Antarctica
120 K6 **Sturgeon** *R* Ontario Canada
94 C1 **Sturgeon** *R* Michigan U.S.A.
110 D2 **Sturgeon** Missouri U.S.A.
119 U6 **Sturgeon B** Manitoba Canada
94 B1 **Sturgeon B** Michigan U.S.A.
99 T5 **Sturgeon Bay** Wisconsin U.S.A.
99 T5 **Sturgeon Bay Canal** Wisconsin U.S.A.
120 K6 **Sturgeon Falls** Ontario Canada
117 P8 **Sturgeon L** Alberta Canada
121 M8 **Sturgeon L** Ontario Canada
119 Q4 **Sturgeon Landing** Manitoba Canada
118 C5 **Sturgeon R** Alberta Canada
118 L5 **Sturgeon R** Saskatchewan Canada
119 P7 **Sturgis** Saskatchewan Canada
110 J4 **Sturgis** Kentucky U.S.A.
94 B5 **Sturgis** Michigan U.S.A.
111 G8 **Sturgis** Mississippi U.S.A.
106 H5 **Sturgis** Oklahoma U.S.A.
98 C5 **Sturgis** South Dakota U.S.A.
44 E3 **Sturla** Italy
8 D6 **Sturminster Newton** England
48 E3 **Štúrovo** Czechoslovakia
9 H5 **Sturry** England
138 D6 **Sturt B** South Australia Australia
142 G4 **Sturt Cr** *R* Western Australia Australia
142 G4 **Sturt Creek** Western Australia Australia
141 F8 **Sturt Des** Qnsld/S Aust Australia
99 T7 **Sturtevant** Wisconsin U.S.A.
138 F3 **Sturt, Mt** New South Wales Australia
138 F3 **Sturt Nat Park** New South Wales Australia
140 C3 **Sturt Plain** N Terr Australia
36 D5 **Stürzelbronn** France
36 E5 **Stutensee** W Germany
89 E9 **Stutterheim** S Africa
111 E7 **Stuttgart** Arkansas U.S.A.
107 L2 **Stuttgart** Kansas U.S.A.
36 G6 **Stuttgart** W Germany
37 K2 **Stützerbach** East Germany
26 H9 **Styggberg** Sweden
28 R9 **Stykkishólmur** Iceland
130 G6 **Suaçui Grande, R** Brazil
71 M9 **Suai** Indonesia
70 C3 **Suai** Sarawak
86 G2 **Suakin** Sudan
99 T5 **Suamico** Wisconsin U.S.A.
124 E3 **Suaqui** Mexico
128 D2 **Suárez** *R* Colombia
70 L9 **Subang** Java
71 F4 **Suban Pt** Philippines
52 C6 **Subate** U.S.S.R.
77 A5 **Subayhīyah, Aş** Kuwait
45 L4 **Subbiano** Italy
80 F5 **Subeihi** Jordan
57 J4 **Subexi** China
69 J11 **Subi** *isld* Indonesia
142 A1 **Subiaco** *dist* Perth, W Aust Australia
42 E7 **Subiaco** Italy
69 J1 **Subi Kecil** *isld* Indonesia
101 M7 **Sublett** Idaho U.S.A.
99 R8 **Sublette** Illinois U.S.A.
107 K4 **Sublette** Kansas U.S.A.
109 L6 **Sublime** Texas U.S.A.
48 F4 **Subotica** Yugoslavia
65 D2 **Subrag** China
118 J8 **Success** Saskatchewan Canada
110 D4 **Success** Missouri U.S.A.
44 H3 **Succiso,Alpe di** *mt* Italy
20 G7 **Sucé** France
48 F1 **Sucha** Poland
Suchan *see* **Partizansk**
31 J2 **Suchan** Poland
31 H7 **Suchdol** Czechoslovakia
31 M4 **Suchedniów** Poland
Süchow *see* **Xuzhou**
31 O2 **Suchowola** Poland
25 F6 **Süchteln** W Germany
100 C1 **Sucia I** Washington U.S.A.
14 C3 **Suck** *R* Ireland
100 H6 **Sucker Cr** Oregon U.S.A.
116 Q7 **Suckling,C** Alaska U.S.A.
33 P6 **Suckow** East Germany
128 E7 **Sucre** Bolivia
126 G10 **Sucre** Colombia
128 G5 **Sucunduri** *R* Brazil
130 D7 **Sucuriu** *R* Brazil
52 E5 **Suda** U.S.S.R.
86 E3 **Sudan** *rep* Africa
108 E1 **Sudan** Texas U.S.A.
52 F5 **Suday** U.S.S.R.
55 B5 **Sud'bodarovka** U.S.S.R.
120 J6 **Sudbury** Ontario Canada
9 G3 **Sudbury** England
86 E4 **Sudd** *dist* Sudan
128 G2 **Suddie** Guyana
33 O6 **Sude** *R* East Germany
28 D7 **Süderbrarup** W Germany
33 M7 **Suderburg** W Germany
32 K4 **Süderhastedt** W Germany
32 J4 **Süderhöft** W Germany
28 B7 **Süder Lügum** W Germany
52 E6 **Sudilova** U.S.S.R.
52 F5 **Sudislavl'** U.S.S.R.
32 E9 **Südlohn** W Germany
52 F6 **Sudogda** U.S.S.R.
54 E4 **Sudost'** *R* U.S.S.R.
83 L13 **Sud Ouest, Pte** Mauritius
79 C9 **Sudr** Egypt
6 F1 **Suðuroy** Faeroes
6 F1 **Suðuroyarfjørður** *fj* Faeroes
54 G5 **Sudzha** U.S.S.R.
59 K3 **Sudzukhe** U.S.S.R.
17 G5 **Sueca** Spain
46 G2 **Süedinenie** Bulgaria
80 G8 **Su'eida** *R* Jordan
80 F8 **Su'eidat** Jordan
117 G8 **Suemez I** Alaska U.S.A.
108 D6 **Sue Pk** Texas U.S.A.
55 E3 **Suer'** *R* U.S.S.R.
21 N6 **Suèvres** France
79 C5 **Suez** Egypt
79 C8 **Suez Canal** Egypt
84 J4 **Suez,G.of** Egypt
80 G4 **Suf** Jordan
118 F8 **Suffield** Alberta Canada
9 H3 **Suffolk** *co* England
101 Q2 **Suffolk** Montana U.S.A.
95 L10 **Suffolk** Virginia U.S.A.
61 K11 **Suga-jima** *isld* Japan
101 O6 **Sugar** Idaho U.S.A.
99 R7 **Sugar** *R* Wisconsin U.S.A.
106 G3 **Sugar City** Colorado U.S.A.
94 H5 **Sugar Grove** Pennsylvania U.S.A.
94 F10 **Sugar Grove** Virginia U.S.A.
109 M6 **Sugar Land** Texas U.S.A.
132 C2 **Sugarloaf** *mt* Brazil
143 C6 **Sugarloaf Hill** Western Australia Australia
113 F13 **Sugarloaf Key** *isld* Florida U.S.A.
139 L4 **Sugarloaf Pt** New South Wales Australia
90 A13 **Sugar Loaf Pt** St Helena
71 G5 **Sugbuhan Pt** Philippines
37 J4 **Sugenheim** W Germany
119 P4 **Suggi L** Saskatchewan Canada
69 F12 **Sugi** Indonesia
60 J10 **Sugi** Japan
78 D3 **Suğla Gölü** *L* Turkey
51 P2 **Sugoy** *R* U.S.S.R.
70 E1 **Sugut** *R* Sabah
70 E1 **Sugut, Tanjung** *C* Sabah
46 G1 **Suhaia, L** Romania
77 E7 **Şuḩār** Oman
37 K2 **Suhl** East Germany
42 H3 **Suhopolje** Yugoslavia
40 H3 **Suhr** *R* Switzerland
47 L6 **Suhut** Turkey
74 C4 **Sui** Pakistan
129 H6 **Suiá-Missu** *R* Brazil
100 E1 **Suiattle Pass** Washington U.S.A.
67 F2 **Suichang** China
67 E3 **Suichuan** China
58 F4 **Suide** China
65 H2 **Suifenhe** China
65 H3 **Suifen He** China
74 D6 **Suigam** India
65 G1 **Suihua** China
67 A2 **Suijiang** China
67 D5 **Sui Jiang** *R* China
59 J2 **Suileng** China
58 E5 **Suining** China
67 C3 **Suining** China
128 E8 **Suipacha** Bolivia
22 G5 **Suippe** *R* France
14 D4 **Suir** *R* Ireland
60 T2 **Suishō tō** *isld* U.S.S.R.
95 L8 **Suitland** Maryland U.S.A.
68 K2 **Suixi** China
67 D1 **Sui Xian** China
65 C7 **Sui Xian** China
67 B2 **Suiyanchang** China
67 B3 **Suiyang** China
40 B2 **Suize** *R* France
59 H3 **Suizhong** China
74 F5 **Sujangarh** India
Suji *see* **Haixing**
70 L9 **Sukabumi** Java
70 K8 **Sukadana** Sumatra
61 O8 **Sukagawa** Japan
70 L9 **Sukanegara** Java
69 K14 **Sukaraja** Indonesia
70 B6 **Sukaramai** Kalimantan
70 F2 **Sukau** Sabah
29 N8 **Sukeva** Finland
51 L2 **Sukhana** U.S.S.R.
65 J1 **Sukhanovka** U.S.S.R.
46 G1 **Sukhindol** Bulgaria
54 G2 **Sukhinichi** U.S.S.R.
54 K3 **Sukhodol'skiy** U.S.S.R.
52 F5 **Sukhona** *R* U.S.S.R.
68 D4 **Sukhothai** Thailand
55 D3 **Sukhoy Log** U.S.S.R.
53 F11 **Sukhumi** U.S.S.R.
115 O4 **Sukkertoppen Iskappe** *ice field* Greenland
74 C5 **Sukkur** Pakistan
76 E1 **Sukma** India
84 E4 **Sūknah** Libya
70 O9 **Sukodadi** Java
70 N9 **Sukohardjo** Java
70 N9 **Sukolilo** Java
71 H5 **Sukon** Sulawesi
69 D9 **Sukon,Ko** *isld* Thailand
33 P5 **Sukow** East Germany
59 L2 **Sukpay Datani** U.S.S.R.
87 C10 **Sukses** Namibia
55 C3 **Suksun** U.S.S.R.
60 F13 **Sukumo** Japan
60 F13 **Sukumo-wan** *B* Japan
117 N8 **Sukunka** *R* British Columbia Canada
26 F8 **Sul** Norway
27 A10 **Sula** *isld* Norway
101 M4 **Sula** Montana U.S.A.
54 D7 **Sula** *R* U.S.S.R.
125 L2 **Sulaco** Honduras
74 C4 **Sulaiman Range** Pakistan
53 G11 **Sulak** U.S.S.R.
71 J6 **Sula,Kep** *isld* Indonesia
52 F4 **Sulanda** *R* U.S.S.R.
15 B1 **Sular Sgeir** *isld* Scotland
70 Q10 **Sulat** *isld* Indonesia
71 G5 **Sulat** Samar Philippines
71 A2 **Sulat, Bukit** *mt* Halmahera Indonesia
116 K4 **Sulatna** *R* Alaska U.S.A.
116 K4 **Sulatna** Alaska U.S.A.
70 **Sulawesi** *isld* Indonesia
70 G7 **Sulawesi Selatan** Sulawesi
71 H4 **Sulawesi Utara** Sulawesi
78 K4 **Sulaymānīyah** Iraq
77 A7 **Şulb, Aş** *plain* Saudi Arabia
27 B12 **Suldal** Norway
27 B12 **Suldalsvatn** Norway
28 D3 **Suldrup** Denmark
31 J3 **Sulechów** Poland
31 J3 **Sulęcin** Poland
77 C1 **Suledeh** Iran
31 M4 **Sulejów** Poland
70 F4 **Suleman Teluk** *B* Kalimantan
27 B12 **Suleskar** Norway
15 D1 **Sule Skerry** *isld* Scotland
32 M5 **Sülfeld** W Germany
66 E4 **Suli Hu** *L* China
69 E13 **Suliki** Sumatra
85 B7 **Sulima** Sierra Leone
48 M5 **Sulina** *R* Romania
48 M5 **Sulina** Romania
32 J7 **Sulingen** W Germany
48 K3 **Sulița** Romania
26 H4 **Sulitjelma** Norway
29 N10 **Sulkava** Finland
128 B4 **Sullana** Peru
111 H8 **Sulligent** Alabama U.S.A.
99 S10 **Sullivan** Illinois U.S.A.
110 E3 **Sullivan** Missouri U.S.A.
117 K10 **Sullivan Bay** British Columbia Canada
Sullivan I *see* **Lanbi Kyun**
118 F6 **Sullivan L** Alberta Canada
15 G12 **Sullom Voe** *B* Shetland Scotland
99 O8 **Sully** Iowa U.S.A.
21 P6 **Sully-la Chapelle** France
21 P6 **Sully-sur-Loire** France
38 N8 **Sulm** *R* Austria
42 F6 **Sulmona** Italy
109 O5 **Sulphur** Louisiana U.S.A.
100 G9 **Sulphur** Nevada U.S.A.
109 L1 **Sulphur** Oklahoma U.S.A.
109 N2 **Sulphur** *R* Texas/Louisiana U.S.A.
103 M3 **Sulphurdale** Utah U.S.A.
109 M2 **Sulphur Springs** Texas U.S.A.
108 E3 **Sulphur Springs Cr** Texas U.S.A.
28 D2 **Sulsted** Denmark
120 H5 **Sultan** Ontario Canada
78 C2 **Sultan Dağları** *mts* Turkey
47 J7 **Sultanhisar** Turkey
75 K5 **Sultanpur** India
33 R5 **Sülten** East Germany
71 G5 **Suluan** *isld* Philippines
70 G1 **Sulu Arch** *islds* Philippines
116 K5 **Sulukna** *R* Alaska U.S.A.
84 G3 **Suluq** Libya
57 D3 **Sulutobe** U.S.S.R.
57 E5 **Sulyukta** U.S.S.R.
36 F7 **Sulz** W Germany
38 H7 **Sulzau** Austria
36 H5 **Sulzbach** Baden-Württemberg W Germany
36 C5 **Sulzbach** Saarland W Germany
37 M5 **Sulzbach-Rosenberg** W Germany
41 L2 **Sulzberg** Austria
41 M2 **Sulzberg** W Germany
146 B10 **Sulzberger B** Antarctica
37 L5 **Sulzbürg** W Germany
37 K3 **Sulzdorf** W Germany
32 M7 **Sülze** W Germany
117 C5 **Sulzer, Mt** Alaska U.S.A.
36 F5 **Sulzfeld** W Germany
37 J4 **Sulzheim** W Germany
37 J3 **Sulzthal** W Germany
71 H4 **Sumalata** Sulawesi Indonesia
70 E1 **Sumangat, Tanjung** *C* Sabah
70 E1 **Sumangat, Tanjung** Sabah
100 C1 **Sumas** Washington U.S.A.
69 D11 **Sumatera** *isld* Indonesia
69 E13 **Sumatera Barat** *prov* Sumatra
69 F14 **Sumatera Selatan** *prov* Sumatra
69 D11 **Sumatera Utara** *prov* Sumatra
Sumatra *see* **Sumatera**
113 C7 **Sumatra** Florida U.S.A.
101 S3 **Sumatra** Montana U.S.A.
128 G5 **Sumaúma** Brazil
71 J9 **Sumba** *isld* Indonesia
71 J9 **Sumba,Selat** *str* Indonesia
71 H9 **Sumbawa** *isld* Indonesia
71 H9 **Sumbawabesar** Indonesia
88 C5 **Sumbawanga** Tanzania
87 B8 **Sumbe** Angola
58 E2 **Sümber** Mongolia
70 N9 **Sumbing, G** *mt* Java
69 E13 **Sumbing Gunung** *mt* Sumatra
15 G2 **Sumburgh Hd** Scotland
117 G7 **Sumdum** Alaska U.S.A.
130 H9 **Sumé** Brazil
70 L9 **Sumedang** Java
48 D4 **Sümeg** Hungary
70 O9 **Sumenep** Indonesia
78 M1 **Sumgait** U.S.S.R.
29 M9 **Sumiainen** Finland
40 G3 **Sumiswald** Switzerland
111 J8 **Sumiton** Alabama U.S.A.
55 E3 **Sumki** U.S.S.R.
55 E2 **Sumkino** U.S.S.R.
98 K10 **Summerfield** Kansas U.S.A.
94 F7 **Summerfield** Ohio U.S.A.
108 E1 **Summerfield** Texas U.S.A.
123 S4 **Summerford** Newfoundland Canada
15 C2 **Summer I** Scotland
99 U4 **Summer I** Michigan U.S.A.
100 E7 **Summer L** Oregon U.S.A.
117 O11 **Summerland** British Columbia Canada
94 B10 **Summer Shade** Kentucky U.S.A.
123 P4 **Summerside** Newfoundland Canada
122 J7 **Summerside** Prince Edward I Canada
110 E4 **Summersville** Missouri U.S.A.
94 G8 **Summersville** West Virginia U.S.A.
112 G4 **Summerton** South Carolina U.S.A.
112 E5 **Summertown** Georgia U.S.A.
123 T5 **Summerville** Newfoundland Canada
112 B3 **Summerville** Georgia U.S.A.
94 H5 **Summerville** Pennsylvania U.S.A.
112 G4 **Summerville** South Carolina U.S.A.
120 F5 **Summit** Ontario Canada
145 F4 **Summit** *mt* New Zealand
116 N5 **Summit** Alaska U.S.A.
101 M1 **Summit** Montana U.S.A.
106 B9 **Summit** New Mexico U.S.A.
100 B5 **Summit** Oregon U.S.A.
98 J4 **Summit** South Dakota U.S.A.
103 M4 **Summit** Utah U.S.A.
94 B2 **Summit City** Michigan U.S.A.
116 P5 **Summit L** Alaska U.S.A.
100 F8 **Summit L** Nevada U.S.A.
117 L6 **Summit Lake** British Columbia Canada
102 H2 **Summit Mt** Nevada U.S.A.
106 D4 **Summit Pk** Colorado U.S.A.
106 D4 **Summitville** Colorado U.S.A.
94 B6 **Summitville** Indiana U.S.A.
110 L6 **Summitville** Tennessee U.S.A.
144 B4 **Sumner** New Zealand
110 J3 **Sumner** Illinois U.S.A.
99 O7 **Sumner** Iowa U.S.A.
110 C2 **Sumner** Missouri U.S.A.
144 D5 **Sumner, L** New Zealand
117 G7 **Sumner Str** Alaska U.S.A.
61 N8 **Sumon-dake** *mt* Japan
48 D5 **Sumony** Hungary
60 H11 **Sumoto** Japan
70 F7 **Sumpangbinangae** Sulawesi
31 K6 **Šumperk** Czechoslovakia
100 G5 **Sumpter** Oregon U.S.A.
111 G10 **Sumrall** Mississippi U.S.A.
52 E3 **Sumskiy Posad** U.S.S.R.
112 G4 **Sumter** South Carolina U.S.A.
54 F6 **Sumy** U.S.S.R.
88 C4 **Suna** Tanzania
52 H5 **Suna** U.S.S.R.
60 P2 **Sunagawa** Japan
101 R9 **Sunbeam** Colorado U.S.A.
101 L5 **Sunbeam** Idaho U.S.A.
94 C10 **Sunbright** Tennessee U.S.A.
101 O1 **Sunburst** Montana U.S.A.
139 G7 **Sunbury** Victoria Australia
95 L10 **Sunbury** North Carolina U.S.A.
94 E6 **Sunbury** Ohio U.S.A.
95 L6 **Sunbury** Pennsylvania U.S.A.
37 N6 **Sünching** W Germany
133 E3 **Suncho Corral** Argentina
89 E5 **Sun City** S Africa
107 M4 **Sun City** Kansas U.S.A.
95 Q3 **Suncook** New Hampshire U.S.A.
98 B5 **Sundance** Wyoming U.S.A.
70 D2 **Sundar** Sarawak
75 N8 **Sundarbans** *tidal forest* India/Bangladesh
70 K9 **Sunda,Selat** *str* Sumatra
140 C3 **Sunday Cr** N Terr Australia
89 D9 **Sundays** *R* S Africa
142 E3 **Sunday Str** Western Australia Australia
28 B3 **Sundby** Denmark
27 J12 **Sundbyberg** Sweden
121 L8 **Sunderland** Ontario Canada
13 G4 **Sunderland** England
32 H10 **Sundern** W Germany
28 D7 **Sundeved** *reg* Denmark
40 F2 **Sundgau** *reg* France
70 N9 **Sundoro, G** *mt* Java
138 C2 **Sundown** South Australia Australia
118 E1 **Sundown** Manitoba Canada
108 E2 **Sundown** Texas U.S.A.
118 C7 **Sundre** Alberta Canada
27 K15 **Sundre** Sweden
121 L7 **Sundridge** Ontario Canada
28 C4 **Sunds** Denmark
26 J9 **Sundsbruk** Sweden
26 H8 **Sundsjö** Sweden
27 C12 **Sundsli** Norway
28 C3 **Sundstrup** Denmark
26 J9 **Sundsvall** Sweden
32 G10 **Sundwig** W Germany
94 E4 **Sunfield** Michigan U.S.A.
111 F8 **Sunflower** Mississippi U.S.A.
69 E12 **Sungaiapit** Sumatra
70 B4 **Sungai Ayak** Kalimantan
69 E13 **Sungaidareh** Sumatra
69 F12 **Sungaiguntung** Sumatra
69 F12 **Sungaikabung** Sumatra
69 H13 **Sungailiat** Indonesia
69 E13 **Sungailimau** Sumatra
70 D5 **Sungaipinang** Kalimantan
69 J12 **Sungaipinyuh** Indonesia
69 B10 **Sungairaya** Sumatra
69 F13 **Sungaisalak** Sumatra
69 G14 **Sungaiselan** Indonesia
Sungari *R see* **Songhua Jiang**
69 E10 **Sungei Patani** Malaysia
70 F7 **Sungguminasa** Sulawesi
86 E3 **Sungikai** Sudan
67 D3 **Sung-pai** China
69 G14 **Sungsang** Sumatra
47 H2 **Sungurlare** Bulgaria
78 E1 **Sungurlu** Turkey
120 C2 **Suni** Ontario Canada
70 E2 **Suniatan Besar, G** *mt* Sabah
65 C5 **Suning** China
37 P3 **Suniperk** Czechoslovakia
42 H3 **Sunja** Yugoslavia
94 B7 **Sunman** Indiana U.S.A.
26 C9 **Sunndal** *R* Norway
26 C9 **Sunndalsöra** Norway
27 F12 **Sunne** Sweden
27 J12 **Sunnersta** Sweden
27 A10 **Sunnfjord** Norway
27 A12 **Sunnhordland** *reg* Norway
113 F11 **Sunniland** Florida U.S.A.
26 B9 **Sunnmöre** Norway
141 K2 **Sunnybank** *dist* Brisbane, Qnsld Australia
122 K8 **Sunnybrae** Nova Scotia Canada
118 C5 **Sunnybrook** Alberta Canada
26 B9 **Sunnylven** Norway
118 F7 **Sunnynook** Alberta Canada
123 T6 **Sunnyside** Newfoundland Canada
103 J3 **Sunnyside** Nevada U.S.A.
103 O2 **Sunnyside** Utah U.S.A.
100 E3 **Sunnyside** Washington U.S.A.
102 B4 **Sunnyvale** California U.S.A.
99 R6 **Sun Prairie** Wisconsin U.S.A.
108 C7 **Sunray** Texas U.S.A.
116 N6 **Sunrise** Alaska U.S.A.
103 O6 **Sunrise** Arizona U.S.A.
98 B7 **Sunrise** Wyoming U.S.A.
101 O2 **Sun River** Montana U.S.A.
111 D11 **Sunset** Louisiana U.S.A.
109 K2 **Sunset** Texas U.S.A.
102 R11 **Sunset Beach** Hawaiian Is
103 N6 **Sunset Crater Nat.Mon** Arizona U.S.A.
117 P8 **Sunset House** Alberta Canada
103 N6 **Sunshine** Arizona U.S.A.
101 Q5 **Sunshine** Wyoming U.S.A.
118 K1 **Sunstrum** Ontario Canada
51 L2 **Suntar** U.S.S.R.
32 K8 **Süntel** *hills* W Germany
85 D7 **Sunyani** Ghana
37 M7 **Sünzhausen** W Germany
67 B6 **Suoi Rut** Vietnam
29 M9 **Suolahti** Finland
26 N2 **Suolovuobme** Norway
29 N10 **Suomenniemi** Finland
119 O2 **Suomi** Ontario Canada
29 O7 **Suomussalmi** Finland
60 E12 **Suō-nada** *sea* Japan
29 N9 **Suonenjoki** Finland
29 M10 **Suonne** *L* Finland
29 N3 **Suorsapää** *mt* Finland
26 K4 **Suorva** Sweden
52 D4 **Suoyarvi** U.S.S.R.
Suozhen *see* **Huantai**
103 M5 **Supai** Arizona U.S.A.
75 M5 **Supaul** India
128 C6 **Supe** Peru
118 H7 **Superb** Saskatchewan Canada
57 D5 **Superfosfatnyy** U.S.S.R.
103 N8 **Superior** Arizona U.S.A.
106 E2 **Superior** Colorado U.S.A.
101 L2 **Superior** Montana U.S.A.
98 J9 **Superior** Nebraska U.S.A.
99 O3 **Superior** Wisconsin U.S.A.
101 R8 **Superior** Wyoming U.S.A.
45 J1 **Superiore,L** Italy
99 R2 **Superior,L** U.S.A./Canada
68 E5 **Suphan Buri** Thailand
78 J2 **Süphan D** *mt* Turkey
45 O6 **Supino** Italy
100 F5 **Suplee** Oregon U.S.A.
54 C7 **Supoy** *R* U.S.S.R.
33 N8 **Süpplingen** W Germany
31 O2 **Supraśl** Poland
48 H3 **Supuru** Romania
72 G6 **Suqutrá** *isld* Indian Oc
27 H12 **Sura** Sweden
52 G3 **Sura** U.S.S.R.
52 G6 **Sura** *R* U.S.S.R.
74 B4 **Surab** Pakistan
70 O9 **Surabaja** Java
77 F7 **Sūrak** Iran
70 N9 **Surakarta** Java
84 E3 **Sūr al Jīn** *watercourse* Libya
70 F5 **Suramana** Sulawesi
40 B5 **Suran** *R* France
79 G3 **Sūrān** Syria
48 E2 **Šurany** Czechoslovakia
141 J7 **Surat** Queensland Australia
74 E8 **Surat** India
74 E4 **Suratgarhi** India
69 D8 **Surat Thani** Thailand
31 O3 **Suraż** Poland
54 D4 **Surazh** U.S.S.R.
141 H6 **Surbiton** Queensland Australia
9 F5 **Surbiton** England
48 F6 **Surčin** Yugoslavia
78 K4 **Sūrdāsh** Iraq
21 L4 **Surdon** France
48 H3 **Surduc** Romania
46 E2 **Surdulica** Yugoslavia
22 L4 **Sure** *R* Luxembourg
48 H5 **Şureanu** Romania
41 K4 **Surettahorn** *mt* Switzerland
102 D7 **Surf** California U.S.A.
95 N7 **Surf City** New Jersey U.S.A.
117 J9 **Surf Inlet** British Columbia Canada
112 J4 **Surfside Beach** South Carolina U.S.A.
18 E6 **Surgères** France
126 C3 **Surgidero de Batabanó** Cuba
55 F1 **Surgut** U.S.S.R.
50 H2 **Surgutikha** U.S.S.R.
76 D2 **Suriapet** India
61 N13 **Suribachi-yama** *mt* Japan
71 G6 **Surigao** Mindanao Philippines
71 G5 **Surigao Str** Philippines
68 F5 **Surin** Thailand
83 L13 **Surinam** Mauritius
129 G3 **Suriname** *rep* S America
129 G2 **Suriname** Suriname
99 S4 **Suring** Wisconsin U.S.A.
128 D2 **Suripá** *R* Venezuela
57 D5 **Surkhandar'inskaya Oblast** *prov* U.S.S.R.
77 C4 **Surmāq** Iran
26 C9 **Surnadalsöra** Norway
117 G6 **Surprise** British Columbia Canada
98 J8 **Surprise** Nebraska U.S.A.
121 Q3 **Surprise,L.de la** Quebec Canada
133 F5 **Sur,Pta** Argentina
112 E6 **Surrency** Georgia U.S.A.
9 F5 **Surrey** *co* England
98 E1 **Surrey** North Dakota U.S.A.
95 L9 **Surry** Virginia U.S.A.
40 H3 **Sursee** Switzerland
84 F3 **Surt** Libya
20 G3 **Surtainville** France
28 S10 **Surtsey** *isld* Iceland
71 N9 **Surubec,Danau** *L* Timor
78 G3 **Suruç** Turkey
61 M11 **Suruga-wan** *B* Japan
69 F14 **Surulangun** Sumatra
71 G7 **Surup** Mindanao Philippines
20 E6 **Surzur** France
28 H6 **Suså** *R* Denmark
44 B1 **Susa** Italy
60 E11 **Susa** Japan
42 G6 **Sušac** *isld* Yugoslavia
84 G3 **Sūsah** Libya
42 F3 **Sušak** Yugoslavia
60 G12 **Susaki** Japan
60 J12 **Susami** Japan
57 G4 **Susamyr** U.S.S.R.
102 D1 **Susan** *R* California U.S.A.
77 A4 **Sūsangerd** Iran
52 F5 **Susanino** U.S.S.R.
102 D1 **Susanville** California U.S.A.
100 G5 **Susanville** Oregon U.S.A.
78 F1 **Suşehri** Turkey
33 N4 **Süsel** W Germany
37 Q5 **Sušice** Czechoslovakia
80 F2 **Susitha** Syria
116 M6 **Susitna** Alaska U.S.A.
116 O5 **Susitna L** Alaska U.S.A.
69 D9 **Suso** Thailand
58 G5 **Susong** China
67 E1 **Susong** China
61 M10 **Susono** Japan
95 M5 **Susquehanna** Pennsylvania U.S.A.
95 L5 **Susquehanna** *R* Pennsylvania U.S.A.
33 P10 **Süsser See** *L* East Germany
Sussex *co see* **West and East Sussex** *counties*
122 G8 **Sussex** New Brunswick Canada
95 N5 **Sussex** New Jersey U.S.A.
101 T6 **Sussex** Wyoming U.S.A.
25 E6 **Susteren** Netherlands
45 K1 **Sustinente** Italy
117 K7 **Sustut Pk** British Columbia Canada
70 E2 **Susul** Sabah
116 K5 **Susulatna** *R* Alaska U.S.A.
51 O2 **Susuman** U.S.S.R.
71 A1 **Susupu** Halmahera Indonesia
47 J5 **Susurluk** Turkey
100 F10 **Sutcliffe** Nevada U.S.A.
48 L5 **Şuteşti** Romania
Sutherland *co see* **Highland** *reg*
87 D12 **Sutherland** S Africa
99 L7 **Sutherland** Iowa U.S.A.
98 E8 **Sutherland** Nebraska U.S.A.
143 F7 **Sutherland Ra** Western Australia Australia
98 E8 **Sutherland Res** Nebraska U.S.A.
144 A6 **Sutherland Sd** New Zealand
100 B6 **Sutherlin** Oregon U.S.A.
56 D5 **Sut-Khol'** U.S.S.R.
74 E3 **Sutlej** *R* Pakistan
79 D2 **Sütluce** Turkey
102 D3 **Sutter Cr** California U.S.A.
9 F2 **Sutterton** England
121 L8 **Sutton** Ontario Canada
121 S7 **Sutton** Quebec Canada
9 F5 **Sutton** England
9 G3 **Sutton** England
144 C6 **Sutton** New Zealand
98 J9 **Sutton** Nebraska U.S.A.
98 H2 **Sutton** North Dakota U.S.A.
94 G8 **Sutton** West Virginia U.S.A.
121 L5 **Sutton Bay** Ontario Canada
9 E2 **Sutton Coldfield** England
9 E1 **Sutton-in-Ashfield** England
94 G8 **Sutton Res** West Virginia U.S.A.
9 E5 **Sutton Scotney** England
141 H5 **Suttor** *R* Queensland Australia
116 J8 **Sutwik I** Alaska U.S.A.
89 D9 **Suurberge** *mts* S Africa
52 C5 **Suure-Jaani** U.S.S.R.
137 Q5 **Suva** Viti Levu Fiji
46 E1 **Suva Pl** *mt* Yugoslavia
46 D2 **Suva Reka** Yugoslavia
29 N9 **Suvasvesi** *L* Finland
Suvla, C *see* **Büyük Kemikli Br.**
54 H2 **Suvorov** U.S.S.R.
47 J1 **Suvorovo** Bulgaria
48 M5 **Suvorovo** U.S.S.R.
61 M9 **Suwa** Japan
61 M9 **Suwa ko** *L* Japan
70 D5 **Suwakong** Kalimantan
31 O1 **Suwałki** Poland
68 F5 **Suwannaphum** Thailand
113 D8 **Suwannee** Florida U.S.A.
119 R2 **Suwannee L** Manitoba Canada
113 E7 **Suwanoochee Cr** Georgia U.S.A.
78 H4 **Suwar** Syria
70 E4 **Suwaran, G** *mt* Kalimantan
79 G6 **Suwaydā', As** Syria
80 G2 **Suwaysah** Syria
80 F6 **Suweima** Jordan
Suweis,El *see* **Suez**
Su Xian *see* **Suzhou**
88 A9 **Suye,L** Zambia
55 D1 **Suyevatpaul** U.S.S.R.
57 E3 **Suzak** U.S.S.R.
83 M14 **Suzanne,Pte** Kerguelen Indian Oc
52 F6 **Suzdal'** U.S.S.R.
19 N16 **Suze la Rousse** France
21 L6 **Suze-sur-Sarthe, la** France
58 G5 **Suzhou** China
59 H5 **Suzhou** China
40 B3 **Suzon** *R* France
121 T4 **Suzor Côté** Quebec Canada
61 L8 **Suzu** Japan
61 K11 **Suzuka** Japan
61 L8 **Suzu-misaki** *C* Japan
56 B4 **Suzun** U.S.S.R.
45 J2 **Suzzara** Italy
27 H10 **Svabensverk** Sweden
28 H6 **Sværdborg** Denmark
26 P1 **Svaerholtklubben** *C* Norway
26 H9 **Svågan** *R* Sweden
26 H5 **Svaipa** *mt* Sweden
147 H12 **Svalbard** *arch* Arctic Oc
28 G5 **Svallerup** Denmark
48 H2 **Svalyava** U.S.S.R.
27 H16 **Svaneke** Denmark
28 E6 **Svanninge** Denmark
27 F12 **Svanskog** Sweden
26 N5 **Svanstein** Sweden
26 R2 **Svanvik** Norway
54 F5 **Svapa** *R* U.S.S.R.
26 M4 **Svappavaara** Sweden
29 K11 **Svartå** Finland
27 G12 **Svartå** Sweden
26 N5 **Svartbyn** Sweden
115 O3 **Svartenhuk Halvö** *pen* Greenland
26 G5 **Svartisen** *mt* Norway
26 M6 **Svartlå** Sweden
27 H11 **Svartnäs** Sweden
26 M6 **Svartöstaden** Sweden
54 K7 **Svatovo** U.S.S.R.
27 D10 **Svatsum** Norway
68 G7 **Svay Rieng** Cambodia
52 G5 **Svecha** U.S.S.R.
27 F16 **Svedala** Sweden
26 L7 **Svedun** Sweden
26 G9 **Sveg** Sweden
26 A10 **Svelgen** Norway
27 D12 **Svelvik** Norway
52 C6 **Švenčionėliai** U.S.S.R.
Svendborg *co see* **Fyn** *co*
28 F6 **Svendborg** Denmark
27 F14 **Svenljunga** Sweden
27 H12 **Svennevad** Sweden
26 F6 **Svenningdal** Norway
100 B3 **Svensen** Oregon U.S.A.
26 J2 **Svensgrunnen** *shoal* Norway
28 D6 **Svenstrup** Sønderjylland Denmark
55 D3 **Sverdlovsk** U.S.S.R.
55 D2 **Sverdlovskaya Oblast'** *prov* U.S.S.R.
115 K1 **Sverdrup Chan** Northwest Territories Canada
50 G1 **Sverdrup, Ostrov** *isld* U.S.S.R.
42 G5 **Sveti Andrija** *isld* Yugoslavia
46 E3 **Sveti Nikola** Yugoslavia
59 L2 **Svetlaya** U.S.S.R.
51 J2 **Svetlogorsk** U.S.S.R.
53 C8 **Svetlogorsk** U.S.S.R.
31 M1 **Svetlogorsk** U.S.S.R.
31 M1 **Svetloye** U.S.S.R.
31 M1 **Svetlyy** U.S.S.R.
51 L3 **Svetlyy** U.S.S.R.
52 C4 **Svetogorsk** U.S.S.R.
46 E1 **Svetozarevo** Yugoslavia
37 P5 **Švihov** Czechoslovakia
48 G6 **Svilajnac** Yugoslavia
47 H3 **Svilengrad** Bulgaria
28 F6 **Svindinge** Denmark
28 G5 **Svinninge** Denmark
Svinø *see* **Svínoy**
6 F1 **Svínoy** *isld* Faeroes
52 D4 **Svir'** *R* U.S.S.R.
52 D4 **Sviritsa** U.S.S.R.
56 F4 **Svirsk** U.S.S.R.
52 D4 **Svir'stroy** U.S.S.R.
46 G1 **Svishtov** Bulgaria
53 C7 **Svisloch'** *R* U.S.S.R.
31 J6 **Svitavy** Czechoslovakia
52 G6 **Sviyaga** *R* U.S.S.R.
59 J1 **Svobodnyy** U.S.S.R.
46 F2 **Svoge** Bulgaria
28 J5 **Svogerslev** Denmark
37 O4 **Svojšin** Czechoslovakia
26 G3 **Svolvaer** Norway
31 J6 **Svratka** *R* Czechoslovakia
46 E1 **Svrljig** Yugoslavia
46 E1 **Svrljiške Pl** *mt* Yugoslavia
52 F5 **Svyatogor'ye** U.S.S.R.
52 E1 **Svyatoy Nos, Mys** *C* U.S.S.R.
52 D4 **Svyatozero** U.S.S.R.
68 C3 **Swa** *R* Burma
9 G2 **Swaffham** England
141 K5 **Swain Reefs** Gt Barrier Reef Aust
112 E5 **Swainsboro** Georgia U.S.A.
134 B4 **Swains I** Pacific Oc
87 B10 **Swakopmund** S Africa
9 G5 **Swale,R** England
137 O4 **Swallow Is** Santa Cruz Is
70 C1 **Swallow Reef** S China Sea
106 F3 **Swallows** Colorado U.S.A.
118 D7 **Swalwell** Alberta Canada
9 E6 **Swanage** England
142 A2 **Swanbourne Beach** *dist* Perth, W Aust Australia
139 G6 **Swan Hill** Victoria Australia
118 B4 **Swan Hills** Alberta Canada
139 J8 **Swan Is** Tasmania Australia
126 C6 **Swan Is** W Indies
117 J8 **Swan, L** British Columbia Canada
98 G4 **Swan L** South Dakota U.S.A.
119 T9 **Swan Lake** Manitoba Canada
101 M2 **Swan Lake** Montana U.S.A.
112 E2 **Swannanoa** North Carolina U.S.A.
119 Q6 **Swan Plain** Saskatchewan Canada
142 E3 **Swan Pt** Western Australia Australia
112 L2 **Swanquarter** North Carolina U.S.A.
143 B9 **Swan R** Western Australia Australia
118 B3 **Swan R** Alberta Canada
138 E5 **Swan Reach** South Australia Australia
119 Q6 **Swan River** Manitoba Canada
99 N2 **Swan River** Minnesota U.S.A.
112 K3 **Swansboro** North Carolina U.S.A.
139 K5 **Swansea** New South Wales Australia
139 J8 **Swansea** Tasmania Australia
103 L7 **Swansea** Arizona U.S.A.
112 F4 **Swansea** South Carolina U.S.A.
8 C4 **Swansea** Wales
95 T2 **Swans I** Maine U.S.A.
118 K7 **Swanson** Saskatchewan Canada
117 J9 **Swanson Bay** British Columbia Canada
98 E9 **Swanson Res** Nebraska U.S.A.
98 J9 **Swanton** Nebraska U.S.A.
94 D5 **Swanton** Ohio U.S.A.
121 R8 **Swanton** Vermont U.S.A.
33 S4 **Swantow** East Germany
139 K3 **Swan Vale** New South Wales Australia
101 O6 **Swan Valley** Idaho U.S.A.
99 M4 **Swanville** Minnesota U.S.A.
89 A10 **Swartberg** *mt* S Africa
103 L2 **Swasey Pk** Utah U.S.A.
120 K4 **Swastika** Ontario Canada
89 G6 **Swaziland** *kingdom* Africa
99 M6 **Swea City** Iowa U.S.A.
26 **Sweden** *kingdom* W Europe
95 M7 **Swedesboro** New Jersey U.S.A.
85 D7 **Swedru** Ghana
12 C2 **Sween, L** Scotland
109 M6 **Sweeny** Texas U.S.A.
140 E3 **Sweers I** Queensland Australia
100 J6 **Sweet** Idaho U.S.A.
101 O1 **Sweetgrass** Montana U.S.A.
111 D7 **Sweet Home** Arkansas U.S.A.
100 C5 **Sweet Home** Oregon U.S.A.
109 L6 **Sweet Home** Texas U.S.A.
110 C3 **Sweet Springs** Missouri U.S.A.
107 L6 **Sweetwater** Oklahoma U.S.A.
112 C2 **Sweet Water** Tennessee U.S.A.
108 G3 **Sweetwater** Texas U.S.A.
101 R7 **Sweetwater** *R* Wyoming U.S.A.
87 D12 **Swellendam** S Africa
108 G2 **Swenson** Texas U.S.A.
31 J5 **Swidnica** Poland
31 J2 **Swidwin** Poland
31 J3 **Swiebodzin** Poland
31 L2 **Swiecie** Poland
116 K6 **Swift** *R* Alaska U.S.A.
95 R2 **Swift** *R* Maine U.S.A.
123 S6 **Swift Current** Newfoundland Canada
118 K8 **Swiftcurrent** Saskatchewan Canada
116 L5 **Swift Fork** *R* Alaska U.S.A.
110 E6 **Swifton** Arkansas U.S.A.
100 C3 **Swift Res** Washington U.S.A.
117 H5 **Swift River** Yukon Territory Canada
100 A1 **Swiftsure Bank Lightship** British Columbia Canada
14 D1 **Swilly,L** Ireland
8 C5 **Swimbridge** England
9 E4 **Swindon** England
Swinemünde *see* **Swinoujście**
9 F2 **Swineshead** England
14 C3 **Swinford** Ireland
106 G3 **Swink** Colorado U.S.A.
31 H2 **Swinoujście** Poland
13 F2 **Swinton** Scotland
40 F4 **Switzerland** *rep* Europe
15 E2 **Swona** *isld* Orkney Scotland
14 E3 **Swords** Ireland
141 F5 **Swords Ra** Queensland Australia
52 D4 **Syamozero, Oz** *L* U.S.S.R.
52 F4 **Syamzha** U.S.S.R.
52 D5 **Syas'** *R* U.S.S.R.
52 D4 **Syas'stroy** U.S.S.R.
52 G5 **Syava** U.S.S.R.
98 A8 **Sybille Cr** Wyoming U.S.A.
14 A4 **Sybil Pt** Ireland
111 K8 **Sycamore** Alabama U.S.A.
99 S8 **Sycamore** Illinois U.S.A.
94 D6 **Sycamore** Ohio U.S.A.
112 F4 **Sycamore** South Carolina U.S.A.
52 D6 **Sychevka** U.S.S.R.
31 K4 **Sycow** Poland
56 D4 **Syda** *R* U.S.S.R.
121 O8 **Sydenham** Ontario Canada
9 G2 **Syderstone** England
139 K5 **Sydney** New South Wales Australia
123 M7 **Sydney** Nova Scotia Canada
98 B2 **Sydney** Montana U.S.A.
140 E3 **Sydney I** Queensland Australia
123 M7 **Sydney Mines** Nova Scotia Canada
115 P5 **Sydproven** Greenland
32 J7 **Syke** W Germany
98 G2 **Sykeston** North Dakota U.S.A.
94 J5 **Sykesville** Pennsylvania U.S.A.
52 H4 **Syktyvkar** U.S.S.R.
111 K8 **Sylacauga** Alabama U.S.A.
110 D6 **Sylamore** Arkansas U.S.A.
26 F8 **Sylene** *mt* Norway
75 O6 **Sylhet** Bangladesh
28 A7 **Sylt** *isld* W Germany
26 B9 **Sylte** Norway
26 S1 **Sylterfjord** *inlet* Norway
112 D2 **Sylva** North Carolina U.S.A.
55 C3 **Sylva** U.S.S.R.
94 J7 **Sylvan** Pennsylvania U.S.A.
107 M2 **Sylvan Grove** Kansas U.S.A.
143 D6 **Sylvania** Western Australia Australia
119 N6 **Sylvania** Saskatchewan Canada
112 F5 **Sylvania** Georgia U.S.A.
94 D5 **Sylvania** Ohio U.S.A.
118 C6 **Sylvan Lake** Alberta Canada
101 P5 **Sylvan Pass** Wyoming U.S.A.
112 D6 **Sylvester** Georgia U.S.A.
140 D4 **Sylvester, L** N Terr Australia
123 R5 **Sylvester,Mt** Newfoundland Canada
107 M4 **Sylvia** Kansas U.S.A.
117 L6 **Sylvia,Mt** British Columbia Canada
56 C1 **Sym** *R* U.S.S.R.
15 E5 **Symington** Scotland
124 H5 **Symon** Mexico
8 D4 **Symonds Yat** England
71 F4 **Syndicate** Philippines
142 F3 **Synnot,Mt** Western Australia Australia
142 F3 **Synnot Ra** Western Australia Australia
56 H3 **Synnyr, Khrebet** *mts* U.S.S.R.
54 N2 **Syntul** U.S.S.R.
52 J2 **Synya** U.S.S.R.
55 E1 **Syn'yakha** *R* U.S.S.R.
Syracuse Italy *see* **Siracusa**
94 B5 **Syracuse** Indiana U.S.A.
107 J3 **Syracuse** Kansas U.S.A.
98 K9 **Syracuse** Nebraska U.S.A.
121 O9 **Syracuse** New York U.S.A.
101 N8 **Syracuse** Utah U.S.A.
57 E4 **Syrdarinsk. Obl** U.S.S.R.
57 E4 **Syrdar'ya** U.S.S.R.
57 D3 **Syrdar'ya** *R* U.S.S.R.
57 D4 **Syr Dar'ya Oblast'** *prov* U.S.S.R.
79 G4 **Syria** *rep* S W Asia
68 C4 **Syriam** Burma
Syrian Desert *see* **Badiet esh Sham**
55 E1 **Syrkovoye, Oz** *L* U.S.S.R.
28 G2 **Syr Odde** *C* Denmark
54 L4 **Syrskiy** U.S.S.R.
55 D3 **Sysert'** U.S.S.R.
95 T1 **Sysladobsis L** Maine U.S.A.
52 H4 **Sysola** *R* U.S.S.R.
9 E2 **Syston** England
56 D4 **Systyg-Khem** U.S.S.R.
52 D6 **Syt'kovo** U.S.S.R.
55 F1 **Sytomino** U.S.S.R.
52 F4 **Syuma** *R* U.S.S.R.
52 H6 **Syumsi** U.S.S.R.
52 H6 **Syun'** *R* U.S.S.R.
46 F3 **Syutkya** *mt* Bulgaria
53 G7 **Syzran'** U.S.S.R.
48 E4 **Szabadszállás** Hungary
48 G2 **Szabolcsszatmár** *co* Hungary
31 L4 **Szadek** Poland
31 K2 **Szamocin** Poland
48 G2 **Szamosszeg** Hungary
31 K3 **Szamotuły** Poland
48 D3 **Szany** Hungary
48 F4 **Szarvas** Hungary
31 O5 **Szczebrzeszyn** Poland
31 H2 **Szczecin** Poland
31 K2 **Szczecinek** Poland
31 M5 **Szczekociny** Poland
31 L4 **Szczerców** Poland
31 N5 **Szczucin** Poland
31 N2 **Szczuczyn** Poland
31 M2 **Szczytno** Poland
Szechwan *prov see* **Sichuan** *prov*
48 F2 **Szécsény** Hungary
48 F4 **Szeged** Hungary
48 G3 **Szeghalom** Hungary
48 E3 **Székesfehérvár** Hungary
48 F2 **Szendrö** Hungary
48 E3 **Szentendre** Hungary
48 F4 **Szentes** Hungary
48 C4 **Szentgotthárd** Hungary
48 D4 **Szentlörinc** Hungary
48 G2 **Szerencs** Hungary
48 D3 **Szigetköz** *dist* Hungary
48 D4 **Szigetvár** Hungary
48 F2 **Szikszó** Hungary
31 N2 **Szkwa** *R* Poland
31 J4 **Szlichtyngowa** Poland
48 E3 **Szob** Hungary
48 F3 **Szolnok** Hungary
48 D3 **Szombathely** Hungary
31 J4 **Szprotawa** Poland
31 M2 **Szreńsk** Poland
31 L2 **Sztum** Poland
31 K2 **Szubin** Poland
31 M4 **Szydłowiec** Poland

T

79 F5 **Taalabaya** Lebanon
71 E3 **Taal,L** Luzon Philippines
48 E4 **Tab** Hungary
71 F4 **Tabaco** Philippines
128 F5 **Tabajara** Brazil
70 P10 **Tabanan** Indonesia
70 P16 **Tabanan** Bali Indonesia
70 E4 **Tabang** Kalimantan
70 D4 **Tabang** *R* Kalimantan
85 E5 **Tabankort** Mali
89 F8 **Tabankulu** S Africa
127 O2 **Tabaquite** Trinidad
137 L2 **Tabar Is** Bismarck Arch
43 B12 **Tabarka** Tunisia
77 G3 **Ţabas** Iran
77 E3 **Ţabas** Iran
125 N8 **Tabasco** *state* Mexico
124 H7 **Tabasco** Mexico
52 G6 **Tabashino** U.S.S.R.
123 N3 **Tabatière,La** Quebec Canada
128 E4 **Tabatinga** Brazil
68 B1 **Tabayin** Burma
71 E2 **Tabayoa, Mt** Philippines
68 G6 **Tabeng** Cambodia
118 E9 **Taber** Alberta Canada
27 G14 **Taberg** Sweden
17 F7 **Tabernas** Spain
17 G5 **Tabernes de Valldigna** Spain

Taberrant — Tatty
83

16 D10 **Taberrant** Morocco
17 G9 **Tabia** Algeria
101 P9 **Tabiona** Utah U.S.A.
69 F13 **Tabir** *R* Sumatra
71 F4 **Tablas** *isld* Philippines
131 B3 **Tablas,C** Chile
71 E4 **Tablas Strait** Philippines
89 A9 **Table B** S Africa
139 H8 **Table C** Tasmania Australia
145 G3 **Table Cape** New Zealand
71 D6 **Table Hd** Philippines
144 A7 **Table Hill** New Zealand
68 A6 **Table I** Andaman Is
68 H2 **Table,I.de la** Vietnam
142 F3 **Tableland** Western Australia Australia
87 C12 **Table Mt** S Africa
116 Q2 **Table Mt** Alaska U.S.A.
71 D5 **Table Pt** Philippines
83 K14 **Table Pt.de la** Réunion Indian Oc
101 R8 **Table Rock** Wyoming U.S.A.
110 C5 **Table Rock Res** Missouri U.S.A.
141 G4 **Tabletop, Mt** Queensland Australia
130 C6 **Taboco,R** Brazil
31 H6 **Tábor** Czechoslovakia
99 L9 **Tabor** Iowa U.S.A.
98 J7 **Tabor** South Dakota U.S.A.
51 P1 **Tabor** U.S.S.R.
88 D4 **Tabora** *reg* Tanzania
88 D4 **Tabora** Tanzania
112 J3 **Tabor City** North Carolina U.S.A.
80 E3 **Tabor, Mt** Israel
118 E9 **Tabor Prov. Park** Alberta Canada
55 D2 **Tabory** U.S.S.R.
85 C8 **Tabou** Ivory Coast
78 L2 **Tabrīz** Iran
68 G2 **Ta Bu** Vietnam
135 U9 **Tabuaeran** *atoll* Pacific Oc
79 G10 **Tabūk** Saudi Arabia
60 E12 **Tabuka** Japan
139 L3 **Tabulam** N S W Australia
71 H5 **Tabulan** Sulawesi
129 G5 **Tabuleiro** Brazil
55 G4 **Tabuny** U.S.S.R.
45 R7 **Taburno, M** *mt* Italy
122 G6 **Tabusintac R** New Brunswick Canada
69 D12 **Tabuyung** Sumatra
88 B6 **Tabwe** Zambia
27 K12 **Täby** Sweden
130 H10 **Tacaratú** Brazil
66 C2 **Tacheng** China
67 G4 **Ta-chia** Taiwan
60 C13 **Tachibana-wan** *B* Japan
61 N10 **Tachikawa** Japan
128 D2 **Táchira** *state* Venezuela
37 O4 **Tachov** Czechoslovakia
70 G7 **Tacipi** Sulawesi
139 L4 **Tacking Pt** N S W Australia
71 G5 **Tacloban** Philippines
133 C1 **Tacna** Peru
103 K9 **Tacna** Arizona U.S.A.
21 O4 **Tacoignières** France
117 M12 **Tacoma** Washington U.S.A.
133 E3 **Tacŏ Pozo** Argentina
128 E7 **Tacora** *mt* Chile
130 E7 **Tacquaritinga** Brazil
130 B10 **Tacuaras** Paraguay
131 G3 **Tacuarembó** Uruguay
131 H4 **Tacuari,R** Uruguay
130 C8 **Tacuati** Paraguay
124 E3 **Tacupeto** Mexico
61 N8 **Tadami** *R* Japan
13 G6 **Tadcaster** England
85 F4 **Tadeinte** *watercourse* Algeria
85 E3 **Tadémaït,Pl.du** Algeria
85 B5 **Tadjakant** Mauritania
85 E3 **Tadjmout** Algeria
86 H3 **Tadjoura** Djibouti
9 E3 **Tadmarton** England
145 D4 **Tadmor** New Zealand
78 G4 **Tadmur** Syria
60 Q2 **Tadoshi** Japan
60 G11 **Tadotsu** Japan
122 C5 **Tadoussec** Quebec Canada
76 D3 **Tadpatri** India
Tadzhikistan *see* **Tadzhikskaya** *S.S.R.*
57 E5 **Tadzhikskaya S.S.R.** U.S.S.R.
65 F6 **Taech'ŏngdo** *isld* S Korea
65 G5 **Taedong** *R* N Korea
65 G7 **Taegu** S Korea
65 F7 **Taehŭksan** *isld* S Korea
65 G6 **Taejon** S Korea
28 J7 **Tæro** *isld* Denmark
137 S5 **Tafahi** *isld* Pacific Oc
17 F2 **Tafalla** Spain
85 F4 **Tafasaset** *watercourse* Algeria
126 A1 **Tafelberg** *mt* Curaçao
16 E9 **Tafersite** Morocco
8 C4 **Taff,R** Wales
79 F8 **Tafila** Jordan
85 C7 **Tafiré** Ivory Coast
26 B9 **Tafjord** Norway
17 F9 **Tafna** *R* Algeria
106 F5 **Tafoya** New Mexico U.S.A.
85 C3 **Tafraoute** Morocco
102 E6 **Taft** California U.S.A.
107 P6 **Taft** Oklahoma U.S.A.
109 K8 **Taft** Texas U.S.A.
77 G5 **Taftan, Kūh-e-** *mt* Iran
95 P5 **Taftville** Connecticut U.S.A.
69 A9 **Tafwap** Nicobar Is
75 N5 **Taga** Bhutan
48 J4 **Ţaga** Romania
77 L2 **Tagab** Afghanistan
116 H4 **Tagagawik** *R* Alaska U.S.A.
61 P7 **Tagajō** Japan
53 E10 **Taganrog** U.S.S.R.
54 K9 **Taganrogskiy Zaliv** *G* U.S.S.R.
85 A4 **Tagarzimat** Western Sahara
71 E3 **Tagaytay City** Philippines
71 F6 **Tagbilaran** Philippines
85 D2 **Taghit** Algeria
117 F6 **Tagish L** British Columbia Canada
45 O5 **Tagliacozzo** Italy
42 E2 **Tagliamento** *R* Italy
45 M1 **Táglio di Po** Italy
22 G5 **Tagnon** France
71 F6 **Tagolo Pt** Philippines
85 C3 **Tagounite** Morocco
26 J8 **Tågsjöberg** Sweden
129 J6 **Taguatinga** Brazil
71 F5 **Tagubanhan** *isld* Philippines
61 L11 **Taguchi** Japan
71 E2 **Tagudin** Philippines
137 L4 **Tagula** *isld* Louisiade Arch
Tagus *R* Portugal *see* **Tejo** *R*
Tagus *R* Spain *see* **Tajo** *R*
98 E1 **Tagus** North Dakota U.S.A.
144 B7 **Tahakopa** New Zealand
69 F10 **Tahan, Gunung** *mt* Malaysia
61 L11 **Tahara** Japan
85 F4 **Tahat** *mt* Algeria
145 D1 **Taheke** New Zealand
77 C6 **Tāheri** Iran
117 G6 **Tahi** *R* British Columbia Canada
135 M10 **Tahiti** *isld* Pacific Oc
110 B6 **Tahlequah** Oklahoma U.S.A.
117 H6 **Tahltan** British Columbia Canada
102 D2 **Tahoe City** California U.S.A.
114 J4 **Tahoe L** Northwest Territories Canada
102 D2 **Tahoe L** California U.S.A.
102 D3 **Tahoe Valley** California U.S.A.
108 F2 **Tahoka** Texas U.S.A.
100 A2 **Taholah** Washington U.S.A.
145 E3 **Tahora** New Zealand
145 F4 **Tahoraiti** New Zealand
85 F6 **Tahoua** Niger
99 V3 **Tahquamenon Falls** Michigan U.S.A.
59 H2 **Ta-hsing-an Ling** China
59 H2 **Ta Hsing-an-Ling Shan-mo** *ra* China
117 K11 **Tahsis** British Columbia Canada
67 F5 **Ta Hsü** *isld* Taiwan
84 J4 **Tahta** Egypt
47 L8 **Tahtali Dağ** *mt* Turkey
117 K9 **Tahtsa** *R* British Columbia Canada
128 D6 **Tahuamanu** *R* Peru
145 E2 **Tahuna** New Zealand
85 C7 **Tai** Ivory Coast
65 E4 **Tai'an** China
65 C6 **Tai'an** China
67 F2 **Taibai** China
106 F7 **Taiban** New Mexico U.S.A.
17 F6 **Taibilla,Sa de** *mts* Spain
65 C4 **Taibus Qi** China
58 G3 **Taibus Qi** China
67 G1 **Taicang** China
67 G4 **T'ai-chung** Taiwan
144 C6 **Taieri** *airport* New Zealand
Taigong *see* **Taijiang**
65 B6 **Taigu** China
65 B5 **Taihang Shan** *mt ra* China
65 B7 **Taihang Shan** *ra* China
145 E3 **Taihape** New Zealand
67 E3 **Taihe** China
61 Q12 **Taiho** Okinawa
67 G1 **Tai Hu** *L* China
67 E1 **Taihu** China
67 C3 **Taijiang** China
Taikang *see* **Dorbod**
65 C7 **Taikang** China
60 R3 **Taiki** Japan
68 B4 **Taikkyi** Burma
59 H2 **Tailai** China
69 D13 **Taileleo** Indonesia
138 E6 **Tailem Bend** South Australia Australia
36 G7 **Tailfingen** W Germany
21 K4 **Taillebois** France
19 P14 **Taillefer** *mt* France
20 H5 **Taillis** France
15 D3 **Tain** Scotland
46 E8 **Tainaron, Akr** *C* Greece
67 F3 **Taining** China
19 N14 **Tain l'Hermitage** France
67 G5 **T'ain-nan** Taiwan
130 G4 **Taiobeiras** Brazil
70 G5 **Taipa** Sulawesi
29 O9 **Taipale** Finland
29 N10 **Taipalsaari** Finland
67 G4 **T'ai-pei** Taiwan
67 C5 **Taiping** China
67 B5 **Taiping** China
67 F1 **Taiping** China
69 E10 **Taiping** Malaysia
59 H3 **Taipingchuan** China
65 G3 **Taipingchuan** China
65 F4 **Taipingshao** China
130 J8 **Taipu** Brazil
61 O8 **Taira** Japan
61 Q12 **Taira** Okinawa
60 O4 **Tairadate kaikyō** Japan
145 E2 **Tairua** New Zealand
60 N3 **Taisei** Japan
60 Q2 **Taisetsuzan Nat.Park** Japan
60 F10 **Taisha** Japan
67 D5 **Taishan** China
67 F3 **Taishun** China
69 E14 **Taitaitanopo** *isld* Indonesia
133 C7 **Taitao, Pen. de** Chile
65 D4 **Taitouying** China
52 C2 **Taivalkoski** Finland
27 M11 **Taivassalo** Finland
67 G5 **Taiwan** *rep* E Asia
Taiwan Haixia *see* **Taiwan Str**
67 F4 **Taiwan Strait** China/Taiwan
67 G1 **Tai Xian** China
67 G1 **Taixing** China
46 E7 **Taïyetos** *mt* Greece
80 E3 **Taiyiba** Israel
80 D4 **Taiyiba** Israel
80 F3 **Taiyiba** *R* Jordan
65 B6 **Taiyuan** China
65 B6 **Taiyue Shan** *mt* China
Taizhou *see* **Linhai**
67 G1 **Taizhou** China
67 G2 **Taizhou Wan** *B* China
65 F4 **Taizi He** *R* China
72 E6 **Ta'izz** N Yemen
86 H3 **Ta'izz** Yemen
84 E5 **Tajarhī** Libya
84 G5 **Tāj, At** Libya
69 H14 **Tajem, Gunung** *mt* Indonesia
43 B13 **Tajerouine** Tunisia
Tajikistan *see* **Tadzhikskaya** *S.S.R.*
61 N8 **Tajima** Japan
61 L10 **Tajimi** Japan
106 D7 **Tajique** New Mexico U.S.A.
124 C2 **Tajito** Mexico
16 E4 **Tajo** *R* Spain
70 N9 **Taju** Java
17 F4 **Tajuna** *R* Spain
68 D4 **Tak** Thailand
71 K8 **Taka' Bonerate, Kepulauan** *islds* Indonesia
61 M8 **Takada** Japan
61 P7 **Takagi** Japan
61 O9 **Takahagi** Japan
61 J10 **Takahama** Japan
60 G11 **Takahashi** Japan
61 O8 **Takahata** Japan
60 E13 **Takajō** Japan
145 D4 **Takaka** New Zealand
46 E7 **Táka, L** Greece
83 K12 **Takamaka** Mahé I Indian Oc
60 H11 **Takamatsu** Japan
60 E13 **Takamori** Japan
61 O5 **Takanosu** Japan
61 K9 **Takaoka** Japan
145 F4 **Takapau** New Zealand
145 F1 **Takapuna** New Zealand
70 F7 **Taka Rewataya** *reef* Indonesia
60 H11 **Takasago** Japan
59 L4 **Takasaki** Japan
60 C12 **Taka shima** *isld* Saga Japan
60 E11 **Taka shima** *isld* Shimane Japan
89 B4 **Takatshwaane** Botswana
61 J11 **Takatsuki** Japan
145 E2 **Takatu Pt.** New Zealand
88 G3 **Takaungu** Kenya
68 D2 **Ta-Kaw** Burma
60 D12 **Takawa** Japan
61 L9 **Takayama** Japan
60 E14 **Takazaki** Japan
60 D14 **Takazaki** Japan
69 F9 **Tak Bai** Thailand
60 E13 **Takeda** Japan
61 K10 **Takefu** Japan
60 F11 **Takehara** Japan
9 G4 **Takeley** England
69 C10 **Takengon** Sumatra
68 G7 **Takeo** Cambodia
60 D12 **Takeo** Japan
60 C11 **Takeshiki** Japan
Take-shima *see* **Tok-to**
77 A1 **Takestān** Iran
60 E12 **Taketazu** Japan
71 C3 **Takeum** W Irian
78 K7 **Takhadid** Iraq
77 L1 **Takhār** *reg* Afghanistan
57 A4 **Takhiatash** U.S.S.R.
117 F5 **Takhini** *R* Yukon Terr Canada
57 A4 **Takhta** U.S.S.R.
57 C6 **Takhta-Bazar** U.S.S.R.
55 E4 **Takhtabrod** U.S.S.R.
57 B3 **Takhtakupyr** U.S.S.R.
77 C5 **Takht-e Jamshīd** Iran
114 H4 **Takijug** *L* N W Terr Canada
60 Q2 **Takikawa** Japan
100 B7 **Takilma** Oregon U.S.A.
60 R1 **Takinoue** Japan
119 R3 **Takipy** Manitoba Canada
70 D6 **Takisung** Kalimantan
144 A6 **Takitimu Mts** New Zealand
117 L8 **Takla Landing** British Columbia Canada
66 B4 **Taklimakan Shamo** *reg* China
57 E5 **Takob** U.S.S.R.
85 D8 **Takoradi** Ghana
116 J5 **Takotna** Alaska U.S.A.
145 D1 **Takou B** New Zealand
116 F6 **Takslesluk L** Alaska U.S.A.
117 G6 **Taku** British Columbia Canada
60 D12 **Taku** Japan
69 D8 **Takua Pa** Thailand
117 F5 **Taku Arm** *L* Br Col/Yukon Terr Canada
69 D8 **Takua Thung** Thailand
117 F6 **Taku Glacier** Br Col/Alaska Canada/U.S.A.
85 F7 **Takum** Nigeria
74 E2 **Talagang** Pakistan
133 D6 **Talagapa** Argentina
68 H7 **Ta Lai** Vietnam
83 J8 **Talaimannar** Sri Lanka
85 F5 **Talak** *reg* Niger
107 P5 **Talala** Oklahoma U.S.A.
16 E10 **Talamagait** Morocco
69 F14 **Talang** Sumatra
70 K8 **Talangbatu** Sumatra
69 G14 **Talangbetutu** Sumatra
69 F14 **Talanglambangantir** Sumatra
69 G14 **Talangpulaukabung** Sumatra
128 B4 **Talara** Peru
77 H7 **Talar-i-Band** *mts* Pakistan
57 F3 **Talas** U.S.S.R.
136 L3 **Talasea** New Britain
57 F4 **Talasskiy Alatau, Khr** *mts* U.S.S.R.
70 G5 **Talatakoh** *isld* Sulawesi
79 G4 **Ţal at Mūsá** *mt* Lebanon
16 D5 **Talavera de la Reina** Spain
130 C10 **Talavera,I** Paraguay
140 F4 **Talawanta** Queensland Australia
71 G7 **Talayan** Philippines
65 G3 **Talazhan** China
79 G4 **Talbīsah** Syria
142 F2 **Talbot, C** Western Australia Australia
113 F7 **Talbot I** Florida U.S.A.
115 M2 **Talbot Inlet** Northwest Territories Canada
119 S4 **Talbot L** Manitoba Canada
143 F7 **Talbot, Mt** Western Australia Australia
139 J4 **Talbragar** New South Wales Australia
131 B5 **Talca** *prov* Chile
131 B5 **Talca** Chile
131 A6 **Talcahuano** Chile
131 B4 **Talca,Pta** Chile
109 M2 **Talco** Texas U.S.A.
94 G9 **Talcott** West Virginia U.S.A.
52 E6 **Taldom** U.S.S.R.
141 F4 **Taldora** Queensland Australia
57 A3 **Taldyk** U.S.S.R.
57 J3 **Taldy-Kurgan** U.S.S.R.
77 B4 **Tal-e Khosravī** Iran
100 C7 **Talent** Oregon U.S.A.
8 C2 **Talerddig** Wales
8 C4 **Talgarth** Wales
76 B3 **Talguppa** India
138 C5 **Talia** South Australia Australia
71 G5 **Talibon** Bohol Philippines
110 A7 **Talihina** Oklahoma U.S.A.
76 C2 **Talikota** India
71 G7 **Talikua** *isld* Mindanao Philippines
86 F4 **Tali Post** Sudan
71 F5 **Talisay** Cebu Philippines
70 F4 **Talisayan** Kalimantan
71 G6 **Talisayan** Philippines
71 J4 **Talisei** *isld* Indonesia
55 D3 **Talitsa** Sverdlovskaya obl U.S.S.R.
55 D1 **Talitsa** Sverdlovskaya obl U.S.S.R.
54 M4 **Talitskiy Chamlyk** U.S.S.R.
33 N5 **Talkau** W Germany
116 N5 **Talkeetna Mts** Alaska U.S.A.
79 B7 **Talkha** Egypt
29 N3 **Talkkunapää** *mt* Finland
77 B3 **Talkuncheh** Iran
45 L4 **Talla** Italy
84 G5 **Ţallāb, Aţ** Libya
111 K8 **Talladega** Alabama U.S.A.
111 G10 **Tallahala** *R* Mississippi U.S.A.
111 M11 **Tallahassee** Florida U.S.A.
111 F7 **Tallahatchie** *R* Mississippi U.S.A.
139 H6 **Tallangatta** Victoria Australia
111 K9 **Tallapoosa** *R* Alabama U.S.A.
111 L8 **Tallapoosa** Georgia U.S.A.
19 Q16 **Tallard** France
26 H10 **Tallåsen** Sweden
80 G1 **Tall ash Sha'ar** *mt* Syria
111 L9 **Tallassee** Alabama U.S.A.
143 B8 **Tallering Pk** Western Australia Australia
8 C4 **Talley** Wales
78 H4 **Tall Fadghāmī** Syria
52 B5 **Tallinn** U.S.S.R.
26 M5 **Talljärv** Sweden
79 G4 **Tall Kalakh** Syria
40 D6 **Talloires** France
14 C4 **Tallow** Ireland
119 P6 **Tall Pines** Saskatchewan Canada
80 G3 **Tall Shihāb** Syria
110 G2 **Tallula** Illinois U.S.A.
111 E9 **Tallulah** Louisiana U.S.A.
119 O9 **Talmage** Saskatchewan Canada
102 A2 **Talmage** California U.S.A.
107 N2 **Talmage** Kansas U.S.A.
99 L9 **Talmage** Nebraska U.S.A.
40 B3 **Talmay** France
56 B4 **Tal'menka** U.S.S.R.
80 B7 **Talmey Yafe** Israel
18 D6 **Talmont** France
48 N2 **Tal'noye** U.S.S.R.
74 F8 **Taloda** India
86 F3 **Talodi** Sudan
107 M5 **Taloga** Oklahoma U.S.A.
70 F4 **Talok** Kalimantan
68 D2 **Ta-Long** Burma
77 L1 **Tāloqān** Afghanistan
106 E5 **Talpa** New Mexico U.S.A.
108 H4 **Talpa** Texas U.S.A.
124 G7 **Talpa de Allende** Mexico
127 O2 **Talparo R** Trinidad
111 M11 **Talquin,L** Florida U.S.A.
80 C6 **Tal Shahar** Israel
52 B6 **Talsi** U.S.S.R.
26 L7 **Tålsmark** Sweden
133 C3 **Taltal** Chile
69 D12 **Talu** Sumatra
71 H4 **Taludaä** Sulawesi
70 G4 **Taluditi** Sulawesi
71 E8 **Talue** *isld* Philippines
68 G3 **Ta Lus,C** Vietnam
41 O4 **Talvera** *R* Italy
26 N1 **Talvik** Norway
141 J8 **Talwood** Queensland Australia
56 F5 **Tal'yany** U.S.S.R.
139 G4 **Talyawalka** *R* New South Wales Australia
8 C3 **Talybont** Wales
8 C1 **Tal-y-cafn** Wales
52 J3 **Talyy** U.S.S.R.
61 M9 **Tama** Japan
61 N10 **Tama** *R* Japan
99 O8 **Tama** Iowa U.S.A.
70 D3 **Tamabo Ra** Sarawak
68 B1 **Tamadaw** Burma
143 A7 **Tamala** Western Australia Australia
85 D7 **Tamale** Ghana
16 C4 **Tamames** Spain
60 D13 **Tamana** Japan
130 J10 **Tamandare** Brazil
140 B4 **Tamani Desert** N Terr Australia
60 G11 **Tamano** Japan
85 F4 **Tamanrasset** Algeria
70 G5 **Tamanusi** Sulawesi
95 M6 **Tamaqua** Pennsylvania U.S.A.
45 L2 **Tamara** Italy
100 J5 **Tamarack** Idaho U.S.A.
99 N3 **Tamarack** Minnesota U.S.A.
60 E13 **Tamarai** Japan
17 H3 **Tamarite de Litera** Spain
110 G3 **Tamaroa** Illinois U.S.A.
41 J5 **Tamaro,Mt** Switzerland
139 H8 **Tamar R** Tasmania Australia
8 B6 **Tamar,R** England
60 G11 **Tamashima** Japan
48 E4 **Tamási** Hungary
Tamatave *see* **Toamasina**
61 O9 **Tamatsukuri** Japan
128 D5 **Tamaya** *R* Peru
85 A4 **Tamayya** Western Sahara
124 F5 **Tamazula** Mexico
124 H8 **Tamazula de Gordiano** Mexico
125 K7 **Tamazunchale** Mexico
37 K2 **Tambach Dietharz** East Germany
85 B6 **Tambacounda** Senegal
71 K8 **Tambalongang** *isld* Indonesia
70 B5 **Tambangmunjul** Kalimantan
69 F14 **Tambangsawah** Sumatra
88 E10 **Tambara** Mozambique
130 J9 **També** Brazil
70 G7 **Tambea** Sulawesi
69 H12 **Tambelan Besar** *isld* Indonesia
69 H12 **Tambelan, Kepulauan** *islds* Indonesia
143 C10 **Tambellup** Western Australia Australia
87 E9 **Tambero** Zambia
70 O9 **Tamberu** Java
131 B2 **Tambillos,Nevado de los** *pk* Chile
141 H6 **Tambo** Queensland Australia
128 D7 **Tambo** *R* Peru
128 C6 **Tambo de Mora** Peru
71 G6 **Tambog Pt** Mindanao Philippines
70 G6 **Tamboli** Sulawesi
124 G5 **Tambor** Mexico
139 H6 **Tamboritha,Mt** Victoria Australia
53 F7 **Tambov** U.S.S.R.
16 B2 **Tambre,R** Spain
142 C5 **Tambrey** Western Australia Australia
70 F5 **Tambulan** Sulawesi
70 E2 **Tambunan** Sabah
86 E4 **Tambura** Sudan
70 F4 **Tambu, Tk** *B* Sulawesi
83 K9 **Tambutta** Sri Lanka
70 E1 **Tambuyukon, G** *mt* Sabah
58 B2 **Tamch** Mongolia
85 B5 **Tamchakett** Mauritania
55 C6 **Tamdy** U.S.S.R.
57 C4 **Tamdybulak** U.S.S.R.
57 C4 **Tamdytau, Gory** *mt* U.S.S.R.
128 D2 **Tame** Colombia
16 B3 **Tâmega** *R* Portugal
133 C7 **Tamel Aike** Argentina
Tamenghest *see* **Tamanrasset**
85 F5 **Tamgak, Mts** Niger
57 E2 **Tamgaly, Ozero** *L* U.S.S.R.
125 L7 **Tamiahua,L.de** Mexico
113 F12 **Tamiami Canal** Florida U.S.A.
69 C10 **Tamiang** *R* Sumatra
76 C5 **Tamil Nadu** *prov* India
41 K4 **Tamina** *R* Switzerland
70 D6 **Taminglayang** Kalimantan
84 G3 **Tamīnī,At** Libya
41 K4 **Tamins** Switzerland
58 D2 **Tamirin Gol** *R* Mongolia
48 F5 **Tamis** *R* Yugoslavia
52 E3 **Tamitsa** U.S.S.R.
57 C1 **Tamkamys** U.S.S.R.
68 J5 **Tam Ky** Vietnam
71 F5 **Tamlang** Negros Philippines
45 R7 **Tammaro** *R* Italy
Tammerfors *see* **Tampere**
110 G4 **Tamms** Illinois U.S.A.
113 E10 **Tampa** Florida U.S.A.
107 N3 **Tampa** Kansas U.S.A.
70 K8 **Tampang** Sumatra
29 K10 **Tampere** Finland
125 L6 **Tampico** Mexico
99 R8 **Tampico** Illinois U.S.A.
101 T1 **Tampico** Montana U.S.A.
69 F11 **Tampin** Malaysia
69 C10 **Tamporbur** Sumatra
68 J5 **Tam Quan** Vietnam
80 D2 **Tamra** Israel
58 G2 **Tamsagbulag** Mongolia
75 Q6 **Tamu** Burma
71 E7 **Tamuk** *isld* Philippines
139 K4 **Tamworth** New South Wales Australia
121 O8 **Tamworth** Ontario Canada
9 E2 **Tamworth** England
95 Q3 **Tamworth** New Hampshire U.S.A.
68 F6 **Tamyong** *R* Cambodia
57 H1 **Tan** U.S.S.R.
116 Q6 **Tana** *R* Alaska U.S.A.
60 J12 **Tanabe** Japan
130 E7 **Tanabi** Brazil
26 Q1 **Tana-Bru** Norway
116 Q5 **Tanacross** Alaska U.S.A.
116 Q5 **Tanada L** Alaska U.S.A.
26 Q1 **Tanafjord** *inlet* Norway
43 G8 **Tanagro** *R* Italy
61 O8 **Tanagura** Japan
86 G3 **Tana Hāyk'** *L* Ethiopia
69 D13 **Tanahbala** *isld* Indonesia
71 K8 **Tanahdjampea** *isld* Indonesia
70 E5 **Tanahgrogot** Kalimantan
71 K10 **Tanahkadukung** Indonesia
68 D13 **Tanahmasa** *isld* Indonesia
70 E3 **Tanahmerah** Kalimantan
69 F9 **Tanah Merah** Malaysia
26 R1 **Tanahorn** *mt* Norway
69 E12 **Tanahputih** Sumatra
70 M9 **Tanah,Tg** *C* Java
70 F7 **Tanakeke** *isld* Sulawesi
70 F6 **Tanambung** Sulawesi
136 J3 **Tanamerah** W Irian
140 A4 **Tanami** N Terr Australia
71 J4 **Tanamon** Sulawesi
68 H7 **Tan An** Vietnam
116 N4 **Tanana** *R* Alaska U.S.A.
116 L4 **Tanana** Alaska U.S.A.
Tananarive *see* **Antananarivo**
18 H8 **Tanargue, Mt** France
44 E2 **Tanaro** *R* Italy
84 E4 **Tanārūt** Libya
71 G5 **Tanauan** Leyte Philippines
141 F7 **Tanbar** Queensland Australia
21 L3 **Tancarville** France
61 P13 **Tancha** Okinawa
65 D7 **Tancheng** China
59 J3 **Tanch'ŏn** N Korea
124 H8 **Tancitario,Cerro de** *mt* Mexico
125 K7 **Tancuayalab** Mexico
75 K5 **Tanda** India
71 G6 **Tandag** Mindanao Philippines
48 L6 **Ţăndărei** Romania
70 E1 **Tandek** Sabah
28 D6 **Tanderup** Denmark
131 F6 **Tandil** Argentina
131 F6 **Tandil, Sa del** *ra* Argentina
70 F3 **Tandjungbatu** Kalimantan
69 J11 **Tandjung Blitung** Indonesia
70 L9 **Tandjungpriok** Java
70 C5 **Tandjungpusu** Kalimantan
74 C6 **Tando Adam** Pakistan
74 C6 **Tando Muhammad Khan** Pakistan
138 F4 **Tandou L** New South Wales Australia
55 G3 **Tandovo, Oz** *L* U.S.S.R.
14 E2 **Tandragee** N Ireland
27 G10 **Tandsjöbörg** Sweden
28 D7 **Tandslet** Denmark
71 E8 **Tandubatu** *isld* Philippines
76 C2 **Tandur** India
145 F3 **Taneatua** New Zealand
59 K5 **Tanega-shima** *isld* Japan
61 P5 **Taneichi** Japan
Tanen *mt see* **Taunggyi** *mt*
71 A3 **Taneti** Halmahera Indonesia
31 O5 **Tanew** *R* Poland
95 K7 **Taneytown** Maryland U.S.A.
85 E4 **Tanezrouft** *reg* Algeria
84 E4 **Tanezzuft** *watercourse* Libya/Algeria
88 G4 **Tanga** Tanzania
75 N6 **Tangail** Bangladesh
137 L2 **Tanga Is** Bismarck Arch
83 K11 **Tangalla** Sri Lanka
Tanganyika *see* **Tanzania**
88 B5 **Tanganyika,L** E Africa
130 D10 **Tangará** Brazil
67 D3 **Tangdukou** China
28 D4 **Tange Å** *R* Denmark
146 K9 **Tange Promontory** *pen* Antarctica
16 D9 **Tanger** Morocco
70 L9 **Tangerang** Java
33 P8 **Tangerhütte** East Germany
33 P7 **Tangermünde** East Germany
28 D4 **Tange Sø** *L* Denmark
58 G4 **Tanggu** China
66 D5 **Tanggula Shan** *ra* China
66 E5 **Tanggula Shankou** *pass* China
58 F5 **Tang He** China
65 C5 **Tang He** *R* China
Tangier *see* **Tanger** Morocco
122 K9 **Tangier** Nova Scotia Canada
122 K9 **Tangier Grand L** Nova Scotia Canada
95 M9 **Tangier I** Virginia U.S.A.
145 E4 **Tangimoana** New Zealand
111 F11 **Tangipahoa** *R* Louisiana U.S.A.
70 G6 **Tangkeleboke, G** *mt* Sulawesi
70 K8 **Tangkittebak, Gunung** *mt* Sumatra
70 L9 **Tangkuban Perahu** *mt* Java
66 D5 **Tang-ku-la-yu-mu Ts'o** *L* China
109 L5 **Tanglewood** Texas U.S.A.
Tanglha Range *see* **Tanggula Shan**
66 F5 **Tangmai** China
141 G5 **Tangorin** Queensland Australia
145 D1 **Tangowahine** New Zealand
67 C6 **Tangpeng** China
66 D5 **Tangra Yumco** *L* China
69 B10 **Tangse** Sumatra
65 D5 **Tangshan** China
67 A3 **Tangtang** China
67 C3 **Tangtou** China
67 E5 **Tangtouxia** China
71 F5 **Tangub** Negros Philippines
85 E6 **Tanguiéta** Benin
56 F3 **Tanguy** U.S.S.R.
59 J2 **Tangwanghe** China
67 F2 **Tangxi** China
65 C5 **Tang Xian** China
67 D1 **Tangxianzhen** China
68 D1 **Tang-Yan** Burma
67 C2 **Tangyan He** *R* China
65 C7 **Tangyin** China
58 F4 **Tangyin** China
65 H1 **Tangyuan** China
29 N4 **Tanhua** Finland
68 G7 **Tani** Cambodia
61 K10 **Tanigumi** Japan
136 G3 **Tanimbar, Kep** *islds* Moluccas Indonesia
40 E5 **Taninges** France
60 D14 **Taniyama** Japan
71 F6 **Tanjay** Philippines
70 D6 **Tanjung** Kalimantan
69 G13 **Tanjung** Sumatra
69 F12 **Tanjungbalai** Kepulauan Riau Indonesia
69 D11 **Tanjungbalai** Sumatra
69 F12 **Tanjungbatu** Indonesia
69 F13 **Tanjungbojo** Sumatra
70 F4 **Tanjungbuaya** *isld* Kalimantan
70 K7 **Tanjungenim** Sumatra
70 E6 **Tanjunggaru** Kalimantan
70 K8 **Tanjungkarang Telukbetung** Sumatra
69 H14 **Tanjung-pandan** Indonesia
69 G12 **Tanjungpinang** Indonesia
69 D11 **Tanjungpura** Sumatra
69 G14 **Tanjungraja** Sumatra
70 E3 **Tanjungredeb** Kalimantan
69 J13 **Tanjungsaleh** *isld* Indonesia
69 J13 **Tanjungsatai** Indonesia
70 E3 **Tanjungselor** Kalimantan
74 D2 **Tank** Pakistan
138 E3 **Tankamarinna,L** South Australia Australia
29 N3 **Tankapirtti** Finland
108 G4 **Tankersly** Texas U.S.A.
56 G5 **Tankhoy** U.S.S.R.
68 B3 **Tanlwe** *R* Burma
68 J7 **Tan My** Vietnam
37 O7 **Tann** Bayern W Germany
37 J2 **Tann** Hessen W Germany
37 M3 **Tanna** East Germany
137 O5 **Tanna** *isld* Vanuatu
15 F4 **Tannadice** Scotland
22 H4 **Tannay** France
33 N9 **Tanne** East Germany
Tannenberg *see* **Stębark**
95 N4 **Tannersville** New York U.S.A.
95 M5 **Tannersville** Pennsylvania U.S.A.
37 N4 **Tännesberg** W Germany
37 J6 **Tannhausen** W Germany
41 M1 **Tannheim** W Germany
29 M6 **Tannila** Finland
119 N1 **Tannin** Ontario Canada
80 C3 **Tanninim** Israel
28 E1 **Tannis Bugt** *B* Denmark
28 E1 **Tannisby** Denmark
37 L2 **Tannroda** East Germany
85 D7 **Tano** *R* Ghana
71 F5 **Tañon Str** Philippines
65 F6 **Tanout** Niger
68 G1 **Tan Quang** Vietnam
124 H4 **Tanque Alvarez** Mexico
125 K7 **Tanquian** Mexico
79 F2 **Tanrıverdi** Turkey
75 K5 **Tansing** Nepal
79 A8 **Tanta** Egypt
68 B1 **Tantabin** Sagaing Burma
68 C3 **Tantabin** Tenasserim Burma
119 Q8 **Tantallon** Saskatchewan Canada
85 B3 **Tan-Tan** Morocco
138 F6 **Tantanoola** South Australia Australia
Tantung *see* **Dandong**
140 C3 **Tanumbirini** N Terr Australia
116 E6 **Tanunak** Alaska U.S.A.
138 E5 **Tanunda** South Australia Australia
55 C3 **Tanyp** *R* U.S.S.R.
88 C4 **Tanzania** *rep* Africa
117 H6 **Tanzilla** *R* British Columbia Canada
65 E2 **Tao'an** China
67 G2 **Taohua Dao** *isld* China
Taohuaping *see* **Longhui**
67 D2 **Taojiang** China
68 D7 **Tao,Ko** *isld* Thailand
65 D7 **Taoluo** China
Taonan *see* **Tao'an**
99 O6 **Taopi** Minnesota U.S.A.
43 G11 **Taormina** Sicily
106 E5 **Taos** New Mexico U.S.A.
85 D4 **Taoudenni** Mali
85 D2 **Taounate** Morocco
85 D2 **Taourirt** Morocco
85 D2 **Taouz** Morocco
67 D2 **Taoyuan** China
55 E3 **Tap** *R* U.S.S.R.
52 C5 **Tapa** U.S.S.R.
71 E8 **Tapaan Passage** Philippines
125 N10 **Tapachula** Mexico
69 E10 **Tapah** Malaysia
129 G5 **Tapajós** *R* Brazil
69 C11 **Tapaktuan** Sumatra
133 E5 **Tapalquén** Argentina
69 E14 **Tapan** Sumatra
129 G3 **Tapanahoni** *R* Suriname
125 M9 **Tapanatapec** Mexico
144 B6 **Tapanui** New Zealand
69 D12 **Tapanuli, Teluk** *B* Sumatra
128 F5 **Tapauá** Brazil
145 D4 **Tapawera** New Zealand
130 H9 **Taperoá** Brazil
131 H3 **Tapes, Pta. de** *C* Brazil
37 K6 **Tapfheim** W Germany
74 F8 **Tāpi** *R* India
71 F7 **Tapiantana** *isld* Philippines
128 D5 **Tapiche** *R* Peru
70 B5 **Tapinbini** Kalimantan
29 L11 **Tapiola** Finland
128 E3 **Tapirapeó, Sa** *mts* Venezuela/Brazil
130 B4 **Tapirapuã** Brazil
69 F10 **Tapis** *mt* Malaysia
124 E4 **Tapizuelas** Mexico
75 M5 **Taplejung** Nepal
48 D4 **Tapolca** Hungary
68 D2 **Ta-Pom** Burma
95 L9 **Tappahannock** Virginia U.S.A.
70 F6 **Tappalang** Sulawesi
94 F6 **Tappan Res** Ohio U.S.A.
98 G3 **Tappen** North Dakota U.S.A.
28 J6 **Tappernøje** Denmark
60 O4 **Tappi zaki** *C* Japan
60 P1 **Tappu** Japan
28 C6 **Taps** Denmark
55 D1 **Tapsuy** *R* U.S.S.R.
145 E2 **Tapu** New Zealand
145 D4 **Tapuaenuku** *mt* New Zealand
71 E8 **Tapul** Philippines
69 D12 **Tapulonanjing** *mt* Sumatra
68 B3 **Tapun** Burma
128 F4 **Tapurucuara** Brazil
133 G3 **Taquara** Brazil
130 D7 **Taquaraçu** *R* Brazil
130 D4 **Taquara,Sa.da** *mts* Brazil
131 H2 **Taquari** *R* Brazil
130 C6 **Taquari,Pantanal do** *swamp* Brazil
112 K2 **Tar** *R* North Carolina U.S.A.
141 K7 **Tara** Queensland Australia
120 J8 **Tara** Ontario Canada
71 E4 **Tara** *isld* Philippines
55 G3 **Tara** *R* U.S.S.R.
55 F3 **Tara** U.S.S.R.
48 E7 **Tara** *mt* Yugoslavia
85 G7 **Taraba** *R* Nigeria
84 E3 **Tarābulus** Libya
128 E3 **Taracua** Brazil
145 F3 **Taradale** New Zealand
84 E4 **Tarāghin** Libya
60 D13 **Taragi** Japan
139 J6 **Tarago** New South Wales Australia
14 E3 **Tara Hill** Ireland
26 L5 **Tårajaure** Sweden
70 E3 **Tarakan** Kalimantan
77 K3 **Tarakki** *reg* Afghanistan
47 L4 **Taraklı** Turkey
48 M4 **Tarakliya** U.S.S.R.
145 D4 **Tarakohe** New Zealand
139 J5 **Taralga** New South Wales Australia
144 C5 **Taramakau R** New Zealand
71 M9 **Taramana** Indonesia
139 J5 **Tarana** New South Wales Australia
145 E3 **Taranaki** *stat area* New Zealand
16 E4 **Tarancón** Spain
145 E1 **Taranga I** New Zealand
76 D5 **Tarangambadi** India
55 D4 **Taranovskoye** U.S.S.R.
15 A3 **Taransay** *isld* Scotland
43 H8 **Taranto** Italy
43 H8 **Taranto,G.di** Italy
128 E7 **Tarapacá** *prov* Chile
145 F3 **Taraponui** *mt* New Zealand
128 C5 **Tarapoto** Peru
18 H7 **Tarare** France
145 E4 **Tararua Range** New Zealand
69 A8 **Tarāsa Dwīp** Nicobar Is
19 N17 **Tarascon** France
48 N1 **Tarashcha** U.S.S.R.
41 M4 **Tarasp** Switzerland
85 F3 **Tarat** Algeria
128 D5 **Tarauacá** Brazil
17 F4 **Taravilla** Spain
145 F3 **Tarawera L** New Zealand
145 F3 **Tarawera, Mt** New Zealand
17 F3 **Tarazona** Spain
17 F5 **Tarazona de la Mancha** Spain
29 K5 **Tårbæk** Denmark
57 K2 **Tarbagatay, Khrebet** *mts* U.S.S.R.
14 B4 **Tarbert** Ireland
15 B3 **Tarbert** Harris Scotland
12 C2 **Tarbert** Strathclyde Scotland
12 B2 **Tarbert,L** Scotland
18 F9 **Tarbes** France
12 D3 **Tarbolton** Scotland
112 K2 **Tarboro** North Carolina U.S.A.
141 F5 **Tarbrax** Queensland Australia
48 K4 **Tarcăului,Munţii** *mts* Romania
138 C4 **Tarcoola** South Australia Australia
139 H4 **Tarcoon** New South Wales Australia
138 C2 **Tarcoonyinna** *R* South Australia Australia
139 J6 **Tarcutta** New South Wales Australia
18 E9 **Tardets-Sorholus** France
17 G3 **Tardienta** Spain
21 J8 **Tardière,la** France
18 F7 **Tardoire** *R* France
59 L2 **Tardoki-Yami, Gora** *mt* U.S.S.R.
143 B8 **Tardun** Western Australia Australia
139 L4 **Taree** New South Wales Australia
139 G4 **Tarella** New South Wales Australia
26 N4 **Tärendö** Sweden
40 E7 **Tarentaise** *dist* France
94 H6 **Tarentum** Pennsylvania U.S.A.
85 B3 **Tarfaya** Morocco
65 F1 **Targan** China
16 E10 **Targuist** Morocco
112 J3 **Tarheel** North Carolina U.S.A.
84 E3 **Tarhūnah** Libya
65 A4 **Tarian Gol** China
16 D8 **Tarifa** Spain
71 F2 **Tarigtig Pt** Philippines
133 E2 **Tarija** *prov* Bolivia
133 E2 **Tarija** Bolivia
76 B4 **Tarikere** India
145 E3 **Tariki** New Zealand
72 F5 **Tarīm** S Yemen
Tarim Basin *see* **Tarim Pendi**
88 F6 **Tarime** Tanzania
66 D3 **Tarim He** *R* China
66 C3 **Tarim Pendi** *basin* China
77 J3 **Tarīn Kowt** Afghanistan
Tari Nor *see* **Dalai Nur** *L*
89 D9 **Tarka** *R* S Africa
87 E12 **Tarkastad** S Africa
110 A1 **Tarkio** Missouri U.S.A.
101 L2 **Tarkio** Montana U.S.A.
50 G2 **Tarko-Sale** U.S.S.R.
85 D7 **Tarkwa** Ghana
133 C7 **Tar,L** Argentina
71 E3 **Tarlac** Philippines
15 F3 **Tarland** Scotland
13 F6 **Tarleton** England
140 D5 **Tarlton Downs** N Terr Australia
28 B5 **Tarm** Denmark
128 C6 **Tarma** Peru
32 K6 **Tarmstedt** W Germany
18 F9 **Tarn** *R* France
18 G9 **Tarn** *dept* France
48 F3 **Tarna** *R* Hungary
26 H6 **Tärnaby** Sweden
77 K3 **Tarnak** *R* Afghanistan
18 F8 **Tarn-et-Garonne** *dept* France
18 H8 **Tarn,Gorges du** France
31 N5 **Tarnobrzeg** Poland
52 F4 **Tarnogskiy Gorodok** U.S.S.R.
119 M6 **Tarnopo** Saskatchewan Canada
33 Q5 **Tarnow** East Germany
31 M5 **Tarnow** Poland
31 L5 **Tarnowskie Gory** Poland
27 J11 **Tärnsjö** Sweden
44 H2 **Taro** *R* Italy
54 F8 **Taromskoye** U.S.S.R.
141 J7 **Taroom** Queensland Australia
85 C2 **Taroudannt** Morocco
28 C7 **Tarp** W Germany
140 D4 **Tarpaulin Swamp** N Terr Australia
109 H6 **Tarpley** Texas U.S.A.
113 E9 **Tarpon Springs** Florida U.S.A.
8 D1 **Tarporley** England
113 L12 **Tarpum Bay** Eleuthera Bahamas
44 L5 **Tarquinia** Italy
80 D7 **Tarqumiya** Jordan
17 H3 **Tarragona** *prov* Spain
17 H3 **Tarragona** Spain
139 H8 **Tarraleah** Tasmania Australia
139 H4 **Tarran Hills** New South Wales Australia
111 K8 **Tarrant City** Alabama U.S.A.
8 D6 **Tarrant Hinton** England
140 E3 **Tarrant,Pt** Queensland Australia
144 B6 **Tarras** New Zealand
17 J3 **Tarrasa** Spain
26 J4 **Tarrekaise** *mt* Sweden
41 N3 **Tarrenz** Austria
106 E2 **Tarryall** Colorado U.S.A.
112 E5 **Tarrytown** Georgia U.S.A.
95 O5 **Tarrytown** New York U.S.A.
17 F9 **Tarsa,C** Algeria
45 P1 **Tarski Zaliv** *B* Yugoslavia
84 F5 **Tarso Taro** *mt* Chad
86 C1 **Tarso Tieroko** *mt* Chad
79 E1 **Tarsus** *R* Turkey
78 E3 **Tarsus** Turkey
133 E2 **Tartagal** Argentina
6 L4 **Tartan** *oil rig* North Sea
45 J1 **Tártaro** *R* Italy
18 E9 **Tartas** France
56 A3 **Tartas** *R* U.S.S.R.
52 C5 **Tartu** U.S.S.R.
79 F4 **Tartūs** Syria
80 C6 **Tarum** Israel
60 P3 **Tarumae-san** *mt* Japan
130 H6 **Tarumirim** Brazil
60 D14 **Tarumizu** Japan
54 J2 **Tarusa** U.S.S.R.
69 D9 **Tarutao,Ko** *isld* Thailand
48 M4 **Tarutino** U.S.S.R.
69 D11 **Tarutung** Sumatra
26 D8 **Tarva** *isld* Norway
38 J9 **Tarvisio** Italy
56 E5 **Tarys-Arzhan** U.S.S.R.
120 K5 **Tarzwell** Ontario Canada
108 B6 **Tasajera, Sa** *mts* Mexico
57 G2 **Tasaral** U.S.S.R.
84 E4 **Tasāwah** Libya
57 D3 **Tas Buget** U.S.S.R.
121 M4 **Taschereau** Quebec Canada
107 K2 **Tasco** Kansas U.S.A.
117 M10 **Taseko, Mt** British Columbia Canada
56 D2 **Taseyeva** *R* U.S.S.R.
76 B2 **Tasgaon** India
58 A2 **Tashanta** U.S.S.R.
57 A4 **Tashauz** U.S.S.R.
75 O5 **Tashigang** Bhutan
57 E4 **Tashkent** U.S.S.R.
57 C6 **Tashkepri** U.S.S.R.
57 F4 **Tash-Kumyr** U.S.S.R.
55 B5 **Tashla** U.S.S.R.
120 C2 **Tashota** Ontario Canada
56 C4 **Tashtagol** U.S.S.R.
56 C4 **Tashtyp** U.S.S.R.
69 F11 **Tasik Dampar** Malaysia
70 M9 **Tasikmalaja** Java
70 L9 **Tasikmalaya** Java
80 G2 **Tasil** Syria
28 F7 **Tåsinge** *isld* Denmark
115 O3 **Tasiusaq** Greenland
26 H7 **Tåsjö** Sweden
26 H7 **Tåsjön** *L* Sweden
85 G5 **Tasker** Niger
47 N11 **Taşkopru** Turkey
56 E5 **Taskyl,Khrebet** *mts* U.S.S.R.
78 J2 **Taşliçay** Turkey
144 D4 **Tasman** New Zealand
145 D4 **Tasman Bay** New Zealand
139 H9 **Tasman Hd** Tasmania Australia
139 H8 **Tasmania** *state* Australia
145 D4 **Tasman Mountains** New Zealand
144 C5 **Tasman, Mt** New Zealand
139 J9 **Tasman Pen** Tasmania Australia
134 G13 **Tasman Plateau** Pacific Oc
137 M9 **Tasman Sea** Pacific Oc
48 H3 **Tăşnad** Romania
85 F5 **Tassara** Niger
19 J5 **Tasselot, Mt** France
115 M6 **Tassialouc,L** Quebec Canada
85 E5 **Tassili du Hoggar** *plateau* Algeria
85 F3 **Tassili-n'-Ajjer** *plateau* Algeria
28 J5 **Tåstrup** Denmark
51 M2 **Tas Tumus** U.S.S.R.
57 E3 **Tasty** U.S.S.R.
79 D2 **Taşucu** Turkey
85 C3 **Tata** Morocco
71 H5 **Tataba** Sulawesi Indonesia
48 E3 **Tatabánya** Hungary
71 E7 **Tatalan** *isld* Philippines
122 J8 **Tatamagouche** Nova Scotia Canada
85 G2 **Tataouine** Tunisia
48 M5 **Tatarbunary** U.S.S.R.
47 H3 **Tatarlar** Turkey
55 G3 **Tatarsk** U.S.S.R.
52 H6 **Tatarskaya A.S.S.R.** U.S.S.R.
59 M1 **Tatarskiy Proliv** *str* U.S.S.R.
70 C3 **Tatau** Sarawak
141 G3 **Tate** *R* Queensland Australia
89 E3 **Tate** *R* Botswana
119 N7 **Tate** Saskatchewan Canada
112 C3 **Tate** Georgia U.S.A.
61 O6 **Tateai** Japan
140 C2 **Tate Bluff** *hill* N Terr Australia
60 O4 **Tateura** Japan
61 L9 **Tate yama** *mt* Japan
61 N11 **Tateyama** Japan
117 P5 **Tathlina L** Northwest Territories Canada
139 K6 **Tathra** New South Wales Australia
116 O6 **Tatitlek** Alaska U.S.A.
117 L10 **Tatla Lake** British Columbia Canada
117 K7 **Tatlatui Prov. Park** British Columbia Canada
116 K5 **Tatlawiksuk** *R* Alaska U.S.A.
117 L10 **Tatlayoko Lake** British Columbia Canada
117 M10 **Tatlow, Mt** British Columbia Canada
101 R5 **Tatman Mt** Wyoming U.S.A.
116 K6 **Tatna L** Alaska U.S.A.
115 K6 **Tatnam,C** Manitoba Canada
139 H6 **Tatong** Victoria Australia
66 D4 **Tatrang** China
31 M6 **Tatry** *mts* Czech/Poland
117 E6 **Tatshenshini** *R* British Columbia Canada
77 K7 **Tatta** Pakistan
9 F1 **Tattershall** England
57 G3 **Tatty** U.S.S.R.

130 F8	Tatuí Brazil	116 K7	Tazimina Lakes Alaska	117 H7	Telegraph Creek British
131 B2	Tatuí,Sa de mts Chile		Columbia Canada		Columbia Canada
108 D2	Tatum New Mexico U.S.A.	84 G4	Tāzirbū Libya	80 F6	Teleilet el Ghassul Jordan
109 N3	Tatum Texas U.S.A.	48 K4	Tazlau R Romania	27 C12	Telemark prov Norway
107 N7	Tatums Oklahoma U.S.A.	116 O6	Tazlina L Alaska U.S.A.	70 E4	Telen R Kalimantan
	Tatung see Datong	50 G2	Tazovskaya Guba G	48 L3	Teleneshty U.S.S.R.
139 H6	Tatura Victoria Australia		U.S.S.R.	48 J6	Teleorman R Romania
129 K5	Tauá Brazil	50 G2	Tazovskiy U.S.S.R.	109 L2	Telephone Texas U.S.A.
128 F4	Tauapeçaçu Brazil	66 F6	Tazungdam Burma	102 G5	Telescope Pk California
37 L2	Taubach East Germany	61 K8	Tazuruhama Japan		U.S.A.
130 F8	Taubaté Brazil	78 K1	Tbilisi U.S.S.R.	127 P5	Telescope Pt Grenada
36 H5	Tauber R W Germany	85 E7	Tchaourou Benin	129 G5	Teles Pires R Brazil
83 R10	Taucha East Germany	86 B6	Tchibanga Gabon	56 C5	Teleskova, Oz L U.S.S.R.
38 H7	Tauern Tunnel Austria	84 E5	Tchigaï, Plat. du Chad/Niger	80 C8	Tel Eyton Israel
37 N7	Taufkirchen W Germany	68 J2	Tching Lan Xan isld Vietnam	142 D5	Telfer Mining Centre
36 G2	Taufstein mt W Germany	85 F5	Tchin-Tabaradene Niger		Western Australia Australia
128 G3	Tauini R Brazil	86 B4	Tchollirè Cameroon	67 C7	Tengqiao China
145 E2	Taukoa New Zealand	111 F8	Tchula Mississippi U.S.A.	67 C5	Teng Xian China
20 C4	Taukè France	31 L1	Tczew Poland	22 J3	Telgte W Germany
19 N16	Taulignan France	128 F4	Tea R Brazil	80 F1	Tel Hazor Israel
28 D5	Taulov Denmark	48 J4	Tea South Dakota U.S.A.	85 B6	Télimélé Guinea
145 E3	Taumarunui New Zealand		Teaca Romania	80 F2	Tel Kinnerot Israel
128 D5	Taumaturgo Brazil	78 J3	Teacapán Mexico	78 J3	Tel Kotchek Syria
110 F4	Taum Sauk Mt Missouri	108 D3	Teague New Mexico U.S.A.	117 K8	Telkwa British Columbia
	U.S.A.	109 L4	Teague Texas U.S.A.		Canada
130 C7	Taunay Brazil	143 D7	Teague,L Western Australia	108 G1	Tell Texas U.S.A.
89 D6	Taung S Africa		Australia	80 C7	Tel Lakhish Israel
68 C5	Taungbon Burma	13 G4	Team Valley England	22 K5	Tellancourt Villers France
68 B2	Taungdwingyi Burma	144 A6	Te Anau New Zealand	110 K4	Tell City Indiana U.S.A.
68 C2	Taung-Gyi Burma	145 E3	Te Anga New Zealand	80 F5	Tell Deir'Alla Jordan
68 D3	Taunggyi mt Burma/Thailand	45 Q7	Teano Italy	54 E1	Telejäkk Sweden
68 C2	Taunglau Burma	101 T6	Teapot Dome hill Wyoming	116 D4	Teller Alaska U.S.A.
68 C4	Taungnyo A ra Burma		U.S.A.	76 B5	Tellicherry India
68 B2	Taungtha Burma	145 E2	Te Araroa New Zealand	112 C2	Tellico L Tennessee U.S.A.
68 B3	Taungup Burma	145 E2	Te Aroha New Zealand	112 C2	Tellico Plains Tennessee
74 D3	Taunsa Pakistan	140 C5	Tea Tree N Terr Australia		U.S.A.
8 C5	Taunton England	145 E3	Te Awamutu New Zealand	122 F3	Tellier Quebec Canada
95 Q5	Taunton Massachusetts	22 J3	Teba Spain	22 J3	Tellin Belgium
	U.S.A.	32 K4	Tebas Indonesia	36 H4	Tellingstedt W Germany
95 R5	Taunton,E Massachusetts	80 C5	Tebessa Algeria	38 H6	Tell Litwinsky Israel
	U.S.A.	130 B10	Tebicuary Paraguay	80 F6	Tell Nimrin Jordan
36 E3	Taunus mts W Germany	69 D13	Tebingtinggi Sumatra	106 C4	Tellurido Colorado U.S.A.
145 E2	Taupiri New Zealand	43 C12	Tebourba Tunisia	80 C7	Tel Maresha Israel
52 B6	Tauraga U.S.S.R.	43 C12	Tébourouba Tunisia	58 C2	Telmen Nuur L Mongolia
145 E3	Taurakawa mt New Zealand	69 F12	Tebrau Malaysia	80 B8	Tel Mifsah Israel
145 F2	Tauranga New Zealand	53 G11	Tebulosmta mt U.S.S.R.	80 C4	Tel Mond Israel
121 R6	Taureau, L Quebec Canada	18 G10	Tech R France	69 D13	Telo Indonesia
145 D1	Tauroa Pt New Zealand	100 H4	Techa U.S.S.R.	29 O4	Telocaset Oregon U.S.A.
55 F2	Taurovy U.S.S.R.	125 K8	Techiman Ghana	144 D5	Teloloapan Mexico
	Taurus Mts see Toroslar	52 J3	Techirghiol Romania	131 B6	Tel'pos'z, Gora mt U.S.S.R.
	Dağlari	144 D5	Technical, Mt New Zealand	70 D2	Telom Sabah
17 G3	Tauste Spain	33 Q6	Teck W Germany	125 O9	Tenosique Mexico
144 B7	Tautuku Peninsula New	133 C6	Tecka Argentina	61 J11	Telsen Argentina
	Zealand	32 G8	Tecklenburg W Germany	61 L11	Teriryū Japan
137 M2	Tauu Is Papua New Guinea	27 F16	Teckomatorp Sweden	111 J11	Tensas R Louisiana U.S.A.
115 K5	Tavani Northwest Territories	124 G7	Tecolotitlan Mexico	111 J11	Tensaw R Alabama U.S.A.
	Canada	124 E3	Tecolotlán Mexico	100 J2	Tensed Idaho U.S.A.
40 F3	Tavannes Switzerland	33 S8	Tecomán Mexico	85 C2	Tensift R Morocco
113 P9	Tavares Florida U.S.A.	103 H6	Tecopa California U.S.A.	99 M2	Tenstrike Minnesota U.S.A.
45 K4	Tavarnelles Val di Pesa Italy	124 E3	Tecorichic Mexico	54 D3	Tenstsa Lusawesi
74 F4	Tavas Turkey	124 E3	Tecoripa Mexico	57 H3	Tentenden Western Australia
22 F4	Tavaux France	125 J9	Tecpan Mexico	143 B10	Tenterden Western Australia
55 E2	Tavda U.S.S.R.	48 L5	Tecuala Mexico	29 G5	Tenterden England
55 D2	Tavda R U.S.S.R.	48 L5	Tecuci Romania	139 K3	Tenterfield New South
26 L7	Tavelsjö Sweden	120 H10	Tecumseh Ontario Canada		Wales Australia
41 J5	Taverne Switzerland	94 D4	Tecumseh Michigan U.S.A.	113 F12	Ten Thousand Is Florida
45 K1	Tavernelle Italy	110 D5	Tecumseh Missouri U.S.A.		U.S.A.
115 M4	Taverner R Northwest	98 K9	Tecumseh Nebraska U.S.A.	70 C4	Tentolomatinan mt Sulawesi
	Territories Canada	107 O6	Tecumseh Oklahoma U.S.A.	124 H7	Tecolatiche Mexico
19 Q17	Taverne France	8 C6	Tedburn St Mary England	45 M3	Teodorano Italy
113 G12	Tavernier Florida U.S.A.	70 P16	Tedjakula Indonesia	116 L1	Teófilo Otōni Brazil
21 P3	Taverny Val d'Oise France	77 G1	Tedzhen U.S.S.R.	48 K1	Teofipol' U.S.S.R.
88 F3	Taveta Kenya	57 B5	Tedzhen U.S.S.R.	60 H11	Teomabal isld Philippines
137 R5	Taveuni isld Fiji	14 K9	Tees R England	61 J9	Teshio R Japan
16 B7	Tavira Portugal	118 D6	Tees England	61 J9	Teshio-sanchi mts Japan
8 B6	Tavistock England	13 G5	Tees,R England	61 J8	Teshio L Japan
43 C8	Tavolara, I Sardinia	120 J9	Teeswater Ontario Canada	69 D7	Teshekpuk L Alaska U.S.A.
55 G4	Tavolzhan U.S.S.R.	71 D6	Teeth,The mt Palawan	73 J3	Thap Put Thailand
16 B4	Távora R Portugal		Philippines	95 B5	Thap Sakae Thailand
68 D5	Tavoy Burma	128 F4	Tefe Brazil	117 F5	Teslin R Yukon Territory
	Tavoy I see Mali Kyun	47 K7	Tefenni Turkey		Canada
68 D6	Tavoy Pt Burma	89 E8	TeGabonoba dist S Africa	117 G5	Teslin L Br Col/Yukon Terr
65 H3	Tavrichanka U.S.S.R.	70 M9	Tegal Java	57 B3	Tesourias R Brazil
55 F4	Tavricheskoye U.S.S.R.	23 K4	Tegel W Berlin	130 D5	Tesouro Brazil
47 N11	Tavşancil Turkey	25 F6	Tegelen Netherlands	37 O4	Tepelská Plošina mts
47 K5	Tavşanli Turkey	N11 P2	Tegernsee L W Germany		Czechoslovakia
47 N11	Tavşanli Turkey	85 F6	Tegina Nigeria	17 G9	Teperon Spain
26 L3	Tavvaätno R Sweden	70 K8	Teginaneng Sumatra	69 F11	Teminlangsat Kalimantan
145 G4	Tawa New Zealand	141 H8	Tego Queensland Australia	69 F10	Teminpul, Bukit hill Malaysia
109 M3	Tawakoni, L Texas U.S.A.	125 L2	Tegucigalpa Honduras	71 C3	Teminabuan W Irian
94 D2	Tawas City Michigan U.S.A.	85 F5	Teguidadam Tessoum Niger	57 A1	Temir U.S.S.R.
118 D4	Tawatinaw Alberta Canada	102 F6	Tehachapi California U.S.A.	48 M2	Temirtau U.S.S.R.
70 E2	Tawau Sabah	102 F6	Tehachapi Mts California	52 J4	Temirgoe U.S.S.R.
		122 A2	Tehachapi Mts California	54 K8	Telpogorsk U.S.S.R.

12 E3 Thornhill Dumfries & Galloway Scotland
13 E6 Thornton England
13 E1 Thornton Scotland
109 P2 Thornton Arkansas U.S.A.
106 F2 Thornton Colorado U.S.A.
99 N7 Thornton Iowa U.S.A.
109 L4 Thornton Texas U.S.A.
100 I4 Thornton Washington U.S.A.
141 F4 Thorntonia Queensland Australia
110 K1 Thorntown Indiana U.S.A.
138 D6 Thorny Passage South Australia Australia
121 L9 Thorold Ontario Canada
Thorout see Torhout
100 E2 Thorp Washington U.S.A.
99 Q5 Thorp Wisconsin U.S.A.
145 D4 Thorpe New Zealand
9 H3 Thorpeness England
28 E4 Thorsager Denmark
118 C5 Thorsby Alberta Canada
146 J8 Thorshavnfjella mts Antarctica
29 T8 Thórshöfn Iceland
28 D4 Thorsø Denmark
119 U1 Thorsteinson L Manitoba Canada
8 C6 Thorverton England
68 Q7 Thot Not Vietnam
21 K7 Thouarcé France
21 K8 Thouaret R France
21 K8 Thouars France
21 J8 Thoursais-Bouildroux France
21 K8 Thouet R France
142 C5 Thouin,C Western Australia Australia
46 E7 Thouria Greece
20 H6 Thourie France
22 D5 Thourotte France
95 L2 Thousand Is Ontario/New York Canada/U.S.A.
103 N3 Thousand Lake Mt Utah U.S.A.
102 F7 Thousand Oaks California U.S.A.
101 L8 Thousand Spring Cr Nevada U.S.A.
101 L7 Thousand Springs Idaho U.S.A.
47 H3 Thrace Turkey
109 K5 Thrall Texas U.S.A.
100 D4 Thrall Washington U.S.A.
9 F3 Thrapston England
139 J6 Thredbo New South Wales Australia
8 C3 Three Cocks Wales
101 K7 Three Creek Idaho U.S.A.
101 O4 Three Forks Montana U.S.A.
118 D7 Three Hills Alberta Canada
139 G8 Three Hummock I Tasmania Australia
110 J5 Three I.Res Tennessee U.S.A.
9 F2 Threekingham England
137 O8 Three Kings Basin Pacific Oc
145 D1 Three Kings Is New Zealand
140 D3 Three Knobs mt N Terr Australia
99 R4 Three Lakes Wisconsin U.S.A.
141 G2 Three Mile Opening, First & Second straits Gt Barrier Reef Aust
98 U3 Three Oaks Michigan U.S.A.
68 D5 Three Pagodas Pass Burma/Thailand
119 T3 Threepoint L Manitoba Canada
85 D8 Three Points, C Ghana
102 F5 Three Rivers California U.S.A.
94 B5 Three Rivers Michigan U.S.A.
106 D8 Three Rivers New Mexico U.S.A.
109 J7 Three Rivers Texas U.S.A.
123 N5 Three Rock Cove Newfoundland Canada
141 G1 Three Sisters islds Queensland Australia
100 D5 Three Sisters mts Oregon U.S.A.
143 B8 Three Springs Western Australia Australia
140 C4 Three Ways Roadhouse N Terr Australia
13 E4 Threlkeld England
109 H2 Throckmorton Texas U.S.A.
73 N7 Throm Cambodia
143 E8 Throssell, L Western Australia Australia
143 E7 Throssell, Mt Western Australia Australia
142 D5 Throssel Ra Western Australia Australia
68 J5 Thu Bon R Vietnam
68 H7 Thu Dao Mot Vietnam
139 J5 Thuddungra New South Wales Australia
18 H8 Thueyte France
40 E6 Thuile, la Italy
22 G3 Thuin Belgium
115 N2 Thule Greenland
115 N2 Thule Air Base Greenland
146 G3 Thule, Southern islds S Sandwich Is Atl Oc
37 O2 Thum East Germany
101 P5 Thumb Wyoming U.S.A.
144 C5 Thumbs, the mt New Zealand
40 G4 Thun Switzerland
141 G4 Thunda Queensland Australia
119 O2 Thunder Ontario Canada
94 D2 Thunder B Michigan U.S.A.
99 R1 Thunder Bay Ontario Canada
98 D4 Thunder Butte Cr South Dakota U.S.A.
120 G2 Thunderhouse Falls Ontario Canada
126 D4 Thunder Knoll Caribbean
118 C4 Thunder L. Prov. Park Alberta Canada
116 G2 Thunder Mt Alaska U.S.A.
66 B4 Thüngen W Germany
69 D8 Thung Maphrao Thailand
69 D8 Thung Song Thailand
70 O5 Thung Wa Thailand
70 O5 Thunkar Bhutan
40 E6 Thurey France
33 R5 Thürikow East Germany
41 L3 Thüringen Austria
37 J2 Thüringer Wald mts East Germany
9 N13 Thurins France
14 D4 Thurles Ireland
8 C7 Thurlestone England
139 G3 Thurloo Downs New South Wales Australia
101 T3 Thurlow Montana U.S.A.
37 L3 Thurnau W Germany
13 E4 Thursby England
141 F1 Thursday I Queensland Australia
121 P7 Thurso Quebec Canada
15 E2 Thurso R Scotland
15 E2 Thurso Scotland
21 K4 Thurston I Antarctica
117 K7 Thutade L British Columbia Canada
146 B8 Thwaites Glacier glacier Antarctica
28 A3 Thy reg Denmark
141 G7 Thylungra Queensland Australia
87 G3 Thyolo Malawi
139 K4 Tia New South Wales Australia
127 J9 Tia R France
65 Q3 Tianbaoshan China
67 B5 Tiandeng China
67 B5 Tiandong China

67 B4 Tian'e China
53 F12 Tianeti U.S.S.R.
67 C4 Tianhe China
65 D5 Tianjin China
58 C4 Tianjun China
67 B4 Tianlin China
67 D1 Tianmen China
65 H3 Tianqiaoling China
Tianshan see Ar Horquin Qi
66 C3 Tian Shan ra China/U.S.S.R.
58 E5 Tianshui China
67 G2 Tiantai China
67 B5 Tianyang China
Tianyi see Ningcheng
67 C4 Tianzhen China
65 C4 Tianzhen China
67 C3 Tianzhu China
134 C11 Tiarei Tahiti Pacific Oc
85 E1 Tiaret Algeria
141 L7 Tiaro Queensland Australia
85 D7 Tiassalé Ivory Coast
130 E9 Tibagi Brazil
86 B4 Tibati Cameroon
13 E3 Tibberton England
80 F2 Tiberias Israel
80 F2 Tiberias, L Israel
86 C1 Tibesti reg Chad
84 F5 Tibesti, Sarir Libya
Tibet aut reg see Xizang Zizhiqu
53 E10 Tiblemont Quebec Canada
46 G9 Tiblelului, Muntii mts Romania
138 F3 Tibooburra New South Wales Australia
75 K4 Tibrikot Nepal
124 C3 Tiburón isld Mexico
71 F4 Ticao isld Philippines
9 G5 Ticehurst England
47 N1 Ticha, Yazovir res Bulgaria
121 O8 Tichborne Ontario Canada
85 C5 Tichitt Mauritania
85 B4 Tichla Western Sahara
44 E1 Ticino R Italy
41 J5 Ticino canton Switzerland
13 G6 Tickhill England
9 E2 Ticknall England
48 H6 Ticleni Romania
95 O3 Ticonderoga New York U.S.A.
27 G13 Tidaholm Sweden
122 F6 Tide Hd New Brunswick Canada
118 F8 Tidenham England
69 A9 Tident Nicobar Is
100 B5 Tidewater Oregon U.S.A.
85 E3 Tidikelt reg Algeria
85 B5 Tidjikja Mauritania
122 H8 Tidnish Nova Scotia Canada
71 A2 Tidore Halmahera Indonesia
33 N5 Tidra, I Mauritania
9 E5 Tidworth England
85 D6 Tiébissou Ivory Coast
33 T7 Tiébélé Burkina
115 P5 Tiefensee East Germany
120 J4 Tieffenbach France
116 P6 Tiekel Alaska U.S.A.
25 D5 Tiel Netherlands
65 G1 Tieli China
65 F3 Tieling China
22 E1 Tielt Belgium
85 C7 Tiémé Ivory Coast
22 E1 Tienen Belgium
Tientsin see Tianjin
67 B6 Tien Yen Vietnam
89 D9 Tier Berg mt S Africa
21 K6 Tiercé France
21 J11 Tierp Sweden
106 D5 Tierra New Mexico U.S.A.
133 D8 Tierra Blanca Mexico
133 D8 Tierra del Fuego, I.Grande de Arg/Chile
101 N9 Tiétar R Spain
130 F8 Tietê R Brazil
130 E7 Tietê Brazil
138 B2 Tietkens, Mt South Australia Australia
100 D3 Tieton Washington U.S.A.
100 D3 Tieton Res Washington U.S.A.
57 H4 Tieyon South Australia Australia
138 C2 Tifariti Western Sahara
45 Q7 Tifata, M mt Italy
6 L4 Tiffany oil rig North Sea
100 F1 Tiffany Mt Washington U.S.A.
99 P8 Tiffin Ohio U.S.A.
94 D5 Tiffin R Ohio U.S.A.
117 H10 Tifrit Algeria
112 D6 Tifton Georgia U.S.A.
70 D2 Tiga Aleutian Is
116 E9 Tigalda I Aleutian Is
100 C4 Tigard Oregon U.S.A.
112 F3 Tiger R South Carolina
99 R6 Tiger Washington U.S.A.
99 R5 Tigerton Wisconsin U.S.A.
15 C5 Tighnabruaich Scotland
51 P3 Tigil U.S.S.R.
56 B5 Tigiretskiy Khrebet mts U.S.S.R.
112 E4 Tignall Georgia U.S.A.
84 B4 Tignère Cameroon
42 A3 Tignes, Bge. de France
122 H7 Tignish Prince Edward I Canada
102 F4 Tigoda R U.S.S.R.
86 H3 Tigray prov Ethiopia
128 C4 Tigre R Peru
83 R8 Tigre R Venezuela
125 K6 Tigre, Cerro del mt Mexico
131 B3 Tigre, Sa ra Argentina
78 J4 Tigris R Iraq
57 A3 Tigrovyy Khvost, Mys C U.S.S.R.
85 F3 Tiguentourine Algeria
86 C2 Tigui Chad
21 P6 Tigy France
79 M9 Tih, Gebel el plateau Egypt
145 C7 Tihoi New Zealand
28 C5 Tihøje hill Denmark
106 C6 Tijeras New Mexico U.S.A.
124 A1 Tijuana Mexico
130 E10 Tijucas Brazil
122 G3 Tika Quebec Canada
133 D4 Tikal anc site Guatemala
74 H6 Tikamgarh India
121 T7 Tikchik Quebec Canada
53 C5 Tikhoretsk U.S.S.R.
52 D5 Tikhvin U.S.S.R.
145 F3 Tikitiki New Zealand
145 F3 Tikokino New Zealand
137 O7 Tikopia isld Santa Cruz Is
78 J3 Tikrit Iraq
51 M1 Tiksha U.S.S.R.
51 M1 Tiksi U.S.S.R.
71 H4 Tikshozero, Oz L U.S.S.R.
69 A4 Tilamuta Sulawesi
115 O5 Tillabéry Niger
100 A4 Tillamook Oregon U.S.A.
100 A4 Tillamook Rock Oregon U.S.A.

112 G2 Tillery, L North Carolina U.S.A.
95 K5 Tilley Alberta Canada
109 L2 Tilley Texas U.S.A.
94 G8 Tillia Niger
69 G11 Tillicoultry Scotland
120 H4 Tillières France
41 N5 Tilone Italy
42 D2 Tione di Trento Italy
112 F5 Tillman South Carolina U.S.A.
113 L11 Tilloo Cay is'd Bahamas
13 G2 Till, R England
120 N10 Tillsonburg Ontario Canada
21 J3 Tilly-sur-Seulles France
14 C4 Tilly France
71 M9 Tilomar Timor
102 E5 Tilos isld Greece
139 G4 Tilpa New South Wales Australia
85 E2 Tilrhemt Algeria
119 Q9 Tilston Manitoba Canada
123 S4 Tilting Newfoundland Canada
110 J1 Tilton Illinois U.S.A.
95 Q3 Tilton New Hampshire U.S.A.
70 G5 Tily mt Sulawesi
28 A4 Tim Denmark
54 J5 Tim U.S.S.R.
121 L5 Timagami Ontario Canada
144 C6 Timaru New Zealand
53 E10 Timashevsk U.S.S.R.
83 K9 Timbákion Crete Greece
53 C10 Timballier I. Louisiana U.S.A.
80 F4 Timbang isld Sabah
54 E2 Timbauba Brazil
145 F4 Timbédra Mauritania
47 J6 Timber Oregon U.S.A.
140 B3 Timber Creek Police Station N Terr Australia
15 B4 Timber L South Dakota U.S.A.
84 B4 Timber Mt Nevada U.S.A.
102 H4 Timboon Victoria Australia
130 E10 Timbo, R Brazil
48 H3 Timbuktu see Tombouctou
48 J4 Timbun Mata Sabah
70 F2 Timellouline Algeria
85 D5 Timetrine Mts Mali
47 K4 Timfi, Óros mt Greece
46 E6 Timfristós mt Greece
65 F5 Timia Niger
85 E3 Timimoun Algeria
48 J4 Timiris, C see Mirik, C
55 C4 Timirova Mare R Romania
55 B3 Timiryazevo U.S.S.R.
48 G5 Timiş R Romania
48 F8 Timişoara Romania
131 A7 Timkapaul U.S.S.R.
33 N5 Timmendorfer Strand W Germany
27 G13 Timmersdala Sweden
85 F5 Timmersoi watercourse Niger
115 P5 Timmiarmiut Greenland
120 J4 Timmins Ontario Canada
112 H3 Timmonsville South Carolina U.S.A.
46 E1 Timok R Romania
129 K5 Timon Brazil
71 M9 Timor isld E Indies
136 E4 Timor Trough Timor Sea
21 M9 Timoshino U.S.S.R.
128 D5 Timoteo Venezuela
128 D5 Timotes Venezuela
103 J4 Timpahute Ra Nevada U.S.A.
101 O9 Timpanogos Cave Nat. Mon Utah U.S.A.
119 N6 Timperley Ra Western Australia Australia
101 N9 Timpie Utah U.S.A.
109 N4 Timpson Texas U.S.A.
26 J9 Timrå Sweden
130 F8 Timré Denmark
130 B2 Timrod Brazil
138 B2 Tims Ford L Tennessee U.S.A.
110 K6 Tim's Ford L Tennessee U.S.A.
31 J6 Timsher U.S.S.R.
57 H4 Timur U.S.S.R.
70 O9 Timur, Jawa prov Java
144 D5 Timuttmu Headland New Zealand
45 Q7 Tiñata, M mt Italy
6 L4 Tiffany oil rig North Sea
79 F8 Tina S Africa
31 N8 Tinaca Pt Mindanao Philippines
83 E3 Tin Algeria
116 K2 Tinaco Venezuela
71 G5 Tinaga isld Philippines
14 E4 Tinahely Ireland
9 E6 Titchfield England
43 F6 Titicaca, L Peru/Bolivia
42 G6 Titograd Yugoslavia
90 P4 Titodohokke Japan
99 M6 Titonka Iowa U.S.A.
129 L6 Titova Mitrovica Yugoslavia
52 D7 Titova Uzice Yugoslavia
52 D1 Titovka R U.S.S.R.
70 O5 Titovo Velenje Yugoslavia
55 E5 Titov Veles Yugoslavia
14 B5 Titran Norway
68 D5 Toe Jaga, Khao mt Burma/Thailand
94 C3 Tittabawassee R Michigan
37 L6 Tittling W Germany
37 L6 Tittmoning W Germany
71 L11 Titu Romania
86 K6 Titule Zaire
113 G9 Titusville Florida U.S.A.
94 H5 Titusville Pennsylvania U.S.A.
85 A6 Tivaouane Senegal
27 G13 Tived Sweden
116 M4 Tiverton Nova Scotia
120 F9 Tiverton Ontario Canada
9 H5 Tiverton England
95 R5 Tiverton Rhode I. U.S.A.
45 K8 Tivoli Italy
116 K2 Tivoli New York U.S.A.
109 L7 Tixkokob Mexico
70 O5 Tizapán el Alto Mexico
72 G7 Tizi-Ifri Morocco
124 G5 Tizimín Mexico
124 H7 Tizi-Ouzou Algeria
124 H7 Tizoc Mexico
56 B4 Tiztoutine Morocco
56 B4 Tizochen U.S.S.R.
129 L6 Tjabang Indonesia
28 B6 Tjæreborg Denmark
56 E4 Tjåmotis Sweden
70 L9 Tjiamis Java
70 L9 Tjiandjur Java
70 L9 Tjilatjap Java
70 R2 Tjirebon Java
70 R2 Tjisomang Java
72 M9 Tjörn isld Sweden
70 L9 Tjieuke Meer Netherlands
68 A7 Tjoinane Andaman Is
55 J7 Tjojala U.S.S.R.
60 H11 Tjokan Java

98 D1 Tioga North Dakota U.S.A.
95 K5 Tioga Pennsylvania U.S.A.
109 L2 Tioga Texas U.S.A.
94 G8 Tioga West Virginia U.S.A.
69 G11 Tioman isld Malaysia
120 H4 Tionaga Ontario Canada
41 N5 Tione Italy
42 D2 Tione di Trento Italy
100 D8 Tionesta California U.S.A.
94 N5 Tionesta Pennsylvania U.S.A.
125 M8 Tipesca Mexico
125 K8 Tippecanoe R Indiana U.S.A.
68 A1 Tippecanoe Indiana U.S.A.
125 L8 Tlapacoyán Mexico
124 H7 Tlaquepaque Mexico
116 Q5 Tippecanoe Indiana U.S.A.
85 E5 Tipperary co Ireland
85 E5 Tipperary Ireland
31 N3 Tipperary Ireland
52 E6 Tippo Mississippi U.S.A.
84 F4 Tipton California U.S.A.
68 C4 Tipton Indiana U.S.A.
73 Q6 Tipton Kansas U.S.A.
60 J1 Tipton Missouri U.S.A.
102 D7 Tipton Oklahoma U.S.A.
103 K6 Tipton, Mt Arizona U.S.A.
68 C4 Tip Top Hill Ontario Canada
9 G4 Tiptree England
117 L6 Tiptur India
128 E3 Tiquié R Brazil
80 C5 Tira Israel
87 H11 Tiracambu, Sa.do mts Brazil
101 L9 Toana mt U.S.A.
45 J3 Toano Italy
95 U9 Toano Virginia U.S.A.
145 F3 Toatoa New Zealand
133 E5 Toay Argentina
70 F5 Toaya Sulawesi
65 K11 Toba Japan
60 D11 Toba, Danau L Sumatra
127 M1 Toba New Zealand
117 L10 Toba Inlet British Columbia Canada
77 K4 Toba & Kakar Ranges Pakistan
80 C4 Tobago Syria
101 L9 Tobar Nevada U.S.A.
87 H13 Tobarra Spain
131 K3 Tobas Argentina
78 K1 Tobelo Indonesia
14 C4 Tobercurry Ireland
71 H7 Tobea isld Indonesia
140 E5 Tobermorey N Terr Australia
141 G7 Tobermory Queensland Australia
120 J7 Tobermory Ontario Canada
15 B4 Tobermory Scotland
61 N14 Tobi isld Pacific Oc
60 P7 Tobi-shima isld Japan
59 K4 Tobin, Kap C Greenland
59 G4 Tobin, L Western Australia Australia
57 K2 Tobin L Saskatchewan Canada
59 K1 Tobin, Mt Nevada U.S.A.
122 F5 Tobique R New Brunswick Canada
62 Tobol' R
69 H14 Toboali Indonesia
54 D5 Tobol U.S.S.R.
54 E2 Tobol' U.S.S.R.
46 J6 To Bong Vietnam
71 F5 Toboso Negros Philippines
Tobruk see Tubruq
95 M5 Tobyhanna Pennsylvania U.S.A.
103 M8 Tobyl R U.S.S.R.
27 G14 Tocantínia Brazil
129 J5 Tocantinópolis Brazil
129 H5 Tocantins R Brazil
57 B3 Tolmachevo U.S.S.R.
52 C5 Toccoa Georgia U.S.A.
45 J2 Toce R Italy
42 F2 Tolmezzo Italy
133 C2 Tochigi Japan
61 M8 Tochio Japan
133 D2 Toco Chile
139 H6 Tocorpuri mt Chile/Bolivia
110 H2 Tocumwal New South Wales Australia
17 F1 Tocuyo R Venezuela
116 N4 Tocuyo de la Costa Venezuela
74 F5 Toda India
15 S2 Todal Norway
28 D3 Todalen Norway
140 B2 Todd R N Terr Australia
122 F7 Todd Mt New Brunswick Canada
140 C6 Todd R N Terr Australia
143 F7 Todd R Western Australia Australia
29 P5 Todmorden England
99 Q6 Todmorden South Australia Australia
99 Q6 Todohokke Japan
60 P4 Todohokke Japan
129 J6 Todos los Santos, L Chile
129 L6 Todos os Santos, B. de Brazil
124 D6 Todos Santos Mexico
55 E5 Todzha, Oz L U.S.S.R.
14 B5 Toe Hd Ireland
68 D5 Toe Jaga, Khao mt Burma/Thailand
90 N3 Tomari Japan
102 G3 Tomari see Golovnino
14 B4 Tomarza Japan
22 F2 Tombador, Sa.do mts Brazil
31 R1 Tombel Cameroon
61 N8 Tombigbee R Mississippi U.S.A.
71 H5 Tomboco Angola
130 Q7 Tombos Brazil
70 O5 Tombouctou Mali
86 B2 Tombstone Arizona U.S.A.
119 Q7 Tombua Angola
131 A6 Tome Chile
71 J7 Tomea isld Indonesia
70 J7 Tomelilla Sweden
121 L6 Tomi Ontario Canada
70 G4 Tomini Sulawesi
70 G5 Tomini, Teluk B Sulawesi
15 E3 Tominoul Scotland
70 G4 Tomioka Japan
143 G7 Tomkinson Ras S/W Australia Australia

70 L9 Tjitarum R Java
27 E12 Tjøme isld Norway
27 E11 Tjørn isld Sweden
28 B4 Tjørn isld Denmark
26 F6 Tjøtta Norway
53 F11 Tkvarcheli U.S.S.R.
125 L9 Tlacolula de Matamoros Mexico
125 M8 Tlacotalpan Mexico
125 K8 Tlalnepantla Mexico
125 K8 Tlalpan Mexico
68 A1 Tlangtlang Burma
125 L8 Tlapacoyán Mexico
125 L8 Tlapa Mexico
124 H7 Tlaquepaque Mexico
125 K8 Tlaxcala Mexico
85 E1 Tlemcen Algeria
85 E5 Tlemcele Niger
48 J2 Tlumach U.S.S.R.
31 N3 Tłuszcz Poland
52 E6 T'ma R U.S.S.R.
84 F4 Tmassat Libya
68 C4 Tni Asia Algeria
73 Q6 To R Burma
117 L6 Toad River British Columbia Canada
87 H1 Toamasina Madagascar
61 N9 Tone R Japan
61 O10 Tone-gawa R Japan
8 C5 Tone, R England
139 G4 Tonga New South Wales Australia
135 S6 Tonga kingdom Pacific Oc
86 F4 Tonga Sudan
88 B10 Tonga Zambia
89 G7 Tongaat S Africa
145 D4 Tonga New Zealand
67 F4 Tonga'an China
110 A2 Tonganoxie Kansas U.S.A.
145 E3 Tongaporutu New Zealand
109 L9 Tongariro New Zealand
145 E3 Tongatapu Group Tonga
137 R6 Tongatapu Group Tonga
58 F5 Tongbai Shan mt ra China
Tongcheng see Dong'e
67 D2 Tongcheng China
67 E1 Tongcheng China
67 E2 Tongchuan China
65 A7 Tongdao China
67 A4 Tonghai China
59 J3 Tonghe China
67 B1 Tonghua China
59 K2 Tongjiang China
59 J3 Tongjiang China
67 B6 Tongjiang China
67 B1 Tongjiang China
59 J2 Tong King, G. of Vietnam
70 D5 Tongla China
12 D4 Tongland Scotland
67 E3 Tongling China
67 B1 Tongliao China
67 E1 Tongnan China
67 E1 Tongnan China
67 B1 Tongren China
71 D12 Tongobory Madagascar
67 B12 Tongobei Bahia Chile
133 C4 Tongquan see Malong
71 E7 Tongquil isld Philippines
67 C3 Tongren China
Tongshan see Xuzhou
67 E2 Tongshan China
68 D2 Tongshi China
68 B7 Tongta Burma
67 E3 Tongtian He R China
15 D2 Tongue Scotland
67 F2 Tongue of the Ocean chan Bahamas
101 T4 Tongue R.Res Montana U.S.A.
65 C5 Tong Xian China
67 G1 Tongxiang China
67 C3 Tongxin China
65 F2 Tongyu China
67 E2 Tongzhou see Nantong
124 E3 Tónichi Mexico
116 D6 Tonk India
86 G7 Tonk Sudan
18 G7 Tonkabon Iran
107 N5 Tonkawa Oklahoma U.S.A.
68 H6 Tonle Kong R Laos/Cambodia
18 G7 Tonle Sap L Cambodia
18 F8 Tonnefins France
29 D5 Tønning Denmark
32 J4 Tønning W Germany
102 G3 Tonopah Nevada U.S.A.
14 D4 Tónquédec France
26 D2 Tønsberg Norway
27 B13 Tønstad Norway
131 G1 Tontal, Sa ra Argentina
130 D8 Tonto Basin Arizona U.S.A.
103 O8 Tonto Nat.Mon Arizona U.S.A.
116 L5 Tonzona R Alaska U.S.A.
141 J8 Toobeah Queensland Australia
141 J8 Toodyay Western Australia Australia
101 N9 Tooele Utah U.S.A.
14 K7 Toogoolawah Queensland Australia
139 G6 Tooleybuc New South Wales Australia
143 B9 Toodyay Western Australia Australia
71 H5 Toolonda Victoria Australia
139 J6 Tooma R New South Wales Australia
73 Q7 Toome Northern Ireland
141 J6 Toompine Queensland Australia
141 J6 Toora Victoria Australia
139 H7 Toora-Khem U.S.S.R.
42 Q3 Toowomba Queensland Australia

59 J5 Tokara-retto islds Japan
55 F5 Tokarevka U.S.S.R.
55 D4 Tokari U.S.S.R.
52 D4 Tokarikha U.S.S.R.
78 F1 Tokat Turkey
145 D2 Tokatoka New Zealand
70 G6 Toke Sulawesi
103 O5 Tokelau islds Pacific Oc
101 P9 Tokewanna Pk Utah U.S.A.
56 E1 Tokhoma R U.S.S.R.
61 L10 Toki Japan
98 H2 Tokio North Dakota U.S.A.
27 D12 Tokke-Vatn L Norway
116 M4 Tokke,L Norway
Tokmak see Eşme
54 G9 Tokmak U.S.S.R.
57 H3 Tokmak U.S.S.R.
70 G4 Toko New Zealand
145 E4 Tokomaru New Zealand
145 E4 Tokomaru Bay New Zealand
145 E4 Tokoroa New Zealand
84 G3 Tokrah Libya
57 H1 Tokrau R U.S.S.R.
88 C10 Toksha-Kuznetsova U.S.S.R.
36 B3 Toksook Bay Alaska U.S.A.
59 K4 Tok-to isld Japan/Korea
59 K4 Toktogul Vdkhr U.S.S.R.
57 G5 Toktomush U.S.S.R.
57 K2 Tokty U.S.S.R.
59 K1 Tokur U.S.S.R.
60 N10 Tokushima Japan
60 H11 Tokuyama Japan
61 J8 Tokwe R Zimbabwe
61 L10 Tōkyō conurbation Japan
61 N10 Tōkyō-wan B Japan
77 N10 Tokzār Afghanistan
145 G3 Tolaga Bay New Zealand
87 H13 Tôlañaro Madagascar
54 N4 Tolar New Mexico U.S.A.
109 K3 Tolar Texas U.S.A.
78 K1 Tolavi U.S.S.R.
55 C4 Tolbazy U.S.S.R.
47 J1 Tolbukhin Bulgaria
133 D9 Toledo Chile
67 E1 Toledo Chile
16 E5 Toledo prov Spain
16 E5 Toledo Spain
22 J2 Toledo Belgium
99 O7 Toledo Illinois U.S.A.
94 D5 Toledo Ohio U.S.A.
65 A7 Toledo Ohio U.S.A.
100 B5 Toledo Oregon U.S.A.
100 C3 Toledo Washington U.S.A.
109 N4 Toledo Bend Res Louisiana U.S.A.
16 D5 Toledo, Montes de mts Spain
42 E5 Tolentino Italy
45 J2 Tolfa, Mt.della Italy
26 G5 Tolga Norway
85 F3 Tolga Algeria
128 E2 Toliara Madagascar
87 G12 Toliara Madagascar
70 G4 Tolitoli Sulawesi
27 G16 Tollarp Sweden
71 E East Germany
17 E7 Tollesee L East Germany
103 M8 Tolleson Arizona U.S.A.
98 H4 Tolley North Dakota U.S.A.
102 E4 Tollhouse California U.S.A.
71 E7 Tolloquil isld Philippines
57 B3 Tolmachevo U.S.S.R.
42 F2 Tolmezzo Italy
42 F2 Tolmin Yugoslavia
28 A2 Tolna Hungary
15 D2 Tolna Hungary
54 A2 Tolochin U.S.S.R.
110 H2 Tolono Illinois U.S.A.
17 F1 Tolosa Spain
116 N4 Tolovana R Alaska U.S.A.
65 O3 Tolsan I S Korea
67 G1 Tolsta Head Scotland
48 K2 Tolstoye U.S.S.R.
103 N9 Toltec Arizona U.S.A.
133 C5 Toltén Chile
133 A7 Toltén, R Chile
124 D5 Toluca Mexico
125 K8 Toluca Mexico
6 L4 Toni oil rig North Sea
29 P5 Tolvand, Ozero L U.S.S.R.
29 P5 Tolwattari U.S.S.R.
52 D4 Tolvuya U.S.S.R.
28 D4 Tol'yatti U.S.S.R.
55 B2 Toma R U.S.S.R.
99 R7 Tomah Wisconsin U.S.A.
68 H6 Tomahawk Wisconsin U.S.A.
60 P1 Tomakomai Japan
70 G5 Tomali Sulawesi
18 G7 Tomar Portugal
16 B5 Tomar Portugal
32 J4 Tomari see Golovnino
90 N3 Tomari Japan
36 B3 Tomari Japan
61 H11 Tomaszów Lubelski Poland
31 O5 Tomaszów Mazowiecki Poland
124 G8 Tomatlán Mexico
57 Y2 Tomazu Yugoslavia
120 B5 Tomball Texas U.S.A.
71 H5 Tombador, Sa.do mts Brazil

95 N6 Toms River New Jersey U.S.A.
116 Q6 Tom White, Mt Alaska U.S.A.
124 F4 Tónachic Mexico
125 N9 Tonalá Mexico
125 N9 Tonalea Arizona U.S.A.
42 D2 Tonale, Pso. di Italy
61 K9 Tonami Japan
128 E4 Tonantins Brazil
100 F1 Tonasket Washington U.S.A.
121 M9 Tonawanda New York U.S.A.
9 G5 Tonbridge England
60 J12 Tonda Japan
71 J4 Tondano Sulawesi
16 B4 Tondela Portugal
Tender co see Sønderjylland
28 B7 Tønder Denmark
120 E3 Tondern Ontario Canada
85 E4 Tondikiwindi Niger
88 C10 Tondongwe mt Zimbabwe
36 B3 Tondorf W Germany
61 N9 Tone R Japan
61 O10 Tone-gawa R Japan
8 C5 Tone, R England
139 G4 Tonga New South Wales Australia
135 S6 Tonga kingdom Pacific Oc
86 F4 Tonga Sudan
88 B10 Tonga Zambia
89 G7 Tongaat S Africa
67 F4 Tonga'an China
110 A2 Tonganoxie Kansas U.S.A.
145 E3 Tongaporutu New Zealand
109 L9 Tongariro New Zealand
145 E3 Tongatapu Group Tonga
137 R6 Tongatapu Group Tonga
58 F5 Tongbai Shan mt ra China
Tongcheng see Dong'e
67 D2 Tongcheng China
67 E1 Tongcheng China
67 E2 Tongchuan China
65 A7 Tongdao China
67 A4 Tonghai China
59 J3 Tonghe China
67 B1 Tonghua China
59 K2 Tongjiang China
59 J3 Tongjiang China
67 B6 Tongjiang China
67 B1 Tongjiang China
59 J2 Tong King, G. of Vietnam
70 D5 Tongla China
12 D4 Tongland Scotland
67 E3 Tongling China
67 B1 Tongliao China
67 E1 Tongnan China
67 B1 Tongren China
71 D12 Tongobory Madagascar
67 E1 Tongren China
Tongshan see Xuzhou
67 E2 Tongshan China
68 D2 Tongshi China
68 B7 Tongta Burma
67 E3 Tongtian He R China
15 D2 Tongue Scotland
67 F2 Tongue of the Ocean chan Bahamas
101 T4 Tongue R.Res Montana U.S.A.
65 C5 Tong Xian China
67 G1 Tongxiang China
67 C3 Tongxin China
65 F2 Tongyu China
67 E2 Tongzhou see Nantong
124 E3 Tónichi Mexico
116 N2 Toolik R Alaska U.S.A.
141 J8 Toogoom Queensland Australia
101 N9 Tooele Utah U.S.A.
14 K7 Toogoolawah Queensland Australia
139 G6 Tooleybuc New South Wales Australia
143 B9 Toodyay Western Australia Australia
71 H5 Toolonda Victoria Australia
139 J6 Tooma R New South Wales Australia
73 Q7 Toome Northern Ireland
141 J6 Toompine Queensland Australia
141 J6 Toora Victoria Australia
139 H7 Toora-Khem U.S.S.R.
141 K7 Toowoomba Queensland Australia
48 L6 Topalu Romania
48 H5 Topana Spain
101 N10 Topawa Arizona U.S.A.
102 E5 Topaz L California U.S.A.
67 G2 Topchihe China
9 E2 Topcliffe England
48 L6 Topile Bulgaria
47 J6 Topla R Czechoslovakia
31 O11 Topľa R Czechoslovakia
48 J6 Toplita Alberta Canada
48 K8 Toplica R Yugoslavia
48 J4 Topolčani Yugoslavia
103 K7 Topocalma, Pta Chile
103 K8 Topock Arizona U.S.A.
46 E4 Topolčane Yugoslavia
48 J5 Topol'čany Czechoslovakia
47 L7 Topolnitsa U.S.S.R.
48 J6 Topoloveni Romania
48 K7 Topoloveni Romania
47 M7 Topolovgrad Bulgaria
42 F2 Topolšica Yugoslavia

106 D1 **Toponas** Colorado U.S.A.
52 E5 **Topornya** U.S.S.R.
52 D2 **Topozero, Ozero** *L* U.S.S.R.
100 E3 **Toppenish** Washington U.S.A.
47 J1 **Topraisar** Romania
57 B4 **Toprak-kala** U.S.S.R.
52 F3 **Topsa** U.S.S.R.
95 U1 **Topsfield** Maine U.S.A.
8 C6 **Topsham** England
95 R3 **Topsham** Maine U.S.A.
140 B3 **Top Springs** N Terr Australia
95 M6 **Topton** Pennsylvania U.S.A.
103 L4 **Toquerville** Utah U.S.A.
102 G3 **Toquima Ra** Nevada U.S.A.
86 F4 **Tor** Ethiopia
6 N6 **Tor** *oil rig* North Sea
17 H3 **Torá** Spain
71 J4 **Torawitan, Tg** *B* Sulawesi
123 L8 **Tor B** Nova Scotia Canada
47 J6 **Torbalı** Turkey
77 F2 **Torbat-e-Ḥeydarīyeh** Iran
77 G2 **Torbat-e Jām** Iran
123 U6 **Torbay** Newfoundland Canada
123 L8 **Tor Bay** Nova Scotia Canada
8 C7 **Torbay** England
143 C11 **Torbay B** Western Australia Australia
27 F10 **Torberget** Norway
116 L6 **Torbert, Mt** Alaska U.S.A.
52 D5 **Torbino** U.S.S.R.
94 B1 **Torch L** Michigan U.S.A.
8 C7 **Torcross** England
21 N2 **Torcy-le-Grand** France
16 D3 **Tordesillas** Spain
26 N6 **Töre** Sweden
27 G13 **Töreboda** Sweden
28 H7 **Toreby** Denmark
27 F15 **Torekov** Sweden
29 K4 **Torekov** Sweden
145 F2 **Torere** New Zealand
27 J12 **Toresund** Sweden
17 F3 **Torete** *R* Spain
54 K8 **Torez** U.S.S.R.
21 H7 **Torfou** France
33 S9 **Torgau** East Germany
33 U5 **Torgelow** East Germany
26 F6 **Torghatten** *isld* Norway
53 G8 **Torgun** *R* U.S.S.R.
27 H15 **Torhamn** Sweden
22 E1 **Torhout** Belgium
61 O10 **Toride** Japan
21 J3 **Torigny-sur-Vire** France
44 C1 **Torino** Italy
86 F5 **Torit** Sudan
130 D5 **Torixoreu** Brazil
52 D5 **Torkovichi** U.S.S.R.
29 N3 **Törmänen** Finland
8 D5 **Tormarton** England
55 G1 **Tormemtor, Ozero** *L* U.S.S.R.
142 E3 **Torment, Pt** Western Australia Australia
16 D4 **Tormes** *R* Spain
117 Q11 **Tornado Mt** Alberta/Br Col Canada
28 D1 **Tornby** Denmark
Torneå *see* **Tornio**
26 M4 **Torne älv** *R* Sweden
32 L5 **Tornesch** W Germany
26 L3 **Torneträsk** Sweden
26 K3 **Torneträsk** *L* Sweden
115 N6 **Torngat Mts** Quebec/Labrador Canada
48 F7 **Tornik** *mt* Yugoslavia
108 A4 **Tornillo** Texas U.S.A.
28 C4 **Torning** Denmark
29 L6 **Tornio** Finland
29 L6 **Tornionjoki** *R* Finland
33 S6 **Tornow** East Germany
133 E5 **Tornquist** Argentina
28 D6 **Torø** *isld* Denmark
60 S2 **Tōro** Japan
16 D3 **Toro** Spain
131 B2 **Toro, Cerro de** *pk* Arg/Chile
48 J3 **Toroiaga** *mt* Romania
48 F3 **Törökszentmiklós** Hungary
46 F4 **Toronaios Kólpos** *G* Greece
139 K5 **Toronto** New South Wales Australia
121 D9 **Toronto** Ontario Canada
107 P4 **Toronto** Kansas U.S.A.
94 G6 **Toronto** Ohio U.S.A.
52 D6 **Toropets** U.S.S.R.
124 H5 **Toro, Pico del** *mt* Mexico
102 H8 **Toro Pk** California U.S.A.
131 B4 **Toro, Pta** Chile
88 E1 **Tororo** Uganda
78 D3 **Toroslar** *mts* Turkey
15 F3 **Torphins** Scotland
52 F6 **Torpino** U.S.S.R.
8 B7 **Torpoint** England
26 H9 **Torpshammar** Sweden
133 G4 **Torquato Severo** Brazil
139 G7 **Torquay** Victoria Australia
98 C1 **Torquay** Saskatchewan Canada
8 C7 **Torquay** England
121 L8 **Torrance** Ontario Canada
102 F8 **Torrance** California U.S.A.
16 B6 **Torrão** Portugal
45 Q8 **Torre Annunziata** Italy
41 O6 **Torrebelvicino** Italy
17 H4 **Torreblanca** Spain
17 F2 **Torrecilla en Cameros** Spain
45 Q8 **Torre del Greco** Italy
44 F1 **Torre del Mangano** Italy
16 C3 **Torre de Moncorvo** Portugal
44 H4 **Torre di Lago Puccini** Italy
16 E7 **Torredonjimeno** Spain
45 L1 **Torréglia** Italy
16 C5 **Torrejoncillo** Spain
16 E1 **Torrelavega** Spain
42 G7 **Torremaggiore** Italy
16 E8 **Torremolinos** Spain
141 H5 **Torrens** *R* Queensland Australia
141 H5 **Torrens Cr** Queensland Australia
138 E4 **Torrens, L** South Australia Australia
17 G5 **Torrente** Spain
124 H5 **Torreón** Mexico
17 G7 **Torre Pacheco** Spain
133 H3 **Tôrres** Brazil
124 D3 **Torres** Mexico
16 E9 **Torres de Alealá** Morocco
137 O4 **Torres Is** Vanuatu
16 B5 **Torres Novas** Portugal
141 F1 **Torres Strait** Queensland Australia
16 A5 **Torres Vedras** Portugal
17 G7 **Torrevieja** Spain
103 N3 **Torrey** Utah U.S.A.
45 N5 **Torricella in Sabina** Italy
8 B6 **Torridge, R** England
45 L1 **Torri di Quartesolo** Italy
28 E5 **Torrild** Denmark
28 C5 **Tørring** Denmark
139 K3 **Torrington** New South Wales Australia
118 D7 **Torrington** Alberta Canada
95 O5 **Torrington** Connecticut U.S.A.
98 B7 **Torrington** Wyoming U.S.A.
98 B7 **Torrington, S** Wyoming U.S.A.
140 C1 **Tor Rock** *mt* N Terr Australia
26 F8 **Torröjen** *L* Sweden
16 E8 **Torrox** Spain
27 H11 **Torsåker** Sweden
27 H15 **Torsås** Sweden
27 G15 **Torsås, V** Sweden
26 F9 **Torsborg** Sweden
27 F11 **Torsby** Sweden
27 H12 **Torshälla** Sweden
6 F1 **Tórshavn** Faeroes
26 J2 **Torsken** Norway
26 L1 **Torsvåg** Norway
57 E3 **Tortkol'** U.S.S.R.
55 F5 **Tortkuduk** U.S.S.R.
43 F11 **Torto** *R* Sicily
113 L7 **Tortola** *isld* Virgin Is
131 B2 **Tortolas, Cerro las** *pk* Arg/Chile
44 E2 **Tortona** Italy
17 H4 **Tortosa** Spain
127 H4 **Tortue, Île de la** Haiti
77 D2 **Ţorūd** Iran
70 G5 **Torue** Sulawesi
31 L2 **Toruń** Poland
27 F15 **Torup** Sweden
52 C5 **Tõrva** U.S.S.R.
27 G13 **Torved** Sweden
13 E5 **Torver** England
26 J7 **Torvsjö** Sweden
121 M8 **Tory Hill** Ontario Canada
14 C1 **Tory I** Ireland
48 G2 **Torysa** *R* Czechoslovakia
31 J3 **Torzym** Poland
60 G12 **Tosa** Japan
60 F13 **Tosa-Shimizu** Japan
60 G12 **Tosa-wan** *B* Japan
60 G12 **Tosa-Yamada** Japan
87 D11 **Tosca** S Africa
45 K4 **Toscana** *reg* Italy
42 C5 **Toscano, Arch** *islds* Italy
124 D5 **Tosca, Pta** *C* Mexico
41 N6 **Toscolano-Moderno** Italy
26 F6 **Tosen** Norway
26 F6 **Tosenfjord** *inlet* Norway
41 N3 **Tösens** Austria
61 K11 **Tōshi-jima** *isld* Japan
61 N11 **To-shima** *isld* Japan
61 P5 **Tōshima-yama** *mt* Japan
52 D5 **Tosno** U.S.S.R.
58 C4 **Toson Hu** *L* China
58 C2 **Tosontsengel** Mongolia
26 F9 **Tossåsen** Sweden
45 L3 **Tossignano** Italy
133 E3 **Tostado** Argentina
101 O3 **Toston** Montana U.S.A.
60 D12 **Tosu** Japan
78 D1 **Tosya** Turkey
31 L5 **Toszek** Poland
17 F7 **Totana** Spain
83 K11 **Totapola** *mt* Sri Lanka
144 C5 **Totara Flat** New Zealand
145 D1 **Totara North** New Zealand
145 D4 **Totaranui** New Zealand
27 E11 **Toten** *reg* Norway
32 L6 **Tötensen** W Germany
21 N2 **Tôtes** France
38 J6 **Totes Gebirge** *mts* Austria
48 F4 **Tótkomlós** Hungary
9 E1 **Totley** England
8 C7 **Totnes** England
129 G2 **Totness** Suriname
89 C6 **Toto** *mt* S Africa
144 B6 **Totoko Pk** New Zealand
125 L9 **Totolápam** Mexico
131 B2 **Totoralillo** Chile
85 C7 **Totota** Liberia
146 G14 **Totten Glacier** Antarctica
139 H4 **Tottenham** New South Wales Australia
121 L8 **Tottenham** Ontario Canada
9 E6 **Totton** England
59 K4 **Tottori** Japan
60 G10 **Tottori** *prefect* Japan
119 M6 **Totzke** Saskatchewan Canada
85 C7 **Touba** Ivory Coast
85 C2 **Toubkal, Jbel** *mt* Morocco
20 H7 **Touches,les** France
100 G3 **Touchet** Washington U.S.A.
119 N7 **Touchwood Hills** Saskatchewan Canada
18 H5 **Toucy** France
65 G3 **Toudao Jiang** *R* China
65 D3 **Toufendi** China
85 D6 **Tougan** Burkina
85 B6 **Tougé** Guinea
85 F2 **Touggourt** Algeria
85 C3 **Touila** Mauritania
19 J4 **Toul** France
85 C7 **Toulépleu** Ivory Coast
20 A5 **Toulinguet,Pte,du** France
122 E3 **Toulnustouc R** Quebec Canada
19 P18 **Toulon** France
99 R8 **Toulon** Illinois U.S.A.
102 F1 **Toulon** Nevada U.S.A.
19 O17 **Touloubre** *R* France
18 F9 **Toulouse** France
84 E5 **Toumma** Niger
85 C7 **Toumodi** Ivory Coast
68 C3 **Toungoo** Burma
21 L3 **Touques** France
21 L3 **Touques** *R* France
22 B2 **Touquet-Paris Plage, le** France
68 F3 **Tourakom** Laos
Tourane *see* **Da Nang**
20 C5 **Tourch** France
22 E2 **Tourcoing** France
21 L7 **Touriane** *reg* France
16 A1 **Touriñan, C** Spain
85 B4 **Tourine** Mauritania
20 G2 **Tourlaville** France
18 F10 **Tourmalet, Col du** France
22 E2 **Tournai** Belgium
128 D5 **Tournavista** Peru
18 F9 **Tournay** France
19 N14 **Tournon** France
21 M8 **Tournon-St.Martin** Indre-et-Loire France
40 A4 **Tournus** France
21 O3 **Tourny** France
130 J8 **Touros** Brazil
21 M4 **Tourouvre** France
21 M7 **Tours** France
21 L7 **Tour-St. Gélin, la** France
40 E5 **Tour Sallière** *mt* Switzerland
22 H4 **Tourteron** France
19 P18 **Tourves** France
21 N3 **Tourville-la-Rivière** France
21 L2 **Tourville-les-Ifs** France
21 O5 **Toury** France
86 C1 **Toussidé Pic** *mt* Chad
21 P1 **Toutencourt** France
119 S7 **Toutes Aides** Manitoba Canada
100 C3 **Toutle** Washington U.S.A.
20 G8 **Touvois** France
89 B9 **Touwsrivier** S Africa
37 O3 **Toužim** Czechoslovakia
127 J10 **Tovar** Venezuela
54 K3 **Tovarkovskiy** U.S.S.R.
27 C13 **Tovdal** Norway
27 C13 **Tovdalselv** *R* Norway
9 F3 **Tove, R** England
61 O5 **Towada-Hachimantai Nat. Park** Japan
61 O5 **Towada ko** *L* Japan
145 E1 **Towai** New Zealand
128 G2 **Towakaima** Guyana
139 J6 **Towamba** New South Wales Australia
110 H1 **Towanda** Illinois U.S.A.
107 O4 **Towanda** Kansas U.S.A.
95 L5 **Towanda** Pennsylvania U.S.A.
70 G7 **Towari** Sulawesi
9 F3 **Towcester** England
99 O2 **Tower** Minnesota U.S.A.
98 J3 **Tower City** North Dakota U.S.A.
95 L6 **Tower City** Pennsylvania U.S.A.
101 P5 **Tower Falls** Wyoming U.S.A.
110 H2 **Tower Hill** Illinois U.S.A.
144 A6 **Towing Head** New Zealand
106 H3 **Towner** Colorado U.S.A.
98 F1 **Towner** North Dakota U.S.A.
102 G5 **Townes Pass** California U.S.A.
111 J8 **Townley** Alabama U.S.A.
95 M7 **Townsend** Delaware U.S.A.
112 F6 **Townsend** Georgia U.S.A.
101 O3 **Townsend** Montana U.S.A.
112 D2 **Townsend** Tennessee U.S.A.
99 S4 **Townsend** Wisconsin U.S.A.
139 J6 **Townsend, Mt** Victoria Australia
141 K5 **Townshend I** Queensland Australia
141 H4 **Townsville** Queensland Australia
94 H5 **Townville** Pennsylvania U.S.A.
70 G6 **Towori, Teluk** *B* Sulawesi
86 F4 **Towot** Sudan
95 L7 **Towson** Maryland U.S.A.
70 G6 **Towuti** *L* Sulawesi
8 C3 **Towy, R** Wales
112 D2 **Toxaway, L** North Carolina U.S.A.
66 B3 **Toxkan He** *R* China
108 D4 **Toyah L** Texas U.S.A.
60 O3 **Tōya-ko** *L* Japan
61 L9 **Toyama** Japan
61 L8 **Toyama wan** *B* Japan
116 A3 **Toygunen** U.S.S.R.
61 L10 **Toyo** Japan
61 L10 **Toyoake** Japan
60 G11 **Toyohama** Japan
61 L11 **Toyohashi** Japan
61 L11 **Toyokawa** Japan
60 R3 **Toyokoro** Japan
61 J11 **Toyonaka** Japan
60 H10 **Toyooka** Japan
61 N8 **Toyosaka** Japan
61 L10 **Toyota** Japan
29 K9 **Töysä** Finland
57 E4 **Toytepa** U.S.S.R.
85 F2 **Tozeur** Tunisia
116 M4 **Tozitna** *R* Alaska U.S.A.
36 C4 **Traben-Trarbach** W Germany
79 F4 **Trâblous** Lebanon
78 G1 **Trabzon** Turkey
122 H6 **Tracadie** New Brunswick Canada
123 L8 **Tracadie** Nova Scotia Canada
122 F8 **Tracey** New Brunswick Canada
69 H8 **Tra Cu** Vietnam
102 C4 **Tracy** California U.S.A.
99 O8 **Tracy** Iowa U.S.A.
99 L5 **Tracy** Minnesota U.S.A.
110 L6 **Tracy City** Tennessee U.S.A.
22 E5 **Tracy-le-Mont** France
41 J6 **Tradate** Italy
119 O3 **Trade L** Saskatchewan Canada
110 J4 **Tradewater** *R* Kentucky U.S.A.
Tradom *see* **Zhongba**
99 O7 **Traer** Iowa U.S.A.
98 F10 **Traer** Kansas U.S.A.
16 C8 **Trafalgar, C** Spain
111 K8 **Trafford** Alabama U.S.A.
113 F11 **Trafford, L** Florida U.S.A.
131 B8 **Traful** *R* Argentina
131 B8 **Traful, L** Argentina
38 L5 **Tragwein** Austria
48 L5 **Traian** Romania
130 J9 **Traição, B. de** Brazil
133 C5 **Traiguén** Chile
133 C7 **Traiguén, I** Chile
100 H1 **Trail** British Columbia Canada
100 C7 **Trail** Oregon U.S.A.
98 F4 **Trail City** South Dakota U.S.A.
115 R3 **Traill Ø** *isld* Greenland
143 D6 **Trainor Hills** Western Australia Australia
117 N5 **Trainor L** Northwest Territories Canada
21 P6 **Traînou** France
130 H10 **Traipu** Brazil
130 J9 **Trairi** *R* Brazil
38 N5 **Traismauer** Austria
21 M3 **Trait,le** France
52 H3 **Trakt** U.S.S.R.
111 F8 **Tralake** Mississippi U.S.A.
14 B4 **Tralee** Ireland
68 J6 **Tram Bo** Vietnam
40 F3 **Tramelan** Switzerland
68 G7 **Tram Kak** Cambodia
68 G7 **Tram Khnan** Cambodia
14 D4 **Tramore** Ireland
118 J6 **Tramping** Saskatchewan Canada
27 H13 **Tranås** Sweden
28 E4 **Tranbjerg** Denmark
133 D3 **Trancas** Argentina
124 G3 **Trancas** Mexico
18 E6 **Tranche, la** France
130 H5 **Trancoso** Brazil
16 C4 **Trancoso** Portugal
27 F14 **Tranemo** Sweden
13 F2 **Tranent** Scotland
69 D9 **Trang** Thailand
139 J4 **Trangie** New South Wales Australia
27 G11 **Trängslet** Sweden
69 H8 **Tranh De, Cua** *R* Vietnam
43 G7 **Trani** Italy
26 J2 **Tranöy** Norway
102 D5 **Tranquillity** California U.S.A.
19 Q18 **Trans** France
20 G4 **Trans** France
20 G5 **Trans** Ille-et-Vilaine France
146 C12 **Transantarctic Mts** Antarctica
118 C1 **Transcona** Manitoba Canada
89 F8 **Transkei** *homeland* S Africa
27 F11 **Transtrand** Sweden
89 E5 **Transvaal** *prov* S Africa
48 J4 **Transylvania** *reg* Romania
Transylvanian Alps *see* **Carpaţii Meridionali** *mts*
68 G8 **Tra On** Vietnam
41 L5 **Traona** Italy
43 E10 **Trapani** Sicily
101 L4 **Trapper Pk** Montana U.S.A.
21 P4 **Trappes** France
131 H3 **Trapua** *R* Brazil
13 E2 **Traquair** Scotland
139 H7 **Traralgon** Victoria Australia
17 F9 **Traras, Mt.des** Algeria
27 G15 **Traryd** Sweden
85 A5 **Trarza** *reg* Mauritania
45 P6 **Trasacco** Italy
42 E5 **Trasimeno, L** Italy
26 L6 **Träskholm** Sweden
109 P1 **Traskwood** Arkansas U.S.A.
16 C3 **Tras os Montes e Alto Douro** *prov* Portugal
16 B1 **Trasparga** Spain
36 B4 **Trassem** W Germany
45 H3 **Trassilico** Italy
68 F6 **Trat** Thailand
38 K5 **Traun** Austria
99 U3 **Traunik** Michigan U.S.A.
38 J6 **Traunsee** *L* Austria
38 J6 **Traunstein** *mt* Austria
38 G6 **Traunstein** W Germany
33 M5 **Trave** *R* W Germany
138 F5 **Travellers L** New South Wales Australia
112 E3 **Travellers Rest** South Carolina U.S.A.
33 N5 **Travemünde** W Germany
33 M5 **Travenberg** W Germany
118 E8 **Travers** Alberta Canada
131 H7 **Traversay Islds** S Sandwich Is
94 B1 **Traverse B.Grand** Michigan U.S.A.
94 B1 **Traverse B.Little** Michigan U.S.A.
94 B2 **Traverse City** Michigan U.S.A.
98 K4 **Traverse, L** South Dakota U.S.A.
116 H4 **Traverse Pk** Alaska U.S.A.
45 H2 **Traversetolo** Italy
122 B5 **Travers, L** Quebec Canada
144 D5 **Travers, Mt** New Zealand
131 C5 **Travesia Puntana** *reg* Argentina
131 C4 **Travesia Tunuyán** *reg* Argentina
68 H8 **Tra Vinh** Vietnam
109 J5 **Travis, L** Texas U.S.A.
42 H4 **Travnik** Yugoslavia
55 G4 **Travnoye** U.S.S.R.
44 F2 **Travo** Italy
70 P10 **Trawangan** Indonesia
14 D1 **Trawbreaga B** Ireland
109 N4 **Trawick** Texas U.S.A.
8 C2 **Trawsfynydd** Wales
143 C9 **Trayning** W Australia
42 G2 **Trbovlje** Yugoslavia
8 B1 **Tre-Arddur B** Wales
127 J3 **Treasure Beach** Jamaica
116 J3 **Treat I** Alaska U.S.A.
44 F2 **Trebbecco, L. di** Italy
44 F2 **Trebbia** *R* Italy
33 S8 **Trebbin** East Germany
33 R4 **Trebel** *R* East Germany
33 O7 **Trebel** W Germany
18 G9 **Trèbes** France
20 C4 **Trébeurden** France
31 J6 **Třebíč** Czechoslovakia
42 J6 **Trebinje** Yugoslavia
42 J6 **Trebišnica** *R* Yugoslavia
48 G2 **Trebišov** Czechoslovakia
42 H5 **Trebižat** *R* Yugoslavia
Trebizond *see* **Trabzon**
144 A7 **Treble Mt** New Zealand
42 G3 **Trebnje** Yugoslavia
31 H6 **Třeboň** Czechoslovakia
20 B5 **Tréboul** France
48 D1 **Třebová** Czechoslovakia
20 D5 **Trébrivan** France
33 R10 **Trebsen** East Germany
36 E4 **Trebur** W Germany
8 C4 **Trecastle** Wales
44 E1 **Trecate** Italy
45 K1 **Trecenta** Italy
106 B7 **Trechado** New Mexico U.S.A.
8 C4 **Tredegar** Wales
41 N6 **Tredici Comuni** *reg* Italy
9 E3 **Tredington** England
20 E6 **Trédion** France
45 L3 **Tredozio** Italy
20 C4 **Trédrez** France
73 L6 **Tree I** Lakshadweep Indian Oc
101 R1 **Treelon** Saskatchewan Canada
20 G6 **Treffieux** France
40 B5 **Treffort** France
8 C1 **Trefnant** Wales
8 C1 **Trefriw** Wales
8 C3 **Tregaron** Wales
119 N8 **Tregarva** Saskatchewan Canada
20 C4 **Trégastel** France
101 L1 **Trego** Montana U.S.A.
102 E1 **Trego** Nevada U.S.A.
99 P4 **Trego** Wisconsin U.S.A.
8 B7 **Tregony** England
20 D4 **Trégorrois** *reg* France
141 K4 **Tregosse Islets & Reefs** Gt Barrier Reef Aust
20 D4 **Treguier** France
20 C6 **Trégunc** France
119 T9 **Treherne** Manitoba Canada
68 G8 **Tre, Hon** *isld* Vietnam
26 K8 **Trehörningsjö** Sweden
20 B5 **Tréhou, le** France
15 D4 **Treig, L** Scotland
18 G7 **Treignac** France
20 G7 **Treillières** France
131 G4 **Treinta y Tres** Uruguay
36 C3 **Treis-Karden** W Germany
140 E5 **Trekelano** Queensland Australia
127 J2 **Trelawney** *parish* Jamaica
89 G1 **Trelawney** Zimbabwe
21 K7 **Trélazé** France
32 L6 **Trelde** W Germany
28 D5 **Trelde Næs** *C* Denmark
133 D6 **Trelew** Argentina
27 F16 **Trelleborg** Sweden
8 D4 **Trelleck** Wales
22 G3 **Trélon** France
8 B2 **Tremadoc** Wales
8 B2 **Tremadoc B** Wales
18 E7 **Tremblade, la** France
20 H5 **Tremblay** France
21 N4 **Tremblay-les-Villages** France
117 L8 **Trembleur L** British Columbia Canada
106 F6 **Trementina** New Mexico U.S.A.
21 J7 **Trémentines** France
37 K3 **Tremersdorf** W Germany
42 G6 **Tremiti, I.di** Italy
110 G1 **Tremont** Illinois U.S.A.
111 H7 **Tremont** Mississippi U.S.A.
95 L6 **Tremont** Pennsylvania U.S.A.
101 N8 **Tremonton** Utah U.S.A.
20 F5 **Trémorel** France
37 P4 **Třemošná** Czechoslovakia
17 H2 **Tremp** Spain
99 P5 **Trempealeau** Wisconsin U.S.A.
33 M5 **Tremsbüttel** W Germany
69 G8 **Trem Trem** *R* Vietnam
99 U3 **Trenary** Michigan U.S.A.
121 S5 **Trenche** *R* Quebec Canada
48 E2 **Trenčin** Czechoslovakia
28 C3 **Trend Å** *R* Denmark
32 K9 **Trendelburg** W Germany
133 E5 **Trenel** Argentina
27 A11 **Trengereid** Norway
70 N9 **Trenggalek** Java
131 E5 **Trenque Lauquen** Argentina
Trent *see* **Trento**
112 K2 **Trent** *R* North Carolina U.S.A.
108 G3 **Trent** Texas U.S.A.
121 L8 **Trent Canal** Ontario Canada
41 N5 **Trentino-Alto Adige** *reg* Italy
41 O5 **Trento** Italy
45 Q8 **Tréntola** Italy
122 K8 **Trenton** Nova Scotia Canada
121 N8 **Trenton** Ontario Canada
113 E8 **Trenton** Florida U.S.A.
94 D4 **Trenton** Michigan U.S.A.
110 C1 **Trenton** Missouri U.S.A.
98 E9 **Trenton** Nebraska U.S.A.
95 N6 **Trenton** New Jersey U.S.A.
95 M3 **Trenton** New York U.S.A.
98 C1 **Trenton** North Dakota U.S.A.
110 M2 **Trenton** Ohio U.S.A.
112 F4 **Trenton** South Carolina U.S.A.
110 H6 **Trenton** Tennessee U.S.A.
13 H6 **Trent, R** England
21 N4 **Tréon** France
46 D2 **Trepča** Yugoslavia
21 N1 **Tréport, le** France
38 H8 **Treppo Carnico** Italy
120 C3 **Treptow L** Ontario Canada
133 F4 **Tres Arboles** Uruguay
131 E7 **Tres Arroyos** Argentina
20 G6 **Tresboeuf** France
128 F5 **Três Casas** Brazil
19 P16 **Trescléoux** France
9 F7 **Tresco** *isld* Isles of Scilly England
130 F7 **Três Corações** Brazil
33 N9 **Treseburg** East Germany
15 B4 **Treshnish I** Scotland
48 E7 **Treskavica** *mt* Yugoslavia
130 D7 **Três Lagoas** Brazil
130 F6 **Três Marias** *dam* Brazil
133 B7 **Tres Montes, Pen** Chile
16 E2 **Trespaderne** Spain
130 D10 **Tres Passos** Brazil
131 E7 **Tres Picos, Cerro** *pk* Argentina
106 E5 **Tres Piedras** New Mexico U.S.A.
102 C5 **Tres Pinos** California U.S.A.
130 F7 **Três Pontas** Brazil
133 C3 **Tres Puentes** Chile
130 G8 **Três Rios** Brazil
21 M6 **Tresson** France
31 J6 **Třešt'** Czechoslovakia
15 G2 **Tresta** Shetland Scotland
125 M8 **Tres Zapotes** Mexico
8 C4 **Tretower** Wales
19 P18 **Trets** France
27 D10 **Trettin** Norway
Treuburg *see* **Olecko**
37 K6 **Treuchtlingen** W Germany
33 N2 **Treuen** W Germany
33 R8 **Treuenbrietzen** East Germany
140 B5 **Treuer Ra** N Terr Australia
27 C12 **Treungen** Norway
20 E5 **Trévé** France
Treves *see* **Trier**
20 C5 **Trévézal,Roc** *mt* France
21 J3 **Trévières** France
41 L6 **Treviglio** Italy
17 F2 **Treviño** Spain
42 E3 **Treviso** Italy
8 A6 **Trevose Head** England
40 A6 **Trévoux** France
36 G2 **Treysa** W Germany
31 H7 **Trhové Sviny** Czechoslovakia
27 H14 **Triabo** Sweden
139 J8 **Triabunna** Tasmania Australia
20 C4 **Triagoz, les** France
140 D2 **Trial B** N Terr Australia
47 V17 **Trianda** Rhodes Greece
117 P8 **Triangle** Alberta Canada
100 J7 **Triangle** Idaho U.S.A.
89 G3 **Triangle** Zimbabwe
47 H8 **Tria Nisiá** *isld* Greece
48 E2 **Tribeč** *R* Czechoslovakia
20 H3 **Tribehou** France
40 H1 **Triberg** W Germany
33 R4 **Tribsees** East Germany
141 H3 **Tribulation, C** Queensland Australia
119 O9 **Tribune** Saskatchewan Canada
107 J3 **Tribune** Kansas U.S.A.
43 G8 **Tricarico** Italy
43 J9 **Tricase** Italy
76 C5 **Trichur** India
9 E6 **Trickett's Cross** England
22 D4 **Tricot** France
139 H5 **Trida** New South Wales Australia
100 G8 **Trident Pk** Nevada U.S.A.
38 K7 **Trieben** Austria
37 N2 **Triebes** East Germany
21 O3 **Trie-Château** France
37 P6 **Triefenried** W Germany
21 P4 **Triel-sur-Seine** France
131 G4 **Trienta-y-Tres** Uruguay
36 B4 **Trier** W Germany
37 K5 **Triesdorf** W Germany
42 F3 **Trieste** Italy
42 E3 **Trieste, G.di** Italy
20 D4 **Trieux** *R* France
22 K5 **Trieux** France
37 P7 **Triftern** W Germany
42 F2 **Triglav** *mt* Yugoslavia
20 F7 **Trignac** France
42 F7 **Trigno** *R* Italy
16 C7 **Trigueròs** Spain
46 F5 **Trikeri** Greece
46 E6 **Trikhonis, L** Greece
46 E5 **Trikkala** Greece
46 E6 **Triklinos** Greece
79 D3 **Trikomo** Cyprus
113 E9 **Trilby** Florida U.S.A.
17 F4 **Trillo** Spain
120 G2 **Trilsbeck L** Ontario Canada
14 E3 **Trim** Ireland
13 G4 **Trimdon** England
9 H4 **Trimley** England
99 M6 **Trimont** Minnesota U.S.A.
142 B5 **Trimouille I** Western Australia Australia
18 F6 **Trimouille, la** France
124 D2 **Trincheras** Mexico
106 F4 **Trinchere** Colorado U.S.A.
83 L9 **Trincomalee** Sri Lanka
90 G11 **Trindade** *isld* Atlantic Oc
9 F4 **Tring** England
46 E5 **Tringia** *mt* Greece
121 T6 **Tring Junction** Quebec Canada
128 F6 **Trinidad** Bolivia
128 D2 **Trinidad** Colombia
126 D4 **Trinidad** Cuba
130 C10 **Trinidad** Paraguay
71 G4 **Trinidad** Philippines
131 G4 **Trinidad** Uruguay
100 A8 **Trinidad** California U.S.A.
106 F4 **Trinidad** Colorado U.S.A.
100 E2 **Trinidad** Washington U.S.A.
127 O2 **Trinidad** *isld* W Indies
127 O9 **Trinidad and Tobago** *rep* W Indies
133 B7 **Trinidad, Canal** Chile
131 E7 **Trinidad, I** Argentina
21 M4 **Trinité-de-Réville, la** France
20 E5 **Trinité-Porhoët, la** France
20 D6 **Trinité-sur-Mer, la** France
123 T5 **Trinity** Newfoundland Canada
109 M5 **Trinity** Texas U.S.A.
109 L3 **Trinity** *R* Texas U.S.A.
141 H3 **Trinity B** Queensland Australia
100 C8 **Trinity Center** California U.S.A.
127 P3 **Trinity Hills** Trinidad
146 C4 **Trinity I** *isld* Antarctica
116 K8 **Trinity Is** Alaska U.S.A.
146 D4 **Trinity Peninsula** *pen* Antarctica
102 F1 **Trinity Ra** Nevada U.S.A.
100 C9 **Trinity Res** California U.S.A.
69 A8 **Trinkat I** Nicobar Is
44 D1 **Trino** Italy
Trinquet, Fort *see* **Bir Moghreim**
83 L12 **Triolet** Mauritius
112 B3 **Trion** Georgia U.S.A.
43 H9 **Trionto, C** Italy
69 C10 **Tripa** *R* Sumatra
Tripoli *see* **Tarābulus** Libya
99 O7 **Tripoli** Iowa U.S.A.
46 E7 **Tripolis** Greece
84 E3 **Tripolitania** *reg* Libya
98 H6 **Tripp** South Dakota U.S.A.
36 D5 **Trippstadt** W Germany
37 M2 **Triptis** East Germany
75 O7 **Tripura** *prov* India
123 N3 **Triquet, L** Quebec Canada
32 J4 **Trischen** *isld* W Germany
37 O4 **Tři Sekery** Czechoslovakia
90 H12 **Tristan da Cunha** Atlantic Oc
68 G7 **Tri Ton** Vietnam
33 M5 **Trittau** W Germany
130 H9 **Triunfo** Brazil
76 C6 **Trivandrum** India
48 D2 **Trnava** Czechoslovakia
21 K3 **Troarn** France
36 G7 **Trochtelfingen** W Germany
26 F5 **Troena** *isld* Norway
28 F6 **Troense** Denmark
38 M7 **Trofaiach** Austria
147 Q9 **Trofimovsk** U.S.S.R.
42 G5 **Trogir** Yugoslavia
42 H5 **Troglav** *mt* Yugoslavia
36 C2 **Troisdorf** W Germany
36 C6 **Troisfontaines** France
85 D1 **Trois Fourches, Cap des** Morocco
21 L7 **Trois Moutiers, les** France
122 C5 **Trois Pistoles** Quebec Canada
22 K3 **Trois Ponts** Belgium
121 S6 **Trois Rivières** Quebec Canada
127 N5 **Trois Rivières** Guadeloupe W Indies
83 M14 **Trois Swains, Les** *islds* Kerguelen Indian Oc
22 K3 **Trois Vierges** Luxembourg
54 M2 **Troitsa** U.S.S.R.
55 E1 **Troitsa** Tyumenskaya obl U.S.S.R.
55 D4 **Troitsk** U.S.S.R.
56 F4 **Troitsk** U.S.S.R.
54 J1 **Troitsk** Moskovskaya Oblast' U.S.S.R.
55 D3 **Troitskiy** U.S.S.R.
52 J3 **Troitsko-Pechorsk** U.S.S.R.
55 F4 **Troitskoye** U.S.S.R.
55 C4 **Troitskoye** Bashkirskaya A.S.S.R. U.S.S.R.
127 L2 **Troja** Jamaica
28 B5 **Troldhede** Denmark
27 F13 **Trollhättan** Sweden
26 D9 **Trollheimen** *mt* Norway
26 C9 **Trolltindane** *mt* Norway
129 G4 **Trombetas** *R* Brazil
133 C5 **Tromen** *mt* Argentina
131 B6 **Tromen, V** Argentina
41 M6 **Trompia, V** Italy
26 K2 **Tromsö** Norway
26 K2 **Tromsöysund** Norway
55 F1 **Trom'yegan** *R* U.S.S.R.
102 G6 **Trona** California U.S.A.
131 B8 **Tronador** *pk* Arg/Chile
20 G4 **Tronchet, le** France
124 G6 **Troncón** Mexico
26 J3 **Trondenes** Norway
26 D8 **Trondheim** Norway
26 D8 **Trondheimsfjord** *inlet* Norway
26 E9 **Tronfjell** *mt* Norway
27 J10 **Trönödal** Sweden
42 F6 **Tronto** *R* Italy
21 M6 **Trôo** France
79 C4 **Troödos, Mt** Cyprus
12 D3 **Trool, L** Scotland
12 D2 **Troon** Scotland
43 G10 **Tropea** Italy
130 G4 **Tropeiros, Sa.dos** *mts* Brazil
103 M4 **Tropic** Utah U.S.A.
46 D2 **Tropojë** Albania
27 J13 **Trosa** Sweden
52 J2 **Trosh** U.S.S.R.
98 K6 **Trosky** Minnesota U.S.A.
119 N9 **Trossachs** Saskatchewan Canada
12 D1 **Trossachs** Scotland
14 E1 **Trostan** *mt* N Ireland
28 E6 **Trøstrup Korup** Denmark
48 M2 **Trostyanets** U.S.S.R.
33 P9 **Trotha** East Germany
98 C2 **Trotters** North Dakota U.S.A.
48 K4 **Trotuş** *R* Romania
101 T9 **Troublesome** Colorado U.S.A.
142 F2 **Troughton I** Western Australia Australia
68 G6 **Troun** Cambodia
109 M3 **Troup** Texas U.S.A.
107 L4 **Trousdale** Kansas U.S.A.
122 F6 **Trousers, L** New Brunswick Canada
117 L6 **Trout** *R* British Columbia Canada
111 D10 **Trout** Louisiana U.S.A.
13 F5 **Troutbeck** England
103 L6 **Trout Cr** Arizona U.S.A.
100 E5 **Trout Cr** Oregon U.S.A.
121 L7 **Trout Creek** Ontario Canada
99 R3 **Trout Creek** Michigan U.S.A.
100 K2 **Trout Creek** Montana U.S.A.
103 L2 **Trout Creek** Utah U.S.A.
117 P10 **Trout L** British Columbia Canada
99 R3 **Trout L** Wisconsin U.S.A.
117 N5 **Trout Lake** Northwest Territories Canada
101 Q5 **Trout Pk** Wyoming U.S.A.
118 C2 **Trout R** Alberta Canada
123 O4 **Trout River** Newfoundland Canada
95 K5 **Trout Run** Pennsylvania U.S.A.
94 J5 **Troutville** Pennsylvania U.S.A.
94 H9 **Troutville** Virginia U.S.A.
21 L3 **Trouville** France
8 D5 **Trowbridge** England
139 H8 **Trowutta** Tasmania Australia
127 J2 **Troy** Jamaica
47 H5 **Troy** Turkey
111 L10 **Troy** Alabama U.S.A.
100 J3 **Troy** Idaho U.S.A.
110 K3 **Troy** Indiana U.S.A.
110 F3 **Troy** Missouri U.S.A.
100 K1 **Troy** Montana U.S.A.
95 P4 **Troy** New Hampshire U.S.A.
95 O4 **Troy** New York U.S.A.
112 H2 **Troy** North Carolina U.S.A.
110 M1 **Troy** Ohio U.S.A.
100 H4 **Troy** Oregon U.S.A.
95 L5 **Troy** Pennsylvania U.S.A.
109 K4 **Troy** Texas U.S.A.
94 G7 **Troy** West Virginia U.S.A.
46 G2 **Troyan** Bulgaria
55 E4 **Troyebratskiy** U.S.S.R.
18 H4 **Troyes** France
95 P2 **Troy, N** Vermont U.S.A.
103 J3 **Troy Pk** Nevada U.S.A.
37 N3 **Tršnice** Czechoslovakia
48 F1 **Trstená** Czechoslovakia
46 D1 **Trstenik** Yugoslavia
140 D1 **Truant I** N Terr Australia
119 N9 **Truax** Saskatchewan Canada
54 E4 **Trubchevsk** U.S.S.R.
54 C6 **Trubezh** *R* U.S.S.R.
124 G5 **Truchas** Mexico
106 E5 **Truchas** New Mexico U.S.A.
36 D6 **Truchtersheim** France
Trucial States *see* **United Arab Emirates**
102 D2 **Truckee** California U.S.A.
102 E2 **Truckee** *R* Nevada U.S.A.
59 K3 **Trudovoye** U.S.S.R.
15 D4 **Truim** *R* Scotland
121 M5 **Truite, L. la** Quebec Canada
125 L2 **Trujillo** Honduras
128 C5 **Trujillo** Peru
16 D5 **Trujillo** Spain
106 F6 **Trujillo** New Mexico U.S.A.
127 J10 **Trujillo** Venezuela
134 F7 **Truk Is** Caroline Is Pacific Oc
99 M6 **Truman** Minnesota U.S.A.
110 F6 **Trumann** Arkansas U.S.A.
95 L4 **Trumansburg** New York U.S.A.
98 H9 **Trumbull** Nebraska U.S.A.
103 L5 **Trumbull, Mt** Arizona U.S.A.
69 C11 **Trumon** Sumatra
9 G3 **Trumpington** England
21 L4 **Trun** France
139 J5 **Trundle** New South Wales Australia
67 B5 **Trung Khanh Phu** Vietnam
69 G8 **Trung Lon,Hon** *isld* Vietnam
69 G8 **Trung Nho,Hon** *isld* Vietnam
138 E5 **Truro** South Australia Australia
122 J8 **Truro** Nova Scotia Canada
8 A7 **Truro** England
99 N8 **Truro** Iowa U.S.A.
95 R4 **Truro** Massachusetts U.S.A.
70 D2 **Trusan** Sarawak
108 H2 **Truscott** Texas U.S.A.
48 K3 **Truşeşti** Romania
37 J2 **Trusetal** East Germany
48 H1 **Truskavets** U.S.S.R.
14 C2 **Truskmore** *mt* Ireland
70 E2 **Trus Madi, G** *mt* Sabah
52 H2 **Trusovo** U.S.S.R.
111 K8 **Trussville** Alabama U.S.A.
46 G1 **Trŭstenik** Bulgaria
28 F4 **Trustrup** Denmark
117 M7 **Trutch** British Columbia Canada
106 C8 **Truth or Consequences** New Mexico U.S.A.
31 J5 **Trutnov** Czechoslovakia
21 J4 **Truttemer-le-Petit** France
95 L4 **Truxton** New York U.S.A.
18 G8 **Truyère** *R* France
46 G2 **Tryavna** Bulgaria
98 F8 **Tryon** Nebraska U.S.A.
145 E2 **Tryphena** New Zealand
27 F10 **Trysil** Norway
27 E10 **Trysilelv** *R* Norway
52 B6 **Tryškiai** U.S.S.R.
31 J2 **Trzcianka** Poland
31 H2 **Trzebiez** Poland
31 K4 **Trzebnica** Poland
31 K3 **Trzemeszno** Poland
42 F2 **Tržič** Yugoslavia
58 C2 **Tsagaain-uul** Mongolia
53 G10 **Tsagan Aman** U.S.S.R.
Tsaidam *basin* *see* **Qaidam Pendi**
46 D5 **Tsamandás** Greece
Tsamkong *see* **Zhanjiang**
Tsangpo *R* *see* **Yarlung Zangbo Jiang** *R*
Tsaochwang *see* **Zaozhuang**
87 H11 **Tsaratanana** Madagascar
87 H10 **Tsaratanana, Massif du** *mt* Madagascar
87 D10 **Tsau** Botswana
88 G3 **Tsavo** Kenya
88 G3 **Tsavo Nat. Park** Kenya
89 A6 **Tsawisis** Namibia
41 M4 **Tschlin** Switzerland
55 D4 **Tselinnoye** U.S.S.R.
55 D5 **Tselinnyy** U.S.S.R.
55 F5 **Tselinograd** U.S.S.R.
54 F3 **Tsementnyy** U.S.S.R.
58 E2 **Tsenhermandal** Mongolia
52 G3 **Tsenogora** U.S.S.R.
56 C3 **Tsentral'nyy** U.S.S.R.
87 C11 **Tses** Namibia
58 C2 **Tsetserieg** Mongolia
58 D2 **Tsetserleg** Mongolia
85 E7 **Tsevié** Togo
87 D11 **Tshabong** Botswana
87 D7 **Tshabuta** Zaire
87 D10 **Tshane** Botswana
87 E8 **Tshangalele, L** Zaire
86 B7 **Tshela** Zaire
87 D7 **Tshibala** Zaire
86 B6 **Tshibobo, Pte** Gabon
86 D7 **Tshikapa** Zaire
87 D7 **Tshimbalanga** Zaire
87 E8 **Tshinsenda** Zaire
86 E7 **Tshofa** Zaire
89 E2 **Tsholotsho** Zimbabwe
Tšhqurghān *see* **Kholm**
86 D6 **Tshuapa** *R* Zaire
87 D10 **Tshwanne** Botswana
52 G2 **Tsil'ma** *R* U.S.S.R.
53 F10 **Tsimlyansk** U.S.S.R.
65 D6 **Tsinan** China
87 D11 **Tsineng** S Africa
46 G3 **Tsinga** *mt* Greece
Tsingtao *see* **Qingdao**
68 F1 **Tsinh Ho** Vietnam
Tsining *see* **Jining** Nei Monggol Zizhiqu
Tsin Ling *mt ra* *see* **Qin Ling** *mt ra*
87 H13 **Tsiombe** Madagascar
46 E5 **Tsiótion** Greece
58 G1 **Tsipa** *R* U.S.S.R.
87 H11 **Tsiroanomandidy** Madagascar
Tsitsihar *see* **Qiqihar**
89 C9 **Tsitsikamaberge** *mts* S Africa
52 G6 **Tsivilsk** U.S.S.R.
87 H12 **Tsivory** Madagascar
53 F12 **Tskhakaya** U.S.S.R.
52 D6 **Tsna** *R* U.S.S.R.
87 D10 **Tsootsha** Botswana
61 K11 **Tsu** Japan
61 M8 **Tsubame** Japan
61 K9 **Tsubata** Japan
61 O9 **Tsuchiura** Japan
60 O4 **Tsugaru-kaikyō** *str* Japan
61 N8 **Tsugawa** Japan
61 P13 **Tsuha** Okinawa
61 L10 **Tsukechi** Japan
61 P13 **Tsuken-jima** *isld* Okinawa
60 P2 **Tsukigata** Japan
61 J12 **Tsukiji** Japan
60 E12 **Tsukumi** Japan
87 C9 **Tsumeb** Namibia
87 C10 **Tsumis** Namibia
61 M10 **Tsuru** Japan
61 K10 **Tsuruga** Japan
61 K10 **Tsuruga-wan** *B* Japan
61 K9 **Tsurugi** Japan
60 H12 **Tsurugi-san** *mt* Japan
61 N7 **Tsuruoka** Japan
59 L4 **Tsururga** Japan
60 E12 **Tsurusaki** Japan
61 K10 **Tsushima** Japan
59 J5 **Tsushima** *isld* Japan
60 C11 **Tsushima-kaikyō** *str* Japan
60 C11 **Tsutsu** Japan
60 E11 **Tsuwano** Japan
60 H10 **Tsuyama** Japan
60 D12 **Tsuyazaki** Japan
48 M1 **Tsybulev** U.S.S.R.
55 E1 **Tsyngaly** U.S.S.R.
52 D1 **Tsyp Navolok** U.S.S.R.
54 K1 **Tsyurupi, Im** U.S.S.R.
16 C3 **Tua** *R* Portugal
145 G3 **Tuahine Pt.** New Zealand
145 F3 **Tuai** New Zealand
145 E2 **Tuakau** New Zealand
14 C3 **Tuam** Ireland
145 D4 **Tuamarina** New Zealand
135 N10 **Tuamotu** *arch* Pacific Oc
135 M10 **Tuamotu Ridge** Pacific Oc
68 F2 **Tuan Giao** Vietnam
69 C11 **Tuangku** *isld* Sumatra
67 B3 **Tuanxi** China
144 B7 **Tuapeka Mouth** New Zealand
125 N2 **Tuapi** Nicaragua
53 E11 **Tuapse** U.S.S.R.
70 E1 **Tuaran** Sabah
144 A7 **Tuatapere** New Zealand
70 K8 **Tua, Tg** *C* Sumatra
56 D4 **Tuba** *R* U.S.S.R.
103 N10 **Tubac** Arizona U.S.A.
103 N5 **Tuba City** Arizona U.S.A.
71 B3 **Tubalai** *isld* Indonesia
78 H5 **Tubal, Wadi** Iraq
70 O9 **Tuban** Java
133 H3 **Tubarão** Brazil
80 E4 **Tubas** Jordan
70 C3 **Tubau** Sarawak
71 D6 **Tubbataha Reefs** Sulu Sea
118 J8 **Tuberose** Saskatchewan Canada
71 E7 **Tubigan** *isld* Philippines
71 E8 **Tubig Puti** Philippines
71 E4 **Tubile Pt** Philippines
36 G7 **Tübingen** W Germany
55 C4 **Tubinskiy** U.S.S.R.
22 G2 **Tubize** Belgium
71 F6 **Tubod** Mindanao Philippines
142 A5 **Tubridgi Pt** Western Australia Australia
84 G3 **Tubruq** Libya
70 E3 **Tubu** *R* Kalimantan
135 M10 **Tubuai Is** Pacific Oc
124 D2 **Tubutama** Mexico
127 K9 **Tucacas** Venezuela
100 H3 **Tucannon** *R* Washington U.S.A.
129 L6 **Tucano** Brazil
128 G7 **Tucavaca** Bolivia
18 G10 **Tuchan** France
67 A3 **Tucheng** China
117 J5 **Tuchitua** Yukon Territory Canada
117 L6 **Tuchodi** *R* British Columbia Canada
31 K2 **Tuchola** Poland
48 G1 **Tuchów** Poland
143 C7 **Tuckanarra** Western Australia Australia
146 C12 **Tucker Glacier** *glacier* Antarctica
103 O9 **Tucson** Arizona U.S.A.
103 N9 **Tucson Mts** Arizona U.S.A.
133 D3 **Tucumán** *prov* Argentina
106 G6 **Tucumcari** New Mexico U.S.A.
129 G5 **Tucunaré** Brazil
127 M10 **Tucupido** Venezuela
127 N10 **Tucupita** Venezuela
129 J4 **Tucurui** Brazil
31 J2 **Tuczno** Poland
25 E6 **Tüddern** W Germany
28 G6 **Tudeå** *R* Denmark
17 F2 **Tudela** Spain
16 D3 **Tudela de Duero** Spain
120 J3 **Tudhope** Ontario Canada
102 C2 **Tudor** California U.S.A.
85 F6 **Tudun Wade** Nigeria
16 C3 **Tuela** *R* Portugal
28 H5 **Tuelsø** Denmark
129 H4 **Tueré** *R* Brazil
21 M5 **Tuffe** France
136 K3 **Tufi** Papua New Guinea
8 B4 **Tufton** Wales
112 D3 **Tugaloo L** South Carolina U.S.A.
118 L8 **Tugaske** Saskatchewan Canada
89 G7 **Tugela** *R* S Africa
94 E9 **Tug Fork** *R* Kentucky U.S.A.

Tuggerah L — Union City 87

139 K5 **Tuggerah L** New South Wales Australia
116 K8 **Tugidak I** Alaska U.S.A.
71 G5 **Tugnug Pt** Samar Philippines
55 D1 **Tugrovskiy** U.S.S.R.
70 F4 **Tuguan Maputi** *isld* Indonesia
71 G7 **Tugubun Pt** Philippines
71 E2 **Tuguegarao** Philippines
55 D3 **Tugulym** U.S.S.R.
59 L1 **Tugur** U.S.S.R.
69 C12 **Tuhemberua** Indonesia
145 D4 **Tui** New Zealand
125 P10 **Tuila** Guatemala
65 A4 **Tui Lamin Sum** China
56 C4 **Tuim** U.S.S.R.
Tujiabu *see* **Yongxiu**
70 E3 **Tujung** Kalimantan
55 C4 **Tukan** U.S.S.R.
79 B8 **Tûkh** Egypt
145 F3 **Tukituki R** New Zealand
68 F6 **Tuk Luy** Cambodia
114 F4 **Tuktoyaktuk** Northwest Territories Canada
52 B6 **Tukums** U.S.S.R.
70 B5 **Tukung, Bt** *mt* Kalimantan
87 F7 **Tukuyu** Tanzania
125 K6 **Tula** Mexico
54 J2 **Tula** U.S.S.R.
119 O4 **Tulabi Lake** Saskatchewan Canada
58 C4 **Tulai Shan** China
117 N11 **Tulameen** British Columbia Canada
125 K7 **Tulancingo** Mexico
70 K8 **Tulangbawang** *R* Sumatra
102 E5 **Tulare** California U.S.A.
98 H5 **Tulare** South Dakota U.S.A.
102 E5 **Tulare Lake Bed** California U.S.A.
108 A2 **Tularosa** New Mexico U.S.A.
106 B8 **Tularosa Mts** New Mexico U.S.A.
106 D9 **Tularosa V** New Mexico U.S.A.
89 B8 **Tulbagh** *mt* S Africa
128 C3 **Tulcán** Ecuador
48 M5 **Tulcea** Romania
48 M2 **Tul'chin** U.S.S.R.
102 E5 **Tule** *R* California U.S.A.
127 H9 **Tulé** Venezuela
Tuléar *see* **Toliara**
108 F1 **Tule Cr** Texas U.S.A.
100 D8 **Tule L** California U.S.A.
100 E8 **Tule L.Res** California U.S.A.
19 N16 **Tulette** France
89 F3 **Tuli** Zimbabwe
31 L3 **Tuliszków** Poland
52 D3 **Tulivaara** Finland
80 D4 **Tulkarm** Jordan
14 C4 **Tulla** Ireland
110 K6 **Tullahoma** Tennessee U.S.A.
139 J5 **Tullamore** New South Wales Australia
14 D3 **Tullamore** Ireland
18 G7 **Tulle** France
28 F7 **Tullebølle** Denmark
139 H5 **Tullibigeal** New South Wales Australia
40 B7 **Tullins** France
48 C2 **Tulln** Austria
38 N5 **Tullnerfeld** *reg* Austria
102 D4 **Tulloch Lake** *res* California U.S.A.
111 D10 **Tullos** Louisiana U.S.A.
14 E4 **Tullow** Ireland
141 H4 **Tully** Queensland Australia
95 L4 **Tully** New York U.S.A.
141 H4 **Tully Falls** Queensland Australia
140 E3 **Tully Inlet** Queensland Australia
52 D1 **Tuloma** *R* U.S.S.R.
65 H1 **Tulongshan** China
52 D3 **Tulos, Oz** *L* U.S.S.R.
29 P8 **Tulos, Oz** *L* U.S.S.R.
47 H2 **Tulovo** Bulgaria
52 J4 **Tulpan** U.S.S.R.
107 P5 **Tulsa** Oklahoma U.S.A.
117 G6 **Tulsequah** British Columbia Canada
14 C3 **Tulsk** Ireland
53 E7 **Tul'skaya Oblast'** *prov* U.S.S.R.
28 D4 **Tulstrup** Denmark
128 C3 **Tuluá** Colombia
125 Q7 **Tulum** Mexico
131 C4 **Tulumaya** *R* Argentina
55 C2 **Tulumbasy** U.S.S.R.
131 C3 **Tulum, V.de** Argentina
56 F4 **Tulun** U.S.S.R.
70 N10 **Tulungagung** Java
71 D5 **Tuluran** Philippines
71 H4 **Tulutu** Indonesia
55 C3 **Tulva** *R* U.S.S.R.
54 M1 **Tuma** U.S.S.R.
103 N10 **Tumacacori Nat.Mon** Arizona U.S.A.
128 C3 **Tumaco** Colombia
71 G7 **Tumadgo Pt** Mindanao Philippines
100 D5 **Tumalo** Oregon U.S.A.
70 C5 **Tumangmiri** Kalimantan
52 D6 **Tumanovo** U.S.S.R.
55 E2 **Tuman, Oz** *L* U.S.S.R.
51 P2 **Tumany** U.S.S.R.
56 E5 **Tumat-Tayga, Khrebet** *mts* U.S.S.R.
128 G2 **Tumatumari** Guyana
86 D6 **Tumba** Zaire
70 C5 **Tumbangmasuki** Kalimantan
70 C5 **Tumbangsamba** Kalimantan
70 C5 **Tumbangsenamang** Kalimantan
70 B5 **Tumbangtiti** Kalimantan
71 G7 **Tumbao** Philippines
139 J6 **Tumbarumba** New South Wales Australia
128 B4 **Tumbes** Peru
124 H8 **Tumbiscatio** Mexico
95 R1 **Tumbledown Mt** Maine U.S.A.
130 B9 **Tumburús** Argentina
9 F1 **Tumby** England
138 D5 **Tumby Bay** South Australia Australia
29 O4 **Tumcha** *R* U.S.S.R.
52 D2 **Tumchaozero, Ozero** *L* U.S.S.R.
65 B4 **Tumd Youqi** China
65 B4 **Tumd Zuoqi** China
80 G4 **Tumeira** Jordan
65 H3 **Tumen** China
59 J3 **Tumen** *R* China/Korea
128 F2 **Tumeremo** Venezuela
70 F2 **Tumindao** *isld* Philippines
130 H6 **Tumiritinga** Brazil
76 C4 **Tumkur** India
15 D4 **Tummel** *R* Scotland
59 M2 **Tumnin** *R* U.S.S.R.
77 H6 **Tump** Pakistan
70 D5 **Tumpah** Kalimantan
69 F9 **Tumpat** Malaysia
71 H5 **Tumputiga, Gunung** *mt* Sulawesi Indonesia
74 H8 **Tumsar** India
85 D6 **Tumu** Ghana
129 G3 **Tumucamaque, Sa** *mts* Brazil
139 J6 **Tumut** New South Wales Australia
52 H6 **Tumutuk** U.S.S.R.
27 F13 **Tun** Sweden
26 J9 **Tuna** Sweden
71 G7 **Tuna Bay** Mindanao Philippines
127 O2 **Tunapuna** Trinidad
128 E7 **Tunari** *mt* Bolivia
126 E4 **Tunas de Zaza** Cuba
131 E5 **Tunas, L** Argentina
77 D6 **Ţunb aş Sughrá** *isld* Iran
77 D6 **Ţunb Kubrá** *isld* Iran
78 G2 **Tunceli** Turkey
67 C7 **Tunchang** China
139 L4 **Tuncurry** New South Wales Australia
52 F3 **Tundra** U.S.S.R.
87 F7 **Tunduma** Zambia
88 F7 **Tunduru** Tanzania
47 H2 **Tundzha** *R* Bulgaria
28 J5 **Tune** Denmark
70 F2 **Tungku** Sabah
29 P6 **Tungozero** U.S.S.R.
67 G5 **Tung Shan** Taiwan
117 J5 **Tungsten** Northwest Territories Canada
102 F1 **Tungsten** Nevada U.S.A.
Tungting Lake *see* **Dongting Hu**
70 C4 **Tungun, Bt** *mt* Kalimantan
56 F1 **Tunguska** *R* U.S.S.R.
58 E2 **Tünhel** Mongolia
27 C11 **Tunhovdfjord** *L* Norway
76 F2 **Tuni** India
110 F7 **Tunica** Mississippi U.S.A.
43 C12 **Tunis** Tunisia
43 D11 **Tunis, G. de** Tunisia
84 D3 **Tunisia** *rep* N Africa
128 D2 **Tunja** Colombia
56 F5 **Tunkinskiye Gol'tsy** *mts* U.S.S.R.
65 B6 **Tunliu** China
26 E9 **Tunna** *R* Norway
120 G6 **Tunnel Dam** Ontario Canada
19 O18 **Tunnel du Rove** France
94 H7 **Tunnelton** West Virginia U.S.A.
26 F7 **Tunnsjö** *L* Norway
28 E5 **Tunø** Denmark
9 H3 **Tunstall** England
8 D1 **Tunstall** England
115 N6 **Tunungayualok I** Labrador, Nfld Canada
131 C4 **Tunuyán, R** Argentina
131 C4 **Tunuyán, Sa. de** *mts* Argentina
67 F2 **Tunxi** China
67 A1 **Tuo Jiang** *R* China
67 D4 **Tuojiang** China
65 E5 **Tuoji Dao** *isld* China
68 G6 **Tuol Khpos** Cambodia
102 D4 **Tuolumne** California U.S.A.
102 E4 **Tuolumne Meadows** California U.S.A.
29 L7 **Tuomioja** Finland
130 E7 **Tupã** Brazil
130 E6 **Tupaciguara** Brazil
128 F4 **Tupanaóca** Brazil
145 G2 **Tuparoa** New Zealand
111 H7 **Tupelo** Mississippi U.S.A.
109 L1 **Tupelo** Oklahoma U.S.A.
111 H7 **Tupelo Nat Battlefield** Mississippi U.S.A.
128 G4 **Tupinambaranas, I** Brazil
130 E4 **Tupiraçaba** Brazil
133 D2 **Tupiza** Bolivia
102 E6 **Tupman** California U.S.A.
29 L7 **Tupos** Finland
117 N8 **Tupper** British Columbia Canada
95 N2 **Tupper Lake** New York U.S.A.
133 D4 **Tupungato** *mt* Arg/Chile
65 E2 **Tuquan** China
128 C3 **Tuquerres** Colombia
67 D7 **Tuqu Wan** *B* China
66 D4 **Tura** China
75 O6 **Tura** India
55 D2 **Tura** *R* U.S.S.R.
145 E4 **Turakina** New Zealand
145 E4 **Turakirae Head** New Zealand
57 K5 **Turakurgan** U.S.S.R.
56 D5 **Turan** U.S.S.R.
59 K1 **Turana, Khrebet** *mt* U.S.S.R.
145 E3 **Turangi** New Zealand
42 E6 **Turano** *R* Italy
45 N5 **Turano, L.di** Italy
126 G9 **Turbaco** Colombia
20 E7 **Turballe, la** France
77 H7 **Turbat** Pakistan
41 J3 **Turbenthal** Switzerland
126 F10 **Turbo** Colombia
17 H2 **Turbón** *mt* Spain
48 M1 **Turbov** U.S.S.R.
48 H6 **Turburea** Romania
52 E3 **Turchasovo** U.S.S.R.
48 H4 **Turda** Romania
143 C6 **Turee Cr** Western Australia Australia
16 E3 **Turégano** Spain
31 L3 **Turek** Poland
79 D10 **Tûr, El** Egypt
127 K10 **Turen** Venezuela
66 D3 **Turfan Depression** China
57 C1 **Turgay** U.S.S.R.
57 B1 **Turgay** *R* U.S.S.R.
55 D5 **Turgayskaya Stolovaya Strana** *dist* U.S.S.R.
121 L3 **Turgeon** *R* Quebec Canada
47 H1 **Tŭrgovishte** Bulgaria
55 D3 **Turgoyak** U.S.S.R.
47 J6 **Turgutlu** Turkey
78 F1 **Turhal** Turkey
52 C5 **Türi** U.S.S.R.
17 G5 **Turia** *R* Spain
129 J4 **Turiaçu** Brazil
127 L9 **Turiamo** Venezuela
31 L7 **Turiec** *R* Czechoslovakia
126 E3 **Turiguano, I** Cuba
Turin *see* **Torino**
118 E9 **Turin** Alberta Canada
95 M3 **Turin** New York U.S.A.
55 D2 **Turinsk** U.S.S.R.
55 D3 **Turinskaya-Sloboda** U.S.S.R.
59 K2 **Turiy Rog** U.S.S.R.
48 D3 **Türje** Hungary
48 H1 **Turka** U.S.S.R.
56 G4 **Turka** *R* U.S.S.R.
86 G5 **Turkana, L** Kenya
47 J4 **Türkeli** *isld* Turkey
41 O1 **Turkenfeld** W Germany
57 E3 **Turkestan** U.S.S.R.
57 E5 **Turkestanskiy Khrebet** *mts* U.S.S.R.
48 F3 **Túrkeve** Hungary
99 P7 **Turkey** *R* Iowa U.S.A.
108 G1 **Turkey** Texas U.S.A.
78 D2 **Turkey** *rep* W Asia
142 G3 **Turkey Creek** Western Australia Australia
106 F6 **Turkey Mts** New Mexico U.S.A.
41 N1 **Türkheim** W Germany
36 C4 **Türkismühle** W Germany
47 L5 **Türkmendağı** *mt* Turkey
Turkmenia *see* **Turkmenskaya** *S.S.R.*
Turkmenistan *see* **Turkmenskaya** *S.S.R.*
57 B5 **Turkmen-Kala** U.S.S.R.
57 B6 **Turkmenkarakul'** U.S.S.R.
50 E4 **Turkmenskaya S.S.R** U.S.S.R.
79 G1 **Türkoğlu** Turkey
127 H4 **Turks and Caicos Is** *isld group* W Indies
127 J4 **Turks Is** W Indies
29 J11 **Turku** Finland
27 M10 **Turku Pori** *reg* Finland
86 G5 **Turkwel** *R* Kenya
16 E5 **Turleque** Spain
102 D4 **Turlock** California U.S.A.
130 G5 **Turmalina** Brazil
117 J6 **Turnagain** *R* Br Col Canada
145 F4 **Turnagain, C** New Zealand
38 M6 **Turnau** Austria
119 Q5 **Turnberry** Manitoba Canada
15 D5 **Turnberry** Scotland
119 S4 **Turnbull** Manitoba Canada
140 B5 **Turnbull, Mt** N Terr Australia
125 P9 **Turneffe Is** Belize
95 R2 **Turner** Maine U.S.A.
94 D2 **Turner** Michigan U.S.A.
101 R1 **Turner** Montana U.S.A.
100 C5 **Turner** Oregon U.S.A.
100 H3 **Turner** Washington U.S.A.
101 U6 **Turnercrest** Wyoming U.S.A.
142 B6 **Turner, Mt** Western Australia
142 G4 **Turner River** W Australia
95 P4 **Turners Falls** Mass U.S.A.
118 C8 **Turner Valley** Alberta Canada
101 P7 **Turnerville** Wyoming U.S.A.
22 H1 **Turnhout** Belgium
38 M6 **Turnitz** Austria
31 J5 **Turnov** Czechoslovakia
46 G1 **Turnu Măgurele** Romania
48 J5 **Turnu Roşu** Romania
57 H1 **Turobay** U.S.S.R.
31 O5 **Turobin** Poland
139 J5 **Turon** *R* New South Wales Australia
107 M4 **Turon** Kansas U.S.A.
139 J5 **Tuross** *R* New South Wales Australia
66 D3 **Turpan** China
108 D7 **Turpin** Oklahoma U.S.A.
126 F4 **Turquino, Pico** *pk* Cuba
106 D9 **Turquoise** New Mexico U.S.A.
116 K6 **Turquoise L** Alaska U.S.A.
38 J8 **Turrach** Austria
110 F6 **Turrell** Arkansas U.S.A.
125 N5 **Turrialba** Costa Rica
19 Q16 **Turriers** France
15 F3 **Turriff** Scotland
55 D1 **Tursuntskiy Tuman, Oz** *L* U.S.S.R.
57 E5 **Tursunzade** U.S.S.R.
55 E2 **Turtas** *R* U.S.S.R.
57 B4 **Turtkul'** U.S.S.R.
99 O1 **Turtle** *R* Ontario Canada
122 H8 **Turtle Cr** New Brunswick Canada
118 J5 **Turtleford** Saskatchewan Canada
141 G1 **Turtlehead I** Queensland Australia
141 K3 **Turtle I** Gt Barrier Reef Aust
142 C5 **Turtle I** Western Australia Australia
70 F1 **Turtle Is** Philippines
85 B7 **Turtle Is** Sierra Leone
118 J5 **Turtle L** Saskatchewan Canada
98 F2 **Turtle L** North Dakota U.S.A.
99 O4 **Turtle L** Wisconsin U.S.A.
98 F1 **Turtle Mts** Manitoba/N Dakota Canada/U.S.A.
29 K5 **Turtola** Finland
98 H4 **Turton** South Dakota U.S.A.
145 E2 **Turua** New Zealand
66 B3 **Turugart** *pass* U.S.S.R.
51 H2 **Turukhansk** U.S.S.R.
55 E1 **Turumeyevo** U.S.S.R.
129 G3 **Turuna** *R* Brazil
28 D6 **Turup** Denmark
9 F3 **Turvey** England
130 D10 **Turvo** *R* Brazil
53 B8 **Tur'ya** *R* U.S.S.R.
31 L6 **Turzovka** Czechoslovakia
111 J8 **Tuscaloosa** Alabama U.S.A.
111 J8 **Tuscaloosa, L** Alabama U.S.A.
42 D6 **Tuscania** Italy
94 F6 **Tuscarawas** *R* Ohio U.S.A.
100 J8 **Tuscarora** Nevada U.S.A.
94 K6 **Tuscarora Mt** Pennsylvania U.S.A.
110 H2 **Tuscola** Illinois U.S.A.
100 K2 **Tuscor** Montana U.S.A.
110 J7 **Tuscumbia** Alabama U.S.A.
110 D3 **Tuscumbia** Missouri U.S.A.
28 H5 **Tuse** Denmark
57 A2 **Tushchibas, Zaliv** *G* U.S.S.R.
14 E4 **Tuskar Rock** Ireland
111 L9 **Tuskegee** Alabama U.S.A.
122 G10 **Tusket** Nova Scotia Canada
54 H5 **Tuskor'** *R* U.S.S.R.
115 O3 **Tussaaq** Greenland
102 G8 **Tustin** California U.S.A.
94 B2 **Tustin** Michigan U.S.A.
26 C8 **Tustna** *isld* Norway
116 M6 **Tustumena L** Alaska U.S.A.
31 M4 **Tuszyn** Poland
78 J2 **Tutak** Turkey
145 D1 **Tutamoe Range** New Zealand
52 E5 **Tutayev** U.S.S.R.
9 E2 **Tutbury** England
98 E6 **Tuthill** South Dakota U.S.A.
76 D6 **Tuticorin** India
46 D1 **Tutin** Yugoslavia
145 F3 **Tutira L** New Zealand
29 O5 **Tutiyarvi** U.S.S.R.
70 D3 **Tutoh** *R* Sarawak
129 K4 **Tutóia** Brazil
70 D2 **Tutong** Brunei
48 L4 **Tutova** *R* Romania
33 S5 **Tutow** East Germany
47 H1 **Tutrakan** Bulgaria
48 K6 **Tutraken** Romania
117 F5 **Tutshi L** Yukon Territory Canada
101 L7 **Tuttle** Idaho U.S.A.
98 F2 **Tuttle** North Dakota U.S.A.
107 N6 **Tuttle** Oklahoma U.S.A.
37 K2 **Tüttleben** W Germany
107 O2 **Tuttle Cr. Lake** Kansas U.S.A.
99 M6 **Tuttle L** Minnesota U.S.A.
41 J2 **Tuttlingen** W Germany
71 N9 **Tutuala** Timor
134 D1 **Tutuila** *isld* Amer Samoa
125 L9 **Tututepec** Mexico
71 O8 **Tutuwawang** Indonesia
111 F7 **Tutwiler** Mississippi U.S.A.
41 O2 **Tutzing** W Germany
58 D2 **Tuul Gol** *R* Mongolia
29 L10 **Tuulos** Finland
29 P9 **Tuupovarra** Finland
29 O9 **Tuusniemi** Finland
137 Q3 **Tuvalu** *islds state* Pacific Oc
137 R6 **Tuvana-i-Ra** *isld* Pacific Oc
137 R6 **Tuvana-i-Tholo** *isld* Pacific Oc
56 E5 **Tuvinskaya A.S.S.R.** U.S.S.R.
70 E4 **Tuwau** *R* Kalimantan
103 L5 **Tuweep** Arizona U.S.A.
65 A5 **Tuwei He** *R* China
116 L6 **Tuxedni B** Alaska U.S.A.
118 A1 **Tuxedo** Manitoba Canada
112 E2 **Tuxedo** North Carolina U.S.A.
41 P3 **Tuxer Gebirge** *mt* Austria
119 M8 **Tuxford** Saskatchewan Canada
9 F1 **Tuxford** England
67 C1 **Tuxiang** China
125 L7 **Tuxpan** Mexico
124 H8 **Tuxpan** Jalisco Mexico
124 G7 **Tuxpan** Nayarit Mexico
125 N9 **Tuxtla Gutiérrez** Mexico
16 B2 **Tuy** Spain
55 F2 **Tuy** *R* U.S.S.R.
117 H6 **Tuya L** British Columbia Canada
68 J6 **Tuy An** Vietnam
67 B6 **Tuyen Quang** Vietnam
68 J6 **Tuy Hoa** Vietnam
52 H6 **Tuymazy** U.S.S.R.
77 A2 **Tūysarkān** Iran
78 D2 **Tuz Gölü** *L* Turkey
103 N7 **Tuzigoot Nat.Mon** Arizona U.S.A.
78 K4 **Tuz Khurmātū** Iraq
78 H2 **Tuzla** *R* Turkey
48 E6 **Tuzla** Yugoslavia
48 N5 **Tuzly** U.S.S.R.
27 F14 **Tvååker** Sweden
26 L7 **Tvärålund** Sweden
26 M6 **Tvärån** Sweden
28 E4 **Tved** Århus Denmark
28 F6 **Tved** Fyn Denmark
28 E3 **Tvede** Denmark
27 C13 **Tvedestrand** Norway
Tver *see* **Kalinin**
28 E1 **Tversted** Denmark
52 E6 **Tvertsa** *R* U.S.S.R.
27 H15 **Tving** Sweden
28 D5 **Tvingstrup** Denmark
28 B4 **Tvis** Denmark
6 F1 **Tvøroyri** Faeroes
47 H2 **Tvŭrditsa** Bulgaria
68 B4 **Twante** Burma
31 K4 **Twardogóra** Poland
85 F4 **Twaret** Niger
121 N8 **Tweed** Ontario Canada
139 L3 **Tweed Heads** New South Wales Australia
118 F4 **Tweedie** Alberta Canada
13 E3 **Tweed, R** Scotland
13 E3 **Tweedsmuir** Scotland
117 K9 **Tweedsmuir Prov.Park** British Columbia Canada
87 D11 **Twee Rivieren** S Africa
118 L9 **Twelvemile L** Saskatchewan Canada
116 P4 **Twelvemile Summit** Alaska U.S.A.
14 B3 **Twelve Pins** *mt* Ireland
103 H7 **Twentynine Palms** California U.S.A.
143 F9 **Twilight Cove** Western Australia Australia
123 S4 **Twillingate** Newfoundland Canada
38 L8 **Twimberg** Austria
100 B1 **Twin** Washington U.S.A.
101 N4 **Twin Bridges** Montana U.S.A.
98 K4 **Twin Brooks** South Dakota U.S.A.
108 G4 **Twin Buttes Res** Texas U.S.A.
119 O2 **Twin City** Ontario Canada
115 N7 **Twin Falls** Labrador, Nfld Canada
101 L7 **Twin Falls** Idaho U.S.A.
142 F5 **Twin Heads** *mt* Western Australia Australia
94 C2 **Twin L** Michigan U.S.A.
99 U6 **Twin Lake** Michigan U.S.A.
117 P7 **Twin Lakes** Alberta Canada
116 K6 **Twin Lakes** Alaska U.S.A.
106 D2 **Twin Lakes** Colorado U.S.A.
101 L6 **Twin Lakes Res** Idaho U.S.A.
123 Q4 **Twin L.,N** Newfoundland Canada
123 R4 **Twin L.,S** Newfoundland Canada
95 Q2 **Twin Mountain** New Hampshire U.S.A.
102 D2 **Twin Peaks** California U.S.A.
101 L5 **Twin Peaks** Idaho U.S.A.
143 C10 **Twin Pks** Western Australia Australia
143 D10 **Twin Rocks** Western Australia Australia
138 E3 **Twins Cr** South Australia Australia
138 D4 **Twins, The** South Australia Australia
145 D4 **Twins, The** *mt* New Zealand
98 K2 **Twin Valley** Minnesota U.S.A.
100 E1 **Twisp** Washington U.S.A.
32 J7 **Twistringen** W Germany
108 D8 **Twitty** Texas U.S.A.
117 J4 **Twitya** *R* Northwest Territories Canada
144 C6 **Twizel** New Zealand
106 H4 **Two Buttes** Colorado U.S.A.
106 H4 **Two Buttes Creek** Colorado U.S.A.
119 R8 **Two Creeks** Manitoba Canada
99 T5 **Two Creeks** Wisconsin U.S.A.
101 P3 **Twodot** Montana U.S.A.
139 K6 **Twofold B** New South Wales Australia
99 P2 **Two Harbors** Minnesota U.S.A.
116 L8 **Two Headed I** Alaska U.S.A.
118 F5 **Two Hills** Alberta Canada
101 P5 **Two Ocean Pass** Wyoming U.S.A.
99 T5 **Two Rivers** Wisconsin U.S.A.
9 E2 **Twycross** England
9 E5 **Twyford** England
9 F5 **Twyford** England
12 D4 **Twynholm** Scotland
48 H2 **Tyachev** U.S.S.R.
28 H6 **Tybjerg** Denmark
28 D6 **Tybrind Vig** *B* Denmark
56 E1 **Tychany** *R* U.S.S.R.
55 G3 **Tychkino** U.S.S.R.
31 J2 **Tychowo** Poland
31 L5 **Tychy** Poland
26 E8 **Tydal** Norway
117 F7 **Tyee** Alaska U.S.A.
100 A1 **Tyee** Washington U.S.A.
94 J9 **Tye River** Virginia U.S.A.
94 H8 **Tygart V** West Virginia U.S.A.
59 J1 **Tygda** U.S.S.R.
101 N7 **Tyhee** Idaho U.S.A.
27 C10 **Tyin** *L* Norway
31 O2 **Tykocin** Poland
98 K5 **Tyler** Minnesota U.S.A.
94 J5 **Tyler** Pennsylvania U.S.A.
109 M3 **Tyler** Texas U.S.A.
100 H2 **Tyler** Washington U.S.A.
111 A9 **Tyler, L** Texas U.S.A.
111 F10 **Tylertown** Mississippi U.S.A.
28 D2 **Tylstrup** Denmark
56 C1 **Tym** *R* U.S.S.R.
48 F1 **Tymbark** Poland
59 M1 **Tymovskoye** U.S.S.R.
55 F2 **Tynay** U.S.S.R.
59 H1 **Tynda** U.S.S.R.
118 E1 **Tyndall** Manitoba Canada
98 J6 **Tyndall** South Dakota U.S.A.
144 C5 **Tyndall, Mt** New Zealand
26 J9 **Tynderö** Sweden
13 G4 **Tyne and Wear** *co* England
13 G3 **Tynemouth** England
118 J7 **Tyner** Saskatchewan Canada
122 J7 **Tyne Valley** Prince Edward I Canada
27 G11 **Tyngsjö** Sweden
31 H6 **Týn nad Vltava** Czechoslovakia
26 E9 **Tynset** Norway
8 C2 **Tyn-y-Groes** Wales
116 O5 **Tyone** *R* Alaska U.S.A.
Tyre *see* **Soûr**
27 D11 **Tyrifjorden** *L* Norway
27 G15 **Tyringe** Sweden
59 K1 **Tyrma** U.S.S.R.
48 L2 **Tyrnovo** U.S.S.R.
112 E2 **Tyron** North Carolina U.S.A.
14 D2 **Tyrone** *co* N Ireland
106 B9 **Tyrone** New Mexico U.S.A.
94 J6 **Tyrone** Pennsylvania U.S.A.
139 G6 **Tyrrell** *R* Victoria Australia
43 D8 **Tyrrhenian Sea** S Europe
28 D5 **Tyrsted** Denmark
26 H3 **Tysfjord** Norway
27 A12 **Tysnesöy** *isld* Norway
27 B11 **Tyssedal** Norway
27 J13 **Tystberga** Sweden
28 H6 **Tystrup** Denmark
31 O5 **Tyszowce** Poland
55 F3 **Tyukalinsk** U.S.S.R.
57 H4 **Tyulek** U.S.S.R.
53 G12 **Tyulen'i, Ostrova** *islds* U.S.S.R.
55 C4 **Tyul'gan** U.S.S.R.
55 E1 **Tyuli** U.S.S.R.
52 J5 **Tyul'kino** U.S.S.R.
55 E3 **Tyumen'** U.S.S.R.
50 F2 **Tyumenskaya Oblast'** *prov* U.S.S.R.
55 E4 **Tyuntyugur** U.S.S.R.
57 C2 **Tyuratam** U.S.S.R.
52 D1 **Tyuva Guba** U.S.S.R.
119 O8 **Tyvan** Saskatchewan Canada
48 M1 **Tyvrov** U.S.S.R.
8 B2 **Tywyn** Wales
25 C3 **t'Zand** Netherlands
87 F10 **Tzaneen** S Africa
Tzepo *see* **Zibo**
46 E5 **Tzoumérka** *mt* Greece
67 G4 **Tz'u-kao Shan** *pk* Taiwan
25 E2 **Tzummarum** Netherlands

U

85 B3 **Uad el Jat** *watercourse* Western Sahara
116 H7 **Ualik, L** Alaska U.S.A.
142 B6 **Uaroo** Western Australia Australia
128 G4 **Uatumã** *R* Brazil
129 L5 **Uaua** Brazil
130 G10 **Uauá** Brazil
128 E4 **Uaupés** Brazil
145 G3 **Uawa R** New Zealand
125 P9 **Uaxactún** Guatemala
130 G7 **Ubá** Brazil
56 B5 **Uba** *R* U.S.S.R.
22 L2 **Ubach o. Worms** Netherlands
55 E4 **Ubagan** *R* U.S.S.R.
130 G5 **Ubaí** Brazil
129 L6 **Ubaitaba** Brazil
86 C5 **Ubangi** *R* Cent Afr Republic/Zaire
Ubari *see* **Awbārī**
78 H6 **Ubayyid, Wadi al** Saudi Arabia
28 G5 **Ubby** Denmark
60 E12 **Ube** Japan
16 E6 **Ubeda** Spain
115 O3 **Ubekendt Ejland** *isld* Greenland
133 H1 **Uberaba** Brazil
130 B5 **Uberaba** *L* Brazil/Bolivia
36 B5 **Überherrn** W Germany
130 E6 **Uberlândia** Brazil
41 K2 **Überlingen** Switzerland
85 F7 **Ubiaja** Nigeria
33 S9 **Ubigau** East Germany
133 D2 **Ubina** *mt* Bolivia
94 E3 **Ubly** Michigan U.S.A.
68 F4 **Ubolratana** *res* Thailand
87 F11 **Ubombo** S Africa
68 G5 **Ubon Ratchathani** Thailand
36 F5 **Ubstadt-Weiher** W Germany
79 C2 **Uçari** Turkey
128 D5 **Ucayali** *R* Peru
47 N11 **Uçburun Yarımada** *pen* Turkey
22 G2 **Uccle** Belgium
16 E3 **Ucero** *R* Spain
47 N11 **Uçgaziler** Turkey
55 C4 **Uchaly** U.S.S.R.
57 K2 **Ucharal** U.S.S.R.
61 O8 **Uchigō** Japan
60 F12 **Uchiko** Japan
115 K7 **Uchi Lake** Ontario Canada
60 O3 **Uchiura wan** *B* Japan
40 A4 **Uchizy** France
57 C4 **Uch Kuduk** U.S.S.R.
57 C4 **Uchkuduk** U.S.S.R.
57 K5 **Uchkurgan** U.S.S.R.
33 P7 **Uchte** *R* East Germany
32 J7 **Uchte** W Germany
51 N3 **Uchur** *R* U.S.S.R.
22 L5 **Uckange** France
30 H2 **Ücker** *R* East Germany
36 C2 **Uckerath** W Germany
33 U4 **Uckeritz** East Germany
9 G6 **Uckfield** England
33 T9 **Uckro** East Germany
117 L11 **Ucluelet** British Columbia Canada
101 O6 **Ucon** Idaho U.S.A.
101 T5 **Ucross** Wyoming U.S.A.
56 G5 **Uda** *R* U.S.S.R.
76 C5 **Udagamandalam** India
74 E6 **Udaipur** India
75 M5 **Udaipur Garhi** Nepal
54 D6 **Uday** *R* U.S.S.R.
76 D3 **Udayagiri** India
77 B7 **Udayd, Khawr al'** *inlet* Qatar/Saudi Arabia
42 G4 **Udbina** Yugoslavia
28 H5 **Udby** Denmark
28 E3 **Udby** Århus Denmark
28 D6 **Udby** Fyn Denmark
28 E3 **Udbyhø** Denmark
28 E3 **Udbyneder** Denmark
27 E13 **Uddevalla** Sweden
12 D2 **Uddingston** Scotland
26 J6 **Uddjaur** *L* Sweden
25 E5 **Uden** Netherlands
32 M10 **Uder** East Germany
76 C1 **Udgir** India
74 F2 **Udhampur** Kashmir
142 E4 **Udialla** Western Australia Australia
42 E2 **Udine** Italy
56 E4 **Udinskiy Khrebet** *mts*
76 B4 **Udipi** India
37 P3 **Udlice** Czechoslovakia
55 B3 **Udmurtskaya A.S.S.R.** U.S.S.R.
52 E5 **Udomlya** U.S.S.R.
61 N11 **Udone-jima** *isld* Japan
68 F4 **Udon Thani** Thailand
140 B6 **Udor, Mt** N Terr Australia
59 L1 **Udskaya Guba** *B* U.S.S.R.
76 C5 **Udumalaipettai** India
47 H2 **Udvoy** *mt* Bulgaria
59 L1 **Udyl, Oz** *L* U.S.S.R.
51 L1 **Udzha** U.S.S.R.
70 G5 **Uëbonti** Sulawesi
33 L5 **Uecker** *R* East Germany
33 T6 **Ueckermark** *reg* East Germany
33 U5 **Ueckermünde** East Germany
61 M9 **Ueda** Japan
25 F5 **Uedem** W Germany
32 G8 **Üeffeln** W Germany
98 K8 **Uehling** Nebraska U.S.A.
60 D13 **Ueki** Japan
70 G5 **Uekuli** Sulawesi
86 E5 **Uele** *R* Zaire
32 E7 **Uelsen** W Germany
33 N7 **Uelzen** W Germany
61 K11 **Ueno** Japan
61 N10 **Uenohara** Japan
86 E5 **Uere** *R* Zaire
36 B3 **Uess** *R* W Germany
32 L5 **Uetersen** W Germany
55 C4 **Ufa** U.S.S.R.
37 J4 **Uffenheim** W Germany
55 C3 **Ufimskiy** U.S.S.R.
87 C10 **Ugab** *R* Namibia
116 J8 **Ugaiushak I** Alaska U.S.A.
116 L8 **Ugak I** Alaska U.S.A.
88 C4 **Ugalla** *R* Tanzania
116 E9 **Ugamak I** Aleutian Is
86 F5 **Uganda** *rep* Africa
116 L8 **Uganik I** Alaska U.S.A.
116 J8 **Ugashik B** Alaska U.S.A.
116 J8 **Ugashik Lakes** Alaska U.S.A.
28 C7 **Uge** Denmark
43 J9 **Ugento** Italy
28 H5 **Ugerløse** Denmark
28 E4 **Uggelhūse** Denmark
28 E1 **Uggerby** Denmark
28 E5 **Uggerslev** Denmark
16 E8 **Ugijar** Spain
28 E2 **Ugilt** Denmark
19 Q13 **Ugine** France
59 M2 **Uglegorsk** U.S.S.R.
55 C2 **Ugleural'skiy** U.S.S.R.
52 E6 **Uglich** U.S.S.R.
42 H5 **Ugljane** Yugoslavia
48 E6 **Ugljevik** Yugoslavia
52 D5 **Uglovka** U.S.S.R.
Ugoi *see* **Ujiji**
54 G2 **Ugra** *R* U.S.S.R.
46 G1 **Ugŭrchin** Bulgaria
55 F1 **Ugut** U.S.S.R.
83 L10 **Uhana** Sri Lanka
31 K6 **Uherské Hradiště** Czechoslovakia
36 H6 **Uhingen** W Germany
87 C10 **Uhlenhorst** Namibia
37 K4 **Uhlfeld** W Germany
119 T2 **Uhlman L** Manitoba Canada
37 L2 **Uhlstädt** East Germany
28 C5 **Uhre** Denmark
94 F6 **Uhrichsville** Ohio U.S.A.
31 O4 **Uhrusk** Poland
15 B3 **Uig** Skye Scotland
87 C7 **Uíge** Angola
65 F4 **Ŭiju** N Korea
55 C6 **Uil** *R* U.S.S.R.
55 B6 **Uil** U.S.S.R.
128 E7 **Uiñamarco, L** Peru/Bolivia
103 L5 **Uinkaret Plat** Arizona U.S.A.
55 C3 **Uinskoye** U.S.S.R.
101 P9 **Uinta Mts** Utah U.S.A.
89 D9 **Uitenhage** S Africa
25 C3 **Uitgeest** Netherlands
25 C4 **Uithoorn** Netherlands
25 G2 **Uithuizen** Netherlands
25 G2 **Uithuizerwad** Netherlands
79 G10 **Ujayyijāt, Abu** *well* Saudi Arabia
31 L5 **Ujazd** Poland
48 G3 **Újfehértó** Hungary
61 J11 **Uji** Japan
74 F7 **Ujiain** India
61 N9 **Ujiie** Japan
88 B4 **Ujiji** Tanzania
70 D4 **Ujohbilang** Kalimantan
48 E3 **Újpest** Hungary
31 K2 **Ujście** Poland
69 E12 **Ujungbatu** Sumatra
70 F7 **Ujung Pandang** Sulawesi
61 Q12 **Uka** Okinawa
61 L8 **Ukawa** Japan
88 D3 **Ukerewe** *isld* Tanzania
75 Q6 **Ukhrul** India
52 E4 **Ukhtoma** U.S.S.R.
89 B4 **Ukhwi Pan** Botswana
100 G4 **Ukiah** Oregon U.S.A.
61 P13 **Ukibaru-jima** *isld* Okinawa
116 D4 **Ukivok** Alaska U.S.A.
Ukkel *see* **Uccle**
115 O3 **Ukkusissat** Greenland
52 B6 **Ukmerge** U.S.S.R.
27 H13 **Ukna** Sweden
55 G3 **Ukrainka** U.S.S.R.
55 F4 **Ukrainka** Omskaya obl U.S.S.R.
54 G7 **Ukrainskaya S.S.R** *rep* U.S.S.R.
42 H4 **Ukrina** *R* Yugoslavia
55 D3 **Uksyanskoye** U.S.S.R.
31 N2 **Ukta** Poland
52 G3 **Uktym** U.S.S.R.
87 B8 **Uku** Angola
87 C8 **Ukuma** Angola
60 B12 **Uku-shima** *isld* Japan
6 M5 **Ula** *oil rig* North Sea
47 J7 **Ula** Turkey
58 E2 **Ulaanbaatar** Mongolia
58 B2 **Ulaangom** Mongolia
139 J4 **Ulan** New South Wales Australia
58 C4 **Ulan** China
Ulan Bator *see* **Ulaanbaatar**
65 C2 **Ulan Hobor** China
Ulan Hot *see* **Horqin Youyi Qianqi**
65 E2 **Ulan Hua** China
53 G10 **Ulan-Khol** U.S.S.R.
48 L1 **Ulanov** U.S.S.R.
65 A4 **Ulansuhai Nur** *L* China
56 G5 **Ulan-Ude** U.S.S.R.
131 C3 **Ulapes, Sa** *mts* Argentina
141 H7 **Ularunda** Queensland Australia
56 B5 **Ul'ba** U.S.S.R.
51 N3 **Ul'banskiy Zaliv** *B* U.S.S.R.
28 C3 **Ulbjerg** Denmark
9 G1 **Ulceby Cross** England
42 J7 **Ulcinj** Yugoslavia
13 E4 **Uldale** England
28 D5 **Uldum** Denmark
Uleåborg *see* **Oulu**
69 B10 **Uleelheue** Sumatra
27 D12 **Ulefoss** Norway
98 K2 **Ulen** Minnesota U.S.A.
52 C6 **Ulena** U.S.S.R.
138 F3 **Ulenia, L** New South Wales Australia
58 F1 **Ulety** U.S.S.R.
28 A4 **Ulfborg** Denmark
28 A4 **Ulfborg Kirke** Denmark
37 J1 **Ulfen** W Germany
65 D2 **Ulgai** China
65 D2 **Ulgain Gol** *R* China
13 G3 **Ulgham** England
76 A1 **Ulhasnagar** India
Uliastai *see* **Dong Ujimqin Qi**
58 C2 **Uliastay** Mongolia
86 E6 **Ulindi** *R* Zaire
42 G4 **Uljan** *isld* Yugoslavia
48 G5 **Uljma** Yugoslavia
56 G3 **Ul'kan** U.S.S.R.
57 C1 **Ul'kayak** *R* U.S.S.R.
28 D7 **Ulkebøl** Denmark
28 C5 **Ulkind** Denmark
56 G3 **Ul'kon** *R* U.S.S.R.
139 K6 **Ulladulla** New South Wales Australia
137 L8 **Ulladulla Trough** Pacific Oc
26 K9 **Ullånger** Sweden
27 F14 **Ullared** Sweden
26 M4 **Ullatti** Sweden
29 K8 **Ullava** Finland
17 H4 **Ulldecona** Spain
27 B11 **Ullensvang** Norway
28 F6 **Ullerslev** Denmark
28 D7 **Ullerup** Denmark
110 G4 **Ullin** Illinois U.S.A.
28 C3 **Ullits** Denmark
26 L2 **Ullsfjord** Norway
13 F4 **Ullswater** *L* England
59 K4 **Ullung Do** *isld* S Korea
111 E7 **Ulm** Arkansas U.S.A.
101 T5 **Ulm** Wyoming U.S.A.
36 H7 **Ulm** W Germany
139 L3 **Ulmarra** New South Wales Australia
36 B3 **Ulmen** W Germany
48 K5 **Ulmeni** Romania
38 L5 **Ulmerfeld** Austria
125 M2 **Ulmukhuas** Nicaragua
70 G7 **Uloe** Sulawesi
48 E7 **Ulog** Yugoslavia
88 E9 **Ulongue** Mozambique
138 E2 **Uloowaranie, L** South Australia Australia
13 E5 **Ulpha** England
56 H1 **Ulqkhan Botuobuya** *R* U.S.S.R.
27 F14 **Ulricehamn** Sweden
143 E7 **Ulrich Ra** Western Australia Australia
36 G2 **Ulrichstein** W Germany
26 H8 **Ulriksfors** Sweden
25 F2 **Ulrum** Netherlands
59 J4 **Ulsan** S Korea
28 D7 **Ulsby** W Germany
15 G1 **Ulsta** Shetland Scotland
28 E2 **Ulsted** Denmark
26 A9 **Ulstein** Norway
14 D2 **Ulster** *prov* N Ireland
95 L5 **Ulster** Pennsylvania U.S.A.
14 D2 **Ulster Canal** N Ireland
28 F5 **Ulstrup** Denmark
26 K4 **Ultevis** *mt* Sweden
139 G6 **Ultima** Victoria Australia
140 D6 **Ultim, Mt** N Terr Australia
41 O4 **Ultimo.V.d'** Italy
47 N10 **Ulu** *R* Turkey
51 M2 **Ulu** U.S.S.R.
125 P10 **Ulua** *R* Honduras
47 K4 **Ulubat Gölü** *L* Turkey
47 K6 **Ulubey** Turkey
79 F2 **Uluçınar** Turkey
47 K4 **Ulu Dağ** *mt* Turkey
71 D5 **Ulugan B** Philippines
88 F5 **Uluguru** *mts* Tanzania
78 E3 **Ulukişla** Turkey
70 C4 **Ululselua, Bt** *mt* Kalimantan
66 D2 **Ulungur He** *R* China
66 D2 **Ulungur Hu** *L* China
Ulun Hua *see* **Siziwang Qi**
58 F1 **Ulunkhan** U.S.S.R.
140 B7 **Uluru Nat Park** N Terr Australia
47 J5 **Ulus Dağı** *mt* Turkey
56 C2 **Uluyuya** *R* U.S.S.R.
15 B4 **Ulva** *isld* Scotland
13 E5 **Ulverston** England
139 H8 **Ulverstone** Tasmania Australia
27 B11 **Ulvik** Norway
27 M10 **Ulvila** Finland
26 K8 **Ulvön** *isld* Sweden
29 K6 **Ulvshale** *pen* Denmark
28 J7 **Ulv Sund** *chan* Denmark
52 G6 **Ul'yankovo** U.S.S.R.
53 G7 **Ul'yanovsk** U.S.S.R.
55 F5 **Ul'yanovskiy** U.S.S.R.
101 L4 **Ulysses** Idaho U.S.A.
107 J4 **Ulysses** Kansas U.S.A.
98 J8 **Ulysses** Nebraska U.S.A.
57 D1 **Ulytau** U.S.S.R.
57 D2 **Ulytau, Gory** *mts* U.S.S.R.
57 C1 **Uly-Zhylanshyk** *R* U.S.S.R.
Ulzburg *see* **Henstedt-Ulzburg**
48 N2 **Uman'** U.S.S.R.
131 C2 **Umango, Cerro** *pk* Argentina
71 M9 **Umarese** Timor Indonesia
74 J7 **Umaria** India
74 C6 **Umarkot** Pakistan
138 E2 **Umaroona, L** South Australia Australia
113 F9 **Umatilla** Florida U.S.A.
100 F4 **Umatilla** Oregon U.S.A.
71 G6 **Umayan** *R* Philippines
95 Q2 **Umbagog L** New Hampshire U.S.A.
140 D2 **Umbakumba** Northern Territory Australia
108 E1 **Umbarger** Texas U.S.A.
140 C7 **Umbeara** N Terr Australia
42 E5 **Umbertide** Italy
136 K3 **Umboi** *isld* Papua New Guinea
52 D1 **Umbozero, Oz** *L* U.S.S.R.
144 B6 **Umbrella Mts** New Zealand
127 J1 **Umbrella Pt** Jamaica
42 E6 **Umbria** *prov* Italy
26 G5 **Umbukta** Norway
130 J9 **Umbuzeiro** Brazil
26 L8 **Umeå** Sweden
26 K7 **Ume älv** *R* Sweden
80 G5 **Um ed Dananir** Jordan
80 G6 **Um el 'Amad** Jordan
80 G7 **Um el Malid** Jordan
80 G4 **Um el Manabi** Jordan
71 B3 **Umera** Indonesia
80 G7 **Um er Risas** Jordan
26 H6 **Umfors** Sweden
118 L1 **Umfreville** Ontario Canada
88 B10 **Umfuli** *R* Zimbabwe
89 G7 **Umgeni** *R* S Africa
26 K7 **Umgransele** Sweden
41 N3 **Umhausen** Austria
88 B10 **Umi** *R* Zimbabwe
116 L2 **Umiat** Alaska U.S.A.
147 G1 **Umingmakkok** U.S.A.
89 G8 **Umkomaas** *R* S Africa
84 F4 **Umm al Aḥrār** Libya
79 H4 **Umm al'Amad** Syria
84 E4 **Umm al Arānib** Libya
77 D7 **Umm al Qaywayn** U.A.E.
86 E3 **Umm Bel** Sudan
79 D10 **Umm Bugma** Egypt
37 K3 **Ummerstadt** East Germany
86 E3 **Umm Keddada** Sudan
86 E2 **Umm Lahai** Sudan
77 A4 **Umm Qasr** Iran
86 F3 **Umm Ruwaba** Sudan
Umm Sai'd *see* **Musay'īd**
86 F3 **Umm Saiyala** Sudan
77 C7 **Umm Shaif** *oil well* Persian Gulf
79 D10 **Umm Shomar, G** *mt* Egypt
79 C10 **Umm Tinâṣṣib,G** *mt* Egypt
26 H6 **Umnäs** Sweden
37 L2 **Umpferstedt** East Germany
100 B6 **Umpqua** *R* Oregon U.S.A.
87 C8 **Umpulo** Angola
80 G4 **Um Qantara** Jordan
80 F3 **Um Qeis** Jordan
80 G8 **Um Quleib** Jordan
80 G6 **Um Quseir** Jordan
74 H8 **Umred** India
80 G7 **Um Rummana** Jordan
80 G7 **Um Shujeira el Gharbiya** Jordan
89 G2 **Umsweswe** *R* Zimbabwe
Umtali *see* **Mutare**
89 F8 **Umtata** S Africa
86 A4 **Umuahia** Nigeria
47 H4 **Umurbey** Turkey
89 G8 **Umzimkulu** *R* S Africa
89 F3 **Umzingwane** *R* Zimbabwe
130 H4 **Una** Brazil
130 J10 **Una** *R* Brazil
42 G4 **Una** *R* Yugoslavia
60 S2 **Unabetsu-dake** *mt* Japan
128 F6 **Unacurizal** Brazil
112 D5 **Unadilla** Georgia U.S.A.
95 M4 **Unadilla** New York U.S.A.
130 F5 **Unaí** Brazil
116 G5 **Unalakleet** Alaska U.S.A.
116 D10 **Unalaska I** Aleutian Is
144 D5 **Una, Mt** New Zealand
29 T9 **Unaós** Iceland
15 C2 **Unapool** Scotland
128 E2 **Unare** *R* Venezuela
29 M4 **Unari** Finland
70 G5 **Unauna** *isld* Sulawesi
17 G2 **Uncastillo** Spain
133 D1 **Uncia** Bolivia
106 C3 **Uncompahgre Pk** Colorado U.S.A.
106 B3 **Uncompahgre Plateau** Colorado U.S.A.
27 G13 **Unden** *L* Sweden
27 G13 **Undenäs** Sweden
138 F6 **Underbool** Victoria Australia
28 E2 **Understed** Denmark
27 K11 **Understen** *lighthouse* Sweden
27 H10 **Undersvik** Sweden
28 D5 **Underup** Denmark
99 L8 **Underwood** Iowa U.S.A.
98 E2 **Underwood** North Dakota U.S.A.
28 H5 **Undløse** Denmark
71 K10 **Undu,Tg** *C* Sumba Indonesia
54 D4 **Unecha** U.S.S.R.
128 E4 **Uneiuxi** *R* Brazil
79 F8 **Uneiza** Jordan
37 P4 **Uněšov** Czechoslovakia
52 E3 **Unezhma** U.S.S.R.
116 G9 **Unga I** Alaska U.S.A.
116 G4 **Ungalik** Alaska U.S.A.
139 H5 **Ungarie** New South Wales Australia
138 D5 **Ungarra** South Australia Australia
115 N6 **Ungava B** Quebec Canada
115 M5 **Ungava, Pen. d'** Quebec Canada
48 L3 **Ungeny** U.S.S.R.
41 M1 **Ungerhausen** W Germany
59 K3 **Unggi** N Korea
128 D5 **União** Brazil
130 D10 **União da Vitória** Brazil
128 F4 **União do Marmará** Brazil
130 J10 **União dos Palmares** Brazil
112 E1 **Unicoi** Tennessee U.S.A.
48 D1 **Uničov** Czechoslovakia
31 L4 **Uniejów** Poland
42 F4 **Unije** *isld* Yugoslavia
116 E9 **Unimak** Aleutian Is
116 E9 **Unimak I** Aleutian Is
85 C8 **Uni,Mt** Liberia
128 F4 **Unini** *R* Brazil
133 D5 **Unión** Argentina
127 O8 **Union** *isld* Lesser Antilles
130 C9 **Unión** Paraguay
98 C9 **Union** Colorado U.S.A.
99 N7 **Union** Iowa U.S.A.
111 F11 **Union** Louisiana U.S.A.
95 S2 **Union** Maine U.S.A.
111 G9 **Union** Mississippi U.S.A.
110 E3 **Union** Missouri U.S.A.
99 L9 **Union** Nebraska U.S.A.
107 N6 **Union** Oklahoma U.S.A.
100 H4 **Union** Oregon U.S.A.
112 F3 **Union** South Carolina U.S.A.
94 G9 **Union** West Virginia U.S.A.
131 E7 **Unión, B** Argentina
95 K7 **Union Bridge** Maryland U.S.A.
111 F10 **Union Church** Mississippi U.S.A.
110 M1 **Union City** Indiana U.S.A.

88

Union City — Vastorf

94 B4 **Union City** Michigan U.S.A.
94 C6 **Union City** Ohio/Indiana U.S.A.
94 H5 **Union City** Pennsylvania U.S.A.
110 G5 **Union City** Tennessee U.S.A.
100 C7 **Union Creek** Oregon U.S.A.
95 M5 **Uniondale** Pennsylvania U.S.A.
126 D3 **Unión de Reyes** Cuba
100 H3 **Union Flat Cr** Washington U.S.A.
100 E3 **Union Gap** Washington U.S.A.
17 G7 **Unión,La** Spain
112 F2 **Union Mills** North Carolina U.S.A.
103 M7 **Union,Mt** Arizona U.S.A.
50 **Union of Soviet Socialist Republics** Europe/Asia
101 Q6 **Union Pass** Wyoming U.S.A.
112 D4 **Union Point** Georgia U.S.A.
118 D1 **Union Pt** Manitoba Canada
111 L9 **Union Springs** Alabama U.S.A.
95 L4 **Union Springs** New York U.S.A.
99 M10 **Union Star** Missouri U.S.A.
109 M9 **Union Stock Yards** Texas U.S.A.
111 J9 **Uniontown** Alabama U.S.A.
110 J4 **Uniontown** Kentucky U.S.A.
94 H7 **Uniontown** Pennsylvania U.S.A.
99 O9 **Unionville** Iowa U.S.A.
94 D3 **Unionville** Michigan U.S.A.
99 N9 **Unionville** Missouri U.S.A.
102 F1 **Unionville** Nevada U.S.A.
94 K8 **Unionville** Virginia U.S.A.
31 L2 **Unisław** Poland
77 C7 **United Arab Emirates (UAE)** Persian Gulf
6 **United Kingdom of Gt.Britain & N.Ireland (UK)** W Europe
92 **United States of America (USA)** N America
52 D3 **Unitsa** U.S.S.R.
118 H6 **Unity** Saskatchewan Canada
95 S2 **Unity** Maine U.S.A.
100 G5 **Unity** Oregon U.S.A.
17 G4 **Universales** *mt* Spain
17 F4 **Universales, Mts** Spain
111 G7 **University** Mississippi U.S.A.
111 K13 **University City** St Louis
110 F3 **University City** Missouri U.S.A.
109 O9 **University Park** Texas U.S.A.
36 C2 **Unkel** W Germany
38 G6 **Unken** Austria
55 C3 **Unkurda** U.S.S.R.
32 G9 **Unna** W Germany
74 J5 **Unnao** India
27 G14 **Unnaryd** Sweden
60 F12 **Unomachi** Japan
37 L6 **Unsernherrn** W Germany
52 E2 **Unskaya Guba** *B* U.S.S.R.
15 G1 **Unst** Shetland Scotland
33 O10 **Unstrut** *R* East Germany
61 P12 **Unten** Okinawa
38 N6 **Unter Berg** *mt* Austria
39 C2 **Unterbrunn** W Germany
Unter Deufstetten *see* **Fichtenau**
41 M4 **Unter Engadin** *dist* Switzerland
36 H4 **Unterfranken** *dist* W Germany
38 H8 **Untergailtal** *V* Austria
36 F5 **Unter Grombach** W Germany
36 H6 **Untergröningen** W Germany
37 M7 **Unterhaching** W Germany
38 E7 **Unter inn-tal** *V* Austria
33 M7 **Unterlüss** W Germany
37 K3 **Untermerzbach** W Germany
36 H5 **Untermünkheim** W Germany
37 K5 **Untern-Bibert** W Germany
36 F5 **Unter Schwarzach** W Germany
Untersteinbach *see* **Rauhenebrach**
38 J7 **Untertal** *R* Austria
38 J7 **Unter Tavern** Austria
41 H4 **Unterwalden** *canton* Switzerland
36 E2 **Unterwilden** W Germany
37 M7 **Unter Zolling** W Germany
55 E1 **Untor, Oz** *L* U.S.S.R.
27 G10 **Untorp** Sweden
128 E3 **Unturán, Sa. de** *mts* Venezuela
117 H7 **Unuk** *R* Alaska U.S.A.
21 N5 **Unverre** France
118 H6 **Unwin** Saskatchewan Canada
78 F1 **Ünye** Turkey
60 D13 **Unzen-Amakusa Nat. Park** Japan
60 D13 **Unzen dake** *mt* Japan
52 F5 **Unzha** U.S.S.R.
38 K7 **Unzmarkt** Austria
61 L9 **Uozu** Japan
54 H3 **Upa** *R* U.S.S.R.
101 P9 **Upalco** Utah U.S.A.
127 N10 **Upata** Venezuela
9 E5 **Upavon** England
87 E7 **Upemba, L** Zaire
115 O3 **Upernavik** Greenland
12 E2 **Uphall** Scotland
98 F1 **Upham** North Dakota U.S.A.
89 B7 **Upington** S Africa
94 B6 **Upland** Indiana U.S.A.
98 H9 **Upland** Nebraska U.S.A.
9 G4 **Upminster** England
116 H6 **Upnuk L** Alaska U.S.A.
52 D1 **Upolaksha** U.S.S.R.
134 C2 **Upolu** *isld* Western Samoa
135 U4 **Upolu Pt** Hawaiian Is
117 P10 **Upper Arrow L** British Columbia Canada
122 G7 **Upper Blackville** New Brunswick Canada
9 F2 **Upper Broughton** England
8 C3 **Upper Chapel** Wales
123 P4 **Upper Humber R** Newfoundland Canada
145 E4 **Upper Hutt** New Zealand
99 P6 **Upper Iowa** *R* Iowa U.S.A.
122 E7 **Upper Kent** New Brunswick Canada
100 D7 **Upper Klamath L** Oregon U.S.A.
14 B5 **Upper L** Ireland
102 B2 **Upper L** California U.S.A.
117 F5 **Upper Laberge** Yukon Territory Canada
117 J5 **Upper Liard** Yukon Territory Canada
118 J1 **Upper Manitou L** Ontario Canada
127 P2 **Upper Manzanilla** Trinidad
95 L8 **Upper Marlboro** Maryland U.S.A.
145 D4 **Upper Moutere** New Zealand
122 K8 **Upper Musquodoboit** Nova Scotia Canada
99 M1 **Upper Red L** Minnesota U.S.A.
101 O5 **Upper Red Rock L** Montana U.S.A.
94 D6 **Upper Sandusky** Ohio U.S.A.
95 N2 **Upper Saranac L** New York U.S.A.
122 J8 **Upper Stewiacke** Nova Scotia Canada
94 H8 **Upper Tract** West Virginia U.S.A.
94 K7 **Upperville** Virginia U.S.A.
Upper Volta *see* **Burkina**
139 H7 **Upper Yarra Res** Victoria Australia
9 F2 **Uppingham** England
27 J12 **Upplands Väsby** Sweden
27 K12 **Uppsala** Sweden
27 J12 **Uppsala** *county* Sweden
116 C6 **Upright,C** St Matthew I, Alaska U.S.A.
119 N1 **Upsala** Ontario Canada
99 M4 **Upsala** Minnesota U.S.A.
122 F6 **Upsalquitch** New Brunswick Canada
74 G2 **Upshi** Kashmir
99 Q3 **Upson** Wisconsin U.S.A.
141 J4 **Upstart, C** Queensland Australia
9 H5 **Upstreet** England
8 D3 **Upton** England
94 B9 **Upton** Kentucky U.S.A.
98 B5 **Upton** Wyoming U.S.A.
84 F3 **Uqaylah,Al** Libya
79 H3 **Uquayribāt** Syria
126 F10 **Urabá,G.de** Colombia
36 G7 **Urach** W Germany
128 F2 **Uracoa** Venezuela
58 E3 **Urad Zhongqi** China
61 N10 **Uraga** Japan
83 K11 **Uragasmanhandiya** Sri Lanka
60 Q3 **Urakawa** Japan
139 H5 **Ural** *mt* New South Wales Australia
100 K1 **Ural** Montana U.S.A.
55 C4 **Ural** *R* U.S.S.R.
139 K4 **Uralla** New South Wales Australia
5 R3 **Ural Mts** U.S.S.R.
50 E3 **Uralskiy Khrebet** *mts* U.S.S.R.
88 D4 **Urambo** Tanzania
139 H6 **Urana** New South Wales Australia
140 E5 **Urandangie** Queensland Australia
130 G4 **Urandi** Brazil
141 L7 **Urangan** Queensland Australia
111 D10 **Urania** Louisiana U.S.A.
114 J6 **Uranium City** Saskatchewan Canada
83 L10 **Uraniya** Sri Lanka
140 C2 **Urapunga** N Terr Australia
128 F3 **Uraricoera** Brazil
143 E9 **Uraryie Rock** *rock* Western Australia Australia
61 P13 **Urasoe** Okinawa
57 E5 **Ura-Tyube** U.S.S.R.
60 P2 **Urausu** Japan
61 N10 **Urawa** Japan
55 D1 **Uray** U.S.S.R.
55 C4 **Urazmetova** U.S.S.R.
52 G6 **Urazovka** U.S.S.R.
54 K6 **Urazovo** U.S.S.R.
99 S9 **Urbana** Illinois U.S.A.
94 B6 **Urbana** Indiana U.S.A.
99 P7 **Urbana** Iowa U.S.A.
110 C4 **Urbana** Missouri U.S.A.
94 D6 **Urbana** Ohio U.S.A.
45 N4 **Urbania** Italy
95 L9 **Urbanna** Virginia U.S.A.
129 K4 **Urbano Santos** Brazil
16 E2 **Urbel** *R* Spain
45 N4 **Urbino** Italy
17 F2 **Urbión, Sa. de** *mts* Spain
22 F5 **Urcel** France
128 D6 **Urcos** Peru
18 E10 **Urdos** France
52 H2 **Urdyuzhskoye Oz** *L* U.S.S.R.
57 K2 **Urdzhar** U.S.S.R.
52 G5 **Uren** U.S.S.R.
50 G2 **Urengoy** U.S.S.R.
145 E3 **Urenui** New Zealand
137 O4 **Uréparapara** *isld* Vanuatu
13 G5 **Ure,R** England
124 D3 **Ures** Mexico
145 F3 **Urewera Country** New Zealand
55 G3 **Urez** U.S.S.R.
78 G3 **Urfa** Turkey
38 K5 **Urfahr** Austria
41 O2 **Urfeld** W Germany
52 G6 **Urga** *R* U.S.S.R.
59 K1 **Urgal** U.S.S.R.
58 B2 **Urgamal** Mongolia
57 B4 **Urgench** U.S.S.R.
41 J4 **Uri** *canton* Switzerland
19 P14 **Uriage** France
111 J10 **Uriah** Alabama U.S.A.
144 C5 **Uriah, Mt** New Zealand
128 D3 **Uribe** Colombia
127 H9 **Uribia** Colombia
110 B3 **Urich** Missouri U.S.A.
101 P8 **Urie** Wyoming U.S.A.
128 F2 **Urimán** Venezuela
124 F4 **Urique** Mexico
41 H4 **Uri Rothstock** *mt* Switzerland
139 G3 **Urisino** New South Wales Australia
55 E4 **Uritskiy** U.S.S.R.
29 K10 **Urjala** Finland
25 E3 **Urk** Netherlands
47 H6 **Urla** Turkey
48 K6 **Urlaţi** Romania
28 D5 **Urlev** Denmark
79 G6 **'Urmān** Syria
55 C4 **Urman** U.S.S.R.
55 E1 **Urmannyy** U.S.S.R.
52 G6 **Urmary** U.S.S.R.
59 K2 **Urmi** *R* U.S.S.R.
Urmia,L *see* **Orūmīyeh, Daryācheh-ye** *L*
55 F2 **Urninskoye Boloto** U.S.S.R.
52 J5 **Urolka** *R* U.S.S.R.
46 E2 **Uroševac** Yugoslavia
131 D7 **Urre Lauquen, L** Argentina
12 E3 **Urr,L** Scotland
99 P9 **Ursa** Illinois U.S.A.
37 J7 **Ursberg** W Germany
25 C3 **Ursem** Netherlands
37 M5 **Ursensollen** W Germany
52 F6 **Urshelskiy** U.S.S.R.
56 C4 **Ursk** U.S.S.R.
36 H6 **Urspring** W Germany
26 M7 **Ursviken** Sweden
55 C4 **Urtazym** U.S.S.R.
58 B4 **Urt Moron** China
124 E4 **Uruáchic** Mexico
130 E4 **Uruaçu** Brazil
130 E4 **Uruana** Brazil
124 H8 **Uruapan del Progreso** Mexico
128 D6 **Urubamba** Peru
128 G4 **Urubu** *R* Brazil
129 G4 **Urucará** Brazil
127 N10 **Urucoa** Venezuela
128 F4 **Urucu** *R* Brazil
129 K5 **Uruçui** Brazil
130 F5 **Urucuia** Brazil
130 B6 **Urucum** Brazil
129 G4 **Urucurituba** Brazil
131 F2 **Uruguaiana** Brazil
130 D10 **Uruguai,R** Brazil
131 G4 **Uruguay** *rep* S America
131 F4 **Uruguay, R** Argentina
79 G2 **Urūmaş Şughrá** Syria
Urumchi *see* **Ürümqi**
66 D3 **Ürümqi** China
69 C11 **Urung** Indonesia
139 L4 **Urunga** New South Wales Australia
128 F6 **Urupa** *R* Brazil
52 H6 **Urussu** U.S.S.R.
130 F4 **Urutágua** Brazil
130 E5 **Urutai** Brazil
145 E3 **Uruti** New Zealand
77 J3 **Urūzgān** *reg* Afghanistan
146 D3 **Urville I, d'** Antarctica
20 G2 **Urville-Nacqueville** France
136 H2 **Urville, Tg. D'** *C* W Irian
89 B4 **Urwi** Botswana
60 Q2 **Uryū** *R* Japan
60 P2 **Uryū** Japan
60 Q1 **Uryū-ko** *L* Japan
58 G1 **Uryum** *R* U.S.S.R.
56 C3 **Uryup** *R* U.S.S.R.
53 F8 **Uryupinsk** U.S.S.R.
52 G6 **Urzhum** U.S.S.R.
48 K6 **Urziceni** Romania
36 B4 **Urzig** W Germany
21 O3 **Us** France
60 E12 **Usa** Japan
71 E7 **Usada** *isld* Philippines
47 K6 **Uşak** Turkey
87 C10 **Usakos** Namibia
80 E5 **Ūsarīn** Jordan
146 C13 **Usarp Mts** *mts* Antarctica
133 F8 **Usborne** *hill* Falkland Is
33 T5 **Usedom** East Germany
143 A7 **Useless Loop** Western Australia Australia
80 D2 **Usha** Israel
116 L7 **Ushagat I** Alaska U.S.A.
50 G1 **Ushakova, Ostrova** *islds* U.S.S.R.
55 E3 **Ushakovo** U.S.S.R.
Ushant *see* **Ouessant, I. d'**
56 E5 **Ush-Bel'dir** U.S.S.R.
60 D13 **Ushibuka** Japan
48 L2 **Ushitsa** *R* U.S.S.R.
61 L8 **Ushitsu** Japan
60 D12 **Ushizu** Japan
57 J2 **Ushtobe** U.S.S.R.
133 D8 **Ushuaia** *airport* Argentina
129 H5 **Usina** Brazil
36 F3 **Usingen** W Germany
8 D4 **Usk** Wales
27 A12 **Uskedal** Norway
8 C4 **Usk,R** Wales
Üskub *see* **Skopje**
47 N10 **Üsküdar** Turkey
47 J3 **Üsküp** Turkey
32 L9 **Uslar** W Germany
54 L4 **Usman** U.S.S.R.
100 F3 **U.S. Mil. Res. Yakima Firing Range** Washington U.S.A.
56 D3 **Usolka** *R* U.S.S.R.
52 J5 **Usol'ye** U.S.S.R.
55 G4 **Uspenka** U.S.S.R.
57 G1 **Uspenskiy** U.S.S.R.
40 F7 **Usseglio** Italy
18 G7 **Ussel** France
13 H6 **Usselby** England
32 J10 **Usseln** W Germany
29 K5 **Usserød** Denmark
18 F6 **Usson du Poitou** France
59 K2 **Ussuri** *R* U.S.S.R.
59 K3 **Ussuriysk** U.S.S.R.
21 K4 **Ussy** France
52 G6 **Usta** *R* U.S.S.R.
56 D5 **Ust'-Abakan** U.S.S.R.
52 G4 **Ust' Alekseyevo** U.S.S.R.
27 C11 **Ustaoset** Norway
53 G7 **Ust'-Aza** U.S.S.R.
55 D3 **Ust-Bagaryak** U.S.S.R.
56 B3 **Ust'-Bakchar** U.S.S.R.
52 H4 **Ust' Chernaya** U.S.S.R.
48 H2 **Ust-'Chorna** U.S.S.R.
52 J5 **Ust' Dolgaya** U.S.S.R.
41 J3 **Uster** Switzerland
43 E10 **Ustica, I. di** Italy
56 F2 **Ust'Ilimsk** U.S.S.R.
56 F3 **Ust'-Ilimskoye Vodokhranilishche** *res* U.S.S.R.
52 J3 **Ust'-Ilych** U.S.S.R.
30 H5 **Ústí'nad** Czechoslovakia
52 H6 **Ustinov** U.S.S.R.
55 F2 **Ust'-Ishim** U.S.S.R.
55 G3 **Ust'Izes** U.S.S.R.
31 K1 **Ustka** Poland
56 B6 **Ust'-Kamenogorsk** U.S.S.R.
58 G1 **Ust'Karenga** U.S.S.R.
55 C4 **Ust'Katav** U.S.S.R.
58 E1 **Ust'-Kiran** U.S.S.R.
55 C3 **Ust Kishert** U.S.S.R.
52 H3 **Ust'Koin** U.S.S.R.
52 H4 **Ust'Kulom** U.S.S.R.
56 G3 **Ust'-Kut** U.S.S.R.
55 D2 **Ust' Loz'va** U.S.S.R.
52 C5 **Ust' Luga** U.S.S.R.
52 J2 **Ust' Lyzha** U.S.S.R.
51 N2 **Ust'Maya** U.S.S.R.
51 L3 **Ust-Muya** U.S.S.R.
52 H4 **Ust'Nem** U.S.S.R.
59 K1 **Ust'Niman** U.S.S.R.
56 F4 **Ust'-Ordynskiy** U.S.S.R.
56 F4 **Ust'-Ordynskiy Buryatskiy Avtonomyy Okrug** *dist* U.S.S.R.
46 G3 **Ustovo** Bulgaria
52 F4 **Ust' Paden'ga** U.S.S.R.
52 F3 **Ust' Pinega** U.S.S.R.
50 H2 **Ust'-Port** U.S.S.R.
52 F4 **Ust' Puya** U.S.S.R.
52 G4 **Ust' Reka** U.S.S.R.
31 O6 **Ustrzyki Dolne** Poland
52 D4 **Ust'Sara** U.S.S.R.
52 J3 **Ust'-Shchugor** U.S.S.R.
55 D1 **Ust'-Tapsuy** U.S.S.R.
55 F3 **Ust'Tara** U.S.S.R.
55 G3 **Ust'Tarka** U.S.S.R.
55 F3 **Ust' Tava** U.S.S.R.
52 H2 **Ust' Tsil'ma** U.S.S.R.
59 K1 **Ust'Tyrma** U.S.S.R.
56 F4 **Ust'-Uda** U.S.S.R.
52 J4 **Ust' Un'ya** U.S.S.R.
52 F3 **Ust'ura** U.S.S.R.
59 H1 **Ust'urov** U.S.S.R.
56 D5 **Ust' Us** U.S.S.R.
52 J2 **Ust' Usa** U.S.S.R.
55 D4 **Ust'-Uyskoye** U.S.S.R.
52 J3 **Ust'-Voya** U.S.S.R.
52 G3 **Ust' Vyyskaya** U.S.S.R.
52 F4 **Ust'ya** *R* U.S.S.R.
52 E5 **Ust'ye** U.S.S.R.
52 E6 **Ust'ye** *R* U.S.S.R.
50 E4 **Ustyurt,Plato** U.S.S.R.
52 E5 **Ustyuzhna** U.S.S.R.
66 C3 **Usu** China
71 L10 **Usu** *isld* Indonesia
60 E12 **Usuki** Japan
125 P11 **Usulután** El Salvador
125 O9 **Usumacinta** *R* Mexico
70 D3 **Usun Apau Plateau** Sarawak
89 G6 **Usutu** *R* Swaziland
52 D6 **Usvyaty** U.S.S.R.
71 B2 **Uta** *isld* Indonesia
103 M2 **Utah** *state* U.S.A.
103 N1 **Utah L** Utah U.S.A.
29 M7 **Utajärvi** Finland
71 H9 **Utan** Indonesia
69 E14 **Utara Selatan** *isld* Indonesia
60 Q2 **Utashinai** Japan
79 G5 **Utaybah, Buḩayrat al** *L* Syria
99 L7 **Ute** Iowa U.S.A.
17 G3 **Utebo** Spain
106 G6 **Ute Cr** New Mexico U.S.A.
88 G6 **Utenge,L** Tanzania
106 E5 **Ute Park** New Mexico U.S.A.
37 P4 **Uterý** Czechoslovakia
55 G4 **Utes** U.S.S.R.
88 G6 **Utete** Tanzania
68 D5 **U Thai Thani** Thailand
77 K7 **Uthal** Pakistan
32 J6 **Uthlede** W Germany
79 H4 **'Uthmānīyah** Syria
68 G5 **Uthumphon Phisai** Thailand
129 G6 **Utiariti** Brazil
107 K3 **Utica** Kansas U.S.A.
94 D4 **Utica** Michigan U.S.A.
99 P6 **Utica** Minnesota U.S.A.
111 F9 **Utica** Mississippi U.S.A.
110 C2 **Utica** Missouri U.S.A.
101 P3 **Utica** Montana U.S.A.
98 J9 **Utica** Nebraska U.S.A.
95 M3 **Utica** New York U.S.A.
94 E6 **Utica** Ohio U.S.A.
17 G5 **Utiel** Spain
26 K7 **Utifällan** Sweden
119 W3 **Utik L** Manitoba Canada
145 E3 **Utiku** New Zealand
118 B3 **Utikuma L** Alberta Canada
27 H16 **Utklippan** *isld* Sweden
27 C10 **Utla** *R* Norway
27 H15 **Utlängan** *isld* Sweden
109 K5 **Utley** Texas U.S.A.
106 G4 **Utleyville** Colorado U.S.A.
74 D1 **Utmanzai** Pakistan
27 M12 **Utö** *lighthouse* Finland
27 K13 **Utö** Sweden
140 C5 **Utopia** N Terr Australia
109 H6 **Utopia** Texas U.S.A.
75 K5 **Utraula** India
25 D4 **Utrecht** Netherlands
89 G6 **Utrecht** S Africa
16 D7 **Utrera** Spain
27 A12 **Utsira** *lighthouse* Norway
29 N2 **Utsjoki** Finland
61 N9 **Utsunomiya** Japan
53 G10 **Utta** U.S.S.R.
68 E4 **Uttaradit** Thailand
74 H4 **Uttar Pradesh** *prov* India
27 H12 **Uttersberg** Sweden
28 G7 **Utterslev** Denmark
36 H4 **Üttingen** W Germany
9 E2 **Uttoxeter** England
116 G2 **Utukok** *R* Alaska U.S.A.
137 O4 **Utupua** *isld* Santa Cruz Is
55 B5 **Utva** *R* U.S.S.R.
37 O3 **Útvina** Czechoslovakia
52 H6 **Utyashkino** U.S.S.R.
32 M8 **Utze** W Germany
33 S5 **Utzedel** East Germany
17 G3 **uuadalope** *R* Spain
29 O10 **Uukuniem** Finland
58 F2 **Uuldza** *R* Mongolia
115 O3 **Uummannaq** Greenland
Uummannarsuaq Greenland *see* **Farvel,Kap**
29 L9 **Uurainen** Finland
Uusikaarlepyy *see* **Nykarleby**
29 J11 **Uusikaupunki** Finland
29 L11 **Uusimaa** *prov* Finland
52 H6 **Uva** U.S.S.R.
48 F7 **Uvac** *R* Yugoslavia
103 K2 **Uvada** Nevada U.S.A.
128 D3 **Uva, L** Colombia
112 E5 **Uvalda** Georgia U.S.A.
108 H6 **Uvalde** Texas U.S.A.
54 B4 **Uvarovichi** U.S.S.R.
52 E6 **Uvarovka** U.S.S.R.
55 E2 **Uvat** U.S.S.R.
137 O6 **Uvéa** *isld* Îles Loyauté Pacific Oc
137 R4 **Uvea** *isld* Îles Wallis Pacific Oc
55 D4 **Uvel'skiy** U.S.S.R.
55 D3 **Uvil'dy, Oz** *L* U.S.S.R.
88 C4 **Uvinza** Tanzania
88 B3 **Uvira** Zaire
60 E13 **Uwae** Japan
60 F12 **Uwajima** Japan
84 H5 **Uweinat,Jebel** *mt* Sudan
135 V5 **Uwekahuna** Hawaiian Is
69 H12 **Uwi** *isld* Indonesia
121 L8 **Uxbridge** Ontario Canada
9 F4 **Uxbridge** England
65 A5 **Uxin Ju** China
125 P7 **Uxmal** Mexico
55 D4 **Uy** *R* U.S.S.R.
116 K8 **Uyak B** Alaska U.S.A.
57 B3 **Uyaly, Ozero** *L* U.S.S.R.
51 O2 **Uyandina** *R* U.S.S.R.
56 D3 **Uyar** U.S.S.R.
15 G1 **Uyea** *isld* Scotland
15 G1 **Uyeasound** Scotland
50 H1 **Uyedineniya,Ostrov** *isld* U.S.S.R.
52 H2 **Uyeg** U.S.S.R.
47 K8 **Uyluk Tepe** *mt* Turkey
85 F7 **Uyo** Nigeria
47 K6 **Uysal Dağı** *mt* Turkey
55 D4 **Uyskoye** U.S.S.R.
57 F3 **Uyuk** U.S.S.R.
133 D2 **Uyuni** Bolivia
48 G2 **Uz** *R* Czechoslovakia
Uzbekistan *see* **Uzbekskaya S.S.R.**
57 B3 **Uzbekskaya S.S.R** *rep* U.S.S.R.
48 F5 **Uzdin** Yugoslavia
20 E5 **Uzel** France
53 G8 **Uzen', Malyy** *R* U.S.S.R.
57 G4 **Uzgen** U.S.S.R.
48 G2 **Uzh** *R* U.S.S.R.
48 G2 **Uzhgorod** U.S.S.R.
56 C3 **Uzhur** U.S.S.R.
41 J3 **Uznach** Switzerland
52 F6 **Uzola** *R* U.S.S.R.
47 N10 **Uzümce** Turkey
47 K8 **Üzümlü** Turkey
47 H6 **Uzun** *isld* Turkey
88 E6 **Uzungwa** Tanzania
47 H3 **Uzunköprü** Turkey
57 B3 **Uzynkair** U.S.S.R.

V

29 M9 **Vaajakoski** Finland
89 E6 **Vaal** *R* S Africa
29 M7 **Vaala** Finland
89 F6 **Vaal Dam** S Africa
29 N11 **Vaalimaa** Finland
87 E10 **Vaalwater** S Africa
29 M8 **Vaaraslahti** Finland
21 L6 **Vaas** France
29 J8 **Vaasa** Finland
25 E4 **Vaassen** Netherlands
29 L4 **Vaattojärvi** Finland
28 H7 **Våbensted** Denmark
57 C5 **Vabkent** U.S.S.R.
130 C7 **Vacaria,R** Brazil
130 C7 **Vacaria,Sa** *mts* Brazil
131 B4 **Vacas,Pta De** Argentina
102 B3 **Vacaville** California U.S.A.
19 N17 **Vaccarès, Etang de** *L* France
52 F6 **Vacha** U.S.S.R.
126 H5 **Vache, Île-à-** Haiti
40 E5 **Vacheresse** France
19 N16 **Vacqueyras** France
52 F6 **Vad** U.S.S.R.
100 C3 **Vader** Washington U.S.A.
27 A10 **Vadheim** Norway
42 G5 **Vadice** Yugoslavia
106 E5 **Vadito** New Mexico U.S.A.
27 B12 **Vadla** Norway
44 D3 **Vado** Italy
44 D3 **Vado, C. di** Italy
74 E7 **Vadodara** India
124 F2 **Vado de Santa Maria** Mexico
52 D1 **Vadozero, Oz** *L* U.S.S.R.
26 R1 **Vadsö** Norway
27 G13 **Vadstenna** Sweden
48 M6 **Vadu** Romania
28 D2 **Vadum** Denmark
41 L3 **Vaduz** Liechtenstein
26 K3 **Vadvetjåkko Nat. Park** Sweden
28 H7 **Væggerløse** Denmark
26 F4 **Vaeröy** Norway
28 G5 **Værslev** Denmark
26 J9 **Vaga** Sweden
52 F4 **Vaga** *R* U.S.S.R.
26 D10 **Vågåmo** Norway
26 G3 **Vagan** Norway
42 G4 **Vaganski** *mt* Yugoslavia
6 F1 **Vágar** *isld* Faeroes
55 E2 **Vagay** U.S.S.R.
Vağda *see* **Erdemh**
29 O2 **Vaggetem** U.S.S.R.
26 R2 **Vaggetem-javrre** *L* Norway
45 K4 **Vaglia** Italy
27 J13 **Vagnahärad** Sweden
16 B4 **Vagos** Portugal
27 F11 **Vägsjöfors** Sweden
26 A10 **Vågsöy** *isld* Norway
31 L6 **Váh** *R* Czechoslovakia
29 J8 **Vähäkyrö** Finland
79 F8 **Vahal** Israel
111 G8 **Vaiden** Mississippi U.S.A.
21 K5 **Vaiges** France
36 F6 **Vaihingen** W Germany
76 B1 **Vaijapur** India
52 C5 **Väike-Maarja** U.S.S.R.
26 L5 **Vaikijaur** Sweden
103 O9 **Vail** Arizona U.S.A.
106 D2 **Vail** Colorado U.S.A.
15 G2 **Vaila** *isld* Scotland
22 F5 **Vailly-sur-Aisne** France
134 B1 **Vailoa** Western Samoa
29 N11 **Vainikkala** Finland
45 Q7 **Vairano Patenora** Italy
20 G8 **Vairé** France
137 Q3 **Vaitupu** *isld* Tuvalu
46 F2 **Vakarel** Bulgaria
27 G11 **Vakern** Sweden
56 B1 **Vakh** *R* U.S.S.R.
57 F6 **Vakhanskiy Khrebet** *mts* U.S.S.R.
57 E5 **Vakhsh** U.S.S.R.
57 E5 **Vakhsh** *R* U.S.S.R.
57 E5 **Vakhshstroy** U.S.S.R.
52 G5 **Vakhtan** U.S.S.R.
52 D3 **Vaknavolok** U.S.S.R.
27 A11 **Vaksdal** Norway
83 L10 **Valachchenai** Sri Lanka
26 F8 **Vålådalen** Sweden
40 F5 **Valais** *canton* Switzerland
52 H5 **Valamaz** U.S.S.R.
46 F3 **Valandovo** Yugoslavia
20 E4 **Val André, le** France
21 J7 **Valanjou** France
27 G12 **Valåsen** Sweden
95 O4 **Valatie** New York U.S.A.
46 G6 **Valáxa** *isld* Greece
38 E8 **Val Badia** Italy
121 P6 **Val Barrette** Quebec Canada
26 G3 **Valberg** Norway
19 P15 **Valbonnais** France
122 E5 **Val Brilliant** Quebec Canada
25 E5 **Valburg** Netherlands
133 D6 **Valcheta** Argentina
121 S7 **Valcourt** Quebec Canada
41 O6 **Valdagno** Italy
16 D2 **Valdavia** *R* Spain
52 D5 **Valday** U.S.S.R.
52 D6 **Valdayskaya Vozvyshennost'** *uplands* U.S.S.R.
17 G4 **Valde Algorfa** Spain
16 D5 **Valdecañas, Embalse de** *res* Spain
17 F5 **Valdeganga** Spain
21 P4 **Val-de-Marne** *dept* France
52 B6 **Valdemārpils** U.S.S.R.
27 J13 **Valdemarsvik** Sweden
16 E4 **Valdemoro** Spain
17 F4 **Valdemoro-Sierra** Spain
16 E6 **Valdepeñas** Spain
16 D3 **Valderaduey** *R* Spain
17 H4 **Valderrobres** Spain
99 T5 **Valders** Wisconsin U.S.A.
121 P7 **Val des Bois** Quebec Canada
112 F2 **Valdese** North Carolina U.S.A.
133 E6 **Valdés, Pen** Argentina
116 O6 **Valdez** Alaska U.S.A.
106 F4 **Valdez** Colorado U.S.A.
41 M5 **Valdidentro** Italy
131 A8 **Valdivia** *prov* Chile
131 A7 **Valdivia** Chile
20 H5 **Val-d'Izé** France
21 O3 **Val-d'Oise** *dept* France
121 N4 **Val-d'Or** Quebec Canada
113 D7 **Valdosta** Georgia U.S.A.
27 D11 **Valdres** *plateau* Norway
19 P16 **Valdrome** France
20 E3 **Vale** Channel Is
100 H6 **Vale** Oregon U.S.A.
98 C5 **Vale** South Dakota U.S.A.
48 G5 **Valea Bistrei** Romania
48 G3 **Valea Lui Mihai** Romania
48 J3 **Valea Vişeului** Romania
37 P3 **Valeč** Czechoslovakia
45 J1 **Valéggio** Italy
129 L6 **Valença** Brazil
21 O7 **Valençay** France
19 N15 **Valence** France
18 F8 **Valence d'Agen** France
18 F9 **Valence-sur-Baïse** France
17 G5 **Valencia** *prov* Spain
17 G5 **Valencia** Spain
127 K9 **Valencia** Venezuela
16 C5 **Valência de Alcantara** Spain
16 D2 **Valencia de Don Juan** Spain
16 B3 **Valençia do Minho** Portugal
17 H5 **Valencia,G de** Spain
14 A5 **Valencia I** Ireland
127 L9 **Valencia,L.de** Venezuela
22 F3 **Valenciennes** France
19 P17 **Valensole** France
59 K3 **Valentin** U.S.S.R.
103 L6 **Valentine** Arizona U.S.A.
111 F12 **Valentine** Louisiana U.S.A.
101 R2 **Valentine** Montana U.S.A.
98 F7 **Valentine** Nebraska U.S.A.
108 C5 **Valentine** Texas U.S.A.
44 E1 **Valenza** Italy
27 E11 **Våler** Norway
109 H4 **Valera** Texas U.S.A.
127 J10 **Valera** Venezuela
27 A12 **Valestrand** Norway
130 H5 **Vale Verde** Brazil
41 M4 **Valfurva** *R* Italy
52 C5 **Valga** U.S.S.R.
120 K4 **Val Gagné** Ontario Canada
43 F11 **Valguarnera Caropepe** Sicily
6 N6 **Valhall** *oil rig* North Sea
101 N1 **Valier** Montana U.S.A.
29 K4 **Välinge** Sweden
48 F6 **Valjevo** Yugoslavia
26 P2 **Valjok** Norway
19 Q15 **Valjouffrey** France
29 L10 **Valkeakoski** Finland
29 M11 **Valkeala** Finland
29 L5 **Valkeavaara** *mt* Finland
25 E7 **Valkenburg** Netherlands
25 D6 **Valkenswaard** Netherlands
54 G7 **Valki** U.S.S.R.
Valko *see* **Valkom**
29 M11 **Valkom** Finland
146 G8 **Valkyrjedomen** *ice dome* Antarctica
19 N17 **Vallabrègues** France
16 D3 **Valladolid** *prov* Spain
16 D3 **Valladolid** Spain
121 N4 **Val Laflamme** Quebec Canada
41 P4 **Vallarga** Italy
41 O6 **Vallarsa** *R* Italy
27 C12 **Valle** Norway
103 M6 **Valle** Arizona U.S.A.
38 E7 **Valle Aurina** Italy
106 C4 **Vallecito Res** Colorado U.S.A.
106 D5 **Vallecitos** New Mexico U.S.A.
45 O7 **Vallecorsa** Italy
131 B2 **Valle Cura,Rio Del** Argentina
42 A3 **Valle d'Aosta** Italy
40 G6 **Valle d'Aosta** *aut reg* Italy
124 G7 **Valle de Banderas** Mexico
16 E1 **Valle de Cabuérniga** Spain
127 M10 **Valle de la Pascua** Venezuela
128 C3 **Valle del Cauca** *div* Colombia
124 F4 **Valle de Olivos** Mexico
124 F4 **Valle de Rosario** Mexico
124 G4 **Valle de Zaragoza** Mexico
126 H9 **Valledupar** Colombia
85 E5 **Vallée de Zgarat** Mali
122 B7 **Vallée Jonction** Quebec Canada
85 E5 **Vallée L'Azawak** Mali/Niger
131 C3 **Valle Fértil, Sa. de** *mts* Argentina
128 F7 **Valle Grande** Bolivia
40 C5 **Valleiry** France
102 B3 **Vallejo** California U.S.A.
45 P7 **Vallemaio** Italy
40 H6 **Valle Mosso** Italy
26 M7 **Vallen** Västerbotten Sweden
26 J8 **Vallen** Väster Norrland Sweden
131 B2 **Vallenar** Chile
36 D3 **Vallendar** W Germany
28 H6 **Vallensved** Denmark
27 K12 **Vallentuna** Sweden
45 O6 **Vallepretra** Italy
133 E2 **Valle,R.del** Argentina
20 H7 **Vallet** France
43 F13 **Valletta** Malta
122 J8 **Valley** Nova Scotia Canada
111 F9 **Valley** Mississippi U.S.A.
98 K8 **Valley** Nebraska U.S.A.
100 H1 **Valley** Washington U.S.A.
101 Q5 **Valley** Wyoming U.S.A.
8 B1 **Valley** Wales
107 N4 **Valley Center** Kansas U.S.A.
118 K7 **Valley Centre** Saskatchewan Canada
98 J3 **Valley City** North Dakota U.S.A.
107 P2 **Valley Falls** Kansas U.S.A.
100 E7 **Valley Falls** Oregon U.S.A.
121 Q7 **Valleyfield** Quebec Canada
111 L7 **Valley Head** Alabama U.S.A.
94 G8 **Valley Head** West Virginia U.S.A.
109 K4 **Valley Mills** Texas U.S.A.
116 K7 **Valley of Ten Thousand Smokes** Alaska U.S.A.
110 F3 **Valley Park** Missouri U.S.A.
101 L8 **Valley Pass** Nevada U.S.A.
94 B8 **Valley Sta** Kentucky U.S.A.
117 P8 **Valleyview** Alberta Canada
109 K2 **Valley View** Texas U.S.A.
Vallgrund, isld *see* **Raippaluoto**
109 M2 **Valliant** Oklahoma U.S.A.
45 M2 **Valli di Comacchio** *reg* Italy
18 F10 **Vallier, Mt** France
121 P6 **Val Limoges** Quebec Canada
21 M2 **Valliquerville** France
28 J6 **Valløby** Denmark
43 G8 **Vallo di Diano** Italy
43 G8 **Vallo di Lucania** Italy
45 L4 **Vallombrosa** Italy
94 A8 **Vallonia** Indiana U.S.A.
21 K6 **Vallon-sur-Gée** France
40 D4 **Vallorbe** Switzerland
27 D12 **Vallöy** Norway
17 H3 **Valls** Spain
27 H10 **Vallsta** Sweden
41 M3 **Valluga** *mt* Austria
27 J10 **Vallvik** Sweden
118 K9 **Val Marie** Saskatchewan Canada
16 E1 **Valmaseda** Spain
31 K6 **Val. Meziříčí** Czechoslovakia
52 C5 **Valmiera** U.S.S.R.
21 P3 **Valmondois** France
21 M2 **Valmont** France
106 E9 **Valmont** New Mexico U.S.A.
45 N6 **Valmontone** Italy
100 H9 **Valmy** Nevada U.S.A.
16 E1 **Valnera** *mt* Spain
20 H2 **Valognes** France
Valona *see* **Vlorë**
16 D3 **Valoria la Buena** Spain
16 C3 **Valpaços** Portugal
76 C5 **Valparai** India
119 N6 **Valparaiso** Saskatchewan Canada
131 B4 **Valparaiso** *prov* Chile
131 B4 **Valparaiso** Chile
124 H6 **Valparaiso** Mexico
111 K11 **Valparaiso** Florida U.S.A.
99 T8 **Valparaiso** Indiana U.S.A.
98 K8 **Valparaiso** Nebraska U.S.A.
40 F6 **Valpelline** *V* Italy
48 E5 **Valpovo** Yugoslavia
40 G7 **Valprato Soana** Italy
122 A8 **Val-Racine** Quebec Canada
19 N16 **Valréas** France
89 E6 **Vals** *R* S Africa
74 E8 **Valsād** India
28 H7 **Vålse** Denmark
100 B5 **Valsetz** Oregon U.S.A.
28 D3 **Valsgård** Denmark
26 G7 **Valsjö** Sweden
27 H12 **Valskog** Sweden
29 J8 **Valsörarna** *lighthouse* Finland
41 L5 **Valtellina** *V* Italy
29 T9 **Valthjofsstadhur** Iceland
45 M4 **Val Tiberina** Italy
29 O8 **Valtimo** Finland
83 M12 **Valton** Mauritius
54 K6 **Valuyki** U.S.S.R.
85 A3 **Valverde** Canary Is
127 J5 **Valverde** Dominican Rep
17 F5 **Valverde de Júcar** Spain
16 C7 **Valverde del Camino** Spain
26 M5 **Valvträsk** Sweden
48 K3 **Vama** Romania
28 C6 **Vamdrup** Denmark
27 G10 **Våmhus** Sweden
88 H7 **Vamizi** *isld* Mozambique
27 E12 **Vamma** Norway
29 K10 **Vammala** Finland
46 G9 **Vámos** Crete Greece
48 G3 **Vámospéros** Hungary
78 J2 **Van** Turkey
109 M3 **Van** Texas U.S.A.
29 L10 **Vanajanselka** *L* Finland
109 L2 **Van Alstyne** Texas U.S.A.
101 S3 **Vananda** Montana U.S.A.
56 F1 **Vanavara** U.S.S.R.
68 G1 **Van-Ban** Vietnam
121 S5 **Van Bruyssel** Quebec Canada
110 B6 **Van Buren** Arkansas U.S.A.
94 B6 **Van Buren** Indiana U.S.A.
95 T6 **Van Buren** Maine U.S.A.
110 F5 **Van Buren** Missouri U.S.A.
68 J6 **Van Canh** Vietnam
22 K4 **Vance** Belgium
21 M6 **Vancé** France
112 K2 **Vanceboro** North Carolina U.S.A.
94 D8 **Vanceburg** Kentucky U.S.A.
68 G2 **Van Chan** Vietnam
57 F5 **Vanchskiy Khrebet** *mts* U.S.S.R.
117 G11 **Vancouver** British Columbia Canada
100 C4 **Vancouver** Washington U.S.A.
143 C10 **Vancouver,C** Western Australia Australia
116 E6 **Vancouver, C** Alaska U.S.A.
117 K10 **Vancouver I** British Columbia Canada
117 D5 **Vancouver, Mt** Alaska/Yukon Terr U.S.A./Canada
110 G3 **Vandalia** Illinois U.S.A.
110 E2 **Vandalia** Missouri U.S.A.
41 L3 **Vandans** Austria
28 A3 **Vandborg** Denmark
119 Q1 **Vandekerckhove** Saskatchewan Canada
28 C5 **Vandel** Denmark
112 L2 **Vandemere** North Carolina U.S.A.
89 E6 **Vanderbijl Pk** S Africa
94 C1 **Vanderbilt** Michigan U.S.A.
109 L7 **Vanderbilt** Texas U.S.A.
94 H6 **Vandergrift** Pennsylvania U.S.A.
117 M8 **Vanderhoof** British Columbia Canada
140 D3 **Vanderlin I** N Terr Australia
109 N1 **Vandervoort** Arkansas U.S.A.
28 B2 **Vandet Sø** *L* Denmark
140 B1 **Van Dieman, C** N Terr Australia
140 E3 **Van Diemen,C** Queensland Australia
140 B1 **Van Diemen G** N Terr Australia
55 E1 **Vandmtor, Oz** *L* U.S.S.R.
121 R5 **Vandry** Quebec Canada
110 G5 **Vanduser** Missouri U.S.A.
100 A9 **Van Duzen** *R* California U.S.A.
27 F13 **Vänern** *L* Sweden
27 F13 **Vänersborg** Sweden
95 L4 **Van Etten** New York U.S.A.
27 C10 **Vang** Norway
88 G4 **Vanga** Tanzania
87 H12 **Vangaindrano** Madagascar
27 F13 **Vanga,N** Sweden
78 J2 **Van Gölü** *L* Turkey
27 C10 **Vangsmjösa** Norway
118 K9 **Vanguard** Saskatchewan Canada
70 A1 **Vanguard Bank** S China Sea
137 M3 **Vangunu** *isld* Solomon Is
68 F3 **Vang Vieng** Laos
26 S2 **Vanhakylä** U.S.S.R.
98 D2 **Van Hook** North Dakota U.S.A.
108 C4 **Van Horn** Texas U.S.A.
106 F5 **Van Houten** New Mexico U.S.A.
137 O4 **Vanikoro Is** Santa Cruz Is
26 K7 **Vänjaurbäck** Sweden
26 K7 **Vänjaurträsk** Sweden
51 S2 **Vankarem** U.S.S.R.
121 Q7 **Vankleek Hill** Ontario Canada
98 F5 **Van Metre** South Dakota U.S.A.
26 L1 **Vanna** *isld* Norway
26 L8 **Vännäs** Sweden
83 J9 **Vannativillu** Sri Lanka
20 E6 **Vannes** France
21 P6 **Vannes-sur-Cosson** France
68 J6 **Van Ninh** Vietnam
57 F4 **Vannovka** U.S.S.R.
107 O7 **Vanoss** Oklahoma U.S.A.
87 C12 **Vanrhynsdorp** S Africa
141 F3 **Vanrook** Queensland Australia
74 E8 **Vānsada** India
94 E9 **Vansant** Virginia U.S.A.
27 G11 **Vansbro** Sweden
118 L6 **Vanscoy** Saskatchewan Canada
142 F2 **Vansittart B** Western Australia Australia
115 L4 **Vansittart I** Northwest Territories Canada
18 H8 **Vans, les** France
29 L11 **Vantaa** *R* Finland
29 L11 **Vantaa** Finland
118 L9 **Vantage** Saskatchewan Canada
100 F3 **Vantage** Washington U.S.A.
98 B7 **Van Tassell** Wyoming U.S.A.
137 O3 **Vanua Lava** *isld* Vanuatu
137 Q5 **Vanua Levu** *isld* Fiji
137 O5 **Vanuatu** *islds* Pacific Oc
99 N9 **Van Wert** Iowa U.S.A.
94 C6 **Van Wert** Ohio U.S.A.
87 D12 **Vanwyksvlei** S Africa
67 A6 **Van Yen** Vietnam
26 A9 **Vanylven** Norway
26 A9 **Vanylvsgapet** *B* Norway
110 D5 **Vanzant** Missouri U.S.A.
48 M2 **Vapnyarka** U.S.S.R.
44 B4 **Var** *R* France
19 Q18 **Var** *dept* France
44 G3 **Vara** *R* Italy
27 F13 **Vara** Sweden
126 D3 **Varadero** Cuba
21 H7 **Varades** France
19 P17 **Varages** France
44 B2 **Varaita** *R* Italy
42 B3 **Varallo** Italy
41 H6 **Varallo** Italy
77 B2 **Varamin** Iran
75 K6 **Varanasi** India
26 R1 **Varangerfjorden** *inlet* Norway
26 R1 **Varangerhalvöya** *mt* Norway
42 G7 **Varano, L. di** Italy
131 A8 **Varas,Pto** Chile
16 D6 **Varas,R** Spain
21 K3 **Varaville** France
44 E3 **Varazze** Italy
27 F14 **Varberg** Sweden
77 L2 **Vardak** *prov* Afghanistan
111 G8 **Vardaman** Mississippi U.S.A.
46 E6 **Vardhoúsia Óri** *mt* Greece
27 L11 **Vårdö** Finland
26 S1 **Vardö** Norway
52 E5 **Varegovo** U.S.S.R.
32 H6 **Varel** W Germany
21 M2 **Varengeville** France
20 G3 **Varenguebec** France
21 J4 **Varenne** *R* France
19 J3 **Varennes en Argonne** France
40 B5 **Varennes St.Sauveur** France
21 O7 **Varennes-sur-Fouzon** France
48 E6 **Vareš** Yugoslavia
41 J6 **Varese** Italy
40 A7 **Vareze** *R* France
27 F13 **Vårgårda** Sweden
55 E3 **Vargashi** U.S.S.R.
130 G10 **Vargem** *R* Brazil
130 F7 **Varginha** Brazil
18 G9 **Varilhes** France
112 J2 **Varina** North Carolina U.S.A.
27 G13 **Väring** Sweden
21 O5 **Varize** France
26 K5 **Varjisträsk** Sweden
29 N9 **Varkaus** Finland
143 C10 **Varley,L** Western Australia Australia
29 K5 **Værløse** Denmark
27 F12 **Varmland** *reg* Sweden
47 J1 **Varna** Bulgaria
55 D4 **Varna** U.S.S.R.
111 G11 **Varnado** Louisiana U.S.A.
28 D6 **Varnæs** Denmark
27 G14 **Vårnamo** Sweden
27 F11 **Värnäs** Sweden
52 F5 **Varnavino** U.S.S.R.
108 B1 **Varney** New Mexico U.S.A.
31 H5 **Varnsdorf** Czechoslovakia
27 F14 **Varnum** Sweden
112 F5 **Varnville** South Carolina U.S.A.
79 D3 **Varosha** Cyprus
48 D3 **Városlöd** Hungary
48 E3 **Várpalota** Hungary
52 G2 **Varsh, Oz** *L* U.S.S.R.
28 E3 **Vårst** Denmark
78 H2 **Varto** Turkey
27 G13 **Vartofta** Sweden
83 K9 **Varuniya** Sri Lanka
46 E7 **Varvára** *mt* Greece
46 E1 **Varvarin** Yugoslavia
54 C10 **Varvarovka** U.S.S.R.
130 G9 **Várzea Alegre** Brazil
130 G5 **Várzea da Palma** Brazil
129 G7 **Várzea Grande** Brazil
130 E9 **Várzea,R** Brazil
52 E1 **Varzino** U.S.S.R.
52 E2 **Varzuga** *R* U.S.S.R.
52 E2 **Varzuga** U.S.S.R.
18 H5 **Varzy** France
48 D3 **Vas** *co* Hungary
130 H11 **Vasa Barris,R** Brazil
76 A1 **Vasai** India
52 B5 **Vasalemma** U.S.S.R.
48 G2 **Vásárosnamény** Hungary
29 K4 **Väsby** Sweden
16 B7 **Vascão** *R* Portugal
48 G4 **Vaşcău** Romania
17 F2 **Vascongadas** *reg* Spain
21 N3 **Vascœuil** France
52 G3 **Vashka** *R* U.S.S.R.
48 K2 **Vashkovtsy** U.S.S.R.
100 C2 **Vashon I** Washington U.S.A.
98 G2 **Vashti** North Dakota U.S.A.
109 J2 **Vashti** Texas U.S.A.
54 H8 **Vasil'kovka** U.S.S.R.
52 G3 **Vasil'yevo** U.S.S.R.
52 G6 **Vasil'yevo** U.S.S.R.
55 F2 **Vasis** U.S.S.R.
29 P11 **Vaskelovo** U.S.S.R.
52 C5 **Vasknarva** U.S.S.R.
29 M3 **Vaskojoki** *R* Finland
48 E4 **Vaskút** Hungary
21 K8 **Vasles** France
48 L4 **Vaslui** Romania
112 H2 **Vass** North Carolina U.S.A.
118 F1 **Vassar** Manitoba Canada
94 D3 **Vassar** Michigan U.S.A.
27 B12 **Vassdalseggja** *mt* Norway
26 K3 **Vassijuare** Sweden
21 J4 **Vassy** Calvados France
26 J4 **Vastenjaure** *L* Sweden
27 J12 **Västerås** Sweden
26 H7 **Västerbotten** *reg* Sweden
27 F11 **Vasterdalälven** *R* Sweden
26 J5 **Västerfjäll** Sweden
27 K12 **Västerhaninge** Sweden
27 H12 **Västermo** Sweden
26 J7 **Vastermyrriset** Sweden
26 J8 **Väster Norr Land** Sweden
27 J14 **Västervik** Sweden
27 J11 **Västland** Sweden
27 H12 **Västmanland** *reg* Sweden
42 F6 **Vasto** Italy
33 N6 **Vastorf** W Germany

Vastra Kvarken — Vilyuysk 89

26 L8 **Vastra Kvarken** *chan* Sweden
48 D3 **Vasvár** Hungary
55 G2 **Vasyugan** *R* U.S.S.R.
21 O7 **Vatan** France
Vaté *isld see* **Éfaté** *isld*
33 P8 **Väthen** East Germany
47 H7 **Vathí** Greece
46 E8 **Váthia** Greece
45 M6 **Vaticano, Citta del** Italy
28 S9 **Vatnajökull** *ice cap* Iceland
26 B9 **Vatne** Norway
28 R9 **Vatneyri** Iceland
27 K12 **Vätö** Sweden
137 R5 **Vatoa** *isld* Fiji
87 H11 **Vatomandry** Madagascar
48 J3 **Vatra Dornei** Romania
27 G13 **Vättern** *L* Sweden
27 J11 **Vattholma** Sweden
41 K4 **Vättis** Switzerland
26 J10 **Vattrång** Sweden
40 C5 **Vauche Marlioz,Mt.De** France
19 O17 **Vaucluse** *dept* France
112 F4 **Vaucluse** South Carolina U.S.A.
40 C2 **Vauconcourt** France
21 L2 **Vaucottes** France
19 J4 **Vaucouleurs** France
36 B6 **Vaucourt** France
40 D4 **Vaud** *canton* Switzerland
21 N3 **Vaudreuil, le** France
122 H9 **Vaughan** Nova Scotia Canada
140 B5 **Vaughan Springs** N Terr Australia
101 O2 **Vaughn** Montana U.S.A.
108 B1 **Vaughn** New Mexico U.S.A.
128 D3 **Vaupés** *div* Colombia
21 K8 **Vausseroux** France
18 H9 **Vauvert** France
20 G2 **Vauville** France
40 D2 **Vauvillers** France
118 E8 **Vauxhall** Alberta Canada
87 J11 **Vavatenina** Madagascar
137 S5 **Vava'u Group** *islds* Tonga
52 H6 **Vavozh** U.S.S.R.
83 K9 **Vavuniya** Sri Lanka
118 J5 **Vawn** Saskatchewan Canada
27 K12 **Vaxholm** Sweden
27 G15 **Växjö** Sweden
20 G6 **Vay** France
76 D4 **Vayalpod** India
50 F1 **Vaygach, Ostrov** *isld* U.S.S.R.
52 F3 **Vaymuga** *R* U.S.S.R.
129 L5 **Vaza** *R* Brazil
130 F5 **Vazante** Brazil
52 G3 **Vazhgort** U.S.S.R.
54 F1 **Vazuzskoye Vodokhranilishche** *res* U.S.S.R.
129 J6 **Veadeiras** Brazil
68 F7 **Veal Renh** Cambodia
28 D3 **Vebbestrup** Denmark
27 F16 **Veberöd** Sweden
98 J4 **Veblen** South Dakota U.S.A.
26 M7 **Vebomark** Sweden
33 M8 **Vechelde** W Germany
25 F3 **Vecht** *R* Netherlands
32 H7 **Vechta** *R* W Germany
32 H7 **Vechta** W Germany
32 L10 **Veckerhagen** W Germany
29 K5 **Vedbæk** Denmark
27 F14 **Veddige** Sweden
28 E3 **Veddum** Denmark
48 J6 **Vedea** Romania
28 A4 **Vedersø** Denmark
27 H12 **Vedevåg** Sweden
133 E4 **Vedia** Argentina
17 H6 **Vedra** *isld* Balearic Is
22 H3 **Vedrin** Belgium
28 E5 **Vedslet** Denmark
28 C6 **Vedsted** Denmark
28 G6 **Ved Stranden** Denmark
27 F13 **Vedum** Sweden
110 J1 **Veedersburg** Indiana U.S.A.
25 G2 **Veendam** Netherlands
25 E4 **Veenendaal** Netherlands
25 F2 **Veenhuizen** Netherlands
25 E2 **Veenwouden** Netherlands
25 A5 **Veere** Netherlands
25 A5 **Veerse Meer** Netherlands
33 N7 **Veerssen** W Germany
28 E6 **Veflinge** Denmark
26 E6 **Vega** *isld* Norway
16 C2 **Vega de Tera** Spain
27 D13 **Vegårs Vatn** *L* Norway
29 K4 **Vegeån** *R* Sweden
32 J6 **Vegesack** W Germany
28 D3 **Veggerby** Denmark
27 D11 **Veggli** Norway
46 E4 **Vegorritis, L** Greece
118 F5 **Vegreville** Alberta Canada
108 A1 **Veguita** New Mexico U.S.A.
33 Q6 **Vehlow** East Germany
27 M11 **Vehmaa** Finland
26 P1 **Veines** Norway
27 F15 **Veinge** Sweden
120 D3 **Vein L** Ontario Canada
133 D5 **Veinticinco de Mayo** Argentina
45 M5 **Veio** Italy
36 H4 **Veitshöchheim** W Germany
28 J4 **Vejby** Denmark
28 C6 **Vejen** Denmark
28 A5 **Vejers** Denmark
28 D4 **Vejerslev** Denmark
28 E2 **Vejgård** Denmark
28 E4 **Vejlby** Århus Denmark
28 D5 **Vejlby** Vejle Denmark
28 D5 **Vejle** Denmark
28 C5 **Vejle** *co* Denmark
28 D5 **Vejle Fjord** *inlet* Denmark
28 H6 **Vejlø** Denmark
28 E7 **Vejnæs Nokke** *C* Denmark
37 P3 **Vejprty** Czechoslovakia
28 G5 **Vejrhøj** *hill* Denmark
28 F5 **Vejrø** *isld* Århus Denmark
28 G6 **Vejrø** *isld* Storstrøm Denmark
28 B5 **Vejrup** Denmark
28 F6 **Vejstrup** Denmark
28 J5 **Veksø** Denmark
52 F4 **Vel** *R* U.S.S.R.
127 H8 **Vela, C. de la** Colombia
22 E2 **Velaines** Belgium
46 E5 **Velaóra** Greece
106 E5 **Velarde** New Mexico U.S.A.
124 H5 **Velardeña** Mexico
18 H7 **Velay, Mts du** France
32 F10 **Velbert** W Germany
37 M5 **Velburg** W Germany
37 M4 **Velden** W Germany
25 D6 **Veldhoven** Netherlands
47 J2 **Veleka** *R* Bulgaria
32 E9 **Velen** W Germany
48 E3 **Velencei Tó** *L* Hungary
46 F5 **Velestínon** Greece
17 F7 **Vélez Bianco** Spain
16 E8 **Vélez Málaga** Spain
17 F7 **Vélez Rubio** Spain
26 F6 **Velfjord** Norway
33 R4 **Velgast** East Germany
130 G6 **Velhas,R** Brazil
42 H3 **Velika** Yugoslavia
42 G3 **Velika Gorica** Yugoslavia
48 G6 **Velika Gradište** Yugoslavia
42 F3 **Velika Kapela** *dist* Yugoslavia
48 G6 **Velika Plana** Yugoslavia
52 G2 **Velikaya** U.S.S.R.
52 C6 **Velikaya** *R* U.S.S.R.
52 G5 **Velikaya** *R* U.S.S.R.
52 E4 **Velikaya Guba** U.S.S.R.
48 K1 **Veliki Borki** U.S.S.R.
48 K1 **Veliki Glubochek** U.S.S.R.
48 G2 **Velikiy Bereznyy** U.S.S.R.
52 D6 **Velikiye-Luki** U.S.S.R.
52 G4 **Velikiy Ustyug** U.S.S.R.
54 M1 **Velikodvorskiy** U.S.S.R.
54 J6 **Velikomikhaylovka** U.S.S.R.
47 H1 **Veliko Turnovo** Bulgaria
52 H2 **Velikovisochnoye** U.S.S.R.
52 F5 **Velikovo** U.S.S.R.
54 M1 **Velikoye, Oz** *L* U.S.S.R.
85 B6 **Velingara** Senegal
46 F2 **Velingrad** Bulgaria
42 E6 **Velino** *R* Italy
42 E6 **Velino, M** *mt* Italy
54 C1 **Velizh** U.S.S.R.
48 E2 **Velká Fatra** *mt* Czechoslovakia
48 E1 **Vel Karlovice** Czechoslovakia
48 G2 **Vel'ké Kapušány** Czechoslovakia
31 L6 **Velké Karlovice** Czechoslovakia
48 D3 **Velký Žitný Ostrov'** *reg* Czechoslovakia
38 L8 **Vellach** Austria
33 N6 **Vellahn** East Germany
137 M3 **Vella Lavella** *isld* Solomon Is
45 J4 **Vellano** Italy
36 H5 **Vellberg** W Germany
21 O8 **Velles** France
45 N6 **Velletri** Italy
28 D4 **Vellev** Denmark
28 A4 **Velling** Denmark
27 F16 **Vellinge** Sweden
45 O5 **Vellino, M** *mt* Italy
76 D4 **Vellore** India
56 D1 **Vel'minskiye Porogi** *falls* U.S.S.R.
56 D1 **Vel'mo** *R* U.S.S.R.
22 J5 **Velosnes** France
25 E4 **Velp** Netherlands
25 C4 **Velsen** Netherlands
52 F4 **Vel'sk** U.S.S.R.
52 H1 **Vel't** U.S.S.R.
33 S7 **Velten** East Germany
22 D3 **Vélu** France
25 E4 **Veluwe** Netherlands
25 E4 **Veluwemeer** Netherlands
98 F1 **Velva** North Dakota U.S.A.
52 J3 **Vel'yu** *R* U.S.S.R.
90 E7 **Vema Fracture** Atlantic Oc
28 A4 **Vemb** Denmark
26 G9 **Vemdalen** Sweden
28 G6 **Vemmelev** Denmark
28 F7 **Vemmenæs** Denmark
29 K5 **Ven** *isld* Sweden
27 H14 **Vena** Sweden
27 D10 **Venabygd** Norway
12 D1 **Venachar,L** Scotland
131 E4 **Venado Tuerto** Argentina
45 Q7 **Venafro** Italy
128 F2 **Venamo,Cerro** *mt* Venezuela/Guyana
98 E9 **Venango** Nebraska U.S.A.
44 C1 **Venaria** Italy
100 G6 **Venator** Oregon U.S.A.
44 B1 **Venáus** Italy
130 E8 **Venceslau Bráz** Brazil
Venda *see* **Vantaa**
45 L1 **Venda** *mt* Italy
89 G4 **Venda** *homeland* S Africa
16 B6 **Vendas Novas** Portugal
18 E6 **Vendée** *dept* France
52 G3 **Vendenga** U.S.S.R.
36 D6 **Vendenheim** France
22 D3 **Vendin-le-Viel** France
21 N6 **Vendôme** France
21 N8 **Vendœuvres** France
17 H3 **Vendrell** Spain
22 H4 **Vendresse** France
28 D2 **Vendsyssel** *reg* Denmark
45 M1 **Veneta, Laguna** Italy
116 P3 **Venetie Landing** Alaska U.S.A.
45 K1 **Veneto** *reg* Italy
52 F6 **Venets** U.S.S.R.
54 K2 **Venev** U.S.S.R.
45 M1 **Venezia** Italy
42 D3 **Venezia-Euganea** *prov* Italy
42 E3 **Venezia,G.di** Italy
128 E2 **Venezuela** *rep* S America
127 J9 **Venezuela,G.de** Venezuela
28 D4 **Veng** Denmark
55 G3 **Vengerovo** U.S.S.R.
76 A3 **Vengurla** India
16 D3 **Venialbo** Spain
116 H8 **Veniaminof Vol** Alaska U.S.A.
118 E4 **Venice** Alberta Canada
Venice Italy *see* **Venezia**
111 M12 **Venice** St Louis
113 E10 **Venice** Florida U.S.A.
111 G12 **Venice** Louisiana U.S.A.
19 N13 **Vénissieux** France
27 G11 **Venjan** Sweden
76 D4 **Venkataguri** India
76 E1 **Venkatapuram** India
25 F6 **Venlo** Netherlands
98 J3 **Venlo** North Dakota U.S.A.
119 M7 **Venn** Saskatchewan Canada
28 D2 **Vennebjerg** Denmark
32 E7 **Vennebrügge** W Germany
27 C13 **Vennesla** Norway
28 B3 **Venø** Denmark
28 B3 **Venø Bugt** *B* Denmark
19 Q15 **Venosc** France
121 O7 **Venosta** Quebec Canada
41 N4 **Venosta, Val** Italy
41 N4 **Venostie, Alpi** Italy
25 E5 **Venray** Netherlands
27 M14 **Venta** *R* U.S.S.R.
124 E5 **Ventana,Pta de la** *C* Mexico
133 E5 **Ventana,Sa** *ra* Argentina
16 E8 **Ventas de Zafarraya** Spain
19 P16 **Ventavon** France
28 H5 **Vented** Denmark
44 C4 **Ventimiglia** Italy
9 E6 **Ventnor** England
43 E8 **Ventotene, I** Italy
19 O16 **Ventoux, Mt** France
33 P5 **Ventschow** East Germany
27 M14 **Ventspils** U.S.S.R.
128 E3 **Ventuari** *R* Venezuela
102 E7 **Ventura** California U.S.A.
98 G3 **Venturia** North Dakota U.S.A.
113 F10 **Venus** Florida U.S.A.
109 K3 **Venus** Texas U.S.A.
138 C5 **Venus B** South Australia Australia
138 C5 **Venus Bay** South Australia Australia
124 H8 **Venustiano Carranza** Mexico
52 D4 **Vepsovskaya Vozvyshennost'** *uplands* U.S.S.R.
133 E3 **Vera** Argentina
17 F7 **Vera** Spain
109 H2 **Vera** Texas U.S.A.
133 D6 **Vera, B** Argentina
130 E8 **Vera Cruz** Brazil
125 L8 **Veracruz** Mexico
74 D8 **Veraval** India
42 B3 **Verbania** Italy
111 K9 **Verbena** Alabama U.S.A.
22 D5 **Verberie** France
52 E6 **Verbilki** U.S.S.R.
41 H7 **Vercelli** Italy
33 R5 **Verchen** East Germany
21 K7 **Verchers,les** France
19 O15 **Vercors** *reg* France
19 Q16 **Verdaches** France
26 E8 **Verdal** Norway
26 E8 **Verdalsöra** Norway
133 D6 **Verde** *R* Argentina
130 E4 **Verde** *R* Brazil
133 F2 **Verde** *R* Paraguay
71 E4 **Verde** *isld* Philippines
103 N7 **Verde** *R* Arizona U.S.A.
85 A6 **Verde, C** Senegal
126 G3 **Verde, Cay** *isld* Bahamas
130 G4 **Verde Grande** *R* Brazil
98 H7 **Verdel** Nebraska U.S.A.
109 J1 **Verden** Oklahoma U.S.A.
32 K7 **Verden** W Germany
131 E7 **Verde,Pen** Argentina
130 G4 **Verde Pequeno, R** Brazil
130 D7 **Verde,R** Brazil
21 N6 **Verdes** France
98 H7 **Verdigre** Nebraska U.S.A.
107 O3 **Verdigris** *R* Okla/Kansas U.S.A.
118 F9 **Verdigris L** Alberta Canada
130 D5 **Verdinho,Sa.do** *mts* Brazil
19 Q17 **Verdon** *R* France
99 L9 **Verdon** Nebraska U.S.A.
18 E7 **Verdon-sur-Mer, le** France
19 J3 **Verdun** France
18 F9 **Verdun-sur-Garonne** France
19 J6 **Verdun-sur-le-Doubs** France
124 E5 **Verdura** Mexico
52 D6 **Verech'ye** U.S.S.R.
89 E6 **Vereeniging** S Africa
119 P7 **Veregin** Saskatchewan Canada
121 N5 **Vérendrye, Parc Prov. de la** Quebec Canada
52 H5 **Vereshchagino** U.S.S.R.
52 E5 **Verestovo, Oz** *L* U.S.S.R.
54 H1 **Vereya** U.S.S.R.
85 B6 **Verga,C** Guinea
17 F1 **Vergara** Spain
133 G4 **Vergara** Uruguay
45 K3 **Vergato** Italy
36 B6 **Vergaville** France
141 G6 **Vergemont** *R* Queensland Australia
141 G6 **Vergemont** Queensland Australia
95 O2 **Vergennes** Vermont U.S.A.
45 L4 **Verghereto** Italy
45 R8 **Vérgine, M** *mt* Italy
16 C3 **Verín** Spain
41 K1 **Veringenstadt** W Germany
56 H3 **Verkh Angara** *R* U.S.S.R.
55 C3 **Verkhiye Kigi** U.S.S.R.
52 J5 **Verkhnaya Yarva** U.S.S.R.
56 H3 **Verkhneangarskiy Khrebet** *mts* U.S.S.R.
55 C4 **Verkhnearshinskiy** U.S.S.R.
55 C4 **Verkhne-Avzyan** U.S.S.R.
54 F8 **Verkhnedneprovsk** U.S.S.R.
54 E2 **Verkhnedneprovskiy** U.S.S.R.
50 H2 **Verkhneimbatsk** U.S.S.R.
54 M7 **Verkhnemakeyevka** U.S.S.R.
29 Q3 **Verkhnetulomskiy** U.S.S.R.
52 D1 **Verkhnetulomskoye, Vodokhranilishche** *L* U.S.S.R.
55 C4 **Verkhneural'sk** U.S.S.R.
52 H6 **Verkhne Yarkeyevo** U.S.S.R.
54 K8 **Verkhneye** U.S.S.R.
55 G3 **Verkhneye Krasnoyarka** U.S.S.R.
52 D2 **Verkhneye Kuyto, Oz** *L* U.S.S.R.
55 C3 **Verkhniye Tatyshly** U.S.S.R.
55 D3 **Verkhniy Neyvinskiy** U.S.S.R.
52 H1 **Verkhniy Shar** U.S.S.R.
55 C3 **Verkhniy Tagil** U.S.S.R.
55 D1 **Verkhniy Vizhay** U.S.S.R.
55 C1 **Verkhniy Vizhay** U.S.S.R.
55 D3 **Verkhnyaya Pyshma** U.S.S.R.
55 D2 **Verkhnyaya Salda** U.S.S.R.
55 D4 **Verkhnyaya Sanarka** U.S.S.R.
55 G3 **Verkhnyaya Tarka** U.S.S.R.
52 G4 **Verkhnyaya Toyma** U.S.S.R.
52 G4 **Verkhnyaya Toz'ma** U.S.S.R.
55 C2 **Verkhnyaya Tura** U.S.S.R.
52 G5 **Verkhoshizhemye** U.S.S.R.
55 D2 **Verkhotur'ye** U.S.S.R.
52 F4 **Verkhovazh'ye** U.S.S.R.
48 J2 **Verkhovina** U.S.S.R.
54 F8 **Verkhovtsevo** U.S.S.R.
51 M2 **Verkhoyanskiy Khrebet** *mts* U.S.S.R.
55 D2 **Verkhyaya Sinyachikha** U.S.S.R.
54 F8 **Verkne Dneprovsk** U.S.S.R.
55 D3 **Verkniy Ufaley** U.S.S.R.
52 G3 **Verkola** U.S.S.R.
118 J8 **Verlo** Saskatchewan Canada
26 C9 **Verma** Norway
22 E4 **Vermand** France
130 D4 **Vermelho,R** Brazil
18 H5 **Vermenton** France
118 G5 **Vermilion** Alberta Canada
99 T10 **Vermilion** Illinois U.S.A.
111 D11 **Vermilion** *R* Louisiana U.S.A.
94 E5 **Vermilion** Ohio U.S.A.
111 D12 **Vermilion B** Louisiana U.S.A.
118 J1 **Vermilion Bay** Ontario Canada
117 Q6 **Vermilion Chutes** Alberta Canada
103 M4 **Vermilion Cliffs** Utah U.S.A.
118 K1 **Vermilion L** Ontario Canada
99 O2 **Vermilion L** Minnesota U.S.A.
118 F5 **Vermilion Prov. Park** Alberta Canada
99 O2 **Vermilion Ra** Minnesota U.S.A.
107 O2 **Vermillion** Kansas U.S.A.
98 K7 **Vermillion** South Dakota U.S.A.
103 M5 **Vermillion Cliffs** *ra* Arizona U.S.A.
121 R5 **Vermillon** *R* Quebec Canada
46 E4 **Vérmion** *mt* Greece
95 P2 **Vermont** *state* U.S.A.
99 Q9 **Vermont** Illinois U.S.A.
21 J6 **Vern** France
41 N4 **Vernago, Lago di** Italy
101 Q9 **Vernal** Utah U.S.A.
102 C4 **Vernalis** California U.S.A.
21 L7 **Vernantes** France
44 G3 **Vernazza** Italy
101 P8 **Verne** Wyoming U.S.A.
87 D11 **Verneakpan** *L* S Africa
120 K6 **Verner** Ontario Canada
21 M4 **Verneuil** Eure France
18 G4 **Verneuil l'Etang** France
21 N7 **Verneuil sur-Indre** France
89 B7 **Verneuk Pan** S Africa
28 E6 **Verninge** Denmark
45 K3 **Vernio** Italy
21 L7 **Vernoil** France
117 O10 **Vernon** British Columbia Canada
122 K7 **Vernon** Prince Edward I Canada
21 N3 **Vernon** Eure France
46 E4 **Vérnon** *mt* Greece
111 H8 **Vernon** Alabama U.S.A.
103 P7 **Vernon** Arizona U.S.A.
98 D10 **Vernon** Colorado U.S.A.
111 L11 **Vernon** Florida U.S.A.
94 B8 **Vernon** Indiana U.S.A.
95 M3 **Vernon** New York U.S.A.
109 H1 **Vernon** Texas U.S.A.
101 N9 **Vernon** Utah U.S.A.
95 P4 **Vernon** Vermont U.S.A.
100 B4 **Vernonia** Oregon U.S.A.
140 B1 **Vernon Is** N Terr Australia
143 C6 **Vernon,Mt** Western Australia Australia
21 M7 **Vernou** France
127 N4 **Vernou** Guadeloupe
21 O7 **Vernou-en-Sologne** France
20 G5 **Vern-sur-Seiche** France
113 G10 **Vero Beach** Florida U.S.A.
46 E4 **Véroia** Greece
44 H1 **Verolanuova** Italy
45 O6 **Veroli** Italy
121 O8 **Verona** Ontario Canada
45 J1 **Verona** Italy
110 C5 **Verona** Missouri U.S.A.
98 H3 **Verona** North Dakota U.S.A.
99 R7 **Verona** Wisconsin U.S.A.
101 T5 **Verona** Wyoming U.S.A.
19 O13 **Verpillière** France
138 D5 **Verran** South Australia Australia
111 E12 **Verret, L** Louisiana U.S.A.
127 H5 **Verrettes** Haiti
21 J8 **Verrie,la** France
19 N17 **Vers** France
21 P4 **Versailles** France
110 L2 **Versailles** Indiana U.S.A.
110 M3 **Versailles** Kentucky U.S.A.
110 D3 **Versailles** Missouri U.S.A.
94 C6 **Versailles** Ohio U.S.A.
55 D1 **Vershina** U.S.S.R.
58 G1 **Vershino-Darasunskiy** U.S.S.R.
32 H8 **Versmold** W Germany
21 K3 **Verson** France
28 C5 **Verst** Denmark
21 K3 **Ver-sur-Mer** France
41 N4 **Vertana,Cima** *mt* Italy
122 C5 **Verte,I** Quebec Canada
20 C6 **Verte,I** France
18 F7 **Verteillac** France
130 J9 **Vertentes** Brazil
129 H6 **Vertentes** *R* Brazil
48 E3 **Vérteshegység** *mt* Hungary
126 E4 **Vertientes** Cuba
54 C5 **Vertiyevka** U.S.S.R.
123 N2 **Verton,L** Quebec Canada
20 H7 **Vertou** France
22 H2 **Vertrijk** Belgium
18 H4 **Vertus** France
45 M4 **Verucchio** Italy
89 G7 **Verulam** S Africa
22 K2 **Verviers** Belgium
22 F4 **Vervins** France
119 M9 **Verwood** Saskatchewan Canada
8 B7 **Veryan B** England
41 J5 **Verzasca,Val** Switzerland
38 O8 **Veržej** Yugoslavia
29 M9 **Vesanto** Finland
22 L2 **Vesdre** *R* Belgium
21 O4 **Vesegre** *R* France
48 D2 **Veseh** Czechoslovakia
31 K7 **Veseli** Czechoslovakia
55 C2 **Vesëlovka** U.S.S.R.
55 G4 **Veselovskoye** U.S.S.R.
55 E4 **Veselyy Podol** U.S.S.R.
26 F6 **Vesfna** *R* Norway
21 K6 **Vesgre** *R* France
52 F3 **Veshkoma** U.S.S.R.
18 H3 **Vesle** *R* France
28 B2 **Vesløs** Denmark
20 H3 **Vesly** France
52 H3 **Veslyana** U.S.S.R.
52 H4 **Veslyana** *R* U.S.S.R.
40 D2 **Vesoul** France
107 M2 **Vesper** Kansas U.S.A.
99 R5 **Vesper** Wisconsin U.S.A.
27 F15 **Vessige** Sweden
99 L5 **Vesta** Minnesota U.S.A.
27 B13 **Vest Agder** *reg* Norway
95 L4 **Vestal Center** New York U.S.A.
26 H3 **Vestbygd** Norway
28 G7 **Vestenskov** Denmark
28 E6 **Vester Aby** Denmark
26 G3 **Vesterålen** *isld* Norway
147 G14 **Vesterålen** Norway
28 B3 **Vester Assels** Denmark
28 G7 **Vesterborg** Denmark
28 H6 **Vester Egede** Denmark
28 H6 **Vester Egesborg** Denmark
28 E2 **Vester Hassing** Denmark
28 D2 **Vester Hjermitslev** Denmark
29 K4 **Vester Karup** Sweden
28 C5 **Vesterlund** Denmark
28 C5 **Vester Nebel** Denmark
28 B5 **Vester Nykirke** Denmark
28 F2 **Vesterøhavn** Denmark
28 E6 **Vester Skerninge** Denmark
28 D7 **Vester Sottrup** Denmark
28 D3 **Vester Tørslev** Denmark
28 A3 **Vestervig** Denmark
27 C12 **Vestfj-Dal** Norway
146 G6 **Vestfjella** *mts* Antarctica
26 F4 **Vestfjorden** *inlet* Norway
27 D12 **Vestfold** *reg* Norway
146 J12 **Vestfold Hills** Antarctica
130 D7 **Véstia** Brazil
6 F1 **Vestmanna** Faeroes
28 S10 **Vestmannaeyjar** *islds* Iceland
26 B9 **Vestnes** Norway
29 T9 **Vestrahorn** *C* Iceland
28 G5 **Vestsjælland** *co* Denmark
26 G3 **Vestvågöy** Norway
45 Q8 **Vesuvio** *mt* Italy
52 E5 **Ves'yegonsk** U.S.S.R.
48 D3 **Veszprém** *co* Hungary
48 D3 **Veszprém** Hungary
48 D3 **Veszprémvarsány** Hungary
48 G4 **Vésztő** Hungary
89 E7 **Vet** *R* S Africa
98 E6 **Vetal** South Dakota U.S.A.
118 F6 **Veteran** Alberta Canada
98 B8 **Veteran** Wyoming U.S.A.
21 O3 **Vétheuil** France
54 C4 **Vetka** U.S.S.R.
27 H14 **Vetlanda** Sweden
52 G5 **Vetluga** U.S.S.R.
52 G5 **Vetluzhskiy** U.S.S.R.
52 G6 **Vetluzhskiy** U.S.S.R.
47 H1 **Vetovo** Bulgaria
52 C6 **Vetrino** U.S.S.R.
28 H6 **Vetterslev** Denmark
45 H3 **Vetto** Italy
26 M4 **Vetträsjärvi** Sweden
36 B2 **Vettweiss** W Germany
21 L8 **Veude** *R* France
21 M2 **Veules** France
21 M2 **Veulettes** France
27 C12 **Veum** Norway
68 H6 **Veun Kham** Cambodia
22 D1 **Veurne** Belgium
94 B8 **Vevay** Indiana U.S.A.
26 F6 **Vevelstad** Norway
40 E5 **Vevey** Switzerland
46 E4 **Vévi** Greece
19 P15 **Veynes** France
103 L4 **Veyo** Utah U.S.A.
19 K4 **Vézelise** France
18 G7 **Vezère** *R* France
46 G2 **Vezhen** *mt* Bulgaria
52 H3 **Vezh'yudor** U.S.S.R.
22 K5 **Vezin** France
21 J7 **Vezins** Maine-et-Loire France
78 E1 **Vezirkoprü** Turkey
36 B6 **Vezouse** *R* France
44 G3 **Vezzano Ligure** Italy
21 O5 **Viabon** France
45 J2 **Viadana** Italy
44 B1 **Via di Ciamarella** *mt* Italy
107 Q6 **Vian** Oklahoma U.S.A.
130 H7 **Viana** Espírito Santo Brazil
129 J4 **Viana** Maranhão Brazil
16 C2 **Viana del Bollo** Spain
16 B6 **Viana do Alentejo** Portugal
16 B3 **Viana do Castelo** Portugal
22 L4 **Vianden** Luxembourg
25 D5 **Vianen** Netherlands
68 F3 **Viangchan** Laos
45 J2 **Viano** Italy
130 E5 **Vianópolis** Brazil
29 L6 **Viantie** Finland
16 D7 **Viar** *R* Spain
44 H4 **Viareggio** Italy
18 G8 **Viaur** *R* France
119 O8 **Vibank** Saskatchewan Canada
28 C4 **Viborg** Denmark
28 B3 **Viborg** *co* Denmark
98 J6 **Viborg** South Dakota U.S.A.
43 G10 **Vibo Valentia** Italy
21 M5 **Vibraye** France
28 E4 **Viby** Århus Denmark
28 J5 **Viby** Roskilde Denmark
48 D2 **Vičany** Czechoslovakia
45 K4 **Vicchio** Italy
146 D4 **Vicecomodoro Marambio** *Arg Base* Antarctica
18 E9 **Vic en Bigorre** France
130 F8 **Vicente S** Brazil
16 D4 **Vicente,S** *mt* Spain
45 L1 **Vicenza** Italy
119 M9 **Viceroy** Saskatchewan Canada
18 F9 **Vic-Fezensac** France
128 E3 **Vichada** *dept* Colombia
131 G3 **Vichadero** Uruguay
52 F6 **Vichuga** U.S.S.R.
133 C4 **Vichuquén** Chile
18 H6 **Vichy** France
107 L5 **Vici** Oklahoma U.S.A.
109 O9 **Vickery** Texas U.S.A.
103 L8 **Vicksburg** Arizona U.S.A.
94 B4 **Vicksburg** Michigan U.S.A.
111 F9 **Vicksburg** Mississippi U.S.A.
45 Q8 **Vico Equense** Italy
42 E6 **Vico, L. di** Italy
45 J4 **Vicopisano** Italy
17 G3 **Vicort, Sierra de** *mts* Spain
130 H10 **Viçosa** Alagoas Brazil
130 G7 **Viçosa** Minas Gerais Brazil
41 L5 **Vicosoprano** Switzerland
45 N5 **Vicovaro** Italy
48 K3 **Vicovu de Sus** Romania
21 P8 **Vicq Exemplet** France
21 M8 **Vicq-sur-Gartempe** France
22 E5 **Vic-sur-Aisne** France
18 G8 **Vic-sur-Cère** France
7 M9 **Victor** *oil rig* North Sea
106 E3 **Victor** Colorado U.S.A.
101 O6 **Victor** Idaho U.S.A.
99 O8 **Victor** Iowa U.S.A.
101 L3 **Victor** Montana U.S.A.
94 K4 **Victor** New York U.S.A.
138 E6 **Victor Harbour** South Australia Australia
131 E4 **Victoria** *R* Argentina
131 E4 **Victoria** Argentina
138 F6 **Victoria** *state* Australia
140 B3 **Victoria** *R* N Terr Australia
139 G6 **Victoria** Victoria Australia
123 T6 **Victoria** Newfoundland Canada
100 B1 **Victoria** Vancouver I, Br Col Canada
131 A7 **Victoria** Chile
127 P5 **Victoria** Grenada
67 F6 **Victoria** Hong Kong
83 K12 **Victoria** Mahe Indian Oc
43 F12 **Victoria** Malta
71 E3 **Victoria** Luzon Philippines
70 D2 **Victoria** Sabah
127 O3 **Victoria** *co* Trinidad
107 L3 **Victoria** Kansas U.S.A.
109 K7 **Victoria** Texas U.S.A.
94 J10 **Victoria** Virginia U.S.A.
89 G3 **Victoria** *prov* Zimbabwe
119 V8 **Victoria Beach** Manitoba Canada
89 D1 **Victoria Falls** Zambezi R Zimbabwe
121 L8 **Victoria Harb** Ontario Canada
126 G2 **Victoria Hill** San Salvador Bahamas
114 H3 **Victoria I** Northwest Territories Canada
139 G5 **Victoria L** New South Wales Australia
123 P5 **Victoria L** *res* Newfoundland Canada
121 N5 **Victoria, L** Quebec Canada
88 D2 **Victoria, L** E Africa
146 C12 **Victoria Land** Antarctica
73 P4 **Victoria Mt** Burma
145 D4 **Victoria Mt** New Zealand
136 K3 **Victoria, Mt** Papua New Guinea
86 F5 **Victoria Nile** *R* Uganda
142 B2 **Victoria Park** *dist* Perth, W Aust Australia
139 K5 **Victoria Pass** New South Wales Australia
140 B3 **Victoria R** N Terr Australia
123 P5 **Victoria R** Newfoundland Canada
144 D5 **Victoria Range** New Zealand
140 B3 **Victoria River Downs** N Terr Australia
114 J4 **Victoria Str** Northwest Territories Canada
145 D1 **Victoria Valley** New Zealand
121 T6 **Victoriaville** Quebec Canada
89 C8 **Victoria West** S Africa
123 L3 **Victor L** Quebec Canada
146 J8 **Victor, Mt** *mt* Antarctica
102 G7 **Victorville** California U.S.A.
140 C7 **Victory Downs** N Terr Australia
133 E4 **Vicuña** Argentina
133 C4 **Vicuña** Chile
28 B7 **Vidå** *R* Denmark
98 A2 **Vida** Montana U.S.A.
100 C5 **Vida** Oregon U.S.A.
103 K7 **Vidal** California U.S.A.
112 E5 **Vidalia** Georgia U.S.A.
111 E10 **Vidalia** Louisiana U.S.A.
83 K8 **Vidattaltivu** Sri Lanka
19 Q16 **Vidauban** France
109 K7 **Vidauri** Texas U.S.A.
28 B4 **Videbæk** Denmark
130 D10 **Videira** Brazil
48 K6 **Videle** Romania
Viderø *see* **Viðoy**
47 O12 **Vidho** *isld* Greece
16 B6 **Vidigueira** Portugal
56 F3 **Vidim** U.S.S.R.
46 F1 **Vidin** Bulgaria
16 C1 **Vidio, C** Spain
74 G7 **Vidisha** India
52 D4 **Vidlitsa** U.S.S.R.
46 E1 **Vidojevica** *mt* Yugoslavia
31 O3 **Vidomlya** U.S.S.R.
109 N5 **Vidor** Texas U.S.A.
111 E11 **Vidor** Texas U.S.A.
118 H9 **Vidora** Saskatchewan Canada
18 H9 **Vidourle** France
6 F1 **Viðoy** *isld* Faeroes
48 K3 **Vidra** Romania
26 L3 **Vidsel** Sweden
28 D2 **Vidstrup** Denmark
42 J6 **Viduša** *mt* Yugoslavia
52 C6 **Vidzy** U.S.S.R.
52 H4 **Vidz'yuyar** U.S.S.R.
21 L3 **Vie** *R* Calvados France
20 G8 **Vie** *R* Vendée France
37 O5 **Viechtach** W Germany
131 D8 **Viedma** Argentina
133 C7 **Viedma, L** Argentina
20 H8 **Vieillevigne** France
108 C5 **Vieja, Sa** *mts* Texas U.S.A.
128 C6 **Viejas, Islas de las** Peru
17 H2 **Viella** Spain
21 M4 **Vielle-Lyre, la** France
22 K3 **Vielsalm** Belgium
28 J6 **Viemose** Denmark
33 N9 **Vienenburg** W Germany
68 E2 **Vieng Pou Kha** Laos
Vienna Austria *see* **Wien** Austria
110 H4 **Vienna** Illinois U.S.A.
95 M8 **Vienna** Maryland U.S.A.
98 J5 **Vienna** South Dakota U.S.A.
94 F7 **Vienna** West Virginia U.S.A.
21 L7 **Vienne** *R* France
18 F6 **Vienne** *dept* France
19 N13 **Vienne** France
131 B3 **Vientes, P. del** *pk* Arg/Chile
Vientiane *see* **Viangchan**
131 B6 **Viento, Cord. del** *ra* Argentina
127 M5 **Vieques** *isld* Puerto Rico
29 N8 **Vieremä** Finland
32 M6 **Vierlande** *reg* W Germany
25 E5 **Vierlingsbeek** Netherlands
36 F4 **Viernheim** W Germany
25 F6 **Viersen** W Germany
21 J3 **Vierville-sur-Mer** France
41 H3 **Vierwaldstätter See** *L* Switzerland
21 P7 **Vierzon** France
124 H5 **Viesca** Mexico
33 Q6 **Viesecke** East Germany
37 L1 **Vieselbach** East Germany
52 C6 **Viesite Nereta** U.S.S.R.
21 J4 **Viessoix** France
42 G7 **Vieste** Italy
68 G3 **Vietnam** *rep* S E Asia
33 R7 **Vietnitz** East Germany
68 G2 **Vietri** Vietnam
45 R8 **Vietri S. Mare** Italy
127 O8 **Vieux Fort** St Lucia
127 N5 **Vieux Fort,Pte.du** Guadeloupe W Indies
108 H3 **View** Texas U.S.A.
28 H5 **Vig** Denmark
52 F5 **Viga** *R* U.S.S.R.
71 E2 **Vigan** Luzon Philippines
18 H8 **Vigan, le** France
45 L2 **Vigarano Mainarda** Italy
45 J1 **Vigásio** Italy
18 F7 **Vigeois** France
44 E1 **Vigevano** Italy
43 G8 **Viggiano** Italy
129 J4 **Vigia** Brazil
16 B7 **Vigia** *mt* Portugal
133 D7 **Vigía, C** Argentina
71 E3 **Vigia Pt** Luzon Philippines
21 P6 **Viglain** France
45 O6 **Viglio** *mt* Italy
21 P1 **Vignacourt** France
44 D1 **Vignale Mon Ferrato** Italy
18 E10 **Vignemale** *mt* France/Spain
22 G4 **Vigneux Hocquet** France
45 K3 **Vignola** Italy
16 B2 **Vigo** Spain
45 L1 **Vigonza** Italy
142 C5 **Vigors,Mt** Western Australia Australia
26 A9 **Vigra** *isld* Norway
27 A13 **Vigrestad** Norway
28 B2 **Vigsø** Denmark
29 L7 **Vihanti** Finland
21 J7 **Vihiers** France
29 L11 **Vihti** Finland
29 K10 **Viiala** Finland
29 O9 **Viinijärvi** *L* Finland
29 M5 **Viiri** Finland
29 M8 **Viitasaari** Finland
76 A2 **Vijayadrug** India
76 E2 **Vijayawada** India
46 D4 **Vijosë** *R* Albania
28 S10 **Vik** Iceland
26 F6 **Vik** Norway
27 G11 **Vika** Sweden
29 M5 **Vikajärvi** Finland
27 H11 **Vikarbyn** Sweden
27 A12 **Vikedal** Norway
71 N9 **Vikeke** Timor
29 K4 **Viken** Sweden
27 G12 **Vikersvik** Sweden
27 D12 **Vikesund** Norway
46 F3 **Vikhren** *mt* Bulgaria
118 F5 **Viking** Alberta Canada
7 M9 **Viking** *oil rig* North Sea
6 M2 **Viking Bank** North Sea
7 M9 **Viking N** *oil rig* North Sea
7 M9 **Viking S** *oil rig* North Sea
27 H11 **Vikmanshyttan** Sweden
26 E7 **Vikna** *isld* Norway
26 E7 **Vikna** Norway
26 J9 **Viksjö** Sweden
55 F3 **Vikulovo** U.S.S.R.
71 M9 **Vila Armindo Monteiro** Timor
Vila Cabral *see* **Lichinga**
131 E4 **Vila Constitución** Argentina
88 G10 **Vila da Maganje** Mozambique
16 B7 **Vila do Bispo** Portugal
16 B3 **Vila do Conde** Portugal
87 F8 **Vila Gamito** Mozambique
20 H5 **Vilaine** *R* Ille-et-Vilaine France
20 F6 **Vilaine** *R* Morbihan France
17 H2 **Vilaller** Spain
87 F9 **Vila Machado** Mozambique
128 E6 **Vila Murtinho** Brazil
87 G11 **Vilanandro, Tanjona** *C* Madagascar
87 G10 **Vilanculos** Mozambique
52 C6 **Vilāni** U.S.S.R.
16 B5 **Vila Nova da Barquinha** Portugal
16 B3 **Vila Nova de Famalicão** Portugal
16 C3 **Vila Nova de Fozcoa** Portugal
16 B3 **Vila Nova de Gaia** Portugal
71 N9 **Vila Nova de Malaca** Timor
16 B7 **Vila Nova de Mil Fontes** Portugal
16 B4 **Vila Nova de Paiva** Portugal
16 B3 **Vila Pouca de Aguiar** Portugal
16 B3 **Vila Real** Portugal
16 C7 **Vila Real de Santo António** Portugal
16 C4 **Vilar Formoso** Portugal
106 H4 **Vilas** Colorado U.S.A.
111 M11 **Vilas** Florida U.S.A.
98 J5 **Vilas** South Dakota U.S.A.
71 N9 **Vila Salazar** Timor
87 F8 **Vila Vasco da Gama** Mozambique
129 H3 **Vila Velha** Amapá Brazil
130 H7 **Vila Velha** Espírito Santo Brazil
16 B5 **Vila Velha de Ródão** Portugal
16 B3 **Vila Verde** Portugal
128 D6 **Vilcabamba, Cord** *mts* Peru
48 H5 **Vîlcanului Muntii** *mt* Romania
48 J5 **Vîlcea** *reg* Romania
28 B4 **Vildbjerg** Denmark
28 B3 **Vile** Denmark
52 G4 **Viled'** *R* U.S.S.R.
37 P3 **Vilémov** Czechoslovakia
53 C7 **Vileyskoye Vodokhranilishche** *res* U.S.S.R.
52 H4 **Vil'gort** Komi A.S.S.R. U.S.S.R.
52 J4 **Vil'gort** Permskaya obl U.S.S.R.
26 J7 **Vilhelmina** Sweden
128 F6 **Vilhena** Brazil
52 C5 **Viljandi** U.S.S.R.
31 O1 **Vilkaviškis** U.S.S.R.
51 J1 **Vil'kitskogo, Proliv** *str* U.S.S.R.
48 M5 **Vilkovo** U.S.S.R.
128 E8 **Villa Abecia** Bolivia
45 N6 **Villa Adriana** Italy
108 A5 **Villa Ahumada** Mexico
127 J5 **Villa Altagracia** Dominican Rep
133 E3 **Villa Angela** Argentina
131 C5 **Villa Atuel** Argentina
45 K1 **Villa Bartolomea** Italy
38 F8 **Villabassa** Italy
128 E6 **Villa Bella** Bolivia
128 E4 **Villa Bittencourt** Brazil
16 C2 **Villablino** Spain
16 E5 **Villacañas** Spain
16 E1 **Villacarriedo** Spain
16 E6 **Villa Carrillo** Spain
16 E4 **Villacastin** Spain
38 J8 **Villach** Austria
16 C2 **Villachica, L. de** Spain
43 B9 **Villacidro** Sardinia
Villa Cisneros *see* **Dakhla, Ad**
133 D4 **Villa Colón** Argentina
133 E4 **Villa Concepción del Tio** Argentina
133 E4 **Villa Constitucion** Argentina
124 G4 **Villa Coronado** Mexico
16 D2 **Villada** Spain
127 L9 **Villa de Cura** Venezuela
133 E4 **Villa del Rosario** Argentina
16 E2 **Villadiego** Spain
131 D3 **Villa Dolores** Argentina
41 H5 **Villadossola** Italy
45 L1 **Villa Estense** Italy
17 G4 **Villafamés** Spain
130 B10 **Villa Franca** Paraguay
16 C2 **Villafranca del Bierzo** Spain
17 G4 **Villafranca del Cid** Spain
16 C6 **Villafranca de los Barros** Spain
17 J3 **Villafranca del Penedés** Spain
45 J1 **Villafranca di Verona** Italy
45 L1 **Villafranca P** Italy
45 L1 **Villaga** Italy
16 B2 **Villagarcia de Arosa** Spain
109 N5 **Village Cr** Texas U.S.A.
109 N5 **Village Mills** Texas U.S.A.
131 G6 **Villa Gesell** Argentina
99 S10 **Villa Grove** Illinois U.S.A.
131 F3 **Villaguay** Argentina
133 F3 **Villa Guillermina** Argentina
133 F3 **Villa Hayes** Paraguay
125 N9 **Villahermosa** Mexico
133 E4 **Villa Huidobro** Argentina
21 K5 **Villaines-la-Jubel** France
21 M7 **Villaines-les-Rochers** France
21 K6 **Villaines-sous-Malicorne** France
128 F8 **Villa Ingavi** Bolivia
133 E5 **Villa Iris** Argentina
127 J5 **Villa Isabel** Dominican Rep
16 B1 **Villalba** Lugo Spain
16 E4 **Villalba** Madrid Spain
45 Q7 **Villa Literno** Italy
16 D2 **Villalón de Campos** Spain
133 E5 **Villalonga** Argentina
16 D3 **Villalpando** Spain
17 F6 **Villamanriqué** Spain
43 B9 **Villamar** Sardinia
131 D4 **Villa Maria** Argentina
133 D2 **Villa Martín** Bolivia
16 D8 **Villamartín** Spain
124 G4 **Villa Matamoros** Mexico
17 F5 **Villamayor de Santiago** Spain
21 O5 **Villamblain** France
133 D4 **Villa Mercedes** Argentina
133 E3 **Villa Minetti** Argentina
45 H3 **Villaminozzo** Italy
133 E2 **Villa Montes** Bolivia
16 B3 **Villa Nova da Cerveira** Portugal
45 L2 **Villanova March** Italy
127 H9 **Villanueva** Colombia
124 H6 **Villanueva** Mexico
106 E6 **Villanueva** New Mexico U.S.A.
16 D6 **Villanueva de Córdoba** Spain
17 F6 **Villanueva del Arzobispo** Spain
16 D6 **Villanueva de la Serena** Spain
16 D3 **Villanueva del Campo** Spain
16 E6 **Villanueva de los Infantes** Spain
17 J3 **Villanueva y Geltrú** Spain
48 E5 **Villány** Hungary
124 G4 **Villa Ocampo** Durango Mexico
16 C1 **Villaodrid** Spain
124 G4 **Villa Orestes Pereyra** Mexico
124 E3 **Villa Pesqueira** Mexico
43 C9 **Villaputzu** Sardinia
16 E2 **Villarcayo** Spain
19 P14 **Villard** France
19 P14 **Villard de Lans** France
17 G5 **Villar del Arzobispo** Spain
16 C5 **Villar del Rey** Spain
133 D5 **Villa Regina** Argentina
142 D4 **Villaret, C** Western Australia Australia
130 B9 **Villa Rey** Paraguay
111 M8 **Villa Rica** Georgia U.S.A.
17 G4 **Villarluengo** Spain
43 F11 **Villarosa** Sicily
17 G5 **Villarreal** Spain
131 A7 **Villarrica** Chile
130 C9 **Villarrica** Paraguay
131 B7 **Villarrica, Vol** Chile
17 F5 **Villarrobledo** Spain
17 F3 **Villarroya de la Sierra** Spain
16 E5 **Villarubia de los Ojos** Spain
95 N7 **Villas** New Jersey U.S.A.
131 D2 **Villa Sanagasta** Argentina
131 D2 **Villa San Martín** Argentina
38 G9 **Villa Santina** Italy
17 F3 **Villasayas** Spain
133 D3 **Villa Unión** Argentina
108 G7 **Villa Union** Mexico
124 G6 **Villa Unión** Durango Mexico
124 F6 **Villa Unión** Sinaloa Mexico
128 D3 **Villavicencio** Colombia
16 D1 **Villaviciosa** Spain
16 D6 **Villaviciosa de Córdoba** Spain
128 C3 **Villavieja** Colombia
133 D2 **Villazón** Bolivia
36 C7 **Villé** France
21 N6 **Ville-aux-Clèrcs, la** France
21 H4 **Villebaudon** France
40 B6 **Villebois** France
18 F7 **Villebois Lavalette** France
19 Q17 **Villecroze** France
21 H7 **Villedieu-la-Blouère** Maine-et-Loire France
20 H4 **Villedieu-les-Poêtes** France
21 O8 **Villedieu-sur-Indre** France
21 M6 **Villedomer** France
21 M2 **Villedomer** France
18 H8 **Villefort** France
44 B4 **Villefranche** France
19 N13 **Villefranche** Rhône France
18 G9 **Villefranche de Lauragais** France
18 G8 **Villefranche-de-Rouergue** France
18 F8 **Villefranche-du-Perigord** France
21 O7 **Villefranche-sur-Cher** France
17 G4 **Villel** Spain
121 L5 **Ville-Marie** Quebec Canada
21 N4 **Villemeux-sur-Eure** France
121 M4 **Villemontel** Quebec Canada
18 G9 **Villemur sur le Tarn** France
17 G6 **Villena** Spain
19 N12 **Villeneuve** France
40 F6 **Villeneuve** Italy
18 G8 **Villeneuve d'Allier** France
22 E2 **Villeneuve d'Ascq** France
19 N15 **Villeneuve de Berg** France
18 E9 **Villeneuve de Marc** France
18 H4 **Villeneuve l'Archevêque** France
19 N17 **Villeneuve-lès-Avignon** France
21 P3 **Villeneuve-les-Sablons** France
18 G4 **Villeneuve-St Georges** France
18 F8 **Villeneuve-sur-Lot** France
18 H4 **Villeneuve-sur-Yonne** France
21 N7 **Villentrois** France
111 D11 **Ville Platte** Louisiana U.S.A.
21 M2 **Villequier** France
21 N6 **Villeromain** France
121 T6 **Villeroy** Quebec Canada
21 J3 **Villers-Bocage** Calvados France
21 P2 **Villers-Bocage** Somme France
21 P3 **Villers-Bretonneux** France
22 D4 **Villers-Carbonnel** France
22 E5 **Villers Cotterets** France
22 J4 **Villers Devant-Orval** Belgium
21 L4 **Villers-en-Ouche** France
22 J2 **Villers-le-Bouillet** Belgium
22 H3 **Villers-le-Gambon** Belgium
22 E3 **Villers-Outreaux** France
22 K5 **Villerupt-la-Montagne** *mt* France
21 L3 **Villerville** France
19 N13 **Villeurbanne** France
131 C3 **Villicun, Sa** *ra* Argentina
21 N8 **Villiers** France
21 J6 **Villiers-Charlemagne** France
41 J1 **Villingen-Schwenningen** W Germany
99 M9 **Villisca** Iowa U.S.A.
36 E3 **Villmar** W Germany
76 D5 **Villupuram** India
Vilna *see* **Vilnius**
118 F4 **Vilna** Alberta Canada
53 C7 **Vilnius** U.S.S.R.
29 L9 **Vilppula** Finland
41 N2 **Vils** Austria
28 B3 **Vils** Denmark
27 M13 **Vilsandi Saar** *isld* U.S.S.R.
37 N7 **Vilsbiburg** W Germany
37 M4 **Vilseck** W Germany
37 P6 **Vilshofen** W Germany
27 G15 **Vilshult** Sweden
28 B6 **Vilslev** Denmark
28 C3 **Vilsted** Denmark
28 B3 **Vilsund** Denmark
42 J6 **Vilusi** Yugoslavia
52 J5 **Vil'va** U.S.S.R.
22 G2 **Vilvoorde** Belgium
51 L2 **Vilyuy** *R* U.S.S.R.
51 M2 **Vilyuysk** U.S.S.R.

90
Vilyuyskoye Vodokhranilishche — Walkersville

56 H1 **Vilyuyskoye Vodokhranilishche** *res* U.S.S.R.
16 C3 **Vimioso** Portugal
27 H14 **Vimmerby** Sweden
27 G11 **Vimo** Sweden
21 L4 **Vimoutiers** France
29 K8 **Vimpeli** Finland
30 H6 **Vimperk** Czechoslovakia
22 D3 **Vimy** France
111 H7 **Vina** Alabama U.S.A.
102 B2 **Vina** California U.S.A.
131 B4 **Viña de Mar** Chile
17 G6 **Vinalapó** *R* Spain
95 T2 **Vinalhaven** Maine U.S.A.
17 H4 **Vinaroz** Spain
40 B7 **Vinay** France
110 J3 **Vincennes** Indiana U.S.A.
146 G14 **Vincennes Bay** Antarctica
111 K8 **Vincent** Alabama U.S.A.
94 F7 **Vincent** Ohio U.S.A.
16 B7 **Vincente, C. de S** Portugal
128 C4 **Vinces** Ecuador
45 R7 **Vinchiaturo** Italy
133 D3 **Vinchina** Argentina
45 J4 **Vinci** Italy
28 B4 **Vind** Denmark
28 C3 **Vindblæs** Denmark
28 G7 **Vindeby** Denmark
26 H5 **Vindelälven** *R* Sweden
26 K6 **Vindelgransele** Sweden
26 L7 **Vindeln** Sweden
143 B7 **Vinden, Mt** Western Australia Australia
28 C4 **Vinderslev** Denmark
28 B4 **Vinderup** Denmark
74 F7 **Vindhya Range** India
28 B4 **Vinding** Ringkøbing Denmark
28 D4 **Vinding** Vejle Denmark
28 D5 **Vinding** Vejle Denmark
28 F6 **Vindinge** Denmark
21 O8 **Vineuil** Indre France
21 N6 **Vineuil** Loir-et-Cher France
95 R5 **Vineyard Haven** Massachusetts U.S.A.
48 G4 **Vinga** Romania
27 H12 **Vingåker, V** Sweden
40 B2 **Vingeanne** *R* France
21 L4 **Vingt Hanaps** France
68 G3 **Vinh** Vietnam
16 C3 **Vinhais** Portugal
68 J7 **Vinh Cam Ranh** *B* Vietnam
68 J6 **Vinh Giat** Vietnam
Vinh Linh *see* **Ho Xa**
69 G8 **Vinh Loi** Vietnam
68 G7 **Vinh Long** Vietnam
68 H3 **Vinh Son** *B* Vietnam
67 B6 **Vinh Yen** Vietnam
46 E3 **Vinica** Yugoslavia
99 L3 **Vining** Minnesota U.S.A.
107 P5 **Vinita** Oklahoma U.S.A.
27 C12 **Vinje** Norway
26 C8 **Vinjeora** Norway
48 H6 **Vînju Mare** Romania
28 D4 **Vinkel** Denmark
48 E5 **Vinkovci** Yugoslavia
26 M2 **Vinnelys** Norway
48 M1 **Vinnitsa** U.S.S.R.
48 H2 **Vinogradov** U.S.S.R.
19 P17 **Vinon** France
107 L7 **Vinson** Oklahoma U.S.A.
146 C7 **Vinson Massif** *mts* Antarctica
27 D10 **Vinstra** *R* Norway
71 E1 **Vintar** Luzon Philippines
99 O7 **Vinton** Iowa U.S.A.
111 C11 **Vinton** Louisiana U.S.A.
94 E8 **Vinton** Ohio U.S.A.
94 H9 **Vinton** Virginia U.S.A.
27 G12 **Vintrosa** Sweden
133 E6 **Vintter** Argentina
48 H4 **Vinţu de Jos** Romania
76 D2 **Vinukonda** India
33 P7 **Vinzelberg** East Germany
55 E3 **Vinzili** U.S.S.R.
102 C1 **Viola** California U.S.A.
100 H3 **Viola** Idaho U.S.A.
99 Q8 **Viola** Illinois U.S.A.
107 N4 **Viola** Kansas U.S.A.
99 Q6 **Viola** Wisconsin U.S.A.
101 P7 **Viola** Wyoming U.S.A.
118 B5 **Violet Grove** Alberta Canada
87 C11 **Vioolsdrif** Namibia
20 H6 **Vioreau, Grand Res. de** France
41 O4 **Vipiteno** Italy
33 R6 **Vipperow** East Germany
42 F4 **Vir** *isld* Yugoslavia
27 H13 **Virå** Sweden
71 G4 **Virac** Philippines
47 K5 **Virancık** Turkey
52 E3 **Virandozero** U.S.S.R.
48 G6 **Virciorova** Romania
119 R9 **Virden** Manitoba Canada
99 R10 **Virden** Illinois U.S.A.
29 J3 **Virdni** *mt* Finland
20 H3 **Vire** *R* France
21 J4 **Vire** France
27 G14 **Vireda** Sweden
142 B5 **Virehow, Mt** Western Australia Australia
87 B9 **Virei** Angola
22 G3 **Virelles** Belgium
22 H3 **Vireux** Belgium
48 H4 **Vîrfurile** Romania
101 P1 **Virgelle** Montana U.S.A.
130 G5 **Virgem da Lapa** Brazil
17 F3 **Virgen,Sa.de la** *mts* Spain
107 P4 **Virgil** Kansas U.S.A.
98 H5 **Virgil** South Dakota U.S.A.
102 C1 **Virgilia** California U.S.A.
94 J10 **Virgilina** Virginia U.S.A.
45 J1 **Virgilio** Italy
103 L5 **Virgin** *R* Arizona U.S.A.
113 L7 **Virgin Gorda** *isld* Virgin Is
14 D3 **Virginia** Ireland
89 E7 **Virginia** S Africa
94 H9 **Virginia** *state* U.S.A.
101 N7 **Virginia** Idaho U.S.A.
99 Q10 **Virginia** Illinois U.S.A.
99 O2 **Virginia** Minnesota U.S.A.
98 K9 **Virginia** Nebraska U.S.A.
95 M10 **Virginia Beach** Virginia U.S.A.
101 O4 **Virginia City** Montana U.S.A.
102 E2 **Virginia City** Nevada U.S.A.
117 L5 **Virginia Falls** Northwest Territories Canada
121 L4 **Virginiatown** Ontario Canada
113 L7 **Virgin Is** W Indies
103 K5 **Virgin Mts** Nev/Ariz U.S.A.
130 G6 **Virginópolis** Brazil
19 P13 **Virignin** France
26 J4 **Virihaure** Sweden
19 O14 **Viriville** France
133 D8 **Virjenes, C** Argentina
28 D4 **Virklund** Denmark
29 N9 **Virmasvesi** *L* Finland
29 N11 **Virolahti** Finland
99 Q6 **Viroqua** Wisconsin U.S.A.
42 H3 **Virovitica** Yugoslavia
42 J6 **Virpazar** Yugoslavia
29 K9 **Virrat** Finland
27 H12 **Virsbo** Sweden
27 H14 **Virserum** Sweden
29 N9 **Virtasalmi** Finland
48 J6 **Vîrtoapele** Romania
46 G1 **Vîrtoapele de Sus** Romania
22 K4 **Virton** Belgium
128 C5 **Virú** Peru
76 C6 **Virudunagar** India
52 C5 **Viru-Jaagup** U.S.S.R.
27 H14 **Vi, S** Sweden
42 G5 **Vis** *isld* Yugoslavia
102 E5 **Visalia** California U.S.A.
19 N16 **Visan** France
45 J1 **Visano** Italy
71 F5 **Visayan Sea** Philippines
28 E3 **Visborg** Denmark
28 B6 **Visby** Sønderjylland Denmark
28 A3 **Visby** Viborg Denmark
27 K14 **Visby** Sweden
130 G7 **Visconde do Rio Branco** Brazil
119 M7 **Viscount** Saskatchewan Canada
114 J3 **Viscount Melville Sd** Northwest Territories Canada
22 K2 **Visé** Belgium
48 E7 **Višegard** Yugoslavia
45 M3 **Viserba** Italy
16 B4 **Viseu** Portugal
48 J3 **Vişeu** *R* Romania
48 J3 **Vişeu de Sus** Romania
76 F2 **Vishakhapatam** India
52 H4 **Vishera** *R* U.S.S.R.
52 G5 **Vishkil'** U.S.S.R.
48 K1 **Vishnevets** U.S.S.R.
55 F5 **Vishnevka** U.S.S.R.
55 D3 **Vishnevogorsk** U.S.S.R.
55 C2 **Visim** U.S.S.R.
55 D1 **Visim** *R* U.S.S.R.
55 C2 **Visimo-Utkinsk** U.S.S.R.
46 G1 **Vişina Veche** Romania
27 G13 **Visingsö** Sweden
27 F14 **Viskafors** Sweden
27 F14 **Viskan** *R* Sweden
52 C6 **Viški** U.S.S.R.
28 G5 **Viskinge** Denmark
27 G15 **Vislanda** Sweden
124 D3 **Visnaga** Mexico
44 B2 **Viso** *mt* Italy
16 E6 **Viso del Marqués** Spain
46 E3 **Visoko** *mt* Yugoslavia
48 E7 **Visoko** Yugoslavia
146 G2 **Visokoi I** S Sandwich Is S Atlantic Oc
40 G5 **Visp** Switzerland
27 H15 **Vissefjärda** Sweden
32 L7 **Visselhövede** W Germany
28 E6 **Vissenbjerg** Denmark
40 G5 **Vissoie** Switzerland
102 G8 **Vista** California U.S.A.
128 F3 **Vista Alegre** Brazil
101 K8 **Vista Res** Nevada U.S.A.
28 F4 **Vistoft** Denmark
46 G3 **Vistonis, L** Greece
Vistula *R see* **Wisła** *R*
46 G1 **Vit** *R* Bulgaria
119 V9 **Vita** Manitoba Canada
76 B2 **Vita** India
54 B1 **Vitebsk** U.S.S.R.
42 E6 **Viterbo** Italy
42 H4 **Viterog Planina** *mts* Yugoslavia
16 C3 **Vitigudino** Spain
56 H4 **Vitim** *R* U.S.S.R.
58 F1 **Vitimskoye Ploskogor'ye** U.S.S.R.
46 E7 **Vitína** Greece
42 H5 **Vitina** Yugoslavia
130 H7 **Vitória** Brazil
17 F2 **Vitoria** Spain
130 H4 **Vitória da Conquista** Brazil
130 J10 **Vitoria de Sta Antão** Brazil
21 N5 **Vitray-en-Beauce** France
20 H5 **Vitré** France
123 N2 **Vitré,L** Quebec Canada
40 C2 **Vitrey** France
19 O18 **Vitrolles** France
21 P6 **Vitry-aux-Loges** France
22 D3 **Vitry-en-Artois** France
27 F11 **Vitsand** Sweden
Vitsi *mt see* **Vérnon** *mt*
26 M4 **Vittangi** *R* Sweden
28 A5 **Vittarp** Denmark
40 C1 **Vittel** France
28 D4 **Vitten** Denmark
27 J12 **Vittinge** Sweden
120 K10 **Vittoria** Ontario Canada
43 F12 **Vittoria** Sicily
43 F13 **Vittoriosa** Malta
42 E3 **Vittorio Ven** Italy
27 G15 **Vittsjö** Sweden
45 R7 **Vitulano** Italy
26 N5 **Vitvattnet** Sweden
40 F7 **Viu** Italy
28 C5 **Viuf** Denmark
18 H7 **Vivarais, Mts du** France
28 E3 **Vive** Denmark
17 G5 **Viver** Spain
16 B1 **Vivero** Spain
44 D1 **Viverone, L. di** Italy
51 J2 **Vivi** U.S.S.R.
109 O3 **Vivian** Louisiana U.S.A.
98 F6 **Vivian** South Dakota U.S.A.
19 N16 **Viviers** France
20 G4 **Vivier-sur-Mer, Le** France
28 E4 **Vivild** Denmark
21 L5 **Vivoin** France
138 D6 **Vivonne** South Australia Australia
18 F6 **Vivonne** France
133 F5 **Vivorata** Argentina
26 M4 **Vivunki** Sweden
124 C4 **Vizcaino,Des.de** Mexico
124 B4 **Vizcaino,Sa** *mts* Mexico
17 F1 **Vizcaya** *prov* Spain
47 J3 **Vize** Turkey
50 G1 **Vize,Ostrova** *islds* U.S.S.R.
52 G2 **Vizhas** U.S.S.R.
76 F1 **Vizianagaram** India
45 P1 **Vižinada** Yugoslavia
52 H4 **Vizinga** U.S.S.R.
48 L6 **Viziru** Romania
48 D1 **Vizovice** Czechoslovakia
43 F11 **Vizzini** Sicily
25 B5 **Vlaardingen** Netherlands
48 L3 **Vlădeni** Romania
46 E2 **Vladičin Han** Yugoslavia
52 F6 **Vladimir** U.S.S.R.
48 F6 **Vladimirci** Yugoslavia
55 D4 **Vladimirovka** U.S.S.R.
52 E6 **Vladimirskaya Oblast'** *prov* U.S.S.R.
54 E1 **Vladimirskiy Tupik** U.S.S.R.
53 B8 **Vladimir Volynskiy** U.S.S.R.
59 K3 **Vladivostok** U.S.S.R.
52 E5 **Vladychnoye** U.S.S.R.
48 K4 **Vlăhiţa** Romania
46 E2 **Vlajna** *mt* Yugoslavia
142 A5 **Vlaming Hd** Western Australia Australia
48 E6 **Vlasenica** Yugoslavia
48 F6 **Vlašić** *mt* Yugoslavia
46 E2 **Vlasotince** Yugoslavia
31 K7 **Vlčany** Czechoslovakia
25 C2 **Vlieland** *isld* Netherlands
25 D2 **Vliestroom** Netherlands
25 A6 **Vlissingen** Netherlands
25 F6 **Vlodrop** Netherlands
46 C4 **Vlorë** Albania
32 J8 **Vlotho** W Germany
31 H7 **Vltava** *R* Czechoslovakia
52 E6 **Vnukovo** *airport* U.S.S.R.
45 L1 **Vo** Italy
109 H5 **Voca** Texas U.S.A.
38 J6 **Vöcklabruck** Austria
107 K2 **Voda** Kansas U.S.A.
68 H7 **Vo Dat** Vietnam
28 B6 **Vodder** Denmark
47 H1 **Voditsa** Bulgaria
52 E4 **Vodla** *R* U.S.S.R.
52 E4 **Vodlozero, Oz** *L* U.S.S.R.
30 H6 **Vodňany** Czechoslovakia
42 F4 **Vodnjan** Yugoslavia
52 H3 **Vodnyy** U.S.S.R.
28 E2 **Vodskov** Denmark
15 G2 **Voe** Shetland Scotland
28 D4 **Voel** Denmark
28 E3 **Voer** Denmark
32 E9 **Voerde** W Germany
32 F10 **Voerde** W Germany
28 D4 **Voerladegard** Denmark
28 F2 **Voerså** Denmark
85 C7 **Vofnjama** Liberia
86 B4 **Vogemt**Nigeria
41 O3 **Vogelkar Sp** *mt* Austria
36 G2 **Vogelsberg** *mt* W Germany
44 F2 **Voghera** Italy
45 L2 **Voghiera** Italy
28 C3 **Vognsild** Denmark
41 H5 **Vogogna** Italy
Vohemar *see* **Iharaña**
37 N4 **Vohenstrauss** W Germany
Vohibinany *see* **Ampasimanolotra**
87 H13 **Vohimena, Tanjona** *C* Madagascar
36 F1 **Vöhl** W Germany
52 C5 **Võhma** U.S.S.R.
37 J7 **Vöhringen** W Germany
32 F10 **Vohwinkel** W Germany
88 G3 **Voi** Kenya
33 S4 **Voigdehgn** East Germany
12 D1 **Voil,L** Scotland
48 L3 **Voineşti** Romania
40 C7 **Voiron** France
38 M7 **Voitsberg** Austria
46 F5 **Voïvïïs** *L* Greece
28 C6 **Vojens** Denmark
26 H6 **Vojmsjön** *L* Sweden
37 N3 **Vojtanov** Czechoslovakia
48 E5 **Vojvodina** *aut terr* Yugoslavia
52 G5 **Vokhma** *R* U.S.S.R.
29 P7 **Voknavolok** U.S.S.R.
30 H6 **Vokyně** Czechoslovakia
52 H3 **Vol'** *R* U.S.S.R.
30 H7 **Volary** Czechoslovakia
98 A4 **Volborg** Montana U.S.A.
131 B3 **Volcan,Cerro del** *pk* Chile
106 D2 **Volcano** Colorado U.S.A.
Volcano B *see* **Uchiura wan** *B*
135 U5 **Volcanoes Nat. Park** Hawaiian Is
131 F6 **Volcán, Sa. del** *ra* Argentina
55 D2 **Volchansk** U.S.S.R.
55 H4 **Volchikha** U.S.S.R.
52 E5 **Volchina** *R* U.S.S.R.
54 H8 **Volch'ya** *R* U.S.S.R.
28 D4 **Voldby** Denmark
28 F4 **Voldby** Denmark
28 E4 **Voldum** Denmark
25 D4 **Volendam** Netherlands
45 J1 **Volfa Mantovana** Italy
99 P7 **Volga** *R* Iowa U.S.A.
98 K5 **Volga** South Dakota U.S.A.
52 E5 **Volga** U.S.S.R.
52 E6 **Volga** *R* U.S.S.R.
52 E4 **Volgo-Balt** *canal* U.S.S.R.
53 F9 **Volgograd** U.S.S.R.
53 F9 **Volgogradskaya Oblast'** *prov* U.S.S.R.
52 D6 **Volgo, Oz** *L* U.S.S.R.
26 J7 **Volgsele** Sweden
98 J7 **Volin** South Dakota U.S.A.
47 H6 **Volissós** Greece
37 J4 **Volkach** W Germany
25 B5 **Volkerak** Netherlands
38 L8 **Völkermarkt** Austria
37 J3 **Völkershausen** W Germany
52 D5 **Volkhov** U.S.S.R.
36 B5 **Völklingen** W Germany
32 K10 **Volkmarsen** W Germany
48 L1 **Volkovintsy** U.S.S.R.
31 P2 **Volkovysk** U.S.S.R.
32 L8 **Völksen** W Germany
89 F6 **Volksrust** S Africa
25 E3 **Vollenhove** Netherlands
22 G2 **Vollezele** Belgium
32 J9 **Völmerstod** *mt* W Germany
36 C5 **Volmunster** France
21 L6 **Volnay** Sarthe France
99 U6 **Volney** Michigan U.S.A.
44 F3 **Vol Noci, L. di** Italy
54 F8 **Vol'nogorsk** U.S.S.R.
55 F4 **Vol'noye** U.S.S.R.
54 G9 **Vol'nyansk** U.S.S.R.
51 J1 **Volochanka** U.S.S.R.
48 K1 **Volochisk** U.S.S.R.
52 F6 **Volodarsk** U.S.S.R.
55 E4 **Volodarskoye** U.S.S.R.
52 F4 **Volodskaya** U.S.S.R.
52 E5 **Vologda** U.S.S.R.
36 B7 **Vologne** *R* France
52 E4 **Vologodskaya Oblast'** *prov* U.S.S.R.
52 D6 **Volok** U.S.S.R.
52 E6 **Volokolamsk** U.S.S.R.
52 G2 **Volokovaya** U.S.S.R.
52 G2 **Volonga** U.S.S.R.
19 Q16 **Volonne** France
46 F5 **Vólos** Greece
52 E4 **Voloshka** U.S.S.R.
52 C5 **Volosovo** U.S.S.R.
48 H2 **Volosyanka** U.S.S.R.
52 D5 **Volot** U.S.S.R.
48 H2 **Volovets** U.S.S.R.
33 O8 **Völpke** East Germany
33 S5 **Völschow** East Germany
53 G8 **Vol'sk** U.S.S.R.
28 E2 **Volstrup** Denmark
130 H10 **Volta** Brazil
85 E7 **Volta** *R* Ghana
41 N7 **Volta** Italy
85 D6 **Volta Blanche** *R* Burkina/Ghana
98 F1 **Voltaire** North Dakota U.S.A.
142 F2 **Voltaire, C** Western Australia Australia
85 D7 **Volta,L** Ghana
85 D6 **Volta Noire** *R* Burkina
130 G8 **Volta Redonda** Brazil
85 D6 **Volta Rouge** *R* Burkina/Ghana
42 D5 **Volterra** Italy
52 F3 **Volteva** U.S.S.R.
44 E3 **Voltri** Italy
45 R8 **Volturara Irpina** Italy
45 Q7 **Volturno** *R* Italy
46 F4 **Vólvi, L** Greece
19 P17 **Volx** France
52 G6 **Volzhsk** U.S.S.R.
53 F9 **Volzhskiy** U.S.S.R.
42 F6 **Vomano** *R* Italy
106 H2 **Vona** Colorado U.S.A.
118 L6 **Vonda** Saskatchewan Canada
87 H12 **Vondrozo** Madagascar
22 J3 **Vonêche** Belgium
116 K5 **Von Frank Mt** Alaska U.S.A.
52 F3 **Vonga** U.S.S.R.
28 C5 **Vonge** Denmark
40 B3 **Vonges** France
46 D6 **Vónitsa** Greece
129 H5 **Von Martius,Cachoeira** *rapids* Brazil
28 D6 **Vonsbæk** Denmark
28 C6 **Vonsild** Denmark
143 E7 **Von Truer Tableland** Western Australia Australia
25 B4 **Voorburg** Netherlands
25 B5 **Voorne** Netherlands
25 B4 **Voorschoten** Netherlands
25 F4 **Voorst** Netherlands
25 E4 **Voorthuizen** Netherlands
29 T9 **Vopnafjördhur** *inlet* Iceland
29 T9 **Vopnafjördhur** Iceland
25 F6 **Vopst** W Germany
29 J8 **Vörå** Finland
41 K4 **Vorab** *mt* Switzerland
41 L3 **Vorarlberg** *prov* Austria
38 N7 **Vorau** Austria
28 C5 **Vorbasse** Denmark
25 F4 **Vorden** Netherlands
32 H8 **Vörden** W Germany
38 L7 **Vordernberg** Austria
41 J4 **Vorder Rhein** *R* Switzerland
28 H6 **Vordingborg** Denmark
19 P14 **Voreppe** France
54 D3 **Vorga** U.S.S.R.
28 B4 **Vorgod** Denmark
46 G5 **Voriai Sporádhes** *islds* Greece
50 F2 **Vorkuta** U.S.S.R.
27 E11 **Vorma** *R* Norway
28 D3 **Vorning** Denmark
55 G3 **Vorob'yevo** U.S.S.R.
53 F8 **Vorona** *R* U.S.S.R.
54 C3 **Voronevo** U.S.S.R.
54 L4 **Voronezh** *R* U.S.S.R.
54 E5 **Voronezh** Ukrainskaya S.S.R. U.S.S.R.
54 L5 **Voronezh** Voronezhskaya obl U.S.S.R.
53 E8 **Voronezhskaya Oblast'** *prov* U.S.S.R.
48 M1 **Voronovitsa** U.S.S.R.
52 F2 **Voronov, Mys** *C* U.S.S.R.
55 D2 **Vorontsovka** U.S.S.R.
50 H1 **Vorontsovo** U.S.S.R.
52 C6 **Vorontsovo** U.S.S.R.
52 E1 **Voron'ya** *R* U.S.S.R.
52 F5 **Voron'ye** U.S.S.R.
54 L8 **Voroshilovgrad** U.S.S.R.
52 G5 **Voroshno** U.S.S.R.
54 N1 **Vorovskogo, im** U.S.S.R.
54 F5 **Vorozhba** U.S.S.R.
33 S5 **Vorpommern** *reg* East Germany
33 N8 **Vorsfelde** W Germany
54 G6 **Vorskala** *R* U.S.S.R.
52 F6 **Vorsma** U.S.S.R.
52 C5 **Võrtsjäry** U.S.S.R.
52 C5 **Võru** U.S.S.R.
28 E4 **Vorup** Denmark
55 D1 **Vor'ya** *R* U.S.S.R.
55 D1 **Vor'yapaul'** U.S.S.R.
52 H3 **Vorykva** *R* U.S.S.R.
40 E2 **Vosges** *mt* France
36 B7 **Vosges** *dept* France
55 C4 **Voskresenskoye** Bashkirskaya A.S.S.R. U.S.S.R.
52 G6 **Voskresenskoye** Gor'kovskaya obl U.S.S.R.
52 E5 **Voskresenskoye** Vologodskaya obl U.S.S.R.
89 C3 **Vosloosrus** S Africa
55 F4 **Vosnesenka** U.S.S.R.
27 B11 **Voss** Norway
54 D9 **Vossiyatskoye** U.S.S.R.
56 B6 **Vost Kazakhstanskaya Oblast'** *prov* U.S.S.R.
52 E1 **Vostochnaya Litsa** U.S.S.R.
57 H2 **Vostochno-Kounradskiy** U.S.S.R.
56 E4 **Vostochnyy Sayan** *mts* U.S.S.R.
146 F11 **Vostok** *U.S.S.R. Base* Antarctica
135 M9 **Vostok I** Pacific Oc
55 E1 **Vostykhoy** U.S.S.R.
109 N5 **Votaw** Texas U.S.A.
109 N5 **Voth** Texas U.S.A.
31 H6 **Votice** Czechoslovakia
52 H6 **Votkinsk** U.S.S.R.
137 O4 **Vot Tandé** *isld* Vanuatu
130 E7 **Votuporanga** Brazil
16 B4 **Vouga** *R* Portugal
21 L8 **Vouillé** Vienne France
46 E5 **Voulgára** *mt* Greece
46 E5 **Voulgarélion** Greece
19 N15 **Voulte, la** France
68 H6 **Voeune** Cambodia
21 M8 **Vouneuil-sur-Vienne** France
46 E4 **Voúrinos** *mt* Greece
21 K5 **Voutré** France
21 J8 **Vouvant** France
21 M7 **Vouvray** France
21 P7 **Vouzeron** France
22 G5 **Vouziers** France
21 P6 **Vouzon** France
21 O5 **Voves** France
27 H10 **Voxna** Sweden
27 H10 **Voxnan** Sweden
27 G14 **Voxtorp** Sweden
52 H5 **Voya** *R* U.S.S.R.
99 O1 **Voyageurs Nat. Park** Minnesota U.S.A.
51 P3 **Voyampolka** U.S.S.R.
48 J1 **Voynilov** U.S.S.R.
52 D2 **Voynitsa** U.S.S.R.
Vöyri *see* **Vörå**
52 J3 **Voyvozh** U.S.S.R.
52 H3 **Voy Vozh** U.S.S.R.
52 G3 **Vozhayel'** U.S.S.R.
52 F4 **Vozhega** U.S.S.R.
52 E4 **Vozhe, Oz** *L* U.S.S.R.
52 H5 **Vozhgaly** U.S.S.R.
52 G3 **Vozhgora** U.S.S.R.
54 C9 **Voznesensk** U.S.S.R.
52 E4 **Voznesenye** U.S.S.R.
55 F4 **Vozvyshenka** U.S.S.R.
28 D2 **Vrå** Denmark
48 E2 **Vráble** Czechoslovakia
27 C12 **Vrådalsv** *L* Norway
53 D10 **Vradiyevka** U.S.S.R.
28 C4 **Vrads** Denmark
46 E6 **Vrakhnéïka** Greece
42 H5 **Vran** *mt* Yugoslavia
48 K5 **Vrancea** *reg* Romania
48 K5 **Vrancei, Muntii** *mts* Romania
47 O13 **Vranganiótika** Greece
65 J3 **Vrangel'** U.S.S.R.
147 P3 **Vrangelya, Os** *isld* U.S.S.R.
42 H5 **Vranica** *mt* Yugoslavia
46 E2 **Vranje** Yugoslavia
48 G2 **Vranov** Czechoslovakia
22 G1 **Vrasene** Belgium
46 F1 **Vratsa** Bulgaria
55 E1 **Vray** *L* U.S.S.R.
42 H4 **Vrbas** *R* Yugoslavia
31 K5 **Vrbno** Czechoslovakia
31 J5 **Vrchlabi** Czechoslovakia
48 F5 **Vrdnik** Yugoslavia
89 F6 **Vrede** S Africa
32 E8 **Vreden** W Germany
32 G7 **Vrees** W Germany
28 D2 **Vrensted** Denmark
28 F6 **Vresen** *isld* Denmark
22 H4 **Vress** France
20 G3 **Vrétot, le** France
27 G12 **Vretstorp** Sweden
42 H5 **Vrgorac** Yugoslavia
76 D5 **Vriddhachalam** India
28 C4 **Vridsted** Denmark
25 G2 **Vries** Netherlands
25 G4 **Vriezenveen** Netherlands
27 G14 **Vrigstad** Sweden
41 K4 **Vrin** Switzerland
22 H4 **Vringe-aux-Bois** France
28 A3 **Vrist** Denmark
22 F3 **Vrith-St.Léger** France
22 H5 **Vrizy** France
28 A5 **Vrøgum** Denmark
22 B3 **Vron** France
47 H6 **Vrondádhes** Greece
46 F8 **Vrondamás** Greece
25 G4 **Vroomshoop** Netherlands
28 C4 **Vroue** Denmark
48 G5 **Vršac** Yugoslavia
45 P1 **Vrsar** Yugoslavia
48 E1 **Vrútky** Czechoslovakia
89 D6 **Vryburg** S Africa
89 G6 **Vryheid** S Africa
37 O5 **Všeruby** Czechoslovakia
37 P4 **Všeruby** Czechoslovakia
31 K6 **Vsetín** Czechoslovakia
55 C1 **Vsevolodo Blagodatskoye** U.S.S.R.
48 E2 **Vtáčnik** *mt* Czechoslovakia
19 P12 **Vuache, Mt de** France
68 G2 **Vu Ban** Vietnam
46 G3 **Vŭcha** *R* Bulgaria
46 D2 **Vučitrn** Yugoslavia
20 G7 **Vue** France
25 D5 **Vught** Netherlands
48 E5 **Vuka** *R* Yugoslavia
48 E5 **Vukovar** Yugoslavia
118 D8 **Vulcan** Alberta Canada
48 H5 **Vulcan** Romania
43 G10 **Vulcano, I** Italy
46 F1 **Vŭlchedrŭm** Bulgaria
47 J1 **Vŭlchidol** Bulgaria
67 B7 **Vu Liet** Vietnam
48 L5 **Vulkaneshty** U.S.S.R.
43 G8 **Vulture, Monte** Italy
103 M8 **Vulture Mts** Arizona U.S.A.
68 J4 **Vung Da Nang** *B* Vietnam
68 J7 **Vung Phan Thiet** *B* Vietnam
68 H7 **Vung Tau** Vietnam
89 F2 **Vungu** *R* Zimbabwe
26 M5 **Vuodas** Sweden
29 N7 **Vuokatti** Finland
29 O11 **Vuoksa** *L* U.S.S.R.
29 O10 **Vuoksenniska** Finland
29 N7 **Vuolijoki** Finland
26 L5 **Vuollerim** Sweden
29 N5 **Vuostimo** Finland
29 N3 **Vuotso** Finland
26 N2 **Vuovdasoaivve** *mt* Norway
47 H2 **Vŭrbitsa** Bulgaria
52 G6 **Vurnary** U.S.S.R.
46 F1 **Vŭrshets** Bulgaria
28 C2 **Vust** Denmark
48 L4 **Vutcani** Romania
55 D4 **Vvedenka** U.S.S.R.
100 F8 **Vya** Nevada U.S.A.
52 E2 **Vyalozero, Oz** *L* U.S.S.R.
52 F5 **Vyaltsevo** U.S.S.R.
29 P9 **Vyartsilya** U.S.S.R.
52 G5 **Vyatka** *R* U.S.S.R.
52 H6 **Vyatskiye Polyany** U.S.S.R.
59 K2 **Vyazemskiy** U.S.S.R.
54 F1 **Vyaz'ma** U.S.S.R.
54 E1 **Vyazma** *R* U.S.S.R.
52 F6 **Vyazniki** U.S.S.R.
52 C6 **Vybor** U.S.S.R.
29 O11 **Vyborg** U.S.S.R.
29 N11 **Vyborgskiy Zaliv** *G* U.S.S.R.
52 H4 **Vychegda** *R* U.S.S.R.
31 J5 **Vychodočeský** *reg* Czechoslovakia
56 F5 **Vydrino** U.S.S.R.
52 E3 **Vyg** *R* U.S.S.R.
48 N4 **Vygoda** U.S.S.R.
54 F3 **Vygonichi** U.S.S.R.
52 D3 **Vygozero, Oz** *L* U.S.S.R.
48 G2 **Vyhorlát** *mt* Czechoslovakia
52 F6 **Vyksa** U.S.S.R.
52 H3 **Vym'** *R* U.S.S.R.
52 G4 **Vymsk** U.S.S.R.
52 C5 **Vyra** U.S.S.R.
52 D5 **Vyritsa** U.S.S.R.
8 C2 **Vyrnwy, L** Wales
8 C2 **Vyrnwy R** Wales
54 B6 **Vyshgorod** U.S.S.R.
31 K6 **Vyškov** Czechoslovakia
31 L6 **Vysoká** *mt* Czechoslovakia
52 G6 **Vysokaya Gora** U.S.S.R.
52 J4 **Vysokaya Parma** *plateau* U.S.S.R.
31 J6 **Vysoké Mýto** Czechoslovakia
59 L1 **Vysokogornyy** U.S.S.R.
52 E6 **Vysokovsk** U.S.S.R.
31 O3 **Vysokoye** U.S.S.R.
29 O11 **Vysotsk** U.S.S.R.
38 K4 **Vyšši Brod** Czechoslovakia
52 E4 **Vytegra** U.S.S.R.
52 G3 **Vyya** *R* U.S.S.R.
59 M2 **Vzmor'ye** U.S.S.R.

W

85 D6 **Wa** Ghana
86 H5 **Waajid** Somalia
25 D5 **Waal** *R* Netherlands
25 B5 **Waalhaven** Netherlands
25 D5 **Waalwijk** Netherlands
80 H2 **Waamo lidow** Kenya
25 D2 **Waardgronden** Netherlands
22 F1 **Waarschoot** Belgium
120 D2 **Wababimiga L** Ontario Canada
118 C5 **Wabamun** Alberta Canada
123 U6 **Wabana** Newfoundland Canada
118 D3 **Wabasca** Alberta Canada
117 Q7 **Wabasca** *R* Alberta Canada
110 J3 **Wabash** *R* U.S.A.
111 F7 **Wabash** Arkansas U.S.A.
94 B6 **Wabash** Indiana U.S.A.
99 O5 **Wabasha** Minnesota U.S.A.
113 G10 **Wabasso** Florida U.S.A.
99 L5 **Wabasso** Minnesota U.S.A.
120 F4 **Wabatongushi L** Ontario Canada
99 S4 **Wabeno** Wisconsin U.S.A.
Wabern *see* **Egling**
118 K1 **Wabigoon** Ontario Canada
121 R4 **Wabino** *R* Quebec Canada
120 A2 **Wabinosh L** Ontario Canada
120 C2 **Waboose Dam** Ontario Canada
120 F6 **Wabos** Ontario Canada
119 T4 **Wabowden** Manitoba Canada
31 L2 **Wąbrzezno** Poland
58 G5 **Wabu Hu** *L* China
115 N7 **Wabush** Labrador, Nfld Canada
102 E2 **Wabuska** Nevada U.S.A.
112 H4 **Waccamaw** *R* South Carolina U.S.A.
112 J3 **Waccamaw, L** North Carolina U.S.A.
113 D8 **Waccasassa B** Florida U.S.A.
95 M9 **Wachapreague** Virginia U.S.A.
36 H5 **Wachbach** W Germany
36 E5 **Wachenheim** W Germany
37 K4 **Wachenroth** W Germany
33 R7 **Wachow** East Germany
22 F1 **Wachtbeke** Belgium
25 F6 **Wachtendonk** W Germany
36 G3 **Wächtersbach** W Germany
32 G7 **Wachtum** W Germany
95 Q4 **Wachusett Res** Massachusetts U.S.A.
135 M11 **Wachusett Shoal** Pacific Oc
71 H7 **Waci** Indonesia
32 K4 **Wacken** W Germany
122 G2 **Waco** Quebec Canada
98 J9 **Waco** Nebraska U.S.A.
109 K4 **Waco** Texas U.S.A.
99 N5 **Waconia** Minnesota U.S.A.
122 G2 **Wacouno R** Quebec Canada
77 K6 **Wad** Pakistan
142 D6 **Wadara Ra** Western Australia Australia
60 H10 **Wadayama** Japan
86 E3 **Wad Banda** Sudan
139 H8 **Waddamana** Tasmania Australia
84 F4 **Waddān** Libya
25 D2 **Waddenzee** Netherlands
9 F4 **Waddesdon** England
9 F1 **Waddington** England
95 M2 **Waddington** New York U.S.A.
117 L10 **Waddington, Mt** British Columbia Canada
94 B8 **Waddy** Kentucky U.S.A.
141 L7 **Waddy Pt** Queensland Australia
112 J2 **Wade** North Carolina U.S.A.
8 B7 **Wadebridge** England
119 O7 **Wadena** Saskatchewan Canada
99 L3 **Wadena** Minnesota U.S.A.
36 B4 **Wadern** W Germany
32 H9 **Wadersloh** W Germany
112 G3 **Wadesboro** North Carolina U.S.A.
123 T4 **Wadham Is** Newfoundland Canada
117 K10 **Wadhams** British Columbia Canada
9 G5 **Wadhurst** England
80 G6 **Wadi es Sir** Jordan
84 K5 **Wâdi Gimâl I** Egypt
86 F1 **Wadi Halfa** Sudan
79 F8 **Wādi Mūsā** Jordan
111 L8 **Wadley** Alabama U.S.A.
112 E5 **Wadley** Georgia U.S.A.
86 F3 **Wad Medani** Sudan
31 L6 **Wadowice** Poland
102 E2 **Wadsworth** Nevada U.S.A.
94 F5 **Wadsworth** Ohio U.S.A.
13 G6 **Wadworth** England
65 G7 **Waegwan** S Korea
109 K6 **Waelder** Texas U.S.A.
68 F4 **Waeng** Thailand
65 E2 **Wafang** China
Wafangdian *see* **Fu Xian**
77 A5 **Wafra** Iran
61 O6 **Waga-gawa** *R* Japan
120 B2 **Wagaming** Ontario Canada
111 H10 **Wagarville** Alabama U.S.A.
32 J7 **Wagenfeld** W Germany
25 E5 **Wageningen** Netherlands
139 H6 **Wagga Wagga** New South Wales Australia
74 E8 **Waghai** India
36 F5 **Waghäusel** W Germany
143 B10 **Wagin** Western Australia Australia
101 R1 **Wagner** Montana U.S.A.
98 H6 **Wagner** South Dakota U.S.A.
107 P6 **Wagoner** Oklahoma U.S.A.
106 F5 **Wagon Mound** New Mexico U.S.A.
100 F6 **Wagontire** Oregon U.S.A.
106 D4 **Wagon Wheel Gap** Colorado U.S.A.
112 H3 **Wagram** North Carolina U.S.A.
31 K3 **Wągrowiec** Poland
100 J3 **Waha** Idaho U.S.A.
83 K9 **Wahalkada Tank** Sri Lanka
145 E2 **Waharoa** New Zealand
102 R12 **Wahiawa** Hawaiian Is
145 E2 **Wahi,L** New Zealand
36 F4 **Wahlen** W Germany
36 C2 **Wahn** W Germany
32 K7 **Wahnebergen** W Germany
98 K8 **Wahoo** Nebraska U.S.A.
98 K3 **Wahpeton** North Dakota U.S.A.
33 S9 **Wahrenbrück** East Germany
33 N7 **Wahrenholz** W Germany
103 L3 **Wah Wah Mts** Utah U.S.A.
76 A2 **Wai** India
135 U6 **Waiahukini** Hawaiian Is
135 T3 **Waiakoa** Hawaiian Is
135 O1 **Waialeale** *pk* Hawaiian Is
102 R11 **Waialee** Hawaiian Is
102 R11 **Waialua** Hawaiian Is
102 R12 **Waianae** Hawaiian Is
102 R12 **Waianae Ra** Hawaiian Is
144 C6 **Waianakarua** New Zealand
144 B7 **Waianiwa** New Zealand
145 G2 **Waiapu** *R* New Zealand
144 B6 **Waiatoto R** New Zealand
144 D5 **Waiau** New Zealand
144 A6 **Waiau** *R* New Zealand
145 F3 **Waiau R** New Zealand
36 G6 **Waiblingen** W Germany
37 N4 **Waidhaus** W Germany
31 J7 **Waidhofen** Austria
38 L6 **Waidhofen an der Ybbs** Austria
71 B3 **Waigama** Indonesia
143 G8 **Waigen Lakes** Western Australia Australia
71 C3 **Waigeo** W Irian
71 C3 **Waigeo** *isld* W Irian
37 J4 **Waigolshausen** W Germany
144 C6 **Waihao Forks** New Zealand
145 D1 **Waiharara** New Zealand
145 E2 **Waiheke I** New Zealand
145 E2 **Waihi** New Zealand
144 A7 **Waihoaka** New Zealand
144 C7 **Waihola** New Zealand
145 D4 **Waihopai** *R* New Zealand
145 D1 **Waihopo** New Zealand
144 C5 **Waiho R** New Zealand
145 E2 **Waihou** New Zealand
145 E2 **Waihou R** New Zealand
145 F3 **Waihua** New Zealand
71 J9 **Waikabubak** Sumba Indonesia
144 B6 **Waikaia** New Zealand
144 B6 **Waikaka** New Zealand
145 E4 **Waikanae** New Zealand
102 S12 **Waikane** Hawaiian Is
145 F3 **Waikareiti, L** New Zealand
145 E2 **Waikare, L** New Zealand
145 F3 **Waikaremoana, L** New Zealand
145 E2 **Waikaretu** New Zealand
144 D5 **Waikari** New Zealand
145 E3 **Waikato** New Zealand
145 E4 **Waikawa** New Zealand
144 B7 **Waikawa** New Zealand
71 J9 **Waikelo Teluk** *B* Sumba Indonesia
138 E5 **Waikerie** South Australia Australia
135 U5 **Waikii** Hawaiian Is
142 A4 **Waikiki** Western Australia Australia
102 S12 **Waikiki Beach** Hawaiian Is
71 L9 **Waiklibang** Indonesia
145 F3 **Waikohu** New Zealand
145 F3 **Waikokopu** New Zealand
144 B7 **Waikotkoi** New Zealand
144 C6 **Waikouaiti** New Zealand
144 A7 **Waikouro** New Zealand
102 V13 **Wailuku** Hawaiian Is
144 B7 **Waimahaka** New Zealand
144 A4 **Waimakariri R** New Zealand
145 D1 **Waimamaka** New Zealand
145 F3 **Waimana** New Zealand
102 S12 **Waimanalo** Hawaiian Is
144 C4 **Waimangaroa** New Zealand
71 J9 **Waimanguar** Indonesia
145 F3 **Waimarama** New Zealand
144 C4 **Waimarie** New Zealand
144 C6 **Waimate** New Zealand
145 E2 **Waimauku** New Zealand
135 U4 **Waimea** Hawaiian Is
135 Q2 **Waimea** Hawaiian Is
102 R11 **Waimea B** Hawaiian Is
70 G6 **Waimenda** Sulawesi
22 L3 **Waimes** Belgium
145 E3 **Waimiha** New Zealand
9 G1 **Wainfleet** England
71 K9 **Waingapu** Sumba Indonesia
145 E4 **Waingawa** New Zealand
135 O1 **Wainiha** Hawaiian Is
144 C5 **Wainihinihi** New Zealand
99 S3 **Wainola** Michigan U.S.A.
144 C6 **Wainono Lagoon** New Zealand
118 G6 **Wainwright** Alberta Canada
116 G1 **Wainwright** Alaska U.S.A.
145 F3 **Waioeka R** New Zealand
135 U6 **Waiohinu** Hawaiian Is
145 E1 **Waiolira** New Zealand
145 F3 **Waiotapu** New Zealand
145 E3 **Waiouru** New Zealand
144 B7 **Waipahi** New Zealand
102 R12 **Waipahu** Hawaiian Is
145 F3 **Waipaoa** New Zealand
145 D1 **Waipapakauri** New Zealand
145 E2 **Waipa R** New Zealand
144 D5 **Waipara** New Zealand
145 F3 **Waipawa** New Zealand
144 C6 **Waipiata** New Zealand
135 U4 **Waipio** Hawaiian Is
145 G3 **Waipiro** New Zealand
144 C6 **Waipori, L** New Zealand
145 E1 **Waipu** New Zealand
145 F3 **Waipukurau** New Zealand
145 F3 **Wairakei** New Zealand
145 E4 **Wairarapa, L** New Zealand
145 D4 **Wairau Valley** New Zealand
144 B7 **Wairio** New Zealand
145 F3 **Wairoa** New Zealand
145 E2 **Wairoa R** New Zealand
145 E1 **Wairua** *R* New Zealand
144 B7 **Wairuna** New Zealand
71 L9 **Wairunu** Flores Indonesia
37 L4 **Waischenfeld** W Germany
145 F3 **Waitahanui** New Zealand
144 C5 **Waitaha R** New Zealand
144 B6 **Waitahuna** New Zealand
145 E2 **Waitakaruru** New Zealand
144 C6 **Waitaki, L** New Zealand
145 E1 **Waitangi** New Zealand
145 E3 **Waitara** New Zealand
145 E4 **Waitarere** New Zealand
144 D6 **Waitati** New Zealand
140 B5 **Waite** *R* N Terr Australia
145 F1 **Waitemata Harb** New Zealand
143 D8 **Waite, Mt** Western Australia Australia
145 E2 **Waitoa** New Zealand
145 E3 **Waitomo** New Zealand
145 E3 **Waitotara** *R* New Zealand
145 E3 **Waitotara** New Zealand
100 G3 **Waitsburg** Washington U.S.A.
119 M6 **Waitville** Saskatchewan Canada
145 E2 **Waiuku** New Zealand
144 C5 **Waiuta** New Zealand
145 E2 **Waiwera** New Zealand
144 B7 **Waiwera South** New Zealand
71 B1 **Wajabula** Halmahera Indonesia
71 C2 **Wajag** *isld* Indonesia
71 B2 **Wajamli** Indonesia
61 K8 **Wajima** Japan
86 H5 **Wajir** Kenya
86 D5 **Waka** Zaire
60 D12 **Wakamatsu** Japan
60 B12 **Wakamatsu-jima** *isld* Japan
120 H5 **Wakami L** Ontario Canada
144 C5 **Wakanui** New Zealand
145 F3 **Wakarara Range** New Zealand
94 A5 **Wakarusa** Indiana U.S.A.
61 J10 **Wakasa-wan** *B* Japan
144 B6 **Wakatipu, L** New Zealand
119 M6 **Wakaw** Saskatchewan Canada
60 J12 **Wakayama** *prefect* Japan
60 J11 **Wakayama** Japan
61 P7 **Wakayanagi** Japan
107 L2 **Wa Keeney** Kansas U.S.A.
121 P7 **Wakefield** Quebec Canada
13 G6 **Wakefield** England
127 J2 **Wakefield** Jamaica
145 D4 **Wakefield** New Zealand
107 O2 **Wakefield** Kansas U.S.A.
99 R3 **Wakefield** Michigan U.S.A.
98 K7 **Wakefield** Nebraska U.S.A.
95 Q5 **Wakefield** Rhode I U.S.A.
95 K10 **Wakefield** Virginia U.S.A.
112 J2 **Wake Forest** North Carolina U.S.A.
134 H6 **Wake I** Pacific Oc
68 B4 **Wakema** Burma
122 H5 **Wakenam** Quebec Canada
94 A5 **Wakerton** Indiana U.S.A.
74 E1 **Wakhan** *reg* Afghanistan
60 H11 **Waki** Japan
60 O4 **Wakinosawa** Japan
107 N5 **Wakita** Oklahoma U.S.A.
60 P1 **Wakkanai** Japan
87 F11 **Wakkerstroom** S Africa
Wako *see* **Watcomb**
120 G6 **Wakomata L** Ontario Canada
139 G6 **Wakool** New South Wales Australia
119 S9 **Wakopa** Manitoba Canada
71 H7 **Wakoru** Indonesia
98 F4 **Wakpala** South Dakota U.S.A.
71 C3 **Wakre** W Irian
71 K9 **Waku** Indonesia
87 C8 **Waku Kungo** Angola
113 C7 **Wakulla** Florida U.S.A.
120 K2 **Wakwayowkastic** *R* Ontario Canada
103 L6 **Walapai** Arizona U.S.A.
83 K11 **Walawe Ganga** *R* Sri Lanka
33 O8 **Walbeck** East Germany
36 D6 **Walbourg** France
94 D5 **Walbridge** Ohio U.S.A.
31 J5 **Wałbrzych** Poland
36 H1 **Walburg** W Germany
139 K4 **Walcha** New South Wales Australia
38 G7 **Walchen** Austria
41 O2 **Walchensee** *L* W Germany
25 A5 **Walcheren** Netherlands
38 F6 **Walchsee** Austria
117 K8 **Walcott** British Columbia Canada
98 K3 **Walcott** North Dakota U.S.A.
101 T8 **Walcott** Wyoming U.S.A.
142 E3 **Walcott Inlet** W Australia
101 M7 **Walcott, L., Res** Idaho U.S.A.
22 G3 **Walcourt** Belgium
31 J2 **Wałcz** Poland
38 L5 **Wald Aist** *R* Austria
36 F5 **Waldangeloch** W Germany
36 D4 **Waldböckelheim** W Germany
36 C2 **Waldbreitbach** W Germany
36 D2 **Waldbröl** W Germany
36 G5 **Waldbrunn** Baden-Württemberg W Germany
36 G5 **Waldbrunn** Hessen W Germany
143 B6 **Waldburg Ra** W Australia
33 T9 **Walddrehna** East Germany
118 K8 **Waldeck** Saskatchewan Canada
36 G1 **Waldeck** W Germany
101 T9 **Walden** Colorado U.S.A.
95 N5 **Walden** New York U.S.A.
37 O2 **Waldenberg** East Germany
36 G6 **Waldenbuch** W Germany
Waldenburg *see* **Wałbrzych**
110 F6 **Waldenburg** Arkansas U.S.A.
36 H5 **Waldenburg** W Germany
37 N4 **Waldershof** W Germany
36 D5 **Waldfischbach** W Germany
118 L6 **Waldheim** Saskatchewan Canada
37 P1 **Waldheim** East Germany
36 H1 **Waldkappel** W Germany
40 G1 **Waldkirch** W Germany
30 H7 **Waldkirchen** W Germany
36 F4 **Waldmichelbach** W Germany
37 O5 **Waldmünchen** W Germany
37 N4 **Wald Naab** *R* W Germany
25 F6 **Waldniel** W Germany
118 B9 **Waldo** British Columbia Canada
109 O2 **Waldo** Arkansas U.S.A.
113 E8 **Waldo** Florida U.S.A.
107 M2 **Waldo** Kansas U.S.A.
94 D6 **Waldo** Ohio U.S.A.
99 T6 **Waldo** Wisconsin U.S.A.
100 C6 **Waldo L** Oregon U.S.A.
95 L8 **Waldorf** Maryland U.S.A.
99 N6 **Waldorf** Minnesota U.S.A.
100 A5 **Waldport** Oregon U.S.A.
119 P8 **Waldron** Saskatchewan Canada
109 N1 **Waldron** Arkansas U.S.A.
146 G14 **Waldron, C** Antarctica
37 N3 **Waldsassen** W Germany
41 H2 **Waldshut** W Germany
37 J7 **Waldstetten** W Germany
37 N4 **Waldthurn** W Germany
36 B5 **Waldwisse** France
71 H5 **Waleabahi** *isld* Sulawesi
71 H5 **Waleakodi** *isld* Sulawesi
71 H5 **Walea,Selat** *str* Sulawesi
70 N9 **Waleri** Java
8 C3 **Wales** *princ* U.K.
116 C4 **Wales** Alaska U.S.A.
99 P2 **Wales** Minnesota U.S.A.
98 H1 **Wales** North Dakota U.S.A.
103 N2 **Wales** Utah U.S.A.
115 L4 **Wales I** Northwest Territories Canada
85 D6 **Walewale** Ghana
33 O5 **Walfisch** East Germany
139 J4 **Walgett** New South Wales Australia
146 B7 **Walgreen Coast** Antarctica
98 J1 **Walhalla** North Dakota U.S.A.
112 D3 **Walhalla** South Carolina U.S.A.
37 N5 **Walhalla** *mt* W Germany
70 N9 **Walikukun** Java
143 A8 **Walkaway** Western Australia Australia
33 R5 **Walkendorf** East Germany
33 N9 **Walkenried** W Germany
140 B6 **Walker** *R* N Terr Australia
141 F3 **Walker** *R* Queensland Australia
100 C8 **Walker** California U.S.A.
99 P7 **Walker** Iowa U.S.A.
107 L3 **Walker** Kansas U.S.A.
111 F11 **Walker** Louisiana U.S.A.
99 M2 **Walker** Minnesota U.S.A.
110 B4 **Walker** Missouri U.S.A.
102 E2 **Walker** *R* Nevada U.S.A.
98 E4 **Walker** South Dakota U.S.A.
89 A10 **Walker B** S Africa
13 E2 **Walkerburn** Scotland
113 J10 **Walker Cay** *isld* Bahamas
119 V4 **Walker L** Manitoba Canada
122 E3 **Walker L** Quebec Canada
116 K3 **Walker L** Alaska U.S.A.
102 F3 **Walker L** Nevada U.S.A.
146 B7 **Walker Mts** Antarctica
102 G6 **Walker Pk** California U.S.A.
140 D2 **Walker R** N Terr Australia
70 D2 **Walker Ra** Sabah
141 J5 **Walkerston** Queensland Australia
94 G8 **Walkersville** West Virginia U.S.A.

95 K5 **Wellsboro** Pennsylvania U.S.A.
99 O7 **Wellsburg** Iowa U.S.A.
95 L4 **Wellsburg** New York U.S.A.
94 G6 **Wellsburg** West Virginia U.S.A.
145 E2 **Wellsford** New Zealand
117 N9 **Wells Gray Prov. Park** British Columbia Canada
143 E7 **Wells, L** Western Australia Australia
119 R1 **Wells L** Manitoba Canada
142 F3 **Wells, Mt** Western Australia Australia
9 G2 **Wells-next-the-sea** England
95 P2 **Wells River** Vermont U.S.A.
94 E7 **Wellston** Ohio U.S.A.
110 E2 **Wellsville** Missouri U.S.A.
94 K4 **Wellsville** New York U.S.A.
101 O8 **Wellsville** Utah U.S.A.
103 K9 **Wellton** Arizona U.S.A.
119 S8 **Wellwood** Manitoba Canada
86 G3 **Welo** *prov* Ethiopia
38 K5 **Wels** Austria
25 D6 **Welschap** Netherlands
36 B4 **Welschbillig** W Germany
36 E1 **Welschenennest** W Germany
122 F8 **Welsford** New Brunswick Canada
109 P5 **Welsh** Louisiana U.S.A.
8 D2 **Welshampton** England
142 B2 **Welshpool** *dist* Perth, W Aust Australia
122 F9 **Welshpool** New Brunswick Canada
8 C2 **Welshpool** Wales
13 H6 **Welton** England
32 G9 **Welver** W Germany
119 Q8 **Welwyn** Saskatchewan Canada
9 F4 **Welwyn Garden City** England
36 H6 **Welzheim** W Germany
8 D2 **Wem** England
86 D6 **Wema** Zaire
142 A1 **Wembley** *dist* Perth, W Aust Australia
117 O8 **Wembley** Alberta Canada
142 A1 **Wembley Downs** *dist* Perth, W Aust Australia
8 B7 **Wembury** England
37 K6 **Wemding** W Germany
25 A5 **Wemeldinge** Netherlands
12 D2 **Wemyss B** Scotland
126 F2 **Wemyss Bight** Eleuthera Bahamas
65 C5 **Wen'an** China
100 E2 **Wenatchee** Washington U.S.A.
67 C7 **Wenchang** China
67 G3 **Wencheng** China
85 D7 **Wenchi** Ghana
67 A1 **Wenchuan** China
102 D1 **Wendel** California U.S.A.
101 L7 **Wendell** Idaho U.S.A.
98 K3 **Wendell** Minnesota U.S.A.
112 J2 **Wendell** North Carolina U.S.A.
36 D4 **Wendelsheim** W Germany
37 L5 **Wendelstein** W Germany
9 G3 **Wenden** England
103 L8 **Wenden** Arizona U.S.A.
36 D2 **Wenden** W Germany
65 E6 **Wendeng** China
33 Q6 **Wendisch Priborn** East Germany
33 O7 **Wendland** *reg* W Germany
9 G2 **Wendling** England
100 C5 **Wendling** Oregon U.S.A.
86 G4 **Wendo** Ethiopia
33 O5 **Wendorf** East Germany
9 F4 **Wendover** England
101 M9 **Wendover** Utah U.S.A.
98 B7 **Wendover** Wyoming U.S.A.
98 F5 **Wendte** South Dakota U.S.A.
22 E1 **Wenduine** Belgium
120 G5 **Wenebegon L** Ontario Canada
67 B3 **Weng'an** China
36 B4 **Wengerohr** W Germany
67 D2 **Wengjiang** China
67 E4 **Wengyuan** China
65 D7 **Wen He** *R* China
36 G3 **Wenings** W Germany
67 A1 **Wenjiang** China
68 K1 **Wenli** China
67 G2 **Wenling** China
141 G2 **Wenlock** Queensland Australia
141 F1 **Wenlock** *R* Queensland Australia
128 A7 **Wenman** *isld* Galapagos Is
32 L8 **Wennigsen** W Germany
41 N3 **Wenns** Austria
99 R8 **Wenona** Illinois U.S.A.
67 C1 **Wenquan** China
67 A5 **Wenshan** China
65 C7 **Wenshang** China
65 B6 **Wenshui** China
67 B2 **Wenshui** China
57 K4 **Wensu** China
13 G6 **Wentbridge** England
138 F5 **Wentworth** New South Wales Australia
13 G6 **Wentworth** England
95 Q3 **Wentworth** New Hampshire U.S.A.
98 K6 **Wentworth** South Dakota U.S.A.
122 J8 **Wentworth Centre** Nova Scotia Canada
110 F3 **Wentzville** Missouri U.S.A.
65 B7 **Wenxi** China
65 B7 **Wen Xian** China
37 N5 **Wenzenbach** W Germany
67 G3 **Wenzhou** China
113 F10 **Weohyakapka L** Florida U.S.A.
100 B9 **Weott** California U.S.A.
89 E7 **Wepener** S Africa
22 H3 **Wepion** Belgium
69 B10 **We, Pulau** *isld* Sumatra
33 T7 **Werbellin** East Germany
33 T7 **Werbellinsee** *L* East Germany
33 P7 **Werben** East Germany
33 S9 **Werbig** East Germany
22 K3 **Werbomont** Belgium
87 D11 **Werda** Botswana
37 N2 **Werdau** East Germany
33 R8 **Werder** East Germany
86 J4 **Werdër** Ethiopia
32 G10 **Werdohl** W Germany
32 G9 **Werl** W Germany
32 G7 **Werlte** W Germany
36 C1 **Wermelskirchen** W Germany
33 R10 **Wermsdorf** East Germany
36 H4 **Wern** *R* W Germany
37 N4 **Wernberg** W Germany
32 G9 **Werne** W Germany
37 J4 **Werneck** W Germany
117 F3 **Wernecke Mts** Yukon Territory Canada
98 D2 **Werner** North Dakota U.S.A.
33 T7 **Werneuchen** East Germany
36 H3 **Wernfeld** W Germany
119 U2 **Wernham L** Manitoba Canada
25 C6 **Wernhout** Netherlands
33 N9 **Wernigerode** East Germany
37 J1 **Werra** *R* E & W Germany
139 G7 **Werribee** Victoria Australia
138 F5 **Werrimull** Victoria Australia
139 K4 **Werris Cr** New South Wales Australia
32 G9 **Werse** *R* W Germany
37 K7 **Wertach** *R* W Germany
36 H4 **Wertheim** W Germany
37 K6 **Wertingen** W Germany
71 M9 **Werula** Indonesia
25 D3 **Wervershoof** Netherlands
32 E9 **Wesel** W Germany
36 D5 **Weselberg** W Germany
33 R6 **Wesenberg** East Germany
32 L9 **Weser** *R* W Germany
32 H5 **Weser** *est* W Germany
107 J3 **Weskan** Kansas U.S.A.
86 G4 **Weska Weka** Ethiopia
109 K9 **Weslaco** Texas U.S.A.
121 N8 **Weslemkoon L** Ontario Canada
95 U2 **Wesley** Maine U.S.A.
123 T4 **Wesleyville** Newfoundland Canada
94 G4 **Wesleyville** Pennsylvania U.S.A.
32 F5 **Wesse** W Germany
32 J4 **Wesselburen** W Germany
36 B2 **Wesseling** W Germany
140 D1 **Wessel Is** N Terr Australia
98 H5 **Wessington** South Dakota U.S.A.
98 H5 **Wessington Springs** South Dakota U.S.A.
111 D8 **Wesson** Arkansas U.S.A.
111 F10 **Wesson** Mississippi U.S.A.
139 G6 **West** Victoria Australia
111 G8 **West** Mississippi U.S.A.
109 K4 **West** Texas U.S.A.
32 G8 **West** W Germany
94 C7 **West Alexandria** Ohio U.S.A.
140 B1 **West Alligator** *R* N Terr Australia
99 S7 **West Allis** Wisconsin U.S.A.
138 C5 **Westall,Pt** South Australia Australia
13 G4 **West Auckland** England
113 B7 **West B** Florida U.S.A.
111 G12 **West B** Louisiana U.S.A.
109 N6 **West B** Texas U.S.A.
140 A3 **West Baines** *R* N Terr Australia
8 D6 **West Bay** England
111 L11 **Westbay** Florida U.S.A.
119 O7 **West Bend** Saskatchewan Canada
99 M7 **West Bend** Iowa U.S.A.
99 S6 **West Bend** Wisconsin U.S.A.
75 M7 **West Bengal** *prov* India
111 J8 **West Blocton** Alabama U.S.A.
99 L9 **Westboro** Missouri U.S.A.
99 Q4 **Westboro** Wisconsin U.S.A.
119 T8 **Westbourne** Manitoba Canada
99 P8 **West Branch** Iowa U.S.A.
94 C2 **West Branch** Michigan U.S.A.
13 G6 **West Bretton** England
117 O11 **Westbridge** British Columbia Canada
9 E2 **West Bridgford** England
9 E2 **West Bromwich** England
95 R3 **Westbrook** Maine U.S.A.
99 L5 **Westbrook** Minnesota U.S.A.
108 F3 **Westbrook** Texas U.S.A.
95 Q2 **West Burke** Vermont U.S.A.
15 G2 **West Burra** Shetland Scotland
139 H8 **Westbury** Tasmania Australia
8 D5 **Westbury** England
101 O1 **West Butte** *mt* Montana U.S.A.
139 H6 **Westby** New South Wales Australia
98 C1 **Westby** North Dakota U.S.A.
99 Q6 **Westby** Wisconsin U.S.A.
144 A6 **West C** New Zealand
127 H4 **West Caicos** *isld* Turks & Caicos Is
12 E2 **West Calder** Scotland
143 C11 **West Cape Howe** Western Australia Australia
99 S8 **West Chicago** Illinois U.S.A.
106 E3 **Westcliffe** Colorado U.S.A.
109 M6 **West Columbia** Texas U.S.A.
99 O5 **West Concord** Minnesota U.S.A.
102 G7 **West Covina** California U.S.A.
9 G6 **Westdean** England
99 N8 **West Des Moines** Iowa U.S.A.
122 J9 **West Dover** Nova Scotia Canada
141 K2 **West End** *dist* Brisbane, Qnsld Australia
126 E1 **West End** Grand Bahama I
102 G6 **Westend** California U.S.A.
112 H2 **West End** North Carolina U.S.A.
22 D1 **Westende** Belgium
113 H11 **West End Pt** Bahamas
113 J11 **West End Settlement** Grand Bahama I
32 L4 **Westensee** *L* W Germany
25 G3 **Westerbork** Netherlands
144 C5 **Westerfield** New Zealand
9 G5 **Westerham** England
22 H1 **Westerlo** Belgium
98 J9 **Western** Nebraska U.S.A.
86 E4 **Western Equatoria** *prov* Sudan
76 A1 **Western Ghats** *mts* India
122 H10 **Western Hd** Nova Scotia Canada
120 K7 **Western Is** Ontario Canada
15 A3 **Western Isles** *reg* Scotland
139 H7 **Western Port** Victoria Australia
94 H7 **Westernport** Maryland U.S.A.
141 G5 **Western R** Queensland Australia
85 B4 **Western Sahara** *reg* Africa
134 A2 **Western Samoa** *islds* Pacific Oc
32 M9 **Westerode** W Germany
32 G6 **Westerstede** W Germany
36 D2 **Westerwald** *reg* W Germany
107 M3 **Westfall** Kansas U.S.A.
100 H6 **Westfall** Oregon U.S.A.
8 D2 **West Felton** England
142 B3 **Westfield** *dist* Perth, W Aust Australia
99 T10 **Westfield** Illinois U.S.A.
95 P4 **Westfield** Massachusetts U.S.A.
94 H4 **Westfield** New York U.S.A.
94 K5 **Westfield** Pennsylvania U.S.A.
99 R6 **Westfield** Wisconsin U.S.A.
122 F8 **Westfield Beach** New Brunswick Canada
110 B6 **West Fork** Arkansas U.S.A.
99 M6 **West Fork** *R* Minnesota U.S.A.
98 A1 **West Fork** *R* Montana U.S.A.
110 H4 **West Frankfort** Illinois U.S.A.
141 H7 **Westgate** Queensland Australia
9 H5 **Westgate** England
West Germany *see* **German Federal Republic**
8 C4 **West Glamorgan** *co* Wales
95 U1 **West Grand L** Maine U.S.A.
112 E6 **West Green** Georgia U.S.A.
9 F6 **West Grinstead** England
141 J7 **Westgrove** Queensland Australia
9 E3 **West Haddon** England
9 G5 **West Ham** England
94 E8 **West Hamlin** West Virginia U.S.A.
95 P6 **Westhampton Beach** Long I, New York U.S.A.
37 K7 **Westheim** W Germany
36 E4 **West Hofen** W Germany
109 K6 **Westhoff** Texas U.S.A.
36 C6 **Westhoffen** France
100 B1 **Westholme** British Columbia Canada
98 E1 **Westhope** North Dakota U.S.A.
68 A6 **West I** Andaman Is
83 M8 **West I** Cocos Is Indian Oc
146 J12 **West Ice Shelf** Antarctica
32 G10 **Westig** W Germany
127 **West Indies** *arch* Caribbean
94 F10 **West Jefferson** North Carolina U.S.A.
94 D7 **West Jefferson** Ohio U.S.A.
22 E1 **Westkapelle** Belgium
25 A6 **Westkapelle** Netherlands
15 D5 **West Kilbride** Scotland
100 F8 **West L** Nevada U.S.A.
110 J1 **West Lafayette** Indiana U.S.A.
94 F6 **West Lafayette** Ohio U.S.A.
100 A6 **Westlake** Oregon U.S.A.
141 G6 **Westland** Queensland Australia
144 B5 **Westland** *stat area* New Zealand
9 H3 **Westleton** England
99 P8 **West Liberty** Iowa U.S.A.
94 D9 **West Liberty** Kentucky U.S.A.
94 D6 **West Liberty** Ohio U.S.A.
13 E2 **West Linton** Scotland
118 D4 **Westlock** Alberta Canada
120 J10 **West Lorne** Ontario Canada
West Lothian *co see* **Lothian and Central** *regions*
122 H2 **West Magpie R** Quebec Canada
9 G5 **West Malling** England
94 C7 **West Manchester** Ohio U.S.A.
141 J8 **Westmar** Queensland Australia
121 O7 **Westmeath** Ontario Canada
14 D3 **Westmeath** *co* Ireland
110 F6 **West Memphis** Arkansas U.S.A.
9 G4 **West Mersea** England
94 G5 **West Middlesex** Pennsylvania U.S.A.
9 E2 **West Midlands** *co* England
94 C7 **West Milton** Ohio U.S.A.
106 E2 **Westminster** Colorado U.S.A.
95 L7 **Westminster** Maryland U.S.A.
112 D3 **Westminster** South Carolina U.S.A.
95 P3 **Westminster** Vermont U.S.A.
140 E3 **Westmoreland** Queensland Australia
107 O2 **Westmoreland** Kansas U.S.A.
95 P4 **Westmoreland** New Hampshire U.S.A.
110 K5 **Westmoreland** Tennessee U.S.A.
Westmorland *co see* **Cumbria**
127 H2 **Westmorland** *parish* Jamaica
103 J8 **Westmorland** California U.S.A.
87 E10 **West Nicholson** Zimbabwe
108 G6 **West Nueces** *R* Texas U.S.A.
8 D2 **Weston** England
144 C6 **Weston** New Zealand
70 D2 **Weston** Sabah
101 O7 **Weston** Idaho U.S.A.
94 C5 **Weston** Michigan U.S.A.
110 B2 **Weston** Missouri U.S.A.
98 K8 **Weston** Nebraska U.S.A.
94 D5 **Weston** Ohio U.S.A.
100 G4 **Weston** Oregon U.S.A.
94 G7 **Weston** West Virginia U.S.A.
98 A5 **Weston** Wyoming U.S.A.
89 E6 **Westonaria** S Africa
8 D5 **Weston-super-Mare** England
109 H2 **Westover** Texas U.S.A.
32 F6 **Westoverledingen** W Germany
113 G11 **West Palm Beach** Florida U.S.A.
95 R2 **West Paris** Maine U.S.A.
110 J3 **Westphalia** Indiana U.S.A.
107 P3 **Westphalia** Kansas U.S.A.
94 K5 **West Pike** Pennsylvania U.S.A.
110 E5 **West Plains** Missouri U.S.A.
139 G8 **West Point** Tasmania Australia
122 H4 **West Point** Quebec Canada
116 P4 **West Point** *mt* Alaska U.S.A.
102 D3 **West Point** California U.S.A.
112 B5 **West Point** Georgia U.S.A.
110 J1 **Westpoint** Indiana U.S.A.-
99 P9 **West Point** Iowa U.S.A.
94 B9 **West Point** Kentucky U.S.A.
111 H8 **West Point** Mississippi U.S.A.
95 N5 **West Point** New York U.S.A.
95 L9 **West Point** Virginia U.S.A.
111 L8 **West Point L** Alabama/Georgia
West Polder *see* **Markerwaard**
123 Q4 **Westport** Newfoundland Canada
14 B3 **Westport** Ireland
144 C4 **Westport** New Zealand
102 A2 **Westport** California U.S.A.
94 B7 **Westport** Indiana U.S.A.
95 O2 **Westport** New York U.S.A.
100 B3 **Westport** Oregon U.S.A.
98 H4 **Westport** South Dakota U.S.A.
110 H6 **Westport** Tennessee U.S.A.
100 A3 **Westport** Washington U.S.A.
118 A3 **West Prairie R** Alberta Canada
123 M10 **West Pt** Nova Scotia Canada
122 H7 **West Pt** Prince Edward I Canada
98 K8 **West Pt** Nebraska U.S.A.
122 G10 **West Pubnico** Nova Scotia Canada
126 A1 **Westpunt** Curaçao
13 G4 **West Rainton** England
119 Q5 **Westray** Manitoba Canada
15 F1 **Westray Firth** Orkney Scotland
120 J5 **Westree** Ontario Canada
36 C5 **Westrich** *reg* W Germany
117 L9 **West Road R** British Columbia Canada
13 F2 **Westruther** Scotland
123 P2 **West St. Modiste** Quebec Canada
110 H3 **West Salem** Illinois U.S.A.
94 E6 **West Salem** Ohio U.S.A.
99 P6 **West Salem** Wisconsin U.S.A.
145 F3 **Westshore** New Zealand
99 L7 **Westside** Iowa U.S.A.
100 E7 **West Side** Oregon U.S.A.
139 J7 **West Sister I** Tasmania Australia
7 L9 **West Sole** *oil rig* North Sea
95 Q2 **West Stewartstown** New Hampshire U.S.A.
9 F6 **West Sussex** *co* England
13 G5 **West Tanfield** England
25 D2 **West Terschelling** Netherlands
110 J2 **West Union** Illinois U.S.A.
99 P7 **West Union** Iowa U.S.A.
94 D8 **West Union** Ohio U.S.A.
94 G7 **West Union** West Virginia U.S.A.
94 C5 **West Unity** Ohio U.S.A.
117 L11 **Westview** British Columbia Canada
122 K8 **Westville** Nova Scotia Canada
111 L11 **Westville** Florida U.S.A.
99 T9 **Westville** Illinois U.S.A.
99 U8 **Westville** Indiana U.S.A.
107 Q6 **Westville** Oklahoma U.S.A.
94 G8 **West Virginia** *state* U.S.A.
22 D1 **West Vlaanderen** Belgium
8 B5 **Westward Ho** England
103 P2 **Westwater** Utah U.S.A.
111 F12 **Westwego** Louisiana U.S.A.
95 M4 **West Winfield** New York U.S.A.
141 K6 **Westwood** Queensland Australia
102 D1 **Westwood** California U.S.A.
109 L9 **Westworth** Texas U.S.A.
139 H5 **West Wyalong** New South Wales Australia
101 O5 **West Yellowstone** Montana U.S.A.
13 G6 **West Yorkshire** *co* England
71 O8 **Wetan** *isld* Indonesia
71 N8 **Wetar** *isld* Indonesia
71 N9 **Wetar, Selat** *str* Indonesia
118 D6 **Wetaskiwin** Alberta Canada
88 G4 **Wete** Tanzania
121 O3 **Wetetnagami** *R* Quebec Canada
37 M1 **Wethau** East Germany
13 G6 **Wetherby** England
68 B1 **Wetlet** Burma
106 E3 **Wetmore** Colorado U.S.A.
109 J6 **Wetmore** Texas U.S.A.
106 E3 **Wet Mts** Colorado U.S.A.
98 H4 **Wetonka** South Dakota U.S.A.
36 F3 **Wetter** *R* W Germany
36 F2 **Wetter** W Germany
32 F10 **Wetter** W Germany
36 F3 **Wetterau** *reg* W Germany
22 F1 **Wetteren** Belgium
41 M3 **Wetter Spitze** *mt* Austria
41 O3 **Wetterstein Geb** *mt* Austria
33 P9 **Wettin** East Germany
32 F8 **Wettringen** W Germany
107 O6 **Wetumka** Oklahoma U.S.A.
111 K9 **Wetumpka** Alabama U.S.A.
68 C1 **Wetwun** Burma
36 F2 **Wetzlar** W Germany
37 L3 **Wetzstein** *mt* East Germany
36 B1 **Wevelinghoven** W Germany
110 E1 **Wever** Iowa U.S.A.
113 B7 **Wewahitchka** Florida U.S.A.
136 J2 **Wewak** Papua New Guinea
107 O6 **Wewoka** Oklahoma U.S.A.
14 E4 **Wexford** *co* Ireland
14 E4 **Wexford** Ireland
14 E4 **Wexford B** Ireland
14 E4 **Wexford Harb** Ireland
118 L4 **Weyakwin L** Saskatchewan Canada
99 S5 **Weyauwega** Wisconsin U.S.A.
9 H2 **Weybourne** England
9 F5 **Weybridge** England
119 O9 **Weyburn** Saskatchewan Canada
38 L6 **Weyer** Austria
36 D2 **Weyerbusch** W Germany
99 P4 **Weyerhauser** Wisconsin U.S.A.
36 D6 **Weyersheim** France
33 M7 **Weyhausen** W Germany
9 E5 **Weyhill** England
122 G9 **Weymouth** Nova Scotia Canada
8 D6 **Weymouth** England
95 R4 **Weymouth** Massachusetts U.S.A.
141 G1 **Weymouth B** Queensland Australia
141 G2 **Weymouth,C** Queensland Australia
9 F5 **Wey, R** England
25 F4 **Wezep** Netherlands
145 E3 **Whakahora** New Zealand
145 E3 **Whakamaru** New Zealand
145 E3 **Whakapapa** New Zealand
145 E1 **Whakapara** New Zealand
145 F3 **Whakapunake** New Zealand
145 F4 **Whakataki** New Zealand
145 F2 **Whakatane** New Zealand
145 F3 **Whakatane** *R* New Zealand
68 D7 **Whale B** Burma
116 D10 **Whalebone C** Aleutian Is
113 K12 **Whale Cay** *isld* Bahamas
Whale I *see* **Motuhora I**
123 P2 **Whale I** Quebec Canada
9 E1 **Whaley Bridge** England
95 L10 **Whaleyville** Virginia U.S.A.
139 J3 **Whallan** *R* New South Wales Australia
13 F6 **Whalley** England
15 G2 **Whalsay** *isld* Shetland Scotland
13 G3 **Whalton** England
145 E4 **Whangaehu** New Zealand
145 E2 **Whangamata** New Zealand
145 E3 **Whangamomona** New Zealand
145 D4 **Whanganui Inlet** New Zealand
145 G2 **Whangaparaoa** New Zealand
145 E2 **Whangaparaoa Pen** New Zealand
145 D1 **Whangape** New Zealand
145 E2 **Whangape, L** New Zealand
145 E1 **Whangarei** New Zealand
145 D1 **Whangaroa** New Zealand
145 E1 **Whangaruru Harbour** New Zealand
145 E4 **Wharanui** New Zealand
145 F4 **Whareama** New Zealand
13 G6 **Wharfe, R** England
95 N6 **Wharton** New Jersey U.S.A.
94 J5 **Wharton** Pennsylvania U.S.A.
109 L6 **Wharton** Texas U.S.A.
144 C5 **Whataroa** New Zealand
145 F3 **Whatatutu** New Zealand
145 E2 **Whatawhata** New Zealand
99 O8 **What Cheer** Iowa U.S.A.
100 C1 **Whatcom, L** Washington U.S.A.
111 J10 **Whatley** Alabama U.S.A.
68 F6 **Whatthana Nakhon** Thailand
102 C2 **Wheatland** California U.S.A.
98 B7 **Wheatland** Wyoming U.S.A.
98 A8 **Wheatland Res** Wyoming U.S.A.
120 H10 **Wheatley** Ontario Canada
9 E4 **Wheatley** England
110 E7 **Wheatley** Arkansas U.S.A.
99 S8 **Wheaton** Illinois U.S.A.
107 O2 **Wheaton** Kansas U.S.A.
98 K4 **Wheaton** Minnesota U.S.A.
110 B5 **Wheaton** Missouri U.S.A.
8 C5 **Wheddon Cross** England
107 J2 **Wheeler** Kansas U.S.A.
100 B4 **Wheeler** Oregon U.S.A.
108 D8 **Wheeler** Texas U.S.A.
117 Q4 **Wheeler L** Northwest Territories Canada
110 J7 **Wheeler L** Alabama U.S.A.
103 K3 **Wheeler Pk** Nevada U.S.A.
106 E5 **Wheeler Pk** New Mexico U.S.A.
102 F6 **Wheeler Ridge** California U.S.A.
94 E8 **Wheelersburg** Ohio U.S.A.
102 E7 **Wheeler Springs** California U.S.A.
94 G6 **Wheeling** West Virginia U.S.A.
98 C1 **Wheelock** North Dakota U.S.A.
94 E9 **Wheelwright** Kentucky U.S.A.
140 E6 **Whelan,Mt** Queensland Australia
13 F5 **Whernside** *mt* England
9 E5 **Wherwell** England
138 C5 **Whidbey I** South Australia Australia
100 C1 **Whidbey I** Washington U.S.A.
111 M11 **Whigham** Georgia U.S.A.
142 C5 **Whim Creek** Western Australia Australia
138 B2 **Whinham, Mt** South Australia Australia
99 M2 **Whipholt** Minnesota U.S.A.
122 F9 **Whipple Pt** Nova Scotia Canada
9 F4 **Whipsnade** England
101 N1 **Whiskey Gap** Alberta Canada
119 T4 **Whiskey Jack Landing** Manitoba Canada
100 C9 **Whiskeytown** California U.S.A.
100 C9 **Whiskeytown-Shasta-Trinity Nat. Rec. Area** California U.S.A.
140 D5 **Whistleduck Creek** N Terr Australia
111 H11 **Whistler** Alabama U.S.A.
9 E2 **Whitacre** England
112 K1 **Whitakers** North Carolina U.S.A.
13 E5 **Whitbeck** England
123 T6 **Whitbourne** Newfoundland Canada
13 G4 **Whitburn** England
12 E2 **Whitburn** Scotland
121 M9 **Whitby** Ontario Canada
13 H5 **Whitby** England
9 F4 **Whitchurch** England
9 E5 **Whitchurch** England
8 D2 **Whitchurch** England
8 C4 **Whitchurch** Wales
111 E7 **White** *R* Arkansas U.S.A.
101 S10 **White** *R* Colorado U.S.A.
99 U6 **White** *R* Michigan U.S.A.
103 J3 **White** *R* Nevada U.S.A.
98 F6 **White** *R* South Dakota U.S.A.
98 K5 **White** South Dakota U.S.A.
108 F2 **White** *R* Texas U.S.A.
103 P2 **White** *R* Utah U.S.A.
100 D2 **White** *R* Washington U.S.A.
99 Q3 **White** *R* Wisconsin U.S.A.
123 Q3 **White B** Newfoundland Canada
118 J8 **White Bear** Saskatchewan Canada
123 P5 **White Bear L** *res* Newfoundland Canada
99 O4 **White Bear L** Minnesota U.S.A.
123 P6 **White Bear R** Newfoundland Canada
100 J4 **White Bird** Idaho U.S.A.
110 J5 **White Bluff** Tennessee U.S.A.
100 F3 **White Bluffs** Washington U.S.A.
122 E6 **White Brook** New Brunswick Canada
98 D4 **White Butte** South Dakota U.S.A.
119 W2 **Whitecap L** Manitoba Canada
111 E11 **White Castle** Louisiana U.S.A.
113 G10 **White City** Florida U.S.A.
107 O3 **White City** Kansas U.S.A.
106 F9 **White City** New Mexico U.S.A.
139 G4 **White Cliffs** New South Wales Australia
99 L10 **White Cloud** Kansas U.S.A.
94 B3 **White Cloud** Michigan U.S.A.
118 B4 **White Court** Alberta Canada
98 D1 **White Earth** North Dakota U.S.A.
108 E2 **Whiteface** Texas U.S.A.
95 O2 **Whiteface Mt** New York U.S.A.
120 J6 **Whitefish** Ontario Canada
117 Q11 **Whitefish** Idaho U.S.A.
99 U4 **Whitefish** *R* Michigan U.S.A.
101 L1 **Whitefish** Montana U.S.A.
99 T6 **Whitefish Bay** Wisconsin U.S.A.
118 E4 **Whitefish L** Alberta Canada
119 O2 **Whitefish L** Ontario Canada
116 K6 **Whitefish L** Alaska U.S.A.
99 V3 **Whitefish L** Michigan U.S.A.
99 M3 **Whitefish L** Minnesota U.S.A.
101 L1 **Whitefish L** Montana U.S.A.
119 N5 **White Fox** Saskatchewan Canada
115 N6 **Whitegull L** Quebec Canada
110 F2 **White Hall** Illinois U.S.A.
99 U6 **Whitehall** Michigan U.S.A.
101 N4 **Whitehall** Montana U.S.A.
99 P5 **Whitehall** Wisconsin U.S.A.
12 E5 **Whitehaven** England
95 M5 **White Haven** Pennsylvania U.S.A.
14 F2 **Whitehead** N Ireland
12 D4 **Whitehill** Scotland
116 N2 **White Hills** Alaska U.S.A.
103 K6 **White Hills** Arizona U.S.A.
117 F5 **Whitehorse** Yukon Territory Canada
100 D8 **White Horse** California U.S.A.
101 L9 **White Horse Pass** Nevada U.S.A.
127 M3 **White Horses** Jamaica
White I *see* **Kvitøya**
146 K9 **White I** Antarctica
115 L4 **White I** Northwest Territories Canada
145 F2 **White I** New Zealand
13 F1 **Whitekirk** Scotland
140 A5 **White L** N Terr/W Aust Australia
142 G5 **White, L** Western Australia Australia
111 D12 **White L** Louisiana U.S.A.
99 U6 **White L** Michigan U.S.A.
98 H6 **White L** South Dakota U.S.A.
99 S4 **White Lake** Wisconsin U.S.A.
94 A7 **Whiteland** Indiana U.S.A.
139 J8 **Whitemark** Tasmania Australia
116 F4 **White Mountain** Alaska U.S.A.
14 E4 **White Mt** Ireland
116 O4 **White Mts** Alaska U.S.A.
102 F4 **White Mts** California U.S.A.
95 Q2 **White Mts** New Hampshire U.S.A.
117 P7 **Whitemud** *R* Alberta Canada
86 F3 **White Nile** *R* Sudan
86 F3 **White Nile** *prov* Sudan
86 F2 **White Nile Dam** Sudan
89 A4 **White Nossob** *R* Namibia
112 K3 **White Oak** North Carolina U.S.A.
109 M2 **White Oak Cr** Texas U.S.A.
109 O2 **White Oak L** Arkansas U.S.A.
118 K1 **White Otter L** Ontario Canada
98 D5 **White Owl** South Dakota U.S.A.
9 E5 **Whiteparish** England
117 F6 **White Pass** Br Col/Alaska Canada/U.S.A.
100 D3 **White Pass** Washington U.S.A.
94 B5 **White Pigeon** Michigan U.S.A.
99 R3 **White Pine** Michigan U.S.A.
100 K2 **Whitepine** Montana U.S.A.
112 D1 **White Pine** Tennessee U.S.A.
103 J2 **White Pine Ra** Nevada U.S.A.
95 N5 **White Plains** New York U.S.A.
112 G1 **White Plains** North Carolina U.S.A.
123 R2 **White Pt** Belle Isle, Nfld
118 B8 **White R** British Columbia Canada
127 L2 **White R** Jamaica
94 B8 **White R** Indiana U.S.A.
98 F6 **White R** South Dakota U.S.A.
120 E4 **White River** Ontario Canada
95 P3 **White River Junc** Vermont U.S.A.
103 J3 **White River Valley** Nevada U.S.A.
100 J8 **White Rock** Nevada U.S.A.
109 O9 **White Rock** Texas U.S.A.
107 M2 **White Rock Cr** Kansas U.S.A.
103 K3 **White Rock Peak** Nevada U.S.A.
White Russia *see* **Belorusskaya S.S.R.**
117 K9 **Whitesail L** British Columbia Canada
100 D4 **White Salmon** Washington U.S.A.
117 P6 **Whitesand** *R* Alberta Canada
8 B7 **Whitesand B** England
119 P7 **Whitesand R** Saskatchewan Canada
108 A3 **White Sands Missile Ra** New Mexico U.S.A.
108 A3 **White Sands Nat. Mon** New Mexico U.S.A.
95 M3 **Whitesboro** New York U.S.A.
109 L2 **Whitesboro** Texas U.S.A.
112 C4 **Whitesburg** Georgia U.S.A.
94 E9 **Whitesburg** Kentucky U.S.A.
White Sea *see* **Beloye More**
109 L9 **White Settlement** Texas U.S.A.
118 F1 **Whiteshell** Manitoba Canada
100 B4 **Whiteson** Oregon U.S.A.
119 U2 **Whitestone L** Manitoba Canada
101 P3 **White Sulphur Springs** Montana U.S.A.
110 K4 **Whitesville** Kentucky U.S.A.
94 K4 **Whitesville** New York U.S.A.
94 F9 **Whitesville** West Virginia U.S.A.
100 E3 **White Swan** Washington U.S.A.
119 M4 **Whiteswan L** Saskatchewan Canada
98 A1 **Whitetail** Montana U.S.A.
112 J3 **Whiteville** North Carolina U.S.A.
110 G6 **Whiteville** Tennessee U.S.A.
85 D7 **White Volta** *R* Ghana
94 B7 **Whitewater** *R* Indiana U.S.A.
101 S1 **Whitewater** Montana U.S.A.
106 B9 **Whitewater** New Mexico U.S.A.
99 S7 **Whitewater** Wisconsin U.S.A.
113 F12 **Whitewater B** Florida U.S.A.
120 A2 **Whitewater L** Ontario Canada
138 B4 **White Well** South Australia Australia
141 G5 **Whitewood** Queensland Australia
119 P8 **Whitewood** Saskatchewan Canada
98 C5 **Whitewood** South Dakota U.S.A.
98 J5 **Whitewood, L** South Dakota U.S.A.
109 L2 **Whitewright** Texas U.S.A.
139 H6 **Whitfield** Victoria Australia
13 F4 **Whitfield Hall** England
127 H2 **Whithorn** Jamaica
12 D4 **Whithorn** Scotland
145 E2 **Whitianga** New Zealand
117 G6 **Whiting** *R* Br Col/Alaska Canada/U.S.A.
107 P2 **Whiting** Kansas U.S.A.
95 N7 **Whiting** New Jersey U.S.A.
12 C3 **Whiting B** Scotland
95 P4 **Whitingham Res** Vermont U.S.A.
118 K6 **Whitkow** Saskatchewan Canada
118 F9 **Whitla** Alberta Canada
8 B4 **Whitland** Wales
101 O1 **Whitlash** Montana U.S.A.
13 G3 **Whitley Bay** England
94 C10 **Whitley City** Kentucky U.S.A.
98 F4 **Whitlocks Crossing** South Dakota U.S.A.
95 R4 **Whitman** Massachusetts U.S.A.
98 E7 **Whitman** Nebraska U.S.A.
98 H1 **Whitman** North Dakota U.S.A.
100 G3 **Whitman Mission Nat. Hist. Site** Washington U.S.A.
112 F3 **Whitmire** South Carolina U.S.A.
146 C8 **Whitmore Mts** *mts* Antarctica
121 M7 **Whitney** Ontario Canada
8 C3 **Whitney** England
98 C7 **Whitney** Nebraska U.S.A.
103 J5 **Whitney** Nevada U.S.A.
100 G5 **Whitney** Oregon U.S.A.
109 K4 **Whitney, L** Texas U.S.A.
102 F5 **Whitney, Mt** California U.S.A.
109 J7 **Whitsett** Texas U.S.A.
9 H5 **Whitstable** England
141 J5 **Whitsunday I** Queensland Australia
109 J3 **Whitt** Texas U.S.A.
94 G7 **Whittaker** West Virginia U.S.A.
99 M6 **Whittemore** Iowa U.S.A.
94 D2 **Whittemore** Michigan U.S.A.
116 N6 **Whittier** Alaska U.S.A.
102 F8 **Whittier** California U.S.A.
13 G3 **Whittingham** England
139 H7 **Whittlesea** Victoria Australia
9 F2 **Whittlesey** England
139 H5 **Whitton** New South Wales Australia
8 C3 **Whitton** Wales
13 G4 **Whittonstall** England
141 F7 **Whitula** *R* Queensland Australia
9 E1 **Whitwell** England
112 B2 **Whitwell** Tennessee U.S.A.
114 J5 **Wholdaia L** Northwest Territories Canada
138 D5 **Whyalla** South Australia Australia
123 L8 **Whycocomagh** Nova Scotia Canada
139 G3 **Whyjonta** New South Wales Australia
68 D3 **Wiang Pa Pao** Thailand
68 D2 **Wiang Phrao** Thailand
120 J8 **Wiarton** Ontario Canada
31 K5 **Wiązów** Poland
98 B2 **Wibaux** Montana U.S.A.
13 G6 **Wibsey** England
107 N4 **Wichita** Kansas U.S.A.
109 J1 **Wichita** *R* Texas U.S.A.
109 J2 **Wichita Falls** Texas U.S.A.
109 J1 **Wichita Mts** Oklahoma U.S.A.
15 E2 **Wick** Scotland
32 G10 **Wickede** W Germany
103 M8 **Wickenburg** Arizona U.S.A.
122 J4 **Wickenden L** Quebec Canada
143 C10 **Wickepin** Western Australia Australia
100 C1 **Wickersham** Washington U.S.A.
108 D4 **Wickett** Texas U.S.A.
9 G4 **Wickford** England
95 Q5 **Wickford** Rhode I U.S.A.
142 B5 **Wickham** Western Australia Australia
9 E6 **Wickham** England
139 G7 **Wickham, C** Tasmania Australia
140 A3 **Wickham Mt** N Terr Australia
121 S7 **Wickham West** Quebec Canada
100 D6 **Wickiup Res** Oregon U.S.A.
110 G5 **Wickliffe** Kentucky U.S.A.
14 E4 **Wicklow** *co* Ireland
14 E4 **Wicklow** Ireland
8 D4 **Wickwar** England
31 L4 **Widawka** *R* Poland
36 G5 **Widdern** W Germany
121 L6 **Widdifield** Ontario Canada
90 A11 **Wideawake** Ascension I
141 L7 **Wide B** Queensland Australia
116 J8 **Wide B** Alaska U.S.A.
8 C6 **Widecombe-in-the-Moor** England
138 B2 **Wide Gum** *R* South Australia Australia
94 G8 **Widen** West Virginia U.S.A.
141 H8 **Widgeegoara** *R* Queensland Australia
143 D9 **Widgiemooltha** Western Australia Australia
71 B3 **Widi, Pulau Pulau** *islds* Indonesia
36 F4 **Wiebelsbach** W Germany
36 C5 **Wiebelskirchen** W Germany
31 K2 **Więcbork** Poland
36 C2 **Wied** W Germany
Wiedenbrück *see* **Rheda-Wiedenbrück**
32 H6 **Wiefelstede** W Germany
33 O10 **Wiehe** East Germany
32 J8 **Wiehengebirge** *hills* W Germany
36 D2 **Wiehl** W Germany
31 M2 **Wielbark** Poland
31 J3 **Wieleń** Poland
31 M6 **Wieliczka** Poland
31 L4 **Wieluń** Poland
38 O5 **Wien** Austria
38 O6 **Wiener Neustadt** Austria
32 M7 **Wienhausen** W Germany
116 M4 **Wien L** Alaska U.S.A.
33 O7 **Wiepke** East Germany
31 O5 **Wieprz** *R* Poland
33 N7 **Wieren** W Germany
109 O4 **Wiergate** Texas U.S.A.
25 D3 **Wieringen** Netherlands
25 C3 **Wieringermeer** Netherlands
31 L4 **Wieruszów** Poland
31 N4 **Wierzbnik** Poland
31 L2 **Wierzchucin** Poland
31 L2 **Wierzyca** *R* Poland
38 M8 **Wies** Austria
37 N4 **Wiesau** W Germany
36 E3 **Wiesbaden** W Germany
40 G2 **Wiese** *R* W Germany
33 Q8 **Wiesenburg** East Germany
36 H6 **Wiesensteig** W Germany
37 L4 **Wiesent** *R* W Germany
37 J4 **Wiesentherd** W Germany
37 L4 **Wiesenttal** W Germany
36 F5 **Wiesloch** W Germany
32 G6 **Wiesmoor** W Germany
32 F7 **Wietmarschen** W Germany
32 L7 **Wietz** W Germany
32 K7 **Wietzen** W Germany
32 L7 **Wietzendorf** W Germany
13 F6 **Wigan** England
98 B9 **Wiggins** Colorado U.S.A.
111 G11 **Wiggins** Mississippi U.S.A.
9 E6 **Wight, I. of** England
8 D3 **Wigmore** England
31 O2 **Wigry, Jezioro** *L* Poland
9 E2 **Wigston** England
13 E4 **Wigton** England
Wigtown *co see* **Dumfries and Galloway** *reg*
12 D4 **Wigtown** Scotland
25 F4 **Wijhe** Netherlands
25 E7 **Wijk** Netherlands
25 C4 **Wijk aan Zee** Netherlands
103 L7 **Wikieup** Arizona U.S.A.
120 J7 **Wikwemikong** Ontario Canada
41 K3 **Wil** Switzerland
83 L11 **Wila Oya** *R* Sri Lanka
98 K9 **Wilber** Nebraska U.S.A.
121 M7 **Wilberforce** Ontario Canada
140 D1 **Wilberforce,C** N Terr Australia
144 C5 **Wilberforce R** New Zealand
101 N3 **Wilborn** Montana U.S.A.
100 B6 **Wilbur** Oregon U.S.A.
100 G2 **Wilbur** Washington U.S.A.
94 E10 **Wilbur Dam** Tennessee U.S.A.
110 A7 **Wilburton** Oklahoma U.S.A.
9 F3 **Wilby** England
139 G4 **Wilcannia** New South Wales Australia
119 N8 **Wilcox** Saskatchewan Canada
99 M9 **Wilcox** Missouri U.S.A.
98 G9 **Wilcox** Nebraska U.S.A.
94 J5 **Wilcox** Pennsylvania U.S.A.
33 T8 **Wildau** East Germany
36 F6 **Wildbad** W Germany
33 R7 **Wildberg** East Germany
36 F6 **Wildberg** W Germany
123 Q4 **Wild Bight** Newfoundland Canada
102 H2 **Wildcat Pk** Nevada U.S.A.
119 V3 **Wilde** Manitoba Canada
37 J2 **Wildeck** W Germany
37 O2 **Wildenfels** East Germany
94 B10 **Wilder** Tennessee U.S.A.
41 O4 **Wilder Freiger** *mt* Austria
117 O9 **Wilderness Prov. Park** Alberta Canada
110 H6 **Wildersville** Tennessee U.S.A.
25 G2 **Wildervank** Netherlands
32 H7 **Wildeshausen** W Germany
36 H3 **Wildflecken** W Germany
120 A4 **Wild Goose** Ontario Canada
40 F5 **Wildhorn** *mt* Switzerland
101 P1 **Wild Horse** Alberta Canada
100 K8 **Wildhorse Res** Nevada U.S.A.
119 P4 **Wildnest L** Saskatchewan Canada
108 B8 **Wildorado** Texas U.S.A.
33 R8 **Wildpark** East Germany
98 K2 **Wild Rice** *R* Minnesota U.S.A.
98 K3 **Wild Rice** *R* North Dakota U.S.A.
98 C1 **Wildrose** North Dakota U.S.A.
99 R5 **Wild Rose** Wisconsin U.S.A.
40 G5 **Wildstrubel** *mt* Switzerland
118 B5 **Wildwood** Alberta Canada
113 E9 **Wildwood** Florida U.S.A.
95 N8 **Wildwood** New Jersey U.S.A.
118 B1 **Wildwood Pk** Manitoba Canada
106 H3 **Wiley** Colorado U.S.A.
36 F6 **Wilferdingen** W Germany
120 E2 **Wilgar** Ontario Canada
89 F6 **Wilge** *R* S Africa
138 C4 **Wilgena** South Australia Australia
146 H12 **Wilhelm II Land** Antarctica
129 G3 **Wilhelmina Geb** *mts* Suriname
25 D5 **Wilhelmina Kanal** Netherlands
136 J3 **Wilhelm, Mt** Papua New Guinea
31 H4 **Wilhelm Pieck Stadt** East Germany
32 H5 **Wilhelmshaven** W Germany
36 F2 **Wilhelmshütte** W Germany
33 O5 **Wiligrad** East Germany
70 N9 **Wilis** *mt* Java
95 M5 **Wilkes-Barre** Pennsylvania U.S.A.
112 F1 **Wilkesboro** North Carolina U.S.A.
146 E14 **Wilkes Coast** Antarctica
146 E13 **Wilkes Land** Antarctica
37 N2 **Wilkhau Hasslau** East Germany
118 J6 **Wilkie** Saskatchewan Canada
146 D5 **Wilkins Coast** Antarctica
146 C5 **Wilkins Ice Shelf** Antarctica
138 C3 **Wilkinson L** South Australia Australia
112 D6 **Willacoochee** Georgia U.S.A.
103 M6 **Willaha** Arizona U.S.A.
100 B4 **Willamette** *R* Oregon U.S.A.
139 G5 **Willangra Billabong** *R* New South Wales Australia
100 B3 **Willapa** *R* Washington U.S.A.
139 G3 **Willara** New South Wales Australia
138 E2 **Willara, L** South Australia Australia
124 D3 **Willard** Mexico
98 C9 **Willard** Colorado U.S.A.
98 B3 **Willard** Montana U.S.A.
106 D7 **Willard** New Mexico U.S.A.
94 E5 **Willard** Ohio U.S.A.
101 N8 **Willard** Utah U.S.A.
95 M8 **Willards** Maryland U.S.A.
142 E4 **Willare Bridge Roadhouse** Western Australia Australia
103 P9 **Willcox** Arizona U.S.A.
32 K9 **Willebadessen** W Germany
22 G1 **Willebroek** Belgium
22 E2 **Willems** France
25 C5 **Willemsdorp** Netherlands
126 B1 **Willemstad** Curaçao
25 B5 **Willemstad** Netherlands

140 B3 Willeroo N Terr Australia
8 D3 Willersley England
22 H4 Willerzie Belgium
9 F4 Willesden England
118 C6 Willesden Green Alberta Canada
120 B2 Willet Ontario Canada
143 B6 Williambury Western Australia Australia
138 D3 William Creek South Australia Australia
119 S5 William L Manitoba Canada
138 F6 William, Mt Victoria Australia
143 B10 William,Mt Western Australia Australia
140 F5 Williams R Queensland Australia
143 B10 Williams Western Australia Australia
103 M6 Williams Arizona U.S.A.
102 B2 Williams California U.S.A.
110 K3 Williams Indiana U.S.A.
99 N7 Williams Iowa U.S.A.
99 L1 Williams Minnesota U.S.A.
99 S7 Williams Bay Wisconsin U.S.A.
99 O8 Williamsburg Iowa U.S.A.
94 C10 Williamsburg Kentucky U.S.A.
95 P4 Williamsburg Massachusetts U.S.A.
94 C7 Williamsburg Ohio U.S.A.
94 J6 Williamsburg Pennsylvania U.S.A.
95 L9 Williamsburg Virginia U.S.A.
127 K2 Williamsfield Jamaica
120 K8 Williamsford Ontario Canada
126 E2 Williams I Bahamas
117 M9 Williams Lake British Columbia Canada
99 N8 Williamson Iowa U.S.A.
95 K3 Williamson New York U.S.A.
94 E9 Williamson West Virginia U.S.A.
123 Q3 Williamsport Newfoundland Canada
99 T9 Williamsport Indiana U.S.A.
94 K7 Williamsport Maryland U.S.A.
95 K5 Williamsport Pennsylvania U.S.A.
94 C4 Williamston Michigan U.S.A.
112 K2 Williamston North Carolina U.S.A.
112 E3 Williamston South Carolina U.S.A.
94 C8 Williamstown Kentucky U.S.A.
95 O4 Williamstown Massachusetts U.S.A.
95 P2 Williamstown Vermont U.S.A.
94 F7 Williamstown West Virginia U.S.A.
110 F5 Williamsville Missouri U.S.A.
141 G8 Willie's Ra Queensland Australia
127 P4 Willkie's Antigua W Indies
95 P5 Willimantic Connecticut U.S.A.
118 E5 Willingdon Alberta Canada
117 P10 Willingdon, Mt Alberta Canada
32 J10 Willingen W Germany
9 G3 Willingham England
13 G4 Willington England
109 M5 Willis Texas U.S.A.
94 G10 Willis Virginia U.S.A.
40 G3 Willisau Switzerland
141 K3 Willis Grp islds Gt Barrier Reef Aust
87 D12 Williston S Africa
113 E8 Williston Florida U.S.A.
98 C1 Williston North Dakota U.S.A.
112 F4 Williston South Carolina U.S.A.
117 M8 Williston L British Columbia Canada
110 G4 Willisville Illinois U.S.A.
8 C5 Williton England
102 A2 Willits California U.S.A.
119 P9 Willmar Saskatchewan Canada
99 L4 Willmar Minnesota U.S.A.
95 F5 Willoughby Ohio U.S.A.
138 E6 Willoughby, C South Australia Australia
117 M9 Willow R British Columbia Canada
116 M6 Willow Alaska U.S.A.
108 E8 Willow Oklahoma U.S.A.
119 P7 Willowbrook Saskatchewan Canada
119 M9 Willow Bunch L Saskatchewan Canada
98 F1 Willow City North Dakota U.S.A.
100 E9 Willow Cr California U.S.A.
100 H5 Willow Cr Oregon U.S.A.
118 D8 Willow Cr. Prov. Park Alberta Canada
117 O4 Willow L Northwest Territories Canada
98 J5 Willow L South Dakota U.S.A.
117 N4 Willowlake R Northwest Territories Canada
89 C9 Willowmore S Africa
140 C5 Willowra N Terr Australia
100 E8 Willow Ranch California U.S.A.
99 R4 Willow Res Wisconsin U.S.A.
99 O3 Willow River Minnesota U.S.A.
94 D4 Willow Run Michigan U.S.A.
119 M9 Willows Saskatchewan Canada
102 B2 Willows California U.S.A.
110 E5 Willow Springs Missouri U.S.A.
139 K4 Willow Tree New South Wales Australia
95 O2 Willsboro New York U.S.A.
142 G5 Wills,L Western Australia Australia
109 L3 Wills Point Texas U.S.A.
138 E6 Willunga South Australia Australia
111 H11 Wilmer Alabama U.S.A.
33 T6 Wilmersdorf East Germany
99 T7 Wilmette Illinois U.S.A.
138 E4 Wilmington South Australia Australia
95 M7 Wilmington Delaware U.S.A.
99 S8 Wilmington Illinois U.S.A.
112 K3 Wilmington North Carolina U.S.A.
94 D7 Wilmington Ohio U.S.A.
95 O4 Wilmington Vermont U.S.A.
99 L6 Wilmont Minnesota U.S.A.
94 C9 Wilmore Kentucky U.S.A.
111 E8 Wilmot Arkansas U.S.A.
94 F6 Wilmot Ohio U.S.A.
144 B6 Wilmot, L New Zealand
144 A6 Wilmot Pass New Zealand
25 C4 Wilnis Netherlands
121 N7 Wilno Ontario Canada
36 E2 Wilnsdorf W Germany
83 J9 Wilpattu Nat.Park Sri Lanka
138 E4 Wilpena R South Australia Australia
138 E4 Wilpena South Australia Australia
22 G1 Wilrijk Belgium
101 P3 Wilsall Montana U.S.A.
37 Q1 Wilsdruff East Germany
32 L6 Wilseder Berg hill W Germany
141 G7 Wilson R Queensland Australia
110 F6 Wilson Arkansas U.S.A.
107 M3 Wilson Kansas U.S.A.
111 E11 Wilson Louisiana U.S.A.
94 J3 Wilson New York U.S.A.
112 K2 Wilson North Carolina U.S.A.
109 K1 Wilson Oklahoma U.S.A.
108 F2 Wilson Texas U.S.A.
101 P6 Wilson Wyoming U.S.A.
138 A4 Wilson Bluff South Australia Australia
115 L4 Wilson, C Northwest Territories Canada
142 F5 Wilson Cliffs hill Western Australia Australia
100 F2 Wilson Creek Washington U.S.A.
103 K3 Wilson Cr. Ra Nevada U.S.A.
146 C13 Wilson Hills Antarctica
106 H3 Wilson Junc Colorado U.S.A.
138 A2 Wilson, L South Australia Australia
110 J7 Wilson L Alabama U.S.A.
142 G5 Wilson,Mt Western Australia Australia
102 G7 Wilson, Mt California U.S.A.
106 C4 Wilson, Mt Colorado U.S.A.
103 K3 Wilson, Mt Nevada U.S.A.
107 M3 Wilson Res Kansas U.S.A.
110 C4 Wilson's Creek Battlefield Nat. Park Missouri U.S.A.
139 H7 Wilson's Promontory Victoria Australia
12 E2 Wilsontown Scotland
98 F9 Wilsonville Nebraska U.S.A.
32 K6 Wilstedt W Germany
32 K5 Wilster W Germany
140 C2 Wilton R N Terr Australia
9 E5 Wilton England
109 N2 Wilton Arkansas U.S.A.
99 P8 Wilton Iowa U.S.A.
95 Q4 Wilton New Hampshire U.S.A.
98 F2 Wilton North Dakota U.S.A.
99 Q6 Wilton Wisconsin U.S.A.
9 E5 Wiltshire co England
22 K4 Wiltz Luxembourg
143 D7 Wiluna Western Australia Australia
22 L4 Wilwerwiltz Luxembourg
119 S3 Wimapedi L Manitoba Canada
113 E10 Wimauma Florida U.S.A.
9 F5 Wimbledon England
145 F4 Wimbledon New Zealand
98 H2 Wimbledon North Dakota U.S.A.
118 D7 Wimborne Alberta Canada
9 E6 Wimborne England
22 B2 Wimereux France
113 B8 Wimico, L Florida U.S.A.
22 B2 Wimille France
38 K8 Wimitz R Austria
36 C6 Wimmenau France
138 F6 Wimmera R Victoria Australia
118 A3 Winagami L Alberta Canada
94 A5 Winamac Indiana U.S.A.
88 E2 Winam Gulf Kenya
139 G4 Winbar New South Wales Australia
87 E11 Winburg S Africa
8 D5 Wincanton England
12 E2 Winchburgh Scotland
9 E4 Winchcomb England
109 H4 Winchell Texas U.S.A.
9 G6 Winchelsea England
95 P4 Winchendon Massachusetts U.S.A.
121 P7 Winchester Ontario Canada
9 E5 Winchester England
144 C6 Winchester New Zealand
100 J3 Winchester Idaho U.S.A.
99 Q10 Winchester Illinois U.S.A.
94 C6 Winchester Indiana U.S.A.
94 C9 Winchester Kentucky U.S.A.
95 P4 Winchester New Hampshire U.S.A.
94 D8 Winchester Ohio U.S.A.
110 K6 Winchester Tennessee U.S.A.
109 K5 Winchester Texas U.S.A.
101 R6 Winchester Wyoming U.S.A.
100 A6 Winchester Bay Oregon U.S.A.
101 R6 Wind R Wyoming U.S.A.
138 D4 Windabout, L South Australia Australia
101 P2 Windam Montana U.S.A.
143 C9 Windarling Pk Western Australia Australia
Windau see Ventspils
94 J6 Windber Pennsylvania U.S.A.
98 C6 Wind Cave Nat. Park South Dakota U.S.A.
36 F3 Windecken W Germany
36 E5 Winden W Germany
112 D4 Winder Georgia U.S.A.
141 K7 Winder Queensland Australia
13 F5 Windermere England
120 G5 Windermere L Ontario Canada
94 B6 Windfall Indiana U.S.A.
95 M6 Wind Gap Pennsylvania U.S.A.
95 R3 Windham, S Maine U.S.A.
32 K8 Windheim W Germany
87 C10 Windhoek Namibia
143 D7 Windich Springs Western Australia Australia
121 R5 Windigo Quebec Canada
107 P7 Winding Stair Mts Oklahoma U.S.A.
37 N4 Windischeschenbach W Germany
38 K6 Windischgarsten Austria
95 M9 Windmill Pt Virginia U.S.A.
107 N3 Windom Kansas U.S.A.
99 L6 Windom Minnesota U.S.A.
106 C4 Windom Pk Colorado U.S.A.
141 G7 Windorah Queensland Australia
37 P6 Windorf W Germany
99 T7 Wind Point Wisconsin U.S.A.
101 Q7 Wind R. Ra Wyoming U.S.A.
37 K5 Windsbach W Germany
141 K1 Windsor dist Brisbane, Qnsld Australia
139 K5 Windsor New South Wales Australia
123 R5 Windsor Newfoundland Canada
122 H9 Windsor Nova Scotia Canada
120 H10 Windsor Ontario Canada
121 T7 Windsor Quebec Canada
9 F5 Windsor England
144 C6 Windsor New Zealand
106 F1 Windsor Colorado U.S.A.
95 P5 Windsor Connecticut U.S.A.
99 S10 Windsor Illinois U.S.A.
95 P4 Windsor Massachusetts U.S.A.
110 C3 Windsor Missouri U.S.A.
95 M4 Windsor New York U.S.A.
112 L2 Windsor North Carolina U.S.A.
112 F4 Windsor South Carolina U.S.A.
95 L10 Windsor Virginia U.S.A.
94 G6 Windsor Heights West Virginia U.S.A.
126 H4 Windsor L. Great Inagua I Bahamas
95 P5 Windsor Locks Connecticut U.S.A.
109 J2 Windthorst Texas U.S.A.
141 F7 Windula R Queensland Australia
127 O7 Windward Is W Indies
126 H5 Windward Passage Cuba/Haiti
116 N5 Windy Alaska U.S.A.
116 K5 Windy Fork R Alaska U.S.A.
119 P4 Windy L Saskatchewan Canada
117 Q5 Windy Pt Northwest Territories Canada
118 G3 Winefred L Alberta Canada
99 R3 Winegar Wisconsin U.S.A.
94 C3 Winegars Michigan U.S.A.
100 E2 Winesap Washington U.S.A.
118 C6 Winfield Alberta Canada
111 J8 Winfield Alabama U.S.A.
107 O4 Winfield Kansas U.S.A.
109 M2 Winfield Texas U.S.A.
8 D6 Winfrith England
98 F2 Wing North Dakota U.S.A.
110 J1 Wingate Indiana U.S.A.
106 B6 Wingate New Mexico U.S.A.
140 B2 Wingate Mts N Terr Australia
139 K4 Wingen New South Wales Australia
22 E1 Wingene Belgium
36 C6 Wingen-sur-Moder France
139 L4 Wingham New South Wales Australia
120 J9 Wingham Ontario Canada
9 H5 Wingham England
110 H5 Wingo Kentucky U.S.A.
32 K5 Wingst W Germany
71 M9 Wini Timor Indonesia
101 Q2 Winifred Montana U.S.A.
98 J6 Winifred South Dakota U.S.A.
142 E5 Winifred,L Western Australia Australia
115 L6 Winisk Ontario Canada
68 D5 Winkana Burma
25 C3 Winkel Netherlands
103 O9 Winkelman Arizona U.S.A.
9 F5 Winkfield England
37 O5 Winklarn W Germany
8 C6 Winkleigh England
119 U9 Winkler Manitoba Canada
38 G8 Winklern Austria
100 C3 Winlock Washington U.S.A.
95 T1 Winn Maine U.S.A.
94 C3 Winn Michigan U.S.A.
140 B6 Winnalls Ridge N Terr Australia
85 D7 Winneba Ghana
99 M6 Winnebago Minnesota U.S.A.
98 K7 Winnebago Nebraska U.S.A.
99 S6 Winnebago, L Wisconsin U.S.A.
142 G6 Winnecke Hills N Terr/W Aust Australia
140 B4 Winnecke,Mt N Terr Australia
142 E6 Winnecke Rock hill Western Australia Australia
99 S5 Winneconne Wisconsin U.S.A.
100 H9 Winnemucca Nevada U.S.A.
102 E1 Winnemucca L Nevada U.S.A.
36 G6 Winnenden W Germany
98 G5 Winner South Dakota U.S.A.
99 T7 Winnetka Illinois U.S.A.
98 H7 Winnetoon Nebraska U.S.A.
101 R2 Winnett Montana U.S.A.
109 P4 Winnfield Louisiana U.S.A.
99 M2 Winnibigoshish L Minnesota U.S.A.
109 N6 Winnie Texas U.S.A.
118 F9 Winnifred Alberta Canada
33 O9 Winnigen East Germany
142 A6 Winning Western Australia Australia
36 D3 Winningen W Germany
118 A1 Winnipeg Manitoba Canada
119 V8 Winnipeg Beach Manitoba Canada
119 T5 Winnipeg, L Manitoba Canada
119 S7 Winnipegosis Manitoba Canada
119 R6 Winnipegosis, L Manitoba Canada
95 Q3 Winnipesaukee, L New Hampshire U.S.A.
111 E9 Winnsboro Louisiana U.S.A.
112 F3 Winnsboro South Carolina U.S.A.
109 M3 Winnsboro Texas U.S.A.
112 E6 Winokur Georgia U.S.A.
103 N6 Winona Arizona U.S.A.
107 J2 Winona Kansas U.S.A.
99 S3 Winona Michigan U.S.A.
99 P5 Winona Minnesota U.S.A.
110 E4 Winona Missouri U.S.A.
109 M3 Winona Texas U.S.A.
100 H3 Winona Washington U.S.A.
109 P1 Winona, L Arkansas U.S.A.
95 P2 Winooski R Vermont U.S.A.
95 O2 Winooski Vermont U.S.A.
25 H2 Winschoten Netherlands
32 M6 Winsen W Germany
32 L7 Winsen W Germany
8 D1 Winsford England
98 J7 Winside Nebraska U.S.A.
9 F4 Winslow England
103 O6 Winslow Arizona U.S.A.
110 B6 Winslow Arkansas U.S.A.
110 J3 Winslow Indiana U.S.A.
95 S2 Winslow Maine U.S.A.
100 C2 Winslow Washington U.S.A.
137 R2 Winslow Reef Phoenix Is Pacific Oc
101 N5 Winsper Idaho U.S.A.
95 O5 Winsted Connecticut U.S.A.
9 E1 Winster England
13 G4 Winston England
101 O3 Winston Montana U.S.A.
106 C8 Winston New Mexico U.S.A.
112 G1 Winston Salem North Carolina U.S.A.
25 G2 Winsum Netherlands
118 H6 Winter Saskatchewan Canada
38 M6 Winterbach Austria
36 F1 Winterberg W Germany
36 D4 Winterberg W Germany
8 D6 Winterbourne Abbas England
9 E5 Winterbourne Stoke England
33 O7 Winterfeld East Germany
113 F9 Winter Garden Florida U.S.A.
114 J3 Winter Harb Northwest Territories Canada
103 K9 Winterhaven California U.S.A.
113 F9 Winter Haven Florida U.S.A.
119 U3 Wintering L Manitoba Canada
36 G7 Winterlingen W Germany
106 E2 Winter Park Colorado U.S.A.
113 F8 Winter Park Florida U.S.A.
95 T2 Winterport Maine U.S.A.
102 C2 Winters California U.S.A.
108 H4 Winters Texas U.S.A.
103 M8 Wintersburg Arizona U.S.A.
99 N8 Winterset Iowa U.S.A.
22 K2 Winterslag Belgium
25 G5 Winterswijk Netherlands
41 J3 Winterthur Switzerland
123 T3 Winterton Newfoundland Canada
13 H6 Winterton England
95 S7 Winterville Maine U.S.A.
95 R4 Winthrop Massachusetts U.S.A.
99 M5 Winthrop Minnesota U.S.A.
95 N2 Winthrop New York U.S.A.
100 E1 Winthrop Washington U.S.A.
99 T7 Winthrop Harbor Illinois U.S.A.
138 C2 Wintinna South Australia Australia
141 G5 Winton Queensland Australia
1 3 M9 Winton New Providence I Bahamas
144 B7 Winton New Zealand
99 P2 Winton Minnesota U.S.A.
112 K1 Winton North Carolina U.S.A.
95 M5 Winton Pennsylvania U.S.A.
100 E2 Winton Washington U.S.A.
101 Q8 Winton Wyoming U.S.A.
40 F1 Wintzenheim France
112 H4 Winyah B South Carolina U.S.A.
37 P6 Winzer W Germany
99 M8 Wiota Iowa U.S.A.
33 N10 Wipper R East Germany
36 C1 Wipperfürth W Germany
33 O9 Wippra East Germany
41 O3 Wipp Tal Austria
83 K11 Wiraketiya Sri Lanka
69 G14 Wiralaga Sumatra
25 E2 Wirdum Netherlands
32 F6 Wirdum W Germany
9 E1 Wirksworth England
145 F2 Wiroa I New Zealand
138 E5 Wirrabara South Australia Australia
138 D4 Wirraminna South Australia Australia
138 F6 Wirrega South Australia Australia
138 C3 Wirrida, L South Australia Australia
138 C4 Wirrulla South Australia Australia
99 N2 Wirt Minnesota U.S.A.
22 B2 Wirwignes France
9 G2 Wisbech England
9 F5 Wisborough Green England
95 S2 Wiscasset Maine U.S.A.
32 K5 Wischhafen W Germany
99 R5 Wisconsin state U.S.A.
99 R4 Wisconsin R Wisconsin U.S.A.
99 R6 Wisconsin Dells Wisconsin U.S.A.
99 R6 Wisconsin, L Wisconsin U.S.A.
99 R5 Wisconsin Rapids Wisconsin U.S.A.
101 M4 Wisdom Montana U.S.A.
94 E9 Wise Virginia U.S.A.
116 M3 Wiseman Alaska U.S.A.
101 N4 Wise River Montana U.S.A.
118 K7 Wiseton Saskatchewan Canada
119 O7 Wishart Saskatchewan Canada
12 E2 Wishaw Scotland
98 G3 Wishek North Dakota U.S.A.
100 E4 Wishram Washington U.S.A.
86 A2 Wisil Dabarow Somalia
31 L2 Wisła R Poland
48 E1 Wisła Poland
31 N6 Wisłok R Poland
33 O5 Wismar East Germany
33 O6 Wismarbucht East Germany
111 E10 Wisner Louisiana U.S.A.
98 K8 Wisner Nebraska U.S.A.
22 B2 Wissant France
36 D5 Wissembourg France
36 D2 Wissen W Germany
9 G2 Wissey, R England
32 H8 Wissingen W Germany
99 P5 Wissota L Wisconsin U.S.A.
31 N4 Wista R Poland
117 K9 Wistaria British Columbia Canada
109 N1 Wister Oklahoma U.S.A.
107 Q7 Wister L Oklahoma U.S.A.
89 F5 Witbank S Africa
89 E8 Witberg mts S Africa
89 A5 Witbooisvlei Namibia
119 U3 Witchai L Manitoba Canada
143 B10 Witchcliffe Western Australia Australia
118 K5 Witchekan L Saskatchewan Canada
87 D11 Witdraai S Africa
9 G4 Witham England
9 F1 Witham, R England
8 C6 Witheridge England
9 G1 Withern England
13 J6 Withernsea England
106 C8 Withington, Mt New Mexico U.S.A.
113 E9 Withlacoochee R Florida U.S.A.
100 F2 Withrow Washington U.S.A.
31 K3 Witkowo Poland
123 U6 Witless B Newfoundland Canada
9 E4 Witney England
89 G5 Witrivier S Africa
22 K4 Witry Belgium
22 G5 Witry-les-Reims France
22 D2 Witschate Belgium
110 G2 Witt Illinois U.S.A.
28 A7 Wittdün W Germany
37 L7 Wittelsbach W Germany
98 F6 Witten South Dakota U.S.A.
32 F10 Witten W Germany
33 S7 Wittenau East Germany
33 R9 Wittenberg East Germany
99 R5 Wittenberg Wisconsin U.S.A.
33 P7 Wittenberge East Germany
33 O5 Wittenburg East Germany
40 F2 Wittenheim France
142 C5 Wittenoom Western Australia Australia
142 G4 Wittenoom,Mt Western Australia Australia
37 O2 Wittgensdorf East Germany
125 N2 Witties, The islds Nicaragua
36 H4 Witthausen W Germany
33 N7 Wittingen W Germany
70 E2 Witti Ra Sabah
32 H8 Wittlage W Germany
36 B4 Wittlich W Germany
32 K7 Wittlohe W Germany
103 M8 Wittmann Arizona U.S.A.
32 G5 Wittmund W Germany
13 G4 Witton Gilbert England
13 G4 Witton-le-Wear England
30 G1 Wittow pen East Germany
33 Q6 Wittstock East Germany
87 C10 Witvlei Namibia
89 E5 Witwatersberg ridge S Africa
89 C2 Witwatersrand S Africa
32 L10 Witzenhausen W Germany
8 C5 Wiveliscombe England
119 W2 Wivenhoe Manitoba Canada
118 L8 Wives Saskatchewan Canada
9 H4 Wix England
31 O1 Wizajny Poland
22 C2 Wizernes France
31 M3 Wkra R Poland
31 L1 Władysławowo Poland
31 J4 Wleń Poland
31 L3 Włocławek Poland
31 O4 Włodawa Poland
31 M5 Włoszczowa Poland
33 O6 Wöbbelin East Germany
9 F4 Woburn England
142 C5 Wodgina Western Australia Australia
139 H6 Wodonga Victoria Australia
31 L5 Wodzisław Poland
25 B6 Woensdrecht Netherlands
25 C4 Woerden Netherlands
94 C10 Wofford Kentucky U.S.A.
25 D3 Wognum Netherlands
41 H3 Wohlen Switzerland
33 O5 Wohlenberg East Germany
40 F4 Wohlen See L Switzerland
146 H7 Wohlthat Massivet mts Antarctica
36 F2 Wohratal W Germany
32 J4 Wöhrden W Germany
121 N7 Woito Ontario Canada
143 A8 Wokarina Western Australia Australia
65 H1 Woken China
65 H1 Woken He R China
117 O8 Woking Alberta Canada
9 F5 Woking England
141 G5 Wokingham R Queensland Australia
9 F5 Wokingham England
33 S6 Wokuhl East Germany
31 L4 Wola Poland
98 H8 Wolbach Nebraska U.S.A.
32 G9 Wolbeck W Germany
101 T10 Wolcott Colorado U.S.A.
95 L3 Wolcott New York U.S.A.
32 E2 Woldbrunn W Germany
33 T6 Woldegk East Germany
141 J7 Woleebee Queensland Australia
117 G5 Wolf R Yukon Territory Canada
111 G11 Wolf R Mississippi U.S.A.
110 G6 Wolf R Tennessee U.S.A.
99 S4 Wolf R Wisconsin U.S.A.
36 E7 Wolfach W Germany
37 P6 Wolfachau W Germany
123 M3 Wolf Bay Quebec Canada
108 D7 Wolf Cr Texas/Okla U.S.A.
94 B10 Wolf Cr. Dam Kentucky U.S.A.
101 N2 Wolf Creek Montana U.S.A.
100 B7 Wolf Creek Oregon U.S.A.
106 D4 Wolf Cr. Pass Colorado U.S.A.
118 J6 Wolfe Saskatchewan Canada
95 Q3 Wolfeboro New Hampshire U.S.A.
109 L2 Wolfe City Texas U.S.A.
121 O8 Wolfe Island Ontario Canada
118 G4 Wolfe L Alberta Canada
33 Q9 Wolfen East Germany
33 N8 Wolfenbüttel W Germany
9 G2 Wolferton England
32 K10 Wolfhagen W Germany
103 L5 Wolf Hole Arizona U.S.A.
123 L6 Wolf I Madeleine Is, Quebec Canada
117 H5 Wolf L Yukon Territory Canada
101 S4 Wolf Mts Wyo/Mont U.S.A.
98 G1 Wolford North Dakota U.S.A.
98 A1 Wolf Pt Montana U.S.A.
37 K5 Wolframs-Eschenbach W Germany
41 O2 Wolfratshausen W Germany
7 G13 Wolf Rock English Chan
38 L8 Wolfsberg Austria
33 N8 Wolfsburg W Germany
37 N2 Wolfsgefärth East Germany
36 E4 Wolfskehlen W Germany
36 D4 Wolfstein W Germany
122 H8 Wolfville Nova Scotia Canada
33 T4 Wolgast East Germany
33 T4 Wolgaster Fähre East Germany
31 H2 Wolin Poland
37 L3 Wolkendorf W Germany
37 P2 Wolkenstein East Germany
33 N10 Wolkramsh East Germany
114 H3 Wollaston, C Northwest Territories Canada
133 D9 Wollaston, Is Chile
114 J6 Wollaston L Saskatchewan Canada
114 J6 Wollaston Lake Saskatchewan Canada
114 H4 Wollaston Pen Northwest Territories Canada
36 B2 Wollersheim W Germany
140 E3 Wollogorang N Terr Australia
139 K5 Wollongong New South Wales Australia
36 D4 Wöllstein W Germany
87 E11 Wolmaransstad S Africa
33 O9 Wolmirsleben East Germany
33 P8 Wolmirstedt East Germany
37 M6 Wolnzach W Germany
31 N3 Wołomin Poland
31 K4 Wołów Poland
71 K9 Wolowaru Flores Indonesia
138 F6 Wolseley South Australia Australia
119 O8 Wolseley Saskatchewan Canada
98 H5 Wolsey South Dakota U.S.A.
36 B4 Wolsfeld W Germany
13 G4 Wolsingham England
115 M5 Wolstenholme, C Quebec Canada
31 J3 Wolsztyn Poland
32 L7 Wolthausen W Germany
33 M8 Woltorf W Germany
25 F3 Wolvega Netherlands
8 D2 Wolverhampton England
94 C1 Wolverine Michigan U.S.A.
22 G2 Wolvertem Belgium
9 E5 Wolverton England
98 K3 Wolverton Minnesota U.S.A.
9 E3 Wolvey England
69 C10 Wolya R Sumatra
120 H5 Woman River Ontario Canada
13 G6 Wombwell England
95 L6 Womelsdorf Pennsylvania U.S.A.
138 F3 Wompah New South Wales Australia
140 D4 Wonarah N Terr Australia
143 E10 Wonberna Rock rock Western Australia Australia
141 K7 Wondai Queensland Australia
22 F1 Wondelgem Belgium
100 B7 Wonder Oregon U.S.A.
116 M5 Wonder L Alaska U.S.A.
140 E6 Wonditti,L Queensland Australia
140 F4 Wondoola Queensland Australia
139 G4 Wongalarroo L New South Wales Australia
141 G5 Wongalee Queensland Australia
143 B9 Wongan Hills Western Australia Australia
70 G4 Wonggarasi Sulawesi
59 J4 Wonju S Korea
70 N9 Wonogiri Java
70 N10 Wonojoyo Java
70 O9 Wonokromo Java
138 F4 Wonominta R New South Wales Australia
70 N9 Wonosari Java
70 M9 Wonosobo Java
71 N9 Wonreli Indonesia
59 J4 Wonsan N Korea
139 H7 Wonthaggi Victoria Australia
143 C6 Wonyulgunna,Mt Western Australia Australia
138 D4 Woocalla South Australia Australia
116 O4 Wood R Alaska U.S.A.
94 J6 Wood Pennsylvania U.S.A.
98 F6 Wood South Dakota U.S.A.
140 D2 Woodah I N Terr Australia
113 F7 Woodbine Georgia U.S.A.
99 L8 Woodbine Iowa U.S.A.
107 N3 Woodbine Kansas U.S.A.
94 C10 Woodbine Kentucky U.S.A.
95 N7 Woodbine New Jersey U.S.A.
121 L9 Woodbridge Ontario Canada
9 H3 Woodbridge England
95 K8 Woodbridge Virginia U.S.A.
117 R6 Wood Buffalo Nat. Park Alberta Canada
139 L3 Woodburn New South Wales Australia
99 N8 Woodburn Iowa U.S.A.
110 K5 Woodburn Kentucky U.S.A.
100 C4 Woodburn Oregon U.S.A.
112 C5 Woodbury Georgia U.S.A.
95 M7 Woodbury New Jersey U.S.A.
110 K6 Woodbury Tennessee U.S.A.
112 F5 Woodcliff Georgia U.S.A.
140 C4 Woodcock,Mt N Terr Australia
139 L3 Woodenbong New South Wales Australia
144 B7 Woodend New Zealand
117 M11 Woodfibre British Columbia Canada
9 G4 Woodford England
127 P5 Woodford Grenada
14 C3 Woodford Ireland
140 C5 Woodforde R N Terr Australia
102 E3 Woodfords California U.S.A.
140 C5 Woodgreen N Terr Australia
9 F4 Wood Green England
9 F1 Woodhall Spa England
13 G6 Woodhead England
99 Q8 Woodhull Illinois U.S.A.
95 K4 Woodhull New York U.S.A.
142 D5 Woodie Woodie Western Australia Australia
100 C2 Woodinville Washington U.S.A.
122 K8 Wood Is Prince Edward I Canada
119 U1 Wood L Manitoba Canada
119 O3 Wood L Saskatchewan Canada
98 F7 Wood L Nebraska U.S.A.
102 E5 Woodlake California U.S.A.
102 C3 Woodland California U.S.A.
110 J1 Woodland Illinois U.S.A.
94 J6 Woodland Pennsylvania U.S.A.
100 C4 Woodland Washington U.S.A.
109 N10 Woodland Hills Texas U.S.A.
106 E3 Woodland Park Colorado U.S.A.
119 U8 Woodlands Manitoba Canada
137 L3 Woodlark isld Papua New Guinea
110 G3 Woodlawn Illinois U.S.A.
142 A3 Woodleigh Western Australia Australia
118 L9 Wood Mt Saskatchewan Canada
117 C5 Wood, Mt Yukon Territory Canada
101 Q4 Wood, Mt Montana U.S.A.
138 D2 Woodmurra Creek South Australia Australia
117 M9 Woodpecker British Columbia Canada
118 E1 Woodridge Manitoba Canada
110 F3 Wood River Illinois U.S.A.
98 H9 Wood River Nebraska U.S.A.
140 E5 Woodroffe R N Terr/Queensland Australia
138 B2 Woodroffe, Mt South Australia Australia
118 L9 Woodrow Saskatchewan Canada
106 G2 Woodrow Colorado U.S.A.
103 O7 Woodruff Arizona U.S.A.
107 L2 Woodruff Kansas U.S.A.
101 O8 Woodruff Utah U.S.A.
101 Q4 Woods mt Montana U.S.A.
109 K7 Woodsboro Texas U.S.A.
94 F7 Woodsfield Ohio U.S.A.
122 G10 Woods Harbour Nova Scotia Canada
139 H7 Woodside Victoria Australia
145 E4 Woodside New Zealand
103 O2 Woodside Utah U.S.A.
140 C4 Woods,L N Terr Australia
118 H1 Woods, Lake of the Minnesota/Ontario U.S.A./Canada
111 D7 Woodson Arkansas U.S.A.
99 Q10 Woodson Illinois U.S.A.
109 H2 Woodson Texas U.S.A.
139 H7 Woods Pt Victoria Australia
141 H4 Woodstock Queensland Australia
122 E7 Woodstock New Brunswick Canada
9 E4 Woodstock England
99 S7 Woodstock Illinois U.S.A.
95 P3 Woodstock Vermont U.S.A.
95 Q2 Woodstock, N New Hampshire U.S.A.
107 M2 Woodston Kansas U.S.A.
95 M7 Woodstown New Jersey U.S.A.
95 Q2 Woodsville New Hampshire U.S.A.
138 E6 Woodswell South Australia Australia
121 M8 Woodville Ontario Canada
145 E4 Woodville New Zealand
110 K7 Woodville Alabama U.S.A.
111 M11 Woodville Florida U.S.A.
111 E10 Woodville Mississippi U.S.A.
94 D5 Woodville Ohio U.S.A.
109 N5 Woodville Texas U.S.A.
107 L5 Woodward Oklahoma U.S.A.
102 D4 Woodward Res California U.S.A.
122 F9 Woodwards Cove New Brunswick Canada
109 P4 Woodworth Louisiana U.S.A.
98 G2 Woodworth North Dakota U.S.A.
8 C5 Woody B England
139 L3 Woody Head New South Wales Australia
116 L8 Woody Island Alaska U.S.A.
123 P4 Woody Point Newfoundland Canada
119 Q6 Woody R Manitoba Canada
8 D3 Woofferton England
71 A3 Wooi Indonesia
8 D6 Wool England
8 B5 Woolacombe England
110 D3 Wooldridge Missouri U.S.A.
139 K5 Woolemi Nat Park New South Wales Australia
13 F3 Wooler England
118 D9 Woolford Prov. Park Alberta Canada
143 D9 Woolgangie Western Australia Australia
141 G4 Woolgar Queensland Australia
143 C6 Woolgathara Western Australia Australia
139 L4 Woolgoolga New South Wales Australia
143 D9 Woolibar Western Australia Australia
140 C5 Woolla Downs N Terr Australia
9 G3 Woolpit England
102 F1 Woolsey Nevada U.S.A.
138 E4 Wooltana South Australia Australia
8 D5 Woolverton England
9 G5 Woolwich England
138 D4 Woomera South Australia Australia
138 B3 Woomera Prohibited Area South Australia Australia
95 Q5 Woonsocket Rhode I U.S.A.
98 H5 Woonsocket South Dakota U.S.A.
13 G3 Wooperton England
141 J6 Woorabinda Queensland Australia
143 A7 Wooramel R Western Australia Australia
8 D2 Woore England
138 C3 Wooroong, L South Australia Australia
94 F6 Wooster Ohio U.S.A.
9 E4 Wootton Bassett England
38 O6 Wopfing Austria
117 O7 Wor Alberta Canada
71 B2 Wor isld Halmahera Indonesia
33 M10 Worbis East Germany
141 F2 Worbody Pt Queensland Australia
Worcester co see Hereford and Worcester co
8 D3 Worcester England
89 A9 Worcester S Africa
95 Q4 Worcester Massachusetts U.S.A.
95 N4 Worcester New York U.S.A.
110 G3 Worden Illinois U.S.A.
100 D7 Worden Oregon U.S.A.
119 P9 Wordsworth Saskatchewan Canada
38 F7 Wörgl Austria
12 E4 Workington England
9 E1 Worksop England
25 D3 Workum Netherlands
101 S5 Worland Wyoming U.S.A.
8 D5 Worle England
33 Q9 Wörlitz East Germany
8 D4 Wormbridge England
25 C4 Wormerveer Netherlands
13 F1 Wormit Scotland
33 P10 Wormlitz East Germany
36 E4 Worms W Germany
8 B4 Worms Head Wales
37 K6 Wörnitz R W Germany
32 J6 Worpswede W Germany
36 B1 Worringen W Germany
36 E4 Wörrstadt W Germany
143 E7 Worsnop,Mt W Australia Australia
38 G7 Wörth Austria
38 O7 Wörth Austria
36 D6 Wœrth France
99 M9 Worth Missouri U.S.A.
37 N6 Wörth Bayern W Germany
36 E5 Wörth Rheinland-Pfalz W Germany
109 L4 Wortham Texas U.S.A.
8 C2 Worthen England
38 K8 Wörther See L Austria
127 P6 Worthing Barbados
9 F6 Worthing England
110 K2 Worthington Indiana U.S.A.
99 L6 Worthington Minnesota U.S.A.
99 O9 Worthington Missouri U.S.A.
94 D6 Worthington Ohio U.S.A.
109 L9 Worth, L Texas U.S.A.
94 B8 Worthville Kentucky U.S.A.
13 G6 Wortley England
71 A3 Wosi Halmahera Indonesia
118 E5 Wostok Alberta Canada
70 G6 Wosu Sulawesi
121 T7 Wotton Quebec Canada
8 D4 Wotton under Edge England
70 G6 Wotu Sulawesi
25 D4 Woudenberg Netherlands
25 C5 Woudrichem Netherlands
98 D6 Wounded Knee South Dakota U.S.A.
25 B5 Wouw Netherlands
22 J5 Wœvre, Forêt de France
141 K6 Wowan Queensland Australia
71 H7 Wowoni isld Indonesia
31 L5 Wożniki Poland
9 F1 Wragby England
Wrangel I see Vrangelya, Os
117 G7 Wrangell Alaska U.S.A.
116 Q6 Wrangell Mts Alaska/Yukon Terr U.S.A./Canada
116 P5 Wrangell-St. Elias Nat Park and Preserve Alaska U.S.A.
9 G1 Wrangle England
106 H1 Wray Colorado U.S.A.
9 F2 Wreak, R England
141 G1 Wreck B Gt Barrier Reef Aust
32 H5 Wremen W Germany
100 B5 Wren Oregon U.S.A.
112 E4 Wrens Georgia U.S.A.
118 E9 Wrentham Alberta Canada
9 H3 Wrentham England
95 Q4 Wrentham Massachusetts U.S.A.
8 D1 Wrexham Wales
30 H3 Wriezen East Germany
121 O6 Wright Quebec Canada
71 G5 Wright Samar Philippines
107 L4 Wright Kansas U.S.A.
112 M1 Wright Bros. Nat. Mem North Carolina U.S.A.
107 P7 Wright City Oklahoma U.S.A.
138 A3 Wright, L South Australia Australia
138 F4 Wright, Mt New South Wales Australia
68 A7 Wrightmyo Andaman Is
109 N2 Wright Patman L Texas U.S.A.
103 O10 Wrightson, Mt Arizona U.S.A.
112 E5 Wrightsville Georgia U.S.A.
95 L6 Wrightsville Pennsylvania U.S.A.
112 K3 Wrightsville Beach North Carolina U.S.A.
102 G7 Wrightwood California U.S.A.
117 M4 Wrigley Northwest Territories Canada
32 L5 Wrist W Germany
118 F9 Writing-on-Stone Prov. Park Alberta Canada
31 K4 Wrocław Poland
119 V6 Wrong L Manitoba Canada
31 J3 Wronki Poland
9 G5 Wrotham England
8 D2 Wroxeter England
9 H2 Wroxham England
119 Q7 Wroxton Saskatchewan Canada
9 E3 Wroxton England
31 J4 Wschowa Poland
65 C6 Wu'an China
143 B9 Wubin Western Australia Australia
65 A6 Wubu China
65 E1 Wuchagou China
65 G2 Wuchang China
67 E1 Wuchang China
65 C6 Wucheng China
65 B6 Wucheng China
Wuchow see Wuzhou
65 B4 Wuchuan China
67 C2 Wuchuan China
67 B5 Wucun China
58 E4 Wuda China
65 E5 Wudao China
65 F3 Wudaogou China
66 E4 Wudaoliang China
67 C2 Wudaoshui China
65 D6 Wudi China
65 A6 Wuding He R China
138 D5 Wudinna South Australia Australia
67 A1 Wudu China
58 D5 Wudu China
67 C1 Wufeng China
67 C3 Wugang China
58 E4 Wuhai China
67 E1 Wuhan China
58 G5 Wuhe China
32 J6 Wuhrden reg W Germany
67 F1 Wuhu China
65 C5 Wuji China
65 G2 Wujia China
67 C6 Wujia China
67 C2 Wu Jiang R China
67 G1 Wujiang China
65 F2 Wujiazhan China
67 F1 Wukang China
85 F7 Wukari Nigeria
65 G2 Wulajie China
33 P9 Wulfen East Germany
32 F9 Wulfen W Germany
33 Q6 Wulfersdorf East Germany
32 F10 Wülfrath W Germany
32 M6 Wulfsen W Germany
32 M9 Wulften W Germany
68 J1 Wuli China
65 D7 Wulian China
67 B1 Wulian China
67 A3 Wulian Feng mts China
65 B8 Wulichuan China
67 C5 Wuli Jiang R China
116 F3 Wulik R Alaska U.S.A.
65 H2 Wulin China
67 C2 Wuling Shan mts China
67 C1 Wulingzhen China
67 B2 Wulong China
71 O8 Wulur Indonesia
37 K5 Wülzburg W Germany
85 G7 Wum Cameroon
139 H5 Wumbulgel New South Wales Australia
67 A3 Wumeng Shan mts China
67 C5 Wuming China
32 K6 Wümme R W Germany
142 C3 Wungang R Western Australia Australia
88 D6 Wungu Tanzania
67 E2 Wuning China
138 F5 Wunkar South Australia Australia
32 J9 Wünnenberg W Germany
33 S8 Wünsdorf East Germany
37 N3 Wunsiedel W Germany
32 K8 Wunstorf W Germany
75 Q7 Wuntho Burma
103 N6 Wupatki Nat. Mon Arizona U.S.A.
67 E4 Wuping China

94 **Wuppertal — Yinmabin**

32 F10 **Wuppertal** W Germany
66 B4 **Wuqia** China
65 C5 **Wuqiang** China
65 C6 **Wuqiao** China
65 D5 **Wuqing** China
143 B8 **Wurarga** Western Australia Australia
37 O7 **Wurmannsquick** W Germany
85 F6 **Wurno** Nigeria
25 F7 **Würselen** W Germany
95 N5 **Wurtsboro** New York U.S.A.
37 M3 **Wurzbach** East Germany
36 H4 **Würzburg** W Germany
33 R10 **Wurzen** East Germany
67 D1 **Wushan** China
67 C1 **Wushan** China
67 C1 **Wu Shan** *mts* China
67 F2 **Wusheng** China
67 B1 **Wusheng** China
67 D1 **Wusheng Guan** *pass* China
68 J2 **Wushi** China
57 J4 **Wushi** China
67 C3 **Wu Shui** *R* China
67 G1 **Wusong** China
36 H3 **Wüstensachsen** W Germany
33 Q7 **Wusterhausen** East Germany
33 R7 **Wustermark** East Germany
32 H6 **Wüsting** W Germany
33 R7 **Wustrau** East Germany
33 P4 **Wustrow** East Germany
33 O7 **Wustrow** W Germany
59 K2 **Wusuli Jiang** *R* China
41 H2 **Wutach** *R* W Germany
65 B5 **Wutai** China
58 F4 **Wutai Shan** *mt ra* China
65 D3 **Wu-tan** China
67 C4 **Wutong** China
67 A2 **Wutongqiao** China
22 H1 **Wuustwezel** Belgium
67 F1 **Wuwei** China
58 D4 **Wuwei** China
67 G1 **Wuxi** China
67 C1 **Wuxi** China
65 B6 **Wuxiang** China
Wuxing *see* **Huzhou**
67 C5 **Wuxuan** China
Wuxue *see* **Guangji**
Wuyang *see* **Zhenyuan**
65 B6 **Wuyang** China
65 C6 **Wuyi** China
67 F1 **Wuyi** China
67 F2 **Wuyi** China
59 J2 **Wuyiling** China
67 E4 **Wuyi Shan** *mts* China
67 F2 **Wuyuan** China
58 E3 **Wuyuan** China
65 B5 **Wuzhai** China
65 G2 **Wuzhan** China
65 A6 **Wuzhen** China
67 D1 **Wuzhen** China
65 B7 **Wuzhi** China
67 C7 **Wuzhi Shan** *pk* China
58 E4 **Wuzhong** China
67 D5 **Wuzhou** China
141 F3 **Wyaaba Cr** Queensland Australia
99 P9 **Wyaconda** *R* Missouri U.S.A.
143 B9 **Wyalkatchem** Western Australia Australia
139 H5 **Wyalong** New South Wales Australia
94 D4 **Wyandotte** Michigan U.S.A.
141 H7 **Wyandra** Queensland Australia
139 J5 **Wyangala Res** New South Wales Australia
141 G8 **Wyara** *L* Queensland Australia
101 T5 **Wyarno** Wyoming U.S.A.
110 G5 **Wyatt** Missouri U.S.A.
9 G5 **Wych Cross** England
139 G6 **Wycheproof** Victoria Australia
9 G5 **Wye** England
143 C8 **Wyemandoo** *mt* W Australia
8 D4 **Wye, R** Wales/England
99 Q5 **Wyeville** Wisconsin U.S.A.
109 L2 **Wylie** Texas U.S.A.
142 B6 **Wyloo** Western Australia Australia
8 D5 **Wylye, R** England
95 S1 **Wyman Dam** Maine U.S.A.
118 K8 **Wymark** Saskatchewan Canada
100 E3 **Wymer** Washington U.S.A.
9 H2 **Wymondham** England
98 K9 **Wymore** Nebraska U.S.A.
142 G3 **Wyndham** Western Australia Australia
144 B7 **Wyndham** New Zealand
142 E3 **Wyndham Ra** Western Australia Australia
98 J3 **Wyndmere** North Dakota U.S.A.
110 F6 **Wynne** Arkansas U.S.A.
142 E4 **Wynne,Mt** Western Australia Australia
107 N7 **Wynnewood** Oklahoma U.S.A.
114 H3 **Wynniatt B** Northwest Territories Canada
141 L7 **Wynnum** Queensland Australia
107 O5 **Wynona** Oklahoma U.S.A.
98 J7 **Wynot** Nebraska U.S.A.
139 H8 **Wynyard** Tasmania Australia
119 N7 **Wynyard** Saskatchewan Canada
99 R6 **Wyocena** Wisconsin U.S.A.
98 A5 **Wyodak** Wyoming U.S.A.
101 S4 **Wyola** Montana U.S.A.
138 B3 **Wyola, L** South Australia Australia
120 H10 **Wyoming** Ontario Canada
101 R6 **Wyoming** *state* U.S.A.
95 M7 **Wyoming** Delaware U.S.A.
99 R8 **Wyoming** Illinois U.S.A.
94 B4 **Wyoming** Michigan U.S.A.
99 N4 **Wyoming** Minnesota U.S.A.
94 J4 **Wyoming** New York U.S.A.
95 Q5 **Wyoming** Rhode I U.S.A.
101 P7 **Wyoming Pk** Wyoming U.S.A.
101 P7 **Wyoming Ra** Wyoming U.S.A.
139 K5 **Wyong** New South Wales Australia
138 F6 **Wyperfeld Nat Park** Victoria Australia
13 F6 **Wyre, R** England
31 K2 **Wyrzysk** Poland
31 O5 **Wysokie** Poland
31 N3 **Wysokie Mazowieckie** Poland
31 N3 **Wyszków** Poland
31 M3 **Wyszogrod** Poland
13 E5 **Wythburn** England
94 F10 **Wytheville** Virginia U.S.A.
83 M14 **Wyville-Thomson** *mt* Kerguelen Indian Oc

X

86 B1 **Xaafuun** Somalia
86 B1 **Xaafuun, Raas** *C* Somalia
86 A1 **Xadeed, Bannaanka** *plain* Somalia
66 B4 **Xaidulla** China
68 E3 **Xaignabouri** Laos
66 D5 **Xainza** China
87 F11 **Xai-Xai** Mozambique
125 P7 **Xal, Cerro de** *mt* Mexico
86 A2 **Xalin** Somalia
Xamba *see* **Hanggin Houqi**
129 J5 **Xambioa** Brazil
68 F2 **Xam Nua** Laos
65 A3 **Xangdin Hural** China
Xangdoring *see* **Xungba**
87 B9 **Xangongo** Angola
25 F5 **Xanten** W Germany
46 G3 **Xánthi** Greece
130 D10 **Xanxerê** Brazil
128 E6 **Xapuri** Brazil
86 A3 **Xarardheere** Somalia
65 C2 **Xar Hudag** China
65 B3 **Xar Moron** China
59 G3 **Xar Moron He** *R* China
65 B3 **Xar Moron Sum** China
87 D10 **Xau, L** Botswana
129 J6 **Xavantes, Sa. dos** *mts* Brazil
57 L4 **Xayar** China
Xêgar *see* **Tingri**
110 H3 **Xenia** Illinois U.S.A.
94 D7 **Xenia** Ohio U.S.A.
128 F4 **Xeriuini** *R* Brazil
46 D5 **Xerovoúni** *R* Greece
67 F3 **Xiabaishi** China
Xiabancheng *see* **Chengde**
65 D4 **Xiabancheng** China
65 H2 **Xiachengzi** China
65 B7 **Xiachuan** China
67 D6 **Xiachuan Dao** *isld* China
Xiacun *see* **Rushan**
65 C4 **Xiahuayuan** China
67 C4 **Xiajiang** China
67 E3 **Xiajiang** China
65 C6 **Xiajin** China
66 F3 **Xiamaya** China
67 F4 **Xiamen** China
58 E5 **Xi'an** China
67 C2 **Xianfeng** China
58 C6 **Xiangcheng** China
65 B8 **Xiangcheng** China
67 D3 **Xiangdong** China
67 B5 **Xiangdu** China
58 F5 **Xiangfan** China
65 B7 **Xiangfen** China
65 D5 **Xianghe** China
65 B3 **Xianghuang Qi** China
67 D3 **Xiang Jiang** *R* China
65 H1 **Xianglan** China
65 A7 **Xiangning** China
66 B5 **Xiangquan He** *R* China
67 G2 **Xiangshan** China
67 G2 **Xiangshan Gang** *B* China
65 D7 **Xiangshui** China
67 D3 **Xiangtan** China
67 D3 **Xiangxiang** China
65 G2 **Xiangyang** China
67 D2 **Xiangyin** China
65 B6 **Xiangyuan** China
67 C5 **Xiangzhou** China
67 G2 **Xianju** China
58 F6 **Xianning** China
Xiannumiao *see* **Jiangdu**
Xiantaozhen *see* **Mianyang**
67 F3 **Xianxia Ling** *mt ra* China
58 E5 **Xianyang** China
67 F4 **Xianyou** China
65 G1 **Xiaobai** China
65 G2 **Xiaocheng** China
65 D3 **Xiaochengzi** China
65 D4 **Xiaochengzi** China
68 J1 **Xiaodong** China
Xiaofan *see* **Wuqiang**
67 D1 **Xiaogan** China
66 C2 **Xiaoguai** China
67 E1 **Xiaohexi** China
59 J1 **Xiao Hinggan Ling** *mt ra* China
Xiaojiang *see* **Pubei**
65 E3 **Xiaojieji** China
66 F4 **Xiao Qaidam** China
67 G1 **Xiaoshan** China
65 A7 **Xiao Shan** *ra* China
65 F4 **Xiaoshi** China
67 D4 **Xiao Shui** *R* China
65 A6 **Xiaosuan** China
65 C5 **Xiaowutai Shan** *mt* China
67 F2 **Xiao Xi** *R* China
65 D7 **Xiao Xian** China
Xiaoxita *see* **Yichang**
Xiaoyi *see* **Gong Xian**
65 B6 **Xiaoyi** China
67 F3 **Xiapu** China
Xiashi *see* **Haining**
65 B7 **Xia Xian** China
65 C7 **Xiayi** China
Xiayingpan *see* **Luzhi**
67 C6 **Xichang** China
58 D6 **Xichang** China
67 C2 **Xiche** China
Xicheng *see* **Yangyuan**
67 B1 **Xichong** China
67 A5 **Xichou** China
65 E2 **Xi Dorolj** China
67 D3 **Xidu** China
Xiedian *see* **Wanrong**
Xiejiaji *see* **Qingyun**
67 D1 **Xiemahe** China
68 F3 **Xieng Khoang** Laos
65 A7 **Xiexian** China
67 C6 **Xieyang Dao** *isld* China
65 F3 **Xifeng** China
67 B3 **Xifeng** China
65 D4 **Xifenqkou** China
66 D6 **Xigazê** China
65 E4 **Xi He** *R* China
65 G1 **Xiji** China
67 D5 **Xi Jiang** *R* China
65 E1 **Xikou** China
67 C2 **Xikou** China
65 B3 **Xil** China
66 E4 **Xiliangzi** China
67 B4 **Xilin** China
65 C2 **Xilin Gol** *R* China
65 H2 **Xilinhe** China
65 C3 **Xilin Hot** China
65 B2 **Xilin Qagan Obo** China
46 F6 **Xilókastron** Greece
65 D3 **Xiluga He** *R* China
67 B3 **Ximahe** China
65 E5 **Ximayi** *isld* China
58 C3 **Ximiao** China
65 E4 **Ximucheng** China
65 B7 **Xin'an** China
67 F2 **Xin'anjiang Shuiku** *res* China
Xin'anzhen *see* **Xinyi**
65 F2 **Xin'anzhen** China
59 H3 **Xinbin** China
Xin Bulag *see* **Xianghuang Qi**
58 G5 **Xincai** China
67 D2 **Xinchang** China
59 H6 **Xinchang** Zhejiang China
65 H1 **Xincheng** China
65 C5 **Xincheng** China
67 C4 **Xincheng** China
65 F3 **Xinchengzi** China
67 C7 **Xincun** China
Xindeng *see* **Chengyang**
65 G2 **Xindian** China
67 C1 **Xindianzi** China
67 A1 **Xindu** China
67 D4 **Xindu** China
67 E4 **Xinfeng** China
67 E3 **Xinfeng** China
67 E3 **Xingan** China
67 C4 **Xing'an** China
65 E4 **Xingcheng** China
65 C5 **Xingchi** China
67 E3 **Xingguo** China
65 B4 **Xinghe** China
65 G1 **Xinghua** China
67 F4 **Xinghua Wan** *B* China
65 J2 **Xingkai Hu** *L* China
65 D4 **Xinglong** China
65 G1 **Xinglongzhen** China
67 E4 **Xingning** China
67 B4 **Xingren** China
67 B3 **Xingren** China
67 C1 **Xingshan** China
65 F1 **Xingshan** China
58 F4 **Xingtai** China
65 C5 **Xingtang** China
67 F3 **Xingtian** China
129 H4 **Xingú** *R* Brazil
67 A2 **Xingwen** China
65 B5 **Xing Xian** China
66 E3 **Xingxingxia** China
65 B7 **Xingyang** China
67 E2 **Xingzi** China
65 C6 **Xinhe** China
57 L4 **Xinhe** China
Xin Hot *see* **Abag Qi**
67 D3 **Xinhua** China
67 C3 **Xinhuang** China
Xinhui *see* **Aohan Qi**
67 D5 **Xinhui** China
46 E5 **Xiniás, L** Greece
58 D4 **Xining** China
Xinji *see* **Shulu**
67 E2 **Xinjian** China
67 E2 **Xin Jiang** *R* China
65 B7 **Xinjiang** Shanxi China
Xinjiangkou *see* **Songzi**
66 C3 **Xinjiang Uygur Zizhiqu** China
67 A1 **Xinjin** China
65 E5 **Xinjin** China
65 E3 **Xinkai He** *R* China
65 C5 **Xinle** China
65 G2 **Xinli** China
65 D3 **Xinlin** China
65 E3 **Xinlitun** China
65 A5 **Xinminzhen** China
67 C3 **Xinning** China
Xinpu *see* **Lianyungang**
67 D2 **Xinqiang** China
67 D3 **Xinshao** China
65 D7 **Xintai** China
67 D1 **Xintankou** China
67 D4 **Xintian** China
65 D7 **Xinwen** China
67 E1 **Xin Xian** China
65 B7 **Xinxiang** China
67 D5 **Xinxing** China
68 J3 **Xinxing** China
67 E1 **Xinyang** China
67 C5 **Xinyi** China
65 D7 **Xinyi** China
65 D7 **Xinyi He** *R* China
67 C7 **Xinying** China
67 E3 **Xinyu** China
66 C3 **Xinyuan** China
65 D6 **Xinzhai** China
65 G3 **Xinzhan** China
65 F2 **Xinzhan** China
65 B7 **Xinzheng** China
65 B5 **Xinzhou** China
67 E1 **Xinzhou** China
58 F5 **Xiong'er Shan** *mt ra* China
65 C5 **Xiong Xian** China
65 E4 **Xiongyuecheng** China
65 B4 **Xiping** China
58 D4 **Xiqing Shan** *mt ra* China
129 K6 **Xique-Xique** Brazil
Xishuanghe *see* **Kenli**
67 B2 **Xishui** Guizhou China
67 E1 **Xishui** Hubei China
65 D2 **Xi Ujimqin Qi** China
67 F2 **Xiuning** China
67 C2 **Xiushan** China
67 E2 **Xiushui** China
67 E2 **Xiu Shui** *R* China
65 B7 **Xiuwu** China
65 F4 **Xiuyan** China
Xiwanzi *see* **Chongli**
66 D6 **Xixabangma Feng** *mt* China
65 A6 **Xi Xian** China
65 B6 **Xiyang** China
67 F3 **Xiyang** China
67 G3 **Xiyang Dao** *isld* China
67 B5 **Xiyang Jiang** *R* China
67 B5 **Xiyangjie** China
75 K1 **Xizang Gaoyuan** *plateau* China
66 C5 **Xizang Zizhiqu** *aut reg* China
65 E5 **Xizhong Dao** *isld* China
125 K8 **Xochimilco** Mexico
58 G5 **Xuancheng** China
67 C1 **Xuan'en** China
67 B1 **Xuanhan** China
58 F3 **Xuanhua** China
68 H7 **Xuan Loc** Vietnam
67 A3 **Xuanwei** China
58 F5 **Xuchang** China
86 H5 **Xuddur** Somalia
67 G2 **Xuedou Shan** *mt* China
67 C3 **Xuefeng Shan** *mts* China
65 A7 **Xuejiaying** China
Xugezhuang *see* **Fengnan**
Xuguit Qi *see* **Yakeshi**
67 E3 **Xu Jiang** *R* China
65 E4 **Xujiatun** China
Xulun Hobot Qagan *see* **Zhengxiangbai Qi**
Xulun Hoh *see* **Zhenglan Qi**
58 C5 **Xümatang** China
67 A4 **Xundian** China
66 C5 **Xungba** China
58 E5 **Xun He** *R* China
59 J2 **Xunke** China
67 E4 **Xunwu** China
65 C7 **Xun Xian** China
67 C3 **Xupu** China
66 D5 **Xuro Co** *L* China
65 C5 **Xushui** China
67 E3 **Xuwan** China
67 C6 **Xuwen** China
68 H7 **Xuyen Moc** Vietnam
58 E6 **Xuyong** China
58 G5 **Xuzhou** China

Y

100 K1 **Yaak** Montana U.S.A.
141 K6 **Yaamba** Queensland Australia
67 A2 **Ya'an** China
138 F6 **Yaapeet** Victoria Australia
71 A3 **Yaba** Indonesia
86 B5 **Yabassi** Cameroon
86 G5 **Yabēlo** Ethiopia
80 F4 **Yabis** *R* Jordan
46 G1 **Yablanitsa** Bulgaria
125 N2 **Yablis** Nicaragua
48 J2 **Yablonitse, Pereval** *pass* U.S.S.R.
48 J2 **Yablonov** U.S.S.R.
54 D6 **Yablonovka** U.S.S.R.
58 E1 **Yablonovyy Khrebet** *mts* U.S.S.R.
79 G5 **Yabrūd** Syria
141 H5 **Yacamunda** Queensland Australia
Yacha *see* **Baisha**
100 A5 **Yachats** Oregon U.S.A.
67 C7 **Yacheng** China
60 D14 **Yachi** Japan
67 B3 **Yachi He** *R* China
130 C10 **Yaciretá** *isld* Paraguay
139 H6 **Yackandandah** Victoria Australia
100 C4 **Yacolt** Washington U.S.A.
133 E2 **Yacuiba** Bolivia
128 E6 **Yacuma** *R* Bolivia
128 E3 **Yacurai** Venezuela
80 D4 **Yad Hanna** Israel
112 F1 **Yadkin** *R* North Carolina U.S.A.
112 G1 **Yadkinville** North Carolina U.S.A.
80 B7 **Yad Mordekhay** Israel
80 C6 **Yad Rambam** Israel
68 H6 **Ya Drang** *R* Cambodia
52 G6 **Yadrin** U.S.S.R.
80 C5 **Yafo** Israel
84 E3 **Yafran** Libya
61 Q12 **Yagaji-jima** *isld* Okinawa
60 C13 **Yagami** Japan
47 J5 **Yağcılar** Turkey
60 P1 **Yagishiri-tō** *isld* Japan
124 G7 **Yago** Mexico
55 E2 **Yagodnyy** U.S.S.R.
52 G4 **Yagrysh** U.S.S.R.
126 E3 **Yaguajay** Cuba
131 G3 **Yaguari** *R* Uruguay
128 D4 **Yaguas** *R* Peru
124 E4 **Yagui** Mexico
80 D3 **Yagur** Israel
69 E9 **Yaha** Thailand
61 L10 **Yahagi-gawa** *R* Japan
100 J1 **Yahk** British Columbia Canada
124 H7 **Yahualica** Mexico
86 D5 **Yahuma** Zaire
78 E2 **Yahyali** Turkey
68 D6 **Yai, Khao** *mt* Burma/Thailand
61 N9 **Yaita** Japan
61 M11 **Yaizu** Japan
80 G5 **Yajuz** Jordan
79 G2 **Yakacık** Turkey
116 Q6 **Yakataga** Alaska U.S.A.
59 H2 **Yakeshi** China
80 B8 **Yakhini** Israel
54 J1 **Yakhroma** U.S.S.R.
55 E2 **Yakhtur, Oz** *L* U.S.S.R.
100 E3 **Yakima** Washington U.S.A.
74 C8 **Yakmach** Pakistan
85 D6 **Yako** Burkina
117 E6 **Yakobi I** Alaska U.S.A.
86 D5 **Yakoma** Zaire
46 F2 **Yakoruda** Bulgaria
86 D4 **Yakossi** Cent Afr Republic
57 K4 **Yakrik** China
52 J4 **Yaksha** U.S.S.R.
52 G5 **Yakshanga** U.S.S.R.
52 H6 **Yakshur-Bod'ya** U.S.S.R.
101 L1 **Yakt** Montana U.S.A.
60 O3 **Yakumo** Japan
59 J5 **Yaku-shima** *isld* Japan
117 D6 **Yakutat** Alaska U.S.A.
117 C6 **Yakutat B** Alaska U.S.A.
51 M2 **Yakutsk** U.S.S.R.
56 H1 **Yakutskaya S.S.R.** U.S.S.R.
69 E9 **Yala** Thailand
47 K4 **Yalakdere** Turkey
83 L11 **Yala Nat. Park** Sri Lanka
138 B4 **Yalatta** South Australia Australia
144 D5 **Yaldhurst** New Zealand
117 N11 **Yale** British Columbia Canada
110 H2 **Yale** Illinois U.S.A.
99 M8 **Yale** Iowa U.S.A.
94 E3 **Yale** Michigan U.S.A.
107 O5 **Yale** Oklahoma U.S.A.
98 H5 **Yale** South Dakota U.S.A.
86 D5 **Yaleko** Zaire
100 C4 **Yale L** Washington U.S.A.
143 B8 **Yalgoo** Western Australia Australia
86 D4 **Yalinga** Cent Afr Republic
127 L2 **Yallahs** *R* Jamaica
127 L3 **Yallahs** Jamaica
141 H6 **Yalleroi** Queensland Australia
143 B10 **Yallingup** Western Australia Australia
139 H7 **Yallourn** Victoria Australia
111 F8 **Yalobusha** *R* Mississippi U.S.A.
86 C4 **Yaloké** Cent Afr Republic
66 F5 **Yalong Jiang** *R* China
47 K4 **Yalova** Turkey
48 M4 **Yalpug** *R* U.S.S.R.
48 M5 **Yalpug, Ozero** *L* U.S.S.R.
138 F3 **Yalpunga** New South Wales Australia
48 L1 **Yaltushkov** U.S.S.R.
65 E1 **Yalu He** *R* China
65 G4 **Yalu River** China/Korea
55 E4 **Yalym** U.S.S.R.
60 Q2 **Yamabe Karikachi Pass** Japan
61 Q6 **Yamada wan** *B* Japan
60 D12 **Yamaga** Japan
61 N7 **Yamagata** *prefect* Japan
61 O7 **Yamagata** Japan
60 D14 **Yamagawa** Japan
60 E11 **Yamaguchi** Japan
59 K1 **Yam-Alin', Khrebet** *mt* U.S.S.R.
50 F1 **Yamal, Poluostrov** *pen* U.S.S.R.
61 M10 **Yamanaka ko** *L* Japan
61 M10 **Yamanashi** *prefect* Japan
47 J6 **Yamanlar Dağı** *mt* Turkey
58 F1 **Yamarovka** U.S.S.R.
60 H10 **Yamasaki** Japan
121 S6 **Yamaska** Quebec Canada
113 G11 **Yamato** Florida U.S.A.
139 L3 **Yamba** New South Wales Australia
138 F5 **Yamba** South Australia Australia
139 G7 **Yambacoona** Tasmania Australia
85 B6 **Yambéring** Guinea
128 D3 **Yambi, Mesa de** Colombia
86 E5 **Yambio** Sudan
47 H2 **Yambol** Bulgaria
136 G3 **Yamdena** *isld* Moluccas Indonesia
Yamdrok Tso *L* *see* **Yamzho Yumco** *L*
68 C2 **Yamethin** Burma
80 E8 **Yam Hamelah** Israel
52 D6 **Yami** U.S.S.R.
61 O9 **Yamizo-san** *mt* Japan
80 F2 **Yam Kinneret** Israel
52 C5 **Yamm** U.S.S.R.
141 F7 **Yamma Yamma L** Queensland Australia
79 E7 **Yammit** Israel
85 D7 **Yamoussoukro** Ivory Coast
101 T9 **Yampa** Colorado U.S.A.
101 R9 **Yampa** *R* Colorado U.S.A.
142 E3 **Yampi Sound** Western Australia Australia
48 K1 **Yampol'** U.S.S.R.
48 L2 **Yampol'** U.S.S.R.
100 D7 **Yamsay Mt** Oregon U.S.A.
52 G4 **Yamskoye** U.S.S.R.
74 G5 **Yamuna** *R* India
74 G3 **Yamunanagar** India
55 G4 **Yamyshevo** U.S.S.R.
66 E6 **Yamzho Yumco** *L* China
51 N2 **Yana** *R* U.S.S.R.
138 F6 **Yanac** Victoria Australia
60 D12 **Yanagawa** Japan
61 O8 **Yanagawa** Japan
61 P12 **Yanaha-jima** *isld* Okinawa
76 F2 **Yanam** India
65 A6 **Yan'an** China
128 D6 **Yanaoca** Peru
56 D2 **Yanashimskiy Polkan** *pk* U.S.S.R.
139 G4 **Yancannia** New South Wales Australia
109 H6 **Yancey** Texas U.S.A.
112 H1 **Yanceyville** North Carolina U.S.A.
65 A6 **Yanchang** China
77 B3 **Yanchashmeh** Iran
Yancheng *see* **Qihe**
67 F1 **Yancheng** China
59 H5 **Yancheng** China
143 B9 **Yanchep** Western Australia Australia
65 A6 **Yanchuan** China
139 H6 **Yanco** *R* New South Wales Australia
139 H5 **Yanco** New South Wales Australia
143 D8 **Yandal** Western Australia Australia
138 F3 **Yandama** *R* South Australia Australia
65 A4 **Yandian** China
143 C7 **Yandil** Western Australia Australia
141 L7 **Yandina** Queensland Australia
68 B4 **Yandoon** Burma
85 C6 **Yanfolila** Mali
86 D5 **Yangambi** Zaire
66 E5 **Yangbajain** China
65 B7 **Yangcheng** China
Yangchuan *see* **Suiyang**
67 D5 **Yangchun** China
Yangcun *see* **Wuqing**
67 E5 **Yangcun** China
65 F3 **Yangdachengzi** China
142 A3 **Yangebup L** Western Australia Australia
65 J2 **Yanggang** China
58 F3 **Yanggao** China
65 C6 **Yanggu** China
57 F4 **Yangibazar** U.S.S.R.
77 B2 **Yangi Emām** Iran
57 D5 **Yangi-Nishan** U.S.S.R.
67 D6 **Yangjiang** China
65 E4 **Yangjiazhangzi** China
67 F3 **Yangkou** China
67 A4 **Yanglin** China
67 D2 **Yangloudong** China
65 C7 **Yangmiao** China
67 D3 **Yangming Shan** *mt* China
52 E3 **Yangory** U.S.S.R.
67 D7 **Yangpu Gang** *inlet* China
67 D3 **Yangquan** China
65 B6 **Yangquan** China
65 C7 **Yangshan** China
67 D4 **Yangshan** China
Yangshe *see* **Shazhou**
67 C4 **Yangshuo** China
67 F1 **Yangtan** China
Yangtze Gorges *see* **Qutang Xia Wu Xia**
Yangtze Kiang *R* *see* **Chang Jiang** *R*
55 E2 **Yangutumskiye** U.S.S.R.
68 D6 **Yangwa** Burma
Yangwu *see* **Yuanyang**
67 E2 **Yangxin** China
65 B4 **Yangyuan** China
67 F1 **Yangzhong** China
67 F1 **Yangzhou** China
67 C2 **Yanhe** China
65 A6 **Yan He** *R* China
138 D5 **Yaninee, L** South Australia Australia
52 D4 **Yanis'yarvi, Oz** *L* U.S.S.R.
65 H3 **Yanji** China
65 C7 **Yanjin** China
67 A2 **Yanjin** China
67 B2 **Yanjing** China
138 F4 **Yanko Glen** New South Wales Australia
98 J7 **Yankton** South Dakota U.S.A.
65 C7 **Yanling** China
142 B6 **Yannarie** *R* Western Australia Australia
Yannina *see* **Ioánnina**
54 B1 **Yanovichi** U.S.S.R.
52 G6 **Yanovo** U.S.S.R.
83 K9 **Yan Oya** *R* Sri Lanka
66 D3 **Yanqi** China
65 C4 **Yanqing** China
142 A5 **Yanrey** Western Australia Australia
65 D5 **Yanshan** China
65 D4 **Yan Shan** *mts* China
67 F2 **Yanshan** China
67 A5 **Yanshan** China
67 F4 **Yanshi** China
65 B7 **Yanshi** China
59 J2 **Yanshou** China
51 N1 **Yanskiy Zaliv** *B* U.S.S.R.
139 H3 **Yantabulla** New South Wales Australia
59 H4 **Yantai** China
138 F3 **Yantara, L** New South Wales Australia
67 B1 **Yanting** China
65 G3 **Yantongshan** China
67 G2 **Yantou** China
47 H1 **Yantra** *R* Bulgaria
80 D2 **Yanūh** Israel
57 D3 **Yany Kurgan** U.S.S.R.
65 C7 **Yanzhou** China
67 B3 **Yanzikou** China
86 C3 **Yao** Chad
61 J11 **Yao** Japan
Yaodu *see* **Dongzhi**
65 A6 **Yaotou** China
86 B5 **Yaoundé** Cameroon
65 D7 **Yaowan** China
65 A7 **Yao Xian** China
69 D9 **Yao Yai, Ko** *isld* Thailand
136 H2 **Yapen** *isld* W Irian
141 F4 **Yappar** *R* Queensland Australia
Yaqian *see* **Yuexi**
127 J5 **Yaque del Sur** *R* Dominican Rep
124 E3 **Yaqui** *R* Mexico
100 A5 **Yaquina Head** Oregon U.S.A.
80 C5 **Yaqum** Israel
52 H5 **Yar** U.S.S.R.
126 F4 **Yara** Cuba
128 E1 **Yaracuy** *state* Venezuela
141 G6 **Yaraka** Queensland Australia
52 G6 **Yaransk** U.S.S.R.
47 K7 **Yaraşlı Gölü** *L* Turkey
47 K6 **Yarbasan** Turkey
8 C6 **Yarcombe** England
138 D4 **Yardea** South Australia Australia
80 F3 **Yardena** Israel
47 L8 **Yardımcı Burun** *C* Turkey
52 H3 **Yarega** U.S.S.R.
48 J2 **Yaremcha** U.S.S.R.
52 G3 **Yarenga** U.S.S.R.
52 G4 **Yarensk** U.S.S.R.
9 H2 **Yare, R** England
128 D3 **Yari** *R* Colombia
61 L9 **Yariga-take** *mt* Japan
47 L5 **Yarimca** Turkey
47 N11 **Yarimca** Turkey
80 D1 **Yârîne** Lebanon
140 E5 **Yaringa** *R* Queensland Australia
128 E1 **Yaritagua** Venezuela
Yarkand *R* *see* **Yarkant He**
Yarkant *see* **Shache**
66 B4 **Yarkant He** *R* China
55 E3 **Yarkovo** U.S.S.R.
138 B4 **Yarle Lakes** South Australia Australia
66 D6 **Yarlung Zangbo Jiang** *R* China
13 G5 **Yarm** England
48 K1 **Yarmolintsy** U.S.S.R.
122 F10 **Yarmouth** Nova Scotia Canada
9 E6 **Yarmouth** England
95 R3 **Yarmouth** Maine U.S.A.
95 R5 **Yarmouth** Massachusetts U.S.A.
80 F3 **Yarmuk** *R* Syria
103 M7 **Yarnell** Arizona U.S.A.
52 E5 **Yaroslavl'** U.S.S.R.
52 E5 **Yaroslavskaya Oblast'** *prov* U.S.S.R.
80 E1 **Yâroûn** Lebanon
54 J7 **Yarovaya** U.S.S.R.
80 C5 **Yarqon** Israel
139 H7 **Yarra** *R* Victoria Australia
141 G2 **Yarraden** Queensland Australia
142 B5 **Yarraloola** Western Australia Australia
139 H7 **Yarram** Victoria Australia
141 K7 **Yarraman** Queensland Australia
140 D4 **Yarran Ra** N Terr Australia
139 H6 **Yarrawonga** Victoria Australia
141 J5 **Yarrawonga Pt** Queensland Australia
143 B8 **Yarra Yarra Ls** Western Australia Australia
142 D5 **Yarrie** Western Australia Australia
141 H7 **Yarronvale** Queensland Australia
15 E5 **Yarrow** *R* Scotland
141 H5 **Yarrowmere** Queensland Australia
55 F1 **Yarsomovy** U.S.S.R.
54 D1 **Yartsevo** U.S.S.R.
128 C2 **Yarumal** Colombia
48 L2 **Yaryshev** U.S.S.R.
86 D5 **Yasanyama** Zaire
137 Q5 **Yasawa Grp** *islds* Fiji
85 F6 **Yashi** Nigeria
85 E7 **Yashikera** Nigeria
60 F12 **Ya-shima** Japan
61 O6 **Yashima** Japan
60 F12 **Yashiro-jima** Japan
55 B4 **Yashkino** U.S.S.R.
54 J8 **Yasinovataya** U.S.S.R.
48 J2 **Yasinya** U.S.S.R.
54 J2 **Yasnogorsk** U.S.S.R.
68 G5 **Yasothon** Thailand
139 J5 **Yass** New South Wales Australia
47 M11 **Yassi** *isld* Turkey
60 G12 **Yasuda** Japan
60 G10 **Yasugi** Japan
77 B4 **Yasuj** Iran
128 E6 **Yata** Bolivia
47 J7 **Yatağan** Turkey
85 E6 **Yatakala** Niger
106 G5 **Yates** New Mexico U.S.A.
94 H6 **Yatesboro** Pennsylvania U.S.A.
107 P4 **Yates Center** Kansas U.S.A.
115 K5 **Yathkyed L** Northwest Territories Canada
80 D5 **Yatma** Jordan
86 D5 **Yatolema** Zaire
Yatou *see* **Rongcheng**
61 M10 **Yatsuga take** *mt* Japan
61 L9 **Yatsuo** Japan
60 D13 **Yatsushiro** Japan
80 D8 **Yatta** Jordan
8 D5 **Yatton** England
128 E3 **Yatua** *R* Venezuela
128 D7 **Yauca** Peru
127 L5 **Yauco** Puerto Rico
112 H4 **Yauhannah** South Carolina U.S.A.
128 C6 **Yauyos** Peru
103 M7 **Yava** Arizona U.S.A.
57 E5 **Yavan** U.S.S.R.
124 E4 **Yavaros** Mexico
128 D6 **Yavero** *R* Peru
128 E8 **Yavi** Argentina
128 E2 **Yavi, Co** *mt* Venezuela
128 E3 **Yavita** Venezuela
55 E4 **Yavlenka** U.S.S.R.
80 B6 **Yavne** Israel
80 F3 **Yavnee** Israel
31 O6 **Yavorov** U.S.S.R.
29 O3 **Yavr** *R* U.S.S.R.
79 H1 **Yavuzeli** Turkey
68 B2 **Yaw** *R* Burma
60 F12 **Yawatahama** Japan
68 C2 **Yawng-hwe** Burma
67 B3 **Yaxi** China
67 C7 **Ya Xian** China
56 C3 **Yaya** U.S.S.R.
52 J5 **Yayva** *R* U.S.S.R.
77 C3 **Yazd** Iran
77 C4 **Yazd-e Khvāst** Iran
57 F5 **Yazgulemskiy Khrebet** *mts* U.S.S.R.
55 C4 **Yazikovo** U.S.S.R.
111 F9 **Yazoo City** Mississippi U.S.A.
52 J4 **Yaz'va** *R* U.S.S.R.
38 M5 **Ybbs** Austria
38 L6 **Ybbsitz** Austria
130 C9 **Ybycúi** Paraguay
28 A3 **Ydby** Denmark
28 G5 **Yderby** Denmark
28 D5 **Yding Skovhøj** *hill* Denmark
52 J3 **Ydzhid Parma** U.S.S.R.
52 J3 **Ydzhyd Patok** *R* U.S.S.R.
68 C5 **Ye** Burma
139 H6 **Yea** Victoria Australia
8 B7 **Yealmpton** England
Yebaishou *see* **Jianping**
86 C1 **Yebbi bou** Chad
21 M2 **Yébleron** France
68 D5 **Yebyu** Burma
66 B4 **Yecheng** China
17 G6 **Yecla** Spain
124 E3 **Yécora** Mexico
68 C3 **Yedashe** Burma
47 K8 **Yedi Burun** *C* Turkey
43 L2 **Yedintsy** U.S.S.R.
52 F3 **Yedoma** Arkhangel'skaya obl U.S.S.R.
52 H2 **Yedoma** Komi A.S.S.R. U.S.S.R.
84 F5 **Yédri** Chad
142 E4 **Yeeda River** Western Australia Australia
138 D5 **Yeelanna** South Australia Australia
143 D7 **Yeelirrie** Western Australia Australia
52 D5 **Yefimovskiy** U.S.S.R.
54 K3 **Yefremov** U.S.S.R.
55 G6 **Yegindybulak** U.S.S.R.
55 E5 **Yegindykol'** U.S.S.R.
56 F3 **Yegirma** *R* U.S.S.R.
53 F10 **Yegorlyk** *R* U.S.S.R.
54 L1 **Yegor'yevsk** U.S.S.R.
130 C10 **Yegros** Paraguay
109 K5 **Yegua Cr** Texas U.S.A.
16 D7 **Yeguas, Sa. de** *mts* Spain
131 B5 **Yeguas, Vol** Chile
86 F5 **Yei** Sudan
67 E1 **Yeji** China
85 D7 **Yeji** Ghana
Yekaterinburg *see* **Sverdlovsk**
55 D1 **Yekaterininka** U.S.S.R.
55 F3 **Yekaterininskoye** U.S.S.R.
59 J1 **Yekaterinoslavka** U.S.S.R.
54 K4 **Yekaterinovka** U.S.S.R.
68 A3 **Ye Kyun** *isld* Burma
52 H6 **Yelabuga** U.S.S.R.
53 F8 **Yelan'** *R* U.S.S.R.
55 D2 **Yelan'** U.S.S.R.
54 N5 **Yelan'-Koleno** U.S.S.R.
141 K8 **Yelarbon** Queensland Australia
58 F1 **Yeleninskiy** U.S.S.R.
54 J9 **Yelenovka** U.S.S.R.
54 G3 **Yelenskiy** U.S.S.R.
54 K4 **Yelets** U.S.S.R.
79 C1 **Yelihüyük** Turkey
55 E1 **Yelizarovo** U.S.S.R.
55 C5 **Yelizavetinka** U.S.S.R.
59 M1 **Yelizavety, Mys** *C* U.S.S.R.
15 G1 **Yell** *isld* Scotland
76 E2 **Yellandu** India
111 K10 **Yellow** *R* Alabama U.S.A.
99 Q5 **Yellow** *R* Wisconsin U.S.A.
119 M6 **Yellow Creek** Saskatchewan Canada
143 C9 **Yellowdine** Western Australia Australia
119 N9 **Yellow Grass** Saskatchewan Canada
117 O9 **Yellowhead Pass** Alberta Canada
114 H5 **Yellowknife** Northwest Territories Canada
117 Q4 **Yellowknife** Northwest Territories Canada
99 L5 **Yellow Medicine** *R* Minnesota U.S.A.
139 H4 **Yellow Mt** New South Wales Australia
100 K5 **Yellow Pine** Idaho U.S.A.
Yellow R *see* **Huang He** *R*
59 H4 **Yellow Sea** China/Korea
110 N2 **Yellow Springs** Ohio U.S.A.
98 B2 **Yellowstone** *R* Montana U.S.A.
101 P5 **Yellowstone L** Wyoming U.S.A.
101 P5 **Yellowstone Nat. Park** Wyoming U.S.A.
15 G1 **Yell Sound** Scotland
110 D5 **Yellville** Arkansas U.S.A.
54 E2 **Yel'nya** U.S.S.R.
56 C1 **Yeloguy** *R* U.S.S.R.
55 E3 **Yeloshnoye** U.S.S.R.
55 C3 **Yelovo Barda** U.S.S.R.
16 C4 **Yeltes** *R* Spain
52 D6 **Yel'tsy** U.S.S.R.
125 M2 **Yelucá** *mt* Nicaragua
52 H3 **Yelva** *R* U.S.S.R.
8 B7 **Yelverton** England
115 L1 **Yelverton B** Northwest Territories Canada
85 E6 **Yelwa** Nigeria
55 D4 **Yemanzhelinsk** U.S.S.R.
112 G5 **Yemassee** South Carolina U.S.A.
72 E5 **Yemen, North** *rep* Arabia
72 F5 **Yemen, South** *rep* Arabia
55 E3 **Yemets** *R* U.S.S.R.
52 F3 **Yemetsk** U.S.S.R.
52 F3 **Yemtsa** U.S.S.R.
52 D1 **Yena** U.S.S.R.
54 K8 **Yenakiyevo** U.S.S.R.
68 B2 **Yenangyat** Burma
68 B2 **Yenangyaung** Burma
68 B3 **Yenanma** Burma
67 A6 **Yen Bai** Vietnam
67 A6 **Yen Chau** Vietnam
139 H5 **Yenda** New South Wales Australia
85 E7 **Yendi** Ghana
58 F1 **Yendondin** U.S.S.R.
55 E1 **Yendra** U.S.S.R.
55 E1 **Yendyr'** U.S.S.R.
68 C2 **Yengan** Burma
66 B4 **Yengisar** China
47 K5 **Yenice** Turkey
47 J5 **Yenice** Turkey
47 H6 **Yenifoça** Turkey
78 A3 **Yenihisar** Turkey
47 J5 **Yeniköy** Turkey
47 N10 **Yeniköy** Turkey
31 M1 **Yenino** U.S.S.R.
47 J7 **Yenipazar** Aydin Turkey
47 L4 **Yenipazar** Bilecik Turkey
47 K4 **Yenişehir** Turkey
56 D2 **Yenisey** *R* U.S.S.R.
56 D2 **Yeniseysk** U.S.S.R.
50 H1 **Yeniseyskiy Zaliv** *G* U.S.S.R.
56 D5 **Yenisey, Verkhn-e** *R* U.S.S.R.
68 G2 **Yen Lap** Vietnam
68 G1 **Yen Minh** Vietnam
47 Q14 **Yennádhi** Rhodes Greece
19 P13 **Yenne** France
52 E1 **Yenozero, Oz** *L* U.S.S.R.
68 G3 **Yen Thanh** Vietnam
116 M5 **Yentna** *R* Alaska U.S.A.
143 E8 **Yeo L** Western Australia Australia
74 F8 **Yeola** India
Yeóryios *isld* *see* **Áyios** *isld*
74 H8 **Yeotmal** India
139 J5 **Yeoval** New South Wales Australia
8 D6 **Yeovil** England
124 E3 **Yepachic** Mexico
54 K3 **Yepifan** U.S.S.R.
141 K6 **Yeppoon** Queensland Australia
46 F7 **Yeráki** Greece
124 J6 **Yerbabuena** Mexico
56 G1 **Yerbogachen** U.S.S.R.
21 N2 **Yère** *R* Seine-Inférieure France
55 F5 **Yerementau** *mt* U.S.S.R.
47 J7 **Yeresik** Turkey
78 K1 **Yerevan** U.S.S.R.
53 F9 **Yergeni** *hills* U.S.S.R.
143 D8 **Yerilla** Western Australia Australia
57 C3 **Yerimbet** U.S.S.R.
102 E3 **Yerington** Nevada U.S.A.
78 E2 **Yerköy** Turkey
55 G5 **Yermak** U.S.S.R.
55 F1 **Yermakovo** U.S.S.R.
56 D4 **Yermakovskoye** U.S.S.R.
55 F5 **Yermentau** U.S.S.R.
52 H2 **Yermitsa** U.S.S.R.
124 G4 **Yermo** Mexico
102 H7 **Yermo** California U.S.A.
55 C4 **Yermolayevo** U.S.S.R.
54 H1 **Yermolino** U.S.S.R.
59 H1 **Yerofey Pavlovich** U.S.S.R.
79 E8 **Yeroham** Israel
141 K2 **Yeronga** *dist* Brisbane, Qnsld Australia
52 H2 **Yersa** *R* U.S.S.R.
25 B6 **Yerseke** Netherlands
52 G3 **Yertom** U.S.S.R.
52 F4 **Yertsevo** U.S.S.R.
128 C6 **Yerupaja** *mt* Peru
80 D6 **Yerushalayim** Israel
21 M2 **Yerville** France
68 B2 **Yesagyo** Burma
67 C1 **Yesanguan** China
52 D6 **Yesenovichi** U.S.S.R.
79 D1 **Yeşidere** Turkey
55 E5 **Yesil'** U.S.S.R.
47 K5 **Yesil Dağı** *mt* Turkey
78 F1 **Yeşilırmak** *R* Turkey
79 G2 **Yeşilkent** Turkey
47 M11 **Yeşilköy** Turkey
47 K7 **Yeşilova** Turkey
79 D1 **Yeşiltepe** Turkey
108 C1 **Yeso** New Mexico U.S.A.
80 C6 **Yesodot** Israel
51 K2 **Yessey** U.S.S.R.
17 F6 **Yeste** Spain
80 F1 **Yesud Ha Ma'ala** Israel
13 F3 **Yetholm** Scotland
139 K3 **Yetman** New South Wales Australia
85 C3 **Yetti** *tribe* Mauritania
68 B1 **Yeu** Burma
20 F8 **Yeu, I.d'** France
55 F3 **Yevgashchino** U.S.S.R.
78 L1 **Yevlakh** U.S.S.R.
21 P7 **Yèvre** *R* France
59 K2 **Yevreyskaya Aut. Oblast** *reg* U.S.S.R.
65 D6 **Ye Xian** China
53 E10 **Yeysk** U.S.S.R.
52 D6 **Yezerishche** U.S.S.R.
52 G5 **Yezhikha** U.S.S.R.
52 G3 **Yezhuga** *R* U.S.S.R.
20 E5 **Yffiniac** France
130 C9 **Yguazu, R** Paraguay
130 C9 **Yhú** Paraguay
47 J8 **Yiali** *isld* Greece
84 J3 **Yi' Allaq, Gebel** Egypt
79 E3 **Yialousa** Cyprus
47 H9 **Yianisádhes** *isld* Crete Greece
47 O12 **Yiannádhes** Greece
46 E4 **Yiannitsá** Greece
68 E1 **Yibang** China
Yibei *see* **Minglun**
67 A2 **Yibin** China
80 B6 **Yibna** Israel
67 D1 **Yichang** China
67 D1 **Yicheng** China
65 D7 **Yicheng** China
65 B7 **Yicheng** China
65 B7 **Yichuan** China
65 A6 **Yichuan** China
67 E3 **Yichun** China
59 J2 **Yichun** China
58 F5 **Yidu** China
65 D6 **Yidu** China
67 E2 **Yifeng** China
80 F1 **Yiftah** Israel
65 B7 **Yi He** *R* China
65 D7 **Yi He** *R* China
67 E3 **Yihuang** China
65 A7 **Yijun** China
65 H1 **Yilan** China
47 J3 **Yıldız Dağları** *mts* Turkey
78 F2 **Yildizeli** Turkey
67 A3 **Yiliang** China
67 A4 **Yiliang** China
66 E4 **Yiliping** China
143 B10 **Yilliminning** Western Australia Australia
67 B1 **Yilong** China
65 G2 **Yimianpo** China
68 B2 **Yin** *R* Burma
65 D7 **Yinan** China
68 C4 **Yinbaing** Burma
65 B7 **Yincheng** China
58 E4 **Yinchuan** China
143 D9 **Yindarlgooda, L** Western Australia Australia
67 D1 **Yindian** China
67 D1 **Yingcheng** China
67 F3 **Yingchuan** China
65 J1 **Yingchun** China
67 D4 **Yingde** China
65 F4 **Ying'ebu** China
Yinggen *see* **Qiongzhong**
65 B7 **Ying He** *R* China
65 E4 **Yingkou** China
67 D1 **Yingshan** China
67 B1 **Yingshan** China
67 E2 **Yingtan** China
65 B5 **Ying Xian** China
65 D3 **Yin He** *R* China
66 C3 **Yining** China
67 C2 **Yinjiang** China
138 F5 **Yinkame** South Australia Australia
68 B1 **Yinmabin** Burma

42 G4 **Zrmanja** *R* Yugoslavia
31 J6 **Zruč** Czechoslovakia
48 G3 **Zsáka** Hungary
33 R10 **Zschepplin** East Germany
37 P2 **Zschopau** East Germany
37 O1 **Zschopau** *R* East Germany
37 O2 **Zschorlau** East Germany
128 E2 **Zuata** *R* Venezuela
127 M10 **Zuata** Venezuela
113 E8 **Zuber** Florida U.S.A.
16 E7 **Zubia** Spain
54 F1 **Zubtsov** U.S.S.R.
80 D3 **Zububa** Israel
37 L6 **Zuchering** W Germany
41 O4 **Zucherkütl** *mt* Austria
133 E1 **Zudañez** Bolivia
33 S4 **Zudar** East Germany
85 C7 **Zuénoula** Ivory Coast
72 G5 **Ẓufār** *prov* Oman
41 H3 **Zug** *canton* Switzerland
58 F1 **Zugdeli** U.S.S.R.
41 H3 **Zuger See** *L* Switzerland
41 O3 **Zugspitze** *mt* W Germany
25 B5 **Zuid Beijerland** Netherlands
25 G2 **Zuidbroek** Netherlands
25 D4 **Zuidelijk-Flevoland** *prov* Netherlands
Zuider Zee *see* **IJsselmeer**
25 C4 **Zuid Holland** *prov* Netherlands
25 F2 **Zuidhorn** Netherlands
25 G2 **Zuidlaarder Meer** Netherlands
25 B5 **Zuidland** Netherlands
25 G2 **Zuidlaren** Netherlands
25 F3 **Zuidwolde** Netherlands
16 D6 **Zújar** *R* Spain
17 F7 **Zújar** Spain
16 D6 **Zújar, Embalse de** *res* Spain
86 G2 **Zula** Ethiopia
128 D2 **Zulia** *state* Venezuela
36 B2 **Zülpich** W Germany
77 A5 **Ẓulūf, Aẓ** *oil well* Persian Gulf
87 F9 **Zumbo** Mozambique
99 O5 **Zumbro** *R* Minnesota U.S.A.
99 O5 **Zumbro Falls** Minnesota U.S.A.
99 O5 **Zumbro R** Minnesota U.S.A.
125 K8 **Zumpango** Mexico
100 J4 **Zumwalt** Oregon U.S.A.
25 C6 **Zundert** Netherlands
85 F7 **Zungeru** Nigeria
58 G3 **Zunhua** China
106 B6 **Zuni** New Mexico U.S.A.
56 F5 **Zun-Morino** U.S.S.R.
67 B3 **Zunyi** China
67 B5 **Zuo Jiang** *R* China
65 B6 **Zuoquan** China
65 B4 **Zuoyun** China
67 B5 **Zuozhou** China
86 H3 **Zuqur, Az** *isld* Red Sea
41 J3 **Zürich** Switzerland
41 J3 **Zürich See** *L* Switzerland
42 G5 **Zut** *isld* Yugoslavia
25 F4 **Zutphen** Netherlands
84 F4 **Zuwaylah** Libya
143 A7 **Zuytdorp Cliffs** Western Australia Australia
56 G3 **Zvezdnyy** U.S.S.R.
89 G3 **Zvishavane** Zimbabwe
85 C7 **Zwedru** Liberia
36 C5 **Zweibrücken** W Germany
37 N2 **Zwickau** East Germany
25 F3 **Zwolle** Netherlands
56 B6 **Zyryanovsk** U.S.S.R.

ACKNOWLEDGEMENTS

PICTURE CREDITS

The sources for the photographs and illustrations appearing on pages 6–43 are listed below. Credits read from top to bottom and left to right on each page.

PAGES

6–19 **Physical Earth maps**
by Duncan Mackay, copyright © Times Books Limited, London.

20–21 **Star Charts**
Copyright © John Bartholomew & Son Limited, Edinburgh.

22–23 **Universe**
Virgo cluster Hale Observatories; *Fornax cluster* and *NGC 6744* copyright © 1979 Royal Observatory, Edinburgh; *Quasar 3C 273 image* by R.J. Davis, T.W.B. Muxlow and R. G. Conway. The Jodrell Bank MERLIN interferometer is operated by the University of Manchester; *Large Magellanic Cloud* copyright © Royal Observatory, Edinburgh; *Lagoon Nebula*, *Veil Nebula* and *Trifid Nebula* Hale Observations; *Space Telescope* Encyclopaedia Universalis.

24–25 **Solar System**
The Sun NASA; *1 Deimos*, *2 Ganymede*, *3 Callisto* NSSDC/NASA; *4 Io* U.S. Geological Survey, Flagstaff, Arizona, *5 Titan*, *6 Enceladus*, *7 Mimas*, *8 Miranda*, *9 Ariel*, *10 Titania*, *11 Oberon* Jet Propulsion Laboratory/NASA; *Jupiter* NSSDC/NASA; *Saturn* NASA; *Uranus* Jet Propulsion Laboratory/NASA; *Mercury* NSSDC/NASA; *Venus* U.S. Geological Survey, Flagstaff, Arizona; *Mars* NSSDC/NASA.

26–27 **Earth's Moon**
Moon Structure Encyclopaedia Universalis; *Moon rock* J.-P. Bibring; *Moon charts* copyright © in this form H.A.G. Lewis OBE.

28–29 **Space flight**
Solar Max repair NASA; NASA, Nimbus Experiment Team for the Coastal Zone Color Scanner; *Jaya* Jet Propulsion Laboratory, California Institute of Technology, Pasadena, California, U.S.A.; *Java* NASA; *Milton Keynes*, *Faro*, *Craters of the Moon* Dr D.A. Rothery, Dept. of Earth Sciences, The Open University; *Voyager probe* Encyclopaedia Universalis; *SPOT* National Remote Sensing Centre Royal Aircraft Establishment

30–31 **Earth Structure**
Magnetosphere Encyclopaedia Universalis.

32–33 **Dynamic Earth**
Rock and hydrological cycles Encyclopaedia Universalis.

34–35 **Climate**
Waterspout Richard Chesher/Planet Earth Pictures.

36–37 **Vegetation and Minerals**
Manganese nodules Robert Hessler/Seaphot Planet Earth Pictures.

38–39 **Energy**
Data from BP Statistical review of world energy June 1986.

40–41 **Food and Population**
Population data copyright © Population Reference Bureau, Inc.

42–43 **Patterns of human settlement**
Cairo provided by NASA.

The publishers would like to thank the following for their help:

American Geographical Society, New York, U.S.A.

Antarctic Place-Names Committee, London and G. Hattersley-Smith

Director of National Mapping, Department of National Development, Canberra, Australia

Institut Géographique Militaire, Brussels, Belgium

Instituto Brasileiro de Geografia e Estatistica, Rio de Janeiro, Brazil

British Tourist Authority, London

Surveys and Mapping Branch, Department of Energy, Mines and Resources, Ottawa, Canada

Ceskoslovenské Akademie Ved, Prague, Czechoslovakia

Columbia University Press, New York, U.S.A.

Kongelig Dansk Geodætisk Institut, Copenhagen, Denmark

Professor P. McL. D. Duff, University of Strathclyde

Esselte Map Service, Stockholm, Sweden

Le Directeur General, Institut Geographique National, Paris, France

Freytag-Berndt und Artaria, Vienna, Austria

General Drafting Company Inc., Convent Station, New Jersey, U.S.A.

Institute of Geological Sciences, Herstmonceux, Sussex

Dr. R. Habel, VEB Hermann Haack, Geographisch-Kartographische Anstalt, Gotha, East Germany

The High Commission of India, London

Survey of India, Dehra Dun, Uttar Pradesh, India

Embassy of the Republic of Indonesia, London

International Hydrographic Bureau, Monaco

International Road Federation, London

International Union of Official Travel Organizations, Geneva

State of Israel Department of Surveys, Tel-Aviv, Israel

Professor P. E. James, Syracuse University, New York

Survey of Kenya, Nairobi, Kenya

Mr. P. Laffitte, Ecole des Mines, Paris, France

Dr R. I. Lawless, Centre for Middle Eastern & Islamic Studies, University of Durham

Dr S. Lippard, Department of Earth Sciences, The Open University, Milton Keynes

Dr D. N. McMaster, University of Edinburgh

Professor R. E. H. Mellor, University of Aberdeen

National Aeronautical and Space Administration, Washington, DC, U.S.A.

National Geographic Society, Washington, DC, U.S.A.

Department of Lands and Survey, Wellington, New Zealand

Nigerian Land and Survey Department, Lagos, Nigeria

Norges Geografiske Oppmaling, Oslo, Norway

Office of the High Commission for Pakistan, London

Palomar Observatory, California Institute of Technology

Dr John Paxton, The Statesman's Year Book, London

Permanent Committee on Geographical Names, London & Mr. P. Woodman

Instituto Geografico Militar, Lima, Peru

Petroleum Information Bureau, London

Petroleum Publishing Co., Tulsa, Oklahoma, U.S.A.

Bureau of Coast and Geodetic Survey, Manila, Republic of the Philippines

Centro de Geografia do Ultramar, Lisbon, Portugal

Instituto Geografico e Cadastral, Lisbon, Portugal

Rand McNally & Co., Chicago, U.S.A.

Mr P. Rouveyrol, Bureau de Recherches Geologiques et Minieres, Paris, France

Dr D. A. Rothery, Department of Earth Sciences, The Open University, Milton Keynes

Royal Geographical Society, London

Royal Scottish Geographical Society, Edinburgh

Scientific American, New York, U.S.A.

National Library of Scotland, Edinburgh

Scottish Development Department, Edinburgh

Mr Theodore Shabad, Editor, Soviet Geography

Survey Department, Singapore

Automobile Association of South Africa, Johannesburg

The Trigonometrical Survey Office, Pretoria, Republic of South Africa

Instituto Geografico y Cadastral, Madrid, Spain

Surveys & Mapping Division, Dar-es-Salaam, United Republic of Tanzania

Touring Club Italiano and Dr S. Toniolo, Milan, Italy

General Directorate of Highways, Ankara, Turkey

Survey, Lands and Mines Department, Entebbe, Uganda

Foreign and Commonwealth Office, London

Hydrographic Department, Ministry of Defence, Taunton

Director-General, Ordnance Survey, Southampton

The Controller, H.M. Stationery Office, London

Office of the Geographer, Department of State, Washington, DC, U.S.A.

Defense Mapping Agency Aerospace Centre, St. Louis, Missouri, U.S.A.

Defense Mapping Agency Hydrographic Center, Washington, DC, U.S.A.

Defense Mapping Agency Topographic Center, Washington, DC, U.S.A.

United States Board on Geographic Names, Washington, DC, U.S.A.

The United States Geological Survey, Washington, DC, U.S.A.
Academy of Sciences of the U.S.S.R. and the National Atlas Committee, Moscow, U.S.S.R.

Dr D. Whitehouse, Farnborough, Hants, England

Surveyor General, Ministry of Lands and Natural Resources, Lusaka, Zambia

Surveyor General, Harare, Zimbabwe

North America
Key to map plates

| 116 | 1:6 000 000 |
| 100 | 1:3 000 000 |